THE PRENTICE-HALL
UNIVERSITY
ATLAS

Prentice-Hall, Inc.,
Englewood Cliffs, New Jersey 07632

Library of Congress Cataloging in Publication Data

Prentice-Hall university atlas.

   Produced and devised by George Philip & Son.
   Includes index.
   1. Atlases.   I. Fullard, Harold.   II. Darby, H. C.
(Henry Clifford), 1909-   III. George Philip & Son.
IV. Title: University atlas.
G1021. P6886 1984   912   84-675201
ISBN 0-13-698259-X

10   9   8   7   6   5   4   3   2   1

ISBN 0-13-698259-X

Printed in Great Britain

This book is available at a special discount when ordered
in bulk quantities. Contact Prentice-Hall, Inc., General
Publishing Division, Special Sales, Englewood Cliffs,
N.J. 07632.

Prentice-Hall International, Inc., *London*

Prentice-Hall of Australia Pty. Limited, *Sydney*

Prentice-Hall Canada Inc., *Toronto*

Prentice-Hall of India Private Limited, *New Delhi*

Prentice-Hall of Japan, Inc., *Tokyo*

Prentice-Hall of Southeast Asia Pte. Ltd., *Singapore*

Whitehall Books Limited, *Wellington, New Zealand*

Editora Prentice-Hall do Brasil Ltda., *Rio de Janeiro*

Edited by
Harold Fullard, M.Sc., Consulting Cartographer,
H. C. Darby, C.B.E., Litt.D., F.B.A., Emeritus Professor of
Geography, University of Cambridge and
B. M. Willett, B.A., Cartographic Editor,
D. Gaylard, Assistant Cartographic Editor

Maps prepared by George Philip Cartographic Services
Ltd under the direction of A. G. Poynter, M.A., Director
of Cartography.

Preface

During the course of over forty-five years since its original publication the University Atlas has been through twenty-one editions, each of which has in its turn been revised and improved.

For the eighth edition in 1958, the atlas was completely redesigned because it was considered that only an entirely new version would meet the needs of the post-war years. In that edition we made two significant changes: a substantial increase in the scale of the sectional maps, and a re-arrangement of the atlas into an easily portable size, convenient for frequent use and able to stand on a bookshelf.

For the twelfth edition in 1967, the style of colouring of the maps was completely changed to provide lighter and clearer layer colours. This in turn made possible the inclusion of hill-shading to complement the layer colouring and bring out clearly relief features without impairing the detail of names, settlements and communications.

For the nineteenth edition in 1978 the content of the atlas was completely re-examined, and the lay-out of a large number of maps was redesigned — in particular those covering Asia, Australasia and Latin America. This enabled larger scales to be provided for (a) China, south-east Asia, Japan, the Tashkent area and the southern Urals; (b) south-east Australia and New Guinea; and (c) Mexico, the West Indies and eastern Brazil. Other new maps covered the Indian Ocean, the North Sea, the French departments, the Benelux countries, Switzerland, Alaska and California. The design of yet other maps was altered to secure a more effective presentation, e.g., the world maps of climate.

As in previous editions, international boundaries have been drawn to show the *de facto* situation where there are rival claims to territory.

Spellings of names are in the forms given in the latest official lists, and generally agree with the rules of the Permanent Committee on Geographical Names and the United States Board on Geographic Names. A list of recent place-name changes and a table showing the transcription of Chinese place-names from the Wade-Giles system into Pinyin appear at the end of the index, which contains over 50,000 entries.

We gratefully acknowledge the help of many official organisations and individuals.

H. FULLARD
H.C. DARBY

Contents

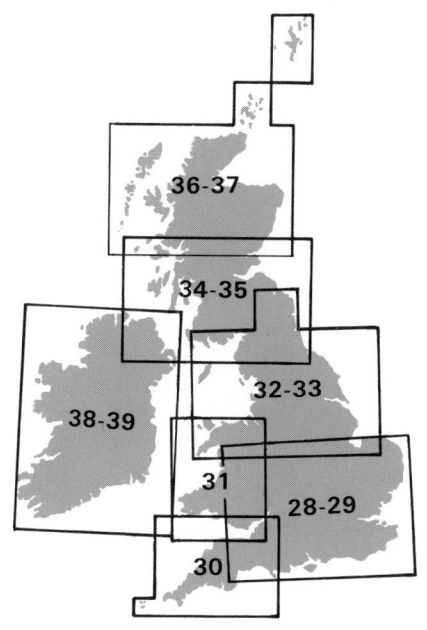

Europe

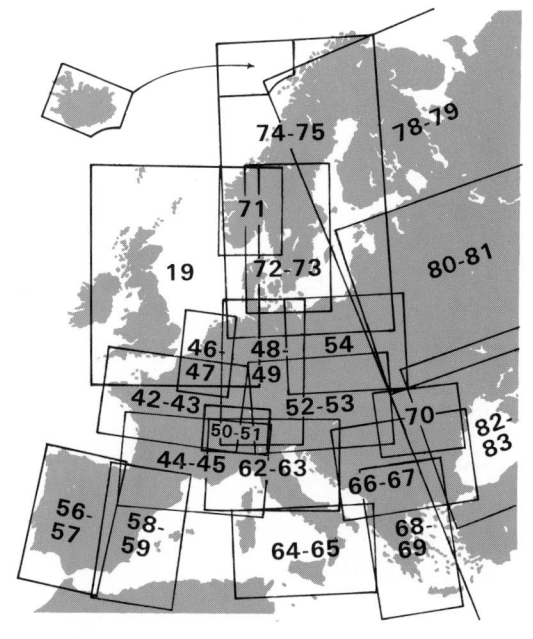

Asia

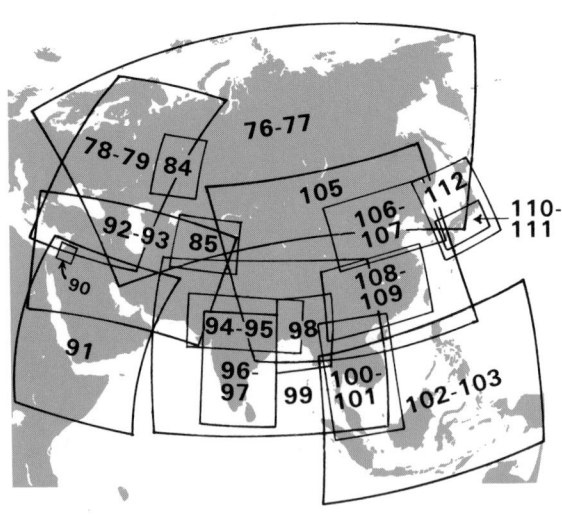

Africa

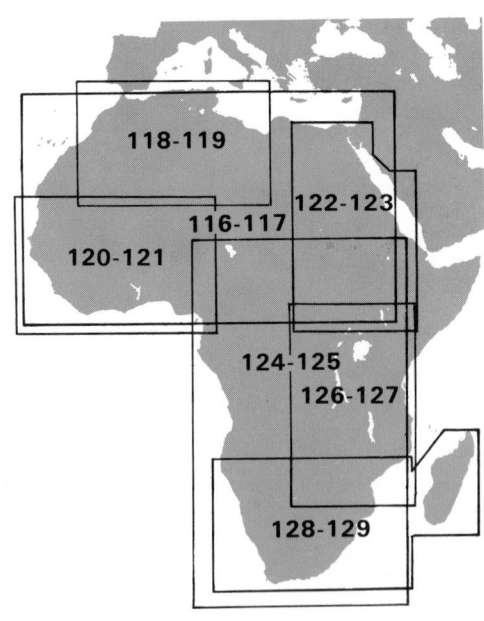

Australasia

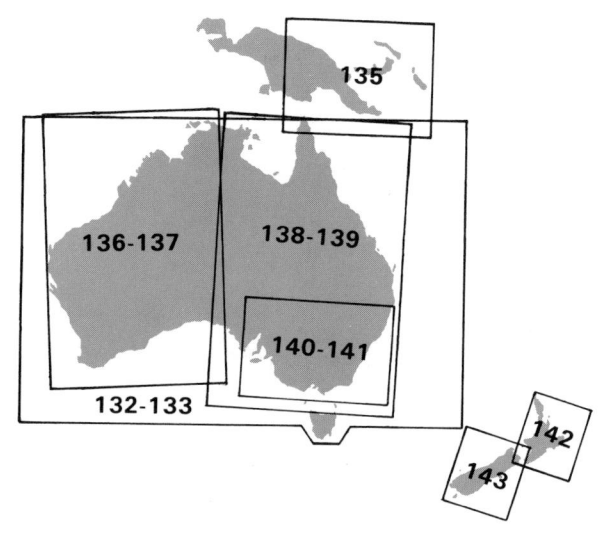

The Americas

Index

Principal Countries of the World

Country	Area in thousands of square km	Population in thousands	Density of population per sq. km.	Capital Population in thousands
Afghanistan	647	15 540	24	Kabul (588)
Albania	29	2 734	94	Tiranë (192)
Algeria	2 382	18 594	8	Algiers (1 503)
Angola	1 247	7 078	6	Luanda (475)
Argentina	2 767	26 863	10	Buenos Aires (8 436)
Australia	7 687	14 727	2	Canberra (227)
Austria	84	7 507	89	Vienna (1 587)
Bangladesh	144	88 656	616	Dacca (1 730)
Belgium	31	9 859	318	Brussels (1 042)
Belize	23	145	6	Belmopan (4)
Benin	113	3 567	32	Porto-Novo (104)
Bhutan	47	1 298	28	Thimphu (60)
Bolivia	1 099	5 600	5	Sucre (63) La Paz (655)
Botswana	600	819	1	Gaborone (37)
Brazil	8 512	119 099	14	Brasilia (763)
Brunei	6	213	37	Bandar Seri Begawan (37)
Bulgaria	111	8 862	80	Sofia (1 032)
Burma	677	35 289	52	Rangoon (2 276)
Burundi	28	4 512	161	Bujumbura (157)
Cambodia	181	8 872	49	Phnom Penh (2 000)
Cameroon	475	8 503	18	Yaoundé (314)
Canada	9 976	23 343	2	Ottawa (718)
Central African Rep.	623	2 370	4	Bangui (187)
Chad	1 284	4 524	4	Ndjamena (179)
Chile	757	11 104	15	Santiago (3 692)
China	9 597	982 550	102	Peking (7 570)
Colombia	1 139	27 520	24	Bogota (2 855)
Congo	342	1 537	5	Brazzaville (290)
Costa Rica	51	2 245	44	San José (563)
Cuba	115	9 833	86	Havana (1 861)
Cyprus	9	629	68	Nicosia (147)
Czechoslovakia	128	15 312	120	Prague (1 176)
Denmark	43	5 124	119	Copenhagen (1 251)
Djibouti	22	119	5	Djibouti (62)
Dominican Republic	49	5 431	111	Santo Domingo (1 103)
Ecuador	284	8 354	29	Quito (743)
Egypt	1 001	41 995	42	Cairo (5 084)
El Salvador	21	4 813	229	San Salvador (366)
Equatorial Guinea	28	363	13	Rey Malabo (37)
Ethiopia	1 222	31 065	25	Addis Abeba (1 210)
Fiji	18	631	35	Suva (118)
Finland	337	4 788	14	Helsinki (893)
France	547	53 788	98	Paris (9 863)
French Guiana	91	64	1	Cayenne (25)
Gabon	268	551	2	Libréville (186)
Gambia	11	601	55	Banjul (48)
Germany, East	108	16 737	155	East Berlin (1 111)
Germany, West	249	61 658	248	Bonn (285)
Ghana	239	11 450	48	Accra (738)
Greece	132	9 599	73	Athens (2 101)
Greenland	2 176	50	0.02	Godthåb (9)
Guatemala	109	7 262	67	Guatemala (793)
Guinea	246	5 014	20	Conakry (526)
Guinea-Bissau	36	777	22	Bissau (109)
Guyana	215	884	4	Georgetown (187)
Haiti	28	5 009	179	Port-au-Prince (791)
Honduras	112	3 691	33	Tegucigalpa (274)
Hong Kong	1	5 068	4827	Victoria (849)
Hungary	93	10 711	115	Budapest (2 060)
Iceland	103	228	2	Reykjavik (83)
India	3 288	683 810	208	Delhi (3 647)
Indonesia	2 027	7 383	73	Jakarta (4 576)
Iran	1 648	37 447	23	Tehran (4 496)
Iraq	435	13 084	28	Baghdad (2 969)
Irish Republic	70	3 440	49	Dublin (525)
Israel	21	3 871	184	Jerusalem (376)
Italy	301	57 140	190	Rome (2 898)
Ivory Coast	322	7 973	25	Abidjan (850)
Jamaica	11	2 192	199	Kingston (573)
Japan	372	117 057	315	Tokyo (8 349)
Jordan	98	2 779	28	Amman (712)
Kenya	583	16 402	28	Nairobi (835)
Korea, North	121	17 914	148	Pyongyang (1 500)
Korea, South	98	37 449	382	Seoul (6 879)
Kuwait	18	1 356	75	Kuwait (775)
Laos	237	3 721	16	Vientiane (177)
Lebanon	10	3 161	316	Beirut (702)
Lesotho	30	1 339	45	Maseru (29)
Liberia	111	1 873	17	Monrovia (172)
Libya	1 760	2 977	2	Tripoli (551)
Luxembourg	3	364	140	Luxembourg (78)
Madagascar	587	8 742	15	Antananarivo (400)
Malawi	118	5 968	51	Lilongwe (103)
Malaysia	330	13 436	41	Kuala Lumpur (452)
Mali	1 240	6 906	6	Bamako (404)
Malta	0.3	369	1 153	Valletta (14)
Mauritania	1 031	1 634	2	Nouakchott (135)
Mauritius	2	959	480	Port Louis (141)
Mexico	1 973	71 911	36	Mexico (13 994)
Mongolia	1 565	1 595	1	Ulan Bator (400)
Morocco	447	20 242	45	Rabat (596)
Mozambique	783	12 130	15	Maputo (384)
Namibia	824	852	1	Windhoek (61)
Nepal	141	14 010	99	Katmandu (210)
Netherlands	41	14 220	347	Amsterdam (965)
New Zealand	269	3 176	12	Wellington (321)
Nicaragua	130	2 703	21	Managua (500)
Niger	1 267	5 305	4	Niamey (130)
Nigeria	924	77 082	83	Lagos (1 477)
Norway	324	4 092	13	Oslo (645)
Oman	212	891	4	Muscat (25)
Pakistan	804	82 441	103	Islamabad (77)
Panama	76	1 837	24	Panama (546)
Papua New Guinea	462	3 082	7	Port Moresby (113)
Paraguay	407	3 067	8	Asunción (565)
Peru	1 285	17 780	14	Lima (3 303)
Philippines	300	48 400	161	Manila (1 438)
Poland	313	35 815	114	Warsaw (1 543)
Portugal	92	9 933	108	Lisbon (1 612)
Puerto Rico	9	3 188	358	San Juan (515)
Romania	238	22 201	93	Bucharest (1 934)
Rwanda	26	5 046	194	Kigali (90)
Saudi Arabia	2 150	8 367	4	Riyadh (667)
Senegal	196	5 661	29	Dakar (799)
Sierra Leone	72	3 474	48	Freetown (214)
Singapore	0.6	2 391	4 122	Singapore (2 308)
Somali Republic	638	3 645	6	Mogadishu (400)
South Africa	1 221	29 285	24	Pretoria (562) Cape Town (1 097)
Spain	505	37 430	74	Madrid (3 520)
Sri Lanka	66	14 738	223	Colombo (1 412)
Sudan	2 506	18 681	8	Khartoum (334)
Surinam	163	352	2	Paramaribo (151)
Swaziland	17	547	32	Mbabane (24)
Sweden	450	8 320	18	Stockholm (1 380)
Switzerland	41	6 329	154	Berne (282)
Syria	185	8 979	49	Damascus (1 142)
Taiwan	36	17 479	486	Taipei (3 050)
Tanzania	945	17 982	19	Dar-es-Salaam (757)
Thailand	514	46 455	90	Bangkok (4 702)
Togo	56	2 699	48	Lomé (135)
Trinidad and Tobago	5	1 156	227	Port of Spain (63)
Tunisia	164	6 363	39	Tunis (944)
Turkey	781	45 218	58	Ankara (2 204)
Uganda	236	13 225	56	Kampala (331)
United Arab Emirates	84	1 040	12	Abu Dhabi (236)
U.S.S.R.	22 402	265 542	12	Moscow (8 011)
United Kingdom	245	55 945	228	London (6 696)
United States	9 363	229 805	25	Washington (3 045)
Upper Volta	274	6 908	25	Ouagadougou (169)
Uruguay	178	2 899	16	Montevideo (1 230)
Venezuela	912	13 913	15	Caracas (2 576)
Vietnam	330	52 742	160	Hanoi (2 571)
Western Samoa	3	156	55	Apia (32)
Yemen, North	195	5 926	30	Sana (448)
Yemen, South	288	1 969	7	Aden (285)
Yugoslavia	256	22 471	88	Belgrade (775)
Zaïre	2 345	28 291	12	Kinshasa (2 008)
Zambia	753	5 680	8	Lusaka (538)
Zimbabwe	391	7 360	19	Harare (633)

SETTLEMENTS

Settlement symbols in order of size

⬠ LONDON   ■ Stuttgart   ● Sevilla   ◎ Bergen   ○ Bath   ○ *Biarritz*   ○ *Srikolayatji*

Settlement symbols and type styles vary according to
the scale of each map and indicate the importance of
towns on the map rather than specific population figures

∴ Sites of Archæological or
Historical importance

BOUNDARIES

——— International Boundaries

— ·· — ·· — International Boundaries
(Undemarcated or Undefined)

··········· Internal Boundaries

International boundaries show the *de facto* situation
where there are rival claims to territory

National and
Provincial Parks

COMMUNICATIONS

═══ Motorways

======= Motorways under construction

——— Principal Roads

⌢ Other Roads

┤---├ Road Tunnels

⌒ Principal Railways

⌒ Other Railways

---- Railways under construction

┤---├ Railway Tunnels

⋈ Passes

··········· Principal Canals

——— Principal Oil Pipelines

_ _3386_ _ Principal Shipping Routes
(Distances in Nautical Miles)

~----~ Tracks and Seasonal Roads

✧ Airports

PHYSICAL FEATURES

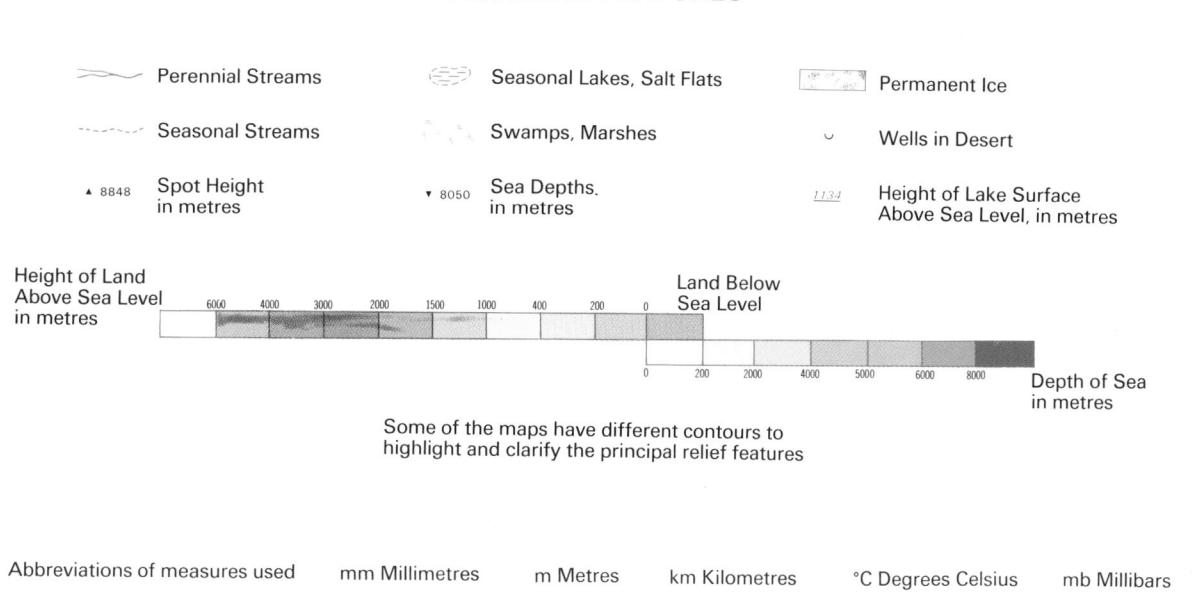

⌒ Perennial Streams

---- Seasonal Streams

▲ 8848 Spot Height
in metres

⊜ Seasonal Lakes, Salt Flats

Swamps, Marshes

▼ 8050 Sea Depths.
in metres

Permanent Ice

◡ Wells in Desert

1134 Height of Lake Surface
Above Sea Level, in metres

Height of Land
Above Sea Level
in metres

| 6000 | 4000 | 3000 | 2000 | 1500 | 1000 | 400 | 200 | 0 |

Land Below
Sea Level

| 0 | 200 | 2000 | 4000 | 5000 | 6000 | 8000 |

Depth of Sea
in metres

Some of the maps have different contours to
highlight and clarify the principal relief features

Abbreviations of measures used   mm Millimetres   m Metres   km Kilometres   °C Degrees Celsius   mb Millibars

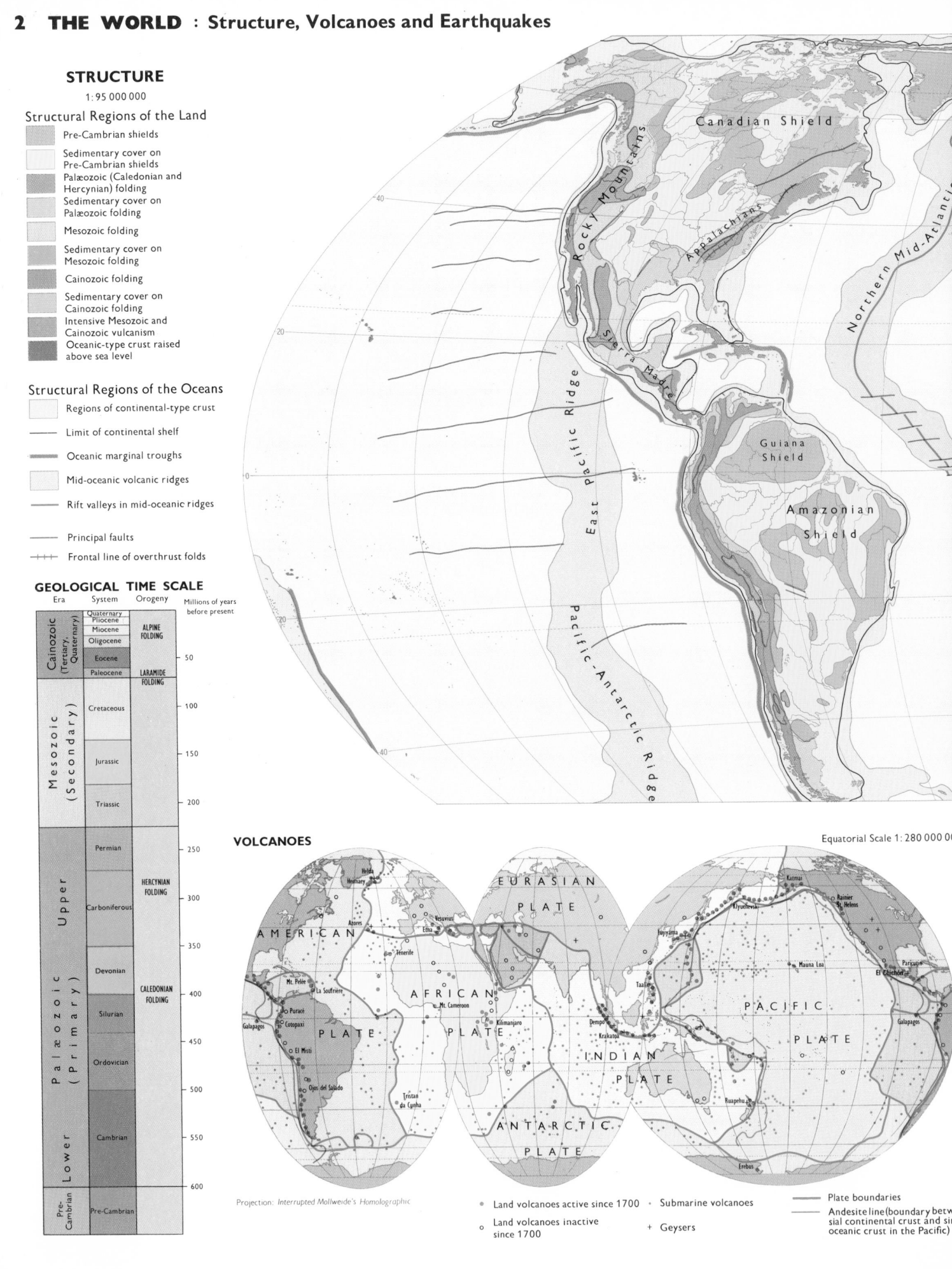

STRUCTURE

1:95 000 000

Structural Regions of the Land

- Pre-Cambrian shields
- Sedimentary cover on Pre-Cambrian shields
- Palæozoic (Caledonian and Hercynian) folding
- Sedimentary cover on Palæozoic folding
- Mesozoic folding
- Sedimentary cover on Mesozoic folding
- Cainozoic folding
- Sedimentary cover on Cainozoic folding
- Intensive Mesozoic and Cainozoic vulcanism
- Oceanic-type crust raised above sea level

Structural Regions of the Oceans

- Regions of continental-type crust
- Limit of continental shelf
- Oceanic marginal troughs
- Mid-oceanic volcanic ridges
- Rift valleys in mid-oceanic ridges
- Principal faults
- Frontal line of overthrust folds

GEOLOGICAL TIME SCALE

Era	System	Orogeny	Millions of years before present
Cainozoic (Tertiary, Quaternary)	Quaternary		
	Pliocene	ALPINE FOLDING	
	Miocene		
	Oligocene		
	Eocene		50
	Paleocene	LARAMIDE FOLDING	
Mesozoic (Secondary)	Cretaceous		100
	Jurassic		150
	Triassic		200
Palæozoic (Primary) — Upper	Permian		250
	Carboniferous	HERCYNIAN FOLDING	300
	Devonian		350
Palæozoic (Primary) — Lower	Silurian	CALEDONIAN FOLDING	400
	Ordovician		450
	Cambrian		500
			550
Pre-Cambrian	Pre-Cambrian		600

VOLCANOES

Equatorial Scale 1 : 280 000 00

EURASIAN PLATE

AMERICAN PLATE

AFRICAN PLATE

PACIFIC PLATE

INDIAN PLATE

ANTARCTIC PLATE

Hekla
Hemavy
Azores
Vesuvius
Etna
Katmai
Rainier
Mt. Helens
Klyuchevski
Fujiyama
Mauna Loa
Paricutín
El Chichón
Mt. Pelée
La Soufrière
Mt. Cameroon
Taal
Purace
Galapagos
Kilimanjaro
Dempo
Cotopaxi
Krakatoa
El Misti
Galapagos
Tenerife
Ojos del Salado
Tristan da Cunha
Ruapehu
Erebus

Projection: *Interrupted Mollweide's Homolographic*

- Land volcanoes active since 1700
- Land volcanoes inactive since 1700
- Submarine volcanoes
- Geysers
- Plate boundaries
- Andesite line (boundary betw sial continental crust and sin oceanic crust in the Pacific)

Canadian Shield
Rocky Mountains
Appalachians
Northern Mid-Atlantic
Sierra Madre
East Pacific Ridge
Guiana Shield
Amazonian Shield
Pacific-Antarctic Ridge

1 : 95 000 000

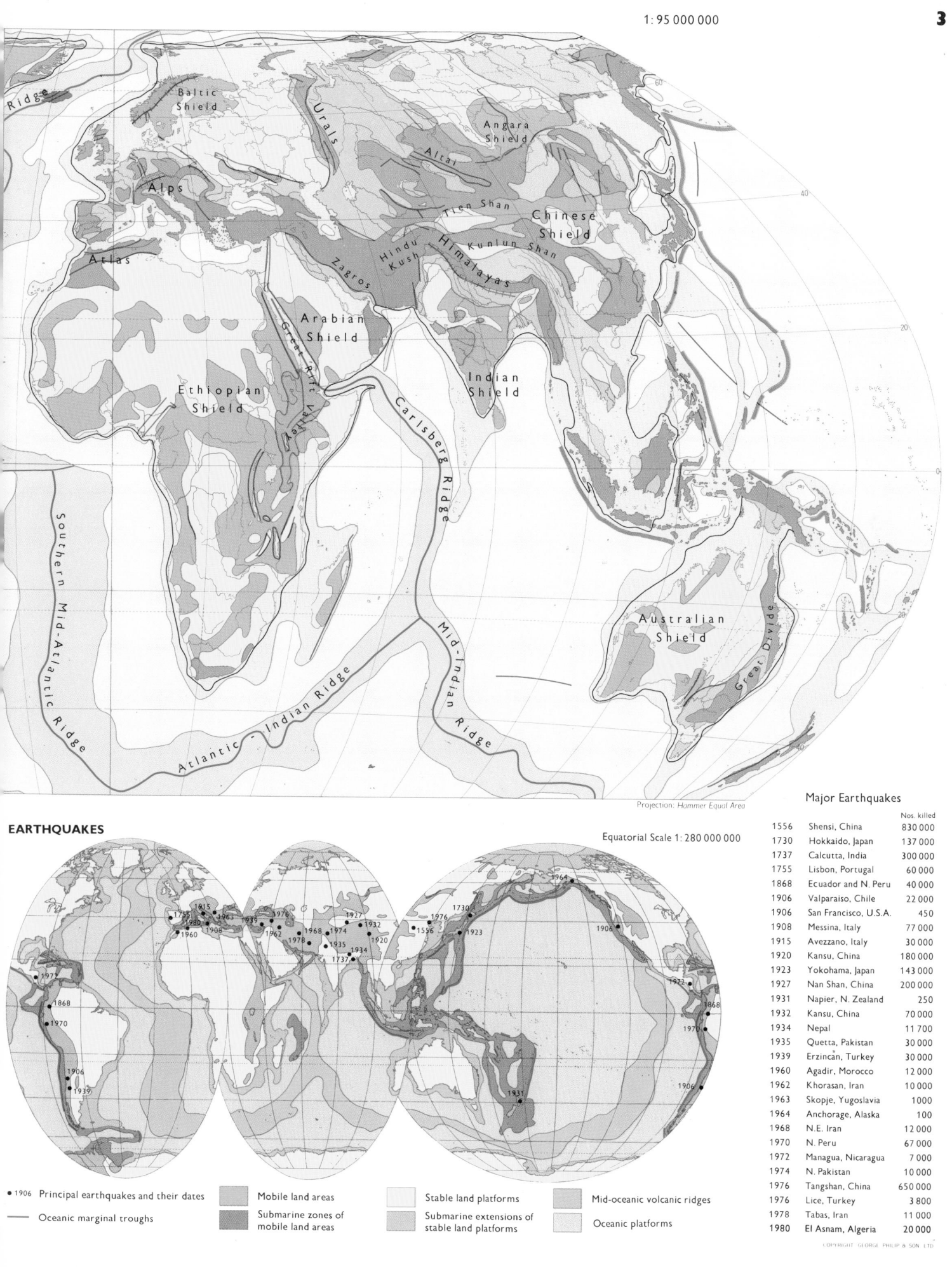

Projection: Hammer Equal Area

EARTHQUAKES

Equatorial Scale 1 : 280 000 000

Major Earthquakes

		Nos. killed
1556	Shensi, China	830 000
1730	Hokkaido, Japan	137 000
1737	Calcutta, India	300 000
1755	Lisbon, Portugal	60 000
1868	Ecuador and N. Peru	40 000
1906	Valparaiso, Chile	22 000
1906	San Francisco, U.S.A.	450
1908	Messina, Italy	77 000
1915	Avezzano, Italy	30 000
1920	Kansu, China	180 000
1923	Yokohama, Japan	143 000
1927	Nan Shan, China	200 000
1931	Napier, N. Zealand	250
1932	Kansu, China	70 000
1934	Nepal	11 700
1935	Quetta, Pakistan	30 000
1939	Erzincan, Turkey	30 000
1960	Agadir, Morocco	12 000
1962	Khorasan, Iran	10 000
1963	Skopje, Yugoslavia	1 000
1964	Anchorage, Alaska	100
1968	N.E. Iran	12 000
1970	N. Peru	67 000
1972	Managua, Nicaragua	7 000
1974	N. Pakistan	10 000
1976	Tangshan, China	650 000
1976	Lice, Turkey	3 800
1978	Tabas, Iran	11 000
1980	El Asnam, Algeria	20 000

● 1906   Principal earthquakes and their dates

——   Oceanic marginal troughs

Mobile land areas

Submarine zones of mobile land areas

Stable land platforms

Submarine extensions of stable land platforms

Mid-oceanic volcanic ridges

Oceanic platforms

Köppen's classification recognises five major climatic regions corresponding broadly to the five principal vegetation types and these are designated by the letters A, B, C, D and E. Each one of these is subdivided on the basis of temperature and rainfall.

CLIMATIC REGIONS   after Köppen
TROPICAL RAINY CLIMATES A

Af	Rain Forest Climate	All mean monthly temperatures above 18°C and an annual variation in temperature of less than 6°C.
Am	Monsoon Climate	
		All monthly temperatures above 18°C but with an annual variation in temperature of less than 12°C.
Aw	Savanna Climate	

The division of the three major A groups as far as rainfall is concerned is illustrated by the graph below:-

DRY CLIMATES B

BS	Steppe Climate
BW	Desert Climate

The principal difference between this grouping and groups A, C, D and E is the combination of a wide range of temperatures with low rainfall.

The differing criteria for separating the Steppe and Desert climates are shown by the graph below:-

WARM TEMPERATE RAINY CLIMATES C

This climatic group is separated from of the coldest month below 18°C but the warmest month is over 10°C.

Cw	Dry Winter Climate
Cs	Dry Summer Climate (Mediterranean)
Cf	Climate with no Dry Season

COLD TEMPERATE RAINY CLIMATES D

Dw	Dry Winter Climate	The mean temperature of the coldest month is below −3°C but the mean temperature of the warmest month is still over 10°C.
Df	Dry Summer Climate	

POLAR CLIMATES E

ET	Tundra Climate	The mean temperature of the warmest month is below 10°C giving permanently frozen subsoil.
EF	Polar Climate	The mean temperature of the warmest month is below 0°C giving permanent ice and snow.

group A by having the mean temperature above −3°C. The mean temperature of

The wettest month of summer has at least en times as much rain as the driest winter month.

The wettest month of winter has at least three times as much rain as the driest month of summer   The driest summer month itself has less than 30mm rainfall.

Even rainfall throughout the year.

The classification is in some cases subdivided by the addition of the following letters after the major types:-

Used with groups C and D
a Hot summer—mean temperature of the hottest month above 22°C and with more than four months of over 10°C.
b Warm summer—mean temperature of the hottest month below 22°C but still with more than four months of over 10°C.
c Cool short summer—mean temperature of the hottest month below 22°C but with less than four months of over 10°C.

Used with group D
d Cool short summer and cold winter—mean temperature of the hottest month below 22°C, and of the coldest month below −38°C.

Used with group B
h Hot dry climate—mean annual temperature above 18°C.
k Cool dry climate—mean annual temperature below 18°C.

Used with group E
H Polar climate due to elevation being over 1500m

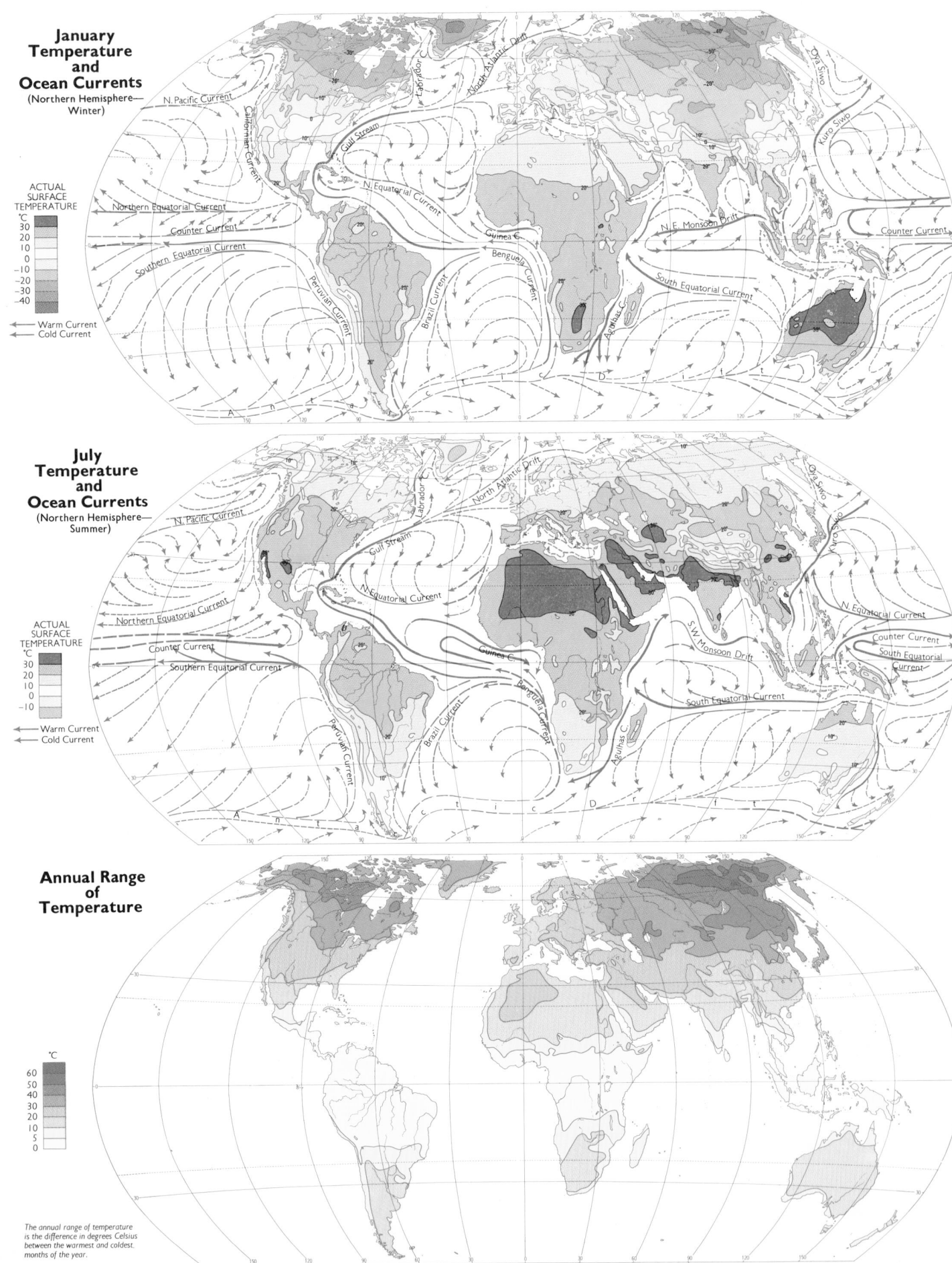

January Temperature and Ocean Currents
(Northern Hemisphere—Winter)

ACTUAL SURFACE TEMPERATURE
°C
30
20
10
0
-10
-20
-30
-40

← Warm Current
← Cold Current

July Temperature and Ocean Currents
(Northern Hemisphere—Summer)

ACTUAL SURFACE TEMPERATURE
°C
30
20
10
0
-10

← Warm Current
← Cold Current

Annual Range of Temperature

°C
60
50
40
30
20
10
5
0

The annual range of temperature is the difference in degrees Celsius between the warmest and coldest months of the year.

Projection : Hammer Equal Area

1:190 000 000

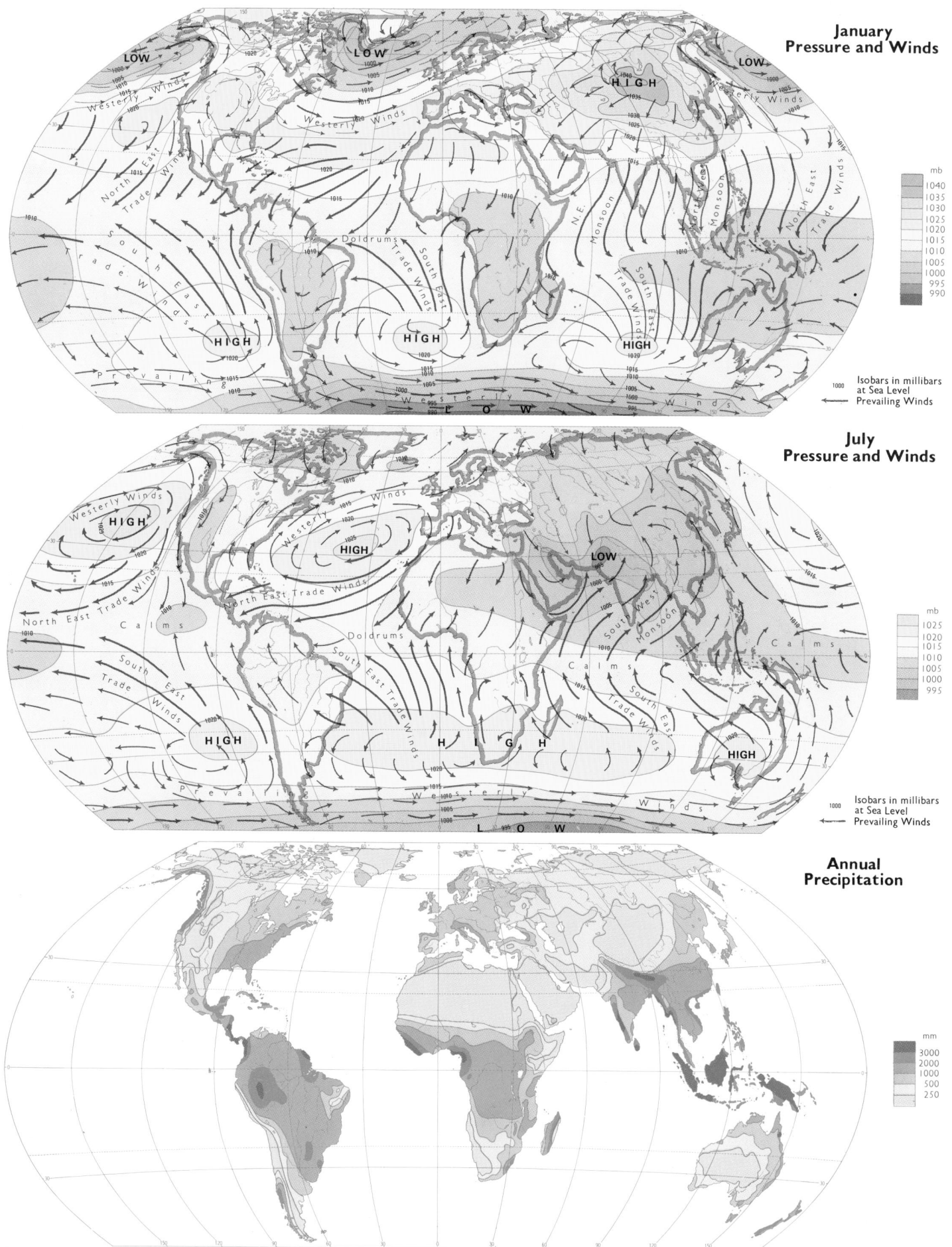

January
Pressure and Winds

	mb
	1040
	1035
	1030
	1025
	1020
	1015
	1010
	1005
	1000
	995
	990

1000 Isobars in millibars
at Sea Level
Prevailing Winds

July
Pressure and Winds

	mb
	1025
	1020
	1015
	1010
	1005
	1000
	995

1000 Isobars in millibars
at Sea Level
Prevailing Winds

Annual
Precipitation

	mm
	3000
	2000
	1000
	500
	250

Projection: *Hammer Equal Area*

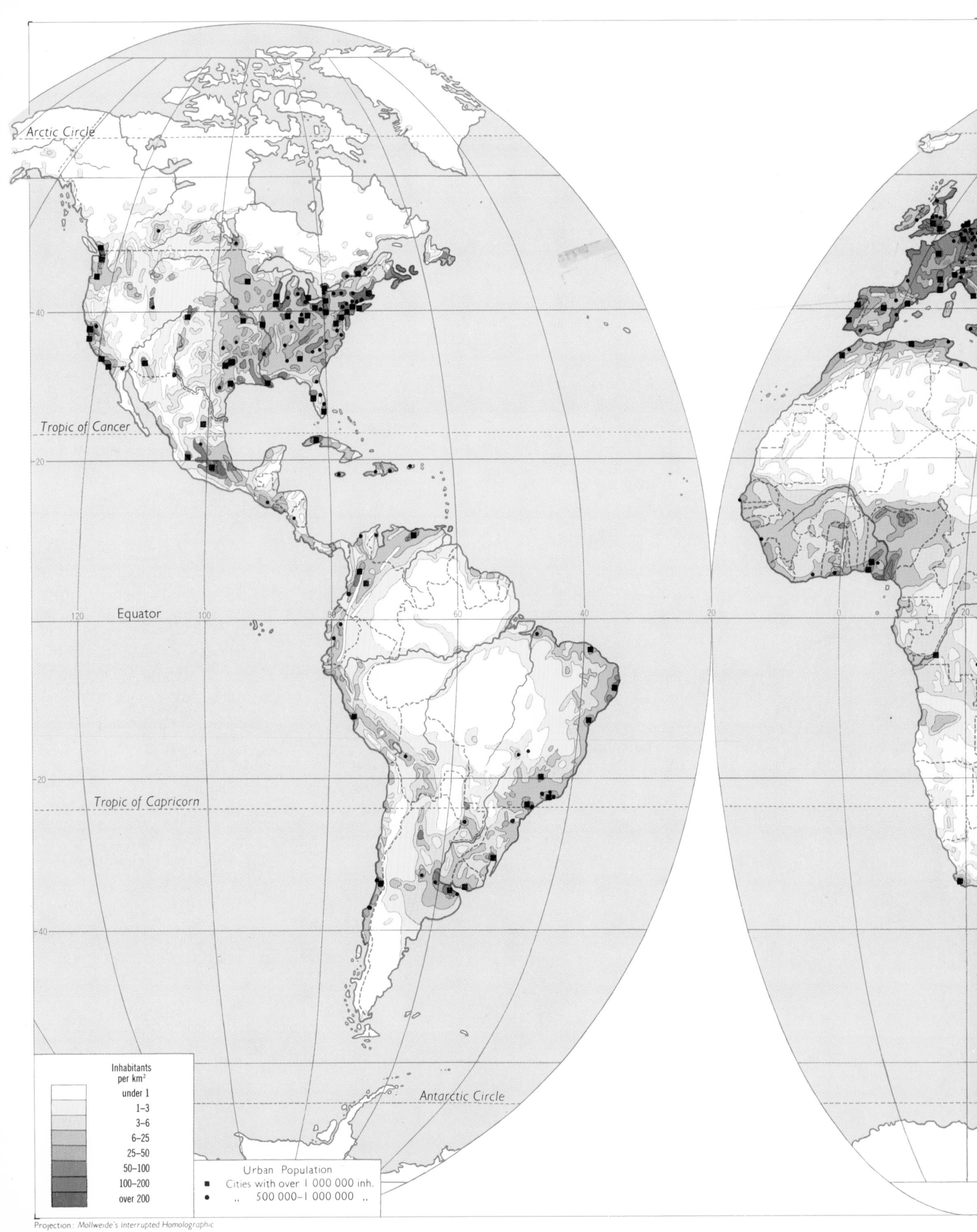

Arctic Circle

40

Tropic of Cancer

20

Equator

120   100   80   60   40   20   0   20

20

Tropic of Capricorn

40

Antarctic Circle

Inhabitants per km²	
	under 1
	1–3
	3–6
	6–25
	25–50
	50–100
	100–200
	over 200

Urban Population
■   Cities with over 1 000 000 inh.
•   ,,   500 000–1 000 000   ,,

Projection: Mollweide's interrupted Homolographic

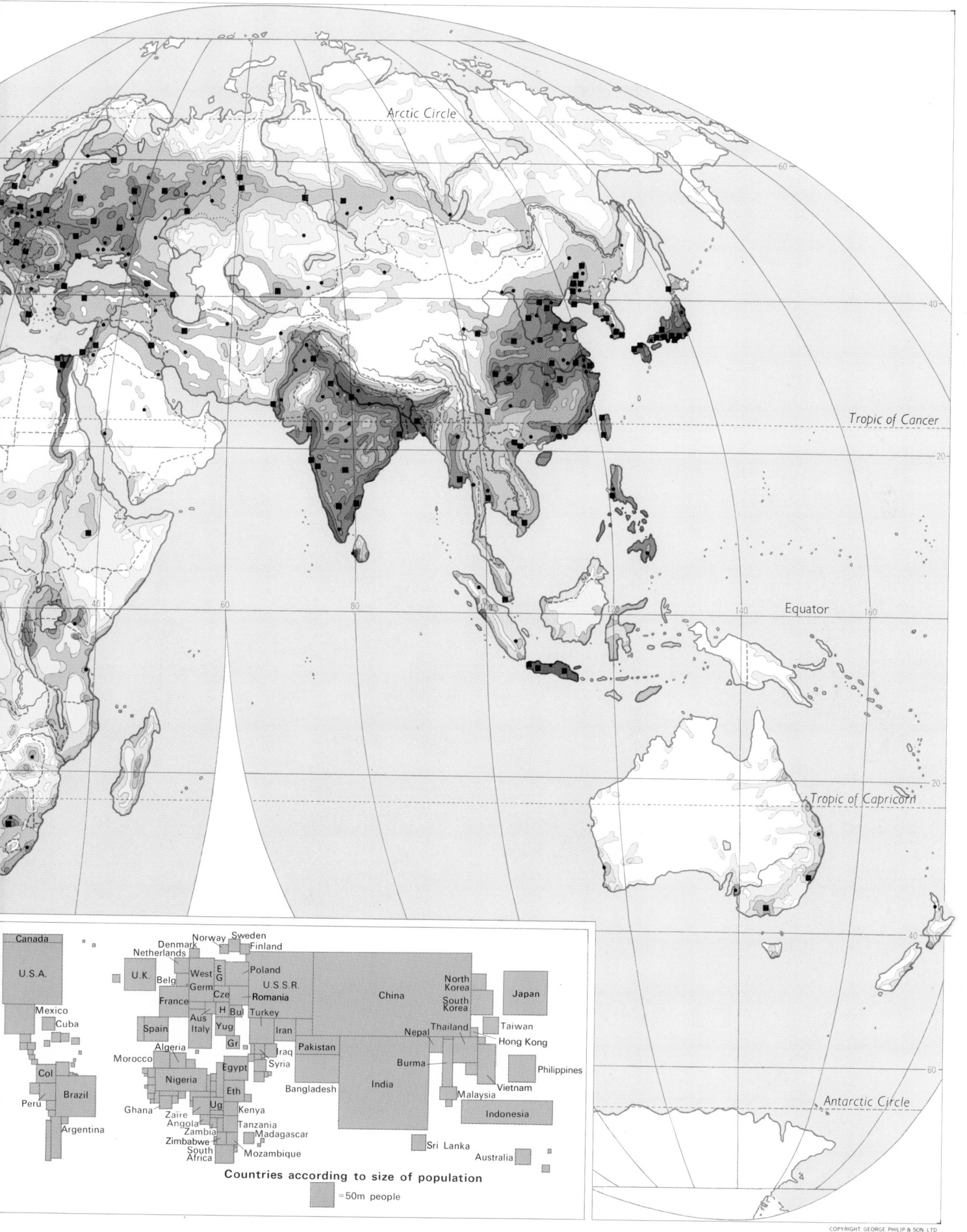

Arctic Circle

Tropic of Cancer

Equator

Tropic of Capricorn

Antarctic Circle

Canada		Denmark	Norway	Sweden		
U.S.A.		Netherlands		Finland		
	U.K.		West	E	Poland	North
	Belg		Germ	G	U.S.S.R.	Korea
Mexico		France	Cze		Romania	China
Cuba			H	Bul	Turkey	South
	Spain	Aus	Italy	Yug		Korea
		Algeria	Gr		Iran	
Morocco			Egypt	Syria	Iraq	Pakistan
Col	Nigeria		Eth			Bangladesh
Peru	Brazil	Ghana		Kenya		India
Argentina		Zaire	Ug			
		Angola	Zambia	Tanzania		
		Zimbabwe		Madagascar		
		South		Mozambique		
		Africa				

Japan

Taiwan

Nepal Thailand

Hong Kong

Burma

Vietnam

Philippines

Malaysia

Indonesia

Sri Lanka

Australia

Countries according to size of population

= 50m people

Projection: *Hammer Equal Area*

1 : 80 000 000

II

COPYRIGHT. GEORGE PHILIP & SON. LTD.

ARCTIC REGIONS

Arctic Explorers

———————	Cook 1778
- - - - - - -	Franklin 1826–47
—·—·—·—·—	McClure 1850–53
—··—··—··—	Nordenskiold ("Vega") 1878–79
—···—···—	De Long 1881
————————	Nansen ("Fram") 1893–96
++++++++++	Abruzzi & Cagni 1899–1900
·-·-·-·-·-	Sverdrup 1902
————————	Peary 1892–1906
—··—··—	Amundsen 1903–6 & 1926
————————	Peary 1908–9
—◦—◦—◦—◦—	Knud Rasmussen 1912
◦—◦—◦—◦—◦	Koch 1913
+—+—+—+	Stefánsson 1914–15
⋋—⋋—⋋—	Byrd 1926 (by air)
⋋—⋋—⋋—	Wilkins 1928 (by air)
—·—·—·—·	Lindsay 1934
—·⊣—·⊣—	Papanin (Drift of Soviet Expedition) 1937–38
···········	"Sedov" 1937–40
—×—×—×—	Knuth (Danish Pearyland Expedition) 1948–49

Projection: Zenithal Equidistant

Progress of Exploration

———————	Coasts explored before 1800
———————	" " between 1800 & 1850
———————	" " between 1850 & 1900
———————	" " since 1900
+ Byrd 1926	Highest latitudes reached by explorers with date

	Seas open all year
	Extreme limits of drift-ice
	Seas covered by pack-ice in Spring
	Seas permanently covered by pack-ice
	Ice-caps and permanent ice shelf

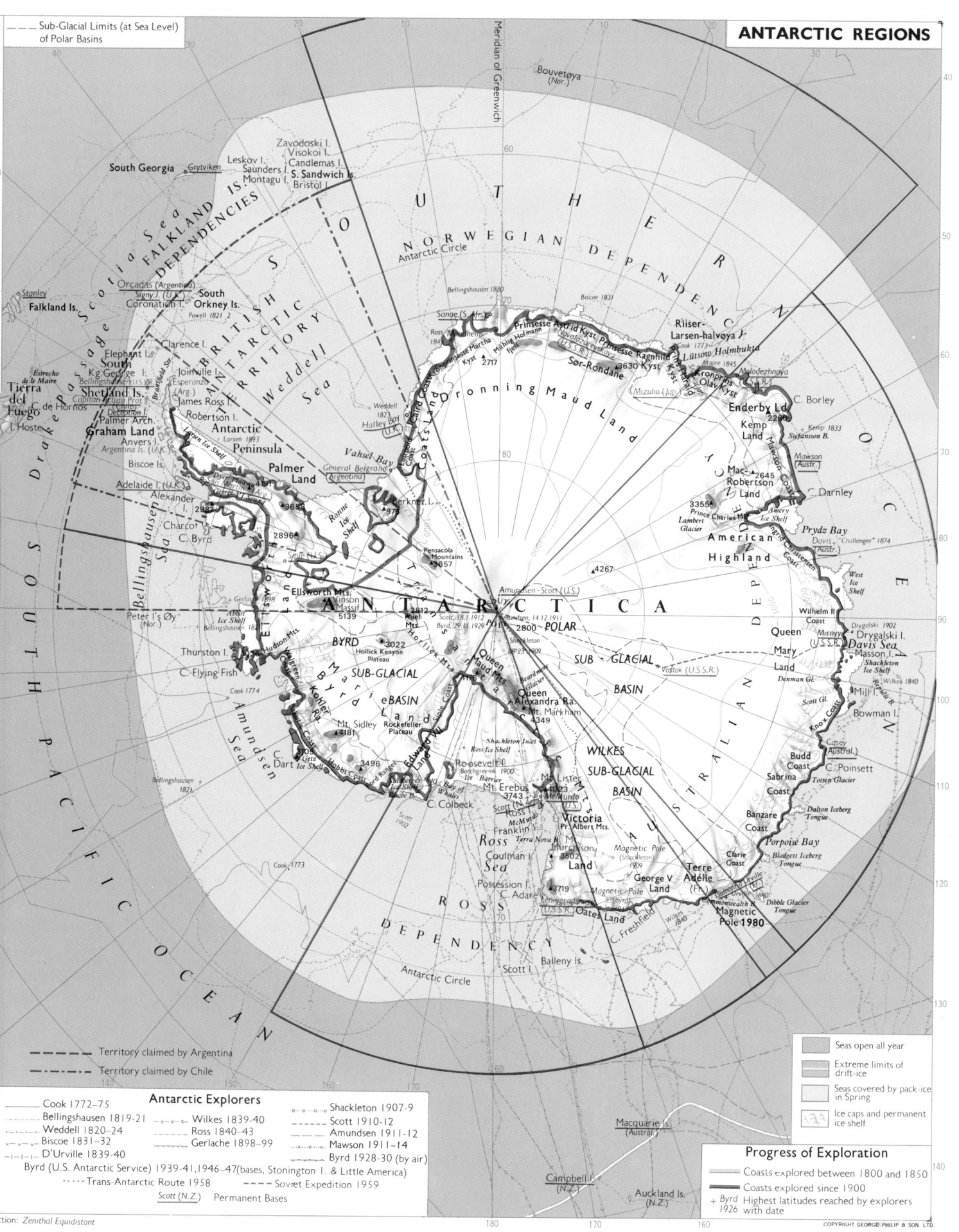

1 : 35 000 000

400   0   400   800   1200 km

Sub-Glacial Limits (at Sea Level) of Polar Basins

ANTARCTIC REGIONS

Territory claimed by Argentina

Territory claimed by Chile

Antarctic Explorers

Cook 1772–75
Bellingshausen 1819–21
Weddell 1820–24
Biscoe 1831–32
D'Urville 1839–40

Wilkes 1839–40
Ross 1840–43
Gerlache 1898–99

Shackleton 1907–9
Scott 1910–12
Amundsen 1911–12
Mawson 1911–14
Byrd 1928–30 (by air)

Byrd (U.S. Antarctic Service) 1939–41, 1946–47 (bases, Stonington I. & Little America)
Trans-Antarctic Route 1958   Soviet Expedition 1959

Scott (N.Z.)   Permanent Bases

Seas open all year

Extreme limits of drift-ice

Seas covered by pack-ice in Spring

Ice caps and permanent ice shelf

Progress of Exploration

Coasts explored between 1800 and 1850

Coasts explored since 1900

+ Byrd   Highest latitudes reached by explorers
1926   with date

Section: Zenithal Equidistant

COPYRIGHT GEORGE PHILIP & SON, LTD.

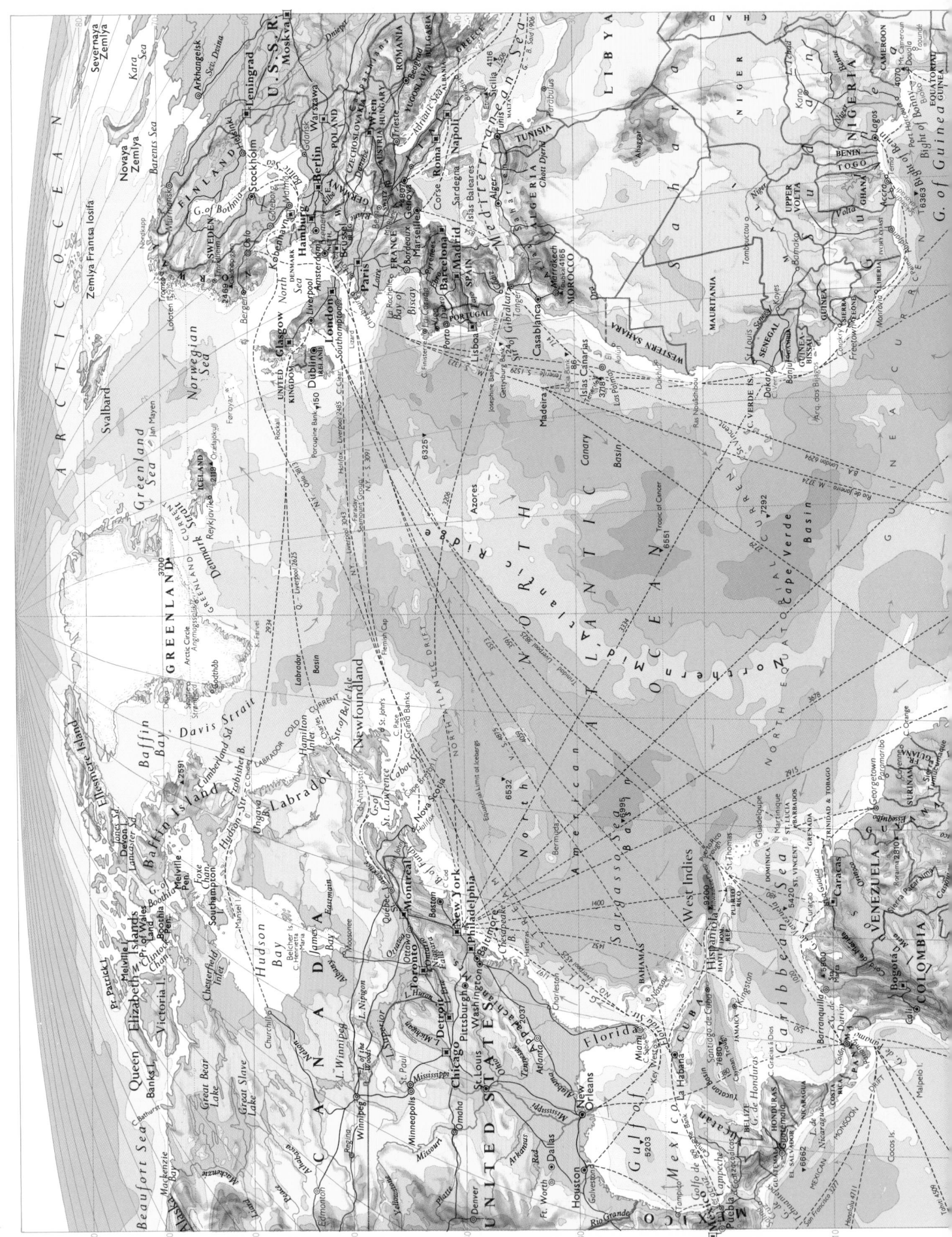

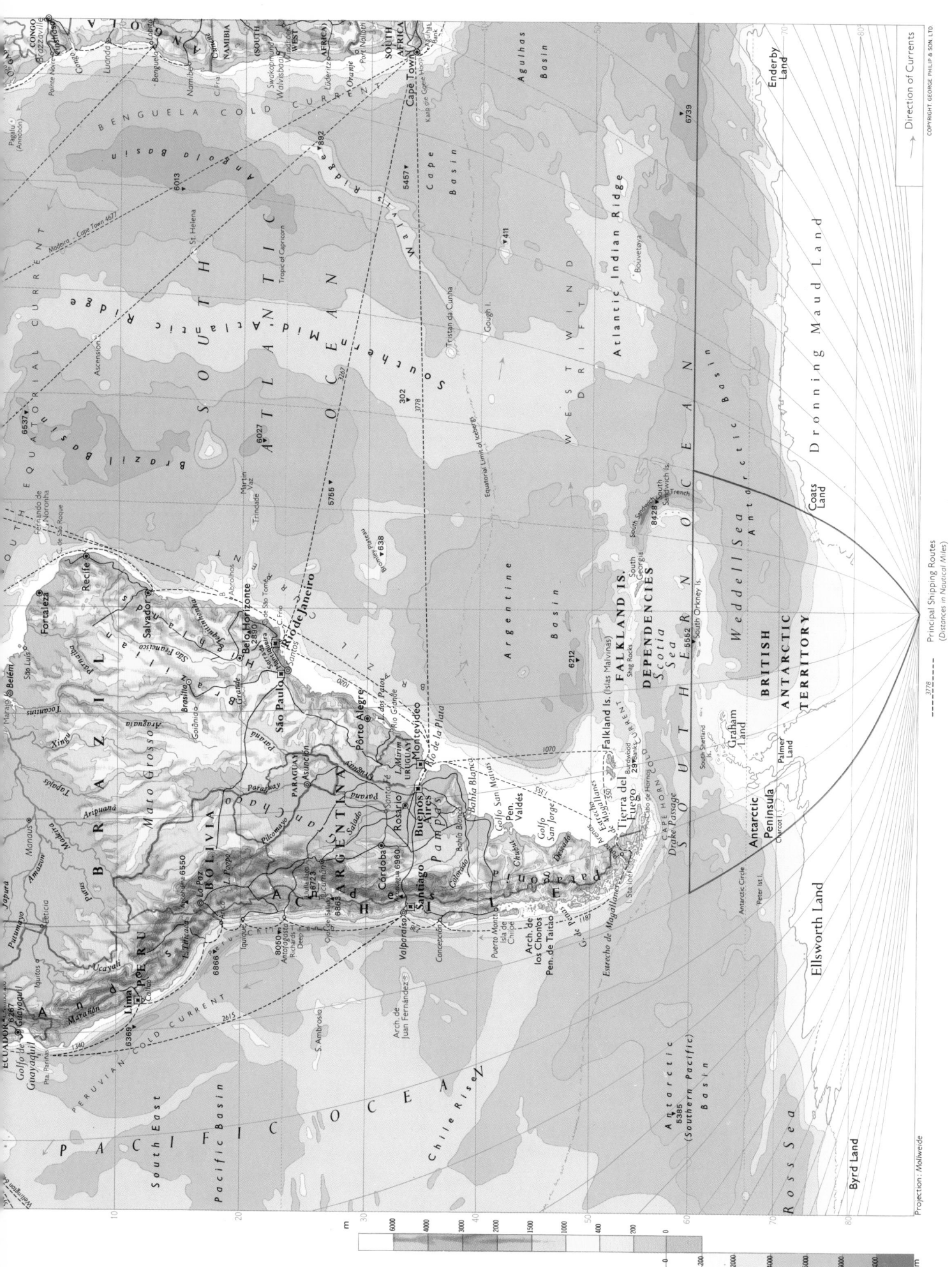

Direction of Currents

COPYRIGHT GEORGE PHILIP & SON LTD

CONGO
Brazzaville
ANGOLA
Luanda
Benguela
NAMIBIA
(SOUTH
WEST
Swakopmund
Walvisbaai
Namibe
Lüderitz
Oranje
SOUTH
AFRICA
Cape Town
Kaap die Goeie Hoop
Port Nolloth
Saldanha
Cape Agulhas

Pagalu (Annobón)

BENGUELA COLD CURRENT

Angola Basin

6013

Madeira - Cape Town 4677

St. Helena

Ascension

Walvis Ridge

Tropic of Capricorn

5457

7892

Cape
Basin

Agulhas
Basin

411

6739

Enderby
Land

Dronning Maud Land

SOUTH ATLANTIC OCEAN

Southern Atlantic Ridge

Mid-Atlantic Ridge

302

3778

Atlantic Indian Ridge

Bouvetøya

Gough I.

Tristan da Cunha

W E S T   W I N D   D R I F T

Equatorial Limit of Icebergs

SOUTH EQUATORIAL CURRENT

Brazil Basin

6537

Fernando de Noronha

Martim Vaz
Trindade

6027

5755

638

Coats
Land

Weddell Sea

Antarctic Basin

8428

South
Sandwich
Trench

South Sandwich Is.

5552

Bouvet

Argentine

Basin

6212

South
Georgia

South Orkney Is.

FALKLAND IS.
DEPENDENCIES

Scotia
Sea

FALKLAND IS.
Falkland Is. (Islas Malvinas)

Shag Rocks

South Shetland
Is.

SOUTH ERN OCEAN

BRITISH
ANTARCTIC
TERRITORY

Graham
Land
Palmer
Land

Antarctic
Peninsula

Charcot I.

Peter I øst I.

3778

Principal Shipping Routes
(Distances in Nautical Miles)

Projection: Mollweide

ECUADOR
Guayaquil
Golfo de
Guayaquil
Pta. Parina
PERU
Lima
Callao

PACIFIC OCEAN

South East

Pacific Basin

Chile Rise

Antarctic
5385
(Southern Pacific)
Basin

Ross Sea

Byrd Land

Ellsworth Land

BRAZIL
Fortaleza
Recife
Salvador
Belém
São Luís
Belo Horizonte
Rio de Janeiro
São Paulo
Santos
Brasília
Goiânia
Pôrto Alegre
Montevideo
URUGUAY
Rio de la Plata
Buenos Aires
Rosario
Córdoba
Santiago
Valparaíso
Concepción
CHILE
ARGENTINA
BOLIVIA
La Paz
PARAGUAY
Asunción
PERU
Iquitos
Antofagasta

A N D E S

Amazon
Putumayo
Iquitos
Manaus
Madeira
Tapajós
Xingu
Araguaia
Tocantins
São Francisco

Mato Grosso

Paraguay
Pilcomayo
Paraná

Pampas

Bahía Blanca

Golfo San Matías
Pen. Valdés
Golfo San Jorge

Estrecho de Magallanes

Tierra del
Fuego

CAPE HORN
Cabo de Hornos
Drake Passage

Antarctic Circle

1:20 000 000

200   0   200   400   600   800 km

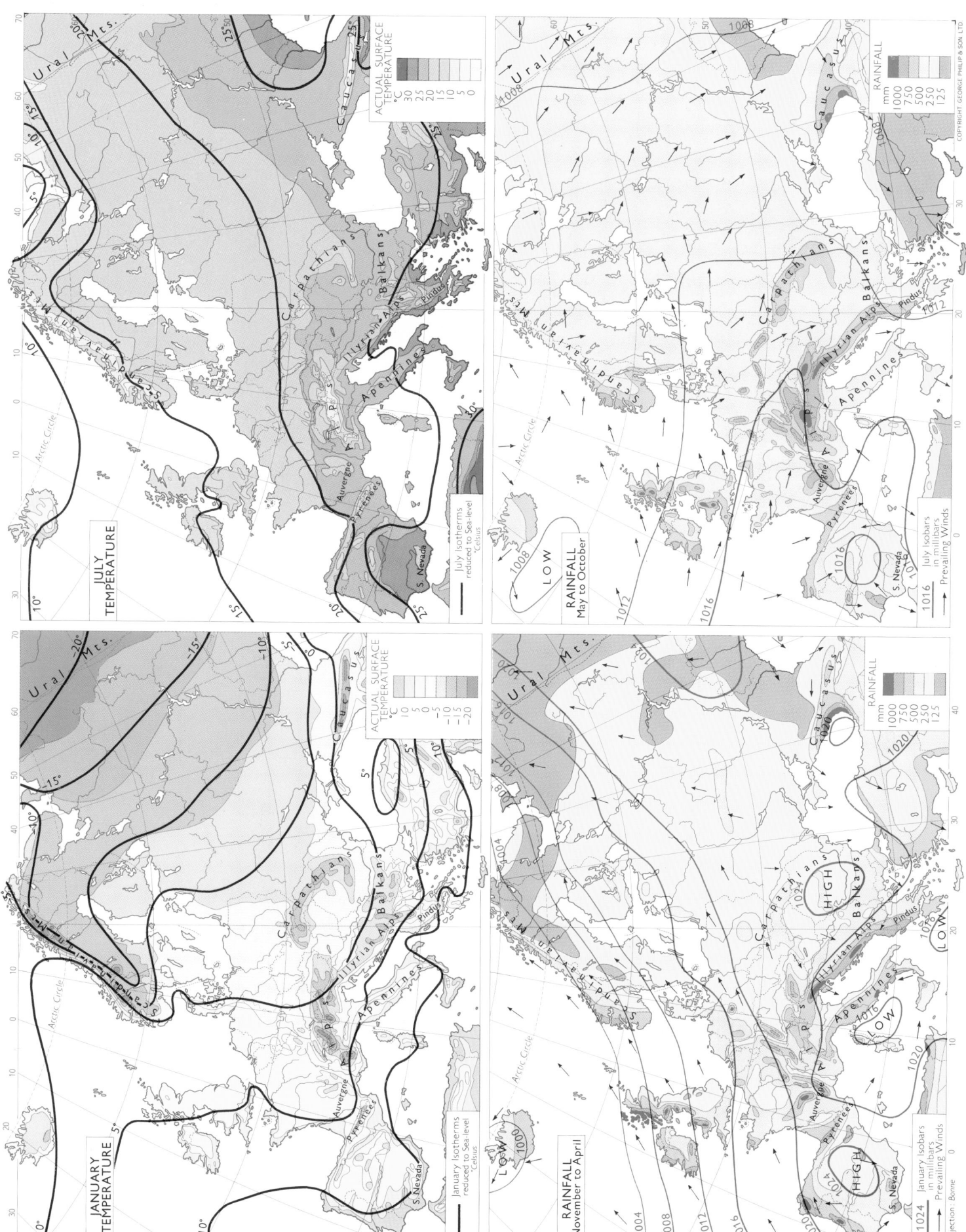

1 : 40 000 000

400   0   400   800   1200   1600 km

JULY
TEMPERATURE

——— July Isotherms
reduced to Sea-level
°Celsius

ACTUAL SURFACE
TEMPERATURE
°C
30
25
20
15
10
5
0

RAINFALL
May to October

LOW

——— July Isobars
in millibars
——→ Prevailing Winds

RAINFALL
mm
1000
750
500
250
125

JANUARY
TEMPERATURE

——— January Isotherms
reduced to Sea-level
°Celsius

ACTUAL SURFACE
TEMPERATURE
°C
10
5
0
-5
-15
-20

RAINFALL
November to April

HIGH

LOW

HIGH

——— January Isobars
in millibars
——→ Prevailing Winds

RAINFALL
mm
1000
750
500
250
125

Projection: Bonne

COPYRIGHT GEORGE PHILIP & SON LTD.

1 : 35 000 000

400   0   400   800   1200 km

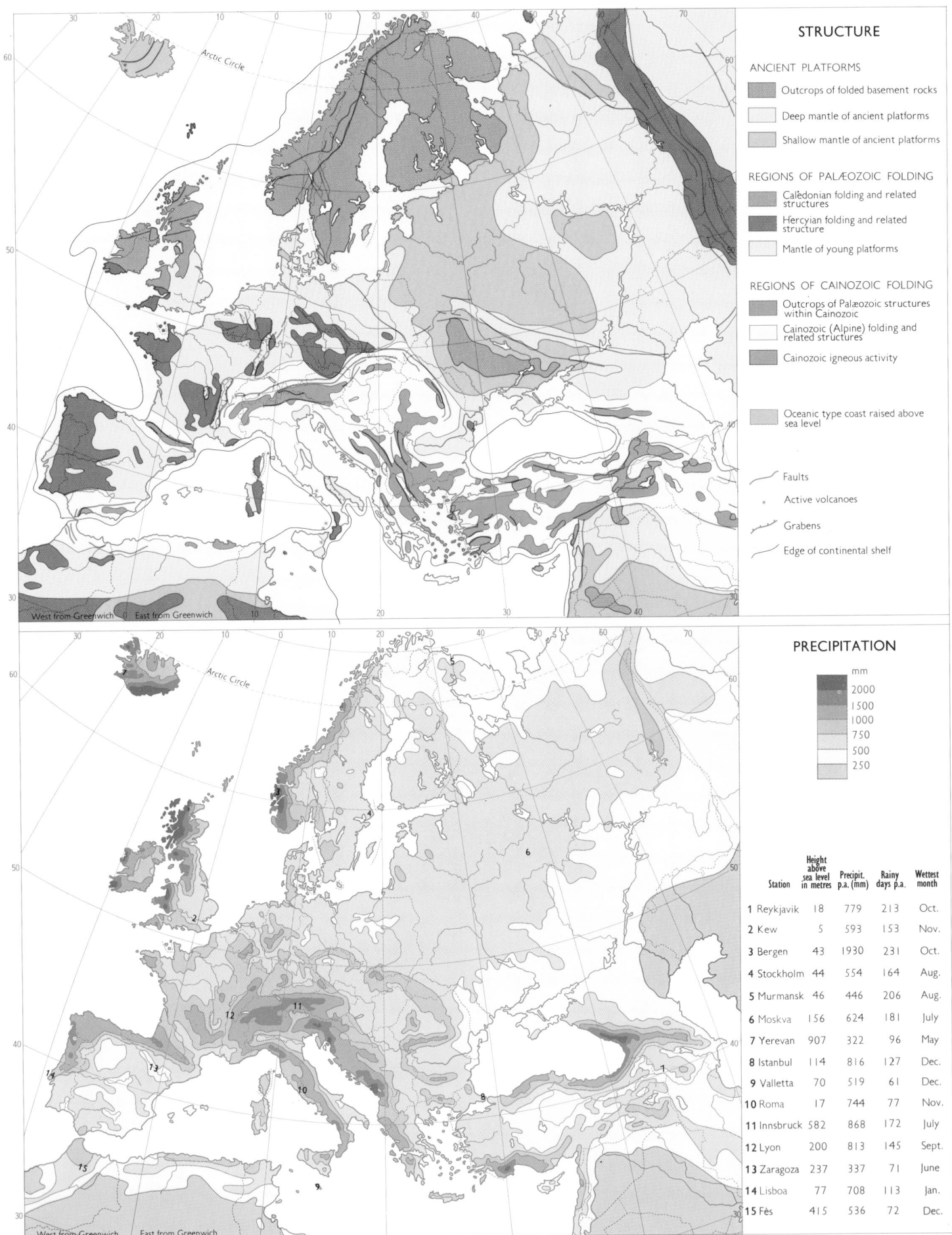

STRUCTURE

ANCIENT PLATFORMS

Outcrops of folded basement rocks

Deep mantle of ancient platforms

Shallow mantle of ancient platforms

REGIONS OF PALÆOZOIC FOLDING

Calèdonian folding and related structures

Hercyian folding and related structure

Mantle of young platforms

REGIONS OF CAINOZOIC FOLDING

Outcrops of Palæozoic structures within Cainozoic

Cainozoic (Alpine) folding and related structures

Cainozoic igneous activity

Oceanic type coast raised above sea level

Faults

* Active volcanoes

Grabens

Edge of continental shelf

West from Greenwich   East from Greenwich

PRECIPITATION

mm

2000
1500
1000
750
500
250

Station	Height above sea level in metres	Precipit. p.a. (mm)	Rainy days p.a.	Wettest month
1 Reykjavik	18	779	213	Oct.
2 Kew	5	593	153	Nov.
3 Bergen	43	1930	231	Oct.
4 Stockholm	44	554	164	Aug.
5 Murmansk	46	446	206	Aug.
6 Moskva	156	624	181	July
7 Yerevan	907	322	96	May
8 Istanbul	114	816	127	Dec.
9 Valletta	70	519	61	Dec.
10 Roma	17	744	77	Nov.
11 Innsbruck	582	868	172	July
12 Lyon	200	813	145	Sept.
13 Zaragoza	237	337	71	June
14 Lisboa	77	708	113	Jan.
15 Fès	415	536	72	Dec.

West from Greenwich   East from Greenwich

Projection: Bonne

1:6 000 000

50   100   150   200   250 km

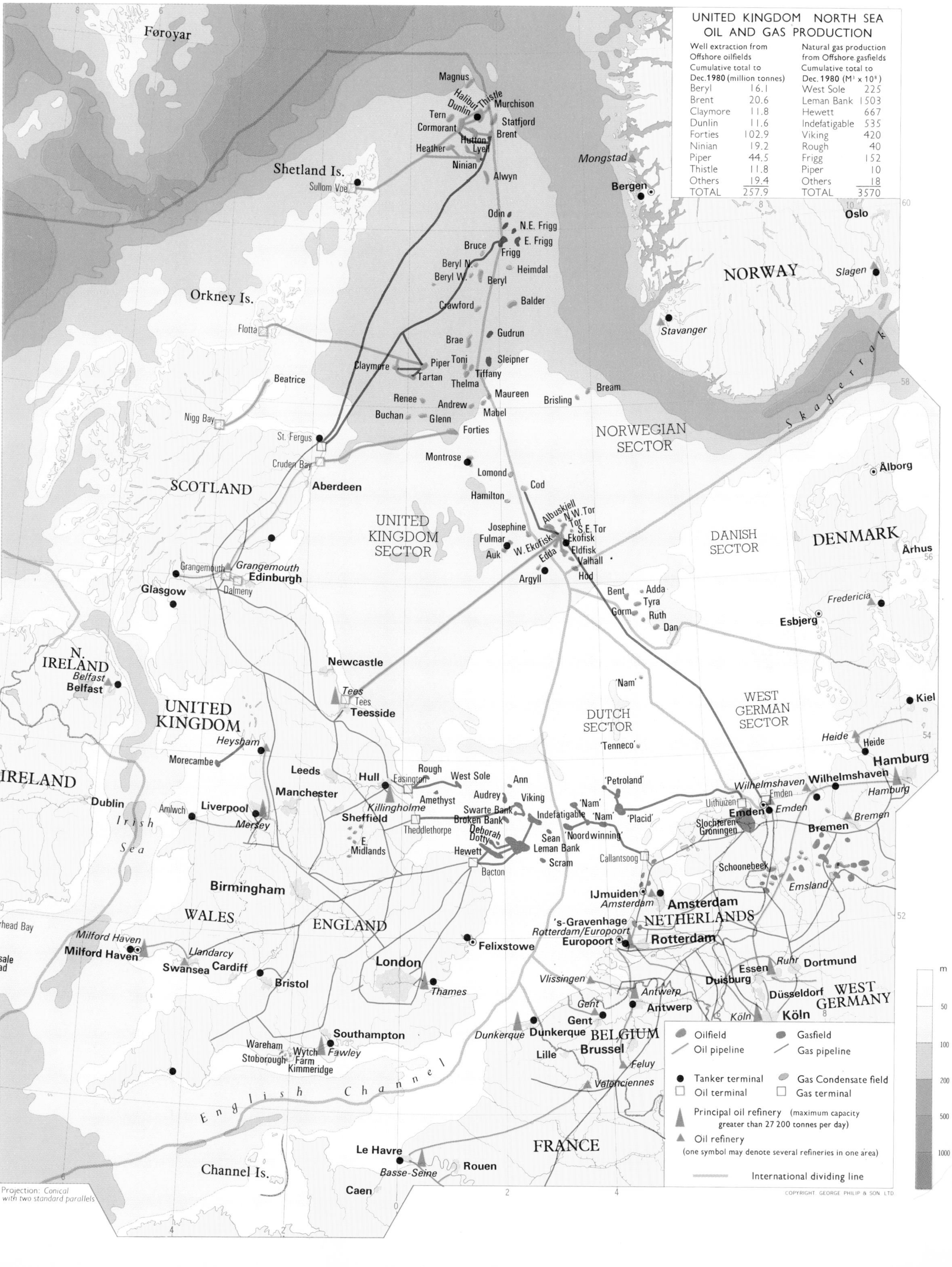

UNITED KINGDOM NORTH SEA OIL AND GAS PRODUCTION

Well extraction from Offshore oilfields Cumulative total to Dec.1980 (million tonnes)		Natural gas production from Offshore gasfields Cumulative total to Dec.1980 (M³ x 10⁸)	
Beryl	16.1	West Sole	225
Brent	20.6	Leman Bank	1503
Claymore	11.8	Hewett	667
Dunlin	11.6	Indefatigable	535
Forties	102.9	Viking	420
Ninian	19.2	Rough	40
Piper	44.5	Frigg	152
Thistle	11.8	Piper	10
Others	19.4	Others	18
TOTAL	257.9	TOTAL	3570

Legend

- ● Oilfield
- ⬮ Gasfield
- ／ Oil pipeline
- ／ Gas pipeline
- ● Tanker terminal
- ⬮ Gas Condensate field
- □ Oil terminal
- □ Gas terminal
- ▲ Principal oil refinery (maximum capacity greater than 27 200 tonnes per day)
- ▲ Oil refinery (one symbol may denote several refineries in one area)
- International dividing line

m — 50, 100, 200, 500, 1000

Projection: Conical with two standard parallels

Map labels (selected):

Føroyar, Shetland Is., Sullom Voe, Orkney Is., Flotta, Beatrice, Nigg Bay, St. Fergus, Cruden Bay, SCOTLAND, Aberdeen, Glasgow, Edinburgh, Grangemouth, Dalmeny, Newcastle, Tees, Teesside, N. IRELAND, Belfast, UNITED KINGDOM, Heysham, Morecambe, Leeds, Manchester, Liverpool, Amlwch, Mersey, IRELAND, Irish Sea, Dublin, Hull, Easington, Killingholme, Sheffield, Theddlethorpe, E. Midlands, Bacton, Birmingham, WALES, ENGLAND, Llandarcy, Swansea, Cardiff, Bristol, Milford Haven, Kinsale Head, Powerhead Bay, Southampton, Wareham, Wytch Farm, Stoborough, Fawley, Kimmeridge, Thames, London, Felixstowe, English Channel, Channel Is., Le Havre, Basse-Seine, Rouen, Caen, FRANCE, Lille, Feluy, Valenciennes, Dunkerque, BELGIUM, Brussel, Gent, Antwerp, Vlissingen, NETHERLANDS, Amsterdam, IJmuiden, 's-Gravenhage, Rotterdam/Europoort, Europoort, Callantsoog, Uithuizen, Schoonebeek, Emden, Groningen, Slochteren, Wilhelmshaven, Bremen, Emsland, Essen, Duisburg, Düsseldorf, Köln, Ruhr, Dortmund, WEST GERMANY, Hamburg, Heide, Kiel, DENMARK, Esbjerg, Fredericia, Århus, Ålborg, DANISH SECTOR, WEST GERMAN SECTOR, DUTCH SECTOR, NORWEGIAN SECTOR, UNITED KINGDOM SECTOR, NORWAY, Oslo, Bergen, Mongstad, Stavanger, Slagen, Skagerrak

Field labels (selected):

Magnus, Halibut, Thistle, Murchison, Dunlin, Tern, Cormorant, Statfjord, Brent, Heather, Hutton, Lyell, Ninian, Alwyn, Odin, N.E. Frigg, E. Frigg, Bruce, Frigg, Heimdal, Beryl N., Beryl W., Beryl, Balder, Crawford, Gudrun, Brae, Piper, Toni, Sleipner, Claymore, Tartan, Tiffany, Thelma, Maureen, Bream, Renee, Andrew, Mabel, Brisling, Buchan, Glenn, Forties, Montrose, Lomond, Cod, Hamilton, Albuskjell, N.W. Tor, Tor, S.E. Tor, Josephine, Fulmar, Ekofisk, Auk, W. Ekofisk, Edda, Eldfisk, Valhall, Argyll, Hod, Bent, Adda, Tyra, Gorm, Ruth, Dan, 'Nam', 'Tenneco', Ann, Viking, Audrey, 'Petroland', West Sole, Rough, Amethyst, Swarte Bank, Indefatigable, 'Placid', Broken Bank, Deborah, Dotty, Sean, 'Noordwinning', Hewett, Leman Bank, Scram

1:20 000 000

200   0   200   400   600   800 km

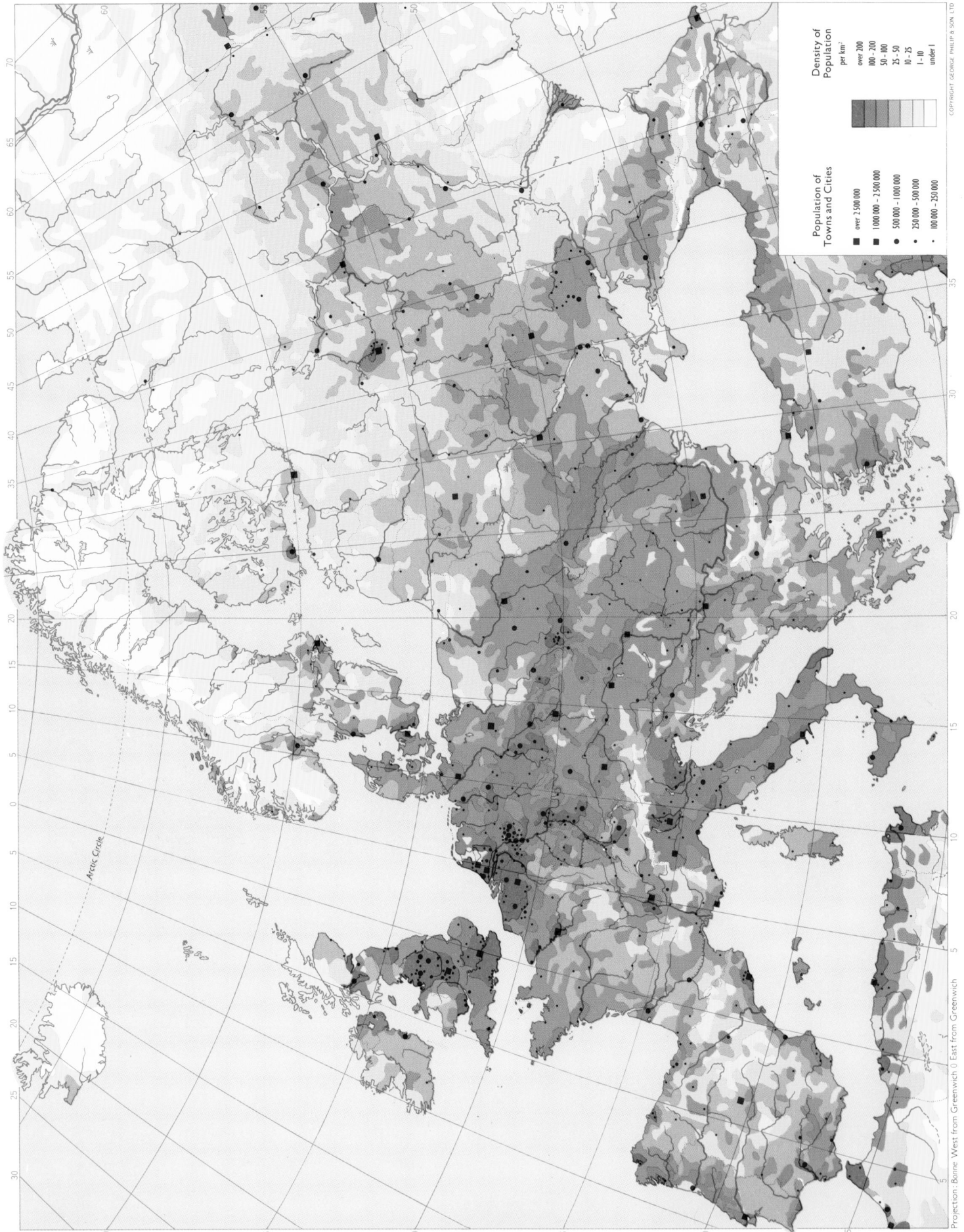

Density of
Population
per km²

over 200
100 - 200
50 - 100
25 - 50
10 - 25
1 - 10
under 1

Population of
Towns and Cities

over 2 500 000
1 000 000 - 2 500 000
500 000 - 1 000 000
250 000 - 500 000
100 000 - 250 000

Arctic Circle

Projection: Bonne West from Greenwich 0 East from Greenwich

COPYRIGHT GEORGE PHILIP & SON LTD

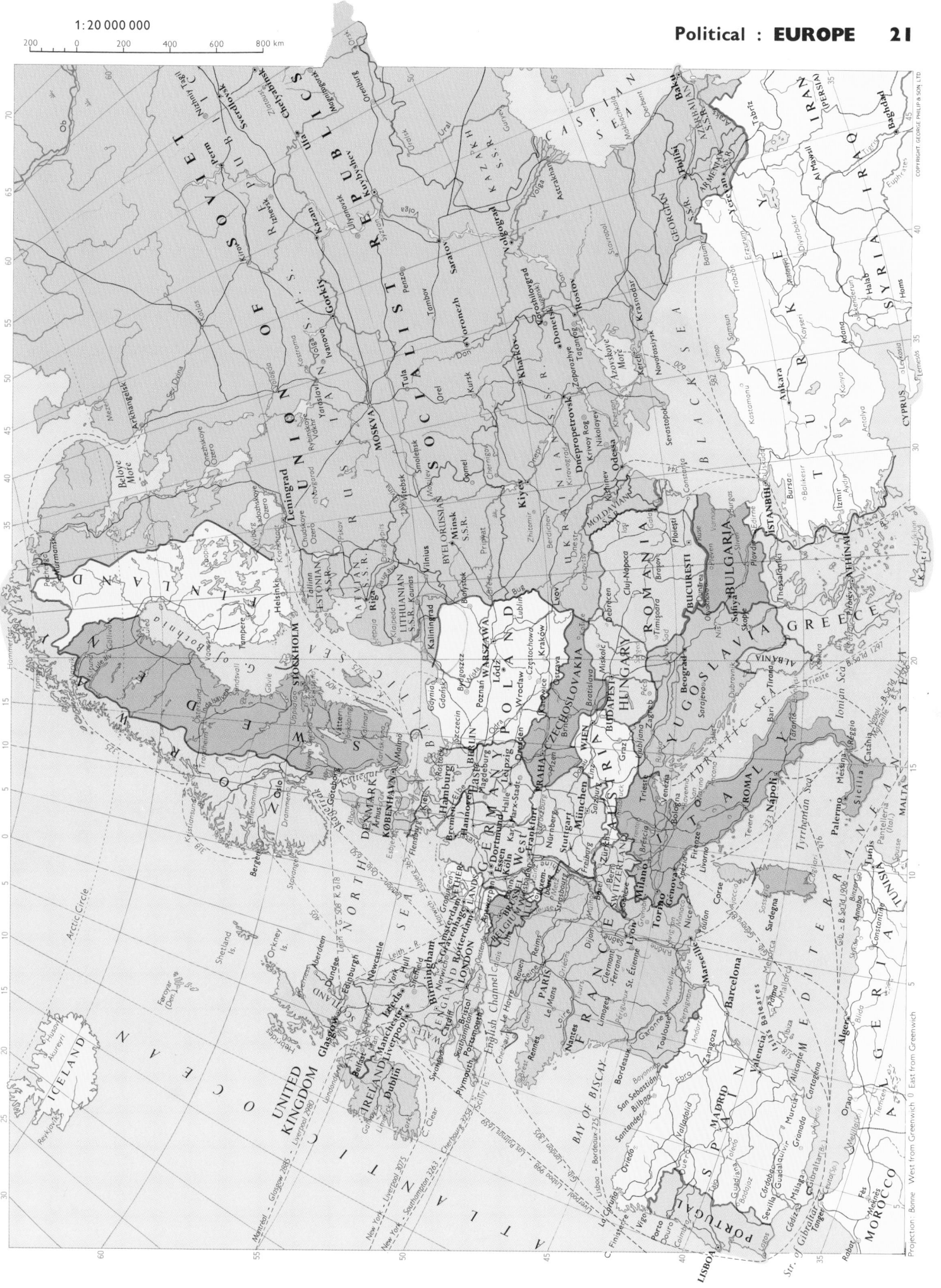

1:20 000 000

200   0   200   400   600   800 km

Projection: Bonne   West from Greenwich 0 East from Greenwich   Projection: Bonne

BRITISH ISLES : Solid Geology

1:4 000 000

50 0 50 100 150 km

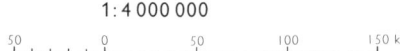

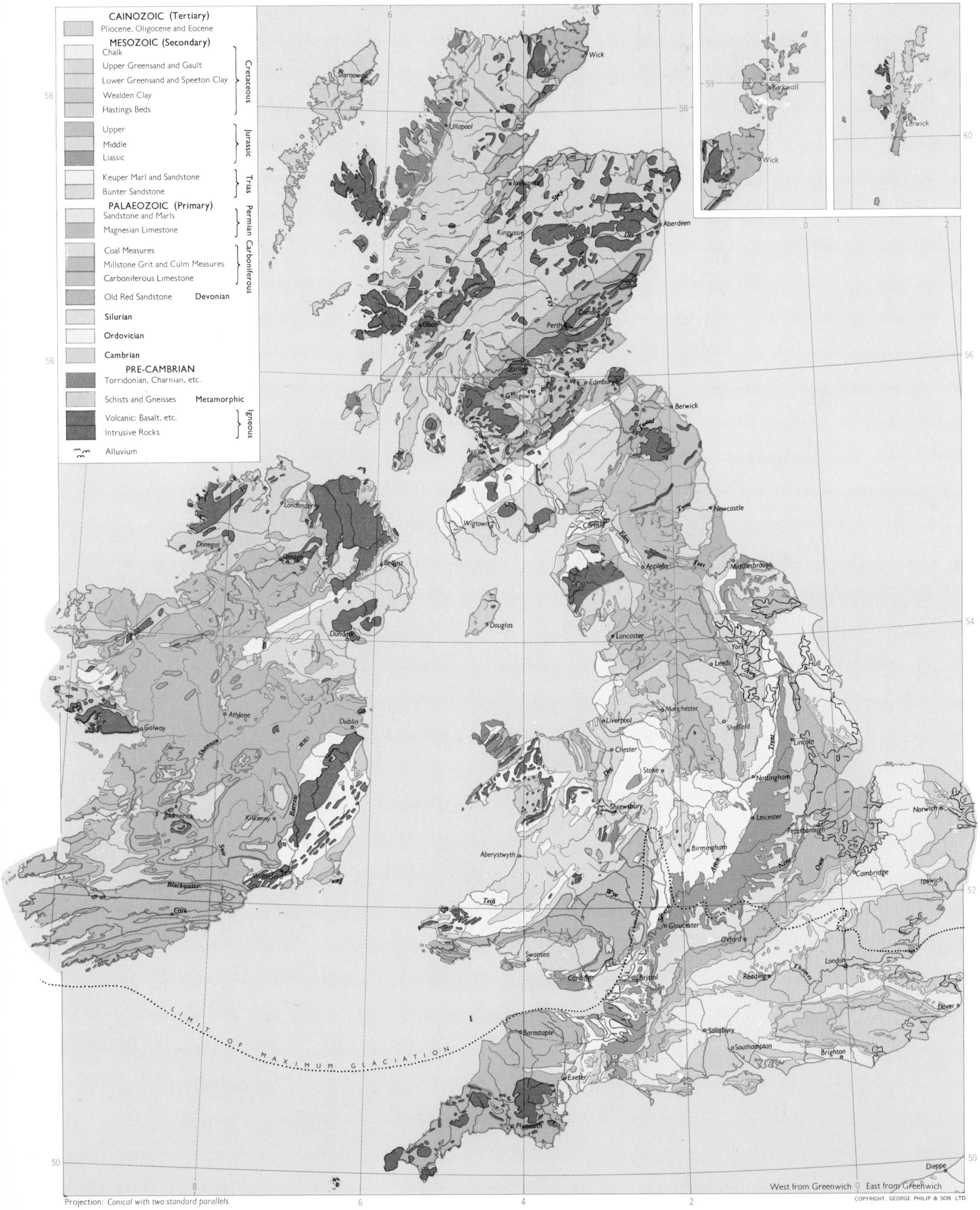
CAINOZOIC (Tertiary)
Pliocene, Oligocene and Eocene
MESOZOIC (Secondary)
Chalk
Upper Greensand and Gault
Lower Greensand and Speeton Clay
Wealden Clay
Hastings Beds
Cretaceous
Upper
Middle
Liassic
Jurassic
Keuper Marl and Sandstone
Bunter Sandstone
Trias
PALAEOZOIC (Primary)
Sandstone and Marls
Magnesian Limestone
Permian
Coal Measures
Millstone Grit and Culm Measures
Carboniferous Limestone
Carboniferous
Old Red Sandstone
Devonian
Silurian
Ordovician
Cambrian
PRE-CAMBRIAN
Torridonian, Charnian, etc.
Schists and Gneisses
Metamorphic
Volcanic: Basalt, etc.
Intrusive Rocks
Igneous
Alluvium
Wick
Stornoway
Ullapool
Kirkwall
Lerwick
Inverness
Spey
Aberdeen
Kingussie
Dee
Tay
Dundee
Perth
Oban
Stirling
Edinburgh
Glasgow
Berwick
Tweed
Ayr
Londonderry
Donegal
Omagh
Belfast
Wigtown
Carlisle
Eden
Tyne
Newcastle
Appleby
Tees
Middlesbrough
Dundalk
Douglas
Lancaster
York
Leeds
Aire
Hull
Galway
Athlone
Dublin
Shannon
Manchester
Liverpool
Sheffield
Trent
Lincoln
Chester
Stoke
Dee
Nottingham
Limerick
Kilkenny
Barrow
Shrewsbury
Leicester
Norwich
Peterborough
Aberystwyth
Birmingham
Suir
Waterford
Avon
Nene
Ouse
Cambridge
Ipswich
Blackwater
Cork
Teifi
Wye
Severn
Gloucester
Oxford
Swansea
London
Thames
Cardiff
Bristol
Reading
Dover
LIMIT OF MAXIMUM GLACIATION
Barnstaple
Salisbury
Southampton
Brighton
Exeter
Plymouth
Dieppe
West from Greenwich
East from Greenwich

Projection: *Conical with two standard parallels*

1 : 4 000 000

50   0   50   100   150 km

ATLANTIC

OCEAN

NORTH

SEA

Dogger
Bank

IRISH SEA

CELTIC

SEA

ENGLISH CHANNEL

St. George's Channel

West from Greenwich 0 East from Greenwich

Projection: Conical with two standard parallels

COPYRIGHT GEORGE PHILIP & SON LTD.

m
1000
400
200
100
0
50
100
200
m

1 : 4 000 000

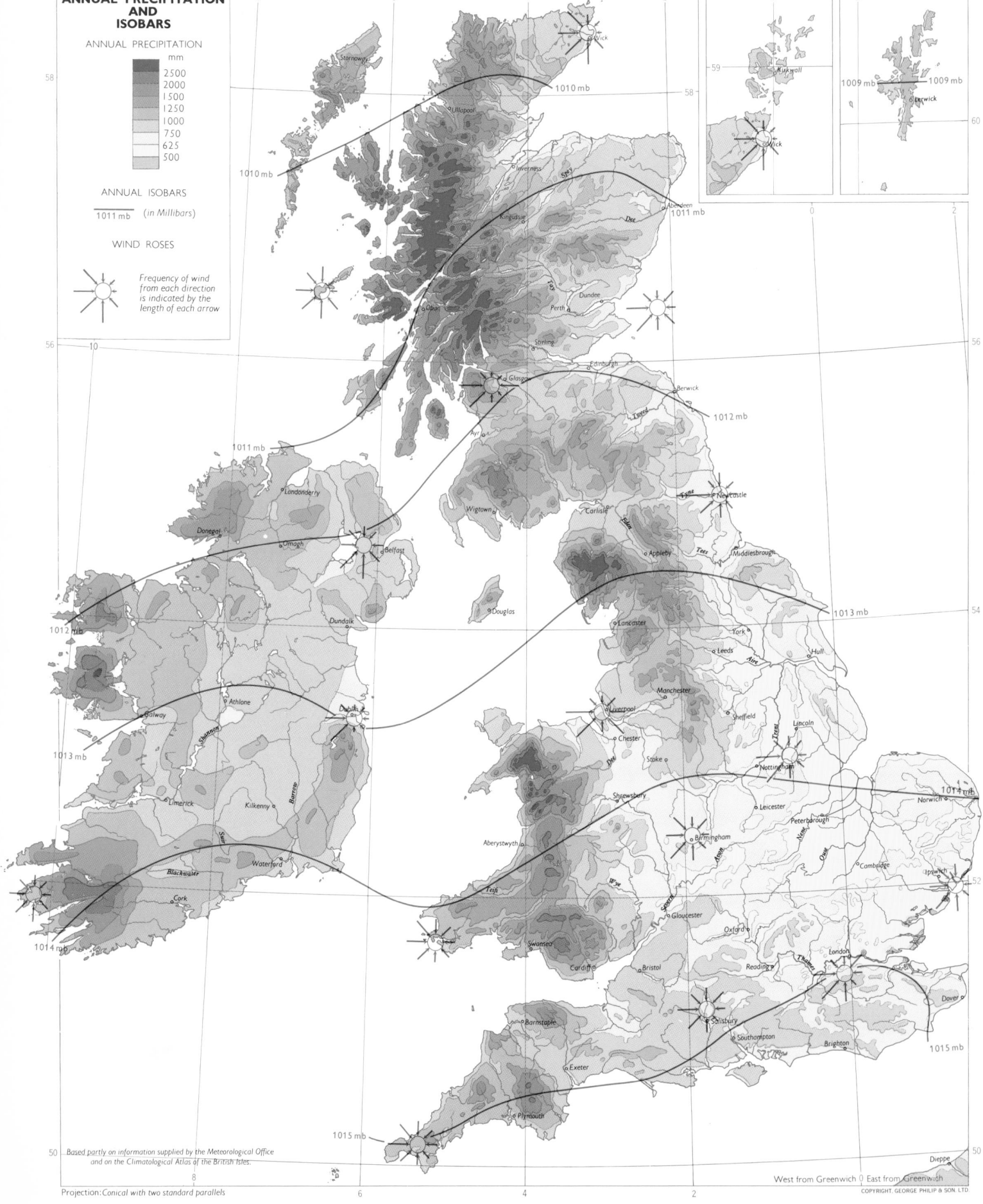

ANNUAL PRECIPITATION
AND
ISOBARS

ANNUAL PRECIPITATION
mm
2500
2000
1500
1250
1000
750
625
500

ANNUAL ISOBARS

1011 mb (in Millibars)

WIND ROSES

Frequency of wind
from each direction
is indicated by the
length of each arrow

Based partly on information supplied by the Meteorological Office
and on the Climatological Atlas of the British Isles.

Projection: Conical with two standard parallels

West from Greenwich 0 East from Greenwich

COPYRIGHT. GEORGE PHILIP & SON. LTD.

1:8 500 000

50 0 50 100 150 200 250 300 km

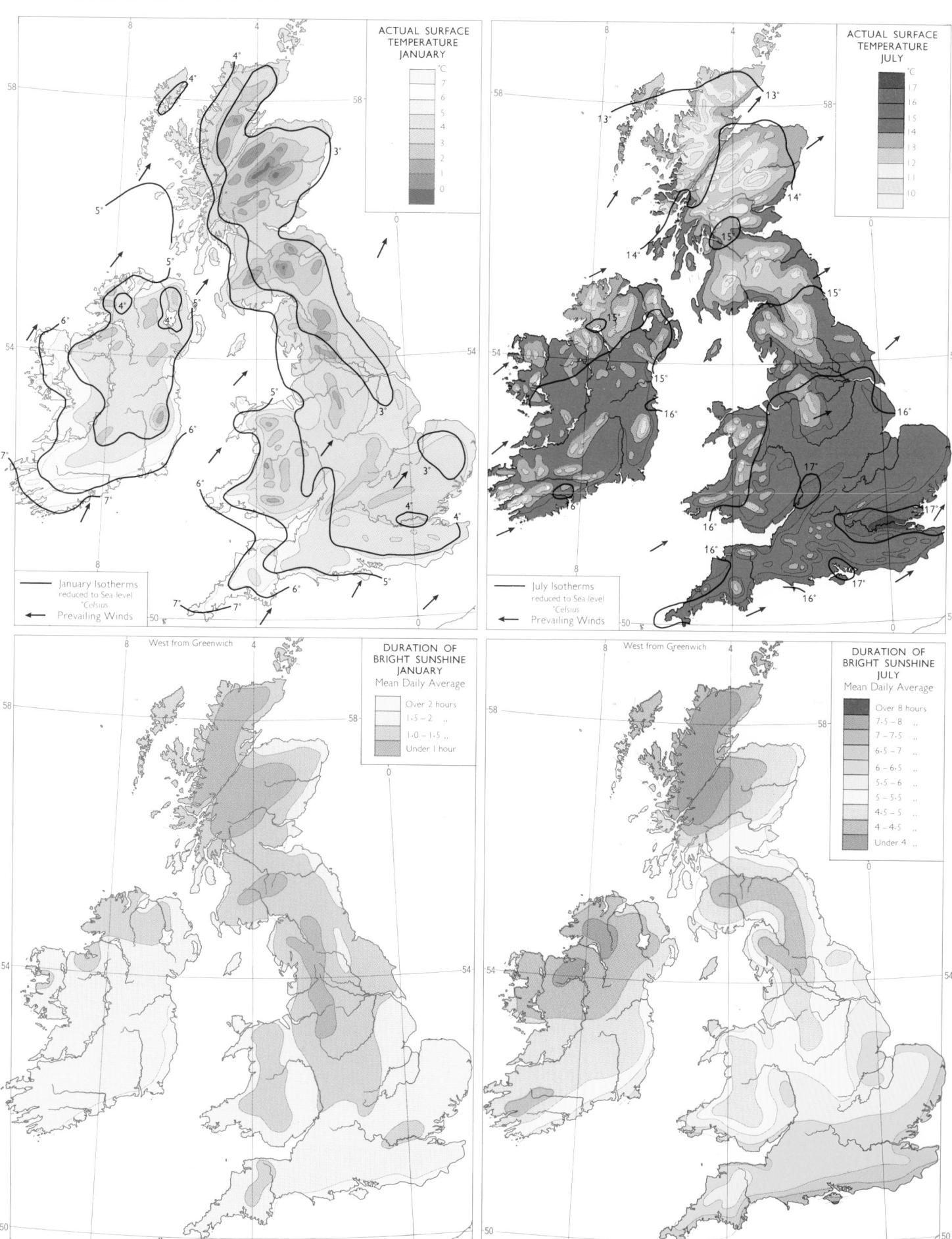

ACTUAL SURFACE
TEMPERATURE
JANUARY
°C
7
6
5
4
3
2
1
0

—— January Isotherms
reduced to Sea-level
°Celsius
←— Prevailing Winds

ACTUAL SURFACE
TEMPERATURE
JULY
°C
17
16
15
14
13
12
11
10

—— July Isotherms
reduced to Sea-level
°Celsius
←— Prevailing Winds

West from Greenwich

DURATION OF
BRIGHT SUNSHINE
JANUARY
Mean Daily Average

Over 2 hours
1·5 – 2 ,,
1·0 – 1·5 ,,
Under 1 hour

West from Greenwich

DURATION OF
BRIGHT SUNSHINE
JULY
Mean Daily Average

Over 8 hours
7·5 – 8 ,,
7 – 7·5 ,,
6·5 – 7 ,,
6 – 6·5 ,,
5·5 – 6 ,,
5 – 5·5 ,,
4·5 – 5 ,,
4 – 4·5 ,,
Under 4 ,,

Projection: Conical with two standard parallels

COPYRIGHT GEORGE PHILIP & SON LTD

1 : 4 000 000

50   100   150 km

SCOTLAND

SUTHERLAND
CAITHNESS
Thurso
Wick
Pentland Firth
Lewis
Stornoway
Harris
North Minch
Ullapool
Lairg
Golspie
ROSS AND CROMARTY
Invergordon
Dingwall
Elgin
Lossiemouth
MORAY
Fraserburgh
Banff
Peterhead
NAIRN
Inverness
BANFF
ABERDEEN
North Uist
Benbecula
South Uist
Barra
Portree
Skye
Kyle
Lochalsh
Rhum
Mallaig
Eigg
Kingussie
Ballater
Balmoral
Stonehaven
Aberdeen
KINCARDINE
INVERNESS
Fort William
Coll
Tiree
Staffa
Iona
Mull
Oban
Ballachulish
Blair Atholl
ANGUS
Forfar
Montrose
Arbroath
PERTH
Crieff
Dundee
ARGYLL
Colonsay
Islay
Campbeltown
Lochgilphead
Perth
Kinross
FIFE
St. Andrews
Cupar
CL.-Clackmannan
KIN.-Kinross
W. Loth.-West Lothian
Leven
Kirkcaldy
STIRLING
Stirling
Dunfermline
Forth
Dunbar
Falkirk
Helensburgh
Greenock
Dumbarton
Edinburgh
Paisley
Glasgow
Motherwell
Hamilton
Berwick-on-Tweed
BERWICK
Duns
Kilmarnock
Saltcoats
Irvine
Prestwick
LANARK
Peebles
Salashiels
SELKIRK
ROXBURGH
Jedburgh
Hawick
Alnwick
Ayr
Sanquhar
AYR
DUMFRIES
Dumfries
NORTHUMBERLAND
WIGTOWN
KIRKCUDBRIGHT
Stranraer
Kirkcudbright
Solway Firth
Carlisle
Newcastle
Tynemouth
South Shields
Gateshead
Sunderland
Mull of Galloway
Whitehaven
CUMBERLAND
Appleby
DURHAM
Durham
Hartlepool
Stockton
TEESSIDE
Middlesbrough
Darlington
Whitby
St. Bee's Hd.
WESTMORLAND
Kendal
Windermere
NORTH RIDING
Northallerton
Scarborough
ISLE OF MAN
Douglas
Barrow
Lancaster
YORKSHIRE
Ripon
York
Flamborough Hd.
Morecambe Bay
EAST RIDING
Beverley
Hull
WEST RIDING
Keighley
Leeds
Bradford
Blackpool
LANCASHIRE
Preston
Burnley
Halifax
Wakefield
Huddersfield
Barnsley
Grimsby
Spurn Hd.
Blackburn
Bolton
Oldham
Doncaster
LINDSEY
Liverpool
St. Helens
Salford
Manchester
Rotherham
Sheffield
Birkenhead
Stockport
Macclesfield
Chesterfield
Lincoln
LINCOLN
Chester
DERBY
Matlock
Mansfield
FLINT
CHESHIRE
Crewe
Stoke-on-Trent
NOTTS
Nottingham
Derby
KESTEVEN
Grantham
Boston
HOLLAND
The Wash
Denbigh
Wrexham
DENBIGH
Caernarvon
Bangor
ANGLESEY
Holyhead
Caernarvon Bay
CAERNARVON
MERIONETH
Dolgelley
MONTGOMERY
Welshpool
Shrewsbury
STAFFORD
Stafford
Wolverhampton
Walsall
LEICESTER
Leicester
Oakham
RUTLAND
Kings Lynn
NORFOLK
Norwich
Gt. Yarmouth
Lowestoft
SHROPSHIRE
Montgomery
Birmingham
Kidderminster
WARWICK
Coventry
Rugby
Leamington
Peterborough
HUNTS
NORTHAMPTON
Northampton
SOKE OF PETERBOROUGH
CAMBRIDGE
CAMBS
SUFFOLK
EAST
WEST
Ipswich
RADNOR
Presteigne
Llandrindod Wells
WORCESTER
Worcester
HEREFORD
Hereford
Stratford-on-Avon
Bedford
BEDFORD
ISLE OF ELY
Cambridge
Bury St. Edmunds
Colchester
Harwich
The Naze
CARDIGAN
Aberystwyth
Cardigan
Cardigan Bay
BRECKNOCK
Brecon
GLOUCESTER
Gloucester
Cheltenham
OXFORD
Oxford
BUCKS
Aylesbury
Luton
HERTFORD
St. Albans
Watford
Hertford
Chelmsford
ESSEX
PEMBROKE
Fishguard
St. David's
Milford Haven
Haverfordwest
CARMARTHEN
MONMOUTH
Monmouth
Newport
MERTHYR TYDFIL
RHONDDA
GLAMORGAN
Llanelli
Swansea
Port Talbot
Cardiff
Bristol
Bath
Swindon
BERKS
Reading
Windsor
Slough
LONDON
Kingston
SURREY
Reigate
Guildford
Aldershot
KENT
Maidstone
Ashford
Chatham
Gillingham
Margate
Canterbury
Dover
Folkestone
Southend
WILTS
Trowbridge
Weston-super-Mare
Bristol Channel
Ilfracombe
Lundy
SOMERSET
Wells
Taunton
Yeovil
Salisbury
Winchester
HANTS
Southampton
Chichester
WEST
SUSSEX
EAST
Lewes
Hastings
Eastbourne
Brighton
Worthing
Newhaven
Barnstaple
Hartland Point
Bude
DEVON
DORSET
Dorchester
Poole
Bournemouth
Weymouth
Isle of Wight
Newport
Portsmouth
Axminster
CORNWALL
Devonport
Plymouth
St. Austell
Camborne
Penzance
Falmouth
Torquay
Start Pt.
Exeter
Land's End
Isles of Scilly
Lizard
Thurso (inset)
Westray
N. Ronaldsay
Sanday
Orkney Is.
ORKNEY
Mainland
Stronsay
Hoy
Kirkwall
South Ronaldsay
CAITHNESS
Wick
Shetland Is.
Unst
Yell
Mainland
ZETLAND
Foula
Lerwick
Fair I.

ATLANTIC
OCEAN

NORTH
SEA

IRISH SEA

St. George's Channel

ENGLISH CHANNEL
Dieppe

IRELAND

NORTHERN IRELAND
ULSTER
DONEGAL
Letterkenny
Donegal
Donegal Bay
Londonderry
LONDONDERRY
ANTRIM
Coleraine
Portrush
Ballymena
Larne
Lifford
TYRONE
Omagh
FERMANAGH
Enniskillen
Sligo
SLIGO
LEITRIM
Ballina
Killala Bay
MAYO
Castlebar
Westport
Achill
Clare
MONAGHAN
Monaghan
ARMAGH
Armagh
Newry
DOWN
Downpatrick
Dundrum
Belfast
Lisburn
Bangor
L. Neagh
CAVAN
Cavan
Clones
LONGFORD
Longford
ROSCOMMON
Roscommon
CONNACHT
Connemara
Corrib
GALWAY
Galway
Athenry
Galway Bay
MEATH
WESTMEATH
Mullingar
Athlone
Tullamore
OFFALY
Birr
LEINSTER
DUBLIN
Dublin (Baile Átha Cliath)
Dún Laoghaire
Bray
Drogheda
Dundalk
LOUTH
KILDARE
Naas
LAOIS
Port Laoise
CLARE
Ennis
TIPPERARY
Nenagh
Thurles
KILKENNY
Kilkenny
CARLOW
Carlow
WICKLOW
Wicklow
Arklow
WEXFORD
Wexford
Enniscorthy
New Ross
Rosslare
Carnsore Pt.
LIMERICK
Limerick
Tipperary
Clonmel
Carrick
WATERFORD
Waterford
Dungarvan
Youghal
MUNSTER
KERRY
Tralee
Killarney
CORK
Cork
Cobh
Cork Harbour
Mallow
Fermoy
Blarney
Bandon
Kinsale
Bantry
C. Clear
Loop Hd.
Kilrush
Listowel
Rath Luirc

1:1 000 000

10   0   10   20   30   40 km

West from Greenwich   0   East from Greenwich

Based upon the Ordnance Survey Map with the permission
of the Controller of Her Majesty's Stationery Office.
Crown Copyright Reserved.

COPYRIGHT GEORGE PHILIP & SON LTD.

Motorways
Motorways under construction

1:1 000 000

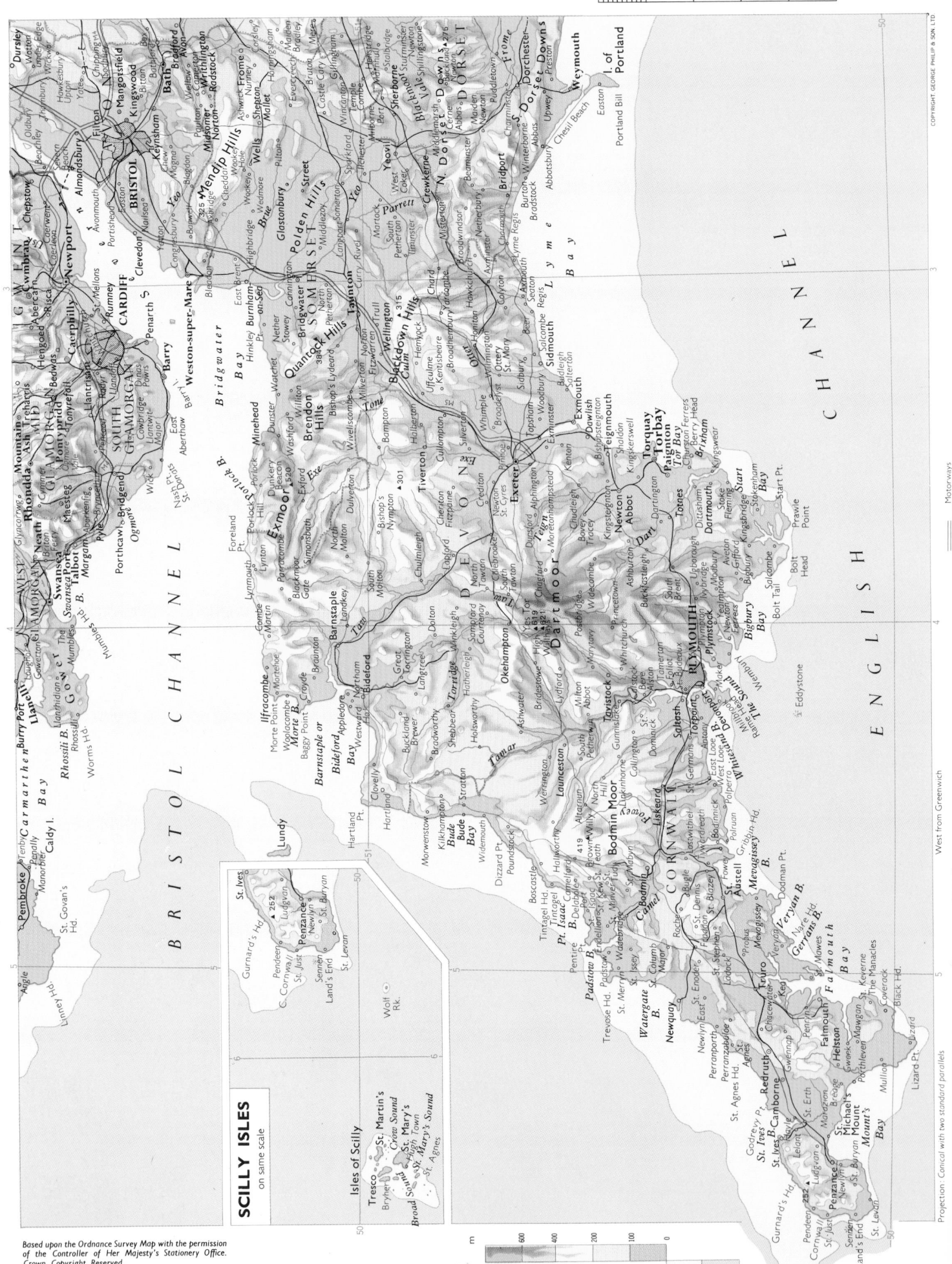

SCILLY ISLES
on same scale

Projection: Conical with two standard parallels

1:1 000 000

10   0   10   20   30   40 km

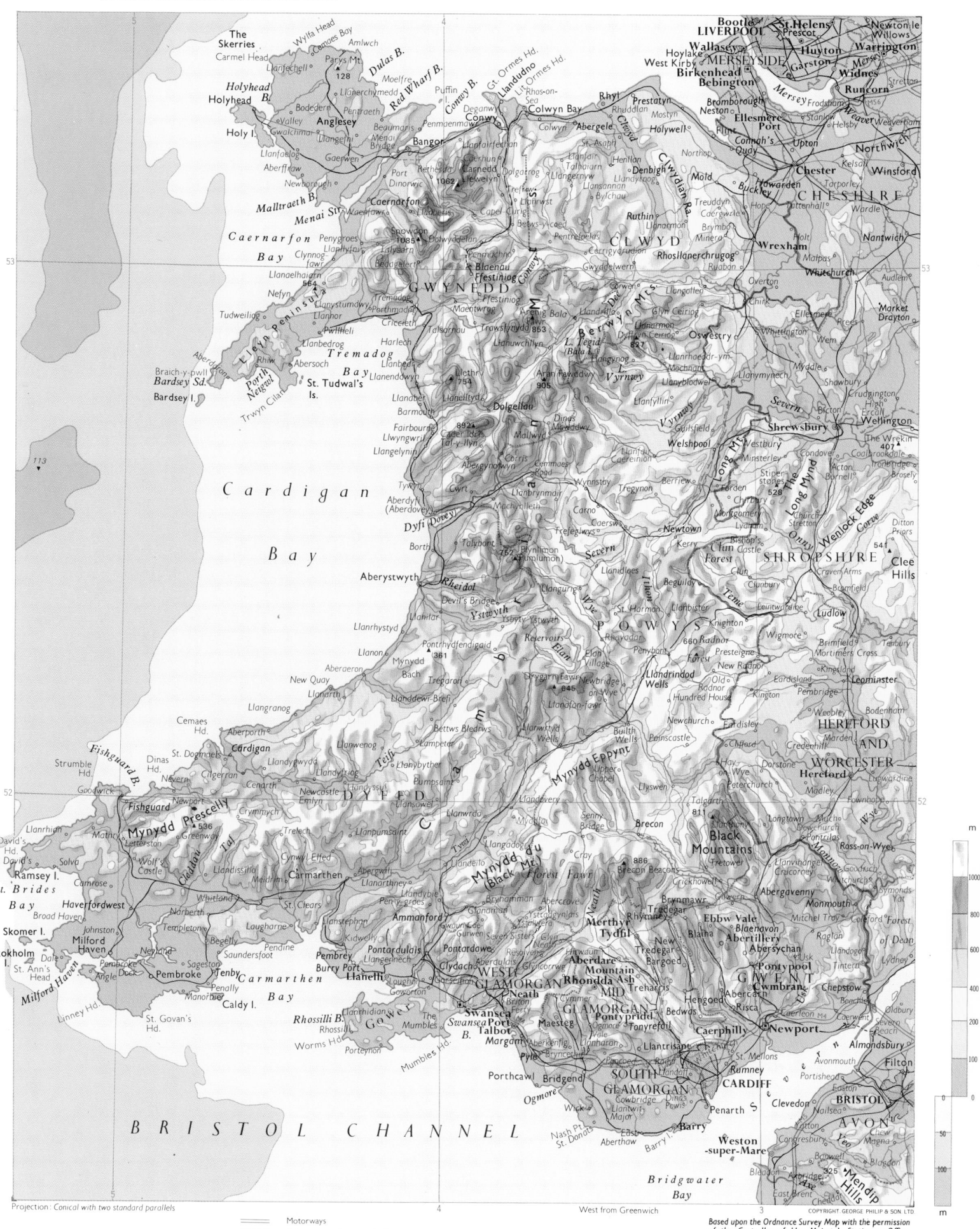

Projection: Conical with two standard parallels

—— Motorways
==== Motorways under construction

West from Greenwich

COPYRIGHT GEORGE PHILIP & SON, LTD.

Based upon the Ordnance Survey Map with the permission
of the Controller of Her Majesty's Stationery Office.
Crown Copyright Reserved.

Projection: Conical with two standard parallels

Motorways

Motorways under construction

1:1 000 000

10   0   10   20   30   40 km

Continuation
Northwards
on same scale

NORTH
SEA

TYNE AND WEAR

BORDERS

NORTHUMBERLAND

HADRIAN'S WALL

TYNE AND
WEAR

CLEVELAND

North York
Moors

Cleveland Hills

YORKSHIRE

Vale of Pickering

Scarborough

Filey Bay

Bridlington
Bay

Flamborough
Head

Harrogate

York

LEEDS

WEST
YORKSHIRE

Wakefield

HUMBERSIDE

KINGSTON-UPON-HULL

Holderness

Hornsea

Beverley

Humber

Scunthorpe

Mouth of the Humber

Great Grimsby

Cleethorpes

Donna Nook

SOUTH YORKSHIRE

SHEFFIELD

Doncaster

ROTHERHAM

Isle
of
Axholme

LINCOLNSHIRE

Lincoln

Louth

Mablethorpe

Sutton-on-Sea

Skegness

WORKSOP

East
Retford

Gainsborough

Market Rasen

Horncastle

Spilsby

Ingoldmells Pt.

DERBYSHIRE

CHESTERFIELD

Mansfield

Newark-
on-Trent

Sleaford

Boston

The Wash

NOTTINGHAM

DERBY

Grantham

NORFOLK

West from Greenwich

East from Greenwich

1 : 1 000 000

10   0   10   20   30   40 km

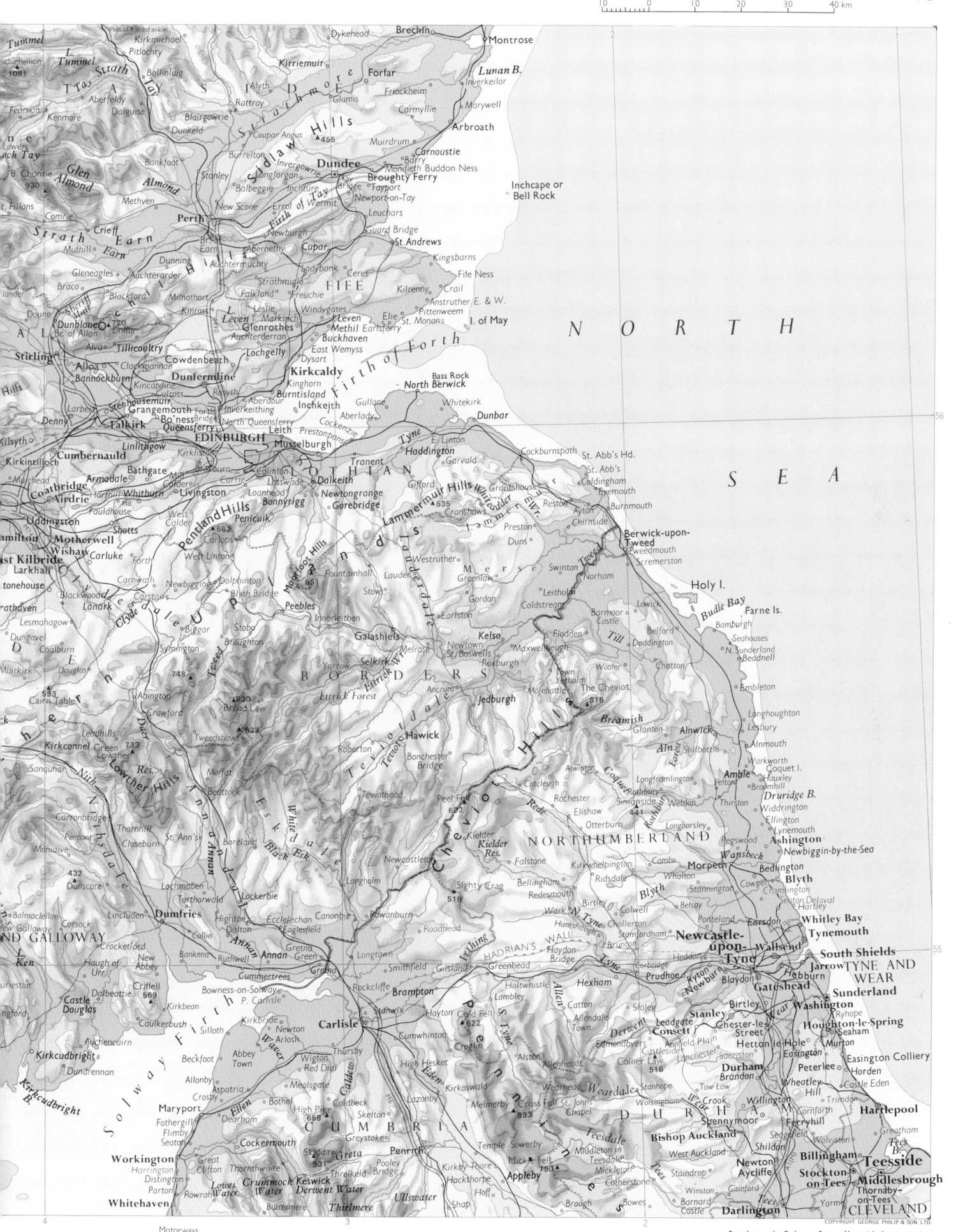

NORTH

SEA

Motorways

Motorways under construction

Based upon the Ordnance Survey Map with the permission
of the Controller of Her Majesty's Stationery Office.
Crown Copyright Reserved.

COPYRIGHT GEORGE PHILIP & SON LTD.

SHETLAND ISLANDS
on same scale

Hecma Ness
Haroldswick
Baltasound
Bluemull Sd.
Balta
Unst
Cullivoe
Uyeasound
Mu Ness
Ramna Stacks
Whale Firth
Fetlar
Point of Fethaland
Mid Yell
The Snap
North Roe
Colgrave Sd.
The Faither
Ronas Hill
450
Yell
Burravoe
Esha Ness
Lunna Ness
Hillswick
Skaw
Out Skerries
Brae
Taing
St. Magnus Bay
SHETLAND
Voe
Whalsay
Muckle Roe
The Häa
Papa Stour
Papa
S Nesting Bay
Sandness
Walls
Eastery
Vaila
Skeld
Lerwick
I. of Noss
Gruting Voe
Bressay
Scalloway
Bard Hd.
West Burra
293
Hamnavoe
Hellis Ness
Kettla Ness
Mousa
Hoswick
St. Ninian's I.
Scousburgh
Boddam
Fitful Hd.
B. of Quendale
Sumburgh Hd.

C. Wrath
Kyle
Kinlochbervie
L. Inchard
L. Laxford
Handa I.
Scourie
72
B. Sta
Eddrachillis Bay
Drumbeg
Quinag
809
Rhu Coigach
Stoer
Assynt
L. Assynt
Enard Bay
Lochinver
Canisp
847
Summer Isles
Elphin
Ledmo
L. Lurgainn
Cromalt Hills
Strathkanaird
Gruinard B.
Coigach
Ullapool
Greenstone Pt.
Strathkanaird
Mellon Charles
L. Broom
An Teallach
1062
L. Ewe
Aultbea
Ardcharni
Poolewe
Fionn Loch
Melvaig
L. na Sealga
Gairloch
L. Gairloch
Bruemore
Kerrysdale
Fannich
W
Talladale
981
L. Maree
Slioch
1093
Kinlochewe
Achnasheen
Longa I.
L. Torridon
Fasag
Torridon
Shieldaig
1053
Henderson
Rona
Sound of Raasay
Kinlochellan
Lochcarron
Coulags
Carron
Applecross Forest
Monar Forest
1062
L. Monar
Applecross
Kishorn
Stromemore
Plockton
Toscaig
Lochcarron
Seguir na Lapal
Narrows
Crowlin Is.
Carron
1150
Raasay
Plockton
Stromeferry
Mullardoch
Scalpay
Kyle of Lochalsh
Auchtertyre
Dornie
L. Alsh
Carn Eige
1183
Kyleakin
Glen Affri
Glenelg
Inverinel
Chalraig
1120
The Saddle
1010
Glen Shiel
Glen Mo
Eilean Iarmain
Teangue
L. Hourn
Cluanie
Tomdoun
Quoich
Armadale
Sound of Sleat
L. Hourn
Glen Garry
Ardvasar
Knoydart
Glen Loyne
Pt. of Sleat
L. Nevis
Mallaig
983
L. Arkaig
Culvain
Culvain
Caledonian Canal
Morar
1040
Loch Morar
Segurr na Clche
Kinlocheil
Corpach
Lochy
Lochailort
Glenfinnan
Misaig
882
Moidart
Kinlochmoidart
Shona
L. Eil
S
Kinlochmoidart
Ben Nevis
L. Moidart
Loch Shiel
Moidart
1134
Ardgour
Fort William
888
Corran
North Ballac
888
Salen
Strontian
L. Leven
Sunart
Glen Co
Sunart
South Laggan
Pt. of Ardnamurchan
Ardnamurchan
Kilchoan
Sorisdale
527
Mingary
Morvern
Drimnin
Strontian
STRATH
L. Eive

Butt of Lewis
Port of Ness
South Dell
Ness
Borve
Cellar Hd.
Barvas
North Tolsta
Tolsta Hd.
Catloway
Shawbost
Back
Broad Bay
Gallan Hd.
Great Bernera
291
Newmarket
Tiumpan Hd.
Uig
Callanish
Stornoway
Portoguiran
Eye Peninsula
L. Roag
Melbost
Bayble
Lewis
Gisla
Lochs
Chicken Hd.
Aird Brenish
575
Balallan
Crossbost
Scarp
Loch Langavat
Cromore
L. Erisort
Kintaravay
Park
Gravir
Kebock Hd.
Husinish
N. Harris
Ardhasig
571
L. Shell
Husinish Pt.
Ardvourlie Castle
Beinn Mhor
809
W. L. Tarbert
Sd. of Shiant
Taransay
L. Seaforth
Shiant Is.
Tarbert
WESTERN
Sd. of Taransay
Harris
Scalpay
Toe Hd.
Scarastavore
H. L. Tarbert
Pabbay
S. Harris
ISLES
Sd. of Pabbay
Leverburgh
Berneray
Rodel
Haskeir Is.
Renish Pt.
Rubha Hunish
Sound of Harris
Kilmaluag
Griminish Pt.
Sollas
Vaternish Pt.
North Uist
Chmaddy
Loch Snizort
Uig
Paible
L. Maddy
Vaternish Pt.
Clachan
Dunvegan Head
Sound of Monach
Carinish
L. Eport
Stein
Trotternish
Rona
Monach Is.
Baleshare
347 Eaval
488
The Storr
719
Grimsay
Ronay
Milovaig
Lephin
Portree
Gramsdale
Dunvegan
Roskhill
Benbecula
Coillore
Ardivachar Pt.
L. Harport
L. Bee
Bracadale
L. Bracadale
Fernilea
Sligachan
Bagh nam Faoileann
Carbost
Drynoch
Scalpay
Howmore
South
Hecla
L. Harport
Bla Bheinn
Kyle of
605
Uist
Minginish
928
Broadford
Rubha Ardvule
620
B. Mhor
Cuillin Hills
L. Eynort
1009
Rubh' an
Daliburgh
Glenbrittle
Dunain
Lochboisdale
L. Boisdale
Soay Sd.
Soay
L. Scavaig
L. Eishort
Eilean
Iarmain
Sound of Eriskay
Sd. of Eriskay
Canna
Teangue
Eriskay
Armadale
Greian Hd.
Cuillin Sound
Ardvasar
Barra
Sanday
Pt. of
384
Sd. of Canna
Sleat
Castlebay
Bruernish Pt.
Kinloch
Mallaig
Vatersay
Rhum
810
Sandray
Eigg
Pabbay
394
Mingulay
Sd. of Eigg
Berneray
Muck
Barra Head
Sd. of Arisaig

Canna
Coll
Clabhach
Pt. of Ardnamurchan
241
Inner
Sorisdale
Coll
Arinagour Pt.
Tobermory
Calgary
Dervaig
Caliach Pt.
L. Frisa
Hebrides
Treshnish Isles
L. Tuath
Drimnin
Tiree
Scarinish
Coll
Hynish B. Passage of Tiree
Caoles
Sd. of Mull
Lochaline
Lismore I.
Hynish
Salen

Outer
Hebrides
Little Minch
North Minch
North Minch
Minch

m
1000
800
600
400
200
100
0
0
50
100
m

Projection: Conical with two standard parallels

1:1 000 000

ORKNEY
ISLANDS
on same scale

Pentland Firth

N O R T H

S E A

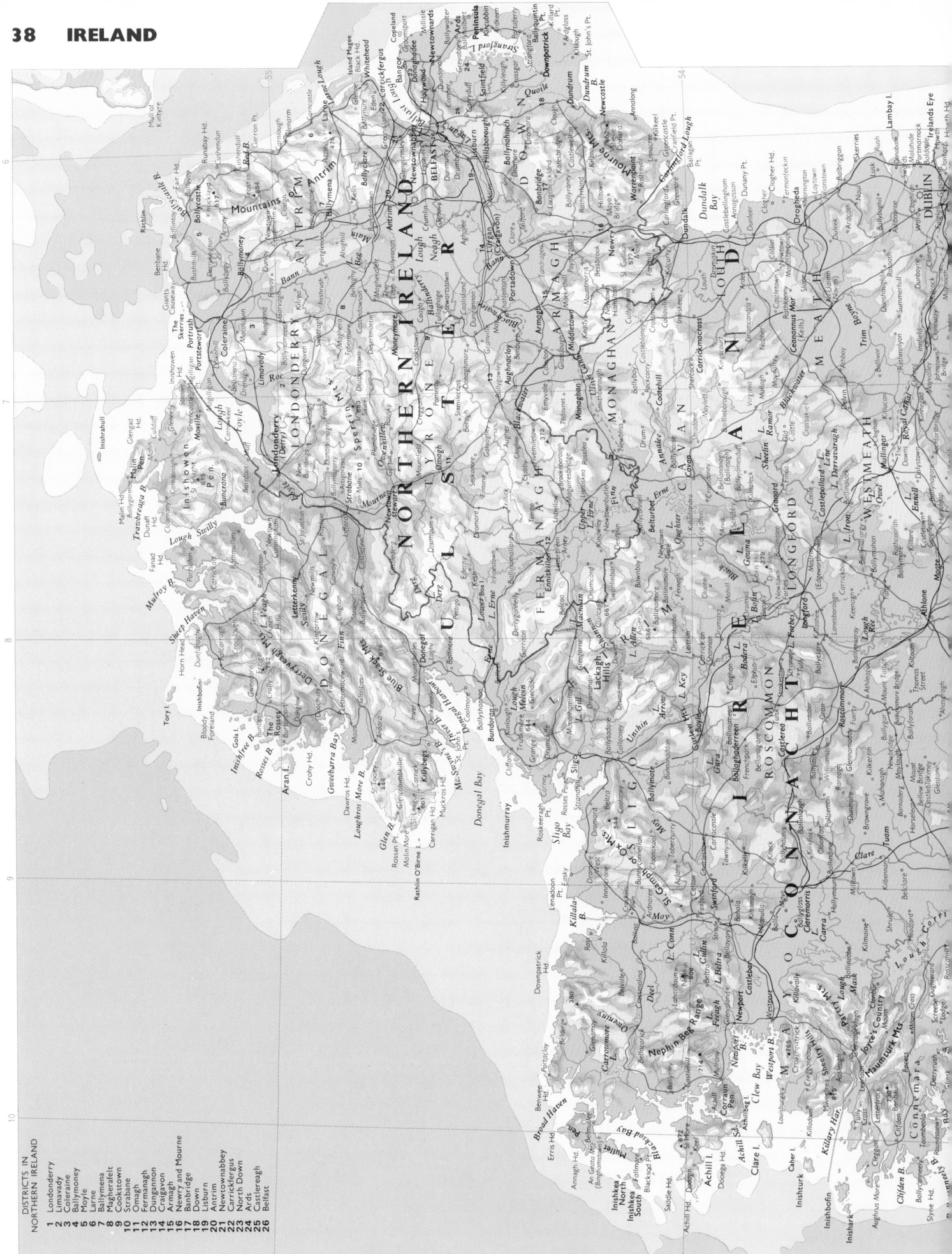

DISTRICTS IN
NORTHERN IRELAND

1 Londonderry
2 Limavady
3 Coleraine
4 Ballymoney
5 Moyle
6 Larne
7 Ballymena
8 Magherafelt
9 Cookstown
10 Strabane
11 Omagh
12 Fermanagh
13 Dungannon
14 Craigavon
15 Armagh
16 Newry and Mourne
17 Banbridge
18 Down
19 Lisburn
20 Antrim
21 Newtownabbey
22 Carrickfergus
23 North Down
24 Ards
25 Castlereagh
26 Belfast

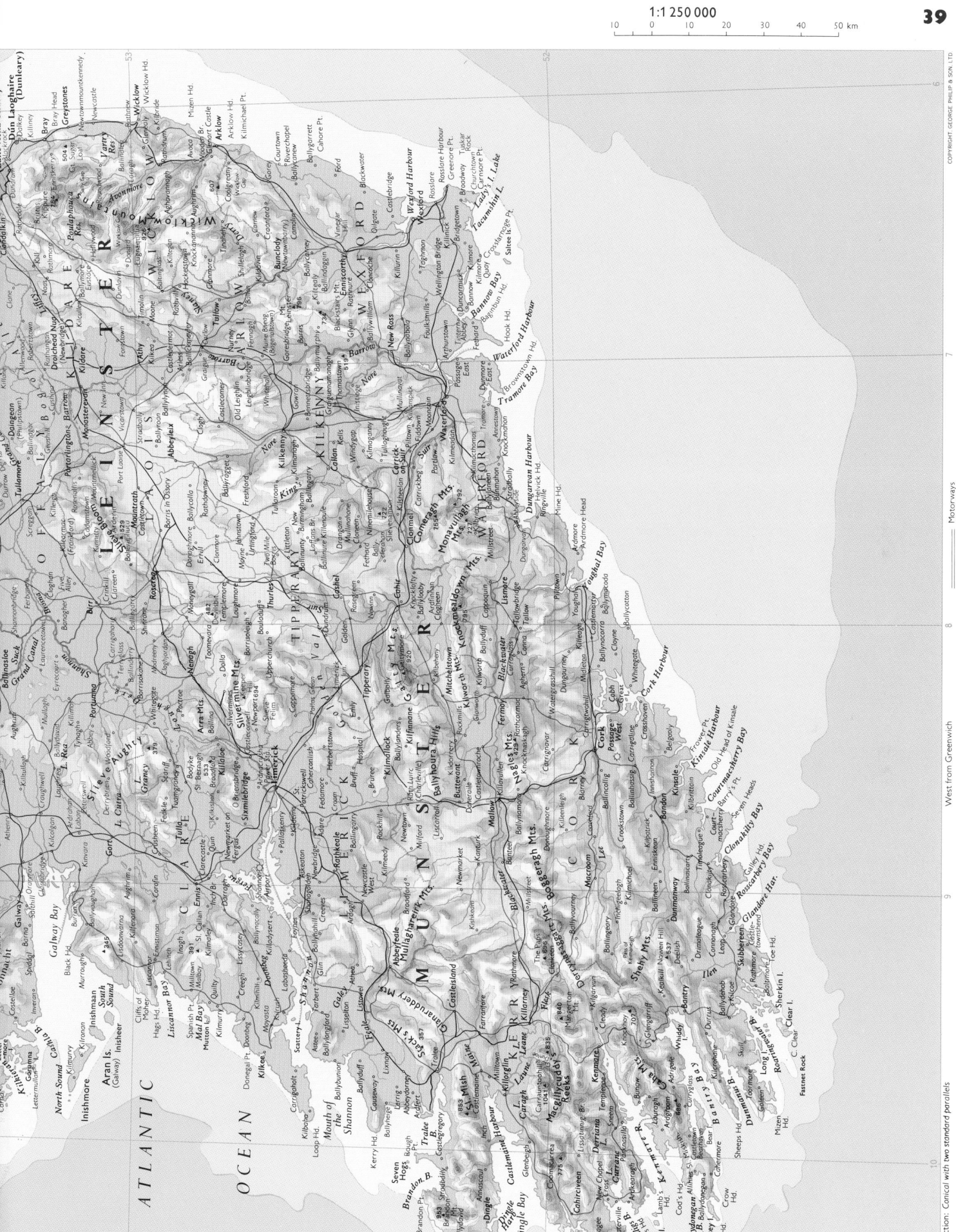

39

1:1 250 000

10   0   10   20   30   40   50 km

COPYRIGHT GEORGE PHILIP & SON. LTD

Projection: Conical with two standard parallels

West from Greenwich

Motorways

m

1000 800 600 400 200 100 0

m 50 100

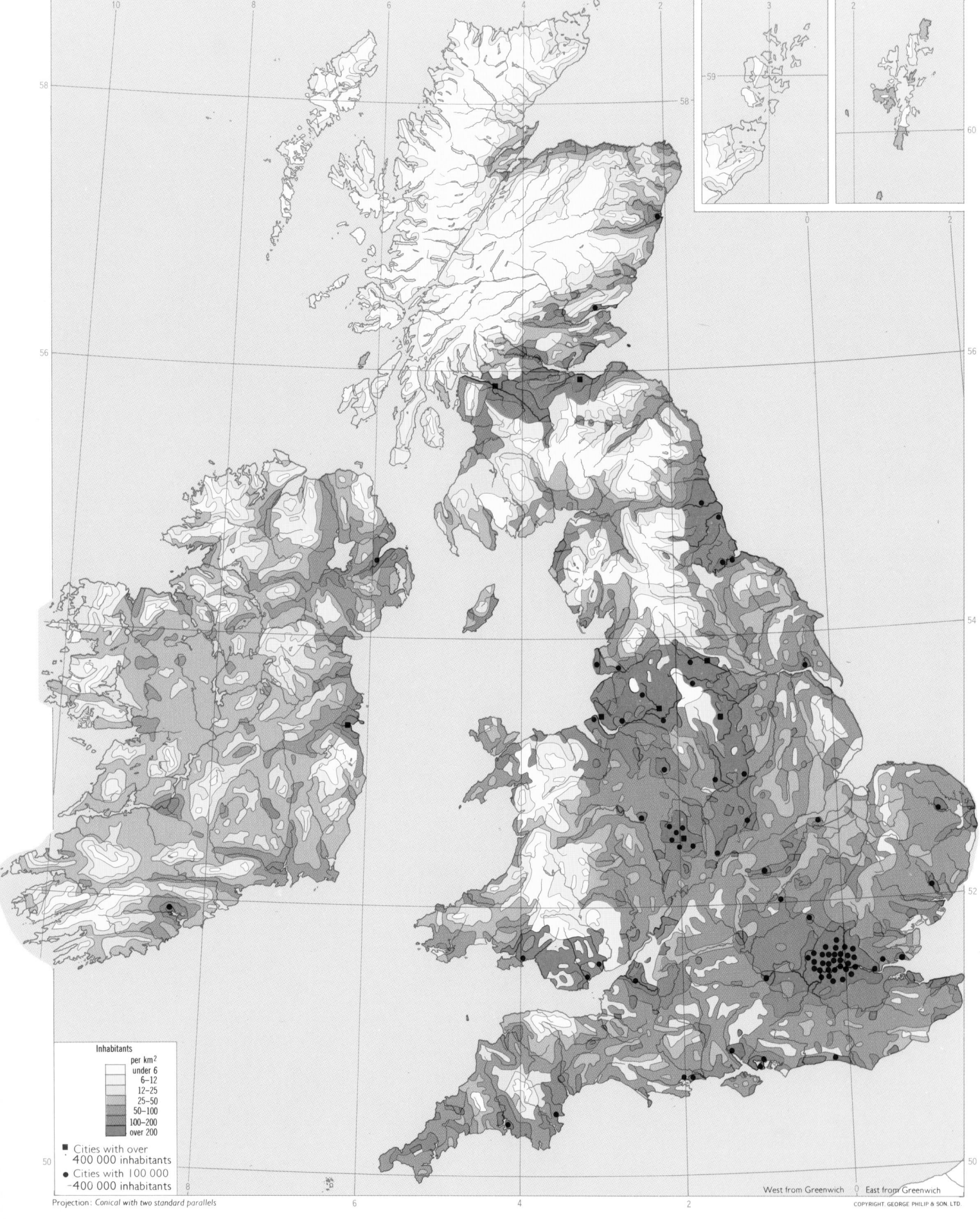

1 : 4 000 000

50   0   50   100   150 km

Inhabitants

per km²
under 6
6–12
12–25
25–50
50–100
100–200
over 200

■ Cities with over
   400 000 inhabitants

● Cities with 100 000
   –400 000 inhabitants

Projection: Conical with two standard parallels

West from Greenwich   East from Greenwich

COPYRIGHT. GEORGE PHILIP & SON. LTD.

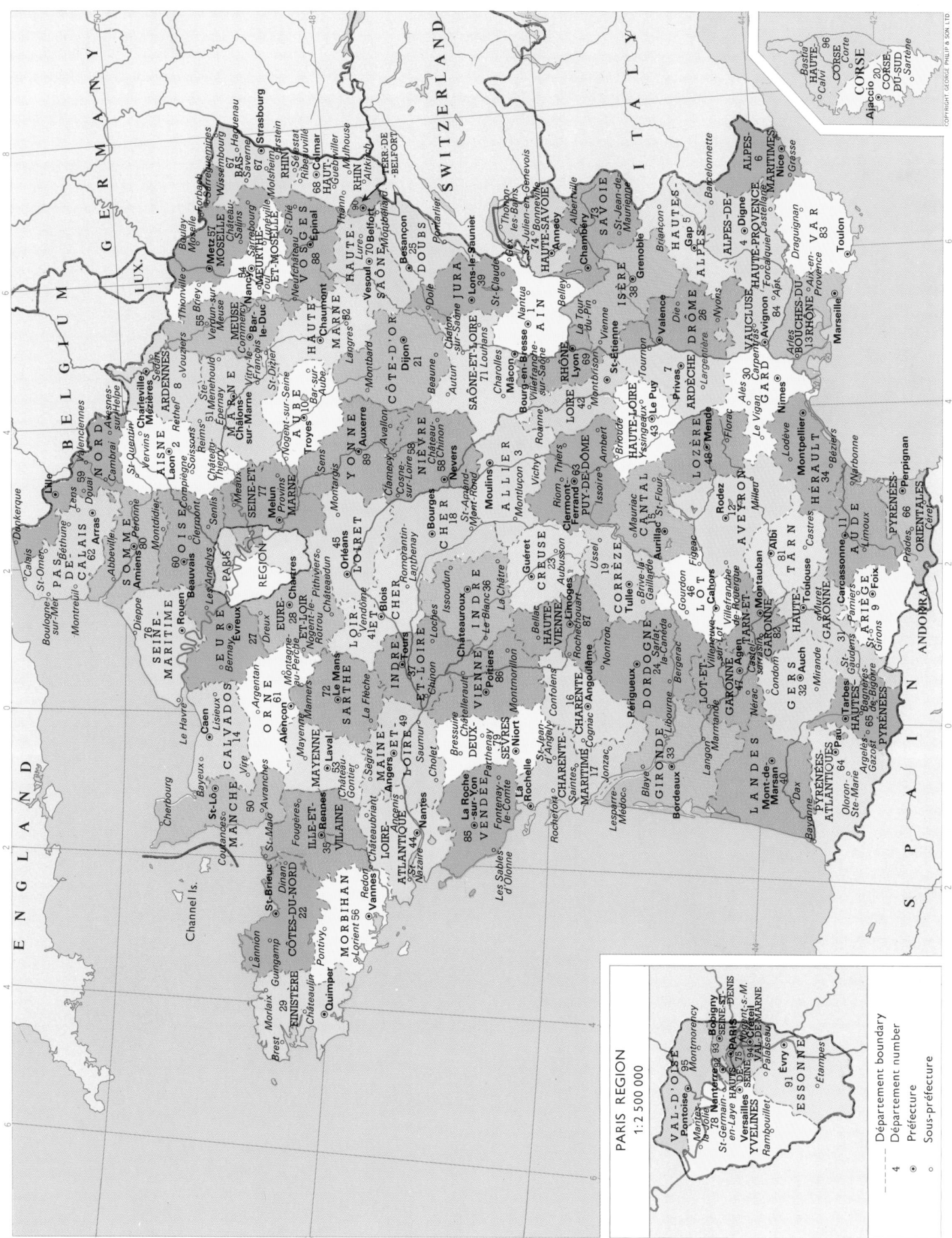

1:5 000 000

50 0 50 100 150 200 km

PARIS REGION
1:2 500 000

- - - - - Département boundary
4 Département number
◉ Préfecture
○ Sous-préfecture

DÉPARTEMENTS IN THE PARIS AREA
1 Ville de Paris   3 Val-de-Marne
2 Seine-St-Denis   4 Hauts-de-Seine

Projection: Conical with two standard parallels

West from Greenwich   East from Greenwich

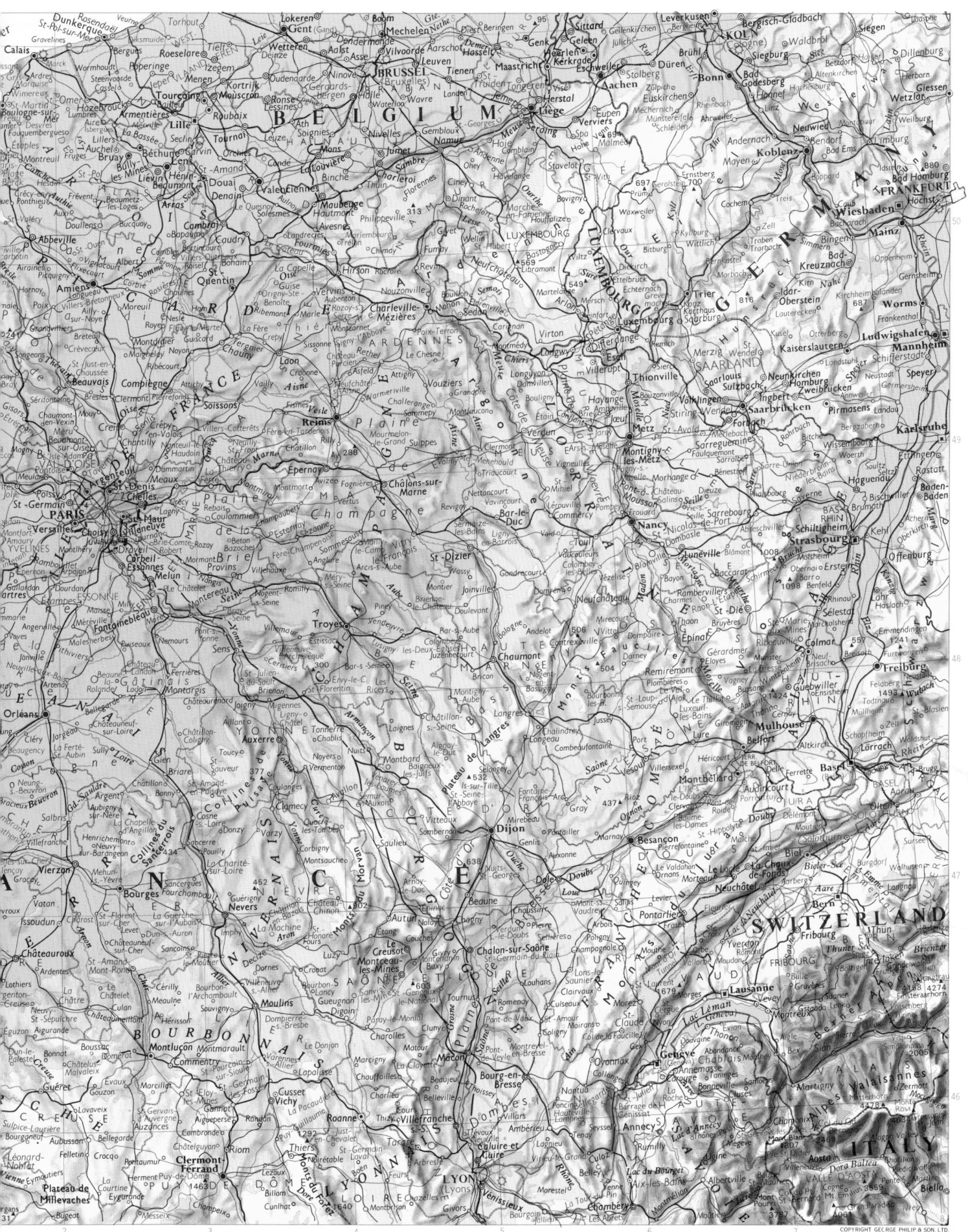

1:2 500 000

Projection: Conical with two standard parallels
West from Greenwich   East from Greenwich

1 : 2 500 000

10 0 10 20 30 40 50 60 70 80 90 100 km

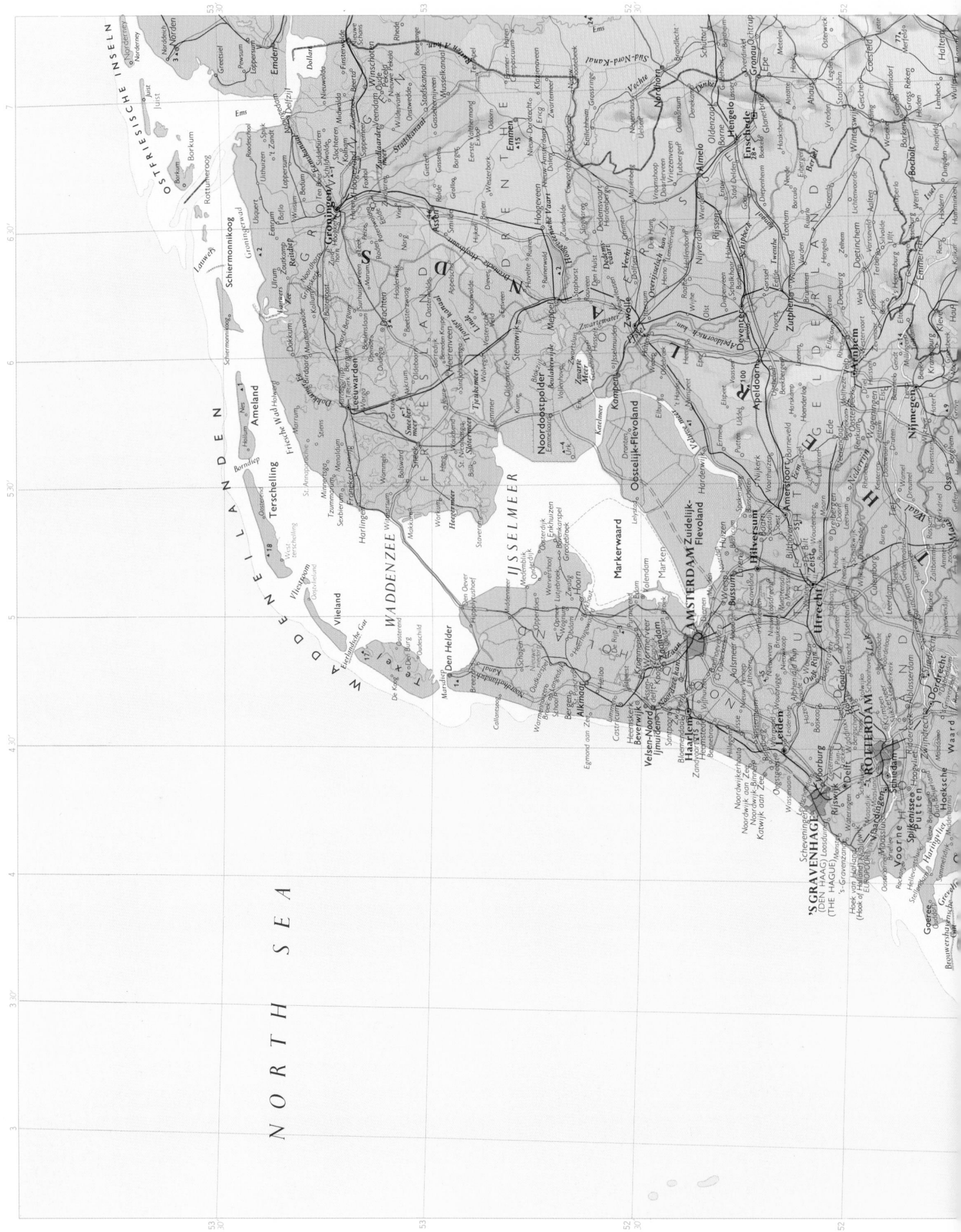

1:1 250 000

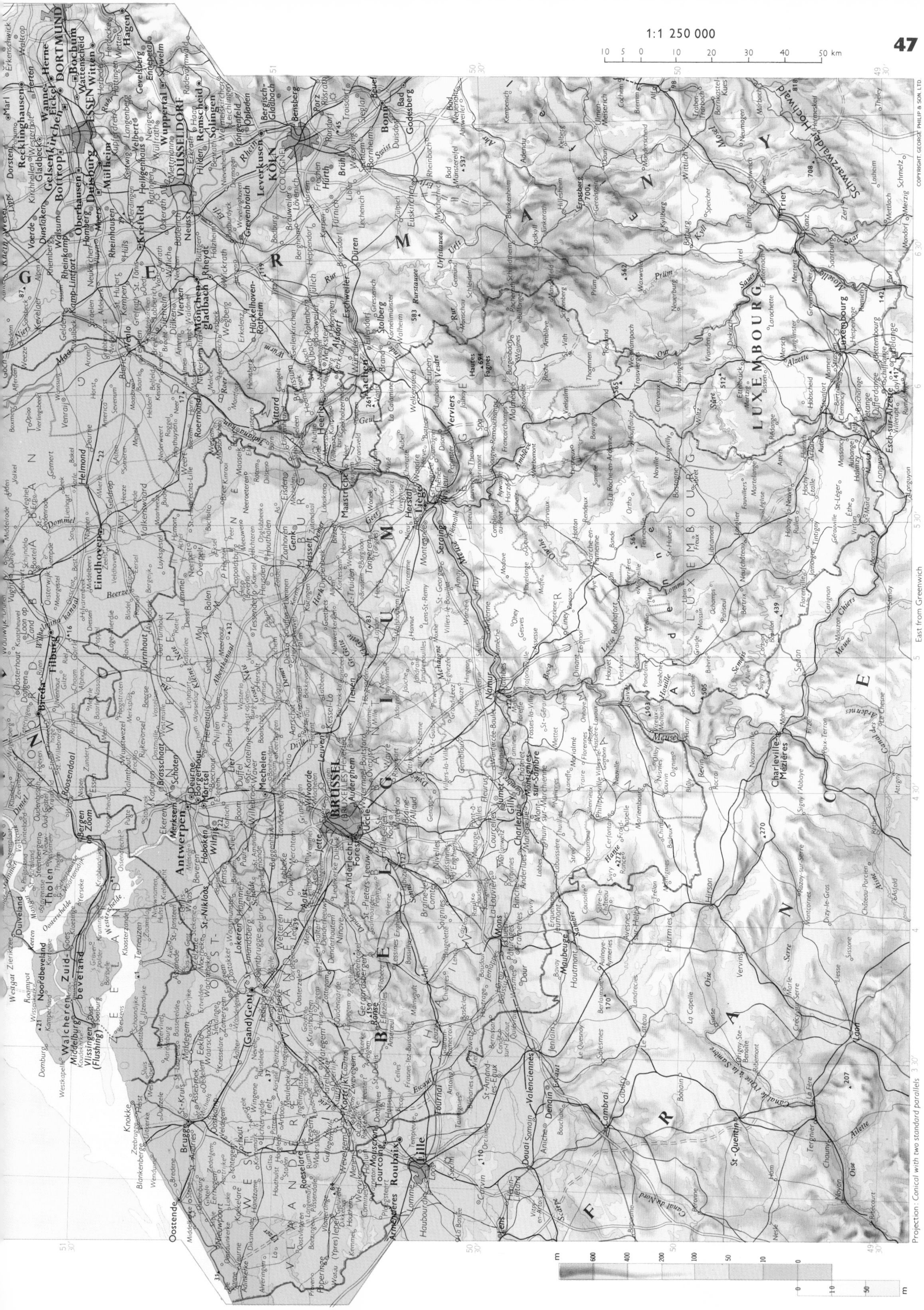

10 5 0 10 20 30 40 50 km

COPYRIGHT GEORGE PHILIP & SON, LTD.

East from Greenwich

Projection: Conical with two standard parallels

GERMANY

BELGIUM

NETHERLAND

LUXEMBOURG

FRANCE

DÜSSELDORF
DORTMUND
ESSEN
KÖLN (COLOGNE)
Bonn
Aachen
Liège
Namur
Charleroi
Mons
BRUSSEL (BRUXELLES)
Antwerpen
Gent (Gand)
Brugge
Eindhoven
Tilburg
Breda
Lille
Roubaix
Tourcoing
Valenciennes
Cambrai
St-Quentin
Charleville-Mézières
Luxembourg
Trier
Maastricht
Hasselt
Leuven
Mechelen
Oostende

m 600 400 200 100 50 10 0

m

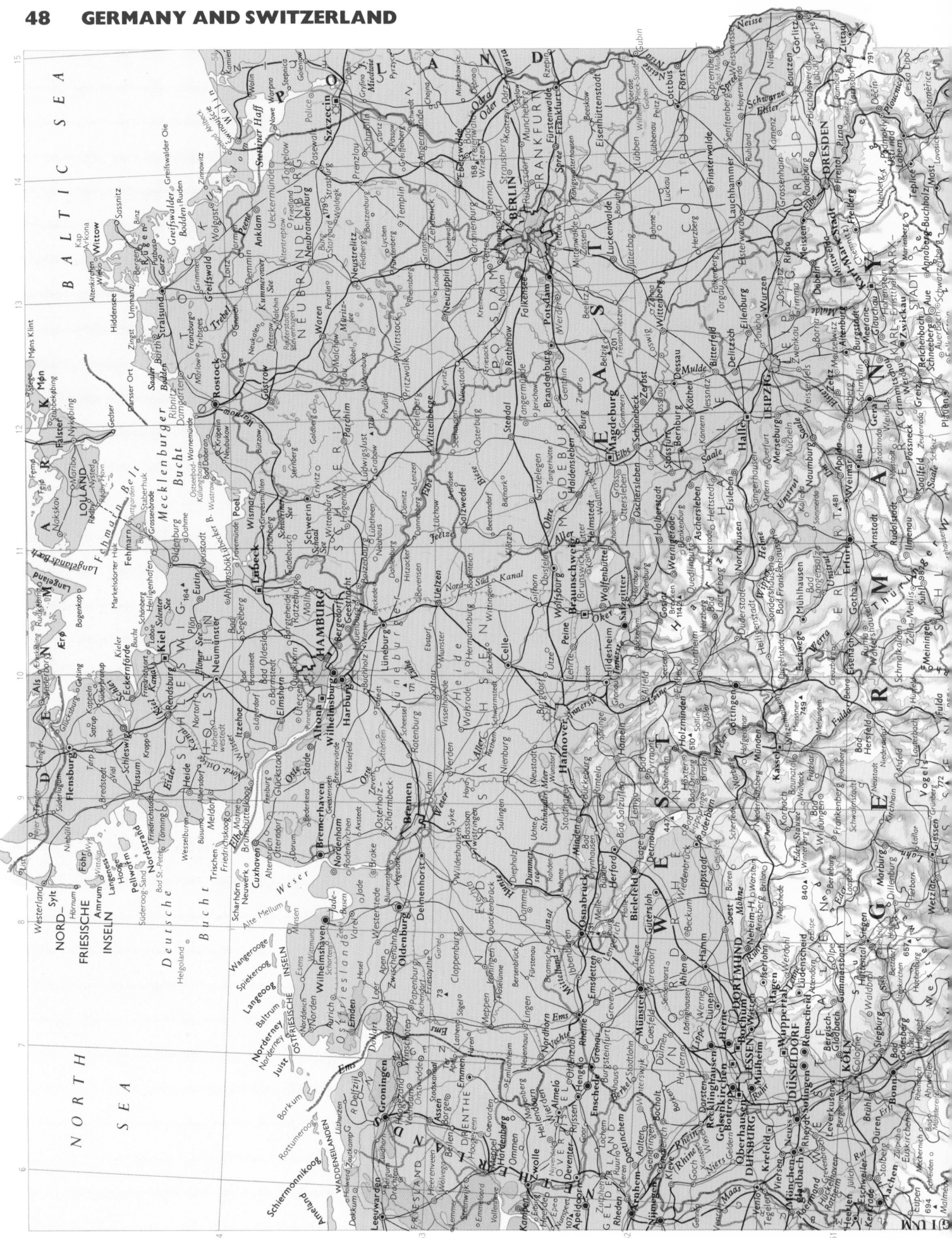

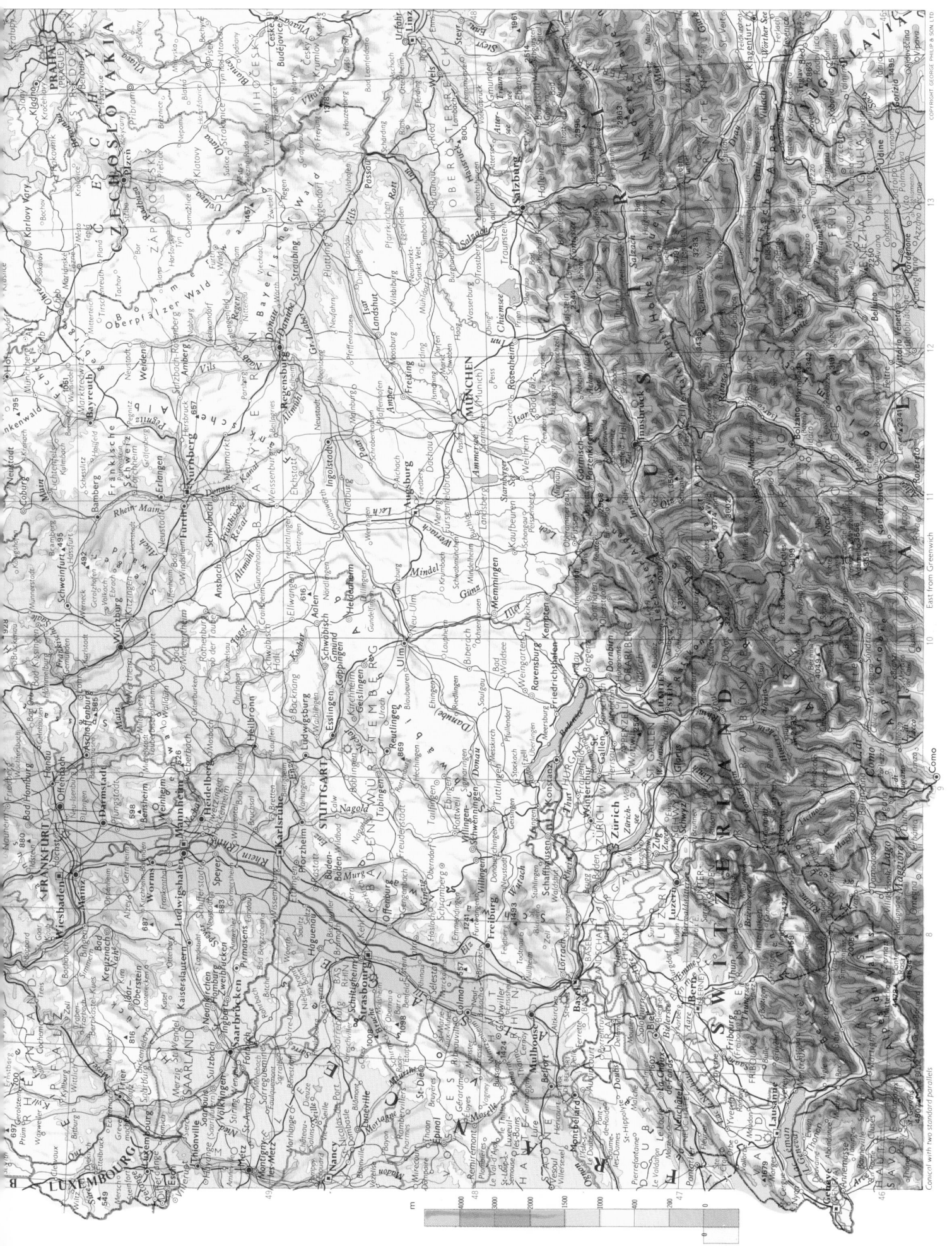

1:2 500 000

10 0 10 20 30 40 50 60 70 80 90 100 km

East from Greenwich

Conical with two standard parallels

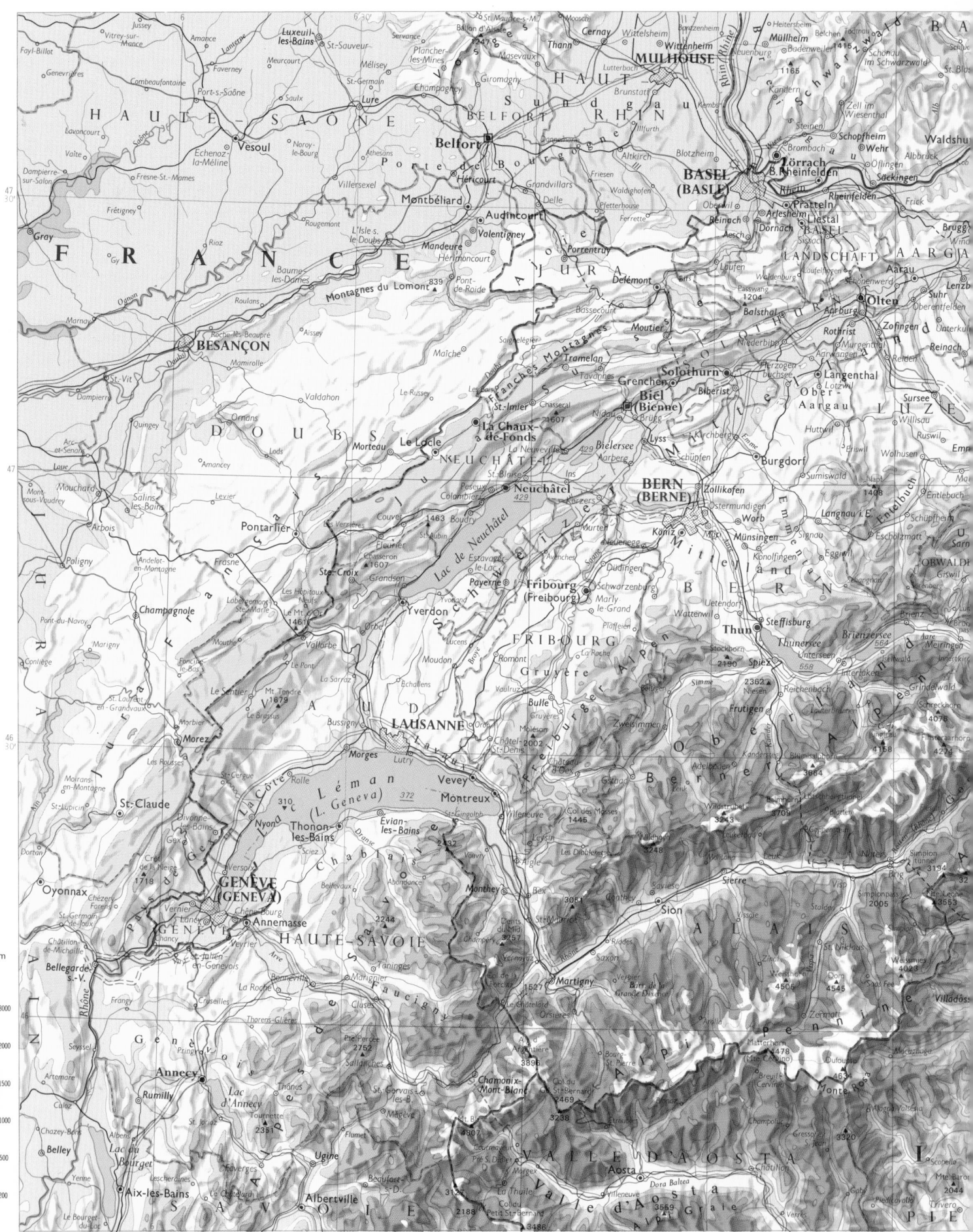

Projection: *Conical with two standard parallels*

1:1 000 000

10   0   10   20   30   40 km

East from Greenwich

COPYRIGHT. GEORGE PHILIP & SON. LTD.

1:2 500 000

10 0 10 20 30 40 50 60 70 80 90 100 km

COPYRIGHT. GEORGE PHILIP & SON. LTD.

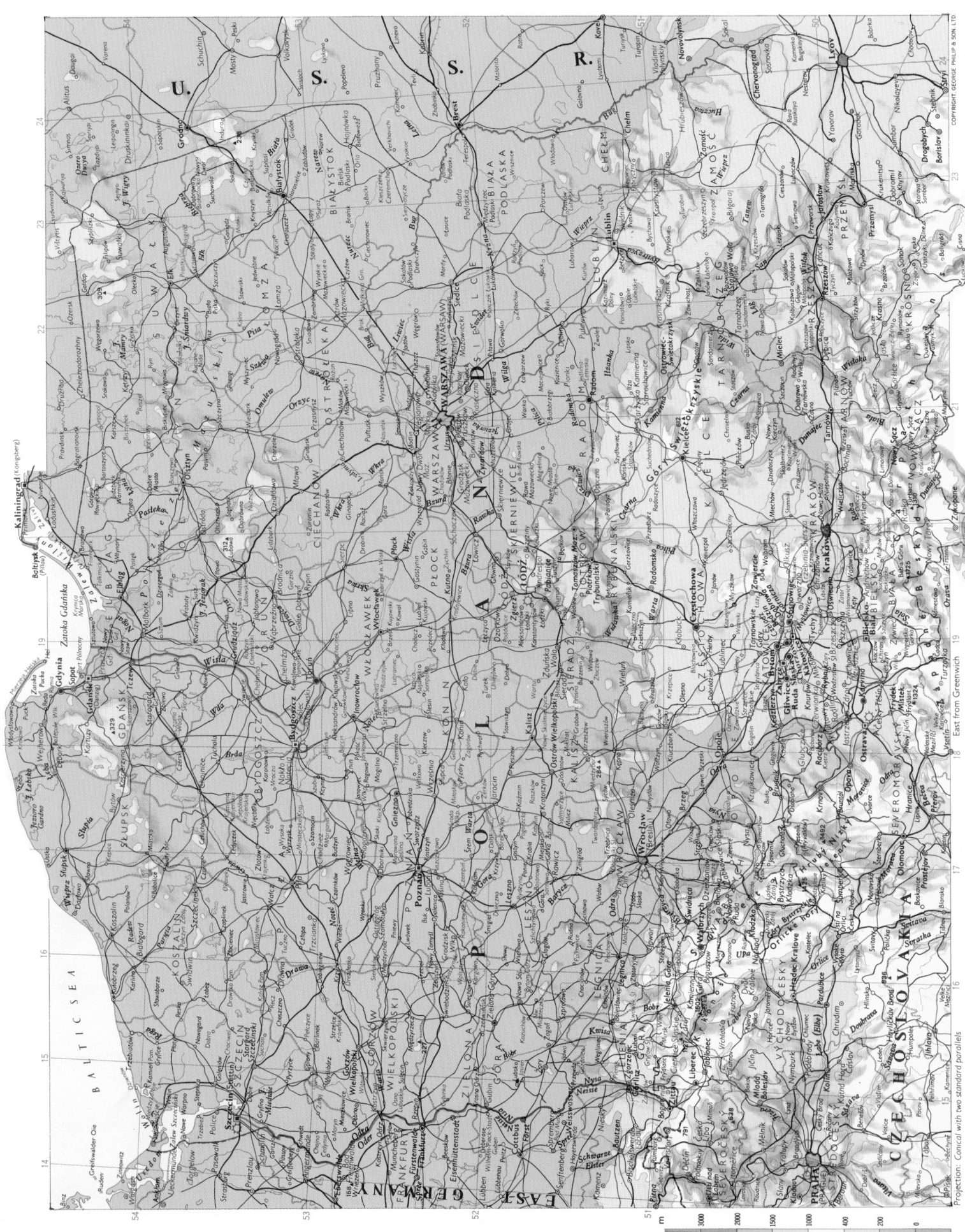

1:3 000 000

1:5 000 000

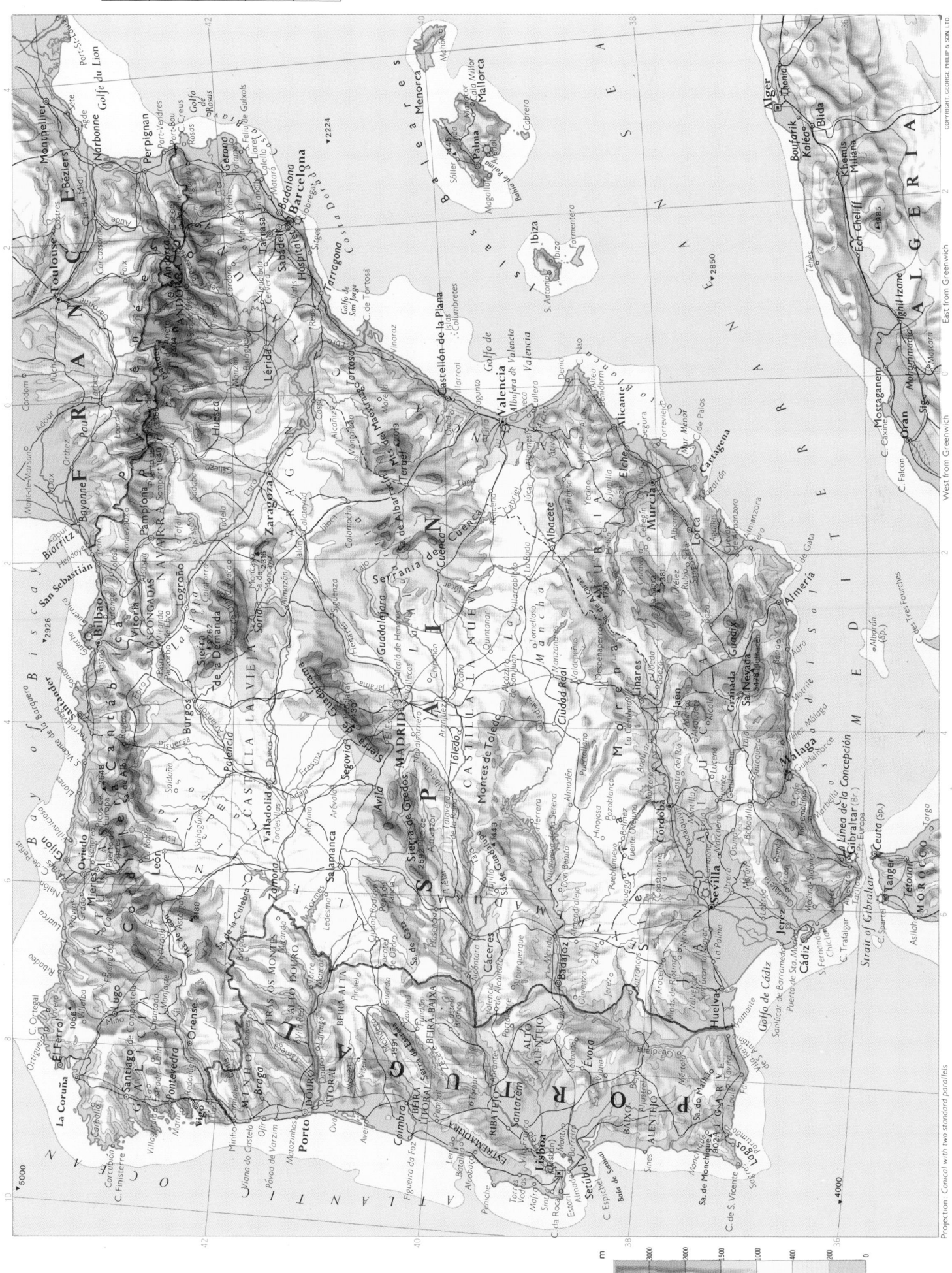

East from Greenwich

West from Greenwich

Projection: Conical with two standard parallels

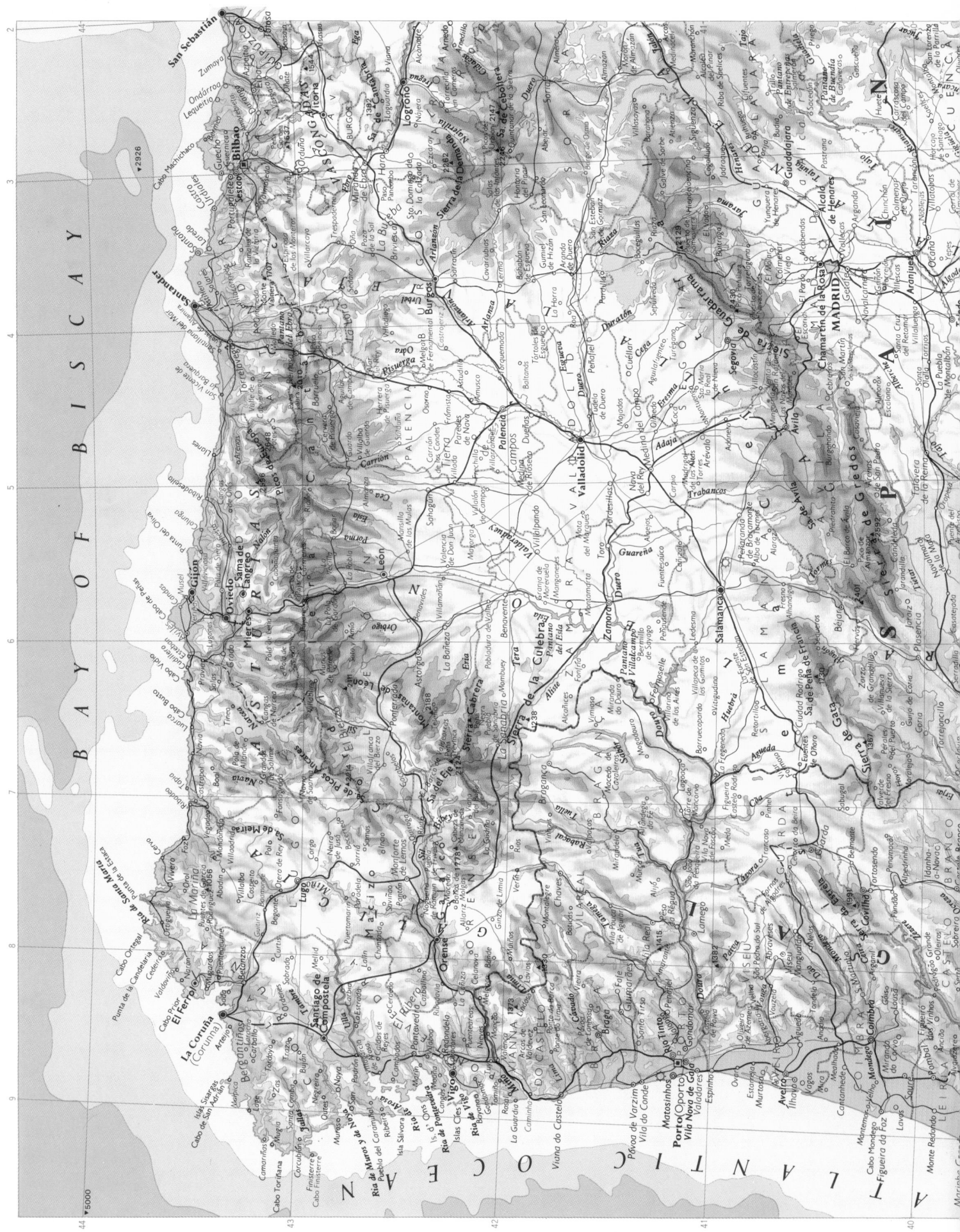

1 : 2 500 000

10 0 10 20 30 40 50 60 70 80 90 100 km

MEDITERRANEAN SEA

MOROCCO

Málaga

Granada

Sevilla

Córdoba

Jaén

Cádiz

Huelva

Gibraltar (Br.)

Ceuta

Tánger (Tanger)

Melilla (Sp.)

Tétouan

Larache

Golfo de Cádiz

LISBOA (LISBON)

Badajoz

Cáceres

Évora

Mérida

Golfo de Almería

Strait of Gibraltar

West from Greenwich

COPYRIGHT GEORGE PHILIP & SON LTD

Projection: Conical with two standard parallels

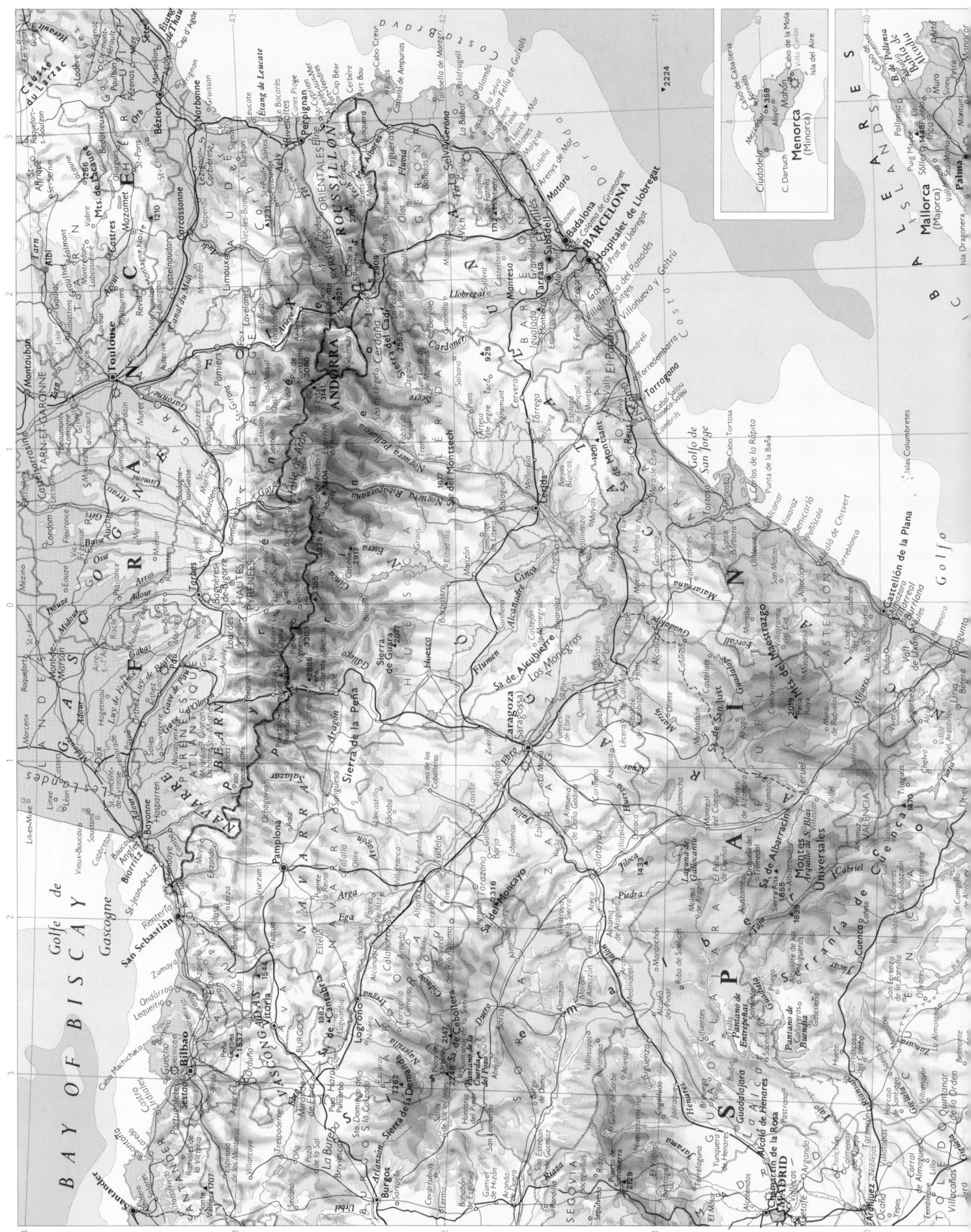

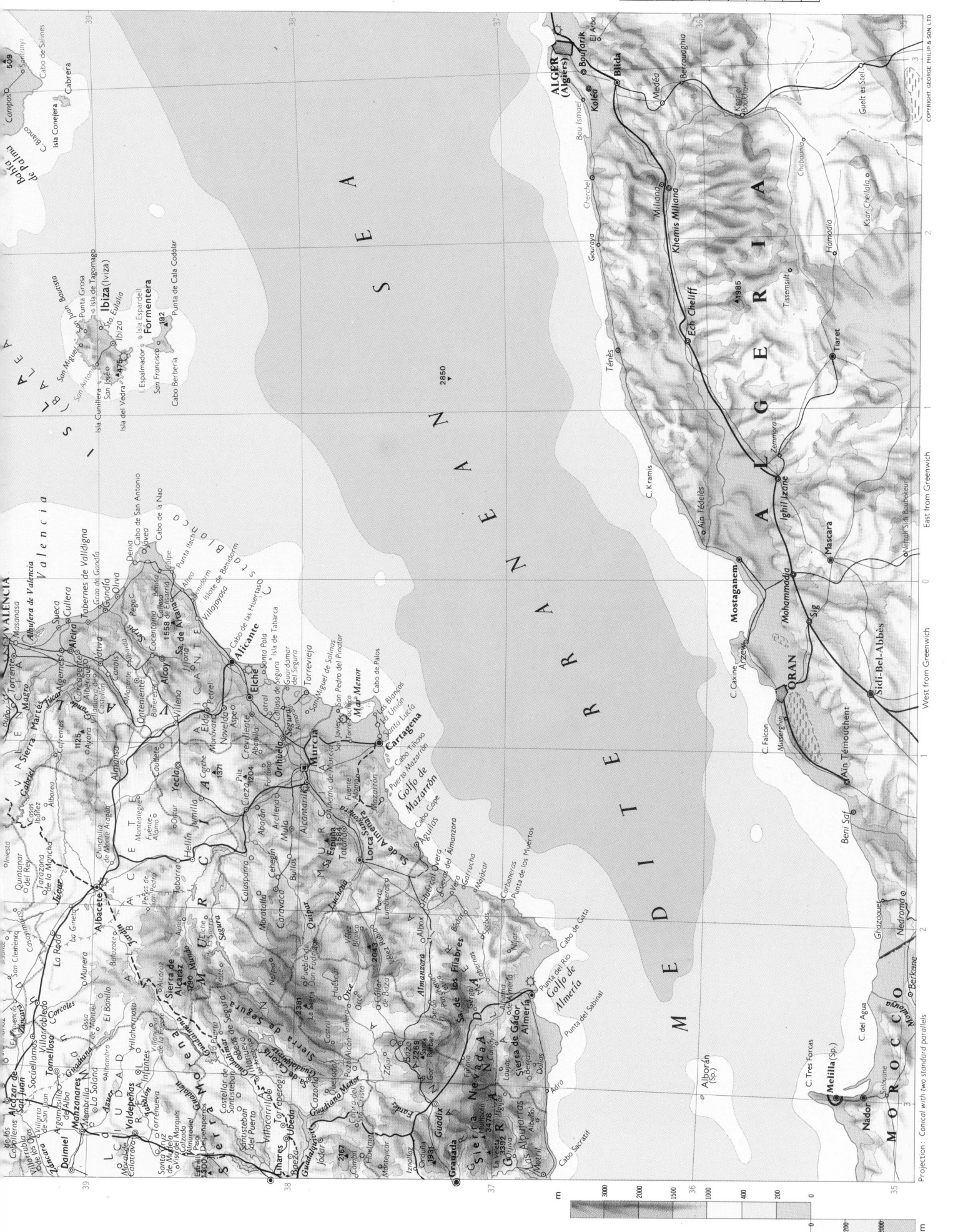

1 : 2 500 000

10 0 10 20 30 40 50 60 70 80 90 100 km

COPYRIGHT GEORGE PHILIP & SON LTD.

Projection: Conical with two standard parallels

East from Greenwich

West from Greenwich

M E D I T E R R A N E A N   S E A

A L G E R I A

M O R O C C O

B A L E A R I C   I S L A N D S

Valencia

Ibiza (Iviza)

Formentera

ALGER (Algiers)

Blida

ORAN

Murcia

Cartagena

Alicante

Albacete

Granada

Melilla (Sp.)

Nador

m 3000 2000 1500 1000 400 200 0

m 0 200 2000

1:10 000 000

100   0   100   200   300   400 km

POLAND

Poznań
Łódź
Warszawa
Brest
Pinsk
Polesye
Chernigov
Sumy
Belgorod
Volgograd

Legnica
Wrocław
Radom
Bug
Pripyat
Konotop
Nezhin
Kremenchug

Chorzów
Kielce
Lublin
Lutsk
Rovno
Zhitomir
Belaya Tserkov
Kiyev
Poltava
Voroshilovgrad
Kamensk-Shakhtinskiy
Tsimlyanskoye
Vdkhr

Kraków
Tarnów
Przemyśl
Lvov
Vinnitsa
U.   S.   S.   R.
Berdichev
Cherkassy
Pereyaslav-Khmelnitskiy
Slavyansk
Artemovsk
Shakhty
Novocherkassk

Ostrava
Jablunkovský pr.
Tatra
Carpathians
Kamenets-Podol'skiy
Uman
Kirovograd
Dnepropetrovsk
Pavlograd
Gorlovka
Makeyevka
Donetsk
Rostov

CZECHOSLOVAKIA
Kolomyya
Chernovtsy
Mogilev-Podolskiy
Pervomaysk
Krivoy Rog
Zaporozhye
Taganrog
Don
Manych

Bratislava
Banská Stiavnica
Tokaj
Botoşani
Beltsy
Tiraspol
U.   K.   R.   A.   I.   N.   E.
Nikolayev
Zhdanov (Mariupol)
Yeisk
Oz. Manych Gudilo
Stavropol

HUNGARY
Miskolc
Debrecen
Iaşi
Kishinev
Bendery
Odessa
Kherson
Melitopol
Berdyansk
Tikhoretsk

Budapest
Kecskemét
MOLDAVIAN S.S.R.
Belgorod Dnestrovskiy
Perekop
Sea of Azov
Krasnodar

Szeged
Hódmezővásárhely
Arad
ROMANIA
Karkinitskiy Zaliv
Krymskaya (Crimea)
Kerch
Kuban

Pécs
Subotica
Timişoara
Cluj-Napoca
Brăila
Sulina
Yevpatoriya
Simferopol
Feodosiya
Novorossiysk
Tuapse

Zagreb
Novi Sad
Petrovaradin
Sibiu
Braşov (Oraşul Stalin)
1545
Sevastopol
Yalta
Sukhumi

YUGOSLAVIA
Beograd
Craiova
Bucureşti
Constanţa
BLACK   SEA
2211
Poti

BOSNA
Sarajevo
Niš
Pleven
Ruse
Varna
Ince Burnu
Sinop
Batumi

Sofiya
BULGARIA
Plovdiv
Edirne
Istanbul
Karadeniz Boğazı (Bosporus)
Zonguldak
Ereğli
Trabzon
Rize

Skopje
Rhodopi Planina
Üsküdar
İzmit
Bolu
Kastamonu
2565
Amasya
Kuzey Anadolu Dağları

Tiranë
Bitola
Thessaloníki
Tekirdağ
Marmara Denizi
Bursa
Ankara
Çankırı
Çorum
Sivas

ALBANIA
GREECE
Sérrai
Kavála
Gallipoli
Çanakkale
Eskişehir
Sivrihisar
Kirşehir
TURKEY
Kayseri

Límnos
Troy
Balıkesir
Kütahya
Afyon Karahisar
Aksaray
Erciyas Dağı 3770

Vóvriai Sporádhes
Lésvos
Ayvalık
Büyük Menderes
Eğridir
Konya
Nigde
Maraş
Gaziantep

Évvoia
Khíos
İzmir
Aydın
Denizli
Burdur
TOROS DAĞLARI
Tarsus
Adana
Halab

Athínai
Piraievs
Sámos
İkaría
Muğla
Antalya
Mersin
İskenderun Körfezi
Antakya
SYRIA

Pátrai
Kikládhes
Náxos
Ródhos
CYPRUS
Lefkosía (Nicosia)
Tarabulus
Hamā

Peloponnisos
Spárti
Thíra
Kárpathos
Iráklion
Kríti
Lemesós
Bayrût (Beirut)
Dimashq (Damascus)
Homs

IONIAN SEA
MEDITERRANEAN   SEA
Haifa
Tel Aviv-Yafo
ISRAEL
Jerusalem
Ammān
JORDAN

Cyrene
Derna
Bûr Saîd
Gaza
Bahr el Miyet

Banghāzī
Tobruq
El Iskandariya
Tanta
Dumyât
El 'Arîsh
Petra

Khalij Surt
Barqa
Salûm
Matrûh
El 'Alamein
EGYPT
El Qâhira (Cairo)
El Suweis
Gebel el Tîh

LIBYA
El Faiyûm
Beni Suêf
Nîle
Khalîg el 'Aqaba
Es Sinâ

COPYRIGHT. GEORGE PHILIP & SON, LTD.

------- Division between Greeks
and Turks in Cyprus;
Turks to the north.

FOR CONTINUATION SEE PAGE 66

m
3000
2000
1500
1000
400
200
0
0
200
2000
4000
m

Projection: Conical with two standard parallels

East from Greenwich

ADRIATIC

SEA

IONIAN

SEA

Golfo di Táranto

Strait of Otranto

G. di Manfredónia

G. di Salerno

G. di Policastro

Golfo di Sant'Eufémia

Golfo di Squillace

G. di Gióia

Isole Eólie o Lípari (Æolian Is.)

Str. di Messina

Golfo di Catánia

G. di Noto

BASILICATA

CALABRIA

SICILIA

ALBANIA

Kérkira (Corfu)

RANEAN SEA

Channel

Projection: Conical with two standard parallels

East from Greenwich

1:2 500 000

10 0 10 20 30 40 50 60 70 80 90 100 km

1:2 500 000

10 0 10 20 30 40 50 60 70 80 90 100 km

COPYRIGHT GEORGE PHILIP & SON LTD

Mitilíni

Káre Burun

968 Ayíassos
Plomárion

Kólpos Kallonís

Omoúsa
Palaióhóra

1297
Vrondádhos
Khíos (Chios)
Ákra Mésta
Ákra Mástikho

Psará

Andípsara

A

E

G

E

A

N

Skántzoúra

(Northern Sporades)

Skíros
Skíros
792

Skiropoúla

Skópelos
Skópelos

S

Foúrnoi
Áyios
Kírikos

1262

Ikaría

957

Mélissa

Dhragonísi

Mikonos

Náxos

Dhragonísi
Khtapodhná

Náxos
1001

Koronís
Koufonísia

Skhinoúsa

Iráklia
N.Náxos

Dhílos
Rínia

Páros
Páros
706

Andíparos
Dhespótiko

Síros
(Ermoúpolis)

Sífnos

Sériphos
560

Kéa

Gávrion

994

Kíthnos

Apóllonia
Kímolos
Mílos
751

Andímilos

Thíra
Thíra

Thirasía

Khristianá

Sikinos

Folégandros

Anáfi

Makrá

Astipálaia
Astipálaia

Amorgós
822
Amorgós

Dhenoúsa

Kínaros
Lévitha

Kríos

Kikládhes
(C Y C L A D E S)

Arkhipélagos

A

Khamilónísion

Dhía

Iráklion
(Candia)

C

R

E

T

E

SEA OF CRETE
(Sea of Candia)

5015

Gávdhos

East from Greenwich

Continuation Eastwards
on same scale

Ródhos
(Rhodes)

D

O

D

H

E

K

A

N

I

S

O

S

(DODECANESE)

Kárpathos
Kárpathos

Stenón Karpathos

Stenón Kasos

m   3000   2000   1500   1000   400   200   0

m   0   200   2000

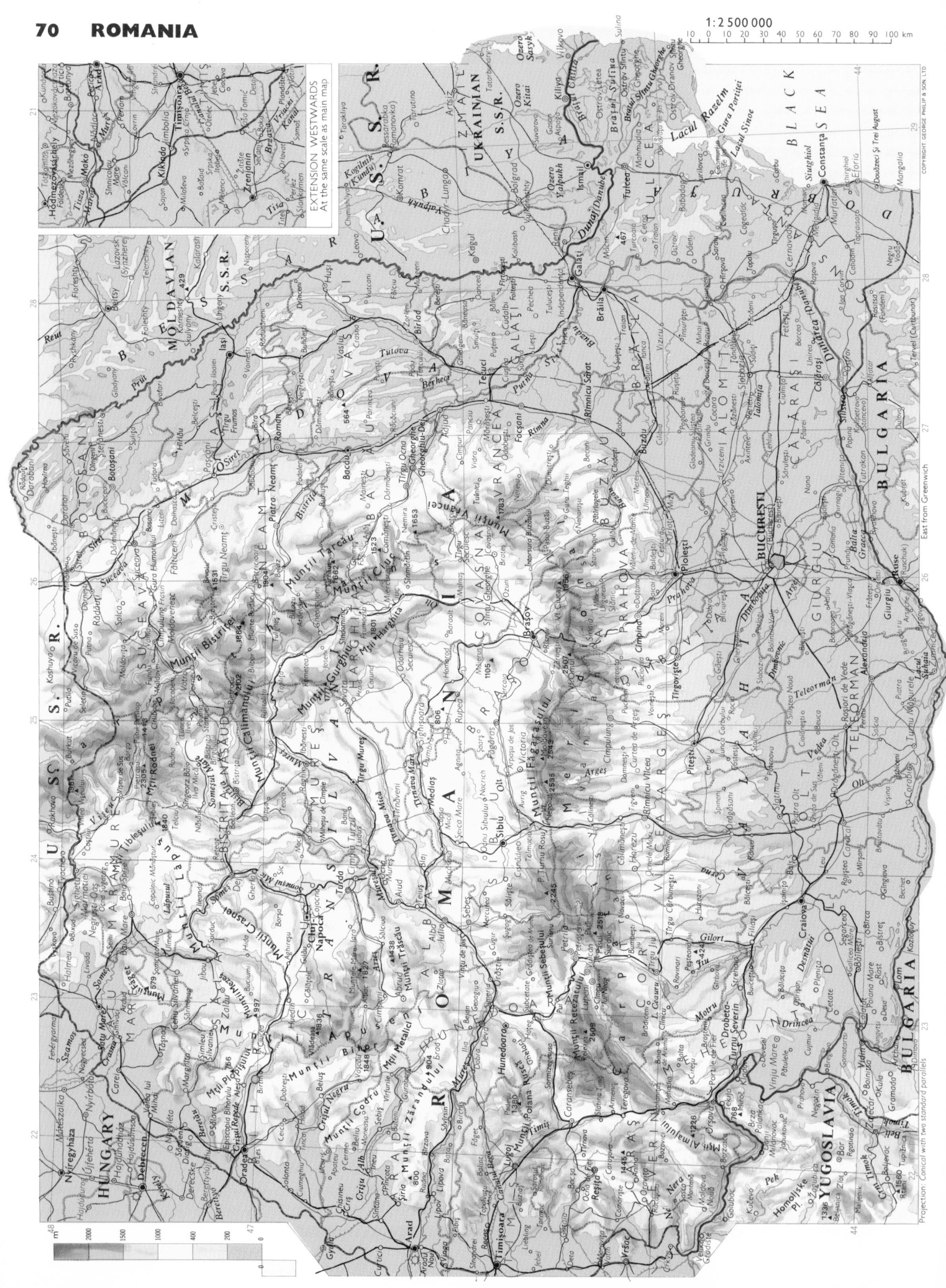

1:2 500 000

EXTENSION WESTWARDS
At the same scale as main map

1 : 2 500 000

10 0 10 20 30 40 50 60 70 80 90 100 km

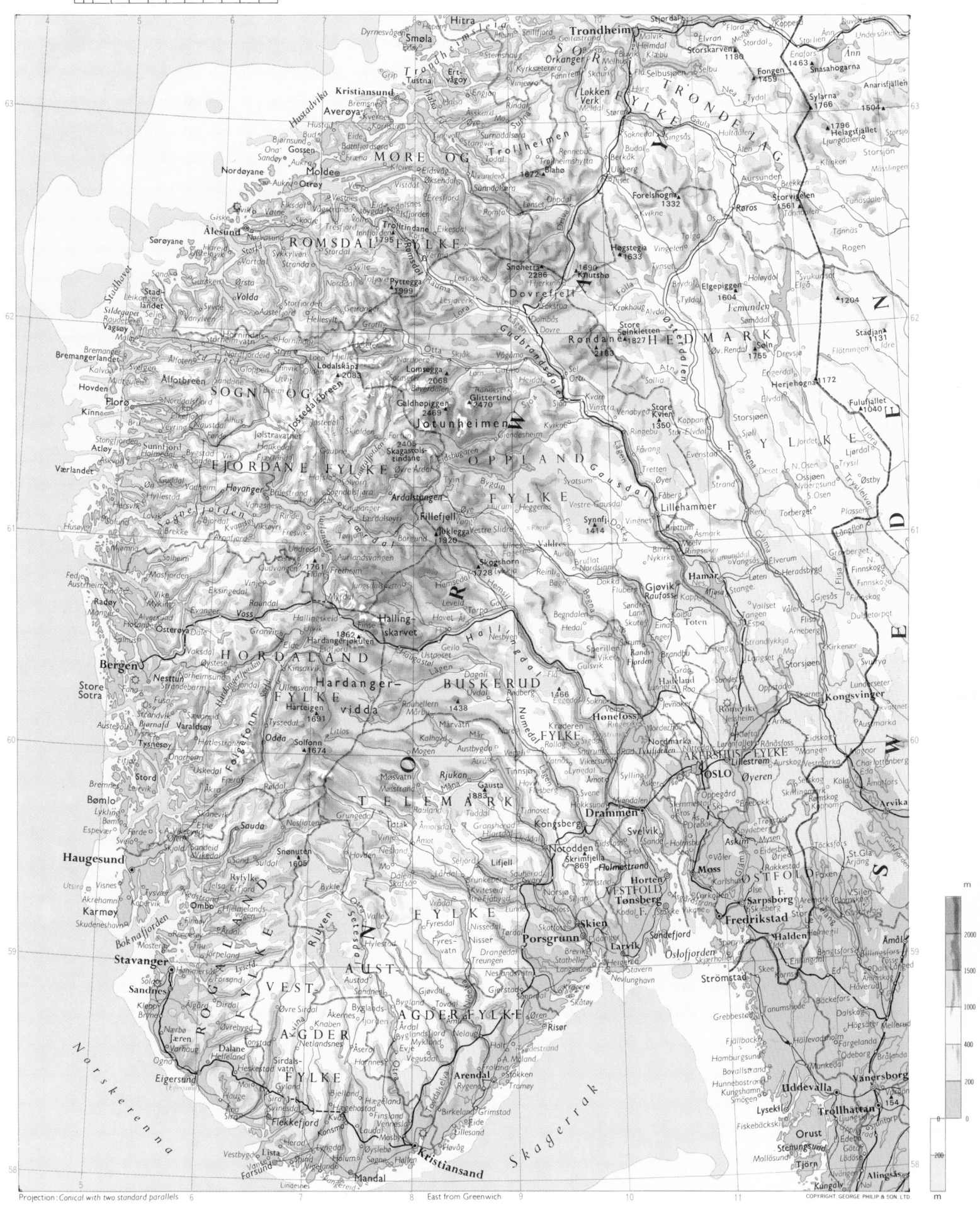

Projection : Conical with two standard parallels   East from Greenwich   COPYRIGHT GEORGE PHILIP & SON LTD.

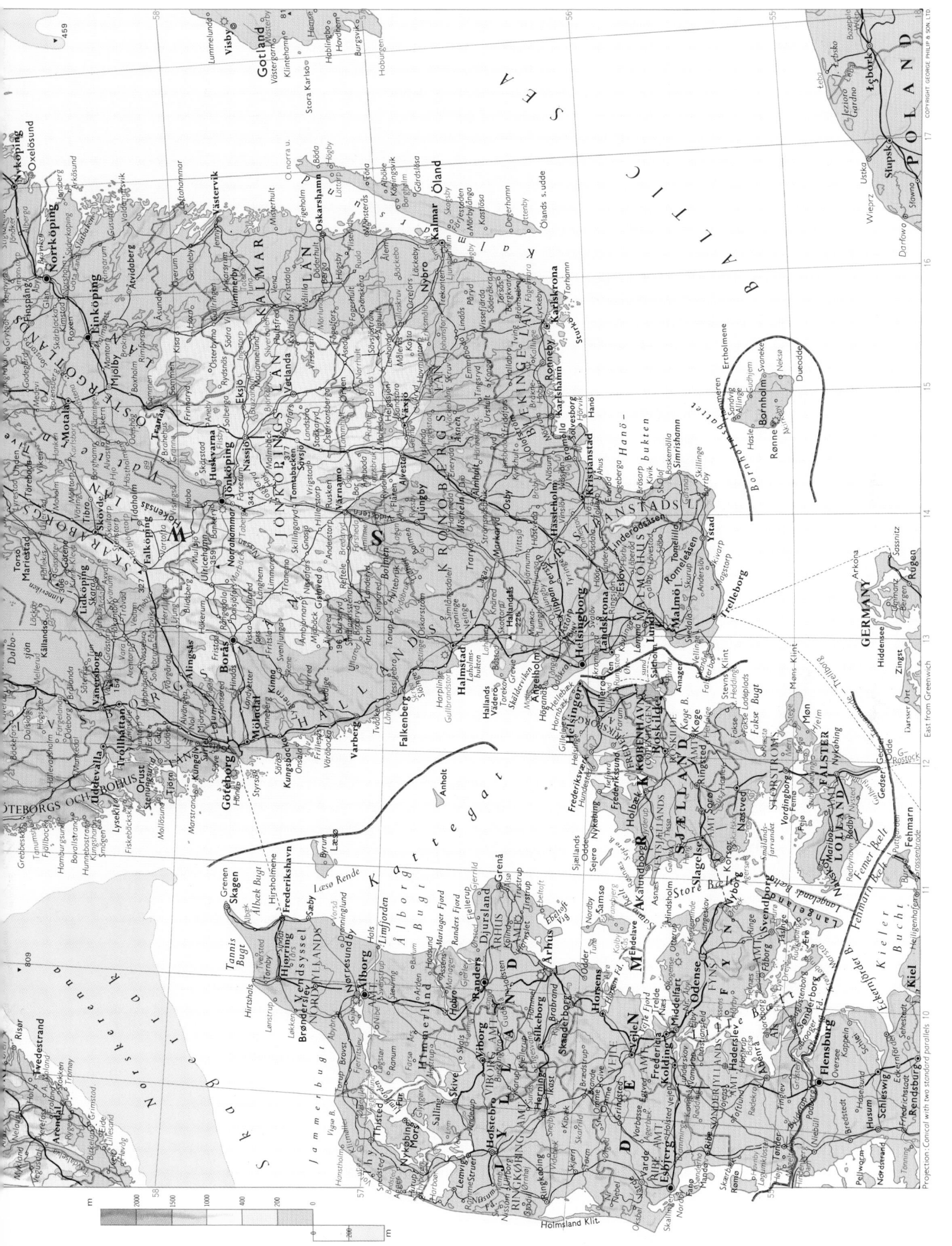

1 : 2 500 000

10 0 10 20 30 40 50 60 70 80 90 100 km

Projection Conical with two standard parallels

East from Greenwich

BALTIC SEA

POLAND

GERMANY

D E N M A R K

J Y L L A N D

SJÆLLAND

Göteborg

Malmö

København

Bornholm

Gotland

Öland

m   2000   1500   1000   400   200   0

Holmsland Klit

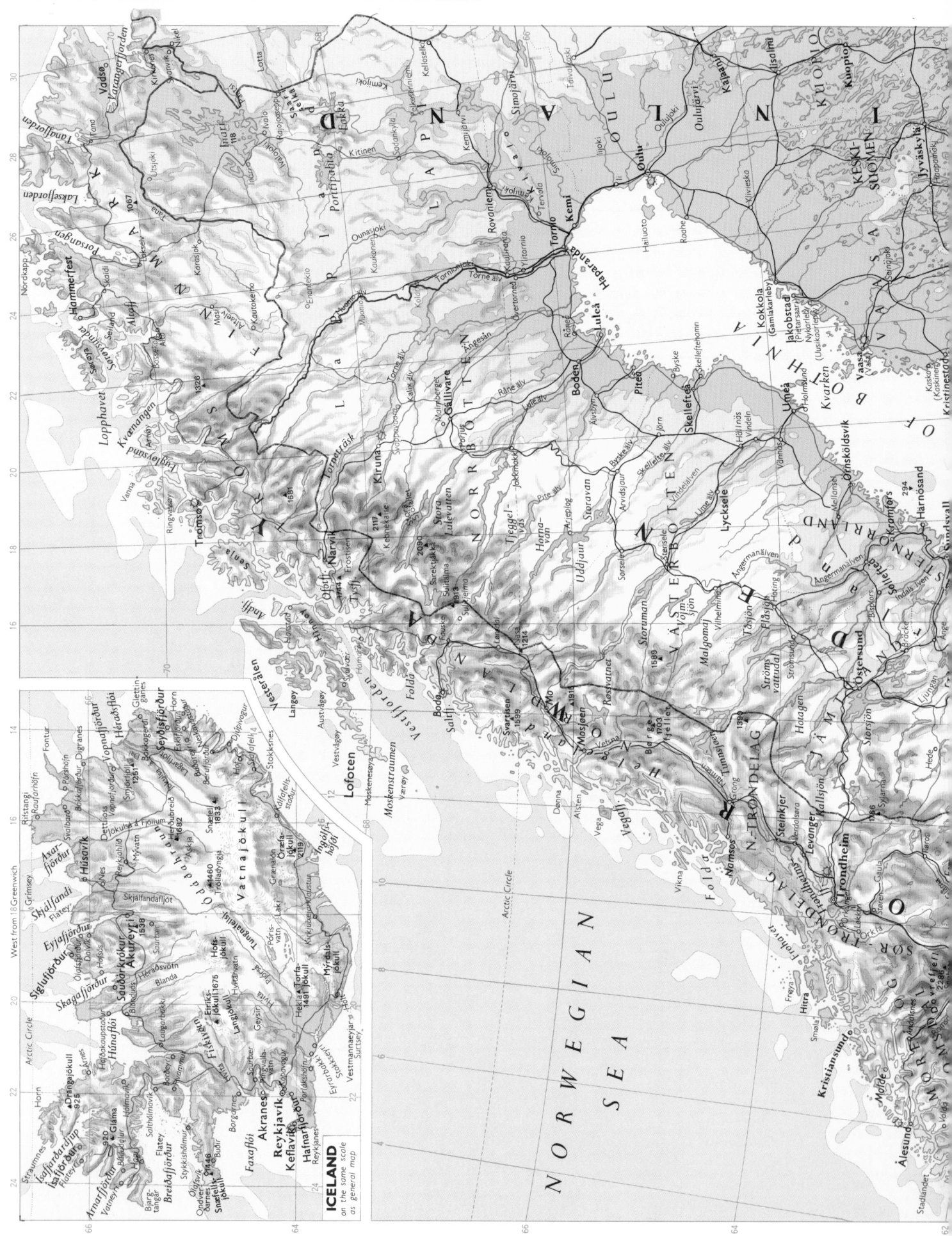

ICELAND
on the same scale
as general map

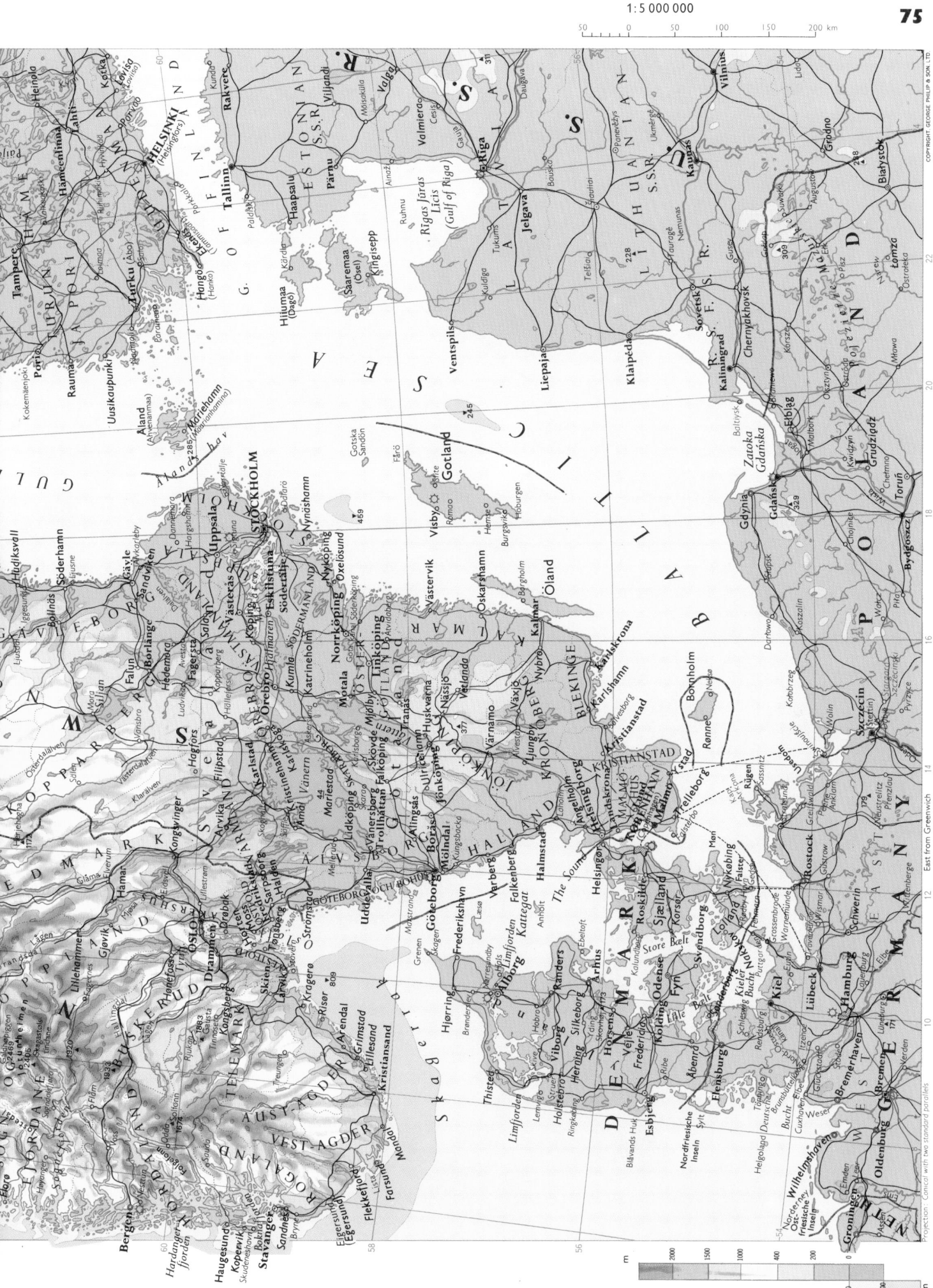

1 : 5 000 000

50   0   50   100   150   200 km

R.S.F.S.R.
1. Daghestan A.S.S.R.
2. Kabardino–Balkar A.S.S.R.
3. Mari A.S.S.R.
4. Mordovian A.S.S.R.
5. North Ossetian A.S.S.R.
6. Tatar A.S.S.R.
7. Udmurt A.S.S.R.
8. Chuvash A.S.S.R.
9. Checheno–Ingush A.S.S.R.
AZERBAIJAN
10. Nakhichevan A.S.S.R.
GEORGIA
11. Abkhaz A.S.S.R.
12. Adzhar A.S.S.R.

1 : 20 000 000

200   0   200   400   600   800 km

O C E A N

Severnaya
Zemlya

Poluostrov
Taymyr
Gory
Taymyr

L a p t e v

S e a

East Siberian Sea

Ostrov Vrangelya

Mys Dezhneva
(East C.)

St. Lawrence I.
(U.S.A.)

Chukotskoye
More

Tiksi

Nordvik

Y A K U T

Verkhoyansk

Khrebet Cherskogo

Bering

Sea

Poluostrov
Kamchatka

A. S. S. R.

Yakutsk

Vilyuysk

Olekminsk

Sea of
Okhotsk

Sakhalin

Magadan

Nikolayevsk-
na-Am.

Okhotsk

Komsomolsk

Khabarovsk

Sovetskaya Gavan

Yuzhno-Sakhalinsk

Krasnoyarsk

Nizhneudinsk

Bratsk

Kirensk

Chita

UlanUde

Irkutsk

Blagoveshchensk

Birobidzhan

Hokkaido

Sapporo

Hakodate

Cheremkhovo

Angarsk

Ussuriysk

Vladivostok

Nakhodka

Sea of JAPAN

M O N G O L I A

Ulaanbaatar
(Ulan Bator)

Haerhpin

Ch'ang ch'un
(Manchuria)

Chilin

Chongjin

Honshu

Ni-gata

I N N E R   M O N G O L I A

S E R   P U B L I C

Shenyang   Fushun

Anshan

Antung

North

Wŏnsan

P'yongyang

Lüta

Sŏul

Inch'on

Taejŏn

South

Pusan

Peip'ing

Paot'ou

Changchiak'ou

COPYRIGHT GEORGE PHILIP & SON LTD.

	Boundaries of U.S.S.R.
	Boundaries of S.S.R.
	Boundaries of A.S.S.R.

1 : 10 000 000

100   0   100   200   300   400 km

1 Kabardino-Balkar A.S.S.R.
2 North Ossetian A.S.S.R.
3 Nakhichevan A.S.S.R. (Azer.)
4 Checheno-Ingush A.S.S.R.
Kargiyè Depression

C A S P I A N   S E A

Kara Bogaz Gol.

B L A C K   S E A

Azovskoye More
(Sea of Azov)

M E D I T E R R A N E A N   S E A

Levant

U K R A I N E

R O M A N I A

B U L G A R I A

MOLDAVIAN S.S.R.

K i r g i z   S t e p p e

K A Z A K H   S.S.R.

Privolzhskaya Vozvyshennost

KALMYK A.S.S.R.

GEORGIAN S.S.R.

ARMENIAN S.S.R.

AZERBAIJAN S.S.R.

T U R K E Y

S Y R I A

I R A Q

I R A N   (P E R S I A)

CYPRUS

Kuzey Anadolu Dağları

Toros Dağları

Anadolu

KIYEV (Kiev)
KHARKOV
Rostov
Volgograd (Stalingrad)
Astrakhan
Guryev
BAKU
Tbilisi
Yerevan
Tabrīz
TEHRĀN
Qom
Hamadān
Baghdad
Al Mawsil
Dimashq (Damascus)
LEBANON
Bayrūt (Beirut)
Halab
Hamā
Homs
Adana
Konya
Ankara
İzmir
İSTANBUL
BUCUREŞTI (Bucharest)
Odessa
Sevastopol
Simferopol
Krasnodar
Novorossiysk
Sochi
Sukhumi
Batumi
Trabzon
Samsun
Krymskiy P-ov. (Crimea)
Rhodos
Dhodhekanísos

Demavend 5604

Division between Greeks and Turks
in Cyprus; Turks to the North.

Projection: Conical with two standard parallels

East from Greenwich

m 4000 2000 1000 400 200 0

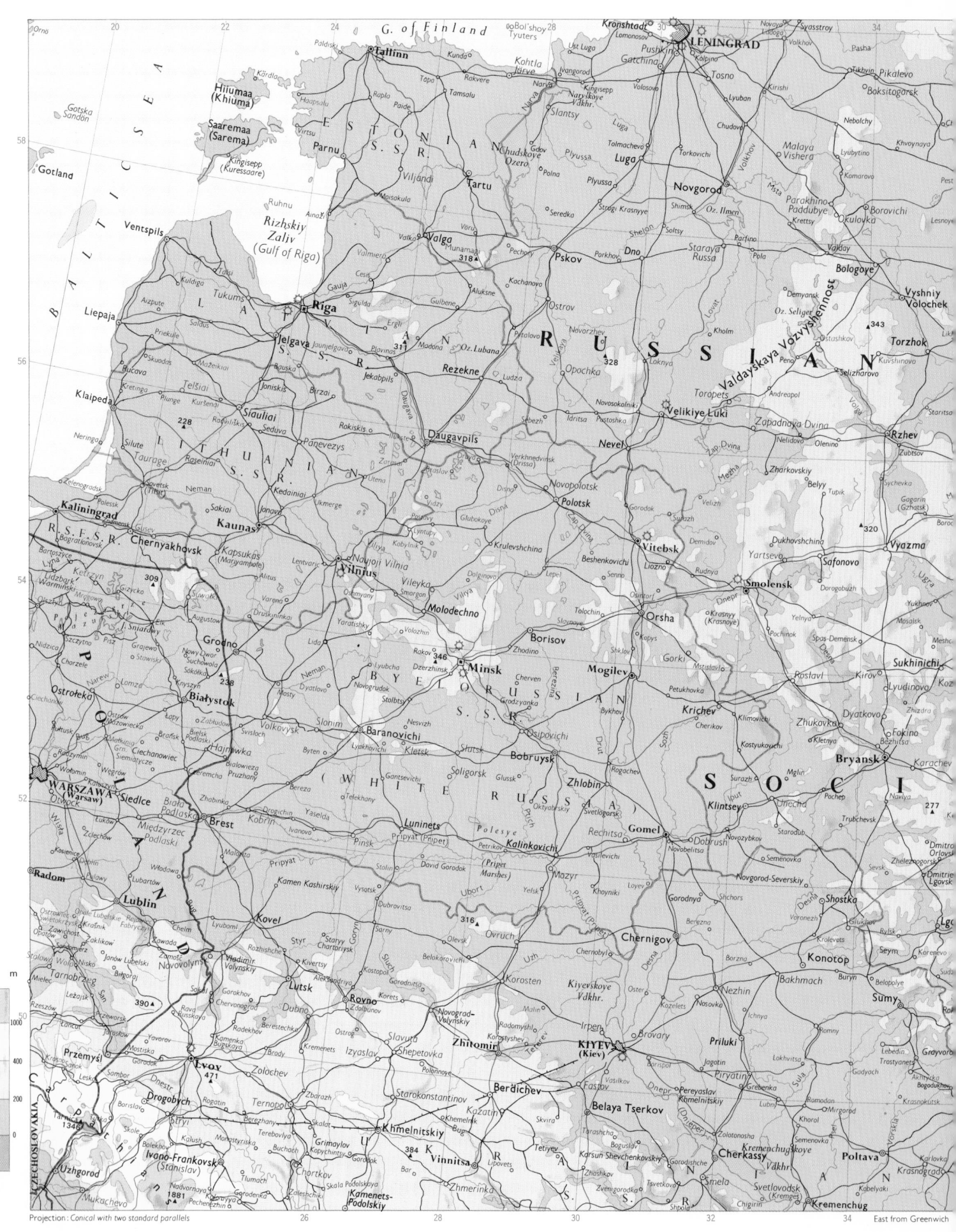

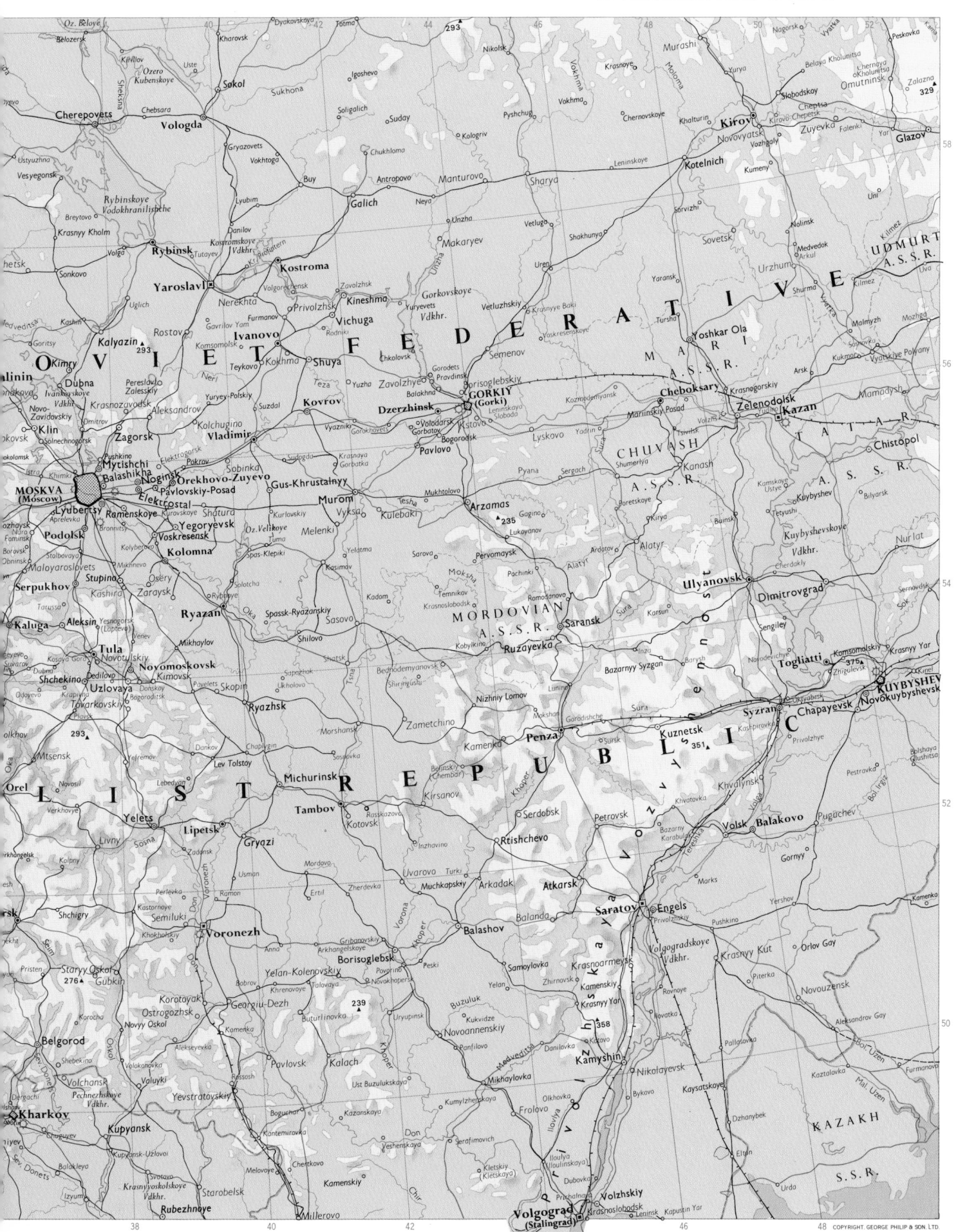

1:5 000 000

50 0 50 100 150 200 km

Projection: Conical with two standard parallels

1:5 000 000

50　0　50　100　150　200 km

Yelan-Kolenovskiy
Bobrov
Povorino
Peski
Krasnoarmeysk
Krasnyy Kut
Orlov Gay
Oz. Chalkar
Chalkar
Dzhambeyty
Georgiu-Dezh
Ostrogozhsk
Kamenka
Buturlinovka
239
Uryupinsk
Novokhoperek
Samoylovka
Zhirnovsk
Ravnoye
Novouzensk
Kushum
Krasnyy Yar
358
Vozyshennost
Volgogradskoye
Vdkhr.
Aleksandrov Gay
Mergenevskiy
Karsha
Ural
Bazartobe
Pavlovsk
Kalach
Novoannenskiy
Panfilovo
Medveditsa
Danilovka
Yelan
Bykovo
Furmanovo
Antonovo

Volgograd
(Stalingrad)
Volzhskiy
Krasnoslobodsk
Kamyshin
Nikolayevsk
Kapustin Yar
Shungay
Zelënyy
Topol

Astrakhan
KALMYK A.S.S.R.
Elista (Stepnoi)
Guryev

Rostov
Bataysk
Azov
Novocherkassk
Shakhty
Novoshakhtinsk

CASPIAN SEA

Krasnodar
Armavir
Stavropol
Nevinnomyssk
Maykop
Cherkessk
Mineralnyye Vody
Pyatigorsk
Kislovodsk
Nalchik
KABARDINO-BALKAR A.S.S.R.
Mozdok
CHECHENO-INGUSH A.S.S.R.
Groznyy
Gudermes
Makhachkala
DAGESTAN A.S.S.R.
Ordzhonikidze
Kizlyar

Sochi
Adler
Gagra
ABKHAZ A.S.S.R.
Sukhumi
Ochamchire
GEORGIAN S.S.R.
Kutaisi
Poti
Batumi
ADZHAR A.S.S.R.
Tskhinvali
Tbilisi
Rustavi
Mingechaur
AZERBAIJAN S.S.R.
Sumgait
BAKU
Derbent

Trabzon
Rize
Leninakan
Kirovakan
Kars
ARMENIAN S.S.R.
Yerevan
Kirovabad

East from Greenwich　40　42　44　46　48

COPYRIGHT. GEORGE PHILIP & SON. LTD

1 : 5 000 000

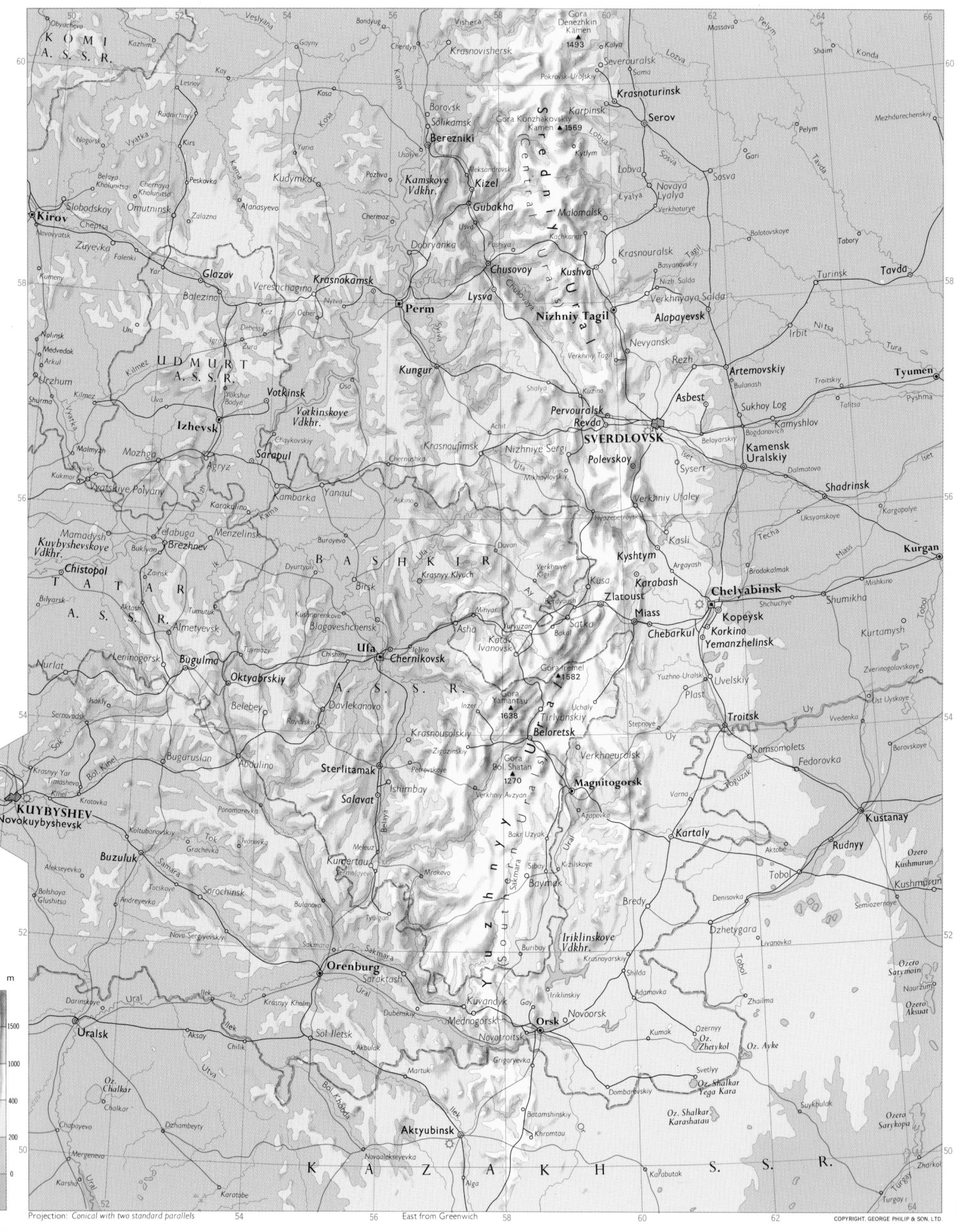

Projection: Conical with two standard parallels   East from Greenwich   COPYRIGHT. GEORGE PHILIP & SON. LTD.

1:5 000 000

50   0   50   100   150   200 km

COPYRIGHT GEORGE PHILIP & SON LTD.

East from Greenwich

Projection: Conical with two standard parallels.

m   6000 4000 3000 2000 1500 1000 400 200   0

1:50 000 000

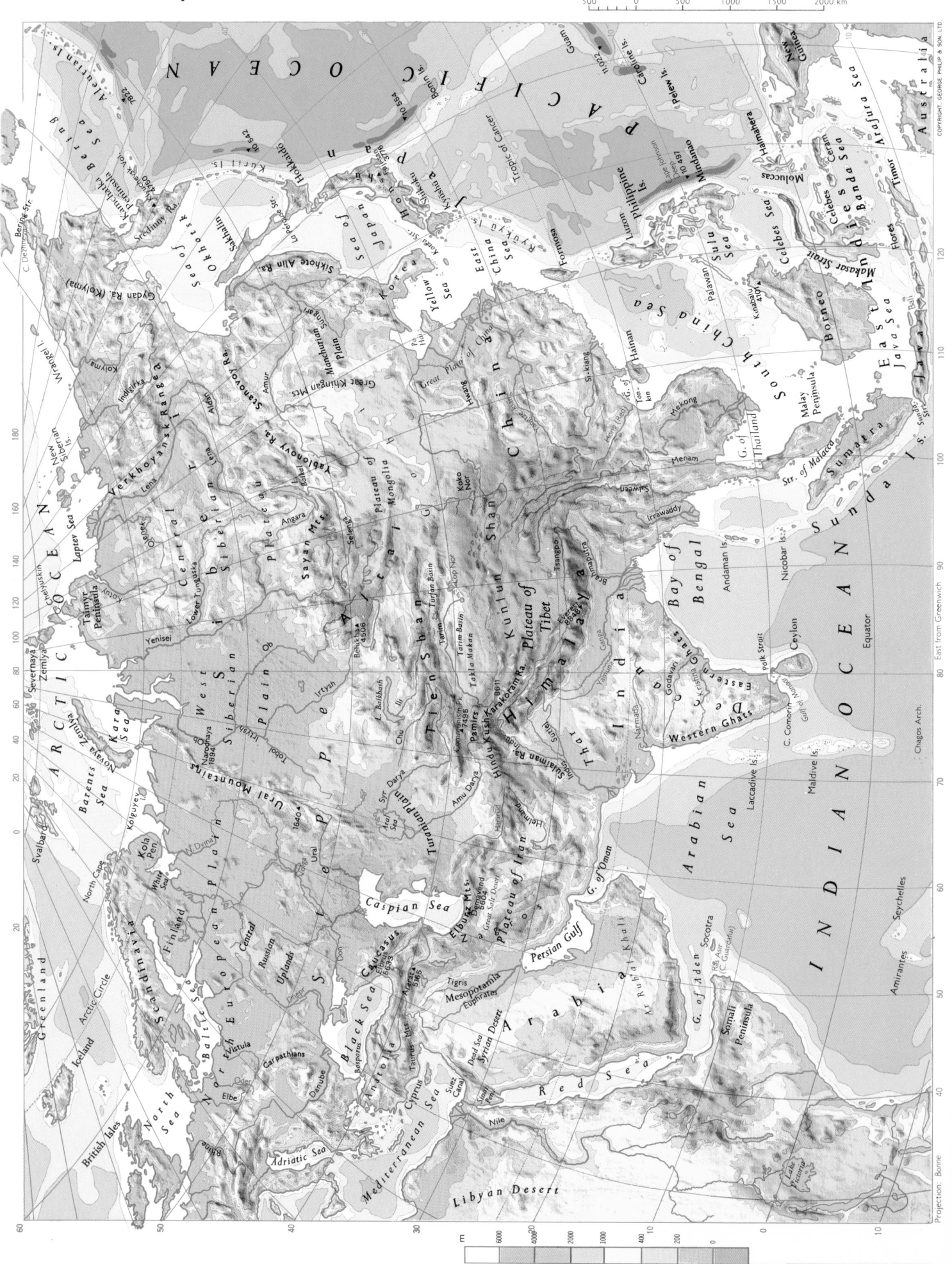

Projection: Bonne

1:50 000 000

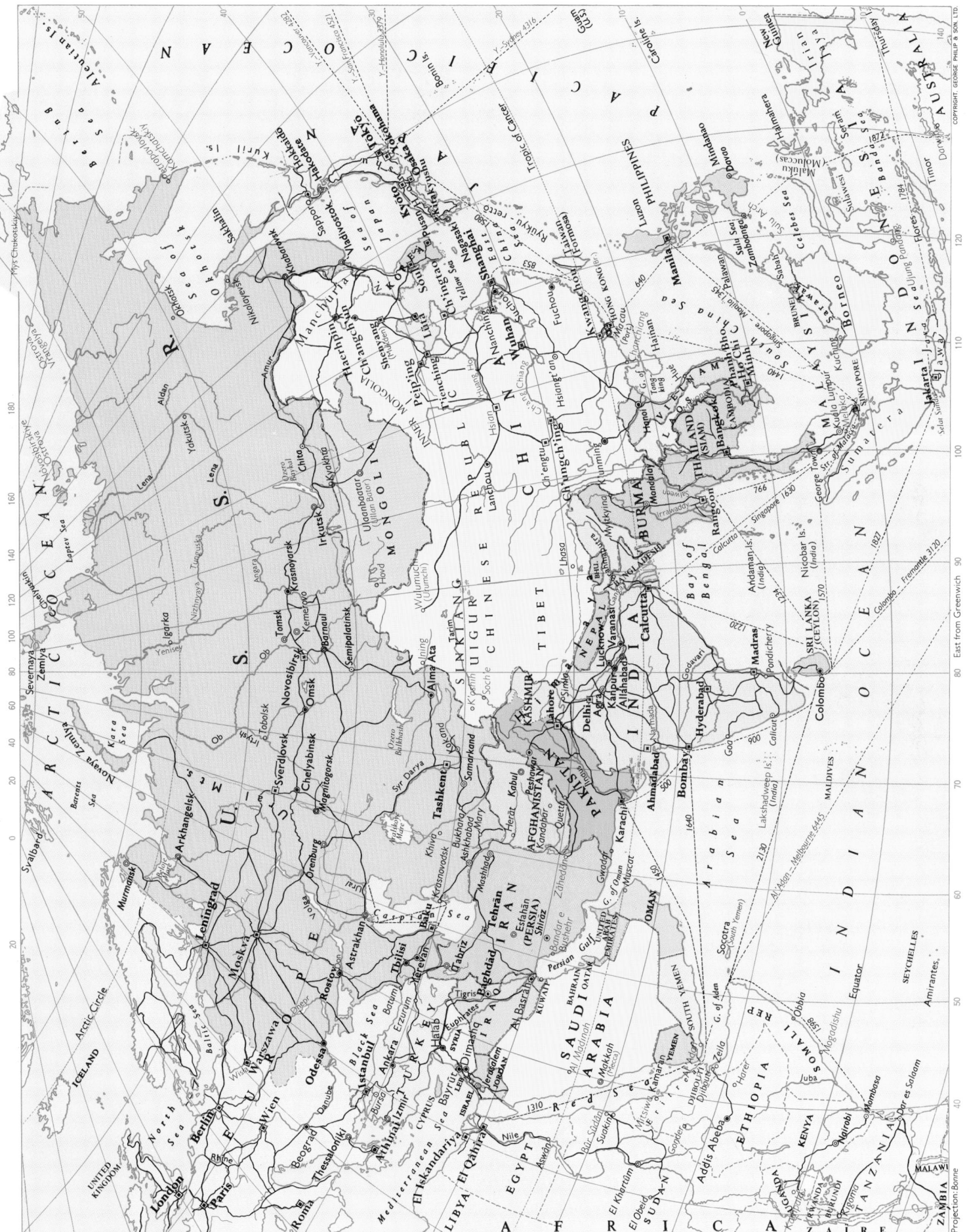

Projection: Bonne

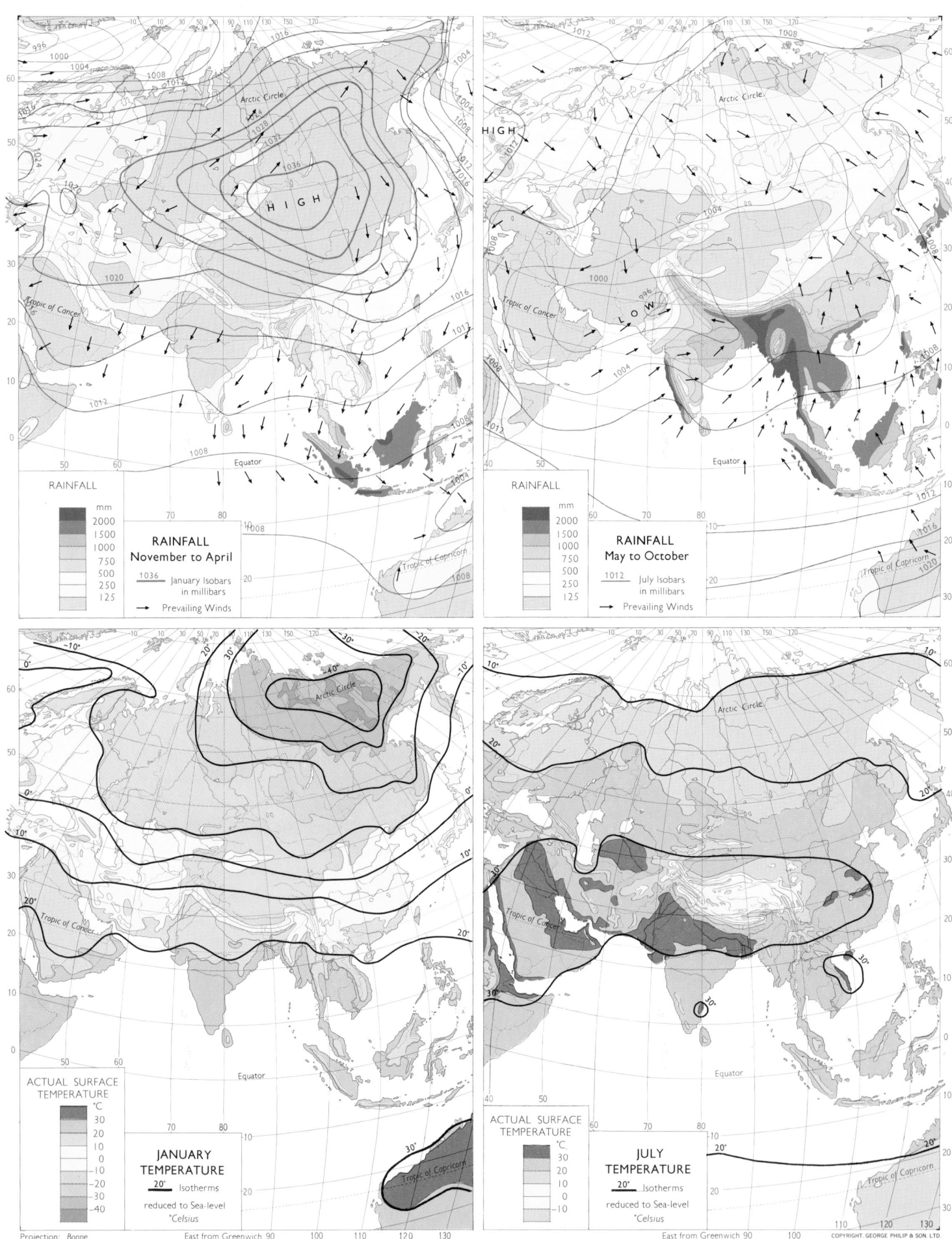

RAINFALL

mm
2000
1500
1000
750
500
250
125

RAINFALL
November to April

1036 January Isobars
        in millibars
→ Prevailing Winds

RAINFALL

mm
2000
1500
1000
750
500
250
125

RAINFALL
May to October

1012 July Isobars
        in millibars
→ Prevailing Winds

ACTUAL SURFACE
TEMPERATURE

°C
30
20
10
0
-10
-20
-30
-40

**JANUARY
TEMPERATURE**

20° Isotherms
reduced to Sea-level
°Celsius

ACTUAL SURFACE
TEMPERATURE

°C
30
20
10
0
-10

**JULY
TEMPERATURE**

20° Isotherms
reduced to Sea-level
°Celsius

Projection: *Bonne*   East from Greenwich 90   100   110   120   130

East from Greenwich 90   100   COPYRIGHT. GEORGE PHILIP & SON. LTD.

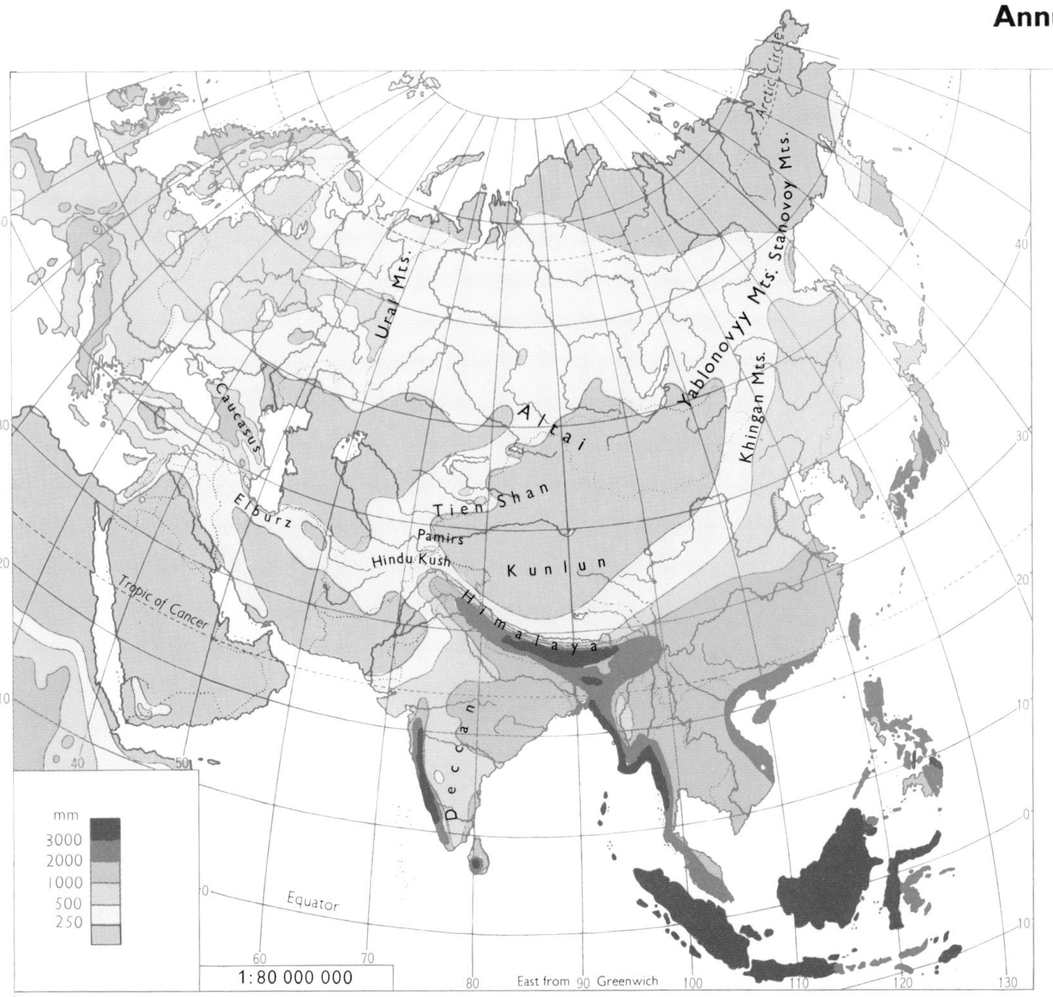

INDIA: MONSOONS

THEIR EVOLUTION
IS SHOWN BY
MONTHLY
CLIMATE
MAPS

RAINFALL
mm per month

mm
25
50
100
200
400

— ISOTHERMS
*Temperature in
degrees Celsius*

— ISOBARS
(Pressure in millibars)

← WINDS

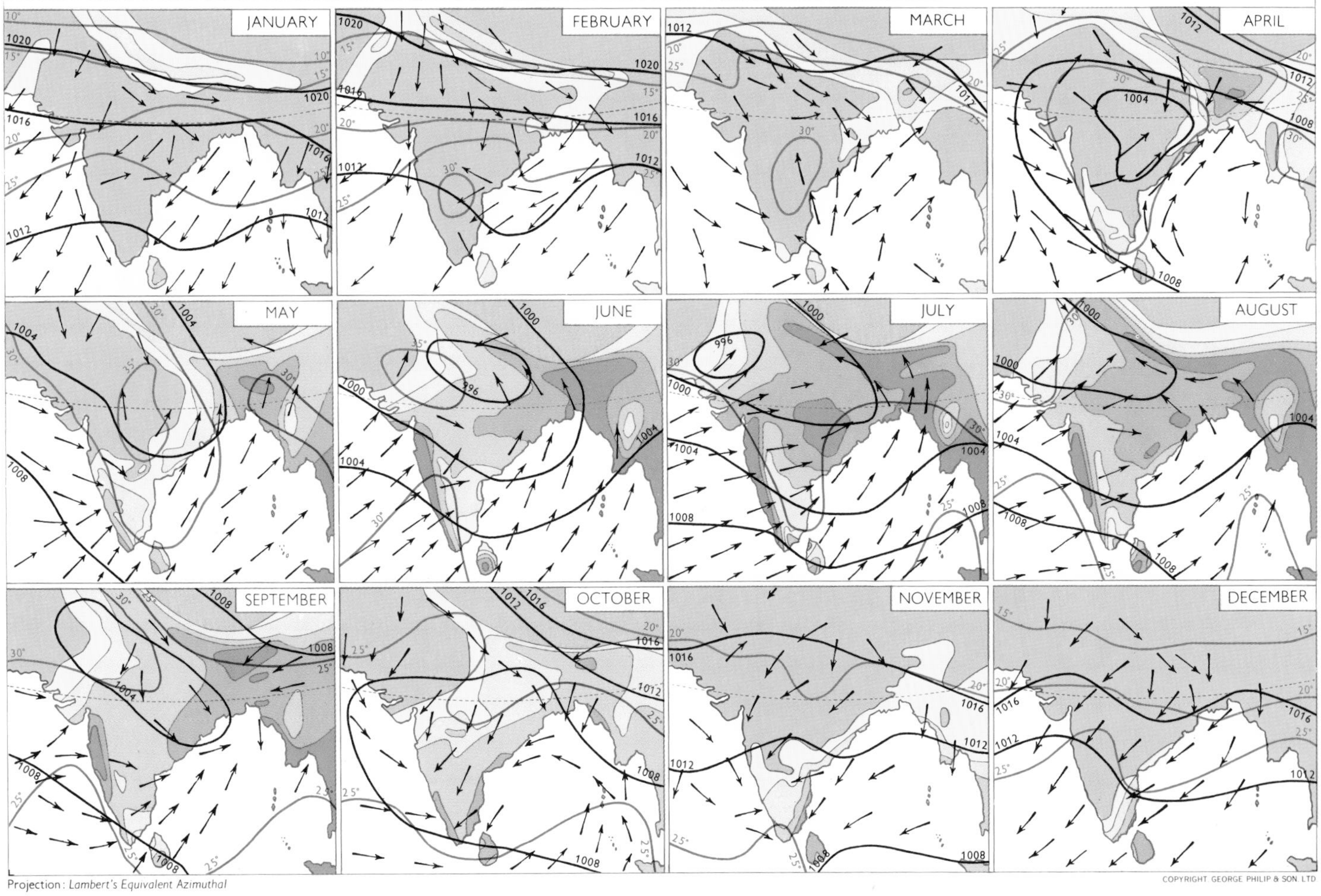

mm
3000
2000
1000
500
250

1:80 000 000

Equator

East from Greenwich

Projection: *Lambert's Equivalent Azimuthal*

COPYRIGHT. GEORGE PHILIP & SON LTD

1:1 000 000

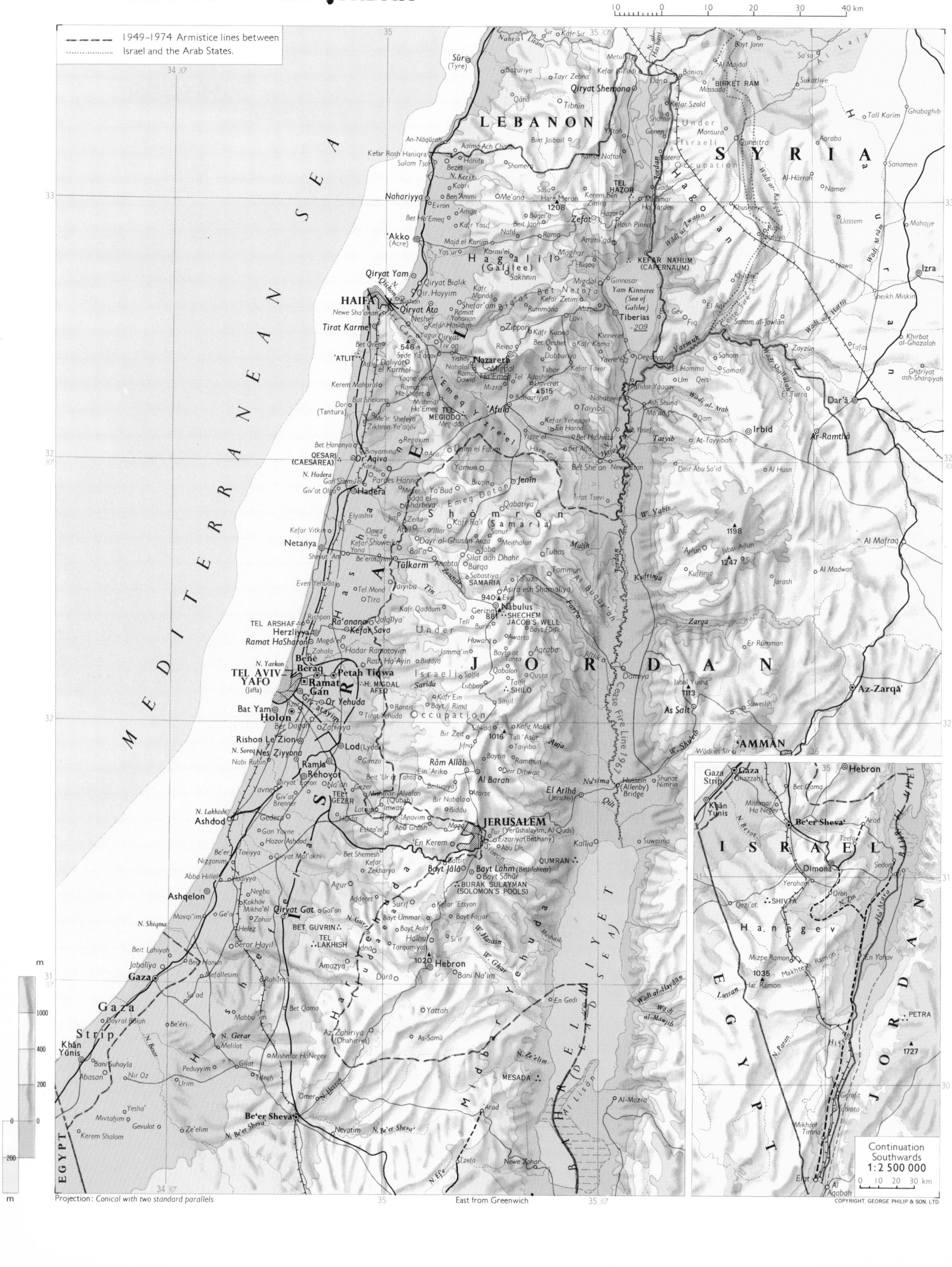

10   0   10   20   30   40 km

1949–1974 Armistice lines between
Israel and the Arab States.

LEBANON

SYRIA

MEDITERRANEAN SEA

JORDAN

EGYPT

ISRAEL

Gaza Strip

Major place names:

Sūr (Tyre), Qiryat Shemona, BIRKET RAM, Nahariyya, Akko (Acre), Qiryat Yam, HAIFA, Qiryat Ata, Tirat Karmel, 'ATLIT, Hagalil (Galilee), KEFAR NAHUM (CAPERNAUM), Tiberias, Yam Kinneret (Sea of Galilee), Nazareth, Afula, TEL MEGIDDO, Emeq Yizre'el, Shomron (Samaria), Netanya, Hadera, QESARI (CAESAREA), Or Aqiva, Jenin, Tülkarm, SAMARIA, NABULUS, SHECHEM, JACOB'S WELL, TEL ARSHAF, Herzliyya, Ramat HaSharon, Bene Beraq, TEL AVIV-YAFO (Jaffa), Ramat Gan, Bat Yam, Holon, Rishon Le Zion, Nes Ziyyona, Ramla, Rehovot, Lod (Lydda), TEL GEZER, Ashdod, Râm Allâh, Al Bareh, El Arihā (Jericho), JERUSALEM (Yerushalayim, Al Quds), Ashqelon, Qiryat Gat, BET GUVRIN, TEL LAKHISH, Bayt Lahm (Bethlehem), QUMRAN, BURAK SULAYMAN (SOLOMON'S POOLS), Gaza, Khān Yūnis, Hebron, MESADA, Be'er Sheva', Dimona, Az Zarqā', 'AMMAN, As Salt, Irbid, Ar-Ramthā, Al Mafraq

'AMMAN

Az-Zarqā'

Inset (Continuation Southwards):

Continuation Southwards
1:2 500 000
0 10 20 30 km

ISRAEL

JORDAN

EGYPT

Gaza Strip, Khān Yūnis, Gaza, Hebron, Be'er Sheva', Dimona, SHIVTA, Ha negev, Mizpe Ramon, Har Ramon 1035, En Yahav, PETRA, 1727, Elat, Al 'Aqaba

Scale bar (elevation, left):

m
1000
400
200
0
200
m

Projection: Conical with two standard parallels

East from Greenwich

1:15 000 000

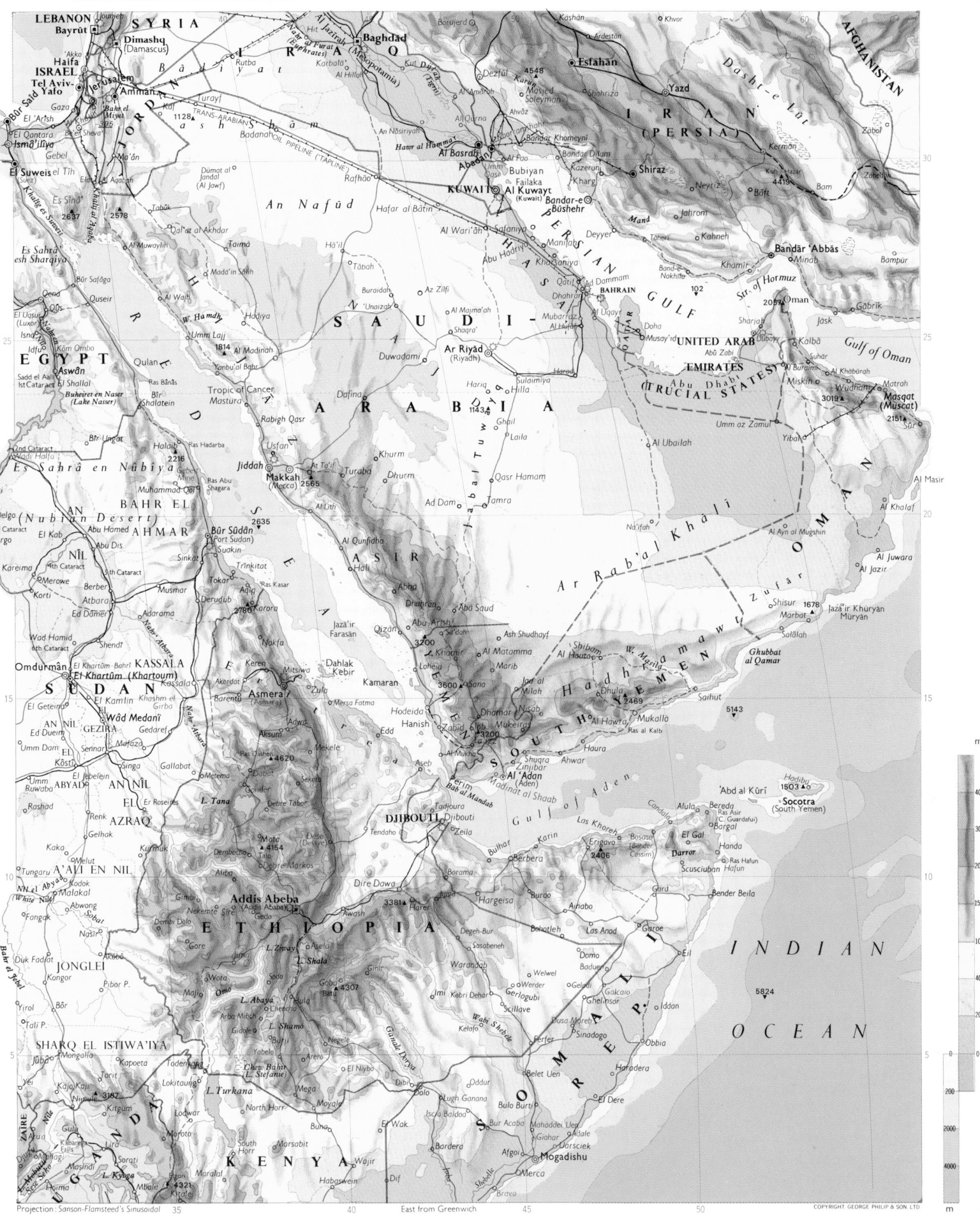

Projection: Sanson-Flamsteed's Sinusoidal

East from Greenwich

COPYRIGHT GEORGE PHILIP & SON LTD

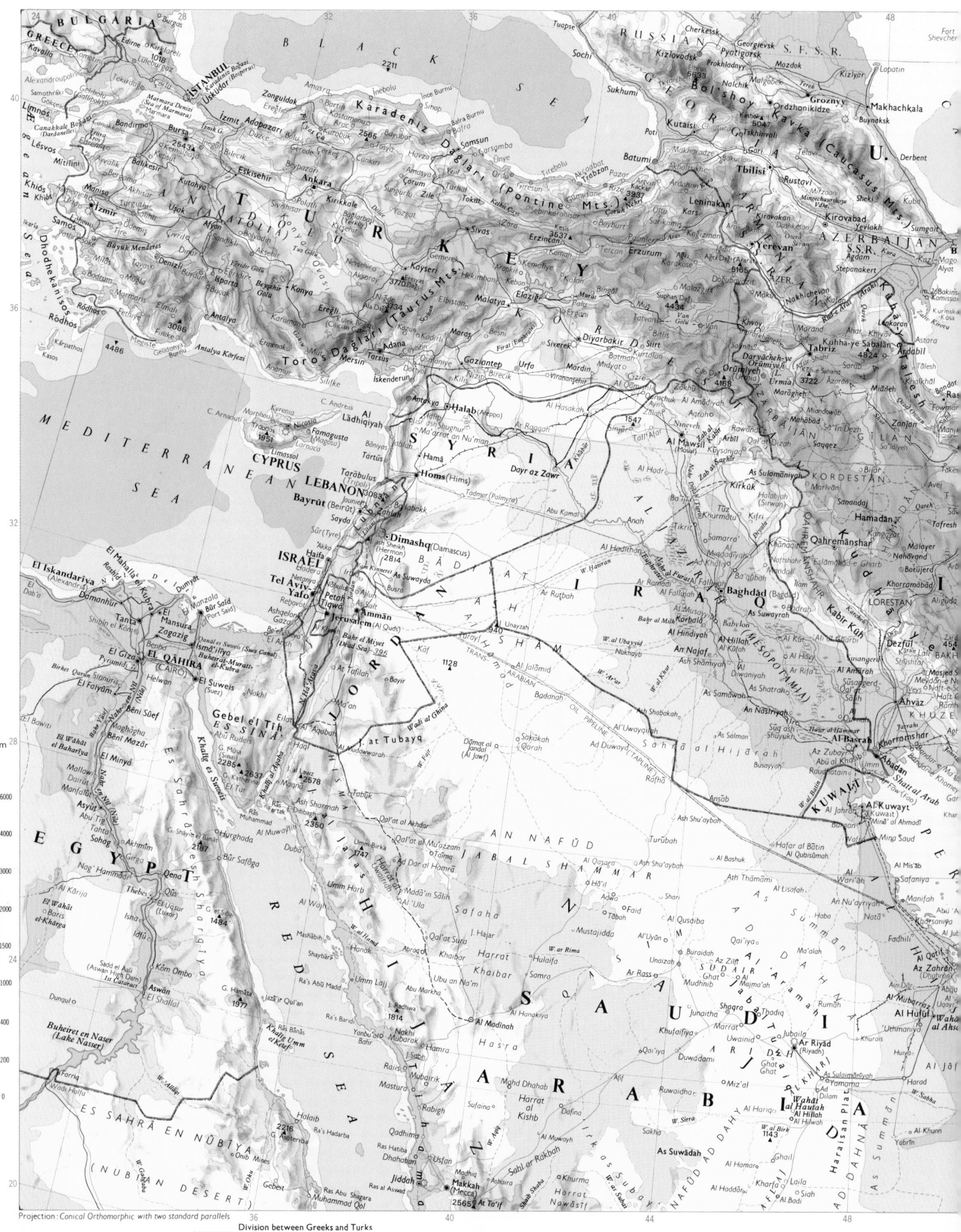

Projection: Conical Orthomorphic with two standard parallels

---------- Division between Greeks and Turks
in Cyprus; Turks to the North.

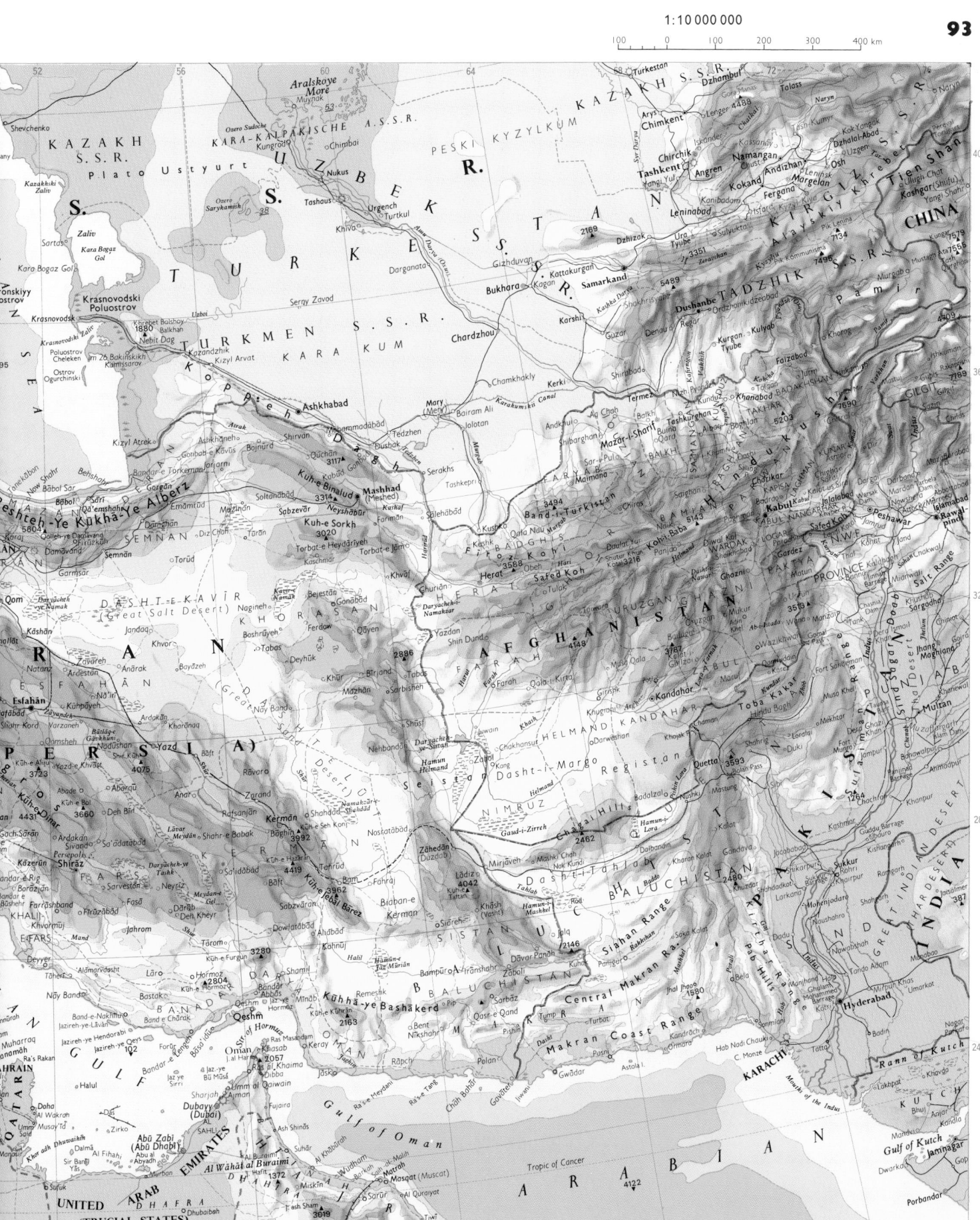

1:10 000 000

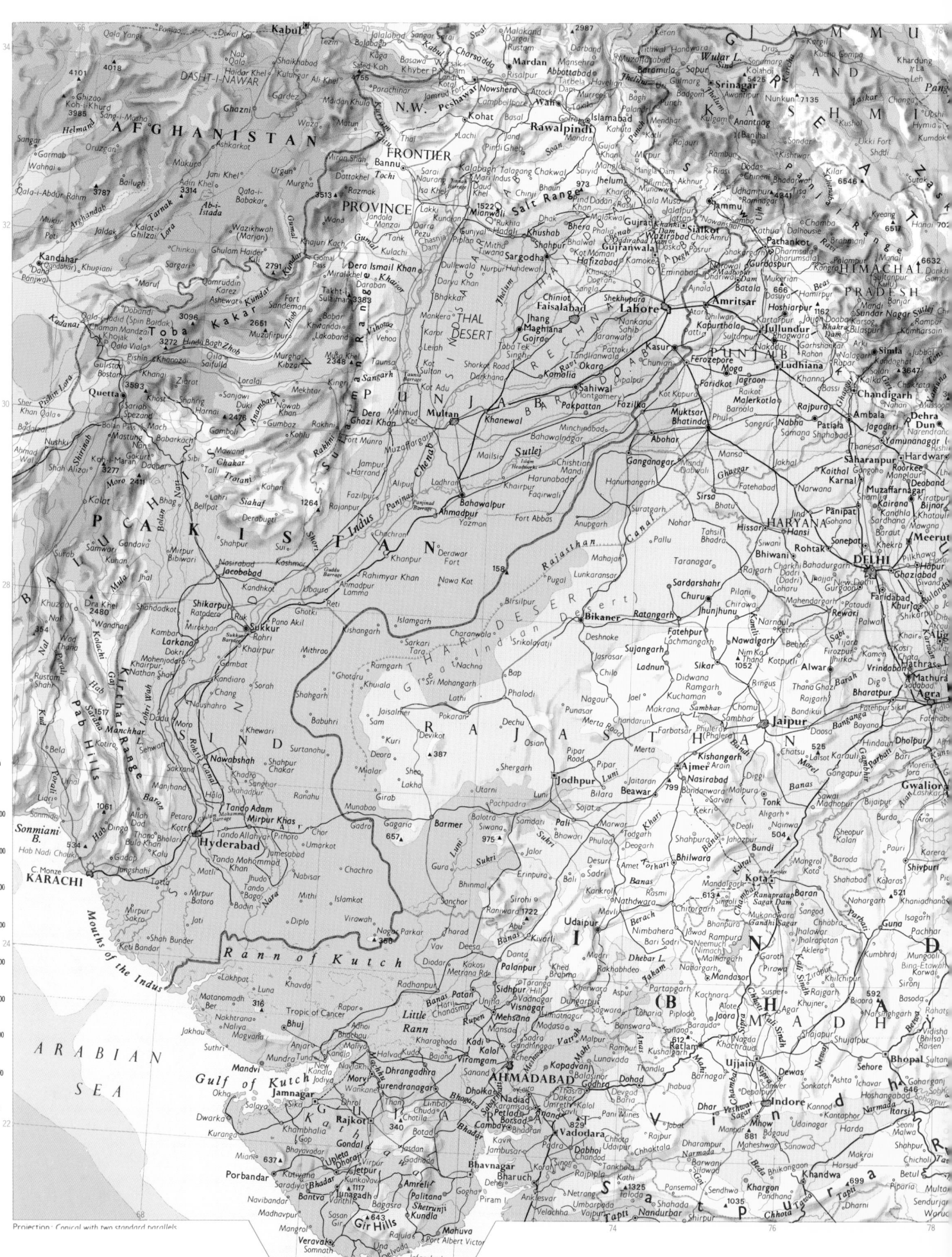

1:6 000 000

50   0   50   100   150   200   250 km

East from Greenwich

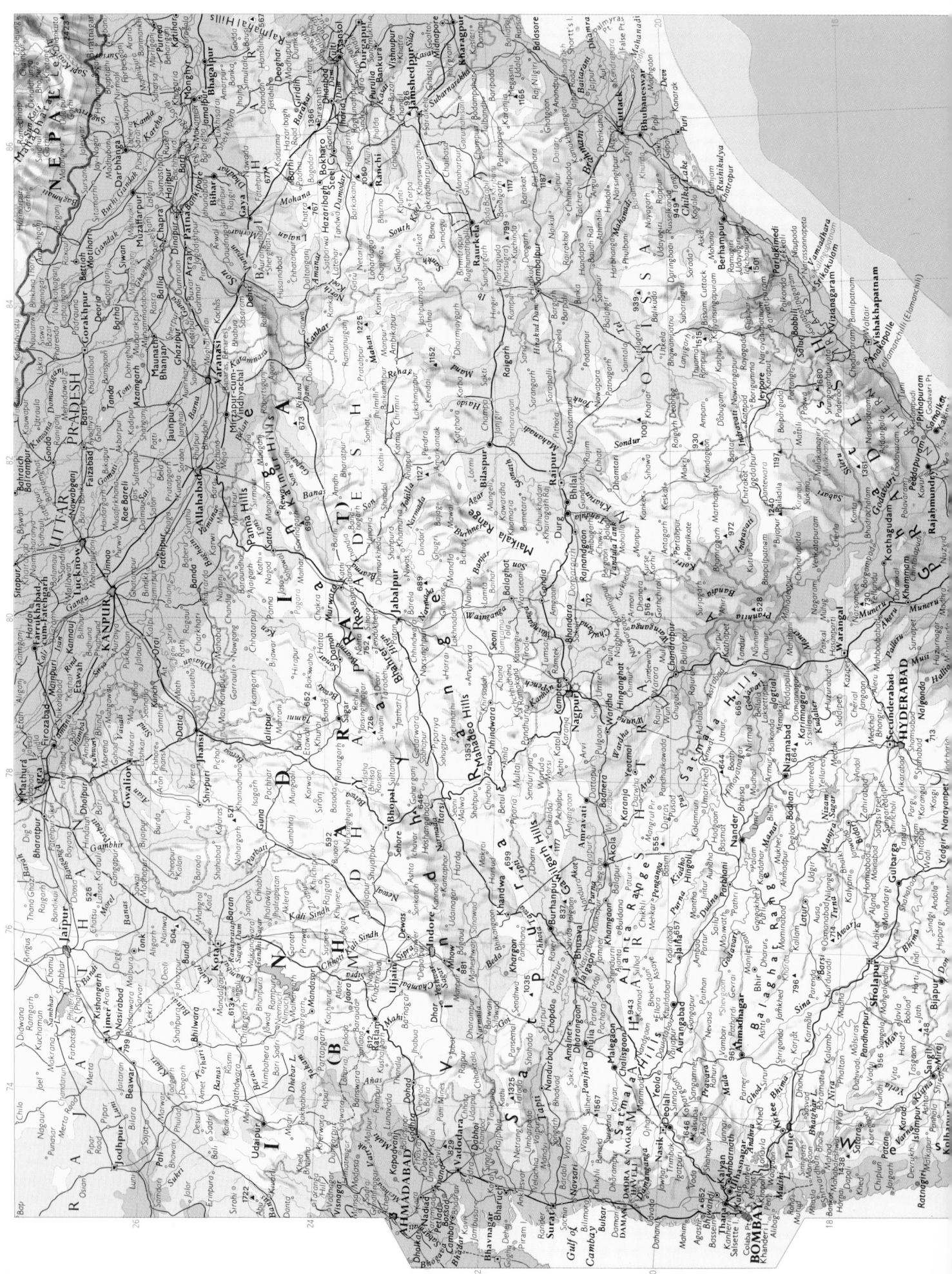

1 : 6 000 000

50 0 50 100 150 200 250 km

BAY OF BENGAL

ARABIAN SEA

Coromandel Coast

MADRAS

ANDHRA PRADESH

KARNATAKA

GOA

TAMIL NADU

Bangalore

Mysore

KERALA

SRI LANKA (CEYLON)

Gulf of Mannar

Palk Strait

Colombo

Trincomalee

Jaffna

C. Comorin

East from 80 Greenwich

COPYRIGHT GEORGE PHILIP & SON LTD

Projection. Conical with two standard parallels
CIB

m 3000 2000 1500 1000 400 200 0 200 2000 4000 m

1:6 000 000

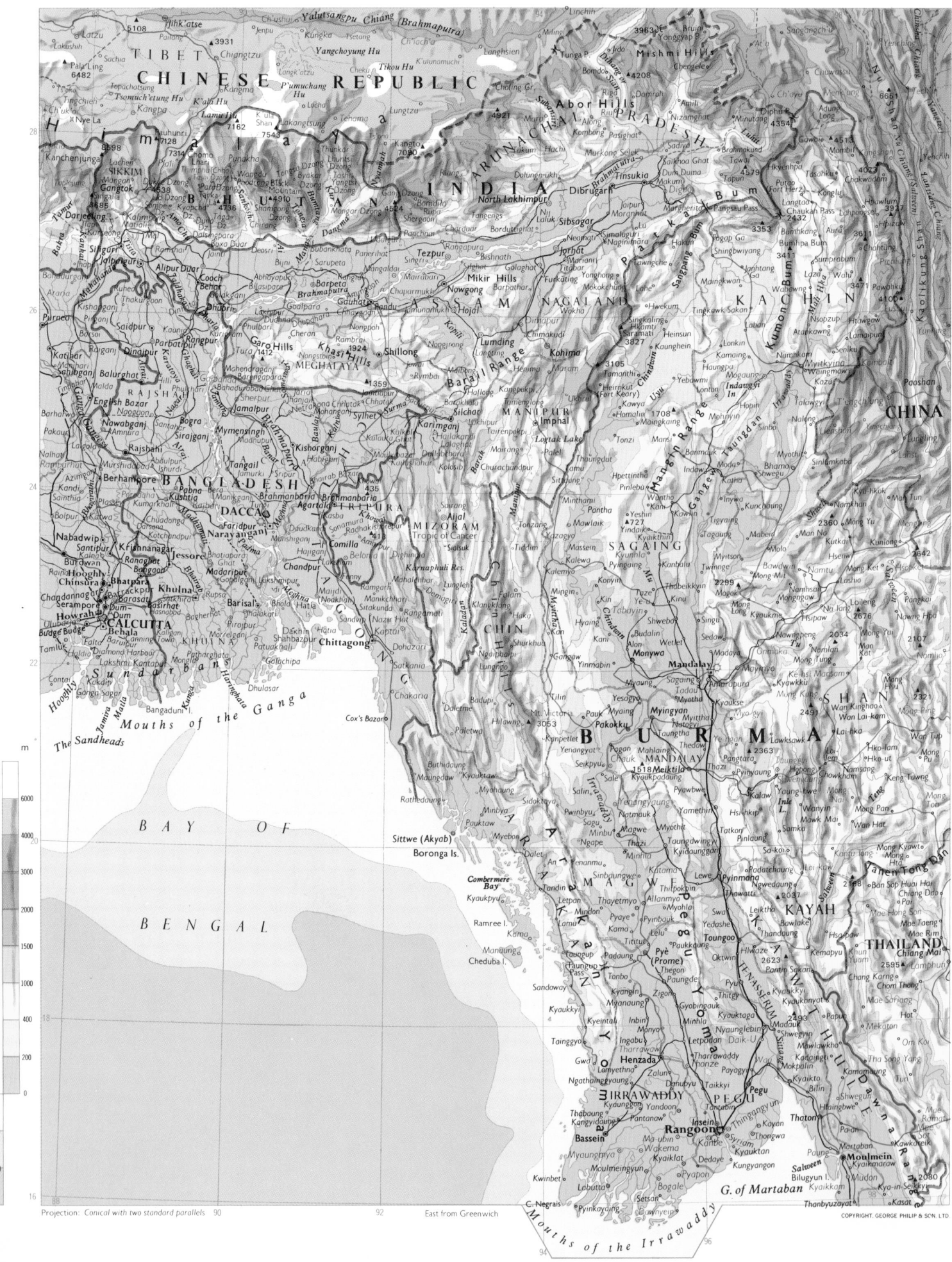

Projection: Conical with two standard parallels   East from Greenwich

1 : 20 000 000

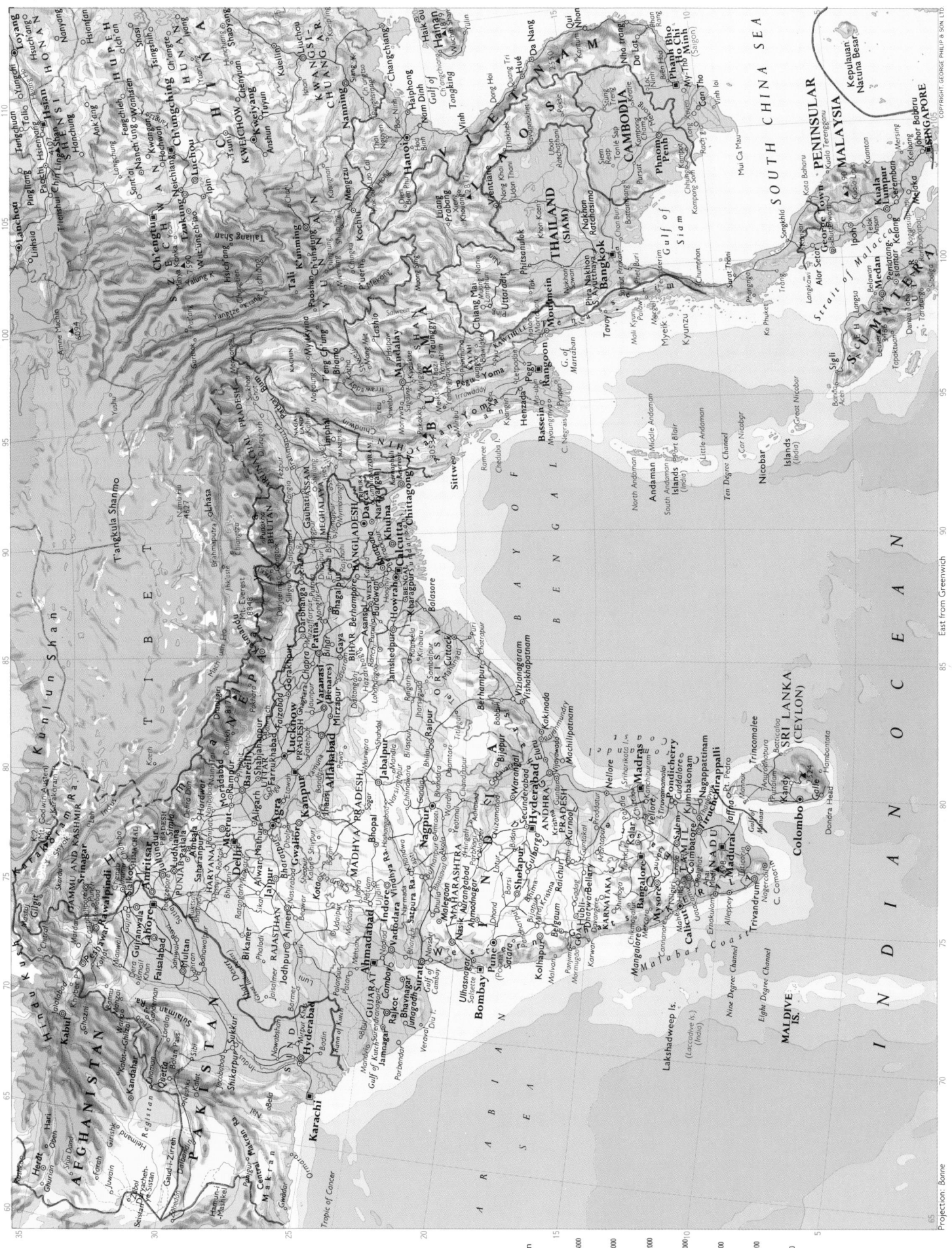

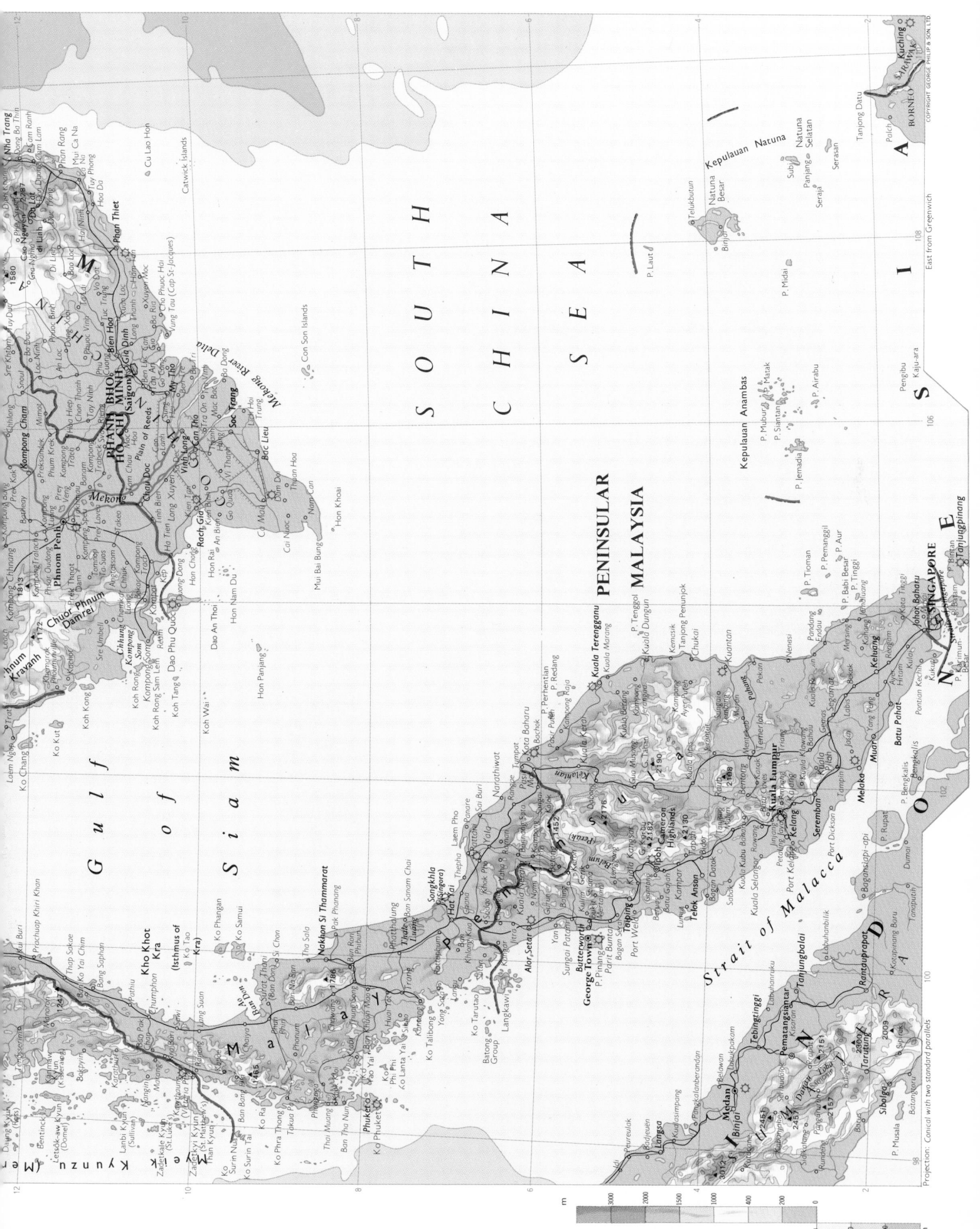

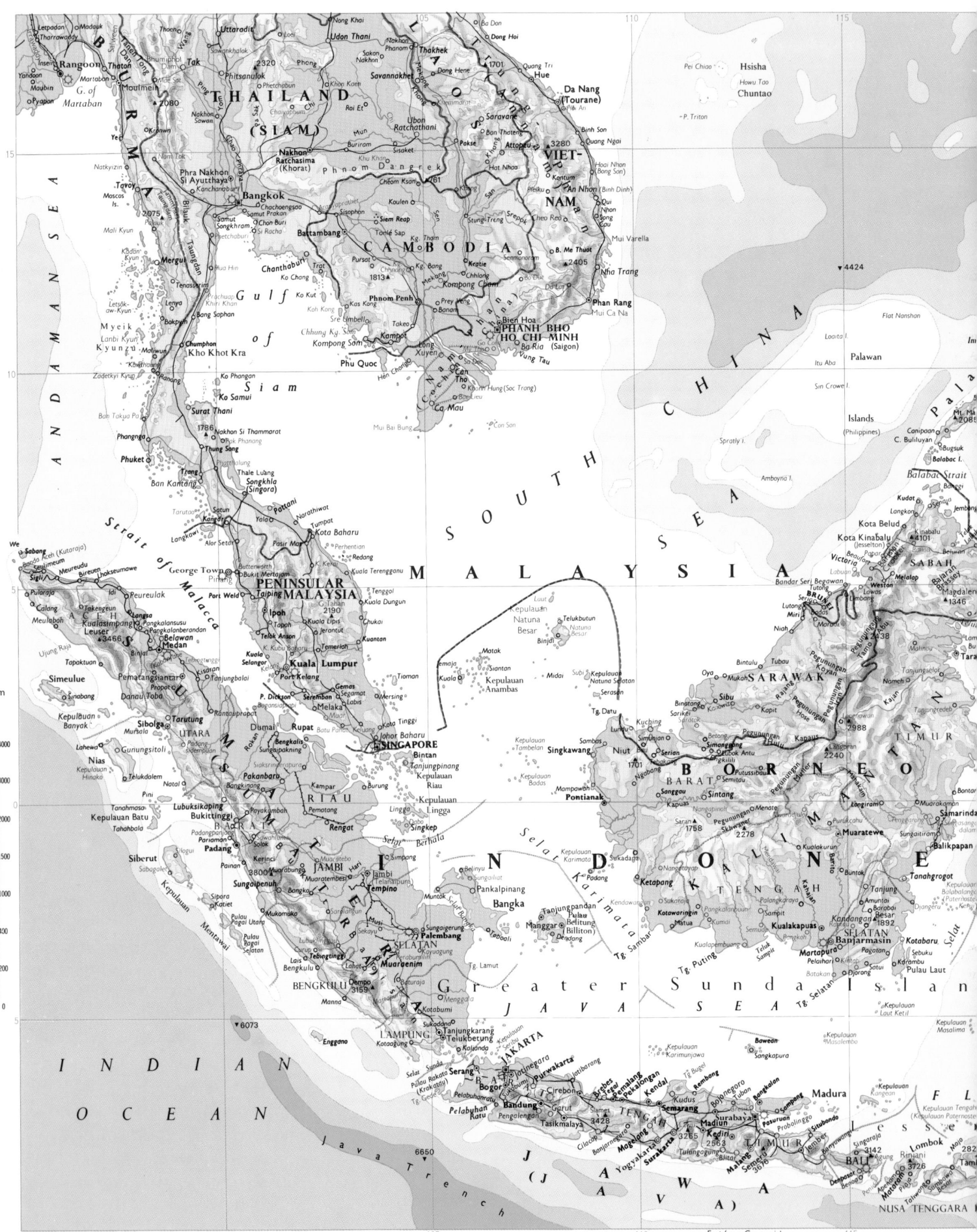

BURMA

Letpadan Madauk
Tharrawaddy Thoona
  Insein Rangoon Thaton
Yandoon Thaton Moulmein
Maubin Martaban
Pyapon G. of
  Martaban
Kadan
Kyun Moscos Is.
Mali Kyun

Thone Nang Khai
Uttaradit Udon Thani
Loei Phon Sakon Nakhon
  Phitsanulok Khon Kaen Phanom
Tak 2320
Sawankhalok
Bhumiphol Dam

THAILAND
(SIAM)

Nakhon Phra Nakhon Nakhon
Ratchasima
(Khorat)

Bangkok
Samut Prakan
Chachoengsao Chon Buri
Si Racha

Gulf

of

Siam

LAOS
Thakhek
Savannakhet
Dong Hene

Dong Hoi
Quang Tri
Hue

Da Nang
(Tourane)

VIET-
NAM

SOUTH CHINA

SEA

MALAYSIA

INDIAN

OCEAN

Java Trench

INDONESIA

JAKARTA

NUSA TENGGARA

Projection: Mercator   East from Greenwich

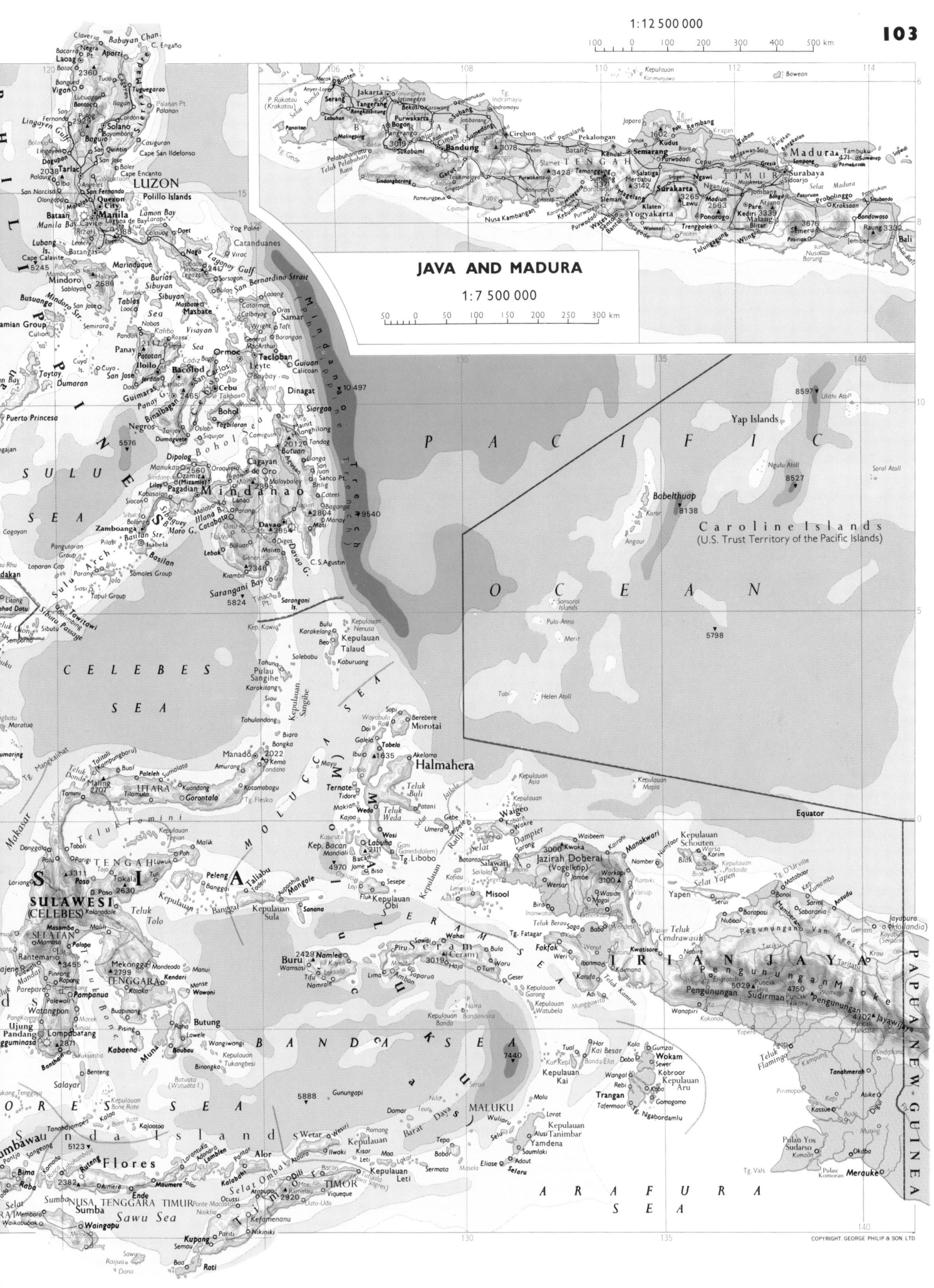

1:12 500 000

100 0 100 200 300 400 500 km

JAVA AND MADURA

1:7 500 000

50 0 50 100 150 200 250 300 km

P A C I F I C

O C E A N

Yap Islands

Caroline Islands
(U.S. Trust Territory of the Pacific Islands)

Babelthuap

P H I L I P P I N E S

LUZON

Manila

Manila Bay

Lubang Is.

Mindoro

Sibuyan Sea

Panay

Iloilo

Bacolod

Negros

Cebu

Bohol

Mindanao

Davao

S U L U   S E A

Zamboanga

Sulu Arch.

Jolo

C E L E B E S   S E A

Manado

UTARA

Gorontalo

M O L U C C A   S E A

Ternate
Tidore

Halmahera

Morotai

Tobelo

Kepulauan Talaud

Pulau Sangihe

S U L A W E S I
(CELEBES)

TENGAH

Teluk Tomini

Kendari

TENGGARA

SELATAN

Ujung Pandang

B A N D A   S E A

Butung

Muna

Buru

Ambon

Seram (Ceram)

Misool

Waigeo

Sorong

Jazirah Doberai
(Vogelkop)

Manokwari

Yapen

I R I A N   J A Y A

Pegunungan Maoke

Pegunungan Sudirman

Jayapura

Teluk Cendrawasih

Kepulauan Aru

Kepulauan Kai

Kepulauan Tanimbar

MALUKU

A R A F U R A

S E A

F L O R E S   S E A

Flores

Sumbawa

Bima

S U M B A

N U S A   T E N G G A R A   T I M U R

T I M O R

Kupang

Sawu Sea

Selat Ombai

Alor

P A P U A   N E W   G U I N E A

Merauke

Madura

Surabaya

Jakarta

Bandung

Semarang

Surakarta

Yogyakarta

TENGAH

Bali

Equator

COPYRIGHT. GEORGE PHILIP & SON. LTD

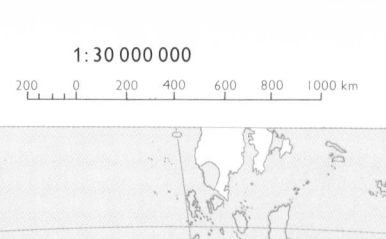

1 : 30 000 000

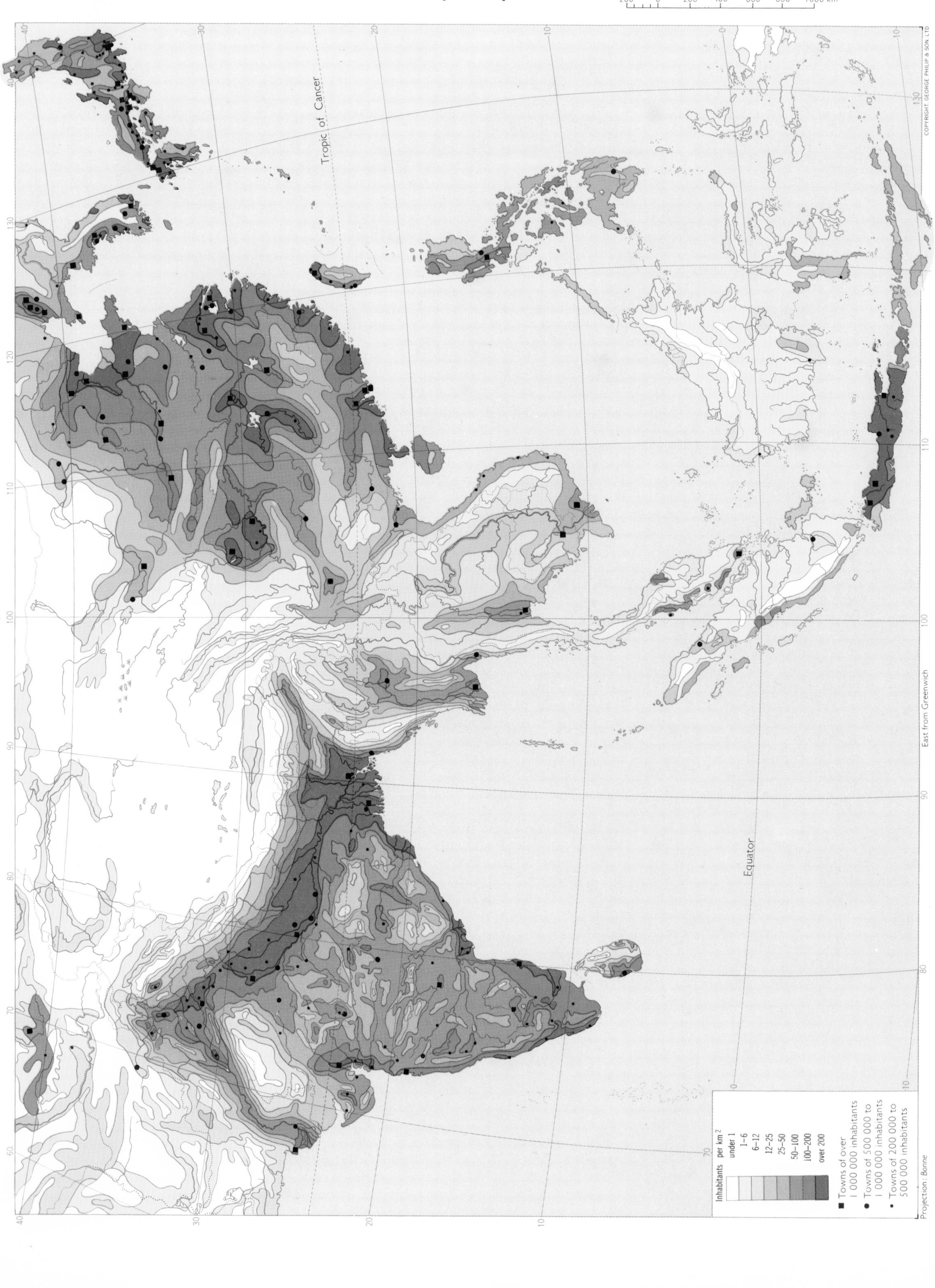

200   0   200   400   600   800   1000 km

COPYRIGHT GEORGE PHILIP & SON, LTD

Tropic of Cancer

Equator

East from Greenwich

Projection: Bonne

Inhabitants per km²	
under 1	
1–6	
6–12	
12–25	
25–50	
50–100	
100–200	
over 200	

■ Towns of over 1 000 000 inhabitants

● Towns of 500 000 to 1 000 000 inhabitants

• Towns of 200 000 to 500 000 inhabitants

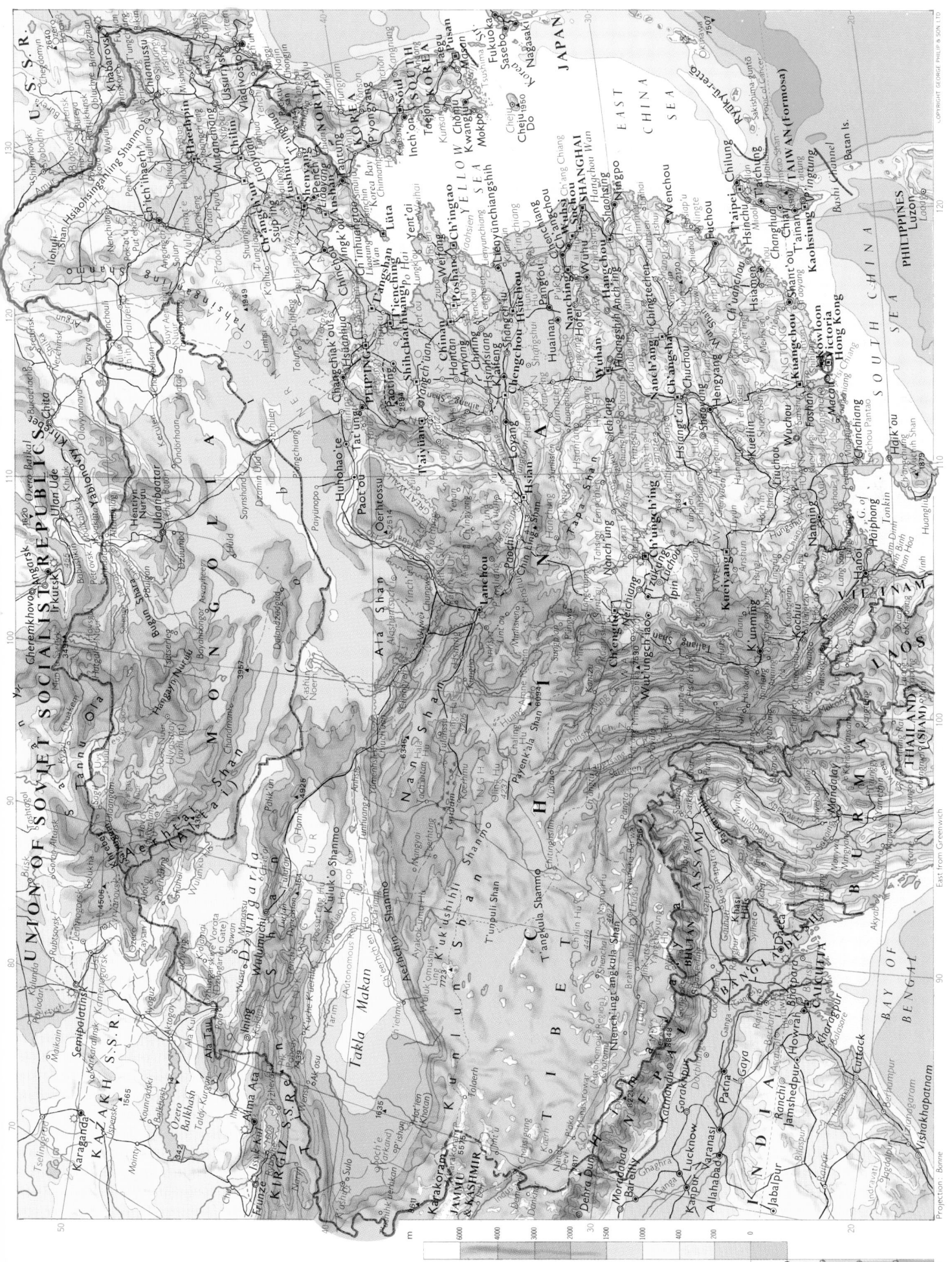

1 : 20 000 000

200   0   200   400   600   800 km

Projection: Bonne

East from Greenwich

COPYRIGHT GEORGE PHILIP & SON LTD

K'oerch'inyuich'iench'i
Chenlai
HAERHPIN
(Harbin)
Pinhsien
Chihsi
Turiy Rog
Ozero
Khanka
U.S.S.R.

HEILUNGKIANG

Paich'eng
Maoshing
Chaoyang
Shuangch'eng
A'ch'eng
Holo Ho
Shuangch'eng

Ankuang
Ch'ienkuehrlossu
Fuyü
Sunghua Chiang (Sungari)
Sanch'aho
Shiht'ouhotzu
Changkuangts'ai Ling
Mutanchiang
Suiyang
Sifenho
Pogranichnyy

T'ungyü
Shenchingtzu
Yüshu
Wuch'ang
Shulan
Shanhot'un
Changkuangts'ai Ling
Ningan
Mulengchen
1758
Pokrovka

KIRIN

Ch'angch'un
Huitechen
Fanchiat'un
Fengman Dam
1812
Tunhua
Huaping
Tungching'eng
Vladivostok

Huaice
Shuangyang
Sunghua Hu
Wang'ch'ing
Kayaho
Hunch'un
Slavyanka

Chilin
(Kirin)
Chiaoho
Ömu
Hsinchan
Ch'unyang
Yenchi
Tumen
Posyet

Ssup'ing
It'ung
Panshih
Chingyü
Fusung
Hoeryöng
Ungga

NORTH
KOREA

P'yŏngyang

SEA OF
JAPAN

SOUTH
KOREA
SEOUL
(Seoul)
Inch'ŏn
Taejŏn

Taegu

PUSAN

YELLOW
SEA

Po Hai
(Gulf of Chihli)

Korea
Bay

Cheju Do
Cheju

JAPAN
Nagasaki

Projection: Conical with two standard parallels

SOUTH CHINA SEA

Luzon Strait

TAIWAN (FORMOSA)

T'AIPEI
Chilung
Hsinchu
T'aichung
Changhua
Chiai
T'ainan
Kaohsiung
P'ingtung

KIANGSU
SHANGHAI
NANCHING (Nanking)
Wuhsi
Suchou (Soochow)
Hangchou
Ningpo

CHEKIANG
Wenchou
Foochou (Foochow)

ANHWEI
Hofei
WUHAN
Wuch'ang
Hanyang

HONAN

HUPEH
Ich'ang

KIANGSI
Nanch'ang
Chiuchiang

FUKIEN
Hsiamen (Amoy)
Chinmen Tao (Quemoy)
Ch'uanchou

HUNAN
Ch'angsha
Hengyang
Shaoyang

KWANGTUNG
KUANGCHOU (Canton)
Foshan
HONG KONG (U.K.)
Kowloon
VICTORIA
Macao (Port.)
Shant'ou (Swatow)

Tropic of Cancer

Chanchiang (Tsamkong)

COPYRIGHT, GEORGE PHILIP & SON LTD.

SEA OF JAPAN

SOUTH KOREA

Oki-Shotō Daimanji-San
Dōgo ▲608
Saigō

H O N S

CHŪGOKU-DISTRICT

Shimane-Hantō Jizō-Zaki Iwami Kasumi Toyooka
Hi-no-Misaki Hirata Shinji Ka Matsue Sakaiminato Yonago Kurayoshi Tottori Hidaka
Taisha Yasugi Dai-Sen Wakasa Suga-no-Sen Wadayama
Izumo Daito Tsuyama Yanahara Nishiwa
Ōda ▲1126 Sanbe-San Dōgo-San Tōjō Niimi Ochiai HYŌG
Gōtsu Yunotsu Shōbara Takahashi Katsuyama OKAYAMA Tatsuno Aioi Himeji Or
Hamada SHIMANE Miyoshi Ibara Sōja Bizen Akō Takasago Kakogawa
Masuda Ōra-Gawa Kake Fuchū Okayama Saidaiji Harima-
Ōmi-Shima Hagi Aono-Yama ▲908 Kammuri-yama Saijō Mihara Onomichi Kurashiki Tamano Shōdo-Shima Nada
Mi-Shima Nagato ▲339 Teshima Shōtō Akas
Tsuno-Shima YAMAGUCHI HIROSHIMA Takehara In'no-shima Tonoshō Awaji-Shima Sumoto
Hibiki- Mine Yamaguchi HIROSHIMA Itsukaichi Kure Marugame Sakaide Takamatsu
Nada Toyoura Tokui Nan'yō Ōtake Hiroshima-Wan Ō-Shima Zentsūji KAGAWA Naruto
Genkai- Hōfu Iwakuni Nigata Aki-Nada Takuma Kotohira Miki Hiketa Tokushim
Nada Onoda Ube Hikari Tokuyama Kudamatsu Kurahashi- Hiuchi- Kan'onji Sanyuki Sammyaku Kamojima
Shimonoseki Yanai Naga-Shima Jima Yashiro- Nada Hōjō Imabari Kawanoe Anabuki Tokushim
Ō-Shima KITAKYŪSHŪ Iwai-Jima Jima Niihama Iyo-mishima TOKUSHIMA Anan
Iki Katsumoto Suō-Nada Heigun-Tō Matsuyama Nyūgawa Saijō Gamō
Kō-ura Fukuma Hime-Jima Matsusaki Iyo Shikoku-Sanchi ▲1981 Iyo-mishima
Higasi-Suidō Nakama Yukuhashi Futago-Yama Kunisaki Iyo-Nada Nagahama Ōzu Kōchi Naruto
Iki-Kaikyō Iizuka Takawa Buzen ▲1200 Uchiko E'HIME Tosa-yamada Nankoku
Ō-Shima FUKUOKA Nōgata Yamada Usa Yufu-Dake Sada-Misaki-Hantō Yawatahama SHIKOKU Aki Tōyō
Ikitsuki- Yobuko Umi FUKUOKA Amagi ▲1584 Kitsuki Sagawa Tosa Muroto
Shima Karatsu Tsukushi Sanchi Hita Beppu-Wan Uwa Susaki Muroto-Misaki
Hirado Matsuura Tosu Kuroki Ōita Tsurusaki Uwajima Hiromi Kubokawa
Hirado- Imari SAGA Kurume Yame Beppu Ōita Saganoseki Tosa - Wan Ashizuri-Zaki
Shima Yoshii Taku Yanagawa Chikugo Usuki Bungo Ekawasaki
Sasebo Kashima Okawa Ōmuta Yamaga Takeda Saiki Saga SHIKOKU
Takeo Tara Omuta Yamaga Aso Tsukumi Sukumo Nakamura SHIKOKU-DISTRICT
Ōmura- ▲983 Tara-Dake Araō ▲1787 Oku-no-Shima Tosa-shimizu
Wan Isahaya Kikuchi Sobo-Yama Kamae Ōita Tosa-shimizu
NAGASAKI Ōmura Tamana KUMAMOTO Mashiki ▲1738 Saiki
Nagasaki Unzen-Dake Kumamoto Ichinomiya Takachiho Nobeoka
Tachibana-Wan ▲1360 Shimabara Uto Takachiho Oki-no-Shima
Amakusa- Kuchinotsu Obama Misumi Kunimi-Dake ▲739 Hinokage
Amakusa- Hondo Kami- Yatsushiro Hyūga Hososhima
Shotō Shimo- Jima Itsuki Shiiba Hyūga
Nada Jima Yatsushiro-Kai Yunomae MIYAZAKI Saito KYŪSHŪ
Ushibuka Minamata Hitoyoshi Takanabe KYŪSHŪ-DISTRICT
Naga-Shima Izumi Ebino Kobayashi Saito
Akune Ōkuchi Yoshimatsu ▲1700 Miyazaki
Kami-koshiki Miyanojō Kurino Kirishima-Yama
Jima Sendai Kajiki Kokubu Miyakonojō Nichinan
Koshiki- Kushikino Jūni Hayato Miyakonojō Aburatsu
Rettō Shimo-koshiki- Kagoshima On-Take Kushima
Jima ▲118 Tarumizu Shibushi
Kagoshima KAGOSHIMA Shibushi-Wan
Taniyama Fukiage Kanoya Kōyama
Noma-Saki Kaseda Chiran Kagoshima- Tarumizu
Makurazaki Kaimon-Dake Wan Yamagawa
Bō-no-Misaki 924 Ibusuki Ōsumi-Hantō
Sata-Misaki

Projection:
Lambert's Conformal
Conic

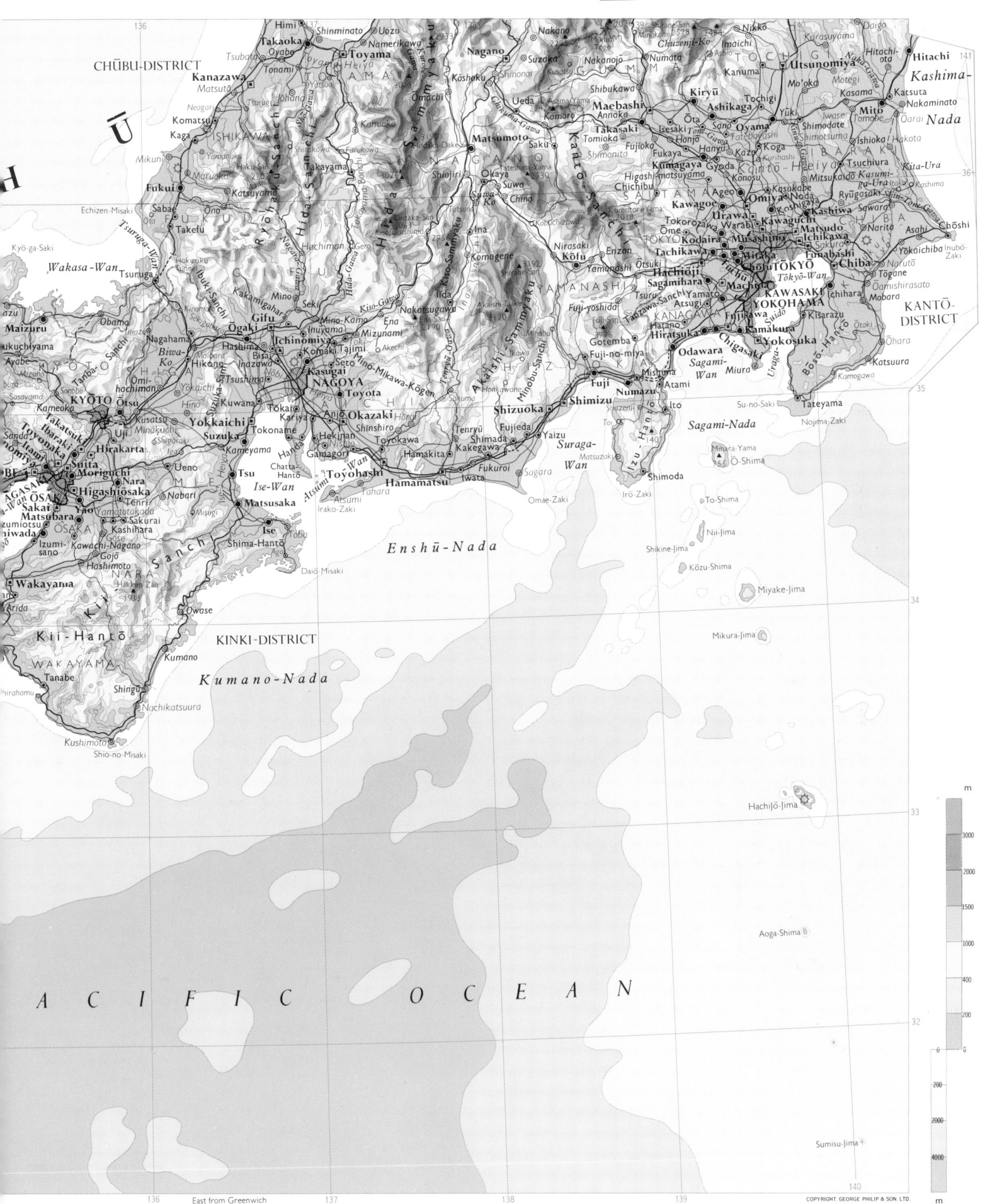

1:2 500 000

10 0 10 20 30 40 50 60 70 80 90 100 km

III

CHŪBU-DISTRICT

Himi Shinminato Uozu Namerikawa Nakano Nikko Daigo
Takaoka Oyabe Toyama Heiya Nagano Chuzenji-Ko Imaichi Karasuyama Hitachi
Kanazawa Tsubata Tonami Kōshoku Suzaka Kusatu Numata Utsunomiya Hitachiōta Kashima-
Matsutō Shimonoi Shibukawa Kiryū Tochigi Kanuma Moka Motegi Kasama Mito Nada
Komatsu Kamioka Ueda Asama-Yama Maebashi Annaka Takasaki Isesaki Ōta Sano Oyama Yūki Shimodate Iwase Tomobe Ōarai
Kaga Takayama Matsumoto Komoro Tomioka Fujioka Honjo Hanyū Kazo Kurihashi Mitsukaido Kasumi- Ishioka Hakota
Fukui Katsuyama Shiojiri Okaya Suwa Chichibu Kumagaya Gyoda Konosu Ryūgasaki Kita-Ura
Echizen-Misaki Sabae Ono Chino Higashi-matsuyama Ageo Kasukabe Kashiwa Sawara
Takefu Ina Komogane Nirasaki Enzan Kōfu Ōme Kawagoe Warabi Kawaguchi Matsudo Narita
Tsuruga-Wan Hachiman Gero Komogane Yamanashi Ōtsuki Tōkyō Kodaira Musashino Ichikawa Chiba
Wakasa-Wan Tsuruga Hokuriku Tunnel Seki Iida Tachikawa Fuchū TŌKYŌ Yokaichiba Inubō-Zaki
Kyō-ga-Saki Obama Mino Kakamigahara Nakatsugawa Hachiōji Machida Tōkyō-Wan Chōshi
Gifu Mino-Kamo Ena Akechi Kōfu Sagamihara Yamato KAWASAKI Naruto Tōgane
Maizuru Ōgaki Ichinomiya Mizunami Tajimi Tsuru Tanzawa-Sanchi YOKOHAMA Kisarazu Mobara
Fukuchiyama Nagahama Hashima Inazawa Komaki Seto Atsugi Fujisawa Kamakura Ōtaki Katsuura
Ayabe Biwa-Ko Hikone Bisai Kasugai Toyota Gotemba Hadano Hiratsuka Yokosuka
Sasayama Sonobe Omi-hachiman Yokkaichi NAGOYA Toyota Fuji-no-miya Odawara Chigasaki Miura Kamogawa
Kameoka KYŌTO Ōtsu Kuwana Tōkai Kariya Anjō Okazaki Shinshiro Fuji Numazu Atami Sagami- Uraga
Ibaraki Uji Kusatsu Tsushima Suzuka Tokoname Hekinan Toyokawa Shimizu Mishima Wan
Takatsuki Minakuchi Shigaraki Kameyama Handa Nishio Toyohashi Shizuoka Ito Izu-Hantō Su-no-Saki Tateyama
Toyonaka Ikoma Shigaraki Tsu Chatta-Hantō Gamagori Hamakita Shimada Yaizu Shimoda Nojima-Zaki
Suita Moriguchi Nara Ueno Ise-Wan Atsumi-Wan Hamamatsu Kakegawa Suraga- Iro-Zaki
OSAKA Higashiōsaka Tenri Nabari Matsusaka Fukuroi Sagara Wan Mihara-Yama Ō-Shima
Sakai Yao Yamatotakada Sakurai Irako-Zaki Iwata Omae-Zaki
Matsubara Kashihara Kawachi-Nagano Ise Tahara Enshū-Nada
Izumiōtsu Gojō Hashimoto Shima-Hantō Ago Shikine-Jima Nii-Jima
Kishiwada Wakayama Hakken-Zan Daio-Misaki Kōzu-Shima
Arida

Kii-Hantō KINKI-DISTRICT Miyake-Jima
WAKAYAMA Kumano Mikura-Jima
Tanabe Kumano-Nada
Shingū
Nachikatsuura
Kushimoto Hachijō-Jima
Shio-no-Misaki

Aoga-Shima

P A C I F I C   O C E A N

Sumisu-Jima

East from Greenwich COPYRIGHT. GEORGE PHILIP & SON. LTD.

136   137   138   139   140

KANTŌ-
DISTRICT

m
3000
2000
1500
1000
400
200
0
0
200
2000
4000
m

1 : 7 500 000

50   0   50   100   150   200   250   300 km

130
135
140
145

CHINA

U.S.S.R.

Turii Rog
Ozero
Khanka

Mutankiang
Ningan
Motoshih
Spassk-Dalni
Varfolomeyevka
Verkhove
Tetyukhe

Ussurysk
(Voroshilov)
Uglovaya
Najin
Suchan
Nakhodka

Vladivostok

Hunchun

Yenki

NORTH
KOREA
Chongjin

Songjin

Tanchon

Zaliv Petra
Velikogo

45

Rebun-Tō
Rishiri-Tō
Wakkanai
Sea of Okhotsk

HOKKAIDŌ
Teshio
Otoineppu
Monbetsu
Yūbetsu
Kitami
Abashiri
Nemuro-Kaikyō

Rumoi
Shibatsu
Daisetsu 2290

Asahigawa
Bibai
Iwanai
Iwamisawa
Otaru
Yūbari
Tokachi
Obihiro
Kushiro

Sapporo
Tomakomai
Poroshiri-Dake

Nemuro

Kamui-
Misaki
Ishikari-Wan
(Otaru-Wan)
Shiraoi
Mombetsu
Muroran
Urakawa
Samani

Setana
Uchiura
Wan
Erimo-Misaki

Okushiri-Tō

Esashi
Matsumae
Hakodate
Esan-Misaki
Tsugaru
Kaikyō
Shiriya-Zaki
Mutsu-
Wan
Mutsu

40

SEA   OF

Kosŏng

SOUTH
KOREA

Ullung Do

OF   JAPAN

Aomori
Hirosaki
Towada
Odate
Hachinohe
Kuji
Noshiro
Tsuneshiro
Iwate-San 2041
Akita
Morioka
Miyako
Honjō
Hanamaki
Yokote
Kamaishi
Kitakami
Ichinoseki
TŌHOKU
Sakata
Mogami
Shinjō
Ishinomaki
Tsuruoka
Kogota
Shiogama
Yamagata
Sendai
Iwanuma
Sado
Niigata
Shibata
Agano
Yonezawa
Fukushima
Bandai-San 1819

35

Pusan

Tsushima Kaikyō
Tsushima

KOREA STRAIT

Oki-Shotō

Wajima
Suzu-Misaki
Nagaoka
Azuma-yama 1819
Kōriyama
Nanao
Himi
Noto-Hantō
Naoetsu
Takada
Tajima
Iwaki
Kashiwazaki
Nikkō
Hitachi
Kanazawa
Toyama
Nagano
Maebashi
Kiryū
Utsunomiya
CHŪBU
Matsumoto
Ueda
Takasaki
Tochigi
Mito
Fukui
Takayama
Chichibu
Kawagoe
Gyoda
Tsuchiura
Takefu
Ontake 3063
Suwa
Ōmiya
KANTŌ
Tsuruga
N
Gifu
Ichinomiya
Kōfu
Urawa
Sawara
Chōshi
Matsue
Tottori
Toyooka
Hikone
Ichikawa
Hino-Misaki
Maizuru
Ōtsu
Fuji-no-miya
TŌKYŌ
Chiba
Izumo
Yonago
Ayabe
Kyōto
Okkaichi
Fuji-San 3776
Kawasaki
Yokohama
Yokosuka
CHŪGOKU
Hamada
Tsuyama
Amagas.
Kōbe
Osaka
Tsu
Shizuoka
Numazu
Fujisawa
Hokayama
Himeji
Akashi
Nara
Matsusaka
Atami
Hamada
Masuda
Kurashiki
Sakai
Kishiwada
Toba
Hamamatsu
Ō-Shima
Tateyama
HŌ
Okayama
Onomichi
Wakayama
Owase
Ise-Wan
Ito
Yamaguchi
Hiroshima
Mihara
Daiō-Misaki
Toyohashi
Ni-jima
Shimonoseki
Tokuyama
Kure
Takamatsu
Marugame
KINKI
Miyake-Jima
Ube
Iki
Suō-Nada
Seto-Naikai
Tokushima
Shingu
Shio-no-Misaki
Mikura-Jima
Fukuoka
Kitakyūshū
Nakatsu
Niihama
Matsuyama
Karatsu
Kurume
Beppu
Kōchi
SHIKOKU
Sasebo
Saga
Ōita
Yawatahama
Muroto-Misaki
Hachijō-Jima
Nakadori-Jima
Ōmuta
Usuki
Uwajima
Nakamura
SHIKOKU
Kashima
Aso-San 1592
Saiki
Ashizuri-zaki
Bungo-Suidō
Nagasaki
Kumamoto
Isahaya
Shimabara
Yatsushiro
Aoga-Shima
Fukue-Jima
Shimo-Jima
Minamata
Nobeoka
Sendai
Miyazaki
Kobayashi
Miyakonojō
Kagoshima
Kanoya
KYŪSHŪ
Makurazaki
Kushibi-Wan
Kagoshima-Wan
Ōsumi-Kaikyō
Ōsumi-Shotō
Nishinoomote
Tane-ga-Shima
Kuchinoerabu-Jima
Tokara-Kaikyō
Naka-no-Shima
Yaku-Jima
Suwanose-Jima

SEA   OF   JAPAN

PACIFIC

OCEAN

PACIFIC   OCEAN

RYŪKYŪ ISLANDS
Continuation southwards
in same scale

Ōsumi-Shotō
Kuchinoerabu-Jima
Tokara-Kaikyō
Yaku-Jima
Naka-no-Shima
Suwanose-Jima
Tokara-Kaikyō
Satsuna-Shotō
Nansei-Shotō (Ryūkyū Islands)
Ōkinawa-Shotō
Naze
Kikai-Jīma
Amami Ō Shima
Setouchi
Tokunoshima
Okinoerabu-
Jima
Okinawa-
Jima
Ishikawa
Koza
Ginowan
Kerama-
Shotō
Naha
Nansei-Shotō Trench 7507
Yaeyama-
Shotō
Miyako-Jima
Hirara
Yonaguni-
Jima
Ishigaki-
Jima
Iriomote-
Jima
Ishigaki

130

m
1500
1000
400
200   30
0
200
m

Projection: Bonne
East from Greenwich
COPYRIGHT GEORGE PHILIP & SON LTD

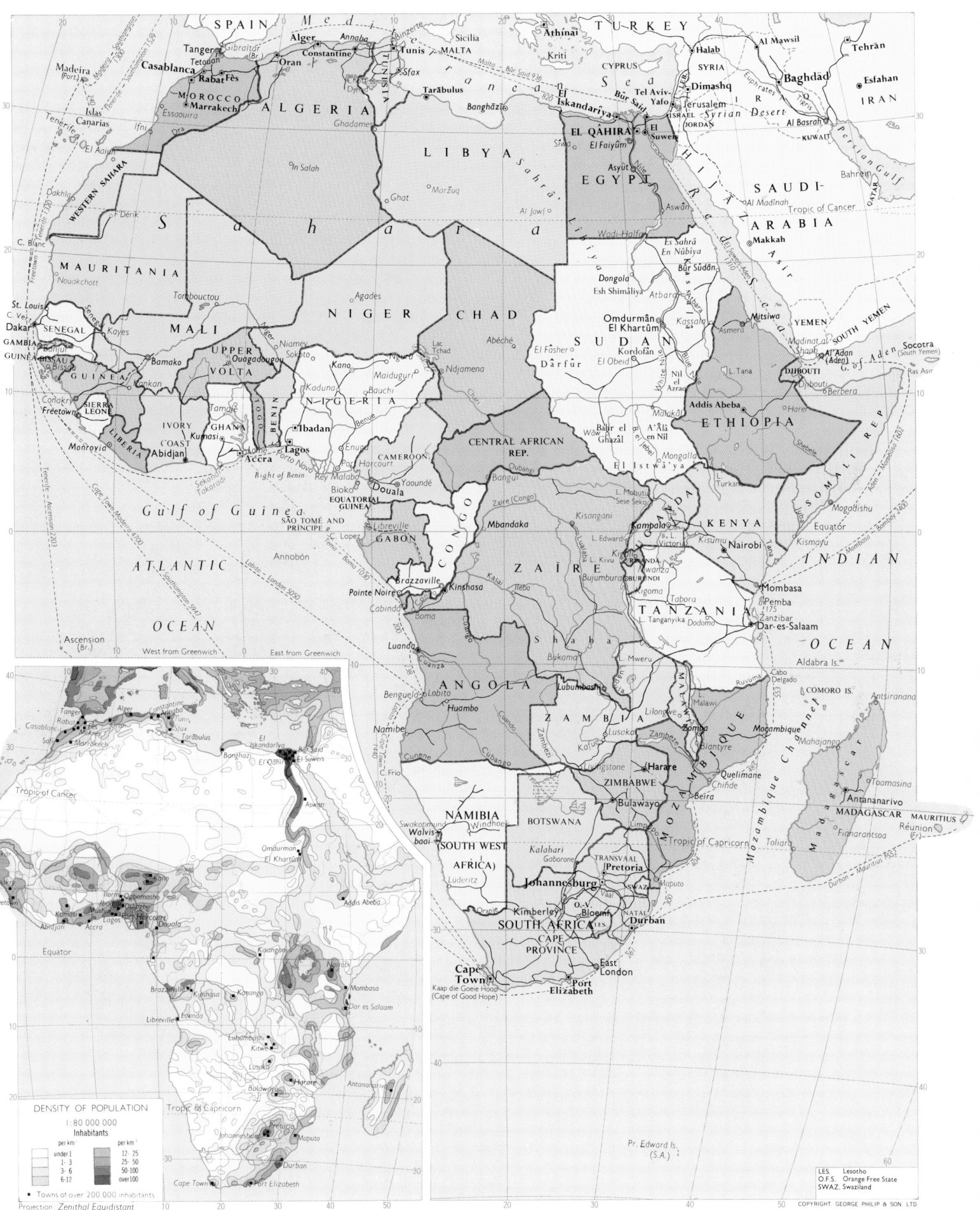

1:40 000 000

400   200   0   400   800   1200   1600 km

SPAIN

Madeira (Port.)
Tanger
Casablanca
Rabat Fès
Tetouan
MOROCCO
Marrakech
Essaouira
Ifni
WESTERN SAHARA
Dakhla
C. Blanc
Nouakchott
MAURITANIA

Islas Canarias
Tenerife
El Aaiún
F'Dérik

Mediterranean Sea

Alger
Annaba
Constantine
Oran
Djebel
TUNISIA
Tunis
Bizerte
Sfax

MALTA
Sicilia

ALGERIA
In Salah
Ghadames
Ghat
Marzuq

LIBYA
Tarabulus
Banghazi

TURKEY
Athínai
Kriti
CYPRUS

Halab
SYRIA
Dimashq
Tel Aviv-Yafo
Jerusalem
El Iskandaríya
El Qâhira
El Suweis
El Faiyûm
EGYPT
Siwa
Asyût
Aswân

Al Mawsil
Tehrân
Baghdâd
Esfahan
IRAN

SAUDI-
ARABIA

Sahara

Tombouctou
MALI
Kayes
SENEGAL
Bamako

St. Louis
Dakar
GAMBIA Banjul
GUINEA-BISSAU Bissau
Conakry
Freetown
SIERRA LEONE
Monrovia
LIBERIA

NIGER
Agades
Niamey
Sokoto

CHAD
Abéché
Ndjamena
Lac Tchad

SUDAN
El Fâsher
Dârfûr
Kordofan
El Obeid
Dongola
Esh Shimâliya
Omdurmân
El Khartûm

Es Sahrâ En Nûbiya
Wadi Halfa
Bûr Sûdân

YEMEN
Makkah
Al Madînah

Tropic of Cancer

UPPER VOLTA
Ouagadougou
Kano
Kaduna
Maiduguri
Bauchi

NIGERIA
Ibadan
Lagos
Enugu
Port Harcourt
Benue

BENIN
TOGO
GHANA
Kumasi
IVORY COAST
Tamale
Accra
Abidjan

Asmera
Mitsiwa
Kassala
L. Tana
Addis Abeba
ETHIOPIA
DJIBOUTI
Berbera

G. of Aden
Socotra (South Yemen)
Ras Asir

SOMALI REP

CAMEROON
Yaoundé
Douala
Bioko
EQUATORIAL GUINEA
SÃO TOMÉ AND PRÍNCIPE
Libreville
GABON
Annobón

CENTRAL AFRICAN REP.
Bangui
Oubangui

Congo
Zaïre (Congo)
Mbandaka
ZAIRE
Kisangani
L. Mobutu Sese Seko

El Istwâ'ya
Mongalla
UGANDA
Kampala
L. Victoria
Nairobi
KENYA
Kismayu
Mogadishu

INDIAN
OCEAN

ATLANTIC
OCEAN

Ascension (Br.)

West from Greenwich   East from Greenwich

Gulf of Guinea

Bight of Benin

CONGO
Brazzaville
Pointe Noire
Kinshasa
Cabinda
Boma
Luanda
ANGOLA
Benguela Lobito
Huambo
Namibe

L. Edward
RWANDA
Bujumbura
BURUNDI
Kigoma
TANZANIA
Dodoma
Tabora
Dar-es-Salaam
Zanzibar
Mombasa
Pemba

L. Tanganyika
Shaba
Bukama
L. Mweru
Lubumbashi

Cabo Delgado
COMORO IS.

ZAMBIA
Lusaka
Livingstone
MALAWI
Lilongwe
Zomba
Blantyre
MOZAMBIQUE
Quelimane
Chinde
Beira

Antsiranana
Mahajanga
MADAGASCAR
Antananarivo
MAURITIUS
Réunion (Fr.)

NAMIBIA
Windhoek
(SOUTH WEST AFRICA)
Swakopmund
Walvis baai
Lüderitz

BOTSWANA
Gaborone
Kalahari

ZIMBABWE
Bulawayo
Harare

Tropic of Capricorn

Maputo
TRANSVAAL
Pretoria
Johannesburg
Kimberley
O.V.
Bloemfontein
SOUTH AFRICA
CAPE PROVINCE
Cape Town
Kaap die Goeie Hoop (Cape of Good Hope)
Port Elizabeth
East London
Durban
NATAL

Pr. Edward Is. (S.A.)

DENSITY OF POPULATION
1:80 000 000
Inhabitants
per km²   per km²
under 1   12- 25
1- 3   25- 50
3- 6   50-100
6-12   over 100
■ Towns of over 200 000 inhabitants

Projection Zenithal Equidistant

Tanger
Casablanca
Rabat Meknès
Marrakech
Alger
Constantine
Tunis
Sfax
Tarabulus
Banghazi
El Iskandaríya
Bûr Saíd
El Qâhira
El Suweis

Tropic of Cancer

Aswân

Omdurman
El Khartûm

Ilorin Ogbomosho
Kumasi
Ibadan
Mushin
Lagos
Port Harcourt
Douala
Abidjan
Accra

Addis Abeba

Equator

Brazzaville Kinshasa
Libreville
Kananga
Kisangani
Nairobi
Mombasa
Dar es Salaam

Lubumbashi
Kitwe
Lusaka

Harare
Bulawayo
Antananarivo

Tropic of Capricorn

Johannesburg
Pretoria
Maputo
Durban
Cape Town
Port Elizabeth

LES.   Lesotho
O.F.S. Orange Free State
SWAZ. Swaziland

COPYRIGHT GEORGE PHILIP & SON LTD

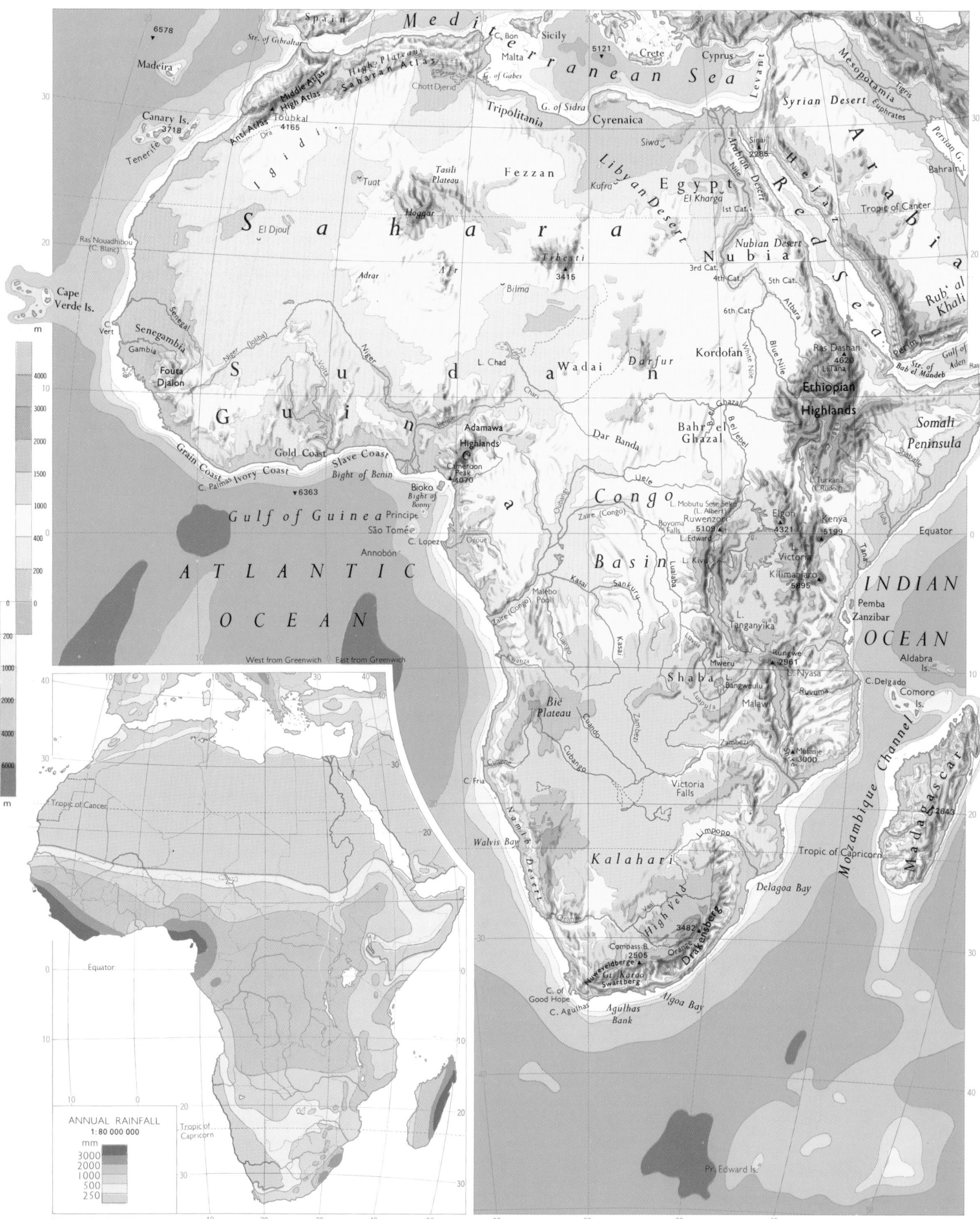

1:40 000 000

400   0   400   800   1200   1600 km

m

4000
3000
2000
1500
1000
400
200
0
0
200
1000
2000
4000
6000

m

Mediterranean Sea

Spain
Madeira
6578
Str. of Gibraltar
Middle Atlas
High Atlas
Saharan Atlas
High Plateaus
Canary Is.
Tenerife
3718
Anti Atlas
Toubkal
4165
Ora
Chott Djerid
G. of Gabes
Bon
Malta
Sicily
Crete
5121
Cyprus
Levant
Syrian Desert
Mesopotamia
Tigris
Euphrates
Persian G.
Bahrain I.

Ras Nouadhibou
(C. Blanc)
Igidi
El Djouf
Sahara
Tuat
Tasili Plateau
Hoggar
Adrar
Air
Bilma
Fezzan
Libyan Desert
Egypt
Kufra
El Kharga
1st Cat.
Siwa
Nile
Tibesti
3415
Nubian Desert
3rd Cat.
4th Cat.
5th Cat.
6th Cat.
Nubia
Arabian Desert
Sinai
2285
Red Sea
Hejaz
Tropic of Cancer
Rub' al Khali
Gulf of Aden
Str. of Bab el Mandeb
Perim

Cape Verde Is.
C. Vert
Senegambia
Gambia
Fouta Djalon
Senegal
Niger (Joliba)
Sudan
Guinea
Volta
Niger
Benue
L. Chad
Chari
Wadai
Darfur
Kordofan
White Nile
Blue Nile
Atbara
Ras Dashan
4620
L.Tana
Ethiopian Highlands
Somali Peninsula
Shabelle

Grain Coast
Gold Coast
Slave Coast
Ivory Coast
C. Palmas
Bight of Benin
Adamawa Highlands
Cameroon Peak
4070
Bioko
Bight of Bonny
6363
Principe
São Tomé
C. Lopez
Annobón
Uele
Dar Banda
Bahr el Ghazal
Bahr el Ghazal
Bahr el Jebel
Turkana
(L. Rudolf)

Gulf of Guinea
ATLANTIC
OCEAN
West from Greenwich   East from Greenwich
Ogooué
Zaire (Congo)
Congo Basin
L. Mobutu Sese Seko
(L. Albert)
Boyoma Falls
Ruwenzori
5109
L. Edward
L. Kivu
Elgon
4321
Kenya
5199
Victoria
Kilimanjaro
5895
INDIAN
OCEAN
Pemba
Zanzibar
Equator
Aldabra Is.

Kasai
Sankuru
Lualaba
L. Tanganyika
Lukuga
Malebo Pool
Kwango
Kasai
Kwanza
Shaba
Mweru
L.
Rungwe
2961
L. Nyasa
Bangweulu
Malawi
Ruvuma
C. Delgado
Comoro Is.

Bié Plateau
Cuango
Cubango
Zambezi
Zambezi
Mlanje
3000
Mozambique Channel
Madagascar
2843

C. Frio
Cunene
Victoria Falls
Limpopo
Tropic of Capricorn

Namib Desert
Walvis Bay
Orange
Kalahari
High Veld
Vaal
Orange
3482
Drakensberg
Delagoa Bay

Compass B.
2505
Nuweveldberge
Gt. Karoo
Swartberg
C. of Good Hope
C. Agulhas
Agulhas Bank
Algoa Bay

40   30   20   10   0   10   20   30   40   50
Tropic of Cancer
Equator
Tropic of Capricorn

ANNUAL RAINFALL
1:80 000 000
mm
3000
2000
1000
500
250

Projection: Lambert's Equivalent Azimuthal

Pr. Edward Is.

COPYRIGHT. GEORGE PHILIP & SON. LTD.

1:80 000 000

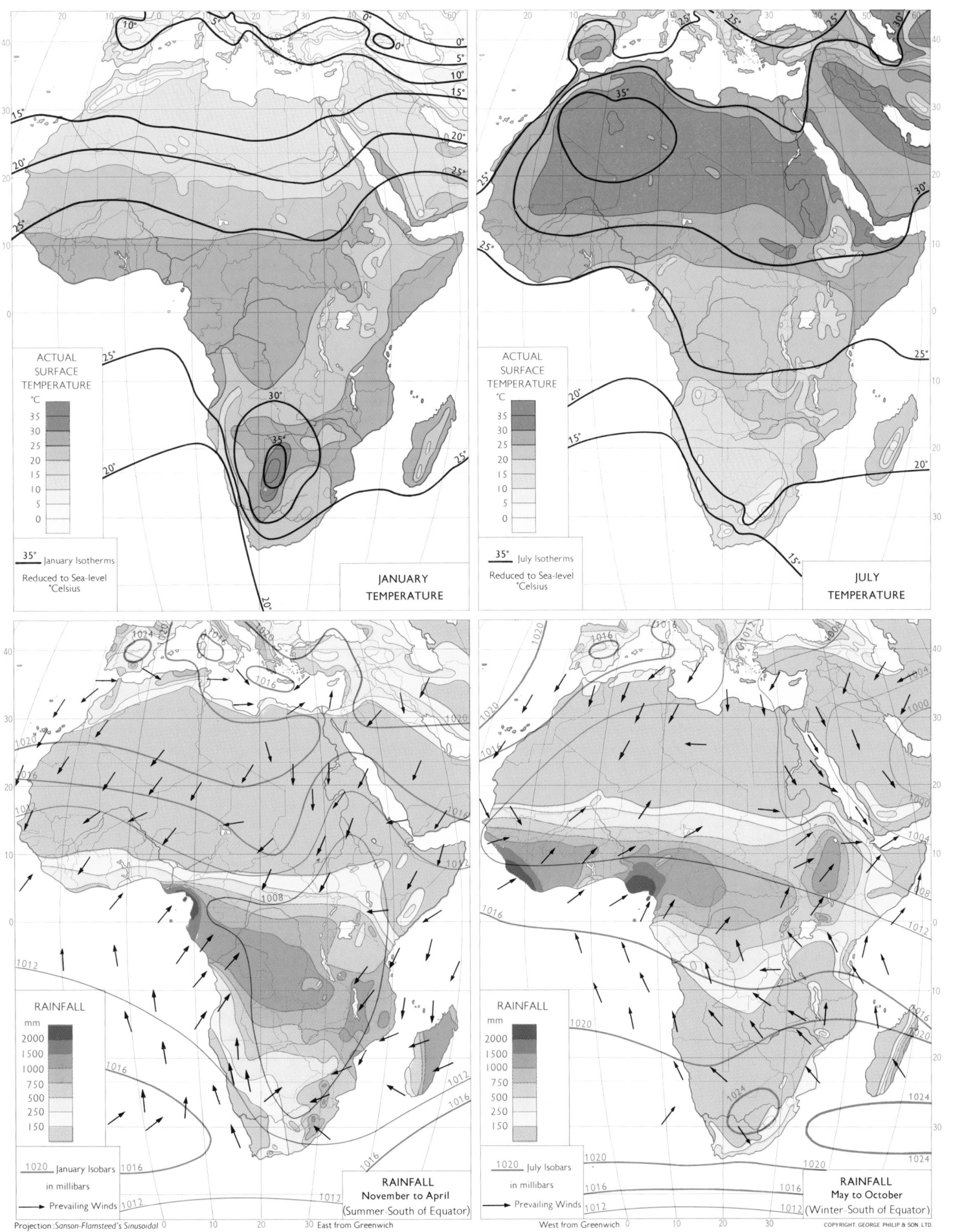

ACTUAL
SURFACE
TEMPERATURE
°C
35
30
25
20
15
10
5
0

35° January Isotherms

Reduced to Sea-level
°Celsius

JANUARY
TEMPERATURE

ACTUAL
SURFACE
TEMPERATURE
°C
35
30
25
20
15
10
5
0

35° July Isotherms

Reduced to Sea-level
°Celsius

JULY
TEMPERATURE

RAINFALL
mm
2000
1500
1000
750
500
250
150

1020 January Isobars
in millibars
Prevailing Winds

RAINFALL
November to April
(Summer-South of Equator)

RAINFALL
mm
2000
1500
1000
750
500
250
150

1020 July Isobars
in millibars
Prevailing Winds

RAINFALL
May to October
(Winter-South of Equator)

Projection: Sanson-Flamsteed's Sinusoidal   0   10   20   30   East from Greenwich

West from Greenwich   0   10   20   30

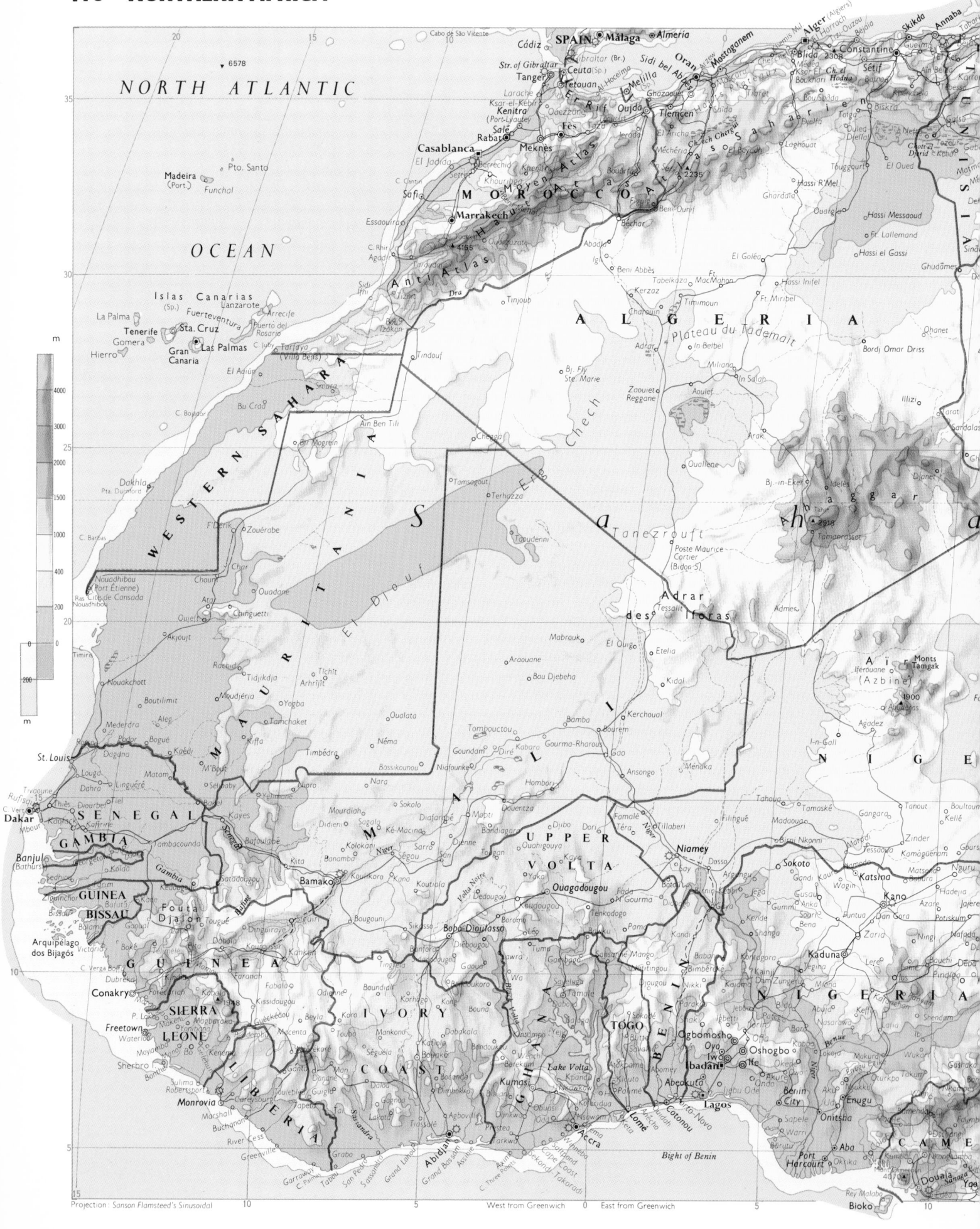

NORTH ATLANTIC

OCEAN

Madeira
(Port.)   Pto. Santo
          Funchal

Islas Canarias
(Sp.)   Lanzarote
La Palma   Fuerteventura   Arrecife
Tenerife Sta. Cruz   Puerto del
Gomera   Las Palmas   Rosario
Hierro   Gran
         Canaria

SPAIN   Málaga   Almería
Cádiz   Gibraltar (Br.)
Str. of Gibraltar   Ceuta (Sp.)
Tanger   Melilla
Larache   Tetouan   Al Hoceima
Ksar-el-Kebir   Sidi bel Abbès   Oran
Kenitra   Oujda   Tlemcen
(Port-Lyautey)   Fes   Taza
Rabat
Casablanca   Meknès
El Jadida   Berréchid
Safi   MOROCCO
Marrakech

Alger (Algiers)
Blida   Constantine
Sétif
Mostaganem
Skikda   Annaba

ALGERIA
Plateau du Tademait

WESTERN SAHARA

MAURITANIA

Nouadhibou
(Port Étienne)
Nouakchott

MALI

SENEGAL
Dakar
GAMBIA
Banjul
(Bathurst)
GUINEA
BISSAU
Bissau

GUINEA
Conakry

SIERRA
LEONE
Freetown

LIBERIA
Monrovia

IVORY
COAST

UPPER
VOLTA
Ouagadougou

GHANA
Accra

TOGO

BENIN

Lomé   Cotonou   Porto-Novo
Lagos

NIGERIA

Kano
Kaduna

NIGER
Niamey

Ibadan

CAMEROON

Projection: Sanson Flamsteed's Sinusoidal

West from Greenwich   East from Greenwich

Bight of Benin

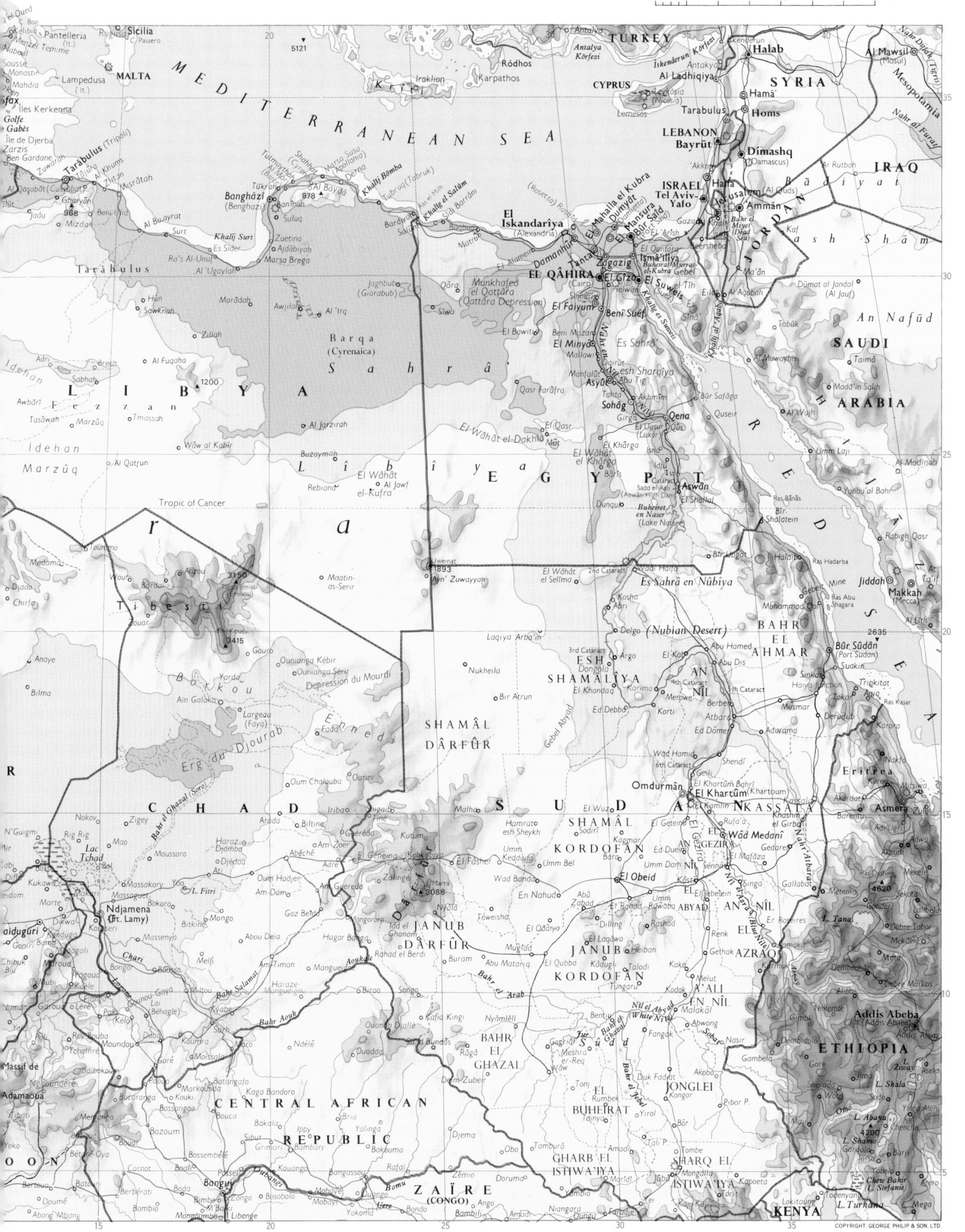

1:15 000 000

100   0   100   200   300   400   500   600 km

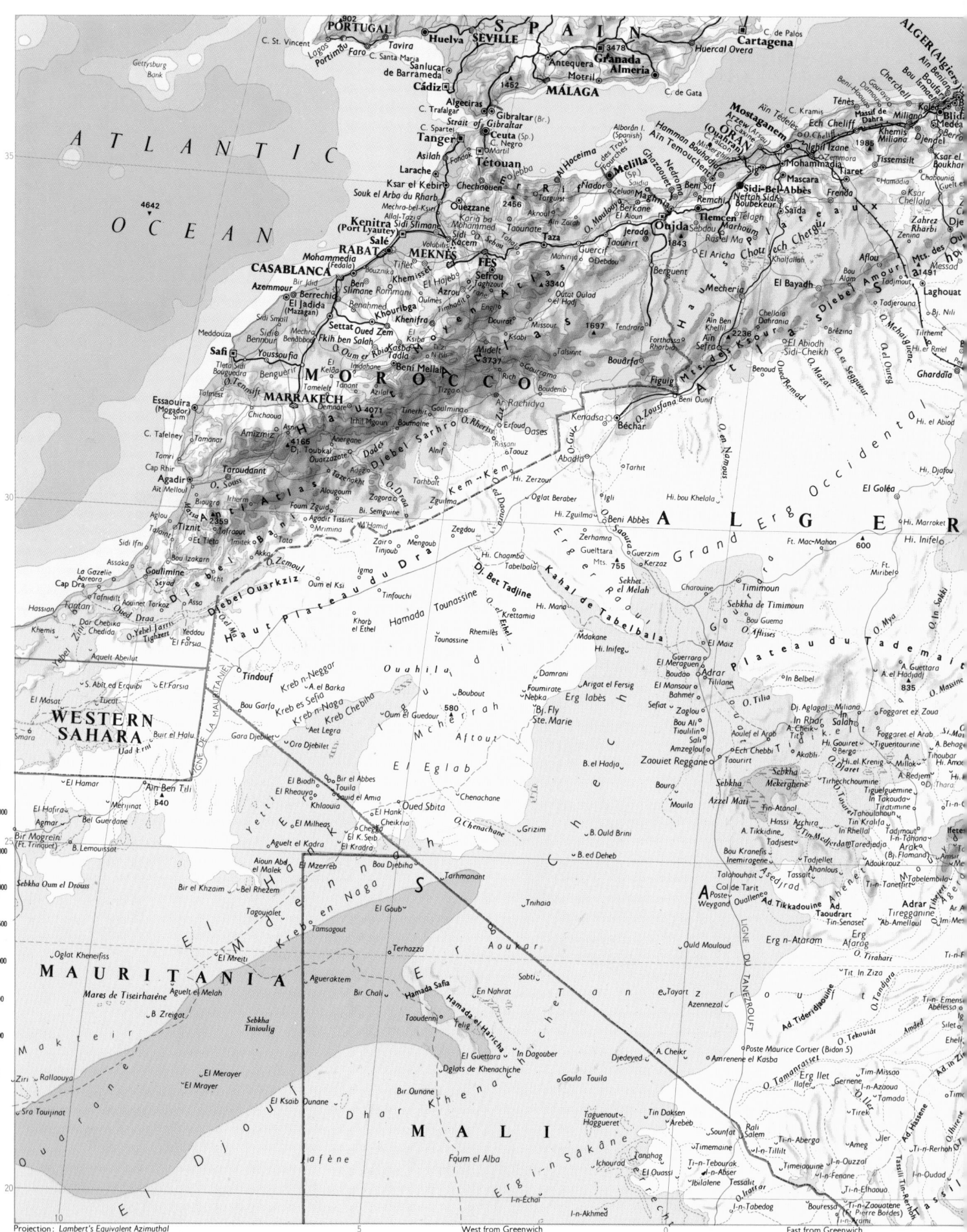

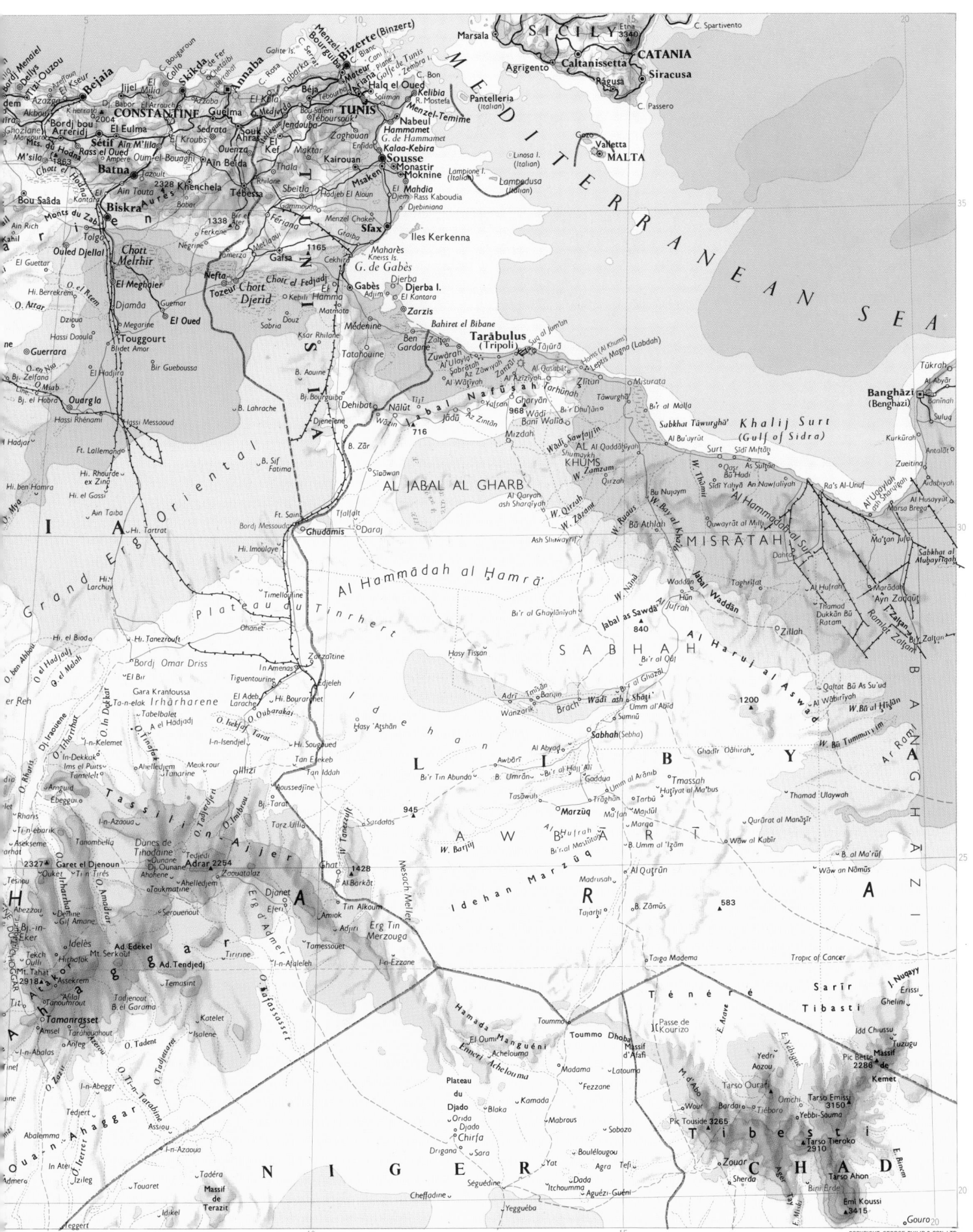

1:8 000 000

50 0 50 100 150 200 250 300 km

MEDITERRANEAN SEA

SICILY
Etna 3340
C. Spartivento
Marsala
Agrigento
Caltanissetta
CATANIA
Ragusa
Siracusa
C. Passero

Pantelleria (Italian)

Linosa I. (Italian)
Lampione I. (Italian)
Lampedusa (Italian)

Valletta
MALTA

Bejaia
Tizi-Ouzou
Dellys
Bordj Menaiel
Jijel
Skikda
Annaba
El Kala

CONSTANTINE
Guelma
Souk Ahras

Bizerte (Binzert)
TUNIS
Nabeul
Hammamet
G. de Hammamet
Menzel-Temime
Kelibia
R. Mostefa
Soliman
Halq el Oued
Zaghouan
Enfidaville

Sétif
Batna
Biskra
Khenchela 2328
Tébessa
Kairouan
Sousse
Monastir
Moknine
El Mahdia
Sfax
Iles Kerkenna

Bou Saâda
Chott Melrhir
Ouled Djellal
El Meghaier
Djamâa
El Oued
Gafsa
Tozeur
Chott Djerid
Gabès
Djerba I.
Zarzis

Touggourt
Ouargla

TUNISIA

Ghudāmis

Tarābulus (Tripoli)
Tājūrā
Misurata
Khalij Surt (Gulf of Sidra)
Surt
Banghāzī (Benghazi)

Jabal Nafūsah
AL JABAL AL GHARB
AL KHUMS
MISRĀTAH

Al Hammādah al Hamrā'

Plateau du Tinrhert

Grand Erg Oriental

Bordj Omar Driss
In Amenas
Edjeleh

Ghat

SABHAH
Al Harūj al Aswad

Sabhah (Sebha)
Marzūq

L I B Y A

Ar Ramlah

Idehan Marzūq

Tassili-n-Ajjer

Djanet

Adrar 2254

Tamanrasset
Mt. Tahat 2918
AHAGGAR

Tropic of Cancer

Taiga Madema

Ténéré
Sarir Tibasti

Plateau du Djado

NIGER

CHAD

Tibesti
Emi Koussi 3415
Pic Touside 3265
Zouar
Gouro

Massif de Kemet
Pic Bette 2286

COPYRIGHT. GEORGE PHILIP & SON. LTD.

Gambia and Senegal have agreed to the
amalgamation of their economies and armies.
This new confederation is known as Senegambia.

West from Greenwich

1:8 000 000

50 0 50 100 150 200 250 300 km

N. E. NIGERIA
on same scale
as general map

NIGER

NIGER

CHAD

CAMEROON

Maiduguri

Maroua

Garoua

ALGERIA

Adrar des Iforhas

Aïr
(Azbine)

Agadez
(Agadés)

NIGER

Tahoua

Niamey

Sokoto

Maradi

Zinder

Gashua

Nguru

UPPER VOLTA

BENIN

Kaduna

Kano

Zaria

Jos
Plateau

BAUCHI

BORNO

NIGERIA

Bauchi

Yola

GONGOLA

Bida

Abuja

Minna

Ilorin

Ogbomosho

OYO

Oyo

IBADAN

Abeokuta

Makurdi

BENUE

Lafia

PLATEAU

KADUNA

GHANA

TOGO

Tamale

Sokodé

Parakou

Accra

Tema

Lomé

Cotonou

Porto-Novo

LAGOS

Benin City

BENDEL

ANAMBRA

Enugu

Onitsha

Warri

Owerri

Aba

Port-Harcourt

Calabar

CROSS RIVER

IMO

CAMEROON

Douala

Yaoundé

Slave Coast

Bight of Benin

Niger Delta

EQUATORIAL GUINEA

BIOKO

Bight of Bonny

OF GUINEA

East from Greenwich

COPYRIGHT GEORGE PHILIP & SON LTD

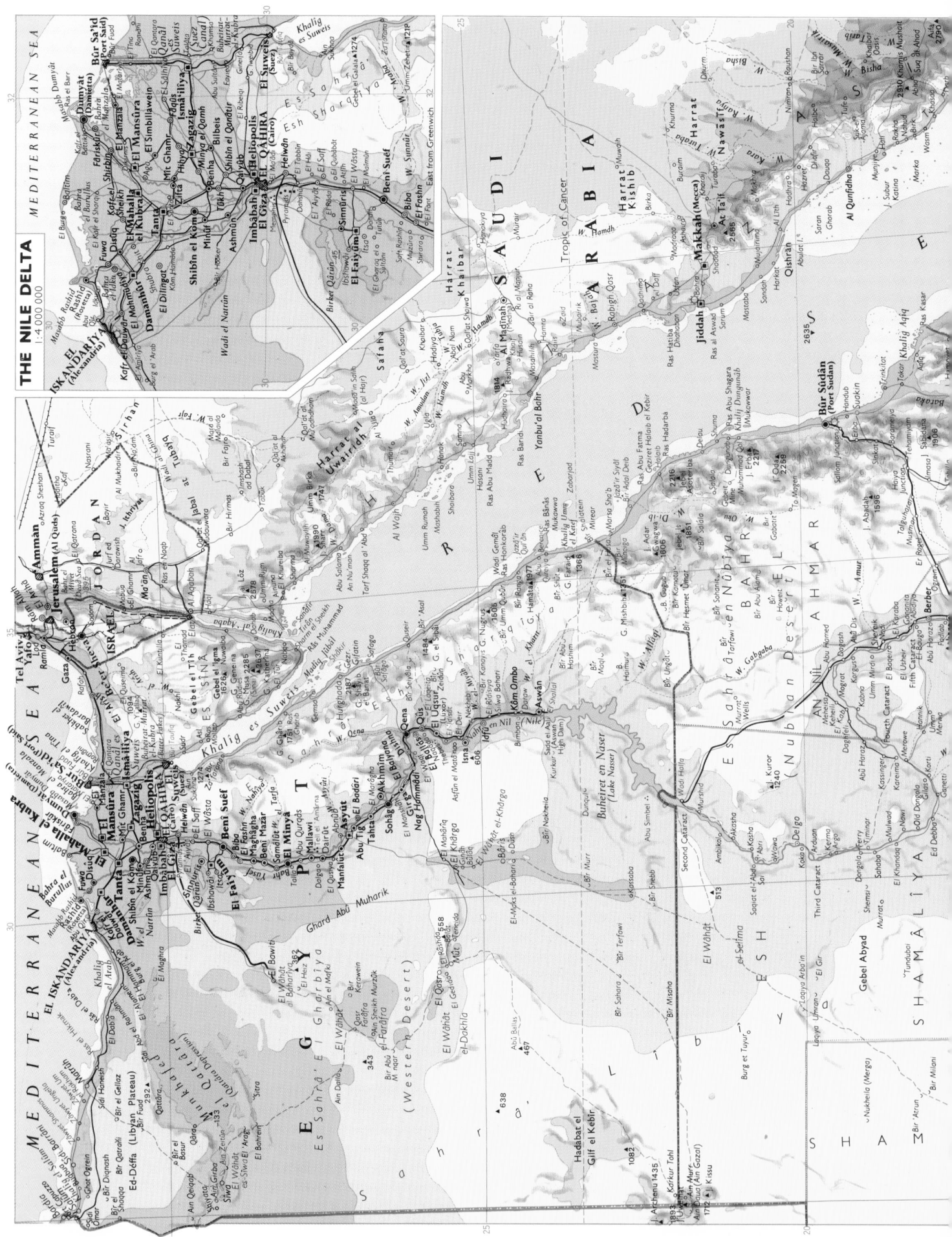

THE NILE DELTA
1:4 000 000

1:8 000 000

50 0 50 100 150 200 250 300 km

COPYRIGHT GEORGE PHILIP & SON LTD

East from Greenwich

Projection: Lambert's Equivalent Azimuthal

m 4000 3000 2000 1500 400 200 0 m

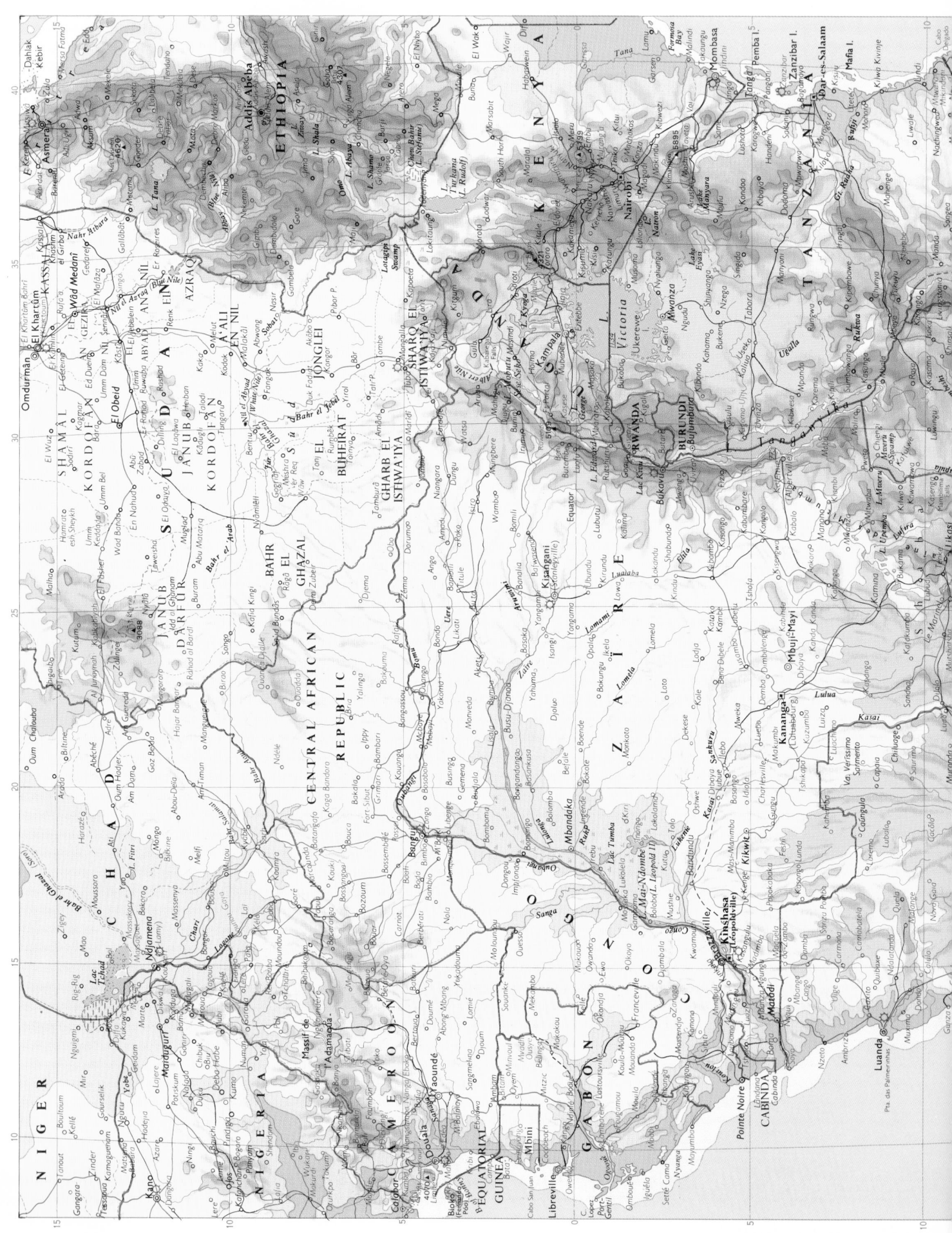

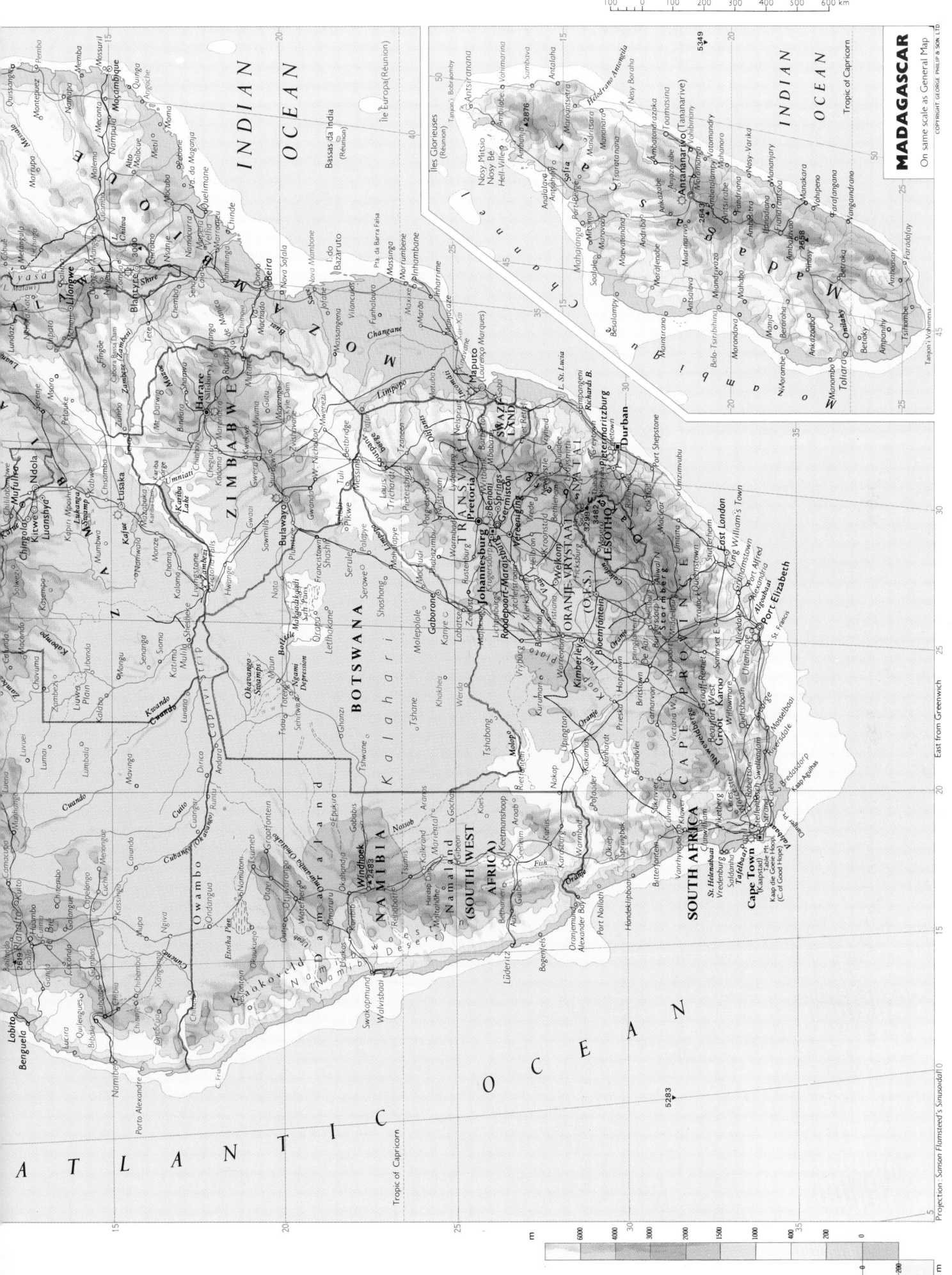

1:15 000 000

100   0   100   200   300   400   500   600 km

COPYRIGHT GEORGE PHILIP & SON, LTD.

MADAGASCAR
On same scale as General Map

INDIAN OCEAN

Tropic of Capricorn

INDIAN OCEAN

ATLANTIC OCEAN

Tropic of Capricorn

East from Greenwich

Projection - Sanson Flamsteed's Sinusoidal

m
6000
4000
3000
2000
1500
1000
400
200
0
200

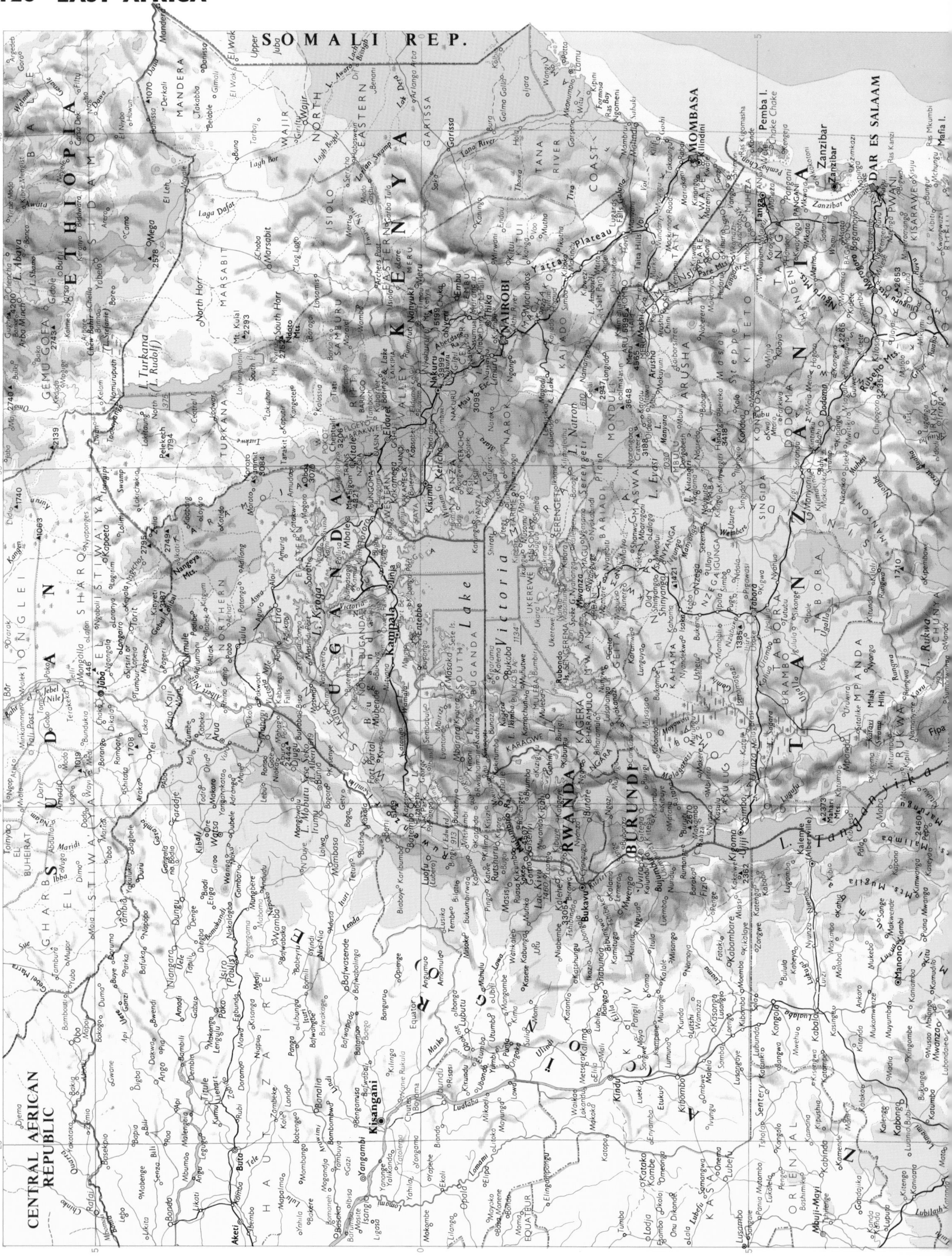
SOMALI REP.
ETHIOPIA
KENYA
UGANDA
SUDAN
TANZANIA
RWANDA
BURUNDI
ZAIRE
CENTRAL AFRICAN REPUBLIC
NAIROBI
MOMBASA
DAR ES SALAAM
Zanzibar
Pemba I.
Mafia I.
Kampala
Kisangani
L. Turkana (L. Rudolf)
Lake Victoria
L. Tanganyika
L. Kyoga
L. Rukwa
L. Eyasi
L. Natron
Tabora
Dodoma
Arusha
Nakuru
Kisumu
Eldoret
Bukavu
Kigoma
Ujiji
Tanga
Kilindini
Entebbe
Jinja
Juba
Marsabit
Garissa
Mwanza
Bujumbura
Kalemie (Albertville)
Kindu
Manono
Buta
Isiro (Paulis)
Aketi
Mbuji-Mayi
Kabalo
Kongolo
Mandera
Moyale
Lamu

1:8 000 000

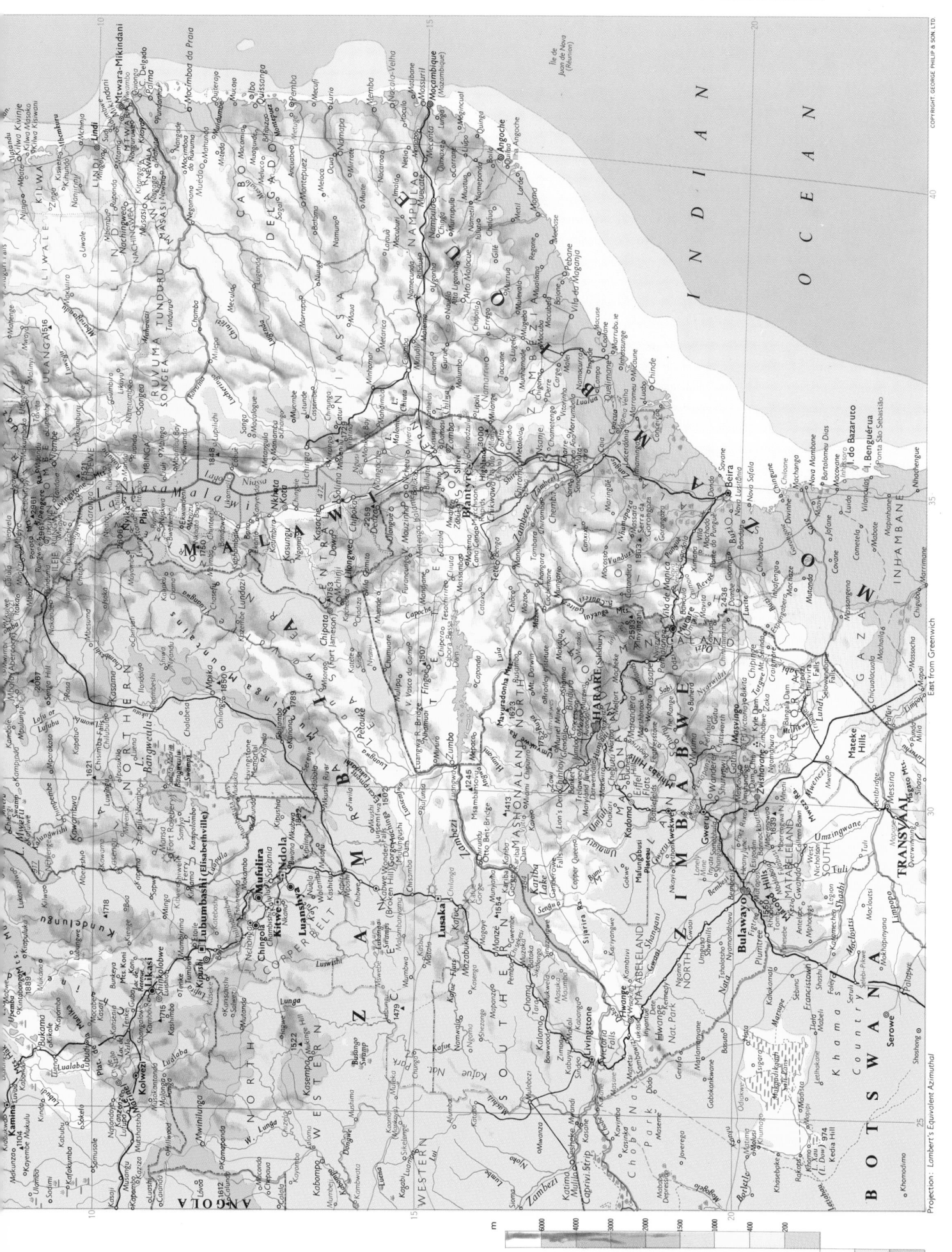

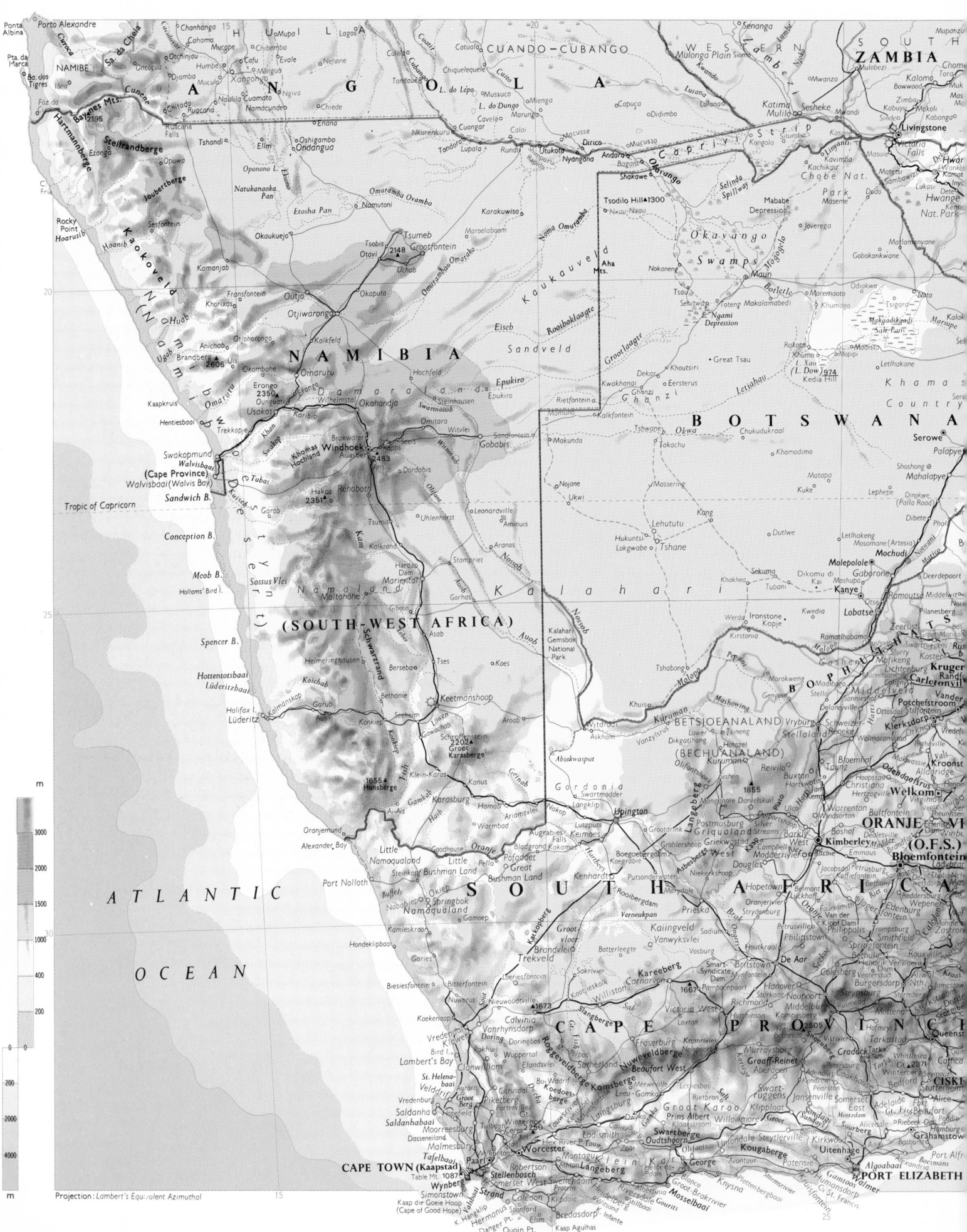

1:8 000 000

50 0 50 100 150 200 250 300 km

MOZAMBIQUE

CHANNEL

ZAMBÉZIA

MALAWI

ZIMBABWE

HARARE

Bulawayo

Gweru

Masvingo

MATABELELAND

SOUTH

VENDA

Pietersburg

TRANSVAAL

PRETORIA

JOHANNESBURG
Springs

SWAZILAND

Maputo
(Lourenço Marques)

MAPUTO

NATAL

PIETERMARITZBURG

DURBAN

Richards Bay

Lake St. Lucia

ESOTHO

East London

INDIAN

OCEAN

East from Greenwich

Beira

Nova Sofala

I. do Bazaruto

I. Benguérua

Inhambane

Xai-Xai

Iles Glorieuses
(Réunion)

Antsiranana

Ambohitra
1475

Nosy Mitsio

Hell-Ville

Ambanja

Tsaratanana
2876

ANTSIR
ANANA

Mahajanga

Maintirano

Morondava

ANTANANARIVO

Antsirabe

Toamasina

Fianarantsoa

FIANARANTSOA

Manakara

Toliara

Tropic of Capricorn

Faradofay

MADAGASCAR

30

45

MADAGASCAR

On same scale as General Map

COPYRIGHT. GEORGE PHILIP & SON, LTD.

East from Greenwich

- - - 5615 - - - Principal Shipping Routes
(Distances in Nautical Miles)

BRITISH
ISLES

A L A S K A

Bristol Bay

Gulf of Alaska

Prince of Wales I.

Queen Charlotte Is.

mak

6741

Mendocino Seascarp

Hawaiian Is.
(U.S.A.)

Honolulu　Oahu

Hawaii

Christmas Island Ridge

CURRENT

P A C I F I C

Palmyra Is. (U.S.)

E A N

Teraina
Tabuaeran
Kirimati

Jarvis I. (U.S.)

Malden I.

Starbuck I.

Vostok
Flint I.

Caroline I.

Marquesas Is.
(Fr.)

bury I.

enix Is.

EQUATORIAL　CURRENT

Tongareva
Penrhyn

Manihiki

apuka

Suwarrow Is.
(Suvorov)

Leeward Is.

ila (U.S.)

OA

Cook
Islands

Society Is. (Fr.)

Windward
Is.

Tahiti (Fr.)

French Polynesia

Manuae

Rarotonga

Tuamotu Archipelago
(Fr.)

vu
avae (N.Z.)

Austral

Tubuai Is.
(Austral Is.)
(Fr.)

Rapa Iti
(Fr.)

Seamount Chain

Pitcairn I. (U.K.)

Ducie I. (U.K.)

Sala-y-Gomez
(Chile)

Easter Is.
(Chile)

Basin

ALASKA
6050
Sitka
Juneau

R　O　C

C A N A D A

Dawson Creek

Prince Rupert

Kitimat

Vancouver

Vancouver I.

Victoria

Seattle
Tacoma
Portland

C. Blanco

C. Mendocino

Sacramento
Oakland
San Francisco

4418

Los Angeles
San Diego

Murray Seascarp

Guadalupe
6225
Pto. Eugenia

Edmonton

Prince Albert

Medicine Hat

Spokane

Helena

Boise

L. Athabaska

Churchill

Lynn Lake

Saskatoon

Regina

Winnipeg

Bismarck

L. Winnipeg

Butte

Cheyenne

Salt Lake City

4711

Tropic of Cancer

Clarion Fracture Zone

Revilla Gigedo Is.
(Mexico)

3666

Clipperton Fracture Zone

Clipperton I. (Fr.)

Equator

Galápagos
(Ecuador)

Cocos I.

Tahiti - Panamá 4570

East Pacific Ridge

PERUVIAN CURRENT

Auckland - Panamá 6510

Southeast

Pacific Basin

6369

Tropic of Capricorn

San Félix (Chile)

San Ambrosio (Chile)

Arch. de Juan Fernández
(Chile)

Alejandro Selkirk

Robinson Crusoe

Chile Rise

Pacific-

Antarctic

Basin

G. of Penas

Wellington
Is.

C. Horn

Str. of Magellan
Tierra del Fuego

Pacific- Antarctic Ridge

WEST WIND DRIFT

CAPE HORN CURRENT

Hudson
Bay

GREENLAND

C. Farewell

Belcher Is.

James
Bay

Scheffeville

Hamilton Inlet

Labrador

N O R T H　A M E R I C A

St. Lawrence

Montréal

Québec

Duluth

L. Superior

Sault Ste. Marie

L. Huron

Ottawa

Toronto

L. Ontario

Buffalo

Minneapolis

Milwaukee

St. Paul

L. Michigan

CHICAGO

Detroit

Pittsburgh

Cincinnati

Indianapolis

Des Moines

Denver

Kansas

St. Louis

Santa Fé

Oklahoma

Little Rock

Memphis

El Paso

Dallas

Austin

Ciudad
Juárez

San Antonio

Houston

Galveston

New
Orleans

Mobile

Torreón

Monterrey

Tampico

C. S. Lucas

Gulf of California

Sierra Madre

M　E　X　I　C　O

Aguascalientes

Guadalajara

San Luis Potosí

México

Puebla

5700

Veracruz

Mérida

Acapulco

3777

S. E. MONSOON DRIFT

GUATEMALA
Guatemala
6669

HONDURAS
Tegucigalpa

El SALVADOR
San Salvador

NICARAGUA
Managua

CENTRAL
AMERICA

COSTA RICA
San José

PANAMÁ
Colón
Panamá Canal

Gulf of Mexico

Tampa

Miami

Florida
Strait

BAHAMAS

La Habana

CUBA

West Indies

Hispaniola

HAITI
JAMAICA
Kingston

DOM.
REP.
Santo
Domingo

PUERTO
RICO
(U.S.)

St. Thomas
Virgin Is.

Leeward
Is.

Guadeloupe
(Fr.)

Martinique
(Fr.)

Caribbean Sea

BELIZE

7680

9200

Barranquilla

San José

BarBarbados

Curaçao (Ne.)

Windward
Is.

TRINIDAD &
TOBAGO

Maracaibo

Caracas

Orinoco

VENEZUELA

Medellín

Bogotá

Cali

COLOMBIA

835

C. S. Francisco

Quito

ECUADOR

Guayaquil

Chimborazo 6267

Cuenca

Iquitos

Manaus

Amazon

BRAZIL

SOUTH

AMERICA

C. Pariñas

Lobos I.

Chiclayo

Trujillo

700

6369

PERU

Lima

Callao

Cuzco

Arequipa

L. Titicaca

Illampú & Ancohuma
6550

La Paz

BOLIVIA

Perú-

6866

Iquique

Chile

8050

Antofagasta
Trench

Salta

Tucumán

Corrientes

PARAGUAY

Asunción

Aconcagua 6960

Córdoba

Rosario

Santa Fe

Paysandú

URUGUAY

Montevideo

Valparaíso

Santiago

Buenos Aires

La Plata

Río de la Plata

Concepción

A R G E N T I N A

Neuquén

Mar del Plata

Patagonia

G. of San Matías

G. of San Jorge

Argentine

Basin

6212

SOUTH

ATLANTIC

OCEAN

Chonos Arch.

Sta. Cruz

Punta Arenas

Falkland Is. (U.K.)

Stanley

South Georgia

ATLANTIC

OCEAN

Newfoundland

Strait of Belle Isle

NORTH

C. Race

Sable I.

UNITED STATES

Cleveland

NEW YORK

Philadelphia

Baltimore

Washington

Richmond

Norfolk

C. Hatteras

Boston

C. Sable

Atlanta

Savannah

Jacksonville

Bermuda (U.K.)

160　　140　　120　　100　West from Greenwich　80　　60　　40　　20

COPYRIGHT. GEORGE PHILIP & SON. LTD.

Java Trench

TIMOR SEA

INDIAN

OCEAN

Croker I.
Cobourg Pen.
Dundas
Melville I. Str.
Van Diemen Gulf
Goulburn Is.
Bathurst I.
Clarence Str.
P. Darwin
Castlereagh
Buc
Arnhem Lar
Pt. Blaze
Anson B.
C. Ford
Batchelor
Rum Jungle
Darwin
Jabiru
Pine Creek
Daly
Katherine
Roper
Matarank a
Ashmore Reef
Cartier I.
C. Londonderry
C. Talbot
Jos. Bonaparte Gulf
Wyndham
Kununurra
Victoria
Victoria River Downs
Larrimah
Birdum
Daly Wate
C. Bougainville B.
Vansittart B.
Admiralty G.
Cambridge G.
Drysdale
Ord
DUNCAN
Bonaparte Archipelago
Montague Sd.
York Sd.
Brunswick B.
Mt. Hann 776
Kimberley
Mt. Ord 1007
King Leopold Ras.
Durack Range
Durack Ord
Wave Hill
Newcastle Waters
STUART
Collier B.
King Sd.
Yampi Sound
Meda
Derby
Hall's Creek
Gordon Downs
Powell Creek
Renner Springs
L. Woods
C. Lévêque
Lacepede Is.
C. Baskerville
Carnot B.
C. Boileau
Broome
Fitzroy
Fitzroy Crossing
GREAT NORTHERN
Sturr
Tanami Desert
Tennant C
Roebuck B.
C. Latouche Treville
C. Bossut
La Grange
Dampier Downs
Gregory Lake
Hordern Hills
The Granites
NORTH
Eighty Mile Beach
Canning Basin
Great Sandy Desert
TERRIT
Barrow Creek
Dampier Archipelago
P. Hedland
Goldsworthy
Port Samson
De Grey
Marble Bar
Shaw
Throssell Ra.
L. Dora
L. Mackay
Reynolds Ra
Mt. Ziel 1510
Hampton Har
Monte Bello Is.
C. Dampier
Preston
Barrow I.
Roebourne
Pilbara
Yule
Nullagine
L. Blanche
Macdonnell Ras.
N.W. Cape
Exmouth G.
Exmouth
Learmonth
Pt. Cloates
Onslow
Fortescue
Hamersley Ra.
Mt. Enid
Wittenoom
Robertson Ra.
L. Disappointment
Gibson Desert
L. Macdonald
James Ra.
Hugh
Palmer
Mt. Bruce 1235
Ophthalmia Range
Ashburton
Mt. Newman 1053
Newman
WESTERN
Rawlinson Ra.
L. Amadeus
Mt. Olga 1151
Ayers Rock 933
Charlotte
Gr. Farquhar
C. Cuvier
Geographe Chan.
Bernier I.
L. McLeod
Lyons
Barlee Ra.
Mt. Augustus 1105
Mt. Egerton 994
Peak Hill
GREAT NORTHERN
Robinson Ras.
L. Buchanan
Barrow Ra.
Musgrave Ranges 1549
Mt. Woodroffe
Hamilte
Alber
Dorre I.
Naturaliste Chan.
Dirk Hartog I.
Denham
Shark B.
S. Passage
Steep Pt.
Carnarvon
Gascoyne
Wooramel
Murchison
Meekatharra
Wiluna
L. Carnegie
L. Wells 712
Everard Ras.
AUSTRALIA
Gantheaume B.
P. Gregory
Houtman
Northampton
Abrolhos
Champion B.
Dongara
Geraldton
Sanford
Cue
Nannine
Mongers Lake
L. Austin
Sandstone
L. Yeo
Great Victoria Desert
L. Maurice
SOUTH AU
Coob
Ped
Tallering Peak 453
Mt. Magnet
Yalgoo
Mt. Barlee
L. Raeside
Leonora
Malcolm
L. Carey
L. Rason
Maralinga
Ooldea
Tarco
Coastal Plains
GERALDTON
L. Moore
Bonnie Rock
Bencubbin
Bullfinch
Menzies
L. Barlee
L. Ballard
Kanowna
Kalgoorlie
Boulder
Zanthus
Premier Downs
Rawlinna
Forrest
Deakin
Nullarbor Plain
Hampton Tableland
EYRE
Eucla Motel
L. Everar
Penong
Cedun
Wedge I.
Basin
Midland Junction
Northam
Kellerberrin
Merredin
Southern Cross
Coolgardie
L. Lefroy
L. Cowan
Norseman
Eucla
C. Adieu
Fowlers B.
Nuyts Archipelago
C. Radstock
Swan
Perth
Fremantle
Kwinana
Toodyay
Beverley
Brookton
Norogin
The Johnston Lakes
L. Dundas
Pt. Dover
Pt. Culver
Great Australian Bight
Investigator Group
Streaky B.
Anxious
Pinjarra
Newdegate
Ravensthorpe
Hopetoun
Esperance
Rocky Pt.
Coffin B. Pe
Whidbe
Bunbury
Collie
Wagin
Nyabing
Gnowangerup
C. Pasley
C. Arid Archipelago of the Recherche
C. le Grand
Geographe B.
C. Naturaliste
Busselton
Bridgetown
Katanning
Stirling Ra.
Pt. Hood
Doubtful B.
C. Knob
Augusta
Manjimup
Pemberton
Mt. Barker
Albany
C. Leeuwin
Flinders B.
Denmark
Tor B.
King George Sound
Pt. d'Entrecasteaux
Pt. Nuyts

m
2000
1500
1000
400
200
0
200
2000
4000
6000
m
30
35

1:14 000 000

100 0 100 200 300 400 500 600 km

CORAL

SEA

CORAL
SEA ISLANDS

SEA TERRITORY

Gulf of

Carpentaria

PACIFIC

Louisiade
Archipelago

QUEENSLAND

Simpson
Desert

Tropic of Capricorn

OCEAN

TRALIA

NEW SOUTH WALES

Lord Howe I.

VICTORIA

MELBOURNE

Australian Alps

TASMAN

Bass Strait

SEA

Furneaux
Group

TASMANIA

Hobart

COPYRIGHT GEORGE PHILIP & SON, LTD.

1:60 000 000

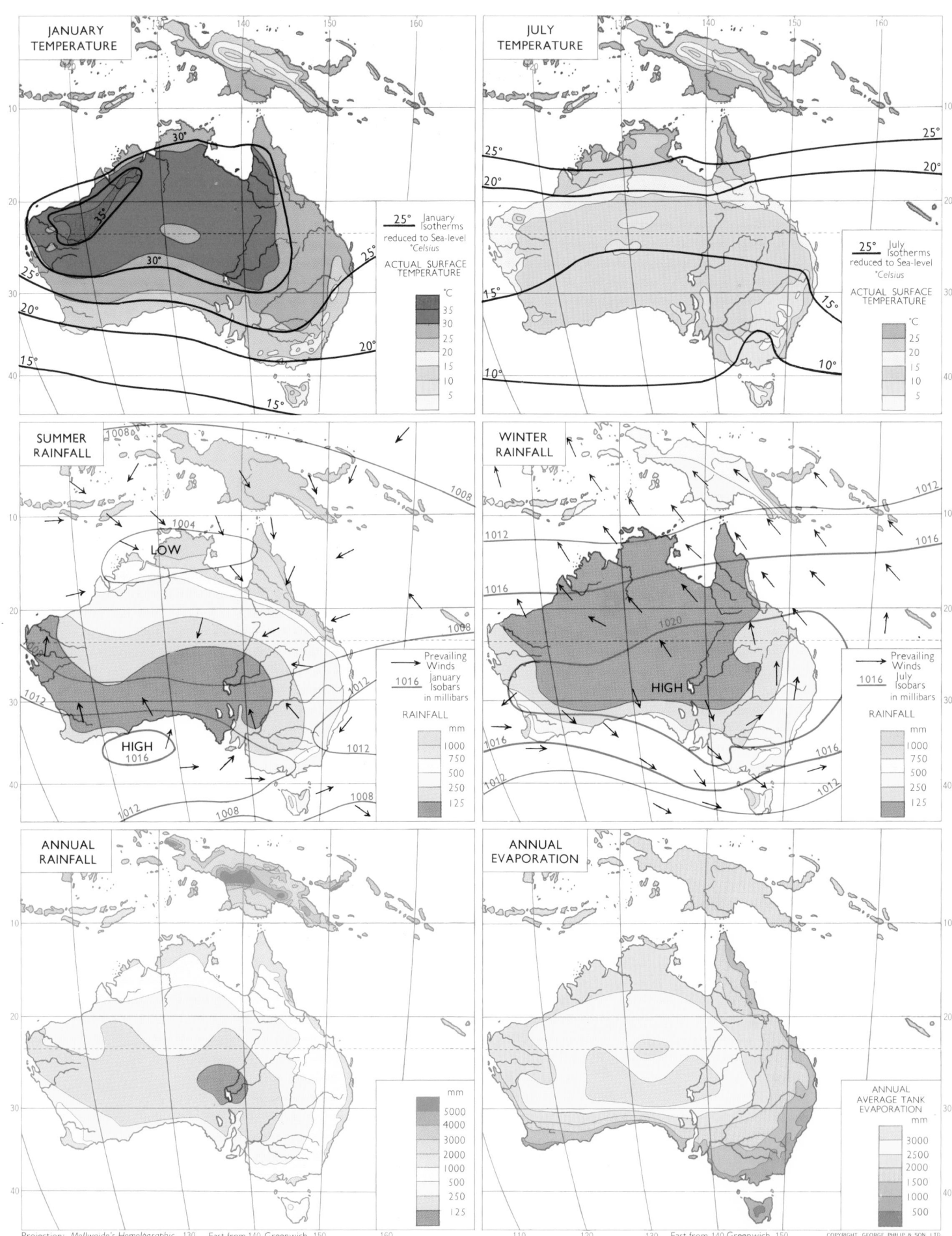

JANUARY
TEMPERATURE

25° January
Isotherms
reduced to Sea-level
°Celsius
ACTUAL SURFACE
TEMPERATURE

°C
35
30
25
20
15
10
5

JULY
TEMPERATURE

25° July
Isotherms
reduced to Sea-level
°Celsius
ACTUAL SURFACE
TEMPERATURE

°C
25
20
15
10
5

SUMMER
RAINFALL

LOW

HIGH
1016

Prevailing
Winds
1016 January
Isobars
in millibars
RAINFALL
mm
1000
750
500
250
125

WINTER
RAINFALL

HIGH

Prevailing
Winds
1016 July
Isobars
in millibars
RAINFALL
mm
1000
750
500
250
125

ANNUAL
RAINFALL

mm
5000
4000
3000
2000
1000
500
250
125

ANNUAL
EVAPORATION

ANNUAL
AVERAGE TANK
EVAPORATION
mm
3000
2500
2000
1500
1000
500

Projection: *Mollweide's Homolographic* 130   East from 140 Greenwich 150   160

110   120   130   East from 140 Greenwich 150   COPYRIGHT GEORGE PHILIP & SON LTD

1:6 500 000

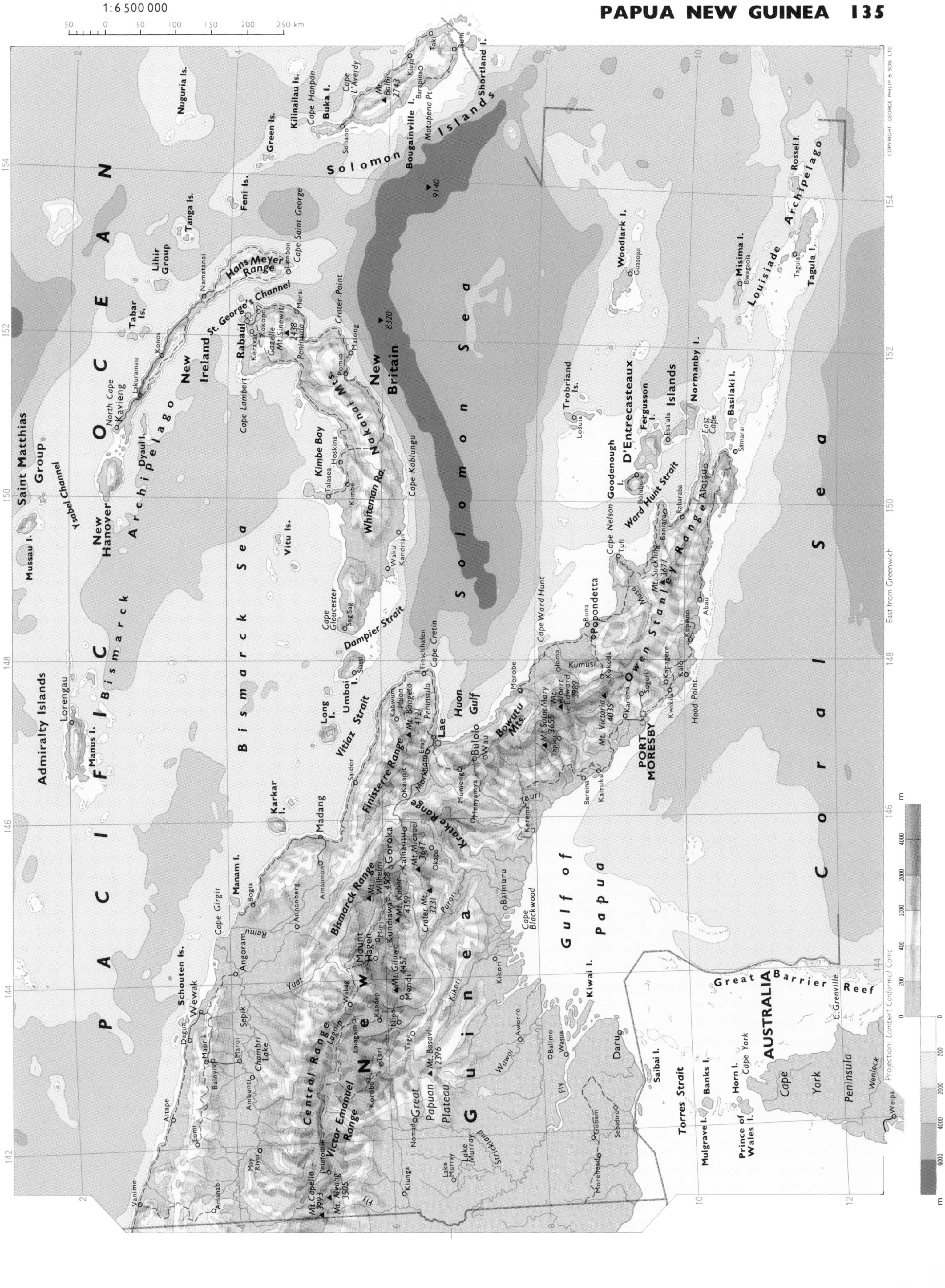

50   0   50   100   150   200   250 km

P A C I F I C   O C E A N

Nuguria Is.

Kilinailau Is.
Cape Hanpan
Buka I.
Cape L'Averdy
Mt. Balbi 2743
Taki
Kieta
Bara
Barpimao
Bem

Green Is.
Tanga Is.
Feni Group

Solomon   Islands

Bougainville I.
Motupena Pt

9140

Shortland I.

Lihir Group

Tabar Is.

Saint Matthias Group

Mussau I.

New Hanover

Ysabel Channel

Bismarck   Archipelago

Hans Meyer Range

New   Ireland

St. George's Channel
Cape Saint George

Namatanai
Lemkamin
Konos

North Cape
Kavieng
Dyaull I.

New   Britain

Rabaul
Kokopo
Keravat
Gazelle Peninsula
Mt. Sinewit 2438
Merai
Pomio
Matong
Crater Point

8320

Solomon   Sea

Cape Lambert

Nakanai   Mts.

Whiteman   Ra.

Kimbe Bay
Talasea
Hoskins

Cape Kablungu

Cape Gloucester
Cape Sag-Sag
Waku
Kandrian

Dampier Strait

B i s m a r c k   S e a

Vitu Is.

Long I.
Umboi I.

Vitiaz Strait

Sio
Saidor

Finisterre Range

Admiralty Islands
Lorengau
Manus I.

Schouten Is.

Cape Girgir

Karkar I.
Manam I.
Bogia
Amalmon
Aiabang

Madang

Ramu

Huon Peninsula
Finschhafen
Cape Cretin

Kabwum
Mt. Bangeta 4121

Lae   Huon   Gulf

Morobe

Wewak

Angoram
Sepik
Marui
Maprik
Bainyik
Ambunti
Chambri Lake

Dagua

Bismarck Range
Mount Hagen
Mt. Wilhelm 4508
Mt. Giluwe 4359
Mendi
Mt. Kubor 4359
Mt. Michael 3647
Okapa
Crater Mts. 3231
Pyraru

Goroka
Kainantu
Kratke Range

Bulolo
Wau
Mumeng

Bowutu Mts.

Mt. Scott
Mt. Suckling 3677
Mt. Albert Edward 3989
Mt. Victoria 4035

Owen   Stanley   Range

Cape Ward Hunt
Buna
Popondetta
Kokoda
Kumusi
Oiloma
Sagari
Okapagere
Kaia
Kupiano
Abau

PORT   MORESBY

Hood Point

Cape Nelson

Tufi

Ward Hunt Strait

Trobriand Is.
Kiriwina
Losuia

D'Entrecasteaux Islands
Goodenough I.
Fergusson I.
Normanby I.
Esa'ala
Bolubolu
Baniara
East Cape
Samarai
Basilaki I.

Woodlark I.
Guasopa

Misima I.
Bwagaoia

Louisiade   Archipelago

Tagula I.
Tagula

Rossel I.

C o r a l   S e a

N e w   G u i n e a

Central Range
Victor Emanuel Range
Mt. Capella 3993
Mt. Alyang 3505
Telefomin

Great Papuan Plateau

Mt. Bosavi 2396

Lake Murray
Fly

Kikori

Gulf   of   Papua

Cape Blackwood

Kiwai I.

Daru

Torres Strait

Mulgrave I.
Banks I.
Saibai I.
Horn I.
Cape York
Prince of Wales I.

AUSTRALIA

Great   Barrier   Reef

Cape York Peninsula

C. Grenville

Weipa

East from Greenwich

Projection: Lambert Conformal Conic

m
6000
4000
2000
1000
400
200
0
200
2000
4000
6000
m

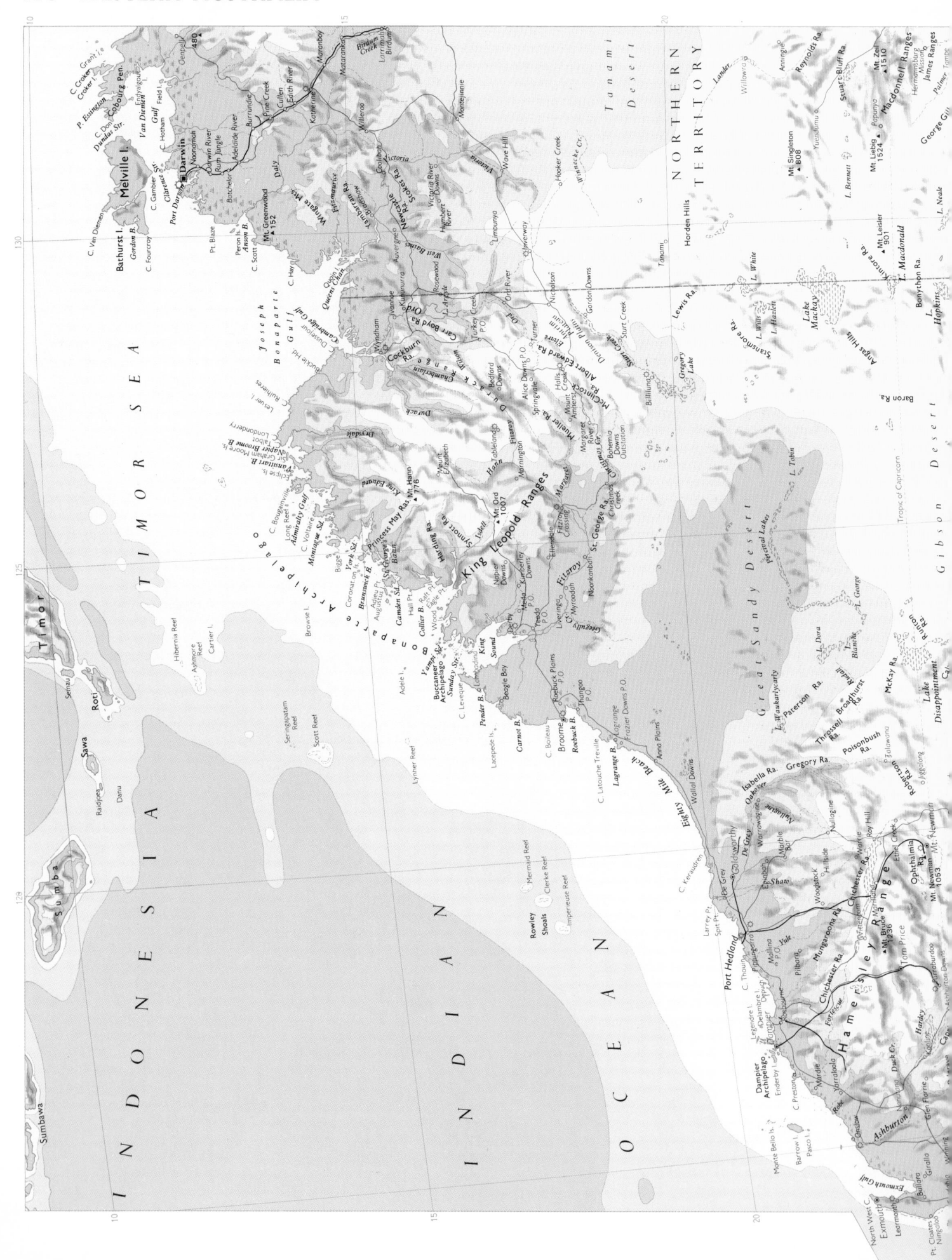

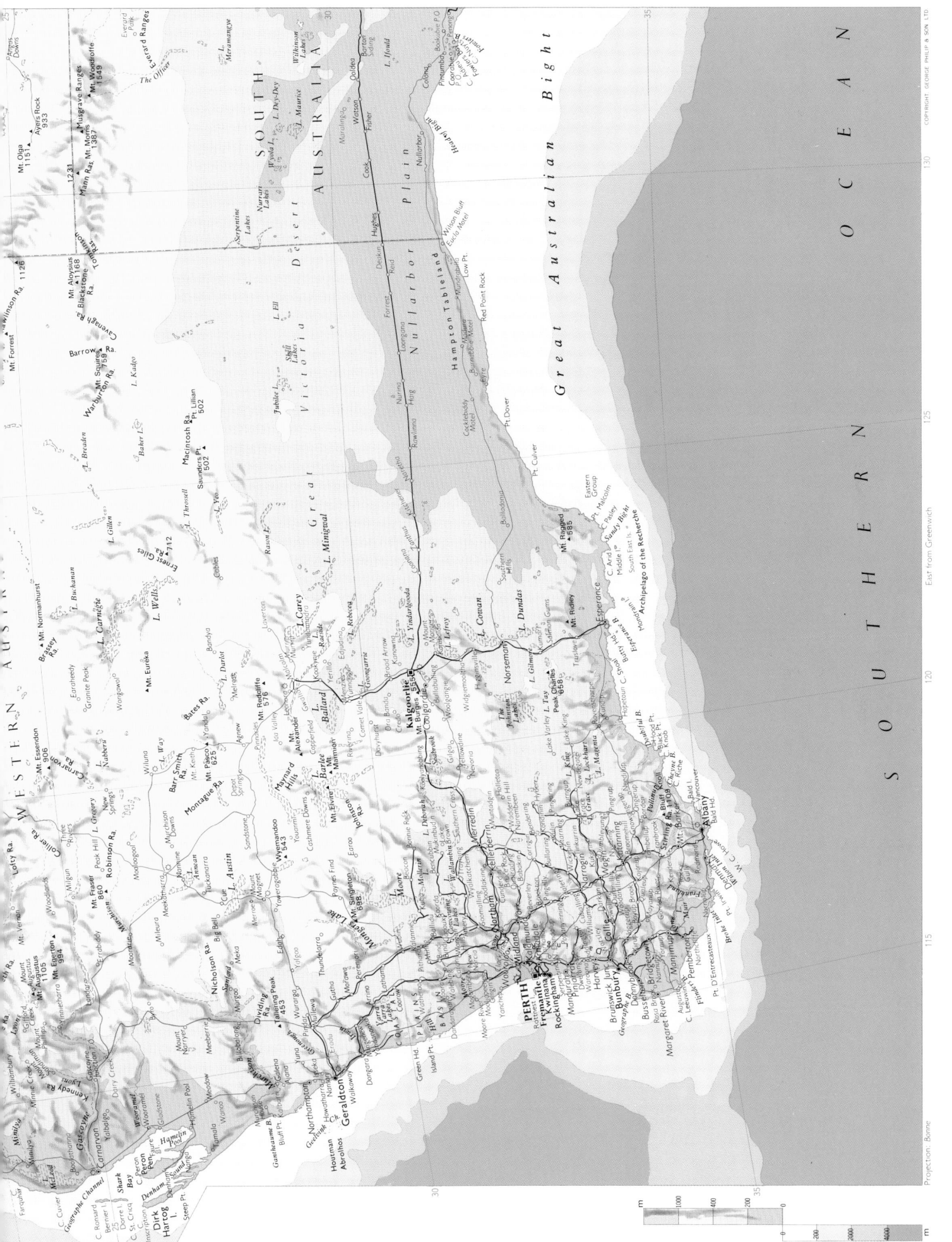

1 : 8 000 000

50   0   50   100   150   200   250   300 km

S O U T H E R N

O C E A N

Great *Australian* *Bight*

S O U T H

A U S T R A L I A

W E S T E R N   A U S T R A L I A

Nullarbor Plain

Hampton Tableland

Great Victoria Desert

PERTH

Kalgoorlie

Geraldton

Bunbury

Albany

Norseman

Esperance

Archipelago of the Recherche

Ayers Rock 933

Mt. Olga 1151

Musgrave Ranges

Mt. Woodroffe 1549

Projection: Bonne

East from Greenwich

COPYRIGHT GEORGE PHILIP & SON LTD

m   1000   400   200   0   200   2000   4000   m

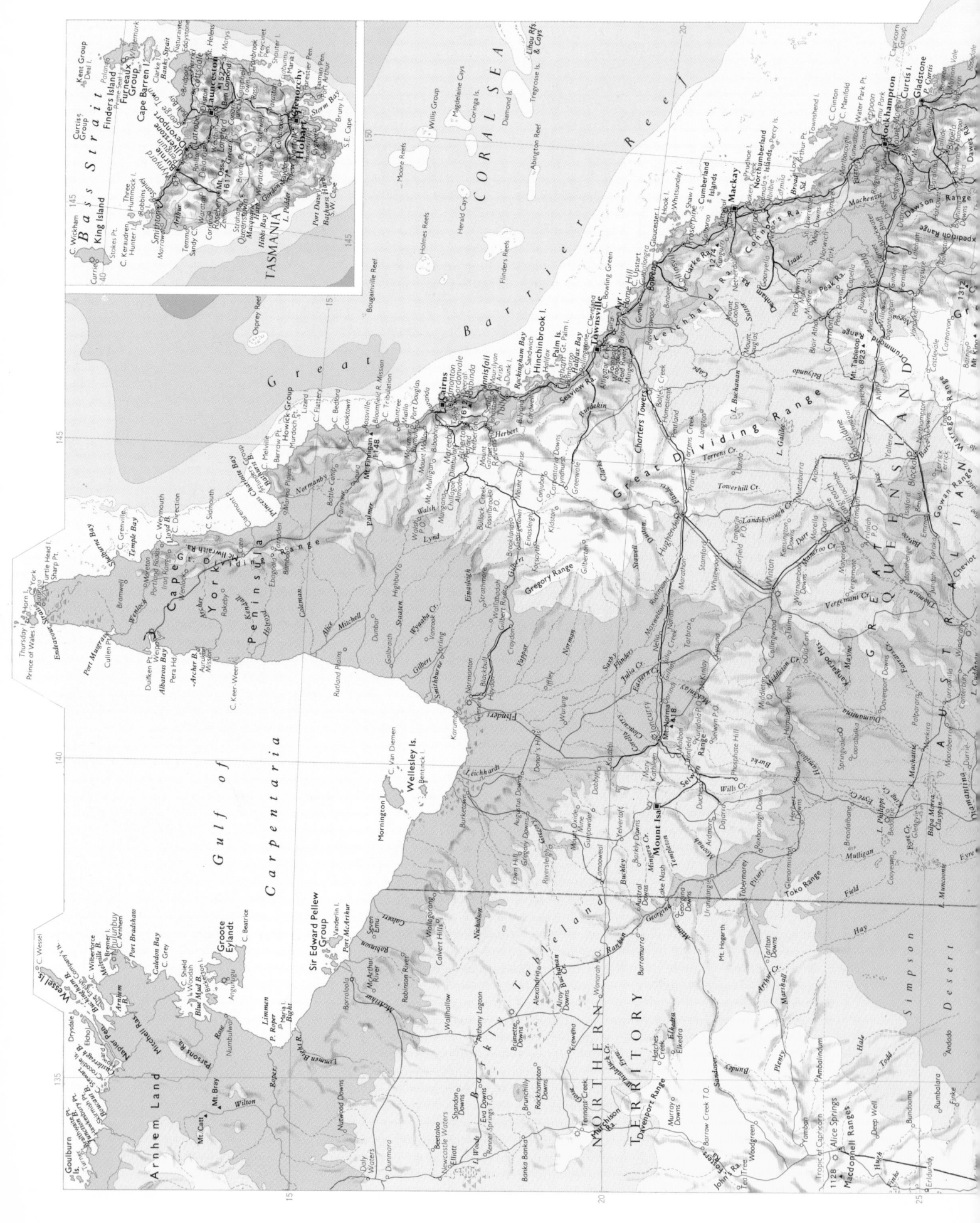

1:8 000 000

50   0   50   100   150   200   250   300 km

T A S M A N   S E A

B A S S I N

D i v i d i n g   R a n g e

Brisbane

N E W   S O U T H   W A L E S

SYDNEY

CANBERRA

V I C T O R I A

MELBOURNE

S O U T H   A U S T R A L I A

ADELAIDE

B a r r i e r   R a n g e

Broken Hill

Lake Eyre North

Lake Torrens

Lake Gairdner

Spencer   Gulf

Kangaroo

Bass   Strait

King Island

Furneaux Group

Flinders Island

Cape Barren I.

Projection: Bonne

East from Greenwich

m

2000
1500
1000
400
200
0 0
200
2000
4000
m

Projection: Alber's Equal area with two standard parallels

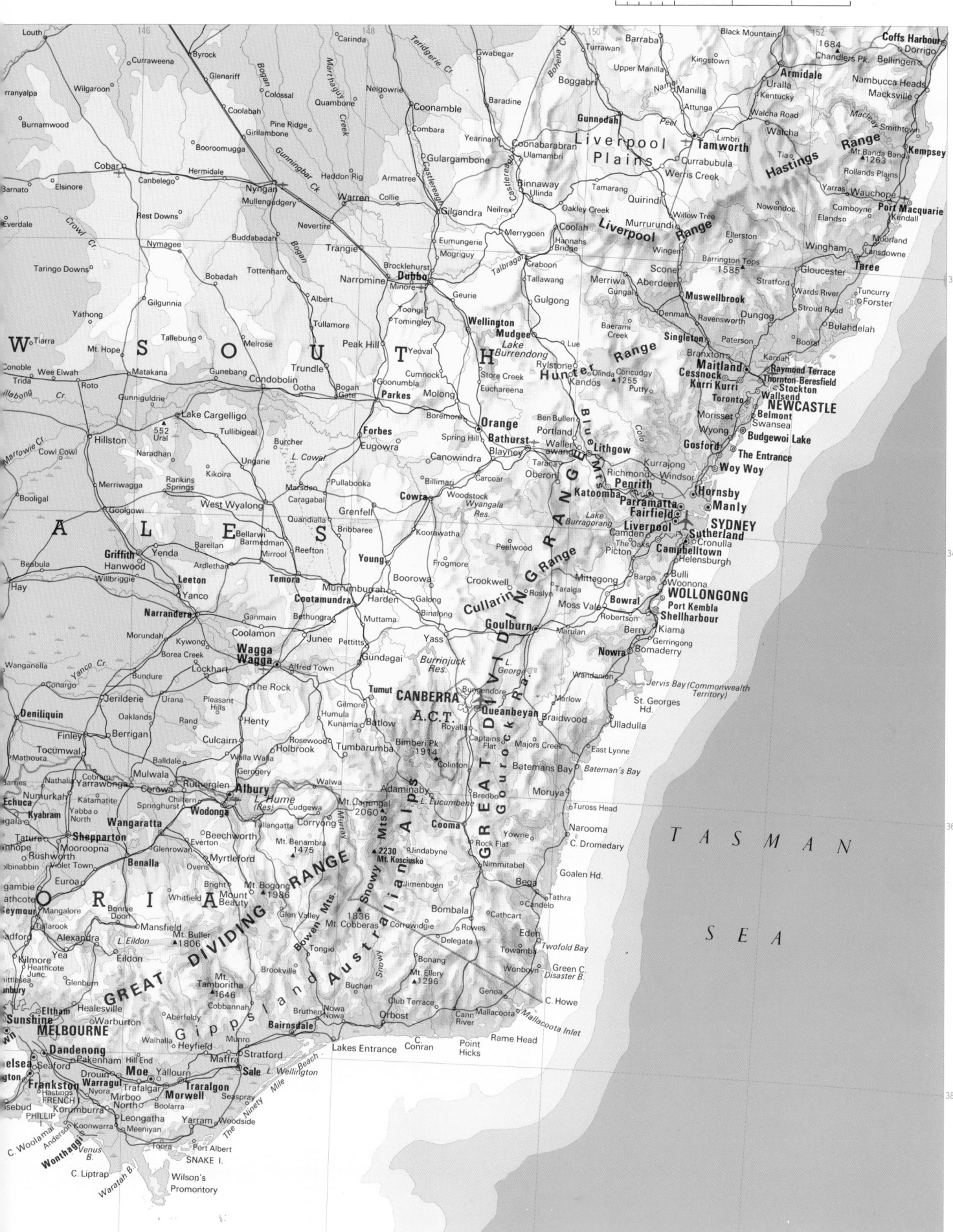

50   0   50   100   150 km

1:3 500 000

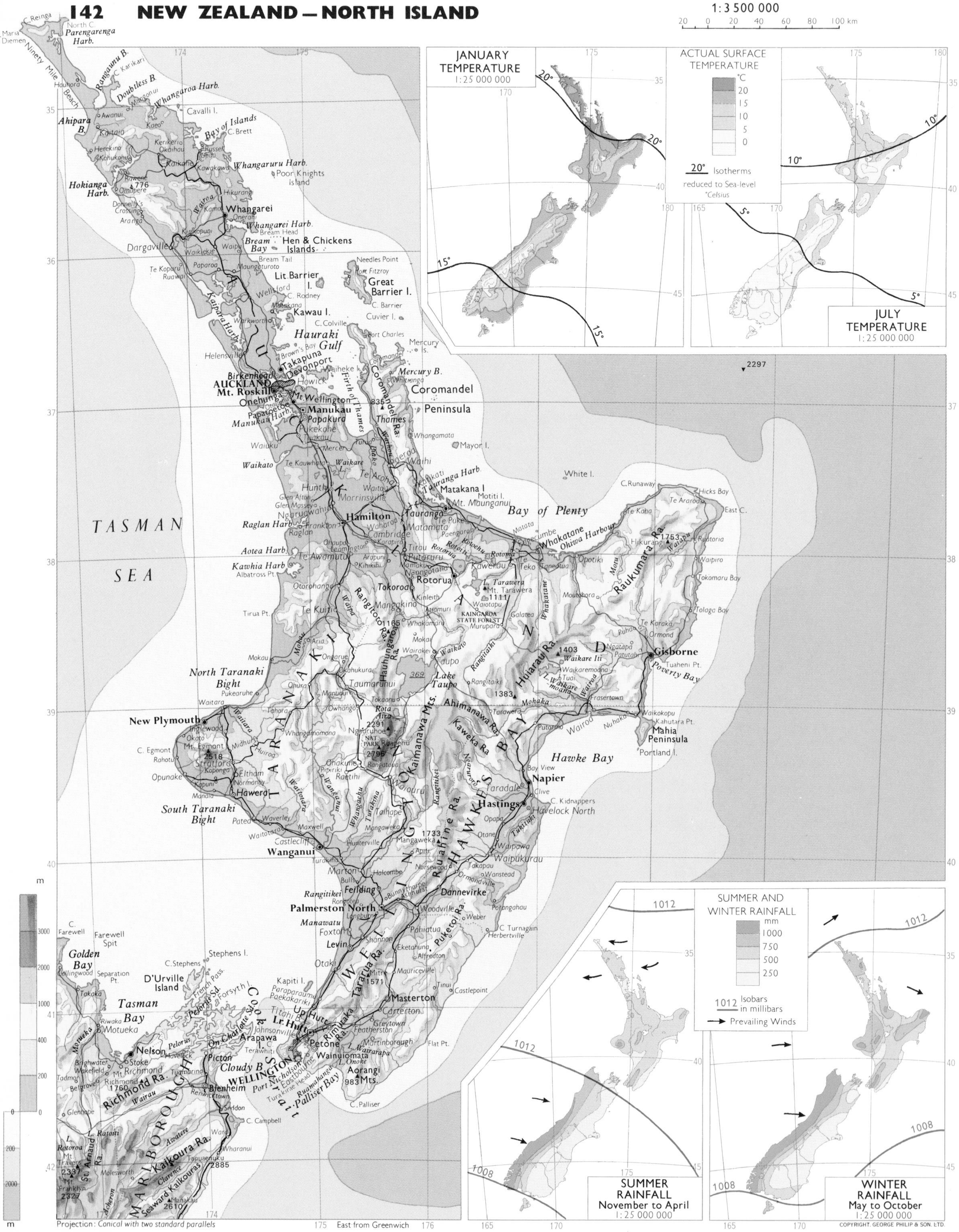

20 0 20 40 60 80 100 km

JANUARY TEMPERATURE
1:25 000 000

ACTUAL SURFACE TEMPERATURE
°C
20
15
10
5
0

20° Isotherms
reduced to Sea-level
°Celsius

JULY TEMPERATURE
1:25 000 000

Place names and features

C. Reinga
C. Maria van Diemen
North C.
Parengarenga Harb.
Rangaunu B.
C. Karikari
Doubtless B.
Whangaroa Harb.
Cavalli I.
Ahipara B.
Ninety Mile Beach
Kaitaia
Kaeo
Kerikeri
Okaihau
Kaikohe
Bay of Islands
C. Brett
Russell
Kawakawa
Poor Knights Island
Hokianga Harb.
Rawene
Omapere
Kaikohe
Hikurangi
Whangaruru Harb.
Dargaville
Te Kopuru
Ruawai
Maungaturoto
Whangarei
Onerahi
Whangarei Harb.
Bream Head
Hen & Chickens Islands
Bream Bay
Bream Tail
Paparoa
Te Hana
Wellsford
Lit. Barrier I.
Port Fitzroy
Great Barrier I.
C. Rodney
Warkworth
Kawau I.
C. Colville
Cuvier I.
Mercury Is.
Helensville
Hauraki Gulf
Brown's Bay
Coromandel
Mercury B.
Whitianga
Coromandel Peninsula
Birkenhead
Takapuna
Devonport
AUCKLAND
Mt. Roskill
Howick
Firth of Thames
Onehunga
Mt. Wellington
Manukau
Papatoetoe
Papakura
Thames
Whangamata
Manukau Harb.
Pukekohe
Mayor I.
Waiuku
Mercer
Waihi
Te Kauwhata
Waikato
Tauranga Harb.
White I.
C. Runaway
Huntly
Te Aroha
Matakana I.
Mt. Maunganui
Hicks Bay
Te Araroa
Ngaruawahia
Morrinsville
Tauranga
Bay of Plenty
Te Kaha
Glen Afton
Glen Massey
Te Puke
Hamilton
Cambridge
Matamata
Paengaroa
Whakatane
Ohiwa Harbour
Hikurangi 1753
Raglan Harb.
Raglan
Frankton
Leamington
Tirau
Rotorua
Kawerau
Opotiki
Te Awamutu
Putaruru
Mamaku
Rotorua
Waipiro
Tokomaru Bay
Aotea Harb.
Kihikihi
Tokoroa
L. Tarawera
Mt. Tarawera 1111
Waiotapu
Galatea
Tolaga Bay
Kawhia Harb.
Albatross Pt.
Otorohanga
Mangakino
Kaingaroa State Forest
Murupara
Te Koraha
Ormond
Tirua Pt.
Te Kuiti
Waitomo
Mokai
Taupo
Ngatapa 1403
Waikare Iti
Gisborne
Tuaheni Pt.
Poverty Bay
Mokau
Ongarue
Taumarunui
Lake Taupo
Rangitaiki
1383
Mohaka
Waikaremoana
Frasertown
North Taranaki Bight
Pukearuhe
Ohura
Manunui
Tokaanu
Ahimanawa Ra.
Wairoa
Waikokopu
Kahutara Pt.
Mahia Peninsula
Portland I.
New Plymouth
Inglewood
Okato
Egmont 2291
Ngauruhoe 2291
Nat. Park
Ruapehu 2796
Kaweka Ra.
Hawke Bay
C. Egmont
Mt. Egmont 2518
Rahotu
Stratford
Kaponga
Eltham
Ohakune
Raetihi
Rangataua
Napier
Taradale
Clive
Opunake
Kapuni
Normanby
Hawera
Manaia
Taihape
Hastings
Havelock North
C. Kidnappers
South Taranaki Bight
Patea
Waverley
Maxwell
Hunterville
1733
Mangaweka
Waipawa
Otane
Waipukurau
Castlecliff
Wanganui
Turakina
Marton
Bulls
Halcombe
Rangitikei Ra.
Dannevirke
Woodville
Weber
Rangitikei
Feilding
Palmerston North
Ruahine Ra.
Pongaroa
Manawatu
Foxton
Shannon
Eketahuna
Alfredton
Herbertville
Levin
Otaki
Mauriceville
Tararua Ra.
Castlepoint
Golden Bay
C. Farewell
Farewell Spit
Collingwood
Separation Pt.
Takaka
Kapiti I.
Paraparaumu
Paekakariki
Mitre 1571
Tinui
Stephens I.
D'Urville Island
French Pass
Pelorus Sd.
Forsyth
Carterton
Masterton
Featherston
Riwaka
Motueka
Titahi B.
Up. Hutt
Greytown
Flat Pt.
Tasman Bay
Brightwater
Stoke
Richmond
Lr. Hutt
Petone
Martinborough
Nelson
Pelorus
Queen Charlotte Sd.
Johnsonville
Wainuiomata
Wanganui Inlet
Picton
Terawhiti
Port Nicholson
Eastbourne
Onoke
Palliser Bay
Richmond Ra.
Havelock
Mt. Richmond
Arapawa
WELLINGTON
Aorangi 983 Mts.
Blenheim
Renwick
Port Underwood
Turakirae Head
C. Palliser
Marlborough
Tasman Sea
Kaikoura Ra.
Seaward Kaikoura Ra.
Tapuaenuku 2885
Wharanui
Clarence
Kaikoura 2610
St. Arnaud Ra.
Nelson Lakes
L. Rotoroa
Travers 2338
Molesworth
Wairau

TASMAN SEA

SUMMER AND WINTER RAINFALL
mm
1000
750
500
250

1012 Isobars in millibars
→ Prevailing Winds

SUMMER RAINFALL
November to April
1:25 000 000

WINTER RAINFALL
May to October
1:25 000 000

m
3000
2000
1000
400
200
0
0
200
2000
m

Projection: Conical with two standard parallels
East from Greenwich
COPYRIGHT. GEORGE PHILIP & SON. LTD.

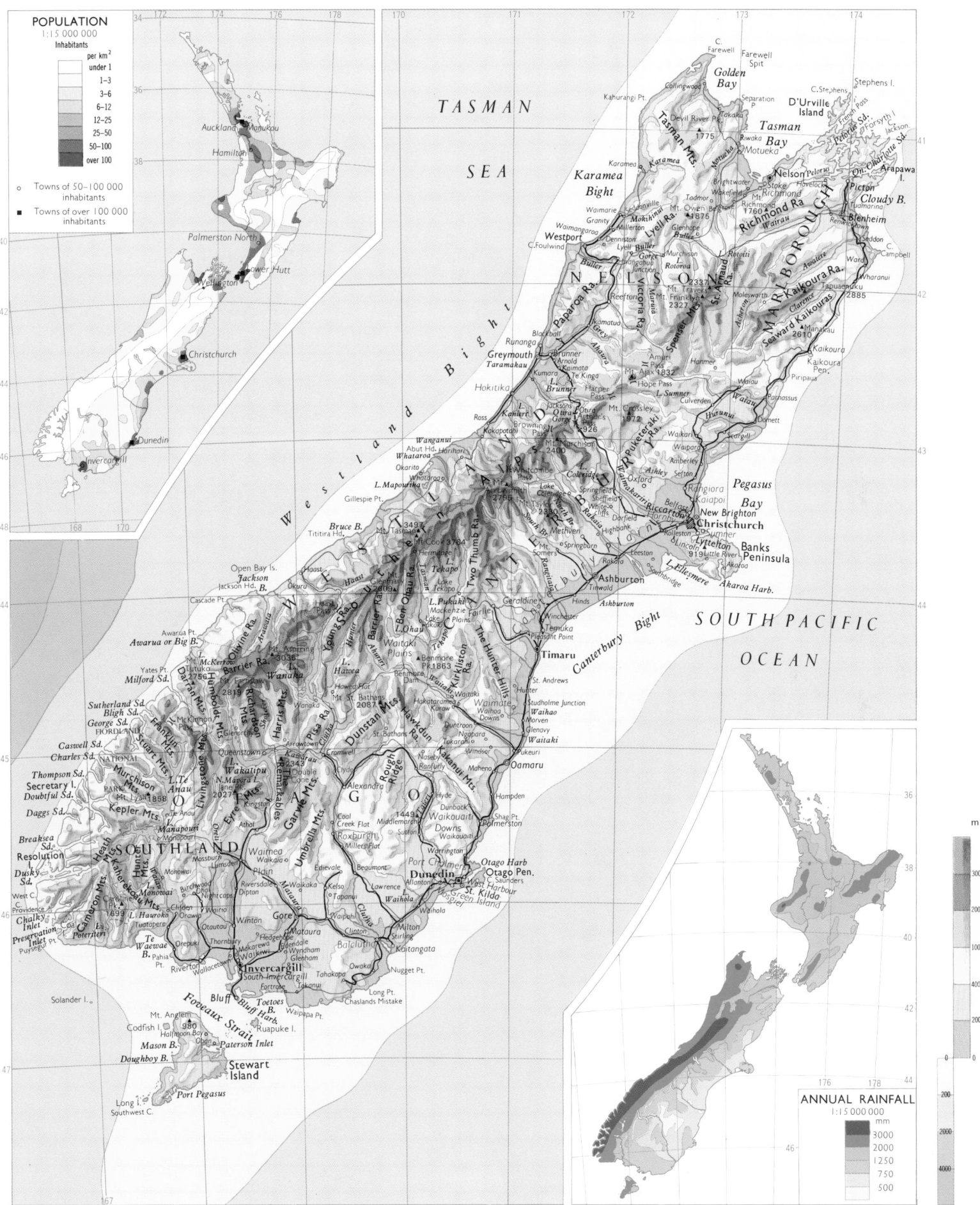

1:3 500 000

20 0 20 40 60 80 100 km

POPULATION
1:15 000 000
Inhabitants
per km²
under 1
1–3
3–6
6–12
12–25
25–50
50–100
over 100

○ Towns of 50–100 000 inhabitants
■ Towns of over 100 000 inhabitants

ANNUAL RAINFALL
1:15 000 000
mm
3000
2000
1250
750
500

m
3000
2000
1000
400
200
0

Projection: Conical with two standard parallels   East from Greenwich   COPYRIGHT. GEORGE PHILIP & SON. LTD.

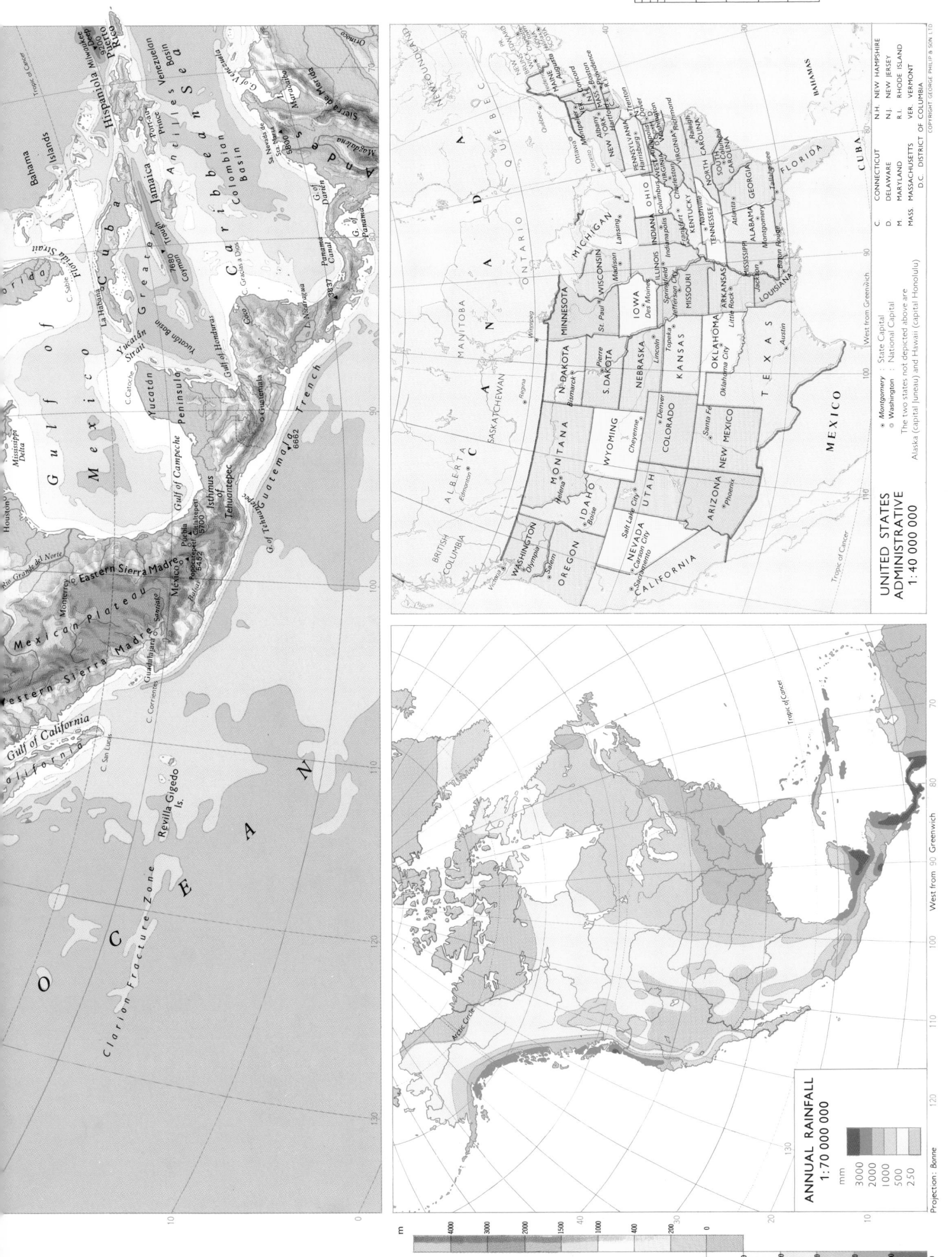

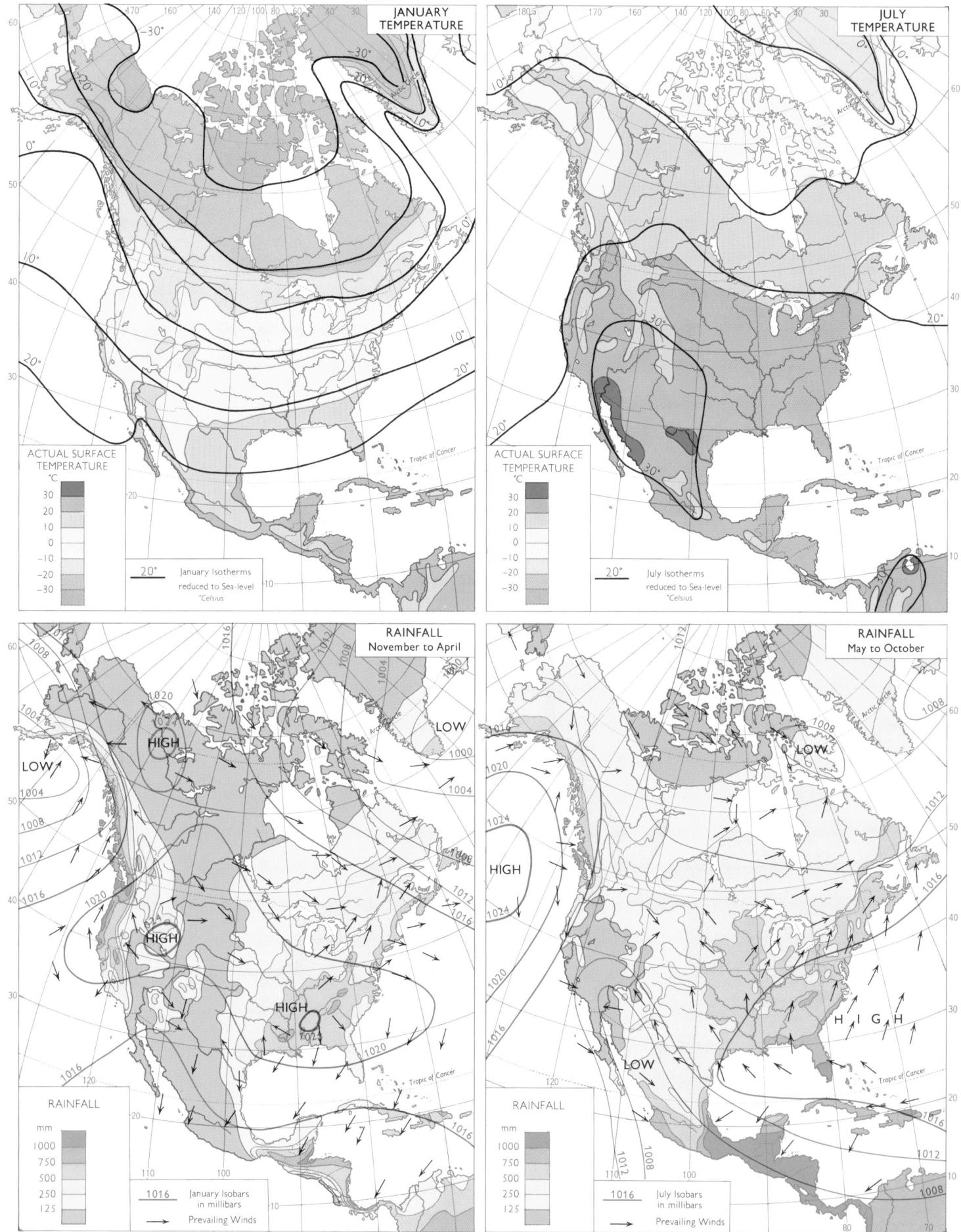

1 : 70 000 000

500   0   500   1000   1500   2000   2500 km

JANUARY
TEMPERATURE

ACTUAL SURFACE
TEMPERATURE
°C

	30
	20
	10
	0
	-10
	-20
	-30

20°   January Isotherms
reduced to Sea-level
°Celsius

JULY
TEMPERATURE

ACTUAL SURFACE
TEMPERATURE
°C

	30
	20
	10
	0
	-10
	-20
	-30

20°   July Isotherms
reduced to Sea-level
°Celsius

RAINFALL
November to April

RAINFALL

mm

	1000
	750
	500
	250
	125

1016   January Isobars
in millibars

→   Prevailing Winds

RAINFALL
May to October

RAINFALL

mm

	1000
	750
	500
	250
	125

1016   July Isobars
in millibars

→   Prevailing Winds

Projection: Lambert's Equivalent Azimuthal   West from 70 Greenwich   COPYRIGHT. GEORGE PHILIP & SON. LTD.

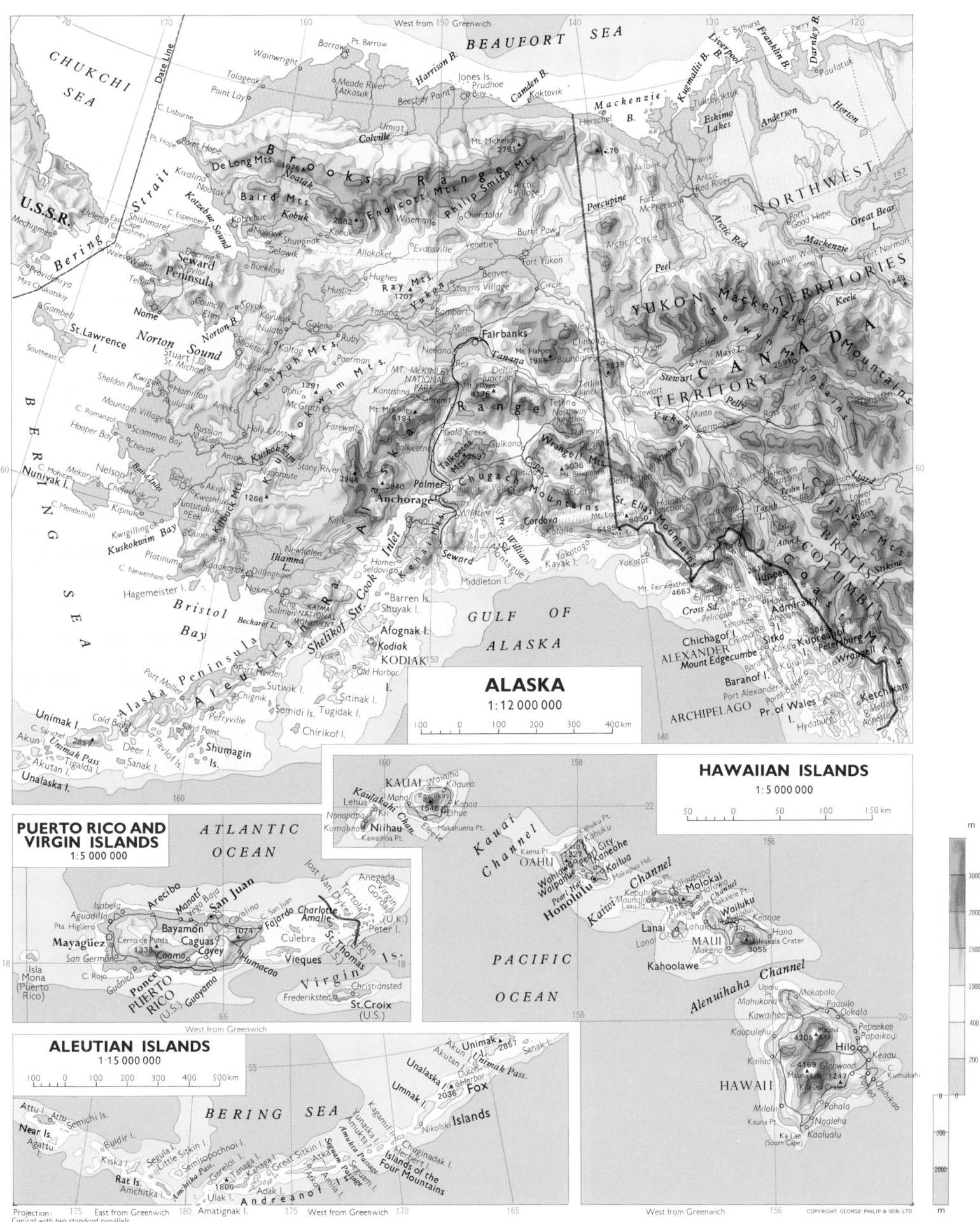

ALASKA

1:12 000 000

100 0 100 200 300 400km

HAWAIIAN ISLANDS

1:5 000 000

50 0 50 100 150 km

PUERTO RICO AND VIRGIN ISLANDS

1:5 000 000

ALEUTIAN ISLANDS

1:15 000 000

100 0 100 200 300 400 500km

Projection:
Conical with two standard parallels

COPYRIGHT. GEORGE PHILIP & SON LTD.

Projection: Bonne

1:15 000 000

100   0   100   200   300   400   500   600 km

Devon Island
Lancaster Sound
Brodeur
Peninsula
Arctic Bay
1890
Bylot I.
Pond Inlet
Milne
Inlet
Pond Inlet
Scott I.
C. Hewett
Clyde
2136
B a f f i n   B a y
Svartenhuk
Halvø
Disko
Christianshåb
Disko B.

G R E E N L A N D

Angmagssalik

60

2850
Kong Frederik VI's Kyst
Sandre Strømfjord
Sukkertoppen

Holsteinsborg
Godthåb
Frederikshåb
Ivigtut
Julianehåb
Nanortalik
Kap Farvel

A T L A N T I C

Broughton
Island
Padloping Island
C. Dyer
Cumberland
Peninsula
Hoare B.
C. Mercy
Cumberland Sd.

Melville
Prince
Charles
Foxe
I.
Hall
Lake
Igloolik
Island
Fury & Hecla Str.
Nettilling
L.

C. Dorchester
Foxe
Basin
Foxe
Penin.
Amadjuak
Amadjuak
L.
Lake
Harbour
Frobisher
Bay
Resolution I.

Pelly
Bay
Committee
B.
Rae Isthmus
Repulse
Bay
Wager
B.
Ross Welcome Sd.
Southampton
I.
Coral Harbour
Coats
I.
Belt
Pen.
Mansel
I.
Digges Is.
Invujivik
Sugluk (Saglouc)
Koartac
Notre Dame
de Koartac
Akpatok
I.
Maricourt
(Wakeham)
C. Chidley

H u d s o n   S t r a i t

Hudson

Bay

257

Ottawa
Is.
Portland
Promontory
Inoucdjouac
(Port Harrison)
Payne L.
P e n i n s u l a
Arnaud
(Bellin)
Payne (Bay)
Ungava
Bay
Port Nouveau Quebec
(George R.)
Hebron
Nain

Sleeper Is.
King
George Is.
King George Is.
Baker's
Dozen
Is.
Belcher
Is.
L'Eau Claire
L. Minto
Mélèzes
Kaniapiskau
Feuilles
Kooksoak
Ft. Chimo
George
Whale
Nutak
Hopedale

1676

N E W

Harrison
C. Harrison
Indian Harbour

C. Henrietta
Maria
Pte.
Louis-XIV
Grand Baleine
Poste-de-
la-Baleine
(Great Whale River)
Kanaaupscow
La Grande
L. Bienville
Lac Bienville
Petitsikapau
L.
Scheffervile
COAST OF LABRADOR
Smallwood
Reservoir
North West R.
Churchill
Falls
Churchill
Rigolet
Cartwright
Battle Harb.
Belle Isle
L. Melville

Winisk
Big
Trout
L.
James
Bay
Akimiski
I.
Nouveau Comptoir
(Paint Hills)
Eastmain
Eastmain
Ft. George
1128
Gagnon
Q U E B E C
Ashuanipi
L.
Romaine
St-Augustin
Natashquan
Moisie
Mingan
d'Anticosti

Ft. Severn
Severn
Attawapiskat
Ft. Albany
Albany
Charlton I.
Fort Rupert
(Rupert
House)
Rupert
L. Albanel
Mistassini
Chibougamau
Rés. de Gouin
Péribonca
Manicouagan
Baie-Comeau
Sept Iles
Port-Cartier
Gulf of
St. Lawrence
NEWFOUNDLAND
St. John's

TARIO
St. Joseph
Albany
St. Joseph
Moosonee
Harricana
Nottaway
Rés. de
Cabonga
L. Tuque
Matagami
Rouyn
Val d'Or
Kirkland Lake
3809

Nakina
Armstrong
L.
Nipigon
Longlac
Geraldton
Hearst
Kapuskasing
Cochrane
L. Abitibi
Taschereau
Senneterre
Dolbeau
St-Jean
Roberval
Chicoutimi
1190
Saguenay
Rivière-
du-Loup
Rimouski
Matane
Pén. de Gaspé
C. Gaspé
Campbellton
Îs. de la Madeleine
PR. EDWARD I.
Tignish
Summerside
Charlottetown
Cape Breton I.
ST-PIERRE
et MIQUELON
(Fr.)
Port aux Basques

Thunder Bay
Michipicoten
Heron Bay
Oba
Franz
Timmins
Iroquois
Falls
Haileybury
Cobalt
Témiscamingue
Shawinigan
Trois-Rivières
Québec
Lévis
Thetford Mines
Woodstock
Edmundston
St. Léonard
Newcastle
Bathurst
Chatham
Dalhousie
NEW
BRUNSWICK
Moncton
Amherst
Springhill
New Glasgow
Antigonish
Pictou
NOVA
SCOTIA
Truro
Sydney
Glace Bay
Port Hawkesbury
Mulgrave
Sable I.
(Nova Scotia)
6309

L. Superior
Sault Ste. Marie
Copper Cliff
Sudbury
North
Bay
Ottawa
Pembroke
Arnprior
Hull
Lachute
Joliette
MONTRÉAL
Lachine
Granby
St-Hyacinthe
Sherbrooke
MAINE
Fredericton
Saint
John
Kentville
Windsor
Dartmouth
Halifax
Bridgewater
Liverpool
Shelburne
B. of Fundy
Digby
Yarmouth
C. Sable

ES'
Georgian
Bay
Parry
Sound
Orillia
Peterboro
Belleville
Cornwall
Ottawa
Kingston
L. Champlain
VERMONT
Lewiston
Bangor
Augusta
Portland
NEW
HAMPSHIRE
Concord
Manchester
Lowell
C. Cod

Sault Ste. Marie
North Chan.
Cheboygan
Lake
Huron
Owen Sound
Oshawa
TORONTO
L. Ontario
Niagara
Falls
Buffalo
Rochester
Syracuse
Utica
Albany
Springfield
Worcester
Boston
Providence
R.I.
New Haven
CONN.

Manistique
Traverse
City
Cadillac
Saginaw
Kitchener
Stratford
Guelph
Hamilton
St. Catharines
Brantford
London
Sarnia
Woodstock
Chatham
Windsor
Erie
Jamestown
Elmira
Williamsport
PENNSYLVANIA
Scranton
Allentown
Reading
Trenton
NEW JERSEY
NEW YORK
Jersey City
Bridgeport
Newark
Stamford
Waterbury

Milwaukee
Racine
Kenosha
Madison
Rockford
Evanston
CHICAGO
South Bend
DETROIT
Toledo
Cleveland
Akron
Youngstown
OHIO
INDIANA
Gary
ILLINOIS
Grand
Rapids
Kalamazoo

West from Greenwich

COPYRIGHT. GEORGE PHILIP & SON. LTD.

80

70

60

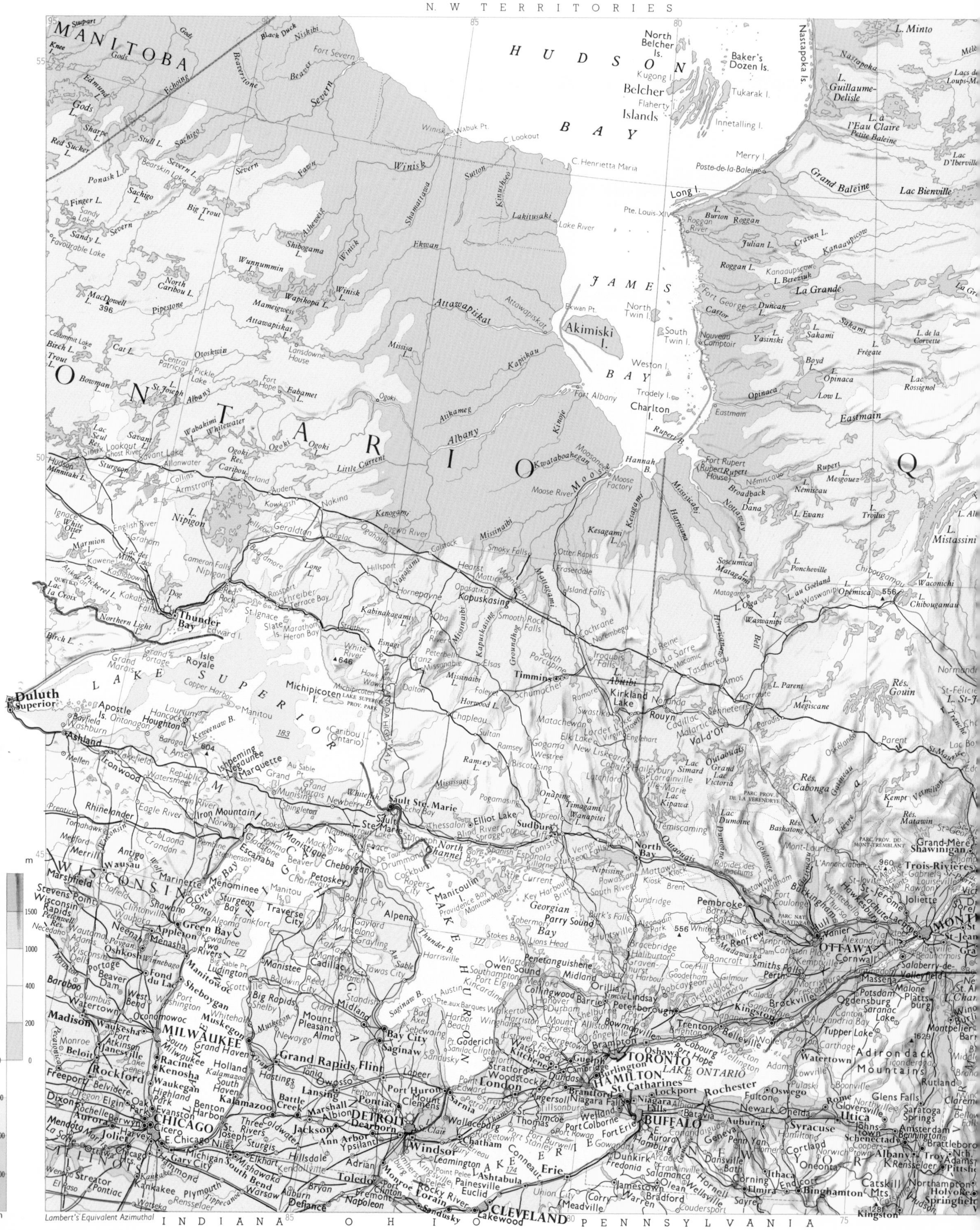

N.W. TERRITORIES

MANITOBA

ONTARIO

HUDSON BAY

JAMES BAY

QUÉBEC

North Belcher Is.
Baker's Dozen Is.
Belcher Islands
Kugong I.
Tukarak I.
Innetalling I.

L. Minto
L. Guillaume-Delisle
L. à l'Eau Claire
Petite Baleine
Lac D'Iberville
Lac Bienville

Grand Baleine

Merry I.
Poste-de-la-Baleine
Long I.
Pte. Louis-XIV

C. Henrietta Maria

Akimiski I.
Ekwan Pt.
North Twin I.
South Twin I.
Weston I.
Trodely I.
Charlton I.

Fort George
La Grande
Nouveau Comptoir
Eastmain
Opinaca

LAKE SUPERIOR

Isle Royale

Duluth
Superior
Apostle Is.
Ashland
Ironwood

Thunder Bay

WISCONSIN

MICHIGAN

LAKE MICHIGAN

LAKE HURON

Georgian Bay

Manitoulin I.

MILWAUKEE
Madison
Beloit
Rockford
CHICAGO

Green Bay
Oshkosh
Fond du Lac

Sault Ste. Marie
Sudbury
North Bay
Timmins
Kirkland Lake
Rouyn
Val-d'Or

Traverse City
Cadillac
Saginaw
Bay City
Flint
DETROIT
Grand Rapids
Kalamazoo
Lansing
Windsor

Parry Sound
Barrie
TORONTO
HAMILTON
London
Sarnia
St. Catharines
Niagara Falls
BUFFALO

OTTAWA
MONTRÉAL
Cornwall
Kingston
Belleville
Peterborough

LAKE ONTARIO
LAKE ERIE

Rochester
Syracuse
Utica
Binghamton

CLEVELAND
Toledo
Erie

INDIANA   OHIO   PENNSYLVANIA

Lambert's Equivalent Azimuthal

1:7 000 000

151

50 0 50 100 150 200 250 300 km

QUEBEC · LABRADOR · NEWFOUNDLAND

COAST OF LABRADOR

South Aulatsivik I. · High I. · Paul I. · Nain · Voisey B. · Davis Inlet · Nunaksaluk I. · Hopedale · Kaipokok B. · Aillik · Makkovik · C. Harrison · Holton · Indian Harbour · Groswater B.

Erlandson · Whale · Nachicapau L. · Kogaluk · Big Bay · Harp L. · Kanairiktok · Naskaupi · Seal L. · Nipishish · L. Melville · Mealy Mts. · 1128 · Separation Point · Cartwright · Sandwich B. · Island of Ponds · Square Islands

Fort McKenzie · Chakonipau L. · Otelnuk L. · Wheeler · L. Tudor · 610 · Whitegull L. · Wakuach · Attikamagen L. · Schefferville · Smallwood Reservoir · Churchill Falls · North-West River · Goose Bay · Happy Valley · Churchill · Eagle · Paradise · St. Lewis · Mary's H. · Battle Harbour

Lac Verneuil · Lac Petitsikapau · Lac Clairambault · Kaniapiskau · L. Néret · Lac Delorme · L. Bermen · Nitchequon · Opiscoteo · Menihek Lakes · Labrador City · Wabush · Lac Joseph · Atikonak L. · Ashuanipi · Burnt L. · Little Mecatina · Minipi L. · St-Augustin · Red Bay · Blanc-Sablon · Str. of Belle Isle · Belle I. · L'Anse-au-Loup · Forteau · Flower's Cove · L'Anse-au-Clair

Naococane · Shabogamo · Opiskotish · Labrador City · Gagnon · Rés. Manicouagan · 1048 · L. Manitou · Romaine · St-Jean · Magpie L. · Natashquan · Musquaro · Kegaska · Etamamu · St-Augustin-Saguenay · Outer I. · I. du Petit-Mécatina · Harrington Harbour · Daniel's Harbour · Port Saunders · White B. · Horse Is. · C. St John · Groais I. · Conche · Englee · Bell I. · Roddickton · St. Lunaire-Griquet · St. Anthony · Hare B.

QUEBEC · LABRADOR · NEWFOUNDLAND

Rés. Pipmuacan · Péribonca · Manouane · Bersimis · Betsiamites · Godbout · Rés. Forteau · Baie-Comeau · Hauterive · Franquelin · Pointe-des-Monts · Cap-Chat · Ste-Anne · Matane · Mont-Louis · Grande-Vallée · Sud Ouest · Pte-Cap · Rivière-au-Renard · Gaspé · Percé · Douglastown · Chandler · Grande-Rivière · Bonaventure

Sept-Îles · Clarke City · Moisie · Port-Cartier · Rivière-Pentecôte · Port-Menier · Î. d'Anticosti · Jupiter · Heath Pt. · Dét. de Jacques-Cartier

GULF OF ST. LAWRENCE · Î. Brion · Î. d'Anticosti · Îs. de la Madeleine (Quebec) · Cap-aux-Meules · Havre-Aubert · St. Paul · C. North

NEWFOUNDLAND · Long Range Mts. · Trout River · Bay of Islands · Corner Brook · Long Pt. · Port au Port B. · Stephenville · St. George's B. · St. George's · St. David's · South Branch · St. Andrew's · C. Ray · Channel-Port aux Basques · Burgeo · Ramea · Grey Res. · Red Indian L. · Buchans · Victoria · White Bear Res. · Bay d'Espoir · Hermitage B. · Fortune B. · Harbour Breton · Grand Falls · Windsor · Bishop's Falls · Botwood · Grand L. · Howley · Springdale · Baie Verte · Notre Dame B. · Twillingate · Fogo I. · Musgrave Harbour · Gander · Glenwood · Gambo · Glovertown · Dark Cove · Lewisporte · Wesleyville · Bonavista B. · Bonavista · Catalina · C. Bonavista · Trinity B. · Clarenville · Content · Carbonear · Harbour Grace · Conception B. · Bay Roberts · Torbay · St. John's · Mt. Pearl · Holyrood · Avalon Peninsula · Placentia B. · Placentia · St. Mary's B. · C. St Mary's · C. Race · Trepassey · Argentia · Long Harbour · Terrenceville · Marystown · Burin · Fortune · Grand Bank · Lamaline · St. Lawrence · St-Pierre · Miquelon · Langlade · SAINT-PIERRE ET MIQUELON (Fr.)

St. Lawrence · Rimouski · Trois-Pistoles · Rivière-du-Loup · Cabano · Kedgwick · Campbellton · Dalhousie · Chaleur B. · Belledune · Bathurst · Tracadie · Lamèque · Miscou I. · North Pt. · Tignish · Alberton · PRINCE EDWARD ISLAND · Summerside · Kensington · Charlottetown · Montague · Souris · East Pt. · Georgetown · Murray Hr. · Pictou · Antigonish · Cape George · Chéticamp · Inverness · Ingonish · Sydney Mines · North Sydney · New Waterford · Glace Bay · Sydney · Louisbourg · Cape Breton Island · Bras d'Or · St. Peters · Port Hawkesbury · Mulgrave · Canso · Chedabucto B.

QUEBEC · Lévis · Montmagny · Thetford Mines · Lac-Mégantic · Sherbrooke · St-Georges · Plessisville · Asbestos · St. Leonard · Grand Falls · NEW BRUNSWICK · Edmundston · Van Buren · Caribou · Presque Isle · Houlton · Hartland · Woodstock · Stanley · Fredericton · Chipman · Newcastle · Chatham · Miramichi B. · Bouctouche · Richibucto · Moncton · Sackville · Amherst · Springhill · New Glasgow · Stellarton · Truro · NOVA SCOTIA · Sherbrooke · Guysborough

MAINE · Moosehead L. · Millinocket · Mattawamkeag · Lincoln · Greenville · Old Town · Brewer · Bangor · Ellsworth · Machias · Eastport · Calais · St. Stephen · Saint John · Bay of Fundy · St. Martins · Sussex · Hampton · St. John · Digby · Annapolis Royal · Bridgetown · Middleton · Windsor · Kentville · Dartmouth · Halifax · Chester · Mahone Bay · Lunenburg · Bridgewater · Liverpool · Shelburne · Yarmouth · Wedgeport · Clark's Harbour · C. Sable · L. Rossignol · Port Mouton · Lockeport · Weymouth · Freeport · St. Mary's B.

Waterville · Augusta · Belfast · Camden · Rockland · Bar Harbor · Mt. Desert I. · Bath · Brunswick · Portland · Saco · Biddeford · Sanford · Rochester · Dover · Portsmouth · Berlin · Rumford · Lewiston · Auburn · Manchester · Nashua · Lawrence · Haverhill · Lynn · BOSTON · Brockton · Lowell · Waltham · Gloucester · C. Ann

ATLANTIC OCEAN · Sable I. (Nova Scotia)

West from Greenwich · COPYRIGHT. GEORGE PHILIP & SON. LTD

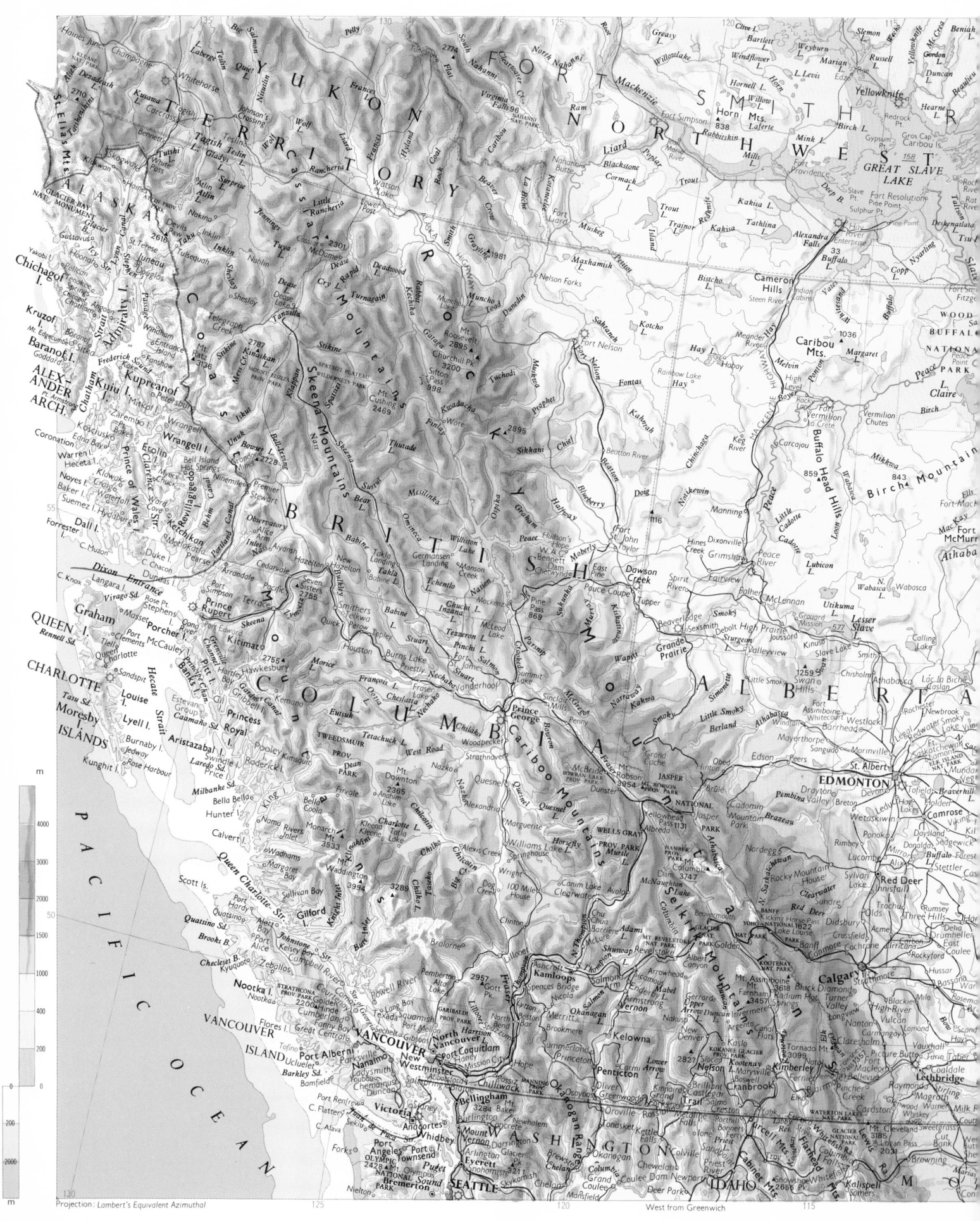

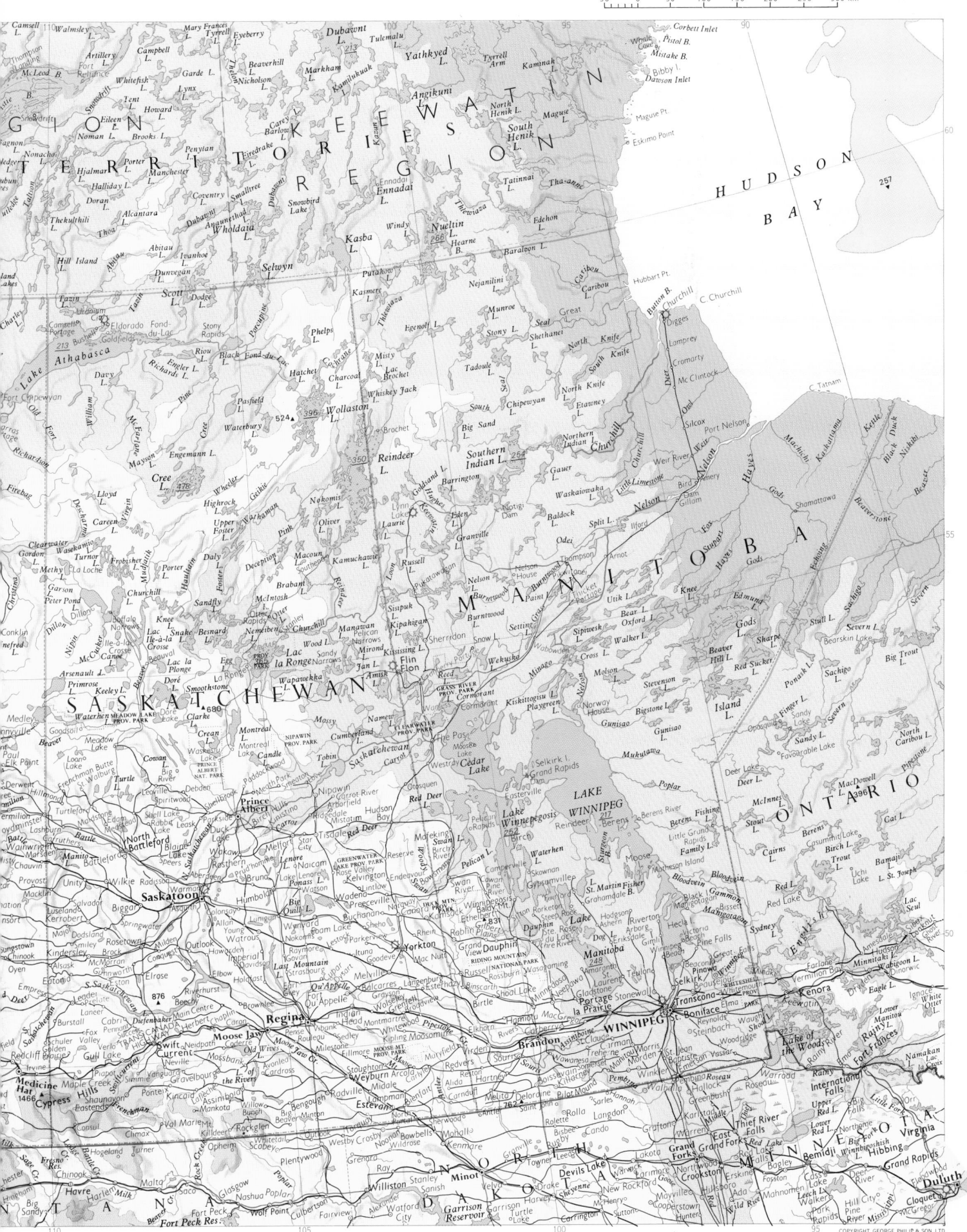

Projection: Albers' Equal Area with two standard parallels

West from Greenwich

CANADA

Lake Winnipeg Berens 95 Albany 90 85 Moosonee A D A

Trout Lake L. St. Joseph Nakina Kenogami Hearst L. Matagami St-Jean Chicoutimi NEW BRUNSWICK

Winnipeg Kenora Sioux Lookout Longlac Oba Cobalt Rés. de Gouin Roberval Edmundston 45

Lake of the Woods Rainy L. St. Ignace Michipicoten I. Timmins Témiscaming L. Abitibi Rouyn Grand-Mère Trois-Rivières Québec MAINE

Thunder Bay Wawa Sudbury North Bay Ottawa Buckingham Hull MONTRÉAL Sherbrooke Penobscot Bay

Thief River Falls Lake Superior 183 Whitefish Bay Sault Ste. Marie L. Nipissing Pembroke Smith's Falls Ottawa St-Hyacinthe Rockland Bar Harbor

MINNESOTA Duluth Marquette Manitoulin Parry Sound Gravenhurst Huntsville Kingston Adirondack Mts. Watertown Burlington VERMONT N. HAMPSHIRE Manchester

Moorhead Fargo Superior Ashland Escanaba Cheboygan Georgian Bay Orillia Peterborough Oswego Glens Falls Rutland Portland

Fergus Falls St. Cloud Rhinelander Iron Mt. Traverse City Owen Sound Barrie Lake Ontario Rochester Syracuse Schenectady Albany MASS. Boston

Minneapolis St. Paul WISCONSIN Green Bay Appleton Manistee TORONTO Hamilton Niagara Falls Buffalo Utica NEW YORK Worcester Providence

Willmar Eau Claire Wausau Stevens Point Cadillac Ludington Stratford London Brantford Jamestown Binghamton Scranton Hartford New Haven

Madison Milwaukee Grand Rapids Lansing DETROIT Lake Erie Erie Warren Wilkes Barre Allentown Reading NEW YORK

IOWA Waterloo Cedar Rapids Rockford CHICAGO Kalamazoo Ann Arbor Windsor Toledo Cleveland Akron Youngstown PENNSYLVANIA Newark NEW JERSEY Jersey City

Des Moines Davenport Moline Gary Ft. Wayne Findlay Lima Massillon Canton Pittsburgh Altoona Harrisburg York PHILADELPHIA Camden Atlantic City

Council Bluffs Oskaloosa Peoria Bloomington Lafayette Kokomo Marion Muncie OHIO Steubenville Wheeling Johnstown Wilmington DEL. Delaware Bay

Omaha Kansas City ILLINOIS Springfield Decatur INDIANA Indianapolis Terre Haute Dayton Kettering Columbus Lancaster Zanesville Clarksburg WEST VIRGINIA Washington Baltimore

Lincoln St. Joseph Hannibal Mexico Cincinnati Covington Portsmouth Charleston Richmond Newport News Norfolk

Topeka Kansas City MISSOURI St. Louis E. St. Louis Evansville Louisville Lexington Huntington Roanoke VIRGINIA Petersburg Albemarle Sd.

Emporia Sedalia Jefferson City Rolla Mt. Vernon KENTUCKY Frankfort Danville Bluefield Lynchburg Roanoke Raleigh 35

Wichita Springfield L. of the Ozarks Lebanon Bowling Green Somerset Middlesboro Winston Greensboro Durham Pamlico

Arkansas City Joplin Carthage Cairo Hopkinsville Cumberland Knoxville Asheville Salem NORTH CAROLINA Wilson C. Hatteras

Tulsa Bartlesville Boston Mts. Jonesboro Clarksville Oak Ridge Charlotte Greensboro Raleigh Pamlico Bay

OKLAHOMA CITY Fort Smith ARKANSAS Little Rock TENNESSEE Nashville Chattanooga Greenville SOUTH CAROLINA Columbia Florence Onslow Bay

McAlester Ouachita Mts. Hot Springs Pine Bluff Memphis Huntsville Rome Greenville Columbia Wilmington C. Fear

Durant Hope Camden El Dorado Greenwood Birmingham Gadsden Anniston Marietta Atlanta Augusta Charleston Long Bay Georgetown

Texarkana Shreveport MISSISSIPPI ALABAMA Bessemer Newnan La Grange GEORGIA Milledgeville Savannah 30

DALLAS Tyler Monroe Jackson Meridian Selma Montgomery Columbus Macon Dublin Altamaha Brunswick

Corsicana Longview Vicksburg Natchez Brookhaven Laurel Troy Dothan Valdosta Jacksonville

Houston Beaumont LOUISIANA Baton Rouge Lafayette Mobile Biloxi Gulfport Pensacola Tallahassee St. Augustine

Galveston Port Arthur New Orleans Delta of the Mississippi Panama City Apalachee B. Gainesville Daytona Beach FLORIDA

Freeport Marsh I. Chandeleur Is. Orlando C. Canaveral

Aransas Pass GULF OF MEXICO Tampa St. Petersburg Lakeland Ft. Pierce Grand Bahama I. Gt. Abaco BAHAMAS

Sarasota Arcadia L. Okeechobee West Palm Beach Freeport N.W. Providence Channel 25

Charlotte Harb. Ft. Myers Fort Lauderdale Miami Eleuthera I.

Florida Bay Key West Florida Keys Andros I. Exuma Sound

ATLANTIC OCEAN

COPYRIGHT GEORGE PHILIP & SON, LTD.

QUEBEC
CANADA
ONTARIO
MONTREAL
Ottawa
TORONTO
BUFFALO
LAKE ONTARIO
LAKE ERIE
LAKE HURON
LAKE SUPERIOR
Georgian Bay
MICHIGAN
DETROIT
CLEVELAND
PITTSBURGH
PHILADELPHIA
NEW YORK
BOSTON
BALTIMORE
WASHINGTON
CHICAGO
MILWAUKEE
CINCINNATI
INDIANAPOLIS
OHIO
INDIANA
ILLINOIS
WISCONSIN
KENTUCKY
WEST VIRGINIA
VIRGINIA
MARYLAND
DELAWARE
NEW JERSEY
PENNSYLVANIA
VERMONT
NEW HAMPSHIRE
Chesapeake Bay

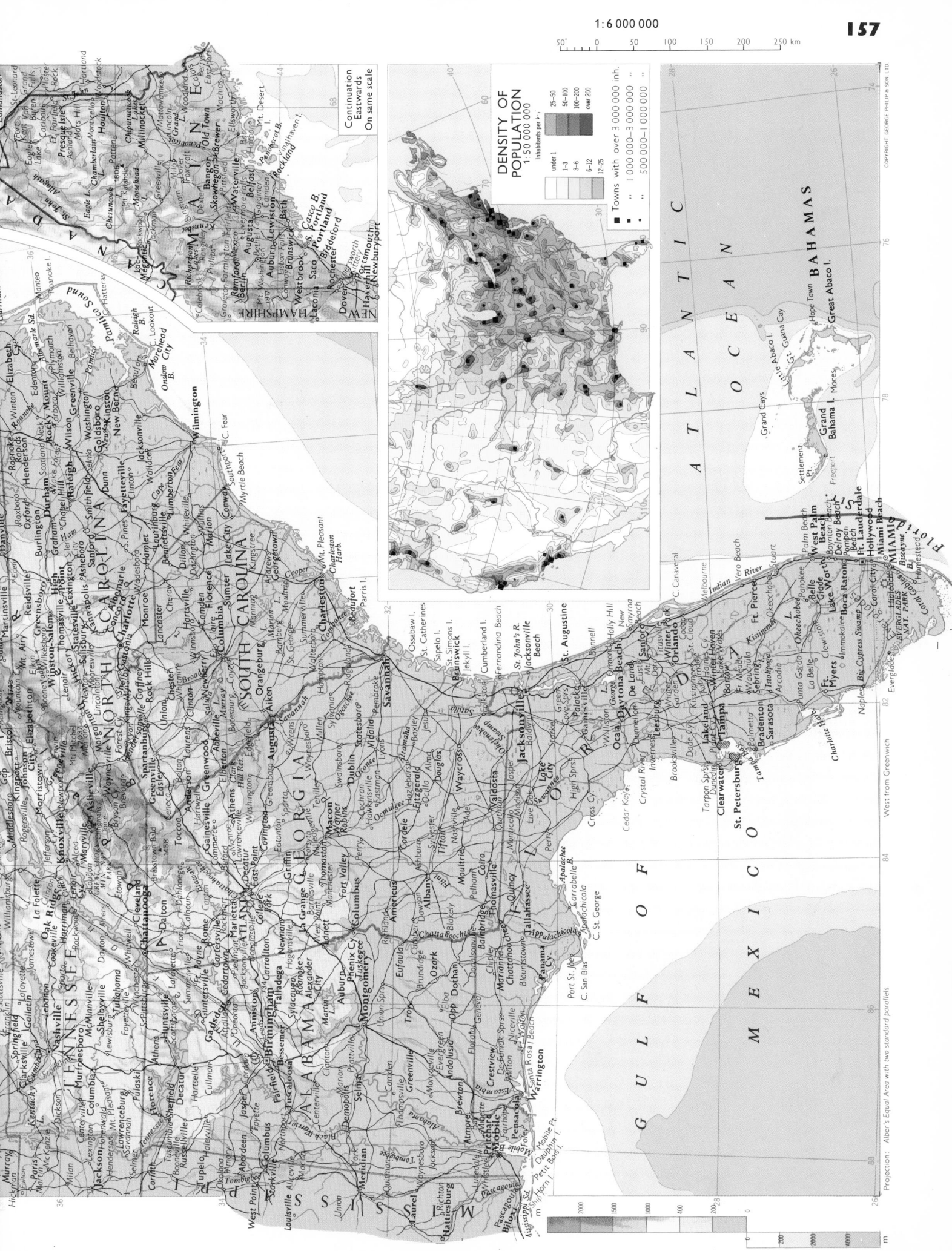

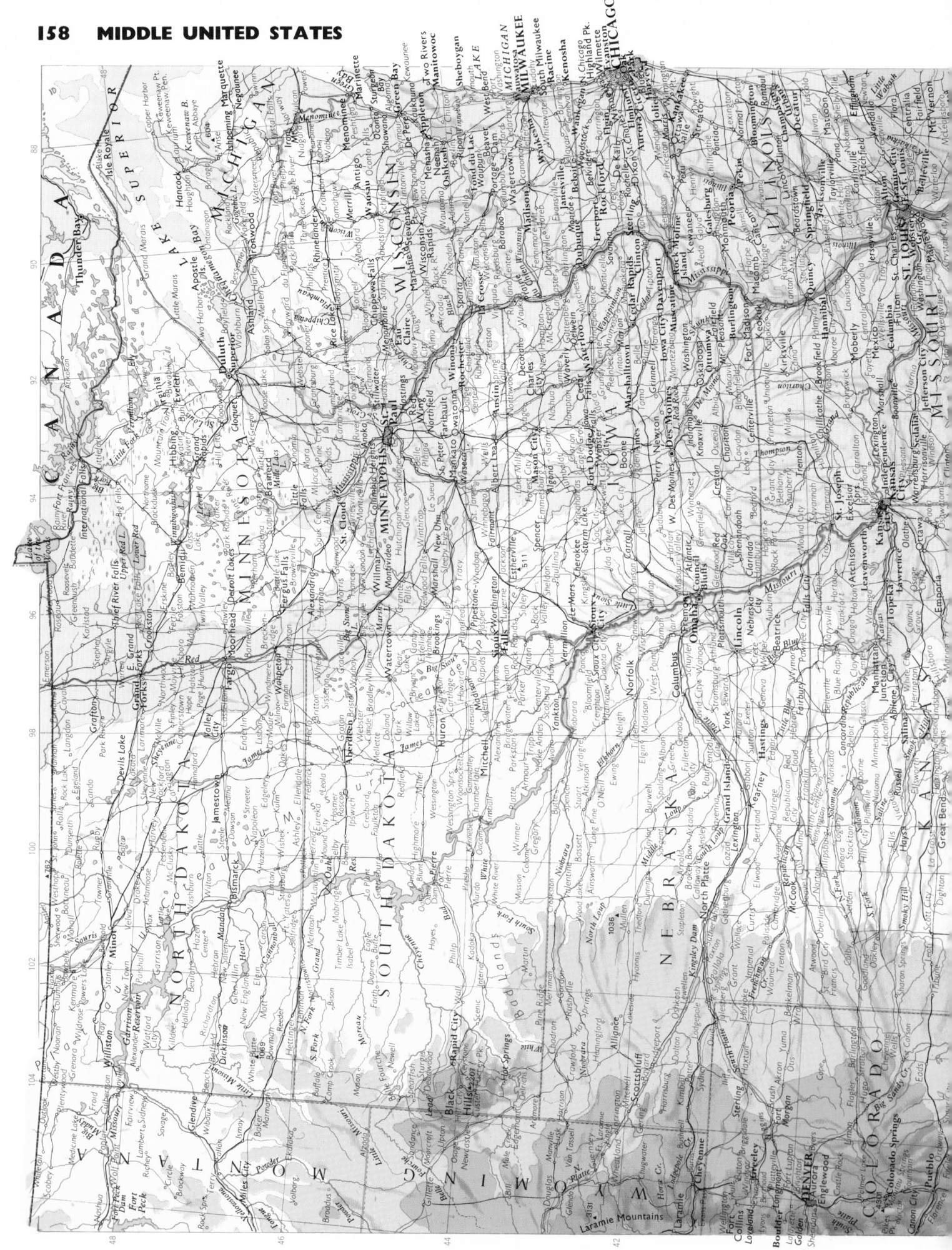

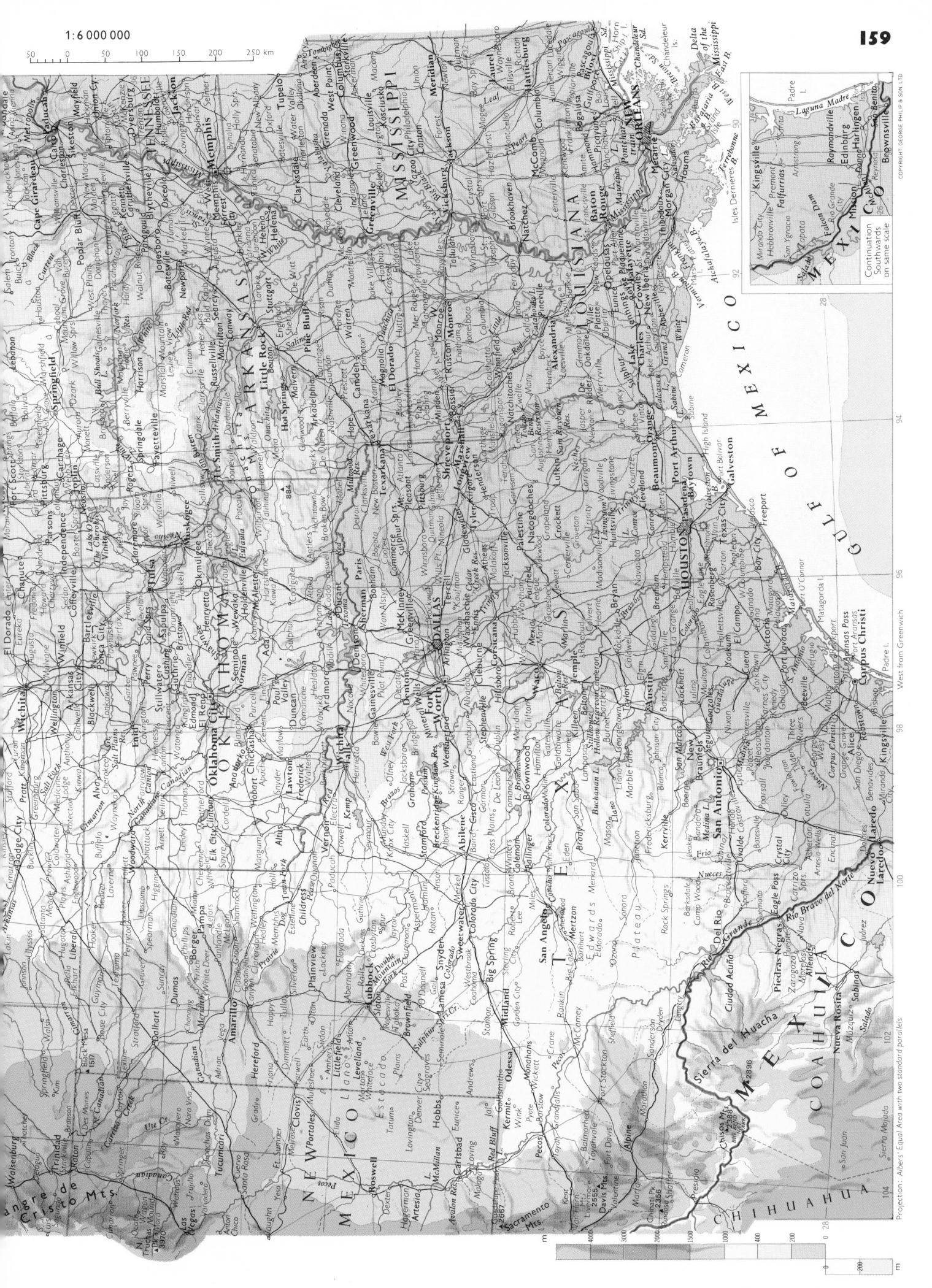

1:6 000 000

50 0 50 100 150 200 250 km

GULF OF MEXICO

TENNESSEE

MISSISSIPPI

ARKANSAS

LOUISIANA

OKLAHOMA

TEXAS

NEW MEXICO

COAHUILA

CHIHUAHUA

MEXICO

NEW ORLEANS

Baton Rouge

Houston

San Antonio

Corpus Christi

DALLAS

Fort Worth

Wichita

Oklahoma City

Tulsa

Memphis

Little Rock

Amarillo

Laguna Madre

Brownsville

West from Greenwich

Projection: Albers' Equal Area with two standard parallels

Continuation Southwards on same scale

COPYRIGHT GEORGE PHILIP & SON, LTD

1 : 6 000 000

1 : 3 000 000

20 0 20 40 60 80 100 120 km

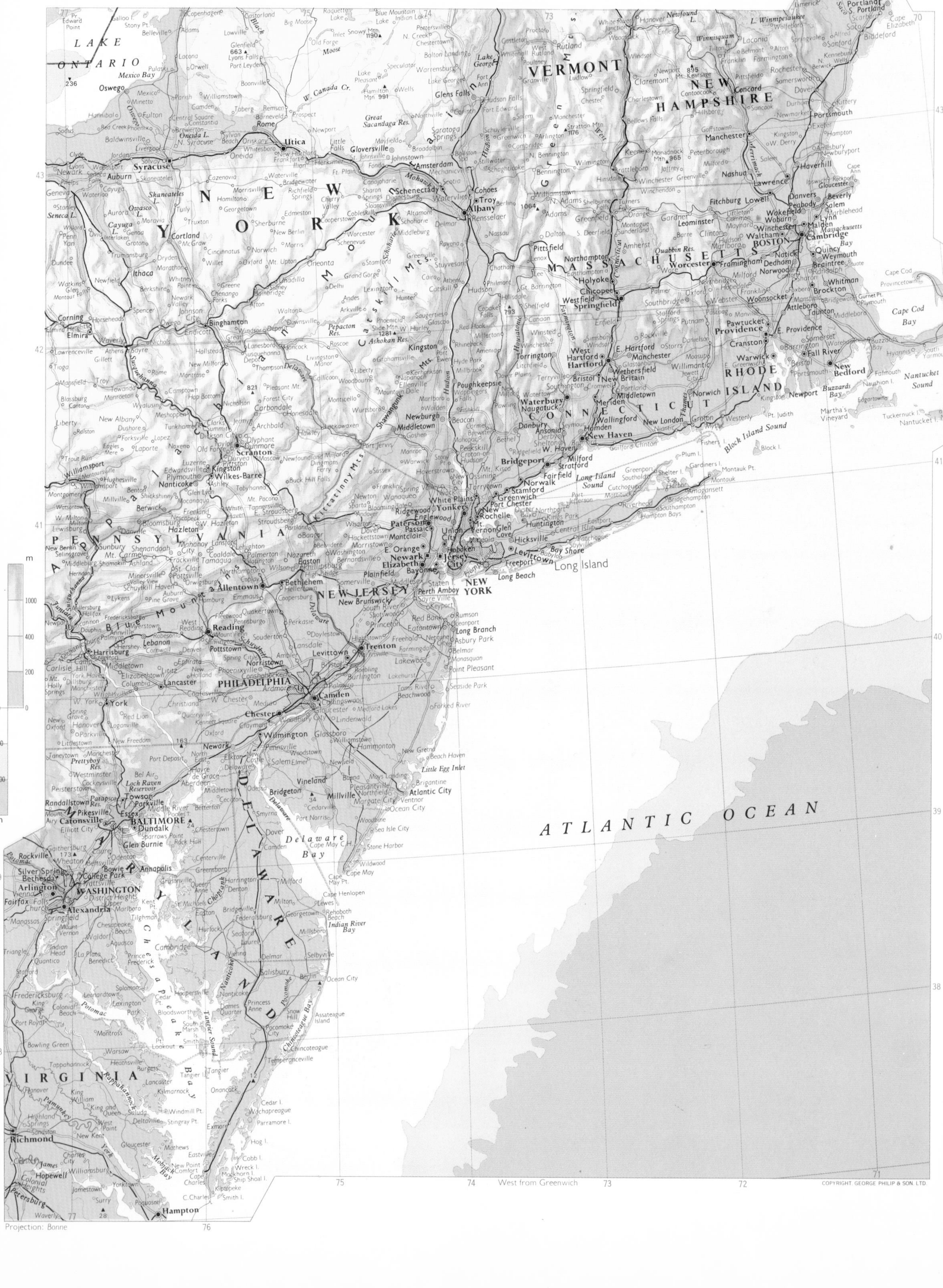

LAKE ONTARIO

VERMONT

NEW HAMPSHIRE

NEW YORK

MASSACHUSETTS

RHODE ISLAND

CONNECTICUT

PENNSYLVANIA

NEW JERSEY

NEW YORK

Long Island

ATLANTIC OCEAN

DELAWARE

MARYLAND

VIRGINIA

Chesapeake Bay

Delaware Bay

Cape Cod Bay

Long Island Sound

Block Island Sound

Nantucket Sound

Buzzards Bay

m
1000
400
200
0
−200
−2000
m

Projection: Bonne

West from Greenwich

COPYRIGHT GEORGE PHILIP & SON LTD.

1:3 000 000

20 0 20 40 60 80 100 120 140 km

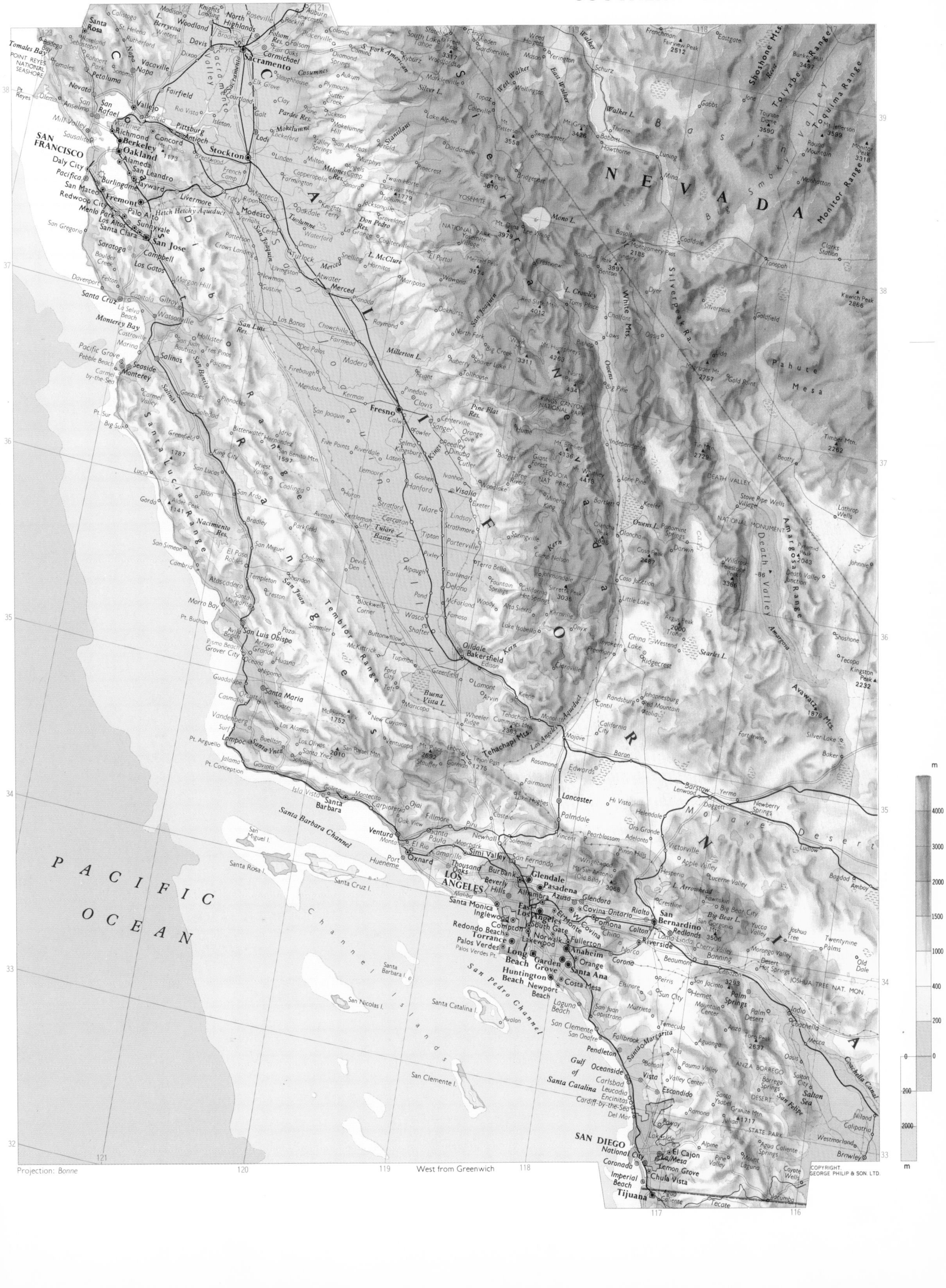

PACIFIC OCEAN

NEVADA

CALIFORNIA

SAN FRANCISCO
Santa Rosa
Point Reyes National Seashore
Novato
Petaluma
San Rafael
Vallejo
Napa
Vacaville
Fairfield
Berkeley
Oakland
Richmond
Concord
San Leandro
Hayward
Fremont
Palo Alto
San Mateo
Redwood City
Daly City
Pacifica
Sunnyvale
Santa Clara
San Jose
Los Gatos
Campbell
Saratoga
Santa Cruz
Watsonville
Monterey Bay
Monterey
Seaside
Salinas
Pacific Grove
Carmel-by-the-Sea
Gilroy
Hollister

Sacramento
Carmichael
Stockton
Modesto
Lodi
Galt
Elk Grove
Woodland
Davis
Dixon
Antioch
Pittsburg
Brentwood
Tracy
Livermore
Manteca
Turlock
Merced
Atwater
Los Banos
Chowchilla
Madera
Fresno
Clovis
Sanger
Reedley
Dinuba
Selma
Kingsburg
Hanford
Visalia
Tulare
Lindsay
Porterville
Delano
Wasco
Shafter
Oildale
Bakersfield
Edison
Arvin
Lamont

San Luis Obispo
Pismo Beach
Grover City
Arroyo Grande
Santa Maria
Guadalupe
Lompoc
Santa Ynez
Buellton
Solvang
Santa Barbara
Montecito
Carpinteria
Ventura
Oxnard
Port Hueneme
Thousand Oaks
Simi Valley
Fillmore
Santa Paula
Newhall
San Fernando
Burbank
Glendale
Pasadena
LOS ANGELES
Beverly Hills
Santa Monica
Inglewood
Compton
Torrance
Redondo Beach
Palos Verdes
Long Beach
Huntington Beach
Newport Beach
Anaheim
Santa Ana
Costa Mesa
Garden Grove
Fullerton
Orange
Norwalk
Whittier
El Monte
Alhambra
Azusa
Glendora
Covina
Pomona
Ontario
Chino
Corona
Riverside
San Bernardino
Colton
Redlands
Rialto
Fontana
Beaumont
Banning
Palm Springs
Indio
Coachella

Lancaster
Palmdale
Edwards
Mojave
Rosamond
Barstow
Victorville
Hesperia
Apple Valley
Lucerne Valley
Twentynine Palms
Yucca Valley

Mojave Desert

Salton Sea

San Diego
National City
Chula Vista
Coronado
Imperial Beach
La Mesa
El Cajon
Lemon Grove
Escondido
Oceanside
Carlsbad
Encinitas
Del Mar
Vista
San Marcos
Ramona
Poway
Tijuana

JOSHUA TREE NAT. MON.

ANZA BORREGO DESERT STATE PARK

SEQUOIA NAT. PARK
KINGS CANYON NATIONAL PARK
YOSEMITE NATIONAL PARK

DEATH VALLEY
DEATH VALLEY NATIONAL MONUMENT

Projection: Bonne

West from Greenwich

COPYRIGHT GEORGE PHILIP & SON LTD.

m
4000
3000
2000
1500
1000
400
200
0
0
200
2000
m

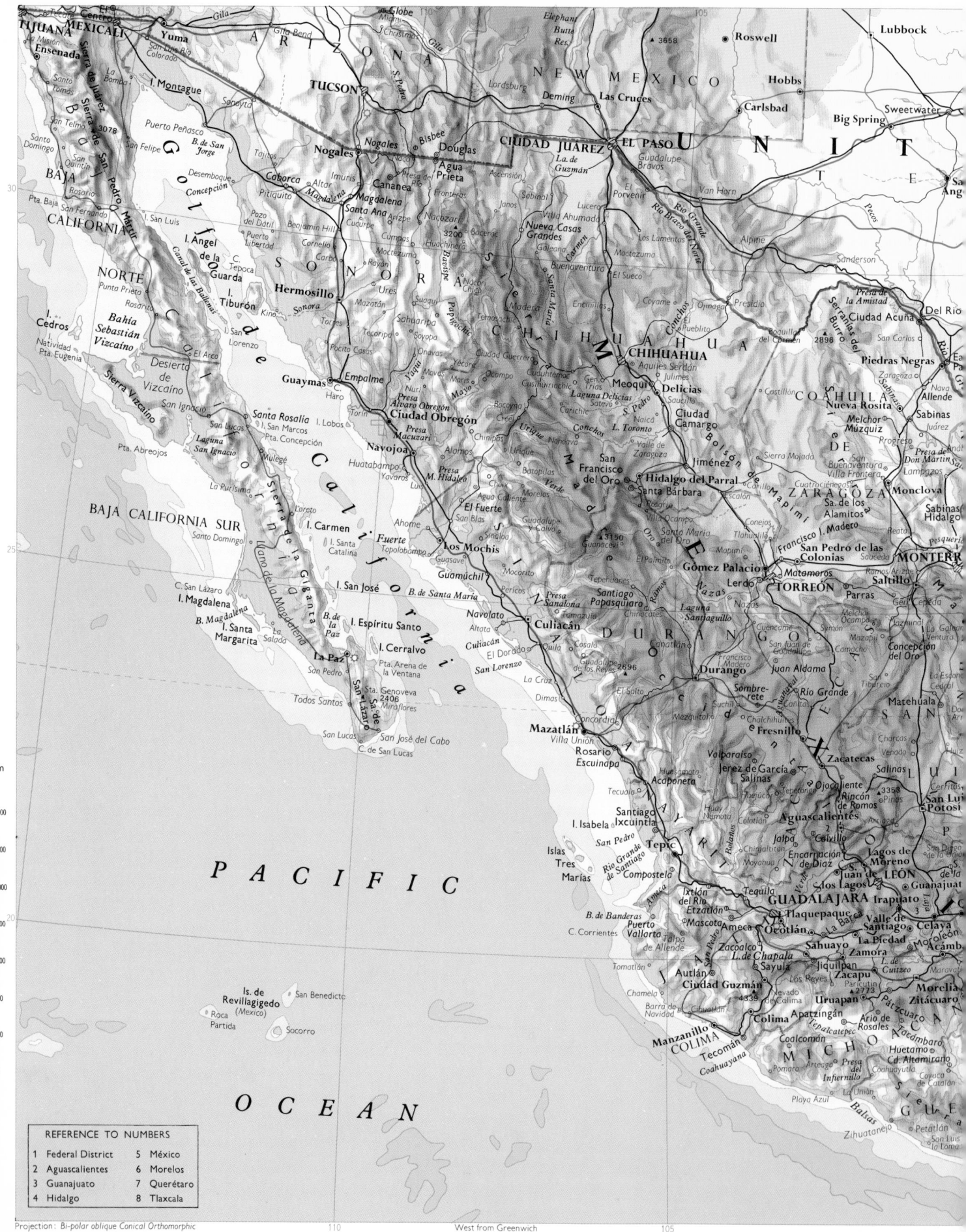

REFERENCE TO NUMBERS

1 Federal District   5 México
2 Aguascalientes   6 Morelos
3 Guanajuato   7 Querétaro
4 Hidalgo   8 Tlaxcala

Projection: Bi-polar oblique Conical Orthomorphic   West from Greenwich

1:8 000 000

50   0   50   100 150 200 250 300 km

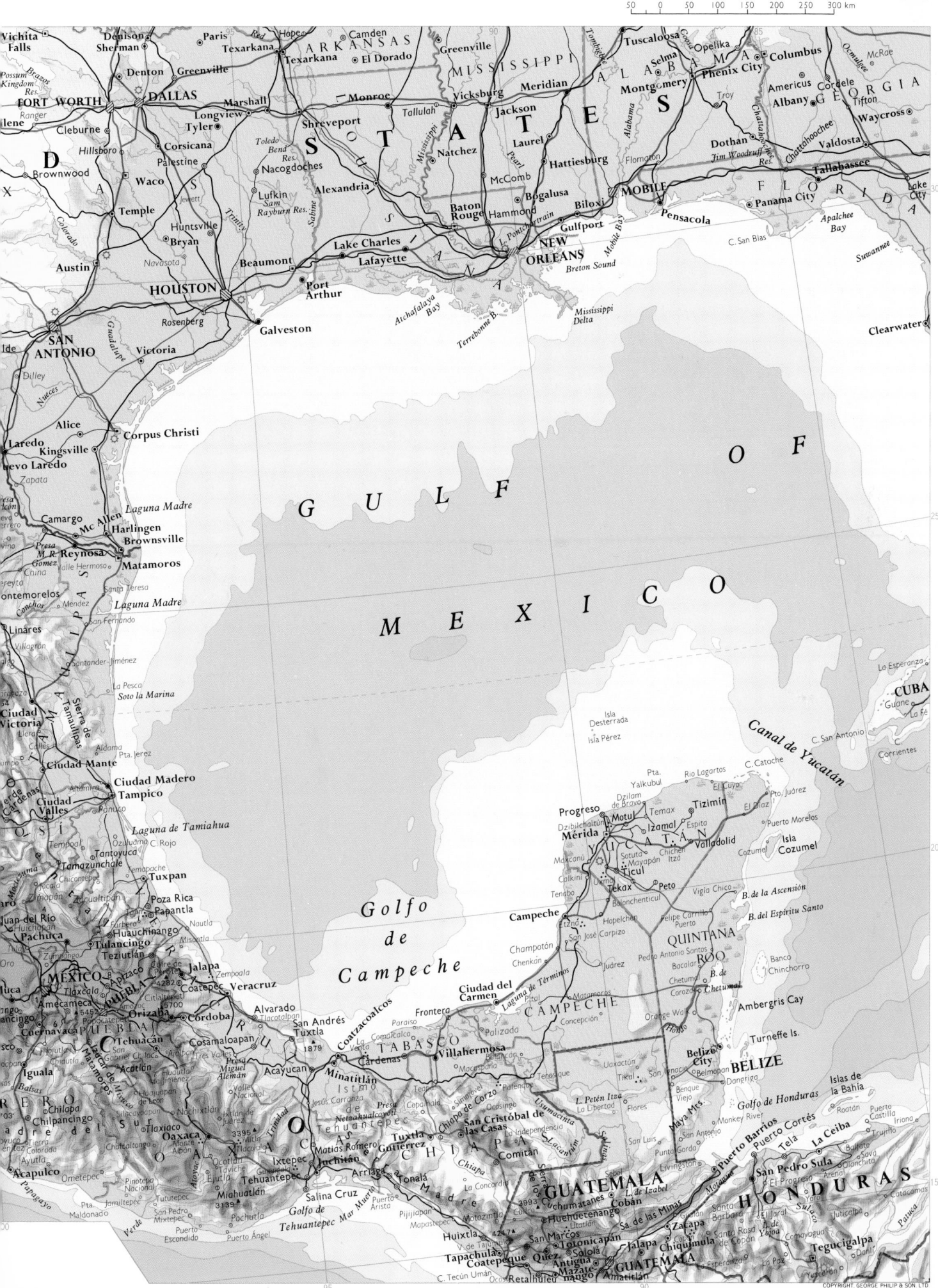

UNITED STATES

Vichita Falls · Denison · Sherman · Paris · Red · Hope · Camden · Greenville · Tuscaloosa · Opelika · Columbus · McRae
Brazos · Denton · Greenville · Texarkana · El Dorado · ARKANSAS · MISSISSIPPI · Selma · Phenix City · Americus · Cordele
Possum Kingdom Res. · Sherman
FORT WORTH · **DALLAS** · Marshall · Monroe · Vicksburg · Meridian · Montgomery · Troy · Albany · GEORGIA · Tifton
Ranger · Cleburne · Longview · Tallulah · ALABAMA · Chattahoochee · Waycross
lene · Tyler · Shreveport · Jackson · Dothan · Valdosta
Hillsboro · Corsicana · Toledo Bend Res. · Natchez · Laurel · Jim Woodruff Res. · Tallahassee · Lake City
Brownwood · Palestine · Nacogdoches · Alexandria · McComb · Hattiesburg · Flomaton · FLORIDA
Waco · Lufkin · Sam Rayburn Res. · Baton Rouge · Bogalusa · Biloxi · **MOBILE** · Panama City · Apalachee Bay
Temple · Huntsville · Baton Rouge · Hammond · Gulfport · Pensacola · C. San Blas · Suwannee
Austin · Bryan · LOUISIANA · Lake Charles · NEW ORLEANS · Mobile Bay · Breton Sound · Clearwater
Lafayette · L. Pontchartrain · Mississippi Delta
HOUSTON · Beaumont · Port Arthur · Atchafalaya Bay · Terrebonne B.
SAN ANTONIO · Rosenberg · Galveston
Victoria

GULF OF MEXICO

Laredo · Alice · Corpus Christi
Kingsville
nuevo Laredo · Zapata · Laguna Madre
Camargo · Mc Allen · Harlingen · Brownsville
M. R. Reynosa · Brownsville
China · Valle Hermoso · Matamoros
Laguna Madre
Linares · San Fernando

Golfo de Campeche

Ciudad Victoria · Isla Desterrada · **CUBA**
Isla Pérez · Guane · La Fé
Canal de Yucatán · C. San Antonio · Corrientes
Ciudad Mante · Pta. Jerez · Rio Lagartos · C. Catoche
Ciudad Madero · Pta. Yalkubul · El Cuyo · Pto. Juárez
Tampico · Progreso · Dzilam de Bravo · Temax · Tizimín · El Díaz · Puerto Morelos
Ciudad Valles · Dzibilchaltún · **Mérida** · Izamal · Espita · Valladolid · Isla Cozumel
Laguna de Tamiahua · Motul · YUCATÁN · Chichén Itzá · Cozumel
Maxcanú · Sotuta · Mayapán · Tekax · Peto · Vigía Chico · B. de la Ascensión
Tuxpan · Calkiní · Tenabo · Bolonchenticul · B. del Espíritu Santo
Poza Rica · Papantla · Nautla · Hecelchakán · Hopelchén · QUINTANA ROO · Banco Chinchorro
Huauchinango · Campeche · Etzná · Felipe Carrillo Puerto
Tulancingo · San José Carpizo · Bacalar · Chetumal
Pachuca · Teziutlán · Jalapa · Champotón · Juárez · Pedro Antonio Santos · B. de Corozal · Chetumal · Ambergris Cay
MÉXICO · Orizaba · Veracruz · Chenkán · Ciudad del Carmen · Frontera · CAMPECHE · Orange Walk · Turneffe Is.
Tlaxcala · **PUEBLA** · Coatepec · Alvarado · Laguna de Términos · Matamoros · Hondo
Córdoba · San Andrés Tuxtla · Paraíso · Palizada · Concepción · **Belize City** · **BELIZE**
Cuernavaca · Tehuacán · Cosamaloapan · Coatzacoalcos · Villahermosa · Uaxactún · Belmopán · Dangriga · Islas de la Bahía
Orizaba · TABASCO · Macuspana · Tikal · Benque Viejo · Roatán · Puerto Castilla
Iguala · Acatlán · Minatitlán · Cárdenas · Tenosique · Maya Mts. · Monkey River · Puerto Cortés · La Ceiba
Chilapa · Nochixtlán · Istmo · Usumacinta · Palenque · L. Petén Itzá · Puerto Barrios · Tela
Chilpancingo · Tlaxiaco · Tehuantepec · San Cristóbal de las Casas · Flores · San Pedro Sula
Oaxaca · CHIAPAS · Tuxtla Gutiérrez · Comitán · **GUATEMALA** · **HONDURAS**
Acapulco · Ixtepec · Juchitán · Arriaga · Tonalá · Chiapa · Sierra Madre · Cobán · Zacapa · Tegucigalpa
Salina Cruz · Golfo de Tehuantepec · Huixtla · Huehuetenango · Sa. de las Minas
Tapachula · Coatepeque · Quez. · Totonicapán · Jalapa · Chiquimula · El Progreso
GUATEMALA · Amatitlán · Retalhuleu

COPYRIGHT GEORGE PHILIP & SON, LTD

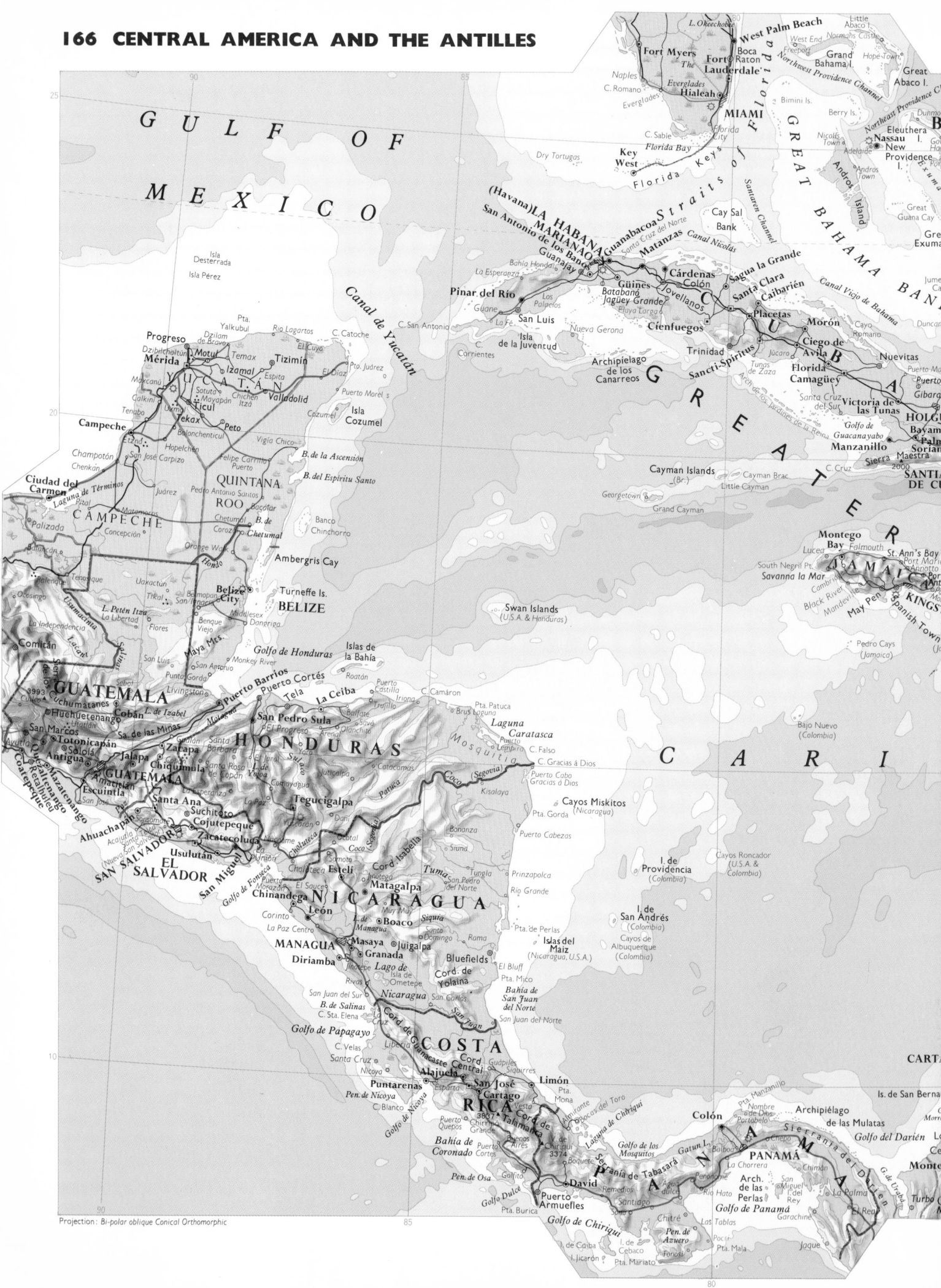

GULF OF MEXICO

Isla Desterrada

Isla Pérez

Pta. Yalkubul

Progreso
Dzilam de Bravo
Río Lagartos
Pta. Catoche

Motul
Temax
Tizimín

Dzibichaltún
Mérida
Izamal
Espita
El Cuyo
Pto. Juárez

Sotuta
Chichén Itzá
Valladolid
Isla
Cozumel

Maxcanú
Ticul

Calkiní
Tekax
Peto

Tenabo
Uxmal
Bolonchenticul

Campeche
Hopelchén
San José Carpizo
Felipe Carrillo
Puerto

Champotón
Chenkan
QUINTANA

Ciudad del
Carmen
CAMPECHE
Juárez
Pedro Antonio Santos
ROO
Bacalar

Laguna de Términos
Matamoros
Chetumal
B. de
Corozal
Chetumal

Palizada
Concepción
Orange Walk
B. de la Ascensión

B. del Espíritu Santo

Banco
Chinchorro

Balancán
Tenosique
Uaxactún
Tikal
Belmopan
San Ignacio
Ambergris Cay

Palenque
L. Petén Itzá
La Libertad
Belize
City
Turneffe Is.

Ocosingo
Flores
Benque
Viejo
Middlesex
BELIZE
Dangriga

Comitán
San Luis
Maya Mts.
Monkey River

La Independencia
San Antonio
Punta Gorda
Golfo de Honduras
Islas de
la Bahía

8993
Cuchumatanes
Cobán
L. de Izabal
Livingston
Puerto Barrios
Roatán
Puerto
Castilla
Trujillo
Irlona
C. Camarón

GUATEMALA
Huehuetenango
Sa. de las Minas
Motagua
Tela
La Ceiba
El Progreso
Balfate
Savá
Olanchito
Pta. Patuca
Brus Laguna

San Marcos
Totonicapán
Zacapa
Santa Bárbara
San Pedro Sula
Arenal
Laguna
Caratasca

Sololá
Jalapa
Chiquimula
Santa Rosa
de Copán
HONDURAS
Comayagua
Juticalpa
Catacamas
Lempira
C. Falso

Antigua
GUATEMALA
Esquipulas
La Esperanza
La Paz
Choluteca
Patuca
Mosquitia
C. Gracias á Dios

Mazatenango
Retalhuleu
Amatitlán
Yupiltepeque
Danlí
Coco
Gracias á Dios

Coatepeque
Escuintla
Santa Ana
Suchitoto
Cojutepeque
Yuscarán
Coco
Segovia
Kisalaya

Ahuachapán
Sonsonate
SAN SALVADOR
Zacatecoluca
La Unión
Cord. Isabelia
Bonanza
Puerto Cabezas

Acajutla
EL SALVADOR
San Miguel
Chinandega
Estelí
Jinotega
Tunla
Siuna
Prinzapolca

Usulután
Golfo de Fonseca
NICARAGUA
Matagalpa
Muy Muy
Río Grande

Corinto
León
Boaco
Santo
Domingo
Pta. de Perlas

La Paz Centro
L. de
Managua
Siquia
Rama

MANAGUA
Masaya
Juigalpa
Bluefields
El Bluff
Pta. Mico

Diriamba
Granada
Cord. de
Yolaina

Jinotepe
Lago de
Nicaragua
Isla de
Ometepe
San Carlos
Bahía de
San Juan
del Norte

Rivas
San Juan del Sur
B. de Salinas
C. STA. ELENA
San Juan
San Juan del Norte

Golfo de Papagayo
Liberia
Cord. de Guanacaste
COSTA
Guápiles
Siquirres
Limón

C. Velas
Santa Cruz
Cord. Central
Pta.
Mona

Puntarenas
Alajuela
San José
Cartago
Colón

Pen. de Nicoya
RICA
Cord. de Talamanca
3807

C. Blanco
Puerto
Quepos
Buenos
Aires
Boquete
PANAMÁ
La Chorrera

Bahía de
Coronado
Puerto
Cortés
3374
David
Santiago
Chitré

Golfo
Dulce
Puerto
Armuelles
Pta. Burica
Golfo de Chiriquí
Pen. de
Azuero
Pta. Mala

Projection: Bi-polar oblique Conical Orthomorphic

Fort Myers
West Palm Beach
Fort
Lauderdale

Naples
Boca
Raton

MIAMI
Bimini Is.

Key
West
Florida Bay
Florida City

Dry Tortugas

(Havana) **LA HABANA**
MARIANAO
San Antonio de los Baños
Matanzas
Cárdenas
Colón

Pinar del Río
Güines
Jovellanos
Santa Clara
Caibarién

San Luis
Batabanó
Jagüey Grande
Placetas
Morón

Cienfuegos
Trinidad
Sancti-Spíritus
Ciego de
Avila

Isla
de la Juventud
Archipiélago
de los
Canarreos
GREATER

Cayman Islands
(Br.)
Cayman Brac
Little Cayman

Georgetown
Grand Cayman

Montego
Bay
JAMAICA
KINGST

Swan Islands
(U.S.A. & Honduras)

Cayos Miskitos
(Nicaragua)

Bajo Nuevo
(Colombia)

CARI

I. de
Providencia
(Colombia)

Cayos Roncador
(U.S.A. &
Colombia)

San Andrés
(Colombia)

Cayos de
Albuquerque
(Colombia)

Islas del
Maíz
(Nicaragua, U.S.A.)

Colón
Archipiélago
de las Mulatas

Golfo de los
Mosquitos
PANAMÁ
Golfo del Darién

Serranía del Darién

1:8 000 000

50   0   50   100   150   200   250   300 km

m
4000
3000
2000
1500
1000
400
0
0
200
2000
4000
6000
8000
m

ATLANTIC

OCEAN

Tropic of Cancer

MAS

Cat I.
The Bight
San Salvador
(Watling I., Guanahani)
Conception I.
Rum Cay
Long I.
Clarence Town
Atwood or
Samana Cay
Crooked I. Passage
Richmond
Crooked I.
Plana Cays
Albert Town
Snug Corner
Acklins I.
Mayaguana I.
Cay Verde
Mira por vos Cay
Hogsty Reef
Little Inagua I.
Caicos Islands
(Br.)
Turks I. Passage
Turks Islands
(Br.)
Lake Rose
Great Inagua I.
Matthew Town
y Santa
mingo
ma
yari
Moa
Baracoa
Pta. de Maisí
I. de la Tortue
Monte Cristi
La Isabela
Puerto Plata
Paso de los Vientos
(Windward) Jean-Rabel
Cap-Haïtien
Fort-Liberté
La Vega
San Frances Viejo
Santo Domingo de Macoris
Cap-à-Foux
Port-de-Paix
Santiago de los Cabelleros
La Vega
Sánchez
Guantánamo
Golfe de la Gonâve
Gonaïves
Hinche
Cordillera Central
3175
Sabana de La Mar
Hato Mayor
Aguadilla
Arecibo
Bayamón
SAN JUAN
Virgin Gorda
Virgin Is. (Br.)
Anegada
Sombrero (Anguilla)
St.-March
St. Thomas
Anegada Passage
Jérémie
I. de la Gonâve
San Juan
Azua de Compostela
San Pedro de Macoris
C. Engano
Road Town
Anguilla (Br.)
Damea
HAITI
PORT-AU-PRINCE
2280
Enriquillo
B. de Yuma
Higüay
La Romana
Mayagüez
Isla Mona
Ponce
Caguas
Virgin Is. (U.S.A.)
St. Maarten (Neth.)
St.-Martin (Guad.)
St.-Barthélemy (Fr.)
Massif de la Hotte
Jacmel
Bani
San Cristóbal
DOMINICAN REP.
1338
Charlotte Amalie
St. Croix
St. Eustatius (Neth.)
Barbuda
Vassa I. (U.S.A.)
C. Carcasse
Les Cayes
Aquin
La Vache
Pedernales
Barahona
SANTO DOMINGO
PUERTO RICO
(U.S.A.)
Guayama
Frederiksted
Saba (Neth.)
Basseterre
ST. KITTS-NEVIS
ANTIGUA & BARBUDA
Pointe-à-Gravois
L. Beata
C. Beata
Christiansted
Nevis
Redonda (Br.)
St. Johns
Antigua
HISPANIOLA
Montserrat (Br.)
Guadeloupe Passage
ANTILLES
LEEWARD ISLANDS
Ste-Rose
Moule
Desirade
I. de Aves (Bird I.) (Venezuela)
GUADELOUPE (Fr.)
Pointe-à-Pitre
Marie-Galante (Fr.)
Basse-Terre
Grand-Bourg
I. des Saintes (Guad.)
Dominica Passage
Portsmouth
DOMINICA
Roseau
Martinique Passage
B   **E**   **A**   **N**   **S**   **E**   **A**
Ste Marie
Mt. Pelée
1397
François
Rivière-Pilot
Fort-de-France
MARTINIQUE
St. Lucia Channel (Fr.)
Castries
ST. LUCIA
Soufrière
St. Vincent Passage
Soufrière 1234
ST. VINCENT
Speightstown
Kingstown
Bridgetown
BARBADOS
Hillsborough
WINDWARD ISLANDS
LESSER ANTILLES
The Grenadines
St. George's
GRENADA
Neth. Antilles
Aruba (Neth.)
Curaçao (Neth.)
Bonaire (Neth.)
Pta. Gallinas
Pen. de Paraguaná
Willemstad
Is. de Aves (Ven.)
Is. Los Roques (Ven.)
I. Orchila (Ven.)
I. Blanquilla (Ven.)
I. Los Hermanos (Ven.)
Is. Los Testigos (Ven.)
Tobago
Scarborough
C. San Román
Punto Fijo
Puerto Cumarebo
Pen. de la Guajira
Pta. Espada
Punta Cardón
Coro
La Vela de Coro
I. Margarita
La Asunción
NUEVA ESPARTA
Porlamar
I. La Tortuga
Pen. de Paria
Galera
Dragon's Mouth
Port of Spain
Ríohacha
Uribia
San Juan de Guía
GUAJIRA
Golfo de Venezuela
Tucacas
Puerto Cabello
Maiquetía
La Guaira
CARACAS
Carúpano
Río Caribe
Güiria
Arima
Trinidad
BARRAN-QUILLA
Santa Marta
San Rafael
Altagracia
Mene de Mauroa
Maracay
DISTRITO FEDERAL
Guatire
Higuerote
Cumaná
SUCRE
Golfo de Paria
San Fernando
TRINIDAD & TOBAGO
Baranoa
Soledad
Ciénaga
Sierra Nevada de Santa Marta
La Concepción
FALCON
Tocuyo
Puerto La Cruz
Caripito
Serpent's Mouth
ATLANTICO
Sabanalarga
Fundación
5800
Cabimas
Santa Rita
Baragua
San Felipe
CARABOBO
Villa de Cura
Ocumare del Tuy
Río Chico
La Cruz
Barcelona
Caicara
Maturín
Calamar
Agustín Codazzi
Villa del Rosario
Ciudad Ojeda
Mene Grande
Carora
Valencia
LARA
BARQUISIMETO
Maritagua de los Morros
S. Juan de los Morros de Orituco
Aragua de Barcelona
Anaco
MONAGAS
MAGDALENA
Valledupar
Machiques
Lago de Maracaibo
Corora
YARACUY
San Carlos
COJEDES
El Sombrero
Cantaura
El Tigre
Tucupita
Carmen
Bolívar
Zambrano
CÉSAR
ZULIA
TRUJILLO
Acarigua
Valle de la Pascua
Pariaguán
Santa María de Ipire
DELTA-
Plato
Agustín Codazzi
Betijoque
Trujillo
PORTUGUESA
El Baúl
GUÁRICO
ANZOÁTEGUI
Ciudad Guayana
Corozal
Sincé
El Banco
El Difícil
Valera
Guanare
Portuguesa
Calabozo
Soledad
AMA-
Sahagún
Magangué
Mompós
NORTE DE SANTANDER
MÉRIDA
Barinas
Libertad
San Fernando de Apure
El Pao
Ciudad Guayana
Sierra Imataca
San Marcos
Planeta Rica
Ayapel
Ocaña
MÉRIDA
Mérida
Ciudad Bolivia
BARINAS
de Nutrias
San Fernando de Apure
Apure
Achaguas
Orinoco
Ciudad Bolívar
Upata
Guasipati
BOLÍVAR
Caucasia
Simití
TÁCHIRA
Barbacoa
Brusual
Caicara
Embalse de Guri
Caroní
El Callao
Tumeremo
San Marcos
VENEZUELA
Mapire
Maturín

1:30 000 000

200 0 200 400 600 800 1000 km

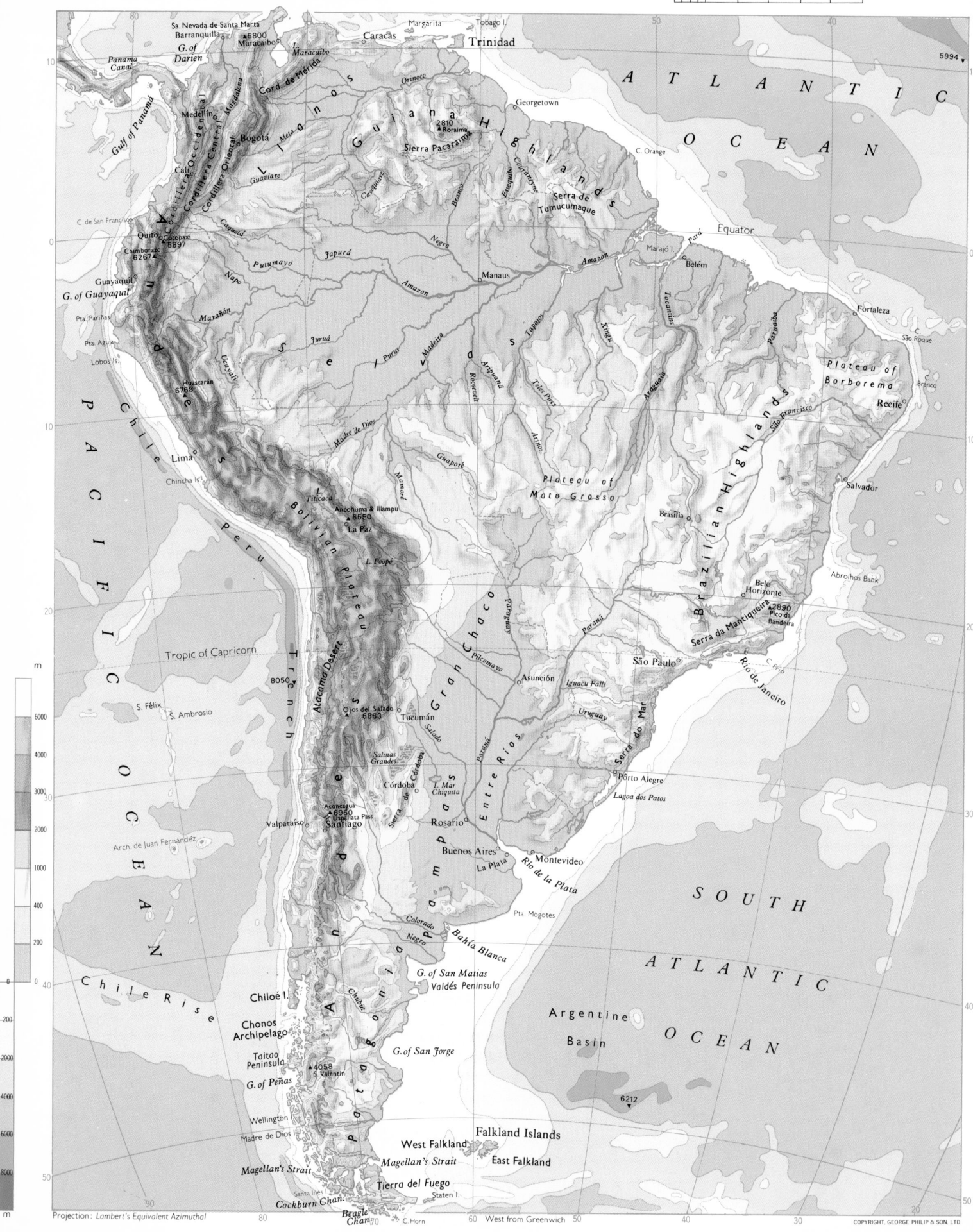

m
6000
4000
3000
2000
1000
400
200
0
200
2000
4000
6000
8000
m

Projection: Lambert's Equivalent Azimuthal

COPYRIGHT. GEORGE PHILIP & SON. LTD.

ATLANTIC OCEAN

Sa. Nevada de Santa Marta
Barranquilla
5800 Maracaibo
L. Maracaibo
Margarita
Tobago I.
Caracas
Trinidad
5994

Panama Canal
G. of Darien
Cord. de Mérida
Orinoco
Georgetown
C. Orange

Medellín
Bogotá
Guiana Highlands
2810 Roraima
Sierra Pacaraima
Serra de Tumucumaque

Cali
Cordillera Occidental
Cordillera Central
Cordillera Oriental
Llanos
Guaviare
Casiquiare
Branco
Essequibo
Corantyne

C. de San Francisco
Quito
Cotopaxi 5897
Putumayo
Japurá
Negro
Equator
Marajó I.
Pará
Belém

Chimborazo 6267
Napo
Amazon
Manaus
Tapajós
Tocantins

Guayaquil
G. of Guayaquil
Marañón
Amazon
Madeira
Xingu
Araguaia
Parnaíba
Fortaleza
São Roque

Pta. Pariñas
Pta. Aguja
Lobos Is.
Jurúa
Purus
Roosevelt
Aripuanã
Teles Pires
Arinos
São Francisco
Plateau of Borborema
Recife
Branco

Huascarán 6768
Ucayali
Madr de Dios
Guaporé
Plateau of Mato Grosso
Brazilian Highlands
Salvador

Chile
Peru
Lima
Chincha Is.
L. Titicaca
Bolivian Plateau
Mamoré
Brasília
Abrolhos Bank

Ancohuma & Illampu 6550
La Paz
L. Poopó
Belo Horizonte
2890 Pico da Bandeira
Serra da Mantiqueira

Tropic of Capricorn
8050
Atacama Desert
Gran Chaco
Pilcomayo
Paraná
São Paulo
C. Frio
Rio de Janeiro

S. Félix
S. Ambrosio
Ojos del Salado 6863
Tucumán
Salado
Asunción
Iguaçu Falls
Uruguay
Serra do Mar
Abrolhos Bank

Salinas Grandes
Córdoba
Sierra de Córdoba
L. Mar Chiquita
Paraná
Entre Rios
Porto Alegre
Lagoa dos Patos

Arch. de Juan Fernández
Aconcagua 6960
Uspallata Pass
Rosario
Buenos Aires
La Plata
Montevideo
Rio de la Plata
Pta. Mogotes

Valparaíso
Santiago
Pampas
Colorado
Bahía Blanca

Chile Rise
Chiloé I.
Negro
G. of San Matias
Valdés Peninsula

Chonos Archipelago
Patagonia
Chubut
G. of San Jorge
Argentine Basin

Taitao Peninsula
G. of Peñas
4058 S. Valentín
6212

Wellington
Madre de Dios I.
Falkland Islands
West Falkland
East Falkland

Magellan's Strait
Magellan's Strait
Santa Inés I.
Cockburn Chan.
Beagle Chan.
C. Horn
Tierra del Fuego
Staten I.

PACIFIC OCEAN
Chile Peru Trench

SOUTH ATLANTIC OCEAN

West from Greenwich

1:80 000 000

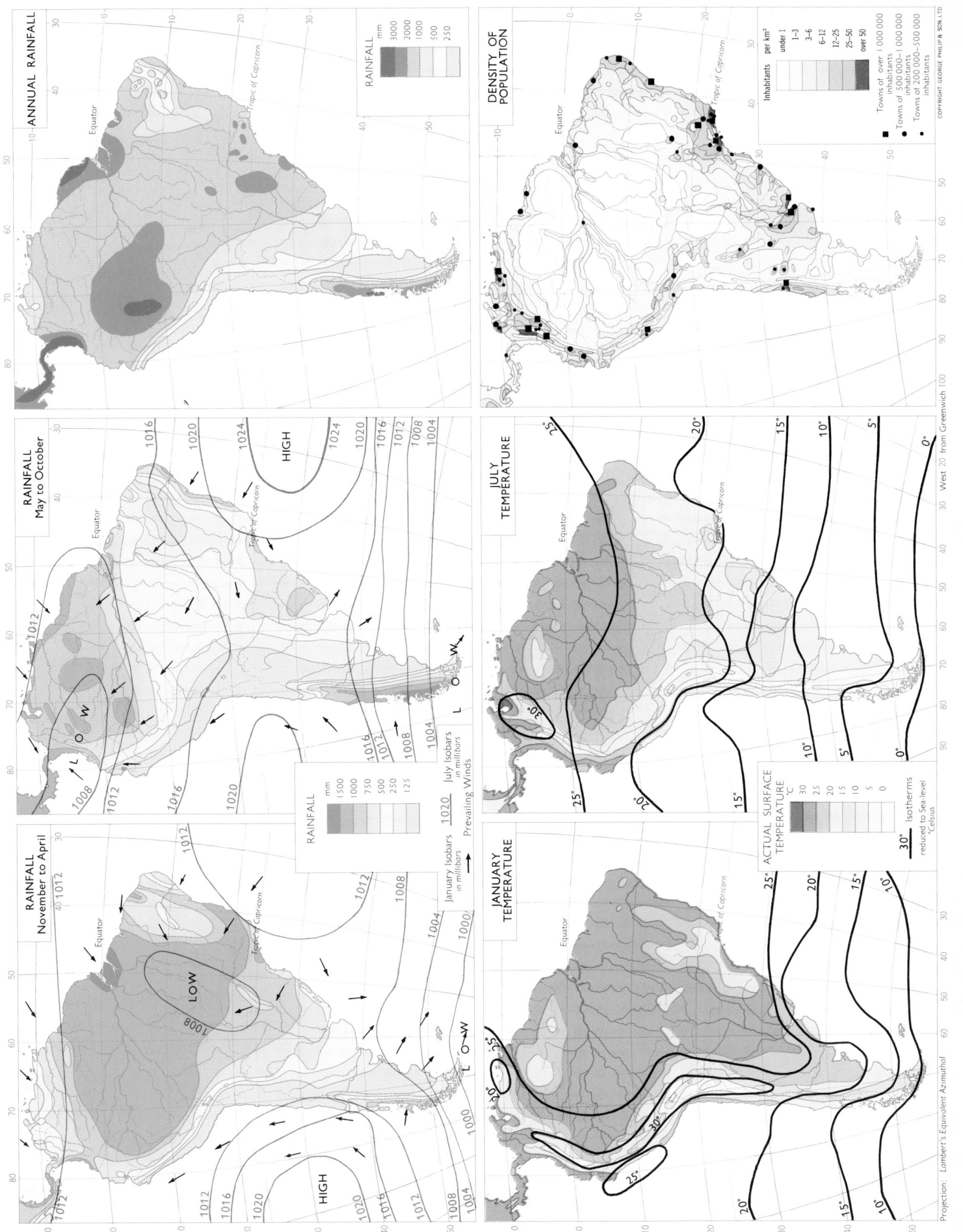

ANNUAL RAINFALL

RAINFALL
3000
2000
1000
500
250
mm

DENSITY OF POPULATION

Inhabitants per km²
under 1
1–3
3–6
6–12
12–25
25–50
over 50

Towns of over 1 000 000 inhabitants
Towns of 500 000–1 000 000 inhabitants
Towns of 200 000–500 000 inhabitants

COPYRIGHT GEORGE PHILIP & SON, LTD.

RAINFALL
May to October

HIGH
1016
1020
1024
1024
1020
1016
1012
1008
1004

1012
LOW
1008
1012
1016
1020

JULY TEMPERATURE

25°
20°
15°
10°
5°
0°

West 20 from Greenwich 100

RAINFALL
1500
1000
750
500
250
125
mm

1020 January Isobars in millibars
July Isobars in millibars
Prevailing Winds

ACTUAL SURFACE TEMPERATURE
°C
30
25
20
15
10
5
0

30° Isotherms reduced to Sea-level Celsius

RAINFALL
November to April

LOW
1008

1012
HIGH
1012
1016
1020
1016
1012
1008
1004
1000
1004
1008

JANUARY TEMPERATURE

25°
20°
15°
10°

Projection: Lambert's Equivalent Azimuthal

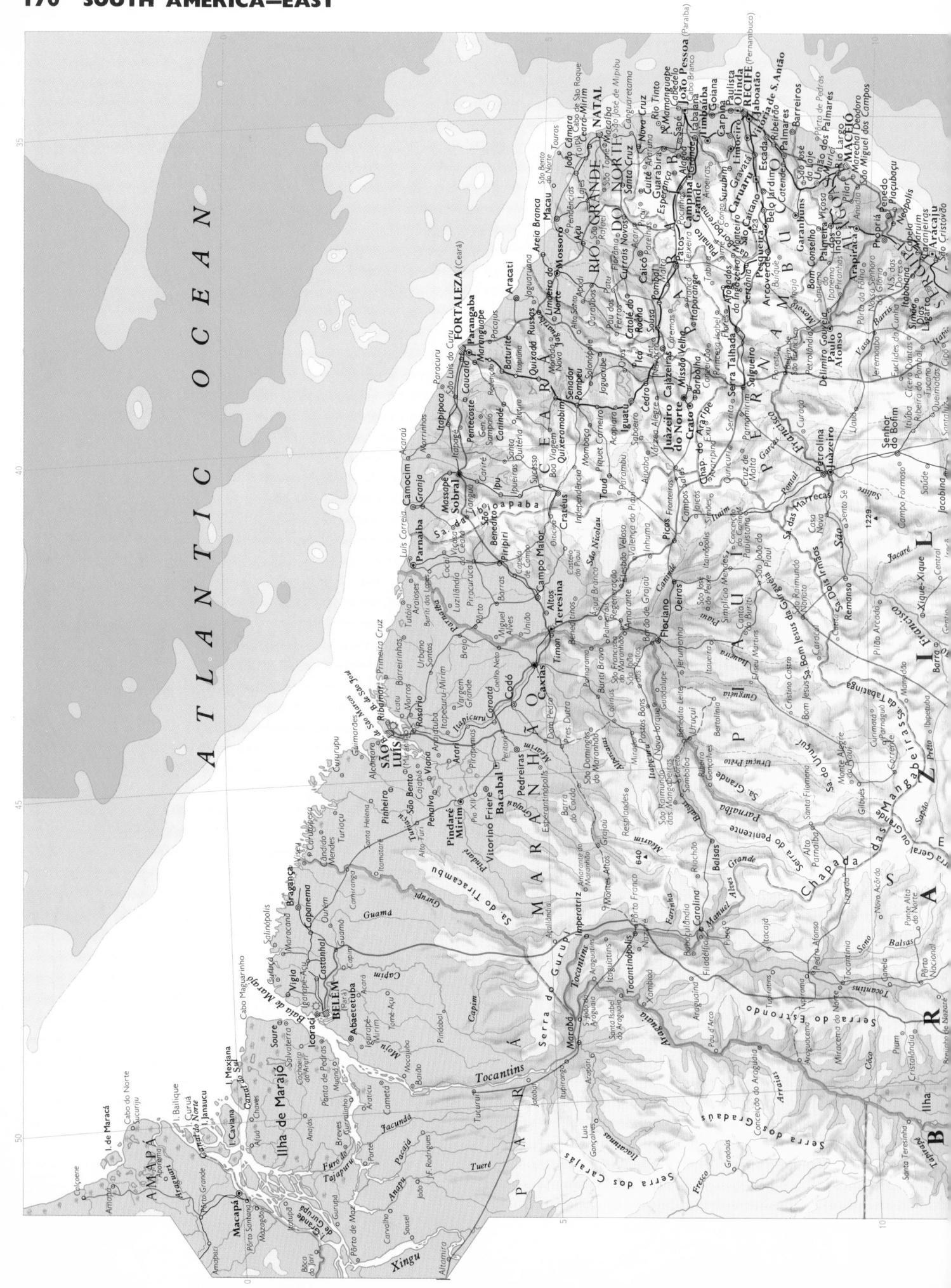

ATLANTIC OCEAN

Tropic of Capricorn

1:8 000 000

50 0 50 100 150 200 250 300 km

COPYRIGHT GEORGE PHILIP & SON LTD

West from Greenwich

Projection: Lambert's Equivalent Azimuthal 50

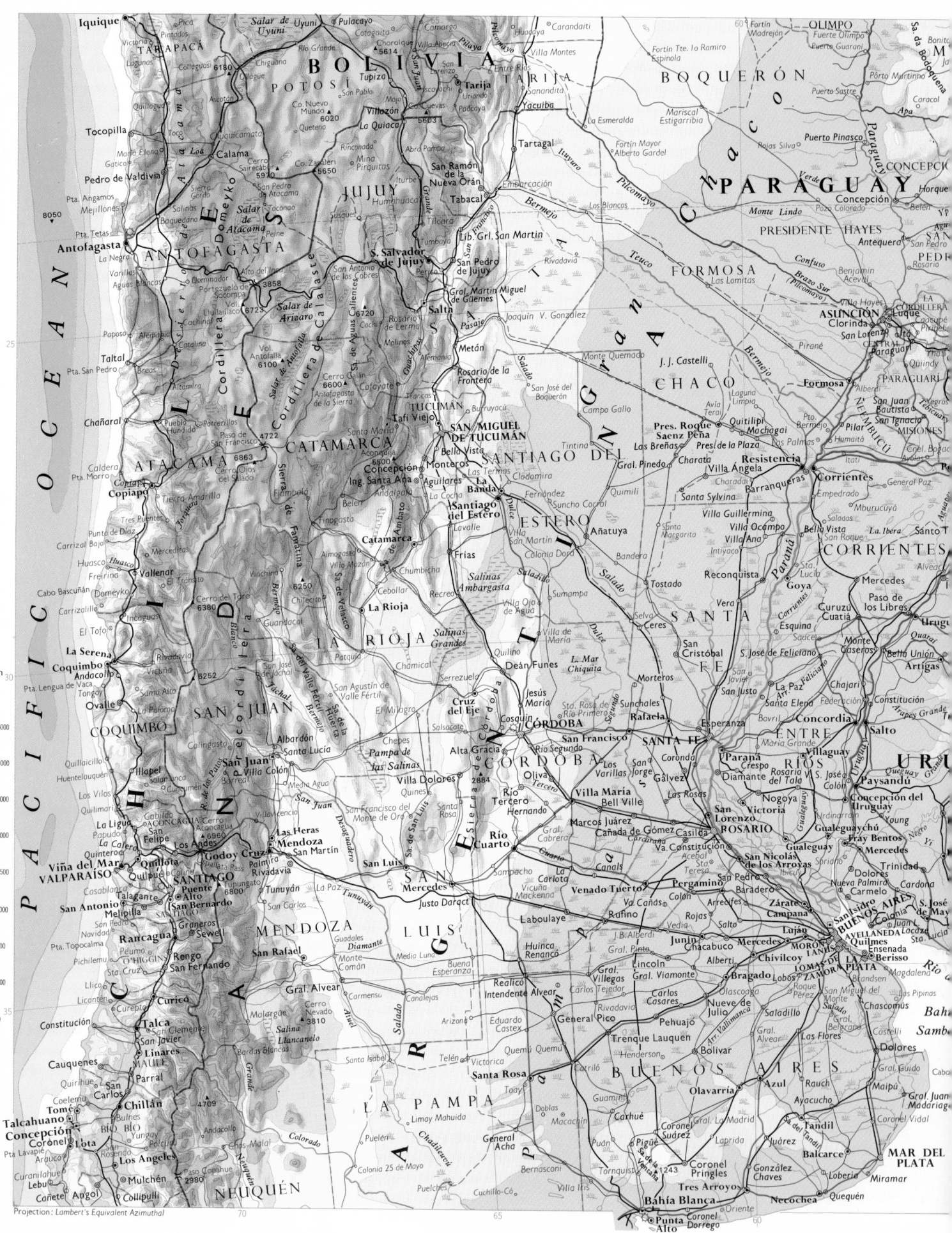

1:8 000 000

50 0 50 100 150 200 250 300 km

BELO
HORIZONTE

N. Lima
Itabirito

Oliveira

Cons.
Lafaiete
Ouro
Prêto

Ponte Nova

Vitória
Itaquari
Vila
Velha
Guaraparí

Campo Belo

São João
del Rei

Carangola
Alegre

Castelo
Cachoeiro
de Itapemirim

Três Lagoas
Andradina
Mirassol
S. José
do Rio Prêto
Olímpia
Batatais

Passos

São Seb.
do Paraíso

São João
del Rei
Ubá
Muriaé
Itaperuna

Xavantina
Mirandópolis
Araçatuba
Catanduva
Bebedouro
Ribeirão
Prêto

Represa de
Furnas

Barbacena
Cataguases

Leopoldina
Cambuci

Guarus
CAMPOS
Cabo de
São Tomé

Panorama
Birigui
Tietê
Penápolis
Jaboticabal
Mococa

Guaxupé

Três
Pontas
Lavras
Além Paraíba
Paraíba

SÃO
PAULO
Adamantina
Lins
Novo
Horizonte
Araraquara
São
Carlos
São João
da Boa Vista
Poços de
Caldas
Pouso
Alegre
Três
Corações
Juiz de Fora

Varginha

RIO DE JANEIRO

Presidente
Prudente
Martinópolis
Tupã
Garça
Bariri
Jaú
Rio Claro
Limeira

Alfenas

Itajubá
2787
Volta
Barra do Pirai
Nova Friburgo
Macaé

Rancharia
Marília
Paraguaçu
Paulista
Bauru
Ouro Fino
Americana
Mogi-Mirim
Redonda
Barra
Mansa
Petrópolis
DUQUE DE CAXIAS

Assis
Santa Cruz
do Rio Pardo
Piracicaba
CAMPINAS
Bragança
Paulista
Guaratinguetá
Cruzeiro
Nova Iguaçu
SÃO GONÇALO

Londrina
Ourinhos
Avaré
Botucatu
Itu
Jundiai
Taubaté
Angra dos Reis
NITERÓI
Cabo Frio

Maringá
Arapongas
Cornélio
Procópio
Jacarèzinho
Itapetininga
Sorocaba
S. J. dos Campos
Jacareí
Ilha Grande
Baía da Ilha Grande
RIO DE JANEIRO
La de Araruama

Apucarana
Tatuí
SÃO PAULO
SANTO ANDRÉ
Ilha de São Sebastião
Tropic of Capricorn

PARANÁ
Itararé
Itapeva
Paranapiacaba
São Vicente
SANTOS
Guarujá
Ilha de São Sebastião
Pta. do Boi

BRAZIL
Castro
Apiaí
Itanhaém

Ponta Grossa
Iguape
Ilha Comprida

Guarapuava
Palmeira
1889
Ilha do Cardoso

CURITIBA
Antonina
Paranaguá
25

União da
Vitória
Irati
Lapa
Guaratuba

Rio Negro
Mafra
São Francisco do Sul

Caçador
São
Paulo
Joinvile

1340
SANTA CATARINA
Blumenau
Itajaí

Chapecó
Joaçaba
Campos Novos
Brusque

Erechim
Rio do Sul
Ilha de Santa Catarina
Florianópolis

Lajes
1808

Caràzinho
Passo Fundo
Vacaria
Tubarão
Laguna
Cabo Santa Marta Grande

Cruz Alta
Criciúma
Araranguá

RIO GRANDE
Bento Gonçalves
Caxias do Sul

Santa Maria
Santa Cruz
do Sul
Nôvo Hamburgo
Taquara

Montenegro
São
Leopoldo
Osorio

Cachoeira do Sul
Rio Pardo
PÔRTO ALEGRE

DO SUL

Santana do
Livramento
São
Gabriel
Dom Pedrito
Camaquã

Rivera
Bagé
Lagoa dos Patos
Mostardas

Pelotas

UGUAY
Melo
Jaguarão
Rio Grande

Santa Vitória do Palmar

ATLANTIC

Treinta y Tres

OCEAN

Minas
Rocha

San Carlos
Maldonado
MONTEVIDEO
Plata

5304

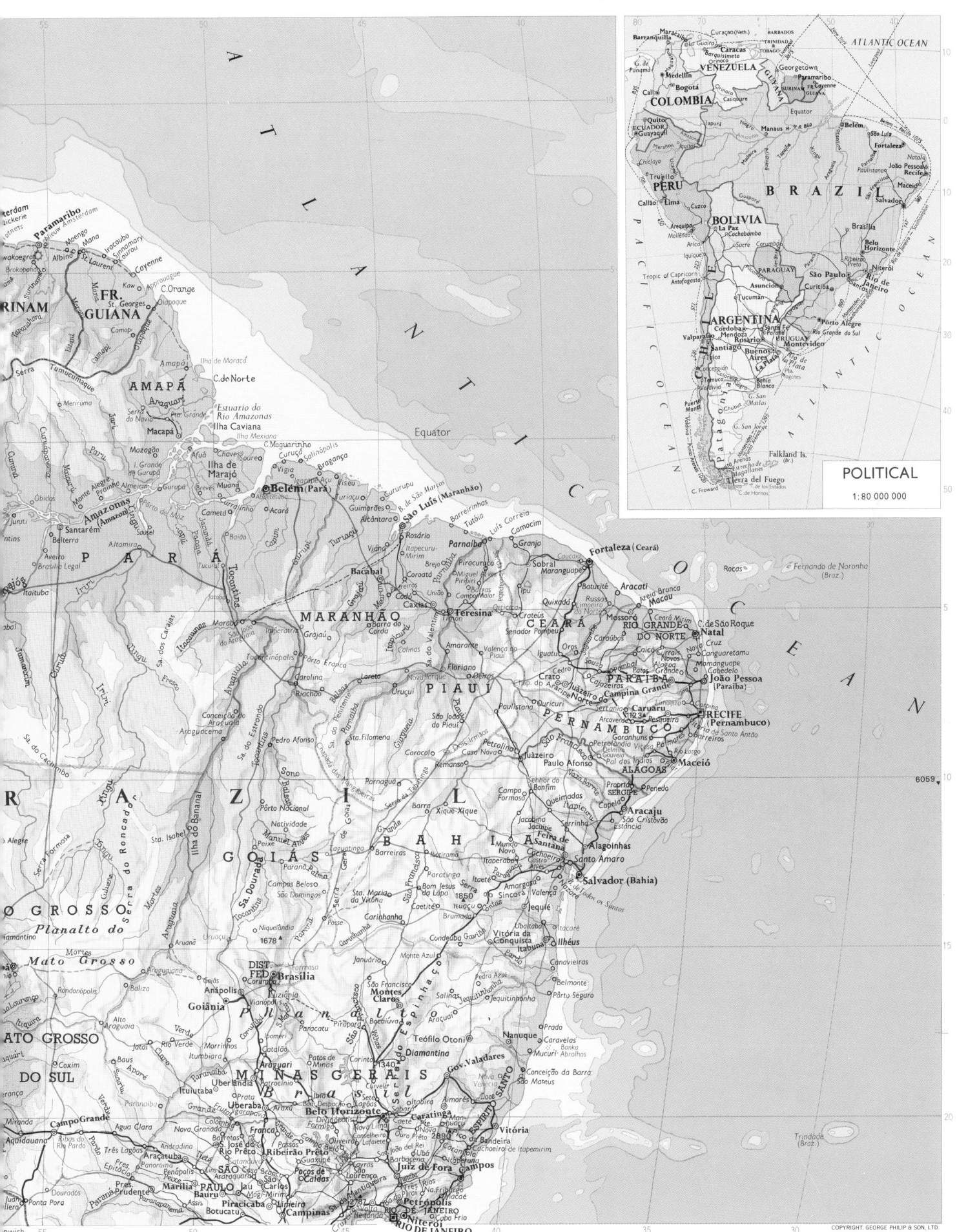

1:16 000 000

200 100 0 200 400 600 km

POLITICAL
1:80 000 000

ATLANTIC OCEAN

Barranquilla
Maracaibo Curaçao (Neth.) BARBADOS
TRINIDAD
Caracas TOBAGO
VENEZUELA GUYANA Georgetown Paramaribo
Medellín Orinoco SURINAM FR.
Bogotá GUIANA Cayenne
COLOMBIA
Quito Equator
ECUADOR Manaus Belém São Luís
Guayaquil Fortaleza
PERU B R A Z I L João Pessoa
Recife
Lima Maceió
Cuzco Salvador
La Paz Brasília
BOLIVIA Belo
Sucre Horizonte
São Paulo Niterói
PARAGUAY Rio de
Tropic of Capricorn Asunción Curitiba Janeiro
A R G E N T I N A Pôrto Alegre
Córdoba Rio Grande do Sul
Valparaíso Santa Fe
Rosario URUGUAY
Santiago Buenos Montevideo
Aires
Bahía Blanca

Falkland Is.
(Br.)
Terra del Fuego
C. de Hornos

ATLANTIC
O C E A N

PARAMARIBO
SURINAM
FR. GUIANA
Cayenne
AMAPÁ
Macapá
Estuario do Rio Amazonas
Ilha de Marajó
Belém (Pará)
Amazonas (Amazon)
Santarém
P A R Á
São Luís (Maranhão)
Parnaíba
Fortaleza (Ceará)
Sobral
MARANHÃO
Teresina
CEARÁ
RIO GRANDE Natal
DO NORTE
PIAUÍ
PARAÍBA João Pessoa (Paraíba)
Campina Grande
PERNAMBUCO Caruaru
RECIFE (Pernambuco)
ALAGOAS Maceió
SERGIPE
Aracaju
B R A Z I L
Feira de Santana
BAHIA
Salvador (Bahia)
MATO GROSSO
Planalto do Mato Grosso
GOIÁS
Vitória da Conquista Ilhéus
DIST. FED. Brasília
Goiânia Planalto Brasil
Montes Claros
MATO GROSSO DO SUL
Campo Grande
Teófilo Otoni Nanuque
Diamantina
Araguari Gov. Valadares
Uberlândia MINAS GERAIS ESPÍRITO SANTO
Uberaba Belo Horizonte Vitória
Ribeirão Preto Juiz de Fora Campos
SÃO PAULO Petrópolis
Marília Campinas Niterói
Piracicaba RIO DE JANEIRO

Fernando de Noronha (Braz.)

O C E A N

Trindade (Braz.)

COPYRIGHT, GEORGE PHILIP & SON, LTD.

1:16 000 000

200 100 0   200   400   600 km

Projection: Sanson-Flamsteed's Sinusoidal

60 West from Greenwich 55

COPYRIGHT GEORGE PHILIP & SON. LTD

INDEX

The number printed in bold type against each index entry indicates the map page where the feature will be found. The geographical coordinates which follow the name are sometimes only approximate but are close enough for the place name to be located.

An open square □ signifies that the name refers to an administrative subdivision of a country while a solid square ■ follows the name of a country. (□) follows the old county names of the U.K.

The alphabetical order of names composed of two or more words is governed primarily by the first word and then by the second. This rule applies even if the second word is a description or its abbreviation, R.,L.,I. for example. Names composed of a proper name (Gibraltar) and a description (Strait of) are positioned alphabetically by the proper name. If the same place name occurs twice or more times in the index and all are in the same country, each is followed by the name of the administrative subdivision in which it is located. The names are placed in the alphabetical order of the subdivisions. If the same place name occurs twice or more in the index and the places are in different countries they will be followed by their country names, the latter governing the alphabetical order. In a mixture of these situations the primary order is fixed by the alphabetical sequence of the countries and the secondary order by that of the country subdivisions.

A. C. T. – Australian Capital Territory
A. R. – Autonomous Region
A. S. S. R. – Autonomous Soviet Socialist Republic
Afghan. – Afghanistan
Afr. – Africa
Ala. – Alabama
Alas. – Alaska
Alg. – Algeria
Alta. – Alberta
Amer. – America
And. P. – Andhra Pradesh
Ang. – Angola
Arch. – Archipelago
Arg. – Argentina
Ariz. – Arizona
Ark. – Arkansas
Atl. Oc. – Atlantic Ocean
Austral. – Australia
B. – Baie, Bahía, Bay, Bucht, Bugt
B.A. – Buenos Aires
B.C. – British Columbia
Bangla. – Bangladesh
Barr. – Barrage
Bay. – Bayern
Belg. – Belgium
Berks. – Berkshire
Bol. – Bolshoi
Bots. – Botswana
Br. – British
Bri. – Bridge
Bt. – Bight
Bucks. – Buckinghamshire
Bulg. – Bulgaria
C. – Cabo, Cap, Cape
C. Prov. – Cape Province
Calif. – California
Camb. – Cambodia
Cambs. – Cambridgeshire
Can. – Canada
Cat. – Cataract, Cataracta
Cent. – Central
Chan. – Channel
Co. – Country
Colomb. – Colombia
Colo. – Colorado
Conn. – Connecticut
Cord. – Cordillera
Cr.. – Creek
Cumb. – Cumbria
Czech. – Czechoslovakia
D.C. – District of Columbia
Del. – Delaware
Dep. – Dependency
Derby. – Derbyshire
Des. – Desert
Dist. – District
Dj. – Djebel
Dumf. & Gall. – Dumfries and Galloway
E. – East
Eng. – England
Fed. – Federal, Federation
Fla. – Florida

For. – Forest
Fr. – France, French
Fs. – Falls
Ft. – Fort
G. – Golf, Golfo, Gulf, Guba
Ga. – Georgia
Germ. – Germany
Glam. – Glamorgan
Glos. – Gloucestershire
Gr. – Grande, Great, Greater, Group
H.K. – Hong Kong
H.P. – Himachal Pradesh
Hants. – Hampshire
Harb. – Harbor, Harbour
Hd. – Head
Here. & Worcs. – Hereford and Worcester
Herts. – Hertfordshire
Holl. – Holland
Hung. – Hungary
I.o.M. – Isle of Man
I. of W. – Isle of Wight
I.(s). – Île, Ilha, Insel, Isla, Island
Id. – Idaho
Ill. – Illinois
Ind. – Indiana
Ind. Oc. – Indian Ocean
J. – Jabal, Jabel, Jazira
Junc. – Junction
K. – Kap, Kapp
K. – Kuala
Kal. – Kalmyk A.S.S.R.
Kans. – Kansas
Kpl. – Kapell
Ky. – Kentucky
L. – Lac, Lacul, Lago, Lagoa, Lake, Limni, Loch, Lough
La. – Lousiana
Lancs. – Lancashire
Leb. – Lebanon
Leics. – Leicestershire
Lim. – Limerick
Lincs. – Lincolnshire
Lit. – Little
Lr. – Lower
Lt. Ho. – Light House
Mad. P. – Madhya Pradesh
Madag. – Madagascar
Malay. – Malaysia
Man. – Manitoba
Manch. – Manchester
Maran. – Maranhão
Mass. – Massachusetts
Md. – Maryland
Me. – Maine
Mend. – Mendoza
Mer. – Méridionale
Mich. – Michigan
Mid. – Middle
Minn. – Minnesota
Miss. – Mississippi
Mo. – Missouri
Mong. – Mongolia
Mont. – Montana

Moroc. – Morocco
Mozam. – Mozambique
Mt.(e). – Mont, Monte, Monti, Montaña, Mountain
Mys. – Mysore
N. – North, Northern, Nouveau
N.B. – New Brunswick
N.C. – North Carolina
N.D. – North Dakota
N.H. – New Hampshire
N.I. – North Island
N.J. – New Jersey
N. Mex. – New Mexico
N.S. – Nova Scotia
N.S.W. – New South Wales
N.T. – Northern Territory
N.W.T. – North West Territory
N.Y. – New York
N.Z. – New Zealand
Nat. – National
Nat Park. – National Park
Nebr. – Nebraska
Neth. – Netherlands
Nev. – Nevada
Newf. – Newfoundland
Nic. – Nicaragua
Northants. – Northamptonshire
Northumb. – Northumberland
Notts. – Nottinghamshire
O. – Oued, ouadi
O.F.S. – Orange Free State
Okla. – Oklahoma
Ont. – Ontario
Or. – Orientale
Oreg. – Oregon
Os. – Ostrov
Oxon. – Oxfordshire
Oz. – Ozero
P. – Pass, Passo, Pasul, Pulau
P.E.I. – Prince Edward Island
P.N.G. – Papua New Guinea
P.O. – Post Office
P. Rico. – Puerto Rico
Pa. – Pennsylvania
Pac. Oc. – Pacific Ocean
Pak. – Pakistan
Pass. – Passage
Pen. – Peninsula, Peninsule
Phil. – Philippines
Pk. – Park, Peak
Plat. – Plateau
P-ov. – Poluostrov
Port. – Portugal, Portuguese
Prom. – Promontory
Prov. – Province, Provincial
Pt. – Point
Pta. – Ponta, Punta
Pte. – Pointe
Què. – Québec
Queens. – Queensland
R. – Rio, River
R.I. – Rhode Island
R.S.F.S.R. – Russian Soviet Federal Socialist Republic
Ra.(s). – Range(s)
Raj. – Rajasthan

Reg. – Region
Rep. – Republic
Res. – Reserve, Reservoir
Rhld. – Pfz. – Rheinland – Pfalz
S. – San, South
S. Afr. – South Africa
S. Austral. – South Australia
S.D. – South Dakota
S.-Holst. – Schleswig-Holstein
S.I. – South Island
S. Leone – Sierra Leone
S.S.R. – Soviet Socialist Republic
S.-U. – Sinkiang-Uighur
Sa. – Serra, Sierra
Sard. – Sardinia
Sask. – Saskatchewan
Scot. – Scotland
Sd. – Sound
Sept. – Septentrionale
Sib. – Siberia
Som. – Somerset
Span. – Spanish
Sprs. – Springs
St. – Saint
Sta. – Santa, Station
Staffs. – Staffordshire
Ste. – Sainte
Sto. – Santo
Str. – Strait, Stretto
Switz. – Switzerland
T.O. – Telegraph Office
Tas. – Tasmania
Tenn. – Tennessee
Terr. – Territory
Tex. – Texas
Tg. – Tanjung
Thai. – Thailand
Tipp. – Tipperary
Trans. – Transvaal
U.K. – United Kingdom
U.S.A. – United States of America
U.S.S.R. – Union of Soviet Socialist Republics
Ukr. – Ukraine
Ut.P. – Uttar Pradesh
Utd. – United
Va. – Virginia
Vdkhr. – Vodokhranilishche
Venez. – Venezuela
Vic. – Victoria
Viet. – Vietnam
Vol. – Volcano
Vt. – Vermont
W. – Wadi, West
W.A. – Western Australia
W. Isles – Western Isles
Wash. – Washington
Wilts. – Wiltshire
Wis. – Wisconsin
Wlkp. – Wielkopolski
Wyo. – Wyoming
Yorks. – Yorkshire
Yug. – Yugoslavia
Zimb. – Zimbabwe

Please refer to the table at the end of the index for recent placename changes in Angola, Iran, Madagascar, Mozambique, Vietnam and Zimbabwe. There is also a table giving the Pin Yin equivalents of the modified Wade-Giles nameforms for the principal Chinese placenames which appear in this Atlas.

Aabenraa-Sønderborg Amt □ Afognak I

A

Aabenraa-Sønderborg Amt □ 73 55 0N 9 30 E
Aachen 48 50 47N 6 4 E
Aadorf 15 47 30N 8 55 E
Aaiun 116 27 9N 13 12W
Aal 73 55 39N 8 18 E
Aâlâ en Nîl □ 123 8 50N 29 55 E
Aalen 49 48 49N 10 6 E
Aalma ech Chaab 90 33 7N 35 9 E
Aalsmeer 46 52 17N 4 43 E
Aalsö 73 56 23N 10 52 E
Aalst, Belg. 47 50 56N 4 2 E
Aalst, Neth. 152 50 57N 4 20 E
Aalten 46 51 56N 6 35 E
Aalter 47 51 5N 3 28 E
Aarau 50 47 23N 8 4 E
Aarburg 50 47 2N 7 16 E
Aardenburg 47 51 16N 3 28 E
Aare, R. 50 47 33N 8 14 E
Aareavaara 74 67 27N 23 29 E
Aargau □ 50 47 26N 8 10 E
Aarhus Amt □ 73 56 15N 10 15 E
Aarle 47 51 30N 5 38 E
Aarschot 47 50 59N 4 49 E
Aarsele 47 51 0N 3 26 E
Aartrijke 47 51 7N 3 6 E
Aarwangen 50 47 15N 7 46 E
Aasleagh 38 53 37N 9 40W
Aastrup 73 55 34N 8 49 E
Aba, Congo 126 3 58N 30 17 E
Aba, Nigeria 121 5 10N 7 19 E
Abâ, Jazîrat 123 13 30N 32 31 E
Abadan 92 30 22N 48 20 E
Abade, Ethiopia 123 9 22N 38 3 E
Abade, Iran 93 31 8N 52 40 E
Abadin 56 43 21N 7 29W
Abadla 118 31 2N 2 45W
Abaeté 171 19 9 S 45 27W
Abaeté, R. 171 18 2 S 45 12W
Abaetetuba 170 1 40 S 48 50W
Abai 173 25 58 S 55 54W
Abak 121 4 58N 7 50 E
Abakaliki 121 6 22N 8 2 E
Abakan 77 53 40N 91 10 E
Abal Nam 122 25 20N 38 37 E
Abalemma 121 16 12N 7 50 E
Aballetuba 170 1 40 S 51 15W
Abanilla 59 38 12N 1 3W
Abano Terme 63 45 22N 11 46 E
Abarán 59 38 12N 1 23W
Abarqu 93 31 10N 53 20 E
Abasan 90 31 19N 34 21 E
Abasberes 123 11 33N 35 23 E
Abashiri 112 44 0N 144 15 E
Abashiri-Wan 112 44 0N 144 30 E
Abau 135 10 11 S 148 46 E
Abaújszántó 53 48 16N 21 12 E
Abaya L. 123 6 30N 37 50 E
Abbadia San Salvatore 63 42 53N 11 40 E
Abbay, R., (Nîl el Azraq) 123 10 17N 35 22 E
Abbaye, Pt. 156 46 58N 88 4W
Abbetorp 73 56 57N 16 8 E
Abbeville, France 43 50 6N 1 49 E
Abbeville, La., U.S.A. 159 30 0N 92 7W
Abbeville, S.C., U.S.A. 157 34 12N 82 21W
Abbey 39 53 7N 8 25W
Abbey Town 32 54 50N 3 18W
Abbeydorney 39 52 21N 9 40W
Abbeyfeale 39 52 23N 9 20W
Abbeyleix 39 52 55N 7 20W
Abbeyside 39 52 5N 7 36W
Abbiategrasso 62 45 23N 8 55 E
Abbieglassie 139 27 15 S 147 28 E
Abbotabad 94 34 10N 73 15 E
Abbots Bromley 28 52 50N 1 52W
Abbots Langley 29 51 43N 0 25W
Abbotsbury 28 50 40N 2 36W
Abbotsford, Can. 152 49 0N 122 10W
Abbotsford, U.S.A. 158 44 55N 90 20W
Abcoude 46 52 17N 4 59 E
'Abd al Kuri 91 12 5N 52 20 E
Abdulino 84 53 42N 53 40 E
Abe, L. 123 11 8N 41 47 E
Abéché 117 13 50N 20 35 E
Abejar 58 41 48N 2 47W
Abekr 123 12 45N 28 50 E
Abêlessa 118 22 58N 4 47 E
Abelti 123 8 10N 37 30 E
Abengourou 120 6 42N 3 27W
Åbenrå 73 55 3N 9 25 E
Abeokuta 121 7 3N 3 19 E
Aber 126 2 12N 32 25 E
Aber-soch 31 52 50N 4 31W
Aberaeron 31 52 15N 4 16W
Aberayron = Aberaeron 31 52 15N 4 16W
Abercarn 31 51 39N 3 9W
Aberchirder 37 57 34N 2 40W
Abercorn 139 25 12 S 151 5 E
Abercorn = Mbala 127 8 46 S 31 17 E
Abercrave 31 51 48N 3 42W
Aberdare 31 51 43N 3 27W
Aberdare Ra. 126 0 15 S 36 50 E
Aberdaron 31 52 48N 4 41W
Aberdeen, Austral. 141 32 9 S 150 56 E
Aberdeen, Can. 153 52 20N 106 8W
Aberdeen, S. Afr. 128 32 28 S 24 2 E
Aberdeen, U.K. 37 57 9N 2 6W
Aberdeen, Md., U.S.A. 162 39 30N 76 14W
Aberdeen, S.D., U.S.A. 158 45 30N 98 30W
Aberdeen, Wash., U.S.A. 160 47 0N 123 50W
Aberdeen (□) 26 57 18N 2 30W
Aberdour 35 56 2N 3 18W
Aberdovey 31 52 33N 4 3W
Aberdulais 31 51 41N 3 46W
Aberfeldy, Austral. 141 37 42 S 146 22 E
Aberfeldy, U.K. 37 56 37N 3 50W
Aberffraw 31 53 11N 4 28W
Aberfoyle 34 56 10N 4 23W
Abergaria-a-Velha 56 40 41N 8 32W
Abergavenny 31 51 49N 3 1W
Abergele 31 53 17N 3 35W
Abergwili 31 51 52N 4 18W
Abergynolwyn 31 52 39N 3 58W
Aberkenfig 31 51 33N 3 36W
Aberlady 35 56 0N 2 51W
Abernathy 159 33 49N 101 49W
Abernethy 35 56 19N 3 18W
Aberporth 31 52 8N 4 32W
Abersychan 31 51 44N 3 3W
Abertillery 31 51 44N 3 9W
Aberystwyth 31 52 25N 4 6W
Abha 122 18 0N 42 34 E
Abhayapuri 98 26 24N 90 38 E
Abidiya 122 18 18N 34 3 E
Abidjan 120 5 26N 3 58W
Abilene, Kans., U.S.A. 158 39 0N 97 16W
Abilene, Texas, U.S.A. 159 32 22N 99 40W
Abingdon, U.K. 28 51 40N 1 17W
Abingdon, Ill., U.S.A. 158 40 53N 90 23W
Abingdon, Va., U.S.A. 157 36 46N 81 56W
Abington 35 55 30N 3 42W
Abington Reef 138 18 0 S 149 35 E
Abitan L. 153 60 27N 107 15W
Abitan, R. 153 59 53N 109 3W
Abitibi L. 150 48 40N 79 40W
Abiy Adi 123 13 39N 39 3 E
Abkhaz A.S.S.R. □ 83 43 0N 41 0 E
Abkit 77 64 10N 157 10 E
Abnûb 122 27 18N 31 4 E
Åbo = Turku 75 60 27N 22 14 E
Abo, Massif d' 119 21 41N 16 8 E
Abocho 121 7 35N 6 56 E
Abohar 94 30 10N 74 10 E
Aboisso 120 5 30N 3 5W
Abomey 121 7 10N 2 5 E
Abondance 45 46 18N 6 42 E
Abong Mbang 124 4 0N 13 8 E
Abonnema 121 4 41N 6 49 E
Abony 53 47 12N 20 3 E
Aboso 120 5 23N 1 57W
Abou Deïa 117 11 20N 19 20 E
Aboyne 37 57 4N 2 48W
Abqaiq 92 26 0N 49 45 E
Abra Pampa 172 22 43 S 65 42W
Abrantes 57 39 24N 8 7W
Abraveses 56 40 41N 7 55 E
Abreojos, Pta. 164 26 50N 113 40W
Abreschviller 43 48 39N 7 6 E
Abrets, Les 45 45 32N 5 35 E
Abri, Esh Shimâliya, Sudan 123 20 50N 30 27 E
Abri, Kordofân, Sudan 123 11 40N 30 21 E
Abrolhos, Arquipélago dos 171 18 0 S 38 30W
Abrolhos, banka 171 18 0 S 38 0W
Abrud 70 46 19N 23 5 E
Abruzzi □ 63 42 15N 14 0 E
Absaroka Ra. 160 44 40N 110 0W
Abû al Khasib 92 30 25N 48 0 E
Abû 'Ali 92 27 20N 49 27 E
Abu Arish 91 16 53N 42 48 E
Abû Ballas 122 24 26N 27 36 E
Abu Deleiq 123 15 57N 33 48 E
Abû Dhabî 93 24 28N 54 36 E
Abû Dis 90 31 47N 35 16 E
Abu Dis 122 19 12N 33 38 E
Abu Dom 123 16 18N 32 25 E
Abû Gabra 123 11 2N 26 50 E
Abû Ghôsh 90 31 48N 35 6 E
Abû Gubeiha 123 11 30N 31 15 E
Abu Habl, W. 123 12 37N 31 0 E
Abu Hamed 122 19 32N 33 13 E
Abû Haraz, Esh Shimâliya, Sudan 122 19 8N 32 18 E
Abû Haraz, Nîl el Azraq, Sudan 123 14 35N 34 30 E
Abû Higar 123 12 50N 33 59 E
Abu Kamal 92 34 30N 41 0 E
Abu Markha 92 25 4N 38 22 E
Abu Qîr 122 31 18N 30 0 E
Abu Qireiya 122 24 5N 35 28 E
Abu Qurqâs 122 28 1N 30 44 E
Abu Salama 122 27 10N 35 51 E
Abû Simbel 122 22 18N 31 40 E
Abu Tig 122 27 4N 31 15 E
Abu Tiga 123 12 47N 34 12 E
Abû Zabad 123 12 25N 29 10 E
Abu Zenîma 122 29 0N 33 15 E
Abuja 121 9 16N 7 2 E
Abunã 174 9 40 S 65 20W
Abunã, R. 174 9 41 S 65 20W
Aburatsu 110 31 34N 131 24 E
Aburo, Mt. 126 2 4N 30 53 E
Abut Hd. 143 43 7 S 170 15 E
Abwong 123 9 2N 32 14 E
Åby 73 58 40N 16 10 E
Aby, Lagune 120 5 15N 3 14W
Acacías 174 3 59N 73 46W
Acajutla 166 13 36N 89 50W
Açallândia 170 5 0 S 47 50W
Acámbaro 164 20 0N 100 40W
Acaponeta 164 22 30N 105 20W
Acapulco de Juárez 165 16 51N 99 56W
Acarai, Serra 175 1 50N 57 50W
Acaraú 170 2 53 S 40 7W
Acari 170 6 31 S 36 38W
Acarigua 174 9 33N 69 12W
Acatlan 165 18 10N 98 3W
Acayucán 165 17 59N 94 58W
Accéglio 62 44 28N 6 59 E
Accomac 156 37 43N 75 40W
Accra 121 5 35N 0 6W
Accrington 32 53 46N 2 22W
Acebal 172 33 20 S 60 50W
Aceh □ 102 4 0N 97 30 E
Acerenza 65 40 50N 15 58 E
Acerra 65 40 57N 14 22 E
Aceuchal 57 38 39N 6 30W
Achaguas 174 7 46N 68 14W
Achak Gomba 99 33 30N 96 25 E
Achalpur 96 21 22N 77 32 E
Achavanich 37 58 22N 3 25W
Achel 47 51 15N 5 29 E
A'ch'eng 107 45 33N 127 0 E
Achenkirch 52 47 32N 11 45 E
Achensee 52 47 26N 11 45 E
Acher 94 23 10N 72 32 E
Achern 49 48 37N 8 5 E
Acheron, R. 143 42 16 S 173 4 E
Achill 38 53 56N 9 55W
Achill Hd. 38 53 59N 10 15W
Achill I. 38 53 58N 10 5W
Achill Sd. 38 53 53N 9 55W
Achillbeg I. 38 53 51N 9 58W
Achim 48 53 1N 9 2 E
Achimota 121 5 35N 0 15W
Achinsk 77 56 20N 90 20 E
Achisay 85 43 35N 68 53 E
Achit 84 56 48N 57 54 E
Achnasheen 36 57 35N 5 5W
Achnashellach 36 57 28N 5 20W
Achol 123 6 35N 31 32 E
A'Chralaig, Mt. 36 57 11N 5 10W
Acireale 65 37 37N 15 9 E
Ackerman 159 33 20N 89 8W
Acklin's I. 167 22 30N 74 0W
Acland, Mt. 133 24 50 S 148 20 E
Aclare 38 54 4N 8 54W
Acle 29 52 38N 1 32 E
Acme 152 51 33N 113 30W
Aconcagua 172 32 50 S 70 0W
Aconcagua □ 172 32 15 S 70 30W
Aconcagua, Cerro 172 32 39 S 70 0W
Aconquija, Mt. 172 27 0 S 66 0W
Acopiara 170 6 6 S 39 27W
Açores, Is. dos 14 38 44N 29 0W
Acquapendente 63 42 45N 11 50 E
Acquasanta 63 42 46N 13 24 E
Acquaviva delle Fonti 65 40 53N 16 50 E
Acqui 62 44 40N 8 28 E
Acre = 'Akko 90 32 35N 35 4 E
Acre □ 174 9 1 S 71 0W
Acre, R. 174 10 45 S 68 25W
Acri 65 39 29N 16 23 E
Acs 53 47 42N 18 0 E
Acton Burnell 28 52 37N 2 41W
Açu 170 5 34 S 36 54W
Ad Dam 91 20 33N 44 45 E
Ad Dammam 92 26 20N 50 5 E
Ad Dar al Hamra 92 27 20N 37 45 E
Ad Dawhah 93 25 15N 51 35 E
Ad Dilam 92 23 55N 47 10 E
Ada, Ethiopia 123 8 48N 38 51 E
Ada, Ghana 121 5 44N 0 40 E
Ada, Minn., U.S.A. 158 47 20N 96 30W
Ada, Okla., U.S.A. 159 34 50N 96 45W
Ada, Yugo. 66 45 49N 20 9 E
Adair C. 12 71 50N 71 0W
Adaja, R. 56 41 15N 4 50W
Adale 91 2 58N 46 27 E
Ådalslinden 72 63 27N 16 55 E
Adam 93 22 15N 57 28 E
Adamantina 171 21 42 S 51 4W
Adamaoua, Massif de l' 121 7 20N 12 20 E
Adamawa Highlands = Adamaoua 121 7 20N 12 20 E
Adamello, Mt. 62 46 10N 10 34 E
Adami Tulu 123 7 53N 38 41 E
Adaminaby 141 36 0 S 148 45 E
Adamovka 84 51 32N 59 56 E
Adams, Mass., U.S.A. 162 42 38N 73 8W
Adams, N.Y., U.S.A. 162 43 50N 76 3W
Adams, Wis., U.S.A. 158 43 59N 89 50W
Adam's Bridge 97 9 15N 79 40 E
Adams L. 152 51 10N 119 40W
Adams Mt. 160 46 10N 121 28W
Adam's Peak 97 6 55N 80 45 E
Adamuz 57 38 2N 4 32W
Adana 92 37 0N 35 16 E
Adanero 56 40 56N 4 36W
Adapazari 92 40 48N 30 25 E
Adarama 123 17 10N 34 52 E
Adare 39 52 34N 8 48W
Adare, C. 13 71 0 S 171 0 E
Adavale 139 25 52 S 144 32 E
Adayio 123 14 29N 40 50 E
Adda, R. 62 45 25N 9 30 E
Addis Ababa = Addis Abeba 123 9 2N 38 42 E
Addis Abeba 123 9 2N 38 42 E
Addis Alem 123 9 0N 38 17 E
Addlestone 29 51 22N 0 30W
Addo 29 33 32 S 25 44 E
Addu Atoll 87 0 30 S 73 0 E
Adebour 121 13 17N 11 50 E
Adel 157 31 10N 83 28W
Adelaide, Austral. 140 34 52 S 138 30 E
Adelaide, Bahamas 166 25 0N 77 31W
Adelaide I. 13 67 15 S 68 30W
Adelaide Pen. 148 68 15N 97 30W
Adelaide River 136 13 15 S 131 7 E
Adelanto 163 34 35N 117 22W
Adelboden 50 46 29N 7 33 E
Adele, I. 136 15 32 S 123 9 E
Adélie, Terre 13 67 0 S 140 0 E
Ademuz 58 40 5N 1 13W
Aden 91 12 50N 45 0 E
Aden, G. of 91 13 0N 50 0 E
Adendorp 128 33 25 S 24 30 E
Adhoi 94 23 26N 70 32 E
Adi 103 4 15 S 133 30 E
Adi Daro 123 14 20N 38 14 E
Adi Keyih 123 14 51N 39 22 E
Adi Kwala 123 14 38N 38 48 E
Adi Ugri 123 14 58N 38 48 E
Adieu, C. 137 32 0 S 132 10 E
Adieu Pt. 136 15 14 S 124 35 E
Adigala 123 10 24N 42 15 E
Adige, R. 63 45 9N 11 25 E
Adigrat 123 14 20N 39 26 E
Adilabad 96 19 33N 78 35 E
Adin 160 41 10N 121 0W
Adin Khel 93 32 45N 68 5 E
Adinkerke 47 51 5N 2 36 E
Adirampattinam 97 10 28N 79 20 E
Adirondack Mts. 156 44 0N 74 15W
Adis Dera 123 10 12N 38 46 E
Adjohon 121 6 41N 2 32 E
Adjud 70 46 7N 27 10 E
Adjumani 126 3 20N 31 50 E
Adlavik Is. 151 55 2N 58 45W
Adler 83 43 28N 39 52 E
Adliswil 51 47 19N 8 32 E
Admer 119 20 21N 5 27 E
Admer, Erg d' 119 24 0N 9 5 E
Admiralty B. 13 62 0 S 59 0W
Admiralty G. 136 14 20 S 125 55 E
Admiralty I. 147 57 40N 134 35W
Admiralty Inlet 160 48 0N 122 40W
Admiralty Is. 135 2 0 S 147 0 E
Admiralty Ra. 13 72 0 S 164 0 E
Ado 121 6 36N 2 56 E
Ado Ekiti 121 7 38N 5 12 E
Adok 123 8 10N 30 20 E
Adola 123 11 14N 41 44 E
Adonara 103 8 15 S 123 5 E
Adoni 97 15 33N 77 18W
Adony 53 47 6N 18 52 E
Adour, R. 44 43 32N 1 32W
Adra, India 95 23 30N 86 42 E
Adra, Spain 59 36 43N 3 3W
Adraj 91 20 1N 51 0 E
Adrano 65 37 40N 14 49 E
Adrar 118 27 51N 0 11W
Adrar des Iforhas 121 19 40N 1 40 E
Adrasman 85 40 38N 69 58 E
Adré 117 13 40N 22 20 E
Adri 119 27 32N 13 2 E
Ádria 63 45 4N 12 3 E
Adrian, Mich., U.S.A. 156 41 55N 84 0W
Adrian, Tex., U.S.A. 159 35 19N 102 37W
Adriatic Sea 60 43 0N 16 0 E
Adrigole 39 51 44N 9 42W
Adua 103 1 45 S 129 50 E
Aduku 126 2 03N 32 45 E
Adula 51 46 30N 9 3 E
Adung Long 98 28 7N 97 42 E
Adur 97 9 8N 76 40 E
Adwa, Ethiopia 123 14 15N 38 52 E
Adwa, Si Arab. 92 27 15N 42 35 E
Adwick le Street 33 53 35N 1 12W
Adzhar A.S.S.R. □ 83 42 0N 42 0 E
Adzopé 120 6 7N 3 49W
Æbelø I. 73 55 39N 10 10 E
Æbeltoft 73 56 12N 10 41 E
Æbeltoft Vig. B. 73 56 9N 10 35 E
Ægean Is. 61 38 0N 25 0 E
Ægean Sea 61 37 0N 25 0 E
Aenemuiden 47 51 30N 3 40 E
Ænes 71 60 5N 6 8 E
Æolian Is. = Eólie, I. 65 38 40N 15 7 E
Aerhchin Shanmo 105 38 0N 88 0 E
Aerhshan 105 47 93N 119 59 E
Aerht'ai Shan 105 48 0N 90 0 E
Æro 73 54 53N 10 20 E
Ærø 73 54 52N 10 25 E
Ærøskøbing 73 54 53N 10 24 E
Aesch 50 47 28N 7 36 E
Aëtós 69 37 15N 21 50 E
Afafi, Massif d' 119 22 11N 14 48 E
Afanasyevo 84 58 52N 53 15 E
Afándou 69 36 18N 28 12 E
Afarag, Erg 118 23 50N 2 47 E
Afdera, Mt. 123 13 16N 41 5 E
Affreville = Khemis Miliania 118 36 11N 2 14 E
Affric, L. 36 57 15N 5 5W
Affric, R. 37 57 15N 4 50W
Afghanistan ■ 93 33 0N 65 0 E
Afgoi 91 2 7N 44 59 E
Afif 92 23 53N 42 56 E
Afikpo 121 5 53N 7 54 E
Aflisses, O. 118 28 30N 0 50 E
Aflou 118 34 7N 2 3 E
Afodo 123 10 18N 34 48 E
Afogados da Ingàzeira 170 7 45 S 37 39W
Afognak I. 147 58 10N 152 50W

Afragola Al Wakrah

Afragola 65 40 54N 14 15 E
Africa 114 10 0N 20 0 E
Afton 162 42 14N 75 31W
Aftout 118 26 50N 3 45W
Afuá 170 0 15 S 50 10W
Afula 90 32 37N 35 17 E
Afyon Karahisar 92 38 20N 30 15 E
Agadès 121 16 58N 7 59 E
Agadir 118 30 28N 9 35W
Agadir Tissint 118 29 57N 7 16W
Agano, R. 112 37 50N 139 30 E
Agapa 77 71 27N 89 15 E
Agapovka 84 53 18N 59 8 E
Agar 94 23 40N 76 2 E
Agaro 123 7 50N 36 38 E
Agartala 98 23 50N 91 23 E
Agassiz 152 49 14N 121 46W
Agat 123 15 38N 38 16 E
Agattu I. 147 52 25N 172 30 E
Agbelouvé 121 6 35N 1 14 E
Agboville 120 5 55N 4 15W
Agdam 83 40 0N 46 58 E
Agdash 83 40 44N 47 22 E
Agde 44 43 19N 3 28 E
Agde, C. d' 44 43 16N 3 28 E
Agdz 118 30 47N 6 30W
Agen 44 44 12N 0 38 E
Ageo 111 35 58N 139 36 E
Ager Tay 119 20 0N 17 41 E
Agersø 73 55 13N 11 12 E
Agger 73 56 47N 8 13 E
Aggersborg 73 57 0N 9 16 E
Aggius 64 40 56N 9 4 E
Aghalee 38 54 32N 6 17W
Aghavannagh 39 52 55N 6 25W
Aghern 39 52 5N 8 10W
Aghil Mts. 93 36 0N 77 0 E
Aghil Pass 93 36 15N 76 35 E
Aginskoye 77 51 6N 114 32 E
Agira 65 37 40N 14 30 E
Aglou 118 29 50N 9 50W
Agly, R. 44 42 46N 3 3 E
Agna Branca 170 7 57 S 47 19W
Agnes 137 28 0 S 120 30 E
Agnew 137 28 1 S 120 30 E
Agnews Hill 38 54 51N 5 55W
Agnibilékrou 120 7 10N 3 11W
Agnita 70 45 59N 24 40 E
Agnone 65 41 49N 14 20 E
Ago 111 33 36N 135 29 E
Agofie 121 8 27N 0 15 E
Agogna, R. 62 45 8N 8 42 E
Agogo, Ghana 121 6 50N 1 1W
Agogo, Sudan 123 7 50N 28 45 E
Agon 42 49 2N 1 34W
Agön 72 61 33N 17 25 E
Agon I. 72 61 34N 17 23 E
Agordo 63 46 18N 12 2 E
Agout, R. 44 43 47N 1 41 E
Agra 94 27 17N 77 58 E
Agrado 174 2 15N 75 46W
Agramunt 58 41 48N 1 6 E
Agreda 58 41 51N 1 55W
Agri 73 56 14N 10 32 E
Ağri Daği 92 39 50N 44 15 E
Agri, R. 65 40 17N 16 15 E
Agrigento 64 37 19N 13 33 E
Agrínion 69 38 37N 21 27 E
Agrøpoli 65 40 23N 14 59 E
Agryz 84 56 33N 53 2 E
Agua Caliente, Mexico 164 26 30N 108 20W
Agua Caliente, U.S.A. 163 32 29N 116 59W
Agua Caliente Springs 163 32 56N 116 19W
Agua Clara 175 20 25 S 52 45W
Agua Prieta 164 31 20N 109 32W
Aguadas 174 5 40N 75 38W
Aguadilla 147 18 27N 67 10W
Aguadulce 166 8 15N 80 32W
Aguanaval, R. 164 23 45N 103 10W
Aguanga 163 33 27N 116 51W
Aguanus, R. 151 50 13N 62 5W
Aguapeí, R. 171 21 0 S 51 0W
Aguapey, R. 172 29 7 S 56 36W
Aguaray Guazú, R. 172 24 47 S 57 19W
Aguarico, R. 174 0 0 77 30W
Aguas Blancas 172 24 15 S 69 55W
Aguas Calientes, Sierra de 172 25 26 S 67 27W
Águas Formosas 171 17 5 S 40 57W
Aguas, R. 58 41 20N 0 30W
Aguascalientes 164 22 0N 102 12W
Aguascalientes □ 164 22 0N 102 20W
Agudo 57 38 59N 4 52W
Agueda 56 40 34N 8 27W
Agueda, R. 56 40 45N 6 37W
Aguelt el Kadra 118 25 3N 7 6W
Agueni N'Ikko 118 32 29N 5 47W
Aguié 121 13 31N 7 46 E
Aguilafuente 56 41 13N 4 7W
Aguilar 57 37 31N 4 40W
Aguilar de Campóo 56 42 47N 4 15W
Aguilares 172 27 26 S 65 35W
Aguilas 59 37 23N 1 35W
Aguja, C. de la 174 11 18N 74 12W
Aguja, Pta. 174 6 0 S 81 0W
Agulaa 123 13 40N 39 40 E
Agulhas, Kaap 128 34 52 S 20 0 E
Agung 102 8 20 S 115 28 E
Agur, Israel 90 31 42N 34 55 E
Agur, Uganda 126 2 28N 32 55 E
Agůš 70 46 28N 26 15 E
Agusan, R. 103 9 20N 125 50 E
Agvali 83 42 36N 46 8 E
Aha Mts. 128 19 45 S 21 0 E
Ahaggar 119 23 0N 6 30 E
Ahamansu 121 7 38N 0 35 E
Ahar 92 38 35N 47 0 E
Ahascragh 38 53 24N 8 20W
Ahaura 143 42 20 S 171 32 E
Ahaura, R. 143 42 21 S 171 34 E
Ahaus 48 52 4N 7 1 E
Ahelledjem 119 26 37N 6 58 E
Ahimanawa Ra. 130 39 5 S 176 30 E
Ahipara B. 142 35 5 S 173 5 E
Ahiri 96 19 30N 80 0 E
Ahlen 48 51 45N 7 52 E
Ahmad Wal 94 29 18N 65 58 E
Ahmadabad (Ahmedabad) 94 23 0N 72 40 E
Ahmadnagar (Ahmednagar) 96 19 7N 74 46 E
Ahmadpur 94 29 12N 71 10 E
Ahmar Mts. 123 9 20N 41 15 E
Ahoada 121 5 8N 6 36 E
Ahoghill 38 54 52N 6 23W
Ahome 164 25 55N 109 11W
Ahr, R. 48 50 25N 6 52 E
Ahrensbök 48 54 0N 10 34 E
Ahrweiler 48 50 31N 7 3 E
Ahsā, Wahatāal 92 25 50N 49 0 E
Ahuachapán 166 13 54N 89 52W
Ahuriri, R. 143 44 31 S 170 12 E
Åhus 73 55 56N 14 18 E
Ahvāz 92 31 20N 48 40 E
Ahvenanmaa 75 60 15N 20 0 E
Ahzar 121 15 30N 3 20 E
Aibaq 93 36 15N 68 5 E
Aichach 49 48 28N 11 9 E
Aichi-ken □ 111 35 0N 137 15 E
Aidone 65 37 26N 14 26 E
Aiello Cálabro 65 39 6N 16 12 E
Aigle 50 46 18N 6 58 E
Aignay-le-Duc 43 47 40N 4 43 E
Aigre 44 45 54N 0 1 E
Aigua 173 34 13 S 54 46W
Aigueperse 44 46 3N 3 13 E
Aigues-Mortes 45 43 35N 4 12 E
Aiguilles 45 44 47N 6 51 E
Aiguillon 44 44 18N 0 21 E
Aiguillon, L' 44 46 20N 1 16W
Aigurande 44 46 27N 1 49 E
Aihui 105 50 16N 127 28 E
Aija 174 9 50 S 77 45W
Aijal 98 23 40N 92 44 E
Aiken 157 33 34N 81 50W
Ailao Shan 108 24 0N 101 30 E
Aillant-sur-Tholon 43 47 52N 3 20 E
Aillik 151 55 11N 59 18W
Ailly-sur-Noye 43 49 45N 2 20 E
Ailsa Craig, I. 34 55 15N 5 7W
Aim 77 59 0N 133 55 E
Aimere 103 8 45 S 121 3 E
Aimogasta 172 28 33 S 66 50W
Aimorés 171 19 30 S 41 4W
Aimorés, Serra dos 171 17 50 S 40 30W
Ain □ 45 46 5N 5 20 E
Ain Banaiyah 93 23 0N 51 0 E
Aïn-Beïda 119 35 50N 7 35 E
Ain ben Khellil 118 33 15N 0 49W
Ain Ben Tili 118 25 59N 9 27W
Aïn Benian 118 36 48N 2 55 E
'Ain Dalla 122 27 20N 27 23 E
Ain Dar 92 25 55N 49 10 E
Ain el Mafki 122 27 30N 28 15 E
Ain Girba 122 29 20N 25 14 E
Aïn M'lila 119 36 2N 6 35 E
Ain Qeiqab 122 29 42N 24 55 E
Ain, R. 45 45 52N 5 11 E
Aïn Rich 118 34 38N 24 55 E
Aïn-Sefra 118 32 47N 0 37W
Ain Sheikh Murzûk 122 26 47N 27 45 E
Ain Sukhna 122 29 32N 32 20 E
Aïn Tédelès 118 36 0N 0 21 E
Aïn-Témouchent 118 35 16N 1 8W
Aïn Touta 119 35 26N 5 54 E
Ain Zeitûn 122 29 10N 25 48 E
Aïn Zorah 118 34 37N 3 32W
Ainabo 91 9 0N 46 25 E
Ainazi 80 57 50N 24 24 E
Aine Galakka 117 18 10N 18 30 E
Aínos Óros 69 38 10N 20 35 E
Ainsdale 32 53 37N 3 2W
Ainsworth 158 42 33N 99 52W
Aioi 110 34 48N 134 28 E
Aion 77 69 50N 169 0 E
Aipe 174 3 13N 75 15W
Aïr 121 18 30N 8 0 E
Airaines 43 49 58N 1 55 E
Aird Brenish, C. 36 58 8N 7 8W
Aird, The, dist. 37 57 26N 4 30W
Airdrie 35 55 53N 3 57W
Aire 43 50 37N 2 22 E
Aire, Isla del 58 39 48N 4 16 E
Aire, R. 43 49 18N 5 0 E
Aire-sur-l'Adour 44 43 42N 0 15W
Aireys Inlet 140 38 29 S 144 5 E
Airolo 51 46 32N 8 37 E
Airvault 42 46 50N 0 8W
Aisgill 32 54 23N 2 21W
Aishihik 147 61 40N 137 46W
Aisne □ 43 49 42N 3 40 E
Aisne, R. 43 49 26N 2 50 E
Aït Melloul 118 30 25N 9 29W
Aitana, Sierra de 59 38 35N 0 24W
Aitape 135 3 11 S 142 22 E
Aith 37 59 8N 2 38W
Aitkin 158 46 32N 93 43W
Aitolía Kai Akarnania □ 69 38 45N 21 18 E
Aitolikón 69 38 26N 21 21 E
Aitoska Planina 67 42 45N 27 30 E
Aiuaba 170 6 38 S 40 7W
Aiud 70 46 19N 23 44 E
Aix-en-Provence 45 43 32N 5 27 E
Aix-la-Chapelle = Aachen 48 50 47N 6 4 E
Aix-les-Bains 45 45 41N 5 53 E
Aix-les-Thermes 44 42 43N 1 51 E
Aix-sur-Vienne 44 45 48N 1 8 E
Aiyang, Mt. 135 5 10 S 141 20 E
Aiyangpienmen 107 40 55N 124 30 E
Aiyansh 152 55 17N 129 2W
Aiyina 69 37 45N 23 26 E
Aiyinion 68 40 28N 22 28 E
Aiyion 69 38 15N 22 5 E
Aizenay 42 46 44N 1 38W
Aizpute 80 56 43N 21 40 E
Aizuwakamatsu 112 37 30N 139 56 E
Ajaccio 45 41 55N 8 40 E
Ajaccio, G. d' 45 41 52N 8 40 E
Ajalpán 165 18 22N 97 15W
Ajana 137 27 56 S 114 35 E
Ajanta Ra. 96 20 28N 75 50 E
Ajax, Mt. 143 42 35 S 172 5 E
Ajdabiyah 119 30 54N 20 4 E
Ajdīr, Raīs 119 33 4N 11 44 E
Ajdovščina 63 45 54N 13 54 E
Ajibar 123 10 35N 38 36 E
'Ajlun 90 32 18N 35 47 E
Ajman 93 25 25N 55 30 E
Ajmer 94 26 28N 74 37 E
Ajo 161 32 18N 112 54W
Ajoie 50 47 22N 7 0 E
Ajok 123 9 15N 28 28 E
Ajua 120 4 50N 1 55W
Ak Dağ 92 36 30N 30 0 E
Akaba 121 8 10N 1 2 E
Akabli 118 26 49N 1 31 E
Akaishi-Dake 111 35 27N 138 9 E
Akaishi-Sammyaku 111 35 25N 138 10 E
Akaki Beseka 123 8 55N 38 45 E
Akala 123 15 39N 36 13 E
Akaroa 143 43 49 S 172 59 E
Akaroa Harb. 131 43 54 S 172 59 E
Akasha 122 21 10N 30 32 E
Akashi 110 34 45N 135 0 E
Akbou 119 36 31N 4 31 E
Akbulak 84 51 1N 55 37 E
Akdala 85 45 2N 74 35 E
Akechi 111 35 18N 137 23 E
Akegbe 121 6 17N 7 28 E
Akelamo 103 1 35N 129 40 E
Akershus Fylke □ 71 60 10N 11 15 E
Akeru, R. 96 17 25N 80 0 E
Aketi 124 2 38N 23 47 E
Akhaïa □ 69 38 5N 21 45 E
Akhalkalaki 83 41 27N 43 25 E
Akhaltsikhe 83 41 40N 43 0 E
Akharnai 69 38 5N 23 44 E
Akhelóös, R. 69 39 5N 21 25 E
Akhendriá 69 34 58N 25 16 E
Akhéron, R. 68 39 31N 20 29 E
Akhisar 92 38 56N 27 48 E
Akhladhókambos 69 37 31N 22 35 E
Akhmîm 122 26 31N 31 47 E
Akhnur 95 32 52N 74 45 E
Akhtopol 67 42 6N 27 56 E
Akhtubinsk (Petropavlovskiy) 83 48 27N 46 7 E
Akhty 83 41 30N 47 45 E
Akhtyrka 80 50 25N 35 0 E
Aki 110 33 30N 133 54 E
Aki-Nada 110 34 5N 132 40 E
Akiak 147 60 50N 161 12W
Akimiski I. 150 52 50N 81 30W
Akimovka 82 46 44N 35 0 E
Akincilar 69 37 57N 27 25 E
Akinum 138 6 15 S 149 30 E
Åkirkeby 73 55 4N 14 55 E
Akita 112 39 45N 140 0 E
Akita-ken □ 112 39 40N 140 30 E
Akjoujt 120 19 45N 14 15W
Akka 118 29 28N 8 9W
'Akko 90 32 35N 35 4 E
Akkol, Kazakh, U.S.S.R. 85 45 0N 75 39 E
Akkol, Kazakh, U.S.S.R. 85 43 36N 70 45 E
Akköy 69 37 30N 27 18 E
Akkrum 46 53 3N 5 50 E
Aklampa 121 8 15N 2 10 E
Aklavik, Can. 147 68 12N 135 0W
Aklavik, N.W.T., Can. 147 68 12N 135 0W
Akmuz 85 41 15N 76 10 E
Aknoul 118 34 40N 3 55W
Akō 110 34 45N 134 24 E
Ako 121 10 19N 10 48 E
Akobo, R. 123 7 10N 34 25 E
Akola 96 20 42N 77 2 E
Akonolinga 121 3 50N 12 18 E
Akordat 123 15 30N 37 40 E
Akosombo Dam 121 6 20N 0 5 E
Ak'osu 105 41 15N 80 14 E
Akot, India 96 21 10N 77 10 E
Akot, Sudan 123 6 31N 30 9 E
Akpatok I. 149 60 25N 68 8W
Åkranes 74 64 19N 22 6W
Åkrehamn 71 59 15N 5 10 E
Akreïjit 120 18 19N 9 11W
Akritas Venétiko, Ákra 69 36 43N 21 54 E
Akron, Colo., U.S.A. 158 40 13N 103 15W
Akron, Ohio, U.S.A. 156 41 7N 81 31W
Akrotiri, Ákra 68 40 26N 25 27W
Aksai Chih, L. 95 35 15N 79 55 E
Aksaray 92 38 25N 34 2 E
Aksarka 76 66 31N 67 50 E
Aksehir 92 38 18N 31 30 E
Aksenovo Zilovskoye 77 53 20N 117 40 E
Aksuat, Ozero 84 51 32N 64 34 E
Aksum 123 14 5N 38 40 E
Aktash, R.S.F.S.R., U.S.S.R. 84 52 2N 52 7 E
Aktash, Uzbek S.S.R., U.S.S.R. 85 39 55N 65 55 E
Aktobe 84 52 55N 62 22 E
Aktogay 85 44 25N 76 44 E
Aktyubinsk 79 50 17N 57 10 E
Aktyuz 85 42 54N 76 7 E
Aku 121 6 40N 7 18 E
Akulurak 147 62 40N 164 35W
Akun I. 147 54 15N 165 30W
Akune 110 32 1N 130 12 E
Akure 121 7 15N 5 5 E
Akureyri 74 65 40N 18 6W
Akusha 83 42 18N 47 30 E
Akutan I. 147 53 30N 166 0W
Akzhar 85 43 8N 71 37 E
Al Abyār 119 32 9N 20 29 E
Al Amadiyah 92 37 5N 43 30 E
Al Amārah 92 31 55N 47 15 E
Al Aqabah 92 29 37N 35 0 E
Al Ashkhara 93 21 50N 59 30 E
Al Ayn al Mugshin 91 19 35N 54 40 E
Al 'Azīzīyah 119 32 30N 13 1 E
Al Badi 92 22 0N 46 35 E
Al Barah 90 31 55N 35 12 E
Al Barkāt 119 24 56N 10 14 E
Al Basrah 92 30 30N 47 50 E
Al Baydā 117 32 30N 21 40 E
Al Bu'ayrāt 119 31 24N 15 44 E
Al Buqay'ah 90 32 15N 35 30 E
Al Dīwaniyah 92 32 0N 45 0 E
Al Fallujah 92 33 20N 43 55 E
Al Fāw 92 30 0N 48 30 E
Al Hadithan 92 34 0N 41 13 E
Al Hamad 92 31 30N 39 30 E
Al Hamar 92 22 23N 46 6 E
Al Hariq 92 23 29N 46 27 E
Al Hasakah 92 36 35N 40 45 E
Al Hauta 91 16 5N 48 20 E
Al Havy 92 32 5N 46 5 E
Al Hillah, Iraq 92 32 30N 44 25 E
Al Hillah, Si Arab. 92 23 35N 46 50 E
Al Hilwah 92 23 24N 46 48 E
Al Hindiya 92 32 30N 44 10 E
Al Hoceïma 118 35 8N 3 58W
Al Hufrah, Awbārī, Libya 119 25 32N 14 1 E
Al Hufrah, Misrātah, Libya 119 29 5N 18 3 E
Al Hufuf 92 25 25N 49 45 E
Al Husayyāt 119 30 24N 20 37 E
Al Husn 90 32 29N 35 52 E
Al Irq 117 29 5N 21 35 E
Al Ittihad = Madinat al Shaab 91 12 50N 45 0 E
Al Jahrah 92 29 25N 47 40 E
Al Jalāmid 92 31 20N 39 45 E
Al Jarzirah 117 26 10N 21 20 E
Al Jawf 117 24 10N 23 24 E
Al Jazir 91 18 30N 56 31 E
Al Jubail 92 27 0N 49 50 E
Al Juwara 91 19 0N 57 13 E
Al Khābūrah 93 23 57N 57 5 E
Al Khalih 90 31 32N 35 6 E
Al Khums (Homs) 119 32 40N 14 17 E
Al Kut 92 32 30N 46 0 E
Al Kuwayt 92 29 20N 48 0 E
Al Ladhiqiyah 92 35 30N 35 45 E
Al Līth 122 20 9N 40 15 E
Al Madīnah 92 24 35N 39 52 E
Al-Mafraq 90 32 17N 36 14 E
Al Majma'ah 92 25 57N 45 22 E
Al Manamah 93 26 10N 50 30 E
Al Marj 117 32 25N 20 30 E
Al Masīrah 91 20 25N 58 50 E
Al Mawsil 92 36 15N 43 5 E
Al Miqdadīyah 92 34 0N 45 0 E
Al Mubarraz 92 25 30N 49 40 E
Al Muharraq 93 26 15N 50 40 E
Al Mukha 91 13 18N 43 15 E
Al Musayyib 92 32 40N 44 25 E
Al Muwaylih 92 27 40N 35 30 E
Al Qaddāhīyah 119 31 15N 15 9 E
Al Qamishli 92 37 10N 41 10 E
Al Qaryah ash Sharqīyah 119 30 28N 13 40 E
Al Qaşabāt 119 32 39N 14 1 E
Al Qatif 92 26 35N 50 0 E
Al Qaţrun 119 24 56N 15 3 E
Al Quaisūmah 92 28 10N 46 20 E
Al Quds 90 31 47N 35 10 E
Al Qunfidha 122 19 3N 41 4 E
Al Quraiyat 93 23 17N 58 53 E
Al Qurnah 92 31 1N 47 25 E
Al 'Ula 92 26 35N 38 0 E
Al Uqaylah 119 30 12N 19 10 E
Al Uqayr 92 25 40N 50 15 E
Al' Uwayqilah 92 30 30N 42 10 E
Al 'Uyūn 92 26 30N 43 50 E
Al Wajh 122 26 10N 36 30 E
Al Wakrah 93 25 10N 51 40 E

Al Warīah Almaden

Al Warīah 92 27 50N 47 30E
Al Wātīyah 119 32 28N 11 57E
Ala, Italy 62 45 46N 11 0E
Ala, Sweden 72 61 13N 17 9E
Ala Shan 105 40 0N 104 0E
Alabama □ 157 31 0N 87 0W
Alabama, R. 157 31 30N 87 35W
Alaçati 69 38 16N 26 23E
Alaejos 56 41 18N 5 13W
Alagna Valsésia 62 45 51N 7 56E
Alagôa Grande 170 7 3S 35 35W
Alagôas □ 170 9 0S 36 0W
Alagoinhas 171 12 0S 38 20W
Alagón 58 41 46N 1 12W
Alagón, R. 56 39 50N 6 50W
Alajuela 166 10 2N 84 8W
Alakamisy 129 21 19S 47 14E
Alakurtti 78 67 0N 30 30E
Alam Ajaib 122 25 55N 27 14E
Alameda, Spain 57 37 12N 4 39W
Alameda, Calif., U.S.A. 163 37 46N 122 15W
Alameda, N. Mex., U.S.A. 161 35 10N 106 43W
Alameda, S.D., U.S.A. 160 43 2N 112 30W
Alamitos, Sierra de los 164 26 30N 102 20W
Alamo 161 37 21N 115 10W
Alamogordo 161 32 59N 106 0W
Alamos 164 27 0N 109 0W
Alamosa 161 37 30N 106 0W
Åland 75 60 15N 20 0E
Aland 96 17 36N 76 35E
Alandroal 57 38 41N 7 24W
Ålands hav 75 60 10N 19 30E
Alange, Presa de 57 38 45N 6 18W
Alangouassou 120 7 30N 4 34W
Alanis 57 38 3N 5 43W
Alanya 92 36 38N 32 0E
Alaotra, L. 129 17 30S 48 30E
Alapayevsk 84 57 52N 61 42E
Alar del Rey 56 42 38N 4 20W
Alaraz 56 40 45N 5 17W
Alaşehir 79 38 23N 28 30E
Alashantsoch'i 106 38 59N 105 45E
Alaska □ 147 65 0N 150 0W
Alaska, G. of 147 58 0N 145 0W
Alaska Highway 152 60 0N 130 0W
Alaska Pen. 147 56 0N 160 0W
Alaska Range 147 62 50N 151 0W
Alássio 62 44 1N 8 10E
Alatri 64 41 44N 13 21E
Alatyr 81 54 45N 46 35E
Alatyr, R. 81 54 45N 45 30E
Alausí 174 2 0S 78 50W
Álava □ 58 42 48N 2 28W
Alava, C. 160 48 10N 124 40W
Alaverdi 83 41 2N 44 37E
Alawoona 140 34 45S 140 30E
Alaykel 85 40 15N 74 25E
Alayor 58 39 57N 4 8E
Alayskiy Khrebet 85 39 45N 72 0E
Alazan, R. 83 41 25N 46 35E
Alba 62 44 41N 8 1E
Alba □ 70 46 10N 23 30E
Alba de Tormes 56 40 50N 5 30W
Alba-Iulia 70 46 8N 23 39E
Albac 70 46 28N 23 1E
Albacete 59 39 0N 1 50W
Albacete □ 59 38 50N 2 0W
Albacutya, L. 140 35 45S 141 58E
Albæk 73 57 36N 10 25E
Ålbæk Bugt 73 57 35N 10 40E
Albaida 59 38 51N 0 31W
Albalate de las Nogueras 58 40 22N 2 18W
Albalate del Arzobispo 58 41 6N 0 31W
Albania ■ 68 41 0N 20 0E
Albano Laziale 64 41 44N 12 40E
Albany, Austral. 137 35 1S 117 58E
Albany, Ga., U.S.A. 157 31 40N 84 10W
Albany, Minn., U.S.A. 158 45 37N 94 38W
Albany, N.Y., U.S.A. 162 42 29N 73 47W
Albany, Oreg., U.S.A. 160 44 41N 123 0W
Albany, Tex., U.S.A. 159 32 45N 99 20W
Albany, R. 150 52 17N 81 31W
Albardón 172 31 20S 68 30W
Albarracín 58 40 25N 1 26W
Albarracín, Sierra de 58 40 30N 1 30W
Albatross B. 138 12 45S 141 30E
Albatross Pt. 142 38 7S 174 44E
Albegna, R. 63 42 40N 11 28E
Albemarle 157 35 27N 80 15W
Albemarle Sd. 157 36 0N 76 30W
Albenga 62 44 3N 8 12E
Alberche, R. 56 40 10N 4 30W
Alberdi 172 26 14S 58 20W
Alberes, Mts. 58 42 28N 2 56W
Alberga 139 27 12S 135 28E
Alberga, R. 136 26 50S 133 40E
Alberique 59 39 7N 0 31W
Alberni 152 49 20N 124 50W
Albersdorf 48 54 8N 9 19E
Albert, Austral. 141 32 22S 147 30E
Albert, Can. 151 45 51N 64 38W
Albert, France 43 50 0N 2 38E
Albert Canyon 152 51 8N 117 41W
Albert Edward, Mt. 135 8 20S 147 24E
Albert Edward Ra. 136 18 17S 127 57E
Albert L., Austral. 140 35 30S 139 10E
Albert L., U.S.A. 160 42 40N 120 8W
Albert Lea 158 43 32N 93 20W
Albert, L. = Mobutu Sese Seko, L. 126 1 30N 31 0E
Albert Nile, R. 126 3 16N 31 38E
Albert Town 167 22 37N 74 33E
Alberta □ 152 54 40N 115 0W
Alberti 172 35 1S 60 16W
Albertinia 128 34 11S 21 34E
Albertirsa 53 47 14N 19 37E
Albertkanaal 47 51 14N 4 26E
Alberton 151 46 50N 64 0W
Albertville 45 45 40N 6 22E
Albertville = Kalemie 126 5 55S 29 9E
Albi 44 43 56N 2 9E
Albia 158 41 0N 92 50W
Albina 175 5 37N 54 15W
Albina, Pta. 128 15 52S 11 44E
Albino 62 45 47N 9 48E
Albion, Idaho, U.S.A. 160 42 21N 113 37W
Albion, Mich., U.S.A. 156 42 15N 84 45W
Albion, Nebr., U.S.A. 158 41 47N 98 0W
Alblasserdam 46 51 52N 4 40E
Albocácer 58 40 21N 0 1E
Alböke 73 56 57N 16 47E
Alborán, I. 57 35 57N 3 0W
Alborea 59 39 17N 1 24W
Ålborg 73 57 2N 9 54E
Ålborg Bugt 73 56 50N 10 35E
Alborz, Reshteh-Ye Kūkhā-Ye 93 36 0N 52 0E
Albox 59 37 23N 2 8W
Albreda 152 52 35N 119 10W
Albrighton 28 52 38N 2 17W
Albuera, La 57 38 45N 6 49W
Albufeira 57 37 5N 8 15W
Albula, R. 51 46 38N 9 30E
Albuñol 59 36 48N 3 11W
Albuquerque 161 35 5N 106 47W
Albuquerque, Cayos de 166 12 10N 81 50W
Alburno, Mte. 65 40 32N 15 20E
Alburquerque 57 39 15N 6 59W
Albury 141 36 3S 146 56E
Albuskjell, oilfield 19 56 40N 3 0E
Alby 72 62 30N 15 28E
Alcácer do Sal 57 38 22N 8 33W
Alcalá de Chisvert 58 40 19N 0 13E
Alcalá de Guadaira 57 37 20N 5 50W
Alcalá de Henares 58 40 28N 3 22W
Alcalá de los Gazules 57 36 29N 5 43W
Alcalá la Real 57 37 27N 3 57W
Alcamo 64 37 59N 12 55E
Alcanadre 58 42 24N 2 7W
Alcanadre, R. 58 41 43N 0 12W
Alcanar 58 40 33N 0 28E
Alcanede 57 39 25N 8 49W
Alcanena 57 39 27N 8 40W
Alcañices 57 41 41N 6 21W
Alcaníz 58 41 2N 0 8W
Alcântara 170 2 20S 44 30W
Alcántara 57 39 41N 6 57W
Alcantara L. 153 60 57N 108 9W
Alcantarilla 59 37 59N 1 12W
Alcaracejos 57 38 24N 4 58W
Alcaraz 59 38 40N 2 29W
Alcaraz, Sierra de 59 38 40N 2 20W
AlcáRovas 57 38 23N 8 9W
Alcarria, La 58 40 31N 2 45W
Alcaudete 57 37 35N 4 5W
Alcázar de San Juan 59 39 24N 3 12W
Alcester 28 52 13N 1 52W
Alcira 59 39 9N 0 30W
Alcoa 157 35 50N 84 0W
Alcobaça, Brazil 171 17 30S 39 13W
Alcobaça, Port. 57 39 32N 9 0W
Alcobendas 58 40 32N 3 38W
Alcolea del Pinar 58 41 2N 2 28W
Alcora 58 40 5N 0 14W
Alcoutim 57 37 25N 7 28W
Alcova 160 42 37N 106 52W
Alcoy 59 38 43N 0 30W
Alcubierre, Sierra de 58 41 45N 0 22W
Alcublas 58 39 48N 0 43W
Alcudia 58 39 51N 3 9E
Alcudia, Bahía de 58 39 45N 3 14E
Alcudia, Sierra de la 57 38 34N 4 30W
Aldabra Is. 11 9 22S 46 28E
Aldama 165 22 25N 98 4W
Aldan 77 58 40N 125 30E
Aldan, R. 77 62 30N 135 10E
Aldborough 33 54 6N 1 21W
Aldbourne 28 51 28N 1 38W
Aldbrough 33 53 50N 0 7W
Aldeburgh 29 52 9N 1 35E
Aldeia Nova 57 37 55N 7 24W
Alden I. 71 61 19N 4 45E
Alder 160 45 27N 112 3W
Alder Pk. 163 35 53N 12 22W
Alderbury 28 51 4N 1 45W
Alderley Edge 32 53 18N 2 15W
Aldermaston 28 51 23N 1 9W
Alderney, I. 42 49 42N 2 12W
Aldershot 29 51 15N 0 43W
Aldersyde 152 50 40N 113 53W
Aldingham 32 54 8N 3 3W
Aledo 158 41 10N 90 50W
Alefa 123 11 55N 36 55E
Aleg 120 17 3N 13 55W
Alegre 173 20 50S 41 30W
Alegrete 173 29 40S 56 0W
Aleisk 76 52 40N 83 0E
Alejandro Selkirk, I. 131 33 50S 80 15W
Aleksandriya, U.S.S.R. 79 50 45N 26 22E
Aleksandriya, U.S.S.R. 82 48 42N 33 3E
Aleksandriyskaya 83 43 59N 47 0E
Aleksandrov 81 56 23N 38 44E
Aleksandrov Gay. 81 50 15N 48 35E
Aleksandrovac 66 44 28N 21 13E
Aleksandrovka 82 48 55N 32 20E
Aleksandrovo 67 43 14N 24 51E
Aleksandrovsk 84 59 9N 57 33E
Aleksandrovsk-Sakhaliniskiy 77 50 50N 142 20E
Aleksandrovskiy Zavod 77 50 40N 117 50E
Aleksandrovskoye 76 60 35N 77 50E
Aleksandrów Kujawski 54 52 53N 18 43E
Aleksandrów Łódzki 54 51 49N 19 17E
Alekseyevka, R.S.F.S.R., U.S.S.R. 81 50 43N 38 40E
Alekseyevka, R.S.F.S.R., U.S.S.R. 84 52 35N 51 17E
Aleksin 81 54 31N 37 9E
Aleksinac 66 43 31N 21 42E
Além Paraíba 173 21 52S 42 41W
Alemania, Argent. 172 25 40S 65 30W
Alemania, Chile 172 25 10S 69 55W
Ålen 71 62 51N 11 17E
Alençon 42 48 27N 0 4E
Alentejo, Alto- 55 39 0N 7 40W
Alentejo, Baixo- 55 38 0N 8 30W
Alenuihaha Chan. 147 20 25N 156 0W
Aleppo 92 36 10N 37 15E
Aléria 45 42 5N 9 26E
Alert B. 152 50 30N 127 35W
Alès 45 44 9N 4 5E
Aleşd 70 47 3N 22 22E
Alessándria 62 44 54N 8 37E
Ålestrup 73 56 42N 9 29E
Ålesund 71 62 28N 6 12E
Alet 123 8 14N 29 2E
Alet-les-Bains 44 43 0N 2 14E
Aletschgletscher 50 46 28N 8 2E
Aletschhorn 50 46 28N 8 0E
Aleutian Is. 147 52 0N 175 0W
Aleutian Ra. 147 55 0N 155 0W
Alexander 158 47 51N 103 40W
Alexander Arch. 147 57 0N 135 0W
Alexander B. 128 28 36S 16 33E
Alexander City 157 32 58N 85 57W
Alexander I. 13 69 0S 70 0W
Alexander, Mt. 137 28 58S 120 16E
Alexandra, Austral. 141 37 8S 145 40E
Alexandra, N.Z. 143 45 14S 169 25E
Alexandra Falls 152 60 29N 116 18W
Alexandria, Austral. 138 19 5S 136 40E
Alexandria, Brazil 171 6 25S 38 1W
Alexandria, B.C., Can. 152 52 35N 122 27W
Alexandria, Ont., Can. 150 45 19N 74 38W
Alexandria, Rumania 70 43 57N 25 24E
Alexandria, S. Afr. 128 33 38S 26 28E
Alexandria, U.K. 34 55 59N 4 40W
Alexandria, Ind., U.S.A. 156 40 18N 85 40W
Alexandria, La., U.S.A. 159 31 20N 92 30W
Alexandria, Minn., U.S.A. 158 45 50N 95 20W
Alexandria, S.D., U.S.A. 158 43 40N 97 45W
Alexandria, Va., U.S.A. 162 38 47N 77 1W
Alexandria = El Iskandarîya 122 31 0N 30 0E
Alexandria Bay 156 44 20N 75 52W
Alexandrina, L. 140 35 25S 139 10E
Alexandroúpolis 68 40 50N 25 54E
Alexis Creek 152 52 0N 123 20W
Alexis, R. 151 52 33N 56 8W
Alfambra 58 40 33N 1 5W
Alfândega da Fé 56 41 20N 6 59W
Alfaro 58 42 10N 1 50W
Alfatar 67 43 59N 27 13E
Alfeld 48 52 0N 9 49E
Alfenas 173 21 40S 44 0W
Alfiós, R. 69 37 36N 21 54E
Alfonsine 63 44 30N 12 1E
Alford, Grampian, U.K. 37 57 13N 2 42W
Alford, Lincs., U.K. 33 53 16N 0 10E
Alfred 162 43 28N 70 40W
Alfred Town 141 35 8S 147 30E
Alfredton 142 40 41S 175 54E
Alfreton 33 53 6N 1 22W
Alfriston 29 50 48N 0 10E
Alfta 72 61 21N 16 4E
Alftanes 74 64 29N 22 10W
Alga 84 49 53N 57 20E
Algaba, La 57 37 27N 6 1W
Algar 57 36 40N 5 39W
Ålgård 71 58 46N 5 53E
Ålgård 71 58 46N 5 53E
Algarinejo 57 37 19N 4 9W
Algarve 57 37 15N 8 10W
Algeciras 57 36 9N 5 28W
Algemesí 59 39 11N 0 27W
Alger 118 36 42N 3 8E
Algeria ■ 118 35 10N 3 11E
Alghero 64 40 34N 8 20E
Algiers = Alger 118 36 42N 3 8E
Algoabaai 128 33 50S 25 45E
Algodonales 57 36 54N 5 24W
Algodor, R. 56 39 51N 3 48W
Algoma, Mich., U.S.A. 156 44 35N 87 27W
Algoma, Oreg., U.S.A. 160 42 25N 121 54W
Algonquin Prov. Pk. 150 45 50N 78 30W
Alhama de Almería 59 36 57N 2 34W
Alhama de Aragón 58 41 18N 1 54W
Alhama de Granada 57 37 0N 3 59W
Alhama de Murcia 59 37 51N 1 25W
Alhambra, Spain 59 38 54N 3 4W
Alhambra, U.S.A. 163 34 8N 118 10W
Alhaurín el Grande 57 36 39N 4 41W
Alhucemas = Al-Hoceïma 118 35 8N 3 58W
Ali al Gharbi 92 32 30N 46 45E
Ali Bayramly 83 39 43N 48 52E
Ali Khel 94 33 56N 69 35E
Ali Sabieh 123 11 10N 42 44E
Ália 64 37 47N 13 42E
Aliabad 93 28 10N 57 35E
Aliaga 58 40 40N 0 42W
Aliakmon, R. 68 40 10N 22 0E
Alibag 96 18 38N 72 56E
Alibo 123 9 52N 37 5E
Alibunar 66 45 5N 20 57E
Alicante 59 38 23N 0 30W
Alicante □ 59 38 30N 0 37W
Alice, S. Afr. 128 32 48S 26 55E
Alice, U.S.A. 159 27 47N 98 1W
Alice Arm 152 55 29N 129 31W
Alice Downs 136 17 45S 127 56E
Alice, Punta dell' 65 39 23N 17 10E
Alice, R., Queens., Austral. 138 15 35S 142 20E
Alice, R., Queens., Austral. 138 24 2S 144 50E
Alice Springs 138 23 40S 135 50E
Alicedale 128 33 15S 26 4E
Aliceville 157 33 9N 88 10W
Alick Cr. 138 20 35S 142 10E
Alicudi, I. 65 38 33N 14 20E
Alida 153 49 25N 101 55W
Aligarh, India 93 27 55N 78 10E
Aligarh, Raj., India 94 25 55N 76 15E
Aligarh, Ut. P., India 94 27 55N 78 10E
Aligudarz 92 33 25N 49 45E
Alijó 56 41 16N 7 27W
Alimena 65 37 42N 14 4E
Alimnía 69 36 16N 27 43E
Aling Kangri 99 31 45N 84 45E
Alingaabro 73 56 56N 10 32E
Alingsås 73 57 56N 12 31E
Alipore 95 22 32N 88 24E
Alipur 94 29 25N 70 55E
Alipur Duar 98 26 30N 89 35E
Aliquippa 156 40 38N 80 18W
Aliste, R. 56 41 48N 6 14W
Alivérion 69 38 24N 24 2E
Aliwal North 128 30 45S 26 45E
Alix 152 52 24N 113 11W
Aljezur 57 37 18N 8 49W
Aljustrel 57 37 55N 8 10W
Alkamari 121 13 27N 11 10E
Alken 47 50 53N 5 18E
Alkhalaf 91 20 30N 58 13E
Alkmaar 46 52 37N 4 45E
All American Canal 161 32 45N 115 0W
Allada 121 6 41N 2 9E
Allah Dad 94 25 38N 67 34E
Allahabad 95 25 25N 81 58E
Allakaket 147 66 30N 152 45W
Allakh Yun 77 60 50N 137 5E
Allal Razi 118 34 30N 6 39W
Allan 153 51 53N 106 4W
Allanche 44 45 14N 2 57E
Allanmyo 98 19 16N 95 17E
Allanridge 128 27 45S 26 40E
Allansford 140 38 26S 142 39E
Allanton 143 45 55S 170 15E
Allanwater 150 50 14N 90 10W
Allaqi, Wadi 122 22 15N 34 55E
Allard Lake 151 50 40N 63 10W
Allariz 56 42 11N 7 50W
Allassac 44 45 15N 1 29E
Alle 47 49 51N 4 58E
Allegan 156 42 32N 85 52W
Allegheny Mts. 156 38 0N 80 0W
Allegheny, R. 156 41 14N 79 50W
Allègre 44 45 12N 3 41E
Allen, Bog of 39 53 15N 7 0W
Allen, L. 38 54 30N 8 5W
Allen R. 35 54 53N 2 13W
Allenby (Hussein) Bridge 90 31 53N 35 33E
Allendale 35 54 55N 2 15W
Allende 164 28 20N 100 50W
Allenheads 35 54 49N 2 12W
Allentown 162 40 36N 75 30W
Allentsteig 52 48 41N 15 20E
Allenwood 39 53 16N 6 53W
Alleppey 97 9 30N 76 28E
Allerōd 73 55 54N 12 19E
Alleur 47 50 39N 5 31E
Allevard 45 45 24N 6 5E
Alliance, Nebr., U.S.A. 158 42 10N 102 50W
Alliance, Ohio, U.S.A. 156 40 53N 81 7W
Allier □ 44 46 25N 3 0E
Allier, R. 43 46 57N 3 4E
Alligator Cr., Queens., Austral. 138 21 20S 149 12E
Alligator Cr., Queens., Austral. 138 19 23S 146 58E
Allihies 39 51 39N 10 4W
Allingåbrl 73 56 28N 10 20E
Allingåbro 73 56 28N 10 20E
Allinge 73 55 17N 14 50E
Alliston 150 44 9N 79 52W
Alloa 35 56 7N 3 49W
Allonby 32 54 45N 3 27W
Allos 45 44 15N 6 38E
Alma, Can. 151 48 35N 71 40W
Alma, Kans., U.S.A. 158 39 1N 96 22W
Alma, Mich., U.S.A. 156 43 25N 84 40W
Alma, Nebr., U.S.A. 158 40 10N 99 25W
Alma, Wis., U.S.A. 158 44 19N 91 54W
Alma Ata 85 43 15N 76 57E
Almada 57 38 40N 9 9W
Almaden 138 17 22S 144 40E

Almadén **Amungen**

Almadén	**57**	38 49N	4 52W
Almagro	**57**	38 50N	3 45W
Almalyk	**85**	40 50N	69 35E
Almanor, L.	**160**	40 15N	121 11W
Almansa	**59**	38 51N	1 5W
Almanza	**56**	42 39N	5 3W
Almanzor, Pico de	**56**	40 15N	5 18W
Almanzora, R.	**59**	37 22N	2 21W
Almarcha, La	**58**	39 41N	2 24W
Almas	**171**	11 33S	47 9W
Almaş, Mţii	**70**	44 49N	22 12E
Almazán	**58**	41 30N	2 30W
Almazora	**58**	39 57N	0 3W
Almeirim, Brazil	**175**	1 30S	52 0W
Almeirim, Port.	**57**	39 12N	8 37W
Almelo	**46**	52 22N	6 42E
Almenar	**58**	41 43N	2 12W
Almenara, Brazil	**171**	16 11S	40 42W
Almenara, Spain	**58**	39 46N	0 14W
Almenara, Sierra de	**59**	37 34N	1 32W
Almendralejo	**57**	38 41N	6 26W
Almería	**59**	36 52N	2 32W
Almería □	**59**	37 20N	2 20W
Almería, G. de	**59**	36 41N	2 28W
Almetyevsk	**84**	54 53N	52 20E
Almhult	**73**	56 32N	14 10E
Almirante	**166**	9 10N	82 30W
Almiropótamos	**69**	38 16N	24 11E
Almirós	**69**	39 11N	22 45E
Almodôvar	**57**	37 31N	8 2W
Almodóvar del Campo	**57**	38 43N	4 10W
Almogia	**57**	36 50N	4 32W
Almonaster la Real	**57**	37 52N	6 48W
Almond R.	**35**	56 27N	3 27W
Almondsbury	**28**	51 33N	2 34W
Almonte, R.	**57**	39 41N	6 12W
Almora	**95**	29 38N	79 4E
Almoradi	**59**	38 7N	0 46W
Almorox	**56**	40 14N	4 24W
Almoustarat	**121**	17 35N	0 8E
Älmult	**73**	56 33N	14 8E
Almuñécar	**57**	36 43N	3 41W
Almunia, La de Doña Godina	**58**	41 29N	1 23W
Almvik	**73**	57 49N	16 30E
Aln, R.	**35**	55 24N	1 35W
Alness	**37**	57 41N	4 15W
Alness R.	**37**	57 45N	4 20W
Alnif	**118**	31 10N	5 8W
Alnmouth	**35**	55 24N	1 37W
Alnön I.	**72**	62 26N	17 33E
Alnwick	**35**	55 25N	1 42W
Aloi	**126**	2 16N	33 10E
Alon	**98**	22 12N	95 5E
Alonsa	**153**	50 50N	99 0W
Alor, I.	**103**	8 15S	124 30E
Alor Setar	**101**	6 7N	100 22E
Alora	**57**	36 49N	4 46W
Alosno	**57**	37 33N	7 7W
Alot'ai	**105**	47 52N	88 7E
Alotau	**135**	10 16S	150 30E
Alougoum	**118**	30 17N	6 56W
Aloysius Mt.	**137**	26 0S	128 38E
Alpaugh	**163**	35 53N	119 29W
Alpedrinha	**56**	40 6N	7 27W
Alpena	**156**	45 6N	83 24W
Alpercatas, R.	**170**	6 2S	44 19W
Alpes-de-Haute-Provence □	**45**	44 8N	6 10E
Alpes-Maritimes □	**45**	43 55N	7 10E
Alpes Valaisannes	**50**	46 4N	7 30E
Alpha	**138**	23 39S	146 37E
Alphen	**47**	51 29N	4 58E
Alphen aan den Rijn	**46**	52 7N	4 40E
Alphington	**30**	50 41N	3 32W
Alpi Apuan	**62**	44 7N	10 14E
Alpi Craie	**43**	45 40N	7 0E
Alpi Lepontine	**51**	46 22N	8 27E
Alpi Orobie	**62**	46 7N	10 0E
Alpi Retiche	**51**	46 45N	10 0E
Alpiarça	**57**	39 15N	8 35W
Alpine, Ariz., U.S.A.	**161**	33 57N	109 4W
Alpine, Calif., U.S.A.	**163**	32 50N	116 46W
Alpine, Tex., U.S.A.	**159**	30 35N	103 35W
Alpnach	**51**	46 57N	8 17E
Alrewas	**28**	52 43N	1 44W
Alrø	**73**	55 52N	10 5E
Alroy Downs	**138**	19 20S	136 5E
Als	**73**	56 46N	10 18E
Alsace	**43**	48 15N	7 25E
Alsager	**32**	53 7N	2 20W
Alsask	**153**	51 21N	109 59W
Alsásua	**58**	42 54N	2 10W
Alseda	**73**	57 27N	15 20E
Alsen	**72**	63 23N	13 56E
Alsfeld	**48**	50 44N	9 19E
Alsh, L.	**36**	57 15N	5 39W
Alsónémedi	**53**	47 34N	19 15E
Alsten	**74**	65 58N	12 40E
Alston	**32**	54 48N	2 26W
Alta	**74**	69 57N	23 10E
Alta Gracia	**172**	31 40S	64 30W
Alta Lake	**152**	50 10N	123 0W
Alta, Sierra	**58**	40 31N	1 30W
Alta Sierra	**163**	35 42N	118 33W
Altaelva	**74**	69 46N	23 45E
Altafjorden	**74**	70 5N	23 5E
Altagracia	**174**	10 45N	71 30W
Altai = Aerht'ai Shan	**105**	48 0N	90 0E
Altamaha, R.	**157**	31 50N	82 0W
Altamira, Brazil	**175**	3 0S	52 10W
Altamira, Chile	**172**	25 47S	69 51W
Altamira, Colomb.	**174**	2 3N	75 47W
Altamira, Mexico	**165**	22 24N	97 55W
Altamira, Cuevas de	**56**	43 20N	4 5W
Altamont	**162**	42 43N	74 3W
Altamura	**65**	40 50N	16 33E
Altanbulag	**54**	50 19N	106 30E
Altar	**164**	30 40N	111 50W
Altarnun	**30**	50 35N	4 30W
Altata	**164**	24 30N	108 0W
Altavista	**156**	37 9N	79 22W
Altdorf	**51**	46 52N	8 36E
Altea	**59**	38 38N	0 2W
Altenberg	**48**	50 46N	13 47E
Altenbruch	**48**	53 48N	8 44E
Altenburg	**48**	50 59N	12 28E
Altenkirchen	**48**	50 41N	7 38E
Altenmarkt	**52**	47 43N	14 39E
Alter do Chão	**57**	39 12N	7 40W
Altkirch	**43**	47 37N	7 15E
Altnaharra	**37**	58 17N	4 27W
Alto Adige = Trentino-Alto Adige	**62**	46 5N	11 0E
Alto Araguaia	**175**	17 15S	53 20W
Alto Chindio	**127**	16 19S	35 25E
Alto Cuchumatanes	**164**	15 30N	91 10W
Alto del Inca	**172**	24 10S	68 10W
Alto Ligonha	**127**	15 30S	38 11E
Alto Molocue	**127**	15 50S	37 35E
Alto Paraná □	**173**	25 0S	54 50W
Alto Parnaíba	**170**	9 6S	45 57W
Alto Santo	**170**	5 31S	38 15W
Alto Turi	**170**	2 54S	45 38W
Alto Uruguay, R.	**173**	27 0S	53 30W
Alton, U.K.	**29**	51 8N	0 59W
Alton, Ill., U.S.A.	**158**	38 55N	90 5W
Alton, N.H., U.S.A.	**162**	43 27N	71 13W
Alton Downs	**139**	26 7S	138 57E
Altona	**48**	53 32N	9 56E
Altoona	**156**	40 32N	78 24W
Altopáscio	**62**	43 50N	10 40E
Altos	**170**	5 3S	42 28W
Altrincham	**32**	53 25N	2 21W
Altstätten	**51**	47 22N	9 33E
Alturas	**160**	41 36N	120 37W
Altus	**159**	34 30N	99 25W
Alucra	**83**	40 22N	38 47E
Aluksône	**80**	57 24N	27 3E
Alula	**91**	11 50N	50 45E
Alupka	**82**	44 23N	34 2E
Alushta	**82**	44 40N	34 25E
Alusi	**103**	7 35S	131 40E
Alustante	**58**	40 36N	1 40W
Alva, U.K.	**35**	56 9N	3 49W
Alva, U.S.A.	**159**	36 50N	98 50W
Alvaiázere	**56**	39 49N	8 23W
Älvangen	**73**	58 0N	12 7E
Alvängen	**73**	57 58N	12 8E
Alvarado, Mexico	**165**	18 40N	95 50W
Alvarado, U.S.A.	**159**	32 25N	97 15W
Alvaro Obregón, Presa	**164**	27 55N	109 52W
Alvastra	**73**	58 20N	14 44E
Alvdal	**71**	62 6N	10 37E
Alvear	**172**	29 5S	56 30W
Alvechurch	**28**	52 22N	1 58W
Alverca	**57**	38 56N	9 1W
Alveringen	**47**	51 1N	2 43E
Älvesta	**73**	56 54N	14 35E
Alvho	**72**	61 30N	14 45E
Alvie, Austral.	**140**	38 14S	143 30E
Alvie, U.K.	**37**	57 10N	3 50W
Alvin	**159**	29 23N	95 12W
Alvito	**57**	38 15N	8 0W
Älvkarleby	**75**	60 32N	17 40E
Alvra, Pic d'	**51**	46 35N	9 50E
Alvros	**72**	62 3N	14 38E
Älvsborgs län □	**73**	58 30N	12 30E
Älvsby	**74**	65 42N	20 52E
Älvsbyn	**74**	65 40N	20 0E
Alvsered	**73**	57 14N	12 51E
Alwar	**94**	27 38N	76 34E
Alwaye	**97**	10 8N	76 24E
Alwinton	**35**	55 20N	2 7W
Alwyn, oilfield	**19**	60 30N	1 45E
Alyangula	**133**	13 55S	136 30E
Alyaskitovyy	**77**	64 45N	141 30E
Alyata	**83**	39 58N	49 25E
Alyth	**37**	56 38N	3 15W
Alzada	**158**	45 3N	104 22W
Alzano Lombardo	**62**	45 44N	9 43E
Alzette, R.	**47**	49 45N	6 6E
Alzey	**49**	49 48N	8 4E
Am-Dam	**117**	12 40N	20 35E
Am Djeress	**117**	16 15N	22 50E
Am Guereda	**117**	12 53N	21 14E
Am Timan	**117**	11 0N	20 10E
Am-Zoer	**124**	14 13N	21 23E
Amadeus, L.	**137**	24 54S	131 0E
Amadi, Congo	**126**	3 40N	26 40E
Amadi, Sudan	**123**	5 29N	30 25E
Amadi, Zaïre	**126**	3 40N	26 40E
Amadia	**92**	37 6N	43 30E
Amadjuak	**149**	64 0N	72 39W
Amadjuak L.	**149**	65 0N	71 8W
Amadora	**57**	38 45N	9 13W
Amaga	**174**	6 3N	75 42W
Amagansett	**162**	40 58N	72 8W
Amagasaki	**111**	34 42N	135 20E
Amager	**73**	55 37N	12 35E
Amagi	**110**	33 25N	130 39E
Amagunze	**121**	6 20N	7 40E
Amaimon	**135**	5 12S	145 30E
Amakusa-Nada	**110**	32 35N	130 5E
Amakusa-Shotō	**110**	32 15N	130 10E
Amål	**72**	59 2N	12 40E
Åmål	**72**	59 3N	12 42E
Amalapuram	**96**	16 35N	81 55E
Amalfi, Colomb.	**174**	6 55N	75 4W
Amalfi, Italy	**65**	40 39N	14 34E
Amaliás	**69**	37 47N	21 22E
Amalner	**96**	21 5N	75 5E
Amambaí	**173**	23 5S	55 13W
Amambaí, R.	**173**	23 22S	53 56W
Amambay □	**173**	23 0S	56 0W
Amambay, Cordillera de	**173**	20 30S	56 0W
Amami-O-Shima	**112**	28 0N	129 0E
Amanab	**135**	3 40S	141 14E
Amandola	**63**	42 59N	13 21E
Amanfrom	**121**	7 20N	0 25E
Amangeldy	**76**	50 10N	65 10E
Amantea	**65**	39 8N	16 3E
Amapá	**170**	2 5N	50 50W
Amapá □	**170**	1 40N	52 0W
Amar Gedid	**123**	14 27N	25 13E
Amara, Iraq	**92**	31 57N	47 12E
Amara, Sudan	**123**	10 25N	34 10E
Amarante, Brazil	**170**	6 14S	42 50W
Amarante, Port.	**56**	41 16N	8 5W
Amarante do Maranhão	**170**	5 36S	46 45W
Amaranth	**153**	50 36N	98 43W
Amarapura	**98**	21 54N	96 3E
Amaravati, R.	**97**	10 50N	77 42E
Amaravati = Amraoti	**96**	20 55N	77 45E
Amareleja	**57**	38 12N	7 13W
Amargosa	**171**	13 2S	39 36W
Amargosa, R.	**163**	36 14N	116 51W
Amargosa Ra., mts	**163**	36 25N	116 40W
Amarillo	**159**	35 14N	101 46W
Amaro Leite	**171**	13 58S	49 9W
Amaro, Mt.	**63**	42 5N	14 6E
Amarpur, India	**99**	23 30N	91 45E
Amarpur, Bihar, India	**95**	25 5N	87 0E
Amarpur, Tripura, India	**99**	23 30N	91 45E
Amasra	**92**	41 45N	32 30E
Amassama	**121**	5 1N	6 2E
Amasya	**92**	40 40N	35 50E
Amatignak I.	**147**	51 19N	179 10W
Amatikulu	**129**	29 3S	31 33E
Amatitlán	**166**	14 29N	90 38W
Amatrice	**63**	42 38N	13 16E
Amay	**47**	50 33N	5 19E
Amazon, R.	**175**	2 0S	53 30W
Amazonas □, Brazil	**174**	4 20S	64 0W
Amazonas □, Colomb.	**174**	1 0S	72 0W
Amazonas □, Venez.	**174**	3 30N	66 0W
Amazonas, R.	**175**	2 0S	53 30W
Ambad	**96**	19 38N	75 50E
Ambahakily	**129**	21 36S	43 41E
Ambala	**94**	30 23N	76 56E
Ambalangoda	**97**	6 15N	80 5E
Ambalapuzha	**97**	9 25N	76 25E
Ambalavao	**129**	21 50S	46 56E
Ambalindum	**138**	23 23S	134 40E
Ambam	**124**	2 20N	11 15E
Ambanifilao	**129**	12 48S	49 47E
Ambanja	**129**	13 40S	48 27E
Ambararata	**129**	13 41S	48 27E
Ambarchik	**77**	69 40N	162 20E
Ambarijeby	**129**	14 56S	47 41E
Ambarnath	**96**	19 12N	73 22E
Ambaro, B. d'	**129**	13 23S	48 38E
Ambasamudram	**97**	8 43N	77 25E
Ambato	**174**	1 5S	78 42W
Ambato-Boéni	**129**	16 28S	46 43E
Ambato, Sierra de	**172**	28 25N	66 10W
Ambatolampy	**129**	19 20S	47 35E
Ambatondrazaka	**129**	17 55S	48 28E
Ambatosoratra	**129**	17 37S	48 31E
Ambenja	**129**	15 17S	46 58E
Ambeno	**103**	9 20S	124 30E
Amberg	**49**	49 25N	11 52E
Ambergris Cay	**165**	18 0N	88 0W
Ambérieu-en-Bugey	**45**	45 57N	5 20E
Amberley	**143**	43 9S	172 44E
Ambert	**44**	45 33N	3 44E
Ambevongo	**129**	15 25S	42 26E
Ambia	**129**	16 11S	45 33E
Ambidédi	**120**	14 35N	11 47W
Ambikapur	**95**	23 15N	83 15E
Ambikol	**122**	21 20N	30 50E
Ambilobé	**125**	13 10S	49 3E
Ambinanindrano	**129**	20 5S	48 23E
Ambjörnarp	**73**	57 25N	13 17E
Amble	**35**	55 20N	1 36W
Ambler	**162**	40 9N	75 13W
Ambleside	**32**	54 26N	2 58W
Amblève	**47**	50 21N	6 10E
Amblève, R.	**47**	50 25N	5 45E
Ambo, Begemdir & Simen, Ethiopia	**123**	12 20N	37 30E
Ambo, Shewa, Ethiopia	**123**	9 0N	37 48E
Ambo, Peru	**174**	10 5S	76 10W
Ambodifototra	**129**	16 59S	49 52E
Ambodilazana	**129**	18 6S	49 10E
Ambohimahasoa	**129**	21 7S	47 13E
Ambohimanga du Sud	**129**	20 52S	47 36E
Ambon	**103**	3 35S	128 20E
Ambongao, Cones d'	**129**	17 0S	45 0E
Amboseli L.	**126**	2 40S	37 10E
Ambositra	**129**	20 31S	47 25E
Amboy	**163**	34 33N	115 51W
Ambre, C. d'	**129**	12 40S	49 10E
Ambre, Mt. d'	**125**	12 30S	49 10E
Ambriz	**124**	7 48S	13 8E
Ambrizete	**124**	7 10S	12 52E
Ambunti	**135**	4 13S	142 52E
Ambut	**97**	12 48N	78 43E
Amby	**139**	26 30S	148 11E
Amchitka I.	**147**	51 30N	179 0W
Amchitka P.	**147**	51 30N	179 0W
Amderma	**76**	69 45N	61 30E
Ameca	**164**	20 30N	104 0W
Ameca, R.	**164**	20 40N	105 15W
Amecameca	**165**	19 10N	98 57W
Ameland	**46**	53 27N	5 45E
Amélia	**63**	42 34N	12 25E
Amèlie-les-Bains-Palalda	**44**	42 29N	2 41E
Amen	**77**	68 45N	180 0E
Amendolaro	**65**	39 58N	16 34E
Amenia	**162**	41 51N	73 33W
America	**47**	51 27N	5 59E
American Falls	**160**	42 46N	112 56W
American Falls Res.	**160**	43 0N	112 50W
American Highland	**13**	73 0S	75 0E
Americana	**173**	22 45S	47 20W
Americus	**157**	32 0N	84 10W
Amersfoort, Neth.	**46**	52 9N	5 23E
Amersfoort, S. Afr.	**129**	26 59S	29 53E
Amersham	**29**	51 40N	0 38W
Amery, Austral.	**137**	31 9S	117 5E
Amery, Can.	**153**	56 34N	94 3W
Ames	**158**	42 0N	93 40W
Amesbury, U.K.	**28**	51 10N	1 46W
Amesbury, U.S.A.	**162**	42 50N	70 52W
Amesdale	**153**	50 2N	92 55W
Ameson	**150**	49 50N	84 35W
Amethyst, gasfield	**19**	53 38N	0 40E
Amfiklia	**69**	38 38N	22 35E
Amfilokhía	**69**	38 52N	21 9E
Amfipolis	**68**	40 48N	23 52E
Ámfissa	**69**	38 32N	22 22E
Amga, R.	**77**	61 0N	132 0E
Amgu	**77**	45 45N	137 15E
Amherst, Burma	**99**	16 2N	97 20E
Amherst, Can.	**151**	45 48N	64 8W
Amherst, Mass., U.S.A.	**162**	42 21N	72 30W
Amherst, Tex., U.S.A.	**159**	34 0N	102 24W
Amherst, Mt.	**136**	18 11S	126 59E
Amherstburg	**150**	42 6N	83 6W
Amiata Mte.	**63**	42 54N	11 40E
Amiens	**43**	49 54N	2 16E
Amigdhalokefáli	**69**	35 23N	23 30E
Amili	**98**	28 25N	95 52E
Amindaion	**68**	40 42N	21 42E
Amirante Is.	**11**	6 0S	53 0E
Amisk L.	**153**	54 35N	102 15W
Amistati, Presa	**164**	29 24N	101 0W
Amite	**159**	30 47N	90 31W
Åmli	**71**	58 45N	8 32E
Amlia I.	**147**	52 5N	173 30W
Amlwch	**31**	53 24N	4 21W
Amm Adam	**123**	16 20N	36 1E
'Ammān	**90**	32 0N	35 52E
Ammanford	**31**	51 48N	4 0W
Ammerån	**72**	63 9N	16 13E
Ammerån	**72**	63 9N	16 13E
Ammersee	**49**	48 0N	11 7E
Ammerzoden	**46**	51 45N	5 13E
Ammi'ad	**90**	32 55N	35 32E
Amnat Charoen	**100**	15 51N	104 38E
Amne Machin	**105**	34 30N	100 0E
Amnéville	**43**	49 16N	6 9E
Amo Chiang, R.	**108**	22 56N	101 47E
Amorebieta	**58**	43 13N	2 44W
Amorgós	**69**	36 50N	25 57E
Amory	**57**	33 59N	88 30W
Amos	**150**	48 35N	78 5W
Åmot	**71**	59 54N	9 54E
Åmot	**71**	59 34N	8 0E
Åmotsdal	**71**	59 37N	8 26E
Amour, Djebel	**118**	33 42N	1 37E
Amoy = Hsiamen	**109**	24 25N	118 4E
Amozoc	**165**	19 2N	98 3W
Ampang	**101**	3 8N	101 45E
Ampanihy	**129**	24 40S	44 45E
Amparihy Est.	**129**	23 57S	47 20E
Ampasindava, B. d'	**129**	13 40S	48 15E
Ampasindava, Presqu'île d'	**129**	13 42S	47 55W
Amper	**121**	9 25N	9 40E
Ampère	**119**	35 44N	5 27E
Ampleforth	**33**	54 13N	1 8W
Ampombiantambo	**129**	12 42S	48 57E
Amposta	**58**	40 43N	0 34E
Ampotaka	**129**	25 3S	44 41E
Ampoza	**129**	22 20S	44 44E
Ampthill	**29**	52 3N	0 30W
Amqa	**90**	32 59N	35 10E
Amqui	**151**	48 28N	67 27W
Amraoti	**96**	20 55N	77 45E
Amreli	**94**	21 35N	71 17E
Amrenene el Kasba	**118**	22 10N	0 30E
Amriswil	**51**	47 33N	9 18E
Amritsar	**94**	31 35N	74 57E
Amroha	**95**	28 53N	78 30E
Amrum	**48**	54 37N	8 21E
Amsel	**119**	22 47N	5 29E
Amsterdam, Neth.	**46**	52 23N	4 54E
Amsterdam, U.S.A.	**162**	42 58N	74 10W
Amsterdam, Ī.	**11**	37 30S	77 30E
Amstetten	**52**	48 7N	14 51E
Amu Darya, R.	**76**	37 50N	65 0E
Amuay	**174**	11 50N	70 10W
Amukta I.	**147**	52 29N	171 20W
Amund Ringnes I.	**12**	78 20N	96 25W
Amundsen Gulf	**148**	71 0N	124 0W
Amundsen Sea	**13**	72 0S	115 0W
Amungen	**72**	61 10N	15 40E

Amuntai Anza

Amuntai 102 2 28S 115 25E
Amur, R. 77 53 30N 122 30E
Amurang 103 1 5N 124 40E
Amuri Pass 143 42 31S 172 11E
Amurrio 58 43 3N 3 0W
Amurzet 77 47 50N 131 5E
Amusco 56 42 10N 4 28W
Amvrakikós Kólpos 69 39 0N 20 55E
Amvrosiyvka 83 47 43N 38 30E
Amzeglouf 118 26 50N 0 1E
An 98 22 29N 96 54E
An Bien 101 9 45N 105 0E
An Geata Mór, (Binghamstown) 38 54 13N 10 0W
An Hoa 100 15 30N 108 20E
An Loc 101 11 40N 106 50E
An Nafud 92 28 15N 41 0E
An Najaf 92 32 3N 44 15E
An-Nāqūrah 90 33 7N 35 8E
An Nasiriyah 92 31 0N 46 15E
An Nawfaliyah 119 30 54N 17 58E
An Nhon (Binh Dinh) 100 13 55N 109 7E
An Nîl □ 123 17 30N 33 0E
An Nîl el Abyad □ 123 14 0N 32 15E
An Nu'ayriyah 92 27 30N 48 30E
An Teallach, Mt. 36 57 49N 5 18W
An Thoi, Dao 101 9 58N 104 0E
An Tuc 100 13 57N 108 39E
An Uaimh 38 53 39N 6 40W
Ana-Sira 71 58 17N 6 25E
Anabta 90 32 19N 35 7E
Anabuki 110 34 2N 134 11E
Anaco 174 9 27N 64 28W
Anaconda 160 46 7N 113 0W
Anacortes 160 48 30N 122 40W
Anadarko 159 35 4N 98 15W
Anadia, Brazil 170 9 42S 36 18W
Anadia, Port. 56 40 26N 8 27W
Anadolu 92 38 0N 29 0E
Anadyr 77 64 35N 177 20E
Anadyr, R. 77 66 50N 171 0E
Anadyrskiy Zaliv 77 64 0N 180 0E
Anáfi 69 36 22N 25 48E
Anafópoulo 69 36 17N 25 50E
Anagni 64 41 44N 13 8E
Anah 92 34 25N 42 0E
Anaheim 163 33 50N 118 0W
Anahim Lake 152 52 28N 125 18W
Anáhuac 164 27 14N 100 9W
Anai Mudi, Mt. 97 10 12N 77 20E
Anaimalai Hills 97 10 20N 76 40E
Anajás 170 0 59S 49 57W
Anajatuba 170 3 16S 44 37W
Anakapalle 96 17 42N 83 06E
Anakie 138 23 32S 147 45E
Anaklia 83 42 22N 41 35E
Analalava 129 14 35S 48 0E
Analapasy 129 25 11S 46 40E
Anam 121 6 19N 6 41E
Anambar, R. 94 30 10N 68 50E
Anambas, Kepulauan 102 3 20N 106 30E
Anamoose 158 47 55N 100 7W
Anamosa 158 42 7N 91 17W
Anamur 92 36 8N 32 58E
Anan 110 33 54N 134 40E
Anand 94 22 32N 72 59E
Anandpur 96 21 16N 86 13E
Anánes 69 36 33N 24 9E
Anantapur 97 14 39N 77 42E
Anantnag 95 33 45N 75 10E
Ananyev 82 47 44N 29 57E
Anapa 82 44 55N 37 25E
Anápolis 171 16 15S 48 50W
Anar 93 30 55N 55 13E
Anarak 93 33 25N 53 40E
Anatolia = Anadolu 92 38 0N 29 0E
Anatone 160 46 9N 117 4W
Añatuya 172 28 20S 62 50W
Anaunethad L. 153 60 55N 104 25W
Anaye 117 19 15N 12 50E
Anbyŏn 107 39 1N 127 35E
Ancaster 33 52 59N 0 32W
Ancenis 42 47 21N 1 10W
Anch'i 109 25 3N 118 13E
Anch'ing 109 30 37N 117 0E
Anch'iu 107 36 25N 119 10E
Ancholme, R. 33 53 42N 0 32W
Anchorage 147 61 10N 149 50W
Anciăo 56 39 56N 8 27W
Ancohuma, Nevada 174 16 0S 68 50W
Ancon 164 8 57N 79 33W
Ancón 174 11 50S 77 10W
Ancona 63 43 37N 13 30E
Ancrum 35 55 31N 2 35W
Ancud 176 42 0S 73 50W
Ancud, G. de 176 42 0S 73 0W
Andacollo, Argent. 172 37 10S 70 42W
Andacollo, Chile 172 30 15S 71 10W
Andado 138 25 25S 135 15E
Andalgalá 172 27 40S 66 30W
Åndalsnes 71 62 35N 7 43E
Andalucía 57 37 35N 5 0W
Andalusia 157 31 51N 86 30W
Andalusia = Andalucía 57 37 35N 5 0W
Andaman Is. 101 12 30N 92 30E
Andaman Sea 101 13 0N 96 0E
Andaman Str. 101 12 15N 92 20E
Andara 128 18 2S 21 9E
Andarai 171 12 48S 41 20W
Andeer 51 46 36N 9 26E
Andelfingen 51 47 36N 8 41E
Andelot 43 46 51N 5 56E
Andelys, Les 42 49 15N 1 25E
Andenne 47 50 30N 5 5E
Andéranboukane 121 15 26N 3 2E
Anderlecht 47 50 50N 4 19E
Anderlues 47 50 25N 4 16E
Andermatt 51 46 38N 8 35E
Andernach 48 50 24N 7 25E
Andernos 44 44 44N 1 6W
Anderslöv 73 55 26N 13 19E
Anderson, Austral. 141 38 32S 145 27E
Anderson, Calif., U.S.A. 160 40 30N 122 19W
Anderson, Ind., U.S.A. 156 40 5N 85 40W
Anderson, Mo., U.S.A. 159 36 43N 94 29W
Anderson, S.C., U.S.A. 157 34 32N 82 40W
Anderson, Mt. 129 25 5S 30 42E
Anderson, R. 147 69 42N 129 0W
Anderstorp 73 57 19N 13 39E
Andes 162 42 12N 74 47W
Andes, mts. 174 20 0S 68 0W
Andfjorden 74 69 10N 16 20E
Andhra, L. 96 18 30N 73 32E
Andhra Pradesh □ 97 15 0N 80 0E
Andikithira 69 35 52N 23 15E
Andimilos 69 36 47N 24 12E
Andiparos 69 37 0N 25 3E
Andipaxoi 69 39 9N 20 13E
Andipsara 69 38 30N 25 29E
Andizhan 76 41 10N 72 0E
Andkhui 93 36 52N 65 8E
Andohararo 129 22 58S 43 45E
Andol 96 17 51N 78 4E
Andong 107 36 40N 128 43E
Andorra ■ 58 42 30N 1 30E
Andorra La Vella 58 42 31N 1 32E
Andover, U.K. 28 51 13N 1 29W
Andover, U.S.A. 162 40 59N 74 44W
Andradina 171 20 54S 51 23W
Andrahary, Mt. 129 13 37S 49 17E
Andraitx 58 39 35N 2 25E
Andramasina 129 19 11S 47 35E
Andrano-Velona 129 18 10S 46 52E
Andranopasy 129 21 17S 43 44E
Andreanof Is. 147 51 0N 178 0W
Andreapol 80 56 40N 32 17E
Andreas 32 54 23N 4 25W
Andrespol 54 51 45N 19 34E
Andrew, oilfield 19 58 4N 1 24E
Andrews, S.C., U.S.A. 157 33 29N 79 30W
Andrews, Tex., U.S.A. 159 32 18N 102 33W
Andreyevka 84 52 19N 51 55E
Ándria 65 41 13N 16 17E
Andrian 65 46 30N 11 13E
Andriba 129 17 30S 46 58E
Andrijevica 66 42 45N 19 48E
Andrítsaina 69 37 29N 21 52E
Androka 129 24 58S 44 2E
Ándros 69 37 50N 24 50E
Andros I. 166 24 30N 78 0W
Andros Town 166 24 43N 77 47W
Andrychów 54 49 51N 19 18E
Andújar 57 38 3N 4 5W
Aneby 73 57 48N 14 49E
Anécho 121 6 12N 1 34E
Anegada I. 167 18 45N 64 20W
Anergane 118 31 4N 7 14W
Aneto, Pico de 58 42 37N 0 40E
Anfeg 119 22 29N 5 58E
Anfu 109 27 23N 114 37E
Ang Thong 100 14 35N 100 31E
Anga 77 60 35N 132 0E
Angamos, Punta 172 23 1S 70 32W
Anganch'i 98 47 9N 123 48E
Angara, R. 77 58 30N 97 0E
Angarsk 77 52 30N 104 0E
Angas Downs 137 24 49S 132 14E
Angas Ra. 137 23 0S 127 50E
Angaston 140 34 30S 139 8E
Ånge 72 62 31N 15 35E
Ångebo 72 61 58N 16 22E
Ángel de la Guarda, I. 164 29 30N 113 30W
Ängelholm 73 56 15N 12 58E
Angellala 139 26 24S 146 54E
Angels Camp 163 38 8N 120 30W
Ångelsberg 72 59 58N 16 0E
Angenong 99 31 57N 94 10E
Anger, R. 123 9 30N 36 35E
Angereb 123 13 11N 37 7E
Angereb, R. 123 14 0N 36 0E
Ångermanälven 72 62 40N 18 0E
Angermünde 48 53 1N 14 0E
Angers 42 47 30N 0 35W
Angerville 43 48 19N 2 0E
Angesån 74 66 50N 22 15E
Anghiari 63 43 32N 12 3E
Angical 171 12 0S 44 42W
Angical do Piauí 171 6 5S 42 44W
Angikuni L. 153 62 0N 100 0W
Angkor 100 13 22N 103 50E
Angle 31 51 40N 5 3W
Anglem Mt. 143 46 45S 167 53E
Anglès 58 41 57N 2 38E
Anglesey (□) 26 53 17N 4 20W
Anglesey, I. 31 53 17N 4 20W
Anglet 44 43 29N 1 31W
Angleton 159 29 12N 95 23W
Angleur 47 50 36N 5 35E
Anglure 43 48 35N 3 50E
Angmagssalik 12 65 40N 37 20W
Angmering 29 50 48N 0 28W
Ango 126 4 10N 26 5E
Angoche 127 16 8S 40 0E
Angoche, I. 127 16 20S 39 50E
Angol 172 37 56S 72 45W
Angola 156 41 40N 85 0W
Angola ■ 125 12 0S 18 0E
Angoon 147 57 40N 134 40W
Angoram 135 4 4S 144 4E
Angoulême 44 45 39N 0 10E
Angoumois 44 45 30N 0 25E
Angra dos Reis 173 23 0S 44 10W
Angra-Juntas 128 27 39S 15 31E
Angran 76 80 59N 69 3E
Angren 85 41 1N 70 12E
Angtassom 101 11 1N 104 41E
Angu 126 3 25N 24 28E
Anguilla ■ 167 18 14N 63 5W
Angurugu 138 14 0S 136 25E
Angus (□) 26 56 45N 2 55W
Angus, Braes of 37 56 51N 3 0W
Anhanduí, R. 173 21 46S 52 9W
Anhée 47 50 18N 4 53E
Anholt 73 56 42N 11 33E
Anhsi 105 40 30N 96 0E
Anhsiang 109 29 24N 112 9E
Anhua, Hunan, China 109 28 22N 111 10E
Anhua, Kwangsi-Chuang, China 108 25 10N 108 21E
Anhwei □ 109 33 15N 116 50E
Ani, Kiangsi, China 109 28 50N 115 32E
Ani, Shansi, China 106 35 3N 111 2E
Aniak 147 61 58N 159 50W
Anicuns 171 16 28S 49 58W
Ánidhros 69 36 38N 25 43E
Anié 121 7 42N 1 8E
Animas 161 31 58N 108 58W
Ånimskog 73 58 53N 12 35E
Anin 101 15 36N 97 50E
Anivorano 129 18 44S 48 58E
Anjangaon 96 21 10N 77 20E
Anjar 94 23 6N 70 10E
Anjen 109 26 42N 113 19E
Anjiabé 129 12 7S 49 20E
Anjidiv I. 97 14 40N 74 10E
Anjō 111 34 57N 137 5E
Anjou 42 47 20N 0 15W
Anjozorobe 129 18 22S 47 52E
Anju 107 39 36N 125 40E
Anka 121 12 13N 5 58E
Ank'ang 108 32 38N 109 5E
Ankara 92 40 0N 32 54E
Ankaramena 129 21 57S 46 39E
Ankazoabo 129 22 18S 44 31E
Ankazobé 129 18 20S 47 10E
Ankazotokana 129 21 20S 48 9E
Ankisabé 129 19 17S 46 29E
Anklesvar 96 21 38N 73 3E
Ankober 123 9 35N 39 40E
Ankoro 126 6 45S 26 55E
Ankuang 107 45 19N 123 40E
Ankuo 106 38 25N 115 19E
Anlu 109 31 12N 113 38E
Anlung 108 25 6N 106 31E
Anmyŏn Do 107 36 25N 126 25E
Ånn 72 63 19N 12 34E
Ann Arbor 156 42 17N 83 45W
Ann C., Antarct. 13 66 30S 50 30E
Ann C., U.S.A. 162 42 39N 70 37W
Ann, gasfield 19 53 40N 2 5E
Ånn L. 72 63 15N 12 35E
Anna, U.S.A. 159 37 28N 89 10W
Anna, U.S.S.R. 81 51 38N 40 23E
Anna Branch, R. 139 34 2S 141 50E
Anna Plains 136 19 17S 121 37E
Annaba 119 36 50N 7 46E
Annaberg-Buchholz 48 50 34N 12 58E
Annagassan 38 53 53N 6 20W
Annagh Hd. 38 54 15N 10 5W
Annaka 111 36 19N 138 54E
Annalee, R. 38 54 3N 7 15W
Annalong 38 54 7N 5 55W
Annam = Trung-Phan 101 16 30N 107 30E
Annamitique, Chaîne 100 17 0N 106 0E
Annan 35 55 0N 3 17W
Annan, R. 35 54 58N 3 18W
Annanberg 135 4 52S 144 42E
Annandale 35 55 10N 3 25W
Annapolis 162 39 0N 76 30W
Annapolis Royal 151 44 44N 65 32W
Annapurna 95 28 34N 83 50E
Annascaul 39 52 10N 10 3W
Anne, oilfield 19 55 24N 5 7E
Annean, L. 137 26 54S 118 14E
Anneberg 73 57 32N 12 6E
Annecy 45 45 55N 6 8E
Annecy, L. d' 45 45 52N 6 10E
Annemasse 45 46 12N 6 16E
Annestown 39 52 8N 7 18W
Annette 147 55 2N 131 35W
Annfield Plain 33 54 52N 1 45W
Annie Peak 137 33 53S 119 59E
Anning 108 24 58N 102 30E
Anningle 136 21 50S 133 7E
Anniston 157 33 45N 85 50W
Annobón 114 1 35S 3 35E
Annonay 45 45 15N 4 40E
Annonciation, L' 150 46 25N 74 55W
Annot 45 43 58N 6 38E
Annotto Bay 166 18 17N 77 3W
Annuello 140 34 53S 142 55E
Annville 162 40 18N 76 32W
Áno Arkhánai 69 35 16N 25 11E
Áno Porróia 68 41 17N 23 2E
Áno Viánnos 69 35 2N 25 21E
Anoka 158 45 10N 93 26W
Anorotsangana 129 13 56S 47 55E
Anp'ing, Hopei, China 106 38 13N 115 31E
Anp'ing, Liaoning, China 107 41 10N 123 30E
Ans 47 50 39N 5 32E
Ansai 106 36 54N 109 10E
Ansbach 49 49 17N 10 34E
Anse au Loup, L' 151 51 32N 56 50W
Anse, L' 150 46 47N 88 28W
Anseba, R. 123 16 15N 37 45E
Anserma 174 5 13N 75 48W
Anseroeul 47 50 43N 3 32E
Anshan 107 41 3N 122 58E
Anshun 105 26 2N 105 57E
Ansley 158 41 19N 99 24W
Ansó 58 42 51N 0 48W
Anson 159 32 46N 99 54W
Anson B. 136 13 20S 130 6E
Ansongo 121 15 25N 0 35E
Ansonia 162 41 21N 73 6W
Ansonville 150 48 46N 80 43W
Anstey 28 52 41N 1 14W
Anstey Hill 109 34 51S 138 44E
Anstruther 35 56 14N 2 40W
Ansudu 103 2 11S 139 22E
Antabamba 174 14 40S 73 0W
Antakya 92 36 14N 36 10E
Antalaha 129 14 57S 50 20E
Antalya 92 36 52N 30 45E
Antalya Körfezi 92 36 15N 31 30E
Antananarivo 125 18 55S 47 35E
Antanimbaribé 129 21 30S 44 48E
Antarctic Pen. 13 67 0S 60 0W
Antarctica 125 90 0S 0 0
Antela, Laguna 56 42 7N 7 40W
Antelope 127 21 2S 28 31E
Anten 73 58 5N 12 22E
Antenor Navarro 170 6 44S 38 27W
Antequera, Parag. 172 24 8S 57 7W
Antequera, Spain 57 37 5N 4 33W
Antero Mt. 161 38 45N 106 43W
Anthemoús 68 40 31N 23 15E
Anthony, Kans., U.S.A. 159 37 8N 98 2W
Anthony, N. Mex., U.S.A. 161 32 1N 106 37W
Anthony Lagoon 138 18 0S 135 30E
Anti Atlas, Mts. 118 30 30N 6 30W
Antibes 45 43 34N 7 6E
Antibes, C, d' 45 43 31N 7 7E
Anticosti, Î. de 151 49 30N 63 0W
Antifer, C. d' 42 49 41N 0 10E
Antigo 158 45 8N 89 5W
Antigonish 151 45 38N 61 58W
Antigua 166 14 34N 90 41W
Antigua Bahama, Canal de la 166 22 10N 77 30W
Antigua, I. 167 17 0N 61 50W
Antilla 166 20 40N 75 50W
Antimony 161 38 7N 112 0W
Antioch 163 38 7N 121 45W
Antioquia 174 6 40N 75 55W
Antioquia □ 174 7 0N 75 30W
Antipodes Is. 130 49 45S 178 40E
Antler 158 48 58N 101 18W
Antler, R. 153 49 8N 101 0W
Antlers 159 34 15N 95 35W
Antofagasta 172 23 50S 70 30W
Antofagasta □ 172 24 0S 69 0W
Antofagasta de la Sierra 172 26 5S 67 20W
Antofallá 172 25 30S 68 5W
Antofalla, Salar de 172 25 40S 67 45W
Antoing 47 50 34N 3 27E
Anton 159 33 49N 102 5W
Anton Chico 161 35 12N 105 5W
Antongil, B. d' 129 15 30S 49 50E
Antonibe 129 15 7S 47 24E
Antonibe, Presqu'île d' 129 15 30S 49 50E
Antonina 173 25 26S 48 42W
Antonito 161 37 4N 106 1W
Antonovo 83 49 25N 51 42E
Antony 30 50 22N 4 13W
Antrain 42 48 28N 1 30W
Antrim 38 54 43N 6 13W
Antrim □ 38 54 42N 6 20W
Antrim Co. 38 54 58N 6 20W
Antrim, Mts. of 38 54 57N 6 8W
Antrim Plateau 136 18 8S 128 20E
Antrodoco 63 42 25N 13 4E
Antropovo 81 58 26N 42 51E
Antsalova 129 18 40S 44 37E
Antse 106 36 15N 112 15E
Antsirabé 129 19 55S 47 2E
Antsohihy 129 14 50S 47 50E
Ant'u 107 43 6N 128 54E
Antung 107 40 10N 124 18E
Antungwei 107 35 10N 119 20E
Antwerp 140 36 17S 142 4E
Antwerp = Antwerpen 47 51 13N 4 25E
Antwerpen 47 51 13N 4 25E
Antwerpen □ 47 51 15N 4 40E
Antz'u 106 39 31N 116 41E
Anupgarh 94 29 10N 73 10E
Anuradhapura 97 8 22N 80 28E
Anvaing 47 50 41N 3 34E
Anvers = Antwerp(en) 47 51 13N 4 25E
Anvers I. 13 64 30S 63 40W
Anvik 147 62 37N 160 20W
Anxious B. 139 33 24S 134 45E
Anyama 120 5 30N 4 3W
Anyang 106 36 7N 114 26E
Anyer-Lor 103 6 6S 105 56E
Anyüan 109 25 9N 115 21E
Anza, Jordan 90 32 22N 35 12E
Anza, U.S.A. 163 33 35N 116 39W

Anza Borrego Desert State Park — Arizpe

Anza Borrego Desert State Park 163 33 0N 116 26W
Anzhero-Sudzhensk 76 56 10N 83 40 E
Ánzio 64 41 28N 12 37 E
Aoga-Shima 111 32 28N 139 46 E
Aoiz 58 42 46N 1 22W
Aomori 112 40 45N 140 45 E
Aomori-ken □ 112 40 45N 140 40 E
Aonla 95 28 16N 79 11 E
Aono-Yama 110 34 28N 131 48 E
Aorangi Mts. 142 41 49 S 175 22 E
Aoreora 118 28 51N 10 53W
Aosta 62 45 43N 7 20 E
Aoudéras 121 17 45N 8 20 E
Aouinet Torkoz 118 28 31N 9 46W
Aoukar □ 118 23 50N 2 45W
Aouker 120 23 48N 4 0W
Aoulef el Arab 118 26 55N 1 2 E
Aoullouz 118 30 44N 8 1W
Apa 108 32 55N 101 40 E
Apa, R. 172 22 6 S 58 2W
Apache, Ariz., U.S.A. 161 31 46N 109 6W
Apache, Okla., U.S.A. 159 34 53N 98 22W
Apahanuerhch'i 106 43 58N 116 2 E
Apalachee B. 157 30 0N 84 0W
Apalachicola 157 29 40N 85 0W
Apalachicola, R. 157 30 0N 85 0W
Apapa 121 6 25N 3 25 E
Apaporis, R. 174 0 30 S 70 30W
Aparecida do Taboado 171 20 5 S 51 5W
Aparri 103 18 22N 121 38 E
Aparurén 174 5 6N 62 8W
Apateu 70 46 36N 21 47 E
Apatin 66 45 40N 19 0 E
Apatzingán 164 19 0N 102 20W
Apeldoorn 46 52 13N 5 57 E
Apeldoornsch Kanal 46 52 29N 6 5 E
Apen 48 53 12N 7 47 E
Apenam 102 8 35 S 116 13 E
Apennines 16 44 20N 10 20 E
Apía 174 5 5N 75 58W
Apiacás, Serra dos 174 9 50 S 57 0W
Apiaí 174 24 31 S 48 50W
Apinajé 171 11 31 S 48 18W
Apiti 142 39 58 S 175 54 E
Apizaco 165 19 26N 98 9W
Aplahové 121 6 56N 1 41 E
Aplao 174 16 0 S 72 40W
Apo, Mt. 103 6 53N 125 14 E
Apodi 170 5 39 S 37 48W
Apolda 48 51 1N 11 30 E
Apollo Bay 140 38 45 S 143 40 E
Apollonia, Greece 69 36 58N 24 43 E
Apollonia, Libya 117 32 52N 21 59 E
Apolo 174 14 30 S 68 30W
Aporé, R. 171 19 27 S 50 57W
Aporema 170 1 14N 50 49W
Apostle Is. 158 46 50N 90 30W
Apóstoles 173 28 0 S 56 0W
Apostolovo 82 47 39N 33 39 E
Apoteri 174 4 2N 58 32W
Appalachian Mts. 156 38 0N 80 0W
Appelscha 46 52 57N 6 21 E
Appeninni 65 41 0N 15 0 E
Appeninno Ligure 62 44 30N 9 0 E
Appenzell 51 47 20N 9 25 E
Appenzell-Ausser Rhoden □ 51 47 23N 9 23 E
Appenzell-Inner Rhoden □ 51 47 20N 9 25 E
Appiano 63 46 27N 11 17 E
Appingedam 46 53 19N 6 51 E
Apple Valley 163 34 30N 117 11W
Appleby 32 54 35N 2 29W
Applecross 36 57 26N 5 50W
Applecross For. 36 57 27N 5 40W
Appledore, Devon, U.K. 30 51 3N 4 12W
Appledore, Kent, U.K. 29 51 2N 0 47 E
Appleton 156 44 17N 88 25W
Approuague 170 4 20N 52 0W
Apreivka 81 55 33N 37 4 E
Apricena 65 41 47N 15 25 E
Aprigliano 65 39 17N 16 19 E
Aprília 64 41 38N 12 38 E
Apsheronsk 83 44 28N 39 42 E
Apsley Str. 136 11 35 S 130 28 E
Apt 45 43 53N 5 24 E
Apucarana 173 23 55 S 51 33W
Apulia = Puglia 65 41 0N 16 30 E
Apure □ 174 7 10N 68 50W
Apure, R. 174 8 0N 69 20W
Apurímac, R. 174 12 10 S 73 30W
Apurito, R. 174 7 50N 67 0W
Apuseni, Munţii 70 46 30N 22 45 E
Aq Chah 93 37 0N 66 5 E
'Aqaba 122 29 31N 35 0 E
'Aqaba, Khalīj al 92 28 15N 33 20 E
Aqîq 122 18 14N 38 12 E
Aqîq, Khalîg 122 18 20N 38 10 E
'Aqraba 90 32 9N 35 20 E
'Aqrah 92 36 46N 43 45 E
Aquanish 151 50 14N 62 2W
Aquasco 162 38 35N 76 43W
Aquidaba 171 10 17 S 37 2W
Aquidauana 175 20 30 S 55 50W
Aquila, L' 63 42 21N 13 24 E
Aquiles Serdán 164 28 37N 105 54W
Aquin 167 18 16N 73 24W
Ar Ramadi 92 33 25N 43 20 E
Ar-Ramthā 90 32 34N 36 0 E
Ar Rass 92 25 50N 43 40 E
Ar Rifai 92 31 50N 46 10 E
Ar Riyād 92 24 41N 46 42 E
Ar Rub 'al Khālī 91 21 0N 51 0 E
Ar Rutbah 92 33 0N 40 15 E
Arab, Khalîg el 122 30 55N 29 0 E
Arab, Shott al 92 30 0N 48 31 E
Araba 121 13 7N 5 0 E
Arabatskaya Strelka 82 45 40N 35 0 E
Arabba 63 46 30N 11 51 E
Arabelo 174 4 55N 64 13W
Arabia 86 25 0N 45 0 E
Arabian Desert 122 28 0N 32 20 E
Arabian Sea 86 16 0N 65 0 E
Aracajú 170 10 55 S 37 4W
Aracataca 174 10 38N 74 9W
Aracati 170 4 30 S 37 44W
Araçatuba 173 21 10 S 50 30W
Aracena 57 37 53N 6 38W
Aracruz 171 19 49 S 40 16W
Araçuaí 171 16 52 S 42 4W
Araçuaí, R. 171 16 46 S 42 2W
Arad 66 46 10N 21 20 E
Arada 117 15 0N 20 20 E
Aradu Nou 66 46 8N 21 20 E
Arafura Sea 103 10 0 S 135 0 E
Aragats 83 40 30N 44 15 E
Aragón 58 41 25N 1 0W
Aragón, R. 58 42 35N 0 50W
Aragona 64 37 24N 13 36 E
Aragua □ 174 10 0N 67 10W
Aragua de Barcelona 174 9 28N 64 49W
Araguacema 170 8 50 S 49 20W
Araguaçu 171 12 49 S 49 51W
Araguaia, R. 170 7 0 S 49 15W
Araguaína 170 7 12 S 48 12W
Araguari 171 18 38 S 48 11W
Araguari, R. 170 1 0N 51 40W
Araguatins 170 5 38 S 48 7W
Araioses 170 2 53 S 41 55W
Arak 118 25 20N 3 45 E
Arāk 92 34 0N 49 40 E
Arakan □ 98 19 0N 94 15 E
Arakan Coast 99 19 0N 94 0 E
Arakan Yoma 98 20 0N 94 30 E
Arákhova 69 38 28N 22 35 E
Araks, R. = Aras, Rud-e 92 39 10N 47 10 E
Aral Sea = Aralskoye More 76 44 30N 60 0 E
Aralsk 76 46 50N 61 20 E
Aralskoye More 76 44 30N 60 0 E
Aramac 138 22 58 S 145 14 E
Arambagh 95 22 53N 87 48 E
Aramů, Mţii de 70 47 10N 22 30 E
Aran Fawddwy, Mt. 31 52 48N 3 40W
Aran, I. 38 55 0N 8 30W
Aran Is. 39 53 5N 9 42W
Aranci 64 41 5N 3 40W
Aranci, Golfo 64 41 0N 9 35 E
Aranda de Duero 58 41 39N 3 42W
Aranđelovac 66 44 18N 20 37 E
Aranga 142 35 44 S 173 40 E
Aranjuez 56 40 1N 3 40W
Aranos 125 24 9 S 19 7 E
Aransas Pass 159 28 0N 97 9W
Aranyaprathet 101 13 41N 102 30 E
Aranzazu 174 5 16N 75 30W
Arao 110 32 59N 130 25 E
Araouane 120 18 55N 3 30W
Arapahoe 158 40 22N 99 53W
Arapari 170 5 34 S 49 15W
Arapawa I. 131 41 13 S 174 20 E
Arapey Grande, R. 172 30 55 S 57 49W
Arapiraca 170 9 45 S 36 39W
Arapkir 92 39 5N 38 30 E
Arapongas 173 23 29 S 51 28W
Arapuni 130 38 3 S 175 37 E
Araranguá 173 29 0 S 49 30W
Araraquara 171 21 50 S 48 0W
Araras 173 5 15 S 60 35W
Ararás, Serra dos 173 25 0 S 53 10W
Ararat, Austral. 140 37 16 S 143 0 E
Ararat, Turkey 92 39 50N 44 15 E
Ararat, Mt. = Ağri Daği 92 39 50N 44 15 E
Arari 170 3 28 S 44 47W
Araria 95 26 9N 87 33 E
Araripe 171 7 12 S 40 8W
Araripe, Chapada do 170 7 20 S 40 0W
Araripina 170 7 33 S 40 34W
Araro 123 4 41N 38 50 E
Araruama, Lagoa de 173 22 53 S 42 12W
Araruna 170 6 52 S 35 44W
Åras 71 59 42N 10 31 E
Aras, Rud-e 92 39 10N 47 10 E
Araticu 170 1 58 S 49 51W
Arauca 174 7 0N 70 40W
Arauca □ 174 6 40N 71 0W
Arauca, R. 174 7 30N 69 0W
Arauco 172 37 16 S 73 25W
Arauco □ 172 37 40 S 73 25W
Araújos 171 19 56 S 45 14W
Arauquita 174 7 2N 71 25W
Araure 174 9 34N 69 13W
Arawa 123 9 57N 41 58 E
Arawhata 143 43 59 S 168 38 E
Arawhata, R. 143 44 0 S 168 40 E
Araxá 171 19 35 S 46 55W
Araya, Pen. de 174 10 40N 64 0W
Arba 123 9 0N 40 20 E
Arba Jahan 126 2 5N 39 2 E
Arba, L' 118 36 40N 3 9 E
Arba Minch 123 6 0N 37 30 E
Arbah, Wadi al 90 30 30N 35 5 E
Arbatax 64 39 57N 9 42 E
Arbedo 51 46 12N 9 3 E
Arbeláez 174 4 17N 74 26W
Arbīl 92 36 15N 44 5 E
Arboga 72 59 24N 15 52 E
Arbois 43 46 55N 5 46 E
Arbon 51 47 31N 9 26 E
Arbore 123 5 3N 36 50 E
Arborea 64 39 46N 8 34 E
Arborfield 153 53 6N 103 39W
Arborg 153 50 54N 97 13W
Arbrå 72 61 28N 16 22 E
Arbresle, L' 45 45 50N 4 26 E
Arbroath 37 56 34N 2 35W
Arbuckle 160 39 3N 122 2W
Arbus 64 39 30N 8 33 E
Arbuzinka 82 47 52N 31 25 E
Arc 43 47 28N 5 34 E
Arcachon 44 44 40N 1 10W
Arcachon, Bassin d' 44 44 42N 1 10W
Arcadia, Fla., U.S.A. 157 27 20N 81 50W
Arcadia, La., U.S.A. 159 32 34N 92 53W
Arcadia, Nebr., U.S.A. 158 41 29N 99 4W
Arcadia, Wis., U.S.A. 158 44 13N 91 29W
Arcata 160 40 55N 124 4W
Arcévia 63 43 29N 12 58 E
Archangel = Arkhangelsk 78 64 40N 41 0 E
Archar 66 43 50N 22 54 E
Archbald 162 41 30N 75 31W
Archena 59 38 9N 1 16W
Archer B. 138 13 20 S 141 30 E
Archer, R. 138 13 25 S 142 50 E
Archers Post 126 0 35N 37 35 E
Archidona 57 37 6N 4 22W
Archiestown 37 57 28N 3 20W
Arci, Monte 64 39 47N 8 44 E
Arcidosso 63 42 51N 11 30 E
Arcila = Asilah 118 35 29N 6 0W
Arcis-sur-Aube 43 48 32N 4 10 E
Arckaringa 139 27 56 S 134 45 E
Arckaringa Cr. 139 28 10 S 135 22 E
Arco, Italy 62 45 55N 10 54 E
Arco, U.S.A. 160 43 45N 113 16W
Arcola 153 49 40N 102 30W
Arcoona 140 31 2 S 137 1 E
Arcos, Brazil 171 20 17 S 45 32W
Arcos, Spain 58 41 12N 2 16W
Arcos de los Frontera 57 36 45N 5 49W
Arcot 97 12 53N 79 20 E
Arcoverde 170 8 25 S 37 4W
Arctic Ocean 12 78 0N 160 0W
Arctic Red, R. 147 66 0N 132 0W
Arctic Red River 147 67 15N 134 0W
Arctic Village 147 68 5N 145 45W
Arda, R., Bulg. 67 41 40N 25 40 E
Arda, R., Italy 62 44 53N 9 52 E
Ardabil 92 38 15N 48 18 E
Ardagh 39 52 30N 9 5W
Ardakan 93 30 20N 52 5 E
Årdal 71 59 9N 6 13 E
Ardales 57 36 53N 4 51W
Årdalstangen 71 61 14N 7 43 E
Ardara 38 54 47N 8 25W
Ardatov 81 54 51N 46 15 E
Ardavasar 36 57 3N 5 54 E
Ardbeg 34 55 38N 6 6W
Ardcath 38 53 36N 6 21W
Ardcharnich 36 57 52N 5 5W
Ardchyle 34 56 26N 4 24W
Ardèche □ 45 44 42N 4 16 E
Ardee 38 53 51N 6 32W
Arden Stby. 73 56 46N 9 52 E
Ardennes 47 49 30N 5 10 E
Ardennes □ 43 49 35N 4 40 E
Ardentes 43 46 45N 1 50 E
Ardentinny 34 56 3N 4 56 E
Arderin, Mt. 39 53 3N 7 40W
Ardestan 93 33 20N 52 25 E
Ardfert 39 52 20N 9 49W
Ardfinnan 39 52 20N 7 53W
Ardglass 38 54 16N 5 38W
Ardgour 36 56 45N 5 25W
Ardgroom 39 51 44N 9 53W
Árdhas, R. 68 41 36N 26 25 E
Ardhasig 36 57 55N 6 51W
Ardhéa 68 40 58N 22 3 E
Ardila, R. 57 38 10N 7 20W
Ardingly 29 51 3N 0 3W
Ardino 67 41 34N 25 9 E
Ardivachar Pt. 36 57 23N 7 25W
Ardkearagh 39 51 48N 10 11W
Ardkeen 38 54 27N 5 31W
Ardlethan 141 34 22 S 146 53 E
Ardlui 34 56 19N 4 43W
Ardmore, Austral. 138 21 39 S 139 11 E
Ardmore, Okla., U.S.A. 159 34 10N 97 5W
Ardmore, Pa., U.S.A. 162 39 58N 75 18W
Ardmore, S.D., U.S.A. 158 43 0N 103 40W
Ardmore Hd. 39 51 58N 7 43W
Ardmore Pt. 34 55 40N 6 0W
Ardnacrusha 39 52 43N 8 38W
Ardnamurchan, Pen. 36 56 43N 6 0W
Ardnamurchan Pt. 36 56 44N 6 14W
Ardnaree 38 54 6N 9 8W
Ardnave Pt. 34 55 54N 6 20W
Ardooie 47 50 59N 3 13 E
Ardore Marina 65 38 11N 16 10 E
Ardrahan 39 53 10N 8 48W
Ardres 43 50 50N 2 0 E
Ardrishaig 34 56 0N 5 27W
Ardrossan, Austral. 140 34 26 S 137 53 E
Ardrossan, U.K. 34 55 39N 4 50W
Ards □ 38 54 35N 5 30W
Ards Pen. 38 54 30N 5 25W
Ardud 70 47 37N 22 52 E
Ardunac 83 41 8N 42 5 E
Ardvoulie Castle 36 58 0N 6 45W
Ardwell 37 57 20N 3 5W
Åre 72 63 22N 13 15 E
Arecibo 147 18 29N 66 42W
Areia Branca 170 5 0 S 37 0W
Aremark 71 59 15N 11 42 E
Arena de la Ventana, Punta 164 24 4N 109 52W
Arenales, Cerro 176 47 5 S 73 40W
Arenas 56 43 17N 4 50W
Arenas de San Pedro 56 40 12N 5 5W
Arenas, Pta. 174 10 20N 62 39W
Arendal 71 58 28N 8 46 E
Arendonk 47 51 19N 5 5 E
Arendsee 48 52 52N 11 27 E
Arenig Fach, Mt. 31 52 55N 3 45 E
Arenig Fawr, Mt. 31 52 56N 3 45W
Arenys de Mar 58 41 35N 2 33 E
Arenzano 62 44 24N 8 40 E
Areópolis 69 36 40N 22 22 E
Arequipa 174 16 20 S 71 30W
Arero 123 4 41N 38 50 E
Arês 171 6 11 S 35 9W
Arès 44 44 47N 1 8W
Arévalo 56 41 3N 4 43W
Arezzo 63 43 28N 11 50 E
Arga, R. 58 42 30N 1 50W
Argalastí 68 39 13N 23 13 E
Argamasilla de Alba 59 39 8N 3 5W
Arganda 58 40 19N 3 26W
Arganil 56 40 13N 8 3W
Argayash 84 55 29N 60 52 E
Argelès-Gazost 44 43 0N 0 6W
Argelès-sur-Mer 44 42 34N 3 1 E
Argent-sur-Sauldre 43 47 33N 2 25 E
Argenta, Can. 152 50 20N 116 55W
Argenta, Italy 63 44 37N 11 50 E
Argentan 42 48 45N 0 1W
Argentário, Mte. 63 42 23N 11 11 E
Argentat 44 45 6N 1 56 E
Argentera 62 44 23N 6 58 E
Argenteuil 43 48 57N 2 14 E
Argentia 151 47 18N 53 58W
Argentiera, C. dell' 64 40 44N 8 8 E
Argentière, Aiguilles d' 50 45 58N 7 2 E
Argentina 174 0 34N 74 17W
Argentina ■ 176 35 0 S 66 0W
Argentino, L. 176 50 10 S 73 0W
Argenton-sur-Creuse 44 46 36N 1 30 E
Argentré 42 48 5N 0 40W
Argeş □ 70 45 0N 24 45 E
Argeş, R. 70 44 30N 25 50 E
Arghandab, R. 94 32 15N 66 23 E
Argo 122 19 28N 30 30 E
Argo, I. 122 19 28N 30 30 E
Argolikós Kólpos 69 37 20N 22 52 E
Argolís □ 69 37 38N 22 50 E
Argonne 43 49 0N 5 20 E
Árgos 69 37 40N 22 43 E
Árgos Orestikón 68 40 27N 21 26 E
Argostólion 69 38 12N 20 33 E
Arguedas 58 42 11N 1 36W
Arguello, Pt. 163 34 34N 120 40W
Argun, R. 77 53 20N 121 28 E
Argungu 121 12 40N 4 31 E
Argus Pk. 163 35 52N 117 26W
Argyle 158 48 23N 96 49W
Argyle Downs 136 16 17 S 128 47 E
Argyle, L. 136 16 20 S 128 40 E
Argyll (□) 26 56 18N 5 15W
Argyll, Dist. 34 56 14N 5 10W
Argyll, oilfield 19 56 8N 3 5 E
Argyrádhes 68 39 27N 19 58 E
Århus 73 56 8N 10 11 E
Aria 142 38 33 S 175 0 E
Ariamsvlei 128 28 9 S 19 51 E
Ariana 119 36 52N 10 12 E
Ariano Irpino 65 41 10N 15 4 E
Ariano nel Polèsine 63 44 56N 12 5 E
Aribinda 121 14 17N 0 52W
Arica, Chile 174 18 32 S 70 20W
Arica, Colomb. 174 2 0 S 71 50W
Arica, Peru 174 1 30 S 75 30W
Arid, C. 137 34 1 S 123 10 E
Arida 111 33 29N 135 44 E
Ariège □ 44 42 56N 1 30 E
Ariège, R. 44 42 56N 1 25 E
Arieş, R. 70 46 24N 23 20 E
Arilje 66 43 44N 20 7 E
Arima 167 10 38N 61 17W
Arinagour 34 56 38N 6 31W
Arinos, R. 174 11 15 S 57 0W
Ario de Rosales 164 19 12N 101 42W
Aripuanã 174 9 25 S 60 30W
Aripuanã, R. 174 7 30 S 60 25W
Ariquemes 174 9 55 S 63 6W
Arisaig 36 56 55N 5 50W
Arisaig, Sd. of 36 56 50N 5 50W
Arîsh, W. el 122 30 25N 34 52 E
Arismendi 174 8 29N 68 22W
Arissa 123 11 10N 41 35 E
Aristazabal, I. 152 52 40N 129 10W
Arita 110 33 11N 129 54 E
Arivaca 161 31 37N 111 25W
Arivonimamo 129 19 1 S 47 11 E
Ariyalur 97 11 8N 79 8 E
Ariza 58 41 19N 2 3W
Arizaro, Salar de 172 24 40 S 67 50W
Arizona 172 35 45 S 65 25W
Arizona □ 161 34 20N 111 30W
Arizpe 164 30 20N 110 11W

Arjang Atalaia

Arjang	72	59 24N	12 9E
Arjäng	72	59 24N	12 8E
Arjeplog	74	66 3N	18 2E
Arjona, Colomb.	174	10 14N	75 22W
Arjona, Spain	57	37 56N	4 4W
Arjuno	103	7 49S	112 19E
Arka	77	60 15N	142 0E
Arkadak	81	51 58N	43 19E
Arkadelphia	159	34 5N	93 0W
Arkadhia □	69	37 30N	22 20E
Arkaig, L.	36	56 58N	5 10W
Arkansas □	159	35 0N	92 30W
Arkansas City	159	37 4N	97 3W
Arkansas, R.	159	35 20N	93 30W
Árkathos, R.	68	39 20N	21 4E
Arkhángelos	69	36 13N	28 7E
Arkhangelsk	78	64 40N	41 0E
Arkhangelskoye	81	51 32N	40 58E
Arkiko	123	15 33N	39 30E
Arkle R.	32	54 25N	2 0W
Arklow	39	52 48N	6 10W
Arklow Hd.	39	52 46N	6 10W
Árkoi	69	37 24N	26 44E
Arkona, Kap	48	54 41N	13 26E
Arkonam	97	13 7N	79 43E
Arkösund	73	58 29N	16 56E
Arkoúdhi	69	38 33N	20 43E
Arkticheskiy, Mys	77	81 10N	95 0E
Arkul	84	57 17N	50 3E
Arkville	162	42 9N	74 37W
Arlanc	44	45 25N	3 42E
Arlanza, R.	56	42 6N	4 0W
Arlanzón, R.	56	42 12N	4 0W
Arlberg Pass	49	49 9N	10 12E
Arlee	160	47 10N	114 4W
Arles	45	43 41N	4 40E
Arlesheim	50	47 30N	7 37E
Arless	39	52 53N	7 1W
Arlington, S. Afr.	129	28 1S	27 53E
Arlington, Oreg., U.S.A.	160	45 48N	120 6W
Arlington, S.D., U.S.A.	158	44 25N	97 4W
Arlington, Va., U.S.A.	162	38 52N	77 5W
Arlington, Vt., U.S.A.	162	43 5N	73 9W
Arlington, Wash., U.S.A.	160	48 11N	122 4W
Arlon	47	49 42N	5 49E
Arlöv	73	55 38N	13 5E
Arly	121	11 35N	1 28E
Armadale, Austral.	137	32 12S	116 0E
Armadale, Lothian, U.K.	35	55 54N	3 42W
Armadale, Skye, U.K.	36	57 24N	5 54W
Armagh, Can.	137	46 41N	70 32W
Armagh, U.K.	38	54 22N	6 40W
Armagh □	38	54 18N	6 37W
Armagh Co.	38	54 16N	6 35W
Armagnac	44	43 44N	0 10E
Armançon, R.	43	47 51N	4 7E
Armavir	83	45 2N	41 7E
Armenia	174	4 35N	75 45W
Armenian S.S.R. □	83	40 0N	41 0E
Armeniş	70	45 13N	22 17E
Armentières	43	50 40N	2 50E
Armero	174	4 58N	74 54W
Armidale	141	30 30S	151 40E
Armour	158	43 20N	98 25W
Armoy	38	55 8N	6 20W
Arms	150	49 34N	86 3W
Armstead	160	45 0N	112 56W
Armstrong, B.C., Can.	152	50 25N	119 10W
Armstrong, Ont., Can.	150	50 18N	89 4W
Armstrong, U.S.A.	159	26 59N	90 48W
Armstrong Cr.	136	16 35S	131 40E
Armur	96	18 48N	78 16E
Arnaia	68	40 30N	23 40E
Arnarfjörður	74	65 48N	23 40W
Arnay-le-Duc	43	47 10N	4 27E
Arnedillo	58	42 13N	2 14W
Arnedo	58	42 12N	2 5W
Árnes	74	66 1N	21 31W
Årnes	71	60 7N	11 28E
Arnett	159	36 9N	99 44W
Arney	38	54 17N	7 41W
Arnhem	46	51 58N	5 55E
Arnhem B.	138	12 20S	136 10E
Arnhem, C.	138	12 20S	137 0E
Arnhem Ld.	138	13 10S	135 0E
Arni	97	12 43N	79 19E
Árnissa	68	40 47N	21 49E
Arno Bay	140	33 54S	136 34E
Arno, R.	62	43 44N	10 20E
Arnold, N.Z.	143	42 29S	171 25E
Arnold, U.K.	33	53 0N	1 8W
Arnold, Calif., U.S.A.	163	38 15N	120 20W
Arnold, Nebr., U.S.A.	158	41 29N	100 10W
Arnoldstein	52	46 33N	13 43E
Arnot	153	55 46N	96 41W
Arnøy	74	70 9N	20 40E
Arnprior	150	45 26N	76 21W
Arnsberg	48	51 25N	8 10E
Arnside	32	54 12N	2 49W
Arnstadt	48	50 50N	10 56E
Aroa	174	10 26N	68 54W
Aroab	125	26 41S	19 39E
Aroánia Óri	69	37 56N	22 12E
Aroche	57	37 56N	6 57W
Aroeiras	170	7 31S	35 41W
Arolla	50	46 2N	7 29E
Arolsen	48	51 23N	9 1E
Arona	62	45 45N	8 32E
Arosa	51	46 47N	9 41E
Arosa, Ría de	56	42 28N	8 57W
Arpajon, Cantal, France	44	44 54N	2 28E
Arpajon, Seine et Oise, France	43	48 37N	2 12E
Arpino	64	41 40N	13 35E
Arra Mts.	39	52 50N	8 22W
Arrabury	139	26 45S	141 0E
Arrah	95	25 35N	84 32E
Arraias	171	12 56S	46 57W
Arraias, R.	170	7 30S	49 20W
Arraiolos	57	38 44N	7 59W
Arran, I.	34	55 34N	5 12W
Arrandale	152	54 57N	130 0W
Arras	43	50 17N	2 46E
Arreau	44	42 54N	0 22E
Arrecife	116	28 59N	13 40W
Arrecifes	172	34 06S	60 9W
Arrée, Mts. d'	42	48 26N	3 55W
Arriaga, Chiapas, Mexico	165	16 15N	93 52W
Arriaga, San Luís de Potosí, Mexico	164	21 55N	101 23W
Arrild	73	55 8N	8 58E
Arrilalah P.O.	138	23 43S	143 54E
Arrino	137	29 30S	115 40E
Arrochar	34	56 12N	4 45W
Arrojado, R.	171	13 24S	44 20W
Arromanches-les-Bains	42	49 20N	0 38W
Arronches	57	39 8N	7 16W
Arrou	42	48 6N	1 8E
Arrow L.	38	54 3N	8 20W
Arrow Rock Res.	160	43 45N	115 50W
Arrowhead	152	50 40N	117 55W
Arrowhead, L.	163	34 16N	117 10W
Arrowsmith, Mt.	143	30 7N	141 38E
Arrowtown	143	44 57S	168 50E
Arroyo de la Luz	57	39 30N	6 38W
Arroyo Grande	163	35 9N	120 32W
Års	73	56 48N	9 30E
Ars	44	46 13N	1 30W
Ars-sur-Moselle	43	49 5N	6 4E
Arsenault L.	153	53 6N	108 32W
Arsiero	63	45 49N	11 22E
Arsikere	97	13 15N	76 15E
Arsk	81	56 10N	49 50E
Årskogen	72	62 8N	17 20E
Árta	69	39 8N	21 2E
Artá	58	39 40N	3 20E
Árta □	68	39 15N	26 0E
Arteaga	164	18 50N	102 20W
Arteijo	56	43 19N	8 29W
Artem,Os.	83	40 28N	50 20E
Artémou	120	15 38N	12 16W
Artemovsk	82	48 35N	37 55E
Artemovski	83	54 45N	93 35E
Artemovskiy	84	57 21N	61 54E
Artenay	43	48 5N	1 50E
Artern	48	51 22N	11 18E
Artesa de Segre	58	41 54N	1 3E
Artesia	159	32 55N	104 25W
Artesia Wells	159	28 17N	99 18W
Artesian	158	44 2N	97 54W
Arth	51	47 4N	8 31E
Arthez-de-Béarn	44	43 29N	0 38W
Arthington	120	6 35N	10 45W
Arthur Cr.	138	22 30S	136 25E
Arthur Pt.	138	22 7S	150 3E
Arthur, R.	138	41 2S	144 40E
Arthur's Pass	143	42 54S	171 35E
Arthur's Town	167	24 38N	75 42W
Arthurstown	39	52 15N	6 58W
Artigas	172	30 20S	56 30W
Artigavan	38	54 51N	7 24W
Artik	83	40 38N	44 50E
Artillery L.	153	63 9N	107 52W
Artois	43	50 20N	2 30E
Artotína	69	38 42N	22 2E
Artvin	92	41 14N	41 44E
Aru, Kepulauan	103	6 0S	134 30E
Arua	126	3 1N	30 58E
Aruanã	171	15 0S	51 10W
Aruba I.	167	12 30N	70 0W
Arudy	44	43 7N	0 28W
Arumpo	140	33 48S	142 55E
Arun, R.	95	27 30N	87 15E
Arun R.	29	50 48N	0 33W
Arunachal Pradesh □	98	28 0N	95 0E
Arundel	29	50 52N	0 32W
Aruppukottai	97	9 31N	78 8E
Arusha	126	3 20S	36 40E
Arusha □	126	4 0S	36 30E
Arusha Chini	126	3 32S	37 20E
Arusi □	123	7 45N	39 00E
Aruvi	97	8 48N	79 53E
Aruwimi, R.	126	1 30N	25 0E
Arva	38	53 57N	7 35W
Arvada	160	44 43N	106 6W
Arvaklu	97	8 20N	79 58E
Arvayheer	105	46 15N	102 48E
Arve, R.	45	46 11N	6 8E
Arvi	96	20 59N	78 16E
Arvida	151	48 25N	71 14W
Arvidsjaur	74	65 35N	19 10E
Arvika	72	59 40N	12 36E
Arvin	163	35 12N	118 50W
Arys	85	42 26N	68 48E
Arys, R.	85	42 45N	68 15E
Arzachena	64	41 5N	9 27E
Arzamas	81	55 27N	43 55E
Arzew	118	35 50N	0 23W
Arzgir	83	45 18N	44 23E
Arzignano	63	45 30N	11 20E
As	47	51 1N	5 35E
Aš	52	50 13N	12 12E
As Salt	90	32 2N	35 43E
As Samawah	92	31 15N	45 15E
As-Samū	90	31 24N	35 4E
As Sulaimānīyah	92	35 35N	45 29E
As Sulṭon	119	31 4N	17 8E
As Suwaih	93	22 10N	59 33E
As Suwayda	92	32 40N	36 30E
As Suwayrah	92	32 55N	45 0E
Asab	128	25 30S	18 0E
Asaba	121	6 12N	6 38E
Asadabad	92	34 50N	48 10E
Asafo	120	6 20N	2 40W
Asahi	111	35 43N	140 39E
Asahi-Gawa, R.	110	34 36N	133 58E
Asahikawa	112	43 45N	142 30E
Asale, L.	123	14 0N	40 20E
Asama-Yama	111	36 24N	138 31E
Asamankese	121	5 50N	0 40W
Asankrangwa	120	5 45N	2 30W
Asansol	95	23 40N	87 1E
Åsarna	72	62 40N	14 20E
Åsarna	72	62 39N	14 22E
Asbe Teferi	123	9 4N	40 49E
Asbesberge	128	29 0S	23 0E
Asbest	84	57 0N	61 30E
Asbestos	151	45 47N	71 58W
Asbury Park	162	40 15N	74 1W
Ascensión	164	31 6N	107 59W
Ascensión, B. de la	165	19 50N	87 20W
Ascension, I.	15	8 0S	14 15W
Aschach	49	48 23N	14 0E
Aschaffenburg	49	49 58N	9 8E
Aschendorf	48	53 2N	7 22E
Aschersleben	48	51 45N	11 28E
Asciano	63	43 14N	11 32E
Áscoli Piceno	63	42 51N	13 34E
Áscoli Satriano	65	41 11N	15 32E
Ascona	51	46 9N	8 46E
Ascope	174	7 46S	79 8W
Ascot	29	51 24N	0 41W
Ascotán	172	21 45S	68 17W
Aseb	123	13 0N	42 40E
Åseda	73	57 10N	15 20E
Åseda	73	57 10N	15 20E
Asedjrad	118	24 51N	1 29E
Asela	123	8 0N	39 0E
Asenovgrad	67	42 1N	24 51E
Åseral	71	58 37N	7 25E
Åseral	71	58 38N	7 26E
Asfeld	43	49 27N	4 5E
Asfordby	29	52 45N	0 57W
Asfûn el Matâ'na	122	25 26N	32 30E
Åsgårdstrand	71	59 22N	10 27E
Ash	29	51 17N	1 16E
Ash Fork	161	35 14N	112 32W
Ash Grove	159	37 21N	93 36W
Ash Shām,Bādiyat	92	31 30N	40 0E
Ash Shāmīyah	92	31 55N	44 35E
Ash Shatrah	92	31 30N	46 10E
Ash Shuna	90	32 32N	35 34E
Asha	84	55 0N	57 16E
Ashaira	122	21 40N	40 40E
Ashanti	121	7 30N	2 0W
Ashau	100	16 6N	107 22E
Ashbourne, Ireland	38	53 31N	6 24W
Ashbourne, U.K.	33	53 2N	1 44W
Ashburn	157	31 42N	83 40W
Ashburton, N.Z.	143	43 53S	171 48E
Ashburton, U.K.	30	50 31N	3 45W
Ashburton Downs	136	23 25S	117 4E
Ashburton, R., Austral.	136	21 40S	114 56E
Ashburton, R., N.Z.	131	44 2S	171 50E
Ashby-de-la-Zouch	28	52 45N	1 29W
Ashchurch	28	52 0N	2 7W
Ashcroft	152	50 40N	121 20W
Ashdod	90	31 49N	34 35E
Ashdot Ya'aqov	90	32 39N	35 35E
Ashdown Forest	29	51 4N	0 2E
Asheboro	157	35 43N	79 46W
Asherton	159	28 25N	99 43W
Asheville	157	35 39N	82 30W
Asheweig, R.	150	54 17N	87 12W
Ashford, Austral.	139	29 15S	151 3E
Ashford, Derby., U.K.	33	53 13N	1 43W
Ashford, Kent, U.K.	29	51 8N	0 53E
Ashford, U.S.A.	160	46 45N	122 2W
Ashikaga	111	36 28N	139 29E
Ashington	35	55 12N	1 35W
Ashio	111	36 38N	139 27E
Ashizuri-Zaki	110	32 35N	132 50E
Ashkarkot	94	33 3N	67 58E
Ashkhabad	76	38 0N	57 50E
Ashland, Kans., U.S.A.	159	37 13N	99 43W
Ashland, Ky., U.S.A.	156	38 25N	82 40W
Ashland, Me., U.S.A.	151	46 34N	68 26W
Ashland, Mont., U.S.A.	160	45 41N	106 12W
Ashland, Nebr., U.S.A.	158	41 5N	96 27W
Ashland, Ohio, U.S.A.	156	40 52N	82 20W
Ashland, Oreg., U.S.A.	160	42 10N	122 38W
Ashland, Pa., U.S.A.	162	40 45N	76 22W
Ashland, Va., U.S.A.	156	37 46N	77 30W
Ashland, Wis., U.S.A.	158	46 40N	90 52W
Ashley, N.D., U.S.A.	158	46 3N	99 23W
Ashley, Pa., U.S.A.	162	41 14N	75 53W
Ashmont	152	54 7N	111 29W
Ashmore Is.	136	12 14S	123 50E
Ashmore Reef	136	12 14S	123 5E
Ashmûn	122	30 18N	30 55E
Ashokan Res.	162	41 56N	74 13W
Ashquelon	90	31 42N	34 55E
Ashtabula	156	41 52N	80 50W
Ashti	96	18 50N	75 15E
Ashton, S. Afr.	128	33 50S	20 5E
Ashton, U.S.A.	160	44 6N	111 30W
Ashton-in-Makerfield	32	53 29N	2 39W
Ashton-u.-Lyne	32	53 30N	2 8E
Ashuanipi, L.	151	52 45N	66 15W
Ashurst	142	40 16S	175 45E
Ashurstwood	29	51 6N	0 2E
Ashwater	30	50 43N	4 18W
Ashwick	28	51 13N	2 31W
Asia	86	45 0N	75 0E
Asia, Kepulauan	103	1 0N	131 13E
Asiago	63	45 52N	11 30E
Asifabad	96	19 30N	79 24E
Asilah	118	35 29N	6 0W
Asinara	64	41 5N	8 15E
Asinara, G. dell'	64	41 0N	8 30E
Asinara I.	64	41 5N	8 15E
Asino	76	57 0N	86 0E
Asir	91	18 40N	42 30E
Asir, Ras	91	11 55N	51 10E
Aska	96	19 37N	84 42E
Askeaton	39	52 37N	8 58W
Asker	71	59 50N	10 26E
Askersund	73	58 53N	14 55E
Askim	71	59 35N	11 10E
Askino	84	56 5N	56 34E
Askja	74	65 3N	16 48W
Åskloster	73	57 13N	12 11E
Askrigg	32	54 19N	2 6W
Asl	122	29 33N	32 44E
Aslackby	33	52 53N	0 23W
Asmar	93	35 10N	71 27E
Asmera (Asmara)	123	15 19N	38 55E
Asnæs	73	55 40N	11 0E
Åsnen	73	56 35N	15 45E
Åsnes	71	60 37N	11 59E
Asni	118	31 17N	7 58W
Aso	110	33 0N	130 42E
Aso-Zan	110	32 53N	131 6E
Asoa	126	4 35N	25 48E
Asola	62	45 12N	10 25E
Asotin	60	46 14N	117 2W
Aspatria	32	54 45N	3 20W
Aspe	59	38 20N	0 40W
Aspen	161	39 12N	106 56W
Aspermont	159	33 11N	100 15W
Aspiring, Mt.	143	44 23S	168 46E
Aspres	45	44 32N	5 44E
Aspur	94	23 58N	74 7E
Asquith	153	52 8N	107 13W
Assa	118	28 35N	9 6W
Assaba, Massif de l'	120	16 10N	11 45W
Assam □	98	25 45N	92 30E
Assamakka	121	19 21N	5 38E
Assateague I.	162	38 5N	75 6W
Asse	47	50 54N	4 6E
Assebroek	47	51 11N	3 17E
Assekrem	119	23 16N	5 49E
Assémini	64	39 18N	9 0E
Assen	46	53 0N	6 35E
Assendelft	46	52 29N	4 45E
Assenede	47	51 14N	3 46E
Assens, Odense, Denmark	73	56 41N	10 3E
Assens, Randers, Denmark	73	55 16N	9 55E
Assesse	47	50 22N	5 2E
Assiniboia	153	49 40N	105 59W
Assiniboine, R.	153	49 53N	97 8W
Assinica L.	150	50 30N	75 20W
Assinie	120	5 9N	3 17W
Assis	173	22 40S	50 20W
Assisi	63	43 4N	12 36E
Ássos	69	38 22N	20 33E
Assynt	36	58 25N	5 10W
Assynt, L.	36	58 25N	5 15W
Astakidha	69	35 53N	26 50E
Astalfort	44	44 4N	0 40E
Astara	79	38 30N	48 50E
Astee	39	52 33N	9 36W
Asten	47	51 24N	5 45E
Asti	62	44 54N	8 11E
Astillero	56	43 24N	3 49W
Astipálaia	69	36 32N	26 22E
Aston, C.	149	70 10N	67 40W
Aston Clinton	29	51 48N	0 44W
Astorga	56	42 29N	6 8W
Astoria	160	46 16N	123 50W
Åstorp	73	56 6N	12 55E
Astrakhan	83	46 25N	48 5E
Astudillo	56	42 12N	4 22W
Asturias	56	43 15N	6 0W
Astwood Bank	28	52 15N	1 55W
Asunción	172	25 21S	57 30W
Asunción, La	174	11 2N	63 53W
Åsunden	73	57 47N	13 18E
Asutri	123	15 25N	35 45E
Aswa, R.	126	2 30N	33 5E
Aswad,Rasal	122	21 20N	39 0E
Aswân	122	24 4N	32 57E
Aswân High Dam = Sadd el Aali	122	24 5N	32 54E
Asyût	122	27 11N	31 4E
Asyûti, Wadi	122	27 18N	31 20E
Aszód	53	47 39N	19 28E
At Tafilah	92	30 45N	35 30E
At Ta'if	122	21 5N	40 27E
Atacama	172	25 40S	67 40W
Atacama □	172	27 30S	70 0W
Atacama, Desierto de	176	24 0S	69 20W
Atacama, Salar de	172	24 0S	68 20W
Ataco	174	3 35N	75 23W
Atakor	119	23 27N	5 31E
Atakpamé	121	7 31N	1 13E
Atalaia	114	9 25S	36 0W

Atalándi **Ayutla**

Name	Page	Lat.	Long.
Atalándi	69	38 39N	22 58E
Atalaya	174	10 45S	73 50W
Ataléia	171	18 3S	41 6W
Atami	111	35 0N	139 55E
Atankawng	98	25 50N	97 47E
Atar	116	20 30N	13 5W
Atara	77	63 10N	129 10E
Ataram, Erg d'	118	23 57N	2 0E
Atarfe	57	37 13N	3 40W
Atascadero	163	35 32N	120 44W
Atasu	76	48 30N	71 0E
Atauro	103	8 10S	125 30E
Atbara	122	17 42N	33 59E
Atbara, R.	122	17 40N	33 56E
Atbashi	85	41 10N	75 48E
Atbashi, Khrebet	85	40 50N	75 30E
Atchafalaya B.	159	29 30N	91 20W
Atchison	158	39 40N	95 0W
Atebubu	121	7 47N	1 0W
Ateca	58	41 20N	1 49W
Aterno, R.	63	42 18N	13 45E
Atesine, Alpi	62	46 55N	11 30E
Atessa	63	42 5N	14 27E
Ath	47	50 38N	3 47E
Ath Thamami	92	27 45N	35 30E
Athabasca	152	54 45N	113 20W
Athabasca, L.	153	59 15N	109 15W
Athabasca, R.	153	58 40N	110 50W
Athboy	38	53 37N	6 55W
Athea	39	52 27N	9 18W
Athenry	39	53 18N	8 45W
Athens, Ala., U.S.A.	157	34 49N	86 58W
Athens, Ga., U.S.A.	157	33 56N	83 24W
Athens, N.Y., U.S.A.	162	42 15N	73 48W
Athens, Ohio, U.S.A.	156	39 52N	82 6W
Athens, Pa., U.S.A.	162	41 57N	76 36W
Athens, Tex., U.S.A.	159	32 11N	95 48W
Athens = Athínai	69	37 58N	23 46E
Atherstone	28	52 35N	1 32W
Atherton, Austral.	138	17 17S	145 30E
Atherton, U.K.	32	53 32N	2 30W
Athiéme	121	6 37N	1 40E
Athínai	69	37 58N	23 46E
Athleague	38	53 34N	8 17W
Athlone	38	53 26N	7 57W
Athni	96	16 44N	75 6E
Athol	143	45 30S	168 35E
Atholl, Forest of	37	56 51N	3 50W
Atholville	151	47 59N	66 43W
Áthos, Mt.	68	40 9N	24 22E
Athus	47	49 34N	5 50E
Athy	39	53 0N	7 0W
Ati	123	13 5N	29 2E
Atiak	126	3 12N	32 2E
Atiamuri	142	38 24S	176 5E
Atico	174	16 14S	73 40W
Atienza	58	41 12N	2 52W
Atikokan	150	48 45N	91 37W
Atikonak L.	151	52 40N	64 32W
Atka, U.S.A.	147	52 5N	174 40W
Atka, U.S.S.R.	77	60 50N	151 48E
Atkarsk	81	51 55N	45 2E
Atkasuk (Meade River)	147	70 30N	157 20W
Atkinson	158	42 35N	98 59W
Atlanta, Ga., U.S.A.	157	33 50N	84 24W
Atlanta, Tex., U.S.A.	159	33 7N	94 8W
Atlantic	158	41 25N	95 0W
Atlantic City	162	39 25N	74 25W
Atlantic Ocean	14	0 0	20 0W
Atlántico □	174	10 45N	75 0W
Atlas, Great, Mts.	114	33 0N	5 0W
Atlin	147	59 31N	133 41W
Atlin Lake	147	59 26N	133 45W
'Atlit	90	32 42N	34 56E
Atløy	71	61 21N	4 58E
Atmakur	97	14 37N	79 40E
Atmore	157	31 2N	87 30W
Atnarko	152	52 25N	126 0W
Atō	110	34 25N	131 40E
Atoka	159	34 22N	96 10W
Átokos	69	38 28N	20 49E
Atolia	163	35 19N	117 37W
Atotonilco el Alto	164	20 20N	98 40W
Atouguia	57	39 20N	9 20W
Atoyac, R.	165	16 30N	97 31W
Ätrafors	73	57 02N	12 40E
Atrak, R.	93	37 50N	57 0E
Ätran	73	57 7N	12 57E
Atrato, R.	174	6 40N	77 0W
Atrauli	94	28 2N	78 20E
Atri	63	42 35N	14 0E
Atsbi	122	13 52N	39 50E
Atsumi	111	34 35N	137 4E
Atsumi-Wan	111	34 44N	137 13E
Atsuta	112	43 24N	141 26E
Attalla	157	34 2N	86 5W
Attawapiskat	150	52 56N	82 24W
Attawapiskat, L.	150	52 18N	87 54W
Attawapiskat, R.	150	52 57N	82 18W
Attendorn	48	51 8N	7 54E
Attersee	52	47 55N	13 31E
Attert	47	49 45N	5 47E
Attica	156	40 20N	87 15W
Attichy	43	49 25N	3 3E
Attigny	43	49 28N	4 35E
Attikamagen L.	151	55 0N	66 30W
Attikí Kai Arkhipélagos □	69	38 10N	23 40E
Attil	90	32 23N	35 4E
Attleboro	162	41 56N	71 18W
Attleborough	29	52 32N	1 1E
Attock	94	33 52N	72 20E
Attopeu	100	14 48N	106 50E
Attu	147	52 55N	173 10W
Attunga	141	30 55S	150 50E
Attur	97	11 35N	78 30E
Attymon	39	53 20N	8 37W
Atuel, R.	172	36 17S	66 50W
Atvidaberg	73	58 12N	16 0E
Atwater	163	37 21N	120 37W
Atwood	158	39 52N	101 3W
Au Sable Pt.	150	46 0N	86 0W
Au Sable, R.	156	44 25N	83 20W
Aubagne	45	43 17N	5 37E
Aubange	47	49 34N	5 48E
Aubarede Pt.	103	17 15N	122 20E
Aube □	43	48 15N	4 0E
Aubel	47	50 42N	5 51E
Aubenas	45	44 37N	4 24E
Aubenton	43	49 50N	4 12E
Auberry	163	37 7N	119 29W
Aubigny-sur-Nère	43	47 30N	2 24E
Aubin	44	44 33N	2 15E
Aubrac, Mts. d'	44	44 38N	2 58E
Auburn, Ala., U.S.A.	157	32 37N	85 30W
Auburn, Calif., U.S.A.	160	38 50N	121 4W
Auburn, Ind., U.S.A.	156	41 20N	85 0W
Auburn, Nebr., U.S.A.	158	40 25N	95 50W
Auburn, N.Y., U.S.A.	162	42 57N	76 39W
Auburn, Penn., U.S.A.	162	40 36N	76 6W
Auburn Range	139	25 15S	150 30E
Auburndale	157	28 5N	81 45W
Aubusson	44	45 57N	2 11E
Auch	44	43 39N	0 36E
Auchel	43	50 30N	2 29E
Auchenblae	37	56 54N	2 26W
Auchencairn	35	54 51N	3 52W
Auchi	121	7 6N	6 13E
Auchinleck	34	55 28N	4 18W
Auchness	37	58 0N	4 36W
Auchterarder	35	56 18N	3 43W
Auchterderran	35	56 8N	3 16W
Auchtermuchty	35	56 18N	3 15W
Auchtertyre	36	57 17N	5 35W
Auckland	142	36 52S	174 46E
Auckland □	142	38 35S	177 0E
Auckland Is.	142	51 0S	166 0E
Aude □	44	43 8N	2 28E
Aude, R.	44	44 13N	3 15E
Auden	150	50 14N	87 53W
Auderghem	47	50 49N	4 26E
Auderville	42	49 43N	1 57W
Audierne	42	48 1N	4 34W
Audincourt	43	47 30N	6 50E
Audlem	32	52 59N	2 31W
Audo Ra.	123	6 20N	41 50E
Audrey, gasfield	19	53 35N	2 0E
Audubon	158	41 43N	94 56W
Aue	48	50 34N	12 43E
Auerbach	48	50 30N	12 25E
Auffay	42	49 43N	1 07E
Augathella	139	25 48S	146 35E
Augher	38	54 25N	7 10W
Aughnacloy	38	54 25N	6 58W
Aughrim, Clare, Ireland	39	53 0N	8 57W
Aughrim, Galway, Ireland	39	53 18N	8 19W
Aughrim, Wicklow, Ireland	39	52 52N	6 20W
Aughrus More	38	53 34N	10 10W
Augrabies Falls	128	28 35S	20 20E
Augsburg	49	48 22N	10 54E
Augusta, Italy	65	37 14N	15 12E
Augusta, Ark., U.S.A.	159	35 17N	91 25W
Augusta, Ga., U.S.A.	157	33 29N	81 59W
Augusta, Kans., U.S.A.	159	37 40N	97 0W
Augusta, Me., U.S.A.	151	44 20N	69 46E
Augusta, Mont., U.S.A.	160	47 30N	112 29W
Augusta, Wis., U.S.A.	158	44 41N	91 8W
Augustenborg	73	54 57N	9 53E
Augustine	159	31 30N	94 37W
Augusto Cardosa	127	12 40S	34 50E
Augustów	54	53 51N	23 00E
Augustus Downs	138	18 35S	139 55E
Augustus I.	136	15 20S	124 30E
Augustus, Mt.	137	24 20S	116 50E
Auk, oilfield	19	56 25N	2 15E
Aukan	123	15 29N	40 50E
Aukum	163	38 34N	120 43W
Auld, L.	136	22 32S	123 44E
Auldearn	37	57 34N	3 50W
Aulla	62	44 12N	9 57E
Aulnay	44	46 2N	0 22W
Aulne, R.	42	48 17N	4 16W
Ault	158	40 40N	104 42W
Ault-Onival	42	50 5N	1 29E
Aultbea	36	57 50N	5 36W
Aulus-les-Bains	44	42 49N	1 19E
Aumale	43	49 46N	1 46E
Aumont-Aubrac	44	44 43N	3 17E
Auna	121	10 9N	4 43E
Aundh	96	17 33N	74 23E
Aunis	44	46 0N	0 50W
Auponhia	103	1 58S	125 27E
Aups	45	43 37N	6 15E
Aur, P.	101	2 35N	104 10E
Aura	98	26 59N	97 57E
Aurahorten, Mt.	71	59 15N	6 53E
Auraiya	95	26 28N	79 33E
Aurangabad, Bihar, India	95	24 45N	84 18E
Aurangabad, Maharashtra, India	96	19 50N	75 23E
Auray	42	47 40N	3 0W
Aurès	119	35 8N	6 30E
Aurich	48	53 28N	7 30E
Aurilândia	171	16 44S	50 28W
Aurillac	44	44 55N	2 26E
Aurlandsvangen	71	60 55N	7 12E
Auronza	63	46 33N	12 27E
Aurora, Brazil	171	6 57S	38 58W
Aurora, S. Afr.	128	32 40S	18 29E
Aurora, Colo., U.S.A.	158	39 44N	104 55W
Aurora, Ill., U.S.A.	156	41 42N	88 12W
Aurora, Mo., U.S.A.	159	36 58N	93 42W
Aurora, Nebr., U.S.A.	158	40 55N	98 0W
Aurora, N.Y., U.S.A.	162	42 45N	76 42W
Aurskog	71	59 55N	11 26E
Aurukun Mission	138	13 20S	141 45E
Aus	128	26 35S	16 12E
Auskerry I.	37	59 2N	2 35W
Aust-Agder fylke □	75	58 55N	7 40E
Austad	71	58 58N	7 37E
Austerlitz = Slavikov	53	49 10N	16 52E
Austevoll	71	60 5N	5 13E
Austin, Austral.	137	27 40S	117 50E
Austin, Minn., U.S.A.	158	43 37N	92 59W
Austin, Nev., U.S.A.	160	39 30N	117 1W
Austin, Tex., U.S.A.	159	30 20N	97 45W
Austin, L.	137	27 40S	118 0E
Austral Downs	138	20 30S	137 45E
Austral Is. = Tubuai, Îles	143	25 0S	150 0E
Australia ■	133	23 0S	135 0E
Australian Alps	141	36 30S	148 8E
Australian Cap. Terr.	139	35 15S	149 8E
Australian Dependency	13	73 0S	90 0E
Austria ■	52	47 0N	14 0E
Austvågøy	74	68 20N	14 40E
Autelbas	47	49 39N	5 52E
Auterive	44	43 21N	1 29E
Authie, R.	43	50 22N	1 38E
Autlan	164	19 40N	104 30W
Autun	43	46 58N	4 17E
Auvelais	47	50 27N	4 38E
Auvergne, Austral.	136	15 39S	130 1E
Auvergne, France	44	45 20N	3 0E
Auxerre	43	47 48N	3 32E
Auxi-le-Château	43	50 15N	2 8E
Auxonne	43	47 10N	5 20E
Auzances	44	46 2N	2 30E
Avaldsnes	71	59 21N	5 20E
Avallon	43	47 30N	3 53E
Avalon	163	33 21N	118 20W
Avalon Pen.	151	47 30N	53 20W
Avalon Res.	159	32 30N	104 30W
Avanigadda	97	16 0N	80 56E
Avaré	173	23 4S	48 58W
Ávas	68	40 57N	25 56E
Avawata Mts.	163	35 30N	116 20W
Avebury	28	51 25N	1 52W
Aveh	92	35 40N	49 15E
Aveiro, Brazil	175	3 10S	55 5W
Aveiro, Port.	56	40 37N	8 38W
Aveiro □	56	40 40N	8 35W
Avelgem	47	50 47N	3 27E
Avellaneda	172	34 50S	58 10W
Avellino	65	40 54N	14 46E
Avenal	163	36 0N	120 8W
Avenchen	50	46 53N	7 2E
Averøya	71	63 0N	7 35E
Aversa	65	40 58N	14 11E
Avery	160	47 22N	115 56W
Aves, Islas de	174	12 0N	67 40W
Avesnes-sur-Helpe	43	50 8N	3 55E
Avesta	72	60 9N	16 10E
Aveton Gifford	30	50 17N	3 51W
Aveyron □	44	44 22N	2 45E
Avezzano	63	42 2N	13 24E
Avgó	69	35 33N	25 37E
Aviá Terai	172	26 45S	60 50W
Aviano	63	46 3N	12 35E
Avich, L.	34	56 17N	5 25W
Aviemore	37	57 11N	3 50W
Avigliana	62	45 7N	7 13E
Avigliano	65	40 44N	15 41E
Avignon	45	43 57N	4 50E
Ávila	56	40 39N	4 43W
Ávila □	56	40 30N	5 0W
Avila Beach	163	35 11N	120 44W
Ávila, Sierra de	56	40 40N	5 0W
Avilés	56	43 35N	5.57W
Avionárion	69	38 31N	24 8E
Avisio, R.	63	46 14N	11 18E
Aviz	57	39 4N	7 53W
Avize	43	48 59N	4 0E
Avoca, Austral.	139	37 5S	143 26E
Avoca, Ireland	39	52 52N	6 13W
Avoca, R., Austral.	140	35 40S	143 43E
Avoca, R., Ireland	39	52 48N	6 10W
Avoch	37	57 34N	4 10W
Avola, Can.	152	51 45N	119 19W
Avola, Italy	65	36 56N	15 7E
Avon	158	43 0N	98 3W
Avon □	28	51 30N	2 40W
Avon Downs	133	19 58S	137 25E
Avon Is.	133	19 37S	158 17E
Avon, R., Austral.	137	31 40S	116 7E
Avon, R., Avon, U.K.	28	51 30N	2 43W
Avon, R., Grampian, U.K.	37	57 25N	3 25W
Avon, R., Hants., U.K.	28	50 44N	1 45W
Avon, R., Warwick, U.K.	28	52 0N	2 9W
Avondale, N.Z.	142	36 54S	174 42E
Avondale, Rhod.	127	17 43S	30 58E
Avonlea	153	50 0N	105 0W
Avonmouth	28	51 30N	2 42W
Avranches	42	48 40N	1 20W
Avrig	70	45 43N	24 21E
Avrillé	44	46 28N	1 28W
Avtovac	66	43 9N	18 35E
Avu Meru □	126	3 20S	36 50E
Awag el Baqar	123	10 10N	33 10E
Awaji	111	34 32N	135 1E
Awaji-Shima	110	34 30N	134 50E
Awali	93	26 0N	50 30E
Awantipur	95	33 55N	75 3E
Awanui	142	35 4S	173 17E
Awarja, R.	96	18 0N	76 15E
Awarta	90	32 10N	35 17E
Awarua Pt.	143	44 15S	168 5E
Awasa, L.	123	7 0N	38 30E
Awash	123	9 1N	40 10E
Awash, R.	123	11 30N	42 0E
Awaso	120	6 15N	2 22W
Awatere, R.	143	41 37S	174 10E
Awbārī	119	26 46N	12 57E
Awe, L.	34	56 15N	5 15W
Aweil	123	8 42N	27 20E
Awgu	121	6 4N	7 24E
Awjilah	117	29 8N	21 7E
Aworro	135	7 43S	143 11E
Ax-les-Thermes	44	42 44N	1 50E
Axarfjörður	74	66 15N	16 45W
Axbridge	28	51 17N	2 50W
Axe Edge	32	53 14N	2 2W
Axe R.	28	51 17N	2 52W
Axel	47	51 16N	3 55E
Axel Heiberg I.	12	80 0N	90 0W
Axelfors	73	57 26N	13 7E
Axholme, Isle of	33	53 30N	1 10E
Axim	120	4 51N	2 15W
Axintele	70	44 37N	26 47E
Axiós, R.	68	40 57N	22 35E
Axmarsbruk	72	61 3N	17 10E
Axminster	30	50 47N	3 1W
Axmouth	30	50 43N	3 2W
Axstedt	48	53 26N	8 43E
Axvall	73	58 23N	13 34E
Ay	43	49 3N	4 0E
Ay, R.	84	56 8N	57 40E
Ayabaca	174	4 40S	79 53W
Ayabe	111	35 20N	135 20E
Ayacucho, Argent.	172	37 5S	58 20W
Ayacucho, Peru	174	13 0S	74 0W
Ayaguz	76	48 10N	80 0E
Ayakkuduk	85	41 12N	65 12E
Ayakok'umu Hu	105	37 30N	89 20E
Ayakudi	97	10 57N	77 6E
Ayamonte	57	37 12N	7 24W
Ayan	77	56 30N	138 16E
Ayancık	82	41 57N	34 18E
Ayapel	174	8 19N	75 9W
Ayapel, Sa. de	174	7 45N	75 30W
Ayaş	82	40 10N	32 14E
Ayaviri	174	14 50S	70 35W
Aydın □	92	37 40N	27 40E
Aye	47	50 14N	5 18E
Ayenngré	121	8 40N	1 1E
Ayer Hitam	101	1 55N	103 11E
Ayeritam	101	5 24N	100 15E
Ayers Rock	136	25 23S	131 5E
Ayiá	68	39 43N	22 45E
Áyia Anna	69	38 52N	23 24E
Ayia Marína, Kásos, Greece	69	35 27N	26 53E
Ayía Marína, Leros, Greece	69	37 11N	26 48E
Ayía Paraskeví	68	39 14N	26 16E
Ayía Rouméli	69	35 14N	23 58E
Ayiássos	69	39 5N	26 23E
Áyios Andréas	69	37 21N	22 45E
Áyios Evstrátios	68	39 34N	24 58E
Áyios Ioánnis, Ákra	69	35 20N	25 40E
Áyios Kírikos	69	37 34N	26 17E
Áyios Matthaíos	68	39 30N	19 47E
Áyios Míron	69	35 15N	25 1E
Áyios Nikólaos	69	35 11N	25 41E
Áyios Pétros	69	38 38N	20 33E
Áyios Yeóryios	69	37 28N	23 57E
Aykathonisi	69	37 28N	27 0E
Ayke, Ozero	84	51 57N	61 36E
Aylesbury	29	51 48N	0 49W
Aylesford	29	51 18N	0 29E
Aylmer L.	148	64 0N	108 30W
Aylsham	29	52 48N	1 16E
Ayn Zālah	92	36 45N	42 35E
'Ayn Zaqqūt	119	29 0N	19 30E
Ayna	59	38 34N	2 3W
Aynho	28	51 59N	1 15W
Ayni	85	39 23N	68 32E
Ayolas	172	27 10S	56 59W
Ayom	123	7 49N	28 23E
Ayon, Ostrov	77	69 50N	169 0E
Ayora	59	39 3N	1 3W
Ayr, Austral.	138	19 35S	147 25E
Ayr, U.K.	34	55 28N	4 37W
Ayr (□)	26	55 25N	4 25W
Ayr, Heads of	34	55 25N	4 43W
Ayr, R.	34	55 29N	4 40W
Ayre, Pt. of	37	58 55N	2 43W
Ayre, Pt. of I.o.M.	32	54 27N	4 21W
Aysgarth	32	54 18N	2 0W
Aysha	123	10 50N	42 23E
Ayton	138	15 45S	145 25E
Ayton, Borders, U.K.	35	55 51N	2 6W
Ayton, N. Yorks., U.K.	33	54 15N	0 29W
Aytos	67	42 47N	27 16E
Aytoska Planina	67	42 45N	27 30E
Ayu, Kepulauan	103	0 35N	131 5E
Ayutla, Guat.	166	14 40N	92 10W

Ayutla Balasore

Ayutla, Mexico 165 16 58N 99 17W
Ayutthaya = Phra Nakhon Si A. 101 14 25N 100 30E
Ayvalık 92 39 20N 26 46E
Aywaille 47 50 28N 5 40E
Az Zahiriya 90 31 25N 34 58E
Az Zahran 92 26 10N 50 7E
Az-Zarqā 90 32 5N 36 4E
Az Zāwiyah 119 32 52N 12 56E
Az-Zilfī 92 26 12N 44 52E
Az Zintān 119 31 59N 12 9E
Az Zubayr 92 30 20N 47 50E
Azambuja 57 39 4N 8 51W
Azamgarh 95 26 35N 83 13E
Azaouak, Vallée de l' 121 15 50N 3 20E
Azārbāijān □ 92 37 0N 44 30E
Azare 121 11 55N 10 10E
Azay-le-Rideau 42 47 16N 0 30E
Azazga 119 36 48N 4 22E
Azbine = Aïr 121 18 0N 8 0E
Azeffoun 119 36 51N 4 26E
Azemmour 118 33 14N 9 20W
Azerbaijan S.S.R. □ 83 40 20N 48 0E
Azezo 123 12 28N 37 15E
Azilal,Beni Mallal 118 32 0N 6 30W
Azimganj 95 24 14N 84 16E
Aznalcóllar 57 37 32N 6 17W
Azogues 174 2 35S 78 0W
Azor 90 32 2N 34 48E
Azores, Is. 14 38 44N 29 0W
Azov 83 47 3N 39 25E
Azov Sea = Azovskoye More 82 46 0N 36 30E
Azovskoye More 82 46 0N 36 30E
Azovy 76 64 55N 64 35E
Azpeitia 58 43 12N 2 19W
Azrou 118 33 28N 5 19W
Aztec 161 36 54N 108 0W
Azúa de Compostela 167 18 25N 70 44W
Azuaga 57 38 16N 5 39W
Azuara 58 41 15N 0 53W
Azuara, R. 58 41 12N 0 55W
Azúcar, Presa del 165 26 0N 99 5W
Azuer, R. 57 38 50N 3 15W
Azuero, Pen. de 166 7 30N 80 30W
Azul 172 36 42S 59 43W
Azusa 163 34 8N 117 52W
Azzaba 119 36 48N 7 6E
Azzano Décimo 63 45 53N 12 46E

B

B. Curri 68 42 22N 20 5E
Ba Don 100 17 45N 106 26E
Ba Dong 101 9 40N 106 33E
Ba Ngoi = Cam Lam 101 11 50N 109 10E
Ba, R. 56 13 5N 109 0E
Ba Tri 101 10 2N 106 36E
Baa 103 10 50S 123 0E
Baamonde 56 43 7N 7 44W
Baar 51 47 12N 8 32E
Baarle Nassau 47 51 27N 4 56E
Baarlo 47 51 20N 6 6E
Baarn 46 52 12N 5 17E
Bāb el Māndeb 91 12 35N 43 25E
Baba Burnu 68 39 29N 26 2E
Baba dag 83 41 0N 48 55E
Baba, Mt. 67 42 44N 23 59E
Babaçulândia 170 7 13S 47 46W
Babadag 70 44 53N 28 44E
Babaeski 67 41 26N 27 6E
Babahoyo 174 1 40S 79 30W
Babakin 137 32 7S 118 1E
Babana 121 10 31N 3 46E
Babar, Alg. 119 35 10N 7 6E
Babar, Pak. 94 31 7N 69 32E
Babar, I. 103 8 0S 129 30E
Babarkach 94 29 45N 68 0E
Babayevo 81 59 24N 35 55E
Babb 160 48 56N 113 27W
Babbitt 163 38 32N 118 39W
Babenhausen 49 49 57N 8 56E
Babi Besar, P. 101 2 25N 103 59E
Babia Gora 54 49 38N 19 38E
Babile 123 9 16N 42 11E
Babinda 138 17 20S 145 56E
Babine 152 55 20N 126 35W
Babine L. 152 54 48N 126 0W
Babine, R. 152 55 45N 127 44W
Babo 103 2 30S 133 30E
Babócsa 53 46 2N 17 21E
Babol 93 36 40N 52 50E
Babol Sar 93 36 45N 52 45E
Baboma 126 2 30N 28 10E
Baborówo Kietrz 53 50 7N 18 1E
Baboua 124 5 49N 14 58E
Babuna, mts. 66 41 30N 21 40E
Babura 121 12 51N 8 59E
Babusar Pass 95 35 12N 73 59E
Babushkin 81 55 45N 37 40E
Babušnica 66 43 7N 22 27E
Babylon, Iraq 92 32 40N 44 30E
Babylon, U.S.A. 162 40 42N 73 20W
Bač 66 45 29N 19 17E
Bac Can 100 22 08N 105 49E
Bac Giang 100 21 16N 106 11E
Bac Kan 101 22 5N 105 50E
Bac Lieu = Vinh Loi 101 9 17N 105 43E
Bac Ninh 100 21 13N 106 4E
Bac Phan 100 22 0N 105 0E
Bac Quang 100 22 30N 104 48E
Bacabal 170 4 15N 44 45W
Bacalar 165 18 12N 87 53W
Bacan,Pulau 103 0 50S 127 30E
Bacarès, Le 44 42 47N 3 3E
Bacarra 103 18 15N 120 37E
Baccarat 43 48 28N 6 42E
Bacchus Marsh 140 37 43S 144 27E
Bacerac 164 30 18N 108 50W
Bach Long Vi,Dao 100 20 10N 107 40E
Bachaquero 174 9 56N 71 8W
Bacharach 49 50 3N 7 46E
Bachclina 76 57 45N 67 20E
Bachok 101 6 4N 102 25E
Bachuma 123 6 31N 36 1E
Bačina 66 43 42N 21 23E
Back 36 58 17N 6 20W
Back, R. 148 65 10N 104 0W
Bačka Palanka 66 45 17N 19 27E
Bačka Topola 66 45 49N 19 39E
Bäckefors 73 58 48N 12 9E
Bački Petrovac 66 45 29N 19 32E
Backnang 49 48 57N 9 26E
Backstairs Passage 133 35 40S 138 5E
Bacolod 103 10 40N 122 57E
Bacqueville 42 49 47N 1 0E
Bacs-Kiskun □ 53 46 43N 19 30E
Bácsalmás 53 46 8N 19 17E
Bacton 29 52 50N 1 29E
Bacuit 103 11 20N 119 20E
Bacup 32 53 42N 2 12W
Bacŭu 70 46 35N 26 55E
Bacŭu □ 70 46 30N 26 45E
Bad Aussee 52 47 43N 13 45E
Bad Axe 150 43 48N 82 59W
Bad Bergzabem 49 49 6N 8 0E
Bad Bramstedt 48 53 56N 9 53E
Bad Doberan 48 54 6N 11 55E
Bad Driburg 48 51 44N 9 0E
Bad Ems 49 50 22N 7 44E
Bad Frankenhausen 48 51 21N 11 3E
Bad Freienwalde 52 52 46N 14 2E
Bad Godesberg 48 50 41N 7 4E
Bad Hersfeld 48 50 52N 9 42E
Bad Hofgastein 52 47 17N 13 6E
Bad Homburg 49 50 17N 8 33E
Bad Honnef 48 50 39N 7 13E
Bad Ischl 52 47 44N 13 38E
Bad Kissingen 49 50 11N 10 5E
Bad Kreuznach 49 49 47N 7 47E
Bad Lands 158 43 40N 102 10W
Bad Lauterberg 48 51 38N 10 29E
Bad Leonfelden 52 48 31N 14 18E
Bad Lippspringe 48 51 47N 8 46E
Bad Mergentheim 49 49 29N 9 47E
Bad Münstereifel 48 50 33N 6 46E
Bad Nauheim 49 50 24N 8 45E
Bad Oeynhausen 48 52 16N 8 45E
Bad Oldesloe 48 53 56N 10 17E
Bad Orb 49 50 16N 9 21E
Bad Pyrmont 48 51 59N 9 5E
Bad, R. 158 44 10N 100 50W
Bad Ragaz 51 47 0N 9 30E
Bad St. Peter 48 54 23N 8 32E
Bad Salzuflen 48 52 8N 8 44E
Bad Segeberg 48 53 58N 10 16E
Bad Tölz 49 47 43N 11 34E
Bad Waldsee 49 47 56N 9 46E
Bad Wildungen 48 51 7N 9 10E
Bad Wimpfen 49 49 12N 9 10E
Bad Windsheim 49 49 29N 10 25E
Badagara 97 11 35N 75 40E
Badagri 121 6 25N 2 55E
Badajoz 57 38 50N 6 59W
Badajoz □ 57 38 40N 6 30W
Badakhshan □ 93 36 30N 71 0E
Badalona 58 41 26N 2 15E
Badalzai 94 29 50N 65 35E
Badampahar 96 22 10N 86 10E
Badanah 92 30 58N 41 30E
Badas 102 4 33N 114 25E
Badas, Kepulauan 102 0 45N 107 5E
Baddo, R. 93 28 15N 65 0E
Bade 103 7 10S 139 35E
Baden, Austria 53 48 1N 16 13E
Baden, Switz. 51 47 28N 8 18E
Baden-Baden 49 48 45N 8 15E
Baden Park 140 32 8S 144 12E
Baden-Württemberg □ 49 48 40N 9 0E
Badenoch 37 58 16N 4 5W
Badenscoth 37 57 27N 2 30W
Badeso 123 9 58N 40 52E
Badgastein 52 47 7N 13 9E
Badger, Can. 151 49 0N 56 4W
Badger, U.S.A. 163 36 38N 119 1W
Badghis □ 93 35 0N 63 0E
Badgom 95 34 1N 74 45E
Badhoevedorp 46 52 20N 4 47E
Badia Polesine 63 45 6N 11 30E
Badin 94 24 38N 68 54E
Badnera 96 20 48N 77 44E
Badogo 120 11 2N 8 13W
Badrinath 95 30 45N 79 30E
Baduen 91 7 15N 47 40E
Badulla 97 7 1N 81 7E
Badupi 98 21 36N 93 27E
Bække 73 55 35N 9 6E
Baena 57 37 37N 4 20W
Baerami Creek 141 32 27S 150 27E
Baetas 174 6 5S 62 15W
Baexem 47 51 13N 5 53E
Baeza, Ecuador 174 0 25S 77 45W
Baeza, Spain 59 37 57N 3 25W
Bafa 93 31 40N 55 25E
Bafa Gölü 69 37 30N 27 29E
Bafatá 120 12 8N 15 20W
Baffin Bay 12 72 0N 64 0W
Baffin I. 149 68 0N 75 0W
Bafia 121 4 40N 11 10E
Bafilo 121 9 22N 1 22E
Bafing, R. 120 11 40N 10 45W
Baflo 46 53 22N 6 31E
Bafoulabé 120 13 50N 10 55W
Bafq 93 31 40N 55 20E
Bafra 82 41 34N 35 54E
Baft 93 29 15N 56 38E
Bafut 121 6 6N 10 2E
Bafwakwandji 126 1 12N 26 52E
Bafwasende 126 1 3N 27 5E
Bagalkot 96 16 10N 75 40E
Bagamoyo 126 6 28S 38 55E
Bagamoyo □ 126 6 20S 38 30E
Bagan Datok 101 3 59N 100 47E
Bagan Serai 101 5 1N 100 32E
Bagan Siapiapi 102 2 12N 100 50E
Baganga 103 7 34N 126 33E
Bagasra 94 21 59N 71 77E
Bagawi 123 12 20N 34 18E
Bagdad 163 34 35N 115 53W
Bagdarin 77 54 26N 113 36E
Bagè 173 31 20S 54 15W
Bagenalstown = Muine Bheag 39 52 42N 6 57W
Baggs 160 41 8N 107 46W
Baggy Pt. 30 51 11N 4 12W
Bagh 95 33 59N 73 45E
Bagh nam Faoileann, B. 36 57 22N 7 13W
Baghdād 92 33 20N 44 30E
Bagherhat 98 22 40N 89 47E
Bagheria 64 38 5N 13 30E
Baghin 93 30 12N 56 45E
Baghlan 93 36 12N 69 0E
Baghlan □ 93 36 0N 68 30E
Baginbun Hd. 39 52 10N 6 50W
Bagley 158 47 30N 95 22W
Bagnacavallo 63 44 25N 11 58E
Bagnara Cálabra 65 38 16N 15 49E
Bagnères-de-Bigorre 44 43 5N 0 9E
Bagnères-de-Luchon 44 42 47N 0 38E
Bagni di Lucca 62 44 1N 10 37E
Bagno di Romagna 63 43 50N 11 59E
Bagnoles-de-l'Orne 42 48 32N 0 25W
Bagnolo Mella 62 45 27N 10 14E
Bagnols-les-Bains 44 44 30N 3 40E
Bagnols-sur-Cèze 45 44 10N 4 36E
Bagnorégio 63 42 38N 12 7E
Bagolino 62 45 49N 10 28E
Bagotville 151 48 22N 70 54W
Bagrdan 66 44 5N 21 11E
Bagshot 29 51 22N 0 41W
Baguio 103 16 26N 120 34E
Bahabón de Esgueva 58 41 52N 3 43W
Bahadurabad 98 25 11N 89 44E
Bahadurgarh 94 28 40N 76 57E
Bahama, Canal Viejo de 166 22 10N 77 30W
Bahama Is. 167 24 40N 74 0W
Bahamas ■ 167 24 0N 74 0W
Baharîya,El Wâhât el 122 28 0N 28 50E
Bahau 101 2 48N 102 26E
Bahawalnagar 94 30 0N 73 15E
Bahawalpur 94 29 37N 71 40E
Bahawalpur □ 94 29 5N 71 3E
Baheri 95 28 45N 79 34E
Baheta 123 13 27N 42 10E
Bahi 126 5 58S 35 21E
Bahi Swamp 126 6 10S 35 0E
Bahia = Salvador 171 13 0S 38 30W
Bahia □ 171 12 0S 42 0W
Bahía Blanca 172 38 35S 62 13W
Bahía de Caráquez 174 0 40S 80 27W
Bahía Honda 166 22 54N 83 10W
Bahía, Islas de la 166 16 45N 86 15W
Bahía Laura 176 48 10S 66 30W
Bahía Negra 174 20 5S 58 5W
Bahir Dar Giyorgis 123 11 33N 37 25E
Bahmer 118 27 32N 0 10W
Bahönye 53 46 25N 17 28E
Bahr Aouk 124 9 20N 20 40E
Bahr Dar 123 11 37N 37 10E
Bahr el Abiad 123 9 30N 31 40E
Bahr el Ahmer □ 122 20 0N 35 0E
Bahr el Arab 123 9 50N 27 10E
Bahr el Azraq 123 10 30N 35 0E
Bahr el Ghazâl □ 123 7 0N 28 0E
Bahr el Ghazâl, R. 123 9 0N 30 0E
Bahr el Jebel 123 7 30N 30 30E
Bahr Salamat 124 10 0N 19 0E
Bahr Yûsef 122 28 25N 30 35E
Bahra 92 21 25N 39 32E
Bahra el Burullus 122 31 28N 30 48E
Bahra el Manzala 122 31 28N 32 01E
Bahraich 95 27 38N 81 50E
Bahrain ■ 93 26 0N 50 35E
Bahramabad 93 30 28N 56 2E
Bahu Kalat 93 25 50N 61 20E
Bai 120 13 35N 3 28W
Bai Bung, Mui 101 8 38N 104 44E
Bai Duc 100 18 3N 105 49E
Bai Thuong 100 19 54N 105 23E
Baia-Mare 70 47 40N 23 17E
Baia-Sprie 70 47 41N 23 43W
Baião 170 2 40S 49 40W
Baïbokoum 117 7 40N 14 45E
Baidoa 91 3 8N 43 30E
Baie Comeau 151 49 12N 68 10W
Baie de l'Abri 151 50 3N 67 0W
Baie Johan Beetz 151 50 18N 62 50W
Baie St. Paul 151 47 28N 70 32W
Baie Trinité 151 49 25N 67 20W
Baie Verte 151 49 55N 56 12W
Baignes 44 45 28N 0 25W
Baigneux-les-Juifs 43 47 31N 4 39E
Ba'ījī 92 35 0N 43 30E
Baikal, L. 77 53 0N 108 0E
Bailadila, Mt. 96 18 43N 81 15E
Baildon 33 53 52N 1 46W
Baile Atha Cliath = Dublin 39 53 20N 6 18W
Bailei 123 6 44N 40 18E
Bailén 57 38 8N 3 48W
Baileux 47 50 2N 4 23E
Bailhongal 97 15 55N 74 53E
Bailique, Ilha 170 1 2N 49 58W
Bailleul 43 50 44N 2 41E
Baillieborough 38 53 55N 7 0W
Baimuru 135 7 35S 144 51E
Bain-de-Bretagne 42 47 50N 1 40W
Bainbridge, U.K. 32 54 18N 2 7W
Bainbridge, Ga., U.S.A. 157 30 53N 84 34W
Bainbridge, N.Y., U.S.A. 162 42 17N 75 29W
Baing 103 10 14S 120 34E
Bainville 158 48 8N 104 10W
Bainyik 135 3 40S 143 4E
Baird 159 32 25N 99 25W
Baird Inlet 147 64 49N 164 18W
Baird Mts. 147 67 10N 160 15W
Bairnsdale 141 37 48S 147 36E
Baissa 121 7 14N 10 38E
Baitadi 95 29 35N 80 25E
Baixa Grande 171 11 57S 40 11W
Baiyuda 122 17 35N 32 07E
Baja 53 46 12N 18 59E
Baja California 164 32 10N 115 12W
Baja, Pta. 164 29 50N 116 0W
Bajah, Wadi 122 23 14N 39 20E
Bajana 94 23 7N 71 49E
Bajimba 139 29 22S 152 0E
Bajimba, Mt. 139 29 17S 152 6E
Bajina Bašta 66 43 58N 19 35E
Bajitpur 95 24 13N 91 0E
Bajmok 66 45 57N 19 24E
Bajo Boquete 167 8 49N 82 27W
Bajoga 121 10 57N 11 20E
Bajool 138 23 40S 150 35E
Bak 53 46 43N 16 51E
Bakal 84 54 56N 58 48E
Bakala 117 6 15N 20 20E
Bakanas 85 44 50N 76 15E
Bakar 63 45 18N 14 32E
Bakel, Neth. 47 51 30N 5 45E
Bakel, Senegal 120 14 56N 12 20W
Baker, Calif., U.S.A. 163 35 16N 116 8W
Baker, Mont., U.S.A. 158 46 22N 104 12W
Baker, Nev., U.S.A. 160 38 59N 114 7W
Baker, Oreg., U.S.A. 160 44 50N 117 55W
Baker Is. 130 0 10N 176 35E
Baker, L., Austral. 137 26 54S 126 5E
Baker, L., Can. 148 64 0N 96 0W
Baker Lake 148 64 20N 96 3W
Baker Mt. 160 48 50N 121 49W
Baker's Dozen Is. 150 56 45N 78 45W
Bakersfield 163 35 25N 119 0W
Bakewell 33 53 13N 1 40W
Bakhchisaray 82 44 40N 33 45E
Bakhmach 80 51 10N 32 45E
Bakhtiari □ 92 32 0N 49 0E
Bakia 123 5 18N 25 45E
Bakinskikh Komissarov 92 39 20N 49 15E
Bakırköy 67 40 59N 28 53E
Bakkafjörðr 74 66 2N 14 48W
Bakkagerði 74 65 31N 13 49W
Bakke 71 58 25N 6 39E
Bakony Forest = Bakony Hegység 53 47 10N 17 30E
Bakony Hegység 53 47 10N 17 30E
Bakony, R. 53 47 35N 17 54E
Bakori 121 11 34N 7 25E
Bakouma 117 5 40N 22 56E
Bakov 52 50 27N 14 55E
Bakpakty 85 44 35N 76 40E
Bakr Uzyak 84 52 59N 58 38E
Baku 83 40 25N 49 45E
Bakwanga = Mbuji Mayi 124 6 9S 23 40E
Bal'a 90 32 20N 35 6E
Bala, L. = Tegid, L. 31 52 53N 3 38W
Balabac I. 102 8 0N 117 0E
Balabac, Selat 102 7 53N 117 5E
Balabagh 94 34 25N 70 12E
Balabakk 92 34 0N 36 10E
Balabalangan, Kepulauan 102 2 20S 117 30E
Balaghat 96 21 49N 80 12E
Balaghat Ra. 96 18 50N 76 30E
Balaguer 58 41 50N 0 50E
Balakhna 81 56 35N 43 32E
Balaklava, Austral. 140 34 7S 138 22E
Balaklava, U.S.S.R. 82 44 30N 33 30E
Balakleya 82 49 28N 36 55E
Balakovo 81 52 4N 47 55E
Balallan 36 58 5N 6 35W
Balancán 165 17 48N 91 32W
Balanda 81 51 30N 44 40E
Balangir 96 20 43N 83 35E
Balapur 96 21 22N 76 45E
Balashikha 81 55 49N 37 59E
Balashov 81 51 30N 43 10E
Balasinor 94 22 57N 73 23E
Balasore 96 21 35N 87 3E

Balassagyarmat Bangor

Balassagyarmat	53	48 4N	19 15 E
Balât	122	25 36N	29 19 E
Balaton	53	46 50N	17 40 E
Balatonfüred	53	46 58N	17 54 E
Balatonszentgyörgy	53	46 41N	17 19 E
Balazote	59	38 54N	2 09W
Balbeggie	35	56 26N	3 19W
Balbi, Mt.	135	5 55 S	154 58 E
Balblair	37	57 39N	4 11W
Balboa	166	9 0N	79 30W
Balbriggan	38	53 35N	6 10W
Balcarce	172	38 0 S	58 10W
Balcarres	153	50 50N	103 35W
Balchik	67	43 28N	28 11 E
Balclutha	143	46 15 S	169 45 E
Bald Hd.	137	35 6 S	118 1 E
Bald Hill, W. Australia, Austral.	137	31 36 S	116 13 E
Bald Hill, W. Australia, Austral.	137	24 55 S	119 57 E
Bald I.	137	34 57 S	118 27 E
Bald Knob	159	35 20N	91 35W
Baldegger-See	51	47 12N	8 17 E
Balder, oilfield	19	59 10N	2 20 E
Balderton	33	53 3N	0 46W
Baldock	29	51 59N	0 11W
Baldock L.	153	56 33N	97 57W
Baldoyle	38	53 24N	6 10W
Baldwin, Fla., U.S.A.	156	30 15N	82 10W
Baldwin, Mich., U.S.A.	156	43 54N	85 53W
Baldwinsville	162	43 10N	76 19W
Bale	63	45 4N	13 46 E
Baleares □	58	39 30N	3 0 E
Baleares, Islas	58	39 30N	3 0 E
Balearic Is. = Baleares, Islas	58	39 30N	3 0 E
Baleia, Ponta da	171	17 40 S	39 7W
Balen	47	51 10N	5 10 E
Baler	103	15 46N	121 34 E
Balerna	51	45 52N	9 0 E
Baleshare I.	36	57 30N	7 21W
Balezino	84	58 2N	53 6 E
Balfate	166	15 48N	86 25W
Balfe's Creek	138	20 12 S	145 55 E
Balfour, S. Afr.	129	26 38 S	28 35 E
Balfour, U.K.	37	59 2N	2 54W
Balfour Downs	137	22 45 S	120 50 E
Balfouriyya	90	32 38N	35 18 E
Balfron	34	56 4N	4 20W
Bali	121	5 54N	10 0 E
Bali □	102	8 20 S	115 0 E
Bali, I.	102	8 20 S	115 0 E
Bali, Selat	103	8 30 S	114 35 E
Baligród	54	49 20N	22 17 E
Balikesir	92	39 35N	27 58 E
Balikpapan	102	1 10 S	116 55 E
Balimbing	103	5 10N	120 3 E
Balimo	135	8 6 S	142 57 E
Baling	101	5 41N	100 55 E
Balintore	37	57 45N	3 55W
Balipara	99	26 50N	92 45 E
Balit	95	36 15N	74 40 E
Baliza	175	16 0 S	52 20W
Balk	46	52 54N	5 35 E
Balkan Mts. = Stara Planina	67	43 15N	23 0 E
Balkan Pen.	16	42 0N	22 0 E
Balkh = Wazirabad	93	36 44N	66 47 E
Balkh □	93	36 30N	67 0 E
Balkhash	76	46 50N	74 50 E
Balkhash, Ozero	76	40 0N	74 50 E
Balla, Ireland	38	53 48N	9 7W
Balla, Pak.	99	24 10N	91 35 E
Ballachulish	36	56 40N	5 10W
Balladonia	137	32 27 S	123 51 E
Ballagan Pt.	38	54 0N	6 6W
Ballaghaderreen	38	53 55N	8 35W
Ballantrae	34	55 6N	5 0W
Ballara	140	32 19 S	140 45 E
Ballarat	139	37 33 S	143 50 E
Ballard, L.	137	29 20 S	120 10 E
Ballarpur	96	19 50N	79 23 E
Ballater	37	57 2N	3 2W
Ballaugh	32	54 20N	4 32W
Balldale	141	36 20N	146 33 E
Ballenas, Canal de las	164	29 10N	113 45W
Balleni	70	45 48N	27 51 E
Balleny Is.	13	66 30 S	163 0 E
Ballia	95	25 46N	84 12 E
Ballickmoyler	39	52 54N	7 2W
Ballidu	137	30 35 S	116 45 E
Ballina, Austral.	139	28 50 S	153 31 E
Ballina, Mayo, Ireland	38	54 7N	9 10W
Ballina, Tipp., Ireland	39	52 49N	8 27W
Ballinagar	39	53 15N	7 21W
Ballinagh = Bellananagh	38	53 55N	7 25W
Ballinalack	38	53 38N	7 28W
Ballinalea	39	53 0N	6 8W
Ballinalee	38	53 46N	7 40W
Ballinamallard	38	54 30N	7 36W
Ballinameen	38	53 54N	8 19W
Ballinamore	38	54 3N	7 48W
Ballinamore Bridge	38	53 30N	8 24W
Ballinascarty	39	51 40N	8 52W
Ballinasloe	39	53 20N	8 12W
Ballincollig	39	51 52N	8 35W
Ballindaggin	39	52 33N	6 43W
Ballinderry	38	53 2N	8 13W
Ballinderry R.	38	54 40N	6 32W
Ballindine	38	53 40N	8 57W
Ballineen	39	51 43N	8 57W
Balling	73	56 38N	8 51 E
Ballingarry, Lim., Ireland	39	53 1N	8 3W
Ballingarry, Tipp., Ireland	39	52 29N	8 50W
Ballingarry, Tipp., Ireland	39	52 35N	7 32W
Ballingeary	39	51 51N	9 13W
Ballinger	159	31 45N	99 58W
Ballinhassig	39	51 48N	8 33W
Ballinlough	38	53 45N	8 39W
Ballinluig	37	56 40N	3 40W
Ballinrobe	38	53 36N	9 13W
Ballinskelligs	39	51 50N	10 17W
Ballinskelligs B.	39	51 46N	10 11W
Ballintober	38	53 43N	8 25W
Ballintoy	38	55 13N	6 20W
Ballintra	38	54 35N	8 9W
Ballinunty	39	52 36N	7 40W
Ballinure	39	52 34N	7 46W
Ballivian	172	22 41 S	62 10W
Ballivor	38	53 32N	6 50W
Ballo Pt.	79	8 55N	13 18W
Balloch	34	56 0N	4 35W
Ballon	39	48 10N	0 16 E
Ballston Spa	162	43 0N	73 51W
Ballybay	38	54 8N	6 52W
Ballybofey	38	54 48N	7 47W
Ballyboghil	38	53 32N	6 16W
Ballybogy	38	55 8N	6 33W
Ballybunion	39	52 30N	9 40W
Ballycanew	39	52 37N	6 18W
Ballycarney	39	52 35N	6 44W
Ballycastle	38	55 12N	6 15W
Ballycastle B.	38	55 12N	6 15W
Ballyclare, Ireland	38	53 40N	8 0W
Ballyclare, U.K.	38	54 46N	6 0W
Ballyclerahan	39	52 25N	7 48W
Ballycolla	39	52 53N	7 27W
Ballyconneely	38	53 27N	10 5W
Ballyconneely B.	38	53 23N	10 8W
Ballyconnell	38	54 7N	7 35W
Ballycotton	39	51 50N	8 0W
Ballycroy	38	54 2N	9 49W
Ballydavid	39	53 12N	8 28W
Ballydavid Hd.	39	52 15N	10 20W
Ballydehob	39	51 34N	9 28W
Ballydonegan	39	51 37N	10 12W
Ballydonegan B.	39	51 38N	10 6W
Ballyduff, Kerry, Ireland	39	52 27N	9 40W
Ballyduff, Waterford, Ireland	39	52 9N	8 2W
Ballyforan	38	53 29N	8 18W
Ballygar	38	53 33N	8 20W
Ballygarrett	39	52 34N	6 15W
Ballygawley	38	54 27N	7 2W
Ballyglass	38	53 45N	9 9W
Ballygorman	38	55 23N	7 20W
Ballyhahill	39	52 33N	9 13W
Ballyhaise	38	54 3N	7 20W
Ballyhalbert	38	54 30N	5 28W
Ballyhaunis	38	53 47N	8 47W
Ballyheige I.	39	52 22N	9 51W
Ballyhoura Hills	39	52 18N	8 33W
Ballyjamesduff	38	53 52N	7 11W
Ballylanders	39	52 25N	8 21W
Ballylaneen	39	52 10N	7 25W
Ballylongford	39	52 34N	9 30W
Ballylooby	39	52 20N	7 59W
Ballylynan	39	52 57N	7 02W
Ballymacoda	39	51 53N	7 56W
Ballymagorry	38	54 52N	7 26W
Ballymahon	39	53 35N	7 45W
Ballymena	38	54 53N	6 18W
Ballymena □	38	54 53N	6 18W
Ballymoe	38	53 41N	8 28W
Ballymoney	38	55 5N	6 30W
Ballymoney □	38	55 5N	6 23W
Ballymore	39	53 30N	7 40W
Ballymore Eustace	39	53 8N	6 38W
Ballymote	38	54 5N	8 30W
Ballymurphy	39	52 33N	6 52W
Ballymurray	38	53 36N	8 8W
Ballynabola	39	52 21N	6 50W
Ballynacally	39	52 42N	9 7W
Ballynacargy	38	53 35N	7 32W
Ballynacorra	39	51 53N	8 10W
Ballynagore	38	53 24N	7 29W
Ballynahinch	38	54 24N	5 55W
Ballynahown	38	53 21N	7 52W
Ballynameen	38	54 58N	6 41W
Ballynamona	39	52 5N	8 39W
Ballynure	38	54 47N	5 59W
Ballyquintin, Pt.	38	54 20N	5 30W
Ballyragget	39	52 47N	7 20W
Ballyroan	39	52 57N	7 20W
Ballyronan	38	54 43N	6 32W
Ballyroney	38	54 17N	6 8W
Ballysadare	38	54 12N	8 30W
Ballyshannon	38	54 30N	8 10W
Ballyvaughan	39	53 7N	9 10W
Ballyvourney	39	51 57N	9 10W
Ballyvoy	38	55 11N	6 11W
Ballywalter	38	54 33N	5 30W
Ballywilliam	39	52 27N	6 52W
Balmaceda	176	46 0 S	71 50W
Balmaclellan	35	55 6N	4 5W
Balmazújváros	53	47 37N	21 21 E
Balmedie	37	57 14N	2 4W
Balmhorn	50	46 26N	7 42 E
Balmoral	140	37 15 S	141 48 E
Balmoral For.	37	57 0N	3 15W
Balmorhea	159	31 2N	103 41W
Balnapaling	37	57 42N	4 2W
Balonne, R.	139	28 47 S	147 56 E
Balovale	125	13 30 S	23 15 E
Balquhidder	34	56 22N	4 22W
Balrampur	95	27 30N	82 20 E
Balranald	140	34 38 S	143 33 E
Balş	70	44 22N	24 5 E
Balsas	165	18 0N	99 40W
Balsas, R., Goias, Brazil	170	9 0 S	48 0W
Balsas, R., Maranhão, Brazil	170	7 15 S	44 35W
Balsas, R., Mexico	164	18 30N	101 20W
Bålsta	72	59 35N	17 30 E
Balsthal	50	47 19N	7 41 E
Balta, Rumania	70	44 54N	22 38 E
Balta, U.S.A.	158	48 12N	100 7W
Balta, U.S.S.R.	82	48 2N	29 45 E
Balta, I.	36	60 44N	0 49W
Baltanás	56	41 56N	4 15W
Baltasound	36	60 47N	0 53W
Baltic Sea	75	56 0N	20 0 E
Baltiisk	75	54 38N	19 55 E
Baltim	122	31 35N	31 10 E
Baltimore, Ireland	39	51 29N	9 22W
Baltimore, U.S.A.	162	39 18N	76 37W
Baltinglass	39	52 57N	6 42W
Baltrum	48	53 43N	7 25 E
Baluchistan □	93	27 30N	65 0 E
Balurghat	95	25 15N	88 44 E
Balvicar	34	56 17N	5 38W
Balygychan	77	63 56N	154 12 E
Bam	93	29 7N	58 14 E
Bam La	99	29 25N	98 35 E
Bama	121	11 33N	13 33 E
Bamako	120	12 34N	7 55W
Bamba	121	17 5N	1 0W
Bambari	117	5 40N	20 35 E
Bambaroo	107	18 50 S	146 11 E
Bamberg, Ger.	49	49 54N	10 53 E
Bamberg, U.S.A.	157	33 19N	81 1W
Bambesi	123	9 45N	34 40 E
Bambey	120	14 42N	16 28W
Bambili	126	3 40N	26 0 E
Bamboo	138	14 34 S	143 20 E
Bambouti	126	5 25N	27 12 E
Bambuí	171	20 1 S	45 58W
Bamburgh	35	55 36N	1 42W
Bamenda	121	5 57N	10 11 E
Bamfield	152	48 45N	125 10W
Bamford	33	53 21N	1 41W
Bamian □	93	35 0N	67 0 E
Bamkin	121	6 3N	11 27 E
Bampton, Devon, U.K.	30	50 59N	3 29W
Bampton, Oxon., U.K.	28	51 44N	1 33W
Bampur	93	27 15N	60 21 E
Bampur, R.	93	27 20N	59 30 E
Ban Aranyaprathet	100	13 41N	102 30 E
Ban Ban	100	19 31N	103 15 E
Ban Bang Hin	101	9 32N	98 35 E
Ban Bua Chum	101	15 11N	101 12 E
Ban Bua Yai	100	15 33N	102 26 E
Ban Chiang Klang	100	19 15N	100 55 E
Ban Chik	100	17 15N	102 22 E
Ban Choho	100	15 2N	102 9 E
Ban Dan Lan Hoi	100	17 0N	99 35 E
Ban Don	100	12 53N	107 48 E
Ban Don = Surat Thani	101	9 8N	99 20 E
Ban Don, Go	101	9 20N	99 25 E
Ban Dong	100	19 14N	100 3 E
Ban Hong	100	18 18N	98 50 E
Ban Houei Sai	101	20 22N	100 32 E
Ban Kaeng	100	17 29N	100 7 E
Ban Kantang	101	7 25N	99 31 E
Ban Keun	100	18 22N	102 35 E
Ban Khai	100	12 46N	101 18 E
Ban Khe Bo	101	19 10N	104 39 E
Ban Kheun	100	20 13N	101 7 E
Ban Khlong Kua	101	6 57N	100 8 E
Ban Khuan Mao	101	7 50N	99 37 E
Ban Khun Yuam	100	18 49N	97 57 E
Ban Ko Yai Chim	101	11 17N	99 26 E
Ban Kok	100	16 40N	103 40 E
Ban Laem	100	13 13N	99 59 E
Ban Lao Ngam	100	15 28N	106 10 E
Ban Le Kathe	100	15 49N	98 53 E
Ban Mae Chedi	100	19 11N	99 31 E
Ban Mae Laeng	100	20 1N	99 17 E
Ban Mae Sariang	100	18 0N	97 56 E
Ban Me Thuot	100	12 40N	108 3 E
Ban Mi	100	15 3N	100 32 E
Ban Muong Mo	100	19 4N	103 58 E
Ban Na Mo	100	17 7N	105 40 E
Ban Na San	101	8 33N	99 52 E
Ban Na Tong	100	20 56N	101 47 E
Ban Nam Bac	100	20 38N	102 20 E
Ban Nam Ma	100	22 2N	101 37 E
Ban Ngang	100	15 59N	106 11 E
Ban Nong Bok	100	17 5N	104 48 E
Ban Nong Boua	100	15 40N	106 33 E
Ban Nong Pling	100	15 40N	100 10 E
Ban Pak Chan	101	10 32N	98 51 E
Ban Phai	100	16 4N	102 44 E
Ban Pong	100	13 50N	99 55 E
Ban Ron Phibun	101	8 9N	99 51 E
Ban Sanam Chai	101	7 33N	100 25 E
Ban Sangkha	100	14 37N	103 52 E
Ban Tak	100	17 2N	99 4 E
Ban Tako	100	14 5N	102 40 E
Ban Takua Pa	101	8 55N	98 25 E
Ban Tha Dua	100	17 59N	98 39 E
Ban Tha Li	100	17 37N	101 25 E
Ban Tha Nun	101	8 12N	98 18 E
Ban Thahine	100	14 12N	105 33 E
Ban Thateng	101	15 25N	106 27 E
Ban Xien Kok	100	20 54N	100 39 E
Ban Yen Nhan	100	20 57N	106 2 E
Baña, La, Punta de	58	40 33N	0 40 E
Banadar Daryay Oman □	93	25 30N	56 0 E
Banadia	174	6 54N	71 49W
Banagher	39	53 12N	8 0W
Banalia	126	1 32N	25 5 E
Banam	101	11 20N	105 17 E
Banamba	120	13 29N	7 22W
Banana	138	24 28 S	150 8 E
Bananal, I. do	171	11 30 S	50 30W
Banaras = Varanasi	95	25 22N	83 8 E
Banas, R., Gujarat, India	94	24 25N	72 30 E
Banas, R., Madhya Pradesh, India	95	24 15N	81 30 E
Bânâs, Ras.	122	23 57N	35 50 E
Banat □	66	45 45N	21 15 E
Banbridge	38	54 21N	6 17W
Banbridge □	38	54 21N	6 16W
Banbury	28	52 4N	1 21W
Banchory	37	57 3N	2 30W
Bancroft	150	45 3N	77 51W
Bancroft = Chililabombwe	127	12 18 S	27 43 E
Band	67	46 30N	24 25 E
Band-i-Turkistan, Ra.	93	35 2N	64 0 E
Banda	95	25 30N	80 26 E
Banda Aceh	102	5 35N	95 20 E
Banda Banda, Mt.	141	31 10 S	152 28 E
Banda Elat	103	5 40 S	133 5 E
Banda, Kepulauan	103	4 37 S	129 50 E
Banda, La	172	27 45 S	64 10W
Banda, Punta	164	31 47N	116 50W
Banda Sea	103	6 0 S	130 0 E
Bandama, R.	120	6 32N	5 30W
Bandanwara	94	26 9N	74 38 E
Bandar = Masulipatnam	97	16 12N	81 12 E
Bandar 'Abbās	93	27 15N	56 15 E
Bandar-e Būshehr	93	28 55N	50 55 E
Bandar-e Chārak	93	26 45N	54 20 E
Bandar-e Deylam	92	30 5N	50 10 E
Bandar-e Lengeh	93	26 35N	54 58 E
Bandar-e Ma'shur	92	30 35N	49 10 E
Bandar-e-Nakhīlu	93	26 58N	53 30 E
Bandar-e-Pahlavi	92	37 30N	49 30 E
Bandar-e Rīg	93	29 30N	50 45 E
Bandar-e Shah	93	37 0N	54 10 E
Bandar-e-Shahpur	92	30 30N	49 5 E
Bandar Maharani = Muar	101	2 3N	102 34 E
Bandar Penggaram = Batu Pahat	101	1 50N	102 56 E
Bandar Seri Begawan	102	4 52N	115 0 E
Bandawe	127	11 58 S	34 5 E
Bande, Belg.	47	50 10N	5 25 E
Bande, Spain	56	42 3N	7 58W
Bandeira, Pico da	173	20 26 S	41 47W
Bandeirante	171	13 41 S	50 48W
Bandera, Argent.	172	28 55 S	62 20W
Bandera, U.S.A.	159	29 45N	99 3W
Banderas, Bahia de	164	20 40N	105 30W
Bandi-San	112	37 36N	140 4 E
Bandia, R.	96	19 30N	80 25 E
Bandiagara	120	14 12N	3 29W
Bandirma	92	40 20N	28 0 E
Bandon	39	51 44N	8 45W
Bandon, R.	39	51 40N	8 11W
Bandula	127	19 0 S	33 7 E
Bandundu	124	3 15 S	17 22 E
Bandung	103	6 36 S	107 48 E
Bandya	137	27 40 S	122 5 E
Bañeres	59	38 44N	0 38W
Banes	167	21 0N	75 42W
Bañeza, La	56	42 17N	5 54W
Banff, Can.	152	51 10N	115 34W
Banff, U.K.	37	57 40N	2 32W
Banff Nat. Park	152	51 30N	116 15W
Banfora	120	10 40N	4 40W
Bang Fai, R.	100	16 57N	104 45 E
Bang Hieng, R.	100	16 24N	105 40 E
Bang Krathum	100	16 34N	100 18 E
Bang Lamung	100	13 3N	100 56 E
Bang Mun Nak	100	16 2N	100 23 E
Bang Pa In	100	14 14N	100 35 E
Bang Rakam	100	16 45N	100 7 E
Bang Saphan	101	11 14N	99 28 E
Bangala Dam	127	21 7 S	31 25 E
Bangalore	97	12 59N	77 40 E
Bangangte	121	5 8N	10 32 E
Bangaon	95	23 0N	88 47 E
Bangassou	124	4 55N	23 55 E
Bangeta, Mt.	135	6 21 S	147 3 E
Banggai	103	1 40 S	123 30 E
Banggi, P.	102	7 50N	117 0 E
Banghāzī	119	32 11N	20 3 E
Bangil	103	7 36 S	112 50 E
Bangjang	123	11 23N	32 41 E
Bangka, Pulau, Celebes, Indon.	103	1 50N	125 5 E
Bangka, Pulau, Sumatera, Indon.	102	2 0 S	105 50 E
Bangka, Selat	102	3 30 S	105 30 E
Bangkalan	103	7 2 S	112 46 E
Bangkinang	102	0 18N	100 5 E
Bangko	102	2 5 S	102 9 E
Bangkok	100	13 45N	100 31 E
Bangladesh ■	98	24 0N	90 0 E
Bangolo	120	7 1N	7 29W
Bangor, Me., U.S.A.	151	44 48N	68 42W

Bangor **Bassevelde**

Bangor, Pa., U.S.A.	**162**	40 51N	75 13W
Bangor, N.I., U.K.	**38**	54 40N	5 40W
Bangor, Wales, U.K.	**31**	53 13N	4 9W
Bangued	**103**	17 40N	120 37 E
Bangui	**124**	4 23N	18 35 E
Banguru	**126**	0 30N	27 10 E
Bangweulu, L.	**127**	11 0 S	30 0 E
Bangweulu Swamp	**127**	11 20 S	30 15 E
Banham	**29**	52 27N	1 3 E
Bani	**167**	18 16N	70 22W
Bani Bangou	**121**	15 3N	2 42 E
Bani, Djebel	**118**	29 16N	8 0W
Bani Na'im	**90**	31 31N	35 10 E
Bani, R.	**120**	12 40N	6 30W
Bani Suhayla	**90**	31 21N	34 19 E
Bania	**120**	9 4N	3 6W
Baniara	**135**	9 44 S	149 54 E
Banihal Pass	**95**	33 30N	75 12 E
Banīnah	**119**	32 0N	20 12 E
Baniyas	**92**	35 10N	36 0 E
Banja Luka	**66**	44 49N	17 26 E
Banjak, Kepulauan	**102**	2 10N	97 10 E
Banjar	**103**	7 24 S	108 30 E
Banjarmasin	**102**	3 20 S	114 35 E
Banjarnegara	**103**	7 24 S	109 42 E
Banjul	**120**	13 28N	16 40W
Banka Banka	**138**	18 50 S	134 0 E
Bankend	**35**	55 2N	3 31W
Bankeryd	**73**	57 53N	14 6 E
Banket	**127**	17 27 S	30 19 E
Bankfoot	**35**	56 30N	3 31W
Bankhead	**37**	57 11N	2 10W
Bankilaré	**121**	14 35N	0 44 E
Bankipore	**95**	25 35N	85 10 E
Banks I., B.C., Can.	**152**	53 20N	130 0W
Banks I., N. W. Terr., Can.	**12**	73 15N	121 30W
Banks I., P.N.G.	**135**	10 10 S	142 15 E
Banks Peninsula	**143**	43 45 S	173 15 E
Banks Str.	**138**	40 40 S	148 10 E
Bankura	**95**	23 11N	87 18 E
Bankya	**66**	42 43N	23 8 E
Bann R., Down, U.K.	**38**	54 30N	6 31W
Bann R., Londonderry, U.K.	**38**	55 10N	6 34W
Bannalec	**42**	47 57N	3 42W
Bannang Sata	**101**	6 16N	101 16 E
Bannerton	**140**	34 42 S	142 47 E
Banning, Can.	**150**	48 44N	91 56W
Banning, U.S.A.	**163**	33 58N	116 58W
Banningville = Bandundu	**124**	3 15 S	17 22 E
Bannockburn, Zimb.	**127**	20 17 S	29 48 E
Bannockburn, U.K.	**35**	56 5N	3 55W
Bannow	**39**	52 12N	6 50W
Bannow B.	**39**	52 13N	6 48W
Bannu	**93**	33 0N	70 18 E
Bañolas	**58**	42 16N	2 44 E
Banon	**45**	44 2N	5 38 E
Baños de la Encina	**57**	38 10N	3 46W
Baños de Molgas	**56**	42 15N	7 40W
Bánovce	**53**	48 44N	18 16 E
Banská Bystrica	**53**	48 46N	19 14 E
Banská Stiavnica	**53**	48 25N	18 55 E
Bansko	**67**	41 52N	23 28 E
Banswara	**94**	23 32N	74 24 E
Bantama	**121**	7 48N	0 42W
Bante	**121**	8 25N	1 53 E
Banteer	**39**	52 8N	8 53W
Banten	**103**	6 5 S	106 8 E
Bantry	**39**	51 40N	9 28W
Bantry, B.	**39**	51 35N	9 50W
Bantul	**103**	7 55 S	110 19 E
Bantva	**94**	21 29N	70 12 E
Bantval	**97**	12 55N	75 0 E
Banu	**93**	35 35N	69 5 E
Banwell	**28**	51 19N	2 51W
Banya	**67**	42 33N	24 50 E
Banyo	**121**	6 52N	11 45 E
Banyuls	**44**	42 29N	3 8 E
Banyumas	**103**	7 32 S	109 18 E
Banyuwangi	**103**	8 13 S	114 21 E
Banzare Coast	**13**	66 30 S	125 0 E
Banzyville = Mobayi	**124**	4 15N	21 8 E
Bao Ha	**100**	22 11N	104 21 E
Bao Lac	**100**	22 57N	105 40 E
Bao Loc	**101**	11 32N	107 48 E
Bap	**94**	27 23N	72 18 E
Bapatla	**97**	15 55N	80 30 E
Bapaume	**43**	50 7N	2 50 E
Bâqa el Gharbiya	**90**	32 25N	35 2 E
Baqūbah	**92**	33 45N	44 50 E
Baquedano	**172**	23 20 S	69 52W
Bar, U.S.S.R.	**82**	49 4N	27 40 E
Bar, Yugo.	**66**	42 8N	19 8 E
Bar Harbor	**151**	44 15N	68 20W
Bar-le-Duc	**43**	48 47N	5 10 E
Bar-sur-Aube	**43**	48 14N	4 40 E
Bar-sur-Seine	**43**	48 7N	4 20 E
Barabai	**102**	2 32 S	115 34 E
Barabinsk	**76**	55 20N	78 20 E
Baraboo	**158**	43 28N	89 46W
Baracoa	**167**	20 20N	74 30W
Baradero	**172**	33 52 S	59 29W
Baradine	**141**	30 56 S	149 4 E
Baraga	**158**	46 49N	88 29W
Barahona, Dom. Rep.	**167**	18 13N	71 7W
Barahona, Spain	**58**	41 17N	2 39W
Barail Range	**99**	25 15N	93 20 E
Barakhola	**99**	25 0N	92 45 E
Barakot	**95**	21 33N	84 59 E
Barakula	**139**	26 30 S	150 33 E
Baralaba	**138**	24 13 S	149 50 E
Baralzon L.	**153**	60 0N	98 3W
Baramati	**96**	18 11N	74 33 E
Baramba	**96**	20 25N	85 23 E
Barameiya	**122**	18 32N	36 38 E
Baramula	**95**	34 15N	74 20 E
Baran	**94**	25 9N	76 40 E
Baranoa	**174**	10 48N	74 55W
Baranof I.	**147**	57 0N	135 10W
Baranovichi	**80**	53 10N	26 0 E
Baranów Sandomierski	**54**	50 29N	21 30 E
Baranya □	**53**	46 0N	18 15 E
Barão de Cocais	**171**	19 56 S	43 28W
Barão de Grajaú	**170**	6 45 S	43 1W
Barão de Melgaço	**174**	11 50 S	60 45W
Baraolt	**70**	46 5N	25 34 E
Barapasi	**103**	2 15 S	137 5 E
Barapina	**135**	6 21 S	155 25 E
Barasat	**95**	22 46N	88 31 E
Barasoli	**123**	13 38N	42 0W
Barat Daya, Kepuluan	**103**	7 30 S	128 0 E
Barataria B.	**159**	29 15N	89 45W
Baraut	**94**	29 13N	77 7 E
Baraya	**174**	3 10N	75 4W
Barbacena	**173**	21 15 S	43 56W
Barbacoas, Colomb.	**174**	1 45N	78 0W
Barbacoas, Venez.	**174**	9 29N	66 58W
Barbados ■	**167**	13 0N	59 30W
Barbalha	**170**	7 19 S	39 17W
Barban	**63**	45 0N	14 4 E
Barbastro	**58**	42 2N	0 5 E
Barbate	**57**	36 13N	5 56W
Barberton, S. Afr.	**129**	25 42 S	31 2 E
Barberton, U.S.A.	**156**	41 0N	81 40W
Barbigha	**95**	25 21N	85 47 E
Barbourville	**157**	36 57N	83 52W
Barbuda I.	**167**	17 30N	61 40W
Barca d'Alva	**56**	41 0N	7 0W
Barca, La	**164**	20 20N	102 40W
Barcaldine	**138**	23 33 S	145 13 E
Barcarrota	**57**	38 31N	6 51W
Barce = Al Marj	**117**	32 25N	20 40 E
Barcellona Pozzo di Gotto	**65**	38 8N	15 15 E
Barcelona, Spain	**58**	41 21N	2 10 E
Barcelona, Venez.	**174**	10 10N	64 40W
Barcelona □	**58**	41 30N	2 0 E
Barcelonette	**45**	44 23N	6 40 E
Barcelos	**174**	1 0 S	63 0W
Barcin	**54**	52 52N	17 55 E
Barcoo, R.	**138**	28 29 S	137 46 E
Barcs	**53**	45 58N	17 28 E
Barczewo	**54**	53 50N	20 42 E
Bard, Hd.	**36**	60 6N	1 5W
Barda	**83**	40 25N	47 10 E
Bardai	**119**	21 25N	17 0 E
Bardas Blancas	**172**	35 49 S	69 45W
Bardejov	**53**	49 18N	21 15 E
Bardera	**91**	2 20N	42 27 E
Bardi	**62**	44 38N	9 43 E
Bardiyah	**117**	31 45N	25 0 E
Bardney	**33**	53 13N	0 19W
Bardo	**54**	50 31N	16 42 E
Bardoc	**137**	30 18 S	121 12 E
Bardoli	**96**	21 12N	73 5 E
Bardsey, I.	**31**	52 46N	4 47W
Bardsey Sound	**31**	52 47N	4 46W
Bardstown	**156**	37 50N	85 29W
Bareilly	**95**	28 22N	79 27 E
Barellan	**141**	34 16 S	146 24 E
Barengapara	**98**	25 14N	90 14 E
Barentin	**42**	49 33N	0 58 E
Barenton	**42**	48 38N	0 50W
Barents Sea	**12**	73 0N	39 0 E
Barentu	**123**	15 2N	37 35 E
Barfleur	**42**	49 40N	1 17W
Barford	**28**	52 15N	1 35W
Barga	**62**	44 5N	10 30 E
Bargal	**91**	11 25N	51 0 E
Bargara	**138**	24 50 S	152 25 E
Barge	**62**	44 43N	7 19 E
Barge, La	**160**	41 12N	110 4W
Bargnop	**123**	9 32N	28 25 E
Bargo	**141**	34 18 S	150 35 E
Bargoed	**31**	51 42N	3 22W
Bargteheide	**48**	53 42N	10 13 E
Barguzin	**77**	53 37N	109 37 E
Barh	**95**	25 29N	85 46 E
Barhaj	**95**	26 18N	83 44 E
Barham	**29**	51 12N	1 10 E
Barhi	**95**	24 15N	85 25 E
Bari, India	**94**	26 39N	77 39 E
Bari, Italy	**65**	41 6N	16 52 E
Bari Doab	**94**	30 20N	73 0 E
Baria = Phuoc Le	**101**	10 39N	107 19 E
Bariadi □	**126**	2 45 S	34 40 E
Barika	**118**	35 23N	5 22 E
Barinas	**174**	8 36N	70 15W
Barinas □	**174**	8 10N	69 50W
Baring C.	**148**	70 0N	117 30W
Baringo	**126**	0 47N	36 16 E
Baringo □	**126**	0 55N	36 0 E
Baringo, L.	**126**	0 47N	36 16 E
Barinitas	**174**	8 45N	70 25W
Baripada	**96**	21 57N	86 45 E
Bariri	**171**	22 4 S	48 44W
Bârîs	**122**	24 42N	30 31 E
Barisal	**98**	22 30N	90 20 E
Barisan, Bukit	**102**	3 30 S	102 15 E
Barito, R.	**102**	2 50 S	114 50 E
Barjac	**45**	44 20N	4 22 E
Barjols	**45**	43 34N	6 2 E
Barjūji, W.	**119**	25 26N	12 12 E
Bark L.	**150**	46 58N	82 25W
Barka	**122**	17 30N	37 34 E
Barkah	**93**	23 40N	58 0 E
Barker, Mt.	**139**	35 4 S	138 55 E
Barking	**29**	51 31N	0 10 E
Barkley Sound	**152**	48 50N	125 10W
Barkly Downs	**138**	20 30 S	138 30 E
Barkly East	**129**	30 58 S	27 33 E
Barkly Tableland	**138**	19 50 S	138 40 E
Barkly West	**128**	28 5 S	24 31 E
Barkol, Wadi	**122**	17 40N	32 0 E
Barksdale	**159**	29 47N	100 2W
Barlborough	**33**	53 17N	1 17W
Barlby	**33**	53 48N	1 3W
Barlee, L.	**137**	29 15 S	119 30 E
Barlee, Mt.	**137**	24 35 S	128 10 E
Barlee Ra.	**137**	23 30 S	116 0 E
Barlett	**163**	36 29N	118 2W
Barletta	**65**	41 20N	16 17 E
Barlinek	**54**	53 0N	15 15 E
Barlingbo	**73**	57 35N	18 27 E
Barlow L.	**153**	62 00N	103 0W
Barmby Moor	**33**	53 55N	0 47W
Barmedman	**141**	34 9 S	147 21 E
Barmer	**94**	25 45N	71 20 E
Barmera	**140**	34 15 S	140 28 E
Barmoor	**35**	55 38N	2 0W
Barmouth	**31**	52 44N	4 3W
Barmstedt	**48**	53 47N	9 46 E
Barna	**39**	53 14N	9 10W
Barnaderg	**38**	53 29N	8 43W
Barnagar	**94**	23 7N	75 19 E
Barnard Castle	**32**	54 33N	1 55W
Barnato	**141**	31 38 S	145 0 E
Barnaul	**76**	53 20N	83 40 E
Barnby Moor	**33**	53 21N	1 0W
Barne Inlet	**13**	80 15 S	160 0 E
Barnes	**141**	36 2 S	144 47 E
Barnesville	**157**	33 6N	84 9W
Barnet	**29**	51 37N	0 15W
Barnetby le Wold	**33**	53 34N	0 24W
Barneveld, Neth.	**96**	52 7N	5 36 E
Barneveld, U.S.A.	**162**	43 16N	75 14W
Barneville	**42**	49 23N	1 46W
Barney, Mt.	**133**	28 17 S	152 44 E
Barngo	**138**	25 3 S	147 20 E
Barnhart	**159**	31 10N	101 8W
Barnoldswick	**32**	53 55N	2 11W
Barnsley	**33**	53 33N	1 29W
Barnstaple	**30**	51 5N	4 3W
Barnstaple B.	**30**	51 5N	4 25W
Barnsville	**158**	46 43N	96 28W
Baro	**121**	8 35N	6 18 E
Baro, R.	**123**	8 25N	33 40 E
Baroda	**94**	25 29N	76 35 E
Baroda = Vadodara, India	**93**	22 20N	73 10 E
Baroda = Vadodara, Gujarat, India	**94**	22 20N	73 10 E
Baron Ra.	**136**	23 30 S	127 45 E
Barpali	**96**	21 11N	83 35 E
Barpathar	**98**	26 17N	93 53 E
Barpeta	**95**	26 20N	91 10 E
Barqa	**117**	27 0N	20 0 E
Barqin	**119**	27 33N	13 34 E
Barques, Pte. aux	**156**	44 5N	82 55W
Barquinha	**57**	39 28N	8 25W
Barquisimeto	**174**	9 58N	69 13W
Barr, France	**43**	48 25N	7 28 E
Barr, U.K.	**34**	55 13N	4 44W
Barr Smith Ra.	**137**	27 10 S	120 15 E
Barra, Brazil	**170**	11 5 S	43 10W
Barra, Gambia	**120**	13 21N	16 36W
Barra da Estiva	**171**	13 38 S	41 19W
Barra de Navidad	**164**	19 12N	104 41W
Barra do Corda	**170**	5 30 S	45 10W
Barra do Mendes	**171**	11 43 S	42 4W
Barra do Piraí	**173**	22 30 S	43 50W
Barra Falsa, Pta. da	**129**	22 58 S	35 37 E
Barra Hd.	**36**	56 47N	7 40W
Barra, I.	**36**	57 0N	7 30W
Barra Mansa	**173**	22 35 S	44 12W
Barra, Sd. of	**36**	57 4N	7 25W
Barraba	**141**	30 21 S	150 35 E
Barrackpur	**95**	22 44N	88 30 E
Barrafranca	**65**	37 22N	14 10 E
Barranca, Lima, Peru	**174**	10 45 S	77 50W
Barranca, Loreto, Peru	**174**	4 50 S	76 50W
Barrancabermeja	**174**	7 0N	73 50W
Barrancas, Colomb.	**174**	10 57N	72 50W
Barrancas, Venez.	**174**	8 55N	62 5W
Barrancos	**57**	38 10N	6 58W
Barranqueras	**172**	27 30 S	59 0W
Barranquilla, Atlántico, Colomb.	**174**	11 0N	74 50W
Barranquilla, Vaupés, Colomb.	**174**	1 39N	72 19W
Barras, Brazil	**170**	4 15 S	42 18W
Barras, Colomb.	**174**	1 45 S	73 13W
Barraute	**150**	48 26N	77 38W
Barre, U.S.A.	**156**	44 15N	72 30W
Barre, U.S.A.	**162**	42 26N	72 6W
Barreal	**172**	31 33 S	69 28W
Barreiras	**171**	12 8 S	45 0W
Barreirinhas	**170**	2 30 S	42 50W
Barreiro	**57**	38 40N	9 6W
Barreiros	**170**	8 49 S	35 12W
Barrême	**45**	43 57N	6 23 E
Barren I.	**101**	12 17N	95 50 E
Barren Is., Madag.	**129**	18 25 S	43 40 E
Barren Is., U.S.A.	**147**	58 45N	152 0W
Barren Junc.	**139**	30 5 S	149 0 E
Barretos	**171**	20 30 S	48 35W
Barrhead, Can.	**152**	54 10N	114 24W
Barrhead, U.K.	**34**	55 48N	4 23W
Barrhill	**34**	55 7N	4 46W
Barrie	**150**	44 24N	79 40W
Barrier, C.	**142**	36 25 S	175 32 E
Barrier Ra., Austral.	**140**	31 0 S	141 30 E
Barrier Ra., N.Z.	**143**	44 5 S	169 42 E
Barrier Rf., Gt.	**138**	19 0 S	149 0 E
Barrière	**152**	51 12N	120 7W
Barrington, Austral.	**133**	31 58 S	151 55 E
Barrington, Ill., U.S.A.	**156**	42 8N	88 5W
Barrington, R.I., U.S.A.	**162**	41 43N	71 20W
Barrington L.	**153**	56 55N	100 15W
Barrington Tops.	**141**	32 6 S	151 28 E
Barringun	**139**	29 1 S	145 41 E
Barrow	**147**	71 16N	156 50W
Barrow Creek T.O.	**138**	21 30 S	133 55 E
Barrow I.	**136**	20 45 S	115 20 E
Barrow-in-Furness	**32**	54 8N	3 15W
Barrow Pt.	**138**	14 20 S	144 40 E
Barrow, Pt.	**147**	71 22N	156 30W
Barrow, R.	**39**	52 10N	6 57W
Barrow Ra.	**137**	26 0 S	127 40 E
Barrow Strait	**12**	74 20N	95 0W
Barrow upon Humber	**33**	53 41N	0 22W
Barrowford	**32**	53 51N	2 14W
Barruecopardo	**56**	41 4N	6 40W
Barruelo	**56**	42 54N	4 17W
Barry, S. Glam., U.K.	**31**	51 23N	3 19W
Barry, Tayside, U.K.	**35**	56 29N	2 45W
Barry I.	**31**	51 23N	3 17W
Barry's Bay	**150**	45 29N	77 41W
Barry's Pt.	**39**	51 36N	8 40W
Barsalogho	**121**	13 25N	1 3W
Barsat	**95**	36 10N	72 45 E
Barsi	**96**	18 10N	75 50 E
Barsø	**73**	55 7N	9 33 E
Barsoi	**99**	25 48N	87 57 E
Barstow, Calif., U.S.A.	**163**	34 58N	117 2W
Barstow, Tex., U.S.A.	**170**	31 30N	103 25W
Barthélemy, Col	**100**	19 26N	104 6 E
Bartica	**174**	6 25N	58 40W
Bartle Frere, Mt.	**138**	17 27 S	145 50 E
Bartlesville	**159**	36 50N	95 58W
Bartlett	**159**	30 46N	97 30W
Bartlett, L.	**152**	63 5N	118 20W
Bartolomeu Dias	**127**	21 10 S	35 8 E
Barton	**33**	54 28N	1 38W
Barton Siding	**137**	30 31 S	132 39 E
Barton-upon-Humber	**33**	53 41N	0 27W
Bartoszyce	**54**	54 15N	20 55 E
Bartow	**157**	27 53N	81 49W
Barú, I. de	**174**	10 15N	75 35W
Baruth	**48**	52 3N	13 31 E
Barvas	**36**	58 21N	6 31W
Barvaux	**47**	50 21N	5 29 E
Barvenkovo	**82**	48 57N	37 0 E
Barwani	**94**	22 2N	74 57 E
Barwell	**28**	52 35N	1 22W
Barysh	**81**	49 2N	25 18 E
Bas-Rhin □	**43**	48 40N	7 30 E
Bašaid	**66**	45 38N	20 25 E
Basa'idu	**93**	26 35N	55 20 E
Basal	**94**	33 33N	72 13 E
Basalt	**163**	38 0N	118 15W
Basankusa	**124**	1 5N	19 50 E
Basawa	**94**	34 15N	70 50 E
Bascharage	**47**	49 34N	5 55 E
Bascuñán, Cabo	**172**	28 52 S	71 35W
Basècles	**47**	50 32N	3 39 E
Basel (Basle)	**50**	47 35N	7 35 E
Basel Landschaft □	**50**	47 26N	7 45 E
Basel-Stadt □	**50**	47 35N	7 35 E
Basento, R.	**65**	40 35N	16 10 E
Bashi Channel	**105**	21 15N	122 0 E
Bashkir A.S.S.R. □	**84**	54 0N	57 0 E
Basilaki, I.	**135**	10 35 S	151 0 E
Basilan, Selat	**103**	6 50N	122 0 E
Basilanl, I.	**103**	6 35N	122 0 E
Basildon	**29**	51 34N	0 29 E
Basilicata □	**65**	40 30N	16 0 E
Basim	**96**	20 3N	77 0 E
Basin	**160**	44 22N	108 2W
Basing	**28**	51 16N	1 3W
Basingstoke	**28**	51 15N	1 5W
Basirhat	**98**	22 40N	88 54 E
Baskatong Res.	**150**	46 46N	75 50W
Baskerville C.	**136**	17 10 S	122 15 E
Basle = Basel	**50**	47 35N	7 35 E
Basmat	**96**	19 15N	77 12 E
Basoda	**94**	23 52N	77 54 E
Basodino	**51**	46 25N	8 28 E
Basoka	**126**	1 16N	23 40 E
Basongo	**124**	4 15 S	20 20 E
Basque Provinces = Vascongadas	**58**	42 50N	2 45W
Basra = Al Basrah	**92**	30 30N	47 50 E
Bass Rock	**35**	56 5N	2 40W
Bass Strait	**138**	39 15 S	146 30 E
Bassano, del Grappa	**63**	45 45N	11 45 E
Bassari	**121**	9 19N	0 57 E
Bassas da India	**125**	22 0 S	39 0 E
Basse	**120**	13 13N	14 15W
Basse-Terre, I.	**167**	16 0N	61 40W
Bassecourt	**50**	47 20N	7 15 E
Bassée, La	**43**	50 31N	2 49 E
Bassein, Burma	**98**	16 30N	94 30 E
Bassein, India	**96**	19 26N	72 48 E
Bassein Myit	**99**	16 45N	94 30 E
Bassenthwaite, L.	**32**	54 40N	3 14W
Basseterre	**167**	17 17N	62 43W
Bassett, Nebr., U.S.A.	**158**	42 37N	99 30W
Bassett, Va., U.S.A.	**157**	36 48N	79 59W
Bassevelde	**47**	51 15N	3 41 E

Bassi Bekkjarvik

Bassi 94 30 44N 76 21 E
Bassigny 43 48 0N 5 10 E
Bassikounou 120 15 55N 6 1W
Bassilly 47 50 40N 3 56 E
Bassum 48 52 50N 8 42 E
Båstad 73 56 25N 12 51 E
Båstad 73 56 25N 12 51 E
Bastak 93 27 15N 54 25 E
Bastar 96 19 25N 81 40 E
Basti 95 26 52N 82 55 E
Bastia 45 42 40N 9 30 E
Bastia Umbra 63 43 4N 12 34 E
Bastide, La 44 44 35N 3 55 E
Bastogne 47 50 1N 5 43 E
Baston 29 52 43N 0 19W
Bastrop 159 30 5N 97 22W
Basuto 128 19 50 S 26 25 E
Basutoland = Lesotho 129 29 0 S 28 0 E
Basyanovskiy 84 58 19N 60 44 E
Bat Yam 90 32 2N 34 44 E
Bata, Eq. Guin. 124 1 57N 9 50 E
Bata, Rumania 70 46 1N 22 4 E
Bataan 103 14 40N 120 25 E
Bataan Pen. 103 14 38N 120 30 E
Batabanó 166 22 40N 82 20W
Batabanó, G. de 167 22 30N 82 30W
Batac 103 18 3N 120 34 E
Batagoy 77 67 38N 134 38 E
Batak 67 41 57N 24 12 E
Batalha 57 39 40N 8 50W
Batama 126 0 58N 26 33 E
Batamay 77 63 30N 129 15 E
Batamshinskiy 84 50 36N 58 16 E
Batang 103 6 55 S 109 40 E
Batangafo 117 7 25N 18 20 E
Batangas 103 13 35N 121 10 E
Batanta, I. 103 0 55N 130 40 E
Bataszék 66 46 10N 18 44 E
Batatais 173 20 54 S 47 37W
Batavia 156 43 0N 78 10W
Bataysk 83 47 3N 39 45 E
Batchelor 136 13 4 S 131 1 E
Bateman's B. 141 35 40 S 150 12 E
Batemans Bay 141 35 44 S 150 11 E
Bates Ra. 137 27 25 S 121 0 E
Batesburg 157 33 54N 81 32W
Batesville, Ark., U.S.A. 159 35 48N 91 40W
Batesville, Miss., U.S.A. 159 34 17N 89 58W
Batesville, Tex., U.S.A. 159 28 59N 99 38W
Batetski 80 58 47N 30 16 E
Bath, U.K. 28 51 22N 2 22W
Bath, Maine, U.S.A. 151 43 50N 69 49W
Bath, N.Y., U.S.A. 156 42 20N 77 17W
Batheay 101 11 59N 104 57 E
Bathford 28 51 23N 2 18W
Bathgate 35 55 54N 3 38W
Bâthie, La 46 45 37N 6 28 E
Bathmen 46 52 15N 6 29 E
Bathurst, Austral. 141 33 25 S 149 31 E
Bathurst, Can. 151 47 37N 65 43W
Bathurst B. 138 14 16 S 144 25 E
Bathurst C. 147 70 30N 128 30W
Bathurst, C. 147 70 34N 128 0W
Bathurst, Gambia = Banjul 120 13 28N 16 40W
Bathurst Harb. 138 43 15 S 146 10 E
Bathurst I., Austral. 136 11 30 S 130 10 E
Bathurst I., Can. 12 76 30N 130 10W
Bathurst Inlet 148 66 50N 108 1W
Batie 120 9 53N 2 53W
Batley 33 53 43N 1 38W
Batlow 141 35 31 S 148 9 E
Batman 92 37 55N 41 5 E
Batna 119 35 34N 6 15 E
Batoka 127 16 45 S 27 15 E
Baton Rouge 159 30 30N 91 5W
Batong, Ko 101 6 32N 99 12 E
Batopilas 164 27 45N 107 45W
Batouri 124 4 30N 14 25 E
Battambang 100 13 7N 103 12 E
Batticaloa 97 7 43N 81 45 E
Battice 47 50 39N 5 50 E
Battipáglia 65 40 38N 15 0 E
Battir 90 31 44N 35 8 E
Battle, Can. 153 52 58N 110 52W
Battle, U.K. 29 50 55N 0 30 E
Battle Camp 138 15 20 S 144 40 E
Battle Creek 156 42 20N 85 36W
Battle Harbour 151 52 16N 55 35W
Battle Lake 158 46 20N 95 43W
Battle Mountain 160 40 45N 117 0W
Battle, R. 153 52 43N 108 15W
Battlefields 127 18 37 S 29 47 E
Battleford 153 52 45N 108 15W
Battonya 53 46 16N 21 3 E
Batu Caves 101 3 15N 101 40 E
Batu Gajah 101 4 28N 101 3 E
Batu, Kepulauan 102 0 30 S 98 25 E
Batu, Mt. 123 6 55N 39 45 E
Batu Pahat 101 1 50N 102 56 E
Batuata, P. 103 6 30 S 122 20 E
Batulaki 103 5 40N 125 30 E
Batumi 83 41 30N 41 30 E
Baturadja 102 4 11 S 104 15 E
Baturité 170 4 28 S 38 45W
Baturité, Serra de 170 4 25 S 39 0W
Baubau 103 5 25 S 123 50 E
Bauchi 121 10 22N 9 48 E
Bauchi □ 121 10 0N 10 0 E
Baud 42 47 52N 3 1W
Baudette 158 48 46N 94 35W
Baudouinville = Moba 126 7 0 S 29 48 E
Baudour 47 50 29N 3 50 E
Bauer, C. 139 32 44 S 134 4 E
Baugé 42 47 31N 0 8W
Bauhinia Downs 138 24 35 S 149 18 E
Baule, La 42 47 18N 2 23W
Bauma 51 47 3N 8 53 E
Baume les Dames 43 47 22N 6 22 E
Baunei 64 40 2N 9 41 E
Bauru 173 22 10 S 49 0W
Baús 175 18 22 S 52 47W
Bauska 80 56 25N 25 15 E
Bautzen 48 51 11N 14 25 E
Baux, Les 45 43 45N 4 51 E
BavaniSte 66 44 49N 20 53 E
Bavaria = Bayern 49 49 7N 11 30 E
Båven 72 59 35N 17 30 E
Bavispe, R. 164 29 30N 109 11W
Bawdsey 29 52 1N 1 27 E
Bawdwin 98 23 5N 97 50 E
Bawean 102 5 46 S 112 35 E
Bawku 121 11 3N 0 19W
Bawlake 98 19 11N 97 21 E
Bawnboy 38 54 8N 7 40W
Bawtry 33 53 25N 1 1W
Baxley 157 31 43N 82 23W
Baxter Springs 159 37 3N 94 45W
Bay Bulls 151 47 19N 52 50W
Bay City, Mich., U.S.A. 156 43 35N 83 51W
Bay City, Oreg., U.S.A. 160 45 45N 123 58W
Bay City, Tex., U.S.A. 159 28 59N 95 55W
Bay de Verde 151 48 5N 52 54W
Bay, Laguna de 103 14 20N 121 11 E
Bay of Islands 142 35 15 S 174 6 E
Bay St. Louis 159 30 18N 89 22W
Bay Shore 162 40 44N 73 15W
Bay Springs 159 31 58N 89 18W
Bay View 142 39 25 S 176 50 E
Baya 127 11 53 S 27 25 E
Bayamo 166 20 20N 76 40W
Bayamón 147 18 24N 66 10W
Bayan Kara Shan 99 34 0N 98 0 E
Bayan-Ovoo 106 47 47N 112 5 E
Bayana 94 26 55N 77 18 E
Bayanaul 76 50 45N 75 45 E
Bayandalay 106 43 30N 103 29 E
Bayanga 124 2 53N 16 19 E
Bayanhongor 105 46 8N 100 43 E
Bayard 158 41 48N 103 17W
Baybay 103 10 40N 124 55 E
Bayble 36 58 12N 6 13W
Bayburt 92 40 15N 40 20 E
Bayerischer Wald 49 49 0N 13 0 E
Bayern □ 49 49 7N 11 30 E
Bayeux 42 49 17N 0 42W
Bayfield 158 46 50N 90 48W
Bayir 92 30 45N 36 55 E
Baykadam 85 43 48N 69 58 E
Baykal, Oz. 77 53 0N 108 0 E
Baykit 77 61 50N 95 50 E
Baykonur 76 47 48N 65 50 E
Baymak 84 52 36N 58 19 E
Baynes Mts. 128 17 15 S 13 0 E
Bayombong 103 16 30N 121 10 E
Bayon 43 48 30N 6 20 E
Bayona 56 42 6N 8 52W
Bayonne, France 44 43 30N 1 28W
Bayonne, U.S.A. 162 40 41N 74 7W
Bayovar 174 5 50 S 81 0W
Baypore, R. 97 11 10N 75 47 E
Bayram-Ali 76 37 37N 62 10 E
Bayreuth 49 49 56N 11 35 E
Bayrischzell 49 47 39N 12 1 E
Bayrūt 92 33 53N 35 31 E
Baysun 85 38 12N 67 12 E
Bayt Aula 90 31 37N 35 2 E
Bayt Fajjar 90 31 38N 35 9 E
Bayt Fūrīk 90 32 11N 35 20 E
Bayt Jala 90 31 43N 35 11 E
Bayt Lahm 90 31 43N 35 12 E
Bayt Rīma 90 32 2N 35 6 E
Bayt Sāhūr 90 31 42N 35 13 E
Bayt Ummar 90 31 38N 35 7 E
Bayta at Tahtā 90 32 9N 35 18 E
Baytin 90 31 56N 35 14 E
Baytown 159 29 42N 94 57W
Bayzhansay 85 43 14N 69 54 E
Bayzo 121 13 52N 4 35 E
Baza 59 37 30N 2 47W
Bazar Dyuzi 83 41 12N 48 10 E
Bazarny Karabulak 81 52 30N 46 20 E
Bazarnyy Syzgan 81 53 45N 46 40 E
Bazartobe 83 49 26N 51 45 E
Bazaruto, I. do 129 21 40 S 35 28 E
Bazas 44 44 27N 0 13W
Bazuriye 90 33 15N 35 16 E
Beabula 141 34 26 S 145 9 E
Beach 158 46 57N 104 0W
Beach Haven 162 39 34N 74 14W
Beachley 28 51 37N 2 39W
Beachport 140 37 29 S 140 0 E
Beachwood 162 39 55N 74 8W
Beachy Head 29 50 44N 0 16 E
Beacon, Austral. 137 30 26 S 117 52 E
Beacon, U.S.A. 162 41 32N 73 58W
Beaconia 153 50 25N 96 31W
Beaconsfield, Austral. 133 41 11 S 146 48 E
Beaconsfield, U.K. 29 51 36N 0 39W
Beadnell 35 55 33N 1 38W
Beagle Bay 136 16 32 S 122 54 E
Beagle, Canal 176 55 0 S 68 30W
Bealanana 129 14 33N 48 44 E
Bealey 143 43 2 S 171 36 E
Beaminster 28 50 48N 2 44W
Bear I. 39 51 38N 9 50W
Bear I. Nor. 12 74 30N 19 0 E
Bear L., B.C., Can. 152 56 10N 126 52W
Bear L., Man., Can. 153 55 8N 96 0W
Bear L., U.S.A. 160 42 0N 111 20W
Bearcreek 160 45 11N 109 6W
Beardmore 150 49 36N 87 57W
Beardmore Glacier 13 84 30 S 170 0 E
Beardstown 158 40 0N 90 25W
Bearn 44 43 28N 0 36W
Bearpaw Mt. 160 48 15N 109 55W
Bearsden 34 55 55N 4 21W
Bearskin Lake 150 53 58N 91 2W
Bearsted 29 51 15N 0 35 E
Beas de Segura 59 38 15N 2 53W
Beasain 58 43 3N 2 11W
Beata, C. 167 17 40N 71 30W
Beata, I. 167 17 34N 71 31W
Beatrice, Zimb. 127 18 15 S 30 55 E
Beatrice, U.S.A. 158 40 20N 96 40W
Beatrice, C. 138 14 20 S 136 55 E
Beatrice, oilfield 19 58 7N 3 6W
Beattock 35 55 19N 3 27W
Beatton, R. 152 56 15N 120 45W
Beatton River 152 57 26N 121 20W
Beatty 163 36 58N 116 46W
Beaucaire 45 43 48N 4 39 E
Beauce, Plaines de 43 48 10N 2 0 E
Beauceville 151 46 13N 70 46W
Beaudesert 139 27 59 S 153 0 E
Beaufort, Austral. 140 37 25 S 143 25 E
Beaufort, Malay. 102 5 30N 115 40 E
Beaufort, N.C., U.S.A. 157 34 45N 76 40W
Beaufort, S.C., U.S.A. 157 32 25N 80 40W
Beaufort Sea 12 72 0N 140 0W
Beaufort-West 128 32 18 S 22 36 E
Beaugency 43 47 47N 1 38 E
Beauharnois 150 45 20N 73 52W
Beaujeu 45 46 10N 4 35 E
Beaujolais 45 46 0N 4 25 E
Beaulieu, Loiret, France 44 47 31N 2 49 E
Beaulieu, Vendée, France 45 46 41N 1 37W
Beaulieu, U.K. 28 50 49N 1 27W
Beaulieu, R. 152 62 3N 113 11W
Beauly 37 57 29N 4 27W
Beauly Firth 37 57 30N 4 20W
Beauly, R. 37 57 26N 4 28W
Beaumaris 31 53 16N 4 7W
Beaumetz-les-Loges 43 50 15N 2 40 E
Beaumont, Belg. 47 50 15N 4 14 E
Beaumont, France 44 44 45N 0 46 E
Beaumont, N.Z. 143 45 50 S 169 33 E
Beaumont, Calif., U.S.A. 163 33 56N 116 58W
Beaumont, Tex., U.S.A. 159 30 5N 94 8W
Beaumont-le-Roger 42 49 4N 0 47 E
Beaumont-sur-Oise 43 49 9N 2 17 E
Beaune 43 47 2N 4 50 E
Beaune-la-Rolande 43 48 4N 2 25 E
Beauraing 47 50 7N 4 57 E
Beausejour 153 50 5N 96 35 E
Beausset, Le 45 43 10N 5 46 E
Beauvais 43 49 25N 2 8 E
Beauval 153 55 9N 107 37W
Beauvoir, Deux Sèvres, France 44 46 12N 0 30W
Beauvoir, Vendée, France 42 46 55N 2 1W
Beaver, Alaska, U.S.A. 147 66 20N 147 30W
Beaver, Okla., U.S.A. 159 36 52N 100 31W
Beaver, Utah, U.S.A. 161 38 20N 112 45W
Beaver City 158 40 13N 99 50W
Beaver Dam 158 43 28N 88 50W
Beaver Falls 156 40 44N 80 20W
Beaver Hill L. 153 54 16N 94 59W
Beaver I. 150 45 40N 85 31W
Beaver, R. 152 59 52N 124 20W
Beaver, R 150 55 55N 87 48W
Beaver, R. 153 55 26N 107 45W
Beaverhill L., Man., Can. 153 54 5N 94 50W
Beaverhill L., N.W.T., Can. 153 63 2N 111 22W
Beaverhill L., Alb., 152 53 27N 112 32W
Beaverlodge 152 55 11N 119 29W
Beavermouth 152 51 32N 117 23W
Beaverstone, R. 150 54 59N 89 25W
Beawar 94 26 3N 74 18 E
Bebedouro 173 21 0 S 48 25W
Bebington 32 53 23N 3 1W
Beboa 129 17 22 S 44 33 E
Bebra 48 50 59N 9 48 E
Beccles 29 52 27N 1 33 E
Bečej 66 45 36N 20 3 E
Beceni 70 45 23N 26 48 E
Becerreá 56 42 51N 7 10W
Béchar 118 31 38N 2 18 E
Becharof L. 147 58 0N 156 30W
Bechuanaland = Botswana 125 23 0 S 24 0 E
Bechyně 52 49 17N 14 29 E
Beckermet 32 54 26N 3 31W
Beckfoot 32 54 50N 3 25W
Beckingham 33 53 24N 0 49W
Beckley 156 37 50N 81 8W
Bécon 42 47 30N 0 50W
Bečva, R. 53 49 31N 17 40 E
Bedale 33 54 18N 1 35W
Bédar 59 37 11N 1 59W
Bédarieux 44 43 37N 3 10 E
Bédarrides 45 44 2N 4 54 E
Beddone, Mt. 138 25 50 S 134 20 E
Bedele 123 8 31N 35 44 E
Bedel,Pereval 85 41 26N 78 26 E
Bederkesa 48 53 37N 8 50 E
Bedford, Can. 150 45 7N 72 59W
Bedford, S. Afr. 128 32 40 S 26 10 E
Bedford, U.K. 29 52 8N 0 29W
Bedford, Ind., U.S.A. 156 38 50N 86 30W
Bedford, Iowa, U.S.A. 158 40 40N 94 41W
Bedford, Ohio, U.S.A. 156 41 23N 81 32W
Bedford, Va., U.S.A. 156 37 25N 79 30W
Bedford □ 29 52 4N 0 28W
Bedford, C. 138 15 14 S 145 21 E
Bedford Downs 136 17 19 S 127 20 E
Bedford Level 29 52 25N 0 5 E
Bedków 54 51 36N 19 44 E
Bedlington 35 55 8N 1 35W
Bednesti 152 53 50N 123 10W
Bednja, R. 63 46 12N 16 25 E
Bednodemyanovsk 81 53 55N 43 15 E
Bedourie 138 24 30 S 139 30 E
Bedretto 51 46 31N 8 31 E
Bedum 47 53 18N 6 36 E
Bedwas 31 51 36N 3 10W
Bedworth 28 52 28N 1 29W
Bedzin 54 50 19N 19 7 E
Bee L. 36 57 22N 7 21W
Beebyn 137 27 0 S 117 48 E
Beech Grove 156 39 40N 86 2W
Beechey Point 147 70 27N 149 18W
Beechworth 141 36 22 S 146 43 E
Beechy 153 50 53N 107 24W
Beeford 33 53 58N 0 18W
Beek, Gelderland, Neth. 46 51 55N 6 11 E
Beek, Limburg, Neth. 47 50 57N 5 48 E
Beek, Noord Brabant, Neth. 47 51 32N 5 38 E
Beekbergen 46 52 10N 5 58 E
Beelitz 48 52 14N 12 58 E
Beemem 47 51 9N 3 21 E
Beenleigh 139 27 43 S 153 10 E
Beer 30 50 41N 3 5W
Be'er Sheva' 90 31 15N 34 48 E
Be'er Sheva', N. 90 31 12N 34 40 E
Be'er Toviyyao 90 31 44N 34 42 E
Be'eri 90 31 25N 34 30 E
Be'erotayim 90 32 19N 34 59 E
Beersheba = Be'er Sheva' 90 31 15N 34 48 E
Beerta 46 53 11N 7 6 E
Beerze, R. 46 51 39N 5 20 E
Beesd 46 51 53N 5 11 E
Beesel 47 51 16N 6 2 E
Beeskow 48 52 9N 14 14 E
Beeston 33 52 55N 1 11W
Beetaloo 138 17 15 S 133 50 E
Beetsterzwaag 46 53 4N 6 5 E
Beetzendorf 48 52 42N 11 6 E
Beeville 159 28 27N 97 44W
Befale 124 0 25N 20 45 E
Befandriana 125 21 55 S 44 0 E
Befotaka, Diégo-Suarez, Madag. 129 14 30 S 48 0 E
Befotaka, Fianarantsoa, Madag. 129 23 49 S 47 0 E
Beg, L. 38 54 48N 6 28W
Bega 141 36 41 S 149 51 E
Bega, Canalul 66 45 37N 20 46 E
Begelly 31 51 45N 4 44W
*Begemdir & Simen □ 123 13 55N 37 30 E
Begna 71 60 41N 9 42 E
Begonte 56 43 10N 7 40W
Begu-Sarai 95 25 24N 86 9 E
Beguildy 31 52 25N 3 11W
Béhagle = Lai 117 9 25N 16 30 E
Behara 125 24 55 S 46 20 E
Behbehan 92 30 30N 50 15 E
Behror 94 27 51N 76 20 E
Behshahr 93 36 45N 53 35 E
Beida (Al Bayda) 117 32 30N 21 40 E
Beighton 33 53 21N 1 21W
Beilen 46 52 52N 6 27 E
Beilngries 49 49 1N 11 27 E
Beilpajah 140 32 54 S 143 52 E
Beilul 123 13 2N 42 20 E
Beinn a' Ghlo, Mt. 37 56 51N 3 42W
Beinn Mhor, Mt. 36 57 59N 6 39W
Beira 127 19 50 S 34 52 E
Beira-Alta 55 40 35N 7 35W
Beira-Baixa 55 40 2N 7 30W
Beira-Litoral 55 40 5N 8 30W
Beirut = Bayrūt 92 33 53N 35 31 E
Beit Bridge 127 14 58 S 30 15 E
Beit Hanum 90 31 32N 34 32 E
Beit Lahiya 90 31 32N 34 30 E
Beit 'Ur et Tahta 90 31 54N 35 5 E
Beit Yosef 90 32 34N 35 33 E
Beitbridge 127 22 12 S 30 0 E
Beith 34 55 45N 4 38W
Beituniya 90 31 54N 35 10 E
Beiuş 70 46 40N 22 21 E
Beja 57 38 2N 7 53W
Béja 119 36 43N 9 12 E
Beja □ 57 37 55N 7 55W
Béjaïa 119 36 42N 5 2 E
Béjar 56 40 23N 5 46W
Bejestan 93 34 30N 58 5 E
Bekabad 85 40 13N 69 14 E
Bekasi 103 6 20 S 107 0 E
Békés 53 46 47N 21 9 E
Békés □ 53 46 45N 21 0 E
Békéscsaba 53 46 40N 21 10 E
Bekily 129 24 13 S 45 19 E
Bekkevoort 47 50 57N 4 58 E
Bekkjarvik 71 60 1N 5 13 E

*Renamed Gonder

Bekoji Berghem

Bekoji	123	7 40N	38 20 E
Bekok	101	2 20N	103 7 E
Bekopaka	129	19 9 S	44 45 E
Bekwai	121	6 30N	1 34W
Bel Air	162	39 32N	76 21W
Bela, India	95	25 50N	82 0 E
Bela, Pak.	94	26 12N	66 20 E
Bela Crkva	66	44 55N	21 27 E
Bela Palanka	66	43 13N	22 17 E
Bela Vista, Brazil	173	22 12 S	56 20W
Bela Vista, Mozam.	129	26 10 S	32 44 E
Bélâbre	44	46 34N	1 8 E
Belaia, Mt.	123	11 25N	36 8 E
Belalcázar	57	38 35N	5 10W
Belanovica	66	44 15N	20 23 E
Belavenona	129	24 50 S	47 4 E
Belawan	102	3 33N	98 32 E
Belaya Glina	83	46 5N	40 48 E
Belaya Kalitva	83	48 13N	40 50 E
Belaya Kholunitsa	84	58 41N	50 13 E
Belaya, R.	84	55 54N	53 33 E
Belaya Tserkov	80	49 45N	30 10 E
Belbroughton	28	52 23N	2 5W
Belceşti	70	47 19N	27 7 E
Bełchatów	54	51 21N	19 22 E
Belcher, C.	12	75 0N	160 0W
Belcher Is.	150	56 15N	78 45W
Belchite	58	41 18N	0 43W
Belclare	38	53 29N	8 55W
Belcoo	38	54 18N	7 52W
Belderg	38	54 18N	9 33W
Beldringe	73	55 28N	10 21 E
Belebey	84	54 7N	54 7 E
Belém de São Francisco	170	8 46 S	38 58W
Belém (Pará)	170	1 20 S	48 30W
Belén, Argent.	172	27 40 S	67 5W
Belén, Colomb.	174	1 26N	75 56W
Belén, Parag.	172	23 30 S	57 6W
Belen	161	34 40N	106 50W
Belene	67	43 39N	25 10 E
Bélesta	44	42 55N	1 56 E
Belet Uen	91	4 30N	45 5 E
Belev	81	53 50N	36 5 E
Belfast, N.Z.	143	43 27 S	172 39 E
Belfast, S. Afr.	129	25 42 S	30 2 E
Belfast, U.K.	38	54 35N	5 56W
Belfast, U.S.A.	151	44 30N	69 0W
Belfast □	38	54 35N	5 56W
Belfast, L.	38	54 40N	5 50W
Belfeld	47	51 18N	6 6 E
Belfeoram	151	47 32N	55 30W
Belfield	158	46 54N	103 11W
Belford	35	55 36N	1 50W
Belfort	43	47 38N	6 50 E
Belfort □	43	47 38N	6 52 E
Belfry	160	45 10N	109 2W
Belgaum	97	15 55N	74 35 E
Belgioioso	62	45 9N	9 21 E
Belgium ■	47	51 30N	5 0 E
Belgooly	138	51 44N	8 30W
Belgorod	82	50 35N	36 35 E
Belgorod Dnestrovskiy	82	46 11N	30 23 E
Belgrade	160	45 50N	111 10W
Belgrade = Beograd	66	44 50N	20 37 E
Belgrove	143	41 27 S	172 59 E
Belhaven	157	35 34N	76 35W
Beli	121	7 52N	10 58 E
Beli Drim, R.	66	42 25N	20 34 E
Beli Manastir	66	45 45N	18 36 E
Beli Timok, R.	66	43 39N	22 14 E
Belice, R.	64	37 44N	12 58 E
Belinga	124	1 10N	13 2 E
Belingwe	127	20 29 S	29 57 E
Belingwe, N., mt.	127	20 37 S	29 55 E
Belinsky (Chembar)	81	53 0N	43 25 E
Belinţ	66	45 48N	21 54 E
Belinyu	102	1 35 S	105 50 E
Beliton, Is.	102	3 10 S	107 50 E
Belitung, I.	102	3 10 S	107 50 E
Beliu	70	46 30N	22 0 E
Belize ■	165	17 0N	88 30W
Belize City	165	17 25N	88 0W
Beljanica	66	44 08N	21 43 E
Bell	151	53 50N	53 10 E
Bell Bay	138	41 6 S	146 53 E
Bell I.	151	50 46N	55 35W
Bell Irving, R.	152	56 12N	129 5W
Bell Peninsula	149	63 50N	82 0W
Bell, R.	150	49 48N	77 38W
Bell Rock = Inchcape Rock	35	56 26N	2 24W
Bell Ville	172	32 40 S	62 40W
Bella Bella	152	52 10N	128 10W
Bella Coola	152	52 25N	126 40W
Bella Unión	172	30 15 S	57 40W
Bella Vista, Corrientes, Argent.	172	28 33 S	59 0W
Bella Vista, Tucuman, Argent.	172	27 10 S	65 25W
Bella Yella	120	7 24N	10 9W
Bellacorick	38	54 8N	9 35W
Bellaghy	38	54 50N	6 31W
Bellágio	62	45 59N	9 15 E
Bellaire	156	40 1N	80 46W
Bellananagh	38	53 55N	7 25W
Bellarena	38	55 7N	6 57W
Bellarwi	141	34 6 S	147 13 E
Bellary	97	15 10N	76 56 E
Bellata	139	29 53 S	149 46 E
Bellavary	38	53 54N	9 9W
Belle Fourche	158	44 43N	103 52W
Belle Fourche, R.	158	44 25N	105 0W
Belle Glade	157	26 43N	80 38W
Belle Ile	42	47 20N	3 10W
Belle Isle	151	51 57N	55 25W
Belle-Isle-en-Terre	42	48 33N	3 23W
Belle Isle, Str. of	151	51 30N	56 30W
Belle, La	157	26 45N	81 22W
Belle Plaine, Iowa, U.S.A.	158	41 51N	92 18W
Belle Plaine, Minn., U.S.A.	158	44 35N	93 48W
Belledonne	45	45 11N	6 0 E
Belledune	151	47 55N	65 50W
Belleek	38	54 30N	8 6W
Bellefontaine	156	40 20N	83 45W
Bellefonte	156	40 56N	77 45W
Bellegarde, Ain, France	45	46 4N	5 49 E
Bellegarde, Creuse, France	43	45 59N	2 19 E
Bellegarde, Loiret, France	43	48 0N	2 26 E
Belleoram	151	47 31N	55 25W
Belleville, Can.	150	44 10N	77 23W
Belleville, Rhône, France	45	46 7N	4 45 E
Belleville, Vendée, France	42	46 48N	1 28W
Belleville, Ill., U.S.A.	158	38 30N	90 0W
Belleville, Kans., U.S.A.	158	39 51N	97 38W
Belleville, N.Y., U.S.A.	162	43 46N	76 10W
Bellevue, Can.	152	49 35N	114 22W
Bellevue, U.S.A.	160	43 25N	144 23W
Belley	45	45 46N	5 41 E
Bellin (Payne Bay)	149	60 0N	70 0W
Bellingen	141	30 25 S	152 50 E
Bellingham, U.K.	35	55 09N	2 16W
Bellingham, U.S.A.	160	48 45N	122 27W
Bellingshausen Sea	13	66 0 S	80 0W
Bellinzona	51	46 11N	9 1 E
Bello	174	6 20N	75 33W
Bellona Reefs	133	21 26 S	159 0 E
Bellows Falls	162	43 10N	72 30W
Bellpat	94	29 0N	68 5 E
Bellpuig	58	41 37N	1 1 E
Belluno	63	46 8N	12 6 E
Bellville	159	29 58N	96 18W
Belmar	162	40 10N	74 2W
Bélmez	57	38 17N	5 17W
Belmont, Austral.	141	33 4 S	151 42 E
Belmont, U.S.A.	162	43 27N	71 29W
Belmonte, Brazil	171	16 0 S	39 0W
Belmonte, Port.	56	40 21N	7 20W
Belmonte, Spain	58	39 34N	2 43W
Belmopan	165	17 18N	88 30W
Belmore	140	33 34 S	141 13 E
Belmullet	38	54 13N	9 58W
Belo Horizonte	171	19 55 S	43 56W
Belo Jardim	170	8 20 S	36 26W
Belo-sur-Mer	129	20 42 S	44 33 E
Belo-sur-Tsiribihana	129	19 40 S	43 30 E
Belogorsk, R.S.F.S.R., U.S.S.R.	77	51 0N	128 20 E
Belogorsk, Ukraine, U.S.S.R.	82	45 3N	34 35 E
Belogradchik	66	43 37N	22 40 E
Belogradets	67	43 22N	27 18 E
Beloha	129	25 10 S	45 3 E
Beloit, Kans., U.S.A.	158	39 32N	98 9W
Beloit, Wis., U.S.A.	158	42 35N	89 0W
Belokholunitskiy	81	58 55N	50 43 E
Belomorsk	78	64 35N	34 30 E
Belonia	98	23 15N	91 30 E
Belopolye	80	51 14N	34 20 E
Beloretsk	84	53 58N	58 24 E
Belovo	76	54 30N	86 0 E
Beloyarskiy	84	56 45N	61 24 E
Beloye More	78	66 0N	38 0 E
Beloye, Oz.	78	60 10N	37 35 E
Beloye Ozero	83	45 15N	46 50 E
Belozersk	81	60 0N	37 30 E
Belpasso	65	37 37N	15 0 E
Belper	33	53 2N	1 29W
Belsay	35	55 6N	1 53W
Belsele	47	51 9N	4 6 E
Belsito	64	37 50N	13 47 E
Beltana	140	30 48 S	138 25 E
Belterra	175	2 45 S	55 0W
Beltinci	63	46 37N	16 20 E
Belton, Humberside, U.K.	33	53 33N	0 49W
Belton, Norfolk, U.K.	29	52 35N	1 39 E
Belton, S.C., U.S.A.	157	34 31N	82 39W
Belton, Tex., U.S.A.	159	31 4N	97 30W
Beltra, Mayo, Ireland	38	53 57N	9 24W
Beltra, Sligo, Ireland	38	54 12N	8 36W
Beltra L.	38	53 56N	9 28W
Beltsy	82	47 48N	28 0 E
Belturbet	38	54 6N	7 28W
Belukha	76	49 50N	86 50 E
Beluran	102	5 48N	117 35 E
Beluša	53	49 5N	18 27 E
Belušió	66	43 50N	21 10 E
Belvedere Maríttimo	65	39 37N	15 52 E
Belvès	44	44 46N	1 0 E
Belvidere, Ill., U.S.A.	158	42 15N	88 55W
Belvidere, N.J., U.S.A.	162	40 48N	75 5W
Belville	38	54 40N	9 22W
Belvis de la Jara	57	39 45N	4 57W
Belyando, R.	138	21 38 S	146 50 E
Belyj Jar	76	58 26N	84 39 E
Belyy	80	55 48N	32 51 E
Belyy, Ostrov	76	73 30N	71 0 E
Belyye Vody	85	42 25N	69 50 E
Belz	80	50 23N	24 1 E
Belzig	48	52 8N	12 36 E
Belzoni	159	33 12N	90 30W
Bemaraha, Plat. du	129	18 40 S	44 45 E
Bemarivo, Majunga, Madag.	129	17 6 S	44 31 E
Bemarivo, Tuléar, Madag.	129	21 45 S	44 45 E
Bemarivo, R.	129	21 45 S	44 45 E
Bemavo	129	21 33 S	45 25 E
Bembéréke	121	10 11N	2 43 E
Bembesi	127	20 0 S	28 58 E
Bembesi, R.	127	20 0 S	28 58 E
Bembézar, R.	57	38 0N	5 20W
Bembridge	28	50 41N	1 4W
Bemidji	158	47 30N	94 50W
Bemmel	46	51 54N	5 54 E
Ben Alder	37	55 59N	4 30W
Ben Avon	37	57 6N	3 28W
Ben Bheigeir, Mt.	34	55 43N	6 6W
Ben Bullen	141	33 12 S	150 2 E
Ben Chonzine	35	56 27N	4 0W
Ben Cruachan, Mt.	34	56 26N	5 8W
Ben Dearg	37	57 47N	4 58W
Ben Dearg, mt.	37	56 54N	3 49W
Ben Dhorain	37	58 7N	3 50W
Ben Dorian	34	56 30N	4 42W
Ben Gardane	119	33 11N	11 11 E
Ben Hee	37	58 16N	4 43W
Ben Hope, mt.	37	58 24N	4 36W
Ben Klibreck	37	58 14N	4 25W
Ben Lawers, mt.	37	56 33N	4 13W
Ben Lomond, mt.	139	30 1 S	151 43 E
Ben Lomond mt.	138	41 38 S	147 42 E
Ben Lomond, mt.	34	56 12N	4 39W
Ben Loyal	37	58 25N	4 25W
Ben Luc	101	10 39N	106 29 E
Ben Lui, mt.	34	56 24N	4 50W
Ben Macdhui	37	57 4N	3 40W
Ben Mhor	36	57 16N	7 21W
Ben More, Mull, U.K.	34	56 26N	6 2W
Ben More, Perth, U.K.	34	56 23N	4 31W
Ben More Assynt	37	58 7N	4 51W
Ben Nevis, mt., N.Z.	143	45 15 S	169 0 E
Ben Nevis, mt., U.K.	36	56 48N	5 0W
Ben Ohau Ra.	143	44 1 S	170 4 E
Ben Quang	100	17 3N	106 55 E
Ben Stack	36	58 20N	4 58W
Ben Tharsiunn	37	57 47N	4 20W
Ben Venue	34	56 13N	4 28W
Ben Vorlich	34	56 22N	4 15W
Ben Wyvis, mt.	37	57 40N	4 35W
Bena	121	11 20N	5 50 E
Bena Dibele	124	4 4 S	22 50 E
Benagalbón	57	36 45N	4 15W
Benagerie	140	31 25 S	140 22 E
Benahmed	118	33 4N	7 9W
Benalla	141	36 30 S	146 0 E
Benambra, Mt.	141	36 31 S	147 34 E
Benameji	57	37 16N	4 33W
Benanee	140	34 31 S	142 52 E
Benares = Varanasi	95	25 22N	83 8 E
Benavente, Port.	57	38 59N	8 49W
Benavente, Spain	56	42 2N	5 43W
Benavides, Spain	56	42 30N	5 54W
Benavides, U.S.A.	159	27 35N	98 28W
Benbane Hd.	38	55 15N	6 30W
Benbaun, Mt.	38	53 30N	9 50W
Benbecula, I.	36	57 26N	7 21W
Benbonyathe, Mt.	140	30 25 S	139 11 E
Benburb	38	54 25N	6 42W
Bencubbin	137	30 48 S	117 52 E
Bend	160	44 2N	121 15W
Bendel □	121	6 0N	6 0 E
Bender Beila	91	9 30N	50 48 E
Bender Cassim	91	11 12N	49 18 E
Bendering	137	32 23 S	118 18 E
Bendery	82	46 50N	29 50 E
Bendigo	140	36 40 S	144 15 E
Beneden Knijpe	46	52 58N	5 59 E
Benedick	162	38 31N	76 41W
Beneditinos	170	5 27 S	42 22W
Benedito Leite	170	7 13 S	44 34W
Benei Beraq	129	32 5N	34 50 E
Bénéna	120	13 9N	4 17W
Beneraird, Mt.	34	55 4N	4 57W
Benešov	52	49 46N	14 41 E
Bénestroff	43	48 54N	6 45 E
Benet	44	46 22N	0 35W
Benevento	65	41 7N	14 45 E
Benfeld	43	48 22N	7 34 E
Beng Lovea	100	12 36N	105 34 E
Benga	127	16 11 S	33 40 E
Bengal, Bay of	99	15 0N	90 0 E
Bengawan Solo	103	7 5 S	112 25 E
Benghazi = Banghāzī	119	32 11N	20 3 E
Bengkalis	102	1 30N	102 10 E
Bengkulu	102	3 50 S	102 12 E
Bengkulu □	102	3 48 S	102 16 E
Bengough	153	49 25N	105 10W
Benguela	125	12 37 S	13 25 E
Benguerir	118	32 16N	7 56W
Benguérua, Î.	129	21 58 S	35 28 E
Benha	122	30 26N	31 8 E
Beni	126	0 30N	29 27 E
Beni Abbès	118	30 5N	2 5W
Beni Haoua	118	36 30N	1 30 E
Benî Mazâr	122	28 32N	30 44 E
Beni Mellal	118	32 21N	6 21W
Beni Ounif	118	32 0N	1 10W
Beni, R.	174	10 30 S	66 0W
Beni Saf	118	35 17N	1 15W
Benî Suêf	122	29 5N	31 6 E
Beniah L.	152	63 23N	112 17W
Benicarló	58	40 23N	0 23 E
Benicia	163	38 3N	122 9W
Benidorm	59	38 33N	0 9W
Benidorm, Islote de	59	38 31N	0 9W
Benin ■	121	10 0N	2 0 E
Benin, Bight of	121	5 0N	3 0 E
Benin City	121	6 20N	5 31 E
Benington	33	52 59N	0 5 E
Benisa	59	38 43N	0 03 E
Benjamin Aceval	172	24 58 S	57 34W
Benjamin Constant	174	4 40 S	70 15W
Benjamin Hill	164	30 10N	111 10W
Benkelman	158	40 7N	101 32W
Benlidi	138	24 35 S	144 50 E
Benmore Pk.	143	44 25 S	170 8 E
Bennane Hd.	34	55 9N	5 2W
Bennebroek	46	52 19N	4 36 E
Bennekom	46	52 0N	5 41 E
Bennett	147	59 56N	134 53W
Bennettsbridge	39	52 36N	7 12W
Bennettsville	157	34 38N	79 39W
Bennington	162	42 52N	73 12W
Benoa	102	8 50 S	115 20 E
Bénodet	42	47 53N	4 7W
Benoni	129	26 11 S	28 18 E
Benoud	118	32 20N	0 16 E
Benque Viejo	165	17 5N	89 8W
Bensheim	49	49 40N	8 38 E
Benson, U.K.	28	51 37N	1 6W
Benson, U.S.A.	161	31 59N	110 19W
Bent	93	26 20N	59 25 E
Benteng	103	6 10 S	120 30 E
Bentinck I.	138	17 3 S	139 35 E
Bentiu	123	9 10N	29 55 E
Bentley, Hants., U.K.	29	51 12N	0 52W
Bentley, S. Yorks, U.K.	33	53 33N	1 9W
Bento Gonçalves	173	29 10 S	51 31W
Benton, Ark., U.S.A.	159	34 30N	92 35W
Benton, Calif., U.S.A.	163	37 48N	118 32W
Benton, Ill., U.S.A.	158	38 0N	88 55W
Benton, Pa., U.S.A.	162	41 12N	76 23W
Benton Harbor	156	42 10N	86 28W
Bentong	101	3 31N	101 55 E
Bentu Liben	123	8 32N	38 21 E
Benue □	121	7 30N	7 30 E
Benue Plateau □	121	8 0N	8 30 E
Benue, R.	121	7 50N	6 30 E
Benwee Hd.	38	54 20N	9 50W
Beo	103	4 25N	126 50 E
Beograd	66	44 50N	20 37 E
Beowawe	160	40 45N	117 0W
Beppu	110	33 15N	131 30 E
Beppu-Wan	110	33 18N	131 34 E
Ber Dagan	90	32 1N	34 49 E
Bera	98	24 5N	89 37 E
Beragh	38	54 34N	7 10W
Berakit	123	14 38N	39 29 E
Berati	68	40 43N	19 59 E
Berber	122	18 0N	34 0 E
Berbéra	117	10 33N	16 35 E
Berbera	91	10 30N	45 2 E
Berbérati	124	4 15N	15 40 E
Berberia, Cabo	59	38 39N	1 24 E
Berbice, R.	174	5 20N	58 10W
Berceto	62	44 30N	10 0 E
Berchtesgaden	49	47 37N	13 1 E
Berck-sur-Mer	43	50 25N	1 36 E
Berdichev	82	49 57N	28 30 E
Berdsk	76	54 47N	83 2 E
Berdyansk	82	46 45N	36 50 E
Berdyaush	84	55 9N	59 9 E
Bere Alston	30	50 29N	4 11W
Bere Regis	28	50 45N	2 13W
Berea	156	37 35N	84 18W
Berebere	103	2 25N	128 45 E
Bereda	91	11 45N	51 0 E
Bereina	135	8 39 S	146 30 E
Berekum	120	7 29N	2 34W
Berenice	122	24 2N	35 25 E
Berens I.	153	52 18N	97 18W
Berens, R.	153	51 21N	97 0W
Berens River	153	52 25N	97 0W
Berestechko	80	50 22N	25 5 E
Bereşti	70	46 6N	27 50 E
Berettyo, R.	53	47 32N	21 47 E
Berettyóújfalu	53	47 13N	21 33 E
Beretŭu, R.	70	47 30N	22 7 E
Berevo	129	19 44 S	44 58 E
Berevo-sur-Ranobe	129	17 14 S	44 17 E
Bereza	80	52 31N	24 51 E
Berezhany	80	49 26N	24 58 E
Berezina, R.	80	54 10N	28 10 E
Berezna	80	51 35N	30 46 E
Berezniki	84	59 24N	56 46 E
Berezovka	82	47 25N	30 55 E
Berezovo	76	64 0N	65 0 E
Berg	71	59 10N	11 18 E
Berga, Spain	58	42 6N	1 48 E
Berga, Kalmar, Sweden	73	57 14N	16 3 E
Berga, Kronoberg, Sweden	73	56 55N	14 0 E
Bergama	92	39 8N	27 15 E
Bergambacht	46	51 56N	4 48 E
Bérgamo	62	45 42N	9 40 E
Bergantiños	56	43 20N	8 40W
Bergedorf	48	53 28N	10 12 E
Bergeijk	47	51 19N	5 21 E
Bergen, Ger.	48	54 24N	13 26 E
Bergen, Norway	71	60 23N	5 20 E
Bergen-Binnen	46	52 40N	4 43 E
Bergen-op-Zoom	47	51 30N	4 18 E
Bergerac	44	44 51N	0 30 E
Bergheim	48	50 57N	6 38 E
Berghem	46	51 46N	5 33 E

Bergisch-Gladbach **Billesdon**

Bergisch-Gladbach	**48**	50 59N	7 9 E
Bergkvara	**73**	56 23N	16 5 E
Bergschenhoek	**46**	51 59N	4 30 E
Bergsjö	**72**	61 59N	17 3 E
Berguent	**118**	34 1N	2 0W
Bergues	**43**	50 58N	2 24 E
Bergum	**46**	53 13N	5 59 E
Bergvik	**72**	61 16N	16 50 E
Berhala, Selat	**102**	1 0 S	104 15 E
Berhampore	**95**	24 2N	88 27 E
Berhampur	**96**	19 15N	84 54 E
Berheci, R.	**70**	46 7N	27 19 E
Berhungra	**139**	34 46 S	147 52 E
Bering Sea	**130**	58 0N	167 0 E
Bering Str.	**147**	66 0N	170 0W
Beringarra	**137**	26 0 S	116 55 E
Beringen, Belg.	**47**	51 3N	5 14 E
Beringen, Switz.	**51**	47 38N	8 34 E
Beringovskiy	**77**	63 3N	179 19 E
Berislav	**82**	46 50N	33 30 E
Berisso	**172**	34 40 S	58 0W
Berja	**59**	36 50N	2 56W
Berkane	**118**	34 52N	2 20W
Berkel, R.	**46**	52 8N	6 12 E
Berkeley	**163**	37 52N	122 20W
Berkeley Springs	**156**	39 38N	78 12W
Berkhamsted	**29**	51 45N	0 33W
Berkhout	**46**	52 38N	4 59 E
Berkner I.	**13**	79 30 S	50 0W
Berkovitsa	**67**	43 16N	23 8 E
Berkshire	**162**	42 19N	76 11W
Berkshire □	**28**	51 30N	1 20W
Berkshire Downs	**28**	51 30N	1 30W
Berkyk	**71**	62 50N	9 59 E
Berlaar	**47**	51 7N	4 39 E
Berland, R.	**152**	54 0N	116 50W
Berlanga	**57**	38 17N	5 50W
Berlave	**47**	51 2N	4 0 E
Berleburg	**48**	51 3N	8 22 E
Berlenga, I.	**75**	39 25N	9 30W
Berlick	**47**	51 22N	6 9 E
Berlin, Ger.	**48**	52 32N	13 24 E
Berlin, Md., U.S.A.	**162**	38 19N	75 12W
Berlin, N.H., U.S.A.	**156**	44 29N	71 10W
Berlin, N.Y., U.S.A.	**162**	42 42N	73 23W
Berlin, E. □	**48**	52 30N	13 30 E
Berlin, W. □	**48**	52 30N	13 20 E
Bermeja, Sierra	**57**	36 45N	5 11W
Bermejo, R., Formosa, Argent.	**172**	26 30 S	58 50W
Bermejo, R., San Juan, Argent.	**172**	30 0 S	68 0W
Bermeo	**58**	43 25N	2 47W
Bermillo de Sayago	**56**	41 22N	6 8W
Bermuda, I.	**10**	32 45N	65 0W
Bern (Berne)	**50**	46 57N	7 28 E
Bern (Berne) □	**50**	46 45N	7 40 E
Bernalda	**65**	40 24N	16 44 E
Bernalillo	**161**	35 17N	106 37W
Bernam, R.	**101**	3 45N	101 5 E
Bernardo de Irigoyen	**173**	26 15 S	53 40W
Bernardsville	**162**	40 43N	74 34W
Bernasconi	**172**	37 55 S	63 44W
Bernau	**49**	47 53N	12 20 E
Bernay	**42**	49 5N	0 35 E
Berndorf	**52**	47 59N	16 1 E
Berne = Bern	**50**	46 57N	7 28 E
Berner Alpen	**50**	46 27N	7 35 E
Berneray, I.	**36**	56 47N	7 38W
Bernese Oberland = Oberland	**50**	46 27N	7 35 E
Bernier I.	**137**	24 50 S	113 12 E
Bernina Pass	**51**	46 22N	9 54 E
Bernina, Piz	**51**	46 20N	9 54 E
Bernissart	**47**	50 28N	3 39 E
Beroroha	**125**	21 40 S	45 10 E
Bérouboucy	**121**	10 34N	2 46 E
Beroun	**52**	49 57N	14 5 E
Berounka, R.	**52**	50 0N	13 47 E
Berovo	**66**	41 42N	22 51 E
Berrahal	**119**	36 54N	7 33 E
Berre	**45**	43 28N	5 11 E
Berre, Étang de	**45**	43 27N	5 5 E
Berrechid	**118**	33 18N	7 36W
Berri	**140**	34 14 S	140 35 E
Berriedale	**37**	58 12N	3 30W
Berriew	**31**	52 36N	3 12W
Berrigan	**141**	35 38 S	145 49 E
Berrouaghia	**118**	36 10N	2 53 E
Berrwillock	**140**	35 36 S	142 59 E
Berry, Austral.	**141**	34 46 S	150 43 E
Berry, France	**43**	47 0N	2 0 E
Berry Hd.	**30**	50 24N	3 29W
Berry Is.	**166**	25 40N	77 50W
Berryville	**159**	36 23N	93 35W
Bersenbrück	**48**	52 33N	7 56 E
Berst Ness	**37**	59 16N	3 0W
Berthaund	**158**	40 21N	105 5W
Berthier Is.	**136**	14 29 S	124 59 E
Berthold	**158**	48 19N	101 45W
Bertincourt	**43**	50 5N	2 58 E
Bertoua	**124**	4 30N	13 45 E
Bertraghboy, B.	**38**	53 22N	9 54W
Bertrand	**158**	40 35N	99 38W
Bertrange	**47**	49 37N	6 3 E
Bertrix	**47**	49 51N	5 15 E
Beruas	**101**	4 30N	100 47 E
Berufjörður	**74**	64 48N	14 29W
Berur Hayil	**90**	31 34N	34 38 E
Berwick	**162**	41 4N	76 17W
Berwick (□)	**26**	55 46N	2 30W
Berwick-upon-Tweed	**35**	55 47N	2 0W
Berwyn Mts.	**31**	52 54N	3 26W

Beryl N., oilfield	**19**	59 37N	1 30 E
Beryl, oilfield	**19**	59 28N	1 30 E
Beryl W., oilfield	**19**	59 32N	1 20 E
Berzasca	**66**	44 39N	21 58 E
Berzence	**53**	46 12N	17 11 E
Besal	**95**	35 4N	73 56 E
Besalampy	**129**	16 43 S	44 29 E
Besançon	**43**	47 9N	6 0 E
Besar	**102**	2 40 S	116 0 E
Beserah	**101**	3 50N	103 21 E
Beshenkovichi	**80**	55 2N	29 29 E
Beška	**66**	45 8N	20 6 E
Beskids, Mts.	**53**	49 35N	18 40 E
Beslan	**83**	43 22N	44 28 E
Besna Kobila	**66**	42 31N	22 10 E
Besnard L.	**153**	55 25N	106 0W
Beşparmak Daği	**69**	37 32N	27 30 E
Bessarabiya	**70**	46 20N	29 0 E
Bessarabka	**82**	46 21N	28 51 E
Bessbrook	**38**	54 12N	6 25W
Bessèges	**45**	44 18N	4 8 E
Bessemer	**158**	46 27N	90 0W
Bessin	**42**	49 21N	1 0W
Bessines-sur-Gartempe	**42**	46 6N	1 22 E
Best	**47**	51 31N	5 23 E
Bet Alfa	**90**	32 31N	35 25 E
Bet Guvrin	**90**	31 37N	34 54 E
Bet Hashitta	**90**	32 31N	35 27 E
Bet Ha'tmeq	**90**	32 58N	35 8 E
Bet Qeshet	**90**	32 41N	35 21 E
Bet She'an	**90**	32 30N	35 30 E
Bet Tadjine, Djebel	**118**	29 0N	3 30W
Bet Yosef	**90**	32 34N	35 33 E
Betafo	**129**	19 50 S	46 51 E
Betanzos	**56**	43 15N	8 12W
Bétaré-Oya	**124**	5 40N	14 5 E
Betekom	**47**	50 59N	4 47 E
Bétera	**58**	39 35N	0 28W
Bethal	**129**	26 27 S	29 28 E
Bethanien	**125**	26 31 S	17 8 E
Bethany, S. Afr.	**128**	29 34 S	25 59 E
Bethany, U.S.A.	**158**	40 18N	94 0W
Bethany = Eizarilya	**90**	31 47N	35 15 E
Bethel, U.S.A.	**147**	60 50N	161 50W
Bethel, Conn., U.S.A.	**162**	41 22N	73 25W
Bethesda, U.K.	**31**	53 11N	4 3W
Bethesda, U.S.A.	**162**	38 59N	77 6W
Bethlehem, S. Afr.	**129**	28 14 S	28 18 E
Bethlehem, U.S.A.	**162**	40 39N	75 24W
Bethlehem = Bayt Lahm	**90**	31 43N	35 12 E
Bethulie	**128**	30 30 S	25 59 E
Béthune	**43**	50 30N	2 38 E
Béthune, R.	**42**	49 56N	1 5 E
Bethungra	**141**	34 45 S	147 51 E
Betijoque	**174**	9 23N	70 44W
Betim	**171**	19 58 S	44 13W
Betioky	**129**	23 48 S	44 20 E
Beton Bazoches	**43**	48 42N	3 15 E
Betong	**101**	5 45N	101 5 E
Betoota	**138**	25 40 S	140 42 E
Betroka	**129**	23 16 S	46 0 E
Betsiamites	**151**	48 56N	68 40W
Betsiamites, R.	**151**	48 56N	68 40W
Betsiboka, R.	**129**	17 0 S	47 0 E
Betsjoeanaland	**128**	26 30 S	22 30 E
Bettembourg	**47**	49 31N	6 6 E
Betterton	**162**	39 52N	76 4W
Betteshanger	**29**	51 14N	1 20 E
Bettiah	**95**	26 48N	84 33 E
Bettles	**147**	66 54N	150 50W
Bèttola	**62**	44 46N	9 35 E
Bettws Bledrws	**31**	52 9N	4 2W
Bettyhill	**37**	58 31N	4 12W
Betul	**96**	21 48N	77 59 E
Betung	**102**	2 0 S	103 10 E
Betws-y-Coed	**31**	53 4N	3 49W
Beuca	**70**	44 14N	24 56 E
Beuil	**45**	44 6N	7 0 E
Beulah, Can.	**153**	50 16N	101 02W
Beulah, U.S.A.	**158**	47 18N	101 47W
Beuvronne, La	**46**	48 59N	2 41 E
Bevensen	**48**	53 5N	10 34 E
Beveren	**47**	51 12N	4 16 E
Beverley, Austral.	**137**	32 9 S	116 56 E
Beverley, U.K.	**33**	53 52N	0 26W
Beverlo	**47**	51 7N	5 13 E
Beverly, Can.	**152**	53 36N	113 21W
Beverly, Mass., U.S.A.	**162**	42 32N	70 50W
Beverly, Wash., U.S.A.	**160**	46 55N	119 59W
Beverly Hills	**163**	34 4N	118 29W
Beverwijk	**46**	52 28N	4 38 E
Bewdley	**28**	52 23N	2 19W
Bex	**50**	46 15N	7 0 E
Bexhill	**29**	50 51N	0 29 E
Bexley	**29**	51 26N	0 10 E
Beyin	**120**	5 1N	2 41W
Beykoz	**67**	41 8N	29 7 E
Beyla	**120**	8 30N	8 38W
Beynat	**44**	45 8N	1 44 E
Beyneu	**76**	45 10N	55 3 E
Beypazaı	**92**	40 10N	31 48 E
Beyşehir Gölü	**92**	37 40N	31 45 E
Bezdan	**66**	45 28N	18 57 E
Bezerros	**171**	8 14 S	35 45W
Bezet	**90**	33 4N	35 8 E
Bezhitsa	**80**	53 19N	34 17 E
Béziers	**44**	43 20N	3 12 E
Bezwada = Vijayawada	**97**	16 31N	80 39 E
Bhachau	**93**	23 20N	70 16 E
Bhadarwah	**95**	32 58N	75 46 E
Bhadra, R.	**97**	13 0N	76 0 E
Bhadrakh	**96**	21 10N	86 30 E

Bhadravati	**97**	13 49N	76 15 E
Bhagalpur	**95**	25 10N	87 0 E
Bhairab	**98**	22 51N	89 34 E
Bhairab Bazar	**98**	24 4N	90 58 E
Bhaisa	**96**	19 10N	77 58 E
Bhakkar	**94**	31 40N	71 5 E
Bhakra Dam	**95**	31 30N	76 45 E
Bhamo	**98**	24 15N	97 15 E
Bhamragarh	**96**	19 30N	80 40 E
Bhandara	**96**	21 5N	79 42 E
Bhanrer Ra.	**94**	23 40N	79 45 E
Bharat = India	**93**	24 0N	78 0 E
Bharatpur	**94**	27 15N	77 30 E
Bharuch	**96**	21 47N	73 0 E
Bhatghar L.	**96**	18 10N	73 48 E
Bhatiapara Ghat	**98**	23 13N	89 42 E
Bhatkal	**97**	13 58N	74 35 E
Bhatpara	**95**	22 50N	88 25 E
Bhattiprolu	**97**	16 7N	80 45 E
Bhaun	**94**	32 55N	72 40 E
Bhaunagar = Bhavnagar	**94**	21 45N	72 10 E
Bhavani	**97**	11 27N	77 43 E
Bhavani, R.	**97**	11 30N	77 15 E
Bhavnagar	**94**	21 45N	72 10 E
Bhawanipatna	**96**	19 55N	83 30 E
Bhera	**94**	32 29N	72 57 E
Bhilsa = Vidisha	**94**	23 28N	77 53 E
Bhilwara	**94**	25 25N	74 38 E
Bhima, R.	**96**	17 20N	76 30 E
Bhimber	**95**	32 59N	74 3 E
Bhimvaram	**96**	16 30N	81 30 E
Bhind	**95**	26 30N	78 46 E
Bhir	**96**	19 4N	75 58 E
Bhiwandi	**96**	19 15N	73 0 E
Bhiwani	**94**	28 50N	76 9 E
Bhola	**98**	22 45N	90 35 E
Bhongir	**96**	17 30N	78 56 E
Bhopal	**94**	23 20N	77 53 E
Bhor	**96**	18 12N	73 53 E
Bhubaneswar	**96**	20 15N	85 50 E
Bhuj	**94**	23 15N	69 49 E
Bhumibol Dam	**100**	17 15N	98 58 E
Bhusaval	**96**	21 15N	69 49 E
Bhutan ■	**98**	27 25N	89 50 E
Biafra, B. of = Bonny, Bight of	**121**	3 30N	9 20 E
Biak	**103**	1 0 S	136 0 E
Biała	**54**	50 24N	17 40 E
Biała Piska	**54**	53 37N	22 5 E
Biała Podlaska	**54**	52 4N	23 6 E
Biała Podlaska □	**54**	52 0N	23 0 E
Biała, R.	**54**	49 46N	20 53 E
Białogard	**54**	54 2N	15 58 E
Biały Bór	**54**	53 53N	16 51 E
Białystok	**54**	53 10N	23 10 E
Białystok □	**54**	53 9N	23 10 E
Biancavilla	**65**	37 39N	14 50 E
Biano Plateau = Manika Plateau	**127**	9 55 S	26 24 E
Biaro	**103**	2 5N	125 26 E
Biarritz	**44**	43 29N	1 33W
Biasca	**51**	46 22N	8 58 E
Biba	**122**	28 55N	31 0 E
Bibaī	**112**	43 19N	141 52 E
Bibby I.	**153**	61 55N	93 0W
Biberach	**49**	48 5N	9 49 E
Biberist	**50**	47 11N	7 34 E
Bibey, R.	**56**	42 24N	7 13W
Bibiani	**120**	6 30N	2 8W
Bibile	**97**	7 10N	81 25 E
Biboohra	**138**	16 56 S	145 25 E
Bibungwa	**126**	2 40 S	28 15 E
Bibury	**28**	51 46N	1 50W
Bic	**151**	48 20N	68 41W
Bicaj	**68**	42 0N	20 25 E
Bicaz	**70**	46 53N	26 5 E
Biccari	**65**	41 23N	15 12 E
Bicester	**28**	51 53N	1 9W
Biche, La, R.	**152**	59 57N	123 50W
Bichena	**123**	10 28N	38 10 E
Bickerton I.	**138**	13 45 S	136 10 E
Bicknell, Ind., U.S.A.	**156**	38 50N	87 20W
Bicknell, Utah, U.S.A.	**161**	38 16N	111 35W
Bicsad	**70**	47 56N	23 28 E
Bicton	**28**	52 43N	2 47W
Bida	**121**	9 3N	5 58 E
Bidar	**96**	17 55N	77 35 E
Biddeford	**151**	43 30N	70 28W
Biddenden	**29**	51 7N	0 40 E
Biddu	**90**	31 50N	35 8 E
Biddulph	**32**	53 8N	2 11W
Biddwara	**123**	5 11N	38 34 E
Biddya	**90**	32 7N	35 4 E
Bideford	**30**	51 1N	4 13W
Bideford Bay	**30**	51 5N	4 20W
Bidford on Avon	**28**	52 9N	1 53W
Bidor	**101**	4 6N	101 15 E
Bidura	**140**	34 10 S	143 21 E
Bié	**125**	12 22 S	16 55 E
Bié Plateau	**125**	12 0 S	16 0 E
Bieber	**160**	41 4N	121 6W
Biel (Bienne)	**50**	47 8N	7 14 E
Bielawa	**54**	50 43N	16 37 E
Bielė Karpaty	**53**	49 5N	18 0 E
Bielefeld	**48**	52 2N	8 31 E
Bielersee	**50**	47 6N	7 5 E
Biella	**62**	45 33N	8 3 E
Bielsk Podlaski	**54**	52 47N	23 12 E
Bielsko-Biała	**54**	49 50N	19 8 E
Bielsko-Biała □	**54**	49 45N	19 15 E
Bien Hoa	**101**	10 57N	106 49 E
Bienfait	**153**	49 10N	102 50W

Bienne = Biel	**50**	47 8N	7 14 E
Bienvenida	**57**	38 18N	6 12W
Bienville, L.	**150**	55 5N	72 40W
Biescas	**58**	42 37N	0 20W
Biesiesfontein	**128**	30 57 S	17 58 E
Bietigheim	**49**	48 57N	9 8 E
Bievre	**47**	49 57N	5 1 E
Biferno, R.	**65**	41 40N	14 38 E
Big B.	**151**	55 43N	60 35W
Big Bear City	**163**	34 16N	116 51W
Big Bear L.	**163**	34 15N	116 56W
Big Beaver	**153**	49 10N	105 10W
Big Beaver House	**150**	52 59N	89 50W
Big Bell	**137**	27 21 S	117 40 E
Big Belt Mts.	**160**	46 50N	111 30W
Big Bend	**129**	26 50 S	32 2 E
Big Bend Nat. Park	**159**	29 15N	103 15W
Big Black, R.	**159**	32 35N	90 30W
Big Blue, R.	**158**	40 20N	96 40W
Big Cr.	**152**	51 42N	122 41W
Big Creek	**163**	37 11N	119 14W
Big Cypress Swamp	**157**	26 12N	81 10W
Big Delta	**147**	64 15N	145 0W
Big Falls	**158**	48 11N	93 48W
Big Horn	**160**	46 11N	107 25W
Big Horn Mts. = Bighorn Mts.	**160**	44 30N	107 30W
Big Horn R.	**160**	45 30N	108 10W
Big Lake	**159**	31 12N	101 25W
Big Moose	**162**	43 49N	74 58W
Big Muddy, R.	**158**	48 25N	104 45W
Big Pine	**163**	37 12N	118 17W
Big Piney	**160**	42 32N	110 3W
Big Quill L.	**153**	51 55N	105 22W
Big, R.	**151**	54 50N	58 55W
Big Rapids	**156**	43 42N	85 27W
Big River	**153**	53 50N	107 0W
Big Sable Pt.	**156**	44 5N	86 30W
Big Salmon	**147**	61 50N	136 0W
Big Sand L.	**153**	57 45N	99 45W
Big Sandy	**160**	48 12N	110 9W
Big Sandy Cr.	**158**	38 52N	103 11W
Big Sioux, R.	**158**	44 20N	96 53W
Big Smoky Valley	**163**	38 30N	117 15W
Big Snowy Mt.	**160**	46 50N	109 15W
Big Spring	**159**	32 10N	101 25W
Big Springs	**158**	41 4N	102 3W
Big Stone City	**158**	45 20N	96 30W
Big Stone Gap	**157**	36 52N	82 45W
Big Stone L.	**158**	44 25N	96 35W
Big Sur	**163**	36 15N	121 48W
Big Trout L.	**150**	53 40N	90 0W
Biganos	**44**	44 39N	0 59W
Bigbury	**30**	50 17N	3 52W
Bigbury B.	**30**	50 18N	3 58W
Bigerymunal, Mt.	**137**	27 25 S	120 40 E
Bigfork	**160**	48 3N	114 2W
Biggar	**153**	52 4N	108 0W
Bigge I.	**136**	14 35 S	125 10 E
Biggenden	**139**	25 31 S	152 4 E
Biggleswade	**29**	52 6N	0 16W
Bighorn Mts.	**160**	44 30N	107 30W
Bignona	**120**	12 52N	16 23W
Bigorre	**44**	43 5N	0 2 E
Bigstone L.	**153**	53 42N	95 44W
Bigtimber	**160**	45 53N	110 0W
Bigwa	**126**	7 10 S	39 10 E
Bihaó	**63**	44 49N	15 57 E
Bihar	**95**	25 5N	85 40 E
Bihar □	**95**	25 0N	86 0 E
Biharamulo	**126**	2 25 S	31 25 E
Biharamulo □	**126**	2 30 S	31 20 E
Biharkeresztes	**53**	47 8N	21 44 E
Bihé Plateau	**125**	12 0 S	16 0 E
Bihor □	**70**	47 0N	22 10 E
Bihor, Munţii	**70**	46 29N	22 47 E
Bijagós, Arquipélago dos	**120**	11 15N	16 10W
Bijaipur	**94**	26 2N	77 36 E
Bijapur, Mad. P., India	**96**	18 50N	80 50 E
Bijapur, Mysore, India	**96**	16 50N	75 55 E
Bijar	**92**	35 52N	47 35 E
Bijeljina	**66**	44 46N	19 17 E
Bijni	**98**	26 30N	90 40 E
Bijnor	**94**	29 27N	78 11 E
Bikaner	**94**	28 2N	73 18 E
Bikapur	**95**	26 30N	82 7 E
Bikin	**77**	46 50N	134 20 E
Bikini, atoll	**130**	12 0N	167 30 E
Bikoro	**124**	0 48 S	18 15 E
Bikoué	**121**	5 55 S	11 50 E
Bilād Banī Bū 'Ali	**93**	22 0N	59 20 E
Bilara	**94**	26 14N	73 53 E
Bilaspara	**98**	26 13N	90 14 E
Bilaspur, India	**99**	22 2N	82 15 E
Bilaspur, Mad. P., India	**95**	22 2N	82 15 E
Bilaspur, Punjab, India	**94**	31 19N	76 50 E
Bilauk Taungdan	**100**	13 0N	99 0 E
Bilbao	**58**	43 16N	2 56W
Bilbor	**70**	47 18N	25 30 E
Bildudalur	**74**	65 41N	23 36W
Bilecik	**92**	40 5N	30 5 E
Bileóa	**66**	42 53N	18 27 E
Bilibino	**77**	68 3N	166 20 E
Bilibiza	**127**	12 30 S	40 20 E
Bilin	**98**	17 14N	97 15 E
Bilir	**77**	65 40N	131 20 E
Bilishti	**68**	40 37N	20 59 E
Bill	**158**	43 18N	105 18W
Billa	**121**	8 55N	12 15 E
Billabalong	**137**	27 25 S	115 49 E
Billericay	**29**	51 38N	0 25 E
Billesdon	**29**	52 38N	0 56W

CIB

Bramon **Brøttum**

Bramon 72 62 14N 17 40E
Brampton, Can. 150 43 45N 79 45W
Brampton, Cambs., U.K. 29 52 19N 0 13W
Brampton, Cumb., U.K. 32 54 56N 2 43W
Bramsche 48 52 25N 7 58E
Bramshott 29 51 5N 0 47W
Bramwell 138 12 8S 142 37E
Brancaster 29 52 58N 0 40E
Branco, Cabo 170 7 9S 34 47W
Branco, R. 174 0 0 61 15W
Brande 73 55 57N 9 8E
Brandenburg 48 52 24N 12 33E
Brander, Pass of 34 56 25N 5 10W
Branderburgh 37 57 43N 3 17W
Brandfort 128 28 40S 26 30E
Brandon, Can. 153 49 50N 99 57W
Brandon, Durham, U.K. 33 54 46N 1 37W
Brandon, Suffolk, U.K. 29 52 27N 0 37E
Brandon, U.S.A. 156 43 48N 73 4W
Brandon, U.S.A. 162 44 2N 73 5W
Brandon B. 39 52 17N 10 8W
Brandon, Mt. 39 52 15N 10 15W
Brandon Pt. 39 52 18N 10 10W
Brandsen 172 35 10S 58 15W
Brandval 71 60 19N 12 1E
Brandvlei 128 30 25S 20 30E
Brandýs 52 50 10N 14 40E
Branford 162 41 15N 72 48W
Braniewo 54 54 25N 19 50E
Brännarp 73 56 46N 12 38E
Bransby 139 28 10S 142 0E
Bransfield Str. 13 63 0S 59 0W
Branson, Colo., U.S.A. 159 37 4N 103 53W
Branson, Mo., U.S.A. 159 36 40N 93 18W
Branston 33 53 13N 0 28W
Brantford 150 43 15N 80 15W
Brantôme 44 45 22N 0 39E
Branxholme 140 37 52S 141 49E
Branxton 141 32 38S 151 21E
Branzi 62 46 0N 9 46E
Bras d'or, L. 151 45 50N 60 50W
Brasiléia 174 11 0S 68 45W
Brasília 171 15 47S 47 55E
Braslav 80 55 38N 27 0E
Braslovče 63 46 21N 15 3E
Braşov 70 45 38N 25 35E
Braşov □ 70 45 45N 25 15E
Brass 121 4 35N 6 14E
Brass, R. 121 4 15N 6 13E
Brasschaat 47 51 19N 4 27E
Brassey, Barisan 102 5 0N 117 15E
Brassey Ra. 137 25 8S 122 15E
Brasstown Bald, Mt. 157 34 54N 83 45W
Brassus, Le 50 46 35N 6 13E
Brasted 29 51 16N 0 8E
Bratislava 53 48 10N 17 7E
Bratsk 77 56 10N 101 30E
Bratteborg 73 57 37N 14 4E
Brattleboro 162 42 53N 72 37W
Brattvær 71 63 25N 7 48E
Braţul Chilia, R. 70 45 25N 29 20E
Braţul Sfîntu Gheorghe, R. 70 45 0N 29 20E
Braţul Sulina, R. 70 45 10N 29 20E
Bratunac 66 44 13N 19 21E
Braunau 52 48 15N 13 3E
Braunschweig 48 52 17N 10 28E
Braunton 30 51 6N 4 9W
Brava 91 1 20N 44 8E
Bråvikeh 72 58 38N 16 32E
Bravo del Norte, R. 164 30 30N 105 0W
Brawley 163 32 58N 115 30W
Bray, France 43 49 15N 1 40E
Bray, Ireland 39 53 12N 6 6W
Bray, U.K. 29 51 30N 0 42W
Bray Hd. 39 51 52N 10 26W
Bray, Mt. 138 14 0N 134 30E
Bray-sur-Seine 43 48 25N 3 14E
Brazeau, R. 152 52 55N 115 14W
Brazil 156 39 30N 87 8W
Brazil ■ 174 5 0N 20 0W
Brazilian Highlands 170 18 0S 46 30W
Brazo Sur, R. 172 25 30S 58 0W
Brazos, R. 159 30 30N 96 20W
Brazzaville 124 4 9S 15 12E
Brčko 66 44 54N 18 46E
Breadalbane, Austral. 138 23 50S 139 35E
Breadalbane, U.K. 34 56 30N 4 15W
Breaden, L. 137 25 51S 125 28E
Breage 30 50 6N 5 17W
Breaksea Sd. 143 45 35S 166 35E
Bream Bay 142 35 56S 174 28E
Bream Head 142 35 51S 174 36E
Bream Tail 142 36 3S 174 36E
Breamish, R. 35 55 30N 1 55W
Breas 172 25 29S 70 24W
Brebes 103 6 52S 109 3E
Brechin 37 56 44N 2 40W
Brecht 47 51 21N 4 38E
Breckenridge, Colo., U.S.A. 160 39 30N 106 2W
Breckenridge, Minn., U.S.A. 158 46 20N 96 36W
Breckenridge, Tex., U.S.A. 159 32 48N 98 55W
Breckland 23 52 30N 0 40E
Brecknock (□) 26 51 58N 3 25W
Břeclav 53 48 46N 16 53E
Brecon 31 51 57N 3 23W
Brecon Beacons 31 51 53N 3 27W
Breda 47 51 35N 4 45E
Bredaryd 73 57 10N 13 45E
Bredasdorp 128 34 33S 20 2E
Bredbo 141 35 58S 149 10E
Brede 29 50 56N 0 37E
Bredene 47 51 14N 2 59E
Bredon Hill 28 52 3N 2 2W
Bredy 84 52 26N 60 21E
Bree 47 51 8N 5 35E
Breezand 46 52 53N 4 49E
Bregalnica, R. 66 41 50N 22 20E
Bregenz 52 47 30N 9 45E
Bregning 73 56 8N 8 30E
Bréhal 42 48 53N 1 30W
Bréhat, I. de 42 48 51N 3 0W
Breiðafjörður 74 65 15N 23 15W
Breil 45 43 56N 7 31E
Breisach 49 48 2N 7 37E
Brejinho de Nazaré 170 11 1S 48 34W
Brejo 170 3 41S 42 47W
Brekke 71 61 1N 5 26E
Bremangerlandet 71 61 51N 5 0E
Bremangerpollen 71 61 51N 5 0E
Bremen 48 53 4N 8 47E
Bremen □ 48 53 6N 8 46E
Bremer I. 138 12 5S 136 45E
Bremerhaven 48 53 34N 8 35E
Bremerton 160 47 30N 122 38W
Bremervörde 48 53 28N 9 10E
Bremgarten 51 47 21N 8 21E
Bremnes 71 59 47N 5 8E
Bremsnes 71 63 6N 7 40E
Brendon Hills 28 51 6N 3 25W
Brenes 57 37 32N 5 54W
Brenham 159 30 5N 96 27W
Brenner Pass 52 47 0N 11 30E
Breno 62 45 57N 10 20E
Brent, Can. 150 46 2N 78 29W
Brent, U.K. 29 51 33N 0 18W
Brent, oil and gasfield 19 61 0N 1 45E
Brenta, R. 63 45 11N 12 18E
Brentwood, U.K. 29 51 37N 0 19W
Brentwood, U.S.A. 163 37 55N 121 42W
Bréscia 62 45 33N 10 13E
Breskens 47 51 23N 3 33E
Breslau = Wrocław. 54 51 5N 17 5E
Bresle, R. 43 50 4N 1 21E
Bresles 43 49 25N 2 13E
Bressanone 63 46 43N 11 40E
Bressay 36 60 10N 1 6W
Bressay I. 36 60 10N 1 5W
Bressay Sd. 36 60 8N 1 10W
Bresse, La 43 48 0N 6 53E
Bresse, Plaine de 43 46 20N 5 10E
Bressuire 42 46 51N 0 30W
Brest, France 42 48 24N 4 31W
Brest, U.S.S.R. 80 52 10N 23 40E
Bretagne 42 48 0N 3 0W
Bretçu 70 46 7N 26 18E
Breteuil 43 49 38N 2 18E
Breton 152 53 7N 114 28W
Breton Sd. 159 29 40N 89 12W
Brett, C. 142 35 10S 174 20E
Bretten 49 49 2N 8 43E
Bretuil 42 48 50N 0 53E
Breukelen 46 52 10N 5 0E
Brevard 157 35 19N 82 42W
Breves 170 1 40S 50 29W
Brevik 71 59 4N 9 42E
Brewarrina 139 30 0S 146 51E
Brewer 151 44 43N 68 50W
Brewer, Mt. 163 36 44N 118 28W
Brewerton 162 43 14N 76 9W
Brewood 28 52 41N 2 10W
Brewster, N.Y., U.S.A. 162 41 23N 73 37W
Brewster, Wash., U.S.A. 160 48 10N 119 51W
Brewster, Kap 12 70 7N 22 0W
Brewton 157 31 9N 87 2W
Breyten 129 26 16S 30 0E
Breytovo 81 58 18N 37 50E
Brézina 118 33 4N 1 14E
Březnice 52 49 32N 13 57E
Breznik 66 42 44N 22 50E
Brezno 53 48 50N 19 40E
Bria 117 6 30N 21 58E
Briançon 45 44 54N 6 39E
Briare 43 47 38N 2 45E
Bribbaree 141 34 10S 147 51E
Bribie I. 139 27 0S 152 58E
Brickaville 129 18 49S 49 4E
Bricon 43 48 5N 5 0E
Bricquebec 42 49 29N 1 39W
Bride 32 54 24N 4 23W
Bridestowe 30 50 41N 4 7W
Bridge 29 51 14N 1 8E
Bridge of Allan 35 56 9N 3 57W
Bridge of Don 37 57 10N 2 8W
Bridge of Earn 35 56 20N 3 25W
Bridge of Orchy 34 56 29N 4 48W
Bridge of Weir 34 55 51N 4 35W
Bridge, R. 152 50 50N 122 40W
Bridgehampton 162 40 56N 72 18W
Bridgend, Islay, U.K. 34 55 46N 6 15W
Bridgend, Mid Glam., U.K. 31 51 30N 3 35W
Bridgeport, Calif., U.S.A. 163 38 14N 119 15W
Bridgeport, Conn., U.S.A. 162 41 12N 73 12W
Bridgeport, Nebr., U.S.A. 158 41 42N 103 10W
Bridgeport, Tex., U.S.A. 159 33 15N 97 45W
Bridger 160 45 20N 108 58W
Bridgeton 162 39 29N 75 10W
Bridgetown, Austral. 137 33 58S 116 7E
Bridgetown, Barbados 167 13 0N 59 30W
Bridgetown, Can. 151 44 55N 65 18W
Bridgetown, Ireland 39 52 13N 6 33W
Bridgeville 162 38 45N 75 36W
Bridgewater, Austral. 140 36 36S 143 59E
Bridgewater, Can. 151 44 25N 64 31W
Bridgewater, Mass., U.S.A. 162 41 59N 70 56W
Bridgewater, N.Y., U.S.A. 162 42 58N 75 15W
Bridgewater, S.D., U.S.A. 158 43 34N 97 29W
Bridgewater, C. 140 38 23S 141 23E
Bridgnorth 28 52 33N 2 25W
Bridgwater 28 51 7N 3 0W
Bridgwater B. 28 51 15N 3 15W
Bridlington 33 54 6N 0 11W
Bridlington B. 33 54 4N 0 10W
Bridport, Austral. 138 40 59S 147 23E
Bridport, U.K. 28 50 43N 2 45W
Brie-Comte-Robert 43 48 40N 2 35E
Brie, Plaine de 43 48 35N 3 10E
Briec 42 48 6N 4 0W
Brielle 46 51 54N 4 10E
Brienne-le-Château 43 48 24N 4 30E
Brienon 43 48 0N 3 35E
Brienz 50 46 46N 8 2E
Brienzersee 50 46 44N 7 53E
Brierfield 32 53 49N 2 15W
Brierley Hill 28 52 29N 2 7W
Briey 43 49 14N 5 57E
Brig 50 46 18N 7 59E
Brigantine 162 39 24N 74 22W
Brigg 33 53 33N 0 30W
Briggsdale 158 40 40N 104 20W
Brigham City 160 41 30N 112 1W
Brighouse 33 53 42N 1 47W
Brighstone 29 50 38N 1 36W
Bright 141 36 42S 146 56E
Brightlingsea 29 51 49N 1 1E
Brighton, Austral. 140 35 5S 138 30E
Brighton, Can. 150 44 2N 77 44W
Brighton, U.K. 29 50 50N 0 9W
Brighton, U.S.A. 158 39 59N 104 50W
Brightstone 29 50 38N 1 23W
Brightwater 143 41 22S 173 9E
Brignogan-Plage 42 48 40N 4 20W
Brignoles 45 43 25N 6 5E
Brigstock 29 52 27N 0 38W
Brihuega 58 40 45N 2 52W
Brikama 120 13 15N 16 45W
Brill 28 51 49N 1 3W
Brilliant 152 49 19N 117 38W
Brilon 48 51 23N 8 32E
Brim 140 36 3S 142 27E
Brimfield 28 52 18N 2 42W
Bríndisi 65 40 39N 17 55E
Brinkley 159 34 55N 91 15W
Brinklow 28 52 25N 1 22W
Brinkworth, Austral. 140 33 42S 138 26E
Brinkworth, U.K. 28 51 33N 1 59W
Brinyan 37 59 8N 3 0W
Brion I. 151 47 46N 61 26W
Brionne 42 49 11N 0 43E
Brionski, I. 63 44 55N 13 45E
Brioude 44 45 18N 3 23E
Briouze 42 48 42N 0 23W
Brisbane 139 27 25S 153 2E
Brisbane, R. 139 27 24S 153 9E
Brisignella 63 44 14N 11 46E
Bristol, U.K. 28 51 26N 2 35W
Bristol, Conn., U.S.A. 162 41 44N 72 57W
Bristol, Pa., U.S.A. 162 40 6N 74 52W
Bristol, R.I., U.S.A. 162 41 40N 71 15W
Bristol, S.D., U.S.A. 158 45 25N 97 43W
Bristol B. 147 58 0N 160 0W
Bristol Channel 30 51 18N 4 30W
Bristol I. 13 58 45S 28 0W
Bristol L. 161 34 23N 116 0W
Briston 29 52 52N 1 4E
Bristow 159 35 5N 96 28W
British Antarctic Territory 13 66 0S 45 0W
British Columbia □ 152 55 0N 125 15W
British Guiana = Guyana 174 5 0N 59 0W
British Honduras = Belize 165 17 0N 88 30W
British Isles 16 55 0N 4 0W
Briton Ferry 31 51 37N 3 50W
Brits 129 25 37S 27 48E
Britstown 128 30 37S 23 30E
Britt 150 45 46N 80 34W
Brittany = Bretagne 42 48 0N 3 0W
Brittas 39 53 14N 6 29W
Brittatorp 73 57 3N 14 58E
Britton 158 45 50N 97 47W
Brive-la-Gaillarde 44 45 10N 1 32E
Briviesca 58 42 32N 3 19W
Brixham 30 50 24N 3 31W
Brixton 138 23 32S 144 57E
Brixworth 29 52 20N 0 54W
Brize Norton 28 51 46N 1 35W
Brlik, U.S.S.R. 76 44 0N 74 5E
Brlik, Kazakh S.S.R., U.S.S.R. 85 44 5N 73 31E
Brlik, Kazakh S.S.R., U.S.S.R. 85 43 40N 73 49E
Brno 53 49 10N 16 35E
Bro 72 59 13N 13 2E
Broach = Bharuch 96 21 47N 73 0E
Broad Arrow 137 30 23S 121 15E
Broad B. 36 58 14N 6 16W
Broad Chalke 28 51 2N 1 54W
Broad Clyst 30 50 46N 3 27W
Broad Haven, Ireland 38 54 20N 9 55W
Broad Haven, U.K. 31 51 46N 5 6W
Broad Law, Mt. 35 55 30N 3 22W
Broad, R. 157 34 30N 81 26W
Broad Sd., Austral. 138 22 0S 149 45E
Broad Sd., U.K. 30 49 56N 6 19W
Broadalbin 162 43 3N 74 12W
Broadford, Austral. 141 37 14S 145 4E
Broadford, Clare, Ireland 39 52 48N 8 38W
Broadford, Limerick, Ireland 39 52 21N 8 59W
Broadford, U.K. 36 57 14N 5 55W
Broadhembury 30 50 49N 3 16W
Broadhurst Ra. 136 22 30S 122 30E
Broads, The 29 52 45N 1 30E
Broadsound Ra. 133 22 50S 149 30E
Broadstairs 29 51 21N 1 28E
Broadus 158 45 28N 105 27W
Broadview 153 50 22N 102 35W
Broadway, Ireland 39 52 13N 6 23W
Broadway, U.K. 28 52 2N 1 51W
Broadwindsor 28 50 49N 2 49W
Broager 73 54 53N 9 40E
Broaryd 73 57 7N 13 15E
Brochet, Man., Can. 153 57 53N 101 40W
Brochet, Manitoba, Can. 153 57 55N 101 40W
Brochet, Québec, Can. 150 47 12N 72 42W
Brochet, L. 153 58 36N 101 35W
Brock 153 51 26N 108 43W
Brocken 48 51 48N 10 40E
Brockenhurst 28 50 49N 1 34W
Brocklehurst 141 32 9S 148 38E
Brockman Mt. 137 22 25S 117 15E
Brockville 150 44 35N 75 41W
Brockway 158 47 18N 105 46W
Brockworth 28 51 51N 2 9W
Brod 66 41 35N 21 17E
Brodarevo 66 43 14N 19 44E
Brodeur Pen. 149 72 30N 88 10W
Brodick 34 55 34N 5 9W
Brodnica 54 53 15N 19 25E
Brodokalmak 84 55 35N 62 6E
Brody 80 50 5N 25 10E
Broechem 47 51 11N 4 38E
Broek 46 52 26N 5 0E
Broek op Langedijk 46 52 41N 4 49E
Brogan 160 44 14N 117 32W
Broglie 42 49 0N 0 30E
Brok 54 52 43N 21 52E
Broke Inlet 137 34 55S 116 25E
Broken Bank, gasfield 19 53 20N 2 4E
Broken Bow, Nebr., U.S.A. 158 41 25N 99 35W
Broken Bow, Okla., U.S.A. 159 34 2N 94 43W
Broken Hill 140 31 58S 141 29E
Broken Hill = Kabwe 127 14 27S 28 28E
Brokind 73 58 13N 15 42E
Bromborough 32 53 20N 3 0W
Bromham 28 51 23N 2 3W
Bromhead 153 49 18N 103 40W
Bromley 29 51 20N 0 5E
Bromölla 73 56 5N 14 28E
Brompton 33 54 22N 1 25W
Bromsgrove 28 52 20N 2 3W
Bromyard 28 52 12N 2 30W
Brønderslev 73 57 16N 9 57E
Brong Ahafo 120 7 50N 2 0E
Bronkhorstspruit 129 25 46S 28 45E
Bronnitsy 81 55 27N 38 10E
Bronte, Italy 65 37 48N 14 49E
Bronte, U.S.A. 159 31 54N 100 18W
Bronte Park 138 42 8S 146 30E
Brookeborough 38 54 19N 7 23W
Brookfield 158 39 50N 93 4W
Brookhaven 159 31 40N 90 25W
Brookings, Oreg., U.S.A. 160 42 4N 124 10W
Brookings, S.D., U.S.A. 158 44 20N 96 45W
Brooklands 138 18 5S 144 0E
Brookmere 152 49 52N 120 53W
Brooks 152 50 35N 111 55W
Brooks B. 152 50 15N 127 55W
Brooks L. 153 61 55N 106 35W
Brooks Ra. 147 68 40N 147 0W
Brooksville 157 28 32N 82 21W
Brookton 137 32 22S 116 57E
Brookville 156 39 25N 85 0W
Brooloo 139 26 30S 152 43E
Broom, L. 36 57 55N 5 15W
Broome 136 18 0S 122 15E
Broomehill 137 31 51S 117 39E
Broomfield 28 51 46N 0 28E
Broomhill 35 55 19N 1 36W
Broons 42 48 20N 2 16W
Brora 37 58 0N 3 50W
Brora L. 37 58 3N 3 58W
Brora, R. 37 58 4N 3 52W
Brosarp 73 55 44N 14 8E
Brösarp 73 55 43N 14 6E
Broseley 28 52 36N 2 30W
Brosna, R. 39 53 8N 8 0W
Broşteni 70 47 14N 25 43E
Brotas de Macaúbas 171 12 0S 42 38W
Brothers 160 43 56N 120 39W
Brothertoft 33 53 0N 0 5W
Brotton 33 54 34N 0 55W
Brøttum 71 61 2N 10 34E

Brough **Bura**

Brough, Cumbria, U.K.	**32**	54 32N	2 19W
Brough, Humberside, U.K.	**33**	53 44N	0 35W
Brough Hd.	**37**	59 8N	3 20W
Broughams Gate	**140**	30 51 S	140 59 E
Broughshane	**38**	54 54N	6 12W
Broughton, Austral.	**138**	20 10 S	146 20 E
Broughton, Borders, U.K.	**35**	55 37N	3 25W
Broughton, Humberside, U.K.	**33**	53 33N	0 36W
Broughton, Northampton, U.K.	**29**	52 22N	0 45W
Broughton, Yorkshire, U.K.	**33**	54 26N	1 8W
Broughton-in-Furness	**32**	54 17N	3 12W
Broughty Ferry	**35**	56 29N	2 50W
Broumov	**53**	50 35N	16 20 E
Brouwershaven	**46**	51 45N	3 55 E
Brouwershavensche Gat	**46**	51 46N	3 50 E
Brovary	**80**	50 34N	30 48 E
Brovst	**73**	57 6N	9 31 E
Browerville	**158**	46 3N	94 50W
Brown, Mt.	**140**	32 30 S	138 0 E
Brown, Pt.	**139**	32 32 S	133 50 E
Brown Willy, Mt.	**30**	50 35N	4 34W
Brownfield	**159**	33 10N	102 15W
Browngrove	**38**	53 33N	8 49W
Brownhills	**28**	52 38N	1 57W
Browning	**160**	48 35N	113 10W
Brownlee	**153**	50 43N	106 1W
Browns Bay	**142**	36 40 S	174 40 E
Brownstown Hd.	**39**	52 8N	7 8W
Brownsville, Oreg., U.S.A.	**160**	44 29N	123 0W
Brownsville, Tenn., U.S.A.	**159**	35 35N	89 15W
Brownsville, Tex., U.S.A.	**159**	25 56N	97 25W
Brownwood	**159**	31 45N	99 0W
Brownwood, L.	**159**	31 51N	98 35W
Browse I.	**136**	14 7 S	123 33 E
Broxburn	**35**	55 56N	3 23W
Broye, R.	**50**	46 52N	6 58 E
Brozas	**57**	39 37N	6 47W
Bruas	**101**	4 31N	100 46 E
Bruay-en-Artois	**43**	50 29N	2 33 E
Bruce Bay	**143**	43 35 S	169 42 E
Bruce, gasfield	**19**	59 45N	1 32 E
Bruce Mines	**150**	46 20N	83 45W
Bruce, Mt.	**136**	22 37 S	118 8 E
Bruce Rock	**137**	31 52 S	118 8 E
Bruchsal	**49**	49 9N	8 39 E
Bruck a.d. Leitha	**53**	48 1N	16 47 E
Bruck a.d. Mur	**52**	47 24N	15 16 E
Brückenau	**49**	50 17N	9 48 E
Brůdiceni	**70**	45 3N	23 4 E
Brue, R.	**28**	51 10N	2 59W
Bruernish Pt.	**36**	57 0N	7 22W
Bruff	**39**	52 29N	8 35W
Brugelette	**47**	50 35N	3 52 E
Bruges = Brugge	**47**	51 13N	3 13 E
Brugg	**50**	47 29N	8 11 E
Brugge	**47**	51 13N	3 13 E
Brühl	**48**	50 49N	6 51 E
Bruinisse	**47**	51 40N	4 5 E
Brûlé	**152**	53 15N	117 58W
Brûlon	**42**	47 58N	0 15W
Brûly	**47**	49 58N	4 32 E
Brumado	**171**	14 14 S	41 40W
Brumado, R.	**171**	14 13 S	41 40W
Brumath	**43**	48 43N	7 40 E
Brummen	**46**	52 5N	6 10 E
Brumunddal	**71**	60 53N	10 56 E
Brunchilly	**138**	18 50 S	134 30 E
Brundidge	**157**	31 43N	85 45W
Bruneau	**160**	42 57N	115 55W
Bruneau, R.	**160**	42 45N	115 50W
Brunei = Bandar Seri Begawan	**102**	4 52N	115 0 E
Brunei ■	**102**	4 50N	115 0 E
Brunette Downs	**138**	18 40 S	135 55 E
Brunflo	**72**	63 5N	14 50 E
Brunico	**63**	46 50N	11 55 E
Brünig, Col de	**50**	46 46N	8 8 E
Brunkeberg	**71**	59 26N	8 28 E
Brunna	**72**	59 52N	17 25 E
Brunnen	**51**	46 59N	8 37 E
Brunner	**143**	42 27 S	171 20 E
Brunner, L.	**143**	42 27 S	171 20 E
Brunnsvik	**72**	60 12N	15 8 E
Bruno	**153**	52 20N	105 30W
Brunsberg	**72**	59 38N	12 52 E
Brunsbüttelkoog	**48**	53 52N	9 13 E
Brunssum	**47**	50 57N	5 59 E
Brunswick, Ga., U.S.A.	**157**	31 10N	81 30W
Brunswick, Md., U.S.A.	**156**	39 20N	77 38W
Brunswick, Me., U.S.A.	**151**	43 53N	69 50W
Brunswick, Mo., U.S.A.	**158**	39 26N	93 10W
Brunswick = Braunschweig	**48**	52 17N	10 28 E
Brunswick B.	**136**	15 15 S	124 50 E
Brunswick Junction	**137**	33 15 S	115 50 E
Brunswick, Pen. de	**176**	53 30 S	71 30W
Bruntál	**53**	50 0N	17 27 E
Brunton	**35**	55 2N	2 6W
Bruny I.	**138**	43 20 S	147 15 E
Bruree	**39**	52 25N	8 40W
Brus Laguna	**166**	15 47N	84 35W
Brusartsi	**66**	43 40N	23 5 E
Brush	**158**	40 17N	103 33W
Brusio	**51**	46 14N	10 8 E
Brusque	**173**	27 5 S	49 0W
Brussel	**47**	50 51N	4 21 E
Brussels = Bruxelles	**47**	50 51N	4 21 E
Brustem	**47**	50 48N	5 14 E
Bruthen	**141**	37 42 S	147 50 E
Bruton	**28**	51 6N	2 28W
Bruvik	**71**	60 29N	5 40 E
Bruxelles	**47**	50 51N	4 21 E
Bruyères	**43**	48 10N	6 40 E
Brwinow	**54**	52 9N	20 40 E
Bryagovo	**67**	41 58N	25 8 E
Bryan, Ohio, U.S.A.	**156**	41 30N	84 30W
Bryan, Texas, U.S.A.	**159**	30 40N	96 27W
Bryan, Mt.	**140**	33 30 S	139 0 E
Bryansk	**80**	53 13N	34 25 E
Bryanskoye	**83**	44 9N	47 10 E
Bryant	**58**	44 39N	97 26W
Bryggja	**71**	61 56N	5 27 E
Bryher I.	**30**	49 57N	6 21W
Brymbo	**31**	53 4N	3 5W
Brynamman	**31**	51 49N	3 52W
Bryncethin	**31**	51 33N	3 34W
Bryne	**71**	58 44N	5 38 E
Brynmawr	**31**	51 48N	3 11W
Bryrup	**73**	56 2N	9 30 E
Bryson City	**157**	35 28N	83 25W
Bryte	**163**	38 35N	121 33W
Brza Palanka	**66**	44 28N	22 37 E
Brzava, R.	**66**	45 21N	20 45 E
Brzeg	**54**	50 52N	17 30 E
Brzeg Dln	**54**	51 16N	16 41 E
Brzesko	**54**	49 59N	20 34 E
Brześć Kujawski	**54**	52 36N	18 55 E
Brzeszcze	**54**	49 59N	19 10 E
Brzeziny	**54**	51 49N	19 42 E
Brzozów	**54**	49 41N	22 3 E
Bu Athiah	**119**	30 1N	15 30 E
Bu Craa	**116**	26 45N	17 2 E
Buapinang	**103**	4 40 S	121 30 E
Buayan	**103**	5 3N	125 28 E
Buba	**120**	11 40N	14 59W
Bubanza	**126**	3 6 S	29 23 E
Bucaramanga	**174**	7 0N	73 0W
Buccaneer Arch.	**136**	16 7 S	123 20 E
Bucchiánico	**63**	42 20N	14 10 E
Bucecea	**70**	47 47N	26 28 E
Bŭceşti	**70**	46 50N	27 11 E
Buchach	**80**	49 5N	25 25 E
Buchan, Austral.	**141**	37 30 S	148 12 E
Buchan, U.K.	**37**	57 32N	2 8W
Buchan Ness	**37**	57 29N	1 48W
Buchan, oilfield	**19**	57 55N	0 0
Buchanan, Can.	**153**	51 40N	102 45W
Buchanan, Liberia	**120**	5 57N	10 2W
Buchanan Cr.	**138**	17 10 S	138 6 E
Buchanan, L., Queens., Austral.	**138**	21 35 S	145 52 E
Buchanan, L., W. Australia, Austral.	**137**	25 33 S	123 2 E
Buchanan, L., U.S.A.	**159**	30 50N	98 25W
Buchans	**151**	49 50N	56 52W
Bucharest = Bucureşti	**70**	44 27N	26 10 E
Buchholz	**48**	53 19N	9 51 E
Buchloe	**49**	48 3N	10 45 E
Buchlyvie	**34**	56 7N	4 20W
Buchon, Pt.	**163**	35 15N	120 54W
Buchs	**51**	47 10N	9 28 E
Buck Hill Falls	**162**	41 11N	75 16W
Buck, The, mt.	**37**	57 19N	3 0W
Buckden	**29**	52 17N	0 16W
Bückeburg	**48**	52 16N	9 2 E
Buckeye	**161**	33 28N	112 40W
Buckfastleigh	**30**	50 28N	3 47W
Buckhannon	**156**	39 2N	80 10W
Buckhaven	**35**	56 10N	3 2W
Buckie	**37**	57 40N	2 58W
Buckingham, Can.	**150**	45 37N	75 24W
Buckingham, U.K.	**29**	52 0N	0 59W
Buckingham □	**29**	51 50N	0 55W
Buckingham B.	**138**	12 10 S	135 40 E
Buckingham Can.	**97**	14 0N	80 5 E
Buckinguy	**139**	31 3 S	147 30 E
Buckland	**147**	66 0N	161 5W
Buckland Brewer	**30**	50 56N	4 14W
Buckle Hd.	**136**	14 26 S	127 52 E
Buckleboo	**140**	32 54 S	136 12 E
Buckley, U.K.	**31**	53 10N	3 5W
Buckley, U.S.A.	**160**	47 10N	122 2W
Bucklin	**159**	37 37N	99 40W
Bucksburn	**37**	57 10N	2 10W
Bucquoy	**43**	50 9N	2 43 E
Buctouche	**151**	46 30N	64 45W
Bucureşti	**70**	44 27N	26 10 E
Bucyrus	**156**	40 48N	83 0W
Budacul, Munte	**41**	47 5N	25 40 E
Budafok	**53**	47 26N	19 2 E
Budalin	**98**	22 20N	95 10 E
Budapest	**53**	47 29N	19 5 E
Budaun	**95**	28 5N	79 10 E
Budd Coast	**13**	67 0 S	112 0 E
Buddabadah	**141**	31 56 S	147 14 E
Buddon Ness	**35**	56 29N	2 42W
Buddusò	**64**	40 35N	9 18 E
Bude	**30**	50 49N	4 33W
Bude Bay	**30**	50 50N	4 40W
Budel	**47**	51 17N	5 34 E
Budeşti	**70**	44 13N	26 30 E
Budge Budge	**95**	22 30N	88 25 E
Budgewoi Lake	**141**	33 13 S	151 34 E
Budia	**58**	40 38N	2 46W
Búdir	**74**	64 49N	23 23W
Budjala	**124**	2 50N	19 40 E
Budle B.	**35**	55 37N	1 45W
Budleigh Salterton	**30**	50 37N	3 19W
Búdrio	**63**	44 31N	11 31 E
Budva	**66**	42 17N	18 50 E
Budzyn	**54**	52 54N	16 59 E
Buea	**121**	4 10N	9 9 E
Buellton	**163**	34 37N	120 12W
Buena	**162**	39 31N	74 56W
Buena Vista, Colo., U.S.A.	**161**	38 56N	106 6W
Buena Vista, Va., U.S.A.	**156**	37 47N	79 23W
Buena Vista L.	**163**	35 15N	119 21W
Buenaventura	**164**	29 50N	107 30W
Buenaventura, B. de	**174**	3 48N	77 17W
Buendía, Pantano de	**58**	40 25N	2 43W
Buenópolis	**171**	17 54 S	44 11W
Buenos Aires, Argent.	**172**	34 30 S	58 20W
Buenos Aires, Colomb.	**174**	1 36N	73 18W
Buenos Aires, C. Rica	**166**	9 10N	83 20W
Buenos Aires □	**172**	36 30 S	60 0W
Buenos Aires, Lago	**176**	46 35 S	72 30W
Buesaco	**174**	1 23N	77 9W
Buffalo, Can.	**153**	50 49N	110 42W
Buffalo, Mo., U.S.A.	**159**	37 40N	93 5W
Buffalo, Okla., U.S.A.	**159**	36 55N	99 42W
Buffalo, S.D., U.S.A.	**159**	45 39N	103 31W
Buffalo, Wyo., U.S.A.	**160**	44 25N	106 50W
Buffalo Center	**147**	64 2N	145 50W
Buffalo Head Hills	**152**	57 25N	115 55W
Buffalo L.	**152**	52 27N	112 54W
Buffalo Narrows	**153**	55 51N	108 29W
Buffalo, R.	**152**	57 50N	117 1W
Buffels, R.	**129**	29 36 S	17 15 E
Buford	**157**	34 5N	84 0W
Bug, R., Poland	**54**	51 20N	23 40 E
Bug, R., U.S.S.R.	**82**	48 0N	31 0 E
Buga	**174**	4 0N	77 0W
Buganda □	**126**	0 0N	31 30 E
Buganga	**126**	0 25N	32 0 E
Bugeat	**44**	45 36N	1 55 E
Buggenhout	**47**	51 1N	4 12 E
Buggs I. L.	**157**	36 20N	78 30W
Buglawton	**32**	53 12N	2 11W
Bugle	**30**	50 23N	4 46W
Bugojno	**66**	44 2N	17 25 E
Bugsuk, I.	**102**	8 15N	117 15 E
Bugue, Le	**44**	44 55N	0 56 E
Bugulma	**84**	54 33N	52 48 E
Buguma	**121**	4 42N	6 55 E
Bugun Shara	**105**	49 0N	104 0 E
Buguruslan	**84**	53 39N	52 26 E
Buheirat-Murrat-el-Kubra	**122**	30 15N	32 40 E
Buhl, Idaho, U.S.A.	**160**	42 35N	114 54W
Buhl, Minn., U.S.A.	**158**	47 30N	92 46W
Buhŭeşti	**70**	46 47N	27 32 E
Buhuşi	**70**	46 41N	26 45 E
Buick	**159**	37 8N	91 2W
Bŭicoi	**70**	45 3N	25 52 E
Buie L.	**34**	56 20N	5 55W
Bŭileşti	**70**	44 01N	23 20 E
Builth Wells	**31**	52 10N	3 26W
Buina Qara	**93**	36 20N	67 0 E
Buinsk	**81**	55 0N	48 18 E
Buíque	**170**	8 37 S	37 9W
Buis-les-Baronnies	**45**	44 17N	5 16 E
Buit, L.	**151**	50 59N	63 13W
Buitenpost	**46**	53 15N	6 9 E
Buitrago	**56**	41 0N	3 38W
Bujalance	**57**	37 54N	4 23W
Buján	**56**	42 59N	8 36W
Bujaraloz	**58**	41 29N	0 10W
Buje	**63**	45 24N	13 39 E
Buji	**135**	9 8 S	142 11 E
Bujnurd	**93**	37 35N	57 15 E
Bujumbura (Usumbura)	**126**	3 16 S	29 18 E
Bük	**53**	47 22N	16 45 E
Buk	**54**	52 21N	16 17 E
Buka I.	**135**	5 10 S	154 35 E
Bukachacha	**77**	52 55N	116 50 E
Bukama	**127**	9 10 S	25 50 E
Bukandula	**126**	0 13N	31 50 E
Bukavu	**126**	2 20 S	28 52 E
Bukene	**126**	4 15 S	32 48 E
Bukhara	**85**	39 48N	64 25 E
Bukima	**126**	1 50 S	33 25 E
Bukit Mertajam	**101**	5 22N	100 28 E
Bukittinggi	**102**	0 20 S	100 20 E
Bukkapatnam	**97**	14 14N	77 46 E
Buklyan	**84**	55 42N	52 10 E
Bukoba	**126**	1 20 S	31 49 E
Bukoba □	**126**	1 30 S	32 0 E
Bukowno	**54**	50 17N	19 35 E
Bukrale	**123**	4 32N	42 0 E
Bukuru	**121**	9 42N	8 48 E
Bukuya	**126**	0 40N	31 52 E
Bula	**120**	12 7N	15 43W
Bülach	**51**	47 31N	8 32 E
Bulahdelah	**141**	32 23 S	152 13 E
Bulan	**103**	12 40N	123 52 E
Bulanash	**84**	57 16N	62 0 E
Bulandshahr	**94**	28 28N	77 58 E
Bulanovo	**84**	52 27N	55 10 E
Bulantai	**99**	36 33N	92 18 E
Bûlâq	**122**	25 10N	30 38 E
Bulawayo	**127**	20 7 S	28 32 E
Buldana	**96**	20 30N	76 18 E
Buldir I.	**147**	52 20N	175 55 E
Bulford	**28**	51 11N	1 45W
Bulgan	**105**	48 45N	103 34 E
Bulgaria ■	**67**	42 35N	25 30 E
Bulgroo	**138**	25 47 S	143 58 E
Bulgunnia	**139**	30 10 S	134 53 E
Bulhar	**91**	10 25N	44 30 E
Buli, Teluk	**103**	1 5N	128 25 E
Buliluyan, C.	**102**	8 20N	117 15 E
Bulki	**123**	6 11N	36 31 E
Bulkington	**163**	52 29N	1 25W
Bulkley, R.	**152**	55 15N	127 40W
Bulkur	**77**	71 50N	126 30 E
Bull Shoals L.	**159**	36 40N	93 5W
Bullabulling	**137**	31 1 S	120 32 E
Bullange	**47**	50 24N	6 15 E
Bullaque, R.	**57**	39 20N	4 13W
Bullara	**136**	22 40 S	114 3 E
Bullaring	**137**	32 30 S	117 45 E
Bullas	**59**	38 2N	1 40W
Bulle	**50**	46 37N	7 3 E
Buller Gorge	**143**	41 40 S	172 10 E
Buller, Mt.	**141**	37 10 S	146 28 E
Buller, R.	**143**	41 44 S	171 36 E
Bullfinch	**137**	30 58 S	119 3 E
Bulli	**141**	34 15 S	150 57 E
Bullock Cr.	**138**	17 51 S	143 45 E
Bulloo Downs, Queens., Austral.	**139**	28 31 S	142 57 E
Bulloo Downs, W.A., Austral.	**137**	24 0 S	119 32 E
Bulloo L.	**139**	28 43 S	142 25 E
Bulloo, R.	**139**	28 43 S	142 30 E
Bulls	**142**	40 10 S	175 24 E
Bully-les-Mines	**43**	50 27N	2 44 E
Bulnes	**172**	36 42 S	72 19W
Bulo Burti	**91**	3 50N	45 33 E
Bulolo	**135**	7 10 S	146 40 E
Bulpunga	**140**	33 47 S	141 45 E
Bulqiza	**68**	40 30N	20 21 E
Bulsar	**96**	20 40N	72 58 E
Bultfontein	**128**	28 18 S	26 10 E
Bulu Karakelong	**103**	4 35N	126 50 E
Buluan	**103**	9 0N	125 30 E
Bŭlŭciţa	**70**	44 23N	23 8 E
Bulukumba	**103**	5 33 S	120 11 E
Bulun	**77**	70 37N	127 30 E
Bulwell	**33**	53 1N	1 12W
Bumba	**124**	2 13N	22 30 E
Bumbiri I.	**126**	1 40 S	31 55 E
Bumble Bee	**161**	34 8N	112 18W
Bumbum	**121**	14 10N	8 10 E
Bumhkang	**98**	26 51N	97 40 E
Bumhpa Bum	**98**	26 51N	97 14 E
Bumi, R.	**127**	17 30 S	28 30 E
Bumtang, R.	**98**	26 56N	90 53 E
Buna, Kenya	**124**	2 58N	39 30 E
Buna, P.N.G.	**135**	8 42 S	148 27 E
Bunaiyin	**92**	23 10N	51 8 E
Bunaw	**39**	51 47N	9 50W
Bunazi	**126**	1 3 S	31 23 E
Bunbeg	**38**	55 4N	8 18W
Bunbury	**132**	33 20 S	115 35 E
Bunclody	**39**	52 40N	6 40W
Buncrana	**38**	55 8N	7 28W
Bundaberg	**139**	24 54 S	152 22 E
Bünde	**48**	52 11N	8 33 E
Bundey, R.	**138**	21 46 S	135 37 E
Bundi	**94**	25 30N	75 35 E
Bundooma	**138**	24 54 S	134 16 E
Bundoran	**38**	54 24N	8 17W
Bundukia	**123**	5 14N	30 55 E
Bundure	**141**	35 10 S	146 1 E
Bŭneasa	**70**	45 56N	27 55 E
Bunessan	**34**	56 18N	6 15W
Bung Kan	**100**	18 23N	103 37 E
Bungay	**29**	52 27N	1 26 E
Bungendore	**141**	35 14 S	149 30 E
Bungil Cr.	**138**	27 5 S	149 5 E
Bungō-Suidō	**110**	33 0N	132 15 E
Bungoma	**126**	0 34N	34 34 E
Bungotakada	**110**	33 35N	131 25 E
Bungu	**126**	7 35 S	39 0 E
Bunguran N. Is.	**102**	4 45N	108 0 E
Bunia	**126**	1 35N	30 20 E
Bunji	**95**	35 45N	74 40 E
Bunju	**102**	3 35N	117 50 E
Bunker Hill	**163**	39 15N	117 8W
Bunkerville	**161**	36 47N	114 6W
Bunkie	**159**	31 1N	92 12W
Bunmahon	**39**	52 8N	7 22W
Bunnanaddan	**38**	54 3N	8 35W
Bunnell	**157**	29 28N	81 12W
Bunnik	**46**	52 4N	5 12 E
Bunnyconnellan	**38**	54 7N	9 1W
Bunnythorpe	**142**	40 16 S	175 39 E
Buñol	**59**	39 25N	0 47W
Bunsbeek	**47**	50 50N	4 56 E
Bunschoten	**46**	52 14N	5 22 E
Buntingford	**29**	51 57N	0 1W
Buntok	**102**	1 40 S	114 58 E
Bununu	**121**	9 51N	9 32 E
Bununu Doss	**121**	10 6N	9 25 E
Bunwell	**29**	52 30N	1 9 E
Bunyoro □ = Western □	**126**	1 45N	31 30 E
Bunza	**121**	12 8N	4 0 E
Búoareyri	**74**	65 2N	14 13W
Buol	**103**	1 15N	121 32 E
Buon Brieng	**100**	13 9N	108 12 E
Buong Long	**100**	13 44N	106 59 E
Buorkhaya, Mys	**77**	71 50N	133 10 E
Buqbuq	**122**	31 29N	25 29 E
Buqei'a	**90**	32 58N	35 20 E
Bur Acaba	**91**	3 12N	44 20 E
Bûr Fuad	**122**	31 15N	32 20 E
Bûr Safâga	**122**	26 43N	33 57 E
Bûr Sa'îd	**122**	31 16N	32 18 E
Bûr Sûdân	**122**	19 32N	37 9 E
Bûr Taufiq	**122**	29 54N	32 32 E
Bura	**126**	1 4 S	39 58 E

Buraidah **Caithness, Ord of, C**

Buraidah	92	26 20N	44 8 E
Buraimī, Al Wāhāt al	93	24 15N	55 43 E
Burak Sulayman	90	31 42N	35 7 E
Burama	91	9 55N	43 7 E
Burao	91	9 32N	45 32 E
Buras	159	29 20N	89 33W
Burayevo	84	55 50N	55 24 E
Burbage, Derby, U.K.	32	53 15N	1 55W
Burbage, Leics., U.K.	28	52 31N	1 20W
Burbage, Wilts., U.K.	28	51 21N	1 40W
Burbank	163	34 9N	118 23W
Burcher	141	33 30 S	147 16 E
Burdekin, R.	138	19 38 S	147 25 E
Burdett	152	49 50N	111 32W
Burdur	92	37 45N	30 22 E
Burdwan	95	23 16N	87 54 E
Bure	123	10 40N	37 4 E
Bure, R.	29	52 38N	1 45 E
Bureba, La	58	42 36N	3 24W
Buren	46	51 55N	5 20 E
Burfell	74	64 5N	20 56W
Burford	28	51 48N	1 38W
Burg, Magdeburg, Ger.	48	52 16N	11 50 E
Burg, Schleswig-Holstein, Ger.	48	54 25N	11 10 E
Burg el Arab	122	30 54N	29 32 E
Burg et Tuyur	122	20 55N	27 56 E
Burgan	92	29 0N	47 57 E
Burgas	67	42 33N	27 29 E
Burgaski Zaliv	67	42 30N	27 39 E
Burgdorf, Ger.	48	52 27N	10 0 E
Burgdorf, Switz.	50	47 3N	7 37 E
Burgenland □	53	47 20N	16 20 E
Burgeo	151	47 37N	57 38W
Burgersdorp	128	31 0 S	26 20 E
Burges, Mt.	137	30 50 S	121 5 E
Burgess	162	37 53N	76 21W
Burgess Hill	29	50 57N	0 7W
Burgh-le-Marsh	33	53 10N	0 15 E
Burghclere	28	51 19N	1 20W
Burghead	37	57 42N	3 30W
Burghead B.	37	57 40N	3 33W
Búrgio	64	37 35N	13 18 E
Bürglen	51	46 53N	8 40 E
Burglengenfeld	49	49 11N	12 2 E
Burgo de Osma	58	41 35N	3 4W
Burgohondo	56	40 26N	4 47W
Burgos	58	42 21N	3 41W
Burgos □	58	42 21N	3 42W
Burgstädt	48	50 55N	12 49 E
Burgsteinfurt	48	52 9N	7 23 E
Burgsvik	73	57 3N	18 19 E
Burguillos del Cerro	57	38 23N	6 35W
Burgundy = Bourgogne	43	47 0N	4 30 E
Burhanpur	96	21 18N	76 20 E
Burhou Rocks	42	49 45N	2 15W
Buri Pen.	123	15 25N	39 55 E
Burias, I.	103	12 55N	123 5 E
Buribay	84	51 57N	58 10 E
Burica, Punta	166	8 3N	82 51W
Burigi, L.	126	2 2 S	31 22 E
Burin, Can.	151	47 1N	55 14W
Burin, Jordan	90	32 11N	35 15 E
Buriram	100	15 0N	103 0 E
Buriti Alegre	171	18 9 S	49 3W
Buriti Bravo	170	5 50 S	43 50W
Buriti dos Lopes	170	3 10 S	41 52W
Burji	123	5 29N	37 51 E
Burkburnett	159	34 7N	98 35W
Burke	160	47 31N	115 56W
Burke, R.	138	23 12 S	139 33 E
Burketown	138	17 45 S	139 33 E
Burk's Falls	150	45 37N	79 24W
Burley, Hants, U.K.	28	50 49N	1 41W
Burley, N. Yorks., U.K.	33	53 55N	1 46W
Burley, U.S.A.	160	42 37N	113 55W
Burlingame	163	37 35N	122 21W
Burlington, Colo., U.S.A.	158	39 21N	102 18W
Burlington, Iowa, U.S.A.	158	40 50N	91 5W
Burlington, Kans., U.S.A.	158	38 15N	95 47W
Burlington, N.C., U.S.A.	157	36 7N	79 27W
Burlington, N.J., U.S.A.	162	40 5N	74 50W
Burlington, Wash., U.S.A.	160	48 29N	122 19W
Burlington, Wis., U.S.A.	156	42 41N	88 18W
Burlyu-Tyube	76	46 30N	79 10 E
Burma ■	98	21 0N	96 30 E
Burnabbie	137	32 7 S	126 21 E
Burnaby I.	152	52 25N	131 19W
Burnamwood	141	31 7 S	144 53 E
Burnet	159	30 45N	98 11W
Burnett, R.	133	24 45 S	152 23 E
Burney	160	40 56N	121 41W
Burnfoot	38	55 4N	7 15W
Burngup	137	33 2 S	118 42 E
Burnham, Essex, U.K.	29	51 37N	0 50 E
Burnham, Somerset, U.K.	28	51 14N	3 0W
Burnham Market	29	52 57N	0 43 E
Burnie	138	41 4 S	145 56 E
Burnley	32	53 47N	2 15W
Burnmouth	35	55 50N	2 4W
Burnoye	85	42 36N	70 47 E
Burns, Oreg., U.S.A.	160	43 40N	119 4W
Burns, Wyo., U.S.A.	158	41 13N	104 18W
Burns Lake	152	54 20N	125 45W
Burnside, L.	137	25 25 S	123 0 E
Burnt Paw	147	67 2N	142 43W
Burntisland	35	56 4N	3 14W
Burntwood L.	153	55 22N	100 26W
Burntwood, R.	153	56 8N	96 34W
Burqa	90	32 18N	35 11 E
Burra	140	33 40 S	138 55 E
Burragorang, L.	141	33 52 S	150 37 E
Burramurra	138	20 25N	137 15 E
Burravoe	36	60 30N	1 3W
Burray I.	37	58 50N	2 54W
Burreli	68	41 36N	20 1 E
Burrelton	35	56 30N	3 16W
Burren	39	53 9N	9 5W
Burren Junction	139	30 7 S	148 59 E
Burrendong Dam	139	32 39 S	149 6 E
Burrendong Res.	141	32 45 S	149 10 E
Burriana	58	39 50N	0 4W
Burrinjuck Res.	141	35 0 S	148 36 E
Burro, Serranías del	164	29 0N	102 0W
Burrow Hd.	34	54 40N	4 23W
Burrundie	136	13 32 S	131 42 E
Burruyacú	172	26 30 S	64 40W
Burry Port	31	51 41N	4 17W
Bursa	92	40 15N	29 5 E
Burseryd	73	57 12N	13 17 E
Burstall	153	50 39N	109 54W
Burstwick	33	53 43N	0 6W
Burton	32	54 10N	2 43W
Burton Agnes	33	54 4N	0 18W
Burton Bradstock	28	50 42N	2 43W
Burton Fleming	33	54 8N	0 20W
Burton L.	150	54 45N	78 20W
Burton Latimer	29	52 23N	0 41W
Burton upon Stather	33	53 39N	0 41W
Burton-upon-Trent	28	52 48N	1 39W
Burtonport	38	54 59N	8 26W
Burtundy	140	33 45 S	142 15 E
Burtville	137	28 42 S	122 33 E
Buru, I.	103	3 30 S	126 30 E
Burufu	120	10 25N	2 50W
Burujird	92	33 58N	48 41 E
Burullus, Bahra el	122	31 25N	31 0 E
Burunday	85	43 20N	76 51 E
Burundi ■	126	3 15 S	30 0 E
Burung	102	0 21N	108 25 E
Bururi	126	3 57 S	29 37 E
Burutu	121	5 20N	5 29 E
Burwash	29	50 59N	0 24 E
Burwash Landing	147	61 21N	139 0W
Burwell, U.K.	29	52 17N	0 20 E
Burwell, U.S.A.	158	41 49N	99 8W
Bury	32	53 36N	2 19W
Bury St. Edmunds	29	52 15N	0 42 E
Buryat A.S.S.R. □	77	53 0N	110 0 E
Burzenin	54	51 28N	18 47 E
Busalla	62	44 34N	8 58 E
Busango Swamp	127	14 15 S	25 45 E
Busayyah	92	30 0N	46 10 E
Busby	152	53 55N	114 0W
Bushati	68	41 58N	19 34 E
Bushell	153	59 31N	108 45W
Bushenyi	126	0 35 S	30 10 E
Bushey	29	51 38N	0 20W
Bushman Land	128	29 30 S	19 30 E
Bushmills	38	55 14N	6 32W
Bushnell, Ill., U.S.A.	158	40 32N	90 30W
Bushnell, Nebr., U.S.A.	158	41 18N	103 50W
Busia □	126	0 25N	34 6 E
Busie	120	10 29N	2 22W
Businga	124	3 16N	20 59 E
Buskerud fylke □	75	60 13N	9 0 E
Busko Zdrój	54	50 28N	20 42 E
Busovača	66	44 6N	17 53 E
Busra	92	32 30N	36 25 E
Bussa	121	10 11N	4 32 E
Bussang	43	47 50N	6 50 E
Busselton	137	33 42 S	115 15 E
Bussigny	50	46 33N	6 33 E
Bussum	46	52 16N	5 10 E
Bustard Hd.	133	24 0 S	151 48 E
Busto Arsizio	62	45 40N	8 50 E
Busto, C.	56	43 34N	6 28W
Busu-Djanoa	124	1 50N	21 5 E
Busuangal, I.	103	12 10N	120 0 E
Büsum	48	54 7N	8 50 E
Buta	126	2 50N	24 53 E
Butare	126	2 31 S	29 52 E
Bute	140	33 51 S	138 2 E
Bute (□)	26	55 40N	5 10W
Bute, I.	34	55 48N	5 2W
Bute Inlet	152	50 40N	124 53W
Bute, Kyles of	34	55 55N	5 10W
Bute, Sd. of	34	55 43N	5 8W
Butemba	126	1 9N	31 37 E
Butembo	126	0 9N	29 18 E
Butera	65	37 10N	14 10 E
Bütgenbach	47	50 26N	6 12 E
Buthidaung	98	20 52N	92 32 E
Butiaba	126	1 50N	31 20 E
Butler	158	38 17N	94 18W
Bütschwil	51	47 23N	9 5 E
Butte, Mont., U.S.A.	160	46 0N	112 31W
Butte, Nebr., U.S.A.	158	42 56N	98 54W
Butterfield, Mt.	137	24 45 S	128 7 E
Buttermere	32	54 32N	3 17W
Butterworth	101	5 24N	100 23 E
Buttevant	39	52 14N	8 40 E
Buttfield, Mt.	137	24 45 S	128 9 E
Button B.	153	58 45N	94 23W
Buttonwillow	163	35 24N	119 28W
Butty Hd.	137	33 54 S	121 39 E
Butuan	103	8 57N	125 33 E
Butuku-Luba	121	3 29N	8 33 E
Butung, I.	103	5 0 S	122 45 E
Buturlinovka	81	50 50N	40 35 E
Butzbach	48	50 24N	8 40 E
Buxar	95	25 34N	83 58 E
Buxton, S. Afr.	128	27 38 S	24 42 E
Buxton, U.K.	32	53 16N	1 54W
Buxy	43	46 44N	4 40 E
Buyaga	77	59 50N	127 0 E
Buynaksk	83	42 36N	47 42 E
Buyr Nuur	105	47 50N	117 42 E
Büyük çekmece	67	41 2N	28 35 E
Büyük Kemikli Burun	68	40 20N	26 15 E
Büyük Menderes, R.	79	37 45N	27 40 E
Buzançais	42	46 54N	1 25 E
Buzau, Pasul	70	45 35N	26 12 E
Buzaymah	117	24 35N	22 0 E
Buzen	110	33 35N	131 5 E
Buzet	63	45 24N	13 58 E
Buzi, R.	127	19 52 S	34 30 E
Buziaş	66	45 38N	21 36 E
Buzuluk	84	52 48N	52 12 E
Buzuluk, R.	81	50 50N	52 12 E
Buzŭu	70	45 10N	26 50 E
Buzŭu □	70	45 20N	26 30 E
Buzŭu, R.	70	45 10N	27 20 E
Buzzards Bay	162	41 45N	70 38W
Bwagaoia	135	10 40 S	152 52 E
Bwana Mkubwe	127	13 8 S	28 38 E
Byala, Ruse, Bulg.	67	43 28N	25 44 E
Byala, Varna, Bulg.	67	42 53N	27 55 E
Byala Slatina	67	43 26N	23 55 E
Byandovan, Mys	83	39 45N	49 28 E
Bychawa	54	51 1N	22 36 E
Byczyha	54	51 7N	18 12 E
Bydgoszcz	54	53 10N	18 0 E
Bydgoszcz □	54	53 16N	17 33 E
Byelorussian S.S.R. □	80	53 30N	27 0 E
Byers	158	39 46N	104 13W
Byfield	28	52 10N	1 15W
Bygland	71	58 50N	7 48 E
Byglandsfjord	71	58 40N	7 50 E
Byglandsfjorden	71	58 44N	7 50 E
Byhalia	159	34 53N	89 41W
Bykhov	80	53 31N	30 14 E
Bykle	71	59 20N	7 22 E
Bykovo	83	49 50N	45 25 E
Bylas	161	33 11N	110 9W
Bylchau	31	53 9N	3 32W
Bylderup	73	54 57N	9 6 E
Bylot I.	149	73 13N	78 34W
Byrd Land = Marie Byrd Land	13	79 30 S	125 0W
Byrd Sub-Glacial Basin	13	82 0 S	120 0W
Byro	137	26 5 S	116 11 E
Byrock	141	30 40 S	146 27 E
Byron B.	151	54 42N	57 40W
Byron, C.	133	28 38 S	153 40W
Byrranga, Gory	77	75 0N	100 0 E
Byrum	73	57 16N	11 0 E
Byske	74	64 57N	21 11 E
Byske, R.	74	65 20N	20 0 E
Bystrovka	85	42 47N	75 42 E
Bystrzyca Kłodzka	54	50 19N	16 39 E
Byten	80	52 50N	25 27 E
Bytom	54	50 25N	19 0 E
Bytom Ordz.	54	51 44N	15 48 E
Bytów	54	54 10N	17 30 E
Byumba	126	1 35 S	30 4 E
Byvalla	72	61 22N	16 27 E
Bzéma	117	24 50N	22 20 E
Bzenec	53	48 58N	17 18 E
C			
Ca Mau = Quan Long	101	9 7N	105 8 E
Ca Mau, Mui = Bai Bung	101	8 35N	104 42 E
Ca Na	101	11 20N	108 54 E
Ca, R.	100	18 45N	105 45 E
Caacupé	172	25 23N	57 5W
Caamano Sd.	152	52 55N	129 25W
Caatingas	170	7 0 S	52 30W
Caazapá	172	26 8 S	56 19W
Caazapá □	173	26 10 S	56 0W
Caballería, Cabo de	58	40 5N	4 5 E
Cabañaquinta	56	43 10N	5 38W
Cabanatuan	103	15 30N	121 5 E
Cabanes	58	40 9N	0 2 E
Cabano	151	47 40N	68 56 E
Cabazon	163	33 55N	116 47W
Cabbage Tree Hd.	108	27 20 S	153 5 E
Cabedelo	170	7 0 S	34 50W
Cabeza del Buey	57	38 44N	5 13W
Cabildo	172	32 30 S	71 5W
Cabimas	174	10 30N	71 25W
Cabinda	124	5 40 S	12 11 E
Cabinda □	124	5 0 S	12 30 E
Cabinet Mts.	160	48 0N	115 30W
Cables	137	27 55 S	123 25 E
Cableskill	162	42 39N	74 30W
Cabo Blanco	176	47 56 S	65 47W
Cabo Delgado □	127	10 35 S	40 35 E
Cabo Frio	173	22 51 S	42 3W
Cabo Pantoja	174	1 0 S	75 10W
Cabonga Reservoir	150	47 20N	76 40W
Cabool	159	37 10N	92 8W
Caboolture	139	27 5 S	152 58 E
Cabora Bassa Dam	127	15 20 S	32 50 E
Caborca (Heroica)	164	30 40N	112 10W
Cabot Strait	151	47 15N	59 40W
Cabra	57	37 30N	4 28W
Cabra del Santo Cristo	59	37 42N	3 16W
Cabrach	37	57 20N	3 0W
Cabras	64	39 57N	8 30 E
Cabrera, I.	59	39 6N	2 59 E
Cabrera, Sierra	56	42 12N	6 40W
Cabri	153	50 35N	108 25W
Cabriel, R.	59	39 20N	1 20W
Cabruta	174	7 50N	66 10W
Caburan	103	6 3N	125 45 E
Cabuyaro	174	4 18N	72 49W
Çacabelos	56	42 36N	6 44W
Čačak	66	43 54N	20 20 E
Cáceres, Brazil	174	16 5 S	57 40W
Cáceres, Colomb.	174	7 35N	75 20W
Cáceres, Spain	57	39 26N	6 23W
Cáceres □	57	39 45N	6 0W
Cache B.	150	46 26N	80 1W
Cache Bay	150	46 22N	80 0W
Cachepo	57	37 20N	7 49W
Cacheu	120	12 14N	16 8W
Cachi	172	25 5 S	66 10W
Cachimbo, Serra do	175	9 30 S	55 0W
Cáchira	174	7 21N	73 17W
Cachoeira	171	12 30 S	39 0W
Cachoeira Alta	171	18 48 S	50 58W
Cachoeira de Itapemirim	173	20 51 S	41 7W
Cachoeira do Sul	173	30 3 S	52 53W
Cachoeiro do Arari	170	1 1 S	48 58W
Cachopo	57	37 20N	7 49W
Cacolo	124	10 9 S	19 21 E
Caconda	125	13 48 S	15 8 E
Caçu	171	18 37 S	51 4W
Caculé	171	14 30 S	42 13W
Cadamstown	39	53 7N	7 39W
Cadarga	139	26 8 S	150 58 E
Çadaux	137	30 48 S	117 15 E
Čadca	53	49 26N	18 45 E
Caddo	159	34 8N	96 18W
Cadenazzo	51	46 9N	8 57 E
Cader Idris	31	52 43N	3 56W
Cadereyta Jiménez	165	25 40N	100 0W
Cadí, Sierra del	58	42 17N	1 42 E
Cadibarrawirracanna, L.	139	28 52 S	135 27 E
Cadillac, Can.	150	48 14N	78 23W
Cadillac, France	44	44 38N	0 20W
Cadillac, U.S.A.	156	44 16N	85 25W
Cadiz	103	11 30N	123 15 E
Cádiz	57	36 30N	6 20W
Cádiz □	57	36 36N	5 45W
Cádiz, G. de	57	36 40N	7 0W
Cadomin	152	53 2N	117 20W
Cadotte, R.	152	56 43N	117 10W
Cadours	44	43 44N	1 2 E
Cadoux	137	30 46 S	117 7 E
Caen	42	49 10N	0 22W
Caenby Corner	33	53 23N	0 32W
Caergwrle	29	53 6N	3 3W
Caerhun	31	53 14N	3 50W
Caerleon	31	51 37N	2 57W
Caernarfon	31	53 8N	4 17W
Caernarfon B.	31	53 4N	4 40W
Caernarvon = Caernarfon	31	53 8N	4 17W
Caernarvon (□)	26	53 8N	4 17W
Caerphilly	31	51 34N	3 13W
Caersws	31	52 32N	3 27W
Caerwent	31	51 37N	2 47W
Cæsarea = Qesari	90	32 30N	34 53 E
Caeté	171	20 0 S	43 40W
Caetité	171	13 50 S	42 50W
Cafayate	172	26 2 S	66 0W
Cafu	128	16 30 S	15 8 E
Cagayan de Oro	103	8 30N	124 40 E
Cagayan, R.	103	18 25N	121 42 E
Cagli	63	43 32N	12 38 E
Cágliari	64	39 15N	9 6 E
Cágliari, G. di	64	39 8N	9 10 E
Cagnano Varano	65	41 49N	15 47 E
Cagnes-sur-Mer	45	43 40N	7 9 E
Caguas	147	18 14N	66 4W
Caha Mts.	39	51 45N	9 40W
Caher I.	38	53 44N	10 1W
Caherconlish	39	52 36N	8 30W
Cahermore	39	51 35N	10 2W
Cahir	39	52 23N	7 56W
Cahirciveen	39	51 57N	10 13W
Cahore Pt.	39	52 34N	6 11W
Cahors	44	44 27N	1 27 E
Cahuapanas	174	5 15 S	77 0W
Cai Ban, Dao	100	21 10N	107 27 E
Cai Nuoc	101	8 56N	105 1 E
Caianda	127	11 29 S	23 31 E
Caibarién	166	22 30N	79 30W
Caicara	174	7 38N	66 10W
Caicó	170	6 20 S	37 0W
Caicos Is.	167	21 40N	71 40W
Caicos Passage	167	22 45N	72 45W
Caihaique	176	45 30 S	71 45W
Caird Coast	13	75 0 S	25 0W
Cairn Gorm	37	57 7N	3 40W
Cairn Table	35	55 30N	4 0W
Cairngorm Mts.	37	57 6N	3 42W
Cairnryan	34	54 59N	5 0W
Cairns	138	16 57 S	145 45 E
Cairo, Ga., U.S.A.	157	30 52N	84 12W
Cairo, Illinois, U.S.A.	159	37 0N	89 10W
Cairo, N.Y., U.S.A.	162	42 18N	74 0W
Cairo = El Qâhira	122	30 1N	31 14 E
Cairo Montenotte	62	44 23N	8 16 E
Caister-on-Sea	29	52 38N	1 43 E
Caistor	33	53 29N	0 20W
Caithness (□)	26	58 25N	3 25W
Caithness, Ord of, C.	37	58 35N	3 37W

Caiundo Canton

Caiundo 125 15 50S 17 52E
Caiza 174 20 2S 65 40W
Cajamarca 174 7 5S 78 28W
Cajapió 170 2 58S 44 48W
Cajarc 44 44 29N 1 50E
Çajàzeiros 170 7 0S 38 30W
Ćajetina 66 43 47N 19 42E
Čajniče 66 43 34N 19 5E
Çakirgöl 83 40 33N 39 40E
Cala 57 37 59N 6 21W
Cala Cadolar 59 38 38N 1 35E
Cala, R. 57 37 50N 6 8W
Calabar 121 4 57N 8 20E
Calabozo 174 9 0N 67 20W
Calábria □ 65 39 24N 16 30E
Calaburras, Pta. de 57 36 30N 4 38W
Calaceite 58 41 1N 0 11E
Calafat 70 43 58N 22 59E
Calafate 176 50 25S 72 25W
Calahorra 58 42 18N 1 59W
Calais, France 43 50 57N 1 56E
Calais, U.S.A. 151 45 5N 67 20W
Calais, Pas de 160 50 57N 1 20E
Calalaste, Sierra de 172 25 0S 67 0W
Calama, Brazil 174 8 0S 62 50W
Calama, Chile 172 22 30S 68 55W
Calamar, Bolívar, Colomb. 174 10 15N 74 55W
Calamar, Vaupés, Colomb. 174 1 58N 72 32W
Calamian Group 103 11 50N 119 55E
Calamocha 58 40 50N 1 17W
Calanaque 174 0 5S 64 0W
Calañas 57 37 40N 6 53W
Calanda 58 40 56N 0 15W
Calang 102 4 30N 95 43E
Calangiánus 64 40 56N 9 12E
Calapan 103 13 25N 121 7E
Calasparra 59 38 14N 1 41W
Calatafimi 64 37 56N 12 50E
Calatayud 58 41 20N 1 40W
Calauag 103 13 55N 122 15E
Calavà, C. 65 38 11N 14 55E
Calavite, Cape 103 13 26N 120 10E
Calbe 48 51 57N 11 47E
Calca 174 13 10S 72 0W
Calci 62 43 44N 10 31E
Calcidica = Khalkidhikí □ 170 40 25N 23 40E
Calcutta 95 22 36N 88 24E
Caldaro 63 46 23N 11 15E
Caldas □ 174 5 15N 75 30W
Caldas da Rainha 57 39 24N 9 8W
Caldas de Reyes 56 42 36N 8 39W
Caldas Novas 171 17 45S 48 38W
Caldbeck 32 54 45N 3 3W
Calder Bridge 32 54 27N 3 31W
Calder Hall 32 54 26N 3 31W
Calder, R. 33 53 44N 1 21W
Caldera 172 27 5S 70 55W
Caldew R. 32 54 54N 2 59W
Caldiran 92 39 7N 44 0E
Caldwell, Idaho, U.S.A. 160 43 45N 116 42W
Caldwell, Kans., U.S.A. 159 37 5N 97 37W
Caldwell, Texas, U.S.A. 159 30 30N 96 42W
Caldy I. 31 51 38N 4 42W
Caledon, S. Afr. 128 34 14S 19 26E
Caledon, U.K. 38 54 22N 6 50W
Caledon B. 138 12 45S 137 0E
Caledon, R. 128 30 0S 26 46E
Caledonian Can. 37 56 50N 5 6W
Calella 58 41 37N 2 40E
Calemba 128 16 0S 15 38E
Calera, La 172 32 50S 71 10W
Calexico 161 32 40N 115 33W
Calf of Man 32 54 4N 4 48W
Calgary, Can. 152 51 0N 114 10W
Calgary, U.K. 34 56 34N 6 17W
Calhoun 157 34 30N 84 55W
Cali 174 3 25N 76 35W
Caliach Pt. 34 56 37N 6 20W
Calicoan, I. 103 10 59N 125 50E
Calicut 93 11 15N 75 43E
Calicut, (Kozhikode) 97 11 15N 75 43E
Caliente 161 37 43N 114 34W
California 158 38 37N 92 30W
California □ 160 37 25N 120 0W
California, Baja 164 32 10N 115 12W
California, Baja, T.N. □ 164 30 0N 115 0W
California, Baja, T.S. □ 164 25 50N 111 50W
California City 163 35 7N 117 57W
California, Golfo de 164 27 0N 111 0W
California Hot Springs 163 35 51N 118 41W
California, Lr. = California, Baja 164 25 50N 111 50W
Calilegua 172 23 45S 64 42W
Călimăneşti 70 45 14N 24 20E
Calingasta 172 31 15S 69 30W
Calipatria 161 33 8N 115 30W
Calistoga 160 38 36N 122 32W
Calitri 65 40 54N 15 25E
Calkini 165 20 21N 90 3W
Callabonna, L. 139 29 40S 140 5E
Callac 42 48 25N 3 27W
Callafo 91 6 48N 43 47E
Callan 39 52 33N 7 25W
Callanish 36 58 12N 6 43W
Callantsoog 46 52 50N 4 42E
Callao 174 12 0S 77 0W
Callaway 158 41 20N 99 56W
Calles 165 23 2N 98 42W
Callicoon 162 41 46N 75 3W
Callide 138 24 18S 150 28E
Calling Lake 152 55 15N 113 12W
Callington 30 56 30N 4 19W
Calliope 138 24 0S 151 16E
Callosa de Ensarriá. 59 38 40N 0 8W
Callosa de Segura 59 38 1N 0 53W
Callow 38 53 58N 9 2W
Calne 28 51 26N 2 0W
Calola 128 16 25S 17 48E
Calore, R. 65 41 8N 14 45E
Caloundra 139 26 45S 153 10E
Calpe 59 38 39N 0 3E
Calshot 28 50 49N 1 18W
Calstock, Can. 150 49 47N 84 9W
Calstock, U.K. 30 50 30N 4 13W
Caltabellotta 64 37 36N 13 11E
Caltagirone 65 37 13N 14 30E
Caltanissetta 65 37 30N 14 3E
Caluire-et-Cuire 45 45 49N 4 51E
Calulo 124 10 1S 14 56E
Calumbo 124 9 0S 13 20E
Caluso 62 45 18N 7 52E
Calvados □ 42 49 5N 0 15W
Calvert 159 30 59N 96 50W
Calvert Hills 138 17 15S 137 20E
Calvert I. 152 51 30N 128 0W
Calvert, R. 138 16 17S 137 44E
Calvert Ra. 136 24 0S 122 30E
Calvillo 164 21 51N 102 43W
Calvinia 128 31 28S 19 45E
Calwa 163 36 42N 119 46W
Calzada Almuradiel 59 38 32N 3 28W
Calzada de Calatrava 57 38 42N 3 46W
Cam Lam 101 11 54N 109 10E
Cam Pha 100 21 1N 107 18E
Cam, R. 29 52 21N 0 16E
Cam Ranh 101 11 54N 109 12E
Cam Xuyen 100 18 15N 106 0E
Camabatela 124 8 20S 15 26E
Camacã 171 15 24S 39 30W
Camaçari 171 12 41S 38 18W
Camacho 164 24 25N 102 18W
Camaguán 174 8 6N 67 36W
Camagüey 166 21 20N 78 0W
Camaiore 62 43 57N 10 18E
Camamu 171 13 57S 39 7W
Camaná 174 16 30S 72 50W
Camaquã, R. 173 30 50S 52 50W
Camaret 42 48 16N 4 37W
Camargo 174 20 38S 65 15E
Camargue 45 43 34N 4 34E
Camarillo 163 34 13N 119 2W
Camariñas 56 43 8N 9 12W
Camarón, C. 166 16 0N 85 0W
Camarones, Argent. 176 44 50S 65 40W
Camarones, Chile 174 19 0S 69 58W
Camas 160 45 35N 122 24W
Camas Valley 160 43 0N 123 46W
Cambados 56 42 31N 8 49W
Cambará 173 23 2S 50 5W
Cambay 94 22 23N 72 33E
Cambay, G. of 94 20 45N 72 30E
Camberley 29 51 20N 0 44W
Cambil 59 37 40N 3 33W
Cambo 35 55 9N 1 57W
Cambo-les-Bains 44 43 22N 1 23W
Cambodia ■ 100 12 15N 105 0E
Camborne 30 50 13N 5 18W
Cambrai 43 50 11N 3 14E
Cambria 163 35 44N 121 6W
Cambrian Mts. 31 52 25N 3 52W
Cambridge, Can. 150 43 23N 80 15W
Cambridge, Jamaica 166 18 18N 77 54W
Cambridge, N.Z. 142 37 54S 175 29E
Cambridge, U.K. 29 52 13N 0 8E
Cambridge, Idaho, U.S.A. 160 44 36N 116 52W
Cambridge, Mass., U.S.A. 162 42 20N 71 8W
Cambridge, Md., U.S.A. 162 38 33N 76 2W
Cambridge, Minn., U.S.A. 158 45 34N 93 15W
Cambridge, Nebr., U.S.A. 158 40 20N 100 12W
Cambridge, N.Y., U.S.A. 162 43 2N 73 22W
Cambridge, Ohio, U.S.A. 156 40 1N 81 22W
Cambridge Bay 148 69 10N 105 0W
Cambridge Gulf 136 14 45S 128 0E
Cambridgeshire □ 29 52 12N 0 7E
Cambrils 58 41 8N 1 3E
Cambuci 173 21 35S 41 55W
Camden, Austral. 141 34 1S 150 43E
Camden, U.K. 29 51 33N 0 10W
Camden, Ala., U.S.A. 157 31 59N 87 15W
Camden, Ark., U.S.A. 159 33 30N 92 50W
Camden, Del., U.S.A. 162 39 7N 75 33W
Camden, Me., U.S.A. 151 44 14N 69 6W
Camden, N.J., U.S.A. 162 39 57N 75 1W
Camden, N.Y., U.S.A. 162 43 20N 75 45W
Camden, S.C., U.S.A. 157 34 17N 80 34W
Camden, B. 147 71 0N 145 0W
Camden Sound 136 15 27S 124 25E
Camel R. 30 50 28N 4 49W
Camelford 30 50 37N 4 41W
Camembert 42 48 53N 0 10E
Cámeri 62 45 30N 8 40E
Camerino 63 43 10N 13 4E
Cameron, Ariz., U.S.A. 161 35 55N 111 31W
Cameron, La., U.S.A. 159 29 50N 93 18W
Cameron, Mo., U.S.A. 158 39 42N 94 14W
Cameron, Tex., U.S.A. 159 30 53N 97 0W
Cameron Falls 150 49 8N 88 19W
Cameron Highlands 101 4 27N 101 22E
Cameron Hills 152 59 48N 118 0W
Cameron Mts. 143 46 1S 167 0E
Cameroon ■ 124 3 30N 12 30E
Camerota 65 40 2N 15 21E
Cameroun, Mt. 121 4 45N 8 55E
Cameroun, R. 121 4 0N 9 35E
Camerton 28 51 18N 2 27W
Cametá 170 2 0S 49 30W
Caminha 56 41 50N 8 50W
Camino 163 38 47N 120 40W
Camira Creek 139 29 15S 152 58E
Camiranga 170 1 48S 46 17W
Cammachmore 37 57 2N 2 9W
Camocim 170 2 55S 40 50W
Camogli 62 44 21N 9 9E
Camolin 39 52 37N 6 26W
Camooweal 138 19 56S 138 7E
Camopi, R. 175 3 12N 52 17W
Camp Crook 158 45 36N 103 59W
Camp Hill 162 40 15N 76 56W
Camp Nelson 163 36 8N 118 39W
Camp Wood 159 29 47N 100 0W
Campagna 65 40 40N 15 5E
Campana 172 34 10S 58 55W
Campana, I. 176 48 20S 75 10W
Campanario 57 38 52N 5 36W
Campania □ 65 40 50N 14 45E
Campbell 163 37 17N 121 57W
Campbell, C. 143 41 47S 174 18E
Campbell I. 142 52 30S 169 0E
Campbell L. 153 63 14N 106 55W
Campbell River 152 50 5N 125 20W
Campbell Town 138 41 52S 147 30E
Campbellpur 94 33 46N 72 20E
Campbellsville 156 37 23N 85 12W
Campbellton, Alta., Can. 152 53 32N 113 15W
Campbellton, N.B., Can. 151 47 57N 66 43W
Campbelltown, Austral. 141 34 4S 150 49E
Campbelltown, U.K. 37 57 34N 4 2W
Campbeltown 34 55 25N 5 36W
Campeche 165 19 50N 90 32W
Campeche □ 165 19 50N 90 32W
Campeche, Golfo de 165 19 30N 93 0W
Camperdown 140 38 14S 143 9E
Camperville 153 51 59N 100 9W
Campi Salentina 65 40 22N 18 2E
Campidano 64 39 30N 8 40E
Campillo de Altobuey 58 39 36N 1 49W
Campillo de Llerena 57 38 30N 5 50W
Campillos 57 37 4N 4 51W
Campina Grande 170 7 20S 35 47W
Campiña, La 57 37 45N 4 45W
Campina Verde 171 19 31S 49 28W
Campinas 173 22 50S 47 0W
Campine 47 51 8N 5 20E
Campinho 170 14 30S 39 10W
Campli 63 42 44N 13 40E
Campo 124 2 15N 9 58E
Campo Beló 171 21 0S 45 30W
Campo de Criptana 59 39 25N 3 7W
Campo de Gibraltar 57 36 15N 5 25W
Campo Flórido 171 19 47S 48 35W
Campo Formoso 170 10 30S 40 20W
Campo Grande 175 20 25S 54 40W
Campo Maior, Brazil 170 4 50S 42 12W
Campo Maior, Port. 57 38 59N 7 7W
Campo Mourão 171 24 3S 52 22W
Campo Tencia 51 46 26N 8 43E
Campo Túres 63 46 53N 11 55E
Campoalegre 174 2 41N 75 20W
Campobasso 65 41 34N 14 40E
Campobello di Licata 64 37 16N 13 55E
Campobello di Mazara 64 37 38N 12 45E
Campofelice 64 37 54N 13 53E
Camporeale 64 37 53N 13 3E
Campos 173 21 50S 41 20W
Campos Altos 171 19 41S 46 10W
Campos Belos 171 13 10S 46 45W
Campos del Puerto 59 39 26N 3 1E
Campos Novos 173 27 21S 51 20W
Campos Sales 170 7 4S 40 23W
Camprodón 58 42 19N 2 23E
Campsie Fells 23 56 2N 4 20W
Camptown 162 41 44N 76 14W
Campuya, R. 174 1 10S 74 0W
Camrose, Can. 152 53 0N 112 50W
Camrose, U.K. 31 51 50N 5 2W
Camsall L. 153 72 32N 106 47W
Camsell Portage 153 59 37N 109 15W
Camurra 139 29 21S 149 52E
Can Gio 101 10 25N 106 58E
Can Tho 101 10 2N 105 46E
Canada ■ 148 60 0N 100 0W
Cañada de Gómez 73 32 55S 61 30W
Canadian 159 35 56N 100 25W
Canadian, R. 159 36 0N 98 45W
Canairiktok, R. 151 54 30N 62 30W
Canajoharie 162 42 54N 74 35W
Çanakkale 68 40 8N 26 30E
Çanakkale Boğazi 68 40 0N 26 0E
Canal de l'Est 43 48 45N 5 35E
Canal Flats 152 50 10N 115 48W
Canal latéral à la Garonne 44 44 25N 0 15E
Canalejas 172 35 15S 66 34W
Canals 172 33 35S 62 40W
Canals 59 38 58N 0 35W
Canandaigua 156 42 55N 77 18W
Cananea 164 31 0N 110 20W
Canarias, Islas 116 29 30N 17 0W
Canarreos, Arch. de los 166 21 35N 81 40W
Canary Is. = Canarias, Islas 116 29 30N 17 0W
Canastra, Serra da 171 20 0S 46 20W
Canatlán 164 24 31N 104 47W
Canaveral, C. 157 28 28N 80 31W
Cañaveras 58 40 27N 2 14W
Canavieiras 171 15 39S 39 0W
Canbelego 141 31 32S 146 18E
Canberra 141 35 15S 149 8E
Canby, Calif., U.S.A. 160 41 26N 120 58W
Canby, Minn., U.S.A. 158 44 44N 96 15W
Canby, Oregon, U.S.A. 160 45 24N 122 45W
Cancale 42 48 40N 1 50W
Candala 91 11 30N 49 58E
Candas 56 43 35N 5 45W
Candé 42 47 34N 1 0W
Candea = Iráklion 69 35 20N 25 12E
Candela 65 41 8N 15 31E
Candelaria 173 27 29S 55 44W
Candelaria, Pta. de la 56 43 45N 8 0W
Candeleda 56 40 10N 5 14W
Candelo 141 36 47S 149 43E
Candia = Iráklion 69 35 20N 25 12E
Cândido de Abreu 171 24 35S 51 20W
Cândido Mendes 170 1 27S 45 43W
Candle L. 153 53 50N 105 18W
Cando 158 48 30N 99 14W
Canea = Khaniá 69 35 30N 24 4E
Canela 170 10 15S 48 25W
Canelli 62 44 44N 8 18E
Canelones 172 34 32S 56 10W
Canet-Plage 44 42 41N 3 2E
Cañete, Chile 172 37 50S 73 30W
Cañete, Cuba 167 20 36N 74 43W
Cañete, Peru 174 13 0S 76 30W
Cañete, Spain 58 40 3N 1 54W
Cañete de las Torres 57 37 53N 4 19W
Canfranc 58 42 42N 0 31W
Cangamba 125 13 40S 19 54E
Cangas 56 42 16N 8 47W
Cangas de Narcea 56 43 10N 6 32W
Cangas de Onís 56 43 21N 5 8W
Canguaretama 170 6 20S 35 5W
Canguçu 173 31 22S 52 43W
Canhotinho 171 8 53S 36 12W
Cani, Is. 119 36 21N 10 5E
Canicado 125 24 2S 33 2E
Canicatti 64 37 21N 13 50E
Canicattini 65 37 1N 15 3E
Canim, L. 152 51 45N 120 50W
Canim Lake 152 51 17N 120 54W
Canindé 170 4 22S 39 19W
Canindé, R. 170 6 15S 42 52W
Canipaan 102 8 33N 117 15E
Canisbay 37 58 38N 3 6W
Canisp Mt. 36 58 8N 5 5W
Cañitas 164 23 36N 102 43W
Cañiza, La 56 42 13N 8 16W
Cañizal 56 41 20N 5 22W
Canjáyar 59 37 1N 2 44W
Cankırı 92 40 40N 33 30E
Cankuzo 126 3 10S 30 31E
Canlaon, Mt. 103 9 27N 118 25E
Canmore 152 51 7N 115 18W
Cann River 141 37 35S 149 7E
Canna I. 36 57 3N 6 33W
Canna, Sd. of 36 57 1N 6 30W
Cannanore 97 11 53N 75 27E
Cannes 45 43 32N 7 0E
Cannich 37 57 20N 4 48W
Canning Basin 136 19 50S 124 0E
Canning Town 95 22 23N 88 40E
Cannington 28 51 8N 3 4W
Cannock 28 52 42N 2 2W
Cannock Chase, hills 23 52 43N 2 0W
Cannon Ball, R. 158 46 20N 101 20W
Cannondale, Mt. 138 25 13S 148 57E
Caño Colorado 174 2 18N 68 22W
Canoe L. 153 55 10N 108 15W
Canol 147 65 15N 126 50W
Canon City 158 39 30N 105 20W
Canonbie 35 55 4N 2 58W
Canopus 140 33 29S 140 42E
Canora 153 51 40N 102 30W
Canosa di Púglia 65 41 13N 16 4E
Canourgue, Le 44 44 26N 3 13E
Canowindra 141 33 35S 148 38E
Canso 151 45 20N 61 0W
Cantabria, Sierra de 58 42 40N 2 30W
Cantabrian Mts. = Cantábrica 56 43 0N 5 10W
Cantábrica, Cordillera 56 43 0N 5 10W
Cantal □ 44 45 4N 2 45E
Cantanhede 56 40 20N 8 36W
Cantaura 174 9 19N 64 21W
Çantavieja 58 40 31N 0 25W
Čantavir 66 45 55N 19 46E
Canterbury, Austral. 138 25 23S 141 53E
Canterbury, U.K. 29 51 17N 1 5E
Canterbury □ 143 43 45S 171 19E
Canterbury Bight 143 44 16S 171 55E
Canterbury Plains 143 43 55S 171 22E
Cantil 163 35 18N 117 58W
Cantillana 57 37 36N 5 50W
Canto do Buriti 170 8 7S 42 58W
Canton, Ga., U.S.A. 157 34 13N 84 29W
Canton, Ill., U.S.A. 158 40 32N 90 0W
Canton, Mass., U.S.A. 162 42 9N 71 9W
Canton, Miss., U.S.A. 159 32 40N 90 1W
Canton, Mo., U.S.A. 158 40 10N 91 33W
Canton, Ohio, U.S.A. 156 40 47N 81 22W
Canton, Okla., U.S.A. 159 36 5N 98 36W

Canton Cascade

Canton, Pa., U.S.A. 162 41 39N 76 51W
Canton, S.D., U.S.A. 158 43 20N 96 35W
Canton = Kuangchou 109 23 10N 113 10 E
*Canton I. 130 2 30 S 172 0W
Canton L. 159 36 12N 98 40W
Cantù 62 45 44N 9 8 E
Canudos 174 7 13 S 58 5W
Canulloit 161 31 58N 106 36W
Canutama 174 6 30 S 64 20W
Canvey 29 51 32N 0 35 E
Canyon, Can. 147 47 25N 84 36W
Canyon, Texas, U.S.A. 159 35 0N 101 57W
Canyon, Wyo., U.S.A. 160 44 43N 110 36W
Canyonlands Nat. Park 161 38 25N 109 30W
Canyonville 160 42 55N 123 14W
Canzo 62 45 54N 9 18 E
Cao Bang 100 22 40N 106 15 E
Cao Lanh 101 10 27N 105 38 E
Caoles 34 56 32N 6 43W
Caolisport, Loch 34 55 54N 5 40W
Cáorle 63 45 36N 12 51 E
Cap-aux-Meules 151 47 23N 61 52W
Cap Chat 151 49 6N 66 40W
Cap-de-la-Madeleine 150 46 22N 72 31W
Cap Haïtien 167 19 40N 72 20W
Cap St.-Jacques = Vung Tau 101 10 21N 107 4 E
Capa Stilo 65 38 25N 16 25 E
Capáccio 65 40 26N 15 4 E
Capaia 124 8 27 S 20 13 E
Capanaparo, R. 174 7 0N 67 30W
Capanema 170 1 12 S 47 11W
Caparo, R. 174 7 30N 70 30W
Capatárida 174 11 11N 70 37W
Capbreton 44 43 39N 1 26W
Capdenac 44 44 34N 2 5 E
Cape Barren I. 138 40 25 S 148 15 E
Cape Breton Highlands Nat. Park 151 46 50N 60 40W
Cape Breton I. 151 46 0N 60 30W
Cape Charles 162 37 15N 75 59W
Cape Coast 121 5 5N 1 15W
Cape Cod B. 162 41 50N 70 18W
Cape Dorset 149 64 14N 76 32W
Cape Dyer 149 66 40N 61 22W
Cape Fear, R. 157 34 30N 78 25W
Cape Girardeau 159 37 20N 89 30W
Cape Jervis 140 35 40 S 138 5 E
Cape May 162 39 1N 74 53W
Cape May C.H. 162 39 5N 74 50W
Cape May Pt. 162 38 56N 74 56W
Cape Montague 151 46 5N 62 25W
Cape Palmas 120 4 25N 7 49W
Cape Preston 136 20 51 S 116 12 E
Cape Province □ 128 32 0 S 23 0 E
Cape, R. 138 20 37 S 147 1 E
Cape Tormentine 151 46 8N 63 47W
Cape Town (Kaapstad) 128 33 55 S 18 22 E
Cape Verde Is. 14 17 10N 25 20W
Cape York Peninsula 138 33 34 S 115 33 E
Capel 29 51 8N 0 18W
Capel Curig 31 53 6N 3 55W
Capela 170 10 30 S 37 0W
Capela de Campo 170 4 40 S 41 55W
Capelinha 171 17 42 S 42 31W
Capella 138 23 2 S 148 1 E
Capella, G. 138 4 45 S 140 50 E
Capella, Mt. 135 5 4 S 141 8 E
Capelle, La 43 49 59N 3 50 E
Capendu 44 43 11N 2 31 E
Capernaum = Kefar Nahum 90 32 54N 35 32 E
Capestang 44 43 20N 3 2 E
Capim 170 1 41 S 47 47W
Capim, R. 170 3 0 S 48 0W
Capinópolis 171 18 41 S 49 35W
Capitan 161 33 40N 105 41W
Capitola 163 36 59N 121 57W
Capivara, Serra da 171 14 35 S 45 0W
Çapizzi 65 37 50N 14 26 E
Capljina 66 43 35N 17 43 E
Capoche, R. 127 15 0 S 32 45 E
Cappamore 39 52 38N 8 20W
Cappoquin 39 52 9N 7 46W
Capraia, I. 62 43 2N 9 50 E
Caprarola 63 42 21N 12 11 E
Capreol 150 46 43N 80 56W
Caprera, I. 64 41 12N 9 28 E
Capri, I. 65 40 34N 14 15 E
Capricorn, C. 133 23 30 S 151 13 E
Capricorn Group 138 23 30 S 151 55 E
Capricorn Ra. 136 23 20 S 117 0 E
Caprino Veronese 62 45 37N 10 47 E
Caprivi Strip 128 18 0 S 23 0 E
Captainganj 95 26 55N 83 45 E
Captain's Flat 141 35 35 S 149 27 E
Captieux 44 44 18N 0 16W
Cápua 65 41 7N 14 15 E
Capulin 159 36 48N 103 59W
Caquetá □ 174 1 0N 74 0W
Caquetá, R. 174 1 0N 76 20W
Cáqueza 174 4 25N 73 57W
Carabobo 174 10 10N 68 5W
Caracal 70 44 8N 24 22 E
Caracaraí 174 1 50N 61 8W
Caracas 174 10 30N 66 55W
Caracol, Piauí, Brazil 170 9 15 S 43 45W
Caracol, Rondonia, Brazil 174 9 15 S 64 20W
Caradoc 140 30 35 S 143 5 E
Caragabal 141 33 49 S 147 45 E
Caragh L. 39 52 3N 9 50W
Caràglio 62 44 25N 7 25 E
*Renamed Abariringa
Caraí 171 17 12 S 41 42W
Carajás, Serra dos 170 6 0 S 51 30W
Caramanta 174 5 33N 75 38W
Carangola 173 20 50 S 42 5W
Carani 137 30 57 S 116 28 E
Caransebeş 70 45 28N 22 18 E
Carapelle, R. 65 41 20N 15 35 E
Caraş Severin □ 66 45 10N 22 10 E
Caraşova 66 45 11N 21 51 E
Caratasca, Laguna 166 15 30N 83 40W
Caratec 42 48 40N 3 55W
Caratinga 171 19 50 S 42 10W
Caratunk 151 45 13N 69 55W
Caraúbas 170 7 43 S 36 31W
Caravaca 59 38 8N 1 52W
Caravággio 62 45 30N 9 39 E
Caravelas 171 17 45 S 39 15W
Caraveli 174 15 45 S 73 25W
Caràzinho 173 28 0 S 53 0W
Carballino 56 42 26N 8 5W
Carballo 56 43 13N 8 41W
Carberry 153 49 50N 99 25W
Carbia 56 42 48N 8 14W
Carbó 164 29 42N 110 58W
Carbon 152 51 30N 113 9W
Carbonara, C. 64 39 8N 9 30 E
Carbondale, Colo, U.S.A. 160 39 30N 107 10W
Carbondale, Ill., U.S.A. 159 37 45N 89 10W
Carbondale, Pa., U.S.A. 162 41 37N 75 30W
Carbonear 151 47 42N 53 13W
Carboneras 59 37 0N 1 53W
Carboneras de Guadazaón 58 39 54N 1 50W
Carbonia 64 39 10N 8 30 E
Carbost 36 57 19N 6 21W
Carbury 38 53 22N 6 58W
Carcabuey 57 37 27N 4 17W
Carcagente 59 39 8N 0 28W
Carcajou 152 57 47N 117 6W
Carcasse, C. 167 18 30N 74 28W
Carcassonne 44 43 13N 2 20 E
Carche 59 38 26N 1 9W
Carcoar 141 33 36 S 149 8 E
Carcross 147 60 13N 134 45W
Cardabia 136 23 2 S 113 55 E
Cardamom Hills 97 9 30N 77 15 E
Cárdenas, Cuba 166 23 0N 81 30W
Cárdenas, San Luis Potosí, Mexico 166 22 0N 99 41W
Cárdenas, Tabasco, Mexico 165 17 59N 93 21W
Cardenete 58 39 46N 1 41W
Cardiff 31 51 28N 3 11W
Cardiff-by-the-Sea 163 33 1N 117 17W
Cardigan 31 52 6N 4 41W
Cardigan (□) 26 52 6N 4 41W
Cardigan B. 31 52 30N 4 30W
Cardington 29 52 7N 0 23W
Cardón 174 11 37N 70 14W
Cardona, Spain 58 41 56N 1 40 E
Cardona, Uruguay 172 33 53 S 57 18W
Cardoner, R. 58 42 0N 1 33 E
Cardross 153 49 50N 105 40W
Cardston 152 49 15N 113 20W
Cardwell 138 18 14 S 146 2 E
Careen L. 153 57 0N 108 11W
Carei 70 47 40N 22 29 E
Carentan 42 49 19N 1 15W
Carey, Idaho, U.S.A. 160 43 19N 113 58W
Carey, Ohio, U.S.A. 156 40 58N 83 22W
Carey, L. 137 29 0 S 122 15 E
Carey L. 153 62 12N 102 55W
Careysburg 120 6 34N 10 30W
Cargados Garajos, Is. 11 17 0 S 59 0 E
Cargelligo, L. 139 33 17 S 146 24 E
Cargèse 45 42 7N 8 35 E
Carhaix-Plouguer 42 48 18N 3 36W
Carhué 172 37 10 S 62 50W
Cariacica 171 20 16 S 40 25W
Cariaco 174 10 29N 63 33W
Caribaná, Pta. 174 8 37N 76 52W
Caribbean Sea 167 15 0N 75 0W
Cariboo Mts. 152 53 0N 121 0W
Caribou, Can. 153 53 15N 121 55W
Caribou, U.S.A. 151 46 55N 68 0W
Caribou I. 150 47 22N 85 49W
Caribou Is. 152 61 55N 113 15W
Caribou L., Man., Can. 153 59 21N 96 10W
Caribou L., Ont., Can. 150 50 25N 89 5W
Caribou Mts. 152 59 12N 115 40W
Caribou, R., Man., Can. 153 59 20N 94 44W
Caribou, R., N.W.T., Can. 152 61 27N 125 45W
Carichic 164 27 56N 107 3W
Carignan 43 49 38N 5 10 E
Carignano 62 44 55N 7 40 E
Carillo 164 26 50N 103 55W
Carinda 141 30 28 S 147 41 E
Cariñena 58 41 20N 1 13W
Carinhanha 171 14 15 S 44 0W
Carinhanha, R. 171 14 20 S 43 47W
Carini 64 38 9N 13 10 E
Carinish 36 57 31N 7 20W
Carinola 64 41 11N 13 58 E
Carinthia □ = Kärnten 52 46 52N 13 30 E
Caripito 174 10 8N 63 6W
Caririacu 171 7 2 S 39 17W
Carisbrooke 28 50 42N 1 19W
Caritianas 174 9 20 S 63 0W
Cark 32 54 11N 2 59W
Carlentini 65 37 15N 15 2 E
Carleton Place 150 45 8N 76 9W
Carleton Rode 29 52 30N 1 6 E
Carletonville 128 26 23 S 27 22 E
Carlin 160 40 50N 116 5W
Carlingford 38 54 3N 6 10W
Carlingford, L. 38 54 0N 6 5W
Carlinville 158 39 20N 89 55W
Carlisle, U.K. 32 54 54N 2 55W
Carlisle, U.S.A. 162 40 12N 77 10W
Carlitte, Pic 44 42 35N 1 43 E
Carloforte 64 39 10N 8 18 E
Carlops 35 55 47N 3 20W
Carlos Casares 172 35 53 S 61 20W
Carlos Chagas 171 17 43 S 40 45W
Carlos Tejedor 172 35 25 S 62 25W
Carlota, La 172 33 30 S 63 20W
Carlow 39 52 50N 6 58W
Carlow □ 39 52 43N 6 50W
Carloway 36 58 17N 6 48W
Carlsbad, Calif., U.S.A. 163 33 11N 117 25W
Carlsbad, N. Mex., U.S.A. 159 32 20N 104 7W
Carlton 33 52 58N 1 6W
Carlton Colville 29 52 27N 1 41 E
Carlton Miniott 33 54 13N 1 22W
Carluke 35 55 44N 3 50W
Carlyle, Can. 153 49 40N 102 20W
Carlyle, U.S.A. 158 38 38N 89 23W
Carmacks 147 62 5N 136 16W
Carmagnola 62 44 50N 7 42 E
Carman 153 49 30N 98 0W
Carmangay 152 50 10N 113 10W
Carmanville 151 49 23N 54 19W
Carmarthen 31 51 52N 4 20W
Carmarthen (□) 26 53 40N 4 18W
Carmarthen B. 31 51 40N 4 30W
Carmaux 44 44 3N 2 10 E
Carmel, Calif., U.S.A. 163 36 38N 121 55W
Carmel, N.Y., U.S.A. 162 41 25N 73 38W
Carmel Hd. 31 53 24N 4 34W
Carmel Mt. 90 32 45N 35 3 E
Carmel Valley 163 36 29N 121 43W
Carmelo 172 34 0 S 58 10W
Carmen, Colomb. 174 9 43N 75 8W
Carmen, Parag. 173 27 13 S 56 12W
Carmen de Patagones 176 40 50 S 63 0W
Carmen, I. 164 26 0N 111 20W
Carmen, R. 164 30 42N 106 29W
Cármenes 56 42 58N 5 34W
Carmensa 172 35 15 S 67 40W
Carmi 156 38 6N 88 10W
Carmichael 163 38 38N 121 19W
Carmila 138 21 55 S 149 24 E
Carmo do Paranaiba 171 18 59 S 46 21W
Carmona 57 37 28N 5 42W
Carmyllie 37 56 36N 2 41W
Carn Ban 37 57 6N 4 15W
Carn Eige 36 57 17N 5 9W
Carn Glas Chorie 37 57 20N 3 50W
Carn Mor 37 57 14N 3 13W
Carn na Saobhaidh 37 57 12N 4 20W
Carna 39 53 20N 9 50W
Carnarvon, Queens., Austral. 138 24 48 S 147 45 E
Carnarvon, W. Austral., Austral. 137 24 51 S 113 42 E
Carnarvon, S. Afr. 128 30 56 S 22 8 E
Carnarvon Ra., Queensland, Austral. 138 25 15 S 148 30 E
Carnarvon Ra., W.A., Austral. 137 25 0 S 120 45 E
Carnaxide 57 38 43N 9 14W
Carncastle 38 54 55N 5 52W
Carndonagh 38 55 15N 7 16W
Carnduff 153 49 10N 101 50W
Carnedd Llewelyn, Mt. 31 53 9N 3 58W
Carnegie, L. 137 26 5 S 122 30 E
Carnew 39 52 43N 6 30W
Carney 38 54 20N 8 30W
Carnforth 32 54 8N 2 47W
Carnic Alps = Karnische Alpen 63 46 34N 12 50 E
Carnlough 38 55 0N 6 0W
Carno 31 52 34N 3 31W
Carnon 44 43 32N 3 59 E
Carnot 124 4 59N 15 56 E
Carnot B. 136 17 20 S 121 30 E
Carnoustie 35 56 30N 2 41W
Carnsore Pt. 39 52 10N 6 20W
Carnwath 35 55 42N 3 38W
Caro 156 43 29N 83 27W
Carolina, Brazil 170 7 10 S 47 30W
Carolina, S. Afr. 129 26 5 S 30 6 E
Carolina, La 57 38 17N 3 38W
Caroline I. 131 9 15 S 150 3W
Caroline Is. 130 8 0N 150 0 E
Caroline Pk. 143 45 57 S 167 15 E
Carolside 152 51 20N 111 40W
Caron 153 50 30N 105 50W
Caroni, R. 174 6 0N 62 40W
Carora 174 10 11N 70 5W
Carovigno 65 40 42N 17 40 E
Carpathians, Mts. 53 49 40N 19 30 E
Carpaţii Meridionali 70 45 30N 25 0 E
Carpenédolo 62 45 22N 10 25 E
Carpentaria Downs 138 18 44 S 144 20 E
Carpentaria, G. of 133 14 0 S 139 0 E
Carpentras 45 44 3N 5 2 E
Carpi 62 44 47N 10 52 E
Carpina 170 7 51 S 35 15W
Carpino 65 41 50N 15 51 E
Carpinteria 163 34 25N 119 31W
Carpio 56 41 13N 5 7W
Carpolac = Morea 140 36 45 S 141 18 E
Carr Boyd Ra. 136 16 15 S 128 35 E
Carra L. 38 53 41N 9 12W
Carrabelle 157 29 52N 84 40W
Carracastle 38 53 57N 8 42W
Carradale 34 55 35N 5 30W
Carraipia 174 11 16N 72 22W
Carrara 62 44 5N 10 7 E
Carrascosa del Campo 58 40 2N 2 45W
Carrauntohill, Mt. 39 52 0N 9 49W
Carraweena 139 29 10 S 140 0 E
Carrbridge 37 57 17N 3 50W
Carriacou, I. 167 12 30N 61 28W
Carribee 140 35 7 S 136 57 E
Carrick 38 54 40N 8 39W
Carrick, dist. 34 55 12N 4 38W
Carrick-on-Shannon 38 53 57N 8 7W
Carrick-on-Suir 39 52 22N 7 30W
Carrick Ra. 143 45 15 S 169 8 E
Carrickart 38 55 10N 7 47W
Carrickbeg 39 52 20N 7 25W
Carrickboy 38 53 36N 7 40W
Carrickfergus 36 54 43N 5 50W
Carrickfergus □ 38 54 43N 5 49W
Carrickmacross 38 54 0N 6 43W
Carrieton 140 32 25 S 138 31 E
Carrigaholt 39 52 37N 9 42W
Carrigahorig 39 53 4N 8 10W
Carrigaline 39 51 49N 8 22W
Carrigallen 38 53 59N 7 40W
Carrigan Hd. 38 54 38N 8 40W
Carrignavar 39 52 0N 8 29W
Carrigtwohill 39 51 55N 8 15W
Carrington 158 47 30N 99 7W
Carrión de los Condes 56 42 20N 4 37W
Carrión, R. 56 42 42N 4 47W
Carrizal 174 12 1N 72 11W
Carrizal Bajo 172 28 5 S 71 20W
Carrizalillo 172 29 0 S 71 30W
Carrizo Cr. 159 36 30N 103 40W
Carrizo Springs 159 28 28N 99 50W
Carrizozo 161 33 40N 105 57W
Carroll 158 42 2N 94 55W
Carrollton, Ga., U.S.A. 157 33 36N 85 5W
Carrollton, Ill., U.S.A. 158 39 20N 90 25W
Carrollton, Ky., U.S.A. 156 38 40N 85 10W
Carrollton, Mo., U.S.A. 158 39 19N 93 24W
Carron L. 36 57 22N 5 35W
Carron R., U.K. 36 57 30N 5 30W
Carron R., U.K. 37 57 51N 4 21W
Carrot, R. 153 53 50N 101 17W
Carrot River 153 53 17N 103 35W
Carrouges 42 48 34N 0 10W
Carrowkeel 38 55 7N 7 12W
Carrowmore L. 38 54 12N 9 48W
Carruthers 153 52 52N 109 16W
Carryduff 38 54 32N 5 52W
Çarşamba 92 41 15N 36 45 E
Carsoli 63 42 7N 13 3 E
Carson 158 46 27N 101 29W
Carson City 160 39 12N 119 46W
Carson Sink 160 39 50N 118 40W
Carsonville 156 43 25N 82 39W
Carsphairn 34 55 13N 4 15W
Carstairs 35 55 42N 3 41W
Cartagena, Colomb. 174 10 25N 75 33W
Cartagena, Spain 59 37 38N 0 59W
Cartago, Colomb. 174 4 45N 75 55W
Cartago, C. Rica 166 9 50N 84 0W
Cartaret 42 49 23N 1 47W
Cartaxo 57 39 10N 8 47W
Cartaya 57 37 16N 7 9W
Cartersville 157 34 11N 84 48W
Carterton 142 41 2 S 175 31 E
Carthage, Ark., U.S.A. 159 34 4N 92 32W
Carthage, Ill., U.S.A. 158 40 25N 91 10W
Carthage, Mo., U.S.A. 159 37 10N 94 20W
Carthage, N.Y., U.S.A. 156 43 59N 75 37W
Carthage, S.D., U.S.A. 158 44 14N 97 38W
Carthage, Texas, U.S.A. 159 32 8N 94 20W
Cartier I. 136 12 31 S 123 29 E
Cartmel 32 54 13N 2 57W
Cartwright 151 53 41N 56 58W
Caruaru 170 8 15 S 35 55W
Carúpano 174 10 45N 63 15W
Carutapera 170 1 13 S 46 1W
Caruthersville 159 36 10N 89 40W
Carvarzere 63 45 8N 12 7 E
Carvin 43 50 30N 2 57 E
Carvoeiro 174 1 30 S 61 59W
Carvoeiro, Cabo 57 39 21N 9 24W
Casa Agapito 174 2 3N 73 58W
Casa Branca, Brazil 171 21 46 S 47 4W
Casa Branca, Port. 57 38 29N 8 12W
Casa Grande 161 32 53N 111 51W
Casa Nova 170 9 10 S 41 5W
Casablanca, Chile 172 33 20 S 71 25W
Casablanca, Moroc. 118 33 36N 7 36W
Casacalenda 65 41 45N 14 50 E
Casalbordino 63 42 10N 14 34 E
Casale Monferrato 62 45 8N 8 28 E
Casalmaggiore 62 44 59N 10 25 E
Casalpusterlengo 62 45 10N 9 40 E
Casamance, R. 120 12 54N 15 0W
Casamássima 65 40 58N 16 55 E
Casanare, R. 174 6 30N 71 20W
Casarano 65 40 0N 18 10 E
Casares 57 36 27N 5 16W
Casas Grandes 164 30 22N 108 0W
Casas IbáPez 59 39 17N 1 30W
Casasimarro 59 39 22N 2 3W
Casatejada 56 39 54N 5 40W
Casavieja 56 40 17N 4 46W
Cascade, Idaho, U.S.A. 160 44 30N 116 2W

Cascade **Cepin**

Cascade, Mont., U.S.A. **160** 47 16N 111 46W
Cascade Locks **160** 45 44N 121 54W
Cascade Pt. **143** 44 1S 168 20E
Cascade Ra. **160** 45 0N 121 30W
Cascais **57** 38 41N 9 25W
Cascina **62** 43 40N 10 32E
Caselle Torinese **62** 45 12N 7 39E
Caserta **65** 41 5N 14 20E
Cashel **39** 52 31N 7 53W
Cashla B. **39** 53 12N 9 37W
Cashmere **160** 47 31N 120 30W
Cashmere Downs **137** 28 57S 119 35E
Casigua **174** 11 2N 71 1W
Casiguran **103** 16 15N 122 15E
Casilda **172** 33 10S 61 10W
Casimcea **70** 44 45N 28 23E
Casino **139** 28 52S 153 3E
Casiquiare, R. **174** 2 45N 66 20W
Caslan **152** 54 38N 112 31W
Casma **174** 9 30S 78 20W
Casmalia **163** 34 50N 120 32W
Casola Valsenio **63** 44 12N 11 40E
Cásoli **63** 42 7N 14 18E
Caspe **58** 41 14N 0 1W
Casper **160** 42 52N 106 27W
Caspian Sea **79** 43 0N 50 0E
Casquets **42** 49 46N 2 15W
Cass City **156** 43 34N 83 15W
Cass Lake **158** 47 23N 94 38W
Cassá de la Selva **58** 41 53N 2 52E
Cassano Iónio **65** 39 47N 16 20E
Cassel **43** 50 48N 2 30E
Casselton **158** 47 0N 97 15W
Cássia **171** 20 36S 46 56W
Cassiar **152** 59 16N 129 40W
Cassiar Mts. **152** 59 30N 130 30W
Cassils **152** 50 29N 112 15W
Cassinga **125** 15 5S 16 23E
Cassino **64** 41 30N 13 50E
Cassiporé, C. **170** 3 50N 51 5W
Cassis **45** 43 14N 5 32E
Cassville **159** 36 45N 93 59W
Cástagneto Carducci **62** 43 9N 10 36E
Castaic **163** 34 30N 118 38W
Castanhal **170** 1 18S 47 55W
Castanheiro **174** 0 17S 65 38W
Casteau **47** 50 32N 4 2E
Castéggio **62** 45 1N 9 8E
Castejón de Monegros **58** 41 37N 0 15W
Castel di Sangro **65** 41 41N 14 5E
Castel San Giovanni **62** 45 4N 9 25E
Castel San Pietro **63** 44 23N 11 30E
Castelbuono **65** 37 56N 14 4E
Casteldelfino **62** 44 35N 7 4E
Castelfiorentino **62** 43 36N 10 58E
Castelfranco Emília **62** 44 37N 11 2E
Castelfranco Veneto **63** 45 40N 11 56E
Casteljaloux **44** 44 19N 0 6E
Castellabate **65** 40 18N 14 55E
Castellammare del Golfo **64** 38 2N 12 53E
Castellammare di Stábia **65** 40 47N 14 29E
Castellammare, G. di **64** 38 5N 12 55E
Castellamonte **62** 45 23N 7 42E
Castellana Grotte **65** 40 53N 17 10E
Castellane **45** 43 50N 6 31E
Castellaneta **65** 40 40N 16 57E
Castellar de Santisteban **59** 38 16N 3 8W
Castelleone **62** 45 19N 9 47E
Castelli **172** 36 7S 57 47W
Castelló de Ampurias **58** 42 15N 3 4E
Castellón □ **58** 40 15N 0 5W
Castellón de la Plana **58** 39 58N 0 3W
Castellote **58** 40 48N 0 15W
Castelltersol **58** 41 45N 2 8E
Castelmáuro **65** 41 50N 14 40E
Castelnau-de-Médoc **44** 45 2N 0 48W
Castelnaudary **44** 43 20N 1 58E
Castelnovo ne' Monti **62** 44 27N 10 26E
Castelnuovo di Val di Cécina **62** 43 12N 10 54E
Castelo **173** 20 53S 41 42E
Castelo Branco **56** 39 50N 7 31W
Castelo Branco □ **56** 39 52N 7 45W
Castelo de Paiva **56** 41 2N 8 16W
Castelo de Vide **57** 39 25N 7 27W
Castelo do Piauí **170** 5 20S 41 33W
Castelsarrasin **44** 44 2N 1 7E
Casteltérmini **64** 37 32N 13 38E
Castelvetrano **64** 37 40N 12 46E
Casterton **140** 37 30S 141 30E
Castets **44** 43 52N 1 6W
Castiglione del Lago **63** 43 7N 12 3E
Castiglione della Pescáia **62** 42 46N 10 53E
Castiglione della Stiviere **62** 45 23N 10 30E
Castiglione Fiorentino **63** 43 20N 11 55E
Castilblanco **57** 39 17N 5 5W
Castilla La Nueva **57** 39 45N 3 20W
Castilla La Vieja **56** 41 55N 4 0W
Castilla, Playa de **57** 37 0N 6 33W
Castille = Castilla **56** 40 0N 3 30W
Castilletes **174** 11 51N 71 19W
Castillón **164** 28 20N 103 38W
Castillon-en-Couserans **44** 42 56N 1 1E
Castillon-la-Bataille **44** 44 51N 0 2W
Castillonès **44** 44 39N 0 37E
Castillos **173** 34 12S 53 52W
Castle Acre **29** 52 42N 0 42W
Castle Cary **28** 51 5N 2 32W
Castle Dale **160** 39 11N 111 1W
Castle Donington **28** 52 50N 1 20W
Castle Douglas **35** 54 57N 3 57W
Castle Eden **54** 54 45N 1 20W
Castle Point **142** 40 54N 176 15E
Castle Rock, Colo., U.S.A. **158** 39 26N 104 50W
Castle Rock, Wash., U.S.A. **160** 46 20N 122 58W
Castlebar **38** 53 52N 9 17W
Castlebay **36** 56 57N 7 30W
Castlebellingham **38** 53 53N 6 22W
Castleblakeney **38** 53 26N 8 28W
Castleblayney **38** 54 7N 6 44W
Castlebridge **39** 52 23N 6 28W
Castlecliff **142** 39 57S 174 59E
Castlecomer **39** 52 49N 7 13W
Castleconnell **39** 52 44N 8 30W
Castledawson **38** 54 47N 6 35W
Castlederg **38** 54 43N 7 35W
Castledermot **39** 52 55N 6 50W
Castlefinn **38** 54 47N 7 35W
Castleford **33** 53 43N 1 21W
Castlegar **152** 49 20N 117 40W
Castlegate **160** 39 45N 110 57W
Castlegregory **39** 52 16N 10 0W
Castlehill **38** 51 1N 9 49W
Castleisland **39** 52 14N 9 28W
Castlemaine, Austral. **140** 37 2S 144 12E
Castlemaine, Ireland **39** 52 10N 9 42W
Castlemaine Harb. **39** 52 8N 9 50W
Castlemartyr **39** 51 54N 8 3W
Castlepollard **38** 53 40N 7 20W
Castlereagh **38** 53 47N 8 30W
Castlereagh □ **38** 54 33N 5 33W
Castlereagh B. **138** 12 10S 135 10E
Castlereagh, R. **141** 30 12S 147 32E
Castleside **32** 54 50N 1 52W
Castleton, Derby., U.K. **33** 53 20N 1 47W
Castleton, N. Yorks., U.K. **33** 54 27N 0 57W
Castleton, U.S.A. **162** 43 37N 73 11W
Castletown, Geoghegan, Ireland **38** 53 27N 7 30W
Castletown, Laois, Ireland **38** 52 58N 7 31W
Castletown, Meath, Ireland **39** 53 47N 6 41W
Castletown, I. of Man **32** 54 4N 4 40W
Castletown, U.K. **37** 58 35N 3 22W
Castletown Bearhaven **39** 51 40N 9 54W
Castletownroche **39** 52 10N 8 28W
Castletownshend **39** 51 31N 9 11W
Castlevale **138** 24 30S 146 48E
Castlewellan **38** 54 16N 5 57W
Castor **152** 52 15N 111 50W
Castorland **162** 43 53N 75 31W
Castres **44** 43 37N 2 13E
Castricum **46** 52 33N 4 40E
Castries **167** 14 0N 60 50W
Castril **59** 37 48N 2 46W
Castro, Brazil **173** 24 45S 50 0W
Castro, Chile **176** 42 30S 73 50W
Castro Alves **171** 12 46S 39 26W
Castro del Río **57** 37 41N 4 29W
Castro Marim **57** 37 13N 7 26W
Castro Urdiales **58** 43 23N 3 19W
Castro Verde **57** 37 41N 8 4W
Castrojeriz **56** 42 17N 4 9W
Castropol **56** 43 32N 7 0W
Castroreale **65** 38 5N 15 15E
Castrovillari **65** 39 49N 16 11E
Castroville, Calif., U.S.A. **163** 36 46N 121 45W
Castroville, Tex, U.S.A. **159** 29 20N 98 53W
Castuera **57** 38 43N 5 37W
Casummit L. **150** 51 29N 92 22W
Cat Ba **100** 20 50N 107 0E
Cat I., Bahamas **167** 24 30N 75 30W
Cat I., U.S.A. **159** 30 15N 89 7W
Çat L. **150** 51 40N 91 50W
Çata **53** 47 58N 18 38E
Catacamas **166** 14 54N 85 56W
Catacaos **174** 5 20S 80 45W
Cataguases **173** 21 23S 42 39W
Catahoula L. **159** 31 30N 92 5W
Catalão **171** 18 10S 47 57W
Çatalca **92** 41 9N 28 28E
Catalina **151** 48 31N 53 4W
Catalonia = Cataluña **58** 41 40N 1 15E
Cataluña **58** 41 40N 1 15E
Catamarca **172** 28 30S 65 50W
Catamarca □ **172** 28 30S 65 50W
Catanduanas, Is. **103** 13 50N 124 20E
Catanduva **173** 21 5S 48 58W
Catánia **65** 37 31N 15 4E
Catánia, G. di **65** 37 25N 15 8E
Catanzaro **65** 38 54N 16 38E
Catarman **103** 12 28N 124 1E
Catastrophe C. **136** 34 59S 136 0E
Catcleugh **35** 55 19N 2 22W
Cateau, Le **43** 50 6N 3 30E
Cateel **103** 7 47N 126 24E
Catende **170** 8 40S 35 43W
Caterham **29** 51 16N 0 4W
Cathcart, Austral. **141** 36 2S 149 24E
Cathcart, S. Afr. **128** 32 18S 27 10E
Catine **41** 46 30N 0 15W
Catio **120** 11 17N 15 15W
Catismiña **174** 4 5N 63 52W
Catita **170** 9 31S 43 1W
Catlettsburg **156** 38 23N 82 38W
Cato I. **133** 23 15S 155 32E
Catoche, C. **165** 21 40N 87 0W
Catolé **171** 7 19S 36 1W
Catolé do Rocha **170** 6 21S 37 45W
Caton **32** 54 5N 2 41W
Catonsville **162** 39 16N 76 44W
Catral **59** 38 10N 0 47W
Catria, Mt. **63** 43 28N 12 42E
Catrimani **174** 0 27N 61 41W
Catrine **34** 55 30N 4 20W
Catsfield **29** 50 53N 0 28E
Catskill **162** 42 14N 73 52W
Catskill Mts. **162** 42 15N 74 15W
Catt, Mt. **138** 13 49S 134 23E
Catterick **33** 54 23N 1 38W
Cattólica **63** 43 58N 12 43E
Cattólica Eraclea **64** 37 27N 13 24E
Catton **35** 54 56N 2 16W
Catu **171** 12 21S 38 23W
Catuala **128** 16 25S 19 2E
Catur **127** 13 45S 35 30E
Catwick Is. **101** 10 0N 109 0E
Cauca □ **174** 2 30N 76 50W
Cauca, R. **174** 7 25N 75 30W
Caucasia **174** 8 0N 75 12W
Caucasus Mts. = Bolshoi Kavkas **83** 42 50N 44 0E
Caucaia **170** 3 40S 38 35W
Caudebec-en-Caux **42** 49 30N 0 42E
Caudete **59** 38 42N 1 2W
Caudry **43** 50 7N 3 22E
Caulkerbush **35** 54 54N 3 40W
Caulnes **42** 48 18N 2 10W
Caulónia **65** 38 23N 16 25E
Caungula **124** 8 15S 18 50E
Cáuquenes **172** 36 0S 72 30W
Caura, R. **174** 6 20N 64 30W
Cauresi, R. **127** 17 40S 33 10E
Causapscal **151** 48 19N 67 12W
Causeway **39** 52 25N 9 45W
Caussade **44** 44 10N 1 33E
Cauterets **44** 42 52N 0 8W
Cauvery, R. **93** 12 0N 77 45E
Caux **42** 49 38N 0 35E
Cava dei Tirreni **65** 40 42N 14 42E
Cávado, R. **56** 41 37N 8 15W
Cavaillon **45** 43 50N 5 2E
Cavalaire-sur-Mer **45** 43 10N 6 33E
Cavalcante **171** 13 48S 47 30W
Cavalerie, La **44** 44 0N 3 10E
Cavalese **63** 46 17N 11 29E
Cavalier **158** 48 50N 97 39W
Cavalli Is. **142** 35 0S 173 58E
Cavallo, I. **45** 41 22N 9 16E
Cavally, R. **120** 5 0N 7 40W
Cavan **38** 54 0N 7 22W
Cavan □ **38** 53 58N 7 10W
Cavanagh Ra. **137** 26 10S 122 50E
Cavárzere **63** 45 8N 12 6E
Cave City **156** 37 13N 85 57W
Cavenagh Range **137** 26 12S 127 55E
Cavendish **140** 37 31S 142 2E
Cavers **150** 48 55N 87 41W
Caviana, Ilha **170** 0 15N 50 0W
Cavite **103** 14 20N 120 55E
Cavour **62** 44 47N 7 22E
Cavtat **66** 42 35N 18 13E
Cawdor **37** 57 31N 3 56W
Cawkers Well **140** 31 41S 142 57E
Cawndilla, L. **140** 32 30S 142 15E
Cawnpore = Kanpur **95** 26 35N 80 20E
Cawood **33** 53 50N 1 7W
Cawston **29** 52 47N 1 10E
Caxias **174** 5 0S 43 27W
Caxias do Sul **173** 29 10S 51 10W
Caxine, C. **118** 35 56N 0 27W
Caxito **124** 8 30S 13 30E
Cay Sal Bank **166** 23 45N 80 0W
Cayambe **174** 0 3N 78 22W
Cayce **157** 33 59N 81 2W
Cayenne **175** 5 0N 52 18W
Cayes, Les **167** 18 15N 73 46W
Cayeux-sur-Mer. **43** 50 10N 1 30E
Cayey **147** 18 7N 66 10W
Caylus **44** 44 15N 1 47E
Cayman Brac, I. **166** 19 43N 79 49W
Cayman Is. **166** 19 40N 79 50W
Cayo **165** 17 10N 89 0W
Cayo Romano, I. **167** 22 0N 73 30W
Cayuga **162** 42 28N 76 30W
Cayuga L. **162** 42 45N 76 45W
Cazalla de la Sierra **57** 37 56N 5 45W
Cazaux et de Sanguinet, Étang de **44** 44 29N 1 10W
Cazenovia **162** 42 56N 75 51W
Cazères **44** 43 13N 1 5E
Çazin **63** 44 57N 15 57E
Cazma **63** 45 45N 16 39E
Cazombo **125** 12 0S 22 48E
Cazorla, Spain **59** 37 55N 3 2W
Cazorla, Venez. **174** 8 1N 67 0W
Cazorla, Sierra de **59** 38 5N 2 55W
Cea, R. **56** 42 40N 5 5W
Ceamurlia de Jos **67** 44 43N 28 47E
Ceanannas Mor **38** 53 42N 6 53W
Ceará = Fortaleza **170** 3 35S 38 35W
Ceará □ **170** 5 0S 40 0W
Ceará Mirim **170** 5 38S 35 25W
Ceauru, L. **70** 44 58N 23 11E
Cebaco, I. **166** 7 33N 81 9W
Cebollar **172** 29 10S 66 35W
Cebollera, Sierra de **58** 42 0N 2 30W
Cebreros **56** 40 27N 4 28W
Cebú **103** 10 18N 123 54E
Cebú, I. **103** 10 15N 123 40E
Ceccano **64** 41 34N 13 18E
Cece **53** 46 46N 18 39E
Cechi **120** 6 15N 4 25W
Cecil Plains **139** 27 30S 151 11E
Cecilton **162** 39 24N 75 52W
Cécina **62** 43 19N 10 33E
Cécina, R. **62** 43 19N 10 40E
Ceclavin **56** 39 50N 6 45W
Cedar City **161** 37 41N 113 3W
Cedar Creek Res. **159** 32 15N 96 0W
Cedar Falls **158** 42 39N 92 29W
Cedar I. **162** 37 35N 75 32W
Cedar Key **157** 29 9N 83 5W
Cedar L. **153** 53 20N 100 10W
Cedar Pt. **162** 38 18N 76 25W
Cedar, R. **158** 41 50N 91 20W
Cedar Rapids **158** 42 0N 91 38W
Cedarburg **156** 43 18N 87 55W
Cedartown **157** 34 1N 85 15W
Cedarvale **152** 55 1N 128 22W
Cedarville **160** 41 37N 120 13W
Cedeira **56** 43 39N 8 2W
Cedral **164** 23 50N 100 42W
Cedrino, R. **64** 40 8N 9 25E
Cedro **170** 6 34S 39 3W
Cedros, I. de **164** 28 10N 115 20W
Ceduna **139** 32 7S 133 46E
Cedynia **54** 52 53N 14 12E
Ceepeecee **152** 49 52N 126 42W
Cefalù **65** 38 3N 14 1E
Cega, R. **56** 41 17N 4 10W
Cegléd **53** 47 11N 19 47E
Céglie Messápico **65** 40 39N 17 31E
Cehegín **59** 38 6N 1 48W
Cehu-Silvaniei **70** 47 24N 23 9E
Ceiba, La **166** 15 40N 86 50W
Ceica **70** 46 53N 22 10E
Ceira, R. **56** 40 15N 7 55W
Cekhira **119** 34 20N 10 5E
Celano **63** 42 6N 13 30E
Celanova **56** 42 9N 7 58W
Celaya **164** 20 31N 100 37W
Celbridge **39** 53 20N 6 33W
Celebes I. = Sulawesi **103** 2 0S 120 0E
Celebes Sea **103** 3 0N 123 0E
Celga **123** 12 38N 37 3E
Çelina **156** 40 32N 84 31W
Čelió **66** 44 43N 18 47E
Celje **63** 46 16N 15 18E
Cellar Hd. **36** 58 25N 6 10W
Celldömölk **53** 47 16N 17 10E
Celle **48** 52 37N 10 4E
Celles **47** 50 42N 3 28E
Celorica da Beira **56** 40 38N 7 24W
Cemaes Bay **31** 53 24N 4 27W
Cemaes Hd. **31** 52 7N 4 44W
Çement **159** 34 56N 98 8W
Čemerno **66** 43 26N 20 26E
Cemmaes Road **31** 52 39N 3 41W
Cenarth **31** 52 3N 4 32W
Cenis, Col du Mt. **45** 45 15N 6 55E
Ceno, R. **62** 44 40N 9 52E
Cenon **44** 44 50N 0 33W
Centallo **62** 44 30N 7 35E
Centenário do Sul **171** 22 48S 51 57W
Center, N.D., U.S.A. **158** 47 9N 101 17W
Center, Texas, U.S.A. **159** 31 50N 94 10W
Centerfield **160** 39 9N 111 56W
Centerville, Ala., U.S.A. **157** 32 55N 87 7W
Centerville, Calif., U.S.A. **163** 36 44N 119 30W
Centerville, Iowa, U.S.A. **158** 40 45N 92 57W
Centerville, Miss., U.S.A. **159** 31 10N 91 3W
Centerville, S.D., U.S.A. **158** 43 10N 96 58W
Centerville, Tenn., U.S.A. **157** 35 46N 87 29W
Centerville, Tex., U.S.A. **159** 31 15N 95 56W
Cento **63** 44 43N 11 16E
Central **170** 11 8S 42 8W
Central □, Kenya **126** 0 30S 33 30E
Central □, Malawi **126** 13 30S 33 30E
Central □, U.K. **34** 56 10N 4 30W
Central □, Zambia **127** 14 25S 28 50E
Central African Republic ■ **124** 7 0N 20 0E
Central Auckland □ **142** 37 30S 175 30E
Central City, Ky., U.S.A. **156** 37 20N 87 7W
Central City, Nebr., U.S.A. **158** 41 8N 98 0W
Central, Cordillera, C. Rica **166** 10 10N 84 5W
Central, Cordillera, Dom. Rep. **167** 19 15N 71 0W
Central I., L. Turkana **126** 3 30N 36 0E
Central Islip **162** 40 49N 73 13W
Central Makran Range **93** 26 30N 64 15E
Central Patricia **150** 51 30N 90 9W
Central Ra. **135** 5 0S 143 0E
Central Russian Uplands **16** 54 0N 36 0E
Central Siberian Plateau **77** 65 0N 105 0E
Central Square **162** 43 17N 76 9W
Centralia, Ill., U.S.A. **158** 38 32N 89 5W
Centralia, Mo., U.S.A. **158** 39 12N 92 6W
Centralia, Wash., U.S.A. **160** 46 46N 122 59W
Centúripe **65** 37 37N 14 41E
Cephalonia = Kefallinia **69** 38 28N 20 30E
Cepin **66** 45 32N 18 34E

Ceprano Château d'Oex

Ceprano	64	41 33N	13 30E
Ceptura	70	45 1N	26 21E
Ceram I. = Seram I.	103	3 10S	129 0E
Ceram Sea	103	2 30S	128 30E
Cerbère	44	42 26N	3 10E
Cerbicales, Îles	45	41 33N	9 22E
Cerbu	70	44 46N	24 46E
Cercal	57	37 48N	8 40W
Cercemaggiore	65	41 27N	14 43E
Cerdaña	58	42 22N	1 35E
Cerdedo	56	42 33N	8 23W
Cerea	63	45 12N	11 13E
Ceres, Argent.	172	29 55S	61 55W
Ceres, Brazil	171	15 17S	49 35W
Ceres, Italy	62	45 19N	7 22E
Ceres, S. Afr.	128	33 21S	19 18E
Ceres, U.K.	35	56 18N	2 57W
Ceres, U.S.A.	163	37 35N	120 57W
Céret	44	42 30N	2 42E
Cereté	174	8 53N	75 48W
Cerfontaine	47	50 11N	4 26E
Cerignola	65	41 17N	15 53E
Cerigo = Kithira	69	36 9N	23 0E
Cérilly	44	46 37N	2 50E
Cerisiers	43	48 8N	3 30E
Cerizay	42	46 50N	0 40W
Çerkeş	92	40 40N	32 58E
Cerknica	63	45 48N	14 21E
Çermerno	66	43 35N	20 25E
Cerna	70	44 4N	28 17E
Cerna, R.	70	44 45N	24 0E
Cernavodů	70	44 22N	28 3E
Cernay	43	47 44N	7 10E
Cerne Abbas	28	50 49N	2 29W
Cernik	66	45 17N	17 22E
Cerralvo, I.	164	24 20N	109 45E
Cerreto Sannita	65	41 17N	14 34E
Cerrig-y-druidion	31	53 2N	3 34W
Cerritos	164	22 20N	100 20W
Cerro	161	36 47N	105 36W
Cêrro Corá	171	6 3S	36 21W
Cerro de Punta, Mt.	147	18 10N	67 0W
Certaldo	62	43 32N	11 2E
Cervaro, R.	65	41 21N	15 30E
Cervera	58	41 40N	1 16E
Cervera de Pisuerga	56	42 51N	4 30W
Cervera del Río Alhama	58	42 2N	1 58W
Cérvia	63	44 15N	12 20E
Cervignano del Friuli	63	45 49N	13 20E
Cervinara	65	41 2N	14 36E
Cervo	56	43 40N	7 24W
Cervoine	45	42 20N	9 29E
Cesanâtico	63	44 12N	12 22E
César □	174	9 0N	73 30W
Cesaro	65	37 50N	14 38E
Cesena	63	44 9N	12 14E
Cesenático	63	44 12N	12 22E
Cēsis	80	57 17N	25 28E
Česká Třebová	53	49 54N	16 27E
Česke Budějovice	52	48 55N	14 25E
České Velenice	52	48 45N	15 1E
Českézemě	52	50 0N	14 0E
Ceskomoravská Vrchovina	52	49 20N	15 45E
Český Brod	52	50 4N	14 52E
Český Krumlov	52	48 43N	14 21E
Český Těšin	53	49 45N	18 39E
Çeşme	69	38 20N	26 23E
Cess, R.	120	5 25N	9 35W
Cessnock	141	32 50S	151 21E
Cestos, R.	120	5 30N	9 30W
Cetate	70	44 7N	23 2E
Cetina, R.	63	43 50N	16 30E
Cetinje	66	42 23N	18 59E
Cetraro	65	39 30N	15 56E
Ceuta	118	35 52N	5 18W
Ceva	62	44 23N	8 0E
Cévennes, mts.	44	44 10N	3 50E
Ceylon = Sri Lanka ■	97	7 30N	80 50E
Cha-am	100	12 48N	99 58E
Cha Pa	100	22 21N	103 50E
Chaam	47	51 30N	4 52E
Chabeuil	45	44 54N	5 1E
Chabjuwardoo B.	137	23 0S	113 30E
Chablais	45	46 20N	6 36E
Chablis	43	47 47N	3 48E
Chabounia	118	35 30N	2 38E
Chacabuco	172	34 40S	60 27W
Chacewater	30	50 15N	5 8W
Chachapoyas	174	6 15S	77 50W
Chachoengsao	100	13 42N	101 5E
Chachran	93	28 55N	70 30E
Chachro	94	25 5N	70 15E
Chaco □	172	25 0S	61 0W
Chaco Austral	176	27 30S	61 40W
Chaco Boreal	172	22 30S	60 10W
Chaco Central	176	24 0S	61 0W
Chad ■	117	12 30N	17 15E
Chadan	77	51 17N	91 35E
Chadileuvú, R.	172	37 0S	65 55W
Chadiza	127	14 10S	33 34E
Chadron	158	42 50N	103 0W
Chadyr-Lunga	82	46 3N	28 51E
Chae Hom	100	18 43N	99 35E
Chaem, R.	100	18 11N	98 38E
Chaeryŏng	107	38 24N	125 36E
Chafurray	174	3 10N	73 14W
Chagai	93	29 30N	63 0E
Chagai Hills	93	29 30N	63 0E
Chagda	77	58 45N	130 30E
Chagford	30	50 40N	3 50W
Chagny	43	46 57N	4 45E
Chagoda	80	59 10N	35 25E
Chagos Arch.	86	6 0S	72 0E
Chāh Bahār	93	25 20N	60 40E
Ch'ahaerhyuichungch'i	106	41 18N	112 48E
Ch'ahanch'elo	106	41 41N	114 15E
Chahar Buriak	93	30 15N	62 0E
Chāhr-e Babak	93	30 10N	55 20E
Chahsikiang	105	32 32N	79 41E
Chahtung	98	26 41N	98 10E
Chai-nat	100	15 11N	100 8E
Chaibasa	99	22 42N	85 49E
Chaillé-les-Marais	44	46 25N	1 2W
Chaise Dieu, La	44	45 20N	3 40E
Chaiya	101	9 23N	99 14E
Chaiyaphum	100	15 48N	102 2E
Chaize-le-Vicomté, La	42	46 40N	1 18W
Chaj Doab	94	32 0N	73 0E
Chajari	172	30 42N	58 0W
Chakaria	98	21 45N	92 5E
Chake Chake	126	5 15S	39 45E
Chakhansur	93	31 10N	62 0E
Chaklashi	94	22 40N	72 52E
Chakonipau, L.	151	56 18N	68 30W
Chakradharpur	95	22 45N	85 40E
Chakwadam	98	27 29N	98 31E
Chakwal	94	32 50N	72 45E
Chala	174	15 48S	74 20W
Chalais	44	45 16N	0 3E
Chalakudi	97	10 18N	76 20E
Chalcatongo	165	17 4N	97 34W
Chalchihuites	164	23 29N	103 53W
Chalcis = Khalkis	69	38 27N	23 42E
Chale	28	50 35N	1 19W
Chaleur B.	151	47 55N	65 30W
Chalfant	163	37 32N	118 21W
Chalfont St. Peter	29	51 36N	0 33W
Chalhuanca	174	14 15S	73 5W
Ch'aling	109	26 47N	113 45E
Chaling Hu	105	34 55N	98 0E
Chalisgaon	96	20 30N	75 10E
Chalkar	83	50 35N	51 52E
Chalkar Oz.	83	50 33N	51 45E
Chalky Inlet	143	46 3S	166 31E
Challans	42	46 50N	1 52W
Challapata	174	19 0S	66 50W
Challerange	43	49 18N	4 46E
Challis	160	44 32N	114 25W
Chalna	95	22 36N	89 35E
Chalon-sur-Saône	43	46 48N	4 50E
Chalonnes	42	47 20N	0 45W
Châlons-sur-Marne	43	48 58N	4 20E
Châlus	44	45 39N	0 58E
Cham, Ger.	49	49 12N	12 40E
Cham, Switz.	51	47 11N	8 28E
Cham, Cu Lao	100	15 57N	108 30E
Chama, R.	127	36 57N	106 37W
Chaman	93	30 58N	66 25E
Chamarajanagar-Ramasamudram	97	11 52N	76 52E
Chamartín de la Rosa	58	40 28N	3 40W
Chamba, India	94	32 35N	76 10E
Chamba, Tanz.	125	11 37S	37 0E
Chambal, R.	94	26 0N	76 55E
Chamberlain, Austral.	136	15 58S	127 54E
Chamberlain, U.S.A.	158	43 50N	99 21W
Chambers	161	35 13N	109 30W
Chambersburg	156	39 53N	77 41W
Chambéry	45	45 34N	5 55E
Chambeshi	127	12 39S	28 1E
Chambeshi, R.	124	10 20S	31 58E
Chambois	42	48 48N	0 6E
Chambon-Feugerolles, Le	45	45 24N	4 18E
Châmbon, Le	45	45 35N	4 26E
Chambord	151	48 25N	72 6W
Chamboulive	44	45 26N	1 42E
Chambri L.	135	4 15S	143 10E
Chamela	164	19 32N	105 5W
Chamical	172	30 22S	66 27W
Chamkar Luong	101	11 0N	103 45E
Chamonix	45	45 55N	6 51E
Champa	95	22 2N	82 43E
Champagne, Can.	152	60 49N	136 30W
Champagne, France	43	49 0N	4 40E
Champagnole	43	46 45N	5 55E
Champaign	156	40 8N	88 14W
Champassak	100	14 53N	105 52E
Champaubert	43	48 50N	3 45E
Champdeniers	44	46 29N	0 25W
Champeix	44	45 37N	3 8E
Champerico	166	14 18N	91 55W
Champier	50	45 27N	5 17E
Champion B.	137	28 44S	114 36E
Champlain	151	46 27N	72 24W
Champotón	165	19 20N	90 50W
Chamusca	57	39 21N	8 29W
Chana	101	6 55N	100 44E
Chañaral	172	26 15S	70 50W
Chanasma	94	23 44N	72 5E
Chanca, R.	57	37 49N	7 15W
Chanchiang	109	21 15N	110 20E
Chancy	50	46 8N	6 0E
Chanda	96	19 57N	79 25E
Chandalar	147	67 30N	148 35W
Chandausi	95	28 27N	78 49E
Chandeleur Is.	159	29 45N	88 53W
Chandeleur Sd.	159	29 58N	88 40W
Chandernagore	95	22 52N	88 24E
Chandigarh	94	30 30N	76 58E
Chandler, Can.	151	48 18N	64 46W
Chandler, Ariz., U.S.A.	161	33 20N	111 56W
Chandler, Okla., U.S.A.	159	35 43N	97 20W
Chandler's Ford	28	50 59N	1 23W
Chandlers Peak	141	30 24S	152 10E
Chandmani	105	45 20N	97 59E
Chandpur, Bangla.	98	22 8N	90 55E
Chandpur, India	94	29 8N	78 19E
Chang	94	26 59N	68 30E
Ch'ang Chiang, R.	109	31 40N	121 50E
Chang, Ko	101	12 0N	102 23E
Changa	95	33 53N	77 35E
Changanacheri	97	9 25N	76 31E
Changane, R.	125	23 30S	33 50E
Ch'anganpao	108	26 9N	109 42E
Changchiak'ou	106	40 50N	114 53E
Ch'angchiang	100	19 19N	108 43E
Ch'angchih	106	36 11N	113 6E
Ch'angchou	109	31 47N	119 58E
Changchou	109	24 31N	117 40E
Ch'angch'un	107	43 58N	125 19E
Ch'angch'unling	107	45 22N	125 28E
Changdori	107	38 30N	127 40E
Ch'angfeng	109	32 27N	117 9E
Changhsing	109	31 0N	119 56E
Ch'anghua	109	30 10N	119 15E
Changhua	109	24 2N	120 30E
Changhŭng	107	34 41N	126 52E
Changhŭngni	107	40 24N	128 19E
Ch'angi	107	36 51N	119 23E
Changjin	107	40 23N	127 15E
Changjin-chŏsuji	107	40 30N	127 15E
Changkuangts'ai Ling	107	45 50N	128 50E
Changli	107	39 40N	119 19E
Ch'angling	107	44 16N	123 57E
Ch'anglo, Fukien, China	109	25 58N	119 31E
Ch'anglo, Fukien, China	109	26 40N	117 20E
Ch'anglo, Kwangtung, China	109	24 4N	115 37E
Changlun	101	6 25N	100 26E
Changming	108	31 44N	104 44E
Ch'angning, Hunan, China	109	26 25N	112 15E
Ch'angning, Szechwan, China	108	28 38N	104 57E
Ch'angning, Yunnan, China	108	24 50N	99 36E
Ch'angpai	107	41 26N	128 0E
Ch'angpai Shan	107	42 25N	129 0E
Changpei	106	41 7N	114 51E
Ch'angp'ing	106	40 12N	116 12E
Changp'ing	109	25 18N	117 24E
Changpu	109	24 2N	117 31E
Ch'angsha	109	28 15N	113 0E
Ch'angshan	109	28 57N	118 31E
Ch'angshou	108	29 50N	107 2E
Ch'angshu	109	31 33N	120 45E
Ch'angshun	108	25 59N	106 25E
Ch'angt'ai	109	24 34N	117 50E
Ch'angte	109	29 5N	111 42E
Ch'angt'ing	109	25 52N	116 20E
Ch'angt'u	107	42 47N	124 0E
Ch'angtu	108	31 10N	97 14E
Ch'angt'u Shan	109	30 15N	122 20E
Ch'angwu	106	35 9N	107 42E
Changwu	107	42 24N	122 30E
Ch'angyang	109	30 28N	111 9E
Ch'angyatien	106	40 40N	108 46E
Changyeh	105	38 56N	100 37E
Changyŏn	107	38 15N	125 6E
Ch'angyüan	106	35 17N	114 50E
Chanhanga	128	16 0S	14 8E
Chanhua	107	37 42N	118 8E
Chani	108	25 36N	103 49E
Channapatna	97	12 40N	77 15E
Channel Is.	42	49 30N	2 40W
Channel Islands	163	33 30N	119 0W
Channing, Mich., U.S.A.	156	46 9N	88 1W
Channing, Tex., U.S.A.	159	35 45N	102 20W
Chantada	56	42 36N	7 46W
Chanthaburi	100	12 38N	102 12E
Chantilly	43	49 12N	2 29E
Chantonnay	42	46 40N	1 3W
Chantrey Inlet	148	67 48N	96 20W
Chanute	159	37 45N	85 25W
Chanyü	107	44 39N	122 45E
Chanza, R.	57	37 49N	7 15W
Ch'ao Hu	109	31 40N	117 30E
Chao Phraya Lowlands	100	15 30N	100 0E
Chao Phraya, R.	100	13 32N	100 36E
Ch'aoan	109	23 41N	116 33E
Chaoan	109	23 47N	117 5E
Chaoch'eng, Shansi, China	106	36 26N	111 43E
Chaoch'eng, Shantung, China	106	36 3N	115 35E
Chaochiao	108	28 1N	102 49E
Chaoch'ing	109	23 7N	112 24E
Chaohsien	106	37 45N	114 46E
Ch'aohsien	109	31 41N	117 49E
Chaop'ing	109	24 1N	110 59E
Chaot'ung	108	27 19N	103 42E
Ch'aoyang, Kwangtung, China	109	23 10N	116 30E
Ch'aoyang, Liaoning, China	107	41 46N	120 16E
Chaoyüan, Heilungkiang, China	107	45 30N	125 8E
Chaoyüan, Shantung, China	107	37 22N	120 24E
Chap Kuduk	76	48 45N	55 5E
Chapala	127	15 50S	37 35E
Chapala, Lago de	164	20 10N	103 20W
Chaparmukh	98	26 12N	92 31E
Chapayevo	83	50 25N	51 10E
Chapayevsk	81	53 0N	49 40E
Chapecó	173	27 14S	52 41W
Chapel-en-le-Frith	32	53 19N	1 54W
Chapel Hill	157	35 53N	79 3W
Chapelle-d'Angillon, La	43	47 21N	2 25E
Chapelle Glain, La	42	47 38N	1 11W
Chapeyevo	84	50 12N	51 10E
Chapleau	150	47 50N	83 24W
Chaplin	153	50 28N	106 40W
Chaplino	82	48 8N	36 15E
Chaplygin	81	53 15N	39 55E
Chapra	95	25 48N	84 50E
Char	116	21 40N	12 45W
Chara	77	56 54N	118 12E
Charadai	172	27 35S	60 0W
Charagua	174	19 45S	63 10W
Charak	93	26 46N	54 18E
Charalá	174	6 17N	73 10W
Charaña	174	17 30S	69 35W
Charapita	174	0 37S	74 21W
Charata	172	27 13S	61 14W
Charcas	164	23 10N	101 20W
Charcoal L.	153	58 49N	102 22W
Charcot I.	13	70 0S	75 0W
Chard, Can.	153	55 55N	111 10W
Chard, U.K.	28	50 52N	2 59W
Chardara	76	41 16N	67 59E
Chardara, Step	85	42 20N	68 0E
Charduar	98	26 51N	92 46E
Chardzhou	85	39 6N	63 34E
Charente-Maritime □	44	45 50N	0 35W
Charente □	44	45 50N	0 16W
Charente, R.	44	45 41N	0 30W
Charentsavan	83	40 35N	44 41E
Chârib, G.	122	28 6N	32 54E
Charikar	93	35 0N	69 10E
Charing	29	51 12N	0 49E
Charité, La	43	47 10N	3 0E
Chariton R.	158	39 19N	92 58W
Charkhari	95	25 24N	79 45E
Charkhi Dadri	94	28 37N	76 17E
Charlbury	28	51 52N	1 29W
Charlemont	38	54 26N	6 40W
Charleroi	47	50 24N	4 27E
Charles, C.	162	37 10N	75 52W
Charles City, Iowa, U.S.A.	158	43 2N	92 41W
Charles City, Va., U.S.A.	162	37 20N	77 4W
Charles L.	153	59 50N	110 33W
Charles, Pk.	137	32 53S	121 8E
Charles Town	156	39 20N	77 50W
Charleston, Miss., U.S.A.	159	34 2N	90 3W
Charleston, Mo., U.S.A.	159	36 52N	89 20W
Charleston, S.C., U.S.A.	157	32 47N	79 56W
Charleston, W. Va., U.S.A.	157	38 24N	81 36W
Charlestown, Ireland	38	53 58N	8 48W
Charlestown, S. Afr.	129	27 26S	29 53E
Charlestown, Ind., U.S.A.	156	38 29N	85 40W
Charlestown, N.H., U.S.A.	162	43 14N	72 24W
Charlestown of Aberlour	37	57 27N	3 13W
Charlesville	124	5 27S	20 59E
Charleville	139	26 24S	146 15E
Charleville-Mézières	43	49 44N	4 40E
Charleville = Rath Luirc	39	52 21N	8 40W
Charlevoix	156	45 19N	85 14W
Charlieu	45	46 10N	4 10E
Charlotte, Mich., U.S.A.	156	42 36N	84 48W
Charlotte, N.C., U.S.A.	157	35 16N	80 46W
Charlotte Amalie	147	18 22N	64 56W
Charlotte Harb.	157	26 45N	82 10W
Charlotte Waters	136	25 56N	134 54E
Charlottenberg	72	59 54N	12 17E
Charlottesville	156	38 1N	78 30W
Charlottetown	151	46 14N	63 8W
Charlton, Austral.	140	36 16S	143 24E
Charlton, U.S.A.	158	40 59N	93 20W
Charlton I.	150	52 0N	79 20W
Charlton Kings	28	51 52N	2 3W
Charlwood	29	51 8N	0 12W
Charmes	43	48 22N	6 17E
Charminster	28	50 43N	2 28W
Charmouth	28	50 45N	2 54W
Charnwood Forest	23	52 43N	1 18W
Charny	151	46 43N	71 15W
Charolles	45	46 27N	4 16E
Charost	43	47 0N	2 7E
Charouïne	118	29 0N	0 15W
Charre	127	17 19S	35 10E
Charroux	44	46 9N	0 25E
Charsadda	94	34 7N	71 45E
Charters Towers	138	20 5S	146 13E
Chartham	29	51 14N	1 1E
Chartre, La	42	47 42N	0 34E
Chartres	42	48 29N	1 30E
Chascomús	172	35 30S	58 0W
Chasefu	127	11 55N	32 58E
Chaslands Mistake	143	46 38S	169 22E
Chasseneuil-sur-Bonnieure	44	45 52N	0 29E
Chata	94	27 42N	77 30E
Châtaigneraie, La	42	46 38N	0 45W
Chatal Balkan = Udvoy Balkan	67	42 50N	26 50E
Château-Chinon	43	47 4N	3 56E
Château d'Oex	50	46 28N	7 8E

Château-du-Loir Ch'iench'engchen

Château-du-Loir 42 47 40N 0 25 E
Château Gontier 42 47 50N 0 42W
Château-la-Vallière 42 47 30N 0 20 E
Château-Landon 43 48 8N 2 40 E
Château, Le 44 45 52N 1 12W
Château Porcien 43 49 31N 4 13 E
Château Renault 42 47 36N 0 56 E
Château-Salins 43 48 50N 6 30 E
Château-Thierry 43 49 3N 3 20 E
Châteaubourg 43 48 7N 1 25W
Châteaubriant 42 47 43N 1 23W
Châteaudun 42 48 3N 1 20 E
Châteaugiron 42 48 3N 1 30W
Châteaulin 42 48 11N 4 8W
Châteaumeillant 44 46 35N 2 12 E
Châteauneuf 42 48 35N 1 15 E
Châteauneuf-du-Faou 42 48 11N 3 50W
Châteauneuf-sur-Charente 44 45 36N 0 3W
Châteauneuf-sur-Cher 43 46 52N 2 18 E
Châteauneuf-sur-Loire 43 47 52N 2 13 E
Châteaurenard 45 43 53N 4 51 E
Châteauroux 43 46 50N 1 40 E
Châtel-Guyon 44 45 55N 3 4 E
Châtel St. Denis 50 46 32N 6 54 E
Châtelaillon-Plage 44 46 5N 1 5W
Châtelard, Le 50 46 4N 6 57 E
Châtelaudren 42 48 33N 2 59W
Chatelet 47 50 24N 4 32 E
Châtelet, Le, Cher, France 44 46 40N 2 20 E
Châtelet, Le, Seine et Marne, France 43 48 30N 2 47 E
Châtellerault 42 46 50N 0 30 E
Châtelus-Malvaleix 44 46 18N 2 1 E
Chatham, N.B., Can. 151 47 2N 65 28W
Chatham, Ont., Can. 150 42 24N 82 11W
Chatham, U.K. 29 51 22N 0 32 E
Chatham, Alaska, U.S.A. 147 57 30N 135 0W
Chatham, La., U.S.A. 159 32 22N 92 26W
Chatham, N.Y., U.S.A. 162 42 21N 73 32W
Chatham Is. 130 44 0 S 176 40W
Chatham Str. 152 57 0N 134 40W
Châtillon, Loiret, France 43 47 36N 2 44 E
Châtillon, Marne, France 43 49 5N 3 43 E
Chatillon 62 45 45N 7 40 E
Châtillon-Coligny 43 47 50N 2 51 E
Châtillon-en-Bazois 43 47 3N 3 39 E
Châtillon-en-Diois 45 44 41N 5 29 E
Châtillon-sur-Seine 43 47 50N 4 33 E
Châtillon-sur-Sèvre 42 46 56N 0 45W
Chatkal, R. 85 41 38N 70 1 E
Chatkalskiy Khrebet 85 41 30N 70 45 E
Chatmohar 95 24 15N 89 26 E
Chatra 95 24 12N 84 56 E
Chatrapur 96 19 22N 85 2 E
Châtre, La 44 46 35N 1 59 E
Chatsworth 127 19 32 S 30 46 E
Chatta-Hantō 111 34 45N 136 55 E
Chattahoochee 157 30 43N 84 51W
Chattanooga 157 35 2N 85 17W
Chatteris 29 52 27N 0 3 E
Chatton 35 55 34N 1 55W
Chaturat 100 15 34N 101 51 E
Chatyrkel, Ozero 85 40 40N 75 18 E
Chatyrtash 85 40 55N 76 25 E
Chau Phu 101 10 42N 105 7 E
Chaudes-Aigues 44 44 51N 3 1 E
Chauffailes 44 46 13N 4 20 E
Chauk 98 20 53N 94 49 E
Chaukan La 99 27 0N 97 15 E
Chaukan Pass 98 27 8N 97 10 E
Chaulnes 43 49 48N 2 47 E
Chaumont 43 48 7N 5 8 E
Chaumont-en-Vexin 43 49 16N 1 53 E
Chaumont-sur-Loire 42 47 29N 1 11 E
Chaunay 44 46 13N 0 9 E
Chauny 43 49 37N 3 12 E
Chausey, Îs. 42 48 52N 1 49W
Chaussin 43 46 59N 5 22 E
Chauvin 153 52 45N 110 10W
Chaux de Fonds, La 50 47 7N 6 50 E
Chaves, Brazil 170 0 15 S 49 55W
Chaves, Port. 56 41 45N 7 32W
Chavuma 125 13 10 S 22 55 E
Chawang 101 8 25N 99 30 E
Ch'aya 108 30 35N 98 3 E
Chayan 85 43 5N 69 25 E
Chayek 85 41 55N 74 30 E
Chaykovskiy 84 56 47N 54 9 E
Chazelles-sur-Lyon 45 45 39N 4 22 E
Cheadle, Gr. Manchester, U.K. 32 53 23N 2 14W
Cheadle, Staffs., U.K. 32 52 59N 1 59W
Cheadle Hulme 32 53 22N 2 12W
Cheb (Eger) 52 50 9N 12 20 E
Chebarkul 84 55 0N 60 25 E
Cheboksary 81 56 8N 47 30 E
Cheboygan 156 45 38N 84 29W
Chebsara 81 59 10N 38 45 E
Chech, Erg 118 25 0N 2 15W
Chechaouen 118 35 9N 5 15W
Chechen 83 43 59N 47 40 E
Chech'eng 106 34 4N 115 13 E
Checheno-Ingush, A.S.S.R. □ 83 43 30N 45 29 E
Chechon 107 37 8N 128 12 E
Checiny 54 50 46N 20 37 E
Checleset B. 152 50 5N 127 35W
Checotah 159 35 31N 95 30W
Chedabucto B. 151 45 25N 61 8W
Cheddar 28 51 16N 2 47W
Cheddleton 32 53 5N 2 2W
Cheduba I. 98 18 45N 93 40 E
Cheepie 139 26 43 S 144 59 E
Ch'eerhch'en Ho, R. 105 39 30N 88 15 E
Chef-Boutonne 44 46 7N 0 4W
Chefoo = Yent'ai 107 37 30N 121 12 E
Chefornak 147 60 10N 164 15W
Chegdomyn 77 51 7N 132 52 E
Chegga 118 25 15N 5 40W
Chehalis 160 46 44N 122 59W
Cheju 107 33 28N 126 30 E
Cheju Do 107 33 29N 126 34 E
Chejung 109 27 13N 119 52 E
Chekalin 81 54 10N 36 10 E
Chekao 109 31 46N 117 45 E
Chekiang □ 109 29 30N 120 0 E
Chela, Sa. da 128 16 20 S 13 20 E
Chelan, Can. 153 52 38N 103 22 E
Chelan, U.S.A. 160 47 49N 120 0W
Chelan, L. 152 48 5N 120 30W
Cheleken 76 39 26N 53 7 E
Chelforó 176 39 0 S 66 40W
Chéliff, O. 118 36 0N 0 8 E
Chelkar 76 47 40N 59 32 E
Chelkar Tengiz, Solonchak 76 48 0N 62 30 E
Chellala Dahrania 118 33 2N 0 1 E
Chelles 43 48 52N 2 33 E
Chełm 54 51 8N 23 30 E
Chełm □ 54 51 15N 23 30 E
Chelmarsh 28 52 29N 2 25W
Chełmek 54 50 6N 19 16 E
Chelmer, R. 29 51 45N 0 42 E
Chełmno 54 53 20N 18 30 E
Chelmsford 29 51 44N 0 29 E
Chełmża 54 53 10N 18 39 E
Chelsea, Austral. 141 38 5 S 145 8 E
Chelsea, Okla., U.S.A. 159 36 35N 95 25W
Chelsea, Vermont, U.S.A. 162 43 59N 72 27W
Cheltenham 28 51 55N 2 5W
Chelva 58 39 45N 1 0W
Chelyabinsk 84 55 10N 61 24 E
Chelyuskin, C. 86 77 30N 103 0 E
Chemainus 152 48 55N 123 48W
Chemikovsk 78 56 31N 58 11 E
Chemillé 42 47 14N 0 45W
Chemnitz = Karl-Marx-Stadt 48 50 50N 12 55 E
Chemor 101 4 44N 101 6 E
Chemult 160 43 14N 121 54W
Chen, Gora 77 65 10N 141 20 E
Chenab, R. 94 30 40N 73 30 E
Chenachane, O. 118 25 30N 3 30W
Chenan 106 33 16N 109 1 E
Chenango Forks 162 42 15N 75 51W
Chencha 123 6 15N 37 32 E
Ch'ench'i 109 28 1N 110 13 E
Ch'enchiachiang 107 34 25N 119 50 E
Chenchiang 109 32 12N 119 27 E
Chenchieh 108 23 15N 107 9 E
Chênée 47 50 37N 5 37 E
Cheney 160 47 38N 117 34W
Chenfeng 108 25 25N 105 51 E
Chengan 108 28 30N 107 30 E
Ch'engch'eng 106 35 6N 109 52 E
Ch'engchiang 108 24 40N 102 55 E
Chengchou 106 34 38N 113 43 E
Chengchow = Chengchou 106 34 38N 113 43 E
Chengelee 98 28 47N 96 16 E
Chengho 109 27 25N 118 46 E
Ch'enghsi Hu 109 32 22N 116 12 E
Ch'enghsien, Chekiang, China 109 29 30N 120 48 E
Ch'enghsien, Kansu, China 106 33 42N 105 36 E
Ch'engk'ou 108 31 58N 108 48 E
Ch'engku 106 33 9N 107 22 E
Ch'engkung 108 24 53N 102 45 E
Ch'engmai 100 19 44N 109 59 E
Ch'engpu 109 26 12N 110 5 E
Ch'engte 107 41 0N 117 58 E
Chengting 106 38 8N 114 37 E
Ch'engtu 108 30 45N 104 0 E
Ch'engtung Hu 109 32 17N 116 23 E
Ch'engtzut'uan 107 39 30N 122 30 E
Ch'engwu 106 35 0N 115 56 E
Ch'engyang 107 36 20N 120 16 E
Chengyang 109 32 36N 114 23 E
Chengyangkuan 109 32 29N 116 37 E
Chenhai 109 29 57N 121 42 E
Ch'enhsien 109 25 48N 113 2 E
Chenhsiung 108 27 27N 104 50 E
Chenhsü 109 27 6N 120 16 E
Chenkán 165 19 8N 90 58W
Chenk'ang 108 24 4N 99 18 E
Chenlai 107 45 52N 123 12 E
Chenning 108 25 57N 105 51 E
Chenp'ing 106 33 2N 112 14 E
Ch'enp'ing 108 31 52N 109 31 E
Chenyüan, Kansu, China 106 35 59N 107 2 E
Chenyüan, Kweichow, China 108 27 0N 108 20 E
Cheo Reo = Hau Bon 101 13 25N 108 28 E
Cheom Ksan 100 14 13N 104 56 E
Chepelare 67 41 44N 24 40 E
Chepén 174 7 10 S 79 15W
Chepes 172 31 20 S 66 35W
Chepo 166 9 10N 79 6W
Chepstow 31 51 38N 2 40W
Cheptsa, R. 81 58 36N 50 4 E
Cheptulil, Mt. 126 1 25N 35 35 E
Chequamegon B. 158 46 40N 90 30W
Chequeche 127 14 13 S 38 30 E
Cher □ 43 47 10N 2 30 E
Chér, R. 43 47 10N 2 10 E
Cheran 98 25 45N 90 44 E
Cherasco 62 44 39N 7 50 E
Cheratte 47 50 40N 5 41 E
Cheraw 157 34 42N 79 54W
Cherbourg 42 49 39N 1 40W
Cherchell 118 36 35N 2 12 E
Cherdakly 81 54 25N 48 50 E
Cherdyn 84 60 24N 56 29 E
Cheremkhovo 77 53 32N 102 40 E
Cherepanovo 76 54 15N 83 30 E
Cherepovets 81 59 5N 37 55 E
Chergui, Chott Ech 118 34 10N 0 25 E
Cheri 121 13 26N 11 21 E
Cherikov 80 53 32N 31 20 E
Cheriton 28 51 3N 1 9W
Cheriton Fitzpaine 30 50 51N 3 38W
Cherkessk 83 44 25N 42 10 E
Cherlak 76 54 15N 74 55 E
Chermoz 84 58 46N 56 10 E
Chernak 85 43 24N 68 2 E
Chernaya Kholunitsa 84 58 51N 51 52 E
Cherni, Mt. 67 42 35N 23 18 E
Chernigov 80 51 28N 31 20 E
Chernikovsk 84 54 48N 56 8 E
Chernobyl 80 51 13N 30 15 E
Chernogorsk 77 54 5N 91 10 E
Chernomorskoye 82 45 31N 32 46 E
Chernovskoye 81 58 48N 47 20 E
Chernovtsy 82 48 0N 26 0 E
Chernoye 77 70 30N 89 10 E
Chernushka 84 56 29N 56 3 E
Chernyakhovsk 80 54 29N 21 48 E
Chernyshevskiy 77 62 40N 112 30 E
Chernyshkovskiy 83 48 30N 42 28 E
Cherokee, Iowa, U.S.A. 158 42 40N 95 30W
Cherokee, Okla., U.S.A. 159 36 45N 98 25W
Cherokees, L. of the 159 36 50N 95 12W
Cherquenco 176 38 35 S 72 0W
Cherrapunji 99 25 17N 91 47 E
Cherry Creek 160 39 50N 114 58W
Cherry Valley, U.S.A. 162 42 48N 74 45W
Cherry Valley, U.S.A. 163 33 59N 116 57W
Cherryvale 159 37 20N 95 33W
Cherskiy 77 68 45N 161 18 E
Cherskogo Khrebet 77 65 0N 143 0 E
Chertkovo 83 49 25N 40 19 E
Chertsey 29 51 23N 0 30W
Cherven 80 53 45N 28 13 E
Cherven-Bryag 67 43 17N 24 7 E
Cherwell, R. 28 51 46N 1 18W
Chesapeake Bay 162 38 0N 76 12W
Chesapeake Beach 162 38 41N 76 32W
Chesha B. = Cheshskaya G. 78 67 20N 47 0 E
Chesham 29 51 42N 0 36W
Cheshire □ 32 53 14N 2 30W
Cheshunt 29 51 42N 0 1W
Chesil Beach 23 50 37N 2 33W
Cheslatta L. 152 53 49N 125 20W
Chesne, Le 43 49 30N 4 45 E
Cheste 59 39 30N 0 41W
Chester, U.K. 32 53 12N 2 53W
Chester, Calif., U.S.A. 160 40 22N 121 22W
Chester, Ill., U.S.A. 158 37 58N 89 50W
Chester, Mont., U.S.A. 160 48 31N 111 0W
Chester, Pa., U.S.A. 162 39 54N 75 20W
Chester, S.C., U.S.A. 157 34 44N 81 13W
Chester, Va., U.S.A. 162 37 21N 77 27W
Chester, Vt., U.S.A. 162 43 16N 72 36W
Chester-le-Street 33 54 53N 1 34W
Chesterfield, Can. 148 63 0N 91 0W
Chesterfield, U.K. 33 53 14N 1 26W
Chesterfield, U.S.A. 162 37 23N 77 31W
Chesterfield I. 129 16 20 S 43 58 E
Chesterfield, Îles 133 19 52 S 158 15 E
Chesterfield Inlet 148 63 30N 90 45W
Chesterton Range 138 25 30 S 147 27 E
Chestertown 162 39 13N 76 4W
Chesuncook L. 151 46 0N 69 10W
Chetaibi 119 37 1N 7 20 E
Cheticamp 151 46 37N 60 59W
Chetumal 165 18 30N 88 20W
Chetumal, Bahía de 165 18 40N 88 10W
Chetwynd 152 55 45N 121 45W
Chevanceaux 44 45 18N 0 14W
Cheviot Hills 35 55 20N 2 30W
Cheviot Ra. 138 25 20 S 143 45 E
Cheviot, The 35 55 29N 2 8W
Chew Bahir 123 4 40N 30 50 E
Chew Magna 28 51 21N 2 37W
Chewelah 160 48 17N 117 43W
Cheyenne, Okla., U.S.A. 159 35 40N 99 40W
Cheyenne, Wyo., U.S.A. 158 41 9N 104 49W
Cheyenne, R. 158 44 50N 101 0W
Cheyenne Wells 158 38 51N 102 23W
Cheylard, Le 45 44 55N 4 25 E
Cheyne B. 137 34 35 S 118 50 E
Chhabra 94 24 40N 76 54 E
Chhang 102 12 15N 104 14 E
Chhatak 95 25 5N 91 37 E
Chhatarpur 95 24 55N 79 43 E
Chhep 100 13 45N 105 24 E
Chhindwara 95 22 2N 78 59 E
Chhlong 101 12 15N 105 58 E
Chhuk 101 10 46N 104 8 E
Chi, R. 100 15 11N 104 43 E
Chiaho 109 25 33N 112 15 E
Chiahsiang 106 35 25N 116 21 E
Chiahsien, Hensi, China 106 38 6N 110 28 E
Chiahsien, Honan, China 106 33 58N 113 13 E
Chiahsing 109 30 45N 120 43 E
Chiai 109 23 29N 120 25 E
Chiali 109 23 10N 120 11 E
Chialing Chiang, R. 108 30 2N 106 19 E
Chiamussu 105 46 50N 130 21 E
Chian, Kiangsi, China 109 27 8N 115 0 E
Chian, Kirin, China 107 41 6N 126 10 E
Chiang Dao 100 19 22N 98 58 E
Chiang Kham 100 19 32N 100 18 E
Chiang Khan 100 17 52N 101 36 E
Chiang Khong 100 20 17N 100 24 E
Chiang Mai 100 18 47N 98 59 E
Chiang Saen 100 20 16N 100 5 E
Chiangch'eng 108 22 36N 101 50 E
Chiangchiat'un 107 40 54N 120 36 E
Chiangching 108 29 13N 106 15 E
Chiangchun 109 23 5N 120 5 E
Chianghua 109 25 2N 111 45 E
Chiangk'ou 108 27 42N 108 50 E
Chiangling 109 30 21N 112 5 E
Chiangmen 109 22 37N 113 3 E
Chiangpei 108 29 47N 106 29 E
Chiangp'ing 108 21 36N 108 8 E
Chiangshan 109 28 45N 118 37 E
Chiangta 108 31 28N 99 12 E
Chiangti 108 27 1N 103 37 E
Chiangyin 109 31 50N 120 18 E
Chiangyü 108 31 47N 104 45 E
Chiangyung 109 25 16N 111 20 E
Chianie 125 15 35 S 13 40 E
Ch'iaochia 108 26 57N 103 3 E
Chiaochou Wan 107 36 10N 120 15 E
Chiaoho, Hopei, China 106 38 1N 116 17 E
Chiaoho, Kirin, China 107 43 42N 127 19 E
Chiaohsien 107 36 20N 120 0 E
Chiaoling 109 24 40N 117 10 E
Chiaotso 106 35 17N 113 18 E
Chiapa de Corzo 165 16 42N 93 0W
Chiapa, R. 165 16 42N 93 0W
Chiapas □ 165 17 0N 92 45W
Chiaramonte Gulfi 65 37 1N 14 41 E
Chiaravalle 63 38 41N 16 24 E
Chiaravalle Centrale 65 38 41N 16 25 E
Chiari 62 45 31N 9 55 E
Chiashan 109 32 37N 118 8 E
Chiasso 51 45 50N 9 0 E
Chiating 109 31 21N 121 15 E
Chiautla 165 18 18N 98 34W
Chiávari 62 44 20N 9 20 E
Chiavenna 62 46 18N 9 23 E
Chiawang 107 34 30N 117 22 E
Chiayü 109 29 59N 113 54 E
Chiba 111 35 30N 140 7 E
Chiba-ken □ 111 35 30N 140 20 E
Chibabava 129 20 25 S 33 35 E
Chibemba 125 15 48 S 14 8 E
Chibougamau 150 49 56N 74 24W
Chibougamau L. 150 49 50N 74 20W
Chibougamau, R. 150 49 50N 75 40W
Chibuk 121 10 52N 12 50 E
Chibuto 129 24 40 S 33 33 E
Chic-Chocs, Mts. 151 48 55N 66 0W
Chic-Chocs, Parc Prov. des 151 48 55N 66 20W
Chicacole = Srikakulam 97 18 14N 84 4 E
Chicago 156 41 53N 87 40W
Chicago Heights 156 41 29N 87 37W
Chicago North 156 42 20N 87 50W
Chichagof I. 152 58 0N 136 0W
Chichaoua 118 31 32N 8 44W
Chichén Itzá 165 20 40N 88 32W
Chichester 29 50 50N 0 47W
Chichester Ra. 136 21 35 S 117 45 E
Chich'i 109 30 4N 118 34 E
Ch'ichiang 108 29 0N 106 40 E
Chichibu 111 36 5N 139 10 E
Ch'ich'ihaerh 105 47 22N 123 57 E
Chichiriviche 174 10 56N 68 16W
Ch'ich'un 109 30 14N 115 25 E
Chickasha 159 35 0N 98 0W
Chicken Hd. 31 58 10N 6 15W
Chiclana de la Frontera 57 36 26N 6 9W
Chiclayo 174 6 42 S 79 50W
Chico 160 39 45N 121 54W
Chico, R., Chubut, Argent. 160 44 0 S 67 0W
Chico, R., Santa Cruz, Argent. 176 49 30 S 69 30W
Chicoa 125 15 35 S 32 20 E
Chicomo 129 24 31 S 34 6 E
Chicontepec 165 20 58N 98 10W
Chicopee 162 42 6N 72 37W
Chicoutimi 151 48 28N 71 5W
Chidambaram 97 11 20N 79 45 E
Chiddingfold 29 51 6N 0 37W
Chidenguele 129 24 55 S 34 2 E
Chidley C. 149 60 23N 64 26W
Chiehhsiu 106 37 0N 111 55 E
Ch'iehmo 105 38 8N 85 32 E
Chiehshou 106 33 20N 115 24 E
Chiehyang 109 23 37N 116 19 E
Chiem Hoa 100 22 12N 105 17 E
Chiemsee 49 47 53N 12 27 E
Chiench'ang 107 41 16N 124 28 E
Chiench'angying 107 40 48N 119 40 E
Ch'iench'engchen 108 27 12N 109 50 E

Ch'ienchiang **Chomen Swamp**

Ch'ienchiang, Hupeh, China	**109**	30 25N	112 51 E
Ch'ienchiang, Kwangsi-Chuang, China	**108**	23 40N	108 58 E
Ch'ienchiang, Szechwan, China	**108**	29 31N	108 46 E
Chiench'uan	**108**	26 28N	99 52 E
Chiengi	**124**	8 45 S	29 10 E
Chienho	**108**	26 39N	108 35 E
Ch'ienhsi	**108**	27 3N	106 0 E
Ch'ienhsien	**106**	34 30N	108 10 E
Chienko	**108**	32 0N	105 23 E
Chienli	**109**	29 49N	112 53 E
Chienou	**109**	27 5N	118 20 E
Ch'ienshan, Anhwei, China	**109**	30 41N	116 35 E
Ch'ienshan, Kiangsi, China	**109**	28 18N	117 40 E
Chienshih	**108**	30 40N	109 43 E
Chienshui	**108**	23 37N	102 49 E
Chiente	**109**	29 29N	119 16 E
Chienti, R.	**63**	43 15N	13 30 E
Chienwei	**108**	29 13N	103 56 E
Chienyang	**109**	27 21N	118 5 E
Ch'ienyang, Hunan, China	**109**	27 18N	110 10 E
Ch'ienyang, Kansu, China	**106**	34 35N	107 2 E
Chienyang	**108**	30 24N	104 33 E
Chierhkalang	**107**	43 6N	122 54 E
Chieri	**62**	45 0N	7 50 E
Chiese, R.	**62**	45 45N	10 35 E
Chieti	**63**	42 22N	14 10 E
Chièvres	**47**	50 35N	3 48 E
Chigasaki	**111**	35 19N	139 24 E
Chignecto B.	**151**	45 48N	64 40W
Chignik	**147**	56 15N	158 27W
Chigorodó	**174**	7 41N	76 42W
Chiguana	**172**	21 0 S	67 50W
Chihari	**107**	38 40N	126 30 E
Ch'ihch'i	**109**	21 59N	112 58 E
Chihchiang, Hunan, China	**108**	27 27N	109 41 E
Chihchiang, Hupei, China	**109**	30 19N	111 30 E
Chihchin	**108**	26 42N	105 45 E
Ch'ihfeng	**107**	42 18N	118 57 E
Chihkou	**107**	35 55N	119 13 E
Chihli, G. of = Po Hai	**107**	38 40N	119 0 E
Ch'ihshui	**108**	29 29N	105 38 E
Ch'ihshui Ho, R.	**108**	28 53N	105 48 E
Chihsi	**107**	45 20N	130 55 E
Ch'ihsien	**106**	34 33N	114 47 E
Chihsien, Honan, China	**106**	35 25N	114 5 E
Chihsien, Hopei, China	**106**	37 34N	115 34 E
Chihsien, Shansi, China	**106**	36 8N	110 39 E
Chihtan	**106**	36 56N	108 47 E
Chihte	**109**	30 9N	117 0 E
Chihuahua	**164**	28 40N	106 3W
Chihuahua □	**164**	28 40N	106 3W
Chihuatlán	**164**	19 14N	104 35W
Chiili	**85**	44 20N	66 15 E
Chik Ballapur	**97**	13 25N	77 45 E
Chikawawa	**127**	16 2 S	34 50 E
Chikhli	**96**	20 20N	76 18 E
Chikmagalur	**97**	13 15N	75 45 E
Chikodi	**96**	16 26N	74 38 E
Chikonde	**127**	12 16 S	31 38 E
Ch'ik'ou	**107**	38 37N	117 35 E
Chikugo	**110**	33 14N	130 28 E
Chikuma-Gawa, R.	**111**	36 59N	138 35 E
Chilac	**165**	18 20N	97 24W
Chilako, R.	**152**	53 53N	122 57W
Chilam Chavki	**95**	35 5N	75 5 E
Chilanga	**127**	15 33 S	28 16 E
Chilant'ai	**106**	39 45N	105 45 E
Chilapa	**165**	17 40N	99 20W
Chilas	**95**	35 25N	74 5 E
Chilaw	**93**	7 30N	79 50 E
Chilcotin, R.	**152**	51 44N	122 23W
Childers	**139**	25 15 S	152 17 E
Childress	**159**	34 30N	100 50W
Chile ■	**176**	35 0 S	71 15W
Chilecito	**172**	29 0 S	67 40W
Chilete	**174**	7 10 S	78 50W
Chilham	**29**	51 15N	0 59 E
Chilik, Kazakh S.S.R., U.S.S.R.	**84**	51 7N	53 55 E
Chilik, Kirgiz S.S.R., U.S.S.R.	**85**	43 33N	78 17 E
Chililabombwe (Bancroft)	**125**	12 18 S	27 43 E
Chilin	**105**	43 53N	126 38 E
Ch'ilin Hu	**105**	31 50N	89 0 E
Chilka L.	**96**	19 40N	85 25 E
Chilko, L.	**152**	52 60N	124 10W
Chilko, R.	**152**	52 6N	124 9W
Chillagoe	**138**	17 14 S	144 33 E
Chillán	**172**	36 40 S	72 10W
Chillicothe, Ill., U.S.A.	**158**	40 55N	89 32W
Chillicothe, Mo., U.S.A.	**158**	39 45N	93 30W
Chillicothe, Ohio, U.S.A.	**156**	39 53N	82 58W
Chilliwack	**152**	49 10N	122 0W
Chilo	**94**	27 12N	73 32 E
Chiloane, Î.	**129**	20 40 S	34 55 E
Chiloé, I. de	**176**	42 50 S	73 45W
Chilpancingo	**165**	17 30N	99 40W
Chiltern	**141**	36 10 S	146 36 E
Chiltern Hills	**29**	51 44N	0 42W
Chilton	**156**	44 1N	88 12W
Chiluage	**124**	9 15 S	21 42 E
Chilubula	**127**	10 14 S	30 51 E
Chilumba	**127**	10 28 S	34 12 E
Chilung	**109**	25 3N	121 45 E
Chilwa, L. (Shirwa)	**127**	15 15 S	35 40 E
Chimacum	**160**	48 1N	122 53W
Chimaltitán	**164**	21 46N	103 50W
Chimán	**166**	8 45N	78 40W
Chimay	**47**	50 3N	4 20 E
Chimbay	**76**	42 57N	59 47 E
Chimborazo	**174**	1 20 S	78 55W
Chimbote	**174**	9 0 S	78 35W
Ch'imen	**109**	29 56N	117 47 E
Chimion	**85**	40 15N	71 32 E
Chimishliya	**70**	46 34N	28 44 E
Chimkent	**85**	42 18N	69 36 E
Chimo	**107**	36 23N	120 27 E
Chimpembe	**127**	9 31 S	29 33 E
Chin □	**98**	22 0N	93 0 E
Chin Chiang, R.	**109**	28 23N	115 48 E
Chin Hills	**98**	22 30N	93 30 E
Chin Ho, R.	**106**	35 2N	113 25 E
Chin Ling Shan	**106**	34 0N	107 0 E
Ch'in Shui, R.	**109**	26 13N	115 15 E
China	**164**	25 40N	99 20W
China ■	**105**	30 0N	110 0 E
China Lake	**163**	35 44N	117 37W
Chinacates	**164**	25 0N	105 14W
Chinacota	**174**	7 37N	72 36W
Ch'inan	**106**	34 50N	105 35 E
Chinan	**106**	36 32N	117 0 E
Chinandega	**166**	12 30N	87 0W
Chinati Pk.	**159**	30 0N	104 25W
Chincha Alta	**174**	13 20 S	76 0W
Chinch'eng	**106**	35 30N	112 50 E
Chinchi	**106**	37 57N	106 6 E
Chinch'i	**109**	27 54N	116 44 E
Chinchiang, Fukien, China	**109**	24 54N	118 35 E
Chinchiang, Kiangsi, China	**109**	29 44N	115 59 E
Chinchiang, Yunnan, China	**108**	26 14N	100 34 E
Chinchilla	**139**	26 45 S	150 38 E
Chinchilla de Monte Aragón	**59**	38 53N	1 40W
Chinchón	**58**	40 9N	3 26W
Chinchorro, Banco	**165**	18 35N	87 20W
Ch'inchou	**108**	21 58N	108 35 E
Chinchou	**107**	41 8N	121 6 E
Chinch'uan	**108**	31 30N	101 55 E
Chincoteague	**162**	37 58N	75 21W
Chincoteague B.	**162**	38 5N	75 8W
Chinde	**127**	18 45 S	36 30 E
Chindo	**107**	34 28N	126 15 E
Chindwin, R.	**98**	21 26N	95 15 E
Chineni	**95**	33 2N	75 15 E
Ch'ing Chiang, R.	**109**	29 51N	112 22 E
Ch'ing Hai	**105**	37 0N	100 20 E
Ching Ho, R.	**106**	34 29N	109 5 E
Ching Shan	**109**	31 40N	111 30 E
Chinga	**127**	15 13 S	38 35 E
Chingan	**109**	28 52N	115 22 E
Ch'ingchen	**108**	26 32N	106 30 E
Ch'ingch'eng	**107**	37 11N	117 42 E
Chingchiang	**109**	32 2N	120 16 E
Ch'ingchiang, Kiangsi, China	**109**	28 5N	115 30 E
Ch'ingchiang, Kiangsu, China	**107**	33 33N	119 4 E
Ch'ingchien	**106**	37 12N	110 6 E
Chingch'uan	**106**	35 15N	107 22 E
Ch'ingfeng	**106**	35 54N	115 7 E
Chinghai	**106**	38 56N	116 55 E
Ch'inghomen	**107**	41 45N	121 25 E
Chinghsi	**108**	23 8N	106 25 E
Ch'inghsien	**106**	38 35N	116 48 E
Chinghsien	**109**	30 42N	118 23 E
Ch'inghsü	**106**	37 40N	112 20 E
Chinghung	**108**	22 0N	100 49 E
Chingi Chiang, R.	**108**	29 32N	103 44 E
Chingku	**108**	23 28N	100 42 E
Chingleput	**97**	12 42N	79 58 E
Ch'ingliu	**109**	26 12N	116 48 E
Chinglo	**106**	38 24N	111 54 E
Ch'inglung	**108**	25 48N	105 14 E
Chingmen	**109**	30 58N	112 6 E
Chingning, Chekiang, China	**109**	27 58N	119 38 E
Chingning, Kansu, China	**106**	35 30N	105 45 E
Chingola	**127**	12 31 S	27 53 E
Chingole	**127**	13 4 S	34 17 E
Chingpien	**106**	37 24N	108 36 E
Chingpo Hu	**107**	43 50N	128 50 E
Ch'ingp'u	**109**	31 9N	121 6 E
Chingshan	**109**	31 2N	113 3 E
Chingshih	**109**	29 40N	111 50 E
Ch'ingshui	**106**	34 44N	106 2 E
Chingsing	**106**	38 5N	114 8 E
Chingt'ai	**106**	37 10N	104 8 E
Ch'ingtao	**107**	36 5N	120 25 E
Chingte	**109**	30 19N	118 31 E
Chingtechen	**109**	29 19N	117 15 E
Ch'ingt'ien	**109**	28 9N	120 17 E
Chingtung	**108**	24 22N	100 50 E
Chingtzukuan	**106**	33 13N	111 2 E
Chinguar	**125**	12 18 S	16 45 E
Chinguetti	**116**	20 25N	12 15W
Chingune	**129**	20 33 S	35 0 E
Ch'ingyang	**105**	36 5N	107 40 E
Chingyang	**106**	34 32N	108 52 E
Ch'ingyang, Anhwei, China	**109**	30 38N	117 50 E
Ch'ingyang, Ningsia Hui, China	**106**	36 5N	107 40 E
Chingyü	**107**	42 22N	126 45 E
Chingyüan	**106**	36 35N	104 40 E
Ch'ingyüan, Chekiang, China	**109**	27 37N	119 3 E
Ch'ingyüan, Kwangtung, China	**109**	23 42N	112 58 E
Ch'ingyüan, Liaoning, China	**107**	42 6N	124 55 E
Ch'ingyün	**107**	37 53N	117 23 E
Chinhae	**107**	35 9N	128 40 E
Chinhanguanine	**129**	25 21 S	32 30 E
Chinhsi	**107**	40 49N	120 55 E
Chinhsiang	**106**	35 5N	116 18 E
Chinhsien, Hopei, China	**106**	38 2N	115 2 E
Chinhsien, Kiangsi, China	**109**	28 22N	116 14 E
Chinhsien, Liaoning, China	**107**	39 6N	121 3 E
Chinhua	**109**	29 9N	119 41 E
Ch'inhuangtao	**107**	39 57N	119 40 E
Chining, Inner Mongolia, China	**106**	41 2N	113 8 E
Chining, Shantung, China	**106**	35 19N	116 36 E
Chiniot	**94**	31 45N	73 0 E
Chinipas	**164**	27 22N	108 32W
Chinju	**107**	35 12N	128 2 E
Chink'ou	**109**	30 20N	114 7 E
Chinle	**161**	36 14N	109 38W
Chinmen	**109**	24 27N	118 21 E
Chinmen Tao, I.	**109**	24 25N	118 25 E
Chinnamanur	**97**	9 50N	77 16 E
Chinnampo	**107**	38 52N	125 28 E
Chinning	**108**	24 40N	102 35 E
Chinnur	**96**	18 57N	79 43 E
Chino, Japan	**111**	35 59N	138 9 E
Chino, U.S.A.	**163**	34 1N	117 41W
Chino Valley	**161**	34 54N	112 28W
Chinon	**42**	47 10N	0 15 E
Chinook, Can.	**153**	51 28N	110 59W
Chinook, U.S.A.	**160**	48 35N	109 19W
Chinp'ing, Kweichow, China	**108**	26 40N	109 7 E
Chinp'ing, Yunnan, China	**108**	22 46N	103 15 E
Chinsali	**124**	10 30 S	32 2 E
Chinsha	**108**	27 29N	106 15 E
Chinsha Chiang, R. = Yangtze Chiang, R.	**108**	27 30N	99 30 E
Chinshan	**109**	30 3N	121 13 E
Ch'inshui	**106**	35 41N	112 11 E
Chintamani	**97**	13 26N	78 3 E
Chint'an	**109**	31 45N	119 35 E
Chint'ang	**108**	30 51N	104 27 E
Chinwangtao = Ch'inhuangtao	**107**	39 57N	119 40 E
Ch'inyang	**106**	35 5N	112 55 E
Ch'inyüan	**106**	36 31N	112 15 E
Chióggia	**63**	45 13N	12 15 E
Chios = Khíos	**69**	38 27N	26 9 E
Chip Lake	**152**	53 35N	115 35W
Chipai L.	**150**	52 56N	87 53W
Chipata (Ft. Jameson)	**127**	13 38 S	32 28 E
Chipewyan L.	**153**	58 0N	98 27W
Chipinga	**127**	20 13 S	32 36 E
Chipiona	**57**	36 44N	6 26W
Chipley	**157**	30 45N	85 32W
Chiplun	**96**	17 31N	73 34 E
Chipman	**151**	46 6N	65 53W
Chipoka	**127**	13 57 S	34 28 E
Chiporovtsi	**66**	43 24N	22 52 E
Chippenham	**28**	51 27N	2 7W
Chippewa Falls	**158**	44 55N	91 22W
Chippewa, R.	**158**	44 45N	91 55W
Chipping Campden	**28**	52 4N	1 48W
Chipping Norton	**28**	51 56N	1 32W
Chipping Ongar	**29**	51 43N	0 15 E
Chipping Sodbury	**28**	51 31N	2 23W
Chiquian	**174**	10 10 S	77 0W
Chiquimula	**166**	14 51N	89 37W
Chiquinquirá	**174**	5 37N	73 50W
Chir, R.	**83**	48 45N	42 10 E
Chirala	**97**	15 50N	80 20 E
Chiramba	**127**	16 55 S	34 39 E
Chiran	**110**	31 22N	130 27 E
Chiras	**93**	35 14N	65 40 E
Chirawa	**94**	28 14N	75 42 E
Chirayinkil	**97**	8 41N	76 49 E
Chirbury	**28**	52 35N	3 6W
Chirchik	**85**	41 29N	69 35 E
Chirfa	**117**	20 55N	12 14 E
Chiricahua Pk.	**161**	31 53N	109 14W
Chirikof I.	**147**	55 50N	155 40W
Chiriqui, Golfo de	**166**	8 0N	82 10W
Chiriquí, Lago de	**166**	9 10N	82 0W
Chiriquí, Vol.	**166**	8 55N	82 35W
Chirivira Falls	**127**	21 10 S	32 12 E
Chirk	**31**	52 57N	3 4W
Chirmiri	**99**	23 15N	82 20 E
Chirnogi	**70**	44 7N	26 32 E
Chirnside	**35**	55 47N	2 11W
Chiromo	**125**	16 30 S	35 7 E
Chirpan	**67**	42 10N	25 19 E
Chirripó Grande, cerro	**166**	9 29N	83 29W
Chisamba	**127**	14 55 S	28 20 E
Chisapani Garhi	**99**	27 30N	84 2 E
Ch'ishan	**106**	34 28N	107 35 E
Chishan	**106**	35 36N	110 59 E
Ch'ishan	**109**	22 44N	120 31 E
Chishmy	**84**	54 35N	55 23 E
Chisholm	**152**	54 55N	114 10W
Chishou	**108**	28 12N	109 43 E
Chishui	**109**	27 14N	115 10 E
Chisimba Falls	**127**	10 12 S	30 56 E
Chisineu Criş	**66**	46 32N	21 37 E
Chisledon	**28**	51 30N	1 44W
Chisone, R.	**62**	45 0N	7 5 E
Chisos Mts.	**159**	29 20N	103 15W
Chistian Mandi	**94**	29 50N	72 55 E
Chistopol	**81**	55 25N	50 38 E
Chita, Colomb.	**174**	6 11N	72 28W
Chita, U.S.S.R.	**77**	52 0N	113 25 E
Chitado	**125**	17 10 S	14 8 E
Ch'it'ai	**105**	44 1N	89 28 E
Chitapur	**96**	17 10N	76 50 E
Chitembo	**125**	13 30 S	16 50 E
Chitina	**147**	61 30N	144 30W
Chitinghsilin	**105**	32 51N	92 28 E
Chitipa	**127**	9 41 S	33 19 E
Chitokoloki	**125**	13 43 S	23 4 E
Chitorgarh	**94**	24 52N	74 43 E
Chitrakot	**96**	19 20N	81 40 E
Chitral	**93**	35 50N	71 56 E
Chitravati, R.	**97**	14 30N	78 0 E
Chitré	**167**	7 59N	80 27W
Chitse	**106**	36 54N	114 52 E
Chittagong	**98**	22 19N	91 55 E
Chittagong □	**98**	24 5N	91 25 E
Chittoor	**97**	13 15N	79 5 E
Chittur	**97**	10 40N	76 45 E
Chitu	**123**	8 38N	37 58 E
Ch'itung, Hunan, China	**109**	26 47N	112 7 E
Ch'itung, Kiangsu, China	**109**	31 49N	121 40 E
Chiuant'u	**107**	42 33N	128 19 E
Chiuchaohua	**108**	32 20N	105 45 E
Chiuch'engch'i	**108**	27 10N	108 42 E
Chiuchiang, Kiangsi, China	**109**	29 43N	115 55 E
Chiuchiang, Kwangtung, China	**109**	22 50N	112 50 E
Chiuch'üan	**105**	39 46N	98 34 E
Chiuhsiangch'eng	**109**	33 13N	114 50 E
Chiukuanch'eng	**106**	35 50N	115 22 E
Chiuling Shan	**109**	28 50N	114 20 E
Chiuliuch'eng	**108**	24 32N	109 15 E
Chiulung	**108**	28 59N	101 32 E
Ch'iungchou Haihsia	**100**	20 10N	110 15 E
Ch'iunghai	**100**	19 15N	110 26 E
Chiunglai	**108**	30 25N	103 30 E
Chiunglai Shan	**108**	31 20N	102 50 E
Ch'iungshan	**100**	19 51N	110 26 E
Chiuningkang	**109**	26 48N	114 6 E
Ch'iupei	**108**	24 3N	104 12 E
Chiushench'iu	**106**	33 10N	115 8 E
Chiushengch'i	**108**	27 31N	109 12 E
Chiusi	**63**	43 1N	11 58 E
Chiut'ai	**107**	44 10N	125 49 E
Chiutaosha	**106**	35 39N	103 45 E
Chiuwuch'ing	**106**	39 23N	116 53 E
Chiva	**59**	39 27N	0 41W
Chivasso	**62**	45 10N	7 52 E
Chivilcoy	**172**	35 0 S	60 0W
Chiwanda	**127**	11 23 S	34 55 E
Chiwefwe	**127**	13 37 S	29 31 E
Chiyang	**107**	37 0N	117 13 E
Ch'iyang	**109**	20 35N	111 52 E
Chiyüan	**106**	35 5N	112 39 E
Chiyün	**109**	28 35N	120 2 E
Chizera	**127**	13 10 S	25 0 E
Chkalov = Orenburg	**78**	52 0N	55 5 E
Chkolovsk	**81**	56 50N	43 10 E
Chlumec	**52**	50 9N	15 29 E
Chmielnik	**54**	50 37N	20 43 E
Cho Bo	**100**	20 46N	105 10 E
Cho Do	**107**	38 30N	124 40 E
Cho Phuoc	**101**	10 26N	107 18 E
Choba	**126**	2 30N	38 5 E
Chobe National Park	**128**	21 30 S	25 0 E
Chobe, R.	**128**	18 10 S	24 10 E
Chobol	**121**	11 53N	13 1 E
Chochiwŏn	**107**	36 37N	127 18 E
Chocianów	**54**	51 35N	15 33 E
Chociwel	**54**	53 29N	15 21 E
Chocó □	**174**	6 0N	77 0W
Chocontá	**174**	5 9N	73 41W
Chodaków	**54**	52 16N	20 18 E
Chodavaram	**96**	17 40N	82 50 E
Chodecz	**54**	52 56N	19 2 E
Chodziez	**54**	52 58N	17 0 E
Choele Choel	**176**	39 11 S	65 40W
Chōfu	**111**	35 39N	139 33 E
Chohsien	**106**	39 30N	116 0 E
Choiseul I.	**130**	7 0 S	156 40 E
Choisy-le-Roi	**43**	48 45N	2 24 E
Choix	**164**	26 40N	108 10W
Chojna	**54**	52 58N	14 25 E
Chojnice	**54**	53 42N	17 40 E
Chojnów	**54**	51 25N	15 58 E
Choke Mts.	**123**	11 18N	37 15 E
Chokurdakh	**77**	70 38N	147 55 E
Cholame	**163**	35 44N	120 18W
Cholet	**42**	47 4N	0 52W
Chollerton	**35**	55 4N	2 7W
Cholpon-Ata	**85**	42 40N	77 6 E
Cholsey	**28**	51 34N	1 10W
Cholu	**106**	40 19N	115 5 E
Choluteca	**166**	13 20N	87 14W
Choluteca, R.	**166**	13 5N	87 20W
Chom Bung	**100**	13 37N	99 36 E
Chom Thong	**100**	18 25N	98 41 E
Choma	**127**	16 48 S	26 59 E
Chomen Swamp	**123**	9 20N	37 10 E

Chomu **Clee Hills**

Chomu	**94**	27 15N	75 40 E
Chomutov	**52**	50 28N	13 23 E
Chon Buri	**100**	13 22N	100 59 E
Chon Thanh	**101**	11 24N	106 36 E
Chŏnan	**107**	36 48N	127 9 E
Chonburi	**101**	13 21N	101 1 E
Chone	**174**	0 40 S	80 0W
Chong Kai	**100**	13 57N	103 35 E
Chong Mek	**100**	15 10N	105 27 E
Chŏngdo	**107**	35 38N	128 42 E
Chŏngha	**107**	36 12N	129 21 E
Chŏngjin	**107**	41 47N	129 50 E
Chŏngju	**107**	39 40N	125 5 E
Chŏngułp	**107**	35 35N	126 50 E
Chŏnju	**107**	35 50N	127 4 E
Chonos, Arch. de los	**176**	45 0 S	75 0W
Chopda	**96**	21 20N	75 15 E
Chopim, R.	**173**	25 35 S	53 5W
Choptank, R.	**162**	38 41N	76 0W
Chorbat La	**95**	34 42N	76 37 E
Chorley	**32**	53 39N	2 39W
Chormet el Melah	**119**	30 11N	16 29 E
Chorolque, Cerro	**172**	20 59 S	66 5W
Choroszcz	**54**	53 10N	22 59 E
Chortkov	**80**	49 2N	25 46 E
Chorul Tso	**95**	32 30N	82 30 E
Chŏrwŏn	**107**	38 15N	127 10 E
Chorzele	**54**	53 15N	21 2 E
Chorzów	**54**	50 18N	19 0 E
Chos-Malal	**172**	37 15 S	70 5W
Chosan	**107**	40 50N	125 47 E
Choshi	**111**	35 45N	140 45 E
Choszczno	**54**	53 7N	15 25 E
Choteau	**160**	47 50N	112 10W
Chotila	**94**	22 30N	71 15 E
Chotzu	**106**	40 52N	112 33 E
Chou Shan	**109**	30 2N	122 6 E
Chouchih	**106**	34 8N	108 14 E
Chouch'ü	**106**	33 46N	104 18 E
Chouning	**109**	27 15N	119 13 E
Chouts'un	**107**	36 48N	117 52 E
Ch'ouyang	**108**	23 14N	104 35 E
Chowchilla	**163**	37 11N	120 12W
Chowkham	**98**	20 52N	97 28 E
Choybalsan	**105**	48 4N	114 30 E
Christchurch, N.Z.	**143**	43 33 S	172 47 E
Christchurch, U.K.	**28**	50 44N	1 47W
Christiana, S. Afr.	**128**	27 52 S	25 8 E
Christiana, U.S.A.	**162**	39 40N	75 40W
Christiansfeld	**73**	55 21N	9 29 E
Christiansö, I.	**73**	55 19N	15 12 E
Christiansted	**147**	17 45N	64 42W
Christie B.	**153**	62 32N	111 10W
Christina, R.	**153**	56 40N	111 3W
Christmas Cr.	**136**	18 53 S	125 55 E
Christmas Creek	**136**	18 29 S	125 23 E
Christmas I., Ind. Oc.	**142**	10 0 S	105 40 E
Christmas I., Pac. Oc.	**131**	1 58N	157 27W
Christopher L.	**137**	24 49 S	127 42 E
Chrudim	**52**	49 58N	15 43 E
Chrzanów	**54**	50 10N	19 21 E
Chtimba	**127**	10 35 S	34 13 E
Chu	**85**	43 36N	73 42 E
Ch'u Chiang, R.	**108**	30 2N	106 19 E
Chu Chua	**152**	51 22N	120 10W
Chu Lai	**100**	15 28N	108 45 E
Chu, R., U.S.S.R.	**85**	45 0N	67 44 E
Chu, R., Viet.	**100**	19 53N	105 45 E
Chuadanga	**98**	23 38N	88 51 E
Ch'üanchou, Fukien, China	**109**	24 56N	118 35 E
Ch'üanchou, Kwangsi-Chuang, China	**109**	25 59N	111 4 E
Chuangho	**107**	39 42N	123 0 E
Chüannan	**109**	24 50N	114 40 E
Chūbu ☐	**112**	36 45N	137 30 E
Chubut, R.	**176**	43 0 S	70 0W
Chuch'eng	**107**	36 0N	119 16 E
Chuch'i	**108**	32 19N	109 52 E
Chuchi, Chekiang, China	**109**	29 43N	120 14 E
Chuchi, Honan, China	**106**	34 27N	115 39 E
Chuchi L.	**152**	55 12N	124 30W
Ch'uching	**108**	25 34N	103 45 E
Chuchou	**109**	27 50N	113 10 E
Chudleigh	**30**	50 35N	3 36W
Chudovo	**80**	59 10N	31 30 E
Chudskoye, Oz.	**80**	58 13N	27 30 E
Ch'üehshan	**109**	32 48N	114 1 E
Chugach Mts.	**147**	62 0N	146 0W
Chugiak	**147**	61 7N	149 10W
Chuginadak I.	**147**	52 50N	169 45W
Chūgoku ☐	**110**	35 0N	133 0 E
Chūgoku-Sanchi	**110**	35 0N	133 0 E
Chuguyev	**82**	49 55N	36 45 E
Chugwater	**158**	41 48N	104 47W
Chuhai	**109**	22 17N	113 34 E
Chühsien	**107**	35 35N	118 49 E
Ch'uhsien, China	**109**	28 57N	118 58 E
Ch'uhsien, China	**109**	32 18N	118 18 E
Chuhsien	**105**	28 57N	118 58 E
Ch'ühsien	**108**	30 51N	107 1 E
Ch'uhsiung	**108**	25 2N	101 32 E
Chüjung	**109**	31 56N	119 10 E
Chukai	**101**	4 13N	103 25 E
Chukhloma	**81**	58 45N	42 40 E
Chūko	**111**	36 44N	139 27 E
Chukotskiy Khrebet	**77**	68 0N	175 0 E
Chukotskiy, Mys	**77**	66 10N	169 3 E
Chukotskoye More	**77**	68 0N	175 0W
Chula Vista	**163**	32 39N	117 8W
Chulak-Kurgan	**85**	43 46N	69 9 E
Chülu	**106**	37 13N	115 1 E

Chulucanas	**174**	5 0 S	80 0W
Chum Phae	**100**	16 32N	102 6 E
Chum Saeng	**100**	15 55N	100 15 E
Chumar	**95**	32 40N	78 35 E
Chumatien	**109**	33 0N	114 4 E
Chumbicha	**172**	29 0 S	66 10W
Chumerna	**67**	42 45N	25 55 E
Chumikan	**77**	54 40N	135 10 E
Chumphon	**101**	10 35N	99 14 E
Chumuare	**127**	14 31 S	31 50 E
Chumunjin	**107**	37 55N	127 44 E
Chunchŏn	**107**	37 58N	127 44 E
Chunga	**127**	15 0 S	26 2 E
Ch'ungan	**109**	27 45N	118 0 E
Ch'ungch'ing, Szechwan, China	**108**	29 30N	106 30 E
Ch'ungch'ing, Szechwan, China	**108**	30 27N	103 43 E
Chungch'üantzu	**106**	39 22N	102 42 E
Chunggang üp	**107**	41 48N	126 48 E
Chunghsiang	**109**	31 10N	112 35 E
Chunghsien	**108**	30 17N	108 4 E
Chunghwa	**107**	38 52N	125 47 E
Ch'ungi	**109**	25 42N	114 19 E
Ch'ungjen	**109**	27 44N	116 2 E
Chungju	**107**	36 58N	127 58 E
Chungkang	**107**	43 42N	127 37 E
Chungking = Ch'ungch'ing	**108**	29 30N	106 30 E
Ch'ungli	**106**	40 5N	115 12 E
Chungli	**109**	24 57N	121 13 E
Ch'ungming	**109**	31 27N	121 24 E
Ch'ungming Tao, I.	**109**	31 35N	121 40 E
Chungmu	**107**	34 50N	128 20 E
Chungning	**106**	35 22N	105 40 E
Chungshan, Kwangsi-Chuang, China	**109**	24 30N	111 17 E
Chungshan, Kwangtung, China	**109**	22 31N	113 20 E
Ch'ungshuiho	**106**	39 54N	111 34 E
Ch'ungte	**109**	30 32N	120 26 E
Chungt'iaoshan	**106**	35 0N	111 30 E
Chungtien	**108**	27 51N	99 42 E
Ch'ungtso	**108**	22 20N	107 20 E
Chungtu	**108**	24 41N	109 42 E
Chungwei	**106**	37 35N	105 10 E
Chungyang	**106**	37 24N	111 10 E
Chungyang Shanmo	**109**	23 10N	121 0 E
Chungyüan	**100**	19 9N	110 28 E
Chünhsien	**109**	32 40N	111 15 E
Chunian	**94**	31 10N	74 0 E
Chunya	**127**	8 30 S	33 27 E
Chunya ☐	**126**	7 48 S	33 0 E
Ch'unyang	**107**	43 42N	129 26 E
Chuquibamba	**174**	15 47N	72 44W
Chuquicamata	**172**	22 15 S	69 0W
Chuquisaca ☐	**172**	23 30 S	63 30W
Chur	**51**	46 52N	9 32 E
Churachandpur	**98**	24 20N	93 40 E
Church Hill	**38**	55 0N	7 53W
Church House	**152**	50 20N	125 10W
Church Stretton	**28**	52 32N	2 49W
Churchdown	**28**	51 53N	2 9W
Churchill	**153**	58 47N	94 11W
Churchill, C.	**153**	58 46N	93 12W
Churchill Falls	**151**	53 36N	64 19W
Churchill L.	**153**	55 55N	108 20W
Churchill Pk.	**152**	58 10N	125 10W
Churchill, R., Man., Can.	**153**	58 47N	94 12W
Churchill, R., Newf., Can.	**151**	53 19N	60 10W
Churchill, R., Sask., Can.	**153**	58 47N	94 12W
Churchtown	**39**	52 12N	6 20W
Churfisten	**51**	47 8N	9 17 E
Churston Ferrers	**30**	50 23N	3 32W
Churu	**94**	28 20N	75 0 E
Churuguaro	**174**	10 49N	69 32W
Churwalden	**51**	46 47N	9 33 E
Chusan	**109**	32 13N	110 24 E
Chushul	**95**	33 40N	78 40 E
Chusovaya, R.	**84**	58 18N	56 22 E
Chusovoy	**84**	58 15N	57 40 E
Chust	**85**	41 0N	71 13 E
Ch'ützu	**106**	36 24N	107 27 E
Chuuronjang	**107**	41 35N	129 40 E
Chuvash A.S.S.R. ☐	**81**	55 30N	48 0 E
Chuwassu	**108**	28 48N	97 27 E
Ch'üwu	**106**	35 35N	111 23 E
Ch'üyang	**106**	38 37N	114 41 E
Chüyeh	**106**	35 23N	116 6 E
Ciacova	**66**	45 35N	21 10 E
Cicero	**156**	41 48N	87 48W
Cicero Dantas	**170**	10 36 S	38 23W
Cidacos, R.	**58**	42 15N	2 10W
Cide	**82**	41 40N	32 50 E
Ciechanów	**54**	52 52N	20 38 E
Ciechanów ☐	**54**	53 0N	20 30 E
Ciechocinek	**54**	52 53N	18 45 E
Ciego de Avila	**166**	21 50N	78 50W
Ciénaga	**174**	11 1N	74 15W
Ciénaga de Oro	**174**	8 53N	75 37W
Cienfuegos	**166**	22 10N	80 30W
Cieplice Śląskie Zdrój	**54**	50 50N	15 40 E
Cierp	**44**	42 55N	0 40 E
Cies, Islas	**56**	42 12N	8 55W
Cieszyn	**54**	49 45N	18 35 E
Cieza	**59**	38 17N	1 23W
Cifuentes	**58**	40 47N	2 37W
Ciha Pa.	**101**	22 20N	103 47 E
Cijara, Pantano de	**57**	39 18N	4 52W
Cijulang	**103**	7 42 S	108 27 E

Cikampek	**103**	6 23 S	107 28 E
Cilacap	**103**	7 43 S	109 0 E
Cıldır	**83**	41 10N	43 20 E
Cilgerran	**31**	52 4N	4 39W
Cilician Gates P.	**92**	37 20N	34 52 E
Cilician Taurus	**92**	36 40N	34 0 E
Cilnicu	**70**	44 54N	23 4 E
Cimarron, Kans., U.S.A.	**159**	37 50N	100 20W
Cimarron, N. Mex., U.S.A.	**159**	36 30N	104 52W
Cimarron, R.	**159**	37 10N	102 10W
Cimpia Turzii	**70**	46 34N	23 53 E
Cimpina	**70**	45 10N	25 45 E
Cîmpulung, Argeş, Rumania	**70**	45 17N	25 3 E
Cîmpulung, Suceava, Rumania	**70**	47 32N	25 30 E
Cimpuri	**67**	46 0N	26 50 E
Cinca, R.	**58**	42 20N	0 9 E
Cincer	**66**	43 55N	17 5 E
Cinch, R.	**157**	36 0N	84 15W
Cincinnati	**156**	39 10N	84 26W
Cincinnatus	**162**	42 33N	75 54W
Cinderford	**28**	51 49N	2 30W
Cîndeşti	**70**	45 15N	26 42 E
Ciney	**47**	50 18N	5 5 E
Cinigiano	**63**	42 53N	11 23 E
Cinogli	**63**	43 23N	13 10 E
Cinto, Mt.	**45**	42 24N	8 54 E
Cioranii	**70**	44 45N	26 25 E
Ciotat, La	**45**	43 12N	5 36 E
Čiovo	**63**	43 30N	16 17 E
Cipó	**171**	11 6 S	38 31W
Circle, Alaska, U.S.A.	**147**	65 50N	144 10W
Circle, Montana, U.S.A.	**158**	47 26N	105 35W
Circleville, Ohio, U.S.A.	**156**	39 35N	82 57W
Circleville, Utah, U.S.A.	**161**	38 12N	112 24W
Cirebon	**103**	6 45 S	108 32 E
Cirencester	**28**	51 43N	1 59W
Cireşu	**70**	44 47N	22 31 E
Cirey-sur-Vezouze	**43**	48 35N	6 57 E
Ciriè	**62**	45 14N	7 35 E
Cirò	**65**	39 23N	17 3 E
Cisco	**159**	32 25N	99 0W
Cislău	**70**	45 14N	26 33 E
Cisna	**54**	49 12N	22 20 E
Cisneros	**174**	6 33N	75 4W
Cisnădie	**70**	45 42N	24 9 E
Cisterna di Latina	**64**	41 35N	12 50 E
Cisternino	**65**	40 45N	17 26 E
Cité de Cansado	**116**	20 51N	17 0W
Citega (Kitega)	**126**	3 30 S	29 58 E
Citeli-Ckaro	**83**	41 33N	46 0 E
Citlaltépetl, mt.	**165**	19 0N	97 20W
Citrusdal	**128**	32 35 S	19 0 E
Città della Pieve	**63**	42 57N	12 0 E
Città di Castello	**63**	43 27N	12 14 E
Città Sant' Angelo	**63**	42 32N	14 5 E
Cittadella	**63**	45 39N	11 48 E
Cittaducale	**63**	42 24N	12 58 E
Cittanova	**65**	38 22N	16 0 E
Ciucaş, mt.	**70**	45 31N	25 56 E
Ciudad Acuña	**164**	29 20N	101 10W
Ciudad Altamirano	**164**	18 20N	100 40W
Ciudad Bolívar	**174**	8 5N	63 30W
Ciudad Camargo	**164**	27 41N	105 10W
Ciudad de Valles	**165**	22 0N	98 30W
Ciudad del Carmen	**165**	18 20N	97 50W
Ciudad Delicias = Delicias	**164**	28 10N	105 30W
Ciudad Guerrero	**164**	28 33N	107 28W
Ciudad Guzmán	**164**	19 40N	103 30W
Ciudad Juárez	**164**	31 40N	106 28W
Ciudad Madero	**165**	22 19N	97 50W
Ciudad Mante	**165**	22 50N	99 0W
Ciudad Obregón	**164**	27 28N	109 59W
Ciudad Piar	**174**	7 27N	63 19W
Ciudad Real	**57**	38 59N	3 55W
Ciudad Real ☐	**57**	38 50N	4 0W
Ciudad Rodrigo	**56**	40 35N	6 32W
Ciudad Trujillo = Sto. Domingo	**167**	18 30N	70 0W
Ciudad Victoria	**165**	23 41N	99 9W
Ciudadela	**58**	40 0N	3 50 E
Ciulniţa	**70**	44 26N	27 22 E
Civa, B.	**82**	41 20N	36 40 E
Cividale del Friuli	**63**	46 6N	13 25 E
Civita Castellana	**63**	42 18N	12 24 E
Civitanova Marche	**63**	43 18N	13 41 E
Civitavécchia	**63**	42 6N	11 46 E
Civitella del Tronto	**63**	42 48N	13 40 E
Civray	**44**	46 10N	0 17 E
Çivril	**92**	38 20N	29 55 E
Cixerri, R.	**64**	39 45N	8 40 E
Cizre	**92**	37 19N	42 10 E
Clabach	**34**	56 38N	6 36W
Clabby	**38**	54 24N	7 22W
Clach Leathad	**34**	56 36N	7 52W
Clachan, N. Uist., U.K.	**36**	57 33N	7 20W
Clachan, Strathclyde, U.K.	**34**	55 45N	5 35W
Clackline	**137**	31 40 S	116 32 E
Clackmannan	**35**	56 10N	3 50W
Clackmannan (☐)	**26**	56 10N	3 47W
Clacton-on-Sea	**29**	51 47N	1 10 E
Cladich	**34**	56 21N	5 5W
Claire, L.	**152**	58 35N	112 5W
Clairemont	**159**	33 9N	100 44W
Clairvaux-les-Laes	**45**	46 35N	5 45 E
Clamecy	**43**	47 28N	3 30 E

Clane	**39**	53 18N	6 40W
Clanfield	**29**	50 56N	1 0W
Clanton	**157**	32 48N	86 36W
Clanwilliam	**128**	32 11 S	18 52 E
Clar, L. nan	**37**	58 17N	4 8W
Clara	**39**	53 20N	7 38W
Clara, R.	**138**	19 8 S	142 30 E
Claraville	**163**	35 24N	118 20W
Clare, N.S.W., Austral.	**140**	33 24 S	143 54 E
Clare, S. Austral., Austral.	**140**	33 50 S	138 37 E
Clare, N. Ireland, U.K.	**38**	54 25N	6 19W
Clare, Suffolk, U.K.	**29**	52 5N	0 36 E
Clare, U.S.A.	**156**	43 47N	84 45W
Clare ☐	**39**	52 20N	7 38W
Clare I.	**38**	53 48N	10 0W
Clare, R.	**38**	53 20N	9 0W
Clarecastle	**39**	52 50N	8 58W
Clareen	**39**	53 4N	7 49W
Claregalaway	**39**	53 20N	8 57W
Claremont	**162**	43 23N	72 20W
Claremont Pt.	**138**	14 1 S	143 41 E
Claremore	**159**	36 20N	95 20W
Claremorris	**38**	53 45N	9 0W
Clarence I.	**13**	61 30 S	53 50W
Clarence, I.	**176**	54 0 S	72 0W
Clarence, R., Austral.	**139**	29 25 S	153 22 E
Clarence, R., N.Z.	**143**	42 10 S	173 56 E
Clarence Str., Austral.	**136**	12 0 S	131 0 E
Clarence Str., U.S.A.	**152**	55 40N	132 10W
Clarence Town	**167**	23 6N	74 59W
Clarendon, Ark., U.S.A.	**159**	34 41N	91 20W
Clarendon, Tex., U.S.A.	**159**	34 58N	100 54W
Clarenville	**151**	48 10N	54 1W
Claresholm	**152**	50 0N	113 45W
Clarie Coast	**13**	67 0 S	135 0 E
Clarinbridge	**39**	53 13N	8 55W
Clarinda	**158**	40 45N	95 0W
Clarion	**158**	42 41N	93 46W
Clark	**158**	44 55N	97 45W
Clark Fork	**160**	48 9N	116 9W
Clark Fork, R.	**160**	48 0N	115 40W
Clark Hill Res.	**157**	33 45N	82 20W
Clarkdale	**161**	34 53N	112 3W
Clarke City	**151**	50 12N	66 38W
Clarke, I.	**138**	40 32 S	148 10 E
Clarke L.	**153**	54 24N	106 54W
Clarke Ra.	**138**	20 45 S	148 20 E
Clarks Fork, R.	**160**	45 0N	109 30W
Clark's Harbour	**151**	43 25N	65 38W
Clarks Station	**163**	38 8N	116 42W
Clarks Summit	**162**	41 31N	75 44W
Clarksburg	**156**	39 18N	80 21W
Clarksdale	**159**	34 12N	90 33W
Clarkston	**160**	46 28N	117 2W
Clarksville, Ark., U.S.A.	**159**	35 29N	93 27W
Clarksville, Tenn., U.S.A.	**157**	36 32N	87 20W
Clarksville, Tex., U.S.A.	**159**	33 37N	94 59W
Claro, R.	**171**	19 8 S	50 40W
Clashmore	**37**	57 53N	4 8W
Clatskanie	**160**	46 9N	123 12W
Clatteringshaws L.	**34**	55 3N	4 17W
Claude	**159**	35 8N	101 22W
Claudio	**171**	20 26 S	44 46W
Claudy	**38**	54 55N	7 10W
Claunie L.	**36**	57 8N	5 6W
Claveria	**103**	18 37N	121 15 E
Claverley	**28**	52 32N	2 19W
Clay	**163**	38 17N	121 10W
Clay Center	**158**	39 27N	97 9W
Clay Cross	**33**	53 11N	1 26W
Clay Hd.	**32**	54 13N	4 23W
Claydon	**29**	52 6N	1 7 E
Clayette, La	**45**	46 17N	4 19 E
Claymont	**162**	39 48N	75 28W
Claymore, oilfield	**19**	58 30N	0 15W
Claypool	**161**	33 27N	110 55W
Clayton, Idaho, U.S.A.	**160**	44 12N	114 31W
Clayton, N. Mex., U.S.A.	**159**	36 30N	103 10W
Cle Elum	**160**	47 15N	120 57W
Cleady	**39**	51 53N	9 32W
Clear C.	**39**	51 26N	9 30W
Clear I.	**39**	51 26N	9 30W
Clear Lake, Calif., U.S.A.	**160**	39 5N	122 47W
Clear Lake, S.D., U.S.A.	**158**	44 48N	96 41W
Clear Lake, Wash., U.S.A.	**160**	48 27N	122 15W
Clear Lake Res.	**160**	41 55N	121 10W
Clearfield, Pa., U.S.A.	**156**	41 0N	78 27W
Clearfield, Utah, U.S.A.	**160**	41 10N	112 0W
Clearmont	**160**	44 43N	106 29W
Clearwater, Can.	**152**	51 38N	120 2W
Clearwater, U.S.A.	**157**	27 58N	82 45W
Clearwater Cr.	**152**	61 36N	125 30W
Clearwater L.	**150**	56 10N	75 0W
Clearwater, Mts.	**160**	46 20N	115 30W
Clearwater Prov. Park	**153**	54 0N	101 0W
Clearwater, R., Alta., Can.	**152**	52 22N	114 57W
Clearwater, R., Alta., Can.	**153**	56 44N	111 23W
Clearwater, R., B.C., Can.	**152**	51 38N	120 3W
Cleat	**37**	58 45N	2 56W
Cleator Moor	**32**	54 30N	3 32W
Cleburne	**159**	32 18N	97 25W
Cleddau R.	**31**	51 46N	4 44W
Clee Hills	**23**	52 26N	2 35W

Cleethorpes Columbia

Cleethorpes **33** 53 33N 0 2W
Cleeve Cloud **28** 51 56N 2 0W
Cleggan **38** 53 33N 10 7W
Clelles **45** 44 50N 5 38E
Clemency **47** 49 35N 5 53E
Clent **28** 52 25N 2 6W
Cleobury Mortimer **28** 52 23N 2 28W
Clerke Reef **136** 17 22S 119 20E
Clerks Rocks **13** 56 0S 36 30W
Clermont **133** 22 49S 147 39E
Clermont-en-Argonne **43** 49 5N 5 4E
Clermont-Ferrand **44** 45 46N 3 4E
Clermont-l'Hérault **44** 43 38N 3 26E
Clerval **43** 47 25N 6 30E
Cléry-Saint-André **43** 47 50N 1 46E
Cles **62** 46 21N 11 4E
Clevedon **28** 51 26N 2 52W
Cleveland, Austral. **139** 27 30S 153 15E
Cleveland, Miss., U.S.A. **159** 33 43N 90 43W
Cleveland, Ohio, U.S.A. **156** 41 28N 81 43W
Cleveland, Okla., U.S.A. **159** 36 21N 96 33W
Cleveland, Tenn., U.S.A. **157** 35 9N 84 52W
Cleveland, Tex., U.S.A. **159** 30 18N 95 0W
Cleveland □ **33** 54 35N 1 8E
Cleveland, C. **138** 19 11S 147 1E
Cleveland Hills **33** 54 25N 1 11W
Clevelândia **173** 26 24S 52 23W
Clevvaux **47** 50 4N 6 2E
Clew Bay **38** 53 54N 9 50W
Clewiston **157** 26 44N 80 50W
Cley **29** 52 57N 1 3E
Clifden, Ireland **38** 53 30N 10 2W
Clifden, N.Z. **143** 46 1S 167 42E
Clifden B. **38** 53 29N 10 5W
Cliff **161** 33 0N 108 44W
Cliffe **29** 51 27N 0 31E
Cliffony **38** 54 25N 8 28W
Clifford **28** 52 6N 3 6W
Clift Sound **36** 60 4N 1 17W
Clifton, Austral. **139** 27 59S 151 53E
Clifton, Ariz., U.S.A. **161** 33 8N 109 23W
Clifton, Tex., U.S.A. **159** 31 46N 97 35W
Clifton Forge **156** 37 49N 79 51W
Climax **153** 49 10N 108 20W
Clingmans Dome **157** 35 35N 83 30W
Clint **161** 31 37N 106 11W
Clinton, B.C., Can. **152** 51 6N 121 35W
Clinton, Ont., Can. **150** 43 37N 81 32W
Clinton, N.Z. **143** 46 12S 169 23E
Clinton, Ark., U.S.A. **159** 35 37N 92 30W
Clinton, Conn., U.S.A. **162** 41 17N 72 32W
Clinton, Ill., U.S.A. **158** 40 8N 89 0W
Clinton, Ind., U.S.A. **156** 39 40N 87 22W
Clinton, Iowa, U.S.A. **158** 41 50N 90 12W
Clinton, Mass., U.S.A. **162** 42 26N 71 40W
Clinton, Mo., U.S.A. **158** 38 20N 93 46W
Clinton, N.C., U.S.A. **157** 35 5N 78 15W
Clinton, Okla., U.S.A. **159** 35 30N 99 0W
Clinton, S.C., U.S.A. **157** 34 30N 81 54W
Clinton, Tenn., U.S.A. **157** 36 6N 84 10W
Clinton C. **138** 22 30S 150 45E
Clinton Colden L. **148** 64 58N 107 27W
Clintonville **158** 44 35N 88 46W
Clipperton, I. **143** 10 18N 109 13W
Clipston **29** 52 26N 0 58W
Clisson **42** 47 5N 1 16W
Clitheroe **32** 53 52N 2 23W
Clive **142** 39 36S 176 58E
Clive L. **152** 63 13N 118 54W
Cloates, Pt. **136** 22 43S 113 40E
Clocolan **129** 28 55S 27 34E
Clodomira **172** 27 35S 64 14W
Clogh **39** 52 51N 7 11W
Cloghan, Donegal, Ireland **38** 54 50N 7 56W
Cloghan, Offaly, Ireland **39** 53 13N 7 53W
Cloghan, W'meath, Ireland **38** 53 33N 7 15W
Clogheen **39** 52 17N 8 0W
Clogher **38** 54 25N 7 10W
Clogher Hd. **38** 53 48N 6 15W
Cloghjordan **39** 52 57N 8 2W
Cloghran **38** 53 26N 6 14W
Clonakilty **39** 51 37N 8 53W
Clonakilty B. **39** 51 33N 8 50W
Clonbur **38** 53 32N 9 21W
Cloncurry, Austral. **138** 20 40S 140 28E
Cloncurry, Ireland **38** 53 26N 6 47W
Cloncurry, R. **138** 18 37S 140 40E
Clondalkin **39** 53 20N 6 25W
Clonee **38** 53 25N 6 28W
Cloneen **39** 52 28N 7 36W
Clones **38** 54 10N 7 13W
Clonkeen **39** 51 59N 9 20W
Clonmany **38** 55 16N 7 24W
Clonmel **39** 52 22N 7 42W
Clonmore **39** 52 49N 6 35W
Clonroche **39** 52 27N 6 42W
Clontarf **38** 53 22N 6 10W
Cloonakool **38** 54 6N 8 47W
Cloone **38** 53 57N 7 47W
Cloonfad **38** 53 41N 8 45W
Cloppenburg **48** 52 50N 8 3E
Cloquet **158** 46 40N 92 30W
Clorinda **172** 25 16S 57 45W
Closeburn **35** 55 13N 3 45W
Cloud Peak **160** 44 30N 107 10W
Cloudcroft **161** 33 0N 105 48W
Cloudy B. **143** 41 25S 174 10E
Clough, Ballymena, U.K. **38** 54 58N 6 16W
Clough, Down, U.K. **38** 54 18N 5 50W
Cloughton **33** 54 20N 0 27W
Clova **37** 56 50N 3 4W
Clovelly **30** 51 0N 4 25W
Cloverdale **160** 38 49N 123 0W
Clovis, Calif., U.S.A. **163** 36 54N 119 45W
Clovis, N. Mex., U.S.A. **159** 34 20N 103 10W
Clowne **33** 53 18N 1 16W
Cloyne **39** 51 52N 8 7W
Club Terrace **141** 37 35S 148 58E
Cluj-Napoca **70** 46 47N 23 38E
Cluj □ **70** 46 45N 23 30E
Clun **28** 52 26N 3 2W
Clun Forest **28** 52 27N 3 7W
Clunbury **28** 52 25N 2 55W
Clunes, Austral. **140** 37 20S 143 45E
Clunes, U.K. **36** 56 57N 4 58W
Cluny **45** 46 26N 4 38E
Cluses **45** 46 5N 6 35E
Clusone **62** 45 54N 9 58E
Clutha, R. **143** 46 20S 169 49E
Clwyd □ **31** 53 5N 3 20W
Clwyd, R. **31** 53 12N 3 30W
Clwydian Ra. **31** 53 10N 3 15W
Clydach **31** 51 42N 3 54W
Clyde, Austral. **139** 28 48S 143 40E
Clyde, Can. **149** 70 30N 68 30W
Clyde, N.Z. **143** 45 12S 169 20E
Clyde, Firth of **34** 55 20N 5 0W
Clyde, R. **34** 55 46N 4 58W
Clydebank **34** 55 54N 4 25W
Clydesdale **35** 55 42N 3 50W
Clynnog-fawr **31** 53 2N 4 22W
Cõa, R. **56** 40 45N 7 0W
Coachella **163** 33 44N 116 13W
Coachella Canal **163** 32 43N 114 57W
Coachford **39** 51 54N 8 48W
Coachman's Cove **151** 50 6N 56 20W
Coagh **38** 54 39N 6 37W
Coahoma **159** 32 17N 101 20W
Coahuayana, R. **164** 18 41N 103 45W
Coahuayutla **164** 18 19N 101 42W
Coahuila □ **164** 27 0N 112 30W
Coal Creek Flat **143** 45 27S 169 19E
Coal I. **143** 46 8S 166 40E
Coal, R. **152** 59 39N 126 57W
Coalane **127** 17 48S 37 2E
Coalbrookdale **28** 52 38N 2 30W
Coalburn **35** 55 35N 3 55W
Coalcomán **164** 18 40N 103 10W
Coaldale, Can. **152** 49 45N 112 35W
Coaldale, U.S.A. **163** 38 2N 117 55W
Coaldale, Pa., U.S.A. **162** 40 50N 75 54W
Coalgate **159** 34 35N 96 13W
Coalinga **163** 36 10N 120 21W
Coalisland **38** 54 33N 6 42W
Coalspur **152** 53 15N 117 0W
Coalville, U.K. **28** 52 43N 1 21W
Coalville, U.S.A. **160** 40 58N 111 24W
Coamo **147** 18 5N 66 22W
Coaraci **171** 14 38S 39 32W
Coari **174** 4 8S 63 7W
Coast □ **126** 2 40S 39 45E
Coast Mts. **152** 52 0N 126 0W
Coast Range **163** 40 0N 124 0W
Coastal Plains Basin **137** 30 10S 115 30E
Coatbridge **35** 55 52N 4 2W
Coatepec **165** 19 27N 96 58W
Coatepeque **166** 14 46N 91 55W
Coatesville **162** 39 59N 75 30W
Coaticook **151** 45 10N 71 46W
Coats I. **149** 62 30N 83 0W
Coats Land **13** 77 0S 25 0W
Coatzacoalcos **165** 18 7N 94 35W
Cobadin **70** 44 5N 28 13E
Cobalt **150** 47 25N 79 42W
Cobán **166** 15 30N 90 21W
Cobar **141** 31 27S 145 48E
Cobb I. **162** 37 17N 75 42W
Cobbannah **141** 37 37S 147 12E
Cobberas, Mt. **141** 36 53S 148 12E
Cobden **140** 38 20S 143 3E
Cóbh **39** 51 50N 8 18W
Cobija **174** 11 0S 68 50W
Cobourg **150** 43 58N 78 10W
Cobourg Pen. **136** 11 20S 132 15E
Cobram **141** 35 54S 145 40E
Cobre **160** 41 6N 114 25W
Cóbuè **125** 12 0S 34 58E
Coburg **49** 50 15N 10 58E
Coca **56** 41 13N 4 32W
Coca, R. **174** 0 25S 77 5W
Cocal **170** 3 28S 41 34W
Cocanada = Kakinada **96** 16 55N 82 20E
Cocentaina **59** 38 45N 0 27W
Cocha, La **172** 27 50S 65 40W
Cochabamba **174** 17 15S 66 20W
Coche, I. **174** 10 47N 63 56W
Cochem **49** 50 8N 7 7E
Cochemane **127** 17 0S 32 54E
Cochilha Grande de Albardão **173** 28 30S 51 30W
Cochin **97** 9 55N 76 22E
Cochin China **101** 10 30N 106 0E
Cochin China = Nam-Phan **101** 10 30N 106 0E
Cochise **161** 32 6N 109 58W
Cochran **157** 32 25N 83 23W
Cochrane, Alta., Can. **152** 51 11N 114 30W
Cochrane, Ont., Can. **150** 49 0N 81 0W
Cochrane, L. **176** 47 10S 72 0W
Cochrane, R. **153** 57 53N 101 34W
Cockatoo I. **136** 16 6S 123 37E
Cockburn **140** 32 5S 141 0E
Cockburn, Canal **176** 54 30S 72 0W
Cockburn, C. **136** 11 20S 132 52E
Cockburn I. **150** 45 55N 83 22W
Cockburn Ra. **136** 15 46S 128 0E
Cockburnspath **35** 55 56N 2 23W
Cockenzie **35** 55 58N 2 59W
Cockerham **32** 53 58N 2 49W
Cockermouth **32** 54 40N 3 22W
Cockeysville **162** 39 29N 76 39W
Cockfield **29** 52 8N 0 47E
Cocklebiddy **137** 32 0S 126 3E
Coco Chan. **101** 13 50N 93 25E
Coco Is. **101** 14 0N 93 12E
Coco, Pta. **174** 2 58N 77 43W
Coco, R. (Wanks) **166** 14 10N 85 0W
Cocoa **157** 28 22N 80 40W
Cocobeach **124** 0 59N 9 34E
Cocoli, R. **120** 12 0N 14 0W
Cocora **70** 44 45N 27 3E
Côcos **171** 14 10S 44 33W
Cocos (Keeling) Is. **11** 12 12S 96 54E
Côcos, R. **171** 12 44S 44 48W
Cod, C. **162** 42 8N 70 10W
Cod, gasfield **19** 57 8N 2 35E
Codajás **174** 3 40S 62 0W
Coddenham **29** 52 8N 1 8E
Codera, C. **174** 10 35N 66 4W
Coderre **153** 50 11N 106 31W
Codigoro **63** 44 50N 12 5E
Codó **170** 4 30S 43 55W
Codogno **62** 45 10N 9 42E
Codróipo **63** 45 57N 13 0E
Codru, Munţii **70** 46 30N 22 15E
Cods Hd. **39** 51 40N 10 7W
Cody **160** 44 35N 109 0W
Coe Hill **150** 44 52N 77 50W
Coelemu **172** 36 30S 72 48W
Coelho Neto **170** 4 15S 43 0W
Coen **138** 13 52S 143 12E
Coesfeld **48** 51 56N 7 10E
Coeur d'Alene **160** 47 45N 116 51W
Coevorden **46** 52 40N 6 44E
Coffeyville **159** 37 0N 95 40W
Coffin B. Pen. **136** 34 20S 135 10E
Coffs Harbour **141** 30 16S 153 5E
Cofre de Perote, Cerro **165** 19 30N 97 10W
Cofrentes **59** 39 13N 1 5W
Cogealac **70** 44 36N 28 36E
Coggeshall **29** 51 53N 0 41E
Coghinas, R. **64** 40 55N 8 48E
Cognac **44** 45 41N 0 20W
Cogne **62** 45 37N 7 21E
Cogolludo **58** 40 59N 3 10W
Cohagen **160** 47 2N 106 45W
Cohoes **162** 42 47N 73 42W
Cohuna **140** 35 45S 144 15E
Coiba I. **166** 7 30N 81 40W
Coig, R. **176** 51 0S 70 20W
Coigach, dist. **36** 58 0N 5 10W
Coillore **36** 57 21N 6 23W
Coimbatore **97** 11 2N 76 59E
Coimbra **56** 40 15N 8 27W
Coimbra □ **56** 40 12N 8 25W
Coin **57** 36 40N 4 48W
Cojedes □ **174** 9 20N 68 20W
Cojimies **174** 0 20N 80 0W
Cojocna **70** 46 45N 23 50E
Cojutepequé **166** 13 41N 88 54W
Čoka **66** 45 57N 20 12E
Cokeville **160** 42 4N 111 0W
Col di Tenda **62** 44 7N 7 36E
Colaba Pt. **96** 18 54N 72 47E
Colac **140** 38 21S 143 35E
Colachel **97** 8 10N 77 15E
Colares **57** 38 48N 9 30W
Colatina **171** 19 32S 40 37W
Colbinabbin **141** 36 38S 144 48E
Colby, U.K. **32** 54 6N 4 42W
Colby, U.S.A. **158** 39 27N 101 2W
Colchagua □ **172** 34 30S 71 0W
Colchester **29** 51 54N 0 55E
Cold Fell **32** 54 54N 2 40W
Coldingham **35** 55 53N 2 10W
Coldstream **35** 55 39N 2 14W
Coldwater **159** 37 18N 99 24W
Coldwell **150** 48 45N 86 30W
Colebrook **138** 42 31S 147 12E
Colebrooke **30** 50 45N 3 44W
Coleford **28** 51 46N 2 38W
Coleman, Can. **152** 49 40N 114 30W
Coleman, U.S.A. **159** 31 52N 99 30W
Coleman, R. **138** 15 6S 141 38E
Colenso **129** 28 44S 29 50E
Coleraine, Austral. **140** 37 36S 141 40E
Coleraine, U.K. **38** 55 8N 6 40E
Coleraine □ **38** 55 8N 6 40E
Coleridge, L. **143** 43 17S 171 30E
Coleroon, R. **97** 11 0N 79 0E
Colesberg **128** 30 45S 25 5E
Coleshill **28** 52 30N 1 42W
Coleville **163** 38 44N 119 30W
Colfax, La., U.S.A. **159** 31 35N 92 39W
Colfax, Wash., U.S.A. **160** 46 57N 117 28W
Colgrave Sd. **36** 60 35N 1 0W
Colhué Huapi, L. **176** 45 30S 69 0W
Cólico **62** 46 8N 9 22E
Coligny **128** 46 24N 5 21E
Colima **164** 19 10N 103 40W
Colima □ **164** 19 10N 103 40W
Colima, Nevado de **164** 19 30N 103 40W
Colina **172** 33 13S 70 45W
Colina do Norte **120** 12 28N 15 0W
Colinas, Goiás, Brazil **171** 14 15S 48 2W
Colinas, Maranhão, Brazil **170** 6 0S 44 10W
Colinton, Austral. **141** 35 50S 149 10E
Colinton, U.K. **35** 55 54N 3 17W
Coll, I. **34** 56 40N 6 35W
Collaguasi **172** 21 5S 68 45W
Collarada, Peña **58** 42 43N 0 29W
Collarenebri **139** 29 33S 148 36E
Collbran **161** 39 16N 107 58W
Colle Salvetti **62** 43 34N 10 27E
Colle Sannita **65** 41 22N 14 48E
Colléchio **62** 44 23N 10 10E
Colleen Bawn **127** 21 0S 29 12E
College Park, Ga., U.S.A. **157** 33 42N 84 27W
College Park, Md., U.S.A. **162** 39 0N 76 55W
Collette **151** 46 40N 65 30W
Collie, N.S.W., Austral. **141** 31 41S 148 18E
Collie, W. Austral., Austral. **137** 33 22S 116 8E
Collier B. **136** 16 10S 124 15E
Collier Law Pk. **32** 54 47N 1 59W
Collier Ra. **137** 24 45S 119 10E
Collin **35** 55 4N 3 30W
Colline Metallifere **62** 43 10N 11 0E
Collingbourne **28** 51 16N 1 39W
Collingswood **162** 39 55N 75 4W
Collingwood, Austral. **138** 22 20S 142 31E
Collingwood, Can. **150** 44 29N 80 13W
Collingwood, N.Z. **143** 40 25S 172 40E
Collingwood B. **138** 9 30S 149 30E
Collins **150** 50 17N 89 27W
Collinsville **138** 20 30S 147 56E
Collipulli **172** 37 55S 72 30W
Collison Ra. **136** 14 49S 127 25E
Collo **119** 36 58N 6 37E
Collon **38** 53 46N 6 29W
Collonges **45** 46 9N 5 52E
Collooney **38** 54 11N 8 28W
Colmar **43** 48 5N 7 20E
Colmars **45** 44 11N 6 39E
Colmenar **57** 36 54N 4 20W
Colmenar de Oreja **58** 40 6N 3 25W
Colmenar Viejo **56** 40 39N 3 47W
Colmor **159** 36 18N 104 36W
Colne **32** 53 51N 2 11W
Colne, R., Essex, U.K. **29** 51 55N 0 50E
Colne, R., Herts., U.K. **29** 51 36N 0 30W
Colnett, Cabo **164** 31 0N 116 20W
Colo, R. **141** 33 25S 150 52E
Cologna Vèneta **63** 45 19N 11 21E
Colomb-Béchar = Béchar **118** 31 38N 2 18E
Colombey-les-Belles **43** 48 32N 5 54E
Colombey-les-deux Églises **43** 48 20N 4 50E
Colômbia **171** 20 10S 48 40W
Colombia **174** 3 24N 79 49W
Colombia ■ **174** 3 45N 73 0W
Colombier **50** 46 58N 6 53E
Colombo **97** 6 56N 79 58E
Colombus, Kans., U.S.A. **159** 37 15N 94 30W
Colombus, Nebr., U.S.A. **158** 41 30N 97 25W
Colombus, N.Mex., U.S.A. **161** 31 54N 107 43W
Colome **158** 43 20N 99 44W
Colón, Argent. **172** 32 12S 58 30W
Colón, Cuba **166** 22 42N 80 54W
Colón, Panama **166** 9 20N 80 0W
Colonel Hill **167** 22 50N 74 21W
Colonella **63** 42 52N 13 50E
Colonia del Sacramento **173** 34 25S 57 50W
Colonia Dora **172** 28 34S 62 59W
Colonia Las Heras **176** 46 30S 69 0W
Colonia Sarmiento **176** 45 30S 68 15W
Colonial Hts. **162** 37 15N 77 25W
Colonne, C. delle **65** 39 2N 17 11E
Colonsay **153** 51 59N 105 52W
Colonsay, I. **34** 56 4N 6 12W
Colorado □ **154** 37 40N 106 0W
Colorado Aqueduct **163** 34 17N 114 10W
Colorado City **159** 32 25N 100 50W
Colorado Desert **154** 34 20N 116 0W
Colorado Plateau **161** 36 40N 110 30W
Colorado, R., Argent. **172** 37 30S 69 0W
Colorado, R., Ariz., U.S.A. **161** 33 30N 114 30W
Colorado, R., Calif., U.S.A. **161** 34 0N 114 33W
Colorado, R., Tex., U.S.A. **159** 29 40N 96 30W
Colorado Springs **158** 38 55N 104 50W
Colorno **62** 44 55N 10 21E
Colossal **141** 30 52S 147 3E
Colotepec **165** 15 47N 97 3W
Colotlán **164** 22 6N 103 16W
Colpy **37** 57 23N 2 35W
Colsterworth **29** 52 48N 0 37W
Coltishall **29** 52 44N 1 21E
Colton, Calif., U.S.A. **163** 34 4N 117 20W
Colton, Wash., U.S.A. **160** 46 41N 117 6W
Columbia, La., U.S.A. **159** 32 7N 92 5W
Columbia, Miss., U.S.A. **159** 31 16N 89 50W
Columbia, Mo., U.S.A. **158** 38 58N 92 20W
Columbia, Pa., U.S.A. **162** 40 2N 76 30W
Columbia, S.C., U.S.A. **157** 34 0N 81 0W

Columbia Coroaci

Columbia, Tenn., U.S.A. 157 35 40N 87 0W
Columbia, C. 12 83 0N 70 0W
Columbia City 156 41 8N 85 30W
Columbia, District of □ 156 38 55N 77 0W
Columbia Falls 160 48 25N 114 16W
Columbia Heights 158 45 5N 93 10W
Columbia, Mt. 152 52 8N 117 20W
Columbia Basin 160 47 30N 118 30W
Columbia, R. 160 45 49N 120 0W
Columbretes, Is. 58 39 50N 0 50 E
Columbus, Ga., U.S.A. 157 32 30N 84 58W
Columbus, Ind., U.S.A. 156 39 14N 85 55W
Columbus, Miss., U.S.A. 157 33 30N 88 26W
Columbus, Mont., U.S.A. 160 45 45N 109 14W
Columbus, N.D., U.S.A. 158 48 52N 102 48W
Columbus, Ohio, U.S.A. 156 39 57N 83 1W
Columbus, Tex., U.S.A. 159 29 42N 96 33W
Columbus, Wis., U.S.A. 158 43 20N 89 2W
Colunda 125 12 7 S 23 36 E
Colunga 56 43 29N 5 16W
Colusa 160 39 15N 122 1W
Colville 160 48 33N 117 54W
Colville, C. 142 36 29 S 175 21 E
Colville, R. 147 69 15N 152 0W
Colwell 35 55 4N 2 4W
Colwich 28 52 48N 1 58W
Colwyn 31 53 17N 3 43W
Colwyn Bay 31 53 17N 3 44W
Colyton 30 50 44N 3 4W
Comácchio 63 44 41N 12 10 E
Comalcalco 165 18 16N 93 13W
Comallo 176 41 0 S 70 5W
Comana 70 44 10N 26 10 E
Comanche, Okla., U.S.A. 159 34 27N 97 58W
Comanche, Tex., U.S.A. 159 31 55N 98 35W
Comăneşti 70 46 25N 26 26 E
Comayagua 166 14 25N 87 37W
Combahee, R. 157 32 45N 80 50W
Combara 141 31 10 S 148 22 E
Combe Martin 30 51 12N 4 2W
Combeaufontaine 43 47 38N 5 54 E
Comber 38 54 33N 5 45W
Combermere Bay 98 19 37N 93 34 E
Comblain 47 50 29N 5 35 E
Combles 43 50 0N 2 50 E
Combourg 42 48 25N 1 46W
Comboyne 141 31 34 S 152 34 E
Combronde 44 45 58N 3 5 E
Comeragh Mts. 39 52 17N 7 35W
Comercinho 171 16 19 S 41 47W
Comet 138 23 36 S 148 38 E
Comet Vale 137 29 55 S 121 4 E
Comilla 98 23 28N 91 10 E
Comines 47 50 46N 3 0 E
Comino, C. 64 40 28N 9 47 E
Cómiso 65 36 57N 14 35 E
Comitán 165 16 18N 92 9W
Commentry 44 46 20N 2 46 E
Commerce, Ga., U.S.A. 157 34 10N 83 25W
Commerce, Tex., U.S.A. 159 33 15N 95 50W
Commercy 43 48 40N 5 34 E
Committee B. 149 68 30N 86 30W
Commonwealth B. 13 67 0 S 144 0 E
Commoron Cr., R. 139 28 22 S 150 8 E
Communism Pk. = Kommunizma, Pk. 93 38 40N 72 20 E
Como 62 45 48N 9 5 E
Como, L. di 62 46 5N 9 17 E
Comodoro Rivadavia 176 45 50 S 67 40W
Comores, Arch. des 11 10 0 S 50 0 E
Comores, Is. 11 12 10 S 44 15 E
Comorin, C. 97 8 3N 77 40 E
Comorişte 70 45 10N 21 35 E
Comoro Is. 11 12 10 S 44 15 E
Comox 152 49 42N 124 55W
Compiègne 43 49 24N 2 50 E
Compíglia Maríttima 62 43 4N 10 37 E
Comporta 57 38 22N 8 46W
Compostela 164 21 15N 104 53W
Comprida, I. 173 24 50 S 47 42W
Compton, U.K. 28 51 2N 1 19W
Compton, U.S.A. 163 33 54N 118 13W
Compton Downs 139 30 28 S 146 30 E
Comrie 35 56 22N 4 0W
Con Cuong 100 19 2N 104 54 E
Côn Dao 101 8 45N 106 45 E
Con Son, Is. 101 8 41N 106 37 E
Conakry 120 9 29N 13 49W
Conara Junction 138 41 50 S 147 26 E
Conargo 141 35 16 S 145 10 E
Conatlán 164 24 30N 104 42W
Concarneau 42 47 52N 3 56W
Conceição, Brazil 170 7 33 S 38 31W
Conceição, Mozam. 127 18 47 S 36 7 E
Conceição da Barra 171 18 35 S 39 45W
Conceição do Araguaia 170 8 0 S 49 2W
Conceição do Canindé 170 7 54 S 41 34W
Conceição do Mato Dentro 171 19 1 S 43 25W
Concepcián 165 18 15N 90 5W
Concepción, Argent. 172 27 20 S 65 35W
Concepción, Boliv. 174 15 50 S 61 40W
Concepción, Chile 172 36 50 S 73 0W
Concepción, Colomb. 174 0 5N 75 37W
Concepción, Parag. 172 23 30 S 57 20W
Concepción, Venez. 174 10 48N 71 46W
Concepción □ 172 37 0 S 72 30W
Concepcion, C. 154 34 30N 120 34W
Concepción del Oro 164 24 40N 101 30W
Concepción del Uruguay 172 32 35 S 58 20W
Concepción, L. 174 17 20 S 61 10W
Concepción, La = Ri-Aba 121 3 28N 84 0 E
Concepción, Punta 164 26 55N 111 50W
Concepción, R. 164 30 32N 113 2W
Conception B. 128 23 55 S 14 22 E
Conception I. 167 23 52N 75 9W
Conception, Pt. 163 34 27N 120 28W
Concession 127 17 27 S 30 56 E
Conchas Dam 159 35 25N 104 10W
Conche 151 50 48N 55 58W
Conches-en-Ouche 50 48 58N 0 58 E
Concho 161 34 32N 109 43W
Concho, R. 159 31 30N 100 8W
Conchos, R., Chihnahua, Mexico 164 29 20N 105 0W
Conchos, R., Tamaulipas, Mexico 165 25 0N 97 32W
Concon 172 32 56 S 71 33W
Concord, Calif., U.S.A. 163 37 59N 122 2W
Concord, N.C., U.S.A. 157 35 28N 80 35W
Concord, N.H., U.S.A. 162 43 12N 71 30W
Concórdia, Argent. 172 31 20 S 58 2W
Concórdia, Brazil 174 4 36 S 66 36W
Concordia, Colomb. 174 2 39N 72 47W
Concordia, Mexico 164 23 18N 106 2W
Concordia, U.S.A. 158 39 35N 97 40W
Concordia, La 165 16 8N 92 38W
Concots 44 44 26N 1 40 E
Concrete 160 48 35N 121 49W
Condah 140 37 57 S 141 44 E
Condamine, R. 133 27 7 S 149 48 E
Condat 44 45 21N 2 46 E
Conde 171 11 49 S 37 37W
Condé 43 50 26N 3 34 E
Conde 158 45 13N 98 5W
Condé-sur-Noireau 42 48 51N 0 33W
Condeúba 171 15 0 S 42 0W
Condobolin 141 33 4 S 147 6 E
Condom 44 43 57N 0 22 E
Condon 160 45 15N 120 8W
Condove 62 45 8N 7 19 E
Condover 28 52 39N 2 46W
Conegliano 63 45 53N 12 18 E
Conejera, I. 59 39 11N 2 58 E
Conejos 164 26 14N 103 53W
Conflans-en-Jarnisy 43 49 10N 5 52 E
Confolens 44 46 2N 0 40 E
Confuso, R. 172 24 10 S 59 0W
Congleton 32 53 10N 2 12W
Congo 170 7 48 S 36 40W
Congo ■ 124 1 0 S 16 0 E
Congo Basin 114 0 10 S 24 30 E
Congo, Democratic Rep. of = Zaïre ■ 124 3 0 S 22 0 E
Congo (Kinshasa) ■ = Zaïre ■ 124 1 0 S 16 0 E
Congo, R. = Zaïre, R. 124 1 30N 28 0 E
Congonhas 173 20 30 S 43 52W
Congresbury 28 51 20N 2 49W
Congress 161 34 11N 112 56W
Congucu 113 31 25 S 52 30W
Conil 57 36 17N 6 10W
Coningsby 33 53 7N 0 9W
Conisbrough 33 53 29N 1 12W
Coniston, Can. 150 46 29N 80 51W
Coniston, U.K. 32 54 22N 3 6W
Coniston Water 32 54 20N 3 5W
Conjeevaram = Kancheepuram 97 12 52N 79 45 E
Conjuboy 138 18 35 S 144 45 E
Conklin 153 55 38N 111 5W
Conlea 139 30 7 S 144 35 E
Conn, L. 38 54 3N 9 15W
Conna 39 52 5N 8 8W
Connacht 38 53 23N 8 40W
Connah's Quay 31 53 13N 3 6W
Conneaut 156 41 55N 80 32W
Connecticut □ 162 41 40N 72 40W
Connecticut, R. 162 41 17N 72 21W
Connel 34 56 27N 5 24W
Connel Park 34 55 22N 4 15W
Connell 160 46 45N 118 58W
Connemara 38 53 29N 9 45W
Conner, La 160 48 22N 122 27W
Connersville 156 39 40N 85 10W
Connonagh 39 51 35N 9 8W
Connor, Mt. 136 14 34 S 126 4 E
Connors Ra. 138 21 40 S 149 10 E
Conoble 141 32 55 S 144 42 E
Cononaco, R. 174 1 20 S 76 30W
Conquest 153 51 32N 107 14W
Conquet, Le 42 48 21N 4 46W
Conrad 160 48 11N 112 0W
Conran, C. 141 37 49 S 148 44 E
Conroe 159 30 15N 95 28W
Conselheiro Lafaiete 173 20 40 S 43 48W
Conselheiro Pena 171 19 10 S 41 30W
Consett 32 54 52N 1 50W
Conshohocken 162 40 5N 75 18W
Consort 153 52 1N 110 46W
Constance = Konstanz 49 47 39N 9 10 E
Constance, L. = Bodensee 51 47 35N 9 25 E
Constanţa 70 44 14N 28 38 E
Constanţa □ 70 44 15N 28 15 E
Constantia 162 43 15N 76 1W
Constantina 57 37 51N 5 40W
Constantine 119 36 25N 6 42 E
Constitución, Chile 172 35 20 S 72 30W
Constitución, Uruguay 172 31 0 S 58 10W
Consuegra 57 39 28N 3 43W
Consul 153 49 20N 109 30W
Contact 160 41 50N 114 56W
Contai 95 21 54N 87 55 E
Contamana 174 7 10 S 74 55W
Contarina 63 45 2N 12 13 E
Contas, R. 171 13 5 S 41 53W
Contes 45 43 49N 7 19 E
Conthey 50 46 14N 7 28 E
Contin 37 57 34N 4 35W
Contoocook 162 43 13N 71 45W
Contra Costa 129 25 9 S 33 30 E
Contres 43 47 24N 1 26 E
Contrexéville 43 48 6N 5 53 E
Convención 174 8 28N 73 21W
Conversano 65 40 57N 17 8 E
Convoy 38 54 52N 7 40W
Conway, Ark., U.S.A. 159 35 5N 92 30W
Conway, N.H., U.S.A. 162 43 58N 71 8W
Conway, S.C., U.S.A. 157 33 49N 79 2W
Conway = Conwy 31 53 17N 3 50W
Conway, L. 139 28 17 S 135 35 E
Conwy 31 53 17N 3 50W
Conwy Bay 31 53 17N 3 57W
Conwy, R. 31 53 18N 3 50W
Coober Pedy 136 29 1 S 134 43 E
Coobina 137 23 22 S 120 10 E
Cooch Behar 98 26 22N 89 29 E
Cook, Austral. 137 30 37 S 130 25 E
Cook, U.S.A. 158 47 49N 92 39W
Cook, Bahia 176 55 10 S 70 0W
Cook Inlet 147 59 0N 151 0W
Cook Is. 131 20 0 S 160 0W
Cook, Mount 143 43 36 S 170 9 E
Cook Strait 143 41 15 S 174 29 E
Cooke Plains 140 35 23 S 139 34 E
Cookeville 157 36 12N 85 30W
Cookham 29 51 33N 0 42W
Cookhouse 128 32 44 S 25 47 E
Cookstown 38 54 40N 6 43W
Cookstown □ 38 54 40N 6 43W
Cooktown 138 15 30 S 145 16 E
Coolabah 141 31 1 S 146 43 E
Cooladdi 139 26 37 S 145 23 E
Coolah 141 31 48 S 149 41 E
Coolamon 141 34 46 S 147 8 E
Coolaney 38 54 10N 8 36W
Coolangatta 139 28 11 S 153 29 E
Coole 38 53 42N 7 23W
Coolgardie 137 30 55 S 121 8 E
Coolgreany 39 52 46N 6 14W
Coolibah 136 15 33 S 130 56 E
Coolidge 161 33 1N 111 35W
Coolidge Dam 161 33 10N 110 30W
Coolmore 38 54 33N 8 12W
Cooma 141 36 12 S 149 8 E
Coomacarrea Mts. 39 51 59N 10 0W
Coonabarabran 141 31 14 S 149 18 E
Coonalpyn 140 35 43 S 139 52 E
Coonamble 141 30 56 S 148 27 E
Coonana 137 31 0 S 123 0 E
Coondapoor 97 13 42N 74 40 E
Coongie 139 27 9 S 140 8 E
Coongoola 139 27 43 S 145 47 E
Cooninie, L. 139 26 4 S 139 59 E
Coonoor 97 11 10N 76 45 E
Cooper 159 33 20N 95 40W
Cooper Cr. 139 28 29 S 137 46 E
Cooper, R. 157 33 0N 79 55W
Coopersburg 162 40 31N 75 23W
Cooperstown, N.D., U.S.A. 158 47 30N 98 14W
Cooperstown, New York, U.S.A. 162 42 42N 74 57W
Coorabie P.O. 137 31 54 S 132 18 E
Coorabulka 138 23 41 S 140 20 E
Coorong, The 133 35 50 S 139 20 E
Coorow 137 29 53 S 116 2 E
Cooroy 139 26 22 S 152 54 E
Coos Bay 160 43 26N 124 7W
Cootamundra 141 34 36 S 148 1 E
Cootehill 38 54 5N 7 5W
Cooyar 139 26 59 S 151 51 E
Cooyeana 138 24 29 S 138 45 E
Copahué, Paso 172 37 49 S 71 8W
Copainalá 165 17 8N 93 11W
Copake Falls 162 42 7N 73 31W
Copán 166 14 50N 89 9W
Cope 158 39 44N 102 50W
Cope, Cabo 59 37 26N 1 28W
Cope Cope 140 36 27 S 143 5 E
Copeland I. 38 54 38N 5 33W
Copenhagen 162 43 54N 75 41W
Copenhagen = København 73 55 41N 12 34 E
Copertino 65 40 17N 18 2W
Copeville 140 34 47 S 139 51 E
Copiapó 172 27 15 S 70 20 E
Copiapó, R. 172 27 19 S 70 56W
Copinsay I. 37 58 54N 2 40W
Coplay 162 40 44N 75 29W
Copley 140 30 24 S 138 26 E
Copp L. 152 60 14N 114 40W
Copparo 63 44 52N 11 49 E
Copper Center 147 62 10N 145 25W
Copper Cliff 150 46 28N 81 4W
Copper Harbor 156 47 31N 87 55W
Copper Mountain 152 49 20N 120 30W
Copper Queen 127 17 29 S 29 18 E
Copper R. 147 61 30N 144 30W
Copperbelt □ 127 13 15N 27 30 E
Copperfield 137 29 1 S 120 26 E
Coppermine 148 67 50N 115 5W
Coppermine, R. 148 67 49N 115 4W
Copperopolis 163 37 58N 120 38W
Cöppingen 49 48 42N 9 40 E
Copythorne 28 50 56N 1 34W
Coquet, I. 35 55 21N 1 30W
Coquet, R. 35 55 18N 1 45W
Coquilhatville = Mbandaka 124 0 1N 18 18 E
Coquille 160 43 15N 124 6W
Coquimbo 172 30 0 S 71 20W
Coquimbo □ 172 31 0 S 71 0W
Cora, oilfield 19 55 45N 4 45 E
Corabia 70 43 48N 24 30 E
Coraçáo de Jesus 171 11 39 S 39 56W
Coracora 174 15 5 S 73 45W
Coradi, Is. 65 40 27N 17 10 E
Coral Harbour 149 64 8N 83 10W
Coral Rapids 150 50 20N 81 40W
Coral Sea 142 15 0 S 150 0 E
Coral Sea Islands Terr. 133 20 0 S 155 0 E
Corato 65 41 12N 16 22 E
Corbeil-Essonnes 43 48 36N 2 26 E
Corbie 43 49 54N 2 30 E
Corbières, mts. 44 42 55N 2 35 E
Corbigny 43 47 16N 3 40 E
Corbin 156 37 0N 84 3W
Corbion 47 49 48N 5 0 E
Corbones, R. 57 37 25N 5 35W
Corbridge 35 54 58N 2 0W
Corby, Lincs., U.K. 29 52 49N 0 31W
Corby, Northants., U.K. 29 52 29N 0 41W
Corcoles, R. 59 39 12N 2 40W
Corcoran 163 36 6N 119 35W
Corcubión 56 42 56N 9 12W
Cord. de Caravaya 174 14 0 S 70 30W
Cordele 157 31 55N 83 49W
Cordell 159 35 18N 99 0W
Cordenons 63 45 59N 12 42 E
Cordes 44 44 5N 1 57 E
Cordillera Oriental 174 5 0N 74 0W
Cordisburgo 171 19 7 S 44 21W
Córdoba 172 31 20 S 64 10W
Córdoba 164 26 20N 103 20W
Córdoba, Mexico 165 18 50N 97 0W
Córdoba, Spain 57 37 50N 4 50W
Córdoba □, Argent. 172 31 22 S 64 15W
Córdoba □, Colomb. 174 8 20N 75 40W
Córdoba □, Spain 57 38 5N 5 0W
Córdoba, Sierra de 172 31 10 S 64 25W
Cordon 103 16 42N 121 32 E
Cordova, Ala., U.S.A. 157 33 45N 87 12W
Cordova, Alaska, U.S.A. 147 60 36N 145 45W
Corella 58 42 7N 1 48W
Corella, R. 138 19 34 S 140 47 E
Coremas 170 7 1 S 37 58W
Corfe Castle 28 50 58N 2 3W
Corfe Mullen 28 50 45N 2 0W
Corfield 138 21 40 S 143 21 E
Corfu = Kerkira 68 39 38N 19 50 E
Corgo 56 42 56N 7 25W
Cori 64 41 39N 12 53 E
Coria 56 40 0N 6 33W
Coricudgy, Mt. 141 32 51 S 150 24 E
Corigliano Cálabro 65 39 36N 16 31 E
Coringa Is. 138 16 58 S 149 58 E
Corinna 138 41 35 S 145 10 E
Corinth, Miss., U.S.A. 157 34 54N 88 30W
Corinth, N.Y., U.S.A. 162 43 15N 73 50W
Corinth = Korinthos 69 37 56N 22 55 E
Corinth Canal 69 37 48N 23 0 E
Corinth, G. of = Korinthiakós 69 38 16N 22 30 E
Corinto, Brazil 171 18 20 S 44 30W
Corinto, Nic. 166 12 30N 87 10W
Corj □ 70 45 5N 23 25 E
Cork 39 51 54N 8 30W
Cork □ 39 51 50N 8 50W
Cork Harbour 39 51 46N 8 16W
Corlay 42 48 20N 3 5W
Corleone 64 37 48N 13 16 E
Corleto Perticara 65 40 23N 16 2 E
Çorlu 67 41 11N 27 49 E
Cormack L. 152 60 56N 121 37W
Cormóns 63 45 58N 13 29 E
Cormorant 153 54 14N 100 35W
Cormorant L. 153 54 15N 100 50W
Cormorant, oilfield 19 61 0N 1 10 E
Corn Hill, Mt. 38 53 48N 7 43W
Corn Is. 167 12 0N 83 0W
Cornelio 164 29 55N 111 8W
Cornélio Procópio 173 23 7 S 50 40W
Cornell 158 45 10N 91 8W
Corner Brook 151 48 57N 57 58W
Corner Inlet 133 38 45 S 146 20 E
Cornforth 33 54 42N 1 28W
Corniglio 62 44 29N 10 5 E
Corning, Ark., U.S.A. 159 36 27N 90 34W
Corning, Calif., U.S.A. 160 39 56N 122 9W
Corning, Iowa, U.S.A. 158 40 57N 94 40W
Corning, N.Y., U.S.A. 162 42 10N 77 3W
Cornwall, Austral. 138 41 33 S 148 7 E
Cornwall, Can. 150 45 2N 74 44W
Cornwall, U.S.A. 162 40 17N 76 25W
Cornwall □ 30 50 26N 4 40W
Cornwall, C. 30 50 8N 5 42W
Cornwallis I. 12 75 8N 95 0W
Corny Pt. 140 34 55 S 137 0 E
Coro 174 11 25N 69 41W
Coroaci 171 18 35 S 42 17W

Coroatá **Crooksville**

Coroatá	170	4 20S	44 0W
Corocoro	174	17 15S	69 19W
Corofin	39	53 27N	8 50W
Coroico	174	16 0S	67 50W
Coromandel, Brazil	171	18 28S	47 13W
Coromandel, N.Z.	142	36 45S	175 31E
Coromandel Coast	97	12 30N	81 0E
Coromandel Pen.	142	37 0S	175 45E
Coromandel Ra.	142	37 0S	175 40E
Coromorant, L.	153	54 20N	100 50W
Corona, Austral.	139	31 16S	141 24E
Corona, Calif., U.S.A.	163	33 49N	117 36W
Corona, N. Mex., U.S.A.	161	34 15N	105 32W
Coronada B.	166	9 0N	83 40W
Coronado	163	32 45N	117 9W
Coronado, Bahía de	166	9 0N	83 40W
Coronation	152	52 5N	111 27W
Coronation Gulf	148	68 25N	112 0W
Coronation I., Antarct.	13	60 45S	46 0W
Coronation I., U.S.A.	152	55 52N	134 20W
Coronation Is.	136	14 57S	124 55E
Coronda	172	31 58S	60 56W
Coronel	172	37 0S	73 10W
Coronel Bogado	172	27 11S	56 18W
Coronel Dorrego	172	38 40S	61 10W
Coronel Fabriciano	171	19 31S	42 38W
Coronel Murta	171	16 37S	42 11W
Coronel Oviedo	172	25 24S	56 30W
Coronel Pringles	172	38 0S	61 30W
Coronel Suárez	172	37 30S	62 0W
Coronel Vidal	172	37 28S	57 45W
Coronie	170	5 55N	56 25W
Corovoda	68	40 31N	20 14E
Corowa	141	35 58S	146 21E
Corozal, Belize	165	18 30N	88 30W
Corozal, Colomb.	174	9 19N	75 18W
Corpach	36	56 50N	5 9W
Corps	45	44 50N	5 56E
Corpus	173	27 10S	55 30W
Corpus Christi	159	27 50N	97 28W
Corpus Christi L.	159	28 5N	97 54W
Corque	174	18 10S	67 50W
Corral de Almaguer	58	39 45N	3 10W
Corran	36	56 44N	5 14W
Corrandibby Ra.	137	26 0S	115 20E
Corraun Pen.	38	53 58N	10 15W
Corrégio	62	44 46N	10 47E
Corrente	170	10 27S	45 10W
Corrente, R.	170	13 8S	43 28W
Correntes, C. das	129	24 6S	35 34E
Correntina	171	13 20S	44 39W
Corrèze □	44	45 20N	1 45E
Corrib, L.	38	53 25N	9 10W
Corrie	34	55 39N	5 10W
Corrientes	172	27 30S	58 45W
Corrientes □	172	28 0S	57 0W
Corrientes, C., Colomb.	174	5 30N	77 34W
Corrientes, C., Cuba	166	21 43N	84 30W
Corrientes, C., Mexico	164	20 25N	105 42W
Corrientes, R., Argent.	172	30 21S	59 33W
Corrientes, R., Colomb.	174	3 15S	75 58W
Corrigan	159	31 0N	94 48W
Corrigin	137	32 20S	117 53E
Corringham	33	53 25N	0 42W
Corris	31	52 41N	3 49W
Corrowidgie	141	36 56S	148 50E
Corry	156	41 55N	79 39W
Corryong	141	36 12S	147 53E
Corryvrecken, G. of	34	56 10N	5 44W
Corse, C.	45	43 1N	9 25E
Corse-du-Sud □	45	41 45N	9 0E
Corse, Î	45	42 0N	9 0E
Corsewall Pt.	34	55 0N	5 10W
Corsham	28	51 25N	2 11W
Corsica = Corse	45	42 0N	9 0E
Corsicana	159	32 5N	96 30W
Corsley	28	51 12N	2 14W
Corsock	35	55 54N	3 56W
Corté	45	42 19N	9 11E
Corte do Pinto	57	37 42N	7 29W
Cortegana	57	37 52N	6 49W
Cortez	161	37 24N	108 35W
Cortina d'Ampezzo	63	46 32N	12 9E
Cortland	162	42 35N	76 11W
Corton	29	52 31N	1 46E
Cortona	63	43 16N	12 0E
Coruche	57	38 57N	8 30W
Çorum	92	40 30N	35 5E
Corumbá, Goias, Brazil	171	16 0S	48 50W
Corumbá, Mato Grosso, Brazil	174	19 0S	57 30W
Corumbá R.	171	17 25S	48 30W
Corumbaiba	171	18 9S	48 34W
Coruña □	56	43 0N	8 37E
Coruña, La	56	43 20N	8 25W
Coruña, La □	56	43 10N	8 30W
Corund	70	46 30N	25 13E
Corunna = La Coruña	56	43 20N	8 25W
Coruripe	171	10 5S	36 10W
Corvallis	160	44 36N	123 15W
Corve, R.	28	52 22N	2 43W
Corvette, L. de la	150	53 25N	73 55W
Corwen	31	52 59N	3 23W
Corydon	158	40 42N	93 22W
Cosalá	164	24 28N	106 40W
Cosamaloapán	165	18 23N	95 50W
Coseley	28	52 33N	2 6W
Cosenza	65	39 17N	16 14E
Coşereni	70	44 38N	26 35E
Cosham	28	50 51N	1 3W
Coshocton	156	40 17N	81 51W
Cosne-s.-Loire	43	47 24N	2 54E
Coso Junction	163	36 3N	117 57W
Coso Pk.	163	36 13N	117 44W
Cospeito	56	43 12N	7 34W
Cosquín	172	31 15S	64 30W
Cossato	62	45 34N	8 10E
Cossé-le-Vivien	42	47 57N	0 54W
Costa Azul	50	43 25N	6 50E
Costa Blanca	59	38 25N	0 10W
Costa Brava	58	41 30N	3 0E
Costa del Sol	57	36 30N	4 30W
Costa Dorada	58	40 45N	1 15E
Costa Mesa	163	33 39N	117 55W
Costa Rica	164	31 20N	112 40W
Costa Rica ■	166	10 0N	84 0W
Costa Smeralda	64	41 5N	9 35E
Costelloe	39	53 20N	9 33W
Costessey	29	52 40N	1 11E
Costigliole d'Asti	62	44 48N	8 11E
Costilla	161	37 0N	105 30W
Coştiui	70	47 53N	24 2E
Cosumnes, R.	163	38 14N	121 25W
Coswig	48	51 52N	12 31E
Cotabato	103	7 14N	124 15E
Cotabena	140	31 42S	138 11E
Cotagaita	172	20 45S	65 30W
Côte d'Azur	45	43 25N	6 50E
Côte d'Or	43	47 10N	4 50E
Côte d'Or □	43	47 30N	4 50E
Côte, La	50	46 25N	6 15E
Côte-St. André, La	45	45 24N	5 15E
Coteau des Prairies	158	44 30N	97 0W
Coteau du Missouri, Plat. du	154	47 0N	101 0W
Cotegipe	171	12 2S	44 15W
Cotentin	42	49 30N	1 30W
Côtes de Meuse	43	49 15N	5 22E
Côtes-du-Nord □	42	48 25N	2 40W
Cotherstone	32	54 34N	1 59W
Cotiella	58	42 31N	0 19E
Cotina, R.	66	43 36N	19 9E
Cotonou	121	6 20N	2 25E
Cotopaxi, Vol.	174	0 30S	78 30W
Cotronei	65	39 9N	16 27E
Cotswold Hills	28	51 42N	2 10W
Cottage Grove	160	43 48N	123 2W
Cottbus	48	51 44N	14 20E
Cottbus □	48	51 43N	13 30E
Cottenham	29	52 18N	0 8E
Cottingham	36	53 47N	0 23W
Cottonwood, Can.	152	53 5N	121 50W
Cottonwood, U.S.A.	161	34 48N	112 1W
Coubre, Pte. de la	44	45 42N	1 15W
Couches	43	46 53N	4 30E
Couço	57	38 59N	8 17W
Coudersport	156	41 45N	78 1W
Couedic, C. du	140	36 5S	136 40E
Couëron	42	47 13N	1 44W
Coueson, R.	42	48 20N	1 15W
Couhé-Vérac	44	46 18N	0 12E
Couillet	47	50 23N	4 28E
Coulags	36	57 26N	5 24W
Coulanges, Deux Sèvres, France	44	46 58N	0 35W
Coulanges, Yonne, France	43	47 30N	3 30E
Coulee City	160	47 44N	119 12W
Coulman I.	13	73 35S	170 0E
Coulommiers	43	48 50N	3 3E
Coulonge, R.	150	45 52N	76 46W
Coulport	34	56 3N	4 53W
Coulterville	163	37 42N	120 12W
Council	147	64 55N	163 45W
Council Bluffs	158	41 20N	95 50W
Council Grove	158	38 41N	96 30W
Coupar Angus	35	56 33N	3 17W
Courantyne, R.	174	5 0N	57 45W
Courçon	44	46 15N	0 50W
Cours	45	46 7N	4 19E
Courseulles	42	49 20N	0 29W
Court-St.-Etienne	47	50 38N	4 34E
Courtenay	152	49 45N	125 0W
Courtine, La	44	45 43N	2 16E
Courtland	163	38 20N	121 34W
Courtmacsherry	39	51 38N	8 43W
Courtmacsherry B.	39	51 37N	8 37W
Courtown	39	52 39N	6 14W
Courtrai = Kortrijk	47	50 50N	3 17E
Courville	42	48 28N	1 15E
Coutances	42	49 3N	1 28W
Couterne	42	48 30N	0 25W
Coutras	44	45 3N	0 8W
Coutts	152	49 0N	111 57W
Couvet	50	46 57N	6 38E
Couvin	47	50 3N	4 29E
Covarrubias	58	42 4N	3 31W
Covasna	70	45 50N	26 10E
Covasna □	70	45 50N	26 0E
Cove Bay	37	57 5N	2 5W
Coventry	28	52 25N	1 31W
Coventry L.	153	61 15N	106 15W
Cover R.	32	54 14N	1 45W
Coverack	30	50 2N	5 6W
Covilhã	56	40 17N	7 31W
Covina	163	34 5N	117 52W
Covington, Ga., U.S.A.	157	33 36N	83 50W
Covington, Ky., U.S.A.	156	39 5N	84 30W
Covington, Okla., U.S.A.	159	36 21N	97 36W
Covington, Tenn., U.S.A.	159	35 34N	89 39W
Cowal Creek Settlement	138	10 54S	142 20E
Cowal, dist.	34	56 5N	5 8W
Cowal, L.	141	33 40S	147 25E
Cowan	153	52 5N	100 45W
Cowan, L.	137	31 45S	121 45E
Cowan L.	153	54 0N	107 15W
Cowangie	140	35 12S	141 26E
Coward Springs	139	29 24S	136 48E
Cowarie	139	27 45S	138 15E
Cowarna	137	30 55S	122 40E
Cowbridge	31	51 28N	3 28W
Cowcowing Lakes	137	30 55S	117 20E
Cowdenbeath	35	56 7N	3 20W
Cowell	140	33 39S	136 56E
Cowes	28	50 45N	1 18W
Cowfold	29	50 58N	0 16W
Cowl Cowl	141	33 36S	145 18E
Cowley	28	51 43N	1 12W
Cowpen	35	55 8N	1 34W
Cowra	141	33 49S	148 42E
Coxim	175	18 30S	54 55W
Cox's Bazar	98	21 26N	91 59E
Cox's Cove	151	49 7N	58 5W
Coyame	164	29 28N	105 6W
Coylton	34	55 26N	4 31W
Coyuca de Benítez	165	17 1N	100 8W
Coyuca de Catalán	164	18 58N	100 41W
Cozad	158	40 55N	99 57W
Cozie, Alpi	62	44 50N	6 59E
Cozumel	165	20 31N	86 55W
Cozumel, Isla de	165	20 30N	86 40W
Craanford	39	52 40N	6 23W
Craboon	141	32 3S	149 30E
Cracow	139	25 17S	150 17E
Cradock	128	32 8S	25 36E
Craggie	37	57 25N	4 6W
Craig, Alaska, U.S.A.	147	55 30N	133 5W
Craig, Colo., U.S.A.	160	40 32N	107 44W
Craigavon = Portadown	38	54 27N	6 26W
Craigavon = Lurgan	38	54 28N	6 20W
Craigellachie	37	57 29N	3 9W
Craighouse	34	55 50N	5 58W
Craigmore	127	20 28S	32 30E
Craignish, L.	34	56 11N	5 32W
Craigtown	37	58 30N	3 53W
Crail	35	56 16N	2 38W
Crailsheim	49	49 7N	10 5E
Craiova	70	44 21N	23 48E
Cramlington	35	55 5N	1 36W
Crampel	117	7 8N	19 81E
Cramsie	138	23 20S	144 15E
Cranberry Portage	153	54 35N	101 23W
Cranborne	28	50 55N	1 55W
Cranborne Chase	29	50 56N	2 6W
Cranbrook, Tas., Austral.	138	42 0S	148 5E
Cranbrook, W. Austral., Austral.	137	34 18S	117 33E
Cranbrook, Can.	152	49 30N	115 46W
Cranbrook, U.K.	29	51 6N	0 33E
Crandon	158	45 32N	88 52W
Crane, Oregon, U.S.A.	160	43 21N	118 39W
Crane, Texas, U.S.A.	159	31 26N	102 27W
Cranfield Pt.	38	54 1N	6 3W
Cranleigh	29	51 8N	0 29W
Cranshaws	35	55 51N	2 30W
Cranston	162	41 47N	71 27W
Cranwell	33	53 4N	0 29W
Craon	42	47 50N	0 58W
Craonne	43	49 27N	3 46E
Crasna	70	46 32N	27 51E
Crasna, R.	70	47 44N	27 35E
Crater Lake	160	42 55N	122 3W
Crater Mt.	135	6 37S	145 7E
Crater Pt.	135	5 25S	152 9E
Crateús	170	5 10S	40 50W
Crathie	37	57 3N	3 12W
Crati, R.	65	39 41N	16 30E
Crato, Brazil	171	7 10S	39 25W
Crato, Port.	57	39 16N	7 39W
Crau	45	43 32N	4 40E
Craughwell	39	53 15N	8 44W
Craven Arms	28	52 27N	2 49W
Crawford, U.K.	35	55 28N	3 40W
Crawford, U.S.A.	158	42 40N	103 25W
Crawford, oilfield	19	59 7N	1 30E
Crawfordsville	156	40 2N	86 51W
Crawley	29	51 7N	0 10W
Cray	31	51 55N	3 38W
Crazy Mts.	160	46 14N	110 30W
Creag Meagaidh, mt.	37	56 57N	4 38W
Crean L.	153	54 5N	106 9W
Crèche, La	44	46 23N	0 19W
Crécy-en-Brie	43	48 50N	2 53E
Crécy-en-Ponthieu	43	50 15N	1 53E
Crécy-sur-Serre	43	49 40N	3 32E
Credenhill	28	52 6N	2 49W
Crediton	30	50 47N	3 39W
Credo	137	30 28S	120 45E
Cree L.	153	57 30N	106 30W
Cree, R., Can.	153	58 57N	105 47W
Cree, R., U.K.	34	54 51N	4 24W
Creede	161	37 56N	106 59W
Creegh	39	52 45N	9 25W
Creel	164	27 45N	107 38W
Creeside	34	55 4N	4 41W
Creeslough	38	55 8N	7 55W
Creetown	34	54 54N	4 23W
Creeves	39	52 33N	9 3W
Creggan	38	54 39N	7 0W
Cregganbaun	38	53 42N	9 48W
Creighton	158	42 30N	97 52W
Creil	43	49 15N	2 34E
Crema	62	45 21N	9 40E
Cremona	62	45 8N	10 2E
Crepaja	66	45 1N	20 38E
Crépy	43	49 37N	3 32E
Crépy-en-Valois	43	49 14N	2 54E
Cres	63	44 58N	14 25E
Cresbard	158	45 13N	98 57W
Crescent, Okla., U.S.A.	159	35 38N	97 36W
Crescent, Oreg., U.S.A.	160	43 30N	121 37W
Crescent City	160	41 45N	124 12W
Crescentino	62	45 11N	8 7E
Crespino	63	44 59N	11 51E
Crespo	172	32 2S	60 19W
Cressman	150	47 40N	72 55W
Cressy	140	38 2S	143 40E
Crest	45	44 44N	5 2E
Crested Butte	161	38 57N	107 0W
Crestline	163	34 14N	117 18W
Creston, Can.	152	49 10N	116 31W
Creston, Calif., U.S.A.	163	35 32N	120 33W
Creston, Iowa, U.S.A.	158	41 0N	94 20W
Creston, Wash., U.S.A.	160	47 47N	118 36W
Creston, Wyo., U.S.A.	160	41 46N	107 50W
Crestone	161	35 2N	106 0W
Crestview, Calif., U.S.A.	163	37 46N	118 58W
Crestview, Fla., U.S.A.	157	30 45N	86 35W
Creswick	140	37 25S	143 51E
Crete	158	40 38N	96 58W
Crete = Kriti	69	35 15N	25 0E
Crete, La, Can.	152	58 10N	116 29W
Crete, La, Alta., Can.	152	58 11N	116 24W
Crete, Sea of	69	26 0N	25 0E
Cretin, C.	135	6 40S	147 53E
Creus, C.	58	42 20N	3 19E
Creuse □	44	46 0N	2 0E
Creuse, R.	44	47 0N	0 34E
Creusot, Le	43	46 50N	4 24E
Creuzburg	48	51 3N	10 15E
Crevalcore	63	44 41N	11 10E
Crèvecœur-le-Grand	43	49 37N	2 5E
Crevillente	59	38 12N	0 48W
Crewe	32	53 6N	2 28W
Crewkerne	28	50 53N	2 48W
Crianlarich	34	56 24N	4 37W
Crib Point	139	38 22S	145 13E
Criccieth	31	52 55N	4 15W
Criciúma	173	28 40S	49 23W
Crick	28	52 22N	1 9W
Crickhowell	31	51 52N	3 8W
Cricklade	28	51 38N	1 50W
Crieff	35	56 22N	3 50W
Criffell Mt.	35	54 56N	3 38W
Crikvenica	63	45 11N	14 40E
Crillon, Mt.	152	58 39N	137 14W
Crimea = Krymskaya	82	45 0N	34 0E
Crimmitschau	48	50 48N	12 23E
Crimond	37	57 35N	1 53W
Crinan Canal	34	56 4N	5 30W
Crinkill	39	53 5N	7 55E
Cristalândia	170	10 36S	49 11W
Cristeşti	70	47 15N	26 33E
Cristino Castro	170	8 49S	44 13W
Crişul Alb, R.	66	46 25N	21 40E
Crişul Negru, R.	70	46 38N	22 26E
Crişul Repede, R.	70	47 20N	22 25E
Crivitz	48	53 35N	11 39E
Crixás	171	14 27S	49 58W
Crna Gora □	66	42 40N	19 20E
Crna Trava	66	42 49N	22 19E
Crni Drim, R.	66	41 17N	20 40E
Crni Timok, R.	66	43 53N	22 0E
Črnoljeva Planina	66	42 20N	21 0E
Črnomeij	63	45 33N	15 10E
Croagh Patrick, mt.	38	53 46N	9 40W
Croatia = Hrvatska	63	45 20N	16 0E
Crocker, Barisan	102	5 0N	116 30E
Crocketford	35	55 3N	3 49W
Crockets Town	38	54 8N	9 7W
Crockett	159	31 20N	95 30W
Crocodile Is.	138	11 43S	135 8E
Crocodile, R.	129	25 30S	31 15E
Crocq	44	45 52N	2 21E
Croghan	38	53 55N	8 13W
Croglin	32	54 50N	2 37W
Crohy Hd.	38	54 55N	8 28W
Croisic, Le	42	47 18N	2 30W
Croisic, Pte. du.	42	47 19N	2 31W
Croix, La, L.	150	48 20N	92 15W
Croker, C.	136	10 58S	132 35E
Croker, I.	136	11 12N	132 32E
Crolly	38	55 2N	8 16W
Cromalt Hills	36	58 0N	5 2W
Cromarty, Can.	153	58 3N	94 9W
Cromarty, U.K.	37	57 40N	4 2W
Cromarty Firth	37	57 40N	4 15W
Cromdale, Hills of	37	57 20N	3 28W
Cromer	29	52 56N	1 18E
Cromore	36	58 6N	6 23W
Cromwell, N.Z.	143	45 3S	169 14E
Cromwell, U.S.A.	162	41 36N	72 39W
Cronat	43	46 43N	3 40E
Crondall	29	51 13N	0 51W
Cronulla	141	34 3S	151 8E
Crook	33	54 43N	1 45W
Crooked I.	167	22 50N	74 10W
Crooked Island Passage	167	23 0N	74 30W
Crooked, R., Can.	152	54 10N	122 35W
Crooked, R., U.S.A.	160	44 30N	121 0W
Crooklands	32	54 16N	2 43W
Crookston, Minn., U.S.A.	158	47 50N	96 40W
Crookston, Nebr., U.S.A.	158	42 56N	100 45W
Crookstown	39	51 50N	8 50W
Crooksville	156	39 45N	82 8W

Crookwell Dalandzadgad

Crookwell 141 34 28S 149 24E
Croom 39 52 32N 8 43W
Crosby, Cumb., U.K. 32 54 45N 3 25W
Crosby, Merseyside, U.K. 32 53 30N 3 2W
Crosby, Minn., U.S.A. 158 46 28N 93 57W
Crosby, N.D., U.S.A. 153 48 55N 103 18W
Crosby Ravensworth 32 54 34N 2 35W
Crosbyton 159 33 37N 101 12W
Cross City 157 29 35N 83 5W
Cross Fell 32 54 44N 2 29W
Cross L. 153 54 45N 97 30W
Cross Plains 159 32 8N 99 7W
Cross, R. 121 4 46N 8 20E
Cross River □ 121 6 0N 8 0E
Cross Sound 147 58 20N 136 30W
Crossakiel 38 53 43N 7 2W
Crossbost 36 58 8N 6 27W
Crossdoney 38 53 57N 7 27W
Crosse, La, Kans., U.S.A. 158 38 33N 99 20W
Crosse, La, Wis., U.S.A. 158 43 48N 91 13W
Crossett 159 33 10N 91 57W
Crossfarnoge Pt. 39 52 10N 6 37W
Crossfield 152 51 25N 114 0W
Crossgar 38 54 22N 5 46W
Crosshaven 39 51 48N 8 19W
Crosshill 34 55 19N 4 39W
Crossley, Mt. 143 42 50S 172 5E
Crossmaglen 38 54 5N 6 37W
Crossmolina 38 54 6N 9 21W
Croton-on-Hudson 162 41 12N 73 55W
Crotone 65 39 5N 17 6E
Crouch, R. 29 51 37N 0 53E
Crow Agency 160 45 40N 107 30W
Crow Hd. 39 51 34N 10 9W
Crow, R. 152 59 41N 124 20W
Crow Sound 30 49 56N 6 16W
Crowborough 29 51 3N 0 9E
Crowell 159 33 59N 99 45W
Crowl Creek 141 32 0S 145 30E
Crowland 29 52 41N 0 10W
Crowle 33 53 36N 0 49W
Crowley 159 30 15N 92 20W
Crowley, L. 163 37 53N 118 42W
Crowlin Is. 36 57 20N 5 50W
Crown Point 156 41 24N 87 23W
Crows Landing 163 37 23N 121 6W
Crows Nest 139 27 16S 152 4E
Crowsnest Pass 152 49 40N 114 40W
Croyde 30 51 7N 4 13W
Croydon, Austral. 138 18 13S 142 14E
Croydon, U.K. 29 51 18N 0 5W
Crozet, Île 11 46 27S 52 0E
Crozon 42 48 15N 4 30W
Cruces, Pta. 174 6 39N 77 32W
Cruden Bay 37 57 25N 1 50W
Crudgington 28 52 46N 2 33W
Crumlin 38 54 38N 6 12W
Crummer Peaks 138 6 40S 144 0E
Crummock Water L. 32 54 33N 3 18W
Crusheen 39 52 57N 8 52W
Cruz, C. 166 19 50N 77 50W
Cruz das Almas 171 12 40S 39 6W
Cruz de Malta 170 8 15S 40 20W
Cruz del Eje 172 30 45S 64 50W
Cruz, La, Colomb. 174 1 35N 76 58W
Cruz, La, C. Rica 166 11 4N 85 39W
Cruz, La, Mexico 164 23 55N 106 54W
Cruzeiro 173 22 50S 45 0W
Cruzeiro do Oeste 173 23 46S 53 4W
Cruzeiro do Sul 174 7 35S 72 35W
Cry L. 152 58 45N 128 5W
Cryfow Sl. 54 51 2N 15 24E
Crymmych 31 51 59N 4 40W
Crystal Brook 140 33 21S 138 12E
Crystal City, Mo., U.S.A. 158 38 15N 90 23W
Crystal City, Tex., U.S.A. 159 28 40N 99 50W
Crystal Falls 156 46 9N 88 11W
Crystal River 157 28 54N 82 35W
Crystal Springs 159 31 59N 90 25W
Čáslav 52 49 54N 15 22E
Csongrád 53 46 43N 20 12E
Csongrád □ 53 46 32N 20 15E
Csorna 53 47 38N 17 18E
Csurgo 53 46 16N 17 9E
Ctesiphon 92 33 9N 44 35E
Cu Lao Hon 101 10 54N 108 18E
Cua Rao 100 19 16N 104 27E
Cuácua, R. 127 18 0S 36 0E
Cuamato 128 17 2S 15 7E
Cuamba = Nova Preixo 127 14 45S 36 22E
Cuando 128 16 25S 22 2E
Cuando Cubango □ 128 16 25S 20 0E
Cuando, R. 125 14 0S 19 30E
Cuangar 128 17 28S 14 40E
Cuango 124 6 15S 16 35E
Cuarto, R. 172 33 25S 63 2W
Cuatrociénegas de Carranza 164 26 59N 102 5W
Cuauhtémoc 164 28 25N 106 52W
Cuba, Port. 57 38 10N 7 54W
Cuba, U.S.A. 161 36 0N 107 0W
Cuba ■ 166 22 0N 79 0W
Cuballing 137 32 50S 117 10E
Cubango, R. 128 16 15S 17 45E
Cuchi 125 14 37S 17 10E
Cuchumatanes, Sierra de los 166 15 35N 91 25W
Cuckfield 29 51 0N 0 8W
Cucurpe 164 30 20N 110 43W
Cucurrupí 174 4 23N 76 56W
Cúcuta 174 7 54N 72 31W
Cudahy 156 42 54N 87 50W
Cudalbi 70 45 46N 27 41E
Cuddalore 97 11 46N 79 45E
Cuddapah 97 14 30N 78 47E
Cuddapan, L. 138 25 45S 141 26E
Cudgewa 141 36 10S 147 42E
Cudillero 56 43 33N 6 9W
Cudworth 33 53 35N 1 25W
Cue 137 27 25S 117 54E
Cuéllar 56 41 23N 4 21W
Cuenca, Ecuador 174 2 50S 79 9W
Cuenca, Spain 58 40 5N 2 10W
Cuenca □ 58 40 0N 2 0W
Cuenca, Serranía de 58 39 55N 1 50W
Cuencamé 164 24 53N 103 41W
Cuerda del Pozo, Pantano de la 58 41 51N 2 44W
Cuernavaca 165 18 50N 99 20W
Cuero 159 29 5N 97 17W
Cuers 45 43 14N 6 5E
Cuervo 159 35 5N 104 25W
Cuesmes 47 50 26N 3 56E
Cuevas de Altamira 56 43 20N 4 5W
Cuevas del Almanzora 59 37 18N 1 58W
Cuevo 174 20 25N 63 30W
Cugir 70 43 48N 23 25E
Cugno 123 6 14N 42 31E
Cuhimbre 174 0 10S 75 23W
Cuiabá 175 15 30S 56 0W
Cuiabá, R. 175 16 50S 56 30W
Cuidad Bolivar 174 8 21N 70 34W
Cuilcagh, Mt. 38 54 12N 7 50W
Cuilco 166 15 24N 91 58W
Cuillin Hills 36 57 14N 6 15W
Cuillin Sd. 36 57 4N 6 20W
Cuima 125 13 0S 15 45E
Cuiseaux 45 46 30N 5 22E
Cuité 170 6 29S 36 9W
Cuito, R. 128 16 50S 19 30E
Cuitzeo, L. 164 19 55N 101 5W
Cujmir 70 44 13N 22 57E
Culan 44 46 34N 2 20E
Cǔlaraşi 43 44 14N 27 23E
Culbertson 158 48 9N 104 30W
Culburra 140 35 50S 139 58E
Culcairn 141 35 41S 147 3E
Culdaff 38 55 17N 7 10W
Culebra, I. 147 18 19N 65 17W
Culebra, Sierra de la 56 41 55N 6 20W
Culemborg 46 51 58N 5 14E
Culgoa 140 35 44S 143 6E
Culgoa, R. 139 29 56S 146 20E
Culiacán 164 24 50N 107 40W
Culiacán, R. 164 24 30N 107 42W
Cǔlimani, Munţii 70 47 12N 25 0E
Cǔlineşti 70 45 21N 24 18E
Culion, I. 103 11 54N 120 1E
Cúllar de Baza 59 37 35N 2 34W
Cullarin Range 141 34 30S 149 30E
Cullaville 38 54 4N 6 40W
Cullen, Austral. 136 13 58S 131 54E
Cullen, U.K. 37 57 45N 2 50W
Cullen Pt. 138 11 57S 141 54E
Cullera 59 39 9N 0 17W
Cullin L. 38 53 58N 9 12W
Cullivoe 36 60 43N 1 0W
Cullman 157 34 13N 86 50W
Culloden Moor 37 57 29N 4 7W
Cullompton 30 50 52N 3 23W
Cullyhanna 38 54 8N 6 35W
Culm, R. 30 50 46N 3 31W
Culoz 45 45 47N 5 46E
Culpataro 140 33 40S 144 22E
Culpeper 156 38 29N 77 59W
Culrain 37 57 55N 4 25W
Culross 35 56 4N 3 38W
Cults 37 57 8N 2 10W
Culuene, R. 175 12 15S 53 10W
Culvain Mt. 36 56 55N 5 19W
Culver, Pt. 137 32 54S 124 43E
Culverden 143 42 47S 172 49E
Cumali 69 36 42N 27 28E
Cumaná 174 10 30N 64 5W
Cumari 171 18 16S 48 11W
Cumberland, Can. 152 49 40N 125 0W
Cumberland, Md., U.S.A. 156 39 40N 78 43W
Cumberland, Wis., U.S.A. 158 45 32N 92 3W
Cumberland (□) 26 54 44N 2 55W
Cumberland I. 157 30 52N 81 30W
Cumberland Is. 138 20 35S 149 10E
Cumberland L. 153 54 3N 102 18W
Cumberland Pen. 149 67 0N 64 0W
Cumberland Plat. 157 36 0N 84 30W
Cumberland, R. 157 36 15N 87 0W
Cumberland Sd. 149 65 30N 66 0W
Cumborah 139 29 40S 147 45E
Cumbrae Is. 34 55 46N 4 54W
Cumbres Mayores 57 38 4N 6 39W
Cumbria □ 32 54 35N 2 55W
Cumbrian Mts. 32 54 30N 3 0W
Cumbum 97 15 40N 79 10E
Cuminestown 37 57 32N 2 17W
Cummerower See 48 53 47N 12 52E
Cummertrees 35 55 0N 3 20W
Cummings Mtn. 163 35 2N 118 34W
Cummins 139 34 16S 135 43E
Cumnock, Austral. 141 32 59S 148 46E
Cumnock, U.K. 34 55 27N 4 18W
Cumnor 28 51 44N 1 20W
Cumpas 164 30 0N 109 48W
Cumuruxatiba 171 17 6S 39 13W
Cumwhinton 32 54 51N 2 49W
Cuñaré 174 0 49N 72 32W
Cuncumén 172 31 53S 70 38W
Cunderdin 137 31 37S 117 12E
Cundinamarca □ 174 5 0N 74 0W
Cunene, R. 128 17 0S 15 0E
Cúneo 62 44 23N 7 31E
Cunillera, I. 59 38 59N 1 13E
Cunlhat 44 45 38N 3 32E
Cunnamulla 139 28 2S 145 38E
Cunninghame, Reg. 34 55 38N 4 35W
Cuorgnè 62 45 23N 7 39E
Cupar, Can. 153 50 57N 104 10W
Cupar, U.K. 35 56 20N 3 0W
Cupica 174 6 50N 77 30W
Cupica, Golfo de 174 6 25N 77 30W
Ćuprija 66 43 57N 21 26E
Curaçá 170 8 59S 39 54W
Curaçao, I. 167 12 10N 69 0W
Curanilahue 172 37 29S 73 28W
Curaray, R. 174 1 30S 75 30W
Curatabaca 174 6 19N 62 51W
Curbarado 174 7 3N 76 54W
Curbur 137 26 28S 115 55E
Cure, La 50 46 28N 6 4E
Curepto 172 35 8S 72 1W
Curiapo 174 8 33N 61 5W
Curicó 172 34 55S 71 20W
Curicó □ 172 34 50S 71 15W
Curimatá 170 10 2S 44 17W
Curiplaya 174 0 16N 74 52W
Curitiba 173 25 20S 49 10W
Curlew Mts. 38 54 0N 8 20W
Curoca Norte 128 16 15S 12 58E
Currabubula 141 31 16S 150 44E
Curracunya 139 28 29S 144 9E
Curraglass 39 52 5N 8 4W
Currais Novos 170 6 13S 36 30W
Curralinho 170 1 35S 49 30W
Curran, L. = Terewah, L. 139 29 50S 147 24E
Currane L. 39 51 50N 10 8W
Currant 160 38 51N 115 32W
Curranyalpa 141 30 53S 144 39E
Curraweena 141 30 47S 145 54E
Currawilla 138 25 10S 141 20E
Current, R. 159 37 15N 91 10W
Currie, Austral. 138 39 56S 143 53E
Currie, U.K. 35 55 53N 3 17W
Currie, U.S.A. 160 40 16N 114 45W
Currie, Mt. 129 30 29S 29 21E
Currituck Sd. 157 36 20N 75 50W
Curry Rivel 28 51 2N 2 52W
Curryglass 39 51 40N 9 50W
Curtea-de-Argeş 70 45 12N 24 42E
Curtis, Spain 56 43 7N 8 4W
Curtis, U.S.A. 158 40 41N 100 32W
Curtis, I. 138 23 35S 151 10E
Curtis, Pt. 138 23 53S 151 21E
Curuá, I. 170 0 48N 50 10W
Curuapanema, R. 175 7 0S 54 30W
Curuçá 170 0 35S 47 50W
Curuguaty 173 24 19S 55 49W
Curupira, Serra 174 1 25N 64 30W
Cururupu 170 1 50S 44 50W
Curuzú Cuatiá 172 29 50S 58 5W
Curvelo 171 18 45S 44 27W
Curyo 140 35 50S 142 47E
Cushendall 38 55 5N 6 3W
Cushendun 38 55 8N 6 3W
Cushina 39 53 11N 7 10W
Cushing, Mt. 152 57 35N 126 57W
Cusihuiriáchic 164 28 10N 106 50W
Cussabat 119 32 39N 14 1E
Cusset 44 46 8N 3 28E
Custer 158 43 45N 103 38W
Cut Bank 160 48 40N 112 15W
Cutchogue 162 41 1N 72 30W
Cuthbert 157 31 47N 84 47W
Cutler 163 36 31N 119 17W
Cutra L. 39 53 2N 8 48W
Cutro 65 39 1N 16 58E
Cuttaburra, R. 139 29 43S 144 22E
Cuttack 96 20 25N 85 57E
Cuvier, C. 137 23 14S 113 22E
Cuvier I. 142 36 27S 175 50E
Cuxhaven 48 53 51N 8 41E
Cuyabeno 174 0 16S 75 53W
Cuyahoga Falls 156 41 8N 81 30W
Cuyo 103 10 50N 121 5E
Cuyuni, R. 175 7 0N 59 30W
Cuzco 174 13 32S 72 0W
Cuzco, Mt. 174 20 0S 66 50W
Čǔzǔneşti 70 44 36N 27 3E
Čvrsnica, Mt. 66 43 36N 17 35E
Cwmbran 31 51 39N 3 0W
Cwrt 31 52 35N 3 55W
Cyangugu 126 2 29S 28 54E
Cybinka 54 52 12N 14 46E
Cyclades = Kikladhes 69 37 20N 24 30E
Cygnet 138 43 8S 147 1E
Cymmer 31 51 37N 3 38W
Cynthiana 156 38 23N 84 10W
Cynwyl Elfed 31 51 55N 4 22W
Cypress Hills 153 49 40N 109 30W
Cyprus ■ 92 35 0N 33 0E
Cyrenaica □ 117 27 0N 20 0E
Cyrene 117 32 39N 21 18E
Czaplinek 54 53 34N 16 14E
Czar 153 52 27N 110 50W
Czarne 54 53 42N 16 58E
Czarnków 54 52 55N 16 38E
Czechoslovakia ■ 53 49 0N 17 0E
Czechowice-Dziedzice 54 49 54N 18 59E
Czeladz 54 50 16N 19 2E
Czempin 54 52 9N 16 33E
Czersk 54 53 46N 17 58E
Czerwiensk 54 52 1N 15 13E
Czerwionka 54 50 7N 18 37E
Częstochowa 54 50 49N 19 7E
Częstochowa □ 54 50 45N 19 0E
Czlopa 54 53 6N 16 6E
Człuchów 54 53 41N 17 22E

D

Da Lat 101 11 56N 108 25E
Da Nang 100 16 4N 108 13E
Da, R. 100 21 15N 105 20E
Daarlerveen 46 52 26N 6 34E
Dab'a, Ras el 122 31 3N 28 31E
Dabai 121 11 25N 5 15E
Dabajuro 174 11 2N 70 40W
Dabakala 120 8 15N 4 20W
Dabatou 120 11 50N 9 20W
Dabburiya 90 32 42N 35 22E
Daberas 128 25 27S 18 30E
Dabhoi 94 22 10N 73 20E
Dabie 54 53 27N 14 45E
Dabola 120 10 50N 11 5W
Dabong 101 5 23N 103 1E
Dabou 120 5 20N 4 23W
Daboya 121 9 30N 1 20W
Dabra Berhan 123 9 42N 39 15E
Dabra Sina 123 9 51N 39 45E
Dabra Tabor 123 11 50N 37 58E
Dabra Zabit 123 11 48N 38 30E
Dabrowa Górnicza 54 50 15N 19 10E
Dabrowa Tarnówska 54 50 10N 20 59E
Dabrówno 54 53 27N 20 2E
Dabus, R. 123 10 12N 35 0E
Dacca 98 23 43N 90 26E
Dacca □ 98 24 0N 90 25E
Dachau 49 48 16N 11 27E
Dadanawa 174 3 0N 59 30W
Daday 82 41 28N 33 35E
Daddato 123 12 24N 42 45E
Dade City 157 28 20N 82 12W
Dadiya 121 9 35N 11 24E
Dadra and Nagar Haveli □ 96 20 5N 73 0E
Dadri = Charkhi Dadri 94 28 37N 76 17E
Dadu 94 26 45N 67 45E
Daer R. 35 55 23N 3 39W
Daet 103 14 2N 122 55E
Dagaio 123 6 8N 40 40E
Dagana 120 16 30N 15 20W
Dagash 122 19 19N 33 25E
Dagestan, A.S.S.R. □ 83 42 30N 47 0E
Daggett 163 34 43N 116 52W
Daggs Sd. 143 45 23S 166 45E
Daghfeli 122 19 18N 32 40E
Daghirie 123 11 40N 41 50E
Dagö = Hiiumaa 80 58 50N 22 45E
Dagoreti 126 1 18S 36 4E
Dagua 135 3 27S 143 20E
Dagupan 103 16 3N 120 20E
Dahab 122 28 30N 34 31E
Dahlak Kebir 123 15 50N 40 10E
Dahlenburg 48 53 11N 10 43E
Dahlonega 157 34 35N 83 59W
Dahme 48 51 51N 13 25E
Daho 121 10 28N 11 18E
Dahomey ■ = Benin ■ 121 8 0N 2 0E
Dahra 120 15 22N 15 30W
Dahra, Massif de 118 36 7N 1 21E
Dai Hao 100 18 1N 106 25E
Dai-Sen 110 35 22N 133 32E
Daigo 111 36 46N 140 21E
Dailly 34 55 16N 4 44W
Daimanji-San 110 36 14N 133 20E
Daimiel 59 39 5N 3 35W
Daintree 138 16 20S 145 20E
Daiō-Misaki 111 34 15N 136 45E
Dairen = Lüta 107 38 55N 121 40E
Dairût 122 27 34N 30 43E
Dairymple 34 55 24N 4 36W
Daisetsu-Zan 112 43 30N 142 57E
Daitari 96 21 10N 85 46E
Daitō 110 35 19N 132 58E
Dajarra 138 21 42S 139 30E
Dak Dam 100 12 20N 107 21E
Dak Nhe 100 15 28N 107 48E
Dak Pek 100 15 4N 107 44E
Dak Song 101 12 19N 107 35E
Dak Sui 100 14 55N 107 43E
Dakala 121 14 27N 2 27E
Dakar 120 14 34N 17 29W
Dakhla 116 23 50N 15 53W
Dakhla, El Wâhât el- 122 25 30N 28 50E
Dakhovskaya 83 44 13N 40 13E
Dakingari 121 11 37N 4 1E
Dakor 94 22 45N 73 11E
Dakoro 121 14 31N 6 46E
Dakota City 158 42 27N 96 28W
Dakota, North 158 47 30N 100 0W
Đakovica 66 42 22N 20 26E
Dakovo 66 45 19N 18 24E
Dakra 120 15 22N 15 30W
Dalaba 120 10 42N 12 15W
Dalälven, L. 72 61 27N 17 15E
Dalandzadgad 106 43 27N 104 30E

Dalarö **Degeh-Bur**

Dalarö	**75**	59 8N	18 24 E
Dalat	**101**	12 3N	108 32 E
Dalbandin	**93**	29 0N	4 23 E
Dalbeattie	**35**	54 55N	3 50W
Dalbosjön, L.	**73**	58 40N	12 45 E
Dalby, Austral.	**139**	27 10 S	151 17 E
Dalby, Sweden	**73**	55 42N	13 22 E
Dale, Sogn og Fjordane, Norway	**71**	61 27N	7 28 E
Dale, Sogn og Fjordane, Norway	**71**	61 22N	5 23 E
Dale, U.K.	**31**	51 42N	5 11W
Dalen, Neth.	**46**	52 42N	6 46 E
Dalen, Norway	**71**	59 26N	8 0 E
Dalet	**98**	19 59N	93 51 E
Daletme	**98**	21 36N	92 46 E
Dalfsen	**46**	52 31N	6 16 E
Dalga	**122**	27 39N	30 41 E
Dalgaranger, Mt.	**137**	27 50 S	117 5 E
Dalhalvaig	**37**	58 28N	3 53W
Dalhart	**159**	36 0N	102 30W
Dalhousie, Can.	**151**	48 0N	66 26W
Dalhousie, India	**94**	32 38N	76 0 E
Daliburgh	**36**	57 10N	7 23W
Dalj	**174**	45 28N	18 58 E
Dalkeith	**35**	55 54N	3 5W
Dalkey	**39**	53 16N	6 7W
Dall I.	**152**	54 59N	133 25W
Dallarnil	**139**	25 19 S	152 2 E
Dallas, U.K.	**37**	57 33N	3 32W
Dallas, Oregon, U.S.A.	**160**	45 0N	123 15W
Dallas, Texas, U.S.A.	**159**	32 50N	96 50W
Dallol	**123**	14 14N	40 17 E
Dalmacija	**66**	43 20N	17 0 E
Dalmally	**34**	56 25N	5 0W
Dalmatia = Dalmacija	**66**	43 20N	17 0 E
Dalmatovo	**84**	56 16N	62 56 E
Dalmellington	**34**	55 20N	4 25W
Dalneretchensk	**77**	45 50N	133 40 E
Daloa	**120**	7 0N	6 30W
Dalry	**34**	55 44N	4 42W
Dalrymple, Mt.	**133**	21 1 S	148 39 E
Dalsjöfors	**73**	57 46N	18 5 E
Dalskog	**73**	58 44N	12 18 E
Dalton, Can.	**150**	48 11N	84 1W
Dalton, Cumbria, U.K.	**33**	54 9N	3 11W
Dalton, Dumfries, U.K.	**35**	55 3N	3 22W
Dalton, N. Yorks., U.K.	**33**	54 28N	1 32W
Dalton, Ga., U.S.A.	**103**	34 45N	85 0W
Dalton, Mass., U.S.A.	**162**	42 28N	73 11W
Dalton, Nebr., U.S.A.	**158**	41 27N	103 0W
Dalton Post	**152**	66 42N	137 0W
Daltonganj	**95**	24 0N	84 4 E
Dalvík	**74**	65 58N	18 32W
Dalwhinnie	**37**	56 56N	4 14W
Daly City	**163**	37 42N	122 28W
Daly L.	**153**	56 32N	105 39W
Daly, R.	**136**	13 21 S	130 18 E
Daly Waters	**138**	16 15 S	133 24 E
Dalystown	**38**	53 26N	7 23W
Dam	**170**	4 45N	55 0W
Dam Doi	**101**	8 59N	105 12 E
Dam Gillan	**153**	56 20N	94 40W
Dam Ha	**100**	21 21N	107 36 E
Dama, Wadi	**122**	27 12N	35 50 E
Daman	**96**	20 25N	72 57 E
Daman □	**96**	20 25N	72 58 E
Damanhûr	**122**	31 0N	30 30 E
Damar, I.	**103**	7 15 S	128 30 E
Damaraland	**128**	21 0 S	17 0 E
Damascus = Dimashq	**92**	33 30N	36 18 E
Damaturu	**121**	11 45N	11 55 E
Damãvand	**93**	36 0N	52 0 E
Damãvand, Qolleh-ye	**93**	35 45N	52 10 E
Damba, Angola	**124**	6 44 S	15 29 E
Damba, Ethiopia	**123**	15 10N	38 47 E
Dâmbovnic, R.	**70**	44 28N	25 18 E
Dame Marie	**167**	18 36N	74 26W
Damerham	**28**	50 57N	1 52W
Dames Quarter	**162**	38 11N	75 54W
Damghan	**93**	36 10N	54 17 E
Damietta = Dumyât	**122**	31 24N	31 48 E
Damin	**93**	27 30N	60 40 E
Damiya	**90**	32 6N	35 34 E
Damman	**92**	26 25N	50 2 E
Dammarie	**43**	48 20N	1 30 E
Dammartin	**43**	49 3N	2 41 E
Dammastock	**51**	46 38N	8 24 E
Damme	**48**	52 32N	8 12 E
Damodar, R.	**95**	23 17N	87 35 E
Damoh	**95**	23 50N	79 28 E
Dampier	**136**	20 41 S	116 42 E
Dampier Arch.	**136**	20 38 S	116 32 E
Dampier Downs	**136**	18 24 S	123 5 E
Dampier, Selat	**103**	0 40 S	131 0 E
Dampier Str.	**135**	5 50 S	148 0 E
Damrei, Chuor Phnum	**101**	12 30N	103 0 E
Damville	**42**	48 51N	1 5 E
Damvillers	**43**	49 20N	5 21 E
Dan Chadi	**121**	12 47N	5 17 E
Dan Dume	**121**	11 28N	7 8 E
Dan Gora	**121**	11 30N	8 7 E
Dan Gulbi	**121**	11 40N	6 15 E
Dan, oilfield	**19**	55 30N	5 10 E
Dan Sadau	**121**	11 25N	6 20 E
Dana	**103**	11 0 S	122 52 E
Dana, Lac	**150**	50 53N	77 20W
Dana, Mt	**163**	37 54N	119 12W
Danakil Depression	**123**	12 45N	41 0 E
Danao	**103**	10 31N	124 1 E
Danbury	**162**	41 23N	73 29W
Danby L.	**161**	34 17N	115 0W
Dand	**94**	31 28N	65 32 E
Dandaragan	**137**	30 40 S	115 40 E
Dandeldhura	**95**	29 20N	80 35 E
Dandeli	**93**	15 5N	74 30 E
Dandenong	**141**	38 0 S	145 15 E
Dandkandi	**98**	23 32N	90 43 E
Danforth	**151**	45 39N	67 57W
Dang Raek	**101**	14 40N	104 0 E
Dangara	**85**	38 6N	69 22 E
•Danger Is.	**131**	10 53 S	165 49W
Danger Pt.	**128**	34 40 S	19 17 E
Dangla	**123**	11 18N	36 56 E
Dangora	**121**	11 30N	8 7 E
Dangrek, Phnom	**100**	14 15N	105 0 E
Daniel	**160**	42 56N	110 2W
Daniel's Harbour	**151**	50 13N	57 35W
Danielskull	**128**	28 11 S	23 33 E
Danielson	**162**	41 50N	71 52W
Danilov	**81**	58 16N	40 13 E
Danilovgrad	**66**	42 38N	19 9 E
Danilovka	**81**	50 25N	44 12 E
Danissa	**126**	3 15N	40 58 E
Danja	**121**	11 29N	7 30 E
Dankalwa	**121**	11 52N	12 12 E
Dankama	**121**	13 20N	7 44 E
Dankhar Gompa	**93**	32 10N	78 10 E
Dankov	**81**	53 20N	39 5 E
Danlí	**166**	14 4N	86 35W
Dannemora	**75**	60 12N	17 51 E
Dannenberg	**48**	53 7N	11 4 E
Dannevirke	**142**	40 12 S	176 8 E
Dannhauser	**129**	28 0 S	30 3 E
Dansalan	**103**	8 2N	124 30 E
Dansville	**156**	42 32N	77 41W
Dantan	**95**	21 57N	87 20 E
Danube, R.	**53**	45 0N	28 20W
Danubyo	**98**	17 15N	95 35 E
Danvers	**162**	42 34N	70 55 E
Danville, Ill., U.S.A.	**156**	40 10N	87 40W
Danville, Ky., U.S.A.	**156**	37 40N	84 45W
Danville, Pa., U.S.A.	**162**	40 58N	76 37W
Danville, Va., U.S.A.	**157**	36 40N	79 20W
Danzig = Gdansk	**54**	54 22N	18 40 E
Dão	**103**	10 30N	122 6 E
Dão, R.	**56**	40 28N	8 0W
Daosa	**94**	26 52N	76 20 E
Daoud = Aïn Beida	**119**	35 50N	7 29 E
Daoulas	**42**	48 22N	4 17W
Dapango	**121**	10 55N	0 16 E
Dar al Hamra, Ad	**92**	27 22N	37 43 E
Dar es Salaam	**126**	6 50 S	39 12 E
Dar'á	**90**	32 36N	36 7 E
Darab	**93**	28 50N	54 30 E
Darabani	**70**	48 10N	26 39 E
Daraj	**119**	30 10N	10 28 E
Daraut Kurgan	**85**	39 33N	72 11 E
Daravica	**66**	42 32N	20 8 E
Daraw	**121**	24 22N	32 51 E
Darazo	**121**	11 1N	10 24W
Darband	**94**	34 30N	72 50 E
Darbhanga	**95**	26 15N	86 8 E
Darby	**160**	46 2N	114 7W
D'Arcy	**152**	50 35N	122 30W
Darda	**66**	45 40N	18 41 E
Dardanelle	**163**	38 2N	119 50W
Dardanelles = Canakkale Bogłazi	**92**	40 0N	26 20 E
Dardenelle	**159**	35 12N	93 9W
Darent, R.	**29**	51 22N	0 12 E
Darfield	**143**	43 29 S	172 7 E
Darfo	**62**	45 43N	10 11 E
Dargai	**94**	34 25N	71 45 E
Dargan Ata	**76**	40 40N	62 20 E
Dargaville	**142**	35 57 S	173 52 E
Darharala	**120**	8 23N	4 20W
Dari	**123**	5 48N	30 26 E
Darién, G. del	**174**	9 0N	77 0W
Darién, Serranía del	**174**	8 30N	77 30W
Dariganga	**106**	45 5N	113 45 E
Darinskoye	**84**	51 20N	51 44 E
Darjeeling	**95**	27 3N	88 18 E
Dark Cove	**151**	48 47N	54 13W
Darkan	**137**	33 20 S	116 43 E
Darke Peak	**140**	33 27 S	136 12 E
Darkot Pass	**95**	36 45N	73 26 E
Darlaston	**28**	52 35N	2 1W
Darling Downs	**139**	28 30 S	152 0 E
Darling, R.	**140**	34 4 S	141 54 E
Darling Ra.	**137**	32 30 S	116 0 E
Darlington, U.K.	**33**	54 33N	1 33W
Darlington, S.C., U.S.A.	**157**	34 18N	79 50W
Darlington, Wis., U.S.A.	**158**	42 43N	90 7W
Darlot, L.	**137**	27 48 S	121 35 E
Darłowo	**54**	54 25N	16 25 E
Darmstadt	**49**	49 51N	8 40 E
Darnall	**129**	29 23 S	31 18 E
Darnétal	**42**	49 25N	1 10 E
Darney	**43**	48 5N	6 0 E
Darnick	**140**	32 48 S	143 38 E
Darnley B.	**147**	69 30N	123 30W
Darnley, C.	**13**	68 0 S	69 0 E
Daroca	**58**	41 9N	1 25W
Darr	**138**	23 13 S	144 7 E
Darr, R.	**138**	23 39 S	143 50 E
Darragh	**39**	52 47N	9 7W
Darran Mts.	**143**	44 37 S	167 59 E
Darrington	**160**	48 14N	121 37W
Darror, R.	**91**	10 30N	50 0 E
Darsana	**98**	23 35N	88 48 E
Darsi	**97**	15 46N	79 44 E
Darsser Ort	**48**	44 27N	12 30 E
Dart, R., N.Z.	**143**	44 20 S	168 20 E
Dart, R., U.K.	**30**	50 24N	3 36W
Dartford	**29**	51 26N	0 15 E
Dartington	**30**	50 26N	3 42W
Dartmoor, Austral.	**140**	37 56N	141 19 E
Dartmoor, U.K.	**30**	50 36N	4 0W
Dartmouth, Austral.	**138**	23 31 S	144 44 E
Dartmouth, Can.	**151**	44 40N	63 30W
Dartmouth, U.K.	**30**	50 21N	3 35W
Dartmouth, L.	**139**	26 4 S	145 18 E
Darton	**33**	53 36N	1 32W
Dartuch, C.	**58**	39 55N	3 49 E
Daru, P.N.G.	**135**	9 3 S	143 13 E
Daru, S. Leone	**120**	8 0N	10 52W
Darvel	**34**	55 37N	4 20W
Darvel Bay	**103**	4 50N	118 20 E
Darwen	**32**	53 42N	2 29W
Darwha	**96**	20 15N	77 45 E
Darwin, Austral.	**136**	12 25 S	130 51 E
Darwin, U.S.A.	**163**	36 15N	117 35W
Darwin, Mt.	**127**	16 45 S	31 33 E
Darwin River	**136**	12 50 S	130 58 E
Daryacheh-ye-Sistan	**93**	31 0N	61 0 E
Daryapur	**96**	20 55N	77 20 E
Dase	**123**	14 53N	37 15 E
Dashato, R.	**123**	7 25N	42 40 E
Dashkesan	**83**	40 40N	46 0 E
Dasht-e Kavīr	**93**	34 30N	55 0 E
Dasht-e Lut	**93**	31 30N	58 0 E
Dasht-i-Khash	**93**	32 0N	62 0 E
Dasht-i-Margo	**93**	30 40N	62 30 E
Dasht-i-Nawar	**94**	33 52N	68 0 E
Dasht, R.	**93**	25 40N	62 20 E
Daska	**94**	32 20N	74 20 E
Dassa-Zoume	**121**	7 46N	2 14 E
Dasseneiland	**128**	33 37 S	18 3 E
Datça	**69**	36 46N	27 40 E
Datia	**95**	25 39N	78 27 E
Dattapur	**96**	20 45N	78 15 E
Daugava	**80**	57 0N	24 0 E
Daugavpils	**80**	55 53N	26 32 E
Daulat Yar	**93**	34 30N	65 45 E
Daulatabad	**96**	19 57N	75 15 E
Daun	**49**	50 5N	6 53 E
Dauphin, Can.	**153**	51 9N	100 5W
Dauphin, U.S.A.	**162**	40 22N	76 56W
Dauphin I.	**157**	30 16N	88 10W
Dauphin L.	**153**	51 20N	99 45W
Dauphiné	**45**	45 15N	5 25 E
Dauqa	**122**	19 30N	41 0 E
Daura, Kano, Nigeria	**121**	13 2N	8 21 E
Daura, N.-E., Nigeria	**121**	11 31N	11 24 E
Davadi	**120**	14 10N	16 3W
Davangere	**97**	14 25N	75 50 E
Davao	**103**	7 0N	125 40 E
Davao, G. of	**103**	6 30N	125 48 E
Davar Panab	**93**	27 25N	62 15 E
Dave	**74**	52 55N	1 50W
Davenport, Calif., U.S.A.	**163**	37 1N	122 12W
Davenport, Iowa, U.S.A.	**158**	41 30N	90 40W
Davenport, Wash., U.S.A.	**160**	47 40N	118 5W
Davenport Downs	**138**	24 8 S	141 7 E
Davenport Ra.	**138**	20 28 S	134 0 E
Daventry	**28**	52 16N	1 10W
David	**166**	8 30N	82 30W
David City	**158**	41 18N	97 10W
David Gorodok	**80**	52 4N	27 8 E
Davidson	**153**	51 16N	105 59W
Davik	**71**	61 53N	5 33 E
Davis	**163**	38 33N	121 45W
Davis Dam	**161**	35 11N	114 35W
Davis Inlet	**151**	55 50N	60 45W
Davis Mts.	**159**	30 42N	104 15W
Davis Str.	**149**	65 0N	58 0W
Davlekanovo	**84**	54 13N	55 3 E
Davos	**51**	46 48N	9 49 E
Davy L.	**153**	58 53N	108 18W
Davyhurst	**137**	30 2 S	120 40 E
Dawa, R.	**123**	5 0N	39 5 E
Dawaki, Jos, Nigeria	**121**	9 25N	9 33 E
Dawaki, Kano, Nigeria	**121**	12 5N	8 23 E
Dawayima	**90**	31 33N	34 55 E
Dawes Ra.	**138**	24 40 S	150 40 E
Dawley	**28**	52 40N	2 29W
Dawlish	**30**	50 34N	3 28W
Dawna Range	**98**	16 30N	98 30 E
Dawnyein	**98**	15 54N	95 36 E
Dawros Hd.	**38**	54 48N	8 32W
Dawson, Can.	**147**	64 10N	139 30W
Dawson, Ga., U.S.A.	**157**	31 45N	84 28W
Dawson, N.D., U.S.A.	**158**	46 56N	99 45W
Dawson Creek	**152**	55 45N	120 15W
Dawson, I.	**176**	53 50 S	70 50W
Dawson Inlet	**153**	61 50N	93 25W
Dawson, R.	**133**	23 25 S	150 10 E
Dawson Range	**138**	24 30 S	149 48 E
Dawson's	**127**	17 0 S	30 57 E
Daylesford	**140**	37 21 S	144 9 E
Dayr al-Ghusūn	**90**	32 21N	35 4 E
Dayr az Zawr	**92**	35 20N	40 5 E
Daysland	**152**	52 50N	112 20W
Dayton, Ohio, U.S.A.	**156**	39 45N	84 10W
Dayton, Tenn., U.S.A.	**157**	35 30N	85 1W
Dayton, Wash., U.S.A.	**160**	46 20N	118 0W
Daytona Beach	**157**	29 14N	81 0W
Dayville	**160**	44 33N	119 37W
De Aar	**128**	30 39 S	24 0 E
De Bilt	**46**	52 6N	5 11 E
De Funiak Springs	**157**	30 42N	86 10W
De Grey	**136**	20 12 S	119 12 E
De Grey, R.	**136**	20 0 S	119 13 E
De Kalb	**158**	41 55N	88 45W
De Koog	**46**	53 6N	4 46 E
De Land	**157**	29 1N	81 19W
De Leon	**159**	32 9N	98 35W
De Long Mts.	**147**	68 10N	163 0W
De Long, Ostrova	**77**	76 40N	149 20 E
De Panne	**47**	51 6N	2 34 E
De Pere	**156**	44 28N	88 1W
De Queen	**159**	34 3N	94 24W
De Quincy	**159**	30 30N	93 27W
De Ridder	**159**	30 48N	93 15W
De Rijp	**46**	52 33N	4 51 E
De Smet	**158**	44 25N	97 35W
De Tour Village	**156**	45 49N	83 56W
De Witt	**159**	34 19N	91 20W
Dead Sea = Miyet, Bahr el	**92**	31 30N	35 30 E
Deadwood	**58**	44 25N	103 43W
Deadwood L.	**152**	59 10N	128 30W
Deaf Adder Cr.	**136**	13 0 S	132 47 E
Deakin	**137**	30 46 S	129 58 E
Deal	**29**	51 13N	1 25 E
Dealesville	**128**	28 41 S	25 44 E
Dean, Forest of	**28**	51 50N	2 35W
Deán Funes	**172**	30 20 S	64 20W
Dearborn	**150**	42 18N	83 15W
Dearham	**32**	54 43N	3 28W
Dease L.	**152**	58 40N	130 5W
Dease Lake	**152**	58 25N	130 6W
Dease, R.	**152**	59 56N	128 32W
Death Valley	**163**	36 27N	116 52W
Death Valley Junc.	**163**	36 21N	116 30W
Death Valley Nat. Monument	**163**	36 30N	117 0W
Deauville	**42**	49 23N	0 2 E
Deba Habe	**121**	10 14N	11 20 E
Debaltsevo	**82**	48 22N	38 26 E
Debar	**66**	41 21N	20 37 E
Debba	**123**	14 20N	41 18 E
Debden	**153**	53 30N	106 50W
Debdou	**118**	33 59N	3 0W
Debeeti	**128**	23 45 S	26 32 E
Deben, R.	**29**	52 4N	1 19 E
Debenham	**29**	52 14N	1 10 E
Debessy	**84**	57 39N	53 49 E
Dębica	**54**	50 2N	21 25 E
Deblin	**54**	51 34N	21 50 E
Debo, L.	**120**	15 14N	3 57W
Debolt	**152**	55 12N	118 1W
Deborah, gasfield	**19**	53 4N	1 50 E
Deborah, L.	**137**	30 45 S	119 0 E
Debrc	**66**	44 38N	19 53 E
Debre Birhan	**123**	9 41N	39 31 E
Debre Markos	**123**	10 20N	37 40 E
Debre May	**123**	11 20N	37 25 E
Debre Sina	**123**	9 51N	39 50 E
Debre Tabor	**123**	11 50N	38 26 E
Debrecen	**53**	47 33N	21 42 E
Dečani	**66**	42 30N	20 10 E
Decatur, Ala., U.S.A.	**157**	34 35N	87 0W
Decatur, Ga., U.S.A.	**157**	33 47N	84 17W
Decatur, Ill., U.S.A.	**158**	39 50N	89 0W
Decatur, Ind., U.S.A.	**156**	40 52N	85 28W
Decatur, Texas, U.S.A.	**159**	33 15N	97 35W
Decazeville	**44**	44 34N	2 15 E
Deccan	**97**	14 0N	77 0 E
Deception I.	**13**	63 0 S	60 15W
Deception L.	**153**	56 33N	104 13W
Deception, Mt.	**140**	30 42 S	138 16 E
Decize	**43**	46 50N	3 28 E
Decollatura	**65**	39 2N	16 21 E
Decorah	**158**	43 20N	91 50W
Deda	**70**	46 56N	24 50 E
Dedaye	**98**	16 24N	95 53 E
Deddington	**28**	51 58N	1 19W
Dedemsvaavt	**46**	52 36N	6 28 E
Dedham	**162**	42 14N	71 10W
Dedilovo	**81**	53 59N	37 50 E
Dédougou	**120**	12 30N	3 35W
Deduru Oya	**97**	7 32N	81 45 E
Dedza	**127**	14 20 S	34 20 E
Dee, R., Eng.-Wales, U.K.	**31**	53 15N	3 7W
Dee, R., Scot., U.K.	**37**	57 4N	2 7W
Deel R.	**38**	53 35N	7 9W
Deelish	**39**	51 41N	9 18W
Deep B.	**152**	61 15N	116 35W
Deep Lead	**140**	37 0 S	142 43 E
Deep Well	**138**	24 20 S	134 0 E
Deepdale	**136**	26 22 S	114 20 E
Deeping Fen	**29**	52 45N	0 15W
Deeping, St. Nicholas	**29**	52 44N	0 11W
Deepwater	**139**	29 25 S	151 51 E
Deer I.	**147**	54 55N	162 20W
Deer Lake, Newf., Can.	**151**	49 11N	57 27W
Deer Lake, Ontario, Can.	**153**	52 36N	94 20W
Deer Lodge	**160**	46 25N	112 40W
Deer Park	**160**	47 55N	117 21W
Deer, R.	**153**	58 23N	94 13W
Deer River	**158**	47 21N	93 44W
Deer Sound	**37**	58 58N	2 50W
Deeral	**138**	17 14 S	145 55 E
Deerdepoort	**128**	24 37 S	26 27 E
Deering	**147**	66 5N	162 50W
Deerlijk	**47**	50 51N	3 22 E
Deerness	**37**	58 57N	2 44W
Deesa	**94**	24 18N	72 10 E
Deferiet	**162**	44 2N	75 41W
Defiance	**156**	41 20N	84 20W
Deganwy	**31**	53 18N	3 49W
Deganya	**90**	32 43N	35 34 E
Degebe, R.	**57**	38 21N	7 37W
Degeh-Bur	**91**	8 11N	43 31 E

*Renamed Pukapuka

CIB

Degema Dieuze

Degema 121 4 50N 6 48 E
Degerfors 74 64 16N 19 46 E
Degersfor 73 59 20N 14 28 E
Degersheim 51 47 23N 9 12 E
Degersiö 72 63 13N 18 3 E
Deggendorf 49 48 49N 12 59 E
Degloor 96 18 34N 77 33 E
Deh Bīd 93 30 39N 53 11 E
Deh Kheyr 93 28 45N 54 40 E
Deh Titan 93 33 45N 63 50 E
Dehibat 119 32 0N 10 47 E
Dehiwala 97 6 50N 79 51 E
Dehkhvareqan 92 37 50N 45 55 E
Dehra Dun 94 30 20N 78 4 E
Dehri 95 24 50N 84 15 E
Deinze 47 50 59N 3 32 E
Deir Abu Sa'id 90 32 30N 38 42 E
Deir Dibwan 90 31 55N 35 15 E
Dej 70 47 10N 23 52 E
Deje 72 59 35N 13 29 E
Dekar 128 18 30 S 23 10 E
Dekemhare 123 15 6N 39 0 E
Dekese 124 3 24 S 21 24 E
Dekhkanabad 85 38 21N 66 30 E
Del Mar 163 32 58N 117 16W
Del Norte 161 37 47N 106 27W
Del Rey, Rio 121 4 30N 8 48 E
Del Rio, Mexico 164 29 22N 100 54W
Del Rio, U.S.A. 159 29 15N 100 50W
Delabole 30 50 37N 4 45W
Delagoa B. 129 25 50 S 32 45 E
Delagua 159 32 35N 104 40W
Delai 122 17 21N 36 6 E
Delambre I. 136 20 27 S 117 4 E
Delano 163 35 48N 119 13W
Delareyville 128 26 41 S 25 26 E
Delavan 158 42 40N 88 39W
Delaware 156 40 20N 83 0W
Delaware □ 162 39 0N 75 40W
Delaware B. 162 38 50N 75 0W
Delaware City 162 39 34N 75 36W
Delaware, R. 162 39 20N 75 25W
Delčevo 66 41 58N 22 46 E
Delchirach 37 57 23N 3 20W
Delegate 141 37 4 S 148 56 E
Delémont 50 47 22N 7 20 E
Delft 46 52 1N 4 22 E
Delft I. 97 9 30N 79 40 E
Delfzijl 46 53 20N 6 55 E
Delgado, C. 127 10 45 S 40 40 E
Delgerhet 106 45 50N 110 30 E
Delgo 122 20 6N 30 40 E
Delhi, India 94 28 38N 77 17 E
Delhi, U.S.A. 162 42 17N 74 56W
Deli Jovan 66 44 13N 22 9 E
Delia 152 51 38N 112 23W
Delice, R. 92 39 45N 34 15 E
Delicias 164 28 10N 105 30W
Delicias, Laguna 164 28 7N 105 40W
Delimiro Gouveia 170 9 23 S 37 59W
Delitzsch 48 51 32N 12 22 E
Dell City 161 31 58N 105 19W
Dell Rapids 158 43 53N 96 44W
Delle 43 47 30N 7 2 E
Dellys 119 36 50N 3 57 E
Delmar, Del., U.S.A. 162 38 27N 75 34W
Delmar, N.Y., U.S.A. 162 42 5N 73 50W
Delmenhorst 48 53 3N 8 37 E
Delmiro 170 9 24 S 38 6W
Delnice 63 45 23N 14 50 E
Deloraine, Austral. 138 41 30 S 146 40 E
Deloraine, Can. 153 49 15N 100 29W
Delorme, L. 151 54 31N 69 52W
Delovo 66 44 55N 20 52 E
Delphi 156 40 37N 86 40W
Delphos 156 40 51N 84 17W
Delportshoop 128 28 22 S 24 20 E
Delray Beach 157 26 27N 80 4W
Delsbo 72 61 48N 16 32 E
Delta, Colo., U.S.A. 161 38 44N 108 5W
Delta, Utah, U.S.A. 160 39 21N 112 29W
Delta Amacuro □ 174 8 30N 61 30W
Deltaville 162 37 33N 76 20W
Delungra 139 29 39 S 150 51 E
Delvin 38 53 37N 7 8W
Delvina 68 39 59N 20 4 E
Delvinákion 68 39 57N 20 32 E
Demak 103 6 50 S 110 40 E
Demanda, Sierra de la 58 42 15N 3 0W
Demba 124 5 28 S 22 15 E
Dembecha 123 10 32N 37 30 E
Dembi 123 8 5N 36 25 E
Dembia 126 3 33N 25 48 E
Dembidolo 123 8 34N 34 50 E
Demchok 93 32 40N 79 29 E
Demer, R. 47 51 0N 5 8 E
Demerais, L. 150 47 35N 77 0W
Demerara, R. 174 7 0N 58 0W
Demidov 80 55 10N 31 30 E
Deming 161 32 10N 107 50W
Demini, R. 174 0 46N 62 56W
Demmin 48 53 54N 13 2 E
Demmit 152 55 20N 119 50W
Demnate 118 31 44N 6 59W
Demonte 62 44 18N 7 18 E
Demopolis 157 32 30N 87 48W
Dempo, Mt. 102 4 10 S 103 15 E
Demyansk 80 57 30N 32 27 E
Den Bemmel 46 51 43N 4 26 E
Den Burg 46 53 3N 4 47 E
Den Chai 100 17 59N 100 4 E
Den Dungen 47 51 41N 5 22 E
Den Haag = 's Gravenhage 46 52 7N 4 17 E
Den Ham 46 52 28N 6 30 E
Den Helder 46 52 57N 4 45 E
Den Hulst 46 52 36N 6 16 E
Den Oever 46 52 56N 5 2 E
Denain 43 50 20N 3 22 E
Denair 163 37 32N 120 48W
Denau 85 38 16N 67 54 E
Denbigh 31 53 12N 3 26W
Denbigh (□) 26 53 8N 3 30W
Denby Dale 33 53 35N 1 40W
Denchin 99 31 35N 95 15 E
Dendang 102 3 7 S 107 56 E
Dender, R. 47 51 2N 4 6 E
Denderhoutem 47 50 53N 4 2 E
Denderleeuw 47 50 54N 4 5 E
Dendermonde 47 51 2N 4 5 E
Deneba 123 9 47N 39 10 E
Denekamp 46 52 22N 7 1 E
Denezhkin Kamen, Gora 84 60 25N 59 32 E
Denge 121 12 52N 5 21 E
Dengi 121 9 25N 9 55 E
Denham 137 25 56 S 113 31 E
Denham Ra. 138 21 55 S 147 46 E
Denham Sd. 137 25 45 S 113 15 E
Denholm 153 52 40N 108 0W
Denia 59 38 49N 0 8 E
Denial B. 139 32 14 S 133 32 E
Deniliquin 141 35 30 S 144 58 E
Denison, Iowa, U.S.A. 158 42 0N 95 18W
Denison, Texas, U.S.A. 159 33 50N 96 40W
Denison Plains 136 18 35 S 128 0 E
Denison Range 136 28 30 S 136 5 E
Denisovka 84 52 28N 61 46 E
Denizli 92 37 42N 29 2 E
Denkez Iyesus 123 12 27N 37 43 E
Denman 141 32 24 S 150 42 E
Denmark 137 34 59 S 117 18 E
Denmark ■ 73 55 30N 9 0 E
Denmark Str. 14 66 0N 30 0W
Dennis Hd. 37 59 23N 2 26W
Denniston 143 41 45 S 171 49 E
Denny 35 56 1N 3 55W
Denpasar 102 8 45 S 115 5 E
Dent 32 54 17N 2 28W
Denton, E. Sussex, U.K. 29 50 48N 0 5 E
Denton, Gr. Manchester, U.K. 32 53 26N 2 10W
Denton, Lincs., U.K. 33 52 52N 0 42W
Denton, Md., U.S.A. 162 38 53N 75 50W
Denton, Mont., U.S.A. 160 47 25N 109 56W
Denton, Texas, U.S.A. 159 33 12N 97 10W
D'Entrecasteaux, C. 137 34 50 S 115 59 E
D'Entrecasteaux Is. 135 9 0 S 151 0 E
D'Entrecasteaux Pt. 137 34 50 S 115 57 E
Dents du Midi 50 46 10N 6 56 E
Denu 121 6 4N 1 8 E
Denver, Colo., U.S.A. 158 39 45N 105 0W
Denver, Pa., U.S.A. 162 40 14N 76 8W
Denver City 159 32 58N 102 48W
Deoband 94 29 42N 77 43 E
Deobhog 96 19 53N 82 44 E
Deogarh 96 21 32N 84 45 E
Deoghar 95 24 30N 86 59 E
Deolali 96 19 50N 73 50 E
Deoli 94 25 50N 75 50 E
Deoria 95 26 31N 83 48 E
Deosai, Mts. 95 35 40N 75 0 E
Deposit 162 42 5N 75 23W
Depot Spring 137 27 55 S 120 3 E
Depuch I. 136 20 35 S 117 44 E
Deputatskiy 77 69 18N 139 54 E
Dera Ghazi Khan 94 30 5N 70 43 E
Dera Ismail Khan 94 31 50N 70 50 E
Dera Ismail Khan □ 94 32 30N 70 0 E
Derati Wells 126 3 52N 36 37 E
Derbent 74 42 5N 48 15 E
Derby, Austral. 136 17 18 S 123 38 E
Derby, U.K. 33 52 55N 1 28W
Derby, U.S.A. 162 41 20N 73 5W
Derby □ 33 52 55N 1 28W
Derecske 53 47 20N 21 33 E
Derg, L. 39 53 0N 8 20W
Derg, R. 38 54 42N 7 26W
Dergachi 81 50 3N 36 3 E
Dergaon 99 26 45N 94 0 E
Dermantsi 67 43 8N 24 17 E
Derna 117 32 40N 22 35 E
Dernieres Isles 159 29 0N 90 45W
Derriana, L. 39 51 54N 10 1W
Derrinallum 140 37 57 S 143 15 E
Derry R. 39 52 43N 6 35W
Derrybrien 39 53 4N 8 38W
Derrygonnelly 38 54 25N 7 50W
Derrygrogan 39 53 19N 7 23W
Derrykeighan 38 55 8N 6 30W
Derrylin 38 54 12N 7 34W
Derry = Londonderry 38 55 0N 7 19W
Derrynasaggart Mts. 39 51 58N 9 15W
Derryrush 38 53 23N 9 40W
Derryveagh Mts. 38 55 0N 8 40W
Derudub 122 17 31N 36 7 E
Dervaig 34 56 35N 6 13W
Derval 42 47 40N 1 41W
Dervéni 69 38 8N 22 25 E
Derwent 153 53 41N 110 58W
Derwent, R., Derby, U.K. 33 52 53N 1 17W
Derwent, R., N. Yorks., U.K. 33 53 45N 0 57W
Derwent, R., Tyne & Wear, U.K. 35 54 58N 1 40W
Derwentwater, L. 32 53 34N 3 9W
Des Moines, Iowa, U.S.A. 158 41 35N 93 37W
Des Moines, N. Mex., U.S.A. 159 36 50N 103 51W
Des Moines, R. 158 40 23N 91 25W
Desaguadero, R., Argent. 172 33 28 S 67 15W
Desaguadero, R., Boliv. 174 17 30 S 68 0W
Desborough 29 52 27N 0 50W
Deschaillons 151 46 32N 72 7W
Descharme, R. 153 56 51N 109 13W
Deschutes, R. 160 45 30N 121 0W
Dese 123 11 5N 39 40 E
Deseado, R. 176 40 0 S 69 0W
Desemboque 164 30 30N 112 27W
Desenzano del Gardo 62 45 28N 10 32 E
Desert Center 161 33 45N 115 27W
Desert Hot Springs 163 33 58N 116 30W
Desertmartin 38 54 47N 6 40W
Desford 28 52 38N 1 19W
Désirade, I. 167 16 18N 61 3W
Deskenatlata L. 152 60 55N 112 3W
Desna, R. 80 52 0N 33 15 E
Desnŭtui, R. 70 44 15N 23 27 E
Desolación, I. 176 53 0 S 74 0W
Despeñaperros, Paso 59 38 24N 3 30W
Despotovac 66 44 6N 21 30 E
Dessa 121 14 44N 1 6 E
Dessau 48 51 49N 12 15 E
Dessel 47 51 15N 5 7 E
Dessye = Dese 123 11 5N 39 40 E
D'Estress B. 140 35 55 S 137 45 E
Desuri 94 25 18N 73 35 E
Desvrès 43 50 40N 1 48 E
Det Udom 100 14 54N 105 5 E
Detinjá, R. 66 43 51N 19 45 E
Detmold 48 51 55N 8 50 E
Detour Pt. 156 45 37N 86 35W
Detroit, Mich., U.S.A. 150 42 13N 83 22W
Detroit, Tex., U.S.A. 159 33 40N 95 10W
Detroit Lakes 158 46 50N 95 50W
Dett 127 18 32 S 26 57 E
Dettifoss 74 65 49N 16 24W
Děčin 52 50 47N 14 12 E
Deurne, Belg. 47 51 12N 4 24 E
Deurne, Neth. 47 51 27N 5 49 E
Deutsche Bucht 48 54 10N 7 51 E
Deutschlandsberg 52 46 49N 15 14 E
Deux-Acren, Les 47 50 44N 3 51 E
Deux-Sèvres □ 42 46 35N 0 20W
Deva 70 45 53N 22 55 E
Devakottai 97 9 55N 78 45 E
Devaprayag 95 30 13N 78 35 E
Dévaványa 53 47 2N 20 59 E
Deveci Daği 82 40 10N 36 0 E
Devecser 53 47 6N 17 26 E
Deventer 46 52 15N 6 10 E
Deveron, R. 37 57 40N 2 31W
Devesel 70 44 28N 22 41 E
Devgad, I. 97 14 48N 74 5 E
Devil R., Pk. 143 40 56 S 172 37 E
Devils Bridge 31 52 23N 3 50W
Devils Den 163 35 46N 119 58W
Devils Lake 158 48 5N 98 50W
Devils Paw, mt. 152 58 47N 134 0W
Devils Pt. 97 9 26N 80 6 E
Devilsbit Mt. 39 52 50N 7 58W
Devin 67 41 44N 24 24 E
Devizes 28 51 21N 2 0W
Devnya 67 43 13N 27 33 E
Devolli, R. 68 40 57N 20 15 E
Devon 152 53 24N 113 44W
Devon I. 12 75 47N 88 0W
Devonport, Austral. 138 41 10 S 146 22 E
Devonport, N.Z. 142 36 49 S 174 49 E
Devonport, U.K. 30 50 23N 4 11W
Devonshire □ 30 50 50N 3 40W
Dewas 94 22 59N 76 3 E
Dewetsdorp 128 29 33 S 26 39 E
Dewgad Baria 94 22 40N 73 55 E
Dewsbury 33 53 42N 1 38W
Dexter, Mo., U.S.A. 159 36 50N 90 0W
Dexter, N. Mex., U.S.A. 159 33 15N 104 25W
Dey-Dey, L. 137 29 12 S 131 4 E
Deyhuk 93 33 15N 104 25W
Deyyer 93 27 55N 51 55 E
Dezadeash L. 152 60 28N 136 58W
Dezfūl 92 32 20N 48 30 E
Dezh Shahpur 92 35 30N 46 25 E
Dezhneva, Mys 77 66 10N 169 3 E
Dhaba 92 27 25N 35 40 E
Dháfni 69 37 48N 22 1 E
Dhahaban 122 21 58N 39 3 E
Dhahiriya = Qz Zahiriya 90 31 25N 34 58 E
Dhahran 92 26 9N 50 10 E
Dhama Dzong 99 28 15N 91 15 E
Dhamási 68 39 43N 22 11 E
Dhampur 95 29 19N 78 33 E
Dhamtari 96 20 42N 81 35 E
Dhanbad 95 23 50N 86 30 E
Dhangarhi 99 28 55N 80 40 E
Dhankuta 95 26 55N 87 20 E
Dhanora 96 20 20N 80 22 E
Dhar 94 22 35N 75 26 E
Dharampur, Mad. P., India 94 22 13N 75 18 E
Dharampur, Maharashtra, India 96 20 32N 73 17 E
Dharapuram 97 10 45N 77 34 E
Dharmapuri 97 12 10N 78 10 E
Dharmavaram 97 14 29N 77 44 E
Dharmsala, (Dharamsala) 94 32 16N 73 23 E
Dhaulagiri Mt. 95 28 45N 83 45 E
Dhebar, L. 94 24 10N 74 0 E
Dhenkanal 96 20 45N 85 35 E
Dhenoúsa 69 37 8N 25 48 E
Dhesfina 69 38 25N 22 31 E
Dheskáti 68 39 55N 21 49 E
Dhespotikó 69 36 57N 24 58 E
Dhidhimótikhon 68 41 22N 26 29 E
Dhikti, Mt. 69 35 8N 25 29 E
Dhilianáta 69 38 15N 20 34 E
Dhílos 69 37 23N 25 15 E
Dhimitsána 69 37 36N 22 3 E
Dhirfis, Mt. 69 38 40N 23 54 E
Dhodhekánisos 69 36 35N 27 0 E
Dhofar 91 17 0N 54 10 E
Dhokós 69 37 20N 23 20 E
Dholiana 68 39 54N 20 32 E
Dholka 94 22 44N 72 29 E
Dholpur 94 26 45N 77 59 E
Dhomokós 69 39 10N 22 18 E
Dhond 96 18 26N 74 40 E
Dhoraji 94 21 45N 70 37 E
Dhoxáthon 68 41 9N 24 16 E
Dhragonisi 69 37 27N 25 29 E
Dhrangadhra 94 22 59N 71 31 E
Dhriopós 69 37 35N 24 35 E
Dhrol 94 22 40N 70 25 E
Dhubaibah 93 23 25N 54 35 E
Dhubri 98 26 2N 90 2 E
Dhulasar 98 21 52N 90 14 E
Dhulia 96 20 58N 74 50 E
Dhupdhara 98 25 58N 91 4 E
Dhurm 122 20 18N 42 53 E
Di Linh 101 11 35N 108 4 E
Di Linh, Cao Nguyen 101 11 30N 108 0 E
Día, I. 69 35 26N 25 13 E
Diable, Mt. 163 37 53N 121 56W
Diablerets, Les 50 46 22N 7 10 E
Diablo Range 163 37 0N 121 5W
Diafarabé 120 14 17N 4 57W
Diala 120 13 59N 10 0W
Dialakoro 120 12 18N 7 54W
Diallassagou 120 13 47N 3 41W
Diamante 172 32 5 S 60 40W
Diamante, R. 172 34 31 S 66 56W
Diamantina 171 18 5 S 43 40W
Diamantina, R. 138 22 25 S 142 20 E
Diamantino 175 14 30 S 56 30W
Diamond Harbour 95 22 11N 88 14 E
Diamond Is. 138 17 25 S 151 5 E
Diamond Mts. 160 40 0N 115 58W
Diamond Springs 163 38 42N 120 49W
Diamondville 160 41 51N 110 30W
Diano Marina 62 43 55N 8 3 E
Dianópolis 171 11 38 S 46 50W
Dianra 120 8 45N 6 14W
Diaole, Î. du. 170 5 15N 52 45W
Diapaga 121 12 5N 1 46 E
Diapangou 121 12 5N 0 10 E
Diapur 140 36 19 S 141 29 E
Diariguila 120 10 35N 10 2W
Dibai (Dubai) 93 25 15N 55 20 E
Dibaya 124 6 20 S 22 0 E
Dibaya Lubue 124 4 12 S 19 54 E
Dibba 93 25 45N 56 16 E
Dibbi 123 4 10N 41 52 E
Dibden 28 50 53N 1 24W
Dibega 92 35 50N 43 46 E
Dibër 68 41 38N 20 15 E
Dibete 128 23 45 S 26 32 E
Dibi 123 4 10N 41 52 E
Dibrugarh 98 27 29N 94 55 E
Dibulla 174 11 17N 73 19W
Dickinson 158 46 50N 102 40W
Dickson 157 36 5N 87 22W
Dickson City 162 41 29N 75 40W
Dicomano 63 43 53 S 11 30 E
Didam 46 51 57N 6 8 E
Didcot 28 51 36N 1 14W
Didesa, W. 123 9 40N 35 50 E
Didiéni 120 14 5N 7 50W
Didsbury 152 51 35N 114 10W
Didwana 94 27 17N 74 25 E
Die 45 44 47N 5 22 E
Diébougou 120 11 0N 3 15W
Diefenbaker L. 153 51 0N 106 55W
Diego Garcia, I. 11 9 50 S 75 0 E
Diégo Suarez 129 12 25 S 49 20 E
Diekirch 47 49 52N 6 10 E
Diélette 42 49 33N 1 52W
Diéma 120 14 32N 9 3W
Diemen 46 52 21N 4 58 E
Diemering 120 12 29N 16 47W
Dien Ban 100 15 53N 108 16 E
Diên Biên Phu 100 21 20N 103 0 E
Dien Khanh 101 12 15N 109 6 E
Diepenheim 46 52 12N 6 33 E
Diepenveen 46 52 18N 6 9 E
Diepholz 48 52 37N 8 22 E
Diepoldsau 51 47 23N 9 40 E
Dieppe 42 49 54N 1 4 E
Dieren 46 52 3N 6 6 E
Dierks 159 34 9N 94 0W
Diessen 47 51 29N 5 10 E
Diessenhofen 51 47 42N 8 46 E
Diest 47 50 58N 5 4 E
Dietikon 51 47 24N 8 24 E
Dieulefit 45 44 32N 5 4 E
Dieuze 43 48 30N 6 40 E

Diever Donskoy

Diever 46 52 51N 6 19E
Diffa 121 13 34N 12 33E
Differdange 47 49 81N 5 54E
Dig 94 27 28N 77 20E
Digba 126 4 25N 25 42E
Digboi 98 27 23N 95 38E
Digby 151 44 41N 65 50W
Digges 153 58 40N 94 0W
Digges Is. 149 62 40N 77 50W
Digges Lamprey 153 58 33N 94 8W
Dighinala 98 23 15N 92 5E
Dighton 158 38 30N 100 26W
Digne 45 44 5N 6 12E
Digoin 44 46 29N 3 58E
Digos 103 6 45N 125 20E
Digranes 74 66 4N 14 44E
Digras 96 20 6N 77 45E
Dihang, R. 99 27 30N 96 30E
Dijlah 92 37 0N 42 30E
Dijle, R. 47 50 58N 4 41E
Dijon 43 47 20N 5 0E
Dikala 123 4 45N 31 28E
Dikhal 123 11 8N 42 20E
Dikomu di Kai, Mt. 128 24 51S 24 36E
Diksmuide 47 51 2N 2 52E
Dikson 76 73 40N 80 5E
Dikumbiya 123 14 45N 37 30E
Dikwa 121 12 4N 13 30E
Dila 123 6 14N 38 22E
Dilam 92 23 55N 47 10E
Dilbeek 47 50 51N 4 17E
Dili 103 8 39S 125 34E
Dilizhan 83 41 46N 44 57E
Dillenburg 48 50 44N 8 17E
Dilley 159 28 40N 99 12W
Dilling 123 12 3N 29 35E
Dillingen 49 49 22N 6 42E
Dillingham 147 59 5N 158 30W
Dillon, Can. 153 55 56N 108 56W
Dillon, Mont., U.S.A. 160 45 9N 112 36W
Dillon, S.C., U.S.A. 157 34 26N 79 20W
Dillon, R. 153 55 56N 108 56W
Dillsburg 162 40 7N 77 2W
Dilolo 14 10 28S 22 18E
Dilsen 47 51 2N 5 44E
Dilston 138 41 22S 147 10E
Dima 123 6 19N 36 15E
Dimapur 98 25 54N 93 45E
Dimas 164 23 43N 106 47W
Dimashq 92 33 30N 36 18E
Dimbelenge 124 4 30N 23 0E
Dimbokro 120 6 45N 4 30W
Dimboola 140 36 28S 142 0E
Dîmbovița □ 70 45 0N 25 30E
Dîmbovita, R. 70 44 40N 26 0E
Dimbulah 138 17 2S 145 4E
Dimitriya Lapteva, Proliv 77 73 0N 140 0E
Dimitrovgrad, Bulg. 67 42 5N 25 35E
Dimitrovgrad, U.S.S.R. 81 54 25N 49 33E
Dimitrovgrad, Yugo. 66 43 0N 22 48E
Dimmitt 159 34 36N 102 16W
Dimo 123 5 19N 29 10E
Dimona 90 31 2N 35 1E
Dimovo 66 43 43N 22 50E
Dinagat I. 103 10 10N 125 40E
Dinajpur 98 25 33N 88 43E
Dinan 42 48 28N 2 2W
Dinant 47 50 16N 4 55E
Dinapore 95 25 38N 85 5E
Dinar 92 38 5N 30 15E
Dinard 42 48 38N 2 6W
Dinaric Alps 16 44 0N 17 30E
Dinas Hd. 31 52 2N 4 56W
Dinas Mawddwy 31 52 44N 3 41W
Dinas Powis 31 51 25N 3 14W
Dinder, Nahr ed 123 12 32N 35 0E
Dindi, R. 96 16 24N 78 15E
Dindigul 97 10 25N 78 0E
Dingelstädt 48 51 19N 10 19E
Dingila 126 3 25N 26 25E
Dingle 39 52 9N 10 17W
Dingle B. 39 52 3N 10 20W
Dingle Harbour 39 52 7N 10 12W
Dingmans Ferry 162 41 13N 74 55W
Dingo 138 23 38S 149 19E
Dingolfing 49 48 38N 12 30E
Dinguiraye 120 11 30N 10 35W
Dingwall 37 57 36N 4 26W
Dingyadi 121 13 0N 0 53E
Dinh Lap 100 21 33N 107 6E
Dinh, Mui 101 11 22N 109 1E
Dinhata 98 26 8N 89 27E
Dinkel 46 52 30N 6 58E
Dinokwe (Palla Road) 128 23 29S 26 37E
Dinosaur National Monument 160 40 30N 108 45W
Dinslaken 47 51 34N 6 41E
Dintel, R. 47 51 39N 4 22E
Dinuba 163 36 37N 119 22W
Dinxperlo 46 51 52N 6 30E
Dio 73 56 37N 14 15E
Diosgyör 53 48 7N 20 43E
Diosig 70 47 18N 22 2E
Dioundiou 121 12 37N 3 33E
Diourbel 120 14 39N 16 12W
Diphu Pass 98 28 9N 97 20E
Diplo 94 24 25N 69 35E
Dipolog 103 8 36N 123 20E
Dipșa 70 46 58N 24 27E
Dipton 143 45 54S 168 22E
Dir 93 35 08N 71 59E
Diré 120 15 20N 3 25W
Dire Dawa 123 9 35N 41 45E
Direction, C. 138 12 51S 143 32E
Diriamba 166 11 51N 86 19W
Dirico 125 17 50S 20 42E
Dirk Hartog I. 137 25 50S 113 5E
Dirranbandi 139 28 33S 148 17E
Disa 123 12 5N 34 15E
Disappointment, C. 160 46 20N 124 0W
Disappointment L. 136 23 20S 122 40E
Disaster B. 141 37 15S 150 0E
Discovery 148 63 0N 115 0W
Discovery B. 140 38 10S 140 40E
Disentis 51 46 42N 8 50E
Dishna 122 26 9N 32 32E
Disina 121 11 35N 9 50E
Disko 12 69 45N 53 30W
Disko Bugt 12 69 10N 52 0W
Disna 80 55 32N 28 11E
Disna, R. 80 55 20N 27 30E
Dison 47 50 37N 5 51E
Diss 29 52 23N 1 6E
Disteghil Sar 95 36 20N 75 5E
Distington 32 54 35N 3 33W
District Heights 162 38 51N 76 53W
District of Columbia □ 162 38 55N 77 0W
Distrito Federal □, Brazil 171 15 45S 47 45W
Distrito Federal □, Venez. 174 10 30N 66 55W
Disûq 122 31 8N 30 35E
Ditchingham 29 52 28N 1 26E
Ditchling & Beacon 29 50 59N 0 7W
Ditinn 120 10 53N 12 11W
Dittisham 30 50 22N 3 36W
Ditton Priors 28 52 30N 2 33W
Diu, I. 94 20 45N 70 58E
Diver 150 46 44N 79 30W
Dives 42 49 18N 0 8W
Dives, R. 42 49 18N 0 7W
Divi Pt. 97 15 59N 81 9E
Divichi 83 41 15N 48 57E
Divide 160 45 48N 112 47W
Dividing Ra. 137 27 45S 116 0E
Divinópolis 171 20 10S 44 54W
Divisões, Serra dos 171 17 0S 51 0W
Divnoye 83 45 55N 43 27E
Divo 120 5 48N 5 15W
Diwal Kol 94 34 23N 67 52E
Dixie 160 45 37N 115 27W
Dixon, Calif., U.S.A. 163 38 27N 121 49W
Dixon, Ill., U.S.A. 158 41 50N 89 30W
Dixon, Mont., U.S.A. 160 47 19N 114 25W
Dixon, N. Mex., U.S.A. 161 36 15N 105 57W
Dixon Entrance 153 54 30N 132 0W
Dixonville 152 56 32N 117 40W
Diyarbakir 92 37 55N 40 18E
Dizzard Pt. 30 50 46N 4 38W
Djabotaoure 121 8 35N 0 58E
Djado 119 21 4N 12 14E
Djado, Plateau du 119 21 29N 12 21E
Djakarta = Jakarta 103 6 9S 106 49E
Djakovo 66 45 19N 18 24E
Djamâa 119 33 32N 5 59E
Djamba 128 16 45S 13 58E
Djambala 124 2 20S 14 30E
Djanet 119 24 35N 9 32E
Djang 121 5 30N 10 5E
Djaul I. 135 2 58S 150 57E
Djawa = Jawa 103 7 0S 110 0E
Djebiniana 119 35 1N 11 0E
Djelfa 118 34 40N 3 15E
Djema 126 6 9N 25 15E
Djeneïene 119 31 45N 10 9E
Djenné 120 14 0N 4 30W
Djenoun, Garet el 119 25 4N 5 31E
Djerba 119 33 52N 10 51E
Djerba, Île de 119 33 56N 11 0E
Djerid, Chott 119 33 42N 8 30E
Djibo 121 14 15N 1 35W
Djibouti 123 11 30N 43 5E
Djibouti ■ 123 11 30N 42 15E
Djidjelli 119 36 52N 5 50E
Djirlange 101 11 44N 108 15E
Djofra 119 28 59N 15 47E
Djolu 124 0 45N 22 5E
Djorf el Youdi 118 32 14N 9 8W
Djougou 121 9 40N 1 45E
Djoum 124 2 41N 12 35E
Djourab, Erg du 117 16 40N 18 50E
Djugu 126 1 55N 30 35E
Djúpivogur 74 64 39N 14 17W
Djursholm 72 59 25N 18 6E
Djursland 73 56 27N 10 45E
Dmitriev-Lgovskiy 80 52 10N 35 0E
Dmitriya Lapteva, Proliv 77 73 0N 140 0E
Dmitrov 81 56 25N 37 32E
Dmitrovsk Orlovskiy 80 52 29N 35 10E
Dneiper, R. = Dnepr 82 52 29N 35 10E
Dnepr, R. 82 50 0N 31 0E
Dneprodzerzhinsk 82 48 32N 34 30E
Dneprodzerzhinskoye Vdkhr. 77 49 0N 34 0E
Dnepropetrovsk 82 48 30N 35 0E
Dneprorudnoye 82 47 21N 34 58E
Dnestr, R. 82 48 30N 26 30E
Dnestrovski = Belgorod 82 50 35N 36 35E
Dniester = Dnestr 82 48 30N 26 30E
Dno 80 57 50N 29 58E
Doan Hung 100 21 38N 105 10E
Doba 117 8 40N 16 50E
Dobané 126 6 20N 24 39E
Dobbiaco 63 46 44N 12 13E
Dobbyn 138 19 44S 139 59E
Dobczyce 54 49 52N 20 25E
Döbeln 48 51 7N 13 10E
Doberai, Jazirah 103 1 25S 133 0E
Dobiegniew 54 52 59N 15 45E
Doblas 172 37 5S 64 0W
Dobo 103 5 45S 134 15E
Doboj 66 44 46N 18 6E
Dobra, Poland 54 53 34N 15 20E
Dobra, Dîmbovița, Rumania 67 44 52N 25 40E
Dobra, Hunedoara, Rumania 70 45 54N 22 36E
Dobre Miasto 54 53 58N 20 26E
Dobrinishta 67 41 49N 23 34E
Dobriš 52 49 46N 14 10E
Dobrodzien 54 50 45N 18 25E
Dobrogea 70 44 30N 28 15E
Dobruja = Dobrogea 70 44 30N 28 15E
Dobrush 80 52 28N 30 35E
Dobryanka 84 58 27N 56 25E
Dobrzyn n. Wisła 54 52 39N 19 22E
Dobtong 123 6 25N 31 40E
Doc, Mui 100 17 58N 106 30E
Doce, R. 171 19 37S 39 49W
Docking 29 52 55N 0 39E
Doda 95 33 10N 75 34E
Döda Fallet 72 63 4N 16 35E
Doddington 29 52 29N 0 3E
Dodecanese = Dhodhekánisos 69 36 35N 27 0E
Dodewaard 46 51 55N 5 39E
Dodge Center 158 44 1N 92 57W
Dodge City 159 37 42N 100 0W
Dodge L. 153 59 50N 105 36W
Dodgeville 158 42 55N 90 8W
Dodman Pt. 30 50 13N 4 49W
Dodo 123 5 10N 29 57E
Dodola 123 6 59N 39 11E
Dodoma 126 6 8S 35 45E
Dodoma □ 126 6 0S 36 0E
Dodsland 153 51 50N 108 45W
Dodson 160 48 23N 108 4W
Doesburg 46 52 1N 6 9E
Doetinchem 46 51 59N 6 18E
Doftana 70 45 17N 25 45E
Dog Creek 152 51 35N 122 14W
Dog L., Man., Can. 152 51 2N 98 31W
Dog L., Ont., Can. 150 48 12N 89 16W
Dog, R. 152 57 50N 94 40W
Doganbey 69 37 40N 27 10E
Dogi 93 32 20N 62 50E
Dogliani 62 44 35N 7 55E
Dōgo 110 36 15N 133 16E
Dōgo-San 110 35 2N 133 13E
Dògondoutchi 121 13 38N 4 2E
Dogoraoua 121 14 0N 5 31E
Dogran 94 31 48N 73 35E
Dohad 94 22 50N 74 15E
Dohazari 99 22 10N 92 5E
Doheny 150 47 4N 72 35W
Doherty 150 46 58N 79 44W
Doi, I. 103 2 21N 127 49E
Doi Luang 101 18 20N 101 30E
Doi Saket 100 18 52N 99 9E
Doig, R., Alta., Can. 152 56 57N 120 0W
Doig, R., B.C., Can. 152 56 25N 120 40W
Dois Irmãos, Serra 171 8 30S 41 5W
Dokka 71 60 49N 10 7E
Dokka, R. 71 61 7N 10 0E
Dokkum 46 53 20N 5 59E
Dokkumer Ee, R. 46 53 18N 5 52E
Dokri Mohenjodaro 94 27 25N 68 7E
Dol 42 48 34N 1 47W
Dolak, Pulau = Kolepom, P. 103 8 0S 138 30E
Doland 158 44 55N 98 5W
Dolbeau 151 48 53N 72 18W
Dôle 43 47 7N 5 31E
Doleib, W. 123 10 30N 33 15E
Dolgarrog 31 53 11N 3 50W
Dolgellau 31 52 44N 3 53W
Dolgelly = Dolgellau 31 52 44N 3 53W
Dolginovo 80 54 39N 27 29E
Dolianovo 64 39 23N 9 11E
Dolinskaya 82 48 16N 32 36E
Dolisie 124 4 0S 13 10E
Dolj □ 70 44 10N 23 30E
Dolla 39 52 47N 8 12W
Dollar 35 56 9N 3 41W
Dollart 46 53 20N 7 10E
Dolna Banya 67 42 18N 23 44E
Dolni Dubnik 67 43 24N 24 26E
Dolo 63 45 25N 12 4E
Dolo Bay 123 4 11N 42 3E
Dolomites = Dolomiti 63 46 30N 11 40E
Dolomiti 63 46 30N 11 40E
Dolores, Argent. 172 36 20S 57 40W
Dolores, Mexico 164 28 53N 108 27W
Dolores, Uruguay 172 33 34S 58 15W
Dolores, Colo., U.S.A. 161 37 30N 108 30W
Dolores, Tex., U.S.A. 159 27 40N 99 38W
Dolores, R. 159 38 30N 108 55W
Đolovo 66 44 55N 20 52E
Dolphin and Union Str. 148 69 5N 114 45W
Dolphin C. 176 51 10S 50 0W
Dolphinton 35 55 42N 3 28W
Dolsk 54 51 59N 17 3E
Dolton 30 50 53N 4 2W
Dolwyddelan 31 53 3N 3 53W
Dom 50 46 6N 7 50E
Dom Joaquim 171 18 57S 43 16W
Dom Pedrito 173 31 0S 54 40W
Dom Pedro 170 4 29S 44 27W
Doma 121 8 25N 8 18E
Domasi 127 15 22S 35 10E
Domat Ems 51 46 50N 9 27E
Domazlice 52 49 28N 13 0E
Dombarovskiy 84 50 46N 59 32E
Dombås 71 62 6N 9 4E
Dombasle 43 49 8N 5 10E
Dombe Grande 125 12 56S 13 8E
Dombes 45 46 3N 5 0E
Dombóvár 53 46 21N 18 9E
Dombrád 53 48 13N 21 54E
Domburg 47 51 34N 3 30E
Domel, I = Letsok-aw-kyun 101 11 30N 98 25E
Domérat 44 46 21N 2 32E
Domett 143 42 53S 173 12E
Domeyko 172 29 0S 71 30W
Domeyko, Cordillera 172 24 30S 69 0W
Domfront 42 48 37N 0 40W
Dominador 172 24 21S 69 20W
Dominica I. 167 15 20N 61 20W
Dominica Passage 167 15 10N 61 20W
Dominican Rep. ■ 167 19 0N 70 30W
Dömitz 48 53 9N 11 13E
Domme 44 44 48N 1 12E
Dommel, R. 47 51 30N 5 20E
Dommerby 73 56 33N 9 5E
Domo 91 7 50N 47 10E
Domodossóla 62 46 6N 8 19E
Dompaire 43 48 14N 6 14E
Dompierre 44 46 31N 3 41E
Dompin 120 5 10N 2 5W
Domrémy 43 48 26N 5 40E
Domsjö 72 63 16N 18 41E
Domville, Mt. 139 28 1S 151 15E
Domvraina 69 38 15N 22 59E
Domzale 63 46 9N 3 6E
Don Benito 57 38 53N 5 51W
Don, C. 136 11 18S 131 46E
Don Duong 101 11 51N 108 35E
Don Martin, Presa de 164 27 30N 100 50W
Don Pedro Res. 163 37 43N 120 24W
Don, R., India 97 16 40N 75 55W
Don, R., Eng., U.K. 33 53 41N 0 51W
Don, R., Scot., U.K. 37 57 14N 2 5W
Don, R., U.S.S.R. 83 49 35N 41 40E
Dona Ana 127 17 25S 35 17E
Donabate 38 53 30N 6 9W
Donadea 38 53 20N 6 45W
Donaghadee 38 54 38N 5 32W
Donaghmore, Ireland 39 52 54N 7 37W
Donaghmore, U.K. 38 54 33N 6 50W
Donald 140 36 23S 143 0E
Donalda 152 52 35N 112 34W
Donaldsonville 159 30 2N 91 50W
Donalsonville 157 31 3N 84 52W
Donard 39 53 1N 6 37W
Donau-Kanal 49 49 1N 11 27E
Donau, R. 53 47 55N 17 20E
Donaueschingen 49 47 57N 8 30E
Donawitz 52 47 22N 15 4E
Doncaster 33 53 31N 1 9W
Dondo, Angola 74 9 45S 14 25E
Dondo, Mozam. 127 19 33S 34 46E
Dondo, Teluk 103 0 29N 120 45E
Dondra Head 97 5 55N 80 40E
Donegal 38 54 39N 8 8W
Donegal □ 38 54 53N 8 0W
Donegal B. 38 54 30N 8 35W
Donegal Har. 38 54 35N 8 15W
Donegal Pt. 39 52 44N 9 38W
Doneraile 39 52 13N 8 37W
Donets, R. 81 48 50N 38 45E
Donetsk 82 48 0N 37 45E
Dong 121 9 20N 12 15E
Dong Ba Thin 101 12 8N 109 13E
Dong Dang 100 21 4N 106 57E
Dong Giam 100 19 15N 105 31E
Dong Ha 100 16 49N 107 8E
Dong Hene 100 16 16N 105 18E
Dong Hoi 100 17 29N 106 36E
Dong Khe 100 22 26N 106 27E
Dong Van 100 23 16N 105 22E
Dong Xoai 101 11 32N 106 55E
Donga 121 7 45N 10 2E
Dongara 137 29 14S 114 57E
Dongargarh 96 21 10N 80 40E
Dongen 47 51 38N 4 56E
Donges 42 47 18N 2 4W
Donggala 103 0 30S 119 40E
Dongola 122 19 9N 30 22E
Dongou 124 2 0N 18 5E
Donhead 28 51 1N 2 8W
Donington 33 52 54N 0 12W
Donington, C. 140 34 45S 136 0E
Doniphan 159 36 40N 90 50W
Donja Stubica 63 45 59N 16 0E
Donji Dušnik 66 43 12N 22 5E
Donji Miholjac 66 45 45N 18 10E
Donji Milanovac 66 44 28N 22 6E
Donji Vakuf 66 44 8N 17 24E
Donjon, Le 44 46 22N 3 48E
Dønna 74 66 6N 12 30E
Donna 74 66 6N 12 30E
Donna 159 26 12N 98 2W
Donna Nook, Pt. 33 53 29N 0 9E
Donnaconna 151 46 41N 71 41W
Donnelly's Crossing 142 35 42S 173 38E
Donnybrook 137 33 34S 115 48E
Donor's Hills 138 18 42S 140 33E
Donoughmore 39 52 0N 8 42W
Donskoy 81 53 55N 38 15W

Donya Lendava **Duncan Town**

Donya Lendava 63 46 35N 16 25 E
Donzère 45 44 28N 4 43 E
Donzy 43 47 20N 3 6 E
Dooagh 38 53 59N 10 7W
Doochary 38 54 54N 8 10W
Doodlakine 137 31 34 S 117 51 E
Dooega Hd. 38 53 54N 10 3W
Doon L. 34 55 15N 4 22W
Doon, R. 34 55 26N 4 41W
Doonbeg 39 52 44N 9 31W
Doonbeg R. 39 52 42N 9 20W
Doorn 46 52 2N 5 20 E
Dor (Tantura) 90 32 37N 34 55 E
Dora Báltea, R. 62 45 42N 7 25 E
Dora, L. 136 22 0 S 123 0 E
Dora Riparia, R. 62 45 7N 7 24 E
Dorada, La 174 5 30N 74 40W
Dorading 123 8 30N 33 5 E
Doran L. 153 61 13N 108 6W
Dorat, Le 44 46 14N 1 5 E
Dörby 73 56 20N 16 12 E
Dorchester, Dorset, U.K. 28 50 42N 2 28W
Dorchester, Oxon., U.K. 28 51 38N 1 10W
Dorchester, C. 149 65 27N 77 27W
Dordogne □ 44 45 5N 0 40 E
Dordogne, R. 44 45 2N 0 36W
Dordrecht, Neth. 46 51 48N 4 39 E
Dordrecht, S. Afr. 128 31 20 S 27 3 E
Doré L. 153 54 46N 107 17W
Doré Lake 153 54 38N 107 54W
Dore, Mt. 44 45 32N 2 50 E
Dore, R. 44 45 59N 3 28 E
Dores 37 57 22N 4 20W
Dores do Indaiá 171 19 27 S 45 36W
Dorfen 49 48 16N 12 10 E
Dorgali 64 40 18N 9 35 E
Dori 121 14 3N 0 2W
Doring, R. 128 32 30 S 19 30 E
Dorion 150 45 23N 74 3W
Dorking 29 51 14N 0 20W
Dormaa-Ahenkro 120 7 15N 2 52W
Dormo, Ras 123 13 14N 42 35 E
Dornach 50 47 29N 7 37 E
Dornberg 63 45 45N 13 50 E
Dornbirn 52 47 25N 9 45 E
Dornes 43 46 48N 3 18 E
Dornie 36 57 17N 5 30W
Dornoch 37 57 52N 4 0W
Dornoch, Firth of 37 57 52N 4 0W
Dornogovi □ 106 44 0N 110 0 E
Doro 121 16 9N 0 51W
Dorog 53 47 42N 18 45 E
Dorogobuzh 80 54 50N 33 10 E
Dorohoi 70 47 56N 26 30 E
Döröö Nuur 105 47 40N 93 30 E
Dorre I. 137 25 13 S 113 12 E
Dorrigo 141 30 20 S 152 44 E
Dorris 160 41 59N 121 58W
Dorset □ 28 50 48N 2 25W
Dorsten 48 51 40N 6 55 E
Dorstone 28 52 4N 3 0W
Dortmund 48 51 32N 7 28 E
Dörtyol 92 36 52N 36 12 E
Dorum 48 53 40N 8 33 E
Doruma 126 4 42N 27 33 E
Dorya, W. 123 5 15N 41 30 E
Dos Bahias, C. 176 44 58 S 65 32W
Dos Cabezas 161 32 1N 109 37W
Dos Hermanas 57 37 16N 5 55W
Dos Palos 163 36 59N 120 37W
Dosara 121 12 20N 6 5 E
Doshi 93 35 35N 68 50 E
Dosso 121 13 0N 3 13 E
Döstrup 73 56 41N 9 42 E
Dot 152 50 12N 121 25W
Dothan 157 31 10N 85 25W
Dottignies 47 50 44N 3 19 E
Dotty, gasfield 19 53 3N 1 48 E
Douai 43 50 21N 3 4 E
Douala 121 4 0N 9 45 E
Douarnenez 42 48 6N 4 21W
Double Island Pt. 139 25 56 S 153 11 E
Doubrava, R. 52 49 40N 15 30 E
Doubs □ 43 47 10N 6 20 E
Doubs, R. 43 46 53N 5 1 E
Doubtful B. 137 34 15 S 119 28 E
Doubtful Sd. 143 45 20 S 166 49 E
Doubtless B. 142 34 55 S 173 26 E
Doucet 150 48 15N 76 35W
Doudeville 42 49 43N 0 47 E
Doué 42 47 11N 0 20W
Douentza 120 14 58N 2 48W
Douglas, S. Afr. 128 29 4 S 23 46 E
Douglas, U.K. 32 54 9N 4 29W
Douglas, U.K. 35 55 33N 3 50W
Douglas, Alaska, U.S.A. 147 58 23N 134 32W
Douglas, Ariz., U.S.A. 161 31 21N 109 30W
Douglas, Ga., U.S.A. 157 31 32N 82 52W
Douglas, Wyo., U.S.A. 158 42 45N 105 20W
Douglas Hd. 32 54 9N 4 28W
Douglastown 151 48 46N 64 24W
Douglasville 157 33 46N 84 43W
Douirat 118 33 2N 4 11W
Doukáton, Ákra 69 38 34N 20 30 E
Doulevant 43 48 22N 4 53 E
Doullens 43 50 10N 2 20 E
Doulus Hd. 39 51 57N 10 19W
Doumé 124 4 15N 13 25 E
Douna 120 12 40N 6 0W
Dounby 37 59 4N 3 13W
Doune 35 56 12N 4 3W
Dounreay 37 58 40N 3 28W
Dour 47 50 24N 3 46 E
Dourada, Serra 171 13 10 S 48 45W
Dourados 173 22 9 S 54 50W
Dourados, R. 173 21 58 S 54 18W
Dourdan 43 48 30N 2 0 E
Douro Litoral □ 55 41 10N 8 20W
Douro, R. 56 41 1N 8 16W
Douăzeci Si Trei August 70 43 50N 28 40 E
Douvaine 45 46 19N 6 16 E
Douz 119 33 25N 9 0 E
Dove 32 52 51N 1 36W
Dove Brook 151 53 40N 57 40W
Dove Creek 161 37 53N 108 59W
Dove Dale 33 53 10N 1 47W
Dove, R. 33 54 20N 0 55W
Dover, Austral. 138 43 18 S 147 2 E
Dover, U.K. 29 51 7N 1 19 E
Dover, Del., U.S.A. 162 39 10N 75 31W
Dover, N.H., U.S.A. 162 43 5N 70 51W
Dover, N.J., U.S.A. 162 40 53N 74 34W
Dover, Ohio, U.S.A. 156 40 32N 81 30W
Dover-Foxcroft 151 45 14N 69 14W
Dover Plains 162 41 43N 73 35W
Dover, Pt. 137 32 32 S 125 32 E
Dover, Str. of 16 51 0N 1 30 E
Doveridge 32 52 54N 1 49 E
Dovey, R. 31 52 32N 4 0W
Dovre 71 62 0N 9 15 E
Dovrefjell 71 62 15N 9 33 E
Dowa 127 13 38 S 33 58 E
Dowagiac 156 42 0N 86 8W
Dowlatabad 93 28 20N 50 40 E
Down □ 38 54 20N 5 50W
Down, Co. 38 54 20N 6 0W
Downey 160 42 29N 112 3W
Downham 29 52 26N 0 15 E
Downham Market 29 52 36N 0 22 E
Downhill 38 55 10N 6 48W
Downieville 160 39 34N 120 50W
Downpatrick 38 54 20N 5 43W
Downpatrick Hd. 38 54 20N 9 21W
Downs Division 139 27 10 S 150 44 E
Downs, The 38 53 30N 7 15W
Downsville 162 42 5N 74 60W
Downton 28 51 0N 1 44W
Dowra 38 54 11N 8 2W
Doylestown 162 40 21N 75 10W
Doyung 99 33 40N 99 25 E
Dra, Cap 118 28 58N 11 0W
Draa, O. 118 30 29N 6 1W
Drachten 46 53 7N 6 5 E
Drăgăneşti 70 44 9N 24 32 E
Drăgăneşti-Viaşca 70 44 5N 25 33 E
Dragaš 66 42 5N 20 35 E
Drăgăsani 70 44 39N 24 17 E
Dragina 66 44 30N 19 25 E
Dragocvet 66 44 0N 21 15 E
Dragonera, I. 58 39 35N 2 19 E
Dragon's Mouth 174 11 0N 61 50W
Dragovistica, (Berivol) 66 42 22N 22 39 E
Draguignan 45 43 30N 6 27 E
Drain 160 43 45N 123 17W
Drake, Austral. 139 28 55 S 152 25 E
Drake, U.S.A. 158 47 56N 100 31W
Drake Passage 13 58 0 S 68 0W
Drakensberg 129 31 0 S 25 0 E
Dráma 68 41 9N 24 10 E
Dráma □ 68 41 10N 24 0 E
Drammen 71 59 42N 10 12 E
Drangajökull 74 66 9N 22 15W
Drangan 39 52 32N 7 36W
Drangedal 71 59 6N 9 3 E
Dranov, Ostrov 70 44 55N 29 30 E
Draperstown 38 54 48N 6 47 E
Dras 95 34 25N 75 48 E
Drau, R. 52 47 46N 13 33 E
Drava, R. 66 45 50N 18 0W
Draveil 43 48 41N 2 25 E
Dravograd 63 46 36N 15 5 E
Drawa, R. 54 53 6N 15 56 E
Drawno 54 53 13N 15 46 E
Drawsko Pom 54 53 35N 15 50 E
Drayton Valley 152 53 25N 114 58W
Dreghorn 34 55 36N 4 30W
Dreibergen 46 52 3N 5 17 E
Drejö 73 54 58N 10 25 E
Dren 66 43 8N 20 44 E
Drenagh 38 55 3N 6 55W
Drenthe □ 54 52 52N 6 40 E
Drentsche Hoofdvaart 46 52 39N 6 4 E
Dresden 48 51 2N 13 45 E
Dresden □ 48 51 12N 14 0 E
Dreumel 47 51 51N 5 26 E
Dreux 42 48 44N 1 23 E
Drezdenko 54 52 50N 15 49 E
Driel 46 51 57N 5 49 E
Driffield 33 54 0N 0 25W
Driftwood 150 49 8N 81 23 E
Drigana 119 20 51N 12 17 E
Driggs 160 43 50N 111 8W
Drimnin 36 56 36N 6 0W
Drimoleague 39 51 40N 9 15W
Drin-i-zi, R. 68 41 37N 20 28 E
Drina, R. 66 44 30N 19 10 E
Drincea, R. 70 44 20N 22 55 E
Drînceni 70 46 49N 28 10 E
Drini, R. 68 42 20N 20 0 E
Drinjača, R. 66 44 20N 19 0 E
Driva 71 62 33N 9 38 E
Driva, R. 71 62 34N 9 33 E
Drivstua 71 62 26N 9 37 E
Drniš 63 43 51N 16 10 E
Drøbak 71 59 39N 10 39 E
Dröbak 75 59 39N 10 48 E
Drobbakk 71 59 39N 10 39 E
Drobin 54 52 42N 19 58 E
Drogheda 38 53 45N 6 20W
Drogichin 80 52 15N 25 8 E
Drogobych 80 49 20N 23 30 E
Droichead Nua 39 53 11N 6 50W
Droitwich 28 52 16N 2 10W
Dromahair 38 54 13N 8 18W
Dromara 38 54 21N 6 1W
Dromard 38 54 14N 8 40W
Drôme □ 45 44 38N 5 15 E
Drôme, R. 45 44 46N 4 46 E
Dromedary, C. 141 36 17 S 150 10 E
Dromiskin 38 53 56N 6 25W
Dromod 38 53 52N 7 55W
Dromore, Down, U.K. 38 54 24N 6 10W
Dromore, Tyrone, U.K. 38 54 31N 7 28W
Dromore West 38 54 15N 8 50W
Dronero 62 44 29N 7 22 E
Dronfield, Austral. 138 21 12 S 140 3 E
Dronfield, U.K. 33 53 18N 1 29W
Dronninglund 73 57 10N 10 19 E
Dronrijp 46 53 11N 5 39 E
Drosendorf 52 48 52N 15 37 E
Drouin 141 38 10 S 145 53 E
Drouzhba 67 43 22N 28 0 E
Drum 38 54 6N 7 9W
Drumbeg, N. Ire., U.K. 38 54 33N 6 0W
Drumbeg, Scot., U.K. 36 58 15N 5 12W
Drumcard 38 54 14N 7 42W
Drumcliffe 38 54 20N 8 30W
Drumcondra 38 53 50N 6 40W
Drumheller 152 51 25N 112 40W
Drumjohn 34 55 14N 4 15W
Drumkeerin 38 54 10N 8 8W
Drumlish 38 53 50N 7 47W
Drummond 160 46 46N 113 4W
Drummond I. 150 46 0N 83 40W
Drummond Pt. 139 34 9 S 135 16 E
Drummond Ra. 138 23 45 S 147 10 E
Drummondville 150 45 55N 72 25W
Drummore 34 54 41N 4 53W
Drumquin 38 54 38N 7 30W
Drumright 159 35 59N 96 38W
Drumshanbo 38 54 2N 8 4W
Drumsna 38 53 57N 8 0W
Drunen 47 51 41N 5 8 E
Druridge B. 35 55 16N 1 32W
Druskinankaj 80 54 3N 23 58 E
Drut, R. 80 52 32N 30 0 E
Druten 46 51 53N 5 36 E
Druya 80 55 45N 27 15 E
Druzhina 77 68 14N 145 18 E
Drvar 63 44 21N 16 2 E
Drvenik 63 43 27N 16 3 E
Dry Tortugas 166 24 38N 82 55W
Dryanovo 67 42 59N 25 28 E
Dryden, Can. 153 49 50N 92 50W
Dryden, N.Y., U.S.A. 162 42 30N 76 18W
Dryden, Tex., U.S.A. 159 30 3N 102 3W
Drygalski I. 13 66 0 S 92 0 E
Drygarn Fawr 31 52 13N 3 39W
Drymen 70 56 4N 4 28W
Drynoch 36 57 17N 6 18W
Drysdale I. 138 11 41 S 136 0 E
Drysdale, R. 136 13 59 S 126 51 E
Dschang 121 5 32N 10 3 E
Du 121 10 26N 1 34W
Du Bois 156 41 8N 78 46W
Du Quoin 158 38 0N 89 10W
Duanesburg 162 42 45N 74 11W
Duaringa 138 23 42 S 149 42 E
Duba 92 27 10N 35 40 E
Dubai = Dubayy 93 25 18N 55 20 E
Dubawnt, L. 153 63 4N 101 42W
Dubawnt, R. 153 64 33N 100 6W
Dubayy 93 25 18N 55 20 E
Dubbeldam 46 51 47N 4 43 E
Dubbo 141 32 11 S 148 35 E
Dubele 126 2 56N 29 35 E
Dübendorf 51 47 24N 8 37 E
Dubenskiy 84 51 27N 56 38 E
Dubh Artach 34 56 8N 6 40W
Dubica 63 45 17N 16 48 E
Dublin, Ireland 38 53 20N 6 18W
Dublin, Ga., U.S.A. 157 32 30N 83 0W
Dublin, Tex., U.S.A. 159 32 0N 98 20W
Dublin □ 38 53 24N 6 20W
Dublin, B. 39 53 24N 6 20W
Dubna 81 54 8N 36 52 E
Dubno 80 50 25N 25 45 E
Dubois 160 44 7N 112 9W
Dubossary 82 47 15N 29 10 E
Dubossasy Vdkhr. 82 47 30N 29 0 E
Dubovka 83 49 5N 44 50 E
Dubovskoye 83 47 28N 42 40 E
Dubrajpur 95 23 48N 87 25 E
Dubrékah 120 9 46N 13 31W
Dubrovitsa 80 51 31N 26 35 E
Dubrovnik 66 42 39N 18 6 E
Dubrovskoye 77 58 55N 111 0 E
Dubuque 158 42 30N 90 41W
Duchesne 160 40 14N 110 22W
Duchess 138 21 20 S 139 50 E
Ducie I. 131 24 47 S 124 40W
Duck Cr., N.S.W., Austral. 139 31 4 S 147 6 E
Duck Cr., W. Australia, Austral. 136 22 37 S 116 53 E
Duck Lake 153 52 50N 106 16W
Duck, Mt. 153 51 27N 100 35W
Duck Mt. Prov. Parks 153 51 45N 101 0W
Duckwall Mtn. 163 37 58N 120 7W
Duddington 29 52 36N 0 32W
Duddon R. 32 54 12N 3 15W
Düdelange 47 49 29N 6 5 E
Duderstadt 48 51 30N 10 15 E
Dudhi 99 24 15N 83 10 E
Dudhnai 98 25 59N 90 47 E
Düdingen 50 46 52N 7 12 E
Dudinka 77 69 30N 86 0 E
Dudley 28 52 30N 2 5W
Dudna, R. 96 19 36N 76 20 E
Dueñas 56 41 52N 4 33W
Düeni 70 44 51N 28 10 E
Dueodde 73 54 59N 15 4 E
Dueré 171 11 20 S 49 17W
Duero, R. 56 41 37N 4 25W
Duff Is. 142 9 0 S 167 0 E
Duffel 47 51 6N 4 30 E
Duffield 33 52 59N 1 30W
Dufftown 37 57 26N 3 9W
Dufourspitz 50 45 56N 7 52 E
Dugi, I. 63 44 0N 15 0 E
Dugo Selo 63 45 51N 16 18 E
Duhak 93 33 20N 57 30 E
Duifken Pt. 138 12 33 S 141 38 E
Duisburg 48 51 27N 6 42 E
Duitama 174 5 50N 73 2W
Duiveland 47 51 38N 4 0 E
Duiwelskloof 129 23 42 S 30 10 E
Dukana 126 3 59N 37 20 E
Dukati 68 40 16N 19 32 E
Duke I. 152 54 50N 131 20W
Dukhan 93 25 25N 50 50 E
Dukhovshchina 80 55 15N 32 27 E
Duki 93 30 14N 68 25 E
Dukla 54 49 30N 21 35 E
Duku, North-Eastern, Nigeria 121 10 43N 10 43 E
Duku, North-Western, Nigeria 121 11 11N 4 55 E
Dulas B. 31 53 22N 4 16W
Dulawan 103 7 5N 124 20 E
Dulce, Golfo 166 8 40N 83 20W
Dulce, R. 172 29 30 S 63 0W
Duleek 38 53 40N 6 24W
Dülgopol 67 43 3N 27 22 E
Dullewala 94 31 50N 71 25 E
Dülmen 48 51 49N 7 18 E
Dulnain Bridge 37 57 19N 3 40W
Dulovo 67 43 48N 27 9 E
Dululu 138 23 48 S 150 15 E
Duluth 158 46 48N 92 10W
Dulverton 28 51 2N 3 33W
Dum Dum 95 22 39N 88 26 E
Dum Duma 99 27 40N 95 40 E
Dumaguete 103 9 17N 123 15 E
Dumai 102 1 35N 101 20 E
Dumaran I. 103 10 33N 119 50 E
Dumaring 103 1 46N 118 10 E
Dumas, Ark., U.S.A. 159 33 52N 91 30W
Dumas, Okla., U.S.A. 159 35 50N 101 58W
Dūmat al Jandal 92 29 55N 39 40 E
Dumba I. 71 61 43N 4 50 E
Dumbarton 34 55 58N 4 35W
Dumbleyung 137 33 17 S 117 42 E
Dumbrăveni 70 46 14N 24 34 E
Dumfries 35 55 4N 3 37W
Dumfries & Galloway □ 35 54 30N 4 0W
Dumfries (□) 26 55 0N 3 30W
Dumienesti 70 46 44N 27 1 E
Dumka 95 24 0N 87 22 E
Dumoine L. 150 46 55N 77 55W
Dumoine, R. 150 46 13N 77 51W
Dumraon 95 25 33N 84 8 E
Dumyât 122 31 24N 31 48 E
Dumyât, Masabb 122 31 28N 32 0 E
Dun Laoghaire, (Dunleary) 39 53 17N 6 9W
Dun-le-Palestel 44 46 18N 1 39 E
Dun-sur-Auron 43 46 53N 2 33 E
Duna, R. 53 45 51N 18 48 E
Dunaff Hd. 38 55 18N 7 30W
Dunaföldvár 53 46 50N 18 57 E
Dunai, R. 53 47 50N 18 52 E
Dunaj, R. 67 45 17N 29 32 E
Dunajec, R. 54 50 12N 20 52 E
Dunajska Streda 53 48 0N 17 37 E
Dunamanagh 38 54 53N 7 20W
Dunans 34 56 4N 5 9W
Dunany Pt. 38 53 51N 6 15W
Dunapatai 53 46 39N 19 4 E
Dunaszekcsö 53 46 22N 18 45 E
Dunaújváros 53 47 0N 18 57 E
Dunav, R. 66 45 0N 20 21 E
Dunavtsi 66 43 57N 22 53 E
Dunback 143 45 23 S 170 36 E
Dunbar, Austral. 138 16 0 S 142 22 E
Dunbar, U.K. 35 56 0N 2 32W
Dunbarton (□) 26 56 4N 4 42W
Dunbeath 37 58 15N 3 25W
Dunblane 35 56 10N 3 58W
Dunboyne 38 53 25N 6 30W
Duncan, Can. 152 48 45N 123 40W
Duncan, Ariz., U.S.A. 161 32 46N 109 6W
Duncan, Okla., U.S.A. 159 34 25N 98 0W
Duncan L. 152 62 51N 113 58W
Duncan, L., Brit. Col., Can. 150 50 20N 117 0W
Duncan, L., Qué., Can. 152 53 29N 77 58W
Duncan Pass. 101 11 0N 92 30 E
Duncan Town 166 22 15N 75 45W

Duncansby **Ecoporanga**

Duncansby 37 58 37N 3 3W
Duncansby Head 37 58 39N 3 0W
Dunchurch 28 52 21N 1 19W
Duncormick 39 53 14N 6 40W
Dundalk, Ireland 38 53 55N 6 45W
Dundalk, U.S.A. 162 39 15N 76 31W
Dundalk, B. 38 53 55N 6 15W
Dundas 150 43 17N 79 59W
Dundas I. 152 54 30N 130 50W
Dundas, L. 137 32 35S 121 50E
Dundas Str. 136 11 15S 131 35E
Dundee, S. Afr. 129 28 11S 30 15E
Dundee, U.K. 35 56 29N 3 0W
Dundee, U.S.A. 162 42 32N 76 59W
Dundgovi □ 106 45 10N 106 0E
Dundo 124 7 23S 20 48E
Dundonald 38 54 37N 5 50W
Dundoo 139 27 40S 144 37E
Dundrennan 35 54 49N 3 56W
Dundrum, Ireland. 39 53 17N 6 15W
Dundrum, U.K. 38 54 17N 5 50W
Dundwara 95 27 48N 79 9E
Dunedin, N.Z. 143 45 50S 170 33E
Dunedin, U.S.A. 157 28 1N 82 45W
Dunedin, R. 152 59 30N 124 5W
Dunfanaghy 38 55 10N 7 59W
Dunfermline 35 56 5N 3 28W
Dungannon 38 54 30N 6 47W
Dungannon □ 38 54 30N 6 55W
Dungarpur 94 23 52N 73 45E
Dungarvan 39 52 6N 7 40W
Dungarvan Harb. 39 52 5N 7 35W
Dungas 121 13 4N 9 20E
Dungavel 35 55 37N 4 7W
Dungbura La 99 34 41N 93 18E
Dungeness 29 50 54N 0 59E
Dungiven 38 54 55N 6 56W
Dunglow 38 54 57N 8 20W
Dungo, L. do 128 17 15S 19 0E
Dungog 141 32 22S 151 40E
Dungourney 39 51 58N 8 5W
Dungu 124 2 32N 28 22E
Dungunâb 122 21 10N 37 9E
Dungunâb, Khalîg 122 21 5N 37 12E
Dunhinda Falls 97 7 5N 81 6E
Dunières 45 45 13N 4 20E
Dunk I. 138 17 59S 146 14E
Dunkeld, Austral. 140 37 40S 142 22E
Dunkeld, U.K. 37 56 34N 3 36W
Dunkerque 43 51 2N 2 20E
Dunkery Beacon 28 51 15N 3 37W
Dunkineely 38 54 38N 8 22W
Dunkirk 156 42 30N 79 18W
Dunkirk = Dunkerque 43 51 2N 2 20E
Dunkuj 123 11 15N 33 0E
Dunkur 123 11 58N 35 58E
Dunkwa, Central, Ghana 120 6 0N 1 47W
Dunkwa, Central, Ghana 121 5 30N 1 0W
Dunlap 158 41 50N 95 30W
Dunlavin 39 53 3N 6 40W
Dunleary = Dun Laoghaire 39 53 17N 6 8W
Dunleer 38 53 50N 6 23W
Dunlin, oilfield 19 61 12N 1 40E
Dunloe, Gap of 39 52 2N 9 40W
Dunlop 34 55 43N 4 32W
Dunloy 38 55 1N 6 25W
Dunmanus B. 39 51 31N 9 50W
Dunmanway 39 51 43N 9 8W
Dunmara 138 16 42S 133 25E
Dunmod 105 47 45N 106 58E
Dunmore, Ireland 38 53 37N 8 44W
Dunmore, U.S.A. 162 41 27N 75 38W
Dunmore East 39 52 9N 7 0W
Dunmore Town 166 25 30N 76 39W
Dunmurry 38 54 33N 6 0W
Dunn 157 35 18N 78 36W
Dunnellon 157 29 4N 82 28W
Dunnet 37 58 37N 3 20W
Dunnet B. 37 58 37N 3 23W
Dunnet Hd. 37 58 38N 3 22W
Dunning, U.K. 35 56 18N 3 37W
Dunning, U.S.A. 158 41 52N 100 4W
Dunolly 140 36 51S 143 44E
Dunoon 34 55 57N 4 56W
Dunqul 122 23 40N 31 10E
Duns 35 55 47N 2 20W
Dunscore 35 55 8N 3 48W
Dunseith 158 48 49N 100 2W
Dunsford 30 50 41N 3 40W
Dunshaughlin 38 53 31N 6 32W
Dunsmuir 160 41 0N 122 10W
Dunstable 29 51 53N 0 31W
Dunstan Mts. 143 44 53S 169 35E
Dunster, Can. 152 53 8N 119 50W
Dunster, U.K. 28 51 11N 3 28W
Dunston 28 52 46N 2 7W
Duntelchaig, L. 37 57 20N 4 18W
Dunton Green 29 51 17N 0 11E
Duntroon 143 44 51S 170 40E
Dunûrea, R. 70 45 0N 29 40E
Dunvegan 36 57 26N 6 35W
Dunvegan Hd. 36 57 30N 6 42W
Dunvegan L. 153 60 8N 107 10W
Duong Dong 101 10 13N 103 58E
Dupree 158 45 4N 101 35W
Dupuyer 160 48 11N 112 31W
Duque de Caxias 173 22 45S 43 19W
Dura 90 31 31N 35 1E
Durack 136 15 33S 127 52E
Durack Ra. 136 16 50S 127 40E
Durance, R. 45 43 55N 4 45E
Durand 156 42 54N 83 58W
Durango, Mexico 164 24 3N 104 39W
Durango, Spain 58 43 13N 2 40W
Durango, U.S.A. 161 37 10N 107 50W
Durango □ 164 25 0N 105 0W
Duranillin 137 33 30S 116 45E
Durant 159 34 0N 96 25W
Duratón, R. 56 41 27N 4 0W
Durazno 172 33 25S 56 38W
Durazzo = Durrësi 68 41 19N 19 28E
Durban, France 44 43 0N 2 49W
Durban, S. Afr. 129 29 49S 31 1E
Dúrcal 57 37 0N 3 34W
Đurdevac 66 46 2N 17 3E
Düren 48 50 48N 6 30E
Durg 96 21 15N 81 22E
Durgapur 95 23 30N 87 9E
Durham, Can. 150 44 10N 80 49W
Durham, U.K. 33 54 47N 1 34W
Durham, N.C., U.S.A. 157 36 0N 78 55W
Durham, N.H., U.S.A. 162 43 8N 70 56W
Durham □ 32 54 42N 1 45W
Durham Downs 139 26 6S 149 3E
Durlstone Hd. 28 50 35N 1 58W
Durmitor Mt. 66 43 18N 19 0E
Dûrmŭneşti 70 46 21N 26 33E
Durness 37 58 34N 4 45W
Durness, Kyle of 37 58 35N 4 55W
Durrandella 138 24 3S 146 35E
Durrësi 68 41 19N 19 28E
Durrie 138 25 40S 140 15E
Durrington 28 51 12N 1 47W
Durrow 39 53 20N 7 31W
Durrus 39 51 37N 9 32W
Dursey Hd. 39 51 34N 10 41W
Dursey I. 39 51 36N 10 12W
Dursley 28 51 41N 2 21W
Durtal 42 47 40N 0 18W
Duru 126 4 20N 28 50E
Durup 73 56 45N 8 57E
D'Urville Island 143 40 50S 173 55E
Duryea 162 41 20N 75 45W
Dusa Mareb 91 5 40N 46 33E
Dûsh 122 24 35N 30 41E
Dushak 76 37 20N 60 10E
Dushanbe 85 38 33N 68 48E
Dusheti 83 42 0N 44 55E
Dushore 162 41 31N 76 24W
Dusky Sd. 143 45 47S 166 30E
Dussejour, C. 136 14 45S 128 13E
Düsseldorf 48 51 15N 6 46E
Dussen 46 51 44N 4 59E
Duszniki Zdrój 54 51 26N 16 22E
Dutch Harbour 147 53 54N 166 35W
Dutlhe 128 23 58S 23 46E
Dutsan Wai 121 10 50N 8 10E
Dutton, R. 138 20 44S 143 10E
Duvan 84 55 42N 57 54E
Duved 72 63 24N 12 55E
Duvno 66 43 42N 17 13E
Duwadami 92 24 35N 44 15E
Duzdab = Zāhedān 93 29 30N 60 50E
Dve Mogili 67 43 47N 25 55E
Dvina, Sev. 78 56 30N 24 0E
Dvina, Zap. 80 61 40N 45 30E
Dvinsk = Daugavpils 80 55 33N 26 32E
Dvinskaya Guba 78 65 0N 39 0E
Dvor 63 45 4N 16 22E
Dvorce 53 49 50N 17 34E
Dvur Králové 52 50 27N 15 50E
Dwarka 94 22 18N 69 8E
Dwellingup 137 32 43S 116 4E
Dwight 156 41 5N 88 25W
Dyakovskoya 81 60 5N 41 12E
Dyatkovo 80 53 48N 34 27E
Dyaul, I. 138 3 0S 150 55E
Dyce 37 57 12N 2 11W
Dyer 163 37 40N 118 5W
Dyer, C. 149 67 0N 61 0W
Dyerbeldzhin 85 41 13N 74 54E
Dyersburg 159 36 2N 89 20W
Dyfed □ 31 52 0N 4 30W
Dyje, R. 53 48 50N 16 45E
Dyke Acland Bay 138 8 45S 148 45E
Dykehead 37 56 43N 3 0W
Dyle, R. 47 50 58N 4 41E
Dymchurch 29 51 2N 1 0E
Dymock 28 51 58N 2 27W
Dynevor Downs 139 28 10S 144 20E
Dynów 54 49 50N 22 11E
Dypvag 71 79 40N 9 8E
Dyrnes 71 63 25N 7 52E
Dysart, Can. 153 50 57N 104 2W
Dysart, U.K. 35 56 8N 3 8W
Dysjön 72 62 38N 15 31E
Dyulgeri 67 42 18N 27 23E
Dyurtyuli 84 55 9N 54 4E
Dzambeyty 83 50 15N 52 30E
Dzaudzhikau = Ordzhonikidze 83 43 0N 44 35E
Dzerzhinsk 80 53 40N 27 7E
Dzhailma 76 51 30N 61 50E
Dzhalal-Abad 84 40 56N 73 0E
Dzhalinda 77 53 40N 124 0E
Dzhambeyty 84 50 16N 52 35E
Dzhambul 85 42 54N 71 22E
Dzhambul, Gora 85 44 54N 73 0E
Dzhankoi 82 45 40N 34 30E
Dzhanybek 83 49 25N 46 50E
Dzhardzhan 77 68 10N 123 5E
Dzharkurgan 85 37 31N 67 25E
Dzhelinde 77 70 0N 114 20E
Dzherzhinsk 80 53 48N 27 19E
Dzhetygara 84 52 11N 61 12E
Dzhetym, Khrebet 85 41 30N 77 0E
Dzhezkazgan 76 47 10N 67 40E
Dzhizak 85 40 6N 67 50E
Dzhugdzur, Khrebet 77 57 30N 138 0E
Dzhuma 85 39 42N 66 40E
Dzhumgoltau, Khrebet 85 42 15N 74 30E
Dzhungarskiye Vorota 76 45 0N 82 0E
Dzhvari 83 42 42N 42 4E
Działdowo 54 53 15N 20 15E
Działoszyce 54 50 22N 20 20E
Działoszyn 54 51 6N 18 50E
Dzibilchaltún 165 21 5N 89 36W
Dzierzgon 54 53 58N 19 20E
Dzierzoniow 54 50 45N 16 39E
Dzilam de Bravo 165 21 24N 88 53W
Dzioua 119 33 14N 5 14E
Dziwnów 54 54 2N 14 45E
Dzungaria 105 44 10N 88 0E
Dzungarian Gates = Dzhungarskiye V. 105 45 0N 82 0E

E

Eabamet, L. 150 51 30N 87 46W
Eads 158 38 30N 102 46W
Eagle, Alaska, U.S.A. 147 64 44N 141 29W
Eagle, Colo., U.S.A. 160 39 45N 106 55W
Eagle Butt 158 45 1N 101 12W
Eagle Grove 158 42 37N 93 53W
Eagle L., Calif., U.S.A. 160 40 35N 120 50W
Eagle L., Me., U.S.A. 151 46 23N 69 22W
Eagle Lake 159 29 35N 96 21W
Eagle Nest 161 36 33N 105 13W
Eagle Pass 159 28 45N 100 35W
Eagle Pk. 163 38 10N 119 25W
Eagle Pt. 136 16 11S 124 23E
Eagle, R. 151 53 36N 57 26W
Eagle River 158 45 55N 89 17W
Eaglehawk 140 36 43S 144 16E
Eagles Mere 162 41 25N 76 33W
Eaglesfield 35 55 3N 3 12W
Eagleshan 34 55 44N 4 18W
Eakring 33 53 9N 0 59W
Ealing 29 51 30N 0 19W
Earaheedy 137 25 34S 121 29E
Earby 32 53 55N 2 8W
Eardisland 28 52 14N 2 50W
Eardisley 28 52 8N 3 0W
Earith 29 52 21N 0 1E
Earl Grey 153 50 57N 104 43W
Earl Shilton 28 52 35N 1 20W
Earl Soham 29 52 14N 1 15E
Earle 159 35 18N 90 26W
Earlimart 163 35 53N 119 16W
Earls Barton 29 52 16N 0 44W
Earl's Colne 29 51 56N 0 43E
Earlsferry 35 56 11N 2 50W
Earlston 35 55 39N 2 40W
Earn, L. 34 56 23N 4 14W
Earn, R. 35 56 20N 3 19W
Earnslaw, Mt. 143 44 32S 168 27E
Earoo 137 29 34S 118 22E
Earsdon 35 55 4N 1 30W
Earth 159 34 18N 102 30W
Easebourne 29 51 0N 0 42W
Easington, Durham, U.K. 33 54 50N 1 24W
Easington, Yorks., U.K. 33 54 40N 0 7W
Easington Colliery 33 54 49N 1 19W
Easingwold 33 54 8N 1 11W
Easky 38 54 17N 8 58W
Easley 157 34 52N 82 35W
East Aberthaw 31 51 23N 3 23W
East Anglian Hts. 29 52 10N 0 17E
East Angus 151 45 30N 71 40W
East, B. 159 29 2N 89 16W
East Barming 29 51 15N 0 29E
East Bathurst 151 47 35N 65 40W
East Bengal 99 24 0N 90 0E
East Bergholt 29 51 58N 1 2E
East Beskids, mts. 53 49 30N 18 45E
East Brent 28 51 14N 2 55W
East C., N.Z. 142 37 42S 178 35E
East C., P.N.G. 135 10 13S 150 53E
East Chicago 156 41 40N 87 30W
East China Sea 105 30 5N 126 0E
East Coulee 152 51 23N 112 27W
East Cowes 28 50 45N 1 17W
East Dereham 29 52 40N 0 57E
East Falkland 176 51 30S 58 30W
East Fen 33 53 4N 0 5E
East Florenceville 151 46 26N 67 36W
East Grand Forks 158 47 55N 97 5W
East Greenwich 162 41 40N 71 27W
East Grinstead 29 51 8N 0 1W
East Harling 29 52 26N 0 55E
East Hartford 162 41 46N 72 39W
East Helena 160 46 37N 111 58W
East Ilsley 28 51 33N 1 15W
East Indies 102 0 0 120 0E
East Jordan 156 45 10N 85 7W
East Kilbride 35 55 46N 4 10W
East Kirkby 33 53 5N 1 15W
East Lansing 156 42 44N 84 37W
East Linton 35 56 0N 2 40W
East Liverpool 156 40 39N 80 35W
East London 129 33 0S 27 55E
East Looe 30 50 22N 4 28W
East Los Angeles 163 34 1N 118 9W
East Lynne 141 35 35S 150 16E
East Main (Eastmain) 151 52 20N 78 30W
East Markham 33 53 15N 0 53W
East Midlands, oilfield 19 53 20N 0 45W
East Moor 33 53 15N 1 30W
East, Mt. 137 29 0S 122 30E
East Orange 162 40 46N 74 13W
East P. 151 46 27N 61 58W
East Pakistan = Bangladesh 99 24 0N 90 0E
East Pine 152 55 48N 120 5W
East Point 157 33 40N 84 28W
East Providence 162 41 49N 71 23W
East Retford 33 53 19N 0 55W
East St. Louis 158 38 36N 90 10W
East Schelde, R. 47 51 38N 3 40E
E. Siberian Sea 77 73 0N 160 0E
East Stroudsburg 162 41 0N 75 11W
East Sussex □ 29 50 55N 0 20E
East Tawas 156 44 17N 83 31W
East Toorale 139 30 27S 145 28E
East Walker, R. 163 38 52N 119 10W
East Wemyss 35 56 8N 3 5W
East Woodhay 28 51 21N 1 26W
Eastbourne, N.Z. 142 41 19S 174 55E
Eastbourne, U.K. 29 50 46N 0 18E
Eastchurch 29 51 23N 0 53E
Eastend 153 49 32N 108 50W
Easter Islands 143 27 0S 109 0W
Easter Ross, dist. 37 57 50N 4 35W
Easter Skeld 36 60 12N 1 27W
Eastern □ 126 0 0S 38 30E
Eastern Cr. 138 20 40S 141 35E
Eastern Ghats 97 15 0N 80 0E
Eastern Group, Is. 137 33 30S 124 30E
Eastern Province □ 120 8 15N 11 0W
Easterville 153 53 8N 99 49W
Easthampton 162 42 16N 72 40W
Eastland 159 32 26N 98 45W
Eastleigh 28 50 58N 1 21W
Eastmain (East Main) 150 52 20N 78 30W
Eastmain, R. 150 52 27N 72 26W
Eastman 157 32 13N 83 41W
Eastnor 28 52 2N 2 22W
Easton, Dorset, U.K. 28 50 32N 2 27W
Easton, Northants., U.K. 29 52 37N 0 31W
Easton, Somerset, U.K. 28 51 28N 2 42W
Easton, Md., U.S.A. 162 38 47N 76 7W
Easton, Pa., U.S.A. 162 40 41N 75 15W
Easton, Wash., U.S.A. 160 47 14N 121 8W
Eastport, Maine, U.S.A. 151 44 57N 67 0W
Eastport, N.Y., U.S.A. 162 40 50N 72 44W
Eastry 29 51 15N 1 19E
Eastview 150 45 27N 75 40W
Eastville 162 37 21N 75 57W
Eastwood 33 53 2N 1 17W
Eaton, U.K. 29 52 52N 0 46W
Eaton, U.S.A. 158 40 35N 104 42W
Eaton, L. 136 22 55S 130 57E
Eaton Socon 29 52 13N 0 18W
Eatonia 153 51 13N 109 25W
Eatonton 157 33 22N 83 24W
Eatontown 162 40 18N 74 7W
Eau Claire, S.C., U.S.A. 157 34 5N 81 2W
Eau Claire, Wis., U.S.A. 158 44 46N 91 30W
Eauze 44 43 53N 0 7E
Eaval, Mt. 36 57 33N 7 12W
Ebagoola 138 14 15S 143 12E
Eban 121 9 40N 4 50E
Ebberston 33 54 14N 0 35W
Ebbw Vale 31 51 47N 3 12W
Ebeggui 119 26 2N 6 0E
Ebeltoft 75 56 12N 10 41E
Ebensee 52 47 48N 13 46E
Eberbach 49 49 27N 8 59E
Eberswalde 48 52 49N 13 50E
Ebikon 51 47 5N 8 21E
Ebingen 49 48 13N 9 1E
Ebino 110 32 2N 130 48E
Ebnat-Kappel 51 47 16N 9 7E
Eboli 65 40 39N 15 2E
Ebolowa 121 2 55N 11 10E
Ebony 128 22 6S 15 15E
Ébrié, Lagune 120 5 12N 4 40W
Ebro, Pantano del 56 43 0N 3 58W
Ebro, R. 58 41 49N 1 5W
Ebstorf 48 53 2N 10 23E
Ecaussines-d' Enghien 47 50 35N 4 11E
Ecclefechan 35 55 3N 3 18W
Eccleshall 28 52 52N 2 14W
Eceabat 68 40 11N 26 21E
Ecueillé 42 47 10N 1 19E
Ech Chebbi 118 26 41N 0 29E
Echallens 50 46 38N 6 38E
Echaneni 77 27 33S 32 6E
Echelles, Les 45 45 27N 5 45E
Echizen-Misaki 111 35 59N 135 57E
Echmiadzin 83 40 12N 44 19E
Echo Bay, N.W.T., Can. 148 66 10N 117 40W
Echo Bay, Ont., Can. 150 46 29N 84 4W
Echoing, R. 153 55 51N 92 5W
Echt, Neth. 47 51 7N 5 52E
Echt, U.K. 37 57 8N 2 26W
Echternach 47 49 49N 6 3E
Echuca 141 36 3S 144 46E
Ecija 57 37 30N 5 10W
Eck L. 34 56 5N 5 0W
Eckernförde 48 54 26N 9 50E
Eckington 33 53 19N 1 21W
Éclipse Is. 136 13 54S 126 19E
Écommoy 42 47 50N 0 17E
Ecoporanga 171 18 23S 40 50W

Écos Eldorado

Écos 43 49 9N 1 35E
Écouché 42 48 42N 0 10W
Ecuador ■ 174 2 0S 78 0W
Ed 73 58 55N 11 55E
Ed Dabbura 122 17 40N 34 15E
Ed Damer 122 17 27N 34 0E
Ed Debba 122 18 0N 30 51E
Ed-Déffa 122 30 40N 26 30E
Ed Deim 123 10 10N 28 20E
Ed Dueim 123 14 0N 32 10E
Ed Dzong 99 32 11N 90 12E
Edah 137 28 16S 117 10E
Edam, Can. 153 53 11N 108 46W
Edam, Neth. 46 52 31N 5 3E
Edapally 97 11 19N 78 3E
Eday, I. 37 59 11N 2 47W
Eday Sd. 37 59 12N 2 45W
Edd 123 14 0N 41 30E
Edda, oilfield 19 56 25N 3 15E
Edderton 37 57 50N 4 10W
Eddrachillis B. 36 58 16N 5 10W
Eddystone 30 50 11N 4 16W
Eddystone Pt. 138 40 59S 148 20E
Ede, Neth. 46 52 4N 5 40E
Ede, Nigeria 121 7 45N 4 29E
Ęde, Sweden 72 62 10N 16 50E
Édea 121 3 51N 10 9E
Edegem 47 51 10N 4 27E
Edehon L. 153 60 25N 97 15W
Edekel, Adrar 119 23 56N 6 47E
Eden, Austral. 141 37 3S 149 55E
Eden, U.K. 38 54 44N 5 47W
Eden, Tex., U.S.A. 159 31 16N 99 50W
Eden, Wyo., U.S.A. 160 42 2N 109 27W
Eden L. 153 56 38N 100 15W
Eden, R. 32 54 57N 3 2W
Edenbridge 29 51 12N 0 4E
Edenburg 128 29 43S 25 58E
Edendale 143 46 19S 168 48E
Edenderry 39 53 21N 7 3W
Edenton 157 36 5N 76 36W
Edenville 129 27 37S 27 34E
Ederny 38 54 32N 7 40W
Edgar 158 40 25N 98 0W
Edgartown 162 41 22N 70 28W
Edge Hill 28 52 7N 1 28W
Edge I. 12 77 45N 22 30E
Edgecumbe 142 37 59S 176 47E
Edgefield 157 33 43N 81 59W
Edgeley 158 46 27N 98 41W
Edgemont 158 43 15N 103 53W
Edgeøya 12 77 45N 22 30E
Edgeworthstown = Mostrim 38 53 42N 7 36W
Edhessa 68 40 48N 22 5E
Edievale 143 45 49S 169 22E
Edina, Liberia 120 6 0N 10 19W
Edina, U.S.A. 158 40 6N 92 10W
Edinburg 159 26 22N 98 10W
Edinburgh 35 55 57N 3 12W
Edington 28 51 17N 2 6W
Edirne 67 41 40N 26 45E
Edison 163 35 21N 118 52W
Edithburgh 140 35 5S 137 43E
Edjeleh 119 28 25N 9 40E
Edjudina 137 29 48S 122 23E
Edmeston 162 42 42N 75 15W
Edmond 159 35 37N 97 30W
Edmondbyers 32 54 50N 1 59W
Edmonds 160 47 47N 122 22W
Edmonton, Austral. 138 17 2S 145 46E
Edmonton, Can. 152 53 30N 113 30W
Edmund L. 153 54 45N 93 17W
Edmundston 151 47 23N 68 20W
Edna 159 29 0N 96 40W
Edna Bay 152 55 55N 133 40W
Edolo 62 46 10N 10 21E
Edouard, L. 126 0 25S 29 40E
Edremit 92 39 40N 27 0E
Edsbyn 72 61 23N 15 49E
Edsel Ford Ra. 13 77 0S 143 0W
Edsele 72 63 25N 16 32E
Edson 152 53 40N 116 28W
Eduardo Castex 172 35 50S 64 25W
Edward I. 150 48 22N 88 37W
Edward, L. (Idi Amin Dada, L.) 126 0 25S 29 40E
Edward, R. 140 35 0S 143 30E
Edward VII Pen. 13 80 0S 160 0W
Edwards 163 34 55N 117 51W
Edwards Plat. 159 30 30N 101 5W
Edwardsville 162 41 15N 75 56W
Edzell 37 56 49N 2 40W
Edzo 152 62 49N 116 4W
Eefde 46 52 10N 6 13E
Eek 147 60 10N 162 0W
Eekloo 47 51 11N 3 33E
Eelde 46 53 8N 6 34E
Eem, R. 46 52 16N 5 20E
Eems Kanaal 46 53 18N 6 46E
Eems, R. 46 53 26N 6 57E
Eenrum 46 53 22N 6 28E
Eernegem 47 51 8N 3 2E
Eerste Valthermond 46 52 53N 6 58E
Eersterivier 128 34 0S 18 45E
Efate, I. (Vate) 46 17 40S 168 25E
Eferding 52 48 18N 14 1E
Eferi 119 24 30N 9 28E
Effingham 156 39 8N 88 30W
Effiums 121 6 35N 8 0E
Effretikon 51 47 25N 8 42E
Efiduasi 121 6 45N 1 25W
Eforie Sud 70 44 1N 28 37E
Ęga, R. 58 42 32N 1 58W
Ęgadi, Ísole 64 37 55N 12 10E
Eganville 150 45 32N 77 5W
Egeland 158 48 42N 99 6W
Egenolf L. 153 59 3N 100 0W
Eger 53 47 53N 20 27E
Eger, R. 53 47 43N 20 32E
Egersund = Eigersund 75 58 26N 6 1E
Egerton, Mt. 137 24 42S 117 44E
Egg L. 153 55 5N 105 30W
Eggenburg 52 48 38N 15 50E
Eggiwil 50 46 52N 7 47E
Egham 29 51 25N 0 33W
Egilsay I. 37 59 10N 2 56W
Eginbah 136 20 53S 119 47E
Egletons 44 45 24N 2 3E
Eglisau 51 47 35N 8 31E
Egmond-aan-Zee 46 52 37N 4 38E
Egmont, C. 142 39 16S 173 45E
Egmont, Mt. 142 39 17S 174 5E
Egogi Bad 123 13 10N 41 30E
Egremont 32 54 28N 3 33W
Eğridir Gölü 92 37 53N 30 50E
Egton 33 54 27N 0 45W
Egtved 73 55 38N 9 18E
Ęgua 174 5 5N 68 0W
Ęguas, R. 171 13 26S 44 14W
Ęgume 121 7 30N 7 14E
Éguzon 44 46 27N 1 33E
Egvekinot 77 66 19N 179 50W
Egyek 53 47 39N 20 52E
Egypt ■ 122 28 0N 31 0E
Eha Amufu 121 6 30N 7 40E
Ehime-ken □ 110 33 30N 132 40E
Ehingen 49 48 16N 9 43E
Ehrwald 52 47 24N 10 56E
Eibar 58 43 11N 2 28W
Eibergen 46 52 6N 6 39E
Eichstätt 49 48 53N 11 12E
Eidanger 71 59 7N 9 43E
Eide 71 60 31N 6 44E
Eider, R. 48 54 15N 8 50E
Eidsberg 71 59 32N 11 16E
Eidsfoss 71 59 36N 10 2E
Eidsvold 139 25 25S 151 12E
Eidsvoll 75 60 19N 11 14E
Eifel 49 50 10N 6 45E
Eiffel Flats 127 18 20S 30 0E
Eigersund 71 58 26N 6 1E
Eigg, I. 36 56 54N 6 10W
Eigg, Sd. of 36 56 52N 6 15W
Eighty Mile Beach 136 19 30S 120 40E
Eil 91 8 0N 49 50E
Eil, L. 36 56 50N 5 15W
Eilat 90 29 30N 34 56E
Eildon 141 37 14S 145 55E
Eildon, L. 139 37 10S 146 0E
Eileen L. 153 62 16N 107 37W
Eilenburg 48 51 28N 12 38E
Ein 'Arik 90 31 54N 35 8E
Ein el Luweiqa 123 14 5N 33 50E
Einasleigh 138 18 32S 144 5E
Einasleigh, R. 138 17 30S 142 17E
Einbeck 48 51 48N 9 50E
Eindhoven 47 51 26N 5 30E
Einsiedeln 51 47 7N 8 46E
Eiriksjökull 74 64 46N 20 24W
Eirlandsche Gat 46 53 12N 4 54E
Eirunepé 174 6 35S 70 0W
Eisden 47 50 59N 5 42E
Eisenach 48 50 58N 10 18E
Eisenberg 48 50 59N 11 50E
Eisenerz 52 47 32N 15 54E
Eisenhüttenstadt 48 52 9N 14 41E
Eisenkappel 52 46 29N 14 36E
Eisenstadt 53 47 51N 16 31E
Eiserfeld 47 50 50N 8 0E
Eisfeld 49 50 25N 10 54E
Eishort, L. 36 57 9N 6 0W
Eisleben 48 51 31N 11 31E
Eizariya (Bethany) 90 31 47N 35 15E
Ejby 73 55 25N 9 56E
Eje, Sierra del 56 42 24N 6 54W
Ejea de los Caballeros 58 42 7N 1 9W
Ejido 174 8 33N 71 14W
Ejura 121 7 25N 1 25E
Ejutla 165 16 34N 96 44W
Ekalaka 158 45 55N 104 30E
Ekawasaki 110 33 13N 132 46E
Ekeryd 73 57 37N 14 6E
Eket 121 4 38N 7 56W
Eketahuna 142 40 38S 175 43E
Ekhinos 68 41 16N 25 1W
Ekibastuz 76 51 40N 75 22E
Ekimchan 77 53 0N 133 0W
Ekofisk, oilfield 19 56 35N 3 30E
Ekofisk, W., oilfield 19 56 35N 3 5E
Ekoli 126 0 23S 24 13E
Ekoln, I. 72 59 45N 17 40E
Eksjö 73 57 40N 14 58W
Ekwan Pt. 150 53 16N 82 7W
Ekwan, R. 150 53 12N 82 15W
El Abiodh 118 32 53N 0 31E
El Aïoun 118 34 33N 2 30W
El 'Aiyat 122 29 36N 31 15E
El Alamein 122 30 48N 28 58E
El Aqaba 90 29 31N 35 0E
El Arahal 57 37 15N 5 33W
El Araq 122 28 40N 26 20E
El Arba 118 36 28N 3 12E
El Arba du Rharb 118 34 50N 5 59W
El Aricha 118 34 13N 1 16W
El Arīhā 90 31 52N 35 27E
El Arish 138 17 49S 146 1E
El 'Arîsh 122 31 8N 33 50E
El Arnaud 119 36 7N 5 49E
El Arrouch 119 36 37N 6 53E
*El Asnam 118 36 10N 1 20E
El Astillero 56 43 24N 3 49W
El Badâri 122 27 4N 31 25E
El Bahrein 122 28 30N 26 25E
El Ballâs 122 26 2N 32 43E
El Balyana 122 26 10N 32 3E
El Baqeir 122 18 40N 33 40E
El Barco de Ávila 56 40 21N 5 31W
El Barco de Valdeorras 56 42 23N 7 0W
El Bauga 122 18 18N 33 52E
El Baúl 174 8 57N 68 17W
El Bawiti 122 28 25N 28 45E
El Bayadh 118 33 40N 1 1E
El Bierzo 56 42 45N 6 30W
El Biodh 118 26 0N 6 32W
El Bluff 166 11 59N 83 40W
El Bonillo 59 38 57N 2 35W
El Cajon 163 32 49N 117 0W
El Callao 174 7 25N 61 50W
El Camp 58 41 5N 1 10E
El Campo 159 29 10N 96 20W
El Carmen 174 1 16N 66 52W
El Castillo 57 37 41N 6 19W
El Centro 161 32 50N 115 40W
El Cerro, Boliv. 174 17 30S 61 40W
El Cerro, Spain 57 37 45N 6 57W
El Cocuy 174 6 25N 72 27W
El Coronil 57 37 5N 5 38W
El Cuy 176 39 55S 68 25W
El Cuyo 165 21 30N 87 40W
El Dab'a 122 31 0N 28 27E
El Dátil 164 30 7N 112 15W
El Deir 122 25 25N 32 20E
El Dere 91 3 50N 47 8E
El Díaz 165 21 1N 87 17W
El Difícul 174 9 51N 74 14W
El Díos 164 20 40N 87 20W
El Diviso 174 1 22N 78 14W
El Djouf 120 20 0N 11 30E
El Dorado, Colomb. 174 1 11N 71 52W
El Dorado, Ark., U.S.A. 159 33 10N 92 40W
El Dorado, Kans., U.S.A. 159 37 55N 96 56W
El Dorado, Venez. 174 6 55N 61 30W
El Dorado Springs 159 37 54N 93 59W
El Eglab 118 26 20N 4 30W
El Escorial 56 40 35N 4 7W
El Faiyûm 122 29 19N 30 50E
El Fâsher 123 13 33N 25 26E
El Fashn 122 28 50N 30 54E
El Ferrol 56 43 29N 3 14W
El Fifi 123 10 4N 25 0E
El Fuerte 164 26 30N 108 40W
El Gal 91 10 58N 50 20E
El Gebir 123 13 40N 29 40E
El Gedida 122 25 40N 28 30E
El Geneina 117 13 27N 22 45E
El Geteina 123 14 50N 32 27E
El Gezira 123 14 0N 33 0E
El Gezira □ 123 15 0N 33 0E
El Gîza 122 30 0N 31 10E
El Goléa 118 30 30N 2 50E
El Guettar 119 34 5N 4 38E
El Hadjire 119 32 36N 5 30E
El Hagiz 123 15 15N 35 50E
El Hajeb 118 33 41N 5 23W
El Hammâm 122 30 52N 29 25E
El Hank, Alg. 118 25 38N 5 29W
El Hank, Maurit. 118 24 37N 7 0W
El Haql 122 29 15N 34 59E
El Hawata 123 13 25N 34 42E
El Heiz 122 27 50N 28 40E
El 'Idisât 122 25 30N 32 35E
El Iskandarîya 122 31 0N 30 0E
El Istwâ'ya □ 123 5 0N 30 0E
El Jadida 118 33 16N 9 31W
El Jorf Lasfar, C. 118 33 5N 8 54W
El Kab 122 19 27N 32 46E
El Kala 119 36 50N 8 30E
El Kamlin 123 15 3N 33 11E
El Kantara, Alg. 119 35 14N 5 45E
El Kantara, Tunisia 119 33 45N 10 58E
El Karaba 122 18 32N 33 41E
El Kef 119 36 12N 8 47E
El Kelâa des Srarhna 118 32 4N 7 27W
El Khandaq 122 18 30N 30 30E
El Khârga 122 25 30N 30 33E
El Khartûm 123 15 31N 32 35E
El Khartûm Bahrî 123 15 40N 32 31E
El-Khroubs 119 36 10N 6 55E
El Khureiba 122 28 3N 35 10E
El Kseur 119 36 46N 4 49E
El Ksiba 118 32 45N 6 1W
El Kuntilla 122 30 1N 34 45E
El Ladhiqiya 92 35 20N 35 30E
El Laqeita 122 25 50N 33 15E
El Leiya 123 16 15N 35 28E
El Mafâza 123 13 38N 34 30E
El Mahalla el Kubra 122 31 0N 31 0E
El Mahâriq 122 25 35N 30 35E
El Maiz 118 28 19N 0 9W
El-Maks el-Bahari 122 24 30N 30 40E
El Manshâh 122 26 26N 31 50E
El Mansour 118 27 47N 0 14W
El Mansûra 122 31 0N 31 19E
El Mantico 174 7 27N 62 32W
El Manzala 122 31 10N 31 50E
El Marâgha 122 26 35N 31 10E
El Masid 123 15 15N 33 0E
El Matariya 122 31 15N 32 0E
El Meghaier 119 33 55N 5 58E
El Melfa 119 31 58N 15 18E
El Meraguen 118 28 0N 0 7W
El Metemma 123 16 50N 33 10E
El Miamo 174 7 39N 61 46W
El Milagro 172 30 59S 65 59W
El Milheas 118 25 27N 6 57W
El Milia 119 36 51N 6 13E
El Minyâ 122 28 7N 30 33E
El Molar 58 40 42N 3 45W
El Monte 163 34 4N 118 2W
El Mreyye 120 18 0N 6 0W
El Obeid 123 13 8N 30 10E
El Oro = Sta. María del Oro 164 25 50N 105 20W
El Oro de Hidalgo 165 19 48N 100 8W
El Oued 119 33 20N 6 58E
El Ouig 120 19 31N 0 27E
El Palmar 174 7 58N 61 53W
El Palmito, Presa 164 25 40N 105 3W
El Panadés 58 41 10N 1 30E
El Pao 174 9 38N 68 8W
El Pardo 56 40 31N 3 47W
El Paso 161 31 50N 106 30W
El Paso Robles 163 35 38N 120 41W
El Pedernoso 59 39 29N 2 45W
El Pedroso 57 37 51N 5 45W
El Pilar 174 10 32N 63 9W
El Pobo de Dueñas 58 40 46N 1 39W
El Portal 163 37 44N 119 49W
El Porvenir, Mexico 164 31 15N 105 51W
El Porvenir, Venez. 174 4 42N 71 19W
El Prat de Llobregat 58 41 18N 2 3E
El Progreso 166 15 26N 87 51W
El Provencío 59 39 23N 2 35W
El Pueblito 164 29 3N 105 4W
El Qahîra 122 30 1N 31 14E
El Qantara 122 30 51N 32 20E
El Qasr 122 25 44N 28 42E
El Qubba 123 11 10N 27 5E
El Quseima 122 30 40N 34 15E
El Qusîya 122 27 29N 30 44E
El Râshda 122 25 36N 28 57E
El Reno 159 35 30N 98 0W
El Rheauya 118 25 52N 6 30W
El Ribero 56 42 30N 8 30W
El Ridisiya 122 24 56N 32 51E
El Rio 163 34 14N 119 10W
El Ronquillo 57 37 44N 6 10W
El Rubio 57 37 22N 5 0W
El Saff 122 29 34N 31 16E
El Salado 174 8 56N 73 55W
El Salto 164 23 47N 105 22W
El Salvador ■ 166 13 50N 89 0W
El Sancejo 57 37 4N 5 6W
El Sauce 166 13 0N 86 40W
El Shallal 122 24 0N 32 53E
El Suweis 122 29 58N 32 31E
El Temblador 174 8 59N 62 44W
El Thamad 122 29 40N 34 28E
El Tigre 174 8 55N 64 15W
El Tocuyo 174 9 47N 69 48W
El Tofo 172 29 22S 71 18W
El Tránsito 172 28 52S 70 17W
El Tûr 122 28 14N 33 36E
El Turbio 176 51 30S 72 40W
El Uqsur 122 25 41N 32 38E
El Vado 58 41 2N 3 18W
El Vallés 58 41 35N 2 20E
El Vigía 174 8 38N 71 39W
El Wak 124 2 49N 40 56E
El Waqf 122 25 45N 32 15E
El Wâsta 122 29 19N 31 12E
El Weguet 123 5 28N 42 17E
Ela 123 12 50N 42 20E
Elafónisos 69 36 29N 22 56E
Elaine 140 37 44S 144 2E
Elamanchili = Yellamanchilli 96 17 26N 82 50E
Elan R. 31 52 17N 3 40W
Elan Village 31 52 18N 3 34W
Elands 141 31 37S 152 20E
Ęlandsvlei 128 32 19S 19 31E
Elassa 69 35 18N 26 21E
Elassón 68 39 53N 22 12E
Elat 103 5 40S 133 5E
Elateia 69 38 37N 22 46E
Elâziğ 92 38 37N 39 22E
Elba 157 31 27N 86 4W
Elba, I. 62 42 48N 10 15E
Elbasani 68 41 9N 20 9E
Elbasani-Berati 68 40 58N 20 0E
Elbe, R. 48 53 15N 10 7E
Elbert, Mt. 161 39 12N 106 36W
Elberta 156 44 35N 86 14W
Elberton 157 34 7N 82 51W
Elbeuf 42 49 17N 1 2E
Elbląg □ 54 54 15N 19 30E
Elblag (Elbing) 54 54 10N 19 25E
Elbow 153 51 7N 106 35W
Elbrus, Mt. 83 43 30N 42 30E
Elburg 46 52 26N 5 50E
Elburz Mts. = Alborz 93 36 0N 52 0E
Elche 59 38 15N 0 42W
Elche de la Sierra 59 38 27N 2 3W
Elcho I. 138 11 55S 135 45E
Elda 59 38 29N 0 47W
Eldfisk, oilfield 19 56 25N 3 30E
Eldon, Iowa, U.S.A. 97 40 50N 92 12W
Eldon, Mo., U.S.A. 158 38 20N 92 38W
Eldora 158 42 20N 93 5W
Eldorado, Argent. 173 26 28S 54 43W

*Renamed Ech Cheliff

Eldorado **Ermelo**

Eldorado, Ont., Can. 97 44 40N 77 32W
Eldorado, Sask., Can. 153 59 35N 108 30W
Eldorado, Mexico 164 24 0N 107 30W
Eldorado, Ill., U.S.A. 156 37 50N 88 25W
Eldorado, Tex., U.S.A. 159 30 52N 100 35W
Eldoret 126 0 30N 35 25 E
Electra 159 34 0N 99 0W
Eleele 147 21 54N 159 35W
Elefantes, R. 129 24 0 S 32 30 E
Elektrogorsk 81 55 56N 38 50 E
Elektrostal 81 55 41N 38 32 E
Elele 121 5 5N 6 50 E
Elena 67 42 55N 25 53 E
Elephant Butte Res. 161 33 45N 107 30W
Elephant I. 13 61 0 S 55 0W
Elephant Pass 97 9 35N 80 25 E
Elesbão Veloso 170 6 13 S 42 8W
Eleshnitsa 67 41 52N 23 36 E
Eleuthera I. 166 25 0N 76 20W
Elevsís 69 38 4N 23 26 E
Elevtheroúpolis 68 40 52N 24 20 E
Elfin Cove 147 58 11N 136 20W
Elgåhogna, Mt. 72 62 7N 12 7 E
Elgepiggen 71 62 10N 11 21 E
Elgeyo-Marakwet □ 126 0 45N 35 30 E
Elgg 51 47 29N 8 52 E
Elgin, Can. 151 45 48N 65 10W
Elgin, U.K. 37 57 39N 3 20W
Elgin, Ill., U.S.A. 156 42 0N 88 20W
Elgin, N.D., U.S.A. 158 46 24N 101 46W
Elgin, Nebr., U.S.A. 158 41 58N 98 3W
Elgin, Nev., U.S.A. 161 37 27N 114 36W
Elgin, Oreg., U.S.A. 160 45 37N 118 0W
Elgin, Texas, U.S.A. 159 30 21N 97 22W
Elgol 36 57 9N 6 6W
Elgon, Mt. 126 1 10N 34 30 E
Elham 29 51 9N 1 7 E
Eliase 103 8 10 S 130 55 E
Elida 159 33 56N 103 41W
Elie 153 49 48N 97 52W
Elie de Beaumont, Mt. 143 43 30 S 170 20 E
Elikón, Mt. 69 38 18N 22 45 E
Elim 147 64 35N 162 20W
Elin Pelin 126 42 40N 23 38 E
Elisabethville = Lubumbashi 127 11 32 S 27 38 E
Eliseu Martins 170 8 13 S 43 42W
Elishaw 35 55 16N 2 14W
Elista 83 46 16N 44 14 E
Elit 123 15 10N 37 0 E
Elizabeth, Austral. 140 34 42 S 138 41 E
Elizabeth, U.S.A. 162 40 37N 74 12W
Elizabeth City 157 36 18N 76 16W
Elizabetha 126 1 3N 23 37 E
Elizabethton 157 36 20N 82 13W
Elizabethtown, Ky., U.S.A. 156 37 40N 85 54W
Elizabethtown, Pa., U.S.A. 162 40 8N 76 36W
Elizondo 58 43 12N 1 30W
Elk City 159 35 25N 99 25W
Elk Grove 163 38 25N 121 22W
Elk Island Nat. Park 152 53 47N 112 59W
Elk Lake 150 47 40N 80 25W
Elk Point 153 53 54N 110 55W
Elk River, Idaho, U.S.A. 160 46 50N 116 8W
Elk River, Minn., U.S.A. 158 45 17N 93 34W
Elkedra 138 21 9 S 135 26 E
Elkedra, R. 138 21 8 S 136 22 E
Elkhart, Ind., U.S.A. 156 41 42N 85 55W
Elkhart, Kans., U.S.A. 159 37 3N 101 54W
Elkhorn 153 49 59N 101 14W
Elkhorn, R. 158 42 0N 98 15W
Elkhotovo 83 43 19N 44 15 E
Elkhovo 67 42 10N 26 40 E
Elkin 157 36 17N 80 50W
Elkins 156 38 53N 79 53W
Elko, Can. 152 49 20N 115 10W
Elko, U.S.A. 160 40 40N 115 50W
Elkton 162 39 36N 75 50W
Ell, L. 137 29 13 S 127 46 E
Elland 33 53 41N 1 49W
Ellecom 46 52 2N 6 6 E
Ellef Ringnes I. 12 78 30N 102 2W
Ellen, Mt. 161 38 4N 110 56W
Ellen R. 32 54 44N 3 24W
Ellendale, Austral. 136 17 56 S 124 48 E
Ellendale, U.S.A. 158 46 3N 98 30W
Ellensburg 160 47 0N 120 30W
Ellenville 162 41 42N 74 23W
Eller Beck Bri. 33 54 23N 0 40W
Ellerston 141 31 49 S 151 20 E
Ellery, Mt. 141 37 28 S 148 40 E
Ellesmere 32 52 55N 2 53W
Ellesmere I. 12 79 30N 80 0W
Ellesmere, L. 131 43 46 S 172 27 E
Ellesmere Port 32 53 17N 2 55W
Ellesworth Land 13 74 0 S 85 0W
Ellezelles 47 50 44N 3 42 E
Ellice Is. 130 8 0 S 176 0 E
Ellicott City 162 39 16N 76 48W
Ellington 35 55 14N 1 34W
Ellinwood 158 38 27N 98 37W
Elliot, Austral. 138 17 33 S 133 32 E
Elliot, S. Afr. 129 31 22 S 27 48 E
Elliot Lake 150 46 35N 82 35W
Ellis 158 39 0N 99 39W
Ellisville 157 31 38N 89 12W
Ellon 37 57 21N 2 5W
Ellore = Eluru 96 16 48N 81 8 E
Ells, R. 152 57 18N 111 40W
Ellsworth 158 38 47N 98 15W
Ellsworth Land 13 76 0 S 89 0W
Ellwangen 49 48 57N 10 9 E
Ellwood City 156 40 52N 80 19W
Elm 51 46 54N 9 10 E
Elma, Can. 153 49 52N 95 55W
Elma, U.S.A. 160 47 0N 123 30 E
Elmer 162 39 36N 75 10W
Elmhurst 156 41 52N 87 58W
Elmina 121 5 5N 1 21W
Elmira, Can. 151 46 30N 61 59W
Elmira, U.S.A. 162 42 8N 76 49W
Elmira Heights 162 42 8N 76 50W
Elmore, Austral. 140 36 30 S 144 37 E
Elmore, U.S.A. 163 33 7N 115 49W
Elmshorn 48 53 44N 9 40 E
Elmswell 29 52 14N 0 53 E
Elorza 174 7 3N 69 31W
Eloy 161 32 46N 111 46W
Éloyes 43 48 6N 6 36 E
Elphin, Ireland 38 53 50N 8 11W
Elphin, U.K. 36 58 4N 5 3W
Elphinstone 138 21 30 S 148 17 E
Elrose 153 51 12N 108 0W
Elsas 150 48 32N 82 55W
Elsinore, Austral. 141 31 35 S 145 11 E
Elsinore, Cal., U.S.A. 163 33 40N 117 15W
Elsinore, Utah, U.S.A. 161 38 40N 112 2W
Elsinore = Helsingor 73 56 2N 12 35 E
Elspe 48 51 10N 8 1 E
Elspeet 46 52 17N 5 48 E
Elst 46 51 55N 5 51 E
Elsterwerda 48 51 27N 13 32 E
Elstree 29 51 38N 0 16W
Elten 46 51 52N 6 9 E
Eltham, Austral. 141 37 43 S 145 12 E
Eltham, N.Z. 142 39 26 S 174 19 E
Elton 83 49 5N 46 52 E
Eluru 96 16 48N 81 8 E
Elvas 57 38 50N 7 17W
Elven 42 47 44N 2 36W
Elverum 71 60 53N 11 34 E
Elvire, Mt. 137 21 52 S 116 50 E
Elvire, R. 136 17 51 S 128 11 E
Elvo, R. 62 45 32N 8 14 E
Elvran 71 63 24N 11 3 E
Elwood, Ind., U.S.A. 156 40 20N 85 50W
Elwood, Nebr., U.S.A. 158 40 38N 99 51W
Ely, U.K. 29 52 24N 0 16 E
Ely, Minn., U.S.A. 158 47 54N 91 52W
Ely, Nev., U.S.A. 160 39 10N 114 50W
Elyashiv 90 32 23N 34 55 E
Elyria 156 41 22N 82 8W
Emådalen 72 61 20N 14 44 E
Emaiygi, R. 80 58 30N 26 30 E
Emba 76 48 50N 58 8 E
Embarcación 172 23 10 S 64 0W
Embarras Portage 153 58 27N 111 28W
Embleton 35 55 30N 1 38W
Embo 37 57 55N 4 0W
Embóna 69 36 13N 27 51 E
Embrach 51 47 30N 8 36 E
Embrun 45 44 34N 6 30 E
Embu 126 0 32 S 37 38 E
Embu □ 126 0 30 S 37 35 E
Emden 48 53 22N 7 12 E
Emeq Hula 90 33 5N 35 8 E
'Emeq Yizre'el 90 32 35N 35 12 E
Emerald 138 23 32 S 148 10 E
Emerson 153 49 0N 97 10W
Emery 161 38 59N 111 17W
Emery Park 161 32 10N 110 59W
Emi Koussi, Mt. 117 20 0N 18 55 E
Emilia-Romagna □ 62 44 33N 10 40 E
Emilius, Mt. 62 45 41N 7 23 E
Eminabad 94 32 2N 74 8 E
Emine 67 42 40N 27 56 E
Emlichheim 48 52 37N 6 51 E
Emly 39 52 28N 8 20W
Emmaboda 73 56 37N 15 32 E
Emmaus 162 40 32N 75 30W
Emme, R. 50 47 0N 7 42 E
Emmeloord 46 52 44N 5 46 E
Emmen, Neth. 47 52 48N 6 57 E
Emmen, Switz. 51 47 4N 8 17 E
Emmendingen 49 48 7N 7 51 E
Emmental 50 47 0N 7 35 E
Emmer-Compascum 46 52 49N 7 2 E
Emmerich 48 51 50N 6 12 E
Emmet 138 24 45 S 144 30 E
Emmetsburg 158 43 3N 94 40W
Emmett 160 43 51N 116 33W
Emöd 53 47 57N 20 47 E
Emona 67 42 43N 27 53 E
Empalme 164 28 1N 110 49W
Empangeni 129 28 50 S 31 52 E
Empedrado 172 28 0 S 58 46W
Empoli 62 43 43N 10 57 E
Emporia, Kans., U.S.A. 158 38 25N 96 16W
Emporia, Va., U.S.A. 157 36 41N 77 32W
Emporium 156 41 30N 78 17W
Empress 153 50 57N 110 0W
Emptinne 47 50 19N 5 8 E
Ems, R. 48 52 37N 7 16 E
Emsdetten 48 52 11N 7 31 E
Emsworth 29 50 51N 0 56 E
Emu 140 36 44 S 143 26 E
Emu Park 138 23 13 S 150 50 E
Emu Ra. 136 23 0 S 122 0 E
Emyvale 38 54 20N 6 57W
En Gedi 90 31 28N 35 25 E
En Harod 90 32 33N 35 22 E
'En Kerem 90 31 47N 35 6 E
En Nahud 123 12 45N 28 25 E
en Namous, O. 118 31 15N 0 10W
Ena 111 35 25N 137 25 E
Ena-San 111 35 26N 137 36 E
Enafors 72 63 17N 12 20 E
Enambú 174 1 1N 70 17W
Enana 128 17 30 S 16 23 E
Enånger 72 61 30N 17 9 E
Enard B. 36 58 5N 5 20W
Enbetsu 112 44 44N 141 47 E
Encantadas, Serra 173 30 40 S 53 0W
Encanto, Cape 103 20 20N 121 40 E
Encarnación 173 27 15 S 56 0W
Encarnación de Diaz 164 21 30N 102 20W
Ench'eng 106 37 9N 116 16 E
Enchi 120 5 53N 2 48W
Encinal 159 28 3N 99 25W
Encinillas 164 33 3N 117 17W
Encinitas 163 33 3N 117 17W
Encino 161 34 46N 106 16W
Encounter B. 140 35 45 S 138 45 E
Encruzilhada 171 15 31 S 40 54W
Endau 101 2 40N 103 38 E
Endau, R. 101 2 30N 103 30 E
Ende 103 8 45 S 121 30 E
Endeavour 153 52 10N 102 39W
Endeavour Str. 138 10 45 S 142 0 E
Endelave 73 55 46N 10 18 E
Enderbury I. 131 3 8 S 171 5W
Enderby, Can. 152 50 35N 119 10W
Enderby, U.K. 28 52 35N 1 15W
Enderby I. 136 20 35 S 116 30 E
Enderby Land 13 66 0 S 53 0 E
Enderlin 158 46 45N 97 41W
Endicott, N.Y., U.S.A. 162 42 6N 76 2W
Endicott, Wash., U.S.A. 160 47 0N 117 45W
Endicott Mts. 147 68 0N 152 30W
Endröd 53 46 55N 20 47 E
Endyalgout I. 136 11 40 S 132 35 E
Enebakk 71 59 46N 11 9 E
Enez 68 40 45N 26 5 E
Enfida 119 36 6N 10 28 E
Enfield, U.K. 29 51 39N 0 4W
Enfield, U.S.A. 162 43 34N 71 57W
Engadin 51 46 45N 10 10 E
Engadine, Lower = Engiadina Bassa 51 46 51N 10 18 E
Engadine, Upper = Engiadin 'Ota 51 46 38N 10 0 E
Engano, C. 167 18 30N 68 20W
Engaño, C. 103 18 35N 122 23 E
Engeddi 90 31 28N 35 25 E
Engelberg 51 46 48N 8 26 E
Engels 81 51 28N 46 6 E
Engemann L. 153 55 55N 106 55W
Enger 71 60 35N 10 20 E
Enggano, I. 102 5 20 S 102 40 E
Enghien 47 50 37N 4 2 E
Engiadin 'Ota 51 46 38N 10 0 E
Engiadina Bassa 51 46 51N 10 18 E
Engkilili 102 1 3N 111 42 E
England 159 34 30N 91 58W
England □ 27 53 0N 2 0W
Englee 151 50 45N 56 5W
Englefield 140 37 21 S 141 48 E
Englehart 150 47 49N 79 52W
Engler L. 153 59 8N 106 52W
Englewood, Colo., U.S.A. 158 39 40N 105 0W
Englewood, Kans., U.S.A. 159 37 7N 99 59W
Englewood, N.J., U.S.A. 162 40 54N 73 59W
English Bazar 95 24 58N 88 21 E
English Channel 42 50 0N 2 0W
English Company Is. 133 12 0 S 137 0 E
English, R. 153 50 30N 93 50W
English River 150 49 20N 91 0W
Enid 159 36 26N 97 52W
Enipévs, R. 68 39 22N 22 17 E
Eniwetok 131 11 30N 152 16 E
Enjil 118 33 12N 4 32W
Enkeldoorn 127 19 2 S 30 52 E
Enkhuizen 46 52 42N 5 17 E
Enköping 72 59 37N 17 4 E
Enlo 108 24 0N 107 7 E
Enna 65 37 34N 14 15 E
Ennadai 153 61 8N 100 53W
Ennadai L. 153 61 0N 101 0W
Ennedi 117 17 15N 22 0 E
Ennell L. 38 53 29N 7 25W
Ennerdale Water 32 54 32N 3 24W
Enngonia 139 29 21 S 145 50 E
Enningdal 71 58 59N 11 33 E
Ennis, Ireland 39 52 51N 8 59W
Ennis, Mont., U.S.A. 160 45 27N 111 48W
Ennis, Texas, U.S.A. 159 32 15N 96 40W
Enniscorthy 39 52 30N 6 35W
Enniskean 39 51 44N 8 56W
Enniskerry 39 53 12N 6 10W
Enniskillen 38 54 20N 7 40W
Ennistimon 39 52 56N 9 18W
Enns 52 48 12N 14 28 E
Enns, R. 52 48 14N 14 27 E
Enoggera Range 108 27 26 S 152 56 E
Enoggera Res. 109 27 27 S 152 55 E
Enontekiö 74 68 23N 23 37 E
Enp'ing 109 22 11N 112 18 E
Enriquillo, L. 167 18 20N 72 5W
Ens 46 52 38N 5 50 E
Enschede 46 52 13N 6 53 E
Ensenada, Argent. 172 34 55 S 57 55W
Ensenada, Mexico 164 31 50N 116 50W
Enshih 108 30 18N 109 27 E
Enshū-Nada 111 34 27N 137 38 E
Ensisheim 43 47 50N 7 20 E
Enstone 28 51 55N 1 25W
Entebbe 126 0 4N 32 28 E
Enter 46 52 17N 6 35 E
Enterprise, Can. 152 60 47N 115 45W
Enterprise, Oreg., U.S.A. 160 45 30N 117 11W
Enterprise, Utah, U.S.A. 161 37 37N 113 36W
Entlebuch 50 46 59N 8 4 E
Entrance 152 53 25N 117 50W
Entre Ríos, Boliv. 172 21 30 S 64 25W
Entre Ríos, Mozam. 127 14 57 S 37 20 E
Entre Ríos □ 172 30 30 S 58 30W
Entre Rios, Bahia 171 11 56 S 38 5W
Entrecasteaux, Pt. d' 137 34 50 S 115 56 E
Entrepeñas, Pantano de 58 40 34N 2 42W
Entwistle 152 53 30N 115 0W
Enugu 121 6 30N 7 30 E
Enugu Ezike 121 7 0N 7 29 E
Enumclaw 160 47 12N 122 0W
Envermeu 42 49 53N 1 15 E
Envigado 174 6 10N 75 35W
Enza, R. 62 44 33N 10 22 E
Enzan 111 35 42N 138 44 E
Eólie o Lípari, Is. 65 38 30N 14 50 E
Epa 138 8 28 S 146 52 E
Epanomí 68 40 25N 22 59 E
Epe, Neth. 47 52 21N 5 59 E
Epe, Nigeria 121 6 36N 3 59 E
Épernay 43 49 3N 3 56 E
Épernon 43 48 35N 1 40 E
Ephesus 92 38 0N 27 30 E
Ephraim 160 39 30N 111 37W
Ephrata, Pa., U.S.A. 162 40 11N 76 11W
Ephrata, Wash., U.S.A. 160 47 28N 119 32W
Epila 58 41 36N 1 17W
Épinac-les-Mines 43 46 59N 4 31 E
Épinal 43 48 19N 6 27 E
Episcopia Bihorului 70 47 12N 21 55 E
Epitálion 69 37 37N 21 30 E
Eport L. 36 57 33N 7 10W
Epping 29 51 42N 0 8 E
Epping Forest 29 51 40N 0 5 E
Epsom 29 51 19N 0 16W
Epukiro 125 21 30 S 19 0 E
Epworth 33 53 30N 0 50W
Equatorial Guinea ■ 124 2 0 S 78 0W
Équeurdreville-Hainneville 42 49 40N 1 40W
Er Rahad 123 12 45N 30 32 E
Er Rif 118 35 1N 4 1W
Er Roseires 123 11 55N 34 30 E
Er Rumman 90 32 9N 35 48 E
Eradu 137 28 40 S 115 2 E
Erandol 96 20 56N 75 20 E
Erap 135 6 37 S 146 51 E
Erāwadī Myit, R. = Irrawaddy, R. 98 19 30N 95 15 E
Erba, Italy 62 45 49N 9 12 E
Erba, Sudan 122 19 5N 36 40 E
Ercha 77 69 45N 147 20 E
Erciyas Daği 92 38 30N 35 30 E
Erdene 106 44 30N 111 10 E
Erding 49 48 18N 11 55 E
Erebus, Mt. 13 77 35 S 167 0 E
Erechim 173 27 35 S 52 15W
Ereğli 92 41 15N 31 30 E
Erei, Monti 65 37 20N 14 20 E
Erembodegem 47 50 56N 4 4 E
Eresma, R. 56 41 13N 4 30W
Eressós 69 39 11N 25 57 E
Erewadi Myitwanya 99 15 30N 95 0 E
Erfenis Dam 128 28 30 S 26 50 E
Erfjord 71 59 20N 6 14 E
Erfoud 118 31 30N 4 15W
Erfurt 48 50 58N 11 2 E
Erfurt □ 48 51 10N 10 30 E
Ergani 92 38 26N 39 49 E
Ergene, R. 67 41 20N 27 0 E
Ergeni Vozyshennost 83 47 0N 44 0 E
Erhlien 106 43 42N 112 2 E
Erhlin 109 23 54N 120 22 E
Erhtao Chiang, R. 107 42 35N 128 10 E
Erhyüan 108 26 7N 99 57 E
Eria, R. 56 42 10N 6 8W
Eriba 123 16 40N 36 10 E
Eriboll, L. 37 58 28N 4 41W
Érica 46 52 43N 6 56 E
Érice 64 38 4N 12 34 E
Ericht, L. 37 56 50N 4 25W
Erie 156 42 10N 80 7W
Erigavo 91 10 35N 47 35 E
Erikoúsa 68 39 55N 19 14 E
Eriksdale 153 50 52N 98 7W
Erikslund 72 62 31N 15 54 E
Erímanthos 69 37 57N 21 50 E
Erimo-misaki 112 41 50N 143 15 E
Eriskay I. 36 57 4N 7 18W
Eriskay, Sd. of 36 57 5N 7 20W
Erisort L. 36 58 5N 6 30W
Eriswil 50 47 5N 7 46 E
Erith 152 53 25N 116 46W
Erithraí 69 38 13N 23 20 E
Eritrea □ 123 14 0N 41 0 E
Erjas, R. 56 39 45N 6 52W
Erker, L. 72 59 51N 18 29 E
Erlangen 49 49 35N 11 0 E
Erldunda 138 25 14 S 133 12 E
Ermelo, Neth. 46 52 35N 5 35 E
Ermelo, S. Afr. 129 26 31 S 29 59 E

Ermenak **Fairmount**

Ermenak 92 36 44N 33 0 E
Ermióni 69 37 23N 23 15 E
Ermoúpolis = Siros 69 37 28N 24 57 E
Ernakulam 97 9 59N 76 19 E
Erne, Lough 38 54 26N 7 46W
Erne, R. 38 54 30N 8 16W
Ernée 42 48 18N 0 56W
Ernest Giles Ra. 137 27 0 S 123 45 E
Erode 97 11 24N 77 45 E
Eromanga 139 26 40 S 143 11 E
Erongo 128 21 39 S 15 58 E
Erongoberg 128 21 45 S 15 32 E
Erp 47 51 36N 5 37 E
Erquelinnes 47 50 19N 4 8 E
Erquy 42 48 38N 2 29W
Erquy, Cap d' 42 48 39N 2 29W
Err, Piz d' 51 46 34N 9 43 E
Errabiddy 137 25 25 S 117 5 E
Erramala Hills 97 15 30N 78 15 E
Errer, R. 123 42 35N 8 40 E
Errigal, Mt. 38 55 2N 8 8W
Errill 39 52 52N 7 40W
Erris Hd. 38 54 19N 10 0W
Errochty, L. 37 56 45N 4 10W
Errogie 37 57 16N 4 23W
Errol 35 56 24N 3 13W
Erseka 68 40 22N 20 40 E
Erskine 158 47 37N 96 0W
Erstein 43 48 25N 7 38 E
Erstfeld 51 46 50N 8 38 E
Ertil 81 51 55N 40 50 E
Ertvågøy 71 63 12N 8 25 E
Ertvelde 47 51 11N 3 45 E
Erundu 128 20 39 S 16 26 E
Eruwa 121 7 33N 3 26 E
Ervalla 72 59 28N 15 16 E
Ervy-le-Châtel 43 48 2N 3 55 E
Erwin 157 36 10N 82 28W
Erzgebirge 48 50 25N 13 0 E
Erzin 77 50 15N 95 10 E
Erzincan 92 39 46N 39 30 E
Erzurum 92 39 57N 41 15 E
Es Sahrâ' Esh Sharqîya 122 26 0N 33 30 E
Es Sider 119 30 50N 18 21 E
Es Sînâ' 122 29 0N 34 0 E
Es Souk 121 18 48N 1 2 E
Es Sûkî 123 13 20N 34 58 E
Esa'ala 135 9 45 S 150 49 E
Esambo 126 3 48 S 23 30 E
Esan-misaki 112 41 40N 141 10 E
Esbjerg 73 55 29N 8 29 E
Escada 170 8 22 S 35 14W
Escalante 161 37 47N 111 37W
Escalante, R. 161 37 45N 111 0W
Escalón 164 26 40N 104 20W
Escalona 56 40 9N 4 29W
Escambia, R. 157 30 45N 87 15W
Escanaba 156 45 44N 87 5W
Escant, R. 47 51 2N 3 45 E
Esch-sur-Alzette 47 49 32N 6 0 E
Eschallens 50 46 39N 6 38 E
Eschede 48 52 44N 10 13 E
Escholzmatt 50 46 55N 7 56 E
Eschwege 48 51 10N 10 3 E
Eschweiler 48 50 49N 6 14 E
Escondida, La 164 24 6N 99 55W
Escondido 163 33 9N 117 4W
Escrick 33 53 53N 1 3W
Escuinapa 164 22 50N 105 50W
Escuintla 166 14 20N 90 48W
Escuminac 151 48 0N 67 0W
Escutillas = Ceba 174 6 33N 70 24W
Eséka 121 3 41N 10 44 E
Esens 48 53 40N 7 35 E
Esera, R. 58 42 24N 0 22 E
Esfahan □ 93 33 0N 53 0 E
Esgueva, R. 56 41 46N 4 14W
Esh Sham = Dimashq 92 33 30N 36 18 E
Esh Shamâlîya □ 122 19 0N 31 0 E
Esha Ness 36 60 30N 1 36W
Eshowe 129 28 50 S 31 30 E
Eshta' ol 90 31 47N 35 0 E
Esiama 120 4 48N 2 25W
Esino, R. 63 43 28N 13 8 E
Esk R. 32 54 23N 3 21W
Esk, R., Dumfries, U.K. 35 54 58N 3 4W
Esk, R., N. Yorks., U.K. 33 54 27N 0 36W
Eskdale 35 55 12N 3 4W
Eskifjördur 74 65 3N 13 55W
Eskilstuna 72 59 22N 16 32 E
Eskimo Ls. 147 69 15N 132 17W
Eskimo Pt. 153 61 10N 94 3W
Eskişehir 92 39 50N 30 35 E
Esla, R. 56 41 45N 5 50W
Eslöv 73 55 50N 13 20 E
Esmeralda, La 172 22 16 S 62 33W
Esmeraldas 174 1 0N 79 40W
Esneux 47 50 32N 5 33 E
Espa 71 60 35N 11 15 E
Espada, Pta. 174 12 5N 71 7W
Espalion 44 44 32N 2 47 E
Espalmador, I. 59 38 48N 1 26 E
Espanola 150 46 15N 81 46W
Espardell, I. del 59 38 47N 1 25 E
Esparraguera 58 41 33N 1 52 E
Esparta 166 9 59N 84 40W
Espejo 57 37 40N 4 34W
Espenberg, C. 147 66 35N 163 40W
Esperança 170 7 1 S 35 51W
Esperance 137 33 45 S 121 55 E
Esperance B. 137 33 48 S 121 55 E
Esperantinópolis 170 4 53 S 44 53W
Esperanza 172 31 29 S 61 3W
Esperanza, La, Argent. 172 24 9 S 64 52W
Esperanza, La, Boliv. 174 14 20 S 62 0W
Esperanza, La, Cuba 166 22 46N 83 44W
Esperanza, La, Hond. 166 14 15N 88 10W
Espéraza 44 42 56N 2 14 E
Espevær Lt. Ho. 71 59 35N 5 7 E
Espichel, C. 57 38 22N 9 16W
Espiel 57 38 11N 5 1W
Espigão, Serra do 173 26 35 S 50 30W
Espinal 174 4 9N 74 53W
Espinazo, Sierra del = Espinhaço, Serra do 171 17 30 S 43 30W
Espinhaço, Serra do 171 17 30 S 43 30W
Espinho 56 41 1N 8 38W
Espinilho, Serra do 173 28 30 S 55 0W
Espino 174 8 34N 66 1W
Espinosa de los Monteros 56 43 5N 3 34W
Espírito Santo □ 171 20 0 S 40 45W
Espíritu Santo, B. del 165 19 15N 79 40W
Espíritu Santo, I. 164 24 30N 110 23W
Espita 165 21 1N 88 19W
Esplanada 171 11 47 S 37 57W
Espluga de Francolí 58 41 24N 1 7 E
Espuña, Sierra de 59 37 51N 1 35W
Espungabera 129 20 29 S 32 45 E
Esquel 176 42 40 S 71 20W
Esquimalt 148 48 30N 123 23W
Esquina 172 30 0 S 59 30W
Essaouira (Mogador) 118 31 32N 9 42W
Essarts, Les 42 46 47N 1 12W
Essebie 126 2 58N 30 40 E
Essen, Belg. 47 51 28N 4 28 E
Essen, Ger. 48 51 28N 6 59 E
Essendon, Mt. 137 25 0 S 120 30 E
Essequibo, R. 174 5 45N 58 50W
Essex 162 39 18N 76 29W
Essex □ 29 51 48N 0 30 E
Esslingen 49 48 43N 9 19 E
Essonne □ 43 48 30N 2 20 E
Essvik 72 62 18N 17 24 E
Estadilla 58 42 4N 0 16 E
Estados, I. de los 176 54 40 S 64 30W
Estagel 44 42 47N 2 40 E
Estância 170 11 16 S 37 26W
Estancia 161 34 50N 106 1W
Estarreja 56 40 45N 8 35W
Estats, P. d' 44 42 40N 1 40 E
Estavayer le Lac 50 46 51N 6 51 E
Estcourt 129 28 58 S 29 53 E
Este 63 45 12N 11 40 E
Esteban 56 43 33N 6 5W
Esteli 166 13 9N 86 22W
Estella 58 42 40N 2 0W
Estelline, S.D., U.S.A. 158 44 39N 96 52W
Estelline, Texas, U.S.A. 159 34 35N 100 27W
Estena, R. 57 39 23N 4 44W
Estepa 57 37 17N 4 52W
Estepona 57 36 24N 5 7W
Esterhazy 153 50 37N 102 5W
Esternay 43 48 44N 3 33 E
Esterri de Aneu 58 42 38N 1 5 E
Estevan 153 49 10N 102 59W
Estevan Group 152 53 3N 129 38W
Estherville 158 43 25N 94 50W
Estissac 43 48 16N 3 48 E
Eston, Can. 153 51 8N 108 40W
Eston, U.K. 33 54 33N 1 6W
Estonian S.S.R. □ 80 48 30N 25 30 E
Estoril 57 38 42N 9 23W
Estrada, La 56 42 43N 8 27W
Estrêla, Serra da 56 40 10N 7 45W
Estrella 59 38 25N 3 35W
Estremadura 57 39 0N 9 0W
Estremoz 57 38 51N 7 39W
Estrondo, Serra do 170 7 20 S 48 0W
Esztergom 53 47 47N 18 44 E
Et Tieta 118 29 37N 9 15W
Et Turra 90 32 39N 35 39 E
Étables-sur-Mer 42 48 38N 2 51W
Etah 95 27 35N 78 40 E
Étain 43 49 13N 5 38 E
Etalle 47 49 40N 5 36 E
Etamamu 151 50 18N 59 59W
Étampes 43 48 26N 2 10 E
Étang 43 46 52N 4 10 E
Etanga 128 17 55 S 13 00 E
Étaples 43 50 30N 1 39 E
Etawah 95 26 48N 79 6 E
Etawah, R. 157 34 20N 84 15W
Etawney L. 153 57 50N 96 50W
Etchingham 29 51 0N 0 27 E
Eteh 121 7 2N 7 28 E
Etelia 121 19 10N 0 55 E
Éthe 47 49 35N 5 35 E
Ethel Creek 136 22 55 S 120 11 E
Ethel, Oued el 118 28 31N 3 37W
Ethelbert 153 51 32N 100 25W
Ethiopia ■ 91 8 0N 40 0 E
Ethiopian Highlands 114 10 0N 37 0 E
Etive, L. 34 56 30N 5 12W
Etna, Mt. 65 37 45N 15 0 E
Etne 71 59 40N 5 56 E
Etoile 127 11 33 S 27 30 E
Etolin I. 152 56 5N 132 20W
Eton 29 51 29N 0 37W
Etoshapan 128 18 40 S 16 30 E
Etowah 157 35 20N 84 30W
Étrépagny 42 49 18N 1 36 E
Étretat 42 49 42N 0 12 E
Etroits, Les 151 47 24N 68 54W
Etropole 68 43 50N 24 0 E
Ettelbrüch 47 49 50N 6 5 E
Ettelbruck 47 49 51N 6 5 E
Etten 47 51 34N 4 38 E
Ettington 28 52 8N 1 38W
Ettlingen 49 48 58N 8 25 E
Ettrick Forest 35 55 30N 3 0W
Ettrick Water 35 55 31N 2 55W
Etuku 126 3 42 S 25 45 E
Etzatlán 164 20 48N 104 5W
Etzna 165 19 35N 90 15W
Eu 42 50 3N 1 26 E
Euboea = Évvoia 69 38 40N 23 40 E
Euchareena 141 32 57 S 149 6 E
Eucla Basin 137 31 19 S 126 9 E
Euclid 156 41 32N 81 31W
Euclides da Cunha 170 10 31 S 39 1W
Eucumbene, L. 141 36 2 S 148 40 E
Eudora 159 33 5N 91 17W
Eudunda 140 34 12 S 139 7 E
Eufaula, Ala., U.S.A. 157 31 55N 85 11W
Eufaula, Okla., U.S.A. 159 35 20N 95 33W
Eufaula, L. 159 35 15N 95 28W
Eugene 160 44 0N 123 8W
Eugenia, Punta 164 27 50N 115 5W
Eugowra 141 33 22 S 148 24 E
Eulo 139 28 10 S 145 3 E
Eumungerie 141 31 56N 148 36 E
Eunice, La., U.S.A. 159 30 35N 92 28W
Eunice, N. Mex., U.S.A. 159 32 30N 103 10W
Eupen 47 50 37N 6 3 E
Euphrates = Furat, Nahr al 92 33 30N 43 0 E
Eure □ 42 49 6N 1 0 E
Eure-et-Loir □ 42 48 22N 1 30 E
Eureka, Can. 12 80 0N 85 56W
Eureka, Calif., U.S.A. 160 40 50N 124 0W
Eureka, Kans., U.S.A. 159 37 50N 96 20W
Eureka, Mont., U.S.A. 160 48 53N 115 6W
Eureka, Nev., U.S.A. 160 39 32N 116 2W
Eureka, S.D., U.S.A. 158 45 49N 99 38W
Eureka, Utah, U.S.A. 160 40 0N 112 0W
Eureka, Mt. 137 26 35 S 121 35 E
Eurelia 140 32 33 S 138 35 E
Euroa 141 36 44 S 145 35 E
Europa, Île 125 22 20 S 40 22 E
Europa, Picos de 56 43 10N 5 0W
Europa Pt. 55 36 2N 6 32W
Europa Pt. = Europa, Pta. de 57 36 3N 5 21W
Europa, Pta. de 57 36 3N 5 21W
Europe 16 20 0N 20 0 E
Europoort 46 51 57N 4 10 E
Euskirchen 48 50 40N 6 45 E
Eustis 157 28 54N 81 36W
Eutin 48 54 7N 10 38 E
Eutsuk L. 152 53 20N 126 45W
Euxton 32 53 41N 2 42W
Eva Downs 138 18 1 S 134 52 E
Eval, Mt. 90 32 15N 35 15 E
Evanger 71 60 39N 6 7 E
Evans 158 40 25N 104 43W
Evans Head 139 29 7 S 153 27 E
Evans L. 150 50 50N 77 0W
Evans P. 158 41 0N 105 35W
Evanston, Ill., U.S.A. 156 42 0N 87 40W
Evanston, Wy., U.S.A. 160 41 10N 111 0W
Evansville, Ind., U.S.A. 156 38 0N 87 35W
Evansville, Wis., U.S.A. 158 42 47N 89 18W
Evanton 37 57 40N 4 20W
Evato 129 20 37 S 47 10 E
Évaux-les-Bains 44 46 12N 2 29 E
Eveleth 158 47 35N 92 40W
Even Yahuda 90 32 16N 34 53 E
Evensk 77 61 57N 159 14 E
Evenstad 71 61 25N 11 7 E
Everard, C. 141 37 49 S 149 17 E
Everard, L. 139 31 30 S 135 0 E
Everard Ras. 137 27 5 S 132 28 E
Evercreech 28 51 8N 2 30W
Everdale 141 31 52 S 144 46 E
Evere 47 50 52N 4 25 E
Everest, Mt. 95 28 5N 86 58 E
Everett 160 48 0N 122 10W
Evergem 47 51 7N 3 43 E
Everglades 157 26 0N 80 30W
Evergreen 157 31 28N 86 55W
Everöd 73 55 53N 14 5 E
Everson 160 48 57N 122 22W
Everton 141 36 25 S 146 33 E
Evesham 28 52 6N 1 57W
Evian-les-Bains 45 46 24N 6 35 E
Evinayong 124 1 50N 10 35 E
Évinos, R. 69 38 27N 21 40 E
Evisa 45 42 15N 8 48 E
Évora 57 38 33N 7 57W
Évora □ 57 38 33N 7 50W
Évreux 42 49 0N 1 8 E
Évritania □ 69 39 5N 21 30 E
Évron 42 48 23N 1 58W
Évros □ 68 41 10N 26 0 E
Evrótas, R. 69 36 50N 22 40 E
Évvoia 69 38 30N 24 0 E
Évvoia □ 69 38 40N 23 40 E
Ewe, L. 36 57 49N 5 38W
Ewell 29 51 20N 0 15W
Ewhurst 29 51 9N 0 25W
Ewing 158 42 18N 98 22W
Ewo 124 0 48 S 14 45 E
Exaltación 174 13 10 S 65 20W
Excelsior 139 33 6 S 149 59W
Excelsior Springs 158 39 20N 94 10W
Excideuil 44 45 20N 1 4 E
Exe, R. 30 50 38N 3 27W
Exeter, U.K. 30 50 43N 3 31W
Exeter, Calif., U.S.A. 163 36 17N 119 9W
Exeter, Nebr., U.S.A. 158 40 43N 97 30W
Exeter, N.H., U.S.A. 162 43 0N 70 58W
Exford 28 51 8N 3 39W
Exloo 46 52 53N 6 52 E
Exmes 42 48 45N 0 10 E
Exminster 30 50 40N 3 29W
Exmoor 30 51 10N 3 59W
Exmore 162 37 32N 75 50W
Exmouth, Austral. 136 22 6 S 114 0 E
Exmouth, U.K. 30 50 37N 3 26W
Exmouth G. 136 22 15 S 114 15 E
Expedition Range 138 24 30 S 149 12 E
Exton 29 52 42N 0 38W
Extremadura 57 39 30N 6 5W
Exu 171 7 31 S 39 43W
Exuma Sound 166 24 30N 76 20W
Eyam 33 53 17N 1 40W
Eyasi, L. 126 3 30 S 35 0 E
Eyawaddi Myii 98 15 50N 95 6 E
Eye, Camb., U.K. 29 52 36N 0 11W
Eye, Norfolk, U.K. 29 52 19N 1 9 E
Eye Pen. 36 58 13N 6 10W
Eyeberry L. 153 63 8N 104 43W
Eyemouth 35 55 53N 2 5W
Eygurande 44 45 40N 2 26 E
Eyhatten 47 50 43N 6 1 E
Eyisen 82 41 0N 36 50 E
Eyjafjorður 74 66 15N 18 30W
Eymet 44 44 40N 0 25 E
Eymoutiers 44 45 40N 1 45 E
Eynhallow Sd. 37 59 8N 3 7W
Eynort, L. 36 57 13N 7 18W
Eynsham 28 51 47N 1 21W
Eyrarbakki 74 63 52N 21 9W
Eyre 137 32 15 S 126 18 E
Eyre Cr. 138 26 40 S 139 0 E
Eyre, L. 133 29 30 S 137 26 E
Eyre L., (North) 139 28 30 S 137 20 E
Eyre L., (South) 139 29 18 S 137 25 E
Eyre Mts. 143 45 25 S 168 25 E
Eyre Pen. 139 33 30 S 137 17 E
Eyrecourt 39 53 12N 8 8W
Ez Zeidab 122 17 25N 33 55 E
Ez Zergoun, W. 118 32 45N 2 25 E
Ezcaray 58 42 19N 3 0W
Ezine 68 39 48N 26 12 E

F

Fabens 161 31 30N 106 8W
Fåborg 73 55 6N 10 15 E
Fabriano 63 43 20N 12 52 E
Fabrizia 43 38 29N 16 19 E
Făcăeni 70 44 32N 27 53 E
Facatativá 174 4 49N 74 22W
Facture 44 44 39N 0 58W
Fada 117 17 13N 21 34 E
Fada-n-Gourma 121 12 10N 0 30 E
Fadd 53 46 28N 18 49 E
Faddeyevski, Ostrov 77 76 0N 150 0 E
Fadhili 92 26 55N 49 10 E
Fadlab 122 17 42N 34 2 E
Faenza 63 44 17N 11 53 E
Fafa 121 15 22N 0 48 E
Fafe 56 41 27N 8 11W
Fagam 121 11 1N 10 1 E
Fågelsjö 72 61 50N 14 35 E
Fagerhult 73 57 8N 15 40 E
Fagernes 75 60 59N 9 14 E
Fagersta 72 60 1N 15 46 E
Fåglavik 73 58 6N 13 6 E
Fagnano Castello 65 39 31N 16 4 E
Fagnano, L. 176 54 30 S 68 0W
Fagnières 43 48 58N 4 20 E
Fahral 93 29 0N 59 0 E
Fahūd 93 22 18N 56 28 E
Faid 92 27 1N 42 52 E
Faido 51 46 29N 8 48 E
Fair, C. 138 12 24 S 143 16 E
Fair Hd. 38 55 14N 6 10W
Fair Isle 23 59 30N 1 40W
Fair Oaks 163 38 39N 121 16W
Fairbank 161 31 44N 110 12W
Fairbanks 147 64 59N 147 40W
Fairbourne 31 52 42N 4 3W
Fairbury 158 40 5N 97 5W
Fairfax, Okla., U.S.A. 159 36 37N 96 45W
Fairfax, Va., U.S.A. 162 38 51N 77 18W
Fairfield, Austral. 141 33 53 S 150 57 E
Fairfield, Ala., U.S.A. 157 33 30N 87 0W
Fairfield, Calif., U.S.A. 163 38 14N 122 1W
Fairfield, Conn., U.S.A. 162 41 8N 73 16W
Fairfield, Idaho, U.S.A. 160 43 27N 114 52W
Fairfield, Ill., U.S.A. 156 38 20N 88 20W
Fairfield, Iowa, U.S.A. 158 41 0N 91 58W
Fairfield, Mont., U.S.A. 160 47 40N 112 0W
Fairfield, Texas, U.S.A. 159 31 40N 96 0W
Fairford, Can. 153 51 37N 98 38W
Fairford, U.K. 28 51 42N 1 48W
Fairhope 157 30 35N 87 50W
Fairlie, N.Z. 143 44 5 S 170 49 E
Fairlie, U.K. 34 55 44N 4 52W
Fairlight 29 50 53N 0 40 E
Fairmead 163 37 5N 120 10W
Fairmont, Minn., U.S.A. 158 43 37N 94 30W
Fairmont, W. Va., U.S.A. 156 39 29N 80 10W
Fairmount Hot Springs 152 50 20N 115 56W
Fairmount 163 34 45N 118 26W

Fairplay **Field**

Fairplay	161	39 9N	107 0W
Fairport	156	43 8N	77 29W
Fairview, Austral.	138	15 31S	144 17E
Fairview, Can.	152	56 5N	118 25W
Fairview, N. Dak., U.S.A.	158	47 49N	104 7W
Fairview, Okla., U.S.A.	159	36 19N	98 30W
Fairview, Utah, U.S.A.	160	39 50N	111 0W
Fairweather, Mt.	147	58 55N	137 45W
Faith	158	45 2N	102 4W
Faither, The, C.	36	60 34N	1 30W
Faizabad, Afghan.	93	37 7N	70 33E
Faizabad, India	95	26 45N	82 10E
Faizpur	96	21 14N	75 49E
Fajardo	147	18 20N	65 39W
Fakenham	29	52 50N	0 51E
Fakfak	103	3 0S	132 15E
Fakiya	170	42 10N	27 4E
Fakobli	120	7 23N	7 23W
Fakse	73	55 15N	12 8E
Fakse B.	73	55 11N	12 15E
Fakse Ladeplads	73	55 16N	12 9E
Fak'u	107	42 31N	123 26E
Falaise	42	48 54N	0 12W
Falaise, Mui	100	19 6N	105 45E
Falakrón Óros	68	41 15N	23 58E
Falam	98	23 0N	93 45E
Falcarragh	38	55 8N	8 8W
Falces	58	42 24N	1 48W
Falcón □	174	11 0N	69 50W
Falcon, C.	118	35 50N	0 50W
Falcón Dam	159	26 50N	99 20W
Falconara Marittima	63	43 37N	13 23E
Faldingworth	33	53 21N	0 22W
Faléa	120	12 16N	11 17W
Falelatai	84	13 55S	171 59W
Falenki	84	58 22N	51 35E
Faleshty	82	47 32N	27 44E
Falfurrias	159	27 8N	98 8W
Falher	152	55 44N	117 15W
Falkenberg, Ger.	48	51 34N	13 13E
Falkenberg, Sweden	73	56 54N	12 30E
Falkensee	48	52 35N	13 6E
Falkenstein	48	50 27N	12 24E
Falkirk	35	56 0N	3 47W
Falkland	35	56 15N	3 13W
Falkland Is.	176	51 30S	59 0W
Falkland Is. Dep.	13	57 0S	40 0W
Falkland Sd.	176	52 0S	60 0W
Falkonéra	69	36 50N	23 52E
Falköping	73	58 12N	13 33E
Fall Brook	161	33 25N	117 12W
Fall River	162	41 45N	71 5W
Fall River Mills	160	41 1N	121 30W
Fallbrook	163	33 23N	117 15W
Fallmore	38	54 6N	10 5W
Fallon, Mont., U.S.A.	158	46 52N	105 8W
Fallon, Nev., U.S.A.	160	39 31N	118 51W
Falls Church	162	38 53N	77 11W
Falls City, Nebr., U.S.A.	158	40 0N	95 40W
Falls City, Oreg., U.S.A.	160	44 54N	123 29W
Falmey	121	12 36N	2 51E
Falmouth, Jamaica	166	18 30N	77 40W
Falmouth, U.K.	30	50 9N	5 5W
Falmouth, Ky., U.S.A.	156	38 40N	84 20W
Falmouth, Mass., U.S.A.	162	41 34N	70 38W
Falmouth B.	30	50 7N	5 3E
False B.	128	34 15S	18 40E
False Divi Pt.	97	15 35N	80 50E
Falset	58	41 7N	0 50E
Falso, C.	166	15 12N	83 21W
Falster	73	54 45N	11 55E
Falsterbo	73	55 23N	12 50E
Falsterbokanalen	73	55 25N	12 56E
Falstone	35	55 10N	2 26W
Faluja	90	31 48N	31 37E
Falun	72	60 37N	15 37E
Famagusta	92	35 8N	33 55E
Famaka	123	11 24N	34 52E
Famatina, Sierra, de	172	29 5S	68 0W
Family L.	153	51 54N	95 27W
Famoso	163	35 37N	119 12W
Fampotabe	129	15 56S	50 8E
Fan i Madh, R.	68	41 56N	20 16E
Fana, Mali	120	13 0N	6 56W
Fana, Norway	71	60 16N	5 20E
Fanad Hd.	38	55 17N	7 40W
Fanambana	129	13 34S	50 0E
Fanárion	68	39 24N	21 47E
Fanch'ang	109	31 2N	118 13E
Fanchiat'un	107	43 42N	125 5E
Fanchih	106	39 14N	113 19E
Fandriana	129	20 14S	47 21E
Fang	100	19 55N	99 13E
Fangch'eng, Honan, China	106	33 16N	112 59E
Fangch'eng, Kwangsi-Chuang, China	108	21 46N	108 21E
Fanghsien	109	32 0N	111 0E
Fangliao	109	22 22N	130 35E
Fangshan	106	38 0N	111 16E
Fangtzu	107	36 39N	119 15E
Fannich, L.	36	57 40N	5 0W
*Fanning I.	131	3 51N	159 22W
Fanny Bay	152	49 27N	124 48W
Fanø	73	55 25N	8 25E
Fano	63	43 50N	13 0E
Fanø, I.	73	55 25N	8 25E
Fanshaw	152	57 11N	133 30W
Fao (Al Fāw)	92	30 0N	48 30E
Faqirwali	94	29 27N	73 0E
Fara in Sabina	63	42 13N	12 44E
Farab	85	39 9N	63 36E
Faraday Seamount Group	14	50 0N	27 0W
Faradje	126	3 50N	29 45E
Farafangana	129	22 49S	47 50E
Farâfra, El Wâhât el-	122	27 15N	28 20E
Farah	93	32 20N	62 7E
Farah □	93	32 25N	62 10E
Farahalana	129	14 26S	50 10E
Faraid, Gebel	122	23 33N	35 19E
Faraid Hd.	37	58 35N	4 48W
Faramana	120	11 56N	4 45W
Faranah	120	10 3N	10 45W
Farasān, Jazā'ir	91	16 45N	41 55E
Farasan Kebir	91	16 40N	42 0E
Faratsiho	129	19 24S	46 57E
Fardes, R.	59	37 25N	3 10W
Fareham	28	50 52N	1 11W
Farewell	147	62 30N	154 0W
Farewell, C.	143	40 29S	172 43E
Farewell C. = Farvel, K.	12	59 48N	43 55W
Farewell Spit	143	40 35S	173 0E
Farfán	174	0 16N	76 41W
Fargo	158	47 0N	97 0W
Faria, R.	90	32 12N	35 27E
Faribault	158	44 15N	93 19W
Faridkot	94	30 44N	74 45E
Faridpur, Bangla.	98	23 15N	90 0E
Faridpur, India	95	18 14N	79 34E
Farila	72	61 48N	15 50E
Färila	72	61 48N	15 50E
Farim	120	12 27N	15 17W
Farimān	93	35 40N	60 0E
Farina	139	30 3S	138 15E
Faringdon	28	51 39N	1 34W
Faringe	72	59 55N	18 7E
Farinha, R.	170	6 15S	47 30W
Färjestaden	73	56 38N	16 25E
Farmakonisi	69	37 17N	27 8E
Farmerville	159	32 48N	92 23W
Farmingdale	162	40 12N	74 10W
Farmington, Calif., U.S.A.	163	37 56N	121 0W
Farmington, N. Mex., U.S.A.	161	36 45N	108 28W
Farmington, N.H., U.S.A.	162	43 25N	71 3W
Farmington, Utah, U.S.A.	160	41 0N	111 58W
Farmington, R.	162	41 51N	72 38W
Farmville	156	37 19N	78 22W
Farnborough	29	51 17N	0 46W
Farne Is.	35	55 38N	1 37W
Farnham	29	51 13N	0 49W
Farnham, Mt.	152	45 20N	72 55W
Farnworth	32	53 33N	2 24W
Faro, Brazil	175	2 0S	56 45W
Faro, Port.	57	37 2N	7 55W
Fårö	75	58 0N	19 10E
Faro □	57	37 12N	8 10W
Faroe Is.	16	62 0N	7 0W
Farquhar, C.	137	23 38S	113 36E
Farquhar, Mt.	136	22 18S	116 53E
Farr	37	57 21N	4 13W
Farranfore	39	52 10N	9 32W
Farrars, Cr.	138	25 35S	140 43E
Farrashband	93	28 57N	52 5E
Farrell	156	41 13N	80 29W
Farrell Flat	140	33 48S	138 48E
Farrukhabad	95	27 30N	79 32E
Fars □	93	29 30N	55 0E
Fársala	68	39 17N	22 23E
Farsø	73	56 46N	9 19E
Farsö	73	56 48N	9 20E
Farstrup	73	56 59N	9 28E
Farsund	71	58 5N	6 55E
Fartura, Serra da	173	26 21S	52 52W
Faru	121	12 48N	6 12E
Farum	73	55 49N	12 21E
Farvel, Kap	12	59 48N	43 55W
Farwell	159	34 25N	103 0W
Faryab	93	28 7N	57 14E
Fasa	93	29 0N	53 32E
Fasag	36	57 33N	5 32W
Fasano	65	40 50N	17 20E
Fashoda	123	9 50N	32 2E
Faskari	79	11 42N	6 58E
Faslane	34	56 3N	4 49W
Fastnet Rock	39	51 22N	9 37W
Fastov	80	50 7N	29 57E
Fatehgarh	95	27 25N	79 35E
Fatehpur, Raj., India	94	28 0N	75 4E
Fatehpur, Ut. P., India	95	27 8N	81 7E
Fatick	120	14 19N	16 27W
Fatima	151	47 24N	61 53W
Fátima	57	39 37N	8 39W
Fatoya	120	11 37N	9 10W
Faucilles, Monts	43	48 5N	5 50E
Fauldhouse	35	55 50N	3 44W
Faulkton	158	45 4N	99 8W
Faulquemont	43	49 3N	6 36E
Fauquembergues	43	50 36N	2 5E
Faure I.	137	25 52S	113 50E
Fauresmith	128	29 44S	25 17E
Fauske	74	67 17N	15 25E
Fauvillers	47	49 51N	5 40E
Faux-Cap	129	25 33S	45 32E
Favara	64	37 19N	13 39E
Faversham	29	51 18N	0 54E
Favignana	64	37 56N	12 18E
Favone	45	41 47N	9 26E
Favourable Lake	150	52 50N	93 39W
Fawley	28	50 49N	1 20W
Fawn, R.	150	52 22N	88 20W
Fawnskin	163	34 16N	116 56W
Faxaflói	74	64 29N	23 0W
Faxäiven	72	63 13N	17 13E
Faya = Largeau	117	17 58N	19 6E
Fayence	45	43 38N	6 42E
Fayette, Ala., U.S.A.	157	33 40N	87 50W
Fayette, La., U.S.A.	156	40 22N	86 52W
Fayette, Mo., U.S.A.	158	39 10N	92 40W
Fayetteville, Ark., U.S.A.	159	36 0N	94 5W
Fayetteville, N.C., U.S.A.	157	35 0N	78 58W
Fayetteville, Tenn., U.S.A.	157	35 0N	86 30W
Fayón	58	41 15N	0 20E
Fazeley	28	52 36N	1 42W
Fazenda Nova	171	16 11S	50 48W
Fazilka	94	30 27N	74 2E
Fazilpur	94	29 18N	70 29E
F'Derik	116	22 40N	12 45W
Fé, La	166	22 2N	84 15W
Feakle	39	52 56N	8 41W
Feale, R.	39	52 26N	9 28W
Fear, C.	157	33 45N	78 0W
Fearn	37	57 47N	4 0W
Fearnan	37	56 34N	4 6W
Feather, R.	160	39 30N	121 20W
Featherston	142	41 6S	175 20E
Featherstone	127	18 42S	30 55E
Fécamp	42	49 45N	0 22E
Fedala = Mohammeda	118	33 44N	7 21W
Fedamore	39	52 33N	8 36W
Federación	172	31 0S	57 55W
Federalsburg	162	38 42N	75 47W
Fedjadj, Chott el	119	33 52N	9 14E
Fedje	71	60 47N	4 43E
Fedorovka	84	53 38N	62 42E
Feeagh L.	38	53 56N	9 35W
Feeny	38	54 54N	7 0W
Fehérgyarmat	53	48 0N	22 30E
Fehmarn	48	54 26N	11 10E
Fehmarn Bælt	73	54 35N	11 20E
Feihsiang	106	36 32N	114 47E
Feihsien	107	35 12N	118 0E
Feilding	142	40 13S	175 35E
*Feira	65	15 35S	30 16E
Feira de Santana	171	12 15S	38 57W
Fejér □	53	47 9N	18 30E
Fejø	73	54 55N	11 30E
Felanitx	59	39 27N	3 7E
Feldbach	52	46 57N	15 52E
Feldberg	48	53 20N	13 26E
Feldberg, mt.	49	47 51N	7 58E
Feldis	51	46 48N	9 26E
Feldkirch	52	47 15N	9 37E
Feldkirchen	52	46 44N	14 6E
Felhit	123	16 40N	38 1E
Felipe Carrillo Puerto	165	19 38N	88 3W
Felixlândia	171	18 47S	44 55W
Felixstowe	29	51 58N	1 22W
Felletin	44	45 53N	2 11E
Felpham	29	50 47N	0 38W
Felton, U.K.	35	55 18N	1 42W
Felton, U.S.A.	163	37 3N	122 4W
Feltre	63	46 1N	11 55E
Feltwell	29	52 29N	0 32E
Femø	73	54 58N	11 53E
Femunden	71	62 10N	11 53E
Fen Ho, R.	106	35 36N	110 42E
Fench'ing	108	24 35N	99 54E
Fénérive	129	17 22S	49 25E
Fenerwa	123	13 5N	39 3E
Fengári	68	40 25N	25 32E
Fengchen	106	40 30N	113 0E
Fengch'eng, Kiangsi, China	109	28 10N	115 43E
Fengch'eng, Liaoning, China	107	40 30N	124 2E
Fengchieh	108	31 3N	109 28E
Fengch'iu	106	35 2N	114 24E
Fenghsiang	106	34 26N	107 18E
Fenghsien, Kiangsu, China	106	34 42N	116 34E
Fenghsien, Shanghai, China	109	30 55N	121 27E
Fenghsien, Shensi, China	106	33 56N	106 41E
Fenghsin	109	28 42N	115 23E
Fenghua	109	29 40N	121 24E
Fenghuang	108	27 58N	109 19E
Fenghuangtsui	106	33 30N	109 27E
Fengi	108	25 35N	100 18E
Fengjun	107	39 51N	118 8E
Fengk'ai	109	23 26N	111 30E
Fengkang	108	27 58N	107 47E
Fengloho	109	31 29N	112 29E
Fengning	106	41 12N	116 32E
Fengshan, Hopei, China	107	41 13N	117 6E
Fengshan, Kwangsi-Chuang, China	108	24 32N	107 3E
Fengt'ai, Anhwei, China	109	32 44N	116 43E
Fengt'ai, Peip'ing, China	106	39 51N	116 17E
Fengteng	106	36 25N	114 14E
Fengtu	108	29 58N	107 59E
Fengyuang	109	32 52N	117 32E
Fenhsi	106	36 38N	111 31E
Feni	109	27 48N	114 41E
Feni Is.	135	4 0S	153 40E
Fenit	39	52 17N	9 51W
Fennagh	39	52 42N	6 50W
Fennimore	158	42 58N	90 41W
Fenny	98	22 55N	91 32E
Fenny Bentley	33	53 4N	1 43W
Fenny Compton	28	52 9N	1 20W
Fenny Stratford	29	51 59N	0 42W
Feno, C. de	45	41 58N	8 33E
Fenoarivo	129	18 26S	46 34E
Fens, The	29	52 45N	0 2E
Fenton, Can.	153	53 0N	105 35W
Fenton, U.S.A.	156	42 47N	83 44W
Fenwick	34	55 38N	4 25W
Fenyang	106	37 19N	111 46E
Feodosiya	82	45 2N	35 28E
Fer, C. de	119	37 3N	7 10E
Ferbane	39	53 17N	7 50W
Ferdows	93	33 58N	58 2E
Fère-Champenoise	43	48 45N	4 0E
Fère-en-Tardenois	43	49 10N	3 30E
Fère, La	43	49 40N	3 20E
Ferentino	64	41 42N	13 14E
Ferfer	91	5 18N	45 20E
Fergana	85	40 23N	71 46E
Ferganskaya Dolina	85	40 50N	71 30E
Ferganskiy Khrebet	85	41 0N	73 50E
Fergus	150	43 43N	80 24W
Fergus Falls	158	46 25N	96 0W
Fergus, R.	39	52 45N	9 0W
Ferguson	150	47 50N	73 30W
Fergusson I.	135	9 30S	150 45E
Fériana	119	34 59N	8 33E
Feričanci	66	45 32N	18 0E
Ferkane	119	34 37N	7 26E
Ferkéssédougou	120	9 35N	5 6W
Ferlach	52	46 32N	14 18E
Ferland	150	50 19N	88 27W
Ferlo, Vallée du	120	15 15N	14 15W
Fermanagh (□)	38	54 21N	7 40W
Fermo	63	43 10N	13 42E
Fermoselle	56	41 19N	6 27W
Fermoy	39	52 4N	8 18W
Fernagh	38	54 2N	7 51W
Fernan Nuñ,z	57	37 40N	4 44W
Fernández	172	27 55S	63 50W
Fernandina	157	30 40N	81 30W
Fernando de Noronha, I.	170	4 0S	33 10W
Fernando do Noronho □	170	4 0S	33 10W
Fernando Póo = Bioko	113	3 30N	8 40E
Fernandópolis	171	20 16S	50 14W
Ferndale, Calif., U.S.A.	160	40 37N	124 12W
Ferndale, Wash., U.S.A.	160	48 51N	122 41W
Ferness	37	57 28N	3 44W
Fernhurst	29	51 3N	0 43W
Fernie	152	49 30N	115 5W
Fernilea	36	57 18N	6 24W
Fernlees	138	23 51S	148 7E
Fernley	160	39 42N	119 20W
Feroke	97	11 9N	75 46E
Ferozepore	94	30 55N	74 40E
Férrai	68	40 53N	26 10E
Ferrandina	65	40 30N	16 28E
Ferrara	63	44 50N	11 36E
Ferrato, C.	64	39 18N	9 39E
Ferreira do Alentejo	57	38 4N	8 6W
Ferreñafe	174	6 35S	79 50W
Ferret, C.	44	44 38N	1 15W
Ferrette	43	47 30N	7 20E
Ferriday	159	31 35N	91 33W
Ferrières	43	48 5N	2 48E
Ferriete	62	44 40N	9 30E
Ferrol	56	43 29N	8 15W
Ferron	160	39 3N	111 3W
Ferros	171	19 14S	43 2W
Ferryhill	33	54 42N	1 32W
Ferryland	151	47 2N	52 53W
Ferté Bernard, La	42	48 10N	0 40E
Ferté, La	43	48 57N	3 6E
Ferté-Mace, La	42	48 35N	0 21W
Ferté-St. Aubin, La	43	47 42N	1 57E
Ferté-Vidame, La	42	48 37N	0 53E
Fertile	158	47 37N	96 18W
Fertilia	64	40 37N	8 13E
Fertöszentmiklós	53	47 35N	16 53E
Fès	118	34 0N	5 0W
Feschaux	47	50 9N	4 54E
Feshi	124	6 0S	18 10E
Fessenden	158	47 42N	99 44W
Fet	71	59 57N	11 12E
Feteşti	70	44 22N	27 51E
Fethaland, Pt.	36	60 39N	1 20W
Fethard	39	52 29N	7 42W
Fethiye	92	36 36N	29 10E
Fetlar, I.	36	60 36N	0 52W
Fettercairn	37	56 50N	2 33W
Feuerthalen	51	47 32N	8 38E
Feurs	45	45 45N	4 13E
Fezzan	117	27 0N	15 0E
Ffestiniog	31	52 58N	3 56W
Fforest Fawr, mt.	31	51 52N	3 35W
Fiambalá	172	27 45S	67 37W
Fianarantsoa	125	21 20S	46 45E
Fianarantsoa □	129	19 30S	47 0E
Fianga	117	9 55N	15 20E
Fibiş	66	45 57N	21 26E
Fichot, I.	151	51 12N	55 40W
Fichtelgebirge	49	50 10N	12 0E
Ficksburg	129	28 51S	27 53E
Fiddown	39	52 20N	7 20W
Fidenza	62	44 51N	10 3E
Field	150	46 31N	80 1W

*Renamed Tubuaeran

*Renamed Luangwa

Field I | Fort Garland

Field I. 136 12 5S 132 23E
Field, R. 138 23 48S 138 0E
Fields Finds 137 29 0S 117 10E
Fierenana 129 18 29S 48 24E
Fiéri 68 40 43N 19 33E
Fiesch 50 46 25N 8 12E
Fife □ 35 56 13N 3 2W
Fife Ness 35 56 17N 2 35W
Fifth Cataract 123 18 15N 33 50E
Figeac 44 44 37N 2 2E
Figline Valdarno 63 43 37N 11 28E
Figtree 127 20 22S 28 20E
Figueira da Foz 56 40 7N 8 54W
Figueiró dos Vinhos 56 39 55N 8 16W
Figueras 58 42 18N 2 58E
Figuig 118 32 5N 1 11W
Fihaonana 129 18 36S 47 12E
Fiherenana, R. 129 22 50S 44 0E
Fiji ■ 142 17 20S 179 0E
Fiji Is. 130 17 20S 179 0E
Fik 90 32 46N 35 41E
Fika 121 11 15N 11 13E
Filabres, Sierra de los 59 37 13N 2 20W
Filadélfia, Brazil 170 7 21S 47 30W
Filadélfia, Italy 65 38 47N 16 17E
Filadelfia 172 22 25S 60 0W
Fil'akovo 53 48 17N 19 50E
Filby 29 52 40N 1 39E
Filchner Ice Shelf 13 78 0S 60 0W
Filer 160 42 30N 114 35W
Filey 33 54 13N 0 18W
Filey B. 33 54 12N 0 15W
Filiaşi 70 44 32N 23 31E
Filiátes 68 39 38N 20 16E
Filiatrá 69 37 9N 21 35E
Filicudi, I. 65 38 35N 14 33E
Filiouri, R. 68 41 15N 25 40E
Filipstad 72 59 43N 14 9E
Filisur 51 46 41N 9 40E
Fillmore, Can. 153 49 50N 103 25W
Fillmore, U.S.A. 163 34 23N 118 58W
Filottrano 63 43 28N 13 20E
Filton 28 51 29N 2 34E
Filyos 82 41 34N 32 4E
Filyos çayi 92 41 35N 32 10E
Finale Ligure 62 44 10N 8 21E
Finale nell' Emília 63 44 50N 11 18E
Fiñana 59 37 10N 2 50W
Fincham 29 52 38N 0 30E
Findhorn 37 57 39N 3 36W
Findhorn, R. 37 57 38N 3 38W
Findlay 156 41 0N 83 41W
Findon 29 50 53N 0 24W
Finea 38 53 46N 7 23W
Finedon 29 52 20N 0 40W
Finger L. 153 53 9N 93 30W
Fingest 29 51 35N 0 52W
Finglas 38 53 22N 6 18W
Fingõe 127 15 12S 31 50E
Finike 92 36 21N 30 10E
Finistère □ 42 48 20N 4 0W
Finisterre 56 42 54N 9 16W
Finisterre, C. 56 42 50N 9 19W
Finisterre Ra. 135 6 0S 146 30E
Finke 138 25 34S 134 35E
Finke, R. 138 24 54S 134 16E
Finland ■ 78 70 0N 27 0E
Finland, G. of 78 60 0N 26 0E
Finlay, R. 152 55 50N 125 10W
Finley, Austral. 141 35 38S 145 35E
Finley, U.S.A. 158 47 35N 97 50W
Finn, R. 38 54 50N 7 55W
Finnart 34 56 7N 4 48W
Finnigan, Mt. 138 15 49S 145 17E
Finniss 140 35 24S 138 48E
Finniss, C. 139 33 38S 134 51E
Finnmark fylke □ 74 69 30N 25 0E
Finschhafen 135 6 33S 147 50E
Finse 71 60 36N 7 30E
Finspång 73 58 45N 15 43E
Finsta 72 59 45N 18 34E
Finsteraarhorn 50 46 31N 8 10E
Finsterwalde 48 51 37N 13 42E
Finsterwolde 46 53 12N 7 6E
Finstown 37 59 0N 3 8W
Fintona 38 54 30N 7 20W
Fintown 38 54 52N 8 8W
Finucanel I. 132 20 19S 118 30E
Finvoy 38 55 0N 6 29W
Fionn L. 36 57 46N 5 30W
Fionnphort 34 56 19N 6 23W
Fiora, R. 63 42 25N 11 35E
Fiordland National Park 143 45 0S 167 50E
Fiorenzuola d'Arda 62 44 56N 9 54E
Fiq 90 32 46N 35 41E
Fire River 150 48 47N 83 36W
Firebag, R. 153 57 45N 111 21W
Firebaugh 163 36 52N 120 27W
Firedrake L. 153 61 25N 104 30W
Firenze 63 43 47N 11 15E
Firkessédougou 120 9 35N 5 6W
Firmi 44 44 32N 2 19E
Firminy 45 45 23N 4 18E
Firoz Kohi 93 34 45N 63 0E
Firozabad 95 27 10N 78 25E
First Cataract 122 24 1N 32 51E
Fīrūzābād 93 28 52N 52 35E
Firuzkuh 93 35 50N 52 40E
Firvale 152 52 27N 126 13W
Fish, R. 128 27 40S 17 30E
Fisher 137 30 30S 131 0E
Fisher B. 153 51 35N 97 13W
Fishguard 31 51 59N 4 59W
Fishguard B. 31 52 2N 4 58W
Fishing L. 153 52 10N 95 24W
Fishkill 162 41 32N 73 53W
Fishtoft 33 52 27N 0 2E
Fishtown 120 4 24N 7 45E
Fiskivötn 74 64 50N 20 45W
Fiskum 71 59 42N 9 46E
Fismes 43 49 20N 3 40E
Fister 71 59 10N 6 5E
Fitchburg 162 42 35N 71 47W
Fitero 58 42 4N 1 52W
Fitful Hd. 36 59 54N 1 20W
Fitjar 71 59 55N 5 17E
Fitri, L. 124 12 50N 17 28E
Fitz Roy 176 47 10S 67 0W
Fitzgerald, Can. 152 59 51N 111 36W
Fitzgerald, U.S.A. 157 31 45N 83 10W
Fitzmaurice, R. 136 14 50S 129 50E
Fitzpatrick 150 47 29N 72 46W
Fitzroy Crossing 136 18 9S 125 38E
Fitzroy, R., Queens., Austral. 138 23 32S 150 52E
Fitzroy, R., W. Australia, Austral. 136 17 25S 124 0E
Fiume = Rijeka 63 45 20N 14 21E
Fiumefreddo Brúzio 65 39 14N 16 4E
Five Alley 39 53 9N 7 51W
Five Points 163 36 26N 120 6W
Fivemiletown 38 54 23N 7 20W
Fizi 126 4 17S 28 55E
Fjæra 71 59 52N 6 22E
Fjaere 71 58 23N 8 36E
Fjellerup 73 56 29N 10 34E
Fjerritslev 73 57 5N 9 15E
Fkih ben Salah 118 32 45N 6 45W
Fla 71 60 25N 9 26E
Flå 71 63 13N 10 18E
Flagler 158 39 20N 103 4W
Flagstaff 161 35 10N 111 40W
Flagstone 152 49 4N 115 10W
Flaherty, I. 150 56 15N 79 15W
Flåm 75 60 52N 7 14E
Flambeau, R. 158 45 40N 90 50W
Flamborough 33 54 7N 0 7W
Flamborough Hd. 33 54 8N 0 4W
Flaming Gorge Dam 160 40 50N 109 25W
Flaming Gorge L. 160 41 15N 109 30W
Flamingo, Teluk 103 5 30S 138 0E
Flanders = Flandres 47 51 10N 3 15E
Flandre Occidental □ 47 51 0N 3 0E
Flandre Orientale □ 47 51 0N 4 0E
Flandreau 158 44 5N 96 38W
Flandres, Plaines des 47 51 10N 3 15E
Flannan Is. 23 58 9N 7 52W
Flaren L. 73 57 2N 14 5E
Flåsjön 74 64 5N 15 50E
Flat, R. 152 61 51N 128 0W
Flat River 159 37 50N 90 30W
Flatey, Barðastrandarsýsla, Iceland 74 66 10N 17 52W
Flatey, Suður-þingeyjarsýsla, Iceland 74 65 22N 22 56W
Flathead L. 160 47 50N 114 0W
Flattery, C., Austral. 138 14 58S 145 21E
Flattery, C., U.S.A. 160 48 21N 124 43W
Flavy-le-Martel 43 49 43N 3 12E
Flawil 51 47 26N 9 11E
Flaxton 158 48 52N 102 24W
Flèche, La 42 47 42N 0 5W
Fleeming, C. 136 11 15S 131 21E
Fleet 29 51 16N 0 50W
Fleetwood, U.K. 32 53 55N 3 1W
Fleetwood, U.S.A. 162 40 27N 75 49W
Flekkefjord 71 58 18N 6 39E
Flémalle 47 50 36N 5 28E
Flensburg Fjord 73 54 50N 9 40E
Flensburg 48 54 46N 9 28E
Flers 42 48 47N 0 33W
Flesberg 71 59 51N 9 22E
Fletton 29 52 34N 0 13W
Fleurance 44 43 52N 0 40E
Fleurier 50 46 54N 6 35E
Fleurus 47 50 29N 4 32E
Flickerbäcken 72 61 47N 12 34E
Flims 51 46 50N 9 17E
Flin Flon 153 54 46N 101 53W
Flinders B. 137 34 19S 115 9E
Flinders Group, Is. 138 14 11S 144 15E
Flinders I. 138 40 0S 148 0E
Flinders, R. 138 17 36S 140 36E
Flinders Ranges 140 31 30S 138 30E
Flinders Reefs 138 17 37S 148 31E
Flint 156 43 5N 83 19W
Flint (□) 26 53 15N 3 12W
Flint, I. 131 11 26S 151 48W
Flint, R. 157 31 20N 84 10W
Flinton 139 27 55S 149 32E
Fliseryd 73 57 6N 16 15E
Flitwick 29 51 59N 0 30W
Flix 58 41 14N 0 32E
Flixecourt 43 50 0N 2 5E
Flobecq 47 50 44N 3 45E
Floda 72 60 30N 14 53E
Flodden 35 55 37N 2 8W
Floodwood 158 46 55N 92 55W
Flora, N. Tröndelag, Norway 71 63 27N 11 22E
Flora, Sogn & Fjordane, Norway 71 61 35N 5 1E
Flora, U.S.A. 156 38 40N 88 30W
Florac 44 44 20N 3 37E
Florala 157 31 0N 86 20W
Florânia 170 6 8S 36 49W
Floreffe 47 50 26N 4 46E
Florence, Ala., U.S.A. 157 34 50N 87 50W
Florence, Ariz., U.S.A. 161 33 0N 111 25W
Florence, Colo., U.S.A. 158 38 26N 105 0W
Florence, Oreg., U.S.A. 160 44 0N 124 3W
Florence, S.C., U.S.A. 157 34 5N 79 50W
Florence = Firenze 63 43 47N 11 15E
Florence, L. 139 28 53S 138 9E
Florennes 47 50 15N 4 35E
Florensac 44 43 23N 3 28E
Florenville 47 49 40N 5 19E
Flores, Azores 16 39 13N 31 13W
Flores, Brazil 170 7 51S 37 59W
Flores, Guat. 166 16 50N 89 40W
Flores I. 152 49 20N 126 10W
Flores, I. 103 8 35S 121 0E
Flores Sea 102 6 30S 124 0E
Floresta 170 9 46S 37 26W
Floresville 159 29 10N 98 10W
Floriano 170 6 50S 43 0W
Florianópolis 173 27 30S 48 30W
Florida, Cuba 166 21 32N 78 14W
Florida, Uruguay 173 34 7S 56 10W
Florida □ 157 28 30N 82 0W
Florida B. 167 25 0N 81 20W
Florida Keys 167 25 0N 80 40W
Florida, Strait of 167 25 0N 80 0W
Florídia 65 37 6N 15 9E
Flórina 68 40 48N 21 26E
Flórina □ 68 40 45N 21 20E
Florningen 72 61 50N 12 16E
Florø 71 61 35N 5 1E
Flosta 71 58 32N 8 56E
Flower's Cove 151 51 14N 56 46W
Floydada 159 33 58N 101 18W
Flüela Pass 51 46 45N 9 57E
Fluk 103 1 42S 127 38E
Flumen, R. 58 41 50N 0 25W
Flumendosa, R. 64 39 30N 9 25E
Fluminimaggiore 64 39 25N 8 30E
Flums 51 47 6N 9 21E
Flushing = Vlissingen 47 51 26N 3 34E
Fluviá, R. 58 42 12N 3 7E
Fly, R. 135 8 25S 143 0E
Foam Lake 153 51 40N 103 32W
Foča 66 43 31N 18 47E
Focşani 70 45 41N 27 15E
Fofo Fofo 138 8 9S 147 6E
Foggaret el Arab 118 27 3N 2 59E
Foggaret ez Zoua 118 27 20N 3 0E
Fóggia 65 41 28N 15 31E
Foggo 121 11 21N 9 57E
Foglia, R. 63 43 50N 12 32E
Fogo 151 49 43N 54 17W
Fogo I. 151 49 40N 54 5W
Fohnsdorf 52 47 12N 14 40E
Föhr 48 54 40N 8 30E
Foia, Cerro da 57 37 19N 8 10W
Foix 44 42 58N 1 38E
Fojnica 66 43 59N 17 51E
Fokang 109 23 52N 113 31E
Fokino 80 53 30N 34 10E
Fokís □ 69 38 30N 22 15E
Fokstua 71 62 8N 9 16E
Folda, Nord-Trøndelag, Norway 74 64 41N 10 50E
Folda, Nordland, Norway 74 67 38N 14 50E
Földeák 53 46 19N 20 30E
Folette, La 157 36 23N 84 9W
Foley 128 30 25N 87 40W
Foleyet 150 48 15N 82 25W
Folgefonni 71 60 23N 6 34E
Foligno 63 42 58N 12 40E
Folkestone 29 51 5N 1 11E
Folkston 157 30 55N 82 0W
Follett 159 36 30N 100 12W
Follónica 62 42 55N 10 45E
Folsom 160 38 41N 121 7W
Fond-du-Lac 153 59 19N 107 12W
Fond du Lac 158 43 46N 88 26W
Fond-du-Lac, R. 153 59 17N 106 0W
Fondak 118 35 34N 5 35W
Fondi 64 41 21N 13 25E
Fonfría 56 41 37N 6 9W
Fongen 71 63 11N 11 38E
Fonni 64 40 5N 9 16E
Fonsagrada 56 43 8N 7 4W
Fonseca, G. de 166 13 10N 87 40W
Fontaine-Française 43 47 32N 5 21E
Fontainebleau 43 48 24N 2 40E
Fontas, R. 152 58 14N 121 48W
Fonte Boa 174 2 25S 66 0W
Fontem 121 5 32N 9 52E
Fontenay-le-Comte 44 46 28N 0 48W
Fontenelle 151 48 54N 64 33W
Fontur 74 66 23N 14 32W
Fonyód 53 46 44N 17 33E
Foochow = Fuchou 109 26 5N 119 18E
Foping 106 33 22N 108 19E
Foppiano 62 46 21N 8 24E
Föra 73 57 1N 16 51E
Forbach 43 49 10N 6 52E
Forbes 141 33 22S 148 0E
Forbesganj 95 26 17N 87 18E
Forcados 121 5 26N 5 26E
Forcados, R. 121 5 25N 5 20E
Forcall, R. 58 40 40N 0 12W
Forcalquier 45 43 58N 5 47E
Forchheim 49 49 42N 11 4E
Forclaz, Col de la 50 46 3N 7 1E
Ford City 163 35 9N 119 27W
Førde 71 61 27N 5 53E
Fordingbridge 28 50 56N 1 48W
Fordongianus 44 40 0N 8 50E
Fords Bridge 139 29 41S 145 29E
Fordyce 159 33 50N 92 20W
Forécariah 120 9 20N 13 10W
Forel 12 66 52N 36 55W
Foremost 152 49 26N 111 25W
Forenza 65 40 50N 15 50E
Forest, Belg. 47 50 49N 4 20E
Forest, U.S.A. 159 32 21N 89 27W
Forest City, Ark., U.S.A. 159 35 0N 90 50W
Forest City, Iowa, U.S.A. 158 43 12N 93 39W
Forest City, N.C., U.S.A. 157 35 23N 81 50W
Forest Grove 160 45 31N 123 4W
Forest Lawn 152 51 4N 114 0W
Forest Row 29 51 6N 0 3E
Forestburg 152 52 35N 112 1W
Forestier Pen. 138 43 0S 148 0E
Forestville, Can. 151 48 48N 69 20W
Forestville, U.S.A. 156 44 41N 87 29W
Forez, Mts. du 44 45 40N 3 50E
Forfar 37 56 40N 2 53W
Forges-les-Eaux 43 49 37N 1 30E
Forget 150 49 40N 102 50W
Forked River 162 39 50N 74 12W
Forks 160 47 56N 124 23W
Forksville 162 41 29N 76 35W
Forlì 63 44 14N 12 2E
Forman 158 46 9N 97 43W
Formazza 62 46 23N 8 26E
Formby Pt. 32 53 33N 3 7W
Formentera, I. 59 38 40N 1 30E
Formentor, C. de 58 39 58N 3 13E
Fórmia 64 41 15N 13 34E
Formiga 171 20 27S 45 25W
Formigine 62 44 37N 10 51E
Formiguères 44 42 37N 2 5E
Formosa, Argent. 172 26 15S 58 10W
Formosa, Brazil 171 15 32S 47 20W
Formosa = Taiwan ■ 109 24 0N 121 0E
Formosa □ 172 26 5S 58 10W
Formosa Bay 126 2 40S 40 20E
Formosa Strait 109 24 40N 120 0E
Formoso, R. 171 10 34S 49 56W
Fornaes, C. 73 56 27N 10 58E
Fornells 58 40 4N 4 4E
Fornos de Algodres 56 40 38N 7 32W
Fornovo di Taro 62 44 42N 10 7E
Forres 37 57 37N 3 38W
Forrest, Vic., Austral. 140 38 22S 143 40E
Forrest, W. Australia, Austral. 137 30 51S 128 6E
Forrest Lakes 137 29 12S 128 46E
Forrest, Mt. 137 24 48S 127 45E
Forrières 47 50 8N 5 17E
Fors, Jämtland, Sweden 72 63 0N 16 40E
Fors, Kopparberg, Sweden 72 60 14N 16 20E
Forsa 72 61 44N 16 55E
Forsand 71 58 54N 6 5E
Forsayth 138 18 33S 143 34E
Forsbacka 72 60 39N 16 54E
Forse 72 63 8N 17 1E
Forserum 73 57 42N 14 30E
Forshaga 72 59 33N 13 29E
Forshem 73 58 38N 13 30E
Forsmo 72 63 16N 17 11E
Forst 48 51 43N 14 37E
Forster 141 32 12S 152 31E
Forsyth, Ga., U.S.A. 157 33 4N 83 55W
Forsyth, Mont., U.S.A. 160 46 14N 106 37W
Forsyth I. 143 40 58S 174 5E
Fort Albany 150 52 15N 81 35W
Fort Ann 162 43 25N 73 30W
Fort Apache 161 33 50N 110 0W
Fort Archambault = Sarh 117 9 5N 18 23E
Fort Assiniboine 152 54 20N 114 45W
Fort Augustus 37 57 9N 4 40W
Fort Babine 152 55 22N 126 37W
Fort Beaufort 128 32 46S 26 40E
Fort Benton 160 47 50N 110 40W
Fort Bragg 160 39 28N 123 50W
Fort Bretonnet = Bousso 117 10 34N 16 52E
Fort Bridger 160 41 22N 110 20W
Fort Charlet = Djanet 121 24 35N 9 32E
Fort Chimo 149 58 6N 68 25W
Fort Chipewyan 153 58 42N 111 8W
Fort Collins 158 40 30N 105 4W
Fort Coulonge 150 45 50N 76 45W
Fort Crampel = Kaga Bandoro 117 7 8N 19 18E
Fort-Dauphin 129 25 2S 47 0E
Fort Davis 159 30 38N 103 53W
Fort-de-France 167 14 36N 61 2W
Fort de Polignac = Illizi 119 26 31N 8 32E
Fort de Possel = Possel 124 5 5N 19 10E
Fort Defiance 161 35 47N 109 4W
Fort Dodge 158 42 29N 94 10W
Fort Flatters = Bordj Omar Driss 119 27 10N 6 40E
Fort Foureau = Kousseri 117 12 0N 14 55E
Fort Frances 153 48 35N 93 25W
Fort Franklin 148 65 30N 123 45W
Fort Garland 161 37 28N 105 30W

Fort George Frýdek-Místek

Fort George 151 53 50N 79 0W
Fort George, R. 150 53 50N 77 0W
Fort Good-Hope 147 66 14N 128 40W
Fort Gouraud = F'Dérik 116 22 40N 12 45W
Fort Grahame 152 56 30N 124 35W
Fort Hancock 161 31 19N 105 56W
Fort Hauchuca 161 31 32N 110 30W
Fort Hertz (Putao) 99 27 28N 97 30E
Fort Hope 150 51 30N 88 10W
Fort Irwin 163 35 16N 116 34W
Fort Jameson = Chipata 127 13 38S 32 38E
Fort Johnston 127 14 25S 35 16E
Fort Kent 151 47 12N 68 30W
Fort Klamath 160 42 45N 122 0W
Fort Lallemand 119 31 13N 6 17E
Fort-Lamy = Ndjamena 117 12 4N 15 8E
Fort Lapperrine = Tamanrasset 119 22 56N 5 30E
Fort Laramie 158 42 15N 104 30W
Fort Lauderdale 157 26 10N 80 5W
Fort Liard 152 60 20N 123 30W
Fort Liberté 167 19 42N 71 51W
Fort Lupton 158 40 8N 104 48W
Fort Mackay 152 57 12N 111 41W
Fort McKenzie 151 57 20N 69 0W
Fort Macleod 152 49 45N 113 30W
Fort MacMahon 118 29 51N 1 45E
Fort McMurray 152 56 44N 111 23W
Fort McPherson 147 67 30N 134 55W
Fort Madison 158 40 39N 91 20W
Fort Meade 157 27 45N 81 45W
Fort Miribel 118 29 31N 2 55E
Fort Morgan 158 40 10N 103 50W
Fort Myers 157 26 30N 82 0W
Fort Nelson 152 58 50N 122 38W
Fort Nelson, R. 152 59 32N 124 0W
Fort Norman 147 64 57N 125 30W
Fort Pacot (Chirfa) 119 20 55N 12 14E
Fort Payne 157 34 25N 85 44W
Fort Peck 160 47 1N 105 30W
Fort Peck Dam 160 48 0N 106 20W
Fort Peck Res. 160 47 40N 107 0W
Fort Pierce 158 27 29N 80 19W
Fort Pierre 158 44 25N 100 25W
Fort Pierre Bordes 118 20 0N 2 55E
Fort Portal 126 0 40N 30 20E
Fort Providence 152 61 21N 117 40W
Fort Qu'Appelle 153 50 45N 103 50W
Fort Randall 147 55 10N 162 48W
Fort Reliance 153 63 0N 109 20W
Fort Resolution 152 61 10N 113 40W
Fort Rixon 127 20 2S 29 17E
Fort Roseberry = Mansa 127 11 10S 28 50E
Fort Rupert (Rupert House) 150 51 30N 78 40W
Fort Saint 119 30 13N 9 31E
Fort St. James 152 54 30N 124 10W
Fort St. John 152 56 15N 120 50W
Fort Sandeman 94 31 20N 69 25E
Fort Saskatchewan 152 53 40N 113 15W
Fort Scott 159 38 0N 94 40W
Fort Selkirk 147 62 43N 137 22W
Fort Severn 150 56 0N 87 40W
Fort Shevchenko 83 44 30N 50 10W
Fort Sibut = Sibut 117 5 52N 19 10E
Fort Simpson 152 61 45N 121 23W
Fort Smith, Can. 152 60 0N 111 51W
Fort Smith, U.S.A. 159 35 25N 94 25W
Fort Stanton 161 33 33N 105 36W
Fort Stockton 159 30 48N 103 2W
Fort Sumner 159 34 24N 104 8W
Fort Thomas 161 33 2N 109 59W
Fort Trinquet = Bir Mogrein 116 25 10N 11 25W
Fort Valley 157 32 33N 83 52W
Fort Vermilion 152 58 24N 116 0W
Fort Victoria 127 20 8S 30 55E
Ft. Walton Beach 157 30 25N 86 40W
Fort Wayne 156 41 5N 85 10W
Fort William 36 56 48N 5 8W
Fort William = Thunder Bay 150 48 20N 89 10W
Fort Worth 159 32 45N 97 25W
Fort Yates 158 46 8N 100 38W
Fort Yukon 147 66 35N 145 12W
Fortaleza 170 3 35S 38 35W
Forte Coimbra 174 19 55S 57 48W
Forte Rocadas 125 16 38S 15 22E
Forteau 151 51 28N 57 1W
Fortescue 136 21 4S 116 4E
Fortescue, R. 136 21 20S 116 5E
Forth, Firth of 35 56 5N 2 55W
Forthassa Rharbia 118 32 52N 1 11W
Forties, oilfield 19 57 40N 1 0E
Fortín Corrales 174 22 21S 60 35W
Fortín Guachalla 174 22 22S 62 23W
Fortín Rojas Silva 172 22 40S 59 3W
Fortín Siracuas 174 21 3S 61 46W
Fortín Teniente Montania 172 22 1S 59 45W
Fortore, R. 63 41 40N 15 0E
Fortrose 143 46 38S 168 45E
Fortuna, Spain 59 38 11N 1 7W
Fortuna, Cal., U.S.A. 160 48 38N 124 8W
Fortuna, N.D., U.S.A. 158 48 55N 103 48W
Fortune Bay 151 47 30N 55 22W
Forty Mile 147 64 20N 140 30W
Forūr 93 26 20N 54 30E
Fos 62 43 20N 4 57E
Fos do Jordão 174 9 30S 72 14W
Fos-sur-Mer 45 43 26N 4 56E
Foshan 109 23 4N 113 5E
Fossacesia 63 42 15N 14 30E
Fossano 62 44 39N 7 40E
Fosses-la-Ville 47 50 24N 4 41E
Fossil 160 45 0N 120 9W
Fossilbrook 138 17 47S 144 29E
Fossombrone 63 43 41N 12 49E
Fosston 158 47 33N 95 39W
Foster, R. 153 55 47N 105 49W
Fosters Ra. 138 21 35S 133 48E
Fostoria 156 41 8N 83 25W
Fou Chiang, R. 108 30 3N 106 21E
Fouch'eng 106 37 52N 116 8E
Fougamou 124 1 38S 11 39E
Fougères 42 48 21N 1 14W
Fouhsinshih 107 42 13N 121 51E
Foul Pt. 97 8 35N 81 25E
Foula, I. 23 60 10N 2 5W
Fouling 108 29 40N 107 20E
Foulpointe 129 17 41S 49 31E
Foum el Alba 118 20 45N 3 0W
Foum el Kreneg 118 29 0N 0 58W
Foum Tatahouine 119 32 57N 10 29E
Foum Zguid 118 30 2N 6 59W
Foumban 121 5 45N 10 50E
Foundiougne 120 14 5N 16 32W
Founing 107 33 47N 119 48E
Fountain, Colo., U.S.A. 158 38 42N 104 40W
Fountain, Utah, U.S.A. 160 39 41N 111 50W
Fountain Springs 163 35 54N 118 51W
Foup'ing 106 38 55N 114 13E
Four Mts., Is. of the 147 52 0N 170 30W
Fourchambault 43 47 0N 3 3E
Fourchu 151 45 43N 60 17W
Fourcroy, C. 136 11 45S 130 2E
Fourmies 43 50 1N 4 2E
Fournás 69 39 3N 21 52E
Foúrnoi 69 37 36N 26 32E
Fours 43 46 50N 3 42E
Foushan 106 35 58N 111 51E
Fouta Djalon 120 11 20N 12 10W
Foux, Cap-à- 167 19 43N 73 27W
Fouyang 109 32 55N 115 52E
Foveaux Str. 143 46 42S 168 10E
Fowler, Calif., U.S.A. 163 36 41N 119 41W
Fowler, Colo., U.S.A. 158 38 10N 104 0W
Fowler, Kans., U.S.A. 159 37 28N 100 7W
Fowlers B. 137 31 59S 132 34E
Fowlers Bay 137 32 0S 132 29E
Fowlerton 159 28 26N 98 50W
Fox Is. 147 52 30N 166 0W
Fox, R. 153 56 3N 93 18W
Fox Valley 153 50 30N 109 25W
Foxboro 162 42 4N 71 16W
Foxe Basin 149 68 30N 77 0W
Foxe Channel 149 66 0N 80 0W
Foxe Pen. 149 65 0N 76 0W
Foxen, L. 72 59 25N 11 55E
Foxhol 46 53 10N 6 43E
Foxpark 160 41 4N 106 6W
Foxton 142 40 29S 175 18E
Foyle, Lough 38 55 6N 7 8W
Foynes 38 52 30N 9 5W
Foz 56 43 33N 7 20W
Foz do Cunene 128 17 15S 11 55E
Foz do Gregório 174 6 47S 71 0W
Foz do Iguaçu 173 25 30S 54 30W
Frackville 162 40 46N 76 15W
Fraga 58 41 32N 0 21E
Fraire 47 50 16N 4 31E
Frameries 47 50 24N 3 54E
Framlingham 29 52 14N 1 20E
Franca 171 20 25S 47 30W
Francavilla al Mare 63 42 25N 14 16E
Francavilla Fontana 65 40 32N 17 35E
France ■ 41 47 0N 3 0E
Frances 140 36 41S 140 55E
Frances Creek 136 13 25S 132 3E
Frances L. 152 61 23N 129 30W
Frances, R. 152 60 16N 129 10W
Francés Viejo, C. 167 19 40N 70 0W
Franceville 124 1 40S 13 32E
Franche Comté □ 43 46 30N 5 50E
Franches Montagnes 50 47 10N 7 0E
Francis-Garnier 118 36 30N 1 30E
Francis Harbour 151 52 34N 55 44W
Francisco I. Madero, Coahuila, Mexico 164 25 48N 103 18W
Francisco I. Madero, Durango, Mexico 164 24 32N 104 22W
Francisco Sá 171 16 28S 43 30W
Francistown 125 21 7S 27 33E
Francofonte 65 37 13N 14 50E
François 151 47 35N 56 45W
Francois L. 152 54 0N 125 30W
François, Le 167 14 38N 60 57W
Francorchamps 47 50 27N 5 57E
Franeker 46 53 12N 5 33E
Frankado 123 12 30N 43 12E
Frankenberg 48 51 3N 8 47E
Frankenthal 49 49 32N 8 21E
Frankford = Kilcormac 39 53 10N 7 43W
Frankfort, Ind., U.S.A. 156 40 20N 86 33W
Frankfort, Kans., U.S.A. 158 39 42N 96 26W
Frankfort, Ky., U.S.A. 156 38 12N 84 52W
Frankfort, Mich., U.S.A. 156 44 38N 86 14W
Frankfort, N.Y., U.S.A. 162 43 2N 75 4W
Frankfurt □ 48 52 30N 14 0E
Frankfurt am Main 49 50 7N 8 40E
Frankfurt an der Oder 48 52 50N 14 31E
Fränkische Alb 49 49 20N 11 30E
Fränkische Saale 49 50 7N 9 49E
Fränkische Saale, R. 49 50 7N 9 49E
Fränkische Schweiz 49 49 45N 11 10E
Frankland, R. 137 35 0S 116 48E
Franklin, Ky., U.S.A. 157 36 40N 86 30W
Franklin, La., U.S.A. 159 29 45N 91 30W
Franklin, Mass., U.S.A. 162 42 4N 71 23W
Franklin, Nebr., U.S.A. 158 40 9N 98 55W
Franklin, N.H., U.S.A. 162 43 28N 71 39W
Franklin, N.J., U.S.A. 162 41 9N 74 38W
Franklin, Pa., U.S.A. 156 41 22N 79 45W
Franklin, Tenn., U.S.A. 157 35 54N 86 53W
Franklin, Va., U.S.A. 157 36 40N 76 58W
Franklin, W. Va., U.S.A. 156 38 38N 79 21W
*Franklin □ 149 71 0N 99 0W
Franklin B. 147 69 45N 126 0W
Franklin D. Roosevelt L. 160 48 30N 118 16W
Franklin I. 13 76 10S 168 30E
Franklin, L. 160 40 20N 115 26W
Franklin Mts., Can. 148 66 0N 125 0W
Franklin Mts., N.Z. 143 44 55S 167 45E
Franklin Str. 148 72 0N 96 0W
Franklinton 159 30 53N 90 10W
Franklyn Mt. 143 42 4S 172 42E
Franks Peak 160 43 50N 109 5W
Frankston 141 38 8S 145 8E
Frankton Junc. 142 37 47S 175 16E
Fränsta 72 62 30N 16 11E
Frant 29 51 5N 0 17E
Frantsa Josifa, Zemlya 76 76 0N 62 0E
Franz 150 48 25N 84 30W
Franz Josef Fd. 12 73 20N 22 0E
Franz Josef Land = Frantsa Josifa 76 76 0N 62 0E
Franzburg 48 54 9N 12 52E
Frascati 64 41 48N 12 41E
Fraser I. 139 25 15S 153 10E
Fraser L. 152 54 0N 124 50W
Fraser, Mt. 137 25 35S 118 20E
Fraser, R., B.C., Can. 152 49 7N 123 11W
Fraser, R., Newf., Can. 151 56 39N 63 10W
Fraserburg 128 31 55S 21 30E
Fraserburgh 37 57 41N 2 0W
Fraserdale 150 49 55N 81 37W
Frasertown 142 38 58S 177 28E
Frashëri 68 40 23N 20 26E
Frasne 43 46 50N 6 10E
Frater 150 47 20N 84 25W
Frauenfeld 51 47 34N 8 54E
Fray Bentos 172 33 10S 58 15W
Frazier Downs P.O. 136 18 48S 121 42E
Frechilla 56 42 8N 4 50W
Fredericia 73 55 34N 9 45E
Frederick, Md., U.S.A. 162 39 25N 77 23W
Frederick, Okla., U.S.A. 159 34 22N 99 0W
Frederick, S.D., U.S.A. 158 45 55N 98 29W
Frederick Reef 133 20 58S 154 23E
Frederick Sd. 153 57 10N 134 0W
Fredericksburg, Tex., U.S.A. 159 30 17N 98 55W
Fredericksburg, Va., U.S.A. 162 38 16N 77 29W
Frederickstown 159 37 35N 90 15W
Fredericton 151 45 57N 66 40W
Fredericton Junc. 151 45 41N 66 40W
Frederiksberg 72 60 12N 14 25E
Frederiksborg Amt □ 73 55 50N 12 10E
Frederikshåb 12 62 0N 49 30W
Frederikshavn 73 57 28N 10 31E
Frederikssund 73 55 50N 12 3E
Frederiksted 147 17 43N 64 53W
Fredonia, Ariz., U.S.A. 161 36 59N 112 36W
Fredonia, Kans., U.S.A. 159 37 34N 95 50W
Fredonia, N.Y., U.S.A. 156 42 26N 79 20W
Fredrikstad 71 59 13N 10 57E
Freehold 162 40 15N 74 18W
Freel Pk. 163 38 52N 119 53W
Freeland 162 41 3N 75 48W
Freeling, Mt. 136 22 35S 133 06E
Freels, C. 151 49 15N 53 30W
Freeman, Calif., U.S.A. 163 35 35N 117 53W
Freeman, S.D., U.S.A. 158 43 25N 97 20W
Freeport, Bahamas 167 25 45N 88 30E
Freeport, Can. 151 44 15N 66 20W
Freeport, Ill., U.S.A. 158 42 18N 89 40W
Freeport, N.Y., U.S.A. 162 40 39N 73 35W
Freeport, Tex., U.S.A. 159 28 55N 95 22W
Freetown 120 8 30N 13 10W
Freevater Forest 37 57 51N 4 45W
Fregenal de la Sierra 57 38 10N 6 39W
Fregene 64 41 50N 12 12E
Fregeneda, La 56 40 58N 6 54W
Fréhel C. 42 48 40N 2 20W
Freiberg 48 50 55N 13 20E
Freibourg = Fribourg 50 46 49N 7 9E
Freiburg, Baden, Ger. 49 48 0N 7 52E
Freiburg, Sachsen, Ger. 48 53 49N 9 17E
Freiburger Alpen 50 46 37N 7 10E
Freire 176 39 0S 72 50W
Freirina 172 28 30S 70 27W
Freising 49 48 24N 11 47E
Freistadt 52 48 30N 14 30E
Freital 48 51 0N 13 40E
Fréjus 45 43 25N 6 44E
Fremantle 137 32 1S 115 47E
Fremont, Calif., U.S.A. 163 37 32N 122 57W
Fremont, Mich., U.S.A. 156 43 29N 85 59W
Fremont, Nebr., U.S.A. 158 41 30N 96 30W
Fremont, Ohio, U.S.A. 156 41 20N 83 5W
Fremont, L. 160 43 0N 109 50W
Fremont, R. 161 38 15N 110 20W
French Camp 163 37 53N 121 16W
French Cr. 156 41 30N 80 2W
French Guiana ■ 175 4 0N 53 0W
French I. 141 38 20S 145 22E
French Terr. of Afars & Issas □ = Djibouti 123 11 30N 42 15E
Frenchglen 160 42 56N 119 0W
Frenchman Butte 153 53 36N 109 36W
Frenchman Creek, R. 158 40 34N 101 35W
Frenchman, R. 160 49 25N 108 20W
Frenchpark 38 53 53N 8 25W
Frenda 118 35 2N 1 1E
Fresco, R. 175 7 15S 51 30W
Freshfield, C. 13 68 25S 151 10E
Freshford 39 52 45N 7 25W
Freshwater 28 50 42N 1 31W
Fresnillo 164 23 10N 103 0W
Fresno 163 36 47N 119 50W
Fresno Alhandiga 56 40 42N 5 37W
Fresno Res. 160 48 47N 110 0W
Freswick 37 58 35N 3 5W
Freuchie 35 56 14N 3 8W
Freudenstadt 49 48 27N 8 25E
Freux 47 49 59N 5 27E
Frévent 43 50 15N 2 17E
Frew, R. 138 20 0S 135 38E
Frewena 138 19 50S 135 50E
Freycinet, C. 137 34 9S 115 0E
Freycinet Pen. 138 42 10S 148 25E
Fria 120 10 27N 13 32W
Fria, La 174 8 13N 72 15W
Friant 163 36 59N 119 43W
Frias 172 28 40S 65 5W
Fribourg 50 46 49N 7 9E
Fribourg □ 50 45 40N 7 0E
Frick 50 47 31N 8 1E
Fridafors 73 56 25N 14 39E
Fridaythorpe 33 54 2N 0 40W
Friedberg, Bayern, Ger. 49 48 21N 10 59E
Friedberg, Hessen, Ger. 10 50 19N 8 45E
Friedland 49 53 40N 13 33E
Friedrichshafen 49 47 39N 9 29E
Friedrichskoog 48 54 1N 8 52E
Friedrichsort 48 54 24N 10 11E
Friedrichstadt 48 54 23N 9 6E
Friendly (Tonga) Is. 130 19 50S 174 30W
Friesach 52 46 57N 14 24E
Friesack 48 52 43N 12 35E
Friesche Wad 46 53 22N 5 44E
Friesland □ 46 53 5N 5 50E
Friesoythe 48 53 1N 7 51E
Frigate, L. 150 53 15N 74 45W
Frigg E., gasfield 19 59 50N 2 20E
Frigg, gasfield 19 59 50N 2 15E
Frigg N.E., gasfield 19 60 0N 2 17E
Frillesås 73 57 20N 12 12E
Frimley 29 51 18N 0 43W
Frinnaryd 73 57 55N 14 50E
Frinton-on-Sea 29 51 50N 1 16E
Frio, C. 128 18 0S 12 0E
Frio, R. 159 29 40N 99 40W
Friockheim 37 56 39N 2 40W
Friona 159 34 40N 102 42W
Frisa, Loch 34 56 34N 6 5W
Frisian Is. 48 53 30N 6 0E
Fristad 73 57 50N 13 0E
Fritch 159 35 40N 101 35W
Fritsla 73 57 33N 12 47E
Fritzlar 48 51 8N 9 19E
Friuli-Venezia-Giulia □ 63 46 0N 13 0E
Frizington 32 54 33N 3 30W
Frobisher B. 149 63 0N 67 0W
Frobisher L. 153 56 20N 108 15W
Frobisher Sd. 149 62 30N 66 0W
Frodsham 32 53 17N 2 45W
Frogmore 141 34 15S 148 52E
Frohavet 74 64 5N 9 35E
Froid 158 48 20N 104 29W
Froid-Chapelle 47 50 9N 4 19E
Frolovo 83 49 45N 43 30E
Fromberg 160 45 19N 108 58W
Frombork 54 54 21N 19 41E
Frome 28 51 16N 2 17W
Frome Downs 140 31 13S 139 46E
Frome, L. 140 30 45S 139 45E
Frome, R. 28 50 44N 2 5W
Fromentine 42 46 53N 2 9W
Frómista 56 42 16N 4 25W
Front Range 160 40 0N 105 10W
Front Royal 158 38 55N 78 10W
Fronteira 57 39 3N 7 39W
Fronteiras 170 7 5S 40 37W
Frontera 165 18 30N 92 40W
Frontignan 44 43 27N 3 45E
Frosinone 64 41 38N 13 20E
Frosolone 65 41 34N 14 27E
Frostburg 156 39 43N 78 57W
Frostisen 74 68 14N 17 10E
Frouard 43 48 47N 6 8E
Frövi 72 59 28N 15 24E
Frower Pt. 39 51 40N 8 30W
Froya 71 63 43N 8 40E
Frøya 71 63 43N 8 40E
Fröya I. 74 63 45N 8 45E
Fruges 43 50 30N 2 8E
Frumoasa 70 46 28N 25 48E
Frunze 85 42 54N 74 36E
Fruška Gora 66 45 7N 19 30E
Frutal 171 20 0S 49 0W
Frutigen 50 46 35N 7 38E
Frýdek-Místek 53 49 40N 18 20E

*Now part of Central Arctic and Baffin

Frýdlant Garibaldi Prov. Park

Frýdlant, Severočeský, Czech.	52	50 56N	15 9E
Frýdlant, Severomoravsky, Czech.	53	49 35N	18 20E
Fryvaldov = Jesenik	53	50 0N	17 8E
Fthiótis □	69	38 50N	22 25E
Fu	72	60 57N	14 44E
Fuan	109	27 9N	119 38E
Fucécchio	62	43 44N	10 51E
Fuch'ing	109	25 43N	119 22E
Fuchou, Fukien, China	109	26 5N	119 18E
Fuchou, Liaoning, China	107	39 45N	121 45E
Fuchū	110	34 34N	133 14E
Fūchū	111	35 40N	139 29E
Fuch'üan	108	26 42N	107 33E
Fuch'uan	109	24 50N	111 16E
Fucino, L.	44	42 0N	13 30E
Fuencaliente	57	38 25N	4 18W
Fuengirola	57	36 32N	4 41W
Fuente-Alamo	59	38 44N	1 24W
Fuente de Cantos	57	38 15N	6 18W
Fuente de San Esteban, La	56	40 49N	6 15W
Fuente del Maestre	57	38 31N	6 28W
Fuente el Fresno	57	39 14N	3 46W
Fuente Ovejuna	57	38 15N	5 25W
Fuentes de Andalucía	57	37 28N	5 20W
Fuentes de Ebro	58	41 31N	0 38W
Fuentes de León	57	38 5N	6 32W
Fuentes de Oñoro	56	40 33N	6 52W
Fuentesaúco	56	41 15N	5 30W
Fuerte Olimpo	172	21 0S	58 0W
Fuerte, R.	164	26 0N	109 0W
Fuerteventura, I.	116	28 30N	14 0W
Fuertey	38	53 37N	8 16W
Fufeng	106	34 20N	107 51E
Fûget	70	45 52N	22 10E
Fûget, Munţii	70	45 50N	22 9E
Fugløysund	74	70 15N	20 20E
Fûgûraş	70	45 48N	24 58E
Fûgûraş, Munţii	70	45 40N	24 40E
Fuhai	105	47 6N	87 23E
Fuhsien, Liaoning, China	107	39 38N	122 0E
Fuhsien, Shensi, China	106	36 2N	109 20E
Fuhsingchen	108	22 47N	101 5E
Fujaira	93	25 7N	56 18E
Fuji	111	35 9N	138 39E
Fuji-no-miya	111	35 20N	138 40E
Fuji-San	111	35 22N	138 44E
Fuji-yoshida	111	35 50N	138 46E
Fujieda	111	34 52N	138 16E
Fujioka	111	36 15N	139 5E
Fujisawa	111	35 22N	139 29E
Fukien □	109	26 0N	117 30E
Fukou	106	34 3N	114 27E
Fuku	106	39 2N	111 3E
Fukuchiyama	111	35 25N	135 9E
Fukui	111	36 0N	136 10E
Fukui-ken □	111	36 0N	136 12E
Fukuma	110	33 46N	130 28E
Fukung	108	26 58N	98 54E
Fukuoka	110	33 30N	130 30E
Fukuoka-ken □	110	33 30N	131 0E
Fukuroi	111	34 45N	137 55E
Fukushima	112	37 30N	140 15E
Fukushima-ken □	112	37 30N	140 15E
Fukuyama	110	34 35N	133 20E
Fûlciu	70	46 17N	28 7E
Fulda	48	50 32N	9 41E
Fullerton, Calif., U.S.A.	163	33 52N	117 58W
Fullerton, Nebr., U.S.A.	158	41 25N	98 0W
Fulmar, oilfield	19	56 30N	2 8E
Fülöpszállás	53	46 49N	19 16E
Fûlticeni	70	47 21N	26 20W
Fulton, Mo., U.S.A.	158	38 50N	91 55W
Fulton, N.Y., U.S.A.	162	43 20N	76 22W
Fuluälven	72	61 18N	13 4E
Fulufjället	72	61 32N	12 41E
Fulungch'üan	107	44 24N	124 37E
Fülüpszállás	53	46 49N	19 16E
Fumay	43	50 0N	4 40E
Fumbusi	121	10 25N	1 20W
Fumel	44	44 30N	0 58E
Fumin	108	25 14N	102 29E
Funabashi	111	35 45N	140 0E
Funafuti, I.	130	8 30S	179 0E
Funchal	116	32 45N	16 55W
Fundación	174	10 31N	74 11W
Fundão, Brazil	171	19 55S	40 24W
Fundão, Port.	56	40 8N	7 30W
Fundu	127	14 58S	30 14E
Fundy, B. of	151	45 0N	66 0W
Funes	174	1 0N	77 28W
Funing, Hopei, China	107	39 54N	119 12E
Funing, Yunnan, China	108	23 37N	105 36E
Funiu Shan	106	33 40N	112 30E
Funsi	120	10 21N	1 54W
Funtua	121	11 30N	7 18E
Fupien	108	31 45N	102 27E
Fup'ing	106	34 47N	109 7E
Fur	73	56 50N	9 0E
Furat, Nahr al	92	33 30N	43 0E
Furbero	165	20 22N	97 31W
Furka Pass	51	46 34N	8 35E
Furmanov	81	57 25N	41 3E
Furmanovka	85	44 17N	72 57E
Furmanovo	83	49 42N	49 25E
Furnas, Représa de	173	20 50S	45 0W
Furneaux Group	138	40 10S	147 50E
Furness, Pen.	32	54 12N	3 10W
Fürstenau	48	52 32N	7 40E
Fürstenfeld	52	47 3N	16 3E
Fürstenfeldbruck	49	48 10N	11 15E
Fürstenwalde	48	52 20N	14 3E
Fürth	49	49 29N	11 0E
Fürth i. Wald	49	49 19N	12 51E
Furtwangen	49	48 3N	8 14E
Furudal	72	61 10N	15 11E
Furukawa	111	36 14N	137 11E
Furusund	72	59 40N	18 55E
Fury and Hecla Str.	149	69 56N	84 0W
Fusa	71	60 12N	5 37E
Fusagasugá	174	4 21N	74 22W
Fuscaldo	65	39 25N	16 1E
Fushan	107	37 30N	121 5E
Fushë Arrëzi	68	42 4N	20 2E
Fushun, Liaoning, China	107	41 50N	123 55E
Fushun, Szechwan, China	108	29 13N	105 0E
Fush'un Chiang, R.	109	30 5N	120 5E
Fusio	51	46 27N	8 40E
Füssen	49	47 35N	10 43E
Fusui	108	22 35N	107 58E
Fusung	107	42 15N	127 20E
Futago-Yama	110	33 35N	131 36E
Futing	109	27 15N	120 10E
Futuk	121	9 45N	10 56E
Futuna I.	130	14 25S	178 20E
Fŭurei	70	45 6N	27 19E
Fuwa	122	31 12N	30 33E
Fuyang	109	30 5N	119 56E
Fuyang Ho, R.	106	38 14N	116 5E
Fuyü	107	45 10N	124 50E
Fuyüan	105	47 40N	132 30E
Füzesgyarmat	53	47 6N	21 14E
Fwaka	125	12 5S	29 25E
Fylde	32	53 50N	2 58W
Fylingdales Moor	33	54 22N	0 32W
Fyn	73	55 20N	10 30E
Fyne, L.	34	56 0N	5 20W
Fyns Amt □	73	55 15N	10 30E
Fynshav	73	54 59N	9 59E
Fyresvatn	71	59 6N	8 10E
Fyvie	37	57 26N	2 24W

G

Gaanda	121	10 10N	12 27E
Gaba	123	6 20N	35 7E
Gaba Tula	82	0 20N	38 35E
Gabah, C.	91	8 0N	50 0E
Gabarin	121	11 8N	10 27E
Gabbs	163	38 52N	117 55W
Gabela	124	11 0S	14 37E
Gaberones = Gaborone	128	24 37S	25 57E
Gabès	119	33 53N	10 2E
Gabès, Golfe de	119	34 0N	10 30E
Gabgaba, W.	122	22 10N	33 5E
Gabin	54	52 23N	19 41E
Gabon ■	124	0 10S	10 0E
Gaborone	128	24 37S	25 57E
Gabrovo	67	42 52N	25 27E
Gacé	42	48 49N	0 20E
Gach Saran	93	30 15N	50 45E
Gacko	66	43 10N	18 33E
Gada	121	13 38N	5 36E
Gadag	97	15 30N	75 45E
Gadamai	123	17 11N	36 10E
Gadap	94	25 5N	67 28E
Gadarwara	95	22 50N	78 50E
Gäddede	74	64 30N	14 15E
Gadebusch	48	53 41N	11 6E
Gadein	123	8 10N	28 45E
Gadhada	94	22 0N	71 35E
Gadmen	51	46 45N	8 16E
Gádor, Sierra de	59	36 57N	2 45W
Gadsden, Ala., U.S.A.	157	34 1N	86 0W
Gadsden, Ariz., U.S.A.	161	32 35N	114 47W
Gadwal	96	16 10N	77 50E
Gaerwen	31	53 13N	4 17W
Gaeta	64	41 12N	13 35E
Gaeta, G. di	64	41 0N	13 25E
Gaffney	157	35 10N	81 31W
Gafsa	119	34 24N	8 51E
Gagarin (Gzhatsk)	80	55 30N	35 0E
Gagetown	151	45 46N	66 29W
Gagino	81	55 15N	45 10E
Gagliano del Capo	65	39 50N	18 23E
Gagnef	72	60 36N	15 5E
Gagnoa	120	6 4N	5 55W
Gagnon	151	51 50N	68 5W
Gagnon, L.	153	62 3N	110 27W
Gagra	83	43 20N	40 10E
Gah	44	43 12N	0 27W
Gahini	126	1 50S	30 30E
Gahmar	95	25 27N	83 55E
Gaibandha	98	25 20N	89 36E
Gaïdhouronísi	69	34 53N	25 41E
Gail	159	32 48N	101 25W
Gail, R.	52	46 37N	13 15E
Gaillac	44	43 54N	1 54E
Gaillon	42	49 10N	1 20E
Gaima	135	8 9S	142 59E
Gainesville, Fla., U.S.A.	157	29 38N	82 20W
Gainesville, Ga., U.S.A.	157	34 17N	83 47W
Gainesville, Mo., U.S.A.	159	36 35N	92 26W
Gainesville, Tex., U.S.A.	159	33 40N	97 10W
Gainford	33	54 34N	1 44W
Gainsborough	33	53 23N	0 46W
Gairdner L.	140	31 30S	136 0E
Gairloch	36	57 42N	5 40W
Gairloch L.	36	57 43N	5 45W
Gairlochy	36	56 55N	5 0W
Gairsay, I.	37	59 4N	2 59W
Gais	51	47 22N	9 27E
Gaithersburg	162	39 9N	77 12W
Gaj	66	45 28N	17 3E
Gajale	121	11 25N	8 10E
Gajiram	121	12 29N	13 9E
Gakuch	95	36 7N	73 45E
Gal Oya Res.	97	8 5N	80 55E
Galachipa	98	22 8N	90 26E
Galadi	121	13 5N	6 20E
Galán, Cerro	172	25 55S	66 52W
Galana, R.	126	3 0S	39 10E
Galangue	125	13 48S	16 3E
Galanta	53	48 11N	17 45E
Galápagos, Is.	131	0 0	89 0W
Galas, R.	101	4 55N	101 57E
Galashiels	35	55 37N	2 50W
Galatás	69	37 30N	23 26E
Galatea	142	38 24S	176 45E
Galaţi	70	45 27N	28 2E
Galaţi □	70	45 45N	27 30E
Galatina	65	40 10N	18 10E
Galátone	65	40 8N	18 3E
Galax	157	36 42N	80 57W
Galaxidhion	69	38 22N	22 23E
Galbally	39	52 24N	8 17W
Galbraith	138	16 25S	141 30E
Galdhøpiggen	71	61 38N	8 18E
Galeana	164	24 50N	100 4W
Galela	103	1 50N	127 55E
Galena, Austral.	137	27 48S	114 42E
Galena, U.S.A.	147	64 42N	157 0W
Galeota Point	167	10 8N	61 0W
Galera	59	37 45N	2 33W
Galera, Pta. de la	174	10 48N	75 16W
Galesburg	158	40 57N	90 23W
Galey R.	39	52 30N	9 23W
Galgate	32	53 59N	2 47W
Galheirão, R.	171	12 23S	45 5W
Galheiros	171	13 18S	46 25W
Galicea Mare	70	44 4N	23 19E
Galich, R.S.F.S.R., U.S.S.R.	81	58 23N	42 18E
Galich, Uk., U.S.S.R.	80	49 10N	24 40E
Galiche	67	43 34N	23 50E
Galicia	56	42 43N	8 0W
Galijp	46	53 10N	5 58E
Galilee = Hagalil	90	32 53N	35 18E
Galilee, L.	138	22 20S	145 50E
Galite, Is. de la	119	37 30N	8 59E
Galivro Mts.	161	32 40N	110 30W
Gallan Hd.	36	58 14N	7 0W
Gallarate	62	45 40N	8 48E
Gallatin	157	36 24N	86 27W
Galle	97	6 5N	80 10E
Gallego	164	29 49N	106 22W
Gállego, R.	58	42 23N	0 30W
Gallegos, R.	176	51 50S	71 0W
Galley Hd.	39	51 32N	8 56W
Galliate	62	45 27N	8 44E
Gallinas, Pta.	174	12 28N	71 40W
Gallipoli	65	40 8N	18 0E
Gallipoli = Gelibolu	68	40 28N	26 43E
Gallipolis	156	38 50N	82 10W
Gällivare	74	67 9N	20 40E
Gällö	72	62 56N	15 15E
Gallo, C. di	64	38 13N	13 19E
Gallocanta, Laguna de	58	40 58N	1 30W
Galloway	34	55 0N	4 25W
Galloway, Mull of	34	54 38N	4 50W
Gallup	161	35 30N	108 54W
Gallur	58	41 52N	1 19W
Gallyaaral	85	40 2N	67 35E
Galmi	121	13 58N	5 41E
Gal'on	90	31 38N	34 51E
Galong	141	34 37S	148 34E
Galoya	93	8 10N	80 55E
Galston	34	55 36N	4 22W
Galt, Can.	150	43 21N	80 19W
Galt, U.S.A.	163	38 15N	121 18W
Galtström	72	62 10N	17 30E
Galtür	52	46 58N	10 11E
Galty Mts.	39	52 22N	8 10W
Galtymore, Mt.	39	52 22N	8 12W
Galva	158	41 10N	90 0W
Galve de Sorbe	58	41 13N	3 10W
Galveston	159	29 15N	94 48W
Galveston B.	159	29 30N	94 50W
Gálvez, Argent.	172	32 0S	61 20W
Gálvez, Spain	57	39 42N	4 16W
Galway	39	53 16N	9 4W
Galway □	38	53 16N	9 3W
Galway B.	39	53 10N	9 20W
Gam, R.	100	21 55N	105 12E
Gamagōri	111	34 50N	137 14E
Gamare, L.	123	11 32N	41 40E
Gamarra	174	8 20N	73 45W
Gamawa	121	12 10N	10 31E
Gambaga	121	10 30N	0 28W
Gambat	94	27 17N	68 26E
Gambela	123	8 14N	34 38E
Gambell	147	63 55N	171 50W
Gambia ■	120	13 25N	16 0W
Gambia, R.	120	13 20N	15 45W
Gambier, C.	136	11 56S	130 57E
Gambier Is.	140	35 3S	136 30E
Gamboli	94	29 53N	68 24E
Gamboma	124	1 55S	15 52E
Gamboola	138	16 29S	143 43E
Gameleira	170	7 50S	50 0W
Gamerco	161	35 33N	108 56W
Gamleby	73	57 54N	16 20W
Gamlingay	29	52 9N	0 11W
Gammelgarn	171	57 24N	18 49E
Gammon, R.	153	51 24N	95 44W
Gamōda-Saki	110	33 50N	134 45E
Gan (Addu Atoll)	87	0 10S	71 10E
Gan Shemu'el	90	32 28N	34 56E
Gan Yavne	90	31 48N	34 42E
Ganado, Ariz., U.S.A.	161	35 46N	109 41W
Ganado, Tex., U.S.A.	159	29 4N	96 31W
Gananoque	150	44 20N	76 10W
Ganaveh	93	29 35N	50 35E
Gand	47	51 2N	3 37E
Gandak, R.	95	27 0N	84 8E
Gandava	94	28 32N	67 32E
Gander	151	48 18N	54 29W
Gander L.	151	48 58N	54 35W
Ganderowe Falls	127	17 20S	29 10E
Gandesa	58	41 3N	0 26E
Gand = Gent	47	51 2N	3 37E
Gandhi Sagar	94	24 40N	75 40E
Gandi	121	12 55N	5 49E
Gandia	59	38 58N	0 9W
Gandino	62	45 50N	9 52E
Gandole	121	8 28N	11 35E
Gandu	171	13 45S	39 30W
Ganedidalem = Gani	103	0 48S	128 14E
Ganetti	122	18 0N	31 10E
Ganga, Mouths of the	95	21 30N	90 0E
Ganga, R.	95	25 0N	88 0E
Ganganagar	94	29 56N	73 56E
Gangapur	94	26 32N	76 37E
Gangara	121	14 35N	8 40E
Gangavati	97	15 30N	76 36E
Gangaw	98	22 5N	94 15E
Ganges	44	43 56N	3 42E
Ganges = Ganga, R.	95	25 0N	88 0E
Gangoh	94	29 46N	77 18E
Gangtok	98	27 20N	88 37E
Ganj	95	27 45N	78 47E
Ganmain	141	34 47S	147 1E
Gannat	44	46 7N	3 11E
Gannett Pk.	160	43 15N	109 47W
Gannvalley	158	44 3N	98 57W
Ganserdorf	53	48 20N	16 43E
Ganta (Gompa)	120	7 15N	8 59W
Gantheaume B.	137	27 40S	114 10E
Gantheaume, C.	140	36 4S	137 25E
Gantsevichi	80	52 42N	26 30E
Ganyushkino	83	46 35N	49 20E
Ganzi	123	4 30N	31 15E
Gao □	121	18 0N	1 0E
Gao Bang	101	22 37N	106 18E
Gaoua	120	10 20N	3 8W
Gaoual	120	11 45N	13 25W
Gaouz	118	31 52N	4 20W
Gap	45	44 33N	6 5E
Gar Dzong	93	32 20N	79 55E
Gara, L.	38	53 57N	8 26W
Garachiné	166	8 0N	78 12W
Garanhuns	170	8 50S	36 30W
Garawe	120	4 35N	8 0W
Garba Tula	126	0 30N	38 32E
Garber	159	36 30N	97 36W
Garberville	160	40 11N	123 50W
Garboldisham	29	52 24N	0 57E
Garça	171	22 14S	49 37W
Garças, R.	170	8 43S	39 41W
Gard □	45	44 2N	4 10E
Garda, L. di	62	45 40N	10 40E
Gardanne	45	43 27N	5 27E
Garde L.	153	62 50N	106 13W
Gardelegen	48	52 32N	11 21E
Garden City, Kans., U.S.A.	159	38 0N	100 45W
Garden City, Tex., U.S.A.	159	31 52N	101 28W
Garden Grove	163	33 47N	117 55W
Gardenstown	37	57 40N	2 20W
Gardez	94	33 31N	68 59E
Gardhiki	69	38 50N	21 55E
Gardian	117	15 45N	19 40E
Gardiner, Can.	150	49 19N	81 2W
Gardiner, Mont., U.S.A.	160	45 3N	110 53W
Gardiner, New Mexico, U.S.A.	159	36 55N	104 29W
Gardiners I.	162	41 4N	72 5W
Gardner	162	42 35N	72 0W
Gardner Canal	152	53 27N	128 8W
Gardnerville	160	38 59N	119 47W
Gardo	91	9 18N	49 20E
Gare, L.	34	56 1N	4 50W
Garelochhead	34	56 7N	4 50W
Gareloi I.	147	51 49N	178 50W
Garešnica	66	45 36N	16 56E
Garéssio	62	44 12N	8 1E
Garey	163	34 53N	120 19W
Garfield, Utah, U.S.A.	160	40 45N	112 15W
Garfield, Wash., U.S.A.	160	47 3N	117 8W
Garforth	33	53 48N	1 22W
Gargaliánoi	69	37 4N	21 38E
Gargano, Mte.	65	41 43N	15 43E
Gargans, Mt.	44	45 37N	1 39E
Gargantua, C.	150	47 35N	85 0W
Gargoune	121	15 56N	0 13E
Gargrave	32	53 58N	2 7W
Garhshankar	94	31 13N	76 11E
Gari	84	59 26N	62 21E
Garibaldi	152	49 56N	123 15W
Garibaldi Prov. Park	152	49 50N	122 40W

Garies	**125**	30 32 S	17 59 E
Garigliano, R.	**64**	41 13N	13 44 E
Garissa	**126**	0 25 S	39 40 E
Garissa □	**126**	0 20 S	40 0 E
Garkida	**121**	10 27N	12 36 E
Garko	**121**	11 45N	8 53 E
Garland	**160**	41 47N	112 10W
Garlasco	**62**	45 11N	8 55 E
Garlieston	**34**	54 47N	4 22W
Garm	**85**	39 0N	70 20 E
Garmab	**94**	32 50N	65 30 E
Garmisch-Partenkirchen	**49**	47 30N	11 5 E
Garmo	**126**	61 51N	8 48 E
Garmouth	**37**	57 40N	3 8W
Garmsar	**93**	35 20N	52 25 E
Garner	**158**	43 4N	93 37W
Garnett	**158**	38 18N	95 12W
Garo Hills	**95**	25 30N	90 30 E
Garoe	**91**	8 35N	48 40 E
Garoke	**139**	36 45 S	141 30 E
Garona, R.	**58**	42 55N	0 45 E
Garonne, R.	**44**	45 2N	0 36W
Garoua (Garwa)	**121**	9 19N	13 21 E
Garraway	**120**	4 35N	8 0W
Garrel	**48**	52 58N	7 59 E
Garrigues	**44**	43 40N	3 30 E
Garrison, Ireland	**38**	54 25N	8 5W
Garrison, Mont., U.S.A.	**160**	46 37N	112 56W
Garrison, N.D., U.S.A.	**158**	31 50N	94 28W
Garrison, Tex., U.S.A.	**159**	47 39N	101 27W
Garrison Res.	**158**	47 30N	102 0W
Garron Pt.	**38**	55 3N	6 0W
Garrovillas	**57**	39 40N	6 33W
Garrucha	**59**	37 11N	1 49W
Garry L., Can.	**148**	65 58N	100 18W
Garry L., U.K.	**37**	57 5N	4 52W
Garry, R.	**37**	56 47N	3 47W
Garsdale Head	**32**	54 19N	2 19W
Garsen	**124**	2 20 S	40 5 E
Garson L., Alta., Can.	**153**	56 19N	110 2W
Garson L., Sask., Can.	**153**	56 20N	110 1W
Garstang	**32**	53 53N	2 47W
Garston	**32**	53 21N	2 55W
Gartempe, R.	**44**	46 47N	0 49 E
Gartok	**93**	31 59N	80 30 E
Gartz	**48**	54 17N	13 21 E
Garu, Ghana	**121**	10 55N	0 20W
Garu, Nigeria	**121**	13 35N	5 25 E
Garub	**128**	26 37 S	16 0 E
Garupá	**170**	1 25 S	51 35W
Garut	**103**	7 14 S	107 53 E
Garvagh	**38**	55 0N	6 41W
Garvaghey	**38**	54 29N	7 8W
Garvald	**35**	55 55N	2 39W
Garváo	**57**	37 42N	8 21W
Garvellachs, Is.	**34**	56 14N	5 42W
Garvie Mts.	**143**	45 30 S	168 50 E
Garwa	**95**	24 11N	83 47 E
Garwolin	**54**	51 55N	21 38 E
Gary	**156**	41 35N	87 20W
Garzón	**174**	2 10N	75 40W
Gasan Kuli	**76**	37 40N	54 20 E
Gascogne	**44**	43 45N	0 20 E
Gascogne, G. de	**58**	44 0N	2 0W
Gascony = Gascogne	**44**	43 45N	0 20 E
Gascoyne Junc. Teleg. Off.	**137**	25 2 S	115 17 E
Gascoyne, R.	**137**	24 52 S	113 37 E
Gascueña	**58**	40 18N	2 31W
Gash, W.	**123**	15 0N	37 15 E
Gashaka	**121**	7 20N	11 29 E
Gasherbrum	**95**	35 40N	76 40 E
Gashua	**121**	12 54N	11 0 E
Gasmata	**138**	6 15 S	150 30 E
Gaspé	**151**	48 52N	64 30W
Gaspé, C.	**151**	48 48N	64 7W
Gaspé Pass.	**151**	49 10N	64 0W
Gaspé Pen.	**151**	48 45N	65 40W
Gaspésie, Parc Prov. de la	**151**	48 55N	65 50W
Gaspesian Prov. Park	**151**	49 0N	66 45W
Gassaway	**156**	38 42N	80 43W
Gasselte	**46**	52 58N	6 48 E
Gasselternijveen	**46**	52 59N	6 51 E
Gássino Torinese	**62**	45 8N	7 50 E
Gassol	**121**	8 34N	10 25 E
Gastonia	**157**	35 17N	81 10W
Gastoúni	**69**	37 51N	21 15 E
Gastoúri	**68**	39 34N	19 54 E
Gastre	**176**	42 10 S	69 15W
Gata, C. de	**59**	36 41N	2 13W
Gata, Sierra de	**56**	40 20N	6 20W
Gataga, R.	**152**	58 35N	126 59W
Gatchina	**80**	59 35N	30 0 E
Gatehouse of Fleet	**34**	54 53N	4 10W
Gateshead	**35**	54 57N	1 37W
Gatesville	**159**	31 29N	97 45W
Gaths	**127**	26 2 S	30 32 E
Gatico	**172**	22 40 S	70 20W
Gatinais	**43**	48 5N	2 40 E
Gâtine, Hauteurs de	**44**	46 35N	0 45W
Gatineau, Parc de la	**150**	45 20N	76 0W
Gatineau, R.	**150**	45 27N	75 42W
Gatley	**32**	53 25N	2 15W
Gatooma	**125**	18 20 S	29 52 E
Gattinara	**62**	45 37N	8 22 E
Gatun, L.	**166**	9 7N	79 56W
Gaucín	**57**	36 31N	5 19W
Gaud-i-Zirreh	**93**	29 45N	62 0 E
Gauer L.	**153**	57 0N	97 50W
Gauhati	**98**	26 10N	91 45 E
Gauja, R.	**80**	57 10N	24 45 E
Gaula, R.	**71**	62 57N	11 0 E
Gaurain-Ramecroix	**47**	50 36N	3 30 E
Gaurdak	**85**	37 50N	66 4 E
Gaussberg, Mt.	**13**	66 45 S	89 0 E
Gausta	**71**	59 50N	8 37 E
Gausta, Mt.	**75**	59 48N	8 40 E
Gavá	**58**	41 18N	2 0 E
Gavarnie	**44**	42 44N	0 3W
Gavater	**93**	25 10N	61 23 E
Gavdhopoúla	**69**	34 56N	24 0 E
Gávdhos	**69**	34 50N	24 5 E
Gavere	**47**	50 55N	3 40 E
Gavião	**57**	39 28N	7 50W
Gaviota	**163**	34 29N	120 13W
Gavle	**72**	60 41N	17 13 E
Gävle	**72**	60 40N	17 9 E
Gävleborgs Lan □	**72**	61 20N	16 15 E
Gavorrano	**62**	42 55N	10 55 E
Gavray	**42**	49 55N	1 20W
Gavrilov Yam	**81**	57 10N	39 37 E
Gávrion	**69**	37 54N	24 44 E
Gawachab	**128**	27 4 S	17 55 E
Gawai	**98**	27 56N	97 40 E
Gawilgarh Hills	**96**	21 15N	76 45 E
Gawler	**140**	34 30 S	138 42 E
Gawler Ranges	**136**	32 30 S	135 45 E
Gawthwaite	**32**	54 16N	3 6W
Gay	**84**	51 27N	58 27 E
Gaya, India	**95**	24 47N	85 4 E
Gaya, Niger	**121**	11 58N	3 28 E
Gaya, Nigeria	**121**	11 57N	9 0 E
Gaylord	**156**	45 1N	84 35W
Gayndah	**139**	25 35 S	151 39 E
Gayny	**84**	60 18N	54 19 E
Gaysin	**82**	48 57N	28 25 E
Gayton	**29**	52 45N	0 35 E
Gayvoron	**82**	48 22N	29 45 E
Gaywood	**29**	52 46N	0 26 E
Gaza	**90**	31 30N	34 28 E
Gaza □	**129**	23 10 S	32 45 E
Gaza Strip	**90**	31 29N	34 25 E
Gazaoua	**121**	13 32N	7 55 E
Gazelle Pen.	**135**	4 40 S	152 0 E
Gazi	**126**	1 3N	24 30 E
Gaziantep	**92**	37 6N	37 23 E
Gbanga	**120**	7 19N	9 13W
Gbekebo	**121**	6 26N	4 48 E
Gboko	**121**	7 17N	9 4 E
Gbongan	**121**	7 28N	4 20 E
Gcuwa	**129**	32 20 S	28 11 E
Gdansk	**54**	54 22N	18 40 E
Gdansk □	**54**	54 10N	18 30 E
Gdanska, Zatoka	**54**	54 30N	19 20 E
Gdov	**80**	58 40N	27 55 E
Gdynia	**54**	54 35N	18 33 E
Geashill	**39**	53 14N	7 20W
Gebe, I.	**103**	0 5N	129 25 E
Gebeit Mine	**122**	21 3N	36 29 E
Gecoa	**123**	7 30N	35 18 E
Gedaref	**123**	14 2N	35 28 E
Gedera	**90**	31 49N	34 46 E
Gedinne	**47**	49 59N	4 56 E
Gedney	**29**	52 47N	0 5W
Gedo	**123**	9 2N	37 25 E
Gèdre	**44**	42 47N	0 2 E
Gedser	**73**	54 35N	11 55 E
Gedser Odde, C.	**73**	54 30N	12 5 E
Geel	**47**	51 10N	4 59 E
Geelong	**140**	38 10 S	144 22 E
Geelvink Chan.	**137**	28 30 S	114 0 E
Geer, R.	**47**	50 51N	5 42 E
Geestenseth	**48**	53 31N	8 51 E
Geesthacht	**48**	53 25N	10 20 E
Geffen	**46**	51 44N	5 28 E
Geh	**126**	26 10N	60 0 E
Geia	**90**	31 38N	34 37 E
Geidam	**121**	12 57N	11 57 E
Geikie, R.	**153**	57 45N	103 52W
Geilenkirchen	**48**	50 58N	6 8 E
Geili	**123**	16 1N	32 37 E
Geilo	**71**	60 32N	8 14 E
Geinica	**53**	48 51N	20 55 E
Geisingen	**49**	47 55N	8 37 E
Geita	**126**	2 48 S	32 12 E
Geita □	**126**	2 50 S	32 10 E
Gel, R.	**123**	7 5N	29 10 E
Gel River	**123**	7 5N	29 10 E
Gela, Golfo di	**65**	37 0N	14 8 E
Geladi	**91**	6 59N	46 30 E
Gelderland □	**46**	52 5N	6 10 E
Geldermalsen	**46**	51 53N	5 17 E
Geldern	**48**	51 32N	6 18 E
Geldrop	**47**	51 25N	5 32 E
Geleen	**47**	50 57N	5 49 E
Gelehun	**120**	8 20N	11 40W
Gelendzhik	**82**	44 33N	38 17 E
Gelibolu	**68**	40 28N	26 43 E
Gelnhausen	**49**	50 12N	9 12 E
Gelsenkirchen	**48**	51 30N	7 5 E
Gelting	**48**	54 43N	9 53 E
Gemas	**101**	2 37N	102 36 E
Gembloux	**47**	50 34N	4 43 E
Gembu	**121**	8 58N	12 31 E
Gemena	**124**	3 20N	19 40 E
Gemerek	**92**	39 15N	36 10 E
Gemert	**47**	51 33N	5 41 E
Gemiston	**128**	26 15 S	28 10 E
Gemlik	**92**	40 28N	29 13 E
Gemmi	**50**	46 25N	7 37 E
Gemona del Friuli	**63**	46 16N	13 7 E
Gemsa	**122**	27 39N	33 35 E
Gemu-Gofa □	**123**	5 40N	36 40 E
Gemünden	**49**	50 3N	9 43 E
Genale	**123**	6 0N	39 30 E
Genappe	**47**	50 37N	4 27 E
Gençay	**44**	46 23N	0 23 E
Gendringen	**46**	51 52N	6 21 E
Gendt	**46**	51 53N	5 59 E
Geneina, Gebel	**122**	29 2N	33 55 E
Genemuiden	**46**	52 38N	6 2 E
General Acha	**172**	37 20 S	64 38W
General Alvear, B. A., Argent.	**172**	36 0 S	60 0W
General Alvear, Mend., Argent.	**172**	35 0 S	67 40W
General Artigas	**172**	26 52 S	56 16W
General Belgrano	**172**	36 0 S	58 30W
General Cabrera	**172**	32 53 S	63 58W
General Cepeda	**164**	25 23N	101 27W
General Guido	**172**	36 40 S	57 50W
General Juan Madariaga	**172**	37 0 S	57 0W
General La Madrid	**172**	37 30 S	61 10W
General MacArthur	**103**	11 18N	125 28 E
General Martin Mignuel de Güemes	**172**	24 50 S	65 0W
General Paz	**172**	27 45 S	57 36W
General Paz, L.	**176**	44 0 S	72 0W
General Pico	**172**	35 45 S	63 50W
General Pinedo	**172**	27 15 S	61 30W
General Pinto	**172**	34 45 S	61 50W
General Roca	**176**	30 0 S	67 40W
General Sampaio	**170**	4 2 S	39 29W
General Santos	**103**	6 12N	125 14 E
General Toshevo	**67**	43 42N	28 6 E
General Treviño	**165**	26 14N	99 29W
General Trías	**164**	28 21N	106 22W
General Viamonte	**172**	35 1 S	61 3W
General Villegas	**172**	35 0 S	63 0W
Generoso, Mte.	**51**	45 56N	9 2 E
Genesee	**160**	46 31N	116 59W
Genesee, R.	**156**	41 35N	78 0W
Geneseo, Ill., U.S.A.	**158**	41 25N	90 10W
Geneseo, Kans., U.S.A.	**158**	38 32N	98 8W
Geneva, Ala., U.S.A.	**157**	31 2N	85 52W
Geneva, Nebr., U.S.A.	**158**	40 35N	97 35W
Geneva, N.Y., U.S.A.	**162**	42 53N	77 0W
Geneva, Ohio, U.S.A.	**156**	41 49N	80 58W
Geneva = Genève	**50**	46 12N	6 9 E
Geneva, L.	**156**	42 38N	88 30W
Geneva, L. = Léman, Lac	**50**	46 26N	6 30 E
Genève	**50**	46 12N	6 9 E
Genève □	**50**	46 10N	6 10 E
Gengenbach	**49**	48 25N	8 0 E
Genichesk	**82**	46 12N	34 50 E
Genil, R.	**57**	37 12N	3 50W
Génissiat, Barrage de	**45**	46 1N	5 48 E
Genk	**47**	50 58N	5 32 E
Genkai-Nada	**110**	34 0N	130 0 E
Genlis	**43**	47 15N	5 12 E
Gennargentu, Mt. del	**64**	40 0N	9 10 E
Gennep	**47**	51 41N	5 59 E
Gennes	**42**	47 20N	0 17W
Genoa, Austral.	**141**	37 29 S	149 35 E
Genoa, Nebr., U.S.A.	**158**	41 31N	97 44W
Genoa, N.Y., U.S.A.	**162**	42 40N	76 32W
Genoa = Génova	**62**	44 24N	8 57 E
Génova	**62**	44 24N	8 56 E
Génova, Golfo di	**62**	44 0N	9 0 E
Gent	**47**	51 2N	3 37 E
Gentbrugge	**47**	51 3N	3 47 E
Genteng	**103**	7 25 S	106 23 E
Genthin	**48**	52 24N	12 10 E
Gentio do Ouro	**170**	11 25 S	42 30W
Geographe B.	**137**	33 30 S	113 20 E
Geographe Chan.	**137**	24 30 S	113 0 E
Geokchay	**83**	40 42N	47 43 E
George, Can.	**151**	46 12N	62 32W
George, S. Afr.	**128**	33 58 S	22 29 E
George, L., New South Wales, Austral.	**141**	35 10 S	149 25 E
George, L., S. Austral., Austral.	**140**	37 25 S	140 0 E
George, L., W. A., Austral.	**137**	22 45 S	123 40 E
George, L., Uganda	**126**	0 5N	30 10 E
George, L., Fla., U.S.A.	**157**	29 15N	81 35W
George, L., N.Y., U.S.A.	**162**	43 30N	73 30W
George, Mt.	**137**	25 17 S	119 0 E
George, R.	**151**	58 49N	66 10W
George River = Port Nouveau	**149**	58 30N	65 50W
George Sound	**143**	44 52 S	167 25 E
George Town, Austral.	**138**	41 5 S	146 49 E
George Town, Bahamas	**166**	23 33N	75 47W
George Town, Malay.	**101**	5 25N	100 19 E
George V Coast	**13**	67 0 S	148 0 E
George West	**159**	28 18N	98 5W
Georgetown, Austral.	**133**	18 17 S	143 33 E
Georgetown, Ont., Can.	**150**	43 40N	80 0W
Georgetown, P.E.I., Can.	**151**	46 13N	62 24W
Georgetown, Cay. Is.	**166**	19 20N	81 24W
Georgetown, Gambia	**120**	13 30N	14 47W
Georgetown, Guyana	**174**	6 50N	58 12W
Georgetown, Colo., U.S.A.	**160**	39 46N	105 49W
Georgetown, Del., U.S.A.	**162**	38 42N	75 23W
Georgetown, N.Y., U.S.A.	**162**	42 46N	75 44W
Georgetown, Ohio, U.S.A.	**156**	38 50N	83 50W
Georgetown, S.C., U.S.A.	**157**	33 22N	79 15W
Georgetown, Tex., U.S.A.	**159**	30 45N	98 10W
Georgi Dimitrov	**67**	42 15N	23 54 E
Georgia □	**156**	32 0N	82 0W
Georgia, Str. of	**152**	49 25N	124 0W
Georgian B.	**150**	45 15N	81 0W
Georgian S.S.R. □	**83**	41 0N	45 0 E
Georgievsk	**83**	44 12N	43 28 E
Georgina Downs	**138**	21 10 S	137 40 E
Georgina, R.	**138**	23 30 S	139 47 E
Georgiu-Dezh	**81**	51 3N	39 20 E
Georgiyevka	**85**	43 3N	74 43 E
Gera	**48**	50 53N	12 5 E
Gera □	**48**	50 45N	11 30 E
Geraardsbergen	**47**	50 45N	3 53 E
Geral de Goias, Serra	**171**	12 0 S	46 0W
Geral do Paranã Serra	**171**	15 0 S	47 0W
Geral, Serra, Bahia, Brazil	**171**	14 0 S	41 0W
Geral, Serra, Goiás, Brazil	**170**	11 15 S	46 30W
Geral, Serra, Santa Catarina, Brazil	**173**	26 25 S	50 0W
Geraldine, N.Z.	**143**	44 5 S	171 15 E
Geraldine, U.S.A.	**160**	47 45N	110 18W
Geraldton, Austral.	**137**	28 48 S	114 32 E
Geraldton, Can.	**150**	49 44N	86 59W
Geranium	**140**	35 23 S	140 11 E
Gerardmer	**43**	48 3N	6 50 E
Gerdine, Mt.	**147**	61 32N	152 30W
Gerede	**82**	40 45N	32 10 E
Gérgal	**59**	37 7N	2 31W
Geriban	**91**	7 10N	48 55 E
Gerik	**101**	5 25N	100 8 E
Gering	**158**	41 51N	103 40W
Gerizim	**90**	32 13N	35 15 E
Gerlach	**160**	40 43N	119 27W
Gerlachovka, Mt.	**53**	49 11N	20 7 E
Gerlafingen	**50**	47 10N	7 34 E
Gerlev	**73**	56 36N	10 9 E
Gerlogubi	**91**	6 53N	45 3 E
German Planina	**66**	42 33N	22 0 E
Germansen Landing	**152**	55 43N	124 40W
Germany, East ■	**48**	52 0N	12 0 E
Germany, West ■	**48**	52 0N	9 0 E
Germersheim	**49**	49 13N	8 0 E
Germiston	**125**	26 11 S	28 10 E
Gernsheim	**49**	49 44N	8 29 E
Gero	**111**	35 48N	137 14 E
Gerogery	**141**	35 50 S	147 1 E
Gerolstein	**49**	50 12N	6 24 E
Gerona	**58**	41 58N	2 46 E
Gerona □	**58**	42 11N	2 30 E
Gérouville	**47**	49 37N	5 26 E
Gerrans B.	**30**	50 12N	4 57W
Gerrard	**152**	50 30N	117 17W
Gerrards Cross	**29**	51 35N	0 32W
Gerrild	**73**	56 30N	10 50 E
Gerringong	**141**	34 46 S	150 47 E
Gers □	**44**	43 35N	0 38 E
Gersau	**51**	47 0N	8 32 E
Gersoppa Falls	**97**	14 12N	74 46 E
Gerufa	**128**	19 8 S	26 0 E
Gerze	**92**	41 45N	35 10 E
Geseke	**48**	51 38N	8 29 E
Geser	**103**	3 50N	130 35 E
Gesso, R.	**62**	44 21N	7 20 E
Gesves	**47**	50 24N	5 4 E
Getafe	**56**	40 18N	3 44W
Gethsémani	**151**	50 13N	60 40W
Gettysburg, Pa., U.S.A.	**156**	39 47N	77 18W
Gettysburg, S.D., U.S.A.	**158**	45 3N	99 56W
Getz Ice Shelf	**13**	75 0 S	130 0W
Geul, R.	**47**	50 53N	5 43 E
Geurie	**141**	32 22 S	148 50 E
Gevaudan	**44**	44 40N	3 40 E
Gevgelija	**66**	41 9N	22 30 E
Gévora, R.	**57**	38 53N	6 57W
Gex	**45**	46 21N	6 3 E
Geyikli	**68**	39 50N	26 12 E
Geyser	**160**	47 17N	110 30W
Geysir	**74**	64 19N	20 18W
Geyve	**82**	40 32N	30 18 E
Ghaghara, R.	**95**	26 0N	84 20 E
Ghail	**92**	21 40N	46 20 E
Ghalla, Wadi el	**123**	12 0N	28 58 E
Ghana ■	**121**	6 0N	1 0W
Ghandhi Dam	**93**	24 30N	75 35 E
Ghansor	**93**	22 39N	80 1 E
Ghanzi	**128**	21 50 S	21 45 E
Ghanzi □	**128**	21 50 S	21 45 E
Gharbîya, Es Sahrâ el	**122**	27 40N	26 30 E
Ghard Abû Muharik	**122**	26 50N	30 0 E
Ghardaïa	**118**	32 31N	3 37 E
Gharyãn	**119**	32 10N	13 0 E
Ghât	**119**	24 59N	10 19 E
Ghat Ghat	**92**	26 0N	45 5 E
Ghatal	**95**	22 40N	87 46 E
Ghatampur	**95**	26 8N	80 13 E
Ghatprabha, R.	**96**	16 15N	75 20 E
Ghazal, Bahr el	**117**	15 0N	17 0 E
Ghazaouet	**118**	35 8N	1 50W
Ghaziabad	**94**	28 42N	77 35 E
Ghazipur	**95**	25 38N	83 35 E
Ghazni	**94**	33 30N	68 17 E
Ghazni □	**93**	33 0N	68 0 E
Ghedi	**62**	45 24N	10 16 E
Ghelari	**70**	45 42N	22 45 E
Ghelinsor	**91**	6 35N	46 55 E
Ghent = Gand	**47**	51 4N	3 43 E

Gheorghe Gheorghiu-Dej Gobo

Gheorghe Gheorghiu-Dej 70 46 17N 26 47 E
Gheorgheni 70 46 43N 25 41 E
Ghergani 70 44 37N 25 37 E
Gherla 70 47 0N 23 57 E
Ghilarza 64 40 8N 8 50 E
Ghisonaccia 45 42 1N 9 26 E
Ghizao 94 33 30N 65 59 E
Ghizar, R. 95 36 10N 73 4 E
Ghod, R. 96 18 40N 74 15 E
Ghorat □ 93 34 0N 64 20 E
Ghost River, Can. 150 50 10N 91 27W
Ghost River, Ont., Can. 150 51 25N 83 20W
Ghot Ogrein 122 31 10N 25 20 E
Ghotaru 94 27 20N 70 1 E
Ghotki 94 28 5N 69 30 E
Ghudâmis 119 30 11N 9 29 E
Ghugri 95 22 39N 80 41 E
Ghugus 96 20 0N 79 0 E
Ghulam Mohammad Barrage 94 25 30N 67 0 E
Ghuriân 93 34 17N 61 25 E
Gia Dinh 101 10 49N 106 42 E
Gia Lai = Pleiku 101 14 3N 108 0 E
Gia Nghia 101 12 0N 107 42 E
Gia Ngoc 100 14 50N 108 58 E
Gia Vuc 100 14 42N 108 34 E
Giamda Dzong 99 30 3N 93 2 E
Giannutri, I. 62 42 16N 11 5 E
Giant Forest 163 36 36N 118 43W
Giant Mts. = Krkonose 52 50 50N 16 10 E
Giant's Causeway 38 55 15N 6 30W
Giarabub = Jaghbub 117 29 42N 24 38 E
Giarre 65 37 44N 15 10 E
Giaveno 62 45 3N 7 20 E
Gibara 166 21 0N 76 20W
Gibbon 158 40 49N 98 45W
Gibe, R. 123 6 25N 36 10 E
Gibellina 64 37 48N 13 0 E
Gibeon 128 25 7 S 17 45 E
Gibraléon 57 37 23N 6 58W
Gibraltar 57 36 7N 5 22W
Gibraltar Pt. 33 53 6N 0 20 E
Gibraltar, Str. of 57 35 55N 5 40W
Gibson Des. 136 24 0 S 126 0 E
Gibsons 152 49 24N 123 32W
Gida. G. 12 72 30N 77 0 E
Giddalur 97 15 20N 78 57 E
Gidde 123 5 40N 37 25 E
Giddings 159 30 11N 96 58W
Gide 123 9 52N 35 5 E
Gien 43 47 40N 2 36 E
Giessen 48 50 34N 8 40 E
Gieten 46 53 0N 6 46 E
Gif-sur-Yvette 46 48 42N 2 8 E
Gifatin, Geziret 122 27 10N 33 50 E
Gifford 35 55 54N 2 45W
Gifford Creek 137 24 3 S 116 16 E
Gifhorn 48 52 29N 10 32 E
Gifu 111 35 30N 136 45 E
Gifu-ken □ 111 36 0N 137 0 E
Gigant 83 46 28N 41 30 E
Giganta, Sa. de la 164 25 30N 111 30W
Gigen 67 43 40N 24 28 E
Giggleswick 32 54 5N 2 19W
Gigha, I. 39 55 42N 5 45W
Giglio, I. 62 42 20N 10 52 E
Gignac 44 43 39N 3 32 E
Gigüela, R. 58 39 47N 3 0W
Gijón 56 43 32N 5 42W
Gil I. 152 53 12N 129 15W
Gila Bend 161 33 0N 112 46W
Gila Bend Mts. 161 33 15N 113 0W
Gila, R. 161 33 5N 108 40W
Gilau 138 5 38 S 149 3 E
Gilbedi 121 13 40N 5 45 E
• Gilbert Is. 130 1 0 S 176 0 E
Gilbert Plains 153 51 9N 100 28W
Gilbert, R. 138 16 35 S 141 15 E
Gilbert River 138 18 9 S 142 52 E
Gilberton 138 19 16 S 143 35 E
Gilbués 170 9 50 S 45 21W
Gilford 38 54 23N 6 20W
Gilford I. 152 50 40N 126 30W
Gilgai 137 31 15 S 119 56 E
Gilgandra 141 31 43 S 148 39 E
Gilgil 126 0 30 S 36 20 E
Gilgit 95 35 50N 74 15 E
Gilgit, R. 95 35 50N 74 25 E
Gilgunnia 141 32 26 S 146 2 E
Giligulgul 139 26 26 S 150 0 E
Gilima 126 3 53N 28 15 E
Giljeva Planina 66 43 9N 20 0 E
Gill L. 38 54 15N 8 25W
Gillam 153 56 20N 94 40W
Gilleleje 73 56 8N 12 19 E
Gillen, L. 137 26 11 S 124 38 E
Gilles, L. 140 32 50 S 136 45 E
Gillespie Pt. 143 43 24 S 169 49 E
Gillett 162 41 57N 76 48W
Gillette 158 44 20N 105 38W
Gilliat 138 20 40 S 141 28 E
Gillingham, Dorset, U.K. 28 51 2N 2 15W
Gillingham, Kent, U.K. 29 51 23N 0 34 E
Gilmer 159 32 44N 94 55W
Gilmore 141 35 14 S 148 12 E
Gilmore, L. 137 32 29 S 121 37 E
Gilmour 150 44 48N 77 37W
Gilo 123 7 35N 34 30 E
Gilo, R. 161 33 5N 108 40W
Gilort, R. 70 44 38N 23 32 E
Gilroy 163 37 1N 121 37W

• *Renamed Kiribati*

Gilsland 32 55 0N 2 34W
Gilău 70 46 45N 23 23W
Giluwe, Mt. 135 6 8 S 143 52 E
Gilwern 31 51 49N 3 5W
Gilze 47 51 32N 4 57 E
Gimâfors 72 62 40N 16 25 E
Gimbi 123 9 3N 35 42 E
Gimigliano 65 38 53N 16 32 E
Gimli 153 50 40N 97 10W
Gimmi 123 9 0N 37 20 E
Gimo 72 60 11N 18 12 E
Gimont 44 43 38N 0 52 E
Gimzo 90 31 56N 34 56 E
Gin Ganga 97 6 5N 80 7 E
Gin Gin 139 25 0 S 151 44 E
Ginâh 122 25 21N 30 30 E
Gindie 138 23 44 S 148 8 E
Gineta, La 59 39 8N 2 1W
Gingin 137 31 22 S 115 54 E
Gîngiova 70 43 54N 23 50 E
Ginir 123 7 12N 40 40 E
Ginosa 65 40 35N 16 45 E
Ginowan 112 26 15N 127 47 E
Ginzo de Limia 56 42 3N 7 47W
Giohar 91 2 20N 45 15 E
Gióia del Colle 65 40 49N 16 55 E
Gióia, G. di 65 38 30N 15 50 E
Gióia Táuro 65 38 26N 15 53 E
Gioiosa Jónica 65 38 20N 16 19 E
Gióna, Óros 69 38 38N 22 14 E
Giong, Teluk 103 4 50N 118 20 E
Giovi, P. dei 45 44 30N 8 55 E
Giovinazzo 65 41 10N 16 40 E
Gippsland 133 37 45 S 147 15 E
Gir Hills 94 21 0N 71 0 E
Girab 94 26 2N 70 38 E
Giralla 136 22 31 S 114 15 E
Giraltovce 53 49 7N 21 32 E
Girard 159 37 30N 94 50W
Girardot 174 4 18N 74 48W
Girdle Ness 37 57 9N 2 2W
Giresun 92 40 45N 38 30 E
Girga 122 26 17N 31 55 E
Girgir, C. 135 3 50 S 144 35 E
Giridih 95 24 10N 86 21 E
Girifalco 65 38 49N 16 25 E
Girilambone 141 31 16 S 146 57 E
Girishk 93 31 47N 64 24 E
Giro 121 11 7N 4 42 E
Giromagny 43 47 44N 6 50 E
Gironde □ 44 44 45N 0 30W
Gironde, R. 44 45 27N 0 53W
Gironella 58 42 2N 1 53 E
Giru 138 19 30 S 147 5 E
Girvan 34 55 15N 4 50W
Girvan R. 34 55 18N 4 51W
Gisborne 142 38 39 S 178 5 E
Gisburn 32 53 56N 2 16W
Gisenyi 126 1 41 S 29 30 E
Giske 71 62 30N 6 3 E
Gisla 36 58 7N 6 53W
Gislaved 73 57 19N 13 32 E
Gisors 43 49 15N 1 40 E
Gissarskiy, Khrebet 85 39 0N 69 0 E
Gistel 47 51 9N 2 59 E
Giswil 50 46 50N 8 11 E
Gitega (Kitega) 126 3 26 S 29 56 E
Gits 47 51 0N 3 6 E
Giubiasco 51 46 11N 9 1 E
Giugliano in Campania 65 40 55N 14 12 E
Giulianova 63 42 45N 13 58 E
Giurgeni 70 44 45N 27 38 E
Giurgiu 70 43 52N 25 57 E
Giv'at Brenner 90 31 52N 34 47 E
Give 73 55 51N 9 13 E
Givet 43 50 8N 4 49 E
Givors 45 45 35N 4 45 E
Givry, Belg. 47 50 23N 4 2 E
Givry, France 43 46 41N 4 46 E
Giza (El Giza) 122 30 1N 31 11 E
Gizhduvan 85 40 6N 64 41 E
Gizhiga 77 62 0N 150 27 E
Gizhiginskaya, Guba 77 61 0N 158 0 E
Gizycko 54 54 2N 21 48 E
Gizzeria 65 38 57N 16 10 E
Gjegjan 68 41 58N 20 3 E
Gjerpen 71 59 15N 9 33 E
Gjerstad 71 58 54N 9 0 E
Gjiri-i-Vlorës 68 40 29N 19 27 E
Gjirokastër 68 40 7N 20 16 E
Gjoa Haven 148 68 20N 96 0W
Gjovdal 71 58 52N 8 19 E
Gjøvik 71 60 47N 10 43 E
Glace Bay 151 46 11N 59 58W
Glacier B. 152 58 30N 136 10W
Glacier Nat. Park 152 51 15N 117 30W
Glacier National Park 160 48 35N 113 40W
Glacier Peak Mt. 160 48 7N 121 7W
Gladewater 159 32 30N 94 58W
Gladstone, Queens., Austral. 74 23 52 S 151 16 E
Gladstone, S.A., Austral. 140 33 15 S 138 22 E
Gladstone, W. Australia, Austral. 137 25 57 S 114 17 E
Gladstone, Can. 153 50 13N 98 57W
Gladstone, U.S.A. 156 45 52N 87 1W
Gladwin 156 43 59N 84 29W
Gladys L. 152 59 50N 133 0W
Glafsfjorden 72 59 30N 12 45 E
Głagów Małapolski 53 50 10N 21 56 E
Gláma 74 65 48N 23 0W
Gláma, R. 71 60 30N 12 8 E
Glamis 37 56 37N 3 0W
Glamorgan (□) 26 51 37N 3 35W
Glamorgan, Vale of 23 50 45N 3 15W
Glan, Phil. 103 5 45N 125 20 E
Glan, Sweden 73 58 37N 16 0 E
Glanaman 31 51 48N 3 56W
Glanaruddery Mts. 39 52 20N 9 27W
Glandore 39 51 33N 9 7W
Glandore Harb. 39 51 33N 9 8W
Glanerbrug 46 52 13N 6 58 E
Glanton 35 55 25N 1 54W
Glanworth 39 52 10N 8 25W
Glarner Alpen 51 46 50N 9 0 E
Glärnisch 51 47 0N 9 0 E
Glarus 51 47 3N 9 4 E
Glarus □ 51 47 0N 9 5 E
Glas Maol 37 56 52N 3 20W
Glasco, Kans., U.S.A. 158 39 25N 97 50W
Glasco, N.Y., U.S.A. 162 42 3N 73 57W
Glasgow, U.K. 34 55 52N 4 14W
Glasgow, Ky., U.S.A. 156 37 2N 85 55W
Glasgow, Mont., U.S.A. 160 48 12N 106 35W
Glasnevin 38 53 22N 6 18W
Glassboro 162 39 42N 75 7W
Glasslough 38 54 20N 6 53W
Glastonbury, U.K. 28 51 9N 2 42W
Glastonbury, U.S.A. 162 41 42N 72 27W
Glatt, R. 51 47 28N 8 32 E
Glattfelden 51 47 33N 8 30 E
Glauchau 48 50 50N 12 33 E
Glazov 81 58 9N 52 40 E
Glbovo 67 42 1N 24 43 E
Gleichen 152 50 50N 113 0W
Gleisdorf 52 47 6N 15 44 E
Glemsford 29 52 6N 0 41 E
Glen Affric 37 57 15N 5 0W
Glen Afton 142 37 46 S 175 4 E
Glen Almond 35 56 28N 3 50W
Glen B. 38 54 43N 8 45W
Glen Burnie 162 39 10N 76 37W
Glen Canyon Dam 161 37 0N 111 25W
Glen Canyon Nat. Recreation Area 161 37 30N 111 0W
Glen Coe 23 56 40N 5 0W
Glen Cove 162 40 51N 73 37W
Glen Esk 37 56 53N 2 50W
Glen Etive 34 56 37N 5 0W
Glen Florrie 136 22 55 S 115 59 E
Glen Garry, Inv., U.K. 36 57 3N 5 7W
Glen Garry, Per., U.K. 37 56 47N 4 5W
Glen Gowrie 140 31 4 S 143 10 E
Glen Helen 32 54 14N 4 35W
Glen Innes 139 29 40 S 151 39 E
Glen Lyon, U.K. 37 56 35N 4 20W
Glen Lyon, U.S.A. 162 41 10N 76 7W
Glen Massey 142 37 38 S 175 2 E
Glen Mor 37 57 12N 4 37 E
Glen Moriston 36 57 10N 4 58W
Glen Orchy 34 56 27N 4 52W
Glen Orrin 37 57 30N 4 45W
Glen Oykel 37 58 5N 4 50W
Glen, R. 29 52 50N 0 7W
Glen Shee 37 56 45N 3 25W
Glen Shiel 36 57 8N 5 20W
Glen Spean 37 56 53N 4 40W
Glen Trool Lodge 34 55 5N 4 30W
Glen Ullin 158 46 48N 101 46W
Glen Valley 141 36 54 S 147 28 E
Glenade 38 54 22N 8 17W
Glenamoy 38 54 14N 9 40W
Glénans, Îs. de 42 47 42N 4 0W
Glenariff 141 30 50 S 146 33 E
Glenarm 38 54 58N 5 58W
Glenart Castle 39 52 48N 6 12W
Glenavy, N.Z. 143 44 54 S 171 7 E
Glenavy, U.K. 38 54 36N 6 12W
Glenbarr 34 55 34N 5 40W
Glenbeigh 39 52 3N 9 57W
Glenbrittle 36 57 13N 6 18W
Glenbrook 142 33 46 S 150 37 E
Glenburn 141 37 37 S 145 26 E
Glencoe, S. Afr. 129 28 11 S 30 11 E
Glencoe, U.S.A. 158 44 45N 94 10W
Glencolumbkille 38 54 43N 8 41W
Glendale, Can. 150 46 45N 84 2W
Glendale, Zimb. 127 17 22 S 31 5 E
Glendale, Ariz., U.S.A. 161 33 40N 112 8W
Glendale, Calif., U.S.A. 163 34 7N 118 18W
Glendale, Oreg., U.S.A. 160 42 44N 123 29W
Glendive 158 47 7N 104 40W
Glendo 158 42 30N 105 0W
Glendora 163 34 8N 117 52W
Gleneagles 35 56 16N 3 44W
Glenealy 39 52 59N 6 10W
Gleneely 38 52 14N 7 8W
Glenelg, Austral. 140 34 58 S 138 31 E
Glenelg, U.K. 36 57 13N 5 37W
Glenelg, R. 140 38 4 S 140 59 E
Glenfarne 38 54 17N 8 0W
Glenfield 162 43 43N 75 24W
Glenfinnan 36 56 52N 5 28W
Glengad Hd. 38 55 19N 7 11W
Glengariff 39 51 45N 9 33W
Glengormley 38 54 41N 5 57W
Glengyle 138 24 48 S 139 37 E
Glenham 143 46 26 S 168 52 E
Glenhope 143 41 40 S 172 39 E
Glenisland 38 53 54N 9 24W
Glenkens, The 34 55 10N 4 15W
Glenluce 34 54 53N 4 50W
Glenmary, Mt. 143 44 0 S 169 55 E
Glenmaye 32 54 11N 4 42W
Glenmora 159 31 1N 92 34W
Glenmorgan 139 27 14 S 149 42 E
Glenn, oilfield 19 57 55N 0 15 E
Glennagevlagh 38 53 36N 9 41W
Glennamaddy 38 53 37N 8 33W
Glenn's Ferry 160 43 0N 115 15W
Glenoe 38 54 47N 5 50W
Glenorchy, S. Austral., Austral. 140 31 55 S 139 46 E
Glenorchy, Tas., Austral. 138 42 49 S 147 18 E
Glenorchy, Vic., Austral. 140 36 55 S 142 41 E
Glenore 138 17 50 S 141 12 E
Glenormiston 138 22 55 S 138 50 E
Glenreagh 139 30 2 S 153 1 E
Glenrock 160 42 53N 105 55W
Glenrothes 35 56 12N 3 11W
Glenrowan 141 36 29 S 146 13 E
Glenroy, S. Australia, Austral. 140 37 13 S 140 48 E
Glenroy, W. Australia, Austral. 136 17 16 S 126 14 E
Glenroy, S. Afr. 132 26 23 S 28 17 E
Glens Falls 162 43 19N 73 39W
Glentane 38 53 25N 8 30W
Glenties 38 54 48N 8 18W
Glenville 156 38 56N 80 50W
Glenwood, Alta., Can. 152 49 21N 113 31W
Glenwood, Newf., Can. 151 49 0N 54 47W
Glenwood, Ark., U.S.A. 159 34 20N 93 30W
Glenwood, Hawaii, U.S.A. 147 19 29N 155 10W
Glenwood, Iowa, U.S.A. 158 41 7N 95 41W
Glenwood, Minn., U.S.A. 158 45 38N 95 21W
Glenwood Sprs. 160 39 39N 107 15W
Gletsch 51 46 34N 8 22 E
Glettinganes 51 65 30N 13 37W
Glin 39 52 34N 9 17W
Glina 63 45 20N 16 6 E
Glinojeck 54 52 49N 20 21 E
Glinsk 39 53 23N 9 49W
Glittertind 71 61 40N 8 32 E
Gliwice (Gleiwitz) 54 50 22N 18 41 E
Globe 161 33 25N 110 53W
Glodeanu-Siliştea 70 44 50N 26 48 E
Glödnitz 52 46 53N 14 7 E
Glodyany 70 47 45N 27 31 E
Gloggnitz 52 47 41N 15 56 E
Głogów 54 51 37N 16 5 E
Głogowek 54 50 21N 17 53 E
Gloria, La 174 8 37N 73 48W
Glorieuses, Îs. 129 11 30 S 47 20 E
Glossop 32 53 27N 1 56W
Gloucester, Austral. 141 32 0 S 151 59 E
Gloucester, U.K. 28 51 52N 2 15W
Gloucester, U.S.A. 162 42 38N 70 39W
Gloucester, Va., U.S.A. 162 37 25N 76 32W
Gloucester, C. 135 5 26 S 148 21 E
Gloucester City 162 39 54N 75 8W
Gloucester, I. 138 20 0 S 148 30 E
Gloucestershire □ 28 51 44N 2 10W
Gloversville 162 43 5N 74 18W
Glovertown 151 48 40N 54 03W
Głubczyce 54 50 13N 17 52 E
Glubokiy 83 48 35N 40 25 E
Glubokoye 80 55 10N 27 45 E
Głucholazy 54 50 19N 17 24 E
Glücksburg 48 54 48N 9 34 E
Glückstadt 48 53 46N 9 28 E
Gluepot 140 33 45 S 140 0 E
Glukhov 80 51 40N 33 50 E
Glussk 80 52 53N 28 41 E
Gł ó wno 54 51 59N 19 42 E
Glyn-ceiriog 31 52 56N 3 12W
Glyn Neath 31 51 45N 3 37W
Glyncorrwg 31 51 40N 3 39W
Glyngøre 73 56 46N 8 52 E
Glynn 39 52 29N 6 55W
Gmünd, Kärnten, Austria 52 46 54N 13 31 E
Gmünd, Niederösterreich, Austria 52 48 45N 15 0 E
Gmunden 52 47 55N 13 48 E
Gnarp 72 62 3N 17 16 E
Gnesta 72 59 3N 17 17 E
Gniew 54 53 50N 18 50 E
Gniewkowo 54 52 54N 18 25 E
Gniezno 54 52 30N 17 35 E
Gnoien 48 53 58N 12 41 E
Gnopp 123 8 47N 29 50 E
Gnosall 28 52 48N 2 15W
Gnosjö 73 57 22N 13 43 E
Gnowangerup 137 33 58 S 117 59 E
Go Cong 101 10 22N 106 40 E
Gō-no-ura 110 33 44N 129 40 E
Goa 97 15 33N 73 59 E
Goa □ 97 15 33N 73 59 E
Goageb 128 26 49 S 17 15 E
Goalen Hd. 141 36 33 S 150 4 E
Goalpara 98 26 10N 90 40 E
Goalundo 95 23 50N 89 47 E
Goaso 120 6 48N 2 30W
Goat Fell 34 55 37N 5 11W
Goba, Ethiopia 123 7 1N 39 59 E
Goba, Mozam. 125 26 15 S 32 13 E
Gobabis 128 22 16 S 19 0 E
Gobi, desert 105 44 0N 111 0 E
Gobichettipalayam 97 11 31N 77 21 E
Gobō 111 33 53N 135 10 E
Gobo 123 5 40N 30 10 E

Goch Grand Bassa

Goch 48 51 40N 6 9E
Gochas 125 24 59S 19 25E
Godalming 29 51 12N 0 37W
Godavari Point 96 17 0N 82 20E
Godavari, R. 96 19 5N 79 0E
Godbout 151 49 20N 67 38W
Godda 95 24 50N 87 20E
Goddua 119 26 26N 14 19E
Godech 66 43 1N 23 4E
Godegård 73 58 43N 15 8E
Goderich 150 43 45N 81 41W
Goderville 42 49 38N 0 22E
Godhavn 12 69 15N 53 38W
Godhra 94 22 49N 73 40E
Godmanchester 29 52 19N 0 11W
Gödöllö 53 47 38N 19 25E
Godoy Cruz 172 32 56S 68 52W
Godrevy Pt. 30 50 15N 5 24W
Gods L. 153 54 40N 94 15W
Gods, R. 153 56 22N 92 51W
Godshill 28 50 38N 1 13W
Godstone 29 51 15N 0 3W
Godthåb 12 64 10N 51 46W
Godwin Austen (K2) 93 36 0N 77 0E
Goeie Hoop, Kaap die 128 34 24S 18 30E
Goeland, L. 150 49 50N 76 48W
Goeree 46 51 50N 4 0E
Goes 47 51 30N 3 55E
Goffstown 162 43 1N 71 36W
Gogama 150 47 35N 81 43W
Gogango 138 23 40S 150 2E
Gogebic, L. 158 46 30N 89 34W
Gogha 94 21 32N 72 9E
Gogolin 54 50 30N 18 0E
Gogra, R. = Ghaghara 99 26 0N 84 20E
Gogriâl 123 8 30N 28 0E
Goiana 170 7 33S 34 59W
Goiandira 171 11 46S 46 40W
Goianésia 171 15 18S 49 7W
Goiânia 171 16 35S 49 20W
Goiás 171 15 55S 50 10W
Goiás □ 170 12 10S 48 0W
Goiatuba 171 18 1S 49 23W
Goil L. 34 56 8N 4 52W
Goirle 47 51 31N 5 4E
Góis 56 40 10N 8 6W
Goisern 52 47 38N 13 38E
Gojam □ 123 10 55N 36 30E
Gojeb, W. 123 7 12N 36 40E
Gojō 111 34 21N 135 42E
Gojra 94 31 10N 72 40E
Gokak 97 16 11N 74 52E
Gokarannath 95 27 57N 80 39E
Gokarn 97 14 33N 74 17E
Gökçeada 68 40 10N 26 0E
Gokteik 99 22 26N 97 0E
Gokurt 94 29 47N 67 26E
Gøl 73 57 4N 9 42E
Gola 95 28 3N 80 32E
Gola I. 38 55 4N 8 20W
Golaghat 98 26 30N 94 0E
Golakganj 95 26 8N 89 52E
Golaya Pristen 82 46 29N 32 23E
Golchikha 12 71 45N 84 0E
Golconda 160 40 58N 117 32W
Gold Beach 160 42 25N 124 25W
Gold Coast, Austral. 139 28 0S 153 25E
Gold Coast, W. Afr. 121 4 0N 1 40W
Gold Creek 147 62 45N 149 45W
Gold Hill 160 42 28N 123 2W
Gold Point 163 37 21N 117 21W
Gold River 152 49 40N 126 10E
Goldach 51 47 28N 9 28E
Goldau 51 47 3N 8 33E
Goldberg 48 53 34N 12 6E
Golden, Can. 152 51 20N 117 0W
Golden, Ireland 39 52 30N 8 0W
Golden, U.S.A. 158 39 42N 105 30W
Golden Bay 143 40 40S 172 50E
Golden Gate 160 37 54N 122 30W
Golden Hinde, mt. 152 49 40N 125 44W
Golden Prairie 153 50 13N 109 37W
Golden Rock 97 10 45N 78 48E
Golden Vale 39 52 33N 8 17W
Goldendale 160 45 53N 120 48W
Goldfield 163 37 45N 117 13W
Goldfields 153 59 28N 108 29W
Goldpines 153 50 45N 93 05W
Goldsand L. 153 57 2N 101 8W
Goldsboro 157 35 24N 77 59W
Goldsmith 159 32 0N 102 40W
Goldsworthy 136 20 21S 119 30E
Goldsworthy, Mt. 136 20 23S 119 31E
Goldthwaite 159 31 25N 98 32W
Goleen 39 51 30N 9 43W
Golegã 57 39 24N 8 29W
Goleniów 54 53 35N 14 50E
Goleta 163 34 27N 119 50W
Golfito 166 8 41N 83 5W
Golfo degli Aranci 65 41 0N 9 38E
Goliad 159 28 40N 97 22W
Golija 66 43 22N 20 15E
Golija, Mts. 66 43 5N 18 45E
Golina 54 52 15N 18 4E
Golo, R. 45 42 31N 9 32E
Golovanesvsk 82 48 25N 30 30E
Gölpazari 82 40 17N 30 17E
Golra 94 33 37N 72 56E
Golspie 37 57 58N 3 58W
Golub Dobrzyn 54 53 7N 19 2E
Golubac 66 44 38N 21 38E
Golyama Kamchiya, R. 67 43 2N 27 18E
Goma, Ethiopia 123 8 29N 36 53E
Goma, Rwanda 126 2 11S 29 18E
Goma, Zaïre 126 1 37S 29 10E
Gomare 128 19 25S 22 8E
Gomati, R. 95 26 30N 81 50E
Gombari 126 2 45N 29 3E
Gombe 121 10 19N 11 2E
Gombe, R. 126 4 30S 32 50E
Gombi 121 10 12N 12 45E
Gomel 80 52 28N 31 0E
Gomera, I. 116 28 10N 17 5W
Gometra I. 34 56 30N 6 18W
Gómez Palacio 164 25 40N 104 40W
Gommern 48 52 54N 11 47E
Gomogomo 103 6 25S 134 53E
Gomoh 99 23 52N 86 10E
Gomotartsi 66 44 6N 22 57E
Goms 50 46 30N 8 15E
Gonābād 93 34 15N 58 45E
Gonaïves 167 19 20N 72 50W
Gonâve, G. de la 167 19 29N 72 42W
Gonâve, I. de la 167 18 45N 73 0W
Gönc 53 48 28N 21 14E
Gonda 95 27 9N 81 58E
Gondab-e Kāvūs 93 37 20N 55 25E
Gondal 94 21 58N 70 52E
Gonder 123 12 23N 37 30E
Gondia 96 21 30N 80 10E
Gondola 127 19 4S 33 37E
Gondomar, Port. 56 41 10N 8 35W
Gondomar, Spain 56 42 7N 8 45W
Gondrecourt-le-Château 43 48 26N 5 30E
Gongola □ 121 8 0N 12 0E
Gongola, R. 121 10 30N 10 22E
Goniadz 54 53 30N 22 44E
Goniri 121 11 30N 12 15E
Gonnesa 64 39 17N 8 27E
Gonno-Altaysk 76 51 50N 86 5E
Gonnos 68 39 52N 22 29E
Gonnosfanadiga 64 39 30N 8 39E
Gonzales, Calif., U.S.A. 163 36 35N 121 30W
Gonzales, Tex., U.S.A. 159 29 30N 97 30W
González Chaves 172 38 02S 60 05W
Good Hope, C. of = Goeie Hoop 128 34 24S 18 30E
Goode 139 31 58S 133 45E
Goodenough I. 135 9 20S 150 15E
Gooderham 150 44 54N 78 21W
Goodeve 153 51 4N 103 10W
Gooding 160 43 0N 114 50W
Goodland 158 39 22N 101 44W
Goodnight 159 35 4N 101 13W
Goodooga 139 29 1S 147 28E
Goodrich 28 51 52N 2 38W
Goodsoil 153 54 24N 109 13W
Goodsprings 161 35 51N 115 30W
Goodwick 31 52 0N 5 0W
Goodwin, Mt. 136 14 13S 129 32E
Goodwood 29 50 53N 0 44W
Goole 33 53 42N 0 52W
Goolgowi 141 33 58S 145 41E
Goolwa 140 35 30S 138 47E
Goomalling 137 31 15S 116 42E
Goombalie 139 29 59S 145 26E
Goonalga 140 31 45S 143 37E
Goonda 127 19 48S 33 57E
Goondiwindi 139 28 30S 150 21E
Goongarrie 137 30 2S 121 8E
Goonumbla 141 32 59S 148 11E
Goonyella 138 21 47S 147 58E
Goor 46 52 13N 6 33E
Gooray 139 28 25S 150 2E
Goose Bay 151 53 15N 60 20W
Goose L. 160 42 0N 120 30W
Goose R. 151 53 20N 60 35W
Goothinga 138 17 36S 140 50E
Gooty 97 15 7N 77 41E
Gop 93 22 5N 69 50E
Gopalganj, Bangla. 98 23 1N 89 50E
Gopalganj, India 95 26 28N 84 30E
Goppenstein 50 46 23N 7 46E
Göppingen 49 48 42N 9 40E
Gor 59 37 23N 2 58W
Góra 54 51 40N 16 31E
Gorakhpur 95 26 47N 83 32E
Gorbatov 81 56 12N 43 2E
Gorbea, Peña 58 43 1N 2 50W
Gorda 163 35 53N 121 26W
Gorda, Punta 166 14 10N 83 10W
Gordon, Austral. 140 32 7S 138 20E
Gordon, U.K. 35 55 41N 2 32W
Gordon, U.S.A. 158 42 49N 102 6W
Gordon B. 136 11 35S 130 10E
Gordon Downs 136 18 48S 128 40E
Gordon L., Alta., Can. 153 56 30N 110 25W
Gordon L., N.W.T., Can. 152 63 5N 113 11W
Gordon, R. 138 42 27S 145 30E
Gordon River 137 34 10S 117 15E
Gordonia 128 28 13S 21 10E
Gordonvale 138 17 5S 145 50E
Gore 139 28 17S 151 30E
Goré 117 7 59N 16 49E
Gore, Ethiopia 123 8 12N 35 32E
Gore, N.Z. 143 46 5S 168 58E
Gore B. 150 45 57N 82 28W
Gorebridge 35 55 51N 3 2W
Goresbridge 39 52 38N 7 0W
Gorey 39 52 41N 6 18W
Gorgan 93 36 55N 54 30E
Gorge, The 138 18 27S 145 30E
Gorgona, I. 174 3 0N 78 10W
Gorgona I. 62 43 27N 9 52E
Gorgora 123 12 15N 37 17E
Gori 83 42 0N 44 7E
Gorinchem 46 51 50N 4 59E
Goring, Oxon, U.K. 28 51 31N 1 8W
Goring, Sussex, U.K. 29 50 49N 0 26W
Gorinhatã 171 19 15S 49 45W
Goritsy 81 57 4N 36 43E
Gorízia 63 45 56N 13 37E
Gorka 54 51 39N 16 58E
Gorki = Gorkiy 81 56 20N 44 0E
Gorkiy 81 57 20N 44 0E
Gorkovskoye Vdkhr. 81 57 2N 43 4E
Gorleston 29 52 35N 1 44E
Gorlev 73 55 30N 11 15E
Gorlice 54 49 35N 21 11E
Görlitz 54 51 10N 14 59E
Gorlovka 81 48 25N 37 58E
Gorman, Calif., U.S.A. 163 34 47N 118 51W
Gorman, Tex., U.S.A. 159 32 15N 98 43W
Gorna Oryakhovitsa 67 43 7N 25 40E
Gorna Radgona 63 46 40N 16 2E
Gornja Tuzla 66 44 35N 18 46E
Gornji Grad 63 46 20N 14 52E
Gornji Milanovac 66 44 00N 20 29E
Gornji Vafuk 66 43 57N 17 34E
Gorno Ablanovo 67 43 37N 25 43E
Gorno Filinskoye 76 60 5N 70 0E
Gornyy 81 51 50N 48 30E
Gorodenka 82 48 41N 25 29E
Gorodets 81 56 38N 43 28E
Gorodische 81 53 13N 45 40E
Gorodnitsa 80 50 46N 27 26E
Gorodnya 80 51 55N 31 33E
Gorodok, Byelorussia, U.S.S.R. 80 55 30N 30 3E
Gorodok, Ukraine, U.S.S.R. 80 49 46N 23 32E
Goroka 135 6 7S 145 25E
Goroke 140 36 43S 141 29E
Gorokhov 80 50 15N 24 45E
Gorokhovets 81 56 13N 42 39E
Gorom Gorom 121 14 26N 0 14W
Goromonzi 127 17 52S 31 22E
Gorong, Kepulauan 103 4 5S 131 15E
Gorongosa, Sa. da 127 18 27S 32 2E
Gorongose, R. 129 20 40S 34 30E
Gorontalo 103 0 35N 123 13E
Goronyo 121 13 29N 5 39E
Gorredijk 46 53 0N 6 3E
Gorron 42 48 25N 0 50W
Gorseinon 31 51 40N 4 2W
Gorssel 46 52 12N 6 12E
Gort 39 53 4N 8 50W
Gortin 38 54 43N 7 13W
Gorumahisani 96 22 20N 86 24E
Gorumna I. 39 53 15N 9 44W
Gorzkowice 54 51 13N 19 36E
Gorzno 54 53 12N 19 38E
Gorzów Slaski 54 51 3N 18 22E
Gorzów Wielkopolski 54 52 43N 15 15E
Gorzów Wielkopolski □ 54 52 45N 15 30E
Gosainthan, Mt. 99 28 20N 85 45E
Gosberton 33 52 52N 0 10W
Göschenen 51 46 40N 8 36E
Gōse 111 34 27N 135 44E
Gosford 141 33 23N 151 18E
Gosforth 32 54 24N 3 27W
Goshen, S. Afr. 128 25 50S 25 0E
Goshen, Calif., U.S.A. 163 36 21N 119 25W
Goshen, Ind., U.S.A. 156 41 36N 85 46W
Goshen, N.Y., U.S.A. 162 41 23N 74 21W
Goslar 48 51 55N 10 23E
Gospič 63 44 35N 15 23E
Gosport 28 50 48N 1 8W
Gossa, I. 71 62 52N 6 50E
Gossau 51 47 25N 9 15E
Gosse, R. 138 19 32S 134 37E
Gostivar 66 41 48N 20 57E
Gostyn 54 51 50N 17 3E
Gostynin 54 52 26N 19 29E
Göta 73 58 6N 12 10E
Göta älv 73 57 42N 11 54E
Göta Kanal 73 58 35N 14 15E
Götaland, reg. 73 58 0N 14 0E
Göteborg 73 57 43N 11 59E
Göteborg & Bohus □ 75 58 20N 11 50E
Gotemba 111 35 18N 138 56E
Götene 73 58 32N 13 30E
Gotha 48 50 56N 10 42E
Gothenburg 158 40 58N 100 8W
Gothenburg = Göteborg 73 57 43N 11 59E
Gotse Delchev (Nevrokop) 67 41 43N 23 46E
Gotska Sandön 75 58 24N 19 15E
Gōtsu 110 35 0N 132 14E
Göttingen 48 51 31N 9 55E
Gottwaldov (Zlin) 53 49 14N 17 40E
Gouda 46 52 1N 4 42E
Goudhurst 29 51 7N 0 28E
Goudiry 120 14 15N 12 45E
Gough I. 15 40 10S 9 45W
Gouin Res. 150 48 35N 74 40W
Gouitafla 120 7 30N 5 53W
Goula Touila 118 21 50N 1 57E
Goulburn 141 34 44S 149 44E
Goulburn Is. 138 11 40S 133 20E
Gould, mt. 137 25 46S 117 18E
Goulia 120 10 1N 7 11W
Goulimine 118 28 50N 10 0W
Goulmima 118 31 41N 4 57W
Gouménissa 68 40 56N 22 37E
Goumeur 119 20 40N 18 30E
Goundam 135 16 25N 3 45W
Gounou-Gaya 124 9 38N 15 31E
Goúra 69 37 56N 22 20E
Gourara 118 29 0N 0 30E
Gouraya 118 36 31N 1 56E
Gourdon, France 44 44 44N 1 23E
Gourdon, U.K. 37 56 50N 2 15W
Gouré 121 14 0N 10 10E
Gourits, R. 128 34 15S 21 45E
Gourma Rharous 121 16 55N 2 5W
Gournay-en-Bray 43 49 29N 1 44E
Gouro 117 19 30N 19 30E
Gourock 34 55 58N 4 49W
Gourock Ra. 141 36 0S 149 25E
Gourselik 121 13 31N 10 52E
Goursi 120 12 42N 2 37W
Gouvêa 171 18 27S 43 44W
Gouzon 44 46 12N 2 14E
Govan 153 51 20N 105 0W
Gove 133 12 25S 136 55E
Goverla 82 49 9N 24 30E
Governador Valadares 171 18 15S 41 57W
Governor's Harbour 166 25 10N 76 14W
Gowan 138 25 0S 145 0E
Gowanda 156 42 29N 78 58W
Gower, The 31 51 35N 4 10W
Gowerton 31 51 38N 4 2W
Gowna, L. 38 53 52N 7 35W
Gowran 39 52 38N 7 5W
Goya 172 29 10S 59 10W
Goyder's Lagoon 139 27 3S 139 58E
Goyllarisquizga 174 10 19S 76 31W
Goz Beïda 117 12 20N 21 30E
Goz Regeb 123 16 3N 35 33E
Gozdnica 54 51 28N 15 4E
Gozo (Ghaudex) 60 36 0N 14 13E
Graaff-Reinet 128 32 13S 24 32E
Graasten 73 54 57N 9 34E
Grabow 48 53 17N 11 31E
Grabów 54 51 31N 18 7E
Grabs 51 47 11N 9 27E
Gračac 63 44 18N 15 57E
Gračanica 66 44 43N 18 18E
Graçay 43 47 10N 1 50E
Grace 160 42 38N 111 46W
Grace, L., (North) 137 33 10S 118 20E
Grace, L., (South) 137 33 15S 118 25E
Graceville 158 45 36N 96 23W
Grachevka 84 52 55N 52 52E
Gracias a Dios, C. 166 15 0N 83 20W
Gradačac 66 44 52N 18 26E
Gradaús 170 7 43S 51 11W
Gradaús, Serra dos 170 8 0S 50 45W
Gradeska Planina 66 41 30N 22 15E
Gradets 67 42 46N 26 30E
Gradignan 44 44 47N 0 36W
Gradnitsa 67 42 57N 24 58E
Grado, Italy 63 45 40N 13 20E
Grado, Spain 56 43 23N 6 4W
Gradule 139 28 32S 149 15E
Grady 159 34 52N 103 15W
Graeca, Lacul 70 44 5N 26 10E
Graemsay I. 37 58 56N 3 17W
Graénalon, L. 74 64 10N 17 20W
Grafham Water 29 52 18N 0 17W
Grafton, Austral. 139 29 38S 152 58E
Grafton, U.S.A. 158 48 30N 97 25W
Grafton, C. 133 16 51S 146 0E
Gragnano 65 40 42N 14 30E
Graham, Can. 150 49 20N 90 30W
Graham, N.C., U.S.A. 157 36 5N 79 22W
Graham, Tex., U.S.A. 159 33 7N 98 38W
Graham Bell, Os. 76 80 5N 70 0E
Graham I. 152 53 40N 132 30W
Graham Land 13 65 0S 64 0W
Graham Mt. 161 32 46N 109 58W
Graham, R. 152 56 31N 122 17W
Grahamdale 153 51 23N 98 30W
Grahamstown 128 33 19S 26 31E
Grahamsville 162 41 51N 74 33W
Grahovo 66 42 40N 18 4E
Graïba 119 34 30N 10 13E
Graide 47 49 58N 5 4E
Graigue 39 52 51N 6 56W
Graiguenamanagh 39 52 32N 6 58W
Grain Coast 120 4 20N 10 0W
Grainthorpe 33 53 27N 0 5E
Graivoron 80 50 29N 35 39E
Grajaú 170 5 50S 46 30W
Grajaú, R. 170 3 41S 44 48W
Grajewo 54 53 39N 22 30E
Gramada 66 43 49N 22 39E
Gramat 44 44 48N 1 43E
Gramisdale 36 57 29N 7 18W
Grammichele 65 37 12N 14 37E
Grampian □ 37 57 0N 3 0W
Grampians, Mts. 140 37 0S 142 20E
Gran Canaria 116 27 55N 15 35W
Gran Chaco 156 25 0S 61 0W
Gran Paradiso 62 49 33N 7 17E
Gran Sabana, La 174 5 30N 61 30W
Gran Sasso d'Italia, Mt. 63 42 25N 13 30E
Granada, Nic. 166 11 58N 86 0W
Granada, Spain 59 37 10N 3 35W
Granada, U.S.A. 158 38 5N 102 13W
Granada □ 57 37 5N 4 30W
Granard 38 53 47N 7 30W
Granbo 72 61 16N 16 33E
Granbury 159 32 28N 97 48W
Granby 150 45 25N 72 45W
Grand Bahama I. 166 26 40N 78 30W
Grand Bank 151 47 6N 55 48W
Grand Bassa 120 6 0N 10 2W

Grand Bassam Grillby

Grand Bassam 120 5 10N 3 49W
Grand Béréby 120 4 38N 6 55W
Grand-Bourg 167 15 53N 61 19W
Grand Canal 39 53 15N 8 10W
Grand Canyon National Park 161 36 15N 112 20W
Grand Cayman 166 19 20N 81 20W
Grand Cess 120 4 40N 8 12W
Grand 'Combe, La 45 44 13N 4 2 E
Grand Coulee 160 47 48N 119 1W
Grand Coulee Dam 160 48 0N 118 50W
Grand Erg Occidental 118 30 20N 1 0 E
Grand Erg Oriental 119 30 0N 6 30 E
Grand Falls 151 47 2N 67 46W
Grand Forks, Can. 152 49 0N 118 30W
Grand Forks, U.S.A. 158 48 0N 97 3W
Grand-Fougeray 42 47 43N 1 44W
Grand Fougeray, Le 42 47 44N 1 43W
Grand Haven 156 43 3N 86 13W
Grand I. 150 46 30N 86 40W
Grand Island 158 40 59N 98 25W
Grand Isle 159 29 15N 89 58W
Grand Junction 161 39 0N 108 30W
Grand L., N.B., Can. 151 45 57N 66 7W
Grand L., Newf., Can. 151 48 45N 57 45W
Grand L., Newf., Can. 151 53 40N 60 30W
Grand L., Newf., Can. 151 49 0N 57 30W
Grand L., U.S.A. 159 29 55N 92 45W
Grand Lac 150 47 35N 77 35W
Grand Lahou 120 5 10N 5 0W
Grand Lake 160 40 20N 105 54W
Grand-Leez 47 50 35N 4 45 E
Grand Lieu, Lac de 42 47 6N 1 40W
Grand Manan I. 151 44 45N 66 52W
Grand Marais, Can. 158 47 45N 90 25W
Grand Marais, U.S.A. 156 46 39N 85 59W
Grand Mère 150 46 36N 72 40W
Grand Motte, La 45 48 35N 1 4 E
Grand Popo 121 6 15N 1 44 E
Grand Portage 150 47 58N 89 41W
Grand Pressigny, Le 42 46 55N 0 48 E
Grand, R., Mo., U.S.A. 160 39 23N 93 27W
Grand, R., S.D., U.S.A. 160 45 45N 101 30W
Grand Rapids, Can. 153 53 12N 99 19W
Grand Rapids, Mich., U.S.A. 156 42 57N 85 40W
Grand Rapids, Minn., U.S.A. 158 47 19N 93 29W
Grand St.-Bernard, Col. du 50 45 53N 7 11 E
Grand Teton 160 43 45N 110 57W
Grand Valley 160 39 30N 108 2W
Grand View 153 51 11N 100 51W
Grandas de Salime 56 43 13N 6 53W
Grande 170 11 30 S 44 30W
Grande, B. 176 50 30 S 68 20W
Grande Baie 151 48 19N 70 52W
Grande Cache 152 53 53N 119 8W
Grande, Coxilha 173 28 18 S 51 30W
Grande de Santiago, R. 164 21 20N 105 50W
Grande Dixence, Barr. de la 50 46 5N 7 23 E
Grande-Entrée 151 47 30N 61 40W
Grande, I. 171 23 9 S 44 14W
Grande, La 160 45 15N 118 0W
Grande Prairie 152 55 15N 118 50W
Grande, R., Jujuy, Argent. 172 23 9 S 65 52W
Grande, R., Mendoza, Argent. 172 36 52 S 69 45W
Grande R. 174 18 35 S 63 0W
Grande, R., Brazil 171 20 0 S 50 0W
Grande, R., Spain 59 39 6N 0 48W
Grande, R., U.S.A. 159 29 20N 100 40W
Grande Rivière 151 48 26N 64 30W
Grande, Serra, Goiás, Brazil 170 11 15 S 46 30W
Grande, Serra, Maranhao, Brazil 170 4 30 S 41 20W
Grande, Serra, Piauí, Brazil 170 8 0 S 45 0W
Grande Vallée 151 49 14N 65 8W
Grandes Bergeronnes 151 48 16N 69 35W
Grandfalls 159 31 21N 102 51W
Grandglise 47 50 30N 3 42 E
Grandoe Mines 152 56 29N 129 54W
Grândola 57 38 12N 8 35W
Grandpré 43 49 20N 4 50 E
Grandson 50 46 49N 6 39 E
Grandview, Can. 153 51 10N 100 42W
Grandview, U.S.A. 160 46 13N 119 58W
Grandvilliers 43 49 40N 1 57 E
Graneros 172 34 5 S 70 45W
Graney L. 39 53 0N 8 40W
Grange 38 54 24N 8 32W
Grange, La, Austral. 136 18 45 S 121 43 E
Grange, La, U.S.A. 163 37 42N 120 27W
Grange, La, Ga., U.S.A. 157 33 4N 85 0W
Grange, La, Ky., U.S.A. 156 38 20N 85 20W
Grange, La, Tex., U.S.A. 159 29 54N 96 52W
Grange-over-Sands 32 54 12N 2 55W
Grangemouth 35 56 1N 3 43W
Granger 160 46 25N 120 5W
Grangesberg 72 60 6N 15 1 E
Grängesberg 72 60 6N 15 1 E
Grangetown 33 54 36N 1 7W
Grangeville 160 45 57N 116 4W
Granite City 158 38 45N 90 3W
Granite Falls 158 44 45N 95 35W
Granite Mtn. 163 33 5N 116 28W
Granite Peak 137 25 40 S 121 20 E
Granite Pk., mt. 160 45 8N 109 52W
Granitnyy, Pik 85 39 32N 70 20 E
Granity 143 41 39 S 171 51 E
Granja 170 3 17 S 40 50W
Granja de Moreruela 56 41 48N 5 44W
Granja de Torrehermosa 57 38 19N 5 35W
Gränna 73 58 1N 14 28 E
Granollers 58 41 39N 2 18 E
Gransee 48 53 0N 13 10 E
Grant, Can. 150 50 6N 86 18W
Grant, U.S.A. 158 40 53N 101 42W
Grant City 158 40 30N 94 25W
Grant, I. 136 11 10 S 132 52 E
Grant, Mt. 163 38 34N 118 48W
Grant Range Mts. 161 38 30N 115 30W
Grantham 33 52 55N 0 39W
Grantown-on-Spey 37 57 19N 3 36W
Grants 161 35 14N 107 57W
Grant's Pass 160 42 30N 123 22W
Grantsburg 158 45 46N 92 44W
Grantshouse 35 55 53N 2 17W
Grantsville 160 40 35N 112 32W
Granville, France 42 48 50N 1 35W
Granville, U.K. 38 54 30N 6 47W
Granville, N.D., U.S.A. 158 48 18N 100 48W
Granville, N.Y., U.S.A. 162 43 24N 73 16W
Granville L. 153 56 18N 100 30W
Grao de Gandía 59 39 0N 0 27W
Grapeland 159 31 30N 95 25W
Gras, L. de 148 64 30N 110 30W
Graskop 129 24 56 S 30 49 E
Gräsmark 72 59 58N 12 44 E
Grasmere, Austral. 139 35 1 S 117 45 E
Grasmere, U.K. 32 54 28N 3 2W
Gräsö 72 60 21N 18 28 E
Graso 72 60 28N 18 35 E
Grasonville 162 38 57N 76 13W
Grass, R. 153 56 3N 96 33W
Grass Range 160 47 0N 109 0W
Grass River Prov. Park 153 54 40N 100 50W
Grass Valley, Calif., U.S.A. 160 39 18N 121 0W
Grass Valley, Oreg., U.S.A. 160 45 28N 120 48W
Grassano 65 40 38N 16 17 E
Grasse 45 43 38N 6 56 E
Grassington 32 54 5N 2 0W
Grassmere 140 31 24 S 142 38 E
Grate's Cove 151 48 8N 53 0W
Graubünden (Grisons) □ 51 46 45N 9 30 E
Graulhet 44 43 45N 1 58 E
Graus 58 42 11N 0 20 E
Gravatá 170 6 59 S 35 29W
Grave 46 51 46N 5 44 E
Grave, Pte. de 44 45 34N 1 4W
's-Graveland 46 52 15N 5 7 E
Gravelbourg 153 49 50N 106 35W
Gravelines 43 51 0N 2 10 E
's-Gravendeel 46 51 47N 4 37 E
's-Gravenhage 46 52 7N 4 17 E
's-Gravenpolder 47 51 28N 3 54 E
's-Gravensance 46 52 0N 4 9 E
Graversfors 73 58 42N 16 8 E
Gravesend, Austral. 139 29 35 S 150 20 E
Gravesend, U.K. 29 51 25N 0 22 E
Gravina di Púglia 65 40 48N 16 25 E
Gravir 36 58 2N 6 25W
Gravois, Pointe-à 167 16 15N 73 45W
Gravone, R. 45 42 3N 8 54 E
Grävsnäs 73 58 5N 12 29 E
Gray 43 47 27N 5 35 E
Grayling 156 44 40N 84 42W
Grayling, R. 152 59 21N 125 0W
Grayrigg 32 54 22N 2 40W
Grays Harbor 160 46 55N 124 8W
Grays L. 160 43 8N 111 30W
Grays Thurrock 29 51 28N 0 23 E
Grayson 153 50 45N 102 40W
Grayvoron 80 50 29N 35 39 E
Graz 52 47 4N 15 27 E
Grazalema 57 36 46N 5 23W
Grdelica 66 42 55N 22 3 E
Greasy L. 152 62 55N 122 12W
Great Abaco I. 166 26 15N 77 10W
Great Australia Basin 133 26 0 S 140 0 E
Great Australian Bight 137 33 30 S 130 0 E
Great Ayton 33 54 29N 1 8W
Great Baddow 29 51 43N 0 31 E
Great Bahama Bank 166 23 15N 78 0W
Great Barrier I. 142 36 11 S 175 25 E
Great Barrier Reef 138 19 0 S 149 0 E
Great Barrington 162 42 11N 73 22W
Great Basin 154 40 0N 116 30W
Great Bear L. 148 65 0N 120 0W
Great Bear, R. 148 65 0N 124 0W
Great Belt 73 55 20N 11 0 E
Great Bena 162 41 57N 75 45W
Great Bend 158 38 25N 98 55W
Great Bentley 29 51 51N 1 5 E
Great Bernera, I. 137 58 15N 6 50W
Great Bitter Lake 122 30 15N 32 40 E
Great Blasket, I. 39 52 5N 10 30W
Great Britain 16 54 0N 2 15W
Great Bushman Land 128 29 20 S 19 20 E
Great Central 152 49 20N 125 10W
Great Chesterford 29 52 4N 0 11 E
Great Clifton 32 54 39N 3 29W
Great Coco I. 101 14 10N 93 25 E
Great Divide 141 23 0 S 146 0 E
Great Dunmow 29 51 52N 0 22 E
Great Exuma I. 166 23 30N 75 50W
Great Falls, Can. 153 50 27N 96 1W
Great Falls, U.S.A. 160 47 27N 111 12W
Great Fish R., S. Afr. 128 33 28 S 27 5 E
Great Fish R., S. Afr. 128 31 30 S 20 16 E
Great Gonerby 33 52 56N 0 40W
Great Guana Cay 166 24 0N 76 20W
Great Hanish 123 13 40N 43 0 E
Great Harbour Deep 151 50 35N 56 25W
Great Harwood 32 52 41N 2 49W
Great I., Can. 153 58 53N 96 35W
Great I., Ireland 39 51 52N 8 15W
Great Inagua I. 167 21 0N 73 20W
Gt. Indian Desert = Thar Desert 94 28 0N 72 0 E
Great Jarvis 151 47 39N 57 12W
Great Karoo = Groot Karoo 128 32 30 S 23 0 E
Great Lake 138 41 50 S 146 30 E
Great Lakes 153 44 0N 82 0W
Great Malvern 28 52 7N 2 19W
Great Massingham 29 52 47N 0 41 E
Great Missenden 29 51 42N 0 42W
Gt. Namaqualand = Groot Namakwaland 128 26 0 S 18 0 E
Great Orme's Head 31 53 20N 3 52W
Great Ouse, R. 29 52 20N 0 8 E
Great Palm I. 138 18 45 S 146 40 E
Great Papuan Plateau 135 6 30 S 142 25 E
Great Plains 50 45 0N 100 0W
Great Ruaha, R. 126 7 30 S 35 0 E
Great Salt Lake 160 41 0N 112 30W
Great Salt Lake Desert 160 40 20N 113 50W
Great Salt Plains Res. 159 36 40N 98 15W
Great Sandy Desert 136 21 0 S 124 0 E
Great Sandy I. = Fraser I. 139 25 15 S 153 0 E
Great Scarcies, R. 120 9 30N 12 40W
Great Shefford 28 51 29N 1 27W
Great Shelford 29 52 9N 0 9 E
Great Shunner Fell 32 54 22N 2 16W
Great Sitkin I. 147 52 0N 176 10W
Great Slave L. 152 61 23N 115 38W
Great Stour, R. 29 51 21N 1 15 E
Gt. Sugar Loaf, mt. 39 53 10N 6 10W
Great Torrington 30 50 57N 4 9W
Gt. Victoria Des. 137 29 30 S 126 30 E
Great Wall 106 38 30N 109 30 E
Gt. Waltham 29 51 47N 0 29 E
Great Whale, R. 150 55 20N 75 30W
Great Whernside, mt. 147 54 9N 1 59W
Great Winterhoek, mt. 128 33 07 S 19 10 E
Great Wyrley 28 52 40N 2 1W
Great Yarmouth 29 52 40N 1 45 E
Great Yeldham 29 52 1N 0 33 E
Greater Antilles 167 17 40N 74 0W
Greater Manchester □ 32 53 30N 2 15W
Greatham 33 54 38N 1 14W
Grebbestad 73 58 42N 11 15 E
Grebenka 80 50 9N 32 22 E
Greco, Mt. 64 41 48N 14 0 E
Gredos, Sierra de 56 40 20N 5 0W
Greece ■ 68 40 0N 23 0 E
Greeley, Colo., U.S.A. 158 40 30N 104 40W
Greeley, Nebr., U.S.A. 158 41 36N 98 32W
Green B. 156 45 0N 87 30W
Green Bay 156 44 30N 88 0W
Green C. 141 37 13 S 150 1 E
Green Cove Springs 157 29 59N 81 40W
Green Hammerton 33 54 2N 1 17W
Green Hd. 137 30 5 S 114 56 E
Green Is. 135 4 35 S 154 10 E
Green Island 143 45 55 S 170 26 E
Green Lowther, Mt. 35 55 22N 3 44W
Green R., Ky., U.S.A. 156 37 54N 87 30W
Green R., Utah, U.S.A. 161 39 0N 110 6W
Green R., Wyo., U.S.A. 160 43 2N 110 2W
Green R., Wyo., U.S.A. 160 41 44N 109 28W
Greenbush 158 48 46N 96 10W
Greencastle, U.K. 38 54 2N 6 5W
Greencastle, U.S.A. 156 39 40N 86 48W
Greene 162 42 20N 75 45W
Greenfield, Calif., U.S.A. 163 35 15N 119 0W
Greenfield, Calif., U.S.A. 163 36 19N 121 15W
Greenfield, Ind., U.S.A. 156 39 47N 85 51W
Greenfield, Iowa, U.S.A. 158 41 18N 94 28W
Greenfield, Mass., U.S.A. 162 42 38N 72 38W
Greenfield, Miss., U.S.A. 159 37 28N 93 50W
Greenhead 35 54 58N 2 31W
Greening 150 48 10N 74 55W
Greenisland 38 54 42N 5 50W
Greenland 12 66 0N 45 0W
Greenland Sea 12 73 0N 10 0W
Greenlaw 35 55 42N 2 28W
Greenock 34 55 57N 4 46W
Greenodd 32 54 14N 3 3W
Greenore 38 54 2N 6 8W
Greenore Pt. 39 52 15N 6 20W
Greenough, R. 137 28 54 S 115 36 E
Greenport 162 41 5N 72 23W
Greensboro, Ga., U.S.A. 157 33 34N 83 12W
Greensboro, Md., U.S.A. 162 38 59N 75 48W
Greensboro, N.C., U.S.A. 157 36 7N 79 46W
Greensburg, Ind., U.S.A. 156 39 20N 85 30W
Greensburg, Kans., U.S.A. 159 37 38N 99 20W
Greensburg, Pa., U.S.A. 156 40 18N 79 31W
Greenstone Pt. 36 57 55N 5 38W
Greenville, Liberia 120 5 7N 9 6W
Greenville, Ala., U.S.A. 157 31 50N 86 37W
Greenville, Calif., U.S.A. 160 40 8N 121 0W
Greenville, Ill., U.S.A. 158 38 53N 89 22W
Greenville, Me., U.S.A. 151 45 30N 69 32W
Greenville, Mich., U.S.A. 156 43 12N 85 14W
Greenville, Miss., U.S.A. 159 33 25N 91 0W
Greenville, N.C., U.S.A. 157 35 37N 77 26W
Greenville, N.H., U.S.A. 162 42 46N 71 49W
Greenville, N.Y., U.S.A. 162 42 25N 74 1W
Greenville, Ohio, U.S.A. 156 40 5N 84 38W
Greenville, Pa., U.S.A. 156 41 23N 80 22W
Greenville, S.C., U.S.A. 157 34 54N 82 24W
Greenville, Tenn., U.S.A. 157 36 13N 82 51W
Greenville, Tex., U.S.A. 159 33 5N 96 5W
Greenwater Lake Prov. Park 153 52 32N 103 30W
Greenway 31 51 56N 4 49W
Greenwich, U.K. 29 51 28N 0 0
Greenwich, Conn., U.S.A. 162 41 1N 73 38W
Greenwich, N.Y., U.S.A. 162 43 2N 73 36W
Greenwood, Can. 152 49 10N 118 40W
Greenwood, Miss., U.S.A. 159 33 30N 90 4W
Greenwood, S.C., U.S.A. 157 34 13N 82 13W
Greenwood, Mt. 136 13 48 S 130 4 E
Gregory 158 43 14N 99 20W
Gregory Downs 138 18 35 S 138 45 E
Gregory, L. 139 28 55 S 139 0 E
Gregory L. 136 20 5 S 127 0 E
Gregory, L. 137 25 38 S 119 58 E
Gregory Lake 136 20 10 S 127 30 E
Gregory, R. 138 17 53 S 139 17 E
Gregory Ra., Queens., Austral. 138 19 30 S 143 40 E
Gregory Ra., W. Austral., Austral. 136 21 20 S 121 12 E
Greian Hd. 36 57 1N 7 30W
Greiffenberg 48 53 6N 13 57 E
Greifswald 48 54 6N 13 23 E
Greifswalder Bodden 48 54 12N 13 35 E
Greifswalder Oie 48 54 15N 13 55 E
Grein 52 48 14N 14 51 E
Greiner Wald 52 48 30N 15 0 E
Greiz 48 50 39N 12 12 E
Gremikha 78 67 50N 39 40 E
Grenå 73 56 25N 10 53 E
Grenada 159 33 45N 89 50W
Grenada I. ■ 167 12 10N 61 40W
Grenade 44 43 47N 1 17 E
Grenadines 167 12 40N 61 20W
Grenchen 50 47 12N 7 24 E
Grenen 73 57 44N 10 40 E
Grenfell, Austral. 141 33 52 S 148 8 E
Grenfell, Can. 153 50 30N 102 56W
Grenoble 45 45 12N 5 42 E
Grenora 158 48 38N 103 54W
Grenville, C. 138 12 0 S 143 13 E
Grenville Chan. 152 53 40N 129 46W
Gréoux-les-Bains 45 43 55N 5 52 E
Gresham 160 45 30N 122 31W
Gresik 103 9 13 S 112 38 E
Gressoney St. Jean 62 45 49N 7 47 E
Greta 32 54 9N 2 36W
Greta R. 32 54 36N 3 5W
Gretna, U.K. 35 54 59N 3 4W
Gretna, U.S.A. 159 30 0N 90 2W
Gretna Green 35 55 0N 3 3W
Gretton 29 52 33N 0 40W
Grevelingen Krammer 46 51 44N 4 0 E
Greven 48 52 7N 7 36 E
Grevená 68 40 4N 21 25 E
Grevená □ 68 40 2N 21 25 E
Grevenbroich 48 51 6N 6 32 E
Grevenmacher 47 49 41N 6 26 E
Grevesmühlen 48 53 51N 11 10 E
Grevie 73 56 22N 12 46 E
Grevinge 73 55 48N 11 34 E
Grey, C. 138 13 0 S 136 35 E
Grey, R. 143 42 27 S 171 12 E
Grey Range 133 27 0 S 143 30 E
Grey Res. 151 48 20N 56 30W
Greyabbey 38 54 32N 5 35W
Greybull 160 44 30N 108 3W
Greystone 32 54 39N 2 52W
Greystones 39 53 9N 6 4W
Greytown, N.Z. 142 41 5 S 175 29 E
Greytown, S. Afr. 129 29 1 S 30 36 E
Gribanovskiy 81 51 28N 41 50 E
Gribbell I. 152 53 23N 129 0W
Gribbin Head 30 50 18N 4 41W
Gridley 160 39 27N 121 47W
Griekwastad 128 28 49 S 23 15 E
Griffin 157 33 17N 84 14W
Griffith 141 34 18 S 146 2 E
Griffith Mine 153 50 47N 93 25W
Grigoryevka 84 50 48N 58 18 E
Grijalva, R. 164 16 20N 92 20W
Grijpskerk 46 53 16N 6 18 E
Grillby 72 59 38N 17 15 E

Grim, C Gus

Grim, C.	133	40 45 S	144 45 E
Grimaïlov	80	49 20N	26 5 E
Grimari	117	5 43N	20 0 E
Grimbergen	47	50 56N	4 22 E
Grimeton	73	57 6N	12 25 E
Griminish Pt.	36	57 40N	7 30W
Grimma	48	51 14N	12 44 E
Grimmen	48	54 6N	13 2 E
Grimsay I.	36	57 29N	7 12W
Grimsby	33	53 35N	0 5W
Grimsel Pass	51	46 34N	8 23 E
Grímsey	74	66 33N	18 0W
Grimshaw	152	56 10N	117 40W
Grimstad	71	58 22N	8 35 E
Grindelwald	50	46 38N	8 2 E
Grindsted	73	55 46N	8 55 E
Grindstone Island	151	47 25N	62 0W
Grindu	70	44 44N	26 50 E
Grinduşul, Mt.	70	46 40N	26 7 E
Griñón	56	40 13N	3 51W
Grinnell	158	41 45N	92 43W
Grip	71	63 16N	7 37 E
Griqualand East	129	30 30 S	29 0 E
Griqualand West	128	28 40 S	23 30 E
Griquet	151	51 30N	55 35W
Grisolles	44	43 49N	1 19 E
Grisons □	49	46 40N	9 30 E
Grisslehamm	72	60 5N	18 49 E
Grita, La	174	8 8N	71 59W
Gritley	37	58 56N	2 45W
Grivegnée	47	50 37N	5 36 E
Griz Nez	43	50 50N	1 35 E
Grizebeck	32	54 16N	3 10W
Grmeč Planina	63	44 43N	16 16 E
Groais I.	151	50 55N	55 35W
Groblersdal	129	25 15 S	29 25 E
Grobming	52	47 27N	13 54 E
Grocka	66	44 40N	20 42 E
Grodek	80	52 46N	23 38 E
Grodkow	54	50 43N	17 40 E
Grodno	80	53 42N	23 52 E
Grodzisk Mazowiecki	54	52 7N	20 37 E
Grodzisk Wlkp.	54	52 15N	16 22 E
Grodzyanka	80	53 31N	28 42 E
Groenlo	46	52 2N	6 37 E
Groesbeck	159	31 32N	96 34W
Groesbeek	46	51 47N	5 58 E
Groix	42	47 38N	3 29W
Groix, I. de	42	47 38N	3 28W
Grójec	54	51 50N	20 58 E
Grolloo	46	52 56N	6 41 E
Gronau	48	52 13N	7 2 E
Grong	74	64 25N	12 8 E
Groningen	46	53 15N	6 35 E
Groningen □	46	53 16N	6 40 E
Groninger Wad	46	53 27N	6 30 E
Grönskåra	73	57 5N	15 43 E
Gronsveld	47	50 49N	5 44 E
Groom	159	35 12N	100 59W
Groomsport	38	54 41N	5 37W
Groot Berg, R.	128	32 50 S	18 20 E
Groot-Brakrivier	128	34 2 S	22 18 E
Groot Karoo	128	32 35 S	23 0 E
Groot Namakwaland = Namaland	128	26 0 S	18 0 E
Groot, R.	128	33 10 S	23 35 E
Groote Eylandt	138	14 0 S	136 50 E
Grootebroek	46	52 41N	5 13 E
Grootfontein	128	19 31 S	18 6 E
Grootlaagte, R.	128	21 10 S	21 20 E
Gros C.	152	61 59N	113 32W
Grosa, Punta	59	39 6N	1 36 E
Grósio	62	46 18N	10 17 E
Grosne, R.	45	46 30N	4 40 E
Gross Glockner	52	47 5N	12 40 E
Gross Ottersleben	48	52 5N	11 33 E
Grossa, Pta.	170	1 20N	50 0W
Grossenbrode	48	54 21N	11 4 E
Grossenhain	48	51 17N	13 32 E
Grosseto	62	42 45N	11 7 E
Grossgerungs	52	48 34N	14 57 E
Grosswater B.	151	54 20N	57 40W
Grote Gette, R.	47	50 51N	5 6 E
Grote Nete, R.	47	51 8N	4 34 E
Groton, U.S.A.	162	41 22N	72 12W
Groton, U.S.A.	162	42 36N	76 22W
Grottaglie	65	40 32N	17 25 E
Grottaminarda	65	41 5N	15 4 E
Grouard Mission	152	55 33N	116 9W
Grouin, Pointe du	42	48 43N	1 51W
Groundhog, R.	150	48 45N	82 20W
Grouse Creek	160	41 51N	113 57W
Grouw	46	53 5N	5 51 E
Groveland	163	37 50N	120 14W
Grovelsjön	72	62 6N	12 16 E
Grover City	163	35 7N	120 37W
Groveton	159	31 5N	95 4W
Groznjan	63	45 22N	13 43 E
Groznyy	83	43 20N	45 45 E
Grubbenvorst	47	51 25N	6 9 E
Grubišno Polje	66	45 44N	17 12 E
Grudusk	54	53 3N	20 38 E
Grudziadz	54	53 30N	18 47 E
Gruinard B.	36	57 56N	5 35W
Gruissan	44	43 8N	3 7 E
Grumo Appula	65	41 2N	16 43 E
Grums	72	59 22N	13 5 E
Grünau	125	27 45 S	18 26 E
Grünberg	48	50 37N	8 55 E
Grundy Center	158	42 22N	92 45W
Grungedal	71	59 44N	7 43 E
Gruting Voe	36	60 12N	1 32W
Gruver	159	36 19N	101 20W
Gruyères	50	46 35N	7 4 E
Gruza	66	43 54N	20 46 E
Gryazi	81	52 30N	39 58 E
Gryazovets	81	58 50N	40 20 E
Grybów	54	49 36N	20 55 E
Grycksbo	72	60 40N	15 29 E
Gryfice	54	53 55N	15 13 E
Gryfino	54	53 16N	14 29 E
Grytgöl	73	58 49N	15 33 E
Grythyttan	72	59 41N	14 32 E
Grytviken	13	53 50 S	37 10W
Gstaad	50	46 28N	7 18 E
Gua	99	22 18N	85 20 E
Gua Musang	101	4 53N	101 58 E
Guacanayabo, Golfo de	166	20 40N	77 20W
Guacara	174	10 14N	67 53W
Guachípas	172	25 40 S	65 30W
Guachiría, R.	174	5 30N	71 30W
Guadajoz, R.	57	37 50N	4 51W
Guadalajara, Mexico	164	20 40N	103 20W
Guadalajara, Spain	58	40 37N	3 12W
Guadalajara □	58	40 47N	3 0W
Guadalcanal	57	38 5N	5 52W
Guadalcanal, I.	130	9 32 S	160 12 E
Guadalén, R.	59	38 30N	3 7W
Guadales	172	34 30 S	67 55W
Guadalete, R.	57	36 45N	5 47W
Guadalhorce, R.	57	36 50N	4 42W
Guadalimar, R.	59	38 10N	2 53W
Guadalmena, R.	59	38 31N	2 50W
Guadalmez, R.	57	38 33N	4 42W
Guadalope, R.	58	41 0N	0 13W
Guadalquivir, R.	57	38 0N	4 0W
Guadalupe, Brazil	170	6 44 S	43 47W
Guadalupe, Spain	57	39 27N	5 17W
Guadalupe, U.S.A.	163	34 59N	120 33W
Guadalupe Bravos	164	31 20N	106 10W
Guadalupe de los Reyes	164	25 23N	104 15W
Guadalupe I.	131	29 0N	118 50W
Guadalupe Pk.	161	31 50N	105 30W
Guadalupe, R.	159	29 25N	97 30W
Guadalupe, Sierra de	55	39 28N	5 30W
Guadalupe y Calvo	164	26 6N	106 58W
Guadarrama, Sierra de	56	41 0N	4 0W
Guadeloupe, I.	167	16 20N	61 40W
Guadeloupe Passage	167	16 50N	68 15W
Guadiamar, R.	57	37 9N	6 20W
Guadiana Menor, R.	59	37 45N	3 7W
Guadiana, R.	57	37 45N	7 35W
Guadiaro, R.	57	36 39N	5 17W
Guadiato, R.	57	37 55N	4 53W
Guadiela, R.	58	40 30N	2 23W
Guadix	59	37 18N	3 11W
Guafo, Boca del	176	43 35 S	74 0W
Guaina	174	5 9N	63 36W
Guainía □	174	2 30N	69 00W
Guaíra	173	24 5 S	54 10W
Guaira, La	174	10 36N	66 56W
Guaitecas, Islas	176	44 0 S	74 30W
Guajará-Mirim	174	10 50 S	65 20W
Guajira, La □	174	11 30N	72 30W
Guajira, Pen. de la	167	12 0N	72 0W
Gualan	166	15 8N	89 22W
Gualdo Tadino	63	43 14N	12 46 E
Gualeguay	172	33 10 S	59 20W
Gualeguaychú	172	33 3 S	58 31W
Guam I.	130	13 27N	144 45 E
Guamá	170	1 37 S	47 29W
Guama	174	10 16N	68 49W
Guamá, R.	170	1 29 S	48 30W
Guamareyes	174	0 30 S	73 0W
Guaminí	172	37 1 S	62 28W
Guampí, Sierra de	174	6 0N	65 35W
Guamuchil	164	25 25N	108 3W
Guanabacoa	166	23 8N	82 18W
Guanabara □	173	23 0 S	43 25W
Guanacaste	166	10 40N	85 30W
Guanacaste, Cordillera del	166	10 40N	85 4W
Guanacevío	164	25 40N	106 0W
Guanajay	166	22 56N	82 42W
Guanajuato	164	21 0N	101 20W
Guanajuato □	164	20 40N	101 20W
Guanambi	171	14 13 S	42 47W
Guanare	174	8 42N	69 12W
Guanare, R.	174	8 50N	68 50W
Guandacol	172	29 30 S	68 40W
Guane	166	22 10N	84 0W
Guanhães	171	18 47 S	42 57W
Guanica	147	17 58N	66 55W
Guanipa, R.	174	9 20N	63 30W
Guanta	174	10 14N	64 36W
Guantánamo	167	20 10N	75 20W
Guapí	174	2 36N	77 54W
Guápiles	166	10 10N	83 46W
Guaporé	173	12 0 S	64 0W
Guaporé, R.	173	13 0 S	63 0W
Guaqui	174	16 41 S	68 54W
Guara, Sierra de	58	42 19N	0 15W
Guarabira	170	6 51 S	35 29W
Guarapari	173	20 40 S	40 30W
Guarapuava	171	25 20 S	51 30W
Guaratinguetá	173	22 49 S	45 9W
Guaratuba	173	25 53 S	48 38W
Guard Bridge	35	56 21N	2 52W
Guarda	56	40 32N	7 20W
Guarda □	56	40 40N	7 20W
Guardafui, C. = Asir, Ras	91	11 55N	51 10 E
Guardamar del Segura	59	38 5N	0 39W
Guardavalle	65	38 31N	16 30 E
Guardia, La	56	41 56N	8 52W
Guardiagrele	63	42 11N	14 11 E
Guardo	56	42 47N	4 50W
Guareña	57	38 51N	6 6W
Guareña, R.	56	41 25N	5 25W
Guaria □	172	25 45N	56 30W
Guárico □	174	8 40N	66 35W
Guarujá	173	24 2 S	46 25W
Guarus	173	21 30 S	41 20W
Guasave	164	25 34N	108 27W
Guasdualito	174	7 15N	70 44W
Guasipati	174	7 28N	61 54W
Guasopa	135	9 12 S	152 56 E
Guastalla	62	44 55N	10 40 E
Guatemala	166	14 40N	90 30W
Guatemala ■	166	15 40N	90 30W
Guatire	174	10 28N	66 32W
Guaviare, R.	174	3 30N	71 0W
Guaxupé	173	21 10 S	47 5W
Guayabal	174	4 43N	71 37W
Guayama	147	17 59N	66 7W
Guayaquil	174	2 15 S	79 52W
Guayaquil, Golfo de	174	3 10 S	81 0W
Guaymallen	172	32 50 S	68 45W
Guaymas	164	27 50N	111 0W
Guba, Ethiopia	123	4 52N	39 18 E
Guba, Zaïre	127	10 38 S	26 27 E
Gubakha	84	58 52N	57 36 E
Gubam	135	8 39 S	141 53 E
Gúbbio	63	43 20N	12 34 E
Gubio	121	12 30N	12 42 E
Gubkin	81	51 17N	37 32 E
Guča	66	43 46N	20 15 E
Guchil	101	5 35N	102 10 E
Gudalur	97	11 30N	76 29 E
Gudata	83	43 7N	40 32 E
Gudbrandsdal	75	61 33N	10 0 E
Guddu Barrage	93	28 30N	69 50 E
Gudenå	73	56 27N	9 40 E
Gudermes	83	43 24N	46 20 E
Gudhjem	73	55 12N	14 58 E
Gudiña, La	56	42 4N	7 8W
Gudivada	96	16 30N	81 15 E
Gudiyatam	97	12 57N	78 55 E
Gudmundra	72	62 56N	17 47 E
Gudrun, gasfield	19	58 50N	1 48 E
Gudur	97	14 12N	79 55 E
Guebwiller	43	47 55N	7 12 E
Guecho	58	43 21N	2 59W
Guéckédou	120	8 40N	10 5W
Guelma	119	36 25N	7 29 E
Guelph	150	43 35N	80 20W
Guelt es Stel	118	35 12N	3 1 E
Guelttara	118	29 23N	2 10W
Guemar	119	33 30N	6 57 E
Guéméné-Penfao	42	47 38N	1 50W
Guéméné-sur-Scorff	42	48 4N	3 13W
Güemes	172	24 50 S	65 0W
Guéné	121	11 44N	3 16 E
Guer	42	47 54N	2 8W
Guérande	42	47 20N	2 26W
Guerche, La	42	47 57N	1 16W
Guerche-sur-l'Aubois, La	43	46 58N	2 56 E
Guercif	118	34 14N	3 21W
Guéréda	124	14 31N	22 5 E
Guéret	44	46 11N	1 51 E
Guérigny	43	47 6N	3 10 E
Guernica	58	43 19N	2 40W
Guernsey	158	42 19N	104 45W
Guernsey I.	42	49 30N	2 35W
Guerrara, Oasis, Alg.	119	32 51N	4 35 E
Guerrara, Saoura, Alg.	118	28 5N	0 8W
Guerrero □	165	17 30N	100 0W
Guerzim	118	29 45N	1 47W
Güeş ti	70	44 48N	25 19 E
Guestling Green	29	50 53N	0 40 E
Gueugnon	45	45 36N	4 3 E
Gueydan	159	30 3N	92 30W
Guezendi = Ghesendor	119	21 14N	18 14 E
Guglia, P. dal	51	46 28N	9 45 E
Guglionesi	63	51 55N	14 54 E
Guhra	93	27 36N	56 8 E
Guia Lopes da Laguna	173	21 26 S	56 7W
Guiana Highlands	174	5 0N	60 0W
Guibes	128	26 41 S	16 49 E
Guider	121	9 55N	13 59 E
Guidimouni	121	13 42N	9 31 E
Guiglo	120	6 45N	7 30W
Guija	125	34 35 S	33 15 E
Guijo de Coria	56	40 6N	6 28W
Guildford	29	51 14N	0 34W
Guilford, Conn., U.S.A.	162	41 15N	72 40W
Guilford, Me., U.S.A.	151	45 12N	69 25W
Guillaumes	45	44 5N	6 52 E
Guillestre	45	44 39N	6 40 E
Guilsfield	31	52 42N	3 9W
Guilvinec	42	47 48N	4 17W
Guimarães, Braz.	170	2 9 S	44 35W
Guimarães, Port.	56	41 28N	8 24W
Guimaras I.	103	10 35N	122 37 E
Guinea ■	120	10 20N	10 0W
Guinea Bissau ■	120	12 0N	15 0W
Guinea, Gulf of	121	3 0N	2 30 E
Guinea, Port. = Guinea Bissau	120	12 0N	15 0W
Güines	166	22 50N	82 0W
Guingamp	42	48 34N	3 10W
Guipavas	42	48 26N	4 29W
Guipúzcoa □	58	43 12N	2 15W
Guir, O.	118	39 29N	2 58W
Guirgo	121	11 54N	1 21W
Güiria	174	10 32N	62 18W
Guisborough	33	54 32N	1 2W
Guiscard	43	49 40N	3 0 E
Guise	43	49 52N	3 35 E
Guitiriz	56	43 11N	7 50W
Guivan	103	11 5N	125 55 E
Gujan-Mestras	44	44 38N	1 4W
Gujar Khan	84	33 15N	73 21 E
Gujarat □	94	23 20N	71 0 E
Gujranwala	94	32 10N	74 12 E
Gujrat	94	32 40N	74 2 E
Gukhothae	101	17 2N	99 50 E
Gukovo	83	48 1N	39 58 E
Gulak	121	10 50N	13 30 E
Gulargambone	141	31 20 S	148 30 E
Gulbahar	93	35 5N	69 10 E
Gulbargâ	96	17 20N	76 50 E
Gulbene	80	57 8N	26 52 E
Gulcha	85	40 19N	73 26 E
Guldborg Sd.	73	54 39N	11 50 E
Guledgud	97	16 3N	75 48 E
Gulf Basin	136	15 20 S	129 0 E
Gulfport	159	30 28N	89 3W
Gulgong	141	32 20 S	149 30 E
Gulistan, Pak.	94	30 36N	66 35 E
Gulistan, U.S.S.R.	85	40 29N	68 46 E
Gulkana	147	62 15N	145 48W
Gull Lake	153	50 10N	108 29W
Gullane	35	56 2N	2 50W
Gullegem	47	50 51N	3 13 E
Gullringen	73	57 48N	15 44 E
Güllük	69	37 12N	27 36 E
Gulma	121	12 40N	4 23 E
Gulmarg	95	34 3N	74 25 E
Gulnam	123	6 55N	29 30 E
Gulnare	140	33 27 S	138 27 E
Gulpaigan	92	33 26N	50 20 E
Gulpen	47	50 49N	5 53 E
Gülpinar	68	39 32N	26 10 E
Gulshad	76	46 45N	74 25 E
Gulsvik	71	60 24N	9 38 E
Gulu	126	2 48N	32 17 E
Gulwe	126	6 30 S	36 25 E
Gulyaypole	82	47 45N	36 21 E
Gum Lake	140	32 42 S	143 9 E
Gumal, R.	94	32 5N	70 5 E
Gumbaz	94	30 2N	69 0 E
Gumel	121	12 39N	9 22 E
Gumiel de Hizán	58	41 46N	3 41W
Gumlu	138	19 53 S	147 41 E
Gumma-ken □	111	36 30N	138 20 E
Gummersbach	48	51 2N	7 32 E
Gummi	121	12 4N	5 9 E
Gümüşane	92	40 30N	39 30 E
Gümüşhaciköy	82	40 50N	35 18 E
Gumzai	103	5 28 S	134 42 E
Guna	94	24 40N	77 19 E
Guna Mt.	123	11 50N	37 40 E
Gundagai	141	35 3 S	148 6 E
Gundih	103	7 10 S	110 56 E
Gundlakamma, R.	97	15 30N	80 15 E
Gunebang	141	33 5 S	146 38 E
Gungal	141	32 17 S	150 32 E
Gungi	123	10 20N	38 3 E
Gungu	124	5 43 S	19 20 E
Gunisao L.	153	53 33N	96 15W
Gunisao, R.	153	53 56N	97 53W
Gunnedah	141	30 59 S	150 15 E
Gunniguldrie	141	33 12 S	146 8 E
Gunningbar Cr.	141	31 14 S	147 6 E
Gunnison, Colo., U.S.A.	161	38 32N	106 56W
Gunnison, Utah, U.S.A.	160	39 11N	111 48W
Gunnison, R.	161	38 50N	108 30W
Gunnworth	153	51 20N	108 9W
Guntakal	97	15 11N	77 27 E
Guntersville	157	34 18N	86 16W
Guntong	101	4 36N	101 3 E
Guntur	96	16 23N	80 30 E
Gunungapi	103	6 45 S	126 30 E
Gunungsitoli	102	1 15N	97 30 E
Gunungsugih	102	4 58 S	105 7 E
Gunupur	96	19 5N	83 50 E
Gunworth	153	51 20N	108 10W
Gunza	124	10 50 S	13 50 E
Gunzenhausen	49	49 6N	10 45 E
Gupis	95	36 15N	73 20 E
Gura	94	25 12N	71 39 E
Gura Humorului	70	47 35N	25 53 E
Gura Teghii	70	45 30N	26 25 E
Gurage, mt.	123	8 20N	38 20 E
Gurchan	92	34 55N	49 25 E
Gurdaspur	94	32 5N	75 25 E
Gurdon	159	33 55N	93 10W
Gurdzhaani	83	41 43N	45 52 E
Gurgan	93	36 51N	54 25 E
Gurgaon	94	28 33N	77 10 E
Gurghiu, Munţii	70	46 41N	25 15 E
Gurguéia, R.	170	6 50 S	43 24W
Guria	62	44 30N	9 0 E
Gurk, R.	52	46 48N	14 20 E
Gurkha	95	28 5N	84 40 E
Gurla Mandhata	95	30 30N	81 10 E
Gurley	139	29 45 S	149 48 E
Gurnard's Head	30	50 12N	5 37W
Gurnet Pt.	162	42 1N	70 34W
Gurrumbah	138	17 30 S	144 55 E
Gurun	101	5 49N	100 27 E
Gürün	92	38 41N	37 22 E
Gurupá	175	1 20 S	51 45W
Gurupá, I. Grande de	175	1 0 S	51 45W
Gurupi	171	11 43 S	49 4W
Gurupi, R.	170	3 20 S	47 20W
Gurupi, Serra do	170	5 0 S	47 30W
Guryev	83	47 5N	52 0 E
Gus	126	3 2N	36 57 E

Gus-Khrsutalnyy	81	55 42N	40 35 E
Gusau	121	12 18N	6 31 E
Gusev	80	54 35N	22 20 E
Gushiago	121	9 55N	0 15W
Gusinje	66	42 35N	19 50 E
Gúspini	64	39 32N	8 38 E
Gusselby	72	59 38N	15 14 E
Güssing	53	47 3N	16 20 E
Gustanj	63	46 36N	14 49 E
Gustavus	147	58 25N	135 58W
Gustine	163	37 21N	121 0W
Güstrow	48	53 47N	12 12 E
Gusum	73	58 16N	16 30 E
Gŭtaia	70	45 26N	21 30 E
Gütersloh	48	51 54N	8 25 E
Gutha	137	28 58 S	115 55 E
Guthalungra	138	19 52 S	147 50 E
Guthrie	159	35 55N	97 30W
Guttannen	51	46 38N	8 18 E
Guttenberg	158	42 46N	91 10W
Guyana ■	174	5 0N	59 0W
Guyenne	44	44 30N	0 40 E
Guyman	159	36 45N	101 30W
Guyra	139	30 15 S	151 40 E
Guzar	85	38 36N	66 15 E
Guzmán, Laguna de	164	31 25N	107 25W
Gwa	98	17 30N	94 40 E
Gwaai	127	19 15 S	27 45 E
Gwabegar	141	30 31 S	149 0 E
Gwadabawa	121	13 20N	5 15 E
Gwādar	93	25 10N	62 18 E
Gwagwada	121	10 15N	7 15 E
Gwalchmai	31	53 16N	4 23W
Gwalia	137	28 54 S	121 20 E
Gwalior	94	26 12N	78 10 E
Gwanara	121	18 55N	3 10 E
Gwanda	127	20 55 S	29 0 E
Gwandu	121	12 30N	4 41 E
Gwane	126	4 45N	25 48 E
Gwaram	121	11 15N	9 51 E
Gwarzo	121	12 20N	8 55 E
Gwasero	121	9 30N	8 30 E
Gwaun-Cae-Gurwen	31	51 46N	3 51W
Gweebarra B.	38	54 52N	8 21W
Gweedore	38	55 4N	8 15W
Gweek	30	50 6N	5 12W
Gwelo	125	19 28 S	29 45 E
Gwennap	30	50 12N	5 9W
Gwent □	31	51 45N	2 55W
Gweta	128	20 12 S	25 17 E
Gwi	121	9 0N	7 10 E
Gwinn	156	46 15N	87 29W
Gwio Kura	121	12 40N	11 2 E
Gwolu	120	10 58N	1 59W
Gwoza	121	11 12N	13 40 E
Gwyddelwern	31	53 2N	3 23W
Gwydir, R.	139	29 27 S	149 48 E
Gwynedd □	31	53 0N	4 0W
Gya La	95	28 45N	84 45 E
Gyangtse	99	28 50N	89 33 E
Gydanskiy P-ov.	76	70 0N	78 0 E
Gyland	71	58 24N	6 45 E
Gympie	139	26 11 S	152 38 E
Gyobingauk	98	18 13N	95 39 E
Gyoda	111	36 10N	139 30 E
Gyoma	53	46 56N	20 58 E
Gyöngyös	53	47 48N	20 15 E
Györ	53	47 41N	17 40 E
Györ-Sopron □	53	47 40N	17 20 E
Gypsum Palace	140	32 37 S	144 9 E
Gypsum Pt.	152	61 53N	114 35W
Gypsumville	153	51 45N	98 40W
Gyttorp	72	59 31N	14 58 E
Gyula	53	46 38N	21 17 E
Gzhatsk = Gagarin	80	55 30N	35 0 E

H

Ha Coi	100	21 26N	107 46 E
Ha Dong	100	20 58N	105 46 E
Ha Giang	100	22 50N	104 59 E
Ha Nam = Phu-Ly	100	20 35N	105 50 E
Ha Tien	101	10 23N	104 29 E
Ha Tinh	100	18 20N	105 54 E
Ha Trung	100	20 0N	105 50 E
Haa, The	36	60 20N	1 0 E
Haacht	47	50 59N	4 37 E
Haag	49	48 11N	12 12 E
Haaksbergen	46	52 9N	6 45 E
Haaltert	47	50 55N	4 1 E
Haamstede	47	51 42N	3 45 E
Haapamäki	74	62 18N	24 28 E
Haapsalu	80	58 56N	23 30 E
Haarby	73	55 13N	10 8 E
Haarlem	46	52 23N	4 39 E
Haast	143	43 51 S	169 1 E
Haast P.	143	44 6 S	169 21 E
Haast, R.	143	43 50 S	169 2 E
Haastrecht	46	52 0N	4 47 E
Hab Nadi Chauki	94	25 0N	66 50 E
Hab, R.	93	25 15N	67 8 E
Haba	92	27 10N	47 0 E
Habana, La	166	23 8N	82 22W
Habaswein	126	1 2N	39 30 E
Habay	152	58 50N	118 44W
Habay-la-Neuve	47	49 44N	5 38 E
Habiganj	98	24 24N	91 30 E
Hablingbo	73	57 12N	18 16 E
Habo	73	57 55N	14 6 E
Haccourt	47	50 44N	5 40 E
Hachenburg	48	50 40N	7 49 E
Hachijō-Jima	111	33 5N	139 45 E
Hachinohe	112	40 30N	141 29 E
Hachiōji	111	35 30N	139 30 E
Hachŏn	107	40 29N	129 2 E
Hachy	47	49 42N	5 41 E
Hacketstown	39	52 52N	6 35W
Hackett	152	52 9N	112 28W
Hackettstown	162	40 51N	74 50W
Hackney	29	51 33N	0 2W
Hackthorpe	32	54 37N	2 42W
Hadali	94	32 16N	72 11 E
Hadarba, Ras	122	22 4N	36 51 E
Hadd, Ras al	93	22 35N	59 50 E
Haddenham	29	51 46N	0 56W
Haddington	35	55 57N	2 48W
Haddon Rig	141	31 27 S	147 52 E
Hadeija	121	12 30N	10 5 E
Hadeija, R.	121	12 20N	9 30W
Haden	139	27 13 S	151 54 E
Hadera	90	32 27N	34 55 E
Haderslev	73	55 15N	9 30 E
Hadhra	122	20 10N	41 5 E
Hadhramaut = Hadramawt	91	15 30N	49 30 E
Hadibu	91	12 35N	54 2 E
Hadjeb el Aïoun	119	35 21N	9 32 E
Hadleigh	29	52 3N	0 58 E
Hadley	28	52 42N	2 28W
Hadlow	29	51 12N	0 20 E
Hadong	107	35 5N	127 44 E
Hadramawt	91	15 30N	49 30 E
Hadrians Wall	35	55 0N	2 30W
Hadsten	73	56 19N	10 3 E
Hadsund	73	56 44N	10 8 E
Haeju	107	38 3N	125 45 E
Haenam	107	34 34N	126 15 E
Haerhpin	107	45 45N	126 45 E
Hafar al Batin	92	28 25N	46 50 E
Hafizabad	94	32 5N	73 40 E
Haflong	98	25 10N	93 5 E
Hafnarfjörður	74	64 4N	21 57W
Haft-Gel	92	31 30N	49 32 E
Hafun	91	10 25N	51 16 E
Hafun, Ras	91	10 29N	51 20 E
Hagalil	90	32 53N	35 18 E
Hagar Banga	117	10 40N	22 45 E
Hagari, R.	97	14 0N	76 45 E
Hagemeister I.	147	58 42N	161 0W
Hagen	48	51 21N	7 29 E
Hagenow	48	53 25N	11 10 E
Hagerman	159	33 5N	104 22W
Hagerstown	156	39 39N	77 46W
Hagetmau	44	43 39N	0 37W
Hagfors	72	60 3N	13 45 E
Häggenås	72	63 24N	14 55 E
Hagi, Iceland	74	65 28N	23 25W
Hagi, Japan	110	34 30N	131 30 E
Hagion Evstratios	68	39 30N	25 0 E
Hagion Oros	68	40 37N	24 6 E
Hags Hd.	39	52 57N	9 30W
Hague, C. de la	42	49 44N	1 56W
Hague, The = s'-Gravenhage	47	52 7N	4 17 E
Haguenau	43	48 49N	7 47 E
Hai □	126	3 10 S	37 10 E
Hai Duong	100	20 56N	106 19 E
Haian, Kiangsu, China	109	32 37N	120 33 E
Haian, Kwangtung, China	109	20 18N	110 11 E
Haich'eng, Fukien, China	109	24 24N	117 51 E
Haich'eng, Liaoning, China	107	40 52N	122 45 E
Haichou	107	34 34N	119 6 E
Haichou Wan	107	35 0N	119 30 E
Haidar Khel	94	33 58N	68 38 E
Haifa	90	32 46N	35 0 E
Haifeng	109	22 59N	115 21 E
Haig	137	30 55 S	126 10 E
Haiger	48	50 44N	8 12 E
Haik'ang	109	20 56N	110 4 E
Haik'ou	100	20 5N	110 20 E
Hā'il	92	27 28N	42 2 E
Hailaerh	105	49 12N	119 42 E
Hailakandi	98	24 42N	92 34 E
Hailey	160	43 30N	114 15W
Haileybury	150	47 30N	79 38W
Hailin	107	44 32N	129 24 E
Hailing Tao	109	21 37N	111 65 E
Hailsham	29	50 52N	0 17 E
Hailun	105	47 27N	126 56 E
Hailung	107	42 30N	125 40 E
Hailuoto	74	65 3N	24 45 E
Haimen, Chekiang, China	109	28 39N	121 25 E
Haimen, Kwangtung, China	109	23 15N	116 35 E
Hainan	100	19 0N	110 0 E
Hainan Str. = Ch'iungcho Haihsia	100	20 10N	110 15 E
Hainaut □	47	50 30N	4 0 E
Hainburg	53	48 9N	16 56 E
Haines, Alaska, U.S.A.	147	59 20N	135 36W
Haines, Oreg., U.S.A.	160	44 51N	117 59W
Haines City	157	28 6N	81 35W
Haines Junction	147	60 45N	137 30W
Hainfeld	52	48 3N	15 48 E
Haining	109	30 23N	120 30 E
Hainton	33	53 21N	0 13W
Haiphong	100	20 47N	106 35 E
Hait'an Tao	109	25 35N	119 45 E
Haiti ■	167	19 0N	72 30W
Haiya Junc.	122	18 20N	36 40 E
Haiyang	107	36 45N	121 15 E
Haiyen	109	30 28N	120 57 E
Haiyüan, Kwangsi-Chuang, China	108	22 6N	107 25 E
Haiyüan, Ningsia Hui, China	106	36 32N	105 40 E
Haja	103	3 19 S	129 37 E
Hajdú-Bihar □	53	47 30N	21 30 E
Hajdúböszörmény	53	47 40N	21 30 E
Hajdúdurog	53	47 48N	21 30 E
Hajdúhadház	53	47 40N	21 40 E
Hajdúnánás	53	47 50N	21 26 E
Hajdúsámson	53	47 37N	21 42 E
Hajdúszobaszló	53	47 27N	21 22 E
Haji Langar	93	35 50N	79 20 E
Hajiganj	98	23 15N	90 50 E
Hajipur	95	25 45N	85 20 E
Hajr	93	24 0N	56 34 E
Haka	98	22 39N	93 37 E
Hakansson, Mts.	127	8 40 S	25 45 E
Hakantorp	73	58 18N	12 55 E
Håkantorp	73	58 18N	12 55 E
Hakataramea	143	44 30 S	170 30 E
Hakataramea, R.	143	44 35 S	170 40 E
Hakken-Zan	111	34 10N	135 54 E
Hakodate	112	41 45N	140 44 E
Hakota	111	36 5N	140 30 E
Haku-San	111	36 9N	136 46 E
Hakun	98	26 46N	95 42 E
Hala	93	25 43N	68 20 E
Hala Hu	105	38 15N	97 40 E
Halab = Aleppo	92	36 10N	37 15 E
Halabjah	92	35 10N	45 58 E
Halaib	122	22 5N	36 30 E
Halanzy	47	49 33N	5 44 E
Halawa	147	21 9N	156 47W
Halbe	122	19 40N	42 15 E
Halberstadt	48	51 53N	11 2 E
Halberton	30	50 55N	3 24W
Halcombe	142	40 8 S	175 30 E
Halcyon, Mt.	103	13 0N	121 30 E
Halden	72	59 7N	11 23 E
Haldensleben	48	52 17N	11 30 E
Haldia	99	22 5N	88 3 E
Haldwani	95	29 25N	79 30 E
Hale	32	53 24N	2 21W
Hale, R.	138	24 56 S	135 53 E
Haleakala Crater	147	20 43N	156 12W
Halen	47	50 57N	5 6 E
Halesowen	28	52 27N	2 2W
Halesworth	29	52 21N	1 30 E
Haleyville	157	34 15N	87 40W
Half Assini	120	5 1N	2 50W
Halfmoon B.	143	46 50 S	168 5 E
Halfway	160	44 56N	117 8W
Halfway, R.	152	56 12N	121 32W
Halhul	90	31 35N	35 7 E
Hali	122	18 40N	41 15 E
Haliburton	150	45 3N	78 30W
Halibut, oilfield	19	61 20N	1 36 E
Halifax, Austral.	138	18 32 S	146 22 E
Halifax, Can.	151	44 38N	63 35W
Halifax, U.K.	32	53 43N	1 51W
Halifax, U.S.A.	162	40 25N	76 55W
Halifax B.	138	18 50 S	147 0 E
Halifax I.	128	26 38 S	15 4 E
Halil, R.	93	27 40N	58 30 E
Halkirk	37	58 30N	3 30W
Hall	52	47 17N	11 30 E
Hall Land	12	81 20N	60 0W
Hall Pt.	136	15 40 S	124 23 E
Hallabro	73	56 22N	15 5 E
Halland	73	56 55N	12 50 E
Hallands län □	73	56 50N	12 50 E
Hallands Väderö	73	56 27N	12 34 E
Hallandsås	73	56 22N	13 0 E
Halle, Belg.	47	50 44N	4 13W
Halle, Nordrhein-Westfalen, Ger.	48	52 4N	8 20 E
Halle, Sachsen-Anhalt, Ger.	48	51 29N	12 0 E
Halle □	48	51 28N	11 58 E
Hällefors	72	59 47N	14 31 E
Hallein	52	47 40N	13 5 E
Hällekis	73	58 38N	13 27 E
Hallett	140	33 25 S	138 55 E
Hallettsville	159	29 28N	96 57W
Hallevadsholm	73	58 37N	11 33 E
Hällevadsholm	73	58 35N	11 33 E
Halley Bay	13	75 31 S	26 36W
Hallia, R.	96	16 55N	79 10 E
Halliday	158	47 20N	102 25W
Halliday L.	153	61 21N	108 56W
Hallim	107	33 24N	126 15 E
Hallingdal, R.	75	60 34N	9 12 E
Hallingskeid	71	60 40N	7 17 E
Hällnäs	74	64 19N	19 36 E
Hallock	153	48 47N	97 57W
Hallow	28	52 14N	2 15W
Hall's Creek	136	18 16 S	127 46 E
Hallsberg	72	59 5N	15 7 E
Hallstahammar	72	59 38N	16 15 E
Hallstatt	52	47 33N	13 38 E
Hallstavik	72	60 5N	18 37 E
Hallstead	162	41 56N	75 45W
Hallwiler See	50	47 16N	8 12 E
Hallworthy	30	50 38N	4 34W
Halmahera, I.	103	0 40N	128 0 E
Halmeu	70	47 57N	23 2 E
Halmstad	73	56 41N	12 52 E
Halq el Oued	119	36 53N	10 10 E
Hals	73	56 59N	10 18 E
Halsa	71	63 3N	8 14 E
Halsafjorden	71	63 5N	8 10 E
Hälsingborg = Helsingborg	73	56 3N	12 42 E
Halstad	158	47 21N	96 41W
Halstead	29	51 59N	0 39 E
Haltdalen	71	62 56N	11 8 E
Haltern	48	51 44N	7 10 E
Haltwhistle	35	54 58N	2 27W
Ham	128	49 44N	3 3 E
Ham Tan	101	10 40N	107 45 E
Ham Yen	100	22 4N	105 3 E
Hamā	92	35 5N	36 40 E
Hamab	128	28 7 S	19 16 E
Hamad	123	15 20N	33 32 E
Hamada	110	34 50N	132 10 E
Hamadān	92	34 52N	48 32 E
Hamadān □	92	35 0N	49 0 E
Hamadh	122	24 55N	39 3 E
Hamadia	118	35 28N	1 57 E
Hamakita	111	34 45N	137 47 E
Hamale	120	10 56N	2 45W
Hamamatsu	111	34 45N	137 45 E
Hamar	71	60 48N	11 7 E
Hamar Koke	123	51 5N	36 45 E
Hamarøy	74	68 5N	15 38 E
Hamâta, Gebel	122	24 17N	35 0 E
Hambantota	93	6 10N	81 10 E
Hamber Prov. Park	152	52 20N	118 0W
Hambledon	28	50 56N	1 6W
Hambleton Hills	33	54 17N	1 12W
Hamburg, Ger.	48	53 32N	9 59 E
Hamburg, Ark., U.S.A.	159	33 15N	91 47W
Hamburg, Iowa, U.S.A.	158	40 37N	95 38W
Hamburg, Pa., U.S.A.	162	40 33N	76 0W
Hamburg □	48	53 30N	10 0 E
Hamden	162	41 21N	72 56W
Hame	75	61 30N	24 0 E
Hämeen Lääni	75	61 24N	24 10 E
Hämeenlinna	75	61 0N	24 28 E
Hamelin Pool	137	26 22 S	114 20 E
Hamelin Pool Bay	137	26 10 S	114 5 E
Hameln	48	52 7N	9 24 E
Hamersley	136	22 20 S	117 37 E
Hamersley Ra.	136	22 0 S	117 45 E
Hamhung	107	40 0N	127 30 E
Hami	105	42 47N	93 32 E
Hamilton, Austral.	140	37 45 S	142 2 E
Hamilton, Can.	150	43 20N	79 50W
Hamilton, N.Z.	142	37 47 S	175 19 E
Hamilton, U.K.	35	55 47N	4 2W
Hamilton, Alas., U.S.A.	147	62 55N	164 0W
Hamilton, Mont., U.S.A.	160	46 20N	114 6W
Hamilton, N.Y., U.S.A.	162	42 49N	75 31W
Hamilton, Ohio, U.S.A.	156	39 20N	84 35W
Hamilton, Tex., U.S.A.	159	31 40N	98 5W
Hamilton Downs	106	21 25 S	142 23 E
Hamilton, gasfield	19	56 54N	2 13 E
Hamilton Hotel	138	22 45 S	140 40 E
Hamilton Inlet	151	54 0N	57 30W
Hamilton Mt.	162	43 25N	74 22W
Hamilton, R., Queens., Austral.	138	23 30 S	139 47 E
Hamilton, R., S. Austral., Austral.	136	26 40 S	134 20 E
Hamiota	153	50 11N	100 38W
Hamlet	157	34 56N	79 40W
Hamley Bridge	140	34 17 S	138 35 E
Hamlin	159	32 58N	100 8W
Hamm	48	51 40N	7 58 E
Hammam bou Hadjar	118	35 23N	0 58W
Hammamet	119	36 24N	10 38 E
Hammamet, G. de	119	36 10N	10 48 E
Hammarö, I.	72	59 20N	13 30 E
Hammarstrand	72	63 7N	16 20 E
Hamme	47	51 6N	4 8 E
Hamme-Mille	47	50 47N	4 43 E
Hammel	73	56 16N	9 52 E
Hammelburg	49	50 7N	9 54 E
Hammenton	156	39 40N	74 47W
Hammeren	73	55 18N	14 47 E
Hammerfest	74	70 39N	23 41 E
Hammersmith	29	51 30N	0 15W
Hammond, Ind., U.S.A.	156	41 40N	87 30W
Hammond, La., U.S.A.	159	30 32N	90 30W
Hammonton	162	39 38N	74 48W
Hamnavoe	36	60 25N	1 5W
Hamneda	73	56 41N	13 51 E
Hamoir	47	50 25N	5 32 E
Hamont	47	51 15N	5 32 E
Hampden	143	45 18 S	170 50 E
Hampshire □	28	51 3N	1 20W
Hampshire Downs	28	51 10N	1 10W
Hampton, Ark., U.S.A.	159	33 35N	92 29W
Hampton, Iowa, U.S.A.	158	42 42N	93 12W
Hampton, N.H., U.S.A.	162	42 56N	70 48W
Hampton, S.C., U.S.A.	157	32 52N	81 2W
Hampton, Va., U.S.A.	162	37 4N	76 18W
Hampton Bays	162	40 53N	72 31W
Hampton Harbour	136	20 30 S	116 30 E
Hampton in Arden	28	52 26N	1 42W
Hampton Tableland	137	32 0N	127 0 E
Hamra	92	24 2N	38 55 E
Hamrange	72	60 59N	17 5 E
Hamrat esh Sheykh	123	14 45N	27 55 E
Hamre	71	60 33N	5 20 E
Hamun Helmand	93	31 15N	61 15 E
Hamun-i-Lora, Pak.	93	29 38N	64 58 E
Hamun-i-Lora, Pak.	93	29 38N	64 58 E
Hamun-i-Mashkel	93	28 30N	63 0 E
Hamyang	107	35 32N	127 42 E
Han Chiang, R., Hupeh, China	109	30 35N	114 15 E

Han Chiang, R **Hawzen**

Han Chiang, R., Kwangtung, China **109** 23 30N 116 48 E
Hana **147** 20 45N 155 59W
Hanak **122** 25 32N 37 0 E
Hanamaki **112** 39 23N 141 7 E
Hanang □ **126** 4 10 S 35 40 E
Hanang, mt. **126** 4 30 S 35 25 E
Hanau **49** 50 8N 8 56 E
Hanbogd **106** 43 11N 107 10 E
Hanch'eng **106** 35 30N 110 30 E
Hanchiang **109** 25 29N 119 5 E
Hanch'uan **109** 30 39N 113 46 E
Hanchuang **107** 34 36N 117 22 E
Hanchung **106** 33 10N 107 2 E
Hancock, Mich., U.S.A. **158** 47 10N 88 35W
Hancock, Minn., U.S.A. **158** 45 26N 95 46W
Hancock, Pa., U.S.A. **162** 41 57N 75 19W
Handa, Japan **111** 34 53N 137 0 E
Handa, Somalia **91** 10 37N 51 2 E
Handa I. **36** 58 23N 5 10W
Handen **72** 59 12N 18 12 E
Handeni **124** 5 25 S 38 2 E
Handeni □ **126** 5 30 S 38 0 E
Handlová **155** 48 45N 18 35 E
Handub **122** 19 15N 37 25 E
Handwara **95** 34 21N 74 20 E
Handzame **47** 51 2N 3 0 E
Hanegev **90** 30 50N 35 0 E
Haney **152** 49 12N 122 40W
Hanford **163** 36 25N 119 39W
Hang Chat **100** 18 20N 99 21 E
Hang Dong **100** 18 41N 98 55 E
Hangang, R. **107** 37 50N 126 30 E
Hangayn Nuruu **105** 47 30N 100 0 E
Hangchinch'i **106** 39 54N 108 56 E
Hangchinhouch'i **106** 41 55N 107 15 E
Hangchou **109** 30 15N 120 8 E
Hangchou Wan **109** 30 30N 121 30 E
Hanger **73** 57 6N 13 58 E
Hangklip, K. **128** 34 26 S 18 48 E
Hangö (Hanko) **75** 59 59N 22 57 E
Hanhongor **106** 43 55N 104 28 E
Hanish J. **91** 13 45N 42 46 E
Hanita **90** 33 5N 35 10 E
Hankinson **158** 46 9N 96 58W
Hanko = Hangö **75** 59 59N 22 57 E
Hank'ou **109** 30 40N 114 18 E
Hankow = Hank'ou **109** 30 40N 114 18 E
Hanksville **161** 38 19N 110 45W
Hanku **107** 39 16N 117 50 E
Hanle **95** 32 42N 79 4 E
Hanmer **143** 42 32 S 172 50 E
Hann, Mt. **136** 16 0 S 126 0 E
Hann, R. **136** 17 26 S 126 17 E
Hanna **152** 51 40N 111 54W
Hannaford **158** 47 23N 98 18W
Hannah **158** 48 58N 98 42W
Hannah B. **150** 51 40N 80 0W
Hannahs Bridge **141** 31 55 S 149 41 E
Hannibal, Mo., U.S.A. **158** 39 42N 91 22W
Hannibal, N.Y., U.S.A. **162** 43 19N 76 35W
Hannik **122** 18 12N 32 20 E
Hanningfield Water **29** 51 40N 0 30 E
Hannover **48** 52 23N 9 43 E
Hannut **47** 50 40N 5 4 E
Hanö **73** 56 0N 14 50 E
Hanö, I. **73** 56 2N 14 50 E
Hanöbukten **73** 55 35N 14 30 E
Hanoi **100** 21 5N 105 55 E
Hanover, S. Afr. **128** 31 4 S 24 29 E
Hanover, N.H., U.S.A. **162** 43 43N 72 17W
Hanover, Pa., U.S.A. **162** 39 46N 76 59W
Hanover, Va., U.S.A. **162** 37 46N 77 22W
Hanover = Hannover **48** 52 23N 9 43 E
Hanover, I. **176** 51 0 S 74 50W
Hanpan, C. **135** 5 0 S 154 35 E
Hans Meyer Ra. **135** 4 20 S 152 55 E
Hansholm **73** 57 8N 8 38 E
Hanshou **109** 28 55N 111 58 E
Hansi **94** 29 10N 75 57 E
Hansjö **72** 61 10N 14 40 E
Hanson, L. **140** 31 0 S 136 15 E
Hanson Range **136** 27 0 S 136 30 E
Hansted **73** 57 8N 8 36 E
Hantan **105** 36 42N 114 30 E
Hante **47** 50 19N 4 11 E
Hanton **106** 36 42N 114 30 E
Hanwood **141** 34 26 S 146 3 E
Hanyang **109** 30 35N 114 0 E
Hanyin **108** 32 53N 108 37 E
Hanyū **111** 36 10N 139 32 E
Hanyüan **108** 29 21N 102 43 E
Haoch'ing **108** 26 34N 100 12 E
Haokang **105** 47 25N 132 8 E
Haopi **106** 35 57N 114 13 E
Haparanda **74** 65 52N 24 8 E
Hapert **47** 51 22N 5 15 E
Happy **159** 34 47N 101 50W
Happy Camp **160** 41 52N 123 30W
Happy Valley **151** 53 15N 60 20W
Hapsu **107** 41 13N 128 51 E
Hapur **94** 28 45N 77 45 E
Haql **92** 29 10N 35 0 E
Har **103** 5 16 S 133 14 E
Har-Ayrag **106** 45 47N 109 16 E
Har Tuv **90** 31 46N 35 0 E
Har Us Nuur **105** 48 0N 92 10 E
Har Yehuda **90** 31 35N 34 57 E
Harad **92** 24 15N 49 0 E
Haradera **91** 4 33N 47 38 E
Haradh **92** 24 15N 49 0 E
Haramsøya **71** 62 39N 6 12 E
Haran **92** 36 48N 39 0 E
Harat **123** 16 5N 39 26 E
Haraze **117** 14 20N 19 12 E
Haraze-Mangueigne **117** 7 22N 17 3 E
Harbin = Haerhpin **107** 45 45N 126 45 E
Harboør **73** 56 38N 8 10 E
Harbor Beach **156** 43 50N 82 38W
Harbor Springs **156** 45 28N 85 0W
Harbour Breton **151** 47 29N 55 50W
Harbour Deep **151** 50 25N 56 30W
Harbour Grace **151** 47 40N 53 22W
Harburg **48** 53 27N 9 58 E
Hårby **73** 55 13N 10 7 E
Harcourt **138** 24 17 S 149 55 E
Harda **94** 22 27N 77 5 E
Hardangerfjorden. **71** 60 15N 6 0 E
Hardangerjøkulen **71** 60 30N 7 0 E
Hardangervidda **71** 60 20N 7 20 E
Hardap Dam **128** 24 32 S 17 50 E
Hardegarijp **46** 53 13N 5 57 E
Harden **141** 34 32 S 148 24 E
Hardenberg **46** 52 34N 6 37 E
Harderwijk **46** 52 21N 5 38 E
Hardey, R. **136** 22 45 S 116 8 E
Hardin **160** 45 50N 107 35W
Harding **129** 30 22 S 29 55 E
Harding Ra. **136** 16 17 S 124 55 E
Hardisty **152** 52 40N 111 18W
Hardman **160** 45 12N 119 49W
Hardoi **95** 27 26N 80 15 E
Hardwar **94** 29 58N 78 16 E
Hardy **159** 36 20N 91 30W
Hardy, Pen. **176** 55 30 S 68 20W
Hare B. **151** 51 15N 55 45W
Hare Gilboa **90** 32 31N 35 25 E
Hare Meron **90** 32 59N 35 24 E
Harelbeke **47** 50 52N 3 20 E
Haren, Ger. **48** 52 47N 7 18 E
Haren, Neth. **46** 53 11N 6 36 E
Harer **123** 9 20N 42 8 E
Harer □ **123** 7 12N 42 0 E
Hareto **123** 9 23N 37 6 E
Harfleur **42** 49 30N 0 10 E
Hargeisa **91** 9 30N 44 2 E
Hargshamn **72** 60 12N 18 30 E
Hari, R., Afghan. **93** 34 20N 64 30 E
Hari, R., Indon. **102** 1 10 S 101 50 E
Haricha, Hamada el **118** 22 40N 3 15W
Harihar **97** 14 32N 75 44 E
Harim, J. al **60** 26 0N 56 10 E
Harima-Nada **110** 34 30N 134 35 E
Haringey **29** 51 35N 0 7W
Haringhata, R. **98** 22 0N 89 58 E
Haringvliet **46** 51 48N 4 10 E
Haripad **97** 9 14N 76 28 E
Harirúd **93** 35 0N 61 0 E
Harkat **122** 20 25N 39 40 E
Harlan, Iowa, U.S.A. **158** 41 37N 95 20W
Harlan, Tenn., U.S.A. **157** 36 58N 83 20W
Harlech **31** 52 52N 4 7W
Harlem **160** 48 29N 108 39W
Harleston **29** 52 25N 1 18 E
Harlingen, Neth. **46** 53 11N 5 25 E
Harlingen, U.S.A. **159** 26 30N 97 50W
Harlow **29** 51 47N 0 9 E
Harlowton **160** 46 30N 109 54W
Harmånger **72** 61 55N 17 20 E
Harmil **123** 16 30N 40 10 E
Harney Basin **160** 43 30N 119 0W
Harney L. **160** 43 0N 119 0W
Harney Pk. **158** 43 52N 103 33W
Härnön **72** 62 36N 18 0 E
Harnösand **72** 62 38N 18 5 E
Haro **58** 42 35N 2 55W
Haro, C. **164** 27 50N 110 55W
Haroldswick **36** 60 48N 0 50W
Håroy **73** 55 13N 10 8 E
Harp L. **151** 55 5N 61 50W
Harpe, La **158** 40 30N 91 0W
Harpenden **29** 51 48N 0 20W
Harpenhalli **97** 14 47N 76 2 E
Harper **120** 4 25N 7 43 E
Harper Mt. **147** 64 15N 143 57W
Harplinge **73** 56 45N 12 45 E
Harport L. **36** 57 20N 6 20W
Harput **92** 38 48N 39 15 E
Harrand **94** 29 28N 70 3 E
Harrat al Kishb **92** 22 30N 40 15 E
Harrat al Umuirid **92** 26 50N 38 0 E
Harrat Khaibar **122** 25 45N 40 0 E
Harrat Nawāsīf **122** 21 30N 42 0 E
Harray, L. of **37** 59 0N 3 15W
Harricana, R. **150** 50 30N 79 10W
Harrietsham **29** 51 15N 0 41 E
Harriman **157** 36 0N 84 35W
Harrington, U.K. **32** 54 37N 3 55W
Harrington, U.S.A. **162** 38 56N 75 35W
Harrington Harbour **151** 50 31N 59 30W
Harris **36** 57 50N 6 55W
Harris L. **136** 31 10 S 135 10 E
Harris Mts. **143** 44 49 S 168 49 E
Harris, Sd. of **36** 57 44N 7 6W
Harrisburg, Ill., U.S.A. **159** 37 42N 88 30W
Harrisburg, Nebr., U.S.A. **158** 41 36N 103 46W
Harrisburg, Oreg., U.S.A. **160** 44 25N 123 10W
Harrisburg, Pa., U.S.A. **162** 40 18N 76 52W
Harrismith **129** 28 15 S 29 8 E
Harrison, Ark., U.S.A. **159** 36 10N 93 4W
Harrison, Idaho, U.S.A. **160** 47 30N 116 51W
Harrison, Nebr., U.S.A. **158** 42 42N 103 52W
Harrison B. **147** 70 25N 151 0W
Harrison, C. **151** 55 0N 58 0W
Harrison L. **152** 49 33N 121 50W
Harrisonburg **156** 38 28N 78 52W
Harrisonville **158** 38 45N 93 45W
Harriston **150** 43 57N 80 53W
Harrisville **150** 44 40N 83 19W
Harrogate **33** 53 59N 1 32W
Harrow **29** 51 35N 0 15W
Harry, L. **139** 29 23 S 138 19 E
Harsefeld **48** 53 26N 9 31 E
Harskamp **46** 52 8N 5 46 E
Harstad **74** 68 48N 16 30 E
Hart **156** 43 42N 86 21W
Hart, L. **140** 31 10 S 136 25 E
Hartbees, R. **128** 29 8 S 20 48 E
Hartberg **52** 47 17N 15 58 E
Harteigen, Mt. **71** 60 11N 7 5 E
Hartest **29** 52 7N 0 41 E
Hartford, Conn., U.S.A. **162** 41 47N 72 41W
Hartford, Ky., U.S.A. **156** 37 26N 86 50W
Hartford, S.D., U.S.A. **158** 43 40N 96 58W
Hartford, Wis., U.S.A. **158** 43 18N 88 25W
Hartford City **156** 40 22N 85 20W
Harthill **35** 55 52N 3 45W
Hartland, Can. **151** 46 20N 67 32W
Hartland, U.K. **30** 50 59N 4 29W
Hartland Pt. **30** 51 2N 4 32W
Hartlebury **28** 52 20N 2 13W
Hartlepool **33** 54 42N 1 11W
Hartley, Zimb. **127** 18 10 S 30 7 E
Hartley, U.K. **35** 55 5N 1 27W
Hartley Bay **152** 53 25N 129 15W
Hartmannberge **128** 17 0 S 13 0 E
Hartney **153** 49 30N 100 35W
Hartpury **28** 51 55N 2 18W
Hartselle **157** 34 25N 86 55W
Hartshorne **159** 34 51N 95 30W
Hartsville **157** 34 23N 80 2W
Hartwell **157** 34 21N 82 52W
Harunabad **94** 29 35N 73 2 E
Harur **97** 12 3N 78 29 E
Harvard, Mt. **161** 39 0N 106 5W
Harvey, Austral. **137** 33 5 S 115 54 E
Harvey, Ill., U.S.A. **156** 41 40N 87 50W
Harvey, N.D., U.S.A. **158** 47 50N 99 58W
Harwell **28** 51 40N 1 17W
Harwich **29** 51 56N 1 18 E
Harwood **33** 53 54N 1 30W
Haryana □ **94** 29 0N 76 10 E
Harz **48** 51 40N 10 40 E
Harzé **47** 50 27N 5 40 E
Harzgerode **48** 51 38N 11 8 E
Hasa **92** 26 0N 49 0 E
Hasaheisa **123** 14 25N 33 20 E
Hasani **122** 25 0N 37 8 E
Hasanpur **94** 28 51N 78 9 E
Haselünne **48** 52 40N 7 30 E
Hasharon **90** 32 12N 34 49 E
Hashefela **90** 31 30N 34 43 E
Hashima **111** 35 20N 136 40 E
Hashimoto **111** 34 19N 135 37 E
Hasjö **72** 63 2N 16 20 E
Håsjö **72** 63 1N 16 5 E
Haskell, Kans., U.S.A. **159** 35 51N 95 40W
Haskell, Tex., U.S.A. **159** 33 10N 99 45W
Haskier Is. **36** 57 42N 7 40W
Haslach **49** 48 16N 8 7 E
Hasle **73** 55 11N 14 44 E
Haslemere **29** 51 5N 0 41W
Haslev **73** 55 18N 11 57 E
Haslingden **32** 53 43N 2 20W
Hasparren **44** 43 24N 1 18W
Hassan **92** 13 0N 76 5 E
Hasselt, Belg. **47** 50 56N 5 21 E
Hasselt, Neth. **46** 52 36N 6 6 E
Hassene, Ad. **118** 21 0N 4 0 E
Hassfurt **49** 50 2N 10 30 E
Hassi Berrekrem **119** 33 45N 5 16 E
Hassi Daoula **119** 33 4N 5 38 E
Hassi el Biod **119** 28 30N 6 0 E
Hassi el Heïda **74** 29 34N 0 14W
Hassi Inifel **118** 29 50N 3 41 E
Hassi Marroket **119** 30 10N 3 0 E
Hassi Messaoud **119** 31 43N 6 8 E
Hassi Taguenza **172** 29 8N 0 23W
Hassi Zerzour **118** 30 51N 3 56W
Hässleby **73** 57 37N 15 30 E
Hässleholmen **73** 56 9N 13 45 E
Hastière-Lavaux **47** 50 13N 4 49 E
Hastigrow **37** 58 32N 3 15W
Hastings, Austral. **141** 38 18 S 145 12 E
Hastings, N.Z. **142** 39 39 S 176 52 E
Hastings, U.K. **29** 50 51N 0 36 E
Hastings, Mich., U.S.A. **156** 42 40N 82 20W
Hastings, Minn., U.S.A. **158** 44 41N 92 51W
Hastings, Nebr., U.S.A. **158** 40 34N 98 22W
Hastings Ra. **141** 31 15 S 152 14 E
Hästveda **73** 56 17N 13 55 E
Hat Nhao **101** 14 46N 106 32 E
Hat Yai **101** 7 1N 100 27 E
Hatanbulag **106** 43 8N 109 14 E
Hatano **111** 35 22N 139 14 E
Hatch **161** 32 45N 107 8W
Hatches Creek **138** 20 56 S 135 12 E
Hatchet L. **153** 58 36N 103 40W
Haţeg **70** 45 36N 22 55 E
Haţeg, Mţii **70** 45 25N 23 0 E
Hatert **46** 51 49N 5 50 E
Hatfield **29** 51 46N 0 11W
Hatfield Broad Oak **29** 51 48N 0 16 E
Hatfield Post Office **140** 33 54N 143 49 E
Hatgal **105** 50 26N 100 9 E
Hatherleigh **30** 50 49N 4 4W
Hathersage **33** 53 20N 1 39W
Hathras **94** 27 36N 78 6 E
Hatia **99** 22 30N 91 5 E
Hato de Corozal **174** 6 11N 71 45W
Hato Mayor **167** 18 46N 69 15W
Hattah **140** 34 48N 142 17 E
Hattem **46** 52 28N 6 4 E
Hatteras, C. **157** 35 10N 75 30W
Hattiesburg **159** 31 20N 89 20W
Hatton, Can. **153** 50 2N 109 50W
Hatton, U.K. **37** 57 24N 1 57W
Hatvan **53** 47 40N 19 45 E
Hau Bon (Cheo Reo) **100** 13 25N 108 28 E
Hau Duc **100** 15 20N 108 13 E
Hauchinango **164** 20 12N 97 45W
Haug **71** 60 23N 10 26 E
Haugastøl **71** 60 30N 7 50 E
Haugesund **71** 59 23N 5 13 E
Haugh of Urr **35** 55 0N 3 51W
Haughangaroa Ra. **142** 38 42 S 175 40 E
Haughley **29** 52 13N 0 59 E
Haukelisæter **71** 59 51N 7 9 E
Haulerwijk **46** 53 4N 6 20 E
Haultain, R. **153** 55 51N 106 46W
Haungpa **98** 25 29N 96 7 E
Haura **91** 13 50N 47 35 E
Hauraki Gulf **142** 36 35 S 175 5 E
Hausruck **52** 48 6N 13 30 E
Haut Atlas **118** 32 0N 7 0W
Haut-Rhin □ **43** 48 0N 7 15 E
Haut Zaïre □ **126** 2 20N 26 0 E
Hauta Oasis **92** 23 40N 47 0 E
Hautah, Wahāt al **92** 23 40N 47 0 E
Haute-Corse □ **45** 42 30N 9 30 E
Haute-Garonne □ **44** 43 28N 1 30 E
Haute-Loire □ **44** 45 5N 3 50 E
Haute-Marne □ **43** 48 10N 5 20 E
Haute-Saône □ **43** 47 45N 6 10 E
Haute-Savoie □ **45** 46 0N 6 20 E
Haute-Vienne □ **44** 45 50N 1 10 E
Hauterive **151** 49 10N 68 16W
Hautes-Alpes □ **45** 44 42N 6 20 E
Hautes Fagnes **47** 50 34N 6 6 E
Hautes-Pyrénées □ **44** 43 0N 0 10 E
Hauteville-Lompnes **45** 45 59N 5 35 E
Hautmont **43** 50 15N 3 55 E
Hautrage **47** 50 29N 3 46 E
Hauts-de-Seine □ **43** 48 52N 2 15 E
Hauts Plateaux **118** 34 14N 1 0 E
Hauxley **35** 55 21N 1 35W
Havana **158** 40 19N 90 3W
Havana = La Habana **166** 23 8N 82 22W
Havant **29** 50 51N 0 59W
Havasu, L. **161** 34 18N 114 8W
Havdhem **73** 57 10N 18 20 E
Havelange **47** 50 23N 5 15 E
Havelian **94** 34 2N 73 10 E
Havelock, N.B., Can. **151** 46 2N 65 24W
Havelock, Ont., Can. **150** 44 26N 77 53W
Havelock, N.Z. **143** 41 17 S 173 48 E
Havelock I. **101** 11 55N 93 2 E
Havelte **46** 52 46N 6 14 E
Haverfordwest **31** 51 48N 4 59W
Haverhill, U.K. **29** 52 6N 0 27 E
Haverhill, U.S.A. **162** 42 50N 71 2W
Haveri **97** 14 53N 75 24 E
Haverigg **32** 54 12N 3 16W
Havering **29** 51 33N 0 20 E
Haverstraw **162** 41 12N 73 58W
Håverud **73** 58 50N 12 28 E
Havîrna **70** 48 4N 26 43 E
Havlíčkuv Brod **52** 49 36N 15 33 E
Havnby **73** 55 5N 8 34 E
Havre **160** 48 40N 109 34W
Havre-Aubert **151** 47 12N 62 0W
Havre de Grace **162** 39 33N 76 6W
Havre, Le **42** 49 30N 0 5 E
Havre St. Pierre **151** 50 18N 63 33W
Havza **92** 41 0N 35 35 E
Haw, R. **157** 37 43N 80 52W
Hawaii □ **147** 20 30N 157 0W
Hawaii I. **147** 20 0N 155 0W
Hawaiian Is. **147** 20 30N 156 0W
Hawarden, Can. **153** 51 25N 106 36W
Hawarden, U.K. **31** 53 11N 3 2W
Hawarden, U.S.A. **158** 43 2N 96 28W
Hawea Flat **143** 44 40 S 169 19 E
Hawea Lake **143** 44 28 S 169 19 E
Hawera **142** 39 35 S 174 19 E
Hawes **32** 54 18N 2 12W
Hawes Water, L. **32** 54 32N 2 48W
Hawick **35** 55 25N 2 48W
Hawk Junction **150** 48 30N 84 38W
Hawkchurch **30** 50 47N 2 56W
Hawkdun Ra. **143** 44 53 S 170 5 E
Hawke B. **142** 39 25N 177 20 E
Hawker **28** 31 59 S 138 22 E
Hawke's Bay □ **142** 39 45 S 176 35 E
Hawke's Harbour **151** 53 2N 55 50W
Hawkesbury **150** 45 35N 74 40W
Hawkesbury I. **152** 53 37N 129 3W
Hawkesbury Pt. **138** 11 55 S 134 5 E
Hawkesbury River **133** 33 50 S 151 44W
Hawkesbury Upton **28** 51 34N 2 19W
Hawkhurst **29** 51 2N 0 31 E
Hawkinsville **157** 32 17N 83 30W
Hawkshead **32** 54 23N 3 0W
Hawkwood **139** 25 45 S 150 50 E
Hawley, Minn., U.S.A. **158** 46 58N 96 20W
Hawley, Pa., U.S.A. **162** 41 28N 75 11W
Haworth **32** 53 50N 1 57W
Hawsker **33** 54 27N 0 34W
Hawthorne **163** 38 31N 118 37W
Hawzen **123** 13 58N 39 28 E

Haxby **Higashiōsaka**

Place	Page	Lat.	Long.
Haxby	33	54 1N	1 4W
Haxtun	158	40 40N	102 39W
Hay, Austral.	141	34 30S	144 51E
Hay, U.K.	31	52 4N	3 9W
Hay, C.	136	14 5S	129 29E
Hay L.	152	58 50N	118 50W
Hay Lakes	152	53 12N	113 2W
Hay, R., Austral.	138	24 10S	137 20E
Hay, R., Can.	152	60 0N	116 56W
Hay River	152	60 51N	115 44W
Hay Springs	158	42 40N	102 38W
Hayange	43	49 20N	6 2E
Hayato	110	31 40N	130 43E
Hayburn Wyke	33	54 22N	0 28W
Haycock	147	65 10N	161 20W
Hayden, Ariz., U.S.A.	161	33 2N	110 54W
Hayden, Wyo., U.S.A.	160	40 30N	107 22W
Haydenville	162	42 22N	72 42W
Haydon	138	18 0S	141 30E
Haydon Bridge	35	54 58N	2 15W
Haye Descartes, La	42	46 58N	0 42E
Haye-du-Puits, La	42	49 17N	1 33W
Hayes	158	44 22N	101 1W
Hayes Pen.	12	75 30N	65 0W
Hayes, R.	153	57 3N	92 12W
Hayle	30	50 12N	5 25W
Haymana	92	39 30N	32 35E
Haynesville	159	33 0N	93 7W
Hays, Can.	152	50 6N	111 48W
Hays, U.S.A.	158	38 55N	99 25W
Hayton	32	54 55N	2 45W
Hayward, Calif., U.S.A.	163	37 40N	122 5W
Hayward, Wis., U.S.A.	158	46 2N	91 30W
Hayward's Heath	29	51 0N	0 5W
Hazard	156	37 18N	83 10W
Hazaribagh	95	23 58N	85 26E
Hazaribagh Road	95	24 12N	85 57E
Hazebrouck	43	50 42N	2 31E
Hazelton, Can.	152	55 20N	127 42W
Hazelton, U.S.A.	158	46 30N	100 15W
Hazen	160	39 37N	119 2W
Hazerswoude	46	52 5N	4 36E
Hazlehurst	157	31 50N	82 35W
Hazleton	156	40 58N	76 0W
Hazlett, L.	136	21 30S	128 48E
Hazrat Imam	93	37 15N	68 50E
Heacham	29	52 55N	0 30E
Head of Bight	137	31 30S	131 25E
Headcorn	29	51 10N	0 39E
Headford	38	53 28N	9 6W
Headington	28	51 46N	1 13W
Headlands	127	18 15S	32 2E
Healdsburg	160	38 33N	122 51W
Healdton	159	34 16N	97 31W
Healesville	141	37 35S	145 30E
Heanor	33	53 1N	1 20W
Heard I.	11	53 0S	74 0E
Hearne	159	30 54N	96 35W
Hearne B.	153	60 10N	99 10W
Hearne L.	152	62 20N	113 10W
Hearst	150	49 40N	83 41W
Heart, R.	158	46 40N	101 30W
Heart's Content	151	47 54N	53 27W
Heath Mts.	143	45 39S	167 9E
Heath Pt.	151	49 8N	61 40W
Heath Steele	151	47 17N	66 5W
Heathcote	141	36 56S	144 45E
Heather, oilfield	19	60 55N	0 50E
Heathfield	29	50 58N	0 18E
Heathsville	162	37 55N	76 28W
Heavener	159	34 54N	94 36W
Hebbronville	159	27 20N	98 40W
Hebburn	35	54 59N	1 30W
Hebden Bridge	32	53 45N	2 0W
Hebel	139	28 58S	147 47E
Heber Springs	159	35 29N	91 39W
Hebgen, L.	160	44 50N	111 15W
Hebrides, U.K.	36	57 30N	7 0W
Hebrides, Inner Is., U.K.	36	57 20N	6 40W
Hebrides, Outer Is., U.K.	36	57 50N	7 25W
Hebron, Can.	149	58 12N	62 38W
Hebron, N.D., U.S.A.	158	46 56N	102 2W
Hebron, Nebr., U.S.A.	158	40 15N	97 33W
Hebron (Al Khalil)	90	31 32N	35 6E
Heby	72	59 56N	16 53E
Hecate Str.	152	53 10N	130 30W
Hechingen	49	48 20N	8 58E
Hechtel	47	51 8N	5 22E
Heckington	33	52 59N	0 17W
Hecla	158	45 56N	98 8W
Hecla I.	153	51 10N	96 43W
Hecla Mt.	36	57 18N	7 15W
Heddal	71	59 36N	9 20E
Heddon	35	55 0N	1 47W
Hédé	42	48 18N	1 49W
Hede	72	62 23N	13 30E
Hedemora	72	60 18N	15 58E
Hedgehope	143	46 12S	168 34E
Hedley	159	34 53N	100 39W
Hedmark □	75	61 17N	11 40E
Hedmark fylke □	71	61 17N	11 40E
Hednesford	28	52 43N	2 0W
Hedon	33	53 44N	0 11W
Hedrum	71	59 7N	10 5E
Heeg	46	52 58N	5 37E
Heegermeer	46	52 56N	5 32E
Heemskerk	46	52 31N	4 40E
Heemstede	46	52 22N	4 37E
Heer	47	50 50N	5 43E
Heerde	46	52 24N	6 2E
's Heerenburg	46	51 53N	6 16E
's Heerenloo	46	52 19N	5 36E
Heerenveen	46	52 57N	5 55E
Heerhugowaard	46	52 40N	4 51E
Heerlen	47	50 55N	6 0E
Heerlerheide	47	50 54N	5 58E
Heers	47	50 45N	5 18E
Heesch	46	51 44N	5 32E
Heestert	47	50 47N	3 25E
Heeze	47	51 23N	5 35E
Hegyalja, Mts.	53	48 25N	21 25E
Heich'engchen	106	36 16N	106 19E
Heide	48	54 10N	9 7E
Heide, oilfield	19	54 5N	9 5E
Heidelberg, Ger.	49	49 23N	8 41E
Heidelberg, C. Prov., S. Afr.	128	34 6S	20 59E
Heidelberg, Trans., S. Afr.	129	26 30S	28 23E
Heidenheim	49	48 40N	10 10E
Heigun-To	110	33 47N	132 14E
Heikant	47	51 15N	4 1E
Heilam	37	58 31N	4 40W
Heilbron	129	27 16S	27 59E
Heilbronn	49	49 8N	9 13E
Heiligenblut	52	47 2N	12 51E
Heiligenhafen	48	54 21N	10 58E
Heiligenstadt	48	51 22N	10 9E
Heilungkiang □	46	48 0N	128 0E
Heim	71	63 26N	9 5E
Heimdal, gasfield	19	59 35N	2 15E
Heino	46	52 26N	6 14E
Heinola	75	61 13N	26 24E
Heinsburg	153	53 50N	110 30W
Heinsch	47	49 42N	5 44E
Heinsun	98	25 52N	95 35E
Heinze Is.	101	14 25N	97 45E
Heirnkut	98	25 14N	94 44E
Heishan	107	41 40N	122 3E
Heishui, Liaoning, China	107	42 6N	119 22E
Heishui, Szechwan, China	108	32 15N	103 0E
Heist	47	51 20N	3 15E
Heist-op-den-Berg	47	51 5N	4 44E
Heistad	71	59 5N	9 40E
Hejaz = Hijāz	92	26 0N	37 30E
Hekelegem	47	50 55N	4 7E
Hekimhan	92	38 50N	38 0E
Hekinan	111	34 52N	137 0E
Hekla	74	63 56N	19 35W
Hel	54	54 38N	18 50E
Helagsfjället	72	62 54N	12 25E
Helchteren	47	51 4N	5 22E
Helden	47	51 19N	6 0E
Helechosa	57	39 22N	4 53W
Helena, Ark., U.S.A.	159	34 30N	90 35W
Helena, Mont., U.S.A.	160	46 40N	112 0W
Helendale	163	34 45N	117 19W
Helensburgh, Austral.	141	34 11S	151 1E
Helensburgh, U.K.	34	56 0N	4 44W
Helensville	142	36 41S	174 29E
Helets	90	31 36N	34 39E
Helgasjön	73	57 0N	14 50E
Helgeland	74	66 20N	13 30E
Helgeroa	71	59 0N	9 45E
Helgoland, I.	48	54 10N	7 51E
Helgum	72	63 25N	16 50E
Heligoland = Helgoland	48	54 10N	7 51E
Heliopolis	122	30 6N	31 17E
Hell-Ville	129	13 25S	48 16E
Hellebæk	73	56 4N	12 32E
Helleland	71	58 33N	6 7E
Hellendoorn	46	52 24N	6 27E
Hellertown	162	40 35N	75 21W
Hellevoetsluis	46	51 50N	4 8E
Helli Ness	36	60 3N	1 10W
Hellick Kenyón Plateau	13	82 0S	110 0W
Hellifield	32	54 0N	2 13W
Hellín	59	38 31N	1 40W
Hellum	73	57 16N	10 10E
Helmand □	93	31 20N	64 0E
Helmand, R.	94	34 0N	67 0E
Helmond	47	51 29N	5 41E
Helmsdale	37	58 7N	3 40W
Helmsley	33	54 15N	1 2W
Helmstedt	48	52 16N	11 0E
Helnæs	73	55 9N	10 0E
Helper	160	39 44N	110 56W
Helperby	33	54 8N	1 20W
Helsby	32	53 16N	2 47W
Helsingborg	73	56 3N	12 42E
Helsinge	73	56 2N	12 12E
Helsingfors = Helsinki	75	60 15N	25 3E
Helsingør	73	56 2N	12 35E
Helsinki (Helsingfors)	75	60 15N	25 3E
Helston	30	50 7N	5 17W
Helvick Hd.	39	52 3N	7 33W
Helvoirt	47	51 38N	5 14E
Helwân	122	29 50N	31 20E
Hem	71	59 26N	10 0E
Hemavati, R.	97	12 50N	67 0E
Hemel Hempstead	29	51 45N	0 28W
Hemet	163	33 45N	116 59W
Hemingford	158	42 21N	103 4W
Hemphill	159	31 21N	93 49W
Hempstead	159	30 5N	96 5W
Hempton	29	52 50N	0 49E
Hemse	73	57 15N	18 22E
Hemsö, I.	72	62 43N	18 5E
Hemsön	72	62 42N	18 5E
Hemsworth	33	53 37N	1 21W
Hemyock	30	50 55N	1 13W
Hen & Chicken Is.	142	35 58S	174 45E
Henares, R.	58	40 55N	3 0W
Hendaye	44	43 23N	1 47W
Henderson, Argent.	172	36 18S	61 43W
Henderson, U.K.	36	57 42N	5 47W
Henderson, Ky., U.S.A.	156	37 50N	87 38W
Henderson, Nev., U.S.A.	161	36 2N	115 0W
Henderson, Pa., U.S.A.	157	35 25N	88 40W
Henderson, Tex., U.S.A.	159	32 5N	94 49W
Hendersonville	157	35 21N	82 28W
Hendon	139	28 5S	151 50E
Hendorf	70	46 4N	24 5E
Henfield	29	50 56N	0 17W
Hengch'eng	106	38 26N	106 26E
Hengelo, Gelderland, Neth.	46	52 3N	6 19E
Hengelo, Overijssel, Neth.	46	52 16N	6 48E
Hengfeng	109	28 25N	117 35E
Henghsien	108	22 36N	109 16E
Hengoed	31	51 39N	3 14W
Hengshan, Hunan, China	109	27 15N	112 51E
Hengshan, Shansi, China	106	37 56N	108 53E
Hengshui	106	37 43N	115 42E
Hengtaohotze	107	44 55N	129 3E
Hengyang	109	26 51N	112 30E
Hengyanghsien	109	26 58N	112 21E
Hénin-Beaumont	43	50 25N	2 58E
Henley	29	51 32N	0 53W
Henley-in-Arden	28	52 18N	1 47W
Henllan	31	53 13N	3 29W
Henlopen, C.	162	38 48N	75 5W
Henlow	29	51 2N	0 18W
Hennan, L.	72	62 3N	15 55E
Henne	73	55 44N	8 11E
Hennebont	42	47 49N	3 19W
Hennenman	128	27 59S	27 1E
Hennessy	159	36 8N	97 53W
Hennigsdorf	48	52 38N	13 13E
Henribourg	153	53 25N	105 38W
Henrichemont	43	47 20N	2 21E
Henrietta	159	33 50N	98 15W
Henrietta Maria C.	150	55 9N	82 20W
Henry	158	41 5N	89 20W
Henryetta	159	35 2N	96 0W
Henstridge	28	50 59N	2 24W
Hentiyn Nuruu	105	48 30N	108 30E
Henty	141	35 30N	147 0E
Henzada	98	17 38N	95 35E
Heppner	160	45 27N	119 34W
Herad	71	58 8N	6 47E
Héraðsflói	74	65 42N	14 12W
Héradsvötn	74	65 25N	19 5W
Herald Cays	138	16 58S	149 9E
Herät	93	34 20N	62 7E
Herät □	93	35 0N	62 0E
Hérault □	44	43 34N	3 15E
Hérault, R.	44	43 20N	3 32E
Herbert	153	50 30N	107 10W
Herbert Downs	138	23 7S	139 9E
Herbert I.	147	52 49N	170 10W
Herbert, R.	138	18 31S	146 17E
Herberton	138	17 28S	145 25E
Herbertstown	39	52 32N	8 29W
Herbiers, Les	42	46 52N	1 0W
Herbignac	42	47 27N	2 18W
Herborn	48	50 40N	8 19E
Herby	54	50 45N	18 50E
Hercegnovi	66	42 30N	18 33E
Herðubreið	74	65 11N	16 21W
Herdla	71	60 34N	4 56E
Hereford, U.K.	28	52 4N	2 42W
Hereford, U.S.A.	159	34 50N	102 28W
Hereford and Worcester □	28	52 10N	2 30W
Herefordshire □	26	52 15N	2 50W
Herefoss	71	58 32N	8 32E
Herekino	142	35 18S	173 11E
Herent	47	50 54N	4 40E
Herentals	47	51 12N	4 51E
Herenthout	47	51 8N	4 45E
Herfølge	73	55 26N	12 9E
Herford	48	52 7N	8 40E
Héricourt	43	47 32N	6 55E
Herington	158	38 43N	97 0W
Herisau	51	47 22N	9 17E
Hérisson	44	46 32N	2 42E
Herjehogna	75	61 43N	12 7E
Herk, R.	47	50 56N	5 12E
Herkenbosch	47	51 9N	6 4E
Herkimer	162	43 0N	74 59W
Herm I.	42	49 30N	2 28W
Herma Ness	36	60 50N	0 54W
Hermagor	52	46 38N	13 23E
Herman	158	45 51N	96 8W
Hermandez	163	36 24N	120 46W
Hermann	158	38 40N	91 25W
Hermannsburg	48	52 49N	10 6E
Hermannsburg Mission	136	23 57S	132 45E
Hermanus	128	34 27S	19 12E
Herment	44	45 45N	2 24E
Hermidale	141	31 30S	146 42E
Hermiston	160	45 50N	119 16W
Hermitage	143	43 44S	170 5E
Hermitage B.	151	47 33N	56 10W
Hermite, Is.	176	55 50S	68 0W
Hermon, Mt. = Sheikh, J. ash	92	33 20N	36 0E
Hermosillo	164	29 10N	111 0W
Hernad, R.	53	48 20N	21 15E
Hernandarias	173	25 20S	54 40W
Hernando, Argent.	172	32 28S	63 40W
Hernando, U.S.A.	159	34 50N	89 59W
Herndon	162	40 43N	76 51W
Herne, Belg.	47	50 44N	4 2E
Herne, Ger.	48	51 33N	7 12E
Herne Bay	29	51 22N	1 8E
Herne Hill	137	31 45S	116 5E
Herning	73	56 8N	8 58E
Heroica Nogales	164	31 14N	110 56W
Heron Bay	150	48 40N	85 25W
Heröy	71	62 18N	5 45E
Herreid	158	45 53N	100 5W
's Herrenbroek	46	52 32N	6 1E
Herrera	57	39 12N	4 50W
Herrera de Alcántar	57	39 39N	7 25W
Herrera de Pisuerga	56	42 35N	4 20W
Herrera del Duque	57	39 10N	5 3W
Herrero, Punta	165	19 17N	87 27W
Herrick	138	41 5S	147 55E
Herrin	159	37 50N	89 0W
Herrljunga	73	58 5N	13 1E
Hersbruck	49	49 30N	11 25E
Herschel I.	147	69 35N	139 5W
Herseaux	47	50 43N	3 15E
Herselt	47	51 3N	4 53E
Herserange	47	49 30N	5 48E
Hershey	162	40 17N	76 39W
Herstal	47	50 40N	5 38E
Herstmonceux	29	50 53N	0 21E
Hersvik	71	61 10N	4 53E
Hertford	29	51 47N	0 4W
Hertford □	29	51 51N	0 5W
's Hertogenbosch	47	51 42N	5 18E
Hertzogville	128	28 9S	25 30E
Hervás	56	40 16N	5 52W
Herve	47	50 38N	5 48E
Hervey B.	133	25 0S	152 52E
*Hervey Is.	131	19 30S	159 0W
Hervey Junction	150	46 50N	72 29W
Herwijnen	46	51 50N	5 7E
Herzberg, Cottbus, Ger.	48	51 40N	13 13E
Herzberg, Niedersachsen, Ger.	48	51 38N	10 20E
Herzele	47	50 53N	3 53E
Herzliyya	90	32 10N	34 50E
Herzogenbuchsee	50	47 11N	7 42E
Herzogenburg	52	48 17N	15 41E
Hesdin	43	50 21N	2 0E
Hesel	48	53 18N	7 36E
Heskestad	71	58 28N	6 22E
Hesperange	47	49 35N	6 10E
Hesperia	163	34 25N	117 18W
Hesse = Hessen	48	50 57N	9 20E
Hessen □	48	50 57N	9 20E
Hessle	33	53 44N	0 28E
Hetch Hetchy Aqueduct	163	37 36N	121 25W
Heteren	46	51 58N	5 46E
Hethersett	29	52 35N	1 10E
Hettinger	158	46 8N	102 38W
Hetton-le-Hole	35	54 49N	1 26W
Hettstedt	48	51 39N	11 30E
Heugem	47	50 49N	5 42E
Heule	47	50 51N	3 15E
Heusden, Belg.	47	51 2N	5 17E
Heusden, Neth.	46	51 44N	5 8E
Hève, C. de la	42	49 30N	0 5E
Heverlee	47	50 52N	4 42E
Heves □	53	47 50N	20 0E
Hevron, N.	90	31 28N	34 52E
Hewett, C.	149	70 16N	67 45W
Hewett, gasfield	19	53 5N	1 50E
Hex River	128	33 30S	19 35E
Hexham	35	54 58N	2 7W
Heybridge	29	51 44N	0 42E
Heyfield	141	37 59S	146 47E
Heysham	32	54 5N	2 53W
Heytesbury	28	51 11N	2 7W
Heythuysen	47	51 15N	5 55E
Heywood, Austral.	140	38 8S	141 37E
Heywood, U.K.	32	53 36N	2 13W
Hi-no-Misaki	110	35 26N	132 38E
Hi Vista	163	34 44N	117 46W
Hiamen	109	31 52N	121 15E
Hiawatha, Kans., U.S.A.	158	39 55N	95 33W
Hiawatha, Utah, U.S.A.	160	39 37N	111 1W
Hibbing	158	47 30N	93 0W
Hibbs B.	138	42 35S	145 15E
Hibbs, Pt.	138	42 38S	145 15E
Hibernia Reef	136	12 0S	123 23E
Hibiki-Nada	110	34 0N	130 0E
Hickman	159	36 35N	89 8W
Hickory	157	35 46N	81 17W
Hicks Bay	142	37 34S	178 21E
Hicksville	162	40 46N	73 30W
Hida-Gawa	70	47 10N	23 9E
Hida-Gawa, R.	111	35 26N	137 3E
Hida-Sammyaku	111	36 30N	137 40E
Hida-Sanchi	111	36 10N	137 0E
Hidaka	110	35 30N	134 44E
Hidalgo □	164	20 30N	99 10W
Hidalgo del Parral	164	26 58N	105 40W
Hidalgo, Presa M.	164	26 30N	108 35W
Hiddensee	48	54 30N	13 6E
Hidrolândia	171	17 0S	49 15W
Hieflau	52	47 36N	14 46E
Hiendelaencina	58	41 5N	3 0W
Hierro I.	116	27 57N	17 56E
Higashi-matsuyama	111	36 2N	139 25E
Higashiōsaka	111	34 40N	135 37E

*Renamed Manuae

Higasi-Suidō
Hong Kong ■

Higasi-Suidō 110 34 0N 129 30E
Higgins 159 36 9N 100 1W
Higginsville 137 31 42S 121 38E
Higgs I. L. 157 36 20N 78 30W
High Atlas = Haut Atlas 118 32 30N 5 0W
High Bentham 32 54 8N 2 31W
High Borrow Bri. 32 54 26N 2 43W
High Bridge 162 40 40N 74 54W
High Ercall 28 52 46N 2 37W
High Hesket 32 54 47N 2 49W
High I. 151 56 40N 61 10W
High Island 159 29 32N 94 22W
High Level 152 58 31N 117 8W
High Pike, mt. 32 54 43N 3 4W
High Point 157 35 57N 79 58W
High Prairie 152 55 30N 116 30W
High River 152 50 30N 113 50W
High Springs 157 29 50N 82 40W
High Tatra 53 49 30N 20 00E
High Veld = Hoëveld 129 26 30S 30 0E
High Willhays, hill 30 50 41N 3 59W
High Wycombe 29 51 37N 0 45W
Higham Ferrers 29 52 18N 0 36W
Highbank 138 47 34S 171 45E
Highbridge 28 51 13N 2 59W
Highbury 138 16 25S 143 9E
Highclere 28 51 20N 1 22W
Highland □ 36 57 30N 5 0W
Highland Pk. 156 42 10N 87 50W
Highland Springs 162 37 33N 77 20W
Highley 28 52 25N 2 23W
Highmore 158 44 35N 99 26W
Highrock L. 153 57 5N 105 32W
Hightae 35 55 5N 3 27W
Hightstown 162 40 16N 74 31W
Highworth 28 51 38N 1 42W
Higley 161 33 27N 111 46W
Higüay 167 18 37N 68 42W
Higüero, Pta. 147 18 22N 67 16W
Hiiumaa 80 58 50N 22 45E
Hijar 58 41 10N 0 27W
Hijãz 91 26 0N 37 30E
Hiji 110 33 22N 131 32E
Hijken 46 52 54N 6 30E
Hikari 110 33 58N 131 58E
Hiketa 110 34 13N 134 24E
Hiko 161 37 30N 115 13W
Hikone 111 35 15N 136 10E
Hikurangi, East Court 142 37 55S 178 4E
Hikurangi, Mt. 142 37 55S 178 4E
Hilawng 98 21 23N 93 48E
Hildburghhausen 49 50 24N 10 43E
Hildesheim 48 52 9N 9 55E
Hilgay 29 52 34N 0 23E
Hill 150 45 40N 74 45W
Hill City, Idaho, U.S.A. 160 43 20N 115 2W
Hill City, Kans., U.S.A. 158 39 25N 99 51W
Hill City, Minn., U.S.A. 158 46 57N 93 35W
Hill City, S.D., U.S.A. 158 43 58N 103 35W
Hill End 141 38 1S 146 9E
Hill Island L. 153 60 30N 109 50W
Hill, R. 137 30 23S 115 3E
Hilla, Iraq 92 32 30N 44 27E
Hilla, Si Arab. 92 23 35N 46 50E
Hillared 73 57 37N 13 10E
Hillegom 46 52 18N 4 35E
Hillerød 73 55 56N 12 19E
Hillerstorp 73 57 20N 13 52E
Hilli 98 25 17N 89 1E
Hillingdon 29 51 33N 0 29W
Hillman 156 45 5N 83 52W
Hillmond 153 53 26N 109 41W
Hillsboro, Kans., U.S.A. 158 38 28N 97 10W
Hillsboro, N. Mex., U.S.A. 161 33 0N 107 35W
Hillsboro, N. Mex., U.S.A. 161 33 0N 107 35W
Hillsboro, N.D., U.S.A. 158 47 23N 97 9W
Hillsboro, N.H., U.S.A. 156 43 8N 71 56W
Hillsboro, Oreg., U.S.A. 160 45 31N 123 0W
Hillsboro, Tex., U.S.A. 159 32 0N 97 10W
Hillsborough, U.K. 38 54 28N 6 6W
Hillsborough, W. Indies 167 12 28N 61 28W
Hillsdale, Mich., U.S.A. 156 41 55N 84 40W
Hillsdale, N.Y., U.S.A. 162 42 11N 73 30W
Hillside 136 21 45S 119 23E
Hillsport 150 49 27N 85 34W
Hillston 141 33 30S 145 31E
Hillswick 36 60 29N 1 28W
Hilltown 38 54 12N 6 8W
Hilo 147 19 44N 155 5W
Hilonghilong, mt. 103 9 10N 125 45E
Hilpsford Pt. 32 54 4N 3 12W
Hilvarenbeek 47 51 29N 5 8E
Hilversum 46 52 14N 5 10E
Himachal Pradesh □ 94 31 30N 77 0E
Himalaya 99 29 0N 84 0E
Himara 68 40 8N 19 43E
Himatnagar 93 23 37N 72 57E
Hime-Jima 110 33 43N 131 40E
Himeji 110 34 50N 134 40E
Himi 111 36 50N 137 0E
Himmerland 73 56 45N 9 30E
Hims = Homs 92 34 40N 36 45E
Hinako, Kepulauan 102 0 50N 97 20E
Hinche 167 19 9N 72 1W
Hinchinbrook I. 138 18 20S 146 15E
Hinckley, U.K. 28 52 33N 1 21W
Hinckley, U.S.A. 160 39 18N 112 41W
Hindås 73 57 42N 12 27E
Hindaun 94 26 44N 77 5E
Hinde Rapids (Hells Gate) 126 5 25S 27 3E
Hinderwell 33 54 32N 0 45W
Hindhead 29 51 6N 0 42W
Hindley 32 53 32N 2 35W
Hindmarsh L. 140 36 5S 141 55E
Hindol 95 20 40N 85 10E
Hinds 143 43 59S 171 36E
Hindsholm 73 55 30N 10 40E
Hindu Bagh 94 30 56N 67 57E
Hindu Kush 93 36 0N 71 0E
Hindubagh 93 30 56N 67 57E
Hindupur 97 13 49N 77 32E
Hines Creek 152 56 20N 118 40W
Hinganghat 96 20 30N 78 59E
Hingeon 47 50 32N 4 59E
Hingham, U.K. 29 52 35N 0 59E
Hingham, U.S.A. 160 48 40N 110 29W
Hingol, R. 93 25 30N 65 30E
Hingoli 96 19 41N 77 15E
Hinkley Pt. 28 50 59N 3 32W
Hinlopenstretet 12 79 35N 18 40E
Hinna 121 10 25N 11 28E
Hinnøy 74 68 40N 16 28E
Hino 111 35 0N 136 15E
Hinojosa 55 38 30N 5 17W
Hinojosa del Duque 57 38 30N 5 17W
Hinokage 110 32 39N 131 24E
Hinsdale 160 48 26N 107 2W
Hinstock 28 52 50N 2 28W
Hinterrhein, R. 51 46 40N 9 25E
Hinton, Can. 152 53 26N 117 34W
Hinton, U.S.A. 156 37 40N 80 51W
Hinwil 51 47 18N 8 51E
Hippolytushoef 46 52 54N 4 58E
Hirado 110 33 22N 129 33E
Hirado-Shima 110 33 20N 129 30E
Hirakarta 111 34 48N 135 40E
Hirakud 96 21 32N 83 51E
Hirakud Dam 96 21 32N 83 45E
Hirara 112 24 48N 125 17E
Hirata 110 35 24N 132 49E
Hiratsuka 111 35 19N 139 21E
Hirhafok 119 23 49N 5 45E
Hirlǔu 70 47 23N 27 0E
Hiromi 110 33 13N 132 36E
Hirosaki 112 40 34N 140 28E
Hiroshima 110 34 30N 132 30E
Hiroshima-ken □ 112 34 50N 133 0E
Hiroshima-Wan 110 34 5N 132 20E
Hirsoholmene 73 57 30N 10 36E
Hirson 43 49 55N 4 4E
Hîrşova 70 44 40N 27 59E
Hirtshals 73 57 36N 9 57E
Hirwaun 31 51 43N 3 30W
Hisoy 71 58 26N 8 44E
Hispaniola, I. 165 19 0N 71 0W
Hissar 94 29 12N 75 45E
Histon 29 52 15N 0 6E
Hita 110 33 20N 130 58E
Hitachi 111 36 36N 140 39E
Hitachiota 111 36 30N 140 30E
Hitchin 29 51 57N 0 16W
Hitoyoshi 110 32 13N 130 45E
Hitra 71 63 30N 8 45E
Hitzacker 48 53 9N 11 1E
Hiuchi-Nada 110 34 5N 133 20E
Hjalmar L. 153 61 33N 109 25W
Hjälmare Kanal 72 59 20N 15 59E
Hjälmaren 72 59 18N 15 40E
Hjartdal 71 59 37N 8 41E
Hjärtsäter 73 58 35N 12 3E
Hjerkinn 71 62 13N 9 33E
Hjerpsted 73 55 2N 8 39E
Hjo 73 58 22N 4 17E
Hjørring 73 57 29N 9 59E
Hjorted 73 57 37N 16 19E
Hjortkvarn 73 58 54N 15 26E
Hko-ut 98 21 40N 97 46E
Hkyenhpa 98 27 43N 97 25E
Hlaingbwe 98 17 8N 97 50E
Hlinsko 52 49 45N 15 54E
Hlohovec 53 48 26N 17 49E
Hlwaze 98 18 54N 96 37E
Ho 121 6 37N 0 27E
Ho Chi Minh, Phanh Bho 101 10 58N 106 40E
Ho Thuong 100 19 32N 105 48E
Hoa Binh 100 20 50N 105 20E
Hoa Da (Phan Ri) 100 11 16N 108 40E
Hoa Hiep 101 11 34N 105 51E
Hoadley 152 52 45N 114 30W
Hoai Nhon (Bon Son) 100 14 28N 109 1E
Hoare B. 149 65 17N 62 55W
Hobart, Austral. 138 42 50S 147 21E
Hobart, U.S.A. 159 35 0N 99 5W
Hobbs 159 32 40N 103 3W
Hobjærg 73 56 19N 9 32E
Hobo 174 2 35N 75 30W
Hoboken, Belg. 47 51 11N 4 21E
Hoboken, U.S.A. 162 40 45N 74 4W
Hobro 73 56 39N 9 46E
Hobscheid 47 49 42N 5 57E
Hoburg C. 73 56 54N 18 8E
Hoburgen 73 56 55N 18 7E
Hochang 108 27 8N 104 45E
Hochatown 159 34 11N 94 39W
Hochdorf 51 47 10N 8 17E
Hochiang 108 28 48N 105 48E
Hochien 106 38 26N 116 5E
Hoch'ih 108 24 43N 108 2E
Hoching 106 35 37N 110 43E
Hoch'iu 109 32 21N 116 13E
Höchst 49 50 6N 8 33E
Hoch'ü 106 39 26N 111 8E
Hoch'uan 108 30 2N 106 18E
Hockenheim 49 49 18N 8 33E
Hod, oilfield 19 56 10N 3 25E
Hodaka-Dake 111 36 17N 137 39E
Hodde 73 55 42N 8 39E
Hodder R. 32 53 57N 2 27W
Hoddesdon 29 51 45N 0 1W
Hodeïda 91 14 50N 43 0E
Hodge, R. 33 54 14N 0 55W
Hodgson 153 51 13N 97 36W
Hódmezóvásárhely 53 46 28N 20 22E
Hodna, Chott el 119 35 30N 5 0E
Hodonín 53 48 50N 17 0E
Hodsager 73 56 19N 8 51E
Hoeamdong 107 42 30N 130 16E
Hoëdic, I. 42 47 21N 2 52W
Hoegaarden 47 50 47N 4 53E
Hoek van Holland 46 52 0N 4 7E
Hoeksche Waard 46 51 46N 4 25E
Hoenderloo 46 52 7N 5 52E
Hoengsŏng 107 37 29N 127 59E
Hoensbroek 47 50 55N 5 55E
Hoeryong 107 42 30N 129 58E
Hoeselt 47 50 51N 5 29E
Hoëveld 129 26 30S 30 0E
Hoeven 47 51 35N 4 35E
Hoeyang 107 38 43N 127 36E
Hof, Ger. 49 50 18N 11 55E
Hof, Iceland 74 64 33N 14 40W
Höfðakaupstaður 74 65 50N 20 19W
Hofei 109 31 52N 117 15E
Hoff 32 54 34N 2 31W
Hofgeismar 48 51 29N 9 23E
Hofors 72 60 35N 16 15E
Hofsjökull 74 64 49N 18 48W
Hofsós 74 65 53N 19 26W
Hōfu 110 34 3N 131 34E
Hofuf 92 25 20N 49 40E
Hög-Gia, Mt. 71 62 23N 10 7E
Hog I. 162 37 26N 75 42W
Hogan Group 139 39 13S 147 1E
Höganäs 73 56 13N 12 34E
Hogansville 157 33 14N 84 50W
Hogarth, Mt. 138 21 50S 137 0E
Hogeland 160 48 51N 108 40W
Högen 72 61 47N 14 11E
Hogenaki Falls 97 12 6N 77 50E
Högfors, Örebro, Sweden 72 59 58N 15 3E
Högfors, Västmanlands, Sweden 72 60 2N 16 3E
Hoggar = Ahaggar 119 23 0N 6 30E
Hōgo-Kaikyo 110 33 20N 131 58E
Hog's Back, hill 29 51 13N 0 40W
Hogs Hd. 39 51 46N 10 13W
Högsäter 73 58 38N 12 5E
Högsby 73 57 10N 16 1E
Högsjo 72 59 4N 15 44E
Hogsthorpe 33 53 13N 0 19E
Hogsty Reef 167 21 41N 73 48W
Hohe Rhön 49 50 24N 9 58E
Hohe Tauern 52 47 11N 12 40E
Hohenau 53 48 36N 16 55E
Hohenems 52 47 22N 9 42E
Hohenstein Ernstthal 48 50 48N 12 43E
Hohenwald 157 35 35N 87 30W
Hohenwestedt 48 54 6N 9 40E
Hohoe 121 7 8N 0 32E
Hohsi 108 24 9N 102 38E
Hohsien, Anhwei, China 109 31 43N 118 22E
Hohsien, Kwangsi-Chuang, China 109 24 25N 111 31E
Hohsüeh 109 30 2N 112 25E
Hôi An 100 15 30N 108 19E
Hoi Xuan 100 20 25N 105 9E
Hoisington 158 38 33N 98 50W
Højer 73 54 58N 8 42E
Hōjō 110 33 58N 132 46E
Hok 73 57 31N 14 16E
Hokensås 73 58 0N 14 5E
Hökensås 73 58 0N 14 5E
Hökerum 73 57 51N 13 16E
Hokianga Harbour 142 35 31S 173 22E
Hokitika 143 42 42S 171 0E
Hokkaidō 112 43 30N 143 0E
Hokkaidō □ 112 43 30N 143 0E
Hokksund 71 59 44N 9 59E
Hok'ou, Kansu, China 106 36 9N 103 29E
Hok'ou, Kwantang, China 109 23 13N 112 45E
Hok'ou, Yunnan, China 108 22 39N 103 57E
Hokow 101 22 39N 103 57E
Hol-Hol. 123 11 20N 42 50E
Holan Shan 106 38 50N 105 50E
Holbæk 73 55 43N 11 43E
Holbeach 29 52 48N 0 1E
Holbeach Marsh 29 52 52N 0 5E
Holborn Hd. 37 58 37N 3 30W
Holbrook, Austral. 141 35 42S 147 18E
Holbrook, U.S.A. 161 35 0N 110 0W
Holden 152 53 13N 112 11W
Holden Fillmore 160 39 0N 112 26W
Holdenville 159 35 5N 96 25W
Holder 140 34 21S 140 0E
Holderness 33 53 45N 0 5W
Holdfast 153 50 58N 105 25W
Holdrege 153 40 25N 99 30W
Hole 71 60 6N 10 12E
Hole-Narsipur 97 12 48N 76 16E
Holešov 53 49 20N 17 35E
Holguín 166 20 50N 76 20W
Holinkoerh 106 40 23N 111 53E
Holíč 53 48 49N 17 10E
Holkham 29 52 57N 0 48E
Holla, Mt. 123 7 5N 36 35E
Hollabrunn 52 48 34N 16 5E
Hollams Bird I. 128 24 40S 14 30E
Holland 156 42 47N 86 7W
Holland Fen 33 53 0N 0 8W
Holland-on-Sea 29 51 48N 1 12E
Hollandia = Jajapura 103 2 28S 140 38E
Hollands Bird I. 128 24 40S 14 30E
Hollandsch Diep 47 51 41N 4 30E
Hollandsch IJssel, R. 46 51 55N 4 34E
Hollandstoun 37 59 22N 2 25W
Höllen 71 58 6N 7 49E
Holleton 137 31 55S 119 0E
Hollidaysburg 156 40 26N 78 25W
Hollis 159 34 45N 99 55W
Hollister 161 36 51N 121 24W
Hollum 46 53 26N 5 38E
Holly 158 38 7N 102 7W
Holly Hill 157 29 15N 81 3W
Holly Springs 159 34 45N 89 25W
Hoîlymount 38 53 40N 9 7W
Hollywood, Ireland 39 53 6N 6 35W
Hollywood, Calif., U.S.A. 154 34 7N 118 25W
Hollywood, Fla., U.S.A. 157 26 0N 80 9W
Holm 72 62 40N 16 40E
Holman Island 148 71 0N 118 0W
Hólmavík 74 65 42N 21 40W
Holme, Humberside,, U.K. 33 53 50N 0 48W
Holme, N. Yorks., U.K. 32 53 34N 1 50W
Holmedal 71 59 46N 5 50E
Holmedal, Fjordane 71 61 22N 5 11E
Holmegil 72 59 10N 11 44E
Holmes Chapel 32 53 13N 2 21W
Holmes Reefs 138 16 27S 148 0E
Holmestrand 71 59 31N 10 14E
Holmfirth 33 53 34N 1 48W
Holmsbu 71 59 32N 10 27E
Holmsjön 72 62 26N 15 20E
Holmsland Klit 73 56 0N 8 5E
Holmsund 74 63 41N 20 20E
Holmwood 29 51 12N 0 19W
Hölö 72 59 3N 17 36E
Holo Ho, R. 107 44 54N 122 22E
Holod 70 46 49N 22 8E
Holon 90 32 2N 34 47E
Holroyd, R. 138 14 10S 141 36E
Holsen 71 61 25N 6 8E
Holstebro 73 56 22N 8 37E
Holsworthy 30 50 48N 4 21W
Holt, Iceland 74 63 33N 19 48W
Holt, Clwyd, U.K. 31 53 4N 2 52W
Holt, Norfolk, U.K. 29 52 55N 1 4E
Holte 73 55 50N 12 29E
Holten 46 52 17N 6 26E
Holton Harbour 151 54 31N 57 12W
Holton le Clay 33 53 29N 0 3W
Holtville 161 32 50N 115 27W
Holum 71 58 6N 7 32E
Holwerd 46 53 22N 5 54E
Holy Cross 147 62 10N 159 52W
Holy I., England, U.K. 35 55 42N 1 48W
Holy I., Scotland, U.K. 34 55 31N 5 4W
Holy I., Wales, U.K. 31 53 17N 4 37W
Holyhead 31 53 18N 4 38W
Holyhead B. 31 53 20N 4 35W
Holyoke, Mass., U.S.A. 162 42 14N 72 37W
Holyoke, Nebr., U.S.A. 158 40 39N 102 18W
Holyrood 151 47 27N 53 8W
Holywell 31 53 16N 3 14W
Holywood 38 54 38N 5 50W
Holzminden 48 51 49N 9 31E
Homa Bay 126 0 36S 34 22E
Homa Bay □ 126 0 50S 34 30E
Homalin 98 24 55N 95 0E
Homberg 48 51 2N 9 20E
Hombori 121 15 20N 1 38W
Homburg 49 49 19N 7 21E
Home B. 149 68 40N 67 10W
Home Hill 138 19 43S 147 25E
Homedale 160 43 42N 116 59W
Homer, Alaska, U.S.A. 147 59 40N 151 35W
Homer, La., U.S.A. 159 32 50N 93 4W
Homestead, Austral. 138 20 20S 145 40E
Homestead, U.S.A. 157 25 29N 80 27W
Hominy 159 36 26N 96 24W
Homnabad 96 17 45N 77 5E
Homoine 129 23 55S 35 8E
Homorod 70 46 5N 25 15E
Homs = Al Khums 119 32 40N 14 17E
Homs (Hims) 92 34 40N 36 45E
Hon Chong 101 10 16N 104 38E
Hon Me 100 19 23N 105 56E
Honan □ 106 34 10N 113 10E
Honbetsu 112 43 7N 143 37E
Honda 174 5 12N 74 45W
Hondeklipbaai 125 30 19S 17 17E
Hondo, Japan 110 32 27N 130 12E
Hondo, U.S.A. 159 29 22N 99 6W
Hondo, R. 165 18 25N 88 21W
Honduras ■ 166 14 40N 86 30W
Honduras, Golfo de 166 16 50N 87 0W
Hönefoss 71 60 10N 10 12E
Honey L. 160 40 13N 120 14W
Honfleur 42 49 25N 0 13E
Höng 73 55 30N 11 14E
Hong Gai 100 20 57N 107 5E
Hong Kong ■ 109 22 11N 114 14E

Hong, R Hsiushui

Hong, R. 100 20 17N 106 34 E
Hongchŏn 107 37 44N 127 53 E
Hongha, R. 101 22 0N 104 0 E
Hongor 106 45 56N 112 50 E
Hongsa 100 19 43N 101 20 E
Hongsŏng 107 36 37N 126 38 E
Honguedo, Détroit d' 151 49 15N 64 0W
Hongwon 107 40 0N 127 56 E
Honiara 142 9 30 S 160 0 E
Honington 33 52 58N 0 35W
Honiton 30 50 48N 3 11W
Honjo, Akita, Japan 112 39 23N 140 3 E
Honjo, Gumma, Japan 111 36 14N 139 11 E
Honkawane 111 35 5N 138 5 E
Honkorâb, Ras 122 24 35N 35 10 E
Honolulu 147 21 19N 157 52W
Honshū 112 36 0N 138 0 E
Hontoria del Pinar 58 41 50N 3 10W
Hoo 29 51 25N 0 33 E
Hood Mt. 160 45 15N 122 0W
Hood, Pt. 137 34 23 S 119 34 E
Hood Pt. 135 10 4 S 147 45 E
Hood River 160 45 45N 121 37W
Hoodsport 160 47 24N 123 7W
Hooge 48 54 31N 8 36 E
Hoogerheide 47 51 26N 4 20 E
Hoogeveen 46 52 44N 6 30 E
Hoogeveensche Vaart 46 52 42N 6 12 E
Hoogezand 46 53 11N 6 45 E
Hooghly-Chinsura 95 22 53N 88 27 E
Hooghly, R. 95 21 59N 88 10 E
Hoogkerk 46 53 13N 6 30 E
Hooglede 47 50 59N 3 5 E
Hoogstraten 47 51 24N 4 46 E
Hoogvliet 46 51 52N 4 21 E
Hook 29 51 17N 0 55W
Hook Hd. 39 52 8N 6 57W
Hook I. 138 20 4 S 149 0 E
Hook of Holland = Hoek v. Holland 47 52 0N 4 7 E
Hooker 159 36 55N 101 10W
Hooker Cr. 136 18 23 S 130 50 E
Hoonah 147 58 15N 135 30W
Hooper Bay 147 61 30N 166 10W
Hoopersville 162 38 16N 76 11W
Hoopeston 156 40 30N 87 40W
Hoopstad 128 27 50 S 25 55 E
Höör 73 55 55N 13 33 E
Hoorn 46 52 38N 5 4 E
Hoover Dam 161 36 0N 114 45W
Hop Bottom 162 41 41N 75 47W
Hopà 83 41 28N 41 30 E
Hope, Can. 152 49 25N 121 25 E
Hope, U.K. 31 53 7N 3 2W
Hope, Ark., U.S.A. 159 33 40N 93 30W
Hope, N.D., U.S.A. 158 47 21N 97 42W
Hope Bay 13 65 0 S 55 0W
Hope, L. 139 28 24 S 139 18 E
Hope L. 37 58 24N 4 38W
Hope Pt. 147 68 20N 166 50W
Hope Town 157 26 30N 76 30W
Hopedale, Can. 151 55 28N 60 13W
Hopedale, U.S.A. 162 42 8N 71 33W
Hopefield 128 33 3 S 18 22 E
Hopei □ 107 39 25N 116 45 E
Hopelchén 165 19 46N 89 50W
Hopeman 37 57 42N 3 26W
Hopen 71 63 27N 8 2 E
Hopetoun 137 33 57 S 120 7 E
Hopetown, Austral. 140 35 42 S 142 22 E
Hopetown, S. Afr. 128 29 34 S 24 3 E
Hopewell 162 37 18N 77 17W
Hopien-Ts'un 108 27 40N 101 55 E
Hopin 98 21 14N 96 53 E
Hop'ing 109 24 26N 114 56 E
Hopkins 158 40 31N 94 45W
Hopkins, L. 136 24 15 S 128 35 E
Hopkinsville 157 36 52N 87 26W
Hopland 160 39 0N 123 7W
Hopo 108 31 24N 99 0 E
Hoptrup 73 55 11N 9 28 E
Hop'u 108 21 41N 109 10 E
Hoquiam 160 46 50N 123 55W
Hōrai 111 34 58N 137 32 E
Horazdovice 52 49 19N 13 42 E
Hörby 73 55 50N 13 44 E
Horcajo de Santiago 58 39 50N 3 1W
Hordaland fylke □ 71 60 25N 6 15 E
Horden 33 54 45N 1 17W
Hordern Hills 136 20 40 S 130 20 E
Hordio 91 10 36N 51 8 E
Horezu 70 45 6N 24 0 E
Horgen 51 47 15N 8 35 E
Horgoš 66 46 10N 20 0 E
Horice 52 50 21N 15 39 E
Horley 29 51 10N 0 10W
Horlick Mts. 13 84 0 S 102 0W
Hormoz 93 27 35N 55 0 E
Hormuz, I. 93 27 8N 56 28 E
Hormuz Str. 93 26 30N 56 30 E
Horn, Austria 52 48 39N 15 40 E
Horn, Isafjarðarsýsla, Iceland 74 66 28N 22 28W
Horn, Suður-Múlasýsla, Iceland 74 65 10N 13 31W
Horn, Neth. 47 51 12N 5 57 E
Horn, Cape = Hornos, C. de 176 55 50 S 67 30W
Horn Head 38 55 13N 8 0W
Horn I., Austral. 138 10 37 S 142 17 E
Horn I., P.N.G. 135 10 35 S 142 20 E
Horn, I. 157 30 17N 88 40W
Horn Mts. 152 62 15N 119 15W
Horn, R. 152 61 30N 118 1W
Hornachuelos 57 37 50N 5 14W
Hornavan 74 66 15N 17 30 E
Hornbæk, Frederiksborg, Denmark 73 56 5N 12 26 E
Hornbæk, Viborg, Denmark 73 56 28N 9 58 E
Hornbeck 159 31 22N 93 20W
Hornbrook 160 41 58N 122 37W
Hornburg 48 52 2N 10 36 E
Hornby 143 43 33 S 172 33 E
Horncastle 33 53 13N 0 8W
Horndal 72 60 18N 16 23 E
Horndean 29 50 56N 1 5W
Hornell 156 42 23N 77 41W
Hornell L. 152 62 20N 119 25W
Hornepayne 150 49 14N 84 48W
Hornindal 71 61 58N 6 30 E
Horningsham 28 51 11N 2 16W
Hornitos 163 37 30N 120 14W
Hornnes 71 58 34N 7 45 E
Hornos, Cabo de 176 55 50 S 67 30 E
Hornoy 43 49 50N 1 54 E
Hornsberg, Jamtland, Sweden 72 63 14N 14 40 E
Hornsberg, Kronobergs, Sweden 72 56 37N 13 47 E
Hornsby 141 33 42 S 151 2 E
Hornsea 33 53 55N 0 10W
Hornslandet Pen. 72 61 35N 17 37 E
Hornslet 73 56 18N 10 19 E
Hornu 47 50 26N 3 50 E
Hörnum 73 54 44N 8 18 E
Horovice 52 49 48N 13 53 E
Horqueta 172 23 15 S 56 55W
Horra, La 56 41 44N 3 53W
Horred 73 57 22N 12 28 E
Horse Cr. 158 41 33N 104 45W
Horse Is. 151 50 15N 55 50W
Horsefly L. 152 52 25N 121 0W
Horseheads 162 42 10N 76 49W
Horseleap 38 53 25N 7 34W
Horsens 73 55 52N 9 51 E
Horsens Fjord 73 55 50N 10 0 E
Horseshoe 137 25 27 S 118 31 E
Horseshoe Dam 161 33 45N 111 35W
Horsforth 33 53 50N 1 39W
Horsham, Austral. 140 36 44 S 142 13 E
Horsham, U.K. 29 51 4N 0 20W
Horsham St. Faith 29 52 41N 1 15 E
Horsovsky Tyn 52 49 31N 12 58 E
Horst 47 51 27N 6 3 E
Horsted Keynes 29 51 2N 0 1W
Horten 71 59 25N 10 32 E
Hortobágy, R. 53 47 30N 21 6 E
Horton 158 39 42N 95 30W
Horton-in-Ribblesdale 32 54 9N 2 19W
Horton, R. 147 69 56N 126 52W
Hörvik 73 56 2N 14 45 E
Horw 51 47 1N 8 19 E
Horwich 32 53 37N 2 33W
Horwood, L. 150 48 10N 82 20W
Hosaina 123 7 30N 37 47 E
Hosdurga 97 13 40N 76 17 E
Hose, Pegunungan 102 2 5N 114 6 E
Hoshan 109 31 24N 116 20 E
Hoshangabad 94 22 45N 77 45 E
Hoshiarpur 94 31 30N 75 58 E
Hoshui 106 36 0N 107 59 E
Hoshun 106 37 19N 113 34 E
Hosingen 47 50 1N 6 6 E
Hoskins 135 5 29 S 150 27 E
Hosmer 158 45 36N 99 29W
Hososhima 110 32 26N 131 40 E
Hospental 51 46 37N 8 34 E
Hospet 97 15 15N 76 20 E
Hospital 39 52 30N 8 28W
Hospitalet de Llobregat 58 41 21N 2 6 E
Hospitalet, L' 44 42 36N 1 47 E
Hoste, I. 176 55 0 S 69 0W
Hostens 44 44 30N 0 40W
Hoswick 36 60 0N 1 15W
Hot 100 18 8N 98 29 E
Hot Creek Ra. 160 39 0N 116 0W
Hot Springs, Ark, U.S.A. 159 34 30N 93 0W
Hot Springs, S.D., U.S.A. 158 43 25N 103 30W
Hotagen, L. 74 63 50N 14 30 E
Hotazel 128 27 17 S 23 00 E
Hotchkiss 161 38 55N 107 47W
Hotham, C. 136 12 2 S 131 18 E
Hot'ien 105 37 7N 79 55 E
Hoting 74 64 8N 16 15 E
Hotolishti 68 41 10N 20 25 E
Hotse 106 35 14N 115 27 E
Hotte, Massif de la 167 18 30N 73 45W
Hottentotsbaai 128 26 8 S 14 59 E
Hotton 47 50 16N 5 26 E
Houat, I. 42 47 24N 2 58W
Houck 161 35 15N 109 15W
Houdan 43 48 48N 1 35 E
Houdeng-Goegnies 47 50 29N 4 10 E
Houei Sai 100 20 18N 100 26 E
Houffalize 47 50 8N 5 48 E
Houghton 158 47 9N 88 39W
Houghton L. 156 44 20N 84 40W
Houghton-le-Spring 35 54 51N 1 28W
Houghton Regis 29 51 54N 0 32W
Houhora 142 34 49 S 173 9 E
Houille, R. 47 50 8N 4 50 E
Houlton 151 46 5N 68 0W
Houma 159 29 35N 90 50W
Houmt Souk = Djerba 119 33 53N 10 37 E
Houndé 120 11 34N 3 31W
Hounslow 29 51 29N 0 20W
Hourn L. 36 57 7N 5 35W
Hourtin 44 45 11N 1 4W
Housatonic, R. 162 41 10N 73 7W
Houston, Can. 152 54 25N 126 30W
Houston, Mo., U.S.A. 159 37 20N 92 0W
Houston, Tex., U.S.A. 159 29 50N 95 20W
Houten 46 52 2N 5 10 E
Houthalen 47 51 2N 5 23 E
Houthem 47 50 48N 2 57 E
Houthulst 47 50 59N 2 57 E
Houtman Abrolhos 137 28 43 S 113 48 E
Houyet 47 50 11N 5 1 E
Hova 73 58 53N 14 14 E
Høvag 71 58 10N 8 15 E
Hövåg 71 58 10N 8 16 E
Hovd 105 48 1N 91 39 E
Hovden 71 59 33N 7 22 E
Hove 29 50 50N 0 10W
Hoveton 29 52 45N 1 23 E
Hovingham 33 54 10N 0 59W
Hovmantorp 73 56 47N 15 7 E
Hövsgöl 106 43 37N 109 39 E
Hovsta 72 59 22N 15 15 E
Howakil 123 15 10N 40 16 E
Howar, W., (Shau) 123 17 0N 25 30 E
Howard, Austral. 139 25 16 S 152 32 E
Howard, Kans., U.S.A. 159 37 30N 96 16W
Howard, S.D., U.S.A. 158 44 2N 97 30W
Howard I. 138 12 10 S 135 24 E
Howard L. 153 62 15N 105 57W
Howatharra 137 28 29 S 114 33 E
Howden 33 53 45N 0 52W
Howe 160 43 48N 113 0W
Howe, C. 141 37 30 S 150 0 E
Howell 156 42 38N 84 0W
Howick, N.Z. 142 36 54 S 174 48 E
Howick, S. Afr. 129 29 28 S 30 14 E
Howick Group 138 14 20 S 145 30 E
Howitt, L. 139 27 40 S 138 40 E
Howley 151 49 12N 57 2W
Howmore 36 57 18N 7 23W
Howrah 95 22 37N 88 27 E
Howth 38 53 23N 6 3W
Howth Hd. 38 53 21N 6 0W
Hoxne 29 52 22N 1 11 E
Höxter 48 51 45N 9 26 E
Hoy I. 37 58 50N 3 15W
Hoy Sd. 37 58 57N 3 20W
Hoya 48 52 47N 9 10 E
Høyanger 71 61 25N 6 50 E
Höydalsmo 71 59 30N 8 15 E
Hoyerswerda 48 51 26N 14 14 E
Hoylake 32 53 24N 3 11W
Höyland 71 58 50N 5 43 E
Hoyleton 140 34 2 S 138 34 E
Hoyos 56 40 9N 6 45W
Hoyüan 109 23 50N 114 40 E
Hpawlum 98 27 12N 98 12 E
Hpettintha 98 24 14N 95 23 E
Hpizow 98 26 57N 98 24 E
Hpungan Pass 99 27 30N 96 55 E
Hrádec Králové 52 50 15N 15 50 E
Hrádek 53 48 46N 16 16 E
Hranice 53 49 34N 17 45 E
Hron, R. 53 48 0N 18 4 E
Hrubieszów 54 50 49N 23 51 E
Hrubý Nizký Jeseník 53 50 7N 17 10 E
Hrvatska 63 45 20N 16 0 E
Hsenwi 98 23 22N 97 55 E
Hsi Chiang, R. 109 22 20N 113 20 E
Hsiach'engtzu, Heilungkiang, China 107 44 41N 130 27 E
Hsiach'engtzu, Schechwan, China 108 29 24N 101 46 E
Hsiachiang 109 27 33N 115 10 E
Hsiaching 106 36 57N 115 59 E
Hsiach'uan Shan 109 21 40N 112 37 E
Hsiahsien 106 35 12N 111 11 E
Hsiai 106 34 17N 116 11 E
Hsiakuan 108 25 39N 100 9 E
Hsiamen 109 24 30N 118 7 E
Hsian 106 34 17N 109 0 E
Hsiang Chiang, R. 109 29 30N 113 10 E
Hsiangch'eng, Honan, China 106 33 50N 113 29 E
Hsiangch'eng, Honan, China 106 33 13N 114 50 E
Hsiangch'eng, Szechwan, China 108 29 0N 99 46 E
Hsiangchou 108 23 58N 109 41 E
Hsiangfan 109 32 7N 112 9 E
Hsianghsiang 109 27 46N 112 30 E
Hsiangning 106 36 1N 110 47 E
Hsiangshan 109 29 18N 121 37 E
Hsiangshuik'ou 107 34 12N 119 34 E
Hsiangt'an 109 27 55N 112 52 E
Hsiangtu 108 23 14N 106 57 E
Hsiangyang 109 32 2N 112 6 E
Hsiangyin 109 28 40N 112 53 E
Hsiangyüan 106 36 32N 113 2 E
Hsiangyün 108 25 29N 100 35 E
Hsiaochin 108 31 1N 102 23 E
Hsiaofeng 109 30 36N 119 33 E
Hsiaohsien 106 34 2N 116 56 E
Hsiaohsinganling Shanmo 105 48 45N 127 0 E
Hsiaoi 106 37 7N 111 46 E
Hsiaokan 109 30 57N 113 53 E
Hsiaoshan 109 30 10N 120 15 E
Hsiaot'ai Shan 107 36 18N 116 38 E
Hsiap'u 109 26 58N 119 57 E
Hsiawa 107 42 38N 120 31 E
Hsich'ang 108 27 50N 102 18 E
Hsichiehť'o 108 30 24N 108 13 E
Hsich'uan 109 33 0N 111 24 E
Hsich'ung 108 31 0N 105 48 E
Hsiehch'eng 107 34 48N 117 15 E
Hsiehmaho 109 31 38N 111 12 E
Hsienchü 109 28 51N 120 44 E
Hsienfeng 108 29 40N 109 7 E
Hsienhsien 106 38 2N 116 12 E
Hsienning 109 29 51N 114 15 E
Hsienshui Ho, R. 108 30 5N 101 5 E
Hsienyang 106 34 22N 108 48 E
Hsienyu 109 25 24N 118 40 E
Hsifei Ho, R. 109 32 38N 116 39 E
Hsifeng, Kweichow, China 108 27 5N 106 42 E
Hsifeng, Liaoning, China 107 42 44N 124 42 E
Hsifengchen 106 35 40N 107 42 E
Hsifengk'ou 107 40 24N 118 19 E
Hsiho 106 34 2N 105 12 E
Hsihsia, Honan, China 106 33 30N 111 30 E
Hsihsia, Shantung, China 107 37 25N 120 48 E
Hsihsiang 108 33 1N 107 40 E
Hsihsien, Honan, China 109 32 24N 114 52 E
Hsihsien, Shensi, China 106 36 41N 110 56 E
Hsihua 106 33 47N 114 31 E
Hsilamunlun Ho, R. 107 43 24N 123 42 E
Hsiliao Ho, R. 107 43 24N 123 42 E
Hsilin 108 24 30N 105 3 E
Hsin Chiang, R. 109 28 50N 116 40 E
Hsin Ho, R. 107 43 33N 123 31 E
Hsinchan 107 43 52N 127 20 E
Hsinch'ang 109 29 30N 120 54 E
Hsincheng 106 34 25N 113 46 E
Hsinch'eng, Hopei, China 106 39 15N 115 59 E
Hsinch'eng, Kwangsi-Chuang, China 108 24 4N 108 40 E
Hsinchiang 106 35 40N 111 15 E
Hsinchien 108 23 58N 102 47 E
Hsinchin 107 39 25N 121 59 E
Hsinching 108 30 25N 103 49 E
Hsinchi'u 107 41 53N 119 40 E
Hsinchou 109 30 52N 114 48 E
Hsinchu 109 24 48N 120 58 E
Hsinfeng, Kiangsi, China 109 25 27N 114 58 E
Hsinfeng, Kiangsi, China 109 26 7N 116 11 E
Hsinfeng, Kwangtung, China 109 24 4N 114 12 E
Hsingan 109 25 39N 110 39 E
Hsingch'eng 107 40 40N 120 48 E
Hsingho 106 40 52N 113 58 E
Hsinghsien 106 38 31N 111 4 E
Hsinghua 107 32 55N 119 52 E
Hsinghua Wan 109 25 20N 119 20 E
Hsingi 108 25 5N 104 55 E
Hsinging 109 26 25N 110 44 E
Hsingjen 108 25 25N 105 13 E
Hsingjenp'ao 106 37 0N 105 0 E
Hsingkuo 109 26 26N 115 16 E
Hsinglung 107 40 29N 117 32 E
Hsingning 109 24 8N 115 43 E
Hsingp'ing 106 34 18N 108 26 E
Hsingshan 109 31 10N 110 51 E
Hsingt'ai 106 37 5N 114 38 E
Hsingyeh 108 22 45N 109 52 E
Hsinhailien = Lienyünchiangshih 107 34 37N 119 13 E
Hsinhsiang 106 35 15N 113 54 E
Hsinhsien, Shansi, China 106 38 24N 112 47 E
Hsinhsien, Shantung, China 106 36 15N 115 40 E
Hsinhsing 109 22 45N 112 11 E
Hsinhua 109 27 43N 111 18 E
Hsinhui 109 22 32N 113 0 E
Hsini 109 22 12N 110 53 E
Hsining 105 36 37N 101 46 E
Hsink'ai Ho, R. 107 41 10N 122 5 E
Hsinkan 109 27 45N 115 21 E
Hsinkao Shan 109 23 25N 120 52 E
Hsinlit'un 107 42 2N 122 19 E
Hsinlo 106 38 15N 114 40 E
Hsinmin 107 42 0N 122 52 E
Hsinpaoan 106 40 27N 115 23 E
Hsinpin 107 41 43N 125 2 E
Hsinp'ing 108 24 6N 101 58 E
Hsinshao 109 27 20N 111 26 E
Hsint'ai 107 35 54N 117 44 E
Hsint'ien 109 25 56N 112 13 E
Hsints'ai 109 32 44N 114 59 E
Hsinyang 109 32 10N 114 6 E
Hsinyeh 109 32 31N 112 21 E
Hsinyü 109 27 48N 114 56 E
Hsipaw 98 22 37N 97 18 E
Hsip'ing, Honan, China 106 33 34N 110 45 E
Hsip'ing, Honan, China 106 33 23N 114 2 E
Hsishni 109 30 27N 115 13 E
Hsitalahai 106 40 38N 109 38 E
Hsiu Shui, R. 109 29 13N 116 0 E
Hsiujen 109 24 26N 110 14 E
Hsiunghsien 106 38 50N 116 11 E
Hsiungyüeh 107 40 12N 122 12 E
Hsiuning 109 29 51N 118 15 E
Hsiushan 108 28 27N 108 59 E
Hsiushui 109 29 2N 114 34 E

Hsiuwen Ibara

Hsiuwen 108 26 52N 106 35 E
Hsiuyen 107 40 19N 123 15 E
Hsiyang 106 37 27N 113 46 E
Hsüanch'eng 109 30 54N 118 41 E
Hsüanen 108 29 59N 109 24 E
Hsüanhan 108 31 25N 107 38 E
Hsüanhua 106 40 38N 115 5 E
Hsüanwei 108 26 13N 104 5 E
Hsüch'ang 106 34 1N 113 53 E
Hsüchou 107 34 15N 117 10 E
Hsüehfeng Shan 109 27 0N 110 30 E
Hsüehweng Shan 109 24 24N 121 12 E
Hsun Chiang, R. 109 23 30N 111 30 E
Hsünhsien 106 35 40N 114 32 E
Hsüni 106 35 6N 108 20 E
Hsüntien 108 25 33N 103 15 E
Hsünwu 109 24 57N 115 28 E
Hsünyang 108 32 48N 109 27 E
Hsüp'u 109 27 56N 110 36 E
Hsüshui 106 39 1N 115 39 E
Hsüwen 109 20 20N 110 9 E
Hsüyung 108 28 6N 105 21 E
Htawgaw 98 25 57N 98 23 E
Hua Hin 100 12 34N 99 58 E
Huaan 109 25 1N 117 33 E
Huachacalla 164 18 45 S 68 17W
Huachinera 164 30 9N 108 55W
Huachipato 172 36 45 S 73 09W
Huacho 174 11 10 S 77 35W
Huachón 174 10 35 S 76 0W
Huachou 109 21 38N 110 35 E
Huacrachuco 174 8 35 S 76 50W
Huahsien, Honan, China 106 35 33N 114 34 E
Huahsien, Shensi, China 106 34 31N 109 46 E
Huai Yot 101 7 45N 99 37 E
Huaiachen 106 40 33N 114 30 E
Huaian, Hopei, China 106 40 33N 114 30 E
Huaian, Kiangsu, China 107 33 31N 119 8 E
Huaichi 109 24 0N 112 8 E
Huaihua 109 27 34N 109 56 E
Huaijen 106 39 50N 113 7 E
Huaijou 106 40 20N 116 37 E
Huainan 109 32 39N 117 2 E
Huaining 109 30 21N 116 42 E
Huaite 107 43 30N 124 50 E
Huaitechen 107 43 52N 124 45 E
Huaiyang 106 33 50N 115 2 E
Huaiyüan, Anhwei, China 109 32 58N 117 13 E
Huaiyüan, Kwangsi-Chuang, China 108 24 36N 108 27 E
Huajuapan 165 17 50N 98 0W
Huajung 109 29 34N 112 34 E
Hualien 109 24 0N 121 30 E
Huallaga, R. 174 5 30 S 76 10W
Hualpai Pk. 161 35 8N 113 58W
Huan Chiang, R. 106 36 4N 107 40 E
Huancabamba 174 5 10 S 79 15W
Huancané 174 15 10 S 69 50W
Huancapi 174 13 25 S 74 0W
Huancavelica 174 12 50 S 75 5W
Huancayo 174 12 5 S 75 0W
Huanchiang 108 24 50N 108 15 E
Huang Ho, R. 107 36 50N 118 20 E
Huangchiakopa 106 40 20N 109 18 E
Huangch'uan 109 32 8N 115 4 E
Huanghsien, Hunen, China 108 27 22N 109 10 E
Huanghsien, Shantung, China 107 37 38N 120 30 E
Huangkang 109 30 27N 114 50 E
Huanglienp'u 108 25 32N 99 44 E
Huangling 106 35 36N 109 17 E
Huangliu 105 18 20N 108 50 E
Huanglung 106 35 37N 109 58 E
Huanglungt'an 109 32 38N 110 33 E
Huangmei 109 30 4N 115 56 E
Huangshih 109 30 10N 115 2 E
Huangt'uan 107 36 55N 121 41 E
Huangyang 109 26 37N 111 42 E
Huangyen 109 28 37N 121 12 E
Huanhsien 106 36 32N 107 10 E
Huaning 108 24 12N 102 55 E
Huanjen 107 41 16N 125 21 E
Huanp'ing 108 26 54N 107 55 E
Huant'ai 107 36 57N 118 5 E
Huánuco 174 9 55 S 76 15W
Huap'ing 108 26 37N 101 13 E
Huap'itientzu 107 43 30N 130 2 E
Huaraz 174 9 30 S 77 32W
Huarmey 174 10 5 S 78 5W
Huasamota 164 22 30N 104 30W
Huascarán 174 9 0 S 77 30W
Huasco 172 28 24 S 71 15W
Huasco, R. 172 28 27 S 71 13W
Huasna 163 35 6N 120 24W
Huatabampo 164 26 50N 109 50W
Huate 106 41 57N 114 4 E
Huatien 107 42 58N 126 50 E
Huauchinango 165 20 11N 98 3W
Huautla 164 18 20N 96 50W
Huautla de Jiménez 165 18 8N 96 51W
Huay Namota 164 21 56N 104 30W
Huayin 106 34 36N 110 2 E
Huayllay 174 11 03 S 76 21W
Huayüan 108 28 30N 109 25 E
Hubbard 159 31 50N 96 50W
Hubbart Pt. 153 59 21N 94 41W
Hubli-Dharwar 97 15 22N 75 15 E
Huchang 107 41 25N 127 2 E
Huchuetenango 164 15 25N 91 30W
Hückelhoven-Ratheim 48 51 6N 6 3 E
Hucknall 33 53 3N 1 12W
Huddersfield 33 53 38N 1 49W
Hudi 122 17 43N 34 28 E
Hudiksvall 72 61 43N 17 10 E
Hudson, Can. 153 50 6N 92 09W
Hudson, Mich., U.S.A. 156 41 50N 84 20W
Hudson, N.H., U.S.A. 162 42 46N 71 26W
Hudson, N.Y., U.S.A. 162 42 15N 73 46W
Hudson, Wis., U.S.A. 158 44 57N 92 45W
Hudson, Wyo., U.S.A. 160 42 54N 108 37W
Hudson B. 153 59 0N 91 0W
Hudson Bay, Can. 149 60 0N 86 0W
Hudson Bay, Sask., Can. 153 52 51N 102 23W
Hudson Falls 162 43 18N 73 34W
Hudson, R. 162 40 42N 74 2W
Hudson Str. 148 62 0N 70 0W
Hudson's Hope 152 56 0N 121 54W
Hué 100 16 30N 107 35 E
Huebra, R. 56 40 54N 6 28W
Huedin 70 46 52N 23 2 E
Huehuetenango 166 15 20N 91 28W
Huejúcar 164 22 21N 103 13W
Huelgoat 42 48 22N 3 46W
Huelma 59 37 39N 3 28W
Huelva 57 37 18N 6 57W
Huelva □ 57 37 40N 7 0W
Huelva, R. 57 37 46N 6 15W
Huentelauquén 172 31 38 S 71 33W
Huércal Overa 59 37 23N 1 57W
Huerta, Sa. de la 172 31 10 S 67 30W
Huertas, C. de las 59 38 21N 0 24W
Huerva, R. 58 41 13N 1 15W
Huesca 58 42 8N 0 25W
Huesca □ 58 42 20N 0 1 E
Huéscar 59 37 44N 2 35W
Huétamo 164 18 36N 100 54W
Huete 58 40 10N 2 43W
Hugh, R. 138 25 1 S 134 10 E
Hugh Town 30 49 55N 6 19W
Hughenden 138 20 52 S 144 10 E
Hughes, Austral. 137 30 42 S 129 31 E
Hughes, U.S.A. 147 66 0N 154 20W
Hughesville 162 41 14N 76 44W
Hugo, Colo., U.S.A. 158 39 12N 103 27W
Hugo, Okla., U.S.A. 159 34 0N 95 30W
Hugoton 159 37 18N 101 22W
Huhehot = Huhohaot'e 106 40 50N 110 39 E
Huhohaot'e 106 40 50N 110 39 E
Huhsien 106 34 8N 108 34 E
Huian 109 25 4N 118 47 E
Huianp'u 106 37 30N 106 40 E
Huiarau Ra. 142 38 45 S 176 55 E
Huich'ang 109 25 32N 115 45 E
Huichapán 165 20 24N 99 40W
Huichou 109 23 5N 114 24 E
Huifa Ho, R. 107 43 6N 126 53 E
Huihsien, Honan, China 106 35 32N 113 54 E
Huihsien, Kansu, China 106 33 46N 106 6 E
Huila 128 15 30 S 15 0 E
Huila □ 174 2 30N 75 45W
Huila, Nevado del 174 3 0N 76 0W
Huilai 109 23 4N 116 18 E
Huili 108 26 39N 102 11 E
Huimin 107 37 29N 117 29 E
Huinan 107 42 40N 126 5 E
Huinca Renancó 172 34 51 S 64 22W
Huining 106 35 41N 105 8 E
Huinung 106 39 0N 106 45 E
Huiroa 142 39 15 S 174 30 E
Huise 47 50 54N 3 36 E
Huishui 108 26 8N 106 35 E
Huissen 46 51 57N 5 57 E
Huiting 106 34 6N 116 4 E
Huitse 108 26 22N 103 15 E
Huit'ung 108 26 56N 109 36 E
Huixtla 165 15 9N 92 28W
Huiya 92 24 40N 49 15 E
Huizen 46 52 18N 5 14 E
Hukawng Valley 99 26 30N 96 30 E
Hukou 109 29 45N 116 13 E
Hukuma 123 14 55N 36 2 E
Hukuntsi 128 23 58 S 21 45 E
Hula 123 6 33N 38 30 E
Hulaifa 92 25 58N 41 0 E
Hulan 105 46 0N 126 44 E
Huld 106 45 5N 105 30 E
Hülda 90 31 50N 34 51 E
Hull, Can. 150 45 20N 75 40W
Hull, U.K. 33 53 45N 0 20W
Hullavington 28 51 31N 2 9W
Hulme End 32 53 8N 1 51W
Hulst 47 51 17N 4 2 E
Hultsfred 73 57 30N 15 52 E
Hulun Ch'ih 105 49 1N 117 32 E
Humacao 147 18 9N 65 50W
Humahuaca 172 23 10 S 65 25W
Humaitá 174 7 35 S 62 40W
Humaita 172 27 2 S 58 31W
Humansdorp 128 34 2 S 24 46 E
Humber, Mouth of 33 53 32N 0 8 E
Humber, R. 33 53 40N 0 10W
Humberside □ 33 53 50N 0 30W
Humbert River 136 16 30 S 130 45 E
Humble 159 29 59N 95 10W
Humboldt, Can. 153 52 15N 105 9W
Humboldt, Iowa, U.S.A. 158 42 42N 94 15W
Humboldt, Tenn., U.S.A. 157 35 50N 88 55W
Humboldt Gletscher 12 79 30N 62 0W
Humboldt, R. 160 40 55N 116 0W
Humbolt Mts. 143 44 30 S 168 15 E
Hume 163 36 48N 118 54W
Hume, L. 141 36 0 S 147 0 E
Humenné 53 48 55N 21 50 E
Humphreys, Mt. 163 37 17N 118 40W
Humphreys Pk. 161 35 24N 111 38W
Humpolec 52 49 31N 15 20 E
Humshaugh 35 55 3N 2 8W
Humula 141 35 30 S 147 46 E
Hün 119 29 2N 16 0 E
Hun Chiang, R. 107 40 52N 125 42 E
Huna Floi 74 65 50N 20 50W
Hunan □ 109 27 30N 111 30 E
Hunch'un 107 42 52N 130 21 E
Hundested 73 55 58N 11 52 E
Hundred House 31 52 11N 3 17W
Hundred Mile House 152 51 38N 121 18W
Hundshögen, mt. 72 62 57N 13 46 E
Hunedoara 70 45 40N 22 50 E
Hunedoara □ 70 45 45N 22 54 E
Hünfeld 48 50 40N 9 47 E
Hung Chiang, R. 108 27 7N 109 57 E
Hung Ho, R. 109 32 24N 115 32 E
Hung Liu Ho, R. 106 38 3N 109 10 E
Hung Yen 100 20 39N 106 4 E
Hungan 109 31 18N 114 33 E
Hungary ■ 53 47 20N 19 20 E
Hungary, Plain of 16 47 0N 20 0 E
Hungchiang 109 27 6N 110 0 E
Hungerford, Austral. 139 28 58 S 144 24 E
Hungerford, U.K. 28 51 25N 1 30W
Hunghai Wan 109 22 45N 115 15 E
Hunghu 109 29 49N 113 30 E
Hüngnam 107 39 55N 127 45 E
Hungshui Ho, R. 108 23 24N 110 12 E
Hungtech'eng 106 36 48N 107 6 E
Hungt'ou Hsü 109 22 4N 121 25 E
Hungt'se Hu 107 33 15N 118 45 E
Hungtung 106 36 15N 111 37 E
Hungya 108 29 56N 103 25 E
Hungyüan 108 32 46N 102 42 E
Huni Valley 120 5 33N 1 56W
Hunmanby 33 54 12N 0 19W
Hunsberge 128 27 58 S 17 5 E
Hunsrück, mts. 49 50 0N 7 30 E
Hunstanton 29 52 57N 0 30 E
Hunsur 97 12 16N 76 16 E
Hunte, R. 48 52 47N 8 28 E
Hunter, N.Z. 143 44 36 S 171 2 E
Hunter, N.D., U.S.A. 158 47 12N 97 17W
Hunter, N.Y., U.S.A. 162 42 13N 74 13W
Hunter Hills, The 143 44 26 S 170 46 E
Hunter, I. 138 40 30 S 144 54 E
Hunter I. 152 51 55N 128 0W
Hunter Mts. 143 45 43 S 167 25 E
Hunter, R. 143 44 21 S 169 27 E
Hunter Ra. 141 32 45 S 150 15 E
Hunters Road 127 19 9 S 29 49 E
Hunterston 34 55 43N 4 55W
Hunterton 139 26 12 S 148 30 E
Hunterville 142 39 56 S 175 35 E
Huntingburg 156 38 20N 86 58W
Huntingdon, Can. 150 45 10N 74 10W
Huntingdon, U.K. 29 52 20N 0 11W
Huntingdon, N.Y., U.S.A. 162 40 52N 73 25W
Huntingdon, Pa., U.S.A. 156 40 28N 78 1W
Huntingdon & Peterborough (□) 26 52 23N 0 10W
Huntingdon I. 151 53 48N 56 45W
Huntington, U.K. 33 54 0N 1 4W
Huntington, Id., U.S.A. 160 44 22N 117 21W
Huntington, Ind., U.S.A. 156 40 52N 85 30W
Huntington, Ut., U.S.A. 160 39 24N 111 1W
Huntington, W. Va., U.S.A. 156 38 20N 82 30W
Huntington Beach 163 33 40N 118 0W
Huntington Park 161 34 58N 118 15W
Huntly, N.Z. 142 37 34 S 175 11 E
Huntly, U.K. 37 57 27N 2 48W
Huntsville, Can. 150 45 20N 79 14W
Huntsville, Ala., U.S.A. 157 34 45N 86 35W
Huntsville, Tex., U.S.A. 159 30 50N 95 35W
Hunyani Dams. 127 18 0 S 31 10 E
Hunyani, R. 127 18 0 S 31 10 E
Hunyüan 106 39 44N 113 42 E
Hunza, R. 95 36 24N 75 50 E
Huohsien 106 36 38N 111 43 E
Huon, G. 135 7 0 S 147 30 E
Huon Pen. 135 6 20 S 147 30 E
Huong Hoa 100 16 37N 106 45 E
Huong Khe 100 18 13N 105 41 E
Huonville 138 43 0 S 147 5 E
Huoshaop'u 107 43 23N 130 26 E
Hupei □ 109 31 5N 113 5 E
Hurbanovo 53 47 51N 18 11 E
Hurezani 70 44 49N 23 40 E
Hurghada 122 27 15N 33 50 E
Hŭrghita □ 70 46 30N 25 30 E
Hŭrghita Mţii 70 46 25N 25 35 E
Hurley, N. Mex., U.S.A. 161 32 45N 108 7W
Hurley, Wis., U.S.A. 158 46 26N 90 10W
Hurlford 34 55 35N 4 29W
Hurliness 37 58 47N 3 15W
Hurlock 162 38 38N 75 52W
Huron, Calif., U.S.A. 163 36 12N 120 6W
Huron, S.D., U.S.A. 158 44 30N 98 20W
Hurricane 161 37 10N 113 12W
Hursley 28 51 1N 1 23W
Hurso 123 9 35N 41 33 E
Hurstbourne Tarrant 28 51 17N 1 27W
Hurstpierpoint 29 50 56N 0 11W
Hurum, Buskerud, Norway 71 59 36N 10 23 E
Hurum, Oppland, Norway 71 61 9N 8 46 E
Hurunui, R. 143 42 54 S 173 18 E
Hurup 73 56 46N 8 25 E
Husaby 73 58 35N 13 25 E
Húsavík 74 66 3N 17 21W
Husband's Bosworth 28 52 27N 1 3W
Husi 70 46 41N 28 7 E
Husinish Pt. 36 57 59N 7 6W
Huskvarna 73 57 47N 14 15 E
Huslia 147 65 40N 156 30W
Husøy 71 61 3N 4 44 E
Hussar 152 51 3N 112 41W
Hussein (Allenby) Br. 90 31 53N 35 33 E
Hustopéce 53 48 57N 16 43 E
Husum, Ger. 48 54 29N 9 3 E
Husum, Sweden 72 63 21N 19 12 E
Hutchinson, Kans., U.S.A. 159 38 3N 97 59W
Hutchinson, Minn, U.S.A. 158 44 50N 94 22W
Huttenberg 52 46 56N 14 33 E
Hüttental 47 50 53N 8 1 E
Huttig 159 33 5N 92 10W
Hutton, Mt. 139 25 51 S 148 20 E
Hutton, oilfield 19 61 0N 1 30 E
Hutton Ra. 137 24 45 S 124 30 E
Huttwil 50 47 7N 7 50 E
Huwarã 90 32 9N 35 15 E
Huwun 123 4 23N 40 6 E
Huy 47 50 31N 5 15 E
Huyton 32 53 25N 2 52W
Hvaler 71 59 4N 11 1 E
Hvammsfjörður 74 65 4N 22 5W
Hvammur 74 65 13N 21 49W
Hvar 63 43 10N 16 45 E
Hvar, I. 63 43 11N 16 28 E
Hvarski Kanal 63 43 15N 16 35 E
Hvítá, Arnessýsla, Iceland 74 64 0N 20 58W
Hvítá, Mýrasýsla, Iceland 74 64 40N 21 5W
Hvítárvatn 74 63 37N 19 50W
Hvitsten 71 59 35N 10 42 E
Hwachon-chŏsuji 107 38 5N 127 50 E
Hwang Ho = Huang Ho, R. 107 36 50N 118 20 E
Hwekum 98 26 7N 95 22 E
Hyannis, Mass., U.S.A. 162 41 39N 70 17W
Hyannis, Nebr., U.S.A. 158 41 60N 101 45W
Hyargas Nuur 105 49 12N 93 34 E
Hyattsville 162 38 59N 76 55W
Hybo 72 61 49N 16 15 E
Hydaburg 147 55 15N 132 45W
Hyde, N.Z. 143 45 18 S 170 16 E
Hyde, U.K. 32 53 26N 2 6W
Hyde Park 162 41 47N 73 56W
Hyden 137 32 24 S 118 46 E
Hyderabad, India 96 17 10N 78 29 E
Hyderabad, Pak. 94 25 23N 68 36 E
Hyderabad □ 94 25 3N 68 24 E
Hyères 45 43 8N 6 9 E
Hyères, Is. d' 45 43 0N 6 28 E
Hyesan 107 41 20N 128 10 E
Hyland Post 139 57 40N 128 10W
Hyland, R. 152 59 52N 128 12W
Hylestad 71 59 6N 7 29 E
Hyllested 71 56 17N 10 46 E
Hyltebruk 73 56 59N 13 15 E
Hymia 95 33 40N 78 2 E
Hyndman Pk. 160 44 4N 114 0W
Hynish 34 56 27N 6 54W
Hynish B. 34 56 29N 6 40W
Hyōgo-ken □ 110 35 15N 135 0 E
Hyrum 160 41 35N 111 56W
Hysham 160 46 21N 107 11W
Hythe 29 51 4N 1 5 E
Hyūga 110 32 25N 131 35 E
Hyvinkä 75 60 38N 24 50 E

I

I Ho, R. 107 34 10N 118 4 E
I-n-Azaoua 119 20 45N 7 31 E
I-n-Échaïe 118 20 10N 2 5W
I-n-Gall 121 6 51N 7 1 E
I-n-Tabedog 118 19 54N 1 3 E
Iabès, Erg 118 27 30N 2 2W
Iaco, R. 174 10 25 S 70 30W
Iaçu 171 12 45 S 40 13W
Iakora 129 23 6 S 46 40 E
Ialomiţa □ 70 44 30N 27 30 E
Ianca 70 45 6N 27 29 E
Iar Connacht 39 53 20N 9 20W
Iara 70 46 31N 23 35 E
Iaşi □ 70 47 20N 27 0 E
Iaşi (Jassy) 70 47 10N 27 40 E
Iauaretê 174 0 30N 69 5W
Iaucdjovac, (Port Harrison) 149 58 25N 78 15W
Iba 103 15 22N 120 0 E
Ibadan 121 7 22N 3 58 E
Ibagué 174 4 27N 73 14W
Ibaiti 171 23 50 S 50 10W
Iballja 68 42 12N 20 0 E
Ibar, R. 66 43 15N 20 40 E
Ibara 110 34 36N 133 28 E

Ibaraki-ken □ **Inhambane**

Ibaraki-ken □ **111** 36 10N 140 10 E
Ibararaki **111** 34 49N 135 34 E
Ibarra **174** 0 21N 78 7W
Ibba **123** 4 49N 29 2 E
Ibba, Bahr el **123** 5 30N 28 55 E
Ibbenbüren **48** 52 16N 7 41 E
Ibembo **126** 2 35N 23 35 E
Ibera, Laguna **172** 28 30 S 57 9W
Iberian Peninsula **16** 40 0N 5 0W
Iberville **150** 45 19N 73 17W
Iberville, Lac d' **150** 55 55N 73 15W
Ibi **121** 8 15N 9 50 E
Ibiá **171** 19 30 S 46 30W
Ibicaraí **171** 14 51 S 39 36W
Ibicuí **171** 14 51 S 39 59W
Ibicuy **172** 33 55 S 59 10W
Ibioapaba, Serra da **170** 20 14 S 40 25W
Ibipetuba **171** 11 0 S 44 32W
Ibiracu **171** 19 50 S 40 30W
Ibitiara **171** 12 39 S 42 13W
Ibiza **59** 38 54N 1 26 E
Ibiza, I. **59** 39 0N 1 30 E
Iblei, Monti **65** 37 15N 14 45 E
Ibo **127** 12 22 S 40 32 E
Ibonma **103** 3 22 S 133 31 E
Ibotirama **171** 12 13 S 43 12W
Ibriktepe **68** 41 2N 26 33 E
Ibshawâi **122** 29 21N 30 40 E
Ibstock **28** 52 42N 1 23W
Ibu **103** 1 35N 127 25 E
Ibuki-Sanchi **111** 35 25N 136 34 E
Ibǔneşti **70** 46 45N 24 50 E
Iburg **48** 52 10N 8 3 E
Ibusuki **110** 31 12N 130 32 E
Ibwe Munyama **127** 16 5 S 28 31 E
Ica **174** 14 0 S 75 30W
Ica, R. **174** 2 55 S 69 0W
Icabarú **174** 4 20N 61 45W
Içana **174** 1 21N 69 0W
Icatu **170** 2 46 S 44 4W
Iceland, I. ■ **74** 65 0N 19 0W
Icha **77** 55 30N 156 0 E
Ichang **109** 25 25N 112 55 E
Ich'ang **109** 30 40N 111 20 E
Ichchapuram **96** 19 10N 84 40 E
Icheng **109** 32 16N 119 12 E
Ich'eng, Hupeh, China **109** 31 43N 112 12 E
Ich'eng, Shansi, China **106** 35 42N 111 40 E
Ichihara **111** 35 28N 140 5 E
Ichikawa **111** 35 44N 139 55 E
Ichilo, R. **174** 16 30 S 64 45W
Ichinomiya, Gifu, Japan **111** 35 18N 136 48 E
Ichinomiya, Kumamoto, Japan **110** 32 58N 131 5 E
Ichinoseki **112** 38 55N 141 8 E
Ichŏn **107** 37 17N 127 27 E
Icht **118** 29 6N 8 54W
Ichtegem **47** 51 5N 3 1 E
Ich'uan **106** 36 4N 110 6 E
Ich'un **105** 47 42N 128 54 E
Ichün **106** 35 23N 109 7 E
Ich'un, Heilungkiang, China **105** 47 42N 128 54 E
Ich'un, Kiangsi, China **109** 27 47N 114 22 E
Icó **170** 6 24 S 38 51W
Icoraci **170** 1 18 S 48 28W
Icy C. **12** 70 25N 162 0W
Icy Str. **153** 58 20N 135 30W
Ida Grove **158** 42 20N 95 25W
Ida Valley **137** 28 42 S 120 29 E
Idabel **159** 33 53N 94 50W
Idaga Hamus **123** 14 13N 39 35 E
Idah **121** 6 10N 6 40 E
Idaho □ **160** 44 10N 114 0W
Idaho City **160** 43 50N 115 52W
Idaho Falls **160** 43 30N 112 10W
Idaho Springs **160** 39 49N 105 30W
Idanha-a-Nova **56** 39 50N 7 15W
Idanre **121** 7 8N 5 5 E
Idar-Oberstein **49** 49 43N 7 19 E
Idd el Ghanam **117** 11 30N 24 25 E
Iddan **91** 6 10N 49 5 E
Idehan **119** 27 10N 11 30 E
Idehan Marzūq **119** 24 50N 13 51 E
Idelès **119** 23 58N 5 53 E
Idfû **122** 25 0N 32 49 E
Idhi Oros **69** 35 15N 24 45 E
Idhra **69** 37 20N 23 28 E
Idi **102** 4 55N 97 45 E
Idi Amin Dada, L. **93** 0 25 S 29 40 E
Idiofa **124** 4 55 S 19 42 E
Idkerberget **72** 60 22N 15 15 E
Idle **33** 53 50N 1 45W
Idle, R. **33** 53 27N 0 49W
Idmiston **28** 51 8N 1 43W
Idna **90** 31 34N 34 58 E
Idria **163** 36 25N 120 41W
Idrija **63** 46 0N 14 5 E
Idritsa **80** 56 25N 28 57 E
Idstein **49** 50 13N 8 17 E
Idsworth **29** 50 56N 0 56W
Idutywa **125** 32 8 S 28 18 E
Ieper **47** 50 51N 2 53 E
Ierápetra **69** 35 0N 25 44 E
Ierissós **68** 40 22N 23 52 E
Ierissóu Kólpos **68** 40 27N 23 57 E
Ierzu **64** 39 48N 9 32 E
Ieshima-Shotō **110** 34 40N 134 32 E
Iesi **63** 43 32N 13 12 E
Ifach, Punta **59** 38 38N 0 5 E
Ifanadiana **129** 21 29 S 47 39 E
Ife **121** 7 30N 4 31 E
Iférouâne **121** 19 5N 8 35 E
Ifni **118** 29 25N 10 10W
Ifon **121** 6 58N 5 40 E
Iga **111** 34 45N 136 10 E
Iganga **126** 0 30N 33 28 E
Igarapava **171** 20 3 S 47 47W
Igarapé Açu **170** 1 4 S 47 33W
Igarapé-Mirim **170** 1 59 S 48 58W
Igarka **77** 67 30N 87 20 E
Igatimi **173** 24 5 S 55 30W
Igatpuri **96** 19 40N 73 35 E
Igbetti **121** 8 44N 4 8 E
Igbo-Ora **121** 7 10N 3 15 E
Igboho **121** 8 40N 3 50 E
Iggesund **72** 61 39N 17 10 E
Igherm **118** 30 7N 8 18W
Ighil Izane **118** 35 44N 0 31 E
Iglene **118** 22 57N 4 58 E
Iglésias **64** 39 19N 8 27 E
Igli **118** 30 25N 2 12W
Iglino **84** 54 50N 56 26 E
Igloolik Island **149** 69 20N 81 30W
Igma **118** 29 9N 6 11W
Igma, Gebel el **122** 28 55N 34 0 E
Ignace **150** 49 30N 91 40W
Igoshevo **81** 59 25N 42 35 E
Igoumenitsa **68** 39 32N 20 18 E
Igra **84** 57 33N 53 7 E
Iguaçu, Cat. del **173** 25 41N 54 26W
Iguaçu, R. **173** 25 30 S 53 10W
Iguala **165** 18 20N 99 40W
Igualada **58** 41 37N 1 37 E
Iguape **171** 24 43 S 47 33W
Iguape, R. **173** 24 40 S 48 0W
Iguassu = Iguaçu **173** 25 41N 54 26W
Iguatu **170** 6 20 S 39 18W
Iguéla **124** 2 0 S 9 16 E
Igumale **121** 6 47N 7 55 E
Igunga □ **126** 4 20 S 33 45 E
Ihiala **121** 5 40N 6 55 E
Ihosy **129** 22 24 S 46 8 E
Ihotry, L. **129** 21 56 S 43 41 E
Ihsien, Anwhei, China **109** 29 53N 117 57E
Ihsien, Hopeh, China **106** 39 21N 115 29E
Ihsien, Liaoning, China **107** 41 34N 121 15E
Ihsien, Shantung, China **107** 37 11N 119 55E
Ihuang **109** 27 32N 115 57 E
Ii **74** 65 15N 25 30 E
Iida **111** 35 35N 138 0 E
Iiey **138** 18 53 S 141 12 E
Iijoki **74** 65 20N 26 15 E
Iisalmi **74** 63 32N 27 10 E
Iizuka **110** 33 38N 130 42 E
Ijebu-Igbo **121** 6 56N 4 1 E
Ijebu-Ode **121** 6 47N 3 52 E
IJmuiden **46** 52 28N 4 35 E
IJssel, R. **46** 52 35N 5 50 E
IJsselmeer **46** 52 45N 5 20 E
IJsselmuiden **46** 52 34N 5 57 E
IJsselstein **46** 52 1N 5 2 E
Ijuí, R. **173** 27 58 S 55 20W
Ijûin **110** 31 37N 130 24 E
IJzendijke **47** 51 19N 3 37 E
IJzer, R. **47** 51 9N 2 44 E
Ik, R. **84** 55 55N 52 36 E
Ikamatua **141** 42 15 S 171 41 E
Ikare **121** 7 18N 5 40 E
Ikaria, I. **69** 37 35N 26 10 E
Ikast **73** 56 8N 9 10 E
Ikawa **111** 35 13N 138 15 E
Ikeda **111** 34 1N 133 48 E
Ikeja **121** 6 28N 3 45 E
Ikela **124** 1 0 S 23 35 E
Ikerre **121** 7 25N 5 19 E
Ikhtiman **67** 42 27N 23 48 E
Iki **110** 33 45N 129 42 E
Iki-Kaikyō **110** 33 40N 129 45 E
Ikimba L. **126** 1 30 S 31 20 E
Ikire **121** 7 10N 4 15 E
Ikirun **121** 7 54N 4 40 E
Ikitsuki-Shima **110** 33 23N 129 26 E
Ikole **121** 7 40N 5 37 E
Ikom **121** 6 0N 8 42 E
Ikopa, R. **129** 17 45 S 46 40 E
Ikot Ekpene **121** 5 12N 7 40 E
Ikungu **126** 1 33 S 33 42 E
Ikuno **110** 35 10N 134 48 E
Ila **121** 8 0N 4 51 E
Ilam **95** 26 58N 87 58 E
Ilan, China **105** 46 14N 129 33 E
Ilan, Taiwan **109** 24 45N 121 44 E
Ilanskiy **77** 56 14N 96 3 E
Ilanz **51** 46 46N 9 12 E
Ilaomita, R. **47** 44 47N 27 0 E
Ilaro Agege **121** 6 53N 3 3 E
Ilayangudi **97** 9 34N 78 37 E
Ilbilbie **138** 21 45 S 149 20 E
Ilchester **28** 51 0N 2 41W
Ile-à-la Crosse **153** 55 27N 107 53W
Ile-à-la-Crosse, Lac **153** 55 40N 107 45W
Ile Bouchard, L' **42** 47 7N 0 26 E
Ile de France □ **43** 49 0N 2 20 E
Ilebo **124** 4 17 S 20 47 E
Ileje □ **127** 9 30 S 33 25 E
Ilek **84** 51 32N 53 21 E
Ilek, R. **84** 51 30N 53 22 E
Ilen R. **39** 51 38N 9 19W
Ilero **121** 8 0N 3 20 E
Ilesha, West-Central, Nigeria **121** 7 37N 4 40 E
Ilesha, Western, Nigeria **121** 8 57N 3 28E
Ilford **153** 56 4N 95 35W
Ilfov □ **70** 44 20N 26 0 E
Ilfracombe, Austral. **138** 23 30 S 144 30 E
Ilfracombe, U.K. **30** 51 13N 4 8W
Ilha Grande, Baia da **171** 23 9S 44 30W
Ílhavo **56** 40 33N 8 43W
Ilheus **171** 14 49 S 39 2W
Ili **85** 45 53N 77 10 E
Ilia **70** 45 57N 22 40 E
Ilia □ **69** 37 45N 21 35 E
Iliamna L. **147** 59 35N 155 30W
Iliang, Yunnan, China **108** 24 54N 103 9E
Iliang, Yunnan, China **108** 27 35N 104 1E
Ilich **85** 40 50N 68 27 E
Ilico **172** 34 50 S 72 20W
Iliff **158** 40 50N 103 3W
Iliki **69** 38 24N 23 15 E
Ilio Pt. **147** 21 13N 157 16W
Iliodhrómia **68** 39 12N 23 50 E
Ilion **162** 43 0N 75 3W
Ilirska Bistrica **63** 45 34N 14 14 E
Iliysk **76** 44 10N 77 20 E
Ilkal **97** 15 57N 76 8 E
Ilkeston **33** 52 59N 1 19W
Ilkley **21** 53 56N 1 49W
Illana B. **103** 7 35N 123 45 E
Illapel **172** 32 0 S 71 10W
'Illar **90** 32 23N 35 7 E
Ille **44** 42 40N 2 37 E
Ille-et-Vilaine □ **42** 48 10N 1 30W
Iller, R. **49** 47 53N 10 10 E
Illescás **56** 40 8N 3 51W
Illig **91** 7 47N 49 45 E
Illimani, Mte. **174** 16 30 S 67 50W
Illinois □ **155** 40 15N 89 30W
Illinois, R. **155** 40 10N 90 20W
Illizi **119** 26 31N 8 32 E
Illora **57** 37 17N 3 53W
Ilmen, Oz. **80** 58 15N 31 10 E
Ilmenau **48** 50 41N 10 55 E
Ilminster **28** 50 55N 2 56W
Ilo **174** 17 40 S 71 20W
Ilobu **121** 7 45N 4 25 E
Ilohuli Shan **105** 51 20N 124 20 E
Iloilo **103** 10 45N 122 33 E
Ilok **66** 45 15N 19 20 E
Ilora **121** 7 45N 3 50 E
Ilorin **121** 8 30N 4 35 E
Ilovatka **81** 50 30N 46 50 E
Ilovlya **83** 49 15N 44 2 E
Ilovlya, R. **83** 49 38N 44 20 E
Iłowa **54** 51 30N 15 10 E
Ilubabor □ **123** 7 25N 35 0 E
Ilukste **80** 55 55N 26 20 E
Ilung **108** 31 34N 106 24 E
Ilva Micá **70** 47 17N 24 40 E
Ilwaki **103** 7 55 S 126 30 E
Ilyichevsk **82** 46 10N 30 35 E
Imabari **110** 34 4N 133 0 E
Imadahane **118** 32 8N 7 0W
Imaichi **111** 36 6N 139 16 E
Imaloto, R. **129** 23 10 S 45 15 E
Iman = Dalneretchensk **77** 45 50N 133 40 E
Imari **110** 33 15N 129 52 E
Imasa **122** 18 0N 36 12 E
Imathía □ **68** 40 30N 22 15 E
Imbâbah **122** 30 5N 31 12 E
Imbler **160** 45 31N 118 0W
Imbros = Imroz **68** 40 10N 26 0 E
Imen **108** 24 40N 102 9 E
Imeni Panfilova **85** 43 23N 77 7 E
Imeni Poliny Osipenko **77** 55 25N 136 29 E
Imeri, Serra **174** 0 50N 65 25W
Imerimandroso **129** 17 26 S 48 35 E
Imi (Hinna) **123** 6 35N 42 30 E
Imi n'Tanoute **118** 31 13N 8 51 E
Imienp'o **107** 45 0N 128 16 E
Imishly **83** 39 49N 48 4 E
Imiteg **118** 29 43N 8 10W
Imlay **160** 40 45N 118 9W
Immingham **33** 53 37N 0 12W
Immokalee **157** 26 25N 81 20W
Imo □ **121** 5 15N 7 20 E
Imola **63** 44 20N 11 42 E
Imotski **66** 43 27N 17 21 E
Imperatriz **170** 5 30 S 47 29W
Impéria **62** 43 52N 8 0 E
Imperial, Can. **153** 51 21N 105 28W
Imperial, Calif., U.S.A. **161** 32 52N 115 34W
Imperial, Nebr., U.S.A. **158** 40 38N 101 39W
Imperial Beach **163** 32 35N 117 8W
Imperial Dam **161** 32 50N 114 30W
Imperial Valley **163** 32 55N 115 30W
Imperieuse Reef **136** 17 36 S 118 50 E
Impfondo **124** 1 40N 18 0 E
Imphal **98** 24 48N 93 56 E
Imphy **43** 46 56N 3 15 E
Imroz = Gökçeada **68** 40 10N 26 0 E
Imst **52** 47 15N 10 44 E
Imuruan B. **103** 10 40N 119 10 E
In Belbel **118** 27 55N 1 12 E
In Delimane **121** 15 52N 1 31 E
In-Gall **121** 16 51N 7 1 E
In Rhar **118** 27 10N 1 59 E
In Salah **118** 27 10N 2 32 E
In Tallak **121** 16 19N 3 15 E
Ina **111** 35 50N 138 0 E
Ina-Bonchi **111** 35 45N 137 58 E
Inagh **39** 52 53N 9 11W
Inajá **170** 8 54 S 37 49W
Inangahua Junc. **143** 41 52 S 171 59 E
Inanwatan **103** 2 10 S 132 5 E
Iñapari **174** 11 0 S 69 40W
Inari **74** 68 54N 27 5 E
Inari, L. **74** 69 0N 28 0 E
Inazawa **111** 35 15N 136 47 E
Inca **58** 39 43N 2 54 E
Incaguasi **172** 29 12 S 71 5W
İnce **32** 53 32N 2 38W
İnce Burnu **92** 42 2N 35 0 E
Inch **39** 52 42N 8 8W
Inch Br. **39** 52 49N 9 6W
Inchard, Loch **36** 58 28N 5 2W
Inchcape Rock **35** 56 26N 2 24W
Inchigeelagh **39** 51 50N 9 8W
Inchini **123** 8 55N 37 37 E
Inchkeith, I. **35** 56 2N 3 8W
Inchnadamph **36** 58 9N 5 0W
Inch'ŏn **107** 37 27N 126 40 E
Inchture **35** 56 26N 3 8W
Incio **56** 42 39N 7 21W
Incomáti, R. **129** 25 15 S 32 35 E
Incudine, Mte. l' **45** 41 50N 9 12 E
Inda Silase **123** 14 10N 38 15 E
Indaal L. **34** 55 44N 6 20W
Indalsälven **72** 62 36N 17 30 E
Indaw **98** 24 15N 96 5 E
Indbir **123** 8 7N 37 52 E
Indefatigable, gasfield **19** 53 20N 2 40 E
Independence, Calif., U.S.A. **163** 36 51N 118 7W
Independence, Iowa, U.S.A. **158** 42 27N 91 52W
Independence, Kans., U.S.A. **159** 37 10N 95 50W
Independence, Mo., U.S.A. **158** 39 3N 94 25W
Independence, Oreg., U.S.A. **160** 44 53N 123 6W
Independence Fjord **12** 82 10N 29 0W
Independence Mts. **160** 41 30N 116 2W
Independência **170** 5 23 S 40 19W
Independencia, La **165** 16 31N 91 47W
Independenţa **70** 45 25N 27 42 E
Inderborskly **83** 48 30N 51 42 E
India ■ **87** 20 0N 80 0 E
Indian Cabins **152** 59 52N 117 2W
Indian Harbour **151** 54 27N 57 13W
Indian Head **153** 50 30N 103 35W
Indian House L. **151** 56 30N 64 30W
Indian Lake **162** 43 47N 74 16W
Indian Ocean **11** 5 0 S 75 0 E
Indian River B. **162** 38 36N 75 4W
Indiana **156** 40 38N 79 9W
Indiana □ **156** 40 0N 86 0W
Indianapolis **156** 39 42N 86 10W
Indianola, Iowa, U.S.A. **158** 41 20N 93 38W
Indianola, Miss., U.S.A. **159** 33 27N 90 40W
Indianópolis **171** 19 2 S 47 55 E
Indiapora **171** 19 57 S 50 17W
Indiaroba **171** 11 32 S 37 31W
Indiga **78** 67 50N 48 50 E
Indigirka, R. **77** 69 0N 147 0 E
Indija **66** 45 6N 20 7 E
Indio **163** 33 46N 116 15W
Indonesia ■ **102** 5 0 S 115 0 E
Indore **94** 22 42N 75 53 E
Indramaju **103** 6 21 S 108 20 E
Indramaju, Tg. **103** 6 20 S 108 20 E
Indravati, R. **96** 19 0N 81 15 E
Indre □ **43** 47 12N 1 39 E
Indre-et-Loire □ **42** 47 12N 0 40 E
Indre, R. **42** 47 2N 1 8 E
Indre Söndeled **71** 58 46N 9 5 E
Indus, Mouth of the **94** 24 00N 68 00 E
Indus, R. **94** 28 40N 70 10 E
İnebolu **92** 41 55N 33 40E
Infante, Kaap **128** 34 27 S 20 51 E
Infantes **59** 38 43N 3 1W
Infiernillo, Presa del **164** 18 9N 102 0W
Infiesto **56** 43 21N 5 21W
Ingá **171** 7 17 S 35 36W
Ingatestone **29** 51 40N 0 23W
Ingelmunster **47** 50 56N 3 16 E
Ingende **124** 0 12 S 18 57 E
Ingenio Santa Ana **172** 27 25 S 65 40W
Ingesvang **73** 56 10N 9 20 E
Ingham **138** 18 43 S 146 10 E
Ingichka **85** 39 47N 65 58 E
Ingleborough, mt. **32** 54 11N 2 23W
Inglefield Land **143** 78 30N 70 0W
Ingleton **32** 54 9N 2 29W
Inglewood, Queensland, Austral. **139** 28 25 S 151 8 E
Inglewood, Vic., Austral. **140** 36 29 S 143 53 E
Inglewood, N.Z. **142** 39 9 S 174 14 E
Inglewood, U.S.A. **163** 33 58N 118 21W
Ingoldmells, Pt. **33** 53 11N 0 21 E
Ingólfshöfði **74** 63 48N 16 39W
Ingolstadt **49** 48 45N 11 26 E
Ingomar **160** 46 43N 107 37W
Ingonish **151** 46 42N 60 18W
Ingore **120** 12 24N 15 48W
Ingul, R. **82** 47 30N 32 15 E
Ingulec **82** 47 42N 33 4 E
Ingulets, R. **82** 47 20N 33 20 E
Inguri, R. **83** 42 58N 42 17 E
Inhaca, I. **129** 26 1 S 32 57 E
Inhafenga **129** 20 36 S 33 47 E
Inhambane **125** 23 54 S 35 30 E

Itaueira, R Jedrzejów

Itaueira, R. 170 6 41 S 42 55 W
Itaúna 171 20 4 S 44 34 W
Itchen, R. 28 50 57 N 1 20 W
Itéa 69 38 25 N 22 25 E
Ithaca 162 42 25 N 76 30 W
Ithaca = Itháki 69 38 25 N 20 43 E
Itháki, I. 69 38 25 N 20 40 E
Ithon R. 31 52 16 N 3 23 W
It'iaoshan 106 37 10 N 104 2 E
Itinga 171 16 36 S 41 47 W
Itiruçu 171 13 31 S 40 9 W
Itiúba 171 10 43 S 39 51 W
Ito 111 34 58 N 139 5 E
Itonamas, R. 174 13 0 S 64 25 W
Itsa 122 29 15 N 30 40 E
Itsukaichi 110 34 22 N 132 8 E
Itsuki 110 32 24 N 130 50 E
Itteville 46 48 31 N 2 21 E
Ittiri 64 40 38 N 8 32 E
Itu, Brazil 173 23 10 S 47 15 W
Itu, Hupeh, China 109 30 24 N 111 26 E
Itu, Shantung, China 107 36 41 N 118 28 E
Itu, Nigeria 121 5 10 N 7 58 E
Ituaçu 171 13 50 S 41 18 W
Ituango 174 7 4 N 75 45 W
Ituiutaba 171 19 0 S 49 25 W
Itumbiara 171 18 20 S 49 10 W
Ituna 153 51 10 N 103 30 W
It'ung 107 43 20 N 125 17 E
Itunge Port 127 9 40 S 33 55 E
Itupiranga 170 5 9 S 49 20 W
Iturama 171 19 44 S 50 11 W
Iturbe 172 23 0 S 65 25 W
Ituri, R. 126 1 45 N 26 45 E
Iturup, Ostrov 77 45 0 N 148 0 E
Ituverava 171 20 20 S 47 47 W
Ituyuro, R. 172 22 40 S 63 50 W
Itzehoe 48 53 56 N 9 31 E
Ivalo 74 68 38 N 27 35 E
Ivalojoki 74 68 30 N 27 0 E
Ivanaj 68 42 17 N 19 25 E
Ivanhoe, N.S.W., Austral. 140 32 56 S 144 20 E
Ivanhoe, N.T., Austral. 136 15 41 S 128 41 E
Ivanhoe, U.S.A. 163 36 23 N 119 13 W
Ivanhoe L. 153 60 25 N 106 30 W
Ivanió Grad 63 45 41 N 16 25 E
Ivanjica 66 43 35 N 20 12 E
Ivanjscie 63 46 12 N 16 13 E
Ivankovskoye Vdkhr. 81 56 48 N 36 55 E
Ivano-Frankovsk, (Stanislav) 80 49 0 N 24 40 E
Ivanovka 84 52 34 N 53 23 E
Ivanovo, Byelorussia, U.S.S.R. 80 52 7 N 25 29 E
Ivanovo, R.S.F.S.R., U.S.S.R. 81 57 5 N 41 0 E
Ivato 129 20 37 S 47 10 E
Ivaylovgrad 67 41 32 N 26 8 E
Ivinghoe 29 51 50 N 0 38 W
Ivinheima, R. 173 21 48 S 54 15 W
Iviza = Ibiza 59 39 0 N 1 30 E
Ivohibe 129 22 31 S 46 57 E
Ivolândia 171 16 34 S 50 51 W
Ivory Coast ■ 120 7 30 N 5 0 W
Ivösjön 73 56 8 N 14 25 E
Ivrea 62 45 30 N 7 52 E
Ivugivik, (N.D. d'Ivugivic) 149 62 24 N 77 55 W
Ivybridge 30 50 24 N 3 56 W
Iwahig 102 8 35 N 117 32 E
Iwai-Jima 110 33 47 N 131 58 E
Iwaki 112 37 3 N 140 55 E
Iwakuni 110 34 15 N 132 8 E
Iwami 110 35 32 N 134 15 E
Iwamisawa 112 43 12 N 141 46 E
Iwanai 112 42 58 N 140 30 E
Iwanuma 112 38 7 N 140 58 E
Iwase 110 36 21 N 140 6 E
Iwata 111 34 49 N 137 59 E
Iwate-ken □ 112 39 30 N 141 30 E
Iwate-San 112 39 51 N 141 0 E
Iwo 121 7 39 N 4 9 E
Iwonicz-Zdroj 54 49 37 N 21 47 E
Iximas 174 13 50 S 68 5 W
Ixopo 129 30 11 S 30 5 E
Ixtepec 165 16 40 N 95 10 W
Ixtlán de Juárez 165 17 23 N 96 28 W
Ixtlán del Rio 164 21 5 N 104 28 W
Ixworth 29 52 18 N 0 50 E
Iyang, Honan, China 106 34 9 N 112 25 E
Iyang, Hunan, China 109 28 36 N 112 20 E
Iyang, Kiangsi, China 109 28 23 N 117 25 E
Iyo 110 33 45 N 132 45 E
Iyo-mishima 110 33 58 N 133 30 E
Iyo-Nada 110 33 40 N 132 20 E
Izabal, L. 166 15 30 N 89 10 W
Izamal 165 20 56 N 89 1 W
Izberbash 83 42 35 N 47 45 E
Izbica Kujawski 54 52 25 N 18 30 E
Izegem 47 50 55 N 3 12 E
Izgrev 67 43 36 N 26 58 E
Izh, R. 84 55 58 N 52 38 E
Izhevsk 84 56 51 N 53 14 E
Izmail 82 45 22 N 28 46 E
Izmir (Smyrna) 79 38 25 N 27 8 E
Izmit 92 40 45 N 29 50 E
Izola 63 45 32 N 13 39 E
Izu-Hantō 111 34 45 N 139 0 E
Izuhara 110 34 12 N 129 17 E
Izumi 110 32 5 N 130 22 E
Izumiotsu 111 34 30 N 135 24 E
Izumisano 111 34 40 N 135 43 E
Izumo 110 35 20 N 132 55 E
Izyaslav 80 50 5 N 25 50 E
Izyum 82 49 12 N 37 28 E

J

Jaba 123 6 20 N 35 7 E
Jaba' 90 32 20 N 35 13 E
Jabaliya 90 31 32 N 34 27 E
Jabalón, R. 59 38 45 N 3 35 W
Jabalpur 95 23 9 N 79 58 E
Jablah 92 35 20 N 36 0 E
Jablanac 63 44 42 N 14 56 E
Jablonec 52 50 43 N 15 10 E
Jablonica 53 48 37 N 17 26 E
Jabłonowo 54 53 23 N 19 10 E
Jaboatão 170 8 7 S 35 1 W
Jaboticabal 173 21 15 S 48 17 W
Jabukovac 66 44 22 N 22 21 E
Jaburu 174 5 30 S 64 0 W
Jaca 58 42 35 N 0 33 W
Jacala 165 21 1 N 99 11 W
Jacaré, R. 170 10 3 S 42 13 W
Jacareí 173 23 20 S 46 0 W
Jacarèzinho 173 23 5 S 50 0 W
Jáchal 172 30 5 S 69 0 W
Jáchymov 52 50 22 N 12 55 E
Jacinto 171 16 10 S 40 17 W
Jack Lane B. 151 55 45 N 60 35 W
Jackfish 150 48 45 N 87 0 W
Jackman 151 45 35 N 70 17 W
Jacksboro 159 33 14 N 98 15 W
Jackson, Austral. 139 26 39 S 149 39 E
Jackson, Ala., U.S.A. 157 31 32 N 87 53 W
Jackson, Calif., U.S.A. 159 37 25 N 89 42 W
Jackson, Ill., U.S.A. 163 38 25 N 120 47 W
Jackson, Ky., U.S.A. 156 37 35 N 83 22 W
Jackson, Mich., U.S.A. 156 42 18 N 84 25 W
Jackson, Minn., U.S.A. 158 43 35 N 95 30 W
Jackson, Miss., U.S.A. 159 32 20 N 90 10 W
Jackson, Ohio, U.S.A. 156 39 0 N 82 40 W
Jackson, Tenn., U.S.A. 157 35 40 N 88 50 W
Jackson, Wyo., U.S.A. 160 43 30 N 110 49 W
Jackson Bay, Can. 152 50 32 N 125 57 W
Jackson Bay, N.Z. 143 43 58 S 168 42 E
Jackson, C. 143 40 59 S 174 20 E
Jackson, L. 160 43 55 N 110 40 W
Jacksons 143 42 46 S 171 32 E
Jacksonville, Ala., U.S.A. 157 33 49 N 85 45 W
Jacksonville, Calif., U.S.A. 163 37 52 N 120 24 W
Jacksonville, Fla., U.S.A. 157 30 15 N 81 38 W
Jacksonville, Ill., U.S.A. 158 39 42 N 90 15 W
Jacksonville, N.C., U.S.A. 157 34 50 N 77 29 W
Jacksonville, Oreg., U.S.A. 160 42 13 N 122 56 W
Jacksonville, Tex., U.S.A. 159 31 58 N 95 12 W
Jacksonville Beach 157 30 19 N 81 26 W
Jacmel 167 18 20 N 72 40 W
Jacob Lake 161 36 45 N 112 12 W
Jacobabad 94 28 20 N 68 29 E
Jacobeni 70 47 25 N 25 20 E
Jacobina 170 11 11 S 40 30 W
Jacob's Well 90 32 13 N 35 13 E
Jacques Cartier, Mt. 151 48 57 N 66 0 W
Jacques Cartier Pass 151 49 50 N 62 30 W
Jacqueville 120 5 12 N 4 25 W
Jacuí, R. 173 30 2 S 51 15 W
Jacuipe, R. 171 12 30 S 39 5 W
Jacundá, R. 170 1 57 S 50 26 W
Jade 48 53 22 N 8 14 E
Jadebusen, B. 48 53 30 N 8 15 E
Jadoigne 47 50 43 N 4 52 E
Jadotville = Likasi 127 10 55 S 26 48 E
Jadovnik 66 43 20 N 19 45 E
Jadraque 58 40 55 N 2 55 W
Jādū 119 32 0 N 12 0 E
Jaén, Peru 174 5 25 S 78 40 W
Jaén, Spain 57 37 44 N 3 43 W
Jaén □ 57 37 50 N 3 30 W
Jafène 118 20 35 N 5 30 W
Jaffa = Tel Aviv-Yafo 90 32 4 N 34 48 E
Jaffa, C. 140 36 58 S 139 40 E
Jaffna 97 9 45 N 80 2 E
Jaffrey 162 42 50 N 72 4 W
Jagadhri 94 30 10 N 77 20 E
Jagadishpur 95 25 30 N 84 21 E
Jagdalpur 96 19 3 N 82 6 E
Jagersfontein 128 29 44 S 25 27 E
Jaghbub 117 29 42 N 24 38 E
Jagraon 93 30 50 N 75 25 E
Jagst, R. 49 49 13 N 10 0 E
Jagtial 96 18 50 N 79 0 E
Jaguaquara 171 13 32 S 39 58 W
Jaguariaíva 173 24 10 S 49 50 W
Jaguaribe 170 5 53 S 38 37 W
Jaguaribe, R. 170 6 0 S 38 35 W
Jaguaruana 170 4 50 S 37 47 W
Jagüey 166 22 35 N 81 7 W
Jagungal, Mt. 141 36 8 S 148 22 E
Jahangirabad 94 28 19 N 78 4 E
Jahrom 93 28 30 N 53 31 E
Jaicós 170 7 21 S 41 8 W
Jainti 98 26 45 N 89 40 E
Jaintiapur 98 25 8 N 92 7 E
Jaipur 94 27 0 N 76 10 E
Jajarm 93 37 5 N 56 20 E
Jajce 66 44 19 N 17 17 E
Jajere 121 11 58 N 11 25 E
Jajpur 96 20 53 N 86 22 E
Jakarta 103 6 9 S 106 49 E
Jakobstad (Pietarsaari) 74 63 40 N 22 43 E
Jakupica 66 41 45 N 21 22 E
Jal 159 32 8 N 103 8 W
Jala 93 27 30 N 62 40 E
Jalalabad, Afghan. 94 34 30 N 70 29 E
Jalalabad, India 95 26 41 N 79 42 E
Jalalpur Jattan 94 32 38 N 74 19 E
Jalama 163 34 29 N 120 29 W
Jalapa, Guat. 166 14 45 N 89 59 W
Jalapa, Mexico 165 19 30 N 96 50 W
Jalas, Jabal al 92 27 30 N 36 30 E
Jalaun 95 26 8 N 79 25 E
Jales 171 20 16 S 50 33 W
Jaleswar 95 26 38 N 85 48 E
Jalgaon, Maharashtra, India 96 21 2 N 76 31 E
Jalgaon, Maharashtra, India 96 21 0 N 75 42 E
Jalhay 47 50 33 N 5 58 E
Jalingo 121 8 55 N 11 25 E
Jalisco □ 164 20 0 N 104 0 W
Jalkot 95 35 20 N 73 24 E
Jallas, R. 56 42 57 N 9 0 W
Jallumba 140 36 55 S 141 57 E
Jalna 96 19 48 N 75 57 E
Jalón, R. 58 41 20 N 1 40 W
Jalpa 164 21 38 N 102 58 W
Jalpaiguri 98 26 32 N 88 46 E
Jalq 93 27 35 N 62 33 E
Jaluit I. 130 6 0 N 169 30 E
Jamaari 121 11 44 N 9 53 E
Jamaica, I. ■ 166 18 10 N 77 30 W
Jamalpur, Bangla. 98 24 52 N 90 2 E
Jamalpur, India 95 25 18 N 86 28 E
Jamalpurganj 95 23 2 N 88 1 E
Jamanxim, R. 175 6 30 S 55 50 W
Jambe 103 1 15 S 132 10 E
Jambes 47 50 27 N 4 52 E
Jambi 102 1 38 S 103 30 E
Jambusar 94 22 3 N 72 51 E
Jamdena, I. = Yamdena 103 7 45 S 131 20 E
James B. 150 53 30 N 80 0 W
James, R., Dak., U.S.A. 158 44 50 N 98 0 W
James, R., Va., U.S.A. 162 37 0 N 76 27 W
James Ranges 136 24 10 S 132 0 E
James Ross I. 13 63 58 S 50 94 W
Jamestown, Austral. 140 33 10 S 138 32 E
Jamestown, S. Afr. 128 31 6 S 26 45 E
Jamestown, Ky., U.S.A. 156 37 0 N 85 5 W
Jamestown, N.D., U.S.A. 158 47 0 N 98 30 W
Jamestown, N.Y., U.S.A. 156 42 5 N 79 18 W
Jamestown, Tenn., U.S.A. 157 36 25 N 85 0 W
Jamestown, Va., U.S.A. 162 37 12 N 76 46 W
Jamiltepec 165 16 17 N 97 49 W
Jamkhandi 97 16 30 N 75 15 E
Jamma'in 90 32 8 N 35 12 E
Jammalamadugu 97 14 51 N 78 25 E
Jammerbugt 73 57 15 N 9 20 E
Jammu 94 32 43 N 74 54 E
Jammu & Kashmir □ 95 34 25 N 77 0 E
Jamnagar 94 22 30 N 70 0 E
Jamner 96 20 45 N 75 45 E
Jamoigne 47 49 41 N 5 24 E
Jampur 94 29 39 N 70 32 E
Jamrud 94 34 2 N 71 24 E
Jamshedpur 95 22 44 N 86 20 E
Jamtara 95 23 59 N 86 41 E
Jämtlands län □ 72 62 40 N 13 50 E
Jamuna, R. 98 23 51 N 89 45 E
Jamurki 98 24 9 N 90 2 E
Jan Kemp 128 27 55 S 24 51 E
Jan L. 153 54 56 N 102 55 W
Jan Mayen Is. 12 71 0 N 11 0 W
Janaúba 171 15 48 S 43 19 W
Janaucu, I. 170 0 30 S 50 10 W
Jand 94 33 30 N 72 0 E
Janda, Laguna de la 57 36 15 N 5 45 W
Jandaia 171 17 6 S 50 7 W
Jandaq 92 34 3 N 54 22 E
Jandola 94 32 20 N 70 9 E
Jandowae 139 26 45 S 151 7 E
Jandrain-Jandrenouilles 47 50 40 N 4 58 E
Jándula, R. 57 38 25 N 3 55 W
Jane Pk. 142 45 15 S 168 20 E
Janesville 158 42 39 N 89 1 W
Janga 121 10 5 N 1 0 W
Jangaon 96 17 44 N 79 5 E
Janhtang Ga 98 26 32 N 96 38 E
Jani Khel 93 32 45 N 68 25 E
Janja 66 44 40 N 19 17 E
Janjevo 66 42 35 N 21 19 E
Janjina 66 42 58 N 17 25 E
Janos 164 30 45 N 108 10 W
Jánoshalma 53 46 18 N 19 21 E
Jánosháza 53 47 8 N 17 12 E
Jánossomorja 53 47 47 N 17 11 E
Janów 54 50 44 N 19 27 E
Janów Lubelski 54 50 48 N 22 23 E
Janów Podlaski 54 52 11 N 23 11 E
Janowiec Wlkp. 54 52 45 N 17 30 E
Januária 171 15 25 S 44 25 W
Janub Dârfûr □ 123 11 0 N 25 0 E
Janub Kordofân □ 123 12 0 N 30 0 E
Janville 43 48 10 N 1 50 E
Janzé 42 47 55 N 1 28 W
Jaop'ing 109 23 43 N 117 0 E
Jaora 94 23 40 N 75 10 E
Jaoyang 106 38 14 N 115 44 E
Japan ■ 112 36 0 N 136 0 E
Japan, Sea of 112 40 0 N 135 0 E
Japan Trench 142 28 0 N 145 0 E
Japara 103 6 30 S 110 40 E
Japen, I. = Yapen 103 1 50 S 136 0 E
Japero 103 4 59 S 137 11 E
Japurá 174 1 48 S 66 30 W
Japurá, R. 174 3 8 S 64 46 W
Jaque 174 7 27 N 78 15 W
Jaques Cartier, Détroit de 151 50 0 N 63 30 W
Jara, La 161 37 16 N 106 0 W
Jaraguá 171 15 45 S 49 20 W
Jaraicejo 57 39 40 N 5 49 W
Jaraiz 56 40 4 N 5 45 W
Jarales 161 34 44 N 106 51 W
Jarama, R. 58 40 50 N 3 20 W
Jarandilla 56 40 8 N 5 39 W
Jaranwala 94 31 15 N 73 20 E
Jarash 90 32 17 N 35 54 E
Järbo 72 60 42 N 16 38 E
Jarbridge 160 41 56 N 115 27 W
Jardim 172 21 28 S 56 9 W
Jardin, R. 59 38 50 N 2 10 W
Jardines de la Reina, Is. 166 20 50 N 78 50 W
Jargalant = Hovd 105 48 1 N 91 38 E
Jargeau 43 47 50 N 2 7 E
Jarmen 48 53 56 N 13 20 E
Järna, Kopp., Sweden 72 60 33 N 14 26 E
Järna, Stockholm, Sweden 72 59 7 N 17 35 E
Jarnac 44 45 40 N 0 11 W
Jarny 43 49 9 N 5 53 E
Jarocin 54 51 59 N 17 29 E
Jaroměr 52 50 22 N 15 52 E
Jarosław 54 50 2 N 22 42 E
Järpås 73 58 23 N 12 57 E
Järpås 73 58 23 N 12 57 E
Järpen 72 63 21 N 13 26 E
Jarrahdale 137 32 24 S 116 5 E
Jarres, Plaine des 100 19 27 N 103 10 E
Jarrow 35 54 58 N 1 28 W
Jarso 123 5 15 N 37 30 E
Järved 72 63 16 N 18 43 E
Jarvis I. 131 0 15 S 159 55 W
Jarvornik 53 50 23 N 17 2 E
Jarwa 95 27 45 N 82 30 E
Jaša Tomió 66 45 26 N 20 50 E
Jasien 54 51 46 N 15 0 E
Jasin 101 2 20 N 102 26 E
Jäsk 93 25 38 N 57 45 E
Jasło 54 49 45 N 21 30 E
Jasper, Can. 152 52 55 N 118 5 W
Jasper, Ala., U.S.A. 157 33 48 N 87 16 W
Jasper, Ark., U.S.A. 97 36 0 N 93 10 W
Jasper, Fla., U.S.A. 157 30 31 N 82 58 W
Jasper, La., U.S.A. 159 30 59 N 93 58 W
Jasper, S.D., U.S.A. 158 43 52 N 96 22 W
Jasper Nat. Park 152 52 50 N 118 8 W
Jasper Place 152 53 33 N 113 25 W
Jastrebarsko 63 45 41 N 15 39 E
Jastrowie 54 53 26 N 16 49 E
Jastrzebie Zdroj 54 49 57 N 18 35 E
Jászapáti 53 47 32 N 20 10 E
Jászárokszállás 53 47 39 N 20 1 E
Jászberény 53 47 30 N 19 55 E
Jászkiser 53 47 27 N 20 20 E
Jászladány 53 47 23 N 20 18 E
Jataí 171 17 50 S 51 45 W
Jati 94 24 27 N 68 19 E
Jatibarang 103 6 28 S 108 18 E
Jatinegara 103 6 13 S 106 52 E
Játiva 59 39 0 N 0 32 W
Jatobal 170 4 35 S 49 33 W
Jatt 90 32 24 N 35 2 E
Jaú 173 22 10 S 48 30 W
Jau al Milah 91 15 15 N 45 40 E
Jauche 47 50 41 N 4 57 E
Jauja 174 11 45 S 75 30 W
Jaunelgava 80 56 35 N 25 0 E
Jaunpur 95 25 46 N 82 44 E
Java = Jawa 103 7 0 S 110 0 E
Java Sea 102 4 35 S 107 15 E
Javadi Hills 97 12 40 N 78 40 E
Jávea 59 38 48 N 0 10 E
Javhlant = Ulyasutay 105 47 45 N 96 49 E
Javla 96 17 18 N 75 9 E
Javron 42 48 25 N 0 25 W
Jawa 103 7 0 S 110 0 E
Jawor 54 51 4 N 16 11 E
Jaworzno 54 50 13 N 19 22 E
Jay 159 33 17 N 94 46 W
Jayawijaya, Pengunungan 103 7 0 S 139 0 E
Jaydot 153 49 15 N 110 15 W
Jaynagar 99 26 43 N 86 9 E
Jayton 159 33 17 N 100 35 W
Jazminal 164 24 56 N 101 25 W
Jean 161 35 47 N 115 20 W
Jean Marie River 152 61 32 N 120 38 W
Jean Rabel 167 19 50 N 73 30 W
Jeanerette 159 29 52 N 91 38 W
Jebba, Moroc. 118 35 11 N 4 43 W
Jebba, Nigeria 121 9 9 N 4 48 E
Jebel 66 40 35 N 21 15 E
Jebel Aulia 123 15 10 N 32 31 E
Jebel Qerri 123 16 16 N 32 50 E
Jedburgh 35 55 28 N 2 33 W
Jedlicze 54 49 43 N 21 40 E
Jedlnia-Letnisko 54 51 25 N 21 19 E
Jedrzejów 54 50 35 N 20 15 E

Jedway Kaboudia, Rass

Jedway	152	52 17N	131 14W
Jeetze, R.	48	52 58N	11 6 E
Jefferson, Iowa, U.S.A.	158	42 3N	94 25W
Jefferson, Tex., U.S.A.	159	32 45N	94 23W
Jefferson, Wis., U.S.A.	158	43 0N	88 49W
Jefferson City	157	36 8N	83 30W
Jefferson, Mt., Calif., U.S.A.	163	38 51N	117 0W
Jefferson, Mt., Oreg., U.S.A.	160	44 45N	121 50W
Jeffersonville	156	38 20N	85 42W
Jega	121	12 15N	4 23 E
Jekabpils	80	56 29N	25 57 E
Jelenia Góra	54	50 50N	15 45 E
Jelenia Góra □	54	51 0N	15 30 E
Jelgava	80	56 41N	22 49 E
Jelica	66	43 50N	20 17 E
Jelli	123	5 25N	31 45 E
Jellicoe	150	49 40N	87 30W
Jelšava	53	48 37N	20 15 E
Jemaja	103	3 5N	105 45 E
Jemaluang	101	2 16N	103 52 E
Jemappes	47	50 27N	3 54 E
Jember	103	8 11 S	113 41 E
Jembongan, I.	102	6 45N	117 20 E
Jemmapes = Azzaba	119	36 48N	7 6 E
Jemnice	52	49 1N	15 34 E
Jena, Ger.	48	50 56N	11 33 E
Jena, U.S.A.	159	31 41N	92 7W
Jench'iu	106	38 43N	116 5 E
Jendouba	119	36 29N	8 47 E
Jenhochieh	108	26 29N	101 45 E
Jenhsien	106	37 8N	114 37 E
Jenhua	109	25 5N	113 45 E
Jenhuai	108	27 53N	106 17 E
Jenin	90	32 28N	35 18 E
Jenkins	156	37 13N	82 41W
Jennings	159	30 10N	92 45W
Jennings, R.	152	59 38N	132 5W
Jenny	73	57 47N	16 35 E
Jeparit	140	36 8 S	142 1 E
Jequié	171	13 51 S	40 5W
Jequitaí, R.	171	17 4 S	44 50W
Jequitinhonha	171	16 30 S	41 0W
Jequitinhonha, R.	171	15 51 S	38 53W
Jerada	118	34 40N	2 10W
Jerantut	101	3 56N	102 22 E
Jérémie	167	18 40N	74 10W
Jeremoabo	170	10 4 S	38 21W
Jerez de García Salinas	164	22 39N	103 0W
Jerez de la Frontera	57	36 41N	6 7W
Jerez de los Caballeros	57	38 20N	6 45W
Jerez, Punta	165	22 58N	97 40W
Jericho	138	23 38 S	146 6 E
Jericho = El Arīhā	90	31 52N	35 27 E
Jerichow	48	52 30N	12 2 E
Jerilderie	141	35 20 S	145 41 E
Jermyn	162	41 31N	75 31W
Jerome	161	34 50N	112 0W
Jersey City	162	40 41N	74 8W
Jersey, I.	42	49 13N	2 7W
Jersey Shore	156	41 17N	77 18W
Jerseyville	158	39 5N	90 20W
Jerumenha	171	7 5 S	43 30W
Jerusalem	90	31 47N	35 10 E
Jervaulx	33	54 19N	1 41W
Jervis B.	141	35 8 S	150 46 E
Jervis, C.	139	35 38 S	138 6 E
Jesenice	63	46 28N	14 3 E
Jesenik	53	50 0N	17 8 E
Jeseník (Frývaldov)	53	50 15N	17 11 E
Jesenske	53	48 20N	20 10 E
Jesselton = Kota Kinabalu	102	6 0N	116 12 E
Jessnitz	48	51 42N	12 19 E
Jessore	98	23 10N	89 10 E
Jesup	157	31 30N	82 0W
Jesús Carranza	165	17 28N	95 1W
Jesús María	172	30 59 S	64 5W
Jetmore	159	38 10N	99 57W
Jetpur	94	21 45N	70 10 E
Jette	47	50 53N	4 20 E
Jevnaker	71	60 15N	10 26 E
Jewett	159	31 20N	96 8W
Jewett City	162	41 36N	72 0W
Jeypore	96	18 50N	82 38 E
Jeziorany	54	53 58N	20 46 E
J.F. Rodrigues	170	2 55 S	50 20W
Jhajjar	94	28 37N	76 14 E
Jhal Jhao	93	26 20N	65 35 E
Jhalakati	98	22 39N	90 12 E
Jhalawar	94	24 35N	76 10 E
Jhang Maghiana	94	31 15N	72 15 E
Jhansi	95	25 30N	78 36 E
Jharia	95	23 45N	86 18 E
Jharsaguda	99	21 50N	84 5 E
Jharsuguda	96	21 50N	84 5 E
Jhelum	94	33 0N	73 45 E
Jhelum, R.	95	31 50N	72 10 E
Jhunjhunu	94	28 10N	75 20 E
Jiangshan	95	28 45N	118 37 E
Jibão, Serra do	171	14 48 S	45 0W
Jibiya	121	13 5N	7 12 E
Jibou	70	47 15N	23 17 E
Jicín	52	50 25N	15 20 E
Jicarón, I.	166	7 10N	81 50W
Jiddah	92	21 29N	39 16 E
Jido	99	29 2N	94 58 E
Jifna	90	31 58N	35 13 E
Jiggalong	136	23 24 S	120 47 E
Jihk'atse	107	29 15N	88 53 E
Jihlava	52	49 28N	15 35 E
Jihočeský □	52	49 8N	14 35 E
Jihomoravský □	53	49 5N	16 30 E
Jiht'u	105	33 27N	79 42 E
Jijiga	91	9 20N	42 50 E
Jijona	59	38 34N	0 30W
Jikamshi	121	12 12N	7 45 E
Jiloca, R.	58	41 0N	1 20W
Jílové	52	49 52N	14 29 E
Jim Jim Cr.	136	12 50 S	132 32 E
Jima	123	7 40N	36 55 E
Jimbolia	66	45 47N	20 57 E
Jimena de la Frontera	57	36 27N	5 24W
Jimenbuen	141	36 42 S	148 53 E
Jiménez	164	27 10N	105 0W
Jind	94	29 19N	76 16 E
Jindabyne	141	36 25 S	148 35 E
Jindrichuv Hradeç	52	49 10N	15 2 E
Jinja	126	0 25N	33 12 E
Jinjang	101	3 13N	101 39 E
Jinjini	120	7 20N	3 42W
Jinnah Barrage	93	32 58N	71 33 E
Jinotega	166	13 6N	85 59W
Jinotepe	166	11 50N	86 10W
Jiparaná (Machado), R.	174	8 45 S	62 20W
Jipijapa	174	1 0 S	80 40W
Jiquilpán	164	19 57N	102 42W
Jisresh Shughur	92	35 49N	36 18 E
Jitarning	137	32 48 S	117 57 E
Jitra	101	6 16N	100 25 E
Jiu, R.	70	44 50N	23 20 E
Jiuchin	109	25 53N	116 0 E
Jiuli	108	24 6N	97 54 E
Jizera, R.	52	50 21N	14 48 E
Jizl Wadi	122	26 30N	38 0 E
Jizō-zaki	110	35 34N	133 20 E
Joaçaba	173	27 5 S	51 31W
Joaíma	171	16 39 S	41 2W
João	170	2 46 S	50 59W
João Amaro	171	12 46 S	40 22W
João Câmara	170	5 32 S	35 48W
João de Almeida	125	15 10 S	13 50 E
João Pessoa	170	7 10 S	34 52W
João Pinheiro	171	17 45 S	46 10W
Joaquim Távora	171	23 30 S	49 58W
Joaquín V. González	172	25 10 S	64 0W
Jobourg, Nez de	42	49 41N	1 57W
Joch'iang	105	39 2N	88 0 E
Jódar	59	37 50N	3 21W
Jodhpur	94	26 23N	73 2 E
Joe Batt's Arm	151	49 44N	54 10W
Joensuu	78	62 37N	29 49 E
Joeuf	43	49 12N	6 1 E
Jofane	125	21 15 S	34 18 E
Joggins	151	45 42N	64 27W
Jogjakarta = Yogyakarta	103	7 49 S	110 22 E
Jōhana	111	36 37N	136 57 E
Johannesburg, S. Afr.	129	26 10 S	28 8 E
Johannesburg, U.S.A.	163	35 22N	117 38W
Johannisnäs	72	62 45N	16 15 E
Johansfors, Halland, Sweden	73	56 50N	12 58 E
Johansfors, Kronoberg, Sweden	73	56 42N	15 32 E
John Days, R.	160	45 0N	120 0W
John o' Groats	37	58 39N	3 3W
Johnshaven	37	56 48N	2 20W
Johnson	159	37 35N	101 48W
Johnson City, N.Y., U.S.A.	162	42 7N	75 57W
Johnson City, Tenn., U.S.A.	157	36 18N	82 21W
Johnson City, Tex., U.S.A.	159	30 15N	98 24W
Johnson Cy.	156	42 9N	67 0W
Johnson Ra.	137	29 40 S	119 15 E
Johnsondale	163	35 58N	118 32W
Johnsons Crossing	152	60 29N	133 18W
Johnsonville	142	41 13 S	174 48 E
Johnston	31	51 45N	5 5W
Johnston Falls = Mambilima Falls	127	10 31 S	28 45 E
Johnston I.	131	17 10N	169 8 E
Johnston Lakes	137	32 20 S	120 45 E
Johnston Ra.	137	29 40 S	119 20 E
Johnstone	34	55 50N	4 31W
Johnstone Str.	152	50 28N	126 0W
Johnstown, Ireland	39	52 46N	7 34W
Johnstown, N.Y., U.S.A.	162	43 1N	74 20W
Johnstown, Pa., U.S.A.	156	40 19N	78 53W
Johnstown Bridge	38	53 23N	6 53W
Johor □	101	2 5N	103 20 E
Johor Baharu	101	1 28N	103 46 E
Johor, S.	101	1 45N	103 47 E
Joigny	43	48 0N	3 20 E
Joinvile	173	26 15 S	48 55 E
Joinville	43	48 27N	5 10 E
Joinville I.	13	63 15N	55 30W
Jojutla	165	18 37N	99 11W
Jokkmokk	74	66 35N	19 50 E
Jökulsá á Brú	74	65 40N	14 16W
Jökulsá Fjöllum	74	65 30N	16 15W
Jökulsa R.	74	65 30N	16 15W
Jolan	163	35 58N	121 9W
Joliet	156	41 30N	88 0W
Joliette	150	46 3N	73 24W
Jolo I.	103	6 0N	121 0 E
Jome, I.	103	1 16 S	127 30 E
Jönåker	73	58 44N	16 40 E
Jönaker	73	58 44N	16 43 E
Jones C.	150	54 33N	79 35W
Jones Sound	12	76 0N	89 0W
Jonesboro, Ark., U.S.A.	159	35 50N	90 45W
Jonesboro, Ill., U.S.A.	159	37 26N	89 18W
Jonesboro, La., U.S.A.	159	32 15N	92 41W
Jonesport	151	44 32N	67 38W
Jönköping	73	57 45N	14 10 E
Jönköpings län □	75	57 30N	14 30 E
Jonquière	151	48 27N	71 14W
Jonsberg	73	58 30N	16 48 E
Jonsered	73	57 45N	12 10 E
Jonzac	44	45 27N	0 28W
Joplin	159	37 0N	94 25W
Jordan, Phil.	103	10 41N	122 38 E
Jordan, Mont., U.S.A.	160	47 25N	106 58W
Jordan, N.Y., U.S.A.	162	43 4N	76 29W
Jordan ■	92	31 0N	36 0 E
Jordan, R.	90	32 10N	35 32 E
Jordan Valley	160	43 0N	117 2W
Jordânia	171	15 45 S	40 11W
Jordanów	54	49 41N	19 49 E
Jorhat	98	26 45N	94 20 E
Jörn	74	65 4N	20 1 E
Jørpeland	71	59 3N	6 1 E
Jorquera, R.	172	28 3 S	69 58W
Jos	121	9 53N	8 51 E
Jošanička Banja	66	43 24N	20 47 E
José Batlle y OrdóPez	173	33 20 S	55 10W
Josefow	54	52 10N	21 11 E
Joseni	70	47 42N	25 29 E
Joseph	160	45 27N	117 13W
Joseph Bonaparte G.	136	14 35 S	128 50 E
Joseph City	161	35 0N	110 16W
Joseph, Lac	151	52 45N	65 18W
Josephine, oilfield	19	58 35N	2 45 E
Joshua Tree	163	34 8N	116 19W
Joshua Tree Nat. Mon.	163	33 56N	116 5W
Josselin	42	47 57N	2 33W
Jostedal	71	61 35N	7 15 E
Jostedalsbre, Mt.	71	61 45N	7 0 E
Jotunheimen	71	61 35N	8 25 E
Jounieh	92	33 59N	35 30 E
Jourdanton	159	28 54N	98 32W
Journe	46	52 58N	5 48 E
Joussard	152	55 22N	115 57W
Joux, Lac de	50	46 39N	6 18 E
Jouzjan □	93	36 10N	66 0 E
Jovellanos	166	22 40N	81 10W
Jowai	98	25 26N	92 12 E
Joyce's Country, dist.	38	53 32N	9 30W
Joyeuse	45	44 29N	4 16 E
Jozini Dam	129	27 27 S	32 7 E
Ju Shui, R.	109	28 36N	116 4 E
Juan Aldama	164	24 20N	103 23W
Juan Bautista	161	36 55N	121 33W
Juan Bautista Alberdi	172	34 26 S	61 48W
Juan de Fuca Str.	160	48 15N	124 0W
Juan de Nova, I.	129	17 3 S	42 45 E
Juan Fernández, Arch. de	131	33 50 S	80 0W
Juan José Castelli	172	25 57 S	60 37W
Juan L. Lacaze	172	34 26 S	57 25W
Juárez, Argent.	172	37 40 S	59 43W
Juárez, Mexico	164	27 37N	100 44W
Juárez, Sierra de	164	32 0N	116 0W
Juatinga, Ponta de	171	23 17 S	44 30W
Juàzeiro	170	9 30 S	40 30W
Juàzeiro do Norte	170	7 10 S	39 18W
Jûbâ	123	4 57N	31 35 E
Juba, R.	91	1 30N	42 35 E
Jubaila	92	24 55N	46 25 E
Jûbâl	122	27 30N	34 0 E
Jubbulpore = Jabalpur	95	23 9N	79 58 E
Jübek	54	54 31N	9 24 E
Jubga	83	44 19N	38 48 E
Jubilee L.	137	29 0 S	126 50 E
Juby, C.	116	28 0N	12 59W
Júcar, R.	58	40 8N	2 13W
Júcaro	166	21 37N	78 51W
Juch'eng	109	25 32N	113 39 E
Juchitán	165	16 27N	95 5W
Judaea = Yehuda	90	31 35N	34 57 E
Judenburg	52	47 12N	14 38 E
Judith Gap	160	46 48N	109 46W
Judith Pt.	162	41 20N	71 30W
Judith, R.	160	47 30N	109 30W
Juian	109	27 45N	120 38 E
Juich'ang	109	29 40N	115 39 E
Juigalpa	166	12 6N	85 26W
Juillac	44	45 20N	1 19 E
Juist, I.	48	53 40N	7 0 E
Juiz de Fora	171	21 43 S	43 19W
Jujuy	172	24 10 S	65 25W
Jujuy □	172	23 20 S	65 40W
Jukao	109	32 24N	120 35 E
Julesberg	158	41 0N	102 20W
Juli	174	16 10 S	69 25W
Julia Cr.	138	20 0 S	141 11 E
Julia Creek	138	20 39 S	141 44 E
Juliaca	174	15 25 S	70 10W
Julian	163	33 4N	116 38W
Julian Alps = Julijske Alpe	63	46 15N	14 1 E
Julianakanaal	47	51 6N	5 52 E
Julianehåb	12	60 43N	46 0W
Julianstown	38	53 40N	6 16W
Jülich	48	50 55N	6 20 E
Julier P.	51	46 28N	9 32 E
Julijske Alpe	63	46 15N	14 1 E
Julimes	164	28 25N	105 27W
Jullundur	94	31 20N	75 40 E
Jumbo	127	17 30 S	30 58 E
Jumento, Cayos	167	23 0N	75 40 E
Jumet	47	50 27N	4 25 E
Jumilla	59	38 28N	1 19W
Jumla	95	29 15N	82 13 E
Jumna, R. = Yamuna	94	27 0N	78 30 E
Junagadh	94	21 30N	70 30 E
Junan	109	32 58N	114 31 E
Junction, Tex., U.S.A.	159	30 29N	99 48W
Junction, Utah, U.S.A.	161	38 10N	112 15W
Junction B.	138	11 52 S	133 55 E
Junction City, Kans., U.S.A.	158	39 4N	96 55W
Junction City, Oreg., U.S.A.	160	44 20N	123 12W
Jundah	138	24 46 S	143 2 E
Jundiaí	173	23 10 S	47 0W
Juneau	147	58 26N	134 30W
Junee	141	34 53 S	147 35 E
Jung Chiang, R.	108	23 25N	110 0 E
Jungan	108	25 14N	109 23 E
Jungch'ang	108	29 27N	105 33 E
Jungch'eng	107	37 9N	122 23 E
Jungchiang	108	25 56N	108 31 E
Jungching	108	29 49N	102 55 E
Jungfrau	50	46 32N	7 58 E
Jungho	106	35 21N	110 32 E
Junghsien, Kwangsi-Chuang, China	109	22 52N	110 33 E
Junghsien, Szechwan, China	108	29 29N	104 22 E
Junglinster	47	49 43N	6 15 E
Jungshahi	94	24 52N	67 44 E
Jungshui	108	24 14N	109 23 E
Juniata, R.	162	40 30N	77 40W
Junín	172	34 33 S	60 57W
Junín de los Andes	176	39 45 S	71 0W
Junnar	96	19 12N	73 58 E
Junquera, La	58	42 25N	2 53 E
Junta, La	159	38 0N	103 30W
Juntura	160	43 44N	119 4W
Juparanã, Lagoa	171	19 35 S	40 18W
Jupiter, R.	151	49 29N	63 37W
Juquiá	171	24 19 S	47 38W
Jur, Nahr el	123	8 45N	29 0 E
Jura	43	46 35N	6 5 E
Jura □	43	46 47N	5 45 E
Jura, I.	34	56 0N	5 50W
Jura, Paps of, mts.	34	55 55N	6 0W
Jura, Sd. of	34	55 57N	5 45W
Jura Suisse	50	47 10N	7 0 E
Jurado	174	7 7N	77 46W
Jurby Hd.	32	54 23N	4 31W
Jurien B.	132	30 17 S	115 0 E
Jurilovca	70	44 46N	28 52W
Jurm	93	36 50N	70 45 E
Juruá, R.	174	2 30 S	66 0W
Juruena, R.	174	7 20 S	58 3W
Juruti	175	2 9 S	56 4W
Jushan	107	36 54N	121 30 E
Jussey	43	47 50N	5 55 E
Justo Daract	172	33 52 S	65 12W
Jüterbog	48	51 59N	13 6 E
Juticalpa	166	14 40N	85 50W
Jutland	16	56 0N	8 0 E
Jutphaas	46	52 2N	5 6 E
Jutung	109	32 19N	121 14 E
Juvigny-sous-Andaine	42	48 32N	0 30W
Juvisy	43	48 43N	2 23 E
Juwain	93	31 45N	61 30 E
Juyüan	109	24 46N	113 16 E
Juzennecourt	43	48 10N	5 0 E
Jye-kundo	99	33 0N	96 50 E
Jylhama	74	64 34N	26 40 E
Jylland	73	56 15N	9 20 E
Jylland (Jutland)	73	56 25N	9 30 E
Jyväskylä	74	62 14N	25 44 E

K

K. Sedili Besar	101	1 55N	104 5 E
K2, Mt.	95	36 0N	77 0 E
Ka Lae (South C.)	147	18 55N	155 41W
Kaaia, Mt.	147	21 31N	158 9W
Kaap die Goeie Hoop	128	34 24 S	18 30 E
Kaap Plato	128	28 30 S	24 0 E
Kaapkruis	128	21 43 S	14 0 E
Kaapstad = Cape Town	125	33 56 S	18 27 E
Kaatsheuvel	47	51 39N	5 2 E
Kabaena, I.	103	5 15 S	122 0 E
Kabala	120	9 38N	11 37W
Kabale	126	1 15 S	30 0 E
Kabalo	126	6 0 S	27 0 E
Kabambare	126	4 41 S	27 39 E
Kabango	127	8 35 S	28 30 E
Kabanjahe	102	8 2N	98 27 E
Kabara	120	16 40N	2 50W
Kabardinka	82	44 40N	37 57 E
Kabardino-Balkar, A.S.S.R. □	83	43 30N	43 30 E
Kabarega Falls	126	2 15N	31 38 E
Kabasalan	103	7 47N	122 44 E
Kabba	121	7 57N	6 3 E
Kabe	110	34 31N	132 31 E
Kabi	121	13 30N	12 35 E
Kabin Buri	100	13 57N	101 43 E
Kabinakagami L.	150	48 54N	84 25W
Kabinda	126	6 23 S	24 28 E
Kablungu, C.	135	6 20 S	150 1 E
Kabna	122	19 6N	32 40 E
Kabompo	127	13 30 S	24 14 E
Kabompo, R.	127	13 50 S	24 10 E
Kabondo	127	8 58 S	25 40 E
Kabongo	126	7 22 S	25 33 E
Kabou	121	9 28N	0 55 E
Kaboudia, Rass	119	35 13N	11 10 E

Kabra	138	23 25S	150 25E
Kabūd Gonbad	93	37 5N	59 45E
Kabuiri	121	11 30N	13 30E
Kabul	94	34 28N	69 18E
Kabul □	93	34 0N	68 30E
Kabul, R.	94	34 30N	69 13E
Kabunga	126	1 38S	28 3E
Kaburuang	103	3 50N	126 30E
Kabushiya	123	16 54N	33 41E
Kabwe	127	14 30S	28 29E
Kabwum	135	6 11S	147 15E
Kačanik	66	42 13N	21 12E
Kachanovo	80	57 25N	27 38E
Kachebera	127	13 56S	32 50E
Kachin □	98	26 0N	97 0E
Kachira, Lake	126	0 40S	31 0E
Kachiry	76	53 10N	75 50E
Kachisi	123	9 40N	37 57E
Kachkanar	84	58 42N	59 33E
Kachot	101	11 30N	103 3E
Kaçkar	83	40 45N	41 30E
Kadaingti	98	17 37N	97 32E
Kadan Kyun, I.	101	12 30N	98 20E
Kadanai, R.	94	32 0N	66 10E
Kadarkút	53	46 13N	17 39E
Kadayanallur	97	9 3N	77 22E
Kaddi	121	13 40N	5 40E
Kade	121	6 7N	0 56W
Kadgo, L.	137	25 30S	125 30E
Kadi	94	23 18N	72 23E
Kadina	140	34 0S	137 43E
Kadiri	97	14 12N	78 13E
* Kadiyevka	83	48 35N	38 40E
Kadoka	158	43 50N	101 31W
Kadom	81	54 37N	42 24E
Kaduna	121	10 30N	7 21E
Kaduna □	121	11 0N	7 30E
Kaduna, R.	121	10 5N	8 10E
Kadyoha	120	8 58N	5 53W
Kadzhi-Say	85	42 8N	77 10E
Kaedi	120	16 9N	13 28W
Kaelé	121	10 15N	14 15E
Kaena Pt.	147	21 35N	158 17W
Kaeng Khoï	100	14 35N	101 0E
Kaeo	142	35 6S	173 49E
Kaerh, China	105	31 45N	80 22E
Kaerh, Sudan	123	5 35N	31 20E
Kaesŏng	107	37 58N	126 35E
Kaf	92	31 25N	37 20E
Kafakumba	124	9 38S	23 46E
Kafan	79	39 18N	46 15E
Kafanchan	121	9 40N	8 20E
Kafareti	121	10 25N	11 12E
Kaffrine	120	14 8N	15 36W
Kafia Kingi	117	9 20N	24 25E
Kafinda	127	12 32S	30 20E
Kafirévs, Ákra	69	38 9N	24 8E
Kafiristan	93	35 0N	70 30E
Kafr Ana	70	32 2N	34 48E
Kafr 'Ein	90	32 3N	35 7E
Kafr el Dauwâr	122	31 8N	30 8E
Kafr Kama	90	32 44N	35 26E
Kafr Kannā	90	32 45N	35 20E
Kafr Malik	90	32 0N	35 18E
Kafr Mandā	90	32 49N	35 15E
Kafr Quaddum	90	32 14N	35 7E
Kafr Ra'i	90	32 23N	35 9E
Kafr Sir	90	33 19N	35 23E
Kafr Yasif	90	32 58N	35 10E
Kafue	127	15 46S	28 9E
Kafue Flats	127	15 32S	27 0E
Kafue Gorge	127	16 0S	28 0E
Kafue Hook	127	14 58S	26 0E
Kafue Nat. Park	65	15 30S	25 40E
Kafue, R.	125	15 30S	26 0E
Kafulwe	127	9 0S	29 1E
Kaga, Afghan.	94	34 14N	70 10E
Kaga, Japan	111	36 16N	136 15E
Kagamil I.	147	53 0N	169 40W
Kagan	85	39 43N	64 33E
Kagawa-ken □	110	34 15N	134 0E
Kagera R.	126	1 15S	31 20E
Kagoshima	110	31 36N	130 40E
Kagoshima-ken □	110	30 0N	130 0E
Kagoshima-Wan	110	31 0N	130 40E
Kagul	82	45 50N	28 15E
Kahajan, R.	102	2 10S	114 0E
Kahama	126	4 8S	32 30E
Kahama □	126	3 40S	32 0E
Kahang	101	2 12N	103 32E
Kahe	126	3 30S	37 25E
Kahemba	124	7 18S	18 55E
Kaherekoua Mts.	143	45 45S	167 15E
Kahniah, R.	152	58 15N	120 55W
Kahnuj	93	27 55N	57 40E
Kahoka	158	40 25N	91 42W
Kahoolawe, I.	147	20 33N	156 35W
Kahuku & Pt.	147	21 41N	157 57W
Kahului	147	20 54N	156 28W
Kahurangi, Pt.	143	40 50S	172 10E
Kahuta	94	33 35N	73 24E
Kai Kai	128	19 52S	21 15E
Kai, Kepulauan	103	5 55S	132 45W
Kaiama	121	9 36N	4 1E
Kaiapit	135	6 18S	146 18E
Kaiapoi	143	42 24S	172 40E
Kaibara	111	35 8N	135 5E
K'aichien	109	23 45N	111 47E
K'aifeng	106	34 50N	114 27E
Kaihsien	107	40 25N	122 25E
K'aihsien	108	31 12N	108 25E
K'aihua	109	29 9N	118 24E
Kaiingveld	128	30 0S	22 0E

Kaikohe	142	35 25S	173 49E
Kaikoura	143	42 25S	173 43E
Kaikoura Pen.	143	42 25S	173 43E
Kaikoura Ra.	143	41 59S	173 41E
Kailahun	120	8 18N	10 39W
Kailashahar	98	25 19N	92 0E
Kaili	108	26 32N	107 57E
K'ailu	107	43 35N	121 12E
Kailua	147	19 39N	156 0W
Kaimana	103	3 30S	133 45E
Kaimanawa Mts.	142	39 15S	175 56E
Kaimata	143	42 34S	171 28E
Kaimganj	95	27 33N	79 24E
Kaimon-Dake	110	31 11N	130 32E
Kaimur Hill	95	24 30N	82 0E
Kainan	110	34 9N	135 12E
Kainantu	135	6 18S	145 52E
Kaingaroa Forest	142	38 30S	176 30E
Kainji Res.	121	10 1N	4 40E
Kaipara Harb.	142	36 25S	174 14E
K'aip'ing	109	22 31N	112 32E
Kaipokok B.	151	54 54N	59 47W
Kairana	94	29 33N	77 15E
Kairiru, I.	138	3 20S	143 20E
Kaironi	103	0 47S	133 40E
Kairouan	119	35 45N	10 5E
Kairuku	135	8 51S	146 35E
Kaiserslautern	49	49 30N	7 43E
Kaitaia	142	35 8S	173 17E
Kaitangata	143	46 17S	169 51E
Kaithal	94	29 48N	76 26E
Kaitu, R.	94	33 20N	70 20E
Kaiwi Channel	147	21 13N	157 30W
K'aiyang	108	27 4N	106 55E
K'aiyüan, Liaoning, China	107	42 33N	124 4E
K'aiyüan, Yunnan, China	108	23 47N	103 10E
Kaiyuh Mts.	147	63 40N	159 0W
Kajaani	74	64 17N	27 46E
Kajabbi	138	20 0S	140 1E
Kajan, R.	102	2 40N	116 40E
Kajang	101	2 59N	101 48E
Kajeli	103	3 20S	127 10E
Kajiado	126	1 53S	36 48E
Kajiki	110	31 44N	130 40E
Kajo Kaji	123	3 58N	31 40E
Kajoa, I.	103	0 1N	127 28E
Kajuagung	102	3 8S	104 46E
Kakabeka Falls	150	48 24N	89 37W
Kakamas	125	28 45S	20 33E
Kakamega	126	0 20N	34 46E
Kakamega □	126	0 20N	34 46E
Kakamigahara	111	35 28N	136 48E
Kakanj	66	44 9N	18 7E
Kakanui Mts.	143	45 10S	170 30E
Kakapotahi	143	43 0S	170 45E
Kake, Japan	110	34 36N	132 19E
Kake, U.S.A.	147	57 0N	134 0W
Kakegawa	111	34 45N	138 1E
Kakhib	83	42 28N	46 34E
Kakhovskoye Vdkhr.	82	47 5N	34 16E
Kakia	125	24 48S	23 22E
Kakinada = Cocanada	99	16 50N	82 11E
Kakinada (Cocanada)	96	16 50N	82 11E
Kakisa L.	152	60 56N	117 43W
Kakisa, R.	152	61 3N	117 10W
Kakogawa	110	34 46N	134 51E
Kaktovik	147	70 8N	143 50W
Kakwa, R.	152	54 37N	118 28W
Kala	121	12 2N	14 40E
Kala Oya.	97	8 15N	80 0E
Kala Shank'ou	95	35 42N	78 20E
Kalaa-Kebira	119	35 59N	10 32E
Kalabagh	94	33 0N	71 28E
Kalabáka	68	39 42N	21 39E
Kalabo	125	14 58S	22 33E
Kalach	81	50 22N	41 0E
Kaladan, R.	99	21 30N	92 45E
Kalahari, Des.	128	24 0S	22 0E
Kalahari Gemsbok Nat. Pk.	128	26 0S	20 30E
Kalahasti	97	13 45N	79 44E
Kalai-Khumb	85	38 28N	70 46E
Kalaja e Turrës	68	41 10N	19 28E
Kalakamati	129	20 40S	27 25E
Kalakan	77	55 15N	116 45E
K'alak'unlun Shank'ou	95	35 33N	77 46E
Kalam	95	35 34N	72 30E
Kalama, U.S.A.	160	46 0N	122 55W
Kalama, Zaïre	126	2 52S	28 35E
Kalamariá	68	40 33N	22 55E
Kalamata	69	37 3N	22 10E
Kalamazoo	156	42 20N	85 35W
Kalamazoo, R.	156	42 40N	86 12W
Kalamb	96	18 3N	74 48E
Kalambo Falls	127	8 37S	31 35E
Kálamos, I.	69	38 37N	20 55E
Kalamoti	69	38 15N	26 4E
Kalamunda	137	32 0S	116 0E
Kalangadoo	140	37 34S	140 41E
Kalannie	137	30 22S	117 5E
Kalao, I.	103	7 21S	121 0E
Kalaotoa, I.	103	7 20S	121 50E
Kälarne	72	62 59N	16 8E
Kalárovo	53	47 54N	18 0E
Kalasin	100	16 26N	103 30E
Kalat	93	29 8N	66 31E
Kalat □	93	27 0N	64 30E
Kalat-i-Ghilzai	93	32 15N	66 58E
Kálathos (Calato)	69	36 9N	28 8E
Kalaupapa	147	21 12N	156 59W
Kalaus, R.	83	45 40N	43 30E

Kalávrita	69	38 3N	22 8E
Kalaw	98	20 37N	96 35E
Kalba	120	9 30N	2 42W
Kalbarri	137	27 40S	114 10E
Kaldhovd	71	60 5N	8 20E
Kalecik	82	40 4N	33 26E
Kalegauk Kyun	99	15 33N	97 35E
Kalehe	126	2 6S	28 50E
Kalema	126	1 12S	31 55E
Kalemie	124	5 55S	29 9E
Kalemyo	98	23 11N	94 4E
Kalety	54	50 35N	18 52E
Kalewa	98	22 41N	95 32E
Kálfafellsstaður	74	64 11N	15 53W
Kalgan = Changchiak'ou	106	40 50N	114 53E
Kalgoorlie	137	30 40S	121 22E
Kaliakra, Nos	67	43 21N	28 30E
Kalianda	102	5 50S	105 45E
Kalibo	103	11 43N	122 22E
Kaliganj Town	98	23 25N	89 8E
Kalima	126	2 33S	26 32E
Kalimantan Barat □	102	0 0	110 30E
Kalimantan Selatan □	102	4 10S	115 30E
Kalimantan Tengah □	102	2 0S	113 30E
Kalimantan Timor □	102	1 30N	116 30E
Kálimnos, I.	69	37 0N	27 0E
Kalimpong	95	27 4N	88 35E
Kalinadi, R.	97	14 50N	74 20E
Kalinin	81	56 55N	35 55E
Kaliningrad	80	54 42N	20 32E
Kalinino	83	45 12N	38 59E
Kalininskoye	85	42 50N	73 49E
Kalinkovichi	80	52 12N	29 20E
Kalinovik	66	43 31N	18 29E
Kalipetrovo (Starčevo)	67	44 5N	27 14E
Kaliro	126	0 56N	33 30E
Kalirrákhi	68	40 40N	24 35E
Kalispell	160	48 10N	114 22W
Kalisz	54	51 45N	18 8E
Kalisz □	54	51 30N	18 0E
Kalisz Pom	54	53 17N	15 55E
Kaliua	126	5 5S	31 48E
Kaliveli Tank	97	12 5N	79 50E
Kalix R.	74	67 0N	22 0E
Kalka	94	30 56N	76 57E
Kalkaroo	140	31 12S	143 54E
Kalkaska	150	44 44N	85 11W
Kalkfeld	128	20 57S	16 14E
Kalkfontein	128	22 4S	20 57E
Kalkfontein Dam	128	29 30S	24 15E
Kalkrand	128	24 1S	17 35E
Kall L.	72	63 35N	13 10E
Kallakurichi	97	11 44N	79 1E
Kållandsö	73	58 40N	13 5E
Källby	73	58 30N	13 8E
Kallia	86	31 46N	35 30E
Kallidaikurichi	97	8 38N	77 31E
Kallinge	73	56 15N	15 18E
Kallithéa	69	37 55N	23 41E
Kallmeti	68	41 51N	19 41E
Kallonís, Kólpos	69	39 10N	26 10E
Kallsjön	74	63 38N	13 0E
Kalltorp	73	58 23N	13 20E
Kalmalo	121	13 40N	5 20E
Kalmar	73	56 40N	16 20E
Kalmar län □	73	57 25N	16 15E
Kalmar sund	73	56 40N	16 25E
Kalmthout	47	51 23N	4 29E
Kalmyk A.S.S.R. □	83	46 5N	46 1E
Kalmykovo	83	49 0N	51 35E
Kalna	95	23 13N	88 25E
Kalo	135	10 1S	147 48E
Kalocsa	53	46 32N	19 0E
Kalofer	67	42 37N	24 59E
Kalol, Gujarat, India	94	23 15N	72 33E
Kalol, Gujarat, India	94	22 37N	73 31E
Kalola	127	10 0S	28 0E
Kalolímnos	69	37 4N	27 8E
Kalomo	127	17 0S	26 30E
Kalonerón	69	37 20N	21 38E
Kalpi	95	26 8N	79 47E
Kalrayan Hills	97	11 45N	78 40E
Kalsubai, Mt.	96	17 35N	73 45E
Kaltbrunn	51	47 13N	9 2E
Kaltungo	121	9 48N	11 19E
Kalu	94	25 5N	67 39E
Kaluga	81	54 35N	36 10E
Kalulushi	127	12 50S	28 3E
Kalundborg	73	55 41N	11 5E
Kalush	80	42 9N	24 12E
Kałuszyn	54	52 13N	21 52E
Kalutara	97	6 35N	80 0E
Kalwaria	54	49 53N	19 41E
Kalya	84	60 15N	59 59E
Kalyan, Austral.	140	34 55S	139 49E
Kalyan, India	96	20 30N	74 3E
Kalyani	174	17 53N	76 59E
Kalyazin	81	57 15N	37 45E
Kam Keut	101	18 20N	104 48E
Kama, Burma	98	22 10N	95 10E
Kama, Zaïre	126	3 30S	27 5E
Kama, R.	84	60 0N	53 0E
Kamachumu	126	1 37S	31 37E
Kamae	110	32 48N	131 56E
Kamaguenam	121	13 36N	10 30E
Kamaing	98	24 26N	94 55E
Kamaishi	112	39 20N	142 0E
Kamakura	111	35 19N	139 33E
Kamalia	94	30 44N	72 42E
Kamalino	147	21 50N	160 14W
Kamamaung	98	17 21N	97 40E
Kamango	126	0 40N	29 52E

Kamapanda	127	12 5S	24 0E
Kamaran	91	15 28N	42 35E
Kamashi	85	38 51N	65 23E
Kamativi	127	18 15S	0 27E
Kamba	121	11 50N	3 45E
Kambalda	137	31 10S	121 37E
Kambam	97	9 45N	77 16E
Kambar	94	27 37N	68 1E
Kambarka	84	56 15N	54 11E
Kambia	120	9 3N	12 53W
Kambolé	127	8 47S	30 48E
Kambove	127	10 51S	26 33E
Kamchatka, P-ov.	77	57 0N	160 0E
Kamde	138	8 0S	140 58E
Kamen	76	53 50N	81 30E
Kamen Kashirskiy	80	51 39N	24 56E
Kamenica	66	44 25N	19 40E
Kamenice	52	49 18N	15 2E
Kamenjak, Rt.	63	44 47N	13 55E
Kamenka, R.S.F.S.R., U.S.S.R.	78	65 58N	44 0E
Kamenka, R.S.F.S.R., U.S.S.R.	81	50 47N	39 20E
Kamenka Bugskaya	80	50 8N	24 16E
Kamenka Dneprovskaya	82	47 29N	34 14E
Kamensk	76	56 25N	62 45E
Kamensk Shakhtinskiy	83	48 23N	40 20E
Kamensk-Uralskiy	84	56 25N	62 2E
Kamenskiy	81	50 48N	45 25E
Kamenskoye	77	62 45N	165 30E
Kamenyak	67	43 24N	26 57E
Kamenz	48	51 17N	14 7E
Kameoka	111	35 0N	135 35E
Kames	34	55 53N	5 15W
Kameyama	111	34 51N	126 27E
Kami	68	42 17N	20 18E
Kami-Jima	110	32 27N	130 20E
Kami-koshiki-Jima	110	31 50N	129 52E
Kamiah	160	46 12N	116 2W
Kamien Krajenskie	54	53 32N	17 32E
Kamien Pomorski	54	53 57N	14 43E
Kamiensk	54	51 12N	19 29E
Kamiita	110	34 6N	134 22E
Kamilonision	69	35 50N	26 15E
Kamilukuak, L.	153	62 22N	101 40W
Kamina	127	8 45S	25 0E
Kaminak L.	153	62 10N	95 0W
Kamioka	111	36 25N	137 15E
Kamituga Mungombe	126	3 2S	28 10E
Kamiyaku	112	30 25N	130 30E
Kamloops	152	50 40N	120 20W
Kamo	143	35 42S	174 20E
Kamogawa	111	35 5N	140 5E
Kamoke	94	32 4N	74 4E
Kamono	124	3 10S	13 20E
Kamp, R.	52	48 35N	15 26E
Kampala	126	0 20N	32 30E
Kampar	101	4 18N	101 9E
Kampar, R.	102	0 30N	102 0E
Kampen	46	52 33N	5 53E
Kamperland	47	51 34N	3 43E
Kamphaeng Phet	100	16 28N	99 30E
Kampolombo, L.	127	11 30S	29 35E
Kampong Ayer Puteh	101	4 15N	103 10E
Kampong Jerangau	101	4 50N	103 10E
Kampong Raja	101	5 45N	102 35E
Kampong Sedili Besar	101	1 56N	104 8E
Kampong To	101	6 3N	101 13E
Kampot	101	10 36N	104 10E
Kamptee	94	21 9N	79 19E
Kampti	120	10 7N	3 25W
Kampuchea ■ = Cambodia	100	12 15N	105 0E
Kamrau, Teluk	103	3 30S	133 45E
Kamsack	153	51 34N	101 54W
Kamskoye Ustye	81	55 10N	49 20E
Kamskoye Vdkhr.	78	58 0N	56 0E
Kamuchawie L.	153	56 18N	101 59W
Kamui-Misaki	112	45 3N	142 30E
Kamyshin	81	50 10N	45 30E
Kamyshlov	84	56 50N	62 43E
Kamyzyak	83	46 4N	48 10E
Kan	98	20 53N	93 49E
Kan Chiang, R.	109	29 45N	116 10E
Kanaaupscow	150	54 2N	76 30W
Kanab	161	37 3N	112 29W
Kanab Creek	161	37 0N	112 40W
Kanaga I.	147	51 45N	177 22W
Kanagawa-ken □	111	35 20N	139 20E
Kanairiktok, R.	151	55 2N	60 18W
Kanakanak	147	59 0N	158 58W
Kanakapura	97	12 33N	77 28E
Kanália	68	39 30N	22 53E
Kananga	124	5 55S	22 18E
Kanarraville	161	37 34N	113 12W
Kanash	81	55 48N	47 32E
Kanawha, R.	156	39 40N	82 0W
Kanayis, Ras el	122	31 30N	28 5E
Kanazawa	111	36 30N	136 38E
Kanbalu	98	17 55N	85 24E
Kanchanaburi	100	14 8N	99 31E
Kanchenjunga, Mt.	95	27 50N	88 10E
Kanchipuram (Conjeeveram)	97	12 52N	79 45E
Kanchou	109	25 51N	114 59E
Kanch'üan	106	36 19N	109 19E
Kanda Kanda	124	6 52S	23 48E
Kandagach	79	49 20N	57 15E
Kandahar	94	31 32N	65 30E
Kandahar □	94	31 0N	65 0E
Kandalaksha	78	67 9N	32 30E
Kandalakshkiyzaliv	78	66 0N	35 0E

* Renamed Stakhanov

Kandalu	93	29 55N	63 20 E
Kandangan	102	2 50S	115 20 E
Kandanos	69	35 19N	23 44 E
Kandé	121	9 57N	1 53 E
Kandep	135	5 54S	143 32 E
Kander, R.	50	46 33N	7 38 E
Kandersteg	50	46 30N	7 40 E
Kandewu	127	14 1S	26 16 E
Kandhíla	69	37 46N	22 22 E
Kandhkot	94	28 16N	69 8 E
Kandhla	94	29 18N	77 19 E
Kandi, Benin	121	11 7N	2 55 E
Kandi, India	95	23 58N	88 5 E
Kandinduna	127	13 58S	24 19 E
Kandira	92	41 5N	30 10 E
Kandla	94	23 0N	70 10 E
Kandos	141	32 45S	149 58 E
Kandrach	93	25 30N	65 30 E
Kandrian	135	6 14S	149 37 E
Kandukur	95	15 12N	79 57 E
Kandy	97	7 18N	80 43 E
Kane	156	41 39N	78 53W
Kane Bassin	12	79 30N	68 0W
Kanel	120	13 18N	14 35W
Kaneohe	147	21 25N	157 48W
Kanevskaya	83	46 3N	39 3 E
Kanfanar	63	45 7N	13 50 E
Kang	93	30 55N	61 55 E
Kangaba	120	11 56N	8 25W
Kangar	101	6 27N	100 12 E
Kangaroo I.	140	35 45S	137 0 E
Kangaroo Mts.	138	23 25S	142 0 E
Kangavar	92	34 40N	48 0 E
Kangean, Kepulauan	102	6 55S	115 23 E
Kangerdlugsuaé	12	68 10N	32 20W
Kanggye	107	41 0N	126 35 E
Kanggyŏng	107	36 10N	126 0 E
Kanghwa	107	37 45N	126 30 E
K'angkang	108	32 46N	101 3 E
Kangnŭng	107	37 45N	128 54 E
Kango	124	0 11N	10 5 E
K'angp'ing	107	43 45N	123 20 E
Kangpokpi	98	25 8N	93 58 E
K'angting	108	30 2N	102 0 E
Kangtissu Shan	95	31 0N	82 0 E
Kangto, Mt.	99	27 50N	92 35 E
Kangyao	107	44 15N	126 40 E
Kangyidaung	98	16 56N	94 54 E
Kanhangad	97	12 21N	74 58 E
Kanheri	96	19 13N	72 50 E
Kani, China	99	29 25N	95 25 E
Kani, Ivory C.	120	8 29N	6 36W
Kaniama	126	7 30S	24 12 E
Kaniapiskau L.	151	54 10N	69 55W
Kaniapiskau, R.	151	57 40N	69 30 E
Kanibadam	85	40 17N	70 25 E
Kanin Nos, Mys	78	68 45N	43 20 E
Kanin, P-ov.	78	68 0N	45 0 E
Kanina	68	40 23N	19 30 E
Kaniva	140	36 22S	141 18 E
Kanjiza	66	46 3N	20 4 E
Kanjut Sar	95	36 15N	75 25 E
Kankakee	156	41 6N	87 50W
Kankakee, R.	156	41 13N	87 0W
Kankan	120	10 30N	9 15W
Kanker	96	20 10N	81 40 E
Kankouchen	107	40 30N	119 27 E
Kanku	106	34 45N	105 12 E
Kankunskiy	77	57 37N	126 8 E
Kanmuri-Yama	110	34 30N	132 4 E
Kannabe	110	34 32N	133 23 E
Kannapolis	157	35 32N	80 37W
Kannauj	95	27 3N	79 26 E
Kannod	93	22 45N	76 40 E
Kano	121	12 2N	8 30 E
Kano □	121	12 30N	9 0 E
Kan'onji	110	34 7N	133 39 E
Kanoroba	120	9 7N	6 8W
Kanowit	102	2 14N	112 20 E
Kanowna	137	30 32S	121 31 E
Kanoya	110	31 25N	130 50 E
Kanózuga	54	49 58N	22 25 E
Kanpetlet	98	21 10N	93 59 E
Kanpur	95	26 35N	80 20 E
Kansas □	158	38 40N	98 0W
Kansas City, Kans., U.S.A.	158	39 0N	94 40W
Kansas City, Mo., U.S.A.	158	39 3N	94 30W
Kansas, R.	158	39 15N	96 20W
Kansenia	127	10 20S	26 0 E
Kansk	77	56 20N	95 37 E
Kansŏng	107	38 24N	128 30 E
Kansu □	105	35 30N	104 30 E
Kant	85	42 53N	74 51 E
Kant'angtzu	106	37 28N	104 33 E
Kantché	121	13 31N	8 30 E
Kantemirovka	83	49 43N	39 55 E
Kantharalak	100	14 39N	104 39 E
Kantishna	147	63 31N	151 5W
Kantō □	111	36 0N	140 0 E
Kantō-Heiya	111	36 0N	139 30 E
Kantō-Sanchi	111	35 50N	138 50 E
Kantu-long	98	19 57N	97 36 E
Kanturk	39	52 10N	8 55W
Kantzu	108	31 37N	100 0 E
Kanuma	111	36 44N	139 42 E
Kanus	128	27 50S	18 39 E
Kanye	128	25 0S	25 28 E
Kanyu	128	20 7S	24 37 E
Kanyü	107	34 53N	119 9 E
Kanzene	127	10 30S	25 12 E
Kanzi, Ras	126	7 1S	39 33 E
Kaoan	109	28 25N	115 22 E
Kaochou	109	21 55N	110 52 E
Kaohofu	109	30 43N	116 49 E
Kaohsien	108	28 21N	104 31 E
Kaohsiung	109	22 35N	120 16 E
Kaok'eng	109	27 39N	114 4 E
Kaoko Otavi	125	18 12S	13 45 E
Kaokoveld	128	19 0S	13 0 E
Kaolack	120	14 5N	16 8W
Kaolan Shan	109	21 55N	113 15 E
Kaolikung Shan	108	26 0N	98 55 E
Kaomi	107	36 25N	119 45 E
Kaopao Hu	109	32 50N	119 15 E
Kaop'ing	106	35 48N	112 55 E
K'aoshant'un	107	44 25N	124 27 E
Kaot'ang	106	36 51N	116 13 E
Kaoyang	106	38 42N	115 47 E
Kaoyu	109	32 46N	119 32 E
Kaoyüan	107	37 7N	118 0 E
Kapaa	147	22 5N	159 19W
Kapadvanj	94	23 5N	73 0 E
Kapagere	135	9 46S	147 42 E
Kapanga	124	8 30S	22 40 E
Kapanovka	83	47 28N	46 50 E
Kapata	127	14 16S	26 15 E
Kapellen	47	51 19N	4 25 E
Kapello, Ákra	69	36 9N	23 3 E
Kapema	127	10 45S	28 22 E
Kapfenberg	52	47 26N	15 18 E
Kapiri Mposhi	127	13 59S	28 43 E
Kapiskau	150	52 50N	82 1W
Kapiskau, R.	150	52 47N	81 55W
Kapit	102	2 0N	113 5 E
Kapiti I.	142	40 50S	174 56 E
Kaplice	52	48 42N	14 30 E
Kapoe	101	9 34N	98 32 E
Kapoeta	123	4 50N	33 35 E
Kápolnásnyék	53	47 16N	18 41 E
Kaponga	143	39 29S	174 9 E
Kapos, R.	53	46 30N	18 20 E
Kaposvár	53	46 25N	17 47 E
Kappeln	48	54 37N	9 56 E
Kapps	128	22 32S	17 18 E
Kaprije	63	43 42N	15 43 E
Kaprijke	47	51 13N	3 38 E
Kapsan	107	41 4N	128 19 E
Kapsukas	80	54 33N	23 19 E
Kapuas Hulu, Pegunungan	102	1 30N	113 30 E
Kapuas, R.	102	0 20N	111 40 E
Kapuka	127	10 30S	32 55 E
Kapulo	127	8 18S	29 15 E
Kapunda	140	34 20S	138 56 E
Kapurthala	94	31 23N	75 25 E
Kapuskasing	150	49 25N	82 30W
Kapuskasing, R.	150	49 49N	82 0W
Kapustin Yar	83	48 37N	45 40 E
Kaputar, Mt.	139	30 15S	150 10 E
Kaputir	126	2 5N	35 28 E
Kapuvár	53	47 36N	17 1 E
Kara, Turkey	69	38 29N	26 19 E
Kara, U.S.S.R.	76	69 10N	65 25 E
Kara Bogaz Gol, Zaliv	76	41 0N	53 30 E
Kara Burun	69	38 41N	26 28 E
Kara, I.	69	36 58N	27 30 E
Kara Kalpak A.S.S.R. □	76	43 0N	60 0 E
Kara Kum	76	39 30N	60 0 E
Kara-Saki	110	34 41N	129 30 E
Kara Sea	76	75 0N	70 0 E
Kara Su	85	40 44N	72 53 E
Kara, Wadi	122	20 40N	42 0 E
Karabash	84	55 29N	60 14 E
Karabekaul	85	38 30N	64 8 E
Karabük	82	41 10N	32 30 E
Karabulak	85	44 54N	78 30 E
Karaburuni	68	40 25N	19 20 E
Karabutak	84	49 59N	60 14 E
Karachala	83	39 45N	48 53 E
Karachayevsk	83	43 50N	42 0 E
Karachev	80	53 10N	35 5 E
Karachi	94	24 53N	67 0 E
Karachi □	94	25 30N	67 0 E
Karad	96	17 15N	74 10 E
Karadeniz Boğazı	92	41 10N	29 5 E
Karadeniz Dağlari	92	41 30N	35 0 E
Karaga	121	9 58N	0 28W
Karagajly	76	49 26N	76 0 E
Karaganda	76	49 50N	73 0 E
Karaginskiy, Ostrov	77	58 45N	164 0 E
Karagwe □	126	2 0S	31 0 E
Karaikal	97	10 59N	79 50 E
Karaikkudi	97	10 0N	78 45 E
Karaitivu I.	97	9 45N	79 52 E
Karaj	93	35 4N	51 0 E
Karak, Jordan	90	31 14N	35 40 E
Karak, Malay.	101	3 25N	102 2 E
Karakas	76	48 20N	83 30 E
Karakitang	103	3 14N	125 28 E
Karakobis	128	22 3S	20 37 E
Karakoram	95	35 20N	76 0 E
Karakoram P. = K'alak'unlun Shank'ou	95	35 33N	77 46 E
Karakoram Pass	93	35 20N	78 0 E
Karakul, Tadzhik, S.S.R., U.S.S.R.	85	39 2N	73 33 E
Karakul, Uzbek S.S.R., U.S.S.R.	85	39 22N	63 50 E
Karakuldzha	85	40 39N	73 26 E
Karakulino	84	56 1N	53 43 E
Karalon	77	57 5N	115 50 E
Karaman	92	37 14N	33 13 E
Karambu	102	3 53S	116 6 E
Karamea	143	41 14S	172 6 E
Karamea Bight	143	41 22S	171 40 E
Karamea, R.	143	41 13S	172 26 E
Karamet Niyaz	85	37 45N	64 34 E
Karamoja □	126	3 0N	34 15 E
Karamsad	94	22 35N	72 50 E
Karanganjar	103	7 38S	109 37 E
Karanja	96	20 29N	77 31 E
Karapoit	142	37 53S	175 32 E
Karaşar	82	40 21N	31 55 E
Karasburg	128	28 0S	18 44 E
Karasino	76	66 50N	86 50 E
Karasjok	74	69 27N	25 30 E
Karasuk	76	53 44N	78 2 E
Karasuk □	126	2 12N	35 15 E
Karasuyama	111	36 39N	140 9 E
Karatau	85	43 10N	70 28 E
Karatau, Khrebet	85	43 30N	69 30 E
Karativu, I.	97	8 22N	79 52 E
Karatiya	90	31 39N	34 43 E
Karatobe	84	49 44N	53 30 E
Karatoya, R.	98	24 7N	89 36 E
Karaturuk	85	43 35N	78 0 E
Karaul-Bazar	85	39 30N	64 48 E
Karauli	94	26 30N	77 4 E
Karavasta	68	40 53N	19 28 E
Karawa	124	3 18N	20 17 E
Karawanken	52	46 30N	14 40 E
Karazhal	76	48 2N	70 49 E
Karbala	92	32 47N	44 3 E
Kårböle	72	61 59N	15 22 E
Karcag	53	47 19N	21 1 E
Karcha, R.	95	34 15N	75 57 E
Kärda	73	57 10N	13 49 E
Kardeljevo	66	43 2N	17 27 E
Kardhámila	69	38 35N	26 5 E
Kardhítsa	68	39 23N	21 54 E
Kardhítsa □	68	39 15N	21 50 E
Kärdla	80	58 50N	22 40 E
Kareeberge	128	30 50S	22 0 E
Kareima	122	18 30N	31 49 E
Karelian A.S.S.R. □	78	65 30N	32 30 E
Karema, P.N.G.	135	9 12S	147 18 E
Karema, Tanz.	126	6 49S	30 24 E
Karen	101	12 49N	92 53 E
Karganrud	92	37 55N	49 0 E
Kargapolye	84	55 57N	64 24 E
Kargasok	76	59 3N	80 53 E
Kargat	76	55 10N	80 15 E
Kargı	82	41 11N	34 30 E
Kargil	95	34 32N	76 12 E
Kargowa	54	52 5N	15 51 E
Karguéri	121	13 36N	10 30 E
Kariai	69	40 14N	24 19 E
Kariba	127	16 28S	28 36 E
Kariba Dam	125	16 30S	28 35 E
Kariba Gorge	127	16 30S	28 50 E
Kariba Lake	127	16 40S	28 25 E
Karibib	128	21 0S	15 56 E
Karikal	97	10 59N	79 50 E
Karikkale	92	39 55N	33 30 E
Karimata, Kepulauan	102	1 40S	109 0 E
Karimata, Selat	102	2 0S	108 20 E
Karimnagar	96	18 26N	79 10 E
Karimundjawa, Kepulauan	102	5 50S	110 30 E
Karin	91	10 50N	45 52 E
Káristos	69	38 1N	24 29 E
Karitane	51	45 38S	170 39 E
Kariya	111	34 58N	137 1 E
Karkal	97	13 15N	74 56 E
Karkar I.	135	4 40S	146 0 E
Karkinitskiy Zaliv	82	45 36N	32 35 E
Karkur	90	32 29N	34 57 E
Karkur Tohl	122	22 5N	25 5 E
Karl Libknekht	80	51 40N	35 45 E
Karl-Marx-Stadt	48	50 50N	12 55 E
Karl-Marx-Stadt □	48	50 45N	13 0 E
Karla, L = Voiviis, Limni	68	39 35N	22 45 E
Karlino	54	54 3N	15 53 E
Karlobag	63	44 32N	15 5 E
Karlovac	63	45 31N	15 36 E
Karlovka	82	49 29N	35 8 E
Karlovy Vary	52	50 13N	12 51 E
Karlsborg	73	58 33N	14 33 E
Karlshamn	73	56 10N	14 51 E
Karlskoga	72	59 22N	14 33 E
Karlskrona	73	56 10N	15 35 E
Karlsruhe	49	49 3N	8 23 E
Karlstad, Sweden	72	59 23N	13 30 E
Karlstad, U.S.A.	158	48 38N	96 30W
Karmøy	71	59 15N	5 15 E
Karnal	94	29 42N	77 2 E
Karnali, R.	95	29 0N	82 0 E
Karnaphuli Res.	98	22 40N	92 20 E
Karnataka □	97	13 15N	77 0 E
Karnes City	159	28 53N	97 53W
Karni	120	10 45N	2 40W
Karnische Alpen	52	46 36N	13 0 E
Karnobat	67	42 40N	27 0 E
Kärnten □	52	46 52N	13 30 E
Karo	120	12 16N	2 22W
Karoi	127	16 48S	29 45 E
Karonga	127	9 57S	33 55 E
Karoonda	140	35 1S	139 59 E
Karos, Is.	69	36 54N	25 40 E
Karousádhes	68	39 47N	19 45 E
Karpalund	73	56 4N	14 5 E
Kárpathos, I.	69	35 37N	27 10 E
Kárpathos, Stenón	69	36 0N	27 30 E
Karpinsk	84	59 45N	60 1 E
Karpogory	78	63 59N	44 27 E
Karrebaek	73	55 12N	11 39 E
Kars	92	40 40N	43 5 E
Karsakpay	76	47 55N	66 40 E
Karsha	83	49 45N	51 35 E
Karshi	85	38 53N	65 48 E
Karsun	81	54 14N	46 57 E
Kartál Óros	68	41 15N	25 13 E
Kartaly	84	53 3N	60 40 E
Kartapur	94	31 27N	75 32 E
Kartuzy	54	54 22N	18 10 E
Karuah	141	32 37S	151 56 E
Karufa	103	3 50S	133 20 E
Karumba	138	17 31S	140 50 E
Karumo	126	2 25S	32 50 E
Karumwa	126	3 12S	32 38 E
Karungu	126	0 50S	34 10 E
Karunjie	136	16 18S	127 12 E
Karup	73	56 19N	9 10 E
Karur	97	10 59N	78 2 E
Karviná	53	49 53N	18 25 E
Karwar	93	14 55N	74 13 E
Karwi	95	25 12N	80 57 E
Kas Kong	101	11 27N	102 12 E
Kasache	127	13 25S	34 20 E
Kasai	110	34 55N	134 52 E
Kasai Occidental □	127	6 30S	22 30 E
Kasai Oriental □	126	5 0S	24 30 E
Kasai, R.	124	8 20S	22 0 E
Kasaji	127	10 25S	23 27 E
Kasama, Japan	111	36 23N	140 16 E
Kasama, Zambia	127	10 16S	31 9 E
Kasandong	107	41 18N	126 55 E
Kasane	128	17 34S	24 50 E
Kasanga	127	8 30S	31 10 E
Kasangulu	124	4 15S	15 15 E
Kasaoka	110	34 30N	133 30 E
Kasaragod	97	12 30N	74 58 E
Kasat	98	15 56N	98 13 E
Kasba	98	25 51N	87 37 E
Kasba L.	153	60 20N	102 10W
Kasba Tadla	118	32 36N	6 17W
Kaschmar	93	35 16N	58 26 E
Kaseberga	73	55 24N	14 8 E
Kaseda	110	31 25N	130 19 E
Kasempa	127	13 30S	25 44 E
Kasenga	127	10 20S	28 45 E
Kasese	126	0 13N	30 3 E
Kasewa	127	14 28S	28 53 E
Kasganj	95	27 48N	78 42 E
Kashabowie	150	48 40N	90 26W
Kashan	93	34 5N	51 30 E
Kashgar = K'oshin	105	39 29N	75 58 E
Kashihara	111	34 35N	135 37 E
Kashima, Ibaraki, Japan	111	35 58N	140 38 E
Kashima, Saga, Japan	110	33 7N	130 6 E
Kashima-Nada	111	36 0N	140 45 E
Kashimbo	127	11 12S	26 19 E
Kashin	81	57 20N	37 36 E
Kashipur, Orissa, India	96	19 16N	83 3 E
Kashipur, Ut. P., India	95	29 15N	79 0 E
Kashira	81	54 45N	38 10 E
Kashiwa	111	35 52N	139 59 E
Kashiwazaki	112	37 22N	138 33 E
Kashkasu	85	39 54N	72 44 E
Kashmir □	95	32 44N	74 54 E
Kashmor	94	28 28N	69 32 E
Kashpirovka	81	53 0N	48 30 E
Kashum Tso	99	34 45N	86 0 E
Kashun Noerh	105	42 25N	101 0 E
Kasimov	81	54 55N	41 20 E
Kasing	126	6 15S	26 58 E
Kaskaskia, R.	158	37 58N	89 57W
Kaskattama, R.	153	57 3N	90 4W
Kaskelan	85	43 20N	76 35 E
Kaskinen (Kaskö)	74	62 22N	21 15 E
Kaskö (Kaskinen)	74	62 22N	21 15 E
Kasli	84	55 53N	60 46 E
Kaslo	152	49 55N	117 0W
Kasmere L.	153	59 34N	101 10W
Kasonawedjo	127	1 50S	137 41 E
Kasongo	126	4 30S	26 33 E
Kasongo Lunda	124	6 35S	17 0 E
Kásos, I.	69	35 20N	26 55 E
Kásos, Stenón	69	35 30N	26 30 E
Kaspi	83	41 54N	44 17 E
Kaspiysk	83	42 45N	47 40 E
Kaspiyskiy	83	45 22N	47 23 E
Kassab ed Doleib	123	13 30N	33 35 E
Kassaba	122	22 40N	29 55 E
Kassala	123	15 23N	36 26 E
Kassala □	123	15 20N	36 26 E
Kassan	85	39 2N	65 35 E
Kassandra	68	40 0N	23 30 E
Kassansay	85	41 15N	71 31 E
Kassel	48	51 19N	9 32 E
Kassinger	122	18 46N	31 51 E
Kassiopi	80	39 48N	19 55 E
Kassue	103	6 58S	139 21 E
Kastamonu	92	41 25N	33 43 E
Kastav	63	45 22N	14 20 E
Kastélli	69	35 29N	23 38 E
Kastéllion	69	35 12N	25 20 E
Kastellorizon = Megiste	61	36 8N	29 34 E
Kastellou, Ákra	69	35 30N	27 15 E
Kasterlee	47	51 15N	4 59 E
Kastlösa	73	56 26N	16 25 E
Kastó, I.	69	38 35N	20 55 E
Kastóri	69	37 10N	22 17 E
Kastoría	68	40 30N	21 15 E
Kastoría □	68	40 30N	21 15 E
Kastorías	68	40 30N	21 20 E
Kastornoye	81	51 55N	38 2 E
Kástron	68	39 53N	25 8 E

Kastrosikiá

Kerman

Kastrosikiá **69** 39 6N 20 36 E
Kasugai **111** 35 12N 136 59 E
Kasukabe **111** 35 58N 139 49 E
Kasulu **126** 4 37 S 30 5 E
Kasulu □ **126** 4 37 S 30 5 E
Kasumi **110** 35 38N 134 38 E
Kasumiga-Ura **111** 36 0N 140 25 E
Kasumkent **83** 41 47N 48 15 E
Kasungu **127** 13 0 S 33 29 E
Kasur **94** 31 5N 74 25 E
Kata **77** 58 46N 102 40 E
Kataba **127** 16 10 S 25 10 E
Katako Kombe **126** 3 25 S 24 20 E
Katákolon **69** 37 38N 21 19 E
Katale **126** 4 52 S 31 7 E
Katalla **147** 60 10N 144 35W
Katama **123** 9 35N 38 36 E
Katamatite **141** 36 6 S 145 41 E
Katanda **126** 0 55 S 29 21 E
Katanga = Shaba **126** 8 0 S 25 0 E
Katanghan □ **93** 36 0N 69 0 E
Katangi **96** 21 56N 79 50 E
Katangli **77** 51 42N 143 14 E
Katanich **123** 6 0N 33 40 E
Katanning **132** 33 40 S 117 33 E
Katastári **69** 37 50N 20 45 E
Katav Ivanovsk **84** 54 45N 58 12 E
Katavi Swamps **126** 6 50 S 31 10 E
Kateríni **68** 40 18N 22 37 E
Katesbridge **38** 54 18N 6 8W
Katha **99** 24 10N 96 30 E
Katherina, Gebel **122** 28 30N 33 57 E
Katherine **136** 14 27 S 132 20 E
Kathiawar, dist. **93** 22 20N 71 0 E
Kathua **95** 32 23N 75 30 E
Kati **120** 12 41N 8 4W
Katiet **102** 2 21 S 99 44 E
Katihar **95** 25 34N 87 36 E
Katima Mulilo **125** 17 28 S 24 13 E
Katima Mulilo Rapids **128** 17 28 S 24 13 E
Katimbira **127** 12 40 S 34 0 E
Katiola **120** 8 10N 5 10W
Katkopberg **128** 30 0 S 20 0 E
Katlanovo **66** 41 52N 21 40 E
Katmai Nat. Monument **147** 58 30N 155 0W
Katmai, vol. **147** 58 20N 154 59W
Katmandu **95** 27 45N 85 12 E
Kato Akhaïa **69** 38 8N 21 33 E
Kato Stazros **68** 40 39N 23 43 E
Katol **96** 21 17N 78 38 E
Katompi **124** 6 2 S 26 23 E
Katonga, R. **126** 0 15N 31 50 E
Katoomba **141** 33 41 S 150 19 E
Katowice **54** 50 17N 19 5 E
Katowice □ **53** 50 15N 19 0 E
Katrine L. **34** 56 15N 4 30W
Katrineholm **72** 59 9N 16 12 E
Katsepe **129** 15 45 S 46 15 E
Katsina **121** 7 10N 9 20 E
Katsina Ala, R. **121** 6 52N 9 40 E
Katsumoto **110** 33 51N 129 42 E
Katsuta **111** 36 25N 140 31 E
Katsuura **111** 35 15N 140 20 E
Katsuyama **111** 36 3N 136 30 E
Kattakurgan **85** 39 55N 66 15 E
Kattawaz **93** 32 48N 68 23 E
Kattawaz-Urgun □ **93** 32 10N 62 20 E
Kattegat **73** 57 0N 11 20 E
Katumba **126** 7 40 S 25 17 E
Katungu **126** 2 55 S 40 3 E
Katwa **95** 23 30N 89 25 E
Katwijk-aan-Zee **46** 52 12N 4 24 E
Katy **54** 51 2N 16 45 E
Kau Tao **101** 10 6N 99 48 E
Kauai Chan. **147** 21 45N 158 50W
Kauai, I. **147** 19 30N 155 30W
Kaufakha **90** 31 29N 34 40 E
Kaufbeuren **49** 47 42N 10 37 E
Kaufman **159** 32 35N 96 20W
Kaukauna **156** 44 20N 88 13W
Kaukauveld **128** 20 0 S 20 15 E
Kaukonen **74** 67 31N 24 53 E
Kaulille **47** 51 11N 5 31 E
Kauliranta **74** 66 27N 23 41 E
Kaunas **80** 54 54N 23 54 E
Kaunghein **98** 25 41N 95 26 E
Kaupulehu **147** 19 43N 155 53W
Kaura Namoda **121** 12 37N 6 33 E
Kautokeino **74** 69 0N 23 4 E
Kavacha **77** 60 16N 169 51 E
Kavadarci **66** 41 26N 22 3 E
Kavaja **68** 41 11N 19 33 E
Kavali **97** 14 55N 80 1 E
Kaválla **68** 40 57N 24 28 E
Kaválla □ **68** 41 05N 24 30 E
Kaválla Kólpos **68** 40 50N 24 25 E
Kavanayén **174** 5 38N 61 48W
Kavarna **67** 43 26N 28 22 E
Kavieng **135** 2 36 S 150 51 E
Kavkaz, Bolshoi **83** 42 50N 44 0 E
Kavousi **69** 35 7N 25 51 E
Kaw = Caux **175** 4 30N 52 15W
Kawa **123** 13 42N 32 34 E
Kawachi-Nagano **111** 34 28N 135 31 E
Kawagoe **111** 35 55N 139 29 E
Kawaguchi **111** 35 52N 138 45 E
Kawaihae **147** 20 3N 155 50W
Kawaihoa Pt. **147** 21 47N 160 12W
Kawaikini, Mt. **147** 22 0N 159 30W
Kawakawa **142** 35 23 S 174 6 E
Kawama **127** 9 30 S 28 30 E
Kawambwa **127** 9 48 S 29 3 E
Kawanoe **110** 34 1N 133 34 E
Kawarau **143** 45 3 S 169 0 E
Kawardha **95** 22 0N 81 17 E
Kawasaki **111** 35 35N 138 42 E
Kawau I. **142** 36 25 S 174 52 E
Kawene **150** 48 45N 91 15W
Kawerau **142** 38 7 S 176 42 E
Kawhia Harbour **142** 38 5 S 174 51 E
Kawick Peak **163** 37 58N 116 57W
Kawkareik **98** 16 33N 98 14 E
Kawlin **98** 23 47N 95 41 E
Kawnro **99** 22 48N 99 8 E
Kawthaung **101** 10 5N 98 36 E
Kawthoolei □ = Kawthuk **98** 18 0N 97 30 E
Kawthuk □ **98** 18 0N 97 30 E
Kawya **98** 16 40N 97 50 E
Kay **84** 59 57N 52 59 E
Kaya **121** 13 25N 1 10W
Kayah □ **98** 19 15N 97 15 E
Kayaho **107** 43 5N 129 46 E
Kayak I. **147** 60 0N 144 30W
Kayan **98** 16 54N 96 34 E
Kayangulam **97** 9 10N 76 33 E
Kaycee **160** 43 45N 106 46W
Kayenta **161** 36 46N 110 15W
Kayes **120** 14 25N 11 30W
Kayima **120** 8 54N 11 15W
Kayl **47** 49 29N 6 2 E
Kayomba **127** 13 11 S 24 2 E
Kayoro **121** 11 0N 1 28W
Kayrakkumskoye Vdkhr. **85** 40 20N 70 0 E
Kayrunnera **139** 30 40 S 142 30 E
Kaysatskoye **83** 49 47N 46 49 E
Kayseri **92** 38 45N 35 30 E
Kaysville **160** 41 2N 111 58W
Kazachinskoye **77** 56 16N 107 36 E
Kazachye **77** 70 52N 135 58 E
Kazakh S.S.R. □ **85** 50 0N 58 0 E
Kazakhstan **84** 51 11N 53 0 E
Kazan **81** 55 48N 49 3 E
Kazan, R. **153** 64 2N 95 30W
Kazanluk **67** 42 38N 25 35 E
Kazanskaya **83** 49 50N 40 30 E
Kazarman **85** 41 24N 73 59 E
Kazatin **82** 49 45N 28 50 E
Kazerun **93** 29 38N 51 40 E
Kazhim **84** 60 21N 51 33 E
Kazi Magomed **83** 40 3N 49 0 E
Kazimierza Wielki **54** 50 15N 20 30 E
Kazincbarcika **53** 48 17N 20 36 E
Kazo **111** 36 7N 139 36 E
Kaztalovka **83** 49 47N 48 43 E
Kazu **98** 25 27N 97 46 E
Kazumba **124** 6 25 S 22 5 E
Kazvin **92** 36 15N 50 0 E
Kazym, R. **76** 63 40N 68 30 E
Kcynia **54** 53 0N 17 30 E
Ké **120** 13 58N 5 18W
Ke-hsi Mansam **98** 21 56N 97 50 E
Ke-Macina **120** 14 5N 5 20W
Kéa **69** 37 35N 24 22 E
Kea **30** 50 13N 5 4W
Kéa, I. **69** 37 30N 24 22 E
Keaau **147** 19 37N 155 3W
Keady **38** 54 15N 6 42W
Keal, Loch na **34** 56 30N 6 5W
Kealkill **39** 51 45N 9 20W
Keams Canyon **161** 35 53N 110 9W
Keanae **147** 20 52N 156 9W
Kearney **158** 40 45N 99 3W
Kearsage, Mt. **162** 43 25N 71 51W
Keban **92** 38 50N 38 50 E
Kebele **123** 12 52N 40 40 E
Kebi **120** 9 18N 6 37W
Kebili **119** 33 47N 9 0 E
Kebkabiya **117** 13 50N 24 0 E
Kebnekaise, mt. **74** 67 54N 18 33 E
Kebock Hd. **36** 58 1N 6 20W
Kebri Dehar **91** 6 45N 44 17 E
Kebumen **103** 7 42 S 109 40 E
Kecel **53** 46 31N 19 16 E
Kechika, R. **152** 59 41N 127 12W
Kecskemét **53** 46 57N 19 35 E
Kedada **123** 5 30N 35 58 E
Kedah □ **101** 5 50N 100 40 E
Kedainiai **80** 55 15N 23 57 E
Kedgwick **151** 47 40N 67 20W
Kedia Hill **128** 21 28 S 24 37 E
Kediri **103** 7 51 S 112 1 E
Kédougou **120** 12 35N 12 10W
Kedzierzyn **54** 50 20N 18 12 E
Keefers **152** 50 0N 121 40W
Keel **38** 53 59N 10 2W
Keelby **33** 53 34N 0 15W
Keele **32** 53 0N 2 17W
Keele, R. **147** 64 15N 127 0W
Keeler **163** 36 29N 117 52W
Keeley L. **153** 54 54N 108 8W
Keeling Is. = Cocos Is. **142** 12 12 S 96 54 E
Keelung = Chilung **109** 25 3N 121 45 E
Keen, Mt. **37** 56 58N 2 54W
Keenagh **38** 53 36N 7 50W
Keene, Calif., U.S.A. **163** 35 13N 118 33W
Keene, N.H., U.S.A. **162** 42 57N 72 17W
Keeper, Mt. **39** 52 46N 8 17W
Keer-Weer, C. **138** 14 0 S 141 32 E
Keerbergen **47** 51 1N 4 38 E
Keeten Mastgat **47** 51 36N 4 0 E
Keetmanshoop **128** 26 35 S 18 8 E
Keewatin **158** 47 23N 93 0W
Keewatin □ **153** 63 20N 94 40W
Keewatin, R. **153** 56 29N 100 46W
Kefa □ **123** 6 55N 36 30 E
Kefallinía, I. **69** 38 28N 20 30 E
Kefamenanu **103** 9 28 S 124 38 E
Kefar Ata **90** 32 48N 35 7 E
Kefar Etsyon **90** 31 39N 35 7 E
Kefar Hasidim **90** 32 47N 35 5 E
Kefar Hittim B. **90** 32 48N 35 27 E
Kefar Nahum **90** 32 54N 35 22 E
Kefar Sava **90** 32 11N 34 54 E
Kefar Szold **90** 33 11N 35 34 E
Kefar Vitkin **90** 32 22N 34 53 E
Kefar Yehezqel **90** 32 34N 35 22 E
Kefar Yona **90** 32 20N 34 54 E
Kefar Zekharya **90** 31 43N 34 57 E
Keffi **121** 8 55N 7 43 E
Keflavík **74** 64 2N 22 35W
Keg River **152** 57 54N 117 7W
Kegalla **97** 7 15N 80 21 E
Kegashka **151** 50 14N 61 18W
Kegworth **28** 52 50N 1 17W
Kehl **49** 48 34N 7 50 E
Keighley **32** 53 52N 1 54W
Keimaneigh, P. of **39** 51 49N 9 17W
Keimoes **128** 28 41 S 21 0 E
Keiss **37** 58 33N 3 6W
Keïta **121** 14 46N 5 56 E
Keith, Austral. **140** 36 0 S 140 20 E
Keith, U.K. **37** 57 33N 2 58W
Keith Arm **148** 65 20N 122 15W
Kekaygyr **85** 40 42N 75 32 E
Kekri **94** 26 0N 75 10 E
Kël **77** 69 30N 124 10 E
Kelamet **123** 16 0N 38 20 E
Kelang **101** 3 2N 101 26 E
Kelani Ganga, R. **97** 6 58N 79 50 E
Kelantan □ **101** 5 10N 102 0 E
Kelantan, R. **101** 6 13N 102 14 E
Këlcyra **68** 40 22N 20 12 E
Keld **32** 54 24N 2 11W
Keles, R. **85** 41 1N 68 37 E
Kelheim **49** 48 58N 11 57 E
Kelibia **119** 36 50N 11 3 E
Kellas **37** 57 33N 3 23W
Kellé, Congo **124** 0 8 S 14 38 E
Kellé, Niger **121** 14 18N 10 10 E
Keller **160** 48 2N 118 44W
Kellerberrin **137** 31 36 S 117 38 E
Kellett C. **12** 72 0N 126 0W
Kellogg **160** 47 30N 116 5W
Kelloselkä **74** 66 56N 28 53 E
Kells, Ireland **39** 52 33N 7 18W
Kells, U.K. **38** 54 48N 6 13W
Kells = Ceanannas Mor **38** 53 42N 6 53W
Kells, Rhinns of **34** 55 9N 4 22W
Kelmentsy **80** 48 30N 26 50 E
Kélo **124** 9 10N 15 45 E
Kelowna **152** 49 50N 119 25W
Kelsale **29** 52 15N 1 30 E
Kelsall **32** 53 14N 2 44W
Kelsey Bay **152** 50 25N 126 0W
Kelso, N.Z. **143** 45 54 S 169 15 E
Kelso, U.K. **35** 55 36N 2 27W
Kelso, U.S.A. **160** 46 10N 122 57W
Keltemashat **85** 42 25N 70 8 E
Keluang **101** 2 3N 103 18 E
Kelvedon **29** 51 50N 0 43 E
Kelvington **153** 52 10N 103 30W
Kem **78** 65 0N 34 38 E
Kem-Kem **118** 30 40N 4 30W
Kem, R. **78** 64 45N 32 20 E
Kema **103** 1 22N 125 8 E
Kemah **92** 39 32N 39 5 E
Kemano **152** 53 35N 128 0W
Kemapyu **98** 18 49N 97 19 E
Kemasik **101** 4 25N 103 25 E
Kembolcha **123** 11 29N 39 42 E
Kemenets-Podolskiy **82** 48 40N 26 30 E
Kemerovo **76** 55 20N 85 50 E
Kemi **74** 65 44N 24 34 E
Kemi älv = Kemijoki **74** 65 47N 24 32 E
Kemijärvi **74** 66 43N 27 22 E
Kemijoki **74** 65 47N 24 32 E
Kemmel **47** 50 47N 2 50 E
Kemmerer **160** 41 52N 110 30W
Kemnay **37** 57 14N 2 28W
Kemp Coast **13** 69 0 S 55 0 E
Kemp L. **159** 33 45N 99 15W
Kempsey, Austral. **141** 31 1 S 152 50 E
Kempsey, U.K. **28** 52 8N 2 11W
Kempston **29** 52 7N 0 30W
Kempt, L. **150** 47 25N 74 22W
Kempten **49** 47 42N 10 18 E
Kemptville **150** 45 0N 75 38W
Ken L. **35** 55 0N 4 8W
Kenadsa **118** 31 48N 2 26W
Kenai **147** 60 35N 151 20W
Kenai Mts. **147** 60 0N 150 0W
Kendal, Indon. **103** 6 56 S 110 14 E
Kendal, U.K. **32** 54 19N 2 44W
Kendall **141** 31 35 S 152 44 E
Kendall, R. **138** 14 4 S 141 35 E
Kendallville **156** 41 25N 85 15W
Kendari **103** 3 50 S 122 30 E
Kendawangan **102** 2 32 S 110 17 E
Kende **121** 11 30N 4 12 E
Kendenup **137** 34 30 S 117 38 E
Kendrapara **96** 20 35N 86 30 E
Kendrick **160** 46 43N 116 41W
Kendrikí Kai Dhitikí Makedhonia □ **68** 40 30N 22 0 E
Kene Thao **100** 17 44N 101 25 E
Kenema **120** 7 50N 11 14W
Keng Kok **100** 16 26N 105 12 E
Keng Tawng **98** 20 45N 98 18 E
Keng Tung, Burma **99** 21 0N 99 30 E
Keng Tung, Burma **99** 21 0N 99 30 E
Kenge **124** 4 50 S 16 55 E
Kengeja **126** 5 26 S 39 45 E
Kengma **108** 23 34N 99 24 E
Kenhardt **128** 29 19 S 21 12 E
Kenilworth **28** 52 22N 1 35W
Kenimekh **85** 40 16N 65 7 E
Kéninkoumou **120** 15 17N 12 18W
Kénitra (Port Lyautey) **118** 34 15N 6 40W
Kenmare, Ireland **39** 51 52N 9 35W
Kenmare, U.S.A. **158** 48 40N 102 4W
Kenmare, R. **39** 51 40N 10 0W
Kenmore **37** 56 35N 4 0W
Kenn Reef **133** 21 12 S 155 46 E
Kennebec **158** 43 56N 99 54W
Kennedy **127** 18 52 S 27 10 E
Kennedy, C. = Canaveral, C. **157** 28 28N 80 31W
Kennedy, Mt. **148** 60 19N 139 0W
Kennedy Ra. **137** 24 45 S 115 10 E
Kennedy Taungdeik **99** 23 35N 94 4 E
Kennet, R. **28** 51 24N 1 7W
Kenneth Ra. **137** 23 50 S 117 8 E
Kennett **159** 36 7N 90 0W
Kennett Square **162** 39 51N 75 43W
Kennewick **160** 46 11N 119 2W
Kenninghall **29** 52 26N 1 0 E
Kénogami **151** 48 25N 71 15W
Kenogami, R. **150** 51 6N 84 28W
Kenora **153** 49 50N 94 35W
Kenosha **156** 42 33N 87 48W
Kensington, Can. **151** 46 28N 63 34W
Kensington, U.S.A. **158** 39 48N 99 2W
Kensington Downs **138** 22 31 S 144 19 E
Kent, Ohio, U.S.A. **156** 41 8N 81 20W
Kent, Oreg., U.S.A. **160** 45 11N 120 45W
Kent, Tex., U.S.A. **159** 31 5N 104 12W
Kent □ **29** 51 12N 0 40 E
Kent Gr. **138** 39 30 S 147 20 E
Kent Pen. **148** 68 30N 107 0W
Kent Pt. **162** 38 50N 76 22W
Kent, Vale of **23** 51 12N 0 30 E
Kentau **85** 43 32N 68 36 E
Kentdale **137** 34 54 S 117 3 E
Kentisbeare **30** 50 51N 3 18W
Kentland **156** 40 45N 87 25W
Kenton, U.K. **30** 50 37N 3 28W
Kenton, U.S.A. **156** 40 40N 83 35W
Kentucky **141** 30 45 S 151 28 E
Kentucky □ **156** 37 20N 85 0W
Kentucky Dam **156** 37 2N 88 15W
Kentucky L. **157** 36 0N 88 0W
Kentucky, R. **156** 38 41N 85 11W
Kentville **151** 45 6N 64 29W
Kentwood **159** 31 0N 90 30W
Kenya ■ **126** 2 20N 38 0 E
Kenya, Mt. **126** 0 10 S 37 18 E
Keo Nena, Deo **100** 18 23N 105 10 E
Keokuk **158** 40 25N 91 24W
Kep, Camb. **101** 10 29N 104 19 E
Kep, Viet. **100** 21 24N 106 16 E
Kep-i-Gjuhëzës **68** 40 28N 19 15 E
Kep-i-Palit **68** 41 25N 19 21 E
Kep-i-Rodonit **68** 41 32N 19 30 E
Kepi **103** 6 32 S 139 19 E
Kepice **54** 54 16N 16 51 E
Kepler Mts. **143** 45 25 S 167 20 E
Kepno **54** 51 18N 17 58 E
Keppel B. **133** 23 21 S 150 55 E
Kepsut **92** 39 40N 28 15 E
Kepuhi **147** 22 13N 159 21W
Kepulauan, R. **103** 5 30 S 139 0 E
Kepulauan Sunda, Ketjil Barat □ **102** 8 50 S 117 30 E
Kepulauan Sunda, Ketjil Timor □ **103** 9 30 S 122 0 E
Kerala □ **97** 11 0N 76 15 E
Kerama-Shotō **112** 26 12N 127 22 E
Keran **95** 34 35N 73 59 E
Kerang **140** 35 40 S 143 55 E
Keratéa **69** 37 48N 23 58 E
Keraudren, C., Tas., Austral. **136** 40 22 S 144 47 E
Keraudren, C., W. Austral., Austral. **138** 19 58 S 119 45 E
Keravat **135** 4 17 S 152 2 E
Keray **93** 26 15N 57 30 E
Kerch **82** 45 20N 36 20 E
Kerchinskiy Proliv **82** 45 10N 36 30 E
Kerchoual **121** 17 20N 0 20 E
Kerem Maharal **90** 32 39N 34 59 E
Kerema **135** 7 58 S 145 50 E
Keren **123** 15 45N 38 28 E
Kerewan **120** 13 35N 16 10W
Kerguelen I. **11** 48 15 S 69 10 E
Kerhonkson **162** 41 46N 74 11W
Keri **69** 37 40N 20 49 E
Keri Kera **123** 12 21N 32 37 E
Kericho **126** 0 22 S 35 15 E
Kericho □ **126** 0 30 S 35 15 E
Kerikeri **143** 35 12 S 173 59 E
Kerinci **102** 2 5 S 101 0 E
Kerkdriel **46** 51 47N 5 20 E
Kerkenna, Iles **119** 34 48N 11 1 E
Kerki **85** 37 50N 65 12 E
Kérkira **68** 39 38N 19 50 E
Kerkrade **47** 50 53N 6 4 E
Kerma **122** 19 33N 30 32 E
Kermadec Is. **130** 31 8 S 175 16W
Kermān **93** 30 15N 57 1 E
Kerman **163** 36 43N 120 4W

Kermān □ **Killavullen**

Kermān □ 93 30 0N 57 0 E
Kermanshah 92 34 23N 47 0 E
Kermanshah □ 92 34 0N 46 30 E
Kerme Körfezi 69 36 55N 27 50 E
Kermen 67 42 30N 26 16 E
Kermit 159 31 56N 103 3W
Kern, R. 163 35 16N 119 18W
Kerns 51 46 54N 8 17 E
Kernville 163 35 45N 118 26W
Keroh 101 5 43N 101 1 E
Kerr, Pt. 142 34 25 S 173 5 E
Kerrera I. 34 56 24N 5 32W
Kerrobert 157 52 0N 109 11W
Kerrville 159 30 1N 99 8W
Kerry 31 52 28N 3 16W
Kerry □ 39 52 7N 9 35W
Kerry Hd. 39 52 26N 9 56W
Kerrysdale 36 57 41N 5 39W
Kersa 123 9 28N 41 48 E
Kerstinbo 72 60 16N 16 58 E
Kerteminde 73 55 28N 10 39 E
Kertosono 103 7 38 S 112 9 E
Keru 123 15 40N 37 5 E
Kerulen, R. 105 48 48N 117 0 E
Kerzaz 118 29 29N 1 25W
Kerzers 50 46 59N 7 12 E
Kesagami L. 150 50 23N 80 15W
Kesagami, R. 150 51 4N 79 45W
Kesan 68 41 49N 26 38 E
Kesch, Piz 51 46 38N 9 53 E
Kesh 38 54 31N 7 43W
Keski Suomen □ 74 62 45N 25 15 E
Kessel, Belg. 47 51 8N 4 38 E
Kessel, Neth. 47 51 17N 6 3 E
Kessel-Lo 47 50 53N 4 43 E
Kessingland 29 52 25N 1 41 E
Kestell 129 28 17 S 28 42 E
Kestenga 78 66 0N 31 50 E
Kesteren 46 51 56N 5 34 E
Keswick 32 54 35N 3 9W
Keszthely 53 46 50N 17 15 E
Keta 121 5 49N 1 0 E
Ketapang 102 1 55 S 110 0 E
Ketchikan 147 55 25N 131 40W
Ketchum 160 43 50N 114 27W
Kete Krachi 121 7 55N 0 1W
Ketef, Khalîg Umm el 122 23 40N 35 35 E
Ketelmeer 46 32 36N 5 46 E
Keti Bandar 94 24 8N 67 27 E
Ketri 94 28 1N 75 50 E
Ketrzyn 54 54 7N 21 22 E
Kettering 29 52 24N 0 44W
Kettla, Ness 36 60 3N 1 20W
Kettle Falls 160 48 41N 118 2W
Kettle Ness 33 54 32N 0 41W
Kettle, R. 153 56 23N 94 34W
Kettleman City 163 36 1N 119 58W
Kettlewell 32 54 8N 2 2W
Kety 54 49 51N 19 16 E
Kevin 160 48 45N 111 58W
Kewanee 158 41 18N 90 0W
Kewaunee 156 44 27N 87 30W
Keweenaw B. 156 46 56N 88 23W
Keweenaw Pen. 156 47 30N 88 0W
Keweenaw Pt. 156 47 26N 87 40W
Kexby 33 53 21N 0 41W
Key Harbour 150 45 50N 80 45W
Key, L. 38 54 0N 8 15W
Key West 166 24 40N 82 0W
Keyingham 33 53 42N 0 7W
Keyling Inlet 136 14 50 S 129 40 E
Keymer 29 50 55N 0 5W
Keynsham 28 51 25N 2 30W
Keynshamburg 127 19 15 S 29 40 E
Keyport 162 40 26N 74 12W
Keyser 156 39 26N 79 0W
Keystone, S.D., U.S.A. 158 43 54N 103 27W
Keystone, W. Va., U.S.A. 156 37 30N 81 30W
Keyworth 28 52 52N 1 8W
Kez 84 57 55N 53 46 E
Kezhma 77 59 15N 100 57 E
Kezmarok 53 49 10N 20 28 E
Khabarovo 76 69 30N 60 30 E
Khabarovsk 77 48 20N 135 0 E
Khachmas 83 41 31N 48 42 E
Khachraud 94 23 25N 75 20 E
Khadari, W. el 123 10 35N 26 16 E
Khadro 94 26 11N 68 50 E
Khadyzhensk 83 44 26N 39 32 E
Khadzhilyangar 95 35 45N 79 20 E
Khagaria 95 25 18N 86 32 E
Khaibar 92 25 38N 39 28 E
Khaibor 122 25 49N 39 16 E
Khaipur, Bahawalpur, Pak. 94 29 34N 72 17 E
Khaipur, Hyderabad, Pak. 94 27 32N 68 49 E
Khair 94 27 57N 77 46 E
Khairabad 95 27 33N 80 47 E
Khairagarh 95 21 27N 81 2 E
Khairpur 93 27 32N 68 49 E
Khairpur □ 94 23 30N 69 8 E
Khakhea 125 24 48 S 23 22 E
Khalach 85 38 4N 64 52 E
Khalfallah 118 34 33N 0 16 E
Khalij-e-Fars □ 93 28 20N 51 45 E
Khalilabad 95 26 48N 83 5 E
Khálki 68 39 36N 22 30 E
Khálki, I. 69 36 15N 27 35 E
Khalkidhikí □ 68 40 25N 23 20 E
Khalkís 69 38 27N 23 42 E
Khalmer-Sede = Tazovskiy 76 67 30N 78 30 E
Khalmer Yu 76 67 58N 65 1 E
Khalturin 81 58 40N 48 50 E
Kham Kent 100 18 15N 104 43 E
Khamaria 96 23 10N 80 52 E
Khama's Country 128 21 45 S 26 30 E
Khamba Dzong 99 28 25N 88 30W
Khambhalia 94 22 14N 69 41 E
Khamgaon 96 20 42N 76 37 E
Khammam 96 17 11N 80 6 E
Khān Yūnis 90 31 21N 34 18 E
Khan Yunus 90 31 21N 34 18 E
Khanabad, Afghan. 93 36 45N 69 5 E
Khanabad, U.S.S.R. 85 40 59N 70 38 E
Khânaqin 92 34 23N 45 25 E
Khandrá 69 35 3N 26 8 E
Khandwa 96 21 49N 76 22 E
Khandyga 77 62 30N 134 50 E
Khanewal 94 30 20N 71 55 E
Khanga Sidi Nadji 119 34 50N 6 50 E
Khanh Duong 100 12 44N 108 44 E
*Khanh Hung 101 9 36N 105 58 E
Khaniá 69 35 30N 24 4 E
Khaniá □ 69 35 0N 24 0 E
Khanion Kólpos 69 35 33N 23 55 E
Khanka, Oz. 76 45 0N 132 30 E
Khanna 94 30 42N 76 16 E
Khanpur 94 28 42N 70 35 E
Khantau 85 44 13N 73 48 E
Khanty-Mansiysk 76 61 0N 69 0 E
Khapalu 95 35 10N 76 20 E
Kharagpur 95 22 20N 87 25 E
Kharaij 122 21 25N 41 0 E
Kharan Kalat 93 28 34N 65 21 E
Kharanaq 93 32 20N 54 45 E
Kharda 96 18 40N 75 40 E
Khardung La 95 34 20N 77 43 E
Kharfa 92 22 0N 46 35 E
Kharg, Jazireh 92 29 15N 50 28 E
Khârga, El Wâhât el 122 25 0N 30 0 E
Khargon, India 93 21 45N 75 35 E
Khargon, India 96 21 45N 75 40 E
Kharit, Wadi el 122 24 5N 34 10 E
Kharkov 82 49 58N 36 20 E
Kharmanli 67 41 55N 25 55 E
Kharovsk 81 59 56N 40 13 E
Kharsaniya 92 27 10N 49 10 E
Khartoum = El Khartûm 123 15 31N 32 35 E
Khartoum □ 123 16 0N 33 0 E
Khasab 93 26 14N 56 15 E
Khasavyurt 83 43 30N 46 40 E
Khasebake 128 20 42 S 24 29 E
Khash 93 28 15N 61 5 E
Khashm el Girba 123 14 59N 35 58 E
Khasi Hills 98 25 30N 91 30 E
Khaskovo 67 41 56N 25 30 E
Khatanga 77 72 0N 102 20 E
Khatanga, Zaliv 12 66 0N 112 0 E
Khatauli 94 29 17N 77 43 E
Khatyrchi 85 40 2N 65 58 E
Khatyrka 77 62 3N 175 15 E
Khavar □ 92 37 20N 46 0 E
Khavast 85 40 10N 68 49 E
Khawa 122 29 45N 40 25 E
Khaydarken 85 39 57N 71 20 E
Khazzân Jabal el Awliyâ 123 15 24N 32 20 E
Khe Bo 100 19 8N 104 41 E
Khe Long 100 21 29N 104 46 E
Khed, Maharashtra, India 96 18 51N 73 56 E
Khed, Maharashtra, India 96 17 43N 73 27 E
Khed Brahma 93 24 7N 73 5 E
Khekra 94 28 52N 77 20 E
Khemarak Phouminville 101 11 37N 102 59 E
Khemis Miliana 118 36 11N 2 14 E
Khemisset 118 33 50N 6 1W
Khemmarat 100 16 10N 105 15 E
Khenchela 119 35 28N 7 11 E
Khenifra 118 32 58N 5 46W
Khenmarak Phouminville 102 11 40N 102 58 E
Kherrata 119 36 27N 5 13 E
Kherson 82 46 35N 32 35 E
Khersónisos Akrotíri 69 35 30N 24 10 E
Khetinsiring 99 32 54N 92 50 E
Khiliomódhion 69 37 48N 22 51 E
Khilok 77 51 30N 110 45 E
Khimki 81 55 50N 37 20 E
Khingan, mts. 86 47 0N 119 30 E
Khios 69 38 27N 26 9 E
Khisar-Momina Banya 67 42 30N 24 44 E
Khiuma = Hiiumaa 80 58 50N 22 45 E
Khiva 76 41 30N 60 18 E
Khiyav 92 38 30N 47 45 E
Khlaouia 118 25 50N 6 32W
Khlong Khlung 100 16 12N 99 43 E
Khlong, R. 101 15 30N 98 50 E
Khmelnitsky 82 49 23N 27 0 E
Khmer Republic ■ = Cambodia 100 12 15N 105 0 E
Khoai, Hon 101 8 26N 104 50 E
Khodzhent 85 40 14N 69 37 E
Khoi 92 38 40N 45 0 E
Khojak P. 93 30 55N 66 30 E
Khok Kloi 101 8 17N 98 19 E
Khok Pho 101 6 43N 101 6 E
Khokholskiy 81 51 35N 38 50 E
Kholm 80 57 10N 31 15 E

**Renamed Soc Trang*

Kholmsk 77 35 5N 139 48 E
Khomas Hochland 128 22 40 S 16 0 E
Khomayn 92 33 40N 50 7 E
Khomo 128 21 7 S 24 35 E
Khon Kaen 100 16 30N 102 47 E
Khong, Camb. 101 13 55N 105 56 E
Khong, Laos 100 14 7N 105 51 E
Khong, R., Laos 101 15 0N 106 50 E
Khong, R., Thai. 101 17 45N 104 20 E
Khong Sedone 100 15 34N 105 49 E
Khonh Hung (Soc Trang) 101 9 37N 105 50 E
Khonu 77 66 30N 143 25 E
Khoper, R. 81 52 0N 43 20 E
Khor el 'Atash 123 13 20N 34 15 E
Khóra 69 37 3N 21 42 E
Khóra Sfákion 69 35 15N 24 9 E
Khorasan □ 93 34 0N 58 0 E
Khorat = Nakhon Ratchasima 100 14 59N 102 12 E
Khorat, Cao Nguyen 100 15 30N 102 50 E
Khorat Plat. 101 15 30N 102 50 E
Khorb el Ethel 118 28 44N 6 11W
Khorog 85 37 30N 71 36 E
Khorol 82 49 48N 33 15 E
Khorramabad 92 33 30N 48 25 E
Khorramshahr 92 30 29N 48 15 E
Khota Kota 127 12 55 S 34 15 E
Khotan = Hot'ien 105 37 7N 79 55 E
Khotin 82 48 31N 26 27 E
Khouribga 118 32 58N 6 50W
Khowai 98 24 5N 91 40 E
Khoyniki 80 51 54N 29 55 E
Khrami, R. 83 41 30N 44 30 E
Khrenovoye 81 51 4N 40 6 E
Khristianá, I. 69 36 14N 25 13 E
Khromtau 84 50 17N 58 27 E
Khtapodhiá, I. 69 37 24N 25 34 E
Khu Khan 100 14 42N 104 12 E
Khufaifiya 92 24 50N 44 35 E
Khugiani 94 31 28N 66 14 E
Khulna 98 22 45N 89 34 E
Khulna □ 98 22 45N 89 35 E
Khulo 83 41 33N 42 19 E
Khunzakh 83 42 35N 46 42 E
Khur 93 32 55N 58 18 E
Khurai 94 24 3N 78 23 E
Khurais 92 24 55N 48 5 E
Khurja 94 28 15N 77 58 E
Khurma 92 21 58N 42 3 E
Khūryān Mūryān, Jazā 'ir 91 17 30N 55 58 E
Khush 93 32 55N 62 10 E
Khushab 94 32 20N 72 20 E
Khuzdar 94 27 52N 66 30 E
Khuzestan □ 92 31 0N 50 0 E
Khvalynsk 81 52 30N 48 2 E
Khvatovka 81 52 24N 46 32 E
Khvor 93 33 45N 55 0 E
Khvormuj 93 28 40N 51 30 E
Khvoy 92 38 35N 45 0 E
Khvoynaya 80 58 49N 34 28 E
Khwaja Muhammad 93 36 0N 70 0 E
Khyber Pass 94 34 10N 71 8 E
Kiabukwa 127 8 40 S 24 48 E
Kiadho, R. 96 19 50N 76 55 E
Kiama 141 34 40 S 150 50 E
Kiamba 126 6 0N 124 40 E
Kiambi 126 7 15 S 28 0 E
Kiambu 126 1 8 S 36 50 E
Kiangsi □ 109 27 20N 115 40 E
Kiangsu □ 109 33 0N 119 50 E
Kiania 129 20 18 S 47 8 E
Kiaohsien = Chiaohsien 107 36 20N 120 0 E
Kibæk 73 56 2N 8 51 E
Kibanga Port 126 0 10 S 32 58 E
Kibangou 124 3 18 S 12 22 E
Kibara 126 2 8 S 33 30 E
Kibara, Mts. 126 8 25 S 27 10 E
Kibombo 126 3 57 S 25 53 E
Kibondo 126 3 35 S 30 45 E
Kibondo □ 126 4 0 S 30 55 E
Kibumbu 126 3 32 S 29 45 E
Kibungu 126 2 10 S 30 32 E
Kibuye, Burundi 126 3 39 S 29 59 E
Kibuye, Rwanda 126 2 3 S 29 21 E
Kibwesa 126 6 30 S 29 58 E
Kibwezi 124 2 27 S 37 57 E
Kibworth Beauchamp 29 52 33N 0 59W
Kičevo 66 41 34N 20 59 E
Kichiga 77 59 50N 163 5 E
Kicking Horse Pass 152 51 27N 116 25W
Kidal 121 17 50N 1 22 E
Kidderminster 28 52 24N 2 13W
Kidete 126 6 25 S 37 17 E
Kidira 120 14 28N 12 13W
Kidlington 28 51 49N 1 18W
Kidnappers, C. 142 39 38 S 177 5 E
Kidsgrove 32 53 6N 2 15W
Kidston 138 18 52 S 144 8 E
Kidstones 32 54 15N 2 2W
Kidugalle 126 6 49 S 38 15 E
Kidwelly 31 51 44N 4 20W
Kiel 48 54 16N 10 8 E
Kiel Canal = Nord-Ostee-Kanal 48 54 15N 9 40 E
Kielce 54 50 58N 20 42 E
Kielce □ 54 51 0N 20 40 E
Kielder 35 55 14N 2 35W
Kieldrecht 47 51 17N 4 11 E
Kieler Bucht 48 54 30N 10 30 E
Kien Binh 101 9 55N 105 19 E
Kien Hung 101 9 43N 105 17 E
Kien Tan 101 10 7N 105 17 E
Kienchwan 99 26 30N 99 45 E
Kienge 127 10 30 S 27 30 E
Kiessé 121 13 29N 4 1 E
Kieta 135 6 12 S 155 36 E
Kiev = Kiyev 80 50 30N 30 28 E
Kiffa 120 16 50N 11 15W
Kifisiá 69 38 4N 23 49 E
Kifissós, R. 69 38 30N 23 0 E
Kifri 92 34 45N 45 0 E
Kigali 126 1 5 S 30 4 E
Kigarama 126 1 1 S 31 50 E
Kigoma □ 126 5 0 S 30 0 E
Kigoma-Ujiji 126 5 30 S 30 0 E
Kigomasha, Ras 126 4 58 S 38 58 E
Kihee 139 27 23 S 142 37 E
Kihikihi 142 38 2 S 175 22 E
Kii-Hantō 111 34 0N 135 45 E
Kii-Sanchi 111 34 20N 136 0 E
Kijik 147 60 20N 154 20W
Kikai-Jima 112 28 19N 129 58 E
Kikinda 66 45 50N 20 30 E
Kikládhes □ 69 37 0N 25 0 E
Kikládhes, Is. 69 37 20N 24 30 E
Kikoira 141 33 59 S 146 40 E
Kikori 135 7 13 S 144 15 E
Kikori, R. 135 7 5 S 144 0 E
Kikuchi 110 32 59N 130 47 E
Kikwit 124 5 5 S 18 45 E
Kil 72 59 30N 13 20 E
Kilafors 72 61 14N 16 36 E
Kilakarai 97 9 12N 78 47 E
Kilauea 147 22 13N 159 25W
Kilauea Crater 147 19 24N 155 17W
Kilbaha 39 52 35N 9 51W
Kilbeggan 38 53 22N 7 30W
Kilbeheny 39 52 18N 8 13W
Kilbennan 38 53 33N 8 54W
Kilbirnie 34 55 46N 4 42W
Kilbrannan Sd. 34 55 40N 5 23W
Kilbride 39 52 56N 6 5W
Kilbrien 39 52 12N 7 40W
Kilbrittain 39 51 40N 8 42W
Kilbuck Mts. 147 60 30N 160 0W
Kilchberg 51 47 18N 8 33 E
Kilchoan 36 56 42N 6 8W
Kilcock 38 53 24N 6 40W
Kilcoe 39 51 33N 9 26W
Kilcogan 39 53 13N 8 52W
Kilconnell 39 53 20N 8 25W
Kilcoo 38 54 14N 6 1W
Kilcormac 39 53 11N 7 44W
Kilcoy 139 26 59 S 152 30 E
Kilcreggan 34 55 59N 4 50W
Kilcrohane 39 51 35N 9 44W
Kilcullen 39 53 8N 6 45W
Kilcurry 38 54 3N 6 26W
Kildare 39 53 10N 6 50W
Kildare □ 39 53 10N 6 50W
Kildavin 39 52 41N 6 42W
Kildemo 39 52 37N 8 50W
Kildonan 37 58 10N 3 50W
Kildorrery 39 52 15N 8 25W
Kilembe 126 0 15N 30 3 E
Kilfenora 39 53 0N 9 13W
Kilfinan 34 55 57N 5 19W
Kilfinnane 39 52 21N 8 30W
Kilgarvan 39 51 54N 9 28W
Kilgore 159 32 22N 94 40W
Kilham 33 54 4N 0 22W
Kilian Qurghan 93 36 52N 78 3 E
Kilifi 126 3 40 S 39 48 E
Kilifi □ 126 3 30 S 39 40 E
Kilimanjaro □ 126 4 0 S 38 0 E
Kilimanjaro, Mt. 126 3 7 S 37 20 E
Kilinailau, Is. 135 4 45 S 155 20 E
Kilindini 126 4 4 S 39 40 E
Kilis 92 36 50N 37 10 E
Kiliya 82 45 28N 29 16 E
Kilju 107 40 57N 129 25 E
Kilkea 39 52 57N 6 55W
Kilkee 39 52 41N 9 40W
Kilkeel 38 54 4N 6 0W
Kilkelly 38 53 53N 8 50W
Kilkenny 39 52 40N 7 17W
Kilkenny □ 39 52 35N 7 15W
Kilkerrin 38 53 32N 8 36W
Kilkhampton 30 50 53N 4 30W
Kilkieran 39 53 20N 9 45W
Kilkieran B. 38 53 18N 9 45W
Kilkis 68 40 58N 22 57 E
Kilkís □ 68 41 5N 22 50 E
Kilkishen 39 52 49N 8 45W
Kilknock 38 53 42N 8 53W
Kill 39 52 11N 7 20W
Killadoon 38 53 44N 9 53W
Killadysert 39 52 40N 9 7W
Killala 38 54 13N 9 12W
Killala B. 38 54 20N 9 12W
Killaloe 39 52 48N 8 28W
Killam 152 52 47N 111 51W
Killane 39 53 20N 7 6W
Killard, Pt. 38 54 18N 5 31W
Killare 38 53 28N 7 34W
Killarney, Man., Can. 150 49 10N 99 40W
Killarney, Ont., Can. 153 45 55N 81 30W
Killarney, Ireland 39 52 2N 9 30W
Killarney, L's. of 39 52 0N 9 30W
Killary Harb. 38 53 38N 9 52W
Killashandra 38 54 1N 7 32W
Killashee 38 53 40N 7 52W
Killavally 38 53 22N 7 23W
Killavullen 39 52 8N 8 32W

Killchianaig Kíthnos

Killchianaig 34 56 2N 5 48W
Killdeer, Can. 153 49 6N 106 22W
Killdeer, U.S.A. 158 47 26N 102 48W
Killeagh 39 51 56N 8 0W
Killean 34 55 38N 5 40W
Killeen 159 31 7N 97 45W
Killeenleigh 39 51 58N 8 49W
Killeigh 39 53 14N 7 27W
Killenaule 39 52 35N 7 40W
Killianspick 39 52 21N 7 18W
Killiecrankie P. 37 56 44N 3 46W
Killimor 39 53 10N 8 17W
Killin 34 56 28N 4 20W
Killiney 39 53 15N 6 8W
Killingdal 71 62 47N 11 26 E
Killinghall 33 54 1N 1 33W
Killini 69 37 55N 21 8 E
Killini, Mts. 69 37 54N 22 25 E
Killinick 39 52 15N 6 29W
Killorglin 39 52 6N 9 48W
Killough 38 54 16N 5 40W
Killtullagh 39 53 17N 8 37W
Killucan 38 53 30N 7 10W
Killurin 39 52 23N 6 35W
Killybegs 38 54 38N 8 26W
Killyleagh 38 54 24N 5 40W
Kilmacolm 34 55 54N 4 39W
Kilmacthomas 39 52 13N 7 27W
Kilmaganny 39 52 26N 7 20W
Kilmaine 38 53 33N 9 10W
Kilmaley 39 52 50N 9 11W
Kilmallock 39 52 22N 8 35W
Kilmaluag 36 57 40N 6 18W
Kilmanagh 39 52 38N 7 28W
Kilmarnock, U.K. 34 55 36N 4 30W
Kilmarnock, U.S.A. 162 37 43N 76 23W
Kilmartin 34 56 8N 5 29W
Kilmaurs 34 55 37N 4 33W
Kilmeaden 39 52 15N 7 15W
Kilmeedy 39 52 25N 8 55W
Kilmelford 34 56 16N 5 30W
Kilmez 84 56 58N 50 55 E
Kilmez, R. 84 56 58N 50 28 E
Kilmichael 39 51 49N 9 4W
Kilmichael Pt. 39 52 44N 6 8W
Kilmihill 39 52 44N 9 18W
Kilmore, Austral. 141 37 25 S 144 53 E
Kilmore, Ireland 39 52 12N 6 35W
Kilmore Quay 39 52 10N 6 36W
Kilmuir 37 57 44N 4 7W
Kilmurry 39 52 47N 9 30W
Kilmurvy 39 53 9N 9 46W
Kilnaleck 38 53 52N 7 21W
Kilninver 34 56 20N 5 30W
Kilombero □ 127 8 0 S 37 0 E
Kilondo 127 9 45 S 34 20 E
Kilosa 126 6 48 S 37 0 E
Kilosa □ 126 6 48 S 37 0 E
Kilpatrick 39 51 46N 8 42W
Kilrea 38 54 58N 6 34W
Kilrenny 35 56 15N 2 40W
Kilronan 39 53 8N 9 40W
Kilrush 39 52 39N 9 30W
Kilsby 28 52 20N 1 11W
Kilsheelan 39 52 23N 7 37W
Kilsmo 72 59 6N 15 35 E
Kilsyth 35 55 58N 4 3W
Kiltamagh 38 53 52N 9 0W
Kiltealy 39 52 34N 6 45W
Kiltegan 39 52 53N 6 35W
Kiltoom 38 53 30N 8 0W
Kilwa □ 127 9 0 S 39 0 E
Kilwa Kisiwani 127 8 58 S 39 32 E
Kilwa Kivinje 127 8 45 S 39 25 E
Kilwa Masoko 127 8 55 S 39 30 E
Kilwinning 34 55 40N 4 41W
Kilworth 39 52 10N 8 15W
Kilworth, mts. 39 52 10N 8 15W
Kim 159 37 18N 103 20W
Kimamba 126 6 45 S 37 10 E
Kimba 140 33 8 S 136 23 E
Kimball, Nebr., U.S.A. 158 41 17N 103 20W
Kimball, S.D., U.S.A. 158 43 47N 98 57W
Kimbe 135 5 33 S 150 11 E
Kimbe B. 135 5 15 S 150 30 E
Kimberley, N.S.W., Austral. 140 32 50 S 141 4 E
Kimberley, W. Australia, Austral. 136 16 20 S 127 0 E
Kimberley, Can. 152 49 40N 115 59W
Kimberley, S. Afr. 128 28 43 S 24 46 E
Kimberley, dist. 132 16 20 S 127 0 E
Kimberley Downs 136 17 24 S 124 22 E
Kimberly 160 42 33N 114 25W
Kimbolton 29 52 17N 0 23W
Kimchŏn 107 36 11N 128 4 E
Kími 69 38 38N 24 6 E
Kimje 107 35 48N 126 45 E
Kimmeridge, oilfield 19 50 36N 2 6W
Kimolos 69 36 48N 24 37 E
Kímolos, I. 69 36 48N 24 35 E
Kimovsk 81 54 0N 38 29 E
Kimparana 120 12 48N 5 0W
Kimry 81 56 55N 37 15 E
Kimsquit 152 52 45N 126 57W
Kimstad 73 58 35N 15 58 E
Kinabalu, mt. 102 6 0N 116 0 E
Kínaros, I. 69 36 59N 26 15 E
Kinaskan L. 152 57 38N 130 8W
Kinawley 38 54 14N 7 40W
Kinbrace 37 58 16N 3 56W
Kincaid 153 49 40N 107 0W
Kincardine, Can. 150 44 10N 81 40W
Kincardine, Fife, U.K. 35 56 4N 3 43W
Kincardine, Highland, U.K. 37 57 52N 4 20W
Kincardine (□) 26 56 56N 2 28W
Kincraig 37 57 8N 3 57W
Kindersley 153 51 30N 109 10W
Kindia 120 10 0N 12 52W
Kindu 126 2 55 S 25 50 E
Kinel 84 53 15N 50 40 E
Kineshma 81 57 30N 42 5 E
Kinesi 126 1 25 S 33 50 E
Kineton 28 52 10N 1 30W
King and Queen 162 37 42N 76 50W
King City 163 36 11N 121 8W
King Cr. 138 24 35 S 139 30 E
King Edward, R. 136 14 14 S 126 35 E
King Frederick VI Land 12 63 0N 43 0W
King Frederick VIII Land 12 77 30N 25 0W
King George 162 38 15N 77 10W
King George B. 176 51 30 S 60 30W
King George I. 13 60 0 S 60 0W
King George Is. 149 53 40N 80 30W
King George Sd. 132 35 5 S 118 0 E
King I., Austral. 138 39 50 S 144 0 E
King I., Can. 152 52 10N 127 40W
King I. = Kadah Kyun 101 12 30N 98 20 E
King, L. 137 33 10 S 119 35 E
King Leopold Ranges 136 17 20 S 124 20 E
King, Mt. 138 25 10 S 147 30 E
King Sd. 136 16 50 S 123 20 E
King William I. 148 69 10N 97 25W
King William, L. 50 42 14 S 146 15 E
King William's Town 128 32 51 S 27 22 E
Kingairloch, dist. 36 56 37N 5 30W
Kingaroy 139 26 32 S 151 51 E
Kingarrow 38 54 55N 8 5W
Kingarth 34 55 45N 5 2W
Kingfisher 159 35 50N 97 55W
Kinghorn 35 56 4N 3 10W
Kingisepp 80 59 25N 28 40 E
Kingisepp (Kuressaare) 80 58 15N 22 15 E
Kingman, Ariz., U.S.A. 161 35 12N 114 2W
Kingman, Kans., U.S.A. 159 37 41N 96 9W
Kings B. 12 78 0N 15 0 E
Kings Canyon National Park 163 37 0N 118 35W
King's Lynn 29 52 45N 0 25 E
Kings Mountain 157 35 13N 81 20W
Kings Park 162 40 53N 73 16W
King's Peak 160 40 46N 110 27W
King's, R. 39 52 32N 7 12W
Kings, R. 163 36 10N 119 50W
King's Sutton 28 52 1N 1 16W
King's Worthy 28 51 6N 1 18W
Kingsbarns 35 56 18N 2 40W
Kingsbridge 30 50 17N 3 46W
Kingsburg 163 36 35N 119 36W
Kingsbury 28 52 33N 1 41W
Kingscote 140 35 33 S 137 31 E
Kingscourt 38 53 55N 6 48W
Kingskerswell 30 50 30N 3 34W
Kingsland 28 52 15N 2 49W
Kingsley 158 42 37N 95 58W
Kingsley Dam 158 41 20N 101 40W
Kingsport 157 36 33N 82 36W
Kingsteignton 30 50 32N 3 35W
Kingston, Can. 150 44 14N 76 30W
Kingston, Jamaica 166 18 0N 76 50W
Kingston, N.Z. 143 45 20 S 168 43 E
Kingston, U.K. 28 51 23N 1 40W
Kingston, N.Y., U.S.A. 162 41 55N 74 0W
Kingston, Pa., U.S.A. 162 41 19N 75 58W
Kingston, R.I., U.S.A. 162 41 29N 71 30W
Kingston South East 140 36 51 S 139 55 E
Kingston-upon-Thames 29 51 23N 0 20W
Kingstown, Austral. 141 30 29 S 151 6 E
Kingstown, St. Vinc. 167 13 10N 61 10W
Kingstree 157 33 40N 79 48W
Kingsville, Can. 150 42 2N 82 45W
Kingsville, U.S.A. 159 27 30N 97 53W
Kingswear 30 50 21N 3 33W
Kingswood 28 51 26N 2 31W
Kington 28 52 12N 3 2W
Kingtung 99 24 30N 100 50 E
Kingussie 37 47 5N 4 2W
Kinistino 153 52 57N 105 2W
Kinkala 124 4 18 S 14 49 E
Kinki □ 111 35 0N 135 30 E
Kinleith 142 38 20 S 175 56 E
Kinloch, N.Z. 143 44 51 S 168 20 E
Kinloch, L. More, U.K. 37 58 17N 4 50W
Kinloch, Rhum, U.K. 36 57 0N 6 18W
Kinloch Rannoch 37 56 41N 4 12W
Kinlochbervie 36 58 28N 5 5W
Kinlochewe 36 57 37N 5 20W
Kinlochiel 36 56 52N 5 20W
Kinlochleven 36 56 42N 4 59W
Kinlochmoidart 36 56 47N 5 43W
Kinloss 37 57 38N 3 37W
Kinlough 38 54 27N 8 16W
Kinn 71 61 34N 4 45 E
Kinna 73 57 32N 12 42 E
Kinnaird 152 49 17N 117 39W
Kinnaird's Hd. 37 57 40N 2 0W
Kinnared 73 57 2N 13 7 E
Kinnegad 38 53 28N 7 8W
Kinneret 90 32 44N 35 34 E
Kinneret, Yam 90 32 45N 35 35 E
Kinneviken, B. 73 58 38N 18 20 E
Kinnitty 39 53 6N 7 44W
Kino 164 28 45N 111 59W
Kinoje, R. 150 52 8N 81 25W
Kinomoto 111 35 30N 136 13 E
Kinoni, C. Afr. 123 5 40N 26 10 E
Kinoni, Uganda 126 0 41 S 30 28 E
Kinping 101 22 56N 103 15 E
Kinrooi 47 51 9N 5 45 E
Kinross 35 56 13N 3 25W
Kinross (□) 26 56 13N 3 25W
Kinsale 39 51 42N 8 31W
Kinsale Harbour 39 51 40N 8 30W
Kinsale Head, gasfield 19 51 20N 8 0W
Kinsale Old Hd. 39 51 37N 8 32W
Kinsarvik 71 60 22N 6 43 E
Kinshasa 124 4 20 S 15 15 E
Kinsley 159 37 57N 99 30W
Kinston 157 35 18N 77 35W
Kintampo 121 8 5N 1 41W
Kintap 102 3 51 S 115 13 E
Kintaravay 36 58 2N 6 42W
Kintore 37 57 14N 2 20W
Kintore Ra. 137 23 15 S 128 47 E
Kintyre, Mull of 34 55 17N 5 4W
Kintyre, pen. 34 55 30N 5 35W
Kinu 98 22 46N 95 37 E
Kinu-Gawa, R. 111 35 36N 139 57 E
Kinushseo, R. 150 55 15N 83 45W
Kinuso 152 55 25N 115 25W
Kinvara 39 53 8N 8 57W
Kinyangiri 126 4 35 S 34 37 E
Kióni 69 38 27N 20 41 E
Kiosk 150 46 6N 78 53W
Kiowa, Kans., U.S.A. 159 37 3N 98 30W
Kiowa, Okla., U.S.A. 159 34 45N 95 50W
Kipahigan L. 153 55 20N 101 55W
Kipanga 126 6 15 S 35 20 E
Kiparissia 69 37 15N 21 40 E
Kiparissiakós Kólpos 69 37 25N 21 25 E
Kipawa Res. Prov. Park 150 47 0N 78 30W
Kipembawe 124 7 38 S 33 27 E
Kipengere Ra. 127 9 12 S 34 15 E
Kipili 126 7 28 S 30 32 E
Kipini 126 2 30 S 40 32 E
Kipling 153 50 6N 102 38W
Kipnuk 147 59 55N 164 7W
Kippen 34 56 8N 4 12W
Kippure, Mt. 39 53 11N 6 23W
Kipushi 127 11 48 S 27 12 E
Kir 124 1 29 S 19 25 E
Kirandul 96 18 33N 81 10 E
Kiratpur 94 29 32N 78 12 E
Kirchberg 50 47 5N 7 35 E
Kirchhain 48 50 49N 8 54 E
Kirchheim 49 48 38N 9 20 E
Kirchheim Bolanden 49 49 40N 8 0 E
Kirchschlag 53 47 30N 16 19 E
Kircubbin 38 54 30N 5 33W
Kirensk 77 57 50N 107 55 E
Kirgiz S.S.R. □ 85 42 0N 75 0 E
Kirgiziya Steppe 79 50 0N 55 0 E
Kiri 124 1 29 S 19 25 E
Kiriburu 96 22 0N 85 0 E
Kirikkale 92 39 51N 33 32 E
Kirikopuni 142 35 50 S 174 1 E
Kirillov 81 59 51N 38 14 E
Kirin □ 107 43 50N 125 45 E
Kirindi, R. 97 6 15N 81 20 E
Kirishi 80 51 28N 31 59 E
Kirishima-Yama 110 31 58N 130 55 E
Kiriwina Is. = Trobriand Is. 138 8 40 S 151 0 E
Kirk Michael 32 54 17N 4 35W
Kirkbean 35 54 56N 3 35W
Kirkbride 32 54 54N 3 13W
Kirkburton 33 53 36N 1 42W
Kirkby 32 53 29N 2 54W
Kirkby-in-Ashfield 33 53 6N 1 15W
Kirkby Lonsdale 32 54 13N 2 36W
Kirkby Malzeard 33 54 10N 1 38W
Kirkby Moorside 33 54 16N 0 56W
Kirkby Steven 32 54 27N 2 23W
Kirkby Thore 32 54 38N 2 34W
Kirkcaldy 35 56 7N 3 10W
Kirkcolm 34 54 59N 5 4W
Kirkconnel 35 55 23N 4 0W
Kirkcowan 34 54 53N 4 38W
Kirkcudbright 35 54 50N 4 3W
Kirkcudbright (□) 26 55 4N 4 0W
Kirkcudbright B. 35 54 46N 4 0W
Kirkeby 73 55 7N 8 33 E
Kirkee 96 18 34N 73 56 E
Kirkenær 71 60 27N 12 3 E
Kirkenes 74 69 40N 30 5 E
Kirkham 32 53 47N 2 52W
Kirkinner 34 54 59N 4 28W
Kirkintilloch 35 55 57N 4 10W
Kirkjubæjarklaustur 74 63 47N 18 4W
Kirkland, Ariz., U.S.A. 161 34 29N 112 46W
Kirkland, Wash., U.S.A. 160 47 40N 122 10W
Kirkland Lake 150 48 9N 80 2W
Kırklareli 67 41 44N 27 15 E
Kirkliston 35 55 55N 3 27W
Kirkliston Ra. 143 44 25 S 170 34 E
Kirkmichael 37 56 43N 3 31W
Kirkoswald 32 54 46N 2 41W
Kirkoswold 34 55 19N 4 48W
Kirkstone P. 32 54 29N 2 55W
Kirksville 158 40 8N 92 35W
Kirkuk 92 35 30N 44 21 E
Kirkwall 37 58 59N 2 59W
Kirkwhelpington 35 55 9N 2 0W
Kirkwood 128 33 22 S 25 15 E
Kirlampudi 96 17 12N 82 12 E
Kirn 49 49 46N 7 29 E
Kirov, R.S.F.S.R., U.S.S.R. 81 54 3N 34 12 E
Kirov, R.S.F.S.R., U.S.S.R. 84 58 35N 49 40 E
Kirovabad 83 40 45N 46 10 E
Kirovakan 83 41 0N 44 0 E
Kirovo 85 40 26N 70 36 E
Kirovo-Chepetsk 81 58 28N 50 0 E
Kirovograd 82 48 35N 32 20 E
Kirovsk, R.S.F.S.R., U.S.S.R. 78 67 48N 33 50 E
Kirovsk, Ukraine, U.S.S.R. 83 48 35N 38 30 E
Kirovski 83 45 51N 48 11 E
Kirovskiy 85 44 52N 78 12 E
Kirovskoye 85 42 39N 71 35 E
Kirriemuir, Can. 153 51 56N 110 20W
Kirriemuir, U.K. 37 56 41N 3 0W
Kirs 84 59 21N 52 14 E
Kirsanov 81 52 35N 42 40 E
Kirşehir 92 39 14N 34 5 E
Kirstonia 128 25 30 S 23 45 E
Kirtachi 121 12 52N 2 30 E
Kirthar Range 93 27 0N 67 0 E
Kirtling 29 52 11N 0 27 E
Kirtlington 28 51 54N 1 9W
Kirton 39 52 56N 0 3W
Kirton-in-Lindsey 33 53 29N 0 35W
Kiruna 74 67 52N 20 15 E
Kirundu 124 0 50 S 25 35 E
Kirup 137 33 40 S 115 50 E
Kiryū 111 36 24N 139 20 E
Kiryu 81 55 5N 46 45 E
Kirzhach 81 56 12N 38 50 E
Kisa 73 58 0N 15 39 E
Kisaga 126 4 30 S 34 23 E
Kisalaya 166 14 40N 84 3W
Kisámou, Kólpos 69 35 30N 23 38 E
Kisanga 126 2 30N 26 35 E
Kisangani 126 0 35N 25 15 E
Kisar, I. 103 8 5 S 127 10 E
Kisaran 102 2 47N 99 29 E
Kisarawe 126 6 53 S 39 0 E
Kisarawe □ 126 7 3 S 39 0 E
Kisarazu 111 35 23N 139 55 E
Kisbér 53 47 30N 18 0 E
Kiselevsk 76 54 5N 86 6 E
Kishanganga, R. 95 34 50N 74 15 E
Kishanganj 95 26 3N 88 14 E
Kishangarh 94 27 50N 70 30 E
Kishi 121 9 1N 3 45 E
Kishinev 82 47 0N 28 50 E
Kishinoi 82 47 1N 28 50 E
Kishiwada 111 34 28N 135 22 E
Kishkeam 39 52 15N 9 12 E
Kishon 90 32 33N 35 12 E
Kishorganj 98 24 26N 90 40 E
Kishorn L. 36 57 22N 5 40W
Kishtwar 95 33 20N 75 48 E
Kisii 126 0 40 S 34 45 E
Kisii □ 126 0 40 S 34 45 E
Kisiju 124 7 23 S 39 19 E
Kısır, Dağ 83 41 0N 43 5 E
Kisizi 126 1 0 S 29 58 E
Kiska I. 147 52 0N 177 30 E
Kiskatinaw, R. 152 56 8N 120 10W
Kiskittogisu L. 153 54 13N 98 20W
Kiskomárom = Zalakomár 53 46 33N 17 10 E
Kiskörös 53 46 37N 19 20 E
Kiskundorozsma 53 46 16N 20 5 E
Kiskunfélegyháza 53 46 42N 19 53 E
Kiskunhalas 53 46 28N 19 37 E
Kiskunmajsa 53 46 30N 19 48 E
Kislovodsk 83 43 50N 42 45 E
Kismayu 113 0 20 S 42 30 E
Kiso-Gawa, R. 111 35 2N 136 45 E
Kiso-Sammyaku 111 35 30N 137 45 E
Kisofukushima 111 35 52N 137 43 E
Kisoro 126 1 17 S 29 48 E
Kispest 53 47 27N 19 9 E
Kissidougou 120 9 5N 10 0W
Kissimmee 157 28 18N 81 22W
Kissimmee, R. 157 27 20N 81 0W
Kississing L. 153 55 34N 100 47W
Kistanje 63 43 58N 15 55 E
Kisterenye 53 48 3N 19 50 E
Kisújszállás 53 47 12N 20 50 E
Kisuki 110 35 17N 132 54 E
Kisumu 126 0 3 S 34 45 E
Kisvárda 53 48 14N 22 4 E
Kiswani 126 4 5 S 37 57 E
Kiswere 127 9 27 S 39 30 E
Kit Carson 158 38 48N 102 45W
Kita 120 13 5N 9 25W
Kita-Ura 111 36 0N 140 34 E
Kitab 85 39 7N 66 52 E
Kitakami, R. 112 38 25N 141 19 E
Kitakyūshū 110 33 50N 130 50 E
Kitale 126 1 0N 35 12 E
Kitami 112 43 48N 143 54 E
Kitangiri, L. 126 4 5 S 34 20 E
Kitano-Kaikyō 110 34 17N 134 58 E
Kitaya 127 10 38 S 40 8 E
Kitchener, Austral. 137 30 55 S 124 8 E
Kitchener, Can. 150 43 27N 80 29W
Kitchigami, R. 150 50 35N 78 5W
Kitega = Citega 126 3 30 S 29 58 E
Kiteto □ 126 5 0 S 37 0 E
Kitgum Matidi 126 3 17N 32 52 E
Kíthira 69 36 9N 23 0 E
Kíthira, I. 69 36 15N 23 0 E
Kíthnos 69 37 26N 24 27 E

Konstantinovski Krokom

Konstantinovski, R.S.F.S.R., U.S.S.R. **83** 47 33N 41 10 E
Konstantynów Łódzki **54** 51 45N 19 20 E
Konstanz **49** 47 39N 9 10 E
Kontagora **121** 10 23N 5 27 E
Kontich **47** 51 8N 4 26 E
Kontum **100** 14 24N 108 0 E
Kontum, Plat. du **100** 14 30N 108 0 E
Konya **92** 37 52N 32 35 E
Konyin **98** 22 58N 94 42 E
Konz Karthaus **49** 49 41N 6 36 E
Konza **124** 1 45 S 37 0 E
Konzhakovskiy Kamen, Gora **84** 59 38N 59 8 E
Koog **12** 52 27N 4 49 E
Kookynie **137** 29 17 S 121 22 E
Koolan I. **136** 16 0 S 123 45 E
Kooline **136** 22 57 S 116 20 E
Kooloonong **140** 34 48 S 143 10 E
Koolyanobbing **137** 30 48 S 119 36 E
Koolymilka P.O. **140** 30 58 S 136 32 E
Koondrook **140** 35 33 S 144 8 E
Koorawatha **141** 34 2 S 148 33 E
Koorda **137** 30 48 S 117 35 E
Kooskia **160** 46 9N 115 59W
Koostatak **153** 51 26N 97 26W
Kootenai, R. **160** 48 30N 115 30W
Kootenay L. **153** 49 45N 117 0W
Kootenay Nat. Park **152** 51 0N 116 0W
Kootingal **173** 31 1 S 151 3 E
Kopa **85** 43 31N 75 50 E
Kopaonik Planina **66** 43 10N 21 0 E
Kopargaon **96** 19 51N 74 28 E
Kópavogur **74** 64 6N 21 55W
Koper **63** 45 31N 13 44 E
Kopervik **71** 59 17N 5 17 E
Kopeysk **84** 55 7N 61 37 E
Kopi **139** 33 24 S 135 40 E
Köping **72** 59 31N 16 3 E
Kopiste **63** 42 48N 16 42 E
Kopliku **68** 42 15N 19 25 E
Köpmanholmen **72** 63 10N 18 35 E
Köpmannebro **73** 58 45N 12 30 E
Koppal **97** 15 23N 76 5 E
Koppang **71** 61 34N 11 3 E
Kopparberg **75** 59 52N 15 0 E
Kopparbergs län □ **147** 61 20N 14 15 E
Koppeh Dāgh **93** 38 0N 58 0 E
Kopperå **71** 63 24N 11 50 E
Kopperå **71** 63 24N 11 52 E
Koppio **140** 34 26 S 135 51 E
Koppom **72** 59 43N 12 10 E
Koprivlen **67** 41 36N 23 53 E
Koprivnica **63** 46 12N 16 45 E
Koprivshtitsa **67** 42 40N 24 19 E
Kopychintsy **80** 49 7N 25 58 E
Korab, mt. **66** 41 44N 20 40 E
Korakiána **68** 39 42N 19 45 E
Koraput **96** 18 50N 82 40 E
Korba **95** 22 20N 82 45 E
Korbach **48** 51 17N 8 50 E
Korbu, G. **101** 4 41N 101 18 E
Korça **68** 40 37N 20 50 E
Korça □ **68** 40 40N 20 50 E
Korčula **63** 42 57N 17 8 E
Korčula, I. **63** 42 57N 17 0 E
Korčulanski Kanal **63** 43 3N 16 40 E
Kordestān □ **92** 36 0N 47 0 E
Korea **107** 40 0N 127 0 E
Korea Bay **107** 39 0N 124 0 E
Korea, South ■ **107** 36 0N 128 0 E
Korea Strait **107** 34 0N 129 30 E
Koregaon **96** 17 40N 74 10 E
Korenevo **80** 51 27N 34 55 E
Korenovsk **83** 45 12N 39 22 E
Korets **80** 50 40N 27 5 E
Korgus **122** 19 16N 33 48 E
Korhogo **120** 9 29N 5 28W
Koribundu **120** 7 41N 11 46W
Koridina **139** 29 42 S 143 25 E
Korim **103** 0 58 S 136 10 E
Korinthía □ **69** 37 50N 22 35 E
Korinthiakós Kólpos **69** 38 16N 22 30 E
Kórinthos **69** 37 56N 22 55 E
Korioumé **120** 16 35N 3 0W
Kōriyama **112** 37 24N 140 23 E
Korkino **84** 54 54N 61 23 E
Körmend **53** 47 5N 16 35 E
Kornat, I. **63** 43 50N 15 20 E
Korneshty **82** 47 21N 28 1 E
Korneuburg **53** 48 20N 16 20 E
Korning **73** 56 30N 9 44 E
Kornsjø **71** 58 57N 11 39 E
Kornstad **71** 62 59N 7 27 E
Koro, Ivory C. **120** 8 32N 7 30W
Koro, Mali **120** 14 1N 2 58W
Koroba **135** 5 44 S 142 47 E
Korocha **81** 50 55N 37 30 E
Korogwe **124** 5 5 S 38 25 E
Korogwe □ **126** 5 0 S 38 20 E
Koroit **140** 38 18 S 142 24 E
Korong Vale **140** 36 22 S 143 45 E
Koróni **69** 36 48N 21 57 E
Korónia, Limni **68** 40 47N 23 37 E
Koronis **69** 37 12N 25 35 E
Koronowo **54** 53 19N 17 55 E
Koror **103** 7 20N 134 28 E
Körös, R. **53** 46 45N 20 20 E
Köröstarcsa **53** 46 53N 21 3 E
Korosten **80** 50 57N 28 25 E
Korotoyak **81** 51 1N 39 2 E
Korraraika, B. de **129** 17 45 S 43 57 E
Korsakov **77** 46 30N 142 42 E
Korshavn **71** 58 2N 7 0 E
Korshunovo **77** 58 37N 110 10 E
Korsör **73** 55 20N 11 9 E
Korsze **54** 54 11N 21 9 E
Kortemark **47** 51 2N 3 3 E
Kortessem **47** 50 52N 5 23 E
Korti **122** 18 0N 31 40 E
Kortrijk **47** 50 50N 3 17 E
Korumburra **141** 38 26 S 145 50 E
Korwai **94** 24 7N 78 5 E
Koryakskiy Khrebet **77** 61 0N 171 0 E
Koryŏng **107** 35 44N 128 15 E
Kos . **69** 36 52N 27 19 E
Kos, I. **69** 36 50N 27 15 E
Kosa, Ethiopia **123** 7 50N 36 50 E
Kosa, U.S.S.R. **84** 59 56N 55 0 E
Kosa, R. **84** 60 11N 55 10 E
Kosaya Gora **81** 54 10N 37 30 E
Koschagy **79** 46 40N 54 0 E
Kosciusko **159** 33 3N 89 34W
Kosciusko, I. **152** 56 0N 133 40W
Kosciusko, Mt. **141** 36 27 S 148 16 E
Kösély, R. **53** 47 25N 21 30 E
Kosgi **96** 16 58N 77 43 E
Kosha **122** 20 50N 30 30 E
Koshigaya **111** 35 54N 139 48 E
K'oshih **105** 39 29N 75 58 E
K'oshihk'ot'engch'i **107** 43 17N 117 24 E
Koshiki-Rettō **110** 31 45N 129 49 E
Kōshoku **111** 36 38N 138 6 E
Koshtëbë **85** 41 5N 74 15 E
Kosi **94** 27 48N 77 29 E
Kosi-meer **129** 27 0 S 32 50 E
Košice **53** 48 42N 21 15 E
Kosjerič **66** 44 0N 19 55 E
Koslan **78** 63 28N 48 52 E
Kosŏng **107** 38 48N 128 24 E
Kosovska-Mitrovica **66** 42 54N 20 52 E
Kosścian **54** 52 5N 16 40 E
Kosścierzyna **54** 54 8N 17 59 E
Kosso **120** 5 3N 5 47W
Kostajnica **63** 45 17N 16 30 E
Kostanjevica **63** 45 51N 15 27 E
Kostelec **53** 50 14N 16 35 E
Kostenets **67** 42 15N 23 52 E
Koster **128** 25 52 S 26 54 E
Kôstî **123** 13 8N 32 43 E
Kostolac **66** 44 43N 21 15 E
Kostroma **81** 57 50N 41 58 E
Kostromskoye Vdkhr. **81** 57 52N 40 49 E
Kostrzyn **54** 52 24N 17 14 E
Kostyukovichi **80** 53 10N 32 4 E
Koszalin **54** 54 12N 16 8 E
Koszalin □ **54** 54 10N 16 10 E
Kószeg **53** 47 23N 16 33 E
Kot Adu **94** 30 30N 71 0 E
Kot Moman **94** 32 13N 73 0 E
Kota **94** 25 14N 75 49 E
Kota Baharu **101** 6 7N 102 14 E
Kota Kinabalu **102** 6 0N 116 12 E
Kota-Kota = Khota Kota **127** 12 55 S 34 15 E
Kota Tinggi **101** 1 44N 103 53 E
Kotaagung **102** 5 38 S 104 29 E
Kotabaru **102** 3 20 S 116 20 E
Kotabumi **102** 4 49 S 104 46 E
Kotamobagu **103** 0 57N 124 31 E
Kotaneelee, R. **152** 60 11N 123 42W
Kotawaringin **102** 2 28 S 111 27 E
Kotchandpur **98** 23 24N 89 1 E
Kotcho L. **152** 59 7N 121 12W
Kotel **67** 42 52N 26 26 E
Kotelnich **81** 58 20N 48 10 E
Kotelnikovo **83** 47 45N 43 15 E
Kotelnyy, Ostrøv **77** 75 10N 139 0 E
Kothagudam **96** 17 30N 80 40 E
Kothapet **96** 19 21N 79 28 E
Köthen **48** 51 44N 11 59 E
Kothi **95** 24 45N 80 40 E
Kotiro **94** 26 17N 67 13 E
Kotka **75** 60 28N 26 58 E
Kotlas **78** 61 15N 47 0 E
Kotlenska Planina **67** 42 56N 26 30 E
Kotli **94** 33 30N 73 55 E
Kotmul **95** 35 32N 75 10 E
Kotohira **110** 34 11N 133 49 E
Kotonkoro **121** 11 3N 5 58 E
Kotor **66** 42 25N 18 47 E
Kotor Varoš **66** 44 38N 17 22 E
Kotoriba **63** 46 23N 16 48 E
Kotovo **81** 50 22N 44 45 E
Kotovsk **82** 47 55N 29 35 E
Kotputli **94** 27 43N 76 12 E
Kotri **94** 25 22N 68 22 E
Kotri, R. **96** 19 45N 80 35 E
Kótronas **69** 36 38N 22 29 E
Kötschach-Mauthen **52** 46 41N 13 1 E
Kottayam **97** 9 35N 76 33 E
Kottur **97** 10 34N 76 56 E
Kotturu **93** 14 45N 76 10 E
Kotuy, R. **77** 70 30N 103 0 E
Kotzebue **147** 66 50N 162 40W
Kotzebue Sd. **147** 66 30N 164 0W
Kouango **124** 5 0N 20 10 E
Koudekerke **47** 51 29N 3 33 E
Koudougou **120** 12 10N 2 20W
Koufonísi, I. **69** 34 56N 26 8 E
Koufonísia, I. **69** 36 57N 25 35 E
Kougaberge **128** 33 48 S 24 20 E
Kouibli **120** 7 15N 7 14W
Kouilou, R. **124** 4 10 S 12 5 E
Kouki **124** 7 22N 17 3 E
Koula Moutou **124** 1 15 S 12 25 E
Koulen **100** 13 50N 104 40 E
Koulikoro **120** 12 40N 7 50W
Koumala **138** 21 38 S 149 15 E
Koumankoun **120** 11 58N 6 6W
Koumbia, Guin. **120** 11 54N 13 40W
Koumbia, Upp. Vol. **120** 11 10N 3 50W
Koumboum **120** 10 25N 13 0W
Koumpenntoum **120** 13 59N 14 34W
Koumra **117** 8 50N 17 35 E
Koumradskiy **76** 47 20N 75 0 E
Koundara **120** 12 29N 13 18W
Kountze **159** 30 20N 94 22W
Koupangtzu **107** 41 22N 121 46 E
Koupéla **121** 12 11N 0 21 E
Kourizo, Passe de **119** 22 28N 15 27 E
Kouroussa **120** 10 45N 9 45W
Koussané **120** 14 53N 11 14W
Kousseri **117** 12 0N 14 55 E
Koutiala **120** 12 25N 5 35W
Kouto **120** 9 53N 6 25W
Kouvé **121** 6 25N 0 59 E
KovaCica **66** 45 5N 20 38 E
Kovel **80** 51 10N 24 20 E
Kovilpatti **97** 9 10N 77 50 E
Kovin **66** 44 44N 20 59 E
Kovrov **81** 56 25N 41 25 E
Kovur, Andhra Pradesh, India **96** 17 3N 81 39 E
Kovur, Andhra Pradesh, India **97** 14 30N 80 1 E
Kowal **54** 52 32N 19 7 E
Kowalewo Pomorskie **54** 53 10N 18 52 E
Kowkash **150** 50 20N 87 20W
Kowloon **109** 22 20N 114 15 E
Kowŏn **107** 39 26N 127 14 E
Kōyama **110** 31 20N 130 56 E
Koyan, Pegunungan **102** 3 15N 114 30 E
Koyang **106** 33 31N 116 11 E
Koytash **85** 40 11N 67 19 E
Koyuk **147** 64 55N 161 20W
Koyukuk, R. **147** 65 45N 156 30W
Koyulhisar **82** 40 20N 37 52 E
Koza **112** 26 19N 127 46 E
Kozan **92** 37 35N 35 50 E
Kozàni **68** 40 19N 21 47 E
Kozàni □ **68** 40 18N 21 45 E
Kozara, Mts. **63** 45 0N 17 0 E
Kozarac **63** 44 58N 16 48 E
Kozelsk **80** 54 2N 35 38 E
Kozhikode = Calicut **97** 11 15N 75 43 E
Kozhva **78** 65 10N 57 0 E
Koziegłowy **54** 50 37N 19 8 E
Kozje **63** 46 5N 15 35 E
Kozle **54** 50 20N 18 8 E
Kozlodui **67** 43 45N 23 42 E
Kozlovets **67** 43 30N 25 20 E
Kozmin **54** 51 48N 17 27 E
Kōzu-Shima **111** 34 13N 139 10 E
Kozuchów **54** 51 45N 15 31 E
Kpabia **121** 9 10N 0 20W
Kpandae **121** 8 30N 0 2W
Kpandu **121** 7 2N 0 18 E
Kpessi **121** 8 4N 1 16 E
Kra Buri **101** 10 22N 98 46 E
Kra, Isthmus of = Kra, Kho Khot **101** 10 15N 99 30 E
Kra, Kho Khot **101** 10 15N 99 30 E
Krabbendijke **47** 51 26N 4 7 E
Krabi **101** 8 4N 98 55 E
Kragan **103** 6 43 S 111 38 E
Kragerø **71** 58 52N 9 25 E
Kragujevac **66** 44 2N 20 56 E
Krajenka **54** 53 18N 16 59 E
Krakatau = Rakata, Pulau **102** 6 10 S 105 20 E
Krakor **100** 12 32N 104 12 E
Kraków **54** 50 4N 19 57 E
Kraków □ **53** 50 0N 20 0 E
Kraksaan **103** 7 43 S 113 23 E
Kraksmala **73** 57 2N 15 20 E
Kråkstad **71** 59 40N 10 50 E
Kråkstad **71** 59 39N 10 55 E
Kralanh **100** 13 35N 103 25 E
Králiky **53** 50 6N 16 45 E
Kraljevo **66** 43 44N 20 41 E
Kralovice **52** 49 59N 13 29 E
Královsky Chlmec **53** 48 27N 22 0 E
Kralupy **52** 50 13N 14 20 E
Kramatorsk **82** 48 50N 37 30 E
Kramer **161** 35 0N 117 38W
Kramfors **72** 62 55N 17 48 E
Kramis, C. **118** 36 26N 0 45 E
Krångede **72** 63 9N 16 10 E
Krångede **72** 63 9N 16 6 E
Kraniá **68** 39 53N 21 18 E
Kranidhion **69** 37 20N 23 10 E
Kranj **63** 46 16N 14 22 E
Kranjska Gora **63** 46 29N 13 48 E
Kranzberg **128** 21 59 S 15 37 E
Krapina **63** 46 10N 15 52 E
Krapina, R. **63** 46 0N 15 55 E
Krapivna **81** 53 58N 37 10 E
Krapkowice **54** 50 29N 17 56 E
Kras Polyana **83** 43 40N 40 25 E
Krashyy Klyuch **84** 55 23N 56 39 E
Kraskino **77** 42 44N 130 48 E
Krāslāva **80** 55 52N 27 12 E
Kraslice **52** 50 19N 12 31 E
Krasnaya Gorbatka **81** 55 52N 41 45 E
Krasnik Fabryezny **54** 50 58N 22 11 E
Krasnoarmeisk **82** 48 18N 37 11 E
Krasnoarmeysk, R.S.F.S.R., U.S.S.R. **81** 50 32N 45 50 E
Krasnoarmeysk, R.S.F.S.R., U.S.S.R. **83** 48 30N 44 25 E
Krasnodar **83** 45 5N 38 50 E
Krasnodonetskaya **83** 48 5N 40 50 E
Krasnog Dardeiskoye **82** 45 32N 34 16 E
Krasnogorskiy **81** 56 10N 48 28 E
Krasnograd **82** 49 27N 35 27 E
Krasnogvardeysk **85** 39 46N 67 16 E
Krasnogvardeyskoye **83** 45 52N 41 33 E
Krasnoïarsk **77** 56 8N 93 0 E
Krasnokamsk **84** 58 4N 55 48 E
Krasnokutsk **80** 50 10N 34 50 E
Krasnoperekopsk **82** 46 0N 33 54 E
Krasnoselkupsk **76** 65 20N 82 10 E
Krasnoslobodsk **83** 48 42N 44 33 E
Krasnoturinsk **84** 59 46N 60 12 E
Krasnoufimsk **84** 56 57N 57 46 E
Krasnouralsk **84** 58 21N 60 3 E
Krasnousolskiy **84** 53 54N 56 27 E
Krasnovishersk **84** 60 23N 57 3 E
Krasnovodsk **79** 40 0N 52 52 E
Krasnoyarsk **77** 56 8N 93 0 E
Krasnoyarskiy **84** 51 58N 59 55 E
Krasnoye, Kal., U.S.S.R. **83** 46 16N 45 0 E
Krasnoye, R.S.F.S.R., U.S.S.R. **81** 59 15N 47 40 E
Krasnoye, Ukr., U.S.S.R. **80** 49 56N 24 42 E
Krasnozavodsk **81** 56 38N 38 16 E
Krasny Liman **82** 48 58N 37 50 E
Krasny Sulin **83** 47 52N 40 8 E
Krasnystaw **54** 50 57N 23 5 E
Krasnyy **80** 49 56N 24 42 E
Krasnyy Kholm, R.S.F.S.R., U.S.S.R. **81** 58 10N 37 10 E
Krasnyy Kholm, R.S.F.S.R., U.S.S.R. **84** 51 35N 54 9 E
Krasnyy Kut **81** 50 50N 47 0 E
Krasnyy Luch **83** 48 13N 39 0 E
Krasnyy Yar, Kal., U.S.S.R. **83** 46 43N 48 23 E
Krasnyy Yar, R.S.F.S.R., U.S.S.R. **81** 50 42N 44 45 E
Krasnyy Yar, R.S.F.S.R., U.S.S.R. **81** 53 30N 50 22 E
Krasnyyoskolskoye, Vdkhr. **82** 49 30N 37 30 E
Kraśnik **54** 50 55N 22 5 E
Kraszna, R. **53** 48 0N 22 20 E
Kratie **100** 12 32N 106 10 E
Kratke Ra. **135** 6 45 S 146 0 E
Kratovo **66** 42 6N 22 10 E
Kravanh, Chuor Phnum **101** 12 0N 103 32 E
Krawang **103** 6 19N 107 18 E
Krefeld **48** 51 20N 6 22 E
Kremaston, Límni **69** 38 52N 21 30 E
Kremenchug **82** 49 5N 33 25 E
Kremenchugskoye Vdkhr. **82** 49 20N 32 30 E
Kremenets **82** 50 8N 25 43 E
Kremenica **66** 40 55N 21 25 E
Kremennaya **82** 49 1N 38 10 E
Kremikovtsi **67** 42 46N 23 28 E
Kremmen **48** 52 45N 13 1 E
Kremmling **160** 40 10N 106 30W
Kremnica **53** 48 45N 18 50 E
Krems **52** 48 25N 15 36 E
Kremsmünster **52** 48 3N 14 8 E
Kretinga **80** 55 53N 21 15 E
Krettamia **118** 28 47N 3 27W
Krettsy **80** 58 15N 32 30 E
Kreuzlingen **51** 47 38N 9 10 E
Kribi **121** 2 57N 9 56 E
Krichem **67** 46 16N 24 28 E
Krichev **80** 53 45N 31 50 E
Kriens **51** 47 2N 8 17 E
Krim, mt. **63** 45 53N 14 30 E
Krimpen **46** 51 55N 4 34 E
Krionéri **69** 38 20N 21 35 E
Krishna, R. **96** 16 30N 77 0 E
Krishnagiri **97** 12 32N 78 16 E
Krishnanagar **95** 23 24N 88 33 E
Krishnaraja Sagara **97** 12 20N 76 30 E
Kristianopel **73** 56 12N 16 0 E
Kristiansand **71** 58 9N 8 1 E
Kristianstad **73** 56 2N 14 9 E
Kristianstad □ **75** 56 15N 14 0 E
Kristiansund **71** 63 7N 7 45 E
Kristiinankaupunki **74** 62 16N 21 21 E
Kristinehamn **72** 59 18N 14 13 E
Kristinestad **74** 62 16N 21 21 E
Kríti, I. **69** 35 15N 25 0 E
Kritsá **69** 35 10N 25 41 E
Kriva Palanka **66** 42 11N 22 19 E
Kriva, R. **66** 42 12N 22 18 E
Krivaja, R. **66** 44 15N 18 22 E
Krivelj **66** 44 8N 22 5 E
Krivoy Rog **82** 47 51N 33 20 E
Krizevci **63** 46 3N 16 32 E
Krk **63** 45 5N 14 36 E
Krk, I. **63** 45 8N 14 40 E
Krka, R. **63** 45 50N 15 30 E
Krkonoše **52** 50 50N 16 10 E
Krnov **53** 50 5N 17 40 E
Krobia **54** 51 47N 16 59 E
Kročehlavy **52** 50 8N 14 9 E
Kroeng Krai **101** 14 55N 98 30 E
Krokawo **54** 54 47N 18 9 E
Krokeaí **69** 36 53N 22 32 E
Kroken, Norway **71** 58 57N 9 8 E
Kroken, Sweden **71** 59 2N 11 23 E
Krokom **72** 63 20N 14 30 E

Krolevets	**80**	51 35N	33 20 E
Kroměříz	**53**	49 18N	17 21 E
Krommenie	**46**	52 30N	4 46 E
Krompachy	**53**	48 54N	20 52 E
Kromy	**80**	52 40N	35 48 E
Kronobergs län □	**73**	56 45N	14 30 E
Kronprins Harald Kyst	**13**	70 0S	35 1 E
Kronprins Olav Kyst	**13**	69 0S	42 0 E
Kronprinsesse Märtha Kyst	**13**	73 30S	10 0W
Kronshtadt	**80**	60 5N	29 35 E
Kroonstad	**125**	27 43S	27 19 E
Kröpelin	**48**	54 4N	11 48 E
Kropotkin	**77**	45 25N	40 35 E
Kropp	**48**	54 24N	9 32 E
Krósniewice	**54**	52 15N	19 11 E
Krosno	**54**	49 35N	21 56 E
Krosno □	**54**	49 30N	22 0 E
Krosno Odrz	**54**	52 3N	15 7 E
Krościenko	**54**	49 29N	20 25 E
Krotoszyn	**54**	51 42N	17 23 E
Krotovka	**84**	53 18N	51 10 E
Krraba	**68**	41 13N	20 0 E
Krško	**63**	45 57N	15 30 E
Krstača, mt.	**66**	42 57N	20 8 E
Kruger Nat. Pk.	**129**	24 0S	31 40 E
Krugersdorp	**129**	26 5S	27 46 E
Kruidfontein	**128**	32 48S	21 59 E
Kruiningen	**47**	51 27N	4 2 E
Kruis, Kaap	**128**	21 55S	13 57 E
Kruishoutem	**47**	50 54N	3 32 E
Kruisland	**47**	51 34N	4 25 E
Kruja	**68**	41 32N	19 46 E
Krulevshchina	**80**	55 5N	27 45 E
Kruma	**68**	42 37N	20 28 E
Krumovgrad	**67**	41 29N	25 38 E
Krung Thep = Bangkok	**100**	13 45N	100 35 E
Krupanj	**66**	44 25N	19 22 E
Krupina	**53**	48 22N	19 5 E
Krupinica, R.	**53**	48 15N	19 5 E
Kruševac	**66**	43 35N	21 28 E
Krušovo	**66**	41 23N	21 19 E
Kruszwica	**54**	52 40N	18 20 E
Kruzof I.	**152**	57 10N	135 40W
Krylbo	**72**	60 7N	16 15 E
Krymsk Abinsk	**82**	44 50N	38 0 E
Krymskaya	**82**	45 0N	34 0 E
Krynica	**54**	49 25N	20 57 E
Krynica Morska	**54**	54 23N	19 28 E
Krynki	**54**	53 17N	23 43 E
Kryulyany	**70**	47 12N	29 9 E
Krzepice	**54**	50 58N	18 50 E
Krzeszowice	**54**	50 8N	19 37 E
Krzywin	**54**	51 58N	16 50 E
Krzyz	**54**	52 52N	16 0 E
Ksabi, Alg.	**118**	29 8N	0 58W
Ksabi, Moroc.	**118**	32 51N	4 13W
Ksar Chellala	**118**	35 13N	2 19 E
Ksar el Boukhari	**118**	35 51N	2 52 E
Ksar el Kebir	**118**	35 0N	6 0W
*Ksar es Souk	**118**	31 58N	4 20W
Ksar Rhilane	**119**	33 0N	9 39 E
Ksiba	**118**	32 46N	6 0W
Ksour, Mts. des	**118**	32 45N	0 30W
Kstovo	**81**	56 12N	44 13 E
Kuachou	**109**	32 14N	119 24 E
Kuala	**102**	2 46N	105 47 E
Kuala Berang	**101**	5 5N	103 1 E
Kuala Dungun	**101**	4 45N	103 25 E
Kuala Kangsar	**101**	4 46N	100 56 E
Kuala Kerai	**101**	5 30N	102 12 E
Kuala Klawang	**101**	2 56N	102 5 E
Kuala Kubu Baharu	**101**	3 34N	101 39 E
Kuala Lipis	**101**	4 10N	102 3 E
Kuala Lumpur	**101**	3 9N	101 41 E
Kuala Marang	**101**	5 12N	103 13 E
Kuala Nerang	**101**	6 16N	100 37 E
Kuala Pilah	**101**	2 45N	102 15 E
Kuala Rompin	**101**	2 49N	103 29 E
Kuala Selangor	**101**	3 20N	101 15 E
Kuala Terengganu	**101**	5 20N	103 8 E
Kuala Trengganu	**101**	5 20N	103 8 E
Kualakahi Chan	**147**	22 2N	159 53W
Kualakapuas	**102**	2 55S	114 20 E
Kualakurun	**102**	1 10S	113 50 E
Kualapembuang, Indon.	**102**	3 14S	112 38 E
Kualapembuang, Indon.	**102**	2 52S	111 45 E
Kuanaan	**107**	34 8N	119 24 E
Kuanch'eng	**107**	40 39N	118 32 E
Kuandang	**103**	0 56N	123 1 E
Kuangan	**108**	30 30N	106 35 E
Kuangch'ang	**109**	26 50N	116 15 E
Kuangchou	**109**	23 12N	113 12 E
Kuangfeng	**109**	28 26N	118 12 E
Kuanghan	**108**	30 56N	104 15 E
Kuanghua	**109**	32 22N	111 43 E
Kuangjao	**107**	37 5N	118 25 E
Kuangling	**106**	39 47N	114 10 E
Kuangnan	**108**	24 3N	105 3 E
Kuangning	**109**	23 40N	112 23 E
Kuangshi	**109**	29 55N	115 25 E
Kuangshun	**108**	26 5N	106 16 E
Kuangte	**109**	30 54N	119 26 E
Kuangtse	**109**	27 30N	117 24 E
Kuangwuch'eng	**106**	37 49N	108 51 E
Kuangyüan	**108**	32 22N	105 50 E
Kuanhsien	**108**	31 0N	103 40 E
Kuanling	**108**	25 55N	105 35 E
Kuanp'ing	**109**	31 39N	110 16 E
Kuantan	**101**	3 49N	103 20 E
Kuant'ao	**106**	36 31N	115 16 E
Kuantaok'ou	**106**	34 18N	111 1 E
K'uantien	**107**	40 47N	124 43 E
Kuanyang	**109**	25 29N	111 9 E
Kuanyün	**107**	34 17N	119 15 E
Kuaram	**123**	12 25N	39 30 E
Kuba	**83**	41 21N	48 32 E
Kubak	**93**	27 10N	63 10 E
Kuban, R.	**82**	45 5N	38 0 E
Kubenskoye, Oz.	**81**	59 40N	39 25 E
Kuberle	**83**	47 0N	42 20 E
Kubokawa	**110**	33 12N	133 8 E
Kubor	**135**	6 10S	144 44 E
Kubrat	**67**	43 49N	26 31 E
Kučevo	**66**	44 30N	21 40 E
Kucha Gompa	**95**	34 25N	76 56 E
Kuchaman	**94**	27 13N	74 47 E
Kuch'ang	**108**	24 58N	102 45 E
Kuchang	**109**	28 37N	109 56 E
K'uche K'uerhlo	**105**	41 43N	82 54 E
Kuchenspitze	**49**	47 3N	10 14 E
Kuchiang	**109**	27 11N	114 47 E
Kuching	**102**	1 33N	110 25 E
Kuchinoerabu-Jima	**112**	30 28N	130 11 E
Kuchinotsu	**110**	32 36N	130 11 E
Kuçove = Qytet Stalin	**68**	40 47N	19 57 E
Kud, R.	**94**	26 30N	66 12 E
Kuda	**93**	23 10N	71 15 E
Kudalier, R.	**96**	18 20N	78 40 E
Kudamatsu	**110**	34 0N	131 52 E
Kudara	**85**	38 25N	72 39 E
Kudat	**102**	6 55N	116 55 E
Kudremukh, Mt.	**97**	13 15N	75 20 E
Kuduarra Well	**136**	20 38S	126 20 E
Kudus	**103**	6 48S	110 51 E
Kudymkar	**84**	59 1N	54 39 E
Kuei Chiang, R.	**109**	23 33N	111 18 E
Kueich'i	**109**	28 17N	117 11 E
Kueich'ih	**109**	30 42N	117 30 E
Kueichu	**108**	26 25N	106 40 E
Kueihsien	**108**	23 6N	109 36 E
Kueilin	**109**	25 20N	110 18 E
Kueip'ing	**108**	23 24N	110 5 E
Kueiting	**108**	26 30N	107 17 E
Kueitung	**109**	26 12N	114 0 E
Kueiyang, Hunan, China	**109**	25 44N	112 43 E
Kueiyang, Kweichow, China	**108**	26 35N	106 43 E
K'uerhlo	**105**	41 44N	86 9 E
Kufra, El Wâhât el	**117**	24 17N	23 15 E
Kufrinja	**90**	32 20N	35 41 E
Kufstein	**52**	47 35N	12 11 E
Kugmallit B.	**147**	29 0N	134 0W
Kugong, I.	**150**	56 18N	79 50W
Kūh-e-Alijuq	**93**	31 30N	51 41 E
Kūh-e-Dinar	**93**	30 10N	51 0 E
Kūh-e-Hazaran	**93**	29 35N	57 20 E
Kūh-e-Jebel Barez	**93**	29 0N	58 0 E
Kūh-e-Sorkh	**93**	35 30N	58 45 E
Kūh-e-Taftan	**93**	28 40N	61 0 E
Kūhak	**93**	27 12N	63 10 E
Kūhha-ye-Bashakerd	**93**	26 45N	59 0 E
Kūhha-ye Sabalān	**93**	38 15N	47 45 E
Kuhnsdorf	**52**	46 37N	14 38 E
Kuhpayeh	**93**	32 44N	52 20 E
Kui Buri	**101**	12 3N	99 52 E
Kuinre	**46**	52 47N	5 51 E
Kuiseb, R.	**125**	23 40S	15 30 E
Kuiu I.	**147**	56 40N	134 15W
Kujangdong	**107**	39 57N	126 1 E
Kuji	**112**	40 11N	141 46 E
Kujū-San	**110**	33 5N	131 15 E
Kujukuri-Heiya	**111**	35 45N	140 30 E
Kukavica, mt.	**66**	42 48N	21 57 E
Kukawa	**121**	12 58N	13 27 E
Kukerin	**137**	33 13S	118 0 E
Kukësi	**68**	42 5N	20 20 E
Kukësi □	**68**	42 25N	20 15 E
Kukko	**123**	8 26N	41 35 E
Kukmor	**84**	56 11N	50 54 E
Kukup	**101**	1 20N	103 27 E
K'uk'ushihli Shanmo	**105**	35 20N	91 0 E
Kukvidze	**81**	50 40N	43 15 E
Kula, Bulg.	**66**	43 52N	22 36 E
Kula, Yugo.	**66**	45 37N	19 32 E
Kulai	**101**	1 44N	103 35 E
Kulal, Mt.	**126**	2 42N	36 57 E
Kulaly, O.	**83**	45 0N	50 0 E
Kulanak	**85**	41 22N	75 30 E
Kulasekharapattanam	**97**	8 20N	78 0 E
Kuldiga	**80**	56 58N	21 59 E
Kuldja = Ining	**105**	43 54N	81 21 E
Kuldu	**123**	12 50N	28 30 E
Kulebaki	**81**	55 22N	42 25 E
Kulen Vakuf	**63**	44 35N	16 2 E
Kulgam	**95**	33 36N	75 2 E
Kuli	**83**	42 2N	46 12 E
Kulim	**101**	5 22N	100 34 E
Kulin	**137**	32 40S	118 2 E
Kulja	**137**	30 28S	117 18 E
Küllük	**69**	37 12N	27 36 E
Kulm	**158**	46 22N	98 58W
K'uloch'akonnoerh	**106**	43 25N	114 50 E
Kulsary	**76**	46 59N	54 1 E
Kultay	**83**	45 5N	51 40 E
Kulti	**95**	23 43N	86 50 E
Kulu	**93**	37 12N	115 2 E
Kulumadau	**138**	9 15S	152 50 E
K'ulunch'i	**107**	42 44N	121 44 E
Kulunda	**76**	52 45N	79 15 E
Kulungar	**94**	34 0N	69 2 E
Kulwin	**140**	35 0S	142 42 E
Kulyab	**85**	37 55N	69 50 E
Kum Tekei	**76**	43 10N	79 30 E
Kuma	**110**	33 39N	132 54 E
Kuma, R.	**83**	44 55N	45 57 E
Kumaganum	**121**	13 8N	10 38 E
Kumagaya	**111**	36 9N	139 22 E
Kumak	**84**	51 10N	60 8 E
Kumamoto	**110**	32 45N	130 45 E
Kumamoto-ken □	**110**	32 30N	130 40 E
Kumano	**111**	33 54N	136 5 E
Kumano-Nada	**111**	33 47N	136 20 E
Kumanovo	**66**	42 9N	21 42 E
Kumara	**143**	42 37S	171 12 E
Kumarkhali	**98**	23 51N	89 15 E
Kumarl	**137**	32 47S	121 33 E
Kumasi	**120**	6 41N	1 38W
Kumba	**121**	4 36N	9 24 E
Kumbakonam	**97**	10 58N	79 25 E
Kumbarilla	**139**	27 15S	150 55 E
Kumbo	**121**	6 15N	10 36 E
Kumbukkan Oya	**97**	6 35N	81 40 E
Kŭmchŏn	**107**	38 10N	126 29 E
Kumdok	**95**	33 32N	78 10 E
Kumeny	**81**	58 10N	49 47 E
Kŭmhwa	**107**	38 17N	127 28 E
Kumi	**126**	1 30N	33 58 E
Kumkale	**68**	40 30N	26 13 E
Kumla	**72**	59 8N	15 10 E
Kumo	**121**	10 1N	11 12 E
Kumon Bum	**98**	26 30N	97 15 E
Kumotori-Yama	**111**	35 51N	138 57 E
Kumta	**97**	14 29N	74 32 E
Kumtorkala	**83**	43 2N	46 50 E
Kumukahi, C.	**147**	19 31N	154 49W
Kumusi, R.	**135**	8 16S	148 13 E
Kumylzhenskaya	**83**	49 51N	42 38 E
Kunágota	**53**	46 26N	21 3 E
Kunama	**141**	35 35S	148 4 E
Kunar	**93**	34 30N	71 3 E
Kunashir, Ostrov	**77**	44 0N	146 0 E
Kunch	**95**	26 0N	79 10 E
Kunda	**80**	59 30N	26 34 E
Kundiawa	**135**	6 2S	145 1 E
Kundip	**137**	33 42S	120 10 E
Kundla	**94**	21 21N	71 25 E
Kunduz	**93**	36 50N	68 50 E
Kunduz □	**93**	36 50N	68 50 E
Kunene, R.	**128**	17 15S	13 40 E
Kungala	**139**	29 58S	153 7 E
Kungälv	**73**	57 53N	11 59 E
Kungan	**109**	30 4N	112 12 E
Kungch'eng	**109**	24 50N	110 49 E
K'ungch'iao Ho	**105**	41 48N	86 47 E
Kŭngdong	**107**	39 9N	126 5 E
Kungey Alatau, Khrebet	**85**	42 50N	77 0 E
Kunghit I.	**152**	52 6N	131 3W
Kungho	**105**	36 28N	100 45 E
Kungka	**108**	28 44N	100 22 E
Kungkuan	**108**	21 51N	109 33 E
Kungrad	**76**	43 6N	58 54 E
Kungsbacka	**73**	57 30N	12 5 E
Kungshan	**108**	27 41N	97 37 E
Kungt'an	**108**	28 49N	108 38 E
Kungur	**84**	57 25N	56 57 E
Kungurri	**138**	21 3S	148 46 E
Kungyangon	**98**	16 27N	96 1 E
Kungyingtzu	**107**	43 38N	121 0 E
Kunhar, R.	**95**	35 0N	73 40 E
Kunhegyes	**53**	47 22N	20 36 E
Kunimi-Dake	**110**	32 33N	131 1 E
Kuningan	**103**	6 59S	108 29 E
Kunisaki	**110**	33 33N	131 45 E
Kunlara	**140**	34 54S	139 55 E
Kunlong	**98**	23 20N	98 50 E
Kunlun Shan	**105**	36 0N	86 30 E
Kunmadaras	**53**	47 28N	20 45 E
K'unming	**108**	25 5N	102 40 E
Kunnamkulam	**97**	10 38N	76 7 E
Kunrade	**47**	50 53N	5 57 E
Kunsan	**107**	35 59N	126 45 E
K'unshan	**109**	31 22N	121 0 E
Kunszentmárton	**53**	46 50N	20 20 E
Kununurra	**136**	15 40S	128 39 E
Kunwarara	**138**	22 55S	150 9 E
Kuohsien	**106**	38 57N	112 46 E
Kuopio	**74**	62 53N	27 35 E
Kuopion Lääni □	**74**	63 25N	27 10 E
Kupa, R.	**63**	45 30N	16 10 E
Kupang	**103**	10 19S	123 39 E
Kupeik'ou	**107**	40 42N	117 9 E
Kupiano	**135**	10 4S	148 14 E
Kupreanof I.	**147**	56 50N	133 30W
Kupres	**66**	44 1N	17 15 E
Kupyansk	**82**	49 45N	37 35 E
Kupyansk-Uzlovoi	**82**	49 52N	37 34 E
Kur, R.	**98**	26 50N	91 0 E
Kura, R.	**83**	40 20N	47 30 E
Kurahashi-Jima	**110**	34 8N	132 31 E
Kuranda	**138**	16 48S	145 35 E
Kurandvad	**96**	16 45N	74 39 E
Kurashiki	**110**	34 40N	133 50 E
Kurayoshi	**110**	35 26N	133 50 E
Kurday	**85**	43 21N	74 59 E
Kurdistan, reg.	**92**	37 30N	42 0 E
Kurduvadi	**96**	18 8N	75 29 E
Kure	**110**	34 14N	132 32 E
Kuressaare = Kingisepp	**80**	58 15N	22 15 E
Kurgaldzhino	**76**	50 35N	70 20 E
Kurgan, R.S.F.S.R., U.S.S.R.	**77**	64 5N	172 50W
Kurgan, R.S.F.S.R., U.S.S.R.	**84**	55 26N	65 18 E
Kurgan-Tyube	**85**	37 50N	68 47 E
Kuria Muria I = Khyryān Muryān J.	**91**	17 30N	55 58 E
Kurichchi	**97**	11 36N	77 35 E
Kuridala	**138**	21 16S	140 29 E
Kurigram	**98**	25 49N	89 39 E
Kurihashi	**111**	36 8N	139 42 E
Kuril Trench	**142**	44 0N	153 0 E
Kurilskiye Ostrova	**77**	45 0N	150 0 E
Kuring Kuru	**128**	17 42S	18 32 E
Kuringen	**47**	50 56N	5 18 E
Kurino	**110**	31 57N	130 43 E
KüRKkkuyu	**68**	39 35N	26 27 E
Kurkur	**122**	23 50N	32 0 E
Kurkûrah	**119**	31 30N	20 1 E
Kurla	**96**	19 5N	72 52 E
Kurlovski	**81**	55 25N	40 40 E
Kurma	**123**	13 55N	24 40 E
Kurmuk	**123**	10 33N	34 21 E
Kurnalpi	**137**	30 29S	122 16 E
Kurnool	**97**	15 45N	78 0 E
Kurobe-Gawe, R.	**111**	36 55N	137 25 E
Kurogi	**110**	33 12N	130 40 E
Kurovskoye	**81**	55 35N	38 55 E
Kurow	**143**	44 4S	170 29 E
Kurrajong, N.S.W., Austral.	**141**	33 33S	150 42 E
Kurrajong, W.A., Austral.	**137**	28 39S	120 59 E
Kurram, R.	**94**	33 30N	70 15 E
Kurri Kurri	**141**	32 50S	151 28 E
Kuršenai	**80**	56 1N	23 3 E
Kurseong	**95**	26 56N	88 18 E
Kursk	**81**	51 42N	36 11 E
Kuršumlija	**66**	43 9N	21 19 E
Kuršumlijska Banja	**66**	43 3N	21 11 E
Kurtalon	**92**	37 55N	41 40 E
Kurtamysh	**84**	54 55N	64 27 E
Kurty, R.	**85**	44 16N	76 42 E
Kuru (Chel), Bahr el	**123**	8 10N	26 50 E
Kuruman	**128**	27 28S	23 28 E
Kurume	**110**	33 15N	130 30 E
Kurunegala	**97**	7 30N	80 18 E
Kurya	**77**	61 15N	108 10 E
Kusa	**84**	55 20N	59 29 E
Kuşadası	**69**	37 52N	27 15 E
Kuşadası Körfezı	**69**	37 56N	27 0 E
Kusatsu, Gumma, Japan	**111**	36 37N	138 36 E
Kusatsu, Shiga, Japan	**111**	34 58N	136 5 E
Kusawa L.	**152**	60 20N	136 13W
Kusel	**49**	49 31N	7 25 E
Kushchevskaya	**83**	46 33N	39 35 E
Kushikino	**110**	31 44N	130 16 E
Kushima	**110**	31 29N	131 14 E
Kushimoto	**111**	33 28N	135 47 E
Kushin	**109**	32 12N	115 48 E
Kushiro	**112**	43 0N	144 25 E
Kushiro, R.	**112**	42 59N	144 23 E
Kushk	**93**	34 55N	62 30 E
Kushka	**76**	35 20N	62 18 E
Kushmurun	**84**	52 27N	64 36 E
Kushmurun, Ozero	**84**	52 40N	64 48 E
Kushnarenkovo	**84**	55 6N	55 22 E
Kushol	**95**	33 40N	76 36 E
Kushrabat	**85**	40 18N	66 32 E
Kushtia	**98**	23 55N	89 5 E
Kushum, R.	**83**	50 40N	50 20 E
Kushva	**84**	58 18N	59 45 E
Kuskokwim Bay	**147**	59 50N	162 56W
Kuskokwim Mts.	**147**	63 0N	156 0W
Kuskokwim, R.	**147**	61 48N	157 0W
Küsnacht	**51**	47 19N	8 15 E
Kussa	**123**	4 9N	38 58 E
Küssnacht	**51**	47 5N	8 26 E
Kustanay	**84**	53 10N	63 35 E
Kusu	**110**	33 16N	131 9 E
Kusung	**108**	28 25N	105 12 E
Kut, Ko	**101**	11 40N	102 35 E
Kutá Horq	**52**	49 57N	15 16 E
Kutahya	**92**	39 30N	30 2 E
Kutaisi	**83**	42 19N	42 40 E
Kutaradja = Banda Aceh	**102**	5 35N	95 20 E
Kutatjane	**102**	3 45N	97 50 E
Kutch, G. of	**94**	22 50N	69 15 E
Kutch, Rann of	**94**	24 0N	70 0 E
Kut'ien	**109**	26 36N	118 48 E
Kutina	**63**	45 29N	16 48 E
Kutiyana	**94**	21 36N	70 2 E
Kutjevo	**66**	45 23N	17 55 E
Kutkai	**98**	23 27N	97 56 E
Kutkashen	**83**	40 58N	47 47 E
Kutná Hora	**52**	49 57N	15 16 E
Kutno	**54**	52 15N	19 23 E
Kuttabul	**138**	21 5S	148 48 E
Kutu	**124**	2 40S	18 11 E
Kutum	**123**	14 20N	24 10 E
Kúty	**53**	48 40N	17 3 E
Kuŭptong	**107**	40 45N	126 1 E
Kuurne	**47**	50 51N	3 18 E
Kuvandyk	**84**	51 28N	57 21 E
Kuvasay	**85**	40 18N	71 59 E
Kuvshinovo	**80**	57 2N	34 11 E
Kuwait = Al Kuwayt	**92**	29 30N	47 30 E
Kuwait ■	**92**	29 30N	47 30 E
Kuwana	**111**	35 0N	136 43 E
Kuyang	**106**	41 8N	110 1 E
Kuybyshev	**81**	55 27N	78 19 E
Kuybyshevo, Ukraine S.S.R., U.S.S.R.	**82**	47 25N	36 40 E
Kuybyshevo, Uzbek S.S.R., U.S.S.R.	**85**	40 20N	71 15 E
Kuybyshevskiy	**85**	37 52N	68 44 E
Kuybyshevskoye Vdkhr.	**81**	55 2N	49 30 E

*Renamed Ar Rachidya,

Kuyeh Ho, R Lambay I

Kuyeh Ho, R. 106 38 30N 110 44 E
Kuylyuk 85 41 14N 69 17 E
Kuyto, Oz. 78 64 40N 31 0 E
Kuyüan, Hopeh, China 106 41 34N 115 38 E
Kuyüan, Ningsia Hui, China 106 36 1N 106 17 E
Kuzhithura 97 8 18N 77 11 E
Kuzino 84 57 1N 59 27 E
Kuzmin 66 45 2N 19 25 E
Kuznetsk 81 53 12N 46 40 E
Kuzomen 78 66 22N 36 50 E
Kvænangen 74 69 55N 21 15 E
Kvam 71 61 40N 9 42 E
Kvamsøy 71 61 7N 6 28 E
Kvarken 74 63 30N 21 0 E
Kvarner 63 44 50N 14 10 E
Kvarnerič 63 44 43N 14 37 E
Kvarnsveden 72 60 32N 15 25 E
Kvarntorp 72 59 8N 15 17 E
Kvås 71 58 16N 7 14 E
Kvernes 71 63 1N 7 44 E
Kvillsfors 73 57 24N 15 29 E
Kvina, R. 71 58 43N 6 52 E
Kvinesdal 71 58 18N 6 59 E
Kviteseid 71 59 24N 8 29 E
Kwabhaca 129 30 51 S 29 0 E
Kwadacha, R. 152 57 28N 125 38W
Kwakhanai 128 21 39 S 21 16 E
Kwakoegron 175 5 25N 55 25W
Kwale, Kenya 126 4 15 S 39 31 E
Kwale, Nigeria 121 6 18N 5 28 E
Kwale □ 126 4 15 S 39 10 E
Kwamouth 124 3 9 S 16 20 E
Kwando, R. 128 16 48 S 22 45 E
Kwangdaeri 107 40 31N 127 32 E
Kwangju 107 35 9N 126 54 E
Kwangsi-Chuang A.R. □ 109 24 0N 109 0 E
Kwangtung □ 109 23 45N 114 0 E
Kwara □ 121 8 0N 5 0 E
Kwaraga 128 20 26 S 24 32 E
Kwataboahegan, R. 150 51 9N 80 50W
Kwatisore 103 3 7 S 139 59 E
Kweichow □ 108 27 20N 107 0 E
Kweiyang = Kueiyang 108 26 35N 106 43 E
Kwethluk 147 60 45N 161 34W
Kwidzyn 54 54 45N 18 58 E
Kwigillingok 147 59 50N 163 10W
Kwiguk 147 63 45N 164 35W
Kwikila 135 9 49 S 147 38 E
Kwimba □ 126 3 0 S 33 0 E
Kwinana 137 32 15 S 115 47 E
Kwitaba 126 3 56 S 29 39 E
Kya-in-Seikkyi 98 16 2N 98 8 E
Kyabe 117 9 30N 19 0 E
Kyabra Cr. 139 25 36 S 142 55 E
Kyabram 139 36 19 S 145 4 E
Kyaiklat 98 16 46N 96 52 E
Kyaikmaraw 98 16 23N 97 44 E
Kyaikthin 98 23 32N 95 40 E
Kyaikto 100 17 20N 97 3 E
Kyakhta 77 50 30N 106 25 E
Kyangin 98 18 20N 95 20 E
Kyaring Tso 99 31 5N 88 25 E
Kyaukhnyat 98 18 15N 97 31 E
Kyaukpadaung 99 20 52N 95 8 E
Kyaukpyu 99 19 28N 93 30 E
Kyaukse 98 21 36N 96 10 E
Kyauktaw 98 21 16N 96 44 E
Kyawkku 98 21 48N 96 56 E
Kyburz 163 38 47N 120 18W
Kybybolite 140 36 53 S 140 55 E
Kyegegwa 126 0 30N 31 0 E
Kyeintali 98 18 0N 94 29 E
Kyela □ 127 9 45 S 34 0 E
Kyenjojo 126 0 40N 30 37 E
Kyidaunggan 98 19 53N 96 12 E
Kyle Dam 127 20 15 S 31 0 E
Kyle, dist. 34 55 32N 4 25W
Kyle of Lochalsh 36 57 17N 5 43W
Kyleakin 36 57 16N 5 44W
Kyneton 140 37 10 S 144 29 E
Kynuna 138 21 37 S 141 55 E
Kyō-ga-Saki 111 35 45N 135 15 E
Kyoga, L. 126 1 35N 33 0 E
Kyogle 139 28 40 S 153 0 E
Kyongju 107 35 51N 129 14 E
Kyongpyaw 99 17 12N 95 10 E
Kyŏngsŏng 107 41 35N 129 36 E
Kyōto 111 35 0N 135 45 E
Kyōto-fu □ 111 35 15N 135 30 E
Kyrínia 92 35 20N 33 20 E
Kyritz 48 52 57N 12 25 E
Kyrkebyn 72 59 18N 13 3 E
Kyrping 71 59 45N 6 5 E
Kyshtym 84 55 42N 60 34 E
Kystatyam 77 67 20N 123 10 E
Kytalktakh 77 65 30N 123 40 E
Kytlym 84 59 30N 59 12 E
Kyu-hkok 98 24 4N 98 4 E
Kyulyunken 77 64 10N 137 5 E
Kyunhla 98 23 25N 95 15 E
Kyuquot 152 50 3N 127 25W
Kyuquot Sd. 83 50 0N 127 25W
Kyurdamir 83 40 25N 48 3 E
Kyūshū 110 33 0N 131 0 E
Kyūshū □ 110 33 0N 131 0 E
Kyūshū-Sanchi 110 32 45N 131 40 E
Kyustendil 66 42 25N 22 41 E
Kyusyur 77 70 39N 127 15 E
Kywong 141 34 58 S 146 44 E
Kyzyl 77 51 50N 94 30 E
Kyzyl-Kiya 85 40 16N 72 8 E
Kyzyl Orda 85 44 56N 65 30 E
Kyzyl Rabat 76 37 45N 74 55 E
Kyzylkum 84 42 30N 65 0 E
Kyzylsu, R. 85 39 11N 72 2 E
Kzyl-orda 85 44 48N 65 28 E

L

Laa 53 48 43N 16 23 E
Laage 48 53 55N 12 21 E
Laasphe 48 50 56N 8 23 E
Laau Pt. 147 21 57N 159 40W
Laba, R. 83 45 0N 40 30 E
Laban, Burma 98 25 52N 96 40 E
Laban, Ireland 39 53 8N 8 50W
Labasheeda 39 52 37N 9 15W
Labastide 44 43 28N 2 39 E
Labastide-Murat 44 44 39N 1 33 E
Labbézenga 121 15 2N 0 48 E
Labdah = Leptis Magna 119 32 40N 14 12 E
Labé 120 11 24N 12 16W
Labe, R. 52 50 3N 15 20 E
Laberec, R. 53 21 57N 49 7 E
Laberge, L. 152 61 11N 135 12W
Labin 63 45 5N 14 8 E
Labinsk 83 44 40N 40 48W
Labis 101 2 22N 103 2 E
Labiszyn 54 52 57N 17 54 E
Laboa 103 8 6 S 122 50 E
Laboe 48 54 25N 10 13 E
Labouheyre 44 44 13N 0 55W
Laboulaye 172 34 10 S 63 30W
Labrador City 151 52 57N 66 55W
Labrador, Coast of ■ 149 53 20N 61 0W
Labranzagrande 174 5 33N 72 34W
Lábrea 174 7 15 S 64 51W
Labrède 44 44 41N 0 32W
Labuan, I. 102 5 15N 115 38W
Labuha 103 0 30 S 127 30 E
Labuhan 103 6 26 S 105 50 E
Labuhanbajo 103 8 28 S 120 1 E
Labuissière 47 50 19N 4 11 E
Labuk, Telok 102 6 10N 117 50 E
Labutta 98 16 9N 94 46 E
Labytnangi 78 66 29N 66 40 E
Lac Allard 151 50 33N 63 24W
Lac Bouchette 151 48 16N 72 11W
Lac du Flambeau 158 46 1N 89 51W
Lac Édouard 151 47 40N 72 16W
Lac la Biche 152 54 45N 111 58W
Lac-Mégantic 151 45 35N 70 53W
Lac Seul 153 50 28N 92 0W
Lac Thien 100 12 25N 108 11 E
Lacanau, Étang de 44 44 58N 1 7W
Lacanau Médoc 44 44 59N 1 5W
Lacantum, R. 165 16 36N 90 40W
Lacara, R. 57 39 7N 6 25W
Lacaune 44 43 43N 2 40 E
Lacaune, Mts. de 44 43 43N 2 50 E
Laccadive Is. = Lakshadweep Is. 86 10 0N 72 30 E
Laceby 33 53 32N 0 10W
Lacepede B. 140 36 40 S 139 40 E
Lacepede Is. 136 16 55 S 122 0 E
Lacerdónia 127 18 3 S 35 35 E
Lachen, Sikkim 98 47 12N 8 51 E
Lachen, Switz. 51 47 12N 8 51 E
Lachi 94 33 25N 71 20 E
Lachine 150 45 30N 73 40W
Lachlan 139 42 50 S 147 3 E
Lachlan, R. 140 34 22 S 143 55 E
Lachmangarh 94 27 50N 75 4 E
Lachute 150 45 39N 74 21 E
Lackagh Hills 38 54 14N 8 0W
Lackawanna 156 42 49N 78 50W
Lackawaxen 162 41 29N 74 59W
Lacock 28 51 24N 2 8W
Lacombe 152 52 30N 113 44W
Lacona 162 43 37N 76 5W
Láconi 64 39 54N 9 4 E
Laconia 162 43 32N 71 30W
Lacq 44 43 25N 0 35W
Lacrosse 160 46 51N 117 58W
Ladainha 171 17 39 S 41 44W
Ladakh Ra. 95 34 0N 78 0 E
Ladder Hills 37 57 14N 3 13W
Ladhar Bheinn 36 57 5N 5 37W
Ladhon, R. 69 37 40N 21 50 E
Lâdik 82 40 57N 35 58 E
Ladismith 128 33 28 S 21 15 E
Lâdiz 93 28 55N 61 15 E
Ladnun 94 27 38N 74 25 E
Ladock 30 50 19N 4 58W
Ladoga, L. = Ladozhskoye Oz. 78 61 15N 30 30 E
Ladon 43 48 0N 2 30 E
Ladozhskoye Ozero 76 61 15N 30 30 E
Ladrone Is. = Mariana Is. 130 17 0N 145 0 E
Lady Babbie 127 18 30 S 29 20 E
Lady Beatrix L. 150 5 20N 76 50W
Lady Edith Lagoon 136 20 36 S 126 47 E
Lady Grey 128 30 43 S 27 13 E
Ladybank 35 56 16N 3 8W
Ladybrand 128 29 9 S 27 29 E
Lady's I. Lake 39 52 12N 6 23W
Ladysmith, Can. 152 49 0N 123 49W
Ladysmith, S. Afr. 128 28 32 S 29 46 E
Ladysmith, U.S.A. 158 45 27N 91 4W
Lae 135 6 40 S 147 2 E
Laem Ngop 101 12 10N 102 26 E
Laem Pho 101 6 55N 101 19 E
Læsø 73 57 15N 10 53 E
Læsø Rende 73 57 20N 10 45 E
Lafayette, Colo., U.S.A. 158 40 0N 105 2W
Lafayette, Ga., U.S.A. 157 34 44N 85 15W
Lafayette, La., U.S.A. 159 30 18N 92 0W
Lafayette, Tenn., U.S.A. 157 36 35N 86 0W
Laferté 150 48 37N 78 48W
Laferte, R. 152 61 53N 117 44W
Laffan's Bridge 39 52 36N 7 45W
Lafia 121 8 30N 8 34 E
Lafiagi 121 8 52N 5 20 E
Lafleche 153 49 45N 106 40W
Lafon 123 5 5N 32 29 E
Laforest 150 47 4N 81 12W
Laforsen 72 61 56N 15 3 E
Lagaip, R. 135 5 4 S 141 52 E
Lagan 73 56 32N 12 58 E
Lagan, R. 38 54 35N 5 55W
Lagarfljót 74 65 40N 14 18W
Lagarto 170 10 54 S 37 41W
Lagarto, Serra do 173 23 0 S 57 15W
Lage, Ger. 48 52 0N 8 47 E
Lage, Spain 56 43 13N 9 0W
Lage-Mierde 47 51 25N 5 9 E
Lågen 71 61 29N 10 2 E
Lågen, R. 75 61 30N 10 20 E
Lägerdorf 48 53 53N 9 35 E
Lagg 34 56 57N 5 50W
Laggan, Grampian, U.K. 37 57 24N 3 6W
Laggan, Highland, U.K. 37 57 3N 4 48W
Laggan B. 34 55 40N 6 20W
Laggan L. 37 56 57N 4 30W
Laggers Pt. 139 30 52 S 153 4 E
Laghman □ 93 34 20N 70 0 E
Laghouat 118 33 50N 2 59 E
Laghy 38 54 37N 8 7W
Lagnieu 45 45 55N 5 20 E
Lagny 43 48 52N 2 40 E
Lago 65 39 9N 16 8 E
Lagôa 57 37 8N 8 27W
Lagoaça 56 41 11N 6 44W
Lagodekhi 83 41 50N 46 22 E
Lagónegro 65 40 8N 15 45 E
Lagonoy Gulf 103 13 50N 123 50 E
Lagos, Nigeria 121 6 25N 3 27 E
Lagos, Port. 57 37 5N 8 41W
Lagos de Moreno 164 21 21N 101 55W
Lagrange 136 14 13 S 125 46 E
Lagrange B. 136 18 38 S 121 42 E
Laguardia 58 42 33N 2 35W
Laguépie 44 44 8N 1 57 E
Laguna, Brazil 173 28 30 S 48 50W
Laguna, U.S.A. 161 35 3N 107 28W
Laguna Beach 163 33 31N 117 52W
Laguna Dam 161 32 55N 114 30W
Laguna de la Janda 57 36 15N 5 45W
Laguna Limpia 172 26 32 S 59 45W
Laguna Madre 165 27 0N 97 20W
Laguna Veneta 63 45 23N 12 25 E
Lagunas, Chile 172 21 0 S 69 45W
Lagunas, Peru 174 5 10 S 75 35W
Lagunillas 174 10 8N 71 16W
Lahad Datu 103 5 0N 118 30 E
Lahaina 147 20 52N 156 41W
Lahan Sai 100 14 25N 102 52 E
Lahanam 100 16 16N 105 16 E
Lahardaun 38 54 2N 9 20W
Laharpur 95 27 43N 80 56 E
Lahat 102 3 45 S 103 30 E
Lahe 98 19 18N 93 36 E
Lahewa 102 1 22N 97 12 E
Lahijan 93 37 10N 50 6 E
Lahn, R. 48 50 52N 8 35 E
Laholm 73 56 30N 13 2 E
Laholmsbukten 73 56 30N 12 45 E
Lahontan Res. 160 39 28N 118 58W
Lahore 94 31 32N 74 22 E
Lahore □ 94 31 55N 74 5 E
Lahpongsel 98 27 7N 98 25 E
Lahr 49 48 20N 7 52 E
Lahti 75 60 58N 25 40 E
Lai (Béhagle) 117 9 25N 16 30 E
Lai Chau 100 22 5N 103 3 E
Lai-hka 98 21 16N 97 40 E
Laiagam 135 5 33 S 143 30 E
Laian 109 32 27N 118 25 E
Laichou Wan 107 37 30N 119 30 E
Laidley 139 27 39 S 152 20 E
Laidon L. 37 56 40N 4 40W
Laifeng 108 29 31N 109 18 E
Laigle 42 48 46N 0 38 E
Laignes 43 47 50N 4 20 E
Laihsi 107 36 51N 120 30 E
Laikipia □ 126 0 30N 36 30 E
Laila 92 22 10N 46 40 E
Laillahue, Mt. 174 17 0 S 69 30W
Laingsburg 128 33 9 S 20 52 E
Laipin 108 23 42N 109 16 E
Lairg 37 58 1N 4 24W
Lais 102 3 35 S 102 0 E
Laishui 106 39 23N 115 42 E
Laiwu 107 36 12N 117 38 E
Laiyang 107 36 58N 120 41 E
Laiyüan 106 39 19N 114 41 E
Laja, R. 164 20 55N 100 46W
Lajes, Rio Grande d. N., Brazil 170 5 41 S 36 14W
Lajes, Sta. Catarina, Brazil 173 27 48 S 50 20W
Lajinha 171 20 9 S 41 37W
Lajkovac 66 44 27N 20 14 E
Lajosmizse 53 47 3N 19 32 E
Lak Sao 100 18 11N 104 59 E
Laka Chih 95 30 40N 81 10 E
Lakaband 94 31 2N 69 15 E
Lakar 103 8 15 S 128 17 E
Lake Alpine 163 38 29N 120 0W
Lake Andes 158 43 10N 98 32W
Lake Anse 156 46 42N 88 25W
Lake Arthur 159 30 8N 92 40W
Lake Brown 137 30 56 S 118 20 E
Lake Cargelligo 141 33 15 S 146 22 E
Lake Charles 159 31 10N 93 10W
Lake City, Colo, U.S.A. 161 38 3N 107 27W
Lake City, Fla., U.S.A. 157 30 10N 82 40W
Lake City, Iowa, U.S.A. 158 42 12N 94 42W
Lake City, Mich., U.S.A. 156 44 20N 85 10W
Lake City, Minn., U.S.A. 158 44 28N 92 21W
Lake City, S.C., U.S.A. 157 33 51N 79 44W
Lake Coleridge 143 43 17 S 171 30 E
Lake District 23 54 30N 3 10W
Lake George 162 43 25N 73 43W
Lake Grace 137 33 7 S 118 28 E
Lake Harbour 149 62 30N 69 50W
Lake Havasu City 161 34 25N 114 29W
Lake Hughes 163 34 41N 118 26W
Lake Isabella 163 35 38N 118 28W
Lake King 137 33 5 S 119 45 E
Lake Lenore 153 52 24N 104 59W
Lake Louise 152 51 30N 116 10W
Lake Mason 137 27 30 S 119 30 E
Lake Mead Nat. Rec. Area 161 36 0N 114 30W
Lake Mills 158 43 23N 93 33W
Lake Murray 135 6 48 S 141 29 E
Lake Nash 138 20 57 S 138 0 E
Lake of the Woods 155 49 0N 95 0W
Lake Pleasant 162 43 28N 74 25W
Lake Providence 159 32 49N 91 12W
Lake River 150 54 22N 82 31W
Lake Superior Prov. Park 150 47 45N 84 45W
Lake Tekapo 143 43 55 S 170 30 E
Lake Traverse 150 45 56N 78 4W
Lake Varley 137 32 48 S 119 30 E
Lake Village 159 33 20N 91 19W
Lake Wales 157 27 55N 81 32W
Lake Worth 157 26 36N 80 3W
Lakefield 150 44 25N 78 16W
Lakehurst 162 40 1N 74 19W
Lakeland 157 28 0N 82 0W
Lakenheath 29 52 25N 0 30 E
Lakes Entrance 141 37 50 S 148 0 E
Lakeside, Ariz., U.S.A. 161 34 12N 109 59W
Lakeside, Calif., U.S.A. 163 32 52N 116 55W
Lakeside, Nebr., U.S.A. 158 42 5N 102 24W
Lakeview, N.Y., U.S.A. 156 42 43N 78 57W
Lakeview, Oreg., U.S.A. 160 42 15N 120 22W
Lakewood, Calif., U.S.A. 163 33 51N 118 8W
Lakewood, N.J., U.S.A. 162 40 5N 74 13W
Lakhaniá 69 35 58N 27 54 E
Lákhi 69 35 24N 23 27 E
Lakhimpur 95 27 14N 94 7 E
Lakhipur, Assam, India 98 24 48N 93 0 E
Lakhipur, Assam, India 98 26 2N 90 18 E
Lakhonpheng 100 15 54N 105 34 E
Lakhpat 94 23 48N 68 47 E
Laki 74 64 4N 18 14W
Lakin 159 37 58N 101 18W
Lakitusaki, R. 150 54 21N 82 25W
Lakki 93 32 38N 70 50 E
Lakonía □ 69 36 55N 22 30 E
Lakonikós Kólpos 69 36 40N 22 40 E
Lakor, I. 103 8 15 S 128 17 E
Lakota, Ivory C. 120 5 50N 5 30W
Lakota, U.S.A. 158 48 0N 98 22W
Laksefjorden 74 70 45N 26 50 E
Lakselv 74 70 2N 24 56 E
Lakselvbukt 74 69 26N 19 40 E
Lakshadweep Is. 86 10 0N 72 30 E
Laksham 98 23 14N 91 8 E
Lakshmi Kantapur 95 22 5N 88 20 E
Lakshmipur 98 22 38N 88 16 E
Lakuramau 135 2 54 S 151 15 E
Lala Ghat 99 24 30N 92 40 E
Lala Musa 94 32 40N 73 57 E
Lalago 126 3 28 S 33 58 E
Lalapanzi 127 19 20 S 30 15 E
Lalganj 95 25 52N 85 13 E
Lalibala 123 12 8N 39 10 E
Lalin 107 45 14N 126 52 E
Lalín 56 42 40N 8 5W
Lalin Ho, R. 107 45 28N 125 43 E
Lalinde 44 44 50N 0 44 E
Lalitapur 99 26 36N 85 32 E
Lalitpur 95 24 42N 78 28 E
Lam 100 21 21N 106 31 E
Lam Pao Res. 100 16 50N 103 15 E
Lama Kara 121 9 30N 1 15 E
Lamaing 99 15 25N 97 53 E
Lamaipum 98 25 40N 97 57 E
Lamar, Colo., U.S.A. 158 38 9N 102 35W
Lamar, Mo., U.S.A. 159 37 30N 94 20W
Lamas 174 6 28 S 76 31W
Lamastre 45 44 59N 4 35 E
Lamaya 108 29 50N 99 56 E
Lamb Hd. 37 59 5N 2 32W
Lambach 52 48 6N 13 51 E
Lamballe 42 48 29N 2 31W
Lambaréné 124 0 20 S 10 12 E
Lambay I. 38 53 30N 6 0W

Lambayeque □ Lawrenceville

Lambayeque □ 174 6 45S 80 0W
Lamberhurst 29 51 5N 0 21E
Lambert 158 47 44N 104 39W
Lambert, C. 135 4 11S 151 31E
Lambert Land 12 79 12N 20 30W
Lambesc 45 43 39N 5 16E
Lambeth 29 51 27N 0 7W
Lambi Kyun, (Sullivan I.) 101 10 50N 98 20E
Lámbia 69 37 52N 21 53E
Lambley 35 54 56N 2 30W
Lambon 135 4 45S 152 48E
Lambourn 28 51 31N 1 31W
Lambro, R. 62 45 18N 9 20E
Lambs Hd. 39 51 44N 10 10W
Lame 121 10 27N 9 12E
Lame Deer 160 45 45N 106 40W
Lamego 56 41 5N 7 52W
Lameque 151 47 45N 64 38W
Lameroo 140 35 19S 140 33E
Lamesa 159 32 45N 101 57W
Lamhult 73 57 12N 14 36E
Lamía 69 38 55N 22 41E
• Lamitan 103 6 40N 122 10E
Lammermuir 35 55 50N 2 25W
Lammermuir Hills 35 55 50N 2 40W
Lamoille 160 40 47N 115 31W
Lamon Bay 103 14 30N 122 20E
Lamont, Can. 152 53 46N 112 50W
Lamont, U.S.A. 163 35 15N 118 55W
Lampa 174 15 10S 70 30W
Lampang 100 18 18N 99 31E
Lampasas 159 31 5N 98 10W
Lampaul 42 48 28N 5 7W
Lampazos de Naranjo 164 27 2N 100 32W
Lampedusa, I. 60 35 36N 12 40E
Lampeter 31 52 6N 4 6W
Lampione, I. 119 35 33N 12 20E
Lampman 153 49 25N 102 50W
Lamprechtshausen 52 48 0N 12 58E
Lampung 102 1 48S 115 0E
Lamu, Burma 98 19 14N 94 10E
Lamu, Kenya 126 2 10S 40 55E
Lamy 161 35 30N 105 58W
Lan Tsan Kiang (Mekong) 87 18 0N 104 15E
Lanai City 147 20 50N 156 56W
Lanai I. 147 20 50N 156 55W
Lanak La 95 34 27N 79 32E
Lanaken 47 50 53N 5 39E
Lanak'o Shank'ou = Lanak La 95 34 27N 79 32E
Lanao, L. 103 7 52N 124 15E
Lanark 35 55 40N 3 48W
Lanark (□) 26 55 37N 3 50W
Lancashire □ 32 53 40N 2 30W
Lancaster, Can. 151 45 17N 66 10W
Lancaster, U.K. 32 54 3N 2 48W
Lancaster, Calif., U.S.A. 163 34 47N 118 8W
Lancaster, Ky., U.S.A. 156 37 40N 84 40W
Lancaster, Pa., U.S.A. 162 40 4N 76 19W
Lancaster, S.C., U.S.A. 157 34 45N 80 47W
Lancaster, Va., U.S.A. 162 37 46N 76 28W
Lancaster, Wis., U.S.A. 158 42 48N 90 43W
Lancaster Sd. 12 74 13N 84 0W
Lancer 153 50 48N 108 53W
Lanchester 33 54 50N 1 44W
Lanch'i 109 29 11N 119 30E
Lanchou 106 36 5N 103 55E
Lanciano 63 42 15N 14 22E
Lancing 29 50 49N 0 19W
Łancut 54 50 10N 22 20E
Lancy 50 46 12N 6 8E
Lándana 124 5 11S 12 5E
Landau 49 49 12N 8 7E
Landeck 52 47 9N 10 34E
Landen 47 50 45N 5 3E
Lander, Austral. 136 20 25S 132 0E
Lander, U.S.A. 160 42 50N 108 49W
Landerneau 42 48 28N 4 17W
Landeryd 73 57 7N 13 15E
Landes □ 44 43 57N 0 48W
Landes, Les 44 44 20N 1 0W
Landete 58 39 56N 1 25W
Landi Kotal 94 34 7N 71 6E
Landivisiau 42 48 31N 4 6W
Landkey 30 51 2N 4 0W
Landor 137 25 10S 117 0E
Landquart 51 46 58N 9 32E
Landquart, R. 51 46 50N 9 47E
Landrecies 43 50 7N 3 40E
Land's End, Can. 12 76 10N 123 0W
Land's End, U.K. 30 50 4N 5 43W
Landsberg 49 48 3N 10 52E
Landsborough Cr. 138 22 28S 144 35E
Landsbro 73 57 24N 14 56E
Landschaft 50 47 28N 7 40E
Landshut 48 48 31N 12 10E
Landskrona 73 56 53N 12 50E
Landvetter 73 57 41N 12 17E
Lane 73 58 25N 12 3E
Laneffe 47 50 17N 4 35E
Lanesboro 162 41 57N 75 34W
Lanesborough 38 53 40N 8 0W
Lanett 157 33 0N 85 15W
Lang Bay 152 49 17N 124 21W
Lang Qua 100 22 16N 104 27E
Lang Shan 106 41 0N 106 20E
Lang Suan 101 9 57N 99 4E
Langaa 73 56 23N 9 51E
Lángadhás 68 40 46N 23 2E
Langádhia 69 37 43N 22 1E
Långan 72 63 19N 14 44E

*Renamed Isabela

Langara I. 152 54 14N 133 1W
Langavat L. 36 58 4N 6 48W
Langchen Khambah (Sutlej) 95 31 25N 80 0E
Langch'i 109 31 10N 119 10E
Langchung 108 31 31N 105 58E
Langdon 158 48 47N 98 24W
Langdorp 47 50 59N 4 52E
Langeac 44 45 7N 3 29E
Langeb, R. 122 17 28N 36 50E
Langeberge, C. Prov., S. Afr. 128 28 15S 22 33E
Langeberge, C. Prov., S. Afr. 128 33 55S 21 20E
Langeland 73 54 56N 10 48E
Langelands Bælt 73 54 55N 10 56E
Langemark 47 50 55N 2 55E
Langen 49 53 36N 8 36E
Langenburg 153 50 51N 101 43W
Langeness 48 54 34N 8 35E
Langenlois 52 48 29N 15 40E
Langensalza 48 51 6N 10 40E
Langenthal 50 47 13N 7 47E
Langeoog 48 53 44N 7 33E
Langeskov 73 55 22N 10 35E
Langesund 71 59 0N 9 45E
Langhem 73 57 36N 13 14E
Länghem 73 57 36N 13 14E
Langhirano 62 44 39N 10 16E
Langholm 35 55 9N 2 59W
Langidoon 140 31 36S 142 2E
Langjökull 74 64 39N 20 12W
Langkawi I. 101 6 20N 99 45E
Langkawi, P. 101 6 25N 99 45E
Langkon 102 6 30N 116 40E
Langk'ouhsü 109 26 8N 115 10E
Langlade, Can. 150 48 14N 76 10W
Langlade, St. P. & M. 151 46 50N 56 20W
Langlo 139 26 26S 146 5E
Langlois 160 42 54N 124 26W
Langnau 50 46 56N 7 47E
Langness 32 54 3N 4 37W
Langogne 44 44 43N 3 50E
Langon 44 44 33N 0 16W
Langøya 74 68 45N 15 10E
Langport 28 51 2N 2 51W
Langres 43 47 52N 5 20E
Langres, Plateau de 43 47 45N 5 20E
Langsa 102 4 30N 97 57E
Långsele 72 63 12N 17 4E
Långshyttan 72 60 27N 16 2E
Langson 100 21 52N 106 42E
Langstrothdale Chase 32 54 14N 2 13W
Langtai 108 26 6N 105 20E
Langtao 98 27 15N 97 34E
Langting 98 25 31N 93 7E
Langtoft 29 52 42N 0 19W
Langtree 30 50 55N 4 11W
Langtry 159 29 50N 101 33W
Langu 101 6 53N 99 47E
Languedoc □ 44 43 58N 3 22E
Langwies 51 46 50N 9 44E
Lanhsien 106 38 17N 111 38E
Lanigan 153 51 51N 105 2W
Lank'ao 106 34 50N 114 49E
Lanna 72 59 16N 14 56E
Lannemezan 44 43 8N 0 23E
Lannercost 138 18 35S 146 0E
Lannilis 42 48 35N 4 32W
Lannion 42 48 46N 3 29W
Lanouaille 44 45 24N 1 9E
Lanp'ing 108 26 25N 99 24E
Lansdale 162 40 14N 75 18W
Lansdowne 141 31 48S 152 30E
Lansdowne House 150 52 14N 87 53W
Lansford 162 40 48N 75 55W
Lanshan 109 25 18N 112 6E
Lansing 156 42 47N 84 32W
Lanslebourg-Mont-Cenis 45 45 17N 6 52E
Lanta Yai, Ko 101 7 35N 99 3E
Lant'ien 106 34 3N 109 20E
Lants'ang 108 22 40N 99 58E
Lants'ang Chiang, R. 108 30 0N 98 0E
Lantsien 99 32 4N 96 6E
Lants'un 107 36 24N 120 10E
Lantuna 103 8 19S 124 8E
Lanus 172 34 44S 58 27W
Lanusei 64 39 53N 9 31E
Lanzarote, I. 116 29 0N 13 40W
Lanzo Torinese 62 45 16N 7 29E
Lao Bao 100 16 35N 106 30E
Lao Cai 100 22 30N 103 57E
Lao, R. 65 39 45N 15 45E
Laoag 103 18 7N 120 34E
Laoang 103 12 32N 125 8E
Laoha Ho, R. 107 43 24N 120 39E
Laois □ 39 53 0N 7 20W
Laon 43 49 33N 3 35E
Laona 156 45 32N 88 41W
Laos ■ 100 17 45N 105 0E
Lapa 173 25 46S 49 44W
Lapalisse 44 46 15N 3 44E
Laparan Cap, I. 103 6 0N 120 0E
Lapeer 156 43 3N 83 20W
Lapford 30 50 52N 3 49W
Lapi □ 74 67 0N 27 0E
Lapland = Lappland 74 68 7N 24 0E
Laporte 162 41 27N 76 30W
Lapovo 66 44 10N 21 2E
Lappland 74 68 7N 24 0E
Laprida 172 37 34S 60 45W
Laptev Sea 77 76 0N 125 0E
Lapush 160 47 56N 124 33W
Lâpusu, R. 70 47 25N 23 40E
Lar 93 27 40N 54 14E
Lara 140 38 2S 144 26E
Lara □ 174 10 10N 69 50W
Larabanga 120 9 16N 1 56W
Laracha 56 43 15N 8 35W
Larache 118 35 10N 6 5W
Laragh 39 53 0N 6 20W
Laragne-Montéglin 45 44 18N 5 49E
Laramie 158 41 15N 105 29W
Laramie Mts. 158 42 0N 105 30W
Laranjeiras 170 10 48S 37 10W
Laranjeiras do Sul 173 25 23S 52 23W
Larantuka 103 8 5S 122 55E
Larap 103 14 18N 122 39E
Larat, I. 103 7 0S 132 0E
Larbert 35 56 2N 3 50W
Lärbro 73 57 47N 18 50E
Larch, R. 149 57 30N 71 0W
Lårdal 71 59 20N 8 25E
Lårdal 71 59 25N 8 10E
Larde 127 16 28S 39 43E
Larder Lake 150 48 5N 79 40W
Lárdhos, Ákra 69 36 4N 28 10E
Laredo, Spain 58 43 26N 3 28W
Laredo, U.S.A. 159 27 34N 99 29W
Laredo Sd. 152 52 30N 128 53W
Laren 46 52 16N 5 14E
Largeau (Faya) 117 17 58N 19 6E
Largentière 45 44 34N 4 18E
Largs 34 55 48N 4 51W
Lari 62 43 34N 10 35E
Lariang 103 1 35S 119 25E
Larimore 158 47 55N 97 35W
Larino 65 41 48N 14 54E
Lárisa 68 39 38N 22 28E
Lárisa □ 68 39 39N 22 24E
Larkana 94 27 32N 68 2E
Larkollen 71 59 20N 10 41E
Larnaca 92 35 0N 33 35E
Lárnax 92 35 0N 33 35E
Larne 38 54 52N 5 50W
Larne L. 38 54 52N 5 50W
Larned 158 38 15N 99 10W
Laroch 36 56 40N 5 9W
Larochette 47 49 47N 6 13E
Laroquebrou 44 44 58N 2 12E
Larrey, Pt. 136 19 55S 119 7E
Larrimah 136 15 35S 133 12E
Larsen Ice Shelf 13 67 0S 62 0W
Larteh 121 5 50N 0 5W
Laru 126 2 54N 24 25E
Larvik 71 59 4N 10 0E
Laryak 76 61 15N 80 0E
Larzac, Causse du 44 44 0N 3 17E
Las Animas 159 38 8N 103 18W
Las Anod 91 8 26N 47 19E
Las Blancos 59 37 38N 0 49W
Las Bonitas 174 7 50N 65 40W
Las Brenãs 172 27 5S 61 7W
Las Cabezas de San Juan 57 37 0N 5 58W
Las Cruces 161 32 25N 106 50W
Las Flores 172 36 0S 59 0W
Las Heras, Mendoza, Argent. 173 32 51S 68 49W
Las Heras, Santa Cruz, Argent. 176 46 30S 69 0W
Las Huertas, Cabo de 59 38 22N 0 24W
Las Khoreh 91 11 4N 48 20E
Las Lajas 176 38 30S 70 25W
Las Lajitas 174 6 55N 65 39W
Las Lomitas 172 24 35S 60 50W
Las Marismas 57 37 5N 6 20W
Las Mercedes 174 9 7N 66 24W
Las Navas de la Concepción 57 37 56N 5 30W
Las Navas de Tolosa 57 38 18N 3 38W
Las Palmas, Argent. 172 27 8S 58 45W
Las Palmas, Canary Is. 116 28 10N 15 28W
Las Palmas □ 116 28 10N 15 28W
Las Piedras 173 34 35S 56 20W
Las Plumas 176 43 40S 67 15W
Las Rosas 172 32 30S 61 40W
Las Tablas 166 7 49N 80 14W
Las Termas 172 27 29S 64 52W
Las Tres Marías, Is. 164 20 12N 106 30W
Las Varillas 172 32 0S 62 50W
Las Vegas, Nev., U.S.A. 161 36 10N 115 5W
Las Vegas, N.M., U.S.A. 161 35 35N 105 10W
Lascano 173 33 35S 54 18W
Lascaux 44 45 5N 1 10E
Lashburn 153 53 10N 109 40W
Lashio 98 22 56N 97 45E
Lashkar 94 26 10N 78 10E
Łasin 54 53 30N 19 2E
Lasithi □ 69 35 5N 25 50E
Lask 54 51 34N 19 8E
Laskill 33 54 19N 1 6W
Laško 63 46 10N 15 16E
Lassance 171 17 54S 44 34W
Lassay 42 48 27N 0 30W
Lassen, Pk. 160 40 20N 121 0W
Lasswade 35 55 53N 3 8W
Last Mountain L. 153 51 5N 105 14W
Lastoursville 124 0 55S 12 38E
Lastovo 63 42 46N 16 55E
Lastovo, I. 63 42 46N 16 55E
Lastovski Kanal 63 42 50N 17 0E
Lat Yao 100 15 45N 99 48E
Latacunga 174 0 50S 78 35W
Latakia = Al Ladhiqiya 92 35 30N 35 45E
Latchford 150 47 20N 79 50W
Laterza 65 40 38N 16 47E
Latham 137 29 44S 116 20E
Lathen 48 52 51N 7 21E
Latheron 37 58 17N 3 20W
Lathrop Wells 163 36 39N 116 24W
Latiano 65 40 33N 17 43E
Latina 64 41 26N 12 53E
Latisana 63 45 47N 13 1E
Latium = Lazio 63 42 0N 12 30E
Laton 163 36 26N 119 41W
Latorica, R. 53 48 31N 22 0E
Latouche 147 60 0N 148 0W
Latouche Treville, C. 136 18 27S 121 49E
Latrobe 138 38 8S 146 44E
Latrobe, Mt. 139 39 0S 146 23E
Latrónico 65 40 5N 16 0E
Latrun 90 31 50N 34 58E
Latur 96 18 25N 76 40E
Latvia, S.S.R. □ 80 56 50N 24 0E
Latzu 105 29 10N 87 45E
Lauchhammer 48 51 35N 13 40E
Laudal 71 58 15N 7 30E
Lauder 35 55 43N 2 45W
Lauderdale 35 55 43N 2 44W
Lauenburg 48 53 23N 10 33E
Läufelfingen 50 47 24N 7 52E
Laufen 50 47 25N 7 30E
Laugarbakki 74 65 20N 20 55W
Laugharne 31 51 45N 4 28W
Laujar 59 37 0N 2 54W
Launceston, Austral. 138 41 24S 147 8E
Launceston, U.K. 30 50 38N 4 21W
Laune, R. 39 52 5N 9 40W
Launglon Bok 101 13 50N 97 54E
Laupheim 49 48 13N 9 53E
Laura, Queens., Austral. 133 15 32S 144 32E
Laura, S.A., Austral. 140 33 10S 138 18E
Lauragh 39 51 46N 9 46W
Laureana di Borrello 65 38 28N 16 5E
Laurel, Del., U.S.A. 162 38 33N 75 34W
Laurel, Md., U.S.A. 162 39 6N 76 51W
Laurel, Miss., U.S.A. 159 31 50N 89 0W
Laurel, Mont., U.S.A. 160 45 46N 108 49W
Laurencekirk 37 56 50N 2 30W
Laurencetown 39 53 14N 8 11W
Laurens 157 34 32N 82 2W
Laurentian Plat. 151 52 0N 70 0W
Laurentides, Parc Prov. des 151 47 45N 71 15W
Lauria 65 40 3N 15 50E
Laurie I. 13 60 0S 46 0W
Laurie L. 153 56 35N 101 57W
Lauriston 35 54 57N 4 2W
Laurinburg 157 34 50N 79 25W
Laurium 156 47 14N 88 26W
Lausanne 50 46 32N 6 38E
Laut Kecil, Kepulauan 102 4 45S 115 40E
Laut, Kepulauan 102 4 45N 108 0E
Lauterbach 48 50 39N 9 23E
Lauterbrunnen 50 46 36N 7 55E
Lauterecken 49 49 38N 7 35E
Lauwe 47 50 47N 3 12E
Lauwers 46 53 32N 6 23E
Lauwers Zee 46 53 21N 6 13E
Lauzon 151 46 48N 71 10W
Lava Hot Springs 160 42 38N 112 1W
Lavadores 56 42 14N 8 41W
Lavagna 62 44 18N 9 22E
Laval 42 48 4N 0 48W
Lavalle 172 28 15S 65 15W
Lavandou, Le 45 43 8N 6 22E
Lâvara 68 41 19N 26 22E
Lavardac 44 44 12N 0 20E
Lavaur 44 43 42N 1 49E
Lavaux 50 46 30N 6 45E
Lavaveix 44 46 5N 2 8E
Lavelanet 44 42 57N 1 51E
Lavello 65 41 4N 15 47E
Lavendon 29 52 11N 0 39W
Lavenham 29 52 7N 0 48E
Laverendrye Prov. Park 150 46 15N 17 15W
Laverne 159 36 43N 99 58W
Lavers Hill 140 38 40S 143 25E
Laverton 137 28 44S 122 29E
Lavi 90 32 47N 35 25E
Lavik 71 61 6N 5 25E
Lávkos 69 39 9N 23 14E
Lavos 56 40 6N 8 49W
Lavras 173 21 20S 45 0W
Lavre 57 38 46N 8 22W
Lavrentiya 77 65 35N 171 0W
Lávrion 69 37 40N 24 4E
Lavumisa 129 27 20S 31 55E
Lawas 102 4 55N 115 40E
Lawele 103 5 16S 123 3E
Lawers 35 56 31N 4 9W
Lawksawk 98 21 15N 96 52E
Lawn Hill 138 18 36S 138 33E
Lawng Pit 99 26 45N 98 35E
Lawra 120 10 39N 2 51W
Lawrence, Austral. 173 29 30S 153 8E
Lawrence, Kans., U.S.A. 158 39 0N 95 10W
Lawrence, Mass., U.S.A. 162 42 40N 71 9W
Lawrenceburg, Ind., U.S.A. 156 39 5N 84 50W
Lawrenceburg, Tenn., U.S.A. 157 35 12N 87 19W
Lawrenceville, Ga., U.S.A. 157 33 55N 83 59W

Lawrenceville Lexington

Lawrenceville, Pa., U.S.A. **162** 42 0N 77 8W
Laws **163** 37 24N 118 20W
Lawton **159** 34 33N 98 25W
Lawu Mt. **103** 7 40S 111 13E
Laxa **72** 59 0N 14 37E
Laxey **32** 54 15N 4 23W
Laxfield **29** 52 18N 1 23E
Laxford, L. **36** 58 25N 5 10W
Laxmeshwar **97** 15 9N 75 28E
Laysan I. **143** 25 30N 167 0W
Laytonville **160** 39 44N 123 29W
Laytown **38** 53 40N 6 15W
Laza **98** 26 30N 97 38E
Lazarevac **66** 44 23N 20 17E
Lazio □ **63** 42 10N 12 30E
Lazonby **32** 54 45N 2 42W
Łazy **54** 50 27N 19 24E
Łbzenica **54** 53 18N 17 15E
Lea **33** 53 22N 0 45W
Lea, R. **29** 51 40N 0 3W
Leach **101** 12 21N 103 46E
Lead **158** 44 20N 103 40W
Leadenham **33** 53 5N 0 33W
Leader **153** 50 50N 109 30W
Leadhills **35** 55 25N 3 47W
Leadville **161** 39 17N 106 23W
Leaf, R., Can. **149** 58 47N 70 4W
Leaf, R., U.S.A. **159** 31 45N 89 20W
Leakey **159** 29 45N 99 45W
Leaksville **157** 36 30N 79 49W
Lealui **125** 15 10S 23 2E
Leamington, Can. **150** 42 3N 82 36W
Leamington, N.Z. **130** 37 55S 175 29E
Leamington, U.K. **28** 52 18N 1 32W
Leamington, U.S.A. **160** 39 37N 112 17W
Leandro Norte Alem **173** 27 34S 55 15W
Leane L. **39** 52 2N 9 32W
Leaoto, Mt. **70** 45 20N 25 20E
Leap **39** 51 34N 9 11W
Learmonth **136** 22 40S 114 10E
Leask **153** 53 5N 106 45W
Leatherhead **29** 51 18N 0 20W
Leavenworth, Mo., U.S.A. **158** 39 25N 95 0W
Leavenworth, Wash., U.S.A. **160** 47 44N 120 37W
Łeba **54** 54 45N 17 32E
Lebak **103** 6 32N 124 5E
Lebane **66** 42 56N 21 44E
Lebanon, Ind., U.S.A. **156** 40 3N 86 55W
Lebanon, Kans., U.S.A. **158** 39 50N 98 35W
Lebanon, Ky., U.S.A. **156** 37 35N 85 15W
Lebanon, Mo., U.S.A. **159** 37 40N 92 40W
Lebanon, Oreg., U.S.A. **160** 44 31N 122 57W
Lebanon, Pa., U.S.A. **162** 40 20N 76 28W
Lebanon, Tenn., U.S.A. **157** 36 15N 86 20W
Lebanon ■ **92** 34 0N 36 0E
Lebbeke **47** 51 0N 4 8E
Lebec **163** 34 36N 118 59W
Lebedin **80** 50 35N 34 30E
Lebedyan **81** 53 0N 39 10E
Lebomboberge **129** 24 30S 32 0E
Łebork **54** 54 33N 17 46E
Lebrija **57** 36 53N 6 5W
Lebu **172** 37 40S 73 47W
Lecce **65** 40 20N 18 10E
Lecco **62** 45 50N 9 27E
Lecco, L. di. **62** 45 51N 9 22E
Lécera **58** 41 13N 0 43W
Lech **52** 47 13N 10 9E
Lech, R. **49** 48 45N 10 45E
Lechlade **28** 51 42N 1 40W
Lechtaler Alpen **52** 47 15N 10 30E
Lectoure **44** 43 56N 0 38E
Łeczyca **54** 52 5N 19 45E
Ledbury **28** 52 3N 2 25W
Lede **47** 50 58N 3 59E
Ledeberg **47** 51 2N 3 45E
Ledec **52** 49 41N 15 18E
Ledesma **56** 41 6N 5 59W
Leduc **152** 53 20N 113 30W
Ledyczek **54** 53 33N 16 59E
Lee, U.K. **28** 50 47N 1 11W
Lee, U.S.A. **160** 40 35N 115 36W
Lee Vining **163** 37 58N 119 7W
Leech L. **158** 47 9N 94 23W
Leedey **159** 35 53N 99 24W
Leeds, U.K. **33** 53 48N 1 34W
Leeds, U.S.A. **157** 33 32N 86 30W
Leek, Neth. **46** 53 10N 6 24E
Leek, U.K. **32** 53 7N 2 2W
Leende **47** 51 21N 5 33E
Leer **48** 53 13N 7 29E
Leerdam **46** 51 54N 5 6E
Leersum **46** 52 0N 5 26E
Leesburg **157** 28 47N 81 52W
Leeston **143** 43 45N 172 19E
Leesville **159** 31 12N 93 15W
Leeton **141** 34 23S 146 23E
Leeuwarden **46** 53 15N 5 48E
Leeuwin, C. **137** 34 20S 115 9E
Leeward Is. **167** 16 30N 63 30W
Lefors **159** 35 30N 100 50W
Lefroy, L. **137** 31 21S 121 40E
Legal **152** 53 55N 113 45W
Legendre I. **136** 20 22S 116 55E
Leghorn = Livorno **62** 43 32N 10 18E
Legion **127** 21 25S 28 30E
Legionowo **54** 52 25N 20 50E
Léglise **47** 49 48N 5 32E
Legnago **63** 45 10N 11 19E
Legnano **62** 45 35N 8 55E
Legnica **54** 51 12N 16 10E
Legnica □ **54** 51 30N 16 0E
Legoniel **38** 54 38N 6 0W
Legrad **63** 46 17N 16 51E
Legume **139** 28 20S 152 12E
Leh **95** 34 15N 77 35E
Lehi **160** 40 20N 112 0W
Lehighton **162** 40 50N 75 44W
Lehinch **39** 52 56N 9 21E
Lehliu **70** 44 29N 26 20E
Lehrte **48** 52 22N 9 58E
Lehua, I. **147** 22 1N 160 6W
Lehututu **128** 23 54S 21 55E
Lei Shui, R. **109** 26 56N 112 39E
Leiah **94** 30 58N 70 58E
Leibnitz **52** 46 47N 15 34E
Leicester **28** 52 39N 1 9W
Leicester □ **28** 52 40N 1 10W
Leichhardt, R. **133** 17 50S 139 49E
Leichhardt Ra. **138** 20 46S 147 40E
Leichou Chiang, R. **109** 20 52N 110 10E
Leichou Pantao **108** 20 40N 110 10E
Leiden **46** 52 9N 4 30E
Leiderdorp **46** 52 9N 4 32E
Leidschendam **46** 52 5N 4 24E
Leie, R. **47** 51 2N 3 45E
Leigh, Gr. Manch., U.K. **32** 53 29N 2 31W
Leigh, Here. & Worcs., U.K. **28** 52 10N 2 21W
Leigh Creek **140** 30 28S 138 24E
Leighlinbridge **39** 52 45N 7 2W
Leighton Buzzard **29** 51 55N 0 39W
Leignon **47** 50 16N 5 7E
Leiktho **98** 19 13N 96 35E
Leinster, Mt. **39** 52 38N 6 47W
Leinster, prov. **39** 53 0N 7 10W
Leintwardine **28** 52 22N 2 51W
Leipo **108** 28 15N 103 34E
Leipzig **48** 51 20N 12 23E
Leipzig □ **48** 51 20N 12 30E
Leiria **57** 39 46N 8 53W
Leiria □ **57** 39 46N 8 53W
Leisler, Mt. **136** 23 23S 129 30E
Leiston **29** 52 13N 1 35E
Leith **35** 55 59N 3 10W
Leith Hill **29** 51 10N 0 23W
Leitha, R. **53** 47 57N 17 5E
Leitholm **35** 55 42N 2 16W
Leitrim **38** 54 0N 8 5W
Leitrim □ **38** 54 8N 8 0W
Leiyang **109** 26 24N 112 51E
Leiza **58** 43 5N 1 55W
Lek, R. **46** 51 54N 4 38E
Lekáni **68** 41 10N 24 35E
Leke **47** 51 6N 2 54E
Lekhainá **69** 37 57N 21 16E
Lekkerkerk **46** 51 54N 4 41E
Leknice **61** 51 34N 14 45E
Leksula **103** 3 46S 126 31E
Leland **159** 33 25N 90 52W
Leland Lakes **153** 60 0N 110 59W
Lelant **30** 50 11N 5 26W
Leleque **176** 42 15S 71 0W
Lelu **98** 19 4N 95 30E
Lelystad **46** 52 30N 5 25E
Lema **121** 12 58N 4 13E
Lemagrut, mt. **123** 3 9S 35 22E
Leman Bank, gasfield **19** 53 5N 2 20E
Léman, Lac **50** 46 26N 6 30E
Lemelerveld **46** 52 26N 6 20E
Lemera **126** 3 0S 28 55E
Lemery **103** 13 58N 120 56E
Lemesós **92** 34 42N 33 1E
Lemgo **48** 52 2N 8 52E
Lemhi Ra. **160** 44 30N 113 30W
Lemmer **46** 52 51N 5 43E
Lemmon **158** 45 59N 102 10W
Lemon Grove **163** 32 45N 117 2W
Lemoore **163** 36 23N 119 46W
Lempdes **44** 45 22N 3 17E
Lemvig **73** 56 33N 8 20E
Lemyethna **98** 21 10N 95 52E
Lena, R. **77** 64 30N 127 0E
Lenadoon Pt. **38** 54 19N 9 3W
Lencloître **42** 46 50N 0 20E
Lençóis **171** 12 35S 41 43W
Lendalfoot **34** 55 12N 4 55W
Lendelede **47** 50 53N 3 16E
Lendinara **63** 45 4N 11 37E
Lene L. **38** 53 40N 7 12W
Lengau de Vaca, Punta **172** 30 14S 71 38W
Lenger **85** 42 12N 69 54E
Lengerich **48** 52 12N 7 50E
Lenggong **101** 5 6N 100 58E
Lengyeltóti **53** 46 40N 17 40E
Lenham **29** 51 14N 0 44E
Lenhovda **73** 57 0N 15 16E
Lenia **123** 4 10N 37 25E
Lenin **83** 48 20N 40 56E
Lenina, Pik **85** 39 20N 72 55E
Leninabad **85** 40 17N 69 37E
Leninakan **83** 41 0N 42 50E
Leningrad **80** 59 55N 30 20E
Leninogorsk, Kazakh S.S.R., U.S.S.R. **76** 50 20N 83 30E
Leninogorsk, R.S.F.S.R., U.S.S.R. **84** 54 36N 52 30E
Leninpol **85** 42 29N 71 55E
Leninsk, R.S.F.S.R., U.S.S.R. **83** 48 40N 45 15E
Leninsk, Uzbek S.S.R., U.S.S.R. **85** 40 38N 72 15E
Leninsk-Kuznetskiy **76** 55 10N 86 10E
Leninskaya **81** 56 7N 44 29E
Leninskoye, R.S.F.S.R., U.S.S.R. **77** 47 56N 132 38E
Leninskoye, R.S.F.S.R., U.S.S.R. **81** 58 23N 47 3E
Leninskoye, Uzbek S.S.R., U.S.S.R. **85** 41 45N 69 23E
Lenk **50** 46 27N 7 28E
Lenkoran **79** 39 45N 48 50E
Lenmalu **103** 1 58S 130 0E
Lennard, R. **136** 17 22S 124 20E
Lennox Hills **34** 56 3N 4 12W
Lennoxtown **34** 55 58N 4 14W
Leno **62** 45 24N 10 14E
Lenoir **157** 35 55N 81 36W
Lenoir City **157** 35 40N 84 20W
Lenora **158** 39 39N 100 1W
Lenore L. **153** 52 30N 104 59W
Lenox **162** 42 20N 73 18W
Lens, Belg. **47** 50 33N 3 54E
Lens, France **43** 50 26N 2 50E
Lens St. Remy **47** 50 39N 5 7E
Lensk (Mukhtuya) **77** 60 48N 114 55E
Lenskoye **82** 45 3N 34 1E
Lent **46** 51 52N 5 52E
Lentini **65** 37 18N 15 0E
Lenwood **163** 34 53N 117 7W
Lenzburg **50** 47 23N 8 11E
Lenzen **48** 53 6N 11 26E
Lenzerheide **51** 46 44N 9 34E
Léo **120** 11 3N 2 2W
Leoben **52** 47 22N 15 5E
Leola **158** 45 47N 98 58W
Leominster, U.K. **28** 52 15N 2 43W
Leominster, U.S.A. **162** 42 32N 71 45W
Léon **44** 43 53N 1 18W
León, Mexico **164** 21 7N 101 30W
León, Nic. **166** 12 20N 86 51W
León, Spain **56** 42 38N 5 34W
Leon **158** 40 40N 93 40W
León □ **56** 42 40N 5 55W
León, Montañas de **56** 42 30N 6 18W
Leonardtown **162** 38 19N 76 39W
Leonel, Mte. **50** 46 15N 8 5E
Leonforte **65** 37 39N 14 22E
Leongatha **141** 38 30S 145 58E
Leonidhion **69** 37 9N 22 52E
Leonora **137** 28 49S 121 19E
Leonora Downs **140** 32 29S 142 5E
Léopold II, Lac = Mai-Ndombe **124** 2 0S 18 0E
Leopoldina **173** 21 28S 42 40W
Leopoldo Bulhões **171** 16 37S 48 46W
Leopoldsburg **47** 51 7N 5 13E
Léopoldville = Kinshasa **124** 4 20S 15 15E
Leoti **158** 38 31N 101 19W
Leoville **153** 53 39N 107 33W
Lépa, L. do **128** 17 0S 19 0E
Lepe **57** 37 15N 7 12W
Lepel **80** 54 50N 28 40E
Lephin **36** 57 26N 6 43W
Lepikha **77** 64 45N 125 55E
Lépo, L. do **128** 17 0S 19 0E
Lepontine Alps **62** 46 22N 8 27E
Lepsény **53** 47 0N 18 15E
Leptis Magna **119** 32 40N 14 12E
Lequeitio **58** 43 20N 2 32W
Lerbäck **72** 58 56N 15 2E
Lercara Friddi **64** 37 42N 13 36E
Lerdo **164** 25 32N 103 32W
Léré **124** 9 39N 14 13E
Lere **121** 9 43N 9 18E
Leribe **129** 28 51S 28 3E
Lérici **62** 44 4N 9 48E
Lérida **58** 41 37N 0 39E
Lérida □ **58** 42 6N 1 0E
Lérins, Is. de **45** 43 31N 7 3E
Lerma **56** 42 0N 3 47W
Léros, I. **69** 37 10N 26 50E
Lérouville **43** 48 50N 5 30E
Lerrig **39** 52 22N 9 47W
Lerwick **36** 60 10N 1 10W
Les **70** 46 58N 21 50E
Lesbos, I. = Lésvos **69** 39 0N 26 20E
Lesbury **35** 55 25N 1 37W
Lésina, L. di **63** 41 53N 15 25E
Lesja **71** 62 7N 8 51E
Lesjaverk **71** 62 12N 8 34E
Lesko **54** 49 30N 22 23E
Leskov, I. **13** 56 0S 28 0W
Leskovac **68** 43 0N 21 58E
Leskovec **68** 40 10N 20 34E
Leslie, U.K. **35** 56 12N 3 12W
Leslie, U.S.A. **159** 35 50N 92 35W
Lesmahagow **35** 55 38N 3 55W
Lesna **54** 51 0N 15 15E
Lesneven **42** 48 35N 4 20W
Lesniča **66** 44 39N 19 20E
Lesnoy **84** 59 47N 52 9E
Lesnoye **80** 58 15N 35 31E
Lesotho ■ **129** 29 40S 28 0E
Lesozavodsk **77** 45 30N 133 20E
Lesparre-Médoc **44** 45 18N 0 57W
Lessay **42** 49 14N 1 30W
Lesse, R. **47** 50 15N 4 54E
Lesser Antilles **167** 12 30N 61 0W
Lesser Slave L. **152** 55 30N 115 25W
Lessines **47** 50 42N 3 50E
Lestock **153** 51 19N 103 59W
Lesuer I. **136** 13 50S 127 17E
Lesuma **128** 17 58S 25 12E
Lésvos, I. **69** 39 0N 26 20E
Leswalt **34** 54 56N 5 6W
Leszno **54** 51 50N 16 30E
Leszno □ **54** 51 45N 16 30E
Letchworth **29** 51 58N 0 13W
Letea, Ostrov **70** 45 18N 29 20E
Lethbridge **152** 49 45N 112 45W
Lethero **140** 33 33S 142 30E
Lethlhakeng **128** 24 0S 24 59E
Leti **103** 8 10S 127 40E
Leti, Kepulauan **103** 8 10S 128 0E
Letiahau, R. **128** 21 40S 23 30E
Leticia **174** 4 0S 70 0W
Letpadan **98** 17 45N 96 0E
Letpan **98** 19 28N 93 52E
Letsôk-aw-Kyun (Domel I.) **101** 11 30N 98 25E
Letterbreen **38** 54 18N 7 43W
Letterfrack **38** 53 33N 9 58W
Letterkenny **38** 54 57N 7 42W
Lettermacaward **38** 54 51N 8 18W
Lettermore I. **39** 53 18N 9 40W
Lettermullan **39** 53 15N 9 44W
Letterston **31** 51 56N 5 0W
Lettoch **37** 57 22N 3 30W
Leu **70** 44 10N 24 0E
Leucadia **163** 33 4N 117 18W
Leucate **44** 42 56N 3 3E
Leucate, Étang de **44** 42 50N 3 0E
Leuchars **35** 56 23N 2 53W
Leuk **50** 46 19N 7 37E
Leukerbad **50** 46 24N 7 36E
Leupegem **47** 50 50N 3 36E
Leuser, G. **102** 4 0N 96 51E
Leutkirch **49** 47 49N 10 1E
Leuven (Louvain) **47** 50 52N 4 42E
Leuze, Hainaut, Belg. **47** 50 36N 3 37E
Leuze, Namur, Belg. **47** 50 33N 4 54E
Lev Tolstoy **81** 53 13N 39 29E
Levádhia **69** 38 27N 22 54E
Levan **160** 39 37N 111 32W
Levanger **74** 63 45N 11 19E
Levani **68** 40 40N 19 28E
Lévanto **62** 44 10N 9 37E
Levanzo, I. **64** 38 0N 12 19E
Levelland **159** 33 38N 102 17W
Leven, Fife, U.K. **35** 56 12N 3 0W
Leven, Humb., U.K. **33** 53 54N 0 18W
Leven, Banc du **129** 12 30S 47 45E
Leven, L. **35** 56 12N 3 22W
Leven R. **33** 54 27N 1 15W
Levens **45** 43 50N 7 12E
Leveque C. **136** 16 20S 123 0E
Leverano **65** 40 16N 18 0E
Leverburgh **36** 57 46N 7 0W
Leverkusen **48** 51 2N 6 59E
Levet **43** 46 56N 2 22E
Levice **53** 48 13N 18 35E
Levick, Mt. **13** 75 0S 164 0E
Levico **63** 46 0N 11 18E
Levie **45** 41 40N 9 7E
Levier **43** 46 58N 6 8E
Levin **142** 40 37S 175 18E
Levis **151** 46 48N 71 9W
Levis, L. **152** 62 37N 117 58W
Levitha, I. **69** 37 0N 26 28E
Levittown, N.Y., U.S.A. **162** 40 41N 73 31W
Levittown, Pa., U.S.A. **162** 40 10N 74 51W
Levka **67** 41 52N 26 15E
Lévka, Mt. **69** 35 18N 24 3E
Levkás **69** 38 48N 20 43E
Levkás, I. **69** 38 40N 20 43E
Levkimmi **68** 39 25N 20 3E
Levkôsia = Nicosia **92** 35 10N 33 25E
Levoča **53** 48 59N 20 35E
Levroux **43** 47 0N 1 38E
Levski **67** 43 21N 25 10E
Levskigrad **67** 42 38N 24 47E
Lewe **98** 19 38N 96 7E
Lewellen **158** 41 22N 102 5W
Lewes, U.K. **29** 50 53N 0 2E
Lewes, U.S.A. **156** 38 45N 75 8W
Lewes, L. **148** 60 30N 134 20W
Lewin Brzeski **54** 50 45N 17 37E
Lewis, Butt of **36** 58 30N 6 12W
Lewis, I. **36** 58 10N 6 40W
Lewis, R. **160** 48 0N 113 15W
Lewis Ra. **136** 20 3S 128 50E
Lewisburg, Pa., U.S.A. **162** 40 57N 76 57W
Lewisburg, Tenn., U.S.A. **157** 35 29N 86 46W
Lewisham **29** 51 27N 0 1W
Lewisporte **151** 49 15N 55 3W
Lewiston, U.K. **37** 57 19N 4 30W
Lewiston, Idaho, U.S.A. **160** 45 58N 117 0W
Lewiston, Utah, U.S.A. **160** 42 0N 111 56W
Lewistown, Mont., U.S.A. **160** 47 0N 109 25W
Lewistown, Pa., U.S.A. **156** 40 37N 77 33W
Lexington, Ill., U.S.A. **158** 40 37N 88 47W
Lexington, Ky., U.S.A. **156** 38 6N 84 30W
Lexington, Md., U.S.A. **162** 38 16N 76 27W
Lexington, Miss., U.S.A. **159** 33 8N 90 2W
Lexington, Mo., U.S.A. **158** 39 7N 93 55W
Lexington, N.C., U.S.A. **157** 35 50N 80 13W
Lexington, Nebr., U.S.A. **158** 40 48N 99 45W
Lexington, N.Y., U.S.A. **162** 42 15N 74 22W
Lexington, Oreg., U.S.A. **160** 45 29N 119 46W

Lexington **Litija**

Lexington, Tenn., U.S.A.	**157**	35 38N	88 25W
Leyburn	**33**	54 19N	1 50W
Leyland	**32**	53 41N	2 42W
Leysdown on Sea	**29**	51 23N	0 57E
Leysin	**50**	46 21N	7 0E
Leyte, I.	**103**	11 0N	125 0E
Lezay	**44**	46 17N	0 0E
Lèze, R.	**44**	43 28N	1 25E
Lezha	**68**	41 47N	19 42E
Lézignan-Corbières	**44**	43 13N	2 43E
Lezoux	**44**	45 49N	3 21E
Lgov	**80**	51 42N	35 10E
Lhanbryde	**37**	57 38N	3 12W
Lhariguo	**99**	30 29N	93 4E
Lhasa	**105**	29 39N	91 6E
Lhokseumawe	**102**	5 20N	97 10E
Lhuntsi Dzong	**98**	27 39N	91 10E
Li, Finland	**74**	65 20N	25 20E
Li, Thai.	**100**	17 48N	98 57E
Li Shui, R.	**109**	29 24N	112 1E
Liádhoi, I.	**69**	36 50N	26 11E
Liang Liang	**103**	5 58N	121 30E
Liang Shan	**108**	23 42N	99 48E
Lianga	**103**	8 38N	126 6E
Liangch'eng, Inner Mongolia, China	**106**	40 26N	112 14E
Liangch'eng, Shantung, China	**107**	35 35N	119 32E
Lianghok'ou	**108**	29 10N	108 44E
Lianghsiang	**106**	39 44N	116 8E
Liangp'ing	**108**	30 41N	107 49E
Liangpran, Gunong	**102**	1 0N	114 23E
Liangtang	**106**	33 56N	106 12E
Liao Ho, R.	**107**	40 39N	122 12E
Liaoch'eng	**106**	36 26N	115 58E
Liaochung	**107**	41 30N	122 42E
Liaoning □	**107**	41 15N	122 0E
Liaotung Pantao	**107**	40 0N	122 22E
Liaotung Wan	**107**	40 30N	121 30E
Liaoyang	**107**	41 17N	123 11E
Liaoyüan	**107**	42 55N	125 10E
Liapádhes	**68**	39 42N	19 40E
Liard, R.	**152**	61 51N	121 18W
Liari	**94**	25 37N	66 30E
Libau = Liepaja	**80**	56 30N	21 0E
Libby	**160**	48 20N	115 10W
Libenge	**124**	3 40N	18 55E
Liberal, Kans., U.S.A.	**159**	37 4N	101 0W
Liberal, Mo., U.S.A.	**159**	37 35N	94 30W
Liberec	**52**	50 47N	15 7E
Liberia	**166**	10 40N	85 30W
Liberia ■	**120**	6 30N	9 30W
Libertad	**174**	8 20N	69 37W
Libertad, La	**166**	16 47N	90 7W
Liberty, Mo., U.S.A.	**158**	39 15N	94 24W
Liberty, N.Y., U.S.A.	**162**	41 48N	74 45W
Liberty, Pa., U.S.A.	**162**	41 34N	77 6W
Liberty, Tex., U.S.A.	**159**	30 5N	94 50W
Libiaz	**53**	50 7N	19 21E
Libin	**47**	49 59N	5 15E
Lîbîya, Sahrâ'	**114**	27 35N	25 0E
Libohava	**68**	40 3N	20 10E
Libourne	**44**	44 55N	0 14W
Libramont	**47**	49 55N	5 23E
Librazhdi	**68**	41 12N	20 22E
Libreville	**124**	0 25N	9 26E
Libya ■	**117**	28 30N	17 30E
Libyan Plateau = Ed-Déffa	**122**	30 40N	26 30E
Licantén	**172**	34 55S	72 0W
Licata	**64**	37 6N	13 55E
Lich'eng	**106**	36 59N	113 31E
Lichfield	**28**	52 40N	1 50W
Lichiang	**108**	26 54N	100 12E
Lichin	**107**	37 32N	118 20E
Lichtaart	**47**	51 13N	4 55E
Lichtenburg	**128**	26 8S	26 8E
Lichtenfels	**49**	50 7N	11 4E
Lichtenvoorde	**46**	51 59N	6 34E
Lichtervelde	**47**	51 2N	3 9E
Lich'uan, Hupeh, China	**109**	30 18N	108 51E
Lich'uan, Kiangsi, China	**109**	27 14N	116 51E
Licosa, Punta	**65**	40 15N	14 53E
Lida, U.S.A.	**163**	37 30N	117 30W
Lida, U.S.S.R.	**80**	53 53N	25 15E
Lidhult	**73**	56 50N	13 27E
Lidingö	**73**	59 22N	18 8E
Lidköping	**73**	58 31N	13 14E
Lido, Italy	**63**	45 25N	12 23E
Lido, Niger	**121**	12 54N	3 44E
Lido di Ostia	**64**	41 44N	12 14E
Lidzbark	**54**	53 15N	19 49E
Lidzbark Warminski	**54**	54 7N	20 34E
Liebenwalde	**48**	52 51N	13 23E
Lieberose	**48**	51 59N	14 18E
Liebling	**66**	45 36N	21 20E
Liechtenstein ■	**49**	47 8N	9 35E
Liederkerke	**47**	50 52N	4 5E
Liège	**47**	50 38N	5 35E
Liège □	**47**	50 32N	5 35E
Liegnitz = Legnica	**54**	51 12N	16 10E
Liempde	**47**	51 35N	5 23E
Lienart	**126**	3 3N	25 31E
Lienartville	**126**	3 3N	25 31E
Liench'eng	**109**	25 47N	116 48E
Lienchiang, Fukien, China	**109**	26 11N	119 32E
Lienchiang, Kwangtung, China	**109**	21 36N	110 16E
Lienhsien	**109**	24 50N	112 23E
Lienp'ing	**109**	24 22N	114 30E
Lienshan, Kwangtung, China	**109**	24 37N	112 2E
Lienshan, Yunnan, China	**108**	24 48N	97 54E
Lienshankuan	**107**	40 58N	123 46E
Lienshui	**107**	33 46N	119 18E
Lienyüan	**109**	27 41N	111 40E
Lienyünchiang	**107**	34 47N	119 30E
Lienyünchiangshih	**107**	34 37N	119 13E
Lienz	**52**	46 50N	12 46E
Liepāja	**80**	56 30N	21 0E
Lier	**47**	51 7N	4 34E
Lierneux	**47**	50 17N	5 47E
Lieshout	**47**	51 31N	5 36E
Lieşta	**70**	45 38N	27 34E
Liestal	**50**	47 29N	7 44E
Lieşti	**70**	45 38N	27 34E
Liévin	**43**	50 24N	2 47E
Lièvre, R.	**150**	45 31N	75 26W
Liezen	**52**	47 34N	14 15E
Liffey, R.	**39**	53 21N	6 20W
Lifford	**38**	54 50N	7 30W
Liffré	**42**	48 12N	1 30W
Lifjell	**71**	59 27N	8 45E
Lightning Ridge	**139**	29 22S	148 0E
Lignano	**63**	45 42N	13 8E
Ligny-en-Barrois	**43**	48 36N	5 20E
Ligny-le-Châtel	**43**	47 54N	3 45E
Ligoúrion	**69**	37 37N	23 2E
Ligua, La	**172**	32 30S	71 16W
Liguria □	**62**	44 30N	9 0E
Ligurian Sea	**62**	43 20N	9 0E
Lihir Group	**135**	3 0S	152 35E
Lihou Reefs and Cays	**138**	17 25S	151 40E
Lihsien, Hopeh, China	**106**	38 29N	115 34E
Lihsien, Hunan, China	**109**	29 38N	111 45E
Lihsien, Kansu, China	**106**	34 11N	105 2E
Lihsien, Szechwan, China	**108**	31 28N	103 17E
Lihue	**147**	21 59N	159 24W
Lihwa	**99**	30 4N	100 18E
Likasi	**127**	10 55S	26 48E
Likati	**124**	3 20N	24 0E
Likhoslavl	**80**	57 12N	35 30E
Likhovski	**83**	48 10N	40 10E
Likoma I.	**127**	12 3S	34 45E
Likumburu	**127**	9 43S	35 8E
Liling	**109**	27 40N	113 30E
Lill	**47**	51 15N	4 50E
Lille	**43**	50 38N	3 3E
Lille Bælt	**73**	55 30N	9 45E
Lillebonne	**42**	49 30N	0 32E
Lillehammer	**71**	61 8N	10 30E
Lillers	**43**	50 35N	2 28E
Lillesand	**71**	58 15N	8 23E
Lillestrøm	**71**	59 58N	11 5E
Lillian Point, Mt.	**137**	27 40S	126 6E
Lillo	**58**	39 45N	3 20W
Lillooet, R.	**152**	49 15N	121 57W
Lilongwe	**127**	14 0S	33 48E
Liloy	**103**	8 4N	122 39E
Lilun	**108**	28 3N	100 27E
Lim, R.	**66**	43 0N	19 40E
Lima, Indon.	**103**	3 37S	128 4E
Lima, Peru	**174**	12 0S	77 0W
Lima, Sweden	**72**	60 55N	13 20E
Lima, Mont., U.S.A.	**160**	44 41N	112 38W
Lima, Ohio, U.S.A.	**156**	40 42N	84 5W
Lima, R.	**56**	41 50N	8 18W
Limanowa	**54**	49 42N	20 22E
Limassol	**92**	34 42N	33 1E
Limavady	**38**	55 3N	6 58W
Limavady □	**38**	55 0N	6 55W
Limay Mahuida	**172**	37 10S	66 45W
Limay, R.	**176**	39 40S	69 45W
Limbang	**102**	4 42N	115 6E
Limbara, Monti	**64**	40 50N	9 10E
Limbdi	**94**	22 34N	71 51E
Limbourg	**47**	50 37N	5 56E
Limbourg □	**47**	51 2N	5 25E
Limbri	**141**	31 3S	151 5E
Limbunya	**136**	17 14S	129 50E
Limburg	**49**	50 22N	8 4E
Limburg □	**47**	51 20N	5 55E
Limedsforsen	**72**	60 52N	13 25E
Limeira	**173**	22 35S	47 28W
Limenária	**68**	40 38N	24 32E
Limerick	**39**	52 40N	8 38W
Limerick □	**39**	52 30N	8 50W
Limerick Junction	**39**	52 30N	8 12W
Limestone, R.	**153**	56 31N	94 7W
Limfjorden	**73**	56 55N	9 0E
Limia, R.	**56**	41 55N	8 8W
Limmared	**73**	57 34N	13 20E
Limmat, R.	**51**	47 26N	8 20E
Limmen	**46**	52 34N	4 42E
Limmen Bight	**138**	14 40S	135 35E
Limmen Bight R.	**138**	15 7S	135 44E
Limni	**69**	38 43N	23 18E
Limnos, I.	**68**	39 50N	25 5E
Limoeiro	**170**	7 52S	25 27W
Limoeiro do Norte	**170**	5 5S	38 0W
Limoges	**44**	45 50N	1 15E
Limón	**167**	10 0N	83 2W
Limon	**158**	39 18N	103 38W
Limone	**62**	44 12N	7 32E
Limousin	**44**	46 0N	1 0E
Limousin, Plateau de	**44**	46 0N	1 0E
Limoux	**44**	43 4N	2 12E
Limpopo, R.	**129**	23 15S	32 5E
Limpsfield	**29**	51 15N	0 1E
Limu Ling, mts.	**100**	19 0N	109 20E
Limuru	**126**	1 2S	36 35E
Lin	**68**	41 4N	20 38E
Linan	**109**	30 13N	119 40E
Linares	**172**	35 50S	71 40W
Linàres	**174**	1 23N	77 31W
Linares, Mexico	**165**	24 50N	99 40W
Linares, Spain	**59**	38 10N	3 40W
Linares □	**172**	36 0S	71 0W
Línas Mte.	**64**	39 25N	8 38E
Linchenchen	**106**	36 28N	110 0E
Linch'eng	**106**	37 26N	114 34E
Linch'i	**106**	35 46N	113 53E
Linchiang	**107**	41 50N	126 55E
Linchin	**106**	35 6N	110 33E
Linch'ing	**106**	36 56N	115 45E
Linch'ü	**107**	36 30N	118 32E
Linch'uan	**109**	28 0N	116 20E
Lincluden	**35**	55 5N	3 40W
Lincoln, Argent.	**172**	34 55S	61 30W
Lincoln, N.Z.	**143**	43 38S	172 30E
Lincoln, U.K.	**33**	53 14N	0 32W
Lincoln, Ill., U.S.A.	**158**	40 10N	89 20W
Lincoln, Kans., U.S.A.	**158**	39 6N	98 9W
Lincoln, Maine, U.S.A.	**151**	45 27N	68 29W
Lincoln, N. Mex., U.S.A.	**161**	33 30N	105 26W
Lincoln, Nebr., U.S.A.	**158**	40 50N	96 42W
Lincoln, N.H., U.S.A.	**162**	44 3N	71 40W
Lincoln □	**33**	53 14N	0 32W
Lincoln Sea	**12**	84 0N	55 0W
Lincoln Wolds	**33**	53 20N	0 5W
Lincolnton	**157**	35 30N	81 15W
Lind, Austral.	**138**	18 58S	144 30E
Lind, U.S.A.	**160**	47 0N	118 33W
Lindale	**32**	54 14N	2 54W
Lindås	**71**	60 44N	5 10E
Lindås, Norway	**71**	60 44N	5 9E
Lindås, Sweden	**73**	56 38N	15 35E
Lindau	**49**	47 33N	9 41E
Linde	**46**	52 50N	6 57E
Linden, Guyana	**174**	6 0N	58 10W
Linden, Calif., U.S.A.	**163**	38 1N	121 5W
Linden, Tex., U.S.A.	**159**	33 0N	94 20W
Lindenheuvel	**47**	50 59N	5 48E
Lindenwold	**162**	39 49N	72 59W
Linderöd	**73**	55 56N	13 47E
Linderödsåsen	**73**	55 53N	13 53E
Lindesberg	**72**	59 36N	15 15E
Lindesnes	**71**	57 58N	7 3E
Lindfield	**29**	51 2N	0 5W
Lindi	**127**	9 58S	39 38E
Lindi □	**127**	9 40S	38 30E
Lindi, R.	**126**	1 25N	25 50E
Lindoso	**56**	41 52N	8 11W
Lindow	**48**	52 58N	12 58E
Lindsay, Can.	**150**	44 22N	78 43W
Lindsay, Calif., U.S.A.	**163**	36 14N	119 6W
Lindsay, Okla., U.S.A.	**159**	34 51N	97 37W
Lindsborg	**158**	38 35N	97 40W
Línea de la Concepcion, La	**55**	36 15N	5 23W
Línea de la Concepción, La	**57**	36 15N	5 23W
Linfen	**106**	36 5N	111 32E
Lingakok	**99**	29 55N	87 38E
Lingayer	**103**	16 1N	120 14E
Lingayer G.	**103**	16 10N	120 15E
Lingch'iu	**106**	39 28N	114 10E
Lingch'uan, Kwangsi Chuang, China	**109**	25 25N	110 20E
Lingch'uan, Shansi, China	**106**	35 46N	113 26E
Lingen	**48**	52 32N	7 21E
Lingfield	**29**	51 11N	0 1W
Lingga, Kepulauan	**102**	0 10S	104 30E
Linghed	**72**	60 48N	15 55E
Linghsien, Hunan, China	**109**	26 26N	113 45E
Linghsien, Shantung, China	**106**	37 21N	116 34E
Lingle	**158**	42 10N	104 18W
Lingling	**109**	26 13N	111 37E
Lingpi	**107**	33 33N	117 33E
Lingshan	**108**	22 26N	109 17E
Lingshih	**106**	36 51N	111 47E
Lingshou	**106**	38 18N	114 22E
Lingshui	**100**	18 27N	110 0E
Lingt'ai	**106**	35 4N	107 37E
Linguéré	**120**	15 25N	15 5W
Lingwu	**106**	38 5N	106 20E
Lingyün	**108**	24 24N	106 31E
Linh Cam	**100**	18 31N	105 31E
Linhai	**109**	28 51N	121 7E
Linhares	**171**	19 25S	40 4W
Linho	**106**	40 50N	107 30E
Linhsi	**107**	43 37N	118 8E
Linhsia	**105**	35 36N	103 5E
Linhsiang	**109**	29 29N	113 30E
Linhsien	**106**	37 57N	110 57E
Lini	**107**	35 5N	118 20E
Linju	**106**	34 14N	112 45E
Link	**68**	41 4N	20 38E
Linkao	**100**	19 56N	109 42E
Linkinhorne	**30**	50 31N	4 22W
Linköping	**73**	58 28N	15 36E
Link'ou	**107**	45 18N	130 15E
Linli	**109**	29 27N	111 39E
Linlithgow	**35**	55 58N	3 38W
Linn, Mt.	**160**	40 0N	123 0W
Linney Head	**31**	51 37N	5 4W
Linnhe, L.	**34**	56 36N	5 25W
Linosa	**119**	35 51N	12 50E
Lins	**173**	21 40S	49 44W
Linshui	**108**	30 18N	106 55E
Linslade	**29**	51 55N	0 40W
Lint'ao	**106**	35 20N	104 0E
Linth, R.	**49**	46 54N	9 0E
Linthal	**51**	46 54N	9 0E
Lintlaw	**153**	52 4N	103 14W
Linton, Can.	**151**	47 15N	72 16W
Linton, U.K.	**29**	52 6N	0 19E
Linton, Ind., U.S.A.	**156**	39 0N	87 10W
Linton, N. Dak., U.S.A.	**158**	46 21N	100 12W
Lints'ang	**108**	23 54N	100 0E
Lint'ung	**106**	34 24N	109 13E
Linville	**139**	26 50S	152 11E
Linwu	**109**	25 17N	112 33E
Linxe	**44**	43 56N	1 13W
Linyanti, R.	**128**	18 10S	24 10E
Linyüan	**107**	41 18N	119 15E
Linz, Austria	**52**	48 18N	14 18E
Linz, Ger.	**48**	50 33N	7 18E
Lion-d'Angers, Le	**42**	47 37N	0 43W
Lion, G. du	**44**	43 0N	4 0E
Lioni	**65**	40 52N	15 10E
Lion's Den	**127**	17 15S	30 5E
Lion's Head	**150**	44 58N	81 15W
Liozno	**80**	55 0N	30 50E
Lipali	**127**	15 50S	35 50E
Lípari	**65**	38 26N	14 58E
Lípari, Is.	**65**	38 40N	15 0E
Lipetsk	**81**	52 45N	39 35E
Lipiany	**54**	53 2N	14 58E
Lip'ing	**108**	26 16N	109 8E
Lipkany	**82**	48 14N	26 25E
Lipljan	**66**	42 31N	21 7E
Lipnik	**53**	49 32N	17 36E
Lipno	**54**	52 49N	19 15E
Lipo	**108**	25 25N	107 53E
Lipova	**66**	46 8N	21 42E
Lipovets	**82**	49 12N	29 1E
Lippstadt	**48**	51 40N	8 19E
Lipsco	**54**	51 10N	21 36E
Lipscomb	**159**	36 16N	100 28W
Lipsko	**54**	51 9N	21 40E
Lipsói, I.	**69**	37 19N	26 50E
Liptovsky Svaty Milkula	**53**	49 6N	19 35E
Liptrap C.	**141**	38 50S	145 55E
Lip'u	**109**	24 30N	110 23E
Lira	**126**	2 17N	32 57E
Liri, R.	**64**	41 25N	13 45E
Liria	**58**	39 37N	0 35W
Lisala	**124**	2 12N	21 38E
Lisbellaw	**38**	54 20N	7 32W
Lisboa	**57**	38 42N	9 10W
Lisboa □	**57**	39 0N	9 12W
Lisbon	**158**	46 30N	97 46W
Lisbon = Lisboa	**57**	38 42N	9 10W
Lisburn	**38**	54 30N	6 9W
Lisburne, C.	**147**	68 50N	166 0W
Liscannor	**39**	52 57N	9 24W
Liscannor, B.	**39**	52 57N	9 24W
Liscarroll	**39**	52 15N	8 44W
Liscia, R.	**64**	41 5N	9 17E
Liscomb	**151**	45 2N	62 0W
Lisdoonvarna	**39**	53 2N	9 18W
Lishe Ho, R.	**108**	24 18N	101 32E
Lishih	**106**	37 30N	111 7E
Lishu	**107**	43 20N	124 37E
Lishuchen	**107**	45 5N	130 40E
Lishui, Chekiang, China	**109**	28 27N	119 54E
Lishui, Kiangsu, China	**109**	31 38N	119 2E
Lisianski I.	**130**	25 30N	174 0W
Lisieux	**42**	49 10N	0 12E
Lisischansk	**83**	48 55N	38 30E
Liskeard	**30**	50 27N	4 29W
Lismore, N.S.W., Austral.	**139**	28 44S	153 21E
Lismore, Vic., Austral.	**133**	37 58S	143 21E
Lismore, Ireland	**39**	52 8N	7 58W
Lismore I.	**34**	56 30N	5 30W
Lisnacree	**38**	54 4N	6 5W
Lisnaskea	**38**	54 15N	7 27W
Liss	**29**	51 3N	0 53W
Lissatinning Bri.	**39**	51 55N	10 1W
Lisse	**46**	52 16N	4 33E
Lisselton	**39**	52 30N	9 34W
Lissycasey	**39**	52 44N	9 12W
List	**48**	55 1N	8 26E
Lista, Norway	**71**	58 7N	6 39E
Lista, Sweden	**75**	59 19N	16 16E
Lister, Mt.	**13**	78 0S	162 0E
Liston	**139**	28 39S	152 6E
Listowel, Can.	**150**	43 44N	80 58W
Listowel, Ireland	**39**	52 27N	9 30W
Listowel Dns.	**139**	25 10S	145 12E
Lit-et-Mixe	**44**	44 2N	1 15W
Lit'ang, Kwangsi-Chuang, China	**108**	23 11N	109 5E
Lit'ang, Szechwan, China	**108**	30 4N	100 18E
Litang	**103**	5 27N	118 31E
Lit'ang Ho, R.	**108**	28 5N	101 28E
Litcham	**29**	52 43N	0 49E
Litchfield, Austral.	**140**	36 18S	142 52E
Litchfield, Conn., U.S.A.	**162**	41 44N	73 12W
Litchfield, Ill., U.S.A.	**158**	39 10N	89 40W
Litchfield, Minn., U.S.A.	**158**	45 5N	95 0W
Liteni	**70**	47 32N	26 32E
Litherland	**32**	53 29N	3 0W
Lithgow	**141**	33 25S	150 8E
Líthinon, Ákra	**69**	34 55N	24 44E
Lithuania S.S.R. □	**80**	55 30N	24 0E
Litija	**63**	46 3N	14 50E

Lititz Londonderry

Lititz	162	40 9N	76 18W
Litókhoron	68	40 8N	22 34 E
Litoměrice	52	50 33N	14 10 E
Litomysi	53	49 52N	16 20 E
Litschau	52	48 58N	15 4 E
Little Abaco I.	157	26 50N	77 30W
Little Aden	91	12 41N	45 6 E
Little America	13	79 0N	160 0W
Little Andaman I.	101	10 40N	92 15 E
Little Barrier I.	142	36 12 S	175 8 E
Little Belt	72	55 8N	9 55 E
Little Belt Mts.	160	46 50N	111 0W
Little Blue, R.	158	40 18N	97 45W
Little Bushman Land	128	29 10 S	18 10 E
Little Cadotte, R.	152	56 41N	117 6W
Little Cayman, I.	166	19 41N	80 3W
Little Churchill, R.	153	57 30N	95 22W
Little Coco I.	101	14 0N	93 15 E
Little Colorado, R.	161	36 0N	111 31W
Little Current	150	45 55N	82 0W
Little Current, R.	150	50 57N	84 36W
Little Egg Inlet	162	39 30N	74 20W
Little Falls, Minn., U.S.A.	158	45 58N	94 19W
Little Falls, N.Y., U.S.A.	162	43 3N	74 50W
Lit. Grand Rapids	153	52 0N	95 29W
Lit. Humbaldt, R.	160	41 20N	117 27W
Lit. Inagua I.	167	21 40N	73 50W
Little Lake	163	35 58N	117 58W
Little Longlac	150	49 42N	86 58W
Little Marais	158	47 24N	91 8W
Little Mecatiná I.	151	50 30N	59 25W
Little Minch	36	57 35N	6 45W
Lit. Miquelon I.	151	46 45N	56 25W
Lit. Missouri R.	158	46 40N	103 50W
Little Namaqualand	128	29 0 S	17 9 E
Little Ormes Hd.	31	53 19N	3 47W
Little Ouse, R.	29	52 25N	0 50 E
Little Para, R.	109	34 47 S	138 25 E
Little Rann of Kutch	94	23 25N	71 25 E
Little Red, R.	159	35 40N	92 15W
Little River	143	43 45 S	172 49 E
Little Rock	159	34 41N	92 10W
Little Ruaha, R.	126	7 50 S	35 30 E
Little Sable Pt.	156	43 40N	86 32W
Little Scarcies, R.	125	9 30N	12 25W
Little Sioux, R.	147	42 20N	95 55W
Little Smoky	152	54 44N	117 11W
Little Smoky River	152	55 40N	117 38W
Little Snake, R.	160	40 45N	108 15W
Little Wabash, R.	156	38 40N	88 20W
Little Walsingham	29	52 53N	0 51 E
Little Whale, R.	150	55 50N	75 0W
Littleborough	32	53 38N	2 8W
Littlefield	159	33 57N	102 17W
Littlefork	158	48 24N	93 35W
Littlehampton, Austral.	109	35 3 S	138 52 E
Littlehampton, U.K.	29	50 48N	0 32W
Littlemill	37	57 31N	3 49W
Littleport	29	52 27N	0 18 E
Littlestone-on-Sea	29	50 59N	0 59 E
Littlestown	162	39 45N	77 3W
Littleton Common	162	42 32N	71 28W
Litu	108	28 24N	101 16 E
Liuan	109	31 45N	116 30 E
Liuch'eng	108	24 39N	109 14 E
Liuchou	108	24 15N	109 22 E
Liuchuang	107	33 9N	120 18 E
Liuheng Tao	109	29 43N	122 8 E
Liuho, Kiangsu, China	109	32 20N	118 51 E
Liuho, Kirin, China	107	42 16N	125 42 E
Liukou	107	40 57N	118 18 E
Liuli	127	11 3 S	34 38 E
Liupa	106	33 40N	107 0 E
Liuwa Plain	125	14 20 S	22 30 E
Liuyang	109	28 9N	113 38 E
Livada	70	47 52N	23 5 E
Livadherón	68	40 2N	21 57 E
Livanovka	84	52 6N	61 59 E
Livarot	42	49 0N	0 9 E
Live Oak	157	30 17N	83 0W
Liveringa	136	18 3 S	124 10 E
Livermore	163	37 41N	121 47W
Livermore, Mt.	159	30 45N	104 8W
Liverpool, Austral.	141	33 54 S	150 58 E
Liverpool, Can.	151	44 5N	64 41W
Liverpool, U.K.	32	53 25N	3 0W
Liverpool, U.S.A.	162	43 6N	76 13W
Liverpool Bay, Can.	147	70 0N	128 0W
Liverpool Bay, U.K.	23	53 30N	3 20W
Liverpool Plains	141	31 15 S	150 15 E
Liverpool Ra.	141	31 50 S	150 30 E
Livingston, Guat.	166	15 50N	88 50W
Livingston, U.K.	45	55 52N	3 33W
Livingston, Calif., U.S.A.	163	37 23N	120 43W
Livingston, Mont., U.S.A.	160	45 40N	110 40W
Livingstone	159	30 44N	94 54W
Livingstone Falls	126	5 25 S	13 35 E
Livingstone I.	13	63 0 S	60 15W
Livingstone (Maramba)	127	17 46 S	25 52 E
Livingstone Memorial	127	12 20 S	30 18 E
Livingstone Mts., N.Z.	143	45 15 S	168 9 E
Livingstone Mts., Tanz.	127	9 40 S	34 20 E
Livingstonia	127	10 38 S	34 5 E
Livno	66	43 50N	17 0 E
Livny	81	52 30N	37 30 E
Livorno	62	43 32N	10 18 E
Livramento	173	30 55 S	55 30W
Livramento do Brumado	171	13 39 S	41 50W
Livron-sur-Drôme	45	44 46N	4 51 E
Liwale	127	9 48 S	37 58 E
Liwale □	127	9 0 S	38 0 E
Liwale Chini	127	9 40 S	38 0 E
Lixnaw	39	52 24N	9 37W
Lixoúrion	69	38 14N	20 24 E
Liyang	109	31 22N	119 30 E
Lizard	30	49 58N	5 10W
Lizard I.	138	14 42 S	145 30 E
Lizard Pt.	30	49 57N	5 11W
Lizarda	170	9 36 S	46 41W
Lizzano	65	40 23N	17 25 E
Ljig	66	44 13N	20 18 E
Ljubija	63	44 55N	16 35 E
Ljubinje	66	42 58N	18 5 E
Ljubljana	63	46 4N	14 33 E
Ljubno	63	46 25N	14 46 E
Ljubovija	66	44 11N	19 22 E
Ljubuški	66	43 12N	17 34 E
Ljung	73	58 1N	13 3 E
Ljungan	72	62 18N	17 23 E
Ljungan, R.	74	62 30N	14 30 E
Ljungaverk	72	62 30N	16 5 E
Ljungby	73	56 49N	13 55 E
Ljusdal	72	61 46N	16 3 E
Ljusnan	72	61 12N	17 8 E
Ljusnan, R.	75	62 0N	15 20 E
Ljusne	72	61 13N	17 7 E
Ljutomer	63	46 31N	16 11 E
Lki	67	41 28N	23 43 E
Llagostera	58	41 50N	2 54 E
Llanaber	31	52 45N	4 5W
Llanaelhaiarn	31	52 59N	4 24W
Llanafan-fawr	31	52 12N	3 29W
Llanarmon Dyffryn Ceiriog	31	52 53N	3 15W
Llanarth	31	52 12N	4 19W
Llanarthney	31	51 51N	4 9W
Llanbedr	31	52 40N	4 7W
Llanbedrog	31	52 52N	4 29W
Llanberis	31	53 7N	4 7W
Llanbister	31	52 22N	3 19W
Llanbrynmair	31	52 36N	3 19W
Llancanelo, Salina	172	35 40 S	69 8W
Llandaff	31	51 29N	3 13W
Llanddewi-Brefi	31	52 11N	3 57W
Llandilo	31	51 45N	4 0W
Llandogo	31	51 44N	2 40W
Llandovery	31	51 59N	3 49W
Llandrillo	31	52 56N	3 27W
Llandrindod Wells	31	52 15N	3 23W
Llandudno	31	53 19N	3 51W
Llandybie	31	51 49N	4 0W
Llandyfriog	31	52 2N	4 26W
Llandygwydd	31	52 3N	4 33W
Llandyrnog	31	53 10N	3 19W
Llandyssul	31	52 3N	4 20W
Llanelli	31	51 41N	4 11W
Llanelltyd	31	52 45N	3 54W
Llanenddwyn	31	52 48N	4 7W
Llanerchymedd	31	53 20N	4 22W
Llanes	56	43 25N	4 50W
Llanfaelog	31	53 13N	4 29W
Llanfair Caereinion	31	52 39N	3 20W
Llanfair Talhaiarn	31	53 13N	3 37W
Llanfairfechan	31	53 15N	3 58W
Llanfechell	31	52 23N	4 25W
Llanfyllin	31	52 47N	3 17W
Llangadog	31	51 56N	3 53W
Llangefni	31	53 15N	4 20W
Llangelynin	31	52 39N	4 7W
Llangennech	31	51 41N	4 10W
Llangerniew	31	53 12N	3 41W
Llangollen	31	52 58N	3 10W
Llangranog	31	52 11N	4 29W
Llangurig	31	52 25N	3 36W
Llangynog	31	52 50N	3 24W
Llanharan	31	51 32N	3 28W
Llanidloes	31	52 28N	3 31W
Llanilar	31	52 22N	4 2W
Llanllyfni	31	53 2N	4 18W
Llannor	31	52 55N	4 25W
Llano Estacado	154	34 0N	103 0W
Llano R.	159	30 50N	99 0W
Llanon	31	52 17N	4 9W
Llanos	174	3 25N	71 35W
Llanpumpsaint	31	51 56N	4 19W
Llanrhaedr-ym-Mochnant	31	52 50N	3 18W
Llanrhidian	31	51 36N	4 11W
Llanrhystyd	31	52 19N	4 9W
Llanrwst	31	53 8N	3 49W
Llansannan	31	53 10N	3 35W
Llansawel	31	52 0N	4 1W
Llanstephan	31	51 46N	4 24W
Llanthony	31	51 57N	3 2W
Llantrisant	31	51 33N	3 22W
Llanuwchllyn	31	52 52N	3 41W
Llanvihangel Crucorney	31	51 53N	2 58W
Llanwenog	31	52 6N	4 11W
Llanwrda	31	51 58N	3 52W
Llanwrtyd Wells	31	52 6N	3 39W
Llanyblodwel	28	52 47N	3 8W
Llanybyther	31	52 4N	4 10W
Llanymynech	28	52 48N	3 6W
Llanystymdwy	31	52 56N	4 17W
Llera	165	23 19N	99 1W
Llerena	57	38 17N	6 0W
Llethr Mt.	31	52 47N	3 58W
Lleyn Peninsula	31	52 55N	4 35W
Llico	172	34 46 S	72 5W
Llobregat, R.	58	41 19N	2 9 E
Lloret de Mar	58	41 41N	2 53 E
Lloyd B.	138	12 45 S	143 27 E
Lloyd Barrage	95	27 46N	68 50 E
Lloyd L.	153	57 22N	108 57W
Lloydminster	153	53 20N	110 0W
Lluchmayor	59	39 29N	2 53 E
Llullaillaco, volcán	172	24 30 S	68 30W
Llwyngwril	31	52 41N	4 6W
Llyswen	31	52 2N	3 18W
Lo	47	50 59N	2 45 E
Lo Ho, Honan, China	106	34 48N	113 4 E
Lo Ho, Shensi, China	106	34 41N	110 6 E
Lo, R.	100	21 18N	105 25 E
Loa	161	38 18N	111 46W
Loa, R.	172	21 30 S	70 0W
Loan	109	27 24N	115 49 E
Loanhead	35	55 53N	3 10W
Loano	62	44 8N	8 14 E
Loans	34	55 33N	4 39W
Lobatse	125	25 12 S	25 40 E
Löbau	48	51 5N	14 42 E
Lobaye, R.	128	4 30N	17 0 E
Lobbes	47	50 21N	4 16 E
Lobenstein	48	50 25N	11 39 E
Lobería	172	38 10 S	58 40W
Łobez	54	53 38N	15 39 E
Lobito	125	12 18 S	13 35 E
Lobón, Canal de	57	38 50N	6 55W
Lobos	172	35 2 S	59 0W
Lobos, I.	164	21 27N	97 13W
Lobos, Is.	168	6 35 S	80 45W
Lobstick L.	151	54 0N	65 12W
Lobva	84	59 10N	60 30 E
Lobva, R.	84	59 8N	60 48 E
Loc Binh	100	21 46N	106 54 E
Loc Ninh	101	11 50N	106 34 E
Locarno	51	46 10N	8 47 E
Loch Raven Res.	162	39 26N	76 33W
Lochaber	36	56 55N	5 0W
Lochailort	36	56 53N	5 40W
Lochaline	36	56 32N	5 47W
Loch'ang	109	25 10N	113 20 E
Lochans	34	54 52N	5 1W
Lochboisdale	36	57 10N	7 20W
Lochbuie	34	56 21N	5 52W
Lochcarron	36	57 25N	5 30W
Lochdonhead	34	56 27N	5 40W
Loche L., La	153	56 40N	109 30W
Loche, La	153	56 29N	109 26W
Lochearnhead	34	56 24N	4 19W
Lochem	46	52 9N	6 26 E
Loch'eng	108	24 47N	108 54 E
Loches	42	47 7N	1 0 E
Lochgelly	35	56 7N	3 18W
Lochgilphead	34	56 2N	5 37W
Lochgoilhead	34	56 10N	4 54W
Lochiang	108	31 21N	104 28 E
Lochih	108	30 18N	105 0 E
Loch'ing	109	28 8N	120 57 E
Loch'ing Wan	109	28 4N	121 5 E
Lochinver	36	58 9N	5 15W
Lochlaggan Hotel	37	56 59N	4 25W
Lochmaben	35	55 8N	3 27W
Lochmaddy	36	57 36N	7 10W
Lochnagar, Queens., Austral.	138	24 34 S	144 52 E
Lochnagar, Queens., Austral.	138	23 33 S	145 38 E
Lochnagar, Mt.	37	56 57N	3 14W
Łochow	54	52 33N	21 42 E
Lochranza	34	55 42N	5 18W
Lochs Park, Reg.	36	58 7N	6 33W
Loch'uan	106	35 48N	109 35 E
Lochwinnoch	34	55 47N	4 39W
Lochy, L.	37	56 58N	4 55W
Lochy, R.	36	56 52N	5 3W
Lock	139	33 34 S	135 46 E
Lock Haven	156	41 7N	77 31W
Lockeford	163	38 10N	121 9W
Lockeport	151	43 47N	65 4W
Lockerbie	35	55 7N	3 21W
Lockhart, Austral.	141	35 14 S	146 40 E
Lockhart, U.S.A.	159	29 55N	97 40W
Lockhart, L.	137	33 15 S	119 3 E
Lockington	140	36 16 S	144 34 E
Lockport	156	43 12N	78 42W
Locle, Le	50	47 3N	6 44 E
Locminé	42	47 54N	2 51W
Locri	65	38 14N	16 14 E
Locronan	42	48 7N	4 15W
Loctudy	42	47 50N	4 12W
Lod	90	31 57N	34 54 E
Lodalskåpa	71	61 47N	7 13 E
Loddon	29	52 32N	1 29 E
Lodève	44	43 44N	3 19 E
Lodge Grass	160	45 21N	107 27W
Lodgepole	158	41 12N	102 40W
Lodgepole Cr.	158	41 20N	104 30W
Lodhran	94	29 32N	71 30 E
Lodi, Italy	62	45 19N	9 30 E
Lodi, U.S.A.	163	38 12N	121 16W
Lodja	124	3 30 S	23 23 E
Lodji	103	1 38 S	127 28 E
Lodosa	58	42 25N	2 4W
Lodose	73	58 5N	12 10 E
Lödöse	73	58 2N	12 9 E
Lodwar	126	3 10N	35 40 E
Łodz	54	51 45N	19 27E
Łodz □	54	51 45N	19 27E
Loengo	126	4 48 S	26 30 E
Lofer	52	47 35N	12 41 E
Lofoten	74	68 10N	13 0 E
Lofoten Is.	74	68 30N	15 0 E
Lofsen	72	62 7N	13 57 E
Loftahammar	73	57 54N	16 41 E
Loftsdalen	72	62 10N	13 20 E
Loftus	33	54 33N	0 52W
Lofty Ra.	136	24 15 S	119 30 E
Loga	121	13 37N	3 14 E
Logan, Kans., U.S.A.	158	39 23N	99 35W
Logan, Ohio, U.S.A.	156	39 25N	82 22 E
Logan, Utah, U.S.A.	160	41 45N	111 50W
Logan, Mt.	147	60 41N	140 22W
Logan Pass	152	48 41N	113 44W
Logansport	156	31 58N	93 58W
Loganville	162	39 51N	76 42W
Logo	123	5 20N	30 18 E
Logo Dergo	123	6 10N	29 18 E
Logroño	58	42 28N	2 32W
*Logroño □	58	42 28N	2 27W
Logrosán	57	39 20N	5 32W
Løgstør	73	56 58N	9 14 E
Lohardaga	95	23 27N	84 45 E
Loheia	91	15 45N	42 40 E
Lohja	75	60 12N	24 5 E
Loho	106	33 33N	114 5 E
Lohr	49	50 0N	9 35 E
Loikaw	98	19 40N	97 17 E
Loimaa	75	60 50N	23 5 E
Loir-et-Cher □	43	47 40N	1 20 E
Loire □	45	45 40N	4 5 E
Loire-Atlantique □	42	47 25N	1 40W
Loire, R.	42	47 16N	2 10W
Loiret □	43	47 58N	2 10 E
Loitz	48	53 58N	13 8 E
Loja, Ecuador	174	3 59 S	79 16W
Loja, Spain	57	37 10N	4 10W
Lojung	108	24 27N	109 36 E
Loka	123	4 13N	31 0 E
Lokandu	124	2 30 S	25 45 E
Løken	71	59 48N	11 29 E
Lokerane	128	24 54 S	24 42 E
Lokeren	47	51 6N	3 59 E
Lokhvitsa	80	50 25N	33 18 E
Lokichokio	126	4 19N	34 13 E
Lokitaung	124	4 12N	35 48 E
Lokka	74	67 49N	27 45 E
Løkken, Denmark	73	57 22N	9 41 E
Løkken, Norway	71	63 8N	9 45 E
Loknya	80	56 49N	30 4 E
Lokobo	123	4 20N	30 30 E
Lokoja	121	7 47N	6 45 E
Lokolama	124	2 35 S	19 50 E
Loktung	100	18 41N	109 5 E
Lokuti	123	4 21N	33 15 E
Lokwei	100	19 12N	110 30 E
Lol	123	5 28N	29 36 E
Lol, R.	123	9 0N	28 10 E
Lola	120	7 52N	8 29W
Lolibai, Gebel	123	3 50N	33 50 E
Lolimi	123	4 35N	34 0 E
Loliondo	124	2 2 S	35 39 E
Lolland	73	54 45N	11 30 E
Lollar	48	50 39N	8 43 E
Lolo	160	46 50N	114 8W
Lolodorf	121	3 16N	10 49 E
Lolungchung	126	30 43N	96 7 E
Lom	67	43 48N	23 20 E
Lom Kao	100	16 53N	101 14 E
Lom, R.	66	43 45N	23 7 E
Lom Sak	100	16 47N	101 15 E
Loma	160	47 59N	110 29W
Loma Linda	163	34 3N	117 16W
Lomami, R.	126	1 0 S	24 40 E
Lomas de Zamóra	172	34 45 S	58 25W
Lombadria	136	16 31 S	122 54 E
Lombard	160	46 7N	111 28W
Lombardia □	62	45 35N	9 45 E
Lombardy = Lombardia	62	45 35N	9 45 E
Lombez	44	43 29N	0 55 E
Lomblen, I.	103	8 30 S	123 32 E
Lombok, I.	102	8 35 S	116 20 E
Lomé	121	6 9N	1 20 E
Lomela	124	2 5 S	23 52 E
Lomela, R.	124	1 30 S	22 50 E
Lomello	62	45 11N	8 46 E
Lometa	159	31 15N	98 25W
Lomie	124	3 13N	13 38 E
Loming	123	4 27N	33 40W
Lomma	73	55 43N	13 6 E
Lomme, R.	47	50 8N	5 10 E
Lommel	47	51 14N	5 19 E
Lomond	152	50 24N	112 36W
Lomond, gasfield	19	57 18N	1 12 E
Lomond, L.	34	56 8N	4 38W
Lomond, mt.	139	30 0 S	151 45 E
Lomphat	101	13 30N	106 59 E
Lompobatang, mt.	103	5 24 S	119 56 E
Lompoc	163	34 41N	120 32W
Lomsegga	71	61 49N	8 21 E
Łomza	54	53 10N	22 2 E
Łomza □	54	53 0N	22 30 E
Lonan	106	34 6N	110 10 E
Lonavla	96	18 46N	73 29 E
Loncoche	176	39 20 S	72 50W
Londa	97	15 30N	74 30 E
Londe, La	45	43 8N	6 14 E
Londerzeel	47	51 0N	4 19 E
Londiani	126	0 10 S	35 33 E
Londinières	42	49 50N	1 25 E
London, Can.	150	43 0N	81 15W
London, U.K.	29	51 30N	0 5W
London, Ky., U.S.A.	156	37 11N	84 5W
London, Ohio, U.S.A.	156	39 54N	83 28W
London □	29	51 30N	0 5W
Londonderry	38	55 0N	7 20W

*Renamed La Rioja

Londonderry, C Lugano, L. di

Londonderry, C. 136 13 45 S 126 55 E
Londonderry, Co. 38 55 0N 7 20W
Londonderry, I. 176 55 0 S 71 0W
Londrina 173 23 0 S 51 10W
Lone Pine 163 36 35N 118 2W
Long Beach, Calif., U.S.A. 163 33 46N 118 12W
Long Beach, N.Y., U.S.A. 162 40 35N 73 40W
Long Beach, Wash., U.S.A. 160 46 20N 124 1W
Long Bennington 33 52 59N 0 45W
Long Branch 162 40 19N 74 0W
Long Clawson 29 52 51N 0 56W
Long Crendon 29 51 47N 1 0W
Long Eaton 33 52 54N 1 16W
Long Gully 109 35 1 S 138 40 E
Long I., Austral. 138 22 8 S 149 53 E
Long I., Bahamas 167 23 20N 75 10W
Long I., Can. 150 44 23N 66 19W
Long I., Ireland 39 51 30N 9 35W
Long I., P.N.G. 135 5 20 S 147 5 E
Long I., U.S.A. 162 40 50N 73 20W
Long I. Sd. 162 41 10N 73 0W
Long Itchington 28 52 16N 1 24W
Long L. 150 49 30N 86 50W
Long, L. 34 56 4N 4 50W
Long L. 162 43 57N 74 25W
Long Melford 29 52 5N 0 44 E
Long Mt. 31 52 38N 3 7W
Long Mynd 23 52 35N 2 50W
Long Pine 158 43 33N 99 50W
Long Pocket 138 18 30 S 146 0 E
Long Pt., Can. 151 48 47N 58 46W
Long Pt., N.Z. 143 46 34 S 169 36 E
Long Preston 32 54 0N 2 16W
Long Ra. 151 49 30N 57 30W
Long Range Mts 151 48 0N 58 30W
Long Reef 136 13 55 S 125 45 E
Long Str. 12 70 0N 175 0 E
Long Sutton 29 52 47N 0 9 E
Long Thanh 101 10 47N 106 57 E
Long Xuyen 101 10 19N 105 28 E
Longá 69 36 53N 21 55 E
Longa I. 36 57 45N 5 50W
Longarone 63 46 15N 12 18 E
Longburn 142 40 23 S 175 35 E
Longdam 99 28 12N 98 16 E
Longeau 43 47 47N 5 20 E
Longford, Austral. 138 41 32 S 147 3 E
Longford, Ireland 38 53 43N 7 50W
Longford, U.K. 28 51 53N 2 14W
Longford □ 38 53 42N 7 45W
Longforgan 35 56 28N 3 8W
Longframlington 35 55 18N 1 47W
Longhawan 102 2 15N 114 55 E
Longhorsley 35 55 15N 1 46W
Longhoughton 35 55 26N 1 38W
Longido 126 2 43 S 36 35 E
Longiram 102 0 5 S 115 45 E
Longkin 98 25 39N 96 22 E
Longlac 150 49 45N 86 25W
Longlier 47 49 52N 5 27 E
Longling 99 24 42N 98 58 E
Longmont 158 40 10N 105 4W
Longnawan 102 21 50N 114 55 E
Longobucco 65 39 27N 16 37 E
Longone, R. 117 10 0N 15 40 E
Longreach 138 23 28 S 144 14 E
Longridge 32 53 50N 2 37W
Long's Peak 160 40 20N 105 50W
Longside 37 57 30N 1 57W
Longton, Austral. 138 21 0 S 145 55 E
Longton, Lancs., U.K. 32 53 43N 2 48W
Longton, Stafford, U.K. 32 53 00N 2 8W
Longtown 32 55 1N 2 59W
Longué 42 47 22N 0 8W
Longueau 42 49 52N 2 22 E
Longuyon 43 49 27N 5 35 E
Longview, Can. 152 50 32N 114 10W
Longview, Tex., U.S.A. 159 32 30N 94 45W
Longview, Wash., U.S.A. 160 46 9N 122 58W
Longvilly 47 50 2N 5 50 E
Longwy 43 49 30N 5 45 E
Lonigo 63 45 23N 11 22 E
Loning 106 34 28N 111 42 E
Löningen 44 52 43N 7 44 E
Lonja, R. 63 45 30N 16 40 E
Lonkor Tso 95 32 40N 83 15 E
Lonoke 159 34 48N 91 57W
Lonouaille 44 46 30N 1 35 E
Lons-le-Saunier 43 46 40N 5 31 E
Lønsdal 74 66 46N 15 26 E
Lønstrup 73 57 29N 9 47 E
Looc 103 12 20N 112 5 E
Lookout, C., Can. 150 55 18N 83 56W
Lookout, C., U.S.A. 157 34 30N 76 30W
Lookout, Pt. 162 38 2N 76 21W
Loolmalasin, mt. 126 3 0 S 35 53 E
Loomis 153 49 15N 108 45W
Loon L. 153 44 50N 77 15W
Loon Lake 153 54 2N 109 10W
Loon-op-Zand 47 51 38N 5 5 E
Loon, R., Alta., Can. 152 57 8N 115 3W
Loon, R., Man., Can. 153 55 53N 101 59W
Loongana 137 30 52 S 127 5 E
Loop Hd. 39 52 34N 9 55W
Loosduinen 46 52 3N 4 14 E
Lop Buri 100 14 48N 100 37 E
Lop Nor 105 40 20N 90 10 E
Lopare 66 44 39N 18 46 E
Lopatin 83 43 50N 47 35 E
Lopatina, G. 77 50 0N 143 30 E
Lopaye 123 6 37N 33 40 E
Lopera 57 37 56N 4 14W
Lopez 162 41 27N 76 20W
Lopez C. 124 0 47 S 8 40 E
Lop'ing, Kiangsi, China 109 28 57N 117 5 E
Lop'ing, Yunnan, China 108 24 56N 104 20 E
Lopodi 123 5 5N 33 15 E
Loppem 47 51 9N 3 12 E
Loppersum 46 53 20N 6 44 E
Lopphavet 74 70 27N 21 15 E
Lora Cr. 139 28 10 S 135 22 E
Lora del Río 57 37 39N 5 33W
Lora, La 56 42 45N 4 0W
Lora, R. 93 32 0N 67 15 E
Lorain 156 41 20N 82 5W
Loralai 94 30 29N 68 30 E
Lorca 59 37 41N 1 42W
Lord Howe I. 130 31 33 S 159 6 E
Lordsburg 161 32 15N 108 45W
Lorengau 135 2 1 S 147 15 E
Loreto, Brazil 170 7 5 S 45 30W
Loreto, Italy 63 43 26N 13 36 E
Loreto, Mexico 164 26 1N 111 21W
Loreto Aprutina 63 42 24N 13 59 E
Lorgues 45 43 28N 6 22 E
Lorica 174 9 14N 75 49W
Lorient 42 47 45N 3 23W
Lorne, Austral. 140 38 33 S 143 59 E
Lorne, U.K. 34 56 26N 5 10W
Lorne, Firth of 34 56 20N 5 40W
Lörrach 49 47 36N 7 38 E
Lorraine 43 49 0N 6 0 E
Lorrainville 150 47 21N 79 23W
Los Alamos, Calif., U.S.A. 163 34 44N 120 17W
Los Alamos, N. Mex., U.S.A. 161 35 57N 106 17W
Los Altos 163 37 23N 122 7W
Los Andes 172 32 50 S 70 40W
Los Angeles 172 37 28 S 72 23W
Los Angeles 163 34 0N 118 10W
Los Angeles Aqueduct 163 35 25N 118 0W
Los Banos 163 37 8N 120 56W
Los Barrios 57 36 11N 5 30W
Los Blancos, Argent. 172 23 45 S 62 30W
Los Blancos, Spain 59 37 38N 0 49W
Los Gatos 163 37 15N 121 59W
Los, Îles de 120 9 30N 13 50W
Los Lamentos 164 30 36N 105 50W
Los Lunas 161 34 55N 106 47W
Los Mochis 164 25 45N 109 5W
Los Monegros 58 41 29N 0 3W
Los Muertos, Punta de 59 36 57N 1 54W
Los Olivos 163 34 40N 120 7W
Los Palacios 166 22 35N 83 15W
Los Palacios y Villafranca 57 37 10N 5 55W
Los Reyes 164 19 21N 99 7W
Los Roques, Is. 167 11 50N 66 45W
Los Santos de Maimona 57 38 37N 6 22W
Los Testigos, Is. 174 11 23N 63 6W
Los Vilos 172 32 0 S 71 30W
Los Yébenes 57 39 36N 3 55W
Loshan, Honan, China 109 32 12N 114 32 E
Loshan, Szechwan, China 108 29 34N 103 44 E
Loshkalakh 77 62 45N 147 20 E
Lošinj, I. 63 44 55N 14 45 E
Losser 46 52 16N 7 1 E
Lossiemouth 37 57 43N 3 17W
Lostwithiel 30 50 24N 4 41W
Losuia 135 8 30 S 151 4 E
Lot □ 44 44 39N 1 40 E
Lot-et-Garonne □ 44 44 22N 0 30 E
Lot, R. 44 44 18N 0 20 E
Lota, Austral. 108 27 28 S 153 11 E
Lota, Chile 172 37 5 S 73 10W
Løten 71 60 51N 11 21 E
Lothian, (□) 26 55 55N 3 35W
Lothiers 43 46 42N 1 33 E
Lotien 108 25 29N 106 39 E
Lot'ien 109 30 47N 115 20 E
Lot'ing 107 39 26N 118 56 E
Loting 109 22 46N 111 34 E
Lötschberg 49 46 25N 7 53 E
Lotschbergtunnel 50 46 26N 7 43 E
Lottefors 72 61 25N 16 24 E
Lotung, China 100 18 44N 109 9 E
Lotung, Taiwan 109 24 41N 121 46 E
Lotz'u 108 25 19N 102 18 E
Lotzukou 107 43 44N 130 20 E
Lotzwil 50 47 12N 7 48 E
Loudéac 42 48 11N 2 47W
Loudon 157 35 41N 84 22W
Loudun 42 47 0N 0 5 E
Loué 42 47 59N 0 9W
Loue, R. 42 47 4N 6 10 E
Louga 120 15 45N 16 5W
Loughborough 28 52 46N 1 11W
Loughbrickland 38 54 19N 6 19W
Loughmore 39 52 45N 7 50W
Loughor 31 51 39N 4 5W
Loughrea 39 53 11N 8 33W
Loughros More, B. 38 54 48N 8 30W
Louhans 45 46 38N 5 12 E
Louis Gentil 118 32 16N 8 31W
Louis Trichardt 125 23 0 S 29 55 E
Louis XIV, Pte. 150 54 37N 79 45W
Louisa 156 38 5N 82 40W
Louisbourg 151 45 55N 60 0W
Louisbourg Nat. Historic Park 151 45 58N 60 20W
Louisburgh 38 53 46N 9 49W
Louise I. 152 52 55N 131 40W
Louiseville 150 46 20N 73 0W
Louisiade Arch. 135 11 10 S 153 0 E
Louisiana 158 39 25N 91 0W
Louisiana □ 159 30 50N 92 0W
Louisville, Ky., U.S.A. 156 38 15N 85 45W
Louisville, Miss., U.S.A. 159 33 7N 89 3W
Loulay 44 46 3N 0 30W
Loulé 57 37 9N 8 0W
Lount L. 153 50 10N 94 20W
Louny 52 50 20N 13 48 E
Loup City 158 41 19N 98 57W
Loupe, La 42 48 29N 1 1 E
Lourdes 44 43 6N 0 3W
Lourdes-de-Blanc-Sablon 151 51 24N 57 12W
Lourenço-Marques, B. de 129 25 50 S 32 45 E
Lourenço-Marques = Maputo 129 25 58 S 32 32 E
Loures 57 38 50N 9 9W
Lourinhã 57 39 14N 9 17W
Louroux Béconnais, Le 42 47 30N 0 55W
Lousã 56 40 7N 8 14W
Louth, Austral. 141 30 30 S 145 8 E
Louth, Ireland 38 53 47N 6 33W
Louth, U.K. 33 53 23N 0 0W
Louth □ 38 53 55N 6 30W
Louti 109 27 45N 111 58 E
Loutrá Aidhipsoú 69 38 54N 23 2 E
Loutráki 69 38 0N 22 57 E
Louveigné 47 50 32N 5 42 E
Louvière, La 47 50 27N 4 10 E
Louviers 42 49 12N 1 10 E
Lovat, R. 80 56 30N 31 20 E
Love 153 53 29N 104 10W
Loveland 158 40 27N 105 4W
Lovell 160 44 51N 108 20W
Lovelock 160 40 17N 118 25W
Lóvere 62 45 50N 10 4 E
Loviisa = Lovisa 75 60 31N 26 20 E
Loving 159 32 17N 104 4W
Lovington 159 33 0N 103 20W
Lovios 56 41 55N 8 4W
Lovisa (Loviisa) 75 60 28N 26 12 E
Lovosice 52 50 30N 14 2 E
Lovran 63 45 18N 14 15 E
Lovrin 66 45 58N 20 48 E
Lövstabukten 72 60 35N 17 45 E
Low Pt. 137 32 25 S 127 25 E
Low Rocky Pt. 133 42 59 S 145 29 E
Lowa 124 1 25 S 25 47 E
Lowa, R. 126 1 15 S 27 40 E
Lowell 162 42 38N 71 19W
Lower Arrow L. 152 49 40N 118 5W
Lower Austria = Niederösterreich 52 48 25N 15 40 E
Lower Beeding 29 51 2N 0 15W
Lower Hermitage 109 34 49 S 138 46 E
Lower Hutt 142 41 10 S 174 55 E
Lower L. 160 41 17N 120 3W
Lower Lake 160 38 56N 122 36W
Lower Neguac 151 47 20N 65 10W
Lower Post 152 59 58N 128 30W
Lower Sackville 151 44 45N 63 43W
Lower Saxony = Niedersachsen 48 52 45N 9 0 E
Lower Seal, L. 150 56 30N 74 23W
Lower Woolgar 138 19 47 S 143 27 E
Lowes Water L. 32 54 35N 3 23W
Lowestoft 29 52 29N 1 44 E
Lowick 35 55 38N 1 57W
Łowicz 54 52 6N 19 55 E
Lowther Hills 35 55 20N 3 40W
Lowville 162 43 48N 75 30W
Loxton 140 34 28 S 140 31 E
Loyal L. 37 58 24N 4 20W
Loyalty Is. 130 21 0 S 167 30 E
Loyang 106 34 41N 112 28 E
Loyauté, Îles 130 21 0 S 167 30 E
Loyeh 108 24 48N 106 34 E
Loyev 80 57 7N 30 40 E
Loyoro 126 3 22N 34 14 E
Loyüan 109 26 30N 119 33 E
Loz 63 45 43N 14 14 E
Lozère □ 44 44 35N 3 30 E
Loznica 66 44 32N 19 14 E
Lozovaya 82 49 0N 36 27 E
Lozva, R. 84 59 36N 62 20 E
Lu 98 45 0N 8 29 E
Lü-Tao 109 22 47N 121 20 E
Luabo 147 18 30 S 36 10 E
Luacano 124 11 15 S 21 37 E
Lualaba, R. 126 5 45 S 26 50 E
Luampa 127 15 4 S 24 20 E
Luan 103 6 10N 124 25 E
Luan Chau 100 21 38N 103 24 E
Luan Ho, R. 107 39 25N 119 15 E
Luanch'eng 106 37 53N 114 39 E
Luanda 124 8 58 S 13 9 E
Luang Doi 100 18 30N 101 0 E
Luang Prabang 100 19 45N 102 10 E
Luang Thale 101 7 30N 100 15 E
Luangwa, R. 125 14 25 S 30 25 E
Luangwa Val. 127 13 30 S 31 30 E
Luanho 107 40 56N 117 42 E
Luanhsien 107 39 45N 118 44 E
Luanping 107 40 56N 117 42 E
Luanshya 127 13 3 S 28 28 E
Luapula □ 127 11 0 S 29 0 E
Luapula, R. 127 12 0 S 28 50 E
Luarca 56 43 32N 6 32W
Luashi 127 10 50 S 23 36 E
Lubalo 124 9 10 S 19 15 E
Luban 54 51 5N 15 15 E
Lubana, Osero 80 56 45N 27 0 E
Lubang Is. 103 13 50N 120 12 E
Lubartów 54 51 28N 22 42 E
Lubawa 54 53 30N 19 48 E
Lubban 90 32 9N 35 14 E
Lubbeek 47 50 54N 4 50 E
Lübben 48 51 56N 13 54 E
Lübbenau 48 51 49N 13 59 E
Lubbock 159 33 40N 102 0W
Lubcroy 37 57 58N 4 47W
Lübeck 48 53 52N 10 41 E
Lübecker Bucht 48 54 3N 11 0 E
Lubefu 126 4 47 S 24 27 E
Lubefu, R. 126 4 47 S 24 27 E
Lubero = Luofu 126 0 1 S 29 15 E
Lubicon L. 152 56 23N 115 56W
Lubien Kujawski 54 52 23N 19 9 E
Lubin 54 51 24N 16 11 E
Lublin 54 51 12N 22 38 E
Lublin □ 54 51 5N 22 30 E
Lubliniec 54 50 43N 18 45 E
Lubny 82 50 3N 32 58 E
Lubok Antu 102 1 3N 111 50 E
Lubon 54 52 21N 16 51 E
Lubongola 126 2 35 S 27 50 E
Lubotin 53 49 17N 20 53 E
Lubraniec 54 52 33N 18 50 E
Lubsko 54 51 45N 14 57 E
Lübtheen 48 53 18N 11 4 E
Lubuagan 103 17 21N 121 10 E
Lubudi 124 6 50 S 21 20 E
Lubudi, R. 127 9 30 S 25 0 E
Lubuhanbilik 102 2 33N 100 14 E
Lubuk Linggau 102 3 15 S 102 55 E
Lubuk Sikaping 102 0 10N 100 15 E
Lubumbashi 127 11 32 S 27 28 E
Lubunda 126 5 12 S 26 41 E
Lubungu 127 14 35 S 26 24 E
Lubutu 126 0 45 S 26 30 E
Luc An Chau 100 22 6N 104 43 E
Luc-en-Diois 45 44 36N 5 28 E
Luc, Le 45 43 23N 6 21 E
Lucan 38 53 21N 6 27W
Lucania, Mt. 147 60 48N 141 25W
Lucca 62 43 50N 10 30 E
Luccens 50 46 43N 6 51 E
Luce Bay 138 54 45N 4 48W
Lucea 166 18 25N 78 10W
Lucedale 157 30 55N 88 34W
Lucena, Phil. 103 13 56N 121 37 E
Lucena, Spain 57 37 27N 4 31W
Lucena del Cid 58 40 9N 0 17W
Lučenec 53 48 18N 19 42 E
Lucera 65 41 30N 15 20 E
Lucerne = Luzern 51 47 3N 8 18 E
Lucerne Valley 163 34 27N 116 57W
Lucero 164 30 49N 106 30W
Luchai 108 24 33N 109 48 E
Luchena, R. 59 37 50N 2 0W
Luch'eng 106 36 18N 113 15 E
Lucheringo, R. 127 12 0 S 36 5 E
Luch'i 109 28 17N 110 10 E
Luchiang, China 109 31 14N 117 17 E
Luchiang, Taiwan 109 24 1N 120 22 E
Luchou 108 28 53N 105 22 E
Lüchow 48 52 58N 11 8 E
Luch'uan 109 22 20N 110 14 E
Lucindale 93 36 59 S 140 23 E
Lucira 125 14 0 S 12 35 E
Luckau 48 51 50N 13 43 E
Luckenwalde 48 52 5N 13 11 E
Lucknow 95 26 50N 81 0 E
Lucomagno, Paso del 51 46 34N 8 49 E
Luçon 44 46 28N 1 10W
Luda Kamchiya, R. 67 42 50N 27 0 E
Ludbreg 63 46 15N 16 38 E
Lüdenscheid 48 51 13N 7 37 E
Lüderitz 128 26 41 S 15 8 E
Ludewa □ 127 10 0 S 34 50 E
Ludgershall 28 51 15N 1 38W
Ludgvan 30 50 9N 5 30W
Ludhiana 94 30 57N 75 56 E
Lüdinghausen 48 51 46N 7 28 E
Ludington 156 43 58N 86 27W
Ludlow, U.K. 28 52 23N 2 42W
Ludlow, Calif., U.S.A. 163 34 43N 116 10W
Ludlow, Vt., U.S.A. 162 43 25N 72 40W
Luduş 70 46 29N 24 5 E
Ludvika 72 60 8N 15 14 E
Ludwigsburg 49 48 53N 9 11 E
Ludwigshafen 49 49 27N 8 27 E
Ludwigslust 48 53 19N 11 28 E
Ludza 80 56 32N 27 43 E
Lue 141 32 38 S 149 50 E
Luebo 124 5 21 S 21 17 E
Lüehyang 106 33 20N 106 3 E
Lueki 126 3 20 S 25 48 E
Luena, Zaîre 127 9 28 S 25 43 E
Luena, Zambia 127 10 40 S 30 25 E
Luepa 174 5 43N 61 31W
Lufeng, Kwangtung, China 109 23 2N 115 37 E
Lufeng, Yunnan, China 108 25 10N 102 5 E
Lufira R. 124 9 30 S 27 0 E
Lufkin 159 31 25N 94 40W
Lufupa 127 10 32 S 24 50 E
Luga 80 58 40N 29 55 E
Luga, R. 80 59 5N 28 30 E
Lugano 51 46 0N 8 57 E
Lugano, L. di 51 46 0N 9 0 E

Lugansk

McIlwraith Ra

Lugansk = Voroshilovgrad 83 48 35N 39 29 E
Lugard's Falls 126 3 6S 38 41 E
Lugela 127 16 25S 36 43 E
Lugenda, R. 127 12 35S 36 50 E
Lugh Ganana 91 3 48N 42 40 E
Lugnaquilla, Mt. 39 52 48N 6 28W
Lugnvik 72 62 56N 17 55 E
Lugo, Italy 63 44 25N 11 53 E
Lugo, Spain 56 43 2N 7 35W
Lugo □ 56 43 0N 7 30W
Lugoj 66 45 42N 21 57 E
Lugones 56 43 26N 5 50W
Lugovoy 76 43 0N 72 20 E
Lugovoye 85 42 55N 72 43 E
Lugwardine 28 52 4N 2 38W
Luhe, R. 48 53 7N 10 0 E
Luhsi, Yunan, China 108 24 31N 103 46 E
Luhsi, Yunnan, China 108 24 27N 98 36 E
Luhuo 108 31 24N 100 41 E
Lui 106 33 52N 115 28 E
Luiana 125 17 25S 22 30W
Luichart L. 37 57 36N 4 43W
Luichow Pen. = Leichou Pantao 108 20 40N 110 5 E
Luing I. 34 56 15N 5 40W
Luino 62 46 0N 8 42 E
Luís 164 26 36N 109 11W
Luis Correia 170 3 0S 41 35W
Luís Gomes 171 6 25S 38 23W
Luís Gonçalves 170 5 37S 50 25W
Luisa 124 7 40S 22 30 E
Luiza 124 7 40S 22 30 E
Luizi 126 6 0S 27 25 E
Luján 172 34 45S 59 5W
Lukanga Swamp 127 14 30S 27 40 E
Lukenie, R. 124 3 0S 18 50 E
Lukhisaral 95 27 11N 86 5 E
Lukolela 124 1 10S 17 12 E
Lukosi 127 18 30S 26 30 E
Lukovit 67 43 13N 24 11 E
Lukoyanov 81 55 2N 44 20 E
Lukuhu 108 27 46N 100 50 E
Lukulu 125 14 35S 23 25 E
Lula 126 0 30N 25 10 E
Lule, R. 74 65 35N 22 10 E
Luleå 74 65 35N 22 10 E
Lüleburgaz 67 41 23N 27 28 E
Luliang 108 25 3N 103 39 E
Luling 159 29 45N 97 40W
Lulonga, R. 124 1 0N 19 0 E
Lulua, R. 124 6 30S 22 50 E
Luluabourg = Kananga 124 5 55S 22 18 E
Lulung 107 39 55N 118 57 E
Lumai 125 13 20S 21 25 E
Lumajang 103 8 8S 113 16 E
Lumbala, Angola 125 12 36S 22 30 E
Lumbala, Angola 125 14 18S 21 18 E
Lumberton, Miss., U.S.A. 159 31 4N 89 28W
Lumberton, N. Mex., U.S.A. 161 36 58N 106 57W
Lumberton, N.C., U.S.A. 157 34 37N 78 59W
Lumbres 43 50 40N 2 5 E
Lumbwa 126 0 12S 35 28 E
Lumby 152 50 10N 118 50W
Lumding 98 25 46N 93 10 E
Lumege 125 11 45S 20 50 E
Lumeyen 123 4 55N 33 28 E
Lumi 135 3 30S 142 2 E
Lummen 47 50 59N 5 12 E
Lumphanan 37 57 8N 2 41W
Lumsden, N.Z. 143 45 44S 168 27 E
Lumsden, U.K. 37 57 16N 2 51W
Lumut 101 4 13N 100 37 E
Lumut, Tg. 102 3 50S 105 58 E
Lunan 108 24 47N 103 16 E
Lunan B. 37 56 40N 2 25W
Lunavada 94 23 8N 73 37 E
Lunca 70 47 22N 25 1 E
Lund, Norway 74 68 42N 18 9 E
Lund, Sweden 73 55 41N 13 12 E
Lund, U.S.A. 160 38 53N 115 0W
Lunda 124 9 40S 20 12 E
Lundazi 125 12 20S 33 7 E
Lunde 71 59 17N 9 5 E
Lunderskov 73 55 29N 9 19 E
Lundi, R. 127 21 15S 31 25 E
Lundu 102 1 40N 109 50 E
Lundy, I. 30 51 10N 4 41W
Lune, R. 32 54 0N 2 51W
Lüneburg 48 53 15N 10 23 E
Lüneburg Heath = Lüneburger Heide 48 53 0N 10 0 E
Lüneburger Heide 48 53 0N 10 0 E
Lunel 45 43 39N 4 9 E
Lünen 48 51 36N 7 31 E
Lunenburg 151 44 22N 64 18W
Lunéville 43 48 36N 6 30 E
Lung Chiang, R. 108 24 30N 109 15 E
Lunga, R. 127 13 0S 26 33 E
Lungan 108 23 11N 107 41 E
Lungch'ang 108 29 20N 105 19 E
Lungch'ih 108 29 25N 103 24 E
Lungchou 108 22 24N 106 50 E
Lungch'üan 109 28 5N 119 7 E
Lungch'uan, Kwangtung, China 109 24 6N 115 15 E
Lungch'uan, Yunnan, China 108 24 16N 97 58 E
Lungern 50 46 48N 8 10 E
Lungholt 74 63 35N 18 10 E
Lunghsi 106 35 3N 104 38 E
Lunghsien 106 34 47N 107 0 E
Lunghua 107 41 18N 117 42 E
Lunghui 109 27 18N 110 52 E
Lungi Airport 120 8 40N 16 47 E
Lungk'ou 107 37 42N 120 21 E
Lungkuan 106 40 45N 115 43 E
Lungkukang 108 32 18N 99 7 E
Lungleh 98 22 55N 92 45 E
Lungli 108 26 27N 106 58 E
Lunglin 108 24 43N 105 26 E
Lungling 108 24 38N 98 35 E
Lungmen 109 23 44N 114 15 E
Lungming 108 23 4N 107 14 E
Lungnan 109 24 54N 114 47 E
Lungngo 98 21 57N 93 36 E
Lungshan 108 29 27N 109 23 E
Lungsheng 109 25 48N 110 0 E
Lungte 106 35 38N 106 6 E
Lungyen 109 25 9N 117 0 E
Lungyu 109 29 2N 119 10 E
Luni 94 26 0N 73 6 E
Luni, R. 94 25 40N 72 20 E
Luninets 80 52 15N 27 0 E
Luning 163 38 30N 118 10W
Lunino 81 53 35N 45 6 E
Lunna Ness 36 60 27N 1 4W
Lunner 71 60 19N 10 35 E
Lunsemfwa Falls 127 14 30S 29 6 E
Lunsemfwa, R. 127 14 50S 30 10 E
Lunteren 46 52 5N 5 38 E
Luofu 126 0 1S 29 15 E
Luozi 124 4 54S 14 0 E
Lupeni 70 45 21N 23 13 E
Łupków 53 49 15N 22 4 E
Lupundu 127 14 18S 26 45 E
Luque, Parag. 172 25 19S 57 25W
Luque, Spain 57 37 35N 4 16W
Luray 156 38 39N 78 26W
Lure 43 47 40N 6 30 E
Luremo 124 8 30S 17 50 E
Lurgainn L. 36 58 1N 5 15W
Lurgan 38 54 28N 6 20W
Luristan 92 33 20N 47 0 E
Lusaka 127 15 28S 28 16 E
Lusambo 126 4 58S 23 28 E
Luseland 153 52 5N 109 24W
Lushan, Honan, China 106 33 45N 113 10 E
Lushan, Kweichow, China 108 26 33N 107 58 E
Lushan, Szechwan, China 108 30 10N 102 59 E
Lushih 106 34 4N 110 2 E
Lushnja 68 40 55N 19 41 E
Lushoto 126 4 47S 38 20 E
Lushoto □ 126 4 45S 38 20 E
Lushui 108 25 51N 98 55 E
Lüshun 107 38 48N 121 16 E
Lusignan 44 46 26N 0 8 E
Lusigny-sur-Barse 43 48 16N 4 15 E
Lusk, Ireland 38 53 32N 6 10W
Lusk, U.S.A. 158 42 47N 104 27W
Luss 34 56 6N 4 40W
Lussac-les-Châteaux 44 46 24N 0 43 E
Lussanvira 171 20 42S 51 7W
Lüta 107 38 55N 121 40 E
Luti 108 7 14S 157 0 E
Luting 108 29 56N 102 12 E
Luton 29 51 53N 0 24W
Lutong 102 4 30N 114 0 E
Lutry 50 46 31N 6 42 E
Lutsk 80 50 50N 25 15 E
Lutterworth 28 52 28N 1 12W
Luverne 158 43 35N 96 12W
Luvua 127 8 48S 25 17 E
Luwegu, R. 127 9 30S 36 20 E
Luwingu, Mt. 124 10 15S 30 2 E
Luwuk 103 10 0S 122 40 E
Luxembourg 47 49 37N 6 9 E
Luxembourg □ 47 49 58N 5 30 E
Luxembourg ■ 47 50 0N 6 0 E
Luxeuil-les-Bains 43 47 49N 6 24 E
Luxor = El Uqsur 122 25 41N 32 38 E
Luy de Béarn, R. 44 43 39N 0 48W
Luy de France, R. 44 43 39N 0 48W
Luy, R. 44 43 39N 1 9W
Luyksgestel 47 51 17N 5 20 E
Luz, Brazil 171 19 48S 45 40W
Luz, France 44 42 53N 0 1 E
Luzern 51 47 3N 8 18 E
Luzern □ 50 47 2N 7 55 E
Luzerne 162 41 17N 75 54W
Luziânia 171 16 20S 48 0W
Luzilândia 170 3 28S 42 22W
Luzon, I. 103 16 0N 121 0 E
Luzy 43 46 47N 3 58 E
Luzzi 65 39 28N 16 17 E
Lvov 80 49 40N 24 0 E
Lwówek 54 52 28N 16 10 E
Lwówek Śląski 54 51 7N 15 38 E
Lyakhovichi 80 53 2N 26 32 E
Lyakhovskiye, Ostrova 77 73 40N 141 0 E
Lyaki 83 40 34N 47 22 E
Lyall Mt. 142 45 16S 167 32 E
* Lyallpur 94 31 30N 73 5 E
Lyalya, R. 84 59 9N 61 29 E
Lyaskovets 67 43 6N 25 44 E
Lybster 37 58 18N 3 16W
Lychen 48 53 13N 13 20 E
Lyckeby 73 56 12N 15 37 E
Lycksele 74 64 38N 18 40 E
Lydd 29 50 57N 0 56 E
Lydda = Lod 90 31 57N 34 54 E

*Renamed Faisalabad

Lydenburg 129 25 10S 30 29 E
Lydford 30 50 38N 4 7W
Lydham 28 52 31N 2 59W
Lyell 143 41 48S 172 4 E
Lyell I. 152 52 40N 131 35W
Lyell, oilfield 19 60 55N 1 12 E
Lyell Range 143 41 38S 172 20 E
Lygnern 73 57 30N 12 15 E
Lykens 162 40 34N 76 42W
Lykling 71 59 42N 5 12 E
Lyman 160 41 24N 110 15W
Lyme Bay 23 50 36N 2 55W
Lyme Regis 30 50 44N 2 57W
Lyminge 29 51 7N 1 6 E
Lymington 28 50 46N 1 32W
Lymm 32 53 23N 2 30W
Lympne 29 51 4N 1 2 E
Lynchburg 156 37 23N 79 10W
Lynd, R. 138 16 28S 143 18 E
Lynd Ra. 139 25 30S 149 20 E
Lynden 160 48 56N 122 32W
Lyndhurst, N.S.W., Austral. 138 33 41S 149 2 E
Lyndhurst, Queens., Austral. 138 19 12S 144 20 E
Lyndhurst, S. Australia, Austral. 139 30 15S 138 18 E
Lyndhurst, U.K. 28 50 53N 1 33W
Lyndon, R. 137 23 29S 114 6 E
Lyneham 28 51 30N 1 57W
Lyngdal, Agder, Norway 71 58 8N 7 7 E
Lyngdal, Buskerud, Norway 71 59 54N 9 32 E
Lynher Reef 136 15 27S 121 55 E
Lynmouth 30 51 14N 3 50W
Lynn 162 42 28N 70 57W
Lynn Canal 152 58 50N 135 20W
Lynn L. 153 56 30N 101 40W
Lynn Lake 153 56 51N 101 3W
Lynton 30 51 14N 3 50W
Lyntupy 80 55 4N 26 23 E
Lynx L. 153 62 25N 106 15W
Lyø 73 55 3N 10 9 E
Lyon 45 45 46N 4 50 E
Lyonnais 45 45 45N 4 15 E
Lyons, Colo., U.S.A. 158 40 17N 105 15W
Lyons, Ga., U.S.A. 157 32 10N 82 15W
Lyons, Kans., U.S.A. 158 38 24N 98 13W
Lyons, N.Y., U.S.A. 162 43 3N 77 0W
Lyons = Lyon 45 45 46N 4 50 E
Lyons Falls 162 43 37N 75 22W
Lyons, R. 137 25 2S 115 9 E
Lyrestad 73 58 48N 14 4 E
Lysá 52 50 11N 14 51 E
Lysekil 73 58 17N 11 26 E
Lyskovo 81 56 0N 45 3 E
Lyss 50 47 4N 7 19 E
Lysva 84 58 07N 57 49 E
Lysvik 72 60 1N 13 9 E
Lytchett Minster 28 50 44N 2 3W
Lytham St. Anne's 32 53 45N 2 58W
Lythe 33 54 30N 0 40W
Lytle 159 29 14N 98 46W
Lyttelton 143 43 35S 172 44 E
Lytton 152 50 13N 121 31W
Lyuban 80 59 16N 31 18 E
Lyubim 81 58 20N 40 50 E
Lyubimets 67 41 50N 26 5 E
Lyubomi 81 51 10N 24 2 E
Lyubotin 82 50 0N 36 4 E
Lyubytino 80 58 50N 33 16 E
Lyudinovo 80 53 52N 34 28 E

M

Ma, R. 100 19 47N 105 56 E
Ma'ad 90 32 37N 35 36 E
Maam Cross 38 53 28N 9 32W
Maamba 128 17 17S 26 28 E
Ma'an 92 30 12N 35 44 E
Maanshan 109 31 40N 118 30 E
Maarheeze 47 51 19N 5 36 E
Maarianhamina 75 60 5N 19 55 E
Maarn 47 52 3N 5 22 E
Maarssen 46 52 9N 5 2 E
Maartensdijk 46 52 9N 5 10 E
Maas 38 54 49N 8 21W
Maas, R. 47 51 48N 4 55 E
Maasbracht 47 51 9N 5 54 E
Maasbree 47 51 22N 6 3 E
Maasdan 46 51 48N 4 34 E
Maasdijk 46 51 58N 4 13 E
Maaseik 47 51 6N 5 45 E
Maasin 102 10 5N 124 55 E
Maasland 46 51 57N 4 16 E
Maasniel 47 51 12N 6 1 E
Maassluis 47 51 56N 4 16 E
Maastricht 47 50 50N 5 40 E
Maatin-es-Sarra 117 21 45N 22 0 E
Maave 129 21 4S 34 47 E
Mabein 98 23 29N 96 37 E
Mabel L. 152 50 35N 118 43W
Mabel, oilfield 19 58 6N 1 36 E
Mabenge 126 4 15N 24 12 E
Mablethorpe 33 53 21N 0 14 E
Mabrouk 121 19 29N 1 15W
Mabton 127 46 13N 120 1W
Mac Bac 101 9 46N 106 7 E
Mc Grath 147 62 58N 155 40W
Macachin 172 37 10S 63 43W
Macadam Ra. 136 14 40S 129 50 E
Macaé 173 22 20S 41 55W
Macaguane 174 6 35N 71 43W
Macaíba 170 5 15S 35 21W
Macajuba 171 12 9S 40 22W
McAlester 159 34 57N 95 40W
Macamic 150 48 45N 79 0W
Macão 57 39 35N 7 59W
Macao = Macau ■ 109 22 16N 113 35 E
Macapá 175 0 5N 51 10W
Macarani 171 15 33S 40 24W
Macarena, Serranía de la 174 2 45N 73 55W
Macarthur 140 38 5S 142 0 E
McArthur, R. 136 16 45S 136 0 E
McArthur River 138 16 27S 137 7 E
Macau 170 5 0S 36 40W
Macau ■ 109 22 16N 113 35 E
Macaúbas 171 13 2S 42 42W
McBride 152 53 20N 120 10W
McCamey 159 31 8N 102 15W
McCammon 160 42 41N 112 11W
McCarthy 147 61 25N 143 0W
McCauley I. 152 53 40N 130 15W
Macclesfield 32 53 16N 2 9W
McClintock 153 57 50N 94 10W
McClintock Chan. 148 72 0N 102 0W
McClintock Ra., Mts. 136 18 44S 127 38 E
McCloud 160 41 14N 122 5W
McCluer Gulf 103 2 20S 133 0 E
McCluer I. 136 11 5S 133 0 E
McClure, L. 163 37 35N 120 16W
McClusky 158 47 30N 100 31W
McComb 159 31 20N 90 30W
McConnell Creek 152 56 53N 126 30W
McCook 158 40 15N 100 35W
McCulloch 152 49 45N 119 15W
McCusker, R. 153 55 32N 108 39W
McDame 152 59 44N 128 59W
McDermitt 160 42 0N 117 45W
McDonald I. 11 54 0S 73 0 E
Macdonald L. 137 23 30S 129 0 E
Macdonald Ra. 136 15 35S 124 50 E
Macdonnell Ranges 136 23 40S 133 0 E
McDouall Peak 139 29 51S 134 55 E
Macdougall L. 148 66 00N 98 27W
McDougalls Well 140 31 8S 141 15 E
MacDowell L. 150 52 15N 92 45W
Macduff 37 57 40N 2 30W
Mace 150 48 55N 80 0W
Maceda 56 42 16N 7 39W
Macedo da Cavaleiros 124 11 25S 16 45 E
Macedo de Cavaleiros 56 41 31N 6 57W
Macedonia = Makedonija 66 41 53N 21 40 E
Macedonia = Makhedonía 68 40 39N 22 0 E
Maceió 170 9 40S 35 41W
Maceira 57 39 41N 8 55W
Macenta 120 8 35N 9 20W
Macerata 63 43 19N 13 28 E
McFarland 163 35 41N 119 14W
Macfarlane, L. 140 32 0S 136 40 E
McFarlane, R. 153 59 12N 107 58W
McGehee 159 33 40N 91 25W
McGill 160 39 27N 114 50W
Macgillycuddy's Reeks, mts. 39 52 2N 9 45W
McGraw 162 42 35N 76 4W
MacGregor 153 49 57N 98 48W
McGregor, Iowa, U.S.A. 158 42 58N 91 15W
McGregor, Minn., U.S.A. 158 46 37N 93 17W
McGregor, R. 152 55 10N 122 0W
McGregor Ra. 139 27 0S 142 45 E
Mach 93 29 50N 67 20 E
Machacalis 171 17 5S 40 45W
Machachi 174 0 30S 78 15W
Machado, R. = Jiparana 174 8 45S 62 20W
Machagai 172 26 56S 60 2W
Machakos 126 1 30S 37 15 E
Machakos □ 126 1 30S 37 15 E
Machala 174 3 10S 79 50W
Machanga 129 20 59S 35 0 E
Machar Marshes 123 9 28N 33 21 E
Machattie, L. 138 24 50S 139 48 E
Machava 129 25 54S 32 28 E
Machece 127 19 15S 35 32 E
Machecoul 42 47 0N 1 49W
Machelen 47 50 55N 4 26 E
Mach'eng 109 31 11N 115 2 E
Mcherrah 118 27 0N 4 30W
Machevna 77 61 20N 172 20 E
Machezo, mt. 57 39 21N 4 20W
Machiang 108 26 30N 107 35 E
Mach'iaoho 107 44 41N 130 32 E
Machias 151 44 40N 67 34W
Machichaco, Cabo 58 43 28N 2 47W
Machichi, R. 153 57 3N 92 6W
Machida 111 35 28N 139 23 E
Machilipatnam 99 16 12N 81 12 E
Machilipatnam = Masulipatnam 96 16 12N 131 15 E
Machine, La 43 46 54N 3 27 E
Mchinja 127 9 44S 39 45 E
Mchinji 127 13 47S 32 58 E
Machiques 174 10 4N 72 34W
Machrihanish 34 55 25N 5 42W
Machupicchu 174 13 8S 72 30W
Machynlleth 31 52 36N 3 51W
•Macias Nguema Biyoga 113 3 30N 8 40 E
McIlwraith Ra. 138 13 50S 143 20 E

•Renamed Bioko

Macina **Makgobistad**

Macina **120** 14 40N 4 50W
Macina, Canal de **120** 13 50N 5 40W
McIntosh **158** 45 57N 101 20W
McIntosh L. **153** 55 11N 104 41W
MacIntosh Range, Mts. **137** 24 45S 121 33E
Macintyre, R. **139** 28 37S 149 40E
Macizo Galaico **56** 42 30N 7 30W
Mackay, Austral. **138** 21 8S 149 11E
Mackay, U.S.A. **160** 43 58N 113 37W
Mackay, L. **136** 22 30S 129 0E
Mackay, R. **152** 57 10N 111 38W
McKay Ra. **137** 23 0S 122 30E
McKeesport **156** 40 21N 79 50W
Mackenzie **152** 55 20N 123 05W
McKenzie **157** 36 10N 88 31W
Mackenzie Bay **147** 69 0N 137 30W
Mackenzie City = Linden **174** 6 0N 58 10W
Mackenzie Highway **152** 58 0N 117 15W
Mackenzie Mts. **147** 64 0N 128 0W
Mackenzie Plains **143** 44 10S 170 25W
Mackenzie, R., Austral. **138** 23 38S 149 46E
Mackenzie, R., Can. **148** 69 10N 134 20W
McKenzie, R. **160** 44 2N 122 30W
•Mackenzie, Terr. **149** 61 30N 144 30W
McKerrow L. **143** 44 25S 168 5E
Mackinaw City **156** 45 47N 84 44W
McKinlay **138** 21 16S 141 18E
McKinlay, R. **138** 20 50S 141 28E
McKinley, Mt. **147** 63 10N 151 0W
McKinley Sea **12** 84 0N 10 0W
McKinney **159** 33 10N 96 40W
Mackinnon Road **126** 3 40S 39 1E
Mackintosh Ra. **137** 27 39S 125 32E
McKittrick **163** 35 18N 119 39W
Mackmyra **72** 60 40N 17 3E
Macksville **141** 30 40S 152 56E
McLaren Vale **140** 35 13S 138 31E
McLaughlin **158** 45 50N 100 50W
Maclean **139** 29 26S 153 16E
McLean **159** 35 15N 100 35W
McLeansboro **158** 38 5N 88 30W
Maclear **129** 31 2S 28 23E
Macleay, R. **141** 30 56S 153 0E
McLennan **152** 55 42N 116 50W
MacLeod, B. **152** 62 53N 110 0W
McLeod L. **137** 24 9S 113 47E
McLeod, L. **137** 24 50S 114 0E
MacLeod Lake **152** 54 58N 123 0W
McIlwraith Ra., Mts. **138** 13 43S 143 23E
McLoughlin, Mt. **160** 42 30N 122 30W
McLure **152** 51 2N 120 13W
McMillan L. **159** 32 40N 104 20W
McMinnville, Oreg., U.S.A. **160** 45 16N 123 11W
McMinnville, Tenn., U.S.A. **157** 35 43N 85 45W
McMorran **153** 51 19N 108 42W
McMurdo Sd. **13** 77 0S 170 0E
McMurray = Fort McMurray **152** 56 45N 111 27W
McNary **161** 34 4N 109 53W
McNaughton L. **152** 52 0N 118 10W
Macnean L. **38** 54 19N 7 52W
MacNutt **153** 51 5N 101 36W
Macodoene **129** 23 32S 35 5E
Macomb **158** 40 25N 90 40W
Macomer **64** 40 16N 8 48E
Mâcon **45** 46 19N 4 50E
Macon, Ga., U.S.A. **157** 32 50N 83 37W
Macon, Miss., U.S.A. **157** 33 7N 88 31W
Macon, Mo., U.S.A. **158** 39 40N 92 26W
Macondo **125** 12 37S 23 46E
Macosquink **38** 55 5N 6 43W
Macossa **127** 17 55S 33 56E
Macoun L. **153** 56 32N 103 50W
Macovane **129** 21 30S 35 0E
McPherson **158** 38 25N 97 40W
McPherson Pk. **163** 34 53N 119 53W
Macpherson Ra. **139** 28 15S 153 15E
Macquarie Harbour **138** 42 15S 145 15E
Macquarie Is. **130** 50 0S 160 0E
Macquarie, R. **139** 30 50S 147 30E
McRae, Mt. **136** 22 17S 117 35E
MacRobertson Coast **13** 68 30S 63 0E
Macroom **39** 51 54N 8 57W
McSwyne's B. **38** 54 37N 8 25W
Macu **174** 0 25N 69 15W
Macugnaga **62** 45 57N 7 58E
Macuirima **127** 19 14S 35 5E
Macuiza **127** 8 7S 34 29E
Macujer **174** 0 24N 73 0W
Macumba, R. **133** 27 11S 136 0E
Macuse **127** 17 45S 37 17E
Macuspana **165** 17 46N 92 36W
Macusse **128** 17 48S 20 23E
Mácuzari, Presa **164** 27 10N 109 10W
Macuze **127** 17 45S 37 17E
Madā 'in Sālih **122** 26 51N 37 58E
Madagali **121** 10 56N 13 33E
Madagascar ■ **129** 20 0S 47 0E
Madagascar, I. **129** 20 0S 47 0E
Madam **120** 7 58N 3 32W
Madama **119** 22 0N 14 0E
Madame I. **151** 45 30N 60 58W
Madanapalle **97** 13 33N 78 34E
Madang **135** 5 12S 145 49E
Madaoua **121** 14 5N 6 27E
Madara **121** 11 45N 10 35E
Madaripur **98** 23 2N 90 15E
Madauk **98** 17 56N 96 52E
Madawaska **150** 45 30N 77 55W
Madawaska, R. **150** 45 27N 76 21W
*Now part of Fort Smith □

Madaya **98** 22 20N 96 10E
Madbar **123** 6 17N 30 45E
Maddalena, I. **64** 41 15N 9 23E
Maddalena, La **64** 41 13N 9 25E
Maddaloni **65** 41 4N 14 23E
Maddy, L. **36** 57 36N 7 8W
Made **47** 51 41N 4 49E
Madebele **123** 12 30N 41 10E
Madeira, Is. **116** 32 50N 17 0W
Madeira, R. **174** 5 30S 61 20W
Madeleine, Is. de la **151** 47 30N 61 40W
Madeley **28** 52 38N 2 28W
Madely **32** 52 59N 2 20W
Madenda **127** 13 42S 35 1W
Madera **163** 37 0N 120 1W
Madha **96** 18 0N 75 55E
Madhubani **95** 26 21N 86 7E
Madhumati, R. **98** 22 53N 89 52E
Madhupur **126** 24 18N 86 37E
Madhya Pradesh □ **94** 21 50N 81 0E
Madi Opei **126** 3 47N 33 5E
Madill **159** 34 5N 96 49W
Madimba, Mozam. **127** 4 58S 15 6E
Madimba, Zaïre **124** 5 0S 15 0E
Madinat al Shaab **91** 12 50N 45 0E
Madingou **124** 4 10S 13 33E
Madirovalo **129** 16 26S 46 32E
Madison, Fla., U.S.A. **157** 30 29N 83 26W
Madison, Ind., U.S.A. **156** 38 42N 85 20W
Madison, Nebr., U.S.A. **158** 41 53N 97 25W
Madison, S.D., U.S.A. **158** 44 0N 97 8W
Madison, Wis., U.S.A. **158** 43 5N 89 25W
Madison City **158** 43 5N 93 10W
Madison Junc. **160** 44 42N 110 56W
Madison, R. **160** 45 0N 111 48W
Madisonville **156** 37 42N 87 30W
Madista **128** 21 15S 25 6E
Madiun **103** 7 38S 111 32E
Madol **123** 9 3N 27 45E
Madona **80** 56 53N 26 5E
Madonie, Le, Mts. **64** 37 50N 13 50E
Madoonga **174** 26 56S 117 35E
Madras, India **97** 13 8N 80 19E
Madras, U.S.A. **160** 44 40N 121 10W
Madras = Tamil Nadu □ **97** 11 0N 77 0E
Madre de Dios, I. **176** 50 20N 75 10W
Madre de Dios, R. **174** 11 30S 67 30W
Madre del Sur, Sierra **165** 17 30N 100 0W
Madre, Laguna **165** 25 0N 97 30W
Madre Occidental, Sierra **164** 27 0N 107 0W
Madre Oriental, Sierra **164** 25 0N 100 0W
Madre, Sierra, Mexico **165** 16 0N 93 0W
Madre, Sierra, Phil. **103** 17 0N 122 0E
Madri **94** 24 16N 73 32E
Madrid **56** 40 25N 3 45W
Madrid □ **56** 40 30N 3 45W
Madridejos **57** 39 28N 3 33W
Madrigal de las Altas Torres **56** 41 5N 5 0W
Madrona, Sierra **57** 38 27N 4 16W
Madroñera **57** 39 26N 5 42W
Madu **123** 14 37N 26 4E
Madura Motel **137** 31 55S 127 0E
Madura, Selat **103** 7 30S 113 20E
Madurai **97** 9 55N 78 10E
Madurantakam **97** 12 30N 79 50E
Madurta **109** 35 1S 138 44E
Maduru Oya **97** 7 40N 81 7E
Madzhalis **83** 42 9N 47 47E
Mae Chan **100** 20 9N 99 52E
Mae Hong Son **100** 19 16N 98 8E
Mae Khlong, R. **100** 13 24N 100 0E
Mae Phrik **100** 17 27N 99 7E
Mae Ramat **100** 16 58N 98 31E
Mae Rim **100** 18 54N 98 57E
Mae Sot **100** 16 43N 98 34E
Mae Suai **100** 19 39N 99 33E
Mae Tha **100** 18 28N 99 8E
Maebaru **110** 33 33N 130 12E
Maebashi **111** 36 24N 139 4E
Maella **58** 41 8N 0 7E
Maentwrog **31** 52 57N 4 0W
Maerhk'ang **108** 31 51N 102 28E
Mâeruş **70** 45 53N 25 31E
Maesteg **31** 51 36N 3 40W
Maestra, Sierra **166** 20 15N 77 0W
Maestrazgo, Mts. del **58** 40 30N 0 25W
Maevatanana **125** 16 56N 46 49E
Ma'fan **119** 25 56N 14 56E
Mafeking, Can. **153** 52 40N 101 10W
*Mafeking, S. Afr. **128** 25 50S 25 38E
Maféré **120** 5 30N 3 2W
Mafeteng **128** 29 51S 27 15E
Maffe **47** 50 21N 5 19E
Maffra **141** 37 53S 146 58E
Mafia □ **126** 7 50S 39 45E
Mafia I. **126** 7 45S 39 50E
Mafou **109** 31 34N 115 15E
Mafra, Brazil **173** 26 10N 50 0W
Mafra, Port. **57** 38 55N 9 20W
Mafungabusi Plateau **127** 18 30S 29 8E
Magadan **77** 59 30N 151 0E
Magadi **126** 1 54S 36 19E
Magadi, L. **126** 1 54S 36 19E
Magaliesburg **129** 26 1S 27 32E
Magallanes, Estrecho de **176** 52 30S 75 0W
Magangué **174** 9 14N 74 45W
Magaria **121** 13 4N 9 5W
Magburaka **120** 8 47N 12 0W
Magdal **90** 32 51N 35 30E
*Renamed Mafikeng

Magdalen Is. = Madeleine, Is. de la **151** 47 30N 61 40W
Magdalena, Argent. **172** 35 5S 57 30W
Magdalena, Boliv. **174** 13 13S 63 57W
Magdalena, Mexico **164** 30 50N 112 0W
Magdalena, U.S.A. **161** 34 10N 107 20W
Magdalena □ **174** 10 0N 74 0W
Magdalena, B. **164** 24 30N 112 10W
Magdalena, I. **164** 24 40N 112 15W
Magdalena, Llano de la **164** 25 0N 111 30W
Magdalena, mt. **102** 4 25N 117 55E
Magdalena, R., Colomb. **174** 8 30N 74 0W
Magdalena, R., Mexico **164** 30 50N 112 0W
Magdeburg **48** 52 8N 11 36E
Magdeburg □ **48** 52 20N 11 40E
Magdelaine Cays **138** 16 33S 150 18E
Magdiel **90** 32 10N 34 54E
Magdub **123** 13 42N 25 5E
Magee **159** 31 53N 89 45W
Magee, I. **38** 54 48N 5 44W
Magelang **103** 7 29S 110 13E
Magellan's Str. **176** 52 30S 75 0W
Magellan's Str. = Magallanes, Est. de **176** 52 30S 75 0W
Magenta, Austral. **140** 33 51S 143 34E
Magenta, Italy **62** 45 28N 8 53E
Magenta, L. **137** 33 30S 119 10E
Maggea **140** 34 28S 140 2E
Maggia **51** 46 15N 8 42E
Maggia, R. **51** 46 18N 8 36E
Maggiorasca, Mt. **62** 44 33N 9 29E
Maggiore, L. **62** 46 0N 8 35E
Maghama **120** 15 32N 12 57W
Maghar **90** 32 54N 35 24E
Maghera **38** 54 51N 6 40W
Magherafelt **38** 54 44N 6 37W
Maghnia **118** 34 50N 1 43W
Maghull **32** 53 31N 2 56W
Magilligan **38** 55 10N 6 53W
Magilligan Pt. **38** 55 10N 6 58W
Magione **63** 43 10N 12 12E
Maglaj **66** 44 33N 18 7E
Magliano in Toscana **63** 42 36N 11 18E
Máglie **65** 40 8N 18 17E
Magnac-Laval **44** 46 13N 1 11E
Magnetic Pole, 1976, (South) **13** 68 48S 139 30E
Magnetic Pole, 1976(North) **12** 76 12N 100 12W
Magnisia □ **69** 39 24N 22 46E
Magnitogorsk **84** 53 27N 59 4E
Magnolia, Ark., U.S.A. **159** 33 18N 93 12W
Magnolia, Miss., U.S.A. **159** 31 8N 90 28W
Magnor **71** 59 56N 12 15E
Magnus, oilfield **19** 61 40N 1 20E
Magny-en-Vexin **43** 49 9N 1 47E
Màgoé **127** 15 45S 31 42E
Magog **151** 45 18N 72 9W
Magoro **126** 1 45N 34 12E
Magosta = Famagusta **92** 35 8N 33 55E
Magoye **127** 16 1S 27 30E
Magpie L. **151** 51 0N 64 40W
Magrath **152** 49 25N 112 50W
Magro, R. **59** 39 20N 0 45W
Magruder Mt. **163** 37 25N 117 33W
Magrur, W. **123** 16 5N 26 30E
Magu □ **126** 2 45S 33 15E
Maguarinho, C. **170** 0 15S 48 30W
Maguire's Bri. **38** 54 18N 7 28W
Maguse L. **153** 61 40N 95 10W
Maguse Pt. **153** 61 20N 93 50W
Maguse River **153** 61 20N 94 25W
Magwe **98** 20 10N 95 0E
Maha Sarakham **100** 16 12N 103 16E
Mahābād **92** 36 50N 45 45E
Mahabaleshwar **96** 17 58N 73 50E
Mahabarat Lekh **95** 28 30N 82 0E
Mahabo **129** 20 23S 44 40E
Mahad **96** 18 6N 73 29E
Mahadeo Hills **94** 22 20N 78 30E
Mahadeopur **96** 18 48N 80 0E
Mahagi **126** 2 20N 31 0E
Mahajamba, B. de la **129** 15 24S 47 5E
Mahajamba, R. **129** 17 0S 47 30E
Mahajan **94** 28 48N 73 56E
Mahajilo, R. **129** 19 30S 46 0E
Mahakam, R. **102** 1 0N 114 40E
Mahalapye **128** 23 1S 26 51E
Mahalla el Kubra **122** 31 10N 31 0E
Mahallāt **93** 33 55N 50 30E
Mahanadi R. **96** 20 33N 85 0E
Mahanagh **38** 53 31N 8 42W
Mahanoro **129** 19 54S 48 48E
Mahanoy City **162** 40 48N 76 10W
Maharashtra □ **96** 19 30N 75 30E
Maharès **119** 34 32N 10 29E
Mahari Mts. **126** 6 20S 30 0E
Mahasolo **129** 19 7S 46 22E
Mahaweli Ganga **97** 8 0N 81 10E
Mahaxay **100** 17 22N 105 48E
Mahboobabad **96** 17 42N 80 2E
Mahbubnagar **96** 16 45N 77 59E
Mahd Dhahab **92** 25 55N 45 30E
Mahdia **119** 35 28N 11 0E
Mahé **97** 11 42N 75 34E
Mahe **95** 33 10N 78 32E
Mahendra Giri, mt. **97** 8 20N 77 30E
Mahendraganj **98** 25 20N 89 45E
Mahenge **127** 8 45S 36 35E
Maheno **143** 45 10S 170 50E
Mahia Pen. **142** 39 9S 177 55E
Mahirija **118** 34 0N 3 16W

Mahlaing **98** 21 6N 95 39E
Mahmiya **123** 17 5N 33 50E
Mahmud Kot **94** 30 16N 71 0E
Mahmudia **70** 45 5N 29 5E
Mahnomen **158** 47 22N 95 57W
Mahoba **95** 25 15N 79 55E
Mahón **58** 39 50N 4 18E
Mahone Bay **151** 44 30N 64 20W
Mahopac **162** 41 22N 73 45W
Mahsü **108** 30 31N 100 19E
Mahukona **147** 20 11N 155 52W
Mahuta **121** 11 32N 4 58E
Mai-Ndombe, L. **124** 2 0S 18 0E
Mai-Sai **100** 20 20N 99 55E
Maibara **111** 35 19N 136 17E
Maîche **43** 47 16N 6 48E
Maicuru, R. **175** 1 0S 54 30W
Máida **65** 38 51N 16 21E
Maidan Khula **94** 33 36N 69 50E
Maiden Bradley **28** 51 9N 2 18W
Maiden Newton **28** 50 46N 2 35W
Maidenhead **29** 51 31N 0 42W
Maidi **123** 16 20N 42 45E
Maidstone, Can. **153** 53 5N 109 20W
Maidstone, U.K. **29** 51 16N 0 31E
Maiduguri **121** 12 0N 13 20E
Maignelay **43** 49 32N 2 30E
Maigualida, Sierra **174** 5 30N 65 10W
Maijdi **98** 22 48N 91 10E
Maikala Ra. **96** 22 0N 81 0E
Mailly-le-Camp **43** 48 41N 4 12E
Mailsi **94** 29 48N 72 15E
Maimana **93** 35 53N 64 38E
Main Barrier Ra. **133** 31 10S 141 20E
Main Centre **153** 50 35N 107 21W
Main Coast Ra. **138** 16 22S 145 10E
Main, R., Ger. **49** 50 13N 11 0E
Main, R., U.K. **38** 54 49N 6 20W
Mainburg **49** 48 37N 11 49E
Maindargi **96** 17 33N 74 21E
Maine **42** 48 0N 0 0E
Maine □ **151** 45 20N 69 0W
Maine-et-Loire □ **42** 47 31N 0 30W
Maine, R. **39** 52 10N 9 40W
Maïne-Soroa **121** 13 13N 12 2E
Maingkwan **98** 26 15N 96 45E
Mainit, L. **103** 9 31N 125 30E
Mainkaing **98** 24 48N 95 16E
Mainland, I., Orkneys, U.K. **37** 59 0N 3 10W
Mainland, I., Shetlands, U.K. **36** 60 15N 1 22W
Mainpuri **95** 27 18N 79 4E
Maintenon **43** 48 35N 1 35E
Maintirano **129** 18 3S 44 1E
Mainvault **47** 50 39N 3 43E
Mainz **49** 50 0N 8 17E
Maipú **172** 37 0S 58 0W
Maipures **174** 5 11N 67 49W
Maiquetía **174** 10 36N 66 57W
Maira, R. **62** 44 29N 7 15E
Mairabari **98** 26 30N 92 30E
Mairipotaba **171** 17 18S 49 28W
Maisi **167** 20 17N 74 9W
Maisi, C. **167** 20 10N 74 10W
Maisse **43** 48 24N 2 21E
Maissin **47** 49 58N 5 10E
Maitland, N.S.W., Austral. **141** 32 44S 151 36E
Maitland, S. Australia, Austral. **140** 34 23S 137 40E
Maitland, L. **137** 27 11S 121 3E
Maiyema **121** 12 5N 4 25E
Maíz, Islas del **166** 12 15N 83 4W
Maizuru **111** 35 25N 135 22E
Majagual **174** 8 33N 74 38W
Majalengka **103** 6 55S 108 14E
Majd el Kurum **90** 32 56N 35 15E
Majene **103** 3 27S 118 57E
Majevica Planina **66** 44 45N 18 50E
Maji **123** 6 20N 35 30E
Major **153** 51 52N 109 37W
Majorca, I. = Mallorca, I. **58** 39 30N 3 0E
Majors Creek **141** 35 33S 149 45E
Majunga **125** 15 40S 46 25E
Majunga □ **129** 17 0S 47 0E
Maka **120** 13 40N 14 10W
Makak **121** 3 36N 11 0E
Makale **103** 3 6S 119 51E
Makamba **126** 4 8S 29 49E
Makamik **150** 48 45N 79 0W
Makapuu Hd. **147** 21 19N 157 39W
Makarewa **143** 46 20S 168 21E
Makari **124** 12 35N 14 28E
Makarikari = Makgadikgadi **128** 20 40S 25 45E
Makarovo **77** 57 40N 107 45E
Makarska **66** 43 20N 17 2E
Makaryev **81** 57 52N 43 50E
Makasar = Ujung Pandang **103** 5 10S 119 20E
Makasar, Selat **103** 1 0S 118 20E
Makat **76** 47 39N 53 19E
Makedhonía □ **68** 40 39N 22 0E
Makedonija □ **66** 41 53N 21 40E
Makena **147** 20 39N 156 27W
Makeni **120** 8 55N 12 5W
Maker **30** 50 20N 4 10W
Makeyevka **82** 48 0N 38 0E
Makgadikgadi **128** 20 40S 25 45E
Makgadikgadi Salt Pans **128** 20 40S 25 45E
Makgobistad **128** 25 45S 25 12E

Makhachkala **Manitou I**

Makhachkala 83 43 0N 47 15 E
Makharadze 83 41 55N 42 2 E
Makian, I. 103 0 12N 127 20 E
†Makin, I. 130 3 30N 174 0 E
Makindu 124 2 7 S 37 40 E
Makinsk 76 52 37N 70 26 E
Makkah 122 21 30N 39 54 E
Makkovik 151 55 0N 59 10W
Makkum 46 53 3N 5 25 E
Maklakovo 77 58 16N 92 29 E
Makó 53 46 14N 20 33 E
Makokou 124 0 40N 12 50 E
Makongo 126 3 15N 26 17 E
Makoro 126 3 10N 29 59 E
Makoua 124 0 5 S 15 50 E
Maków Podhal 54 49 43N 19 45 E
Makrá, I. 69 36 15N 25 54 E
Makrai 93 22 2N 77 0 E
Makran 93 26 13N 61 30 E
Makran Coast Range 93 25 40N 4 0 E
Makrana 94 27 2N 74 46 E
Mákri 68 40 52N 25 40 E
Maksimkin Yar 76 58 58N 86 50 E
Maktar 119 35 48N 9 12 E
Mākū 92 39 15N 44 31 E
Makuan 108 23 2N 104 24 E
Makum 98 27 30N 95 23 E
Makumbe 128 20 15 S 24 26 E
Makumbi 124 5 50 S 20 43 E
Makunda 128 22 30 S 20 7 E
Makurazaki 110 31 15N 130 20 E
Makurdi 120 7 43N 8 28 E
Makwassie 128 27 17 S 26 0 E
Mal 98 26 51N 86 45 E
Mal B. 39 52 50N 9 30W
Mal-i-Gjalicës së Lumës 68 42 2N 20 25 E
Mal i Gribës 68 40 17N 9 45 E
Mal i Nemërçkës 68 40 15N 20 15 E
Mal i Tomorit 68 40 42N 20 11 E
Mala Kapela 63 44 45N 15 30 E
Mala, Pta. 166 7 28N 80 2W
Malabang 103 7 36N 124 3 E
Malabar Coast 97 11 0N 75 0 E
Malacca = Melaka 101 2 15N 102 15 E
Malacca, Str. of 101 3 0N 101 0 E
Malacky 53 48 27N 17 0 E
Malad City 160 41 10N 112 20 E
Maladetta, Mt. 59 42 40N 0 30 E
Malafaburi 123 10 37N 40 30 E
Málaga, Colomb. 174 6 42N 72 44W
Málaga, Spain 57 36 43N 4 23W
Malaga 159 32 12N 104 2W
Málaga □ 57 36 38N 4 58W
Malagarasi 126 5 5 S 30 50 E
Malagarasi, R. 126 3 50 S 30 30 E
Malagasy Rep. ■ = Madagascar ■ 129 20 0 S 47 0 E
Malagón 57 39 11N 3 52W
Malagón, R. 57 37 40N 7 20W
Malahide 38 53 26N 6 10W
Malaimbandy 129 20 20 S 45 36 E
Malakâl 123 9 33N 31 50 E
Malakand 94 34 40N 71 55 E
Malakoff 159 32 10N 95 55W
Malakwa 152 50 55N 118 50W
Malamyzh 77 50 0N 136 50 E
Malang 103 7 59 S 112 35 E
Malanje 124 9 30 S 16 17 E
Mälaren 72 59 30N 17 10 E
Malargüe 172 35 40 S 69 30W
Malartic 150 48 9N 78 9W
Malatya 92 38 25N 38 20 E
Malawi ■ 127 13 0 S 34 0 E
Malawi, L. (Lago Niassa) 127 12 30 S 34 30 E
Malay Pen. 101 7 25N 100 0 E
•Malaya □ 101 4 0N 102 0 E
Malaya Belözerka 82 47 12N 34 56 E
Malaya Vishera 80 58 55N 32 25 E
Malaybalay 103 8 5N 125 15 E
Malayer 92 34 19N 48 51 E
Malaysia ■ 102 5 0N 110 0 E
•Malaysia, Western □ 101 5 0N 102 0 E
Malazgirt 92 39 10N 42 33 E
Malbaie, La 151 47 40N 70 10W
Malbon 138 21 5 S 140 17 E
Malbooma 139 30 41 S 134 11 E
Malbork 54 54 3N 19 10 E
Malca Dube 123 6 40N 41 52 E
Malchin 48 53 43N 12 44 E
Malchow 48 53 29N 12 25 E
Malcolm 137 28 51 S 121 25 E
Malcolm, Pt., S. Australia, Austral. 109 34 52 S 138 29 E
Malcolm, Pt., W. Australia, Austral. 137 33 48 S 123 45 E
Malczyce 54 51 14N 16 29 E
Maldegem 47 51 14N 3 26 E
Malden, Mass., U.S.A. 162 42 26N 71 5W
Malden, Mo., U.S.A. 159 36 35N 90 0W
Malden I. 143 4 3 S 155 1W
Maldive Is. ■ 86 2 0N 73 0W
Maldon, Austral. 140 37 0 S 144 6 E
Maldon, U.K. 29 51 43N 0 41 E
Maldonado 173 35 0 S 55 0W
Maldonado, Punta 165 16 19N 98 35W
Malé 62 46 20N 10 55 E
Malé Karpaty 53 48 30N 17 20 E
Maléa, Ákra 69 36 28N 23 7 E
Malegaon 96 20 30N 74 30 E
Malei 127 17 12 S 36 58 E
Malela 126 4 22 S 26 8 E
Malenge 127 12 40 S 26 42 E
Målerås 73 56 54N 15 34 E
Malerkotla 94 30 32N 75 58 E
Máles 69 36 6N 25 35 E
Malesherbes 43 48 15N 2 24 E
Maleske Planina 66 41 38N 23 7 E
Malestroit 42 47 49N 2 25W
Malfa 65 38 35N 14 50 E
Malgobek 83 43 30N 44 52 E
Malgomaj L. 74 64 40N 16 30 E
Malgrat 58 41 39N 2 46 E
Malham Tarn 32 54 6N 2 11W
Malhão, Sa. do 55 37 25N 8 0W
Malheur L. 160 43 19N 118 42W
Malheur, R. 160 43 55N 117 55W
Mali 120 12 10N 12 20W
Mali ■ 121 15 0N 10 0W
Mali H Ka R. 98 25 42N 97 30 E
Mali Kanal 66 45 36N 19 24 E
Mali Kyun, I. 101 13 0N 98 20 E
Mali, R. 99 26 20N 97 40 E
Malibu 163 34 2N 118 41W
Malih, Nahr al 90 32 20N 35 29 E
Malik 103 0 39 S 123 16 E
Malili 103 2 42 S 121 23 E
Malimba, Mts. 126 7 30 S 29 30 E
Malin, Ireland 38 55 18N 7 16W
Malin, U.S.S.R. 80 50 46N 29 15 E
Malin Hd. 38 55 18N 7 16W
Malin Pen. 38 55 20N 7 17W
Malinau 102 3 35N 116 30 E
Malindi 126 3 12 S 40 5 E
Maling, Mt. 103 1 0N 121 0 E
Malingping 103 6 45 S 106 2 E
Malinyi 127 8 56 S 36 0 E
Maliqi 68 40 45N 20 48 E
Malita 103 6 19N 125 39 E
Malkapur, Maharashtra, India 96 16 57N 74 0W
Malkapur, Maharashtra, India 96 20 53N 76 17 E
Małkinia Grn. 54 52 42N 21 58 E
Malko Turnovo 67 41 59N 27 31 E
Mallacoota 141 37 40 S 149 40 E
Mallacoota Inlet 141 37 40 S 149 40 E
Mallaha 90 33 6N 35 35 E
Mallaig 36 57 0N 5 50W
Mallala 140 34 26 S 138 30 E
Mallawan 95 27 4N 80 12 E
Mallawi 122 27 44N 30 44 E
Mallemort 45 43 44N 5 11 E
Málles Venosta 62 46 42N 10 32 E
Mállia 69 35 17N 25 27 E
Mallina P.O. 136 20 53 S 118 2 E
Mallorca, I. 58 39 30N 3 0 E
Mallow 39 52 8N 8 40W
Malltraeth B. 31 53 7N 4 30W
Mallwyd 31 52 43N 3 41W
Malmbäck 73 57 34N 14 28 E
Malmberget 74 67 11N 20 40 E
Malmédy 47 50 25N 6 2 E
Malmesbury, S. Afr. 128 33 28 S 18 41 E
Malmesbury, U.K. 28 51 35N 2 5W
Malmö 75 55 36N 12 59 E
Malmöhus län □ 73 55 45N 13 30 E
Malmslätt 73 58 27N 15 33 E
Malmyzh 84 56 31N 50 41 E
Malmyzh Mozhga 81 56 35N 50 30 E
Malnaş 70 46 2N 25 49 E
Malo Konare 67 42 12N 24 24 E
Maloarkhangelsk 81 52 28N 36 30 E
Maloja 51 46 25N 9 35 E
Maloja Pass 51 46 23N 9 42 E
Malolos 103 14 50N 121 2 E
Malomalsk 84 58 45N 59 53 E
Malombe L. 127 14 40 S 35 15 E
Malomir 67 42 16N 26 30 E
Malone 156 44 50N 74 19W
Malorad 67 43 28N 23 41 E
Malorita 80 51 41N 24 3 E
Maloyaroslovets 81 55 2N 36 20 E
Malozemelskaya Tundra 78 67 0N 50 0 E
Malpartida 57 39 26N 6 30W
Malpas 32 53 3N 2 47W
Malpelo I. 174 4 3N 80 35W
Malpica 56 43 19N 8 50W
Malprabha, R. 97 15 40N 74 50 E
Malta, Brazil 170 6 54 S 37 31W
Malta, Idaho, U.S.A. 160 42 15N 113 50W
Malta, Mont., U.S.A. 160 48 20N 107 55W
Malta ■ 64 35 50N 14 0 E
Maltahöhe 125 24 55 S 17 0 E
Maltby 33 53 25N 1 12W
Malters 50 47 3N 8 11 E
Malton 33 54 9N 0 48W
Maluku □ 103 3 0 S 128 0 E
Maluku, Kepulauan 103 3 0 S 128 0 E
Malumfashi 121 11 48N 7 39 E
Malung, China 108 25 18N 103 20 E
Malung, Sweden 72 60 42N 13 44 E
Malvalli 97 12 28N 77 8 E
Malvan 97 16 2N 73 30 E
Malvern, U.K. 28 52 7N 2 19W
Malvern, U.S.A. 159 34 22N 92 50W
Malvern Hills 28 52 0N 2 19W
Malvern Wells 28 52 4N 2 19W
Malvérnia 129 22 6 S 31 42 E
Malvik 71 63 25N 10 40 E
Malvinas Is. = Falkland Is. 174 51 30 S 59 0W
Malya 126 3 5 S 33 38 E
Malybay 85 43 30N 78 25 E
Mama 77 58 18N 112 54 E
Mamadysh 81 55 44N 51 23 E
Mamaia 70 44 18N 28 37 E
Mamaku 142 38 5 S 176 8 E
Mamanguape 170 6 50 S 35 4W
Mamasa 103 2 55 S 119 20 E
Mambasa 126 1 22N 29 3 E
Mamberamo, R. 103 2 0 S 137 50 E
Mambilima Falls 127 10 31 S 28 45 E
Mambirima 127 11 25 S 27 33 E
Mambo 126 4 52 S 38 22 E
Mambrui 126 3 5 S 40 5 E
Mameigwess L. 150 52 35N 87 50W
Mamer 47 49 38N 6 2 E
Mamers 42 48 21N 0 22 E
Mamfe 121 5 50N 9 15 E
Mammamattawa 150 50 25N 84 23W
Mámmola 65 38 23N 16 13 E
Mammoth 161 32 46N 110 43W
Mamoré, R. 175 9 55 S 65 20W
Mamou 120 10 15N 12 0W
Mampatá 120 11 54N 14 53W
Mampawah 102 0 30N 109 5 E
Mampong 121 7 6N 1 26W
Mamuju 103 2 50 S 118 50 E
Man 120 7 30N 7 40W
Man, I. of 32 54 15N 4 30W
Man Na 98 23 27N 97 19 E
Man O' War Peak 151 56 58N 61 40W
Man, R. 96 17 20N 75 0 E
Man Tun 98 23 2N 98 38 E
Mana, Fr. Gui. 175 5 45N 53 55W
Mana, U.S.A. 147 22 3N 159 45W
Mana, R. 123 6 20N 40 41 E
Måna, R. 71 59 55N 8 50 E
Manaar, Gulf of 97 8 30N 79 0 E
Manacacias, R. 174 4 23N 72 4W
Manacapuru 174 3 10 S 60 50W
Manacles, The 30 50 3N 5 5W
Manacor 58 39 32N 3 12 E
Manage 47 50 31N 4 15 E
Managua 166 12 0N 86 20W
Managua, L. 166 12 20N 86 30W
Manaia 142 39 33 S 174 8 E
Manakana 129 13 45 S 50 4 E
Manakara 129 22 8 S 48 1 E
Manakau Mt. 143 42 15 S 173 42 E
Manam I. 135 4 5 S 145 0 E
Manamâh, Al 93 26 11N 50 35 E
Manambao, R. 129 17 35 S 44 45 E
Manambato 129 13 43 S 49 7 E
Manambolo, R. 129 19 20 S 45 0 E
Manambolosy 129 16 2 S 49 40 E
Mananara 129 16 10 S 49 30 E
Mananara, R. 129 23 25 S 48 10 E
Mananjary 129 21 13 S 48 20 E
Manantenina 129 24 17 S 47 19 E
Manaos = Manaus 174 3 0 S 60 0W
Manapouri 143 45 34 S 167 39 E
Manapouri, L. 143 45 32 S 167 32 E
Manar, R. 96 18 50N 77 20 E
Manas, Gora 85 42 22N 71 2 E
Manas, R. 99 26 12N 90 40 E
Manasarowar, L. 105 30 45N 81 20 E
Manasarowar L. 105 30 45N 81 20 E
Manasir 93 24 30N 51 10 E
Manaslu, Mt. 95 28 33N 84 33 E
Manasquan 162 40 7N 74 3W
Manassa 161 37 12N 105 58W
Manassas 162 38 45N 77 28W
Manassu 105 44 18N 86 13 E
Manati 147 18 26N 66 29W
Manaung Kyun 98 18 45N 93 40 E
Manaus 174 3 0 S 60 0W
Manawan L. 153 55 24N 103 14W
Manawatu, R. 142 40 28 S 175 12 E
Manay 103 7 17N 126 33 E
Manby 33 53 22N 0 6 E
Mancelona 156 44 54N 85 5W
Mancha, La 59 39 10N 2 54W
Mancha Real 57 37 48N 3 39W
Manchaster, L. 108 27 29 S 152 46 E
Manche □ 42 49 10N 1 20W
Manchester, U.K. 32 53 30N 2 15W
Manchester, Conn., U.S.A. 162 41 47N 72 30W
Manchester, Ga., U.S.A. 157 32 53N 84 32W
Manchester, Iowa, U.S.A. 158 42 28N 91 27W
Manchester, Ky., U.S.A. 156 38 40N 83 45W
Manchester, N.H., U.S.A. 162 42 58N 71 29W
Manchester, Pa., U.S.A. 162 40 4N 76 43W
Manchester, Vt., U.S.A. 162 43 10N 73 5W
Manchester L. 153 61 28N 107 29W
Manchouli 105 49 46N 117 24 E
Manchuria = Tung Pei 107 44 0N 126 0 E
Manciano 63 42 35N 11 30 E
Mancifa 123 6 53N 41 50 E
Mand, R. 93 28 20N 52 30 E
Manda, Chunya, Tanz. 127 6 51 S 32 29 E
Manda, Jombe, Tanz. 127 10 30 S 34 40 E
Mandabé 125 21 0 S 44 55 E
Mandaguari 173 23 32 S 51 42W
Mandah 106 44 27N 108 20 E
Mandal 71 58 2N 7 25 E
Mandalay 99 22 0N 96 10 E
Mandalay = Mandale 98 22 0N 96 10 E
Mandale 99 22 0N 96 10 E
Mandalgovi 106 45 45N 106 20 E
Mandali 92 33 52N 45 28 E
Mandalya Körfezi 69 37 15N 27 20 E
Mandan 158 46 50N 101 0W
Mandapeta 96 16 47N 81 56 E
Mandar, Teluk 103 3 35 S 119 4 E
Mandas 64 39 40N 9 8 E
Mandasaur 93 24 3N 75 8 E
Mandasor (Mandsaur) 94 24 3N 75 8 E
Mandawai (Katingan), R. 102 1 30 S 113 0 E
Mandelieu-la-Napoule 45 43 34N 6 57 E
Mandera 126 3 55N 41 42 E
Mandera □ 126 3 30N 41 0 E
Manderfeld 47 50 20N 6 20 E
Mandi, India 94 31 39N 76 58 E
Mandi, Zambia 127 14 30 S 23 45 E
Mandimba 125 14 20 S 35 40 E
Mandioli 103 0 40 S 127 20 E
Mandla 95 22 39N 80 30 E
Mandø 73 55 18N 8 33 E
Mandoto 129 19 34 S 46 17 E
Mandoúdhion 69 38 48N 23 29 E
Mandra 94 33 23N 73 12 E
Mandráki 69 36 36N 27 11 E
Mandrase, R. 129 25 10 S 46 30 E
Mandritsara 129 15 50 S 48 49 E
Mandsaur (Mandasor) 94 24 3N 75 8 E
Mandurah 137 32 36 S 115 48 E
Mandúria 65 40 25N 17 38 E
Mandvi 96 22 51N 69 22 E
Mandya 97 12 30N 77 0 E
Mandzai 94 30 55N 67 6 E
Mané 121 12 59N 1 21W
Manea 29 52 29N 0 10 E
Maner, R. 97 18 30N 79 40 E
Maneroo 138 23 22 S 143 53 E
Maneroo Cr. 138 23 21 S 143 53 E
Manfalût 122 27 20N 30 52 E
Manfred 140 33 19 S 143 45 E
Manfredónia 65 41 40N 15 55 E
Manfredónia, G. di 65 41 30N 16 10 E
Manga, Brazil 171 14 46 S 43 56W
Manga, Upp. Vol. 121 11 40N 1 4W
Mangabeiras, Chapada das 170 10 0 S 46 30W
Mangahan 142 40 26 S 175 48 E
Mangalagiri 96 16 26N 80 36 E
Mangaldai 98 26 26N 92 2 E
Mangalia 70 43 50N 28 35 E
Mangalore, Austral. 141 36 56 S 145 10 E
Mangalore, India 97 12 55N 74 47 E
Manganeses 56 41 45N 5 43W
Mangaon 96 18 15N 73 20 E
Manger 71 60 38N 5 3W
Mangerton Mt. 39 51 59N 9 30W
Manggar 102 2 50 S 108 10 E
Manggawitu 103 4 8 S 133 32 E
Mangin Range 98 24 15N 95 45 E
Mangla Dam 95 33 32N 73 50 E
Manglaur 94 29 44N 77 49 E
Mangoche 125 14 25 S 35 16 E
Mangoky, R. 129 21 29 S 44 40 E
Mangole I. 103 1 50 S 125 55 E
Mangombe 126 1 20 S 26 48 E
Mangonui 142 35 1 S 173 32 E
Mangotsfield 28 51 29N 2 29W
Mangualde 56 40 38N 7 48W
Mangueigne 117 10 40N 21 5 E
Mangueira, Lagoa da 173 33 0 S 52 50W
Manguéni, Hamada 119 22 47N 12 56 E
Mangum 159 34 50N 99 30W
Mangyai 105 37 50N 91 38 E
Mangyshlak P-ov. 83 43 40N 52 30 E
Manhattan, Kans., U.S.A. 158 39 10N 96 40W
Manhattan, Nev., U.S.A. 163 38 31N 117 3W
Manhiça 129 25 23 S 32 49 E
Manhuaçu 171 20 15 S 42 2W
Manhui 106 41 1N 107 14 E
Manhumirim 171 20 22 S 41 57W
Mani 99 34 52N 87 11 E
Maní 174 4 49N 72 17W
Mania, R. 129 19 55 S 46 10 E
Maniago 63 46 11N 12 40 E
Manica 127 18 58 S 32 59 E
Manica e Sofala □ 129 19 10 S 33 45 E
Manicaland □ 127 19 0 S 32 30 E
Manicoré 174 6 0 S 61 10W
Manicouagan L. 151 51 25N 68 15W
Manicouagan, R. 151 49 30N 68 30W
Manifah 92 27 30N 49 0 E
Manifold 138 22 41 S 150 40 E
Manigotagan 153 51 6N 96 8W
Manigotagan L. 153 50 52N 95 37W
Manihiki I. 131 10 24 S 161 1W
Manika, Plat. de 127 10 0 S 25 5 E
Manikganj 98 23 52N 90 0 E
Manila, Phil. 103 14 40N 121 3 E
Manila, U.S.A. 160 41 0N 109 44W
Manila B. 103 14 0N 120 0 E
Manilla 141 30 45 S 150 43 E
Manimpé 120 14 11N 5 28W
Maningory 129 17 9 S 49 30 E
Manipur □ 98 24 30N 94 0 E
Manipur, R. 98 23 45N 93 40 E
Manisa 92 38 38N 27 30 E
Manistee 156 44 15N 86 20W
Manistee, R. 156 44 15N 86 21W
Manistique 156 45 59N 86 18W
Manito L. 153 52 43N 109 43W
Manitoba □ 153 55 30N 97 0W
Manitoba, L. 153 51 0N 98 45W
Manitou 153 49 15N 98 32W
Manitou I. 150 47 22N 87 30W

* Renamed Peninsular Malaysia
† Renamed Butaritari

Manitou Is		Marosakoa

Manitou Is.	156	45 8N	86 0W
Manitou L., Ont., Can.	153	49 15N	93 0W
Manitou L., Qué., Can.	151	50 55N	65 17W
Manitoulin I.	150	45 40N	82 30W
Manitowaning	150	45 46N	81 49W
Manitowoc	156	44 8N	87 40W
Manizales	174	5 5N	75 32W
Manja	129	21 26S	44 20E
Manjacaze	125	24 45S	34 0E
Manjakandriana	129	18 55S	47 47E
Manjeri	97	11 7N	76 11E
Manjhand	94	25 50N	68 10E
Manjil	92	36 46N	49 30E
Manjimup	137	34 15S	116 6E
Manjra, R.	96	18 20N	77 20E
Mankaiana	129	26 38S	31 6E
Mankato, Kans., U.S.A.	158	39 49N	98 11W
Mankato, Minn., U.S.A.	158	44 8N	93 59W
Mankono	120	8 10N	6 10W
Mankota	153	49 25N	107 5W
Manlay	106	44 9N	106 50E
Manlleu	58	42 2N	2 17E
Manly, N.S.W., Austral.	141	33 48S	151 17E
Manly, Queens., Austral.	108	27 27S	153 11E
Manmad	96	20 18N	74 28E
Mann Ranges, Mts.	137	26 6S	130 5E
Manna	102	4 25S	102 55E
Mannahill	140	32 25S	140 0E
Mannar	97	9 1N	79 54E
Mannar, G. of	97	8 30N	79 0E
Mannar I.	97	9 5N	79 45E
Mannargudi	97	10 45N	79 32E
Männedorf	51	47 15N	8 43E
Mannheim	49	49 28N	8 29E
Manning, Can.	152	56 53N	117 39W
Manning, U.S.A.	157	33 40N	80 9W
Manning Prov. Park	152	49 5N	120 45W
Mannington	156	39 35N	80 25W
Manningtree	29	51 56N	1 3E
Mannu, C.	64	40 2N	8 24E
Mannu, R.	64	39 35N	8 56E
Mannum	140	34 57S	139 12E
Mano	120	8 3N	12 12W
Manokwari	103	0 54S	134 0E
Manolás	69	38 4N	21 21E
Manombo	129	22 57S	43 28E
Manono	124	7 15S	27 25E
Manorbier	31	51 38N	4 48W
Manorhamilton	38	54 19N	8 11W
Manosque	45	43 49N	5 47E
Manouane L.	151	50 45N	70 45W
Manpojin	107	41 6N	126 24E
Manresa	58	41 48N	1 50E
Mans, Le	42	48 0N	0 10E
Mansa, Gujarat, India	94	23 27N	72 45E
Mansa, Punjab, India	94	30 0N	75 27E
Mansa, Zambia	127	11 13S	28 55E
Mansel I.	149	62 0N	79 50W
Mansenra	94	34 20N	73 11E
Mansfield, Austral.	141	37 4S	146 6E
Mansfield, U.K.	33	53 8N	1 12W
Mansfield, La., U.S.A.	159	32 2N	93 40W
Mansfield, Mass., U.S.A.	162	42 2N	71 12W
Mansfield, Ohio, U.S.A.	156	40 45N	82 30W
Mansfield, Pa., U.S.A.	162	41 48N	77 4W
Mansfield, Wash., U.S.A.	160	47 51N	119 44W
Mansfield Woodhouse	33	53 11N	1 11W
Mansi	98	24 40N	95 44E
Mansidão	170	10 43S	44 2W
Mansilla de las Mulas	56	42 30N	5 25W
Mansle	44	45 52N	0 9E
Manso, R.	171	14 0S	52 0W
Mansôa	120	12 0N	15 20W
Manson Cr.	152	55 37N	124 25W
Mansoura, Djebel	119	36 1N	4 31E
Manta	174	1 0S	80 40W
Mantalingajan, Mt.	102	8 55N	117 45E
Mantare	126	2 42S	33 13E
Manteca	163	37 50N	121 12W
Mantecal	174	7 34N	69 17W
Mantekomu Hu	99	34 40N	89 0E
Mantena	171	18 47S	40 59W
Manteo	157	35 55N	75 41W
Mantes-la-Jolie	43	49 0N	1 41E
Manthani	96	18 40N	79 35E
Manthelan	42	47 9N	0 47E
Manti	160	39 23N	111 32W
Mantiqueira, Serra da	173	22 0S	44 0W
Manton, U.K.	29	52 37N	0 41W
Manton, U.S.A.	156	44 23N	85 25W
Mantorp	73	58 21N	15 20E
Mántova	62	45 10N	10 47E
Mänttä	74	62 0N	24 40E
Mantua = Mántova	62	45 10N	10 47E
Mantung	140	34 35S	140 3E
Manturova	81	58 10N	44 30E
Manu	174	12 10S	71 0W
Manucan	103	8 14N	123 3E
Manuel Alves Grande, R.	170	7 27S	47 35W
Manuel Alves, R.	171	11 19S	48 28W
Manui I.	103	3 35S	123 5E
Manukau	142	37 1S	174 55E
Manukau Harbour	142	37 3S	174 45E
Manunui	142	38 54S	175 21E
Manus I.	135	2 0S	147 0E
Manvi	97	15 57N	76 59E
Manville, R.I., U.S.A.	162	41 58N	71 28W
Manville, Wyo., U.S.A.	158	42 48N	104 36W
Manwath	96	19 19N	76 32E
Many	159	31 36N	93 28W
Manyane	128	23 21S	21 42E
Manyara L.	126	3 40S	35 50E
Manych-Gudilo, Oz.	83	46 24N	42 38E
Manych, R.	83	47 0N	41 15E
Manyonga, R.	126	4 5S	34 0E
Manyoni	126	5 45S	34 55E
Manyoni □	126	6 30S	34 30E
Manzai	94	32 20N	70 15E
Manzala, Bahra el	122	31 10N	31 56E
Manzanares	59	39 0N	3 22W
Manzaneda, Cabeza de	56	42 12N	7 15W
Manzanillo, Cuba	166	20 20N	77 10W
Manzanillo, Mexico	164	19 0N	104 20W
Manzanillo, Pta.	166	9 30N	79 40W
Manzano Mts.	161	34 30N	106 45W
Manzini	129	26 30S	31 25E
Mao	117	14 4N	15 19E
Maohsing	107	45 31N	124 32E
Maoke, Pengunungan	102	3 40S	137 30E
Maolin	107	43 55N	123 25E
Maoming	109	21 39N	110 54E
Maopi T'ou	109	21 56N	120 43E
Maoping	109	30 51N	110 54E
Maowen	108	31 41N	103 52E
Mapastepec	165	15 26N	92 54W
Mapia, Kepulauan	103	0 50N	134 20E
Mapien	108	28 48N	103 39E
Mapimí	164	25 50N	103 31W
Mapimí, Bolsón de	164	27 30N	103 15W
Map'ing	109	31 36N	113 33E
Mapinga	126	6 40S	39 12E
Mapinhane	129	22 20S	35 0E
Maple Creek	153	49 55N	109 29W
Mapleton	160	44 4N	123 58W
Maplewood	158	38 33N	90 18W
Mappinga	109	34 58S	138 52E
Maprik	135	3 44S	143 3E
Mapuca	97	15 36N	73 46E
Mapuera, R.	174	0 30S	58 25W
Maputo	129	25 58S	32 32E
Maqnā	92	28 25N	34 50E
Maquela do Zombo	124	6 0S	15 15E
Maquinchao	176	41 15S	68 50W
Maquoketa	158	42 4N	90 40W
Mar Chiquita, L.	172	30 40S	62 50W
Mar del Plata	172	38 0S	57 30W
Mar Menor, L.	59	37 40N	0 45W
Mar, Reg.	37	57 11N	2 53W
Mar, Serra do	173	25 30S	49 0W
Mara, Bangla.	98	28 11N	94 7E
Mara, Tanz.	126	1 30S	34 32E
Mara □, Tanz.	126	1 45S	34 20E
Mara □, Tanz.	126	1 30S	34 32E
Maraã	174	1 43S	65 25W
Marabá	170	5 20S	49 5W
Maracá, I. de	170	2 10N	50 30W
Maracaibo	174	10 40N	71 37W
Maracaibo, Lago de	174	9 40N	71 30W
Maracaju	173	21 38S	55 9W
Maracanã	170	0 46S	47 27W
Maracás	171	13 26S	40 27W
Maracay	174	10 15N	67 36W
Marādah	119	29 4N	19 4E
Maradi	121	13 35N	8 10E
Maradun	121	12 35N	6 18E
Marāgheh	92	37 30N	46 12E
Maragogipe	171	12 46S	38 55W
Marajó, B. de	170	1 0S	48 30W
Marajó, Ilha de	170	1 0S	49 30W
Maralal	124	1 0N	36 38E
Maralinga	137	29 45S	131 15E
Marama	140	35 10S	140 10E
Marampa	120	8 45N	10 28W
Maramureş □	70	47 45N	24 0E
Maran	101	3 35N	102 45E
Marana	161	32 30N	111 9W
Maranboy	136	14 40S	132 40E
Maranchón	58	41 6N	2 15W
Marand	92	38 30N	45 45E
Marandellas	127	18 5S	31 42E
Maranguape	170	3 55S	38 50W
Maranhão = São Luis	170	2 31S	44 16W
Maranhão □	170	5 0S	46 0W
Marañón, R.	174	4 50S	75 35W
Marano, L. di	63	45 42N	13 13E
Maranoa R.	139	27 50S	148 37E
Maraş	92	37 37N	36 53E
Mărăşeşti	70	45 52N	27 5E
Maratea	65	39 59N	15 43E
Marateca	57	38 34N	8 40W
Marathókambos	69	37 43N	26 42E
Marathon, Austral.	138	20 51S	143 32E
Marathon, Can.	150	48 44N	86 23W
Marathón	69	38 11N	23 58E
Marathon, N.Y., U.S.A.	162	42 25N	76 3W
Marathon, Tex., U.S.A.	159	30 15N	103 15W
Maratua, I.	103	2 10N	118 35E
Maraú	171	14 6S	39 0W
Marazion	30	50 8N	5 29W
Marbat	91	17 0N	54 45E
Marbella	57	36 30N	4 57W
Marble Bar	136	21 9S	119 44E
Marble Falls	159	30 30N	98 15W
Marblehead	162	42 29N	70 51W
Marburg	48	50 49N	8 44E
Marby	72	63 7N	14 18E
Marcal, R.	53	47 21N	17 15E
Marcali	53	46 35N	17 25E
Marcaria	62	45 7N	10 34E
March	29	52 33N	0 5E
Marchand = Rommani	118	33 20N	6 40W
Marché	44	46 0N	1 20E
Marche □	63	43 22N	13 10E
Marche-en-Famenne	47	50 14N	5 19E
Marchena	57	37 18N	5 23W
Marches = Marche	63	43 22N	13 10E
Marciana Marina	62	42 44N	10 12E
Marcianise	65	41 3N	14 16E
Marcigny	45	46 17N	4 2E
Marcillac-Vallon	44	44 29N	2 27E
Marcillat	44	46 12N	2 38E
Marcinelle	47	50 24N	4 26E
Marck	43	50 57N	1 57E
Marckolsheim	43	48 10N	7 30E
Marcos Juárez	172	32 42S	62 5W
Marcus I.	130	24 0N	153 45E
Mardan	94	34 20N	72 0E
Marden	28	52 7N	2 42W
Mardie	136	21 12S	115 59E
Mardin	92	37 20N	40 36E
Marechal Deodoro	170	9 43S	35 54W
Maree L.	36	57 40N	5 30W
Mareeba	138	16 59S	145 28E
Mareham le Fen	33	53 7N	0 3W
Marek	103	4 41S	120 24E
Marek = Stanke Dimitrov	66	42 27N	23 9E
Maremma	62	42 45N	11 15E
Maréna	120	14 0N	7 30W
Marenberg	63	46 38N	15 13E
Marengo	158	41 42N	92 5W
Marennes	126	45 49N	1 5W
Marenyi	126	4 22S	39 8E
Marerano	129	21 23S	44 52E
Marèttimo, I.	64	37 58N	12 5E
Mareuil-sur-Lay	44	46 32N	1 14W
Marfa	159	30 15N	104 0W
Marfleet	33	53 45N	0 15W
Margable	123	12 54N	42 38E
Margam	31	51 33N	3 45W
Marganets	82	47 40N	34 40E
Margao	97	14 12N	73 58E
Margaree Harbour	151	46 26N	61 8W
Margaret Bay	152	51 20N	127 20W
Margaret L.	152	58 56N	115 25W
Margaret, R.	136	12 57S	131 16E
Margaret River	137	33 57S	115 7E
Margarita, Isla de	174	11 0N	64 0W
Margarítion	68	39 22N	20 26E
Margate, S. Afr.	129	30 50S	30 20E
Margate, U.K.	29	51 23N	1 24E
Margate City	162	39 20N	74 31W
Margelan	85	40 27N	71 42E
Margeride, Mts. de la	44	44 43N	3 38E
Margherita	98	27 16N	95 40E
Margherita di Savola	65	41 25N	16 5E
Marghita	70	47 22N	22 22E
Margonin	54	52 58N	17 5E
Margreten	47	50 49N	5 49E
Marguerite	152	52 30N	122 25W
Marhoum	118	34 27N	0 11W
Mari, A.S.S.R. □	81	56 30N	48 0E
María Elena	172	22 18S	69 40W
María Grande	172	31 45S	59 55W
Maria, I.	138	14 52S	135 45E
Maria I.	138	42 35S	148 0E
Maria van Diemen, C.	142	34 29S	172 40E
Mariager	73	56 40N	10 0E
Mariager Fjord	73	56 42N	10 19E
Mariakani	126	3 50S	39 27E
Marian L.	152	63 0N	116 15W
Mariana	171	20 23S	43 25W
Mariana Is.	130	17 0N	145 0E
Mariana Trench	130	13 0N	145 0W
Marianao	166	23 8N	82 24W
Mariani	98	26 39N	94 19E
Marianna, Ark., U.S.A.	159	34 48N	90 48W
Marianna, Fla., U.S.A.	157	30 45N	85 15W
Mariannelund	73	57 37N	15 35E
Mariánské Lázně	52	49 57N	12 41E
Marias, R.	160	48 26N	111 40W
Mariato, Punta	166	7 12N	80 52W
Mariazell	52	47 47N	15 19E
Marib	91	15 25N	45 20E
Maribo	73	54 48N	11 30E
Maribor	63	46 36N	15 40E
Marico, R.	128	24 25S	26 30E
Maricopa, Ariz., U.S.A.	161	33 5N	112 2W
Maricopa, Calif., U.S.A.	163	35 7N	119 27W
Marîdî	123	4 55N	29 25E
Marîdî, W.	123	5 25N	29 21E
Marie Galante, I.	167	15 56N	61 16W
Mariecourt	149	61 30N	72 0W
Mariefred	72	59 15N	17 12E
Mariehamn (Maarianhamina)	75	60 5N	19 57E
Marienberg, Ger.	48	50 40N	13 10E
Marienberg, Neth.	47	52 30N	6 35E
Marienberg, P.N.G.	138	3 54S	144 10E
Marienbourg	47	50 6N	4 31E
Mariental	128	24 36S	18 0E
Mariestad	73	58 43N	13 50E
Marietta, Ga., U.S.A.	157	34 0N	84 30W
Marietta, Ohio, U.S.A.	156	39 27N	81 27W
Marignane	45	43 25N	5 13E
Mariinsk	76	56 10N	87 20E
Mariinskiy Posad	81	56 10N	47 45E
Marília	173	22 0S	50 0W
Marillana	136	22 37S	119 24E
Marín	56	42 23N	8 42W
Marina	163	36 41N	121 48W
Marina di Cirò	65	39 22N	17 8E
Mariña, La	56	43 30N	7 40W
Marina Plains	138	14 37S	143 57E
Marinduque, I.	103	13 25N	122 0E
Marine City	156	42 45N	82 29W
Marinel, Le	127	10 25S	25 17E
Marineo	64	37 57N	13 23E
Marinette, Ariz., U.S.A.	161	33 41N	112 16W
Marinette, Wis., U.S.A.	156	45 4N	87 40W
Maringá	173	23 35S	51 50W
Marinha Grande	57	39 45N	8 56W
Marino	109	35 3S	138 31E
Marino Rocks	109	35 3S	138 31E
Marion, Austral.	109	34 59S	138 33E
Marion, Ala., U.S.A.	157	32 33N	87 20W
Marion, Ill., U.S.A.	159	37 45N	88 55W
Marion, Ind., U.S.A.	156	40 35N	85 40W
Marion, Iowa, U.S.A.	158	42 2N	91 36W
Marion, Kans., U.S.A.	158	38 25N	97 2W
Marion, Mich., U.S.A.	156	44 7N	85 8W
Marion, N.C., U.S.A.	157	35 42N	82 0W
Marion, Ohio, U.S.A.	156	40 38N	83 8W
Marion, S.C., U.S.A.	157	34 11N	79 22W
Marion, Va., U.S.A.	157	36 51N	81 29W
Marion Bay	140	35 12S	136 59E
Marion, L.	157	33 30N	80 15W
Marion Reef	138	19 10S	152 17E
Maripa	174	7 26N	65 9W
Mariposa	163	37 31N	119 59W
Mariscal Estigarribia	172	22 3S	60 40W
Maritime Alps = Alpes Maritimes	62	44 10N	7 10E
Maritsa	67	42 1N	25 50E
Maritsá	69	36 22N	28 10E
Maritsa, R.	67	42 15N	24 0E
Mariyampole = Kapsukas	80	54 33N	23 19E
Marjan	93	32 5N	68 20E
Mark	34	55 2N	5 1W
Marka	122	18 14N	41 19E
Markapur	97	15 44N	79 19E
Markaryd	73	56 28N	13 35E
Marke	47	50 48N	3 14E
Marked Tree	159	35 35N	90 24W
Markelo	46	52 14N	6 30E
Markelsdorfer Huk	48	54 33N	11 0E
Marken	46	52 26N	5 12E
Markerwaard	46	52 33N	5 15E
Market Bosworth	28	52 37N	1 24W
Market Deeping	29	52 40N	0 20W
Market Drayton	32	52 55N	2 30W
Market Harborough	29	52 29N	0 55W
Market Lavington	28	51 17N	1 59W
Market Rasen	33	53 24N	0 20W
Market Weighton	33	53 52N	0 40W
Markethill	38	54 18N	6 31W
Markfield	28	52 42N	1 18W
Markham I.	12	84 0N	0 45W
Markham L.	153	62 30N	102 35W
Markham Mts.	13	83 0S	164 0E
Markham, R.	135	6 41S	147 2E
Marki	54	52 20N	21 2E
Markinch	35	56 12N	3 9W
Markleeville	163	38 42N	119 47W
Markoupoulon	69	37 53N	23 57E
Markovac	66	44 14N	21 7E
Markovo	77	64 40N	169 40E
Markoye	121	14 39N	0 2E
Marks	81	51 45N	46 50E
Marks Tey	29	51 53N	0 48E
Marksville	159	31 10N	92 2W
Markt Schwaben	49	48 14N	11 49E
Marktredwitz	49	50 1N	12 2E
Marlboro, Can.	152	53 30N	116 50W
Marlboro, U.S.A.	162	42 19N	71 33W
Marlboro, N.Y., U.S.A.	162	41 36N	73 58W
Marlborough, Austral.	138	22 46S	149 52E
Marlborough, U.K.	28	51 26N	1 44W
Marlborough □	143	41 45S	173 33E
Marlborough Downs	28	51 25N	1 55W
Marle	43	49 43N	3 47E
Marlin	159	31 25N	96 50W
Marlow, Austral.	141	35 17S	149 55E
Marlow, Ger.	48	54 8N	12 34E
Marlow, U.K.	29	51 34N	0 47W
Marlow, U.S.A.	159	34 40N	97 58W
Marly-le-Grand	50	46 47N	7 10E
Marmagao	97	15 25N	73 56E
Marmande	44	44 30N	0 10E
Marmara denizi	92	40 45N	28 15E
Marmara, I.	82	40 35N	27 38E
Marmara, Sea of = Marmara denizi	92	40 45N	28 15E
Marmaris	92	36 50N	28 14E
Marmarth	158	46 21N	103 52W
Marmion L.	150	48 55N	91 30W
Marmion Mt.	137	29 16S	119 50E
Marmolada, Mte.	63	46 25N	11 55E
Marmolejo	57	38 3N	4 13W
Marmora	150	44 28N	77 41W
Marnay	43	47 20N	5 48E
Marne	48	53 57N	9 1E
Marne □	43	49 0N	4 10E
Marne, R.	43	48 53N	4 25E
Marnhull	28	50 58N	2 20W
Maro	124	8 30N	19 0E
Maroa	174	2 43N	67 33W
Maroala	129	15 23S	47 59E
Maroantsetra	129	15 26S	49 44E
Marocco ■	129	32 0N	5 50W
Maromandia	129	14 13S	48 5E
Maroni, R.	175	4 0N	52 0W
Marónia	68	40 53N	25 24E
Maroochydore	139	26 29S	153 5E
Maroona	140	37 27S	142 54E
Maros, R.	53	46 25N	20 20E
Marosakoa	129	15 26S	46 38E

Marostica
Maya, R

Marostica 63 45 44N 11 40 E
Maroua 121 10 40N 14 20 E
Marovoay 129 16 6 S 46 39 E
Marple 32 53 23N 2 5W
Marquard 128 28 40 S 27 28 E
Marqueira 57 38 41N 9 9W
Marquesas Is. = Marquises 131 9 30 S 140 0W
Marquette 156 46 30N 87 21W
Marquise 43 50 50N 1 40 E
Marquises, Is. 131 9 30 S 140 0W
Marra 139 31 12 S 144 10 E
Marra, Gebet 123 7 20N 27 35 E
Marradi 63 44 5N 11 37 E
Marrakech 118 31 40N 8 0W
Marrat 92 25 0N 45 35 E
Marrawah 138 40 55 S 144 42 E
Marrecas, Serra das 170 9 0 S 41 0W
Marree 139 29 39 S 138 1 E
Marrimane 129 22 58 S 33 34 E
Marromeu 125 18 40 S 36 25 E
Marroqui, Punta 56 36 0N 5 37W
Marrowie Creek 141 33 23 S 145 40 E
Marrubane 127 18 0 S 37 0 E
Marrum 46 53 19N 5 48 E
Marrupa 127 13 8 S 37 30 E
Mars, Le 158 43 0N 96 0W
Marsa Susa (Apollonia) 117 32 52N 21 59 E
Marsabit 126 2 18N 38 0 E
Marsabit □ 126 2 45N 37 45 E
Marsala 64 37 48N 12 25 E
Marsciano 63 42 54N 12 20 E
Marsden 141 33 47N 147 32 E
Marsdiep 46 52 58N 4 46 E
Marseillan 44 43 23N 3 31 E
Marseille 45 43 18N 5 23 E
Marseilles = Marseille 45 43 18N 5 23 E
Marsh I. 159 29 35N 91 50W
Marshall, Liberia 120 6 8N 10 22W
Marshall, Ark., U.S.A. 159 35 58N 92 40W
Marshall, Mich., U.S.A. 156 42 17N 84 59W
Marshall, Minn., U.S.A. 158 44 25N 95 45W
Marshall, Mo., U.S.A. 158 39 8N 93 15W
Marshall, Tex., U.S.A. 159 32 29N 94 20W
Marshall Is. 130 9 0N 171 0 E
Marshall, R. 138 22 59 S 136 59 E
Marshalltown 158 42 0N 93 0W
Marshfield, U.K. 28 51 27N 2 18W
Marshfield, Mo., U.S.A. 159 37 20N 92 58W
Marshfield, Wis., U.S.A. 158 44 42N 90 10W
Mársico Nuovo 65 40 26N 15 43 E
Marske by the sea 33 54 35N 1 0W
Märsta 72 59 37N 17 52 E
Marstal 73 54 51N 10 30 E
Marston Moor 33 53 58N 1 17W
Marstrand 73 57 53N 11 35 E
Mart 159 31 34N 96 51W
Marta, R. 63 42 18N 11 47 E
Martaban 98 16 30N 97 35 E
Martaban, G. of 98 15 40N 96 30 E
Martano 65 40 14N 18 18 E
Martapura 102 3 22 S 114 56 E
Marte 121 12 23N 13 46 E
Martebo 73 57 45N 18 30 E
Martelange 47 49 49N 5 43 E
Martés, Sierra 59 39 20N 1 0W
Marthaguy Creek 141 30 50 S 147 45 E
Martham 29 52 42N 1 38 E
Martha's Vineyard 162 41 25N 70 35W
Martigné Ferchaud 42 47 50N 1 20W
Martigny 50 46 6N 7 3 E
Martigues 45 43 24N 5 4 E
Martil 118 35 36N 5 15W
Martin, Czech. 53 49 6N 18 48 E
Martin, S.D., U.S.A. 158 43 11N 101 45W
Martin, Tenn., U.S.A. 159 36 23N 88 51W
Martin, L. 157 32 45N 85 50W
Martin, R. 58 41 2N 0 43W
Martina 51 46 53N 10 28 E
Martina Franca 65 40 42N 17 20 E
Martinborough 142 41 14 S 175 29 E
Martinez 163 38 1N 122 8W
Martinho Campos 171 19 20 S 45 13W
Martinique, I. 167 14 40N 61 0W
Martinique Passage 167 15 15N 61 0W
Martinon 69 38 25N 23 15 E
Martinópolis 173 22 11 S 51 12W
Martins 171 6 5 S 37 55W
Martinsberg 52 48 22N 15 9 E
Martinsburg 156 39 30N 77 57W
Martinsville, Ind., U.S.A. 156 39 29N 86 23W
Martinsville, Va., U.S.A. 157 36 41N 79 52W
Martley 28 52 14N 2 22W
Martock 28 50 58N 2 47W
Marton 142 40 4 S 175 23 E
Martorell 58 41 28N 1 56 E
Martos 57 37 44N 3 58W
Martre, La, L. 148 63 8N 117 16W
Martre, La, R. 148 63 0N 118 0W
Martuk 84 50 46N 56 31 E
Martuni 83 40 9N 45 10 E
Maru 121 12 22N 6 22 E
Marudi 102 4 10N 114 25 E
Maruf 93 31 30N 67 0 E
Marugame 110 34 15N 133 55 E
Maruggio 65 40 20N 17 33 E
Marui 135 4 4 S 143 2 E
Maruim 170 10 45 S 37 5W
Marulan 141 34 43 S 150 3 E
Marum 46 53 9N 6 16 E
Marunga 128 17 20 S 20 2 E
Marungu, Mts. 126 7 30 S 30 0 E
Maruoka 111 36 9N 136 16 E
Marvejols 44 44 33N 3 19 E
Marvine Mt. 161 38 44N 111 40W
Marwar 94 25 43N 73 45 E
Mary 76 37 40N 61 50 E
Mary Frances L. 153 63 19N 106 13W
Mary Kathleen 138 20 35 S 139 48 E
Maryborough, Queens., Austral. 139 25 31 S 152 37 E
Maryborough, Vic., Austral. 140 37 0 S 143 44 E
Maryets 81 56 17N 49 47 E
Maryfield 153 49 50N 101 35W
Marykirk 37 56 47N 2 30W
Maryland □ 156 39 10N 76 40W
Maryland Jc. 127 12 45 S 30 31 E
Maryport 32 54 43N 3 30W
Mary's Harbour 151 52 18N 55 51W
Marystown 151 47 10N 55 10W
Marysvale 161 38 25N 112 17W
Marysville, Can. 152 49 35N 116 0W
Marysville, Calif., U.S.A. 160 39 14N 121 40W
Marysville, Kans., U.S.A. 158 39 50N 96 38W
Marysville, Ohio, U.S.A. 156 40 15N 83 20W
Marytavy 30 50 34N 4 6W
Maryvale 139 28 4 S 152 12 E
Maryville 157 35 50N 84 0W
Marywell 37 56 35N 2 31W
Marzo, Punta 174 6 50N 77 42W
Marzuq 119 25 53N 14 10 E
Masada = Mesada 90 31 20N 35 19 E
Masafa 127 13 50 S 27 30 E
Masai 101 1 29N 103 55 E
Masai Steppe 126 4 30 S 36 30 E
Masaka 126 0 21 S 31 45 E
Masakali 121 13 2N 12 32 E
Masalima, Kepulauan 102 5 10 S 116 50 E
Masamba 103 2 30 S 120 15 E
Masan 107 35 11N 128 32 E
Masanasa 59 39 25N 0 25W
Masandam, Ras 93 26 30N 56 30 E
Masasi 127 10 45 S 38 52 E
Masasi □ 127 10 45 S 38 50 E
Masaya 166 12 0N 86 7W
Masba 121 10 35N 13 1 E
Mascara 118 35 26N 0 6 E
Mascota 164 20 30N 104 50W
Masela 103 8 9 S 129 51 E
Maseme 147 18 46 S 25 3 E
Maseru 128 29 18 S 27 30 E
Mashaba 127 20 2 S 30 29 E
Mashabih 92 25 35N 36 30 E
Masham 33 54 15N 1 40W
Mashan 108 23 44N 108 14 E
Masherbrum, mt. 95 35 38N 76 18 E
Mashhad 93 36 20N 59 35 E
Mashi 121 13 0N 7 54 E
Mashiki 110 32 51N 130 53 E
Mashki Chah 93 29 5N 62 30 E
Mashkode 150 47 2N 84 7W
Mashonaland, North, □ 127 16 30 S 30 0 E
Mashonaland, South, □ 127 18 0 S 31 30 E
Mashtagi 83 40 35N 50 0 E
Masi 74 69 26N 23 50 E
Masi-Manimba 124 4 40 S 18 5 E
Masindi 126 1 40N 31 43 E
Masindi Port 126 1 43N 32 2 E
Masirah 91 20 25N 58 50 E
Masisea 174 8 35 S 74 15W
Masisi 126 1 23 S 28 49 E
Masjed Solyman 92 31 55N 49 25 E
Mask, L. 38 53 36N 9 24W
Maski 97 15 56N 76 46 E
Maslen Nos 67 42 18N 27 48 E
Maslinica 63 43 24N 16 13 E
Masnou 58 41 28N 2 20 E
Masoala, C. 129 15 59 S 50 13 E
Masoarivo 129 19 3 S 44 19 E
Masohi 103 3 2 S 128 15 E
Masomeloka 129 20 17 S 48 37 E
Mason, Nev., U.S.A. 163 38 56N 119 8W
Mason, S.D., U.S.A. 158 45 12N 103 27W
Mason, Tex., U.S.A. 159 30 45N 99 15W
Mason B. 143 46 55 S 167 45 E
Mason City 160 48 0N 119 0W
Masqat 93 23 37N 58 36 E
Massa 62 44 2N 10 7 E
Massa Maríttima 62 43 3N 10 52 E
Massa, O. 118 30 0N 9 30W
Massachusetts □ 162 42 25N 72 0W
Massachusetts B. 162 42 30N 70 0W
Massada 90 33 12N 35 45 E
Massafra 65 40 35N 17 8 E
Massaguet 124 12 28N 15 26 E
Massakory 117 13 0N 15 49 E
Massangena 129 21 34 S 33 0 E
Massapê 170 3 31 S 40 19W
Massarosa 62 43 53N 10 17 E
Massat 44 42 53N 1 21 E
Massava 84 60 40N 62 6 E
Massawa = Mitsiwa 123 15 35N 39 25 E
Massena 156 44 52N 74 55W
Massenya 117 11 30N 16 25 E
Masset 152 54 0N 132 0W
Massiac 44 45 15N 3 11 E
Massif Central 44 45 30N 2 21 E
Massillon 156 40 47N 81 30W
Massinga 125 23 15 S 35 22 E
Massingir 129 23 46 S 32 4 E
Mässlingen 98 62 42N 12 48 E
Massman 138 16 25 S 145 25 E
Masson I. 13 66 10 S 93 20 E
Mastaba 122 20 52N 39 30 E
Mastanli = Momchilgrad 21 41 33N 25 23 E
Masterton 142 40 56 S 175 39 E
Mástikho, Ákra 68 38 10N 26 2 E
Mastuj 95 36 20N 72 36 E
Mastung 93 29 50N 66 42 E
Mastura 122 23 7N 38 52 E
Masuda 110 34 40N 131 51 E
Masulipatam 96 16 12N 81 12 E
Maswa □ 126 1 20 S 34 0 E
Mat, R. 68 41 40N 20 0 E
Mata de São João 171 12 31 S 38 17W
Matabeleland North □ 127 20 0 S 28 0 E
Matabeleland South □ 127 19 0 S 29 0 E
Mataboor 103 1 41 S 138 3 E
Matachel, R. 57 38 32N 6 0W
Matachewan 150 47 56N 80 39W
Matad 105 47 12N 115 29 E
Matadi 124 5 52 S 13 31 E
Matador 153 50 49N 107 56W
Matagalpa 166 13 10N 85 40W
Matagami 150 49 45N 77 34W
Matagami, L. 150 49 50N 77 40W
Matagorda 159 28 43N 96 0W
Matagorda, B. 159 28 30N 96 15W
Matagorda I. 159 28 10N 96 40W
Matak, P. 101 3 18N 106 16 E
Matakana 141 32 59 S 145 54 E
Matale 97 7 30N 80 44 E
Matam 120 15 34N 13 17W
Matamata 142 37 48 S 175 47 E
Matameye 121 13 26N 8 28 E
Matamoros, Campeche, Mexico 165 25 53N 97 30W
Matamoros, Coahuila, Mexico 164 25 45N 103 1W
Matamoros, Puebla, Mexico 165 18 2N 98 17W
Matamoros, Tamaulipas, Mexico 165 25 50N 97 30W
Matana, D. 103 2 30 S 121 25 E
Matandu, R. 127 8 35 S 39 40 E
Matane 151 48 50N 67 33W
Mat'ang, Szechwan, China 108 31 54N 102 55 E
Mat'ang, Yunnan, China 108 23 30N 104 4 E
Matankari 121 13 46N 4 1 E
Matanuska 148 61 38N 149 0W
Matanzá 174 7 22N 73 2W
Matanzas 166 23 0N 81 40W
Matapá, Ákra 69 36 22N 22 27 E
Matapedia 151 48 0N 66 59W
Matara 97 5 58N 80 30 E
Mataram 102 8 41 S 116 10 E
Matarani 174 16 50 S 72 10W
Mataranka 136 14 55 S 133 4 E
Mataró 58 41 32N 2 29 E
Matarraña, R. 58 40 55N 0 8 E
Mataruška Banja 66 43 40N 20 45 E
Matata 142 37 54 S 176 48 E
Matatiele 129 30 20 S 28 49 E
Mataura 143 46 11 S 168 51 E
Mataura, R. 143 45 49 S 168 44 E
Matehuala 164 23 40N 100 50W
Mateira 171 18 54 S 50 30W
Mateke Hills 127 21 48 S 31 0 E
Matélica 63 43 15N 13 0 E
Matera 65 40 40N 16 37 E
Mátészalka 53 47 58N 22 20 E
Matetsi 127 18 12 S 26 0 E
Mateur 119 37 0N 9 48 E
Mateyev Kurgan 83 47 35N 38 47 E
Matfors 72 62 21N 17 2 E
Matha 44 45 52N 0 20W
Matheson I. 153 51 45N 96 56W
Mathews 162 37 26N 76 19W
Mathias Pass 143 43 7 S 171 6 E
Mathis 159 28 4N 97 48W
Mathoura 141 35 50 S 144 55 E
Mathry 31 51 56N 5 6W
Mathura 94 27 30N 77 48 E
Mati 103 6 55N 126 15 E
Mati, R. 68 41 40N 20 0 E
Matías Romero 165 16 53N 95 2W
Matibane 127 14 49 S 40 45 E
Matien 109 32 55N 116 26 E
Matlock 33 53 8N 1 32W
Matmata 119 33 30N 9 59 E
Matna 123 13 49N 35 10 E
Mato Grosso □ 175 14 0 S 55 0W
Mato Grosso, Planalto do 174 15 0 S 54 0W
Mato Verde 171 15 23 S 42 52W
Matochkin Shar 76 73 10N 56 40 E
Matong 135 5 36 S 151 50 E
Matopo Hills 127 20 36 S 28 20 E
Matopos 127 20 20 S 28 29 E
Matour 45 46 19N 4 29 E
Matozinhos 56 41 11N 8 42W
Matrah 93 23 37N 58 30 E
Matrûh 122 31 19N 27 9 E
Matsang Tsangpo (Brahmaputra), R. 99 29 25N 88 0 E
Matsena 121 13 5N 10 5 E
Matsesta 83 43 34N 39 44 E
Matsu Tao 109 26 9N 119 56 E
Matsubara 111 34 33N 135 34 E
Matsudo 111 35 47N 139 54 E
Matsue 110 35 25N 133 10 E
Matsumae 112 41 26N 140 7 E
Matsumoto 111 36 15N 138 0 E
Matsusaka 111 34 34N 136 32 E
Matsutō 111 36 31N 136 34 E
Matsuura 110 33 20N 129 49 E
Matsuyama 110 33 45N 132 45 E
Mattagami, R. 150 50 43N 81 29W
Mattancheri 97 9 50N 76 15 E
Mattawa 150 46 20N 78 45W
Mattawamkeag 151 45 30N 68 30W
Matterhorn, mt. 50 45 58N 7 39 E
Mattersburg 53 47 44N 16 24 E
Matthew Town 167 20 57N 73 40W
Matthew's Ridge 174 7 37N 60 10W
Mattice 150 49 40N 83 20W
Mattituck 162 40 58N 72 32W
Mattmar 72 63 18N 13 54 E
Mattoon 156 39 30N 88 20W
Matua 102 2 58 S 110 52 E
Matuba 129 24 28 S 32 49 E
Matucana 174 11 55 S 76 15W
Matun 94 33 22N 69 58 E
Maturín 174 9 45N 63 11W
Matutina 171 19 13 S 45 58W
Matzuzaki 111 34 43N 138 50 E
Mau-é-ele 129 24 18 S 34 2 E
Mau Escarpment 126 0 40 S 36 0 E
Mau Ranipur 95 25 16N 79 8 E
Mauagami, R. 150 49 30N 82 0W
Maubeuge 43 50 17N 3 57 E
Maubourguet 44 43 29N 0 1 E
Mauchline 34 55 31N 4 23W
Maud 37 57 30N 2 8W
Maud, Pt. 137 23 6 S 113 45 E
Maude 140 34 29 S 144 18 E
Maudheim 13 71 5 S 11 0W
Maudin Sun 99 16 0N 94 30 E
Maués 174 3 20 S 57 45W
Mauganj 99 24 50N 81 55 E
Maughold 32 54 18N 4 17W
Maughold Hd. 32 54 18N 4 17W
Maui I. 147 20 45N 156 20 E
Maulamyaing 99 16 30N 97 40 E
Maule □ 172 36 5 S 72 30W
Mauleon 44 43 14N 0 54W
Maulvibazar 98 24 29N 91 42 E
Maum 38 53 31N 9 35W
Maumee 156 41 35N 83 40W
Maumee, R. 156 41 42N 83 28W
Maumere 103 8 38 S 122 13 E
Maumturk Mts. 38 53 32N 9 42W
Maun 128 20 0 S 23 26 E
Mauna Kea, Mt. 147 19 50N 155 28W
Mauna Loa, Mt. 147 19 50N 155 28W
Maunath Bhanjan 95 25 56N 83 33 E
Maungaturoto 142 36 6 S 174 23 E
Maungdow 98 21 14N 94 5 E
Maungmagan Is. 99 14 0 S 97 48 E
Maungmagan Kyunzu 101 14 0N 97 48 E
Maupin 160 45 12N 121 9W
Maure-de-Bretagne 42 47 53N 2 0W
Maureen, oilfield 19 58 5N 1 45 E
Maurepas L. 159 30 18N 90 35W
Maures, mts. 45 43 15N 6 15 E
Mauriac 44 45 13N 2 19 E
Maurice L. 137 29 30 S 131 0 E
Mauriceville 142 40 45 S 175 35 E
Maurienne 45 45 15N 6 20 E
Mauritania ■ 116 20 50N 10 0W
Mauritius ■ 11 20 0 S 57 0 E
Mauron 42 48 9N 2 18W
Maurs 44 44 43N 2 12 E
Maurthe, R. 43 48 47N 6 9 E
Mauston 158 43 48N 90 5W
Mauterndorf 52 47 9N 13 40 E
Mauvezin 44 43 44N 0 53 E
Mauzé-sur le Mignon 44 46 12N 0 41W
Mavelikara 97 9 14N 76 32 E
Mavinga 125 15 50 S 20 10 E
Mavli 94 24 45N 73 55 E
Mavqi'im 90 31 38N 34 32 E
Mavrova 68 40 26N 19 32 E
Mavuradonha Mts. 127 16 30 S 31 30 E
Mawa 126 2 45N 26 33 E
Mawana 94 29 6N 77 58 E
Mawand 94 29 33N 68 38 E
Mawer 153 50 46N 106 22W
Mawgan 30 50 4N 5 10W
Mawkmai 98 20 14N 97 50 E
Mawlaik 98 23 40N 94 26 E
Mawlawkho 98 17 50N 97 38 E
Mawson Base 13 67 30N 65 0 E
Max 158 47 50N 101 20W
Maxcanú 165 20 40N 90 10W
Maxhamish L. 152 59 50N 123 17W
Maxixe 129 23 54 S 35 17 E
Maxwellheugh 35 55 35N 2 23W
Maxwelltown 142 39 51 S 174 49 E
Maxwelton, Queens., Austral. 138 15 45 S 142 30 E
Maxwelton, Queens., Austral. 138 20 43 S 142 41 E
May Downs 138 22 38 S 148 55 E
May, I. of 35 56 11N 2 32W
May Nefalis 123 15 0N 38 12 E
May Pen 166 17 58N 77 15W
May River 135 4 19 S 141 58 E
Maya 58 43 12N 1 29W
Maya Gudo, Mt. 123 7 30N 37 8 E
Maya Mts. 165 16 30N 89 0W
Maya, R. 77 58 20N 135 0 E

Mayaguana Island **Menglien**

Place	Page	Lat.	Long.
Mayaguana Island	167	21 30N	72 44W
Mayagüez	147	18 12N	67 9W
Mayahi	121	13 58N	7 40E
Mayals	58	41 22N	0 30E
Mayang	108	27 53N	109 48E
Mayanup	137	33 58S	116 25E
Mayapán	165	20 38N	89 27W
Mayarf	167	20 40N	75 39W
Mayarí	167	20 40N	75 41W
Mayavaram = Mayuram	97	11 3N	79 42E
Maybell	160	40 30N	108 4W
Maybole	34	55 21N	4 41W
Maychew	123	12 50N	39 42E
Maydena	138	42 45S	146 39E
Maydos	68	40 13N	26 20E
Mayen	49	50 18N	7 10E
Mayenne	42	48 20N	0 38W
Mayenne □	42	48 10N	0 40W
Mayer	161	34 28N	112 17W
Mayerthorpe	152	53 57N	115 8W
Mayfield, Derby., U.K.	33	53 1N	1 47W
Mayfield, E. Sussex, U.K.	29	51 1N	0 17E
Mayfield, Ky., U.S.A.	157	36 45N	88 40W
Mayfield, N.Y., U.S.A.	162	43 6N	74 16W
Mayhill	161	32 58N	105 30W
Maykop	83	44 35N	40 25E
Mayli-Say	85	41 17N	72 24E
Maymyo	100	22 2N	96 28E
Maynard	162	42 30N	71 33W
Maynard Hills	137	28 35S	119 50E
Mayne, Le, L.	151	57 5N	68 30W
Mayne, R.	138	23 40S	142 10E
Maynooth, Can.	150	45 14N	77 56W
Maynooth, Ireland	38	53 22N	6 38W
Mayo	147	63 38N	135 57W
Mayo □	139	53 47N	9 7W
Mayo Bridge	38	54 11N	6 13W
Mayo L.	147	63 45N	135 0W
Mayo, R.	164	26 45N	109 47W
Mayon, Mt.	103	13 15N	123 42E
Mayor I.	142	37 16S	176 17E
Mayorga	56	42 10N	5 16W
Mays Landing	162	39 27N	74 44W
Mayskiy	83	43 47N	43 59E
Mayson L.	153	57 55N	107 10W
Maysville	156	38 43N	84 16W
Mayu, I.	103	1 30N	126 30E
Mayuram	97	11 3N	79 42E
Mayville	158	47 30N	97 23W
Mayya	77	61 44N	130 18E
Mazabuka	127	15 52S	27 44E
Mazagán = El Jadida	118	33 11N	8 17W
Mazagão	175	0 20S	51 50W
Mazama	152	49 43N	120 8W
Mazamet	44	43 30N	2 20E
Mazán	174	3 15S	73 0W
Mazapil	164	24 38N	101 34W
Mazar-i-Sharif	93	36 41N	67 0E
Mazar, O.	118	32 0N	1 38E
Mazara del Vallo	64	37 40N	12 34E
Mazarredo	176	47 10S	66 50W
Mazarrón	59	37 38N	1 19W
Mazarrón, Golfo de	59	37 27N	1 19W
Mazaruni, R.	174	6 15N	60 0W
Mazatán	164	29 0N	110 8W
Mazatenango	166	14 35N	91 30W
Mazatlán	164	23 10N	106 30W
Māzhān	93	32 30N	59 0E
Mazheikyai	80	56 20N	22 20E
Mazinān	93	36 25N	56 48E
Mazoe	127	17 28S	30 58E
Mazoe R.	125	16 45S	32 30E
Mazoi	127	16 42S	33 7E
Mazrûb	123	14 0N	29 20E
Mazurian Lakes = Mazurski, Pojezierze	54	53 50N	21 0E
Mazurski, Pojezierze	54	53 50N	21 0E
Mazzarino	65	37 19N	14 12E
Mbaba	120	14 59N	16 44W
Mbabane	129	26 18S	31 6E
Mbagne	120	16 6N	14 47W
M'bahiakro	120	7 33N	4 19W
M'Baiki	124	3 53N	18 1E
Mbala	127	8 46S	31 17E
Mbale	126	1 8N	34 12E
Mbalmayo	121	3 33N	11 33E
Mbamba Bay	127	11 13S	34 49E
Mbandaka	124	0 1S	18 18E
Mbanga	121	4 30N	9 33E
Mbanza Congo	124	6 18S	14 16E
Mbanza Ngungu	124	5 12S	14 53E
Mbarara	126	0 35S	30 25E
Mbatto	120	6 28N	4 22W
Mbenkuru, R.	127	9 25S	39 50E
Mberubu	121	6 10N	7 38E
Mbesuma	127	10 0S	32 2E
Mbeya	127	8 54S	33 29E
Mbeya □	126	8 15S	33 30E
Mbia	123	6 15N	29 18E
Mbimbi	127	13 25S	23 2E
Mbinga	127	10 50S	35 0E
Mbinga □	127	10 50S	35 0E
Mbini □	124	1 30N	10 0E
Mbiti	123	5 42N	28 3E
Mboki	123	5 19N	25 58E
Mboro	120	15 9N	16 54W
Mboune	120	14 42N	13 34W
Mbour	120	14 22N	16 54W
Mbout	120	16 1N	12 38W
Mbozi □	127	9 0S	32 50E
Mbuji-Mayi	126	6 9S	23 40E
Mbulu	124	3 45S	35 30E
Mbulu □	126	3 52S	35 33E
Mbumbi	128	18 26S	19 59E
Mburucuyá	172	28 1S	58 14W
M'chounech	119	34 57N	6 1E
M'Clure Str., Can.	10	75 0N	118 0W
M'Clure Str., Can.	12	74 0N	120 0W
Mdennah	118	24 37N	6 0W
Mead L.	161	36 1N	114 44W
Meade, Can.	150	49 26N	83 51W
Meade, U.S.A.	159	37 18N	100 25W
Meadow	137	26 35S	114 40E
Meadow Lake	153	54 10N	108 26W
Meadow Lake Prov. Park	153	54 27N	109 0W
Meadville	156	41 39N	80 9W
Meaford	150	44 36N	80 35W
Mealfuarvonie, Mt.	37	57 15N	4 34W
Mealhada	56	40 22N	8 27W
Mealsgate	32	54 46N	3 14W
Mealy Mts.	151	53 10N	60 0W
Meander, R. = Menderes, Büyük	92	37 45N	27 40E
Meander River	152	59 2N	117 42W
Meare's, C.	160	45 37N	124 0W
Mearim, R.	170	3 4S	44 35W
Mearns, Howe of the	37	56 52N	2 26W
Measham	28	52 43N	1 30W
Meath □	38	53 32N	6 40W
Meath Park	153	53 27N	105 22W
Meatian	140	35 34S	143 21E
Meaulne	44	46 36N	2 28E
Meaux	43	48 58N	2 50E
Mecanhelas	127	15 12S	35 54E
Mecca	163	33 37N	116 3W
Mecca = Makkah	122	21 30N	39 54E
Mechanicsburg	162	40 12N	77 0W
Mechanicville	162	42 54N	73 41W
Mechara	123	8 36N	40 20E
Mechelen, Anvers, Belg.	47	51 2N	4 29E
Mechelen, Limbourg, Belg.	47	50 58N	5 41E
Méchéria	118	33 35N	0 18W
Mechernich	48	50 35N	6 39E
Mechetinskaya	83	46 45N	40 32E
Mecidiye	68	40 38N	26 32E
Mecitözü	82	40 32N	35 25E
Mecklenburg B.	48	54 20N	11 40E
Meconta	127	14 59S	39 50E
Meda	56	40 57N	7 18W
Meda P.O.	136	17 22S	123 59E
Meda, R.	136	17 20S	124 30E
Medaguine	118	33 41N	3 26E
Medak	96	18 1N	78 15E
Medan	102	3 40N	98 38E
Medanosa, Pta.	176	48 0S	66 0W
Medawachchiya	97	8 30N	80 30E
Meddouza, cap	118	32 33N	9 9W
Médéa	118	36 12N	2 50E
Mededa	66	43 44N	19 15E
Medeiros Neto	171	17 20S	40 14W
Medel, Pic	51	46 37N	8 55E
Medellín	174	6 15N	75 35W
Medemblik	46	52 46N	5 8E
Meder	123	14 42N	40 44E
Mederdra	120	17 0N	15 38W
Medford, Oreg., U.S.A.	160	42 20N	122 52W
Medford, Wis., U.S.A.	158	45 9N	90 21W
Medford Lakes	162	39 52N	74 48W
Medgidia	70	44 15N	28 19E
Medi	123	5 4N	30 42E
Media	162	39 55N	75 23W
Media Agua	172	31 58S	68 25W
Media Luna	172	34 45S	66 44W
Mediaş	70	46 9N	24 22E
Medical Lake	160	47 41N	117 42W
Medicina	63	44 29N	11 38E
Medicine Bow	160	41 56N	106 11W
Medicine Hat	153	50 0N	110 45W
Medicine Lake	158	48 30N	104 30W
Medicine Lodge	159	37 20N	98 37W
Medina, Brazil	171	16 15S	41 29W
Medina, Colomb.	174	4 30N	73 21W
Medina, N.D., U.S.A.	158	46 57N	99 20W
Medina, N.Y., U.S.A.	156	43 15N	78 27W
Medina, Ohio, U.S.A.	156	41 9N	81 50W
Medina = Al Madīnah	92	24 35N	39 52E
Medina de Rioseco	56	41 53N	5 3W
Medina del Campo	56	41 18N	4 55W
Medina L.	159	29 35N	98 58W
Medina, R.	159	29 10N	98 20W
Medina-Sidonia	57	36 28N	5 57W
Medinaceli	58	41 12N	2 30W
Mediterranean Sea	60	35 0N	15 0E
Medjerda, O.	119	36 35N	8 30E
Medkovets	67	43 37N	23 10E
Medley	153	54 25N	110 16W
Mednogorsk	84	51 24N	57 37E
Médoc	44	45 10N	0 56W
Medstead, Can.	153	53 19N	108 5W
Medstead, U.K.	28	51 7N	1 4W
Medulin	63	44 49N	13 55E
Medveda	66	42 50N	21 32E
Medveditsa, R.	81	50 30N	44 0E
Medvedok	81	57 20N	50 1E
Medvezhi, Ostrava	77	71 0N	161 0E
Medvezhyegorsk	78	63 0N	34 25E
Medway, R.	29	51 12N	0 23E
Medyn	81	54 59N	35 56E
Medzev	53	48 43N	20 55E
Medzilaborce	53	49 17N	21 52E
Meeandh	108	27 26S	153 6E
Meeberrie	137	26 57S	116 0E
Meekatharra	137	26 32S	118 29E
Meeker	160	40 1N	107 58W
Meelpaeg L.	151	48 18N	56 35W
Meeniyan	141	38 35S	146 0E
Meer	47	51 27N	4 45E
Meerane	48	50 51N	12 30E
Meerbeke	47	50 50N	4 3E
Meerle	47	51 29N	4 48E
Meerssen	47	50 53N	5 50E
Meerut	94	29 1N	77 50E
Meeteetsa	160	44 10N	108 56W
Meeuwen	47	51' 6N	5 31E
Mega	123	3 57N	38 30E
Megálo Khorio	69	36 27N	27 24E
Megálo Petali, I.	69	38 0N	24 15E
Megalópolis	69	37 25N	22 7E
Meganisi, I.	69	38 39N	20 48E
Mégantic	151	45 36N	70 56W
Mégara	69	37 58N	23 22E
Megarine	119	33 14N	6 2E
Megdhova, R.	69	39 10N	21 45E
Megen	46	51 49N	5 34E
Mégève	45	45 51N	6 37E
Meghalaya □	98	25 50N	91 0E
Meghalayap	99	25 40N	89 55E
Meghezez, Mt.	123	9 18N	39 26E
Meghna, R.	98	23 45N	90 40E
Megiddo	90	32 36N	35 11E
Mégiscane, L.	150	48 35N	75 55W
Megiste	61	36 8N	29 34E
Mehadia	70	44 56N	22 23E
Mehaigne, R.	47	50 32N	5 13E
Mehaïguene, O.	118	32 20N	2 45E
Meharry, Mt.	132	22 59S	118 35E
Mehedinti □	70	44 40N	22 45E
Meheisa	122	19 38N	32 57E
Mehndawal	95	26 58N	83 5E
Mehsana	94	23 39N	72 26E
Mehun-sur-Yèvre	43	47 10N	2 13E
Mei Chiang, R.	109	24 25N	116 35E
Meia Ponte, R.	171	18 32S	49 36W
Meichuan	109	30 9N	115 33E
Meidrim	31	51 51N	4 3W
Meiganga	124	6 20N	14 10E
Meigh	38	54 8N	6 22W
Meihsien, Kwangtung, China	109	24 18N	116 7E
Meihsien, Shensi, China	106	34 16N	107 42E
Meijel	47	51 21N	5 53E
Meiktila	98	21 0N	96 0E
Meilen	51	47 16N	8 39E
Meiningen	48	50 32N	10 25E
Meio, R.	171	13 36S	49 7W
Meira, Sierra de	56	43 15N	7 15W
Meiringen	50	46 43N	8 12E
Meishan	108	30 3N	103 51E
Meissen	48	51 10N	13 29E
Meit'an	108	27 48N	107 28E
Meithalun	90	32 21N	35 16E
Méjean	44	44 15N	3 30E
Mejillones	172	23 10S	70 30W
Meka	137	27 25S	116 48E
Mekambo	124	1 2N	14 5E
Mekdela	123	11 24N	39 10E
Mekhtar	93	30 30N	69 15E
Meklong = Samut Songkhram	101	13 24N	100 1E
Meknès	118	33 57N	5 33W
Meko	121	7 27N	2 52E
Mekong, R.	101	18 0N	104 15E
Mekongga	103	3 50S	121 30E
Mekoryok	147	60 20N	166 20W
Melagiri Hills	97	12 20N	77 30E
Melah, Sebkhet el	118	29 20N	1 30W
Melaka	101	2 15N	102 15E
Melaka □	101	2 20N	102 15E
Melalap	102	5 10N	116 5E
Mélambes	69	35 8N	24 40E
Melanesia	130	4 0S	155 0E
Melapalaiyam	97	8 39N	77 44E
Melbost	36	58 12N	6 20W
Melbourn	29	52 5N	0 1E
Melbourne, Austral.	141	37 50S	145 0E
Melbourne, U.K.	28	52 50N	1 25W
Melbourne, U.S.A.	157	28 13N	80 14W
Melcésine	62	45 46N	10 48E
Melchor Múzquiz	164	27 50N	101 40W
Melchor Ocampo (San Pedro Ocampo)	164	24 52N	101 40W
Méldola	63	44 7N	12 3E
Meldorf	48	54 5N	9 5E
Mêle-sur-Sarthe, Le	42	48 31N	0 22E
Melegnano	62	45 21N	9 20E
Melekess = Dimitrovgrad	81	54 25N	49 33E
Melenci	66	45 32N	20 20E
Melenki	81	55 20N	41 37E
Meleuz	84	52 58N	55 55E
Melfi, Chad	117	11 0N	17 59E
Melfi, Italy	65	41 0N	15 40E
Melfort, Can.	153	52 50N	104 37W
Melfort, Zimb.	127	18 0S	31 25E
Melfort, Loch	34	56 13N	5 33W
Melgaço	56	42 7N	8 15W
Melgar de Fernamental	56	42 27N	4 17W
Melhus	71	63 17N	10 18E
Melick	47	51 10N	6 1E
Melide	51	45 57N	8 57E
Meligalá	69	37 15N	21 59E
Melilla	118	35 21N	2 57W
Melilot	42	31 22N	34 37E
Melipilla	172	33 42S	71 15W
Mélissa Óros	69	37 32N	26 4E
Melita	153	49 15N	101 5W
Mélito di Porto Salvo	65	37 55N	15 47E
Melitopol	82	46 50N	35 22E
Melk	52	48 13N	15 20E
Melksham	28	51 22N	2 9W
Mellan-Fryken	72	59 45N	13 10E
Mellansel	74	63 25N	18 17E
Melle, Belg.	47	51 0N	3 49E
Melle, France	44	46 14N	0 10W
Melle, Ger.	48	52 12N	8 20E
Mellégue, O.	119	36 32N	8 51E
Mellen	158	46 19N	90 36W
Mellerud	73	58 41N	12 28E
Mellette	158	45 11N	98 29W
Mellid	56	42 55N	8 1W
Mellish Reef	133	17 25S	155 50E
Mellit	123	14 15N	25 40E
Mellon Charles	36	57 52N	5 37W
Melmerby	32	54 44N	2 35W
Melnik	67	41 30N	23 25E
Mělník	52	50 22N	14 23E
Melo	173	32 20S	54 10W
Melolo	103	9 53S	120 40E
Melones Res.	163	37 57N	120 31W
Melouprey	100	13 48N	105 16E
Melovoye	83	49 25N	40 5E
Melrhir, Chott	119	34 25N	6 24E
Melrose, N.S.W., Austral.	141	32 42S	146 57E
Melrose, W. Australia, Austral.	137	27 50S	121 15E
Melrose, U.K.	35	55 35N	2 44W
Melrose, U.S.A.	159	34 27N	103 33W
Mels	51	47 3N	9 25E
Melsele	47	51 13N	4 17E
Melsonby	33	54 28N	1 41W
Melstone	160	46 45N	108 0W
Melsungen	48	51 8N	9 34E
Melton	29	52 51N	1 1E
Melton Constable	29	52 52N	1 1E
Melton Mowbray	29	52 46N	0 52W
Melun	43	48 32N	2 39E
Melunga	128	17 15S	16 22E
Melur	97	10 2N	78 23E
Melut	123	10 30N	32 20E
Melvaig	36	57 48N	5 49W
Melvich	37	58 33N	3 55W
Melville	153	50 55N	102 50W
Melville B.	138	12 0S	136 45E
Melville, C.	138	14 11S	144 30E
Melville I., Austral.	136	11 30S	131 0E
Melville I., Can.	12	75 30N	111 0W
Melville, L., Newf., Can.	151	53 45N	59 40W
Melville, L., Newf., Can.	151	59 30N	53 40W
Melville Pen.	149	68 0N	84 0W
Melvin L.	38	54 26N	8 10W
Melvin, R.	152	59 11N	117 31W
Mélykút	53	46 11N	19 25E
Memaliaj	68	40 25N	19 58E
Memba	127	14 11S	40 30E
Memboro	103	9 30S	119 30E
Membrilla	59	38 59N	3 21W
Memel	129	27 38S	29 36E
Memel = Klaipeda	80	55 43N	21 10E
Memmingen	49	47 59N	10 12E
Memphis, Tenn., U.S.A.	159	35 7N	90 0W
Memphis, Tex., U.S.A.	159	34 45N	100 30W
Mena	159	34 40N	94 15W
Menai Bridge	31	53 14N	4 11W
Menai Strait	31	53 7N	4 20W
Ménaka	121	15 59N	2 18E
Menaldum	46	53 13N	5 40E
Menamurtee	140	31 25S	143 11E
Menarandra, R.	129	25 0S	44 50E
Menard	159	30 57N	99 58W
Menasha	156	44 13N	88 27W
Menate	102	0 12S	112 47E
Mendawai, R.	102	1 30S	113 0E
Mende	44	44 31N	3 30E
Mendebo Mts.	123	7 0N	39 22E
Mendenhall, C.	147	59 44N	166 10W
Menderes, R.	92	37 25N	28 45E
Mendez	165	25 7N	98 34W
Mendhar	95	33 35N	74 10E
Mendi, Ethiopia	123	9 47N	35 4E
Mendi, P.N.G.	135	6 11S	143 47E
Mendip Hills	28	51 17N	2 40W
Mendlesham	29	52 15N	1 4E
Mendocino	160	39 26N	123 50W
Mendong Gompa	95	31 16N	85 11E
Mendota, Calif., U.S.A.	163	36 46N	120 24W
Mendota, Ill., U.S.A.	158	41 35N	89 5W
Mendoza	172	32 50S	68 52W
Mendoza □	172	33 0S	69 0W
Mendrisio	51	45 52N	8 59E
Mene Grande	174	9 49N	70 56W
Menemen	92	38 18N	27 10E
Menen	47	50 47N	3 7E
Menfi	64	37 36N	12 57E
Meng-pan	99	23 5N	100 19E
Meng-so	101	22 33N	99 31E
Meng-wang	99	22 17N	100 32E
Meng Wang	101	22 18N	100 31E
Mengch'eng	106	33 17N	116 34E
Mengeš	63	46 24N	14 35E
Menggala	102	4 20S	105 15E
Menghai	108	21 58N	100 28E
Menghsien	106	34 54N	112 47E
Mengibar	57	37 58N	3 48W
Mengla	108	21 28N	101 35E
Menglien	108	22 21N	99 36E

Mengoub	118	29 49N	5 26W
Mengpolo	108	24 24N	99 14E
Mengshan	109	24 12N	110 31E
Mengting	108	23 33N	98 5E
Mengtz = Mengtzu	108	23 25N	103 20E
Mengtzu	108	23 25N	103 20E
Mengyin	107	35 40N	117 55E
Menihek L.	151	54 0N	67 0W
Menin	47	50 47N	3 7E
Menindee	140	32 20N	142 25E
Menindee, L.	140	32 20N	142 25E
Meningie	140	35 43S	139 20E
Menkúng	99	28 38N	98 24E
Menlo Park	163	37 27N	122 12W
Menominee	156	45 9N	87 39W
Menominee, R.	156	45 30N	87 50W
Menomonie	158	44 50N	91 54W
Menor, Mar	59	37 43N	0 48W
Menorca, I.	58	40 0N	4 0E
Mentawai, Kepulauan	102	2 0S	99 0E
Mentekab	101	3 29N	102 21E
Menton	45	43 50N	7 29E
Menyamya	135	7 10S	145 59E
Menzel-Bourguiba	119	39 9N	9 49E
Menzel Chaker	119	35 0N	10 26E
Menzelinsk	84	55 53N	53 1E
Menzies	137	29 40S	120 58E
Me'ona (Tarshiha)	90	33 1N	35 15E
Meoqui	164	28 17N	105 29W
Mepaco	127	15 57S	30 48E
Meppel	47	52 42N	6 12E
Meppen	48	52 41N	7 20E
Mequinenza	58	41 22N	0 17E
Mer Rouge	159	32 47N	91 48W
Merabéllou, Kólpos	69	35 10N	25 50E
Merai	135	4 52S	152 19E
Merak	103	5 55S	106 1E
Meramangye, L.	137	28 25S	132 13E
Merano (Meran)	63	46 40N	11 10E
Merate	62	45 42N	9 23E
Merauke	103	8 29S	140 24E
Merbabu, Mt.	103	7 30S	110 40E
Merbein	140	34 10S	142 2E
Merca	91	1 48N	44 50E
Mercadal	58	39 59N	4 5E
Mercara	97	12 30N	75 45E
Mercato Saraceno	63	43 57N	12 11E
Merced	163	37 18N	120 30W
Merced Pk.	163	37 36N	119 24W
Merced, R.	163	37 21N	120 58W
Mercedes, Buenos Aires, Argent.	172	34 40S	59 30W
Mercedes, Corrientes, Argent.	172	29 10S	58 5W
Mercedes, San Luis, Argent.	172	33 5S	65 21W
Mercedes, Uruguay	172	33 12S	58 0W
Merceditas	172	28 20S	70 35W
Mercer	142	37 16S	175 5E
Merchtem	47	50 58N	4 14E
Mercy C.	149	65 0N	62 30W
Merdrignac	42	48 11N	2 27W
Mere, Belg.	47	50 55N	3 58E
Mere, U.K.	28	51 5N	2 16W
Meredith C.	176	52 15S	60 40W
Meredith, L.	159	35 30N	101 35W
Merei	70	45 7N	26 43E
Merelbeke	47	51 0N	3 45E
Méréville	43	48 20N	2 5E
Merewa	123	7 40N	36 54E
Mergenevo	84	49 56N	51 18E
Mergenevskiy	83	49 59N	51 15E
Mergui	101	12 30N	98 35E
Mergui Arch. = Myeik Kyunzu	101	11 30N	97 30E
Meribah	140	34 43S	140 51E
Mérida, Mexico	165	20 50N	89 40W
Mérida, Spain	57	38 55N	6 25W
Mérida, Venez.	174	8 36N	71 8W
Mérida □	174	8 30N	71 10W
Mérida, Cord. de	174	9 0N	71 0W
Meriden, U.K.	28	52 27N	1 36W
Meriden, U.S.A.	162	41 33N	72 47W
Meridian, Idaho, U.S.A.	160	43 41N	116 25W
Meridian, Miss., U.S.A.	157	32 20N	88 42W
Meridian, Tex., U.S.A.	159	31 55N	97 37W
Mering	49	48 15N	11 0E
Merioneth (□)	26	52 49N	3 55W
Merirumã	175	1 15N	54 50W
Merke	85	42 52N	73 11E
Merkel	159	32 30N	100 0W
Merkem	47	50 57N	2 51E
Merksem	47	51 16N	4 25E
Merksplas	47	51 22N	4 52E
Merlebach	43	49 5N	6 52E
Merlerault, Le	42	48 41N	0 16E
Mermaid Mt.	138	27 29S	152 49E
Mermaid Reef	136	17 6S	119 36E
Mern	73	55 3N	12 3E
Merowe	122	18 29N	31 46E
Merredin	137	31 28S	118 18E
Merrick, Mt.	34	55 8N	4 30W
Merrill, Oregon, U.S.A.	160	42 2N	121 37W
Merrill, Wis., U.S.A.	158	45 11N	89 41W
Merrimack, R.	162	42 49N	70 49W
Merritt	152	50 10N	120 45W
Merriwa	141	32 6S	150 22E
Merriwagga	141	33 47S	145 43E
Merroe	137	27 53S	117 50E
Merry I.	150	55 29N	77 31W
Merrygoen	141	31 51S	149 12E
Merryville	159	30 47N	93 31W
Mersa Fatma	123	14 57N	40 17E
Mersch	47	49 44N	6 7E
Merse, dist.	35	55 40N	2 30W
Mersea I.	29	51 48N	0 55E
Merseburg	48	51 20N	12 0E
Mersey, R.	32	53 20N	2 56W
Merseyside □	32	53 25N	2 55W
Mersin	92	36 51N	34 36E
Mersing	101	2 25N	103 50E
Merta	94	26 39N	74 4E
Mertert	47	49 43N	6 29E
Merthyr Tydfil	31	51 45N	3 23W
Mértola	57	37 40N	7 40E
Merton	29	51 25N	0 13W
Mertzig	47	49 51N	6 1E
Mertzon	159	31 17N	100 48W
Méru	43	49 13N	2 8E
Meru	126	0 3N	37 40E
Meru □	126	0 3N	37 46E
Meru, mt.	126	3 15S	36 46E
Merville	43	50 38N	2 38E
Méry-sur-Seine	43	48 31N	3 54E
Merzifon	82	40 53N	35 32E
Merzig	49	49 26N	6 37E
Merzouga, Erg Tin	119	24 0N	11 4E
Mesa	161	33 20N	111 56W
Mesa, La, Colomb.	174	4 38N	74 28W
Mesa, La, Calif., U.S.A.	163	32 48N	117 5W
Mesa, La, N. Mex., U.S.A.	161	32 6N	106 48W
Mesach Mellet	119	24 30N	11 30E
Mesada	90	31 20N	35 19E
Mesagne	65	40 34N	17 48E
Mesaras, Kólpos	69	35 6N	24 47E
Meschede	48	51 20N	8 17E
Mesfinto	123	13 30N	37 22E
Mesgouez, L.	150	51 20N	75 0W
Meshchovsk	80	54 22N	35 17E
Meshed = Mashhad	93	36 20N	59 35E
Meshoppen	162	41 36N	76 3W
Mesick	156	44 24N	85 42W
Mesilinka, R.	152	56 6N	124 30W
Mesilla	161	32 20N	107 0W
Meslay-du-Maine	42	47 58N	0 33W
Mesocco	51	46 23N	9 12E
Mesolóngion	69	38 27N	21 28E
Mesopotamia, reg.	92	33 30N	44 0E
Mesoraca	65	39 5N	16 47E
Mésou Volímais	69	37 53N	27 35E
Mess Cr.	152	57 55N	131 14W
Messac	42	47 49N	1 50W
Messad	118	34 8N	3 30E
Méssaména	121	3 48N	12 49E
Messancy	47	49 36N	5 49E
Messeix	44	45 37N	2 33E
Messina, Italy	65	38 10N	15 32E
Messina, S. Afr.	129	22 20S	30 12E
Messina, Str. di	65	38 5N	15 35E
Messíni	69	37 4N	22 1E
Messinia □	69	37 10N	22 0E
Messiniakós, Kólpos	69	36 45N	22 5E
Mestà, Akra	69	38 16N	25 53E
Mesta, R.	67	41 30N	24 0E
Mestanza	57	38 35N	4 4W
Město Teplá	52	49 59N	12 52E
Mestre	63	45 30N	12 13E
Mestre, Espigão	171	12 30S	46 10W
Městys Zelezná Ruda	52	49 8N	13 15E
Meta □	174	3 30N	73 0W
Meta, R.	174	6 20N	68 5W
Metagama	150	47 0N	81 55W
Metaline Falls	160	48 52N	117 22W
Metán	172	25 30S	65 0W
Metauro, R.	63	43 45N	12 59E
Metchosin	152	48 15N	123 37W
Metehara	123	8 58N	39 57E
Metema	123	12 56N	36 13E
Metengobalame	127	14 49S	34 30E
Méthana	69	37 35N	23 23E
Metheringham	33	53 9N	0 22W
Methlick	37	57 26N	2 13W
Methóni	69	36 49N	21 42E
Methuen, Mt.	136	15 54S	124 44E
Methven, N.Z.	143	43 38S	171 40E
Methven, U.K.	35	56 25N	3 35W
Methwin, Mt.	137	25 3S	120 45E
Methwold	29	52 30N	0 33E
Methy L.	153	56 28N	109 30W
Metil	125	16 24S	39 0E
Metkovets	67	43 37N	23 10E
Metković	66	43 6N	17 39E
Metlakatla	147	55 10N	131 33W
Metlaoui	119	34 24N	8 24E
Metlika	63	45 40N	15 20E
Metowra	139	25 3S	146 15E
Metropolis	159	37 10N	88 47W
Métsovon	68	39 48N	21 12E
Mettet	47	50 19N	4 41E
Mettuppalaiyam	97	11 18N	76 59E
Mettur	97	11 48N	77 47E
Mettur Dam	95	11 45N	77 45E
Metulla	90	33 17N	35 34E
Metz	43	49 8N	6 10E
Meulaboh	102	4 11N	96 3E
Meulan	43	49 0N	1 52E
Meung-sur-Loire	43	47 50N	1 40E
Meureudu	102	5 19N	96 10E
Meurthe-et-Moselle □	43	48 52N	6 0E
Meuse □	43	49 8N	5 25E
Meuse, R.	47	50 45N	5 41E
Meuselwitz	48	51 3N	12 18E
Mevagissey	30	50 16N	4 48W
Mevagissey Bay	30	50 15N	4 40W
Mexborough	33	53 29N	1 18W
Mexia	159	31 38N	96 32W
Mexiana, I.	170	0 0	49 30W
Mexicali	164	32 40N	115 30W
México	165	19 20N	99 10W
Mexico, Me., U.S.A.	156	44 35N	70 30W
Mexico, Mo., U.S.A.	158	39 10N	91 55W
Mexico, N.Y., U.S.A.	162	43 28N	76 18W
Mexico ■	164	20 0N	100 0W
México □	164	19 20N	99 10W
Mexico, G. of	165	25 0N	90 0W
Mey	37	58 38N	3 14W
Meyenburg	48	53 19N	12 15E
Meymac	44	45 32N	2 10E
Meyrargues	45	43 38N	5 32E
Meyrueis	44	44 12N	3 27E
Meyssac	44	45 3N	1 40E
Mezdra	67	43 12N	23 35E
Mèze	44	43 27N	3 36E
Mezen	78	65 50N	44 20E
Mezha, R.	80	55 50N	31 45E
Mezhdurechenskiy	84	59 36N	65 56E
Mezidon	42	49 5N	0 1W
Mézières	43	49 45N	4 42E
Mézilhac	45	44 49N	4 21E
Mézin	44	44 4N	0 16E
Mezöberény	53	46 49N	21 3E
Mezöfalva	53	46 55N	18 49E
Mezöhegyes	53	46 19N	20 49E
Mezokovácsháza	53	46 25N	20 57E
Mezökövesd	53	47 49N	20 35E
Mézos	44	44 5N	1 10W
Mezötúr	53	47 0N	20 41E
Mezquital	164	23 29N	104 23W
Mezzolombardo	62	46 13N	11 5E
Mgeta	127	8 22S	38 6E
Mglin	80	53 2N	32 50E
Mhlaba Hills	127	18 30S	30 30E
Mhow	94	22 33N	75 50E
Mi-Shima	110	34 46N	131 9E
Miahuatlán	165	16 21N	96 36W
Miajadas	57	39 9N	5 54W
Mialar	94	26 15N	70 20E
Miallo	138	16 28S	145 22E
Miami, Ariz., U.S.A.	161	33 25N	111 0W
Miami, Fla., U.S.A.	157	25 45N	80 15W
Miami, Tex., U.S.A.	159	35 44N	100 38W
Miami Beach	157	25 49N	80 6W
Miami, R.	156	39 20N	84 40W
Miamisburg	156	39 40N	84 11W
Miandowāb	92	37 0N	46 5E
Miandrivazo	125	19 50S	45 56E
Miāneh	92	37 30N	47 40E
Mianwali	94	32 38N	71 28E
Miaoli	109	24 34N	120 48E
Miarinarivo	129	18 57S	46 55E
Miass	84	54 59N	60 6E
Miass, R.	84	56 6N	64 30E
Miasteczko Kraj	54	53 7N	17 1E
Miastko	54	54 0N	16 58E
Mica Dam	152	54 5N	118 32W
Mica Res.	152	51 55N	118 00W
Michael, Mt.	135	6 27S	145 22E
Michalovce	29	48 44N	21 54E
Micheldever	28	51 7N	1 17W
Michelson, Mt.	147	69 20N	144 20W
Michelstadt	49	49 40N	9 0E
Michigan □	155	44 40N	85 40W
Michigan City	156	41 42N	86 56W
Michigan, L.	156	44 0N	87 0W
Michih	106	37 49N	110 7E
Michikamau L.	151	54 0N	64 0W
Michipicoten	150	47 55N	84 55W
Michipicoten I.	150	47 40N	85 50W
Michoacan □	164	19 0N	102 0W
Michurin	67	42 9N	27 51E
Michurinsk	81	52 58N	40 27E
Mickle Fell	32	54 38N	2 16W
Mickleover	33	52 55N	1 32W
Mickleton, Oxon., U.K.	28	52 5N	1 45W
Mickleton, Yorks., U.K.	32	54 36N	2 3W
Miclere	138	22 34S	147 32E
Micronesia	130	17 0N	160 0E
Micŭsasa	70	46 7N	24 7E
Mid Calder	35	55 53N	3 23W
Mid Glamorgan □	31	51 40N	3 25W
Mid Yell	36	60 36N	1 5W
Midai, P.	101	3 0N	107 47E
Midale	153	49 25N	103 20W
Midas	160	41 14N	116 56W
Middagsfjället	72	63 27N	12 19E
Middelbeers	47	51 28N	5 15E
Middelburg, Neth.	47	51 30N	3 36E
Middelburg, C. Prov., S. Afr.	128	31 30S	25 0E
Middelburg, Trans., S. Afr.	129	25 49N	29 28E
Middelfart	73	55 30N	9 43E
Middelharnis	46	51 46N	4 10E
Middelkerke	47	51 11N	2 49E
Middelrode	47	51 41N	5 26E
Middelveld	128	29 45S	22 30E
Middle Alkali L.	160	41 30N	120 3W
Middle Andaman I.	101	12 30N	92 30E
Middle Brook	151	48 40N	54 20W
Middle I.	137	28 55S	113 55E
Middle River	162	39 19N	76 25W
Middle Zoy	28	51 5N	2 54W
Middleboro	162	41 49N	70 55W
Middleburg, N.Y., U.S.A.	162	42 36N	74 19W
Middleburg, Pa., U.S.A.	162	40 47N	77 3W
Middlebury	162	44 0N	73 9W
Middleham	33	54 17N	1 49W
Middlemarch	143	45 30S	170 9E
Middlemarsh	28	50 51N	2 29W
Middleport	156	39 0N	82 5W
Middlesbrough	33	54 35N	1 14W
Middlesex, Belize	165	17 2N	88 31W
Middlesex, U.S.A.	162	40 36N	74 30W
Middleton, Can.	151	44 57N	65 4W
Middleton, Gr. Manchester, U.K.	32	53 33N	2 12W
Middleton, Norfolk, U.K.	29	52 43N	0 29E
Middleton Cheney	28	52 4N	1 17W
Middleton Cr.	138	22 35S	141 51E
Middleton I.	147	59 30N	146 28W
Middleton-in-Teesdale	32	54 38N	2 5W
Middleton in the Wolds	33	53 56N	0 35W
Middleton P.O.	138	22 22S	141 32E
Middletown, U.K.	38	54 18N	6 50W
Middletown, Conn., U.S.A.	162	41 37N	72 40W
Middletown, Del., U.S.A.	162	39 30N	84 21W
Middletown, N.Y., U.S.A.	162	41 28N	74 28W
Middletown, Pa., U.S.A.	162	40 12N	76 44W
Middlewich	32	53 12N	2 28W
Midelt	118	32 46N	4 44W
Midhurst, N.Z.	142	39 17S	174 18E
Midhurst, U.K.	29	50 59N	0 44W
Midi, Canal du	44	43 45N	1 21E
Midi d'Ossau	58	42 50N	0 25W
Midland, Austral.	137	31 54S	115 59E
Midland, Can.	150	44 45N	79 50W
Midland, Mich., U.S.A.	156	43 37N	84 17W
Midland, Tex., U.S.A.	159	32 0N	102 3W
Midland Junc.	137	31 50S	115 58E
Midlands □	127	19 40S	29 0E
Midleton	39	51 52N	8 12W
Midlothian, Austral.	138	17 10S	141 12E
Midlothian, U.S.A.	159	32 30N	97 0W
Midlothian (□)	26	55 45N	3 15W
Midnapore	95	22 25N	87 21E
Midongy du Sud	129	23 35S	47 1E
Midongy, Massif de	129	23 30S	47 0E
Midskog	73	58 56N	14 5E
Midsomer Norton	28	51 17N	2 29W
Midvale	160	40 39N	111 58W
Midway Is.	130	28 13N	177 22W
Midwest	160	43 27N	106 11W
Midwolda	46	53 12N	6 52E
Midzur	66	43 24N	22 40E
Mie-ken □	111	34 30N	136 10E
Miechów	54	50 21N	20 5E
Miedzyborz	54	51 39N	17 24E
Miedzychód	54	52 35N	15 53E
Miedzylesie	54	50 41N	16 40E
Miedzyrzec Podlaski	54	51 58N	22 45E
Miedzyrzecz	54	52 26N	15 35E
Miedzyzdroje	54	53 56N	14 26E
Miejska Górka	54	51 39N	16 58E
Miélan	44	43 27N	0 19E
Mielelek	138	6 1S	148 58E
Miench'ih	106	34 48N	111 40E
Mienchu	108	31 22N	104 7E
Mienga	128	17 12S	19 48E
Mienhsien	106	33 11N	106 36E
Mienning	108	28 30N	102 10E
Mienyang, Hupei, China	109	30 10N	113 20E
Mienyang, Szechwan, China	108	31 28N	104 46E
Miercurea Ciuc	70	46 21N	25 48E
Mieres	56	43 18N	5 48W
Mierlo	47	51 27N	5 37E
Mieso	123	9 15N	40 43E
Mieszkowice	54	52 47N	14 30E
Migdal	90	32 51N	35 30E
Migdal Afeq	90	32 5N	34 58E
Migennes	43	47 58N	3 31E
Migliarino	63	44 54N	11 56E
Miguel Alemán, Presa	165	18 15N	96 40W
Miguel Alves	170	4 11S	42 55W
Miguel Calmon	170	11 26S	40 36W
Mihara	110	34 24N	133 5E
Mihara-Yama	111	34 43N	139 23E
Mihsien	106	34 31N	113 22E
Mii	108	26 50N	102 3E
Mijares, R.	58	40 15N	0 50W
Mijas	57	36 36N	4 40W
Mijdrecht	46	52 13N	4 53E
Mijilu	121	10 22N	13 19E
Mikese	126	6 48S	37 55E
Mikha Tskhakaya	83	42 15N	42 7E
Mikhailovgrad	67	43 27N	23 16E
Mikhailovka	82	47 16N	35 27E
Mikhaylov	81	54 20N	39 0E
Mikhaylovka, Azerbaijan, U.S.S.R.	83	41 31N	48 52E
Mikhaylovka, R.S.F.S.R., U.S.S.R.	81	50 3N	43 5E
Mikhaylovski	84	56 27N	59 7E
Mikhnevo	81	55 4N	37 59E
Miki, Hyōgo, Japan	110	34 48N	134 59E
Miki, Kagawa, Japan	110	34 12N	134 7E
Mikinai	69	37 43N	22 46E
Mikindani	127	10 15S	40 2E
Mikkeli	75	61 43N	27 25E
Mikkeli □	74	62 0N	28 0E
Mikkelin Lääni □	74	61 56N	28 0E
Mikkwa, R.	152	58 25N	114 46W
Mikniya	123	17 0N	33 45E
Mikołajki	54	53 49N	21 37E

Mikol Mjømna

Mikołów 53 50 10N 18 50 E
Míkonos, I. 69 37 30N 25 25 E
Mikrón Dhérion 68 41 19N 26 6 E
Mikulov 53 48 48N 16 39 E
Mikumi 126 7 26 S 37 9 E
Mikun 78 62 20N 50 0 E
Mikuni 111 36 13N 136 9 E
Mikuni-Tōge 111 36 50N 138 40 E
Mikura-Jima 111 33 52N 139 36 E
Mila 119 36 27N 6 16 E
Milaca 158 45 45N 93 40W
Milagro 174 2 0 S 79 30W
Milan, Mo., U.S.A. 158 40 10N 93 5W
Milan, Tenn., U.S.A. 157 35 55N 88 45W
Milan = Milano 62 45 28N 9 10 E
Milang, S. Australia, Austral. 139 32 2 S 139 10 E
Milang, S. Australia, Austral. 140 35 24 S 138 58 E
Milange 127 16 3 S 35 45 E
Milano 62 45 28N 9 10 E
Milâs 92 37 20N 27 50 E
Milazzo 65 38 13N 15 13 E
Milbank 158 45 17N 96 38W
Milborne Port 28 50 58N 2 28W
Milden 153 51 29N 107 32W
Mildenhall 29 52 20N 0 30 E
Mildura 140 34 13 S 142 9 E
Miléai 68 39 20N 23 9 E
Miles, Austral. 139 26 40 S 150 23 E
Miles, U.S.A. 159 31 39N 100 11W
Miles City 158 46 30N 105 50W
Milestone 153 49 59N 104 31W
Mileto 65 38 37N 16 3 E
Miletto, Mte. 65 41 26N 14 23 E
Mileurà 137 26 22 S 117 20 E
Milevsko 52 49 27N 14 21 E
Milford, Ireland 39 52 20N 8 52W
Milford, Conn., U.S.A. 162 41 13N 73 4W
Milford, Del., U.S.A. 162 38 52N 75 27W
Milford, Mass., U.S.A. 162 42 8N 71 30W
Milford, N.H., U.S.A. 162 42 50N 71 39W
Milford, Pa., U.S.A. 162 41 20N 74 47W
Milford, Utah, U.S.A. 161 38 20N 113 0W
Milford Haven 31 51 43N 5 2W
Milford Haven, B. 31 51 40N 5 10W
Milford on Sea 28 50 44N 1 36W
Milford Sd. 143 44 34 S 167 47 E
Milgun 137 25 6 S 118 18 E
Milh, Ras el 117 32 0N 24 55 E
Miliana, Aïn Salah, Alg. 118 27 20N 2 32 E
Miliana, Médéa, Alg. 118 36 12N 2 15 E
Milicz 54 51 31N 17 19 E
Miling 137 30 30 S 116 17 E
Militello in Val di Catánia 65 37 16N 14 46 E
Milk, R. 160 48 40N 107 15W
Milk River 152 49 10N 112 5W
Mill 47 51 41N 5 48 E
Mill City 160 44 45N 122 28W
Mill, I. 13 66 0 S 101 30 E
Mill Valley 163 37 54N 122 32W
Millau 44 44 8N 3 4 E
Millbrook, U.K. 30 50 19N 4 12W
Millbrook, U.S.A. 162 41 47N 73 42W
Millbrook Res. 109 34 50 S 138 49 E
Mille Lacs, L. 158 46 10N 93 30W
Mille Lacs, L. des 150 48 45N 90 35W
Milledgeville 157 33 7N 83 15W
Millen 157 32 50N 81 57W
Miller 158 44 35N 98 59W
Millerovo 83 48 57N 40 28 E
Miller's Flat 143 45 39 S 169 23 E
Millersburg 162 40 32N 76 58W
Millerton, N.Z. 143 41 39 S 171 54 E
Millerton, U.S.A. 162 41 57N 73 32W
Millerton, L. 163 37 0N 119 42W
Milleur Pt. 34 55 2N 5 5W
Millevaches, Plat. de 44 45 45N 2 0 E
Millicent 140 37 34 S 140 21 E
Millingen 46 51 52N 6 2 E
Millinocket 151 45 45N 68 45W
Millisle 38 54 38N 5 33W
Millmerran 139 27 53 S 151 16 E
Millom 32 54 13N 3 16W
Millport 34 55 45N 4 55W
Mills L. 152 61 30N 118 20W
Millsboro 162 38 36N 75 17W
Millstreet 39 52 4N 9 5W
Milltown, Galway, Ireland 38 53 37N 8 54W
Milltown, Kerry, Ireland 39 52 9N 9 42W
Milltown, U.K. 37 57 33N 4 48W
Milltown Malbay 39 52 51N 9 25W
Millville, N.J., U.S.A. 162 39 22N 75 0W
Millville, Pa., U.S.A. 162 41 7N 76 32W
Millwood Res. 159 33 45N 94 0W
Milly 43 48 24N 2 20 E
Milly Milly 137 26 4 S 116 43 E
Milna 63 43 20N 16 28 E
Milnathort 35 56 14N 3 25W
Milne Inlet 149 72 30N 80 0W
Milne, R. 138 21 10 S 137 33 E
Milngavie 34 55 57N 4 20W
Milnor 158 46 19N 97 29W
Milnthorpe 32 54 14N 2 47W
Milo, Can. 152 50 34N 112 53W
Milo, China 108 24 28N 103 23 E
Milolii 147 22 8N 159 42W
Mílos 69 36 44N 24 25 E
Mílos, I. 69 36 44N 24 25 E
Milo evo 66 45 42N 20 20 E
Miłosław 54 52 12N 17 32 E
Milovaig 36 57 27N 6 45W
Milparinka P.O. 139 29 46 S 141 57 E
Miltenberg 49 49 41N 9 13 E
Milton, N.Z. 143 46 7 S 169 59 E
Milton, Dumf. & Gall., U.K. 34 55 18N 4 50W
Milton, Hants., U.K. 28 50 45N 1 40W
Milton, Northants, U.K. 29 52 12N 0 55W
Milton, Calif., U.S.A. 163 38 3N 120 51W
Milton, Del., U.S.A. 162 38 47N 75 19W
Milton, Fla., U.S.A. 157 30 38N 87 0W
Milton, Pa., U.S.A. 162 41 0N 76 53W
Milton Abbot 30 50 35N 4 16W
Milton-Freewater 160 45 57N 118 24W
Milton Keynes 29 52 3N 0 42W
Milverton 28 51 2N 3 15W
Milwaukee 156 43 9N 87 58W
Milwaukie 160 45 27N 122 39W
Mim 120 6 57N 2 33W
Mimizan 44 44 12N 1 13W
Mimon 52 50 38N 14 43 E
Mimoso 171 15 10 S 48 5W
Min Chiang, R., China 105 28 48N 104 33 E
Min Chiang, R., Fukien, China 109 26 5N 119 37 E
Min Chiang, R., Szechwan, China 108 28 48N 104 33 E
Min-Kush 85 41 4N 74 28 E
Mina 161 38 21N 118 9W
Mina Pirquitas 172 22 40 S 66 40W
Mina Saud 92 28 45N 48 20 E
Minā'al Ahmadī 92 29 5N 48 10 E
Mīnāb 93 27 10N 57 1 E
Minago, R. 153 54 33N 98 13W
Minakami 111 36 49N 138 59 E
Minaki 153 50 0N 94 40W
Minakuchi 111 34 58N 136 10 E
Minamata 110 32 10N 130 30 E
Minamitane 112 30 25N 130 54 E
Minas Basin 151 45 20N 64 12W
Minas de Rio Tinto 57 37 42N 6 22W
Minas de San Quintín 57 38 49N 4 23W
Minas Gerais □ 171 18 50 S 46 0W
Minas Novas 171 17 15 S 42 36W
Minas, Sierra de las 166 15 9N 89 31W
Minatitlán 165 17 58N 94 35W
Minbu 98 20 10N 95 0 E
Minbya 98 20 22N 93 16 E
Mincha 140 36 1 S 144 6 E
Minch'in 106 38 42N 103 11 E
Minch'ing 109 26 13N 118 51 E
Minchinhampton 28 51 42N 2 10W
Mincio, R. 62 45 8N 10 55 E
Mindanao, I. 103 8 0N 125 0 E
•Mindanao Sea 103 9 0N 124 0 E
Mindanao Trench 103 8 0N 128 0 E
Mindelheim 49 48 4N 10 30 E
Minden, Ger. 48 52 18N 8 54 E
Minden, U.S.A. 159 32 40N 93 20W
Mindiptana 103 5 45 S 140 22 E
Mindon 98 19 21N 94 44 E
Mindoro, I. 103 13 0N 121 0 E
Mindoro Strait 103 12 30N 120 30 E
Mindouli 124 4 12 S 14 28 E
Mine 110 34 12N 131 7 E
Mine Hd. 39 52 0N 7 37W
Minehead 28 51 12N 3 29W
Mineola, N.Y., U.S.A. 162 40 45N 73 38W
Mineola, Tex., U.S.A. 159 32 40N 95 30W
Minera 31 53 3N 3 7W
Mineral King 163 36 27N 118 36W
Mineral Wells 159 32 50N 98 5W
Mineralnyye Vody 83 44 18N 43 15 E
Minersville, Pa., U.S.A. 162 40 40N 76 17W
Minersville, Utah, U.S.A. 161 38 14N 112 58W
Minervino Murge 65 41 6N 16 4 E
Minette 157 30 54N 87 43W
Minetto 162 43 24N 76 28W
Mingan 151 50 20N 64 0W
Mingary, Austral. 140 32 8 S 140 45 E
Mingary, U.K. 36 56 42N 6 5W
Mingch'i 109 26 24N 117 12 E
Mingchiang 109 32 28N 114 8 E
Mingechaur 83 40 52N 47 0 E
Mingechaurskoye Vdkhr. 83 40 56N 47 20 E
Mingela 138 19 52 S 146 38 E
Mingenew 137 29 12 S 115 21 E
Mingera Cr. 138 20 38 S 138 10 E
Mingin 98 22 50N 94 30 E
Minginish, Dist. 36 57 14N 6 15W
Minglanilla 58 39 34N 1 38W
Mingulay I. 36 56 50N 7 40W
Minho □ 55 41 25N 8 20W
Minho, R. 55 41 58N 8 40W
Minhou 109 26 0N 119 18 E
Minhow = Fuchou 109 26 5N 119 18 E
Minhsien 106 34 26N 104 2 E
Minidoka 160 42 47N 113 34W
Minigwal L. 137 29 31 S 123 14 E
Minilya 137 23 55 S 114 0 E
Minilya, R. 137 23 45 S 114 0 E
Mininera 140 37 37 S 142 58 E
Minióevo 66 43 42N 22 18 E
Minipi, L. 151 52 25N 60 45W
Minj 135 5 54 S 144 30 E
Mink L. 152 61 54N 117 40W
Minlaton 140 34 45 S 137 35 E
Minna 121 9 37N 6 30 E
Minneapolis, Kans., U.S.A. 158 39 11N 97 40W
Minneapolis, Minn., U.S.A. 158 44 58N 93 20W
Minnesota □ 158 46 40N 94 0W
Minnesund 71 60 23N 11 14 E
Minnie Creek 137 24 3 S 115 42 E
Minnigaff 34 54 58N 4 30W
Minnitaki L. 150 49 47N 91 5W
Mino 111 35 32N 136 55 E
Mino-Kamo 111 35 23N 137 2 E
Mino-Mikawa-Kōgen 111 35 10N 137 30 E
Miño, R. 56 41 58N 8 40W
Minobu 111 35 22N 138 26 E
Minobu-Sanchi 111 35 14N 138 20 E
Minorca = Menorca 58 40 0N 4 0 E
Minore 141 32 14 S 148 27 E
Minot 158 48 10N 101 15W
Minquiers, Les 42 48 58N 2 8W
Minsen 48 53 43N 7 58 E
Minsk 80 53 52N 27 30 E
Minsk Mazowiecki 54 52 10N 21 33 E
Minster 29 51 20N 1 20 E
Minster-on-Sea 29 51 25N 0 50 E
Minsterley 28 52 38N 2 56W
Mintaka Pass 93 37 0N 74 58 E
Minthami 98 23 55N 94 16 E
Mintlaw 37 57 32N 1 59W
Minto 147 64 55N 149 20W
Minto L. 150 48 0N 84 45W
Minton 153 49 10N 104 35W
Minturn 160 39 45N 106 25W
Minturno 64 41 15N 13 43 E
Minûf 122 30 26N 30 52 E
Minusinsk 77 53 50N 91 20 E
Minutang 98 28 15N 96 30 E
Minvoul 124 2 9N 12 8 E
Minya Konka 108 29 34N 101 53 E
Minyar 84 55 4N 57 33 E
Minyip 140 36 29 S 142 36 E
Mionica 66 44 14N 20 6 E
Mios Num, I. 103 1 30 S 135 10 E
Miquelon 151 47 3N 56 20W
Miquelon, St. Pierre et, □ 151 47 8N 56 24W
Mir-Bashir 83 40 11N 46 58 E
Mira, Italy 63 45 26N 12 9 E
Mira, Port. 56 40 26N 8 44W
Mira, R. 57 37 30N 8 30W
Mirabella Eclano 65 41 3N 14 59 E
Miracema do Norte 170 9 33 S 48 24W
Mirador 170 6 22 S 44 22W
Miraflores 164 23 21N 109 45W
Miraj 96 16 50N 74 45 E
Miram 138 21 15 S 148 55 E
Miram Shah 94 33 0N 70 0 E
Miramar, Argent. 172 38 15 S 57 50W
Miramar, Mozam. 129 23 50 S 35 35 E
Miramas 45 43 33N 4 59 E
Mirambeau 44 45 23N 0 35W
Miramichi B. 151 47 15N 65 0W
Miramont-de-Guyenne 44 44 37N 0 21 E
Miranda 175 20 10 S 56 15W
Miranda de Ebro 58 42 41N 2 57W
Miranda do Corvo 56 40 6N 8 20W
Miranda do Douro 56 41 30N 6 16W
Mirando City 159 27 28N 98 59W
Mirandola 62 44 53N 11 2 E
Mirandópolis 173 21 9 S 51 6W
Mirango 127 13 32 S 34 58 E
Mirano 63 45 29N 12 6 E
Miraporvos, I. 167 22 9N 74 30W
Mirassol 173 20 46 S 49 28W
Mirboo North 141 38 24 S 146 10 E
Mirear, I. 122 23 15N 35 41 E
Mirebeau, Côte d'Or, France 43 47 25N 5 20 E
Mirebeau, Vienne, France 42 46 49N 0 10 E
Mirecourt 43 48 20N 6 10 E
Mirgorod 80 49 58N 33 50 E
Miri 102 4 18N 114 0 E
Miriam Vale 138 24 20 S 151 33 E
Mirim, Lagoa 173 32 45 S 52 50W
Mirimire 174 11 10N 68 43W
Mirny 13 66 0 S 95 0 E
Mirnyy 77 62 33N 113 53 E
Mirond L. 153 55 6N 102 47W
Mirosławiec 54 53 20N 16 5 E
Mirpur 95 33 15N 73 50 E
Mirpur Bibiwari 94 28 33N 67 44 E
Mirpur Khas 94 25 30N 69 0 E
Mirpur Sakro 94 24 33N 67 41 E
Mirrool 141 34 19 S 147 10 E
Mirror 152 52 30N 113 7W
Mirsani 70 44 1N 23 59 E
Mirsk 54 50 58N 15 23 E
Miryang 107 35 31N 128 44 E
Mirzaani 83 41 24N 46 5 E
Mirzapur 95 25 10N 82 45 E
Misantla 165 19 56N 96 50W
Miscou I. 151 47 57N 64 31W
Misery, Mt. 108 34 52 S 138 48 E
Mish'ab, Ra'as al 92 28 15N 48 43 E
Mishan 105 45 31N 132 2 E
Mishawaka 156 41 40N 86 8W
Mishbih, Gebel 122 22 48N 34 38 E
Mishima 111 35 10N 138 52 E
Mishkino 84 55 20N 63 55 E
Mishmar Aiyalon 90 31 52N 34 57 E
Mishmar Ha' Emeq 90 32 37N 35 7 E
Mishmar Ha Negev 90 31 22N 34 48 E
Mishmar Ha Yarden 90 33 0N 35 56 E
Mishmi Hills 98 29 0N 96 0 E
Misilmeri 64 38 2N 13 25 E
Misima I. 135 10 40 S 152 45 E
Misión, La 164 32 5N 116 50W
Misiones □, Argent. 173 27 0 S 55 0W
Misiones □, Parag. 172 27 0 S 56 0W
Miskin 93 23 44N 56 52 E
Miskitos, Cayos 166 14 26N 82 50W
Miskolc 53 48 7N 20 50 E
Misoke 126 0 42 S 28 2 E
Misoöl, I. 103 2 0 S 130 0 E
Misrātah 119 32 18N 15 3 E
Missanabie 150 48 20N 84 6W
Missão Velha 170 7 15 S 39 10W
Misserghin 118 35 44N 0 49W
Missinaibi L. 150 48 23N 83 40W
Missinaibi, R. 150 50 30N 82 40W
Mission, S.D., U.S.A. 158 43 21N 100 36W
Mission, Tex., U.S.A. 159 26 15N 98 30W
Mission City 152 49 10N 122 15W
Missisa L. 150 52 20N 85 7W
Mississagi 150 46 15N 83 9W
Mississippi, R. 159 35 30N 90 0W
Mississippi Sd. 159 30 25N 89 0W
Missoula 160 47 0N 114 0W
Missouri □ 158 38 25N 92 30W
Missouri, Little, R. 160 46 0N 111 35W
Missouri, R. 158 40 20N 95 40W
Mistake B. 153 62 8N 93 0W
Mistassini L. 150 51 0N 73 40W
Mistassini, R. 151 48 42N 72 20W
Mistastin L. 151 55 57N 63 20W
Mistatim 153 52 52N 103 22W
Mistelbach 53 48 34N 16 34 E
Misterbianco 65 37 32N 15 0 E
Misterton, Notts., U.K. 33 53 27N 0 49W
Misterton, Som., U.K. 28 50 51N 2 46W
Mistretta 65 37 56N 14 20 E
Misty L. 153 58 53N 101 40W
Misugi 111 34 31N 136 16 E
Misumi 110 32 37N 130 27 E
Mît Ghamr 122 30 42N 31 12 E
Mitaka 111 35 40N 139 33 E
Mitan 85 40 0N 66 35 E
Mitatib 123 15 59N 36 12 E
Mitchel Troy 31 51 46N 2 45W
Mitcheldean 28 51 51N 2 29W
Mitchell, Austral. 139 26 29 S 147 58 E
Mitchell, Ind., U.S.A. 156 38 42N 86 25W
Mitchell, Nebr., U.S.A. 158 41 58N 103 45W
Mitchell, Oreg., U.S.A. 160 44 31N 120 8W
Mitchell, S.D., U.S.A. 158 43 40N 98 0W
Mitchell, Mt. 157 35 40N 82 20W
Mitchell, R. 138 15 12 S 141 35 E
Mitchelstown 39 52 16N 8 18W
Mitchelton 108 27 25 S 152 59 E
Mitha Tiwana 94 32 13N 72 6 E
Míthimna 68 39 20N 26 12 E
Mitiamo 140 36 12 S 144 15 E
Mitilíni 69 39 6N 26 35 E
Mitilíni = Lesvos 68 39 0N 26 20 E
Mitilinoi 69 37 42N 26 56 E
Mitla 165 16 55N 96 24W
Mito 111 36 20N 140 30 E
Mitsinjo 129 16 1 S 45 52 E
Mitsiwa 123 15 35N 39 25 E
Mitsiwa Channel 123 15 30N 40 0 E
Mitsukaidō 111 36 1N 139 59 E
Mittagong 141 34 28 S 150 29 E
Mittelland 50 46 50N 7 23 E
Mittelland Kanal 48 52 23N 7 45 E
Mittenwalde 48 52 16N 13 33 E
Mittweida 48 50 59N 13 0 E
Mitu 108 25 21N 100 32 E
Mitú 174 1 8N 70 3W
Mituas 174 3 52N 68 49W
Mitumba 126 7 8 S 31 2 E
Mitumba, Chaîne des 126 10 0 S 26 20 E
Mitwaba 127 8 2N 27 17 E
Mityana 126 0 23N 32 2 E
Mitzick 124 0 45N 11 40 E
Miura 111 35 12N 139 40 E
Mius, R. 83 47 30N 39 0 E
Mixteco, R. 165 18 11N 98 30W
Miyagi-Ken □ 112 38 15N 140 45 E
Miyâh, W. el 122 25 10N 30 33 E
Miyake-Jima 111 34 0N 139 30 E
Miyako 112 39 40N 141 75 E
Miyako-Jima 112 24 45N 125 20 E
Miyakonojō 110 31 32N 131 5 E
Miyanojō 110 31 54N 130 27 E
Miyanoura-Dake 112 30 20N 130 26 E
Miyata 110 33 49N 130 42 E
Miyazaki 110 31 56N 131 30 E
Miyazaki-ken □ 110 32 0N 131 30 E
Miyazu 110 35 35N 135 10 E
Miyet, Bahr el 92 31 30N 35 30 E
Miyoshi 110 34 48N 132 51 E
Miyūn 106 40 22N 116 49 E
Mizamis = Ozamiz 103 8 15N 123 50 E
Mizdah 119 31 30N 13 0 E
Mizen Hd., Cork, Ireland 39 51 27N 9 50W
Mizen Hd., Wick., Ireland 39 52 52N 6 4W
Mizil 70 44 59N 26 29 E
Mizoram □ 98 23 0N 92 40 E
Mizuho 111 35 6N 135 17 E
Mizunami 111 35 22N 137 15 E
Mjöbäck 73 57 28N 12 53 E
Mjölby 73 58 20N 15 10 E
Mjømna 71 60 55N 4 55 E

*Renamed Bohol Sea

CIB

Mjörn Montcornet

Mjörn **73** 57 55N 12 25 E
Mjøsa **71** 60 40N 11 0 E
Mkata **126** 5 45 S 38 20 E
Mkokotoni **126** 5 55 S 39 15 E
Mkomazi **126** 4 40 S 38 7 E
Mkulwe **127** 8 37 S 32 20 E
Mkumbi, Ras **126** 7 38 S 39 55 E
Mkushi **127** 14 25 S 29 15 E
Mkushi River **127** 13 40 S 29 30 E
Mkuze, R. **129** 27 45 S 32 30 E
Mkwaya **126** 6 17 S 35 40 E
Mladá Boleslav **52** 50 27N 14 53 E
Mladenovac **66** 44 28N 20 44 E
Mlala Hills **126** 6 50 S 31 40 E
Mlange **127** 16 2 S 35 33 E
Mlava, R. **66** 44 35N 21 18 E
Mława **54** 53 9N 20 25 E
Mlinište **63** 44 15N 16 50 E
Mljet, I. **66** 42 43N 17 30 E
Młynary **54** 54 12N 19 46 E
Mme **121** 6 18N 10 14 E
Mo, Hordaland, Norway **71** 60 49N 5 48 E
Mo, Telemark, Norway **71** 59 28N 7 50 E
Mo, Sweden **72** 61 19N 16 47 E
Mo i Rana **74** 66 15N 14 7 E
Moa, I. **103** 8 0 S 128 0 E
Moa, R. **120** 7 0N 11 40W
Moab **161** 38 40N 109 35W
Moabi **124** 2 24 S 10 59 E
Moalie Park **139** 29 42 S 143 3 E
Moaña **56** 42 18N 8 43W
Moanda **124** 1 28 S 13 21 E
Moapo **161** 36 45N 114 37W
Moate **39** 53 25N 7 43W
Moba **126** 7 0 S 29 48 E
Mobara **111** 35 25N 140 18 E
Mobaye **124** 4 25N 21 5 E
Mobayi **124** 4 15N 21 8 E
Moberley **158** 39 25N 92 25W
Moberly, R. **152** 56 12N 120 55W
Mobert **150** 48 41N 85 40W
Mobile **157** 30 41N 88 3W
Mobile B. **157** 30 30N 88 0W
Mobile, Pt. **157** 30 15N 88 0W
Mobjack B. **162** 37 16N 76 22W
Möborg **73** 56 24N 8 21 E
Mobridge **158** 45 40N 100 28W
Mobutu Sese Seko, L. **126** 1 30N 31 0 E
Moc Chav **100** 20 50N 104 38 E
Moc Hoa **101** 10 46N 105 56 E
Mocabe Kasari **127** 9 58 S 26 12 E
Mocajuba **170** 2 35 S 49 30W
Moçambique **127** 15 3 S 40 42 E
Moçambique □ **127** 14 45 S 38 30 E
Mocanaqua **162** 41 9N 76 8W
Mochiang **108** 23 25N 101 44 E
Mochiara Grove **128** 20 43 S 21 50 E
Mochudi **128** 24 27 S 26 7 E
Mocimboa da Praia **127** 11 25 S 40 20 E
Mociu **70** 46 46N 24 3 E
Möckeln **73** 56 40N 14 15 E
Mockhorn I. **162** 37 10N 75 52W
Moclips **160** 47 14N 124 10W
Moçâmedes □ **128** 16 35 S 12 30 E
Mocoa **174** 1 15N 76 45W
Mococa **173** 21 28 S 47 0W
Mocorito **164** 25 20N 108 0W
Moctezuma **164** 30 12N 106 26W
Moctezuma, R. **165** 21 59N 98 34W
Mocuba **125** 16 54 S 37 25 E
Moda **98** 24 22N 96 29 E
Modane **45** 45 12N 6 40 E
Modasa **94** 23 30N 73 21 E
Modave **47** 50 27N 5 18 E
Modbury, Austral. **109** 34 50 S 138 41 E
Modbury, U.K. **30** 50 21N 3 53W
Modder, R. **128** 28 50 S 24 50 E
Modderrivier **128** 29 2 S 24 38 E
Módena **62** 44 39N 10 55 E
Modena **161** 37 55N 113 56W
Modesto **163** 37 43N 121 0W
Módica **65** 36 52N 14 45 E
Modigliana **63** 44 9N 11 48 E
Modjokerto **103** 7 29 S 112 25 E
Modlin **54** 52 24N 20 41 E
Mödling **53** 48 5N 16 17 E
Modo **123** 5 31N 30 33 E
Modra **53** 48 19N 17 20 E
Modreeny **39** 52 57N 8 6W
Modriča **66** 44 57N 18 17 E
Moe **141** 38 12 S 146 19 E
Moebase **127** 17 3 S 38 41 E
Moei, R. **101** 17 25N 98 10 E
Moëlan-s-Mer **42** 47 49N 3 38W
Moelfre **31** 53 21N 4 15W
Moengo **175** 5 45N 54 20W
Moergestel **47** 51 33N 5 11 E
Moësa, R. **51** 46 12N 9 10 E
Moffat **35** 55 20N 3 27W
Moga **94** 30 48N 75 8 E
Mogadiscio = Mogadishu **91** 2 2N 45 25 E
Mogadishu **91** 2 2N 45 25 E
Mogador = Essaouira **118** 31 32N 9 42W
Mogadouro **56** 41 22N 6 47W
Mogami-gawa, R. **112** 38 45N 140 0 E
Mogaung **98** 25 20N 97 0 E
Møgeltønder **73** 54 57N 8 48 E
Mogente **59** 38 52N 0 45W
Moggil **108** 27 34 S 152 52 E
Mogho **123** 4 54N 40 16 E
Mogi das Cruzes **173** 23 45 S 46 20W
Mogi-Guaçu, R. **173** 20 53 S 48 10W
Mogi-Mirim **173** 22 20 S 47 0W
Mogielnica **54** 51 42N 20 41 E
Mogilev **80** 53 55N 30 18 E
Mogilev Podolskiy **82** 48 20N 27 40 E
Mogilno **54** 52 39N 17 55 E
Mogincual **125** 15 35 S 40 25 E
Mogliano Veneto **63** 45 33N 12 15 E
Mogocha **77** 53 40N 119 50 E
Mogoi **103** 1 55 S 133 10 E
Mogok **98** 23 0N 96 40 E
Mogollon **161** 33 25N 108 55W
Mogollon Mesa **161** 43 40N 111 0W
Mogriguy **141** 32 3 S 148 40 E
Moguer **57** 37 15N 6 52W
Mogumber **137** 31 2 S 116 3 E
Mohács **53** 45 58N 18 41 E
Mohaka, R. **142** 39 7 S 177 12 E
Mohall **158** 48 46N 101 30W
Mohammadābād **93** 37 30N 59 5 E
Mohammedia **118** 33 44N 7 21W
Mohave Desert **161** 35 0N 117 30W
Mohawk **161** 32 45N 113 50W
Mohawk, R. **162** 42 47N 73 42W
Moheda **73** 57 1N 14 35 E
Mohembo **125** 18 15 S 21 43 E
Moher, Cliffs of **39** 52 58N 9 30W
Mohican, C. **147** 60 10N 167 30W
Mohill **38** 53 57N 7 52W
Möhne, R. **48** 51 29N 8 10 E
Mohnyin **98** 24 47N 96 22 E
Moholm **73** 58 37N 14 5 E
Mohon **43** 49 45N 4 44 E
Mohoro **126** 8 6 S 39 8 E
Moia **123** 5 3N 28 2 E
Moidart, L. **36** 56 47N 5 40W
Moinabad **96** 17 44N 77 16 E
Moineşti **70** 46 28N 26 21 E
Mointy **76** 47 40N 73 45 E
Moira **38** 54 28N 6 16W
Moirais **69** 35 4N 24 56 E
Moirans **45** 45 20N 5 33 E
Moirans-en-Montagne **45** 46 26N 5 43 E
Moisäkula **80** 58 3N 24 38 E
Moisie **151** 50 7N 66 1W
Moisie, R. **151** 50 6N 66 5W
Moissac **44** 44 7N 1 5 E
Moita **57** 38 38N 8 58W
Mojácar **59** 37 6N 1 55W
Mojados **56** 41 26N 4 40W
Mojave **163** 35 8N 118 8W
Mojave Desert **163** 35 0N 116 30W
Mojo, Boliv. **172** 21 48 S 65 33W
Mojo, Ethiopia **123** 8 35N 39 5 E
Mojo, I. **102** 8 10 S 117 40 E
Moju, R. **170** 1 40 S 48 25W
Mokai **142** 38 32 S 175 56 E
Mokambo **127** 12 25 S 28 20 E
Mokameh **95** 25 24N 85 55 E
Mokau, R. **142** 38 35 S 174 55 E
Mokelumne Hill **163** 38 18N 120 43W
Mokelumne, R. **163** 38 23N 121 25W
Mokhós **69** 35 16N 25 27 E
Mokhotlong **126** 29 22 S 29 2 E
Mokihinui **143** 41 33 S 171 58 E
Moknine **119** 35 35N 10 58 E
Mokokchung **99** 26 15N 94 30 E
Mokpalin **98** 17 26N 96 53 E
Mokpo **107** 34 50N 126 30 E
Mokra Gora **66** 42 50N 20 30 E
Mokronog **63** 45 57N 15 9 E
Moksha, R. **81** 54 45N 43 40 E
Mokshan **81** 52 25N 44 35 E
Mokta Spera **120** 16 38N 9 6W
Moktama Kwe **99** 15 40N 96 30 E
Mol **47** 51 11N 5 5 E
Mola, C. de la **58** 39 53N 4 20 E
Mola di Bari **65** 41 3N 17 5 E
Moland **71** 59 11N 8 6 E
Moláoi **69** 36 49N 22 56 E
Molat, I. **63** 44 15N 14 50 E
Molchanovo **76** 57 40N 83 50 E
Mold **31** 53 10N 3 10W
Moldava nad Bodvou **53** 48 38N 21 0 E
Moldavia = Moldova **70** 46 30N 27 0 E
Moldavian S.S.R.□ **82** 47 0N 28 0 E
Molde **71** 62 45N 7 9 E
Moldotau, Khrebet **85** 41 35N 75 0 E
Moldova **70** 46 30N 27 0 E
Moldova Nouŭ **70** 44 45N 21 41 E
Moldoveanu, mt. **67** 45 36N 24 45 E
Mole Creek **138** 41 32 S 146 24 E
Mole, R. **29** 51 13N 0 15W
Molepolole **125** 24 28 S 25 28 E
Moléson **50** 46 33N 7 1 E
Molesworth **143** 42 5 S 173 16 E
Molfetta **65** 41 12N 16 35 E
Molina de Aragón **58** 40 46N 1 52W
Moline **158** 41 30N 90 30W
Molinella **63** 44 38N 11 40 E
Molinos **172** 25 28 S 66 15W
Moliro **126** 8 12 S 30 30 E
Molise □ **63** 41 45N 14 30 E
Moliterno **65** 40 14N 15 50 E
Mollahat **98** 22 56N 89 48 E
Mölle **73** 56 17N 12 31 E
Molledo **56** 43 8N 4 6W
Mollendo **174** 17 0 S 72 0W
Mollerin, L. **137** 30 30 S 117 35 E
Mollerusa **58** 41 37N 0 54 E
Mollina **57** 37 8N 4 38W
Mölln **48** 53 37N 10 41 E
Mollösund **73** 58 4N 11 30 E
Mölltorp **73** 58 30N 14 26 E
Mölndal **73** 57 40N 12 3 E
Mölnlycke **73** 57 40N 12 8 E
Molo **98** 23 22N 96 53 E
Molochansk **82** 47 15N 35 23 E
Molochaya, R. **82** 47 0N 35 30 E
Molodechno **80** 54 20N 26 50 E
Molokai, I. **147** 21 8N 157 0W
Moloma, R. **81** 59 0N 48 15 E
Molong **141** 33 5 S 148 54 E
Molopo, R. **125** 25 40 S 24 30 E
Mólos **69** 38 47N 22 37 E
Molotov, Mys **77** 81 10N 95 0 E
Moloundou **124** 2 8N 15 15 E
Molsheim **43** 48 33N 7 29 E
Molson L. **153** 54 22N 95 32W
Molteno **128** 31 22 S 26 22 E
Molu, I. **103** 6 45 S 131 40 E
Molucca Sea **103** 4 0 S 124 0 E
Moluccas = Maluku, Is. **103** 1 0 S 127 0 E
Molusi **128** 20 21 S 24 29 E
Moma, Mozam. **127** 16 47 S 39 4 E
Moma, Zaïre **126** 1 35 S 23 52 E
Momanga **128** 18 7 S 21 41 E
Momba **140** 30 58 S 143 30 E
Mombaça **170** 15 43 S 48 43W
Mombasa **126** 4 2 S 39 43 E
Mombetsu, Hokkaido, Japan **112** 42 27N 142 4 E
Mombetsu, Hokkaido, Japan **112** 44 21N 143 22 E
Mombuey **56** 42 3N 6 20W
Momchilgrad **67** 41 33N 25 23 E
Momi **126** 1 42 S 27 0 E
Momignies **47** 50 2N 4 10 E
Mompós **174** 9 14N 74 26W
Møn **73** 54 57N 12 15 E
Mon, R. **99** 20 25N 94 30 E
Mona, Canal de la **167** 18 30N 67 45W
Mona, I. **167** 18 5N 67 54W
Mona Passage **167** 18 0N 67 40W
Mona, Punta, C. Rica **166** 9 37N 82 36W
Mona, Punta, Spain **57** 36 43N 3 45W
Monach Is. **36** 57 32N 7 40W
Monach, Sd. of **36** 57 34N 7 26W
Monaco ■ **44** 43 46N 7 23 E
Monadhliath Mts. **37** 57 10N 4 4W
Monadnock Mt. **162** 42 52N 72 7W
Monagas □ **174** 9 20N 63 0W
Monaghan **38** 54 15N 6 58W
Monaghan □ **38** 54 10N 7 0W
Monahans **159** 31 35N 102 50W
Monapo **127** 14 50 S 40 12 E
Monar For. **36** 57 27N 5 10W
Monar L. **36** 57 26N 5 8W
Monarch Mt. **152** 51 55N 125 57W
Monasterevan **39** 53 10N 7 5W
Monastier-sur-Gazeille, Le **44** 44 57N 3 59 E
Monastir **119** 35 50N 10 49 E
Monastyriska **80** 49 8N 25 14 E
Monavullagh Mts. **39** 52 14N 7 35W
Moncada **58** 39 30N 0 24W
Moncalieri **62** 45 0N 7 40 E
Moncalvo **62** 45 3N 8 15 E
Moncarapacho **57** 37 5N 7 46W
Moncayo, Sierra del **58** 41 48N 1 50W
Mönchengladbach **48** 51 12N 6 23 E
Monchique **57** 37 19N 8 38W
Monchique, Sa. de, **55** 37 18N 8 39W
Monclova **164** 26 50N 101 30W
Monção **56** 42 4N 8 27W
Moncontant **42** 46 43N 0 36W
Moncontour **42** 48 22N 2 38W
Moncton **151** 46 7N 64 51W
Mondego, Cabo **56** 40 11N 8 54W
Mondego, R. **56** 40 28N 8 0W
Mondeodo **103** 3 21 S 122 9 E
Mondolfo **63** 43 45N 13 8 E
Mondoñedo **56** 43 25N 7 23W
Mondoví **62** 44 23N 7 56 E
Mondovi **158** 44 37N 91 40W
Mondragon **45** 44 13N 4 44 E
Mondragone **64** 41 8N 13 52 E
Mondrain I. **137** 34 9 S 122 14 E
Monduli □ **126** 3 0 S 36 0 E
Monemvasía **69** 36 41N 23 3 E
Monessen **156** 40 9N 79 50W
Monesterio **57** 38 6N 6 15W
Monestier-de-Clermont **45** 44 55N 5 38 E
Monet **150** 48 10N 75 40W
Monêtier-les-Bains, Le **45** 44 58N 6 30 E
Monett **159** 36 55N 93 56W
Moneygall **39** 52 54N 7 59W
Moneymore **38** 54 42N 6 40W
Monfalcone **63** 45 49N 13 32 E
Monflanquin **44** 44 32N 0 47 E
Monforte **57** 39 6N 7 25W
Monforte de Lemos **56** 42 31N 7 33W
Mong Cai **101** 21 27N 107 54 E
Möng Hsu **99** 21 54N 98 30 E
Mong Hta **98** 19 50N 98 35 E
Mong Ket **98** 23 8N 98 22 E
Möng Kung **98** 21 35N 97 35 E
Mong Kyawt **98** 19 56N 98 45 E
Mong Lang **101** 20 29N 97 52 E
Möng Nai **98** 20 32N 97 55 E
Möng Pai **98** 19 40N 97 15 E
Mong Pawk **99** 22 4N 99 16 E
Mong Ping **98** 21 22N 99 2 E
Mong Pu **98** 20 55N 98 44 E
Mong Ton **98** 20 25N 98 45 E
Mong Tung **98** 22 2N 97 41 E
Mong Wa **99** 21 26N 100 27 E
Mong Yai **98** 22 28N 98 3 E
Mongalla **123** 5 8N 31 55 E
Monger, L. **137** 29 25 S 117 5 E
Monghyr **95** 25 23N 86 30 E
Mongla **98** 22 8N 89 35 E
Mongngaw **98** 22 47N 96 59 E
Mongo **117** 12 14N 18 43 E
Mongolia ■ **105** 47 0N 103 0 E
Mongonu **121** 12 40N 13 32 E
Mongororo **124** 12 22N 22 26 E
Mongoumba **124** 3 33N 18 40 E
Mongpang **101** 23 5N 100 25 E
Mongu **125** 15 16 S 23 12 E
Mongua **128** 16 43 S 15 20 E
Moniaive **35** 55 11N 3 55W
Monifieth **35** 56 30N 2 48W
Monistral-St.-Loire **45** 45 17N 4 11 E
Monitor, Pk. **163** 38 52N 116 35W
Monitor, Ra. **163** 38 30N 116 45W
Monivea **38** 53 22N 8 42W
Monk **153** 47 7N 69 59W
Monkey Bay **127** 14 7 S 35 1 E
Monkey River **165** 16 22N 88 29W
Monki **54** 53 23N 22 48 E
Monkira **138** 24 46 S 140 30 E
Monkoto **124** 1 38 S 20 35 E
Monmouth, U.K. **31** 51 48N 2 43W
Monmouth, U.S.A. **158** 40 50N 90 40W
Monmouth (□) **26** 51 34N 3 5W
Monnow R. **28** 51 54N 2 48W
Mono, L. **163** 38 0N 119 9W
Mono, Punta del **166** 12 0N 83 30W
Monolith **163** 35 7N 118 22W
Monópoli **65** 40 57N 17 18 E
Monor **53** 47 21N 19 27 E
Monóvar **59** 38 28N 0 53W
Monowai **143** 45 53 S 167 25 E
Monowai, L. **143** 45 53 S 167 25 E
Monreal del Campo **58** 40 47N 1 20W
Monreale **64** 38 6N 13 16 E
Monroe, La., U.S.A. **159** 32 32N 92 4W
Monroe, Mich., U.S.A. **156** 41 55N 83 26W
Monroe, N.C., U.S.A. **157** 35 2N 80 37W
Monroe, Utah, U.S.A. **161** 38 45N 111 39W
Monroe, Wis., U.S.A. **158** 42 38N 89 40W
Monroe City **158** 39 40N 91 40W
Monroeton **162** 41 43N 76 29W
Monroeville **157** 31 33N 87 15W
Monrovia, Liberia **120** 6 18N 10 47W
Monrovia, U.S.A. **161** 34 7N 118 1W
Mons **47** 50 27N 3 58 E
Møns Klint **73** 54 57N 12 33 E
Monsaraz **57** 38 28N 7 22W
Monse **103** 4 0 S 123 10 E
Monségur **44** 44 38N 0 4 E
Monsélice **63** 43 13N 11 45 E
Monster **46** 52 1N 4 10 E
Mont-aux-Sources **129** 28 44 S 28 52 E
Mont-de-Marsin **44** 43 54N 0 31W
Mont d'Or, Tunnel **43** 46 45N 6 18 E
Mont-Dore, Le **44** 45 35N 2 50 E
Mont Joli **151** 48 37N 68 10W
Mont Laurier **150** 46 35N 75 30W
Mont Luis **151** 42 31N 2 6 E
Mont St. Michel **42** 48 40N 1 30W
Mont-sur-Marchienne **47** 50 23N 4 24 E
Mont Tremblant Prov. Park **150** 46 30N 74 30W
Montabaur **48** 50 26N 7 49 E
Montacute **109** 34 53 S 138 45 E
Montagnac **44** 43 29N 3 28 E
Montagnana **63** 45 13N 11 29 E
Montagu **128** 33 45 S 20 8 E
Montagu, I. **164** 58 30 S 26 15W
Montague, Can. **151** 46 10N 62 39W
Montague, Calif., U.S.A. **160** 41 47N 122 30W
Montague, Mass., U.S.A. **162** 42 31N 72 33W
Montague, I. **164** 31 40N 144 46W
Montague I. **147** 60 0N 147 0W
Montague Ra. **137** 29 15 S 119 30 E
Montague Sd. **136** 14 28 S 125 20 E
Montaigu **42** 46 59N 1 18W
Montalbán **58** 40 50N 0 45W
Montalbano di Elicona **65** 38 1N 15 0 E
Montalbano Iónico **65** 40 17N 16 33 E
Montalbo **58** 39 53N 2 42W
Montalcino **63** 43 4N 11 30 E
Montalegre **56** 41 49N 7 47W
Montalto di Castro **63** 42 20N 11 36 E
Montalto Uffugo **65** 39 25N 16 9 E
Montalvo **163** 34 15N 119 12W
Montamarta **56** 41 39N 5 49W
Montaña **174** 6 0 S 73 0W
Montana **50** 46 19N 7 29 E
Montana □ **154** 47 0N 110 0W
Montánchez **57** 39 15N 6 8W
Montañita **174** 1 30N 75 28W
Montargis **43** 48 0N 2 43 E
Montauban **44** 44 0N 1 21 E
Montauk **162** 41 3N 71 57W
Montauk Pt. **162** 41 4N 71 52W
Montbard **43** 47 38N 4 20 E
Montbéliard **43** 47 31N 6 48 E
Montblanch **58** 41 23N 1 4 E
Montbrison **45** 45 36N 4 3 E
Montçalm, Pic de **44** 42 40N 1 25 E
Montceau-les-Mines **43** 46 40N 4 23 E
Montchanin **62** 46 47N 4 30 E
Montclair **162** 40 53N 74 49W
Montcornet **43** 49 40N 4 0 E

Morven **Mukden**

Morven, Austral. 139 26 22S 147 5E
Morven, N.Z. 143 44 50S 171 6E
Morven, dist. 34 56 38N 5 44W
Morven, mt., Grampian, U.K. 37 57 8N 3 1W
Morven, mt., Highland, U.K. 37 58 15N 3 40W
Morvern 36 56 38N 5 44W
Morwell 141 38 10S 146 22E
Moryn 54 52 51N 14 22E
Mosalsk 80 54 30N 34 55E
Mosbach 49 49 21N 9 9E
Mosciano Sant' Ángelo 63 42 42N 13 52E
Moscos Is. 101 14 0N 97 30E
Moscow, Idaho, U.S.A. 160 46 45N 116 59W
Moscow, Pa., U.S.A. 162 41 20N 75 31W
Moscow = Moskva 81 55 45N 37 35E
Mosel, R. 49 50 22N 7 36E
Moselle □ 43 48 59N 6 33E
Moselle, R. 47 50 22N 7 36E
Moses Lake 160 47 16N 119 17W
Mosgiel 143 45 53S 170 21E
Moshi 126 3 22S 37 18E
Moshi □ 126 3 22S 37 18E
Moshupa 128 24 46S 25 29E
Mósina 54 52 15N 16 50E
Mosjøen 74 65 51N 13 12E
Moskenesøya 74 67 58N 13 0E
Moskenstraumen 74 67 47N 13 0E
Moskva 81 55 45N 37 35E
Moskva, R. 81 55 5N 38 51E
Moslavačka Gora 63 45 40N 16 37E
Mošćenice 63 45 17N 14 16E
Mosomane (Artesia) 128 24 2S 26 19E
Mosonmagyaróvár 53 47 52N 17 18E
Mo orin 66 45 19N 20 4E
Mospino 82 47 52N 38 0E
Mosquera 174 2 35N 78 30W
Mosquero 159 35 48N 103 57W
Mosqueruela 58 40 21N 0 27W
Mosquitia 166 15 20N 84 10W
Mosquitos, Golfo de los 166 9 15N 81 10W
Moss 71 59 27N 10 40E
Moss Vale 141 34 32S 150 25E
Mossaka 124 1 15S 16 45E
Mossâmedes, Angola 125 15 7S 12 11E
Mossâmedes, Brazil 171 16 7S 50 11W
Mossbank 153 49 56N 105 56W
Mossburn 143 45 41S 168 15E
Mosselbaai 128 34 11S 22 8E
Mossendjo 124 2 55S 12 42E
Mosses, Col des 50 46 25N 7 7E
Mossgiel 140 33 15S 144 30E
Mossley 32 53 31N 2 1W
Mossman 138 16 28S 145 23E
Mossoró 170 5 10S 37 15W
Mossuril 127 14 58S 40 42E
Mossy, R. 153 54 5N 102 58W
Most 52 50 31N 13 38E
Mostar 66 43 22N 17 50E
Mostardas 173 31 2S 50 51W
Mostefa, Rass 119 36 55N 11 3E
Mosterøy 71 59 5N 5 37E
Mostiska 80 49 48N 23 4E
Mostrim 38 53 42N 7 38W
Mosty 80 53 27N 24 38E
Mostyn 31 53 18N 3 14W
Mosul = Al Mawsil 92 36 20N 43 5E
Mosulpo 107 33 20N 126 17E
Mosvatn, L. 71 59 52N 8 5E
Mota del Cuervo 58 39 30N 2 52W
Mota del Marqués 56 41 38N 5 11W
Motagua, R. 166 15 44N 88 14W
Motala 73 58 32N 15 1E
Motcombe 28 51 1N 2 12W
Motegi 111 36 32N 140 11E
Mothe-Achard, La 42 46 37N 1 40W
Motherwell 35 55 48N 4 0W
Motihari 95 26 37N 85 1E
Motilla del Palancar 58 39 34N 1 55W
Motnik 63 46 14N 14 54E
Motocurunya 174 4 24N 64 5W
Motovun 63 45 20N 13 50E
Motozintea de Mendoza 165 15 21N 92 14W
Motril 59 36 44N 3 37W
Motrul, R. 70 44 44N 22 59E
Mott 158 46 25N 102 14W
Motte-Chalançon, La 45 44 30N 5 21E
Motte, La 45 44 20N 6 3E
Mottisfont 28 51 2N 1 32W
Mottola 65 40 38N 17 0E
Motueka 143 41 7S 173 1E
Motul 165 21 0N 89 20W
Motupena Pt. 135 6 30S 155 10E
Mouchalagane, R. 151 50 56N 68 41W
Moúdhros 68 39 50N 25 18E
Moudjeria 120 17 50N 12 15W
Moudon 50 46 40N 6 49E
Mouila 124 1 50S 11 0E
Moulamein 140 35 3S 144 1E
Moule, Le 167 16 20N 61 22W
Moulins 44 46 35N 3 19E
Moulmein 98 16 30N 97 40E
Moulmeingyun 98 16 23N 95 16E
Moulouya, O. 118 35 8N 2 22W
Moulton, U.K. 29 52 17N 0 51W
Moulton, U.S.A. 159 29 35N 97 8W
Moultrie 157 31 11N 83 47W
Moultrie, L. 157 33 25N 80 10W
Mound City, Mo., U.S.A. 158 40 2N 95 25W
Mound City, S.D., U.S.A. 158 45 46N 100 3W
Moúnda, Ákra 69 38 5N 20 45E
Moundou 117 8 40N 16 10E
Moundsville 156 39 53N 80 43W
Moung 100 12 46N 103 27E
Mount Airy 162 36 31N 80 37W
Mount Amherst 136 18 24S 126 58E
Mount Angel 160 45 4N 122 46W
Mount Augustus 137 24 20S 116 56E
Mount Barker, S.A., Austral. 140 35 5S 138 52E
Mount Barker, W.A., Austral. 137 34 38S 117 40E
Mount Barker Junc. 109 35 1S 138 52E
Mount Beauty 141 36 47S 147 10E
Mount Bellew Bridge 38 53 28N 8 30W
Mount Buckley 138 20 6S 148 0E
Mount Carmel, Ill., U.S.A. 156 38 20N 87 48W
Mount Carmel, Pa., U.S.A. 162 40 46N 76 25W
Mount Clemens 150 42 35N 82 50W
Mount Coolon 138 21 25S 147 25E
Mount Cootatha Park 108 27 29S 152 57E
Mount Crosby 108 27 32S 152 48E
Mount Darwin 125 16 47S 31 38E
Mount Desert I. 151 44 25N 68 25W
Mount Dora 157 28 49N 81 32W
Mount Douglas 138 21 35S 146 50E
Mount Edgecumbe 147 57 8N 135 22W
Mount Elizabeth 136 16 0S 125 50E
Mount Enid 136 21 42S 116 26E
Mount Forest 150 43 59N 80 43W
Mount Fox 138 18 45S 145 45E
Mount Gambier 140 37 50S 140 46E
Mount Garnet 138 17 37S 145 6E
Mount Goldsworthy 132 20 25S 119 39E
Mount Gravatt 108 27 32S 153 5E
Mount Hagen 135 5 52S 144 16E
Mount Hope, N.S.W., Austral. 141 32 51S 145 51E
Mount Hope, S.A., Austral. 139 34 7S 135 23E
Mount Hope, U.S.A. 156 37 52N 81 9W
Mount Horeb 158 43 0N 89 42W
Mount Howitt 139 26 31S 142 16E
Mount Isa 138 20 42S 139 26E
Mount Ive 140 32 25S 136 5E
Mount Keith 137 27 15S 120 30E
Mount Kisco 162 41 12N 73 44W
Mount Laguna 163 32 52N 116 25W
Mount Larcom 138 23 48S 150 59E
Mount Lavinia 93 6 50N 79 50E
Mount Lofty Ra. 133 34 35S 139 5E
Mount McKinley Nat. Pk. 147 64 0N 150 0W
Mount Magnet 137 28 2S 117 47E
Mount Manara 140 32 29S 143 58E
Mount Margaret 139 26 54S 143 21E
Mount Maunganui 142 37 40S 176 14E
Mount Monger 137 31 0S 122 0E
Mount Morgan 138 23 40S 150 25E
Mount Morris 156 42 43N 77 50W
Mount Mulligan 138 16 45S 144 47E
Mount Narryer 137 26 30S 115 55E
Mount Newman 136 23 18S 119 45E
Mount Nicholas 137 22 54S 120 27E
Mount Oxide 138 19 30S 139 29E
Mount Pearl 151 47 31N 52 47W
Mount Penn 162 40 20N 75 54W
Mount Perry 139 25 13S 151 42E
Mount Phillips 137 24 25S 116 15E
Mount Pleasant, Iowa, U.S.A. 158 41 0N 91 35W
Mount Pleasant, Mich., U.S.A. 156 43 35N 84 47W
Mount Pleasant, S.C., U.S.A. 157 32 45N 79 48W
Mount Pleasant, Tenn., U.S.A. 157 35 31N 87 11W
Mount Pleasant, Tex., U.S.A. 159 33 5N 95 0W
Mount Pleasant, Ut., U.S.A. 160 39 40N 111 29W
Mount Pocono 162 41 8N 75 21W
Mount Rainier Nat. Park. 160 46 50N 121 43W
Mount Revelstoke Nat. Park 152 51 5N 118 30W
Mount Robson 152 52 56N 119 15W
Mount Robson Prov. Park 152 53 0N 119 0W
Mount Samson 108 27 18S 152 51E
Mount Sandiman 137 24 25S 115 30E
Mount Shasta 160 41 20N 122 18W
Mount Somers 143 43 45S 171 27E
Mount Sterling, Ill., U.S.A. 158 40 0N 90 40W
Mount Sterling, Ky., U.S.A. 158 38 0N 84 0W
Mount Surprise 138 18 10S 144 17E
Mount Talbot 38 53 31N 8 18W
Mount Tom Price 137 22 50S 117 40E
Mount Upton 162 42 26N 75 23W
Mount Vernon, Austral. 137 24 15S 118 15E
Mount Vernon, D.C., U.S.A. 162 38 47N 77 10W
Mount Vernon, Ill., U.S.A. 162 38 17N 88 57W
Mount Vernon, Ind., U.S.A. 158 38 17N 88 57W
Mount Vernon, N.Y., U.S.A. 156 40 57N 73 49W
Mount Vernon, Ohio, U.S.A. 156 40 20N 82 30W
Mount Vernon, Wash., U.S.A. 160 48 27N 122 18W
Mount Victor 140 32 11S 139 44E
Mount Whaleback 132 23 18S 119 44E
Mount Willoughby 139 27 58S 134 8E
Mountain Ash 31 51 42N 3 22W
Mountain Center 163 33 42N 116 44W
Mountain City, Nev., U.S.A. 160 41 54N 116 0W
Mountain City, Tenn., U.S.A. 157 36 30N 81 50W
Mountain Dale 162 41 41N 74 32W
Mountain Grove 159 37 5N 92 20W
Mountain Home, Ark., U.S.A. 159 36 20N 92 25W
Mountain Home, Idaho, U.S.A. 160 43 11N 115 45W
Mountain Iron 158 47 30N 92 87W
Mountain Park. 152 52 50N 117 15W
Mountain View, Ark., U.S.A. 159 35 52N 92 10W
Mountain View, Calif., U.S.A. 161 37 26N 122 5W
Mountain Village 147 62 10N 163 50W
Mountainair 161 34 35N 106 15W
Mountcharles 38 54 37N 8 12W
Mountfield 38 54 34N 7 10W
Mountmellick 39 53 7N 7 20W
Mountnorris 38 54 15N 6 29W
Mountnorris B. 136 11 25S 132 45E
Mountrath 39 53 0N 7 30W
Mounts Bay 30 50 3N 5 27W
Mountsorrel 28 52 43N 1 9W
Mountvernon 152 48 25N 122 20W
Mouping 107 37 24N 121 35E
Moura, Austral. 138 24 35S 149 58E
Moura, Brazil 174 1 25S 61 45W
Moura, Port. 57 38 7N 7 30W
Mourão 57 38 22N 7 22W
Mourdi, Depression du 117 18 10N 23 0E
Mourdiah 120 14 35N 7 25W
Moure, La 158 46 27N 98 17W
Mourenx 44 43 23N 0 36W
Mouri 121 5 6N 1 14W
Mourilyan 138 17 35S 146 3E
Mourmelon-le-Grand 43 49 8N 4 22E
Mourne Mts. 38 54 10N 6 0W
Mourne, R. 38 54 45N 7 39W
Mouroubra 137 29 42S 117 52E
Mourzouq 119 25 53N 14 10W
Mousa I. 36 60 0N 1 10W
Mouscron 47 50 45N 3 12E
Moussoro 117 13 50N 16 35E
Mouthe 43 46 44N 6 12E
Moutier 50 47 16N 7 21E
Moutiers 45 45 29N 6 31E
Mouting 108 25 22N 101 32E
Moutong 103 0 28N 121 13E
Mouy 43 49 18N 2 20E
Mouzáki 68 39 25N 21 37E
Movas 164 28 10N 109 25W
Moville 38 55 11N 7 3W
Moxhe 47 50 38N 5 5E
Moxotó, R. 170 9 19S 38 14W
Moy, Inverness, U.K. 37 57 22N 4 3W
Moy, Ulster, U.K. 38 54 27N 6 40W
Moy, R. 38 54 5N 8 50W
Moyagee 137 27 48S 117 48E
Moyahua 164 21 16N 103 10W
Moyale, Ethiopia 123 3 34N 39 4E
Moyale, Kenya 126 3 30N 39 0E
Moyamba 120 8 15N 12 30W
Moyasta 39 52 40N 9 31W
Moycullen 39 53 20N 9 10W
Moyie 152 49 17N 115 50W
Moyle □ 38 55 10N 6 15W
Moylett 38 53 57N 7 7W
Moynalty 38 53 48N 6 52W
Moyne 39 52 45N 7 43W
Moyobamba 174 6 0S 77 0W
Moyvalley 38 53 26N 6 55W
Moza 90 31 48N 35 8E
Mozambique = Moçambique 125 15 3S 40 42E
Mozambique ■ 129 19 0S 35 0E
Mozambique Chan. 129 20 0S 39 0E
Mozdok 83 43 45N 44 48E
Mozhaisk 81 55 30N 36 2E
Mozhga 84 56 26N 52 15E
Mozirje 63 46 22N 14 58E
Mozua 126 3 57N 24 2E
Mozyr 80 52 0N 29 15E
Mpanda 126 6 23S 31 40E
Mpanda □ 126 6 23S 31 40E
Mpésoba 120 12 31N 5 39W
Mpika 127 11 51S 31 25E
Mpraeso 121 6 50N 0 50W
Mpulungu 127 8 51S 31 5E
Mpwapwa 124 6 30S 36 30E
Mpwapwa □ 126 6 30S 36 20E
Mragowo 54 53 57N 21 18E
Mrakovo 84 52 43N 56 38E
Mramor 66 43 20N 21 45E
Mrhaïer 119 33 55N 5 58E
Mrimina 118 29 50N 7 9W
Mrkonjió Grad 66 44 26N 17 4E
Mrkopalj 63 45 21N 14 52E
Mrocza 54 53 16N 17 35E
Msab, Oued en 119 32 35N 5 20E
Msaken 119 35 49N 10 33E
M'Salu, R. 127 12 25S 39 15E
Msambansovu, mt. 127 15 50S 30 3E
M'sila 119 35 46N 4 30E
Msoro 125 13 35S 31 50E
Msta, R. 80 58 30N 33 30E
Mstislavl 80 54 0N 31 50E
Mszana Dolna 54 49 41N 20 5E
Mszczonów 54 51 58N 20 33E
Mtama 127 10 17S 39 21E
Mtilikwe, R. 127 21 0S 31 12E
Mtsensk 81 53 25N 36 30E
Mtskheta 83 41 52N 44 45E
Mtwara 124 10 20S 40 20E
Mtwara □ 126 1 0S 39 0E
Mtwara-Mikindani 127 10 20S 40 20E
Mu Gia, Deo 100 17 40N 105 47E
Mu Ness 36 60 41N 0 50W
Mu, R. 98 21 56N 95 38E
Muaná 170 1 25S 49 15W
Muanda 124 6 0S 12 20E
Muang Chiang Rai 100 19 52N 99 50E
Muang Kalasin 101 16 26N 103 30E
Muang Lampang 101 18 16N 99 32E
Muang Lamphun 100 18 40N 98 53E
Muang Nan 101 18 52N 100 42E
Muang Phetchabun 101 16 23N 101 12E
Muang Phichit 101 16 29N 100 21E
Muang Ubon 101 15 15N 104 50E
Muang Yasothon 101 15 50N 104 10E
Muar 101 2 3N 102 34E
Muar, R. 101 2 15N 102 48E
Muarabungo 102 1 40S 101 10E
Muaradjuloi 102 0 12S 114 3E
Muaraenim 102 3 40S 103 50E
Muarakaman 102 0 2S 116 45E
Muaratebo 102 1 30S 102 26E
Muaratembesi 102 1 40S 103 2E
Muaratewe 102 0 50S 115 0E
Mubairik 92 23 22N 39 8E
Mubarakpur 95 26 12N 83 24E
Mubende 126 0 33N 31 22E
Mubi 121 10 18N 13 16E
Mubur, P. 101 3 20N 106 12E
Mucajaí, Serra do 174 2 23N 61 10W
Much Dewchurch 28 51 58N 2 45W
Much Marcle 28 51 59N 2 27W
Much Wenlock 28 52 36N 2 34W
Muchalls 37 57 2N 2 10W
Mücheln 48 51 18N 11 49E
Muchinga Mts. 127 11 30S 31 30E
Muchkapskiy 81 51 52N 42 28E
Mûcin 70 45 16N 28 8E
Muck, I. 36 56 50N 6 15W
Muckadilla 139 26 35S 148 23E
Muckle Roe I. 36 60 22N 1 22W
Muckross Hd. 38 54 37N 8 35W
Mucubela 129 16 53S 37 49E
Mucugê 171 13 5S 37 49E
Mucuri 171 18 0S 40 0W
Mucurici 171 18 6S 40 31W
Mud I. 108 27 20S 153 14E
Mud L. 160 40 15N 120 15W
Mudanya 82 40 25N 28 50E
Muddy, R. 161 38 30N 110 55W
Mudgee 141 32 32S 149 31E
Mudhnib 92 25 50N 44 18E
Mudjatik, R. 153 56 1N 107 36W
Mudon 98 16 15N 97 44E
Muecate 127 14 55S 39 34E
Muêda 127 11 36S 39 28E
Muela, La 58 41 36N 1 7W
Mueller Ra., Mts. 136 18 18S 126 46E
Muerto, Mar 165 16 10N 94 10W
Muff 38 55 4N 7 16W
Mufindi □ 127 8 30S 35 20E
Mufou Shan 109 29 15N 114 20E
Mufulira 127 12 32S 28 15E
Mufumbiro Range 126 1 25S 29 30E
Mugardos 56 43 27N 8 15W
Muge 57 39 3N 8 40W
Muge, R. 57 39 15N 8 18W
Múggia 63 45 36N 13 47E
Mugi 110 33 40N 134 25E
Mugia 56 43 3N 9 17W
Mugila, Mts. 126 7 0S 28 50E
Muğla 92 37 15N 28 28E
Múglizh 67 42 37N 25 32E
Mugu 95 29 45N 82 30E
Muhammad Qol 122 20 53N 37 9E
Muhammad Râs 122 27 50N 34 0E
Muhammadabad 95 26 4N 83 25E
Muharraqa = Sa'ad 90 31 28N 34 33E
Muhesi, R. 126 6 40S 35 5E
Muheza □ 126 5 0S 39 0E
Mühldorf 49 48 14N 12 23E
Mühlhausen 48 51 12N 10 29E
Mühlig-Hofmann-fjella 13 72 30S 5 0E
Muhutwe 126 1 35S 31 45E
Mui Bai Bung 101 8 35N 104 42E
Mui Ron 101 18 7N 106 27E
Muiden 46 52 20N 5 4E
Muine Bheag 39 52 42N 6 59W
Muiños 56 41 58N 7 59W
Muir, L. 137 34 30S 116 40E
Muir of Ord 37 57 30N 4 35W
Muirdrum 35 56 31N 2 40W
Muirkirk 35 55 31N 4 6W
Muja 123 12 2N 39 30E
Mukachevo 80 48 27N 22 45E
Mukah 102 2 55N 112 5E
Mukalla 91 14 33N 49 2E
Mukawwa, Geziret 122 23 55N 35 53E
Mukdahan 100 16 32N 104 43E
Mukden = Shenyang 107 41 48N 123 27E

Mukeiras Nabari

Mukeiras 91 13 59N 45 52E
Mukhtolovo 81 55 29N 43 15E
Mukinbudin 137 30 55S 118 5E
Mukombwe 127 15 48S 26 32E
Mukomuko 102 2 20S 101 10E
Mukomwenze 126 6 49S 27 15E
Mukry 85 37 54N 65 12E
Muktsar 94 30 30N 74 30E
Muktsar Bhatinda 94 30 15N 74 57E
Mukur 94 32 50N 67 50E
Mukutawa, R. 153 53 10N 97 24W
Mukwela 127 17 0S 26 40E
Mula 59 38 3N 1 33W
Mula, R. 96 19 16N 74 20E
Mulanay 103 13 30N 122 30E
Mulange 126 3 40S 27 10E
Mulatas, Arch. de las 166 6 51N 78 31W
Mulchén 172 37 45S 72 20W
Mulde, R. 48 50 55N 12 42E
Mule Creek 158 43 19N 104 8W
Muleba 126 1 50S 31 37E
Muleba □ 126 2 0S 31 30E
Mulegé 164 26 53N 112 1W
Mulegns 51 46 32N 9 38E
Mulengchen 107 44 32N 130 14E
Muleshoe 159 34 17N 102 42W
Mulga Valley 140 31 8S 141 3E
Mulgathing 139 30 15S 134 0E
Mulgrave 151 45 38N 61 31W
Mulgrave I. 135 10 5S 142 10E
Mulhacén 59 37 4N 3 20W
Mülheim 48 51 26N 6 53W
Mulhouse 43 47 40N 7 20E
Muli, China 99 28 21N 100 40E
Muli, China 108 27 50N 101 15E
Mull Head 37 59 23N 2 53W
Mull I. 34 56 27N 6 0W
Mull, Ross of, dist. 34 56 20N 6 15W
Mull, Sound of 34 56 30N 5 50W
Mullagh 39 53 13N 8 25W
Mullaghareirk Mts. 39 52 20N 9 10W
Mullaittvu 97 9 15N 80 55E
Mullardoch L. 36 57 30N 5 0W
Mullen 158 42 5N 101 0W
Mullengudgery 141 31 43S 147 29E
Mullens 156 37 34N 81 22W
Muller, Pegunungan 102 0 30N 113 30E
Muller Ra. 138 5 30S 143 0E
Mullet Pen. 38 54 10N 10 2W
Mullewa 137 28 29S 115 30E
Mullheim 49 47 48N 7 37E
Mulligan, R. 138 26 40S 139 0E
Mullin 159 31 33N 98 38W
Mullinahone 39 52 30N 7 31W
Mullinavat 39 52 23N 7 10W
Mullingar 38 53 31N 7 20W
Mullins 157 34 12N 79 15W
Mullion 30 50 1N 5 15W
Mullsjö 73 57 56N 13 55E
Mullumbimby 139 28 30S 153 30E
Mulobezi 127 16 45S 25 7E
Mulrany 38 53 54N 9 47W
Mulroy B. 38 55 15N 7 45W
Mulshi L. 96 18 30N 73 20E
Multai 96 21 39N 78 15E
Multan 94 30 15N 71 30E
Multan □ 94 30 29N 72 29E
Multrå 72 63 10N 17 24E
Mulumbe, Mts. 127 8 40S 27 30E
Mulungushi Dam 127 14 48S 28 48E
Mulvane 159 37 30N 97 15W
Mulwad 122 18 45N 30 39E
Mulwala 141 35 59S 146 0E
Mumbles 31 51 34N 4 0W
Mumbles Hd. 31 51 33N 4 0W
Mumbwa 125 15 0S 27 0E
Mumeng 135 7 1S 146 37E
Mumra 83 45 45N 47 41E
Mun 101 15 17N 103 0E
Mun, R. 100 15 19N 105 30E
Muna, I. 103 5 0S 122 30E
Muna Sotuta 165 20 29N 89 43W
Munawwar 95 32 47N 74 27E
Münchberg 49 50 11N 11 48E
Müncheberg 48 52 30N 14 9E
München 49 48 8N 11 33E
Munchen-Gladbach = Mönchengladbach 48 51 12N 6 23E
Muncho Lake 152 59 0N 125 50W
Munchŏn 107 39 14N 127 19E
Münchwilen 51 47 38N 8 59E
Muncie 156 40 10N 85 20W
Mundakayam 97 9 30N 76 32E
Mundala, Puncak 103 4 30S 141 0E
Mundare 152 53 35N 112 20W
Munday 159 33 26N 99 39W
Münden 48 51 25N 9 42E
Mundesley 29 52 53N 1 24E
Mundiwindi 136 23 47S 120 9E
Mundo Novo 171 11 50S 40 29W
Mundo, R. 59 38 30N 2 15W
Mundra 94 22 54N 69 26E
Mundrabilla 137 31 52S 127 51E
Munera 59 39 2N 2 29W
Muneru, R. 96 16 45N 80 3E
Mungallala 139 26 25S 147 34E
Mungallala Cr. 139 28 53S 147 5E
Mungana 138 17 8S 144 27E
Mungaoli 94 24 24N 78 7E
Mungari 127 17 12S 33 42E
Mungbere 124 2 36N 28 28E
Mungindi 139 28 58S 149 1E
Munhango 125 12 10S 18 38E
Munhango R. 125 11 30S 19 30E
Munich = München 49 48 8N 11 35E
Munising 156 46 25N 86 39W
Munjiye 122 18 47N 41 20W
Munka-Ljungby 73 56 16N 12 58E
Munkedal 73 58 28N 11 40E
Munkfors 72 59 50N 13 30E
Muñoz Gamero, Pen. 176 52 30S 73 5E
Munro 141 37 56S 147 11E
Munroe L. 153 59 13N 98 35W
Munsan 107 37 51N 126 48E
Munshiganj 98 23 33N 90 32E
Münsingen 50 46 52N 7 32E
Munster 43 48 2N 7 8E
Münster, Niedersachsen, Ger. 48 52 59N 10 5E
Münster, Nordrhein-Westfalen, Ger. 48 51 58N 7 37E
Münster, Switz. 51 46 30N 8 17E
Munster □ 39 52 20N 8 40W
Muntadgin 137 31 45S 118 33E
Muntele Mare 70 46 30N 23 12E
Muntok 102 2 5S 105 10E
Muon Pak Beng 101 19 51N 101 4E
Muong Beng 100 20 23N 101 46E
Muong Boum 100 22 24N 102 49E
Muong Er 100 20 49N 104 1E
Muong Hai 100 21 3N 101 49E
Muong Hiem 100 20 5N 103 22E
Muong Houn 100 20 8N 101 23E
Muong Hung 100 20 56N 103 53E
Muong Kau 100 15 6N 105 47E
Muong Khao 100 19 47N 103 29E
Muong Khoua 100 21 5N 102 31E
Muong La 101 20 52N 102 5E
Muong Liep 100 18 29N 101 40E
Muong May 100 14 49N 106 56E
Muong Ngeun 100 20 36N 101 3E
Muong Ngoi 100 20 43N 102 41E
Muong Nhie 100 22 12N 102 28E
Muong Nong 100 16 22N 106 30E
Muong Ou Tay 100 22 7N 101 48E
Muong Oua 100 18 18N 101 20E
Muong Pak Bang 100 19 54N 101 8E
Muong Penn 100 20 13N 103 52E
Muong Phalane 100 16 39N 105 34E
Muong Phieng 100 19 6N 101 32E
Muong Phine 100 16 32N 106 2E
Muong Sai 100 20 42N 101 59E
Muong Saiapoun 100 18 24N 101 31E
Muong Sen 100 19 24N 104 8E
Muong Sing 100 21 11N 101 9E
Muong Son 100 20 27N 103 19E
Muong Soui 100 19 33N 102 52E
Muong Va 100 21 53N 102 19E
Muong Xia 100 20 19N 104 50E
Muonio 74 67 57N 23 40E
Muonio älv 74 67 48N 23 25E
Muotathal 51 46 58N 8 46E
Muotohora 142 38 18S 177 40E
Mupa 125 16 5S 15 50E
Muqaddam, Wadi 123 17 0N 32 0E
Mur-de-Bretagne 42 48 12N 3 0W
Mur, R. 52 47 7N 13 55E
Mura, R. 63 46 37N 16 9E
Murallón, Cuerro 176 49 55S 73 30W
Muralto 51 46 11N 8 49E
Muranda 126 1 52S 29 20E
Murang'a 126 0 45S 37 9E
Murashi 81 59 30N 49 0E
Murat 44 45 7N 2 53E
Murau 52 47 6N 14 10E
Muravera 64 39 25N 9 35E
Murça 56 41 24N 7 28W
Murchison 143 41 49S 172 21E
Murchison Downs 137 26 45S 118 55E
Murchison Falls = Kabarega Falls 126 2 15N 31 38E
Murchison House 137 27 39S 114 14E
Murchison Mts. 143 45 13S 167 23E
Murchison, oilfield* 19 61 25N 1 40E
Murchison, R. 137 26 45S 116 15E
Murchison Ra. 138 20 0S 134 10E
Murchison Rapids 127 15 55S 34 35E
Murcia 59 38 2N 1 10W
Murcia □ 59 37 50N 1 30W
Murdo 158 43 56N 100 43W
Murdoch Pt. 138 14 37S 144 55E
Murdock Hill 109 34 59S 138 55E
Mure, La 45 44 55N 5 48E
Mureş □ 70 46 45N 24 40E
Mureşul, R. 70 46 15N 20 13E
Muret 44 43 30N 1 20E
Murfatlar 70 44 10N 28 26E
Murfreesboro 157 35 50N 86 21W
Murg 51 47 8N 9 13E
Murgab 85 38 10N 73 59E
Murgeni 70 46 12N 28 1E
Murgenthal 50 47 16N 7 50E
Murgon 139 26 15S 151 54E
Murgoo 137 27 24S 116 28E
Muri 51 47 17N 8 21E
Muriaé 173 21 8S 42 23W
Murias de Paredes 56 42 52N 6 19W
Murici 170 9 19S 35 56W
Muriel Mine 127 17 14S 30 40E
Muritiba 171 12 55S 39 15W
Murits see 48 53 25N 12 40E
Murjo Mt. 103 6 36S 110 53E
Murka 126 3 27S 38 0E
Murmansk 78 68 57N 33 10E
Murmerwoude 46 53 18N 6 0E
Murnau 49 47 40N 11 11E
Muro, France 45 42 34N 8 54E
Muro, Spain 58 39 45N 3 3E
Muro, C. di 45 41 44N 8 37E
Muro Lucano 65 40 45N 15 30E
Murom 81 55 35N 42 3E
Muroran 112 42 25N 141 0E
Muros 56 42 45N 9 5W
Muros y de Noya, Ria de 56 42 45N 9 0W
Muroto 110 33 18N 134 9E
Muroto-Misaki 110 33 15N 134 10E
Murowana Gosślina 54 52 35N 17 0E
Murphy 160 43 11N 116 33W
Murphys 163 38 8N 120 28W
Murphysboro 159 37 50N 89 20W
Murrat 122 18 51N 29 33E
Murray, Ky., U.S.A. 157 36 40N 88 20W
Murray, Utah, U.S.A. 160 40 41N 111 58W
Murray Bridge 140 35 6S 139 14E
Murray Downs 138 21 4S 134 40E
Murray Harb. 151 46 0N 62 28W
Murray, L., P.N.G. 135 7 0S 141 35E
Murray, L., U.S.A. 157 34 8N 81 30W
Murray, R., S. Australia, Austral. 140 35 20S 139 22E
Murray, R., W. Australia, Austral. 133 32 33S 115 45E
Murray, R., Can. 152 56 11N 120 45W
Murraysburg 128 31 58S 23 47E
Murree 94 33 56N 73 28E
Murrieta 163 33 33N 117 13W
Murrin Murrin 137 28 50S 121 45E
Murrough 39 53 7N 9 18W
Murrumbidgee, R. 140 34 40S 143 0E
Murrumburrah 141 34 32S 148 22E
Murrurundi 141 31 42S 150 51E
Murshid 122 21 40N 31 10E
Murshidabad 95 24 11N 88 19E
Murska Sobota 63 46 39N 16 12E
Murtazapur 96 20 40N 77 25E
Murten 50 46 56N 6 7E
Murten-see 50 46 56N 7 4E
Murtle L. 152 52 8N 119 38W
Murtoa 140 36 35S 142 28E
Murton 33 54 51N 1 22W
Murtosa 56 40 44N 8 40W
Muru 123 6 36N 29 16E
Murungu 126 4 12S 31 10E
Murupara 142 38 28S 176 42E
Murwara 95 23 46N 80 28E
Murwillumbah 139 28 18S 153 27E
Mürz, R. 52 47 30N 15 25E
Mürzzuschlag 52 47 36N 15 41E
Muş 92 38 45N 41 30E
Musa, Gebel (Sinai) 122 28 32N 33 59E
Musa Khel 94 30 29N 69 52E
Musa Qala (Musa Kala) 93 32 20N 64 50E
Musa, R. 135 9 3S 148 55E
Musaffargarh 93 30 10N 71 10E
Musairik, Wadi 122 19 30N 43 10E
Musala, I. 102 1 41N 98 28E
Musalla, mt. 67 42 13N 23 37E
Musan 107 42 12N 129 12E
Musangu 127 10 28S 23 55E
Musasa 126 3 25S 31 30E
Musashino 111 35 42N 139 34E
Muscat = Masqat 93 23 37N 58 36E
Muscat & Oman = Oman 91 23 0N 58 0E
Muscatine 158 41 25N 91 5W
Musel 56 43 34N 5 42W
Musetula 127 14 28S 24 1E
Musgrave Ras. 137 26 0S 132 0E
Mushie 124 2 56S 17 4E
Mushin 121 6 32N 3 21E
Musi, R., India 96 17 10N 79 25E
Musi, R., Indon. 102 2 55S 103 40E
Muskeg, R. 152 60 20N 123 20W
Muskegon 156 43 15N 86 17W
Muskegon Hts. 156 43 12N 86 17W
Muskegon, R. 156 43 25N 86 0W
Muskogee 159 35 50N 95 25W
Muskwa, R. 152 58 47N 122 48W
Musmar 122 18 6N 35 40E
Musofu 127 13 30S 29 0E
Musoma 126 1 30S 33 48E
Musoma □ 126 1 50S 34 30E
Musquaro, L. 151 50 38N 61 5W
Musquodoboit Harbour 151 44 50N 63 9W
Mussau I. 135 1 30S 149 40E
Musselburgh 35 55 57N 3 3W
Musselkanaal 46 52 57N 7 0E
Musselshell, R. 160 46 30N 108 15W
Mussidan 44 45 2N 0 22E
Mussomeli 64 37 35N 13 43E
Musson 47 49 33N 5 42E
Mussooree 94 30 27N 78 6E
Mussuco 128 17 2S 19 3E
Mustafa Kemalpaşa 92 40 3N 28 25E
Mustajidda 92 26 30N 41 50E
Mustang 95 29 10N 83 55E
Mustapha, C. 119 36 55N 11 3E
Musters, L. 176 45 20S 69 25W
Musudan 107 40 50N 129 43E
Muswellbrook 141 32 16S 150 56E
Muszyna 53 49 22N 20 55E
Mût 122 25 28N 28 58E
Mut 92 36 40N 33 28E
Mutan Chiang, R. 107 46 18N 129 31E
Mutanchiang 107 44 40N 129 35E
Mutanda, Mozam. 129 21 0S 33 34E
Mutanda, Zambia 127 12 15S 26 13E
Muthill 35 56 20N 3 50W
Mutis 174 1 4N 77 25W
Mutooroo 140 32 26S 140 55E
Mutshatsha 127 10 35S 24 20E
Mutsu-Wan 112 41 5N 140 55E
Muttaburra 138 22 38S 144 29E
Muttama 141 34 46S 148 8E
Mutton Bay 151 50 50N 59 2W
Mutton I. 39 52 50N 9 31W
Mutuáli 127 14 55S 37 0E
Mutung 108 29 35N 106 51E
Mutunópolis 171 13 40S 49 15W
Muvatupusha 97 9 53N 76 35E
Muxima 124 9 25S 13 52E
Muy, Le 45 43 28N 6 34E
Muy Muy 166 12 39N 85 36W
Muya 77 56 27N 115 39E
Muyaga 126 3 14S 30 33E
Muyunkum, Peski 85 44 12N 71 0E
Muzaffarabad 95 34 25N 73 30E
Muzaffargarh 94 30 5N 71 14E
Muzaffarnagar 94 29 26N 77 40E
Muzaffarpur 95 26 7N 85 32E
Muzhi 76 65 25N 64 40E
Muzillac 42 47 35N 2 30W
Muzkol, Khrebet 85 38 22N 73 20E
Muzo 174 5 32N 74 6W
Muzon C. 152 54 40N 132 40W
Mvôlô 123 6 10N 29 53E
Mwadui 126 3 35S 33 40E
Mwandi Mission 127 17 30S 24 51E
Mwango 126 6 48S 24 12E
Mwanza, Katanga, Congo 126 7 55S 26 43E
Mwanza, Kwango, Congo 127 5 29S 17 43E
Mwanza, Malawi 126 16 58S 24 28E
Mwanza, Tanz. 126 2 30S 32 58E
Mwanza □ 126 2 0S 33 0E
Mwaya 126 9 32S 33 55E
Mweelrea, Mt. 38 53 37N 9 48W
Mweka 124 4 50S 21 40E
Mwenga 126 3 1S 28 21E
Mwepo 127 11 50S 26 10E
Mweru, L. 127 9 0S 29 0E
Mweza Range 127 21 0S 30 0E
Mwimbi 127 8 38S 31 39E
Mwinilunga 127 11 43S 24 25E
Mwinilunga, Mt. 127 11 43S 24 25E
My Tho 101 10 29N 106 23E
Mya, O. 119 30 46N 2 44E
Myadh 124 1 16N 13 10E
Myanaung 98 18 25N 95 10E
Myaungmya 98 16 30N 95 0E
Mybster 37 58 27N 3 24W
Myddfai 31 51 59N 3 47W
Myddle 28 52 49N 2 47W
Myerstown 162 40 22N 76 18W
Myingyan 98 21 30N 95 30E
Myitkyina 98 25 30N 97 26E
Myittha, R. 98 16 15N 94 34E
Myjava 53 48 41N 17 37E
Mylor 109 35 3S 138 46E
Mymensingh 98 24 45N 90 24E
Myndmere 158 46 23N 97 7W
Mynydd Bach, Hills 31 52 16N 4 6W
Mynydd Eppynt, Mts. 31 52 4N 3 30W
Mynydd Prescelly, mt. 31 51 57N 4 48W
Mynzhilgi, Gora 85 43 48N 68 51E
Myogi 101 21 24N 96 28E
Myrdal 71 60 43N 7 10E
Mýrdalsjökull 74 63 40N 19 6W
Myrrhee 136 36 46S 146 17E
Myrtle Beach 157 33 43N 78 50W
Myrtle Creek 160 43 0N 123 19W
Myrtle Point 160 43 0N 124 4W
Myrtleford 141 36 34S 146 44E
Myrtletown 108 27 23S 153 8E
Mysen 71 59 33N 11 20E
Myslenice 54 49 51N 19 57E
Myslibórz 54 52 55N 14 50E
Myslowice 54 50 15N 19 12E
Mysore 97 12 17N 76 41E
Mysore □ = Karnataka 142 13 15N 77 0E
Mystic 162 41 21N 71 58W
Mystishchi 81 55 50N 37 50E
Myszkow 54 50 45N 19 22E
Mythen 51 47 2N 8 42E
Myton 160 40 10N 110 2W
Mývatn 74 65 36N 17 0W
Mze, R. 52 49 47N 12 50E
Mzimba 127 11 48S 33 33E
Mzuzu 127 11 30S 33 55E

N

N' Dioum 120 16 31N 14 39W
Na-lang 98 22 42N 97 33E
Na Noi 100 18 19N 100 43E
Na Phao 100 17 35N 105 44E
Na Sam 100 22 3N 106 37E
Na San 100 21 12N 104 2E
Naaldwijk 46 51 59N 4 13E
Naalehu 147 19 4N 155 35W
Na'am 123 9 42N 28 27E
Na'an 90 31 53N 34 52E
Naantali 75 60 29N 22 2E
Naarden 46 52 18N 5 9E
Naas 39 53 12N 6 40W
Nababeep 128 29 36S 17 46E
Nabadwip 95 23 34N 88 20E
Nabari 111 34 37N 136 5E

Nabas Nashville

Nabas 103 11 47N 122 6 E
Nabberu, L. 137 25 30 S 120 30 E
*Naberezhnyye Chelny 84 55 42N 52 19 E
Nabesna 147 62 33N 143 10W
Nabeul 119 36 30N 10 51 E
Nabha 94 30 26N 76 14 E
Nabi Rubin 90 31 56N 34 44 E
Nabire 103 3 15 S 136 27 E
Nabisar 94 25 8N 69 40 E
Nabispi, R. 151 50 14N 62 13W
Nabiswera 126 1 27N 32 15 E
Nablus = Nābulus 90 32 14N 35 15 E
Naboomspruit 129 24 32 S 28 40 E
Nābulus 90 32 14N 35 15 E
Nabúri 127 16 53 S 38 59 E
Nacala-Velha 127 14 32 S 40 34 E
Nacaome 166 13 31N 87 30W
Nacaroa 127 14 22 S 39 56 E
Naches 160 46 48N 120 49W
Nachikatsuura 111 33 33N 135 58 E
Nachingwea 127 10 49 S 38 49 E
Nachingwea □ 127 10 30 S 38 30 E
Nachna 94 27 34N 71 41 E
Náchod 53 50 25N 16 8 E
Nacimento Res. 163 35 46N 120 53W
Nacka 72 59 17N 18 12 E
Nackara 140 32 48 S 139 12 E
Naco, Mexico 164 31 20N 109 56W
Naco, U.S.A. 161 31 24N 109 58W
Nacogdoches 159 31 33N 95 30W
Nácori Chico 164 29 39N 109 1W
Nacozari 164 30 30N 109 50W
Nadi 122 18 40N 33 41 E
Nadiad 94 22 41N 72 56 E
Nador 118 35 14N 2 58W
Nadushan 93 32 2N 53 35 E
Nadvornaya 80 48 40N 24 35 E
Nadym 76 63 35N 72 42 E
Nadym, R. 76 65 30N 73 0 E
Nærbø 71 58 40N 5 39 E
Næstved 73 55 13N 11 44 E
Nafada 121 11 8N 11 20 E
Näfels 51 47 6N 9 4 E
Nafferton 33 54 1N 0 24W
Naft Shāh 92 34 0N 45 30 E
Nafūd ad Dahy 92 22 0N 45 0 E
Nafūsah, Jabal 119 32 12N 12 30 E
Nag Hammâdi 122 26 2N 32 18 E
Naga 103 13 38N 123 15 E
Naga Hills 99 26 0N 94 30 E
Naga, Kreb en 118 24 12N 6 0W
Naga-Shima, Kagoshima, Japan 110 32 10N 130 9 E
Naga-Shima, Yamaguchi, Japan 110 33 55N 132 5 E
Nagagami, R. 150 49 40N 84 40W
Nagahama, Ehime, Japan 111 33 36N 132 29 E
Nagahama, Shiga, Japan 111 35 23N 136 16 E
Nagai Parkar 94 24 28N 70 46 E
Nagaland □ 98 26 0N 94 30 E
Nagambie 141 36 47 S 145 10 E
Nagano 111 36 40N 138 10 E
Nagano-ken □ 111 36 15N 138 0 E
Nagaoka 112 37 27N 138 50 E
Nagappattinam 97 10 46N 79 51 E
Nagar Parkar 93 24 30N 70 35 E
Nagara-Gawa, R. 111 35 1N 136 43 E
Nagari Hills 97 15 30N 79 45 E
Nagarjuna Sagar 96 16 35N 79 17 E
Nagasaki 110 32 47N 129 50 E
Nagasaki-ken □ 110 32 50N 129 40 E
Nagato 110 34 19N 131 5 E
Nagaur 94 27 15N 73 45 E
Nagbhir 96 20 34N 79 42 E
Nagchu Dzong 99 31 22N 91 54 E
Nagercoil 97 8 12N 77 33 E
Nagina 95 29 30N 78 30 E
Nagineh 93 34 20N 57 15 E
Nagold 49 48 38N 8 40 E
Nagoorin 138 24 17 S 151 15 E
Nagorsk 81 59 18N 50 48 E
Nagorum 126 4 1N 34 33 E
Nagoya 111 35 10N 136 50 E
Nagpur 96 21 8N 79 10 E
Nagrong 99 32 46N 84 16 E
Nagua 167 19 23N 69 50W
Nagyatád 53 46 14N 17 22 E
Nagyecsed 53 47 53N 22 24 E
Nagykanizsa 53 46 28N 17 0 E
Nagykörös 53 46 55N 19 48 E
Nagyléta 53 47 23N 21 55 E
Naha 112 26 13N 127 42 E
Nahalal 90 32 41N 35 12 E
Nahanni Butte 152 61 2N 123 20W
Nahanni Nat. Pk. 152 61 15N 125 0W
Naharayim 90 32 28N 35 33 E
Nahariyya 90 33 1N 35 5 E
Nahāvand 92 34 10N 48 30 E
Nahe, R. 49 49 48N 7 33 E
Nahf 90 32 56N 35 18 E
Nahîya, Wadi 122 27 37N 32 0 E
Nahlin 152 58 55N 131 38W
Nahud 122 18 12N 41 40 E
Naiapu 70 44 12N 25 47 E
Naicá 164 27 53N 105 31W
Naicam 153 52 30N 104 30W
Na'ifah 91 19 59N 50 46 E
Naila 49 50 19N 11 43 E
Nailsea 28 51 25N 2 44W
Nailsworth 28 51 41N 2 12W
Nain 151 56 34N 61 40W
*Renamed Brezhnev

Na'in 93 32 54N 53 0 E
Naini Tal 95 29 23N 79 30 E
Nainpur 93 22 30N 80 10 E
Naintré 42 46 46N 0 29 E
Naira, I. 103 4 28 S 130 0 E
Nairn 37 57 35N 3 54W
Nairn (□) 26 57 28N 3 52W
Nairn R. 37 57 32N 3 58W
Nairobi 126 1 17 S 36 48 E
Naivasha 126 0 40 S 36 30 E
Naivasha □ 126 0 40 S 36 30 E
Naivasha L. 126 0 48 S 36 20 E
Najac 44 44 14N 1 58 E
Najafābād 93 32 40N 51 15 E
Najd 92 26 30N 42 0 E
Nájera 58 42 26N 2 48W
Najerilla, R. 58 42 15N 2 45W
Najibabad 94 29 40N 78 20 E
Najin 107 42 12N 130 15 E
Naju 107 35 3N 126 43 E
Naka-Gawa, R. 111 36 20N 140 36 E
Naka-no-Shima 112 29 51N 129 46 E
Nakalagba 126 2 50N 27 58 E
Nakama 110 33 56N 130 43 E
Nakaminato 111 36 21N 140 36 E
Nakamura 110 33 0N 133 0 E
Nakanai Mts. 135 5 40 S 151 0 E
Nakano 111 36 45N 138 22 E
Nakanojō 111 36 35N 138 51 E
Nakatane 112 30 31N 130 57 E
Nakatsu 110 33 40N 131 15 E
Nakatsugawa 111 35 29N 137 30 E
Nakelele Pt. 147 21 2N 156 35W
Nakfa 123 16 40N 38 25 E
Nakhichevan, A.S.S.R. □ 79 39 14N 45 30 E
Nakhl 122 29 55N 33 43 E
Nakhl Mubarak 92 24 10N 38 10 E
Nakhodka 77 43 10N 132 45 E
Nakhon Nayok 100 14 12N 101 13 E
Nakhon Pathom 100 13 49N 100 3 E
Nakhon Phanom 100 17 23N 104 43 E
Nakhon Ratchasima (Khorat) 100 14 59N 102 12 E
Nakhon Sawan 100 15 35N 100 10 E
Nakhon Si Thammarat 100 8 29N 100 0 E
Nakhon Thai 100 17 17N 100 50 E
Nakina, B.C., Can. 152 59 12N 132 52W
Nakina, Ont., Can. 150 50 10N 86 40W
Nakło n. Noteoja 54 53 9N 17 38 E
Naknek 147 58 45N 157 0W
Nakodar 94 31 8N 75 31 E
Nakomis 127 39 19N 89 19W
Nakskov 73 54 50N 11 8 E
Näkten 72 62 48N 14 38 E
Naktong, R. 107 35 7N 128 57 E
Nakur 94 30 2N 77 32 E
Nakuru 126 0 15 S 35 5 E
Nakuru □ 126 0 15 S 35 5 E
Nakuru, L. 126 0 23 S 36 5 E
Nakusp 152 50 20N 117 45W
Nal, R. 94 27 0N 65 50 E
Nalchik 83 43 30N 43 33 E
Nälden 72 63 21N 14 14 E
Näldsjön 72 63 25N 14 15 E
Nalerigu 121 10 35N 0 25W
Nalgonda 96 17 6N 79 15 E
Nalhati 95 24 17N 87 52 E
Nalinnes 47 50 19N 4 27 E
Nallamalai Hills 97 15 30N 78 50 E
Nalón, R. 56 43 35N 6 10W
Nālūt 119 31 54N 11 0 E
Nam Can 101 8 46N 104 59 E
Nam Dinh 100 20 25N 106 5 E
Nam Du, Hon 101 9 41N 104 21 E
'Nam', gasfields 19 53 17N 3 36 E
Nam Ngum 100 18 35N 102 34 E
'Nam', oilfield 19 54 50N 4 40 E
Nam-Phan 101 10 30N 106 0 E
Nam Phong 100 16 42N 102 52 E
Nam Tha 100 20 58N 101 30 E
Nam Tok 100 14 14N 99 4 E
Nam Tso = Namu Hu 105 30 45N 90 30 E
Namacurra 125 17 30 S 36 50 E
Namakkal 97 11 13N 78 13 E
Namaland, Africa 128 26 0 S 18 0 E
Namaland, S. Afr. 128 30 0 S 18 0 E
Namangan 85 41 0N 71 40 E
Namapa 127 13 43 S 39 50 E
Namasagali 126 1 2N 33 0 E
Namatanai 135 3 40 S 152 29 E
Nambala 120 14 1N 5 58W
Namber 103 1 2 S 134 57 E
Nambour 139 26 32 S 152 58 E
Nambucca Heads 141 30 37 S 153 0 E
Namcha Barwa 105 29 40N 95 10 E
Namche Bazar 95 27 51N 86 47 E
Namchonjŏm 107 38 15N 126 26 E
Namêche 47 50 28N 5 0 E
Namecund 127 14 54 S 37 37 E
Nameh 102 2 34N 116 21 E
Nameponda 127 15 50 S 39 50 E
Namerikawa 111 36 46N 137 20 E
Námestovo 53 49 24N 19 25 E
Nametil 127 15 40 S 39 15 E
Náměšt nad Oslavou 53 49 12N 16 10 E
Namew L. 153 54 14N 101 56W
Namhsan 98 22 48N 97 42 E
Nami 101 6 2N 100 46 E
Namib Desert = Namib Woestyn 128 22 30 S 15 0 E
Namib-Woestyn 128 22 30 S 15 0 E
Namibia □ 128 22 0 S 18 9 E

Namiquipa 164 29 15N 107 25W
Namja Pass 95 30 0N 82 25 E
Namkhan 98 23 50N 97 41 E
Namlea 103 3 10 S 127 5 E
Namoi, R. 141 30 12 S 149 30 E
Namous, O. 118 30 44N 0 18W
Nampa 160 43 40N 116 40W
Nampula 127 15 6 S 39 7 E
Namrole 103 3 46 S 126 46 E
Namsen 74 64 27N 11 42 E
Namsen, R. 74 64 40N 12 45 E
Namsos 74 64 28N 11 0 E
Namtu 98 23 5N 97 28 E
Namtumbo 127 10 30 S 36 4 E
Namu 152 51 52N 127 41W
Namu Hu 105 30 45N 90 30 E
Namur 47 50 27N 4 52 E
Namur □ 47 50 17N 5 0 E
Namutoni 128 18 49 S 16 55 E
Namwala 127 15 44 S 26 30 E
Namwŏn 107 35 23N 127 23 E
Namysłow 54 51 6N 17 42 E
Nan 100 18 48N 100 46 E
Nan Ling 109 25 0N 112 30 E
Nan, R. 100 15 42N 100 9 E
Nan Shan 105 38 30N 99 0 E
Nana 70 44 17N 26 34 E
Nānā, W. 119 30 0N 15 24 E
Nanaimo 152 49 10N 124 0W
Nanam 107 41 44N 129 40 E
Nan'an 109 24 58N 118 23 E
Nanango 139 26 40 S 152 0 E
Nanao 109 23 26N 117 1 E
Nanch'ang 109 28 40N 115 50 E
Nanchang, Fukien, China 109 24 26N 117 18 E
Nanchang, Hupei, China 109 31 47N 111 42 E
Nanch'eng 109 27 33N 116 35 E
Nancheng = Hanchung 106 33 10N 107 2 E
Nanchiang 108 32 21N 106 50 E
Nanchiao 108 22 2N 100 15 E
Nanchien 106 25 5N 100 30 E
Nanching 109 32 3N 118 47 E
Nanchishan Liehtao 108 27 28N 121 4 E
Nanch'uan 108 29 7N 107 16 E
Nanch'ung 108 30 50N 106 4 E
Nancy 43 48 42N 6 12 E
Nanda Devi, Mt. 95 30 30N 80 30 E
Nandan 110 34 10N 134 42 E
Nander 96 19 10N 77 20 E
Nandewar Ra. 139 30 15 S 150 35 E
Nandi □ 126 0 15N 35 0 E
Nandikotkur 97 15 52N 78 18 E
Nandura 96 20 52N 76 25 E
Nandurbar 96 21 20N 74 15 E
Nandyal 97 15 30N 78 30 E
Nanfeng 109 27 10N 116 24 E
Nanga 137 26 7 S 113 45 E
Nanga Eboko 121 4 41N 12 22 E
Nanga Parbat, mt. 95 35 10N 74 35 E
Nangade 127 11 5 S 39 36 E
Nangapinoh 102 0 20 S 111 14 E
Nangarhar □ 93 34 20N 70 0 E
Nangatajap 102 1 32 S 110 34 E
Nangeya Mts. 126 3 30N 33 30 E
Nangis 43 48 33N 3 0 E
Nangodi 121 10 58N 0 42W
Nangola 120 12 41N 6 35W
Nangwarry 140 37 33 S 140 48 E
Nanhsien 109 29 22N 112 25 E
Nanhsiung 109 25 10N 114 18 E
Nanhua 108 25 10N 101 20 E
Nanhui 109 31 3N 121 46 E
Nani Hu 109 31 10N 118 55 E
Nanjangud 97 12 6N 76 43 E
Nanjeko 127 5 31 S 23 30 E
Nanjirinji 127 9 41 S 39 5 E
Nankana Sahib 94 31 27N 73 38 E
Nank'ang 109 25 38N 114 45 E
Nanking = Nanching 109 32 5N 118 45 E
Nankoku 110 33 29N 133 38 E
Nankung 106 37 22N 115 20 E
Nanling 109 30 56N 118 19 E
Nannine 137 26 51 S 118 18 E
Nanning 108 22 48N 108 20 E
Nannup 137 33 59 S 115 48 E
Nanpa 108 32 13N 104 51 E
Nanp'an Chiang, R. 108 25 0N 106 11 E
Nanpara 95 27 52N 81 33 E
Nanp'i 106 38 4N 116 34 E
Nanp'ing, Fukien, China 109 26 38N 118 10 E
Nanp'ing, Hupeh, China 109 29 55N 112 2 E
Nanpu 108 31 19N 106 2 E
Nanripe 127 13 52 S 38 52 E
Nansei-Shotō 112 26 0N 128 0 E
Nansen Sd. 12 81 0N 91 0W
Nansio 126 2 3 S 33 4 E
Nanson 137 28 35 S 114 45 E
Nant 44 44 1N 3 18 E
Nantes 42 47 12N 1 33W
Nanteuil-le-Haudouin 43 49 9N 2 48 E
Nantiat 44 46 1N 1 11 E
Nanticoke 162 41 12N 76 1W
Nanticoke, R. 162 38 16N 75 56W
Nanton, Can. 152 50 21N 113 46W
Nanton, China 108 24 59N 107 32 E
Nantua 45 46 10N 5 35 E
Nantucket 162 41 17N 70 6W
Nantucket I. 155 41 16N 70 3W
Nantucket Sd. 162 41 30N 70 15W

Nant'ung 109 32 0N 120 55 E
Nantwich 32 53 5N 2 31W
Nanuque 171 17 50 S 40 21W
Nanutarra 136 22 32 S 115 30 E
Nanyang 106 33 0N 112 32 E
Nan'yō 110 34 3N 131 49 E
Nanyüan 106 39 48N 116 24 E
Nanyuki 126 0 2N 37 4 E
Nao, C. de la 59 38 44N 0 14 E
Nao Chou Tao 109 20 55N 110 35 E
Nao, La, Cabo de 59 38 44N 0 14 E
Naococane L. 151 52 50N 70 45W
Naogaon 98 24 52N 88 52 E
Napa 163 38 18N 122 17W
Napa, R. 163 38 10N 122 19W
Napamute 147 61 30N 158 45W
Napanee 150 44 15N 77 0W
Napanoch 162 41 44N 74 2W
Nape 100 18 18N 105 6 E
Nape Pass = Keo Neua, Deo 100 18 23N 105 10 E
Napf 50 47 1N 7 56 E
Napiéolédougou 120 9 18N 5 35W
Napier 142 39 30 S 176 56 E
Napier Broome B. 136 14 2 S 126 37 E
Napier Downs 136 17 11 S 124 36 E
Napier Pen. 138 12 4 S 135 43 E
Naples 157 26 10N 81 45W
Naples = Nápoli 65 40 50N 14 5 E
Nap'o 108 23 44N 106 49 E
Napo □ 174 0 30 S 77 0W
Napo, R. 174 3 5 S 73 0W
Napoleon, N. Dak., U.S.A. 158 46 32N 99 49W
Napoleon, Ohio, U.S.A. 156 41 24N 84 7W
Nápoli 65 40 50N 14 5 E
Nápoli, G. di 65 40 40N 14 10 E
Napopo 126 4 15N 28 0 E
Napoule, La 45 43 31N 6 56 E
Nappa 32 53 58N 2 14W
Nappa Merrie 139 27 36 S 141 7 E
Naqâda 122 25 53N 32 42 E
Nara, Japan 111 34 40N 135 49 E
Nara, Mali 120 15 25N 7 20W
Nara, Canal 94 26 0N 69 20 E
Nara-ken □ 111 34 30N 136 0 E
Nara Visa 159 35 39N 103 10W
Naracoorte 140 36 58 S 140 45 E
Naradhan 141 33 34 S 146 17 E
Narasapur 96 16 26N 81 50 E
Narasaropet 96 16 14N 80 4 E
Narathiwat 101 6 40N 101 55 E
Narayanganj 98 23 31N 90 33 E
Narayanpet 96 16 45N 77 30 E
Narberth 31 51 48N 4 45W
Narbonne 44 43 11N 3 0 E
Narborough 28 52 34N 1 12W
Narcea, R. 56 43 15N 6 30W
Nardò 65 40 10N 18 0 E
Nare Head 30 50 12N 4 55W
Narembeen 137 32 7 S 118 17 E
Naretha 137 31 0 S 124 45 E
Nari, R. 94 29 10N 67 50 E
Narin 93 36 5N 69 0 E
Narinda, B. de 129 14 55 S 47 30 E
Narino □ 174 1 30N 78 0W
Narita 111 35 47N 140 19 E
Narmada, R. 94 22 40N 77 30 E
Narnaul 94 28 5N 76 11 E
Narni 63 42 30N 12 30 E
Naro, Ghana 120 10 22N 2 27W
Naro, Italy 64 37 18N 13 48 E
Naro Fominsk 81 55 23N 36 32 E
Narodnaya, G. 78 65 5N 60 0 E
Narok 126 1 20 S 33 30 E
Narok □ 126 1 20 S 33 30 E
Narón 56 43 32N 8 9W
Narooma 141 36 14 S 150 4 E
Narowal 94 32 6N 74 52 E
Narrabri 139 30 19 S 149 46 E
Narran, R. 139 28 37 S 148 12 E
Narrandera 141 34 42 S 146 31 E
Narraway, R. 152 55 44N 119 55W
Narrogin 137 32 58 S 117 14 E
Narromine 141 32 12 S 148 12 E
Narrows, str. 36 57 20N 6 5W
Narsampet 96 17 57N 79 58 E
Narsinghpur 95 22 54N 79 14 E
Naruto 110 34 11N 134 37 E
Narutō 111 35 36N 140 25 E
Naruto-Kaikyō 110 34 14N 134 39 E
Narva 80 59 10N 28 5 E
Narva, R. 80 59 10N 27 50 E
Narvik 74 68 28N 17 26 E
Narvskoye Vdkhr. 80 59 10N 28 5 E
Narwana 94 29 39N 76 6 E
Naryan-Mar 78 68 0N 53 0 E
Naryilco 139 28 37 S 141 53 E
Narym 76 59 0N 81 58 E
Narymskoye 76 49 10N 84 15 E
Naryn 85 41 26N 75 58 E
Naryn, R. 85 40 52N 71 36 E
Nasa 74 66 29N 15 23 E
Nasa, mt. 74 66 32N 15 23 E
Nasarawa 121 8 32N 7 41 E
Naseby, N.Z. 143 45 1 S 170 10 E
Naseby, U.K. 29 52 24N 0 59W
Naser, Buheirat en 122 23 0N 32 30 E
Nash Pt. 31 51 24N 3 34W
Nashua, Iowa, U.S.A. 158 42 55N 92 34W
Nashua, Mont., U.S.A. 160 48 10N 106 25W
Nashua, N.H., U.S.A. 162 42 50N 71 25W
Nashville, Ark., U.S.A. 159 33 56N 93 50W

Nashville Nevillé-Pont-Pierre

Nashville, Ga., U.S.A. 157 31 13N 83 15W
Nashville, Tenn., U.S.A. 157 36 12N 86 46W
Našice 66 45 32N 18 4 E
Nasielsk 54 52 35N 20 50 E
Nasik 96 20 2N 73 50 E
Nasirabad, Bangla. 95 24 42N 90 30 E
Nasirabad, India 94 26 15N 74 45 E
Nasirabad, Pak. 96 28 25N 68 25 E
Naskaupi, R. 151 53 47N 60 51W
Naso 65 38 8N 14 46 E
Nass, R. 152 55 0N 129 40W
Nassau, Bahamas 166 25 0N 77 30W
Nassau, U.S.A. 162 42 30N 73 34W
Nassau, Bahía 176 55 20 S 68 0W
Nasser City = Kôm Ombo 122 24 25N 32 52 E
Nasser, L. = Naser, Buheiret en 122 23 0N 32 30 E
Nassian 120 7 58N 2 57W
Nässjö 73 57 38N 14 45 E
Nastopoka Is. 150 57 0N 77 0W
Näsum 73 56 10N 14 29 E
Näsviken 72 61 46N 16 52 E
Nata, Bots. 128 20 7 S 26 4 E
Nata, China 100 19 37N 109 17 E
Nata, Si Arab. 92 27 15N 48 35 E
Nata, Tanz. 125 2 0 S 34 25 E
Natagaima 174 3 37N 75 6W
Natal, Brazil 170 5 47 S 35 13W
Natal, Can. 152 49 43N 114 51W
Natal, Indon. 102 0 35N 99 0 E
Natal □ 129 28 30 S 30 30 E
Natalinci 66 44 15N 20 49 E
Natanz 93 33 30N 51 55 E
Natashquan 151 50 14N 61 46W
Natashquan Pt. 151 50 8N 61 40W
Natashquan, R. 151 50 7N 61 50W
Natchez 159 31 35N 91 25W
Natchitoches 159 31 47N 93 4W
Naters 50 46 19N 8 0 E
Nathalia 141 36 1 S 145 7 E
Nathdwara 94 24 55N 73 50 E
Natick 162 42 16N 71 19W
Natih 93 22 25N 56 30 E
Natimuk 140 36 42 S 142 0 E
Nation, R. 152 55 30N 123 32W
National City 163 32 45N 117 7W
National Mills 153 52 52N 101 40W
Natitingou 121 10 20N 1 26 E
Natividad, I. de 164 27 50N 115 10W
Natkyizin 101 14 57N 97 59 E
Natogyi 98 21 25N 95 39 E
Natoma 158 39 14N 99 0W
Natron L. 126 2 20 S 36 0 E
Natrûn, W. el. 122 30 25N 30 0 E
Natuna Besar, Kepulauan 101 4 0N 108 15 E
Natuna Selatan, Kepulauan 101 2 45N 109 0 E
Naturaliste, C. 132 33 32 S 115 0 E
Naturaliste C. 138 40 50 S 148 15 E
Naturaliste Channel 137 25 20 S 113 0 E
Natya 140 34 57 S 143 13 E
Nau 85 40 9N 69 22 E
Nau-Nau 128 18 57 S 21 4 E
Nau Qala 94 34 5N 68 5 E
Naubinway 150 46 7N 85 27W
Naucelle 44 44 13N 2 20 E
Nauders 52 46 54N 10 30 E
Nauen 48 52 36N 12 52 E
Naujoji Vilnia 80 54 48N 25 27 E
Naumburg 48 51 10N 11 48 E
Nauru I. 130 0 25N 166 0 E
Naurzum 84 51 32N 64 34 E
Naushahra 93 34 0N 72 0 E
Nauta 174 4 20 S 73 35W
Nautanwa 99 27 20N 83 25 E
Nautla 165 20 20N 96 50W
Nava 164 28 25N 100 46W
Nava del Rey 56 41 22N 5 6W
Navacerrada, Puerto de 56 40 47N 4 0W
Navahermosa 57 39 41N 4 28W
Navalcarnero 56 40 17N 4 5W
Navalmoral de la Mata 56 39 52N 5 16W
Navalvillar de Pela 57 39 9N 5 24W
Navan = An Uaimh 38 53 39N 6 40W
Navarino, I. 176 55 0 S 67 30W
Navarra □ 58 42 40N 1 40W
Navarre 44 43 15N 1 20 E
Navarreux 44 43 20N 0 47W
Navasota 159 30 20N 96 5W
Navassa I. 167 18 30N 75 0W
Nave 62 45 35N 10 17 E
Navenby 33 53 7N 0 32W
Naver L. 37 58 18N 4 20W
Naver, R. 37 58 34N 4 15W
Navia 56 43 24N 6 42W
Navia de Suarna 56 42 58N 6 59W
Navia, R. 56 43 15N 6 50W
Navidad 172 33 57 S 71 50W
Navlya 80 52 53N 34 15 E
Navoi 85 40 9N 65 22 E
Navojoa 164 27 0N 109 30W
Navolato 164 24 47N 107 42W
Navolok 78 62 33N 39 57 E
Návpaktos 69 38 23N 21 42 E
Návplion 69 37 33N 22 50 E
Navrongo 121 10 57N 0 58W
Navsari 96 20 57N 72 59 E
Nawa Kot 94 28 21N 71 24 E
Nawabganj 98 24 35N 81 14 E
Nawabganj, Bara Banki 95 26 56N 81 14 E
Nawabganj, Bareilly 95 28 32N 79 40 E
Nawabshah 94 26 15N 68 25 E
Nawada 95 24 50N 85 25 E
Nawakot 95 28 0N 85 10 E
Nawalgarh 96 27 50N 75 15 E
Nawansnahr 95 32 33N 74 48 E
Nawapara 95 20 52N 82 33 E
Nawi 122 18 32N 30 50 E
Nawng Hpa 98 21 52N 97 52 E
Náxos 69 37 8N 25 25 E
Náxos, I. 69 37 5N 25 30 E
Nay 44 43 10N 0 18W
Nay Band 93 27 20N 52 40 E
Naya 174 3 13N 77 22W
Naya, R. 174 3 13N 77 22W
Nayakhan 77 62 10N 159 0 E
Nayarit □ 164 22 0N 105 0W
Nayé 120 14 28N 12 12W
Nayung 108 26 50N 105 17 E
Nazaré, Bahia, Brazil 171 13 0 S 39 0W
Nazaré, Goiás, Brazil 170 6 23 S 47 40W
Nazaré, Port. 57 39 36N 9 4W
Nazaré Antônio de Jesus 171 13 2 S 39 0W
Nazaré da Mata 171 7 44 S 35 14W
Nazareth, Israel 90 32 42N 35 17 E
Nazareth, U.S.A. 162 40 44N 75 19W
Nazas 164 25 10N 104 0W
Nazas, R. 164 25 20N 104 4W
Naze 112 28 22N 129 27 E
Naze, The 29 51 43N 1 19 E
Nazeret 123 8 45N 39 15 E
Nazir Hat 98 22 35N 91 55 E
Nazko 152 53 1N 123 37W
Nazko, R. 152 53 7N 123 34W
Nchacoongo 129 24 20 S 35 9 E
Nchanga 127 12 30 S 27 49 E
Ncheu 127 14 50 S 34 37 E
Ndala 126 4 45 S 33 23 E
Ndali 121 9 50N 2 46 E
Ndareda 126 4 12 S 35 30 E
Ndélé 117 8 25N 20 36 E
Ndendeé 124 2 29 S 10 46 E
Ndjamena 117 12 4N 15 8 E
Ndjolé 124 0 10 S 10 45 E
Ndola 127 13 0 S 28 34 E
Ndoto Mts. 126 2 0N 37 0 E
Ndrhamcha, Sebkra de 120 18 30N 15 55W
Nduguti 126 4 18 S 34 41 E
NE Frt. Agency = Arun. Pradesh □ 98 28 0N 95 0 E
Nea 71 63 15N 11 0 E
Néa Epidhavros 69 37 40N 23 7 E
Néa Filippiás 68 39 12N 20 53W
Néa Kallikrátiá 68 40 21N 23 1 E
Néa Vissi 68 41 34N 26 33 E
Neagari 111 36 26N 136 25 E
Neagh, Lough 38 54 35N 6 25W
Neah Bay 160 48 25N 124 40W
Neale L. 137 24 15 S 130 0 E
Neamarrói 127 15 58 S 36 50 E
Neamţ □ 70 47 0N 26 20 E
Neápolis, Kozan, Greece 68 40 20N 21 24 E
Neápolis, Kriti, Greece 69 35 15N 25 36 E
Neápolis, Lakonia, Greece 69 36 27N 23 8 E
Near Is. 147 53 0N 172 0W
Neath 31 51 39N 3 49W
Neath, R. 23 51 46N 3 35W
Nebbou 121 11 9N 1 51W
Nebine Cr. 139 29 7 S 146 56 E
Nebo 138 21 42 S 148 42 E
Nebolchy 81 59 12N 32 58 E
Nebraska □ 158 41 30N 100 0W
Nebraska City 158 40 40N 95 52W
Necedah 158 44 2N 90 7W
Nechako, R. 152 53 30N 122 44W
Neches, R. 159 31 80N 94 20W
Neckar, R. 49 48 43N 9 15 E
Necochea 172 38 30 S 58 50W
Nectar Brook 140 32 43 S 137 57 E
Nedelišće 63 46 23N 16 22 E
Neder Rijn, R. 46 51 57N 6 2 E
Nederbrakel 47 50 48N 3 46 E
Nederlandsöy I. 71 62 20N 5 35 E
Nederweert 47 51 17N 5 45 E
Nedha, R. 69 37 25N 21 45 E
Nedroma 118 35 1N 1 45W
Nedstrand 71 59 21N 5 49 E
Neede 46 52 8N 6 37 E
Needham Market 29 52 9N 1 2 E
Needilup 137 33 55 S 118 45 E
Needles 161 34 50N 114 35W
Needles, Pt. 142 36 3 S 175 25 E
Needles, The 28 50 48N 1 19W
Ñeembucú □ 172 27 0 S 58 0W
Neemuch (Nimach) 94 24 30N 74 50 E
Neenah 156 44 10N 88 30W
Neepawa 153 50 20N 99 30W
Neer 47 51 16N 5 59 E
Neerheylissem 47 51 5N 5 42 E
Neeroeteren 47 50 44N 4 58 E
Neerpelt 47 51 13N 5 26 E
Nefta 119 33 53N 7 58 E
Neftah Sidi Boubekeur 118 35 1N 0 4 E
Neftegorsk 83 44 25N 39 45 E
Neftenbach 51 47 32N 8 41 E
Neftyannye Kamni 79 40 20N 50 55 E
Nefyn 31 52 57N 4 29W
Negapatam = Nagappattinam 97 10 46N 79 38 E
Negaunee 156 46 30N 87 36W
Negba 90 31 40N 34 41 E
Negele 123 5 20N 39 30 E
Negeri Sembilan □ 101 2 50N 102 10 E
Negev = Hanegev 90 30 50N 35 0 E
Negolu 70 45 48N 24 32 E
Negombo 97 7 12N 79 50 E
Negotin 66 44 16N 22 37 E
Negotino 66 41 29N 22 9 E
Negra, La 172 23 46 S 70 18W
Negra, Peña 56 42 11N 6 30W
Negra Pt. 103 18 40N 120 50 E
Negrais C. 98 16 0N 94 30 E
Negreira 56 42 54N 8 45W
Negreşti 70 46 50N 27 30 E
Négrine 119 34 30N 7 30 E
Negro, C. 118 35 40N 5 11W
Negro, R., Argent. 176 40 0 S 64 0W
Negro, R., Brazil 174 0 25 S 64 0W
Negro, R., Uruguay 173 32 30 S 55 30W
Negros, I. 103 10 0N 123 0 E
Negru Vodă 70 43 47N 28 21 E
Nehbandān 93 31 35N 60 5 E
Neheim-Hüsten 48 51 27N 7 58 E
Nehoiaşu 70 45 24N 26 20 E
Neichiang 108 29 35N 105 0 E
Neich'iu 106 37 17N 114 31 E
Neidpath 153 50 12N 107 20W
Neihart 160 47 0N 110 52W
Neihsiang 106 33 3N 111 53 E
Neilrex 141 31 44 S 149 20 E
Neilston 34 55 47N 4 27W
Neilton 160 47 24N 123 59W
Neira de Jusá 56 42 53N 7 14W
Neisse, R. 48 51 0N 15 0 E
Neiva 174 2 56N 75 18W
Nejanilini L. 153 59 33N 97 48W
Nejo 123 9 30N 35 28 E
Nekemte 123 9 4N 36 30 E
Nêkheb 122 25 10N 33 0 E
Neksø 73 55 4N 15 8 E
Nelas 56 40 32N 7 52W
Nelaug 71 58 39N 8 40 E
Nelgowrie 141 30 54 S 148 7 E
Nelia 138 20 39 S 142 12 E
Nelidovo 80 56 13N 32 49 E
Neligh 158 42 11N 98 2W
Nelkan 77 57 50N 136 15 E
Nellikuppam 97 11 46N 79 43 E
Nellore 97 14 27N 79 59 E
Nelma 77 47 30N 139 0 E
Nelson, Can. 152 49 30N 117 20W
Nelson, N.Z. 143 41 18 S 173 16 E
Nelson, U.K. 32 53 50N 2 14W
Nelson, Ariz., U.S.A. 161 35 35N 113 24W
Nelson, Nev., U.S.A. 161 35 46N 114 55W
Nelson □ 143 42 11 S 172 15 E
Nelson, C., Austral. 140 38 26 S 141 32 E
Nelson, C., P.N.G. 135 9 0 S 149 20 E
Nelson, Estrecho 176 51 30 S 75 0W
Nelson Forks 152 59 30N 124 0W
Nelson House 153 55 47N 98 51W
Nelson I. 147 60 40N 164 40W
Nelson L. 153 55 48N 100 7W
Nelson, R. 153 54 33N 98 2W
Nelspruit 126 25 29 S 30 59 E
Néma 120 16 40N 7 15W
Neman (Nemunas), R. 80 53 30N 25 10 E
Neméa 69 37 49N 22 40 E
Nemegos 150 47 40N 83 15W
Nemeiben L. 153 55 20N 105 20W
Nemira, Mt. 70 46 17N 26 19 E
Nemiscau 150 49 30N 111 15W
Nemours 43 48 16N 2 40 E
Nemunas, R. 80 55 25N 21 10 E
Nemuro 112 43 20N 145 35 E
Nemuro-Kaikyō 112 43 30N 145 30 E
Nemuy 77 55 40N 135 55 E
Nenagh 39 52 52N 8 11W
Nenana 147 64 30N 149 0W
Nenasi 101 3 9N 103 23 E
Nenchiang 105 49 11N 125 13 E
Nene, R. 29 52 38N 0 7 E
Neno 127 15 25 S 34 40 E
Nenusa, Kepulauan 103 4 45N 127 1 E
Neodesha 159 37 30N 95 37W
Néon Petrítsi 68 41 16N 23 15 E
Neópolis 170 10 18 S 36 35W
Neosho 159 36 56N 94 28W
Neosho, R. 159 35 59N 95 10W
Nepal ■ 95 28 0N 84 30 E
Nepalganj 95 28 0N 81 40 E
Nephi 160 39 43N 111 52W
Nephin Beg Ra. 38 54 0N 9 40W
Nephin, Mt. 38 54 1N 9 21W
Nepomuk 52 49 29N 13 35 E
Neptune City 162 40 13N 74 4W
Néra, R. 66 44 52N 21 45 E
Nerac 44 44 19N 0 20 E
Nerchinsk 77 52 0N 116 39 E
Nerchinskiy Zavod 77 51 10N 119 30 E
Nereju 70 45 43N 26 43 E
Nerekhta 81 57 26N 40 38 E
Neret L. 151 54 45N 70 44W
Neretva, R. 66 43 30N 17 50 E
Neretvanski 66 43 7N 17 10 E
Neringa 80 55 21N 21 5 E
Nerja 57 36 43N 3 55W
Nerl, R. 81 56 30N 40 30 E
Nerokoúrou 69 35 29N 24 3 E
Nerpio 59 38 11N 2 16W
Nerva 57 37 42N 6 30W
Nes, Iceland 74 65 53N 17 24W
Nes, Neth. 46 53 26N 5 47 E
Nes Ziyyona 90 31 56N 34 48W
Nesbyen 71 60 34N 9 6 E
Nescopeck 162 41 3N 76 12W
Nesebyr 67 42 41N 27 46 E
Nesflaten 71 59 38N 6 48 E
Neskaupstaður 74 65 9N 13 42W
Nesland 71 59 31N 7 59 E
Neslandsvatn 71 58 57N 9 10 E
Nesle 43 49 45N 2 53 E
Nesodden 71 59 48N 10 40 E
Ness, dist. 36 58 27N 6 20W
Ness, Loch 37 57 15N 4 30W
Nesslau 51 47 14N 9 13 E
Neston 32 53 17N 3 3W
Nestórion Óros 68 40 24N 21 16 E
Néstos, R. 68 41 20N 24 35 E
Nesttun 71 60 19N 5 21 E
Nesvizh 80 53 14N 26 38 E
Netanya 90 32 20N 34 51 E
Nèthe, R. 47 51 5N 4 55 E
Netherdale 138 21 10 S 148 33 E
Netherlands ■ 47 52 0N 5 30 E
Netherlands Guiana = Surinam 170 4 0N 56 0W
Nethy Bridge 37 57 15N 3 40W
Netley 28 50 53N 1 21W
Netley Gap 28 32 43 S 139 59 E
Netley Marsh 28 50 55N 1 32W
Neto, R. 65 39 10N 16 58 E
Netrakong 98 24 53N 90 47 E
Nettancourt 43 48 51N 4 57 E
Nettilling L. 149 66 30N 71 0W
Nettlebed 29 51 34N 0 54W
Nettleham 33 53 15N 0 28W
Nettuno 64 41 29N 12 40 E
Netzahualcoyotl, Presa 165 17 10N 93 30W
Neu-Isenburg 49 50 3N 8 42 E
Neu Ulm 49 48 23N 10 2 E
Neubrandenburg 48 53 33N 13 17 E
Neubrandenburg □ 48 53 30N 13 20 E
Neubukow 48 54 1N 11 40 E
Neuburg 49 48 43N 11 11 E
Neuchâtel 50 47 0N 6 55 E
Neuchâtel □ 50 47 0N 6 55 E
Neuchâtel, Lac de 50 46 53N 6 50 E
Neudau 52 47 11N 16 6 E
Neuenegg 50 46 54N 7 18 E
Neuenhaus 48 52 30N 6 55 E
Neuf-Brisach 43 48 0N 7 30 E
Neufchâteau, Belg. 47 49 50N 5 25 E
Neufchâteau, France 43 48 21N 5 40 E
Neufchâtel 43 49 43N 1 30 E
Neufchâtel-sur-Aisne 43 49 26N 4 0 E
Neuhaus 48 53 16N 10 54 E
Neuhausen 51 47 41N 8 37 E
Neuilly-St. Front 43 49 10N 3 15 E
Neukalen 49 53 49N 12 48 E
Neumarkt 49 49 16N 11 28 E
Neumünster 48 54 4N 9 58 E
Neung-sur-Beuvron 43 47 30N 1 50 E
Neunkirchen, Austria 52 47 43N 16 4 E
Neunkirchen, Ger. 49 49 23N 7 6 E
Neuquén 176 38 0 S 68 0 E
Neuquén □ 172 38 0 S 69 50W
Neuruppin 48 52 56N 12 48 E
Neuse, R. 157 35 5N 77 40W
Neusiedl 53 47 57N 16 50 E
Neusiedler See 53 47 50N 16 47 E
Neuss 48 51 12N 6 39 E
Neussargues-Moissac 44 45 9N 3 1 E
Neustadt, Bay., Ger. 49 49 42N 12 10 E
Neustadt, Bay., Ger. 49 48 48N 11 47 E
Neustadt, Bay., Ger. 49 49 34N 10 37 E
Neustadt, Bay., Ger. 49 50 23N 11 0 E
Neustadt, Gera, Ger. 48 50 45N 11 43 E
Neustadt, Hessen, Ger. 48 50 51N 9 9 E
Neustadt, Niedersachsen, Ger. 48 52 30N 9 30 E
Neustadt, Potsdam, Ger. 48 52 50N 12 27 E
Neustadt, Rhld-Pfz., Ger. 49 49 21N 8 10 E
Neustadt, S.-Holst., Ger. 48 54 6N 10 49 E
Neustrelitz 48 53 22N 13 4 E
Neuveville, La 50 47 4N 7 6 E
Neuvic 44 45 23N 2 16 E
Neuville, Belg. 95 50 11N 4 32 E
Neuville, France 43 45 52N 4 51 E
Neuville-aux-Bois 43 48 4N 2 3 E
Neuvy-St.-Sépulchure 44 46 35N 1 48 E
Neuvy-sur-Barangeon 43 47 20N 2 15 E
Neuwerk, I. 48 53 55N 8 30 E
Neuwied 48 50 26N 7 29 E
Neva, R. 78 59 50N 30 30 E
Nevada 159 37 20N 94 40W
Nevada □ 160 39 20N 117 0W
Nevada City 163 39 20N 121 0W
Nevada de Sta. Marta, Sa. 174 10 55N 73 50W
Nevada, Sierra, Spain 59 37 3N 3 15W
Nevada, Sierra, U.S.A. 160 39 0N 120 30W
Nevado, Cerro 172 35 30 S 68 20W
Nevado de Colima, Mt. 164 19 35N 103 45W
Nevanka 77 56 45N 98 55 E
Nevasa 94 19 34N 75 0 E
Nevel 80 56 0N 29 55 E
Nevele 47 51 3N 3 28 E
Nevern 31 52 2N 4 49W
Nevers 43 47 0N 3 9 E
Nevertire 141 31 50 S 147 44 E
Neville 153 49 58N 107 39W
Nevillé-Pont-Pierre 42 47 33N 0 33 E

Nevinnomyssk **Nîl el Abyad, Bahr**

Name	Page	Lat.	Long.
Nevinnomyssk	**83**	44 40N	42 0 E
Nevis I.	**167**	17 0N	62 30W
Nevis, L.	**36**	57 0N	5 43W
Nevlunghavn	**71**	58 58N	9 53 E
Nevoria	**137**	31 25 S	119 25 E
Nevrokop = Gotse Delchev	**67**	41 43N	23 46 E
Nevşehir	**92**	38 33N	34 40 E
Nevyansk	**84**	57 30N	60 13 E
New Abbey	**35**	54 59N	3 38W
New Aberdour	**37**	57 39N	2 12W
New Adawso	**121**	6 50N	0 2W
New Albany, Ind., U.S.A.	**156**	38 20N	85 50W
New Albany, Miss., U.S.A.	**159**	34 30N	89 0W
New Albany, Pa., U.S.A.	**162**	41 35N	76 28W
New Alresford	**28**	51 6N	1 10W
New Amsterdam	**174**	6 15N	57 30W
New Angledool	**139**	29 10 S	147 55 E
New Bedford	**162**	41 40N	70 52W
New Berlin, N.Y., U.S.A.	**162**	42 38N	75 20W
New Berlin, Pa., U.S.A.	**162**	40 50N	76 57W
New Bern	**157**	35 8N	77 3W
New Birmingham	**39**	52 36N	7 38W
New Boston	**159**	33 27N	94 21W
New Braunfels	**159**	29 43N	98 9W
New Brighton, N.Z.	**143**	43 29 S	172 43 E
New Brighton, U.K.	**32**	53 27N	3 2W
New Britain	**162**	41 41N	72 47W
New Britain, I.	**135**	5 50 S	150 20 E
New Brunswick	**162**	40 30N	74 28W
New Brunswick □	**151**	46 50N	66 30W
New Buildings	**38**	54 57N	7 21W
New Bussa	**121**	9 53N	4 31 E
New Byrd	**13**	80 0 S	120 0W
New Caledonia, I.	**130**	21 0 S	165 0 E
New Castile = Castilla La Neuva	**57**	39 45N	3 20W
New Castle, Del., U.S.A.	**162**	39 40N	75 34W
New Castle, Ind., U.S.A.	**156**	39 55N	85 23W
New Castle, Pa., U.S.A.	**156**	41 0N	80 20W
New Chapel Cross	**39**	51 51N	10 12W
New City	**162**	41 8N	74 0W
New Cumnock	**34**	55 24N	4 13W
New Cuyama	**163**	34 57N	119 38W
New Deer	**37**	57 30N	2 10W
New Delhi	**94**	28 37N	77 13 E
New Denver	**152**	50 0N	117 25W
New England	**158**	46 36N	102 47W
New England Ra.	**139**	30 20 S	151 45 E
New Forest	**28**	50 53N	1 40W
New Freedom	**162**	39 44N	76 42W
New Galloway	**35**	55 4N	4 10W
New Glasgow	**151**	45 35N	62 36W
New Gretna	**162**	39 35N	74 28W
New Guinea, I.	**135**	4 0 S	136 0 E
New Hampshire □	**156**	43 40N	71 40W
New Hampton	**158**	43 2N	92 20W
New Hanover	**129**	29 22 S	30 31 E
New Hanover I.	**135**	2 30 S	150 10 E
New Hartford	**162**	43 4N	75 18W
New Haven	**162**	41 20N	72 54W
New Hazelton	**152**	55 20N	127 30W
*New Hebrides, Is.	**130**	15 0 S	168 0 E
New Holland, U.K.	**33**	53 42N	0 22W
New Holland, U.S.A.	**162**	40 6N	76 5W
New Iberia	**159**	30 2N	91 54W
New Inn	**39**	53 5N	7 10W
New Ireland, I.	**135**	3 20 S	151 50 E
New Jersey □	**162**	39 50N	74 10W
New Kensington	**156**	40 36N	79 43W
New Kent	**162**	37 31N	76 59W
New Lexington	**156**	39 40N	82 15W
New Liskeard	**150**	47 31N	79 41W
New London, Conn., U.S.A.	**162**	41 23N	72 8W
New London, Minn., U.S.A.	**158**	45 17N	94 55W
New London, Wis., U.S.A.	**158**	44 23N	88 43W
New Luce	**34**	54 57N	4 50W
New Madrid	**159**	36 40N	89 30W
New Meadows	**160**	45 0N	116 10W
New Mexico □	**154**	34 30N	106 0W
New Milford, Conn., U.S.A.	**162**	41 35N	73 25W
New Milford, Pa., U.S.A.	**162**	41 50N	75 45W
New Mills	**32**	53 22N	2 0W
New Norcia	**137**	30 57 S	116 13 E
New Norfolk	**138**	42 46 S	147 2 E
New Orleans	**159**	30 0N	90 5W
New Oxford	**162**	39 52N	77 4W
New Philadelphia	**156**	40 29N	81 25W
New Pitsligo	**37**	57 35N	2 11W
New Plymouth, Bahamas	**166**	26 56N	77 20W
New Plymouth, N.Z.	**142**	39 4 S	174 5 E
New Point Comfort	**162**	37 18N	76 15W
New Providence I.	**166**	25 0N	77 30W
New Quay	**31**	52 13N	4 21W
New Radnor	**31**	52 15N	3 10W
New Richmond	**158**	45 6N	92 34W
New Roads	**159**	30 43N	91 30W
New Rockford	**158**	47 44N	99 7W
New Romney	**29**	50 59N	0 57 E
New Ross	**39**	52 24N	6 58W
New Rossington	**33**	53 30N	1 4W

Name	Page	Lat.	Long.
New Salem	**158**	46 51N	101 25W
New Siberian Is. = Novosibirskiye Os.	**77**	75 0N	140 0 E
New Smyrna Beach	**157**	29 0N	80 50W
New South Wales □	**139**	33 0 S	146 0 E
New Springs	**137**	25 49 S	120 1 E
New Tamale	**121**	9 10N	1 10W
New Tredegar	**31**	51 43N	3 15W
New Ulm	**158**	44 15N	94 30W
New Waterford	**151**	46 13N	60 4W
New Westminster	**152**	49 10N	122 52W
New York □	**156**	42 40N	76 0W
New York City	**162**	40 45N	74 0W
New Zealand ■	**143**	40 0 S	176 0 E
Newala	**127**	10 58 S	39 10 E
Newala □	**127**	10 46 S	39 20 E
Newark, U.K.	**33**	53 6N	0 48W
Newark, Del., U.S.A.	**162**	39 42N	75 45W
Newark, N.J., U.S.A.	**162**	40 41N	74 12W
Newark, N.Y., U.S.A.	**162**	43 2N	77 10W
Newark, Ohio, U.S.A.	**156**	40 5N	82 30W
Newark Valley	**162**	42 14N	76 11W
Newberg	**160**	45 22N	123 0W
Newberry	**156**	46 20N	85 32W
Newberry Springs	**163**	34 50N	116 41W
Newbiggin-by-the-Sea	**35**	55 12N	1 31W
Newbigging	**35**	55 42N	3 33W
Newbliss	**38**	54 10N	7 8W
Newborough	**31**	53 10N	4 22W
Newbridge, Kildare, Ireland	**39**	53 11N	6 50W
Newbridge, Limerick, Ireland	**38**	52 33N	9 0W
Newbridge-on-Wye	**31**	52 13N	3 27W
Newbrook	**152**	54 24N	112 57W
Newburgh, Fife, U.K.	**35**	56 21N	3 15W
Newburgh, Grampian, U.K.	**37**	57 19N	2 0W
Newburgh, U.S.A.	**162**	41 30N	74 1W
Newburn	**35**	54 57N	1 45W
Newbury	**28**	51 24N	1 19W
Newburyport	**162**	42 48N	70 50W
Newby Bridge	**32**	54 16N	2 59W
Newbyth	**37**	57 35N	2 17W
Newcastle, Austral.	**141**	33 0 S	151 40 E
Newcastle, Can.	**151**	47 1N	65 38W
Newcastle, Ireland	**39**	53 5N	6 4W
Newcastle, S. Afr.	**125**	27 45 S	29 58 E
Newcastle, U.K.	**38**	54 13N	5 54W
Newcastle, U.S.A.	**158**	43 50N	104 12W
Newcastle Emlyn	**31**	52 2N	4 29W
Newcastle Ra.	**136**	15 45 S	130 15 E
Newcastle-under-Lyme	**32**	53 2N	2 15W
Newcastle-upon-Tyne	**35**	54 59N	1 37W
Newcastle Waters	**136**	17 30 S	133 28 E
Newcastle West	**38**	52 27N	9 3W
Newcastleton	**35**	55 10N	2 50W
Newchurch	**31**	52 9N	3 10W
Newdegate	**137**	33 6 S	119 0 E
Newe Etan	**90**	32 30N	35 32 E
Newe Sha'anan	**90**	32 47N	34 59 E
Newe Zohar	**90**	31 9N	35 21 E
Newell	**158**	44 48N	103 25W
Newenham, C.	**147**	58 40N	162 15W
Newent	**28**	51 56N	2 24W
Newfield, N.J., U.S.A.	**162**	39 33N	75 1W
Newfield, N.Y., U.S.A.	**162**	42 18N	76 33W
Newfound L.	**162**	43 40N	71 47W
Newfoundland	**151**	48 30N	56 0W
Newfoundland □	**151**	48 28N	56 0W
Newhalem	**152**	48 41N	121 16W
Newhalen	**147**	59 40N	155 0W
Newhall	**163**	34 23N	118 32W
Newham	**29**	51 31N	0 2 E
Newhaven	**29**	50 47N	0 4 E
Newington, N. Kent, U.K.	**29**	51 21N	0 40 E
Newington, S. Kent, U.K.	**29**	51 5N	1 8 E
Newinn	**39**	52 28N	7 54W
Newkirk	**159**	36 52N	97 3W
Newlyn	**30**	50 6N	5 33W
Newlyn East	**30**	50 22N	5 3W
Newmachar	**37**	57 16N	2 11W
Newman	**163**	37 19N	121 1W
Newman, Mt.	**137**	23 20 S	119 34 E
Newmarket, Ireland	**39**	52 13N	9 0W
Newmarket, Lewis, U.K.	**36**	58 14N	6 24W
Newmarket, Suffolk, U.K.	**29**	52 15N	0 23 E
Newmarket, U.S.A.	**162**	43 4N	70 57W
Newmarket-on-Fergus	**39**	52 46N	8 54W
Newmill	**37**	57 34N	2 58W
Newmills	**38**	54 56N	7 49W
Newmilns	**34**	55 36N	4 20W
Newnan	**157**	33 22N	84 48W
Newnes	**139**	33 9 S	150 16 E
Newnham	**28**	51 48N	2 27W
Newport, Essex, U.K.	**29**	51 58N	0 13 E
Newport, Gwent, U.K.	**31**	51 35N	3 0W
Newport, I. of W., U.K.	**28**	50 42N	1 18W
Newport, Salop, U.K.	**28**	52 47N	2 22W
Newport, Ark., U.S.A.	**159**	35 38N	91 15W
Newport, Ky., U.S.A.	**156**	39 5N	84 23W
Newport, N.H., U.S.A.	**162**	43 23N	72 8W
Newport, Oreg., U.S.A.	**160**	44 41N	124 2W
Newport, R.I., U.S.A.	**162**	41 30N	71 19W
Newport, Tenn., U.S.A.	**157**	35 39N	83 12W
Newport, Wash., U.S.A.	**160**	48 11N	117 2W
Newport B.	**38**	53 52N	9 38W
Newport Beach	**163**	33 40N	117 58W
Newport News	**162**	37 2N	76 54W

Name	Page	Lat.	Long.
Newport on Tay	**35**	56 27N	2 56W
Newport Pagnell	**29**	52 5N	0 42W
Newquay	**30**	50 24N	5 6W
Newry	**38**	54 10N	6 20W
Newry & Mourne □	**38**	54 10N	6 15W
Newton, Iowa, U.S.A.	**158**	41 40N	93 3W
Newton, Kans., U.S.A.	**159**	38 2N	97 30W
Newton, Mass., U.S.A.	**156**	42 21N	71 10W
Newton, N.C., U.S.A.	**157**	35 42N	81 10W
Newton, N.J., U.S.A.	**162**	41 3N	74 46W
Newton, Texas, U.S.A.	**159**	30 54N	93 42W
Newton Abbot	**30**	50 32N	3 37W
Newton Arlosh	**32**	54 53N	3 15W
Newton-Aycliffe	**33**	54 36N	1 33W
Newton Boyd	**139**	29 45 S	152 16 E
Newton Ferrers	**30**	50 19N	4 3W
Newton le Willows	**32**	53 28N	3 27W
Newton St. Cyres	**30**	50 46N	3 35W
Newton Stewart	**34**	54 57N	4 30W
Newtonabbey □	**38**	54 45N	6 0W
Newtongrange	**35**	55 52N	3 4W
Newtonhill	**37**	57 1N	20 52 E
Newtonmore	**37**	57 4N	4 7W
Newtown, Ireland	**39**	52 20N	8 47W
Newtown, Scot, U.K.	**35**	55 34N	2 38W
Newtown, Wales, U.K.	**31**	52 31N	3 19W
Newtown Crommelin	**38**	54 59N	6 13W
Newtown Cunningham	**38**	55 0N	7 32W
Newtown Forbes	**38**	53 46N	7 50W
Newtown Gore	**38**	54 3N	7 41W
Newtown Hamilton	**38**	54 12N	6 35W
Newtownabbey	**38**	54 40N	5 55W
Newtownards	**38**	54 37N	5 40W
Newtownbutler	**38**	54 12N	7 22W
Newtownmount-kennedy	**39**	53 5N	6 7W
Newtownstewart	**38**	54 43N	7 22W
Nexon	**48**	45 41N	1 10 E
Neya	**81**	58 21N	43 49 E
Neyland	**31**	51 43N	4 58W
Neyrīz	**93**	29 15N	54 55 E
Neyshābūr	**93**	36 10N	58 20 E
Neyyattinkara	**97**	8 26N	77 5 E
Nezhin	**80**	51 5N	31 55 E
Nezperce	**160**	46 13N	116 15W
Ngabang	**102**	0 30N	109 55 E
Ngaiphaipi	**98**	22 14N	93 15 E
Ngambé	**121**	5 48N	11 29 E
Ngami Depression	**128**	20 30 S	22 46 E
Ngamo	**127**	19 3 S	27 25 E
Ngandjuk	**103**	7 32 S	111 55 E
Ngao	**100**	18 46N	99 59 E
Ngaoundéré	**124**	7 15N	13 35 E
Ngapara	**143**	44 57 S	170 46 E
Ngara	**126**	2 29 S	30 40 E
Ngara □	**126**	2 29 S	30 40 E
Ngaruawahia	**142**	37 42 S	175 11 E
Ngatapa	**142**	38 32 S	177 45 E
Ngathainggyaung	**98**	17 24N	95 5 E
Ngauruhoe, Mt.	**142**	39 13 S	175 45 E
Ngawi	**103**	7 24 S	111 26 E
Ngetera	**121**	12 40 S	12 46 E
Ngha Lo	**101**	21 33N	104 28 E
Nghia Lo	**100**	21 33N	104 28 E
Ngoma	**127**	13 8 S	33 45 E
Ngomahura	**127**	20 33 S	30 57 E
Ngomba	**127**	8 20 S	32 53 E
Ngonye Falls	**128**	16 35 S	23 30 E
Ngop	**123**	6 17N	30 9 E
Ngorkou	**120**	15 40N	3 41W
Ngorongoro	**126**	3 11 S	35 32 E
Ngozi	**126**	2 54 S	29 50 E
Ngudu	**126**	2 58 S	33 25 E
N'Guigrai	**117**	14 20N	13 20 E
Nguna, I.	**100**	17 26 S	168 21 E
Ngunga	**126**	3 37 S	33 37 E
Ngungu	**143**	6 15N	28 16 E
Ngunguru	**94**	35 37 S	174 30 E
Nguru	**121**	12 56N	10 29 E
Nguru Mts.	**126**	6 0 S	37 30 E
Nguyen Binh	**100**	22 39N	105 56 E
Ngwenya	**129**	26 5 S	31 7 E
Nha Trang	**101**	12 16N	109 10 E
Nhacoongo	**129**	24 18 S	35 14 E
Nhangutazi, Lago	**129**	24 0 S	34 30 E
Nhill	**140**	36 18 S	141 40 E
Nho Quan	**100**	20 18N	105 45 E
Nhulunbuy	**138**	12 10 S	136 45 E
Nia-nia	**126**	1 30N	27 40 E
Niafounké	**120**	16 0N	4 5W
Niagara	**156**	45 45N	88 0W
Niagara Falls, Can.	**150**	43 7N	79 5W
Niagara Falls, N. Amer.	**150**	43 5N	79 5W
Niah	**102**	3 58N	113 46 E
Niamey	**121**	13 27N	2 6 E
Nianforando	**120**	9 37N	10 36W
Nianfors	**72**	61 36N	16 46 E
Niangara	**126**	3 50N	27 50 E
Niantic	**162**	41 19N	72 12W
Nias, I.	**102**	1 0N	97 40 E
Niassa □	**127**	13 30 S	36 0 E
Niassa, Lago	**127**	12 30 S	34 30 E
Nibbiano	**62**	44 54N	9 20 E
Nibe	**73**	56 59N	9 38 E
Nibong Tebal	**101**	5 10N	100 29 E
Nicaragua ■	**166**	11 40N	85 30W
Nicaragua, Lago de	**166**	12 50N	85 30W
Nicastro	**65**	39 0N	16 18 E
Nice	**45**	43 42N	7 14 E
Niceville	**157**	30 30N	86 30W
Nichinan	**110**	31 38N	131 23 E
Nicholas, Chan.	**166**	23 30N	80 30W
Nicholasville	**156**	37 54N	84 31W

Name	Page	Lat.	Long.
Nichols	**162**	42 1N	76 22W
Nicholson, Austral.	**136**	18 2 S	128 54 E
Nicholson, Can.	**150**	47 58N	83 47W
Nicholson, U.S.A.	**162**	41 37N	75 47W
Nicholson, R.	**138**	17 31 S	139 36 E
Nicholson Ra.	**137**	27 15 S	116 30 E
Nicobar Is.	**86**	9 0N	93 0 E
Nicoclí	**174**	8 26N	76 48W
Nicola	**152**	50 8N	120 40W
Nicolet	**150**	46 17N	72 35W
Nicolls Town	**166**	25 8N	78 0W
Nicosia, Cyprus	**92**	35 10N	33 25 E
Nicosia, Italy	**65**	37 45N	14 22 E
Nicótera	**65**	38 33N	15 57 E
Nicoya	**166**	10 9N	85 27W
Nicoya, Golfo de	**166**	10 0N	85 0W
Nicoya, Pen. de	**166**	9 45N	85 40W
Nidau	**50**	47 7N	7 15 E
Nidd, R.	**33**	54 1N	1 32W
Nidda	**48**	50 24N	9 2 E
Nidda, R.	**49**	50 25N	9 2 E
Nidderdale	**33**	54 5N	1 46W
Nidzica	**54**	53 25N	20 28 E
Niebüll	**48**	54 47N	8 49 E
Niederaula	**48**	50 48N	9 37 E
Niederbipp	**50**	47 16N	7 42 E
Niederbronn	**43**	48 57N	7 39 E
Niedere Tauern	**93**	47 18N	14 0 E
Niedermarsberg	**48**	51 28N	8 52 E
Niederösterreich □	**52**	48 25N	15 40 E
Niedersachsen □	**48**	54 45N	9 0 E
Niel	**47**	51 7N	4 20 E
Niellé	**120**	10 5N	5 38W
Niemba	**126**	5 58 S	28 24 E
Niemcza	**54**	50 42N	16 47 E
Niemodlin	**54**	50 38N	17 38 E
Niemur	**140**	35 17 S	144 9 E
Nienburg	**48**	52 38N	9 15 E
Nienchʼingʼangkula Shan	**105**	30 10N	90 0 E
Niepołomice	**54**	50 3N	20 13 E
Niesen	**50**	46 38N	7 39 E
Niesky	**48**	51 18N	14 48 E
Nieszawa	**54**	52 52N	18 42 E
Nieuw Amsterdam	**46**	52 43N	6 52 E
Nieuw Beijerland	**46**	51 49N	4 20 E
Nieuw-Buinen	**46**	52 58N	6 56 E
Nieuw-Dordrecht	**46**	52 45N	6 59 E
Nieuw Hellevoet	**46**	51 51N	4 8 E
Nieuw Loosdrecht	**46**	52 12N	5 8 E
Nieuw Nickerie	**175**	6 0N	57 10W
Nieuw-Schoonebeek	**46**	52 39N	7 0 E
Nieuw-Vassemeer	**47**	51 34N	4 12 E
Nieuw-Vennep	**46**	52 16N	4 38 E
Nieuw-Weerdinge	**46**	52 51N	6 59 E
Nieuwe-Niedorp	**46**	52 44N	4 54 E
Nieuwe-Pekela	**46**	53 5N	6 58 E
Nieuwe-Schans	**46**	53 11N	7 12 E
Nieuwe-Tonge	**47**	51 43N	4 10 E
Nieuwendijk	**46**	51 46N	4 55 E
Nieuwerkerken	**47**	50 52N	5 12 E
Nieuwkoop	**46**	52 9N	4 48 E
Nieuwleusen	**46**	52 34N	6 17 E
Nieuwnamen	**47**	51 18N	4 9 E
Nieuwolda	**46**	53 15N	6 58 E
Nieuwpoort	**47**	51 8N	2 45 E
Nieuwveen	**46**	52 12N	4 46 E
Nieves	**56**	42 7N	8 26W
Nièvre □	**43**	47 10N	5 40 E
Nigata	**110**	34 13N	132 39 E
Nigde	**92**	38 0N	34 40 E
Nigel	**129**	26 27 S	28 25 E
Niger □	**121**	10 0N	5 0 E
Niger ■	**121**	13 30N	10 0 E
Niger, R.	**121**	10 0N	4 40 E
Nigeria ■	**121**	8 30N	8 0 E
Nigg B.	**37**	57 41N	4 5W
Nightcaps	**143**	45 57 S	168 14 E
Nigrita	**68**	40 56N	23 29 E
Nihtaur	**94**	29 27N	78 23 E
Nii-Jima	**111**	34 20N	139 15 E
Niigata	**112**	37 58N	139 0 E
Niigata-ken □	**112**	37 15N	138 45 E
Niihama	**110**	33 55N	133 10 E
Niihau, I.	**147**	21 55N	160 10W
Niimi	**110**	34 59N	133 28 E
Nijar	**59**	36 53N	2 15W
Nijkerk	**46**	52 13N	5 30 E
Nijlen	**47**	51 10N	4 40 E
Nijmegen	**47**	51 50N	5 52 E
Nijverdal	**46**	52 22N	6 28 E
Nike	**121**	6 26N	7 29 E
Nikel	**74**	69 30N	30 5 E
Nikiniki	**103**	9 40 S	124 30 E
Nikitas	**68**	40 17N	23 34 E
Nikki	**121**	9 58N	3 21 E
Nikkō	**111**	36 45N	139 35 E
Nikolayev	**82**	46 58N	32 7 E
Nikolayevsk-na-Amur	**77**	53 40N	140 50 E
Nikolayevski	**83**	50 10N	45 35 E
Nikolsk	**81**	59 30N	45 28 E
Nikolski	**147**	53 0N	168 50W
Nikolskoye, Amur, U.S.S.R.	**77**	47 50N	131 5 E
Nikolskoye, Kamandorskiye, U.S.S.R.	**77**	55 12N	166 0 E
Nikopol, Bulg.	**67**	43 43N	24 54 E
Nikopol, U.S.S.R.	**82**	47 35N	34 25 E
Niksar	**82**	40 31N	37 2 E
Nīkshah	**93**	26 15N	60 10 E
Nik ió	**66**	42 50N	18 57 E
Nîl el Abyad, Bahr	**123**	9 30N	31 40 E

* Renamed Vanuatu

Nîl el Azraq □ N. Taranaki Bt

Nîl el Azraq □ 123 12 30N 34 30 E
Nîl el Azraq, Bahr 123 10 30N 35 0 E
Nîl, Nahr el 122 27 30N 30 30 E
Nila 103 8 24 S 120 29 E
Niland 161 33 16N 115 30W
Nile □ 126 2 0N 31 30 E
Nile Delta 122 31 40N 31 0 E
Nile, R. = Nîl, Nahr el 122 27 30N 30 30 E
Niles 156 41 8N 80 40W
Nilgiri Hills 97 11 30N 76 30 E
Nilo Peçanha 171 13 37 S 39 6W
Nilpena 140 30 58 S 138 20 E
Nimach = Neemuch 94 24 30N 74 50 E
Nimar 96 21 49N 76 22 E
Nimba, Mt. 120 7 39N 8 30W
Nimbahera 94 24 37N 74 45 E
Nîmes 45 43 50N 4 23 E
Nimfaíon, Ákra 68 40 5N 24 20 E
Nimingarra 132 20 31 S 119 55 E
Nimmitabel 141 36 29 S 149 15 E
Nimneryskiy 77 58 0N 125 10 E
Nimule 123 3 32N 32 3 E
Nimy 47 50 28N 3 57 E
Nin 63 44 16N 15 12 E
Nindigully 139 28 21 S 148 50 E
Ninemile 152 56 0N 130 7W
Ninemilehouse 39 52 28N 7 29W
Ninety Mile Beach 130 34 45 S 173 0 E
Ninety Mile Beach, The 133 38 15 S 147 24 E
Nineveh 92 36 25N 43 10 E
Ninfield 29 50 53N 0 26 E
Ningaloo 136 22 41 S 113 41 E
Ningan 107 44 23N 129 26 E
Ningch'eng 107 41 34N 119 20 E
Ningch'iang 106 32 49N 106 13 E
Ningchin 106 37 37N 114 55 E
Ningching Shan 108 31 45N 97 15 E
Ninghai 109 29 18N 121 25 E
Ninghsiang 109 28 15N 112 30 E
Ninghsien 106 35 35N 107 58 E
Ninghua 109 26 14N 116 36 E
Ningkang 109 26 45N 113 58 E
Ningkuo 109 30 38N 118 58 E
Ninglang 108 27 19N 100 53 E
Ningling 106 34 27N 115 19 E
Ningming 108 22 12N 107 5 E
Ningnan 108 27 7N 102 42 E
Ningpo 109 29 53N 121 33 E
Ningshan 106 33 12N 108 29 E
Ningsia Hui A.R. □ 106 37 45N 106 0 E
Ningte 109 26 45N 120 0 E
Ningtsin 99 29 44N 98 28 E
Ningtu 109 26 22N 115 48 E
Ningwu 106 29 2N 112 15 E
Ningyang, Fukien, China 109 25 44N 117 8 E
Ningyang, Shantung, China 106 35 46N 116 47 E
Ningyüan 109 25 36N 111 54 E
Ninh Binh 100 20 15N 105 55 E
Ninh Giang 100 20 44N 106 24 E
Ninh Hoa 100 12 30N 109 7 E
Ninh Ma 100 12 48N 109 21 E
Ninian, oilfield 19 60 42N 1 30 E
Ninove 47 50 51N 4 2 E
Nioaque 173 21 5 S 55 50W
Niobrara 158 42 48N 97 59W
Niobrara R. 158 42 30N 103 0W
Nioki 124 2 47 S 17 40 E
Niono 120 14 15N 6 0W
Nioro 120 15 30N 9 30W
Nioro du Rip 120 13 40N 15 50W
Nioro du Sahel 120 15 30N 9 30W
Niort 44 46 19N 0 29W
Niou 121 12 42N 2 1W
Nipa 135 6 9 S 143 29 E
Nipan 138 24 45 S 150 0 E
Nipani 96 16 20N 74 25 E
Nipawin 153 53 20N 104 0W
Nipawin Prov. Park 153 54 0N 104 37W
Nipigon 150 49 0N 88 17W
Nipigon, L. 150 49 50N 88 30W
Nipin, R. 153 55 46N 109 2W
Nipishish L. 151 54 12N 60 45W
Nipissing L. 150 46 20N 80 0W
Nipomo 163 35 4N 120 29W
Niquelândia 171 14 33 S 48 23W
Nira, R. 96 18 5N 74 25 E
Nirasaki 111 35 42N 138 27 E
Nirmal 96 19 3N 78 20 E
Nirmali 95 26 20N 86 35 E
Niš 66 43 19N 21 58 E
Nisa 57 39 30N 7 41W
Nisab 91 14 25N 46 29 E
Nišava, R. 66 43 20N 22 10 E
Niscemi 65 37 8N 14 21 E
Nishi-Sonogi-Hantō 110 32 55N 129 45 E
Nishinomiya 111 34 45N 135 20 E
Nishinoomote 112 30 43N 130 59 E
Nishio 111 34 52N 137 3 E
Nishiwaki 110 34 59N 134 48 E
Nísiros, I. 69 36 35N 27 12 E
Niskibi, R. 150 56 29N 88 9W
Nisko 54 50 35N 22 7 E
Nispen 47 51 29N 4 28 E
Nisporeny 70 47 4N 28 10 E
Nissafors 73 57 25N 13 37 E
Nissan 73 56 40N 12 51 E
Nissan I. 138 4 30 S 154 10 E
Nissedal 71 59 10N 8 30 E
Nisser 71 59 7N 8 28 E
Nissum Fjord 73 56 20N 8 11 E
Nistelrode 47 51 42N 5 34 E
Nisutlin, R. 152 60 14N 132 34W
Nitchequon 151 53 10N 70 58W
Niterói 173 22 52 S 43 0W
Nith, R. 35 55 20N 3 5W
Nithsdale 35 55 14N 3 50W
Niton 28 50 35N 1 14W
Nitra 53 48 19N 18 4 E
Nitra, R. 53 48 30N 18 7 E
Nitsa, R. 84 57 29N 64 33 E
Nittedal 71 60 1N 10 57 E
Niuchieh 108 27 47N 104 16 E
Niuchuang 107 40 58N 122 38 E
Niue I. (Savage I.) 130 19 2 S 169 54W
Niulan Chiang, R. 108 27 24N 103 9 E
Niut, Mt. 102 0 55N 109 30 E
Nivelles 47 50 35N 4 20 E
Nivernais 43 47 0N 3 40 E
Nixon, Nev., U.S.A. 160 39 54N 119 22W
Nixon, Tex., U.S.A. 159 29 17N 97 45W
Nizam Sagar 96 18 10N 77 58 E
Nizamabad 96 18 45N 78 7 E
Nizamghat 98 28 20N 95 45 E
Nizhanaya Tunguska 77 64 20N 93 0 E
Nizhiye Sergi 84 56 40N 59 18 E
Nizhne Kolymsk 77 68 40N 160 55 E
Nizhne-Vartovskoye 76 60 56N 76 38 E
Nizhneangarsk 77 56 0N 109 30 E
Nizhnegorskiy 82 45 27N 34 38 E
Nizhneudinsk 77 55 0N 99 20 E
Nizhniy Lomov 81 53 34N 43 38 E
Nizhniy Novgorod = Gorkiy 81 56 20N 44 0 E
Nizhniy Pyandzh 85 37 12N 68 35 E
Nizhniy Tagil 84 57 55N 59 57 E
Nizhny Salda 84 58 8N 60 42 E
Nizké Tatry 53 48 55N 20 0 E
Nizza Monferrato 62 44 46N 8 22 E
Njakwa 127 11 1 S 33 56 E
Njinjo 127 8 34 S 38 44 E
Njombe 124 9 20 S 34 50 E
Njombe □ 127 9 20 S 34 49 E
Njombe, R. 126 7 15 S 34 30 E
Nkambe 121 6 35N 10 40 E
Nkana 127 13 0 S 28 8 E
Nkawkaw 121 6 36N 0 49W
Nkhata Bay 124 11 33 S 34 16 E
Nkhota Kota 127 12 56 S 34 15 E
Nkongsamba 121 4 55N 9 55 E
Nkunka 127 14 57 S 25 58 E
Nkwanta 120 6 10N 2 10W
Nmai Pit, R. 99 25 30N 98 0 E
Nmai, R. 99 25 30N 98 0 E
Nmaushahra 95 33 11N 74 15 E
Nnewi 121 6 0N 6 59 E
Noakhali = Maijdi 98 22 50N 90 45 E
Noatak 147 67 32N 163 10W
Noatak, R. 147 68 0N 161 0W
Nobber 38 53 49N 6 45W
Nobeoka 110 32 36N 131 41 E
Nōbi-Heiya 111 35 15N 136 45 E
Noblejas 58 39 58N 3 26W
Noblesville 156 40 1N 85 59W
Noce, R. 62 46 22N 11 0 E
Nocera Inferiore 65 40 45N 14 37 E
Nocera Terinese 65 39 2N 16 9 E
Nocera Umbra 63 43 8N 12 47 E
Nochixtlán 165 17 28N 97 14W
Noci 65 40 47N 17 7 E
Nockatunga 139 27 42 S 142 42 E
Nocona 159 33 48N 97 45W
Nocrich 70 45 55N 24 26 E
Noda, Japan 111 35 56N 139 52 E
Noda, U.S.S.R. 77 47 30N 142 5 E
Noel 159 36 36N 94 29W
Nogales, Mexico 164 31 36N 94 29W
Nogales, U.S.A. 161 31 33N 115 50W
Nōgata 110 33 48N 130 54 E
Nogent-en-Bassigny 43 48 0N 5 20 E
Nogent-le-Rotrou 42 48 20N 0 50 E
Nogent-sur-Seine 43 48 30N 3 30 E
Noggerup 137 33 32 S 116 5 E
Noginsk, Moskva, U.S.S.R. 81 55 50N 38 25 E
Noginsk, Sib., U.S.S.R. 77 64 30N 90 50 E
Nogoa, R. 138 23 33 S 148 32 E
Nogoyá 172 32 24 S 59 48W
Nógrád □ 53 48 0N 19 30 E
Nogueira de Ramuin 56 42 21N 7 43W
Noguera Pallaresa, R. 58 42 15N 1 0 E
Noguera Ribagorzana, R. 58 42 15N 0 45 E
Nohar 94 29 11N 74 49 E
Noi, R. 101 14 50N 100 15 E
Noire, Mts. 42 48 11N 3 40W
Noirétable 44 45 48N 3 46 E
Noirmoutier 42 47 0N 2 15W
Noirmoutier, Î. de 42 46 58N 2 10W
Nojane 128 23 15 S 20 14 E
Nojima-Zaki 111 34 54N 139 53 E
Nok Kundi 93 28 50N 62 45 E
Nokaneng 128 19 47 S 22 17 E
Nokhtuysk 77 60 0N 117 45 E
Nokomis 153 51 35N 105 0W
Nokomis L. 153 57 0N 103 0W
Nokou 124 14 35N 14 47 E
Nol 73 57 56N 12 5 E
Nola, C. Afr. Emp. 124 3 35N 16 10 E
Nola, Italy 65 40 54N 14 29 E
Nolay 43 46 58N 4 35 E
Nolby 72 62 17N 17 26 E
Noli, C. di 62 44 12N 8 26 E
Nolinsk 84 57 28N 49 57 E
Noma Omuramba, R. 128 19 6 S 20 30 E
Noma-Saki 110 31 25N 130 7 E
Nomad 135 6 19 S 142 13 E
Noman L. 153 62 15N 108 55W
Nombre de Dios 166 9 34N 79 28W
Nome 147 64 30N 165 30W
Nomo-Zaki 110 32 35N 129 44 E
Nonacho L. 153 61 57N 109 28W
Nonancourt 42 48 47N 1 11 E
Nonant-le-Pin 42 48 42N 0 12 E
Nonda 138 20 40 S 142 28 E
Nong Chang 100 15 23N 99 51 E
Nong Het 100 19 29N 103 59 E
Nong Khae 101 14 29N 100 53 E
Nong Khai 100 17 50N 102 46 E
Nonoava 164 27 22N 106 38W
Nonopapa 147 21 50N 160 15W
Nonthaburi 100 13 51N 100 34 E
Nontron 44 45 31N 0 40 E
Noonamah 136 12 40 S 131 4 E
Noonan 158 48 51N 102 59W
Noondoo 139 28 35 S 148 30 E
Noonkanbah 102 18 30 S 124 50 E
Noord-Bergum 46 53 14N 6 1 E
Noord Brabant □ 47 51 40N 5 0 E
Noord Holland □ 46 52 30N 4 45 E
Noordbeveland 47 51 45N 3 50 E
Noordeloos 46 51 55N 4 56 E
Noordhollandsch Kanaal 46 52 55N 4 48 E
Noordhorn 46 53 16N 6 24 E
Noordoostpolder 46 52 45N 5 45 E
Noordwijk aan Zee 46 52 14N 4 26 E
Noordwijk-Binnen 46 52 14N 4 27 E
Noordwijkerhout 46 52 16N 4 30 E
'Noordwinning', gasfield 19 53 13N 3 10 E
Noordzee Kanaal 46 52 28N 4 35 E
Noorvik 147 66 50N 161 14W
Noorwolde 46 52 54N 6 8 E
Nootka 152 49 38N 126 38W
Nootka I. 152 49 40N 126 50W
Noqui 124 5 55 S 13 30 E
Nora, Ethiopia 123 16 6N 40 4 E
Nora, Sweden 72 59 32N 15 2 E
Noranda 150 48 20N 79 0W
Norberg 72 60 4N 15 56 E
Norbottens län □ 74 66 58N 20 0 E
Nórcia 63 42 50N 13 5 E
Norco 163 33 56N 117 33W
Nord □ 43 50 15N 3 30 E
Nord-Ostee Kanal 48 54 5N 9 15 E
Nord-Süd Kanal 48 53 0N 10 32 E
Nord-Trondelag Fylke □ 74 64 20N 12 0 E
Nordagutu 71 59 25N 9 20 E
Nordaustlandet 12 79 55N 23 0 E
Nordborg 73 55 5N 9 50 E
Nordby, Fanø, Denmark 73 55 27N 8 24 E
Nordby, Samsø, Denmark 73 55 58N 10 32 E
Norddal 71 62 15N 7 14 E
Norddalsfjord kpl. 71 61 39N 5 23 E
Norddeich 48 53 37N 7 10 E
Nordegg 152 52 29N 116 5W
Nordelph 29 52 34N 0 18 E
Norden 48 53 35N 7 12 E
Nordenham 48 53 29N 8 28 E
Norderhov 71 60 7N 10 17 E
Norderney 48 53 42N 7 9 E
Norderney, I. 48 53 42N 7 15 E
Nordfjord 71 61 55N 5 30 E
Nordfriesische Inseln 48 54 40N 8 20 E
Nordhausen 48 51 29N 10 47 E
Nordhorn 48 52 27N 7 4 E
Nordjyllands Amt □ 73 57 0N 10 0 E
Nordkapp, Norway 74 71 10N 25 44 E
Nordkapp, Svalb. 12 80 31N 20 0 E
Nordkinn 16 71 3N 28 0 E
Nordland Fylke □ 74 65 40N 13 0 E
Nördlingen 49 48 50N 10 30 E
Nordrhein-Westfalen □ 48 51 45N 7 30 E
Nordstrand, I. 48 54 27N 8 50 E
Nordvik 77 73 40N 110 57 E
Nore 71 60 10N 9 0 E
Nore R. 39 52 40N 7 20W
Noreena Cr. 136 22 20 S 120 25 E
Norefjell 71 60 16N 9 29 E
Norembega 150 48 59N 80 43W
Noresund 71 60 11N 9 37 E
Norfolk, Nebr., U.S.A. 158 42 3N 97 25W
Norfolk, Va., U.S.A. 156 36 52N 76 15W
Norfolk □ 29 52 39N 1 0 E
Norfolk Broads 29 52 30N 1 15 E
Norfolk I. 130 28 58 S 168 3 E
Norfork Res. 159 36 25N 92 0W
Norg 46 53 4N 6 28 E
Norham 35 55 44N 2 9W
Norilsk 77 69 20N 88 0 E
Norley 139 27 45 S 143 48 E
Normal 158 40 30N 89 0W
Norman 159 35 12N 97 30W
Norman, R. 138 19 20 S 142 35 E
Norman Wells 147 65 17N 126 45W
Normanby 142 39 32 S 174 18 E
Normanby I. 135 10 55 S 151 5 E
Normanby, R. 138 14 23 S 144 10 E
Normandie 42 48 45N 0 10 E
Normandie, Collines de 42 48 55N 0 45W
Normandin 150 48 49N 72 31W
Normandy = Normandie 42 48 45N 0 10 E
Normanhurst, Mt. 137 25 13 S 122 30 E
Normanton, Austral. 138 17 40 S 141 10 E
Normanton, U.K. 33 53 41N 1 26W
Normanville 140 35 27 S 138 18 E
Norna, Mt. 138 20 55 S 140 42 E
Nornalup 137 35 0 S 116 48 E
Norquay 153 51 53N 102 5W
Ñorquinco 176 41 51 S 70 55W
Norrahammar 73 57 43N 14 7 E
Norrbottens län □ 74 66 50N 18 0 E
Norrby 74 64 55N 18 15 E
Nørre Åby 73 55 27N 9 52 E
Nørre Nebel 73 55 47N 8 17 E
Nørresundby 73 57 5N 9 52 E
Norris 160 45 40N 111 48W
Norristown 162 40 9N 75 15W
Norrköping 73 58 37N 16 11 E
Norrland □ 74 66 50N 18 0 E
Norrtälje 72 59 46N 18 42 E
Norseman 137 32 8 S 121 43 E
Norsholm 73 58 31N 15 59 E
Norsk 77 52 30N 130 0 E
Norte de Santander □ 174 8 0N 73 0W
North Adams 162 42 42N 73 6W
North America 50 40 0N 70 0W
North Andaman I. 101 13 15N 92 40 E
North Atlantic Ocean 14 30 0N 50 0W
North Ballachulish 36 56 42N 5 9W
North Battleford 153 52 50N 108 17W
North Bay 150 46 20N 79 30W
North Belcher Is. 150 56 50N 79 50W
North Bend, Can. 152 49 50N 121 35W
North Bend, U.S.A. 160 43 28N 124 7W
North Bennington 162 42 56N 73 15W
North Berwick, U.K. 35 56 4N 2 44W
North Berwick, U.S.A. 162 43 18N 70 43W
North Br., Ashburton R. 143 43 30 S 171 30 E
North Buganda □ 126 1 0N 32 0 E
North Canadian, R. 159 36 48N 103 0W
North C., Antarct. 13 71 0N 166 0 E
North C., Can. 151 47 2N 60 20W
North, Cape 151 47 2N 60 25W
North C., N.Z. 142 34 23 S 173 4 E
North C., P.N.G. 135 2 32 S 150 50 E
North C., Spitsbergen 12 80 40N 20 0 E
North Caribou L. 150 52 50N 90 40W
North Carolina □ 157 35 30N 80 0W
North Cerney 28 51 45N 1 58W
North Channel, Br. Is. 34 55 0N 5 30W
North Channel, Can. 150 46 0N 83 0W
North Chicago 156 42 19N 87 50W
North Collingham 33 53 8N 0 46W
North Dakota □ 158 47 30N 100 0W
North Dandalup 137 32 30 S 116 2 E
N. Dorset Downs 28 50 50N 2 30W
North Down □ 38 54 40N 5 45W
North Downs 29 51 17N 0 30W
North East 162 39 36N 75 56W
North Eastern □ 126 1 30N 40 0 E
North Esk, R. 37 56 44N 2 25W
North European Plain 16 55 0N 20 0 E
N. Foreland, Pt. 29 51 22N 1 28 E
North Fork 163 37 14N 119 29W
N. Frisian Is. = Nordfr'sche Inseln 48 54 50N 8 20 E
N. Harris, dist. 36 58 0N 6 55W
North Henik L. 153 61 45N 97 40W
North Hill 30 50 33N 4 26W
North Horr 126 3 20N 37 8 E
North Hykeham 33 53 10N 0 35W
North I., Kenya 126 4 5N 36 5 E
North I., N.Z. 143 38 0 S 175 0 E
North Kamloops 152 50 40N 120 25W
North Kessock 37 57 30N 4 15W
North Knife L., Can. 153 58 0N 97 0W
North Knife L., Man., Can. 153 58 5N 97 5W
North Knife, R. 153 58 53N 94 45W
North Koel, R. 95 23 50N 84 5 E
North Korea ■ 105 40 0N 127 0 E
N. Lakhimpur 99 27 15N 94 10 E
N. Las Vegas 161 36 15N 115 6W
North Mara □ 126 1 20 S 34 20 E
North Minch 36 58 5N 5 55W
North Molton 30 51 3N 3 48W
North Nahanni, R. 152 62 15N 123 20W
North Ossetian A.S.S.R. □ 83 43 30N 44 30 E
North Palisade 163 37 6N 118 32W
North Petherton 28 51 6N 3 1W
North Platte 158 41 10N 100 50W
North Platte, R. 160 42 50N 106 50W
North Pt., Austral. 108 27 23 S 153 14 E
North Pt., Can. 151 47 5N 65 0W
North Pole 12 90 0N 0 0 E
North Portal 153 49 0N 102 33W
North Powder 160 45 2N 117 59W
North Queensferry 35 56 1N 3 22W
North Riding (□) 26 54 22N 1 30W
North Roe, dist. 36 60 40N 1 22W
North Ronaldsay, I. 37 59 20N 2 30W
North Sea 19 56 0N 4 0 E
North Sentinel, I. 101 11 35N 92 15 E
North Somercotes 33 53 28N 0 9 E
North Sound 39 53 10N 9 48W
North Sound, The 37 59 18N 2 45W
North Sporades = Voriai Sporádhes 69 39 0N 24 10 E
North Stradbroke I. 133 27 35 S 153 28 E
North Sunderland 35 55 35N 1 40W
North Sydney 151 46 12N 60 21W
North Syracuse 162 43 8N 76 7W
N. Taranaki Bt. 82 38 45 S 174 20 E

North Tawton **Nyirbátor**

North Tawton **30** 50 48N 3 55W
North Thompson, R. **152** 50 40N 120 20W
North Thoresby **33** 53 27N 0 3W
North Tidworth **28** 51 14N 1 40W
North Tolsta **36** 58 21N 6 13W
N. Tonawanda **156** 43 5N 78 50W
N. Truchas Pk. **161** 36 0N 105 30W
North Twin I. **150** 53 20N 80 0W
North Tyne, R. **35** 54 59N 2 7W
North Uist I. **36** 57 40N 7 15W
North Vancouver **152** 49 25N 123 20W
North Vermilion **152** 58 25N 116 0W
North Vernon **156** 39 0N 85 35W
North Vietnam ■ **100** 22 0N 105 0E
North Wabasca L. **152** 56 0N 113 55W
North Walsham **29** 52 49N 1 22E
North West C. **136** 21 45S 114 9E
North West Highlands **36** 57 35N 5 2W
North West River **151** 53 30N 60 10W
North Western □ **127** 13 30S 25 30E
North York Moors **33** 54 25N 0 50W
North Yorkshire □ **33** 54 15N 1 25W
Northallerton **33** 54 20N 1 26W
Northam, Austral. **132** 31 35S 116 42E
Northam, S. Afr. **137** 24 55S 27 15E
Northam, U.K. **30** 51 2N 4 13W
Northampton, Austral. **137** 28 21S 114 33E
Northampton, U.K. **29** 52 14N 0 54W
Northampton, Mass., U.S.A. **162** 42 22N 72 39W
Northampton, Pa., U.S.A. **162** 40 38N 75 24W
Northampton □ **29** 52 16N 0 55W
Northampton Downs **138** 24 35S 145 48E
Northbridge **162** 42 12N 71 40W
Northcliffe **137** 34 39S 116 7E
N.E. Land **12** 80 0N 24 0E
N.E. Providence Chan. **166** 26 0N 76 0W
Northeast Providence Channel **166** 26 0N 76 0W
Northeim **48** 51 42N 10 0E
Northern □, Malawi **127** 11 0S 34 0E
Northern □, Uganda **126** 3 5N 32 30E
Northern □, Zambia **127** 10 30S 31 0E
Northern Circars **96** 17 30N 82 30E
Northern Indian L. **153** 57 20N 97 20W
Northern Ireland □ **38** 54 45N 7 0W
Northern Light, L. **150** 48 15N 90 39W
Northern Province □ **120** 9 0S 11 30W
Northern Territory □ **136** 16 0S 133 0E
Northfield, Minn., U.S.A. **158** 44 37N 93 10W
Northfield, N.J., U.S.A. **162** 39 22N 74 33W
Northfleet **29** 51 26N 0 20E
Northiam **29** 50 59N 0 39E
Northland □ **143** 35 30S 173 30E
Northleach **28** 51 49N 1 50W
Northome **158** 47 53N 94 15W
Northop **31** 53 13N 3 8W
Northport, Ala., U.S.A. **157** 33 15N 87 35W
Northport, Mich., U.S.A. **156** 45 8N 85 39W
Northport, N.Y., U.S.A. **162** 40 53N 73 20W
Northport, Wash., U.S.A. **160** 48 55N 117 48W
Northrepps **29** 52 53N 1 20E
Northumberland □ **35** 55 12N 2 0W
Northumberland, C. **140** 38 5S 140 40E
Northumberland Is. **138** 21 30S 149 50E
Northumberland Str. **151** 46 20N 64 0W
Northville **162** 43 13N 74 11W
Northway Junction **147** 63 0N 141 55W
N.W. Providence Chan. **166** 26 0N 78 0W
Northwest Terr. **148** 65 0N 100 0W
N.W.Basin **137** 25 45S 115 0E
Northwich **32** 53 16N 2 30W
Northwold **29** 52 33N 0 37E
Northwood, Iowa, U.S.A. **158** 43 27N 93 12W
Northwood, N.D., U.S.A. **158** 47 44N 97 30W
Norton, Rhod. **127** 17 52S 30 40E
Norton, N. Yorks., U.K. **33** 54 9N 0 48W
Norton, Suffolk, U.K. **29** 52 15N 0 52E
Norton, U.S.A. **158** 39 50N 100 0W
Norton B. **147** 64 40N 162 0W
Norton Fitzwarren **28** 51 1N 3 10W
Norton Sd. **147** 64 0N 165 0W
Norton Summit **109** 34 56S 138 43E
Nortorf **48** 54 14N 9 47E
Norwalk, Calif., U.S.A. **163** 33 54N 118 5W
Norwalk, Conn., U.S.A. **162** 41 9N 73 25W
Norwalk, Ohio, U.S.A. **156** 41 13N 82 38W
Norway **156** 45 46N 87 57W
Norway ■ **74** 67 0N 11 0E
Norway House **153** 53 59N 97 50W
Norwegian Dependency **13** 66 0N 15 0E
Norwegian Sea **14** 66 0N 1 0E
Norwich, U.K. **29** 52 38N 1 17E
Norwich, Conn., U.S.A. **162** 41 33N 72 5W
Norwich, N.Y., U.S.A. **162** 42 32N 75 30W
Norwood, Austral. **109** 34 56S 138 39E
Norwood, U.S.A. **162** 42 10N 71 10W
Noshiro **112** 40 12N 140 0E
Noshiro, R. **112** 40 15N 140 15E
Nosok **76** 70 10N 82 20E
Nosovka **80** 50 50N 31 30E
Nosratābād **93** 29 55N 60 0E
Noss Hd. **37** 58 29N 3 4W
Noss, I. of **36** 60 8N 1 1W
Nossa Senhora da Glória **170** 10 14S 37 25W
Nossa Senhora das Dores **170** 10 29S 37 13W
Nossebro **73** 58 12N 12 43E
Nossob **128** 22 15S 17 48E
Nossob, R. **128** 25 15S 20 30E
Nosy Bé, I. **125** 13 25S 48 15E
Nosy Mitsio, I. **125** 12 54S 48 36E
Nosy Varika **125** 20 35S 48 32E
Notigi Dam **153** 56 40N 99 10W
Notikewin **152** 56 55N 117 50W
Notikewin, R. **152** 56 59N 117 38W
Notios Evvoïkós Kólpos **69** 38 20N 24 0E
Noto **65** 36 52N 15 4E
Notò, G. di **65** 36 50N 15 10E
Notodden **71** 59 35N 9 17E
Notre Dame **151** 46 18N 64 46W
Notre Dame B. **151** 49 45N 55 30W
Notre Dame de Koartac **149** 60 55N 69 40W
Notre Dame d'Ivugivic **149** 62 20N 78 0W
Nottaway, R. **150** 51 22N 78 55W
Nøtterøy **71** 59 14N 10 24E
Nottingham **33** 52 57N 1 10W
Nottingham □ **33** 53 10N 1 0W
Nottoway, R. **156** 37 0N 77 45W
Notwani, R. **128** 24 14S 26 20E
Nouadhibou **116** 21 0N 17 0W
Nouakchott **120** 18 20N 15 50W
Nouméa **130** 22 17S 166 30E
Noup Hd. **37** 59 20N 3 2W
Noupoort **128** 31 10S 24 57E
Nouveau Comptoir (Paint Hills) **150** 53 0N 78 49W
Nouvelle Calédonie **142** 21 0S 165 0E
Nouzonville **43** 49 48N 4 44E
Nova-Annenskiy **81** 50 32N 42 39E
Nová Bana **53** 48 28N 18 39E
Nová Bystrice **52** 49 2N 15 8E
Nova Chaves **124** 10 50S 21 15E
Nova Cruz **170** 6 28S 35 25W
Nova Era **171** 19 45S 43 3W
Nova Esperança **173** 23 8S 52 13W
Nova Friburgo **173** 22 10S 42 30W
Nova Gaia **124** 10 10S 17 35E
Nova Gradiška **66** 45 17N 17 28E
Nova Granada **171** 20 30S 49 20W
Nova Iguaçu **173** 22 45S 43 28W
Nova Iorque **170** 7 0S 44 5W
Nova Lamego **120** 12 19N 14 11W
Nova Lima **173** 19 59S 43 51W
Nova Lisboa = Huambo **125** 12 42S 15 54E
Nova Lusitânia **127** 19 50S 34 34E
Nova Mambone **129** 21 0S 35 3E
Nova Mesto **63** 45 47N 15 12E
Nova Paka **52** 50 29N 15 30E
Nova Ponte **171** 19 8S 47 41W
Nova Preixo **127** 14 45S 36 22E
Nova Scotia □ **151** 45 10N 63 0W
Nova Sofala **129** 20 7S 34 48E
Nova Varoš **66** 43 29N 19 48E
Nova Venécia **171** 18 45S 40 24W
Nova Zagora **67** 42 32N 25 59E
Novaci, Rumania **70** 45 10N 23 42E
Novaci, Yugo. **66** 41 5N 21 29E
Novaleksandrovskaya **83** 45 29N 41 17E
Novalorque **171** 6 48S 44 0W
Novara **62** 45 27N 8 36E
Novato **163** 38 6N 122 35W
Novaya Kakhovka **82** 46 42N 33 27E
Novaya Ladoga **78** 60 7N 32 16E
Novaya Lyalya **84** 58 50N 60 35E
Novaya Sibir, O. **77** 75 10N 150 0E
Novaya Zemlya **76** 75 0N 56 0E
Novelda **59** 38 24N 0 45W
Novellara **62** 44 50N 10 43E
Noventa Vicentina **63** 45 18N 11 30E
Novgorod **80** 58 30N 31 25E
Novgorod Severskiy **80** 52 2N 33 10E
Novgorod Volynski **80** 50 38N 27 47E
Novi Bečej. **66** 45 36N 20 10E
Novi Grad **63** 45 19N 13 33E
Novi Knezeva **66** 46 4N 20 8E
Novi Krichim **67** 42 22N 24 31E
Novi Ligure **62** 44 45N 8 47E
Novi-Pazar **67** 43 25N 27 15E
Novi Pazar **66** 43 12N 20 28E
Novi Sad **66** 45 18N 19 52E
Novi Vinodolski **63** 45 10N 14 48E
Novigrad **63** 44 10N 15 32E
Noville **47** 50 4N 5 46E
Novo Acôrdo **170** 13 10S 46 48W
Nôvo Cruzeiro **171** 17 29S 41 53W
Novo Freixo **127** 14 49S 36 30E
Nôvo Hamburgo **173** 29 37S 51 7W
Novo Horizonte **171** 21 25S 49 10W
Novo Luso **103** 4 3S 126 6E
Novo Redondo **124** 11 10S 13 48E
Novo Selo **66** 44 11N 22 47E
Novo-Sergiyevskiy **84** 52 5N 53 38E
Novo-Zavidovskiy **81** 56 32N 36 29E
Novoalekseyevka **84** 50 8N 55 39E
Novoataysk **76** 53 30N 84 0E
Novoazovsk **82** 47 15N 38 4E
Novobelitsa **80** 52 27N 31 2E
Novobogatinskoye **83** 47 26N 51 17E
Novocherkassk **83** 47 27N 40 5E
Novodevichye **81** 53 37N 48 58E
Novograd Volynskiy **80** 50 40N 27 35E
Novogrudok **80** 53 40N 25 50E
Novokayakent **83** 42 45N 42 52E
Novokazalinsk **76** 45 40N 61 40E
Novokhopersk **81** 51 5N 41 50E
Novokuybyshevsk **84** 53 7N 49 58E
Novokuznetsk **76** 54 0N 87 10E
Novomirgorod **82** 48 57N 31 33E
Novomoskovsk, R.S.F.S.R., U.S.S.R. **81** 54 5N 38 15E
Novomoskovsk, Ukrainian S.S.R., U.S.S.R. **81** 48 33N 35 17E
Novoorsk **84** 51 21N 59 2E
Novopolotsk **80** 55 38N 28 37E
Novorossiysk **82** 44 43N 37 52E
Novorzhev **80** 57 3N 29 25E
Novoselitsa **82** 48 14N 26 15E
Novoshakhtinsk **83** 47 39N 39 58E
Novosibirsk **76** 55 0N 83 5E
Novosibirskiye Ostrava **77** 75 0N 140 0E
Novosil **81** 52 58N 36 58E
Novosokolniki **80** 56 33N 28 42E
Novotroitsk **84** 51 10N 58 15E
Novotroitskoye **85** 43 42N 73 46E
Novotulskiy **81** 54 10N 37 36E
Novoukrainka **82** 48 25N 31 30E
Novouzensk **81** 50 32N 48 17E
Novovolynsk **80** 50 45N 24 4E
Novovyatsk **84** 58 24N 49 45E
Novozybkov **80** 52 30N 32 0E
Novska **66** 45 19N 17 0E
Novy Bug **82** 47 34N 34 29E
Nový Bydzov **52** 50 14N 15 29E
Novy Dwór Mazowiecki **54** 52 26N 20 44E
Nový Jičín **53** 49 15N 18 0E
Novyy Oskol **81** 50 44N 37 55E
Novyy Port **76** 67 40N 72 30E
Novyye Aneny **70** 46 51N 29 13E
Now Shahr **93** 36 40N 51 40E
Nowa Deba **54** 50 26N 21 41E
Nowa Nowa **141** 37 44S 148 3E
Nowa Skalmierzyce **54** 51 43N 18 0E
Nowa Sól **54** 51 48N 15 44E
Nowe **54** 53 41N 18 44E
Nowe Miasteczko **54** 51 42N 15 42E
Nowe Miasto **54** 51 38N 20 34E
Nowe Miasto Lubawskie **54** 53 27N 19 33E
Nowe Warpno **54** 53 42N 14 18E
Nowen Hill **39** 51 42N 9 15W
Nowendoc **141** 31 32S 151 44E
Nowgong **98** 26 20N 92 50E
Nowingi **140** 34 33S 142 15E
Nowogard **54** 53 41N 15 10E
Nowogród **54** 53 14N 21 53E
Nowra **141** 34 53S 150 35E
Nowthanna Mt. **137** 27 0S 118 40E
Nowy Dwór **54** 53 40N 23 0E
Nowy Korczyn **54** 50 19N 20 48E
Nowy Sącz **54** 49 40N 20 41E
Nowy Sącz □ **54** 49 30N 20 30E
Nowy Staw **54** 54 13N 19 2E
Nowy Targ **53** 49 30N 20 2E
Nowy Tomysśl **54** 52 19N 16 10E
Noxen **162** 41 25N 76 4W
Noxon **160** 48 0N 115 54W
Noya **56** 42 48N 8 53W
Noyant **42** 47 30N 0 6E
Noyers **43** 47 40N 4 0E
Noyes, I. **152** 55 30N 133 40W
Noyon **43** 49 34N 3 0E
Nriquinha **125** 16 0S 21 25E
Nsa, O. en **119** 32 23N 5 20E
Nsanje **127** 16 55S 35 12E
Nsawam **121** 5 50N 0 24W
Nsomba **127** 10 45S 29 59E
Nsopzup **98** 25 51N 97 30E
Nsukka **121** 7 0N 7 50E
Nuanetsi **125** 21 15S 30 48E
Nuanetsi, R. **127** 21 10S 31 20E
Nuatja **121** 7 0N 1 10E
Nuba Mts. = Nubāh, Jibālan **123** 12 0N 31 0E
Nubāh, Jibālan **123** 12 0N 31 0E
Nûbîya, Es Sahrâ En **122** 21 30N 33 30E
Ñuble □ **172** 37 0S 72 0W
Nuboai **103** 2 10S 136 30E
Nubra, R. **95** 34 50N 77 25E
Nudgee **108** 27 22S 153 5E
Nudgee Beach **108** 27 21S 153 6E
Nŭdlac **66** 46 10N 20 50E
Nudo Ausangate, Mt. **174** 13 45S 71 10W
Nudo de Vilcanota **174** 14 30S 70 0W
Nueces, R. **159** 28 18N 98 39W
Nueltin L. **153** 60 30N 99 30W
Nuenen **47** 51 29N 5 33E
Nueva Antioquia **174** 6 5N 69 26W
Nueva Casas Grandes **164** 30 25N 107 55W
Nueva Esparta □ **174** 11 0N 64 0W
Nueva Gerona **166** 21 53N 82 49W
Nueva Imperial **176** 38 45S 72 58W
Nueva Palmira **172** 33 52S 58 20W
Nueva Rosita **164** 28 0N 101 20W
Nueva San Salvador **166** 13 40N 89 25W
Nuéve de Julio **172** 35 30S 61 0W
Nuevitas **166** 21 30N 77 20W
Nuevo, Golfo **176** 43 0S 64 30W
Nuevo Guerrero **165** 26 34N 99 15W
Nuevo Laredo **165** 27 30N 99 40W
Nuevo León □ **164** 25 0N 100 0W
Nuevo Rocafuerte **174** 0 55S 76 50W
Nugget Pt. **143** 46 27S 169 50E
Nugrus Gebel **122** 24 58N 39 34E
Nuhaka **142** 39 3S 177 45E
Nuhurowa, I. **103** 5 30S 132 45E
Nuits **43** 47 10N 4 56E
Nuits-St.-Georges **43** 47 10N 4 56E
Nukey Bluff, Mt. **132** 32 32S 135 40E
Nukheila (Merga) **122** 19 1N 26 21E
Nukus **76** 42 20N 59 40E
Nuland **46** 51 44N 5 26E
Nulato **147** 64 40N 158 10W
Nules **58** 39 51N 0 9W
Nullagine **136** 21 53S 120 6E
Nullagine, R. **136** 21 20S 120 20E
Nullarbor **137** 31 28S 130 55E
Nullarbor Plain **137** 30 45S 129 0E
Numalla, L. **139** 28 43S 144 20E
Numan **121** 9 29N 12 3E
Numansdorp **46** 51 43N 4 26E
Numata **111** 36 45N 139 4E
Numatinna, W. **123** 6 38N 27 15E
Numazu **111** 35 7N 138 51E
Numbulwar **138** 14 15S 135 45E
Numfoor, I. **103** 1 0S 134 50E
Numurkah **141** 36 0S 145 26E
Nun, R. **105** 47 30N 124 40E
Nunaksaluk, I. **151** 55 49N 60 20W
Nundah **108** 27 24S 152 54E
Nuneaton **28** 52 32N 1 29W
Nungo **127** 13 23S 37 43E
Nungwe **126** 2 48S 32 2E
Nunivak I. **147** 60 0N 166 0W
Nunkun, Mt. **95** 33 57N 76 8E
Nunney **28** 51 13N 2 20W
Nunspeet **46** 52 21N 5 45E
Nuoro **64** 40 20N 9 20E
Nŭousa **68** 40 42N 22 9E
Nuqayy, Jabal **119** 23 11N 19 30E
Nuqui **174** 5 42N 77 17W
Nurata **85** 40 33N 65 41E
Nuratau, Khrebet **85** 40 40N 66 30E
Nure, R. **62** 44 40N 9 32E
Nuremburg = Nürnberg **49** 49 26N 11 5E
Nuri **164** 28 2N 109 22W
Nurina **137** 30 44S 126 23E
Nuriootpa **140** 34 27S 139 0E
Nurlat **84** 54 29N 50 45E
Nürnberg **49** 49 26N 11 5E
Nurrari Lakes **137** 29 1S 130 5E
Nurri **64** 39 43N 9 13E
Nusa Barung **103** 8 22S 113 20E
Nusa Kambangan **103** 7 47S 109 0E
Nusa Tenggara □ **102** 7 30S 117 0E
Nusa Tenggara Barat **102** 8 50S 117 30E
Nusa Tenggara Timur **103** 9 30S 122 0E
Nushki **94** 29 35N 65 65E
Nûsûud **70** 47 19N 24 29E
Nutak **149** 57 28N 61 52W
Nuth **47** 50 55N 5 53E
Nutwood Downs **138** 15 49S 134 10E
Nuwaiba **122** 28 58N 34 40E
Nuwakot **95** 28 10N 83 55E
Nuwara Eliya **97** 6 58N 80 55E
Nuwefontein **128** 28 1S 19 6E
Nuweveldberge **128** 32 10S 21 45E
Nuyts Arch. **139** 32 12S 133 20E
Nuyts, C. **137** 32 2S 132 21E
Nuyts, Pt. **132** 35 4S 116 38E
Nuzvid **96** 16 47N 80 53E
NW Tor, oilfield **19** 56 42N 3 13E
Nyaake (Webo) **120** 4 52N 7 37W
Nyabing **137** 33 30S 118 7E
Nyack **162** 41 5N 73 57W
Nyadal **72** 62 48N 17 59E
Nyagyn **76** 62 8N 63 36E
Nyah West **140** 35 11S 143 21E
Nyahanga **126** 2 20S 33 37E
Nyahua **126** 5 25S 33 23E
Nyahururu **126** 0 2N 36 27E
Nyahururu Falls **126** 0 2N 36 27E
Nyakanazi **126** 3 2S 31 10E
Nyakasu **126** 3 58S 30 6E
Nyakrom **121** 5 40N 0 50W
Nyâlâ **123** 12 2N 24 58E
Nyamandhlovu **127** 19 55S 28 16E
Nyambiti **126** 2 48S 33 27E
Nyamwaga **126** 1 27S 34 33E
Nyandekwa **126** 3 57S 32 32E
Nyanga, L. **137** 29 57S 126 10E
Nyangana **128** 18 0S 20 40E
Nyanguge **126** 2 30S 33 12E
Nyangwena **127** 15 18S 28 45E
Nyanji **127** 14 25S 31 46E
Nyankpala **121** 9 21N 0 58W
Nyanza, Burundi **126** 4 21S 29 36E
Nyanza, Rwanda **126** 2 10S 29 42E
Nyanza □ **126** 0 10S 34 15E
Nyarling, R. **152** 60 41N 113 23W
Nyasa, L. = Malawi, L. **127** 12 0S 34 30E
Nyaunglebin **98** 17 52N 96 42E
Nyazepetrovsk **84** 56 3N 59 36E
Nyazwidzi, R. **127** 19 35S 32 0E
Nyborg **73** 55 18N 10 47E
Nybro **73** 56 44N 15 55E
Nybster **37** 58 34N 3 6W
Nyda **76** 66 40N 73 10E
Nyenchen Tanglha Shan **99** 30 30N 95 0E
Nyeri **126** 0 23S 36 56E
Nyeri □ **126** 0 25S 56 55E
Nyerol **123** 8 41N 32 1E
Nyhem **72** 62 54N 15 37E
Nyiel **123** 6 9N 31 4E
Nyika Plat. **127** 10 30S 36 0E
Nyilumba **127** 10 30S 40 22E
Nyinahin **120** 6 43N 2 3W
Nyirbátor **53** 47 49N 22 9E

Nyíregyháza Oldmeldrum

Nyíregyháza 53 48 0N 21 47 E
Nykarleby (Uusikaarlepyy) 74 63 32N 22 31 E
Nykobing 73 54 56N 11 52 E
Nykøbing, Falster, Denmark 73 54 56N 11 52 E
Nykøbing, Mors, Denmark 73 56 48N 8 51 E
Nykøbing, Sjælland, Denmark 73 55 55N 11 40 E
Nyköbing 73 56 49N 8 50 E
Nyköping 73 58 45N 17 0 E
Nykroppa 72 59 37N 14 18 E
Nykvarn 72 59 11N 17 25 E
Nyland 72 63 1N 17 45 E
Nylstroom 129 24 42 S 28 22 E
Nymagee 141 32 7 S 146 20 E
Nymburk 52 50 10N 15 1 E
Nymindegab 73 55 50N 8 12 E
Nynäshamn 72 58 54N 17 57 E
Nyngan 141 31 30 S 147 8 E
Nyon 50 46 23N 6 14 E
Nyons 45 44 22N 5 10 E
Nyora 141 38 20 S 145 41 E
Nyord 73 55 4N 12 13 E
Nysa 54 50 40N 17 22 E
Nysa, R. 54 52 4N 14 46 E
Nyssa 160 43 56N 117 2W
Nysted 73 54 40N 11 44 E
Nytva 84 57 56N 55 20 E
Nyūgawa 110 33 56N 133 5 E
Nyunzu 126 5 57 S 27 58 E
Nyurba 77 63 17N 118 20 E
Nzega 126 4 10 S 33 12 E
Nzega □ 126 4 10 S 33 10 E
N'Zérékoré 120 7 49N 8 48W
Nzilo, Chutes de 127 10 18 S 25 27 E
Nzubuka 126 4 45 S 32 50 E

O

O-Shima, Fukuoka, Japan 110 33 54N 130 25 E
O-Shima, Nagasaki, Japan 110 33 29N 129 33 E
O-Shima, Shizuoka, Japan 111 34 44N 139 24 E
Oa, Mull of 34 55 35N 6 20W
Oa, The, Pen. 34 55 36N 6 17W
Oacoma 158 43 50N 99 26W
Oadby 28 52 37N 1 7W
Oahe 158 44 33N 100 29W
Oahe Dam 158 44 28N 100 25W
Oahe Res 158 45 30N 100 15W
Oahu I. 147 21 30N 158 0W
Oak Creek 160 40 15N 106 59W
Oak Harb. 160 48 20N 122 38W
Oak Lake 153 49 45N 100 45W
Oak Park 156 41 55N 87 45W
Oak Ridge 157 36 1N 84 5W
Oak View 163 34 24N 119 18W
Oakbank, S. Australia, Austral. 109 34 59 S 138 51 E
Oakbank, S. Australia, Austral. 140 33 4 S 140 33 E
Oakdale, Calif., U.S.A. 163 37 49N 120 56W
Oakdale, La., U.S.A. 159 30 50N 92 38W
Oakengates 28 52 42N 2 29W
Oakes 158 46 14N 98 4W
Oakesdale 160 47 11N 117 9W
Oakey 139 27 25 S 151 43 E
Oakham 29 52 40N 0 43W
Oakhill 156 38 0N 81 7W
Oakhurst 163 37 19N 119 40W
Oakland 163 37 50N 122 18W
Oakland City 156 38 20N 87 20W
Oaklands, N.S.W., Austral. 141 35 34 S 146 10 E
Oaklands, S. Australia, Austral. 109 35 1 S 138 32 E
Oakley 160 42 14N 113 55W
Oakley Creek 141 31 37 S 149 46 E
Oakover, R. 136 20 43 S 120 33 E
Oakridge 160 43 47N 122 31W
Oakwood 159 31 35N 95 47W
Oamaru 143 45 5 S 170 59 E
Oamishirasato 111 35 23N 140 18 E
Oarai 111 36 21N 140 40 E
Oasis, Calif., U.S.A. 163 33 28N 116 6W
Oasis, Nev., U.S.A. 163 37 29N 117 55W
Oates Coast 13 69 0 S 160 0 E
Oatman 161 35 1N 114 19W
Oaxaca 165 17 2N 96 40W
Oaxaca □ 165 17 0N 97 0W
Ob, R. 76 62 40N 66 0 E
Oba 150 49 4N 84 7W
Obala 121 4 9N 11 32 E
Obama, Eukui, Japan 111 35 30N 135 45 E
Obama, Nagasaki, Japan 110 32 43N 130 13 E
Oban, N.Z. 143 46 55 S 168 10 E
Oban, U.K. 34 56 25N 5 30W
Obatogamau L. 150 49 34N 74 26W
Obbia 91 5 25N 48 30 E
Obdam 46 52 41N 4 55 E
Obed 152 53 30N 117 10W
Obeh 93 34 28N 63 10 E
Ober-Aagau 50 47 10N 7 45 E
Obera 173 27 21 S 55 2W
Oberalppass 51 46 39N 8 35 E
Oberalpstock 51 46 45N 8 47 E
Oberammergau 49 47 35N 11 3 E
Oberdrauburg 52 46 44N 12 58 E
Oberengadin 51 46 35N 9 55 E
Oberentfelden 50 47 21N 8 2 E
Oberhausen 48 51 28N 6 50 E
Oberkirch 49 48 31N 8 5 E
Oberland 50 46 30N 7 30 E
Oberlin, Kans., U.S.A. 158 39 52N 100 31W
Oberlin, La., U.S.A. 159 30 42N 92 42W
Obernai 43 48 28N 7 30 E
Oberndorf 49 48 17N 8 35 E
Oberon 141 33 45 S 149 52 E
Oberösterreich □ 52 48 10N 14 0 E
Oberpfalzer Wald 49 49 30N 12 25 E
Oberseebach 51 48 53N 7 58 E
Obersiggenthal 51 47 29N 8 18 E
Oberstdorf 49 47 25N 10 16 E
Oberwil 50 47 32N 7 33 E
Obi, Kepulauan 103 1 30 S 127 30 E
Obiaruku 121 5 51N 6 9 E
Óbidos, Brazil 175 1 50 S 55 30W
Óbidos, Port. 57 39 19N 9 10W
Obihiro 112 42 25N 143 12 E
Obilnoye 83 47 32N 44 30 E
Obisfelde 48 52 27N 10 57 E
Objat 44 45 16N 1 24 E
Obluchye 77 49 10N 130 50 E
Obninsk 81 55 8N 36 13 E
Obo, C. Afr. Emp. 123 5 20N 26 32 E
Obo, Ethiopia 123 3 34N 38 52 E
Oboa, Mt. 126 1 45N 34 45 E
Obock 123 12 0N 43 20 E
Oborniki 54 52 39N 16 59 E
Oborniki Śl. 54 51 17N 16 53 E
Obot 123 4 32N 37 13 E
Obout 121 3 28N 11 47 E
Oboyan 81 51 20N 36 28 E
Obrenovac 66 44 40N 20 11 E
O'Briensbridge 39 52 46N 8 30W
Obrovac 63 44 11N 15 41 E
Observatory Inlet 152 55 25N 129 45W
Obshchi Syrt 16 52 0N 53 0 E
Obskaya Guba 76 70 0N 73 0 E
Obuasi 121 6 17N 1 40W
Obubra 121 6 8N 8 20 E
Obyachevo 84 60 20N 49 37 E
Obzor 67 42 50N 27 52 E
Ocala 157 29 11N 82 5W
Ocampo 164 28 9N 108 8W
Ocaña 59 39 55N 3 30W
Ocanomowoc 158 43 7N 88 30W
Ocate 159 36 12N 104 59W
Occidental, Cordillera 174 5 0N 76 0W
Ocean City, Md., U.S.A. 162 38 20N 75 5W
Ocean City, N.J., U.S.A. 162 39 18N 74 34W
Ocean Falls 152 52 25N 127 40W
Ocean I. 130 0 45 S 169 50 E
Ocean Park 160 46 30N 124 2W
Oceanlake 160 45 0N 124 0W
Oceano 163 35 6N 120 37W
Oceanside 163 33 13N 117 26W
Ochagavia 58 42 55N 1 5W
Ochakov 82 46 35N 31 30 E
Ochamchire 83 42 46N 41 32 E
Ochamps 47 49 56N 5 16 E
Och'eng 109 30 20N 114 51 E
Ocher 84 57 53N 54 42 E
Ochiai 110 35 1N 133 45 E
Ochil Hills 35 56 14N 3 40W
Ochiltree 34 55 26N 4 23W
Ochre River 153 51 4N 99 47W
Ochsenfurt 49 49 38N 10 3 E
Ocilla 157 31 35N 83 12W
Ockelbo 72 60 54N 16 45 E
Ocmulgee, R. 157 32 0N 83 19W
Ocna Mureş 70 46 23N 23 49 E
Ocna-Sibiului 70 45 52N 24 2 E
Ocnele Mari 70 45 8N 24 18 E
Oconee, R. 157 32 30N 82 55W
Oconto 156 44 52N 87 53W
Oconto Falls 156 44 52N 88 10W
Ocós 166 14 31N 92 11W
Ocosingo 165 18 4N 92 15W
Ocotal 166 13 41N 86 41W
Ocotlán 164 20 21N 102 42W
Ocquier 47 50 24N 5 24 E
Ocreza, R. 56 39 50N 7 35W
Ócsa 53 47 17N 19 15 E
Octave 161 34 10N 112 43W
Octeville 42 49 38N 1 40W
Octyabrskoy Revolyutsii, Os. 77 79 30N 97 0 E
Ocumare del Tuy 174 10 7N 66 46W
Ocussi 103 9 20 S 124 30 E
Oda, Ghana 121 5 50N 1 5W
Oda, Ehime, Japan 110 33 36N 132 53 E
Oda, Shimane, Japan 110 35 11N 132 30 E
Ödåkra 73 56 9N 12 45 E
Ödåkra 73 56 7N 12 45 E
Odanakumadona 128 20 55 S 24 46 E
Odáoahraun 74 65 5N 17 0W
Odate 112 40 16N 140 34 E
Odawara 111 35 20N 139 6 E
Odda 71 60 3N 6 35 E
Odder 73 55 58N 10 10 E
Oddobo 123 12 21N 42 6 E
Oddur 91 4 0N 43 35 E
Ödeborg 73 58 32N 11 58 E
Odei, R. 153 56 6N 96 54W
Odemira 57 37 35N 8 40W
Ödemiş 92 38 15N 28 0 E
Odense 73 55 22N 10 23 E
Odenton 162 39 5N 76 42W
Odenwald 48 49 18N 9 0 E
Oder, R. 48 53 0N 14 12 E
Oderzo 63 45 47N 12 29 E
Odessa, Del., U.S.A. 162 39 27N 75 40W
Odessa, Tex., U.S.A. 159 31 51N 102 23W
Odessa, Wash., U.S.A. 160 47 25N 118 35W
Odessa, U.S.S.R. 82 46 30N 30 45 E
Odiel, R. 57 37 30N 6 55W
Odienné 120 9 30N 7 34W
Odiham 29 51 16N 0 56W
Odin, gasfield 19 60 5N 2 10 E
Odoben 121 5 38N 0 56W
Odobeşti 70 45 43N 27 4 E
Odolanów 54 51 34N 17 40 E
O'Donnell 159 33 0N 101 48W
Odoorn 46 52 51N 6 51 E
Odorheiul Secuiesc 70 46 21N 25 21 E
Odoyevo 81 53 56N 36 42 E
Odra, R., Czech. 53 49 43N 17 47 E
Odra, R., Poland 54 52 40N 14 28 E
Odra, R., Spain 56 42 30N 4 15W
Odzaci 66 45 30N 19 17 E
Odzak 66 45 3N 18 18 E
Odzi 125 19 0 S 32 20 E
Oedelem 47 51 10N 3 21 E
Oegstgeest 46 52 11N 4 29 E
Oeiras, Brazil 170 7 0 S 42 8W
Oeiras, Port. 57 38 41N 9 18W
Oelrichs 158 43 11N 103 14W
Oelsnitz 48 50 24N 12 11 E
Oenpelli 136 12 20 S 133 4 E
Oensingen 50 47 17N 7 43 E
Oerhtossu, reg. 106 39 20N 108 30 E
Ofanto, R. 65 41 8N 15 50 E
Ofen Pass 51 46 37N 10 17 E
Offa 121 8 13N 4 42 E
Offaly □ 39 53 15N 7 30W
Offenbach 49 50 6N 8 46 E
Offenbeek 47 51 17N 6 5 E
Offenburg 126 48 27N 7 56 E
Offerdal 72 63 28N 14 0 E
Offida 63 42 56N 13 40 E
Offranville 42 49 52N 1 0 E
Ofidhousa, I. 69 36 33N 26 8 E
Ofotfjorden 74 68 27N 16 40 E
Oga-Hantō 111 39 58N 139 59 E
Ogahalla 150 50 6N 85 51W
Ogaki 111 35 21N 136 37 E
Ogallala 158 41 12N 101 40W
Ogbomosho 121 8 1N 3 29 E
Ogden, Iowa, U.S.A. 158 42 3N 94 0W
Ogden, Utah, U.S.A. 160 41 13N 112 1W
Ogdensburg 156 44 40N 75 27W
Ogeechee, R. 157 32 30N 81 32W
Oglio, R. 62 45 15N 10 15 E
Ogmore 138 22 37 S 149 35 E
Ogmore, R. 31 51 29N 3 37W
Ogmore Vale 30 51 35N 3 32W
Ogna 71 58 31N 5 48 E
Ognon, R. 43 47 43N 6 32 E
Ogoja 121 6 38N 8 39 E
Ogoki 150 51 35N 86 0W
Ogoki L. 150 50 50N 87 10W
Ogoki, R. 150 51 38N 85 57W
Ogoki Res. 150 50 45N 88 15W
Ogooué, R. 124 1 0 S 10 0 E
Ogori 110 34 6N 131 24 E
Ogosta, R. 67 43 35N 23 35 E
Ogowe, R. = Ogooué, R. 124 1 0 S 10 0 E
Ograzden 66 41 30N 22 50 E
Ogrein 122 17 55N 34 50 E
Ogulin 63 45 16N 15 16 E
Ogun □ 121 7 0N 3 0 E
Oguni 110 33 4N 131 2 E
Oguta 121 5 44N 6 44 E
Ogwashi-Uku 121 6 15N 6 30 E
Ogwe 121 5 0N 7 14 E
Ohai 143 44 55 S 168 0 E
Ohakune 142 39 24 S 175 24 E
Ohara 111 35 15N 140 23 E
Ohau, L. 143 44 15 S 169 53 E
Ohaupo 142 37 56 S 175 20 E
Ohey 47 50 26N 5 8 E
O'Higgins □ 172 34 15 S 71 1W
Ohio □ 156 40 20N 83 0W
Ohio, R. 156 38 0N 86 0W
Ohiwa Harbour 142 37 59 S 177 10 E
Ohre, R. 52 50 10N 12 30 E
Ohrid 66 41 8N 20 52 E
Ohridsko, Jezero 66 41 8N 20 52 E
Ohrigstad 129 24 41 S 30 36 E
Öhringen 49 49 11N 9 31 E
Oi Ho 108 28 37N 98 16 E
Oignies 47 50 28N 3 0 E
Oil City 156 41 26N 79 40W
Oildale 163 35 25N 119 1W
Oilgate 39 52 25N 6 30W
Oinousa, I. 69 38 33N 26 14 E
Oirschot 47 51 30N 5 18 E
Oise □ 43 49 28N 2 30 E
Oise, R. 43 49 53N 3 50 E
Oisterwijk 47 51 35N 5 12 E
Oita 110 33 14N 131 36 E
Oita-ken □ 110 33 15N 131 30 E
Oiticica 170 5 3 S 41 5W
Ojai 163 34 28N 119 16W
Ojinaga 164 29 34N 104 25W
Ojocaliente 164 30 25N 106 30W
Ojos del Salado 172 27 0 S 68 40W
Oka, R. 81 56 20N 43 59 E
Okahandja 128 22 0 S 16 59 E
Okahukura 142 38 48N 175 14 E
Okaihau 142 35 19 S 173 36 E
Okakune 142 39 26 S 175 24 E
Okanagan L. 152 50 0N 119 30W
Okanogan 160 48 22N 119 35W
Okanogan, R. 160 48 40N 119 24W
Okány 53 46 52N 21 21 E
Okapa 135 6 38 S 145 39 E
Okaputa 128 20 5 S 17 0 E
Okara 94 30 50N 73 25 E
Okarito 143 43 15 S 170 9 E
Okato 142 39 12 S 173 53 E
Okaukuejo 125 19 10 S 16 0 E
Okavango, R. = Cubango, R. 125 16 15 S 18 0 E
Okavango Swamp 128 19 30 S 23 0 E
Okawa 110 33 9N 130 21 E
Okaya 111 36 0N 138 10 E
Okayama 110 34 40N 133 54 E
Okayama-ken □ 110 35 0N 133 50 E
Okazaki 111 34 57N 137 10 E
Oke-Iho 121 8 1N 3 18 E
Okeechobee 157 27 16N 80 46W
Okeechobee L. 157 27 0N 80 50W
Okefenokee Swamp 157 30 50N 82 15W
Okehampton 30 50 44N 4 1W
Okene 121 7 32N 6 11 E
Oker, R. 48 52 7N 10 34 E
Okha 77 53 40N 143 0 E
Okhi Óros 69 38 5N 24 25 E
Okhotsk 77 59 20N 143 10 E
Okhotsk, Sea of 77 55 0N 145 0 E
Okhotskiy Perevoz 77 61 52N 135 35 E
Okhotsko Kolymskoy 77 63 0N 157 0 E
Oki-no-Shima 110 32 44N 132 33 E
Oki-Shotō 110 36 15N 133 15 E
Okiep 128 29 39 S 17 53 E
Okigwi 121 5 52N 7 20 E
Okija 121 5 54N 6 55 E
Okinawa-Jima 112 26 32N 128 0 E
Okinawa-Shotō 112 27 0N 128 0 E
Okinoerabu-Jima 112 27 21N 128 33 E
Okitipupa 121 6 31N 4 50 E
Oklahoma □ 159 35 20N 97 30W
Oklahoma City 159 35 25N 97 30W
Okmulgee 159 35 38N 96 0W
Oknitsa 82 48 25N 27 20 E
Okolo 126 2 37N 31 8 E
Okondeka 128 21 38 S 15 37 E
Okondja 124 0 35 S 13 45 E
Okonek 54 53 32N 16 51 E
Okrika 121 4 47N 7 4 E
Oksby 73 55 33N 8 8 E
Oktyabr 85 43 41N 77 12 E
Oktyabrskiy 84 54 28N 53 28 E
Okuchi 110 32 4N 130 37 E
Okulovka 80 58 19N 33 28 E
Okuru 143 43 55 S 168 55 E
Okushiri-Tō 112 42 15N 139 30 E
Okuta 121 9 14N 3 12 E
Okwa, R. 128 22 25 S 22 30 E
Okwoga 121 7 3N 7 42 E
Ola 159 35 2N 93 10W
Ólafsfjörður 74 66 4N 18 39W
Ólafsvík 74 64 53N 23 43W
Olancha 163 36 15N 118 1W
Olancha Pk. 163 36 15N 118 7W
Olanchito 167 15 30N 86 30W
Öland 73 56 45N 16 50 E
Olargues 44 43 34N 2 53 E
Olary 140 32 18 S 140 19 E
Olascoaga 172 35 15 S 60 39W
Olathe 158 38 50N 94 50W
Olavarría 172 36 55 S 60 20W
Oława 54 50 57N 17 20 E
Olbia 64 40 55N 9 30 E
Olbia, G. di 64 40 55N 9 35 E
Old Bahama Chan. 166 22 10N 77 30W
Old Baldy Pk = San Antonio, Mt. 163 34 17N 117 38W
Old Castile = Castilla la Vieja 56 41 55N 4 0W
Old Castle 38 53 46N 7 10W
Old Cork 138 22 57 S 142 0 E
Old Dale 163 34 8N 115 47W
Old Deer 37 57 30N 2 3W
Old Dongola 122 18 11N 30 44 E
Old Factory 150 52 36N 78 43W
Old Forge, N.J., U.S.A. 162 43 43N 74 58W
Old Forge, N.Y., U.S.A. 162 43 43N 74 58W
Old Forge, Pa., U.S.A. 162 41 20N 75 46W
Old Fort, R. 152 58 36N 110 24W
Old Harbor 147 57 12N 153 22W
Old Kilpatrick 34 55 56N 4 34W
Old Leake 33 53 2N 0 6 E
Old Leighlin 39 52 46N 7 2W
Old Man of Hoy 37 58 53N 3 25W
Old Point Comfort 162 37 0N 76 20W
Old Radnor 31 52 14N 3 7W
Old Serenje 127 13 7 S 30 45 E
Old Shinyanga 126 3 33 S 33 27 E
Old Town 151 45 0N 68 50W
Old Wives L. 153 50 5N 106 0W
Oldbury 28 52 30N 2 0W
Oldeani 126 3 22 S 35 35 E
Oldenburg, Niedersachsen, Ger. 48 53 10N 8 10 E
Oldenburg, S.-Holst, Ger. 48 54 16N 10 53 E
Oldenzaal 46 52 19N 6 53 E
Oldham 32 53 33N 2 8W
Oldman, R. 152 49 57N 111 42W
Oldmeldrum 37 57 20N 2 19W

Olds Örken, L

Olds 152 51 50N 114 10W
Olean 156 42 8N 78 25W
Oléggio 62 45 36N 8 38 E
Oleiros 56 39 56N 7 56W
Olekma, R. 77 58 0N 121 30 E
Olekminsk 77 60 40N 120 30 E
Olema 163 38 3N 122 47W
Olen 47 51 9N 4 52 E
Olenek 77 68 20N 112 30 E
Olenek, R. 77 71 0N 123 50 E
Olenino 80 56 15N 33 20 E
Oléron, I. d' 44 45 55N 1 15W
Olesno 54 50 51N 18 26 E
Oleśnica 54 51 13N 17 22 E
Olevsk 80 51 18N 27 39 E
Olga 77 43 50N 135 0 E
Olga, L. 150 49 47N 77 15W
Olga, Mt. 137 25 20 S 130 40 E
Olgastretet 12 78 35N 25 0 E
Ølgod 73 55 49N 8 36 E
Olgrinmole 37 58 29N 3 33W
Olhão 57 37 3N 7 48W
Olib 63 44 23N 14 44 E
Olib, I. 63 44 23N 14 44 E
Oliena 64 40 18N 9 22 E
Oliete 58 41 1N 0 41W
Olifants, R. 125 24 5 S 31 20 E
Olifantshoek 128 27 57 S 22 42 E
Ólimbos 69 35 44N 27 11 E
Ólimbos, Óros 68 40 6N 22 23 E
Olímpia 173 20 44 S 48 54W
Olimpo□ 172 20 30 S 58 45W
Olinda 170 8 1 S 34 51W
Olindiná 170 11 22 S 38 21W
Oling Hu 105 34 52N 97 30 E
Olite 58 42 29N 1 40W
Oliva, Argent. 172 32 0 S 63 38W
Oliva, Spain 59 38 58N 0 15W
Oliva de la Frontera 57 38 17N 6 54W
Oliva, Punta del 56 43 37N 5 28W
Olivares 58 39 46N 2 20W
Oliveira, Bahia, Brazil 171 12 23 S 38 35W
Oliveira, Minas Gerais, Brazil 171 20 50 S 44 50W
Oliveira de Azemeis 56 40 49N 8 29W
Oliveira dos Brejinhos 171 12 19 S 42 54W
Olivença 127 11 47 S 35 13 E
Olivenza 57 38 41N 7 9W
Oliver 152 49 20N 119 30W
Oliver L. 153 56 56N 103 22W
Olivine Ra. 143 44 15 S 168 30 E
Olivone 51 46 32N 8 57 E
Olkhovka 83 49 48N 44 32 E
Olkusz 54 50 18N 19 33 E
Ollagüe 172 21 15 S 68 10W
Ollerton 33 53 12N 1 1W
Olloy 47 50 5N 4 36 E
Olmedo 56 41 20N 4 43W
Olmos, L. 172 33 25 S 63 19W
Olney, U.K. 29 52 9N 0 42W
Olney, Ill., U.S.A. 156 38 40N 88 0W
Olney, Tex., U.S.A. 159 33 25N 98 45W
Olofström 73 56 17N 14 32 E
Oloma 121 3 29N 11 19 E
Olomane, R. 151 50 14N 60 37W
Olomouc 53 49 38N 17 12 E
Olonets 78 61 10N 33 0 E
Olongapo 103 14 50N 120 18 E
Oloron-Ste.-Marie 44 43 11N 0 38W
Olot 58 42 11N 2 30 E
Olovo 66 44 8N 18 35 E
Olovyannaya 77 50 50N 115 10 E
Olpe 48 51 2N 7 50 E
Olsene 47 50 58N 3 28 E
Olshanka 82 48 16N 30 58 E
Olst 46 52 20N 6 7 E
Olsztyn 54 53 48N 20 29 E
Olsztyn□ 54 54 0N 21 0 E
Olsztynek 54 53 34N 20 19 E
Olt□ 70 44 20N 24 30 E
Olt, R. 70 43 50N 24 40 E
Olten 50 47 21N 7 53 E
Oltenita 70 44 7N 26 42 E
Olton 159 34 16N 102 7W
Oltu 92 40 35N 41 50 E
Oluanpi 109 21 54N 120 51 E
Oluego 58 41 47N 2 0W
Olvera 57 36 55N 5 18W
Olympia, Greece 69 37 39N 21 39 E
Olympia, U.S.A. 160 47 0N 122 58W
Olympic Mts. 160 47 50N 123 45W
Olympic Nat. Park 160 47 48N 123 30W
Olympus, Mt. 160 47 52N 123 40W
Olympus, Mt. = Ólimbos, Oros 68 40 6N 22 23 E
Olyphant 162 41 28N 75 37W
Om Hajer 123 14 20N 36 41 E
Om Koï 100 17 48N 98 22 E
Omachi 111 36 30N 137 50 E
Omae-Zaki 111 34 36N 138 14 E
Omagh 38 54 36N 7 20W
Omagh□ 38 54 35N 7 15W
Omaha 158 41 15N 96 0W
Omak 160 48 24N 119 31W
Oman ■ 92 23 0N 58 0 E
Oman, G. of 93 24 30N 58 30 E
Omaruru 128 21 26 S 16 0 E
Omaruru, R. 128 21 44 S 14 30 E
Omate 174 16 45 S 71 0W
Ombai, Selat 103 8 30 S 124 50 E
Ombersley 28 52 17N 2 12W
Ombo 71 59 18N 6 0 E
Ombombo 128 18 43 S 13 57 E
Omboué 124 1 35 S 9 15 E
Ombrone, R. 62 42 48N 11 15 E
Omchi 119 21 22N 17 53 E
Omdraai 128 20 5 S 21 56 E
Omdurmân 121 15 40N 32 28 E
Ome 111 35 47N 139 15 E
Omegna 62 45 52N 8 23 E
Omeonga 126 3 40 S 24 22 E
Ometepe, Isla de 166 11 32N 85 35W
Ometepec 165 16 39N 98 23W
Omez 90 32 22N 35 0 E
Omi-Shima, Ehime, Japan 110 34 15N 133 0 E
Omi-Shima, Yamaguchi, Japan 110 34 15N 131 9 E
Omihachiman 111 35 7N 136 3 E
Omineca, R. 152 56 3N 124 16W
Omiš 63 43 28N 16 40 E
Omisalj 63 45 13N 14 32 E
Omitara 128 22 16 S 18 2 E
Ōmiya 111 35 54N 139 38 E
Omme 73 55 56N 8 32 E
Ommen 46 52 31N 6 26 E
Ömnöovi□ 106 43 15N 104 0 E
Omono, R. 112 39 46N 140 3 E
Omsk 76 55 0N 73 38 E
Omsukchan 77 62 32N 155 48 E
Omul, Mt. 70 45 27N 25 29 E
Omura 110 33 8N 130 0 E
Omura-Wan 110 32 57N 129 52 E
Omuramba, R. 125 19 10 S 19 20 E
Omurtag 67 43 8N 26 26 E
Ōmuta 110 33 0N 130 26 E
Omutninsk 84 58 45N 52 4 E
On 47 50 11N 5 18 E
On-Take 110 31 35N 130 39 E
Oña 58 42 43N 3 25W
Onaga 158 39 32N 96 12W
Onalaska 158 43 53N 91 14W
Onamia 158 46 4N 93 38W
Onancock 162 37 42N 75 49W
Onang 103 3 2 S 118 55 E
Onaping L. 150 47 3N 81 30W
Onarheim 71 59 57N 5 35 E
Oñate 58 43 3N 2 25W
Onavas 164 28 28N 109 30W
Onawa 158 42 2N 96 2W
Onaway 156 45 21N 84 11W
Oncesti 70 43 56N 25 52 E
Onchan 32 54 11N 4 27W
Oncocua 128 16 30 S 13 40 E
Onda 58 39 55N 0 17W
Ondaejin 107 41 34N 129 40 E
Ondangua 128 17 57 S 16 4 E
Ondárroa 58 43 19N 2 25W
Ondas, R. 171 12 8 S 45 0W
Ondava, R. 53 48 50N 21 40 E
Onderdijk 46 52 45N 5 8 E
Ondo, Japan 110 24 11N 132 32 E
Ondo, Nigeria 121 7 4N 4 47 E
Ondo□ 121 7 0N 5 0 E
Ondombo 128 21 3 S 16 5 E
Öndörhaan 105 47 19N 110 39 E
Ondörshil 106 45 33N 108 5 E
Ondverdarnes 74 64 52N 24 0W
One Tree Hill 109 34 43 S 138 46 E
Onega 78 64 0N 38 10 E
Onega, G. of = Onezhskaya G. 78 64 30N 37 0 E
Onega, L. = Onezhskoye Oz. 78 62 0N 35 30 E
Onega, R. 78 63 0N 39 0 E
Onehunga 142 36 55N 174 30 E
Oneida 162 43 5N 75 40W
Oneida L. 162 43 12N 76 0W
O'Neill 158 42 30N 98 38W
Onekotan, Ostrov 77 49 59N 154 0 E
Onema 126 4 35 S 24 30 E
Oneonta, Ala., U.S.A. 157 33 58N 86 29W
Oneonta, N.Y., U.S.A. 162 42 26N 75 5W
Onerahi 142 35 45 S 174 22 E
Onezhskaya Guba 78 64 30N 37 0 E
Onezhskoye Ozero 78 62 0N 35 30 E
Ongarue 142 38 42 S 175 19 E
Ongerup 137 33 58 S 118 28 E
Ongjin 107 37 56N 125 21 E
Ongkharak 100 14 8N 101 1 E
Ongoka 126 1 20 S 26 0 E
Ongole 97 15 33N 80 2 E
Ongon 106 45 41N 113 5 E
Onhaye 47 50 15N 4 50 E
Oni 83 42 33N 43 26 E
Onida 158 44 42N 100 5W
Onilahy, R. 129 23 30 S 44 0 E
Onitsha 121 6 6N 6 42 E
Onkaparinga, R. 109 35 2 S 138 47 E
Onmaka 98 22 17N 96 41 E
Onny, R. 28 52 30N 2 50W
Ono, Japan 110 34 51N 134 56 E
Ono, Japan 111 35 59N 136 29 E
Onoda 110 33 59N 131 11 E
Onomichi 110 34 25N 133 12 E
Onpyŏngni 107 33 25N 126 55 E
Ons, Islas de 56 42 23N 8 55W
Onsala 73 57 26N 12 0 E
Onslow 136 21 40 S 115 0 E
Onslow B. 157 34 10N 77 0W
Onstwedde 46 52 2N 7 4 E
Ontake-San 111 35 53N 137 29 E
Ontaneda 56 43 12N 3 57W
Ontario, Calif., U.S.A. 163 34 2N 117 40W
Ontario, Oreg., U.S.A. 160 44 1N 117 1W
Ontario□ 150 52 0N 88 10W
Ontario, L. 150 43 40N 78 0W
Onteniente 59 38 50N 0 35W
Ontonagon 158 46 52N 89 19W
Ontur 59 38 38N 1 29W
Onyx 163 35 41N 118 14W
Oodnadatta 139 27 33 S 135 30 E
Ooglaamie 12 72 1N 157 0W
Ookala 147 20 1N 155 17W
Ooldea 137 30 27 S 131 50 E
Ooltgensplaat 47 51 41N 4 21 E
Oona River 152 53 57N 130 16W
Oordegem 47 50 58N 3 54 E
Oorindi 138 20 40 S 141 1 E
Oost-Vlaanderen□ 47 51 5N 3 50 E
Oost-Vlieland 46 53 18N 5 4 E
Oostakker 47 51 6N 3 46 E
Oostburg 47 51 19N 3 30 E
Oostduinkerke 47 51 7N 2 41 E
Oostelijk-Flevoland 46 52 31N 5 38 E
Oostende 47 51 15N 2 50 E
Oosterbeek 46 51 59N 5 51 E
Oosterdijk 46 52 44N 5 14 E
Oosterend, Frise, Neth. 46 53 24N 5 23 E
Oosterend, Holl. Sept., Neth. 46 53 5N 4 52 E
Oosterhout, Brabank, Neth. 47 51 39N 4 52 E
Oosterhout, Gueldre, Neth. 46 51 53N 5 50 E
Oosterschelde 47 51 33N 4 0 E
Oosterwolde 46 53 0N 6 17 E
Oosterzele 47 50 57N 3 48 E
Oostkamp 47 51 9N 3 14 E
Oostmalle 47 51 18N 4 44 E
Oostrozebekke 47 50 55N 3 21 E
Oostvleteven 47 50 56N 2 45 E
Oostvoorne 46 51 55N 4 5 E
Oostzaan 46 52 26N 4 52 E
Ootacamund 97 11 30N 76 44 E
Ootha 141 33 6 S 147 29 E
Ootmarsum 46 52 24N 6 54 E
Ootsa L. 152 53 50N 126 20W
Ootsi 128 25 2 S 25 45 E
Opaka 67 43 28N 26 10 E
Opala, U.S.S.R. 77 52 15N 156 15 E
Opala, Zaïre 124 1 11 S 24 45 E
Opalenica 54 52 18N 16 24 E
Opalton 138 23 15 S 142 46 E
Opan 67 42 13N 25 41 E
Opanake 97 6 35N 80 40 E
Opapa 142 39 47 S 176 42 E
Opasatika 150 49 30N 82 50W
Opasquia 153 53 16N 93 34W
Opatija 63 45 21N 14 17 E
Opatów 54 50 50N 21 27 E
Opava 53 49 57N 17 58 E
Opawica, L. 150 49 35N 75 55W
Opeinde 46 53 8N 6 4 E
Opelousas 159 30 35N 92 0W
Opémisca L. 150 50 0N 75 0W
Open Bay Is. 143 43 51 S 168 51 E
Opglabbeek 47 51 3N 5 35 E
Opheim 160 48 52N 106 30W
Ophir, U.K. 147 58 56N 3 11W
Ophir, U.S.A. 147 63 10N 156 40W
Ophthalmia Ra. 136 23 15 S 119 30 E
Opi 121 6 36N 7 28 E
Opien 108 29 15N 103 24 E
Opinaca L. 150 52 39N 76 20W
Opinaca, R. 150 52 15N 78 2W
Opioo 47 51 37N 5 54 E
Opiskotish, L. 151 53 10N 67 50W
Opmeer 46 52 42N 4 57 E
Opobo 121 4 35N 7 34 E
Opochka 80 56 42N 28 45 E
Opoczno 54 51 22N 20 18 E
Opole 54 50 42N 17 58 E
Opole□ 54 50 40N 17 56 E
Oporto = Porto 56 41 8N 8 40W
Opotiki 142 38 1 S 177 19 E
Opp 157 31 19N 86 13W
Oppegård 71 59 48N 10 48 E
Oppenheim 49 49 50N 8 22 E
Opperdoes 46 52 45N 5 4 E
Oppido Mamertina 65 38 16N 15 59 E
Oppland fylke□ 71 61 15N 9 30 E
Oppstad 71 60 17N 11 40 E
Opua 142 35 19 S 174 9 E
Opunake 142 39 26 S 173 52 E
Opuzen 66 43 1N 17 34 E
Or Yehuda 90 32 2N 34 50 E
Ora 63 46 20N 11 19 E
Ora Banda 137 30 20 S 121 0 E
Oracle 161 32 45N 110 46W
Oradea 70 47 2N 21 58 E
Öræfajökull 74 64 2N 16 39W
Orahovac 66 42 24N 20 40 E
Orahovica 66 45 35N 17 52 E
Orai 95 25 58N 79 30 E
Oraison 45 43 55N 5 55 E
Oran, Alg. 118 35 37N 0 39W
Oran, Argent. 172 23 10 S 64 20W
Oran, Ireland 38 53 40N 8 20W
Orange, Austral. 141 33 15 S 149 7 E
Orange, France 45 44 8N 4 47 E
Orange, Calif., U.S.A. 163 33 47N 117 51W
Orange, Mass., U.S.A. 162 42 35N 72 15W
Orange, Tex., U.S.A. 159 30 0N 93 40W
Orange, Va., U.S.A. 156 38 17N 78 5W
Orange, C. 175 4 20N 51 30W
Orange Cove 163 36 38N 119 19W
Orange Free State = Oranje Vrystaat 128 28 30 S 27 0 E
Orange Free State□ 128 28 30 S 27 0 E
Orange Grove 159 27 57N 97 57W
Orange, R. = Oranje, R. 128 28 30 S 18 0 E
Orange Walk 165 18 6N 88 33W
Orangeburg 157 33 27N 80 53W
Orangerie B. 138 10 30 S 149 30 E
Orangeville 150 43 55N 80 5W
Oranienburg 48 52 45N 13 15 E
Oranje, R. 128 28 30 S 18 0 E
Oranje Vrystaat□ 128 28 30 S 27 0 E
Oranjemund (Orange Mouth) 128 28 32 S 16 29 E
Oranmore 39 53 16N 8 57W
Orapa 128 21 13 S 25 25 E
Oras 103 12 9N 125 22 E
Orašje 66 45 1N 18 42 E
Oraşul Stalin = Braşov 70 45 7N 25 39 E
Orava, R. 53 49 24N 19 20 E
Oraviţa 66 45 6N 21 43 E
Orb, R. 44 43 28N 3 5 E
Orba, R. 62 44 45N 8 40 E
Ørbæk 73 55 17N 10 39 E
Orbe 50 46 43N 6 32 E
Orbec 42 49 1N 0 23 E
Orbetello 63 42 26N 11 11 E
Órbigo, R. 56 42 40N 5 45W
Orbost 141 37 40 S 148 29 E
Örbyhus 72 60 15N 17 43 E
Orbyhus 72 60 13N 17 43 E
Orce 59 37 44N 2 28W
Orce, R. 59 37 45N 2 30W
Orchies 43 50 28N 3 14 E
Orchila, Isla 167 11 48N 66 10W
Orco, R. 62 45 20N 7 45 E
Orcutt 163 34 52N 120 27W
Ord 136 17 23 S 128 51 E
Ord, Mt. 136 17 20 S 125 34 E
Ord, R. 136 15 33 S 128 35 E
Ordenes 56 43 5N 8 29W
Orderville 161 37 18N 112 43W
Ordhead 37 57 10N 2 31W
Ordie 37 57 6N 2 54W
Ordos (Oerhtossu) 106 39 0N 108 0 E
Ordu 92 40 55N 37 53 E
Orduña 58 42 58N 2 58W
Orduña, Mte. 59 37 20N 3 30W
Ordway 158 38 15N 103 42W
Ordzhonikidze, R.S.F.S.R., U.S.S.R. 83 43 0N 44 35 E
Ordzhonikidze, Ukraine S.S.R., U.S.S.R. 82 47 32N 34 3 E
Ordzhonikidze, Uzbek S.S.R., U.S.S.R. 85 41 21N 69 22 E
Ordzhonikidzeabad 85 38 34N 69 1 E
Ore, Sweden 72 61 8N 15 10 E
Ore, Zaïre 126 3 17N 29 30 E
Ore Mts. = Erzgebirge 49 50 25N 13 0 E
Orebic 66 43 0N 17 11 E
Örebro 72 59 20N 15 18 E
Örebro län□ 72 59 27N 15 0 E
Oregon 158 42 1N 89 20W
Oregon□ 160 44 0N 120 0W
Oregon City 160 45 21N 122 35W
Öregrund 72 60 21N 18 30 E
Öregrundsgrepen 72 60 25N 18 15 E
Orekhov 82 47 30N 35 32 E
Orekhovo-Zuyevo 81 55 50N 38 55 E
Orel 81 52 57N 36 3 E
Orel, R. 82 49 5N 35 25 E
Orellana, Canal de 57 39 2N 6 0W
Orellana la Vieja 57 39 1N 5 32W
Orellana, Pantano de 57 39 5N 5 10W
Orem 160 40 27N 111 45W
Oren 69 37 3N 27 57 E
Orenburg 84 51 45N 55 6 E
Orense 56 42 19N 7 55W
Orense□ 56 42 15N 7 30W
Orepuki 143 46 19 S 167 46 E
Orestiás 68 41 30N 26 33 E
Øresund 73 55 45N 12 45 E
Oreti, R. 143 45 39 S 168 14 E
Orford 29 52 6N 1 31 E
Orford Ness 29 52 6N 1 31 E
Orgañá 58 42 13N 1 20 E
Orgaz 57 39 39N 3 53W
Orgeyev 82 47 9N 29 10 E
Orgon 45 43 47N 5 3 E
Orhon Gol, R. 105 50 21N 106 5 E
Ória 65 40 30N 17 38 E
Orient 139 28 7 S 143 3 E
Orient Bay 150 49 20N 88 10W
Oriente 172 38 44 S 60 37W
Origny 43 49 50N 3 30 E
Origny-Ste.-Benoîte 43 49 50N 3 30 E
Orihuela 59 38 7N 0 55W
Orihuela del Tremedal 58 40 33N 1 39W
Oriku 68 40 20N 19 30 E
Orinoco, Delta del 167 8 30N 61 0W
Orinoco, R. 174 5 45N 67 40W
Orion 153 49 28N 110 49W
Oriskany 162 43 9N 75 20W
Orissa□ 96 21 0N 85 0 E
Oristano 64 39 54N 8 35 E
Oristano, Golfo di 64 39 50N 8 22 E
Orizaba 165 18 50N 97 10W
Orizare 67 42 44N 27 39 E
Orizona 171 17 3 S 48 18W
Ørje 71 59 29N 11 39 E
Orjen, mt. 66 42 35N 18 34 E
Orjiva 59 36 53N 3 24W
Orkanger 71 63 18N 9 52 E
Orkelljunga 73 56 17N 13 17 E
Örken, L. 73 57 11N 15 0 E

Örkény Owen

Name	Page	Lat.	Long.
Örkény	**53**	47 9N	19 26 E
Orkla	**71**	63 18N	9 51 E
Orkla, R.	**74**	63 18N	9 51 E
Orkney	**128**	26 42 S	26 40 E
Orkney □	**37**	59 0N	3 0W
Orkney Is.	**37**	59 0N	3 0W
Orland	**160**	39 46N	122 12W
Orlando	**157**	28 30N	81 25W
Orlando, C.d'	**65**	38 10N	14 43 E
Orléanais	**43**	48 0N	2 0 E
Orléans	**43**	47 54N	1 52 E
Orleans, I. d'	**156**	46 54N	70 58W
Orlice, R.	**52**	50 5N	16 10 E
Orlické Hory	**53**	50 15N	16 30 E
Orlov	**53**	49 17N	20 51 E
Orlov Gay	**81**	51 4N	48 19 E
Orlovat	**66**	45 14N	20 33 E
Ormara	**93**	25 16N	64 33 E
Ormea	**62**	44 9N	7 54 E
Ormesby St. Margaret	**29**	52 39N	1 42 E
Ormilia	**68**	40 16N	23 33 E
Ormoc	**103**	11 0N	124 37 E
Ormond, N.Z.	**142**	38 33 S	177 56 E
Ormond, U.S.A.	**157**	29 13N	81 5W
Ormondville	**142**	40 5 S	176 19 E
Ormoz	**63**	46 25N	16 10 E
Ormskirk	**32**	53 35N	2 53W
Ornans	**43**	47 7N	6 10 E
Orne □	**42**	48 40N	0 0 E
Orneta	**54**	54 8N	20 9 E
Ørnhøj	**73**	56 13N	8 34 E
Ornö	**72**	59 4N	18 24 E
Örnsköldsvik	**72**	63 17N	18 40 E
Oro Grande	**163**	34 36N	117 20W
Oro, R.	**164**	26 8N	105 58W
Orocué	**174**	4 48N	71 20W
Orodo	**121**	5 34N	7 4 E
Orogrande	**161**	32 20N	106 4W
Orol	**56**	43 34N	7 39W
Oromocto	**151**	45 54N	66 29W
Oron, Israel	**90**	30 55N	35 1 E
Oron, Nigeria	**121**	4 48N	8 14 E
Oron, Switz.	**50**	46 34N	6 50 E
Oron, R.	**77**	69 21N	95 43 E
Oronsay I.	**34**	56 0N	6 14W
Oronsay, Pass of	**34**	56 0N	6 10W
Oropesa	**56**	39 57N	5 10W
Oroquieta	**103**	8 32N	123 44 E
Orori	**107**	40 1N	127 27 E
Orós	**170**	6 15 S	38 55W
Orosei, G. di	**64**	40 15N	9 40 E
Orosháza	**53**	46 32N	20 42 E
Orotukan	**77**	62 16N	151 42 E
Oroville, Calif., U.S.A.	**160**	39 31N	121 30W
Oroville, Wash., U.S.A.	**160**	48 58N	119 30W
Orowia	**143**	46 1 S	167 50 E
Orphir	**37**	58 56N	3 8W
Orrefors	**73**	56 50N	15 45 E
Orroroo	**140**	32 43 S	138 38 E
Orsa	**72**	61 7N	14 37 E
Orsara di Puglia	**65**	41 17N	15 16 E
Orsasjön	**72**	61 7N	14 37 E
Orsha	**80**	54 30N	30 25 E
Orsières	**50**	46 2N	7 9 E
Orsk	**84**	51 12N	58 34 E
Ørslev	**73**	55 23N	11 56 E
Orsogna	**63**	42 13N	14 17 E
Orşova	**70**	44 41N	22 25 E
Ørsted	**73**	56 30N	10 20 E
Orta, L. d'	**62**	45 48N	8 21 E
Orta Nova	**65**	41 20N	15 40 E
Orte	**63**	42 28N	12 23 E
Ortegal, C.	**56**	43 43N	7 52W
Orthez	**44**	43 29N	0 48W
Ortho	**47**	50 8N	5 37 E
Ortigueira	**56**	43 40N	7 50W
Ortles, mt.	**62**	46 31N	10 33 E
Orto, Tokay	**85**	42 20N	76 1 E
Ortón, R.	**174**	10 50 S	67 0W
Orton Tebay	**32**	54 28N	2 35W
Ortona	**63**	42 21N	14 24 E
Orune	**64**	40 25N	9 20 E
Oruro	**174**	18 0 S	67 19W
Orust	**73**	58 10N	11 40 E
Orûştie	**70**	45 50N	23 10 E
Oruzgan	**94**	32 30N	66 35 E
Orvault	**42**	47 17N	1 38 E
Orvieto	**63**	42 43N	12 8 E
Orwell	**162**	43 35N	75 60W
Orwell, R.	**29**	52 2N	1 12 E
Orwigsburg	**162**	40 38N	76 6W
Oryakhovo	**66**	43 40N	23 57 E
Orzinuovi	**62**	45 24N	9 55 E
Orzysz	**54**	53 50N	21 58 E
Os	**71**	60 9N	5 30 E
Osa	**84**	57 17N	55 26 E
Osa, Pen. de	**166**	8 0N	84 0W
Osage, Iowa, U.S.A.	**158**	43 15N	92 50W
Osage, Wyo., U.S.A.	**158**	43 59N	104 25W
Osage City	**158**	38 43N	95 51W
Osage, R.	**158**	38 15N	92 30W
Ōsaka	**111**	34 30N	135 30 E
Osaka-fu □	**111**	34 40N	135 30 E
Osaka-Wan	**111**	34 30N	135 18 E
Osan	**107**	37 11N	127 4 E
Osawatomie	**158**	38 30N	94 55W
Osborne	**158**	39 30N	98 45W
Osby	**73**	56 23N	13 59 E
Osceola, Ark., U.S.A.	**159**	35 40N	90 0W
Osceola, Iowa, U.S.A.	**158**	41 0N	93 20W
Oschatz	**48**	51 17N	13 8 E
Oschersleben	**48**	52 2N	11 13 E
Öschiri	**64**	40 43N	9 7 E
Osečina	**66**	44 23N	19 34 E
Ösel = Saaremaa	**80**	58 30N	22 30W
Osenovka	**66**	70 40N	120 50 E
Osëry	**81**	54 52N	38 28 E
Osh	**85**	40 37N	72 49 E
Oshan	**108**	24 11N	102 24 E
Oshawa	**150**	43 50N	78 45W
Oshikango	**128**	17 9 S	16 10 E
Oshima	**110**	33 11N	132 24 E
Oshkosh, Nebr., U.S.A.	**156**	41 27N	102 20W
Oshkosh, Wis., U.S.A.	**156**	44 3N	88 35W
Oshmyany	**80**	54 26N	25 58 E
Oshogbo	**121**	7 48N	4 37 E
Oshwe	**124**	3 25 S	19 28 E
Osica de Jos	**70**	44 14N	24 20 E
Osieczna	**54**	51 55N	16 40 E
Osijek	**66**	45 34N	18 41 E
Osilo	**64**	40 45N	8 41 E
Osimo	**63**	43 40N	13 30 E
Osintorf	**80**	54 34N	30 31 E
Osipovichi	**80**	53 25N	28 33 E
Oskaloosa	**158**	41 18N	92 40W
Oskarshamn	**73**	57 15N	16 27 E
Oskelaneo	**150**	48 5N	75 15W
Oskol, R.	**81**	50 20N	38 0 E
Oslo	**71**	59 55N	10 45 E
Oslob	**103**	9 31N	123 26 E
Oslofjorden	**71**	59 20N	10 35 E
Osmanabad	**96**	18 5N	76 10 E
Osmancık	**82**	40 45N	34 47 E
Osmand Ra.	**136**	17 10 S	128 45 E
Osmaniye	**92**	37 5N	36 10 E
Osmo	**72**	58 58N	17 55 E
Osmotherley	**33**	54 22N	1 18W
Osnabrück	**48**	52 16N	8 2 E
Osobláha	**53**	50 17N	17 44 E
Osolo	**71**	59 53N	10 52 E
Osona	**128**	22 3 S	16 59 E
Osorio	**173**	29 53 S	50 17W
Osorno, Chile	**176**	40 25 S	73 0W
Osorno, Spain	**56**	42 24N	4 22W
Osorno, Vol.	**176**	41 0N	72 30W
Osoyoos	**152**	49 0N	119 30W
Ospika, R.	**152**	56 20N	124 0W
Osprey Reef	**138**	13 52 S	146 36 E
Oss	**46**	51 46N	5 32 E
Ossa de Montiel	**59**	38 58N	2 45W
Ossa, Mt.	**138**	41 52 S	146 3 E
Ossa, Oros	**68**	39 47N	22 42 E
Ossabaw I.	**157**	31 45N	81 8W
Ossendrecht	**47**	51 24N	4 20 E
Ossett	**33**	53 40N	1 35W
Ossining	**162**	41 9N	73 50W
Ossipee	**162**	43 41N	71 9W
Ośsno Lubuskie	**54**	52 28N	14 51 E
Ossokmanuan L.	**151**	53 25N	65 0W
Ossora	**77**	59 20N	163 13 E
Ośświecim	**54**	50 2N	19 11 E
Ostashkov	**80**	57 4N	33 2 E
Oste, R.	**48**	53 30N	9 12 E
Ostend = Oostende	**47**	51 15N	2 50 E
Oster	**80**	50 57N	30 46 E
Osterburg	**48**	52 47N	11 44 E
Østerby	**72**	60 13N	17 55 E
Østerbymo	**73**	57 49N	15 15 E
Österdalälven	**72**	61 30N	13 45 E
Östergötlands Län □	**73**	58 35N	15 45 E
Osterholz-Scharmbeck	**48**	53 14N	8 48 E
Østerild	**73**	57 3N	8 50 E
Østerild	**73**	57 2N	8 51 E
Österkorsberga	**73**	57 18N	15 6 E
Ostermundigen	**50**	46 58N	7 30 E
Østerøya	**71**	60 32N	5 30 E
Östersund	**72**	63 10N	14 38 E
Østfold fylke □	**71**	59 25N	11 25 E
Ostfriesische Inseln	**48**	53 45N	7 15 E
Ostia Lido (Lido di Roma)	**64**	41 43N	12 17 E
Ostiglia	**63**	45 4N	11 9 E
Ostrava	**53**	49 51N	18 18 E
Ostrgrog	**54**	52 37N	16 33 E
Ostróda	**54**	53 42N	19 58 E
Ostrog	**80**	50 20N	26 30 E
Ostrogozhsk	**81**	50 55N	39 7 E
Ostrołeka	**54**	53 4N	21 38 E
Ostrołeka □	**54**	53 0N	21 30 E
Ostrov, Bulg.	**67**	43 40N	24 9 E
Ostrov, Rumania	**70**	44 6N	27 24 E
Ostrov, U.S.S.R.	**80**	57 25N	28 20 E
Ostrów Mazowiecka	**54**	52 50N	21 51 E
Ostrów Wielkopolski	**54**	51 36N	17 44 E
Ostrowiec-Swietokrzyski	**54**	50 55N	21 22 E
Ostrozac	**66**	43 43N	17 49 E
Ostrzeszów	**54**	51 25N	17 52 E
Ostseebad-Kühlungsborn	**48**	54 10N	11 40 E
Östsinni	**71**	60 53N	10 3 E
Ostuni	**65**	40 44N	17 34 E
Osum, R.	**67**	43 35N	25 0 E
Osumi-Hanto	**110**	31 20N	130 55 E
Osumi-Kaikyō	**112**	30 55N	131 0 E
Osumi, R.	**68**	40 40N	20 10 E
Osumi-Shoto	**112**	30 30N	130 40 E
Osuna	**57**	37 14N	5 8W
Oswaldtwistle	**32**	53 44N	2 27W
Oswego	**162**	43 29N	76 30W
Oswestry	**28**	52 52N	3 3W
Ota, Japan	**111**	35 11N	136 38 E
Ota, Japan	**111**	36 18N	139 22 E
Ota-Gawa	**110**	34 21N	132 18 E
Otago □	**143**	45 20 S	169 20 E
Otago Harb.	**143**	45 47 S	170 42 E
Otago Pen.	**143**	45 48 S	170 45 E
Otahuhu	**142**	36 56 S	174 51 E
Otake	**110**	34 12N	132 13 E
Otaki, Japan	**111**	35 17N	140 15 E
Otaki, N.Z.	**142**	40 45 S	175 10 E
Otane	**142**	39 54 S	176 39 E
Otar	**85**	43 32N	75 12 E
Otaru	**112**	43 10N	141 0 E
Otaru-Wan	**112**	43 25N	141 1 E
Otautau	**143**	46 9 S	168 1 E
Otava, R.	**52**	49 16N	13 32 E
Otavalo	**174**	0 20N	78 20W
Otavi	**128**	19 40 S	17 24 E
Otchinjau	**128**	16 30 S	13 56 E
Otelec	**66**	45 36N	20 50 E
Otero de Rey	**56**	43 6N	7 36W
Othello	**160**	46 53N	119 8W
Othonoi, I.	**68**	39 52N	19 22 E
Othris, Mt.	**69**	39 4N	22 42 E
Otira	**143**	42 49 S	171 35 E
Otira Gorge	**143**	42 53 S	171 33 E
Otis	**158**	40 12N	102 58W
Otjiwarongo	**128**	20 30 S	16 33 E
Otley	**33**	53 54N	1 41W
Otmuchow	**54**	50 28N	17 10 E
Otočac	**63**	44 53N	15 12 E
Otoineppu	**112**	44 44N	142 16 E
Otorohanga	**142**	38 12 S	175 14 E
Otoskwin, R.	**150**	52 13N	88 6W
Otosquen	**153**	53 17N	102 1W
Otoyo	**110**	33 43N	133 45 E
Otra	**71**	58 8N	8 1 E
Otranto	**65**	40 9N	18 28 E
Otranto, C.d'	**65**	40 7N	18 30 E
Otranto, Str. of	**65**	40 15N	18 40 E
Otrøy	**71**	62 43N	6 50 E
Otsuki	**111**	35 36N	138 57 E
Otta	**71**	61 46N	9 32 E
Ottapalam	**97**	10 46N	76 23 E
Ottawa, Can.	**150**	45 27N	75 42W
Ottawa, Ill., U.S.A.	**156**	41 20N	88 55W
Ottawa, Kans., U.S.A.	**158**	38 40N	95 10W
Ottawa Is.	**149**	59 35N	80 16W
Ottawa, R.	**150**	47 45N	78 35W
Ottélé	**121**	3 38N	11 19 E
Ottenby	**73**	56 15N	16 24 E
Otter L.	**153**	55 35N	104 39W
Otter R.	**30**	50 47N	3 12W
Otter Rapids, Ont., Can.	**150**	50 11N	81 39W
Otter Rapids, Sask., Can.	**153**	55 38N	104 44W
Otterburn	**35**	55 14N	2 12W
Otterndorf	**48**	53 47N	8 52 E
Otteröy, I.	**71**	62 45N	6 50 E
Ottersheim	**52**	48 21N	14 12 E
Otterup	**73**	55 30N	10 22 E
Ottery St. Mary	**30**	50 45N	3 16W
Ottignies	**47**	50 40N	4 33 E
Otto Beit Bridge	**127**	15 59 S	28 56 E
Ottosdal	**128**	26 46 S	25 59 E
Ottoshoop	**128**	25 45 S	26 58 E
Ottsjö	**72**	63 13N	13 2 E
Ottter Ferry	**34**	56 1N	5 20W
Ottumwa	**158**	41 0N	92 25W
Otu	**121**	8 14N	3 22 E
Otukpa (Al Owuho)	**121**	7 9N	7 41 E
Oturkpo	**121**	7 10N	8 15 E
Otway, Bahía	**176**	53 30 S	74 0W
Otway, C.	**140**	38 52 S	143 30 E
Otwock	**54**	52 5N	21 20 E
Ötz	**52**	47 13N	10 53 E
Ötz, Fl.	**52**	47 13N	10 53 E
Ötz, R.	**52**	47 14N	10 50 E
Ötztaler Alpen	**52**	46 58N	11 0 E
Ou, Neua	**100**	22 18N	101 48 E
Ou, R.	**100**	20 4N	102 13 E
Ouachita Mts.	**159**	34 50N	94 30W
Ouachita, R.	**159**	33 0N	92 15W
Ouadane	**116**	20 50N	11 40W
Ouadda	**117**	8 15N	22 20 E
Ouagadougou	**121**	12 25N	1 30W
Ouahigouya	**120**	13 40N	2 25W
Ouahila	**118**	27 50N	5 0W
Ouahran = Oran	**118**	35 37N	0 39W
Oualâta	**121**	17 20N	6 55W
Ouallene	**118**	24 41N	1 11 E
Ouanda Djallé	**117**	8 55N	22 53 E
Ouango	**124**	4 19N	22 30 E
Ouargla	**119**	31 59N	5 25 E
Ouarkziz, Djebel	**118**	28 50N	8 0W
Ouarzazate	**118**	30 55N	6 55W
Ouatagouna	**121**	15 11N	0 43 E
Oubangi, R.	**124**	1 0N	17 50 E
Oubarakai, O.	**119**	27 20N	9 0 E
Ouche, R.	**43**	47 11N	5 10 E
Oud-Gastel	**47**	51 35N	4 28 E
Oud Turnhout	**47**	51 19N	5 0 E
Ouddorp	**46**	51 50N	3 57 E
Oude-Pekela	**46**	53 6N	7 0 E
Oude Rijn, R.	**46**	52 12N	4 24 E
Oudega	**46**	53 8N	6 0 E
Oudenaarde	**47**	50 50N	3 37 E
Oudenbosch	**47**	51 35N	4 32 E
Oudenburg	**47**	51 11N	3 1 E
Ouderkerk, Holl. Mérid., Neth.	**46**	51 56N	4 38 E
Ouderkerk, Utrecht, Neth.	**46**	52 18N	4 55 E
Oudeschild	**46**	53 2N	4 50 E
Oudewater	**46**	52 2N	4 52 E
Oudkarspel	**46**	52 43N	4 49 E
Oudon	**42**	47 22N	1 19W
Oudon, R.	**42**	47 47N	1 2W
Oudtshoorn	**128**	33 35 S	22 14 E
Oued Sbita	**118**	25 50N	5 2W
Ouellé	**120**	7 26N	4 1W
Ouessa	**120**	11 4N	2 47W
Ouessant, Île d'	**42**	48 28N	5 6W
Ouesso	**124**	1 37N	16 5 E
Ouezzane	**118**	34 51N	5 42W
Ouffet	**47**	50 26N	5 28 E
Oughter L.	**38**	54 2N	7 30W
Oughterard	**38**	53 26N	9 20W
Ougrée	**47**	50 36N	5 32 E
Ouidah	**121**	6 25N	2 0 E
Ouimet	**150**	48 43N	88 35W
Ouistreham	**42**	49 17N	0 18W
Ouj, R.	**118**	51 15N	29 45 E
Oujda □	**118**	33 18N	1 25W
Oujeft	**116**	20 2N	13 0W
Oulad Naïl, Mts. des	**118**	34 30N	3 30 E
Ouled Djellal	**119**	34 28N	5 2 E
Oulmès	**118**	33 17N	6 0W
Oulton	**29**	52 29N	1 40 E
Oulton Broad	**29**	52 28N	1 43 E
Oulu	**74**	65 1N	25 29 E
Oulu □	**74**	65 10N	27 20 E
Oulujärvi	**74**	64 25N	27 0 E
Oulujoki	**74**	64 45N	26 30 E
Oulun Lääni □	**74**	64 36N	27 20 E
Oulx	**62**	45 2N	6 49 E
Oum el Bouaghi	**119**	35 55N	7 6 E
Oum el Ksi	**118**	29 4N	6 59W
Oum-er-Rbia	**118**	32 30N	6 30W
Oum-er-Rbia, O.	**118**	32 30N	6 30W
Oumè	**120**	5 21N	5 27W
Ounane, Dj.	**119**	25 4N	7 10 E
Ounasjoki	**74**	66 31N	25 44 E
Oundle	**29**	52 28N	0 28W
Ounguati	**128**	21 54 S	15 46 E
Ounianga Kébir	**117**	19 4N	20 29 E
Ounlivou	**121**	7 20N	1 34 E
Our, R.	**47**	49 55N	6 5 E
Ouray	**161**	38 3N	107 48W
Oureg, Oued el	**118**	32 34N	2 10 E
Ourém	**170**	1 33 S	47 6W
Ouricuri	**170**	7 53 S	40 5W
Ourinhos	**173**	23 0 S	49 54W
Ourini	**117**	16 7N	22 25 E
Ourique	**57**	37 38N	8 16W
Ouro Fino	**173**	22 16 S	46 25W
Ouro Prêto	**173**	20 20 S	43 30W
Ouro Sogui	**120**	15 36N	13 19W
Oursi	**121**	14 41N	0 27W
Ourthe, R.	**47**	50 29N	5 35 E
Ouse	**138**	42 25 S	146 42 E
Ouse, R., Sussex, U.K.	**29**	50 58N	0 3 E
Ouse, R., Yorks., U.K.	**33**	54 3N	0 7 E
Oust	**44**	42 52N	1 13 E
Oust, R.	**42**	48 8N	2 49W
Out Skerries, Is.	**36**	60 25N	0 50W
Outardes, R.	**151**	50 0N	69 4W
Outer Hebrides, Is.	**36**	57 30N	7 40W
Outer I.	**151**	51 10N	58 35W
Outes	**56**	42 52N	8 55W
Outjo	**128**	20 5 S	16 7 E
Outlook, Can.	**153**	51 30N	107 0W
Outlook, U.S.A.	**158**	48 53N	104 46W
Outreau	**43**	50 40N	1 36 E
Outwell	**29**	52 36N	0 14 E
Ouyen	**140**	35 1 S	142 22 E
Ouzouer-le-Marché	**42**	47 54N	1 32 E
Ovada	**62**	44 39N	8 40 E
Ovalle	**172**	30 33 S	71 18W
Ovamboland = Owambo	**128**	17 20 S	16 30 E
Ovar	**56**	40 51N	8 40W
Ovejas	**174**	9 32N	75 14W
Ovens	**141**	36 35 S	146 46 E
Over Flakkee, I.	**47**	51 45N	4 5 E
Over Wallop	**28**	51 9N	1 35W
Overbister	**37**	59 16N	2 33W
Overdinkel	**46**	52 14N	7 2 E
Overflakkee	**46**	51 44N	4 10 E
Overijse	**47**	50 47N	4 32 E
Overijssel	**46**	50 46N	4 32 E
Overijssel □	**46**	52 25N	6 35 E
Overijsselsch Kanaal	**46**	52 31N	6 6 E
Överkalix	**74**	66 19N	22 50 E
Overpelt	**47**	51 12N	5 20 E
Overstand	**29**	52 55N	1 20W
Overton, Clwyd, U.K.	**31**	52 58N	2 56W
Overton, Hants, U.K.	**28**	51 14N	1 16W
Overton, U.S.A.	**161**	36 32N	114 31W
Övertorneå	**74**	66 23N	23 40 E
Overum	**73**	58 0N	16 20 E
Ovid, Colo., U.S.A.	**158**	41 0N	102 17W
Ovid, N.Y., U.S.A.	**162**	42 41N	76 49W
Ovidiopol	**82**	46 15N	30 30 E
Oviedo	**56**	43 25N	5 50W
Oviedo □	**56**	43 20N	6 0W
Oviken	**72**	63 0N	14 23 E
Oviksfjällen	**72**	63 0N	13 49 E
Övör Hangay □	**106**	45 0N	102 30 E
Ovoro	**121**	5 26N	7 16 E
Øvre Sirdal	**71**	58 48N	6 43 E
Øvre Sirdal	**71**	58 48N	6 47 E
Ovruch	**80**	51 25N	28 45 E
Owaka	**143**	46 27 S	169 40 E
Owambo	**128**	17 20 S	16 30 E
Owasco L.	**162**	42 50N	76 31W
Owase	**111**	34 7N	136 5 E
Owatonna	**158**	44 3N	93 17W
Owego	**162**	42 6N	76 17W
Owel, L.	**38**	53 34N	7 24W
Owen	**140**	34 15 S	138 32 E

Name	Pg	°	′		°	′	
Owen Falls	126	0	30	N	33	5	E
Owen Mt.	143	41	35	S	152	33	E
Owen Sound	150	44	35	N	80	55	W
Owen Stanley Range	135	8	30	S	147	0	E
Owendo	124	0	17	N	9	30	E
Oweniny R.	38	54	13	N	9	32	W
Owenkillew R.	38	54	44	N	7	15	W
Owens L.	163	36	20	N	118	0	W
Owens, R.	163	36	32	N	117	59	W
Owensboro	156	37	40	N	87	5	W
Owensville	158	38	20	N	91	30	W
Owerri	121	5	29	N	7	0	E
Owhango	142	39	51	S	175	20	E
Owl, R.	153	57	51	N	92	44	W
Owo	121	7	18	N	5	30	E
Owosso	156	43	0	N	84	10	W
Owston Ferry	33	53	28	N	0	47	W
Owyhee	160	42	0	N	116	3	W
Owyhee, R.	160	43	10	N	117	37	W
Owyhee Res.	160	43	30	N	117	30	W
Ox Mts.	38	54	6	N	9	0	W
Oxberg	72	61	7	N	14	11	E
Oxelösund	73	58	43	N	17	15	E
Oxford, N.Z.	143	43	18	S	172	11	E
Oxford, U.K.	28	51	45	N	1	15	W
Oxford, Mass., U.S.A.	162	42	7	N	71	52	W
Oxford, Miss., U.S.A.	159	34	22	N	89	30	W
Oxford, N.C., U.S.A.	157	36	19	N	78	36	W
Oxford, N.Y., U.S.A.	162	42	27	N	75	36	W
Oxford, Ohio, U.S.A.	156	39	30	N	84	40	W
Oxford, Pa., U.S.A.	162	39	47	N	75	59	W
Oxford □	28	51	45	N	1	15	W
Oxford L.	153	54	51	N	95	37	W
Oxilíthos	69	38	35	N	24	7	E
Oxley	140	34	11	S	144	6	E
Oxley Cr.	108	27	35	S	153	0	E
Oxnard	163	34	10	N	119	14	W
Oya	102	2	55	N	111	55	E
Oyabe	111	36	47	N	136	56	E
Oyama	111	36	18	N	139	48	E
Oyana	110	32	32	N	130	18	E
Oyem	124	1	42	N	11	43	E
Oyen	153	51	22	N	110	28	W
Øyeren	71	59	48	N	11	14	E
Øyeren	71	59	50	N	11	15	E
Oykel Bridge	37	57	58	N	4	45	W
Oykell, R.	37	57	55	N	4	26	W
Oymyakon	77	63	25	N	143	10	E
Oyo	121	7	46	N	3	56	E
Oyo □	121	8	0	N	3	30	E
Oyonnax	45	46	16	N	5	40	E
Oyster B.	138	42	15	S	148	5	E
Øystese	71	60	22	N	6	9	E
Øystese	71	60	24	N	6	12	E
Oytal	85	42	54	N	73	17	E
Ozamis (Mizamis)	103	8	15	N	123	50	E
Ozark, Ala., U.S.A.	157	31	29	N	85	39	W
Ozark, Ark., U.S.A.	159	35	30	N	93	50	W
Ozark, Mo., U.S.A.	159	37	0	N	93	15	W
Ozark Plateau	159	37	20	N	91	40	W
Ozarks, L. of	158	38	10	N	93	0	W
Ózd	53	48	14	N	20	15	E
Ozerhinsk	80	53	40	N	27	7	E
Ozërnyy	84	51	8	N	60	50	E
Ozieri	64	40	35	N	9	0	E
Ozimek	54	50	41	N	18	11	E
Ozona	159	30	43	N	101	11	W
Ozorków	54	51	57	N	19	16	E
Ozren, Mt.	66	43	55	N	18	29	E
Ozu	110	33	30	N	132	33	E
Ozu Kumamoto	110	32	52	N	130	52	E
Ozuluama	165	21	40	N	97	50	W
Ozun	70	45	47	N	25	50	E

P

Name	Pg	°	′		°	′	
Pa	120	11	33	N	3	19	W
Pa-an	98	16	45	N	97	40	E
Pa Mong Dam	100	18	0	N	102	22	E
Pa Sak, R.	101	15	30	N	101	0	E
Paal	47	51	2	N	5	10	E
Paar, R.	49	48	42	N	11	27	E
Paarl	128	33	45	S	18	56	E
Paatsi, R.	74	68	55	N	29	0	E
Paauilo	147	20	3	N	155	22	W
Pab Hills	94	26	30	N	66	45	E
Pabbay I.	36	57	46	N	7	12	W
Pabbay, Sd. of	36	57	45	N	7	4	W
Pabianice	54	51	40	N	19	20	E
Pabna	98	24	1	N	89	18	E
Pabo	126	2	56	N	32	3	E
Pacajá, R.	170	1	56	S	50	50	W
Pacajus	170	4	10	S	38	38	W
Pacasmayo	174	7	20	S	79	35	W
Pacaudière, La	43	46	11	N	3	52	E
Paceco	64	37	59	N	12	32	E
Pachhar	94	24	40	N	77	42	E
Pachino	65	36	43	N	15	4	E
Pacho	174	5	8	N	74	10	W
Pachora	96	20	38	N	75	29	E
Pachpadra	93	25	58	N	72	10	E
Pachuca	165	20	10	N	98	40	W
Pachung	108	31	58	N	106	40	E
Pacific	152	54	48	N	128	28	W
Pacific Grove	163	36	38	N	121	58	W
Pacific Ocean	143	10	0	N	140	0	W
Pacifica	163	37	36	N	122	30	W
Packsaddle	140	30	36	S	141	58	E
Pacoh	152	53	0	N	132	30	W
Pacov	52	49	27	N	15	0	E
Pacsa	53	46	44	N	17	2	E

Name	Pg	°	′		°	′	
Pacuí, R.	171	16	46	S	45	1	W
Pacy-sur-Eure	171	49	1	N	1	23	E
Paczkow	54	50	28	N	17	0	E
Padaido, Kepulauan	103	1	5	S	138	0	E
Padalarang	103	7	50	S	107	30	E
Padang	102	1	0	S	100	20	E
Padang, I.	102	1	0	S	100	10	E
Padangpanjang	102	0	30	S	100	20	E
Padangsidimpuan	102	1	30	N	99	15	E
Padatchuang	98	19	41	N	96	35	E
Padborg	73	54	49	N	9	21	E
Paddock Wood	29	51	13	N	0	24	E
Paddockwood	153	53	30	N	105	30	W
Paderborn	48	51	42	N	8	44	E
Padesul	70	45	40	N	22	22	E
Padiham	32	53	48	N	2	20	W
Padina	70	44	50	N	27	8	E
Padlei	153	62	10	N	97	5	W
Padloping Island	149	67	0	N	63	0	W
Padma, R.	98	23	22	N	90	32	E
Padmanabhapuram	97	8	16	N	77	17	E
Pádova	63	45	24	N	11	52	E
Padra	94	22	15	N	73	7	E
Padrauna	95	26	54	N	83	59	E
Padre I.	159	27	0	N	97	20	W
Padrón	56	42	41	N	8	39	W
Padstow	32	50	33	N	4	57	W
Padstow Bay	30	50	35	N	4	58	W
Padua = Pádova	63	45	24	N	11	52	E
Paducah, Ky., U.S.A.	156	37	0	N	88	40	W
Paducah, Tex., U.S.A.	159	34	3	N	100	16	W
Padul	57	37	1	N	3	38	W
Padula	65	40	20	N	15	40	E
Padwa	96	18	27	N	82	37	E
Paekakariki	142	40	59	S	174	58	E
Paektu-san	107	42	0	N	128	3	E
Paengaroa	142	37	49	S	176	29	E
Paengnyŏng Do	107	37	57	N	124	40	E
Paeroa	142	37	23	S	175	41	E
Paesana	62	44	40	N	7	18	E
Pag	63	44	27	N	15	5	E
Pag, I.	63	44	50	N	15	0	E
Paga	121	11	1	N	1	8	W
Pagadian	103	7	55	N	123	30	E
Pagai Selatan, I.	102	3	0	S	100	15	W
Pagai Utara, I.	102	2	35	S	100	0	E
Pagalu, I.	114	1	35	S	3	35	E
Pagaralam	102	4	0	S	103	17	E
Pagastikós Kólpos	68	39	15	N	23	12	E
Pagatan	102	3	33	S	115	59	E
Page	158	47	11	N	97	37	W
Paglieta	63	42	10	N	14	30	E
Pagnau	123	8	15	N	34	7	E
Pagny-sur-Moselle	43	48	59	N	6	2	E
Pagosa Springs	161	37	16	N	107	4	W
Pagwa River	150	50	2	N	85	14	W
Pahala	147	20	25	N	156	0	W
Pahang □	101	3	40	N	102	20	E
Pahang, R.	101	3	30	N	103	9	E
Pahang, st.	101	3	30	N	103	9	E
Pahiatua	142	40	27	S	175	50	E
Pahoa	147	19	30	N	154	57	W
Pahokee	157	26	50	N	80	30	W
Pahrump	161	36	15	N	116	0	W
Pahsien	106	39	10	N	116	20	E
Pahsientung	107	43	11	N	120	57	E
Pai	100	19	19	N	98	27	E
Paia	147	20	54	N	156	22	W
Paible	36	57	35	N	7	30	W
Paich'eng	105	45	40	N	122	52	E
Paich'i	109	28	2	N	111	18	E
P'aichou	109	30	12	N	113	56	E
Paicines	163	36	44	N	121	17	W
Paide	80	58	57	N	25	31	E
Paignton	30	50	26	N	3	33	W
Paiho, China	109	32	49	N	110	3	E
Paiho, Taiwan	109	23	21	N	120	25	E
Paihok'ou	109	31	46	N	110	13	E
Päijänne	75	61	30	N	25	30	E
Pailin	101	12	46	N	102	36	E
Pailolo Chan.	147	21	5	N	156	42	W
Paimbœuf	42	47	17	N	2	0	W
Paimboeuf	44	47	17	N	2	2	W
Paimpol	42	48	48	N	3	4	W
Painan	102	1	15	S	100	40	E
Painesville	156	41	42	N	81	18	W
Painiu	109	32	51	N	112	10	E
Painscastle	31	52	7	N	3	13	W
Painswick	28	51	47	N	2	11	W
Paint l.	153	55	28	N	97	57	W
Painted Desert	161	36	40	N	112	0	W
Paintsville	156	37	50	N	82	50	W
Paipa	174	5	47	N	73	7	W
Paise	108	23	55	N	106	28	E
Paisha	106	34	23	N	112	32	E
Paisley, U.K.	34	55	51	N	4	27	W
Paisley, U.S.A.	160	42	43	N	120	40	W
Paita	174	5	5	S	81	0	W
Paiva, R.	56	40	50	N	7	55	W
Paiyin	105	36	45	N	104	4	E
Paiyü	99	31	12	N	98	45	E
Paiyunopo	106	41	46	N	109	58	E
Pajares	56	39	57	N	1	48	W
Pak Lay	100	18	15	N	101	27	E
Pak Phanang	101	8	21	N	100	12	E
Pak Sane	100	18	22	N	103	39	E
Pak Song	100	15	11	N	106	14	E
Pak Suong	100	19	58	N	102	15	E
Pakala	97	13	29	N	79	8	E
Pakanbaru	102	0	30	N	101	15	E
Pakaraima, Sierra	174	6	0	N	60	0	W
Pakemba	127	13	3	N	29	58	E
Pakenham	141	38	6	S	145	30	E

Name	Pg	°	′		°	′	
Pakhoi = Peihai	108	21	30	N	109	5	E
Pakhtakor	85	40	2	N	65	46	E
Pakistan ■	93	30	0	N	70	0	E
Pakistan, East = Bangladesh ■	99	24	0	N	90	0	E
Pakkading	100	18	19	N	103	59	E
Paknam = Samut Prakan	100	13	36	N	100	36	E
P'ako	105	30	52	N	81	19	E
Pakokku	98	21	30	N	95	0	E
Pakpattan	94	30	25	N	73	16	E
Pakrac	66	45	27	N	17	12	E
Paks	53	46	38	N	18	55	E
Pakse	100	15	5	N	105	52	E
Paksikori	107	42	27	N	130	31	E
Paktya □	93	33	0	N	69	30	E
Pakwach	126	2	28	N	31	27	E
Pal	93	33	45	N	79	33	E
Pala, Chad	117	9	25	N	15	5	E
Pala, U.S.A.	163	33	22	N	117	5	W
Pala, Zaïre	126	6	45	S	29	30	E
Palabek	126	3	22	N	32	33	E
Palacious	159	28	44	N	96	12	W
Palafrugell	58	41	55	N	3	10	E
Palagiano	65	40	35	N	17	0	E
Palagonía	65	37	20	N	14	43	E
Palagruza	63	42	24	N	16	15	E
Palaiókastron	69	35	12	N	26	18	E
Palaiokhóra	69	35	16	N	23	39	E
Pálairos	69	38	45	N	20	51	E
Palais, Le	42	47	20	N	3	10	W
Palakol	96	16	31	N	81	46	E
Palam	96	19	0	N	77	0	E
Palamás	68	39	26	N	22	4	E
Palamós	58	41	50	N	3	10	E
Palampur	94	32	10	N	76	30	E
Palana, Austral.	138	39	45	S	147	55	E
Palana, U.S.S.R.	77	59	10	N	160	10	E
Palanan	103	17	8	N	122	29	E
Palandri	95	33	42	N	73	40	E
Palanpur	94	24	10	N	72	25	E
Palapye	128	22	30	S	27	7	E
Palar, R.	97	12	27	N	80	13	E
Palas	95	35	4	N	73	4	E
Palatka	157	29	40	N	81	40	W
Palau Is.	130	7	30	N	134	30	E
Palauig	103	15	26	N	119	54	E
Palauk	101	13	10	N	98	40	E
Palavas	44	43	32	N	3	56	E
Palawan, I.	102	10	0	N	119	0	E
Palayancottai	97	8	45	N	77	45	E
Palazzo San Gervásio	65	40	53	N	15	58	E
Palazzolo Acreide	65	37	4	N	14	43	E
Paldiski	80	59	23	N	24	9	E
Pale	66	43	50	N	18	38	E
Palel	98	24	27	N	94	2	E
Paleleh	103	1	10	N	121	50	E
Palembang	102	3	0	S	104	50	E
Palencia	56	42	1	N	4	34	W
Palencia □	56	42	31	N	4	33	W
Palermo, Colomb.	174	2	54	N	75	26	W
Palermo, Italy	64	38	8	N	13	20	E
Palermo, U.S.A.	160	39	30	N	121	37	W
Palestine, Asia	90	32	0	N	35	0	E
Palestine, U.S.A.	159	31	42	N	95	35	W
Palestrina	64	41	50	N	12	52	E
Paletwa	98	21	30	N	92	50	E
Palghat	97	10	46	N	76	42	E
Palgrave	29	52	22	N	1	7	E
Palgrave, Mt.	136	23	22	S	115	58	E
P'ali	105	27	45	N	89	10	E
Pali	94	25	50	N	73	20	E
Palik'un	105	43	30	N	92	51	E
Palimé	121	6	57	N	0	37	E
Palintaoch'i	107	43	59	N	119	20	E
Palinuro, C.	65	40	1	N	15	14	E
Palinyuch'i (Tapanshang)	107	43	40	N	118	20	E
Palisade	158	40	35	N	101	10	W
Paliseul	47	49	54	N	5	8	E
Palitana	94	21	32	N	71	49	E
Palizada	165	18	18	N	92	8	W
Palizzi	65	37	58	N	15	59	E
Palk Bay	97	9	30	N	79	30	E
Palk Strait	97	10	0	N	80	0	E
Palkonda	96	18	36	N	83	48	E
Palkonda Ra.	97	13	50	N	79	20	E
Pallasgreen	39	52	35	N	8	22	W
Pallaskenry	39	52	39	N	8	53	W
Pallasovka	81	50	4	N	47	0	E
Palleru, R.	96	17	30	N	79	40	E
Pallinup	137	34	0	S	117	55	E
Pallisa	126	1	12	N	33	43	E
Palliser, C.	142	41	26	S	175	5	E
Palliser, Is.	142	41	37	S	175	14	E
Pallu	94	28	59	N	74	14	E
Palm Beach	157	26	46	N	80	0	W
Palm Desert	163	33	43	N	116	22	W
Palm Is.	138	18	40	S	146	35	E
Palm Springs	163	33	51	N	116	35	W
Palma, Canary Is.	16	28	40	N	17	50	W
Palma, Mozam.	127	10	46	S	40	29	E
Palma, Spain	58	39	33	N	2	39	E
Palma, Bahía de	59	39	30	N	2	39	E
Palma del Río	57	37	43	N	5	17	W
Palma di Montechiaro	64	37	12	N	13	46	E
Palma, I.	116	28	45	N	17	50	W
Palma, La, Panama	166	8	15	N	78	0	W
Palma, La, Spain	57	37	21	N	6	38	W
Palma, R.	171	10	10	N	71	50	W
Palma Soriano	166	20	15	N	76	0	W
Palmanova	63	45	54	N	13	18	E
Palmares	170	8	41	S	35	36	W

*Renamed Belau

Name	Pg	°	′		°	′	
Palmarito	174	7	37	N	70	10	W
Palmarola, I.	64	40	57	N	12	50	E
Palmas	173	26	29	S	52	0	W
Palmas, C.	120	4	27	N	7	46	W
Palmas de Monte Alto	171	14	16	S	43	10	W
Pálmas, G. di	64	39	0	N	8	30	E
Palmdale	163	34	36	N	118	7	W
Palmeira	171	25	25	S	50	0	W
Palmeira dos Índios	170	9	25	S	36	37	W
Palmeirais	170	12	31	S	41	34	W
Palmeiras, R.	171	12	22	S	47	8	W
Palmeirinhas, Pta. das	124	9	2	S	12	57	E
Palmela	57	38	32	N	8	57	W
Palmelo	171	17	20	S	48	27	W
Palmer, Alaska, U.S.A.	147	61	35	N	149	10	W
Palmer, Mass., U.S.A.	162	42	9	N	72	21	W
Palmer Arch	13	64	15	S	65	0	W
Palmer Lake	158	39	10	N	104	52	W
Palmer Pen.	13	73	0	S	60	0	W
Palmer, R., N. Terr., Austral.	138	24	30	S	133	0	E
Palmer, R., Queens., Austral.	138	16	5	S	142	43	E
Palmerston	142	45	29	S	170	43	E
Palmerston, C.	133	21	32	S	149	29	E
Palmerston North	143	40	21	S	175	39	E
Palmerton	162	40	47	N	75	36	W
Palmetto	157	27	33	N	82	33	W
Palmi	65	38	21	N	15	51	E
Palmira, Argent.	172	32	59	S	68	25	W
Palmira, Colomb.	174	3	32	N	76	16	W
Palmyra, Mo., U.S.A.	158	39	45	N	91	30	W
Palmyra, N.J., U.S.A.	162	40	0	N	75	1	W
Palmyra, Pa., U.S.A.	162	40	18	N	76	36	W
Palmyra = Tadmor	92	34	30	N	37	55	E
Palni	97	10	30	N	77	30	E
Palni Hills	97	10	14	N	77	33	E
Palo Alto	163	37	25	N	122	8	W
Palo del Colle	65	41	4	N	16	43	E
Paloe	103	8	20	S	121	43	E
Paloma, La	172	30	35	S	71	0	W
Palombara Sabina	63	42	4	N	12	45	E
Palopo	103	3	0	S	120	16	E
Palos, Cabo de	59	37	38	N	0	40	W
Palos Verdes	163	33	48	N	118	23	W
Palos Verdes, Pt.	163	33	43	N	118	26	W
Palouse	160	46	59	N	117	5	W
Palparara	138	24	47	S	141	22	E
Pålsboda	73	59	3	N	15	22	E
Palu, Indon.	103	1	0	S	119	59	E
Palu, Turkey	92	38	45	N	40	0	E
Paluan	103	13	35	N	120	29	E
Palwal	94	28	8	N	77	19	E
Pama, China	108	24	9	N	107	15	E
Pama, Upp. Vol.	121	11	19	N	0	44	E
Pamanukan	103	6	16	S	107	49	E
Pamban I.	97	9	24	N	79	35	E
Pamekasan	103	7	10	S	113	29	E
Pameungpeuk	103	7	38	S	107	44	E
Pamiench'eng	107	43	13	N	124	2	E
Pamiers	44	43	7	N	1	39	E
Pamir, R.	85	37	1	N	72	41	E
Pamirs, Ra.	85	37	40	N	73	0	E
Pamlico, R.	157	35	25	N	76	40	W
Pamlico Sd.	157	35	20	N	76	0	W
Pampa	159	35	35	N	100	58	W
Pampa de las Salinas	172	32	1	S	66	58	W
Pampa, La □	172	36	50	S	66	0	W
Pampanua	103	4	22	S	120	14	E
Pamparato	62	44	16	N	7	54	E
Pampas, Argent.	172	34	0	S	64	0	W
Pampas, Peru	174	12	20	S	74	50	W
Pamplona, Colomb.	174	7	23	N	72	39	W
Pamplona, Spain	58	42	48	N	1	38	W
Pampoenpoort	128	31	3	S	22	40	E
Pamunkey, R.	162	37	32	N	76	50	W
Pana	158	39	25	N	89	0	W
Panaca	161	37	51	N	114	50	W
Panagyurishte	67	42	49	N	24	15	E
Panaitan, I.	103	6	35	S	105	10	E
Panaji (Panjim)	97	15	25	N	73	50	E
Panamá	166	9	0	N	79	25	W
Panama ■	166	8	48	N	79	55	W
Panama Canal	166	9	10	N	79	56	W
Panama Canal Zone	166	9	10	N	79	56	W
Panama City	157	30	10	N	85	41	W
Panamá, Golfo de	166	8	4	N	79	20	W
Panamint Mts.	161	36	15	N	117	20	W
Panamint Springs	163	36	20	N	117	28	W
Panão	174	9	55	S	75	55	W
Panare	101	6	51	N	101	30	E
Panarea, I.	65	38	38	N	15	3	E
Panaro, R.	62	44	48	N	11	5	E
Panarukan	103	7	40	S	113	52	E
Panay, G.	103	11	0	N	122	30	E
Panay I.	103	11	10	N	122	30	E
Pancake Ra.	161	38	30	N	116	0	W
Pančevo	66	44	52	N	20	41	E
Panciu	70	45	54	N	27	8	E
Pancorbo, Paso	58	42	32	N	3	5	W
Pandan	103	11	45	N	122	10	E
Pandangpanjang	102	0	40	S	100	20	E
Pandeglang	103	6	25	S	106	0	E
Pandharpur	96	17	41	N	75	20	E
Pandhurna	96	21	36	N	78	35	E
Pandilla	58	41	32	N	3	43	W
Pando	174	34	30	S	56	0	W
Pando, L. = Hope L.	139	28	24	S	139	18	E
Panevězys	80	55	42	N	24	25	E
Panfilov	76	44	30	N	80	0	E
Panfilovo	81	50	25	N	42	46	E
Pang-Long	99	23	11	N	98	45	E
Pang-Yang	99	22	7	N	98	48	E

Panga **Paulista**

Panga	**126**	1 52N	26 18 E
Pangaion Óros	**68**	40 50N	24 0 E
Pangalanes, Canal des	**129**	22 48 S	47 50 E
Pangani	**126**	5 25 S	38 58 E
Pangani □	**126**	5 25 S	39 0 E
Pangani, R.	**126**	4 40 S	37 50 E
Pangbourne	**28**	51 28N	1 5W
P'angchiang	**106**	42 50N	113 1 E
Pangfou	**109**	32 55N	117 25 E
Pangi	**126**	3 10 S	26 35 E
Pangkai	**98**	22 40N	97 31 E
Pangkalanberandan	**102**	4 1N	98 20 E
Pangkalansusu	**102**	4 2N	98 42 E
Pangkoh	**102**	3 5 S	114 8 E
Pangnirtung	**149**	66 0N	66 0W
Pangong Tso, L.	**95**	34 0N	78 20 E
Pangrango	**103**	6 46 S	107 1 E
Pangsau Pass	**98**	27 15N	96 10 E
Pangta	**105**	30 14N	97 24 E
Pangtara	**98**	20 57N	96 40 E
Panguitch	**161**	37 52N	112 30W
Pangutaran Group	**103**	6 18N	120 34 E
Panhandle	**159**	35 23N	101 23W
P'anhsien	**108**	25 46N	104 39 E
Pani Mines	**94**	22 29N	73 50 E
Panipat	**94**	29 25N	77 2 E
Panjal Range	**94**	32 30N	76 50 E
Panjgur	**93**	27 0N	64 5 E
Panjim = Panaji	**93**	15 25N	73 50 E
Panjinad Barrage	**93**	29 22N	71 15 E
Panjwai	**94**	31 26N	65 27 E
Pankadjene	**103**	4 46 S	119 34 E
Pankal Pinang	**102**	2 0 S	106 0 E
Pankshin	**121**	9 25N	9 25 E
P'anlung Chiang, R.	**108**	21 18N	105 25 E
Panmunjŏm	**107**	37 59N	126 38 E
Panna	**95**	24 40N	80 15 E
Panna Hills	**95**	24 40N	81 15 E
Pannuru	**97**	16 5N	80 34 E
Panorama	**173**	21 21 S	51 51W
Panruti	**97**	11 46N	79 35 E
P'anshan	**107**	41 12N	122 4 E
P'anshih	**107**	42 55N	126 3 E
Pant'anching	**106**	39 7N	103 52 E
Pantano	**161**	32 0N	110 32W
Pantar, I.	**103**	8 28 S	124 10 E
Pantelleria	**64**	36 52N	12 0 E
Pantelleria, I.	**64**	36 52N	12 0 E
Pantha	**98**	24 7N	94 17 E
Pantin Sakan	**98**	18 38N	97 33 E
Pantjo	**103**	8 42 S	118 40 E
Pantón	**56**	42 31N	7 37W
Pantukan	**103**	7 17N	125 58 E
Panuco	**165**	22 0N	98 25W
Panyam	**121**	9 27N	9 8 E
P'anyü	**109**	23 2N	113 20 E
Pão de AçIcar	**171**	9 45 S	37 26W
Paoan	**109**	22 32N	114 8 E
Paoch'eng	**106**	33 14N	106 56 E
Paochi	**106**	34 25N	107 11 E
Paochiatun	**107**	33 56N	120 12 E
Paoching	**108**	28 41N	109 35 E
Paok'ang	**109**	31 57N	111 20 E
Paokuot'u	**107**	42 20N	120 42 E
Páola	**65**	39 21N	16 2 E
Paola	**158**	38 36N	94 50W
Paonia	**161**	38 56N	107 37W
Paoshan, Shanghai, China	**109**	31 25N	121 29 E
Paoshan, Yunnan, China	**105**	25 7N	99 9 E
Paote	**106**	39 7N	111 13 E
Paoti	**107**	39 44N	117 18 E
Paoting	**106**	38 50N	115 30 E
Paot'ou	**106**	40 35N	110 3 E
Paoua	**117**	7 25N	16 30 E
Paoying	**107**	33 15N	119 20 E
Papá	**53**	47 22N	17 30 E
Papa Sd.	**37**	59 20N	2 56W
Papa, Sd. of	**36**	60 19N	1 40W
Papa Stour I.	**36**	60 20N	1 40W
Papa Stronsay I.	**37**	59 10N	2 37W
Papa Westray I.	**37**	59 20N	2 55W
Papagayo, Golfo de	**166**	10 4N	85 50W
Papagayo, R., Brazil	**164**	12 30 S	58 10W
Papagayo, R., Mexico	**165**	16 36N	99 43W
Papagni R.	**97**	14 10N	78 30 E
Papaikou	**147**	19 47N	155 6W
Papakura	**142**	37 4 S	174 59 E
Papaloapan, R.	**164**	18 2N	96 51W
Papantla	**165**	20 45N	97 21W
Papar	**102**	5 45N	116 0 E
Paparoa	**142**	36 6 S	174 16 E
Paparoa Range	**143**	42 5 S	171 35 E
Pápas, Ákra	**69**	38 13N	21 6 E
Papatoetoe	**142**	36 59 S	174 51 E
Papenburg	**48**	53 7N	7 25 E
Papien Chiang, R. (Da)	**108**	22 56N	101 47 E
Papigochic, R.	**164**	29 9N	109 40W
Paposo	**172**	25 0 S	70 30W
Paps, The, mts.	**39**	52 0N	9 15W
Papua, Gulf of	**135**	9 0 S	144 50 E
Papua New Guinea ■	**135**	8 0 S	145 0 E
PapuCa	**63**	44 22N	15 30 E
Papudo	**172**	32 29 S	71 27W
Papuk, mts.	**66**	45 30N	17 30 E
Papun	**98**	18 0N	97 30 E
Pará = Belém	**170**	1 20 S	48 30W
Pará □	**175**	3 20 S	52 0W
Parábita	**65**	40 3N	18 8 E
Paracatú	**171**	17 10 S	46 50W
Paracatu, R.	**171**	16 30 S	45 4W
Paracel Is.	**102**	16 49N	111 2 E
Parachilna	**140**	31 10 S	138 21 E
Parachinar	**94**	34 0N	70 5 E
Paracombe	**109**	34 51 S	138 47 E
Paracuru	**170**	3 24 S	39 4W
Paradas	**57**	37 18N	5 29W
Paradela	**56**	42 44N	7 37W
Paradip	**95**	20 15N	86 35 E
Paradise	**160**	47 27N	114 54W
Paradise, R.	**151**	53 27N	57 19W
Paradise Valley	**160**	41 30N	117 28W
Parado	**103**	8 42 S	118 30 E
Paradyz	**54**	51 19N	20 2 E
Parafield	**109**	34 47 S	138 38 E
Parafield Airport	**109**	34 48 S	138 38 E
Paragould	**159**	36 5N	90 30W
Paragua, La	**174**	6 50N	63 20W
Paragua, R.	**174**	6 30N	63 30W
Paraguaçu Paulista	**173**	22 22 S	50 35W
Paraguaçu, R.	**171**	12 45 S	38 54W
Paraguai, R.	**174**	16 0 S	57 52W
Paraguaipoa	**174**	11 21N	71 57W
Paraguana, Pen. de	**174**	12 0N	70 0W
Paraguarí	**172**	25 36 S	57 0W
Paraguarí □	**172**	26 0 S	57 10W
Paraguay ■	**172**	23 0 S	57 0W
Paraguay, R.	**172**	27 18 S	58 38W
Paraíba = Joéo Pessoa	**164**	7 10 S	35 0W
Paraiba □	**170**	7 0 S	36 0W
Paraíba do Sul, R.	**173**	21 37 S	41 3W
Paraibano	**171**	6 30 S	44 1W
Parainen	**75**	60 18N	22 18 E
Paraíso	**165**	19 3 S	52 59W
Paraiso	**165**	18 24N	93 14W
Parakhino Paddubye	**80**	58 46N	33 10 E
Parakou	**121**	9 25N	2 40 E
Parakylia	**140**	30 24 S	136 25 E
Paralion-Astrous	**69**	37 25N	22 45 E
Paramagudi	**97**	9 31N	78 39 E
Paramaribo	**175**	5 50N	55 10W
Parambu	**170**	6 13 S	40 43W
Paramillo, Nudo del	**174**	7 4N	75 55W
Paramirim	**171**	13 26 S	42 15W
Paramirim, R.	**171**	11 34 S	43 18W
Paramithiá	**68**	39 30N	20 35 E
Paramushir, Ostrov	**77**	40 24N	156 0 E
Paran, N.	**90**	30 14N	34 48 E
Paraná	**172**	32 0 S	60 30W
Paranã	**171**	12 30 S	47 40W
Paraná □	**173**	24 30 S	51 0W
Paraná, R.	**172**	33 43 S	59 15W
Paranã, R.	**171**	22 25 S	53 1W
Paranaguá	**173**	25 30 S	48 30W
Paranaíba, R.	**171**	18 0 S	49 12W
Paranapanema, R.	**173**	22 40 S	53 9W
Paranapiacaba, Serra do	**173**	24 31 S	48 35W
Paranavaí	**173**	23 4 S	52 28W
Parang, Jolo, Phil.	**103**	5 55N	120 54 E
Parang, Mindanao, Phil.	**103**	7 23N	124 16 E
Parangaba	**170**	3 45 S	38 33W
Paraóin	**66**	43 54N	21 27 E
Paraparanma	**143**	40 57 S	175 3 E
Parapóla, I.	**69**	36 55N	23 27 E
Paraspóri, Ákra	**69**	35 55N	27 15 E
Paratinga	**171**	12 40 S	43 10W
Paratoo	**140**	32 42 S	139 22 E
Parattah	**138**	42 22 S	147 23 E
Paraúna	**171**	17 2 S	50 26W
Paray-le-Monial	**45**	46 27N	4 7 E
Parbati, R.	**94**	25 51N	76 34 E
Parbatipur	**98**	25 39N	88 55 E
Parbhani	**96**	19 8N	76 52 E
Parchim	**48**	53 25N	11 50 E
Parczew	**54**	51 9N	22 52 E
Pardee Res.	**163**	38 16N	120 51W
Pardes Hanna	**90**	32 28N	34 57 E
Pardilla	**56**	41 33N	3 43W
Pardo, R., Bahia, Brazil	**171**	15 40 S	39 0W
Pardo, R., Mato Grosso, Brazil	**171**	21 0 S	53 25W
Pardo, R., Minas Gerais, Brazil	**171**	15 48 S	44 48W
Pardo, R., São Paulo, Brazil	**171**	20 45 S	48 0W
Pardubice	**52**	50 3N	15 45 E
Pare	**103**	7 43 S	112 12 E
Pare □	**126**	4 10 S	38 0 E
Pare Mts.	**126**	4 0 S	37 45 E
Pare Pare	**103**	4 0 S	119 45 E
Parecis, Serra dos	**174**	13 0 S	60 0W
Paredes de Nava	**56**	42 9N	4 42W
Parelhas	**170**	6 41 S	36 39W
Paren	**77**	62 45N	163 0 E
Parengarenga Harbour	**142**	34 31 S	173 0 E
Parent	**150**	47 55N	74 35W
Parent, Lac.	**150**	48 31N	77 1W
Parentis-en-Born	**44**	44 21N	1 4W
Parepare	**103**	4 0 S	119 40 E
Parfino	**80**	57 59N	31 34 E
Parfuri	**129**	22 28 S	31 17 E
Paria, Golfo de	**174**	10 20N	62 0W
Paria, Pen. de	**174**	10 50N	62 30W
Pariaguán	**174**	8 51N	64 43W
Pariaman	**102**	0 47 S	100 11 E
Paricutín, Cerro	**164**	19 28N	102 15W
Parigi	**103**	0 50 S	120 5 E
Parika	**174**	6 50N	58 20W
Parima, Serra	**174**	2 30N	64 0W
Parinari	**174**	4 35 S	74 25W
Parincea	**70**	46 27N	27 9 E
Parîng, mt.	**70**	45 20N	23 37 E
Parintins	**175**	2 40 S	56 50W
Pariparit Kyun	**99**	14 55 S	93 45 E
Paris, Can.	**150**	43 12N	80 25W
Paris, France	**43**	48 50N	2 20 E
Paris, Idaho, U.S.A.	**160**	42 13N	111 30W
Paris, Ky., U.S.A.	**156**	38 12N	84 12W
Paris, Tenn., U.S.A.	**157**	36 20N	88 20W
Paris, Tex., U.S.A.	**159**	33 40N	95 30W
Parish	**162**	43 24N	76 9W
Pariti	**103**	9 55 S	123 30 E
Park City	**160**	40 42N	111 35W
Park Falls	**158**	45 58N	90 27 E
Park Range	**160**	40 0N	106 30W
Park Rapids	**158**	46 56N	95 0W
Park River	**158**	48 25N	97 17W
Park Rynie	**129**	30 25 S	30 35 E
Park View	**161**	36 45N	106 37W
Parkent	**85**	41 18N	69 40 E
Parker, Ariz., U.S.A.	**161**	34 8N	114 16W
Parker, S.D., U.S.A.	**158**	43 25N	97 7W
Parker Dam	**161**	34 13N	114 5W
Parkersburg	**156**	39 18N	81 31W
Parkerview	**153**	51 21N	103 18W
Parkes, A.C.T., Austral.	**133**	35 18 S	149 8 E
Parkes, N.S.W., Austral.	**141**	33 9 S	148 11 E
Parkfield	**163**	35 54N	120 26W
Parkhar	**85**	37 30N	69 34 E
Parknasilla	**39**	51 49N	9 50W
Parkside	**153**	53 10N	106 33W
Parkston	**158**	43 25N	98 0W
Parksville	**152**	49 20N	124 21W
Parkville	**162**	39 23N	76 33W
Parlakimedi	**96**	18 45N	84 5 E
Parma, Italy	**62**	44 50N	10 20 E
Parma, U.S.A.	**160**	43 49N	116 59W
Parna, R.	**62**	44 27N	10 3 E
Parnaguá	**170**	10 10 S	44 10W
Parnaíba, Piauí, Brazil	**170**	3 0 S	41 40W
Parnaíba, São Paulo, Brazil	**170**	19 34 S	51 14W
Parnaíba, R.	**170**	3 35 S	43 0W
Parnamirim	**170**	8 5 S	39 34W
Parnarama	**170**	5 41 S	43 6W
Parnassōs, mt.	**69**	38 17N	21 30 E
Parnassus	**143**	42 42 S	173 23 E
Párnis, mt.	**69**	38 14N	23 45 E
Párnon Óros	**69**	37 15N	22 45 E
Pärnu	**80**	58 12N	24 33 E
Parola	**96**	20 47N	75 7 E
Paroo Chan.	**133**	30 50 S	143 35 E
Paroo, R.	**139**	30 0 S	144 5 E
Paropamisus Range = Fī roz Kohi	**93**	34 45N	63 0 E
Páros	**69**	37 5N	25 9 E
Páros, I.	**69**	37 5N	25 12 E
Parowan	**161**	37 54N	112 56W
Parpaillon, mts.	**45**	44 30N	6 40 E
Parracombe	**30**	51 11N	3 55W
Parral	**172**	36 10 S	72 0W
Parramatta	**141**	33 48 S	151 1 E
Parramore I.	**162**	37 32N	75 39W
Parras	**164**	25 30N	102 20W
Parrett, R.	**28**	51 7N	2 58W
Parris I.	**157**	32 20N	80 30W
Parrsboro	**151**	45 30N	64 10W
Parry	**153**	49 47N	104 41W
Parry, C.	**147**	70 20N	123 38W
Parry Is.	**12**	77 0N	110 0W
Parry Sound	**150**	45 20N	80 0W
Parshall	**158**	47 56N	102 11W
Parsnip, R.	**152**	55 10N	123 2W
Parsons	**159**	37 20N	95 10W
Parsons Ra., Mts.	**138**	13 30 S	135 15 E
Partabpur	**96**	20 0N	80 42 E
Partanna	**64**	37 43N	12 51 E
Partapgarh	**94**	24 2N	74 40 E
Parthenay	**42**	46 38N	0 16W
Partille	**73**	57 48N	12 18 E
Partinico	**64**	38 3N	13 6 E
Partney	**33**	53 12N	0 7 E
Parton	**32**	54 34N	3 35W
Partry Mts.	**38**	53 40N	9 28W
Partur	**96**	19 40N	76 14 E
Paru, R.	**175**	0 20 S	53 30W
Parur	**97**	10 13N	76 14 E
Paruro	**174**	13 45 S	71 50W
Parvatipuram	**96**	18 50N	83 25 E
Parwan □	**93**	35 0N	69 0 E
Påryd	**73**	56 34N	15 55 E
Parys	**128**	26 52 S	27 29 E
Parys, Mt.	**31**	53 23N	4 18W
Pas-de-Calais □	**43**	50 30N	2 30 E
Pasadena, Calif., U.S.A.	**163**	34 5N	118 9W
Pasadena, Tex., U.S.A.	**159**	29 45N	95 14W
Pasaje	**174**	3 10 S	79 40W
Pasaje, R.	**172**	25 35 S	64 57W
Pascagoula	**159**	30 30N	88 30W
Pascagoula, R.	**159**	30 40N	88 35W
Paşcani	**70**	47 14N	26 45 E
Pasco	**160**	46 10N	119 0W
Pasco, Cerro de	**174**	10 45 S	76 10W
Pascoag	**162**	41 57N	71 42W
Pascoe, Mt.	**137**	27 25 S	120 40 E
Pasewalk	**48**	53 30N	14 0 E
Pasfield L.	**153**	58 24N	105 20W
Pasha, R.	**80**	60 20N	33 0 E
Pashiwari	**95**	34 40N	75 10 E
Pashiya	**84**	58 33N	58 26 E
Pashmakli = Smolyan	**67**	41 36N	24 38 E
Pasighat	**98**	28 4N	95 21 E
Pasir Mas	**101**	6 2N	102 8 E
Pasir Puteh	**101**	5 50N	102 24 E
Pasirian	**103**	8 13 S	113 8 E
Pasley, C.	**137**	33 52 S	123 35 E
Pasman I.	**63**	43 58N	15 20 E
Pasmore, R.	**140**	31 5 S	139 49 E
Pasni	**93**	25 15N	63 27 E
Paso de Indios	**176**	43 55 S	69 0W
Paso de los Libres	**172**	29 44 S	57 10W
Paso de los Toros	**172**	32 36 S	56 37W
Paso Robles	**161**	35 40N	120 45W
Paspebiac	**151**	48 3N	65 17W
Pasrur	**94**	32 16N	74 43 E
Passage East	**39**	52 15N	7 0W
Passage West	**39**	51 52N	8 20W
Passaic	**162**	40 50N	74 8W
Passau	**49**	48 34N	13 27 E
Passendale	**47**	50 54N	3 2 E
Passero, C.	**65**	36 42N	15 8 E
Passo Fundo	**173**	28 10 S	52 30W
Passos	**171**	20 45 S	46 37W
Passow	**48**	53 13N	14 3 E
Passwang	**50**	47 22N	7 41 E
Passy	**43**	45 55N	6 41 E
Pastaza, R.	**174**	2 45 S	76 50W
Pastek	**54**	54 3N	19 41 E
Pasto	**174**	1 13N	77 17W
Pasto Zootécnico do Cunene	**128**	16 20 S	15 20 E
Pastos Bons	**170**	6 36 S	44 5W
Pastrana	**58**	40 27N	2 53W
Pasuruan	**103**	7 40 S	112 53 E
Pasym	**54**	53 48N	20 49 E
Pásztó	**53**	47 52N	19 43 E
Patagonia, Argent.	**176**	45 0 S	69 0W
Patagonia, U.S.A.	**161**	31 35N	110 45W
Patan, India	**93**	23 54N	72 14 E
Patan, Gujarat, India	**96**	17 22N	73 48 E
Patan, Maharashtra, India	**94**	23 54N	72 14 E
Patan (Lalitapur)	**99**	27 40N	85 20 E
Pat'ang Szechwan	**105**	30 2N	98 58 E
Patani	**103**	0 20N	128 50 E
Pataohotzu	**107**	43 5N	127 33 E
Patapsco Res.	**162**	39 27N	76 55W
Pataudi	**94**	28 18N	76 48 E
Patay	**43**	48 2N	1 40 E
Patcham	**29**	50 52N	0 9W
Patchewollock	**140**	35 22 S	142 12 E
Patchogue	**162**	40 46N	73 1W
Patea	**142**	39 45 S	174 30 E
Pategi	**121**	8 50N	5 45 E
Pateley Bridge	**33**	54 5N	1 45W
Patensie	**128**	33 46 S	24 49 E
Paternò	**65**	37 34N	14 53 E
Paternoster, Kepulauan	**102**	7 5 S	118 15 E
Pateros	**160**	48 4N	119 58W
Paterson, Austral.	**141**	32 37 S	151 39 E
Paterson, U.S.A.	**162**	40 55N	74 10W
Paterson Inlet	**143**	46 56 S	168 12 E
Paterson Ra.	**136**	21 45 S	122 10 E
Paterswolde	**46**	53 9N	6 34 E
Pathankot	**94**	32 18N	75 45 E
Patharghata	**98**	22 2N	89 58 E
Pathfinder Res.	**160**	42 0N	107 0W
Pathiu	**101**	10 42N	99 19 E
Pathum Thani	**100**	14 1N	100 32 E
Páti	**103**	6 45 S	111 3 E
Patiala	**94**	30 23N	76 26 E
Patine Kouta	**120**	12 45N	13 45W
Patjitan	**103**	8 12 S	111 8 E
Patkai Bum	**98**	27 0N	95 30 E
Pátmos	**69**	37 21N	26 36 E
Pátmos, I.	**69**	37 21N	26 36 E
Patna, India	**95**	25 35N	85 18 E
Patna, U.K.	**34**	55 21N	4 30W
Patonga	**126**	2 45N	33 15 E
Patos	**170**	7 1 S	37 16W
Patos de Minas	**171**	18 35 S	46 32W
Patos, Lag. dos	**173**	31 20 S	51 0 E
Patosi	**68**	40 42N	19 38 E
Patquía	**172**	30 0 S	66 55W
Pátrai	**69**	38 14N	21 47 E
Pátraikos, Kólpos	**69**	38 17N	21 30 E
Patrick	**32**	54 13N	4 41W
Patrocínio	**171**	18 57 S	47 0W
Patta	**126**	2 10 S	41 0 E
Patta, I.	**126**	2 10 S	41 0 E
Pattada	**64**	40 35N	9 7 E
Pattanapuram	**97**	9 6N	76 33 E
Pattani	**101**	6 48N	101 15 E
Patten	**151**	45 59N	68 28W
Patterdale	**32**	54 33N	2 55W
Patterson, Calif., U.S.A.	**163**	37 30N	121 9W
Patterson, La., U.S.A.	**159**	29 44N	91 20W
Patterson, Mt.	**163**	38 29N	119 20W
Patti	**94**	31 17N	74 54 E
Patti Castroreale	**65**	38 8N	14 57 E
Pattoki	**94**	31 5N	73 52 E
Pattukkottai	**97**	10 25N	79 20 E
Patu	**170**	6 6 S	37 38W
Patuakhali	**98**	22 20N	90 25 E
Patuca, Punta	**166**	15 49N	84 14W
Patuca, R.	**166**	15 20N	84 40W
Patung	**109**	31 0N	110 30 E
Pâturages	**47**	50 25N	3 52 E
Patutahi	**142**	38 38 S	177 55 E
Pátzcuaro	**164**	19 30N	101 40W
Pau	**44**	43 19N	0 25W
Pau d' Arco	**170**	7 30 S	49 22W
Pau dos Ferros	**170**	6 7 S	38 10W
Pauillac	**44**	45 11N	0 46W
Pauini, R.	**174**	1 42 S	62 50W
Pauk	**98**	21 55N	94 30 E
Paul I.	**151**	56 30N	61 20W
Paulatuk	**147**	69 25N	124 0W
Paulhan	**44**	43 33N	3 28 E
Paulis = Isiro	**126**	2 53N	27 58 E
Paulista	**170**	7 57 S	34 53W

Paulistana **Perryton**

Paulistana	**170**	8 9 S	41 9 W
Paull	**33**	53 42 N	0 12 W
Paullina	**158**	42 55 N	95 40 W
Paulo Afonso	**170**	9 21 S	38 15 W
Paulo de Faria	**171**	20 2 S	49 24 W
Paulpietersburg	**129**	27 23 S	30 50 E
Paul's Valley	**159**	34 40 N	97 17 W
Pauma Valley	**163**	33 16 N	116 58 W
Paungde	**98**	18 29 N	95 30 E
Pauni	**96**	20 48 N	79 40 E
Pavelets	**81**	53 49 N	39 14 E
Pavia	**62**	45 10 N	9 10 E
Pavlikeni	**67**	43 14 N	25 20 E
Pavlodar	**76**	52 33 N	77 0 E
Pavlof Is.	**147**	55 30 N	161 30 W
Pavlograd	**82**	48 30 N	35 52 E
Pavlovo, Gorkiy, U.S.S.R.	**81**	55 58 N	43 5 E
Pavlovo, Yakut A.S.S.R., U.S.S.R.	**77**	63 5 N	115 25 E
Pavlovsk	**81**	50 26 N	40 5 E
Pavlovskaya	**83**	46 17 N	39 47 E
Pavlovskiy Posad	**81**	55 37 N	38 42 E
Pavullo nel Frignano	**62**	44 20 N	10 50 E
Pawahku	**98**	26 11 N	98 40 E
Pawhuska	**159**	36 40 N	96 25 W
Pawling	**162**	41 35 N	73 37 W
Pawnee	**159**	36 24 N	96 50 W
Pawnee City	**158**	40 8 N	96 10 W
Pawtucket	**162**	41 51 N	71 22 W
Paximádhia	**69**	35 0 N	24 35 E
Paxoi, I.	**68**	39 14 N	20 12 E
Paxton, Ill., U.S.A.	**156**	40 25 N	88 0 W
Paxton, Nebr., U.S.A.	**158**	41 12 N	101 27 W
Paya Bakri	**101**	2 3 N	102 44 E
Payakumbah	**102**	0 20 S	100 35 E
Payenhaot'e (Alashantsoch'i)	**106**	38 50 N	105 32 E
Payenk'ala Shan	**105**	34 20 N	97 0 E
Payerne	**50**	46 49 N	6 56 E
Payette	**160**	44 0 N	117 0 W
Paymogo	**57**	37 44 N	7 21 W
Payne L.	**149**	59 30 N	74 30 W
Payne, R.	**149**	60 0 N	70 0 W
Payneham	**109**	34 54 S	138 39 E
Paynes Find	**137**	29 15 S	117 42 E
Paynesville, Liberia	**120**	6 20 N	10 45 W
Paynesville, U.S.A.	**158**	45 21 N	94 44 W
Paysandú	**172**	32 19 S	58 8 W
Payson, Ariz., U.S.A.	**161**	34 17 N	111 15 W
Payson, Utah, U.S.A.	**160**	40 8 N	111 41 W
Paz, Bahía de la	**164**	24 15 N	110 25 W
Paz Centro, La	**166**	12 20 N	86 41 W
Paz, La, Entre Ríos, Argent.	**172**	30 50 S	59 45 W
Paz, La, San Luis, Argent.	**172**	33 30 S	67 20 W
Paz, La, Boliv.	**174**	16 20 S	68 10 W
Paz, La, Hond.	**166**	14 20 N	87 47 W
Paz, La, Mexico	**164**	24 10 N	110 20 W
Paz, La, Bahia de	**164**	24 20 N	110 40 W
Paz, R.	**166**	13 44 N	90 10 W
Pazar	**92**	41 10 N	40 50 E
Pazardzhik	**67**	42 12 N	24 20 E
Pazin	**63**	45 14 N	13 56 E
Pčinja, R.	**66**	42 0 N	21 45 E
Pe Ell	**160**	46 30 N	123 18 W
Peabody	**162**	42 31 N	70 56 W
Peace Point	**152**	59 7 N	112 27 W
Peace, R.	**152**	59 0 N	111 25 W
Peace River	**152**	56 15 N	117 18 W
Peace River Res.	**152**	55 40 N	123 40 W
Peacehaven	**29**	50 47 N	0 1 E
Peach Springs	**161**	35 36 N	113 30 W
Peak Downs	**138**	22 55 S	148 0 E
Peak Downs Mine	**138**	22 17 S	148 11 E
Peak Hill, N.S.W., Austral.	**141**	32 39 S	148 11 E
Peak Hill, W. A., Austral.	**137**	25 35 S	118 43 E
Peak Range	**138**	22 50 S	148 20 E
Peak, The	**32**	53 24 N	1 53 W
Peake	**140**	35 25 S	140 0 E
Peake Cr.	**139**	28 2 S	136 7 E
Peale Mt.	**161**	38 25 N	109 12 W
Pearblossom	**163**	34 30 N	117 55 W
Pearce	**161**	31 57 N	109 56 W
Pearl Banks	**97**	8 45 N	79 45 E
Pearl City	**147**	2 21 N	158 0 W
Pearl Harbor	**147**	21 20 N	158 0 W
Pearl, R.	**159**	31 50 N	90 0 W
Pearsall	**159**	28 55 N	99 8 W
Pearse I.	**152**	54 52 N	130 14 W
Peary Land	**12**	82 40 N	33 0 W
Pease, R.	**159**	34 18 N	100 15 W
Peasenhall	**29**	52 17 N	1 24 E
Pebane	**127**	17 10 S	38 8 E
Pebas	**174**	3 10 S	71 55 W
Pebble Beach	**163**	36 34 N	121 57 W
Peçanha	**171**	18 33 S	42 34 W
Péccioli	**62**	43 32 N	10 43 E
Pechea	**70**	45 36 N	27 49 E
Pechenezhin	**82**	48 30 N	24 48 E
Pechenga	**78**	69 30 N	31 25 E
Pechnezhskoye Vdkhr.	**81**	50 0 N	36 50 E
Pechora, R.	**78**	62 30 N	56 30 E
Pechorskaya Guba	**78**	68 40 N	54 0 E
Pechory	**80**	57-48 N	27 40 E
Pecica	**66**	46 10 N	21 3 E
Pečka	**66**	44 18 N	19 33 E
Pécora, C.	**64**	39 28 N	8 23 E
Pecos	**159**	31 25 N	103 35 W
Pecos, R.	**159**	31 22 N	102 30 W
Pecqueuse	**47**	48 39 N	2 3 E
Pécs	**53**	46 5 N	18 15 E
Pedasí	**166**	7 32 N	80 3 W
Peddapalli	**96**	18 40 N	79 24 E
Peddapuram	**96**	17 6 N	82 5 E
Peddavagu, R.	**96**	16 33 N	79 8 E
Pedder, L.	**138**	42 55 S	146 10 E
Pedernales	**167**	18 2 N	71 44 W
Pedirka	**139**	26 40 S	135 14 E
Pedjantan, I.	**102**	0 5 S	106 15 E
Pedra Azul	**171**	16 2 S	41 17 W
Pedra Grande, Recifes do	**171**	17 45 S	38 58 W
Pedras, Pta. de	**171**	7 38 S	34 47 W
Pedreiras	**170**	4 32 S	44 40 W
Pedrera, La	**174**	1 18 S	69 43 W
Pedro Afonso	**170**	9 0 S	48 10 W
Pedro Antonio Santos	**165**	18 54 N	88 15 W
Pedro Cays	**166**	17 5 N	77 48 W
Pedro Chico	**174**	1 4 N	70 25 W
Pedro de Valdivia	**172**	22 33 S	69 38 W
Pedro Juan Caballero	**173**	22 30 S	55 40 W
Pedro Muñoz	**59**	39 25 N	2 56 W
Pedrógão Grande	**56**	39 55 N	8 0 W
Peebinga	**140**	34 52 S	140 57 E
Peebles	**35**	55 40 N	3 12 W
Peebles (□)	**26**	55 37 N	3 4 W
Peekshill	**162**	41 18 N	73 57 W
Peel, Austral.	**139**	33 20 S	149 38 E
Peel, I. of Man	**32**	54 14 N	4 40 W
Peel Fell, mt.	**35**	55 17 N	2 35 W
Peel, R., Austral.	**141**	30 50 S	150 29 E
Peel, R., Can.	**147**	67 0 N	135 0 W
Peelwood	**141**	34 7 S	149 27 E
Peene, R.	**48**	53 53 N	13 53 E
Peera Peera Poolanna L.	**139**	26 30 S	138 0 E
Peers	**152**	53 40 N	116 0 W
Pegasus Bay	**143**	43 20 S	173 10 E
Peggau	**52**	47 12 N	15 21 E
Pego	**59**	38 51 N	0 8 W
Pegswood	**35**	55 12 N	1 38 W
Pegu	**99**	17 20 N	96 29 E
Pegu Yoma, mts.	**98**	19 0 N	96 0 E
Pegwell Bay	**29**	51 18 N	1 22 E
Pehčevo	**66**	41 41 N	22 55 E
Pehuajó	**172**	36 0 S	62 0 W
Pei Chiang, R.	**109**	23 12 N	112 45 E
Pei Wan	**107**	36 25 N	120 45 E
Peian	**105**	48 16 N	126 36 E
Peichen	**107**	41 38 N	121 50 E
Peichengchen	**107**	44 30 N	123 27 E
Peichiang	**109**	23 0 N	120 0 E
Peihai	**108**	21 30 N	109 5 E
P'eihsien, Kiangsu, China	**106**	34 44 N	116 55 E
P'eihsien, Kiangsu, China	**107**	34 20 N	117 57 E
Peiliu	**109**	22 45 N	110 20 E
Peine, Chile	**172**	23 45 S	68 8 W
Peine, Ger.	**48**	52 19 N	10 12 E
Peip'an Chiang, R.	**108**	25 0 N	106 11 E
Peip'ei	**105**	29 49 N	106 27 E
Peip'iao	**107**	41 48 N	120 44 E
Peip'ing	**106**	39 45 N	116 25 E
Peissenberg	**49**	47 48 N	11 4 E
Peitz	**48**	51 50 N	14 23 E
Peixe	**171**	12 0 S	48 40 W
Peixe, R.	**171**	21 31 S	51 58 W
Peize	**46**	53 9 N	6 30 E
Pek, R.	**66**	44 58 N	21 55 E
Pekalongan	**103**	6 53 S	109 40 E
Pekan	**101**	3 30 N	103 25 E
Pekin	**158**	40 35 N	89 40 W
Peking = Peip'ing	**106**	39 45 N	116 25 E
Pelabuhan Ratu, Teluk	**103**	7 5 S	106 30 E
Pelabuhanratu	**103**	7 0 S	106 32 E
Pélagos, I.	**68**	39 17 N	24 4 E
Pelagruza, Is.	**63**	42 24 N	16 15 E
Pelaihari	**102**	3 55 S	114 45 E
Pełczyce	**54**	53 3 N	15 16 E
Peleaga, mt.	**70**	45 22 N	22 55 E
Pelee I.	**150**	41 47 N	82 40 W
Pelée, Mt.	**167**	14 40 N	61 0 W
Pelee, Pt.	**150**	41 54 N	82 31 W
Pelekech, mt.	**126**	3 52 N	35 8 E
Peleng, I.	**103**	1 20 S	123 30 E
Pelham	**157**	31 5 N	84 6 W
Pelhrimov	**52**	49 24 N	15 12 E
Pelican	**147**	58 12 N	136 28 W
Pelican L.	**153**	52 28 N	100 20 W
Pelican Narrows	**153**	55 10 N	102 56 W
Pelican Portage	**152**	55 51 N	113 0 W
Pelican Rapids	**153**	52 45 N	100 42 W
Peligre, L. de	**167**	19 1 N	71 58 W
Pelkosenniemi	**74**	67 6 N	27 28 E
Pella	**158**	41 20 N	93 0 W
Pélla □	**68**	40 52 N	22 0 E
Péllaro	**65**	38 1 N	15 40 E
Pellworm, I.	**48**	54 30 N	8 40 E
Pelly Bay	**149**	68 0 N	89 50 W
Pelly L.	**148**	66 0 N	102 0 W
Pelly, R.	**147**	62 15 N	133 30 W
Peloponnese = Pelóponnisos	**69**	37 10 N	22 0 E
Pelopónnisos Kai Dhitiktí Iprotikí Ellas □	**69**	37 10 N	22 0 E
Peloritani, Monti	**65**	38 2 N	15 15 E
Peloro, C.	**65**	38 15 N	15 40 E
Pelorus Sound	**143**	40 59 S	173 59 E
Pelotas	**173**	31 42 S	52 23 W
Pelòvo	**67**	43 26 N	24 17 E
Pelvoux, Massif de	**45**	44 52 N	6 20 E
Pelym R.	**84**	59 39 N	63 6 E
Pemalang	**103**	6 53 S	109 23 E
Pematang Siantar	**102**	2 57 N	99 5 E
Pemba, Mozam.	**127**	12 58 S	40 30 E
Pemba, Zambia	**127**	16 30 S	27 28 E
Pemba Channel	**126**	5 0 S	39 37 E
Pemba, I.	**126**	5 0 S	39 45 E
Pemberton, Austral.	**137**	34 30 S	116 0 E
Pemberton, Can.	**152**	50 25 N	122 50 W
Pembina	**153**	48 58 N	97 15 W
Pembina, R.	**153**	49 0 N	98 12 W
Pembine	**156**	45 38 N	87 59 W
Pembrey	**31**	51 42 N	4 17 W
Pembroke, Can.	**150**	45 50 N	77 7 W
Pembroke, N.Z.	**143**	44 33 S	169 9 E
Pembroke, U.K.	**31**	51 41 N	4 57 W
Pembroke, U.S.A.	**157**	32 5 N	81 32 W
Pembroke (□)	**26**	51 40 N	5 0 W
Pembroke Dock	**31**	51 41 N	4 57 W
Pembury	**29**	51 8 N	0 20 E
Pen-y-Ghent	**32**	54 10 N	2 15 W
Pen-y-groes, Dyfed, U.K.	**31**	51 48 N	4 3 W
Pen-y-groes, Gwynedd, U.K.	**31**	53 3 N	4 18 W
Peñíscola	**58**	40 22 N	0 24 E
Peña de Francia, Sierra de	**56**	40 32 N	6 10 W
Peña Roya, mt.	**58**	40 24 N	0 40 W
Peña, Sierra de la	**58**	42 32 N	0 45 W
Penafiel	**56**	41 12 N	8 17 W
Peñafiel	**56**	41 35 N	4 7 W
Peñaflor	**57**	37 43 N	5 21 W
Peñalara, Pico	**56**	40 51 N	3 57 W
Penally	**31**	51 39 N	4 44 W
Penalva	**170**	3 18 S	45 10 W
Penamacôr	**56**	40 10 N	7 10 W
Penang = Pinang	**101**	5 25 N	100 15 E
Penápolis	**173**	21 30 S	50 0 W
Peñaranda de Bracamonte	**56**	40 53 N	5 13 W
Peñarroya-Pueblonuevo	**57**	38 19 N	5 16 W
Penarth	**31**	51 26 N	3 11 W
Peñas, C. de	**56**	43 42 N	5 52 W
Peñas de San Pedro	**59**	38 44 N	2 0 W
Peñas, G. de	**176**	47 0 S	75 0 W
Peñas, Pta.	**174**	11 17 N	70 28 W
Pench'i	**107**	41 20 N	123 48 E
Pencoed	**31**	51 31 N	3 30 W
Pend Oreille, L.	**160**	48 0 N	116 30 W
Pend Oreille, R.	**160**	49 4 N	117 37 W
Pendálofon	**68**	40 14 N	21 12 E
Pendeen	**30**	50 11 N	5 39 W
Pendelikón	**69**	38 5 N	23 53 E
Pendembu	**120**	9 7 N	12 14 W
Pendências	**170**	5 15 S	36 43 W
Pender B.	**136**	16 45 S	122 42 E
Pendine	**31**	51 44 N	4 33 W
Pendle Hill	**32**	53 53 N	2 18 W
Pendleton, Calif., U.S.A.	**163**	33 16 N	117 23 W
Pendleton, Oreg., U.S.A.	**160**	45 35 N	118 50 W
Pendzhikent	**85**	39 29 N	67 37 E
Penedo	**170**	10 15 S	36 36 W
Penetanguishene	**150**	44 50 N	79 55 W
Penfield	**109**	34 44 S	138 38 E
Pengalengan	**103**	7 9 S	107 30 E
P'engch'i	**108**	30 50 N	105 42 E
Penge, Kasai, Congo	**126**	5 30 S	24 33 E
Penge, Kivu, Congo	**126**	4 27 S	28 25 E
P'enghsien	**108**	30 59 N	103 56 E
P'enghu Liehtao	**109**	22 30 N	119 30 E
P'englai	**107**	37 49 N	120 47 E
P'engshui	**108**	29 19 N	108 12 E
P'engtse	**109**	29 53 N	116 32 E
Penguin	**138**	41 8 S	146 6 E
Penhalonga	**127**	18 52 S	32 40 E
Peniche	**57**	39 19 N	9 22 W
Penicuik	**35**	55 50 N	3 14 W
Penida, I.	**102**	8 45 S	115 30 E
Penistone	**33**	53 31 N	1 38 W
Penitentes, Serra dos	**170**	8 45 S	46 20 W
Penkridge	**28**	52 44 N	2 8 W
Penmachno	**31**	53 2 N	3 47 W
Penmaenmawr	**31**	53 16 N	3 55 W
Penmarch	**42**	47 49 N	4 21 W
Penmarch, Pte. de	**42**	47 48 N	4 22 W
Penn Yan	**162**	42 39 N	77 7 W
Pennabilli	**63**	43 50 N	12 17 E
Pennant	**153**	50 32 N	108 14 W
Penne	**63**	42 28 N	13 56 E
Penner, R.	**97**	14 50 N	78 20 E
Penneshaw	**140**	35 44 S	137 56 E
Pennines	**32**	54 50 N	2 20 W
Pennino, Mte.	**63**	43 6 N	12 54 E
Pennsburg	**162**	40 23 N	75 30 W
Pennsville	**162**	39 39 N	75 31 W
Pennsylvania □	**156**	40 50 N	78 0 W
Penny	**152**	53 51 N	121 48 W
Peno	**80**	57 2 N	32 33 E
Penola	**140**	37 25 S	140 47 E
Penong	**139**	31 59 S	133 5 E
Penonomé	**166**	8 31 N	80 21 W
Penpont	**35**	55 14 N	3 49 W
Penrhyn Is.	**131**	9 0 S	150 30 W
Penrith, Austral.	**141**	33 43 S	150 38 E
Penrith, U.K.	**32**	54 40 N	2 45 W
Penryn	**30**	50 10 N	5 7 W
Pensacola	**157**	30 30 N	87 10 W
Pensacola Mts.	**13**	84 0 S	40 0 W
Pense	**153**	50 25 N	104 59 W
Penshurst, Austral.	**140**	37 49 S	142 20 W
Penshurst, U.K.	**29**	51 10 N	0 12 E
Pentecoste	**170**	3 48 S	37 17 W
Penticton	**152**	49 30 N	119 30 W
Pentire Pt.	**30**	50 35 N	4 57 W
Pentland	**138**	20 32 S	145 25 E
Pentland Firth	**37**	58 43 N	3 10 W
Pentland Hills	**35**	55 48 N	3 25 W
Pentland Skerries	**37**	58 41 N	2 53 W
Pentraeth	**31**	53 17 N	4 13 W
Pentre Foelas	**31**	53 2 N	3 41 W
Penukonda	**97**	14 5 N	77 38 E
Penwortham	**32**	53 45 N	2 44 W
Penybont	**31**	52 17 N	3 18 W
Penylan L.	**153**	61 50 N	106 20 W
Penza	**81**	53 15 N	45 5 E
Penzance	**30**	50 7 N	5 32 W
Penzberg	**49**	47 46 N	11 23 E
Penzhinskaya Guba	**77**	61 30 N	163 0 E
Penzlin	**48**	53 32 N	13 6 E
Peó	**66**	42 40 N	20 17 E
Peoria, Ariz., U.S.A.	**161**	33 40 N	112 15 W
Peoria, Ill., U.S.A.	**158**	40 40 N	89 40 W
Pepacton Res.	**162**	42 5 N	74 58 W
Pepingen	**47**	50 46 N	4 10 E
Pepinster	**47**	50 34 N	5 47 E
Pepmbridge	**28**	52 13 N	2 54 W
Pepperwood	**160**	40 23 N	124 0 W
Peqini	**68**	41 4 N	19 44 E
Pera Hd.	**138**	12 55 S	141 37 E
Perabumilih	**102**	3 27 S	104 15 E
Perakhóra	**69**	38 2 N	22 56 E
Peraki, R.	**101**	5 10 N	101 4 E
Perales de Alfambra	**58**	40 38 N	1 0 W
Perales del Puerto	**56**	40 10 N	6 40 W
Peralta	**58**	42 21 N	1 49 W
Pérama	**69**	35 20 N	24 22 E
Perast	**66**	42 31 N	18 47 E
Percé	**151**	48 31 N	64 13 W
Perche	**42**	48 31 N	1 1 E
Perche, Collines de la	**42**	42 30 N	2 5 E
Percival Lakes	**136**	21 25 S	125 0 E
Percy	**42**	48 55 N	1 11 W
Percy Is.	**138**	21 39 S	150 16 E
Percyville	**138**	19 2 S	143 45 E
Perdido, Mte.	**58**	42 40 N	0 50 E
Pereira	**174**	4 49 N	75 43 W
Pereira Barreto	**171**	20 38 S	51 7 W
Pereira de Eóa	**128**	16 48 S	15 50 E
Perekerten	**140**	34 55 S	143 40 E
Perenjori	**137**	29 26 S	116 16 E
Pereslavi-Zelesskiy	**80**	56 45 N	38 58 E
Pereyaslav-Khmelnitskiy	**80**	50 3 N	31 28 E
Perez, I.	**165**	22 24 N	89 42 W
Perg	**52**	48 15 N	14 38 E
Pergamino	**172**	33 52 S	60 30 W
Pergine Valsugano	**63**	46 4 N	11 15 E
Pérgola	**63**	43 35 N	12 50 E
Perham	**158**	46 36 N	95 36 W
Perham Down Camp	**28**	51 14 N	1 38 W
Perhentian, Kepulauan	**101**	5 54 N	102 42 E
Peri, L.	**140**	30 45 S	143 35 E
Periam	**66**	46 2 N	20 59 E
Péribonca, L.	**151**	50 1 N	71 10 W
Péribonca, R.	**151**	48 45 N	72 5 W
Perico	**172**	24 20 S	65 5 W
Pericos	**164**	25 3 N	107 42 W
Périers	**42**	49 11 N	1 25 W
Périgord	**44**	45 0 N	0 40 E
Périgueux	**44**	45 10 N	0 42 E
Perija, Sierra de	**174**	9 30 N	73 3 W
Perim, I.	**91**	12 39 N	43 25 E
Peristera, I.	**69**	39 15 N	23 58 E
Peritoró	**170**	4 20 S	44 18 W
Periyakulam	**97**	10 5 N	77 30 E
Periyar, L.	**97**	9 25 N	77 10 E
Periyar, R.	**97**	10 15 N	78 10 E
Perkam, Tg.	**103**	1 35 S	137 50 E
Perkasie	**162**	40 22 N	75 18 W
Perkovió	**63**	43 41 N	16 10 E
Perlas, Arch. de las	**166**	8 41 N	79 7 W
Perlas, Punta de	**166**	11 30 N	83 30 W
Perleberg	**48**	53 5 N	11 50 E
Perlevka	**81**	51 56 N	38 57 E
Perlez	**66**	45 11 N	20 22 E
Perlis □	**101**	6 30 N	100 15 E
Perm (Molotov)	**84**	58 0 N	57 10 E
Përmeti	**68**	40 15 N	20 21 E
Pernambuco = Recife	**170**	8 0 S	35 0 W
Pernambuco □	**170**	8 0 S	37 0 W
Pernatty Lagoon	**140**	31 30 S	137 12 E
Peron, C.	**137**	25 30 S	113 30 E
Peron Is.	**136**	13 9 S	130 4 E
Peron Pen.	**137**	26 0 S	113 10 E
Péronne	**43**	49 55 N	2 57 E
Péronnes	**47**	50 27 N	4 9 E
Perosa Argentina	**62**	44 57 N	7 11 E
Perouse Str., La	**86**	45 40 N	142 0 E
Perow	**152**	54 35 N	126 10 W
Perpendicular Pt.	**139**	31 37 S	152 52 E
Perpignan	**44**	42 42 N	2 53 E
Perranporth	**30**	50 21 N	5 9 W
Perranzabuloe	**30**	50 18 N	5 7 W
Perris	**163**	33 47 N	117 14 W
Perros-Guirec	**42**	48 49 N	3 28 W
Perry, Fla., U.S.A.	**157**	30 9 N	83 10 W
Perry, Ga., U.S.A.	**157**	32 25 N	83 41 W
Perry, Iowa, U.S.A.	**158**	41 48 N	94 5 W
Perry, Maine, U.S.A.	**157**	44 59 N	67 20 W
Perry, Okla., U.S.A.	**159**	36 20 N	97 20 W
Perry, Mt.	**139**	25 12 S	151 41 E
Perryton	**159**	36 28 N	100 48 W

Perryville **Ping, R**

Perryville, Alas., U.S.A. **147** 55 54N 159 10W
Perryville, Mo., U.S.A. **159** 37 42N 89 50W
Persberg **72** 59 47N 14 15 E
Persepolis **93** 29 55N 52 50 E
Pershore **28** 52 7N 2 4W
Persia = Iran **93** 35 0N 50 0 E
Persian Gulf **93** 27 0N 50 0 E
Perstorp **73** 56 10N 13 25 E
Perth, Austral. **137** 31 57 S 115 52 E
Perth, N.B., Can. **150** 46 43N 67 42W
Perth, Ont., Can. **150** 44 55N 76 15W
Perth, U.K. **35** 56 24N 3 27W
Perth (□) **26** 56 30N 4 0W
Perth Amboy **162** 40 30N 74 25W
Perthus, Le **44** 42 30N 2 53 E
Pertuis **45** 43 42N 5 30 E
Pertuis Breton **44** 46 17N 1 25W
Pertuis d'Antioche **44** 46 6N 1 20W
Peru, Ill., U.S.A. **158** 41 18N 89 12W
Peru, Ind., U.S.A. **156** 40 42N 86 0W
Peru ■ **174** 8 0 S 75 0W
Perúgia **63** 43 6N 12 24 E
Perušió **63** 44 40N 15 22 E
Péruwelz **47** 50 31N 3 36 E
Pervomayskiy **81** 53 20N 40 10 E
Pervouralsk **84** 56 55N 60 0 E
Perwez **47** 50 38N 4 48 E
Pésaro **63** 43 55N 12 53 E
Pesca, La **165** 23 46N 97 47W
Pescadores Is. (P'enghu Liehtao) **109** 23 30N 119 30 E
Pescara **63** 42 28N 14 13 E
Peschanokopskoye **83** 46 14N 41 4 E
Péscia **62** 43 54N 10 40 E
Pescina **63** 42 0N 13 39 E
Peseux **50** 46 59N 6 53 E
Peshawar **94** 34 2N 71 37 E
Peshawar □ **94** 35 0N 72 50 E
Peshkopia **68** 41 41N 20 25 E
Peshovka **84** 59 4N 52 22 E
Peshtera **67** 42 2N 24 18 E
Peshtigo **156** 45 4N 87 46W
Peski **81** 51 14N 42 12 E
Peskovka **81** 59 9N 52 28 E
Pêso da Régua **56** 41 10N 7 47W
Pesqueira **170** 8 20 S 36 42W
Pesquiería **164** 29 23N 110 54W
Pesquieria, R. **164** 25 54N 99 11W
Pessac **44** 44 48N 0 37W
Pessoux **47** 50 17N 5 11 E
Pest □ **53** 47 29N 19 5 E
Pestovo **80** 58 33N 35 18 E
Pestravka **81** 52 28N 49 57 E
Péta **69** 39 10N 21 2 E
Petah Tiqwa **90** 32 6N 34 53 E
Petalídhion, Khóra **69** 36 57N 21 55 E
Petaling Jaya **101** 3 4N 101 42 E
Petaluma **163** 38 13N 122 39W
Petange **47** 49 33N 5 55 E
Petatlán **164** 17 31N 101 16W
Petauke **127** 14 14 S 31 12 E
Petawawa **150** 45 54N 77 17W
Petegem **47** 50 59N 3 32 E
Petén Itza, Lago **166** 16 58N 89 50W
Peter 1st, I. **13** 69 0 S 91 0W
Peter Pond L. **153** 55 55N 108 44W
Peterbell **150** 48 36N 83 21W
Peterboro **162** 42 55N 71 59W
Peterborough, S. Australia, Austral. **140** 32 58 S 138 51 E
Peterborough, Victoria, Austral. **133** 38 37 S 142 50 E
Peterborough, U.K. **29** 52 35N 0 14W
Peterchurch **28** 52 3N 2 57W
Peterculter **37** 57 5N 2 18W
Peterhead **37** 57 30N 1 49W
Peterlee **33** 54 45N 1 18W
Petersburg, Alas., U.S.A. **152** 56 50N 133 0W
Petersburg, Ind., U.S.A. **156** 38 30N 87 15W
Petersburg, Va., U.S.A. **162** 37 17N 77 26W
Petersburg, W. Va., U.S.A. **156** 38 59N 79 10W
Petersfield **29** 51 0N 0 56W
Peterswell **39** 53 7N 8 46W
Petford **138** 17 20 S 144 50 E
Petília Policastro **65** 39 7N 16 48 E
Petit Bois I. **157** 30 16N 88 25W
Petit Cap **151** 48 58N 63 58W
Petit Goâve **167** 18 27N 72 51W
Petit-Quevilly, Le **42** 49 26N 1 0 E
Petitcodiac **151** 45 57N 65 11W
Petite Saguenay **151** 47 59N 70 1W
Petitsikapau, L. **151** 54 37N 66 25W
Petlad **94** 22 30N 72 45 E
Peto **165** 20 10N 89 0W
Petone **142** 41 13 S 174 53 E
Petoskey **150** 45 22N 84 57W
Petra, Jordan **90** 30 20N 35 22 E
Petra, Spain **58** 39 37N 3 6 E
Petra, Ostrova **12** 76 15N 118 30 E
Petralia **65** 37 49N 14 4 E
Petrel **59** 38 30N 0 46W
Petrich **67** 41 24N 23 13 E
Petrijanec **63** 46 23N 16 17 E
Petrikov **80** 52 11N 28 29 E
Petrila **70** 45 29N 23 29 E
Petrinja **63** 45 28N 16 18 E
'Petroland', gasfield **19** 53 35N 4 15 E
Petrolândia **170** 9 5 S 38 20W
Petrolia **150** 42 54N 82 9W
Petrolina **170** 9 24 S 40 30W
Petropavlovsk **76** 55 0N 69 0 E
Petropavlovsk-Kamchatskiy **77** 53 16N 159 0 E
Petrópolis **173** 22 33 S 43 9W
Petroşeni **70** 45 28N 23 20 E
Petrova Gora **63** 45 15N 15 45 E
Petrovac **66** 42 13N 18 57 E
Petrovaradin **66** 45 16N 19 55 E
Petrovsk **81** 52 22N 45 19 E
Petrovsk-Zabaykalskiy **77** 51 26N 108 30 E
Petrovskoye, R.S.F.S.R., U.S.S.R. **83** 45 25N 42 58 E
Petrovskoye, R.S.F.S.R., U.S.S.R. **84** 53 37N 56 23 E
Petrozavodsk **78** 61 41N 34 20 E
Petrus Steyn **129** 27 38 S 28 8 E
Petrusburg **128** 29 4 S 25 26 E
Pettigo **38** 54 32N 7 49W
Pettitts **141** 34 5[illegible] S 148 10 E
Petworth **29** 50 59N 0 37W
Peumo **172** 34 21 S 71 19W
Peureulak **102** 4 48N 97 45 E
Pevek **77** 69 15N 171 0 E
Pevensey **29** 50 49N 0 20 E
Pevensey Levels **29** 50 50N 0 20 E
Peveragno **62** 44 20N 7 37 E
Pewsey **28** 51 20N 1 46W
Pewsey, Vale of **28** 51 20N 1 46W
Peyrehorade **44** 43 34N 1 7W
Peyruis **45** 44 1N 5 56 E
Pézenas **44** 43 28N 3 24 E
Pezinok **53** 48 17N 17 17 E
Pfaffenhofen **49** 48 31N 11 31 E
Pfäffikon **51** 47 13N 8 46 E
Pfarrkirchen **49** 48 25N 12 57 E
Pforzheim **49** 48 53N 8 43 E
Pfungstadt **49** 49 47N 8 36 E
Phagwara **93** 31 10N 75 40 E
Phala **128** 23 45 S 26 50 E
Phalodi **94** 27 12N 72 24 E
Phalsbourg **43** 48 46N 7 15 E
Phan **100** 19 28N 99 43 E
Phan Rang **101** 11 40N 109 9 E
Phan Thiet **101** 11 1N 108 9 E
Phanat Nikhom **100** 13 27N 101 11 E
Phangan, Ko **101** 9 45N 100 0 E
Phangnga **101** 8 28N 98 30 E
Phanh Bho Ho Chi Minh **101** 10 58N 106 40 E
Phanom Dang Raek, mts. **100** 14 45N 104 0 E
Phanom Sarakham **100** 13 45N 101 21 E
Pharenda **95** 27 5N 83 17 E
Phatthalung **101** 7 39N 100 6 E
Phayao **100** 19 11N 99 55 E
Phelps, N.Y., U.S.A. **162** 42 57N 77 5W
Phelps, Wis., U.S.A. **158** 46 2N 89 2W
Phelps L. **153** 59 15N 103 15W
Phenix City **157** 32 30N 85 0W
Phet Buri **100** 13 1N 99 55 E
Phetchabun **100** 16 25N 101 8 E
Phetchabun, Thiu Khao **100** 16 0N 101 20 E
Phetchaburi **101** 13 1N 99 55 E
Phi Phi, Ko **101** 7 45N 98 46 E
Phiafay **100** 14 48N 106 0 E
Phibun Mangsahan **100** 15 14N 105 14 E
Phichai **100** 17 22N 100 10 E
Phïchit **100** 16 26N 100 22 E
Philadelphia, Miss., U.S.A. **159** 32 47N 89 5W
Philadelphia, Pa., U.S.A. **162** 40 0N 75 10W
Philip **158** 44 4N 101 42W
Philip Smith Mts. **147** 68 0N 146 0W
Philippeville **47** 50 12N 4 33 E
Philippi L. **138** 24 20 S 138 55 E
Philippines ■ **103** 12 0N 123 0 E
Philippolis **128** 30 15 S 25 16 E
Philippopolis = Plovdiv **67** 42 8N 24 44 E
Philipsburg **160** 46 20N 113 21W
Philipstown **128** 30 28 S 24 30 E
Phillip, I. **141** 38 30 S 145 12 E
Phillips, Texas, U.S.A. **159** 35 48N 101 17W
Phillips, Wis., U.S.A. **158** 45 41N 90 22W
Phillips Ra. **136** 16 53 S 125 50 E
Phillipsburg, Kans., U.S.A. **158** 39 48N 99 20W
Phillipsburg, Penn., U.S.A. **162** 40 43N 75 12W
Phillott **139** 27 53 S 145 50 E
Philmont **162** 42 14N 73 37W
Philomath **160** 44 28N 123 21W
Phimai **100** 15 13N 102 30 E
Phitsanulok **100** 16 50N 100 12 E
Phnom Penh **101** 11 33N 104 55 E
Phnom Thbeng **101** 13 50N 104 56 E
Phoenicia **162** 42 5N 74 14W
Phoenix, Ariz., U.S.A. **161** 33 30N 112 10W
Phoenix, N.Y., U.S.A. **162** 43 13N 76 18W
Phoenix Is. **130** 3 30 S 172 0W
Phoenixville **162** 40 12N 75 29W
Phon **100** 15 49N 102 36 E
Phon Tiou **100** 17 53N 104 37 E
Phong, R. **100** 16 23N 102 56 E
Phong Saly **100** 21 42N 102 9 E
Phong Tho **100** 22 32N 103 21 E
Phongdo **99** 30 14N 91 14 E
Phonhong **100** 18 30N 102 25 E
Phonum **101** 8 49N 98 48 E
Photharam **100** 13 41N 99 51 E
Phra Chedi Sam Ong **100** 15 16N 98 23 E
Phra Nakhon Si Ayutthaya **100** 14 25N 100 30 E
Phra Thong, Ko **101** 9 5N 98 17 E
Phrae **100** 18 7N 100 9 E
Phrao **101** 19 23N 99 15 E
Phrom Phiram **100** 17 2N 100 12 E
Phu Dien **100** 18 58N 105 31 E
Phu Doan **101** 21 40N 105 10 E
Phu Loi **100** 20 14N 103 14 E
Phu Ly (Ha Nam) **100** 20 35N 105 50 E
Phu Qui **100** 19 20N 105 20 E
Phu Tho **100** 21 24N 105 13 E
Phuc Yen **100** 21 16N 105 45 E
Phuket **100** 8 0N 98 28 E
Phuket, Ko, I. **101** 8 0N 98 22 E
Phulbari **98** 21 52N 88 8 E
Phulera (Phalera) **94** 26 52N 75 16 E
Phun Phin **101** 9 7N 99 12 E
Phuoc Le (Baria) **101** 10 39N 107 19 E
Piabia **138** 25 12 S 152 45 E
Piacá **170** 7 42 S 47 18W
Piacenza **62** 45 2N 9 42 E
Piaçubaçu **170** 10 24 S 36 25W
Piádena **62** 45 8N 10 22 E
Pialba **139** 25 20 S 152 45 E
Pian, Cr. **139** 30 2 S 148 12 E
Piancó **171** 7 12 S 37 57W
Pianella **63** 42 24N 14 5 E
Piangil **140** 35 5 S 143 20 E
Pianoro **63** 44 20N 11 20 E
Pianosa, I., Puglia, Italy **63** 42 12N 15 44 E
Pianosa, I., Toscana, Italy **62** 42 36N 10 4 E
Piapot **153** 49 59N 109 8W
Pias **57** 38 1N 7 29W
Piaseczno **54** 52 5N 21 2 E
Piassabussu **171** 10 24 S 36 25W
Piastow **54** 52 12N 20 48 E
Piatá **171** 13 9 S 41 48W
Piatra Neamţ **70** 46 56N 26 21 E
Piatra Olt **70** 43 51N 25 9 E
Piauí □ **170** 7 0 S 43 0W
Piaui, R. **170** 6 38 S 42 42W
Piave, R. **63** 45 50N 13 9 E
Piazza Armerina **65** 37 21N 14 20 E
Pibor Post **123** 6 47N 33 3 E
Pibor, R. **123** 7 1N 33 0 E
Pica **174** 20 35 S 69 25W
Picard, Plaine de **43** 50 0N 2 0 E
Picardie **43** 50 0N 2 15 E
Picardy = Picardie **43** 50 0N 2 15 E
Picayune **159** 30 40N 89 40W
Piccadilly, Austral. **109** 34 59 S 138 44 E
Piccadilly, Zambia **127** 14 0 S 29 30 E
Picerno **65** 40 40N 15 37 E
Pichiang **108** 26 40N 98 53 E
Pichieh **108** 27 20N 105 20 E
Pichilemu **172** 34 22 S 72 9W
Pickerel L. **150** 48 40N 91 25W
Pickering **33** 54 15N 0 46W
Pickering, Vale of **33** 54 0N 0 45W
Pickle Lake **150** 51 30N 90 12W
Pico **16** 38 28N 28 18W
Pico Truncado **176** 46 40 S 68 10W
Picos **170** 7 5 S 41 28W
Picos Ancares, Sierra de **56** 42 51N 6 52W
Picquigny **43** 49 56N 2 10 E
Picton, Austral. **141** 34 12 S 150 34 E
Picton, Can. **150** 44 1N 77 9W
Picton, N.Z. **143** 41 18 S 174 3 E
Pictou **151** 45 41N 62 42W
Picture Butte **152** 49 55N 112 45W
Picuí **170** 6 31 S 36 21W
Picún-Leufú **176** 39 30 S 69 5W
Pidley **29** 52 33N 0 4W
Pidurutalagala, mt. **97** 7 10N 80 50 E
Piedad, La **164** 20 20N 102 1W
Piedecuesta **174** 6 59N 73 3W
Piedicavallo **62** 45 41N 7 57 E
Piedmont **157** 33 55N 85 39W
Piedmont = Piemonte **62** 45 0N 7 30 E
Piedmont Plat. **157** 34 0N 81 30W
Piedmonte d'Alife **65** 41 22N 14 22 E
Piedra, R. **58** 41 10N 1 45W
Piedrabuena **57** 39 0N 4 10W
Piedrahita **56** 40 28N 5 23W
Piedras Blancas Pt. **161** 35 45N 121 18W
Piedras Negras **164** 28 35N 100 35W
Piedras, R. de las **174** 11 40 S 70 50W
Piemonte **62** 45 0N 7 30 E
Piena **45** 42 15N 8 34 E
Piensk **54** 51 16N 15 2 E
Pier Millan **140** 35 14 S 142 40 E
Pierce **160** 46 46N 115 53W
Piería □ **68** 40 13N 22 25 E
Pierowall **37** 59 20N 3 0W
Pierre, France **43** 46 54N 5 13 E
Pierre, U.S.A. **158** 44 23N 100 20W
Pierrefeu **45** 43 8N 6 9 E
Pierrefonds **43** 49 20N 3 0 E
Pierrefontaine **43** 47 14N 6 32 E
Pierrefort **44** 44 55N 2 50 E
Pierrelatte **45** 44 23N 4 43 E
Pieštany **155** 48 35N 17 50 E
Piesting, R. **53** 48 0N 16 19 E
Pieszyce **54** 50 43N 16 33 E
Piet Retief **129** 27 1 S 30 50 E
Pietarsaari **74** 63 41N 22 40 E
Pietermaritzburg **129** 29 35 S 30 25 E
Pietersburg **129** 23 54 S 29 25 E
Pietraperzia **65** 37 26N 14 8 E
Pietrasanta **62** 43 57N 10 12 E
Pietrosu **70** 47 12N 25 8 E
Pietrosul **70** 47 35N 24 43 E
Pieve di Cadore **63** 46 25N 12 22 E
Pieve di Teco **62** 44 3N 7 54 E
Pievepélago **62** 44 12N 10 35 E
Pigadhítsa **68** 39 59N 21 23 E
Pigadia **69** 35 30N 27 12 E
Pigeon I. **97** 14 2N 74 20 E
Pigeon, R. **150** 48 1N 89 42W
Piggott **159** 36 20N 90 10W
Pigna **62** 43 57N 7 40 E
Pigü **172** 37 36 S 62 25W
Pihani **95** 27 36N 80 15 E
Pijnacker **46** 52 1N 4 26 E
Pikalevo **80** 59 37N 34 0 E
Pikes Peak **158** 38 50N 105 10W
Pikesville **162** 39 23N 76 44W
Piketberg **128** 32 55 S 18 40 E
Pikeville **156** 37 30N 82 30W
Pik'ochi **106** 40 45N 111 17 E
Pikou **106** 32 45N 105 22 E
Pikwitonei **153** 55 35N 97 9W
Piła **54** 53 10N 16 48 E
Piła □ **54** 53 0N 17 0 E
Pila, mte. **59** 38 16N 1 11W
Pilaia **68** 40 32N 22 59 E
Pilani **94** 28 22N 75 33 E
Pilão Arcado **170** 10 9 S 42 26W
Pilar, Brazil **170** 9 36 S 35 56W
Pilar, Parag. **172** 26 50 S 58 10W
Pilas, I. **103** 6 39N 121 37 E
Pilatus **51** 46 59N 8 15 E
Pilbara Cr. **132** 21 15 S 118 22 E
Pilbara Mining Centre **136** 21 15 S 118 16 E
Pilcomayo, R. **172** 25 21 S 57 42W
Píli **69** 36 50N 27 15 E
Pilibhit **95** 28 40N 79 50 E
Pilion, mt. **68** 39 27N 23 7 E
Pilis **53** 47 17N 19 35 E
Pilisvörösvár **53** 47 38N 18 56 E
Pilkhawa **94** 28 43N 77 42 E
Pilling **32** 53 55N 2 54W
Pilltown **39** 51 59N 7 49W
Pílos **69** 36 55N 21 42 E
Pilot Mound **153** 49 15N 98 54W
Pilot Point **159** 33 26N 97 0W
Pilot Rock **160** 45 30N 118 58W
Pilsen = Plzen **52** 49 45N 13 22 E
Pilštanj **63** 46 8N 15 39 E
Pilton **28** 51 0N 2 35W
Piltown **39** 52 22N 7 18W
Pilzno **54** 50 0N 21 16 E
Pimba **140** 31 18 S 136 46 E
Pimenta Bueno **174** 11 35 S 61 10W
Pimentel **174** 6 45 S 79 55W
Pimuacan, Rés. **151** 49 45N 70 30W
Pina **58** 41 29N 0 33W
Pinang, I. **101** 5 25N 100 15 E
Pinar del Río **166** 22 26N 83 40W
Pinawa **149** 50 9N 95 50W
Pince C. **151** 46 38N 53 45W
Pinchbeck **29** 52 48N 0 9W
Pincher Creek **152** 49 30N 113 57W
Pinchi L. **152** 54 38N 124 30W
Pinch'uan **108** 25 51N 100 34 E
Pinckneyville **158** 38 5N 89 20W
Pîncota **66** 46 20N 21 45 E
Pind Dadan Khan **94** 32 55N 73 47 E
Pindar **137** 28 30 S 115 47 E
Pindaré Mirim **170** 3 37 S 45 21W
Pindaré, R. **170** 3 17 S 44 47W
Pindi Gheb **94** 33 14N 72 12 E
Pindiga **121** 9 58N 10 53 E
Pindobal **170** 3 16 S 48 25W
Pindos Óros **68** 40 0N 21 0 E
Pindus Mts. = Pindos Óros **68** 40 0N 21 0 E
Pine **161** 34 27N 111 30W
Pine Bluff **159** 34 10N 92 0W
Pine, C. **151** 46 37N 53 32W
Pine City **158** 45 46N 93 0W
Pine Creek, N.T., Austral. **132** 13 50 S 131 49 E
Pine Creek, Queens., Austral. **138** 13 13 S 142 47 E
Pine Dock **153** 51 38N 96 48W
Pine Falls **153** 50 34N 96 11W
Pine Flat Res. **163** 36 50N 119 20W
Pine Grove **162** 40 33N 76 23W
Pine Hill **138** 23 42 S 147 0 E
Pine, La **160** 40 53N 80 45W
Pine Pass **152** 55 25N 122 42W
Pine Point **152** 60 50N 114 28W
Pine, R., Austral. **108** 27 18 S 153 2 E
Pine, R., Can. **153** 55 20N 107 38W
Pine Ridge, Austral. **141** 31 10 S 147 30 E
Pine Ridge, U.S.A. **158** 42 2N 102 35W
Pine River, Can. **153** 51 45N 100 30W
Pine River, U.S.A. **158** 46 40N 94 20W
Pine Valley **163** 32 50N 116 32W
Pinecrest **163** 38 12N 120 1W
Pinedale, Ariz., U.S.A. **161** 34 23N 110 16W
Pinedale, Calif., U.S.A. **163** 36 50N 119 48W
Pinega **52** 64 45N 43 40 E
Pinega, R. **78** 64 20N 43 0 E
Pinehill **138** 23 38 S 146 57 E
Pinerolo **62** 44 47N 7 21 E
Pineto **63** 42 36N 14 4 E
Pinetop **161** 34 10N 109 57W
Pinetown **129** 29 48 S 30 54 E
Pinetree **158** 43 42N 105 52W
Pineville, Ky., U.S.A. **157** 36 42N 83 42W
Pineville, La., U.S.A. **159** 31 22N 92 30W
Pinewood **153** 48 45N 94 10W
Piney, Can. **153** 49 5N 96 10W
Piney, France **43** 48 22N 4 21 E
Ping, R. **100** 15 42N 100 9 E

CIB

Pingaring **Polcura**

Pingaring	**137**	32 40 S	118 32 E
P'ingch'ang	**108**	31 33N	107 6 E
P'ingchiang	**109**	28 42N	113 35 E
P'ingch'uan	**107**	41 0N	118 36 E
Pingelly	**137**	32 29 S	116 59 E
P'ingho	**109**	24 18N	117 2 E
P'inghsiang, Kiangsi, China	**109**	27 39N	113 50 E
P'inghsiang, Kwangsi Chuang, China	**108**	22 6N	106 44 E
P'inghu	**109**	30 38N	121 0 E
P'ingi, Shantung, China	**107**	35 30N	117 36 E
P'ingi, Yünnan, China	**108**	25 40N	104 14 E
P'ingkuo	**108**	23 20N	107 34 E
P'ingli	**108**	32 26N	109 22 E
P'ingliang	**105**	35 32N	106 50 E
Pinglo, Kwangsi-Chuang, China	**109**	24 30N	110 45 E
Pinglo, Ningsia Hui, China	**106**	38 58N	106 30 E
P'inglu	**106**	37 32N	112 14 E
P'ingluch'eng	**106**	39 46N	112 6 E
P'ingnan, Fukien, China	**109**	26 56N	119 3 E
P'ingnan, Kwangsi-Chiang, China	**109**	23 33N	110 23 E
P'ingpa	**108**	26 25N	106 15 E
P'ingpien	**108**	22 54N	103 40 E
Pingrup	**137**	33 32 S	118 29 E
P'ingt'an	**109**	25 31N	119 47 E
P'ingt'ang	**108**	25 50N	107 19 E
P'ingting	**106**	37 48N	113 37 E
P'ingt'ingshan	**106**	33 43N	113 28 E
P'ingtu	**107**	36 47N	119 56 E
P'ingtung	**105**	22 38N	120 30 E
Pingwu	**105**	32 27N	104 25 E
P'ingwu	**108**	32 25N	104 36 E
P'ingyang	**109**	27 40N	120 33 E
P'ingyangchen	**107**	45 11N	131 15 E
P'ingyao	**106**	37 12N	112 10 E
P'ingyin	**106**	36 18N	116 26 E
P'ingyüan, Kwangtung, China	**109**	24 34N	115 54 E
P'ingyüan, Ningsia Hui, China	**106**	37 9N	116 25 E
Pinhai	**107**	34 0N	119 50 E
Pinhal	**173**	22 10 S	46 46W
Pinheiro	**170**	2 31 S	45 5W
Pinhel	**56**	40 18N	7 0W
Pinhoe	**30**	50 44N	3 29W
Pinhsien, Heilung Kiang, China	**107**	45 44N	127 27 E
Pinhsien, Shensi, China	**106**	35 10N	108 10 E
Pini, I.	**102**	0 10N	98 40 E
Piniós, R., Ilia, Greece	**69**	37 38N	21 20 E
Piniós, R., Trikkala, Greece	**68**	39 55N	22 10 E
Pinjarra	**137**	32 37 S	115 52 E
Pink, R.	**153**	56 50N	103 50W
Pinkafeld	**53**	47 22N	16 9 E
Pinlebu	**98**	24 5N	95 22 E
Pinnacles, Austral.	**137**	28 12 S	120 26 E
Pinnacles, U.S.A.	**163**	36 33N	121 8W
Pinnaroo	**140**	35 13 S	140 56 E
Pinon Hills	**163**	34 26N	117 39W
Pinos	**164**	22 20N	101 40W
Pinos, I. de	**166**	21 40N	82 40W
Pinos, Mt	**163**	34 49N	119 8W
Pinos Pt.	**161**	36 50N	121 57W
Pinos Puente	**57**	37 15N	3 45W
Pinotepa Nacional	**165**	16 25N	97 55W
Pinrang	**103**	3 46 S	119 34 E
Pinsk	**80**	52 10N	26 8 E
Pintados	**174**	20 35 S	69 40W
Pinto Butte Mt.	**153**	49 22N	107 27W
Pintumba	**137**	31 50 S	132 18 E
Pinwherry	**34**	55 9N	4 50W
Pinyang	**108**	23 17N	108 47 E
Pinyug	**78**	60 5N	48 0 E
Pinzolo	**62**	46 9N	10 45 E
Pio XII	**170**	3 53 S	45 17W
Pioche	**161**	38 0N	114 35W
Piombino	**62**	42 54N	10 30 E
Pioner, I.	**77**	79 50N	92 0 E
Pionki	**54**	51 29N	21 28 E
Piorini, L.	**174**	3 15 S	62 35W
Piotrków Trybunalski	**54**	51 23N	19 43 E
Piotrków Trybunalski □	**54**	51 30N	19 45 E
Piove di Sacco	**63**	45 18N	12 1 E
Pip	**93**	26 45N	60 10 E
Pipar	**94**	26 25N	73 31 E
Pipariya	**96**	22 45N	78 23 E
Piper, oilfield	**19**	58 30N	0 15 E
Pipéri, I.	**68**	39 20N	24 19 E
Pipestone	**158**	44 0N	96 20W
Pipestone Cr.	**153**	53 37N	109 46W
Pipestone, R.	**150**	52 53N	89 23W
Pipinas	**172**	35 30 S	57 19W
Pipiriki	**142**	38 28 S	175 5 E
Pipmuacan Res.	**151**	49 40N	70 25W
Pippingarra	**136**	20 27 S	118 42 E
Pipriac	**42**	47 49N	1 58W
Piqua	**156**	40 10N	84 10W
Piquet Carneiro	**171**	5 48 S	39 25W
Piquiri, R.	**173**	24 3 S	54 14W
Piracanjuba	**171**	17 18 S	49 1W
Piracicaba	**173**	22 45 S	47 30W
Piracuruca	**170**	3 50 S	41 50W
Piræus = Piraiévs	**69**	37 57N	23 42 E
Piraiévs	**69**	37 57N	23 42 E
Piraiévs □	**69**	37 0N	23 30 E
Piráino	**65**	38 10N	14 52 E
Pirajui	**173**	21 59 S	49 29W
Piran (Pirano)	**63**	45 31N	13 33 E
Pirane	**172**	25 25 S	59 30W
Piranhas	**170**	9 27 S	37 46W
Pirapemas	**170**	3 43 S	44 14W
Pirapora	**171**	17 20 S	44 56W
Piratyin	**80**	50 15N	32 25 E
Pirbright	**29**	51 17N	0 40W
Pirdop	**67**	42 40N	24 10 E
Pires do Rio	**171**	17 18 S	48 17W
Pirganj	**98**	25 51 S	88 24 E
Pirgos, Ilia, Greece	**69**	37 40N	21 27 E
Pirgos, Messinia, Greece	**69**	36 50N	22 16 E
Pirgovo	**67**	43 44N	25 43 E
Piriac-sur-Mer	**42**	47 22N	2 33W
Piribebuy	**172**	25 26 S	57 2W
Pirin Planina	**67**	41 40N	23 30 E
Pirineos, mts.	**58**	42 40N	1 0 E
Piripiri	**170**	4 15 S	41 46W
Piritu	**174**	9 23N	69 12W
Pirmasens	**49**	49 12N	7 30 E
Pirna	**48**	50 57N	13 57 E
Pirojpur	**98**	22 35N	90 1 E
Pirot	**66**	43 9N	22 39 E
Pirsagat, R.	**83**	40 15N	48 45 E
Pirtleville	**161**	31 25N	109 35W
Piru	**163**	34 25N	118 48W
Piryí	**69**	38 13N	25 59 E
Pisa	**62**	43 43N	10 23 E
Pisa Ra.	**143**	44 52 S	169 12 E
Pisagua	**174**	19 40 S	70 15W
Pisarovina	**63**	45 35N	15 50 E
Pisciotta	**65**	40 7N	15 12 E
Pisco	**174**	13 50 S	76 5W
Piscu	**70**	45 30N	27 43 E
Písek	**52**	49 19N	14 10 E
Pisham	**108**	29 37N	106 13 E
P'ishan	**105**	37 38N	78 19 E
Pishin Lora, R.	**94**	30 15N	66 5 E
Pising	**103**	5 8 S	121 53 E
Pismo Beach	**163**	35 9N	120 38W
Pissos	**44**	44 19N	0 49W
Pisticci	**65**	40 24N	16 33 E
Pistoia	**62**	43 57N	10 53 E
Pistol B.	**153**	62 25N	92 37W
Pisuerga, R.	**56**	42 10N	4 15W
Pisz	**54**	53 38N	21 49 E
Pitalito	**174**	1 51N	76 2W
Pitanga	**171**	24 46 S	51 44W
Pitangui	**171**	19 40 S	44 54 E
Pitarpunga, L.	**140**	34 24 S	143 30 E
Pitcairn I.	**131**	25 5 S	130 5W
Pite älv	**74**	65 44N	20 50W
Piteå	**74**	65 20N	21 25 E
Piteşti	**70**	44 52N	24 54 E
Pithapuram	**96**	17 10N	82 15 E
Pithara	**137**	30 20 S	116 35 E
Píthion	**68**	41 24N	26 40W
Pithiviers	**43**	48 10N	2 13 E
Pitigliano	**63**	42 38N	11 40 E
Pitiquito	**164**	30 42N	112 2W
Pitlochry	**37**	56 43N	3 43W
Pitt I.	**152**	53 30N	129 50W
Pittem	**47**	51 1N	3 13 E
Pittenweem	**35**	56 13N	2 43W
Pittsburg, Calif., U.S.A.	**163**	38 1N	121 50W
Pittsburg, Kans., U.S.A.	**159**	37 21N	94 43W
Pittsburg, Tex., U.S.A.	**159**	32 59N	94 58W
Pittsburgh	**156**	40 25N	79 55W
Pittsfield, Ill., U.S.A.	**158**	39 35N	90 46W
Pittsfield, N.H., U.S.A.	**162**	43 17N	71 18W
Pittston	**162**	41 19N	75 50W
Pittsworth	**139**	27 41 S	151 37 E
Pituri, R.	**138**	22 35 S	138 30 E
Pitzewo	**107**	39 28N	122 30 E
Piuí	**171**	20 28 S	45 58W
Pium	**170**	10 27 S	49 11W
Piura	**174**	5 5 S	80 45W
Piva, R.	**66**	43 15N	18 50 E
Pivijay	**174**	10 28N	74 37W
Piwniczna	**54**	49 27N	20 42 E
Pixariá Óros	**69**	38 42N	23 39 E
Pixley	**163**	35 58N	119 18W
Piyai	**68**	39 17N	21 25 E
Piyang	**109**	32 50N	113 30 E
Piz Bernina	**49**	46 23N	9 45 E
Pizarro	**174**	4 58N	77 22W
Pizol	**51**	46 57N	9 23 E
Pizzo	**65**	38 44N	16 10 E
Placentia	**151**	47 20N	54 0W
Placentia B.	**151**	47 0N	54 40W
Placerville	**160**	38 47N	120 51W
Placetas	**166**	22 15N	79 44W
'Placid', gasfield	**19**	53 25N	4 20 E
Plačkovica, mts.	**66**	41 45N	22 30 E
Pladda, I.	**34**	55 25N	5 7W
Plaffein	**50**	46 45N	7 17 E
Plain Dealing	**159**	32 56N	93 41W
Plainfield	**162**	40 37N	74 28W
Plains, Kans., U.S.A.	**159**	37 20N	100 35W
Plains, Mont., U.S.A.	**160**	47 27N	114 57W
Plains, Tex., U.S.A.	**159**	33 11N	102 50W
Plainview, Nebr., U.S.A.	**158**	42 25N	97 48W
Plainview, Tex., U.S.A.	**159**	34 10N	101 40W
Plainville	**158**	39 18N	99 19W
Plainwell	**156**	42 28N	85 40W
Plaisance	**44**	43 36N	0 3 E
Pláka	**68**	36 45N	24 26 E
Plakhino	**76**	67 45N	86 5 E
Planá	**52**	49 50N	12 44 E
Plana Cays	**167**	22 38N	73 30W
Planada	**163**	37 18N	120 19W
Planaltina	**171**	15 30 S	47 45W
Plancoët	**42**	48 32N	2 13W
Plandište	**66**	45 16N	21 10 E
Planeta Rica	**174**	8 25N	75 36W
Planina, Slovenija, Yugo.	**63**	45 47N	14 19 E
Planina, Slovenija, Yugo.	**63**	46 10N	15 12 E
Plankinton	**158**	43 45N	98 27W
Plano	**159**	33 0N	96 45W
Plant City	**157**	28 0N	82 15W
Plant, La	**158**	45 11N	100 40W
Plaquemine	**159**	30 20N	91 15W
Plasencia	**56**	40 3N	6 8W
Plaški	**63**	45 4N	15 22 E
Plassen	**72**	61 9N	12 30 E
Plast	**84**	54 22N	60 50 E
Plaster Rock	**151**	46 53N	67 22W
Plata, La, Argent.	**172**	35 0 S	57 55W
Plata, La, U.S.A.	**162**	38 32N	76 59W
Plata, La, Rio de	**172**	35 0 S	56 40W
Platani, R.	**64**	37 28N	13 23 E
Plateau	**13**	70 55 S	40 0 E
Plateau □	**121**	9 0N	9 0 E
Plateau du Coteau du Missouri	**158**	47 9N	101 5W
Platí, Akra	**68**	40 27N	24 0 E
Platinum	**147**	59 2N	161 50W
Plato	**174**	9 47N	74 47W
Platte	**158**	43 28N	98 50W
Platte, Piz	**51**	46 30N	9 35 E
Platte, R.	**158**	41 0N	98 0W
Platteville	**158**	40 18N	104 47W
Plattling	**49**	48 46N	12 53 E
Plattsburgh	**156**	44 41N	73 30W
Plattsmouth	**158**	41 0N	96 0W
Plau	**48**	53 27N	12 16 E
Plauen	**48**	50 29N	12 9 E
Plav	**66**	42 38N	19 57 E
Plavnica	**66**	42 10N	19 20 E
Plavsk	**81**	53 40N	37 18 E
Playa Azul	**164**	17 59N	102 24W
Playa de Castilla	**57**	41 25N	0 12W
Playgreen L.	**153**	54 0N	98 15W
Pleasant Bay	**151**	46 51N	60 48W
Pleasant Hill	**158**	38 48N	94 14W
Pleasant Hills	**141**	35 28 S	146 50 E
Pleasant Mount	**162**	41 44N	75 26W
Pleasant Pt.	**143**	44 16 S	171 9 E
Pleasanton	**159**	29 0N	98 30W
Pleasantville	**162**	39 25N	74 30W
Pléaux	**44**	45 8N	2 13 E
Pleiku (Gia Lai)	**101**	14 3N	108 0 E
Plélan-le-Grand	**42**	48 0N	2 7W
Plémet	**42**	48 11N	2 36W
Pléneuf-Val-André	**42**	48 35N	2 32W
Pleniţa	**70**	44 14N	23 10 E
Plenty, Bay of	**142**	37 45 S	177 0 E
Plenty, R.	**138**	23 25 S	136 31 E
Plentywood	**158**	48 45N	104 35W
Plesetsk	**78**	62 40N	40 10 E
Plessisville	**151**	46 14N	71 47W
Plestin-les-Grèves	**42**	48 40N	3 39W
Pleszew	**54**	51 53N	17 47 E
Pleternica	**66**	45 17N	17 48 E
Pletipi L.	**151**	51 44N	70 6W
Pleven	**67**	43 26N	24 37 E
Plevlja	**66**	43 21N	19 21 E
Płock	**54**	52 32N	19 40 E
Płock □	**54**	52 30N	19 45 E
Plöcken Passo	**63**	46 37N	12 57 E
Plockton	**36**	57 20N	5 40W
Ploegsteert	**47**	50 44N	2 53 E
Ploëmeur	**42**	47 44N	3 26W
Ploërmel	**42**	47 55N	2 26W
Ploieşti	**70**	44 57N	26 5 E
Plomárion	**69**	38 58N	26 24 E
Plomb du Cantal	**44**	45 2N	2 48 E
Plombières	**43**	47 59N	6 27 E
Plomin	**63**	45 8N	14 10 E
Plön	**48**	54 8N	10 22 E
Plöner See	**48**	53 9N	15 5 E
Plonge, Lac La	**153**	55 8N	107 20W
Płonsk	**54**	52 37N	20 21 E
Płoty	**54**	53 48N	15 18 E
Plouay	**42**	47 55N	3 21W
Ploudalmézeau	**42**	48 34N	4 41W
Plougasnou	**42**	48 42N	3 49W
Plouha	**42**	48 41N	2 57W
Plouhinec	**42**	48 0N	4 29W
Plovdiv	**67**	42 8N	24 44 E
Plum I.	**162**	41 10N	72 12W
Plumbridge	**38**	54 46N	7 15W
Plummer	**160**	47 21N	116 59W
Plumtree	**127**	20 27 S	27 55 E
Plunge	**80**	55 53N	21 51 E
Pluvigner	**42**	47 46N	3 1W
Plymouth, U.K.	**30**	50 23N	4 9W
Plymouth, Calif., U.S.A.	**163**	38 29N	120 51W
Plymouth, Ind., U.S.A.	**156**	41 20N	86 19W
Plymouth, Mass., U.S.A.	**162**	41 58N	70 40W
Plymouth, N.C., U.S.A.	**157**	35 54N	76 55W
Plymouth, N.H., U.S.A.	**162**	43 44N	71 41W
Plymouth, Pa., U.S.A.	**162**	41 17N	76 0W
Plymouth, Wis., U.S.A.	**156**	43 42N	87 58W
Plymouth Sd.	**30**	50 20N	4 10W
Plympton	**30**	50 24N	4 2W
Plymstock	**30**	50 22N	4 6W
Plynlimon = Pumlumon Fawr	**31**	52 29N	3 47W
Plyussa	**80**	47 40N	29 0 E
Plyussa, R.	**80**	58 40N	28 30 E
Plzen	**52**	49 45N	13 22 E
Pniewy	**54**	52 31N	16 16 E
Pô	**121**	11 14N	1 5W
Po Hai	**107**	38 30N	119 0 E
Po, R.	**62**	45 0N	10 45 E
Poai	**106**	35 10N	113 4 E
Pobé	**121**	7 0N	2 38 E
Pobedino	**76**	49 51N	142 49 E
Pobedy Pik	**76**	40 45N	79 58 E
Pobiedziska	**54**	52 29N	17 19 E
Pobla de Lillet, La	**58**	42 16N	1 59 E
Pobla de Segur	**58**	42 15N	0 58 E
Pobladura de Valle	**56**	42 6N	5 44W
Pocahontas, Arkansas, U.S.A.	**159**	37 18N	81 20W
Pocahontas, Iowa, U.S.A.	**158**	42 41N	94 42W
Pocatello	**160**	42 50N	112 25W
Pochep	**80**	52 58N	33 15 E
Pochinki	**81**	54 41N	44 59 E
Pochinok	**80**	54 28N	32 29 E
Pöchlarn	**52**	48 12N	15 12 E
Pochontas	**152**	53 0N	117 51W
Pochutla	**165**	15 50N	96 31W
Pocinhos	**170**	7 4 S	36 3W
Pocita Casas	**164**	28 32N	111 6W
Pocklington	**33**	53 56N	0 48W
Poções	**171**	14 31 S	40 21W
Pocomoke City	**162**	38 4N	75 32W
Pocomoke, R.	**162**	38 5N	75 34W
Poços de Caldas	**173**	21 50 S	46 45W
Pocrane	**171**	19 37 S	41 37W
PoC!tky	**52**	49 15N	15 14 E
Poddebice	**54**	51 54N	18 58 E
Poděbrady	**52**	50 9N	15 8 E
Podensac	**44**	44 40N	0 22W
Podgorica = Titograd	**66**	42 30N	19 19 E
Podkamennaya Tunguska	**77**	61 50N	90 26 E
Podlapac	**63**	44 45N	15 47 E
Podmokly	**52**	50 48N	14 10 E
Podoleni	**70**	46 46N	26 39 E
Podolínec	**53**	49 16N	20 31 E
Podolsk	**81**	55 25N	37 30 E
Podor	**120**	16 40N	14 50W
Podporozhy	**78**	60 55N	34 2 E
Podravska Slatina	**66**	45 42N	17 45 E
Podsreda	**63**	45 42N	17 41 E
Podu Turcului	**70**	46 11N	27 25 E
Podujevo	**66**	42 54N	21 10 E
Poel, I.	**48**	54 0N	11 25 E
Pofadder	**128**	29 10 S	19 22 E
Pogamasing	**150**	46 55N	81 50W
Poggiardo	**65**	40 3N	18 21 E
Poggibonsi	**63**	43 27N	11 8 E
Pogoanele	**70**	44 55N	27 0 E
Pogorzela	**54**	51 50N	17 12 E
Pogradeci	**68**	40 57N	20 48 E
Poh	**103**	0 46 S	122 51 E
Pohang	**107**	36 1N	129 23 E
Pohorelá	**53**	48 50N	20 2 E
Pohorelice	**53**	48 59N	16 31 E
Pohorje, mts.	**63**	46 30N	15 7 E
Poiana Mare	**70**	43 57N	23 5 E
Poiana Ruscŭi, Munţii	**70**	45 45N	22 25 E
Pt. Augusta	**140**	32 30 S	137 50 E
Point Baker	**147**	56 20N	133 35W
Point Cloates	**137**	22 40 S	113 45 E
Point Edward	**150**	43 10N	82 30W
Point Fortin	**167**	10 9N	61 46W
Point Hope	**147**	68 20N	166 50W
Point Lay	**147**	69 45N	163 10W
Point Pass	**140**	34 5 S	139 5 E
Point Pedro	**97**	9 50N	80 15 E
Point Pleasant, N.J., U.S.A.	**162**	40 5N	74 4W
Point Pleasant, W. Va., U.S.A.	**156**	38 50N	82 7W
Point Reyes Nat. Seashore	**163**	38 0N	122 58W
Point Rock	**159**	31 30N	99 56W
Pointe-à-la Hache	**159**	29 35N	89 55W
Pointe-à-Pitre	**167**	16 10N	61 30W
Pointe-Noire	**124**	4 48 S	12 0 E
Poirino	**62**	44 55N	7 50 E
Poisonbush Ra.	**136**	22 30 S	121 30 E
Poissy	**43**	48 55N	2 0 E
Poitiers	**42**	46 35N	0 20W
Poitou, Plaines du	**44**	46 30N	0 1W
Poix	**43**	49 47N	2 0 E
Poix-Terron	**43**	49 38N	4 38 E
Pojoaque	**161**	35 55N	106 0W
Pojuca	**171**	12 21 S	38 20W
Pokaran	**93**	27 0N	71 50 E
Pokataroo	**139**	29 30 S	148 34 E
Poko, Sudan	**123**	5 41N	31 55 E
Poko, Zaïre	**126**	3 7N	26 52 E
Pok'ot'u	**105**	48 46N	121 54 E
Pokrovka	**85**	42 20N	78 0 E
Pokrovsk	**77**	61 29N	129 6 E
Pokrovsk-Uralskiy	**84**	60 10N	59 49 E
Pol	**56**	43 9N	7 20W
Pola	**80**	57 30N	32 0 E
Pola de Allande	**56**	43 16N	6 37W
Pola de Gordón, La	**56**	42 51N	5 41W
Pola de Lena	**56**	43 10N	5 49W
Pola de Siero	**56**	43 24N	5 39W
Pola de Somiedo	**56**	43 5N	6 15W
Polacca	**161**	35 52N	110 25W
Polan	**93**	25 30N	61 10 E
Poland ■	**54**	52 0N	20 0 E
Polanów	**54**	54 7N	16 41 E
Polar Bear Prov. Park	**150**	54 30N	83 20W
Polcura	**172**	37 10 S	71 50W

Połcyn Zdrój Portel

Połcyn Zdrój 54 53 47N 16 5E
Polden Hills 28 51 7N 2 50W
Polegate 29 50 49N 0 15E
Polessk 80 54 50N 21 8E
Polesworth 28 52 37N 1 37W
Polevskoy 84 56 26N 60 11E
Polewali, Sulawesi, Indon. 103 4 8S 119 43E
Polewali, Sulawesi, Indon. 103 3 21S 119 31E
Polgar 53 47 54N 21 6E
Pŏlgyo-ri 107 34 51N 127 21E
Poli 124 8 34N 12 54E
Políaigos, I. 69 36 45N 24 38E
Policastro, Golfo di 65 39 55N 15 35E
Police 54 53 33N 14 33E
Polička 53 49 43N 16 15E
Polignano a Mare 65 41 0N 17 12E
Poligny 43 46 50N 5 42E
Polikhnitas 69 39 4N 26 10E
Polillo I. 103 14 56N 122 0E
Polis 92 35 3N 32 30E
Polistena 65 38 25N 16 4E
Poliyiros 68 40 23N 23 25E
Polkowice 54 51 29N 16 3E
Polla 65 40 31N 15 27E
Pollachi 97 10 35N 77 0E
Pollensa 58 39 54N 3 2E
Pollensa, B. de 58 39 55N 3 5E
Póllica 65 40 13N 15 3E
Pollino, Mte. 65 39 54N 16 13E
Pollock 158 45 58N 100 18W
Pollremon 38 53 40N 8 38W
Polna 80 58 31N 28 0E
Polnovat 76 63 50N 66 5E
Polo, Kwangtung, China 109 23 9N 114 17E
Polo, S.-U., China 105 44 59N 81 57E
Polo, U.S.A. 158 42 0N 89 38W
Pologi 82 47 29N 36 15E
Polonnoye 80 50 6N 27 30E
Polossu 108 31 12N 98 36E
Polotsk 80 55 30N 28 50E
Polperro 30 50 19N 4 31W
Polruan 30 50 17N 4 36W
Polski Trmbesh 67 43 20N 25 38E
Polsko Kosovo 67 43 23N 25 38E
Polson 160 47 45N 114 12W
Poltava 82 49 35N 34 35E
Polur 97 12 32N 79 11E
Polyarny 78 69 8N 33 20E
Pomarance 62 43 18N 10 51E
Pomarico 65 40 31N 16 33E
Pomaro 164 18 20N 103 18W
Pombal, Brazil 170 6 55S 37 50W
Pombal, Port. 56 39 55N 8 40W
Pómbia 69 35 0N 24 51E
Pomeroy, U.K. 38 54 36N 6 56W
Pomeroy, Ohio, U.S.A. 156 39 0N 82 0W
Pomeroy, Wash., U.S.A. 160 46 30N 117 33W
Pomio 135 5 32S 151 33E
Pomona 163 34 2N 117 49W
Pomorie 67 42 26N 27 41E
Pompano 157 26 12N 80 6W
Pompei 65 40 45N 14 30E
Pompey 43 48 50N 6 2E
Pompeys Pillar 160 46 0N 108 0W
Ponape I. 130 6 55N 158 10E
Ponask, L. 150 54 0N 92 41W
Ponass L. 153 52 16N 103 58W
Ponca 158 42 38N 96 41W
Ponca City 159 36 40N 97 5W
Ponce 147 18 1N 66 37W
Ponchatoula 159 30 27N 90 25W
Poncheville, L. 150 50 10N 76 55W
Poncin 45 46 6N 5 25E
Pond 163 35 43N 119 20W
Pond Inlet 149 72 30N 75 0W
Pondicherry 97 11 59N 79 50E
Pondoland 129 31 10S 29 30W
Pondooma 140 33 29S 136 59E
Pondrôme 47 50 6N 5 0E
Ponds, I. of 151 53 27N 55 52W
Ponferrada 56 42 32N 6 35W
Pongaroa 142 40 33S 176 15E
Póngo , Ponte de 127 19 0S 34 0E
Pongo, W. 123 8 0N 27 20E
Poniatowa 54 51 11N 22 3E
Poniec 54 51 48N 16 50E
Ponnaiyar, R. 97 11 50N 79 45E
Ponnani 97 10 45N 75 59E
Ponnani, R. 97 10 45N 75 59E
Ponneri 97 13 20N 80 15E
Ponnyadaung 99 22 0N 94 10E
Ponoi 78 67 0N 41 0E
Ponoi, R. 78 67 10N 39 0E
Ponoka 152 52 42N 113 40W
Ponomarevka 84 53 19N 54 8E
Ponorogo 103 7 52S 111 29E
Pons, France 44 45 35N 0 34W
Pons, Spain 58 41 55N 1 12E
Ponsul, R. 57 39 54N 8 45E
Pont-à-Celles 47 50 30N 4 22E
Pont-à-Mousson 43 45 54N 6 1E
Pont Audemer 42 49 21N 0 30E
Pont Aven 42 47 51N 3 47W
Pont Canavese 62 45 24N 7 33E
Pont Château 42 47 26N 2 8W
Pont-de-Roide 43 47 23N 6 45E
Pont-de-Salars 44 44 18N 2 44E
Pont-de-Vaux 43 46 26N 4 56E
Pont-de-Veyle 45 46 17N 4 53E
Pont-l'Abbé 42 47 52N 4 15W
Pont Lafrance 151 47 40N 64 58W
Pont, Le 50 46 41N 6 20E
Pont-l'Eveque 42 49 18N 0 11E
Pont-St.-Esprit 45 44 16N 4 40E
Pont-sur-Yonne 43 48 18N 3 10E
Ponta de Pedras 170 1 23S 48 52W
Ponta Grossa 173 25 0S 50 10W
Ponta Pora 173 22 20S 55 35W
Ponta São Sebastião 129 22 2S 35 25E
Pontacq 44 43 11N 0 8W
Pontailler 43 47 18N 5 24E
Pontal, R. 170 9 8S 40 12W
Pontalina 171 17 31S 49 27W
Pontardawe 31 51 43N 3 51W
Pontardulais 31 51 42N 4 3W
Pontarlier 43 46 54N 6 20E
Pontassieve 63 43 47N 11 25E
Pontaubault 42 48 40N 1 20W
Pontaumur 44 45 52N 2 40E
Pontcharra 45 45 26N 6 1E
Pontchartrain, L. 159 30 12N 90 0W
Pontchâteau 42 47 25N 2 5W
Ponte Alta do Norte 170 10 45S 47 34W
Ponte Alta, Serra do 171 19 42S 47 40W
Ponte da Barca 56 41 48N 8 25W
Ponte de Sor 57 39 17N 7 57W
Ponte dell 'Olio 62 44 52N 9 39E
Ponte di Legno 62 46 15N 10 30E
Ponte do Lima 56 41 46N 8 35W
Ponte do Pungué 127 19 30S 34 33E
Ponte Leccia 45 42 28N 9 13E
Ponte nell' Alpi 63 46 10N 12 18E
Ponte Nova 173 20 25S 42 54W
Ponte San Martino 62 45 36N 7 47E
Ponte San Pietro 62 45 42N 9 35E
Pontebba 63 46 30N 13 17E
Pontecorvo 64 41 28N 13 40E
Pontedera 62 43 40N 10 37E
Pontefract 33 53 42N 1 19W
Ponteix 153 49 46N 107 29W
Ponteland 35 53 3N 1 45W
Pontelandolfo 65 41 17N 14 41E
Pontemacassar Naikliu 103 9 30S 123 58E
Pontevedra 56 42 26N 8 40W
Pontevedra □ 56 42 25N 8 39W
Pontevedra, R. de 56 42 22N 8 45W
Pontevico 62 45 16N 10 6E
Ponthierville = Ubundi 126 0 22S 25 30E
Pontiac, Ill., U.S.A. 158 40 50N 88 40W
Pontiac, Mich., U.S.A. 156 42 40N 83 20W
Pontian Kechil 101 1 29N 103 23E
Pontianak 102 0 3S 109 15E
Pontine Is. = Ponziane, Isole 64 40 55N 13 0E
Pontine Mts. = Karadeniz D. 92 41 30N 35 0E
Pontinia 64 41 25N 13 2E
Pontivy 42 48 5N 3 0W
Pontoise 43 49 3N 2 5E
Ponton, R. 152 58 27N 116 11W
Pontorson 42 48 34N 1 30W
Pontrémoli 62 44 22N 9 52E
Pontresina 51 46 29N 9 48E
Pontrhydfendigaid 31 52 17N 3 50W
Pontrieux 28 48 42N 3 10W
Pontrilas 28 51 56N 2 53W
Ponts-de Cé, Les 42 47 25N 0 30W
Pontypool 31 51 42N 3 1W
Pontypridd 31 51 36N 3 21W
Ponza, I. 64 40 55N 12 57E
Ponziane, Isole 64 40 55N 13 0E
Poochera 139 32 43S 134 51E
Poole 28 50 42N 2 2W
Poole Harb. 28 50 41N 2 0W
Poolewe 36 57 45N 5 38W
Pooley Bridge 32 54 37N 2 49W
Pooley I. 152 52 45N 128 15W
Poonamallee 97 13 3N 80 10E
Poona = Pune 96 18 29N 73 57E
Pooncarie 140 33 22S 142 31E
Poonindie 140 34 34S 135 54E
Poopelloe, L. 140 31 40S 144 0E
Poopó, Lago de 174 18 30S 67 35W
Poor Knights Is. 142 35 29S 174 43E
Pooraka 109 34 50S 138 38E
Poorman 147 64 5N 155 48W
Popai 108 22 13N 109 55E
Popak 101 22 15N 109 56E
Popakai, Austral. 170 32 12S 141 46E
Popakai, Surinam 170 3 20N 55 30W
Popanyinning 137 32 40S 117 2E
Popayán 174 2 27N 76 36W
Poperinge 47 50 51N 2 42E
Popigay 77 71 55N 110 47E
Popilta, L. 140 33 10S 141 42E
Popio, L. 140 33 10S 141 52E
Poplar 158 48 3N 105 9W
Poplar Bluff 159 36 45N 90 22W
Poplar, R., Man., Can. 153 53 0N 97 19W
Poplar, R., N.W.T., Can. 152 61 22N 121 52W
Poplarville 159 30 55N 89 30W
Popocatepetl, vol. 165 19 10N 98 40W
Popokabaka 124 5 49S 16 40E
Pópoli 63 42 12N 13 50E
Popondetta 135 8 48S 148 17E
Popovača 63 45 30N 16 41E
Popovo 67 43 21N 26 18E
Poppel 47 51 27N 5 2E
Poprád 53 49 3N 20 18E
Poprád, R. 53 49 15N 20 30E
Poquoson 162 37 7N 76 21W
Poradaha 98 23 51N 89 1E
Porali, R. 94 27 15N 66 24E
Porangahau 142 40 17S 176 37E
Porangatu 171 13 26S 49 10W
Porbandar 94 21 44N 69 43E
Porcher I. 152 53 50N 130 30W
Porcos, R. 171 12 42S 45 7W
Porcuna 57 37 52N 4 11W
Porcupine, R., Can. 153 59 11N 104 46W
Porcupine, R., U.S.A. 147 67 0N 143 0W
Pordenone 63 45 58N 12 40E
Pordim 67 43 23N 24 51E
Pore 174 5 43N 72 0W
Poreč 63 45 14N 13 36E
Porecatu 171 22 43S 51 24W
Poretskoye 81 55 9N 46 21E
Pori 75 61 29N 21 48E
Porirua 142 41 8S 174 52E
Porjus 74 66 57N 19 50E
Porkhov 80 57 45N 29 38E
Porkkala 75 59 59N 24 26E
Porlamar 174 10 57N 63 51W
Porlezza 62 46 2N 9 8E
Porlock 28 51 13N 3 36W
Porlock B. 28 51 14N 3 37W
Porlock Hill 28 51 12N 3 40W
Porma, R. 56 42 45N 5 21W
Pornic 42 47 7N 2 5W
Poronaysk 77 49 20N 143 0E
Póros 69 37 30N 23 30E
Póros, I. 69 37 30N 23 30E
Poroshiri-Dake 112 42 41N 142 52E
Poroszló 53 47 39N 20 40E
Poroto Mts. 127 9 0S 33 30E
Porraburdoo 137 23 15S 117 28E
Porrentruy 50 47 25N 7 6E
Porreras 58 39 29N 3 2E
Porsangen 74 70 40N 25 40E
Porsgrunn 71 59 10N 9 40E
Port 43 47 43N 6 4E
Port Adelaide 140 34 46S 138 30E
Port Alberni 152 49 15N 124 50W
Port Albert 141 38 42S 146 42E
Port Albert Victor 94 21 0N 71 30E
Port Alexander 147 56 13N 134 40W
Port Alfred, Can. 151 48 18N 70 53W
Port Alfred, S. Afr. 125 33 36S 26 55E
Port Alice 152 50 25N 127 25W
Port Allegany 156 41 49N 78 17W
Port Allen 159 30 30N 91 15W
Port Alma 138 23 38S 150 53E
Port Angeles 160 48 7N 123 30W
Port Antonio 166 18 10N 76 30W
Port Aransas 159 27 49N 97 4W
Port Arthur, Austral. 138 43 7S 147 50E
Port Arthur, U.S.A. 159 30 0N 94 0W
Port Arthur = Lüshun 107 38 51N 121 20E
Port Arthur = Thunder Bay 150 48 25N 89 10W
Port Askaig 34 55 51N 6 8W
Port au Port B. 151 48 40N 58 50W
Port-au-Prince 167 18 40N 72 20W
Port Augusta West 140 32 29S 137 47E
Port Austin 150 44 3N 82 59W
Port aux Basques 151 47 32N 59 8W
Port Awanui 142 37 50S 178 29E
Port Bannatyne 34 55 51N 5 4W
Port Bell 126 0 18N 32 35E
Port Bergé Vaovao 129 15 33S 47 40E
Port Blair 101 11 40N 92 30E
Port Blandford 151 48 30N 53 50W
Port Bolivar 159 29 20N 94 40W
Port Bou 58 42 25N 3 9E
Port Bouet 120 5 16N 4 57W
Port Bradshaw 138 12 30S 137 0E
Port Broughton 140 33 37S 137 56E
Port Burwell 150 42 40N 80 48W
Port Campbell 140 35 37S 143 1E
Port Canning 95 22 17N 88 48E
Port Carlisle 32 54 56N 3 12W
Port-Cartier 151 50 10N 66 50W
Port Chalmers 143 45 49S 170 30E
Port Charlotte 34 55 44N 6 22W
Port Chester 162 41 0N 73 41W
Port Clements 152 53 40N 132 10W
Port Clinton 156 41 30N 83 0W
Port Colborne 150 42 50N 79 10W
Port Coquitlam 152 49 20N 122 45W
Port Curtis 138 24 0S 151 34E
Port Darwin, Austral. 136 12 24S 130 45E
Port Darwin, Falk. Is. 176 51 50S 59 0W
Port Davey 138 43 16S 145 55E
Port-de-Bouc 45 43 24N 4 59E
Port de Paix 167 19 50N 72 50W
Port Deposit 162 39 37N 76 5W
Port Dickson 101 2 30N 101 49E
Port Dinorwic 31 53 11N 4 12W
Port Douglas 138 16 30S 145 30E
Port Edward 152 54 12N 130 10W
Port Elgin 150 44 25N 81 25W
Port Elizabeth 128 33 58S 25 40E
Port Ellen 34 55 38N 6 10W
Port Erin 32 54 5N 4 45W
Port Erroll 37 57 25N 1 50W
Port Essington 136 11 15S 132 10E
Port Étienne = Nouadhibou 116 21 0N 17 0W
Port Ewen 162 41 54N 73 59W
Port Fairy 140 38 22S 142 12E
Port Fitzroy 142 36 8S 175 20E
Port Fouâd = Bûr Fuad 122 31 15N 32 20E
Port Francqui 124 4 17S 20 47E
Port-Gentil 124 0 47S 8 40E
Port Gibson 159 31 57N 91 0W
Port Glasgow 34 55 57N 4 40W
Port Gregory 137 27 40S 114 0E
Port Harcourt 121 4 40N 7 10E
Port Hardy 152 50 41N 127 30W
Port Harrison 149 58 25N 78 15W
Port Hawkesbury 151 45 36N 61 22W
Port Hedland 136 20 25S 118 35E
Port Heiden 147 57 0N 158 40W
Port Hood 151 46 0N 61 32W
Port Hope 150 44 0N 78 20W
Port Hueneme 163 34 7N 119 12W
Port Huron 156 43 0N 82 28W
Port Isaac 30 50 35N 4 50W
Port Isaac B. 30 50 36N 4 50W
Port Isabel 159 26 12N 97 9W
Port Jackson 133 33 50S 151 18E
Port Jefferson 162 40 58N 73 5W
Port Jervis 162 41 22N 74 42W
Port Joinville 42 46 45N 2 23W
Port Kaituma 174 8 3N 59 58W
Port Katon 83 46 27N 38 56E
Port Kelang 101 3 0N 101 23E
Port Kembla 141 34 29S 150 56E
Port La Nouvelle 44 43 1N 3 3E
Port Laoise 39 53 2N 7 20W
Port Lavaca 159 28 38N 96 38W
Port Leyden 162 43 35N 75 21W
Port Lincoln 140 34 42S 135 52E
Port Logan 34 54 42N 4 57W
Port Loko 120 8 48N 12 46W
Port Louis 42 47 42N 3 22W
Port Lyautey = Kenitra 118 34 15N 6 40W
Port Lyttelton 143 43 37N 172 50E
Port Macdonnell 140 38 0S 140 39E
Port Macquarie 141 31 25S 152 54E
Port Maitland 151 44 0N 66 2W
Port Maria 166 18 25N 76 55W
Port Mellon 152 49 32N 123 31W
Port Menier 151 49 51N 64 15W
Port Morant 166 17 54N 76 19W
Port Moresby 135 9 24S 147 8E
Port Mouton 151 43 58N 64 50W
Port Musgrave 138 11 55S 141 50E
Port Navalo 42 47 34N 2 54W
Port Nelson 153 57 3N 92 36W
Port Nicholson 142 41 20S 174 52E
Port Nolloth 128 29 17S 16 52E
Port Norris 162 39 15N 75 2W
Port Nouveau-Quebec (George R.) 149 58 30N 65 50W
Port O'Connor 159 28 26N 96 24W
Port of Ness 36 58 29N 6 13W
Port of Spain 167 10 40N 61 20W
Port Orchard 160 47 31N 122 38W
Port Oxford 160 42 45N 124 28W
Port Pegasus 143 47 12S 167 41E
Port Perry 150 44 6N 78 56W
Port Phillip B. 139 38 10S 144 50E
Port Pirie 140 33 10S 137 58E
Port Pólnocny □ 54 54 25N 18 42E
Port Radium = Echo Bay 148 66 10N 117 40W
Port Renfrew 152 48 30N 124 20W
Port Roper 138 14 45S 134 47E
Port Rowan 150 42 40N 80 30W
Port Royal 162 38 10N 77 12W
Port Safaga = Bûr Safâga 122 26 43N 33 57E
Port Said = Bûr Sa'îd 122 31 16N 32 18E
Port St. Joe 157 29 49N 85 20W
Port St. Johns = Umzimvubu 129 31 38S 29 33E
Port-St. Louis 45 43 23N 4 50E
Port St. Louis 129 13 7S 48 48E
Port-St.-Louis-du-Rhône 45 43 23N 4 49E
Port St. Mary 32 54 5N 4 44W
Port St. Servain 151 51 21N 58 0W
Port Sanilac 150 43 26N 82 33W
Port Saunders 151 50 40N 57 18W
Port Shepstone 129 30 44S 30 28E
Port Simpson 152 54 30N 130 20W
Port Stanley 150 42 40N 81 10W
Port Sudan = Bûr Sôdân 122 19 32N 37 9E
Port Sunlight 32 53 22N 3 0W
Port Talbot 31 51 35N 3 48W
Port Taufiq = Bûr Taufiq 122 29 54N 32 32E
Port Townsend 160 48 7N 122 50W
Port-Vendres 44 42 32N 3 8E
Port Victoria 140 34 30S 137 29E
Port Wakefield 140 34 12S 138 10E
Port Washington 156 43 25N 87 52W
Port Weld 101 4 50N 100 38E
Port William 34 54 46N 4 35W
Portachuelo 174 17 10S 63 20W
Portacloy 38 54 20N 9 48W
Portadown (Craigavon) 38 54 27N 6 26W
Portaferry 38 54 23N 5 32W
Portage, Can. 151 46 40N 64 5W
Portage, U.S.A. 158 43 31N 89 25W
Portage la Prairie 153 49 58N 98 18W
Portage Mt. Dam 152 56 0N 122 0W
Portageville 159 36 25N 89 40W
Portaguiran 36 58 15N 6 10W
Portalegre 57 39 19N 7 25W
Portalegre □ 57 39 20N 7 40W
Portales 159 34 12N 103 25W
Portarlington 39 53 10N 7 10W
Porte, La 156 41 40N 86 40W
Porteirinha 171 15 44S 43 2W
Portel, Brazil 170 1 57S 50 49W

Portel Prochowice

Portel, Port.	57	38 19N	7 41W
Porter L., N.W.T., Can.	153	61 41N	108 5W
Porter L., Sask., Can.	153	56 20N	107 20W
Porterville, S. Afr.	128	33 0S	18 57E
Porterville, U.S.A.	163	36 5N	119 0W
Portet	44	43 34N	0 11W
Porteynon	31	51 33N	4 13W
Portglenone	38	54 53N	6 30W
Portgordon	37	57 40N	3 1W
Porth Neigwl	31	52 48N	4 35W
Porth Neigwl, B.	31	52 48N	4 33W
Porthcawl	31	51 28N	3 42W
Porthill	160	49 0N	116 30W
Porthleven	30	50 5N	5 19W
Porthmadog	31	52 55N	4 13W
Portile de Fier	70	44 42N	22 30E
Portimão	57	37 8N	8 32W
Portishead	28	51 29N	2 46W
Portknockle	37	57 40N	2 52W
Portland, N.S.W., Austral.	141	33 20S	150 0E
Portland, Victoria, Austral.	140	38 20S	141 35E
Portland, Conn., U.S.A.	162	41 34N	72 39W
Portland, Me., U.S.A.	151	43 40N	70 15W
Portland, Mich., U.S.A.	156	42 52N	84 58W
Portland, Oreg., U.S.A.	160	45 35N	122 40W
Portland B.	140	38 15S	141 45E
Portland Bill	28	50 31N	2 27W
Portland, C.	133	40 46S	148 0E
Portland I.	142	39 20S	177 51E
Portland, I. of	28	50 32N	2 25W
Portland, Pa.	162	40 55N	75 6W
Portland Prom.	149	58 40N	78 33W
Portlaw	39	52 18N	7 20W
Portmagee	39	51 53N	10 22W
Portmahomack	37	57 50N	3 50W
Portmarnock	38	53 25N	6 10W
Portnacroish	34	56 34N	5 24W
Portnahaven	34	55 40N	6 30W
Portneuf	151	46 43N	71 55W
Pôrto, Brazil	170	3 54S	42 42W
Pôrto, Port.	56	41 8N	8 40W
Pôrto □	56	41 8N	8 20W
Pôrto Alegre, Mato Grosso, Brazil	170	21 40S	53 30W
Pôrto Alegre, Rio Grande do Sul, Brazil	173	30 5S	51 3W
Porto Alexandre	128	15 55S	11 55E
Porto Amboim = Gunza	124	10 50S	13 50E
Porto Amelia = Pemba	127	12 58S	40 30E
Porto Argentera	62	44 15N	7 27E
Porto Azzurro	62	42 46N	10 24E
Porto Botte	64	39 3N	8 33E
Porto Calvo	171	9 4S	35 24W
Porto Civitanova	63	43 19N	13 44E
Pôrto da Fôlha	170	9 55S	37 17W
Pôrto de Moz	170	1 41S	52 22W
Pôrto de Pedras	170	9 10S	35 17W
Porto Empédocle	64	37 18N	13 30E
Pôrto Esperança	174	19 37S	57 29W
Pôrto Franco	170	6 20S	47 24W
Porto Garibaldi	63	44 41N	12 14E
Porto, G. de	45	42 17N	8 34E
Pôrto Lago	68	41 1N	25 6E
Porto Mendes	173	24 30S	54 15W
Pôrto Murtinho	174	21 45S	57 55W
Pôrto Nacional	170	10 40S	48 30W
Porto Novo, Benin	121	6 23N	2 42E
Porto Novo, India	97	11 30N	79 38E
Porto Recanati	63	43 26N	13 40E
Porto San Giorgio	63	43 11N	13 49E
Porto San Stéfano	68	42 26N	11 6E
Porto Santo, I.	116	33 45S	16 25W
Pôrto São José	173	22 43S	53 10W
Pôrto Seguro	171	16 26S	39 5W
Porto Tolle	63	44 57N	12 20E
Porto Tórres	64	40 50N	8 23E
Pôrto União	173	26 10S	51 10W
Pôrto Válter	174	8 5S	72 40W
Porto-Vecchio	45	41 35N	9 16E
Pôrto Velho	174	8 46S	63 54W
Portobelo	166	9 35N	79 42W
Portoferráio	62	42 50N	10 20E
Portogruaro	63	45 47N	12 50E
Portola	160	39 49N	120 28W
Portomaggiore	63	44 41N	11 47E
Porton Camp	28	51 8N	1 42W
Portoscuso	64	39 12N	8 22E
Portovénere	62	44 2N	9 50E
Portovíejo	174	1 0S	80 20W
Portpatrick	34	54 50N	5 7W
Portree	36	57 25N	6 11W
Portroe	39	52 53N	8 20W
Portrush	38	55 13N	6 40W
Portsall	42	48 37N	4 45W
Portsalon	38	55 12N	7 37W
Portskerra	37	58 35N	3 55W
Portslade	29	50 50N	0 11W
Portsmouth, Domin.	167	15 34N	61 27W
Portsmouth, U.K.	28	50 48N	1 6W
Portsmouth, N.H., U.S.A.	162	43 5N	70 45W
Portsmouth, Ohio, U.S.A.	156	38 45N	83 0W
Portsmouth, R.I., U.S.A.	162	41 35N	71 44W
Portsmouth, Va., U.S.A.	156	36 50N	76 20W
Portsoy	37	57 41N	2 41W
Portstewart	38	55 12N	6 43W
Porttipahta	74	68 5N	26 30E
Portugal ■	56	40 0N	7 0W
Portugalete	58	43 19N	3 4W
Portuguesa □	174	9 10N	69 15W
Portuguese Guinea = Guinea Bissau	120	12 0N	15 0W
Portuguese Timor ■ = Timor	103	8 0S	126 30E
Portumna	39	53 5N	8 12W
Porvenir	176	53 10S	70 30W
Porvoo	75	60 24N	25 40E
Porzuna	57	39 9N	4 9W
Posada, R.	64	40 40N	9 35E
Posadas, Argent.	173	27 30S	56 0W
Posadas, Spain	57	37 47N	5 11W
Poschiavo	51	46 19N	10 4E
Posets, mt.	58	42 39N	0 25E
Poshan	107	36 30N	117 50E
Posídhio, Ákra	68	39 57N	23 30E
Poso	103	1 20S	120 55E
Poso Colorado	172	23 30S	58 45W
Poso, D.	103	1 20S	120 55E
Posong	107	34 46N	129 5E
Posse	171	14 4S	46 18W
Possel	124	5 5N	19 10E
Possession I.	13	72 4S	172 0E
Pössneck	48	50 42N	11 34E
Possut'eng Hu	105	42 0N	87 0E
Post	159	33 13N	101 21W
Post Falls	160	47 50N	116 59W
Postavy	80	55 4N	26 58E
Postbridge	30	50 36N	3 54W
Poste-de-la-Baleine	30	50 36N	3 54W
Poste Maurice Cortier (Bidon 5)	118	22 14N	1 2E
Postiljon, Kepulauan	103	6 30S	118 50E
Postmasburg	128	28 18S	23 5E
Postojna	63	45 46N	14 12E
Potamós	69	39 38N	19 53E
Potchefstroom	125	26 41S	27 7E
Potcoava	70	44 30N	24 39E
Poté	171	17 49S	41 49W
Poteau	159	35 5N	94 37W
Poteet	159	29 4N	98 35W
Potelu, Lacul	70	43 44N	24 20E
Potenza	65	40 40N	15 50E
Potenza Picena	63	43 22N	13 37E
Poteriteri, L.	143	46 5S	167 10E
Potes	56	43 15N	4 42W
Potgietersrus	129	24 10S	29 3E
Poti	83	42 10N	41 38E
Potiraguá	171	15 36S	39 53W
Potiskum	121	11 39N	11 2E
Potlogi	70	44 34N	25 34E
Potomac, R.	162	38 0N	76 23W
Potosí	174	19 38S	65 50W
Potosí □	174	20 31S	67 0W
Pot'ou	106	37 57N	116 39E
Potrerillos	172	26 20S	69 30W
Potros, Cerro del	172	28 32S	69 0W
Potsdam, Ger.	48	52 23N	13 4E
Potsdam, U.S.A.	156	44 40N	74 59W
Potsdam □	48	52 40N	12 50E
Potter	158	41 15N	103 20W
Potter Heigham	29	52 44N	1 33E
Potterne	28	51 19N	2 0W
Potters Bar	29	51 42N	0 11W
Potterspury	29	52 5N	0 52W
Pottery Hill = Abu Ballas	122	24 26N	27 36E
Pottstown	162	40 17N	75 40W
Pottsville	162	40 39N	76 12W
Pottuvil	93	6 55N	81 50E
P'otzu	109	23 30N	120 25E
Pouancé	42	47 44N	1 10W
Pouce Coupé	152	55 40N	120 10W
Poughkeepsie	162	41 40N	73 57W
Pouilly	43	47 18N	2 57E
Poulaphouca Res.	39	53 8N	6 30W
Pouldu, Le	42	47 41N	3 36W
Poulsbo	160	47 45N	122 39W
Poultney	162	43 31N	73 14W
Poulton le Fylde	32	53 51N	2 59W
Poundstock	30	50 44N	4 34W
Pouso Alegre, Mato Grosso, Brazil	175	11 55S	57 0W
Pouso Alegre, Minas Gerais, Brazil	173	22 14S	45 57W
Pouzages	44	46 40N	0 50W
Povenets	78	62 50N	34 50E
Poverty Bay	142	38 43S	178 2E
Póvoa de Lanhosa	56	41 33N	8 15W
Póvoa de Varzim	56	41 25N	8 46W
Povorino	81	51 12N	42 28E
Powassan	150	46 5N	79 25W
Poway	163	32 58N	117 2W
Powder, R.	158	46 47N	105 12W
Powell	160	44 45N	108 45W
Powell Creek	136	18 6S	133 46E
Powell River	152	49 22N	125 31W
Powers, Mich., U.S.A.	156	45 40N	87 32W
Powers, Oreg., U.S.A.	160	42 53N	124 2W
Powers Lake	158	48 37N	102 38W
Powick	28	52 9N	2 15W
Powis, Vale of	23	52 40N	3 10W
Powys □	31	52 20N	3 20W
P'oyang	109	29 1N	116 38E
Poyang Hu	109	29 10N	116 10E
Poyarkovo	77	49 36N	128 41E
Poyntzpass	38	54 17N	6 22W
Poysdorf	53	48 40N	16 37E
Poza de la Sal	58	42 35N	3 31W
Poza Rica	165	20 33N	97 27W
Pozarevac	66	44 35N	21 18E
Pozega	66	45 21N	17 41E
Pozhva	84	59 5N	56 5E
Poznan	54	52 25N	17 0E
Pozo	163	35 20N	120 24W
Pozo Alcón	59	37 42N	2 56W
Pozo Almonte	174	20 10S	69 50W
Pozoblanco	57	38 23N	4 51W
Pozzallo	65	36 44N	15 40E
Pra, R.	121	5 30N	1 38W
Prabuty	54	53 47N	19 15E
Prača	66	43 47N	18 43E
Prachatice	52	49 1N	14 0E
Prachin Buri	100	14 0N	101 25E
Prachuap Khiri Khan	101	11 49N	99 48E
Pradelles	44	44 46N	3 52E
Pradera	174	3 25N	76 15W
Prades	44	42 38N	2 23E
Prado	171	17 20S	39 13W
Prado del Rey	57	36 48N	5 33W
Præstø	73	55 8N	12 2E
Pragersko	63	46 27N	15 42E
Prague = Praha	52	50 5N	14 22E
Praha	52	50 5N	14 22E
Prahecq	44	46 19N	0 26W
Prahita, R.	97	19 0N	79 55E
Prahova □	70	44 50N	25 50E
Prahova, R.	70	44 50N	25 50E
Prahova, Reg.	70	44 50N	25 50E
Prahovo	66	44 18N	22 39E
Praid	70	46 32N	25 10E
Prainha, Amazonas, Brazil	174	7 10S	60 30W
Prainha, Pará, Brazil	175	1 45S	53 30W
Prairie, Queens., Austral.	138	20 50S	144 35E
Prairie, S. Australia, Austral.	109	34 51S	138 49E
Prairie City	160	45 27N	118 44W
Prairie du Chien	158	43 1N	91 9W
Prairie, R.	159	34 45N	101 15W
Praja	102	8 39S	116 27E
Prajeczno	54	51 10N	19 0E
Pramánda	68	39 32N	21 8E
Pran Buri	100	12 23N	99 55E
Prang	121	8 1N	0 56W
Prapat	102	2 41N	98 58E
Praszka	54	51 32N	18 31E
Prata, Minas Gerais, Brazil	171	19 25S	49 0W
Prata, Pará, Brazil	170	1 10S	47 35W
Prática di Mare	64	41 40N	12 26E
Prato	62	43 53N	11 5E
Prátola Peligna	63	42 7N	13 51E
Pratovécchio	63	43 44N	11 43E
Prats-de-Molló	44	42 25N	2 27E
Pratt	159	37 40N	98 45W
Pratteln	50	47 31N	7 41E
Prättigau	51	46 56N	9 44E
Prattville	157	32 30N	86 28W
Pravara, R.	96	19 30N	74 28E
Pravdinsk	81	56 29N	43 28E
Pravia	56	43 30N	6 12W
Prawle Pt.	30	50 13N	3 41W
Pré-en-Pail	42	48 28N	0 12W
Pré St. Didier	62	45 45N	7 0E
Precordillera	172	30 0S	69 1W
Predáppio	63	44 7N	11 58E
Predazzo	63	46 19N	11 37E
Predejane	66	42 51N	22 9E
Preeceville	153	51 57N	102 40W
Prees	32	52 54N	2 40W
Preesall	32	53 55N	2 58W
Préfailles	42	47 9N	2 11W
Pregonero	174	8 1N	71 46W
Pregrada	63	46 11N	15 45E
Preko	63	44 7N	15 14E
Prelate	153	50 51N	109 24W
Prelog	63	46 18N	16 32E
Premier	152	56 4N	129 56W
Premier Downs	137	30 30S	126 30E
Premont	159	27 19N	91 8W
Premuda, I.	63	44 20N	14 36E
Prenj, mt.	66	43 33N	17 53E
Prenjasi	68	41 6N	20 32E
Prentice	158	45 31N	90 19W
Prenzlau	48	53 19N	13 51E
Prepansko Jezero	68	40 45N	21 0E
Preparis I.	99	14 55N	93 45E
Preparis North Channel	101	15 12N	93 40E
Preparis South Channel	101	14 36N	93 40E
Prerov	53	49 28N	17 27E
Prescot	32	53 27N	2 49W
Prescott, Can.	150	44 45N	75 30W
Prescott, Ariz., U.S.A.	161	34 35N	112 30W
Prescott, Ark., U.S.A.	159	33 49N	93 22W
Preservation Inlet	143	46 8S	166 35E
Preševo	66	42 19N	21 39E
Presho	158	43 56N	100 4W
Preshute	28	51 24N	1 45W
Presicce	65	39 53N	18 13E
Presidencia de la Plaza	172	27 0S	60 0W
Presidencia Roque Sáenz Peña	172	26 45S	60 30W
Presidente Dutra	164	5 15S	44 30W
Presidente Epitácio	171	21 46S	52 6W
Presidente Hayes □	172	24 0S	59 0W
Presidente Hermes	174	11 0S	61 55W
Presidente Prudente	173	22 5S	51 25W
Presidente Rogue Saena Peña	172	34 33S	58 30W
Presidio, Mexico	164	29 29N	104 23W
Presidio, U.S.A.	159	29 30N	104 20W
Preslav	67	43 10N	26 52E
Prespa, L. = Prepansko Jezero	68	40 45N	21 0E
Prespa, mt.	67	41 44N	25 0E
Presque Isle	151	46 40N	68 0W
Prestatyn	31	53 20N	3 24W
Prestea	120	5 22N	2 7W
Presteigne	31	52 17N	3 0W
Preštice	52	49 34N	13 20E
Preston, Borders, U.K.	35	55 48N	2 18W
Preston, Dorset, U.K.	28	50 38N	2 26W
Preston, Lancs., U.K.	32	53 46N	2 42W
Preston, Idaho, U.S.A.	160	42 0N	112 0W
Preston, Minn., U.S.A.	158	43 39N	92 3W
Preston, Nev., U.S.A.	160	38 59N	115 2W
Preston, C.	136	20 51S	116 12E
Prestonpans	35	55 58N	3 0W
Prestwich	32	53 32N	2 18W
Prestwick	34	55 30N	4 38W
Prêto, R., Bahia	170	11 21S	43 52W
Pretoria	129	25 44S	28 12E
Prettyboy Res.	162	39 37N	76 43W
Preuilly-sur-Claise	42	46 51N	0 56E
Préveza	69	38 57N	20 47E
Préveza □	68	39 20N	20 40E
Prey-Veng	101	11 35N	105 29E
Priazovskoye	82	46 22N	35 28E
Pribilov Is.	12	56 0N	170 0W
Priboj	66	43 35N	19 32E
Pribram	52	49 41N	14 2E
Price	160	39 40N	110 48W
Price I.	152	52 23N	128 41W
Prichalnaya	83	48 57N	44 33E
Priego	58	40 38N	2 21W
Priego de Córdoba	57	37 27N	4 12W
Priekule	80	57 27N	21 45E
Prieska	128	29 40S	22 42E
Priest Gully Cr.	108	27 29S	153 11E
Priest L.	160	48 30N	116 55W
Priest River	160	48 11N	117 0W
Priest Valley	163	36 10N	120 39W
Priestly	152	54 8N	125 20W
Prievidza	53	48 46N	18 36E
Prijedor	63	44 58N	16 41E
Prijepolje	66	43 27N	19 40E
Prilep	66	41 21N	21 37E
Priluki	80	50 30N	32 15E
Prime Seal I.	138	40 3S	147 43E
Primeira Cruz	170	2 30S	43 26W
Primorsko	67	42 15N	27 44E
Primorsko-Akhtarsk	82	46 2N	38 10E
Primrose L.	153	54 55N	109 45W
Prince Albert	153	53 15N	105 50W
Prince Albert Nat. Park	153	54 0N	106 25W
Prince Albert Pen.	148	72 30N	116 0W
Prince Alfred C.	12	74 20N	124 40W
Prince Charles I.	149	67 47N	76 12W
Prince Edward I. □.	151	44 2N	77 20W
Prince Edward Is.	11	45 15S	39 0E
Prince Frederick	162	38 33N	76 35W
Prince George	152	53 50N	122 50W
Prince of Wales, C.	147	65 50N	168 0W
Prince of Wales I.	147	73 0N	99 0W
Prince of Wales, I.	147	53 30N	131 30W
Prince of Wales Is.	135	10 40S	142 10E
Prince Patrick I.	12	77 0N	120 0W
Prince Regent Inlet	12	73 0N	90 0W
Prince Rupert	152	54 20N	130 20W
Prince William Sd.	147	60 20N	146 30W
Princenhage	47	51 9N	4 45E
Princes Risborough	29	51 43N	0 50W
Princesa Isabel	170	7 44S	38 0W
Princess Anne	162	38 12N	75 41W
Princess Charlotte B.	138	14 25S	144 0E
Princess Mary Ranges	136	15 30S	125 30E
Princess Royal I.	152	53 0N	128 40W
Princeton, Can.	152	49 27N	120 30W
Princeton, Ill., U.S.A.	158	41 25N	89 25W
Princeton, Ind., U.S.A.	156	38 20N	87 35W
Princeton, Ky., U.S.A.	156	37 6N	87 55W
Princeton, Mo., U.S.A.	158	40 23N	93 35W
Princeton, N.J., U.S.A.	162	40 18N	74 40W
Princeton, W. Va., U.S.A.	156	37 21N	81 8W
Princetown	30	50 33N	4 0W
Principe Chan.	152	53 28N	130 0W
Principe da Beira	174	12 20S	64 30W
Principe, I. de	114	1 37N	7 27E
Prineville	160	44 17N	120 57W
Prins Albert	128	33 12S	22 2E
Prins Harald Kyst	13	70 0S	35 1E
Prinzapolca	166	13 20N	83 35W
Prior, C.	56	43 34N	8 17W
Pripet Marshes = Polesye	80	52 0N	28 10E
Pripet, R. = Pripyat, R.	80	51 30N	30 0E
Pripyat, R.	80	51 30N	30 0E
Prislop, Pasul	70	47 37N	25 15E
Pristen	81	51 15N	12 40E
Priština	66	42 40N	21 13E
Pritchard	157	30 47N	88 5W
Pritzwalk	48	53 10N	12 11E
Privas	45	44 45N	4 37E
Priverno	64	41 29N	13 10E
Privolzhsk	81	57 9N	14 9E
Privolzhskaya Vozvyshennest	81	51 0N	46 0E
Privolzhskiy	81	51 25N	46 3E
Privolzhye	81	52 52N	48 33E
Privutnoye	83	47 12N	43 30E
Prizren	66	42 13N	20 45E
Prizzi	64	37 44N	13 24E
Prnjavor	66	44 52N	17 43E
Probolinggo	103	7 46S	113 13E
Probus	30	50 17N	4 55W
Prochowice	54	51 17N	16 20E

Procida, I Qattâra, Munkhafed el

Procida, I.	**64**	40 46N	14 0E
Proctor	**162**	43 40N	73 2W
Proddatur	**97**	14 45N	78 30E
Proença-a-Nova	**57**	39 45N	7 54W
Profondeville	**47**	50 23N	4 52E
Progreso	**165**	21 20N	89 40W
Prokhladnyy	**83**	43 50N	44 2E
Prokletije	**68**	42 30N	19 45E
Prokopyevsk	**76**	54 0N	87 3E
Prokuplje	**66**	43 16N	21 36E
Proletarskaya	**83**	46 42N	41 50E
Prome = Pyè	**99**	18 45N	95 30E
Prophet, R.	**152**	58 48N	122 40W
Propriá	**170**	10 13S	36 51W
Propriano	**45**	41 41N	8 52E
Proserpine	**138**	20 21S	148 36E
Prospect, Austral.	**109**	34 53S	138 36E
Prospect, U.S.A.	**162**	43 18N	75 9W
Prosser	**160**	46 11N	119 52W
Prostějov	**53**	49 30N	17 9E
Proston	**139**	26 14S	151 32E
Proszowice	**54**	50 13N	20 16E
Protection	**159**	37 16N	99 30W
Próti, I.	**69**	37 5N	21 32E
Provadija	**67**	43 12N	27 30E
Proven	**47**	50 54N	2 40E
Provence	**45**	43 40N	5 46E
Providence, Ky., U.S.A.	**156**	37 25N	87 46W
Providence, R.I., U.S.A.	**162**	41 41N	71 15W
Providence Bay	**150**	45 41N	82 15W
Providence C.	**143**	45 59S	166 29E
Providence Mts.	**161**	35 0N	115 30W
Providencia	**174**	0 28S	76 28W
Providencia, I. de	**166**	13 25N	81 26W
Provideniya	**77**	64 23N	173 18E
Province Wellesley	**101**	5 15N	100 20E
Provincetown	**162**	42 5N	70 11W
Provins	**43**	48 33N	3 15E
Provo	**160**	40 16N	111 37W
Provost	**153**	52 25N	110 20W
Prozor	**66**	43 50N	17 34E
Prudentópolis	**171**	25 12S	50 57W
Prudhoe	**35**	54 57N	1 52W
Prudhoe Bay, Austral.	**138**	21 30S	149 30W
Prudhoe Bay, U.S.A.	**147**	70 20N	148 20W
Prudhoe I.	**138**	21 23S	149 45E
Prudhoe Land	**12**	78 1N	65 0W
Prud'homme	**153**	52 20N	105 54W
Prudnik	**54**	50 20N	17 38E
Prüm	**49**	50 14N	6 22E
Pruszcz	**54**	54 17N	19 40E
Pruszków	**54**	52 9N	20 49E
Prut, R.	**70**	46 3N	28 10E
Prvič, I.	**63**	44 55N	14 47E
Prvomay	**67**	42 8N	25 17E
Prydz B.	**13**	69 0S	74 0E
Pryor	**159**	36 17N	95 20W
Przasnysz	**54**	53 2N	20 45E
Przedbórz	**54**	51 6N	19 53E
Przedecz	**54**	52 20N	18 53E
Przemyśl	**54**	49 50N	22 45E
Przemyśl □	**54**	80 0N	23 0E
Przeworsk	**54**	50 6N	22 32E
Przewóz	**54**	51 28N	14 57E
Przhevalsk	**85**	42 30N	78 20E
Przysucha	**54**	51 22N	20 38E
Psakhná	**69**	38 34N	23 35E
Psará, I.	**69**	38 37N	25 38E
Psathoúra, I.	**68**	39 30N	24 12E
Psel, R.	**82**	49 25N	33 50E
Pserimos, I.	**69**	36 56N	27 12E
Pskem, R.	**85**	41 38N	70 1E
Pskemskiy Khrebet	**85**	42 0N	70 45E
Pskent	**85**	40 54N	69 20E
Pskov	**80**	57 50N	28 25E
Psunj, mt.	**66**	45 25N	17 19E
Pszczyna	**54**	49 59N	18 58E
Pteleón	**69**	39 3N	22 57E
Ptich, R.	**80**	52 30N	28 45E
Ptolemais	**68**	40 30N	21 43E
Ptuj	**63**	46 28N	15 50E
Ptujska Gora	**63**	46 23N	15 47E
Pua	**100**	19 11N	100 55E
Puán	**172**	37 30S	63 0W
P'uan	**108**	25 47N	104 57E
Puan	**107**	35 44N	126 7E
Pubnico	**151**	43 47N	65 50W
Pucallpa	**174**	8 25S	74 30W
P'uchen	**107**	37 21N	118 1E
P'uch'eng	**109**	27 45N	118 47E
Pucheni	**70**	45 12N	25 17E
P'uch'i	**109**	29 43N	113 53E
Pucisce	**63**	43 22N	16 43E
Puck	**54**	54 45N	18 23E
Puddletown	**28**	50 45N	2 21W
Pudsey	**33**	53 47N	1 40W
Pudukkottai	**97**	10 28N	78 47E
Puebla	**165**	19 0N	98 10W
Puebla □	**165**	18 30N	98 0W
Puebla de Alcocer	**57**	38 59N	5 14W
Puebla de Don Fadrique	**59**	37 58N	2 25W
Puebla de Don Rodrigo	**57**	39 5N	4 37W
Puebla de Guzmán	**57**	37 37N	7 15W
Puebla de los Infantes, La	**57**	37 47N	5 24W
Puebla de Montalbán, La	**56**	39 52N	4 22W
Puebla de Sanabria	**56**	42 4N	6 38W
Puebla de Trives	**56**	42 20N	7 10W
Puebla del Caramiñal	**56**	42 37N	8 56W
Puebla, La	**58**	39 50N	3 0E
Pueblo	**158**	38 20N	104 40W
Pueblo Bonito	**161**	36 4N	107 57W
Pueblo Hundido	**172**	26 20S	69 30W
Pueblo Nuevo	**174**	8 26N	71 26W
Pueblonuevo	**55**	38 16N	5 16W
Puelches	**172**	38 5S	66 0W
Puelén	**172**	37 32S	67 38W
Puente Alto	**172**	33 32S	70 35W
Puente del Arzobispo	**56**	39 48N	5 10W
Puente Genil	**57**	37 22N	4 47W
Puente la Reina	**58**	42 40N	1 49W
Puentearas	**56**	42 10N	8 28W
Puentedeume	**56**	43 24N	8 10W
Puentes de García Rodríguez	**56**	43 27N	7 51W
Puerco, R.	**161**	35 10N	109 45W
Puerh	**105**	23 11N	100 56E
P'uerh	**108**	23 5N	101 5E
Puerhching	**105**	47 43N	86 53E
Puerta, La	**59**	38 22N	2 45W
Puerto Aisén	**176**	45 10S	73 0W
Puerto Angel	**165**	15 40N	96 29W
Puerto Arista	**165**	15 56N	93 48W
Puerto Armuelles	**166**	8 20N	83 10W
Puerto Ayacucho	**174**	5 40N	67 35W
Puerto Barrios	**166**	15 40N	88 40W
Puerto Bermejo	**172**	26 55S	58 34W
Puerto Bermúdez	**174**	10 20S	75 0W
Puerto Bolívar	**174**	3 10S	79 55W
Puerto Cabello	**174**	10 28N	68 1W
Puerto Cabezas	**166**	14 0N	83 30W
Puerto Cabo Gracias a Dios	**166**	15 0N	83 10W
Puerto Capaz = Jebba	**118**	35 11N	4 43W
Puerto Carreño	**174**	6 12N	67 22W
Puerto Casado	**172**	22 19S	57 56W
Puerto Castilla	**166**	16 0N	86 0W
Puerto Chicama	**174**	7 45S	79 20W
Puerto Coig	**176**	50 54S	69 15W
Puerto Columbia	**174**	10 59N	74 58W
Puerto Cortés, C. Rica	**166**	8 20N	82 20W
Puerto Cortés, Hond.	**166**	15 51N	88 0W
Puerto Cuemani	**174**	0 5N	73 21W
Puerto Cumarebo	**174**	11 29N	69 21W
Puerto de Cabras	**116**	28 40N	13 30W
Puerto de Morelos	**165**	20 49N	86 52W
Puerto de Santa María	**57**	36 36N	6 13W
Puerto Deseado	**176**	47 45S	66 0W
Puerto Heath	**174**	12 25S	68 45W
Puerto Huitoto	**174**	0 18N	74 3W
Puerto Juárez	**165**	21 11N	86 49W
Puerto La Cruz	**174**	10 13N	64 38W
Puerto Leguízamo	**174**	0 12S	74 46W
Puerto Libertad	**164**	29 55N	112 41W
Puerto Limón, Meta, Colomb.	**174**	3 23N	73 30W
Puerto Limón, Putumayo, Colomb.	**174**	1 3N	76 30W
Puerto Lobos	**176**	42 0S	65 3W
Puerto López	**174**	4 5N	72 58W
Puerto Lumbreras	**59**	37 34N	1 48W
Puerto Madryn	**176**	42 48S	65 4W
Puerto Maldonado	**174**	12 30S	69 10W
Puerto Manotí	**166**	21 22N	76 50W
Puerto Mazarrón	**59**	37 34N	1 15W
Puerto Mercedes	**174**	1 11N	72 53W
Puerto Montt	**176**	41 22S	72 40W
Puerto Natales	**176**	51 45S	72 25W
Puerto Nuevo	**174**	5 53N	69 56W
Puerto Ordaz	**174**	8 16N	62 44W
Puerto Padre	**166**	21 13N	76 35W
Puerto Páez	**174**	6 13N	67 28W
Puerto Peñasco	**164**	31 20N	113 33W
Puerto Pinasco	**172**	22 43S	57 50W
Puerto Pirámides	**176**	42 35S	64 20W
Puerto Plata	**167**	19 40N	70 45W
Puerto Princesa	**94**	9 44N	118 44E
Puerto Quellón	**176**	43 7S	73 37W
Puerto Quepos	**166**	9 29N	84 6W
Puerto Real	**57**	36 33N	6 12W
Puerto Rico	**174**	1 54N	75 10W
Puerto Rico ■	**147**	18 15N	66 45W
Puerto Rico Trough	**14**	20 0N	63 0W
Puerto Sastre	**172**	22 25S	57 55W
Puerto Suárez	**174**	18 58S	57 52W
Puerto Tejada	**174**	3 14N	76 24W
Puerto Umbria	**174**	0 52N	76 33W
Puerto Vallarta	**164**	20 26N	105 15W
Puerto Villamizar	**174**	8 25N	72 30W
Puerto Wilches	**174**	7 21N	73 54W
Puertollano	**57**	38 43N	4 7W
Puertomarín	**56**	42 48N	7 37W
Pueyrredón, L.	**176**	47 20S	72 0W
Puffin I., Ireland	**39**	51 50N	10 25W
Puffin I., U.K.	**31**	53 19N	4 1W
Pugachev	**81**	52 0N	48 55E
Puge	**126**	4 45S	33 11E
Puget Sd.	**160**	47 15N	123 30W
Puget-Théniers	**45**	43 58N	6 53E
Púglia	**65**	41 0N	16 30E
Pugŏdong	**107**	42 5N	130 0E
Pugu	**126**	6 55S	39 4E
Puha	**142**	38 30S	177 50E
P'uhsien	**106**	36 25N	110 4E
Puhute Mesa	**163**	37 25N	116 50W
Pui	**70**	45 30N	23 4E
Puieşti	**70**	46 25N	27 33E
Puig Mayor, Mte.	**58**	39 49N	2 47E
Puigcerdá	**58**	42 24N	1 50E
Puigmal, Mt.	**58**	42 23N	2 7E
Puisaye, Collines de	**43**	47 34N	3 28E
Puiseaux	**43**	48 11N	2 30E
Pujon-chosuji	**107**	40 35N	127 35E
Puka	**68**	42 2N	19 53E
Pukaki L.	**143**	44 4S	170 1E
Pukatawagan	**153**	55 45N	101 20W
Pukchin	**107**	40 12N	125 45E
Pukchŏng	**107**	40 14N	128 18E
Pukearuhe	**142**	38 55S	174 31E
Pukekohe	**142**	37 12S	174 55E
Puketeraki Ra.	**143**	42 58S	172 13E
Pukeuri	**143**	45 4S	171 2E
P'uko	**108**	27 27N	102 34E
Pukoo	**147**	21 4N	156 48W
P'uk'ou	**109**	32 7N	118 43E
Pula	**64**	39 0N	9 0E
Pula (Pola)	**63**	44 54N	13 57E
Pulaski, N.Y., U.S.A.	**162**	43 32N	76 9W
Pulaski, Tenn., U.S.A.	**157**	35 10N	87 0W
Pulaski, Va., U.S.A.	**156**	37 4N	80 49W
Pulawy	**54**	51 23N	21 59E
Pulborough	**29**	50 58N	0 30W
Pulgaon	**96**	20 44N	78 21E
Pulham Market	**29**	52 25N	1 15E
Pulham St. Mary	**29**	52 25N	1 14E
Pulicat, L.	**97**	13 40N	80 15E
Puliyangudi	**97**	9 11N	77 24E
Pullabooka	**141**	33 44S	147 46E
Pullen Cr.	**108**	27 33S	152 54E
Pullman	**160**	46 49N	117 10W
Pulmakong	**121**	11 2N	0 2E
Pulog, Mt.	**103**	16 40N	120 50E
Puloraja	**102**	4 55N	95 24E
Pultusk	**54**	52 43N	21 6E
Pumlumon Fawr	**31**	52 29N	3 47W
Pumpsaint	**31**	52 3N	3 58W
Puna	**174**	19 45S	65 28W
Puna de Atacama	**172**	25 0S	67 0W
Puná, I.	**174**	2 55S	80 5W
Punakha	**98**	27 42N	89 52E
Punalur	**97**	9 0N	76 56E
Punasar	**94**	27 6N	73 6E
Punata	**174**	17 25S	65 50W
Punch	**95**	33 48N	74 4E
Pune	**96**	18 29N	73 57E
Pungsan	**107**	40 50N	128 9E
P'uning	**109**	23 19N	116 9E
Punjab □	**94**	31 0N	76 0E
Punkatawagon	**153**	55 44N	101 20W
Puno	**174**	15 55S	70 3W
Punt, La	**51**	46 35N	9 56E
Punta Alta	**176**	38 53S	62 4W
Punta Arenas	**176**	53 0S	71 0W
Punta de Díaz	**172**	28 0S	70 45W
Punta de Piedras	**174**	10 54N	64 6W
Punta del Lago Viedma	**176**	49 45S	72 0W
Punta Gorda, Belize	**165**	16 10N	88 45W
Punta Gorda, U.S.A.	**157**	26 55N	82 0W
Punta Prieta	**164**	28 58N	114 17W
Puntabie	**139**	32 12S	134 5E
Puntarenas	**166**	10 0N	84 50W
Puntes de García Rodríguez	**56**	43 27N	7 50W
Punto Fijo	**174**	11 42N	70 13W
Punxsutawney	**156**	40 56N	79 0W
P'upei	**108**	22 16N	109 33E
Puquio	**174**	14 45S	74 10W
Pur, R.	**76**	65 30N	77 40E
Purace, vol.	**174**	2 21N	76 23W
Puračić	**66**	44 33N	18 28E
Purari, R.	**135**	7 49S	145 0E
Purbeck, Isle of	**28**	50 40N	2 5W
Purcell	**159**	35 0N	97 25W
Purchena Tetica	**59**	37 21N	2 21W
Purdy Is.	**138**	3 0S	146 0E
Purfleet	**29**	51 29N	0 15E
Puri	**96**	19 50N	85 58E
Purificación	**174**	3 51N	74 55W
Purísima, La	**164**	26 10N	112 4W
Purley	**28**	51 29N	1 4W
Purli	**96**	18 50N	76 35E
Purmerend	**47**	52 30N	4 58E
Purna, R.	**96**	19 55N	76 20E
Purnea	**95**	25 45N	87 31E
Pursat	**101**	12 34N	103 50E
Puruey	**174**	7 35N	64 48W
Purukcahu	**102**	0 35S	114 35E
Purulia	**95**	23 17N	86 33E
Purus, R.	**174**	5 25S	64 0W
Purwakarta	**103**	6 35S	107 29E
Purwodadi, Jawa, Indon.	**103**	7 7S	110 55E
Purwodadi, Jawa, Indon.	**103**	7 51S	110 0E
Purworejo	**103**	7 43S	110 2E
Puryong	**107**	42 0N	129 43E
Pus, R.	**96**	19 50N	77 45E
Pusad	**96**	19 56N	77 36E
Pusan	**107**	35 5N	129 0E
Pushchino	**77**	54 20N	158 10E
Pushkin	**80**	59 45N	30 25E
Pushkino	**81**	51 16N	47 9E
Puskitamika L.	**150**	49 20N	76 30W
Püspökladány	**53**	47 19N	21 6E
Pussa	**129**	24 30S	33 55E
Pustoshka	**80**	56 11N	29 30E
Puszczykowo	**54**	52 18N	16 49E
Putahow L.	**153**	59 54N	100 40W
Putao	**98**	27 28N	97 30E
Putaruru	**142**	38 2S	175 50E
Putbus	**48**	54 19N	13 29E
Put'ehach'i	**105**	48 0N	122 43E
Puţeni	**70**	45 49N	27 42E
Puthein Myit, R.	**99**	15 56N	94 18E
P'ut'ien	**109**	25 27N	118 59E
Putignano	**65**	40 50N	17 5E
P'uting	**108**	26 19N	105 45E
Putlitz	**48**	53 15N	12 3E
Putna	**70**	47 50N	25 33E
Putna, R.	**70**	45 42N	27 26E
Putnam	**162**	41 55N	71 55W
Putnok	**53**	48 18N	20 26E
P'ut'o	**109**	29 58N	122 15E
Putorana, Gory	**77**	69 0N	95 0E
Putorino	**142**	39 4S	177 9E
Putta	**47**	51 4N	4 38E
Puttalam	**93**	8 1N	79 55E
Puttalam Lagoon	**97**	8 15N	79 45E
Putte	**47**	51 22N	4 24E
Putten	**46**	52 16N	5 36E
Puttgarden	**48**	54 28N	11 15E
Puttur	**97**	12 46N	75 12E
Putty	**141**	32 57S	150 42E
Putumayo □	**174**	1 30S	70 0W
Putumayo, R.	**174**	1 30S	70 0W
Putussibau, G.	**102**	0 45N	113 50E
Pututahi	**142**	38 39S	177 53E
Puurs	**47**	51 5N	4 17E
Puy-de-Dôme	**44**	45 46N	2 57E
Puy-de-Dôme □	**44**	45 47N	3 0E
Puy-de-Sancy	**44**	45 32N	2 41E
Puy Guillaume	**44**	45 57N	3 28E
Puy, Le	**44**	45 3N	3 52E
Puy l'Evêque	**44**	44 31N	1 9E
Puyallup	**160**	47 10N	122 22W
P'uyang	**106**	35 41N	115 0E
Puylaurens	**44**	43 35N	2 0E
Puyôo	**44**	43 33N	0 56W
Pwalagu	**121**	10 38N	0 50W
Pwani □, Tanz.	**126**	7 0S	39 0E
Pwani □, Tanz.	**126**	7 0S	39 30E
Pweto	**127**	8 25S	28 51E
Pwinbyu	**98**	20 23N	94 40E
Pwllheli	**31**	52 54N	4 26W
Pya Ozero	**78**	66 8N	31 22E
Pyana, R.	**81**	55 30N	45 0E
Pyandzh	**85**	37 14N	69 6E
Pyandzh, R.	**85**	37 6N	68 20E
Pyapon	**98**	16 5N	95 50E
Pyasina, R.	**77**	72 30N	90 30E
Pyatigorsk	**83**	44 2N	43 0E
Pyatikhatki	**82**	48 28N	33 38E
Pyaye	**98**	19 12N	95 10E
Pyè	**98**	18 49N	95 13E
Pyinbauk	**98**	19 10N	95 12E
Pyinmana	**98**	19 45N	96 20E
Pyŏktong	**107**	40 37N	125 26E
Pyŏnggang	**107**	38 24N	127 17E
Pyŏngtaek	**107**	37 1N	127 4E
P'yŏngyang	**107**	39 0N	125 45E
Pyote	**159**	31 34N	103 5W
Pyramid L.	**160**	40 0N	119 30W
Pyramid Pk.	**163**	36 25N	116 37W
Pyramids	**122**	29 58N	31 9E
Pyrenees	**44**	42 45N	0 18E
Pyrénées-Atlantiques □	**44**	43 15N	1 0W
Pyrénées-Orientales □	**44**	42 35N	2 26E
Pyrzyce	**54**	53 10N	14 55E
Pyshchug	**81**	58 57N	45 27E
Pyshma, R.	**84**	57 8N	66 18E
Pytalovo	**80**	57 5N	27 55E
Python	**127**	17 56S	29 10E
Pyttegga	**71**	62 13N	7 42E
Pyu	**98**	18 30N	96 35E
Pyzdry	**54**	52 11N	17 42E

Q

Qaar Zeitun	**122**	29 10N	25 48E
Qabalon	**90**	32 8N	35 17E
Qabatiya	**90**	32 25N	35 16E
Qadam	**93**	32 55N	66 45E
Qadhimah	**92**	22 20N	39 13E
Qadian	**94**	31 51N	74 19E
Qal at Shajwa	**122**	25 2N	38 57E
Qala-i-Jadid (Spin Baldak)	**94**	31 1N	66 25E
Qala-i-Kirta	**93**	32 15N	63 0E
Qala Nau	**93**	35 0N	63 5E
Qala Punja	**93**	37 0N	72 40E
Qala Yangi	**94**	34 20N	66 30E
Qal'at al Akhdhar	**92**	28 0N	37 10E
Qal'at Saura	**122**	26 10N	38 40E
Qal'eh Shaharak	**93**	34 10N	64 20E
Qalqīlya	**90**	32 12N	34 58E
Qalyûb	**122**	30 12N	31 11E
Qam	**90**	32 36N	35 43E
Qamar, Ghubbat al	**91**	16 20N	52 30E
Qamruddin Karez	**94**	31 45N	68 20E
Qana	**90**	33 12N	35 17E
Qâra	**122**	29 38N	26 30E
Qara Qash, R.	**95**	35 45N	78 45E
Qara Tagh La = Kala Shank'ou	**95**	35 42N	78 20E
Qarachuk	**92**	37 0N	42 2E
Qarah	**92**	29 55N	40 3E
Qardud	**123**	10 20N	29 56E
Qarrasa	**123**	14 38N	32 5E
Qarsa	**123**	9 28N	41 48E
Qaşr Bū Hadi	**119**	31 1N	16 45E
Qasr-e-Qand	**93**	26 15N	60 45E
Qasr Farâfra	**122**	27 0N	28 1E
Qastina	**90**	31 44N	34 45E
Qatar ■	**93**	25 30N	51 15E
Qattâra	**122**	30 12N	27 3E
Qattara Depression = Q. Munkhafed el	**122**	29 30N	27 30E
Qattâra, Munkhafed el	**122**	29 30N	27 30E

Qayen Rancharia

Qayen 93 33 40N 59 10 E
Qazvin 92 36 15N 50 0 E
Qena 122 26 10N 32 43 E
Qena, Wadi 122 26 57N 32 50 E
Qendrevca 68 40 20N 19 48 E
Qesari 90 32 30N 34 53 E
Qeshm 93 26 55N 56 10 E
Qeshm, I. 93 26 50N 56 0 E
Qila Safed 93 29 0N 61 30 E
Qila Saifulla 94 30 45N 68 17 E
Qiryat 'Anivim 90 31 49N 35 7 E
Qiryat Bialik 90 32 50N 35 5 E
Qiryat 'Eqron 90 31 52N 34 49 E
Qiryat Hayyim 90 32 49N 35 4 E
Qiryat Shemona 90 33 13N 35 35 E
Qiryat Yam 90 32 51N 35 4 E
Qishon, R. 90 32 42N 35 7 E
Qishran 122 20 14N 40 2 E
Qizan 123 16 57N 42 34 E
Qom 93 34 40N 51 0 E
Quabbin Res. 162 42 17N 72 21W
Quabbo 123 12 2N 39 56 E
Quackenbrück 48 52 40N 7 59 E
Quadring 33 52 53N 0 9W
Quainton 29 51 51N 0 53W
Quairading 137 32 0 S 117 21 E
Quakerstown 162 40 27N 75 20W
Qualeup 137 33 48 S 116 48 E
Quambatook 138 35 49 S 143 34 E
Quambone 141 30 57 S 147 53 E
Quan Long 101 9 7N 105 8 E
Quanan 159 34 20N 99 45W
Quandialla 141 34 1 S 147 47 E
Quang Nam 101 15 55N 108 15 E
Quang Ngai 101 15 13N 108 58 E
Quang Yen 100 21 3N 106 52 E
Quantock Hills, The 28 51 8N 3 10W
Quaraí 172 30 15 S 56 20W
Quarré les Tombes 43 47 21N 4 0 E
Quarryville 162 39 54N 76 10W
Quartu Sant' Elena 64 39 15N 9 10 E
Quartzsite 161 33 44N 114 16W
Quatsino 152 50 30N 127 40W
Quatsino Sd. 152 50 42N 127 58W
Qubab = Mishmar Aiyalon 90 31 52N 34 57 E
Qūchān 93 37 10N 58 27 E
Que Que 127 18 58 S 29 48 E
Queanbeyan 141 35 17 S 149 14 E
Québec 151 46 52N 71 13W
Québec □ 151 50 0N 70 0W
Quedlinburg 48 51 47N 11 9 E
Queen Alexandra Ra. 13 85 0 S 170 0 E
Queen Anne 162 38 55N 75 57W
Queen Bess Mt. 152 51 13N 124 35W
Queen Charlotte 152 53 15N 132 2W
Queen Charlotte Is. 152 53 20N 132 10W
Queen Charlotte Sd. 143 41 10 S 174 15 E
Queen Charlotte Str. 152 51 0N 128 0W
Queen Elizabeth Is. 10 78 0N 95 0W
Queen Elizabeth Nat. Pk. 126 0 0 S 30 0 E
Queen Mary Coast 13 70 0 S 95 0 E
Queen Maud G. 148 68 15N 102 30W
Queenborough 29 51 24N 0 46 E
Queen's Chan. 136 15 0 S 129 30 E
Queensbury 32 53 46N 1 50W
Queenscliff 138 38 16 S 144 39 E
Queensferry 35 56 0N 3 25W
Queensland □ 138 15 0 S 142 0 E
Queenstown, Austral. 138 42 4 S 145 35 E
Queenstown, N.Z. 143 45 1 S 168 40 E
Queenstown, S. Afr. 125 31 52 S 26 52 E
Queguay Grande, R. 172 32 9 S 58 9W
Queimadas 170 11 0 S 39 38W
Quela 124 9 10 S 16 56 E
Quelimane 127 17 53 S 36 58 E
Quemado, N. Mex., U.S.A. 161 34 17N 108 28W
Quemado, Tex., U.S.A. 159 28 58N 100 35W
Quemoy, I. = Chinmen Tao, I. 109 24 25N 118 25 E
Quemú-Quemú 172 36 3 S 63 36W
Quendale, B. of 36 59 53N 1 20W
Quequén 172 38 30 S 58 30W
Querein 123 13 30N 34 50 E
Querétaro 164 20 40N 100 23W
Querétaro □ 164 20 30N 100 30W
Querfurt 48 51 22N 11 33 E
Quesada 59 37 51N 3 4W
Quesnel 152 53 5N 122 30W
Quesnel L. 152 52 30N 121 20W
Quesnel, R. 152 52 58N 122 29W
Quest, Pte. 151 49 52N 64 40W
Questa 161 36 45N 105 35W
Questembert 42 47 40N 2 28W
Quetico 150 48 45N 90 55W
Quetico Prov. Park 150 48 30N 91 45W
Quetta 93 30 15N 66 55 E
Quetta □ 93 30 15N 66 55 E
Quezaltenango 166 14 40N 91 30W
Quezon City 103 14 38N 121 0 E
Qui Nhon 101 13 40N 109 13 E
Quiaca, La 172 22 5 S 65 35W
Quibaxi 124 8 24 S 14 27 E
Quibdó 174 5 42N 76 40W
Quiberon 42 47 29N 3 9W
Quibor 174 9 56N 69 37W
Quick 152 54 36N 126 54W
Quickborn 48 53 42N 9 52 E
Quiet L. 152 61 5N 133 5W
Quiévrain 47 50 24N 3 41 E
Quiindy 172 25 58 S 57 14W
Quila 164 24 23N 107 13W
Quilán, C. 176 43 15 S 74 30W
Quilengues 125 14 12 S 14 12 E
Quilimarí 172 32 5 S 70 30W
Quilino 172 30 14 S 64 29W
Quillabamba 174 12 50 S 72 50W
Quillagua 172 21 40 S 69 40W
Quillaicillo 172 31 17 S 71 40W
Quillan 44 42 53N 2 10 E
Quillebeuf 42 49 28N 0 30 E
Quillota 172 32 54 S 71 16W
Quilmes 172 34 43 S 58 15W
Quilon 97 8 50N 76 38 E
Quilpie 139 26 35 S 144 11 E
Quilpué 172 33 5 S 71 33W
Quilty 39 52 50N 9 27W
Quilua 127 16 17 S 39 54 E
Quimilí 172 27 40 S 62 30W
Quimper 42 48 0N 4 9W
Quimperlé 42 47 53N 3 33W
Quin 39 52 50N 8 52W
Quinag 36 58 13N 5 5W
Quincy, Calif., U.S.A. 160 39 56N 121 0W
Quincy, Fla., U.S.A. 157 30 34N 84 34W
Quincy, Ill., U.S.A. 158 39 55N 91 20W
Quincy, Mass., U.S.A. 162 42 14N 71 0W
Quincy, Wash., U.S.A. 160 47 22N 119 56W
Quines 172 32 13 S 65 48W
Quinga 127 15 49 S 40 15 E
Quingey 43 47 7N 5 52 E
Quinhagak 147 59 45N 162 0W
Quintana de la Serena 57 38 45N 5 40W
Quintana Roo □ 165 19 0N 88 0W
Quintanar de la Orden 58 39 36N 3 5W
Quintanar de la Sierra 58 41 57N 2 55W
Quintanar del Rey 59 39 21N 1 56W
Quintero 172 32 45 S 71 30W
Quintin 42 48 26N 2 56W
Quinto 58 41 25N 0 32W
Quinyambie 139 30 15 S 141 0 E
Quípar, R. 59 37 58N 2 3W
Quirihue 172 36 15 S 72 35W
Quirindi 141 31 28 S 150 40 E
Quiriquire 174 9 59N 63 13W
Quiroga 56 42 28N 7 18W
Quirpon I. 151 51 32N 55 28W
Quisiro 174 10 53N 71 17W
Quissac 45 43 55N 4 0 E
Quissanga 127 12 24 S 40 28 E
Quitilipi 172 26 50 S 60 13W
Quitman, Ga., U.S.A. 157 30 49N 83 35W
Quitman, Miss., U.S.A. 157 32 2N 88 42W
Quitman, Tex., U.S.A. 159 32 48N 95 25W
Quito 174 0 15 S 78 35W
Quixadá 170 4 55 S 39 0W
Quixaxe 127 15 17 S 40 4 E
Quixeramobim 170 5 12 S 39 17W
Qul'ân, Jazâ'ir 122 24 22N 35 31 E
Qumran 90 31 43N 35 27 E
Quneitra 90 33 7N 35 48 E
Quoich L. 36 57 4N 5 20W
Quoile, R. 38 54 21N 5 40W
Quoin I. 136 14 54 S 129 32 E
Quoin Pt., N.Z. 143 46 19 S 170 11 E
Quoin Pt., S. Afr. 128 34 46 S 19 37 E
Quondong 140 33 6 S 140 18 E
Quorn, Austral. 140 32 25 S 138 0 E
Quorn, Can. 150 49 25N 90 55W
Quorndon 28 52 45N 1 10W
Qûs 122 25 55N 32 50 E
Quseir 122 26 7N 34 16 E
Qusra 90 32 5N 35 20 E
Quthing 129 30 25 S 27 36 E
Quynh Nhai 100 21 49N 103 33 E
Qytet Stalin (Kuçove) 68 40 47N 19 57 E

R

Ra, Ko 101 9 13N 98 16 E
Raa. 73 56 0N 12 45 E
Råa. 73 56 0N 12 45 E
Raahana 90 32 12N 34 52 E
Raahe 74 64 40N 24 28 E
Raalte 46 52 23N 6 16 E
Raamsdonksveer 47 51 43N 4 52 E
Raasay I. 36 57 25N 6 4W
Raasay, Sd. of 36 57 30N 6 8W
Rab 63 44 45N 14 45 E
Rab, I. 63 44 45N 14 45 E
Raba 103 8 36 S 118 55 E
Rába, R. 54 47 38N 17 38 E
Rabaçal, R. 56 41 41N 7 15W
Rabah 121 13 5N 5 30 E
Rabai 126 3 50 S 39 31 E
Rabaraba 135 9 58 S 149 49 E
Rabastens 44 43 50N 1 43 E
Rabastens, Hautes Pyrénées 44 43 25N 0 10 E
Rabat 118 34 2N 6 48W
Rabaul 135 4 24 S 152 18 E
Rabbalshede 73 58 40N 11 27 E
Rabbit L. 153 47 0N 79 38W
Rabbit Lake 153 53 8N 107 46W
Rabbit, R. 152 59 41N 127 12W
Rabbitskin, R. 152 61 47N 120 42W
Rabigh 92 22 50N 39 5 E
Rabka 54 49 37N 19 59 E
Rača 66 44 14N 21 0 E
Rácale 65 39 57N 18 6 E
Racalmuto 64 37 25N 13 41 E
Racconigi 62 44 47N 7 41 E
Race, C. 151 46 40N 53 5W
Raceview 108 27 38 S 152 47 E
Rach Gia 101 10 5N 105 5 E
Raciaz 54 52 46N 20 10 E
Racibórz (Ratibor) 54 50 7N 18 18 E
Racine 156 42 41N 87 51W
Rackheath 29 52 41N 1 22 E
Rackwick 37 58 52N 3 23W
Radama, Îs. 129 14 0 S 47 47 E
Radama, Presqu'île d' 129 14 16 S 47 53 E
Radan, mt. 66 42 59N 21 29 E
Radbuza, R. 52 49 35N 13 5 E
Radcliffe, Gr. Manch., U.K. 32 53 35N 2 19W
Radcliffe, Notts., U.K. 33 52 57N 1 3W
Rade 71 59 21N 10 53 E
Radeburg 48 51 6N 13 45 E
Radeče 63 46 5N 15 14 E
Radekhov 80 50 25N 24 32 E
Radford 156 37 8N 80 32W
Radhanpur 94 23 50N 71 38 E
Radika, R. 66 41 38N 20 37 E
Radisson 153 52 30N 107 20W
Radium Hill 133 32 30 S 140 42 E
Radium Hot Springs 152 50 48N 116 12W
Radkow 54 50 30N 16 24 E
Radley 28 51 42N 1 14W
Radlin 54 50 3N 18 29 E
Radna 66 46 7N 21 41 E
Radnevo 67 42 17N 25 58 E
Radnice 52 49 51N 13 35 E
Radnor (□) 26 52 20N 3 20W
Radnor Forest 31 52 17N 3 10W
Radom 54 51 23N 21 12 E
Radom □ 54 51 30N 21 0 E
Radomir 66 42 37N 23 4 E
Radomsko 54 51 5N 19 28 E
Radomyshl 80 50 30N 29 12 E
Radomysl Wielki 54 50 14N 21 15 E
Radoszyce 54 51 4N 20 15 E
Radoviš 66 41 38N 22 28 E
Radovljica 63 46 22N 14 12 E
Radöy I. 71 60 40N 4 55 E
Radstadt 52 47 24N 13 28 E
Radstock 28 51 17N 2 25W
Radstock, C. 139 33 12 S 134 20 E
Raduša 66 42 7N 21 15 E
Radviliškis 80 55 49N 23 33 E
Radville 153 49 30N 104 15W
Radymno 54 49 59N 22 52 E
Radyr 31 51 32N 3 16W
Radzanów 54 52 56N 20 8 E
Radziejów 54 52 40N 18 30 E
Radzyn Chełminski 54 53 23N 18 55 E
Rae 152 62 50N 116 3W
Rae Bareli 95 26 18N 81 20 E
Rae Isthmus 149 66 40N 87 30W
Raeside, L. 137 29 20 S 122 0 E
Raetihi 142 39 25 S 175 17 E
Rafaela 172 31 10 S 61 30W
Rafah 122 31 18N 34 14 E
Rafai 126 4 59N 23 58 E
Raffadali 64 37 23N 13 29 E
Rafhā 92 29 35N 43 35 E
Rafid 90 32 57N 35 52 E
Rafsanjān 93 30 30N 56 5 E
Raft Pt. 136 16 4 S 124 26 E
Ragag 123 10 59N 24 40 E
Ragama 97 7 0N 79 50 E
Ragged Mt. 137 33 27 S 123 25 E
Raglan, Austral. 138 23 42 S 150 49 E
Raglan, N.Z. 142 37 55 S 174 55 E
Raglan, U.K. 31 51 46N 2 51W
Ragueneau 151 49 11N 68 18W
Ragunda 72 63 6N 16 23 E
Ragusa 65 36 56N 14 42 E
Raha 103 8 20 S 118 40 E
Rahad el Berdi 117 11 20N 23 40 E
Rahad, Nahr er 123 12 40N 35 30 E
Rahden 48 52 26N 8 36 E
Raheita 123 12 46N 43 4 E
Raheng = Tak 100 17 5N 99 10 E
Rahimyar Khan 94 28 30N 70 25 E
Rahotu 142 39 20 S 173 49 E
Raichur 96 16 10N 77 20 E
Raiganj 95 25 37N 88 10 E
Raigarh, Madhya Pradesh, India 96 21 56N 83 25 E
Raigarh, Orissa, India 96 19 51N 82 6 E
Raiis 92 23 33N 38 43 E
Raijua 103 10 37 S 121 36 E
Railton 138 41 25 S 146 28 E
Rainbow 140 35 55 S 142 0 E
Rainbow Lake 152 58 30N 119 23W
Rainham 29 51 22N 0 36 E
Rainier 160 46 4N 123 0W
Rainier, Mt. 160 46 50N 121 50W
Rainworth 33 53 8N 1 6W
Rainy L. 153 48 30N 92 30W
Rainy River 153 48 50N 94 30W
Raipur 96 21 17N 81 45 E
Raith 150 48 50N 90 0W
Raj Nandgaon 99 21 0N 81 0 E
Raja Empat, Kepulauan 103 0 30 S 129 40 E
Raja-Jooseppi 74 68 28N 28 29 E
Raja, Ujung 102 3 40N 96 25 E
Rajahmundry 96 17 1N 81 48 E
Rajang, R. 102 2 30N 113 30 E
Rajapalaiyarm 97 9 25N 77 35 E
Rajasthan □ 94 26 45N 73 30 E
Rajasthan Canal 94 30 31N 71 0 E
Rajauri 95 33 25N 74 21 E
Rajbari 98 23 47N 89 41 E
Rajgarh, Mad. P., India 94 24 2N 76 45 E
Rajgarh, Raj., India 94 28 40N 75 25 E
Rajgród 54 53 42N 22 42 E
Rajhenburg 63 46 1N 15 29 E
Rajkot 94 22 15N 70 56 E
Rajmahal Hills 95 24 30N 87 30 E
Rajnandgaon 96 21 5N 81 5 E
Rajojooseppi 74 68 25N 28 30 E
Rajpipla 96 21 50N 73 30 E
Rajpura 94 30 32N 76 32 E
Rajshahi 98 24 22N 88 39 E
Rajshahi □ 95 25 0N 89 0 E
Rakaia 143 43 45 S 172 1 E
Rakaia, R. 143 43 26 S 171 47 E
Rakan, Ras 93 26 10N 51 20 E
Rakaposhi 95 36 10N 74 0 E
Rakaposhi, mt. 93 36 20N 74 30 E
Rakha 122 18 25N 41 30 E
Rakhni 94 30 4N 69 56 E
Rakitovo 67 41 59N 24 5 E
Rakkestad 71 59 25N 11 21 E
Rakoniewice 54 52 10N 16 16 E
Rakops 128 21 1 S 24 28 E
Rákospalota 53 47 30N 19 5 E
Rakovica 63 44 59N 15 38 E
Rakovník 52 50 6N 13 42 E
Rakovski 67 42 21N 24 57 E
Raleigh, Can. 150 49 30N 92 5W
Raleigh, U.S.A. 150 35 46N 78 38W
Raleigh B. 157 34 50N 76 15W
Ralja 66 44 33N 20 34 E
Ralls 159 33 40N 101 20W
Ralston 162 41 30N 76 57W
Rām Allāh 90 31 55N 35 10 E
Ram Hd. 141 37 47 S 149 30 E
Ram, R. 152 62 1N 123 41W
Rama, Israel 90 32 56N 35 21 E
Rama, Nic. 166 12 9N 84 15W
Ramacca 65 37 24N 14 40 E
Ramachandrapuram 96 16 50N 82 4 E
Ramadi 92 33 28N 43 15 E
Ramales de la Victoria 58 43 15N 3 28W
Ramalho, Serra do 171 13 45 S 44 0W
Raman 101 6 29N 101 18 E
Ramanathapuram 97 9 25N 78 55 E
Ramanetaka, B. de 129 14 13 S 47 52 E
Ramas C. 97 15 5N 73 55 E
Ramat Gan 90 32 4N 34 48 E
Ramatlhabama 128 25 37 S 25 33 E
Ramban 95 33 14N 75 12 E
Rambervillers 43 48 20N 6 38 E
Rambipudji 103 8 12 S 113 37 E
Rambla, La 57 37 37N 4 45W
Rambouillet 43 48 40N 1 48 E
Rambre Kyun 98 19 0N 94 0 E
Ramdurg 97 15 58N 75 22 E
Rame Head 30 50 19N 4 14W
Ramechhap 95 27 25N 86 10 E
Ramelau, Mte. 103 8 55 S 126 22 E
Ramenskoye 81 55 32N 38 15 E
Ramgarh, Bihar, India 95 23 40N 85 35 E
Ramgarh, Rajasthan, India 94 27 16N 75 14 E
Ramgarh, Rajasthan, India 94 27 30N 70 36 E
Ramhormoz 92 31 15N 49 35 E
Ramla 90 31 55N 34 52 E
Ramlat Zalṭan 119 28 30N 19 30 E
Ramlu Mt. 123 13 32N 41 40 E
Ramme 73 56 30N 8 11 E
Rammun 90 31 55N 35 17 E
Ramna Stacks, Is. 36 60 40N 1 20W
Ramnad = Ramanathapuram 97 9 25N 78 55 E
Ramnagar 95 32 47N 75 18 E
Ramnäs 72 59 46N 16 12 E
Ramon 81 52 8N 39 21 E
Ramona 163 33 1N 116 56W
Ramor L. 38 53 50N 7 5W
Ramore 150 48 30N 80 25W
Ramos Arizpe 164 23 35N 100 59W
Ramos, R. 164 25 35N 105 3W
Ramoutsa 128 24 50 S 25 52 E
Rampart 147 65 0N 150 15W
Rampside 32 54 6N 3 10W
Rampur, H.P., India 94 31 26N 77 43 E
Rampur, M.P., India 94 23 25N 73 53 E
Rampur, Orissa, India 96 21 48N 83 58 E
Rampur, U.P., India 94 28 50N 79 5 E
Rampura 94 24 30N 75 27 E
Rampurhat 95 24 10N 87 50 E
Ramsbottom 32 53 36N 2 20W
Ramsbury 28 51 26N 1 37W
Ramsel 47 51 2N 4 50 E
Ramsele 74 63 31N 16 27 E
Ramsey, Can. 150 47 25N 82 20W
Ramsey, Cambs., U.K. 29 52 27N 0 6W
Ramsey, Essex, U.K. 29 51 55N 1 12 E
Ramsey, I. of M., U.K. 32 54 20N 4 21W
Ramsgate 29 51 20N 1 25 E
Ramshai 98 26 44N 88 51 E
Rämshyttan 72 60 17N 15 15 E
Ramsjö 72 62 11N 15 37 E
Ramtek 96 21 20N 79 15 E
Ramu, R. 135 4 0 S 144 41 E
Ramvik 72 62 49N 17 51 E
Ranaghat 95 23 15N 88 35 E
Ranahu 94 25 55N 69 45 E
Ranau 102 6 2N 116 40 E
Rancagua 172 34 10 S 70 50W
Rance 47 50 9N 4 16 E
Rance, R. 42 48 34N 1 59W
Rancharia 171 22 15 S 50 55W

Rancheria, R Rennell Sd

Rancheria, R. 152 60 13N 129 7W
Ranchester 160 44 57N 107 12W
Ranchi 95 23 19N 85 27E
Rancu 70 44 32N 24 15E
Rand 141 35 33S 146 32E
Randallstown 162 39 22N 76 48W
Randalstown 38 54 45N 6 20W
Randan 44 46 2N 3 21E
Randazzo 65 37 53N 14 56E
Randböl 73 55 43N 9 17E
Randers 73 56 29N 10 1E
Randers Fjord 73 56 37N 10 20E
Randfontein 129 26 8S 27 45E
Randolph, Mass., U.S.A. 162 42 10N 71 3W
Randolph, Utah, U.S.A. 160 41 43N 111 10W
Randolph, Vt., U.S.A. 162 43 55N 72 39W
Randsburg 163 35 26N 117 44W
Randsfjord 71 60 15N 10 25E
Râne älv 74 66 26N 21 10E
Rânea 74 65 53N 22 18E
Ranfurly 143 45 7S 170 6E
Rangae 101 6 19N 101 44E
Rangamati 98 22 38S 92 12E
Rangataua 142 39 26S 175 28E
Rangaunu B. 142 34 51S 173 15E
Rångedala 73 57 47N 13 9E
Rangeley 156 44 58N 70 33W
Rangely 160 40 3N 108 53W
Ranger 159 32 30N 98 42W
Rangia 98 26 15N 91 20E
Rangiora 143 43 19S 172 36E
Rangitaiki 130 38 52S 176 23E
Rangitaiki, R. 142 37 54S 176 49E
Rangitata, R. 143 43 45S 171 15E
Rangitikei, R. 142 40 17S 175 15E
Rangitoto Range 142 38 25S 175 35E
Rangkasbitung 103 6 22S 106 16E
Rangon 99 16 45N 96 20E
Rangon, R. 99 16 28N 96 40E
Rangoon 98 16 45N 96 20E
Rangpur 98 25 42N 89 22E
Rangsit 100 13 59N 100 37E
Ranibennur 97 14 35N 75 30E
Raniganj 95 23 40N 87 15E
Ranipet 97 12 56N 79 23E
Raniwara 93 24 50N 72 10E
Ranken, R. 138 20 31S 137 36E
Rankin 159 31 16N 101 56W
Rankin Inlet 148 62 30N 93 0W
Rankin's Springs 141 33 49S 146 14E
Rannes 138 24 6S 150 11E
Rannoch L. 37 56 41N 4 20W
Rannoch Moor 34 56 38N 4 48W
Rannoch Sta. 37 56 40N 4 32W
Ranobe, B. de 129 23 3S 43 33E
Ranohira 129 22 29S 45 24E
Ranomafana, Tamatave, Madag. 129 18 57S 48 50E
Ranomafana, Tuléar, Madag. 129 24 34S 47 0E
Ranong 101 9 56N 98 40E
Rantau 102 4 15N 98 5E
Rantauprapat 102 2 15N 99 50E
Rantemario 103 3 15S 119 57E
Rantis 90 32 4N 35 3E
Rantoul 156 40 18N 88 10W
Ranum 73 56 54N 9 14E
Ranwanlenau 128 19 37S 22 49E
Raon-l'Étape 43 48 24N 6 50E
Raoui, Erg er 118 29 0N 2 0W
Rapa Iti, I. 131 27 35S 144 20W
Rapallo 62 44 21N 9 12E
Rapang 103 3 45S 119 55E
Rāpch 93 25 40N 59 15E
Raphoe 38 54 52N 7 36W
Rapid City 158 44 0N 103 0W
Rapid, R. 152 59 15N 129 5W
Rapid River 156 45 55N 87 0W
Rapides des Joachims 150 46 13N 77 43W
Rapla 80 58 88N 24 52E
Rapness 37 59 15N 2 51W
Raposos 171 19 57S 43 48W
Rappahannock, R. 162 37 35N 76 17W
Rapperswil 51 47 14N 8 45E
Raqqa 92 36 0N 38 55E
Raquete 127 14 8S 38 13E
Raquette Lake 162 43 49N 74 40W
Rareagh 38 53 37N 8 37W
Rarotonga, I. 131 21 30S 160 0W
Ras al Khaima 93 25 50N 56 5E
Ra's Al-Unūf 119 30 25N 18 15E
Ra's at Tannurah 92 26 40N 50 10E
Ras Dashan, mt. 123 13 8N 37 45E
Ras el Ma 118 34 26N 0 50W
Ras Gharib 122 28 6N 33 18E
Ras Mallap 122 29 18N 32 50E
Rasa, Punta 176 40 50S 62 15W
Rasboda 72 60 8N 16 58E
Raseiniai 80 55 25N 23 5E
Rashad 123 11 55N 31 0E
Rashîd 122 31 21N 30 22E
Rashîd, Masabb 122 31 22N 30 17E
Rasht 92 37 20N 49 40E
Rasi Salai 100 15 20N 104 9E
Rasipuram 97 11 30N 78 25E
Raška 66 43 19N 20 39E
Raso, C. 170 1 50N 50 0W
Rason, L. 137 28 45S 124 25E
Raşova 70 44 15N 27 55E
Rasovo 67 43 42N 23 17E
Rasra 95 25 50N 83 50E
Rass el Oued 119 35 57N 5 2E
Rasskazovo 81 52 35N 41 50E
Rastatt 49 48 50N 8 12E
Rastu 70 43 53N 23 16E
Raszków 54 51 43N 17 40E
Rat Buri 100 13 30N 99 54E
Rat, Is. 147 51 50N 178 15E
Rat, R. 152 56 0N 99 30W
Rat River 152 61 7N 112 36W
Rätan 72 62 27N 14 33E
Ratangarh 94 28 5N 74 35E
Rath 95 25 36N 79 37E
Rath Luirc (Charleville) 39 52 21N 8 40W
Rathangan 39 53 13N 7 0W
Rathconrah 38 53 30N 7 32W
Rathcoole 39 53 17N 6 29W
Rathcormack 39 52 5N 8 19W
Rathdowney 39 52 52N 7 36W
Rathdrum, Ireland 39 52 57N 6 13W
Rathdrum, U.S.A. 160 47 50N 116 58W
Ratheclaung 98 20 29N 92 45E
Rathen 37 57 38N 1 58W
Rathenow 48 52 38N 12 23E
Rathfriland 38 54 12N 6 12W
Rathkeale 39 52 32N 8 57W
Rathkenny 38 53 45N 6 39W
Rathlin I. 38 55 18N 6 14W
Rathlin O'Birne I. 38 54 40N 8 50W
Rathmelton 38 55 3N 7 35W
Rathmolyon 38 53 30N 6 49W
Rathmore, Cork, Ireland 39 51 30N 9 21W
Rathmore, Kerry, Ireland 39 52 5N 9 12W
Rathmore, Kildare, Ireland 39 53 13N 6 35W
Rathmullen 38 55 6N 7 32W
Rathnure 39 52 30N 6 47W
Rathvilly 72 52 54N 6 42W
Ratlam 94 23 20N 75 0E
Ratnagiri 96 16 57N 73 18E
Ratnapura 97 6 40N 80 20E
Ratoath 38 53 30N 6 27W
Raton 159 37 0N 104 30W
Rattaphum 101 7 8N 100 16E
Ratten 52 47 28N 15 44E
Rattray 37 56 36N 3 20W
Rattray Hd. 37 57 38N 1 50W
Rättvik 72 60 52N 15 7E
Ratz, Mt. 152 57 23N 132 12W
Ratzeburg 48 53 41N 10 46E
Raub 101 3 47N 101 52E
Rauch 172 36 45S 59 5W
Raufarhöfn 74 66 27N 15 57W
Raufoss 71 60 44N 10 37E
Raukumara Ra. 142 38 5S 177 55E
Raul Soares 171 20 5S 42 22W
Rauland 71 59 43N 8 0E
Rauma 75 61 10N 21 30E
Rauma, R. 71 62 34N 7 43E
Raundal 71 60 40N 6 37E
Raunds 29 52 20N 0 32W
Raung, Mt. 103 8 8S 114 4E
Raurkela 96 22 14N 84 50E
Rava Russkaya 80 50 15N 23 42E
Ravanusa 64 37 16N 13 58E
Ravar 93 31 20N 56 51E
Ravels 47 51 22N 5 0E
Ravena 162 42 28N 73 49W
Ravenglass 32 54 21N 3 25W
Ravenna, Italy 63 44 28N 12 15E
Ravenna, U.S.A. 158 41 3N 98 58W
Ravensburg 49 47 48N 9 38E
Ravenshoe 138 17 37S 145 29E
Ravenstein 46 51 47N 5 39E
Ravensthorpe 137 33 35S 120 2E
Ravenstonedale 32 54 26N 2 26W
Ravenswood, Austral. 138 20 6S 146 54E
Ravenswood, U.S.A. 156 38 58N 81 47W
Ravensworth 141 32 26S 151 4E
Raventasón 174 6 10S 81 0W
Ravi, R. 94 31 0N 73 0E
Ravna Gora 63 45 24N 14 50E
Ravna Reka 66 43 59N 21 35E
Ravnstrup 73 56 27N 9 17E
Rawa Mazowiecka 54 51 46N 20 12E
Rawalpindi 94 33 38N 73 8E
Rawalpindi □ 93 33 10N 72 50E
Rawāndūz 92 36 40N 44 30E
Rawang 101 3 20N 101 35E
Rawdon 150 46 3N 73 40W
Rawene 142 35 25S 173 32E
Rawicz 54 51 36N 16 52E
Rawlinna 137 30 58S 125 28E
Rawlins 160 41 50N 107 20W
Rawlinson Range 137 24 40S 128 30E
Rawmarsh 33 53 27N 1 20W
Rawson 176 43 15S 65 0W
Rawtenstall 32 53 42N 2 18W
Rawuya 121 12 10N 6 50E
Ray, N. Mex., U.S.A. 159 35 57N 104 8W
Ray, N.D., U.S.A. 158 48 21N 103 6W
Ray, C. 151 47 33N 59 15W
Ray Mts. 147 66 0N 152 10W
Rayachoti 97 14 4N 78 50E
Rayadrug 97 14 40N 76 50E
Rayagada 96 19 15N 83 20E
Raychikhinsk 77 49 46N 129 25E
Rayevskiy 84 54 4N 54 56E
Rayin 93 29 40N 57 22E
Rayleigh 29 51 36N 0 38E
Raymond, Can. 152 49 30N 112 35W
Raymond, Calif., U.S.A. 163 37 13N 119 54W
Raymond, Wash., U.S.A. 160 46 45N 123 48W
Raymond Terrace 141 32 45S 151 44E
Raymondville 159 26 30N 97 50W
Raymore 153 51 25N 104 31W
Rayne 159 30 16N 92 16W
Rayón 164 29 43N 110 35W
Rayong 100 12 40N 101 20E
Rayville 159 32 30N 91 45W
Raz, Pte. du 42 48 2N 4 47W
Razana 66 44 6N 19 55E
Razanj 66 43 40N 21 31E
Razdelna 67 43 13N 27 41E
Razelm, Lacul 70 44 50N 29 0E
Razgrad 67 43 33N 26 34E
Razlog 67 41 53N 23 28E
Razmak 94 32 45N 69 50E
Razole 96 16 56N 81 48E
Razor Back Mt. 152 51 32N 125 0W
Ré, Île de 44 46 12N 1 30W
Rea, L. 39 53 10N 8 32W
Reading, U.K. 29 51 27N 0 57W
Reading, U.S.A. 162 40 20N 75 53W
Realicó 172 35 0S 64 15W
Réalmont 44 43 48N 2 10E
Ream 101 10 34N 103 39E
Reata 164 26 8N 101 5W
Reay 37 58 33N 3 48W
Rebais 43 48 50N 3 10E
Rebecca L. 137 30 0S 122 30E
Rebi 103 5 30S 134 7E
Rebiana 117 24 12N 22 10E
Rebun-Tō 112 45 23N 141 2E
Recanati 63 43 24N 13 32E
Recaş 66 45 46N 21 30E
Recess 38 53 29N 9 4W
Recherche, Arch. of the 137 34 15S 122 50E
Rechitsa 80 52 13N 30 15E
Recht 47 50 20N 6 3E
Recife 170 8 0S 35 0W
Recklinghausen 48 51 36N 7 10E
Reconquista 172 29 10S 59 45W
Recreo 172 29 25S 65 10W
Reculver 29 51 22N 1 12E
Recz 54 53 16N 15 31E
Red B. 38 55 4N 6 2W
Red Bank 162 40 21N 74 4W
Red Bay 151 51 44N 56 25W
Red Bluff 160 40 11N 122 11W
Red Bluff L. 159 31 59N 103 58W
Red Cliffs 140 34 19S 142 11E
Red Cloud 158 40 8N 98 33W
Red Creek 162 43 14N 76 45W
Red Deer 152 52 20N 113 50W
Red Deer L. 153 52 55N 101 20W
Red Deer, R. 152 50 58N 110 0W
Red Deer R. 153 52 53N 101 1W
Red Dial 32 54 48N 3 9W
Red Hook 162 41 55N 73 53W
Red Indian L. 151 48 35N 57 0W
Red L. 158 48 0N 95 0W
Red Lake 153 51 1N 94 1W
Red Lake Falls 158 47 54N 96 30W
Red Lion 162 39 54N 76 36W
Red Lodge 160 45 10N 109 10W
Red Mountain 163 35 37N 117 38W
Red Oak 158 41 0N 95 10W
Red Point Rock 137 32 13S 127 32E
Red, R., Can. 153 50 24N 96 48W
Red, R., Minn., U.S.A. 158 48 10N 97 0W
Red, R., Tex., U.S.A. 159 33 57N 95 30W
Red, R. = Hong, R. 100 20 17N 106 34E
Red Rock 150 48 55N 88 15W
Red Rock, L. 158 41 30N 93 15W
Red Sea 91 25 0N 36 0E
Red Slate Mtn. 163 37 31N 118 52W
Red Sucker L 153 54 9N 93 40W
Red Tower Pass = Turnu Rosu P. 70 45 33N 24 17E
Red Wharf Bay 31 53 18N 4 10W
Red Wing 158 44 32N 92 35W
Reda 54 54 40N 18 19E
Rédange 47 49 46N 5 52E
Redbank 108 27 36S 152 52E
Redbridge 29 51 35N 0 7E
Redcar 33 54 37N 1 4W
Redcliff 153 50 10N 110 50W
Redcliffe 139 27 12S 153 0E
Redcliffe, Mt. 137 28 30S 121 30E
Redcliffs 139 34 16S 142 10E
Reddersburg 128 29 41S 26 10E
Redding 160 40 30N 122 25W
Redditch 28 52 18N 1 57W
Rede, R. 35 55 8N 2 12W
Redenção 170 4 13S 38 43W
Redesmouth 35 55 7N 2 12W
Redfield 158 45 0N 98 30W
Redhill 29 51 14N 0 10W
Redknife, R. 152 61 14N 119 22W
Redland 37 59 6N 3 4W
Redlands 163 34 0N 117 11W
Redlynch 28 50 59N 1 42W
Redmile 33 52 54N 0 48W
Redmire 32 54 19N 1 55W
Redmond, Austral. 137 34 55S 117 40E
Redmond, U.S.A. 160 44 19N 121 11W
Redon 42 47 40N 2 6W
Redonda, I. 167 16 58N 62 19W
Redondela 56 42 15N 8 38W
Redondo 57 38 39N 7 37W
Redondo Beach 163 33 52N 118 26W
Redrock Pt. 152 62 11N 115 2W
Redruth 30 50 14N 5 14W
Redvers 153 49 35N 101 40W
Redwater 152 53 55N 113 6W
Redwood City 163 37 30N 122 15W
Redwood Falls 158 44 30N 95 2W
Ree, L. 38 53 35N 8 0W
Reed City 156 43 52N 85 30W
Reed L. 153 54 38N 100 30W
Reed, Mt. 151 52 5N 68 5W
Reeder 158 47 7N 102 52W
Reedham 29 52 34N 1 33E
Reedley 163 36 36N 119 27W
Reedsburg 158 43 34N 90 5W
Reedsport 160 43 45N 124 4W
Reedy Creek 140 36 58S 140 2E
Reef Pt. 142 35 10S 173 5E
Reefton, N.S.W., Austral. 141 34 15S 147 27E
Reefton, S. Australia, Austral. 109 34 57S 138 55E
Reefton, N.Z. 143 42 6S 171 51E
Reepham 29 52 46N 1 6E
Reeth 32 54 23N 1 56W
Refsnes 71 61 9N 7 14E
Reftele 73 57 11N 13 35E
Refugio 159 28 18N 97 17W
Rega, R. 54 53 52N 15 16E
Regalbuto 65 37 40N 14 38E
Regar 85 38 30N 68 14E
Regavim 90 32 32N 35 2E
Regen 49 48 58N 13 9E
Regeneração 170 6 15S 42 41W
Regensburg 49 49 1N 12 7E
Regensdorf 51 47 26N 8 28E
Réggio di Calábria 65 38 7N 15 38E
Réggio nell' Emilia 62 44 42N 10 38E
Regina 153 50 30N 104 35W
Registan □ 93 30 15N 65 0E
Registro 173 24 29S 47 49W
Reguengos de Monsaraz 57 38 25N 7 32W
Rehar 95 23 36N 82 52E
Rehoboth, Damaraland, Namibia 128 23 15S 17 4E
Rehoboth, Ovamboland, Namibia 128 17 55S 15 5E
Rehoboth Beach 162 38 43N 75 5W
Rehovot 90 31 54N 34 48E
Reichenbach, Ger. 48 50 36N 12 19E
Reichenbach, Switz. 50 46 38N 7 42E
Reid 137 30 49S 128 26E
Reid River 138 19 40S 146 48E
Reiden 50 47 14N 7 59E
Reidsville 157 36 21N 79 40W
Reigate 29 51 14N 0 11W
Reillo 58 39 54N 1 53W
Reims 43 49 15N 4 0E
Reina 90 32 43N 35 18E
Reina Adelaida, Arch. 176 52 20S 74 0W
Reinach, Aargau, Switz. 50 47 14N 8 11E
Reinach, Basel, Switz. 50 47 29N 7 35E
Reinbeck 158 42 18N 92 40W
Reindeer I. 153 52 30N 98 0W
Reindeer L. 153 57 15N 102 15W
Reindeer, R. 153 55 36N 103 11W
Reine, La 150 48 50N 79 30W
Reinga, C. 142 34 25S 172 43E
Reinosa 56 43 2N 4 15W
Reinosa, Paso 56 42 56N 4 10W
Reira 123 15 25N 34 50E
Reiss 37 58 29N 3 7W
Reisterstown 162 39 28N 76 50W
Reitdiep 46 53 20N 6 20E
Reitz 129 27 48S 28 29E
Reivilo 128 27 36S 24 8E
Rejmyra 73 58 50N 15 55E
Reka, R. 63 45 40N 14 0E
Rekovac 66 43 51N 21 3E
Remad, Ouedber 118 33 28N 1 20W
Remanso 170 9 41S 42 4W
Remarkable, Mt. 140 32 48S 138 10E
Rembang 103 6 42S 111 21E
Remchi 118 35 2N 1 26W
Remedios, Colomb. 174 7 2N 74 41W
Remedios, Panama 166 8 15N 81 50W
Remeshk 93 26 55N 58 50E
Remetea 70 46 45N 29 29E
Remich 47 49 32N 6 22E
Remiremont 43 48 0N 6 36E
Remo 123 6 48N 41 20E
Remontnoye 83 47 44N 43 37E
Remoulins 45 43 55N 4 35E
Remscheid 48 51 11N 7 12E
Remsen 162 43 19N 75 11W
Rena 71 61 8N 11 20E
Renda 123 14 30N 40 0E
Rende 65 39 19N 16 11E
Rendeux 47 50 14N 5 30E
Rendina 69 39 4N 21 58E
Rendsburg 48 54 18N 9 41E
Rene 77 66 2N 179 25W
Renee, oilfield 19 58 4N 0 16E
Renens 50 46 31N 6 34E
Renfrew, Can. 150 45 30N 76 40W
Renfrew, U.K. 34 55 52N 4 24W
Renfrew (□) 26 55 50N 4 30W
Rengat 102 0 30S 102 45E
Rengo 172 34 24S 70 50W
Reni 82 45 28N 28 15E
Renigunta 97 13 38N 79 30E
Renish Pt. 36 57 44N 6 59W
Renkum 46 51 58N 5 43E
Renmark 140 34 11S 140 43E
Rennell Sd. 152 53 23N 132 35W

Renner Springs Teleg. Off **Riverton**

Renner Springs Teleg. Off. 138 18 20 S 133 47 E
Rennes 42 48 7N 1 41W
Rennesøy 71 59 6N 5 43 E
Reno 160 39 30N 119 50W
Reno, R. 63 44 45N 11 40 E
Renovo 156 41 20N 77 47W
Rens 55 54 54N 9 5 E
Rensselaer, Ind., U.S.A. 156 41 0N 87 10W
Rensselaer, N.Y., U.S.A. 162 42 38N 73 41W
Rentería 58 43 19N 1 54W
Renton 160 47 30N 122 9W
Renwicktown 143 41 30 S 173 51 E
Réo 120 12 28N 2 35 E
Réole, La 44 44 35N 0 1W
Reotipur 95 25 33N 83 45 E
Repalle 97 16 2N 80 45 E
Répcelak 53 47 24N 17 1 E
Repton 28 52 50N 1 32W
Republic, Mich., U.S.A. 156 46 25N 87 59W
Republic, Wash., U.S.A. 160 48 38N 118 42W
Republican City 158 40 9N 99 20W
Republican, R. 158 40 0N 98 30W
Repulse B., Antarct. 13 64 30 S 99 30 E
Repulse B., Austral. 133 20 31 S 148 45 E
Repulse Bay 149 66 30N 86 30W
Requena, Peru 174 5 5 S 73 52W
Requena, Spain 59 39 30N 1 4W
Resele 72 63 20N 17 5 E
Resen 66 41 5N 21 0 E
Reserve, Can. 153 52 28N 102 39W
Reserve, U.S.A. 161 33 50N 108 54W
Resht = Rasht 92 37 20N 49 40 E
Resistencia 172 27 30 S 59 0W
Reşiţa 66 45 18N 21 53 E
Resko 54 53 47N 15 25 E
Resolution I., Can. 149 61 30N 65 0W
Resolution I., N.Z. 143 45 40 S 166 40 E
Resolven 31 51 43N 3 42W
Resplandes 170 6 17 S 45 13W
Resplendor 171 19 20 S 41 15W
Ressano Garcia 129 25 25 S 32 0 E
Rest Downs 141 31 48 S 146 21 E
Reston, Can. 153 49 33N 101 6W
Reston, U.K. 35 55 51N 2 11W
Restrepo 174 4 15N 73 33W
Reszel 54 54 4N 21 10 E
Retalhuleu 166 14 33N 91 46W
Reteag 70 47 10N 24 0 E
Retem, O. el 119 33 40N 0 40 E
Retenue, Lac de 127 11 0 S 27 0 E
Rethel 43 49 30N 4 20 E
Rethem 48 52 47N 9 25 E
Réthimnon 69 35 15N 24 40 E
Réthimnon □ 69 35 23N 24 28 E
Retie 47 51 16N 5 5 E
Rétiers 42 47 55N 1 25W
Retiro 172 35 59 S 71 47W
Retortillo 56 40 48N 6 21W
Rétság 53 47 58N 19 10 E
Reuland 47 50 12N 6 8 E
Réunion, Î. 11 22 0 S 56 0 E
Reus 58 41 10N 1 5 E
Reusel 47 51 21N 5 9 E
Reuss, R. 51 47 16N 8 24 E
Reuterstadt-Stavenhagen 48 53 41N 12 54 E
Reutlingen 49 48 28N 9 13 E
Reutte 52 47 29N 10 42 E
Reuver 47 51 17N 6 5 E
Revda 84 56 48N 59 57 E
Revel 44 43 28N 2 0 E
Revelganj 95 25 50N 84 40 E
Revelstoke 152 51 0N 118 0W
Revigny 43 48 50N 5 0 E
Revilla Gigedo, Is. de 131 18 40N 112 0W
Revillagigedo I. 152 55 50N 131 20W
Revin 43 49 55N 4 39 E
Revolyutsii, Pix 85 38 31N 72 21 E
Revuè, R. 127 19 30 S 33 35 E
Rewa 95 24 33N 81 25 E
Rewari 94 28 15N 76 40 E
Rex 147 64 10N 149 20W
Rexburg 160 43 45N 111 50W
Rey Bouba 117 8 40N 14 15 E
Rey Malabo 121 3 45N 8 50 E
Reyes, Pt. 163 37 59N 123 2W
Reykjahlið 74 65 40N 16 55W
Reykjanes 74 63 48N 22 40W
Reykjavik 74 64 10N 21 57 E
Reynolds 153 49 40N 95 55W
Reynolds Ra. 136 22 30 S 133 0 E
Reynosa 165 26 5N 98 18W
*Rezā'iyeh 92 37 40N 45 0 E
*Rezā'iyeh, Daryācheh-ye 92 37 30N 45 30 E
Rēzekne 80 56 30N 27 17 E
Rezh 84 57 23N 61 24 E
Rezina 70 47 45N 29 0 E
Rezovo 67 42 0N 28 0 E
Rgotina 67 44 1N 22 18 E
Rhaeadr Ogwen 31 53 8N 4 0W
Rharis, O. 119 26 30N 5 4 E
Rhayader 31 52 19N 3 30W
Rheden 46 52 0N 6 3 E
Rheidol, R. 31 52 25N 3 57W
Rhein 153 51 25N 102 15W
Rhein, R. 48 51 42N 6 20 E
Rheinbach 48 50 38N 6 54 E
Rheine 48 52 17N 7 25 E
Rheineck 51 47 28N 9 31 E
Rheinfelden 50 47 32N 7 47 E
Rheinland-Pfalz □ 49 50 50N 7 0 E
Rheinsberg 48 53 6N 12 52 E
Rheinwaldhorn 51 46 30N 9 3 E
Rhenen 46 51 58N 5 33 E
Rheydt 48 51 10N 6 24 E
Rhin, R. 48 51 42N 6 20 E
Rhinau 43 48 19N 7 43 E
Rhine, R. = Rhein 47 51 42N 6 20 E
Rhinebeck 162 41 56N 73 55W
Rhinelander 158 45 38N 89 29W
Rhino Camp 126 3 0N 31 22 E
Rhisnes 47 50 31N 4 48 E
Rhiw 31 52 49N 4 37W
Rho 62 45 31N 9 2 E
Rhode Island □ 162 41 38N 71 37W
Rhodes = Ródhos 69 36 15N 28 10 E
Rhodes' Tomb 127 20 30 S 28 30 E
Rhodesia = Zimbabwe ■ 127 20 0 S 30 0 E
Rhodope Mts. = Rhodopi Planina 67 41 40N 24 20 E
Rhondda 31 51 39N 3 30W
Rhône □ 45 45 54N 4 35 E
Rhône, R. 45 43 28N 4 42 E
Rhos-on-Sea 31 53 18N 3 46W
Rhosllanerchrugog 31 53 3N 3 4W
Rhossilli 31 51 34N 4 18W
Rhu Coigach, C. 36 58 6N 5 27W
Rhuddlan 31 53 17N 3 28W
Rhum, I. 36 57 0N 6 20W
Rhyl 31 53 19N 3 29W
Rhymney 31 51 45N 3 17W
Rhynie 37 57 20N 2 50W
Ri-Aba 121 3 28N 8 40 E
Riachão 170 7 20 S 46 37W
Riachão do Jacuípe 171 11 48 S 39 21W
Riacho de Santana 171 13 37 S 42 57W
Rialma 171 15 18 S 49 34W
Rialto 163 34 6N 117 22W
Riang 98 27 31N 92 56 E
Riaño 56 42 59N 5 0W
Rians 45 43 37N 5 44 E
Riansares, R. 58 40 0N 3 0W
Riasi 95 33 10N 74 50 E
Riau □ 102 0 0 102 35 E
Riau, Kepulauan 102 0 30N 104 20 E
Riaza 58 41 18N 3 30W
Riaza, R. 58 41 16N 3 29W
Riba de Saelices 58 40 55N 2 18 E
Ribadavia 56 42 17N 8 8W
Ribadeo 56 43 35N 7 5W
Ribadesella 56 43 30N 5 7W
Ribamar 170 2 33 S 44 3W
Ribas 58 42 19N 2 15 E
Ribat 125 29 50N 60 55 E
Ribatejo □ 55 39 15N 8 30W
Ribble, R. 32 54 13N 2 20W
Ribe 73 55 19N 8 44 E
Ribe Amt □ 73 55 34N 8 30 E
Ribeauvillé 43 48 10N 7 20 E
Ribécourt 43 49 30N 2 55 E
Ribeira 56 42 36N 8 58W
Ribeira do Pombal 170 10 50 S 38 32W
Ribeirão Prêto 173 21 10 S 47 50W
Ribeiro Gonçalves 170 7 32 S 45 14W
Ribémont 43 49 47N 3 27 E
Ribera 64 37 30N 13 13 E
Ribérac 44 45 15N 0 20 E
Riberalta 174 11 0 S 66 0W
Ribnica 63 45 45N 14 45 E
Ribnitz-Dangarten 48 54 14N 12 24 E
Ričany 52 50 0N 14 40 E
Riccall 33 53 50N 1 4W
Riccarton 143 43 32 S 172 37 E
Riccia 65 41 30N 14 50 E
Riccione 63 44 0N 12 39 E
Rice Lake 158 45 30N 91 42W
Rich 118 32 16N 4 30W
Rich Hill 159 38 5N 94 22W
Richards B. 129 28 48 S 32 6 E
Richards Deep 15 25 0 S 73 0W
Richards L. 153 59 10N 107 10W
Richardson Mts. 143 44 49 S 168 34 E
Richardson, R. 153 58 25N 111 14W
Richardton 158 46 56N 102 22W
Riche, C. 137 34 36 S 118 47 E
Richelieu 42 47 0N 0 20 E
Richey 158 47 42N 105 5W
Richfield, Idaho, U.S.A. 160 43 2N 114 5W
Richfield, Utah, U.S.A. 161 38 50N 112 0W
Richfield Springs 162 42 51N 74 59W
Richibucto 151 46 42N 64 54W
Richland, Ga., U.S.A. 157 32 7N 84 40W
Richland, Oreg., U.S.A. 160 44 49N 117 9W
Richland, Wash., U.S.A. 160 46 15N 119 15W
Richland Center 158 43 21N 90 22W
Richlands 156 37 7N 81 49W
Richmond, N.S.W., Austral. 141 33 35 S 150 42 E
Richmond, Queens., Austral. 138 20 43 S 143 8 E
Richmond, N.Z. 143 41 4 S 173 12 E
Richmond, S. Afr. 125 29 51 S 30 18 E
Richmond, N. Yorks., U.K. 33 54 24N 1 43W
Richmond, Surrey, U.K. 29 51 28N 0 18W
Richmond, Calif., U.S.A. 163 38 0N 122 21W
Richmond, Ind., U.S.A. 156 39 50N 84 50W
Richmond, Ky., U.S.A. 156 37 40N 84 20W
Richmond, Mo., U.S.A. 158 39 15N 93 58W
Richmond, Tex., U.S.A. 159 29 32N 95 42W
Richmond, Va., U.S.A. 162 37 33N 77 27W
Richmond Gulf 150 56 20N 75 50W
Richmond, Mt. 143 41 32 S 173 22 E
Richmond, Ra. 139 29 0 S 152 45 E
Richmond Ra. 143 41 32 S 173 22 E
Richterswil 51 47 13N 8 43 E
Richton 157 31 23N 88 58W
Richwood 156 38 17N 80 32W
Rickmansworth 29 51 38N 0 28W
Ricla 58 41 31N 1 24W
Riddarhyttan 72 59 49N 15 33 E
Ridderkerk 46 51 52N 4 35 E
Riddes 50 46 11N 7 14 E
Ridgecrest 163 35 38N 117 40W
Ridgedale 153 53 0N 104 10W
Ridgefield 162 41 17N 73 30W
Ridgeland 157 32 30N 80 58W
Ridgelands 138 23 16 S 150 17 E
Ridgetown 150 42 26N 81 52W
Ridgewood 162 40 59N 74 7W
Ridgway 156 41 25N 78 43W
Riding Mt. Nat. Park 153 50 50N 100 0W
Ridley Mt. 137 33 12 S 122 7 E
Ridsdale 35 55 9N 2 8W
Ried 52 48 14N 13 30 E
Riehen 50 47 35N 7 39 E
Riel 47 51 31N 5 1 E
Rienne 47 50 0N 4 53 E
Rienza, R. 63 46 49N 11 47 E
Riesa 48 51 19N 13 19 E
Riesi 65 37 16N 14 4 E
Rietfontein 128 26 44 S 20 1 E
Rieti 63 42 23N 12 50 E
Rieupeyroux 44 44 19N 2 12 E
Rievaulx 33 54 16N 1 7W
Riez 45 43 49N 6 6 E
Rifle 160 39 40N 107 50W
Rifstangi 74 66 32N 16 12W
Rift Valley 126 0 20N 36 0 E
Rig Rig 117 14 13N 14 25 E
Riga 80 56 53N 24 8 E
Riga, G. of = Rīgas Jūras Līcis 80 57 40N 23 45 E
Rīgas Jūras Līcis 80 57 40N 23 45 E
Rigby 160 43 41N 111 58W
Riggins 160 45 29N 116 26W
Rignac 44 44 25N 2 16 E
Rigo 138 9 41 S 147 31 E
Rigolet 151 54 10N 58 23W
Riihimäki 75 60 45N 24 48 E
Riiser-Larsen halvøya 13 68 0 S 35 0 E
Riishiri-Tō 112 45 11N 141 15 E
Rijau 121 11 8N 5 17 E
Rijeka Crnojevica 66 42 24N 19 1 E
Rijeka (Fiume) 63 45 20N 14 21 E
Rijen 47 51 35N 4 55 E
Rijkevorsel 47 51 21N 4 46 E
Rijn, R. 47 52 5N 4 50 E
Rijnsberg 46 52 11N 4 27 E
Rijsbergen 47 51 31N 4 41 E
Rijssen 46 52 19N 6 30 E
Rijswijk 46 52 4N 4 22 E
Rike 123 10 50N 39 53 E
Rikita 123 5 5N 28 29 E
Rila 67 42 7N 23 7 E
Rila Planina 66 42 10N 23 30 E
Rillington 33 54 10N 0 41W
Rilly 43 49 11N 4 3 E
Rima 99 28 35N 97 5 E
Rima, R. 121 13 15N 5 15 E
Rimavská Sobota 53 48 22N 20 2 E
Rimbey 152 52 35N 114 15W
Rimbo 72 59 44N 18 21 E
Rimforsa 73 58 8N 15 42 E
Rimi 121 12 58N 7 43 E
Rimini 63 44 3N 12 33 E
Rîmna, R. 70 45 36N 27 3 E
Rîmnicu Sărat 70 45 26N 27 3 E
Rîmnicu Vîlcece 70 45 9N 24 21 E
Rimouski 151 48 27N 68 30W
Rinca 103 8 45 S 119 35 E
Rincón de Romos 164 22 14N 102 18W
Rinconada 172 22 26 S 66 10W
Ringarum 73 58 21N 16 26 E
Ringe 73 55 13N 10 28 E
Ringel Spitz 51 46 53N 9 19 E
Ringford 35 54 55N 4 3W
Ringim 121 12 13N 9 10 E
Ringkøbing 73 56 5N 8 15 E
Ringkøbing Amt □ 73 56 15N 8 30 E
Ringling 160 46 16N 110 56W
Ringmer 29 50 53N 0 5 E
Ringmoen 71 60 21N 10 6 E
Ringsaker 71 60 54N 10 45 E
Ringsend 38 55 2N 6 45W
Ringsjön L. 73 55 55N 13 30 E
Ringsted 73 55 25N 11 46 E
Ringvassøy 74 69 36N 19 15 E
Ringville 39 52 3N 7 37W
Ringwood 28 50 50N 1 48W
Rinía, I. 69 37 23N 25 13 E
Rinjani 65 8 20 S 116 30 E
Rinns, The, Reg. 34 54 52N 5 3W
Rintein 48 52 11N 9 3 E
Rio Arica 174 1 35 S 75 30W
Rio Branco 174 9 58 S 67 49W
Rio Branco 173 32 40 S 53 40W
Rio Brilhante 173 21 48 S 54 33W
Río Chico 174 10 19N 65 59W
Rio Claro, Brazil 173 22 19 S 47 35W
Rio Claro, Trin 167 10 20N 61 25W
Rio Colorado 176 39 0 S 64 0W
Rio Cuarto 172 33 10 S 64 25W
Rio das Pedras 129 23 8 S 35 28 E
Rio de Contas 171 13 36 S 41 48W
Rio de Janeiro 173 23 0 S 43 12W
Rio de Janeiro □ 173 22 50 S 43 0W
Rio del Rey 121 4 42N 8 37 E
Rio do Prado 171 16 35 S 40 34W
Rio do Sul 173 27 95 S 49 37W
Rio Gallegos 176 51 35 S 69 15W
Río Grande 176 53 50 S 67 45W
Rio Grande 173 32 0 S 52 20W
Río Grande, Mexico 164 23 50N 103 2W
Río Grande, Nic. 166 12 54N 83 33W
Rio Grande City 159 26 30N 91 55W
Rio Grande del Norte, R. 154 26 0N 97 0W
Rio Grande do Norte □ 170 5 40 S 36 0W
Rio Grande do Sul □ 173 30 0 S 53 0W
Rio Grande, R. 161 37 47N 106 15W
Río Hato 166 8 22N 80 10W
Rio Lagartos 165 21 36N 88 10W
Rio Largo 171 9 28 S 35 50W
Rio Maior 57 39 19N 8 57W
Rio Marina 62 42 48N 10 25 E
Rio Mulatos 174 19 40 S 66 50W
Rio Muni □ = Mbini □ 124 1 30N 10 0 E
Rio Negro 173 26 0 S 50 0W
Rio Oriente 166 22 17N 81 13W
Rio Pardo, Minas Gerais, Brazil 171 15 55 S 42 30W
Rio Pardo, Rio Grande do Sul, Brazil 173 30 0 S 52 30W
Rio Prêto, Serra do 171 13 29 S 39 55W
Rio, Punta del 59 36 49N 2 24W
Rio Real 171 11 28 S 37 56W
Río Segundo 172 31 40 S 63 59W
Río Tercero 172 32 15 S 64 8W
Rio Tinto, Brazil 170 6 48 S 35 5W
Rio Tinto, Port. 56 41 11N 8 34W
Rio Verde 170 17 50 S 51 0W
Río Verde 165 21 56N 99 59W
Rio Vista 163 38 11N 121 44W
Riobamba 174 1 50 S 78 45W
Riohacha 174 11 33N 72 55W
Rioja, La, Argent. 172 29 20 S 67 0W
Rioja, La, Spain 58 42 20N 2 20W
Rioja, La □ 172 29 30 S 67 0W
Riom 44 45 54N 3 7 E
Riom-ès-Montagnes 44 45 17N 2 39 E
Rion-des-Landes 44 43 55N 0 56W
Rionegro 174 6 9N 75 22W
Rionero in Vúlture 65 40 55N 15 40 E
Ríos 56 41 58N 7 16W
Riosucio, Caldas, Colomb. 174 5 30N 75 40W
Riosucio, Choco, Colomb. 174 7 27N 77 7W
Riou L. 153 59 7N 106 25W
Riparia, Dora, R. 62 45 7N 7 24 E
Ripatransone 63 43 0N 13 45 E
Ripley, Derby, U.K. 33 53 3N 1 24W
Ripley, N. Yorks, U.K. 33 54 3N 1 34W
Ripley, U.S.A. 159 35 43N 89 34W
Ripoll 58 42 15N 2 13 E
Ripon, Calif., U.S.A. 163 37 44N 121 7W
Ripon, Wis., U.S.A. 156 43 51N 88 50W
Riposto 65 37 44N 15 12 E
Risalpur 94 34 3N 71 59 E
Risan 66 42 32N 18 42 E
Risca 31 51 36N 3 6W
Riscle 44 43 39N 0 5W
Rishon Le Zion 90 31 58N 34 48 E
Rishpon 90 32 12N 34 49 E
Rishton 32 53 46N 2 26W
Riska 71 58 56N 5 52 E
Risle, R. 42 48 55N 0 41 E
Risnov 70 45 35N 25 27 E
Rison 159 33 57N 92 11W
Risør 71 58 43N 9 13 E
Ritchie's Archipelago 101 12 5N 94 0 E
Riti 121 7 57N 9 41 E
Ritzville 160 47 10N 118 21W
Riu 98 28 19N 95 3 E
Riva Bella Ouistreham 42 49 17N 0 18W
Riva del Garda 62 45 53N 10 50 E
Rivadavia, Buenos Aires, Argent. 172 35 29 S 62 59W
Rivadavia, Mendoza, Argent. 172 33 13 S 68 30W
Rivadavia, Salta, Argent. 172 24 5 S 63 0W
Rivadavia, Chile 172 29 50 S 70 35W
Rivarolo Canavese 62 45 20N 7 42 E
Rivas 166 11 30N 85 50W
Rive-de-Gier 45 45 32N 4 37 E
River Cess 120 5 30N 9 25W
Rivera 173 31 0 S 55 50W
Riverchapel 39 52 38N 6 14W
Riverdale 163 36 26N 119 52W
Riverhead 162 40 53N 72 40W
Riverhurst 153 50 55N 106 50W
Riverina 136 29 45 S 120 40 E
Riverina, dist. 133 35 30 S 145 20 E
Rivers 153 50 2N 100 14W
Rivers □ 121 5 0N 6 30 E
Rivers Inlet 152 51 40N 127 20W
Rivers, L. of the 153 49 49N 105 44W
Riversdal 128 34 7 S 21 15 E
Riverside, Calif., U.S.A. 163 34 0N 117 22W
Riverside, Wyo., U.S.A. 160 41 12N 106 57W
Riversleigh 138 19 5 S 138 48 E
Riverton, Austral. 140 34 10 S 138 46 E

*Renamed Orumiyeh

Riverton, Can.	**153**	51 5N	97 0W
Riverton, N.Z.	**143**	46 21S	168 0E
Riverton, U.S.A.	**160**	43 1N	108 27W
Riverview	**108**	27 36S	152 51E
Rives	**45**	45 21N	5 31E
Rivesaltes	**44**	42 47N	2 50E
Riviera	**62**	44 0N	8 30E
Rivière à Pierre	**151**	46 57N	72 12W
Rivière-au-Renard	**151**	48 59N	64 23W
Rivière Bleue	**151**	47 26N	69 2W
Rivière-du-Loup	**151**	47 50N	69 30W
Rivière Pontecôte	**151**	49 57N	67 1W
Rívoli	**62**	45 3N	7 31E
Rivoli B.	**140**	37 32S	140 3E
Rivungo	**128**	16 9S	21 51E
Riwaka	**143**	41 5S	172 59E
Rixensart	**47**	50 43N	4 32E
Riyadh = Ar Riyad	**92**	24 41N	46 42E
Rize	**92**	41 0N	40 30E
Rizzuto, C.	**65**	38 54N	17 5E
Rjukan	**71**	59 54N	8 33E
Roa, Norway	**71**	60 17N	10 37E
Roa, Spain	**56**	41 41N	3 56W
Road Town	**167**	18 27N	64 37W
Road Weedon	**28**	52 14N	1 6W
Roade	**29**	52 10N	0 53W
Roadhead	**32**	55 4N	2 44W
Roag, L.	**36**	58 10N	6 55W
Roan Antelope	**127**	13 2S	28 19E
Roanne	**45**	46 3N	4 4E
Roanoke, Ala., U.S.A.	**157**	33 9N	85 23W
Roanoke, Va., U.S.A.	**156**	37 19N	79 55W
Roanoke I.	**157**	35 55N	75 40W
Roanoke, R.	**157**	36 15N	77 20W
Roanoke Rapids	**157**	36 36N	77 42W
Roaringwater B.	**39**	51 30N	9 30W
Roatán	**166**	16 18N	86 35W
Robbins I.	**138**	40 42S	145 0E
Robe, R., Austral.	**136**	21 42S	116 15E
Robe, R., Ireland	**38**	53 38N	9 10W
Röbel	**48**	53 24N	12 37E
Robert Lee	**159**	31 55N	100 26W
Robert Pt.	**137**	32 34S	115 40E
Roberton	**35**	55 24N	2 53W
Roberts	**160**	43 44N	112 8W
Robertsganj	**95**	24 44N	83 12E
Robertson, Austral.	**132**	34 37S	150 36E
Robertson, S. Afr.	**128**	33 46S	19 50E
Robertson I.	**13**	68 0S	75 0W
Robertson Ra.	**136**	23 15S	121 0E
Robertsport	**120**	6 45N	11 26W
Robertstown, Austral.	**140**	33 58S	139 5E
Robertstown, Ireland	**39**	53 16N	6 50W
Roberval	**150**	48 32N	72 15W
Robeson Kanal	**12**	82 0N	61 30W
Robesonia	**162**	40 21N	76 8W
Robin Hood's B.	**33**	54 26N	0 31W
Robinson Crusoe I.	**143**	33 50S	78 30W
Robinson, R.	**138**	16 3S	137 16E
Robinson Ranges	**137**	25 40S	118 0E
Robinson River	**138**	16 45S	136 58E
Robinvale	**140**	34 40S	142 45E
Robla, La	**56**	42 50N	5 41W
Roblin	**153**	51 14N	101 21W
Roboré	**174**	18 10S	59 45W
Robson, Mt.	**152**	53 10N	119 10W
Robstown	**159**	27 47N	97 40W
Roca, C. da	**57**	38 40N	9 31W
Roca Partida, I.	**164**	19 1N	112 2W
Roçadas	**128**	16 45S	15 0E
Rocas, I.	**170**	4 0S	34 1W
Rocca d'Aspidé	**65**	40 27N	15 10E
Rocca San Casciano	**63**	44 3N	11 30E
Roccalbegna	**63**	42 47N	11 30E
Roccastrada	**63**	43 0N	11 10E
Rocella Iónica	**65**	38 20N	16 24E
Rocester	**32**	52 56N	1 50W
Rocha	**173**	34 30S	54 25W
Rochdale	**32**	53 36N	2 10W
Roche	**30**	50 24N	4 50W
Roche-Bernard, La	**42**	47 31N	2 19W
Roche-Canillac, La	**44**	45 12N	1 57E
Roche-en-Ardenne, La	**47**	50 11N	5 35E
Roche, La, France	**45**	46 4N	6 19E
Roche, La, Switz.	**50**	46 42N	7 7E
Roche-sur-Yon, La	**42**	46 40N	1 25W
Rochechouart	**44**	45 50N	0 49E
Rochefort, Belg.	**47**	50 9N	5 12E
Rochefort, France	**44**	45 56N	0 57W
Rochefort-en-Terre	**42**	47 42N	2 22W
Rochefoucauld, La	**44**	45 44N	0 24E
Rochelle	**158**	41 55N	89 5W
Rochelle, La	**44**	46 10N	1 9W
Rocher River	**152**	61 23N	112 44W
Rocherath	**47**	50 26N	6 18E
Rocheservière	**42**	46 57N	1 30W
Rochester, Austral.	**140**	36 22S	144 41E
Rochester, Can.	**152**	54 22N	113 27W
Rochester, Kent, U.K.	**29**	51 22N	0 30E
Rochester, Northum., U.K.	**35**	55 16N	2 16W
Rochester, Ind., U.S.A.	**156**	41 5N	86 15W
Rochester, Minn., U.S.A.	**158**	44 1N	92 28W
Rochester, N.H., U.S.A.	**162**	43 19N	70 57W
Rochester, N.Y., U.S.A.	**156**	43 10N	77 40W
Rochford	**29**	51 36N	0 42E
Rochfortbridge	**38**	53 25N	7 19W
Rociana	**57**	37 19N	6 35W
Rociu	**70**	44 43N	25 2E
Rock Flat	**141**	36 21S	149 13E
Rock Hall	**162**	39 8N	76 14W
Rock Hill	**157**	34 55N	81 2W
Rock Island	**158**	41 30N	90 35W
Rock Lake	**158**	48 50N	99 13W
Rock, R.	**152**	60 7N	127 7W
Rock Rapids	**158**	43 25N	96 10W
Rock River	**160**	41 49N	106 0W
Rock Sound	**166**	24 54N	76 12W
Rock Sprs., Ariz., U.S.A.	**161**	34 2N	112 11W
Rock Sprs., Mont., U.S.A.	**160**	46 55N	106 11W
Rock Sprs., Tex., U.S.A.	**159**	30 2N	100 11W
Rock Sprs., Wyo., U.S.A.	**160**	41 40N	109 10W
Rock Valley	**158**	43 10N	96 17W
Rockall I.	**16**	57 37N	13 42W
Rockanje	**46**	51 52N	4 4E
Rockcliffe	**32**	54 58N	3 0W
Rockcorry	**38**	54 7N	7 0W
Rockdale	**159**	30 40N	97 0W
Rockefeller Plat.	**13**	84 0S	130 0W
Rockford	**158**	42 20N	89 0W
Rockglen	**153**	49 11N	105 57W
Rockhampton	**138**	23 22S	150 32E
Rockhampton Downs	**138**	18 57S	135 10E
Rockhill	**39**	52 25N	8 44W
Rockingham, Austral.	**137**	32 15S	115 38E
Rockingham, U.K.	**29**	52 32N	0 43W
Rockingham B.	**138**	18 5S	146 10E
Rockingham For.	**29**	52 28N	0 42W
Rockland, Idaho, U.S.A.	**160**	42 37N	112 57W
Rockland, Me., U.S.A.	**151**	44 0N	69 0W
Rockland, Mich., U.S.A.	**158**	46 40N	89 10W
Rockmart	**157**	34 1N	85 2W
Rockmills	**39**	52 13N	8 25W
Rockport, Mass., U.S.A.	**162**	42 39N	70 36W
Rockport, Mo., U.S.A.	**158**	40 26N	95 30W
Rockport, Tex., U.S.A.	**159**	28 2N	97 3W
Rockville, Conn., U.S.A.	**162**	41 51N	72 27W
Rockville, Md., U.S.A.	**162**	39 7N	77 10W
Rockwall	**159**	32 55N	96 30W
Rockwell City	**158**	42 20N	94 35W
Rockwood	**157**	35 52N	84 40W
Rocky Ford	**158**	38 7N	103 45W
Rocky Gully	**137**	34 30S	117 0E
Rocky Lane	**152**	58 31N	116 22W
Rocky Mount	**157**	35 55N	77 48W
Rocky Mountain House	**152**	52 22N	114 55W
Rocky Mts.	**152**	55 0N	121 0W
Rocky Pt.	**137**	33 30S	123 57E
Rockyford	**152**	51 14N	113 10W
Rocroi	**43**	49 55N	4 30E
Rod	**93**	28 10N	63 5E
Roda, La, Albacete, Spain	**59**	39 13N	2 15W
Roda, La, Sevilla, Spain	**57**	37 12N	4 46W
Rødberg	**71**	60 17N	8 56E
Rødby	**73**	54 41N	11 23E
Rødby Havn	**73**	54 39N	11 22E
Roddickton	**151**	50 51N	56 8W
Rødding	**73**	55 23N	9 3E
Rødekro	**73**	55 4N	9 20E
Rodel	**36**	57 45N	6 57W
Roden	**46**	53 8N	6 26E
Rødenes	**71**	59 35N	11 34E
Rodenkirchen	**48**	53 24N	8 26E
Roderick I.	**152**	52 38N	128 22W
Rodez	**44**	44 21N	2 33E
Rodholívas	**68**	40 55N	24 0E
Rodhópi □	**68**	41 10N	25 30E
Ródhos	**69**	36 15N	28 10E
Ródhos, I.	**69**	36 15N	28 10E
Roding R.	**29**	51 31N	0 7E
Rödjenäs	**73**	57 33N	14 50E
Rodna	**70**	47 25N	24 50E
Rodney, C.	**142**	36 17S	174 50E
Rodniki	**81**	57 7N	41 37E
Rodriguez, I.	**11**	20 0S	65 0E
Roe, R.	**38**	55 0N	6 56W
Roebling	**162**	40 7N	74 45W
Roebourne	**136**	20 44S	117 9E
Roebuck B.	**136**	18 5S	122 20E
Roebuck Plains P.O.	**136**	17 56S	122 28E
Roelofarendsveen	**46**	52 12N	4 38E
Roer, R.	**47**	51 12N	5 59E
Roermond	**47**	51 12N	6 0E
Roes Welcome Sd.	**149**	65 0N	87 0W
Roeselare	**47**	50 57N	3 7E
Rœulx	**47**	50 31N	4 7E
Rogachev	**80**	53 8N	30 5E
Rogagua, L.	**174**	14 0S	66 50W
Rogaland fylke □	**75**	59 12N	6 20E
Rogans Seat, Mt.	**32**	54 25N	2 10W
Rogaóica	**66**	44 4N	19 40E
Rogaška Slatina	**63**	46 15N	15 42E
Rogate	**29**	51 0N	0 51W
Rogatec	**63**	46 15N	15 46E
Rogatin	**80**	29 24N	24 36E
Rogers	**159**	36 20N	94 0W
Rogers City	**156**	45 25N	83 49W
Rogerson	**160**	42 10N	114 40W
Rogersville	**157**	36 27N	83 1W
Roggan River	**151**	54 25N	79 32W
Roggel	**47**	51 16N	5 56E
Roggeveldberge	**128**	32 10S	20 10E
Roggiano Gravina	**65**	39 37N	16 9E
Rogliano, France	**45**	42 57N	9 30E
Rogliano, Italy	**65**	39 11N	16 20E
Rogoaguado, L.	**174**	13 0S	65 30W
Rogowo	**54**	52 43N	17 38E
Rogozno	**54**	52 45N	16 59E
Rogue, R.	**160**	42 30N	124 0W
Rohan	**42**	48 4N	2 45W
Rohnert Park	**163**	38 16N	122 40W
Rohrbach	**43**	49 3N	7 15E
Rohri	**94**	27 45N	68 51E
Rohri Canal	**94**	26 15N	68 27E
Rohtak	**94**	28 55N	76 43E
Roi Et	**100**	15 56N	103 40E
Roisel	**43**	49 58N	3 6E
Rojas	**172**	34 10S	60 45W
Rojo, C., Mexico	**165**	21 33N	97 20W
Rojo, C., W. Indies	**147**	17 56N	67 11W
Rokan, R.	**102**	1 30N	100 50E
Rokeby	**138**	13 39S	142 40E
Rokiskis	**80**	55 55N	25 35E
Rokitnoye	**81**	50 57N	35 56E
Rokycany	**52**	49 43N	13 35E
Rolândia	**173**	23 5S	52 0W
Røldal	**71**	59 47N	6 50E
Rolde	**46**	52 59N	6 39E
Rolette	**158**	48 42N	99 50W
Rolfstorp	**73**	57 11N	12 27E
Rolla, Kansas, U.S.A.	**159**	37 10N	101 40W
Rolla, Missouri, U.S.A.	**159**	38 0N	91 42W
Rolla, N. Dak., U.S.A.	**158**	48 50N	99 36W
Rollag	**71**	60 2N	9 18E
Rollands Plains	**141**	31 17S	152 42E
Rolle	**50**	46 28N	6 20E
Rolleston, Austral.	**138**	24 28S	148 35E
Rolleston, N.Z.	**143**	43 35S	172 24E
Rollingstone	**138**	19 2S	146 24E
Rom	**123**	9 54N	32 16E
Roma, Austral.	**139**	26 32S	148 49E
Roma, Italy	**64**	41 54N	12 30E
Roma, Sweden	**73**	57 32N	18 26E
Roman, Bulg.	**67**	43 8N	23 54E
Roman, Rumania	**70**	46 57N	26 55E
Romana, La	**167**	18 27N	68 57W
Romang, I.	**103**	7 30S	127 20E
Romania ■	**61**	46 0N	25 0E
Romanija planina	**66**	43 50N	18 45E
Romano, Cayo	**166**	22 0N	77 30W
Romano di Lombardia	**62**	45 32N	9 45E
Romanovka = Bessarabka	**82**	46 21N	28 51E
Romans	**62**	45 3N	5 3E
Romanshorn	**51**	47 33N	9 22E
Romanzof, C.	**147**	62 0N	165 50W
Rombo □	**126**	3 10S	37 30E
Rome, U.S.A.	**162**	41 51N	76 21W
Rome, Ga., U.S.A.	**157**	34 20N	85 0W
Rome, N.Y., U.S.A.	**162**	43 14N	75 29W
Rome = Roma	**64**	41 54N	12 30E
Romeleåsen	**73**	55 34N	13 33E
Romenây	**45**	46 30N	5 1E
Romeo	**151**	47 28N	57 4W
Romerike	**71**	60 7N	11 10E
Romilly	**43**	48 31N	3 44E
Romîni	**70**	44 59N	24 11E
Rommani	**118**	33 31N	6 40W
Romney	**156**	39 21N	78 45W
Romney Marsh	**29**	51 0N	1 0E
Romny	**80**	50 48N	33 28E
Rømø	**73**	55 10N	8 30E
Romodan	**80**	50 0N	33 15E
Romodanovo	**81**	54 26N	45 23E
Romont	**50**	46 42N	6 54E
Romorantin-Lanthenay	**43**	47 21N	1 45E
Romsdal, R.	**71**	62 25N	8 0E
Romsdalen	**74**	62 25N	7 50E
Romsey	**28**	51 0N	1 29W
Ron	**100**	17 53N	106 27E
Rona I.	**36**	57 33N	6 0W
Ronan	**160**	47 30N	114 11W
Ronas Hill	**36**	60 33N	1 25W
Ronay I.	**36**	57 30N	7 10W
Roncador Cay	**166**	13 40N	80 4W
Roncador, Serra do	**171**	12 30S	52 30W
Roncesvalles, Paso	**58**	43 1N	1 19W
Ronceverte	**156**	37 45N	80 28W
Ronciglione	**63**	42 18N	12 12E
Ronco, R.	**63**	44 26N	12 15E
Ronda	**57**	36 46N	5 12W
Ronda, Serranía de	**57**	36 44N	5 3W
Rondane	**71**	61 57N	9 50E
Rondón	**174**	6 17N	71 6W
Rondônia □	**174**	11 0S	63 0W
Rong, Koh	**101**	10 45N	103 15E
Ronge, La, Can.	**153**	55 5N	105 20W
Ronge, La, Sask., Can.	**153**	55 6N	105 17W
Ronge, Lac La	**153**	55 10N	105 0W
Rongotea	**142**	40 19S	175 25E
Rønne	**73**	55 6N	14 44E
Ronne Land	**13**	83 0S	70 0W
Ronneby	**73**	56 12N	15 17E
Ronsard, C.	**137**	24 46S	113 10E
Ronse	**47**	50 45N	3 35E
Roodepoort-Maraisburg	**125**	26 8S	27 52E
Roodeschool	**46**	53 25N	6 46E
Roof Butte	**161**	36 29N	109 5W
Roompot	**47**	51 37N	3 44E
Roorkee	**94**	29 52N	77 59E
Roosendaal	**47**	51 32N	4 29E
Roosevelt, Minn., U.S.A.	**158**	48 51N	95 2W
Roosevelt, Utah, U.S.A.	**160**	40 19N	110 1W
Roosevelt I.	**13**	79 0S	161 0W
Roosevelt, Mt.	**152**	58 20N	125 20W
Roosevelt Res.	**161**	33 46N	111 0W
Roosky	**38**	53 50N	7 55W
Ropczyce	**54**	50 4N	21 38E
Roper, R.	**138**	14 43S	135 27E
Ropesville	**159**	33 25N	102 10W
Ropsley	**33**	52 53N	0 31W
Roque Pérez	**172**	35 25S	59 24W
Roquefort	**44**	44 2N	0 20W
Roquefort-sur-Souizon	**44**	43 58N	2 59E
Roquemaure	**45**	44 3N	4 48E
Roquetas	**58**	40 50N	0 30E
Roquevaire	**45**	43 20N	5 36E
Roraima □	**174**	2 0N	61 30W
Roraima, Mt.	**174**	5 10N	60 40W
Rorketon	**153**	51 24N	99 35W
Røros	**71**	62 35N	11 23E
Rorschach	**51**	47 28N	9 30E
Rørvik	**74**	64 54N	11 15E
Rosa, U.S.A.	**160**	38 15N	122 16W
Rosa, Zambia	**127**	9 33S	31 15E
Rosa Brook	**137**	33 57S	115 10E
Rosa, C.	**119**	37 0N	8 16E
Rosa, Monte	**50**	45 57N	7 53E
Rosal	**56**	41 57N	8 51W
Rosal de la Frontera	**57**	37 59N	7 13W
Rosalia	**160**	47 26N	117 25W
Rosamund	**163**	34 52N	118 10W
Rosans	**45**	44 24N	5 29E
Rosario	**172**	33 0S	60 50W
Rosário, Maran., Brazil	**170**	3 0S	44 15W
Rosário, Rio Grande do Sul, Brazil	**176**	30 15S	55 0W
Rosario, Baja California, Mexico	**164**	30 0N	116 0W
Rosario, Durango, Mexico	**164**	26 30N	105 35W
Rosario, Sinaloa, Mexico	**164**	23 0N	106 0W
Rosario, Venez.	**174**	10 19N	72 19W
Rosario de la Frontera	**172**	25 50S	65 0W
Rosario de Lerma	**172**	24 59S	65 35W
Rosario del Tala	**172**	32 20S	59 10W
Rosário do Sul	**173**	30 15S	54 55W
Rosarito	**164**	28 38N	114 4W
Rosarno	**65**	38 29N	15 59E
Rosas	**58**	42 19N	3 10E
Rosas, G. de,	**55**	42 10N	3 15E
Rosburgh	**143**	45 33S	169 19E
Roscoe	**162**	41 56N	74 55W
Roscoff	**42**	48 44N	4 0W
Roscommon, Ireland	**38**	53 38N	8 11W
Roscommon, U.S.A.	**156**	44 27N	84 35W
Roscommon □	**38**	53 40N	8 15W
Roscrea	**39**	52 58N	7 50W
Rose Blanche	**151**	47 38N	58 45W
Rose Harbour	**152**	52 15N	131 10W
Rose Ness	**37**	58 52N	2 50W
Rose Pt.	**152**	54 11N	131 39W
Rose, R.	**138**	14 16S	135 45E
Rose Valley	**153**	52 19N	103 49W
Roseau, Domin.	**167**	15 20N	61 30W
Roseau, U.S.A.	**158**	48 51N	95 46W
Rosebery	**138**	41 46S	145 33E
Rosebud, Austral.	**141**	38 21S	144 54E
Rosebud, U.S.A.	**159**	31 5N	97 0W
Roseburg	**160**	43 10N	123 10W
Rosedale, Austral.	**138**	24 38S	151 53E
Rosedale, U.S.A.	**159**	33 51N	91 0W
Rosedale Abbey	**33**	54 22N	0 51W
Rosée	**47**	50 14N	4 41E
Rosegreen	**39**	52 28N	7 51W
Rosehall	**37**	57 59N	4 36W
Rosehearty	**37**	57 42N	2 8W
Rosemarkie	**37**	57 35N	4 8W
Rosemary	**152**	50 46N	112 5W
Rosenallis	**39**	53 10N	7 25W
Rosenberg	**159**	29 30N	95 48W
Rosendaël	**43**	51 3N	2 24E
Rosenheim	**49**	47 51N	12 9E
Roseto degli Abruzzi	**63**	42 40N	14 2E
Rosetown	**153**	51 35N	108 3W
Rosetta = Rashîd	**122**	31 21N	30 22E
Roseville	**160**	38 46N	121 17W
Rosewood, N.S.W., Austral.	**141**	35 38S	147 52E
Rosewood, N.T., Austral.	**136**	16 28S	128 58E
Rosewood, Queens., Austral.	**139**	27 38S	152 36E
Rosh Haniqra, Kefar	**90**	33 5N	35 5E
Rosh Pinna	**90**	32 58N	35 32E
Rosh Ze'ira	**90**	31 14N	35 15E
Roshage C.	**73**	57 7N	8 35E
Rosières	**43**	48 36N	6 20E
Rosignano Marittimo	**62**	43 23N	10 28E
Rosignol	**174**	6 15N	57 30W
Roşiori-de-Vede	**70**	44 9N	25 0E
Rositsa	**67**	43 57N	27 57E
Rositsa, R.	**67**	43 10N	25 30E
Roskeeragh Pt.	**38**	54 22N	8 40W
Roskhill	**36**	57 24N	6 31W
Roskilde	**73**	55 38N	12 3E
Roskilde Amt □	**73**	55 35N	12 5E
Roskilde Fjord	**73**	55 50N	12 2E
Roskill, Mt.	**142**	36 55S	174 45E
Roslavl	**80**	53 57N	32 55E
Roslyn	**141**	34 29S	149 37E
Rosmaninhal	**57**	39 44N	7 5W
Røsnæs	**73**	55 44N	10 55E
Rosneath	**34**	56 1N	4 49W
Rosolini	**65**	36 49N	14 58E
Rosporden	**42**	47 57N	3 50W
Ross, Austral.	**138**	42 2S	147 30E
Ross, N.Z.	**143**	42 53S	170 49E
Ross, U.K.	**28**	51 55N	2 34W
Ross and Cromarty (□)	**26**	57 43N	4 50W

Ross Dependency **Sabang, O**

Ross Dependency	**13**	70	0 S	170	5W
Ross I.	**13**	77	30 S	168	0 E
Ross Ice Shelf	**13**	80	0 S	180	0W
Ross L.	**160**	48	50N	121	0W
Ross on Wye	**28**	51	55N	2	34W
Ross River, Austral.	**138**	19	15 S	146	51 E
Ross River, Can.	**147**	62	30N	131	30W
Ross Sea	**13**	74	0 S	178	0 E
Rossa	**51**	46	23N	9	8 E
Rossall Pt.	**32**	53	55N	3	2W
Rossan Pt.	**38**	54	42N	8	47W
Rossano Cálabro	**65**	39	36N	16	39 E
Rossburn	**153**	50	40N	100	49W
Rosscahill	**38**	53	23N	9	15W
Rosscarbery	**39**	51	39N	9	1W
Rosscarbery B.	**39**	51	32N	9	0W
Rossel I.	**138**	11	30 S	154	30 E
Rosses B.	**38**	55	2N	8	30W
Rosses Point	**38**	54	17N	8	34W
Rosses, The	**38**	55	2N	8	20W
Rossignol, L., N.S., Can.	**151**	44	12N	65	0W
Rossignol, L., Qué., Can.	**150**	52	43N	73	40W
Rossing	**128**	22	30 S	14	50 E
Rossland	**152**	49	6N	117	50W
Rosslare	**39**	52	17N	6	23W
Rosslau	**48**	51	52N	12	15 E
Rosslea	**38**	54	15N	7	11W
Rosso	**120**	16	40N	15	45W
Rossosh	**83**	50	15N	39	20 E
Rossport	**150**	48	50N	87	30W
Rossum	**46**	51	48N	5	20 E
Røssvatnet	**74**	65	45N	14	5 E
Rossville	**138**	15	48 S	145	15 E
Rosthern	**153**	52	40N	106	20W
Rostock	**48**	54	4N	12	9 E
Rostock □	**48**	54	10N	12	30 E
Rostov, Don, U.S.S.R.	**83**	47	15N	39	45 E
Rostov, Moskva, U.S.S.R.	**81**	57	14N	39	25 E
Rostrenen	**42**	48	14N	3	21W
Rostrevor	**38**	54	7N	6	12W
Roswell	**159**	33	26N	104	32W
Rosyth	**35**	56	2N	3	26W
Rota	**57**	36	37N	6	20W
Rotälven	**72**	61	30N	14	10 E
Rotan	**159**	32	52N	100	30W
Rotem	**47**	51	3N	5	45 E
Rotenburg	**48**	53	6N	9	24 E
Rothbury	**35**	55	19N	1	55W
Rothbury Forest	**35**	55	19N	1	50W
Rothenburg	**51**	47	6N	8	16 E
Rothenburg ob der Tauber	**49**	49	21N	10	11 E
Rother, R.	**29**	50	59N	0	40W
Rotherham	**33**	53	26N	1	21W
Rothes	**37**	57	31N	3	12W
Rothesay, Can.	**151**	45	23N	66	0W
Rothesay, U.K.	**34**	55	50N	5	3W
Rothhaar G., mts.	**50**	51	6N	8	10 E
Rothienorman	**37**	57	24N	2	28W
Rothrist	**50**	47	18N	8	54 E
Rothwell, Northants, U.K.	**29**	52	25N	0	48W
Rothwell, W. Yorks., U.K.	**33**	53	46N	1	29W
Roti, I.	**103**	10	50 S	123	0 E
Rotkop	**128**	26	44 S	15	27 E
Roto	**141**	33	0 S	145	30 E
Roto Aira L.	**142**	39	3 S	175	55 E
Rotoehu L.	**142**	38	1 S	176	32 E
Rotoiti L.	**142**	41	51 S	172	49 E
Rotoma L.	**142**	38	2 S	176	35 E
Rotondella	**65**	40	10N	16	30 E
Rotoroa Lake	**143**	41	55 S	172	39 E
Rotorua	**142**	38	9 S	176	16 E
Rotorua, L.	**142**	38	5 S	176	18 E
Rotselaar	**47**	50	57N	4	42 E
Rottal	**37**	56	48N	3	1W
Rotten, R.	**50**	46	18N	7	36 E
Rottenburg	**49**	48	28N	8	56 E
Rottenmann	**52**	47	31N	14	22 E
Rotterdam	**46**	51	55N	4	30 E
Rottingdean	**29**	50	48N	0	3W
Rottnest I.	**137**	32	0 S	115	27 E
Rottumeroog	**46**	53	33N	6	34 E
Rottweil	**49**	48	9N	8	38 E
Rotuma, I.	**130**	12	25 S	177	5 E
Roubaix	**43**	50	40N	3	10 E
Roudnice	**52**	50	25N	14	15 E
Rouen	**42**	49	27N	1	4 E
Rouergue	**45**	44	20N	2	20 E
Rough, gasfield	**19**	53	50N	0	27 E
Rough Pt.	**39**	52	19N	10	0W
Rough Ridge	**143**	45	10 S	169	55 E
Rouillac	**44**	45	47N	0	4W
Rouleau	**153**	50	10N	104	56W
Round Mt.	**139**	30	26 S	152	16 E
Round Mountain	**163**	38	46N	117	3W
Roundstone	**38**	53	24N	9	55W
Roundup	**160**	46	25N	108	35W
Roundwood	**39**	53	4N	6	14W
Rourkela	**95**	22	14N	84	50 E
Rousay, I.	**37**	59	10N	3	2W
Rousky	**38**	54	44N	7	10 E
Rousse, L'Île	**45**	43	27N	8	57 E
Roussillon	**45**	45	24N	4	49 E
Rouveen	**46**	52	37N	6	11 E
Rouxville	**128**	30	11 S	26	50 E
Rouyn	**150**	48	20N	79	0W
Rovaniemi	**74**	66	29N	25	41 E
Rovato	**62**	45	34N	10	0 E
Rovenki	**83**	48	5N	39	27 E
Rovereto	**62**	45	53N	11	3 E
Rovigo	**63**	45	4N	11	48 E
Rovinari	**70**	46	56N	23	10 E
Rovinj	**63**	45	18N	13	40 E
Rovira	**174**	4	15N	75	20W
Rovno	**80**	50	40N	26	10 E
Rovnoye	**81**	50	52N	46	3 E
Rovuma, R.	**127**	11	30 S	36	10 E
Rowanburn	**35**	55	5N	2	54W
Rowena	**139**	29	48 S	148	55 E
Rowes	**141**	37	0 S	149	6 E
Rowley Shoals	**136**	17	40 S	119	20 E
Rowood	**161**	32	18N	112	54W
Rowrah	**32**	54	34N	3	26W
Roxa	**120**	11	15N	15	45W
Roxas	**103**	11	36N	122	49 E
Roxboro	**157**	36	24N	78	59W
Roxborough Downs	**138**	22	20 S	138	45 E
Roxburgh, N.Z.	**143**	45	33 S	169	19 E
Roxburgh, U.K.	**35**	55	34N	2	30W
Roxburgh (□)	**26**	55	30N	2	30W
Roxby	**33**	53	38N	0	37W
Roxen	**73**	58	30N	15	40 E
Roy	**160**	47	17N	109	0W
Roy Hill	**136**	22	37 S	119	58 E
Roy, Le	**159**	38	8N	95	35W
Roya, Peña	**58**	40	25N	0	40W
Royal Canal	**38**	53	29N	7	0W
Royal Oak	**156**	42	30N	83	5W
Royalla	**141**	35	30 S	149	9 E
Royan	**44**	45	37N	1	2W
Roybridge	**37**	56	53N	4	50W
Roye	**43**	47	40N	6	31 E
Røyken	**71**	59	45N	10	23 E
Royston	**29**	52	3N	0	1W
Royton	**32**	53	34N	2	7W
Rozaj	**66**	42	50N	20	15 E
Rozan	**54**	52	52N	21	25 E
Rozdol	**80**	49	30N	24	1 E
Rozier, Le	**44**	44	13N	3	12 E
Roznava	**53**	48	37N	20	35 E
Rozoy	**43**	48	40N	2	56 E
Rozoy-sur-Serre	**43**	49	40N	4	8 E
Rozwadów	**54**	50	37N	22	2 E
Rrësheni	**68**	41	47N	19	49 E
Rtanj, mt.	**66**	43	45N	21	50W
Rtem, Oued el	**119**	33	40N	5	34 E
Rtishchevo	**81**	52	35N	43	50 E
Rúa	**56**	42	24N	7	6W
Ruacaná	**128**	17	20 S	14	12 E
Ruahine Ra.	**142**	39	55 S	176	2 E
Ruamahanga, R.	**142**	41	24 S	175	8 E
Ruapehu	**142**	39	17 S	175	35 E
Ruapuke I.	**143**	46	46 S	168	31 E
Ruatoria	**142**	37	55 S	178	20 E
Ruâus, W.	**119**	30	14N	15	0 E
Ruawai	**142**	36	15 S	173	59 E
Rub 'al Khali	**91**	21	0N	51	0 E
Rubeho, mts.	**126**	6	50 S	36	25 E
Rubery	**28**	52	24N	1	59W
Rubezhnoye	**82**	49	6N	38	25 E
Rubha Ardvule C.	**36**	57	17N	7	32W
Rubha Hunish, C.	**36**	57	42N	6	20W
Rubh'an Dunain, C.	**36**	57	10N	6	20W
Rubiataba	**171**	15	8 S	49	48W
Rubicone, R.	**63**	44	0N	12	20 E
Rubim	**171**	16	23 S	40	32W
Rubinéia	**171**	20	13 S	51	2W
Rubino	**120**	6	4N	4	18W
Rubio	**174**	7	43N	72	22W
Rubona	**126**	0	29N	30	9 E
Rubtsovsk	**76**	51	30N	80	50 E
Ruby	**147**	64	40N	155	35W
Ruby L.	**160**	40	10N	115	28W
Ruby Mts.	**160**	40	30N	115	30W
Rubyvale	**138**	23	25 S	147	45 E
Rucava	**80**	56	9N	20	32 E
Ruciane-Nida	**54**	53	40N	21	32 E
RûcûSdia	**66**	44	59N	21	36 E
Rud	**71**	60	1N	10	1 E
Ruda	**73**	57	6N	16	7 E
Ruda Slaska	**53**	50	16N	18	50 E
Rudall	**140**	33	43 S	136	17 E
Rudbar	**93**	30	0N	62	30 E
Ruden, I.	**48**	54	13N	13	47 E
Rüdersdorf	**48**	52	28N	13	48 E
Rudewa	**127**	10	7 S	34	47 E
Rudgwick	**29**	51	7N	0	54W
Rudkøbing	**73**	54	56N	10	41 E
Rudna	**54**	51	30N	16	17 E
Rudnichnyy	**84**	59	38N	52	26 E
Rudnik, Bulg.	**67**	42	36N	27	30 E
Rudnik, Yugo.	**67**	44	7N	20	35 E
Rudnik, mt.	**67**	44	7N	20	35 E
Rudnogorsk	**77**	57	15N	103	42 E
Rudnya	**80**	54	55N	31	13 E
Rudnyy	**84**	52	57N	63	7 E
Rudo	**66**	43	41N	19	23 E
Rudolstadt	**48**	50	44N	11	20 E
Rudozem	**67**	41	29N	24	51 E
Rudston	**33**	54	6N	0	19W
Rŭducaneni	**70**	46	58N	27	54 E
Rŭdŭuţi	**70**	47	50N	25	59 E
Rudyard	**156**	46	14N	84	35 E
Rue	**43**	50	15N	1	40 E
Ruelle	**44**	45	41N	0	14 E
Rufa'a	**123**	14	44N	33	32 E
Ruffec Charente	**44**	46	2N	0	12W
Rufi	**123**	5	58N	30	18 E
Rufiji □	**126**	8	0 S	38	30 E
Rufiji, R.	**124**	7	50 S	38	15 E
Rufino	**172**	34	20 S	62	50W
Rufisque	**120**	14	40N	17	15W
Rufunsa	**127**	15	4 S	29	34 E
Rugby, U.K.	**28**	52	23N	1	16W
Rugby, U.S.A.	**158**	48	21N	100	0W
Rugeley	**28**	52	47N	1	56W
Rügen, I.	**48**	54	22N	13	25 E
Rugezi	**126**	2	6 S	33	18 E
Rugles	**42**	48	50N	0	40 E
Ruhâma	**90**	31	31N	34	43 E
Ruhea	**98**	26	10N	88	25 E
Ruhengeri	**126**	1	30 S	29	36 E
Ruhla	**48**	50	53N	10	21 E
Ruhland	**48**	51	27N	13	52 E
Ruhr, R.	**48**	51	25N	7	15 E
Ruhuhu, R.	**127**	10	15 S	34	55 E
Rui Barbosa	**171**	12	18 S	40	27W
Ruidosa	**159**	29	59N	104	39W
Ruidoso	**161**	33	19N	105	39W
Ruinen	**46**	52	46N	6	21 E
Ruinen A Kanaal	**46**	52	54N	7	8 E
Ruinerwold	**46**	52	44N	6	15 E
Ruj, mt.	**66**	42	52N	22	42 E
Rujen, mt.	**66**	42	9N	22	30 E
Ruk	**94**	27	50N	68	42 E
Rukwa □, Tanz.	**126**	7	0 S	31	30 E
Rukwa □, Tanz.	**126**	7	0 S	31	30 E
Rukwa L.	**126**	7	50 S	32	10 E
Rulhieres, C.	**136**	13	56 S	127	22 E
Rulles	**47**	49	43N	5	32 E
Rully	**167**	46	52N	4	44 E
Rum Jungle	**136**	13	0 S	130	59 E
Ruma	**66**	45	8N	19	50 E
Rumah	**92**	25	35N	47	10 E
Rumania ■	**61**	46	0N	25	0 E
Rumbalara	**138**	25	20 S	134	29 E
Rumbek	**123**	6	54N	29	37 E
Rumbeke	**47**	50	56N	3	10 E
Rumburk	**52**	50	57N	14	32 E
Rumelange	**47**	49	27N	6	2 E
Rumford	**156**	44	30N	70	30W
Rumia	**54**	54	37N	18	25 E
Rumilly	**45**	45	53N	5	56 E
Rumney	**31**	51	32N	3	7W
Rumoi	**112**	43	56N	141	39W
Rumonge	**126**	3	59 S	29	26 E
Rumsey	**152**	51	51N	112	48W
Rumson	**162**	40	23N	74	0W
Rumula	**138**	16	35 S	145	20 E
Rumuruti	**126**	0	17N	36	32 E
Runabay Hd.	**38**	55	10N	6	2W
Runanga	**143**	42	25 S	171	15 E
Runaway, C.	**142**	37	32 S	178	2 E
Runcorn, Austral.	**108**	27	36 S	153	4 E
Runcorn, U.K.	**32**	53	20N	2	44W
Rungwa	**126**	6	55 S	33	32 E
Rungwa, R.	**126**	7	15 S	33	10 E
Rungwe	**127**	9	11 S	33	32 E
Rungwe □	**127**	9	25 S	33	32 E
Runka	**121**	12	28N	7	20 E
Runn	**72**	60	30N	15	40 E
Rupa	**98**	27	15N	92	30 E
Rupar	**94**	31	2N	76	38 E
Rupat, I.	**102**	1	45N	101	40 E
Rupea	**61**	46	2N	25	13 E
Rupert House = Fort Rupert	**150**	51	30N	78	40W
Rupert, R.	**150**	51	29N	78	45W
Rupsa	**98**	21	44N	87	20 E
Rupununi, R.	**175**	3	30N	59	30W
Ruquka Gie La	**99**	31	35N	97	55 E
Rurrenabaque	**174**	14	30 S	67	32W
Rus, R.	**58**	39	30N	2	30W
Rusambo	**127**	16	30 S	32	4 E
Rusape	**125**	18	35 S	32	8 E
Ruschuk = Ruse	**67**	43	48N	25	59 E
Ruse	**67**	43	48N	25	59 E
Rusetu	**70**	44	57N	27	14 E
Rush	**38**	53	31N	6	7W
Rushden	**29**	52	17N	0	37W
Rushford	**158**	43	48N	91	46W
Rushville, Ill., U.S.A.	**158**	40	6N	90	35W
Rushville, Ind., U.S.A.	**156**	39	38N	85	22W
Rushville, Nebr., U.S.A.	**158**	42	43N	102	35W
Rushworth	**141**	36	32 S	145	1 E
Rusken	**73**	57	15N	14	20 E
Ruskington	**33**	53	5N	0	23W
Russas	**171**	4	56 S	38	2W
Russell, Can.	**153**	50	50N	101	20W
Russell, N.Z.	**142**	35	16 S	174	10 E
Russell, U.S.A.	**158**	38	56N	98	55W
Russell L., Man., Can.	**153**	56	15N	101	30W
Russell L., N.W.T., Can.	**152**	63	5N	115	44W
Russellkonda	**96**	19	57N	84	42 E
Russellville, Ala., U.S.A.	**157**	34	30N	87	44W
Russellville, Ark., U.S.A.	**159**	35	15N	93	0W
Russellville, Ky., U.S.A.	**157**	36	50N	86	50W
Russi	**63**	44	21N	12	1 E
Russian Mission	**147**	61	45N	161	25W
Russian S.F.S.R. □	**77**	62	0N	105	0 E
Russkoye Ustie	**12**	71	0N	149	0 E
Rust	**53**	47	49N	16	42 E
Rustam	**94**	34	25N	72	13 E
Rustam Shahr	**94**	26	58N	66	6 E
Rustavi	**83**	40	45N	44	30 E
Rustenburg	**128**	25	41 S	27	14 E
Ruston	**159**	32	30N	92	40W
Ruswil	**50**	47	5N	8	8 E
Rutana	**126**	3	55 S	30	0 E
Rutba	**92**	33	4N	40	15 E
Rute	**57**	37	19N	4	29W
Ruteng	**103**	8	26 S	120	30 E
Ruth	**160**	39	15N	115	1W
Ruth, oilfield	**19**	55	33N	4	55 E
Rutherglen, Austral.	**141**	36	5 S	146	29 E
Rutherglen, U.K.	**34**	55	50N	4	11W
Ruthin	**31**	53	7N	3	20W
Ruthven	**37**	57	4N	4	2W
Ruthwell	**35**	55	0N	3	24W
Rüti	**51**	47	16N	8	51 E
Rutigliano	**65**	41	1N	17	0 E
Rutland	**162**	43	38N	73	0W
Rutland (□)	**26**	52	38N	0	40W
Rutland I.	**101**	11	25N	92	40 E
Rutland Plains	**138**	15	38 S	141	49 E
Rutledge L.	**153**	61	33N	110	47W
Rutledge, R.	**153**	61	4N	112	0W
Rutshuru	**126**	1	13 S	29	25 E
Ruurlo	**46**	52	5N	6	24 E
Ruvo di Púglia	**65**	41	7N	16	27 E
Ruvu	**126**	6	49 S	38	43 E
Ruvu, R.	**126**	7	25 S	38	15 E
Ruvuma □	**127**	10	20 S	36	0 E
Ruvuma, R.	**127**	11	30 S	36	10 E
Ruwaidha	**92**	23	40N	44	40 E
Ruwandiz	**92**	36	40N	44	32 E
Ruwenzori Mts.	**126**	0	30N	29	55 E
Ruwenzori, mt.	**126**	0	30N	29	55 E
Ruyigi	**126**	3	29 S	30	15 E
Ruzayevka	**81**	54	10N	45	0 E
Ruzhevo Konare	**67**	42	23N	24	46 E
Ruzomberok	**53**	49	3N	19	17 E
Rwanda ■	**126**	2	0 S	30	0 E
Ryaberg	**73**	56	47N	13	15 E
Ryakhovo	**67**	44	0N	26	18 E
Ryan, L.	**34**	55	0N	5	2W
Ryazan	**81**	54	50N	39	40 E
Ryazhsk	**81**	53	45N	40	3 E
Rybache	**76**	46	40N	81	20 E
Rybachi Poluostrov	**78**	69	43N	32	0 E
Rybachye	**85**	42	26N	76	12 E
Rybinsk (Shcherbakov)	**81**	58	5N	38	50 E
Rybinsk Vdkhr.	**81**	58	30N	38	0 E
Rybnik	**54**	50	6N	18	32 E
Rybnitsa	**82**	47	45N	29	0 E
Rychwał	**54**	52	4N	18	10 E
Ryd	**73**	56	27N	14	42 E
Rydal	**34**	54	28N	2	59W
Ryde	**28**	50	44N	1	9W
Rydö	**73**	56	58N	13	10 E
Rydsnäs	**73**	57	47N	15	9 E
Rydułtowy	**54**	50	4N	18	23 E
Rydzyna	**54**	51	47N	16	39 E
Rye, Denmark	**73**	56	5N	9	45 E
Rye, U.K.	**29**	50	57N	0	46 E
Rye Patch Res.	**160**	40	45N	118	20W
Rye, R.	**33**	54	12N	0	53W
Ryegate	**160**	46	21N	109	27W
Ryhope	**35**	54	52N	1	22W
Rylsk	**80**	51	30N	34	51 E
Rylstone	**141**	32	46 S	149	58 E
Rymanów	**54**	49	35N	21	51 E
Ryn	**54**	53	57N	21	34 E
Ryningsnäs	**73**	57	17N	15	58 E
Ryōhaku-Sanchi	**111**	36	0N	136	49 E
Rypin	**54**	53	3N	19	32 E
Ryton, Tyne & Wear, U.K.	**35**	54	58N	1	44W
Ryton, Warwick, U.K.	**28**	52	23N	1	25W
Ryūgasaki	**111**	35	54N	140	11 E
Ryūkyū Is. = Nansei-Shotō	**112**	26	0N	128	0 E
Rzepin	**54**	52	20N	14	49 E
Rzeszów	**54**	50	5N	21	58 E
Rzeszów □	**54**	50	0N	22	0 E
Rzhev	**80**	56	20N	34	20 E

S

s'-Hertogenbosch	**47**	51	42N	5	17 E
Sa	**100**	18	34N	100	45 E
Sa. da Canastra	**125**	19	30 S	46	5W
Sa Dec	**101**	10	20N	105	46 E
Sa-Koi	**98**	19	54N	97	3 E
Sa'ad (Muharraga)	**90**	31	28N	34	33 E
Sa'ādatabād	**93**	30	10N	53	5 E
Saale, R.	**48**	51	25N	11	56 E
Saaler Bodden	**48**	54	20N	12	25 E
Saalfelden	**70**	47	26N	12	51 E
Saalfield	**48**	50	39N	11	21 E
Saane, R.	**50**	46	23N	7	18 E
Saanen	**50**	46	29N	7	15 E
Saar (Sarre), □	**43**	49	20N	6	45 E
Saarbrücken	**49**	49	15N	6	58 E
Saarburg	**49**	49	36N	6	32 E
Saaremaa	**80**	58	30N	22	30 E
Saariselkä	**74**	68	16N	28	15 E
Saarland □	**131**	49	20N	6	45 E
Saarlouis	**49**	49	19N	6	45 E
Saas Fee	**50**	46	7N	7	56 E
Saas-Grund	**50**	46	7N	7	57 E
Saba I.	**167**	17	30N	63	10W
Sabac	**66**	44	48N	19	42 E
Sabadell	**58**	41	28N	2	7 E
Sabae	**111**	35	57N	136	11 E
Sabagalel	**102**	1	36 S	98	40 E
Sabah □	**102**	6	0N	117	0 E
Sabak	**100**	3	46N	100	58 E
Sábana de la Mar	**167**	19	7N	69	40W
Sábanalarga	**174**	10	38N	74	55W
Sabang, O.	**102**	5	50N	95	15 E

Sabará St. Lawrence

Sabará 171 19 55 S 43 55 W
Sabarania 103 2 5 S 138 18 E
Sabari, R. 96 18 0 N 81 25 E
Sabastiya 90 32 17 N 35 12 E
Sabaudia 64 41 17 N 13 2 E
Sabderat 123 15 26 N 36 42 E
Sabhah 119 27 9 N 14 29 E
Sabie 129 25 4 S 30 48 E
Sabinal, Mexico 164 30 50 N 107 25 W
Sabinal, U.S.A. 159 29 20 N 99 27 W
Sabinal, Punta del 59 36 43 N 2 44 W
Sabinas 164 27 50 N 101 10 W
Sabinas Hidalgo 164 26 40 N 100 10 W
Sabinas, R. 164 27 37 N 100 42 W
Sabine 159 29 42 N 93 54 W
Sabine, R. 159 31 30 N 93 35 W
Sabinópolis 171 18 40 S 43 6 W
Sabinov 53 49 6 N 21 5 E
Sabirabad 83 40 0 N 48 30 E
Sabkhat Tawurgha 119 31 48 N 15 30 E
Sablayan 103 12 5 N 120 50 E
Sable 42 47 50 N 0 21 W
Sable, C., Can. 151 43 29 N 65 38 W
Sable, C., U.S.A. 166 25 5 N 81 0 W
Sable I. 151 44 0 N 60 0 W
Sablé-sur-Sarthe 42 47 50 N 0 20 W
Sables-D'Olonne, Les 44 46 30 N 1 45 W
Saboeiro 170 6 32 S 39 54 W
Sabor, R. 56 41 16 N 7 10 W
Sabou 120 12 1 N 2 28 W
Sabrātah 119 32 47 N 12 29 E
Sabrina Coast 13 67 0 S 120 0 E
Sabugal 56 40 20 N 7 5 W
Sabzevar 93 36 15 N 57 40 E
Sabzvaran 93 28 45 N 57 50 E
Sac City 158 42 26 N 95 0 W
Sacandaga Res. 162 43 6 N 74 16 W
Sacedón 58 40 29 N 2 41 W
Sachigo, L. 150 53 50 N 92 12 W
Sachigo, R. 150 55 6 N 88 58 W
Sachinbulako 106 43 5 N 111 47 E
Sachkhere 83 42 25 N 43 28 E
Sachseln 51 46 52 N 8 15 E
Sacile 63 45 58 N 16 7 E
Säckingen 49 47 34 N 7 56 E
Saco, Me., U.S.A. 162 43 30 N 70 27 W
Saco, Mont., U.S.A. 160 48 28 N 107 19 W
Sacquoy Hd. 37 59 12 N 3 5 W
Sacramento, Brazil 171 19 53 S 47 27 W
Sacramento, U.S.A. 163 38 39 N 121 30 E
Sacramento Mts. 161 32 30 N 105 30 W
Sacramento, R. 163 38 3 N 121 56 W
Sacratif, Cabo 59 36 42 N 3 28 W
Sacriston 33 54 49 N 1 38 W
Sada 56 43 22 N 8 15 W
Sada-Misaki-Hantō 110 33 22 N 132 1 E
Sadaba 58 2 19 N 1 12 W
Sa'dani 124 5 58 S 38 35 E
Sadao 101 6 38 N 100 26 E
Sadasivpet 96 17 38 N 77 50 E
Sadberge 33 54 32 N 1 30 W
Sadd el Aali 122 24 5 N 32 54 E
Saddell 34 55 31 N 5 30 W
Saddle, Hd. 38 54 0 N 10 10 W
Saddle, The 36 57 10 N 5 27 W
Sade 121 11 22 N 10 45 E
Sadiba 128 18 53 S 23 1 E
Sadimi 127 9 25 S 23 32 E
Sado 112 38 0 N 138 25 E
Sado, R. 57 38 10 N 8 22 W
Sadon, Burma 99 25 28 N 98 0 E
Sadon, U.S.S.R. 83 42 52 N 43 58 E
Sadri 94 24 28 N 74 30 E
Saduya 98 27 50 N 95 40 E
Sæby 73 57 21 N 10 30 E
Saelices 58 39 55 N 2 49 W
Safâga 122 26 42 N 34 0 E
Safaha 122 26 25 N 39 0 E
Safaniya 92 28 5 N 48 42 E
Safárikovo 53 48 25 N 20 20 E
Safed Koh, Mts. 94 34 15 N 64 0 E
Safford 61 32 54 N 109 52 W
Saffron Walden 29 52 2 N 0 15 E
Safi, Jordan 90 31 2 N 35 28 E
Safi, Moroc. 118 32 18 N 9 14 W
Safiah 42 31 27 N 34 46 E
Safonovo 80 65 40 N 47 50 E
Safranbolu 82 41 15 N 32 34 E
Sag Harbor 162 40 59 N 72 17 W
Sag Sag 135 5 32 S 148 23 E
Saga, Indon. 103 2 40 S 132 55 E
Saga, Kōchi, Japan 110 33 5 N 133 6 E
Saga, Saga, Japan 110 33 15 N 130 16 E
Saga-ken □ 110 33 15 N 130 20 E
Sagâg 71 59 46 N 5 25 E
Sagaing 98 23 30 N 95 30 E
Sagaing □ 98 22 0 N 95 30 E
Sagala 120 14 9 N 6 38 W
Sagami-Nada 111 34 58 N 139 23 E
Sagami-Wan 111 35 15 N 139 25 E
Sagamihara 111 35 33 N 139 25 E
Saganoseki 110 33 15 N 131 53 E
Sagar 93 23 50 N 78 50 E
Sagara, India 97 14 14 N 75 6 E
Sagara, Japan 111 34 41 N 138 12 E
Sagara, L. 126 5 20 S 31 0 E
Sagawa 110 33 28 N 133 11 E
Sågen 72 60 17 N 14 10 E
Sagil 105 50 20 N 91 40 E
Saginaw 156 43 26 N 83 55 W
Saginaw B. 150 43 50 N 83 40 W
Sagleipie 45 45 25 N 7 0 E
Saglouc (Sugluk) 149 62 30 N 74 15 W
Sagone 45 42 7 N 8 42 E
Sagone, G. de 45 42 4 N 8 40 E
Sagori 107 35 25 N 126 49 E
Sagra, La, Mt. 59 38 0 N 2 35 W
Sagres 57 37 0 N 8 58 W
Sagu 98 20 13 N 94 46 E
Sagua la Grande 166 22 50 N 80 10 W
Saguache 161 38 10 N 106 4 W
Saguenay, R. 151 48 22 N 71 0 W
Sagunto 58 39 42 N 0 18 W
Sahaba 122 18 57 N 30 25 E
Sahagún, Colomb. 174 8 57 N 75 27 W
Sahagún, Spain 56 42 18 N 5 2 W
Saham 90 32 42 N 35 46 E
Sahara 118 23 0 N 5 0 W
Saharanpur 94 29 58 N 77 33 E
Saharien Atlas 118 34 9 N 3 29 E
Sahasinaka 129 21 49 S 47 49 E
Sahaswan 95 28 5 N 78 45 E
Sahel, Canal du 120 14 20 N 6 0 W
Sahibganj 95 25 12 N 87 55 E
Sahiwal 94 30 45 N 73 8 E
Sahl Arraba 90 37 26 N 35 12 E
Sahtaneh, R. 152 59 2 N 122 28 W
Sahuaripa 164 29 30 N 109 0 W
Sahuarita 161 31 58 N 110 59 W
Sahuayo 164 20 4 N 102 43 W
Sahy 53 48 4 N 18 55 E
Sai Buri 101 6 43 N 101 39 E
Saibai I. 135 9 25 S 142 40 E
Sa'id Bundas 117 8 24 N 24 48 E
Saïda 118 34 50 N 0 11 E
Sa'idabad 93 29 30 N 55 45 E
Saidapet 97 13 0 N 80 15 E
Saidor 135 5 40 S 146 29 E
Saidu 95 34 50 N 72 15 E
Säle 72 59 8 N 12 55 E
Saighan 93 35 10 N 67 55 E
Saignelégier 50 47 15 N 7 0 E
Saignes 44 45 20 N 2 31 E
Saigō 110 36 12 N 133 20 E
Saigon = Phanh Bho Ho Chi Minh 101 10 58 N 106 40 E
Saih-al-Malih 93 23 37 N 58 31 E
Saihut 91 15 12 N 51 10 E
Saijō, Ehima, Japan 110 33 55 N 133 11 E
Saijō, Hiroshima, Japan 110 34 25 N 132 45 E
Saikhoa Ghat 99 27 50 N 95 40 E
Saiki 110 32 58 N 131 57 E
Saillans 45 44 42 N 5 12 E
Sailolof 103 1 7 S 130 46 E
Saima 107 40 59 N 124 15 E
Saimaa, L. 78 61 15 N 28 15 E
St. Abbs 35 55 54 N 2 7 W
St. Abb's Head 35 55 55 N 2 10 W
St. Aegyd 52 47 52 N 15 33 E
St. Affrique 44 43 57 N 2 53 E
St. Agnes 30 50 18 N 5 13 W
St. Agnes Hd. 30 50 19 N 5 14 W
St. Agnes I. 30 49 53 N 6 20 W
St.-Agrève 45 45 0 N 4 23 E
St.-Aignan 42 47 16 N 1 22 E
St. Albans, Austral. 138 24 43 S 139 56 E
St. Albans, Can. 151 47 51 N 55 50 W
St. Albans, U.K. 29 51 44 N 0 19 W
St. Albans, Vt., U.S.A. 156 44 49 N 73 7 W
St. Albans, W. Va., U.S.A. 156 38 21 N 81 50 W
St. Alban's Head 28 50 34 N 2 3 W
St. Albert 152 53 37 N 113 40 W
St. Amand 43 50 25 N 3 6 E
St.-Amand-en-Puisaye 43 47 32 N 3 5 E
St.-Amand-Mont-Rond 44 46 43 N 2 30 E
St.-Amarin 43 47 54 N 7 0 E
St.-Amour 45 46 26 N 5 21 E
St. Andrä 52 46 46 N 14 50 E
St. André, C. 129 16 11 S 44 27 E
St.-André-de-Cubzac 44 44 59 N 0 26 W
St. André de l'Eure 42 48 54 N 1 16 E
St.-André-les-Alpes 45 43 58 N 6 30 E
St. Andrews, Can. 151 47 45 N 59 15 W
St. Andrews, N.Z. 143 44 33 S 171 10 E
St. Andrews, U.K. 35 56 20 N 2 48 W
St. Ann B. 151 46 22 N 60 25 W
St. Anne 42 49 43 N 2 11 W
St. Anne's 32 53 45 N 3 2 W
St. Ann's 35 55 14 N 3 28 W
St. Ann's Bay 166 18 26 N 77 15 W
St. Ann's Hd. 31 51 41 N 5 11 W
St. Anthony, Can. 151 51 22 N 55 35 W
St. Anthony, U.S.A. 160 44 0 N 111 49 W
St.-Antonin-Noble-Val 44 44 10 N 1 45 E
St. Arnaud 140 36 32 S 143 16 E
St. Arnaud Ra. 143 42 1 S 172 53 E
St. Arthur 151 47 47 N 67 46 W
St. Asaph 31 53 15 N 3 27 W
St. Astier 44 45 8 N 0 31 E
St.-Aubin 50 46 54 N 6 47 E
St.-Aubin-du-Cormier 42 48 15 N 1 26 W
St. Augustin 129 23 33 S 43 46 E
St-Augustin-Saguenay 151 51 13 N 58 38 W
St. Augustine 157 29 52 N 81 20 W
St. Austell 30 50 20 N 4 48 W
St.-Avold 43 49 6 N 6 43 E
St. Barthélemy, I. 167 17 50 N 62 50 W
St. Bathans 143 44 53 S 170 0 E
St. Bathan's Mt. 143 44 45 S 169 45 E
St. Bees 32 54 29 N 3 36 W
St. Bee's Hd. 32 54 30 N 3 38 E
St.-Benoît-du-Sault 44 46 26 N 1 24 E
St. Bernard, Col du Grand 50 45 53 N 7 11 E
St.-Blaise 50 47 1 N 6 59 E
St. Blazey 32 50 22 N 4 48 W
St. Boniface 153 49 50 N 97 10 W
St. Bonnet 45 44 40 N 6 5 E
St. Boswells 35 55 34 N 2 39 W
St.-Brévin-les-Pins 42 47 14 N 2 10 W
St. Briavels 28 51 44 N 2 39 W
St.-Brice-en-Coglès 42 48 25 N 1 22 W
St. Bride's 151 46 56 N 54 10 W
St. Bride's B. 31 51 48 N 5 15 W
St.-Brieuc 42 48 30 N 2 46 W
St. Budeaux 30 50 23 N 4 10 W
St. Buryan 30 50 4 N 5 34 W
St.-Calais 42 47 55 N 0 45 E
St.-Cast 42 48 37 N 2 18 W
St. Catharines 150 43 10 N 79 15 W
St. Catherine's I. 157 31 35 N 81 10 W
St. Catherine's Pt. 28 50 34 N 1 18 W
St.-Céré 44 44 51 N 1 54 E
St. Cergue 50 46 27 N 6 10 E
St. Cernin 44 45 5 N 2 25 E
St.-Chamond 45 45 28 N 4 31 E
St. Charles, Ill., U.S.A. 156 41 55 N 88 21 W
St. Charles, Mo., U.S.A. 158 38 46 N 90 30 W
St.-Chély-d'Apcher 44 44 48 N 3 17 E
St.-Chinian 44 43 25 N 2 56 E
St. Christopher (St. Kitts) 167 17 20 N 62 40 W
St.-Ciers-sur-Gironde 44 45 17 N 0 37 W
St. Clair 162 40 42 N 76 12 W
St. Clair, L. 150 42 30 N 82 45 W
St.-Claud 44 45 54 N 0 28 E
St. Claude 153 49 40 N 98 20 W
St.-Claude 45 46 22 N 5 52 E
St. Clears 31 51 48 N 4 30 W
St.-Cloud 42 48 51 N 2 12 E
St. Cloud, Fla., U.S.A. 157 28 15 N 81 15 W
St. Cloud, Minn., U.S.A. 158 45 30 N 94 11 W
St. Coeur de Marie 151 48 39 N 71 43 W
St. Columb Major 30 50 26 N 4 56 W
St. Combs 37 57 40 N 1 55 W
St. Cricq, C. 137 25 17 S 113 6 E
St. Croix Falls 158 45 18 N 92 22 W
St. Croix, I. 147 17 45 N 64 45 W
St. Croix, R. 158 45 20 N 92 50 W
St. Cyprien 44 42 37 N 3 0 E
St.-Cyr 45 43 11 N 5 43 E
St. Cyrus 36 56 47 N 2 25 W
St. David's, Can. 151 48 12 N 58 52 W
St. David's, U.K. 31 51 54 N 5 16 W
St. David's Head 31 51 54 N 5 16 W
St.-Denis 43 48 56 N 2 22 E
St.-Denis-d'Orques 42 48 2 N 0 17 W
St. Dennis 30 50 23 N 4 53 W
St.-Dié 43 48 17 N 6 56 E
St. Dizier 43 48 40 N 5 0 E
St. Dogmaels 31 52 6 N 4 42 W
St. Dominick 30 50 28 N 4 15 W
St. Donats 31 51 23 N 3 32 W
St.-Egrève 45 45 14 N 5 41 E
St. Elias, Mt. 147 60 20 N 141 59 W
St. Elias Mts. 147 59 30 N 137 30 W
St. Eloy 44 46 10 N 2 51 E
St. Emilon 44 44 53 N 0 9 W
St. Endellion 30 50 33 N 4 49 W
St. Enoder 30 50 22 N 4 57 W
St. Erth 30 50 10 N 5 26 W
St. Étienne 45 45 27 N 4 22 E
St.-Étienne-de-Tinée 45 44 16 N 6 56 E
St. Eustatius I. 167 17 20 N 63 0 W
St. Félicien 150 48 40 N 72 25 W
St. Fergus 37 57 33 N 1 50 W
St. Fillans 35 56 25 N 4 7 W
St. Finian's B. 39 51 50 N 10 22 W
St. Fintan's 151 48 10 N 58 50 W
St.-Florent 45 42 41 N 9 18 E
St.-Florent-sur-Cher 43 46 59 N 2 15 E
St.-Florentin 43 48 0 N 3 45 E
St.-Flour 44 45 2 N 3 6 E
St.-Fons 45 45 42 N 4 52 E
St. Francis 158 39 48 N 101 47 W
St. Francis C. 128 34 14 S 24 49 E
St. Francis, R. 159 32 25 N 90 36 W
St.-Fulgent 42 46 50 N 1 10 W
St. Gabriel de Brandon 150 46 17 N 73 24 W
St.-Gengoux-le-National 45 46 37 N 4 40 E
St.-Geniez-d'Olt 44 44 27 N 2 58 E
St. George, Austral. 139 28 1 S 148 41 E
St. George, Can. 151 45 11 N 66 50 W
St. George, P.N.G. 135 4 10 S 152 20 E
St. George, S.C., U.S.A. 157 33 13 N 80 37 W
St. George, Utah, U.S.A. 161 37 10 N 113 35 W
St. George, C., Can. 151 48 30 N 59 16 W
St. George, C., P.N.G. 135 4 49 S 152 53 E
St. George, C., U.S.A. 157 29 36 N 85 2 W
St. George Hd. 139 35 11 S 150 45 E
St. George Ra., Mts. 136 18 40 S 125 0 E
St. George West 153 50 33 N 96 7 W
St.-Georges 47 50 37 N 4 20 E
St. George's 151 48 26 N 58 31 W
St. Georges, Qué., Can. 151 46 8 N 70 40 W
St. Georges, Quebec, Can. 150 46 42 N 72 35 W
St. Georges, Fr. Gui. 175 4 0 N 52 0 W
St. George's 167 12 5 N 61 43 W
St. George's B. 151 48 24 N 58 53 W
St. George's Channel 147 52 0 N 6 0 W
St. Georges-de-Didonne 44 45 36 N 1 0 W
St. Georges Head 141 35 12 S 150 42 E
St.-Gérard 47 50 21 N 4 44 E
St. Germain 43 48 53 N 2 5 E
St.-Germain-Lembron 44 45 27 N 3 14 E
St.-Germain-de-Calberte 44 44 13 N 3 48 E
St.-Germain-des-Fossés 44 46 12 N 3 26 E
St.-Germain-du-Plain 43 46 42 N 4 58 E
St.-Germain-Laval 45 45 50 N 4 1 E
St. Germans 30 50 24 N 4 19 W
St. Gervais, Haute Savoie, France 45 45 53 N 6 42 E
St. Gervais, Puy de Dôme, France 44 46 4 N 2 50 E
St.-Gervais-les-Bains 43 45 53 N 6 41 E
St.-Gildas, Pte. de 42 47 8 N 2 14 W
St.-Gilles 45 43 40 N 4 26 E
St. Gilles Croix-de-Vie 42 46 41 N 1 55 W
St.-Gingolph 50 46 24 N 6 48 E
St.-Girons 44 42 59 N 1 8 E
St. Gla, L. 72 59 35 N 12 30 E
St. Goar 49 50 31 N 7 43 E
St. Gotthard P. = San Gottardo 51 46 33 N 8 33 E
St. Govan's Hd. 31 51 35 N 4 56 W
St.-Guadens 44 43 6 N 0 44 E
St.-Gualtier 42 46 39 N 1 26 E
St.-Guénolé 42 47 49 N 4 23 W
St. Harmon 31 52 21 N 3 29 W
St. Heddinge 73 55 9 N 12 26 E
St. Helena 160 38 29 N 122 30 W
St. Helena, I. 15 15 55 S 5 44 W
St. Helenabaai 128 32 40 S 18 10 E
St. Helens, Austral. 138 41 20 S 148 15 E
St. Helens, I.o.W., U.K. 28 50 42 N 1 6 W
St. Helens, Merseyside, U.K. 32 53 28 N 2 44 W
St. Helens, U.S.A. 160 45 55 N 122 50 W
St. Helier 42 49 11 N 2 6 W
St. Hilaire 42 48 35 N 1 7 W
St. Hippolyte 43 47 20 N 6 50 E
St. Hippolyte-du-Fort 44 43 58 N 3 52 E
St.-Honoré 43 46 54 N 3 50 E
St.-Hubert 47 50 2 N 5 23 E
St. Hyacinthe 150 45 40 N 72 58 W
St. Ignace 156 45 53 N 84 43 W
St. Ignace I. 150 48 45 N 88 0 W
St. Ignatius 160 47 25 N 114 2 W
St.-Imier 50 47 9 N 6 58 E
St. Issey 30 50 30 N 4 55 W
St. Ives, Cambs., U.K. 29 52 20 N 0 5 W
St. Ives, Cornwall, U.K. 30 50 13 N 5 29 W
St. Ives Bay 30 50 15 N 5 27 W
St.-James 42 48 31 N 1 20 W
St. James 158 43 57 N 94 40 W
St. James C. 152 51 55 N 131 0 W
St. Jean 150 45 20 N 73 50 W
St.-Jean 45 48 57 N 3 1 E
St. Jean Baptiste 153 49 15 N 97 20 W
St. Jean, C. 124 1 5 N 9 20 E
St.-Jean-de-Maurienne 45 45 16 N 6 28 E
St.-Jean-de-Luz 44 43 23 N 1 39 W
St.-Jean-de-Monts 42 46 47 N 2 4 W
St. Jean-du-Gard 44 44 7 N 3 52 E
St.-Jean-en-Royans 45 45 1 N 5 18 E
St.-Jean, L. 151 48 40 N 72 0 W
St. Jean-Port-Joli 151 47 15 N 70 13 W
St.-Jean, R. 151 50 17 N 64 20 W
St. Jérôme, Qué., Can. 150 45 47 N 74 0 W
St. Jérôme, Qué., Can. 151 48 26 N 71 53 W
St. John, Can. 151 45 20 N 66 8 W
St. John, Kans., U.S.A. 159 37 59 N 98 45 W
St. John, N.D., U.S.A. 158 48 58 N 99 40 W
St. John, C. 151 50 0 N 55 32 W
St. John, I. 147 18 20 N 64 45 W
St. John, R. 151 45 15 N 66 4 W
St. Johns 167 17 6 N 61 51 W
St. John's, Can. 151 47 35 N 52 40 W
St. John's, U.K. 32 54 13 N 4 38 W
St. Johns, Ariz., U.S.A. 161 34 31 N 109 26 W
St. Johns, Mich., U.S.A. 156 43 0 N 84 38 W
St. Johns Chapel 32 54 43 N 2 10 W
St. John's Pt., Ireland 38 54 35 N 8 26 W
St. John's Pt., U.K. 38 54 14 N 5 40 W
St. Johns, R. 157 30 20 N 81 30 W
St. Johnsbury 156 44 25 N 72 1 W
St. Johnston 38 54 56 N 7 29 W
St. Johnsville 162 43 0 N 74 43 W
St. Joseph, La., U.S.A. 159 31 55 N 91 15 W
St. Joseph, Mo., U.S.A. 158 39 40 N 94 50 W
St. Joseph, I. 150 46 12 N 83 58 W
St. Joseph, L. 150 51 10 N 90 35 W
St. Joseph, R. 156 42 7 N 86 30 W
St. Joseph's 156 42 5 N 86 30 W
St. Jovite 150 46 8 N 74 38 W
St. Juéry 44 43 55 N 2 42 E
St. Julien 45 46 8 N 6 5 E
St.-Julien-Chapteuil 45 45 2 N 4 4 E
St. Julien du Sault 43 48 1 N 3 17 E
St.-Junien 44 45 53 N 0 55 E
St. Just 30 50 7 N 5 41 W
St.-Just-en-Chaussée 43 49 30 N 2 25 E
St.-Just-en-Chevalet 44 45 55 N 3 50 E
St.-Justin 44 43 59 N 0 14 W
St. Karlsö, I. 73 57 17 N 17 58 E
St. Keverne 30 50 3 N 5 5 W
St. Kew 30 50 34 N 4 48 W
St. Kilda 143 45 53 S 170 31 E
St. Kilda, I. 23 57 40 N 8 50 W
St. Kitts-Nevis ■ 167 17 20 N 62 40 W
St. Laurent 153 50 25 N 97 58 W
St.-Laurent-du-Pont 45 45 23 N 5 45 E
St.-Laurent-en-Grandvaux 45 46 35 N 5 45 E
St. Lawrence, Austral. 138 22 16 S 149 31 E
St. Lawrence, Can. 151 46 54 N 55 23 W

St. Lawrence, Gulf of — Sam Ngao

St. Lawrence, Gulf of	**151**	48 25N	62 0W
St. Lawrence, I.	**147**	63 0N	170 0W
St. Lawrence, R.	**151**	49 30N	66 0W
St.-Léger	**47**	49 37N	5 39E
St. Leonard	**151**	47 12N	67 58W
St.-Léonard-de-Noblat	**44**	45 49N	1 29E
St. Leonards	**29**	50 51N	0 34E
St. Levan	**30**	50 3N	5 36W
St Lewis, R.	**151**	52 26N	56 11W
St. Lin	**150**	45 44N	73 46W
St.-Lô	**42**	49 7N	1 5W
St. Louis, Senegal	**120**	16 8N	16 27W
St. Louis, Mich., U.S.A.	**156**	43 27N	84 38W
St. Louis, Mo., U.S.A.	**158**	38 40N	90 12W
St. Louis R.	**158**	47 15N	92 45W
St.-Loup-sur-Semouse	**43**	47 53N	6 16E
St. Lucia, C.	**129**	28 32S	32 29E
St. Lucia Channel	**167**	14 15N	61 0W
St. Lucia I.	**167**	14 0N	60 50W
St. Lucia, Lake	**129**	28 5S	32 30E
St. Lunaire-Griquet	**151**	51 31N	55 28W
St. Maarten, I.	**167**	18 0N	63 5W
St. Mabyn	**30**	50 30N	4 45W
St. Magnus B.	**36**	60 25N	1 35W
St.-Maixent-l'École	**44**	46 24N	0 12W
St.-Malo	**42**	48 39N	2 1W
St. Malo, G. de	**42**	48 50N	2 30W
St. Mandrier	**45**	43 4N	5 56E
St. Marc	**167**	19 10N	72 50W
St.-Marcellin	**45**	45 9N	5 20E
St. Marcouf, Is.	**42**	49 30N	1 10W
St.-Mard	**47**	49 2N	2 42E
St. Margaret's-at-Cliffe	**29**	51 10N	1 23E
St. Margaret's Hope	**37**	58 49N	2 58W
St. Maries	**160**	47 17N	116 34W
St. Martin	**43**	50 42N	1 38E
St.-Martin, I.	**167**	18 0N	63 0W
St. Martin L.	**153**	51 40N	98 30W
St. Martin-Tende-Vésubie	**45**	44 4N	7 15E
St. Martins	**151**	45 22N	65 25W
St. Martin's I.	**30**	49 58N	6 16W
St. Martinsville	**159**	30 10N	91 50W
St.-Martory	**44**	43 9N	0 56E
St. Mary B.	**151**	46 50N	53 50W
St. Mary Bourne	**28**	51 16N	1 24W
St. Mary C.	**120**	13 24N	13 10E
St. Mary Is.	**97**	13 20N	74 35E
St. Mary, Mt.	**135**	8 8S	146 54E
St. Mary Pk.	**140**	31 32S	138 34E
St. Marys, N.S.W., Austral.	**133**	33 44S	150 49E
St. Marys, Tas., Austral.	**138**	41 32S	148 11E
St. Mary's, Can.	**151**	46 56N	53 34W
St. Mary's, U.K.	**37**	58 53N	2 55W
St. Mary's, Ohio, U.S.A.	**156**	40 33N	84 20W
St. Mary's, Pa., U.S.A.	**156**	41 30N	78 33W
St Marys Bay	**151**	44 25N	66 10W
St. Mary's, C.	**151**	46 50N	54 12W
St. Mary's I.	**30**	49 55N	6 17W
St. Mary's Pk.	**133**	31 30S	138 33E
St. Mary's Sd.	**30**	49 53N	6 19W
St. Mathews I. = Zadetkyi Kyun	**101**	10 0N	48 25E
St.-Mathieu, Pte. de	**42**	48 20N	4 45W
St. Matthias Grp.	**135**	1 30S	150 0E
St.-Maur-des-Fosses	**43**	48 48N	2 30E
St. Maurice	**50**	46 13N	7 0E
St. Maurice R.	**150**	47 20N	72 50W
St. Mawes	**30**	50 10N	5 1W
St.-Médard-de-Guizières	**44**	45 1N	0 4W
St.-Méen-le-Grand	**42**	48 11N	2 12W
St. Merryn	**30**	50 31N	4 58W
St. Michael	**147**	63 30N	162 30W
St. Michaels, Arizona, U.S.A.	**161**	35 45N	109 5W
St. Michaels, Maryland, U.S.A.	**162**	38 47N	76 14W
St. Michael's Mt.	**30**	50 7N	5 30W
St. Michel	**45**	45 15N	6 29E
St. Mihiel	**43**	48 54N	5 30E
St. Minver	**30**	50 34N	4 52W
St. Monans	**35**	56 13N	2 46W
St.-Nazaire	**42**	47 17N	2 12W
St. Neots	**29**	52 14N	0 16W
St.-Nicholas-de-Port	**43**	48 38N	6 18E
St. Niklaus	**50**	46 10N	7 49E
St. Ninian's, I.	**36**	59 59N	1 20W
St. Olaf	**73**	55 40N	14 12E
St.-Omer	**43**	50 45N	2 15E
St. Osyth	**29**	51 47N	1 4E
St. Ouen	**43**	48 50N	2 20E
St. Pacome	**151**	47 24N	69 58W
St. Palais	**44**	45 40N	1 8W
St. Pamphile	**151**	46 58N	69 48W
St.-Pardoux-la-Rivière	**44**	45 29N	0 45E
St. Pascal	**151**	47 32N	69 48W
St. Patrickswell	**39**	52 36N	8 43W
St. Paul, Can.	**152**	54 59N	111 17W
St. Paul, France	**44**	43 44N	1 3W
St. Paul, Minn., U.S.A.	**158**	44 54N	93 5W
St. Paul, Nebr., U.S.A.	**158**	41 15N	98 30W
St. Paul-de-Fenouillet	**44**	42 50N	2 28E
St. Paul, I., Atl. Oc.	**14**	0 50N	31 40W
St. Paul, I., Can.	**151**	47 12N	60 9W
St. Paul, I., Ind. Oc.	**11**	30 40S	77 34E
St. Paul's B.	**151**	49 48N	57 58W
St.-Peray	**45**	44 57N	4 50E
St.-Père-en-Retz	**42**	47 11N	2 2W
St. Peter	**158**	44 15N	93 57W
St. Peter Port	**42**	49 27N	2 31W
St. Peters, N.S., Can.	**151**	45 40N	60 53W
St. Peters, P.E.I., Can.	**151**	46 25N	62 35W
St. Petersburg	**157**	27 45N	82 40W
St.-Philbert-de-Grand-Lieu	**42**	47 2N	1 39W
St Pierre	**151**	46 40N	56 0W
St.-Pierre-d'Oleron	**44**	45 57N	1 19W
St.-Pierre-Église	**42**	49 40N	1 24W
St.-Pierre-en-Port	**42**	49 48N	0 30E
Saint-Pierre et Miquelon □	**151**	46 55N	56 10W
St-Pierre, L.	**150**	46 12N	72 52W
St.-Pierre-le-Moûtier	**43**	46 47N	3 7E
St. Pierre-sur-Dives	**42**	49 2N	0 1W
St.-Pieters Leew	**47**	50 47N	4 16E
St. Pol	**43**	50 21N	2 20E
St.-Pol-de-Léon	**42**	48 41N	4 0W
St.-Pol-sur-Mer	**43**	51 1N	2 20E
St. Pons	**44**	43 30N	2 45E
St.-Pourçain-sur-Sioule	**43**	46 18N	3 18E
St.-Quay-Portrieux	**42**	48 39N	2 51W
St.-Quentin	**43**	49 50N	3 16E
St. Rambert-d'Albon	**45**	45 17N	1 35E
St.-Raphaël	**45**	43 25N	6 46E
St. Regis	**160**	47 20N	115 3W
St.-Rémy-de-Provence	**45**	43 48N	4 50E
St.-Renan	**42**	48 26N	4 37W
St.-Saëns	**42**	49 41N	1 16E
St.-Sauveur-en-Puisaye	**43**	47 37N	3 12E
St.-Sauveur-le-Vicomte	**42**	49 23N	1 32W
St. Savin	**44**	46 34N	0 50E
St.-Savinien	**44**	45 53N	0 42W
St. Sebastien, C.	**129**	12 26S	48 44E
St.-Seine-l'Abbaye	**43**	47 26N	4 47E
St. Sernin	**44**	43 54N	2 35E
St.-Servan-sur-Mer	**42**	48 38N	2 0E
St.-Sever-Calvados	**42**	48 50N	1 3W
St. Simeon	**151**	47 51N	69 54W
St. Stephen, Can.	**151**	45 16N	67 17W
St. Stephen, U.K.	**30**	50 20N	4 52W
St.-Sulpice	**44**	43 46N	1 41E
St.-Sulpice-Laurière	**44**	46 3N	1 29E
St. Teath	**30**	50 34N	4 45W
St.-Thegonnec	**42**	48 31N	3 57W
St. Thomas	**150**	42 45N	81 10W
St. Thomas, I.	**147**	18 21N	64 55W
St. Tite	**150**	46 45N	72 40W
St. Tropez	**45**	43 17N	6 38E
St. Troud	**47**	50 48N	5 10E
St. Tudwal's Is.	**31**	52 48N	4 28W
St. Tudy	**30**	50 33N	4 45W
St.-Vaast-la-Hougue	**42**	49 35N	1 17W
St. Valéry	**43**	50 10N	1 38E
St.-Valéry-en-Caux	**42**	49 52N	0 43E
St.-Vallier	**45**	45 11N	4 50E
St.-Vallier-de-Thiey	**45**	43 42N	6 51E
St.-Varent	**42**	46 53N	0 13W
St. Vincent	**14**	18 0N	26 1W
St. Vincent C.	**125**	21 58S	43 20E
St. Vincent, C. = São Vincente	**57**	37 0N	9 0W
St. Vincent-de-Tyrosse	**44**	43 39N	1 18W
St. Vincent, G.	**140**	35 0S	138 0E
St. Vincent, I.	**167**	13 10N	61 10W
St. Vincent Passage	**167**	13 30N	61 0W
St.-Vith	**47**	50 17N	6 9E
St.-Yrieux-la-Perche	**44**	45 31N	1 12E
Ste.-Adresse	**42**	49 31N	0 5E
Ste.-Agathe-des-Monts	**150**	46 3N	74 17W
Ste. Anne	**167**	14 26N	60 53W
Ste. Anne de Beaupré	**151**	47 2N	70 58W
Ste. Anne de Portneuf	**151**	48 38N	69 8W
Ste.-Anne-des-Monts	**151**	49 8N	66 30W
Ste. Benoîte	**43**	49 47N	3 30E
Ste. Cecile	**151**	47 56N	64 34W
Ste.-Croix	**43**	46 49N	6 34E
Ste.-Enimie	**44**	44 22N	3 26E
Ste.-Foy-la-Grande	**44**	44 50N	0 13E
Ste. Genevieve	**158**	37 59N	90 2W
Ste. Germaine	**151**	46 24N	70 24W
Ste.-Hermine	**44**	46 32N	1 4W
Ste.-Livrade-sur-Lot	**44**	44 24N	0 36E
Ste. Marguerite, R.	**151**	50 9N	66 36W
Ste. Marie	**167**	14 48N	61 1W
Ste.-Marie-aux-Mines	**43**	48 10N	7 12E
Ste. Marie, C.	**129**	25 36S	45 8E
Ste. Marie de la Madeleine	**151**	46 26N	71 0W
Ste. Marie, I.	**129**	16 50S	49 55E
Ste.-Maure-de-Touraine	**42**	47 7N	0 37E
Ste.-Maxime	**45**	43 19N	6 39E
Ste.-Menehould	**43**	49 5N	4 54E
Ste.-Mère-Église	**42**	49 24N	1 19W
Ste. Rose	**167**	16 20N	61 45W
Ste. Rose du lac	**153**	51 41N	99 30W
Ste. Teresa	**172**	33 33S	60 54W
Saintes	**44**	45 45N	0 37W
Saintes, I. des	**167**	15 50N	61 35W
Saintes-Maries-de-la-Mer	**45**	43 26N	4 26E
Saintes Maries, Les	**45**	43 27N	4 25E
Saintfield	**38**	54 28N	5 50W
Saintonge	**44**	45 40N	0 50W
Sairang	**99**	23 50N	92 45E
Sairecábur, Cerro	**172**	22 43S	67 54W
Saitama-ken □	**111**	36 25N	137 0E
Saito	**110**	32 3N	131 18E
Sajama, Nevada	**174**	18 0S	68 55W
Sajan	**66**	45 50N	20 58E
Sajószentpéter	**53**	48 12N	20 44E
Sajum, mt.	**95**	33 20N	79 0E
Saka Ilkalat	**93**	27 20N	64 7E
Sakai	**111**	34 30N	135 30E
Sakaide	**110**	34 15N	133 56E
Sakaiminato	**110**	35 38N	133 11E
Sakaka	**92**	30 0N	40 8E
Sakami, L.	**150**	53 15N	76 45W
Sâkâne, 'Erg i-n	**118**	20 30N	1 30W
Sakania	**127**	12 43S	28 30E
Sakar, I.	**138**	5 30S	148 0E
Sakarya, R.	**82**	40 5N	31 0E
Sakata	**112**	36 38N	138 19E
Sakchu	**107**	40 23N	125 2E
Sakeny, R.	**129**	20 0S	45 25E
Sakété	**121**	6 40N	2 32E
Sakhalin, Ostrov	**77**	51 0N	143 0E
Sakhi Gopal	**96**	19 58N	85 50E
Sakhnin	**90**	32 52N	35 12E
Saki	**82**	45 16N	33 34E
Sakiai	**80**	54 59N	23 0E
Sakmara	**84**	52 0N	55 20E
Sakmara, R.	**84**	51 46N	55 1E
Sakołow Małopolski	**54**	50 10N	22 9E
Sakon Nakhon	**100**	17 10N	104 9E
Sakrand	**94**	26 10N	68 15E
Sakri	**96**	21 2N	74 40E
Sakskøbing	**73**	54 49N	11 39E
Saku	**111**	36 11N	138 31E
Sakuma	**111**	35 3N	137 56E
Sakurai	**111**	34 30N	135 51E
Sakuru	**111**	35 43N	140 14E
Säkylä	**75**	61 4N	22 20E
Sal, R.	**83**	47 25N	42 20E
Sal'a	**53**	48 10N	17 50E
Sala	**72**	59 58N	16 35E
Sala Consilina	**65**	40 23N	15 35E
Sala-y-Gomez, I.	**131**	26 28S	105 28W
Salaberry-de-Valleyfield	**150**	45 15N	74 8W
Salada, La	**164**	24 30N	111 30W
Saladas	**172**	28 15S	58 40W
Saladillo	**172**	35 40S	59 55W
Salado, R., Buenos Aires, Argent.	**172**	35 40S	58 10W
Salado, R., Santa Fe, Argent.	**172**	27 0S	63 40W
Salado, R., Mexico	**164**	26 52N	99 19W
Salaga	**121**	8 31N	0 31W
Salala, Liberia	**120**	6 42N	10 7W
Salala, Sudan	**122**	21 17N	36 16E
Salalah	**91**	16 56N	53 59E
Salama	**90**	32 3N	34 48E
Salamanca, Chile	**172**	32 0S	71 25W
Salamanca, Spain	**56**	40 58N	5 39W
Salamanca, U.S.A.	**156**	42 10N	78 42W
Salamanca □	**56**	40 57N	5 40W
Salamaua	**138**	7 10S	147 0E
Salamina	**174**	5 25N	75 29W
Salamis	**69**	37 56N	23 30E
Salar de Atacama	**176**	23 30S	68 25W
Salar de Uyuni	**174**	20 30S	67 45W
Salard	**70**	47 12N	22 3E
Salas	**56**	43 25N	6 15W
Salas de los Infantes	**58**	42 2N	3 17W
Salavat	**84**	53 21N	55 55E
Salaverry	**174**	8 15S	79 0W
Salawe	**126**	3 17S	32 56E
Salayar, I.	**103**	6 15S	120 30E
Salazar, R.	**58**	42 45N	1 8W
Salbohed	**72**	59 55N	16 22E
Salbris	**43**	47 25N	2 3E
Salcia	**70**	43 56N	24 55E
Salcombe	**30**	50 14N	3 47W
Salcombe Regis	**30**	50 41N	3 11W
Saldaña	**56**	42 32N	4 48W
Saldanha	**128**	33 0S	17 58E
Saldanhabaai	**128**	33 6S	18 0E
Saldus	**80**	56 45N	22 37E
Sale	**141**	38 6S	147 6E
Salé	**118**	34 3N	6 48W
Sale	**32**	53 26N	2 19W
Saléa-koïra	**121**	16 54N	0 46W
Salebabu	**103**	3 45N	125 55E
Salehabad	**93**	35 40N	61 2E
Salekhard	**76**	66 30N	66 25E
Salem, India	**97**	11 40N	78 11E
Salem, Ind., U.S.A.	**156**	38 38N	86 16W
Salem, Mass., U.S.A.	**162**	42 29N	70 53W
Salem, Mo., U.S.A.	**159**	37 40N	91 30W
Salem, N.H., U.S.A.	**162**	42 47N	71 12W
Salem, N.J., U.S.A.	**162**	39 34N	75 29W
Salem, N.Y., U.S.A.	**162**	43 10N	73 20W
Salem, Ohio, U.S.A.	**156**	40 52N	80 50W
Salem, Oreg., U.S.A.	**160**	45 0N	123 0W
Salem, Va., U.S.A.	**156**	37 19N	80 8W
Salembu, Kepulauan	**102**	5 35S	114 30E
Salemi	**64**	37 49N	12 47E
Salen, Norway	**75**	64 41N	11 27E
Salen, Highland, U.K.	**36**	56 42N	5 48W
Salen, Strathclyde, U.K.	**34**	56 31N	5 57W
Salernes	**45**	43 34N	6 15E
Salerno	**65**	40 40N	14 44E
Salerno, G. di	**65**	40 35N	14 45E
Salfit	**90**	32 5N	35 11E
Salford	**32**	53 30N	2 17W
Salford Priors	**28**	52 10N	1 52W
Salgir, R.	**82**	45 30N	34 30E
Salgótarján	**53**	48 5N	19 47E
Salgueiro	**170**	8 4S	39 6W
Salies-de-Béarn	**44**	43 28N	0 56W
Salima	**125**	13 47S	34 28E
Salin	**98**	20 35N	94 40E
Salina	**158**	38 50N	97 40W
Salina Cruz	**165**	16 10N	95 10W
Salina, I.	**65**	38 35N	14 50E
Salina, La	**174**	10 22N	71 27W
Salinas, Brazil	**171**	16 20S	42 10W
Salinas, Chile	**172**	23 31S	69 29W
Salinas, Ecuador	**174**	2 10S	80 50W
Salinas, Mexico	**164**	23 37N	106 8W
Salinas, U.S.A.	**163**	36 40N	121 31W
Salinas Ambargasta	**172**	29 0S	65 30W
Salinas, B. de	**166**	11 4N	85 45W
Salinas, Cabo de	**59**	39 16N	3 4E
Salinas (de Hidalgo)	**164**	22 30N	101 40W
Salinas Grandes	**172**	30 0S	65 0W
Salinas, Pampa de las	**172**	31 58S	66 42W
Salinas, R., Mexico	**165**	16 28N	90 31W
Salinas, R., U.S.A.	**163**	36 45N	121 48W
Saline, R.	**158**	39 10N	99 5W
Salines-les-Bains	**43**	46 58N	5 52E
Salinópolis	**170**	0 40S	47 20W
Salir	**57**	37 14N	8 2W
Salisbury, Austral.	**140**	34 46S	138 40E
•Salisbury, Zimb.	**127**	17 50S	31 2E
Salisbury, U.K.	**28**	51 4N	1 48W
Salisbury, Md., U.S.A.	**162**	38 20N	75 38W
Salisbury, N.C., U.S.A.	**157**	35 42N	80 29W
Salisbury Plain	**28**	51 13N	1 50W
Salitre, R.	**170**	9 29S	40 39W
Salka	**121**	10 20N	4 58E
Salle, La	**158**	41 20N	89 5W
Sallent	**58**	41 49N	1 54E
Salles-Curan	**44**	44 11N	2 48E
Salling	**73**	56 40N	8 55E
Sallisaw	**159**	35 26N	94 45W
Sallom Junc.	**122**	19 23N	37 6E
Sally Gap, Mt.	**39**	53 7N	6 18W
Salmerón	**58**	40 33N	2 29W
Salmo	**152**	49 10N	117 20W
Salmon	**160**	45 12N	113 56W
Salmon Arm	**152**	50 40N	119 15W
Salmon Falls	**160**	42 55N	114 59W
Salmon Gums	**137**	32 59S	121 38E
Salmon, R., Can.	**152**	54 3N	122 40W
Salmon, R., U.S.A.	**160**	46 0N	116 30W
Salmon Res.	**151**	48 05N	56 00W
Salmon River Mts.	**160**	45 0N	114 30W
Salo	**75**	60 22N	23 3E
Salò	**62**	45 37N	10 32E
Salobreña	**57**	36 44N	3 35W
Salome	**161**	33 51N	113 37W
Salon-de-Provence	**45**	43 39N	5 6E
Salonica = Thessaloniki	**68**	40 38N	22 58E
Salonta	**70**	46 49N	21 42E
Salop □	**28**	52 36N	2 45W
Salor, R.	**57**	39 39N	7 3W
Salou, Cabo	**58**	41 3N	1 10E
Salsacate	**172**	31 20S	65 5W
Salsaker	**72**	62 59N	18 20E
Salses	**44**	42 50N	2 55E
Salsette I.	**96**	19 5N	72 50E
Salsk	**83**	46 28N	41 30E
Salso, R.	**65**	37 6N	13 55E
Salsomaggiore	**62**	44 48N	9 59E
Salt	**90**	32 2N	35 43E
Salt Creek	**140**	36 8S	139 38E
Salt Creek Telegraph Office	**139**	36 0S	139 35E
Salt Fork R.	**159**	37 25N	98 40W
Salt Lake City	**160**	40 45N	111 58W
Salt, R., Can.	**152**	60 0N	112 25W
Salt, R., U.S.A.	**161**	33 50N	110 25W
Salt Range	**94**	32 30N	72 25E
Salta	**172**	24 47S	65 25W
Salta □	**172**	24 48S	65 30W
Saltash	**30**	50 25N	4 13W
Saltburn by Sea	**33**	54 35N	0 58W
Saltcoats	**34**	55 38N	4 47W
Saltee Is.	**39**	52 7N	6 37W
Saltergate	**33**	54 20N	0 40W
Saltfjorden	**74**	67 15N	14 20E
Saltfleet	**33**	53 25N	0 11E
Saltfleetby	**33**	53 23N	0 10E
Salthill	**39**	53 15N	9 6W
Saltholm	**73**	55 38N	12 43E
Salthólmavík	**74**	65 24N	21 57W
Saltillo	**164**	25 30N	100 57W
Salto, Argent.	**172**	34 20S	60 15W
Salto, Uruguay	**172**	31 20S	57 59W
Salto □	**172**	31 20S	57 59W
Salto Augusto, falls	**172**	8 30S	58 0W
Salto da Divisa	**171**	16 0S	39 57W
Salton City	**163**	33 21N	115 59W
Salton Sea	**163**	33 20N	115 50W
Saltpond	**121**	5 15N	1 3W
Saltsjöbaden	**73**	59 15N	18 20E
Saltspring	**152**	48 54N	123 37W
Saltwood	**29**	51 4N	1 5E
Saluda	**162**	37 36N	76 36W
Salula, R.	**157**	34 12N	81 45W
Salûm	**122**	31 31N	25 7E
Salûm, Khâlig el	**122**	31 30N	25 9E
Salur	**96**	18 27N	83 18E
Saluzzo	**62**	44 39N	7 29E
Salvador, Brazil	**171**	13 0S	38 30W
Salvador, Can.	**153**	52 10N	109 25W
Salvador ■	**164**	13 50N	89 0W
Salvador, L.	**159**	29 46N	90 16W
Salvaterra	**170**	0 46S	48 31W
Salvaterra de Magos	**57**	39 1N	8 47W
Sálvora, Isla	**56**	42 30N	8 58W
Salwa	**93**	24 45N	50 55E
Salween, R.	**98**	16 31N	97 37E
Salza, R.	**52**	47 43N	15 0E
Salzach, R.	**52**	47 15N	12 25E
Salzburg	**52**	47 48N	13 2E
Salzgitter	**48**	52 2N	10 22E
Salzwedel	**48**	52 50N	11 11E
Sam Neua	**100**	20 29N	104 0E
Sam Ngao	**100**	17 18N	99 0E

*Renamed Harare

Name	Map	Lat °	′	N/S	Long °	′	E/W
Sam Rayburn Res.	159	31	15	N	94	20	W
Sam Son	100	19	44	N	105	54	E
Sam Ten	100	19	59	N	104	38	E
Sama	84	60	12	N	60	22	E
Sama de Langreo	56	43	18	N	5	40	W
Samales Group	103	6	0	N	122	0	E
Samalkot	96	17	3	N	82	13	E
Samâlût	122	28	20	N	30	42	E
Samana	94	30	10	N	76	13	E
Samana Cay	167	23	3	N	73	45	W
Samanco	174	9	10	S	78	30	W
Samanga	127	8	20	S	39	13	E
Samangan	93	36	15	N	67	40	E
Samangwa	126	4	23	S	24	10	E
Samani	112	42	7	N	142	56	E
Samar, I.	103	12	0	N	125	0	E
Samara, R.	84	53	10	N	50	4	E
Samaria	135	10	39	S	150	41	E
Samaria = Shomron	90	32	15	N	35	13	E
Samarkand	85	39	40	N	67	0	E
Samarra	92	34	16	N	43	55	E
Samastipur	95	25	50	N	85	50	E
Samatan	44	43	29	N	0	55	E
Samba, Kashmir	95	32	32	N	75	10	E
Samba, Zaïre	126	4	38	S	26	22	E
Sambaíba	170	7	8	S	45	21	W
Sambaina	129	19	37	S	47	8	E
Sambaise	65	38	58	N	16	16	E
Sambalpur	96	21	28	N	83	58	E
Sambas, S.	102	1	20	N	109	20	E
Sambava	129	14	16	S	50	10	E
Sambawizi	127	18	24	S	26	13	E
Sambhal	95	28	35	N	78	37	E
Sambhar	94	26	52	N	75	10	E
Sambonifacio	62	45	24	N	11	16	E
Sambor, Camb.	100	12	46	N	106	0	E
Sambor, U.S.S.R.	80	49	30	N	23	10	E
Sambre, R.	47	50	27	N	4	52	E
Sambuca	64	37	39	N	13	6	E
Samburu □	126	1	10	N	37	0	E
Sambusu	128	17	55	S	19	21	E
Samchŏk	107	37	30	N	129	10	E
Samchonpo	107	34	54	N	128	6	E
Same	126	4	2	S	37	38	E
Samedan	51	46	32	N	9	52	E
Samer	43	50	38	N	1	44	E
Samfya	127	11	16	S	29	31	E
Sámi	69	38	15	N	20	39	E
Samna	122	25	12	N	37	17	E
Samnager	71	60	23	N	5	39	E
Samnaun	51	46	57	N	10	22	E
Samnu	119	27	15	N	14	55	E
Samo Alto	172	30	22	S	71	0	W
Samoan Is.	10	14	0	S	171	0	W
Samobor	63	45	47	N	15	44	E
Samoëns	45	46	5	N	6	45	E
Samoorombón, Bahía	172	36	5	S	57	20	W
Samorogouan	120	11	21	N	4	57	W
Samos	56	42	44	N	7	20	W
Samoš	66	45	13	N	20	49	E
Sámos, I.	69	37	45	N	26	50	E
Samosir, P.	102	2	35	N	98	50	E
Samothráki	68	40	28	N	25	38	E
Samothráki, I.	68	40	25	N	25	40	E
Sampa	120	8	0	N	2	36	W
Sampacho	172	33	20	S	64	50	W
Sampang	103	7	11	S	113	13	E
Samper de Calanda	58	41	11	N	04	2	W
Sampford Courtenay	30	50	47	N	3	58	W
Sampit	102	2	20	S	113	0	E
Samra	92	25	35	N	41	0	E
Samreboi	120	5	34	N	7	28	E
Samrée	47	50	13	N	5	39	E
Samrong, Camb.	100	14	15	N	103	30	E
Samrong, Thai.	100	15	10	N	100	40	E
Samsø	73	55	50	N	10	35	E
Samsø Bælt	73	55	45	N	10	45	E
Samsonovo	85	37	53	N	65	15	E
Samsun	92	41	15	N	36	15	E
Samsun Daği	69	37	45	N	27	10	E
Samtredia	83	42	7	N	42	24	E
Samui, Ko	101	9	30	N	100	0	E
Samur, R.	83	41	30	N	48	0	E
Samusole	127	10	2	S	24	0	E
Samut Prakan	100	13	32	N	100	40	E
Samut Sakhon	100	13	31	N	100	20	E
Samut Songkhram (Mekong)	100	13	24	N	100	1	E
Samwari	94	28	5	N	66	46	E
Samyo La	99	29	55	N	84	46	E
San	120	13	15	N	4	45	W
San Adrián, C. de	56	43	21	N	8	50	W
San Adrián, G. de	56	43	21	N	8	50	W
San Agustín	174	1	53	N	76	16	W
San Agustín, C.	103	6	20	N	126	13	E
San Agustín de Valle Fértil	172	30	35	S	67	30	W
San Ambrosio, I.	131	26	35	S	79	30	W
San Andreas	163	38	17	N	120	39	W
San Andrés, I. de	166	12	42	N	81	46	W
San Andres Mts.	161	33	0	N	106	45	W
San Andrés Tuxtla	165	18	30	N	95	20	W
San Angelo	159	31	30	N	100	30	W
San Anselmo	163	37	49	N	122	34	W
San Antonio, Belize	165	16	15	N	89	2	W
San Antonio, Chile	172	33	40	S	71	40	W
San Antonio, N. Mex., U.S.A.	161	33	58	N	106	57	W
San Antonio, Tex., U.S.A.	159	29	30	N	98	30	W
San Antonio, Venez.	174	3	30	N	66	44	W
San Antonio Abad	59	38	59	N	1	19	E

Name	Map	Lat °	′	N/S	Long °	′	E/W
San Antonio, C., Argent.	172	36	15	S	56	40	W
San Antonio, C., Cuba	166	21	50	N	84	57	W
San Antonio, C. de	59	38	48	N	0	12	E
San Antonio de Caparo	174	7	35	N	71	27	W
San Antonio de los Baños	166	22	54	N	82	31	W
San Antonio de los Cobres	172	24	16	S	66	2	W
San Antonio do Zaire	124	6	8	S	12	11	E
San Antonio, Mt. (Old Baldy Pk.)	163	34	17	N	117	38	W
San Antonio Oeste	176	40	40	S	65	0	W
San Antonio, R.	159	28	30	N	97	14	W
San Ardo	163	36	1	N	120	54	W
San Bartolomeo in Galdo	65	41	23	N	15	2	E
San Benedetto	62	45	2	N	10	57	E
San Benedetto del Tronto	63	42	57	N	13	52	E
San Benedicto, I.	164	19	18	N	110	49	W
San Benito	159	26	5	N	97	32	W
San Benito Mtn.	163	36	22	N	120	37	W
San Benito, R.	163	36	53	N	121	50	W
San Bernardino	163	34	7	N	117	18	W
San Bernardino, Paso del	51	46	28	N	9	11	E
San Bernardo	172	33	40	S	70	50	W
San Bernardo, I. de	174	9	45	N	75	50	W
San Blas	164	26	10	N	108	40	W
San Blas, C.	157	29	40	N	85	25	W
San Blas, Cord. de	166	9	15	N	78	30	W
San Borja	174	15	0	S	67	12	W
San Buenaventura	164	27	5	N	101	32	W
San Buenaventura = Ventura	163	34	17	N	119	18	W
San Carlos, Argent.	172	33	50	S	69	0	W
San Carlos, Mexico	164	29	0	N	101	10	W
San Carlos, Nic.	166	11	12	N	84	50	W
San Carlos, Phil.	103	10	29	N	123	25	E
San Carlos, Uruguay	173	34	46	S	54	58	W
San Carlos, U.S.A.	161	33	24	N	110	27	W
San Carlos, Amazonas, Venez.	174	1	55	N	67	4	W
San Carlos, Cojedes, Venez.	174	9	40	N	68	36	W
San Carlos de Bariloche	176	41	10	S	71	25	W
San Carlos de la Rápita	58	40	37	N	0	35	E
San Carlos del Zulia	174	9	1	N	71	55	W
San Carlos L.	161	33	20	N	110	10	W
San Carlos = Butuku-Luba	121	3	29	N	8	33	E
San Cataldo	64	37	30	N	13	58	E
San Celoni	58	41	42	N	2	30	E
San Clemente, Chile	172	35	30	S	71	39	W
San Clemente, Spain	59	39	24	N	2	25	W
San Clemente, U.S.A.	163	33	29	N	117	45	W
San Clemente I.	163	32	53	N	118	30	W
San Constanzo	63	43	46	N	13	5	E
San Cristóbal, Argent.	172	30	20	S	61	10	W
San Cristóbal, Dom. Rep.	167	18	25	N	70	6	W
San Cristóbal, Venez.	174	7	46	N	72	14	W
San Cristóbal de las Casas	165	16	50	N	92	33	W
San Damiano d'Asti	62	44	51	N	8	4	E
San Daniel del Friuli	63	46	10	N	13	0	E
San Demétrio Corone	65	39	34	N	16	22	E
San Diego, Calif., U.S.A.	163	32	43	N	117	10	W
San Diego, Tex., U.S.A.	159	27	47	N	98	15	W
San Diego, C.	176	54	40	S	65	10	W
San Diego de la Unión	164	21	28	N	100	52	W
San Donà di Piave	63	45	38	N	12	34	E
San Elpídio a Mare	63	43	16	N	13	41	E
San Estanislao	172	24	39	S	56	26	W
San Esteban de Gormaz	58	41	34	N	3	13	W
San Felice sul Panaro	62	44	51	N	11	9	E
San Felipe, Chile	172	32	43	S	70	50	W
San Felipe, Mexico	164	31	0	N	114	52	W
San Felipe, Venez.	174	10	20	N	68	44	W
San Felipe, R.	163	33	12	N	115	49	W
San Feliu de Guixols	58	41	45	N	3	1	E
San Feliu de Llobregat	58	41	23	N	2	2	E
San Félix	174	8	20	N	62	35	W
San Félix, I.	131	26	30	S	80	0	W
San Fernando, Chile	172	34	30	S	71	0	W
San Fernando, Mexico	164	30	0	N	115	10	W
San Fernando, Luzon, Phil.	103	15	5	N	120	37	E
San Fernando, Luzon, Phil.	103	16	40	N	120	23	E
San Fernando, Spain	57	36	22	N	6	17	W
San Fernando, Trin	167	10	20	N	61	30	W
San Fernando, U.S.A.	163	34	15	N	118	29	W
San Fernando de Apure	174	7	54	N	67	28	W
San Fernando de Atabapo	174	4	3	N	67	42	W
San Fernando di Puglia	65	41	18	N	16	5	E
San Francisco, Córdoba, Argent.	172	31	30	S	62	5	W
San Francisco, San Luis, Argent.	172	32	45	S	66	10	W
San Francisco, U.S.A.	163	37	47	N	122	30	W
San Francisco de Macorís	167	19	19	N	70	15	W
San Francisco del Monte de Oro	172	32	36	S	66	8	W
San Francisco del Oro	164	26	52	N	105	50	W
San Francisco Javier	59	38	40	N	1	25	E
San Francisco, Paso de	172	35	40	S	70	24	W
San Francisco, R.	161	33	30	N	109	0	W

Name	Map	Lat °	′	N/S	Long °	′	E/W
San Francisco Solano, Pta.	174	6	18	N	77	29	W
San Francisville	159	30	48	N	91	22	W
San Fratello	65	38	1	N	14	33	E
San Gabriel	174	0	36	N	77	49	W
San Gavino Monreale	64	39	33	N	8	47	E
San German	147	18	5	N	67	3	W
San Gil	174	6	33	N	73	8	W
San Gimignano	62	43	28	N	11	3	E
San Giórgio di Nogaro	63	45	50	N	13	13	E
San Giórgio Iónico	65	40	27	N	17	23	E
San Giovanni Bianco	62	45	52	N	9	40	E
San Giovanni in Fiore	65	39	16	N	16	42	E
San Giovanni in Persiceto	63	44	39	N	11	12	E
San Giovanni Rotondo	65	41	41	N	15	42	E
San Giovanni Valdarno	63	43	32	N	11	30	E
San Giuliano Terme	62	43	45	N	10	26	E
San Gorgonio Mtn.	163	34	7	N	116	51	W
San Gottardo, Paso del	51	46	33	N	8	33	E
San Gregorio, Uruguay	173	32	37	S	55	40	W
San Gregorio, U.S.A.	163	37	20	N	122	23	W
San Guiseppe Iato	64	37	37	N	13	11	E
San Ignacio, Mexico	164	27	27	N	112	51	W
San Ignacio, Parag.	172	26	52	S	57	3	W
San Ignacio, Laguna	164	26	50	N	113	11	W
San Ildefonso, C.	103	16	0	N	122	10	E
San Isidro	172	34	29	S	58	31	W
San Jacinto, Colomb.	174	9	50	N	75	8	W
San Jacinto, U.S.A.	163	33	47	N	116	57	W
San Jerónimo, Sa. de	174	8	0	N	75	50	W
San Javier, Misiones, Argent.	173	27	55	S	55	5	W
San Javier, Santa Fe, Argent.	172	30	40	S	59	55	W
San Javier, Boliv.	174	16	18	S	62	30	W
San Javier, Chile	172	35	40	S	71	45	W
San Javier, Spain	59	37	49	N	0	50	W
San Jerónimo, Sa. de	174	8	0	N	75	50	W
San Joaquin	163	36	36	N	120	11	W
San Joaquin R.	163	38	4	N	121	51	W
San Joaquin Valley	163	37	0	N	120	30	W
San Jorge	172	31	54	S	61	50	W
San Jorge, Bahía de	164	31	20	N	113	20	W
San Jorge, Golfo de	176	46	0	S	66	0	W
San Jorge, G. de	58	40	50	N	0	55	W
San José, C. Rica	174	17	45	S	60	50	W
San José, C. Rica	166	10	0	N	84	2	W
San José, Guat.	164	14	0	N	90	50	W
San José, Luzon, Phil.	103	15	45	N	120	55	E
San José, Mindoro, Phil.	103	10	50	N	122	5	E
San Jose, Calif., U.S.A.	163	37	20	N	121	53	W
San Jose, N. Mex., U.S.A.	159	35	26	N	105	30	W
San José Carpizo	165	19	26	N	90	32	W
San José de Feliciano	172	30	26	S	58	46	W
San José de Jáchal	172	30	5	S	69	0	W
San José de Mayo	172	34	27	S	56	27	W
San José de Ocuné	174	4	15	N	70	20	W
San José del Cabo	164	23	0	N	109	50	W
San José del Guaviare	174	2	35	N	72	38	W
San José, I.	164	25	0	N	110	50	W
San Juan, Argent.	172	31	30	S	68	30	W
San Juan, Antioquía, Colomb.	174	8	46	N	76	32	W
San Juan, Meta, Colomb.	174	3	26	N	73	50	W
San Juan, Dom. Rep.	147	18	49	N	71	12	W
San Juan, Coahuila, Mexico	164	29	34	N	101	53	W
San Juan, Jalisco, Mexico	164	21	20	N	102	50	W
San Juan, Querétaro, Mexico	164	20	25	N	100	0	W
San Juan, Phil.	103	8	35	N	126	20	E
San Juan, Pto Rico	147	18	28	N	66	37	W
San Juan □	172	31	9	S	69	0	W
San Juan Bautista, Parag.	172	26	37	S	57	6	W
San Juan Bautista, Spain	59	39	5	N	1	31	E
San Juan Bautista, U.S.A.	163	36	51	N	121	32	W
San Juan, C.	147	18	23	N	65	37	W
San Juan Capistrano	163	33	29	N	117	40	W
San Juan de Guadalupe	164	24	38	N	102	44	W
San Juan de los Cayos	174	11	10	N	68	25	W
San Juan de los Morros	174	9	55	N	67	21	W
San Juan de Norte, B. de	166	11	30	N	83	40	W
San Juan del Norte	166	10	58	N	83	40	W
San Juan del Puerto	57	37	20	N	6	50	W
San Juan del Río	165	24	47	N	104	27	W
San Juan del Sur	166	11	20	N	86	0	W
San Juan Mts.	161	38	30	N	108	30	W
San Juan, Presa de	164	17	45	N	95	15	W
San Juan, R., Argent.	172	32	20	S	67	25	W
San Juan, R., Colomb.	174	4	0	N	77	20	W
San Juan, R., Nic.	166	11	0	N	84	30	W
San Juan, R., Calif., U.S.A.	163	36	14	N	121	9	W
San Juan, R., Utah, U.S.A.	161	37	20	N	110	20	W
San Julián	176	49	15	S	68	0	W
San Just, Sierra de	58	40	45	N	0	41	W
San Justo	172	30	55	S	60	30	W
San Kamphaeng	100	18	45	N	99	8	E
San Lázaro, C.	164	24	50	N	112	18	W
San Lázaro, Sa. de	164	23	25	N	110	0	W
San Leandro	163	37	40	N	122	6	W
San Leonardo	58	41	51	N	3	5	W
San Lorenzo, Argent.	172	32	45	S	60	45	W

Name	Map	Lat °	′	N/S	Long °	′	E/W
San Lorenzo, Ecuador	174	1	15	N	78	50	W
San Lorenzo, Parag.	172	25	20	S	57	32	W
San Lorenzo, Venez.	174	9	47	N	71	4	W
San Lorenzo de la Parilla	58	39	51	N	2	22	W
San Lorenzo de Morunys	58	42	8	N	1	35	E
San Lorenzo, I., Mexico	164	28	35	N	112	50	W
San Lorenzo, I., Peru	174	12	20	S	77	35	W
San Lorenzo, Mt.	176	47	40	S	72	20	W
San Lorenzo, R.	164	24	15	N	107	24	W
San Lucas, Boliv.	174	20	5	S	65	0	W
San Lucas, Baja California S., Mexico	164	27	10	N	112	14	W
San Lucas, Baja California S., Mexico	164	22	53	N	109	54	W
San Lucas, U.S.A.	163	36	8	N	121	1	W
San Lucas, C. de	164	22	50	N	110	0	W
San Lucido	65	39	18	N	16	3	E
San Luis, Argent.	172	33	20	S	66	20	W
San Luis, Cuba	166	22	17	N	83	46	W
San Luis, Guat.	166	16	14	N	89	27	W
San Luis, U.S.A.	161	37	14	N	105	26	W
San Luis, Venez.	174	11	7	N	69	42	W
San Luis □	172	34	0	S	66	0	W
San Luis de la Loma	164	17	18	N	100	55	W
San Luis de la Paz	164	21	19	N	100	32	W
San Luis de Potosí	164	22	9	N	100	59	W
San Luis de Potosí □	164	22	10	N	101	0	W
San Luis, I.	164	29	58	N	114	26	W
San Luis Obispo	161	35	21	N	120	38	W
San Luis Res.	163	37	4	N	121	5	W
San Luis Río Colorado	164	32	29	N	114	48	W
San Luis, Sierra de	172	37	25	N	66	10	W
San Marco Argentano	65	39	34	N	16	8	E
San Marco dei Cavoti	65	41	20	N	14	50	E
San Marco in Lámis	65	41	43	N	15	38	E
San Marcos, Guat.	166	14	59	N	91	52	W
San Marcos, U.S.A.	159	29	53	N	98	0	W
San Marcos, I.	164	27	13	N	112	6	W
San Marino	63	43	56	N	12	25	E
San Marino ■	63	43	56	N	12	25	E
San Martín, Argent.	172	33	5	S	68	28	W
San Martín, Colomb.	174	3	42	N	73	42	W
San Martín de Valdeiglesias	56	40	21	N	4	24	W
San Martino de Calvi	62	45	57	N	9	41	E
San Mateo, Spain	58	40	28	N	0	10	E
San Mateo, U.S.A.	163	37	32	N	122	19	W
San Matías	174	16	25	S	58	20	W
San Matías, Golfo de	176	41	30	S	64	0	W
San Miguel, El Sal.	166	13	30	N	88	12	W
San Miguel, Panama	166	8	27	N	78	55	W
San Miguel, Spain	59	39	3	N	1	26	E
San Miguel, U.S.A.	163	35	45	N	120	42	W
San Miguel, Venez.	174	9	40	N	65	11	W
San Miguel de Salinas	59	37	59	N	0	47	W
San Miguel de Tucumán	172	26	50	S	65	20	W
San Miguel del Monte	172	35	23	S	58	50	W
San Miguel I.	163	34	2	N	120	23	W
San Miguel, R., Boliv.	174	16	0	S	62	45	W
San Miguel, R., Ecuador/Ecuador	174	0	25	N	76	30	W
San Miniato	62	43	40	N	10	50	E
San Narciso	103	15	2	N	120	3	E
San Nicolás de los Arroyas	172	33	17	S	60	10	W
San Nicolas I.	154	33	16	N	119	30	W
San Onofre	163	33	22	N	117	34	W
San Onofre	174	9	44	N	75	32	W
San Pablo, Boliv.	172	21	43	S	66	38	W
San Pablo, Colomb.	174	5	27	N	70	56	W
San Paolo di Civitate	65	41	44	N	15	16	E
San Pedro, Buenos Aires, Argent.	173	33	43	S	59	45	W
San Pedro, Jujuy, Argent.	172	24	12	S	64	55	W
San Pedro, Chile	172	21	58	S	68	30	W
San Pedro, Colomb.	174	4	56	N	71	53	W
San Pedro, Dom. Rep.	167	18	30	N	69	18	W
San Pedro, Ivory C.	120	4	50	N	6	33	W
San Pedro, Mexico	164	23	55	N	110	17	W
San Pedro □	172	24	0	S	57	0	W
San Pedro Channel	163	33	35	N	118	25	W
San Pedro de Arimena	174	4	37	N	71	42	W
San Pedro de Atacama	172	22	55	S	68	15	W
San Pedro de Jujuy	172	24	12	S	64	55	W
San Pedro de las Colonias	164	25	50	N	102	59	W
San Pedro de Lloc	174	7	15	S	79	28	W
San Pedro del Norte	166	13	4	N	84	33	W
San Pedro del Paraná	172	26	43	S	56	13	W
San Pedro del Pinatar	59	37	50	N	0	50	W
San Pedro Mártir, Sierra	164	31	0	N	115	30	W
San Pedro Mixtepec	165	16	2	N	97	0	W
San Pedro = Melchor Ocampo	164	24	52	N	101	40	W
San Pedro, Pta.	172	25	30	S	70	38	W
San Pedro, R., Chihuahua, Mexico	164	28	20	N	106	10	W
San Pedro, R., Michoacan, Mexico	164	19	23	N	103	51	W
San Pedro, R., Nayarit, Mexico	164	21	45	N	105	30	W
San Pedro, R., U.S.A.	161	32	45	N	110	35	W
San Pedro Sula	166	15	30	N	88	0	W
San Pedro Tututepec	165	16	9	N	97	38	W
San Pedro,Pta.	172	25	30	S	70	38	W
San Pietro, I.	64	39	9	N	8	17	E
San Pietro Vernotico	65	40	28	N	18	0	E
San Quintín, Mexico	164	30	29	N	115	57	W

San Quintín Santiago

San Quintín, Phil. 103 16 1N 120 56E
San, R. 54 50 25N 22 20E
San Rafael, Argent. 172 34 40S 68 30W
San Rafael, Colomb. 174 6 2N 69 45W
San Rafael, Calif., U.S.A. 163 38 0N 122 32W
San Rafael, N. Mex., U.S.A. 161 35 6N 107 58W
San Rafael, Venez. 174 10 42N 71 46W
San Rafael Mtn. 163 34 41N 119 52W
San Ramón de la Nueva Orán 172 23 10S 64 20W
San Remo 62 43 48N 7 47E
San Román, C. 174 12 12N 70 0W
San Roque, Argent. 172 28 15S 58 45W
San Roque, Spain 57 36 17N 5 21W
San Rosendo 172 37 10S 72 50W
San Saba 159 31 12N 98 45W
San Salvador 166 13 40N 89 20W
San Salvador de Jujuy 172 23 30S 65 40W
San Salvador (Watlings) I. 167 24 0N 74 40W
San Sebastián, Argent. 176 53 10S 68 30W
San Sebastián, Spain 58 43 17N 1 58W
San Sebastián, Venez. 174 9 57N 67 11W
San Serverino 63 43 13N 13 10E
San Severo 63 41 41N 15 23E
San Simeon 163 35 39N 121 11W
San Simon 161 32 14N 109 16W
San Stéfano di Cadore 63 46 34N 12 33E
San Telmo 164 30 58N 116 6W
San Tiburcio 164 24 8N 101 32W
San Valentin, Mte. 176 46 30S 73 30W
San Vicente de Alcántara 57 39 22N 7 8W
San Vicente de la Barquera 56 43 30N 4 29W
San Vicente del Caguán 174 2 7N 74 46W
San Vicenzo 93 43 9N 10 32E
San Vito al Tagliamento 63 45 55N 12 50E
San Vito, C. 64 38 11N 12 41E
San Vito Chietino 63 42 19N 14 27E
San Vito dei Normanni 65 40 40N 17 40E
San Yanaro 174 2 47N 69 42W
San Ygnacio 159 27 6N 92 24W
San Ysidro 161 32 33N 117 5W
San'a 91 15 27N 44 12E
Sana, R. 63 44 40N 16 43E
Sanaba 120 12 25N 3 47W
Sanabria, La 56 42 0N 6 30W
Sanâfir 122 27 49N 34 37E
Sanaga, R. 121 3 35N 9 38E
Sanak I 147 53 30N 162 30W
Sanaloa, Presa 164 24 50N 107 20W
Sanana 103 2 5S 125 50E
Sanand 94 22 59N 72 25E
Sanandaj 92 35 25N 47 7E
Sanandita 172 21 40S 63 35W
Sanary 45 43 7N 5 48E
Sanawad 94 22 11N 76 5E
Sanbe-San 110 35 6N 132 38E
Sancergues 43 47 10N 2 54E
Sancerre 43 47 20N 2 50E
Sanch'a Ho 108 26 55N 106 6E
Sanch'aho 107 44 59N 126 1E
Sánchez 167 19 15N 69 36W
Sanchiang 108 25 22N 109 26E
Sanchor 94 24 52N 71 49E
Sanco, Pt. 103 8 15N 126 24E
Sancoins 43 46 47N 2 55E
Sancti-Spíritus 166 21 52N 79 33W
Sand Lake 150 47 46N 84 31W
Sand Point 147 55 20N 160 32W
Sand, R. 129 22 25S 30 5E
Sand Springs 159 36 12N 96 5W
Sanda 111 34 53N 135 14E
Sanda I. 34 55 17N 5 35W
Sandah 122 20 35N 39 32E
Sandakan 102 5 53N 118 10E
Sandalwood 140 34 55S 140 9E
Sandan 101 12 46N 106 0E
Sandanski 67 41 35N 23 16E
Sandaré 120 14 40N 10 15W
Sanday I. 36 57 2N 6 30W
Sanday, I. 37 59 15N 2 30W
Sanday Sd. 37 59 11N 2 31W
Sandbach 32 53 9N 2 23W
Sandbank 34 55 58N 4 57W
Sande, Möre og Romsdal, Norway 71 62 15N 5 27E
Sande, Sogn og Fjordane, Norway 71 61 20N 5 47E
Sandefjord 71 59 10N 10 15E
Sandeid 71 59 33N 5 52E
Sanders 161 35 12N 109 25W
Sanderson 159 30 5N 102 30W
Sanderston 140 34 46S 139 15E
Sandfell 74 63 57N 16 48W
Sandfly L. 153 55 43N 106 6W
Sandgate, Austral. 139 27 18S 153 3E
Sandgate, U.K. 29 51 5N 1 9E
Sandhammaren, C. 73 55 23N 14 14E
Sandhead 34 54 48N 4 58W
Sandhurst 29 51 21N 0 48W
Sandia 174 14 10S 69 30W
Sandikli 92 38 30N 30 20E
Sandiman, Mt. 137 24 21S 115 20E
Sandnes 71 58 50N 5 45E
Sandness 37 60 18N 1 38W
Sandoa 124 9 48S 23 0E
Sandomierz 54 50 40N 21 43E
Sandona 174 1 17N 77 28W
Sandover, R. 138 21 43S 136 32E
Sandoway 99 18 20N 94 30E
Sandown 28 50 39N 1 9W
Sandpoint 160 48 20N 116 40W
Sandray, I. 36 56 53N 7 30W
Sandringham 29 52 50N 0 30E
Sandslån 72 63 2N 17 49E
Sandspit 152 53 14N 131 49W
Sandston 162 37 31N 77 19W
Sandstone 137 27 59S 119 16E
Sandusky, Mich., U.S.A. 150 43 26N 82 50W
Sandusky, Ohio, U.S.A. 156 41 25N 82 40W
Sandveld 128 32 0S 18 15E
Sandvig, Denmark 73 55 18N 14 48E
Sandvig, Sweden 72 55 32N 14 47E
Sandvika 71 59 54N 10 29E
Sandviken 72 60 38N 16 46E
Sandwich 29 51 16N 1 21E
Sandwich B., Can. 151 53 40N 57 15W
Sandwich B., S. Afr. 128 23 25S 14 20E
Sandwich, C. 138 18 14S 146 18E
Sandwich Group 13 57 0S 27 0W
Sandwip Chan. 99 22 35N 91 35E
Sandy 29 53 8N 0 18W
Sandy Bight 137 33 50S 123 20E
Sandy C., Queens., Austral. 139 24 42S 153 15E
Sandy C., Tas., Austral. 138 41 25S 144 45E
Sandy Cay 167 23 13N 75 18W
Sandy Cr. 160 42 20N 109 30W
Sandy L. 150 53 2N 93 0W
Sandy Lake 150 53 0N 93 15W
Sandy Narrows 153 55 5N 103 4W
Sanford, Fla., U.S.A. 157 28 45N 81 20W
Sanford, Me., U.S.A. 162 43 28N 70 47W
Sanford, N.C., U.S.A. 157 35 30N 79 10W
Sanford, Mt. 136 16 58S 130 32E
Sanford Mt. 148 62 30N 143 0W
Sanford, R. 137 27 22S 115 53E
Sang-i-Masha 94 33 16N 67 5E
Sanga 127 12 22S 35 21E
Sanga, R. 124 1 0N 16 30E
Sanga Tolon 77 61 50N 149 40E
Sangamner 96 19 30N 74 15E
Sangar, Afghan. 94 32 56N 65 30E
Sangar, U.S.S.R. 77 63 55N 127 31E
Sangar Sarcai 94 34 27N 70 35E
Sangasanga 102 0 29S 117 13E
Sangchen La 99 31 30N 84 40E
Sangchih 109 29 25N 109 30E
Sange 126 6 58S 84 40E
Sangeang, I. 103 8 12S 119 6E
Sanger 163 36 47N 119 35W
Sangerhausen 48 51 28N 11 18E
Sanggau 102 0 5N 110 30E
Sangihe, Kep. 103 3 0N 126 0E
Sangihe, P. 103 3 45N 125 30E
Sangju 107 36 25N 128 10E
Sangkan Ho 108 40 24N 115 19E
Sangkapura 102 5 52S 112 40E
Sangkhla 100 15 7N 98 28E
Sangli 96 16 55N 74 33E
Sangmélina 121 2 57N 12 1E
Sangonera, R. 59 37 39N 2 0W
Sangpang Bum 98 26 30N 95 50E
Sangre de Cristo Mts. 159 37 0N 105 0W
Sangro, R. 63 42 10N 14 30E
Sangudo 152 53 50N 114 54W
Sangüesa 58 42 37N 1 17W
Sanguinaires, I. 45 41 51N 8 36E
Sanhala 120 10 3N 6 51W
Sanho 107 39 59N 117 4E
Sani R. 100 13 32N 105 57E
Sanish 158 48 0N 102 30W
Sanje 126 0 49S 31 30E
Sankaranayinarkovil 97 9 10N 77 35E
Sankeshwar 96 16 23N 74 23E
Sankosh, R. 98 26 24N 89 47E
Sankt Andra 52 46 46N 14 50E
Sankt Antönien 51 46 58N 9 48E
Sankt Blasien 49 47 47N 8 7E
Sankt Gallen 51 47 26N 9 22E
Sankt Gallen □ 51 47 25N 9 22E
Sankt Ingbert 49 49 16N 7 6E
Sankt Johann 52 47 22N 13 12E
Sankt Margrethen 51 47 28N 9 37E
Sankt Moritz 51 46 30N 9 50E
Sankt Olof 73 55 37N 14 8E
Sankt Pölten 52 48 12N 15 38E
Sankt Valentin 52 48 11N 14 33E
Sankt Veit 52 46 54N 14 22E
Sankt Wendel 49 49 27N 7 9E
Sankt Wolfgang 52 47 43N 13 27E
Sankuru, R. 124 4 17S 20 25E
Sanlúcar de Barrameda 57 37 26N 6 18W
Sanlucár la Mayor 57 37 26N 6 18W
Sanluri 64 39 35N 8 55E
Sanmártin 70 46 19N 25 58E
Sanmen 109 29 5N 121 35E
Sanmenhsia 106 34 46N 111 30E
Sanming 109 26 13N 117 35E
Sannan 111 35 2N 135 1E
Sannaspos 128 29 6S 26 34E
Sannicandro Gargánico 65 41 50N 15 34E
Sânnicolaul-Maré 66 46 5N 20 39E
Sannidal 71 58 55N 9 15E
Sannieshof 128 26 30S 25 47E
Sano 111 36 19N 139 35E
Sanok 54 49 35N 22 10E
Sanokwelle 120 7 19N 8 38W
Sanpa 108 29 43N 99 33E
Sanpah 139 30 32S 141 12E
Sanquhar 35 55 21N 3 56W
Sansanding Dam 120 13 37N 6 0W
Sansanné-Mango 121 10 20N 0 30E
Sansepolcro 63 43 34N 12 8E
Sanshui 109 23 11N 112 53E
Sanski Most 63 44 46N 16 40E
Sansui 108 26 57N 108 37E
Sant' Ágata de Gati 65 41 6N 14 30E
Sant' Ágata di Militello 65 38 2N 14 40E
Santa Ana, Ecuador 174 1 10S 80 20W
Santa Ana, El Sal. 166 14 0N 89 40W
Santa Ana, Mexico 164 30 31N 111 8W
Santa Ana, U.S.A. 163 33 48N 117 55W
Santa Ana, El Beni 174 13 50S 65 40W
Sant' Ángelo Lodigiano 62 45 14N 9 25E
Sant' Antioco 64 39 2N 8 30E
Sant' Antíoco, I. 64 39 2N 8 30E
Sant' Arcángelo di Romagna 63 44 4N 12 26E
Santa Bárbara, Brazil 171 16 0S 59 0W
Santa Bárbara, Colomb. 174 5 53N 75 35W
Santa Barbara 166 14 53N 88 14W
Santa Bárbara, Mexico 164 26 48N 105 50W
Santa Bárbara, Spain 58 40 42N 0 29E
Santa Barbara 163 34 25N 119 40W
Santa Bárbara 174 7 47N 71 10W
Santa Barbara Channel 163 34 20N 120 0W
Santa Barbara I. 163 33 29N 119 2W
Santa Barbara Is. 161 33 31N 119 0W
Santa Bárbara, Mt. 59 37 23N 2 50W
Santa Catalina 174 10 36N 75 17W
Santa Catalina, G. of 163 33 0N 118 0W
Santa Catalina, I., Mexico 164 25 40N 110 50W
Santa Catalina, I., U.S.A. 163 33 20N 118 30W
Santa Catarina □ 173 27 25S 48 30W
Santa Catarina, I. de 173 27 30S 48 40W
Santa Caterina 65 37 37N 14 1E
Santa Cecília 173 26 56S 50 27W
Santa Clara, Cuba 166 22 20N 80 0W
Santa Clara, Calif., U.S.A. 163 37 21N 122 0W
Santa Clara, Utah, U.S.A. 161 37 10N 113 38W
Santa Clara de Olimar 173 32 50S 54 54W
Santa Clotilde 174 2 25S 73 45W
Santa Coloma de Farnés 58 41 50N 2 39E
Santa Coloma de Gramanet 58 41 27N 2 13E
Santa Comba 56 43 2N 8 49W
Santa Croce Camerina 65 36 50N 14 30E
Santa Cruz, Argent. 176 50 0S 68 50W
Santa Cruz, Boliv. 174 17 43S 63 10W
Santa Cruz, Brazil 170 7 57S 36 12W
Santa Cruz, Canary Is. 116 28 29N 16 26W
Santa Cruz, Chile 172 34 38S 71 27W
Santa Cruz, C. Rica 166 10 15N 85 41W
Santa Cruz, Phil. 103 14 20N 121 30E
Santa Cruz, Calif., U.S.A. 163 36 55N 122 1W
Santa Cruz, N. Mexico, U.S.A. 161 35 59N 106 1W
Santa Cruz □ 174 17 43S 63 10W
Santa Cruz Cabrália 171 16 17S 39 2W
Santa Cruz de Barahona 167 18 12N 71 6W
Santa Cruz de Mudela 59 38 39N 3 28W
Santa Cruz de Tenerife □ 72 28 10N 17 20W
Santa Cruz del Norte 166 23 9N 81 55W
Santa Cruz del Retamar 56 40 8N 4 14W
Santa Cruz del Sur 166 20 50N 78 0W
Santa Cruz do Rio Pardo 173 22 54S 49 37W
Santa Cruz do Sul 173 29 42S 52 25W
Santa Cruz I. 154 34 0N 119 45W
Santa Cruz, Is. 130 10 30S 166 0E
Santa Cruz, R. 176 50 10S 70 0W
Santa Elena, Argent. 172 30 58S 59 47W
Santa Elena, Ecuador 174 2 16S 80 52W
Santa Elena C. 167 10 54N 85 56W
Santa Enimie 44 44 24N 3 26E
Sant' Eufémia, Golfo di 65 38 50N 16 10E
Santa Eulalia 59 40 34N 1 20W
Santa Fe, Argent. 172 31 35S 60 41W
Santa Fe, Spain 57 37 11N 3 43W
Santa Fe, U.S.A. 161 35 40N 106 0W
Santa Fé □ 172 31 50S 60 55W
Santa Filomena 170 9 0S 45 50W
Santa Genoveva, Mt. 164 23 18N 109 52W
Santa Groce di Magliano 65 41 43N 14 59E
Santa Helena 170 2 14S 45 18W
Santa Helena de Goiás 171 17 43S 50 35W
Santa Inês 171 13 17S 39 48W
Santa Inés, I. 176 54 0S 73 0W
Santa Inés, Mt. 57 38 32N 5 37W
Santa Isabel, Argent. 172 36 10S 67 0W
Santa Isabel, Brazil 171 13 45S 56 30W
Santa Isabel = Rey Malabo 121 3 45N 8 50E
Santa Isabel do Araguaia 170 6 7S 48 19W
Santa Isabel, Pico 121 4 43N 8 49E
Santa Juliana 171 19 19S 47 32W
Santa Lucía, Corrientes, Argent. 172 28 58S 59 5W
Santa Lucía, San Juan, Argent. 172 31 30S 68 45W
Santa Lucía, Spain 59 37 35N 0 58W
Santa Lucia 172 34 27S 56 24W
Santa Lucia Range 163 36 0N 121 20W
Santa Luzia 170 6 53S 36 56W
Santa Magdalena, I. 164 24 50N 112 15W
Santa Margarita, Argent. 172 38 18S 61 35W
Santa Margarita, U.S.A. 163 35 23N 120 37W
Santa Margarita, I. 164 24 30N 112 0W
Santa Margarita, R. 163 33 13N 117 23W
Santa Margherita 62 44 20N 9 11E
Santa María, Argent. 172 26 40S 66 0W
Santa Maria, Brazil 173 29 40S 53 40W
Santa Maria 65 41 3N 14 29E
Santa María 164 27 40N 114 40W
Santa María, Spain 58 39 39N 2 45E
Santa Maria, Switz. 51 46 36N 10 25E
Santa Maria, U.S.A. 163 34 58N 120 29W
Santa Maria, Zambia 127 11 5S 29 58E
Santa María, Bahía de 164 25 10N 108 40W
Santa Maria, Cabo de 57 36 39N 7 53W
Santa Maria da Vitória 171 13 24S 44 12W
Santa María del Oro 164 25 30N 105 20W
Santa Maria di Leuca, C. 65 39 48N 18 20E
Santa Maria do Suaçuí 171 18 12S 42 25W
Santa María la Real de Nieva 56 41 4N 4 24W
Santa María, R. 164 31 0N 107 14W
Santa Marta, Colomb. 174 11 15N 74 13W
Santa Marta, Spain 57 38 37N 6 39W
Santa Marta Grande, C. 173 28 43S 48 50W
Santa Marta, Ría de 56 43 44N 7 45W
Santa Marta, Sierra Nevada de 147 10 55N 73 50W
Santa Monica 163 34 0N 118 30W
Santa Napa 160 38 28N 122 45W
Santa Olalla, Huelva, Spain 57 37 54N 6 14W
Santa Olalla, Toledo, Spain 56 40 2N 4 25W
Sant' Onofrio 65 38 42N 16 10E
Santa Paula 163 34 20N 119 2W
Santa Pola 59 38 13N 0 35W
Santa Quitéria 170 4 20S 40 10W
Santa Rita, U.S.A. 161 32 50N 108 0W
Santa Rita, Guarico, Venez. 174 8 8N 66 16W
Santa Rita, Zulia, Venez. 174 10 32N 71 32W
Santa Rosa, La Pampa, Argent. 172 36 40S 64 30W
Santa Rosa, San Luis, Argent. 172 32 30S 65 10W
Santa Rosa, Boliv. 174 10 25S 67 20W
Santa Rosa, Brazil 173 27 52S 54 29W
Santa Rosa, Colomb. 174 3 32N 69 48W
Santa Rosa, Hond. 164 14 40N 89 0W
Santa Rosa, Calif., U.S.A. 163 38 26N 122 43W
Santa Rosa, N. Mexico, U.S.A. 159 34 58N 104 40W
Santa Rosa, Amazonas, Venez. 174 1 29N 66 55W
Santa Rosa, Apure, Venez. 174 6 37N 67 57W
Santa Rosa de Cabal 174 4 52N 75 38W
Santa Rosa de Copán 166 14 47N 88 46W
Santa Rosa de Osos 174 6 39N 75 28W
Santa Rosa de Río Primero 172 31 8S 63 20W
Santa Rosa de Viterbo 174 5 53N 72 59W
Santa Rosa I., Calif., U.S.A. 163 34 0N 120 6W
Santa Rosa I., Fla., U.S.A. 157 30 23N 87 0W
Santa Rosa Mts. 160 41 45N 117 30W
Santa Rosalía 164 27 20N 112 30W
Santa Sofia 63 43 57N 11 55E
Santa Sylvina 172 27 50S 61 10W
Santa Tecla = Nueva San Salvador 164 13 40N 89 25W
Santa Teresa, Argent. 172 33 25S 60 47W
Santa Teresa, Brazil 171 19 55S 40 36W
Santa Teresa, Mexico 165 25 17N 97 51W
Santa Teresa, Venez. 174 4 43N 61 4W
Santa Teresa di Riva 63 37 58N 15 21E
Santa Teresa Gallura 64 41 14N 9 12E
Santa Teresinha 170 12 45S 39 32W
Santa Vitória 171 18 50S 50 8W
Santa Vitória do Palmar 173 33 32S 53 25W
Santa Ynez 163 34 37N 120 5W
Santa Ynez, R. 163 34 37N 120 41W
Santa Ysabel 163 33 7N 116 40W
Sant'ai 108 31 5N 105 2E
Santadi 64 39 5N 8 42E
Santahar 98 24 48N 88 59E
Santaluz 171 11 15S 39 22W
Santana 171 13 2S 44 5W
Santana, Coxilha de 173 30 50S 55 35W
Santana do Ipanema 170 9 22S 37 14W
Santana do Livramento 173 30 55S 55 30W
Santander, Colomb. 174 3 1N 76 28W
Santander, Spain 56 43 27N 3 51W
Santander □ 56 43 25N 4 0W
Santander Jiménez 165 24 11N 98 29W
Santañy 59 39 20N 3 5E
Santaquin 160 40 0N 111 51W
Santarém, Brazil 175 2 25S 54 42W
Santarém, Port. 57 39 12N 8 42W
Santarém □ 57 39 10N 8 40W
Santaren Channel 166 24 0N 79 30W
Santèramo in Colle 65 40 48N 16 45E
Santerno, R. 63 44 10N 11 38E
Santhia 62 45 20N 8 10E
Santiago, Brazil 173 29 11S 54 52W
Santiago, Chile 172 33 24S 70 50W
Santiago, Dom. Rep. 167 19 30N 70 40W

Santiago   Sayville

Santiago, Panama 166 8 0N 81 0W
Santiago □ 172 33 30S 70 50W
Santiago de Compostela 56 42 52N 8 37W
Santiago de Cuba 166 20 0N 75 49W
Santiago del Estero 172 27 50S 64 15W
Santiago del Estero □ 172 27 50S 64 20W
Santiago do Cacém 57 38 1N 8 42W
Santiago Ixcuintla 164 21 50N 105 11W
Santiago Papasquiaro 164 25 0N 105 20W
Santiago, Punta de 121 3 12N 8 40E
Santiaguillo, L. de 164 24 50N 104 50W
Santillana del Mar 56 43 24N 4 6W
Santipur 95 23 17N 88 25E
Säntis 51 47 15N 9 22E
Santisteban del Puerto 59 38 17N 3 15W
Santo Amaro 171 12 30S 38 50W
Santo Anastácio 173 21 58S 51 39W
Santo André 173 23 39S 46 29W
Santo Ângelo 173 28 15S 54 15W
Santo Antonio 170 15 50S 56 0W
Santo Antônio de Jesus 171 12 58S 39 16W
Santo Antonio do Zaire 124 6 7S 12 20E
Santo Corazón 174 18 0S 58 45W
Santo Domingo, Dom. Rep. 167 18 30N 70 0W
Santo Domingo, Baja Calif. N., Mexico 164 30 43N 115 56W
Santo Domingo, Baja Calif. S., Mexico 164 25 32N 112 2W
Santo Domingo, Nic. 166 12 14N 84 59W
Santo Domingo de la Calzada 58 42 26N 2 27W
Santo Isabel do Morro 171 11 34S 50 40W
Santo Stéfano di Camastro 65 38 1N 14 22E
Santo Stino di Livenza 63 45 45N 12 40E
Santo Tirso 56 41 29N 8 18W
Santo Tomas 164 31 33N 116 24W
Santo Tomás 174 14 34S 72 30W
Santo Tomé 173 28 40S 56 5W
Santoña 56 43 29N 3 20W
Santos 173 24 0S 46 20W
Santos Dumont 173 22 55S 43 10W
Santos, Sierra de los 57 38 7N 5 12W
Santport 46 52 26N 4 39E
Santu 108 25 59N 107 52E
Sanur 90 32 22N 35 15E
Sanvignes-les-Mines 43 46 40N 4 18E
San'yō 110 34 2N 131 5E
Sanyuki-Sammyaku 110 34 5N 133 0E
Sanza Pombo 124 7 18S 15 56E
São Anastacio 173 22 0S 51 40W
São Bartolomeu de Messines 57 37 15N 8 17W
São Benedito 170 4 3S 40 53W
São Bento 170 2 42S 44 50W
São Bento do Norte 170 5 4S 36 2W
São Borja 173 28 45S 56 0W
São Bras d'Alportel 57 37 8N 7 58W
São Caitano 170 8 21S 36 6W
São Carlos 173 22 0S 47 50W
São Cristóvão 170 11 15S 37 15W
São Domingos, Brazil 171 13 25S 46 10W
São Domingos, Guin.-Biss. 170 12 22N 16 8W
São Domingos do Maranhão 170 5 42S 44 22W
São Félix, Bahia, Brazil 171 12 38S 38 58W
São Félix, Mato Grosso, Brazil 171 11 36S 50 39W
Sao Francisco 171 16 0S 44 50W
São Francisco do Maranhão 170 6 15S 42 52W
São Francisco do Sul 173 26 15S 48 36W
São Francisco, R. 170 10 30S 36 24W
São Gabriel 173 30 10S 54 30W
São Gabriel da Palha 171 18 47S 40 59W
São Gonçalo 173 22 48S 43 5W
São Gotardo 171 19 19S 46 3W
Sao Hill 127 8 20S 35 18E
São João da Boa Vista 173 22 0S 46 52W
São João da Pesqueira 56 41 8N 7 24W
São João da Ponte 171 15 56S 44 1W
São João del Rei 173 21 8S 44 15W
São João do Araguaia 170 5 23S 48 46W
São João do Paraíso 171 15 19S 42 1W
São João do Piauí 170 8 10S 42 15W
São João dos Patos 170 6 30S 43 42W
São João Evangelista 171 18 32S 42 45W
São Joaquim da Barra 171 20 35S 47 53W
São José, B. de 170 2 38S 44 4W
São José da Laje 170 9 1S 36 3W
São José de Mipibu 170 6 5S 35 15W
São José do Peixe 170 7 24S 42 34W
São José do Rio Prêto 173 20 50S 49 20W
São José dos Campos 173 23 7S 45 52W
São Leopoldo 173 29 50S 51 10W
São Lourenço, Mato Grosso, Brazil 173 16 30S 55 5W
São Lourenço, Minas Gerais, Brazil 171 22 7S 45 3W
São Lourenço, R. 175 16 40S 56 0W
São Luís do Curu 170 3 40S 39 14W
São Luís Gonzaga 173 28 25S 55 0W
São Luís (Maranhão) 170 2 39S 44 15W
São Marcelino 174 1 0N 67 12W
São Marcelino 174 1 0N 67 12W
São Marcos, B. de 170 2 0S 44 0W
São Marcos, R. 171 18 15S 47 37W
São Martinho 56 39 30N 9 8W
São Mateus 171 18 44S 39 50W
São Mateus, R. 171 18 35S 39 44W
São Miguel 16 37 33N 25 27W
São Miguel do Araguaia 171 13 19S 50 13W
São Miguel dos Campos 170 9 47S 36 5W
São Nicolau, R. 170 5 45S 42 2W
São Paulo 173 23 40S 46 50W
São Paulo □ 173 22 0S 49 0W
São Pedro do Piaui 171 5 56S 42 43W
São Pedro do Sul 56 40 46N 8 4W
São Rafael 170 5 47S 36 55W
São Raimundo das Mangabeiras 170 7 1S 45 29W
São Raimundo Nonato 170 9 1S 42 42W
São Romão, Amazonas, Brazil 174 5 53S 67 50W
São Romão, Minas Gerais, Brazil 171 16 22S 45 4W
São Roque, C. de 170 5 30S 35 10W
São Sebastião do Paraíso 173 20 54S 46 59W
São Sebastião, I. 173 23 50S 45 18W
São Simão 171 18 56S 50 30W
São Teotónio 57 37 30N 8 42W
São Tomé 170 5 58S 36 4W
São Tomé, C. de 173 22 0S 41 10W
São Tomé, I. 114 0 10N 7 0E
São Vicente 173 23 57S 46 23W
São Vicente, Cabo de 57 37 0N 9 0W
Saona, I. 167 18 10N 68 40W
Saône-et-Loire □ 43 46 25N 4 50E
Saône, R. 43 46 25N 4 50E
Saonek 103 0 28S 130 47E
Saoura, O. 118 29 55N 1 50W
Sapai 68 41 2N 25 43E
Sapão, R. 170 11 1S 45 32W
Saparua, I. 103 3 33S 128 40E
Sapé 170 7 6S 35 13W
Sapele 121 5 50N 5 40E
Sapelo I. 157 31 28N 81 15W
Sapiéntza I. 69 36 33N 21 43E
Sapodnyy Sayan 77 52 30N 94 0E
Sapone 121 12 3N 1 35W
Saposoa 174 6 55S 76 30W
Sapozhok 81 53 59N 40 51E
Sappemeer 46 53 10N 6 48E
Sapporo 112 43 0N 141 15E
Sapri 65 40 5N 15 37E
Sapudi, I. 103 7 2S 114 17E
Sapulpa 159 36 0N 96 40W
Sapur 95 34 18N 74 27E
Saqota 123 12 40N 39 1E
Saqqez 92 36 15N 46 20E
Sar-i-Pul 93 36 10N 66 0E
Sar Planina 66 42 10N 21 0E
Sara 120 11 40N 3 53W
Sara Buri 100 14 30N 100 55E
Sarab 92 38 0N 47 30E
Sarada, R. 99 28 15N 80 30E
Saragossa = Zaragoza 58 41 39N 0 53W
Saraguro 174 3 35S 79 16W
Sarai 70 44 43N 28 10E
Saraipalli 96 21 20N 82 59E
Sarajevo 66 43 52N 18 26E
Saraktash 84 51 47N 56 22E
Saramati 98 25 44N 95 2E
Saran 122 19 35N 40 30E
Saran, G. 102 0 30S 111 25E
Saranac Lake 156 44 20N 74 10W
Saranda, Alb. 68 39 59N 19 55E
Saranda, Tanz. 126 5 45S 34 59E
Sarandí del Yi 173 33 18S 55 38W
Sarandí Grande 172 33 20S 55 50W
Sarangani B. 103 6 0N 125 13E
Sarangani Is. 103 5 25N 125 25E
Sarangarh 96 21 30N 82 57E
Saransk 81 54 10N 45 10E
Sarapul 84 56 28N 53 48E
Sarasota 157 27 10N 82 30W
Saratoga, Calif., U.S.A. 163 37 16N 122 2W
Saratoga, Wyo., U.S.A. 160 41 30N 106 56W
Saratoga Springs 162 43 5N 73 47W
Saratok 102 3 5S 110 50E
Saratov 81 51 30N 46 2E
Saravane 100 15 43N 106 25E
Sarawak □ 102 2 0N 113 0E
Saraya 120 12 50N 11 45W
Sarbaz 93 26 38N 61 19E
Sarbisheh 93 32 30N 59 40E
Sârbogârd 53 46 55N 18 40E
Sarca, R. 62 46 5N 10 45E
Sardalas 119 25 50N 10 54E
Sardarshahr 94 28 30N 74 29E
Sardegna, I. 64 39 57N 9 0E
Sardhana 94 29 9N 77 39E
Sardinata 174 8 5N 72 48W
Sardinia = Sardegna 64 39 57N 9 0E
Sardo 123 11 56N 41 14E
Sarektjåkkå 74 67 27N 17 43E
Sarengrad 66 45 14N 19 16E
Sarèyamou 120 16 25N 3 10W
Sargasso Sea 14 27 0N 72 0W
Sargent 158 41 42N 99 24W
Sargodha 94 32 10N 72 40E
Sargodha □ 94 31 50N 72 0E
Sarh 117 9 5N 18 23E
Sarhro, Jebel 118 31 6N 5 0W
Sári 93 36 30N 53 11E
Sária, I. 69 35 54N 27 17E
Sarichef C. 147 54 38N 164 59W
Sarida, R. 90 32 4N 35 3E
Sarikamiş 92 40 22N 42 35E
Sarikei 102 2 8N 111 30E
Sarina 138 21 22S 149 13E
Sarine, R. 50 46 32N 7 4E
Sariñena 58 41 47N 0 10W
Sarír Tibasti 119 22 50N 18 30E
Sarita 159 27 14N 90 49W
Sariwŏn 107 38 31N 125 46E
Sariyer 67 41 10N 29 3E
Sark, I. 42 49 25N 2 20W
Sarkad 53 46 47N 21 17E
Sarlat-la-Canéda 44 44 54N 1 13E
Sarles 158 48 58N 98 57W
Sarmi 103 1 49S 138 38E
Särna 72 61 41N 12 58E
Sarnano 63 43 2N 13 17E
Sarnen 50 46 53N 8 13E
Sarnia 150 42 58N 82 23W
Sarno 65 40 48N 14 35E
Sarnowa 54 51 39N 16 53E
Sarny 80 51 17N 26 40E
Särö 73 57 31N 11 57E
Sarolangun 102 2 30S 102 30E
Saronikós Kólpos 69 37 45N 23 45E
Saros Körfezi 68 40 30N 26 15E
Sárospatak 53 48 18N 21 33E
Sarosul Romanesc 66 45 34N 21 43E
Sarpsborg 71 59 16N 11 12E
Sarracín 58 42 15N 3 45W
Sarralbe 43 48 55N 7 1E
Sarraz, La 50 46 38N 6 30E
Sarre, La 150 48 45N 79 15W
Sarre, R. 43 48 49N 7 0E
Sarre-Union 43 48 55N 7 4E
Sarrebourg 43 48 43N 7 3E
Sarreguemines 43 49 1N 7 4E
Sarriá 56 42 41N 7 29W
Sarrión 58 40 9N 0 49W
Sarro 120 13 40N 5 5W
Sarstedt 48 52 13N 9 50E
Sartène 45 41 38N 9 0E
Sarthe □ 42 47 58N 0 10E
Sarthe, R. 42 47 33N 0 31W
Sartilly 42 48 45N 1 28W
Sartynya 76 63 30N 62 50E
Sarum 122 21 11N 39 10E
Sarúr 93 23 17N 58 4E
Sárvár 53 47 15N 16 56E
Sarveston 93 29 20N 53 10E
Särvfjället 72 62 42N 13 30E
Sárviz, R. 53 46 40N 18 40E
Sary Ozek 85 44 22N 77 59E
Sary-Tash 85 39 44N 73 15E
Saryagach 85 41 27N 69 9E
Sarych, Mys. 82 44 25N 33 25E
Sarykolskiy Khrebet 85 38 30N 74 30E
Sarykopa, Ozero 84 50 22N 64 6E
Sarymoin, Ozero 84 51 36N 64 30E
Saryshagan 76 46 12N 73 48E
Sarzana 70 44 7N 9 57E
Sarzeau 42 47 31N 2 48W
Sas van Gent 47 51 14N 3 48E
Sasa 90 33 2N 35 23E
Sasabeneh 91 7 59N 44 43E
Sasaram 95 24 57N 84 5E
Sasayama 111 35 4N 135 13E
Sasca Montanŭ 66 44 41N 21 45E
Sasebo 110 33 10N 129 43E
Saser Mt. 95 34 50N 77 50E
Saskatchewan □ 153 54 40N 106 0W
Saskatchewan, R. 153 53 12N 99 16W
Saskatoon 153 52 10N 106 38W
Sasolburg 129 26 46S 27 49E
Sasovo 81 54 25N 41 55E
Sassandra 120 5 0N 6 8W
Sassandra, R. 120 5 0N 6 8W
Sássari 64 40 44N 8 33E
Sassenheim 46 52 14N 4 31E
Sassnitz 48 54 29N 13 39E
Sasso Marconi 63 44 22N 11 12E
Sassocorvaro 63 43 47N 12 30E
Sassoferrato 63 43 26N 12 51E
Sassuolo 62 44 31N 10 47E
Sástago 58 41 19N 0 21W
Sastown 120 4 45N 8 27W
Sasumua Dam 126 0 54S 36 46E
Sasyk, Ozero 70 45 45N 30 0E
Sasykkul 85 37 41N 73 11E
Sata-Misaki 110 30 59N 130 40E
Satadougou 120 12 40N 11 25W
Satanta 159 37 30N 101 0W
Satara 96 17 44N 73 58E
Satilla, R. 157 31 15N 81 50W
Satka 84 55 3N 59 1E
Satkania 98 22 4N 92 3E
Satkhira 98 22 43N 89 8E
Satmala Hills 96 20 15N 74 40E
Satna 95 24 35N 80 50E
Sator, mt. 63 44 11N 16 43E
Sátoraljaújhely 53 48 25N 21 41E
Satpura Ra. 94 21 40N 75 0E
Satrup 48 54 39N 9 38E
Satsuma-Hantō 110 31 25N 130 25E
Satsuna-Shotō 112 30 0N 130 0E
Sattahip 100 12 41N 100 54E
Sattenpalle 96 16 25N 80 6E
Satu Mare 70 47 46N 22 55E
Satui 102 3 50S 115 20E
Satumare □ 70 47 45N 23 0E
Satun 101 6 43N 100 2E
Saturnina, R. 174 12 15S 58 10W
Sauce 172 30 5S 58 46W
Sauceda 164 25 46N 101 19W
Saucillo 164 28 1N 105 17W
Sauda 71 59 38N 6 21E
Saúde 170 10 56S 40 24W
Sauðarkrókur 74 65 45N 19 40W
Saudi Arabia ■ 92 26 0N 44 0E
Sauerland 48 51 0N 8 0E
Saugerties 162 42 4N 73 58W
Saugues 44 44 58N 3 32E
Sauherad 71 59 25N 9 15E
Sauid el Amia 118 25 57N 6 8W
Saujon 44 45 41N 0 55W
Sauk Center 158 45 42N 94 56W
Sauk Rapids 158 45 35N 94 10W
Saulgau 49 48 4N 9 32E
Saulieu 43 47 17N 4 14E
Sault 45 44 6N 5 24E
Sault Ste. Marie, Can. 150 46 30N 84 20W
Sault Ste. Marie, U.S.A. 156 46 27N 84 22W
Saumlaki 103 7 55S 131 20E
Saumur 42 47 15N 0 5W
Saunders 152 52 58N 115 40W
Saunders C. 143 45 53S 170 45E
Saunders I. 13 57 30S 27 30W
Saunders Point, Mt. 137 27 52S 125 38E
Saundersfoot 31 51 43N 4 42W
Saurbær, Borgarfjarðarsýsla, Iceland 74 64 24N 21 35W
Saurbær, Eyjafjarðarsýsla, Iceland 74 65 27N 18 13W
Sauri 121 11 50N 6 44E
Sausalito 163 37 51N 122 29W
Sautatá 174 7 50N 77 4W
Sauveterre, B. 44 43 25N 0 57W
Sauzé-Vaussais 44 46 8N 0 8E
Savá 166 15 32N 86 15W
Sava 65 40 28N 17 32E
Sava, R. 63 44 40N 19 50E
Savage 158 47 43N 104 20W
Savalou 121 7 57N 2 4E
Savanah Downs 138 19 30S 141 30E
Savane 127 19 37S 35 8E
Savanna 158 42 5N 90 10W
Savanna la Mar 166 18 10N 78 10W
Savannah, Ga., U.S.A. 157 32 4N 81 4W
Savannah, Mo., U.S.A. 158 39 55N 94 46W
Savannah, Tenn., U.S.A. 157 35 12N 88 18W
Savannah Downs 138 19 28S 141 47E
Savannah, R. 157 33 0N 81 30W
Savannakhet 100 16 30N 104 49E
Savant L. 150 50 14N 90 6W
Savant Lake 150 50 30N 90 25W
Savantvadi 97 15 55N 73 54E
Savanur 97 14 59N 75 28E
Savda 96 21 9N 75 56E
Savé 121 8 2N 2 17E
Save R. 125 21 16S 34 0E
Saveh 92 35 2N 50 20E
Savelovo 81 56 51N 37 20E
Savelugu 121 9 38N 0 54W
Savenay 42 47 20N 1 55W
Saverdun 44 43 14N 1 34E
Saverne 43 48 39N 7 20E
Savièse 50 46 17N 7 22E
Savigliano 62 44 39N 7 40E
Savigny-sur-Braye 44 47 53N 0 49E
Saviñao 56 42 35N 7 38W
Savio, R. 63 43 58N 12 10E
Savnik 66 42 59N 19 10E
Savognin 51 46 36N 9 37E
Savoie □ 45 45 26N 6 35E
Savona 62 44 19N 8 29E
Savonlinna 78 61 55N 28 55E
Sävsjö 73 57 20N 14 40E
Sävsjöström 73 57 1N 15 25E
Sawahlunto 102 0 52S 100 52E
Sawai 103 3 0S 129 5E
Sawai Madhopur 94 26 0N 76 25E
Sawang Daen Din 100 17 28N 103 28E
Sawankhalok 100 17 19N 99 50E
Sawara 111 35 55N 140 30E
Sawatch Mts. 161 38 30N 106 30W
Sawbridgeworth 29 51 49N 0 10E
Sawdā, Jabal as 119 28 51N 15 12E
Sawel, Mt. 38 54 48N 7 5W
Sawfajjin, W. 119 31 46N 14 30E
Sawi 101 10 14N 99 5E
Sawmills 127 19 30S 28 2E
Sawston 29 52 7N 0 11E
Sawtry 29 52 26N 0 17W
Sawu, I. 103 10 35S 121 50E
Sawu Sea 103 9 30S 121 50E
Saxby, R. 138 18 25S 140 53E
Saxilby 33 53 16N 0 40W
Saxlingham Nethergate 29 52 33N 1 16E
Saxmundham 29 52 13N 1 29E
Saxon 50 46 9N 7 11E
Saxony, Lower = Niedersachsen 48 52 45N 9 0E
Say 121 13 8N 2 22E
Saya 121 9 30N 3 18E
Sayabec 151 48 35N 67 41W
Sayaboury 100 19 15N 101 45E
Sayán 174 11 0S 77 25W
Sayan, Vostochnyy 77 54 0N 96 0E
Sayan, Zapadnyy 77 52 30N 94 0E
Sayasan 83 42 56N 46 15E
Sayda 92 33 35N 35 25E
Sayhan Ovoo 106 45 27N 103 54E
Sayhandulaan 106 44 40N 109 1E
Saynshand 106 44 55N 110 11E
Sayō 110 34 59N 134 22E
Sayre, Okla., U.S.A. 159 35 20N 99 40W
Sayre, Pa., U.S.A. 162 42 0N 76 30W
Sayula 164 19 50N 103 40W
Sayville 162 40 45N 73 7W

Sazan **Semirara Is**

Sazan **68** 40 30N 19 20 E
Sazin **95** 35 35N 73 30 E
Sazlika, R. **67** 42 15N 25 50 E
Sbeïtla **119** 35 12N 9 7 E
Scaër **42** 48 2N 3 42W
Scalasaig **34** 56 4N 6 10W
Scalby **33** 54 18N 0 26W
Scalby Ness **33** 54 18N 0 25W
Scalea **65** 39 49N 15 47 E
Scalloway **36** 60 9N 1 16W
Scalpay, I., Inner Hebrides, U.K. **36** 57 18N 6 0W
Scalpay, I., Outer Hebrides, U.K. **36** 57 51N 6 40W
Scamblesby **33** 53 17N 0 5W
Scammon Bay **147** 62 0N 165 49W
Scandia **152** 50 20N 112 0W
Scandiano **62** 44 36N 10 40 E
Scandinavia **16** 64 0N 12 0 E
Scansano **63** 42 40N 11 20 E
Scapa Flow **37** 58 52N 3 6W
Scarastovore **36** 57 50N 7 2W
Scarba, I. **34** 56 10N 5 42W
Scarborough, Trin **167** 11 11N 60 42W
Scarborough, U.K. **33** 54 17N 0 24W
Scargill **143** 42 56 S 172 58 E
Scariff **39** 52 55N 8 32W
Scariff I. **39** 51 43N 10 15W
Scarinish **34** 56 30N 6 48W
Scarning **29** 52 40N 0 53W
Scarp, I. **36** 58 1N 7 8W
Scarpe, R. **43** 50 31N 3 27 E
Scarsdale **140** 37 41 S 143 39 E
Scattery I. **39** 52 37N 9 30W
Scavaig, L. **36** 57 8N 6 10W
Scebeli, Uebi **91** 2 0N 44 0 E
Scédro, I. **63** 43 6N 16 43 E
Scenic **158** 43 49N 102 32W
Schaal See **48** 53 40N 10 57 E
Schaan **51** 47 10N 9 31 E
Schaesberg **47** 50 54N 6 0 E
Schaffen **47** 51 0N 5 5 E
Schaffhausen **51** 47 42N 8 39 E
Schaffhausen □ **51** 47 42N 8 36 E
Schagen **47** 52 49N 4 48 E
Schaghticoke **162** 42 54N 73 35W
Schalkhaar **46** 52 17N 6 12 E
Schalkwijk **46** 52 0N 5 11 E
Schangnau **50** 46 50N 7 47 E
Schänis **51** 47 10N 9 3 E
Schärding **52** 48 27N 13 27 E
Scharhörn, I. **48** 53 58N 8 24 E
Scharnitz **52** 47 23N 11 15 E
Scheessel **48** 53 10N 9 33 E
Schefferville **151** 54 48N 66 50W
Scheibbs **52** 48 1N 15 9 E
Schelde, R. **47** 51 10N 4 20 E
Scheldewindeke **47** 50 56N 3 46 E
Schenectady **162** 42 50N 73 58W
Schenevus **162** 42 33N 74 50W
Scherfede **48** 51 32N 9 2 E
Scherpenheuvel **47** 50 58N 4 58 E
Scherpenisse **47** 51 33N 4 6 E
Scherpenzeel **46** 52 5N 5 30 E
Schesaplana **51** 47 5N 9 43 E
Scheveningen **46** 52 6N 4 16 E
Schichallion, Mt. **37** 56 40N 4 6W
Schiedam **46** 51 55N 4 25 E
Schiermonnikoog **46** 53 29N 6 10 E
Schiermonnikoog, I. **46** 53 30N 6 15 E
Schiers **51** 47 58N 9 41 E
Schifferstadt **49** 49 22N 8 23 E
Schifflange **47** 49 30N 6 1 E
Schijndel **47** 51 37N 5 27 E
Schiltigheim **43** 48 35N 7 45 E
Schio **63** 45 42N 11 21 E
Schipbeek **46** 52 14N 6 10 E
Schipluiden **46** 51 59N 4 19 E
Schirmeck **43** 48 29N 7 12 E
Schladming **52** 47 23N 13 41 E
Schlei, R. **48** 54 45N 9 52 E
Schleiden **48** 50 32N 6 26 E
Schleswig **48** 54 32N 9 34 E
Schleswig-Holstein □ **48** 54 10N 9 40 E
Schlieren **51** 47 28N 8 27 E
Schlüchtern **49** 50 20N 9 32 E
Schmalkalden **48** 50 43N 10 28 E
Schmölin **48** 50 54N 12 22 E
Schneeberg, Austria **52** 47 53N 15 55 E
Schneeberg, Ger. **48** 50 35N 12 39 E
Schoenberg **47** 50 17N 6 16 E
Schofield **158** 44 54N 89 39W
Schoharie **162** 42 40N 74 19W
Schoharie, R. **162** 42 56N 74 18W
Schönberg, Rostock, Ger. **48** 53 50N 10 55 E
Schönberg, Schleswig-Holstein, Ger. **48** 54 23N 10 20 E
Schönebeck **48** 52 2N 11 42 E
Schönenwerd **50** 47 23N 8 0 E
Schöningen **48** 52 8N 10 57 E
Schoondijke **47** 51 21N 3 33 E
Schoonebeek **46** 52 39N 6 52 E
Schoonebeek, oilfield **19** 52 45N 6 50 E
Schoonhoven **46** 51 57N 4 51 E
Schoonoord **46** 52 51N 6 46 E
Schoorl **46** 52 42N 4 42 E
Schors **80** 51 48N 31 56 E
Schortens **48** 53 37N 7 51 E
Schoten **47** 51 16N 4 30 E
Schouten, Kepulauan **103** 1 0 S 136 0 E
Schouter I. **138** 42 20 S 148 20 E
Schouwen, I. **47** 51 43N 3 45 E
Schramberg **49** 48 12N 8 24 E
Schrankogl **52** 47 3N 11 7 E
Schreckhorn **50** 46 36N 8 7 E
Schreiber **150** 48 45N 87 20W
Schroon Lake **162** 43 47N 73 46W
Schruns **52** 47 5N 9 56 E
Schuler **153** 50 20N 110 6W
Schuls **51** 46 48N 10 18 E
Schumacher **150** 48 30N 81 16W
Schüpfen **50** 47 2N 7 24 E
Schüpfheim **50** 46 57N 8 2 E
Schurz **163** 38 57N 118 48W
Schuyler **158** 41 30N 97 3W
Schuylerville **162** 43 6N 73 35W
Schuylkill Haven **162** 40 37N 76 11W
Schuylkill, R. **162** 39 53N 75 12W
Schwabach **49** 49 19N 11 3 E
Schwäbisch Gmünd **49** 48 49N 9 48 E
Schwäbisch Hall **49** 49 7N 9 45 E
Schwäbischer Alb **49** 48 30N 9 30 E
Schwanden **51** 47 1N 9 5 E
Schwarzach, R. **52** 50 30N 11 30 E
Schwarzenberg **48** 50 31N 12 49 E
Schwarzenburg **50** 46 49N 7 20 E
Schwarzwald **49** 48 0N 8 0 E
Schwaz **52** 47 20N 11 44 E
Schwedt **48** 53 4N 14 18 E
Schweinfurt **49** 50 3N 10 12 E
Schweizer Mittelland **50** 47 0N 7 15 E
Schweizer Reneke **128** 27 11 S 25 18 E
Schwerin **48** 53 37N 11 22 E
Schwerin □ **48** 53 35N 11 20 E
Schweriner See **48** 53 45N 11 26 E
Schwetzingen **49** 49 22N 8 35 E
Schwyz **51** 47 2N 8 39 E
Schwyz □ **51** 47 2N 8 39 E
Sciacca **64** 37 30N 13 3 E
Scicli **65** 36 48N 14 41 E
Scie, La **151** 49 57N 55 36W
Scillave **91** 6 22N 44 32 E
Scilly, Isles of **30** 49 55N 6 15W
Scinawa **54** 51 25N 16 26 E
Scioto, R. **156** 39 0N 83 0W
Scituate **162** 42 12N 70 44W
Sclayn **47** 50 29N 5 2 E
Scobey **158** 48 47N 105 30W
Scole **29** 52 22N 1 10 E
Scone **141** 32 0 S 150 52 E
Scopwick **33** 53 6N 0 24W
Scórdia **65** 37 19N 14 50 E
Score Hd. **36** 60 12N 1 5W
Scoresby Sund **12** 70 20N 23 0W
Scorno, Punta dello **64** 41 7N 8 23 E
Scotia, Calif., U.S.A. **160** 40 36N 124 4W
Scotia, N.Y., U.S.A. **162** 42 50N 73 58W
Scotia Sea **13** 56 5 S 56 0W
Scotland **158** 43 10N 97 45W
Scotland □ **51** 57 0N 4 0W
Scotland Neck **157** 36 6N 77 24W
Scott **13** 77 0 S 165 0 E
Scott, C., Antarct. **13** 71 30 S 168 0 E
Scott, C., Austral. **136** 13 30 S 129 49 E
Scott City **158** 38 30N 100 52W
Scott, I. **13** 67 0 S 179 0 E
Scott Inlet **149** 71 0N 71 0W
Scott Is. **152** 50 48N 128 40W
Scott L. **153** 59 55N 106 18W
Scott Reef **136** 14 0 S 121 50 E
Scottburgh **129** 30 15 S 30 47 E
Scottsbluff **158** 41 55N 103 35W
Scottsboro **157** 34 40N 86 0W
Scottsburg **156** 38 40N 85 46W
Scottsdale **138** 41 9 S 147 31 E
Scottsville **157** 36 48N 86 10W
Scottville, Austral. **138** 20 33 S 147 49 E
Scottville, U.S.A. **156** 43 57N 86 18W
Scourie **36** 58 20N 5 10W
Scousburgh **36** 59 58N 1 20W
Scrabby **38** 53 53N 7 32W
Scrabster **37** 58 36N 3 31W
Scram, gasfield **19** 52 55N 2 42 E
Scramoge **38** 53 46N 8 4W
Scranton **162** 41 22N 75 41W
Screebe Lodge **38** 53 23N 9 33W
Screggan **42** 53 15N 7 32W
Scremerston **35** 55 44N 1 59W
Scridain, L. **34** 56 23N 6 7W
Scunthorpe **33** 53 35N 0 38W
Scuol **51** 46 48N 10 17 E
Scusciuban **91** 10 28N 50 5 E
SE Tor, oilfield **19** 56 38N 3 27 E
Sea Isle City **162** 39 9N 74 42W
Seabra **171** 12 25 S 41 46W
Seabrook, L. **137** 30 55 S 119 40 E
Seaford, Austral. **141** 38 10 S 145 11 E
Seaford, U.K. **29** 50 46N 0 8 E
Seaford, U.S.A. **162** 38 37N 75 36W
Seaforth **150** 43 35N 81 25W
Seaforth, L. **36** 57 52N 6 36W
Seagraves **159** 32 56N 102 30W
Seaham **35** 54 51N 1 20W
Seahouses **35** 55 35N 1 39W
Seal Cove **151** 49 57N 56 22W
Seal L. **151** 54 20N 61 30W
Seal, R. **153** 58 50N 97 30W
Sealga, L. na **36** 57 50N 5 18W
Sealy **159** 29 46N 96 9W
Seamer **33** 54 14N 0 27W
Sean, gasfield **19** 53 13N 2 50 E
Searchlight **161** 35 31N 114 55W
Searcy **159** 35 15N 91 45W
Searles, L. **163** 35 47N 117 17W
Seascale **32** 54 24N 3 29W
Seaside, Calif., U.S.A. **163** 36 37N 121 50W
Seaside, Oreg., U.S.A. **160** 46 12N 121 55W
Seaside Park **162** 39 55N 74 5W
Seaspray **141** 38 25 S 147 15 E
Seaton, U.K. **30** 50 42N 3 3W
Seaton, U.K. **32** 54 40N 3 31W
Seaton Delaval **35** 55 5N 1 33W
Seattle **160** 47 41N 122 15W
Seaview Ra. **138** 18 40 S 145 45 E
Seaward Kaikouras, Mts. **143** 42 10 S 173 44 E
Sebago Lake **162** 43 50N 70 35W
Sebastián Vizcaino, Bahia **164** 28 0N 114 30W
Sebastopol **160** 38 24N 122 49W
Sebastopol = Sevastopol **82** 44 35N 33 30 E
Sebderat **123** 15 26N 36 42 E
Sebdou **118** 34 38N 1 19W
Sebeşului, Mţii. **70** 45 56N 23 40 E
Sebewaing **156** 43 45N 83 27W
Sebezh **80** 56 14N 28 22 E
Sebi **120** 15 50N 4 12W
Sebinkarahisar **82** 40 22N 38 28 E
Sebiş **70** 46 23N 22 13 E
Sebkra Azzel Mati **118** 26 10N 0 43 E
Sebkra Mekerghene **118** 26 21N 1 30 E
Sebou, Oued **118** 34 16N 6 40W
Sebring **157** 27 36N 81 47W
Sebta = Ceuta **118** 35 52N 5 26W
Sebuku, I. **102** 3 30 S 116 25 E
Sebuku, Teluk **102** 4 0N 118 10 E
Sečanj **66** 45 25N 20 47 E
Secchia, R. **62** 44 30N 10 40 E
Sechelt **152** 49 25N 123 42W
Sechura, Desierto de **174** 6 0 S 80 30W
Seclin **43** 50 33N 3 2 E
Secondigny **42** 46 37N 0 26W
Sečovce **53** 48 42N 21 40 E
Secretary I. **143** 45 15 S 166 56 E
Secunderabad **96** 17 28N 78 30 E
Seda, R. **57** 39 6N 7 53W
Sedalia **158** 38 40N 93 18W
Sedan, Austral. **140** 34 34 S 139 19 E
Sedan, France **43** 49 43N 4 57 E
Sedan, U.S.A. **159** 37 10N 96 11W
Sedano **58** 42 43N 3 49W
Sedbergh **32** 54 20N 2 31W
Seddon **143** 41 40 S 174 7 E
Seddonville **143** 41 33 S 172 1 E
Sede Ya'aqov **90** 32 43N 35 7 E
Sederberg, Mt. **128** 32 22 S 19 7 E
Sedgefield **33** 54 40N 1 27W
Sedgewick **152** 52 48N 111 41W
Sedhiou **120** 12 50N 15 30W
Sedičany **52** 49 40N 14 25 E
Sedico **63** 46 8N 12 6 E
Sedinenie **67** 42 16N 24 33 E
Sedley **153** 50 10N 104 0W
Sedom **90** 31 5N 35 20 E
Sedova, Pik **76** 73 20N 55 10 E
Sédrata **119** 36 7N 7 31 E
Sedro Woolley **160** 48 30N 122 15W
Sedrun **51** 46 36N 8 47 E
Seduva **80** 55 45N 23 45 E
Sedziszów Małapolski **54** 50 5N 21 45 E
Seebad Ahlbeck **48** 53 56N 14 10 E
Seefeld **52** 47 19N 11 13 E
Seehausen **48** 52 52N 11 43 E
Seeheim **128** 26 32 S 17 52 E
Seekoe, R. **128** 30 34 S 24 45 E
Seeland **50** 47 0N 7 6 E
Seelaw **48** 52 32N 14 22 E
Seend **28** 51 20N 2 2W
Sées **42** 48 38N 0 10 E
Seesen **48** 51 53N 10 10 E
Sefadu **120** 8 35N 10 58W
Séfeto **120** 14 8N 9 49W
Sefrou **118** 33 52N 4 52W
Sefton **143** 43 15 S 172 41 E
Sefton Mt. **143** 43 40 S 170 5 E
Sefuri-San **110** 33 28N 130 18 E
Sefwi Bekwai **120** 6 10N 2 25W
Seg-ozero **76** 63 0N 33 10 E
Segamat **101** 2 30N 102 50 E
Segarcea **70** 44 6N 23 43 E
Segbwema **120** 8 0N 11 0W
Segeston **31** 51 41N 4 48W
Seget **103** 1 24 S 130 58 E
Segguer, O. **118** 32 4N 2 4 E
Segid **123** 16 55N 42 0 E
Segonzac **44** 45 36N 0 14W
Segorbe **58** 39 50N 0 30W
Ségou **120** 13 30N 6 10W
Segovia **56** 40 57N 4 10W
Segovia □ **56** 40 55N 4 10W
Segré **42** 47 40N 0 52W
Segre, R. **58** 41 40N 0 43 E
Seguam **147** 52 0N 172 30W
Seguam Pass. **147** 53 0N 175 30W
Séguéla **120** 7 55N 6 40W
Segula I. **147** 52 0N 178 5W
Segundo **159** 37 12N 104 50W
Segundo, R. **172** 30 53 S 62 44W
Segura, R. **59** 38 9N 0 40W
Segura, Sierra de **59** 38 5N 2 45W
Sehithwa **125** 20 30 S 22 30 E
Sehore **94** 23 10N 77 5 E
Sehwan **94** 26 28N 67 53 E
Seica Mare **70** 46 1N 24 7 E
Seikpyu **98** 20 54N 94 48 E
Seil, I. **34** 56 17N 5 37W
Seilandsjøkelen **74** 70 25N 23 16 E
Seiling **159** 36 10N 99 5W
Seille, R. **45** 46 31N 4 57 E
Seilles **47** 50 30N 5 6 E
Sein, I. de **42** 48 2N 4 52W
Seinäjoki **74** 62 48N 22 43 E
Seine-Maritime □ **42** 49 40N 1 0 E
Seine □ **43** 49 0N 3 0 E
Seine-et-Marne □ **43** 48 45N 3 0 E
Seine, R. **42** 49 28N 0 15 E
Seine-Saint-Denis □ **43** 48 58N 2 24 E
Seini **70** 47 44N 23 21 E
Seistan **93** 30 50N 61 0 E
Seiyala **122** 22 57N 32 41 E
Sejal **174** 2 45N 68 0W
Sejerby **73** 55 54N 11 10 E
Sejerø **73** 55 54N 11 15 E
Sejerø Bugt **73** 55 53N 11 9 E
Seka **123** 8 10N 36 52 E
Sekaju **102** 2 58 S 103 58 E
Seke **126** 3 20 S 33 31 E
Sekenke **126** 4 18 S 34 11 E
Seki **111** 35 29N 136 55 E
Sekigahara **111** 35 22N 136 28 E
Sekiu **160** 48 30N 124 29W
Sekkane, Erg in **118** 20 30N 1 30W
Sekondi **120** 5 2N 1 48W
Sekondi-Takoradi **120** 5 0N 1 48W
Sekuma **128** 24 36 S 23 57 E
Sela Dingay **123** 9 58N 39 32 E
Selah **160** 46 44N 120 30W
Selama **101** 5 12N 100 42 E
Selangor □ **101** 3 20N 101 30 E
Selargius **64** 39 14N 9 14 E
Selaru, I. **103** 8 18 S 131 0 E
Selat Bangka **102** 2 30 S 105 30 E
Selawik **147** 66 55N 160 10W
Selb **49** 50 9N 12 9 E
Selborne **29** 51 5N 0 55W
Selby, U.K. **33** 53 47N 1 5W
Selby, U.S.A. **158** 45 34N 99 55W
Selbyville **162** 38 28N 75 13W
Selce **63** 43 20N 16 50 E
Selden **158** 39 24N 100 39W
Seldovia **147** 59 30N 151 45W
Sele, R. **65** 40 27N 15 0 E
Selenica **68** 40 33N 19 39 E
Selenter See **48** 54 19N 10 26 E
Selestat **43** 48 10N 7 26 E
Selet **72** 63 15N 15 45 E
Seletan, Tg. **102** 4 10 S 114 40 E
Seletin **70** 47 50N 25 12 E
Selevac **66** 44 44N 20 52 E
Selfridge **158** 46 3N 100 57W
Sélibaby **120** 15 20N 12 15W
Seliger, Oz. **80** 57 15N 33 0 E
Seligman **161** 35 17N 112 56W
Selim, C. Afr. **126** 5 31N 23 48 E
Selim, Turkey **83** 40 15N 42 58 E
Selîma, El Wâhât el **122** 21 28N 29 31 E
Selinda Spillway **128** 18 35 S 23 10 E
Selinoús **69** 37 35N 21 37 E
Selinsgrove **162** 40 48N 76 52W
Selipuk Gompa **95** 31 23N 82 49 E
Selizharovo **80** 57 1N 33 17 E
Selje **71** 62 3N 5 22 E
Seljord **71** 59 30N 8 40 E
Selkirk, Can. **153** 50 10N 97 20W
Selkirk, U.K. **35** 55 33N 2 50W
Selkirk (□) **26** 55 30N 3 0W
Selkirk I. **153** 53 20N 99 6W
Selkirk Mts. **152** 51 15N 117 40W
Selles-sur-Cher **43** 47 16N 1 33 E
Sellières **43** 46 50N 5 32 E
Sells **161** 31 57N 111 57W
Sellye **53** 45 52N 17 51 E
Selma, Ala., U.S.A. **157** 32 30N 87 0W
Selma, Calif., U.S.A. **163** 36 39N 119 39W
Selma, N.C., U.S.A. **157** 35 32N 78 15W
Selmer **157** 35 9N 88 36W
Sélo, Óros **68** 41 10N 126 0 E
Selongey **43** 47 36N 5 10 E
Selowandoma Falls **127** 21 15 S 31 50 E
Selpele **103** 0 1 S 130 5 E
Selsey **29** 50 44N 0 47W
Selsey Bill **29** 50 44N 0 47W
Seltz **43** 48 48N 8 4 E
Selu, I. **103** 7 26 S 130 55 E
Selukwe **127** 19 40 S 30 0 E
Sélune, R. **42** 48 38N 1 22W
Selva, Argent. **172** 29 50 S 62 0W
Selva, Spain **58** 41 13N 1 8 E
Selva Beach, La **163** 36 56N 121 51W
Selva, La **58** 42 0N 2 45 E
Selvas **174** 6 30 S 67 0W
Selwyn **133** 21 30 S 140 29 E
Selwyn L. **153** 60 0N 104 30W
Selwyn Mts. **147** 63 0N 130 0W
Selwyn P.O. **138** 21 32 S 140 30 E
Selwyn Ra. **138** 21 10 S 140 0 E
Semani, R. **68** 40 45N 19 50 E
Semarang **103** 7 0 S 110 26 E
Sembabule **126** 0 4 S 31 25 E
Semeih **123** 12 43N 30 53 E
Semenov **81** 56 43N 44 30 E
Semenovka **82** 49 37N 33 2 E
Semeru, Mt. **103** 8 4 S 113 3 E
Sémi **120** 15 4N 13 41W
Semiluki **81** 51 41N 39 10 E
Seminoe Res. **160** 42 0N 107 0W
Seminole, Okla., U.S.A. **159** 35 15N 96 45W
Seminole, Tex., U.S.A. **159** 32 41N 102 38W
Semiozernoye **84** 52 22N 64 8 E
Semipalatinsk **76** 50 30N 80 10 E
Semirara Is. **103** 12 0N 121 20 E

Semisopochnoi I **Shawbost**

Semisopochnoi I.	**147**	52 0N	179 40W
Semitau	**102**	0 29N	111 57 E
Semiyarskoye	**76**	50 55N	78 30 E
Semmering Pass.	**52**	47 41N	15 45 E
Semnan	**93**	35 55N	53 25 E
Semnan □	**93**	36 0N	54 0 E
Semois, R.	**47**	49 53N	4 44 E
Semporna	**103**	4 30N	118 33 E
Semuda	**102**	2 51 S	112 58 E
Semur-en-Auxois	**43**	47 30N	4 20 E
Sen. R.	**101**	13 45N	105 12 E
Sena Madureira	**174**	9 5 S	68 45W
Senador Pompeu	**170**	5 40 S	39 20W
Senai	**101**	1 38N	103 38 E
Senaja	**102**	6 49 S	117 2 E
Senanga	**128**	16 2 S	23 14 E
Senatobia	**159**	34 38N	89 57W
Sendafa	**123**	9 11N	39 3 E
Sendai, Kagoshima, Japan	**110**	31 50N	130 20 E
Sendai, Miyagi, Japan	**112**	38 15N	141 0 E
Sendamangalam	**97**	11 17N	78 17 E
Sendeling's Drift	**128**	28 12 S	16 52 E
Sendenhorst	**48**	51 50N	7 49 E
Sendurjana	**96**	21 32N	78 24 E
Senec	**53**	48 12N	17 23 E
Seneca, Oreg., U.S.A.	**160**	44 10N	119 2W
Seneca, S.C., U.S.A.	**157**	34 43N	82 59W
Seneca Falls	**162**	42 55N	76 50W
Seneca L.	**162**	42 40N	76 58W
Seneffe	**47**	50 32N	4 16 E
Senegal ■	**120**	14 30N	14 30W
Senegal, R.	**120**	16 30N	15 30W
Senekal	**129**	28 18 S	27 36 E
Senftenberg	**48**	51 30N	13 51 E
Senga Hill	**127**	9 19 S	31 11 E
Senge Khambab (Indus), R.	**94**	28 40N	70 10 E
Sengerema □	**126**	2 10 S	32 20 E
Sengiley	**81**	53 58N	48 54 E
Sengwa, R.	**127**	17 10 S	28 15 E
Senhor-do-Bonfim	**170**	10 30 S	40 10W
Senica	**53**	48 41N	17 25 E
Senigállia	**63**	43 42N	13 12 E
Seniku	**98**	25 32N	97 48 E
Senio, R.	**63**	44 18N	11 47 E
Senj	**63**	45 0N	14 58 E
Senja	**74**	69 25N	17 20 E
Senlis	**43**	49 13N	2 35 E
Senmonorom	**100**	12 27N	107 12 E
Sennâr	**123**	13 30N	33 35 E
Senne, R.	**47**	50 42N	4 13 E
Sennen	**30**	50 4N	5 42W
Senneterre	**150**	48 25N	77 15W
Senno	**80**	54 45N	29 58 E
Sennori	**64**	40 49N	8 36 E
Senny Bridge	**31**	51 57N	3 35W
Seno	**100**	16 41N	105 1 E
Senonches	**42**	48 34N	1 2 E
Senorbi	**64**	39 33N	9 8 E
Senoze e	**63**	45 43N	14 3 E
Sens	**43**	48 11N	3 15 E
Senta	**66**	45 55N	20 3 E
Sentein	**44**	42 53N	0 58 E
Senteny	**126**	5 17 S	25 42 E
Sentier, Le	**51**	46 37N	6 15 E
Sentinel	**161**	32 56N	113 13W
Sento Sé	**170**	9 40 S	41 18W
Sentolo	**103**	7 55 S	110 13 E
Senya Beraku	**121**	5 28N	0 31W
Seo de Urgel	**58**	42 22N	1 23 E
Seohara	**95**	29 15N	78 33 E
Seoni	**95**	22 5N	79 30 E
Seorinayan	**96**	21 45N	82 34 E
Separation Point	**151**	53 37N	57 25W
Seph, R.	**33**	54 17N	1 9W
Sepik, R.	**135**	3 49 S	144 30 E
Sepólno Krajenskie	**54**	53 26N	17 30 E
Sepone	**100**	16 45N	106 13 E
Sepopa	**128**	18 49 S	22 12 E
Sepopol	**54**	54 16N	21 2 E
Sepori	**107**	38 57N	127 25 E
Sept Îles	**151**	50 13N	66 22W
Septemvri	**67**	42 13N	24 6 E
Septimus	**138**	21 13 S	148 47 E
Sepúlveda	**56**	41 18N	3 45W
Sequeros	**56**	40 31N	6 2W
Sequim	**160**	48 3N	123 9W
Sequoia Nat. Park	**163**	36 30N	118 30W
Serafimovich	**83**	49 30N	42 50 E
Seraing	**47**	50 35N	5 32 E
Seraja	**101**	2 41N	108 35 E
Seram, I.	**103**	3 10 S	129 0 E
Serampore	**95**	22 44N	88 30 E
Serang	**103**	6 8 S	106 10 E
Serasan	**101**	2 31N	109 2 E
Serasan, I.	**102**	2 29N	109 4 E
Seravezza	**62**	43 59N	10 13 E
Serbia = Srbija	**66**	43 30N	21 0 E
Sercaia	**70**	45 49N	25 9 E
Serdo	**123**	11 56N	41 14 E
Serdobsk	**81**	52 28N	44 10 E
Seredka	**80**	58 12N	28 3 E
Seregno	**62**	45 40N	9 12 E
Seremban	**101**	2 43N	101 53 E
Serena, La, Chile	**172**	29 55 S	71 10W
Serena, La, Spain	**57**	38 45N	5 40W
Serengeti □	**126**	2 0 S	34 30 E
Serengeti Plain	**126**	2 40 S	35 0 E
Serenje	**125**	13 14 S	30 15 E
Sergach	**81**	55 30N	45 30 E
Serge, R.	**58**	42 5N	1 21 E
Sergievsk	**81**	54 0N	51 10 E

Sergipe □	**170**	10 30 S	37 30W
Seria	**102**	4 37N	114 30 E
Serian	**102**	1 10N	110 40 E
Seriate	**62**	45 42N	9 43 E
Sérifontaine	**43**	49 20N	1 45 E
Sérifos, I.	**69**	37 9N	24 30 E
Sérignan	**44**	43 17N	3 17 E
Serik	**92**	36 55N	31 10 E
Seringapatam Reef	**136**	13 38 S	122 5 E
Sermaize-les-Bains	**43**	48 47N	4 54 E
Sermata, I.	**103**	8 15 S	128 50 E
Sérmide	**63**	45 0N	11 17 E
Sernovodsk	**76**	61 20N	73 28 E
Sernovodsk	**84**	53 54N	51 16 E
Sero	**120**	14 42N	10 59W
Serón	**59**	37 20N	2 29W
Serós	**58**	41 27N	0 24 E
Serov	**84**	59 36N	60 35 E
Serowe	**128**	22 25 S	26 43 E
Serpa	**57**	37 57N	7 38 E
Serpeddi, Punta	**64**	39 19N	9 28 E
Serpentara	**64**	39 8N	9 38 E
Serpentine	**137**	32 23 S	115 58 E
Serpentine L.	**137**	28 30 S	129 10 E
Serpent's Mouth	**174**	10 0N	61 30W
Serpis, R.	**59**	38 45N	0 21W
Serpukhov	**81**	54 55N	37 28 E
Serra	**171**	20 7 S	40 18W
Serra Capriola	**65**	41 47N	15 12 E
Serra do Salitre	**171**	19 6 S	46 41W
Serra Talhada	**170**	7 59 S	38 18W
Serradilla	**56**	39 50N	6 9W
Sérrai □	**68**	41 5N	23 37 E
Serramanna	**64**	39 26N	8 56 E
Serranía de Cuenca	**58**	40 10N	1 50W
Serrat, C.	**119**	37 14N	9 10 E
Serres	**45**	44 26N	5 43 E
Serrezuela	**172**	30 40 S	65 20W
Serrinha	**171**	11 39 S	39 0W
Serrita	**170**	7 56 S	39 19W
Serro	**171**	18 37 S	43 23W
Sersale	**65**	39 1N	16 44 E
Sertã	**56**	39 48N	8 6W
Sertânia	**170**	8 5 S	37 20W
Sertanópolis	**173**	23 4 S	51 2W
Sertâo	**170**	10 0 S	40 20W
Sertig	**51**	46 44N	9 52 E
Serua, P.	**103**	6 18 S	130 1 E
Serui	**103**	1 45 S	136 10 E
Serule	**128**	21 57 S	27 11 E
Sérvia	**68**	40 9N	21 58 E
Sesajap Lama	**102**	3 32N	117 11 E
Sese Is.	**126**	0 30 S	32 30 E
Sesepe	**103**	1 30 S	127 59 E
Sesfontein	**128**	19 7 S	13 39 E
Sesheke	**128**	17 29 S	24 13 E
Sesia, R.	**62**	45 35N	8 23 E
Sesimbra	**57**	38 28N	9 20W
Seskanore	**38**	54 31N	7 15W
Sessa Aurunca	**64**	41 14N	13 55 E
Sestao	**58**	43 18N	3 0W
Sesto S. Giovanni	**62**	45 32N	9 14 E
Sestri Levante	**62**	44 17N	9 22 E
Sestrières	**62**	44 58N	6 56 E
Sestrunj, I.	**63**	44 10N	15 0 E
Sestu	**64**	39 18N	9 6 E
Sesvenna	**51**	46 42N	10 25 E
Seta	**108**	32 20N	100 41 E
Setaka	**110**	33 9N	130 28 E
Setana	**112**	42 26N	139 51 E
Sète	**44**	43 25N	3 42 E
Sete Lagoas	**171**	19 27 S	44 16W
Sétif	**119**	36 9N	5 26 E
Seto	**111**	35 14N	137 6 E
Seto Naikai	**110**	34 20N	133 30 E
Setouchi	**112**	28 8N	129 19 E
Setsan	**98**	16 3N	95 23 E
Settat	**118**	33 0N	7 40W
Setté Cama	**124**	2 32 S	9 57 E
Séttimo Tor	**62**	45 9N	7 46 E
Setting L.	**153**	55 0N	98 38W
Settle	**32**	54 5N	2 18W
Settlement Pt.	**157**	26 40N	79 0W
Setto Calende	**62**	45 44N	8 37 E
Setúbal	**57**	38 30N	8 58W
Setúbal □	**57**	38 25N	8 35W
Setúbal, B. de	**57**	38 40N	8 56W
Seul L.	**150**	50 25N	92 30W
Seul Reservoir, Lac	**150**	50 25N	92 30W
Seulimeum	**102**	5 27N	95 15 E
Seuzach	**51**	47 32N	8 49 E
Sevastopol	**82**	44 35N	33 30 E
Sevelen	**51**	47 7N	9 30 E
Seven Emu	**138**	16 20 S	137 8 E
Seven Heads	**39**	51 35N	8 43W
Seven Hogs, Is.	**39**	52 20N	10 0W
Seven, R.	**33**	54 11N	0 51W
Seven Sisters	**31**	51 46N	3 43W
Seven Sisters, mt	**152**	54 56N	128 10W
Sevenoaks	**29**	51 16N	0 11 E
Sevenum	**47**	51 25N	6 2 E
Sever, R.	**57**	39 40N	7 32W
Sévérac-le-Chateau	**44**	44 20N	3 5 E
Severn Beach	**28**	51 34N	2 39W
Severn L.	**150**	53 54N	90 48W
Severn, R., Can.	**150**	56 2N	87 36W
Severn, R., U.K.	**28**	51 35N	2 38W
Severn Stoke	**28**	52 5N	2 13W
Severnaya Zemlya	**77**	79 0N	100 0 E
Severnyye Uvaly	**78**	58 0N	48 0 E
Severo-Kurilsk	**77**	50 40N	156 8 E
Severodonetsk	**83**	48 50N	38 30 E
Severodvinsk	**78**	64 27N	39 58 E

Severomoravsky □	**53**	49 38N	17 40 E
Severouralsk	**84**	60 9N	59 57 E
Sevier	**161**	38 39N	112 11W
Sevier L.	**160**	39 0N	113 20W
Sevier, R.	**161**	39 10N	112 50W
Sevilla, Colomb.	**174**	4 16N	75 57W
Sevilla, Spain	**57**	37 23N	6 0W
Sevilla □	**57**	37 0N	6 0W
Seville = Sevilla	**57**	37 23N	6 0W
Sevnica	**63**	46 2N	15 19 E
Sevsk	**80**	52 10N	34 30 E
Seward	**147**	60 0N	149 40W
Seward Pen.	**147**	65 0N	164 0W
Sewell	**172**	34 10 S	70 45W
Sewer	**103**	5 46 S	134 40 E
Sexbierum	**46**	53 13N	5 29 E
Sexsmith	**152**	55 21N	118 47W
Seychelles, Is.	**11**	5 0 S	56 0 E
Seyðisfjörður	**74**	65 16N	14 0W
Seym, R.	**80**	51 45N	35 0 E
Seymchan	**77**	62 40N	152 30 E
Seymour, Austral.	**141**	37 0 S	145 10 E
Seymour, Conn., U.S.A.	**162**	41 23N	73 5W
Seymour, Ind., U.S.A.	**156**	39 0N	85 50W
Seymour, Tex., U.S.A.	**159**	33 35N	99 18W
Seymour, Wis., U.S.A.	**156**	44 30N	88 20W
Seyne	**45**	44 21N	6 22 E
Seyne-sur-Mer, La	**45**	43 7N	5 52 E
Sezana	**63**	45 43N	13 41 E
Sézanne	**43**	48 40N	3 40 E
Sezze	**64**	41 30N	13 3 E
Sfântu Gheorghe	**70**	45 52N	25 48 E
Sfax	**119**	34 49N	10 48 E
Sgurr Mor	**36**	57 42N	5 0W
Sgurr na Ciche	**36**	57 0N	5 29W
Sgurr na Lapaich	**36**	57 23N	5 5W
Sha Ch'i, R.	**109**	26 35N	118 8 E
Shaartuz	**85**	37 16N	68 8 E
Shaba	**126**	8 0 S	25 0 E
Shaba Gamba	**99**	32 8N	88 55 E
Shaballe, R.	**123**	5 0N	44 0 E
Shabani	**127**	20 17 S	30 2 E
Shabbear	**30**	50 52N	4 12W
Shabla	**67**	43 31N	28 32 E
Shabogamo L.	**151**	48 40N	77 0W
Shabunda	**126**	2 40 S	27 16 E
Shackleton	**13**	78 30 S	36 1W
Shackleton Inlet	**13**	83 0 S	160 0 E
Shaddad	**122**	21 25N	40 2 E
Shadi	**95**	33 24N	77 14 E
Shadrinsk	**84**	56 5N	63 58 E
Shadwân	**122**	27 30N	34 0 E
Shaffa	**121**	10 30N	12 6 E
Shafter	**163**	35 32N	119 14W
Shaftesbury	**28**	51 0N	2 12W
Shag Pt.	**143**	45 29 S	170 52 E
Shagamu	**121**	6 23N	3 39 E
Shagram	**95**	36 24N	72 20 E
Shah Bunder	**94**	24 13N	67 50 E
Shahabad, And. P., India	**96**	17 10N	78 11 E
Shahabad, Punjab, India	**94**	30 10N	76 55 E
Shahabad, Raj., India	**94**	25 15N	77 11 E
Shahabad, Uttar Pradesh, India	**95**	27 36N	79 56 E
Shāhābād	**93**	37 40N	56 50 E
Shahada	**96**	21 33N	74 30 E
Shahapur	**96**	15 50N	74 34 E
Shāhbād	**92**	34 10N	46 30 E
Shahdād	**93**	30 30N	57 40 E
Shahdadkot	**94**	27 50N	67 55 E
Shahddpur	**94**	25 55N	68 35 E
Shahganj	**95**	26 3N	82 44 E
Shahgarh	**93**	27 15N	69 50 E
Shahhat (Cyrene)	**117**	32 40N	21 35 E
Shāhī	**93**	36 30N	52 55 E
Shahjahanpur	**95**	27 54N	79 57 E
Shaho	**106**	36 31N	114 35 E
Shahpur, Mad. P., India	**94**	22 12N	77 58 E
Shahpur, Mysore, India	**97**	16 40N	76 48 E
Shahpur, Iran	**92**	38 12N	44 45 E
Shahpur, Pak.	**94**	28 46N	68 27 E
Shahpura	**95**	23 10N	80 45 E
Shahr-e Babak	**93**	30 10N	55 20 E
Shahr Kord	**93**	32 15N	50 55 E
Shahraban	**92**	34 0N	45 0 E
Shahreza	**93**	32 0N	51 55 E
Shahrig	**94**	30 15N	67 40 E
Shahriza	**93**	32 0N	51 50 E
Shahrud	**93**	36 30N	55 0 E
Shahrukh	**93**	33 50N	60 10 E
Shahsavar	**93**	36 45N	51 12 E
Shahsien	**109**	26 25N	117 50 E
Shahuk'ou	**106**	40 20N	112 18 E
Shaibâra	**123**	25 26N	36 47 E
Shaikhabad	**94**	34 0N	68 45 E
Shaim	**84**	60 21N	64 10 E
Shajapur	**94**	23 20N	76 15 E
Shakargarh	**94**	32 17N	75 43 E
Shakawe	**128**	18 28 S	21 49 E
Shakhristan	**85**	39 47N	68 49 E
Shakhrisyabz	**85**	39 3N	66 50 E
Shakhty	**83**	47 40N	40 10 E
Shakhunya	**81**	57 40N	47 0 E
Shaki	**121**	8 41N	3 21 E
Shakopee	**158**	44 45N	93 30W
Shaktolik	**147**	64 30N	161 15W
Shala Lake	**123**	7 30N	38 30 E
Shaldon	**30**	50 32N	3 31W
Shalkar Karashatau, Ozero	**84**	50 26N	61 12 E
Shalkar Yega Kara, Ozero	**84**	50 45N	60 54 E

Sham, J. ash	**93**	23 10N	57 5 E
Shama	**121**	5 1N	1 42W
Shamâl Dâfû □	**123**	15 0N	25 0 E
Shamâl Kordofân □	**123**	15 0N	30 0 E
Shamar, Jabal	**92**	27 40N	41 0 E
Shamattawa	**153**	55 51N	92 5W
Shamattawa, R.	**150**	55 1N	85 23W
Shambe	**123**	7 2N	30 46 E
Shambu	**123**	9 32N	37 3 E
Shamgong Dzong	**98**	27 19N	90 35 E
Shamil, India	**94**	29 32N	77 18 E
Shamil, Iran	**93**	27 30N	56 55 E
Shamkhor	**83**	40 56N	46 0 E
Shamo, L.	**123**	5 45N	37 30 E
Shamokin	**162**	40 47N	76 33W
Shamrock	**159**	35 15N	100 15W
Shamva	**125**	17 20 S	31 32 E
Shan □	**98**	21 30N	98 30 E
Shanagolden	**39**	52 35N	9 6W
Shanan, R.	**123**	8 0N	40 20 E
Shanch'eng	**109**	31 45N	115 30 E
Shandon	**163**	35 39N	120 23W
Shandon Downs	**138**	17 45 S	134 50 E
Shanga	**121**	9 1N	5 2 E
Shangalowe	**127**	10 50 S	26 30 E
Shangani	**127**	19 1 S	28 51 E
Shangani, R.	**127**	18 35 S	27 45 E
Shangchih, (Chuho)	**107**	45 10N	127 59 E
Shangching	**106**	33 9N	110 2 E
Shangch'iu	**105**	34 26N	115 40 E
Shangch'uan Shan, I.	**109**	21 45N	112 45 E
Shanghai	**109**	31 10N	121 25 E
Shanghang	**109**	25 5N	116 30 E
Shangho	**107**	37 19N	117 9 E
Shanghsien	**106**	33 30N	109 58 E
Shangjao	**109**	28 25N	117 57 E
Shangkao	**109**	28 16N	114 50 E
Shanglin	**108**	23 26N	108 36 E
Shangnan	**106**	33 35N	110 49 E
Shangpanch'eng	**107**	40 50N	118 0 E
Shangshui	**106**	33 42N	114 34 E
Shangssu	**108**	22 10N	108 0 E
Shangtsai	**106**	33 15N	114 20 E
Shangtu	**106**	41 31N	113 35 E
Shangyu	**109**	25 59N	114 29 E
Shanhaikuan	**107**	40 2N	119 48 E
Shanhot'un	**107**	44 42N	127 12 E
Shanhsien	**106**	34 51N	116 9 E
Shani	**121**	10 14N	12 2 E
Shaniko	**160**	45 0N	120 15W
Shanklin	**28**	50 39N	1 9W
Shannon, Greenl.	**12**	75 10N	18 30W
Shannon, N.Z.	**142**	40 33 S	175 25 E
Shannon Airport	**39**	52 42N	85 7W
Shannon Bridge	**39**	53 17N	8 2W
Shannon I.	**12**	75 0N	18 0W
Shannon, Mouth of the	**39**	52 30N	9 55W
Shannon, R.	**39**	53 10N	8 10W
Shansi □	**106**	37 30N	112 15 E
Shantar, Ostrov Bolshoi	**77**	55 9N	137 40 E
Shant'ou	**109**	23 28N	116 40 E
Shantung □	**105**	36 0N	117 30 E
Shantung Pantao	**107**	37 5N	121 0 E
Shanyang	**106**	33 39N	110 2 E
Shanyin	**106**	39 34N	112 50 E
Shaohing	**109**	30 0N	120 32 E
Shaokuan	**109**	24 50N	113 35 E
Shaowu	**109**	27 25N	117 30 E
Shaoyang	**109**	27 10N	111 30 E
Shap	**32**	54 32N	2 40W
Shap'ing	**109**	22 46N	112 57 E
Shapinsay, I.	**37**	59 2N	2 50W
Shapinsay Sd.	**37**	59 0N	2 51W
Shaqra	**92**	25 15N	45 16 E
Sharafa (Ogr)	**123**	11 59N	27 7 E
Sharavati, R.	**97**	14 32N	74 0 E
Sharhjui	**93**	32 30N	67 22 E
Shari	**92**	27 20N	43 45 E
Sharjah	**93**	25 23N	55 26 E
Shark B., N. Territory, Austral.	**132**	11 20 S	130 35 E
Shark B., W. Australia, Austral.	**137**	25 55 S	113 32 E
Sharm el Sheikh	**122**	27 53N	34 15 E
Sharon, Mass., U.S.A.	**162**	42 5N	71 11W
Sharon, Pa., U.S.A.	**156**	41 18N	80 30W
Sharon, Plain of = Hasharon	**90**	32 12N	34 49 E
Sharon Springs	**162**	42 48N	74 37W
Sharp Pt.	**138**	10 58 S	142 43 E
Sharpe, L.	**150**	54 10N	93 21W
Sharpe L.	**153**	50 23N	95 30W
Sharpness	**28**	51 43N	2 28W
Sharya	**81**	58 12N	45 40 E
Shasha	**123**	6 29N	35 59 E
Shashemene	**123**	7 13N	38 33 E
Shashi	**125**	21 15 S	27 27 E
Shashi, R.	**127**	21 40 S	28 40 E
Shashih	**109**	30 19N	112 14 E
Shasta, Mt.	**160**	41 45N	122 0W
Shasta Res.	**160**	40 50N	122 15W
Shati	**109**	26 6N	114 51 E
Shatsk	**81**	54 0N	41 45 E
Shattuck	**159**	36 17N	99 55W
Shaumyani	**83**	41 13N	44 45 E
Shaunavon	**153**	49 35N	108 25W
Shaver Lake	**163**	37 9N	119 18W
Shaw I.	**138**	20 30 S	149 2 E
Shaw, R.	**136**	20 21 S	119 17 E
Shawan	**105**	44 21N	85 37 E
Shawangunk Mts.	**162**	41 40N	74 25W
Shawano	**156**	44 45N	88 38W
Shawbost	**36**	58 20N	6 40W

CIB

Shawbury **Siddeburen**

Shawbury	**28**	52 48N	2 40W
Shawinigan	**150**	46 35N	72 50W
Shawnee	**159**	35 15N	97 0W
Shaymak	**85**	37 33N	74 50 E
Shaziz	**99**	33 10N	82 43 E
Shchëkino	**81**	54 1N	37 28 E
Shcherbakov = Rybinsk	**81**	58 5N	38 50 E
Shchigri	**81**	51 55N	36 58 E
Shchuchinsk	**76**	52 56N	70 12 E
Shchuchye	**84**	55 12N	62 46 E
Shchurovo	**81**	55 0N	38 51 E
Shebekino	**81**	50 28N	37 0 E
Shebele, Wabi	**123**	2 0N	44 0 E
Sheboygan	**156**	43 46N	87 45W
Shechem	**90**	32 13N	35 21 E
Shech'i	**106**	33 3N	112 57 E
Shediac	**151**	46 14N	64 32W
Sheefry Hills	**38**	53 43N	9 40W
Sheelin, Lough	**38**	53 48N	7 20W
Sheep Haven	**38**	55 12N	7 55W
Sheeps Hd.	**39**	51 32N	9 50W
Sheerness	**29**	51 26N	0 47 E
Sheet Harbour	**151**	44 56N	62 31W
Shefar'am	**90**	32 48N	35 10 E
Shefeiya	**90**	32 35N	34 58 E
Sheffield, U.K.	**33**	53 23N	1 28W
Sheffield, Ala., U.S.A.	**157**	34 45N	87 42W
Sheffield, Mass., U.S.A.	**162**	42 6N	73 23W
Sheffield, Tex., U.S.A.	**159**	30 42N	101 49W
Shefford	**29**	52 2N	0 20W
Shegaon	**96**	20 48N	76 59 E
Sheho	**153**	51 35N	103 13W
Shehojele	**123**	10 40N	35 27 E
Shehsien, Anhwei, China	**109**	29 52N	118 26 E
Shehsien, Hopeh, China	**106**	36 33N	113 40 E
Shehung	**108**	31 0N	105 12 E
Shehy Mts.	**39**	51 47N	9 15W
Sheikhpura	**95**	25 9N	85 53 E
Shek Hasan	**123**	13 5N	35 58 E
Shekar Dzong	**95**	28 45N	87 0 E
Shekhupura	**94**	31 42N	73 58 E
Sheki	**83**	41 10N	47 5 E
Sheksna, R.	**81**	59 30N	38 30 E
Shelburne, N.S., Can.	**151**	43 47N	65 20W
Shelburne, Ont., Can.	**150**	44 4N	80 15W
Shelburne B.	**133**	11 50 S	143 0 E
Shelburne Falls	**162**	42 36N	72 45W
Shelby, Mich., U.S.A.	**156**	43 34N	86 27W
Shelby, Mont., U.S.A.	**160**	48 30N	111 59W
Shelby, N.C., U.S.A.	**157**	35 18N	81 34W
Shelbyville, Ill., U.S.A.	**158**	39 25N	88 45W
Shelbyville, Ind., U.S.A.	**156**	39 30N	85 42W
Shelbyville, Tenn., U.S.A.	**157**	35 30N	86 25W
Sheldon	**158**	43 6N	95 51W
Sheldon Point	**147**	62 30N	165 0W
Sheldrake	**151**	50 20N	64 51W
Shelikef, Str.	**147**	58 0N	154 0W
Shelikhova, Zaliv	**77**	59 30N	157 0 E
Shell, L.	**36**	58 0N	6 28W
Shell Lake	**153**	53 19N	107 14W
Shell Lakes	**137**	29 20 S	127 30 E
Shellbrook	**153**	53 13N	106 24W
Shellharbour	**141**	34 31 S	150 51 E
Shelon, R.	**80**	58 10N	30 30 E
Shelter Bay	**151**	50 30N	67 20W
Shelter I	**162**	41 5N	72 21W
Shelton, Conn., U.S.A.	**162**	41 18N	73 7W
Shelton, Wash., U.S.A.	**160**	47 15N	123 6W
Shemakha	**83**	40 50N	48 28 E
Shenandoah, Iowa, U.S.A.	**158**	40 50N	95 25W
Shenandoah, Pa., U.S.A.	**162**	40 49N	76 13W
Shenandoah, Va., U.S.A.	**156**	38 30N	78 38W
Shenandoah, R.	**156**	38 30N	78 38W
Shencha	**105**	30 56N	88 38 E
Shench'ih	**106**	39 8N	112 10 E
Shenchingtzu	**107**	44 48N	124 32 E
Shench'iu	**106**	33 26N	115 2 E
Shencottah	**97**	8 59N	77 18 E
Shendam	**121**	9 10N	9 30 E
Shendî	**123**	16 46N	33 33 E
Shendurni	**96**	20 39N	75 36 E
Shenfield	**29**	51 39N	0 21 E
Shengfang	**106**	39 5N	116 42 E
Shëngjergji	**68**	41 2N	20 10 E
Shëngjini	**68**	41 50N	19 35 E
Shenmëria	**68**	42 7N	20 13 E
Shenmu	**106**	38 54N	110 24 E
Shensi □	**106**	34 50N	109 25 E
Shenton, Mt.	**137**	27 57 S	123 22 E
Shenyang	**107**	42 50N	123 25 E
Sheopur Kalan	**93**	25 40N	76 40 E
Shepetovka	**80**	50 10N	27 0 E
Shephelah = Hashefela	**90**	31 30N	34 43 E
Shepparton	**141**	36 23 S	145 26 E
Sheppey, I. of	**29**	51 23N	0 50 E
Shepshed	**28**	52 47N	1 18W
Shepton Mallet	**28**	51 11N	2 31W
Sher Khan Qala	**94**	29 55N	66 10 E
Sher Qila	**95**	36 7N	74 2 E
Sherada	**123**	7 25N	36 30 E
Sherborne	**28**	50 56N	2 31W
Sherborne St. John	**28**	51 18N	1 7W
Sherbro I.	**120**	7 30N	12 40W
Sherbrooke	**151**	45 8N	81 57W
Sherburn, N. Yorks., U.K.	**33**	54 12N	0 32W
Sherburn, N. Yorks., U.K.	**33**	53 47N	1 15W
Sherburne	**162**	42 41N	75 30W
Shercock	**38**	54 0N	6 54W
Sherda	**119**	20 7N	16 46 E
Shere	**29**	51 13N	0 28W
Shereik	**122**	18 52N	33 40 E
Sherfield English	**28**	51 1N	1 35W
Sheridan, Ark., U.S.A.	**159**	34 20N	92 25W
Sheridan, Col., U.S.A.	**158**	39 44N	105 3W
Sheridan, Wyo., U.S.A.	**160**	44 50N	107 0W
Sheriff Hutton	**33**	54 5N	1 0W
Sheriff Muir	**35**	56 12N	3 53W
Sheringham	**29**	52 56N	1 11 E
Sherkin I.	**39**	51 38N	9 25W
Sherkot	**95**	29 22N	78 35 E
Sherman	**159**	33 40N	96 35W
Sherpur	**98**	24 41N	89 25 E
Sherridon	**153**	55 8N	101 5W
Sherston	**28**	51 35N	2 13W
Sherwood, N.D., U.S.A.	**158**	48 59N	101 36W
Sherwood, Tex., U.S.A.	**159**	31 18N	100 45W
Sherwood For.	**33**	53 5N	1 5W
Shesheke	**125**	17 14 S	24 22 E
Sheslay	**152**	58 17N	131 45W
Sheslay, R.	**152**	58 48N	132 5W
Shethanei L.	**153**	58 48N	97 50W
Shetland □	**36**	60 30N	1 30W
Shetland Is.	**36**	60 30N	1 30W
Shevaroy Hills	**97**	11 58N	78 12 E
Shevchenko	**83**	44 25N	51 20 E
Shewa □	**123**	9 33N	38 10 E
Sheyenne	**159**	47 52N	99 8W
Sheyenne, R.	**158**	47 40N	98 15W
Shiant Is.	**36**	57 54N	6 20W
Shiant, Sd. of Scot.	**36**	57 54N	6 30W
Shibam	**91**	16 0N	48 36 E
Shibata	**112**	37 57N	139 20 E
Shiberghan □	**93**	35 45N	66 0 E
Shibetsu	**112**	44 10N	142 23 E
Shibîn El Kôm	**122**	30 31N	30 55 E
Shibogama L.	**150**	53 35N	88 15W
Shibukawa	**111**	36 29N	139 0 E
Shibushi	**110**	31 25N	131 0 E
Shibushi-Wan	**110**	31 24N	131 8 E
Shickshinny	**162**	41 9N	76 9W
Shido	**110**	34 19N	134 10 E
Shiel, L.	**36**	56 48N	5 32W
Shield, C.	**138**	13 20 S	136 20 E
Shieldaig	**36**	57 31N	5 39W
Shifnal	**28**	52 40N	2 23W
Shiga-ken □	**111**	35 20N	136 0 E
Shigaib	**117**	15 5N	23 35 E
Shigaraki	**111**	34 57N	136 2 E
Shihch'eng	**109**	26 19N	116 15 E
Shihchiachuangi	**106**	38 2N	114 30 E
Shihch'ien	**108**	27 30N	108 14 E
Shihchiu Hu	**109**	31 28N	118 53 E
Shihchu	**108**	30 4N	108 10 E
Shihch'üan	**106**	33 3N	108 17 E
Shihhsing	**109**	24 57N	114 4 E
Shihku	**108**	26 52N	99 56 E
Shihkuaikou	**106**	40 42N	110 20 E
Shihlung	**109**	23 55N	113 35 E
Shihmen	**109**	29 36N	111 23 E
Shihmenchien	**109**	29 33N	116 47 E
Shihmien	**108**	29 20N	102 28 E
Shihping	**108**	27 2N	108 7 E
Shihp'ing	**108**	23 43N	102 30 E
Shihshou	**109**	29 43N	112 26 E
Shihtai	**109**	30 22N	117 57 E
Shihtien	**108**	24 44N	99 11 E
Shiht'ouhotzu	**107**	44 52N	128 41 E
Shihtsuishan	**106**	39 15N	106 50 E
Shihtsung	**108**	24 51N	103 59 E
Shiiba	**110**	32 29N	131 4 E
Shijaku	**68**	41 21N	19 33 E
Shikarpur, India	**94**	28 17N	78 7 E
Shikarpur, Pak.	**94**	27 57N	68 39 E
Shikine-Jima	**111**	34 19N	139 13 E
Shikohabad	**93**	27 6N	78 38 E
Shikoku	**110**	33 30N	133 30 E
Shikoku □	**110**	33 30N	133 30 E
Shikoku-Sanchi	**110**	33 30N	133 30 E
Shilbottle	**35**	55 23N	1 42W
Shilda	**84**	51 49N	59 47 E
Shildon	**33**	54 37N	1 39W
Shilka	**77**	52 0N	115 55 E
Shilka, R.	**77**	57 30N	93 18 E
Shillelagh	**39**	52 46N	6 32W
Shillingstone	**28**	50 54N	2 15W
Shillington	**162**	40 18N	75 58W
Shillong	**98**	25 35N	91 53 E
Shiloh	**90**	32 4N	35 10 E
Shilovo	**81**	54 25N	40 57 E
Shima-Hantō	**111**	34 22N	136 45 E
Shimabara	**110**	32 48N	130 20 E
Shimada	**111**	34 49N	138 19 E
Shimane-Hantō	**110**	35 30N	133 0 E
Shimane-ken □	**110**	35 0N	132 30 E
Shimenovsk	**77**	52 15N	127 30 E
Shimizu	**111**	35 0N	138 30 E
Shimo-Jima	**110**	32 15N	130 7 E
Shimo-Koshiki-Jima	**110**	31 40N	129 43 E
Shimoda	**111**	34 40N	138 57 E
Shimodate	**111**	36 20N	139 55 E
Shimoga	**97**	13 57N	75 32 E
Shimoni	**126**	4 38 S	39 20 E
Shimonita	**111**	36 13N	138 47 E
Shimonoseki	**110**	33 58N	131 0 E
Shimotsuma	**111**	36 11N	139 58 E
Shimpuru Rapids	**128**	17 45 S	19 55 E
Shimsha, R.	**97**	13 15N	76 54 E
Shimsk	**80**	58 15N	30 50 E
Shin Dand	**93**	33 12N	62 8 E
Shin, L.	**37**	58 7N	4 30W
Shin, R.	**37**	58 0N	4 26W
Shin-Tone-Gawa	**111**	35 57N	140 27 E
Shingbwiyang	**98**	26 41N	96 13 E
Shingleton	**150**	46 33N	86 33W
Shingu	**111**	33 40N	135 55 E
Shinji	**110**	35 24N	132 54 E
Shinji Ko	**110**	35 26N	132 57 E
Shinjō	**112**	38 46N	140 18 E
Shinkafe	**121**	13 8N	6 29 E
Shinminato	**111**	36 47N	137 4 E
Shinonoi	**111**	36 35N	138 9 E
Shinrone	**39**	53 0N	7 58W
Shinshiro	**111**	34 54N	137 30 E
Shinyanga	**126**	3 45 S	33 27 E
Shinyanga □	**126**	3 30 S	33 30 E
Shio-no-Misaki	**111**	33 25N	135 45 E
Shiogama	**112**	38 19N	141 1 E
Shiojiri	**111**	36 6N	137 58 E
Ship I.	**159**	30 16N	88 55W
Ship Shoal I.	**162**	37 10N	75 45W
Shipbourne	**29**	51 13N	0 19 E
Shipdham	**29**	52 38N	0 53 E
Shipehenski Prokhod	**67**	42 39N	25 28 E
Shipki La	**93**	31 45N	78 40 E
Shipley	**33**	53 50N	1 47W
Shippegan	**151**	47 45N	64 45W
Shippensburg	**156**	40 4N	77 32W
Shiprock	**161**	36 51N	108 45W
Shipston-on-Stour	**28**	52 4N	1 38W
Shipton-under-Wychwood	**28**	51 51N	1 35W
Shir Kūh	**93**	31 45N	53 30 E
Shirabad	**85**	37 40N	67 1 E
Shirahama	**111**	33 41N	135 20 E
Shirakawa	**111**	36 17N	136 56 E
Shirane-San, Gumma, Japan	**111**	36 48N	139 22 E
Shirane-San, Yamanashi, Japan	**111**	35 34N	138 9 E
Shiraoi	**112**	42 33N	141 21 E
Shirati	**126**	1 10 S	34 0 E
Shiraz	**93**	29 42N	52 30 E
Shire, R.	**127**	16 30 S	35 0 E
Shirebrook	**33**	53 13N	1 11W
Shiresh	**85**	39 58N	70 59 E
Shirinab, R.	**94**	29 30N	66 30 E
Shiringushi	**81**	42 54N	53 56W
Shiriya-Zaki	**112**	41 25N	141 30 E
Shirol	**96**	16 47N	74 41 E
Shirpur	**96**	21 21N	74 57 E
Shirvan	**93**	37 30N	57 50 E
Shirwa L. = Chilwa L.	**127**	15 15 S	35 40 E
Shishmanova	**67**	42 58N	23 12 E
Shishmaref	**147**	66 15N	166 10W
Shivali, (Sirkall)	**97**	11 15N	79 41 E
Shivpuri	**94**	25 18N	77 42 E
Shivta	**90**	30 53N	34 40 E
Shiwele Ferry	**127**	11 25 S	28 31 E
Shiyata	**122**	29 25N	25 7 E
Shizuoka	**111**	35 0N	138 30 E
Shizuoka-ken □	**111**	35 15N	138 40 E
Shklov	**80**	54 10N	30 15 E
Shkoder = Shkodra	**68**	42 6N	19 20 E
Shkodra	**68**	42 6N	19 20 E
Shkodra □	**68**	42 5N	19 20 E
Shkumbini, R.	**68**	41 5N	19 50 E
Shmidt, O.	**77**	81 0N	91 0 E
Shō Gawa, R.	**111**	36 47N	137 4 E
Shoa Ghimirra, (Wota)	**123**	7 4N	35 51 E
Shoal, C.	**137**	33 52 S	121 10 E
Shoal Lake	**153**	50 30N	100 35W
Shōbara	**110**	34 51N	133 1 E
Shōdo-Shima	**110**	34 30N	134 15 E
Shoeburyness	**29**	51 31N	0 49 E
Shokpar	**85**	43 49N	74 21 E
Sholapur	**96**	17 43N	75 56 E
Shologontsy	**77**	66 13N	114 14 E
Shomera	**90**	33 4N	35 17 E
Shōmrōn	**90**	32 15N	35 13 E
Shona I.	**36**	56 48N	5 50W
Shongopovi	**161**	35 49N	110 37W
Shoranur	**97**	10 46N	76 19 E
Shorapur	**96**	16 31N	76 48 E
Shoreham-by-Sea	**29**	50 50N	0 17W
Shortland I.	**135**	7 0 S	155 45 E
Shoshone, Calif., U.S.A.	**163**	35 58N	116 16W
Shoshone, Idaho, U.S.A.	**160**	43 0N	114 27W
Shoshone L.	**160**	44 0N	111 0W
Shoshone Mts.	**160**	39 30N	117 30W
Shoshong	**125**	22 56 S	26 31 E
Shoshoni	**160**	43 13N	108 5W
Shostka	**80**	51 57N	33 32 E
Shotts	**35**	55 49N	3 47W
Shouch'ang	**109**	29 22N	119 13 E
Shouhsien	**109**	32 35N	116 48 E
Shoukuang	**107**	36 53N	118 42 E
Shouning	**109**	27 26N	119 27 E
Shouyang	**106**	37 59N	113 9 E
Show Low	**161**	34 16N	110 0W
Shpola	**82**	49 1N	31 30 E
Shreveport	**159**	32 30N	93 50W
Shrewsbury	**28**	52 42N	2 45W
Shrewton	**28**	51 11N	1 55W
Shrivardhan	**96**	18 10N	73 3 E
Shrivenham	**28**	51 36N	1 39W
Shropshire □	**28**	52 36N	2 45W
Shrule	**38**	53 32N	9 7W
Shuangch'eng	**107**	45 25N	126 20 E
Shuangchiang	**108**	23 33N	99 45 E
Shuangfeng	**109**	27 26N	112 15 E
Shuangfeng Tao	**109**	26 35N	120 8 E
Shuangkou	**107**	34 3N	117 34 E
Shuangliao	**105**	43 31N	123 30 E
Shuangpai	**108**	24 50N	101 36 E
Shuangshantzu	**107**	40 21N	119 12 E
Shuangyang	**107**	43 32N	125 40 E
Shuangyashan	**105**	46 37N	131 22 E
Shuch'eng	**109**	31 27N	116 57 E
Shugden Gomba	**99**	29 35N	96 55 E
Shuguri Falls	**127**	8 33 S	37 22 E
Shuich'eng	**108**	26 35N	104 54 E
Shuichi	**109**	27 28N	118 21 E
Shuiyeh	**106**	36 8N	114 6 E
Shujalpur	**94**	23 43N	76 40 E
Shulan	**107**	44 27N	126 57 E
Shumagin Is.	**147**	55 0N	159 0W
Shumerlya	**81**	55 30N	46 10 E
Shumikha	**84**	55 10N	63 15 E
Shunan	**109**	29 37N	119 0 E
Shunch'ang	**109**	26 48N	117 47 E
Shungay	**83**	48 30N	46 45 E
Shungnak	**147**	66 55N	157 10W
Shunning	**99**	24 35N	99 50 E
Shunte	**109**	22 48N	113 17 E
Shuohsien	**106**	39 19N	112 25 E
Shupka Kunzang	**95**	34 22N	78 22 E
Shuqra	**91**	13 22N	45 34 E
Shur, R.	**93**	28 30N	55 0 E
Shurab	**85**	40 3N	70 33 E
Shurchi	**85**	37 59N	67 47 E
Shurkhua	**98**	22 15N	93 38 E
Shurma	**84**	56 58N	50 21 E
Shusf	**93**	31 50N	60 5 E
Shūshtar	**92**	32 0N	48 50 E
Shuswap L.	**152**	50 55N	119 3W
Shuweika	**90**	32 20N	35 1 E
Shuya	**81**	56 50N	41 28 E
Shuyak I.	**147**	58 35N	152 30W
Shuzenji	**111**	34 58N	138 56 E
Shwebo	**98**	22 30N	95 45 E
Shwegu	**98**	18 49N	95 26 E
Shwegun	**98**	17 9N	97 39 E
Shweli Myit	**99**	23 45N	96 45 E
Shweli, R.	**99**	23 45N	96 45 E
Shwenyaung	**98**	20 46N	96 57 E
Shyok	**95**	34 15N	78 5 E
Shyok, R.	**95**	34 30N	78 15 E
Si Chon	**101**	9 0N	99 54 E
Si Kiang = Hsi Chiang, R.	**39**	22 20N	113 20 E
Si Prachan	**100**	14 37N	100 9 E
Si Racha	**101**	13 10N	100 56 E
Siah	**92**	22 0N	47 0 E
Siahan Range	**93**	27 30N	64 40 E
Siaksriinderapura	**102**	0 51N	102 0 E
Sialkot	**94**	32 32N	74 30 E
Sialsuk	**98**	23 24N	92 45 E
Siam	**140**	32 35 S	136 41 E
Siam, G. of	**101**	11 30N	101 0 E
Siam = Thailand ■	**100**	16 0N	102 0 E
Sian = Hsian	**106**	34 17N	109 0 E
Siantan, P.	**101**	3 10N	106 15 E
Siareh	**93**	28 5N	60 20 E
Siargao, I.	**103**	9 52N	126 3 E
Siari	**95**	34 55N	76 40 E
Siasi	**103**	5 34N	120 50 E
Siassi	**135**	5 40 S	147 51 E
Siátista	**68**	40 15N	21 33 E
Siau, I.	**103**	2 50N	125 25 E
Siauliai	**80**	55 56N	23 15 E
Siaya □	**126**	0 0N	34 20 E
Siazan	**83**	41 3N	48 7 E
Sibâi, Gebel el	**122**	25 45N	34 10 E
Sibari	**65**	39 47N	16 27 E
Sibay	**84**	52 42N	58 39 E
Sibaya, L.	**129**	27 20 S	32 45 E
Sibbald	**153**	51 24N	110 10W
Sibenik	**63**	43 48N	15 54 E
Siberia	**77**	60 0N	100 0 E
Siberut, I.	**102**	1 30 S	99 0 E
Sibi	**94**	29 30N	67 48 E
Sibil	**103**	4 59 S	140 35 E
Sibiti	**124**	3 38 S	13 19 E
Sibiu	**70**	45 45N	24 9 E
Sibiu □	**70**	45 50N	24 15 E
Sible Hedingham	**29**	51 58N	0 37 E
Sibley, Iowa, U.S.A.	**158**	43 21N	95 43W
Sibley, La., U.S.A.	**159**	32 34N	93 16W
Sibolga	**102**	1 50N	98 45 E
Sibret	**47**	49 58N	5 38 E
Sibsagar	**98**	27 0N	94 36 E
Sibsey	**33**	53 3N	0 1 E
Sibuco	**103**	7 20N	122 10 E
Sibuguey B.	**103**	7 50N	122 45 E
Sibuko	**103**	7 20N	122 10 E
Sibut	**117**	5 52N	19 10 E
Sibutu, I.	**102**	4 45N	119 30 E
Sibutu Passage	**103**	4 50N	120 0 E
Sibuyan, I.	**103**	12 25N	122 40 E
Sicamous	**152**	50 49N	119 0W
Sicapoo	**103**	18 9N	121 34 E
Sicasica	**154**	17 20 S	67 45W
Siccus, R.	**140**	31 42 S	139 25 E
Sicilia, Canale di	**64**	37 25N	12 30 E
Sicilia, I.	**65**	37 30N	14 30 E
Sicily = Sicilia	**65**	37 30N	14 30 E
Sicuani	**174**	14 10 S	71 10W
Siculiana	**64**	37 20N	13 23 E
Sid	**63**	45 6N	19 16 E
Sidamo □	**123**	5 0N	37 50 E
Sidaouet	**121**	18 34N	8 3 E
Sidaradougou	**120**	10 42N	4 12W
Sidbury	**30**	50 43N	3 12W
Siddeburen	**46**	53 15N	6 52 E

Siddipet **Skaneateles**

Siddipet 96 18 0N 79 0 E
Sidensjo 72 63 20N 18 20 E
Sidéradougou 120 10 42N 4 12W
Siderno Marina 65 38 16N 16 17 E
Sidheros, Ákra 69 35 19N 26 19 E
Sidhirókastron 68 37 20N 21 46 E
Sidhpur 94 23 56N 71 25 E
Sîdi Abd el Rahman 122 30 55N 28 41 E
Sîdi Barrâni 122 31 32N 25 58 E
Sidi-Bel-Abbès 118 35 13N 0 10W
Sidi Bennour 118 32 40N 9 26W
Sidi Haneish 122 31 10N 27 35 E
Sidi Ifni 118 29 29N 10 3W
Sidi Kacem 118 34 11N 5 40W
Sīdī Miftāh 119 31 8N 16 58 E
Sidi Moussa, O. 118 33 0N 8 50W
Sidi Omar 122 31 24N 24 57 E
Sīdī Yahya 119 30 55N 16 30 E
Sidlaw Hills 35 56 32N 3 10W
Sidlesham 29 50 46N 0 46W
Sidmouth 30 50 40N 3 13W
Sidmouth, C. 138 13 25 S 143 36 E
Sidney, Can. 152 48 39N 123 24W
Sidney, Mont., U.S.A. 158 47 51N 104 7W
Sidney, N.Y., U.S.A. 162 42 18N 75 20W
Sidney, Ohio, U.S.A. 156 40 18N 84 6W
Sidoardjo 103 7 30 S 112 46 E
Sidoktaya 98 20 27N 94 15 E
Sidon, (Saida) 92 33 38N 35 28 E
Sidra, G. of = Khalī j Surt 61 31 40N 18 30 E
Siedlce 54 52 10N 22 20 E
Siedlce □ 54 52 0N 22 0 E
Siegburg 48 50 48N 7 12 E
Siegen 48 50 52N 8 2 E
Siem Pang 100 14 7N 106 23 E
Siem Reap 100 13 20N 103 52 E
Siena 63 43 20N 11 20 E
Sieniawa 54 50 11N 22 38 E
Sieradź 54 51 37N 18 41 E
Sieradź □ 54 51 30N 19 0 E
Sieraków 54 52 39N 16 2 E
Sierck-les-Bains 43 49 26N 6 20 E
Sierpc 54 52 55N 19 43 E
Sierpe, Bocas de la 174 10 0N 61 30W
Sierra Alta 58 40 31N 1 30W
Sierra Blanca 161 31 11N 105 17W
Sierra Blanca, mt. 161 33 20N 105 54W
Sierra City 160 39 34N 120 42W
Sierra Colorado 176 40 35 S 67 50W
Sierra de Gädor 59 36 57N 2 45W
Sierra de Yeguas 57 37 7N 4 52W
Sierra Gorda 172 23 0 S 69 15W
Sierra Leone ■ 120 9 0N 12 0W
Sierra Majada 164 27 19N 103 42W
Sierre 50 46 17N 7 31 E
Sifnos 69 37 0N 24 45 E
Sifton 153 51 21N 100 8W
Sifton Pass 152 57 52N 126 15W
Sig 118 35 32N 0 12W
Sigaboy 103 6 39N 126 10 E
Sigdal 71 60 4N 9 38 E
Sigean 44 43 2N 2 58 E
Sighetul Marmatiei 70 47 57N 23 52 E
Sighişoara 70 46 12N 24 50 E
Sighty Crag 35 55 8N 2 37W
Sigli 102 5 25N 96 0 E
Siglufjörður 74 66 12N 18 55W
Sigma 103 11 29N 122 40 E
Sigmaringen 49 48 5N 9 13 E
Signakhi 83 40 52N 45 57 E
Signau 50 46 56N 7 45 E
Signy I. 13 60 45 S 46 30W
Signy-l'Abbaye 43 49 40N 4 25 E
Sigsig 174 3 0 S 78 50W
Sigtuna 72 59 36N 17 44 E
Sigüenza 58 41 3N 2 40W
Siguiri 120 11 31N 9 10W
Sigulda 80 57 10N 24 55 E
Sigurd 161 38 57N 112 0W
Sihanoukville = Kompong Som 101 10 40N 103 30 E
Si'ir 90 31 35N 35 9 E
Siirt 92 37 57N 41 55 E
Sijarira, Ra. 127 17 36 S 27 45 E
Sijsele 13 51 12N 3 20 E
Sikandarabad 94 28 30N 77 39 E
Sikandra Rao 93 27 43N 78 24 E
Sikar 94 27 39N 75 10 E
Sikasso 120 11 7N 5 35W
Sikerete 128 19 0 S 20 48 E
Sikeston 159 36 52N 89 35W
Sikhote Alin, Khrebet 77 46 0N 136 0 E
Sikiá. 68 40 2N 23 56 E
Sikinos, I. 69 36 40N 25 8 E
Sikionia 69 38 0N 22 44 E
Sikkani Chief, R. 152 57 47N 122 15W
Sikkim ■ 98 27 50N 88 50 E
Siklós 53 45 50N 18 19 E
Sikoro 120 12 19N 7 8W
Sikqo 101 7 34N 99 21 E
Sil, R. 56 42 23N 7 30W
Sila, La, Mts. 65 39 15N 16 35 E
Silacayoapán 165 17 30N 98 9W
Silandro 62 46 38N 10 48 E
Silat adh Dhahr 90 32 19N 35 11 E
Silba 63 44 24N 14 41 E
Silba, I. 63 44 24N 14 41 E
Silchar 98 24 49N 92 48 E
Silcox 153 57 12N 94 10W
Silenrieux 47 50 14N 4 27 E
Siler City 157 35 44N 79 30W
Sileru, R. 96 18 0N 82 0 E
Silesia = Slask 54 51 0N 16 30 E
Silet 118 22 44N 4 37 E
Silgarhi Doti 95 29 15N 82 0 E
Silghat 98 26 35N 93 0 E
Silifke 92 36 22N 33 58 E
Siliguri 98 26 45N 88 25 E
Siliqua 64 39 20N 8 49 E
Silistra 67 44 6N 27 19 E
Siljan, L. 72 60 55N 14 45 E
Silkeborg 73 56 10N 9 32 E
Sillajhuay, Cordillera 174 19 40 S 68 40W
Sillé-le Guillaume 42 48 10N 0 8W
Silloth 32 54 53N 3 25W
Siloam Springs 159 36 15N 94 31W
Silogui 102 1 10 S 98 46 E
Silsbee 159 30 20N 94 8W
Silsden 32 53 55N 1 55W
Silute 80 55 21N 21 33 E
Silva Porto = Bié 125 12 22 S 16 55 E
Silvaplana 51 46 28N 9 48 E
Silver City, Calif., U.S.A. 160 36 19N 119 44W
Silver City, N. Mex., U.S.A. 161 32 50N 108 18W
Silver Cr., R. 160 43 30N 119 30W
Silver Creek 156 42 33N 79 9W
Silver L. 163 38 39N 120 6W
Silver Lake, Calif., U.S.A. 163 35 21N 116 7W
Silver Lake, Oreg., U.S.A. 160 43 9N 121 4W
Silver Springs 162 39 2N 77 3W
Silverhojden 72 60 2N 15 0 E
Silvermine, Mts. 39 52 47N 8 15W
Silvermines 39 52 48N 8 15W
Silverpeak, Ra. 163 37 35N 117 45W
Silverstone 28 52 5N 1 3W
Silverton, Austral. 140 31 52 S 141 10 E
Silverton, U.K. 30 50 49N 3 29W
Silverton, Colo., U.S.A. 161 37 51N 107 45W
Silverton, Tex., U.S.A. 159 34 30N 101 16W
Silves 57 37 11N 8 26W
Silvia 174 2 37N 76 21W
Silvies, R. 160 43 57N 119 5W
Silvolde 46 51 55N 6 23 E
Silvretta Gruppe 51 46 50N 10 6 E
Silwa Bahari 122 24 45N 32 55 E
Silwan 90 31 59N 35 15 E
Silwani 93 23 18N 78 27 E
Silz 52 47 16N 10 56 E
Sim, C. 118 31 26N 9 51W
Simanggang 102 1 15N 111 25 E
Simão Dias 170 10 44 S 37 49W
Simard, L. 150 47 40N 78 40W
Simarun 93 31 16N 51 40 E
Simba 126 1 41 S 34 12 E
Simbach 49 48 16N 13 3 E
Simbo 126 4 51 S 29 41 E
Simcoe 150 42 50N 80 20W
Simcoe, L. 150 44 25N 79 20W
Simenga 77 62 50N 107 55 E
Simeon 47 50 45N 5 36 E
Simeulue, I. 102 2 45N 95 45 E
Simferopol 82 44 55N 34 3 E
Sími 69 36 35N 27 50 E
Sími, I. 69 36 35N 27 50 E
Simi Valley 163 34 16N 118 47W
Simikot 95 30 0N 81 50 E
Simiti 174 7 58N 73 57W
Simitli 66 41 52N 23 7 E
Simla 94 31 2N 77 15 E
Simleu-Silvaniei 70 47 17N 22 50 E
Simme, R. 50 46 38N 7 25 E
Simmern 48 49 59N 7 32 E
Simmie 153 49 56N 108 6W
Simmler 163 35 21N 119 59W
Simões 170 7 30 S 40 49W
Simojärvi 74 66 5N 27 10 E
Simojoki 74 65 46N 25 15 E
Simojovel 165 17 12N 92 38W
Simonette, R. 152 55 9N 118 15W
Simonsbath 28 51 8N 3 45W
Simonside, Mt. 35 55 17N 2 0W
Simonstown 128 34 14 S 18 26 E
Simontornya 53 46 45N 18 33 E
Simpang 101 4 50N 100 40 E
Simpleveld 47 50 50N 5 58 E
Simplício Mendes 170 7 51 S 41 54W
Simplon 50 46 12N 8 4 E
Simplon Pass 50 46 15N 8 0 E
Simplon Tunnel 50 46 15N 8 7 E
Simpson Des. 138 25 0 S 137 0 E
Simpungdong 107 41 56N 129 29 E
Simrishamn 73 55 33N 14 22 E
Simsbury 162 41 52N 72 48W
Simunjan 102 1 25N 110 45 E
Sîmŭrtin 70 46 19N 25 58 E
Simushir, Ostrov 77 46 50N 152 30 E
Sina, R. 97 18 25N 75 28 E
Sinaai 47 51 9N 4 2 E
Sinabang 102 2 30N 46 30 E
Sinai = Es Sînâ' 122 29 0N 34 0 E
Sinai, Mt. = Musa, G. 122 28 32N 33 59 E
Sinaia 70 45 21N 25 38 E
Sinaloa 164 25 50N 108 20W
Sinaloa □ 164 25 0N 107 30W
Sinalunga 63 43 12N 11 43 E
Sinamaica 174 11 5N 71 51W
Sînandrei 70 45 52N 21 13 E
Sināwan 119 31 0N 10 30 E
Sinbaung we 98 19 43N 95 10 E
Sinbo 98 24 46N 97 3 E
Sincé 174 9 15N 75 9W
Sincelejo 174 9 18N 75 24W
Sinchangni, Kor., N. 107 40 7N 128 28 E
Sinchangni, Kor., N. 107 39 24N 126 8 E
Sinclair 160 41 47N 107 35W
Sinclair Mills 152 54 5N 121 40W
Sinclair's B. 37 58 30N 3 0W
Sincorá, Serra do 171 13 30 S 41 0W
Sind, R. 95 34 18N 75 0 E
Sind Sagar Doab 94 32 0N 71 30 E
Sinda 127 17 28 S 25 51 E
Sindal 73 57 28N 10 10 E
Sindangan 103 8 10N 123 5 E
Sindangbarang 103 7 27 S 107 9 E
Sindjai 103 5 0 S 120 20 E
Sinelnikovo 82 48 25N 35 30 E
Sines 57 37 56N 8 51W
Sines, Cabo de 57 37 58N 8 53W
Sineu 58 39 39N 3 0 E
Sinewit, Mt. 135 4 44 S 152 2 E
Sinfra 120 6 35N 5 56W
Sing Buri 100 14 53N 100 25 E
Singa 123 13 10N 33 57 E
Singanallurt 97 11 2N 77 1 E
Singaparna 103 7 23 S 108 4 E
Singapore ■ 101 1 17N 103 51 E
Singapore, Straits of 101 1 15N 104 0 E
Singaraja 102 8 15 S 115 10 E
Singen 49 47 45N 8 50 E
Singida 126 4 49 S 34 48 E
Singida □ 126 6 0 S 34 30 E
Singitikós, Kólpos 68 40 6N 24 0 E
Singkaling Hkamti 98 26 0N 95 45 E
Singkang 103 4 8 S 120 1 E
Singkawang 102 1 0N 109 5 E
Singkep, I. 102 0 30 S 104 20 E
Singleton, Austral. 141 32 33 S 151 10 E
Singleton, U.K. 29 50 55N 0 45W
Singleton, Mt. 137 29 27 S 117 15 E
Singö 72 60 12N 18 45 E
Singoli 94 25 0N 75 16 E
Singora = Songkhla 101 7 12N 100 36 E
Singosan 107 38 52N 127 25 E
Sinhailian (Lienyünchiangshih) 107 34 31N 118 15 E
Sinhung 107 40 11N 127 34 E
Siniatsikon, Óros 68 40 25N 21 35 E
Siniscóla 64 40 35N 9 40 E
Sinj 63 43 42N 16 39 E
Sinjajevina, Planina 66 42 57N 19 22 E
Sinjil 90 32 3N 35 15 E
Sinkat 122 18 55N 36 49 E
Sinkiang-Uighur □ 105 42 0N 86 0 E
Sinmark 107 38 25N 126 14 E
Sinnai Sardinia 64 39 18N 9 13 E
Sinnar 96 19 48N 74 0 E
Sinni, R. 65 40 6N 16 15 E
Sinnicolau-Maré 70 46 5N 20 39 E
Sinnûris 122 29 26N 30 31 E
Sinoe, L. 70 44 35N 28 50 E
Sinoia 127 17 20 S 30 8 E
Sinop 92 42 1N 35 11 E
Sinop, R. 82 42 1N 35 2 E
Sinpo 107 40 0N 128 13 E
Sins 51 47 12N 8 24 E
Sinskoye 77 61 8N 126 48 E
Sint Annaland 47 51 36N 4 6 E
Sint Annaparochie 46 53 16N 5 40 E
Sint-Denijs 47 50 45N 3 23 E
Sint Eustatius, I. 167 17 30N 62 59W
Sint-Genesius-Rode 47 50 45N 4 22 E
Sint-Gillis-Waas 47 51 13N 4 6 E
Sint-Huibrechts-Lille 47 51 13N 5 29 E
Sint-Katelinje-Waver 47 51 5N 4 32 E
Sint-Kruis 47 51 13N 3 15 E
Sint-Laureins 47 51 14N 3 32 E
Sint Maarten, I. 167 18 4N 63 4W
Sint-Michiels 47 51 11N 3 15 E
Sint Nicolaasga 46 52 55N 5 45 E
Sint Niklaas 47 51 10N 4 9 E
Sint Oedenrode 47 51 35N 5 29 E
Sint Pancras 46 52 40N 4 48 E
Sint-Pauwels 47 51 11N 3 57 E
Sint Philipsland 47 51 37N 4 10 E
Sint Truiden 47 50 48N 5 12 E
Sint Willebroad 47 51 33N 4 33 E
Sintana Ano 70 46 20N 21 30 E
Sintang 102 0 5N 111 35 E
Sintjohannesga 46 52 55N 5 52 E
Sinton 159 28 1N 97 30W
Sintra 57 38 47N 9 25W
Sinŭiju 107 40 5N 124 24 E
Sinuk 147 64 42N 166 22W
Sinyang = Hsinyang 109 32 10N 114 6 E
Sinyukha, R. 82 48 31N 30 31 E
Siófok 53 46 54N 18 4 E
Sióma 128 16 25 S 23 28 E
Sion 50 46 14N 7 20 E
Sion Mills 38 54 47N 7 29W
Sioua, El Wâhât es 122 29 10N 25 30 E
Sioux City 158 42 32N 96 25W
Sioux Falls 158 43 35N 96 40W
Sioux Lookout 150 50 10N 91 50W
Sip Song Chaw Thai, reg. 100 21 30N 103 30 E
Sipan 66 42 45N 17 52 E
Sipera, I. 102 2 18 S 99 40 E
Sipiwesk L. 153 55 5N 97 35W
Sipul 138 5 50 S 148 28 E
Siquia, R. 166 12 30N 84 30W
Siquijor, I. 103 9 12N 123 45 E
Siquirres 166 10 6N 83 30W
Siquisique 174 10 34N 69 42W
Sir Edward Pellew Group 138 15 40 S 137 10 E
Sir Graham Moore Is. 136 13 53 S 126 34 E
Sir Samuel Mt. 137 27 45 S 120 40 E
Sir Thomas, Mt. 137 27 10 S 129 45 E
Sira 97 13 41N 76 49 E
Sira, R. 71 58 43N 6 40 E
Siracusa 65 37 4N 15 17 E
Sirajganj 95 24 25N 89 47 E
Sirake 138 9 1 S 141 2 E
Sirakoro 120 12 41N 9 14W
Sirasso 120 9 16N 6 6W
Siret 70 47 55N 26 5 E
Siret, R. 70 47 58N 26 5 E
Siria 66 46 16N 21 38 E
Sirinhaém 171 8 35 S 35 7W
Sirkall (Shivali) 97 11 15N 79 41 E
Sirna, I. 69 36 22N 26 42 E
Sirnach 51 47 28N 8 59 E
Sirohi 94 24 52N 72 53 E
Siroki Brijeg 66 43 21N 17 36 E
Sironj 94 24 5N 77 45 E
Siros 69 37 28N 24 57 E
Síros, I. 69 37 28N 24 57 E
Sirretta Pk. 163 35 56N 118 19W
Sirsa 94 29 33N 75 4 E
Sirsi 97 14 40N 74 49 E
Siruela 57 38 58N 5 3W
Sisak 63 45 30N 16 21 E
Sisaket 100 15 8N 104 23 E
Sisante 59 39 25N 2 12W
Sisargas, Islas 56 43 21N 8 50W
Sishen 128 27 55 S 22 59 E
Sisipuk I. 153 55 40N 102 0W
Sisipuk L. 153 55 45N 101 50W
Sisophon 100 13 31N 102 59 E
Sissach 50 47 27N 7 48 E
Sisseton 158 45 43N 97 3W
Sissonne 43 49 34N 3 51 E
Sistan-Baluchistan □ 93 27 0N 62 0 E
Sistema Central 56 40 40N 5 55W
Sistema Ibérico 58 41 0N 2 10W
Sisteron 45 44 12N 5 57 E
Sisters 160 44 21N 121 32W
Sitamarhi 95 26 37N 85 30 E
Sitapur 95 27 38N 80 45 E
Siteki 129 26 32 S 31 58 E
Sitges 58 41 17N 1 47 E
Sithoniá 68 40 0N 23 45 E
Sitía 69 35 13N 26 6 E
Sítio da Abadia 171 14 48 S 46 16W
Sitka 147 57 9N 134 58W
Sitona 123 14 25N 37 23 E
Sitoti 128 23 15 S 23 40 E
Sitra 122 28 40N 26 53 E
Sittang Myit, R. 99 18 20N 96 45 E
Sittang, R. 98 17 10N 96 58 E
Sittard 47 51 0N 5 52 E
Sittaung 98 24 10N 94 35 E
Sittensen 48 53 17N 9 32 E
Sittingbourne 29 51 20N 0 43 E
Sittwe 99 20 15N 92 45 E
Situbondo 103 7 45 S 114 0 E
Siuch'uan 109 26 20N 114 30 E
Siuna 166 13 37N 84 45W
Sivaganga 97 9 50N 78 28 E
Sivagiri 97 9 16N 77 26 E
Sivakasi 97 9 24N 77 47 E
Sivand 93 30 5N 52 55 E
Sivas 92 39 43N 36 58 E
Siverek 92 37 50N 39 25 E
Sivrihisar 92 39 30N 31 35 E
Sivry 47 50 10N 4 12 E
Siwa 122 29 11N 25 31 E
Siwalik Range 95 28 0N 83 0 E
Siwan 95 26 13N 84 27 E
Sixmile Cross 38 54 34N 7 7W
Sixmilebridge 39 52 45N 8 46W
Siyâl, Jazâ'ir 122 22 49N 36 6 E
Siyana 94 28 37N 78 6 E
Sizewell 29 52 13N 1 38 E
Sjaelland 73 55 30N 11 30 E
Sjaellands Odde 73 56 0N 11 15 E
Själevad 72 63 18N 18 36 E
Sjarinska Banja 66 42 45N 21 38 E
Sjenica 66 43 16N 20 0 E
Sjernaröy 71 59 15N 5 50 E
Sjoa 71 61 41N 9 40 E
Sjöbo 73 55 37N 13 45 E
Sjöholt 71 62 27N 6 52 E
Sjönsta 74 67 10N 16 3 E
Sjösa 73 58 47N 17 4 E
Skadovsk 82 46 17N 32 52 E
Skælskör 73 55 16N 11 18 E
Skagafjörður 74 65 54N 19 35W
Skagastölstindane, mt. 75 61 25N 8 10 E
Skagen 75 68 37N 14 27 E
Skagen, pt. 73 57 43N 10 35 E
Skagern 72 59 0N 14 20 E
Skagerrak 73 57 30N 9 0 E
Skagway 147 59 30N 135 20W
Skaidi 74 70 26N 24 30 E
Skala Podolskaya 82 48 50N 26 15 E
Skalat 80 49 23N 25 55 E
Skalbmierz 54 50 22N 12 30 E
Skalderviken 73 56 22N 12 30 E
Skalicd 53 48 50N 17 15 E
Skallingen, Odde 73 55 32N 8 13 E
Skalni Dol = Kamenyak 67 43 24N 26 57 E
Skals 73 56 34N 9 24 E
Skanderborg 73 56 2N 9 55 E
Skaneateles 162 42 57N 76 26W

Skaneateles L Sollentuna

Skaneateles L. 162 42 51N 76 22W
Skånevik 71 59 43N 5 53E
Skanninge 73 58 24N 15 5E
Skanör 73 55 24N 12 50E
Skanor 73 55 24N 12 50E
Skantzoúra I. 69 39 5N 24 6E
Skara 73 58 25N 13 30E
Skaraborgs län □ 73 58 20N 13 30E
Skarblacka 73 58 36N 15 50E
Skardhö 71 62 30N 8 47E
Skardu 95 35 20N 75 35E
Skaresta 73 58 26N 16 22E
Skarszewy 54 54 4N 18 25E
Skarvane, Mt. 71 63 18N 11 27E
Skarzysko Kamienna 54 51 7N 20 52E
Skatöy 71 50 50N 9 30E
Skattungbyn 72 61 10N 14 56E
Skaw (Grenen) 73 57 46N 10 34E
Skaw Taing 36 60 23N 0 57W
Skebo 72 59 58N 18 37E
Skebokvarn 72 59 7N 16 45E
Skeena Mts. 152 56 40N 128 30W
Skeena, R. 152 54 9N 130 5W
Skeggjastadir 74 66 3N 14 50W
Skegness 33 53 9N 0 20E
Skeldon 174 6 0N 57 20W
Skellefte älv 74 65 30N 18 30E
Skellefteå 74 64 45N 20 58E
Skelleftehamn 74 64 41N 21 14E
Skellig Rocks 39 51 47N 10 32W
Skellingthorpe 33 53 14N 0 37W
Skelmersdale 32 53 34N 2 49W
Skelmorlie 34 55 52N 4 53W
Skelton, Cleveland., U.K. 33 54 33N 0 59W
Skelton, Cumb., U.K. 32 54 42N 2 50W
Skender Vakuf 66 44 29N 17 22E
Skene 73 57 30N 12 37E
Skerries, Rks. 38 55 14N 6 40W
Skerries, The 31 53 27N 4 40W
Skhirra, La = Cekhira 119 34 20N 10 5E
Skhíza, I. 69 36 41N 20 40E
Skhoinoúsa, I. 69 36 53N 25 31E
Ski 71 59 43N 10 52E
Skíathos, I. 69 39 12N 23 30E
Skibbereen 39 51 33N 9 16W
Skiddaw, Mt. 32 54 39N 3 9W
Skidegate, Inlet 48 53 20N 132 0W
Skien 71 59 12N 9 35E
Skierniewice 54 51 58N 20 19E
Skikda 119 36 50N 6 58E
Skillingaryd 73 57 27N 14 5E
Skillinge 73 55 30N 14 16E
Skillingmark 72 59 48N 120 1E
Skinari, Akra 69 37 56N 20 40E
Skipness 34 55 46N 5 20W
Skipsea 33 53 58N 0 13W
Skipton, Austral. 140 37 39S 143 21E
Skipton, U.K. 32 53 57N 2 1W
Skirild 73 55 58N 8 53E
Skirmish Pt. 138 11 59S 134 17E
Skiropoúla, I. 69 38 50N 24 21E
Skíros 69 38 55N 24 34E
Skíros, I. 69 38 55N 24 34E
Skivarp 73 55 26N 13 34E
Skive 73 56 33N 9 2E
Skjåk 71 61 52N 8 22E
Skjálfandafljót 74 65 15N 17 25W
Skjálfandi 74 66 5N 17 30W
Skjeberg 71 59 12N 11 12E
Skjern 73 55 57N 8 30E
Skjönne 71 60 16N 9 1E
Skoczów 54 49 49N 18 45E
Skodje 71 62 30N 6 43E
Skofja Loka 63 46 9N 14 19E
Skoger 71 59 42N 10 16E
Skoghall 72 59 20N 13 30E
Skoghult 73 56 59N 15 55E
Skokholm, I. 31 51 42N 5 16W
Skoki 54 52 40N 17 11E
Skole 80 49 3N 23 30E
Skomer, I. 31 51 44N 5 19W
Skonsberg 72 62 25N 17 21E
Skópelos 69 39 9N 23 47E
Skópelos, I. 69 39 9N 23 47E
Skopin 81 53 55N 39 32E
Skopje 66 42 1N 21 32E
Skorcz 54 53 47N 18 30E
Skorped 72 63 23N 17 55E
Skotfoss 71 59 12N 9 30E
Skoudas 80 56 21N 21 45E
Skövde 75 58 15N 13 59E
Skovorodino 77 54 0N 125 0E
Skowhegan 151 44 49N 69 40W
Skowman 153 51 58N 99 35W
Skradin 63 43 52N 15 53E
Skreanäs 73 56 52N 12 35E
Skudeneshavn 71 59 10N 5 10E
Skull 39 51 32N 9 40W
Skultorp 73 58 24N 13 51E
Skulyany 82 47 19N 27 39E
Skunk, R. 158 40 42N 91 7W
Skurup 73 55 28N 13 30E
Skutskär 73 60 37N 17 25E
Skvira 82 49 44N 29 32E
Skwaner, Pegunungan 102 1 0S 112 30E
Skwierzyna 54 52 46N 15 30E
Skye, I. 36 57 15N 6 10W
Skykomish 160 47 43N 121 16W
Skyros (Skíros), L. 69 38 52N 24 37E
Slagelse 73 55 23N 11 19E
Slagharen 46 52 37N 6 34E
Slaidburn 32 53 57N 2 28W
Slaley 35 54 55N 2 4W
Slamannon 140 32 1S 143 41E
Slamet, G. 102 7 16S 109 8E
Slane 38 53 42N 6 32W
Slaney, R. 39 52 52N 6 45W
Slangerup 73 55 50N 12 11E
Slânic 70 45 14N 25 58E
Slankamen 66 45 8N 20 15E
Slano 66 42 48N 17 53E
Slantsy 80 59 7N 28 5E
Slany 52 50 13N 14 6E
Slask 54 51 25N 16 0E
Slatbaken 73 58 28N 16 30E
Slate Is. 150 48 40N 87 0W
Slatina 70 44 28N 24 22E
Slatington 162 40 45N 75 37W
Slaton 159 33 27N 101 38W
Slave Coast 121 6 0N 2 30E
Slave Lake 152 55 17N 114 50W
Slave Pt. 152 61 11N 114 56W
Slave, R. 152 61 18N 113 39W
Slavgorod 76 53 10N 78 50E
Slavinja 66 43 14N 22 50E
Slavkov (Austerlitz) 53 49 10N 16 52E
Slavnoye 80 54 24N 29 15E
Slavonski Brod 66 45 11N 18 0E
Slavonski Pozega 66 45 20N 17 40E
Slavuta 80 50 15N 27 2E
Slavyans 82 48 55N 37 30E
Slavyansk 82 45 15N 38 11E
Sława 54 51 52N 16 2E
Sławno 54 54 20N 16 41E
Sławoborze 54 53 55N 15 42E
Slea Hd. 39 52 7N 10 30W
Sleaford 33 53 0N 0 22W
Sleaford B. 139 34 55S 135 45E
Sleat, Pt. of 36 57 1N 6 0W
Sleat, Sd. of 36 57 5N 5 47W
Sledmere 33 54 4N 0 35W
Sleeper, Is. 149 56 50N 80 30W
Sleepers, The 149 58 30N 81 0W
Sleepy Eye 158 44 15N 94 45W
Sleidinge 47 51 8N 3 41E
Sleights 33 54 27N 0 40W
Sleipner, gasfield 19 58 30N 1 48E
Sleman 103 7 40S 110 20E
Slemmestad 71 59 47N 10 30E
Slemon L. 152 63 13N 116 4W
Slesin 54 52 22N 18 14E
Sletterhage, Kap 73 56 7N 10 31E
Slide Mt. 162 42 0N 74 23W
Slidell 159 30 20N 89 48W
Sliedrecht 46 51 50N 4 45E
Slieve Anierin 38 54 5N 7 58W
Slieve Aughty 39 53 4N 8 30W
Slieve Bernagh 39 52 50N 8 30W
Slieve Bloom 39 53 4N 7 40W
Slieve Callan 39 52 51N 9 16W
Slieve Donard 38 54 10N 5 57W
Slieve Felim 39 52 40N 8 20W
Slieve Gamph 38 54 6N 9 0W
Slieve Gullion 38 54 8N 6 26W
Slieve League 38 54 40N 8 42W
Slieve Mish 39 52 12N 9 50W
Slieve Miskish 39 51 40N 10 10W
Slieve More 38 54 1N 10 3W
Slieve Snaght 38 54 59N 8 7W
Slieve Tooey 38 54 46N 8 39W
Slievenamon Mt. 39 52 25N 7 37W
Sligachan 36 57 17N 6 10W
Sligo 38 54 17N 8 28W
Sligo □ 38 54 10N 8 35W
Sligo B. 38 54 20N 8 40W
Slikkerveer 46 51 53N 4 36E
Slioch, mt. 36 57 40N 5 20W
Slipje 47 51 9N 2 51E
Slite 75 57 42N 18 48E
Sliven 67 42 42N 26 19E
Slivnitsa 66 42 50N 23 0E
Sljeme, mt. 63 45 57N 15 58E
Słupsk □ 54 54 15N 17 30E
Sloansville 162 42 45N 74 22W
Slobodskoy 84 58 40N 50 6E
Slobozia, Ialomiţa, Rumania 70 44 34N 27 23E
Slobozia, Valahia, Rumania 70 44 30N 25 14E
Slocan 152 49 48N 117 28W
Slochteren 46 53 12N 6 48E
Slochteren-Groningen, gasfield 19 53 10N 6 45E
Slöinge 73 56 51N 12 42E
Słomniki 54 50 16N 20 4E
Slonim 80 53 4N 25 19E
Slotermeer 46 52 55N 5 38E
Slough 29 51 30N 0 35W
Sloughhouse 163 38 26N 121 12W
Slovakia □ 53 48 30N 19 0E
Slovenia = Slovenija 63 45 58N 14 30E
Slovenija □ 63 45 58N 14 30E
Slovenska Bistrica 63 46 24N 15 35E
Slovenske Krusnohorie 53 48 45N 20 0E
Slovenské Rhudhorie 52 48 45N 19 0E
Słubice 54 52 22N 14 35E
Sluis 47 51 18N 3 23E
Slunchev Bryag 67 42 40N 27 41E
Slunj 63 45 6N 15 33E
Słupca 54 52 15N 17 52E
Słupsk 54 54 30N 17 3E
Slurry 128 25 49S 25 42E
Slyne Hd. 38 53 25N 10 10W
Slyudyanka 77 51 40N 103 30E
Smål-Taberg 73 57 42N 14 5E
Smålandsfarvandet 73 55 10N 11 20E
Smalandsstenar 73 57 9N 13 24E
Smålandstarvandet 73 55 10N 11 20E
Smalltree L. 153 61 0N 105 0W
Smallwood Reservoir 151 54 20N 63 10W
Smara 118 26 48N 11 31W
Smarje 63 46 15N 15 34E
Smart Syndicate Dam 128 30 45S 23 10E
Smeaton 153 53 30N 105 49W
Smedberg 73 58 35N 12 0E
Smederevo 66 44 40N 20 57E
Smedstorp 73 55 38N 13 58E
Smela 82 49 30N 32 0E
Smerwick Harb. 39 52 12N 10 23W
Smethwick 28 52 29N 1 58W
Smidovich 77 48 36N 133 49E
Smilde 46 52 58N 6 28E
Smiley 153 51 38N 109 29W
Smilyan 67 41 29N 24 46E
Smith 152 55 10N 114 0W
Smith Arm 152 66 15N 123 0W
Smith Center 158 39 50N 98 50W
Smith I. 162 38 0N 76 0W
Smith, R. 152 59 34N 126 30W
Smith Sund 12 78 30N 74 0W
Smithborough 38 54 13N 7 8W
Smithburne, R. 138 17 3S 140 57E
Smithers 152 54 45N 127 10W
Smithfield, U.K. 32 54 59N 2 51W
Smithfield, U.S.A. 157 35 31N 78 16W
Smith's Falls 150 44 55N 76 0W
Smithton, N.S.W., Austral. 139 31 0S 152 48E
Smithton, Tas., Austral. 138 40 53S 145 6E
Smithtown 141 30 58S 152 56E
Smithville 159 30 2N 97 12W
Smjörfjöll 74 65 30N 15 42W
Smoky Bay 139 32 22S 133 56E
Smoky Falls 150 50 4N 82 10W
Smoky Hill, R. 158 38 45N 98 0W
Smoky Lake 152 54 10N 112 30W
Smola 71 63 23N 8 3E
Smolensk 80 54 45N 32 0E
Smolikas, Óros 68 40 9N 20 58E
Smolník 53 48 43N 20 44E
Smolyan 67 41 36N 24 38E
Smooth Rock Falls 150 49 17N 81 37W
Smoothstone L. 153 54 40N 106 50W
Smorgon 80 54 28N 26 24E
Smulţi 70 45 57N 27 44E
Smyadovo 67 43 2N 27 1E
Smyrna 162 39 18N 75 36W
Smyrna = İzmir 92 38 25N 27 8E
Snaefell 30 54 18N 4 26W
Snaefells Jökull 74 64 45N 23 25W
Snainton 33 54 14N 0 33W
Snaith 33 53 42N 1 1W
Snake I. 141 38 47S 146 33E
Snake L. 153 55 32N 106 35W
Snake, R. 160 46 31N 118 50W
Snake Ra., Mts. 160 39 0N 114 30W
Snake River Plain 160 43 13N 113 0W
Snap, The 36 60 35N 0 50W
Snape 29 52 11N 1 29E
Snarum 71 60 1N 9 54E
Snasahogarha 72 63 10N 12 20E
Snedsted 73 56 55N 8 32E
Sneek 46 53 2N 5 40E
Sneeker-meer 46 53 2N 5 45E
Sneem 39 51 50N 9 55W
Snejbjerg 73 56 8N 8 54E
Snĕka 52 50 41N 15 50E
Snelling 163 37 31N 120 26W
Snettisham 29 52 52N 0 30E
Snezhnoye 83 48 0N 38 58E
Sneznik, mt. 63 45 36N 14 35E
Snigirevka 82 47 2N 32 35E
Snina 53 49 0N 22 9E
Snizort, L. 36 57 33N 6 28W
Snohetta 71 62 19N 9 16E
Snohomish 160 47 53N 122 6W
Snonuten 71 59 31N 6 50E
Snoul 101 12 4N 106 26E
Snow Hill 162 38 10N 75 21W
Snow L. 153 54 52N 100 3W
Snowbird L. 153 60 45N 103 0W
Snowdon, Mt. 31 53 4N 4 8W
Snowdrift 153 62 24N 110 44W
Snowdrift, R. 153 62 24N 110 44W
Snowflake 161 34 30N 110 4W
Snowshoe 152 53 43N 121 0W
Snowtown 140 33 46S 138 14E
Snowville 160 41 59N 112 47W
Snowy Mt. 162 43 45N 74 26W
Snowy Mts. 141 36 30S 148 20E
Snowy, R. 141 37 46S 148 30E
Snug Corner 167 22 33N 73 52W
Snyder, Okla., U.S.A. 159 34 4N 99 0W
Snyder, Tex., U.S.A. 159 32 45N 100 57W
Soacha 174 4 35N 74 13W
Soahanina 129 18 42S 44 13E
Soalala 129 16 6S 45 20E
Soan, R. 94 33 20N 72 40E
Soanierana-Ivongo 129 16 55S 49 35E
Soap Lake 160 47 29N 119 31W
Soay, I. 36 57 9N 6 13W
Soay Sd. 36 57 10N 6 15W
Sobat, Nahr 123 8 32N 32 40E
Soběslav 52 49 16N 14 45E
Sobhapur 94 22 47N 78 17E
Sobinka 81 56 0N 40 0E
Sobo-Yama 110 32 51N 131 16E
Sobótka 54 50 54N 16 44E
Sobrado 56 43 2N 8 2W
Sobral 170 3 50S 40 30W
Sobreira Formosa 57 39 46N 7 51W
Soc Giang 100 22 54N 106 1E
Soc Trang = Khonh Hung 101 9 37N 105 50E
Soča, R. 63 46 20N 13 40E
Socha 174 6 0N 72 41W
Sochaczew 54 52 15N 20 13E
Soch'e 105 38 24N 77 20E
Sochi 83 43 35N 39 40E
Société, Is. de la 131 17 0S 151 0W
Socompa, Portezuelo de 172 24 27S 68 18W
Socorro 174 6 29N 73 16W
Socorro, I. 164 18 45N 110 58W
Socotra, I. 91 12 30N 54 0E
Socúellmos 59 39 16N 2 47W
Soda Creek 152 52 25N 122 10W
Soda L. 161 35 7N 116 2W
Soda Plains 94 35 30N 79 0E
Soda Springs 160 42 4N 111 40W
Sodankylä 74 67 29N 26 40E
Söderfjärden 72 62 3N 17 25E
Söderfors 72 60 23N 17 25E
Söderhamn 72 61 18N 17 10E
Söderköping 72 58 31N 16 35E
Södermanlands län □ 72 59 10N 16 30E
Södertälje 72 59 12N 17 50E
Sodium 128 30 15S 15 45E
Sodo 123 7 0N 37 57E
Södra Vi 73 57 45N 15 45E
Sodrazica 63 45 45N 14 39E
Sodus 162 43 13N 77 5W
Soekmekaar 129 23 30S 29 55E
Soest, Ger. 48 51 34N 8 7E
Soest, Neth. 46 52 9N 5 19E
Soestdijk 46 52 11N 5 17E
Sofádhes 68 39 28N 22 4E
Sofara 120 13 59N 4 9W
Sofia = Sofiya 67 42 45N 23 20E
Sofia, R. 129 15 25S 48 40E
Sofievka 82 47 58N 34 14E
Sofikón 69 37 47N 23 3E
Sofila 67 42 45N 23 20E
Sofiya 67 42 45N 23 20E
Sogad 103 10 30N 125 0E
Sogakofe 121 6 2N 0 39E
Sogamoso 174 5 43N 72 56W
Sögel 48 52 50N 7 32E
Sogeri 135 9 26S 147 35E
Sogipo 107 33 13N 126 34E
Sogn og Fjordane fylke □ 71 61 40N 6 0E
Sogndal 71 58 20N 6 15E
Sogndalsfjøra 75 61 14N 7 5E
Sognefjorden 71 61 10N 5 50E
Sohâg 122 26 27N 31 43E
Soham 29 52 20N 0 20E
Sohano 135 5 22S 154 37E
Sŏhori 107 40 7N 128 23E
Soignies 47 50 35N 4 5E
Soira, Mt. 123 14 45N 39 30E
Soissons 43 49 25N 3 19E
Soitava, R. 53 49 30N 16 37E
Sojat 94 25 55N 73 38E
Sok, R. 84 53 24N 50 8E
Sokal 80 50 31N 24 15E
Söke 69 37 48N 27 28E
Sokhós 68 40 48N 23 22E
Sokhta Chinar 93 35 5N 67 35E
Sokna 71 60 16N 9 50E
Soknedal 71 62 57N 10 13E
Soko Banja 66 43 40N 21 51E
Sokodé 121 9 0N 1 11E
Sokó'ka 54 53 25N 23 30E
Sokol 81 59 30N 40 5E
Sokolo 120 14 42N 6 8W
Sokolov 52 50 12N 12 40E
Sokoł ó w Matopolski 53 50 12N 22 7E
Sokoł ó w Podlaski 54 52 25N 22 15E
Sokoto 121 13 2N 5 16E
Sokoto □ 121 12 30N 5 0E
Sokoto, R. 121 12 30N 6 10E
Sokuluk 85 42 52N 74 18E
Sol Iletsk 84 51 10N 55 0E
Sola 71 58 53N 5 36E
Sola, R. 126 49 38N 19 8E
Solai 126 0 2N 36 12E
Solana, La 59 38 59N 3 14W
Solano 103 16 25N 121 15E
Solares 56 43 23N 3 43W
Solberga 73 57 45N 14 43E
Solca 70 47 40N 25 50E
Solec Kujawski 54 53 5N 18 14E
Soledad, Colomb. 174 10 55N 74 46W
Soledad, U.S.A. 163 36 27N 121 16W
Soledad, Venez. 174 8 10N 63 34W
Solemint 163 34 25N 118 27W
Solent, The 28 50 45N 1 25W
Solenzara 45 41 53N 9 23E
Solesmes 43 50 10N 3 30E
Solfonn, Mt. 71 60 2N 6 57E
Soligalich 81 59 5N 42 10E
Solihull 28 52 26N 1 47W
Solikamsk 84 59 38N 56 50E
Solila 129 21 25S 46 37E
Soliman 119 36 42N 10 30E
Solimões, R. 174 2 15S 66 30W
Solingen 48 51 10N 7 4E
Sollas 36 57 39N 7 20W
Sollebrunn 73 58 8N 12 32E
Sollefteå 72 63 12N 17 20E
Sollentuna 72 59 26N 17 56E

Soller Speer

Soller 58 39 43N 2 45 E
Sollerön 72 60 54N 14 38 E
Solna 72 59 22N 18 1 E
Solnechnogorsk 81 56 10N 36 57 E
Sölnkletten, Mt. 71 61 55N 10 18 E
Sologne 59 47 40N 2 0 E
Solojärg 73 56 50N 10 8 E
Solok 102 0 55 S 100 40 E
Sololá 166 14 49N 91 10 E
Solomon Is. ■ 135 6 0 S 155 0 E
Solomon, N. Fork, R. 158 39 45N 99 0W
Solomon Sea 135 7 0 S 150 0 E
Solomon, S. Fork, R. 158 39 25N 99 12W
Solomon's Pools = Burak Sulayman 90 31 42N 35 7 E
Solon Springs 158 46 19N 91 47W
Solonópole 170 5 44 S 39 1W
Solor, I. 103 8 27 S 123 0 E
Solotcha 81 54 48N 39 53 E
Solothurn 50 47 13N 7 32 E
Solothurn □ 50 47 18N 7 40 E
Solotobe 85 44 37N 66 3 E
Solsona 58 42 0N 1 31 E
Solt 53 46 45N 19 1 E
Solta, I. 63 43 24N 16 15 E
Soltanabad 93 36 29N 58 5 E
Soltaniyeh 92 36 20N 48 55 E
Soltau 48 52 59N 9 50 E
Soltsy 80 58 10N 30 10 E
Solun 105 46 40N 120 40 E
Solund 71 61 5N 4 50 E
Solund I. 71 61 7N 4 50 E
Solunska Glava 66 41 44N 21 31 E
Solva 31 51 52N 5 12W
Solvang 163 34 36N 120 8W
Solvay 162 43 5N 76 17W
Solvesborg 73 56 5N 14 35 E
Sölvesborg 73 56 5N 14 35 E
Solway Firth 32 54 45N 3 38W
Solwezi 127 12 20 S 26 21 E
Somali Rep. ■ 91 7 0N 47 0 E
Somaliland 123 12 0N 43 0 E
Sombe Dzong 98 27 13N 89 8 E
Sombernon 43 47 20N 4 40 E
Sombor 66 45 46N 19 17 E
Sombrerete 164 23 40N 103 40W
Sombrero I. 167 18 30N 63 30W
Somerby 29 52 42N 0 49W
Someren 47 51 23N 5 42 E
Somers 160 48 4N 114 18W
Somerset, Austral. 138 10 45 S 142 25 E
Somerset, Can. 153 49 25N 98 39W
Somerset, Colo., U.S.A. 161 38 55N 107 30W
Somerset, Ky., U.S.A. 156 37 5N 84 40W
Somerset, Mass., U.S.A. 162 41 45N 71 10W
Somerset □ 28 51 9N 3 0W
Somerset East 128 32 42 S 25 35 E
Somerset, I. 148 73 30N 93 0W
Somerset West 128 34 8 S 18 50 E
Somersham 29 52 24N 0 0W
Somersworth 162 43 15N 70 51W
Somerton, U.K. 28 51 3N 2 45W
Somerton, U.S.A. 161 32 41N 114 47W
Somerville 162 40 34N 74 36W
Someş, R. 70 47 15N 23 45 E
Someşul Mare, R. 70 47 18N 24 30 E
Somma Lombardo 62 45 41N 8 42 E
Somma Vesuviana 65 40 52N 14 23 E
Sommariva 139 26 24 S 146 36 E
Sommatino 65 37 20N 14 0 E
Somme □ 43 50 0N 2 20 E
Somme, B. de la 42 5 22N 1 30 E
Sommelsdijk 46 51 46N 4 9 E
Sommen 73 58 12N 15 0 E
Sommen, L. 73 58 0N 15 15 E
Sommepy-Tahure 43 49 15N 4 31 E
Sömmerda 48 51 10N 11 8 E
Sommersted 73 55 19N 9 18 E
Sommesous 43 48 44N 4 12 E
Sommières 45 43 47N 4 6 E
Somogy □ 53 46 19N 17 30 E
Somogyszob 53 46 18N 17 20 E
Somoto 166 13 28N 86 37W
Sompolno 54 52 26N 18 45 E
Somport, Paso 58 42 48N 0 31W
Somport, Puerto de 58 42 48N 0 31W
Sompting 29 50 51N 0 20W
Son, Neth. 47 51 31N 5 30 E
Son, Norway 71 59 32N 10 42 E
Son, Spain 56 42 43N 8 58W
Son Hoa 100 13 2N 108 58 E
Son La 100 21 20N 103 50 E
Son Ma 100 15 3N 108 34 E
Son Tay 100 21 8N 105 30 E
Soná 166 8 0N 81 10W
Sonamarg 95 34 18N 75 21 E
Sonamukhi 95 23 18N 87 27 E
Sonamura 98 23 29N 91 15 E
Sŏnchŏn 107 39 48N 124 55 E
Soncino 62 45 24N 9 52 E
Sondags, R. 128 32 10N 24 40 E
Sóndala 62 46 20N 10 20 E
Sondar 95 33 28N 75 56 E
Sönder Hornum 73 56 32N 9 38 E
Sønder Omme 73 55 50N 8 54 E
Sønderborg 73 54 55N 9 49 E
Sonderhausen 48 51 22N 10 50 E
Sonderjyllands Amt □ 73 55 10N 9 10 E
Sondre Höland 71 59 44N 11 30 E
Sondre Land 71 60 44N 10 21 E
Söndre Stromfjord 12 66 30N 50 52W
Sóndrio 62 46 10N 9 53 E
Sone 127 17 23 S 34 55 E
Sonepat 94 29 0N 77 5 E
Sonepur 96 20 55N 83 50 E
Song 100 18 28N 100 11 E
Song Cau 100 13 20N 109 18 E
Songa, R. 71 59 57N 7 30 E
Sŏngchŏn 107 39 12N 126 15 E
Songea 127 10 40 S 35 40 E
Songea □ 127 10 30 S 36 0 E
Songeons 43 49 32N 1 50 E
Songjin 107 40 40N 129 10 E
Songjŏngni 107 35 8N 126 47 E
Songkhla 101 7 13N 100 37 E
Songnim 107 38 45N 125 39 E
Songwe, Malawi 127 9 44 S 33 58 E
Songwe, Zaïre 127 3 20 S 26 16 E
Sonkel, Ozero 85 41 50N 75 12 E
Sonkovo 81 57 50N 37 5 E
Sonmiani 94 25 25N 66 40 E
Sonning 29 51 28N 0 53W
Sonnino 64 41 25N 13 13 E
Sono, R., Goias, Brazil 170 8 58 S 48 11W
Sono, R., Minas Gerais, Brazil 171 17 2 S 45 32W
Sonobe 111 35 6N 135 28 E
Sonogno 51 46 22N 8 47 E
Sonoma 163 38 17N 122 27W
Sonora, Calif., U.S.A. 163 37 59N 120 27W
Sonora, Texas, U.S.A. 159 30 33N 100 37W
Sonora □ 164 28 0N 111 0W
Sonora P. 160 38 17N 119 35W
Sonora, R. 164 28 30N 111 33W
Sonoyta 164 31 51N 112 50W
Sŏnsan 107 36 14N 128 17 E
Sonskyn 128 30 47 S 26 28 E
Sonsonate 166 13 43N 89 44W
Sonthofen 49 47 31N 10 16 E
Soo Junction 156 46 20N 85 14W
Soochow = Suchou 109 31 15N 120 40 E
Söonder Nissum 73 56 19N 8 11 E
Sop Hao 100 20 33N 104 27 E
Sop Prap 100 17 53N 99 20 E
Sopi 103 2 40N 128 28 E
Sopo, Nahr 123 8 40N 26 30 E
Sopot, Poland 54 54 27N 18 31 E
Sopot, Yugo. 66 44 29N 20 30 E
Sopotnica 66 41 23N 21 13 E
Sopron 49 47 41N 16 37 E
Sop's Arm 151 49 46N 56 56W
Sör-Fron 71 61 35N 9 59 E
Sor, R. 57 39 7N 9 52 E
Sør-Rondane 13 72 0 S 25 0 E
Sør Trøndelag fylke □ 71 63 0N 11 0 E
Sora 64 41 45N 13 36 E
Sorada 96 19 32N 84 45 E
Sorah 94 27 13N 68 56 E
Söråker 72 62 30N 17 32 E
Sorano 63 42 40N 11 42 E
Sorata 174 15 50 S 68 50W
Sorbas 59 37 6N 2 7W
Sorbie 34 54 46N 4 26W
Sordale 37 58 33N 3 26W
Sordeval 42 48 44N 0 55W
Sorel 150 46 0N 73 10W
Sörenberg 50 46 50N 8 2 E
Soresina 62 45 17N 9 51 E
Sörfold 74 67 5N 14 20 E
Sorgues 45 44 1N 4 53 E
Soria 58 41 43N 2 32W
Soria □ 58 41 46N 2 28W
Soriano 172 33 24 S 58 19W
Soriano □ 176 33 30 S 58 0W
Sorisdale 34 56 40N 6 28W
Sorn 34 55 31N 4 18W
Sorø 73 55 26N 11 32 E
Soro 120 10 9N 9 48W
Sorocaba 173 23 31 S 47 35W
Sorochinsk 84 52 26N 53 10 E
Soroki 82 48 8N 28 12 E
Soroksár 53 47 24N 19 9 E
Soron 94 27 55N 78 45 E
Sorong 103 0 55 S 131 15 E
Sororoca 174 0 43N 61 31W
Soroti 126 1 43N 33 35 E
Soröy Sundet 74 70 25N 23 0 E
Soröya 74 70 35N 22 45 E
Soroyane 71 62 25N 5 32 E
Sorraia, R. 57 38 55N 8 35W
Sorrento, Austral. 139 38 22 S 144 47 E
Sorrento, Italy 65 40 38N 14 23 E
Sorris Sorris 128 21 0 S 14 46 E
Sorsele 74 65 31N 17 30 E
Sorso 64 40 50N 8 34 E
Sorsogon 103 13 0N 124 0 E
Sortat 37 58 32N 3 12W
Sortino 65 37 9N 15 1 E
Sos 58 42 30N 1 13W
Sŏsan 107 36 47N 126 27 E
Soscumica, L. 150 50 15N 77 27W
Sosdala 73 56 2N 13 41 E
Sosna, R. 81 52 30N 38 0 E
Sosnowiec 54 50 20N 19 10 E
Sospel 45 43 52N 7 27 E
Soštanj 63 46 23N 15 4 E
Sŏsura 107 42 16N 130 36 E
Sosva 84 59 10N 61 50 E
Sosva, R. 84 59 32N 62 20 E
Soto la Marina, R. 165 23 40N 97 40W
Soto y Amío 56 42 46N 5 53W
Sotra I. 71 60 15N 5 0 E
Sotteville 42 49 24N 1 5 E
Souanké 124 2 10N 14 10 E
Souderton 162 40 19N 75 19W
Soufi 120 15 13N 12 17W
Souflíon 68 41 12N 26 18 E
Soufrière 167 13 51N 61 4W
Soufrière, vol. 167 13 10N 61 10W
Sougne-Remouchamps 47 50 29N 5 42 E
Souillac 44 44 53N 1 29 E
Souk-Ahras 119 36 17N 7 57 E
Souk el Arba du Rharb 118 34 50N 5 59W
Souk el Khemis 119 36 36N 8 58 E
Soukhouma 100 14 38N 105 48 E
Sŏul 105 37 31N 127 6 E
Soulac-sur-Mer 44 45 30N 1 7W
Soultz 43 48 57N 7 52 E
Soumagne 47 50 37N 5 44 E
Sound, The 75 56 7N 12 30 E
Soúnion, Ákra 69 37 37N 24 1 E
Sour el Ghozlane 119 36 10N 3 45 E
Sources, Mt. aux 129 28 45 S 28 50 E
Sourdeval 42 48 43N 0 55W
Soure, Brazil 170 0 35 S 48 30W
Soure, Port. 56 40 4N 8 38W
Souris, Man., Can. 153 49 40N 100 20W
Souris, P.E.I., Can. 151 46 21N 62 15W
Souris, R. 153 49 40N 99 34W
Soúrpi 69 39 6N 22 54 E
Sous, R. 118 30 31N 9 27W
Sousa 170 6 45 S 38 10W
Sousel, Brazil 170 2 38 S 52 29W
Sousel, Port. 57 38 57N 7 40W
Souss, O. 118 30 23N 8 24W
Sousse 119 35 50N 10 38 E
Soustons 44 43 45N 1 19W
Souterraine, La 44 46 15N 1 30 E
South Africa, Rep. of, ■ 125 30 0 S 25 0 E
South Amboy 162 40 29N 74 17W
South America 168 10 0 S 60 0W
South Auckland & Bay of Plenty □ 142 38 30 S 177 0 E
South Aulatsivik I. 151 56 45N 61 30W
South Australia □ 136 32 0 S 139 0 E
South Baldy, Mt. 161 34 6N 107 27W
South Bend, Indiana, U.S.A. 156 41 38N 86 20W
South Bend, Wash., U.S.A. 160 46 44N 123 52W
South Benfleet 29 51 33N 0 34 E
South Blackwater 138 24 00 S 148 35 E
South Boston 157 36 42N 78 58W
South Br. Ashburton, R. 143 43 30 S 171 15 E
South Branch, Can. 151 47 55N 59 2W
South Branch, U.S.A. 151 44 30N 83 55W
South Brent 30 50 26N 3 50W
South Brook 151 49 26N 56 5W
South Buganda □ 126 0 15 S 31 30 E
South Cape 147 18 58N 155 24 E
South Carolina □ 157 33 45N 81 0W
South Cave 33 53 46N 0 37W
South Charleston 156 38 20N 81 40W
South China Sea 101 7 0N 107 0 E
South Dakota □ 158 45 0N 100 0W
South Dell 36 58 28N 6 20W
South Dorset Downs 28 50 40N 2 26W
South Downs 29 50 53N 0 10W
South East C. 138 43 40 S 146 50 E
South East Is. 137 34 17 S 123 30 E
South Elkington 33 53 22N 0 5W
South Esk, R. 37 56 44N 3 3W
South Foreland 29 51 7N 1 23 E
S. Fork, American, R. 163 38 45N 121 5W
South Fork, R. 160 47 54N 113 15W
South Gamboa 164 9 4N 79 40W
South Gate 163 33 57N 118 12W
South Georgia 13 54 30 S 37 0W
South Glamorgan □ 31 51 30N 3 20W
South Grafton 139 29 41 S 152 47 E
South Harris, district 36 56 51N 3 10W
South Haven 156 42 22N 86 20W
South Hayling 29 50 47N 0 56W
South Henik, L. 153 61 30N 97 30W
South Horr 126 2 12N 36 56 E
South I., Kenya 126 2 35N 36 35 E
South I., N.Z. 143 43 0 S 170 0 E
South Invercargill 143 46 26N 168 23 E
South Kirby 33 53 35N 1 25W
South Knife, R. 153 58 55N 94 37W
S. Kolok 101 6 2N 101 58 E
South Korea ■ 107 36 0N 128 0 E
S. Lembing 101 3 55N 103 3 E
South Magnetic Pole 13 66 30 S 139 30 E
South Marsh Is. 162 38 6N 76 1W
South Milwaukee 156 42 50N 87 52W
South Molton 30 51 1N 3 50W
South Nahanni, R. 152 61 3N 123 21W
South Nesting B. 36 60 18N 1 5W
South Orkney Is. 13 63 0 S 45 0W
South Pass 160 42 20N 108 58W
South Passage 137 26 07 S 113 09 E
S. Petani 101 5 37N 100 30 E
South Petherton 28 50 57N 2 49W
South Petherwin 30 50 35N 4 22W
South Pines 157 35 10N 79 25W
South Platte, R. 158 40 50N 102 45W
South Pt. 151 49 6N 62 11W
South Pole 13 90 0 S 0 0 E
South Porcupine 150 48 30N 81 12W
South Portland 162 43 38N 70 15W
South River, Can. 150 45 52N 79 29W
South River, U.S.A. 162 40 27N 74 23W
South Ronaldsay, I. 37 58 46N 2 58W
S. Sandwich Is. 15 57 0 S 27 0W
South Saskatchewan, R. 153 53 15N 105 5W
South Sd. 39 53 4N 9 28W
South Seal, R. 153 58 48N 98 8W
South Sentinel, I. 101 11 1N 92 16 E
South Shetland Is. 13 62 0 S 59 0W
South Shields 35 54 59N 1 26W
South Sioux City 158 42 30N 96 30W
South Taranaki Bight 142 39 40 S 174 5 E
South Tawton 30 50 44N 3 55W
South Thompson, R. 152 50 40N 120 20W
South Twin I. 150 53 7N 79 52W
South Tyne, R. 35 54 46N 2 25W
South Uist, I. 37 57 4N 7 21W
South Ulvön, I. 72 63 0N 18 45 E
South Walls, I. 37 58 45N 3 7W
South West Africa ■ = Namibia 128 22 0 S 18 9 E
South West C. 138 43 34 S 146 3 E
South West Cape 143 47 16 S 167 31 E
South Williamsport 162 41 14N 77 0W
South Yarmouth 162 41 35N 70 10W
South Yemen ■ 91 15 0N 48 0 E
South Yorkshire □ 33 53 30N 1 20W
Southam 28 52 16N 1 24W
Southampton, Can. 150 44 30N 81 25W
Southampton, U.K. 28 50 54N 1 23W
Southampton, U.S.A. 162 40 54N 72 22W
Southampton I. 149 64 30N 84 0W
Southampton Water 28 50 52N 1 21W
Southborough 29 51 10N 0 15 E
Southbridge, N.Z. 143 43 48 S 172 16 E
Southbridge, U.S.A. 162 42 4N 72 2W
Southeast C. 147 62 55N 169 40W
Southend, Can. 153 56 19N 103 14W
Southend, U.K. 34 55 18N 5 38W
Southend-on-Sea 29 51 32N 0 42 E
Southern □, Malawi 127 15 0 S 35 0 E
Southern □, S. Leone 120 0 8N 12 30 E
Southern □, Uganda 122 0 30 S 30 30 E
Southern □, Zambia 127 16 20 S 26 20 E
Southern Alps 143 43 41 S 170 11 E
Southern Cross 137 31 12 S 119 15 E
Southern Hills 137 32 15 S 122 40 E
Southern Indian L. 153 57 10N 98 30W
Southern Indian Lake 153 57 0N 99 0W
Southern Ocean 13 62 0 S 160 0W
Southern Uplands 35 55 30N 3 3W
Southery 29 52 32N 0 23 E
Southington 162 41 37N 72 53W
Southland □ 143 45 51 S 168 13 E
Southminster 29 51 40N 0 51 E
Southold 162 41 4N 72 26W
Southport, Austral. 139 27 58 S 153 25 E
Southport, U.K. 32 53 38N 3 1W
Southport, U.S.A. 157 33 55N 78 0W
Southwark 29 51 29N 0 5W
Southwell 33 53 4N 0 57W
Southwick 29 50 50N 0 14W
Southwold 29 52 19N 1 41 E
Soutpansberge 129 23 0 S 29 30 E
Souvigny 44 46 33N 3 10 E
Sovata 70 46 35N 25 3 E
Sovetsk, Lithuania, U.S.S.R. 80 55 6N 21 50 E
Sovetsk, R.S.F.S.R., U.S.S.R. 81 57 38N 48 53 E
Sovetskaya Gavan 77 48 50N 140 0 E
Sovicille 63 43 16N 11 12 E
Sovra 66 42 44N 17 34 E
Sowerby 33 54 13N 1 19W
Sōya-Misaki 112 45 30N 142 0 E
Soyopa 164 28 41N 109 37W
Sozh, R. 80 53 50N 31 50 E
Sozopol 67 42 23N 27 42 E
Spa 47 50 29N 5 53 E
Spain ■ 55 40 0N 5 0W
Spakenburg 46 52 15N 5 22 E
Spalding, Austral. 140 33 30 S 138 37 E
Spalding, U.K. 29 52 47N 0 9W
Spalding, U.S.A. 158 41 45N 98 27W
Spandet 73 55 15N 8 54 E
Spånga 72 59 23N 17 55 E
Spångenäs 73 57 36N 16 7 E
Spangereid 71 58 3N 7 9 E
Spaniard's Bay 151 47 38N 53 20W
Spanish 150 46 12N 82 20W
Spanish Fork 160 40 10N 111 37W
Spanish Pt. 39 52 51N 9 27W
Spanish Sahara □ = Western Sahara 116 25 0N 13 0W
Spanish Town 166 18 0N 77 20W
Sparkford 28 51 2N 2 33W
Sparrows Point 162 39 13N 76 29W
Sparta, Ga., U.S.A. 157 33 18N 82 59W
Sparta, N.J., U.S.A. 162 41 2N 74 38W
Sparta, Wis., U.S.A. 158 43 55N 91 10W
Sparta = Spárti 69 37 5N 22 25 E
Spartanburg 157 35 0N 82 0W
Spartel, C. 118 35 47N 5 56W
Spárti 69 37 5N 22 25 E
Spartivento, C., Calabria, Italy 65 37 56N 16 4 E
Spartivento, C., Sard., Italy 65 38 52N 8 50 E
Spas-Demensk 80 54 20N 34 0 E
Spas-Klepiki 81 54 34N 40 2 E
Spassk-Dalniy 77 44 40N 132 40 E
Spassk-Ryazanskiy 81 54 30N 40 25 E
Spatha Ákra. 69 35 42N 23 43 E
Spatsizi, R. 152 57 42N 128 7W
Spean Bridge 36 56 53N 4 55W
Spearfish 158 44 32N 103 52W
Spearman 159 36 15N 101 10W
Speculator 162 43 30N 74 25W
Speed 140 35 21 S 142 27 E
Speer 51 47 12N 9 8 E

Speers **Stíra**

Speers **153** 52 43N 107 34W
Speightstown **167** 13 15N 59 39W
Speke **32** 53 21N 2 51W
Speke Gulf, L. Victoria **126** 2 20S 32 50E
Spekholzerheide **47** 50 51N 6 2E
Spelve, L. **34** 56 22N 5 45W
Spenard **147** 61 5N 149 50W
Spencer, Idaho, U.S.A. **160** 44 18N 112 8W
Spencer, Iowa, U.S.A. **158** 43 5N 95 3W
Spencer, Nebr., U.S.A. **158** 42 52N 98 43W
Spencer, N.Y., U.S.A. **162** 42 14N 76 30W
Spencer, W. Va., U.S.A. **156** 38 47N 81 24W
Spencer B. **128** 25 30S 14 47E
Spencer Bay **148** 69 32N 93 32W
Spencer, C. **140** 35 20S 136 45E
Spencer G. **140** 34 0S 137 20E
Spences Bridge **152** 50 25N 121 20W
Spennymoor **33** 54 43N 1 35W
Spenser Mts. **143** 42 15S 172 45E
Sperkhiós, R. **69** 38 57N 22 3E
Sperrin Mts. **38** 54 50N 7 0W
Spessart **49** 50 0N 9 20E
Spetsai **69** 37 16N 23 9E
Spétsai, I. **69** 37 15N 23 10E
Spey B. **37** 57 41N 3 0W
Spey Bay **37** 57 39N 3 4W
Spey, R. **37** 57 26N 3 25W
Speyer **49** 49 19N 8 26E
Speyer, R. **41** 49 18N 7 52E
Spezia = La Spézia **62** 44 7N 9 49E
Spézia, La **62** 44 8N 9 50E
Spezzano Albanese **65** 39 41N 16 19E
Spiddal **39** 53 14N 9 19W
Spiekeroog, I. **48** 53 45N 7 42E
Spielfeld **63** 46 43N 15 38E
Spiez **50** 46 40N 7 40E
Spijk **46** 53 24N 6 50E
Spijkenisse **46** 51 51N 4 20E
Spili **69** 35 13N 24 31E
Spilimbergo **63** 46 7N 12 53E
Spillimacheen **152** 51 6N 117 0W
Spilsby **33** 53 10N 0 6E
Spin Baldak **93** 31 3N 66 16E
Spinazzola **65** 40 58N 16 5E
Spincourt **43** 49 20N 5 39E
Spind **71** 58 6N 6 53E
Spineni **70** 44 43N 24 37E
Spirit Lake **160** 47 56N 116 56W
Spirit River **152** 55 45N 118 50W
Spiritwood **153** 53 24N 107 33W
Spišská Nová Ves **53** 48 58N 20 34E
Spišské Podhradie **53** 49 0N 20 48E
Spit Pt. **136** 20 4S 118 59E
Spithead **29** 50 43N 0 56W
Spittal **52** 46 48N 13 31E
Spitzbergen (Svalbard) **12** 78 0N 17 0E
Split **63** 43 31N 16 26E
Split L. **153** 56 8N 96 15W
Splitski Kan **63** 43 31N 16 20E
Splügen **51** 46 34N 9 21E
Splügenpass **51** 46 30N 9 20E
Spoffard **159** 29 10N 100 27W
Spofforth **33** 53 57N 1 28W
Spokane **160** 47 45N 117 25W
Sponvika **71** 59 7N 11 15E
Spooner **158** 45 49N 91 51W
Sporádhes **69** 37 0N 27 0E
Sporyy Navolok, M. **76** 75 50N 68 40E
Spotswood **162** 40 23N 74 23W
Spragge **150** 46 15N 82 40W
Sprague **160** 47 25N 117 59W
Sprague River **160** 42 49N 121 31W
Spratly, I. **102** 8 20N 112 0E
Spray **160** 44 56N 119 46W
Spree, R. **48** 52 23N 13 52E
Sprimont **47** 50 30N 5 40E
Spring City, Pa., U.S.A. **162** 40 11N 75 33W
Spring City, Utah, U.S.A. **160** 39 31N 111 28W
Spring Grove **162** 39 55N 76 56W
Spring Hill **141** 33 23S 149 9E
Spring Mts. **161** 36 20N 115 43W
Spring Valley, Minn., U.S.A. **158** 43 40N 92 30W
Spring Valley, N.Y., U.S.A. **162** 41 7N 74 4W
Springbok **128** 29 42S 17 54E
Springburn **143** 43 40S 171 32E
Springdale, Can. **151** 49 30N 56 6W
Springdale, Ark., U.S.A. **159** 36 10N 94 5W
Springdale, Wash., U.S.A. **160** 48 1N 117 50W
Springe **48** 52 12N 9 35E
Springerville **161** 34 10N 109 16W
Springfield, N.Z. **143** 43 19S 171 56E
Springfield, Colo., U.S.A. **159** 37 26N 102 40W
Springfield, Ill., U.S.A. **158** 39 48N 89 40W
Springfield, Mass., U.S.A. **162** 42 8N 72 37W
Springfield, Mo., U.S.A. **159** 37 15N 93 20W
Springfield, Ohio, U.S.A. **156** 39 50N 83 48W
Springfield, Oreg., U.S.A. **160** 44 2N 123 0W
Springfield, Tenn., U.S.A. **157** 36 35N 86 55W
Springfield, Va., U.S.A. **162** 38 45N 77 13W
Springfield, Vt., U.S.A. **162** 43 20N 72 30W
Springfontein **128** 30 15S 25 40E
Springhill **151** 45 40N 64 4W
Springhouse **152** 51 56N 122 7W
Springhurst **141** 36 10S 146 31E
Springs **129** 26 13S 28 25E
Springsure **138** 24 8S 148 6E
Springvale, Queens., Austral. **138** 23 33S 140 42E
Springvale, W. Australia, Austral. **136** 17 48S 127 41E
Springvale, U.S.A. **162** 43 28N 70 48W
Springville, Calif., U.S.A. **163** 36 8N 118 49W
Springville, N.Y., U.S.A. **156** 42 31N 78 41W
Springville, Utah, U.S.A. **160** 40 14N 111 35W
Springwater **153** 51 58N 108 23W
Sproatley **33** 53 46N 0 9W
Spur **159** 33 28N 100 50W
Spurn Hd. **33** 53 34N 0 8E
Spuz **66** 42 32N 19 10E
Spuzzum **152** 49 37N 121 23W
Spydeberg **71** 59 37N 11 4E
Squam L. **162** 43 45N 71 32W
Squamish **152** 49 45N 123 10W
Square Islands **151** 52 47N 55 47W
Squillace, Golfo di **65** 38 43N 16 35E
Squinzano **65** 40 27N 18 1E
Squires, Mt. **137** 26 14S 127 46E
Sragen **103** 7 28S 110 59E
Srbac **66** 45 7N 17 30E
Srbija □ **66** 43 30N 21 0E
Srbobran **66** 45 32N 19 48E
Sre Khtum **101** 12 10N 106 52E
Sre Umbell **101** 11 8N 103 46E
Srebrnica **66** 44 10N 19 18E
Sredinyy Khrebet **77** 57 0N 160 0E
Središce **63** 46 24N 16 17E
Sredna Gora **67** 42 40N 25 0E
Sredne Tambovskoye **77** 50 55N 137 45E
Srednekolymsk **77** 67 20N 154 40E
Srednevilyuysk **77** 63 50N 123 5E
Sredni Rodopi **67** 41 40N 24 45E
Sredniy Ural, mts. **166** 59 0N 59 0E
Srem **54** 52 6N 17 2E
Srepok, R. **100** 13 33N 106 16E
Sretensk **77** 52 10N 117 40E
Sri Lanka ■ **97** 7 30N 80 50E
Sriharikota, I. **97** 13 40N 81 30E
Srikakulam **96** 18 14N 84 4E
Srinagar **95** 34 12N 74 50E
Sripur **98** 24 14N 90 30E
Srirangam **97** 10 54N 78 42E
Srirangapatnam **97** 12 26N 76 43E
Şrivilliputtur **97** 9 31N 77 40E
Šroda Wlkp. **54** 52 15N 17 19E
Srpska Crnja **66** 45 38N 20 44E
Srpska Itabej **66** 45 35N 20 44E
Ssu Chiao **109** 30 43N 122 28E
Ssuhsien **107** 33 25N 117 54E
Ssuhui **109** 23 20N 112 41E
Ssunan **108** 27 56N 108 14E
Ssup'ing **105** 43 10N 124 25E
Ssushui, Honan, China **106** 34 51N 113 12E
Ssushui, Shantung, China **107** 35 39N 117 15E
Ssutzuwangch'i **106** 41 30N 111 37E
Staaten, R. **138** 16 24S 141 17E
Stabroek **47** 51 20N 4 22E
Stack's Mts. **39** 52 20N 9 34W
Stad Delden **46** 52 16N 6 43E
Stade **48** 53 35N 9 31E
Staden **47** 50 59N 3 1E
Staðarhólskirkja **74** 65 23N 21 58W
Stadil **73** 56 12N 8 12E
Städjan **72** 61 56N 12 30E
Stadlandet **71** 62 10N 5 10E
Stadsforsen **72** 63 0N 16 45E
Stadskanaal **46** 53 4N 6 48E
Stadthagen **48** 52 20N 9 14E
Stadtlohn **48** 51 59N 6 52E
Stadtroda **48** 50 51N 11 44E
Stäfa **51** 47 14N 8 45E
Stafafell **74** 64 25N 14 52W
Staffa, I. **34** 56 26N 6 21W
Stafford, U.K. **28** 52 49N 2 9W
Stafford, Kansas, U.S.A. **159** 38 0N 98 35W
Stafford, Va., U.S.A. **162** 38 2S 77 30W
Stafford □ **28** 52 53N 2 10W
Stafford Springs **162** 41 58N 72 20W
Stagnone, I. **64** 37 50N 12 28E
Staindrop **33** 54 35N 1 49W
Staines **29** 51 26N 0 30W
Stainforth **33** 53 37N 0 59W
Stainmore For. **32** 54 29N 2 5W
Stainton **33** 53 17N 0 23W
Stainz **52** 46 53N 15 17E
Staithes **33** 54 33N 0 47W
Stakkroge **73** 55 53N 8 51E
Stala **66** 43 43N 21 28E
Stalbridge **28** 50 57N 2 22W
Stalden **50** 46 14N 7 52E
Stalham **29** 52 46N 1 31E
Stalingrad = Volgograd **83** 48 40N 44 25E
Staliniri = Tskhinvali **83** 42 14N 44 1E
Stalino = Donetsky **82** 48 0N 37 45E
Stalinogorsk = Novomoskovsk **81** 54 5N 38 15E
Stallingborough **33** 53 36N 0 11W
Stalowa Wola **54** 50 34N 22 3E
Stalybridge **32** 53 29N 1 56W
Stamford, Austral. **138** 21 15S 143 46E
Stamford, U.K. **29** 52 39N 0 29W
Stamford, Conn., U.S.A. **162** 41 5N 73 30W
Stamford, N.Y., U.S.A. **162** 42 25N 74 37W
Stamford, Tex., U.S.A. **159** 32 58N 99 50W
Stamford Bridge **33** 53 59N 0 53W
Stamfordham **35** 55 3N 1 53W
Stampersgat **47** 51 37N 4 26E
Stamps **159** 33 22N 93 30W
Stanberry **158** 40 12N 94 32W
Standerton **129** 26 55S 29 13E
Standish, U.K. **32** 53 35N 2 39W
Standish, U.S.A. **156** 43 58N 83 57W
Standon **29** 51 53N 0 2E
Stanford **160** 47 11N 110 10W
Stanford on Teme **28** 52 17N 2 26W
Stange Hedmark **71** 60 43N 11 11E
Stanger **129** 29 18S 31 21E
Stanhope, Austral. **141** 36 27S 144 59E
Stanhope, U.K. **32** 54 45N 2 0W
Stanišic **53** 45 53N 19 12E
Stanislaus, R. **163** 37 40N 121 15W
Stanislav = Ivano-Frankovsk **80** 49 0N 24 40E
Stanke Dimitrov **66** 42 27N 23 9E
Stanley, Austral. **138** 40 46S 145 19E
Stanley, N.B., Can. **151** 46 20N 66 50W
Stanley, Sask., Can. **153** 55 24N 104 22W
Stanley, Falk. Is. **176** 51 40S 58 0W
Stanley, Durham, U.K. **33** 54 53N 1 42W
Stanley, Tayside, U.K. **35** 56 29N 3 28W
Stanley, Idaho, U.S.A. **160** 44 10N 114 59W
Stanley, N.D., U.S.A. **158** 48 20N 102 23W
Stanley, Wis., U.S.A. **158** 44 57N 91 0W
Stanley Res. **97** 11 50N 77 40E
Stanleyville = Kisangani **126** 0 35N 25 15E
Stanlow **32** 53 17N 2 52W
Stann Creek **165** 17 0N 88 20W
Stannington **35** 55 7N 1 41W
Stanovoy Khrebet **77** 55 0N 130 0E
Stans **51** 46 58N 8 21E
Stansmore Ra. **136** 21 23S 128 33E
Stansted Mountfitchet **29** 51 54N 0 13E
Stanthorpe **139** 28 36S 151 59E
Stanton, Can. **147** 69 45N 128 52W
Stanton, U.S.A. **159** 32 8N 101 45W
Stantsiya Karshi **85** 38 49N 65 47E
Stanwix **32** 54 54N 2 56W
Staphorst **46** 52 39N 6 12E
Stapleford **33** 52 56N 1 16W
Staplehurst **29** 51 9N 0 35E
Stapleton **158** 41 30N 100 31W
Staporkow **54** 51 9N 20 31E
Star City **153** 52 55N 104 20W
Stara-minskaya **83** 46 33N 39 0E
Stara Moravica **66** 45 50N 19 30E
Stara Pazova **66** 45 0N 20 10E
Stara Planina **67** 43 15N 23 0E
Stara Zagora **67** 42 26N 25 39E
Starachowice-Wierzbnik **54** 51 3N 21 2E
Staraya Russa **80** 57 58N 31 10E
Starbuck I. **131** 5 37S 155 55W
Stargard **48** 53 29N 13 19E
Stargard Szczecinski **54** 53 20N 15 0E
Stari Bar **66** 42 7N 19 13E
Stari Trg. **63** 45 29N 15 7E
Staritsa **80** 56 33N 35 0E
Starke **157** 30 0N 82 10W
Starkville, Colo., U.S.A. **159** 37 10N 104 31W
Starkville, Miss., U.S.A. **157** 33 26N 88 48W
Starnberg **49** 48 0N 11 20E
Starnberger See **49** 48 0N 11 0E
Starobelsk **83** 49 27N 39 0E
Starodub **80** 52 30N 32 50E
Starogard **54** 53 55N 18 30E
Start Bay **30** 50 15N 3 35W
Start Pt., Devon, U.K. **30** 50 13N 3 38W
Start Pt., Orkney, U.K. **37** 59 17N 2 25W
Stary Sacz **54** 49 33N 30 26E
Staryy Biryuzyak **83** 44 46N 46 50E
Staryy Kheydzhan **77** 60 0N 144 50E
Staryy Krym **82** 44 48N 35 8E
Staryy Oskol **81** 51 12N 37 55E
Stassfurt **48** 51 51N 11 34E
State College **156** 40 47N 77 49W
State Is. **150** 48 40N 87 0W
Staten I. **162** 40 35N 74 10W
Staten, I. = Los Estados, I. de **176** 54 40S 64 0W
Statesboro **157** 32 26N 81 46W
Statesville **157** 35 48N 80 51W
Statfjord, oilfield **19** 61 15N 1 50E
Stathelle **71** 59 3N 9 41E
Stauffer **163** 34 45N 119 3W
Staunton, U.K. **28** 51 58N 2 19W
Staunton, Ill., U.S.A. **158** 39 0N 89 49W
Staunton, Va., U.S.A. **156** 38 7N 79 4W
Stavanger **71** 58 57N 5 40E
Staveley, Cumbria, U.K. **32** 54 24N 2 49W
Staveley, Derby, U.K. **33** 53 16N 1 20W
Stavelot **47** 50 23N 5 55E
Stavenisse **47** 51 35N 4 1E
Staveren **46** 52 53N 5 22E
Stavern **71** 59 0N 10 1E
Stavfjord **71** 61 30N 5 0E
Stavre **72** 62 51N 15 19E
Stavropol **83** 45 5N 42 0E
Stavroúpolis **68** 41 12N 24 45E
Stavsjö **73** 48 42N 16 30E
Stawell **140** 37 5S 142 47E
Stawell, R. **138** 20 38S 142 55E
Stawiszyn **54** 51 56N 18 4E
Staxigoe **37** 58 28N 3 2W
Steamboat Springs **160** 40 30N 106 58W
Stebark **54** 53 30N 20 10E
Stebleva **68** 41 18N 20 33E
Steckborn **51** 47 44N 8 59E
Steele **158** 46 56N 99 52W
Steelton **162** 40 17N 76 50W
Steelville **159** 37 57N 91 21W
Steen, R. **152** 59 35N 117 10W
Steen River **152** 59 40N 117 12W
Steenbergen **47** 51 35N 4 19E
Steenvoorde **43** 50 48N 2 33E
Steenwijk **46** 52 47N 6 7E
Steep Pt. **137** 26 08S 113 8E
Steep Rock **153** 51 30N 98 48W
Steep Rock Lake **150** 48 50N 91 38W
Stefånesti **70** 47 44N 27 15E
Stefanie L. = Chew Bahir **123** 4 40N 30 50E
Steffisburg **50** 46 47N 7 38E
Stefůnesti **70** 47 44N 27 15E
Stege **73** 55 0N 12 18E
Steierdorf Anina **66** 45 6N 21 51E
Steiermark □ **52** 47 26N 15 0E
Steigerwald **49** 49 45N 10 30E
Stein, Neth. **47** 50 58N 5 45E
Stein, Switz. **51** 47 40N 8 50E
Stein, U.K. **36** 57 30N 6 35W
Steinbach **153** 49 32N 96 40W
Steinfort **47** 49 39N 5 55E
Steinheim **48** 51 50N 9 6E
Steinkjer **74** 63 59N 11 31E
Steinkopf **125** 29 15S 17 48E
Stekene **47** 51 12N 4 2E
Stella Land **128** 26 45S 24 50E
Stellarton **151** 45 32N 62 45W
Stellenbosch **128** 33 58S 18 50E
Stellendam **46** 51 49N 4 1E
Stelvio, Paso dello **51** 46 32N 10 27E
Stemshaug **71** 63 19N 8 44E
Stendal **48** 52 36N 11 50E
Stene **47** 51 12N 2 56E
Stenhousemuir **35** 56 2N 3 46W
Stenmagle **73** 55 49N 11 39E
Stenness, L., of **37** 59 0N 3 15W
Stensele **74** 65 3N 17 8E
Stenstorp **73** 58 17N 13 45E
Stenungsund **73** 58 6N 11 50E
Stepanakert **79** 40 0N 46 25E
Stephan **158** 48 30N 96 53W
Stephens Cr. **140** 32 15S 141 55E
Stephens I., Can. **152** 54 10N 130 45W
Stephens I., N.Z. **143** 40 40S 174 1E
Stephenville, Can. **151** 48 31N 58 30W
Stephenville, U.S.A. **159** 32 12N 98 12W
Stepnica **54** 53 38N 14 36E
Stepnoi = Elista **83** 46 25N 44 17E
Stepnoye **84** 54 4N 60 26E
Sterkstroom **128** 31 32S 26 32E
Sterlego, Mys **12** 80 30N 90 0E
Sterling, Colo., U.S.A. **158** 40 40N 103 15W
Sterling, Ill., U.S.A. **158** 41 45N 89 45W
Sterling, Kans., U.S.A. **158** 38 17N 98 13W
Sterling City **159** 31 50N 100 59W
Sterlitamak **84** 53 40N 56 0E
Sternberg **48** 53 42N 11 48E
Sternberk **53** 49 45N 17 15E
Stettin = Szczecin **54** 53 27N 14 27E
Stettiner Haff **48** 53 50N 14 25E
Stettler **152** 52 19N 112 40W
Steubenville **156** 40 21N 80 39W
Stevenage **29** 51 54N 0 11W
Stevens Port **158** 44 32N 89 34W
Stevens Village **147** 66 0N 149 10W
Stevenson L. **153** 53 55N 95 9W
Stevenson, R. **136** 46 15S 134 10E
Stevenston **34** 55 38N 4 46W
Stevns Klint **73** 55 17N 12 28E
Stewart **152** 55 56N 129 57W
Stewart, C. **138** 11 57S 134 45E
Stewart, I. **176** 54 50S 71 30W
Stewart I. **143** 46 58S 167 54E
Stewart River **147** 63 19N 139 26W
Stewarton **34** 55 40N 4 30W
Stewartstown **38** 54 35N 6 40W
Stewiacke **151** 45 9N 63 22W
Steyning **29** 50 54N 0 19W
Steynsburg **128** 31 15S 25 49E
Steyr **52** 48 3N 14 25E
Steyr, R. **52** 48 57N 14 15E
Steytlerville **128** 33 17S 24 19E
Stia **63** 43 48N 11 41E
Stiens **46** 53 16N 5 46E
Stigler **159** 35 19N 95 6W
Stigliano **65** 40 24N 16 13E
Stigsnæs **73** 55 13N 11 18E
Stigtomta **73** 58 47N 16 48E
Stikine Mts. **148** 59 30N 129 30W
Stikine, R. **147** 58 0N 131 12W
Stilfontein **128** 26 50S 26 50E
Stilís **69** 38 55N 22 37E
Stillington **33** 54 7N 1 5W
Stillwater, Minn., U.S.A. **158** 45 3N 92 47W
Stillwater, N.Y., U.S.A. **162** 42 55N 73 41W
Stillwater, Okla., U.S.A. **159** 36 5N 97 3W
Stillwater Mts. **160** 39 45N 118 6W
Stilwell **159** 35 52N 94 36W
Stimfalias, L. **69** 37 51N 22 27E
Stimson **150** 48 58N 80 30W
Stinchar, R. **34** 55 10N 4 50W
Stingray Pt. **162** 37 35N 76 15W
Stip **66** 41 42N 22 10E
Stiperstones Mt. **28** 52 36N 2 57W
Stíra **69** 38 9N 24 14E

Stiring Wendel Sukkur

Stiring Wendel	43	49 12N	6 57 E
Stirling, Austral.	138	17 12 S	141 35 E
Stirling, Can.	152	49 30N	112 30W
Stirling, N.Z.	143	46 14 S	169 49 E
Stirling, U.K.	35	56 17N	3 57W
Stirling (□)	26	56 3N	4 10W
Stirling Ra.	137	34 0 S	118 0 E
Stjárneborg	73	57 53N	14 45 E
Stjarnsfors	72	60 2N	13 45 E
Stjördalshalsen	71	63 29N	10 51 E
Stobo	35	55 38N	3 18W
Stoborough, oilfield	19	50 38N	2 8W
Stockaryd	73	57 19N	14 36 E
Stockbridge	28	51 7N	1 30W
Stockerau	53	48 24N	16 12 E
Stockett	160	47 23N	111 7W
Stockholm	72	59 20N	18 3 E
Stockholms län □	72	59 30N	18 20 E
Stockhorn	50	46 42N	7 33 E
Stockport	32	53 25N	2 11W
Stocksbridge	33	53 30N	1 36W
Stockton, Austral.	141	32 56 S	151 47 E
Stockton, Calif., U.S.A.	163	38 0N	121 20W
Stockton, Kans., U.S.A.	158	39 30N	99 20W
Stockton, Mo., U.S.A.	159	37 40N	93 48W
Stockton-on-Tees	33	54 34N	1 20W
Stockvik	72	62 17N	17 23 E
Stoczek Łukowski	54	51 58N	22 22 E
Stode	72	62 28N	16 35 E
Stoer	36	58 12N	5 20W
Stogovo, mts.	66	41 31N	20 38 E
Stoke, N.Z.	143	41 19N	173 14 E
Stoke, U.K.	29	51 26N	0 41 E
Stoke Ferry	29	52 34N	0 31 E
Stoke Fleming	30	50 19N	3 36W
Stoke Mandeville	29	51 46N	0 47W
Stoke Prior	28	52 18N	2 5W
Stokenham	30	50 15N	3 40W
Stokes Bay	150	45 0N	81 22W
Stokes Pt.	138	40 10 S	143 56 E
Stokes Ra.	136	15 50 S	130 50 E
Stokesley	33	54 27N	1 12W
Stokke	71	59 13N	10 17 E
Stokkem	47	51 1N	5 45 E
Stokken	71	58 31N	8 53 E
Stokkseyri	74	63 50N	20 58W
Stokksnes	74	64 14N	14 58W
Stolac	66	43 8N	17 59 E
Stolberg, Germ., E.	48	51 33N	11 0 E
Stolberg, Germ., W.	48	50 48N	6 13 E
Stolbovaya, R.S.F.S.R., U.S.S.R.	77	64 50N	153 50 E
Stolbovaya, R.S.F.S.R., U.S.S.R.	81	55 10N	37 32 E
Stolbtsy	80	53 22N	26 43 E
Stolin	80	51 53N	26 50 E
Stolnici	70	44 31N	24 48 E
Stolwijk	46	51 59N	4 47 E
Ston	66	42 51N	17 43 E
Stone, Bucks., U.K.	29	51 48N	0 52W
Stone, Stafford, U.K.	32	52 55N	2 10W
Stone Harbor	162	39 3N	74 45W
Stonecliffe	150	46 13N	77 56W
Stonehaven	37	56 58N	2 11W
Stonehenge, Austral.	138	24 22 S	143 17 E
Stonehenge, U.K.	28	51 9N	1 45W
Stonehouse, Glous., U.K.	28	51 45N	2 18W
Stonehouse, Strathclyde, U.K.	35	55 42N	4 0W
Stonewall	153	50 10N	97 19W
Stongfjord	71	61 28N	14 0 E
Stonham Aspall	29	52 11N	1 7 E
Stony L.	153	58 51N	98 40W
Stony Point	162	41 14N	73 59W
Stony Rapids	153	59 16N	105 50W
Stony River	147	61 48N	156 48W
Stony Stratford	29	52 4N	0 51W
Stony Tunguska = Tunguska, Nizhmaya	77	64 0N	95 0 E
Stopnica	54	50 27N	20 57 E
Stor Elvdal	71	61 30N	11 1 E
Stora Borge Fjell, Mt.	48	65 12N	14 0 E
Stora Gla	72	59 30N	12 30 E
Stora Karlsö	73	57 17N	17 59 E
Stora Lulevatten	74	67 10N	19 30 E
Stora Sjøfallet	74	67 29N	18 40 E
Storavan	74	65 45N	18 10 E
Stord Leirvik, I.	71	59 48N	5 27 E
Store Bælt	73	55 20N	11 0 E
Store Creek	141	32 54 S	149 6 E
Store Heddinge	73	55 18N	12 23 E
Storen	71	63 3N	10 18 E
Storfjorden	71	62 25N	6 30 E
Storm B.	138	43 10 S	147 30 E
Storm Lake	158	42 35N	95 5W
Stormberg	125	31 16 S	26 17 E
Stormsrivier	128	33 59 S	23 52 E
Stornoway	36	58 12N	6 23W
Storozhinets	82	48 14 S	25 45 E
Storr, The, mt.	36	57 30N	6 12W
Storrs	162	41 48N	72 15W
Storsjö	72	62 49N	13 5 E
Storsjöen, Hedmark, Norway	71	60 20N	11 40 E
Storsjöen, Hedmark, Norway	71	61 30N	11 14 E
Storsjön, Gavleborg, Sweden	72	60 35N	16 45 E
Storsjön, Jämtland, Sweden	72	62 50N	13 8 E
Storstroms Amt □	73	49 50N	11 45 E
Stort, R.	29	51 50N	0 7 E
Storuman	74	65 5N	17 10 E
Storuman, L.	74	65 5N	17 10 E
Storvätteshagna, Mt.	72	62 6N	12 30 E
Storvik	72	60 35N	16 33 E
Stotfold	29	52 2N	0 13W
Stoughton	153	49 40N	103 0W
Stour, R., Dorset, U.K.	28	50 48N	2 7W
Stour, R., Heref. & Worcs., U.K.	28	52 25N	2 13W
Stour, R., Kent, U.K.	29	51 15N	0 57 E
Stour, R., Suffolk, U.K.	29	51 55N	1 5 E
Stourbridge	28	52 28N	2 8W
Stourport	28	52 21N	2 18W
Stout, L.	153	52 0N	94 40W
Stove Pipe Wells Village	163	36 35N	117 11W
Stow	35	55 41N	2 50W
Stow Bardolph	29	52 38N	0 24 E
Stow-on-the-Wold	28	51 55N	1 42W
Stowmarket	29	52 11N	1 0 E
Stowupland	29	52 12N	1 3 E
Strabane	38	54 50N	7 28W
Strabane □	38	54 45N	7 25W
Strachan	37	57 1N	2 31W
Strachur	34	56 10N	5 5W
Stracin	66	42 13N	22 2 E
Stradbally, Kerry, Ireland	39	52 15N	10 4W
Stradbally, Laoighis, Ireland	39	53 2N	7 10W
Stradbally, Waterford, Ireland	39	52 7N	7 28W
Stradbroke	29	52 19N	1 16 E
Strade	38	53 56N	9 8W
Stradella	62	45 4N	9 20 E
Stradone	38	54 0N	7 12W
Strahan	138	42 9 S	145 20 E
Straldzha	67	42 35N	26 40 E
Stralkonice	52	49 15N	13 53 E
Stralsund	48	54 17N	13 5 E
Strand, Hedmark, Norway	71	61 18N	11 15 E
Strand, Rogaland, Norway	71	59 3N	5 56 E
Strand, S. Afr.	128	34 9 S	18 48 E
Stranda	71	62 19N	6 58 E
Strandby	73	56 47N	9 13 E
Strandebarm	71	60 17N	6 0 E
Strandhill	38	54 16N	8 34W
Strandvik	71	60 9N	5 41 E
Strangford	38	54 23N	5 34W
Strängnäs	72	59 23N	17 8 E
Stranorlar	38	54 58N	7 47W
Stranraer	34	54 54N	5 0W
Strasbourg, Can.	153	51 4N	104 55W
Strasbourg, France	43	48 35N	7 42 E
Strasburg, Ger.	48	53 30N	13 44 E
Strasburg, U.S.A.	158	46 12N	101 9W
Strassen	47	49 37N	6 4 E
Stratford, N.S.W., Austral.	141	32 7 S	151 55 E
Stratford, Vic., Austral.	141	37 59 S	147 7 E
Stratford, Can.	150	43 23N	81 0W
Stratford, N.Z.	142	39 20 S	174 19 E
Stratford, Calif., U.S.A.	163	36 10N	119 49W
Stratford, Conn., U.S.A.	162	41 13N	73 8W
Stratford, Tex., U.S.A.	159	36 20N	102 3W
Stratford-on-Avon	28	52 12N	1 42W
Stratford St. Mary	29	51 58N	0 59 E
Strath Avon	37	57 19N	3 23W
Strath Dearn	37	57 20N	4 0W
Strath Earn	35	56 20N	3 50W
Strath Glass	37	57 20N	4 40W
Strath Naver	37	58 24N	4 12W
Strath Spey	37	57 15N	3 40W
Strathalbyn	140	35 13 S	138 53 E
Strathaven	35	55 40N	4 4W
Strathbogie, Dist.	37	57 25N	2 45W
Strathclyde □	34	56 0N	4 50W
Strathcona Prov. Park	152	49 38N	125 40W
Strathdon	37	57 12N	3 4W
Strathkanaird	36	57 58N	5 5W
Strathmore, Austral.	138	17 50 S	142 35 E
Strathmore, Can.	152	51 5N	113 25W
Strathmore, Highland, U.K.	37	58 20N	4 40W
Strathmore, Tayside, U.K.	37	56 40N	3 4W
Strathmore, U.S.A.	163	36 9N	119 4W
Strathnaver	152	53 20N	122 33W
Strathpeffer	37	57 35N	4 32W
Strathroy	150	42 58N	81 38W
Strathy	37	58 30N	4 0W
Strathy Pt.	37	58 35N	4 0W
Strathyre	34	56 14N	4 20W
Stratmiglo Scot.	35	56 16N	3 15W
Stratton, U.K.	30	50 49N	4 31W
Stratton, U.S.A.	158	39 20N	102 36W
Stratton St. Margaret	28	51 35N	1 45W
Straubing	49	48 53N	12 35 E
Straumnes	74	66 26N	23 8W
Straumsnes Åsskard	71	63 4N	8 2 E
Strausberg	48	52 40N	13 52 E
Strawberry Res.	160	40 0N	111 0W
Strawn	159	32 36N	98 30W
Strážnice	53	48 54N	17 19 E
Streaky B.	139	32 51 S	134 18 E
Streaky Bay	139	32 48 S	134 13 E
Streatley	28	51 31N	1 9W
Streator	158	41 9N	88 52W
Stredočeský □	52	49 55N	14 30 E
Stredoslovenský □	53	48 30N	19 15 E
Streé	47	50 17N	4 18 E
Street	28	51 7N	2 43W
Strehaia	70	44 37N	23 10 E
Strelcha	67	42 30N	24 19 E
Strelka	77	58 5N	93 10 E
Streng, R.	100	13 12N	103 37 E
Strengelvåg	74	68 58N	15 11 E
Strensall	33	54 3N	1 2W
Stretford	32	53 27N	2 19W
Stretton	32	53 21N	2 34W
Strezhevoy	76	60 42N	77 34 E
Strezhnoye	76	57 45N	84 2 E
Stribro	52	49 44N	13 0 E
Strichen	37	57 35N	2 5W
Strickland, R.	135	7 35 S	141 36 E
Strijen	46	51 45N	4 33 E
Strimón, R.	68	41 0N	23 30 E
Strimonikós Kólpos	68	40 33N	24 0 E
Striven, L.	34	55 58N	5 9W
Strofadhes, I.	69	37 15N	21 0 E
Strokestown	38	53 47N	8 6W
Strom	71	60 17N	11 44 E
Ström	72	61 52N	17 20 E
Stroma, I. of	37	58 40N	3 8W
Strombacka	72	61 58N	16 44 E
Strómboli, I.	65	38 48N	15 12 E
Stromeferry	36	57 20N	5 33W
Stromemore	36	57 22N	5 33W
Stromness	37	58 58N	3 18W
Ströms Vattudal L.	74	64 0N	15 30 E
Stromsberg	72	60 28N	17 44 E
Strömsnäsbruk	73	56 35N	13 45 E
Strömstad	72	58 55N	11 15 E
Stromsund	74	63 51N	15 35 E
Stronachlachar	34	56 15N	4 35W
Strone	34	55 59N	4 54W
Stróngoli	65	39 16N	17 2 E
Stronsay Firth	37	59 4N	2 50W
Stronsay, I.	37	59 8N	2 38W
Strontian	36	56 42N	5 32W
Strood	29	51 23N	0 30 E
Stroove	38	55 13N	6 57W
Stropkov	53	49 13N	21 39 E
Stroud	28	51 44N	2 12W
Stroud Road	141	32 18 S	151 57 E
Stroudsberg	162	40 59N	75 15W
Struer	73	56 30N	8 35 E
Struga	66	41 13N	20 44 E
Strugi Krasnye	80	58 21N	28 51 E
Struma, R.	67	41 50N	23 18 E
Strumble Hd.	31	52 3N	5 6W
Strumica	66	41 28N	22 41 E
Strumica, R.	66	41 26N	27 46 E
Strusshamn	71	60 24N	5 10 E
Struthers	150	48 41N	85 51W
Struy	37	57 25N	4 40W
Stryama	67	42 16N	24 54 E
Stryi	80	49 16N	23 48 E
Stryker	152	48 40N	114 44W
Stryków	54	51 55N	19 33 E
Strzegom	54	50 58N	16 20 E
Strzelce Krajenskie	54	52 52N	15 33 E
Strzelecki Creek	139	29 37 S	139 59 E
Strzelin	54	50 46N	17 2 E
Strzelno	54	52 35N	18 9 E
Strzyżów	54	49 52N	21 47 E
Stuart, Fla., U.S.A.	157	27 11N	80 12W
Stuart, Nebr., U.S.A.	158	42 39N	99 8W
Stuart I.	147	63 55N	164 50W
Stuart L.	152	54 30N	124 30W
Stuart Mts.	143	45 2 S	167 39 E
Stuart, R.	152	54 0N	123 35W
Stuart Range	139	29 10 S	134 56 E
Stuart's Ra.	136	29 10 S	135 0 E
Stubbekøbing	73	54 53N	12 9 E
Stuben	52	46 58N	10 31 E
Stuberhuk	48	54 23N	11 18 E
Studholme Junc.	143	44 42 S	171 9 E
Studland	28	50 39N	1 58W
Studley	28	52 16N	1 54W
Stugsund	72	61 16N	17 18 E
Stugun	72	63 10N	15 40 E
Stull, L.	153	54 24N	92 34W
Stung-Treng	100	13 31N	105 58 E
Stupart, R.	153	56 0N	93 25W
Stupino	81	54 57N	38 2 E
Sturgeon B.	153	52 0N	97 50W
Sturgeon Bay	156	44 52N	87 20W
Sturgeon Falls	150	46 25N	79 57W
Sturgeon L., Alta., Can.	152	55 6N	117 32W
Sturgeon L., Ont., Can.	150	50 0N	90 45W
Sturgis, Mich., U.S.A.	156	41 50N	85 25W
Sturgis, S.D., U.S.A.	158	44 25N	103 30W
Sturko, I.	73	56 5N	15 42 E
Sturminster Marshall	28	50 48N	2 4W
Sturminster Newton	28	50 56N	2 18W
Stúrovo	53	47 48N	18 41 E
Sturt Cr.	136	19 0 S	128 15 E
Sturt Creek	136	19 0 S	128 15 E
Sturt, R.	136	34 58 S	138 31 E
Sturton	33	53 22N	0 39W
Sturts Meadows	140	31 18 S	141 42 E
Stutterheim	128	32 33 S	27 28 E
Stuttgart, Ger.	49	48 46N	9 10 E
Stuttgart, U.S.A.	159	34 30N	91 33W
Stuyvesant	162	42 23N	73 45W
Stykkishólmur	74	65 2N	22 40W
Styr, R.	80	51 4N	25 20 E
Styria = Steiermark	52	47 26N	15 0 E
Su-no-Saki	111	34 58N	139 45 E
Suakin	122	19 0N	37 20 E
Suan	107	38 42N	126 22 E
Suaqui	164	29 12N	109 41W
Suay Rieng	101	11 9N	105 45 E
Subang	103	7 30 S	107 45 E
Subansiri, R.	98	26 48N	93 50 E
Subi	101	2 55N	108 50 E
Subi, I.	102	2 58N	108 50 E
Subiaco	63	41 56N	13 5 E
Subotica	66	46 6N	19 29 E
Success	153	50 28N	108 6W
Suceava	70	47 38N	26 16 E
Suceava □	70	47 37N	26 18 E
Suceava, R.	70	47 38N	26 16 E
Sucha-Beskidzka	54	49 44N	19 35 E
Suchan	54	53 18N	15 18 E
Suchedniów	54	51 3N	20 49 E
Such'i	109	21 23N	110 16 E
Suchien	107	33 58N	118 17 E
Suchil	164	23 38N	103 55W
Suchitoto	166	13 56N	89 0W
Suchou	109	31 15N	120 40 E
Süchow = Hsüchou	107	34 15N	117 10 E
Suchowola	54	53 33N	23 3 E
Sucio, R.	174	6 40N	77 0W
Suck, R.	39	53 17N	8 10W
Suckling, Mt.	135	9 43 S	148 59 E
Sucre, Boliv.	174	19 0 S	65 15W
Sucre, Venez.	174	10 25N	64 5W
Sucre □, Colomb.	174	8 50N	75 40W
Sucre □, Venez.	174	10 25N	63 30W
Sučueni	70	47 20N	22 5 E
Sucunduri, R.	174	6 20N	58 35W
SuCuraj	63	43 10N	17 8 E
Sucuriju	170	1 39N	49 57W
Sud-Ouest, Pte. du	151	49 23N	63 36W
Sud, Pte.	151	49 3N	62 14W
Suda, R.	81	59 40N	36 30 E
Sudak	82	44 51N	34 57 E
Sudan ■	117	15 0N	30 0 E
Sudan, The	114	11 0N	9 0 E
Suday	81	59 0N	43 15 E
Sudbury, Can.	150	46 30N	81 0W
Sudbury, Derby, U.K.	33	52 53N	1 43W
Sudbury, Suffolk, U.K.	29	52 2N	0 44 E
Sûdd	123	8 20N	29 30 E
Süderbrarup	48	54 38N	9 47 E
Süderlügum	48	54 50N	8 46 E
Sudetan Mts. = Sudety	53	50 20N	16 45 E
Sudety	53	50 20N	16 45 E
Sudi	127	10 11 S	39 57 E
Sudirman, Pengunungan	103	4 30N	137 0 E
Suditi	70	44 35N	27 38 E
Sudogda	81	55 55N	40 50 E
Sudr	122	29 40N	32 42 E
Sudzha	80	51 14N	34 25 E
Sueca	59	39 12N	0 21W
Sueur, Le	158	44 25N	93 52W
Suez = Suweis	122	28 40N	33 0 E
Suf	90	32 19N	35 49 E
Sufaina	92	23 6N	40 44 E
Suffield	153	50 12N	111 10W
Suffolk	156	36 47N	76 33W
Suffolk □	29	52 16N	1 0 E
Suffolk, East, □	29	52 16N	1 10 E
Suffolk, West, □	29	52 16N	0 45 E
Sufi-Kurgan	85	40 2N	73 30 E
Sufuk	93	23 50N	51 50 E
Suga no-Sen	110	35 25N	134 25 E
Sugag	70	45 47N	23 37 E
Sugar City	158	38 18N	103 38W
Sugarloaf Pt.	126	32 22 S	152 30 E
Suguk = Sagloue	149	62 10N	75 40W
Sugny	47	49 49N	4 54 E
Suhaia, L.	70	43 45N	25 15 E
Suhãr	93	24 20N	56 40 E
Suhbaatar	105	46 54N	113 25 E
Suhl	48	50 35N	10 40 E
Suhl □	48	50 37N	10 43 E
Suhr	50	47 22N	8 5 E
Suhsien	106	33 40N	117 0 E
Suhum	121	6 5N	0 27W
Suian	109	29 28N	118 44 E
Suica	66	43 52N	17 11 E
Suich'ang	109	28 36N	119 16 E
Suichiang	108	28 40N	103 58 E
Suifenho	107	44 30N	131 2 E
Suihsien	109	31 41N	113 20 E
Suihua	98	46 37N	127 0 E
Suilu	108	22 20N	107 48 E
Suining, Hunan, China	108	26 21N	110 0 E
Suining, Kiangsu, China	107	33 54N	117 56 E
Suining, Szechwan, China	108	30 31N	105 34 E
Suippes	43	49 8N	4 30 E
Suir, R.	39	52 31N	7 59W
Suita	111	34 45N	135 32 E
Suiteh	106	37 35N	110 5 E
Suiyang, Heilungkiang, China	107	44 26N	130 51 E
Suiyang, Kweichow, China	108	27 57N	107 11 E
Sujangarh	94	27 42N	47 31 E
Sukabumi	103	6 56 S	106 57 E
Sukadana	102	1 10 S	110 0 E
Sukandja	102	2 28 S	110 25 E
Sukarnapura = Jajapura	103	2 28N	140 38 E
Sukarno, G. = Jaja, Puncak	103	3 57 S	137 17 E
Sukchŏn	107	39 22N	125 35 E
Sukhinichi	80	54 8N	35 10 E
Sukhona, R.	78	60 30N	45 0 E
Sukhothai	100	17 1N	99 49 E
Sukhoy Log	84	56 55N	62 1 E
Sukhumi	83	43 0N	41 0 E
Sukkur	94	27 50N	68 46 E

Sukkur Barrage Sydra, G. of

Sukkur Barrage 93 27 50N 68 45 E
Sukma 96 18 24N 81 37 E
Sukovo 66 43 4N 22 37 E
Sukumo 110 32 56N 132 44 E
Sukunka, R. 152 55 45N 121 15W
Sul, Canal do 170 0 10 S 48 30W
Sula, Kepulauan 103 1 45 S 125 0 E
Sula, R. 80 50 0N 33 0 E
Sulaco, R. 166 15 2N 87 44W
Sulaiman Range 94 30 30N 69 50 E
Sulaimanke Headworks 94 30 27N 73 55 E
Sûlaj □ 70 47 15N 23 0 E
Sulak, R. 83 43 20N 47 20 E
Sulam Tsor 90 33 4N 35 6 E
Sulawesi □ 103 2 0 S 120 0 E
Sulawesi, I. 103 2 0 S 120 0 E
Sulby 32 54 18N 4 29W
Sulechów 54 52 5N 15 40 E
Sulecin 54 52 26N 15 10 E
Sulejów 54 51 26N 19 53 E
Sulejówek 54 52 13N 21 17 E
Sulgen 51 47 33N 9 7 E
Sulima 120 6 58N 11 32W
Sulina 70 45 10N 29 40 E
Sulingen 48 52 41N 8 47 E
Sûlişte 70 45 45N 23 56 E
Suliţa 70 47 39N 20 59 E
Sulitälma 74 67 17N 17 28 E
Sulitjelma 74 61 7N 16 8 E
Sułkowice 54 49 50N 19 49 E
Sullana 174 5 0 S 80 45W
Sullivan, Ill., U.S.A. 158 39 40N 88 40W
Sullivan, Ind., U.S.A. 156 39 5N 87 26W
Sullivan, Mo., U.S.A. 158 38 10N 91 10W
Sullivan Bay 152 50 55N 126 50W
Sullom Voe 36 60 30N 1 20W
Sully-sur-Loire 43 47 45N 2 20 E
Sulmierzyce 57 51 36N 17 30 E
Sulmona 63 42 3N 13 55 E
Sulo 105 39 25N 76 6 E
Sulphur, La., U.S.A. 159 30 20N 93 22W
Sulphur, Okla., U.S.A. 159 34 35N 97 0W
Sulphur Pt. 152 60 56N 114 48W
Sulphur Springs 159 33 5N 95 30W
Sulphur Springs, Cr. 159 32 50N 102 8W
Sultan 150 47 36N 82 47W
Sultanpur 95 26 18N 82 10 E
Sulu Arch. 103 6 0N 121 0 E
Sulu Sea 103 8 0N 120 0 E
Sululta 123 9 10N 38 43 E
Sulung Shan 108 31 30N 99 30 E
Suluq 119 31 44N 20 14 E
Sulyukta 85 39 56N 69 34 E
Sulzbach-Rosenburg 49 49 30N 11 46 E
Sumalata 103 1 0N 122 37 E
Sumampa 172 29 25 S 63 29W
Sumatera, I. 102 0 40N 100 20 E
Sumatera Selatan □ 102 3 30 S 104 0 E
Sumatera Tengah □ 102 1 0 S 100 0 E
Sumatera Utara □ 102 2 0N 99 0 E
Sumatra 160 46 45N 107 37W
Sumatra = Sumatera 102 0 40N 100 20 E
Sumba, I. 103 9 45 S 119 35 E
Sumba, Selat 103 9 0 S 118 40 E
Sumbawa 102 8 26 S 117 30 E
Sumbawa, I. 103 8 34 S 117 17 E
Sumbawanga □ 126 8 0 S 31 30 E
Sumbing, mt. 103 7 19 S 110 3 E
Sumburgh Hd. 36 59 52N 1 17W
Sumdo 95 35 6N 79 43 E
Sumé 170 7 39 S 36 55W
Sumedang 103 6 49 S 107 56 E
Sümeg 53 46 59N 17 20 E
Sumenep 103 7 3 S 113 51 E
Sumgait 83 40 34N 49 10 E
Sumisu-Jima 111 31 27N 140 3 E
Sumiswald 50 47 2N 7 44 E
Summer Is. 36 58 0N 5 27W
Summer L. 160 42 50N 120 50W
Summerhill 38 53 30N 6 44W
Summerland 152 49 32N 119 41W
Summerside 151 46 24N 63 47W
Summerville, Ga., U.S.A. 157 34 30N 85 20W
Summerville, S.C., U.S.A. 157 33 2N 80 11W
Summit, Can. 150 47 50N 72 20W
Summit, U.S.A. 147 63 20N 149 20W
Summit L. 152 54 20N 122 40W
Summit Pk. 161 37 20N 106 48W
Sumner, N.Z. 143 43 35 S 172 48 E
Sumner, U.S.A. 158 42 49N 92 7W
Sumner L. 143 42 42 S 172 15 E
Sumoto 110 34 21N 134 54 E
Sumperk 53 49 59N 17 0 E
Sumprabum 98 26 33N 97 4 E
Sumter 157 33 55N 80 10W
Sumy 80 50 57N 34 50 E
Sun City 163 33 41N 117 11W
Suna 126 5 23 S 34 48 E
Sunan 107 39 15N 125 40 E
Sunart, dist. 36 56 40N 5 40W
Sunart, L. 36 56 42N 5 43W
Sunburst 160 48 56N 111 59W
Sunbury, Austral. 141 37 35 S 144 44 E
Sunbury, U.S.A. 162 40 50N 76 46W
Sunchales 172 30 58 S 61 35W
Suncho Corral 172 27 55 S 63 14W
Sunchŏn 107 34 52N 127 31 E
Suncook 162 43 8N 71 27W
Sund 71 60 13N 5 10 E
Sunda Ketjil, Kepulauan 102 7 30 S 117 0 E
Sunda, Selat 102 6 20 S 105 30 E
Sundalsöra 71 62 40N 8 36 E
Sundance 158 44 27N 104 27W
Sundarbans, The 98 22 0N 89 0 E
Sundargarh 96 22 10N 84 5 E
Sunday Str. 136 16 25 S 123 18 E
Sundays, R. 128 32 10 S 24 40 E
Sundby 73 56 53N 8 40 E
Sundbyberg 72 59 22N 17 58 E
Sunderland, U.K. 35 54 54N 1 22W
Sunderland, U.S.A. 162 42 27N 72 36W
Sundre 152 51 49N 114 38W
Sundridge, Can. 150 45 45N 79 25W
Sundridge, U.K. 29 51 15N 0 10 E
Sunds 73 56 13N 9 1 E
Sundsjö 72 62 59N 15 9 E
Sundsvall 72 62 23N 17 17 E
Sung Hei 101 10 20N 106 2 E
Sungaipakning 102 1 19N 102 0 E
Sungaipenuh 102 2 1 S 101 20 E
Sungaitiram 102 0 45 S 117 8 E
Sungari, R. = Sunghua Chiang 107 44 30N 126 20 E
Sungch'i 109 27 2N 118 19 E
Sungchiang 109 31 2N 121 14 E
Sungei Lembing 101 2 53N 103 4 E
Sungei Patani 101 5 38N 100 29 E
Sungei Siput 101 4 51N 101 6 E
Sungfou 109 31 5N 114 42 E
Sungguminasa 103 5 17 S 119 30 E
Sunghsien 106 34 10N 112 10 E
Sunghua Chiang, R. 105 47 42N 132 30 E
Sungikai 123 12 20N 29 51 E
Sungk'an 108 28 33N 106 52 E
Sungming 108 25 22N 103 2 E
Sungpan 105 32 50N 103 20 E
Sungp'an 108 32 36N 103 36 E
Sungt'ao 108 28 12N 109 12 E
Sungtzu Hu 109 30 10N 111 45 E
Sungü 129 21 18 S 32 28 E
Sungurlu 82 40 12N 34 21 E
Sungyang 109 28 16N 119 29 E
Sunja 63 45 21N 16 35 E
Sunk Island 33 53 38N 0 7W
Sunkar, Gora 85 44 15N 73 50 E
Sunnäsbruk 72 61 10N 7 12 E
Sunne, Jamtland, Sweden 72 63 7N 14 25 E
Sunne, Varmland, Sweden 72 59 52N 13 12 E
Sunnfjord 71 61 25N 5 18 E
Sunnhordland 71 59 50N 5 30 E
Sunninghill 29 51 25N 0 40W
Sunnmöre 71 62 15N 6 30 E
Sunnyside, Utah, U.S.A. 160 39 40N 110 24W
Sunnyside, Wash., U.S.A. 160 46 24N 120 2W
Sunnyvale 163 37 23N 122 2W
Sunray 159 36 1N 101 47W
Sunshine 141 37 48 S 144 52 E
Sunson 121 9 35N 0 2W
Suntar 77 62 15N 117 30 E
Sunyani 120 7 21N 2 22W
Suō-Nada 110 33 50N 131 30 E
Suolahti 74 62 34N 25 52 E
Suonenjoki 74 62 37N 27 7 E
Supai 161 36 14N 112 44W
Supaul 95 26 10N 86 40 E
Supe 123 8 34N 35 35 E
Superior, Ariz., U.S.A. 161 33 19N 111 9W
Superior, Mont., U.S.A. 160 47 15N 114 57W
Superior, Nebr., U.S.A. 158 40 3N 98 2W
Superior, Wis., U.S.A. 158 46 45N 92 0W
Superior, L. 155 47 40N 87 0W
Supetar 63 43 25N 16 32 E
Suphan Buri 100 14 30N 100 10 E
Suprasśl 54 53 13N 23 19 E
Suq al Jumah 119 32 58N 13 12 E
Sūr, Leb. 90 33 19N 35 16 E
Sūr, Oman 93 22 34N 59 32 E
Sur, Pt. 163 36 18N 121 54W
Sura, R. 81 55 30N 46 20 E
Surab 94 28 25N 66 15 E
Surabaja = Surabaya 103 7 17 S 112 45 E
Surabaya 103 7 17 S 112 45 E
Surahammar 72 59 43N 16 13 E
Suraia 70 45 40N 27 25 E
Surakarta 103 7 35 S 110 48 E
Surakhany 83 40 13N 50 1 E
Surandai 97 8 58N 77 26 E
Surany 53 48 6N 18 10 E
Surat, Austral. 139 27 10 S 149 6 E
Surat, India 96 21 12N 72 55 E
Surat, Khalīj 119 31 40N 18 30 E
Surat Thani 101 9 6N 99 14 E
Suratgarh 94 29 18N 73 55 E
Surazh 80 53 5N 32 27 E
Surduc 70 47 15N 23 25 E
Surduc Pasul 70 45 21N 23 23 E
Surdulica 66 42 41N 22 11 E
Sûre, R. 47 49 51N 6 6 E
Surendranagar 94 22 45N 71 40 E
Surf 163 34 41N 120 36W
Surf Inlet 152 53 8N 128 50W
Surgères 44 46 7N 0 47W
Surhuisterveen 46 53 11N 6 10 E
Suri 95 23 50N 87 34 E
Surianu, mt. 70 45 33N 23 31 E
Suriapet 96 17 10N 79 40 E
Surif 90 31 40N 35 4 E
Surin 100 14 50N 103 34 E
Surin Nua, Ko 101 9 30N 97 55 E
Surinam ■ 175 4 0N 56 15W
Suriname, R. 170 4 30N 55 30W
Surkhandarya, R. 85 37 12N 67 20 E
Sûrmasu 70 46 45N 25 13 E
Sürmene 83 41 0N 40 1 E
Surovikino 83 48 32N 42 55 E
Surprise L. 152 59 40N 133 15W
Surrey □ 29 51 16N 0 30W
Surry 162 37 8N 76 50W
Sursee 50 47 11N 8 6 E
Sursk 81 53 3N 45 40W
Surt 119 31 11N 16 46 E
Surt, Al Hammādah al 119 30 0N 17 50 E
Surtsey 74 63 20N 20 30W
Surubim 170 7 50 S 35 45W
Suruga-Wan 111 34 45N 138 30 E
Surup 103 6 27N 126 17 E
Surur 93 23 20N 58 10 E
Susa 62 45 8N 7 3 E
Susaa, R. 73 55 20N 11 42 E
Sušac, I. 63 42 46N 16 30 E
Susak, I. 63 44 30N 14 28 E
Susaki 110 33 22N 133 17 E
Susamyr 85 42 12N 73 58 E
Susamyrtau, Khrebet 85 42 8N 73 15 E
Susangerd 92 31 35N 48 20 E
Susanino 77 52 50N 140 14 E
Susanville 160 40 28N 120 40W
Susch 51 46 46N 10 5 E
Sušice 52 49 17N 13 30 E
Susquehanna Depot 162 41 55N 75 36W
Susquehanna, R. 156 41 50N 76 20W
Susques 172 23 35 S 66 25W
Sussex, Can. 151 45 45N 65 37W
Sussex, U.S.A. 162 41 12N 74 38W
Sussex (□) 26 50 55N 0 20W
Sussex, E. □ 29 51 0N 0 0 E
Sussex, W. □ 29 51 0N 0 30W
Susten Pass 51 46 43N 8 26 E
Susteren 47 51 4N 5 51 E
Sustut, R. 152 56 20N 127 30W
Susuman 77 62 47N 148 10 E
Susuna 103 3 20 S 133 25 E
Susung 109 30 9N 116 6 E
Susz 54 53 44N 19 20 E
Suţeşti 70 45 13N 27 27 E
Sutherland, Austral. 141 34 2 S 151 4 E
Sutherland, Can. 153 52 15N 106 40W
Sutherland, S. Afr. 125 32 33 S 20 40 E
Sutherland, U.S.A. 158 41 12N 101 11W
Sutherland (□) 26 58 10N 4 30W
Sutherland Falls 143 44 48 S 167 46 E
Sutherland Pt. 133 28 15 S 153 35 E
Sutherland Ra. 137 25 42 S 125 21 E
Sutherlin 160 43 28N 123 16W
Sutivan 63 43 23N 16 30 E
Sutlej, R. 94 30 0N 73 0 E
Sutter Creek 163 38 24N 120 48W
Sutterton 33 52 54N 0 8W
Sutton, N.Z. 143 45 34 S 170 8 E
Sutton, U.K. 29 51 22N 0 13W
Sutton, U.S.A. 158 40 40N 97 50W
Sutton Bridge 29 52 46N 0 12 E
Sutton Coldfield 28 52 33N 1 50W
Sutton Courtenay 28 51 39N 1 16W
Sutton-in-Ashfield 33 52 8N 1 16W
Sutton-on-Sea 33 53 18N 0 18 E
Sutton, R. 150 55 15N 83 45W
Sutton Scotney 28 51 9N 1 20W
Suttor, R. 138 20 36 S 147 2 E
Sutwik I. 147 56 35N 157 10W
Suva 143 17 40 S 178 8 E
Suva Gora 66 41 45N 21 3 E
Suva Planina 66 43 10N 22 5 E
Suva Reka 66 42 21N 20 50 E
Suvarov Is. 131 13 15 S 163 30W
Suvo Rudište 66 43 17N 20 49 E
Suvorovo 67 43 20N 27 35 E
Suwa 111 36 2N 138 8 E
Suwa-Ko 111 36 3N 138 5 E
Suwałki 54 54 8N 22 59 E
Suwałki □ 54 54 0N 22 30 E
Suwannaphum 100 15 33N 105 47 E
Suwannee, R. 157 30 0N 83 0W
Suwanose-Jima 112 29 38N 129 38 E
Suweis, El 122 29 58N 32 31 E
Suweis, Khalîg es 122 28 40N 33 0 E
Suweis, Qanâl es 122 31 0N 32 20 E
Suwŏn 107 37 17N 127 1 E
Suykbulak 84 50 25N 62 33 E
Suzak 85 44 9N 68 27 E
Suzaka 111 36 39N 138 19 E
Sûzava, R. 52 49 50N 15 0 E
Suzdal 81 56 29N 40 26 E
Suze, La 42 47 54N 0 2 E
Suzuka 111 34 55N 136 36 E
Suzuka-Sam 111 35 5N 136 30 E
Suzzara 62 45 0N 10 45 E
Svalbard, Arctica 12 78 0N 17 0 E
Svalbard, Iceland 74 66 12N 15 43W
Svalöv 73 55 57N 13 8 E
Svanå 72 59 46N 15 23 E
Svanvik 74 69 38N 30 3 E
Svappavaari 74 67 40N 21 03 E
Svarstad 71 59 27N 9 56 E
Svartisen 74 66 40N 14 16 E
Svartvik 72 62 19N 17 24 E
Svatovo 82 49 35N 38 5 E
Svay Chek 100 13 48N 102 58 E
Svay Rieng 101 11 5N 105 48 E
Svealand □ 75 59 55N 15 0 E
Svedala 73 55 30N 13 15 E
Sveg 72 62 2N 14 21 E
Sveio 71 59 33N 5 23 E
Svelvik 71 59 37N 10 24 E
Svendborg 73 55 4N 10 35 E
Svene 71 59 45N 9 31 E
Svenljunga 73 57 29N 13 29 E
Svensbro 73 58 15N 13 52 E
Svenstavik 72 62 45N 14 26 E
Svenstrup 73 56 58N 9 50 E
Sverdlovsk 84 56 50N 60 30 E
Sverdrup Is. 12 79 0N 97 0W
Svetac 63 43 3N 15 43 E
Sveti Ivan Zelina 63 45 57N 16 16 E
Sveti Jurij 63 46 14N 15 24 E
Sveti Lenart 63 46 36N 15 48 E
Sveti Nikola 66 41 51N 21 56 E
Sveti Trojica 63 46 37N 15 33 E
Svetlogorsk 80 52 38N 29 46 E
Svetlograd 83 45 25N 42 58 E
Svetlovodsk 80 49 2N 33 13 E
Svetlyy 84 50 48N 60 51 E
Svetozarevo 66 44 0N 21 15 E
Svidník 53 49 20N 21 37 E
Svilaja Pl. 63 43 49N 16 31 E
Svilajnac 66 44 15N 21 11 E
Svilengrad 67 41 49N 26 12 E
Svinö 73 55 6N 11 44 E
Svir, R. 78 61 2N 34 50 E
Svishov 67 43 36N 25 23 E
Svisloch 80 53 26N 24 2 E
Svitavy 53 49 47N 16 28 E
Svobodnyy 77 51 20N 128 0 E
Svoge 67 42 59N 23 23 E
Svolvær 74 68 15N 14 34 E
Svratka, R. 53 49 27N 16 12 E
Svrljig 66 43 25N 22 6 E
Swa 98 19 15N 96 17 E
Swabian Alps 49 48 30N 9 30 E
Swadlincote 28 52 47N 1 34W
Swaffham 29 52 38N 0 42 E
Swain Reefs 138 21 45 S 152 20 E
Swainsboro 157 32 38N 82 22W
Swakopmund 128 22 37 S 14 30 E
Swale, R. 34 54 18N 1 20W
Swallowfield 29 51 23N 0 56W
Swalmen 47 51 13N 6 2 E
Swan Hill 140 35 20 S 143 33 E
Swan Hills 152 54 42N 115 24W
Swan Islands 166 17 22N 83 57W
Swan L. 153 52 30N 100 50W
Swan Pt. 136 16 22 S 123 1 E
Swan, R. 132 32 3 S 115 35 E
Swan Reach 140 34 35 S 139 37 E
Swan River 153 52 10N 101 16W
Swanage 28 50 36N 1 59W
Swanlinbar 38 54 11N 7 42W
Swansea, Austral. 141 33 3 S 151 35 E
Swansea, U.K. 31 51 37N 3 57W
Swansea Bay 31 51 34N 3 55W
Swar, R. 95 35 15N 72 24 E
Swartberg 128 30 15 S 29 23 E
Swartberge 128 33 20 S 22 0 E
Swarte Bank, gasfield 19 53 27N 2 10 E
Swartruggens 128 25 39 S 26 42 E
Swarzedz 54 52 25N 17 4 E
Swastika 150 48 7N 80 6W
Swatow = Shant'ou 109 23 28N 116 40 E
Swatragh 38 54 55N 6 40W
Swaziland ■ 129 26 30 S 31 30 E
Sweden ■ 74 67 0N 15 0 E
Swedru 121 5 32N 0 41W
Sweet Home 160 44 26N 122 38W
Sweetwater, Nev., U.S.A. 163 38 27N 119 9W
Sweetwater, Tex., U.S.A. 159 32 30N 100 28W
Sweetwater, R. 160 42 31N 107 30W
Swellendam 128 34 1 S 20 26 E
Świdin 54 53 47N 15 49 E
Swidnica 54 50 50N 16 30 E
Świdnik 54 51 13N 22 39 E
Świebodzice 54 50 51N 16 20 E
Świebodzin 54 52 15N 15 37 E
Swiecie 54 53 25N 18 30 E
Swietorkrzyskie, Góry 54 51 0N 20 30 E
Swift Current 153 50 20N 107 45W
Swiftcurrent Cr. 153 50 38N 107 44W
Swilly L. 38 55 12N 7 35W
Swilly, R. 38 54 56N 7 50W
Swindle, I. 152 52 30N 128 35W
Swindon 28 51 33N 1 47W
Swinemünde = Świnoujście 54 53 54N 14 16 E
Swineshead 33 57 57N 0 9W
Swinford 38 53 57N 8 57W
Świnoujście 54 53 54N 14 16 E
Swinton, Borders, U.K. 35 55 43N 2 14W
Swinton, Gr. Manch., U.K. 32 53 31N 2 21W
Swinton, S. Yorks., U.K. 33 53 28N 1 20W
Switzerland ■ 49 46 30N 8 0 E
Swona, I. 37 58 30N 3 3W
Swords 38 53 27N 6 15W
Syasstroy 80 60 5N 32 15 E
Sybil Pt. 39 52 12N 10 28W
Sychevka 80 55 45N 34 10 E
Syców 54 51 19N 17 40 E
Sydney, Austral. 141 33 53 S 151 10 E
Sydney, Can. 151 46 7N 60 7W
Sydney, U.S.A. 158 41 12N 103 0W
Sydney Mines 151 46 18N 60 15W
Sydproven 12 60 30N 45 35W
Sydra, G. of = Surt 61 31 40N 18 30 E

Syke
Tambelan, Kepulauan

Syke 48 52 55N 8 50 E
Syktyvkar 78 61 45N 50 40 E
Sylacauga 157 33 10N 86 15W
Sylarna, Mt. 72 63 2N 12 11 E
Sylhet 98 24 54N 91 52 E
Sylt, I. 48 54 50N 8 20 E
Sylva, R. 84 58 0N 56 54 E
Sylvan Beach 162 43 12N 75 44W
Sylvan Lake 152 52 20N 114 10W
Sylvania 157 32 45N 81 37W
Sylvester 157 31 31N 83 50W
Sym 76 60 20N 87 50 E
Symington 35 55 35N 3 36W
Symón 164 24 42N 102 35W
Symonds Yat 28 51 50N 2 38W
Synnott Ra. 136 16 30 S 125 20 E
Syr Darya 76 45 0N 65 0 E
Syracuse, Kans., U.S.A. 159 38 0N 101 40W
Syracuse, N.Y., U.S.A. 162 43 4N 76 11W
Syrdarya 85 40 50N 68 40 E
Syria ■ 92 35 0N 38 0 E
Syriam 98 16 44N 96 19 E
Syrian Des. 92 31 30N 40 0 E
Sysert 84 56 29N 60 49 E
Syston 28 52 42N 1 5W
Syuldzhyukyor 77 63 25N 113 40 E
Syutkya, mt. 67 41 50N 24 16 E
Syzran 81 53 12N 48 30 E
Szabolcs-Szatmár □ 53 48 2N 21 45 E
Szamocin 54 53 2N 17 7 E
Szamotuły 54 52 35N 16 34 E
Szaraz, R. 53 46 28N 20 44 E
Szazhalombatta 53 47 20N 18 58 E
Szczara, R. 53 53 15N 25 10 E
Szczebrzeszyn 54 50 42N 22 59 E
Szczecin 54 53 27N 14 27 E
Szczecin □ 54 53 25N 14 32 E
Szczecinek 54 53 43N 16 41 E
Szczekocimy 54 50 38N 19 48 E
Szczrk 53 49 42N 19 1 E
Szczuczyn 54 53 36N 22 19 E
Szczytno 54 53 33N 21 0 E
Szechwan □ 109 30 15N 103 15 E
Szécsény 53 48 7N 19 30 E
Szeged 53 46 16N 20 10 E
Szeghalom 53 47 1N 21 10 E
Székesfehérvár 53 47 15N 18 25 E
Szekszárd 53 46 22N 18 42 E
Szendrö 53 48 24N 20 41 E
Szentendre 53 47 39N 19 4 E
Szentes 53 46 39N 20 21 E
Szentgotthárd 53 46 58N 16 19 E
Szentlörinc 53 46 3N 18 1 E
Szerencs 53 48 10N 21 12 E
Szeshui 33 34 50N 113 20 E
Szigetvár 53 46 3N 17 46 E
Szlichtyogowa 54 51 42N 16 15 E
Szob 53 47 48N 18 53 E
Szolnok 53 47 10N 20 15 E
Szolnok □ 53 47 15N 20 30 E
Szombathely 53 47 14N 16 38 E
Szprotawa 54 51 33N 15 35 E
Sztum 54 53 55N 19 1 E
Sztuto 54 54 20N 19 15 E
Sztutowo 54 54 20N 19 15 E
Szürvas 53 46 50N 20 38 E
Szydłowiec 54 51 15N 20 51 E
Szypliszki 54 54 17N 23 2 E

T

't Harde 46 52 24N 5 54 E
't Zandt 46 53 22N 6 46 E
Ta-erh Po, L. 106 43 15N 116 35 E
Ta Khli Khok 100 15 18N 100 20 E
Ta Lai 101 11 24N 107 23 E
Taalintehdas 74 60 2N 22 30 E
Taan 107 45 30N 124 18 E
Taavetti 75 60 56N 27 32 E
Taba 92 26 55N 42 30 E
Tabacal 172 23 15 S 64 15W
Tabaco 103 13 22N 123 44 E
Tabagné 120 7 59N 3 4W
Tabar Is. 135 2 50 S 152 0 E
Tabarca, Isla de 59 38 17N 0 30W
Tabarka 119 36 56N 8 46 E
Tabarra 59 38 37N 1 44 E
Tabas, Khorasan, Iran 93 33 35N 56 55 E
Tabas, Khorasan, Iran 93 32 48N 60 12 E
Tabasará, Serranía de 166 8 35N 81 40W
Tabasco □ 165 17 45N 93 30W
Tabatinga 174 4 11 S 69 58W
Tabatinga, Serra da 170 10 30 S 44 0W
Tabayin 98 22 42N 95 20 E
Tabelbala, Kahal de 118 28 47N 2 0W
Taber 152 49 47N 112 8W
Taberg 162 43 18N 75 37W
Tabernas 59 37 4N 2 26W
Tabernas de Valldigna 59 39 5N 0 13W
Tabigha 90 32 53N 35 33 E
Tabira 170 7 35 S 37 33W
Tablas, I. 103 12 25N 122 2 E
Table B. 151 53 40N 56 25W
Table Mt. 128 34 0 S 18 22 E
Table Top, Mt. 138 23 24 S 147 11 E
Tableland 136 17 16 S 126 51 E
Tabletop, mt. 137 22 32 S 123 50 E
Tábor 52 49 25N 14 39 E
Tabor 90 32 42N 35 24 E
Tabora 126 5 2 S 32 57 E
Tabora □ 126 5 0 S 33 0 E
Tabory 84 58 31N 64 33 E
Tabou 120 4 30N 7 20W
Tabouda 118 34 44N 5 14W
Tabrīz 92 38 7N 46 20 E
Tabūk 92 28 30N 36 25 E
Täby 72 59 29N 18 4 E
Tacámbaro 164 19 14N 101 28W
Tacarigua, L. de 174 11 3N 68 25W
Tach'aitan 105 37 50N 95 18 E
T'ach'eng 105 46 45N 82 57 E
Tach'eng 106 38 35N 116 39 E
Tach'engtzu 107 41 44N 118 52 E
Tach'i 109 24 51N 121 14 E
Tachia 109 24 25N 120 28 E
Tachiai 108 23 44N 103 57 E
Tachibana-Wan 110 32 45N 130 7 E
Tachikawa 111 35 42N 139 25 E
Tach'in Ch'uan, R. 108 31 57N 102 11 E
Tach'ing Shan, mts. 106 40 50N 111 0 E
Tachira 174 8 7N 72 21W
Tachira □ 174 8 7N 72 15W
Tachov 52 49 47N 12 39 E
Tachu 108 30 45N 107 13 E
Tacina, R. 65 39 5N 16 51 E
Tacloban 103 11 15N 124 58 E
Tacna 174 18 0 S 70 20W
Tacoma 160 47 15N 122 30W
Tacuarembó 173 31 45 S 56 0W
Tacumshin L. 39 52 12N 6 28W
Tadcaster 33 53 53N 1 16W
Tademaït, Plateau du 118 28 30N 2 30 E
Tadent, O. 119 22 30N 7 0 E
Tadjerdjert, O. 119 26 0N 8 0W
Tadjerouna 118 33 31N 2 3 E
Tadjettaret, O. 119 22 0N 7 30W
Tadjmout, O. 118 25 37N 3 48 E
Tadjoura 123 11 50N 42 55 E
Tadjoura, Golfe de 123 11 50N 43 0 E
Tadley 28 51 21N 1 8W
Tadmor, N.Z. 143 41 27 S 172 45 E
Tadmor, Syria 92 34 30N 37 55 E
Tado 174 5 16N 76 32W
Tadotsu 110 34 16N 133 45 E
Tadoule L 153 58 36N 98 20W
Tadoussac 151 48 11N 69 42W
Tadzhik S.S.R. □ 85 35 30N 70 0 E
Taechŏnni 107 36 21N 126 36 E
Taegu 107 35 50N 128 37 E
Taegwandong 107 40 13N 125 12 E
Taejŏn 107 36 20N 127 28 E
Taerhhanmaoming-anlienhoch'i 106 41 50N 110 27 E
Taerhting 105 37 15N 92 36 E
Taf, R. 31 51 55N 4 36W
Tafalla 58 42 30N 1 41W
Tafang 108 27 10N 105 39 E
Tafar 123 6 52N 28 15 E
Tafas 90 32 44N 36 5 E
Tafassasset, O. 119 23 0N 9 11 E
Tafelbaai 128 33 35 S 18 25 E
Tafelney, C. 118 31 3N 9 51W
Tafermaar 103 6 47 S 134 10 E
Tafí Viejo 172 26 43 S 65 17W
Tafiré 120 9 4N 5 10W
Tafnidilt 118 28 47N 10 58W
Tafraout 118 29 50N 8 58W
Taft, Phil. 103 11 57N 125 30 E
Taft, Ala., U.S.A. 163 35 10N 119 28W
Taft, Tex., U.S.A. 159 27 58N 97 23W
Taga Dzong 98 27 5N 90 0 E
Taganrog 83 47 12N 38 50 E
Taganrogskiy Zaliv 82 47 0N 38 30 E
Tagant 120 18 20N 11 0W
Tagap Ga 98 26 56N 96 13 E
Tagbilaran 103 9 39N 123 51 E
Tage 135 6 19 S 143 20 E
Tággia 62 43 52N 7 50 E
Taghmon 39 52 19N 6 40W
Taghrīfat 119 29 5N 17 26 E
Taghzout 118 33 30N 4 49W
Tagish 152 60 19N 134 16W
Tagish L. 147 60 10N 134 20W
Tagliacozzo 63 42 4N 13 13 E
Tagliamento, R. 63 45 38N 13 5 E
Táglio di Po 63 45 0N 12 12 E
Tagomago, Isla de 59 39 2N 1 39 E
Tagua, La 174 0 3N 74 40W
Taguatinga 171 12 26 S 46 26W
Tagula 135 11 22 S 153 15 E
Tagula I. 135 11 30 S 153 30 E
Tagum (Hijo) 103 7 33N 125 53 E
Tagus = Tajo, R. 55 39 44N 5 50W
Tahahbala, I. 102 0 30 S 98 30 E
Tahakopa 143 46 30 S 169 23 E
Tahala 118 34 0N 4 28W
Tahan, Gunong 101 4 45N 102 25 E
Tahara 111 34 40N 137 16 E
Tahat Mt. 119 23 18N 5 21 E
Tāherī 93 27 43N 52 20 E
Tahiti, I. 131 17 37 S 149 27W
Tahoe 160 39 12N 120 9W
Tahoe, L. 160 39 0N 120 9W
Tahora 142 39 2 S 174 49 E
Tahoua 121 14 57N 5 16 E
Tahsien 108 31 17N 107 30 E
Tahsin 108 22 48N 107 23 E
Tahsinganling Shanmo 105 49 0N 122 0 E
Tahsingkou 107 43 23N 129 39 E
Tahsintien 107 37 37N 120 50 E
Tahsüeh Shan, mts. 108 31 15N 101 20 E
Tahta 122 26 44N 31 32 E
Tahulandang, I. 103 2 27N 125 23 E
Tahuna 103 3 45N 125 30 E
Tahung Shan, mts. 109 31 30N 112 50 E
Tai 108 30 41N 103 29 E
Taï 120 5 55N 7 30W
T'ai Hu 105 31 10N 120 0 E
Tai Shan 109 30 17N 122 10 E
T'aian 107 36 12N 117 7 E
T'aichiang 108 26 40N 108 19 E
T'aichou 109 32 22N 119 45 E
T'aichou Liehtao 109 28 30N 121 53 E
T'aichung 105 24 9N 120 37 E
T'aichunghsien 109 24 15N 120 35 E
Taieri, R. 143 46 3 S 170 12 E
Taiga Madema 119 23 46N 15 25 E
T'aihang Shan, mts. 106 35 40N 113 20 E
Taihape 142 39 41 S 175 48 E
T'aiho, Anhwei, China 109 33 10N 115 36 E
T'aiho, Kiangsi, China 109 26 50N 114 53 E
T'aihsien 109 32 17N 120 10 E
T'aihsing 109 32 10N 120 4 E
Taihu 109 30 30N 116 25 E
T'aik'ang 106 34 4N 114 52 E
Taikkyi 98 17 20N 96 0 E
T'aiku 106 37 23N 112 34 E
Tailem Bend 140 35 12 S 139 29 E
Tailfingen 49 48 15N 9 1 E
Taima 92 27 35N 38 45 E
Taimyr = Taymyr 77 75 0N 100 0 E
Taimyr, Oz. 77 74 20N 102 0 E
Tain 37 57 49N 4 4W
T'ainan 109 23 0N 120 10 E
T'ainanhsien 109 23 21N 120 17 E
Tainaron, Akra 69 36 22N 22 27 E
Tainggya 98 17 49N 94 29 E
T'aining 109 26 55N 117 12 E
Taintignies 47 50 33N 3 22 E
Taiobeiras 171 15 49 S 42 14W
T'aipei 109 25 2N 121 30 E
T'aip'ing 109 30 18N 118 6 E
Taiping 101 4 51N 100 44 E
Taipu 170 5 37 S 35 36W
T'aip'ussuchi 106 41 55N 115 23 E
Taisha 110 35 24N 132 40 E
T'aishan 109 22 17N 112 43 E
Taishun 109 27 33N 119 43 E
Taita □ 126 4 0 S 38 30 E
Taita Hills 126 3 25 S 38 15 E
Taitao, Pen. de 176 46 30 S 75 0W
T'aitung 105 22 43N 121 4 E
Taivalkoski 74 65 33N 28 12 E
Taiwan (Formosa) ■ 109 23 30N 121 0 E
Taiwara 93 33 30N 64 24 E
Taïyetos Óros 69 37 0N 22 23 E
Taiyiba, Israel 90 32 36N 35 27 E
Taiyiba, Jordan 90 31 55N 35 17 E
T'aiyüan 106 37 55N 112 40 E
Ta'izz 91 13 43N 44 7 E
Tajapuru, Furo do 170 1 50 S 50 25W
Tajarhī 119 24 15N 14 46 E
Tajicaringa 164 23 15N 104 44W
Tajima 112 35 19N 135 8 E
Tajimi 111 35 19N 137 8 E
Tajimi Gifu 55 35 25N 137 5 E
Tajitos 164 30 58N 112 18W
Tajo, R. 57 40 35N 1 52W
Tajumulco, Volcán de 165 15 20N 91 50W
Tājūrā 119 32 51N 13 27 E
Tak 100 16 52N 99 8 E
Takachiho 110 32 42N 131 18 E
Takahashi 110 34 51N 133 39 E
Takaka 143 40 51N 172 50 E
Takamatsu 110 34 20N 134 5 E
Takanabe 110 32 8N 131 30 E
Takaoka 111 36 40N 137 0 E
Takapau 142 40 2 S 176 21 E
Takapuna 142 36 47 S 174 47 E
Takasago 110 34 45N 134 48 E
Takasaki 111 36 20N 139 0 E
Takase 110 34 7N 133 48 E
Takatsuki 111 34 51N 135 37 E
Takaungu 126 3 38 S 39 52 E
Takawa 110 33 47N 130 51 E
Takayama 111 36 18N 137 11 E
Takayama-Bonchi 111 36 0N 137 18 E
Takefu 111 35 50N 136 10 E
Takehara 110 34 21N 132 55 E
Takeley 29 51 52N 0 16 E
Takeo, Camb. 101 10 59N 104 47 E
Takeo, Japan 110 33 12N 130 1 E
Tåkern 73 58 22N 14 45 E
Takestan 92 36 0N 49 50 E
Taketa 110 32 58N 131 24 E
Takh 95 33 6N 77 32 E
Takhman 101 11 29N 104 57 E
Taki 135 6 29 S 155 52 E
Takingeun 102 4 45N 96 50 E
Takla L. 152 55 15N 125 45W
Takla Landing 152 55 30N 125 50W
Takla Makan 105 39 0N 83 0 E
Takoradi 120 4 58N 1 55W
Taku, China 107 38 59N 117 41 E
Taku, Japan 110 33 18N 130 3 E
Taku, R. 152 58 30N 133 50W
Takuan 108 27 44N 103 53 E
Takum 121 7 18N 9 36 E
Takuma 110 34 13N 133 40 E
Takushan 107 39 55N 123 30 E
Tal-y-llyn 31 52 40N 3 44W
Tal-y-sarn 31 53 3N 4 12W
Tala, Uruguay 173 34 21 S 55 46W
Tala, U.S.S.R. 77 72 40N 113 30 E
Talach'in 106 36 42N 104 54 E
Talagante 172 33 40 S 70 50W
Talaint 118 29 37N 9 45W
Talak 121 18 0N 5 0 E
Talamanca, Cordillera de 166 9 20N 83 20W
Talara 174 4 30 S 81 10 E
Talas 85 42 45N 72 0 E
Talas, R. 85 44 0N 70 20 E
Talasea 135 5 20 S 150 2 E
Talasskiy, Khrebet 85 42 15N 72 0 E
Talata Mafara 121 12 38N 6 4 E
Talaud, Kepulauan 103 4 30N 127 10 E
Talavera de la Reina 56 39 55N 4 46W
Talawana 136 22 51 S 121 9 E
Talawgyi 98 25 4N 97 19 E
Talayan 103 6 52N 124 24 E
Talbot, C. 136 13 48 S 126 43 E
Talbragar, R. 141 32 5 S 149 15 E
Talca 172 35 20 S 71 46W
Talca □ 172 35 20 S 71 46W
Talcahuano 172 36 40 S 73 10W
Talcher 96 20 55N 85 3 E
Talcho 121 14 35N 3 22 E
Taldom 81 56 45N 37 29 E
Taldy Kurgan 76 45 10N 78 45 E
Taleqan □ 93 36 40N 69 30 E
Talesh, Kūlhā-Ye 92 39 0N 48 30 E
Talfit 90 32 5N 35 17 E
Talga, R. 136 21 2 S 119 51 E
Talgar 85 43 19N 77 15 E
Talgar, Pic 85 43 5N 77 20 E
Talgarth 31 51 59N 3 15W
Talguharai 122 18 19N 35 56 E
Talguppa 93 14 10N 74 45 E
Tali, Shensi, China 106 34 48N 109 48 E
Tali, Yunnan, China 108 25 45N 100 5 E
Tali Post 123 5 55N 30 44 E
Taliabu, I. 103 1 45 S 125 0 E
Taliang Shan 108 28 0N 103 0 E
Talibong, Ko 101 7 15N 99 23 E
Talihina 159 34 45N 95 1W
Talikoti 96 16 29N 76 17 E
Talimardzhan 85 38 23N 65 37 E
Taling Ho, R. 107 40 54N 121 38 E
Taling Sung 101 15 5N 99 11 E
Talitsa 84 57 0N 63 43 E
Taliwang 102 8 50 S 116 55 E
Talkeetna 147 62 20N 150 0W
Talkeetna Mts. 147 62 20N 149 0W
Tall 'Asūr 90 31 59N 35 17 E
Talla 122 28 5N 30 43 E
Talladale 36 57 41N 5 20W
Talladega 157 33 28N 86 2W
Tallahassee 157 30 25N 84 15W
Tallangatta 141 36 15 S 147 10 E
Tallarook 141 37 5 S 145 6 E
Tallåsen 72 61 52N 16 2 E
Tallawang 141 32 12 S 149 28 E
Tällberg 72 60 51N 15 2 E
Tallebung 141 32 42 S 146 34 E
Tallering Pk 137 28 6 S 115 37 E
Tallinn (Reval) 80 59 29N 24 58 E
Tallow 39 52 6N 8 0W
Tallowbridge 39 52 6N 8 1W
Tallulah 159 32 25N 91 12W
Talluza 90 32 17N 35 18 E
Talmage 153 49 46N 103 40W
Talmest 118 31 48N 9 21W
Talmont 44 46 27N 1 37W
Talnoye 82 48 57N 30 35 E
Taloda 96 21 34N 74 19 E
Talodi 123 10 35N 30 22 E
Talou Shan, mts. 108 28 20N 107 10 E
Talovaya 81 51 13N 40 38 E
Talpa de Allende 164 20 23N 104 51W
Talsarnau 31 52 54N 4 4W
Talsinnt 118 32 33N 3 27W
Taltal 172 25 23 S 70 40W
Taltson L. 153 61 30N 110 15W
Taltson R. 152 61 24N 112 46W
Talwood 139 28 29 S 149 29 E
Talyawalka Cr. 140 32 28 S 142 22 E
Talybont 31 52 29N 3 59W
Tam Chau 101 10 48N 105 12 E
Tam Ky 100 15 34N 108 29 E
Tam Quan 100 14 35N 109 3 E
Tama 158 41 56N 92 37W
Tama Abu, Pegunungan 102 3 10N 115 0 E
Tamala 137 26 35 S 113 40 E
Tamalameque 174 8 52N 73 49W
Tamale 121 9 22N 0 50W
Taman 82 45 14N 36 41 E
Tamana 110 32 58N 130 32 E
Tamanar 118 31 1N 9 46W
Tamano 110 34 35N 133 59 E
Tamanrasset 119 22 56N 5 30 E
Tamanrasset, O. 118 22 0N 2 0 E
Tamanthi 98 25 19N 95 17 E
Tamaqua 162 40 46N 75 58W
Tamar, R. 30 50 33N 4 15W
Támara 174 5 50N 72 10W
Tamarang 141 31 27 S 150 5 E
Tamarite de Litera 58 41 52N 0 25 E
Tamashima 110 34 32N 133 40 E
Tamási 53 46 40N 18 18 E
Tamaské 121 14 55N 5 55 E
Tamatave 129 18 10 S 49 25 E
Tamatave □ 129 18 0 S 49 0 E
Tamaulipas □ 165 24 0N 99 0W
Tamaulipas, Sierra de 165 23 30N 98 20W
Tamazula 164 24 55N 106 58W
Tamazunchale 165 21 16N 98 47W
Tambacounda 120 13 55N 13 45W
Tambai 123 16 32N 37 13 E
Tambelan, Kepulauan 102 1 0N 107 30 E

Tambellup **Taunton**

Tambellup	**137**	34 4 S	117 37 E
Tambo	**138**	24 54 S	146 14 E
Tambo de Mora	**174**	13 30 S	76 20W
Tambohorano	**129**	17 30 S	43 58 E
Tambora, G.	**102**	8 12 S	118 5 E
Tamboritha, Mt.	**141**	37 31 S	146 51 E
Tambov	**81**	52 45N	41 20 E
Tambre, R.	**56**	42 55N	8 30W
Tambuku, G.	**103**	7 8 S	113 40 E
Tamburâ	**123**	5 40N	27 25 E
Tamchaket	**120**	17 25N	10 40W
Tamchok Khambab (Brahmaputra)	**99**	29 25N	88 0 E
Tamdybulak	**85**	41 46N	64 36 E
Tame	**174**	6 28N	71 44W
Tame, R.	**28**	52 43N	1 45W
Tamega, R.	**56**	41 12N	8 5W
Tamelelt	**119**	26 30N	6 14 E
Tamenglong	**98**	25 0N	93 35 E
Tamerfors	**75**	61 30N	23 50 E
Tamerlanovka	**85**	42 36N	69 17 E
Tamerton Foliot	**30**	50 25N	4 10W
Tamerza	**119**	34 23N	7 58 E
Tamgak, Mts.	**121**	19 12N	8 35 E
Tamiahua, Laguna de	**165**	21 30N	97 30W
Tamil Nadu □	**97**	11 0N	77 0 E
Tamines	**47**	50 26N	4 36 E
Taming	**106**	36 20N	115 10 E
Tamins	**51**	46 50N	9 24 E
Tamluk	**95**	22 18N	87 58 E
Tammisaari (Ekenäs)	**75**	60 0N	23 26 E
Tammun'	**90**	32 18N	35 23 E
Tamnaren	**72**	60 10N	17 25 E
Tamou	**121**	12 45N	2 11 E
Tampa	**157**	27 57N	82 30W
Tampa B.	**157**	27 40N	82 40W
Tampere	**75**	61 30N	23 50 E
Tampico	**165**	22 20N	97 50W
Tampin	**101**	2 28N	102 13 E
Tamri	**118**	30 49N	9 50W
Tamrida = Hadibu	**91**	12 35N	54 2 E
Tamsagbulag	**105**	47 14N	117 21 E
Tamsagout	**118**	24 5N	6 35W
Tamsalu	**80**	59 11N	26 8 E
Tamsweg	**52**	47 7N	13 49 E
Tamu	**99**	24 13N	94 12 E
Tamuja, R.	**57**	39 33N	6 8W
Tamworth, Austral.	**141**	31 0 S	150 58 E
Tamworth, U.K.	**28**	52 38N	1 41W
Tamyang	**107**	35 19N	126 59 E
Tan An	**101**	10 32N	106 25 E
Tana	**74**	70 7N	28 5 E
Tana Fd.	**74**	70 35N	28 30 E
Tana, L.	**123**	13 5N	37 30 E
Tana, R., Kenya	**126**	0 50 S	39 45 E
Tana, R., Norway	**48**	69 50N	26 0 E
Tanabe	**111**	33 44N	135 22 E
Tanabi	**171**	20 37 S	49 37W
Tanacross	**147**	63 40N	143 30W
Tanafjorden	**74**	70 45N	28 25 E
Tanagro, R.	**65**	40 35N	15 25 E
Tanahdjampea, I.	**103**	7 10 S	120 35 E
Tanahgrogot	**102**	1 55 S	116 15 E
Tanahmasa, I.	**102**	0 5 S	98 29 E
Tanahmerah	**103**	6 0 S	140 7 E
Tanami	**136**	19 59 S	129 43 E
Tanami Des.	**136**	18 50 S	132 0 E
Tanana	**147**	65 10N	152 15W
Tanana, R.	**147**	64 25N	145 30W
Tananarive	**129**	18 55 S	47 31 E
Tananarive □	**129**	19 0 S	47 0 E
Tananarive = Antananarivo	**125**	18 55 S	47 31 E
Tananger	**71**	58 57N	5 37 E
Tanant	**118**	31 54N	6 56W
Tánaro, R.	**62**	44 9N	7 50 E
Tanaunelia	**64**	40 42N	9 45 E
Tanba-Sanchi	**111**	35 7N	135 48 E
Tanbar	**97**	25 55 S	142 0 E
Tancarville	**42**	49 29N	0 28 E
Tanchai	**108**	25 58N	107 49 E
T'anch'eng	**107**	34 38N	118 21 E
Tanda, U.P., India	**95**	26 33N	82 35 E
Tanda, U.P., India	**95**	28 57N	78 56 E
Tanda, Ivory C.	**120**	7 48N	3 10W
Tandag	**103**	9 4N	126 9 E
Tandala	**127**	9 25 S	34 15 E
Tândărei	**70**	44 39N	27 40 E
Tandil	**172**	37 15 S	59 6W
Tandjungpandan	**102**	2 43 S	107 38 E
Tandlianwald	**94**	31 3N	73 9 E
Tando Adam	**94**	25 45N	68 40 E
Tandou L.	**140**	32 40 S	142 5 E
Tandragee	**38**	54 22N	6 23W
Tandsbyn	**72**	63 0N	14 45W
Tandur	**96**	19 11N	79 30 E
Tane-ga-Shima	**112**	30 35N	130 59 E
Taneatua	**142**	38 4 S	177 1 E
Tanen Range	**101**	19 40N	99 0 E
Tanen Tong Dan, Burma	**99**	16 30N	98 30 E
Tanen Tong Dan, Thai.	**100**	19 43N	98 30 E
Taneytown	**162**	39 40N	77 10W
Tanezrouft	**118**	23 9N	0 11 E
Tanfeng	**106**	33 45N	110 18 E
Tang	**38**	53 31N	7 49W
Tang, Koh	**101**	10 16N	103 7 E
Tang Krasang	**101**	12 34N	105 3 E
Tang La	**99**	32 59N	92 17 E
Tang Pass	**99**	32 59N	92 17 E
Tanga	**99**	5 5 S	39 2 E
Tanga □	**126**	5 20 S	38 0 E
Tanga Is.	**135**	3 20 S	153 15 E
Tangail	**98**	24 15N	89 55 E
Tanganyika, L.	**126**	6 40 S	30 0 E
T'angch'i	**109**	29 3N	119 24 E
Tanger	**118**	35 50N	5 49W
Tangerang	**103**	6 12 S	106 39 E
Tangerhütte	**48**	52 26N	11 50 E
Tangermünde	**48**	52 32N	11 57 E
T'angho	**109**	32 10N	112 20 E
Tangier	**162**	37 49N	75 59W
Tangier = Tanger	**118**	35 50N	5 49W
Tangier I.	**162**	37 50N	76 0W
Tangier Sd.	**162**	38 3N	75 5W
Tangkak	**101**	2 18N	102 34 E
T'angku	**107**	39 4N	117 45 E
T'angkula Shanmo	**98**	33 0N	92 0 E
Tanglha Shan	**99**	33 0N	90 0 E
Tangorin P.O.	**138**	21 47 S	144 12 E
Tangra Tso	**99**	31 25N	85 30 E
Tangshan	**106**	34 25N	116 24 E
T'angshan	**107**	39 40N	118 10 E
T'angt'ang	**108**	26 29N	104 12 E
T'angt'ou	**107**	35 21N	118 32 E
Tangt'u	**109**	31 34N	118 29 E
Tanguiéta	**121**	10 40N	1 21 E
Tangyang, Chekiang, China	**109**	29 17N	120 14 E
Tangyang, Hupeh, China	**109**	30 50N	111 45 E
Tangyen Ho, R.	**108**	28 55N	108 36 E
Tanimbar, Kepulauan	**103**	7 30 S	131 30 E
Taning	**106**	36 32N	110 47 E
Taniyama	**110**	31 31N	130 31 E
Tanjay	**103**	9 30N	123 5 E
Tanjore = Thanjavur	**97**	10 48N	79 12 E
Tanjung	**102**	2 10 S	115 25 E
Tanjung Malim	**101**	3 42N	101 31 E
Tanjungbalai	**102**	2 55N	99 44 E
Tanjungbatu	**102**	2 23N	118 3 E
Tanjungkarang	**102**	5 20 S	105 10 E
Tanjungpinang	**102**	1 5N	104 30 E
Tanjungpriok	**103**	6 8 S	106 55 E
Tanjungredeb	**102**	2 9N	117 29 E
Tanjungselor	**102**	2 55N	117 25 E
Tank	**94**	32 14N	70 25 E
Tankan Shan	**109**	22 3N	114 16 E
Tanleng	**108**	30 20N	103 33 E
Tanndalen	**72**	62 33N	12 18 E
Tannin	**150**	49 40N	91 0W
Tannis B.	**73**	57 40N	10 15 E
Tano, R.	**120**	6 0N	2 30W
Tanoumrout	**119**	23 2N	5 31 E
Tanout	**121**	14 50N	8 55 E
Tanquinho	**171**	12 42 S	39 43W
Tanshui	**109**	25 10N	121 28 E
Tanta	**122**	30 45N	30 57 E
Tantan	**118**	28 29N	11 1W
Tantoyuca	**165**	21 21N	98 10W
Tantung	**107**	40 10N	124 23 E
Tantura = Dor	**90**	32 37N	34 55 E
Tanuku	**96**	16 45N	81 44 E
Tanum	**73**	58 42N	11 20 E
Tanunda	**140**	34 30 S	139 0 E
Tanur	**97**	11 1N	75 46 E
Tanus	**44**	44 8N	2 19 E
Tanworth	**28**	52 20N	1 50W
Tanzania ■	**126**	6 40 S	34 0 E
Tanzawa-Sanchi	**111**	35 27N	139 0 E
Tanzilla, R.	**152**	58 8N	130 43W
T'aoan	**107**	45 20N	122 50 E
Taoch'eng	**108**	29 3N	100 10 E
Taoerh Ho	**107**	45 42N	124 5 E
Taofu	**108**	31 0N	101 9 E
Taohsien	**109**	25 37N	111 24 E
T'aohua Tao	**109**	29 48N	122 17 E
T'aolo	**106**	38 45N	106 40 E
Taormina	**65**	37 52N	15 16 E
Taos	**161**	36 28N	105 35W
Taoudenni	**118**	22 40N	3 55W
Taoudrart, Adrar	**118**	24 25N	2 24 E
Taounate	**118**	34 32N	4 41W
Taourirt, Alg.	**118**	26 37N	0 8 E
Taourirt, Moroc.	**118**	34 20N	2 47W
Taouz	**118**	31 2N	4 0W
T'aoyüan, China	**109**	28 54N	111 29 E
T'aoyüan, Taiwan	**109**	25 0N	121 4 E
Tapa	**80**	59 15N	26 0 E
Tapa Shan	**108**	31 45N	109 30 E
Tapachula	**165**	14 54N	92 17W
Tapah	**101**	4 12N	101 15 E
Tapajós, R.	**175**	4 30 S	56 10W
Tapaktuan	**102**	3 30N	97 10 E
Tapanui	**143**	45 56 S	169 18 E
Tapauá	**174**	5 40 S	64 20W
Tapauá, R.	**174**	6 0 S	65 40W
Tapeta	**120**	6 36N	8 52W
Taphan Hin	**100**	16 13N	100 16 E
Tapia	**56**	43 34N	6 56W
Tapieh Shan, mts.	**109**	31 20N	115 30 E
T'ap'ingchen	**106**	33 42N	111 44 E
Tapini	**135**	8 19 S	147 0 E
Tápiószele	**53**	47 45N	19 55 E
Tapiraí	**171**	19 52 S	46 1W
Tapirapé, R.	**170**	10 41 S	50 38W
Tapirapecó, Serra	**174**	1 10N	65 0W
Taplan	**140**	34 33 S	140 52 E
Tapolca	**53**	46 53N	17 29 E
Tappahannock	**162**	37 56N	76 50W
Tapsing	**99**	30 22N	96 25 E
Tapti, R.	**96**	21 25N	75 0 E
Tapu	**109**	24 31N	116 41 E
Tapuaenuku, Mt.	**143**	41 55 S	173 50 E
Tapul Group, Is.	**103**	5 35N	120 50 E
Tapun	**98**	18 22N	95 27 E
Taquara	**173**	29 36N	50 46W
Taquari, R.	**173**	18 10 S	56 0W
Taquaritinga	**171**	21 24 S	48 30W
Tara, Austral.	**139**	27 17 S	150 31 E
Tara, Japan	**110**	33 2N	130 11 E
Tara, U.S.S.R.	**76**	56 55N	74 30 E
Tara, Zambia	**127**	16 58 S	26 45 E
Tara-Dake	**110**	32 58N	130 6 E
Tara, R.	**66**	43 10N	19 20 E
Tarabagatay, Khrebet	**77**	48 0N	83 0 E
Tarābulus, Leb.	**92**	34 31N	33 52 E
Tarābulus, Libya	**119**	32 49N	13 7 E
Taradale	**142**	39 33 S	176 53 E
Tarahouahout	**119**	22 47N	5 59 E
Tarakan	**102**	3 20N	117 35 E
Tarakit, Mt.	**126**	2 2N	35 10 E
Taralga	**141**	34 26 S	149 52 E
Taramakau, R.	**143**	42 34 S	171 8 E
Tarana	**141**	33 31 S	149 52 E
Taranagar	**94**	28 43N	75 9 E
Taranaki □	**142**	39 5 S	174 51 E
Tarancón	**58**	40 1N	3 1W
Taranga	**94**	23 56N	72 43 E
Taranga Hill	**94**	24 0N	72 40 E
Taransay, I.	**36**	57 54N	7 0W
Taransay, Sd. of	**36**	57 52N	7 0W
Táranto	**65**	40 30N	17 11 E
Táranto, G. di	**65**	40 0N	17 15 E
Tarapacá	**174**	2 56 S	69 46W
Tarapacá □	**172**	20 45 S	69 30W
Tarare	**45**	45 54N	4 26 E
Tararua Range	**142**	40 45 S	175 25 E
Tarascon, Ariège, France	**44**	42 50N	1 37 E
Tarascon, Bouches-du-Rhône, France	**45**	43 48N	4 39 E
Tarashcha	**82**	49 30N	30 31 E
Tarat, Bj.	**119**	26 4N	9 7 E
Tarauacá	**174**	8 6 S	70 48W
Tarauacá, R.	**174**	7 30 S	70 30W
Taravo, R.	**45**	41 48N	8 52 E
Tarawera	**142**	39 2 S	176 36 E
Tarawera L.	**142**	38 13 S	176 27 E
Tarawera Mt.	**142**	38 14 S	176 32 E
Tarazat, Massif de	**119**	20 2N	8 30 E
Tarazona	**58**	41 55N	1 43W
Tarazona de la Mancha	**59**	39 16N	1 55W
Tarbat Ness	**37**	57 52N	3 48W
Tarbela Dam	**94**	34 0N	72 52 E
Tarbert, Ireland	**39**	52 34N	9 22W
Tarbert, Strathclyde, U.K.	**34**	55 55N	5 25W
Tarbert, W. Isles, U.K.	**36**	57 54N	6 49W
Tarbert, L. E.	**36**	57 50N	6 45W
Tarbert, L. W., Strathclyde, U.K.	**34**	55 58N	5 30W
Tarbert, L. W., W. Isles, U.K.	**36**	57 55N	6 56W
Tarbes	**44**	43 15N	0 3 E
Tarbet, Highland, U.K.	**36**	56 58N	5 38W
Tarbet, Strathclyde, U.K.	**34**	56 13N	4 44W
Tarbolton	**34**	55 30N	4 30W
Tarboro	**157**	35 55N	77 3W
Tarbrax	**138**	21 7 S	142 26 E
Tarbū	**119**	26 0N	15 5 E
Tarcento	**63**	46 12N	13 12 E
Tarcoola	**139**	30 44 S	134 36 E
Tarcoon	**139**	30 15 S	146 35 E
Tarcău, Munţii	**70**	46 39N	26 7 E
Tardets-Sorholus	**44**	43 17N	0 52W
Taree	**141**	31 50 S	152 30 E
Tarentaise	**45**	45 30N	6 35 E
Tarf Shaqq al Abd	**122**	26 50N	36 6 E
Tarfa, Wadi el	**122**	28 16N	31 15 E
Tarfaya	**116**	27 55N	12 55W
Targon	**44**	44 44N	0 16W
Targuist	**118**	34 59N	4 14W
Tarhbalt	**118**	30 48N	5 10W
Tarhit	**118**	30 58N	2 0W
Tarhūnah	**119**	32 15N	13 28 E
Tari	**135**	5 54 S	142 59 E
Tarib, Wadi	**122**	18 30N	43 23 E
Táriba	**174**	7 49N	72 13W
Tarifa	**57**	36 1N	5 36W
Tarija	**172**	21 30 S	64 40W
Tarija □	**172**	21 30 S	63 30W
Tarim, R.	**105**	41 5N	86 40 E
Tarime □	**126**	1 15 S	34 0 E
Taringo Downs	**141**	32 13 S	145 33 E
Taritoe, R.	**103**	3 0 S	138 5 E
Tarka, R.	**128**	32 10 S	26 0 E
Tarkastad	**128**	32 0 S	26 16 E
Tarkhankut, Mys	**82**	45 25N	32 30 E
Tarko Sale	**76**	64 55N	77 50 E
Tarkwa	**120**	5 20N	2 0W
Tarlac	**103**	15 29N	120 35 E
Tarland	**37**	57 8N	2 51W
Tarleton	**32**	53 41N	2 50W
Tarlsland	**152**	57 03N	111 40W
Tarlton Downs	**138**	22 40 S	136 45 E
Tarm	**73**	55 56N	8 31 E
Tarma	**174**	11 25 S	75 45W
Tarn □	**44**	43 49N	2 8 E
Tarn-et-Garonne □	**44**	44 8N	1 20 E
Tarn, R.	**44**	44 5N	1 2 E
Tärna	**74**	65 45N	15 10 E
Tarna, R.	**53**	48 0N	20 5 E
Tårnby	**73**	55 37N	12 36 E
Tarnobrzeg □	**54**	50 40N	22 0 E
Tarnów	**54**	50 3N	21 0 E
Tarnów □	**54**	50 0N	21 0 E
Tarnowskie Góry	**54**	50 27N	18 54 E
Táro, R.	**62**	44 37N	9 58 E
Tarong	**139**	26 47 S	151 51 E
Taroom	**139**	25 36 S	149 48 E
Taroudannt	**118**	30 30N	8 52W
Tarp	**48**	54 40N	9 25 E
Tarpon Springs	**157**	28 8N	82 42W
Tarporley	**32**	53 10N	2 42W
Tarquinia	**63**	42 15N	11 45 E
Tarqumiyah	**90**	31 35N	35 1 E
Tarragona	**58**	41 5N	1 17 E
Tarragona □	**58**	41 0N	1 0 E
Tarrasa	**58**	41 26N	2 1 E
Tárrega	**58**	41 39N	1 9 E
Tarrytown	**162**	41 5N	73 52W
Tarshiha = Me'ona	**90**	33 1N	35 15 E
Tarso Emissi	**119**	21 27N	18 36 E
Tarso Ovrari	**119**	21 27N	17 27 E
Tarsus	**92**	36 58N	34 55 E
Tartagal	**172**	22 30 S	63 50W
Tartan, oilfield	**19**	58 22N	0 5 E
Tartas	**44**	43 50N	0 49W
Tartna Point	**140**	32 54 S	142 24 E
Tartu	**80**	58 25N	26 58 E
Tartus	**92**	34 55N	35 55 E
Tarumirim	**171**	19 16 S	41 59W
Tarumizu	**110**	31 29N	130 42 E
Tarussa	**81**	54 44N	37 10 E
Tarutao, Ko	**101**	6 33N	99 40 E
Tarutung	**102**	2 0N	99 0 E
Tarves	**37**	57 22N	2 13W
Tarvisio	**63**	46 31N	13 35 E
Tarz Ulli	**119**	25 46N	9 44 E
Tas-Buget	**85**	44 46N	65 33 E
Tasahku	**98**	27 33N	97 52 E
Tasāwah	**119**	26 0N	13 37 E
Taschereau	**150**	48 40N	78 40W
Taseko, R.	**152**	52 4N	123 9W
Tasgaon	**96**	17 2N	74 39 E
Ta'shan	**123**	16 31N	42 33 E
Tashauz	**76**	42 0N	59 20 E
Tashet'ai	**106**	41 0N	109 21 E
Tashi Chho Dzong	**98**	27 31N	89 45 E
Tashihch'iao (Yingk'ou)	**107**	40 38N	122 30 E
T'ashihk'uerhkan	**85**	37 47N	75 14 E
Tashkent	**85**	41 20N	69 10 E
Tashkumyr	**85**	41 40N	72 10 E
Tashkurghan	**93**	36 45N	67 40 E
Tashtagol	**76**	52 47N	87 53 E
Tasikmalaya	**103**	7 18 S	108 12 E
Tasjön	**74**	64 15N	15 45 E
Taşköpru	**82**	41 30N	34 15 E
Tasman Bay	**143**	40 59 S	173 25 E
Tasman Glacier	**143**	43 45 S	170 20 E
Tasman, Mt.	**143**	43 34 S	170 12 E
Tasman Mts.	**143**	41 3 S	172 25 E
Tasman Pen.	**138**	43 10 S	148 0 E
Tasman, R.	**143**	43 48 S	170 8 E
Tasman Sea	**142**	36 0 S	160 0 E
Tasmania, I., □	**138**	49 0 S	146 30 E
Tassil Tin-Rerhoh	**118**	20 5N	3 55 E
Tassili n-Ajjer	**119**	25 47N	8 1 E
Tassili-Oua-Ahaggar	**119**	20 41N	5 30 E
Tasty	**85**	44 47N	69 7 E
Tasu Sd.	**152**	52 47N	132 2W
Tata, Hung.	**53**	47 37N	18 19 E
Tata, Moroc.	**118**	29 46N	7 50W
Tatabánya	**53**	47 32N	18 25 E
Tatar A.S.S.R. □	**84**	55 30N	51 30 E
Tatarsk	**76**	55 20N	75 50 E
*Tatarskiy Proliv	**77**	54 0N	141 0 E
Tatebayashi	**111**	36 15N	139 32 E
Tateshina-Yama	**111**	36 8N	138 11 E
Tateyama	**111**	35 0N	139 50 E
Tathlina L.	**152**	60 33N	117 39W
Tathra	**141**	36 44 S	149 59 E
Tat'ien, Fukien, China	**109**	25 42N	117 50 E
Tat'ien, Szechwan, China	**108**	26 18N	101 45 E
Tatinnai L.	**153**	60 55N	97 40W
Tatlayoka Lake	**152**	51 35N	124 24W
Tatnam, C.	**153**	57 16N	91 0W
Tato Ho, R.	**108**	31 25N	100 42 E
Tatra = Tatry	**54**	49 20N	20 0 E
Tatry	**54**	49 20N	20 0 E
Tatsu	**108**	29 40N	105 45 E
Tatsuno	**110**	34 52N	134 33 E
Tatta	**94**	24 42N	67 55 E
Tattenhall	**32**	53 7N	2 47W
Tatu Ho, R.	**108**	29 35N	103 47 E
Tatuí	**173**	23 25 S	48 0W
Tatum	**159**	33 16N	103 16W
Tat'ung, Anhwei, China	**109**	30 48N	117 44 E
Tat'ung, Shansi, China	**106**	40 9N	113 19 E
Tatura	**141**	36 29 S	145 16 E
Tatvan	**92**	37 28N	42 27 E
Tauá	**170**	6 1 S	40 26W
Taubaté	**173**	23 5 S	45 30W
Tauberbischofsheim	**49**	49 37N	9 40 E
Taucha	**48**	51 22N	12 31 E
Tauern, mts.	**52**	47 15N	12 40 E
Tauern-tunnel	**52**	47 0N	13 12 E
Taufikia	**123**	9 24N	31 37 E
Taumarunui	**142**	38 53 S	175 15 E
Taumaturgo	**174**	9 0 S	73 50W
Taung	**128**	27 33 S	24 47 E
Taungdwingyi	**98**	20 1N	95 40 E
Taunggyi	**98**	20 50N	97 0 E
Taungtha	**98**	20 45N	94 50 E
Taungup	**98**	18 51N	94 14 E
Taungup Pass	**98**	18 40N	94 45 E
Taungup Taunggya	**99**	18 20N	93 40 E
Taunsa Barrage	**95**	31 0N	70 50 E
Taunton, U.K.	**28**	51 1N	3 7W

Renamed Sakhalinskiy Zalir

Taunton **Tetbury**

Taunton, U.S.A. 162 41 54N 71 6W
Taunus 49 50 15N 8 20E
Taupo 142 38 41S 176 7E
Taupo, L. 142 38 46S 175 55E
Tauq 92 35 12N 44 29E
Taurage 80 55 14N 22 28E
Tauramena 174 5 1N 72 45W
Tauranga 142 37 35S 176 11E
Tauranga Harb. 142 37 30S 176 5E
Taureau, Lac 150 46 50N 73 40W
Tauri, R. 135 8 8S 146 8E
Taurianova 65 38 22N 16 1E
Taurus Mts. = Toros Dağlari 92 37 0N 35 0E
Táuste 58 41 58N 1 18W
Tauz 83 41 0N 45 40E
Tavani 153 62 10N 93 30W
Tavannes 50 47 13N 7 12E
Tavas 92 37 35N 29 8E
Tavda 84 58 7N 65 8E
Tavda, R. 84 59 30N 63 0E
Taverny 43 49 2N 2 13E
Taveta 124 3 31N 37 37E
Taviche 165 16 38N 96 32W
Tavignano, R. 45 42 7N 9 33E
Tavira 57 37 8N 7 40W
Tavistock 30 50 33N 4 9W
Tavolara, I. 64 40 55N 9 40E
Távora, R. 56 41 0N 7 30W
Tavoy 101 14 7N 98 18E
Tavoy, I. = Mali Kyun 99 13 0N 98 20E
Taw, R. 30 50 58N 3 58W
Tawang 99 27 37N 91 50E
Tawas City 156 44 16N 83 31W
Tawau 102 4 20N 117 55E
Tawngche 98 26 34N 95 38E
Tawnyinah 38 53 55N 8 45W
Tāworgha' 119 32 1N 15 2E
Taxila 94 33 42N 72 52E
Tay Bridge 35 56 28N 3 0W
Tay, Firth of 35 56 25N 3 8W
Tay, L., Austral. 137 32 55S 120 48E
Tay, L., U.K. 35 56 30N 4 10W
Tay Ninh 101 11 20N 106 5E
Tay, R. 35 56 37N 3 38W
Tay Strath 37 56 38N 3 40W
Tayabamba 174 8 15S 77 10W
Tayao 108 25 41N 101 18E
Tayaparva La 95 31 35N 83 20E
Tayeh 109 30 5N 114 57E
Taylor, Can. 152 56 13N 120 40W
Taylor, Alaska, U.S.A. 147 65 40N 164 50W
Taylor, Pa., U.S.A. 162 41 23N 75 43W
Taylor, Tex., U.S.A. 159 30 30N 97 30W
Taylor, Mt. 143 43 30S 171 20E
Taylor Mt. 161 35 16N 107 50W
Taylorville 158 39 32N 89 20W
Taymyr, Oz. 77 74 50N 102 0E
Taymyr, P-ov. 77 75 0N 100 0E
Taynuilt 34 56 25N 5 15W
Tayport 34 56 27N 2 52W
Tayr Zebna 90 33 14N 35 23E
Tayshet 77 55 58N 97 25E
Tayside □ 35 56 25N 3 30W
Taytay 103 10 45N 119 30E
Tayu 109 25 38N 114 9E
Tayülo 105 29 13N 98 13E
Tayung 109 29 8N 110 30E
Taz, R. 76 65 40N 82 0E
Taza 118 34 10N 4 0W
Taze 98 22 57N 95 24E
Tazenakht 118 30 46N 7 3W
Tazin L. 153 59 44N 108 42W
Tazin, R. 153 60 26N 110 45W
Tazoult 119 35 29N 6 11E
Tazovskiy 76 67 30N 78 30E
Tbilisi (Tiflis) 83 41 50N 44 50E
Tchad (Chad) ■ 117 12 30N 17 15E
Tchad, Lac 117 13 30N 14 30E
Tchaourou 121 8 58N 2 40E
Tchentlo L. 152 55 15N 125 0W
Tchibanga 124 2 45S 11 12E
Tchin Tabaraden 121 15 58N 5 50E
Tczew 54 54 8N 18 50E
Te Anau L. 143 45 15S 167 45E
Te Araroa 142 37 39S 178 25E
Te Aroha 142 37 32S 175 44E
Te Awamutu 142 38 1S 175 20E
Te Horo 142 40 48S 175 6E
Te Kaha 142 37 44S 177 44E
Te Karaka 142 38 26S 177 53E
Te Kauwhata 142 37 25S 175 9E
Te Kinga 143 42 35S 171 31E
Te Kopuru 142 36 2S 173 56E
Te Kuiti 142 38 20S 175 11E
Te Puke 142 37 46S 176 22E
Te Waewae B. 143 46 13S 167 33E
Tea Tree 136 22 11S 133 17E
Teaca 70 46 55N 24 30E
Teague 159 31 40N 96 20W
Tean 109 29 21N 115 42E
Teangue 36 57 7N 5 52W
Teano 65 41 15N 14 1E
Teapa 165 17 35N 92 56W
Teba 57 36 59N 4 55W
Tebay 32 54 25N 2 35W
Teberda 83 43 30N 43 54E
Tébessa 119 35 22N 8 8E
Tebicuary, R. 172 26 36S 58 16W
Tebing Tinggi 102 3 38S 102 1E
Tébourba 119 36 49N 9 51E
Téboursouk 119 36 29N 9 10E
Tebulos 83 42 36N 45 25E
Tecapa 163 35 51N 116 14W
Tecate 164 32 34N 116 38W
Techa, R. 84 56 13N 62 58E
Tech'ang 108 27 22N 102 10E
Techiang 108 28 19N 108 5E
Techiman 120 7 35N 1 58W
Tech'in 108 28 30N 98 52E
Tech'ing 109 23 8N 111 46E
Techirghiol 70 44 4N 28 32E
Techou 106 37 19N 116 19E
Tecomán 164 18 55N 103 53W
Tecoripa 164 28 37N 109 57W
Tecuci 70 45 51N 27 27E
Tecumseh 156 42 1N 83 59W
Tedavnet 38 54 19N 7 2W
Tedesa 123 5 10N 37 40E
Tedzhen 76 37 23N 60 31E
Tees B. 72 54 37N 1 10W
Tees, R. 33 54 36N 1 25W
Teesdale 32 54 37N 2 10W
Teesside 33 54 37N 1 13W
Tefé 174 3 25S 64 50W
Tegal 103 6 52S 109 8E
Tegelen 47 51 20N 6 9E
Teggiano 65 40 24N 15 32E
Teghra 95 25 30N 85 34E
Tegid, L. 31 52 53N 3 38W
Tegina 121 10 5N 6 11E
Tegucigalpa 166 14 10N 87 0W
Tehachapi 163 35 11N 118 29W
Tehachapi Mts. 163 35 0N 118 40W
Tehamiyam 122 18 26N 36 45E
Tehilla 122 17 42N 36 6E
Téhini 120 9 39N 3 32W
Tehrān 93 35 44N 51 30E
Tehrān □ 93 35 0N 49 30E
Tehsing 109 28 54N 117 34E
Tehua 109 25 30N 118 14E
Tehuacán 165 18 20N 97 30W
Tehuantepec 165 16 10N 95 19W
Tehuantepec, Golfo de 165 15 50N 95 0W
Tehuantepec, Istmo de 165 17 0N 94 30W
Tehui 107 44 32N 125 42E
Teich, Le 44 44 38N 0 59W
Teifi, R. 31 52 4N 4 14W
Teign, R. 30 50 41N 3 42W
Teignmouth 30 50 33N 3 30W
Teikovo 81 56 55N 40 30E
Teil, Le 45 44 33N 4 40E
Teilleul, Le 42 48 32N 0 53W
Teishyai 80 55 59N 22 14E
Teiuş 70 46 12N 23 40E
Teixeira 170 7 13S 37 15W
Teixeira de Sousa = Luau 124 10 40S 22 10E
Teixeira Pinto 120 12 10N 13 55E
Tejo, R. 57 39 15N 8 35W
Tejon Pass 163 34 49N 118 53W
Tejung 108 28 46N 99 19E
Tekamah 158 41 48N 96 14W
Tekapo, L. 143 43 53S 170 33E
Tekax 165 20 20N 89 30W
Tekeli 85 44 50N 79 0E
Tekeze, W. 123 13 50N 37 50E
Tekija 66 44 42N 22 26E
Tekirdağ 92 40 58N 27 30E
Tekkali 96 18 43N 84 24E
Teko 108 31 49N 98 40E
Tekoa 160 47 19N 117 4W
Tekoulât, O. 118 22 30N 2 20E
Tel Adashim 90 32 39N 35 17E
Tel Aviv-Yafo 90 32 4N 34 48E
Tel Hanan 90 32 47N 35 3E
Tel Hazor 90 33 2N 35 2E
Tel Lakhish 90 31 34N 34 51E
Tel Malhata 90 31 13N 35 2E
Tel Megiddo 90 32 35N 38 11E
Tel Mond 90 32 15N 34 56E
Tela 166 15 40N 87 28W
Télagh 118 34 51N 0 32W
Telanaipura = Jambi 102 1 38S 103 30E
Telavi 83 42 0N 45 30E
Telciu 70 47 25N 24 24E
Telefomin 135 5 10S 141 40E
Telega = Doftana 70 45 17N 25 45E
Telegraph Cr. 152 58 0N 131 10W
Telekhany 80 52 30N 25 46E
Telemark fylke □ 71 59 25N 8 30E
Telén 172 36 15S 65 31W
Teleneshty 70 47 35N 28 24E
Teleño 56 42 23N 6 22W
Teleorman □ 70 44 0N 25 0E
Teleorman, R. 70 44 15N 25 20E
Teles Pires (São Manuel), R. 174 8 40S 57 0W
Telescope Peak, Mt. 163 36 6N 117 7W
Teletaye 121 16 31N 1 30E
Telford 28 52 42N 2 31W
Telfs 52 47 19N 11 4E
Telgte 48 51 59N 7 46E
Telichie 139 31 45S 139 59E
Télimélé 120 10 54N 13 2W
Telkwa 152 54 41N 126 56W
Tell 90 32 12N 35 12E
Tell City 156 38 0N 86 44W
Teller 147 65 12N 166 24W
Tellicherry 97 11 45N 75 30E
Tellin 47 50 5N 5 13E
Telluride 161 37 58N 107 54W
Telok Anson 101 4 3N 101 0E
Teloloapán 165 18 21N 99 51W
Telom, R. 101 4 20N 101 46E
Telpos Iz. 78 63 35N 57 30E
Telsen 176 42 30S 66 50W
Teltow 48 52 24N 13 15E
Telukbetung 102 5 29S 105 17E
Telukbutun 101 4 5N 108 7E
Telukdalem 102 0 45N 97 50E
Tema 121 5 41N 0 0E
Temagami L. 150 47 0N 80 10W
Temanggung 103 7 18S 110 10E
Temapache 165 21 4N 97 38W
Temax 165 21 10N 88 50W
Tembe 126 0 30S 28 25E
Tembeling, R. 101 4 20N 102 23E
Tembleque 58 39 41N 3 30W
Temblor Ra, mts. 163 35 30N 120 0W
Tembuland □ 129 31 35S 28 0E
Teme, R. 28 52 23N 2 15W
Temecula 163 33 26N 117 6W
Temelelt 118 31 50N 7 32W
Temerloh 101 3 27N 102 25E
Temir Tau 76 53 10N 87 20E
Temirtau 76 50 5N 72 56E
Témiscaming 150 46 44N 79 5W
Temma 138 41 12S 144 42E
Temnikov 81 54 40N 43 11E
Temo, R. 64 40 20N 8 30E
Temora 141 34 30S 147 30E
Temosachic 164 28 58N 107 50W
Tempe, S. Afr. 161 29 1S 26 13E
Tempe, U.S.A. 161 33 26N 111 59W
Tempe Downs 136 24 22S 132 24E
Temperanceville 162 37 54N 75 33W
Tempestad 174 1 20S 74 56W
Tempino 102 1 55S 103 23E
Témpio Pausania 64 40 53N 9 6E
Temple 159 31 5N 97 28W
Temple B. 138 12 15S 143 3E
Temple Combe 28 51 0N 2 25W
Temple Ewell 29 51 9N 1 16W
Temple Sowerby 30 54 38N 2 33W
Templemore 39 52 48N 7 50W
Templenoe 39 51 52N 9 40W
Templeton, Austral. 138 18 30S 142 30E
Templeton, U.K. 31 51 46N 4 45W
Templeton, U.S.A. 163 35 33N 120 42W
Templeton, R. 138 21 0S 138 40E
Templeuve 47 50 39N 3 17E
Templin 48 53 8N 13 31E
Tempo 38 54 23N 7 28W
Tempoal 165 21 31N 98 23W
Temryuk 82 45 15N 37 11E
Temse 47 51 7N 4 13E
Temska, R. 66 43 17N 22 33E
Temuco 176 38 50S 72 50W
Temuka 143 44 14S 171 17E
Ten Boer 46 53 16N 6 42E
Tena 174 0 59S 77 49W
Tenabo 165 20 2N 90 12W
Tenaha 159 31 57N 94 15W
Tenali 96 16 15N 80 35E
Tenancingo 165 19 0N 99 33W
Tenango 165 19 0N 99 40W
Tenasserim 100 12 6N 99 3E
Tenasserim □ 100 14 0N 98 30E
Tenay 45 45 55N 5 30E
Tenbury 28 52 18N 2 35W
Tenby 31 51 40N 4 42W
Tenda 45 44 5N 7 34E
Tenda, Col de 45 44 9N 7 32E
Tendaho 123 11 39N 40 54E
Tende 45 44 5N 7 35E
Tendelti 123 13 1N 31 55E
Tendjedi, Adrar 119 23 41N 7 32E
Tendrara 118 33 3N 1 58W
Tendre, Mt. 50 46 35N 6 18E
Teneida 122 25 30N 29 19E
Ténéré 119 23 2N 16 0E
Tenerife, I. 116 28 20N 16 40W
Tènès 118 36 31N 1 14E
T'eng Ch'ung 99 25 9N 98 22E
Teng, R. 101 20 30N 98 10E
Tengah □ 103 2 0S 122 0E
Tengah Kepulauan 102 7 5S 118 15E
Tengchow = P'englai 107 37 49N 120 47E
Tengch'uan 108 26 0N 100 4E
Tengch'ung 108 25 2N 98 28E
Tengfeng 106 34 27N 113 2E
Tenggara □ 103 3 0S 122 0E
Tenggol, P. 101 4 48N 103 41E
T'enghsien, Honan, China 109 32 41N 112 5E
T'enghsien, Kwangsi Chuang, China 109 23 23N 110 54E
T'enghsien, Shantung, China 105 35 8N 117 9E
Tengiz, Ozero 76 50 30N 69 0E
Tengko 99 32 30N 98 0E
Tengk'o 108 32 32N 97 35E
Tengk'ou 106 40 18N 106 59E
Tenigerbad 51 46 42N 8 57E
Tenille 157 33 58N 82 50W
Tenindewa 137 28 30S 115 20E
Tenkasi 97 8 55N 77 20E
Tenke, Congo 127 11 22S 26 40E
Tenke, Zaîre 127 10 32S 26 7E
Tenkodogo 121 12 0N 0 10W
Tenna, R. 63 43 12N 13 43E
Tennant Creek 136 19 30S 134 0E
'Tenneco', oilfield 19 54 6N 4 42E
Tennessee □ 155 36 0N 86 30W
Tenneville 47 50 6N 5 32E
Tennsift, Oued 118 32 3N 9 28W
Tenom 102 5 4N 115 38E
Tenosique 165 17 30N 91 24W
Tenri 111 34 46N 135 55E
Tenryū 111 34 52N 137 55E
Tent L. 153 62 25N 107 54W
Tenterden 29 51 4N 0 42E
Tenterfield 139 29 0S 152 0E
Teófilo Otôni 171 17 50S 41 30W
Tepa 120 6 57N 2 30W
Tepalcatepec, R. 164 18 35N 101 59W
Tepao 108 23 21N 106 33E
Tepehuanes 164 25 21N 105 44W
Tepetongo 164 22 28N 103 9W
Tepic 164 21 30N 104 54W
Tepi'ng 107 37 28N 116 67E
Teploklyuchenka 85 42 30N 78 30E
Tepoca, C. 164 29 20N 112 25W
Tequila 164 20 54N 103 47W
Ter Apel 46 52 53N 7 5E
Ter, R. 58 42 0N 2 30E
Téra 121 14 0N 0 57E
Tera, R. 56 41 54N 5 44W
Téramo 63 42 40N 13 40E
Terang 140 38 15S 142 55E
Terawhiti, C. 142 41 16S 174 38E
Terborg 46 51 56N 6 22E
Tercan 92 39 50N 40 30E
Terceira 16 38 43N 27 13W
Tercero, R. 172 32 58S 61 47W
Terdal 96 16 33N 75 9E
Terebovlya 80 49 18N 25 44E
Teregova 70 45 10N 22 16E
Terek-Say 85 41 30N 71 11E
Terembone Cr. 139 30 25S 148 50E
Terengganu □ 101 4 55N 103 0E
Tereshka, R. 81 52 0N 46 36E
Teresina 170 5 2S 42 45W
Terewah L. 139 29 52S 147 35E
Terezinha 174 0 44N 69 27W
Terges, R. 57 37 49N 7 41W
Tergnier 43 49 40N 3 17E
Terhazza 118 23 45N 4 59W
Terheijden 47 51 38N 4 45E
Teriang 101 3 15N 102 26E
Terkezi 117 18 27N 21 40E
Terlizzi 65 41 8N 16 32E
Termas de Chillan 172 36 50S 71 31W
Terme 82 41 11N 37 0E
Termez 85 37 0N 67 15E
Términi Imerese 43 37 59N 13 51E
Términos, Laguna de 165 18 35N 91 30W
Termoli 63 42 0N 15 0E
Termon 38 55 3N 7 50W
Termonfeckin 38 53 47N 6 15W
Tern, oilfield 19 61 17N 0 55E
Ternate 103 0 45N 127 25E
Terneuzen 47 51 20N 3 50E
Terney 77 45 3N 136 37E
Terni 63 42 34N 12 38E
Ternitz 52 47 43N 16 2E
Ternopol 80 49 30N 25 40E
Terowie, N.S.W., Austral. 139 32 27S 147 52E
Terowie, Vic., Austral. 140 33 10S 138 50E
Terra Bella 163 35 58N 119 3W
Terra Nova B. 13 74 50S 164 40E
Terrace 152 54 30N 128 35W
Terrace Bay 150 48 47N 87 10W
Terracina 64 41 17N 13 12E
Terralba 64 39 42N 8 38E
Terranuova 63 43 38N 11 35E
Terrasini Favarotta 64 38 10N 13 4E
Terrasson 44 45 7N 1 19E
Terrebonne B. 159 29 15N 90 28W
Terrecht 118 20 10N 0 10W
Terrell 159 32 44N 96 19W
Terrenceville 151 47 40N 54 44W
Terrick Terrick 138 24 44S 145 5E
Terry 158 46 47N 105 20W
Terryglass 39 53 3N 8 14W
Terryville 162 41 41N 73 1W
Terschelling, I. 46 53 25N 5 20E
Terskey Alatau, Khrebet 85 41 50N 77 0E
Terter, R. 83 40 5N 46 15E
Teruel 58 40 22N 1 8W
Teruel □ 58 40 48N 1 0W
Tervel 67 43 45N 27 28E
Tervola 74 66 6N 24 49E
Teryaweyna L. 140 32 18S 143 22E
Tešanj 66 44 38N 17 59E
Teseney 123 15 5N 36 42E
Tesha, R. 81 55 32N 43 0E
Teshio 112 44 53N 141 44E
Teshio-Gawa, R. 112 44 53N 141 45E
Tešica 66 43 27N 21 45E
Tesiyn Gol, R. 105 50 28N 93 4E
Teslin 147 60 10N 132 43W
Teslin L. 152 60 15N 132 57W
Teslin, R. 152 61 34N 134 35W
Teslió 66 44 37N 17 54E
Teso □ = Eastern □ 126 1 50N 33 45E
Tessalit 121 20 12N 1 0E
Tessaoua 121 13 47N 7 56E
Tessenderlo 47 51 4N 5 5E
Tessier 153 51 48N 107 26W
Tessin 48 54 2N 12 28E
Tessit 121 15 13N 0 18E
Test, R. 28 51 7N 1 30W
Testa del Gargano 65 41 50N 16 10E
Teste, La 44 44 37N 1 8W
Tét 53 47 30N 17 33E
Tetachuck L. 152 53 18N 125 55W
Tetas, Pta. 172 23 31S 70 38W
Tetbury 28 51 37N 2 9W

Tete Tijibadok

Tete 127 16 13S 33 33E
Tete □ 127 15 15S 32 40E
Teterev, R. 80 50 30N 29 30E
Teteringen 47 51 37N 4 49E
Teterow 48 53 45N 12 34E
Teteven 67 42 58N 24 17E
Tethull, R. 152 60 35N 112 12W
Tetiyev 82 49 22N 29 38E
Tetlin 147 63 14N 142 50W
Tetlin Junction 147 63 29N 142 55W
Tetney 33 53 30N 0 1W
Teton, R. 160 47 58N 111 0W
Tétouan 118 35 35N 5 21W
Tetovo 66 42 1N 21 2E
Tettenhall 28 52 35N 2 7W
Tetuán = Tétouan 118 35 30N 5 25W
Tetyukhe 77 44 45N 135 40E
Teuco, R. 172 25 30S 60 25W
Teufen 51 47 24N 9 23E
Teulada 64 38 59N 8 47E
Teulon 153 50 23N 97 16W
Tevere, R. 63 42 30N 12 20E
Teviot, R. 35 55 21N 2 51W
Teviotdale 35 55 25N 2 50W
Teviothead 35 55 19N 2 55W
Tewantin 139 26 27S 153 3E
Tewkesbury 28 51 59N 2 8W
Texada I. 152 49 40N 124 25W
Texarkana, Ark., U.S.A. 159 33 25N 94 0W
Texarkana, Tex., U.S.A. 159 33 25N 94 3W
Texas 139 28 49S 151 15E
Texas □ 159 31 40N 98 30W
Texas City 159 27 20N 95 20W
Texel, I. 46 53 5N 4 50E
Texhoma 159 36 32N 101 47W
Texline 159 36 26N 103 0W
Texoma L. 159 34 0N 96 38W
Teyang 108 31 8N 104 24E
Teykovo 81 56 55N 40 30E
Teynham 29 51 19N 0 50E
Teyr Zebna 90 33 14N 35 23E
Teza, R. 81 56 41N 41 45E
Tezin 94 34 24N 69 30E
Teziutlán 165 19 50N 97 30W
Tezpur 98 26 40N 92 45E
Tezzeron L. 152 54 43N 124 30W
Tha-anne, R. 153 60 31N 94 37W
Tha Deua, Laos 100 17 57N 102 38E
Tha Deua, Laos 100 19 26N 101 50E
Tha Nun 101 8 12N 98 17E
Tha Pia 100 17 48N 100 32E
Tha Rua 100 14 34N 100 44E
Tha Sala 101 8 40N 99 56E
Tha Song Yang 101 17 34N 97 55E
Thaba Putsoa, mt. 129 29 45S 28 0E
Thabana Ntlenyana, Mt. 129 29 30S 29 9E
Thabazimbi 129 24 40S 26 4E
Thabeikkyin 98 22 53N 95 59E
Thai Binh 100 20 27N 106 20E
Thai Muang 101 8 24N 98 16E
Thai Nguyen 100 21 35N 105 46E
Thailand (Siam) ■ 100 16 0N 102 0E
Thakhek 100 17 25N 104 45E
Thakurgaon 98 26 2N 88 28E
Thal 94 33 28N 70 33E
Thal Desert 93 31 0N 71 30E
Thala 119 35 35N 8 40E
Thala La 99 28 25N 97 23E
Thalabarivat 100 13 33N 105 57E
Thalkirch 51 46 39N 9 17E
Thallon 139 28 30S 148 57E
Thalwil 51 47 17N 8 35E
Thame 29 51 44N 0 58W
Thame, R. 29 51 52N 0 47W
Thames 142 37 7S 175 34E
Thames, Firth of 142 37 0S 175 25E
Thames, R., Can. 150 42 20N 82 25W
Thames, R., N.Z. 142 37 32S 175 45E
Thames, R., U.K. 28 51 30N 0 35E
Thames, R., U.S.A. 162 41 18N 72 9W
Thāmit, W. 119 30 51N 16 14E
Than Uyen 100 22 0N 103 54E
Thana 96 19 12N 72 59E
Thanbyuzayat 98 15 58N 97 44E
Thanesar 94 30 1N 76 52E
Thanet, I. of 29 51 21N 1 20E
Thang Binh 101 15 50N 108 20E
Thangoo P.O. 136 18 10S 122 22E
Thangool 138 24 29S 150 35E
Thanh Hoa 100 19 48N 105 46E
Thanh Hung 101 9 55N 105 43E
Thanh Thuy 100 22 55N 104 51E
Thanjavur (Tanjore) 97 10 48N 79 12E
Thanlwin myit, R. 99 20 0N 98 0E
Thann 43 47 48N 7 5E
Thaon 43 48 15N 6 25E
Thap Sakae 101 11 30N 99 37E
Thap Than 100 15 27N 99 54E
Thar (Great Indian) Desert 94 28 25N 72 0E
Tharad 94 24 30N 71 30E
Thargomindah 139 27 58S 143 46E
Tharrawaddy 98 17 38N 95 48E
Tharrawaw 98 17 41N 95 28E
Tharthār, Bahr ath 92 34 0N 43 0E
Thasopoúla, I. 68 40 49N 24 45E
Thásos 68 40 50N 24 50E
Thásos, I. 68 40 40N 24 40E
That Khe 100 22 16N 106 28E
Thatcham 28 51 24N 1 17W
Thatcher, Ariz., U.S.A. 161 32 54N 109 46W
Thatcher, Colo., U.S.A. 161 37 38N 104 6W
Thaton 98 16 55N 97 22E
Thau, Étang de 44 43 23N 3 36E
Thaungdut 98 24 30N 94 40E
Thaxted 29 51 57N 0 20E
Thayer 159 36 34N 91 34W
Thayetmyo 98 19 20N 95 18E
Thayngen 51 47 49N 8 43E
Thazi 99 21 0N 96 5E
The Alberga, R. 139 27 6S 135 33E
The Bight 167 24 19N 75 24W
The Corrong 139 36 0S 139 30E
The Dalles 160 45 40N 121 11W
The Diamantina 139 26 45S 139 30E
The English Company's Is. 138 11 50S 136 32E
The Entrance 141 33 21S 151 30E
The Four Archers 138 15 31S 135 22E
The Frome, R. 139 29 8S 137 54E
The Granites 136 20 35S 130 21E
The Great Divide 141 35 0S 149 17E
The Grenadines, Is. 167 12 30N 61 30W
The Hague (s'Gravenhage) 47 52 7N 7 14E
The Hamilton, R. 139 26 40S 135 19E
The Johnston Lakes 137 32 25S 120 30E
The Lake 167 21 5N 73 34W
The Loup 38 54 42N 6 32W
The Macumba, R. 139 27 52S 137 12E
The Neales, R. 139 28 8S 136 47E
The Oaks 141 34 3S 150 34E
The Officer, R. 137 27 46S 129 46E
The Pas 153 53 45N 101 15W
The Range 127 19 2S 31 2E
The Rock 141 35 15S 147 2E
The Salt Lake 139 30 6S 142 8E
The Stevenson, R. 139 27 6S 135 33E
The Thumbs, Mts. 143 43 35S 170 40E
The Warburton, R. 139 28 4S 137 28E
Theale 28 51 26N 1 5W
Thebes 122 25 40N 32 35E
Thedford 158 41 59N 100 31W
Theebine 139 25 57S 152 34E
Thekulthili L. 153 61 3N 110 0W
Thelma, oilfield 19 58 25N 1 18E
Thelon, R. 153 62 35N 104 3W
Thénezay 42 46 44N 0 2W
Thenon 44 45 9N 1 4E
Theodore 138 24 55S 150 3E
Thepha 101 6 52N 100 58E
Thérain, R. 43 49 15N 2 27E
Thermaïkos Kólpos 68 40 15N 22 45E
Thermopílai P. 69 38 48N 22 45E
Thermopolis 160 43 14N 108 10W
Thesprotía □ 68 39 27N 20 22E
Thessalía □ 68 39 30N 22 0E
Thessalon 150 46 20N 83 30W
Thessaloníki 68 40 38N 23 0E
Thessaloníki □ 68 40 45N 23 0E
Thessaly = Thessalía 68 39 30N 22 0E
Thetford 29 52 25N 0 44E
Thetford Mines 151 46 8N 71 18W
Theun, R. 100 18 19N 104 0E
Theunissen 128 28 26S 26 43E
Theux 47 50 32N 5 49E
Thevenard 139 32 9S 133 38E
Thiámis, R. 68 39 34N 20 18E
Thiberville 42 49 8N 0 27E
Thicket Portage 153 55 19N 97 42W
Thief River Falls 159 48 15N 96 10W
Thiel 120 14 55N 15 5W
Thiene 63 45 42N 11 29E
Thierache 43 49 51N 3 45E
Thiers 44 45 52N 3 33E
Thies 120 14 50N 16 51W
Thiet 123 7 37N 28 49E
Thika 126 1 1S 37 5E
Thika □ 126 1 1S 37 5E
Thille-Boubacar 120 16 31N 15 5W
Thillot, Le 43 47 53N 6 46E
Thimphu (Tashi Chho Dzong) 98 27 31N 89 45E
þingvallavatn 74 64 11N 21 9W
Thionville 43 49 20N 6 10E
Thírá 69 36 23N 25 27E
Thirasiá, I. 69 36 26N 25 21E
Thirlmere, L. 32 54 32N 3 4W
Thirsk 33 54 15N 1 20W
Thisted 75 56 58N 8 40E
Thistle I. 140 35 0S 136 8E
Thistle, oilfield 19 61 20N 1 35E
Thitgy 98 18 15N 96 13E
Thitpokpin 98 19 24N 96 1E
Thiu Khao Phetchabun 101 16 20N 100 55E
Thívai 69 38 19N 23 19E
Thiviers 44 45 25N 0 54E
Thizy 45 46 2N 4 18E
þjorsa 74 63 47N 20 48W
Thlewiaza, R., Man., Can. 153 59 43N 100 5W
Thlewiaza, R., N.W.T., Can. 153 60 29N 94 40W
Thmar Puok 100 13 57N 103 4E
Tho Vinh 100 19 16N 105 42E
Thoa, R. 153 60 31N 109 47W
Thoen 100 17 36N 99 12E
Thoeng 100 19 41N 100 12E
Thoissey 45 46 12N 4 48E
Tholdi 95 35 5N 76 6E
Tholen 47 51 32N 4 13E
Thomas, Okla., U.S.A. 159 35 48N 98 48W
Thomas, W. Va., U.S.A. 156 39 10N 79 30W
Thomas, L. 139 26 4S 137 58E
Thomas Street 38 53 27N 8 15W
Thomastown 39 52 32N 7 10W
Thomasville, Ala., U.S.A. 157 31 55N 87 42W
Thomasville, Fla., U.S.A. 157 30 50N 84 0W
Thomasville, N.C., U.S.A. 157 35 5N 80 4W
Thommen 47 50 14N 6 5E
Thompson, Can. 153 55 45N 97 52W
Thompson, U.S.A. 162 41 52N 75 31W
Thompson Falls 160 47 37N 115 26W
Thompson Landing 153 62 56N 110 40W
Thompson, R., Can. 152 50 15N 121 24W
Thompson, R., U.S.A. 158 39 46N 93 37W
Thompsons 161 39 0N 109 50W
Thompsonville 162 42 0N 72 37W
Thomson, R. 138 25 11S 142 53E
Thomson's Falls = Nyahururu Falls 126 0 2N 36 27E
Thon Buri 100 13 43N 100 29E
Thonburi 101 13 50N 100 36E
Thônes 45 45 54N 6 18E
Thongwa 98 16 45N 96 33E
Thonon-les-Bains 45 46 22N 6 29E
Thonze 98 17 38N 95 47E
Thorez 83 48 4N 38 34E
þorlákshöfn 74 63 51N 21 22W
Thornaby on Tees 33 54 36N 1 19W
Thornborough 138 16 54S 145 2E
Thornbury, N.Z. 143 46 17S 168 9E
Thornbury, U.K. 28 51 36N 2 31W
Thorndon 29 52 16N 1 8E
Thorne, U.K. 33 53 36N 0 56W
Thorne, U.S.A. 163 38 36N 118 34W
Thorne Glacier 13 87 30N 150 0E
Thorney 29 52 37N 0 8W
Thornham 29 52 59N 0 35E
Thornhill 35 55 15N 3 46W
Thornthwaite 32 54 36N 3 13W
Thornton-Beresfield 141 32 50S 151 40E
Thornton Celveleys 32 53 52N 3 1W
Thornton Dale 33 54 14N 0 41W
Thorpe 29 52 38N 1 20E
Thorpe le Soken 29 51 50N 1 11E
Thouarcé 43 47 17N 0 30W
Thouin, C. 136 20 20S 118 10E
Thousand Oakes 163 34 10N 118 50W
Thrace = Thráki 68 41 10N 25 30E
Thráki 68 41 9N 25 30E
Thrakikón Pélagos 68 40 30N 25 0E
Thrapston 29 52 24N 0 32W
Three Bridges 29 51 7N 0 9W
Three Forks 160 45 5N 111 40W
Three Hills 152 51 43N 113 15W
Three Hummock I. 138 40 25S 144 55E
Three Kings Is. 142 34 10S 172 10E
Three Lakes 158 45 41N 89 10W
Three Pagodas P. 100 15 16N 98 23E
Three Points, C. 120 4 42N 2 6W
Three Rivers, Austral. 137 25 10S 119 5E
Three Rivers, Calif., U.S.A. 163 36 26N 118 54W
Three Rivers, Tex., U.S.A. 159 28 30N 98 10W
Three Sisters, Mt. 160 44 10N 121 52W
Threlkeld 32 54 37N 3 2W
Threshfield 32 54 5N 2 2W
þ ó risvatn 74 64 50N 19 26W
Throssell, L. 137 27 27S 124 16E
Throssell Ra. 136 17 24S 126 4E
þ ó rshöfn 74 66 12N 15 20W
Thrumster 37 58 24N 3 8W
Thuan Moa 101 8 58N 105 30E
Thubun Lakes 153 61 30N 112 0W
Thueyts 45 44 41N 4 9E
Thuillies 47 50 18N 4 20E
Thuin 47 50 20N 4 17E
Thuir 44 42 38N 2 45E
Thule 12 77 30N 69 0W
Thun 50 46 45N 7 38E
Thundelarra 137 28 53S 117 7E
Thunder B. 156 45 0N 83 20W
Thunder Bay 150 48 20N 89 0W
Thunder River 152 52 13N 119 20W
Thundulda 137 32 15S 126 3E
Thunersee 50 46 43N 7 39E
Thung Song 101 8 10N 99 40E
Thunkar 98 27 55N 91 0E
Thuong Tra 100 16 2N 107 42E
Thur, R. 51 47 32N 9 10E
Thurgau □ 51 47 34N 9 10E
Thüringer Wald 48 50 35N 11 0E
Thurlby 29 52 45N 0 21W
Thurles 39 52 40N 7 53W
Thurloo Downs 139 29 15S 143 30E
Thurmaston 28 52 40N 1 8W
Thurmont 162 39 37N 77 25W
Thurn P. 49 47 20N 12 15E
Thursby 32 54 40N 3 3W
Thursday I. 138 10 30S 142 3E
Thurso, Can. 150 45 36N 75 15W
Thurso, U.K. 37 58 34N 3 31W
Thurso, R. 37 58 36N 3 30W
Thurston I. 13 72 0S 100 0W
Thury-Harcourt 42 49 0N 0 30W
Thusis 51 46 42N 9 26E
Thutade L. 152 57 0N 126 55W
Thuy, Le 100 17 14N 106 49E
Thylungra 139 26 4S 143 28E
Thyolo 127 16 7S 35 5E
Thysville = Mbanza Ngungu 124 5 12S 14 53E
Ti-n-Amzi, O. 121 17 35N 4 20E
Ti-n-Barraouene, O. 121 18 40N 4 5E
Ti-n-Emensan 118 22 59N 4 45E
Ti-n-Geloulet 118 25 58N 4 2E
Ti-n-Medjerdam, O. 118 25 45N 1 30W
Ti-n-Tarabine, O. 119 21 37N 7 11E
Ti-n-Zaouatène 118 48 55S 77 9W
Tia 141 31 10S 151 50E
Tiahualilo 164 26 20N 103 30W
Tianguá 170 3 44S 40 59W
Tiankoura 120 10 47N 3 17W
Tiaret (Tagdent) 118 35 28N 1 21E
Tiarra 141 32 46S 145 1E
Tiassalé 120 5 58N 4 57W
Tibagi 173 24 30S 50 24W
Tibagi, R. 173 22 47S 51 1W
Tibari 123 5 2N 31 48E
Tibati 121 6 22N 12 30E
Tiber = Tevere, R. 63 42 30N 12 20E
Tiber Res. 160 48 20N 111 15W
Tiberias 90 32 47N 35 32E
Tiberias, L. = Kinneret, Yam 90 32 49N 35 36E
Tibesti 119 21 0N 17 30E
Tibet 99 32 30N 86 0E
Tibet □ 105 32 30N 86 0E
Tibiri 121 13 34N 7 4E
Tibleș, mt. 70 47 32N 24 15E
Tibleș, Mţii 70 47 41N 24 6E
Tibnīn 90 33 12N 35 24E
Tibooburra 139 29 26S 142 1E
Tibro 73 58 28N 14 10E
Tibugá, Golfo de 174 5 45N 77 20W
Tiburón, I. 164 29 0N 112 30W
Ticehurst 29 51 2N 0 23E
Tichit 120 18 35N 9 20W
Ticino □ 51 46 20N 8 45E
Ticino, R. 62 45 23N 8 47E
Tickhill 33 53 25N 1 8W
Ticonderoga 162 43 50N 73 28W
Ticul 165 20 20N 89 50W
Tidaholm 73 58 12N 13 55E
Tiddim 98 23 20N 93 45E
Tideridjaouine, Adrar 118 23 0N 2 15E
Tideswell 33 53 17N 1 46W
Tidikelt 118 26 58N 1 30E
Tidjikdja 120 18 4N 11 35W
Tidore 103 0 40N 127 25E
Tidra, I. 120 19 45N 16 20W
Tiébélé 121 11 6N 0 59W
Tiébissou 120 7 9N 5 18W
Tiéboro 119 21 20N 17 7E
Tiefencastel 51 46 40N 9 33E
Tiego 120 12 6N 2 38E
T'iehling 107 42 17N 123 50E
Tiel 46 51 53N 5 26E
Tielt 47 51 0N 3 20E
Tien Shan 85 42 0N 80 0E
Tien Yen 100 21 20N 107 24E
T'iench'ang 107 32 41N 118 59E
T'ienchen 106 40 30N 114 6E
Tiench'eng 109 21 31N 111 18E
T'ienching 107 39 10N 117 15E
T'ienchu 108 26 55N 109 12E
T'iench'üan 108 30 4N 102 50E
T'ienchuangt'ai 107 40 49N 122 6E
Tienen 47 50 48N 4 57E
T'ienho 108 24 47N 108 42E
T'ienhsi 108 24 26N 106 5E
Tiénigbé 120 8 11N 5 43W
Tienkianghsien 69 30 25N 107 30E
T'ienlin 108 24 19N 106 15E
T'ienmen 109 30 37N 113 10E
T'ieno 108 25 9N 106 57E
Tienpai 109 21 30N 111 1E
T'ienshui 105 34 35N 105 15E
T'ient'ai 109 29 9N 121 2E
Tientsin = T'ienching 105 39 10N 117 15E
T'ientung 108 23 39N 107 8E
T'ienyang 108 23 40N 106 44E
Tierp 72 60 20N 17 30E
Tierra Alta 174 8 11N 76 4W
Tierra Amarilla 172 27 28S 70 18W
Tierra Colorada 165 17 10N 99 35W
Tierra de Barros 57 38 40N 6 30W
Tierra de Campos 56 42 10N 4 50W
Tierra del Fuego, I. Gr. de 176 54 0S 69 0W
Tiétar, R. 56 39 55N 5 50W
Tieté, R. 171 20 40S 51 35W
Tieyon 139 26 12S 133 52E
Tiffin 156 41 8N 83 10W
Tifi 123 6 12N 36 55E
Tiflèt 118 33 54N 6 20W
Tiflis = Tbilisi 83 41 50N 44 50E
Tifrah 90 31 19N 34 42E
Tifton 157 31 28N 83 32W
Tifu 103 3 39S 126 18E
Tigalda I. 147 54 9N 165 0W
Tighnabruaich 34 55 55N 5 13W
Tigil 77 58 0N 158 10E
Tignish 151 46 58N 64 2W
Tigre □ 123 13 35N 39 15E
Tigre, R. 174 3 30S 74 58W
Tigu 99 29 48N 91 38E
Tiguentourine 119 28 8N 8 58E
Tiguila 121 14 44N 1 50W
Tigveni 70 45 10N 24 31E
Tigyaing 98 23 45N 96 10E
Tîh, Gebel el 122 29 32N 33 26E
Tihodaine, Dunes de 119 25 15N 7 15E
Tījī 119 32 0N 11 18E
Tijiamis 103 7 16S 108 29E
Tijibadok 103 6 53S 106 47E

Tijirit, O Tolox

Tijirit, O. 120 19 30N 6 15W
Tijuana 164 32 30N 117 3W
Tikal 166 17 2N 89 35W
Tikamgarh 95 24 44N 78 57E
Tikan 138 5 58S 149 2E
Tikhoretsk 83 45 56N 40 5E
Tikhvin 80 59 35N 33 30E
Tikkadouine, Adrar 118 24 28N 1 30E
Tiko 121 4 4N 9 20E
Tikrit 92 34 35N 43 37E
Tiksi 77 71 50N 129 0E
Tilamuta 103 0 40N 122 15E
Tilburg 47 51 31N 5 6E
Tilbury, Can. 150 42 17N 84 23W
Tilbury, U.K. 29 51 27N 0 24E
Tilcara 172 23 30S 65 23W
Tilden 158 42 3N 97 45W
Tilemsès 121 15 37N 4 44E
Tilemsi, Vallée du 121 17 42N 0 15E
Tilghman 162 38 42N 76 20W
Tilhar 95 28 0N 79 45E
Tilia, O. 118 27 32N 0 55E
Tilichiki 77 61 0N 166 5E
Tiligul, R. 82 47 35N 30 30E
Tililane 118 27 49N 0 6W
Tilin 98 21 41N 94 6E
Tilissos 69 38 15N 25 0E
Till, R. 35 55 35N 2 3W
Tillabéri 121 14 7N 1 28E
Tillamook 160 45 29N 123 55W
Tillberga 72 59 42N 16 39E
Tilley 152 50 28N 111 38W
Tillia 121 16 8N 4 47E
Tillicoultry 35 56 9N 3 44W
Tillsonburg 150 42 53N 80 44W
Tilmanstone 29 51 13N 1 18E
Tílos, I. 69 36 27N 27 27E
Tilpa 139 30 57S 144 24E
Tilrhemt 118 33 9N 3 22E
Tilsit = Sovetsk 80 55 6N 21 50E
Tilt, R. 37 56 50N 3 50W
Tilton 162 43 25N 71 36W
Timahoe 39 52 59N 7 12W
Timanskiy Kryazh 78 65 58N 50 5E
Timaru 143 44 23S 171 14E
Timashevo 84 53 22N 51 9E
Timashevsk 83 45 35N 39 0E
Timau 126 0 4N 37 15E
Timbákion 69 35 4N 24 45E
Timbaúba 170 7 31S 35 19W
Timbédra 120 16 17N 8 16W
Timber L. 158 45 29N 101 0W
Timber Mtn. 163 37 6N 116 28W
Timbío 174 2 20N 76 40W
Timbiqui 174 2 46N 77 42W
Timboon 140 38 30S 142 58E
Timbuktu = Tombouctou 120 16 50N 3 0W
Timdjaouine 118 21 47N 4 30E
Timétrine Montagnes 121 19 25N 1 0W
Timfi Óros 68 39 59N 20 45E
Timfristós, Óros 69 38 57N 21 50E
Timhadite 118 33 15N 5 4W
Timimoun 118 29 14N 0 16E
Timimoun, Sebkha de 118 28 50N 0 46E
Timiris, C. 120 19 15N 16 30W
Timiş □ 66 45 40N 21 30E
Timiş, R. 70 45 30N 21 0E
Timişoara 66 45 43N 21 15E
Timmins 150 48 28N 81 25W
Timmoudi 118 29 20N 1 8W
Timok, R. 66 44 10N 22 40E
Timoleague 39 51 40N 8 51W
Timolin 39 52 59N 6 49W
Timon 170 5 8S 42 52W
Timor □ 103 8 0S 126 30E
Timor, I. 103 9 0S 125 0E
Timor Sea 136 10 0S 127 0E
Timur □ 103 9 0S 125 0E
Tin Alkoum 119 24 30N 10 17E
Tin Gornai 121 16 38N 0 38W
Tin Mtn. 163 36 54N 117 28W
Tîna, Khalîg el 122 31 20N 32 42E
Tinaca Pt. 103 5 30N 125 25E
Tinaco 174 9 42N 68 26W
Tinafak, O. 119 27 10N 7 0W
Tinahely 39 52 48N 6 28W
Tinambacan 103 12 5N 124 32E
Tinapagee 139 29 25S 144 15E
Tinaquillo 174 9 55N 68 18W
Tinaroo Falls 138 17 5S 145 4E
Tinca 70 46 46N 21 58E
Tinchebray 42 48 47N 0 45W
Tindivanam 97 12 15N 79 35E
Tindouf 118 27 50N 8 4W
Tindzhe Dzong 95 28 20N 88 8E
Tineo 56 43 21N 6 27W
Tinerhir 118 31 29N 5 31W
Tinfouchi 118 28 58N 5 54W
T'ing Chiang, R. 109 24 24N 116 35E
Tingan 100 19 42N 110 18E
Tingch'u, R. 108 28 20N 99 12E
Tingewick 28 51 59N 1 4W
Tinggi, Pulau, Is. 101 2 18N 104 7E
Tinghai 109 30 0N 122 10E
Tinghsi 106 35 33N 104 32E
Tinghsiang 106 38 32N 112 59E
Tinghsien 106 38 30N 115 0E
Tingkawk Sakun 98 26 4N 96 44E
Tingk'ouchen 106 39 48N 106 36E
Tinglev 73 54 57N 9 13E
Tingnan 109 24 47N 115 2E
Tingo María 174 9 10S 76 0W
Tingpien 106 37 36N 107 38E
Tingshan 109 31 16N 119 51E
Tingsryd 73 56 31N 15 0E
Tingt'ao 106 35 4N 115 34E
Tingvalla 73 58 47N 12 2E
Tingyüan 109 32 32N 117 41E
Tinh Bien 101 10 36N 104 57E
Tinharé, I. de 171 13 30S 38 58W
Tinié 121 14 17N 1 30W
Tinioulig, Sebkra 118 22 30N 6 45W
Tinjoub 118 29 45N 5 40W
Tinkurrin 137 32 59S 117 46E
Tinnia 172 27 0S 62 45W
Tinnoset 71 59 45N 9 3E
Tinnsjø 71 59 55N 8 54E
Tinogasta 172 28 0S 67 40W
Tínos 69 37 33N 25 8E
Tiñoso, C. 59 37 32N 1 6W
Tinsukia 98 27 29N 95 26E
Tintagel 30 50 40N 4 45W
Tintagel Hd. 30 50 40N 4 46W
Tintern 31 51 42N 2 41W
Tintern Abbey 39 52 14N 6 50W
Tintigny 47 49 41N 5 31E
Tintina 172 27 2S 62 45W
Tintinara 140 35 48S 140 2E
Tinto, R. 57 37 30N 5 33W
Tinui 142 40 52S 176 5E
Tinwald 143 43 55S 171 43E
Tioga 162 41 54N 77 9W
Tioman, I. 101 2 50N 104 10E
Tioman, Pulau, Is. 101 2 50N 104 10E
Tionaga 150 48 0N 82 0W
Tione di Trento 62 46 3N 10 44E
Tior 123 6 26N 31 11E
Tioulilin 118 27 1N 0 2W
Tipongpani 99 27 20N 95 55E
Tipperary 39 52 28N 8 10W
Tipperary □ 39 52 37N 7 55W
Tipton, U.K. 28 52 32N 2 4W
Tipton, Calif., U.S.A. 163 36 3N 119 19W
Tipton, Ind., U.S.A. 156 40 17N 86 30W
Tipton, Iowa, U.S.A. 158 41 45N 91 12W
Tiptonville 159 36 22N 89 30W
Tiptree 29 51 48N 0 46E
Tiptur 97 13 15N 76 26E
Tira 90 32 14N 34 56E
Tiracambu, Serra do 170 3 15S 46 30W
Tirahart, O. 118 23 55N 2 0W
Tiran 93 32 45N 51 0E
Tirân 122 27 56N 34 35E
Tirana 68 41 18N 19 49E
Tirana-Durrësi □ 68 41 35N 20 0E
Tirano 62 46 13N 10 11E
Tirarer, Mont 121 19 35N 1 10W
Tiraspol 82 46 55N 29 35E
Tirat Carmel 90 32 46N 34 58E
Tirat Tsevi 90 32 26N 35 31E
Tirat Yehuda 90 32 1N 34 56E
Tiratimine 118 25 56N 3 37E
Tirdout 121 16 7N 1 5W
Tire 92 38 5N 27 50E
Tirebolu 92 40 58N 38 45E
Tiree, I. 34 56 31N 6 55W
Tiree, Passage of 34 56 30N 6 30W
Tîrgoviste 70 44 55N 25 27E
Tîrgu Frumos 70 47 12N 27 2E
Tîrgu-Jiu 70 45 5N 23 19E
Tîrgu Mureş 70 46 31N 24 38E
Tîrgu Neamţ 70 47 12N 26 25E
Tîrgu Ocna 70 46 16N 26 39E
Tîrgu Secuiesc 70 46 0N 26 10E
Tirich Mir Mt. 93 36 15N 71 35E
Tiriola 65 38 57N 16 32E
Tiririca, Serra da 171 17 6S 47 6W
Tirlyanskiy 84 54 14N 58 35E
Tirna, R. 96 18 5N 76 30E
Tîrnava = Botoroaga 70 44 8N 25 32E
Tîrnava Mare, R. 70 46 15N 24 30E
Tîrnava Mica, R. 70 46 17N 24 30E
Tírnavos 68 39 45N 22 18E
Tîrnova 70 45 23N 22 1E
Tîrnăveni 70 46 19N 24 13E
Tirodi 96 21 35N 79 35E
Tirol □ 52 47 3N 10 43E
Tiros 171 19 0S 45 58W
Tirschenreuth 49 49 51N 12 20E
Tirso, L. 64 40 8N 8 56E
Tirso, R. 64 40 33N 9 12E
Tirstrup 73 56 18N 10 42E
Tirua 142 38 25S 174 40E
Tiruchchirappalli 97 10 45N 78 45E
Tiruchendur 97 8 30N 78 11E
Tiruchengodu 97 11 23N 77 56E
Tirumangalam 97 9 49N 77 58E
Tirunelveli (Tinnevelly) 97 8 45N 77 45E
Tirupati 97 13 45N 79 30E
Tiruppattur 97 12 30N 78 30E
Tiruppur 97 11 12N 77 22E
Tiruturaipundi 97 10 32N 79 41E
Tiruvadaimarudur 97 11 2N 79 27E
Tiruvallar 97 13 9N 79 57E
Tiruvannamalai 97 12 10N 79 12E
Tiruvarur (Negapatam) 97 10 46N 79 38E
Tiruvatipuram 97 12 39N 79 33E
Tiruvottiyur 97 13 10N 80 22E
Tisa, R. 66 45 30N 20 20E
Tisdale 153 52 50N 104 0W
Tiseirhatène, Mares de 118 22 51N 9 30W
Tishomingo 159 34 14N 96 38W
Tisjön 72 60 56N 13 0E
Tisnaren 72 58 58N 15 56E
Tisno 63 44 45N 15 41E
Tišnov 53 49 21N 16 25E
Tisovec 53 48 41N 19 56E
Tissemsilt 118 35 35N 1 50E
Tissit, O. 119 27 28N 9 58W
Tissø 73 55 35N 11 18E
Tista, R. 98 25 23N 89 43E
Tisted 73 56 58N 8 40E
Tisza, R. 53 47 38N 20 44E
Tiszaföldvár 53 47 0N 20 14E
Tiszafüred 53 47 38N 20 50E
Tiszalök 53 48 0N 21 10E
Tiszavasvári 53 47 58N 21 18E
Tit, Alg. 118 27 0N 1 37E
Tit, Alg. 119 23 0N 5 10E
Tit-Ary 77 71 50N 126 30E
Titaguas 58 39 53N 1 6W
Titahi Bay 142 41 6S 174 50E
Titai Damer 123 16 43N 37 25E
Titchfield 28 50 51N 1 13W
Titel 66 45 29N 20 18E
Tithwal 95 34 21N 73 50E
Titicaca, L. 174 15 30S 69 30W
Titilagarh 96 20 15N 83 5E
Tititira Head 98 43 38S 169 26E
Titiwa 121 12 14N 12 53E
Titlis 51 46 46N 8 27E
Titograd 66 42 30N 19 19E
Titov Veles 66 41 46N 21 47E
Titova Korenica 63 44 45N 15 41E
Titovo Uzice 66 43 55N 19 50E
Titule 126 3 15N 25 31E
Titumate 174 8 19N 77 5W
Titusville 156 41 35N 79 39W
Tiumpan Hd. 36 58 15N 6 10W
Tivaouane 120 14 56N 16 45W
Tivat 66 42 28N 18 43E
Tiveden 73 58 50N 14 30E
Tiverton 30 50 54N 3 30W
Tivoli 63 41 58N 12 45E
Tiwi 93 22 45N 59 12E
Tiyo 123 14 41N 40 57E
Tizga 118 32 1N 5 9W
Tizi n'Isly 118 32 28N 5 47W
Tizi Ouzou 119 36 42N 4 3E
Tizmín 165 21 0N 88 1W
Tiznados, R. 174 8 50N 67 50W
Tiznit 118 29 48N 9 45W
Tjalang 103 4 30N 95 43E
Tjangkuang, Tg. 102 7 0S 105 0E
Tjareme, G. 103 6 55S 108 27E
Tjeggelvas 74 66 37N 17 45E
Tjepu 103 7 12S 111 31E
Tjeukemeer 46 52 53N 5 48E
Tjiandjur 103 6 51S 107 7E
Tjibatu 103 7 8S 107 59E
Tjikadjang 103 7 25S 107 48E
Tjimahi 103 6 53S 107 33E
Tjirebon = Cirebon 103 6 45S 108 32E
Tjöllong 71 59 6N 10 3E
Tjöme 71 59 8N 10 26E
Tjonger Kanaal 46 52 52N 6 52E
Tjörn 73 58 0N 11 35E
Tjörnes 74 66 12N 17 9W
Tjuls 73 57 30N 18 15E
Tjurup 102 4 26S 102 13E
Tkibuli 83 42 26N 43 0E
Tkvarcheli 83 42 47N 41 52E
Tlacolula 165 16 57N 96 29W
Tlacotalpán 165 18 37N 95 40W
Tlaquepaque 164 20 39N 103 19W
Tlaxcala 165 19 20N 98 14W
Tlaxcala □ 165 19 30N 98 20W
Tlaxiaco 165 17 10N 97 40W
Tlell 152 53 34N 131 56W
Tlemcen 118 34 52N 1 15W
Tleta di Sidi Bouguedra 118 32 16N 9 58W
Tleta Sidi Bouguedra 118 32 16N 9 59W
Tlumach 80 48 46N 25 0E
Tłuszcz 54 52 25N 21 25E
Tlyarata 83 42 9N 46 26E
Tmassah 119 26 19N 15 51E
Tmisan 119 27 23N 13 30E
To Bong 100 12 45N 109 16E
T'o Chiang, R. 108 28 56N 105 33E
To-Shima 111 34 31N 139 17E
Toad, R. 152 59 25N 124 57W
Toay 172 36 50S 64 30W
Toba 111 34 30N 136 45E
Toba Kakar 94 31 30N 69 0E
Toba, L. 102 2 40N 98 50E
Toba Tek Singh 94 30 55N 72 25E
Tobago, I. 167 11 10N 60 30W
Tobarra 59 38 35N 1 41W
Tobelo 103 1 25N 127 56E
Tobercurry 38 54 3N 8 43W
Tobermore 38 54 49N 6 43W
Tobermorey 138 22 12S 138 0E
Tobermory, Can. 150 45 12N 81 40W
Tobermory, U.K. 34 56 37N 6 4W
Tobin, L. 136 21 45S 125 49E
Tobin L. 153 53 35N 103 30W
Toboali 102 3 0S 106 25E
Tobol 84 52 40N 62 39E
Tobol, R. 84 58 10N 68 12E
Toboli 103 0 38S 120 12E
Tobolsk 84 58 0N 68 10E
Tobruk = Tubruq 117 32 7N 23 55E
Tobyhanna 162 41 10N 75 15W
Tocantínia 170 9 33S 48 22W
Tocantinópolis 170 6 20S 47 25W
Tocantins, R. 170 14 30S 49 0W
Tocca 157 34 6N 83 17W
Toce, R. 62 46 5N 8 29E
Tochigi 111 36 25N 139 45E
Tochigi-ken □ 111 36 45N 139 45E
Tocina 57 37 37N 5 44W
Toconao 172 34 35N 83 19W
Toconhão, Serra do 171 14 30S 47 46W
Tocópero 174 11 30N 69 16W
Tocopilla 172 22 5S 70 10W
Tocumwal 141 35 45S 145 31E
Tocuyo, R. 174 10 50N 69 0W
Todd, R. 138 24 52S 135 48E
Toddington 29 51 57N 0 31W
Todeli 103 1 38S 124 34E
Todenyang 126 4 35N 35 56E
Todi 63 42 47N 12 24E
Tödi 51 46 48N 8 55E
Todjo 103 1 20S 121 15E
Todmorden 32 53 43N 2 7W
Todos os Santos, Baía de 171 12 48S 38 38W
Todos Santos 164 23 27N 110 13W
Todos Santos, Bahia de 164 31 48N 116 42W
Todtnau 49 47 50N 7 56E
Toe Hd., Ireland 39 51 29N 9 13W
Toe Hd., U.K. 36 57 50N 7 10W
Toecé 121 11 50N 1 16W
Toetoes B. 143 46 42S 168 41E
Tofield 152 53 25N 112 40W
Tofino 152 49 11N 125 55W
Töfsingdalems National Park 72 62 15N 12 44E
Tofta 73 57 11N 12 20E
Toftlund 73 55 11N 9 2E
Tōgane 111 35 33N 140 22E
Togba 120 17 26N 10 25W
Toggenburg 51 47 16N 9 9E
Togian, Kepulauan 103 0 20S 121 50E
Togliatti 81 53 37N 49 18E
Togo ■ 121 6 15N 1 35E
Toguzak, R. 84 54 3N 62 44E
Tōhoku □ 112 39 50N 141 45E
Toi 111 34 54N 134 47E
Toinya 123 6 17N 29 46E
Toiyabe Dome 163 38 51N 117 22W
Toiyabe, Ra. 163 39 10N 117 10W
Tōjō 110 34 53N 133 16E
Tok, R. 84 52 46N 52 22E
Tokaanu 142 38 58S 175 46E
Tokachi, R. 112 42 44N 143 42E
Tokaj 53 48 8N 21 27E
Tokala, G. 103 1 30S 121 40E
Tokanui 143 46 34S 168 56E
Tokarahi 143 44 56S 170 39E
Tokat 92 40 22N 36 35E
Tŏkchŏn 107 39 45N 126 18E
Tokelau Is. 130 9 0S 172 0W
Toki 111 35 18N 137 8E
Tokmak, Kirgizia, U.S.S.R. 84 42 55N 75 45E
Tokmak, Ukraine, U.S.S.R. 82 47 16N 35 42E
Toko Ra. 138 23 5S 138 20E
Tokomaru Bay 142 38 8S 178 22E
Tokombere 121 11 18N 3 30E
Tokomlós 53 46 24N 20 45E
Tokoname 111 34 53N 136 51E
Tokong 101 5 27N 100 23E
Tokoroa 142 38 20S 175 50E
Tokorozawa 111 35 47N 139 28E
T'ok'ot'o 106 40 15N 111 12E
Toktogul 85 41 50N 72 50E
Tokuii 110 34 11N 131 42E
Tokule 123 14 54N 38 26E
Tokunoshima 112 27 56N 128 55E
Tokushima 110 34 4N 134 34E
Tokushima-ken □ 110 35 50N 134 30E
Tokuyama 110 34 0N 131 50E
Tōkyō 111 35 45N 139 45E
Tōkyō-to □ 111 35 40N 139 30E
Tōkyō-Wan 111 35 25N 139 47E
Tolaerh 105 35 8N 81 33E
Tolaga Bay 142 38 21S 178 20E
Tolageak 147 70 2N 162 50W
Tolbukhin 67 43 37N 27 49E
Toledo, Spain 56 39 50N 4 2W
Toledo, Ohio, U.S.A. 156 41 37N 83 33W
Toledo, Oreg., U.S.A. 160 44 40N 123 59W
Toledo, Wash., U.S.A. 160 42 29N 122 58W
Toledo, Montes de 57 39 33N 4 20W
Tolentino 63 43 12N 13 17E
Tolfino 152 49 6N 125 54W
Tolga, Alg. 119 34 46N 5 22E
Tolga, Norway 71 62 26N 11 1E
Tolima □ 174 3 45N 75 15W
Tolima, Vol. 174 4 40N 75 19W
Tolitoli 103 1 5N 120 50E
Tolkamer 46 51 52N 6 6E
Tolkmicko 54 54 19N 19 31E
Tollarp 73 55 55N 13 58E
Tollesbury 29 51 46N 0 51E
Tolleson 161 33 29N 112 10W
Tollhouse 163 37 1N 119 24W
Tolmachevo 80 58 56N 29 57E
Tolmezzo 63 46 23N 13 0E
Tolmino 63 46 11N 13 45E
Tolna 53 46 25N 18 48E
Tolna □ 53 46 30N 18 30E
Tolne 73 57 28N 10 20E
Tolo 124 2 50S 18 40E
Tolo, Teluk 103 2 20S 122 10E
Tolokiwa I. 138 5 30S 147 30E
Tolon 121 9 26N 1 3W
Tolosa 58 43 8N 2 5W
Tolox 57 36 41N 4 54W

Tolsta Hd Tregnago

Tolsta Hd. 36 58 20N 6 10W
Toluca 165 19 20N 99 50W
Tolun 106 42 22N 116 30E
Tom Burke 129 23 5S 28 4E
Tomahawk 158 45 28N 89 40W
Tomakomai 112 42 38N 141 36E
Tomales 163 38 15N 122 53W
Tomales B. 163 38 15N 123 58W
Tomar 57 39 36N 8 25W
Tómaros Óros 68 39 29N 20 48E
Tomaszów Lubelski 54 50 29N 23 23E
Tomaszów Mazowiecki 54 51 30N 19 57E
Tomatin 37 57 20N 4 0W
Tomatlán 164 19 56N 105 15W
Tombé 123 5 53N 31 40E
Tombigbee, R. 157 32 0N 88 6W
Tombodor, Serra do 171 12 0S 41 30W
Tombouctou 120 16 50N 3 0W
Tombstone 161 31 40N 110 4W
Tomdoun 36 57 4N 5 2W
Tomé 172 36 36S 73 6W
Tomé-Açu 170 2 25S 48 9W
Tomelilla 73 55 33N 13 58E
Tomelloso 59 39 10N 3 2W
Tomingley 141 32 31S 148 16E
Tomini 103 0 30N 120 30E
Tomini, Teluk 103 0 10S 122 0E
Tominian 120 13 17N 4 35W
Tomiño 56 41 59N 8 46W
Tomintoul 37 57 15N 3 22W
Tomioka 111 36 15N 138 54E
Tomkinson Ranges 137 26 11S 129 5E
Tommot 77 58 50N 126 20E
Tomnavoulin 37 57 19N 3 18W
Tomnop Ta Suos 101 11 20N 104 15E
Tomo, Colomb. 174 2 38N 67 32W
Tomo, Japan 110 34 23N 133 23E
Tomobe 111 36 40N 140 41E
Toms Place 163 37 34N 118 41W
Toms River 162 39 59N 74 12W
Tomsk 76 56 30N 85 12E
Tomtabacken 73 57 30N 14 30E
Tonalá 165 16 8N 93 41W
Tonale, Passo del 62 46 15N 10 34E
Tonalea 161 36 17N 110 58W
Tonami 111 36 56N 136 58E
Tonantins 174 2 45S 67 45W
Tonasket 160 48 45N 119 30W
Tonawanda 156 43 0N 78 54W
Tonbridge 29 51 12N 0 18E
Tondano 103 1 35N 124 54E
Tondela 56 40 31N 8 5W
Tønder 73 54 58N 8 50E
Tondi 97 9 45N 79 4E
Tondi Kiwindi 121 14 28N 2 02E
Tondibi 121 16 39N 0 14W
Tone-Gawa, R. 111 35 44N 140 51E
Tone, R. 137 34 23S 116 25E
Tone R. 30 50 59N 3 15W
Tong 28 52 39N 2 18W
Tonga Is. ■ 130 20 0S 173 0W
Tonga Trench 143 18 0S 175 0W
Tongaat 129 29 33S 31 9E
Tongala 141 36 14S 144 56E
Tongaland 129 27 0S 32 0E
Tongareva I 143 9 0S 158 0W
Tongariro, mt. 142 39 7S 175 50E
Tongchŏnni 107 39 50N 127 25E
Tongeren 47 50 47N 5 28E
Tongio 141 37 14S 147 44E
Tongjosŏn Man 107 39 30N 128 0E
Tongking = Bac-Phan 101 21 30N 105 0E
Tongking, G. of 101 20 0N 108 0E
Tongnae 107 35 12N 129 5E
Tongobory 129 23 32S 44 20E
Tongoy 172 30 25S 71 40W
Tongres = Tongeren 47 50 47N 5 28E
Tongsa Dzong 98 27 31N 90 31E
Tongue 37 58 29N 4 25W
Tongue, Kyle of 37 58 30N 4 30W
Tongue, R. 160 48 30N 106 30W
Tongyang 107 39 9N 126 53E
Tonj 123 7 20N 28 44E
Tonk 94 26 6N 75 54E
Tonkawa 159 36 44N 67 22W
Tonkin = Bac-Phan 100 22 0N 105 0E
Tonkin, G. of 100 20 0N 108 0E
Tonlé Sap 100 13 0N 104 0E
Tonnay-Charente 44 45 56N 0 55W
Tonneins 44 44 24N 0 20E
Tonnerre 43 47 51N 3 59E
Tönning 48 54 18N 8 57E
Tonopah 163 38 4N 117 12W
Tonoshō 110 34 29N 134 11E
Tonosí 166 7 20N 80 20W
Tonsberg 71 59 19N 10 25E
Tonstad 71 58 40N 6 45E
Tonto Basin 61 33 58N 111 15W
Tonyrefail 31 51 35N 3 26W
Tonzang 98 23 36N 93 42E
Tonzi 98 24 39N 94 57E
Tooele 160 40 30N 112 20W
Toolona 140 36 58S 141 5E
Toombeolo 38 53 26N 9 52W
Toomevara 39 52 50N 8 2W
Toompine 139 27 15S 144 19E
Toongi 141 32 28S 148 30E
Toonpan 138 19 28S 146 48E
Toora 141 38 39S 146 23E
Toora-Khem 77 52 28N 96 9E
Toormore 39 51 31N 9 41W
Toowoomba 139 27 32S 151 56E
Top 93 34 15N 68 35E
Top Ozero 78 65 35N 32 0E
Topalu 70 44 31N 28 3E
Topaz 163 38 41N 119 30W
Topeka 158 39 3N 95 40W
Topki 76 55 25N 85 20E
Topla, R. 53 49 0N 21 36E
Topley 152 54 32N 126 5W
Toplica, R. 66 43 15N 21 30E
Toplița 70 46 55N 25 27E
Topocalma, Pta. 172 34 10S 72 2W
Topock 161 34 46N 114 29W
Topola 66 44 17N 20 32E
Topol'čany 53 48 35N 18 12E
Topoli 83 47 59N 51 45E
Topolnitsa, R. 67 42 21N 24 0E
Topolobampo 164 25 40N 109 10W
Topolovgrad 67 42 5N 26 20E
TopolvŭT Mare 66 45 46N 21 41E
Toppenish 160 46 27N 120 16W
Topsham 30 50 40N 3 27W
Topusko 63 45 18N 15 59E
Toquima, Ra. 163 39 0N 117 0W
Tor Bay, Austral. 137 35 5S 117 50E
Tor Bay, U.K. 23 50 26N 3 31W
Tor Ness 37 58 47N 3 18W
Tor, oilfield 19 56 40N 3 35E
Torá 58 41 49N 1 25E
Tora Kit 123 11 2N 32 30E
Torata 174 17 3S 70 1W
Torbat-e Heydarīyeh 93 35 15N 59 12E
Torbat-e Jām 93 35 8N 60 35E
Torbay, Can. 151 47 40N 52 42W
Torbay, U.K. 30 50 26N 3 31W
Torchin 80 50 45N 25 0E
Tordal 71 59 10N 8 45E
Tordesillas 56 41 30N 5 0W
Tordoya 56 43 6N 8 36W
Töre 74 65 55N 22 40E
Töreboda 73 58 41N 14 7E
Torfajökull 74 63 54N 19 0W
Torgau 48 51 32N 13 0E
Torgelow 48 53 40N 13 59E
Torhout 47 51 5N 3 7E
Tori 123 7 53N 33 35E
Torigni-sur-Vire 42 49 3N 0 58W
Torija 58 40 44N 3 2W
Torin 164 27 33N 110 5W
Toriñana, C. 56 43 3N 9 17W
Torino 62 45 4N 7 40E
Torit 123 4 20N 32 55E
Torkovichi 80 58 51N 30 30E
Tormac 66 45 30N 21 30E
Tormentine 151 46 6N 63 46W
Tormes, R. 56 41 7N 6 0W
Tornado Mt. 152 49 55N 114 40W
Tornby 73 57 32N 9 56E
Torne älv 74 65 50N 24 12E
Torneå = Tornio 74 65 50N 24 12E
Torness 37 57 18N 4 22W
Torneträsk 74 68 24N 19 15E
Tornio 74 65 50N 24 12E
Tornionjoki 74 65 50N 24 12E
Tornquist 172 38 0S 62 15W
Toro 56 41 35N 5 24W
Torö 73 58 48N 17 50E
Toro, Cerro del 172 29 0S 69 50W
Toro Pk. 163 33 34N 116 24W
Törökszentmjklés 53 47 11N 20 27E
Toronátos Kólpos 68 40 5N 23 30E
Toronto, Austral. 141 33 0S 151 30E
Toronto, Can. 150 43 39N 79 20W
Toronto, U.S.A. 156 40 27N 80 36W
Toronto, L. 164 27 40N 105 30W
Toropets 80 56 30N 31 40E
Tororo 126 0 45N 34 12E
Toros Dağlari 92 37 0N 35 0E
Torphins 37 57 7N 2 37W
Torpoint 30 50 23N 4 12W
Torpshammar 72 62 29N 16 20E
Torquay, Austral. 140 38 20S 144 19E
Torquay, Can. 153 49 9N 103 30W
Torquay, U.K. 30 50 27N 3 31W
Torquemada 56 42 2N 4 19W
Torralba de Calatrava 57 39 1N 3 44W
Torran Rocks 34 56 14N 6 24W
Torrance 163 33 50N 118 19W
Torrão 57 38 16N 8 11W
Torre Annunziata 64 40 45N 14 26E
Tôrre de Moncorvo 56 41 12N 7 8W
Torre del Greco 65 40 47N 14 22E
Torre del Mar 57 36 44N 4 6W
Torre-Pacheco 29 37 44N 0 57W
Torre Pellice 62 44 49N 7 13E
Torreblanca 58 40 14N 0 12E
Torrecampo 57 38 29N 4 41W
Torrecilla en Cameros 58 42 15N 2 38W
Torredembarra 58 41 9N 1 24W
Torredonjimeno 57 37 46N 3 57W
Torrejoncillo 56 39 54N 6 28W
Torrelaguna 58 40 50N 3 38W
Torrelavega 56 43 20N 4 5W
Torremaggiore 65 41 42N 15 17E
Torremolinos 57 36 38N 4 30W
Torrens Cr. 138 22 23S 145 9E
Torrens Creek 138 20 48S 145 3E
Torrens, L. 140 31 0S 137 50E
Torrente 59 39 27N 0 28W
Torrenueva 59 38 38N 3 22W
Torreón 164 25 33N 103 25W
Torreperogil 59 38 2N 3 17W
Torres, Mexico 164 28 46N 110 47W
Torres, Spain 56 41 6N 5 0W
Tôrres Novas 57 39 27N 8 33W
Torres Strait 135 9 50S 142 20E
Torres Vedras 57 39 5N 9 15W
Torrevieja 59 37 59N 0 42W
Torrey 161 38 12N 111 30W
Torridge, R. 30 50 51N 4 10W
Torridon 36 57 33N 5 34W
Torridon, L. 36 57 35N 5 50W
Torrijos 56 39 59N 4 18W
Törring 73 55 52N 9 29E
Torrington, Conn., U.S.A. 162 41 50N 73 9W
Torrington, Wyo., U.S.A. 158 42 5N 104 8W
Torroboll 37 58 0N 4 23W
Torroella de Montgri 58 42 2N 3 8E
Torrox 57 36 46N 3 57W
Torsås 73 56 24N 16 0E
Torsby 72 60 7N 13 0E
Torsjok 72 57 5N 34 55E
Torsö 73 58 48N 13 45E
Torthorwald 35 55 7N 3 30W
Tortola, I. 147 18 19N 65 0W
Tórtoles de Esgueva 56 41 49N 4 2W
Tortona 62 44 53N 8 54E
Tortoreto 63 42 50N 13 55E
Tortorici 65 38 2N 14 48E
Tortosa 58 40 49N 0 31E
Tortosa C. 58 40 41N 0 52E
Tortosendo 56 40 15N 7 31W
Tortue, I. de la 167 20 5N 72 57W
Tortuga, Isla la 167 11 8N 67 2W
Torud 93 35 25N 55 5E
Torugart, Pereval 85 40 32N 75 24E
Torun 54 53 0N 18 39E
Torup 73 56 57N 13 5E
Torvastad 71 59 23N 5 15E
Torver 32 54 20N 3 7W
Tory I. 38 55 17N 8 12W
Torysa, R. 53 48 50N 21 15E
Torzhok 80 57 5N 34 55E
Tosa 110 33 24N 133 23E
Tosa-shimizu 110 32 52N 132 58E
Tosa-Wan 110 33 15N 133 30E
Tosa-yamada 110 33 36N 133 38E
Toscaig 36 57 23N 5 49W
Toscana 62 43 30N 11 5E
Tosno 80 59 30N 30 58E
Töss, R. 51 47 32N 8 39E
Tossa 58 41 43N 2 56E
Tostado 172 29 15S 61 50W
Tostedt 48 53 17N 9 42E
Tosu 110 33 22N 130 31E
Toszek 54 50 27N 18 32E
Totak 71 59 40N 7 45E
Totana 59 37 45N 1 30W
Toten 71 60 37N 10 53E
Toteng 128 20 22S 22 58E
Tôtes 42 49 41N 1 3E
Totland 28 50 41N 1 32W
Totley 33 53 18N 1 32W
Totma 81 60 0N 42 40E
Totnes 30 50 26N 3 41W
Totonicapán 166 14 50N 91 20W
Totskoye 84 52 32N 52 45E
Tottenham 141 32 14S 147 21E
Totton 28 50 55N 1 29W
Tottori 110 35 30N 134 15E
Tottori-ken □ 110 35 30N 134 12E
Touamotou, Archipel des 131 17 0S 144 0W
Touat 118 27 30N 0 30E
Touba 120 8 15N 7 40W
Toubkal, Djebel 118 31 0N 8 0W
Toubouai, Iles 131 25 0S 150 0W
Toucy 43 47 44N 3 15E
Tougan 120 13 11N 2 58W
Touggourt 119 33 10N 6 0E
Tougué 120 11 25N 11 50W
Toukmatine 119 24 49N 7 11E
Toul 43 48 40N 5 53E
Toulepleu 120 6 32N 8 24W
Toulon 45 43 10N 5 55E
Toulouse 44 43 37N 1 27E
Toummo 119 22 45N 14 8E
Toummo Dhoba 119 22 30N 14 31E
Toumodi 120 6 32N 5 4W
Tounan 109 23 41N 120 28E
Tounassine, Hamada 118 28 48N 5 0W
Toungoo 98 19 0N 96 30E
Touques, R. 42 49 22N 0 8E
Touquet, Le 43 50 30N 1 36E
Tour-du-Pin, La 45 45 33N 5 27E
Touraine 42 47 20N 0 30E
Tourane = Da Nang 100 16 4N 108 13E
Tourcoing 43 50 42N 3 10E
Tourcoingbam 121 13 23N 1 33W
Tournai 47 50 35N 3 25E
Tournan-en-Brie 43 48 44N 2 46E
Tournay 44 43 13N 0 13E
Tournon 45 45 4N 4 50E
Tournon-St.-Martin 42 46 45N 0 58E
Tournus 45 46 35N 4 54E
Touros 170 5 12S 35 28W
Tours 42 47 22N 0 40E
Touside, Pic 119 21 1N 16 18E
T'outaokou 107 42 44N 129 12E
Touwsrivier 128 33 20S 20 0E
Tovar 174 8 20N 71 46W
Tovarkovskiy 81 53 40N 38 5E
Tovdal 71 58 47N 8 10E
Tovdalselva 71 58 20N 8 16E
Towamba 141 37 6S 149 43E
Towanda 162 41 46N 76 30W
Towcester 29 52 7N 0 56W
Tower 158 47 49N 92 17W
Towerhill Cr. 138 22 28S 144 35E
Town Yetholm 35 55 33N 2 19W
Towner 158 48 25N 100 26W
Townsend 160 46 25N 111 32W
Townshend, C. 133 22 18S 150 30E
Townshend, I. 138 22 16S 150 31E
Townsville 138 19 15S 146 45E
Towson 162 39 26N 76 34W
Toyah 159 31 20N 103 48W
Toyahvale 159 30 58N 103 45W
Toyama 111 36 40N 137 15E
Toyama-ken □ 111 36 45N 137 30E
Tōyō 110 33 26N 134 16E
Toyohashi 111 34 45N 137 25E
Toyokawa 111 34 48N 137 27E
Toyonaka 111 34 50N 135 28E
Toyooka 110 35 35N 134 55E
Toyota 111 35 3N 137 7E
Toyoura 110 34 6N 130 57E
Toytepa 85 41 3N 69 20E
Tozeur 119 33 56N 8 8E
Tra On 101 9 58N 105 55E
Trabancos, R. 56 41 0N 5 3E
Trabzon 92 41 0N 39 45E
Tracadie 151 47 30N 64 55W
Tracy, Calif., U.S.A. 163 37 46N 121 27W
Tracy, Minn., U.S.A. 158 44 12N 95 3W
Tradate 62 45 43N 8 54E
Trafalgar 141 38 14S 146 12E
Trafalgar, C. 57 36 10N 6 2W
Traghan 119 26 0N 14 30E
Traian 70 45 2N 28 15E
Trail 152 49 5N 117 40W
Trainor L. 152 60 24N 120 17W
Traipu 171 9 58S 37 1W
Tralee 39 52 16N 9 42W
Tralee B. 39 52 17N 9 55W
Tramelan 50 47 13N 7 7E
Tramore 39 52 10N 7 10W
Tramore B. 39 52 9N 7 10W
Tran Ninh, Cao Nguyen 100 19 30N 103 10E
Tranås 73 58 3N 14 59E
Tranås 73 55 37N 13 59E
Trancas 172 26 20S 65 20W
Tranche-sur-Mer, La 42 46 20N 1 27W
Trancoso 56 40 49N 7 21W
Tranebjerg 73 55 51N 10 36E
Tranemo 73 57 30N 13 20E
Tranent 35 55 57N 2 58W
Trang 101 7 33N 99 38E
Trangahy 129 19 7S 44 43E
Trangan, I. 103 6 40S 134 20E
Trangie 141 32 4S 148 0E
Trångsviken 72 63 19N 14 0E
Trani 65 41 17N 16 24E
Tranoroa 129 24 42S 45 4E
Tranquebar 97 11 1N 79 54E
Tranqueras 173 31 8S 56 0W
Trans Nzoia □ 126 1 0N 35 0E
Transcona 153 49 50N 97 0W
Transilvania 70 46 19N 25 0E
Transkei □ 129 32 15S 28 15E
Transtrand 72 61 6N 13 20E
Transvaal □ 128 25 0S 29 0E
Transylvania = Transilvania 70 46 19N 25 0E
Transylvanian Alps 70 45 30N 25 0E
Trápani 64 38 1N 12 30E
Trappe Peak, Mt. 160 45 56N 114 29W
Traqowel 140 35 50S 144 0E
Traralgon 141 38 12S 146 34E
Traryd 73 56 35N 13 45E
Trarza □ 120 17 30N 15 0W
Tras os Montes e Alto-Douro □ 55 41 25N 7 20W
Trasacco 63 41 58N 13 30E
Trasimeno, L. 63 43 10N 12 5E
Träslöv 73 57 8N 12 21E
Trat 101 12 14N 102 33E
Traun 52 48 14N 14 15E
Traun-see 49 47 48N 13 45E
Traunstein 49 47 52N 12 40E
Trâvad 73 58 15N 13 5E
Traveller's L. 140 33 20S 142 0E
Travemünde 48 53 58N 10 52E
Travers, Mt. 143 42 1S 172 45E
Traverse City 156 44 45N 85 39W
Traverse I. 13 48 0S 28 0E
Travnik 66 44 17N 17 39E
Trawbreaga B. 38 55 20N 7 25W
Trawsfynydd 31 52 54N 3 55W
Trayning 137 31 7S 117 46E
Traynor 153 52 20N 108 32W
Trazo 56 43 0N 8 30W
Trbovlje 63 46 12N 15 5E
Trebbia, R. 62 44 52N 9 30E
Trebel, R. 48 54 0N 12 50E
Trebinje 66 42 44N 18 22E
Trebisacce 65 39 52N 16 32E
Trebišnica, R. 66 42 47N 18 8E
Trebišov 53 48 38N 21 41E
Trebizat 66 43 15N 17 30E
Třebon 52 48 59N 14 48E
Trebujena 57 36 52N 6 11W
Trecate 62 45 29N 8 42E
Tredegar 31 51 47N 3 16W
Trefeglwys 31 52 31N 3 31W
Trefriw 31 53 9N 3 50W
Tregaron 31 52 14N 3 56W
Trégastel-Plage 42 48 49N 3 31W
Tregnago 63 45 31N 11 10E

Tregrasse Is Tullow

Tregrasse Is. 138 17 41 S 150 43 E
Tréguier 42 48 47N 3 16W
Trégunc 42 47 51N 3 51W
Tregynon 31 52 32N 3 19W
Treharris 31 51 40N 3 17W
Treherne 153 49 38N 98 42W
Tréia 63 43 30N 13 20 E
Treig, L. 37 56 48N 4 42W
Treignac 44 45 32N 1 48 E
Treinta y Tres 173 33 10 S 54 50W
Treis 49 50 9N 7 19 E
Trekveid 128 30 35 S 19 45 E
Trelde Næs 73 55 38N 9 53 E
Trelech 31 51 56N 4 28W
Trelew 176 43 10 S 65 20W
Trélissac 44 45 11N 0 47 E
Trelleborg 73 55 20N 13 10 E
Trélon 43 50 5N 4 6 E
Tremadoc 31 52 57N 4 9W
Tremadoc, Bay 31 52 51N 4 18W
Tremblade, La 44 45 46N 1 8W
Tremelo 47 51 0N 4 42 E
Trementina 159 35 27N 105 30W
Tremiti, I. 63 42 8N 15 30 E
Tremonton 160 41 45N 112 10W
Tremp 58 42 10N 0 52 E
Trenary 156 46 12N 86 59W
Trenčin 53 48 52N 18 4 E
Trenche, R. 150 47 46N 72 53W
Trenggalek 103 8 5 S 111 44 E
Trenque Lauquen 172 36 0 S 62 45W
Trent, R. 33 53 33N 0 44W
Trentham 32 52 59N 2 12W
Trentino-Alto Adige □ 62 46 5N 11 0 E
Trento 62 46 5N 11 8 E
Trenton, Can. 150 44 10N 77 40W
Trenton, Mo., U.S.A. 158 40 5N 93 37W
Trenton, Nebr., U.S.A. 158 40 14N 101 4W
Trenton, N.J., U.S.A. 162 40 15N 74 41W
Trenton, Tenn., U.S.A. 159 35 58N 88 57W
Trepassey 151 46 43N 53 25W
Tréport, Le 42 50 3N 1 20 E
Treptow 48 53 42N 13 15 E
Trepuzzi 65 40 26N 18 4 E
Tres Arroyos 172 38 20 S 60 20W
Três Corações 173 21 30 S 45 30W
Três Lagoas 171 20 50 S 51 50W
Tres Marías, Is. 164 21 25N 106 28W
Três Marias, Represa 171 18 12 S 45 15W
Tres Montes, C. 176 47 0 S 75 35W
Tres Pinos 163 36 48N 121 19W
Três Pontas 173 21 23 S 45 29W
Tres Puentes 172 27 50 S 70 15W
Três Puntas, C. 176 47 0 S 66 0W
Tres Rios 173 22 20 S 43 30W
Tres Valles 165 18 15N 96 8W
Tresco I. 30 49 57N 6 20W
Treshnish Is. 34 56 30N 6 25W
Treska, R. 66 41 45N 21 11 E
Treskavika Planina 66 43 40N 18 20 E
Trespaderne 58 42 47N 3 24W
Tretower 31 51 53N 3 11W
Trets 45 43 27N 5 41 E
Treuchtlingen 49 48 58N 10 55 E
Treuddyn 31 53 7N 3 8W
Treuenbrietzen 48 52 6N 12 51 E
Treungen 75 59 1N 8 31 E
Treviglio 62 45 31N 9 35 E
Trevinca, Peña 56 42 15N 6 46W
Treviso 63 45 40N 12 15 E
Trevose Hd. 30 50 33N 5 3W
Trévoux 45 45 57N 4 47 E
Trgovište 66 42 20N 22 10 E
Triabunna 138 42 30 S 147 55 E
Triánda 69 36 25N 28 10 E
Triang 101 3 13N 102 27 E
Triangle 162 38 33N 77 20W
Triaucourt-en-Argonne 43 48 59N 5 2 E
Tribsees 48 54 4N 12 46 E
Tribulation, C. 138 16 5 S 145 29 E
Tribune 158 38 30N 101 45W
Tricárico 65 40 37N 16 9 E
Tricase 65 39 56N 18 20 E
Trichinopoly = Tiruchchirappalli 97 10 45N 78 45 E
Trichur 97 10 30N 76 18 E
Trida 141 33 1 S 145 1 E
Trier 49 49 45N 6 37 E
Trieste 63 45 39N 13 45 E
Trieste, G. di 63 45 37N 13 40 E
Triggiano 65 41 4N 16 58 E
Triglav 63 46 30N 13 45 E
Trigno, R. 63 41 55N 14 37 E
Trigueros 57 37 24N 6 50W
Trikeri 69 39 6N 23 5 E
Tríkhonis, Límni 69 38 34N 21 30 E
Tríkkala 68 39 34N 21 47 E
Tríkkala □ 68 39 41N 21 30 E
Trikora, G. 103 4 11 S 138 0 E
Trilj 63 43 38N 16 42 E
Trillick 38 54 27N 7 30W
Trillo 58 40 42N 2 35W
Trim 38 53 34N 6 48W
Trimdon 33 54 43N 1 23W
Trimley 29 51 59N 1 19 E
Trincomalee 97 8 38N 81 15 E
Trindade 171 16 40 S 49 30W
Trindade, I. 15 20 20 S 29 50W
Trinidad, Boliv. 174 14 54 S 64 50W
Trinidad, Colomb. 174 5 25N 71 40W
Trinidad, Cuba 166 21 40N 80 0W
Trinidad, Uruguay 172 33 30 S 56 50W
Trinidad, U.S.A. 159 37 15N 104 30W
Trinidad & Tobago ■ 167 10 30N 61 20W
Trinidad, I., Argent. 176 39 10 S 62 0W
Trinidad, I., S. Amer. 167 10 30N 61 15W
Trinidad, R. 165 17 49N 95 9W
Trinitápoli 65 41 22N 16 5 E
Trinity, Can. 151 48 22N 53 29W
Trinity, U.S.A. 159 30 50N 95 20W
Trinity B., Austral. 133 16 30 S 146 0 E
Trinity B., Can. 151 48 20N 53 10W
Trinity Mts. 159 40 20N 118 50W
Trinity R. 159 30 30N 95 0W
Trino 62 45 10N 8 18 E
Trion 157 34 35N 85 18W
Trionto C. 65 34 38N 16 47 E
Triora 62 44 0N 7 46 E
Tripoli = Tarabulus 92 34 31N 33 52 E
Tripoli = Tarābulus 119 32 49N 13 7 E
Trípolis 69 37 31N 22 25 E
Tripp 158 43 16N 97 58W
Tripura □ 98 24 0N 92 0 E
Trischen, I. 48 54 3N 8 32 E
Tristan da Cunha, I. 15 37 6 S 12 20W
Trivandrum 97 8 31N 77 0 E
Trivento 65 41 48N 14 31 E
Trnava 53 48 23N 17 35 E
Trobriand Is. 135 8 30 S 151 0 E
Trochu 152 51 50N 113 13W
Trodely I. 150 52 15N 79 26W
Trogir 63 43 32N 16 15 E
Troglav, mt. 63 43 56N 16 36 E
Trögstad 71 59 37N 11 16 E
Tróia 65 41 22N 15 19 E
Troilus, L. 150 50 50N 74 35W
Troina 65 37 47N 14 34 E
Trois Fourches, Cap des 118 35 26N 2 58W
Trois Pistoles 151 48 5N 69 10W
Trois-Rivières 150 46 25N 72 40W
Troisvierges 47 50 8N 6 0 E
Troitsk 84 54 10N 61 35 E
Troitskiy 84 55 29N 37 18 E
Troitsko-Pechorsk 78 62 40N 56 10 E
Trölladyngja 74 64 54N 17 15W
Trolladyngja 74 64 49N 17 29W
Trollhättan 73 58 17N 12 20 E
Trollheimen 71 62 46N 9 1 E
Tromöy 71 58 28N 8 53 E
Troms fylke □ 74 68 56N 19 0 E
Tromsø 74 69 40N 18 56 E
Trona 163 35 46N 117 23W
Tronador, Mt. 176 41 53 S 71 0W
Tröndelag, N. □ 74 65 0N 12 0 E
Tröndelag, S. □ 71 62 0N 10 0 E
Trondheim 71 63 25N 10 25 E
Trondheimsfjorden 74 63 35N 10 30 E
Trönninge 73 56 38N 12 59 E
Trönö 72 61 22N 16 54 E
Tronto, R. 63 42 50N 13 46 E
Troodos, mt. 128 34 58N 32 55 E
Troon 34 55 33N 4 40W
Tropea 65 38 40N 15 53 E
Tropic 161 37 44N 112 4W
Tropoja 68 42 23N 20 10 E
Trossachs, The 34 56 14N 4 24W
Trostan Mt. 38 55 4N 6 10W
Trostberg 49 48 2N 12 33 E
Trotternish, dist. 36 57 32N 6 15W
Troup 159 32 10N 95 3W
Troup Hd. 37 57 41N 2 18W
Trout L., N.W. Terr., Can. 152 60 40N 121 40W
Trout L., Ont., Can. 153 51 20N 93 15W
Trout Lake 150 46 10N 85 2W
Trout, R. 152 61 19N 119 51W
Trout River 151 49 29N 58 8W
Trout Run 162 41 23N 77 3W
Trouville 42 49 21N 0 5 E
Trowbridge 28 51 18N 2 12W
Troy, Turkey 69 39 55N 26 20 E
Troy, Alabama, U.S.A. 157 31 50N 85 58W
Troy, Kans., U.S.A. 158 39 47N 95 2W
Troy, Mo., U.S.A. 158 38 56N 90 59W
Troy, Montana, U.S.A. 160 48 30N 115 58W
Troy, N.Y., U.S.A. 162 42 45N 73 39W
Troy, Ohio, U.S.A. 156 40 0N 84 10W
Troy, Pa., U.S.A. 162 41 47N 76 47W
Troyan 67 42 57N 24 43 E
Troyes 43 48 19N 4 3 E
Trpanj 66 43 1N 17 15 E
Trstena 53 49 21N 19 37 E
Trstenik 66 43 36N 21 0 E
Trubchevsk 80 52 33N 33 47 E
Truc Giang 101 10 14N 106 22 E
Trucial States = Utd. Arab Emirates 93 24 0N 54 30 E
Truckee 160 39 20N 120 11W
Trujillo, Colomb. 174 4 10N 76 19W
Trujillo, Hond. 166 16 0N 86 0W
Trujillo, Peru 174 8 0 S 79 0W
Trujillo, Spain 57 39 28N 5 55W
Trujillo, U.S.A. 159 35 34N 104 44W
Trujillo, Venez. 174 9 22N 70 26W
Truk Is. 131 7 25N 151 46 E
Trull 28 50 58N 3 8W
Trumann 159 35 42N 90 32W
Trumansburg 162 42 33N 76 40W
Trumbull, Mt. 161 36 25N 113 32W
Trumpington 29 52 11N 0 6 E
Trûn 66 42 51N 22 38 E
Trun, France 42 48 50N 0 2 E
Trun, Switz. 51 46 45N 8 59 E
Trundle 141 32 53 S 147 42 E
Trung-Phan, reg. 100 16 0N 108 0 E
Truro, Austral. 140 34 24 S 139 9 E
Truro, Can. 151 45 21N 63 14 E
Truro, U.K. 30 50 17N 5 2W
Trùscŭu, Muntii 70 46 14N 23 14 E
Truskmore, mt. 38 54 23N 8 20W
Truslove 137 33 20 S 121 45 E
Trustrup 73 56 20N 10 46 E
Truth or Consequences 161 33 9N 107 16W
Trutnov 52 50 37N 15 54 E
Truxton 162 42 45N 76 2W
Truyère, R. 44 44 38N 2 34 E
Trwyn Cilan 31 52 47N 4 31W
Tryavna 67 42 54N 25 25 E
Tryon 157 35 15N 82 16W
Trzciarka 54 53 3N 16 25 E
Trzciel 54 52 23N 15 50 E
Trzcinsko-Zdroj 54 52 58N 14 35 E
Trzebiez 54 53 38N 14 31 E
Trzebinia 54 50 11N 19 30 E
Trzeblatów 54 54 3N 15 18 E
Trzebnica 54 51 20N 17 1 E
Trzemeszno 54 52 33N 17 48 E
Tržič 63 46 22N 14 18 E
Tsafriya 90 31 59N 34 51 E
Tsaidam 105 37 0N 95 0 E
Tsak'o 108 31 56N 99 35 E
Tsamandás 68 39 46N 20 21 E
Tsamkong = Chanchiang 109 21 15N 110 20 E
Tsana Dzong 99 28 0N 91 55 E
Tsanga 99 30 43N 100 32 E
Ts'angchi 108 31 48N 105 57 E
Ts'angchou 106 38 10N 116 50 E
Tsangpo 99 29 40N 89 0 E
Ts'angyüan 108 23 9N 99 15 E
Ts'ao Ho, R. 107 40 32N 124 11 E
Tsaochuang 107 34 30N 117 49 E
Tsaochwang 174 35 11N 115 28 E
Ts'aohsien 106 34 50N 115 31 E
Tsaoyang 109 32 8N 112 42 E
Tsaratanana 129 16 47 S 47 39 E
Tsaratanana, Mt. de 129 14 0 S 49 0 E
Tsarevo = Michurin 67 42 9N 27 51 E
Tsaring Nor 99 34 40N 97 20 E
Tsaritsáni 68 39 53N 15 14 E
Tsau 128 20 8 S 22 29 E
Tsaukaib 128 26 37 S 15 39 E
Tsebrikovo 82 47 9N 30 10 E
Ts'ehung 108 25 2N 105 47 E
Tselinograd 76 51 10N 71 30 E
Tsengch'eng 109 23 17N 113 49 E
Ts'enkung 108 27 13N 108 45 E
Tsetserleg 105 47 36N 101 32 E
Tshabong 128 26 2 S 22 29 E
Tshane 125 24 5 S 21 54 E
Tshela 124 5 4 S 13 0 E
Tshesebe 129 20 43 S 27 32 E
Tshhinvali 83 42 14N 44 1 E
Tshibeke 126 2 40 S 28 35 E
Tshibinda 126 2 23 S 28 30 E
Tshikapa 124 6 17 S 21 0 E
Tshilenge 126 6 12 S 23 40 E
Tshinsenda 127 12 15N 28 0 E
Tshofa 124 5 8 S 25 8 E
Tshombe 129 25 18 S 45 29 E
Tshwane 128 22 24 S 22 1 E
Tsigara 128 20 22 S 25 54 E
Tsihombe 125 25 10 S 45 41 E
Tsilmamo 123 6 1N 35 10 E
Tsimlyansk 83 47 45N 42 0 E
Tsimlyanskoye Vdkhr. 83 48 0N 43 0 E
Tsinan = Chinan 106 36 32N 117 0 E
Tsineng 128 27 05 S 23 05 E
Tsinga, mt. 68 41 23N 24 44 E
Tsinghai □ 105 36 0N 96 0 E
Tsingtao = Ch'ingtao 107 36 5N 120 25 E
Tsinjomitondraka 129 15 40 S 47 8 E
Tsiroanomandidy 129 18 46 S 46 2 E
Tsivilsk 81 55 50N 47 25 E
Tsivory 129 24 4 S 46 5 E
Tskhinali 79 42 22N 43 52 E
Tso Chiang, R. 108 22 52N 108 5 E
Tso Morari, L. 95 32 50N 78 20 E
Tsochou 108 22 36N 107 36 E
Tsoch'üan 106 37 3N 113 27 E
Tsodilo Hill 128 18 49 S 21 43 E
Tsogttsetsiy 106 43 43N 105 35 E
Tsokung 108 29 55N 97 44 E
Tsona Dzong 99 28 0N 91 55 E
Tsoshui 106 33 40N 109 9 E
Tsouhsien 106 35 24N 116 58 E
Tsu 111 34 45N 136 25 E
Tsu L. 152 60 40N 111 52W
Tsuchiura 111 36 12N 140 15 E
Tsugaru-Kaikyō 112 41 35N 141 0 E
Tsukumi 110 33 4N 131 52 E
Tsukushi-Sanchi 110 33 25N 130 30 E
Tsumeb 128 19 9 S 17 44 E
Tsumis 128 23 39 S 17 29 E
Tsuna 110 34 28N 134 56 E
Ts'ungchiang 108 25 45N 108 54 E
Tsunhua 107 40 12N 117 56 E
Tsuni 108 27 43N 106 52 E
Tsuno-Shima 110 34 21N 130 52 E
Tsuru 111 35 31N 138 57 E
Tsuruga 111 35 45N 136 2 E
Tsuruga-Wan 111 35 50N 136 3 E
Tsurugi 111 36 37N 136 37 E
Tsurugi-San 110 33 51N 134 6 E
Tsurumi-Saki 110 32 56N 132 5 E
Tsuruoka 112 38 44N 139 50 E
Tsurusaki 110 33 14N 131 41 E
Tsushima 111 35 10N 136 43 E
Tsushima, I. 110 34 20N 129 20 E
Tsvetkovo 82 49 15N 31 33 E
Tu, R. 98 22 50N 97 15 E
Tua, R. 57 41 19N 7 15W
Tuai 143 38 47 S 177 15 E
Tuakau 142 37 16 S 174 59 E
Tual 103 5 30 S 132 50 E
Tuam 38 53 30N 8 50W
Tuamarina 143 41 25 S 173 59 E
Tuamgraney 39 52 54N 8 32W
Tuamotu Arch = Touamotou 131 17 0 S 144 0W
Tuan 108 23 59N 108 3 E
T'uanch'i 108 27 28N 107 7 E
T'uanfeng 109 30 38N 114 52 E
Tuao 103 17 47 S 121 30 E
Tuapse 83 44 5N 39 10 E
Tuatapere 143 46 8 S 167 41 E
Tuath, Loch 34 56 30N 6 15W
Tuba City 161 36 8N 111 12W
Tubac 161 31 45N 111 2W
Tubai Is. = Toubouai, Îles 131 25 0 S 150 0W
Tuban 102 6 57 S 112 4 E
Tubarão 173 28 30 S 49 0W
Tubas 90 32 20N 35 22 E
Tubau 102 3 10N 113 40 E
Tubayq, Jabal at 122 29 30N 27 30 E
Tubbergen 46 52 24N 6 48 E
Tübingen 48 48 31N 9 4 E
Tubize 47 50 42N 4 13 E
Tubja, W. 122 25 27N 38 55 E
Tubruq, (Tobruk) 117 32 7N 23 55 E
Tubuai, Îles 131 25 0 S 150 0W
Tuc Trung 101 11 1N 107 12 E
Tucacas 174 10 48N 68 19W
Tucano 170 10 58 S 38 48W
Tuch'ang 109 29 15N 116 13 E
T'uch'ang 109 24 42N 121 25 E
Tuchodi, R. 152 58 17N 123 42W
Tuchola 54 53 33N 17 52 E
Tuchów 54 49 54N 21 1 E
T'uch'üan 107 45 22N 121 41 E
Tuckanarra 137 27 8 S 118 1 E
Tuckernuck I. 162 41 15N 70 17W
Tucson 161 32 14N 110 59W
Tucumán 172 26 50 S 65 20W
Tucumán □ 172 26 48 S 66 2W
Tucumcari 159 35 12N 103 45W
Tucupido 174 9 17N 65 47W
Tucupita 174 9 14N 62 3W
Tucuracas 174 11 45N 72 22W
Tucuruí 170 3 42 S 49 27W
Tuczno 54 53 13N 16 10 E
Tudela 58 42 4N 1 39W
Tudela de Duero 56 41 37N 4 39W
Tudor, Lac 151 55 50N 65 25W
Tudora 70 47 31N 26 45 E
Tudweiliog 31 52 54N 4 37W
Tuella, R. 56 41 50N 7 10W
Tuen 139 28 33 S 145 37 E
Tueré, R. 170 2 48 S 50 59W
Tufi 135 9 8 S 149 19 E
Tugidak I. 147 56 30N 154 40W
Tuguegarao 103 17 35N 121 42 E
Tugur 77 53 50N 136 45 E
Tugwa 128 17 27 S 18 33 E
Tukangbesi, Kepulauan 103 6 0 S 124 0 E
Tukarak I. 150 56 15N 78 45W
Tukobo 120 5 1N 2 47W
Tūkrah 119 32 30N 20 37 E
Tuku, mt. 123 9 10N 36 43 E
Tukums 80 57 2N 23 3 E
Tukuyu 127 9 17 S 33 35 E
Tukzar 93 35 55N 66 25 E
Tula, Hidalgo, Mexico 165 20 0N 99 20W
Tula, Tamaulipas, Mexico 165 23 0N 99 40W
Tula, Nigeria 121 9 51N 11 27 E
Tula, U.S.S.R. 81 54 13N 37 32 E
Tulak 93 33 55N 63 40 E
Tulancingo 165 20 5N 98 22W
Tulanssu 105 36 52N 98 24 E
Tulare 163 36 15N 119 26W
Tulare Basin 163 36 0N 119 48W
Tulare Lake 163 36 0N 119 53W
Tularosa 161 33 4N 106 1W
Tulbagh 128 33 16 S 19 6 E
Tulcán 174 0 48N 77 43W
Tulcea 70 45 13N 28 46 E
Tulcea □ 70 45 0N 29 0 E
Tulchin 82 48 41N 28 55 E
*Tuléar 129 23 21 S 43 40 E
**Tuléar □ 129 21 0 S 45 0 E
Tulemalu L. 153 62 58N 99 25W
Tulgheş 70 4 58N 25 45 E
Tuli, Indon. 103 1 24 S 122 26 E
Tuli, Zimb. 127 21 58 S 29 13 E
Tuliuchen 106 39 1N 116 54 E
Tulkarm 90 32 19N 35 10 E
Tulla, Ireland 39 52 53N 8 45W
Tulla, U.S.A. 159 34 35N 101 44W
Tulla, L. 34 56 33N 4 47W
Tullaghoge 38 54 36N 6 43W
Tullaghought 39 52 25N 7 22W
Tullahoma 157 35 23N 86 12W
Tullamore, Austral. 141 32 39 S 147 36 E
Tullamore, Ireland 39 53 17N 7 30W
Tullaroan 39 52 40N 7 27W
Tulle 44 45 16N 0 47 E
Tullibigeal 141 33 25 S 146 44 E
Tullins 45 45 18N 5 29 E
Tulln 52 48 20N 16 4 E
Tullow 39 52 48N 6 45W

*Renamed Toliara
**Renamed Toliara □

Tullus **Uddingston**

Tullus 123 11 7N 24 40 E
Tully, Austral. 138 17 56 S 145 55 E
Tully, Ireland 38 53 44N 8 9W
Tully, U.S.A. 162 42 48N 76 7W
Tully Cross 38 53 35N 9 59W
Tûlmaciu 70 45 38N 24 19 E
Tulmaythah 117 32 40N 20 55 E
Tulmur 138 22 40 S 142 20 E
Tulnici 70 45 51N 26 38 E
Tulovo 67 42 33N 25 32 E
Tulsa 159 36 10N 96 0W
Tulsequah 152 58 39N 133 35W
Tulsk 38 53 47N 8 15W
Tulu Milki 123 9 55N 38 14 E
Tulu Welel, Mt. 123 8 56N 35 30 E
Tulua 174 4 6N 76 11W
T'ulufan 105 42 56N 89 10 E
Tulun 77 54 40N 100 10 E
Tulungagung 103 8 5 S 111 54 E
Tum 103 3 28 S 130 21 E
Tuma 81 55 10N 40 30 E
Tuma, R. 166 13 18N 84 50W
Tumaco 174 1 50N 78 45W
Tumatumari 174 5 20N 58 55W
Tumba 72 59 12N 17 48 E
Tumba, L. 124 0 50 S 18 0 E
Tumbarumba 141 35 44 S 148 0 E
Tumbaya 172 23 50 S 65 20W
Tumbes 174 3 30 S 80 20W
Tumbwa 127 11 25 S 27 15 E
Tumby B. 140 34 21 S 136 8 E
T'umen 107 42 55N 129 50 E
T'umen Kiang, R. 107 42 18N 130 41 E
Tumeremo 174 7 18N 61 30W
Tumiritinga 171 18 58 S 41 38W
Tumkur 97 13 18N 77 12 E
Tumleberg 73 58 16N 12 52 E
Tummel, L. 37 56 43N 3 55W
Tummel, R. 37 56 42N 4 5W
T'umot'eyuch'i 106 40 42N 111 8 E
Tump 93 26 7N 62 16 E
Tumpat 101 6 11N 102 10 E
Tumsar 96 21 26N 79 45 E
Tumu 120 10 56N 1 56W
Tumucumaque, Serra de 175 2 0N 55 0W
Tumut 141 35 16 S 148 13 E
Tumutuk 84 55 1N 53 19 E
Tumwater 160 47 0N 122 58W
Tuna, Pta. 147 17 59N 65 53W
Tunas de Zaza 166 21 39N 79 34W
Tunbridge Wells 29 51 7N 0 16 E
T'unch'i 105 29 50N 118 26 E
Tuncurry 141 32 9 S 152 29 E
Tunduru 127 11 0 S 37 25 E
Tunduru □ 127 11 5 S 37 22 E
Tundzha, R. 67 42 0N 26 35 E
Tune 71 59 16N 11 2 E
Tung Chiang, R. 109 22 55N 113 35 E
Tung-Pei 77 44 0N 126 0 E
Tunga La 99 29 0N 94 14 E
Tunga Pass 98 29 0N 94 14 E
Tunga, R. 97 13 42N 75 20 E
Tungabhadra Dam 97 15 21N 76 23 E
Tungabhadra, R. 97 15 30N 77 0 E
Tungachen 106 36 15N 165 12 E
Tungan 106 29 24N 111 17 E
T'ungan 109 24 44N 118 9 E
T'ungcheng, Anhwei, China 109 31 3N 116 58 E
T'ungcheng, Hupeh, China 109 29 15N 113 49 E
Tungch'i 108 28 43N 106 42 E
T'ungchiang, Heilungkiang, China 105 47 40N 132 30 E
T'ungchiang, Szechwan, China 108 31 56N 107 15 E
Tungchingch'eng 107 44 9N 129 7 E
Tungchuan 105 35 4N 109 2 E
T'ungch'uan 106 35 95N 109 5 E
Tungch'uan 108 26 9N 103 7 E
Tungfanghsien, (Paso) 100 18 50N 108 33 E
Tungfeng 107 42 40N 125 34 E
T'unghai 108 24 8N 102 43 E
Tunghai Tao 109 21 2N 110 25 E
Tunghsiang 109 28 14N 116 35 E
T'unghsien 105 39 45N 116 43 E
T'unghsin 106 37 9N 106 28 E
T'unghua 107 41 45N 126 0 E
Tungi 98 23 53N 90 24 E
T'ungjen 105 27 43N 109 10 E
Tungkan 108 23 22N 105 9 E
Tungkou 107 39 52N 124 8 E
Tungku 108 31 52N 100 14 E
T'ungku 109 28 32N 114 23 E
Tungkuan 109 23 0N 113 39 E
T'ungkuan 105 34 37N 110 27 E
Tungkuang 106 37 53N 116 32 E
Tungla 166 13 24N 84 15W
Tunglan 108 24 30N 107 23 E
T'ungliang 108 29 52N 106 2 E
T'ungliao 107 43 37N 122 16 E
Tungling 109 31 0N 117 54 E
Tungliu 109 30 13N 116 55 E
T'unglu 109 29 49N 119 40 E
Tungnafellsjökull 74 64 45N 17 55W
T'ungnan 108 30 14N 105 48 E
Tungning 107 44 3N 131 7 E
T'ungpai 109 32 22N 113 24 E
Tungp'ing 106 35 55N 116 18 E
Tungpu 99 31 42N 98 19 E
Tungshan 109 23 40N 117 31 E
Tungshih 109 24 12N 120 43 E
Tungsten, Can. 152 61 57N 128 16W
Tungsten, U.S.A. 160 40 50N 118 10W
Tungt'ai 109 32 50N 120 46 E
T'ungtao 108 26 21N 109 36 E
T'ungtien 108 26 40N 99 32 E
Tungt'ing Hu 109 29 18N 112 45 E
Tungtzu 108 28 8N 106 49 E
Tunguchumuch'inch'i 106 45 33N 116 50 E
Tunguska, Nizhmaya, R. 77 64 0N 95 0 E
Tunguska, Podkammenaya, R. 77 61 0N 98 0 E
T'ungwei 106 35 18N 105 10 E
T'ungyü 107 44 48N 123 6 E
Tunhua 107 43 20N 128 10 E
Tunhuang 105 40 10N 94 50 E
Tuni 96 17 22N 82 43 E
Tunia 174 2 41N 76 31W
Tunica 159 34 43N 90 23W
Tunis 119 36 50N 10 11 E
Tunis, Golfe de 119 37 0N 10 30 E
Tunisia ■ 119 33 30N 9 10 E
Tunja 174 5 40N 73 25W
Tunkhannock 162 41 32N 75 56W
T'unliu 106 36 19N 112 54 E
Tunnsjøen 74 64 45N 13 25 E
Tuno I. 73 55 58N 10 27 E
T'unpuli Shan 105 35 0N 89 30 E
Tunstall 29 52 7N 1 28 E
Tuntatuliag 147 60 20N 162 45W
Tunungayualuk I. 151 56 0N 61 0W
Tunuyán 172 33 55 S 69 0W
Tunuyán, R. 172 33 33 S 67 30W
Tuolumne 163 37 59N 120 16W
Tuolumne, R. 163 37 36N 121 13W
Tuoy-Khaya 77 62 32N 111 18 E
Tupã 173 21 57 S 50 28W
Tupaciguara 171 18 35 S 48 42W
Tuparro, R. 174 5 0N 68 40W
Tupelo 157 34 15N 88 42W
Tupik 77 54 26N 119 57 E
Tupinambaranas, I. 174 3 0 S 58 0W
Tupirama 170 8 58 S 48 12W
Tupiratins 170 8 23 S 48 8W
Tupiza 172 21 30 S 65 40W
Tupman 163 35 18N 119 21W
Tupper 152 55 32N 120 1W
Tupper L. 156 44 18N 74 30W
Tupungato, Cerro 172 33 15 S 69 50W
Tuque, La 150 47 30N 72 50W
Túquerres 174 1 5N 77 37W
Tur 90 31 47N 35 14 E
Tura, India 98 25 30N 90 16 E
Tura, U.S.S.R. 77 64 20N 99 30 E
Tura, R. 84 57 12N 66 56 E
Turaba, W. 122 21 15N 41 32 E
Turagua, Serranía 174 7 20N 64 35W
Turaiyur 97 11 9N 78 38 E
Turakina 142 40 3 S 175 16 E
Turakirae Hd. 142 41 26 S 174 56 E
Tūrān 93 35 45N 56 50 E
Turan 77 51 38N 101 40 E
Turbenthal 51 47 27N 8 51 E
Tureburg 72 59 30N 17 58 E
Turégano 56 41 9N 4 1W
Turek 54 52 3N 18 30 E
Turen 174 9 17N 69 6W
Turfan Depression 105 42 45N 89 0 E
Turgay 84 49 38N 63 30 E
Turgay, R. 84 48 1N 62 45 E
Türgovishte 67 43 17N 26 38 E
Turgutlu 92 38 30N 27 48 E
Turhal 82 40 24N 36 19 E
Turia, R. 58 39 43N 1 0W
TuriaçI 170 1 40 s 45 28W
TuriaçI, R. 170 3 0 s 46 0W
Turigshih 100 18 42N 109 27 E
Turin = Torino 62 45 3N 7 40 E
Turin Taber 152 49 47N 112 24W
Turinsk 84 58 3N 63 42 E
Turkana □ 126 3 0N 35 30 E
Turkana, L. 80 4 10N 32 10 E
Turkestan 76 43 10N 68 10 E
Turkestanskiy, Khrebet 85 39 35N 69 0 E
Túrkeve 53 47 6N 20 44 E
Turkey ■ 92 39 0N 36 0 E
Turkey Creek P.O. 136 17 2 S 128 12 E
Turki 81 52 0N 43 15 E
Turkmen S.S.R. □ 85 39 0N 59 0 E
Turks Is. 167 21 20N 71 20W
Turks Island Passage 167 21 30N 71 20W
Turku (Åbo) 75 60 30N 22 19 E
Turku-Pori □ 75 60 27N 22 15 E
Turkwell, R. 126 2 30N 35 20 E
Turlock 163 37 30N 120 55W
Turnagain, C. 142 40 28 S 176 38 E
Turnagain, R. 152 59 12N 127 35W
Turnberry, Can. 153 53 25N 101 45W
Turnberry, U.K. 34 55 19N 4 50W
Turneffe Is. 165 17 20N 87 50W
Turner 160 48 52N 108 25W
Turner Pt. 138 11 47 S 133 32 E
Turner River 136 17 52 S 128 16 E
Turner Valley 152 50 40N 114 17W
Turners Falls 162 42 36N 72 34W
Turnhout 47 51 19N 4 57 E
Türnitz 52 47 55N 15 29 E
Turnor L. 153 56 35N 108 35W
Turnov 52 50 34N 15 10 E
Turnovo 67 43 5N 25 41 E
Turnovo □ 67 43 4N 25 39 E
Turnu Mŭgurele 70 43 46N 24 56 E
Turnu Roşu Pasul 70 45 33N 24 17 E
Turnu-Severin 70 44 39N 22 41 E
Turö 73 55 2N 10 40 E
Turon 159 37 48N 98 27W
Tuross Head 141 36 3 S 150 8 E
Turriff 37 57 32N 2 28W
Tursha 81 56 50N 47 45 E
Tursi 65 40 15N 16 27 E
Turtle Hd. I. 138 10 50 S 142 37 E
Turtle L., Can. 153 53 36N 108 38W
Turtle L., N.D., U.S.A. 158 47 30N 100 55W
Turtle L., Wis., U.S.A. 158 45 22N 92 10W
Turtleford 153 53 23N 108 57W
Turua 142 37 14 S 175 35 E
Turubah 92 28 20N 43 15 E
Turukhansk 77 65 50N 87 50 E
Turun ja Porin lääni □ 75 60 27N 22 15 E
Turzovka 53 49 25N 18 41 E
Tuscaloosa 157 33 13N 87 31W
Tuscánia 63 42 25N 11 53 E
Tuscany = Toscana 62 43 28N 11 15 E
Tuscola, Ill., U.S.A. 156 39 48N 88 15W
Tuscola, Tex., U.S.A. 159 32 15N 99 48W
Tuscumbia 157 34 42N 87 42W
Tushan 106 25 50N 107 33 E
Tushino 81 55 44N 37 29 E
Tuskar Rock 39 52 12N 6 10W
Tuskegee 157 32 24N 85 39W
Tŭšnad 70 47 30N 22 33 E
Tustna 71 63 10N 8 5 E
Tuszyn 54 51 36N 19 33 E
Tutaryd 73 56 54N 13 59 E
Tutbury 28 52 52N 1 41W
Tutikorin 97 8 50N 78 12 E
Tutin 66 43 0N 20 20 E
Tutóia 170 2 45 S 42 20W
Tutoko Mt. 143 44 35 S 168 1 E
Tutong 102 4 47N 114 34 E
Tutova, R. 70 46 20N 27 30 E
Tutrakan 67 44 2N 26 40 E
Tutshi L. 152 59 56N 134 30W
Tuttlingen 49 47 59N 8 50 E
Tutuaia 103 8 25 S 127 15 E
Tutye 140 35 12 S 141 29 E
Tuva, A.S.S.R. □ 77 51 30N 95 0 E
Tuxford 33 53 14N 0 52W
Tuxpan 165 20 50N 97 30W
Tuxtla Gutiérrez 165 16 50N 93 10W
Tuy 56 42 3N 8 39W
Tuy An 100 13 17N 109 16 E
Tuy Doc 101 12 15N 107 27 E
Tuy Hoa 100 13 5N 109 17 E
Tuy Phong 101 11 14N 108 43 E
Tuya L. 152 59 7N 130 35W
Tuyen Hoa 100 17 50N 106 10 E
Tuyen Quang 100 21 50N 105 10 E
Tuymazy 84 54 36N 53 42 E
Tuyun 108 26 15N 107 32 E
Tuz Gölü 92 38 45N 33 30 E
Tuz Khurmatli 92 34 52N 44 41 E
Tuz Khurmatu 92 34 50N 44 45 E
Tuzkan, Ozero 85 40 35N 67 28 E
Tuzla 66 44 34N 18 41 E
Tuzlov, R. 83 47 28N 39 45 E
Tvåaker 73 57 4N 12 25 E
Tværsted 73 57 36N 10 12 E
Tvarskog 73 56 34N 16 0 E
Tved 73 56 12N 10 25 E
Tvedestrand 71 58 38N 8 58 E
Tveitsund 71 59 2N 8 31 E
Tvelt 71 60 30N 7 11 E
Tvyrditsa 67 42 42N 25 53 E
Twain Harte 163 38 2N 120 14W
Twardogóra 54 51 23N 17 28 E
Twatt 37 59 6N 3 15W
Tweed, R. 35 55 42N 2 10W
Tweede Exploërmond 46 52 55N 6 56 E
Tweedmouth 35 55 46N 2 1W
Tweedshaws 35 55 26N 3 29W
Tweedsmuir Prov. Park 152 52 55N 126 20W
Twello 46 52 14N 6 6 E
Twelve Pins 38 53 32N 9 50W
Twentynine Palms 163 34 10N 116 4W
Twillingate 151 49 42N 54 45W
Twin Bridges 160 45 33N 112 23W
Twin Falls 160 42 30N 114 30W
Twin Valley 158 47 18N 96 15W
Twinnge 98 21 58N 96 23 E
Twisp 160 48 21N 120 5W
Twistringen 48 52 48N 8 38 E
Two Harbors 158 47 1N 91 40W
Two Hills 152 53 43N 111 45W
Two Mile Borris 39 52 41N 7 43W
Two Rivers 156 44 10N 87 31W
Two Thumbs Ra. 143 43 45 S 170 44 E
Two Tree 138 18 25 S 140 3 E
Twofold B. 141 37 8 S 149 59 E
Twong 123 5 18N 28 29 E
Twyford, Berks., U.K. 29 51 29N 0 51W
Twyford, Hants., U.K. 28 51 1N 1 19W
Ty 73 56 27N 8 32 E
Tyborön 73 56 42N 8 12 E
Tychy 54 50 9N 18 59 E
Tyczyn 54 49 58N 22 2 E
Tydd St. Mary 29 52 45N 0 9 E
Tykocin 54 53 13N 22 46 E
Tyldal 71 62 8N 10 48 E
Tyldesley 32 53 31N 2 29W
Tyler, Minn., U.S.A. 158 44 18N 96 15W
Tyler, Tex., U.S.A. 159 44 18N 96 15W
Tylldal 71 62 7N 10 45 E
Tylösand 73 56 33N 12 40 E
Týn nad Vltavou 52 49 13N 14 26 E
Tynagh 39 53 10N 8 22W
Tyndall, Mt. 143 43 15 S 170 55 E
Tyndinskiy 77 55 10N 124 43 E
Tyndrum 34 56 26N 4 41W
Tyne & Wear □ 35 54 55N 1 35W
Tyne, R., Eng., U.K. 35 54 58N 1 28W
Tyne, R., Scot., U.K. 35 55 58N 2 45W
Tynemouth 35 55 1N 1 27W
Tynset 71 62 17N 10 47 E
Tyre = Sūr 90 33 19N 35 16 E
Tyrifjorden 71 60 2N 10 8 E
Tyringe 73 56 9N 13 35 E
Tyristrand 71 60 5N 10 5 E
Tyrnyauz 83 43 21N 42 45 E
Tyrol = Tirol 52 46 50N 11 20 E
Tyrone □ 38 54 40N 7 15W
Tyrone, Co. 38 54 40N 7 15W
Tyrrell Arm 153 62 27N 97 30W
Tyrrell, L. 140 35 20 S 142 50 E
Tyrrell L. 153 63 7N 105 27W
Tyrrell, R. 140 35 26 S 142 51 E
Tyrrhenian Sea 60 40 0N 12 30 E
Tysfjörden 74 68 10N 16 10 E
Tysmenitsa 80 48 58N 24 50 E
Tysnes 71 60 1N 5 30 E
Tyssedal 71 60 7N 6 35 E
Tystberga 73 58 51N 17 15 E
Tyulgan 84 52 22N 56 12 E
Tyumen 84 57 0N 65 18 E
Tyumen-Aryk 85 44 2N 67 1 E
Tyup 85 42 45N 78 20 E
Tyvoll 71 62 43N 11 21 E
Tywardreath 30 50 21N 4 40W
Tywi, R. 31 51 48N 4 20W
Tywyn 31 52 36N 4 5W
Tzaneen 129 23 47 S 30 9 E
Tzefa 90 31 7N 35 12 E
Tzermiadhes Neapolis 69 35 11N 25 29 E
Tzoumérka, Óros 68 39 30N 21 26 E
Tzu Shui, R. 109 29 2N 112 55 E
Tzuch'ang 106 37 12N 109 44 E
Tzuch'eng 107 36 39N 117 56 E
Tzuch'i 109 27 42N 116 58 E
Tz'uch'i 109 29 59N 121 14 E
Tzuchien 99 27 43N 98 34 E
Tzuchin 109 23 38N 115 10 E
Tzuchung 108 29 49N 104 55 E
Tz'uhsien 106 36 22N 114 23 E
Tzuhsing 109 25 58N 113 24 E
Tzukuei 105 31 0N 110 38 E
Tzukung 108 29 20N 104 50 E
Tz'uli 109 29 25N 111 6 E
Tzummarum 46 53 14N 5 32 E
Tzupo 105 36 49N 118 5 E
T'zuyang 108 32 31N 108 32 E
Tzuyang 108 30 7N 104 39 E
Tzuyün 108 25 45N 106 5 E

U

U Taphao 100 12 35N 101 0 E
Uad Erni, O. 118 26 30N 9 30W
Uainambi 174 1 43N 69 51W
Uanda 138 21 37 S 144 55 E
Uarsciek 91 2 28N 45 55 E
Uasadi-jidi, Sierra 174 4 54N 65 18W
Uasin □ 126 0 30N 35 20 E
Uassem 90 32 59N 36 2 E
Uato-Udo 103 4 3 S 126 6 E
Uatumã, R. 174 1 30 S 59 25W
Uauá 170 9 50 S 39 28W
Uaupés 174 0 8 S 67 5W
Uaxactún 166 17 25N 89 29W
Ub 66 44 28N 20 6 E
Ubá 173 21 0 S 43 0W
Ubaitaba 171 14 18 S 39 20W
Ubangi, R. = Oubangi 124 1 0N 17 50 E
Ubaté 174 5 19N 73 49W
Ubauro 94 28 15N 69 45 E
Ube 110 33 56N 131 15 E
Ubeda 59 38 3N 3 23W
Uberaba 171 19 50 S 47 55W
Uberlândia 171 19 0 S 48 20W
Ubiaja 121 6 41N 6 22 E
Ubolratna Phong, L. 100 16 45N 102 30 E
Ubombo 129 27 31 S 32 4 E
Ubon Ratchathani 100 15 15N 104 50 E
Ubondo 126 0 55 S 25 42 E
Ubort, R. 80 51 45N 28 30 E
Ubrique 57 36 41N 5 27W
Ubundi 126 0 22 S 25 30 E
Ucayali, R. 174 6 0 S 75 0W
Uccle 47 50 48N 4 22 E
Uchaly 84 54 19N 59 27 E
Uchi Lake 153 51 10N 92 40W
Uchiko 110 33 33N 132 39 E
Uchiura-Wan 112 42 25N 140 40 E
Uchte 48 52 29N 8 52 E
Uchterek 85 41 45N 73 12 E
Uckerath 48 50 44N 7 22 E
Uckfield 29 50 58N 0 6 E
Ucluelet 152 48 57N 125 32W
Ucolta 107 32 56 S 138 59 E
Ucuriş 70 46 41N 21 58 E
Uda, R. 77 54 42N 135 14 E
Udaipur 94 24 36N 73 44 E
Udaipur Garhi 95 27 0N 86 35 E
Udamalpet 97 10 35N 77 15 E
Udbina 63 44 31N 15 47 E
Uddeholm 72 60 1N 13 38 E
Uddel 46 52 15N 5 48 E
Uddevalla 73 58 21N 11 55 E
Uddingston 35 55 50N 4 3W

Uddjaur Ust Kuyga

Uddjaur 74 65 55N 17 50E
Uden 47 51 40N 5 37E
Udgir 96 18 25N 77 5E
Udhampur 95 33 0N 75 5E
Udi 121 6 23N 7 21E
Údine 63 46 5N 13 10E
Údine □ 63 46 3N 13 13E
Udipi 97 13 25N 74 42E
Udmurt, A.S.S.R. □ 84 57 30N 52 30E
Udon Thani 100 17 29N 102 46E
Udubo 121 11 52N 10 35E
Udvoj Balken 67 42 50N 26 50E
Udzungwa Range 127 11 15S 35 10E
Ueckermünde 48 53 45N 14 1E
Ueda 111 36 24N 138 16E
Uedineniya, Os. 12 78 0N 85 0E
Uele, R. 124 3 50N 22 40E
Uelen 77 66 10N 170 0W
Uelzen 48 53 0N 10 33E
Ueno 111 34 53N 136 14E
Uere, R. 124 3 45N 24 45E
Uetendorf 50 46 47N 7 34E
Ufa 84 54 45N 55 55E
Ufa, R. 84 56 30N 58 10E
Uffculme 30 50 45N 3 19W
Ufford 29 52 6N 1 22E
Ugad R. 125 20 55S 14 30E
Ugalla, R. 126 6 0S 32 0E
Ugamas 128 28 0S 19 41E
Uganda ■ 126 2 0N 32 0E
Ugborough 30 50 22N 3 53W
Ugchelen 46 52 11N 5 56E
Ugento 65 39 55N 18 10E
Ugep 121 5 53N 8 2E
Ugie 129 31 10S 28 13E
Ugijar 59 36 58N 3 7W
Ugine 45 45 45N 6 25E
Ugla 122 25 40N 37 42E
Uglich 81 57 33N 38 13E
Ugljane 63 43 35N 16 46E
Ugra, R. 80 54 45N 35 30E
Ugurchin 67 43 6N 24 26E
Uh, R. 53 48 40N 22 0E
Uherske Hradiště 53 49 4N 17 30E
Uhersky Brod 53 49 1N 17 40E
Uhrichsville 156 40 23N 81 22W
Uig, Lewis, U.K. 36 58 13N 7 1W
Uig, Skye, U.K. 36 57 35N 6 20W
Uinta Mts. 160 40 45N 110 30W
Uitenhage 128 33 40S 25 28E
Uitgeest 46 52 32N 4 43E
Uithoorn 46 52 14N 4 50E
Uithuizen 46 53 24N 6 41E
Uitkerke 47 51 18N 3 9E
Ujda = Oujda 118 34 45N 2 0W
Ujfehértó 53 47 49N 21 41E
Ujh, R. 95 32 40N 75 30E
Ujhani 95 28 0N 79 6E
Uji 111 34 53N 135 48E
Ujjain 94 23 9N 75 43E
Újpest 53 47 22N 19 6E
Ujszász 53 47 19N 20 7E
Ujung Pandang 103 5 10S 119 20E
Uka 77 57 50N 162 0E
Ukara I. 126 1 44S 33 0E
Ukehe 121 6 40N 7 24E
Ukerewe □ 126 2 0S 32 30E
Ukerewe Is. 126 2 0S 33 0E
Ukholovo 81 54 47N 40 30E
Ukhrul 98 25 10N 94 25E
Ukhta 78 63 55N 54 0E
Ukiah 160 39 10N 123 9W
Ukki Fort 95 33 28N 76 54E
Ukmerge 80 55 15N 24 45E
Ukraine S.S.R. □ 82 48 0N 35 0E
Uksyanskoye 84 55 57N 63 1E
Ukwi 128 23 29S 20 30E
Ulaanbaatar 105 47 55N 106 53E
Ulaangom 105 49 58N 92 2E
Ulak I. 147 51 24N 178 58W
Ulamambri 141 31 19S 149 23E
Ulamba 127 9 3S 23 38E
Ulan Bator = Ulaanbaatar 105 47 55N 106 53E
Ulan Ude 77 52 0N 107 30E
Ulanbel 85 44 50N 71 7E
Ulanga □ 127 8 40S 36 50E
Ulanów 54 50 30N 22 16E
Ulaya, Morogoro, Tanz. 126 7 3S 36 55E
Ulaya, Shinyanga, Tanz. 126 4 25S 33 30E
Ulbster 37 58 21N 3 9W
Ulceby Cross 33 53 14N 0 6E
Ulcinj 66 41 58N 19 10E
Ulco 128 28 21S 24 15E
Ulefoss 71 59 17N 9 16E
Ulëza 68 41 46N 19 57E
Ulfborg 73 56 16N 8 20E
Ulft 46 51 53N 6 23E
Ulhasnagar 96 19 15N 73 10E
Ulinda 141 31 35S 149 30E
Uljma 66 45 2N 21 10E
Ulla, R. 56 42 45N 8 30W
Ulladulla 141 35 21S 150 29E
Ullånger 72 62 58N 18 16E
Ullapool 36 57 54N 5 10W
Ullared 73 57 8N 12 42E
Ulldecona 58 40 36N 0 20E
Ullswater, L. 32 54 35N 2 52W
Ullvättern, L. 72 59 30N 14 21E
Ulm 49 48 23N 10 0E
Ulmarra 139 29 37S 153 4E
Ulmeni 70 45 4N 46 40E
Ulricehamn 73 57 46N 13 26E
Ulrum 46 53 22N 6 20E
Ulsberg 71 62 45N 9 59E
Ulsfeinvik 71 62 21N 5 53E
Ulster □ 38 54 45N 6 30W
Ulster Canal 38 54 15N 7 0W
Ulstrem 67 42 1N 26 27E
Ultima 140 35 22S 143 18E
Ulubaria 95 22 31N 88 4E
Ulugh Muztagh 99 36 40N 87 30E
Uluguru Mts. 126 7 15S 37 30E
Ulva, I. 34 56 30N 6 12W
Ulvenhout 47 51 33N 4 48E
Ulverston 32 54 13N 3 7W
Ulverstone 138 41 11S 146 11E
Ulvik 71 60 35N 6 54E
Ulvo 73 56 40N 14 37E
Ulya 77 59 10N 142 0E
Ulyanovsk 81 54 25N 48 25E
Ulyasutay 105 47 45N 96 49E
Ulysses 159 37 39N 101 25W
Ulzio 62 45 2N 6 49E
Um Qeis 90 32 40N 35 41E
Umag 63 45 26N 13 31E
Umala 174 17 25S 68 5W
Uman 82 48 40N 30 12E
Umánaé 12 70 40N 52 10W
Umánaé Fjord 10 70 40N 52 0W
Umaria 99 23 35N 80 50E
Umarkhed 96 19 37N 77 38E
Umarkot 93 25 15N 69 40E
Umatilla 160 45 58N 119 17W
Umba 78 66 50N 34 20E
Umbertide 63 43 18N 12 20E
Umboi I. 135 5 40S 148 0E
Umbrella Mts. 143 45 35S 169 5E
Umbria □ 63 42 53N 12 30E
Ume, R. 74 64 45N 18 30E
Umeå 74 63 45N 20 20E
Umera 103 0 12S 129 30E
Umfuli, R. 127 17 50S 29 40E
Umgusa 127 19 29S 27 52E
Umi 110 33 34N 130 30E
Umiat 147 69 25N 152 20W
Umka 66 44 40N 20 19E
Umkomaas 129 30 13S 30 48E
Umm al Aranib 119 26 10N 14 54E
Umm al Qaiwain 93 25 30N 55 35E
Umm Arda 123 15 17N 32 31E
Umm az Zamul 93 22 35N 55 18E
Umm Bel 123 13 35N 28 0E
Umm Digulgulaya 123 10 28N 24 58E
Umm Dubban 123 15 23N 32 52E
Umm el Fahm 90 32 31N 35 9E
Umm Hagar 123 14 20N 36 41E
Umm Koweika 123 13 10N 32 16E
Umm Lajj 92 25 0N 37 23E
Umm Merwa 122 18 4N 32 30E
Umm Qurein 123 16 3N 28 49E
Umm Rumah 122 25 50N 36 30E
Umm Ruwaba 123 12 50N 31 10E
Umm Said 93 25 0N 51 40E
Umm Sidr 123 14 29N 25 10E
Ummanz I. 48 54 29N 13 9E
Umnak. 147 53 20N 168 20W
Umnak I. 147 53 0N 168 0W
Umniati, R. 127 18 0S 29 0E
Umpang 101 16 3N 98 54E
Umpqua, R. 160 43 30N 123 30W
Umrer 96 20 51N 79 18E
Umreth 94 22 41N 73 4E
Umshandige Dam 127 20 10S 30 40E
Umtali 127 18 58S 32 38E
Umtata 129 31 36S 28 49E
Umuahia-Ibeku 121 5 33N 7 29E
Umvukwe Ra.. 127 16 45S 30 45E
Umvuma 127 19 16S 30 30E
Umzimvubu, R. 129 31 38S 29 33E
Umzingwane, R. 127 21 30S 29 30E
Umzinto 129 30 15S 30 45E
Una 94 20 46N 71 8E
Una, Mt. 143 42 13S 172 36E
Una, R. 63 44 50N 16 15E
Unac, R. 63 44 42N 16 15E
Unadilla 162 42 20N 75 17W
Unalanaska I. 147 54 0N 164 30W
Uncastillo 58 42 21N 1 8W
Uncia 174 18 25S 66 40W
Uncompahgce Pk., Mt. 161 38 5N 107 32W
Unden 73 58 45N 14 25E
Underbool 140 35 10S 141 51E
Undersaker 72 63 19N 13 21E
Undersvik 72 61 36N 16 20E
Undredal 71 60 57N 7 6E
Unecha 80 52 50N 32 37E
Ungarie 141 33 38S 146 56E
Ungarra 140 34 12S 136 2E
Ungava B. 149 59 30N 67 30W
Ungava Pen. 50 60 0N 75 0W
Ungeny 82 47 11N 27 51E
Unggi 105 42 16N 130 28E
Ungwatiri 123 16 52N 36 10E
Uni 84 56 44N 51 47E
União 170 4 50S 37 50W
União da Vitória 173 26 5S 51 0W
União dos Palamares 170 9 10S 36 2W
Uniejów 54 51 59N 18 46E
Unije, I. 63 44 40N 14 15E
Unimak I. 147 54 30N 164 30W
Unimak Pass. 148 53 30N 165 15W
Union, Mo., U.S.A. 158 38 25N 91 0W
Union, S.C., U.S.A. 157 34 49N 81 39W
Union City, N.J., U.S.A. 162 40 47N 74 5W
Union City, Ohio, U.S.A. 156 40 11N 84 49W
Union City, Pa., U.S.A. 156 41 53N 79 50W
Union Gap 157 46 38N 120 29W
Unión, La, Chile 176 40 10S 73 0W
Unión, La, Colomb. 174 1 35N 77 5W
Unión, La, El Sal. 165 13 20N 87 50W
Union, La 164 17 58N 101 49W
Unión, La, Spain 59 37 38N 0 53W
Unión, La, Venez. 174 7 28N 67 53W
Union, Mt. 161 34 34N 112 21W
Union of Soviet Soc. Rep. ■ 77 47 0N 100 0E
Union Springs 157 32 9N 85 44W
Uniondale Road 128 33 39S 23 7E
Uniontown 156 39 54N 79 45W
Unirea 70 44 15N 27 35E
United Arab Emirates ■ 93 23 50N 54 0E
United Arab Republic ■ 113 27 5N 30 0E
United Kingdom ■ 27 55 0N 3 0W
United States of America ■ 155 37 0N 96 0W
Unity 153 52 30N 109 5W
Unjha 94 23 46N 72 24E
Unnao 95 26 35N 80 30E
Uno, Ilha 120 11 15N 16 13W
Unshin, R. 38 54 8N 8 26W
Unst, I. 36 60 50N 0 55W
Unstrut, R. 48 51 16N 11 29E
Unter-Engadin 51 46 48N 10 20E
Unterägeri 51 47 8N 8 36E
Unterkulm 50 47 18N 8 7E
Unterseen 50 46 41N 7 50E
Unterwalden nid dem Wald □ 51 46 50N 8 25E
Unterwalden ob dem Wald □ 51 46 55N 8 15E
Unterwaldner Alpen 51 46 55N 8 15E
Unterwasser 51 46 32N 8 21E
Unturán, Sierra de 174 1 35N 64 40W
Unuk, R. 152 56 5N 131 3W
Ünye 82 41 5N 37 15E
Unzen-Dake 111 32 45N 130 17E
Unzha 81 57 40N 44 8E
Unzha, R. 81 58 0N 43 40E
Uors 51 46 42N 9 12E
Uozu 111 36 48N 137 24E
Upa, R. 53 50 45N 16 15E
Upal 123 6 56N 34 12E
Upata 174 8 1N 62 24W
Upavon 28 51 17N 1 49W
Upemba, L. 127 8 30S 26 20E
Upernavik 12 72 49N 56 20W
Upington 128 28 25S 21 15E
Upleta 94 21 46N 70 16E
Upolu Pt. 147 20 16N 155 52W
Upper Alkali Lake 160 41 47N 120 0W
Upper Arrow L. 152 50 30N 117 50W
Upper Austria = Oberösterreich 52 48 15N 14 10E
Upper Chapel 31 52 3N 3 26W
Upper Foster L. 153 56 47N 105 20W
Upper Heyford 28 51 54N 1 16W
Upper Hutt 142 41 8S 175 5E
Upper Klamath L. 160 42 16N 121 55W
Upper L. Erne 38 54 14N 7 22W
Upper Lake 160 39 10N 122 55W
Upper Manilla 141 30 38S 150 40E
Upper Marlboro 162 38 49N 76 45W
Upper Musquodoboit 151 45 10N 62 58W
Upper Sandusky 156 40 50N 83 17W
Upper Volta ■ 120 12 0N 0 30W
Upperchurch 39 52 43N 8 2W
Upphärad 73 58 9N 12 19E
Uppingham 29 52 36N 0 43W
Uppsala 72 59 53N 17 38E
Uppsala län □ 72 60 0N 17 30E
Upshi 95 33 48N 77 52E
Upstart, C. 138 19 41S 147 45E
Upton, U.K. 32 53 14N 2 52W
Upton, U.S.A. 158 44 8N 104 35W
Upton-upon-Severn 28 52 4N 2 12W
Upwey 28 50 40N 2 29W
Ur 92 30 55N 46 25E
Ura-Tyube 85 39 55N 69 1E
Urabá, Golfo de 174 8 25N 76 53W
Uracará 174 2 20S 57 50W
Urach 49 48 29N 9 25E
Uraga-Suidō 111 35 13N 139 45E
Urakawa 112 42 9N 142 47E
Ural, Mt. 141 33 21S 146 12E
Ural Mts. = Uralskie Gory 78 60 0N 59 0E
Ural, R. 84 49 0N 52 0W
Uralla 141 30 37S 151 29E
Uralsk 84 51 20N 51 20E
Uralskie Gory 78 60 0N 59 0E
Urambo 126 5 4S 32 47E
Urambo □ 126 5 0S 32 0E
Urana 141 35 15S 146 21E
Urandangi 138 21 32S 138 14E
Uranium City 153 59 34N 108 37W
Uraricaá, R. 174 3 20N 61 56W
Uravakonda 97 14 57N 77 12E
Urawa 111 35 50N 139 40E
Uray 76 60 5N 65 15E
Urbana, Ill., U.S.A. 156 40 7N 88 12W
Urbana, Ohio, U.S.A. 156 40 9N 83 44W
Urbana, La 174 7 8N 66 56W
Urbánia 63 43 40N 12 31E
Urbano Santos 170 3 12S 43 23W
Urbel, R. 58 42 30N 3 49W
Urbino 63 43 43N 12 38E
Urbión, Picos de 58 42 1N 2 52W
Urcos 174 13 30S 71 30W
Urda, Spain 57 39 25N 3 43W
Urda, U.S.S.R. 83 48 52N 47 23E
Urdinarrain 172 32 37S 58 52W
Urdos 44 42 51N 0 35W
Urdzhar 76 47 5N 81 38E
Ure, R. 33 54 20N 1 25W
Uren 81 57 35N 45 55E
Ures 164 29 30N 110 30W
Ureshino 110 33 6N 129 59E
Urfa 92 37 12N 38 50E
Urfahr 52 48 19N 14 17E
Urgench 76 41 40N 60 30E
Urgun 93 32 55N 69 12E
Urgut 85 39 23N 67 15E
Uri 95 34 8N 74 2E
Uri □ 51 46 43N 8 35E
Uribante, R. 174 7 25N 71 50W
Uribe 174 3 13N 74 24W
Uribia 174 11 43N 72 16W
Urim 90 31 18N 34 32E
Uriondo 172 21 41S 64 41W
Urique 164 27 13N 107 55W
Urique, R. 164 26 29N 107 58W
Urirotstock 51 46 52N 8 32E
Urk 46 52 39N 5 36E
Urla 92 38 20N 26 55E
Urlati 70 44 59N 26 15E
Urlingford 39 52 43N 7 35W
Urmia, L. 92 37 30N 45 30E
Urmia 92 37 40N 45 0E
Urmston 32 53 28N 2 22W
Urner Alpen 51 46 45N 8 45E
Uroševac 66 42 23N 21 10E
Urrao 174 6 20N 76 11W
Urshult 73 56 31N 14 50E
Urso 123 9 35N 41 33E
Ursus 54 52 21N 20 53E
Uruaca 171 15 30S 49 41W
Uruaçu 171 14 30S 49 10W
Uruapán 164 19 30N 102 0W
Urubamba 174 13 5S 72 10W
Urubamba, R. 174 11 0S 73 0W
Uruçuca 171 14 35S 39 16W
Uruçui 170 7 20S 44 28W
Uruçui Prêto, R. 170 7 20S 44 38W
Uruçui, Serra do 170 9 0S 44 45W
Urucuia, R. 171 16 8S 45 5W
Uruguai, R. 173 24 0S 53 30W
Uruguaiana 172 29 50S 57 0W
Uruguay ■ 172 32 30S 55 30W
Uruguay, R. 172 28 0S 56 0W
Urumchi = Wulumuchi 105 43 40N 87 50E
Urup, I. 77 43 0N 151 0E
Urup, R. 83 44 19N 41 30E
Urutaí 171 17 28S 48 12W
Uruyén 174 5 41N 62 25W
Uruzgan □ 93 33 30N 66 0E
Uryupinsk 81 50 45N 42 3E
Urzhum 81 57 10N 49 56E
Urziceni 70 44 46N 26 42E
Usa 110 33 31N 131 21E
Usa, R. 78 66 20N 56 0E
Uşak 92 38 43N 29 28E
Usakos 128 22 0S 15 31E
Usambara Mts. 126 4 50S 38 20E
Usedom 48 53 50N 13 55E
Useko 124 5 8S 32 24E
Usfan 122 21 58N 39 27E
Ush-Tobe 76 45 16N 78 0E
Ushakova, O. 12 82 0N 80 0E
Ushant = Ouessant, Île d' 42 48 25N 5 5W
Ushashi 126 1 59S 33 57E
Ushat 123 7 59N 29 28E
Ushibuka 110 32 11N 130 1E
Ushuaia 176 54 50S 68 23W
Ushumun 77 52 47N 126 32E
Usk 31 51 42N 2 53W
Usk, R. 31 51 37N 2 56W
Uskedal 71 59 56N 5 53E
Üsküdar 92 41 0N 29 5E
Uslar 48 51 39N 9 39E
Usman 81 52 5N 39 48E
Usoga □ 126 0 5N 33 30E
Usoke 126 5 7S 32 19E
Usolye Sibirskoye 77 52 40N 103 40E
Usoro 121 5 33N 6 11E
Uspallata, P. de 172 32 30S 69 28W
Uspenskiy 76 48 50N 72 55E
Usquert 46 53 24N 6 36E
Ussel 44 45 32N 2 18E
Ussuriysk 77 43 40N 131 50E
Ust 52 50 41N 14 2E
Ust Aldan = Batamay 77 63 30N 129 15E
Ust Amginskoye = Khandyga 77 62 30N 134 50E
Ust-Bolsheretsk 77 52 40N 156 30E
Ust Buzulukskaya 81 50 8N 42 11E
Ust Doneckij 83 47 35N 40 55E
Ust Donetskiy 83 47 35N 40 55E
Ust Ilga 77 55 5N 104 55E
Ust Ilimpeya = Yukti 77 63 20N 105 0E
Ust-Ilimsk 77 58 3N 102 39E
Ust Ishim 76 57 45N 71 10E
Ust Kamchatsk 77 56 10N 162 0E
Ust Kamenogorsk 76 50 0N 82 20E
Ust Karenga 77 54 40N 116 45E
Ust Khayryuzova 77 57 15N 156 55E
Ust Kut 77 56 50N 105 10E
Ust Kuyga 77 70 1N 135 36E

Vatomandry **Vijayadurg**

Vatomandry	129	19 20S	48 59E
Vatra-Dornei	70	47 22N	25 22E
Vats	71	59 29N	5 45E
Vättern, L.	73	58 25N	14 30E
Vättis	51	46 55N	9 27E
Vaucluse □	45	44 3N	5 10E
Vaucouleurs	43	48 37N	5 40E
Vaud □	50	46 35N	6 30E
Vaughan	161	34 37N	105 12W
Vaughn	160	47 37N	111 36W
Vaulruz	50	46 38N	7 0E
Vaupés □	174	1 0N	71 0W
Vaupés, R.	174	1 0N	71 0W
Vauvert	45	43 42N	4 17E
Vauxhall	152	50 5N	112 9W
Vavincourt	43	48 49N	5 12E
Vavoua	120	7 23N	6 29W
Vaxholm	72	59 25N	18 20E
Växjö	73	56 52N	14 50E
Vaygach, Ostrov	76	70 0N	60 0E
Vaza Barris, R.	171	10 0S	37 30W
Veadeiros	171	14 7S	47 31W
Veagh L.	38	55 3N	7 57W
Vechta	48	52 47N	8 18E
Vechte, R.	46	52 34N	6 6E
Vecilla, La	56	42 51N	5 27W
Vecsés	53	47 26N	19 19E
Vedaraniam	97	10 25N	79 50E
Vedbæk	73	55 50N	12 33E
Veddige	73	57 17N	12 20E
Vedea, R.	70	44 0N	25 20E
Vedelgem	47	51 7N	3 10E
Vedia	172	34 30S	61 31W
Vedra, Isla del	59	38 52N	1 12E
Vedrin	47	50 30N	4 52E
Veendam	46	53 5N	6 52E
Veenendaal	46	52 2N	5 34E
Veenwouden	46	53 14N	6 0E
Veerle	47	51 4N	4 59E
Vefsna	74	65 48N	13 10E
Vega, Norway	74	65 40N	11 55E
Vega, U.S.A.	159	35 18N	102 26W
Vega Baja	147	18 27N	66 23W
Vega Fd.	74	65 37N	12 0E
Vega, I.	74	65 42N	11 50E
Vega, La	167	19 20N	70 30W
Vegadeo	56	43 27N	7 4W
Vegesack	48	53 10N	8 38E
Vegfjorden	74	65 37N	12 0E
Veggerby	73	56 54N	9 39E
Veggli	71	60 3N	9 9E
Veghel	47	51 37N	5 32E
Vegorritis, Limni	68	40 45N	21 45E
Vegreville	152	53 30N	112 5W
Vegusdal	71	58 32N	8 10E
Veii	63	42 0N	12 24E
Veinticino de Mayo	172	38 0S	67 40W
Veitch	140	34 39S	140 31E
Vejen	73	55 30N	9 9E
Vejer de la Frontera	57	36 15N	5 59W
Vejle	73	55 43N	9 30E
Vejle Amt □	73	55 2N	11 22E
Vejle Fjord	73	55 40N	9 50E
Vejlo	73	55 10N	11 45E
Vela Luka	63	42 59N	16 44E
Velanai I.	97	9 45N	79 45E
Velarde	161	36 11N	106 1W
Velas, C.	166	10 21N	85 52W
Velasco	159	29 0N	95 20W
Velasco, Sierra de.	172	29 20S	67 10W
Velay, Mts. du	44	45 0N	3 40E
Velb	46	52 0N	5 59E
Velddrif	128	32 42S	18 11E
Velden	47	51 25N	6 10E
Veldhoven	47	51 24N	5 25E
Veldwezelt	47	50 52N	5 38E
Velebit Planina	63	44 50N	15 20E
Velebitski Kanal	63	44 45N	14 55E
Veleka, R.	67	42 4N	27 30E
Velenje	63	46 23N	15 8E
Velestínon	68	39 23N	22 43E
Vélez	174	6 1N	73 41W
Velez	66	43 19N	18 2E
Vélez Blanco	57	37 41N	2 5W
Vélez Málaga	57	36 48N	4 5W
Vélez Rubio	59	37 41N	2 5W
Velhas, R.	171	17 13S	44 49W
Velika	66	45 27N	17 40E
Velika Goricá	63	45 44N	16 5E
Velika Kapela	63	45 10N	15 5E
Velika Kladuša	63	45 11N	15 48E
Velika Morava, R.	66	44 30N	21 9E
Velika Plana	66	44 20N	21 1E
Velikaya, R.	80	56 40N	28 40E
Veliké Kapušany	53	48 34N	22 5E
Velike Lašče	63	45 49N	14 45E
Veliki Backa Kanal	68	45 45N	19 15E
Veliki Jastrebac	66	43 25N	21 30E
Veliki Ustyug	78	60 47N	46 20E
Velikiye Luki	80	56 25N	30 32E
Velíko Turnovo	67	43 5N	25 41E
Velikonda Range	97	14 45N	79 10E
Velikoye, Oz.	81	55 15N	40 0E
Velingrad	67	42 4N	23 58E
Velino, Mt.	63	42 10N	13 20E
Velizh	80	55 30N	31 11E
Velké Karlovice	53	49 20N	18 17E
Velke Mezirici	52	49 21N	16 1E
Velký ostrov Zitný	53	48 5N	17 20E
Vellar, R.	97	11 30N	79 36E
Velletri	64	41 43N	12 43E
Velling	73	56 2N	8 20E
Vellinge	73	55 29N	13 0E
Vellir	74	65 55N	18 28W
Vellore	97	12 57N	79 10E
Velsen-Noord	46	52 27N	4 40E
Velsk	78	61 10N	42 5E
Velten	48	52 40N	13 11E
Veluwe Meer	46	52 24N	5 44E
Velva	158	48 6N	100 56W
Velvendós	68	40 15N	22 6E
Vem	73	56 21N	8 21E
Vembanad Lake	97	9 36N	76 15E
Veme	71	60 14N	10 7E
Ven	73	55 55N	12 45E
Vena	73	57 31N	16 0E
Venado	164	22 50N	101 10W
Venado Tuerto	172	33 50S	62 0W
Venafro	65	41 28N	14 3E
Venarey-les-Laumes	43	47 32N	4 26E
Venaria	62	45 12N	7 39E
Venčane	66	44 24N	20 28E
Vence	45	43 43N	7 6E
Vendas Novas	57	38 39N	8 27W
Vendée	42	46 50N	1 35W
Vendée □	44	46 40N	1 20W
Vendée, Collines de	42	46 35N	0 45W
Vendée, R.	42	46 30N	0 45W
Vendeuvre-sur-Barse	43	48 14N	4 28E
Vendôme	42	47 47N	1 3E
Vendrell	58	41 10N	1 30E
Vendsyssel	73	57 22N	10 0E
Veneta, Laguna	63	45 19N	12 13E
Venetie	147	67 0N	146 30W
Véneto □	63	45 30N	12 0E
Venev	81	54 22N	38 17E
Venézia	63	45 27N	12 20E
Venézia, Golfo di	63	45 20N	13 0E
Venezuela ■	174	8 0N	65 0W
Venezuela, Golfo de	174	11 30N	71 0W
Vengurla	97	15 53N	73 45E
Vengurla Rocks	97	15 50N	73 22E
Venice = Venézia	63	45 27N	12 20E
Vénissieux	45	45 43N	4 53E
Venjansjön	72	60 58N	14 2E
Venkatagiri	97	14 0N	79 35E
Venkatapuram	96	18 20N	80 30E
Venlo	47	51 22N	6 11E
Vennesla	71	58 15N	8 0E
Venø, Is.	73	56 33N	8 38E
Venraij	47	51 31N	6 0E
Venta de Cardeña	57	38 16N	4 20W
Venta de San Rafael	56	40 42N	4 12W
Venta, La	165	18 8N	94 3W
Ventana, Punta de la	164	24 4N	109 48W
Ventersburg	128	28 7S	27 9E
Ventimíglia	62	43 50N	7 39E
Ventnor	28	50 35N	1 12W
Ventotene, I.	64	40 48N	13 25E
Ventry	39	52 8N	10 21W
Ventspils	80	57 25N	21 32E
Ventuari, R.	174	5 20N	66 0W
Ventucopa	163	34 50N	119 29W
Ventura	163	34 16N	119 18W
Ventura, La	164	24 38N	100 54W
Venturosa, La	174	6 8N	68 48W
Venus B.	141	38 40S	145 42E
Veoy	71	62 45N	7 30E
Veoy Is.	71	62 45N	7 30E
Vera, Argent.	172	29 30S	60 20W
Vera, Spain	59	37 15N	1 15W
Veracruz	165	19 10N	96 10W
Veracruz □	165	19 0N	96 15W
Veraval	94	20 53N	70 27E
Verbánia	62	45 50N	8 55E
Verbicaro	65	39 46N	15 54E
Verbier	50	46 6N	7 13E
Vercelli	62	45 19N	8 25E
Verdalsøra	74	63 48N	11 30E
Verde Grande, R.	171	16 13S	43 49W
Verde Pequeno, R.	171	14 48S	43 31W
Verde, R., Argent.	176	41 55S	66 0W
Verde, R., Goiás, Brazil	171	18 1S	50 14W
Verde, R., Goiás, Brazil	171	19 11S	50 44W
Verde, R., Chihuahua, Mexico	164	26 59N	107 58W
Verde, R., Oaxaca, Mexico	164	15 59N	97 50W
Verde, R., Veracruz, Mexico	165	21 10N	102 50W
Verde, R., Parag.	172	23 9S	57 37W
Verden	48	52 58N	9 18E
Verdhikoúsa	68	39 47N	21 59E
Verdigre	158	42 38N	98 0W
Verdon-sur-Mer, Le	44	45 33N	1 4W
Verdun	43	49 12N	5 24E
Verdun-sur-le Doubs	43	46 54N	5 0E
Vereeniging	129	26 38S	27 57E
Vérendrye, Parc Prov. de	150	47 20N	76 40W
Vereshchagino	84	58 5N	54 40E
Verga, C.	120	10 30N	14 10W
Vergara	58	43 9N	2 28W
Vergato	62	44 18N	11 8E
Vergemont	138	23 33S	143 1E
Vergemont Cr.	138	24 16S	143 16E
Vergt	44	45 2N	0 43E
Verín	56	41 57N	7 27W
Veriña	56	43 32N	5 43W
Verkhnedvinsk	80	55 45N	27 58E
Verkhneuralsk	84	53 53N	59 13E
Verkhniy-Avzyan	84	53 32N	57 33E
Verkhniy Baskunchak	83	48 5N	46 50E
Verkhniy Tagil	84	57 22N	59 56E
Verkhniy Ufaley	84	56 4N	60 14E
Verkhniye Kigi	84	55 25N	58 37E
Verkhnyaya Salda	84	58 2N	60 33E
Verkhoturye	84	58 52N	60 48E
Verkhovye	81	52 55N	37 15E
Verkhoyansk	77	67 50N	133 50E
Verkhoyanskiy Khrebet	77	66 0N	129 0E
Verlo	153	50 19N	108 35W
Verma	71	62 21N	8 3E
Vermenton	43	47 40N	3 42E
Vermilion	153	53 20N	110 50W
Vermilion, B.	159	29 45N	91 55W
Vermilion Bay	153	49 50N	93 20W
Vermilion Chutes	152	58 22N	114 51W
Vermilion, R., Alta., Can.	153	53 22N	110 51W
Vermilion, R., Qué., Can.	150	47 38N	72 56W
Vermillion	158	42 50N	96 56W
Vermont □	156	43 40N	72 50W
Vern, oilfield	19	55 35N	4 45E
Vernal	160	40 28N	109 35W
Vernalis	163	37 36N	121 17W
Vernayez	50	46 8N	7 3E
Verner	150	46 25N	80 8W
Verneuil, Bois de	50	48 59N	1 59E
Verneuil-sur-Avre	42	48 45N	0 55E
Vernier	50	46 13N	6 5E
Vernon, Can.	152	50 20N	119 15W
Vernon, France	42	49 5N	1 30E
Vernon, U.S.A.	159	34 0N	99 15W
Vero Beach	157	27 39N	80 23W
Véroia	68	40 34N	22 18E
Verolanuova	62	45 20N	10 5E
Véroli	64	41 43N	13 24E
Verona	62	45 27N	11 0E
Veropol	77	66 0N	168 0E
Verrieres, Les	50	46 55N	6 28E
Versailles	43	48 48N	2 8E
Versoix	50	46 17N	6 10E
Vert, C.	120	14 45N	17 30W
Vertou	42	47 10N	1 28W
Vertus	43	48 54N	4 0E
Verulam	129	29 38S	31 2E
Verviers	47	50 37N	5 52E
Vervins	43	49 50N	3 53E
Verwood, Can.	153	49 30N	105 40W
Verwood, U.K.	28	50 53N	1 53W
Veryan	30	50 13N	4 56W
Veryan Bay	30	50 12N	4 51W
Verzej	63	46 34N	16 13E
Vesdre, R.	47	50 36N	6 0E
Veselí nad Luznicí	52	49 12N	14 15E
Veselie	67	42 18N	27 38E
Veselovskoye Vdkhr.	83	47 0N	41 0E
Veselyy Res.	83	47 0N	41 0E
Veshenskaya	83	49 35N	41 44E
Vesle, R.	43	49 17N	3 50E
Veslyana, R.	84	60 20N	54 0E
Vesoul	43	60 40N	6 11E
Vessigebro	73	56 58N	12 40E
Vest-Agder fylke □	71	58 30N	7 15E
Vest Fjorden	71	68 0N	15 0E
Vesta	166	9 43N	83 3W
Vestby	71	59 37N	10 45E
Vester Hassing	73	57 4N	10 8E
Vesterålen	74	68 45N	14 30E
Vestersche Veld	46	52 52N	6 9E
Vestfjorden	74	67 55N	14 0E
Vestfold fylke □	71	59 15N	10 0E
Vestmannaeyjar	74	63 27N	20 15W
Vestmarka	71	59 56N	11 59E
Vestnes	71	62 39N	7 5E
Vestone	62	45 43N	10 25E
Vestsjaellands Amt □	73	55 30N	11 20E
Vestspitsbergen	12	78 40N	17 0E
Vestvågøy	74	68 18N	13 50E
Vesuvio	65	40 50N	14 22E
Vesuvius, Mt. = Vesuvio	65	40 50N	14 22E
Veszprém	53	47 8N	17 57E
Veszprém □	53	47 5N	17 55E
Vésztő	53	46 55N	21 16E
Vetapalam	97	15 47N	80 18E
Vetlanda	73	57 24N	15 3E
Vetluga	81	57 53N	45 45E
Vetluzhskiy	81	57 17N	45 12E
Vetovo	67	43 42N	26 16E
Vetralia	63	42 20N	12 2E
Vetren	67	42 15N	24 3E
Vettore, Mte.	63	44 38N	7 5E
Veurne	47	51 5N	2 40E
Vevey	50	46 28N	6 51E
Vévi	68	40 47N	21 38E
Veys	92	31 30N	49 0E
Vézelise	43	48 30N	6 5E
Vezhen, mt.	67	42 50N	24 20E
Vi Thanh	101	9 42N	105 26E
Viacha	174	16 30S	68 5W
Viadana	62	44 55N	10 30E
Viana, Brazil	170	3 0S	44 40W
Viana, Port.	55	38 20N	8 0W
Viana, Spain	58	42 31N	2 22W
Viana do Castelo	56	41 42N	8 50W
Vianden	47	49 56N	6 12E
Vianen	46	51 59N	5 5E
Vianna do Castelo □	56	41 50N	8 30W
Vianópolis	171	16 40S	48 35W
Viar, R.	57	37 45N	5 54W
Viaréggio	62	43 52N	10 13E
Vibank	153	50 20N	103 56W
Vibey, R.	56	42 21N	7 15E
Vibo Valéntia	65	38 40N	16 5E
Viborg	73	56 27N	9 23E
Viborg Amt □	73	56 30N	9 20E
Vic-en-Bigorre	44	43 24N	0 3E
Vic-Fezensac	44	43 45N	0 18E
Vic Fézensac	44	43 47N	0 19E
Vic-sur-Cère	44	44 59N	2 38E
Vic-sur-Seille	43	48 45N	6 33E
Vicarstown	39	53 5N	7 7W
Vicenza	63	45 32N	11 31E
Vich	58	41 58N	2 19E
Vichada □	174	5 0N	69 30W
Vichuga	81	57 25N	41 55E
Vichy	44	46 9N	3 26E
Vickerstown	32	54 8N	3 17W
Vicksburg, Mich., U.S.A.	156	42 10N	85 30W
Vicksburg, Miss., U.S.A.	159	32 22N	90 56W
Vico, L. di	63	42 20N	12 10E
Viçosa, Min. Ger., Brazil	170	20 45S	42 53W
Viçosa, Pernambuco, Brazil	170	9 28S	36 14W
Viçosa do Ceará	170	3 34S	41 5W
Vicosoprano	51	46 22N	9 38E
Victor	158	38 43N	105 7W
Victor Emanuel Ra.	135	5 20S	142 15E
Victor Harbour	139	35 30S	138 37E
Victoria, Argent.	172	32 40S	60 10W
Victoria, Austral.	138	21 16S	149 3E
*Victoria, Camer.	121	4 1N	9 10E
Victoria, Can.	152	48 30N	123 25W
Victoria, Chile	176	38 13S	72 20W
Victoria, Guin.	120	10 50N	14 32W
Victoria, H. K.	109	22 25N	114 15E
Victoria, Malay.	102	5 20N	115 20E
Victoria, Tex., U.S.A.	159	28 50N	97 0W
Victoria, Va., U.S.A.	158	38 52N	99 8W
Victoria □, Austral.	131	37 0S	144 0E
Victoria □, Zimb.	127	21 0S	31 30E
Victoria Beach	153	50 40N	96 35W
Victoria de las Tunas	166	20 58N	76 59W
Victoria Falls	127	17 58S	25 45E
Victoria, Grand L.	150	47 31N	77 30W
Victoria Harbour	150	44 45N	79 45W
Victoria I.	148	71 0N	111 0W
Victoria, L., N.S.W., Austral.	140	33 57S	141 15E
Victoria, L., Vic., Austral.	139	38 2S	147 34E
Victoria, L., E. Afr.	126	1 0S	33 0E
Victoria, La	174	10 14N	67 20W
Victoria Ld.	13	75 0S	160 0E
Victoria, Mt., Burma	98	21 15N	93 55E
Victoria, Mt., P.N.G.	135	8 55S	147 32E
Victoria Nile R.	126	2 25N	31 50E
Victoria, R.	136	15 10S	129 40E
Victoria R. Downs	136	16 25S	131 0E
Victoria Ra.	143	42 12S	172 7E
Victoria Res.	151	48 20N	57 27W
Victoria Taungdeik	99	21 15N	93 55E
Victoria West	128	31 25S	23 4E
Victoriaville	151	46 4N	71 56W
Victorica	172	36 20S	65 30W
Victorino	174	2 48N	67 50W
Victorville	163	34 32N	117 18W
Vicuña	172	30 0S	70 50W
Vicuña Mackenna	172	33 53S	64 25W
Vidalia	157	32 13N	82 25W
Vidauban	45	43 25N	6 27E
Videlv, R.	71	58 50N	8 32E
Vidigueira	57	38 12N	7 48W
Vidin	66	43 59N	22 28E
Vidio, Cabo	56	43 35N	6 14W
Vidisha (Bhilsa)	94	23 28N	77 53E
Vidöstern	73	57 5N	14 0E
Vidra	70	45 56N	26 55E
Viduša, mts.	66	42 55N	18 21E
Vidzy	80	54 40N	26 37E
Viedma	176	40 50S	63 0W
Viedma, L.	176	49 30S	72 30W
Vieira	56	41 38N	8 8W
Viejo Canal de Bahama	166	22 10N	77 30W
Viella	58	42 43N	0 44E
Vielsalm	47	50 17N	5 54E
Vien Pou Kha	101	20 45N	101 5E
Vienenburg	48	51 57N	10 35E
Vieng Pou Kha	100	20 41N	101 4E
Vienna, Illinois, U.S.A.	159	37 29N	88 54W
Vienna, Va., U.S.A.	162	38 54N	77 16W
Vienna = Wien	53	48 12N	16 22E
Vienne	45	45 31N	4 53E
Vienne □	44	45 53N	0 42E
Vienne, R.	42	47 5N	0 30E
Vientiane	100	17 58N	102 36E
Vieques, I.	147	18 8N	65 25W
Vierlingsbeek	47	51 36N	6 1E
Viersen	48	51 15N	6 23E
Vierwaldstättersee	51	47 0N	8 30E
Vierzon	43	47 13N	2 5E
Vieux-Boucau-les-Bains	44	43 48N	1 23W
Vif	45	45 5N	5 41E
Vigan	103	17 35N	120 28E
Vigan, Le	44	44 0N	3 36E
Vigevano	62	45 18N	8 50E
Vigia	170	0 50S	48 5W
Vigía Chico	165	19 46N	87 35W
Vignacourt	43	50 1N	2 15E
Vignemale, Pic du	44	42 47N	0 10W
Vigneulles	43	48 59N	5 40E
Vignola	62	44 29N	11 0E
Vigo	56	42 12N	8 41W
Vigo, Ría de	56	42 15N	8 45W
Vihiers	42	47 10N	0 30W
Vijayadurg	96	16 30N	73 25E

*Renamed Limbe

Vijayawada (Bezwada) Voitsberg

Vijayawada (Bezwada)	**96**	16 31N	80 39 E
Vijfhuizen	**46**	52 22N	4 41 E
Vikedal	**71**	59 30N	5 55 E
Viken, L.	**73**	58 40N	10 2 E
Vikersund	**71**	59 58N	10 2 E
Viking	**152**	53 7N	111 50W
Viking, gasfield	**19**	53 30N	2 20 E
Vikna	**74**	64 52N	10 57 E
Vikramasingapuram	**97**	8 40N	76 47 E
Viksjö	**72**	62 45N	17 26 E
Vikulovo	**76**	56 50N	70 40 E
Vila Alferes Chamusca	**129**	24 27 S	33 0 E
Vila Arriaga	**125**	14 35 S	13 30 E
Vila Bittencourt	**174**	1 20 S	69 20W
Vila Cabral = Lichinga	**127**	13 13 S	35 11 E
Vila Caldas Xavier	**127**	14 28 S	33 0 E
Vila Coutinho	**127**	14 37 S	34 19 E
Vila da Maganja	**127**	17 18 S	37 30 E
Vila da Ponte	**125**	14 35 S	16 40 E
Vila de Aljustrel	**125**	13 30 S	19 45 E
Vila de João Belo = Xai-Xai	**129**	25 6 S	33 31 E
Vila de Liquica	**103**	8 40 S	125 20 E
Vila de Manica	**125**	18 58 S	32 59 E
Vila de Rei	**57**	39 41N	8 9W
Vila de Sena = Sena	**127**	17 25 S	35 0 E
Vila do Bispo	**57**	37 5N	8 53W
Vila do Conde	**56**	41 21N	8 45W
Vila Fontes	**125**	17 51 S	35 24 E
Vila Fontes Velha	**127**	17 51 S	35 24 E
Vila Franca de Xira	**57**	38 57N	8 59W
Vila Gamito	**127**	14 12 S	33 0 E
Vila General Machado	**125**	11 58 S	17 22 E
Vila Gomes da Costa	**129**	24 20 S	33 37 E
Vila Henrique de Carvalho = Lunda	**124**	9 40 S	20 12 E
Vila Junqueiro	**127**	15 25 S	36 58 E
Vila Luisa	**129**	25 45 S	32 35 E
Vila Luso = Moxico	**125**	11 53 S	19 55 E
Vila Machado	**127**	19 15 S	34 14 E
Vila Marechal Carmona = Uige	**124**	7 30 S	14 40 E
Vila Mariano Machado	**125**	13 3 S	14 35 E
Vila Moatize	**127**	16 11 S	33 40 E
Vila Mouzinho	**127**	14 48 S	34 25 E
Vila Murtinho	**174**	10 20 S	65 20W
Vila Nova de Fozcôa	**56**	41 5N	7 9W
Vila Nova de Ourém	**57**	39 40N	8 35W
Vila Nova do Seles	**125**	11 35 S	14 22 E
Vila Novo de Gaia	**56**	41 4N	8 40W
Vila Paiva Couceiro	**125**	14 37 S	14 40 E
Vila Paiva de Andrada	**127**	18 37 S	34 2 E
Vila Pery = Chimoio	**127**	19 4 S	33 30 E
Vila Pouca de Aguiar	**56**	41 30N	7 38W
Vila Real	**56**	41 17N	7 48W
Vila Real de Santo Antonio	**57**	37 10N	7 28W
Vila Robert Williams	**125**	12 46 S	15 30 E
Vila Salazar, Angola	**124**	9 12 S	14 48 E
Vila Salazar, Indon.	**103**	5 25 S	123 50 E
Vila Teixeira da Silva	**125**	12 10 S	15 50 E
Vila Vasco da Gama	**127**	14 54 S	32 14 E
Vila Velha	**173**	20 20 S	40 17W
Vila Verissimo Sarmento	**124**	8 15 S	20 50 E
Vila Viçosa	**57**	38 45N	7 27W
Vilaboa	**56**	42 21N	8 39W
Vilaine, R.	**42**	47 35N	2 10W
Vilanculos	**129**	22 1 S	35 17 E
Vilar Formosa	**56**	40 38N	6 45W
Vilareal □	**56**	41 36N	7 35W
Vileyka	**80**	54 30N	27 0 E
Vilhelmina	**74**	64 35N	16 39 E
Vilhena	**174**	12 30 S	60 0W
Viliga	**77**	60 2N	156 56 E
Viliya, R.	**80**	54 57N	24 35 E
Viljandi	**80**	58 28N	25 30 E
Villa Abecia	**172**	21 0 S	68 18W
Villa Ahumada	**164**	30 30N	106 40W
Villa Ana	**172**	28 28 S	59 40W
Villa Angela	**172**	27 34 S	60 45W
Villa Bella	**174**	10 25 S	65 30W
Villa Bens (Tarfaya)	**116**	27 55N	12 55W
Villa Cañas	**172**	34 0 S	61 35W
Villa Cisneros = Dakhla	**116**	23 50N	15 53W
Villa Colón	**172**	31 38 S	68 20W
Villa Constitución	**172**	33 15 S	60 20W
Villa de Cura	**174**	10 2N	67 29W
Villa de María	**172**	30 0 S	63 43W
Villa de Rosario	**172**	24 30 S	57 35W
Villa Dolores	**172**	31 58 S	65 15W
Villa Franca	**172**	26 14 S	58 20W
Villa Frontera	**164**	26 56N	101 27W
Villa Guillermina	**172**	28 15 S	59 29W
Villa Hayes	**172**	25 0 S	57 20W
Villa Iris	**172**	38 12 S	63 12W
Villa Julia Molina	**167**	19 5N	69 45W
Villa Madero	**164**	24 28N	104 10W
Villa Maria	**172**	32 20 S	63 10W
Villa Mazán	**172**	28 40 S	66 30W
Villa Mentes	**172**	21 10 S	63 30W
Villa Minozzo	**62**	44 21N	10 30 E
Villa Montes	**172**	21 10 S	63 30W
Villa Ocampo, Argent.	**172**	28 30 S	59 20W
Villa Ocampo, Mexico	**164**	26 29N	105 30W
Villa Ojo de Agua	**172**	29 30 S	63 44W
Villa San Agustin	**172**	30 35 S	67 30W
Villa San Giovanni	**65**	38 13N	15 38 E
Villa San José	**172**	32 12 S	58 15W
Villa San Martín	**172**	28 9 S	64 9W
Villa Santina	**63**	46 25N	12 55 E
Villa Unión	**164**	23 12N	106 14W
Villablino	**56**	42 57N	6 19W
Villabruzzi	**91**	3 3N	45 18 E
Villacampo, Pantano de	**56**	41 31N	6 0W
Villacañas	**58**	39 38N	3 20W
Villacarlos	**58**	39 53N	4 17 E
Villacarriedo	**58**	43 14N	3 48W
Villacarrillo	**59**	38 7N	3 3W
Villacastín	**56**	40 46N	4 25W
Villach	**52**	46 37N	13 51 E
Villaciaro	**64**	39 27N	8 45 E
Villada	**56**	42 15N	4 59W
Villadiego	**56**	42 31N	4 1W
Villadossóla	**62**	46 4N	8 16 E
Villafeliche	**58**	41 10N	1 30W
Villafranca	**58**	42 17N	1 46W
Villafranca de los Barros	**57**	38 35N	6 18W
Villafranca de los Caballeros	**59**	39 26N	3 21W
Villafranca del Bierzo	**56**	42 38N	6 50W
Villafranca del Cid	**58**	40 26N	0 16W
Villafranca del Panadés	**58**	41 21N	1 40 E
Villafranca di Verona	**62**	45 20N	10 51 E
Villagarcía de Arosa	**56**	42 34N	8 46W
Villagrán	**165**	24 29N	99 29W
Villaguay	**172**	32 0 S	58 45W
Villaharta	**57**	38 9N	4 54W
Villahermosa, Mexico	**165**	17 45N	92 50W
Villahermosa, Spain	**59**	38 46N	2 52W
Villaines-la-Juhel	**42**	48 21N	0 20W
Villajoyosa	**59**	38 30N	0 12W
Villalba	**56**	40 36N	3 59W
Villalba de Guardo	**56**	42 42N	4 49W
Villalón de Campos	**56**	42 5N	5 4W
Villalpando	**56**	41 51N	5 25W
Villaluenga	**56**	40 2N	3 54W
Villamañán	**56**	42 19N	5 35W
Villamartín	**56**	36 52N	5 38W
Villamayor	**58**	41 42N	0 43W
Villamblard	**44**	45 2N	0 32 E
Villanova Monteleone	**64**	40 30N	8 28 E
Villanueva, Colomb.	**174**	10 37N	72 59W
Villanueva, U.S.A.	**161**	35 16N	105 31W
Villanueva de Castellón	**59**	39 5N	0 31W
Villanueva de Córdoba	**57**	38 20N	4 38W
Villanueva de la Fuente	**59**	38 42N	2 42W
Villanueva de la Serena	**57**	38 59N	5 50W
Villanueva de la Sierra	**56**	40 12N	6 24W
Villanueva de los Castillejos	**57**	37 30N	7 15W
Villanueva del Arzobispo	**59**	38 10N	3 0W
Villanueva del Duque	**57**	38 20N	4 38W
Villanueva del Fresno	**57**	38 23N	7 10W
Villanueva y Geltrú	**58**	41 13N	1 40 E
Villaodrid	**56**	43 20N	7 11W
Villaputzu	**64**	39 28N	9 33 E
Villar del Arzobispo	**58**	39 44N	0 50W
Villar del Rey	**57**	39 7N	6 50W
Villarcayo	**58**	42 56N	3 34W
Villard	**45**	45 4N	5 33 E
Villard-Bonnot	**45**	45 14N	5 53 E
Villard-de-Lans	**45**	45 3N	5 33 E
Villarino de los Aires	**56**	41 18N	6 23W
Villarosa	**65**	37 36N	14 9 E
Villarramiel	**56**	42 2N	4 55W
Villarreal	**58**	39 55N	0 3W
Villarrica, Chile	**176**	39 15 S	72 30W
Villarrica, Parag.	**172**	25 40 S	56 30W
Villarrobledo	**59**	39 18N	2 36W
Villarroya de la Sierra	**58**	41 27N	1 46W
Villarrubia de los Ojos	**59**	39 14N	3 36W
Villars	**45**	46 0N	5 2 E
Villarta de San Juan	**59**	39 15N	3 25W
Villasayas	**58**	41 24N	2 39W
Villaseca de los Gamitos	**56**	41 2N	6 7W
Villastar	**58**	40 17N	1 9W
Villatobas	**58**	39 54N	3 20W
Villavicencio, Argent.	**172**	32 28 S	69 0W
Villavicencio, Colomb.	**174**	4 9N	73 37W
Villaviciosa	**56**	43 32N	5 27W
Villazón	**172**	22 0 S	65 35W
Ville de Paris □	**43**	48 50N	2 20 E
Ville Marie	**150**	47 20N	79 30W
Ville Platte	**159**	30 45N	92 17W
Villedieu	**42**	48 50N	1 12W
Villefort	**44**	44 28N	3 56 E
Villefranche	**43**	47 19N	146 0 E
Villefranche-de-Lauragais	**44**	43 25N	1 44 E
Villefranche-de-Rouergue	**44**	44 21N	2 2 E
Villefranche-du-Périgord	**44**	44 38N	1 5 E
Villefranche-sur-Saône	**45**	45 59N	4 43 E
Villel	**58**	40 14N	1 12W
Villemaur	**43**	48 14N	3 40 E
Villemur-sur-Tarn	**44**	43 51N	1 31 E
Villena	**59**	38 39N	0 52W
Villenauxe	**43**	48 36N	3 30 E
Villenave	**44**	44 46N	0 33W
Villeneuve, France	**43**	48 42N	2 25 E
Villeneuve, Italy	**62**	45 40N	7 10 E
Villeneuve, Switz.	**50**	46 24N	6 56 E
Villeneuve-l'Archevèque	**43**	48 14N	3 32 E
Villeneuve-lès-Avignon	**45**	43 57N	4 49 E
Villeneuve-sur-Allier	**44**	46 40N	3 13 E
Villeneuve-sur-Lot	**44**	44 24N	0 42 E
Villeréal	**44**	44 38N	0 45 E
Villers Bocage	**42**	49 3N	0 40W
Villers Bretonneux	**43**	49 50N	2 30 E
Villers-Cotterets	**43**	49 15N	3 4 E
Villers-Farlay	**47**	47 0N	5 45 E
Villers-le-Bouillet	**47**	50 34N	5 15 E
Villers-le-Gambon	**47**	50 11N	4 37 E
Villers-sur-Mer	**42**	49 21N	0 2W
Villersexel	**43**	47 33N	6 26 E
Villerslev	**73**	56 49N	8 29 E
Villerupt	**43**	49 28N	5 55 E
Villerville	**42**	49 26N	0 5 E
Villiers	**129**	27 2 S	28 36 E
Villingen = Schwenningen	**49**	48 3N	8 29 E
Villisca	**158**	40 55N	94 59W
Villupuram	**97**	11 59N	79 31 E
Vilna	**152**	54 7N	111 55W
Vilnius	**80**	54 38N	25 25 E
Vils	**52**	47 33N	10 37 E
Vilsbiburg	**49**	48 27N	12 23 E
Vilslev	**73**	55 24N	8 42 E
Vilusi	**66**	42 44N	18 34 E
Vilvoorde	**47**	50 56N	4 26 E
Vilyuy, R.	**77**	63 58N	125 0 E
Vilyuysk	**77**	63 40N	121 20 E
Vimercate	**62**	45 38N	9 25 E
Vimiosa	**56**	41 35N	6 13W
Vimmerby	**73**	57 40N	15 55 E
Vimo	**72**	60 50N	14 20 E
Vimoutiers	**42**	48 57N	0 10 E
Vimperk	**52**	49 3N	13 46 E
Viña del Mar	**172**	33 0 S	71 30W
Vinaroz	**58**	40 30N	0 27 E
Vincennes	**156**	38 42N	87 29W
Vincent	**163**	34 33N	118 11W
Vinchina	**172**	28 45 S	68 15W
Vindel älv	**74**	64 20N	19 20 E
Vindeln	**74**	64 12N	19 43 E
Vinderup	**73**	56 29N	8 45 E
Vindhya Ra.	**94**	22 50N	77 0 E
Vinegar Hill	**39**	52 30N	6 28W
Vineland	**162**	39 30N	75 0W
Vinga	**66**	46 0N	21 14 E
Vingnes	**71**	61 7N	10 26 E
Vinh	**100**	18 45N	105 38 E
Vinh Linh	**100**	17 4N	107 2 E
Vinh Loi	**101**	9 20N	104 45 E
Vinh Long	**101**	10 16N	105 57 E
Vinh Yen	**100**	21 21N	105 35 E
Vinhais	**56**	41 50N	7 0W
Vinica	**63**	45 28N	15 16 E
Vinita	**159**	36 40N	95 12W
Vinkeveen	**46**	52 13N	4 56 E
Vinkovci	**66**	45 19N	18 48 E
Vinnitsa	**82**	49 15N	28 30 E
Vinstra	**71**	61 37N	9 44 E
Vinton, Iowa, U.S.A.	**158**	42 8N	92 1W
Vinton, La., U.S.A.	**159**	30 13N	93 35W
Vintu de Jos	**70**	46 0N	23 30 E
Viöl	**48**	54 32N	9 12 E
Violet Town	**141**	36 38 S	145 42 E
Vipava	**63**	45 51N	13 38 E
Vipiteno	**63**	46 55N	11 25 E
Viqueque	**103**	8 42 S	126 30 E
Vir	**85**	37 45N	72 5 E
Vir, I.	**63**	44 17N	15 3 E
Virac	**103**	13 30N	124 20 E
Virachei	**100**	13 59N	106 49 E
Virago Sd.	**152**	54 0N	132 42W
Virajpet	**97**	12 15N	75 50 E
Viramgam	**94**	23 5N	72 0 E
Virarajendrapet (Virajpet)	**97**	12 10N	75 50 E
Viravanallur	**97**	8 40N	79 30 E
Virden	**153**	49 50N	100 56W
Vire	**42**	48 50N	0 53W
Virgem da Lapa	**171**	16 49 S	42 21W
Virgenes, C.	**176**	52 19 S	68 21W
Virgin Gorda, I.	**147**	18 45N	64 26W
Virgin Is.	**147**	18 40N	64 30W
Virgin, R., Can.	**153**	57 2N	108 17W
Virgin, R., U.S.A.	**161**	36 50N	114 10W
Virginia, Ireland	**38**	53 50N	7 5W
Virginia, S. Afr.	**128**	28 8 S	26 55 E
Virginia, U.S.A.	**158**	47 30N	92 32W
Virginia □	**156**	37 45N	78 0W
Virginia Beach	**156**	36 54N	75 58W
Virginia City, Mont., U.S.A.	**160**	45 25N	111 58W
Virginia City, Nev., U.S.A.	**160**	39 19N	119 39W
Virginia Falls	**152**	61 38N	125 42W
Virginiatown	**150**	48 9N	79 36W
Virgins, C.	**176**	52 10 S	68 30W
Virieu-le-Grand	**45**	45 51N	5 39 E
Virje	**66**	46 4N	16 59 E
Viroqua	**158**	43 33N	90 57W
Virovitica	**66**	45 51N	17 21 E
Virpaza, R.	**66**	42 14N	19 6 E
Virserum	**73**	57 20N	15 35 E
Virton	**47**	49 35N	5 32 E
Virtsu	**80**	58 32N	23 33 E
Virudhunagar	**97**	9 30N	78 0 E
Vis	**63**	43 0N	16 10 E
Vis, I.	**63**	43 0N	16 10 E
Vis Kanal	**63**	43 4N	16 5 E
Visalia	**163**	36 25N	119 18W
Visayan Sea	**103**	11 30N	123 30 E
Visby	**73**	57 37N	18 18 E
Viscount Melville Sd.	**12**	74 10N	108 0W
Visé	**47**	50 44N	5 41 E
Višegrad	**66**	43 47N	19 17 E
Viseu, Brazil	**170**	1 10 S	46 20W
Viseu, Port.	**56**	40 40N	7 55W
Vişeu	**70**	47 45N	24 25 E
Viseu □	**56**	40 40N	7 55W
Vishakhapatnam	**96**	17 45N	83 20 E
Vishera, R.	**84**	59 55N	56 25 E
Vishnupur	**95**	23 8N	87 20 E
Visikoi I.	**13**	56 30 S	26 40 E
Visingsö	**73**	58 2N	14 20 E
Viskafors	**73**	57 37N	12 50 E
Vislanda	**73**	56 46N	14 30 E
Vislinskil Zaliv (Zalew Wislany)	**54**	54 20N	19 50 E
Visnagar	**94**	23 45N	72 32 E
Višnja Gora	**63**	45 58N	14 45 E
Viso del Marqués	**59**	38 32N	3 34W
Viso, Mte.	**62**	44 38N	7 5 E
Visoko	**66**	43 58N	18 10 E
Visp	**50**	46 17N	7 52 E
Vispa, R.	**50**	46 9N	7 48 E
Visselhovde	**48**	52 59N	9 36 E
Vissoie	**50**	46 13N	7 36 E
Vista	**163**	33 12N	117 14W
Vistonis, Limni	**68**	41 0N	25 7 E
Vistula, R. = Wisła, R.	**54**	53 38N	18 47 E
Vit, R.	**67**	43 30N	24 30 E
Vitanje	**63**	46 40N	15 18 E
Vitebsk	**80**	55 10N	30 15 E
Viterbo	**63**	42 25N	12 8 E
Viti Levu, I.	**143**	17 30 S	177 30 E
Vitiaz Str.	**135**	5 40 S	147 10 E
Vitigudino	**56**	41 1N	6 35W
Vitim	**77**	59 45N	112 25 E
Vitim, R.	**77**	58 40N	112 50 E
Vitína	**69**	37 40N	22 10 E
Vitina	**66**	43 17N	17 29 E
Vitória	**171**	20 20 S	40 22W
Vitoria	**58**	42 50N	2 41W
Vitória da Conquista	**171**	14 51 S	40 51W
Vitória de São Antão	**170**	8 10 S	37 20W
Vitorino Friere	**170**	4 4 S	45 10W
Vitré	**42**	48 8N	1 12W
Vitry-le-François	**43**	48 43N	4 33 E
Vitsi, Mt.	**68**	40 40N	21 25 E
Vittangi	**74**	67 41N	21 40 E
Vitteaux	**43**	47 24N	4 30 E
Vittel	**43**	48 12N	5 57 E
Vittória	**65**	36 58N	14 30 E
Vittório Véneto	**63**	45 59N	12 18 E
Vitu Is.	**135**	4 50 S	149 25 E
Vivegnis	**47**	50 42N	5 39 E
Viver	**58**	39 55N	0 36W
Vivero	**56**	43 39N	7 38W
Viviers	**45**	44 30N	4 40 E
Vivonne, Austral.	**140**	35 59 S	137 9 E
Vivonne, France	**44**	46 36N	0 15 E
Vivonne B.	**140**	35 59 S	137 9 E
Vivsta	**72**	62 30N	17 18 E
Vizcaíno, Desierto de	**164**	27 40N	113 50W
Vizcaíno, Sierra	**164**	27 30N	114 0W
Vizcaya □	**58**	43 15N	2 45W
Vizianagaram	**96**	18 6N	83 10 E
Vizille	**45**	45 5N	5 46 E
Vizinada	**63**	45 20N	13 46 E
Viziru	**70**	45 0N	27 43 E
Vizovice	**53**	49 12N	17 56 E
Vizzini	**65**	37 9N	14 43 E
Vlaardingen	**46**	51 55N	4 21 E
Vladicin Han	**66**	42 42N	22 1 E
Vladimir	**81**	56 0N	40 30 E
Vladimir Volynskiy	**80**	50 50N	24 18 E
Vladimirci	**66**	44 36N	19 45 E
Vladimirovac	**66**	45 1N	20 53 E
Vladimirovka, U.S.S.R.	**83**	44 37N	44 41 E
Vladimirovka, U.S.S.R.	**83**	48 27N	46 5 E
Vladimirovo	**67**	43 32N	23 22 E
Vladislavovka	**82**	45 15N	35 15 E
Vladivostok	**82**	43 10N	131 53 E
Vlamertinge	**47**	50 51N	2 49 E
Vlaming Head	**137**	21 48 S	114 5 E
Vlasenica	**66**	44 11N	18 59 E
Vlasim	**52**	49 40N	14 53 E
Vlasinsko Jezero	**66**	42 44N	22 37 E
Vlašió, mt.	**66**	44 19N	17 37 E
Vlasotinci	**66**	42 59N	22 7 E
Vleuten	**46**	52 6N	5 1 E
Vlieland, I.	**46**	53 30N	4 55 E
Vliestroom	**46**	53 19N	5 8 E
Vlijmen	**47**	51 42N	5 14 E
Vlissingen	**47**	51 26N	3 34 E
Vlora	**68**	40 32N	19 28 E
Vlora □	**68**	40 12N	20 0 E
Vltava, R.	**52**	49 35N	14 10 E
Vlădeasa, mt.	**70**	46 47N	22 50 E
Vo Dat	**101**	11 9N	107 31 E
Vobarno	**62**	45 38N	10 30 E
Voćin	**66**	45 37N	17 33 E
Vodice	**63**	43 47N	15 47 E
Vodnany	**52**	49 9N	14 11 E
Vodnjan	**63**	44 59N	13 52 E
Voe	**36**	60 21N	1 15W
Voga	**121**	6 23N	1 30 E
Vogelkop = Doberai, Jazirah	**103**	1 25 S	133 0 E
Vogelsberg	**48**	50 37N	9 30 E
Voghera	**62**	44 59N	9 1 E
Vohémar	**129**	13 25 S	50 0 E
Vohipeno	**129**	22 22 S	47 51 E
Voi	**126**	3 25 S	38 32 E
Void	**43**	48 40N	5 36 E
Voil, L.	**34**	56 20N	4 25W
Voineşti, Iaşi, Rumania	**70**	47 5N	27 27 E
Voineşti, Ploeşti, Rumania	**70**	45 5N	25 14 E
Voiotia □	**69**	38 20N	23 0 E
Voiron	**45**	45 22N	5 35 E
Voiseys B.	**151**	56 15N	61 50W
Voitsberg	**52**	47 3N	15 9 E

Voiviis Limni, L
Walla Walla

Voiviis Limni, L. 68 39 30N 22 45 E
Vojens 73 55 16N 9 18 E
Vojmsjön 74 64 55N 16 40 E
Vojnió 63 45 19N 15 43 E
Vojvodina, Auton. Pokragina 66 45 20N 20 0 E
Vokhma 81 59 0N 46 45 E
Vokhma, R. 81 59 0N 46 44 E
Vokhtoga 81 58 46N 41 8 E
Volary 52 48 54N 13 52 E
Volborg 158 45 50N 105 44W
Volchansk 81 50 17N 36 58 E
Volchya, R. 82 48 0N 37 0 E
Volda 71 62 9N 6 5 E
Volendam 46 52 30N 5 4 E
Volga 81 57 58N 38 16 E
Volga Hts. = Privolzhskaya V.S. 79 51 0N 46 0 E
Volga, R. 83 52 20N 48 0 E
Volgodonsk 83 47 33N 42 5 E
Volgograd 83 48 40N 44 25 E
Volgogradskoye Vdkhr. 81 50 0N 45 20 E
Volgorechensk 81 57 28N 41 14 E
Volissós 69 38 29N 25 54 E
Volkerak 47 51 39N 4 18 E
Völkermarkt 52 46 39N 14 39 E
Volkhov 80 59 55N 32 15 E
Volkhov, R. 80 59 30N 32 0 E
Völklingen 49 49 15N 6 50 E
Volkovysk 80 53 9N 24 30 E
Volksrust 129 27 24 S 29 53 E
Vollenhove 46 52 40N 5 58 E
Volnovakha 82 47 35N 37 30 E
Volo 140 31 37 S 143 0 E
Volochayevka 77 48 40N 134 30 E
Volodary 81 56 12N 43 15 E
Vologda 81 59 25N 40 0 E
Volokolamsk 81 56 5N 36 0 E
Volokonovka 81 50 33N 37 58 E
Volontirovka 82 46 28N 29 28 E
Vólos 68 39 24N 22 59 E
Volosovo 80 59 27N 29 32 E
Volozhin 80 54 3N 26 30 E
Volsk 81 52 5N 47 28 E
Volstrup 73 57 19N 10 27 E
Volta, L. 121 7 30N 0 15 E
Volta, R. 121 8 0N 0 10W
Volta Redonda 173 22 31 S 44 5W
Voltaire, C. 136 14 16 S 125 35 E
Volterra 62 43 24N 10 50 E
Voltri 62 44 25N 8 43 E
Volturara Áppula 65 41 30N 15 2 E
Volturno, R. 65 41 18N 14 20 E
Volubilis 118 34 2N 5 33W
Vólvi, L. 68 40 40N 23 34 E
Volzhsk 81 55 57N 48 23 E
Volzhskiy 83 48 56N 44 46 E
Vondrozo 129 22 49 S 47 20 E
Vónitsa 69 38 53N 20 58 E
Voorburg 46 52 5N 4 24 E
Voorne Putten 46 51 52N 4 10 E
Voorst 46 52 10N 6 8 E
Voorthuizen 46 52 11N 5 36 E
Vopnafjörður 74 65 45N 14 40W
Vorarlberg □ 52 47 20N 10 0 E
Vóras Óros 68 40 57N 21 45 E
Vorbasse 73 55 39N 9 6 E
Vorden 46 52 6N 6 19 E
Vorderrheim, R. 51 46 49N 9 25 E
Vordingborg 73 55 0N 11 54 E
Voreppe 45 45 18N 5 39 E
Voríai Sporádhes 69 39 15N 23 30 E
Vórios Evvoïkós Kólpos 69 38 45N 23 15 E
Vorkuta 78 67 48N 64 20 E
Vorma 71 60 9N 11 27 E
Vorona, R. 81 52 0N 42 20 E
Voronezh, R.S.S.R., U.S.S.R. 81 51 40N 39 10 E
Voronezh, Ukraine, U.S.S.R. 80 51 47N 33 28 E
Voronezh, R. 81 52 30N 39 30 E
Vorontsovo-Aleksandrovskoïe = Zelenokumsk. 83 44 30N 44 1 E
Voroshilovgrad 83 48 38N 39 15 E
Voroshilovsk = Kommunarsk 83 48 3N 38 40 E
Vorovskoye 77 54 30N 155 50 E
Vorselaar 47 51 12N 4 46 E
Vorskla, R. 82 49 30N 34 31 E
Vorukh 85 39 52N 70 35 E
Vorupør 73 56 58N 8 22 E
Vosges 43 48 20N 7 10 E
Vosges □ 43 48 12N 6 20 E
Voskopoja 68 40 40N 20 33 E
Voskresensk 81 55 27N 38 31 E
Voskresenskoye 81 56 51N 45 30 E
Voss 71 60 38N 6 26 E
Vosselaar 47 51 19N 4 52 E
Vostok I. 131 10 5 S 152 23W
Vostotnyy Sayan 77 54 0N 96 0 E
Votice 52 49 38N 14 39 E
Votkinsk 84 57 0N 53 55 E
Votkinskoye Vdkhr. 78 57 30N 55 0 E
Vouga, R. 56 40 46N 8 10W
Voulte-sur-Rhône, La 45 44 48N 4 46 E
Vouvry 50 46 21N 6 21 E
Voúxa, Ákra 69 35 37N 20 32 E
Vouzela 56 40 43N 8 7W
Vouziers 43 49 22N 4 40 E
Voves 43 48 15N 1 38 E
Voxna 72 61 20N 15 30 E
Voy 37 59 1N 3 16W
Vozhe Oz. 78 60 45N 39 0 E
Vozhgaly 81 58 24N 50 1 E
Voznesensk 82 47 35N 31 15 E
Voznesenye 78 61 0N 35 45 E
Vráble 53 48 15N 18 16 E
Vrácevšnica 66 44 2N 20 34 E
Vrådal 71 59 20N 8 25 E
Vradiyevka 82 49 56N 30 38 E
Vraka 68 42 8N 19 28 E
Vrakhnéika 69 38 10N 21 40 E
Vrancea □ 70 45 50N 26 45 E
Vrancei, Munți 70 46 0N 26 30 E
Vrangelja, Ostrov 77 71 0N 180 0 E
Vrangtjarn 72 62 14N 16 37 E
Vranica, mt. 66 43 59N 18 0 E
Vranje 66 42 34N 21 54 E
Vranjska Banja 66 42 34N 22 1 E
Vranov 53 48 53N 21 40 E
Vransko 63 46 17N 14 58 E
Vratsa 67 43 13N 23 30 E
Vratsa □ 67 43 30N 23 30 E
Vrbas 66 45 0N 17 27 E
Vrbas, R. 66 44 30N 17 10 E
Vrbnik 63 45 4N 14 32 E
Vrboviec 63 45 53N 16 28 E
Vrbovsko 63 45 24N 15 5 E
Vrchlabí 52 49 38N 15 37 E
Vrede 129 27 24 S 29 6 E
Vredefort 128 27 0 S 26 58 E
Vredenburg 128 32 51 S 18 0 E
Vredendal 128 31 41 S 18 35 E
Vreeswijk 46 52 1N 5 6 E
Vrena 73 58 54N 16 41 E
Vrgorac 66 43 12N 17 20 E
Vrhnika 63 45 58N 14 15 E
Vriddhachalam 97 11 30N 79 10 E
Vridi 120 5 15N 4 3W
Vridi Canal 120 5 15N 4 3W
Vries 46 53 5N 6 35 E
Vriezenveen 46 52 25N 6 38 E
Vrindaban 94 27 37N 77 40 E
Vrnograč 63 43 12N 17 20 E
Vrondádhes 69 38 25N 26 7 E
Vroomshoop 46 52 27N 6 34 E
Vrpolje 66 43 42N 16 1 E
Vršac 66 45 8N 21 18 E
Vršački Kanal 66 45 15N 21 0 E
Vrsheto 67 43 15N 23 23 E
Vryburg 128 26 55 S 24 45 E
Vryheid 129 27 54 S 30 47 E
Vsetín 53 49 20N 18 0 E
Vu Liet 100 18 43N 105 23 E
Vůcha, R. 67 41 53N 24 26 E
Vučitrn 66 42 49N 20 59 E
Vught 47 51 38N 5 20 E
Vuka, R. 66 45 28N 18 30 E
Vukovar 66 45 21N 18 59 E
Vulcan, Can. 152 50 25N 113 15W
Vulcan, Rumania 70 45 23N 23 17 E
Vulcan, U.S.A. 156 45 46N 87 51W
Vŭlcani 66 46 0N 20 26 E
Vulcano, I. 65 38 25N 14 58 E
Vulchedrŭma 67 43 42N 23 16 E
Vulci 63 42 23N 11 37 E
Vŭleni 70 44 15N 24 45 E
Vulkaneshty 82 45 35N 28 30 E
Vunduzi, R. 127 18 0 S 33 45 E
Vung Tau 101 10 21N 107 4 E
Vûrbitsa 67 42 59N 26 40 E
Vutcani 70 46 26N 27 59 E
Vuyyuru 96 16 28N 80 50 E
Vvedenka 84 54 0N 63 53 E
Vyara 96 21 8N 73 28 E
Vyasniki 81 56 10N 42 10 E
Vyatka, R. 84 56 30N 51 0 E
Vyatskiye Polyany 84 56 5N 51 0 E
Vyazemskiy 77 47 32N 134 45 E
Vyazma 80 55 10N 34 15 E
Vyborg 78 60 43N 28 47 E
Vychegda R. 78 61 50N 52 30 E
Vychodné Beskydy 53 49 30N 22 0 E
Východočeský □ 52 50 20N 15 45 E
Východoslovenský □ 53 48 50N 21 0 E
Vyg-ozero 78 63 30N 34 0 E
Vyja, R. 81 41 53N 24 26 E
Vypin, I. 97 10 10N 76 15 E
Vyrnwy, L. 31 52 48N 3 30W
Vyrnwy, R. 31 52 43N 3 15W
Vyshniy Volochek 80 57 30N 34 30 E
Vyškov 53 49 17N 17 0 E
Vysoké Mýto 53 49 58N 16 23 E
Vysoké Tatry 53 49 30N 20 0 E
Vysokovsk 81 56 22N 36 30 E
Vysotsk 80 51 53N 36 32 E
Vyssi Brod 92 48 36N 14 20 E
Vytegra 52 61 15N 36 40 E

W

Wa 121 10 7N 2 25W
Waal, R. 46 51 59N 4 8 E
Waalwijk 47 51 42N 5 4 E
Waarschoot 47 51 10N 3 36 E
Waasmunster 47 51 6N 4 5 E
Wabag 135 5 32 S 143 53 E
Wabakimi L. 150 50 38N 89 45W
Wabana 151 47 40N 53 0W
Wabasca 152 55 57N 113 45W
Wabash 156 40 48N 85 46W
Wabash, R. 156 39 10N 87 30W
Wabawng 98 25 18N 97 46 E
Wabeno 156 45 25N 88 40W
Wabi Gestro, R. 123 6 0N 41 35 E
Wabi, R. 123 7 35N 40 5 E
Wabi Shaballe, R. 123 8 0N 40 45 E
Wabigoon, L. 153 49 44N 92 34W
Wabowden 153 54 55N 98 38W
Wabrzezno 54 53 16N 18 57 E
Wabuk Pt. 150 55 20N 85 5W
Wabush City 151 52 55N 66 52W
Wabuska 160 39 16N 119 13W
W.A.C. Bennett Dam 152 56 2N 122 6W
Wachapreague 162 37 36N 75 41W
Wachtebeke 47 51 11N 3 52 E
Waco 159 31 33N 97 5W
Waconichi, L. 150 50 8N 74 0W
Wad ar Rimsa 92 26 5N 41 30 E
Wad Ban Naqa 123 16 32N 33 9 E
Wad Banda 123 13 10N 27 50 E
Wad el Haddad 123 13 50N 33 30 E
Wad en Nau 123 14 10N 33 34 E
Wad Hamid 123 16 20N 32 45 E
Wâd Medanî 123 14 28N 33 30 E
Wad Thana 94 27 22N 66 23 E
Wadayama 110 35 19N 134 52 E
Waddân 119 29 9N 16 45 E
Waddân, Jabal 119 29 0N 16 15 E
Waddeneilanden 46 53 25N 5 10 E
Waddenzee 46 53 6N 5 10 E
Wadderin Hill 137 32 0 S 118 25 E
Waddesdon 29 51 50N 0 54W
Waddingham 33 53 28N 0 31W
Waddington 33 53 10N 0 31W
Waddington, Mt. 152 51 23N 125 15W
Waddinxveen 46 52 2N 4 40 E
Waddy Pt. 139 24 58 S 153 21 E
Wadebridge 30 50 31N 4 51W
Wadena, Can. 153 51 57N 103 38W
Wadena, U.S.A. 158 46 25N 95 2W
Wädenswil 51 47 14N 8 30 E
Wadesboro 157 35 2N 80 2W
Wadhams 152 51 30N 127 30W
Wadhurst 29 51 3N 0 21 E
Wadi 121 13 5N 11 40 E
Wâdi ash Shâfi' 119 27 30N 15 0 E
Wâdi Banî Walîd 119 31 49N 14 0 E
Wadi Gemâl 122 24 35N 35 10 E
Wadi Halfa 122 21 53N 31 19 E
Wadi Masila 91 16 30N 49 0 E
Wadi Sabha 92 23 50N 48 30 E
Wadlew 54 51 31N 19 23 E
Wadowice 54 49 52N 19 30 E
Wadsworth 160 39 44N 119 22W
Waegwan 107 35 59N 128 23 E
Waenfawr 31 53 7N 4 10W
Wafou Hu 109 32 19N 116 56 E
Wafra 92 28 33N 48 3 E
Wagenberg 47 51 40N 4 46 E
Wageningen 46 51 58N 5 40 E
Wager B. 149 65 26N 88 40W
Wager Bay 149 65 56N 90 49W
Wagga Wagga 141 35 7 S 147 24 E
Waghete 103 4 10 S 135 50 E
Wagin, Austral. 137 33 17 S 117 25 E
Wagin, Nigeria 137 12 42N 7 10 E
Wagon Mound 159 36 10N 105 0W
Wagoner 159 36 0N 95 20W
Wagrowiec 54 52 48N 17 19 E
Wah 94 33 45N 72 40 E
Wahai 103 2 48 S 129 35 E
Wahiawa 147 21 30N 158 2W
Wahnai 94 32 40N 65 50 E
Wahoo 158 41 15N 96 35W
Wahpeton 158 46 20N 96 35W
Wahratta 140 31 58 S 141 50 E
Wai 96 17 56N 73 57 E
Wai, Koh 101 9 55N 102 55 E
Waiai, R. 143 45 36 S 167 45 E
Waianae 147 21 25N 158 8W
Waiau 143 42 39 S 173 5 E
Waiau, R. 143 42 47 S 173 22 E
Waiawe Ganga 97 6 15N 81 0 E
Waibeem 103 0 30 S 132 50 E
Waiblingen 49 48 49N 9 20 E
Waidhofen, Niederösterreich, Austria 52 48 49N 15 17 E
Waidhofen, Niederösterreich, Austria 52 47 57N 14 46 E
Waigeo, I. 103 0 20 S 130 40 E
Waihao Downs 143 44 48 S 170 55 E
Waihao, R. 143 44 52 S 171 11 E
Waiheke Islands 142 36 48 S 175 6 E
Waihi 142 37 23 S 175 52 E
Waihola 143 46 1 S 170 8 E
Waihola L. 143 45 59 S 170 8 E
Waihou, R. 143 37 15 S 175 40 E
Waika 126 2 22 S 25 42 E
Waikabubak 103 9 45 S 119 25 E
Waikaka 143 45 55 S 169 1 E
Waikaoti 131 45 36 S 170 41 E
Waikare, L. 142 37 26 S 175 13 E
Waikaremoana 142 38 42 S 177 12 E
Waikaremoana L. 142 38 49 S 177 9 E
Waikari 143 42 58 S 172 41 E
Waikato, R. 142 37 23 S 174 43 E
Waikawa Harbour 143 46 39 S 169 9 E
Waikerie 140 34 9 S 140 0 E
Waikiekie 142 35 57 S 174 16 E
Waikokopu 142 39 3 S 177 52 E
Waikokopu Harb. 142 39 4 S 177 53 E
Waikouaiti 143 45 36 S 170 41 E
Wailuku 147 20 53N 156 26W
Waimakariri, R. 143 42 23 S 172 42 E
Waimangaroa 143 41 43 S 171 46 E
Waimanola 147 21 19N 157 43W
Waimarie 143 41 35 S 171 58 E
Waimarino 143 40 40 S 175 20 E
Waimate 143 44 53 S 171 3 E
Waimea 147 21 57N 159 39W
Waimea Plain 143 45 55 S 168 35 E
Waimes 47 50 25N 6 7 E
Wainfleet All Saints 33 53 7N 0 16 E
Wainganga, R. 96 21 0N 79 45 E
Waingapu 103 9 35 S 120 11 E
Waingmaw 98 25 21N 97 26 E
Wainiha 147 22 9N 159 34W
Wainuiomata 142 41 17 S 174 56 E
Wainwright, Can. 153 52 50N 110 50W
Wainwright, U.S.A. 147 70 39N 160 10W
Waiotapu 142 38 21 S 176 25 E
Waiouru 142 39 28 S 175 41 E
Waipahi 143 46 6 S 169 15 E
Waipahu 147 21 23N 158 1W
Waipapa Pt. 143 46 40 S 168 51 E
Waipara 143 43 3 S 172 46 E
Waipawa 142 39 56 S 176 38 E
Waipiro 142 38 2 S 176 22 E
Waipori 131 45 50 S 169 52 E
Waipu 142 35 59 S 174 29 E
Waipukurau 142 40 1 S 176 33 E
Wairakei 142 38 37 S 176 6 E
Wairarapa I. 142 41 14 S 175 15 E
Wairau, R. 143 41 32 S 174 7 E
Wairio 143 45 59 S 168 3 E
Wairoa 142 39 3 S 177 25 E
Wairoa, R. 142 36 5 S 173 59 E
Waitaki Plains 143 44 22 S 170 0 E
Waitaki, R. 143 44 23 S 169 55 E
Waitara 142 38 59 S 174 15 E
Waitchie 140 35 22 S 143 8 E
Waitoa 142 37 37 S 175 35 E
Waitotara 142 39 49 S 174 44 E
Waitsburg 160 46 15N 118 10W
Waiuku 142 37 15 S 174 45 E
Wajir 126 1 42N 40 20 E
Wajir □ 126 1 42N 40 20 E
Wakaia 143 45 44 S 168 51 E
Wakasa 110 35 20N 134 24 E
Wakasa-Wan 111 34 45N 135 30 E
Wakatipu, L. 143 45 5 S 168 33 E
Wakaw 153 52 39N 105 44W
Wakayama 111 34 15N 135 15 E
Wakayama-ken □ 111 33 50N 135 30 E
Wake 110 34 48N 134 8 E
Wake Forest 157 35 58N 78 30W
Wake I. 130 19 18N 166 36 E
Wakefield, N.Z. 143 41 24 S 173 5 E
Wakefield, U.K. 33 53 41N 1 31W
Wakefield, Mass., U.S.A. 162 42 30N 71 3W
Wakefield, Mich., U.S.A. 158 46 28N 89 53W
Wakema 98 16 40N 95 18 E
Wakhan □ 93 37 0N 73 0 E
Wakkanai 112 45 28N 141 35 E
Wakkerstroom 129 27 24 S 30 10 E
Wako 150 49 50N 91 22W
Wakool 140 35 28 S 144 23 E
Wakool, R. 140 35 5 S 143 33 E
Wakre 103 0 30 S 131 5 E
Waku 135 6 5 S 149 9 E
Wakuach L. 151 55 34N 67 32W
Walachia □ 70 44 0N 25 0 E
Walamba 127 13 30 S 28 42 E
Walberswick 29 52 18N 1 39 E
Wałbrzych 54 50 45N 16 18 E
Walbury Hill 28 51 22N 1 28W
Walcha 141 30 55 S 151 31 E
Walcha Road 141 30 55 S 151 24 E
Walcheren, I. 46 51 30N 3 35 E
Walcott 160 41 50N 106 55W
Walcz 54 53 17N 16 27 E
Wald 51 47 17N 8 56 E
Waldbröl 48 50 52N 7 36 E
Waldeck 48 51 12N 9 4 E
Walden, Colo., U.S.A. 160 40 47N 106 20W
Walden, N.Y., U.S.A. 162 41 32N 74 13W
Waldenburg 50 47 23N 7 45 E
Waldorf 162 38 37N 76 54W
Waldport 160 44 30N 124 2W
Waldron, Can. 153 50 53N 102 35W
Waldron, U.K. 29 50 56N 0 13 E
Waldron, U.S.A. 159 34 52N 94 4W
Waldshut 49 47 37N 8 12 E
Waldya 123 11 50N 39 34 E
Walebing 137 30 40 S 116 15 E
Walembele 120 10 30N 1 14W
Walensee 51 47 7N 9 13 E
Walenstadt 51 47 8N 9 19 E
Wales 147 65 38N 168 10W
Walewale 121 10 21N 0 50W
Walgett 133 30 0 S 148 5 E
Walhalla, Austral. 141 37 56 S 146 29 E
Walhalla, U.S.A. 153 48 55N 97 55W
Waliso 123 8 33N 38 1 E
Walkaway 137 28 59 S 114 48 E
Walker 158 47 4N 94 35W
Walker L., Man., Can. 153 54 42N 96 57W
Walker L., Qué., Can. 151 50 20N 67 11W
Walker L., U.S.A. 163 38 56N 118 46W
Walkerston 138 21 11 S 149 8 E
Wall 158 44 0N 102 14W
Walla Walla, Austral. 141 35 45 S 146 54 E
Walla Walla, U.S.A. 160 46 3N 118 25W

Wallabadah Weaverham

Wallabadah 138 17 57S 142 15E
Wallace, Idaho, U.S.A. 160 47 30N 116 0W
Wallace, N.C., U.S.A. 157 34 50N 77 59W
Wallace, Nebr., U.S.A. 158 40 51N 101 12W
Wallaceburg 150 42 40N 82 23W
Wallacetown 143 46 21S 168 19E
Wallachia = Valahia 70 44 35N 25 0E
Wallal 139 26 32S 146 7E
Wallal Downs 136 19 47S 120 40E
Wallambin, L. 137 30 57S 117 35E
Wallaroo 140 33 56S 137 39E
Wallasey 32 53 26N 3 2W
Walldurn 49 49 34N 9 23E
Wallerawang 141 33 25S 150 4E
Wallhallow 138 17 50S 135 50E
Wallingford 162 43 27N 72 50W
Wallis Arch. 142 13 20S 176 20E
Wallisellen 51 47 25N 8 36E
Wallowa 160 45 40N 117 35W
Wallowa, Mts. 160 45 20N 117 30W
Walls 36 60 14N 1 32W
Wallsend, Austral. 141 32 55S 151 40E
Wallsend, U.K. 35 54 59N 1 30W
Wallula 160 46 3N 118 59W
Wallumbilla 139 26 33S 149 9E
Walmer, S. Afr. 128 33 57S 25 35E
Walmer, U.K. 29 51 12N 1 23E
Walmsley, L. 153 63 25N 108 36W
Walney, Isle of 32 54 5N 3 15W
Walnut Ridge 159 36 7N 90 58W
Walpeup 140 35 10S 142 2E
Walpole 29 52 44N 0 13E
Walsall 28 52 36N 1 59W
Walsenburg 159 37 42N 104 45W
Walsh, Austral. 138 16 40S 144 0E
Walsh, U.S.A. 159 37 28N 102 15W
Walsh, R. 138 16 31S 143 42E
Walshoutem 47 50 43N 5 4E
Walsoken 29 52 41N 0 12E
Walsrode 48 52 51N 9 37E
Waltair 96 17 44N 83 23E
Walterboro 157 32 53N 80 40W
Walters 159 34 25N 98 20W
Waltershausen 48 50 53N 10 33E
Waltham, Can. 150 45 57N 76 57W
Waltham, U.K. 29 53 32N 0 6W
Waltham, U.S.A. 34 42 22N 71 12W
Waltham Abbey 29 51 40N 0 1E
Waltham Forest 29 51 37N 0 2E
Waltham on the Wolds 29 52 49N 0 48W
Waltman 160 43 8N 107 15W
Walton 162 42 12N 75 9W
Walton-le-Dale 32 53 45N 2 41W
Walton-on-the-Naze 29 51 52N 1 17E
Walu 98 23 54N 96 57E
Walvis Ridge 15 30 0S 3 0E
Walvisbaai 128 23 0S 14 28E
Walwa 141 35 59S 147 44E
Wamaza 126 4 12S 27 2E
Wamba, Kenya 126 0 58N 37 19E
Wamba, Nigeria 126 8 58N 8 34E
Wamba, Zaïre 121 2 10N 27 57E
Wamego 158 39 14N 96 22W
Wamena 103 3 58S 138 50E
Wampo 99 31 30N 86 38E
Wamsasi 103 3 27S 126 7E
Wan Hat 98 20 14N 97 53E
Wan Kinghao 98 21 34N 98 17E
Wan Lai-Kam 98 21 21N 98 22E
Wan Tup 98 21 13N 98 42E
Wana 94 32 20N 69 32E
Wanaaring 139 29 38S 144 0E
Wanaka L. 143 44 33S 169 7E
Wanan 109 26 25N 114 50E
Wanapiri 103 4 30S 135 50E
Wanapitei 150 46 30N 80 45W
Wanapitei L. 150 46 45N 80 40W
Wanaque 162 41 3N 74 17W
Wanbi 140 34 46S 140 17E
Wanborough 28 51 33N 1 40W
Wanch'eng 108 22 51N 107 25E
Wanch'üan 106 35 26N 110 50E
Wanch'uan 106 40 50N 114 56E
Wandanian 141 35 6S 150 30E
Wanderer 127 19 36S 30 1E
Wandiwash 97 12 30N 79 30E
Wandoan 139 26 5S 149 55E
Wandre 47 50 40N 5 39E
Wandsworth 29 51 28N 0 15W
Wanfercée-Baulet 47 50 28N 4 35E
Wanfuchuang 107 40 10N 122 34E
Wang Kai (Ghâbat el Arab) 123 9 3N 29 23E
Wang Noi 100 14 13N 100 44E
Wang, R. 100 17 8N 99 2E
Wang Saphung 100 17 18N 101 46E
Wang Thong 100 16 50N 100 26E
Wanga 126 2 58N 29 12E
Wangal 103 6 8S 134 9E
Wanganella 141 35 6S 144 49E
Wanganui 142 39 35S 175 3E
Wanganui, R., N.I., N.Z. 142 39 25S 175 4E
Wanganui, R., S.I., N.Z. 143 43 3S 170 26E
Wangaratta 141 36 21S 146 19E
Wangchiang 109 30 7N 116 41E
Wangch'ing 107 43 14N 129 38E
Wangdu Phodrang 98 27 28N 89 54E
Wangerooge I. 48 53 47N 7 52E
Wangi 126 1 58S 40 58E
Wangiwangi, I. 103 5 22S 123 37E
Wangmo 108 25 14N 105 59E
Wangts'ang 108 32 12N 106 21E
Wangtu 106 38 42N 115 4E
Wanhsien, Hopeh, China 106 38 49N 115 7E
Wanhsien, Kansu, China 105 36 45N 107 24E
Wankaner 94 22 42N 71 0E
Wanki Nat. Park 128 19 0S 26 30E
Wankie 127 18 18S 26 30E
Wankie □ 127 18 18S 26 30E
Wanless 153 54 11N 101 21W
Wanna Lakes 137 28 30S 128 27E
Wannien 109 28 40N 116 55E
Wanon Niwar 100 17 38N 103 46E
Wanshengch'ang 108 28 58N 106 55E
Wanssum 47 51 32N 6 5E
Wanstead 143 40 8S 176 30E
Wantage 28 51 35N 1 25W
Wantsai 109 28 5N 114 22E
Wanyin 98 20 23N 97 15E
Wanyüan 108 32 4N 108 5E
Wanzarik 119 27 3N 13 30E
Wanze 47 50 32N 5 13E
Wapakoneta 156 40 35N 84 10W
Wapato 160 46 30N 120 25W
Wapawekka L. 153 54 55N 104 40W
Wapikopa L. 150 42 50N 88 10W
Wapiti, R. 150 55 5N 118 18W
Wappingers Fs. 162 41 35N 73 56W
Wapsipinican, R. 158 41 44N 90 19W
Warabi 111 35 49N 139 41E
Warandab 91 7 20N 44 2E
Warangal 96 17 58N 79 45E
Waratah 138 41 30S 145 30E
Waratah B. 139 38 54S 146 5E
Warboys 29 52 25N 0 5W
Warburg 48 51 29N 9 10E
Warburton 141 37 47S 145 42E
Warburton, R. 143 27 30S 138 30E
Warburton Ra. 137 25 55S 126 28E
Ward, Ireland 38 53 25N 6 19W
Ward, N.Z. 143 41 49S 174 11E
Ward Cove 152 55 25N 132 10W
Ward Hunt, C. 135 8 2S 148 10E
Ward Hunt Str. 135 9 30S 150 0E
Ward Mtn. 163 37 12N 118 54W
Ward, R. 139 26 32S 146 6E
Warden 129 27 50S 29 0E
Wardha 96 20 45N 78 39E
Wardha, R. 93 19 57N 79 11E
Wardington 28 52 8N 1 17W
Wardle 32 53 7N 2 35W
Wardlow 152 50 56N 111 31W
Wardoan 133 25 59S 149 59E
Wards River 141 32 11S 151 56E
Ward's Stone, mt. 32 54 2N 2 39W
Ware, Can. 152 57 26N 125 41W
Ware, U.K. 29 51 48N 0 2W
Ware, U.S.A. 162 42 16N 72 15W
Waregem 47 50 53N 3 27E
Wareham, U.K. 28 50 41N 2 8W
Wareham, U.S.A. 162 41 45N 70 44W
Wareham, oilfield 19 50 40N 2 8W
Waremme 47 50 43N 5 15E
Waren 48 53 30N 12 41E
Warendorf 48 51 57N 8 0E
Warialda 139 29 29S 150 33E
Wariap 103 1 30S 134 5E
Warin Chamrap 100 15 12N 104 53E
Wark 35 55 5N 2 14W
Warkopi 103 1 12S 134 9E
Warkworth, N.Z. 142 36 24S 174 41E
Warkworth, U.K. 35 55 22N 1 38W
Warley 28 52 30N 2 0W
Warm Springs, Mont., U.S.A. 160 46 11N 112 56W
Warm Springs, Nev., U.S.A. 161 38 16N 116 32W
Warman 153 52 19N 106 30W
Warmbad, Namibia 128 19 14S 13 51E
Warmbad, Namibia 128 28 25S 18 42E
Warmbad, S. Afr. 129 24 51S 28 19E
Warmenhuizen 46 52 43N 4 44E
Warmeriville 43 49 20N 4 13E
Warminster 28 51 12N 2 11W
Warmond 46 52 12N 4 30E
Warnambool Downs 138 22 48S 142 52E
Warnemünde 48 54 9N 12 5E
Warner 152 49 17N 112 12W
Warner Range, Mts. 160 41 30S 120 20W
Warner Robins 157 32 41N 83 36W
Warneton 47 50 45N 2 57E
Warnow, R. 48 54 0N 12 9E
Warnsveld 46 52 8N 6 14E
Waroona 137 32 50S 115 58E
Warora 96 20 14N 79 1E
Warracknabeal 140 36 9S 142 26E
Warragul 141 38 10S 145 58E
Warrawaqine 136 20 51S 120 42E
Warrayelu 123 10 40N 39 28E
Warrego, R. 139 30 24S 145 21E
Warrego Ra. 138 25 15S 146 0E
Warren, Austral. 141 31 42S 147 51E
Warren, Ark., U.S.A. 159 33 35N 92 3W
Warren, Pa., U.S.A. 156 41 52N 79 10W
Warren, R.I., U.S.A. 156 41 43N 71 19W
Warrenpoint 38 54 7N 6 15W
Warrens Landing 153 53 40N 98 0W
Warrensburg 158 38 45N 93 45W
Warrenton, S. Afr. 128 28 9S 24 47E
Warrenton, U.S.A. 160 46 11N 123 59W
Warrenville 139 25 48S 147 22E
Warri 121 5 30N 5 41E
Warrie 136 22 12S 119 40E
Warrina 136 28 12S 135 50E
Warrington, N.Z. 143 45 43S 170 35E
Warrington, U.K. 32 53 25N 2 38W
Warrington, U.S.A. 157 30 22N 87 16W
Warrnambool 140 38 25S 142 30E
Warroad 158 49 0N 95 20W
Warsaw 156 41 14N 85 50W
Warsaw = Warszawa 54 52 13N 21 0E
Warsop 33 53 13N 1 9W
Warstein 48 51 26N 8 20E
Warszawa 54 52 13N 21 0E
Warszawa □ 54 52 30N 17 0E
Warta 54 51 43N 18 38E
Warta, R. 54 52 40N 16 10E
Waru 103 3 30S 130 36E
Warud 96 21 30N 78 16E
Warwick, Austral. 139 28 10S 152 1E
Warwick, U.K. 28 52 17N 1 36W
Warwick, N.Y., U.S.A. 162 41 16N 74 22W
Warwick, R.I., U.S.A. 162 41 43N 71 25W
Warwick □ 28 52 20N 1 30W
Wasa 152 49 45N 115 50W
Wasatch, Mt., Ra. 160 40 30N 111 15W
Wasbank 129 28 15S 30 9E
Wasbister 37 59 11N 3 2W
Wasco, Calif., U.S.A. 163 35 37N 119 16W
Wasco, Oreg., U.S.A. 160 45 45N 120 46W
Waseca 158 44 3N 93 31W
Wasekamio L. 153 56 45N 108 45W
Wash, The 33 52 58N 0 20W
Washburn, N.D., U.S.A. 158 47 23N 101 0W
Washburn, Wis., U.S.A. 158 46 38N 90 55W
Washford 28 51 9N 3 22W
Washington, U.K. 35 54 55N 1 30W
Washington, D.C., U.S.A. 162 38 52N 77 0W
Washington, Ga., U.S.A. 157 33 45N 82 45W
Washington, Ind., U.S.A. 156 38 40N 87 8W
Washington, Iowa, U.S.A. 158 41 20N 91 45W
Washington, Miss., U.S.A. 158 38 35N 91 20W
Washington, N.C., U.S.A. 157 35 35N 77 1W
Washington, N.J., U.S.A. 162 40 45N 74 59W
Washington, Ohio, U.S.A. 156 39 34N 83 26W
Washington, Pa., U.S.A. 156 40 10N 80 20W
Washington, Utah, U.S.A. 161 37 10N 113 30W
Washington □ 160 47 45N 120 30W
Washington Court House 156 39 34N 83 26W
* Washington I., Pac. Oc. 131 4 43N 160 25W
Washington I., U.S.A. 156 45 24N 86 54W
Washington Mt. 156 44 15N 71 18W
Washir 93 32 15N 63 50E
Wasian 103 1 47S 133 19E
Wasilków 54 53 12N 23 13E
Wasior 103 2 43S 134 30E
Waskaiowaka, L. 153 56 33N 96 23W
Waskesiu Lake 153 53 55N 106 5W
Wasm 122 18 2N 41 32E
Waspik 47 51 41N 4 57E
Wassen 51 46 42N 8 36E
Wassenaar 46 52 8N 4 24E
Wasserburg 49 48 4N 12 15E
Wassy 43 48 30N 4 58E
Wast Water, L. 32 54 26N 3 18W
Waswanipi 150 49 40N 75 59W
Waswanipi, L. 150 49 35N 76 40W
Watangpone 103 4 29S 120 25E
Wataroa 143 43 18S 170 24E
Wataroa, R. 143 43 7S 170 16E
Watawaha, P. 103 6 30S 122 20E
Watchet 28 51 10N 3 20W
Water Park Pt. 138 22 56S 150 47E
Water Valley 159 34 9N 89 38W
Waterberg, Namibia 128 20 30S 17 18E
Waterberg, S. Afr. 129 24 14S 28 0E
Waterberg, mt. 128 20 26S 17 13E
Waterbury 162 41 32N 73 0W
Waterbury L. 153 58 10N 104 22W
Waterford, Ireland 39 52 16N 7 8W
Waterford, S. Afr. 128 33 6S 25 0E
Waterford, U.S.A. 163 37 38N 120 46W
Waterford □ 39 51 10N 7 40W
Waterford Harb. 39 52 10N 6 58W
Watergate Bay 30 50 26N 5 4W
Watergrasshill 39 52 1N 8 20W
Waterhen L., Man., Can. 153 52 10N 99 40W
Waterhen L., Sask., Can. 153 54 28N 108 25W
Wateringen 46 52 2N 4 16E
Waterloo, Belg. 47 50 43N 4 25E
Waterloo, Can. 150 43 30N 80 32W
Waterloo, S. Leone 120 8 26N 13 8W
Waterloo, U.K. 32 53 29N 3 2W
Waterloo, Ill., U.S.A. 158 38 22N 90 6W
Waterloo, Iowa, U.S.A. 158 42 27N 92 20W
Waterloo, N.Y., U.S.A. 162 42 54N 76 53W
Watermeal-Boitsfort 47 50 48N 4 25E
Watermeet 158 46 15N 89 12W
Waternish 36 57 32N 6 35W
Waterton Lakes Nat. Park 152 49 5N 114 15W
Watertown, Conn., U.S.A. 162 41 36N 73 7W
Watertown, N.Y., U.S.A. 162 43 58N 75 57W
Watertown, S.D., U.S.A. 158 44 57N 97 5W
Watertown, Wis., U.S.A. 158 43 15N 88 45W
Waterval-Boven 129 25 40S 30 18E
Waterville, Ireland 39 51 49N 10 10W
Waterville, Me., U.S.A. 151 44 35N 69 40W
Waterville, N.Y., U.S.A. 162 42 56N 75 23W
Waterville, Wash., U.S.A. 160 47 45N 120 1W
Watervliet, Belg. 47 51 17N 3 38E
Watervliet, U.S.A. 162 42 46N 73 43W
Wates 103 7 53S 110 6E
Watford 29 51 38N 0 23W
Watford City 158 47 50N 103 23W
Wath 33 53 29N 1 20W
Wathaman, R. 153 57 16N 102 59W
Watheroo 137 30 15S 116 0W
Watien 109 32 45N 112 30E
Wat'ing 106 35 25N 106 46E
Watkins Glen 162 42 25N 76 55W
Watlings I. 167 24 0N 74 35W
Watlington, Norfolk, U.K. 29 52 40N 0 24E
Watlington, Oxford, U.K. 29 51 38N 1 0W
Watonga 159 35 51N 98 24W
Watou 47 50 51N 2 38E
Watraba 139 31 58S 133 13E
Watrous, Can. 153 51 40N 105 25W
Watrous, U.S.A. 159 35 50N 104 55W
Watsa 126 3 4N 29 30E
Watseka 156 40 45N 87 45W
Watson, Austral. 137 30 29S 131 31E
Watson, Can. 153 52 10N 104 30W
Watson Lake 147 60 6N 128 49W
Watsontown 162 41 5N 76 52W
Watsonville 163 36 55N 121 49W
Watten 37 21 1S 144 3E
Wattenwil 50 46 46N 7 30E
Wattiwarriganna Cr. 139 28 57S 136 10E
Watton 29 52 35N 0 50E
Wattwil 51 47 18N 9 6E
Watubela, Kepulauan 103 4 28S 131 54E
Wau 135 7 21S 146 47E
Waubach 47 50 55N 6 3E
Waubay 158 45 42N 97 17W
Waubra 140 37 21S 143 39E
Wauchope 141 31 28S 152 45E
Wauchula 157 27 35N 81 50W
Waugh 153 49 40N 95 20W
Waukegan 156 42 22N 87 54W
Waukesha 156 43 0N 88 15W
Waukon 158 43 14N 91 33W
Wauneta 158 40 27N 101 25W
Waupaca 158 44 22N 89 8W
Waupun 158 43 38N 88 44W
Waurika 159 34 12N 98 0W
Wausau 158 44 57N 89 40W
Wautoma 158 44 3N 89 20W
Wauwatosa 156 43 6N 87 59W
Wave Hill 136 17 32N 131 0E
Waveney, R. 29 52 24N 1 20E
Waver R. 32 54 50N 3 15W
Waverley 142 39 46S 174 37E
Waverly, Iowa, U.S.A. 158 42 40N 92 30W
Waverly, N.Y., U.S.A. 162 42 0N 76 33W
Wavre 47 50 43N 4 38E
Wavreille 47 50 7N 5 15E
Wâw 123 7 45N 28 1E
Waw an Namus 119 24 24N 18 11E
Wawa, Can. 150 47 59N 84 47W
Wawa, Nigeria 121 9 54N 4 27E
Wawa, Sudan 122 20 30N 30 22E
Wawanesa 153 49 36N 99 40W
Wawoi, R. 135 7 48S 143 16E
Wawona 163 37 32N 119 39W
Waxahachie 159 32 22N 96 53W
Waxweiler 49 50 6N 6 22E
Way, L. 137 26 45S 120 16E
Wayabula Rau 103 2 29N 128 17E
Wayatinah 138 42 19S 146 27E
Waycross 157 31 12N 82 25W
Wayi 123 5 8N 30 10E
Wayne, Nebr., U.S.A. 158 42 16N 97 0W
Wayne, W. Va., U.S.A. 156 38 15N 82 27W
Waynesboro, Miss., U.S.A. 157 31 40N 88 39W
Waynesboro, Pa., U.S.A. 156 39 46N 77 32W
Waynesboro, Va., U.S.A. 156 38 4N 78 57W
Waynesburg 156 39 54N 80 12W
Waynesville 157 35 31N 83 0W
Waynoka 159 36 38N 98 53W
Waza 94 33 22N 69 22E
Wâzin 119 31 58N 10 51E
Wazirabad, Afghan. 93 36 44N 66 47E
Wazirabad, Pak. 94 32 30N 74 8E
We 102 6 3N 95 56E
Weald, The 29 51 7N 0 9E
Wear, R. 35 54 55N 1 22W
Weardale 32 54 44N 2 5W
Wearhead 32 54 45N 2 14W
Weatherford, Okla., U.S.A. 159 35 30N 98 45W
Weatherford, Tex., U.S.A. 159 32 45N 97 48W
Weaver, R. 32 53 17N 2 35W
Weaverham 32 53 15N 2 30W

*Renamed Teraina

Webb City **Whitby**

Webb City **159** 37 9N 94 30W
Weber **142** 40 24 S 176 20 E
Webera, Bale, Ethiopia **123** 6 29N 40 33 E
Webera, Shewa, Ethiopia **123** 9 40N 39 0 E
Webster, Mass., U.S.A. **162** 42 4N 71 54W
Webster, S.D., U.S.A. **158** 45 24N 97 33W
Webster, Wis., U.S.A. **158** 45 53N 92 25W
Webster City **158** 42 30N 93 50W
Webster Green **158** 38 38N 90 20W
Webster Springs **156** 38 30N 80 25W
Wecliniec **54** 51 18N 15 10 E
Weda **103** 0 30N 127 50 E
Weda, Teluk **103** 0 30N 127 50 E
Weddell I. **176** 51 50 S 61 0W
Weddell Sea **13** 72 30 S 40 0W
Wedderburn **140** 36 20 S 143 33 E
Wedge I. **132** 30 50 S 115 11 E
Wedgeport **151** 43 44N 65 59W
Wedmore **28** 51 14N 2 50W
Wednesbury **28** 52 33N 2 1W
Wednesfield **28** 52 36N 2 3W
Wedza **127** 18 40 S 31 33 E
Wee Elwah **141** 32 2 S 145 14 E
Wee Waa **139** 30 11 S 149 26 E
Weed **160** 41 29N 122 22W
Weedsport **162** 43 3N 76 35W
Weemelah **139** 29 2 S 149 7 E
Weenen **129** 28 48 S 30 7 E
Weener **48** 53 10N 7 23 E
Weert **47** 51 15N 5 43 E
Weesen **51** 47 7N 9 4 E
Weesp **46** 52 18N 5 2 E
Weggis **51** 47 2N 8 26 E
Wegierska-Gorka **54** 49 36N 19 7 E
Wegorzewo **54** 54 13N 21 43 E
Wegroów **54** 52 24N 22 0 E
Wehl **46** 51 58N 6 13 E
Wei Ho, R., Honan, China **106** 34 58N 113 32 E
Wei Ho, R., Shensi, China **106** 34 38N 110 20 E
Wei-si **99** 27 18N 99 18 E
Weich'ang **107** 41 56N 117 34 E
Weichou Tao **108** 21 3N 109 2 E
Weich'uan **106** 34 19N 114 0 E
Weida **48** 50 47N 12 3 E
Weiden **49** 49 40N 12 10 E
Weifang **107** 36 47N 119 10 E
Weihai **107** 37 30N 122 10 E
Weihsi **108** 27 18N 99 18 E
Weihsin **108** 27 48N 105 5 E
Weilburg **48** 50 28N 8 17 E
Weilheim **49** 47 50N 11 9 E
Weimar **48** 51 0N 11 20 E
Weinan **106** 34 30N 109 35 E
Weinfelden **51** 47 34N 9 6 E
Weingarten **49** 47 49N 9 39 E
Weinheim **49** 49 33N 8 40 E
Weining **108** 26 50N 104 19 E
Weipa **138** 12 24 S 141 50 E
Weir, R., Austral. **139** 28 20 S 149 50 E
Weir, R., Can. **153** 56 54N 93 21W
Weir River **153** 56 49N 94 6W
Weisen **51** 46 42N 9 43 E
Weiser **160** 44 10N 117 0W
Weishan, Shantung, China **107** 34 49N 47 6 E
Weishan, Yunnan, China **108** 25 16N 100 21 E
Weissenburg **49** 49 2N 10 58 E
Weissenfels **48** 51 11N 11 58 E
Weisshorn **50** 46 7N 7 43 E
Weissmies **50** 46 8N 8 1 E
Weisstannen **51** 46 59N 9 22 E
Weisswasser **48** 51 30N 14 36 E
Weiswampach **47** 50 8N 6 5 E
Wéitra **52** 48 41N 14 54 E
Weiyüan **106** 35 6N 104 14 E
Weiyuan **106** 35 10N 104 20 E
Weiz **52** 47 13N 15 39 E
Wejherowo **54** 54 35N 18 12 E
Wekusko **153** 54 45N 99 45W
Wekusko L. **153** 54 40N 99 50W
Welbourn Hill **139** 27 21 S 134 6 E
Welby **153** 50 33N 101 29W
Welch **156** 37 29N 81 36W
Welcome **138** 15 20 S 144 40 E
Weldon **35** 55 16N 1 46W
Welega □ **123** 9 25N 34 20 E
Welford, Berks., U.K. **28** 51 28N 1 24W
Welford, Northampton, U.K. **28** 52 26N 1 5W
Welkenraedt **47** 50 39N 5 58 E
Welkite **123** 8 15N 37 42 E
Welkom **128** 28 0 S 26 50 E
Welland **150** 43 0N 79 10W
Welland, R. **29** 52 43N 0 10W
Wellen **47** 50 50N 5 21 E
Wellesley Is. **138** 17 20 S 139 30 E
Wellin **47** 50 5N 5 6 E
Wellingborough **29** 52 18N 0 41W
Wellington, Austral. **141** 32 35 S 148 59 E
Wellington, Can. **150** 43 57N 77 20W
Wellington, N.Z. **142** 41 19 S 174 46 E
Wellington, S. Afr. **128** 33 38 S 18 57 E
Wellington, U.K. **28** 50 58N 3 13W
Wellington, Col., U.S.A. **158** 40 43N 105 0W
Wellington, Kans., U.S.A. **159** 37 15N 97 25W
Wellington, Nev., U.S.A. **163** 38 47N 119 28W
Wellington, Okla., U.S.A. **159** 34 55N 100 13W
Wellington □ **143** 40 8 S 175 36 E
Wellington Bridge **39** 52 15N 6 45W
Wellington, I. **176** 49 30 S 75 0W
Wellington, L. **141** 38 6 S 147 20 E
Wellington, Mt. **142** 36 55 S 174 52 E
Wellington (Telford) **28** 52 42N 2 31W
Wello, L. **137** 26 43 S 123 10 E
Wellow **28** 51 20N 2 22W
Wells, Norfolk, U.K. **29** 52 57N 0 51 E
Wells, Somerset, U.K. **28** 51 12N 2 39W
Wells, Me., U.S.A. **162** 43 18N 70 35W
Wells, Minn., U.S.A. **158** 43 44N 93 45W
Wells, Nev., U.S.A. **160** 41 8N 115 0W
Wells, N.Y., U.S.A. **162** 43 24N 74 17W
Wells Gray Prov. Park **152** 52 30N 120 15W
Wells L. **137** 26 44 S 123 15 E
Wellsboro **156** 41 46N 77 20W
Wellsford **142** 36 16 S 174 32 E
Wellsville, Mo., U.S.A. **158** 39 4N 91 30W
Wellsville, N.Y., U.S.A. **156** 42 9N 77 53W
Wellsville, Ohio, U.S.A. **156** 40 36N 80 40W
Wellsville, Utah, U.S.A. **160** 41 35N 111 59W
Wellton **161** 32 46N 114 6W
Welmel, W. **123** 6 0N 40 20 E
Welney **29** 52 31N 0 15 E
Welo □ **123** 11 50N 39 48 E
Wels **52** 48 9N 14 1 E
Welshpool **31** 52 40N 3 9W
Welton **33** 53 19N 0 29W
Welwel **91** 7 5N 45 25 E
Welwitschia **128** 20 16 S 14 59 E
Welwyn **153** 50 20N 101 30W
Welwyn Garden City **29** 51 49N 0 11W
Wem **28** 52 52N 2 45W
Wembere, R. **126** 4 45 S 34 0 E
Wembury **30** 50 19N 4 6W
Wemmel **47** 50 55N 4 18 E
Wemyss Bay **34** 55 52N 4 54W
Wenatchee **160** 47 30N 120 17W
Wench'ang **100** 19 38N 110 42 E
Wencheng **109** 27 48N 120 5 E
Wenchi **120** 7 46N 2 8W
Wenchiang **108** 30 43N 103 56 E
Wenchou **109** 28 1N 120 39 E
Wench'uan **108** 31 28N 103 35 E
Wendell **160** 42 50N 114 51W
Wendesi **103** 2 30 S 134 10 E
Wendo **123** 6 40N 38 27 E
Wendover, U.K. **29** 51 46N 0 45W
Wendover, U.S.A. **160** 40 49N 114 1W
Wenduine **47** 51 18N 3 5 E
Wengan **108** 27 0N 107 32 E
Wengch'eng **109** 24 22N 113 50 E
Wenge **126** 0 3N 24 0 E
Wengen **50** 46 37N 7 55 E
Wengniut'ech'i **107** 42 59N 118 48 E
Wengpu **108** 32 55N 98 30 E
Wengyüan **109** 24 21N 114 7 E
Wenhsi **106** 35 23N 111 8 E
Wenhsiang **106** 34 36N 110 34 E
Wenhsien, Honan, China **106** 34 56N 113 4 E
Wenhsien, Kansu, China **106** 58 0N 104 39 E
Wenling **109** 28 22N 121 18 E
Wenlock **138** 13 6 S 142 58 E
Wenlock Edge **23** 52 30N 2 43W
Wenlock, R. **133** 12 2 S 141 55 E
Wenshan **108** 23 22N 104 13 E
Wenshang **106** 35 37N 116 33 E
Wenshui, Kweichow, China **108** 28 27N 106 31 E
Wenshui, Shansi, China **106** 37 25N 112 1 E
Wensleydale **32** 54 18N 2 0W
Wensu **105** 41 15N 80 14 E
Wenteng **107** 37 10N 122 0 E
Wentworth **140** 34 2 S 141 54 E
Wentworth, Mt. **138** 24 12 S 147 1 E
Wenut **103** 3 11 S 133 19 E
Weobley **28** 52 9N 2 52W
Weott **160** 40 19N 123 56W
Wepener **128** 29 42 S 27 3 E
Werbomont **47** 50 23N 5 41 E
Werda **128** 25 24 S 23 15 E
Werdau **48** 50 45N 12 20 E
Werder, Ethiopia **91** 6 58N 45 1 E
Werder, Ger. **48** 52 23N 12 56 E
Werdohl **48** 51 15N 7 47 E
Weri **103** 3 10 S 132 30 E
Werkendam **46** 51 50N 4 53 E
Werne **48** 51 38N 7 38 E
Wernigerode **48** 51 49N 0 45 E
Werribee **140** 37 54 S 144 40 E
Werrimull **140** 34 25 S 141 38 E
Werrington **30** 50 31N 4 22W
Werris Creek **141** 31 18 S 150 38 E
Wersar **103** 1 30 S 131 55 E
Wertheim **49** 49 44N 9 32 E
Wervershoof **46** 52 44N 5 10 E
Wervik **47** 50 47N 3 3 E
Wesel **48** 51 39N 6 34 E
Weser, R. **48** 53 33N 8 30 E
Wesiri **103** 7 30 S 126 30 E
Wesleyville **151** 49 8N 53 36W
Wessel, C. **138** 10 59 S 136 46 E
Wessel Is. **138** 11 10 S 136 45 E
Wesselburen **48** 54 11N 8 53 E
Wessem **47** 51 11N 5 49 E
Wessington **158** 44 30N 98 40W
Wessington Springs **158** 44 10N 98 35W
West **159** 31 50N 97 5W
West Auckland **33** 54 38N 1 42W
West B. **151** 45 53N 82 8W
West, B. **159** 29 5N 89 27W
West Baines, R. **136** 15 36 S 129 58 E
West Bend **156** 43 25N 88 10W
West Bengal □ **95** 25 0N 90 0 E
West Branch **156** 44 16N 84 13W
West Bridgford **33** 52 56N 1 8W
West Bromwich **28** 52 32N 2 1W
West Burra, I. **36** 60 5N 1 21W
West Calder **35** 55 51N 3 34W
West Canada Cr. **162** 43 1N 74 58W
West Cape Howe **137** 35 8 S 117 36 E
West Chester **162** 39 58N 75 36W
West Coker **28** 50 55N 2 40W
West Columbia **159** 29 10N 95 38W
West Covina **163** 34 4N 117 54W
West Derry **162** 42 55N 71 19W
West Des Moines **158** 41 30N 93 45W
West End **166** 26 41N 78 58W
West Falkland Island **176** 51 30 S 60 0W
West Fen **33** 53 5N 0 5W
West Frankfort **158** 37 56N 89 0W
West Glamorgan □ **31** 51 40N 3 55W
West Grinstead **29** 50 58N 0 19W
West Haddon **28** 52 21N 1 5W
West Harbour **131** 45 51 S 170 33 E
West Hartford **162** 41 45N 72 45W
West Haven **162** 41 18N 72 57W
West Hazleton **162** 40 58N 76 0W
West Helena **159** 34 30N 90 40W
West Hurley **162** 41 59N 74 7W
West Indies **158** 15 0N 70 0W
West Kilbride **34** 55 41N 4 50W
West Kirby **32** 53 22N 3 11W
West Lavington **28** 51 16N 1 59W
West Linton **35** 55 45N 3 24W
West Looe **30** 50 21N 4 29W
West Lulworth **28** 50 37N 2 14W
West Lunga, R. **127** 12 35 S 24 45 E
West Magpie R. **151** 51 2N 64 42W
West Malling **29** 51 16N 0 25 E
West Memphis **159** 35 5N 90 3W
West Meon **28** 51 2N 1 3W
West Mersea **29** 51 46N 0 55 E
West Midlands □ **28** 52 30N 1 55W
West Milton **162** 41 1N 76 50W
West Monroe **159** 32 32N 92 7W
West Nicholson **127** 21 2 S 29 20 E
West Pakistan = Pakistan **93** 27 0N 67 0W
West Palm Beach **157** 26 44N 80 3W
West Paris **101** 44 18N 70 30W
West Parley **28** 50 46N 1 52W
West Plains **159** 36 45N 91 50W
West Pt. **140** 35 1 S 135 56 E
West Point, Can. **151** 49 55N 64 30W
West Point, Jamaica **166** 18 14N 78 30W
West Point, Ga., U.S.A. **157** 32 54N 85 10W
West Point, Miss., U.S.A. **157** 33 36N 88 38W
West Point, Nebr., U.S.A. **158** 41 50N 96 43W
West Point, Va., U.S.A. **162** 37 35N 76 47W
West Pokot □ **126** 1 30N 35 40 E
West, R. **162** 42 52N 72 33W
West Rasen **33** 53 23N 0 23W
West Reading **162** 40 20N 75 57W
West Riding (□) **26** 53 50N 1 30W
West Road R. **152** 53 18N 122 53W
West Rutland **162** 43 36N 73 3W
West Schelde = Westerschelde **47** 51 23N 3 50 E
West Sole, gasfield **19** 53 40N 1 15 E
West Spitsbergen **12** 78 40N 17 0 E
West Sussex □ **29** 50 55N 0 30W
West-Terschelling **46** 53 22N 5 13 E
West Virginia □ **156** 39 0N 18 0W
West-Vlaanderen □ **47** 51 0N 3 0 E
West Walker, R. **163** 38 54N 119 9W
West Wittering **29** 50 44N 0 53W
West Wyalong **141** 33 56 S 147 10 E
West Yellowstone **160** 44 47N 111 4W
West York **162** 39 57N 76 46W
West Yorkshire □ **33** 53 45N 1 40W
Westall **139** 32 55 S 134 4 E
Westbank **152** 49 50N 119 25W
Westbourne **29** 50 53N 0 55W
Westbrook, Maine, U.S.A. **162** 43 40N 70 22W
Westbrook, Tex., U.S.A. **159** 32 25N 101 0W
Westbury, Austral. **138** 41 30 S 146 51 E
Westbury, Salop, U.K. **28** 52 40N 2 57W
Westbury, Wilts., U.K. **28** 51 16N 2 11W
Westbury-on-Severn **28** 51 49N 2 24W
Westby **158** 48 52N 104 3W
Westend **163** 35 42N 117 24W
Wester Ross, dist. **36** 57 37N 5 0W
Westerbork **46** 52 51N 6 37 E
Westerham **29** 51 16N 0 5 E
Westerland **48** 54 51N 8 20 E
Western □, Kenya **126** 0 30N 34 30 E
Western □, Uganda **126** 1 45N 31 30 E
Western □, Zambia **127** 13 15N 27 30 E
Western Australia □ **137** 25 0 S 118 0 E
Western Bay **151** 46 50N 52 30W
Western Germany ■ **48** 50 0N 8 0 E
Western Ghats **97** 15 30N 74 30 E
Western Is. □ **36** 57 40N 7 0W
Western River **140** 35 42 S 136 56 E
Western Samoa ■ **130** 14 0 S 172 0W
Westernport **156** 30 30N 79 5W
Westerschelde, R. **47** 51 25N 4 0 E
Westerstede **48** 51 15N 7 55 E
Westervoort **46** 51 58N 5 59 E
Westerwald, mts. **48** 50 39N 8 0 E
Westfield, U.K. **29** 50 53N 0 30 E
Westfield, U.S.A. **162** 42 9N 72 49W
Westgat **47** 51 39N 3 44 E
Westhope **158** 48 55N 101 0W
Westhoughton **32** 53 34N 2 30W
Westkapelle, Belg. **47** 51 19N 3 19 E
Westkapelle, Neth. **47** 51 31N 3 28 E
Westland □ **143** 43 33 S 169 59 E
Westland Bight **143** 42 55 S 170 5 E
Westlock **152** 54 9N 113 55W
Westmalle **47** 51 18N 4 42 E
Westmeath □ **38** 53 30N 7 30W
Westmine **137** 29 2 S 116 8 E
Westminster **162** 39 34 S 77 1W
Westmorland **161** 33 2N 115 42W
Westmorland (□) **26** 54 28N 2 40W
Weston, Malay. **102** 5 10N 115 35 E
Weston, U.K. **28** 52 51N 2 2W
Weston, Oreg., U.S.A. **160** 45 50N 118 30W
Weston, W. Va., U.S.A. **156** 39 3N 80 29W
Weston I. **150** 52 33N 79 36W
Weston-super-Mare **28** 51 20N 2 59W
Westport, Ireland **38** 53 44N 9 31W
Westport, N.Z. **143** 41 46 S 171 37 E
Westport, U.S.A. **160** 46 48N 124 4W
Westport B. **38** 53 48N 9 38W
Westray **153** 53 36N 101 24W
Westray Firth **37** 59 15N 3 0W
Westray, I. **37** 59 18N 3 0W
Westree **150** 47 26N 81 34W
Westruther **35** 55 45N 2 34W
Westview **152** 49 50N 124 31W
Westville, Ill., U.S.A. **156** 40 3N 87 36W
Westville, Okla., U.S.A. **159** 36 0N 94 33W
Westward Ho **30** 51 2N 4 16W
Westwood **160** 40 26N 121 0W
Wetar, I. **103** 7 30 S 126 30 E
Wetaskiwin **152** 52 55N 113 24W
Wetherby **33** 53 56N 1 23W
Wethersfield **162** 41 43N 72 40W
Wetlet **98** 21 13N 95 53 E
Wettingen **51** 47 28N 8 20 E
Wetwang **33** 54 2N 0 35W
Wetzikon **51** 47 19N 8 48 E
Wetzlar **48** 50 33N 8 30 E
Wevelgem **47** 50 49N 3 12 E
Wewak **135** 3 38 S 143 41 E
Wewaka **159** 35 10N 96 35W
Wexford **39** 52 20N 6 28W
Wexford □ **39** 52 20N 6 25W
Wexford Harb. **39** 52 20N 6 25W
Wey, R. **29** 51 19N 0 29W
Weybourne **29** 52 57N 1 9 E
Weybridge **29** 51 22N 0 28W
Weyburn **153** 49 40N 103 50W
Weyburn L. **152** 63 0N 117 59W
Weyer **52** 47 51N 14 40 E
Weymouth, Can. **151** 44 30N 66 1W
Weymouth, U.K. **28** 50 36N 2 28W
Weymouth, U.S.A. **162** 42 13N 70 53W
Weymouth, C. **133** 12 37 S 143 27 E
Wezep **46** 52 28N 6 0 E
Whakamaru **142** 38 23 S 175 63 E
Whakatane **142** 37 57 S 177 1 E
Whale Cove **148** 62 11N 92 36W
Whale Firth **36** 60 40N 1 10W
Whale, R. **151** 58 15N 67 40W
Whales **13** 78 0 S 165 0W
Whaley Bridge **32** 53 20N 2 0W
Whalley **32** 53 49N 2 25W
Whalsay, I. **36** 60 22N 1 0W
Whalton **35** 55 7N 1 46W
Whangamomona **142** 39 8 S 174 44 E
Whangarei **142** 35 43 S 174 21 E
Whangarei Harbour **142** 35 45 S 174 28 E
Whangaroa **142** 35 4 S 173 46 E
Whangumata **142** 37 12 S 175 53 E
Whaplode **29** 52 42N 0 3W
Wharanui **143** 41 55 S 174 6 E
Wharfe, R. **33** 53 55N 1 30W
Wharfedale **31** 54 7N 2 4W
Wharton, N.J., U.S.A. **162** 40 53N 74 36W
Wharton, Tex., U.S.A. **159** 29 20N 96 6W
Whauphill **34** 54 48N 4 31W
Whayjonta **139** 29 40 S 142 35 E
Wheatland **158** 42 4N 105 58W
Wheatley Hill **33** 54 45N 1 23W
Wheaton, Md., U.S.A. **162** 39 3N 77 3W
Wheaton, Minn., U.S.A. **158** 45 50N 96 29W
Wheeler, Oreg., U.S.A. **160** 45 45N 123 57W
Wheeler, Tex., U.S.A. **159** 35 29N 100 15W
Wheeler Peak, Mt. **160** 38 57N 114 15W
Wheeler, R. **153** 57 34N 104 15W
Wheeler Ridge **163** 35 0N 118 57W
Wheeling **156** 40 2N 80 41W
Whichham **32** 54 14N 3 22W
Whidbey I. **152** 48 15N 122 40W
Whidbey Is. **136** 34 30 S 135 3 E
Whiddy, I. **39** 51 41N 9 30W
Whimple **30** 50 46N 3 21W
Whipsnade **29** 51 51N 0 32W
Whiskey Gap **152** 49 0N 113 3W
Whiskey Jack L. **153** 58 23N 101 55W
Whissendine **29** 52 43N 0 46W
Whistleduck Cr. **138** 20 15 S 135 18 E
Whistler **157** 30 50N 88 10W
Whiston **32** 53 25N 2 45W
Whitburn **35** 55 52N 3 41W
Whitby **33** 54 29N 0 37W

Whitchurch **Winterberg**

Whitchurch, U.K.	31	51 32N	3 15W
Whitchurch, Devon, U.K.	30	50 31N	4 7W
Whitchurch, Hants., U.K.	28	51 14N	1 20W
Whitchurch, Here., U.K.	28	51 51N	2 41W
Whitchurch, Salop, U.K.	32	52 58N	2 42W
Whitcombe, Mt.	131	43 12S	171 0E
Whitcombe, P.	131	43 12S	171 0E
White B.	151	50 0N	56 35W
White Bear Res.	151	48 10N	57 05W
White Bird	160	45 46N	116 21W
White Bridge	35	57 11N	4 32W
White Butte	156	46 23N	103 25W
White City	158	38 50N	96 45W
White Cliffs, Austral.	140	30 50S	143 10E
White Cliffs, N.Z.	143	43 26S	171 55E
White Deer	159	35 30N	101 8W
White Esk, R.	35	55 14N	3 11W
White Hall	158	39 25N	90 27W
White Haven	162	41 3N	75 47W
White Horse Hill	28	51 35N	1 35W
White I.	142	37 30S	177 13E
White L., Austral.	136	24 43S	121 44E
White L., U.S.A.	159	29 45N	92 30W
White Mts.	163	37 30N	118 15W
White Nile = Nîl el Abyad, Bahr	123	9 30N	31 40E
White Nile Dam	123	15 24N	32 30E
White Otter L.	150	49 5N	91 55W
White Pass	147	59 40N	135 3W
White Plains, Liberia	120	6 28N	10 40W
White Plains, U.S.A.	162	41 2N	73 44W
White, R., Ark., U.S.A.	159	36 28N	93 55W
White, R., Colo., U.S.A.	160	40 8N	108 52W
White, R., Ind., U.S.A.	156	39 25N	86 30W
White, R., S.D., U.S.A.	158	43 10N	102 52W
White River, Can.	150	48 35N	85 20W
White River, S. Afr.	129	25 20S	31 00E
White River, U.S.A.	158	43 48N	100 5W
White River Junc.	162	43 38N	72 20W
White Russia = Byelorussia, SSR	80	53 30N	27 0E
White Sea = Beloye More	78	66 30N	38 0E
White Sulphur Springs, Mont., U.S.A.	160	46 35N	111 0W
White Sulphur Springs, W. Va., U.S.A.	160	37 50N	80 16W
White Volta, R., (Volta Blanche)	121	10 0N	1 0W
White Well	137	31 25S	131 3E
Whiteadder Water, R.	35	55 47N	2 20W
Whitecourt	152	54 10N	115 45W
Whiteface	159	33 35N	102 40W
Whitefish	160	48 25N	114 22W
Whitefish L.	153	62 41N	106 48W
Whitefish Pt.	156	46 45N	85 0W
Whitegate, Clare, Ireland	39	52 58N	8 24W
Whitegate, Cork, Ireland	39	51 49N	8 15W
Whitegull, L.	151	55 27N	64 17W
Whitehall, Ireland	39	52 42N	7 2W
Whitehall, U.K.	37	59 9N	2 36W
Whitehall, Mich., U.S.A.	156	43 21N	86 20W
Whitehall, Mont., U.S.A.	160	45 52N	112 4W
Whitehall, N.Y., U.S.A.	162	43 32N	73 28W
Whitehall, Wis., U.S.A.	158	44 20N	91 19W
Whitehaven	32	54 33N	3 35W
Whitehead	38	54 45N	5 42W
Whitehorse	147	60 43N	135 3W
Whitehorse, Vale of	28	51 37N	1 30W
Whitekirk	35	56 2N	2 36W
Whiteman Ra.	135	5 55S	150 0E
Whitemark	138	40 7S	148 3E
Whitemouth	153	49 57N	95 58W
Whiten Hd.	37	58 34N	4 35W
Whitesail, L.	152	53 35N	127 45W
Whitesand B.	30	50 18N	4 20W
Whitesboro, N.Y., U.S.A.	162	43 8N	75 20W
Whitesboro, Tex., U.S.A.	159	33 40N	96 58W
Whiteshell Prov. Park	153	50 0N	95 40W
Whitetail	158	48 54N	105 15W
Whiteville	157	34 20N	78 40W
Whitewater	156	42 50N	88 45W
Whitewater Baldy, Mt.	161	33 20N	108 44W
Whitewater L.	150	50 50N	89 10W
Whitewood, Austral.	138	21 28S	143 30E
Whitewood, Can.	153	50 20N	102 20W
Whitfield	141	36 42S	146 24E
Whithorn	162	54 55N	4 25W
Whitianga	142	36 47S	175 41E
Whitland	31	51 49N	4 38W
Whitley Bay	35	55 4N	1 28W
Whitman	162	42 4N	70 55W
Whitmire	157	34 33N	81 40W
Whitney	150	45 31N	78 14W
Whitney, Mt.	163	36 35N	118 14W
Whitney Pt.	162	42 19N	75 59W
Whitstable	29	51 21N	1 2E
Whitsunday I.	138	20 15S	149 4E
Whittier	147	60 46N	148 48W
Whittington, Derby, U.K.	33	53 17N	1 26W
Whittington, Salop, U.K.	28	52 53N	3 0W
Whittle, C.	151	50 11N	60 8W
Whittlesea	141	37 27S	145 9E
Whittlesey	29	52 34N	0 8W
Whittlesford	29	52 6N	0 9E
Whitton	33	53 42N	0 39W
Whitwell, Derby, U.K.	33	53 16N	1 11W
Whitwell, Isle of Wight, U.K.	28	50 35N	1 19W
Whitwell, U.S.A.	157	35 15N	85 30W
Whitwick	28	52 45N	1 23W
Whitworth	32	53 40N	2 11W
Whixley	33	54 2N	1 19W
Wholdaia L.	153	60 43N	104 20W
Whyalla	140	33 2S	137 30E
Whyjonta	139	29 41S	142 28E
Whyte Yarcowie	107	33 13S	138 54E
Wiarton	150	44 50N	81 10W
Wiawso	120	6 10N	2 25W
Wiay I.	36	57 24N	7 12W
Wiazow	54	50 50N	17 10E
Wibaux	158	47 0N	104 13W
Wichian Buri	100	15 39N	101 7E
Wichita	159	37 40N	97 29W
Wichita Falls	159	33 57N	98 30W
Wick, Scot., U.K.	37	58 26N	3 5W
Wick, Wales, U.K.	31	51 24N	3 32W
Wick R.	37	58 28N	3 14W
Wickenburg	161	33 58N	112 45W
Wickepin	137	32 50S	117 30E
Wickett	159	31 37N	102 58W
Wickford	29	51 37N	0 31E
Wickham	28	50 54N	1 11W
Wickham, C.	138	39 35S	143 57E
Wickham Market	29	52 9N	1 21E
Wicklow	39	53 0N	6 2W
Wicklow □	39	52 59N	6 25W
Wicklow Gap	39	53 3N	6 23W
Wicklow Hd.	39	52 59N	6 3W
Wicklow Mts.	39	53 0N	6 30W
Wickwar	28	51 35N	2 23W
Widawa	54	51 27N	18 51E
Widdrington	35	55 15N	1 35W
Wide B.	138	4 52S	152 0E
Wide Firth	37	59 2N	3 0W
Widecombe	30	50 34N	3 48W
Widemouth	30	50 45N	4 34W
Widgiemooltha	137	31 30S	121 34E
Widnes	32	53 22N	2 44W
Wiek	48	54 37N	13 17E
Wielbark	54	53 24N	20 55E
Wielén	54	52 53N	16 9E
Wieliczka	54	50 0N	20 5E
Wielun	54	51 15N	18 40E
Wien	53	48 12N	16 22E
Wiener Neustadt	53	47 49N	16 16E
Wieprz, R., Koszalin, Poland	54	54 26N	16 35E
Wieprz, R., Lublin, Poland	54	51 15N	22 50E
Wierden	46	52 22N	6 35E
Wiers	47	50 30N	3 32E
Wieruszów	54	51 19N	18 9E
Wiesbaden	49	50 7N	8 17E
Wiesental	49	49 15N	8 30E
Wigan	32	53 33N	2 38W
Wiggins, Colo., U.S.A.	158	40 16N	104 3W
Wiggins, Miss., U.S.A.	159	30 53N	89 9W
Wight, I. of	28	50 40N	1 20W
Wigmore	28	52 19N	2 51W
Wigston	28	52 35N	1 6W
Wigton	32	54 50N	3 9W
Wigtown	34	54 52N	4 27W
Wigtown (□)	26	54 53N	4 45W
Wigtown B.	34	54 46N	4 15W
Wihéries	47	50 23N	3 45E
Wijangala	139	33 57S	148 59E
Wijchen	46	51 48N	5 44E
Wijhe	46	52 23N	6 8E
Wijk bij Duurstede	46	51 59N	5 21E
Wil	51	47 28N	9 3E
Wilamowice	53	49 55N	19 9E
Wilangee	140	31 28S	141 20E
Wilber	158	40 34N	96 59W
Wilburton	159	34 55N	95 15W
Wilcannia	140	31 30S	143 26E
Wildbad	49	48 44N	8 32E
Wildervank	46	53 5N	6 52E
Wildeshausen	48	52 54N	8 25E
Wildhorn	50	46 22N	7 21E
Wildon	52	46 52N	15 31E
Wildrose, Calif., U.S.A.	163	36 14N	117 11W
Wildrose, N. Dak., U.S.A.	158	48 36N	103 17W
Wildspitze	52	46 53N	10 53E
Wildstrubel	50	46 24N	7 32E
Wildwood	162	38 59N	74 46W
Wilgaroon	141	30 52S	145 42E
Wilhelm II Coast	13	67 0S	90 0E
Wilhelm Mt.	135	5 50S	145 1E
Wilhelm-Pieck-Stadt Guben	48	51 59N	14 48E
Wilhelmina Kanaal	47	51 36N	5 6E
Wilhelmina, Mt.	175	3 50N	56 30W
Wilhelmsburg, Austria	52	48 6N	15 36E
Wilhelmsburg, Ger.	48	53 28N	10 1E
Wilhelmshaven	48	53 30N	8 9E
Wilhelmstal	128	21 58S	16 21E
Wilkes-Barre	162	41 15N	75 52W
Wilkes Land	13	69 0S	120 0E
Wilkesboro	157	36 10N	81 9W
Wilkie	153	52 27N	108 42W
Wilkinson Lakes	137	29 40S	132 39E
Willamina	160	45 9N	123 32W
Willamulka	140	33 55S	137 52E
Willandra Billabong Creek	140	33 22S	145 52E
Willapa, B.	160	46 44N	124 0W
Willard, N. Mex., U.S.A.	161	34 35N	106 1W
Willard, N.Y., U.S.A.	162	42 40N	76 50W
Willard, Utah, U.S.A.	160	41 28N	112 1W
Willaumez Pen.	138	5 3S	150 3E
Willaura	140	37 31S	142 45E
Willberforce, C.	138	11 54S	136 35E
Willbriggie	141	34 28S	146 2E
Willcox	161	32 13N	109 53W
Willebroek	47	51 4N	4 22E
Willemstad	167	12 5N	69 0W
Willenhall	28	52 36N	2 3W
Willeroo	136	15 14S	131 37E
Willesborough	29	51 8N	0 55E
Willet	162	42 28N	75 55W
William Cr.	139	28 58S	136 22E
William, Mt.	140	37 17S	142 35E
William, R.	153	59 8N	109 19W
Williambury	137	23 45S	115 12E
Williams, Austral.	137	33 2S	116 52E
Williams, U.S.A.	161	35 16N	112 11W
Williams Lake	152	52 2N	122 10W
Williamsburg, Ky., U.S.A.	157	36 45N	84 10W
Williamsburg, Va., U.S.A.	162	37 17N	76 44W
Williamsburg, Va., U.S.A.	162	37 16N	79 43W
Williamson	156	37 46N	82 17W
Williamsport	162	41 18N	77 1W
Williamston	157	35 50N	77 5W
Williamstown, Austral.	141	37 51S	144 52E
Williamstown, Ireland	38	53 41N	8 34W
Williamstown, Mass., U.S.A.	162	42 43N	73 12W
Williamstown, N.Y., U.S.A.	162	43 25N	75 53W
Williamstown, N.Y., U.S.A.	162	43 25N	75 54W
Williamsville	159	37 0N	90 33W
Willimantic	162	41 45N	72 12W
Willingdon	29	50 47N	0 17E
Willis Group	138	16 18S	150 0E
Willisau	50	47 7N	8 0E
Williston, S. Afr.	128	31 20S	20 53E
Williston, Fla, U.S.A.	157	29 25N	82 28W
Williston, N.D., U.S.A.	158	48 10N	103 35W
Williston L.	152	56 0N	124 0W
Williton	28	51 9N	3 20W
Willits	160	39 28N	123 17W
Willmar	158	45 5N	95 0W
Willoughby	33	53 14N	0 12E
Willow Bunch	153	49 20N	105 35W
Willow L.	152	62 10N	119 8W
Willow Lake	158	44 40N	97 40W
Willow River	152	54 6N	122 28W
Willow Springs	159	37 0N	92 0W
Willow Tree	141	31 40S	150 45E
Willow Wall	107	41 30N	120 40E
Willowlake, R.	152	62 42N	123 8W
Willowmore	128	33 15S	23 30E
Willows, Austral.	138	23 45S	147 25E
Willows, U.S.A.	160	39 30N	122 10W
Wills Cr.	138	22 43S	140 2E
Wills, L.	136	21 25S	128 51E
Wills Pt.	159	32 42N	95 57W
Willunga	140	35 15S	138 30E
Wilmete	156	42 6N	87 44W
Wilmington, Austral.	140	32 39S	138 7E
Wilmington, U.K.	30	50 46N	3 8W
Wilmington, Del., U.S.A.	162	39 45N	75 32W
Wilmington, Ill., U.S.A.	156	41 19N	88 10W
Wilmington, N.C., U.S.A.	157	34 14N	77 54W
Wilmington, Ohio, U.S.A.	156	39 29N	83 46W
Wilmington, Vt., U.S.A.	162	42 52N	72 52W
Wilmslow	32	53 19N	2 14W
Wilnecote	28	52 36N	1 40W
Wilpena Cr.	140	31 25S	139 29E
Wilrijk	47	51 9N	4 22E
Wilsall	160	45 59N	110 4W
Wilson, U.S.A.	162	40 41N	75 15W
Wilson, N.C., U.S.A.	157	35 44N	77 54W
Wilson Bluff	137	31 41S	129 0E
Wilson Inlet	137	35 0S	117 20E
Wilson, Mt.	161	37 55N	105 3W
Wilson, R., Queens., Austral.	139	27 38S	141 24E
Wilson, R., W. Australia, Austral.	136	16 48S	128 16E
Wilson's Promontory	141	38 55S	146 25E
Wilster	48	53 55N	9 23E
Wilton, U.K.	28	51 5N	1 52W
Wilton, U.S.A.	158	47 12N	100 53W
Wilton, R.	138	14 45S	134 33E
Wiltshire □	28	51 20N	2 0W
Wiltz	47	49 57N	5 55E
Wiluna	137	26 36S	120 14E
Wimblington	29	52 31N	0 5E
Wimborne Minster	28	50 48N	2 0W
Wimereux	43	50 45N	1 37E
Wimmera	133	36 30S	142 0E
Wimmera, R.	140	36 8S	141 56E
Winam G.	126	0 20S	34 15E
Winburg	128	28 30S	27 2E
Wincanton	28	51 3N	2 24W
Winchelsea, Austral.	140	38 10S	144 1E
Winchelsea, U.K.	29	50 55N	0 43E
Winchendon	162	42 40N	72 3W
Winchester, N.Z.	143	44 11S	171 17E
Winchester, U.K.	28	51 4N	1 19W
Winchester, Conn., U.S.A.	162	41 53N	73 9W
Winchester, Conn., U.S.A.	162	41 55N	73 8W
Winchester, Idaho, U.S.A.	160	46 11N	116 32W
Winchester, Ind., U.S.A.	156	40 10N	84 56W
Winchester, Ky., U.S.A.	156	38 0N	84 8W
Winchester, Mass., U.S.A.	162	42 28N	71 10W
Winchester, N.H., U.S.A.	162	42 47N	72 22W
Winchester, Tenn., U.S.A.	157	35 11N	86 8W
Winchester, Va., U.S.A.	156	39 14N	78 8W
Wind, R.	160	43 30N	109 30W
Wind River Range, Mts.	160	43 0N	109 30W
Windber	156	40 14N	78 50W
Winder	157	34 0N	83 40W
Windera	139	26 17S	151 51E
Windermere	32	54 24N	2 56W
Windermere, L.	32	54 20N	2 57W
Windfall	152	54 12N	116 13W
Windflower L.	152	62 52N	118 30W
Windhoek	128	22 35S	17 4E
Windischgarsten	52	47 42N	14 21E
Windmill Pt.	162	37 35N	76 17W
Windom	158	43 48N	95 3W
Windorah	138	25 24S	142 36E
Window Rock	161	35 47N	109 4W
Windrush, R.	28	51 48N	1 35W
Windsor, Austral.	141	33 37S	150 50E
Windsor, Newf., Can.	151	48 57N	55 40W
Windsor, N.S., Can.	151	44 59N	64 5W
Windsor, Ont., Can.	150	42 18N	83 82W
Windsor, N.Z.	143	44 59S	170 49E
Windsor, U.K.	29	51 28N	0 36W
Windsor, Col., U.S.A.	158	40 33N	104 55W
Windsor, Conn., U.S.A.	162	41 50N	72 40W
Windsor, Miss., U.S.A.	158	38 32N	93 31W
Windsor, N.Y., U.S.A.	162	42 5N	75 37W
Windsor, Vt., U.S.A.	162	43 30N	72 25W
Windsorton	128	28 16S	24 44E
Windward Is.	167	13 0N	63 0W
Windward Passage	167	20 0N	74 0W
Windy L.	153	60 20N	100 2W
Windygap	39	52 28N	7 24W
Windygates	35	56 12N	3 1W
Winefred L.	153	55 30N	110 30W
Winejok	123	9 1N	27 30E
Winfield	159	37 15N	97 0W
Wing	29	51 54N	0 41W
Wingate Mts.	136	14 25S	130 40E
Wingen	141	31 54S	150 54E
Wingene	47	51 3N	3 17E
Wingham, Austral.	141	31 48S	152 22E
Wingham, Can.	150	43 55N	81 20W
Wingham, U.K.	29	51 16N	1 12E
Winifred	160	47 30N	109 28W
Winisk	150	55 20N	85 15W
Winisk L.	150	52 55N	87 22W
Winisk, R.	150	55 17N	85 5W
Wink	159	31 49N	103 9W
Winkleigh	30	50 49N	3 57W
Winkler	153	49 15N	97 56W
Winklern	52	46 52N	12 52E
Winneba	121	5 25N	0 36W
Winnebago	158	43 43N	94 8W
Winnebago L.	156	44 0N	88 20W
Winnecke Cr.	136	18 35S	131 34E
Winnemucca	160	41 0N	117 45W
Winnemucca, L.	160	40 25N	19 21W
Winner	158	43 23N	99 52W
Winnetka	156	42 8N	87 46W
Winnett	160	47 2N	108 28W
Winnfield	159	31 57N	92 38W
Winnibigoshish L.	158	47 25N	94 12W
Winning Pool	136	23 9S	114 30E
Winnipeg	153	49 50N	97 9W
Winnipeg Beach	153	50 30N	96 58W
Winnipeg, L.	153	52 0N	97 0W
Winnipeg, R.	153	50 38N	96 19W
Winnipegosis	153	51 39N	99 55W
Winnipegosis L.	153	52 30N	100 0W
Winnipesaukee, L.	162	43 38N	71 21W
Winnisquam L.	162	43 33N	71 30W
Winnsboro, Lou, U.S.A.	159	32 10N	91 41W
Winnsboro, S.C., U.S.A.	157	34 23N	81 5W
Winnsboro, Tex., U.S.A.	158	32 56N	95 15W
Winokapau, L.	151	53 15N	62 50W
Winona, Miss., U.S.A.	159	33 30N	89 42W
Winona, Wis., U.S.A.	158	44 2N	91 45W
Winooski	156	44 31N	73 11W
Winschoten	46	53 9N	7 3E
Winsen	48	53 21N	10 11E
Winsford	32	53 12N	2 31W
Winslow, U.K.	29	51 57N	0 52W
Winslow, U.S.A.	161	35 2N	110 41W
Winstead	156	41 55N	73 5W
Winster	33	53 9N	1 42W
Winston-Salem	157	36 7N	80 15W
Winsum	46	53 20N	6 32E
Winter Garden	157	28 33N	81 35W
Winter Haven	157	28 0N	81 42W
Winter Park	157	28 34N	81 19W
Winterberg	48	51 12N	8 30E

Winterborne Abbas

Yaapeet

Winterborne Abbas	**28**	50 43N	2 30W
Winters	**159**	31 58N	99 58W
Winterset	**158**	41 18N	94 0W
Winterswijk	**46**	51 58N	6 43 E
Winterthur	**51**	47 30N	8 44 E
Winterton, Humberside, U.K.	**33**	53 39N	0 37W
Winterton, Norfolk, U.K.	**29**	52 43N	1 43 E
Winthrop, Minn., U.S.A.	**158**	44 31N	94 25W
Winthrop, Wash., U.S.A.	**160**	48 27N	120 6W
Winton, Austral.	**138**	22 24 S	143 3 E
Winton, N.Z.	**143**	46 8 S	168 20 E
Winton, U.S.A.	**157**	36 25N	76 58W
Wirksworth	**33**	53 5N	1 34W
Wirral	**23**	53 25N	3 0W
Wirraminna	**140**	31 12 S	136 13 E
Wirrulla	**139**	32 24 S	134 31 E
Wisbech	**29**	52 39N	0 10 E
Wisborough Green	**29**	51 2N	0 30W
Wisconsin □	**158**	44 30N	90 0W
Wisconsin Dells	**158**	43 38N	89 45W
Wisconsin, R.	**158**	45 25N	89 45W
Wisconsin Rapids	**158**	44 25N	89 50W
Wisdom	**147**	45 36N	113 1W
Wiserman	**147**	67 25N	150 15W
Wishaw	**35**	55 46N	3 55W
Wishek	**158**	46 20N	99 35W
Wiske, R.	**33**	54 26N	1 27W
Wisła	**53**	49 38N	18 53 E
Wisła, R.	**54**	53 38N	18 47 E
Wisłok, R.	**53**	50 7N	22 25 E
Wisłoka, R.	**53**	49 50N	21 28 E
Wismar	**48**	53 53N	11 23 E
Wismar B.	**48**	54 0N	11 15 E
Wisner	**158**	42 0N	96 46W
Wissant	**43**	50 52N	1 40 E
Wissembourg	**43**	48 57N	7 57 E
Wissenkerke	**47**	51 35N	3 45 E
Wistoka, R.	**54**	49 50N	21 28 E
Witbank	**129**	25 51 S	29 14 E
Witchita	**159**	37 40N	97 22W
Witchyburn	**37**	57 37N	2 37W
Witdraai	**128**	26 58 S	20 48 E
Witham	**29**	51 48N	0 39 E
Witham, R.	**33**	53 3N	0 8W
Withern	**33**	53 19N	0 9 E
Withernsea	**33**	53 43N	0 2W
Witkowo	**54**	52 26N	17 45 E
Witley	**29**	51 9N	0 39W
Witmarsum	**46**	53 6N	5 28 E
Witney	**28**	51 47N	1 29W
Witnossob, R.	**128**	23 0 S	18 40 E
Wittdün	**48**	54 38N	8 23 E
Witten	**48**	51 26N	7 19 E
Wittenberg	**48**	51 51N	12 39 E
Wittenberge	**48**	53 0N	11 44 E
Wittenburg	**48**	53 30N	11 4 E
Wittenoom, W. Australia, Austral.	**132**	22 15 S	118 20 E
Wittenoom, W. Australia, Austral.	**136**	18 34 S	128 51 E
Wittersham	**29**	51 1N	0 42 E
Wittingen	**48**	52 43N	10 43 E
Wittlich	**49**	50 0N	6 54 E
Wittmund	**48**	53 39N	7 35 E
Wittow	**48**	54 37N	13 21 E
Wittstock	**48**	53 10N	12 30 E
Witzenhausen	**48**	51 20N	9 50 E
Wiveliscombe	**28**	51 2N	3 20W
Wivenhoe	**29**	51 51N	0 59 E
Wiyeb, W.	**123**	7 15N	40 15 E
Wladyslawowo	**54**	52 6N	18 28 E
Wlen	**160**	51 0N	15 39 E
Wlingi	**103**	8 5 S	112 25 E
Włocławek	**54**	52 40N	19 3 E
Włodawa	**54**	51 33N	23 31 E
Włoszczowa	**54**	50 50N	19 55 E
Woburn, U.K.	**29**	51 59N	0 37W
Woburn, U.S.A.	**162**	42 31N	71 7W
Woburn Sands	**29**	51 1N	0 38W
Wodonga	**141**	36 5 S	146 50 E
Wodzisław Sl.	**54**	50 1N	18 26 E
Woerden	**46**	52 5N	4 54 E
Woerht'ukou	**106**	42 35N	112 19 E
Woerth	**43**	48 57N	7 45 E
Woevre	**43**	49 15N	5 45 E
Wognum	**46**	52 40N	5 1 E
Wohlen	**51**	47 21N	8 17 E
Wokam, I.	**103**	5 45 S	134 28 E
Wokha	**98**	26 6N	94 16 E
Woking, Can.	**152**	55 35N	118 50W
Woking, U.K.	**29**	51 18N	0 33W
Wokingham	**29**	51 25N	0 50W
Wolbrom	**54**	50 24N	19 45 E
Woldegk	**48**	53 27N	13 35 E
Wolf Creek	**160**	47 1N	112 2W
Wolf L.	**152**	60 24N	133 42W
Wolf Point	**158**	48 6N	105 40W
Wolf, R.	**152**	60 17N	132 33W
Wolf Rock	**30**	49 56N	5 50W
Wolfe I.	**150**	44 7N	76 20W
Wolfeboro	**162**	43 35N	71 12W
Wolfenbüttel	**48**	52 10N	10 33 E
Wolfenden	**152**	52 0N	119 25W
Wolfheze	**46**	52 0N	5 48 E
Wolfram	**138**	17 6 S	145 0 E
Wolf's Castle	**31**	51 53N	4 57W
Wolfsberg	**52**	46 50N	14 52 E
Wolfsburg	**48**	52 27N	10 49 E
Wolgast	**48**	54 3N	13 46 E
Wolhusen	**50**	47 4N	8 4 E
Wolin	**54**	53 40N	14 37 E
Wollaston, Islas	**176**	55 40 S	67 30W
Wollaston L.	**153**	58 7N	103 10W
Wollaston Pen.	**148**	69 30N	115 0W
Wollogorang	**138**	17 13 S	137 57 E
Wollongong	**141**	34 25 S	150 54 E
Wolmaransstad	**128**	27 12 S	26 13 E
Wolmirstedt	**48**	52 15N	11 35 E
Wołomin	**54**	52 19N	21 15 E
Wołow	**54**	51 20N	16 38 E
Wolseley, Austral.	**140**	36 23 S	140 54 E
Wolseley, Can.	**153**	50 25N	103 15W
Wolseley, S. Afr.	**128**	33 26 S	19 7 E
Wolsingham	**32**	54 44N	1 52W
Wolstenholme Sound	**12**	74 30N	75 0W
Wolsztyn	**54**	52 8N	16 5 E
Wolvega	**46**	52 52N	6 0 E
Wolverhampton	**28**	52 35N	2 6W
Wolverton	**29**	52 3N	0 48W
Wolviston	**33**	54 39N	1 25W
Wombera	**123**	10 45N	35 49 E
Wombwell	**33**	53 31N	1 23W
Wommels	**46**	53 6N	5 36 E
Wonarah P.O.	**138**	19 55 S	136 20 E
Wonboyn	**141**	37 15 S	149 55 E
Wonck	**47**	50 46N	5 38 E
Wondai	**139**	26 20 S	151 49 E
Wondelgem	**47**	51 5N	3 44 E
Wonder Gorge	**127**	14 40 S	29 0 E
Wongalarroo L.	**140**	31 32 S	144 0 E
Wongan	**137**	30 51 S	116 37 E
Wongan Hills	**137**	30 53 S	116 42 E
Wongawal	**137**	25 5 S	121 55 E
Wonosari	**103**	7 38 S	110 36 E
Wŏnsan	**107**	39 11N	127 27 E
Wonston	**28**	51 9N	1 18W
Wonthaggi	**141**	38 37 S	145 37 E
Wonyulgunna Hill, Mt.	**137**	24 52 S	119 44 E
Woocalla	**140**	31 42 S	137 12 E
Wood Buffalo Nat. Park	**152**	56 28N	113 41W
Wood Green	**138**	22 26 S	134 12 E
Wood Is.	**136**	16 24 S	123 19 E
Wood L.	**153**	55 17N	103 17W
Wood Lake	**158**	42 38N	100 14W
Wood Mt.	**153**	49 14N	106 30W
Woodah I.	**138**	13 27 S	136 10 E
Woodanilling	**137**	33 31 S	117 24 E
Woodbine	**162**	39 14N	74 49W
Woodbourne	**162**	41 46N	74 35W
Woodbridge	**29**	52 6N	1 19 E
Woodburn	**139**	29 6 S	153 23 E
Woodbury, U.K.	**30**	50 40N	3 24W
Woodbury, U.S.A.	**162**	39 50N	75 9W
Woodchopper	**147**	65 25N	143 30W
Wooden Bridge	**39**	52 50N	6 13W
Woodend	**140**	37 20N	144 33 E
Woodford	**39**	53 3N	8 23W
Woodfords	**163**	38 47N	119 50W
Woodhall Spa.	**33**	53 10N	0 12W
Woodham Ferrers	**29**	51 40N	0 37 E
Woodlake	**163**	36 25N	119 6W
Woodland	**160**	38 40N	121 50W
Woodlands	**137**	24 46 S	118 8 E
Woodlark I.	**135**	9 10 S	152 50 E
Woodley	**29**	51 26N	0 54W
Woodpecker	**152**	53 30N	122 40W
Woodplumpton	**32**	53 47N	2 46W
Woodridge	**153**	49 20N	96 9W
Woodroffe, Mt.	**137**	26 20 S	131 45 E
Woodruff, Ariz., U.S.A.	**161**	34 51N	110 1W
Woodruff, Utah, U.S.A.	**160**	41 30N	111 4W
Woods, L., Austral.	**138**	17 50 S	133 30 E
Woods, L., Can.	**151**	54 30N	65 13W
Woods, Lake of the	**153**	49 30N	94 30W
Woodside, S. Australia, Austral.	**140**	34 58 S	138 52 E
Woodside, Victoria, Austral.	**141**	38 31 S	146 52 E
Woodstock, N.S.W., Austral.	**141**	33 45 S	148 53 E
Woodstock, Queens., Austral.	**138**	19 35 S	146 50 E
Woodstock, W.A., Austral.	**136**	21 41 S	118 57 E
Woodstock, N.B., Can.	**151**	46 11N	67 37W
Woodstock, Ont., Can.	**150**	43 10N	80 45W
Woodstock, U.K.	**28**	51 51N	1 20W
Woodstock, Ill., U.S.A.	**158**	42 17N	88 30W
Woodstock, Vt., U.S.A.	**162**	43 37N	72 31W
Woodstown	**162**	39 39N	75 20W
Woodville, N.Z.	**142**	40 20 S	175 53 E
Woodville, U.S.A.	**159**	30 45N	94 25W
Woodward	**159**	36 24N	99 28W
Woodward, Mt.	**137**	26 0 S	131 0 E
Woody	**163**	35 42N	118 50W
Wookey	**28**	51 13N	2 41W
Wookey Hole	**28**	51 13N	2 41W
Wool	**28**	50 41N	2 13W
Woolacombe	**30**	51 10N	4 12W
Woolamai, C.	**141**	38 30 S	145 23 E
Wooler	**35**	55 33N	2 0W
Woolgangie	**137**	31 12 S	120 35 E
Woolyeenyer, Mt.	**137**	32 16 S	121 47 E
Woombye	**139**	26 40 S	152 55 E
Woomera	**140**	31 11 S	136 47 E
Woonona	**141**	34 21 S	150 54 E
Woonsocket	**162**	42 0N	71 30W
Woonsockett	**158**	44 5N	98 15W
Wooramel	**137**	25 45 S	114 40 E
Wooramel, R.	**137**	25 30 S	114 30 E
Wooroloo	**137**	31 48 S	116 18 E
Wooroorooka	**139**	29 0 S	145 41 E
Wooster	**156**	40 38N	81 55W
Wootton Bassett	**28**	51 32N	1 55W
Wootton Wawen	**28**	52 16N	1 47W
Worb	**50**	46 56N	7 33 E
Worcester, S. Afr.	**125**	33 39 S	19 27 E
Worcester, U.K.	**28**	52 12N	2 12W
Worcester, Mass., U.S.A.	**162**	42 14N	71 49W
Worcester, N.Y., U.S.A.	**162**	42 35N	74 45W
Worcestershire (□)	**26**	52 13N	2 10W
Worfield	**28**	52 34N	2 22W
Wörgl	**52**	47 29N	12 3 E
Worikambo	**121**	10 43N	0 11W
Workington	**32**	54 39N	3 34W
Worksop	**33**	53 19N	1 9W
Workum	**46**	52 59N	5 26 E
Worland	**160**	44 0N	107 59W
Wormerveer	**46**	52 30N	4 46 E
Wormhoudt	**43**	50 52N	2 28 E
Wormit	**35**	56 26N	2 59W
Worms	**49**	49 37N	8 21 E
Worms Head	**29**	51 33N	4 19W
Worplesdon	**29**	51 16N	0 36W
Worsley	**137**	33 15 S	116 2 E
Wortham, U.K.	**29**	52 22N	1 3 E
Wortham, U.S.A.	**159**	31 48N	96 27W
Wörther See	**52**	46 37N	14 19 E
Worthing	**29**	50 49N	0 21W
Worthington	**158**	43 35N	95 30W
Wosi	**103**	0 15 S	128 0 E
Wota (Shoa Ghimirra)	**123**	7 4N	35 51 E
Wotton-under-Edge	**28**	51 37N	2 20W
Woubrugge	**46**	52 10N	4 39 E
Woudenberg	**46**	52 5N	5 25 E
Woudsend	**46**	52 56N	5 38 E
Wour	**119**	21 14N	16 0 E
Wouw	**47**	51 31N	4 23 E
Wowoni, I.	**103**	4 5 S	123 5 E
Woy Woy	**141**	33 30 S	151 19 E
Wragby	**33**	53 17N	0 18W
Wrangell	**147**	56 30N	132 25W
Wrangell, I.	**152**	56 20N	132 10W
Wrangell Mts.	**147**	61 40N	143 30W
Wrangle	**33**	53 3N	0 9 E
Wrath, C.	**36**	58 38N	5 0W
Wray	**158**	40 8N	102 18W
Wreck I.	**162**	37 12N	75 48W
Wrekin, The, Mt.	**28**	52 41N	2 35W
Wrens	**157**	33 13N	82 23W
Wrentham	**29**	52 24N	1 39 E
Wrexham	**31**	53 5N	3 0W
Wriezen	**48**	52 43N	14 9 E
Wright, Can.	**152**	51 52N	121 40W
Wright, Phil.	**103**	11 42N	125 2 E
Wright, Mt.	**151**	52 40N	67 25W
Wrightlington	**28**	51 18N	2 16W
Wrightson, Mt.	**161**	31 49N	110 56W
Wrightsville	**162**	40 2N	76 32W
Wrightwood	**163**	34 21N	117 38W
Wrigley	**148**	63 16N	123 27W
Writtle	**29**	51 44N	0 27 E
Wrocław	**54**	51 5N	17 5 E
Wrocław □	**54**	51 0N	17 0 E
Wronki	**54**	52 41N	16 21 E
Wrotham	**29**	51 18N	0 20 E
Wroughton	**28**	51 31N	1 47W
Wroxham	**29**	52 42N	1 23 E
Wrzesśnia	**54**	52 21N	17 36 E
Wschowa	**54**	51 48N	16 20 E
Wu Chiang, R.	**108**	29 42N	107 20 E
Wu Shui, R.	**109**	27 7N	109 57 E
Wuan	**106**	36 45N	114 2 E
Wubin	**137**	30 6 S	116 37 E
Wuch'ang, Heilungkiang, China	**107**	44 55N	127 10 E
Wuch'ang, Hupeh, China	**109**	30 30N	114 15 E
Wuch'eng	**108**	30 48N	98 46 E
Wuch'i	**108**	31 28N	109 36 E
Wuchiang	**109**	31 10N	120 37 E
Wuchih Shan, mts.	**100**	18 45N	109 45 E
Wuch'ing	**107**	39 25N	117 7 E
Wuchou	**105**	23 33N	111 18 E
Wuch'uan, Inner Mong., China	**106**	41 8N	111 24 E
Wuch'uan, Kwangsi-Chuang, China	**109**	21 29N	110 49 E
Wuch'uan, Kweichow, China	**108**	28 30N	107 58 E
Wuchung	**106**	38 4N	106 12 E
Wufeng	**109**	30 12N	110 36 E
Wuhan	**109**	30 35N	114 15 E
Wuho	**107**	33 9N	117 53 E
Wuhsi	**105**	31 30N	120 20 E
Wuhsiang	**106**	36 50N	112 52 E
Wuhsing	**109**	30 49N	120 5 E
Wuhsüan	**108**	23 36N	109 39 E
Wuhu	**105**	31 18N	118 20 E
Wuhu (Wou-tou)	**109**	31 21N	118 30 E
Wui, Anhwei, China	**109**	28 53N	119 48 E
Wui, Hopeh, China	**106**	37 49N	115 54 E
Wui Shan, mts.	**105**	27 30N	117 30 E
Wukang	**109**	26 50N	110 15 E
Wukari	**121**	7 57N	9 42 E
Wulachieh	**107**	44 5N	126 27 E
Wulanhaot'e	**105**	46 5N	122 5 E
Wulanpulang	**106**	41 8N	110 56 E
Wulehe	**121**	3 42N	0 0 E
Wuliang Shan, mts.	**108**	24 0N	100 55 E
Wuliaru, I.	**103**	7 10 S	131 0 E
Wulien	**107**	35 45N	119 12 E
Wuluk'omushih Ling	**105**	36 25N	87 25 E
Wulumuchi	**105**	43 40N	87 50 E
Wulunku Ho, R.	**105**	46 58N	87 28 E
Wum	**121**	6 40N	10 2 E
Wuming	**108**	23 11N	108 12 E
Wuneba	**123**	4 49N	30 22 E
Wuning	**109**	29 16N	115 0 E
Wunnummin L.	**150**	52 55N	89 10W
Wunsiedel	**49**	50 2N	12 0 E
Wunstorf	**48**	52 26N	9 29 E
Wuntho, Burma	**98**	21 44N	96 2 E
Wuntho, Burma	**99**	23 55N	95 45 E
Wupao	**106**	37 35N	110 45 E
Wup'ing	**109**	25 9N	116 5 E
Wuppertal, Ger.	**48**	51 15N	7 8 E
Wuppertal, S. Afr.	**128**	32 13 S	19 12 E
Wurarga	**137**	28 25 S	116 15 E
Würenlingen	**51**	47 32N	8 16 E
Wurung	**138**	19 13 S	140 38 E
Würzburg	**49**	49 46N	9 55 E
Wurzen	**48**	51 21N	12 45 E
Wushan, Kansu, China	**106**	34 42N	104 58 E
Wushan, Szechwan, China	**108**	31 3N	109 57 E
Wushench'i	**106**	38 57N	109 15 E
Wustrow	**48**	54 4N	11 33 E
Wusu	**105**	44 27N	84 37 E
Wutai	**106**	38 44N	113 18 E
Wuti	**107**	37 46N	117 39 E
Wuting	**108**	25 33N	102 26 E
Wuting = Huimin	**107**	37 32N	117 33 E
Wuting Ho, R.	**106**	37 8N	110 25 E
Wut'ungch'iao	**108**	29 24N	104 0 E
Wutunghaolan	**107**	42 49N	120 11 E
Wuustwezel	**47**	51 23N	4 36 E
Wuwei, Anhwei, China	**109**	31 22N	117 55 E
Wuwei, Kansu, China	**105**	37 55N	102 48 E
Wuyang	**106**	33 25N	113 36 E
Wuyo	**121**	10 23N	11 50 E
Wuyüan, Inner Mong., China	**106**	41 6N	108 16 E
Wuyüan, Kiangsi, China	**109**	29 17N	117 54 E
Wuyün	**105**	49 17N	129 40 E
Wyaaba Cr.	**138**	16 27 S	141 35 E
Wyalkatchem	**137**	31 8 S	117 22 E
Wyalong	**139**	33 54 S	147 16 E
Wyalusing	**162**	41 40N	76 16W
Wyandotte	**156**	42 14N	83 13W
Wyandra	**139**	27 12 S	145 56 E
Wyangala Res.	**141**	33 54 S	149 0 E
Wyara, L.	**139**	28 42 S	144 14 E
Wych Farm, oilfield	**19**	50 38N	2 2W
Wycheproof	**140**	36 0N	143 17 E
Wye	**29**	51 11N	0 56 E
Wye, R.	**28**	52 0N	2 36W
Wyemandoo, Mt.	**137**	28 28 S	118 29 E
Wyk	**48**	54 41N	8 33 E
Wylfa Hd.	**31**	53 25N	4 28W
Wylye, R.	**28**	51 8N	1 53W
Wymondham, Leicester, U.K.	**29**	52 45N	0 42W
Wymondham, Norfolk, U.K.	**29**	52 34N	1 7 E
Wymore	**158**	40 10N	97 8W
Wynberg	**128**	34 2 S	18 28 E
Wynbring	**139**	30 33 S	133 32 E
Wyndham, Austral.	**136**	15 33 S	128 3 E
Wyndham, N.Z.	**143**	46 20 S	168 51 E
Wynne	**159**	35 15N	90 50W
Wynnstay	**31**	52 36N	3 33W
Wynnum	**139**	27 27 S	153 9 E
Wynyard	**153**	51 45N	104 10W
Wyola, L.	**137**	29 8 S	130 17 E
Wyoming □	**154**	42 48N	109 0W
Wyong	**141**	33 14 S	151 24 E
Wyre Forest	**28**	52 24N	2 24W
Wyre, I.	**37**	59 7N	2 58W
Wyre, R.	**37**	53 52N	2 57W
Wyrzysk	**54**	53 10N	17 17 E
Wysoka	**54**	53 13N	17 2 E
Wyszków	**54**	52 36N	21 25 E
Wyszogród	**54**	52 23N	20 9 E
Wytheville	**156**	37 0N	81 3W

X

Xai-Xai	**129**	25 6 S	33 31 E
Xambioá	**170**	6 25 S	48 40W
Xanten	**48**	51 40N	6 27 E
Xanthí	**68**	41 10N	24 58 E
Xanthí □	**68**	41 10N	24 58 E
Xapuri	**174**	10 35 S	68 35W
Xau	**128**	21 15 S	24 44 E
Xavantina	**173**	21 15 S	52 48W
Xenia	**156**	39 42N	83 57W
Xieng Khouang	**100**	19 17N	103 25 E
Xilókastron	**69**	38 4N	22 43 E
Xinavane	**129**	25 2 S	32 47 E
Xingu, R.	**175**	2 25 S	52 35W
Xiniás, L.	**69**	39 2N	22 12 E
Xique-Xique	**170**	10 50 S	42 40W
Xuan Loc	**101**	10 56N	107 14 E
Xuyen Moc	**101**	10 34N	107 25 E

Y

Ya 'Bud	**90**	32 27N	35 10 E
Yaamba	**138**	23 8 S	150 22 E
Yaan	**108**	30 0N	102 59 E
Yaapeet	**140**	35 45 S	142 3 E

Yabassi	**121**	4 30N	9 57 E
Yabba North	**141**	36 13 S	145 42 E
Yabelo	**123**	4 57N	38 8 E
Yablanitsa	**67**	43 2N	24 5 E
Yablonovyy Khrebet	**77**	53 0N	114 0 E
Yabrīn	**92**	23 7N	48 52 E
Yach'i	**108**	27 35N	106 40 E
Yachiang	**108**	30 4N	101 7 E
Yacuiba	**172**	22 0 S	63 25W
Yadgir	**96**	16 45N	77 5 E
Yadkin, R.	**157**	36 15N	81 0W
Yadrin	**81**	55 57N	46 6 E
Yaeyama-Shotō	**112**	24 25N	124 0 E
Yagaba	**121**	10 14N	1 20W
Yagoua	**124**	10 20N	14 58 E
Yagur	**90**	32 45N	35 4 E
Yaha	**101**	6 29N	101 8 E
Yahk	**152**	49 6N	116 10W
Yahuma	**124**	1 0N	22 5 E
Yaihsien	**100**	18 14N	109 29 E
Yaizu	**111**	34 52N	138 20 E
Yajua	**121**	11 27N	12 49 E
Yakage	**110**	34 37N	133 35 E
Yakataga	**147**	60 5N	142 32W
Yakiang	**99**	30 4N	101 15 E
Yakima	**160**	46 42N	120 30W
Yakima, R.	**160**	47 0N	120 30W
Yako	**120**	12 59N	2 15W
Yakoruda	**67**	42 1N	23 29 E
Yakshur Bodya	**84**	57 11N	53 7 E
Yaku-Jima	**112**	30 20N	130 30 E
Yakut A.S.S.R. □	**77**	62 0N	130 0 E
Yakutat	**147**	59 50N	139 44W
Yakutsk	**77**	62 5N	129 40 E
Yala	**101**	6 33N	101 18 E
Yalabusha, R.	**159**	33 53N	89 50W
Yalbalgo	**137**	25 10 S	114 45 E
Yalboroo	**138**	20 50 S	148 40 E
Yalgoo	**137**	28 16 S	116 39 E
Yalikavak	**69**	37 6N	27 18 E
Yalinga	**117**	6 20N	23 10 E
Yalkubul, Punta	**165**	21 32N	88 37W
Y'allaq, G.	**122**	30 21N	33 31 E
Yalleroi	**138**	24 3 S	145 42 E
Yallourn	**141**	38 10 S	146 18 E
Yalpukh, Oz.	**70**	45 30N	28 41 E
Yalta	**82**	44 30N	34 10 E
Yalu Chiang, R.	**107**	39 45N	124 20 E
Yalung Chiang, R.	**105**	26 35N	101 45 E
Yalutorovsk	**76**	56 30N	65 40 E
Yam Kinneret	**90**	32 49N	35 36 E
Yamada	**110**	33 43N	130 49 E
Yamaga	**110**	33 1N	130 41 E
Yamagata	**112**	38 15N	140 15 E
Yamagata-ken □	**112**	38 30N	140 0 E
Yamagawa	**110**	31 12N	130 39 E
Yamaguchi	**110**	34 10N	131 32 E
Yamaguchi-ken □	**110**	34 20N	131 40 E
Yamal, Poluostrov	**76**	71 0N	70 0 E
Yamana	**92**	24 5N	47 30 E
Yamanaka	**111**	36 15N	136 22 E
Yamanashi-ken □	**111**	35 40N	138 40 E
Yamankhalinka	**83**	47 43N	49 21 E
Yamantau	**78**	54 20N	57 40 E
Yamantau, Gora	**84**	54 15N	58 6 E
Yamato	**111**	35 27N	139 25 E
Yamatotakada	**111**	34 31N	135 45 E
Yamazaki	**110**	35 0N	134 32 E
Yamba, N.S.W., Austral.	**139**	29 26 S	153 23 E
Yamba, S. Australia, Austral.	**140**	34 10 S	140 52 E
Yambah	**138**	23 10 S	133 50 E
Yâmbiô	**123**	4 35N	28 16 E
Yambol	**67**	42 30N	26 36 E
Yamdena	**103**	7 45 S	131 20 E
Yame	**110**	33 13N	130 35 E
Yamethin	**98**	20 29N	96 18 E
Yamil	**121**	12 53N	8 4 E
Yamma-Yamma L.	**139**	26 16 S	141 20 E
Yampa, R.	**160**	40 37N	108 0W
Yampi Sd.	**136**	16 8 S	123 38 E
Yampol	**82**	48 15N	28 15 E
Yamrat	**121**	10 11N	9 55 E
Yamrukohal, Mt.	**67**	42 44N	24 52 E
Yamun	**90**	32 29N	35 14 E
Yamuna (Jumna), R.	**94**	27 0N	78 30 E
Yan	**121**	10 5N	12 11 E
Yan Oya	**97**	9 0N	81 10 E
Yana, R.	**77**	69 0N	134 0 E
Yanac	**140**	36 8 S	141 25 E
Yanagawa	**110**	33 10N	130 24 E
Yanahara	**110**	34 58N	134 2 E
Yanam	**96**	16 47N	82 15 E
Yanaul	**84**	56 25N	55 0 E
Yanbu 'al Bahr	**92**	24 0N	38 5 E
Yancannia	**139**	30 12 S	142 35 E
Yanchep	**137**	31 30 S	115 45 E
Yanco	**141**	34 38 S	146 27 E
Yanco Cr.	**141**	35 14 S	145 35 E
Yandabome	**138**	7 1 S	145 46 E
Yandal	**137**	27 35 S	121 10 E
Yandanooka	**137**	29 18 S	115 29 E
Yandaran	**138**	24 43 S	152 6 E
Yandil	**137**	26 20 S	119 50 E
Yandoon	**98**	17 0N	95 40 E
Yanfolila	**120**	11 11N	8 9W
Yangambi	**126**	0 47N	24 20 E
Yangch'angtzukou	**106**	41 31N	109 1 E
Yangch'eng	**106**	35 32N	112 26 E
Yangchiang	**109**	21 55N	111 55 E
Yangchiaoch'iao	**109**	29 45N	112 49 E
Yangchiapa	**106**	42 6N	113 46 E
Yangchou	**109**	32 24N	119 26 E
Yangchoyung Hu	**105**	29 0N	90 40 E
Yangch'ü = T'aiyüan	**106**	37 55N	112 40 E
Yangch'üan	**106**	37 54N	113 36 E
Yangch'un	**109**	22 10N	111 47 E
Yanghsien	**106**	33 20N	107 30 E
Yanghsin	**109**	29 53N	115 10 E
Yangi-Yer	**76**	40 17N	68 48 E
Yangibazar	**85**	41 40N	70 53 E
Yangikishlak	**85**	40 25N	67 10 E
Yangiyul	**85**	41 0N	69 3 E
Yangku	**106**	36 8N	115 48 E
Yangliuch'ing	**107**	39 11N	117 9 E
Yangp'i	**108**	25 40N	100 0 E
Yangp'ing	**109**	31 13N	111 33 E
Yangp'ingkuan	**106**	33 2N	105 56 E
Yangshan	**109**	24 28N	112 38 E
Yangshuo	**109**	24 45N	110 24 E
Yangtze (Ch'ang Chiang)	**109**	1 48N	121 53 E
Yangyang	**107**	38 4N	128 38 E
Yangyüan	**106**	40 5N	114 12 E
Yanhee Res.	**101**	17 30N	98 45 E
Yanko Cr.	**139**	35 17 S	145 15 E
Yankton	**158**	42 55N	97 25W
Yanna	**139**	26 58 S	146 0 E
Yanonge	**126**	0 35N	24 38 E
Yantabulla	**139**	29 21 S	145 0 E
Yantra, R.	**67**	43 35N	25 37 E
Yany Kurgan	**85**	43 55N	67 15 E
Yao, Chad	**117**	12 56N	17 33 E
Yao, Japan	**111**	34 32N	135 36 E
Yao Yai, Ko	**101**	8 0N	98 35 E
Yaoan	**108**	25 32N	101 12 E
Yaoundé	**121**	3 50N	11 35 E
Yaowan	**107**	34 10N	118 3 E
Yap Is.	**103**	9 30N	138 10 E
Yapen	**103**	1 50 S	136 0 E
Yapen, Selat	**103**	1 20 S	136 10 E
Yapo, R.	**174**	0 30 S	77 0W
Yappar, R.	**138**	18 22 S	141 16 E
Yaqui, R.	**164**	28 28N	109 30W
Yar	**84**	58 14N	52 5 E
Yar-Sale	**76**	66 50N	70 50 E
Yaracuy □	**174**	10 20N	68 45W
Yaraka	**138**	24 53 S	144 3 E
Yaransk	**81**	57 13N	47 56 E
Yaratishky	**80**	54 3N	25 52 E
Yarcombe	**30**	50 51N	3 6W
Yarda	**117**	18 35N	19 0 E
Yardea P.O.	**139**	32 23 S	135 32 E
Yare, R.	**29**	52 36N	1 28 E
Yarensk	**78**	61 10N	49 8 E
Yarfa	**122**	24 40N	38 35 E
Yari, R.	**174**	1 0N	73 40W
Yaringa North	**137**	25 53 S	114 30 E
Yaringa South	**137**	26 3 S	114 28 E
Yarkand = Soch'e	**105**	38 24N	77 20 E
Yarkhun, R.	**95**	36 30N	72 45 E
Yarm	**33**	54 31N	1 21W
Yarmouth, Can.	**151**	43 53N	65 45W
Yarmouth, U.K.	**28**	50 42N	1 29W
Yaroslavl	**81**	57 35N	39 55 E
Yarra Yarra Lakes	**137**	29 40 S	115 45 E
Yarraden	**138**	14 28 S	143 15 E
Yarraloola	**136**	21 33 S	115 52 E
Yarram	**141**	38 29 S	146 40 E
Yarraman	**139**	26 50 S	152 0 E
Yarraman Cr.	**139**	26 46 S	152 1 E
Yarranvale	**139**	26 50 S	145 20 E
Yarras	**141**	31 25 S	152 20 E
Yarrawonga	**141**	36 0 S	146 0 E
Yarrow	**35**	55 32N	3 0W
Yarrowee, R.	**140**	38 18 S	144 30 E
Yarto	**140**	35 28 S	142 16 E
Yartsevo	**77**	60 20N	90 0 E
Yarumal	**174**	6 58N	75 24W
Yaselda, R.	**80**	52 26N	25 30 E
Yashi	**121**	12 23N	7 54 E
Yashiro-Jima	**110**	33 55N	132 15 E
Yasin	**95**	36 24N	73 15 E
Yasinovataya	**82**	48 7N	37 57 E
Yasinski, L.	**150**	53 16N	77 35W
Yasnogorsk	**81**	54 32N	37 38 E
Yasothon	**100**	15 50N	104 10 E
Yass	**141**	34 49 S	148 54 E
Yasugi	**110**	35 26N	133 15 E
Yas'ur	**90**	32 54N	35 10 E
Yatagan	**69**	37 20N	28 10 E
Yate	**28**	51 32N	2 26W
Yates Center	**159**	37 53N	95 45W
Yates Pt.	**143**	44 29 S	167 49 E
Yathkyed L.	**153**	62 40N	98 0W
Yathong	**141**	32 37 S	145 33 E
Yatsuo	**111**	36 34N	137 8 E
Yatsushiro	**110**	32 30N	130 40 E
Yatsushiro-Kai	**110**	32 30N	130 25 E
Yatta	**90**	31 27N	35 6 E
Yatta Plat.	**126**	2 0 S	38 0 E
Yattah	**90**	31 27N	35 6 E
Yatton	**28**	51 23N	2 50W
Yauyos	**174**	12 10 S	75 50W
Yaval	**96**	21 10N	75 42 E
Yavan	**85**	38 19N	69 2 E
Yavari R.	**174**	4 50 S	72 0W
Yavorov	**80**	49 55N	23 20 E
Yawatahama	**110**	33 27N	132 24 E
Yawri B.	**120**	8 22N	13 0W
Yaxley	**29**	52 31N	0 14W
Yazagyo	**98**	23 30N	94 6 E
Yazd (Yezd)	**93**	31 55N	54 27 E
Yazdan	**93**	33 30N	60 50 E
Yazoo City	**159**	32 48N	90 28W
Yazoo, R.	**159**	32 35N	90 50W
Ybbs	**52**	48 12N	15 4 E
Yding Skovhøj	**75**	55 59N	9 46 E
Yea	**141**	37 14 S	145 26 E
Yealering	**137**	32 36 S	117 36 E
Yealmpton	**30**	50 21N	4 0W
Yearinan	**141**	31 10 S	149 11 E
Yebbi-Souma	**119**	21 7N	17 54 E
Yebbigué	**119**	22 30N	17 30 E
Yebel Jarris Tighzert, O.	**118**	28 10N	9 37W
Yebyu	**99**	14 15N	98 13 E
Yechŏn	**107**	36 39N	128 27 E
Yecla	**59**	38 35N	1 5W
Yécora	**164**	28 20N	108 58W
Yedashe	**98**	17 24N	95 50 E
Yeddou	**118**	28 5N	9 2W
Yeeda River	**136**	17 31 S	123 38 E
Yeelanna	**139**	34 9 S	135 45 E
Yefremov	**81**	53 15N	38 3 E
Yegorlyk, R.	**83**	46 15N	41 30 E
Yegorlykskaya	**83**	46 5N	40 35 E
Yegoryevsk	**81**	55 27N	38 55 E
Yegros	**172**	26 20 S	56 25W
Yehchih	**108**	27 39N	99 0 E
Yehsien	**106**	33 37N	113 20 E
Yehud	**90**	32 3N	34 53 E
Yehuda, Midbar	**90**	31 35N	34 57 E
Yei	**123**	4 3N	30 40 E
Yei, Nahr	**123**	5 50N	30 20 E
Yelan	**81**	50 55N	43 43 E
Yelan Kolenovski	**81**	51 16N	40 45 E
Yelandur	**97**	12 6N	77 0 E
Yelanskoye	**77**	61 25N	128 0 E
Yelarbon	**139**	28 33 S	150 49 E
Yelatma	**81**	55 0N	41 52 E
Yelets	**81**	52 40N	38 30 E
Yelimané	**120**	15 9N	22 49 E
Yell, I.	**36**	60 35N	1 5W
Yell Sd.	**36**	60 33N	1 15W
Yellamanchilli (Elamanchili)	**96**	17 26N	82 50 E
Yellow Sea	**105**	35 0N	123 0 E
Yellowdine	**137**	31 17 S	119 40 E
Yellowhead P.	**152**	52 53N	118 25W
Yellowknife	**152**	62 27N	114 21W
Yellowknife, R.	**152**	62 31N	114 19W
Yellowstone L.	**160**	44 30N	110 20W
Yellowstone National Park	**160**	44 35N	110 0W
Yellowstone, R.	**158**	46 35N	105 45W
Yelnya	**80**	54 35N	33 15 E
Yelsk	**80**	51 50N	29 3 E
Yelvertoft	**138**	20 13 S	138 53 E
Yelwa	**122**	10 49N	8 41 E
Yemanzhelinsk	**84**	54 58N	61 18 E
Yemen ■	**91**	15 0N	44 0 E
Yemen, South ■	**91**	15 0N	48 0 E
Yen Bai	**100**	21 42N	104 52 E
Yenakiyevo	**82**	48 15N	38 5 E
Yenan	**106**	36 42N	109 25 E
Yenangyaung	**98**	20 30N	95 0 E
Yenanma	**98**	19 46N	96 48 E
Yenchang	**106**	36 44N	110 2 E
Yench'eng, Honan, China	**106**	33 37N	114 0 E
Yench'eng, Kiangsu, China	**107**	33 24N	120 10 E
Yench'i	**105**	42 4N	86 34 E
Yenchi	**107**	42 53N	129 31 E
Yench'ih	**106**	37 47N	107 24 E
Yenchihsien	**107**	42 46N	129 24 E
Yenchin	**108**	28 4N	104 14 E
Yench'ing	**106**	40 28N	115 58 E
Yenching	**108**	29 7N	98 33 E
Yenchou	**105**	35 40N	116 50 E
Yench'uan	**106**	36 52N	110 11 E
Yenda	**141**	34 13 S	146 14 E
Yendéré	**120**	10 12N	4 59W
Yendi	**121**	9 29N	0 1W
Yenfeng	**108**	25 52N	101 5 E
Yenho	**108**	28 35N	108 28 E
Yenhsing	**108**	25 22N	101 44 E
Yenisaía	**68**	41 1N	24 57 E
Yenisey, R.	**76**	68 0N	86 30 E
Yeniseysk	**77**	58 39N	92 4 E
Yeniseyskiy Zaliv	**76**	72 20N	81 0 E
Yenne	**45**	45 43N	5 44 E
Yenotyevka	**83**	47 15N	47 0 E
Yenpien	**108**	26 54N	101 34 E
Yenshan, Hopeh, China	**107**	38 3N	117 12 E
Yenshan, Yunnan, China	**108**	23 40N	104 22 E
Yenshou	**107**	45 27N	128 19 E
Yent'ai	**107**	37 35N	121 25 E
Yent'ing	**108**	31 19N	105 20 E
Yenyüan	**108**	27 25N	101 33 E
Yenyuka	**77**	58 20N	121 30 E
Yeo, L.	**137**	28 0 S	124 30 E
Yeo, R.	**28**	51 1N	2 46W
Yeola	**96**	20 0N	74 30 E
Yeotmal	**96**	20 20N	78 15 E
Yeoval	**141**	32 41 S	148 39 E
Yeovil	**28**	50 57N	2 38W
Yepes	**56**	39 55N	3 39W
Yeppoon	**138**	23 5 S	150 47 E
Yeráki	**69**	37 0N	22 42 E
Yerbogachen	**77**	61 16N	108 0 E
Yerevan	**83**	40 10N	44 20 E
Yerilla	**137**	29 24 S	121 47 E
Yerington	**163**	38 59N	119 10W
Yerla, R.	**96**	17 35N	74 30 E
Yermakovo	**77**	52 35N	126 20 E
Yermo	**163**	34 58N	116 50W
Yermolayevo	**78**	52 58N	56 12 E
Yerofey Pavlovich	**77**	54 0N	122 0 E
Yerseke	**47**	51 29N	4 3 E
Yershov	**81**	51 15N	48 27 E
Yerūshalayim	**90**	31 47N	35 10 E
Yerville	**42**	49 40N	0 53 E
Yes Tor, Mt.	**30**	50 41N	3 59W
Yesagyo	**98**	21 38N	95 14 E
Yesan	**107**	36 41N	126 51 E
Yeşilirmak	**82**	41 0N	36 40 E
Yeso	**159**	34 29N	104 87W
Yessentuki	**83**	44 0N	42 45 E
Yeste	**59**	38 22N	2 19W
Yeu, I. d'	**42**	46 42N	2 20W
Yevlakh	**83**	40 39N	47 7 E
Yevpatoriya	**82**	45 15N	33 20 E
Yevstratovskiy	**81**	50 11N	39 2 E
Yeya, R.	**83**	46 40N	39 0 E
Yeysk Staro	**82**	46 40N	38 12 E
Yhati	**172**	25 45 S	56 35W
Yhú	**173**	25 0 S	56 0W
Yi, R.	**172**	33 7 S	57 8W
Yialí, I.	**69**	36 41N	27 11 E
Yiáltra	**69**	38 51N	22 59 E
Yiannisádhes, I.	**69**	35 20N	26 10 E
Yiannitsa	**68**	40 46N	22 24 E
Yibal	**91**	22 10N	56 8 E
Yidhá	**68**	40 35N	22 53 E
Yinchiang	**108**	27 58N	108 20 E
Yinch'uan	**105**	38 30N	106 20 E
Yindarlgooda, L.	**137**	30 40 S	121 52 E
Ying Ho, R.	**109**	32 30N	116 32 E
Yingch'eng	**109**	30 55N	113 33 E
Yingchiang	**108**	24 48N	98 5 E
Yinghsien	**106**	39 36N	113 12 E
Yingk'ou	**107**	40 38N	122 30 E
Yingp'an, Chiang, G.	**108**	21 20N	109 30 E
Yingp'anshan	**108**	27 56N	105 34 E
Yingshan, Hupeh, China	**109**	31 37N	113 46 E
Yingshan, Hupeh, China	**109**	30 50N	115 45 E
Yingshan, Szechwan, China	**108**	31 6N	106 35 E
Yingshang	**109**	32 36N	116 16 E
Yingtan	**105**	28 12N	117 0 E
Yingte	**109**	24 10N	113 24 E
Yinkanie	**140**	34 22 S	140 17 E
Yinmabin	**99**	22 10N	94 55 E
Yinnietharra	**137**	24 39 S	116 12 E
Yioúra, I.	**68**	39 23N	24 10 E
Yipang	**101**	22 15N	101 26 E
Yirga Alem	**124**	6 34N	38 29 E
Yithion	**69**	36 46N	22 34 E
Yizre'el	**90**	32 34N	35 19 E
Ylitornio	**74**	66 19N	23 39 E
Ylivieska	**74**	64 4N	24 28 E
Yngaren	**73**	58 50N	16 35 E
Ynykchanskiy	**77**	60 15N	137 43 E
Yoakum	**159**	29 20N	97 10W
Yobuko	**110**	33 32N	129 54 E
Yog Pt.	**103**	13 55N	124 20 E
Yogyakarta	**103**	7 49 S	110 22 E
Yoho Nat. Park	**152**	51 25N	116 30W
Yojoa, L. de	**166**	14 53N	88 0W
Yŏju	**107**	37 20N	127 35 E
Yokadouma	**124**	3 35N	14 50 E
Yōkaichi	**111**	35 6N	136 12 E
Yōkaichiba	**111**	35 42N	140 33 E
Yokkaichi	**111**	35 0N	136 30 E
Yoko	**121**	5 50N	12 20 E
Yokohama	**111**	35 27N	139 39 E
Yokosuka	**111**	35 20N	139 40 E
Yokote	**112**	39 20N	140 30 E
Yola	**121**	9 10N	12 29 E
Yolaina, Cordillera de	**166**	11 30N	84 0W
Yom Mae Nam	**101**	15 15N	100 20 E
Yonago	**110**	35 25N	133 19 E
Yŏnan	**107**	37 55N	126 11 E
Yonezawa	**112**	37 57N	140 4 E
Yong Peng	**101**	2 0N	103 3 E
Yong Sata	**101**	7 8N	99 41 E
Yongampo	**107**	39 56N	124 23 E
Yŏngchon	**107**	35 58N	128 56 E
Yŏngdŏk	**107**	36 24N	129 22 E
Yŏngdŭngpo	**107**	37 31N	126 54 E
Yŏnghŭng	**107**	39 31N	127 18 E
Yŏngju	**107**	36 50N	128 40 E
Yŏngwŏl	**107**	37 11N	128 28 E
Yonibana	**120**	8 30N	12 19W
Yonker	**153**	52 40N	109 40W
Yonkers	**162**	40 57N	73 51W
Yonne □	**43**	47 50N	3 40 E
Yonne, R.	**43**	48 23N	2 58 E
Yonov	**121**	7 33N	8 42 E
Yoqueam	**90**	32 40N	35 6 E
York, Austral.	**137**	31 52 S	116 47 E
York, U.K.	**33**	53 58N	1 7W
York, Ala., U.S.A.	**157**	32 30N	88 18W
York, Nebr., U.S.A.	**158**	40 55N	97 35W
York, Pa., U.S.A.	**162**	39 57N	76 43W
York, C.	**138**	10 42 S	142 31 E
York Factory	**153**	57 0N	92 18W
York Haven	**162**	40 7N	76 46W
York, Kap	**12**	75 55N	66 25W
York, R.	**162**	37 15N	76 23W
York Sd.	**136**	14 50 S	125 5 E
York, Vale of	**23**	54 15N	1 25W
Yorke Pen.	**140**	34 50 S	137 40 E
Yorkshire Wolds	**33**	54 0N	0 30W
Yorkton	**153**	51 11N	102 28W
Yorktown, Tex., U.S.A.	**159**	29 0N	97 29W

Yorktown Zell

Yorktown, Va., U.S.A. 162 37 14N 76 30W
Yornup 137 34 2S 116 10E
Yoro 166 15 9N 87 7W
Yosemite National Park 163 38 0N 119 30W
Yosemite Village 163 37 45N 119 35W
Yoshii 110 33 16N 129 46E
Yoshimatsu 110 32 0N 130 47E
Yoshkar Ola 81 56 49N 47 10E
Yŏsu 107 34 47N 127 45E
Youanmi 137 28 37S 118 49E
Youbou 152 48 53N 124 13W
Youghal 39 51 58N 7 51W
Youghal B. 39 51 55N 7 50W
Youkounkoun 120 12 35N 13 11W
Young, Austral. 141 34 19S 148 18E
Young, Can. 153 51 47N 105 45W
Young, Uruguay 172 32 44S 57 36W
Young, U.S.A. 161 34 9N 110 56W
Young Ra. 143 44 10S 169 30E
Younghusband, L. 140 30 50S 136 5E
Younghusband Pen. 140 36 0S 139 25E
Youngstown, Can. 153 51 35N 111 10W
Youngstown, U.S.A. 156 41 7N 80 41W
Youssoufia 118 32 16N 8 31W
Yoweragabbie 137 28 14S 117 39E
Yowrie 141 36 17S 149 46E
Yoxall 28 52 45N 1 49W
Yoxford 29 52 16N 1 30E
Yozgat 92 39 51N 34 47E
Ypané, R. 172 23 29S 57 19W
Yport 42 49 45N 0 15E
Ypres 47 50 50N 2 52E
Ypsilanti 156 42 18N 83 40W
Yreka 160 41 44N 122 40W
Ysabel Chan. 135 2 0S 150 0E
Ysbyty Ystwyth 31 52 20N 3 50W
Ysleta 161 31 45N 106 24W
Yssingeaux 45 45 9N 4 8E
Ystad 73 55 26N 13 50E
Ystalyfera 31 51 46N 3 48W
Ystradgynlais 31 51 47N 3 45W
Ystwyth, R. 31 52 24N 4 2W
Ythan, R. 37 57 26N 2 12W
Ytre Adal 71 60 15N 10 14E
Ytterhogdal 72 62 12N 14 56E
Ytyk-Kel 77 62 20N 133 28E
Yü Chiang, R., China 105 22 50N 108 6E
Yü Chiang, R., China 108 22 50N 108 6E
Yu Shui, R. 108 28 37N 110 23E
Yüan Chiang, R. 109 29 0N 111 50E
Yüan Chiang, R (Hong.) 108 29 12N 111 43E
Yüanan 109 31 3N 111 34E
Yüanchiang, Hünan, China 109 28 50N 112 23E
Yüanchiang, Yunnan, China 108 23 40N 102 0E
Yüanch'ü 106 35 18N 111 41E
Yüanli 109 24 27N 120 39E
Yüanlin 109 23 45N 120 30E
Yüanling 109 28 30N 110 5E
Yüanmou 108 25 42N 101 32E
Yüanyang 108 23 10N 102 58E
Yüanyang 108 35 3N 113 57E
Yuat, R. 135 4 10S 143 52E
Yuba City 160 39 12N 121 37W
Yūbari 112 43 4N 141 59E
Yūbetsu 112 43 13N 144 5E
Yucatán □ 165 21 30N 86 30W
Yucatán Basin 14 20 0N 84 0W
Yucatán Channel 166 22 0N 86 30W
Yucca 161 34 56N 114 6W
Yucca Valley 163 34 8N 116 30W
Yücha 108 26 55N 101 24E
Yucheng 106 36 55N 116 40E
Yüch'i 108 24 25N 102 35E
Yuch'i 109 26 10N 118 11E
Yüchiang 109 28 24N 116 53E
Yüch'ien 109 30 12N 119 24E
Yüch'ing 108 27 13N 107 54E
Yudino 76 55 10N 67 55E
Yüehhsi, Anhwei, China 109 30 54N 116 22E
Yüehhsi, Szechwan, China 108 28 36N 102 35E
Yüehyang 109 29 20N 113 7E
Yuendumu 136 22 16S 131 49E
Yufu-Dake 110 33 17N 131 33E
Yugoslavia ■ 66 44 0N 20 0E
Yühsien 106 34 10N 113 30E
Yuhsien, Hunan, China 109 27 2N 113 20E
Yuhsien, Shansi, China 106 38 5N 113 24E
Yühuan Tao, I. 109 28 5N 121 15E
Yukan 109 28 43N 116 35E
Yukhnov 80 54 44N 35 15E
Yūki 111 36 18N 139 53E
Yukon □ 147 63 0N 135 0W
Yukon, R. 147 65 30N 150 0W
Yukti 77 63 20N 105 0E
Yukuhashi 110 33 44N 130 59E
Yule, R. 136 20 24S 118 12E
Yuli 122 9 44N 10 12E
Yülin 100 18 10N 109 31E
Yulin, Guangdong, China 109 22 36N 110 7E
Yulin, Shensi, China 105 38 15N 109 30E
Yuma, Ariz., U.S.A. 161 32 45N 114 37W
Yuma, Colo., U.S.A. 158 40 10N 102 43W
Yuma, B. de 167 18 20N 68 35W
Yumali 140 35 32S 139 45E
Yumbe 126 3 28N 31 15E
Yumbi 126 1 12S 26 15E
Yumbo 174 3 35N 76 28W
Yümenhsien 105 40 17N 97 12E
Yün Ho 107 33 16N 118 45E
Yun Ho 109 35 0N 117 0E
Yuna 137 28 20S 115 0E
Yünan 109 23 14N 111 31E
Yunaska I. 147 52 40N 170 40W
Yünch'eng, Shansi, China 106 35 1N 110 59E
Yünch'eng, Shantung, China 106 35 35N 115 56E
Yunfou 109 22 56N 112 2E
Yungan 109 25 50N 117 25E
Yungas 174 17 0S 66 0W
Yungay 172 37 10S 72 5W
Yungch'eng 106 33 56N 116 22E
Yungchi 106 34 52N 110 26E
Yungch'ing 106 39 19N 116 29E
Yungch'uan 108 20 22N 105 52E
Yungch'un 109 25 19N 118 17E
Yungfeng 109 27 20N 115 27E
Yungfu 109 24 59N 109 59E
Yungho 106 36 44N 110 39E
Yunghsin 109 16 55N 114 18E
Yunghsing 109 26 8N 113 6E
Yunghsiu 109 29 8N 115 42E
Yungjen 108 26 4N 101 42E
Yungk'ang, Chekiang, China 109 28 53N 120 2E
Yungk'ang, Kwangsi Chuang Aut. Region, China 108 22 48N 107 51E
Yungnien 106 36 49N 114 33E
Yungning, Kwangsi Chuang A. R., China 108 22 45N 108 29E
Yungning, Ningsia Hui A. R., China 106 38 18N 106 18E
Yungning, Yunnan, China 108 27 50N 100 40E
Yungningchai 106 36 35N 108 51E
Yungp'ing 108 25 25N 99 36E
Yungshan 108 28 11N 103 35E
Yungsheng 108 26 42N 100 45E
Yungshun, Hunan, China 108 29 3N 109 50E
Yungshun, Kwangsi Chuang, China 108 22 48N 108 55E
Yungt'ai 109 25 52N 118 55E
Yungteng 106 36 44N 103 24E
Yungting 109 24 49N 116 46E
Yunho = Lishui 109 28 6N 119 34E
Yünhsi 109 33 0N 110 22E
Yünhsiao 109 24 1N 117 15E
Yünhsien, Hupeh, China 105 32 50N 110 53E
Yünhsien, Yunnan, China 108 24 25N 100 6E
Yünlin 109 23 42N 120 31E
Yunling Shan, mts. 108 28 30N 98 50E
Yunlung 99 25 50N 99 25E
Yünmeng 109 31 1N 113 39E
Yunnan □ 108 25 0N 102 30E
Yunndaga 137 29 45S 121 0E
Yunomae 110 32 12N 130 59E
Yunotso 110 35 5N 132 21E
Yunquera de Henares 58 40 47N 3 11W
Yunta 140 32 34S 139 36E
Yünyang 108 30 55N 108 56E
Yüp'ing 108 27 14N 108 54E
Yupyongdong 107 41 49N 128 53E
Yur 77 59 52N 137 49E
Yurga 76 55 42N 84 51E
Yuria 84 59 22N 54 10E
Yuribei 76 71 20N 76 30E
Yurimaguas 174 5 55S 76 0W
Yurya 81 59 1N 49 13E
Yuryev Polskiy 81 56 30N 59 47E
Yuryevets 81 57 25N 43 2E
Yuryuzan 84 54 27N 58 28E
Yuscarán 166 13 58N 86 51W
Yusha, Jebel 90 32 4N 35 41E
Yüshan 109 28 40N 118 15E
Yüshanchen 108 29 31N 108 25E
Yushe 106 37 4N 112 58E
Yüshu 105 33 1N 96 44E
Yushu 107 44 46N 126 34E
Yüt'ai 106 35 2N 116 40E
Yüt'ien 107 39 53N 117 45E
Yütu 109 26 0N 115 24E
Yütz'u 106 37 42N 112 44E
Yüwang 106 37 9N 106 28E
Yuyang 108 28 44N 108 46E
Yüyang 109 30 12N 119 56E
Yüyao 109 30 3N 121 9E
Yuyao 109 30 0N 121 20E
Yuyu 105 40 20N 112 30E
Yuyü 106 40 10N 112 25E
Yüyuan 109 28 9N 121 11E
Yuzha 81 56 40N 42 10E
Yuzhno-Sakhalinsk 77 47 5N 142 5E
Yuzhno-Surkhanskoye Vodokhranilishehe 85 37 53N 67 42E
Yuzhno-Uralsk 84 54 26N 61 15E
Yuzhnyy Ural, mts. 84 53 0N 58 0E
Yvelines □ 43 48 40N 1 45E
Yverdon 50 46 47N 6 39E
Yvetot 42 49 37N 0 44E
Yvonand 50 46 48N 6 44E

Z

Za, O. 118 34 5N 2 30W
Zaalayskiy Khrebet 85 39 20N 73 0E
Zaamslag 47 51 19N 3 55E
Zaan, R. 46 52 25N 4 52E
Zaandam 47 52 26N 4 49E
Zab, Monts du 119 34 55N 5 0E
Zabalj, Yugo. 66 45 21N 20 5E
Zabalj, Yugo. 66 45 23N 20 5E
Zabari 66 44 22N 21 15E
Zabarjad 122 23 40N 36 12E
Zabaykalskiy 77 49 40N 117 10E
Zabkowice Slaskie 54 50 22N 19 17E
Zabljak 66 42 19N 19 10E
Zabludow 54 53 0N 23 19E
Zabno 54 50 9N 20 53E
Zābol 93 31 0N 61 25E
Zābolī 93 27 10N 61 35E
Zabré 121 11 12N 0 36W
Zabrze 54 50 24N 18 50E
Zacapa 166 14 59N 89 31W
Zacapu 164 19 50N 101 43W
Zacatecas 164 22 49N 102 34W
Zacatecas □ 164 23 30N 103 0W
Zacatecolua 166 13 29N 88 51W
Zacaultipán 165 20 39N 98 36W
Zacoalco 164 20 10N 103 40W
Zadar 63 44 8N 15 8E
Zadawa 121 11 33N 10 19E
Zadetkyi Kyun 101 10 0N 98 25E
Zadonsk 81 52 25N 38 56E
Zafed 90 32 58N 35 29E
Zafora, I. 69 36 5N 26 24E
Zafra 57 38 26N 6 30W
Zagan 54 51 39N 15 22E
Zagazig 122 30 40N 31 12E
Zaghouan 119 36 23N 10 10E
Zaglivérion 68 40 36N 23 15E
Zaglou 118 27 17N 0 3W
Zagnanado 121 7 18N 2 28E
Zagorá 68 39 27N 23 6E
Zagora 118 30 14N 5 51W
Zagórów 54 52 10N 17 54E
Zagorsk 81 56 20N 38 10E
Zagórz 54 49 30N 22 14E
Zagreb 63 45 50N 16 0E
Zāgros, Kudha-ye 93 33 45N 47 0E
Zagubica 66 44 15N 21 47E
Zaguinaso 120 10 1N 6 14W
Zāhedān 93 29 30N 60 50E
Zahirabad 96 17 43N 77 37E
Zahlah 92 33 52N 35 50E
Zahna 48 51 54N 12 47E
Zahrez Chergui 118 35 0N 3 30E
Zahrez Rharbi 118 34 50N 2 55E
Zailiyskiy Alatau, Khrebet 85 43 5N 77 0E
Zainsk 84 55 18N 52 4E
Zaïr 118 29 47N 5 51W
Zaïre, R. 124 1 30N 28 0E
Zaïre, Rep. of ■ 124 3 0S 23 0E
Zaječar 66 43 53N 22 18E
Zakamensk 77 50 23N 103 17E
Zakariya 90 31 43N 34 57E
Zakataly 83 41 38N 46 35E
Zakavkazye 83 42 0N 44 0E
Zakhu 92 37 10N 42 50E
Zákinthos 69 37 47N 20 54E
Zákinthos, I. 69 37 45N 27 45E
Zakopane 54 49 18N 19 57E
Zala □ 53 46 42N 16 50E
Zala, R. 53 46 53N 17 6E
Zalaegerszeg 53 46 53N 16 47E
Zalakomár 53 46 33N 17 10E
Zalalövö 53 46 51N 16 35E
Zalamea de la Serena 57 38 40N 5 38W
Zalamea la Real 57 37 41N 6 38W
Zalau 121 10 30N 8 58E
Zalazna 84 58 39N 52 31E
Zalec 63 46 16N 15 10E
Zaleshchiki 82 48 45N 25 45E
Zalewo 54 53 55N 19 41E
Zalingei 117 13 5N 23 10E
Zalţan, Jabal 119 28 46N 19 45E
Zaltbommel 46 51 48N 5 15E
Zalū 121 47 12N 23 5E
Zambeke 126 2 8N 25 17E
Zambèze, R. 127 18 46S 36 16E
Zambezi, R. 127 18 46S 36 16E
Zambezia □ 127 16 15S 37 30E
Zambia ■ 125 15 0S 28 0E
Zamboanga 103 6 59N 122 3E
Zambrano 174 9 45N 74 49W
Zametchino 81 53 30N 42 30E
Zamora, Mexico 164 20 0N 102 21W
Zamora, Spain 56 41 30N 5 45W
Zamora □ 56 41 30N 5 46W
Zamosść 54 50 50N 23 22E
Zamuro, Sierra del 174 4 0N 62 30W
Zamzam, W. 119 31 0N 14 30E
Zan 121 9 26N 0 17W
Zanaga 124 2 48S 13 48E
Záncara, R. 58 39 20N 3 0W
Zandvoort 46 52 22N 4 32E
Zanesville 156 39 56N 82 2W
Zangue, R. 127 18 5S 35 10E
Zanjan 92 36 40N 48 35E
Zannone, I. 64 40 38N 13 2E
Zante = Zákinthos 69 37 47N 20 54E
Zanthus 137 31 2S 123 34E
Zanzibar 126 6 12S 39 12E
Zanzibar I. 126 6 12S 39 12E
Zanzūr 119 32 55N 13 1E
Zaouatalaz 119 24 57N 8 16E
*Zaouiet El Kahla 119 27 10N 6 40E
Zaouiet Reggane 118 26 32N 0 3E
Zapadna Morava, R. 66 43 50N 20 15E
Zapadnaya Dvina 80 56 15N 32 3E
Západné Beskydy 54 49 30N 19 0E
Zapadočesky □ 52 49 35N 13 0E
Západoslovenský □ 53 48 30N 17 30E
Zapala 176 39 0S 70 5W
Zapaleri, Cerro 172 22 49S 67 11W
Zapata 159 26 56N 92 17W
Zapatón, R. 57 39 0N 6 49W
Zaporozhye 82 47 50N 35 10E
Zapponeta 65 41 27N 15 57E
Zara 92 39 58N 37 43E
Zaragoza, Colomb. 174 7 30N 74 52W
Zaragoza, Coahuila, Mexico 164 28 30N 101 0W
Zaragoza, Nuevo León, Mexico 165 24 0N 99 36W
Zaragoza, Spain 58 41 39N 0 53W
Zaragoza □ 58 41 35N 1 0W
Zarand 93 30 46N 56 34E
Zarasai 80 55 40N 26 12E
Zarate 172 34 7S 59 0W
Zaraysk 81 54 48N 38 53E
Zaraza 174 9 21N 65 19W
Zarembo I. 152 56 20N 132 50W
Zari 73 13 8N 12 37E
Zaria 121 11 0N 7 40E
Zarisberge 128 24 30S 16 15E
Zarki 54 50 38N 19 21E
Zarnów 54 51 16N 20 9E
Zarnuqa 90 31 53N 34 47E
Zarów 54 50 56N 16 29E
Zarqa, R. 90 32 10N 35 37E
Zaruma 174 3 40S 79 30W
Zary 54 51 37N 15 10E
Zarza de Alange 57 38 49N 6 13W
Zarza de Granadilla 56 40 14N 6 3W
Zarza, La 57 37 42N 6 51W
Zarzaîtine 119 28 32N 9 5E
Zarzal 174 4 24N 76 4W
Zarzis 119 33 31N 11 2E
Zas 56 43 4N 8 53W
Zashiversk 77 67 25N 142 40E
Zaskar Mountains 95 33 15N 77 30E
Zaskar, R. 95 33 55N 77 2E
Zastron 128 30 18S 27 7E
Zatec 52 50 20N 13 32E
Zator 54 49 59N 19 28E
Zavala 66 42 50N 17 59E
Zavareh 93 33 35N 52 28E
Zaventem 47 50 53N 4 28E
Zavetnoye 83 47 13N 43 50E
Zavidovići 66 44 27N 18 13E
Zavitinsk 77 50 10N 129 20E
Zavodoski, I. 13 56 0S 27 45W
Zavolzhye 81 56 37N 43 18E
Zawadzkie 54 50 37N 18 28E
Zawidów 54 51 1N 15 1E
Zawiercie 54 50 30N 19 13E
Zâwyet Shammâs 122 31 30N 26 37E
Zâwyet Um el Rakham 122 31 18N 27 1E
Zâwyet Ungeila 122 31 23N 26 42E
Zayandeh, R. 93 32 35N 32 0E
Zayarsk 77 56 20N 102 55E
Zaysan 76 47 28N 84 52E
Zaysan, Oz. 76 48 0N 83 0E
Zāzamt, W. 119 30 29N 14 30E
Zazir, O. 119 22 0N 5 40E
Zázrivá 53 49 16N 19 7E
Zbarazh 80 49 43N 25 44E
Zbaszyn 54 52 14N 15 56E
Zbaszynek 54 52 16N 15 51E
Zblewo 54 53 56N 18 19E
Zdandijk 46 52 82N 4 49E
Zdolbunov 80 50 30N 26 15E
Zdrelo 66 44 16N 21 28E
Zdunska Wola 54 51 37N 18 59E
Zduny 54 51 39N 17 21E
Zeballos 152 49 59N 126 50W
Zebediela 129 24 20S 29 17E
Zedelgem 47 51 8N 3 8E
Zeebrugge 47 51 19N 3 12E
Zeehan 138 41 52S 145 25E
Zeeland 47 51 41N 5 40E
Zeeland □ 47 51 30N 3 50E
Ze'elim 90 31 13N 34 32E
Zeelst 47 51 25N 5 25E
Zeerust 128 25 31S 26 4E
Zefat 90 32 58N 35 29E
Zegdou 118 29 51N 4 53W
Zege 123 11 43N 37 18E
Zegelsem 47 50 49N 3 43E
Zegoua 120 10 32N 5 35W
Zehdenick 48 52 59N 13 20E
Zeil, Mt. 136 23 24S 132 23E
Zeila 91 11 15N 43 30E
Zeist 46 52 5N 5 15E
Zeita 90 32 23N 35 2E
Zeitz 48 51 3N 12 9E
Zele 47 51 4N 4 2E
Zelendolsk 81 55 55N 48 30E
Zelengora, mts. 66 43 22N 18 30E
Zelenika 66 42 27N 18 37E
Zelenogradsk 80 54 53N 20 29E
Zelenokumsk 83 44 30N 44 1E
Zelenovski 83 48 6N 50 45E
Zelhem 47 52 0N 6 21E
Zell 49 47 42N 7 50E

*Renamed Bordj Omar Driss

Name	Map	Lat	Long
Zell am See	52	47 19N	12 47 E
Zella Mehlis	48	50 40N	10 41 E
Zelouane	86	35 1N	2 58W
Zelzate	47	51 13N	3 47 E
Zémio	126	5 2N	25 5 E
Zemmora	118	35 44N	0 51 E
Zemora, I.	119	37 5N	10 56 E
Zemoul, W.	118	29 15N	7 30W
Zemst	47	50 59N	4 28 E
Zemun	66	44 51N	20 25 E
Zenica	66	44 10N	17 57 E
Zenina	118	34 30N	2 37 E
Zentsūji	110	34 14N	133 47 E
Zepce	66	44 28N	18 2 E
Zeravshan	85	39 10N	68 39 E
Zeravshan, R.	85	39 32N	63 45 E
Zeravshanskiy, Khrebet	85	39 20N	69 0 E
Zerbst	48	51 59N	12 8 E
Zerhamra	118	29 58N	2 30W
Zerków	54	52 4N	17 32 E
Zermatt	50	46 2N	7 46 E
Zernez	51	46 42N	10 7 E
Zernograd	83	46 52N	40 11 E
Zeroud, O.	119	35 30N	9 30 E
Zerqani	68	41 30N	20 20 E
Zestafoni	83	42 6N	43 0 E
Zetel	48	53 33N	7 57 E
Zetland (□)	26	60 30N	0 15W
Zetten	46	51 56N	5 44 E
Zeulenroda	48	50 39N	12 0 E
Zeven	48	53 17N	9 19 E
Zevenaar	46	51 56N	6 5 E
Zevenbergen	47	51 38N	4 37 E
Zévio	62	45 23N	11 10 E
Zeya	77	54 2N	127 20 E
Zeya, R.	77	53 30N	127 0 E
Zeyse	123	5 44N	37 23W
Zeytin	92	37 53N	36 53 E
Zêzere, R.	56	40 0N	7 55W
Zgierz	54	51 45N	19 27 E
Zgorzelec	54	51 10N	15 0 E
Zhabinka	80	52 13N	24 2 E
Zhailma	84	51 30N	61 50 E
Zhalanash	85	43 3N	78 38 E
Zhamensk	80	54 37N	21 17 E
Zhanadarya	85	44 45N	64 40 E
Zhanatas	76	43 11N	81 18 E
Zharkol	84	49 57N	64 5 E
Zharkovskiy	80	55 56N	32 19 E
Zhashkov	82	49 15N	30 5 E
Zhdanov	82	47 5N	37 31 E
Zheleznogorsk-Ilimskiy	77	56 34N	104 8 E
Zherdevka	81	51 56N	41 21 E
Zhetykol, Ozero	84	51 2N	60 54 E
Zhigansk	77	66 35N	124 10 E
Zhigulevsk	81	53 28N	49 45 E
Zhirhovsk	81	50 57N	44 49 E
Zhitomir	80	50 20N	28 40 E
Zhizdra	80	53 45N	34 40 E
Zhlobin	80	52 55N	30 0 E
Zhmerinka	82	49 2N	28 10 E
Zhodino	80	54 5N	28 17 E
Zhovtnevoye	82	47 54N	32 2 E
Zhuantobe	85	43 43N	78 18 E
Zhukovka	80	53 35N	33 50 E
Zhupanovo	77	51 59N	15 9 E
Ziarat	94	30 25N	67 30 E
Zichem	47	51 2N	4 59 E
Ziebice	54	50 37N	17 2 E
Ziel, Mt.	136	23 20 S	132 30 E
Zielona Góra	54	51 57N	15 31 E
Zielona Góra □	54	51 57N	15 30 E
Zierikzee	47	51 40N	3 55 E
Ziesar	48	52 16N	12 19 E
Zifta	122	30 43N	31 14 E
Zigazinskiy	84	53 50N	57 20 E
Zigey	117	14 50N	15 50 E
Ziguinchor	120	12 25N	16 20W
Zihuatanejo	164	17 38N	101 33W
Zile	92	40 15N	36 0 E
Zilfi	92	26 12N	44 52 E
Zilina	53	49 12N	18 42 E
Zillah	119	28 40N	17 41 E
Zillertaler Alpen	52	47 6N	11 45 E
Zima	77	54 0N	102 5 E
Zimane, Adrar in	118	22 10N	4 30 E
Zimapán	165	20 40N	99 20W
Zimba	127	17 20 S	26 25 E
Zimbabwe ■	127	20 16 S	31 0 E
Zimovniki	83	47 10N	42 25 E
Zinal	50	46 8N	7 38 E
Zinder	121	13 48N	9 0 E
Zinga	127	9 16 S	38 41 E
Zingem	47	50 54N	3 40 E
Zingst	48	54 24N	12 45 E
Zini, Yebel	118	28 0N	11 0W
Ziniaré	121	12 44N	1 10W
Zinjibar	91	13 5N	46 0 E
Zinkgruvan	73	58 50N	15 6 E
Zinnowitz	48	54 5N	13 54 E
Zion Nat. Park	161	37 25N	112 50W
Zipaquirá	174	5 0N	74 0W
Zippori	90	32 64N	35 16 E
Zirc	53	47 17N	17 42 E
Ziri	63	47 17N	11 14 E
Zirje, I.	63	43 39N	15 42 E
Zirl	52	47 17N	11 14 E
Zisterdorf	53	48 33N	16 45 E
Zitácuaro	164	19 20N	100 30W
Zitava, R.	53	48 14N	18 21 E
Zitiste	66	45 30N	2 32 E
Zitsa	68	39 47N	20 40 E
Zittau	48	50 54N	14 47 E
Zitundo	129	26 48 S	32 47 E
Zivinice	66	44 27N	18 36 E
Ziway, L.	123	8 0N	38 50 E
Ziz, Oued	118	31 40N	4 15W
Zizip	92	37 5N	37 50 E
Zlarin	63	43 42N	15 49 E
Zlatar	63	46 5N	16 3 E
Zlataritsa	67	43 2N	24 55 E
Zlatibor	66	43 45N	19 43 E
Zlatista	67	42 41N	24 7 E
Zlatna	70	46 8N	23 11 E
Zlatograd	67	41 22N	25 7 E
Zlatoust	78	55 10N	59 40 E
Zletovo	66	41 59N	22 17 E
Zlitan	119	32 25N	14 35 E
Złocieniec	54	53 30N	16 1 E
Zloczew	54	51 24N	18 35 E
Zlot	66	44 1N	22 0 E
Złotoryja	54	51 8N	15 55 E
Złotów	54	53 22N	17 2 E
Złoty Stok	54	50 27N	16 53 E
Zmeinogorsk	76	51 10N	82 13 E
Zmigród	54	51 28N	16 53 E
Zmiyev	82	49 45N	36 27 E
Znamenka	82	48 45N	32 30 E
Znin	54	52 51N	17 44 E
Znojmo	52	48 50N	16 2 E
Zoar	128	33 30 S	21 26 E
Zobia	126	3 0N	25 50 E
Zoetermeer	46	52 3N	4 30 E
Zofingen	50	47 17N	7 56 E
Zogno	62	45 49N	9 41 E
Zolder	47	51 1N	5 19 E
Zollikofen	50	47 0N	7 28 E
Zollikon	51	47 21N	8 34 E
Zolochev	80	49 45N	24 58 E
Zolotonosha	82	49 45N	32 5 E
Zomba	127	15 30 S	35 19 E
Zombi	126	3 35N	29 10 E
Zomergem	47	51 7N	3 33 E
Zongo	124	4 12N	18 0 E
Zonguldak	82	41 28N	31 50 E
Zonhoven	47	50 59N	5 23 E
Zorgo	121	12 22N	0 35W
Zorita	57	39 17N	5 39W
Zorleni	70	46 14N	27 44 E
Zornitsa	67	42 23N	26 58 E
Zorritos	174	3 50 S	80 40W
Zory	54	50 3N	18 44 E
Zorzor	120	7 46N	9 28W
Zossen	48	52 13N	13 28 E
Zottegam	47	50 52N	3 48 E
Zouar	119	20 30N	16 32 E
Zouérabe	116	22 35N	12 30W
Zousfana, O.	118	31 51N	1 30W
Zoutkamp	46	53 20N	6 18 E
Zqorzelec	54	51 9N	15 0 E
Zrenjanin	66	45 22N	20 23 E
Zuarungu	121	10 49N	0 52W
Zuba	121	9 11N	7 12 E
Zubair, Jazãir	123	15 0N	42 10 E
Zubia	57	37 8N	3 33W
Zubtsov	80	56 10N	34 34 E
Zueitina	119	30 58N	20 7 E
Zuénoula	120	7 34N	6 3W
Zuera	58	41 51N	0 49W
Zug	51	47 10N	8 31 E
Zug □	51	47 9N	8 35 E
Zugar	123	14 0N	42 40 E
Zugdidi	83	42 30N	41 48 E
Zugersee	51	47 7N	8 35 E
Zugspitze	49	47 25N	10 59 E
Zuid-Holland □	46	52 0N	4 35 E
Zuid-horn	46	53 15N	6 23 E
Zuidbeveland	47	51 30N	3 50 E
Zuidbroek	46	53 10N	6 52 E
Zuidelijk-Flevoland	46	52 22N	5 22 E
Zuidlaarder meer	46	53 8N	6 42 E
Zuidland	46	51 49N	4 15 E
Zuidlaren	46	53 6N	6 42 E
Zuidwolde	46	52 40N	6 26 E
Zújar	59	37 34N	2 50W
Zújar, Pantano del	57	38 55N	5 35W
Zújar, R.	59	38 30N	5 30 E
Zula	123	15 17N	39 40 E
Zulia □	174	10 0N	72 10W
Zülpich	48	50 41N	6 38 E
Zululand	129	43 19N	2 15W
Zumaya	58	43 19N	2 15W
Zumbo	127	15 35 S	30 26 E
Zummo	121	9 51N	12 59 E
Zumpango	165	19 48N	99 6W
Zundert	47	51 28N	4 39 E
Zungeru	121	9 48N	6 8 E
Zuni	161	35 7N	108 57W
Zupania	66	45 4N	18 43 E
Zur	66	42 13N	20 34 E
Zura	84	57 36N	53 24 E
Zŭrandului	70	46 14N	22 7 E
Zürich	51	47 22N	8 32 E
Zürich □	51	47 26N	8 40 E
Zürichsee	51	47 18N	8 40 E
Zuromin	54	53 4N	19 57 E
Zuru	121	11 27N	5 4 E
Zurzach	51	47 35N	8 18 E
Zut, I.	63	43 52N	15 17 E
Zutendaal	47	50 56N	5 35 E
Zutphen	46	52 9N	6 12 E
Zuwárrah	119	32 58N	12 1 E
Zuyevka	84	58 27N	51 10 E
Zuzemberk	63	45 52N	14 56 E
Zvenigorodka	82	49 4N	30 56 E
Zverinogolovskoye	84	55 0N	62 30 E
Zvezdets	67	42 6N	27 26 E
Zvolen	53	48 33N	19 10 E
Zvonce	66	42 57N	22 34 E
Zvornik	66	44 26N	19 7 E
Zwaag	46	52 40N	5 4 E
Zwanenburg	46	52 23N	4 45 E
Zwarte Meer	46	52 38N	5 57 E
Zwarte Waler	46	52 39N	6 1 E
Zwartemeer	46	52 43N	7 2 E
Zwartsluis	46	52 39N	6 4 E
Zwedru (Tchien)	120	5 59N	8 15W
Zweibrücken	49	49 15N	7 20 E
Zwenkau	48	51 13N	12 19 E
Zwetti	52	48 35N	15 9 E
Zwickau	48	50 43N	12 30 E
Zwijnaarde	47	51 0N	3 43 E
Zwijndrecht, Belg.	47	51 13N	4 20 E
Zwijndrecht, Neth.	46	51 50N	4 39 E
Zwolle	46	52 31N	6 6 E
Zymoelz, R.	152	54 33N	128 31W
Zyrardów	54	52 3N	20 35 E
Zywiec	54	44 42N	19 12 E

Recent Place-Name Changes

The following place-name changes have recently occurred in Angola, Iran, Madagascar, Mozambique, Vietnam and Zimbabwe. The new names are given on the maps but the former names are in the index.

Angola

Former Name	New name
Ambrizete	Nzeto
Artur de Paiva	Capelongo
Bié	Kuito
Cassinga	Kassinga
Dundo	Luachimo
General Machado	Camacupa
João de Almeida	Chibia
Macedo do Cavaleiros	Andulo
Mariano Machado	Ganda
Moçâmedes	Namibe
Nova Redondo	Ngunza
Ongiva	Ngiva
Paiva Couceiro	Gambos
Robert Williams	Caála
Roçadas	Xangongo
San António do Zaïre	Soyo
Teixeira da Silva	Bailundo
Vila Ariaga	Bibala
Vila Marechal Carmona	Uíge

Iran

Former name	New name
Bandar-e Pahlavi	Bandar-e Anzalī
Bandar-e Shah	Bandar-e Torkeman
Bandar-e Shahpur	Bandar-e Khomeynī
Dehkhvareqan	Āzar Shahr
Dezh Shahpur	Marīvan
Kermanshah	Qahremānshahr
Khorramshahr	Khorramshahr (Khunīnshahr)
Naft Shah	Naftshahr
Reza'iyeh	Orūmīyeh
Reza'iyeh, Daryacheh-ye	Orūmīyeh, Daryācheh-ye
Sar Eskand Khan	Āzarān
Shāhābād	Eslāmābād-e Gharb
Shāhī	Qā'emshahr
Shahpur	Salmās
Shahreza	Qomsheh
Shāhrud	Emāmrūd
Shahsavar	Tunekābon
Soltaniyeh	Sa'īdīyeh

Madagascar

Former name	New name
Ambre, C. de	Bobaomby, Tanjon' i
Ambre, Mt. d'	Ambohitra
Brickaville	Vohibinany
Chesterfield I.	Vestale, Toraka
Diégo Suarez	Antsiranana
Fénérive	Fenoarivo Atsinanana
Fort-Dauphin	Faradofay
Majunga	Mahajanga
Midongy du Sud	Midongy Atsimo
Ste. Marie, C.	Vohimena, T.' i
Ste. Marie, I.	Boraha, Nosy
Tamatave	Toamasina
Tuléar	Toliara

Mozambique

Former name	New name
Augusto Cardosa	Metangula
Entre Rios	Malema
Malvérnia	Chicualacuala
Mau-é-ele	Marão
Olivença	Lupilichi
Vila Alferes Chamusca	Guijá
Vila Caldas Xavier	Muende
Vila Coutinho	Ulonguè
Vila Fontes	Caia
Vila de Junqueiro	Gurué
Vila Luísa	Marracuene
Vila Paiva de Andrada	Gorongoza

Vietnam

Former name	New name
An Loc	Hon Quan
An Tuc	An Khe
Chau Phu	Chau Doc
Dien Bien Phu	Dien Bien
Hau Bon	Cheo Reo
Khanh Hung	Soc Trang
Kien Hung	Go Quao
Phuoc Le	Ba Ria
Quan Long	Ca Mau
Truc Giang	Ben Tre

Zimbabwe

Former name	New name
Balla Balla	Mbalabala
Belingwe	Mberengwa
Chipinga	Chipinge
Dett	Dete
Enkeldoorn	Chivhu
Essexvale	Esigodini
Fort Victoria	Masvingo
Gwelo	Gweru
Hartley	Chegutu
Gatooma	Kadoma
Inyazura	Nyazura
Marandellas	Marondera
Mashaba	Mashava
Melsetter	Chimanimani
Mrewa	Murewa
Mtoko	Mutoko
Nuanetsi	Mwenezi
Que Que	Kwekwe
Salisbury	Harare
Selukwe	Shurugwi
Shabani	Zvishavane
Sinoia	Chinhoyi
Somabula	Somabhula
Tjolotjo	Tsholotsho
Umvuma	Mvuma
Umtali	Mutare
Wankie	Hwange

Chinese Place-Names

The following list gives the Pin Yin nameform and the modified Wade-Giles nameform for the principal places in China. Pin Yin is officially approved by the Chinese and is gaining in use throughout the world. Wade-Giles is the transcription selected for the maps and index in this atlas and is still extensively used in the West.

Pin Yin	Wade-Giles	Pin Yin	Wade-Giles	Pin Yin	Wade-Giles
Anhui	Anhwei	Jiangxi	Kiangsi	Taizhou	T'aichou
Anqing	Anch'ing	Jiaxing	Chiahsing	Tandong	T'antung
Baoding	Paoting	Jilin	Chilin	Tanggula Shan	T'angkula Shanmo
Baoji	Paochi	Jinan	Chinan	Tian Shan	Tien Shan
Baotou	Paot'ou	Jingdezhen	Chingtechen	Tianjin	T'ienching
Bei'an	Peian	Jinhua	Chinhua	Tianshui	Tienshui
Beihai	Peihai	Jining	Chining	Tongchuan	Tungchwan
Beijing	Peip'ing	Jinxi	Chinhsi	Tonghua	T'unghua
Bengbu	Pangfou	Jinxian	Chinhsien	Tongling	Tungling
Benxi	Pench'i	Jinzhou	Chinchou	Ürümqi	Wulumuchi
Boshan	Poshan	Jiujiang	Chiuchiang	Wanxian	Wanhsien
Cangzhou	Ts'angchou	Jixi	Chihsi	Wenzhou	Wenchou
Changchi	Ch'angchih	Junggur Pendi	Dzungaria	Wutongqiao	Wut'ungchi'ao
Changchun	Ch'angch'un	Kashi	Kashgar	Wuxi	Wuhsi
Changde	Changt'e	Lanzhou	Lanchou	Wuzhou	Wuchou
Changsha	Ch'angsha	Lianyungan	Lienyünchiangshih	Xiaguan	Hsiakuan
Changshu	Ch'angshu	Liuzhou	Liuchou	Xiamen	Hsiamen
Changzhou	Ch'angchou	Lüda	Lüta	Xi'an	Hsian
Chengde	Ch'engte	Luoshan	Loshan	Xiangfan	Hsiangfan
Chengdu	Ch'engtu	Luoyang	Loyang	Xiangtan	Hsiangt'an
Chongqing	Ch'ungch'ing	Luzhou	Luchou	Xianyang	Hsienyang
Da Hinggan Ling	Tahsinganling	Manzhouli	Manchouli	Xiao Hinggan Ling	Hsiaohsinganling
	Shanmo	Meixian	Meihsien		Shanmo
Datong	Tat'ung	Mudanjiang	Mutanchiang	Xingtai	Hsingt'ai
Dezhou	Techou	Nanchong	Nanch'ung	Xining	Hsinging
Dongchuan	Tungch'uan	Nanjing	Nanching	Xinjiang Uygur Zizhiqu	Singkiang-Uigur
Duyun	Tuyün	Nantong	Nant'ung	Xinjin	Hsinchin
Fujian	Fukien	Nanzhang	Nanch'ang	Xinxiang	Hsinhsiang
Fuxin	Fouhsinshin	Neijiang	Neichiang	Xuanhua	Hsüanhua
Fuzhou	Fuchou	Ningbo	Ningpo	Xuchang	Hsüch'ang
Gansu	Kansu	Ningxia Huizu Zizhiqu	Ningsia Hui	Xuzhou	Hsüchou
Ganzhou	Kanchou	Pingdingshan	P'ingt'ingshan	Yangquan	Yangch'üan
Gejiu	Kochiu	Pingxiang	P'inghsiang	Yangzhou	Yangchou
Guangdong	Kwangtung	Qaidam Pendi	Tsaidam	Yanji	Yenchi
Guangxi Zhuangzu Zizhiqu	Kwangsi-Chuang	Qingdao	Ch'ingtao	Yanjin	Yench'eng
Guangzhou	Kuangchou	Qinghai	Tsinghai	Yantai	Yent'ai
Guilin	Kueilin	Qingjiang	Ch'ingchiang	Yibin	Ipin
Guiyang	Kueiyang	Qinhuangdao	Ch'inhuangtao	Yichang	Ich'ang
Guizhou	Kweichow	Qiqihar	Ch'ich'ihaerh	Yingchuan	Yinch'uan
Hangzhou	Hangchou	Quanzhou	Ch'üanchou	Yining	Ining
Harbin	Haerhpin	Rugao	Jukao	Yiyang	Iyang
Hebei	Hopei	Sanmenxia	Sanmenhsia	Yuci	Yutz'ü
Hebi	Haopi	Shaanxi	Shensi	Zaozhuang	Tsaochuang
Hechuan	Hoch'uan	Shandong	Shantung	Zhangjiakou	Changchiak'ou
Hefei	Hofei	Shangqiu	Shangch'iu	Zhangjiang	Chanchiang
Hegang	Haokang	Shangrao	Shangjao	Zhangzhou	Changchou
Heilong Jiang	Heilungkiang	Shanxi	Shansi	Zhao'an	Ch'aoan
Henan	Honan	Shaoguan	Shaokuan	Zhejiang	Chekiang
Hohhot	Huhohaot'e	Shaoxing	Shaohsing	Zhengzhou	Chengchou
Huaide	Huaite	Shijiazhuang	Shihchiachuangi	Zhenjiang	Chenchiang
Huangshi	Huangshih	Shizuishan	Shihtsuishan	Zhuhai	Chuhai
Hubei	Hupei	Shunde	Shunte	Zhuzhou	Chuchou
Jiamusi	Chiamussu	Sichuan	Szechwan	Zigong	Tzukung
Ji'an	Chian	Siping	Ssup'ing	Zunyi	Tsuni
Jiangmen	Chiangmen	Suxian	Suhsien		
Jiangsu	Kiangsu	Suzhou	Suchou		

Geographical Terms

This is a list of some of the geographical words from foreign languages which are found in the place names on the maps and in the index. Each is followed by the language and the English meaning.

Afr. afrikaans
Alb. albanian
Amh. amharic
Ar. arabic
Ber. berber
Bulg. bulgarian
Bur. burmese

Chin. chinese
Cz. czechoslovakian
Dan. danish
Dut. dutch
Fin. finnish
Flem. flemish
Fr. french

Gae. gaelic
Ger. german
Gr. greek
Heb. hebrew
Hin. hindi
I.-C. indo-chinese
Ice. icelandic

It. italian
Jap. japanese
Kor. korean
Lapp. lappish
Lith. lithuanian
Mal. malay
Mong. mongolian

Nor. norwegian
Pash. pashto
Pers. persian
Pol. polish
Port. portuguese
Rum. rumanian
Russ. russian

Ser.-Cr. serbo-croat
Siam. siamese
Sin. sinhalese
Som. somali
Span. spanish
Swed. swedish
Tib. tibetan
Turk. turkish

A. (Ain) Ar. spring
–á Ice. river
a Dan., Nor., Swed. stream
–abad Pers., Russ. town
Abyad Ar. white
Ad. (Adrar) Ar., Ber. mountain
Ada, Adasi Tur. island
Addis Amh. new
Adrar Ar., Ber. mountain
Ain Ar. spring
Ākra Gr. cape
Akrotiri Gr. cape
Alb Ger. mountain
Albufera Span. lagoon
–álen Nor. islands
Alpen Ger. mountain pastures
Alpes Fr. mountains
Alpi It. mountains
Alto Port. high
–älv, –älven Swed. stream, river
Amt Dan. first-order administrative division
Appennino It. mountain range
Arch. (Archipiélago) Span. archipelago
Arcipélago It. archipelago
Arq. (Arquipélago) Port. archipelago
Arr. (Arroyo) Span. stream
–Ås, –åsen Nor., Swed. hill
Autonomna Oblast Ser.-Cr. autonomous region
Ayios Gr. island
Ayn Ar. well, waterhole

B(a). (Baía) Port. bay
B. (Baie) Fr. bay
B. (Bahía) Span. bay
B. (Ben) Gae. mountain
B. (Bir) Ar. well
B. (Bucht) Ger. bay
B. (Bugt.) Dan. bay
Baai, –baai Afr. bay
Bâb Ar. gate
Bäck, –bäcken Swed. stream
Back, backen, Swed. hill
Bad, –baden Ger. spa
Bādiya,-t Ar. desert
Baek Dan. stream
Baelt Dan. strait
Bahía Span. bay
Bahr Ar. sea, river
Bahra Ar. lake
Baía Port. bay
Baie Fr. bay
Bajo, –a, Span. lower
Bakke Nor. hill
Bala Pers. upper
Baltă Rum. marsh, lake
Banc Fr. bank
Bander Ar., Mal. port
Bandar Pers. bay
Banja Ser. Cr. spa resort
Barat Mal. western
Barr. (Barrage) Fr. dam
Barracão Port. dam, waterfall
Bassin Fr. bay
Bayt Heb. house, village
Bazar Hin. market, bazaar
Be'er Ar. well
Beit Heb. village
Belo-, Belyy, Belaya,

Beloye, Russ. white
Ben Gae. mountain
Bender Somal. harbour
Berg,(e) –berg(e) Afr. mountain(s)
Berg, –berg Ger. mountain
–berg, –et Nor., Swed. hill, mountain, rock
Bet Heb. house, village
Bir, Bir Ar. well
Birket Ar. lake, bay, marsh
Bj. (Bordj) Ar. port
–bjerg Dan. hill, point
Boca Span. river mouth
Bodden Ger. bay, inlet
Bogaz, Boğaz, –ı Tur. strait
Boka Ser.-Cr. gulf, inlet
Bol. (Bolshoi) Russ. great, large
Bordj Ar. fort
–borg Dan., Nor., Swed. castle, fort
–botn Nor. valley floor
bouche(s) Fr. mouth
Br. (Burnu) Tur. cape
Braţul Rum. distributary stream
–breen Nor. glacier
–bruck Ger. bridge
–brunn Swed. well, spring
Bucht Ger. bay
Bugt, –bugt Dan. bay
Buheirat Ar. lake
Bukit Mal. hill
Bukten Swed. bay
–bulag Mong. spring
Bûr Ar. port
Burg. Ar. fort
Burg, –burg Ger. castle
Burnu Tur. cape
Burun Tur. cape
Butt Gae. promontory
–by Dan., Nor., Swed. town
–byen Nor., Swed. town

C. (Cabo) Port., Span. headland, cape
C. (Cap) Fr. cape
C. (Capo) It. cape
Cabeza Span. peak, hill
Camp Port., Span. land, field
Campo Span. plain
Campos Span. upland
Can. (Canal) Fr., Span. canal
Canale It. canal
Canalul Ser.-Cr. canal
Cao Nguyên Thai. plateau, tableland
Cap Fr. cape
Capo It. cape
Cataracta Sp. cataract
Cauce Span. intermittent stream
Causse Fr. upland (limestone)
Cayi Tur. river
Cayo Span. rock(s), islet(s)
Cerro Span. hill, peak
Ch. (Chaîne(s)) Fr. mountain range(s)
Ch. (Chott) Ar. salt lake
Chaco Span. jungle
Chaîne(s) Fr. mountain range(s)
Chap. (Chapada) Port. hills, upland

Chapa Span. hills, upland
Chapada Port. hills, upland
Chaung Bur. stream, river
Chen Chin. market town
Ch'eng Chin. town
Chiang Chin. river
Ch'ih Chin. pool
Ch'ŏn Kor. river
–chŏsuji Kor. reservoir
Chott Ar. salt lake, swamp
Chou Chin. district
Chu Tib. river
Chung Chin. middle
Chute Fr. waterfall
Co. (Cerro) Span. hill, peak
Coch. (Cochilla) Port. hills
Col Fr., It. Pass
Colline(s) Fr. hill(s)
Conca It. plain, basin
Cord. (Cordillera) Span. mountain chain
Costa It., Span. coast
Côte Fr. coast, slope, hill
Cuchillas Spain hills
Cu-Lao I.-C. island

D. (Dolok) Mal. mountain
Dágh Pers. mountain
Dağ(ı) Tur. mountain(s)
Dağları Tur. mountain range
Dake Jap. mountain
–dal Nor. valley
–dal, –e Dan., Nor. valley
–dal, –en Swed. valley, stream
Dalay Mong. sea, large lake
–dalir Ice. valley
–dalur Ice. valley
–damm, –en Swed. lake
Danau Mal. lake
Dao I.-O. island
Dar Ar. region
Darya Russ. river
Daryācheh Pers. marshy lake, lake
Dasht Pers. desert, steppe
Daung Bur. mountain, hill
Dayr Ar. depression, hill
Debre Amh. hill
Deli Ser.-Cr. mountain(s)
Denizi Tur. sea
Dépt. (Département) Fr. first-order administrative division
Desierto Span. desert
Dhar Ar. region, mountain chain
Dj. (Djebel) Ar. mountain
Dō Jap., Kor. island
Dong Kor. village, town
Dong Thai. jungle region
–dorf Ger. village
–dorp Afr. village
–drif Afr. ford
–dybet Dan. marine channel
Dzong Tib. town, settlement

Eil.-eiland(en) Afr., Dut. island(s)
–elv Nor. river
–'emeq Heb. plain, valley
'erg Ar. desert with dunes
Estrecho Span. strait
Estuario Span. estuary

Étang Fr. lagoon
–ey(jar) Ice. island(s)

F. (Fiume) It. river
F. Folyó Hung. river
Fd. (Fjord) Nor. Inlet of sea
–feld Ger. field
–fell Ice. mountain, hill
–feng Chin. mountain
Fiume It. river
Fj. (–fjell) Nor. mountain
–fjall Ice. mountain(s), hill(s)
–fjäll(et) Swed. hill(s), mountain(s), ridge
–fjällen Swed. mountains
–fjard(en) Swed. fjord, bay, lake
Fjeld Dan. mountain
–fjell Nor. mountain, rock
–fjord(en) Nor. inlet of sea
–fjorden Dan. bay, marine channel
–fjörður Ice. fjord
Fl. (Fleuve) Fr. river
Fl. (Fluss) Ger. river
–flói Ice. bay, marshy country
Fluss Ger. river
foce,–i It. mouth(s)
Folyó Hung. river
–fontein Afr. fountain, spring
–fors, –en, Swed. rapids, waterfall
Foss Ice., Nor. waterfall
–furt Ger. ford
Fylke Nor. first-order administrative division

G. (Gebel) Ar. mountain
G. (Gebirge) Ger. hills, mountains
G. (Golfe) Fr. gulf
G. (Golfo) It. gulf
G. (Gora) Bulg., Russ., Ser.-Cr. mountain
G. (Gunong) Mal. mountain
–gang Kor. river
Ganga Hin., Sin. river
–gat Dan. sound
–gau Ger. district
Gave Fr. stream
–gawa Jap. river
Geb. (Gebirge) Ger. hills, mountains
Gebel Ar. mountain
Geziret Ar. island
Ghat Hin. range of hills
Ghiol Rum. lake
Ghubbat Ar. bay, inlet
Gji Alb. bay
Gjol Alb. lagoon, lake
Gl. (Glava) Ser.-Cr. mountain, peak
Glen. Gae. valley
Gletscher Ger. glacier
Gobi Mong. desert
Gol Mong. river
Golfe Fr. gulf
Golfo It., Span. gulf
Gomba Tib. settlement
Gora Bulg., Russ., Ser.-Cr. mountain(s)
Góry Pol., Russ. mountain
Gölü Tur. lake
–gorod Russ. small town
Grad Bulg., Russ., Ser-Cr. town, city

Grada Russ. mountain range
Guba Russ. bay
–Guntō Jap. island group
Gunong Mal. mountain
Gură Rum. passage

H. Hadabat Ar. plateau
–hafen Ger. harbour, port
Haff Ger. bay
Hai Chin. sea
Haihsia Chin. strait
–hale Dan. spit, peninsula
Hals Dan., Nor. peninsula, isthmus
Halvø Dan. peninsula
Halvøya Nor. peninsula
Hāmad, Hamada,
Hammādah Ar. stony desert, plain
–hamn Swed., Nor. harbour, anchorage
Hāmūn Ar. plain
Hāmūn Pers. low-lying marshy area
–Hantō Jap. peninsula
Harju Fin. hill
Hassi Ar. well
–haug Nor. hill
Hav Swed. gulf
Havet Nor. sea
–havn Dan., Nor. harbour
Hegyseg Hung. forest
Heide Ger. heath
Hi. (hassi) Ar. well
Ho Chin. river
–hø Nor. peak
Hochland Afr. highland
Hoek, –hoek Afr., Dut. cape
Höfn Ice. harbour, port
–hög, –en, –högar, –högarna Swed. hill(s), peak, mountain
Höhe Ger. hills
Holm Dan. island
–holm, –holme, –holzen, Swed. island
Hon I.-C. island
Hora Cz. mountain
–horn Nor. peak
Hory Cz. mountain range, forest
–hoved Dan. point, headland, peninsula
Hráun Ice. lava
–hsi Chin. mountain, stream
–hsiang Chin. village
–hsien Chin. district
Hu Chin. lake
Huk Dan., Ger. point
Huken Nor. head

I. (Île) Fr. island
I. (Ilha) Port. island
I. (Insel) Ger. island
I. (Isla) Span. island
I. (Isola) It. island
Idehan Ar., Ber. sandy plain
Île(s) Fr. island(s)
Ilha Port. island
Insel(n) Ger. island(s)
Irmak Tur. river
Is. (Inseln) Ger. islands
Is. (Islas) Span. islands
Is. (Isola) It. island
Isola, –e It. island(s)
Istmo Span. isthmus

J. (Jabal) Ar. mountain
J. (Jazira) Ar. island
J. (Jebel) Ar. mountain
J. (Jezioro) Pol. lake
Jabal Ar. mountain, range
–jaur Swed. lake
–järvi Fin. lake, bay, pond
Jasovir Bulg. reservoir
Jazā'ir Ar. islands
Jazira Ar. island
Jazireh Pers. island
Jebel Ar. mountain
Jezero Ser.-Cr. lake
Jezioro Pol. lake
–Jima Jap. island
Jøkelen Nor. glacier
–joki Fin. stream
–jökull Ice. glacier
Jūras Līcis Lat. bay, gulf

K. (Kap) Dan. cape
K (Khalig) Ar. gulf
K. (Kiang) Chin. river
K. (Kuala) Mal. confluence, estuary
Kaap Afr. cape
Kai Jap. sea
Kaikyō Jap. strait
Kamennyy Russ. stony
Kampong Mal. village
Kan. (Kanal) Ser.-Cr. channel, canal
Kanaal Dut., Flem. canal
Kanal Dan. channel, gulf
Kanal Ger., Swed. canal, stream
kanal Ser.-Cr. channel, canal
Kang Kor. river, bay
Kangri Tib. mountain glacier
Kap Dan., Ger. cape
Kapp Nor. cape
Kas I.-C. island
–kaupstaður Ice. market town
–kaupunki Fin. town
Kavir Pers. salt desert
Kébir Ar. great
Kéfar Heb. village, hamlet
–ken Jap. first-order administrative division
Kep Alb. cape
Kepulauan Mal. archipelago
Ketjil Mal. lesser, little
Khalig, Khalij Ar. gulf
khamba, –idg Tib. source, spring
Khawr Ar. wadi
Khirbat Ar. ruins
Kho Khot Thai. isthmus
Khôr Pers. creek, estuary
Khrebet Russ. mountain range
Kiang Chin. river
–klint Dan. cliff
–Klintar Swed. hills
Kloof Afr. gorge
Knude Dan. point
Ko Jap. lake
Ko Thai. island ⌿
Kohi Pash. mountains
Kol Russ. lake
Kolymskoye Russ. mountain range
Kólpos Gr., Tur. gulf, bay
Kompong Mal. landing place
–kop Afr. hill

–köping *Swed.* market town
Körfezi *Tur.* gulf
Kosa *Russ.* spit
–koski *Fin.* cataract, rapids
–kraal *Afr.* native village
Krasnyy *Russ.* red
Kryash *Russ.* ridge, hills
Kuala *Mal.* confluence, estuary
kuan *Chin.* pass
Kuh –hha *Pers.* mountains
Kul *Russ.* lake
Kulle *Swed.* hill, shoal
Kum *Russ.* sandy desert
Kumpu *Fin.* hill
Kurgan *Russ.* mound
Kwe *Bur.* bay, gulf
Kyst *Dan.* coast
Kyun, –zu, –umya *Bur.* island(s)

L. (Lac) *Fr.* lake
L. (Lacul) *Rum.* lake
L. (Lago) *It.*, *Span.* lake, lagoon
L. (Lagoa) *Port.* lagoon
L. (Límni) *Gr.* lake
L. (Loch) *Gae.* (lake, inlet)
L. (Lough) *Gae.* (lake, inlet)
La *Tib.* pass
La (Lagoa) *Port.* lagoon
–laagte *Afr.* watercourse
Läani *Fin.* first-order administrative division
Län *Swed.* first-order administrative division
Lac *Fr.* lake
Lacul *Rum.* lake, lagoon
Lago *It.*, *Span.* lake, lagoon
Lagoa *Port.* lagoon
Laguna *It.*, *Span.* lagoon, intermittent lake
Lagune *Fr.* lake
Lahti *Fin.* bay, gulf, cove
Lakhti *Russ.* bay, gulf
Lampi *Fin.* lake
Land *Ger.* first-order administrative division
–land *Dan.* region
–land *Afr.*, *Nor.* land, province
Lido *It.* beach, shore
Liehtao *Chin.* islands
Lilla *Swed.* small
Límni *Gr.* lake
Ling *Tib.* mountain range, ice
Linna *Fin.* historical fort
Llano *Span.* prairie, plain
Loch *Gae.* (lake)
Lough *Gae.* (lake)
Lum *Alb.* river
Lund *Dan.* forest
–lund, –en *Swed.* wood(s)

M. (Maj, Mai) *Alb.* mountain, peak
M. (Mont) *Fr.* mountain peak
M. (Mys) *Russ.* cape
Madina(h) *Ar.* town, city
Madiq *Ar.* strait
Maj *Alb.* peak
Mäki *Fin.* hill, hillside
Mal *Alb.* mountain
Mal *Russ.* little, small
Mal/a, –i, –o *Ser.-Cr.* small, little
Man *Kor.* bay
Mar *Span.* lagoon, sea
Mare *Rum.* great
Marisma *Span.* marsh
–mark *Dan.*, *Nor.* land
Marsâ *Ar.* anchorage, bay, inlet
Masabb *Ar.* river mouth
Massif *Fr.* upland, plateau
Mato *Port.* forest
Mazar *Pers.* shrine, tomb
Meer *Afr.*, *Dut.*, *Ger.* lake sea

Mi., Mti. (Monti) *It.* mountains
Miao *Chin.* temple, shrine
Midbar *Heb.* wilderness
Mif. (Massif) *Fr.* upland, plateau
Misaki *Jap.* cape, point
–mo *Nor.*, *Swed.* heath, island
–mon *Swed.* heath
Mong *Bur.* town
Mont *Fr.* hill, mountain
Montagna *It.* mountain
Montagne *Fr.* hill, mountain
Montaña *Span.* mountain
Monte *It.*, *Port.*, *Span.* mountain
Monti *It.* mountains
More *Russ.* sea
Mörön *Hung.* river
Mt. (Mont) *Fr.* mountain
Mt. (Monti) *It.* mountain
Mt. (Montaña) *Span.* mountain range
Mte. (Monte) *It.*, *Port.*, *Span.* mountain
Mți. (Munți) *Rum.* mountain
Mts. (Monts) *Fr.* mountains
Muang *Mal.* town
Mui *Ar.*, *I.-C.* cape
Mull *Gae.* (promontory)
Mund, –mund *Afr.* mouth
Munkhafed *Ar.* depression
Munte *Rum.* mount
Munți(i) *Rum.* mountain(s)
Muong *Mal.* village
Myit *Bur.* river
Myitwanya *Bur.* mouths of river
–myri *Ice.* bog
Mys *Russ.* cape

N. (Nahal) *Heb.* river
Naes *Dan.* point, cape
Nafüd *Ar.* sandy desert
Nahal *Heb.* river
Nahr *Ar.* river, stream
Najd *Ar.* plateau, pass
Nakhon *Thai.* town
Nam *I.-C.* river
–nam *Kor.* south
–näs *Swed.* cape
–nes *Ice.*, *Nor.* cape
Ness, –ness *Gae.* promontory, cape
Nez *Fr.* cape
–niemi *Fin.* cape, point, peninsula, island
Nizhne, –iy *Russ.* lower
Nizmennost *Russ.* plain, lowland
Nísos, Nísoi *Gr.* island(s)
Nor *Chin.* lake
Nor *Tib.* peak
Nos *Bulg.*, *Russ.* cape, point
Nudo *Span.* mountain
Nuruu *Mong.* mountain range
Nuur *Mong.* lake

O. (Ostrov) *Russ.* island
O (Ouâdî, Oued) *Ar.* wadi
–ö *Swed.* island, peninsula, point
–öar, (–na) *Swed.* islands
Oblast *Russ.* administrative division
Öbor *Mong.* inner
Occidental *Fr.*, *Span.* western
Odde *Dan.*, *Nor.* point, peninsula, cape
Oji *Alb.* bay
Ojo *Span.* spring
Oki *Jap.* bay
–ön *Swed.* island peninsula
Ondör *Mong.* high, tall

–ör *Swed.* island, peninsula, point
Orașul *Rum.* city
Ord *Gae.* point
Óri *Gr.* mountains
Oriental *Span.* eastern
Órmos *Gr.* bay
Óros *Gr.* mountain
Ort *Ger.* point, cape
Ostrov(a) *Russ.* island(s)
Otok(–i) *Ser.-Cr.* island(s)
Ouadi, –edi *Ar.* dry watercourse, wadi
Ouzan *Pers.* river
Ova (–si) *Tur.* plains, lowlands
–øy, (–a) *Nor.* island(s)
Oya *Hin.* point
Oya *Sin.* river
Oz. (Ozero, a) *Russ.* lake(s)

P. (Passo) *It.* pass
P. (Pasul) *Rum.* pass
P. (Pico) *Span.* peak
P. (Prokhod) *Bulg.* pass
–pää *Fin.* hill(s), mountain
Pahta *Lapp.* hill
Pampa, –s *Span.* plain(s) salt flat(s)
Pan. (Pantano) *Span.* Reservoir
Pantao *Chin.* peninsula
Parbat *Urdu* mountain
Pas *Fr.* gap
Paso *Span.* pass, marine channel
Pass *Ger.* pass
Passo *It.* pass
Pasul *Rum.* pass
Patam *Hin.* small village
Patna, –patnam *Hin.* small village
Pegunungan *Mal.* mountain, range
Pei, –pei *Chin.* north
Pélagos *Gr.* sea
Pen. (Península) *Span.* peninsula
Peña *Span.* rock, peak
Península *Span.* peninsula
Per. (Pereval) *Russ.* pass
Pertuis *Fr.* channel
Peski *Russ.* desert, sands
Phanom *I.-C.*, *Thai.* mountain
Phnom *I.-C.* mountain
Phu *I.-C.* mountain
Pic *Fr.* peak
Pico(s) *Span.* peak(s)
Pik *Russ.* peak
Piz., pizzo *It.* peak
Pl. (Planina) *Ser.-Cr.* mountain, range
Plage *Fr.* beach
Plaine *Fr.* plain
Planalto *Span.* plateau
Planina *Bulg.*, *Ser.-Cr.* mountain, range
Plat. (Plateau) *Fr.* level upland
Plato *Russ.* plateau
Playa *Span.* beach
P-ov. (Poluostrov) *Russ.* peninsula
Pointe *Fr.* point, cape
Pojezierze *Pol.* lakes plateau
Polder *Dut.* reclaimed farmland
–pólis *Gr.* city, town
Poluostrov *Russ.* peninsula
Połwysep *Pol.* peninsula
Pont *Fr.* bridge
Ponta *Port.* point, cape
Ponte *It.* bridge
Poort *Afr.* passage, gate
–poort *Dut.* port
Porta *Port.* pass
Portil, –e *Rum.* gate
Portillo *Span.* pass
Porto *It.* port
Porto *Port.*, *Span.* port

Pot. (Potámi, Potamós) *Gr.* river
Poulo *I.-C.* island
Pr. (Průsmyk) *Cz.* pass
Pradesh *Hin.* state
Presa *Span.* reservoir
Presqu'île *Fr.* peninsula
Prokhod *Bulg.* pass
Proliv *Russ.* strait
Prusmyk *Cz.* pass
Pso. (Passo) *It.* pass
Pta. (Ponta) *Port.* point, cape
Pta. (Punta) *It.*, *Span.* point, cape, peak
Pte. (Pointe) *Fr.* point cape
Puerto *Span.* port, pass
Puig *Cat.* peak
Pulau *Mal.* island
Puna *Span.* desert plateau
Punta *It.*, *Span.* point, peak
Puy *Fr.* hill

Qal'at *Ar.* fort
Qanal *Ar.* canal
Qasr *Ar.* fort
Qiryat *Heb.* town
Qolleh *Pers.* mountain

Ramla *Ar.* sand
Rann *Hin.* swampy region
Rao *I.-C.* river
Ras *Amh.* cape, headland
Rás *Ar.* cape, headland
Recife(s) *Port.* reef(s)
Reka *Bulg.*, *Cz.*, *Russ.* river
Repede *Rum.* rapids
Represa *Port.* dam
Reshteh *Pers.* mountain range
–Rettô *Jap.* group of islands
Ría *Span.* estuary, bay
Ribeirão *Port.* river
Rijeka *Ser.-Cr.* river
Rio *Port.* river
Río *Span.* river
Riv. (Riviera) *It.* coastal plain, coast, river
Rivier *Afr.* river
Riviera *It.* coast
Rivière *Fr.* river
Roche *Fr.* rock
Rog *Russ.* horn
–rück *Ger.* ridge
Rüd *Pers.* stream, river
Rudohorie *Cz.* ore mountains
Rzeka *Pol.* river

S. (Sungei) *Mal.* river
Sa. (Serra) *It.*, *Port.* range of hills
Sa. (Sierra) *Span.* range of hills
–saari *Fin.* island
Sadd *Ar.* dam
Sagar, –ara *Hin.*, *Urdu* lake
Saharā *Ar.* desert
Sahrâ *Ar.* desert
Sa'id *Ar.* highland
Sakar *Fin.* mountain
–Saki *Jap.* point
Sal. (Salar) *Span.* salt pan
Salina(s) *Span.* salt flat(s)
–salmi *Fin.* strait, sound, lake, channel
Saltsjöbad *Swed.* resort
Sammyaku *Jap.* mountain, range
Samut *Thai.* gulf
–San *Jap.* hill, mountain
Sap. (Sapadno) *Russ.* west
Sasso *It.* mountain
Se, Sé *I.-C.* river
Sebkha, –kra *Ar.* salt flats
See *Ger.* lake
–see *Ger.* sea
–șehir *Turk.* town
Selat *Mal.* strait
–selkä *Fin.* bay, lake, sound, ridge, hills

Selva *Span.* forest, wood
Seno *Span.* bay, sound
Serír *Ar.* desert of small stones
Serra *It.*, *Port.* range of hills
Serranía *Span.* mountains
Sev. (Severo) *Russ.* north
–shahr *Pers.* city, town
Shan *Chin.* hills, mountains, pass
Shan-mo *Chin.* mountain range
Shatt *Ar.* river
–Shima *Jap.* island
Shimāli *Ar.* northern
–Shotô *Jap.* group of islands
Shuik'u *Chin.* reservoir
Sierra *Span.* hill, range
Sjö, sjön *Swed.* lake, bay, sea
Sjøen *Dan.* sea
Skär *Swed.* island, rock, cape
Skog *Nor.* forest
–skog, –skogen *Swed.* wood(s)
–skov *Dan.* forest
Slieve *Gae.* range of hills
–sø *Dan.*, *Nor.* lake
Sør *Nor.* south, southern
Solonchak *Russ.* salt lake, marsh
Souk *Ar.* market
Spitze *Ger.* peak, mountain
–spruit *Afr.* stream
–stad *Afr.*, *Nor.*, *Swed.* town
Stadur *Ice.* town
Stausee *Ger.* reservoir
Stenón *Gr.* strait, pass
Step *Russ.* plain
Str. (Stretto) *It.* strait
–strand *Dan.*, *Nor.* beach
–strede *Nor.* straits
Strelka *Russ.* spit
–strete *Nor.* straits
Stretto *It.* strait
Stroedet *Dan.* strait
–ström, –strömmen *Swed.* stream(s)
–stroom *Dut.* large river
Suidô *Jap.* strait, channel
Sûn *Bur.* cape
Sund *Dan.* sound
–sund, –sundet *Swed.* sound, estuary, inlet
–sund(et) *Nor.* sound
Sungai, –ei *Mal.* river
Sungei *Mal.* river
Sur *Span.* south, southern
Sveti *Bulg.* pass
Syd *Dan.*, *Swed.* south

Tai –tai *Chin.* tower
Tal *Mong.* plain, steppe
–tal *Ger.* valley
Tall *Ar.* hills, hummocks
Tandjung *Mal.* cape, headland
Tao *Chin.* island
Tassili *Ar.* rocky plateau
Tau *Russ.* mountain, range
Taung *Bur.* mountain, south
Taunggya *Bur.* pass
Tělok *I.-C.*, *Mal.* bay bight
Teluk *Mal.* bay, gulf
Tg. (Tandjung) *Mal.* cape, headland
–thal *Ger.* valley
Thok *Tib.* town
Tierra *Span.* land, country
–tind *Nor.* peak
Tjärn, –en, –et *Swed.* lake
Tong *Nor.* village, town
Tong *Bur.*, *Thai.* mountain range
Tonle *I.-C.* large river, lake
–träsk *Swed.* bog, swamp
Tsangpo *Tib.* large river
Tso *Tib.* lake

Tsu *Jap.* entrance, bay
Tulur *Ar.* hill
T'un *Chin.* village
Tung *Chin.* east
Tunnel *Fr.* tunnel
Tunturi *Fin.* hill(s), mountain(s), ridge

Uad *Ar.* dry watercourse, wadi
Udjung *Mal.* cape
Udd, udde, udden *Swed.* point, peninsula
Uebi *Somal.* river
Us *Mong.* water
Ust *Russ.* river mouth
Uul *Mong.*, *Russ.* mountain, range

V. (Volcán) *Span.* volcano
–vaara *Fin.* hill, mountain, ridge, peak
–våg *Nor.* bay
Val *Fr.*, *It.* valley
Valea *Rum.* valley
–vall, –vallen *Swed.* mountain
Valle *Span.* valley
Vallée *Fr.* valley
Valli *It.* lake, lagoon
Väst *Swed.* west
–vatn *Ice.*, *Nor.* lake
Vatten *Swed.* lake
Vdkhr. (Vodokhranilishche) *Russ.* reservoir
–ved, –veden *Swed.* range, hills
Veld, –veld *Afr.* field
Velik/a, –e, –i, –o *Ser.-Cr.* large
–vesi *Fin.* water, lake, bay sound, strait
Vest *Dan.*, *Nor.* west
Vf. (vîrful) *Rum.* peak, mountain
–vidda *Nor.* plateau
Vig *Dan.* bay, inlet, cove, lagoon, lake, bight
–vik, –vika, –viken *Nor.*, *Swed.* bay, cove, gulf, inlet, lake
Vila *Port.* small town
Villa *Span.* town
Ville *Fr.* town
Vinh *I.-C.* bay
Virful *Rum.* peak, mountain
–vlei *Afr.* pond, pool
Vodokhranilishche *Russ.* reservoir
Vol. (Volcán) *Span.* volcano, mountain
Vorota *Russ.* gate
Vostochnyy *Russ.* eastern
Vozyshennost *Russ.* heights, uplands
Vrata *Bulg.* gate, pass
Vrchovina *Cz.* mountainous country
Vrchy *Cz.* mountain range
Vung *I.-C.* gulf
–vuori *Fin.* mountain, hill

W. (Wādī) *Ar.* dry watercourse
Wâhât *Ar.* oasis
Wald *Ger.* wood, forest
Wan *Chin.*, *Jap.* bay
Webi *Amh.* river
Woestyn *Afr.* desert

Yam *Heb.* sea
Yang *Chin.* ocean
Yazovir *Bulg.* reservoir
Yoma *Bur.* mountain range
–yüan *Chin.* spring

Zaki *Jap.* peninsula
Zalew *Pol.* lagoon, swamp
Zaliv *Russ.* bay
Zan *Jap.* mountain
Zatoka *Pol.* bay
Zee *Dut.* sea
Zemlya *Russ.* land, island(s)